Microsoft Office XP

Introductory Concepts and Techniques

WORD 2002 EXCEL 2002 ACCESS 2002 POWERPOINT 2002 OUTLOOK 2002

Microsoft

Introductory Concepts and Techniques

WORD 2002 EXCEL 2002 ACCESS 2002 POWERPOINT 2002 OUTLOOK 2002

Gary B. Shelly
Thomas J. Cashman
Misty E. Vermaat

Contributing Authors
Steven G. Forsythe
Jodi L. Groen
Mary Z. Last
Philip J. Pratt
James S. Quasney
Jeffrey J. Quasney
Susan L. Sebok
Jeffrey J. Webb

COURSE TECHNOLOGY
25 THOMSON PLACE
BOSTON MA 02210

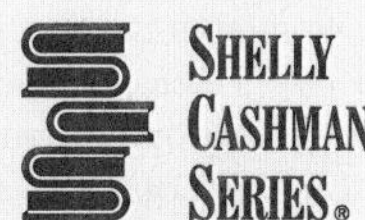
SHELLY
CASHMAN
SERIES®

Australia • Canada • Denmark • Japan • Mexico • New Zealand • Philippines • Puerto Rico • Singapore
South Africa • Spain • United Kingdom • United States

Asia (excluding Japan)
Thomson Learning
60 Albert Street, #15-01
Albert Complex
Singapore 189969

Japan
Thomson Learning
Palaceside Building 5F
1-1-1 Hitotsubashi, Chiyoda-ku
Tokyo 100 0003 Japan

Australia/New Zealand
Nelson/Thomson Learning
102 Dodds Street
Southbank, Victoria 3006
Australia

Latin America
Thomson Learning
Seneca, 53
Colonia Polanco
11560 Mexico D.F. Mexico

South Africa
Thomson Learning
15 Brookwood Street
P.O. Box 1722
Soverset West 7120
South Africa

Canada
Nelson/Thomson Learning
1120 Birchmount Road
Scarborough, Ontario
Canada M1K 5G4

UK/Europe/Middle East
Thomson Learning
Berkshire House
168-173 High Holborn
London, WC1V 7AA United Kingdom

Spain
Thomson Learning
Calle Magallanes, 25
28015-MADRID
ESPANA

For more information, contact Course Technology, 25 Thomson Place, Boston, MA 02210.

Or visit our Internet site at www.course.com

PHOTO CREDITS: **Microsoft Windows 2000** *Project 1, pages INT 1.02-03* Man and computer, computer brain, Courtesy of ArtToday; photo of Bill Gates, Courtesy of Microsoft; **Microsoft Word 2002** *Project 2, pages WD 2.02-03* Boy at computer, caution sign, computer, library, man biting nails, SUV, woman sleeping, Courtesy of ArtToday; *Project 3, pages WD 3.02-03* Drawing of Albert Einstein, girl working on computer, Courtesy of ArtToday; violin, hand with pen, Courtesy of Nova Development; envelopes, handshake, man working, Courtesy of PhotoDisc, Inc.; **Microsoft Excel 2002** *Project 3, pages E 3.02-03* Coins, man working on notebook computer, money, Courtesy of PhotoDisc, Inc.; house and car, light bulb, telephone, television and radio, Courtesy of Corel; **Microsoft Access 2002** *Project 1, pages A 1.04-05* Trojan horse, Trojan horse fresco, Courtesy of ArtToday; adults helping child with headset, silhouettes, Courtesy of Dynamic Graphics; adult and child reading, teacher and students at computers, Courtesy of PhotoDisc, Inc.; *Project 2, pages A 2.02-03* Father holding baby, globe artwork, Courtesy of Nova Development; child's portrait, Courtesy of PhotoDisc, Inc.; **Microsoft PowerPoint 2002** *Project 1, pages PP 1.04-05* Business people, cell phone, circuit boards and gears, fiber optic cable, notebook computer, number printout, telephone jack, utility wires and towers, world on computer screen, Courtesy of PhotoDisc, Inc.; *Project 2, pages PP 2.02-03* Conference room meeting, office meeting, three businesspeople, woman in taxi, woman speaking at a meeting, Courtesy of PhotoDisc, Inc.; **Microsoft Outlook 2002** *Project 1, pages O 1.04-05* Aztec calendar, book, cell phone, clock, hourglass, quill pen, sundial, typewriter, Courtesy of ArtToday; CD, computer, fiber optics, lantern, man in office, world and satellite, Courtesy of PhotoDisc, Inc.; **Office XP Integration** *Project 1, pages I 1.04-05* Computer and equipment, doctor with notebook computer, finger on monitor, hospital clinic, notebook computer, woman at computer workstation, Courtesy of ArtToday; couple at table, doctor in lab coat, eye in background, family dinner, hotel resort, hospital worker at computer workstation, Courtesy of PhotoDisc, Inc.

ISBN 0-7895-6289-8 (perfect bound) ISBN 0-7895-6393-2 (spiral bound)

3 4 5 6 7 8 9 10 BC 06 05 04 03 02

Microsoft Office XP
Introductory Concepts and Techniques
WORD 2002 EXCEL 2002 ACCESS 2002 POWERPOINT 2002 OUTLOOK 2002

Contents

Essential Introduction to Computers

Microsoft Windows 2000 and Office XP

1 PROJECT ONE

AN INTRODUCTION TO WINDOWS 2000 PROFESSIONAL AND OFFICE XP

Microsoft Word 2002

1 PROJECT ONE

Creating and Editing a Word Document

2 PROJECT TWO

Creating a Research Paper

3 PROJECT THREE

Creating a Resume Using a Wizard and a Cover Letter with a Table

WEB FEATURE

Creating Web Pages Using Word

Microsoft Excel 2002

1 PROJECT ONE

Creating a Worksheet and Embedded Chart

2 PROJECT TWO

Formulas, Functions, Formatting, and Web Queries

3 PROJECT THREE

What-If Analysis, Charting, and Working with Large Worksheets

WEB FEATURE

Creating Static and Dynamic Web Pages Using Excel

Microsoft Access 2002

1 PROJECT ONE

Creating a Database Using Design and Datasheet Views

2 PROJECT TWO

Querying a Database Using the Select Query Window

3 PROJECT THREE

Maintaining a Database Using the Design and Update Features of Access

WEB FEATURE

Publishing to the Internet Using Data Access Pages

Microsoft PowerPoint 2002

1 PROJECT ONE

Using a Design Template and Text Slide Layout to Create a Presentation

2 PROJECT TWO

Using the Outline Tab and Clip Art to Create a Slide Show

WEB FEATURE

Creating a Presentation on the Web Using PowerPoint

Microsoft Outlook 2002

1 PROJECT ONE

Schedule and Contact Management Using Outlook

Office XP Integration

1 PROJECT ONE

Integrating Office XP Applications and the World Wide Web

APPENDIX A

Microsoft Office XP Help System

Preface

The Shelly Cashman Series® offers the finest textbooks in computer education. We are proud of the fact that our series of Microsoft Office 4.3, Microsoft Office 95, Microsoft Office 97, and Microsoft Office 2000 textbooks have been the most widely used books in education. With each new edition of our Office books, we have made improvements based on the software and comments made by the instructors and students who use our textbooks. The *Microsoft Office XP* books continue with the innovation, quality, and reliability that you have come to expect from the Shelly Cashman Series.

Office XP is the most significant upgrade ever to the Office suite. It provides a much smarter work experience for users. Microsoft has enhanced Office XP in the following areas: (1) streamlined user interface; (2) smart tags and task panes to help simplify the way people work; (3) speech and handwriting recognition; (4) an improved Help system; (5) enhanced Web capabilities; and (6) application-specific features.

In this *Microsoft Office XP* book, you will find an educationally sound and easy-to-follow pedagogy that combines a step-by-step approach with corresponding screens. All projects and exercises in this book are designed to take full advantage of the Office XP enhancements. The popular Other Ways and More About features offer in-depth knowledge of Office XP. The new Learn It Online page presents a wealth of additional exercises to ensure your students have all the reinforcement they need. The project openers provide a fascinating perspective of the subject covered in the project. The project material is developed carefully to ensure that students will see the importance of learning Office XP for future coursework.

Objectives of This Textbook

Microsoft Office XP: Introductory Concepts and Techniques is intended for a course that includes a brief introduction to Office XP. No experience with a computer is assumed, and no mathematics beyond the high school freshman level is required. The objectives of this book are:

- To teach the fundamentals of Office XP
- To expose students to practical examples of the computer as a useful tool
- To acquaint students with the proper procedures to create documents, worksheets, databases, and presentations suitable for coursework, professional purposes, and personal use
- To help students discover the underlying functionality of Office XP so they can become more productive
- To develop an exercise-oriented approach that allows learning by doing
- To introduce students to new input technologies
- To encourage independent study, and help those who are working alone

Approved by Microsoft as Courseware for the Microsoft Office User Specialist Program Core Level

Microsoft Office XP: Introductory Concepts and Techniques, when used in combination with the companion textbook *Microsoft Office XP: Advanced Concepts and Techniques* in a two-semester sequence, has been approved by

Microsoft as courseware for the Microsoft Office User Specialist (MOUS) program. After completing the projects and exercises in this book and its companion book, students will be prepared to take the Core-level Microsoft Office User Specialist Exams for Microsoft Word 2002, Microsoft Excel 2002, and Microsoft Access 2002, and the Comprehensive-level Microsoft Office User Specialist Exam for Microsoft PowerPoint 2002.

By passing the certification exam for a Microsoft software program, students demonstrate their proficiency in that program to employers. This exam is offered at participating centers, participating corporations, and participating employment agencies. See Appendix E for additional information on the MOUS program and for a table that includes the Word 2002, Excel 2002, Access 2002, and PowerPoint 2002 MOUS skill sets and corresponding page numbers on which a skill is discussed in the book and can be practiced, or visit the Web site mous.net. To purchase a Microsoft Office User Specialist certification exam, visit desktopiq.com.

The Shelly Cashman Series Microsoft Office User Specialist Center Web page (Figure 1) has more than fifteen Web pages you can visit to obtain additional information on the MOUS Certification program. The Web page scsite.com.offxp/cert.htm includes links to general information on certification, choosing an application for certification, preparing for the certification exam, and taking and passing the certification exam.

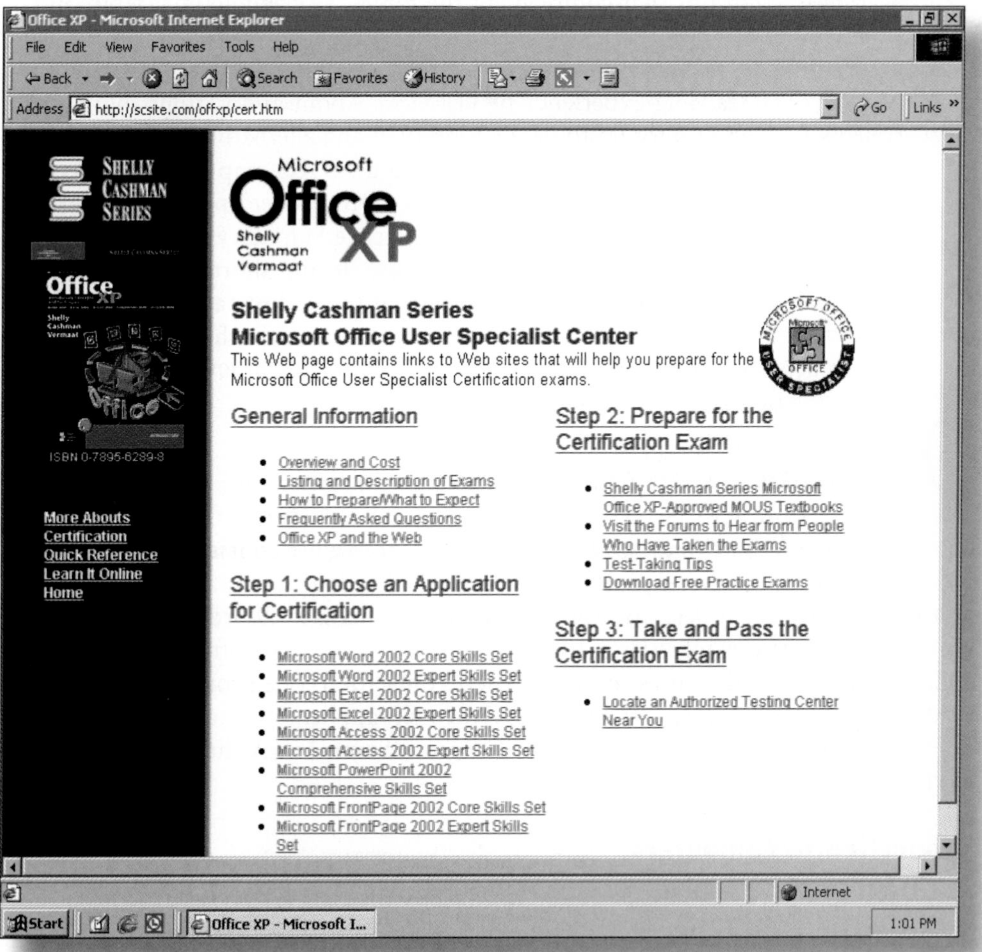

FIGURE 1 The Shelly Cashman Series Microsoft Office User Specialist Center Web Page

The Shelly Cashman Approach

Features of the Shelly Cashman Series *Microsoft Office XP* books include:

- Project Orientation: Each project in the book presents a practical problem and complete solution in an easy-to-understand approach.
- Step-by-Step, Screen-by-Screen Instructions: Each of the tasks required to complete a project is identified throughout the development of the project. Full-color screens accompany the steps.
- Thoroughly Tested Projects: Every screen in the book is correct because it is produced by the author only after performing a step, resulting in unprecedented quality.
- Other Ways Boxes and Quick Reference Summary: Office XP provides a variety of ways to carry out a given task. The Other Ways boxes displayed at the end of most of the step-by-step sequences specify the other ways to do the task completed in the steps. Thus, the steps and the Other Ways box make a comprehensive reference unit. A Quick Reference Summary that summarizes the way specific tasks can be completed can be found at the back of this book or on the Web at scsite.com/offxp/qr.htm.
- More About Feature: These marginal annotations provide background information and tips that complement the topics covered, adding depth and perspective.
- Integration of the World Wide Web: The World Wide Web is integrated into the Office XP learning experience by (1) More About annotations that send students to Web sites for up-to-date information and alternative approaches to tasks; (2) a MOUS information Web page and a MOUS map Web page so students can better prepare for the Microsoft Office User Specialist (MOUS) Certification examinations; (3) a Quick Reference Summary Web page that summarizes the ways to complete tasks (mouse, menu, shortcut menu, and keyboard); and (4) the Learn It Online page at the end of each project, which has project reinforcement exercises, learning games, and other types of student activities.

Other Ways

1. Right-click slide anywhere except text placeholders, click Slide Layout on shortcut menu, double-click desired slide layout
2. Press ALT+O, press L, press ARROW keys to select desired slide layout, press ENTER
3. In Voice Command mode, say "Format, Slide Layout, Title Text and Two Content, Close"

More About

Maintaining a Database: Recovery

If a problem occurs that damages either the data in the database or the structure of the database, the database is recovered by copying the backup copy over it. To do so, use the copy features of Windows to copy the backup version (for example, Alisa Vending Backup) over the actual database (for example, Alisa Vending Services). This will return the database to the state it was in when the backup was made.

Organization of This Textbook

Microsoft Office XP: Introductory Concepts and Techniques consists of a brief introduction to computers, a project on Microsoft Windows 2000 and an introduction to Microsoft Office XP, three projects each on Microsoft Word 2002, Microsoft Excel 2002, and Microsoft Access 2002, two projects on Microsoft PowerPoint 2002, four short Web Features following each application, one project on Microsoft Outlook 2002, one project on integrating Office XP applications and the World Wide Web, five appendices, and a Quick Reference Summary. A short description of each follows.

Introduction to Computers

Many students taking a course in the use of Microsoft Office XP will have little previous experience with computers. For this reason, the book begins with a completely updated 32-page section titled Essential Introduction to Computers that covers essential computer hardware and software concepts and information on how to purchase, install, and maintain desktop, handheld, and notebook computers.

An Introduction to Windows 2000 Professional and Office XP

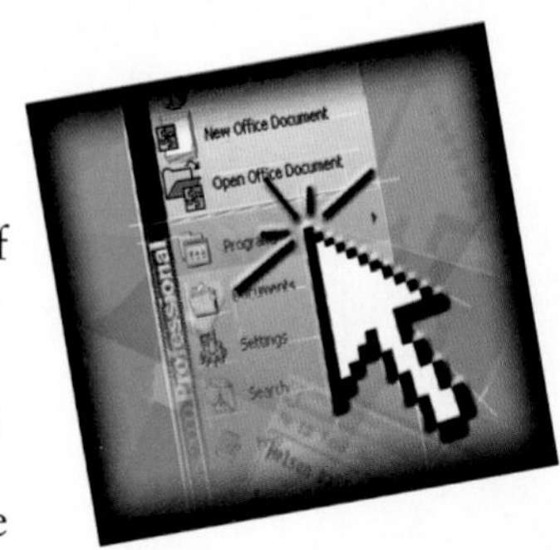

Students learn about user interfaces, Microsoft Windows 2000, Windows Explorer, and each Office XP application. Topics include using the mouse; minimizing, maximizing, and restoring windows; closing and reopening windows; sizing and scrolling windows; launching and quitting an application; displaying the contents of a folder; expanding and collapsing a folder; creating a folder; selecting and copying a group of files; renaming and deleting a file and a folder; using Windows 2000 Help; and shutting down Windows 2000. Topics pertaining to Microsoft Office XP include a brief explanation of Microsoft Word 2002; Microsoft Excel 2002; Microsoft Access 2002; Microsoft PowerPoint 2002; Microsoft Publisher 2002; Microsoft FrontPage 2002; and Microsoft Outlook 2002 and examples of how these applications take advantage of the Internet and World Wide Web.

Microsoft Word 2002

Project 1 – Creating and Editing a Word Document In Project 1, students are introduced to Word terminology and the Word window by preparing an announcement. Topics include starting and quitting Word; entering text; checking spelling while typing; saving a document; selecting characters, words, lines, and paragraphs; changing the font and font size of text; centering, right-aligning, bolding, and italicizing text; undoing commands and actions; inserting clip art into a document; resizing a graphic; printing a document; opening a document; correcting errors; and using the Word Help system.

Project 2 – Creating a Research Paper In Project 2, students use the MLA style of documentation to create a research paper. Topics include changing margins; adjusting line spacing; using a header to number pages; entering text using Click and Type; first-line indenting paragraphs; using the AutoCorrect feature and AutoCorrect Options button; adding a footnote; modifying a style; inserting a symbol automatically; inserting a manual page break; creating a hanging indent; creating a text hyperlink; sorting paragraphs; moving text; using the Paste Options button; finding a synonym; counting and recounting words in a document; checking spelling and grammar at once; and e-mailing a document.

Project 3 – Creating a Resume Using a Wizard and a Cover Letter with a Table In Project 3, students create a resume using Word's Resume Wizard and then create a cover letter with a letterhead. Topics include personalizing the resume; using print preview; adding color to characters; setting and using tab stops; collecting and pasting; adding a bottom border; clearing formatting; inserting the current date; inserting a nonbreaking space; creating and inserting an AutoText entry; creating a bulleted list while typing; inserting a Word table; entering data into a Word table; and formatting a Word table. Finally, students address and print envelopes and mailing labels.

Web Feature – Creating Web Pages Using Word In this Web Feature, students are introduced to creating Web pages. Topics include saving the resume created in Project 3 as a Web page; creating a Web page using the Web Page Wizard; resizing a Web page frame; editing a hyperlink; and editing a Web page from your browser.

Microsoft Excel 2002

Project 1 – Creating a Worksheet and Embedded Chart In Project 1, students are introduced to Excel terminology, the Excel window, speech recognition and speech playback, and the basic characteristics of a worksheet and workbook. Topics include starting and quitting Excel; customizing Excel, entering text and numbers; selecting a range; using the AutoSum button; copying using the fill handle; changing font size and color; formatting in bold; centering across columns; using the AutoFormat command; charting using the ChartWizard; saving and opening a workbook; editing a worksheet; using the AutoCalculate area; and using the Excel Help system.

Project 2 – Formulas, Functions, Formatting, and Web Queries In Project 2, students use formulas and functions to build a worksheet and learn more about formatting and printing a worksheet. Topics include entering dates and formulas; using functions; verifying formulas; changing fonts; formatting text and numbers; conditional formatting; drawing borders; changing the widths of columns and rows; spell checking; changing sheet names; previewing a worksheet; printing a section of a worksheet; and displaying and printing the formulas in a worksheet. This project also introduces students to accessing real-time data using Web Queries and sending the open workbook as an e-mail attachment directly from Excel.

Project 3 – What-If-Analysis, Charting, and Working with Large Worksheets In Project 3, students learn how to work with larger worksheets, how to create a worksheet based on assumptions, how to use the IF function and absolute cell references, charting techniques, and how to perform what-if analysis. Topics include assigning global formats; rotating text; using the fill handle to create a series; deleting, inserting, copying, and moving data on a worksheet; displaying and formatting the system date; displaying and docking toolbars; creating a 3-D Pie chart on a chart sheet, enhancing a 3-D Pie chart; freezing titles; changing the magnification of worksheets; displaying different parts of the worksheet using panes; and simple what-if analysis and goal seeking.

Web Feature – Creating Static and Dynamic Web Pages Using Excel In this Web Feature, students are introduced to creating a new folder, and creating static Web pages (noninteractive pages that do not change) and dynamic Web pages (interactive pages that offer Excel functionality). Topics include, saving and previewing an Excel workbook as a Web page; viewing and manipulating a Web page created in Excel using a browser; and using the Commands and Options dialog box.

Microsoft Access 2002

Project 1 -- Creating a Database Using Design and Datasheet Views In Project 1, students are introduced to the concept of a database and shown how to use Access to create a database. Topics include creating a database; creating a table; defining the fields in a table; opening a table; adding records to a table; closing a table; and previewing and printing the contents of a table. Other topics in this project include using a form to view data; using the Report Wizard to create a report; and using the Access Help system. Students also learn how to design a database to eliminate redundancy.

Project 2 - Querying a Database Using the Select Query Window In Project 2, students learn to use queries to obtain information from the data in their databases. Topics include creating queries, running queries, and printing the results. Specific query topics include displaying only selected fields; using character data in criteria; using wildcards; using numeric data in criteria; using various comparison operators; and creating compound criteria. Other related topics include sorting, joining tables, and restricting records in a join. Students also use calculated fields, statistics, and grouping.

Project 3 – Maintaining a Database Using the Design and Update Features of Access In Project 3, students learn the crucial skills involved in maintaining a database. Topics include using Datasheet view and Form view to add new records, to change existing records, and to delete records; and to locate and filter records. Students also learn the processes of changing the structure of a table; adding additional fields;

changing characteristics of existing fields; creating a variety of validation rules; and specifying referential integrity. Students perform mass changes and deletions using queries, create single-field and multiple-field indexes, and use subdatasheets to view related data.

Web Feature – Publishing to the Internet Using Data Access Pages In this Web Feature, students learn to create a data access page to enable users to access the data in a database via the Internet. Topics include creating a data access page using the Page Wizard; previewing a data access page from within Access 2002; and using a data access page.

Microsoft PowerPoint 2002

Project 1 – Using a Design Template and Text Slide Layout to Create a Presentation In Project 1, students are introduced to PowerPoint terminology, the PowerPoint window, and the basics of creating a bulleted list presentation. Topics include choosing a design template by using a task pane; creating a title slide and text slides; changing the font size and font style; ending a slide show with a black slide; saving a presentation; viewing the slides in a presentation; checking a presentation for spelling errors; printing copies of the slides; and using the PowerPoint Help system.

Project 2 – Using the Outline Tab and Clip Art to Create a Slide Show In Project 2, students create a presentation from an outline, insert clip art, and add animation effects. Topics include creating a slide presentation by indenting paragraphs on the Outline tab; changing slide layouts; inserting clip art; changing clip art size; adding an animation scheme; animating clip art; running an animated slide show; printing audience handouts from an outline; and e-mailing a slide show from within PowerPoint.

Web Feature – Creating a Presentation on the Web Using PowerPoint In this Web Feature, students are introduced to saving a presentation as a Web page. Topics include saving an existing PowerPoint presentation as an HTML file; viewing the presentation as a Web page; editing a Web page through a browser; and viewing the editing changes.

Schedule and Contact Management Using Microsoft Outlook 2002

In this project, students discover the benefits of personal information management systems by using Outlook to create a schedule of classes and extracurricular activities. Students learn how to enter both one-time and recurring appointments and events. Topics include starting and quitting the Calendar and Contacts folders; generating and managing daily, weekly, and monthly schedules; printing and saving a calendar; generating a list of contacts; creating tasks using the TaskPad; printing tasks; and creating, importing, and exporting personal subfolders.

Integrating Microsoft Office XP Applications and the World Wide Web

In this project, students are introduced to the seamless partnership of the Microsoft Office XP applications, which allows the sharing of information among Word, Excel, Access, PowerPoint, Outlook, and the World Wide Web. Topics include embedding an Excel chart into a Word document; creating a Web site home page from a Word document; creating a Web page from a PowerPoint presentation; creating a data access page Web page from an Access database; and creating hyperlinks from the home page created in Word to the Web pages created in PowerPoint and Access, as well as adding an e-mail link.

Appendices

This book includes five appendices. Appendix A presents a detailed step-by-step introduction to the Microsoft Office XP Help system. Appendix B describes how to use the speech and handwriting recognition of Office XP. Appendix C explains how to publish Office Web pages to a Web server. Appendix D shows students how to reset the menus and toolbars. Appendix E introduces students to the Microsoft Office User Specialist (MOUS) Certification program.

Microsoft Office XP Quick Reference Summary

This book concludes with a detailed Quick Reference Summary. In the Microsoft Office XP applications, you can accomplish a task in a number of ways, such as using the mouse, menu, shortcut menu, and keyboard. The Quick Reference Summary provides a quick reference to each task presented in this textbook.

End-of-Project Student Activities

A notable strength of the Shelly Cashman Series *Microsoft Office XP* books is the extensive student activities at the end of each project. Well-structured student activities can make the difference between students merely participating in a class and students retaining the information they learn. The activities in the Shelly Cashman Series *Microsoft Office XP* books include the following.

- What You Should Know A listing of the tasks completed within a project together with the pages on which the step-by-step, screen-by-screen explanations appear. This section provides a perfect study review for students.
- Learn It Online Every project features a Learn It Online page comprised of ten exercises. These exercises utilize the Web to offer project-related reinforcement activities that will help students gain confidence in their Office XP abilities. These exercises include True/False, Multiple Choice, Short Answer, Flash Cards, Practice Test, Learning Games, Tips and Tricks, Newsgroup usage, Expanding Your Horizons, and Search Sleuth.

- Apply Your Knowledge This exercise usually requires students to open and manipulate a file on the Data Disk. To obtain a copy of the Data Disk, follow the instructions on the inside back cover of this textbook.
- In the Lab Three in-depth assignments per project require students to apply the knowledge gained in the project to solve problems on a computer.
- Cases and Places Up to seven unique case studies that require students to apply their knowledge to real-world situations.

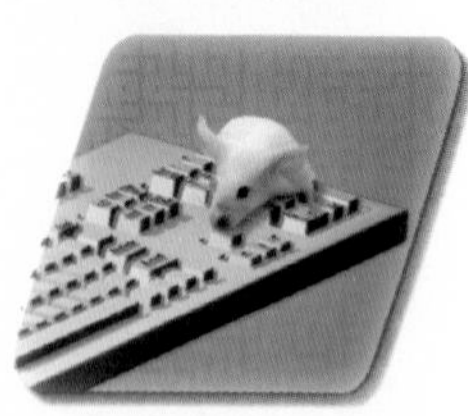

Shelly Cashman Series Teaching Tools

The three basic ancillaries that accompany this textbook are: Teaching Tools (ISBN 0-7895-6323-1), Course Presenter (ISBN 0-7895-6466-1), and MyCourse.com. These ancillaries are available to adopters through your Course Technology representative or by calling one of the following telephone numbers: Colleges and Universities, 1-800-648-7450; High Schools, 1-800-824-5179; Private Career Colleges, 1-800-477-3692; Canada, 1-800-268-2222; and Corporations and Government Agencies, 1-800-340-7450.

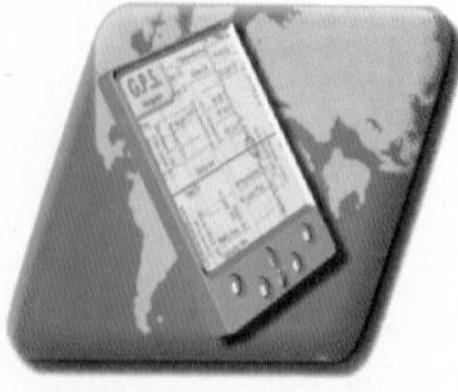

Teaching Tools

The Teaching Tools for this textbook include both teaching and testing aids. The contents of the Teaching Tools CD-ROM are listed below.

- Instructor's Manual The Instructor's Manual is made up of Microsoft Word files. The files include lecture notes, solutions to laboratory assignments, and a large test bank. The files allow you to modify the lecture notes or generate quizzes and exams from the test bank using your own word processing software. Where appropriate, solutions to laboratory assignments are embedded as icons in the files. When an icon appears, double-click it and the application will start and the solution will display on the screen. The Instructor's Manual includes the following for each project: project objectives; project overview; detailed lesson plans with page number references; teacher notes and activities; answers to the end-of-project exercises; a test bank of 110 questions for every project (25 multiple-choice, 50 true/false, and 35 fill-in-the-blank) with page number references; and transparency references. The transparencies are available through the Figures in the Book. The test bank questions are the same as in ExamView and Course Test Manager. Thus, you can print a copy of the project test bank and use the printout to select your questions in ExamView or Course Test Manager.
- Figures in the Book Illustrations for every screen and table in the textbook are available in electronic form. Use this ancillary to present a slide show in lecture or to print transparencies for use in lecture with an overhead projector. If you have a personal computer and LCD device, this ancillary can be an effective tool for presenting lectures.
- ExamView ExamView is a state-of-the-art test builder that is easy to use. ExamView enables you quickly to create printed tests, Internet tests, and computer (LAN-based) tests. You can enter your own test questions or use the test bank that accompanies ExamView. The test bank is the same as the one described in the Instructor's Manual section. Instructors who want to continue to use our earlier generation test builder, Course Test Manager, rather than ExamView, can call Customer Service at 1-800-648-7450 for a copy of the Course Test Manager database for this book.
- Course Syllabus Any instructor who has been assigned a course at the last minute knows how difficult it is to come up with a course syllabus. For this reason, sample syllabi are included that can be customized easily to a course.
- Lecture Success System Lecture Success System files are for use with the application software, a personal computer, and projection device to explain and illustrate the step-by-step, screen-by-screen development of a project in the textbook without entering large amounts of data.
- Instructor's Lab Solutions Solutions and required files for all the In the Lab assignments at the end of each project are available. Solutions also are available for any Cases and Places assignment that supplies data.
- Lab Tests/Test Outs Tests that parallel the In the Lab assignments are supplied for the purpose of testing students in the laboratory on the material covered in the project or testing students out of the course.
- Project Reinforcement True/false, multiple choice, and short answer questions help students gain confidence.
- Student Files All the files that are required by students to complete the Apply Your Knowledge exercises are included.
- Interactive Labs Eighteen completely updated, hands-on Interactive Labs that take students from ten to fifteen minutes each to step through help solidify and reinforce mouse and keyboard usage and computer concepts. Student assessment is available.

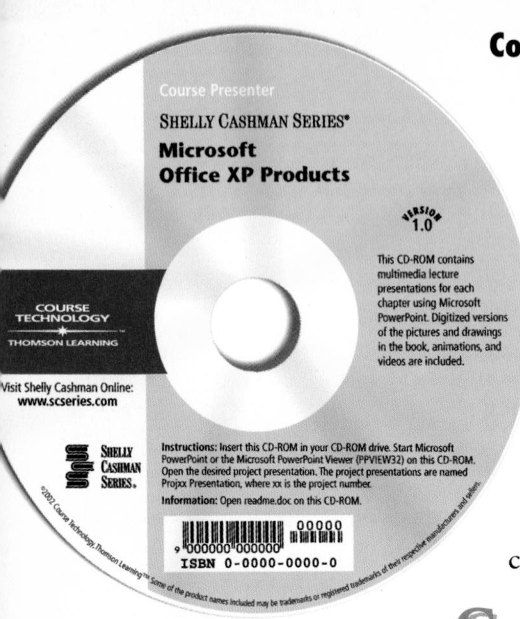

Course Presenter

Course Presenter is a CD-ROM-based multimedia lecture presentation system that provides PowerPoint slides for each project. Presentations are based on the projects' objectives. Use this presentation system to present well-organized lectures that are both interesting and knowledge-based. Course Presenter provides consistent coverage at schools that use multiple lecturers in their applications courses.

MyCourse.com

MyCourse.com offers instructors and students an opportunity to supplement classroom learning with additional course content. You can use MyCourse.com to expand on traditional learning by accessing and completing readings, tests, and other assignments through the customized, comprehensive Web site. For additional information, visit mycourse.com and click the Help button.

Supplements

Two salable supplements that help reinforce the concepts presented can be used in combination with this book.

Workbook

The highly popular *Workbook for Microsoft Office XP: Introductory Concepts and Techniques* (ISBN 0-7895-4690-6) includes a variety of activities that help students recall, review, and master the concepts presented. The *Workbook* complements the end-of-project material with a guided project outline; a self-test consisting of true/false, multiple-choice, short answer, and matching questions; and activities calculated to help students develop a deeper understanding of the information presented.

SAM XP

SAM XP is a powerful skills-based testing and reporting tool that measures your students' proficiency in Microsoft Office applications through real-world, performance-based questions.

Shelly Cashman Online

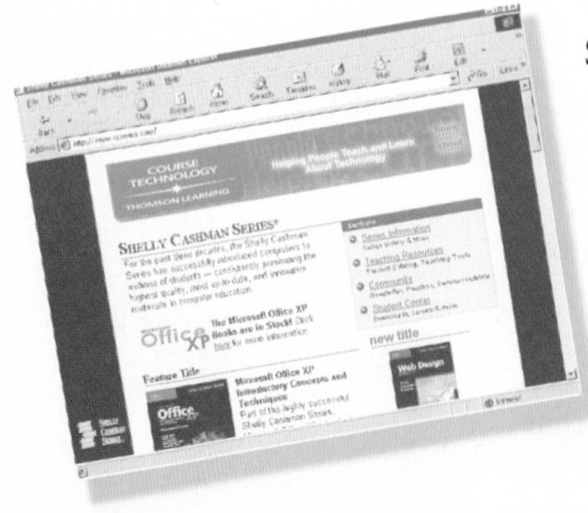

Shelly Cashman Online is a World Wide Web service available to instructors and students of computer education. Visit Shelly Cashman Online at scseries.com. Shelly Cashman Online is divided into four areas:

- **Series Information** Information on the Shelly Cashman Series products.
- **Teaching Resources** This area includes password-protected data, Series information, teaching tools, and certification and electronic aids.
- **Community** Opportunities to discuss your course and your ideas with instructors in your field and with the Shelly Cashman Series team.
- **Student Center** Dedicated to students learning about computers with Shelly Cashman Series textbooks and software. This area includes cool links and much more.

Acknowledgments

The Shelly Cashman Series would not be the leading computer education series without the contributions of outstanding publishing professionals. First, and foremost, among them is Becky Herrington, director of production and designer. She is the heart and soul of the Shelly Cashman Series, and it is only through her leadership, dedication, and tireless efforts that superior products are made possible.

Under Becky's direction, the following individuals made significant contributions to these books: Doug Cowley, production manager; Ginny Harvey, series specialist and developmental editor; Ken Russo, senior Web and graphic designer; Mike Bodnar, associate production manager; Mark Norton, Web designer; Betty Hopkins and Richard Herrera, interior design; Michelle French, Christy Otten, Kellee LaVars, Stephanie Nance, Chris Schneider, Sharon Lee Nelson, Sarah Boger, Amanda Lotter, Michael Greco, and Ryan Ung, graphic artists; Jeanne Black and Betty Hopkins, QuarkXPress compositors; Lyn Markowicz, Nancy Lamm, Kim Kosmatka, Pam Baxter, Eva Kandarpa, Ellana Russo, and Marilyn Martin, copy editors/proofreaders; Cristina Haley, proofreader/indexer; Sarah Evertson of Image Quest, photo researcher; Ginny Harvey, Rich Hansberger, Kim Clark, and Nancy Smith, contributing writers; and Richard Herrera, cover art.

Finally, we would like to thank Richard Keaveny, associate publisher; Cheryl Ouellette, managing editor; Jim Quasney, series consulting editor; Alexandra Arnold, product manager; Erin Runyon, associate product manager; Francis Schurgot and Marc Ouellette, Web product managers; Rachel VanKirk, marketing manager; and Reed Cotter, editorial assistant.

Gary B. Shelly
Thomas J. Cashman
Misty E. Vermaat

Shelly Cashman Series – Traditionally Bound Textbooks

The Shelly Cashman Series presents the following computer subjects in a variety of traditionally bound textbooks. For more information, see your Course Technology representative or call 1-800-648-7450. For Shelly Cashman Series information, visit Shelly Cashman Online at **scseries.com**

COMPUTERS	
Computers	Discovering Computers 2002: Concepts for a Digital World, Web Enhanced, Complete Edition Discovering Computers 2002: Concepts for a Digital World, Web Enhanced, Introductory Edition Discovering Computers 2002: Concepts for a Digital World, Web Enhanced, Brief Edition Teachers Discovering Computers: Integrating Technology in the Classroom Exploring Computers: A Record of Discovery 4e Study Guide for Discovering Computers 2002: Concepts for a Digital World, Web Enhanced Essential Introduction to Computers 4e (32-page)
WINDOWS APPLICATIONS	
Microsoft Office	Microsoft Office XP: Essential Concepts and Techniques (5 projects) Microsoft Office XP: Brief Concepts and Techniques (9 projects) Microsoft Office XP: Introductory Concepts and Techniques (15 projects) Microsoft Office XP: Advanced Concepts and Techniques (11 projects) Microsoft Office XP: Post Advanced Concepts and Techniques (11 projects) Microsoft Office 2000: Essential Concepts and Techniques (5 projects) Microsoft Office 2000: Brief Concepts and Techniques (9 projects) Microsoft Office 2000: Introductory Concepts and Techniques, Enhanced Edition (15 projects) Microsoft Office 2000: Advanced Concepts and Techniques (11 projects) Microsoft Office 2000: Post Advanced Concepts and Techniques (11 projects)
Integration	Integrating Microsoft Office XP Applications and the World Wide Web: Essential Concepts and Techniques
PIM	Microsoft Outlook 2002: Essential Concepts and Techniques
Microsoft Works	Microsoft Works 6: Complete Concepts and Techniques[1] • Microsoft Works 2000: Complete Concepts and Techniques[1] • Microsoft Works 4.5[1]
Microsoft Windows	Microsoft Windows 2000: Complete Concepts and Techniques (6 projects)[2] Microsoft Windows 2000: Brief Concepts and Techniques (2 projects) Microsoft Windows 98: Essential Concepts and Techniques (2 projects) Microsoft Windows 98: Complete Concepts and Techniques (6 projects)[2] Introduction to Microsoft Windows NT Workstation 4 Microsoft Windows 95: Complete Concepts and Techniques[1]
Word Processing	Microsoft Word 2002[2] • Microsoft Word 2000[2] • Microsoft Word 97[1] • Microsoft Word 7[1]
Spreadsheets	Microsoft Excel 2002[2] • Microsoft Excel 2000[2] • Microsoft Excel 97[1] • Microsoft Excel 7[1] Microsoft Excel 5[1]
Database	Microsoft Access 2002[2] • Microsoft Access 2000[2] • Microsoft Access 97[1] • Microsoft Access 7[1]
Presentation Graphics	Microsoft PowerPoint 2002[2] • Microsoft PowerPoint 2000[2] • Microsoft PowerPoint 97[1] Microsoft PowerPoint 7[1]
Desktop Publishing	Microsoft Publisher 2002[1] • Microsoft Publisher 2000[1]
PROGRAMMING	
Programming	Microsoft Visual Basic 6: Complete Concepts and Techniques[1] • Programming in QBasic Java Programming: Complete Concepts and Techniques[1] • Structured COBOL Programming 2e
INTERNET	
Browser	Microsoft Internet Explorer 5: An Introduction • Microsoft Internet Explorer 4: An Introduction Netscape Navigator 6: An Introduction • Netscape Navigator 4: An Introduction
Web Page Creation and Design	Web Design: Introductory Concepts and Techniques • HTML: Complete Concepts and Techniques[1] Microsoft FrontPage 2002: Essential Concepts and Techniques • Microsoft FrontPage 2002[2] Microsoft FrontPage 2000[1] • JavaScript: Complete Concepts and Techniques[1]
SYSTEMS ANALYSIS	
Systems Analysis	Systems Analysis and Design 4e
DATA COMMUNICATIONS	
Data Communications	Business Data Communications: Introductory Concepts and Techniques 3e

[1]Also available as an Introductory Edition, which is a shortened version of the complete book
[2]Also available as an Introductory Edition, which is a shortened version of the complete book and also as a Comprehensive Edition, which is an extended version of the complete book

Essential INTRODUCTION TO COMPUTERS

and How to Purchase, Install, and Maintain a Personal Computer

OBJECTIVES

After completing this material, you will be able to:

- Define the term computer and discuss the four basic computer operations: input, processing, output, and storage
- Define data and information
- Explain the principal components of the computer and their use
- Describe the use and handling of floppy disks and hard disks
- Discuss computer software and explain the difference between system software and application software
- Identify several types of personal computer application software
- Discuss computer communications channels and equipment and the Internet and World Wide Web
- Explain how to purchase, install, and maintain a personal computer, a notebook computer, and a handheld computer
- Define e-commerce

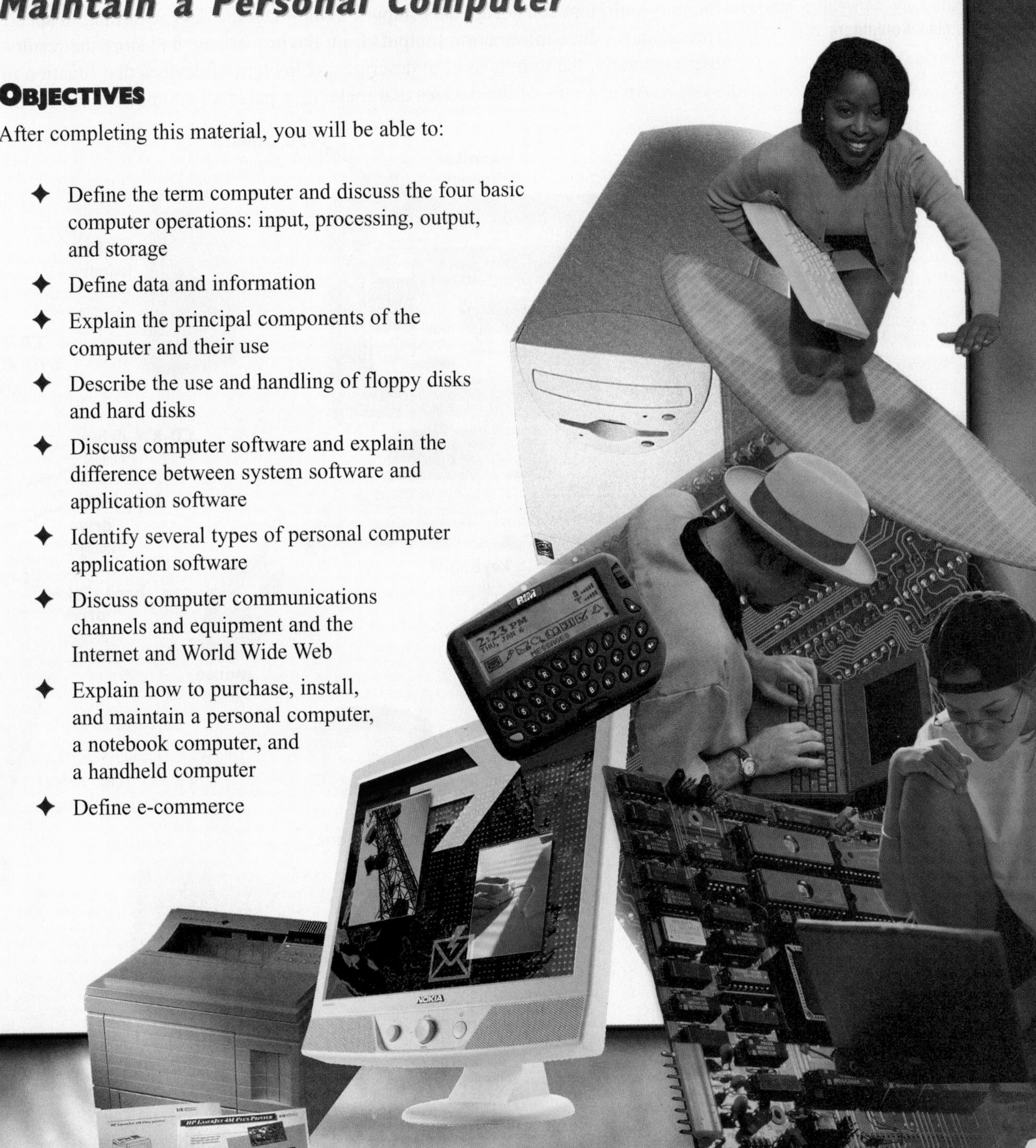

Computers are everywhere... at home, at work, and at school. Every day, computers impact how individuals work and how they live. The use of personal computers continues to increase and has made computing available to almost anyone. In addition, advances in communications technology allow people to use personal computers to access and send information easily and quickly to other computers and computer users. At home, at work, and in the field, computers are helping people to do their work faster, more accurately, and in some cases, in ways that previously would not have been possible.

Web Link

For more information on computers, visit the Introduction to Computers WEB LINK page (scsite.com/ic4/weblink.htm) and click **Computers**.

What Is a Computer?

The most obvious question related to understanding computers is, *What is a computer?* A **computer** is an electronic device, operating under the control of instructions stored in its own memory unit, that can accept data (input), manipulate the data according to specified rules (process), produce information (output) from the processing, and store the results for future use. Generally, the term is used to describe a collection of devices that function together as a system. An example of the devices that make up a personal computer is shown in Figure 1.

Figure 1
Devices that comprise a personal computer.

What Does a Computer Do?

Whether small or large, computers can perform four general operations. These operations comprise the **information processing cycle** and are input, process, output, and storage. Collectively, these operations describe the procedures a computer performs to process data into information and store it for future use.

All computer processing requires **data**. Data is a collection of raw facts, figures, and symbols, such as numbers, words, images, video, and sounds, given to a computer during the input operation. Computers manipulate data to create information. **Information** is data that is organized, meaningful, and useful. During the output operation, the information that has been created is put into some form, such as a printed report, a paycheck, an invoice, a Web page, or spoken words. The information also can be placed in computer storage for future use.

These operations occur through the use of electronic circuits contained on small silicon chips inside the computer (Figure 2). Because these electronic circuits rarely fail and the data flows along these circuits at close to the speed of light, processing can be accomplished in billionths of a second.

People who use the computer directly or use the information it provides are called **computer users**, **end users**, or sometimes, just **users**.

Web Link

For more information on information, visit the Introduction to Computers WEB LINK page (scsite.com/ic4/weblink.htm) and click **Information**.

Figure 2
Inside a computer are chips and other electronic components that process data in billionths of a second.

Why Is a Computer so Powerful?

A computer derives its power from its capability to perform the information processing cycle with amazing speed, reliability (low failure rate), and accuracy; its capacity to store huge amounts of data and information; and its ability to communicate with other computers.

How Does a Computer Know What to Do?

For a computer to perform operations, it must be given a detailed set of instructions that tells it exactly what to do. These instructions are called a **computer program**, or **software**. Before processing for a specific job begins, the computer program corresponding to that job is stored in the computer. Once the program is stored, the computer can begin to operate by executing the program's first instruction. The computer executes one program instruction after another until the job is complete.

Web Link

For more information on computer programs, visit the Introduction to Computers WEB LINK page (scsite.com/ic4/weblink.htm) and click **Computer Programs**.

What Are the Components of a Computer?

To understand how computers process data into information, you need to examine the primary components of the computer. The five primary components of a computer are input devices, the central processing unit (control unit and arithmetic/logic unit), memory, output devices, and storage devices as shown in Figure 3. The next five sections describe these primary components.

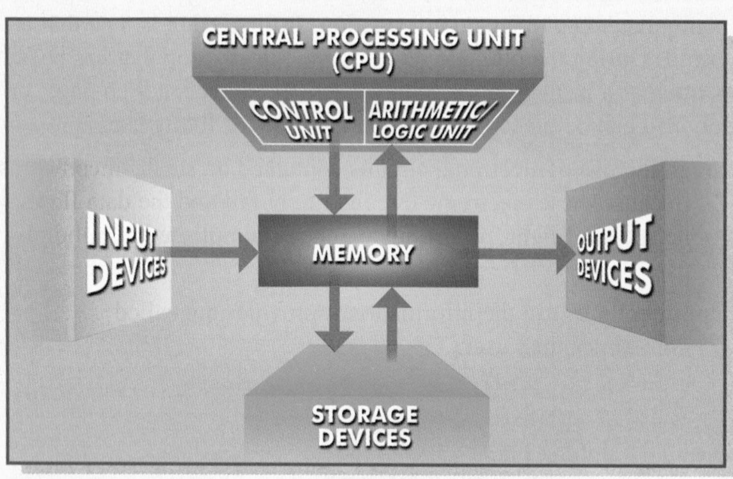

Figure 3
A computer is composed of input devices through which data is entered into memory, the central processing unit (CPU) that processes data stored in memory, output devices through which the results of the processing are made available, and storage devices that store data for future processing.

Web Link
For more information on input devices, visit the Introduction to Computers WEB LINK page (scsite.com/ic4/weblink.htm) and click **Input Devices**.

Input Devices

An **input device** is any hardware component that allows you to enter data, programs, commands, and user responses into a computer. Depending on your particular application and requirement, the input device you use may vary. Popular input devices include the keyboard, mouse, digital camera, scanner, and microphone. The two primary input devices used are the keyboard and the mouse. This section discusses both of these input devices.

The Keyboard

A keyboard is an input device that contains keys you press to enter data into the computer. A desktop computer keyboard (Figure 4) typically has 101 to 105 keys. Keyboards for smaller computers, such as notebooks, contain fewer keys. A computer keyboard includes keys that allow you to type letters of the alphabet, numbers, spaces, punctuation marks, and other symbols such as the dollar sign ($) and asterisk (*). A keyboard also contains other keys that allow you to enter data and instructions into the computer.

Figure 5 shows an onscreen keyboard available with Microsoft Office XP. You use a mouse to select keys on an onscreen keyboard.

Figure 4
A desktop computer keyboard. You type using keys in the typing area and on the numeric keypad.

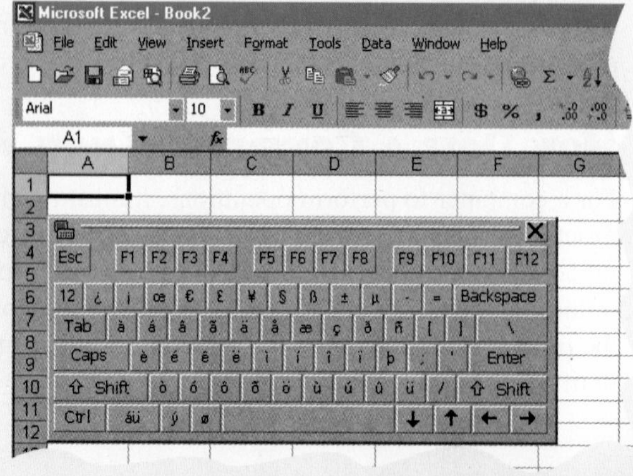

Figure 5
The Microsoft Office XP onscreen keyboard allows you to enter numbers and text using a mouse.

Most handheld computers (left in Figure 6) use an onscreen keyboard. With handheld computers, you use a stylus to select keys on the onscreen keyboard. A notebook computer (right in Figure 6) has the keyboard built into the top of the unit.

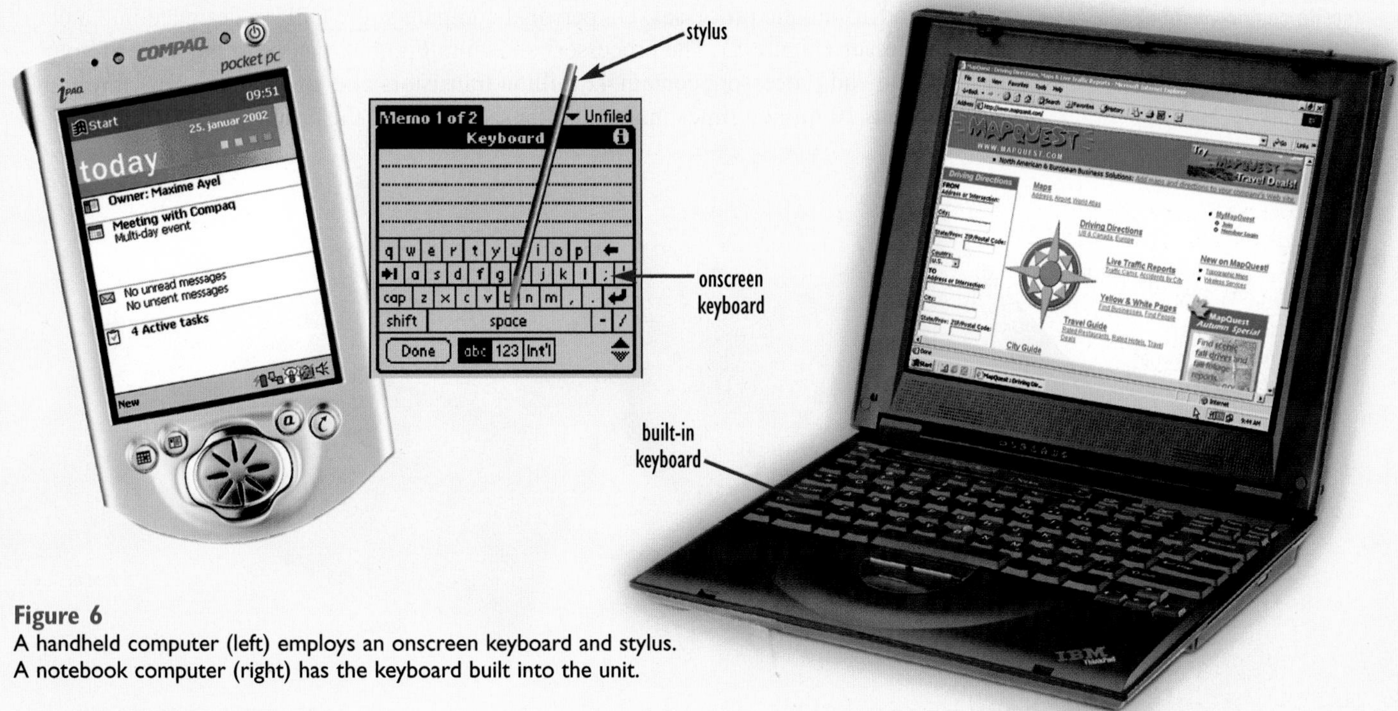

Figure 6
A handheld computer (left) employs an onscreen keyboard and stylus. A notebook computer (right) has the keyboard built into the unit.

The Mouse

A **mouse** (Figure 7) is a pointing device that fits comfortably under the palm of your hand. With a mouse, you control the movement of the pointer, often called the mouse pointer, on the screen and make selections from the screen. A mouse has one to five buttons. The bottom of a mouse is flat and contains a mechanism that detects movement of the mouse.

Notebook computers come with a pointing device built into the keyboard so that you can select items on the screen without requiring additional desktop space.

Web Link
For more information on a mouse, visit the Introduction to Computers WEB LINK page (scsite.com/ic4/weblink.htm) and click **Mouse**.

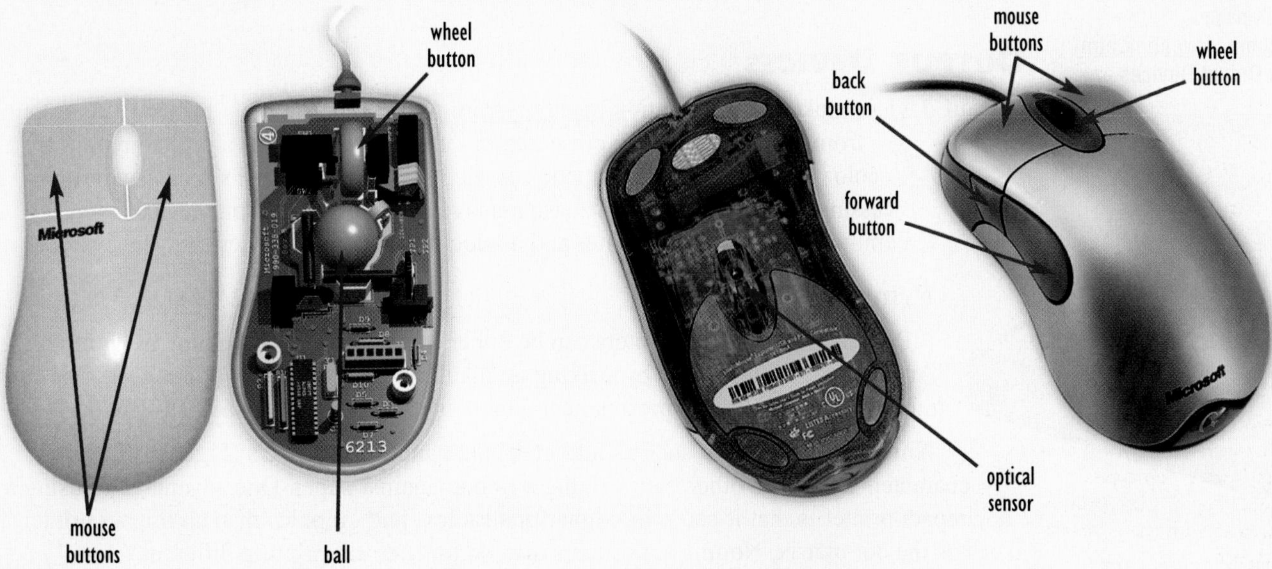

Figure 7
A mechanical mouse (left) contains a small ball. An optical mouse (right) uses an optical sensor, rather than a ball.

Web Link

For more information on CPUs, visit the Introduction to Computers WEB LINK page (scsite.com/ic4/weblink.htm) and click **CPUs**.

The Central Processing Unit

The **central processing unit** (**CPU**) contains the electronic circuits that cause processing to occur. The CPU is made up of the **control unit** and **arithmetic/logic unit** (see Figure 3 on page COM4). The control unit interprets the instructions. The arithmetic/logic unit performs the logical and arithmetic processes. On personal computers, the CPU is designed into a chip called a **processor** (Figure 8). The processors shown in Figure 8 can fit in the palm of your hand. The high-end processors contain 42 million transistors and are capable of performing some operations 10 million times in a tenth of a second, or in the time it takes to blink your eye.

Figure 8
Basic personal computers have a Celeron™ or Duron™ processor. Higher-performance personal computers use Athlon™ and Pentium® processors.

Memory

Memory, also called **random access memory**, or **RAM**, consists of electronic components that store data including numbers, letters of the alphabet, graphics, and sound. Any data to be processed must be stored in memory. The amount of memory in computers typically is measured in kilobytes or megabytes. One **kilobyte** (**K or KB**) equals approximately 1,000 memory locations and one **megabyte** (**M or MB**) equals approximately one million memory locations. A **memory location**, or **byte**, usually stores one character. Therefore, a computer with 96 MB of memory can store approximately 96 million characters. One megabyte can hold approximately 500 pages of text information.

Web Link

For more information on output devices, visit the Introduction to Computers WEB LINK page (scsite.com/ic4/weblink.htm) and click **Output Devices**.

Output Devices

Output devices make the information resulting from processing available for use. The output from computers can be presented in many forms, such as a printed report or color graphics. When a computer is used for processing tasks such as word processing, spreadsheets, or database management, the two output devices more commonly used are the printer and a television-like display device.

Figure 9
Dot matrix printers are capable of handling wide paper and printing multipart forms.

Printers

Printers used with computers can be either impact printers or nonimpact printers. An **impact printer** prints by striking an inked ribbon against the paper. One type of impact printer used with personal computers is the dot matrix printer (Figure 9).

Nonimpact printers, such as ink-jet printers and laser printers (Figure 10), form characters by means other than striking a ribbon against paper. One advantage of using a nonimpact printer is that it can print higher-quality text and graphics than an impact printer, such as the dot matrix. Nonimpact printers also do a better job printing different fonts (Figure 11), are quieter, and can print in color. The popular and affordable ink-jet printer forms a character or graphic by using a nozzle that sprays drops of ink onto the page.

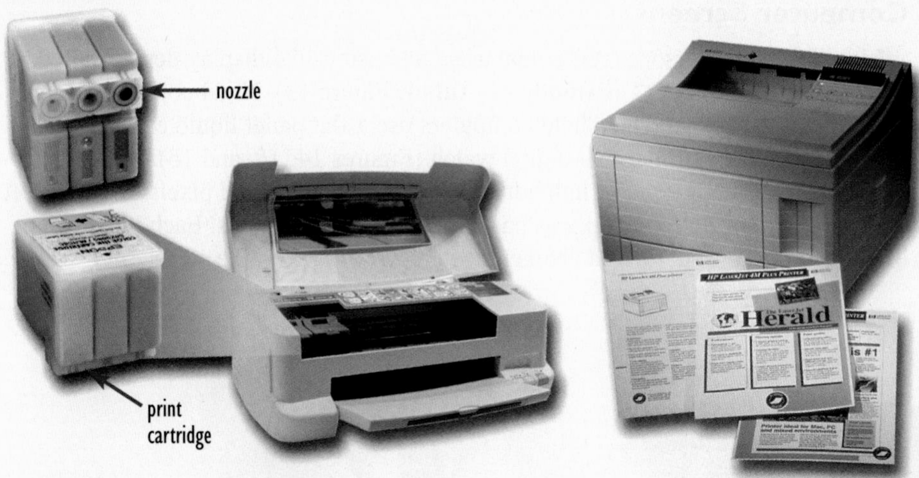

Figure 10
Two types of nonimpact printers are the ink-jet printer (left) and the laser printer (right). Nonimpact printers are excellent for printing work that includes graphics.

Ink-jet printers produce excellent images. The speed of an ink-jet printer is measured by the number of pages per minute (ppm) it can print. Most ink-jet printers print from one to eight pages per minute. Graphics and colors print at the slower rate.

Laser printers work similarly to a copying machine by converting data from the computer into a beam of light that is focused on a photoconductor drum, forming the images to be printed (Figure 12). The photoconductor attracts particles of toner that are fused by heat and pressure onto paper to produce an image. Laser printers produce high-quality black-and-white or color output and are used for applications that combine text and graphics such as desktop publishing. Laser printers for personal computers can cost from several hundred dollars to several thousand dollars. The more expensive the laser printer, the more pages it can print per minute.

Figure 11
A variety of typefaces (fonts) are commonly available on personal computers.

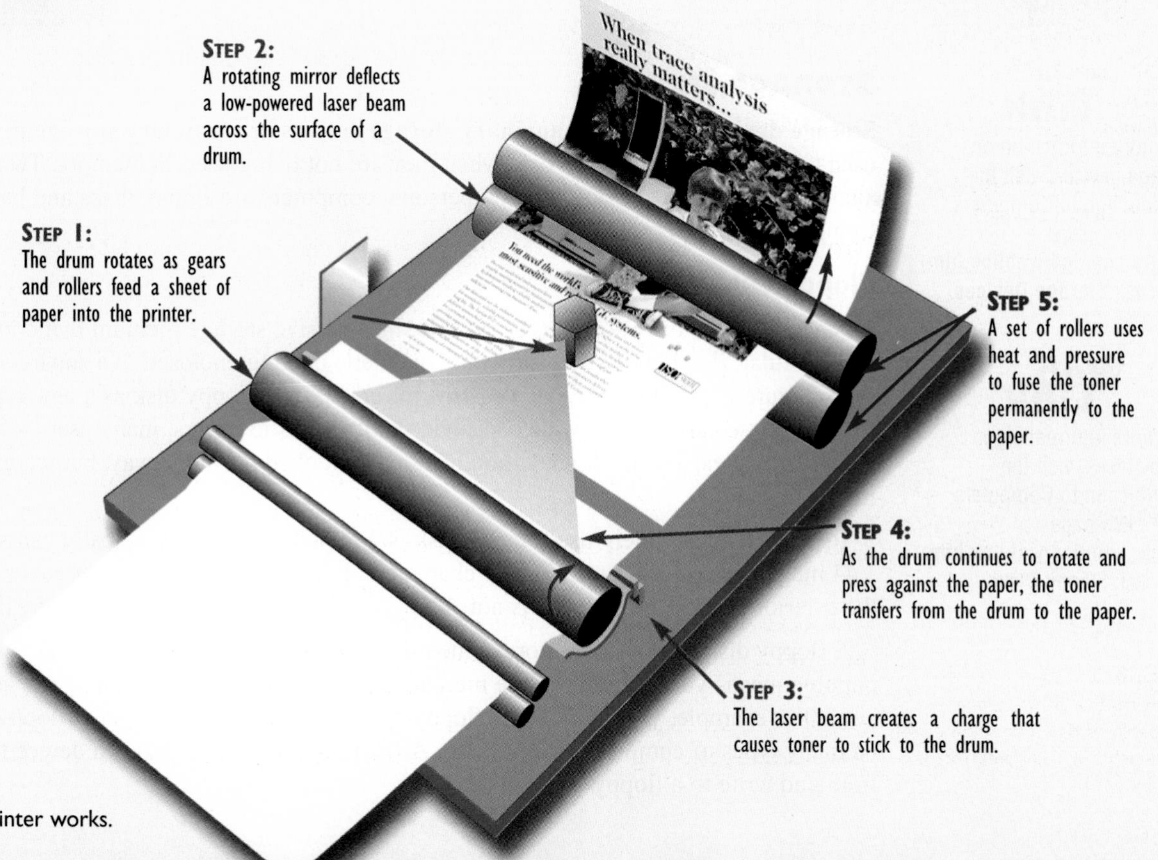

STEP 2:
A rotating mirror deflects a low-powered laser beam across the surface of a drum.
STEP 1:
The drum rotates as gears and rollers feed a sheet of paper into the printer.
STEP 5:
A set of rollers uses heat and pressure to fuse the toner permanently to the paper.
STEP 4:
As the drum continues to rotate and press against the paper, the toner transfers from the drum to the paper.
STEP 3:
The laser beam creates a charge that causes toner to stick to the drum.
When trace analysis really matters...

Figure 12
How a laser printer works.

Computer Screens

Figure 13
The core of many desktop monitors is a cathode ray tube (CRT).

Most full-sized personal computers use a television-like display device called a **screen**, **monitor**, or **CRT** (**cathode ray tube**) (Figure 13). Notebook computers, flat screen displays, and handheld computers use a flat panel liquid crystal display (LCD) technology similar to a digital watch (Figures 14, 15, and 16). The surface of the screen is composed of individual picture elements called pixels. A screen set to a resolution of 800 x 600 pixels has a total of 480,000 pixels. Each pixel can be illuminated to form parts of a character or graphic shape on the screen.

Figure 14
Most notebook computers use a liquid crystal display (LCD) display because it is lightweight and thin.

Figure 15
An LCD monitor is much thinner than a CRT monitor.

Figure 16
Handheld computers use LCD displays.

Web Link
For more information on storage devices, visit the Introduction to Computers WEB LINK page (scsite.com/ic4/weblink.htm) and click **Storage Devices**.

Storage Devices

Storage devices, also called **auxiliary storage** devices or **secondary storage devices**, are used to store instructions and data when they are not being used in memory. Two types of auxiliary storage more often used on personal computers are floppy disks and hard disks. Compact discs also are common.

Web Link
For more information on floppy disks, visit the Introduction to Computers WEB LINK page (scsite.com/ic4/weblink.htm) and click **Floppy Disks**.

Floppy Disks

A **floppy disk**, or **diskette**, is a portable, inexpensive storage medium that consists of a thin, circular, flexible plastic disk with a magnetic coating enclosed in a square-shaped plastic shell (Figure 17). In the early 1970s, IBM introduced the floppy disk as a new type of storage. Because these early 8-inch wide disks had flexible plastic covers, many users referred to them as floppies. The next generation of floppies looked the same way, but were only 5.25 inches wide.

Today, the most widely used floppy disk is 3.5 inches wide and typically can store up to 1.44 megabytes of data or 1,457,664 characters. It has a rigid plastic outer cover. Although the exterior of the 3.5-inch disk is not floppy, users still refer to them as floppy disks.

A floppy disk is a portable storage medium. When discussing a storage medium, the term portable means you can remove the medium from one computer and carry it to another computer. For example, you can insert a floppy disk into and remove it from a floppy disk drive on many types of computers (Figure 18). A floppy disk drive (FDD) is a device that can read from and write to a floppy disk.

A floppy disk is a type of a magnetic disk, which means it uses magnetic patterns to store items such as data, instructions, and information on the disk's surface. Most magnetic disks are read/write storage media; that is, you can access (read) data from and place (write) data on a magnetic disk any number of times, just as you can with an audiocassette tape. Most floppy disks that you purchase are already formatted. If they are not formatted, then before you can write on a new floppy disk, it must be formatted.

Formatting is the process of preparing a disk (floppy disk or hard disk) for reading and writing by organizing the disk into storage locations called tracks and sectors (Figure 19). A **track** is a narrow recording band that forms a full circle on the surface of the disk. The disk's storage locations then are divided into pie-shaped sections, which break the tracks into small arcs called sectors. A **sector** is capable of holding 512 bytes of data. A typical floppy disk stores data on both sides and has 80 tracks on each side of the recording surface with 18 sectors per track.

Data stored in sectors on a floppy disk must be retrieved and placed into memory to be processed. The time required to access and retrieve data is called the **access time**. The access time for floppy disks varies from about 175 milliseconds (one millisecond equals 1/1000 of a second) to approximately 300 milliseconds. On average, data stored in a single sector on a floppy disk can be retrieved in approximately 1/15 to 1/3 of a second.

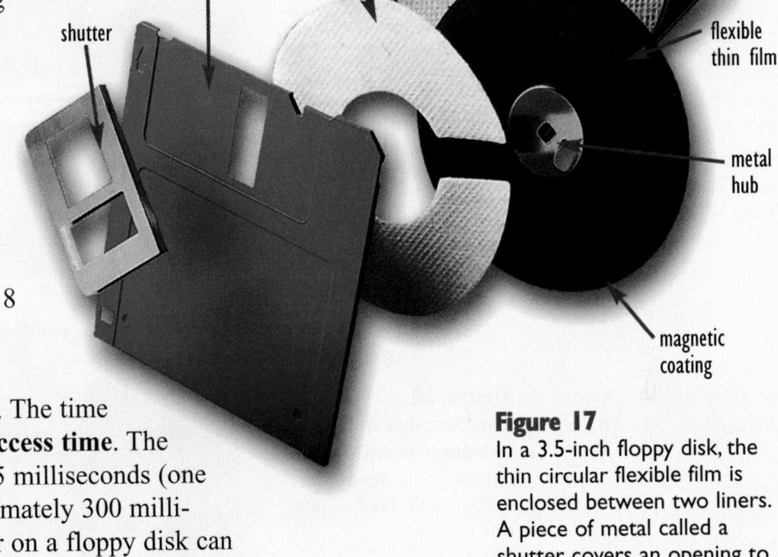

Figure 17
In a 3.5-inch floppy disk, the thin circular flexible film is enclosed between two liners. A piece of metal called a shutter covers an opening to the recording surface in the rigid plastic shell.

Figure 18
On a computer, you insert and remove a floppy disk from a floppy disk drive.

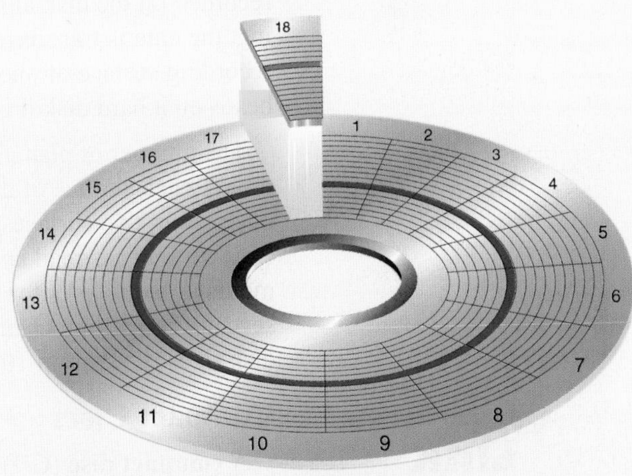

Figure 19
A track is a narrow recording band that forms a full circle on the surface of a disk. The disk's storage locations then are divided into pie-shaped sections, which break the tracks into small arcs called sectors.

Web Link

For more information on hard disks, visit the Introduction to Computers WEB LINK page (scsite.com/ic4/weblink.htm) and click **Hard Disks**.

Hard Disks

Another form of auxiliary storage is a **hard disk**. A hard disk consists of one or more rigid metal platters coated with a metal oxide material that allows data to be recorded magnetically on the surface of the platters (Figure 20). Although hard disks are available in removable cartridge form, most disks cannot be removed from the computer. As with floppy disks, the data is recorded on hard disks on a series of tracks. The tracks are divided into sectors when the disk is formatted.

Figure 20
The hard disk in a desktop computer normally resides permanently inside the system unit. That is, it is not portable.

The hard disk platters spin at a high rate of speed, typically 5,400 to 7,200 revolutions per minute. When reading data from the disk, the read head senses the magnetic spots that are recorded on the disk along the various tracks and transfers that data to memory. When writing, the data is transferred from memory and is stored as magnetic spots on the tracks on the recording surface of one or more of the disk platters. When reading or writing, the read/write heads on a hard disk drive do not actually touch the surface of the disk.

The number of platters permanently mounted on the spindle of a hard disk varies. On most drives, each surface of the platter can be used to store data. Thus, if a hard disk drive uses one platter, two surfaces are available for data. If the drive uses two platters, four sets of read/write heads read and record data from the four surfaces. Storage capacities of internally mounted fixed disks for personal computers range from one billion characters to more than seventy-five billion characters. One billion bytes are called a **gigabyte (GB)**. Typical hard disk sizes range from 10 GB to 75 GB.

Web Link

For more information on compact discs, visit the Introduction to Computers WEB LINK page (scsite.com/ic4/weblink.htm) and click **Compact Discs**.

Compact Discs

A **compact disc (CD)**, also called an optical disc, is a flat, round, portable, metal storage medium that usually is 4.75 inches in diameter and less than 1/20 of an inch thick. Just about every desktop computer and notebook computer includes some type of compact disc drive installed in a drive bay. These drives read compact discs, including audio discs.

On these drives, you push a button to slide out a tray, insert your compact disc with the label side up, and then push the same button to close the tray (Figure 21). Other convenient features on most of these drives include a volume control button and a headphone jack so you can use stereo headphones to listen to audio without disturbing others nearby.

Compact discs are available in a variety of formats, including CD-ROM, CD-R, CD-RW, and DVD-ROM.

CD-ROMs

A **CD-ROM** (pronounced SEE-DEE-rom), or **compact disc read-only memory**, is a compact disc that uses the same laser technology as audio CDs for recording music. In addition to audio, a CD-ROM can contain text, graphics, and video. The manufacturer writes, or records, the contents of standard CD-ROMs. You can only read the contents of these discs. That is, you cannot erase or modify their contents — hence the name read-only.

A typical CD-ROM holds about 650 MB of data, instructions, and information. This is about 450 times more than you can store on a 3.5-inch floppy disk.

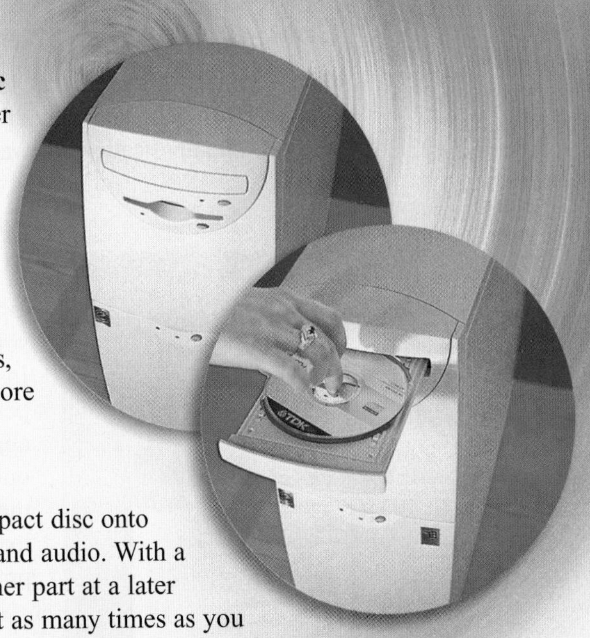

CD-R and CD-RW

A **CD-R** (**compact disc-recordable**) is a multisession compact disc onto which you can record your own items such as text, graphics, and audio. With a CD-R, you can write on part of the disc at one time and another part at a later time. Once you have recorded the CD-R, you can read from it as many times as you wish. You can write on each part only one time, and you cannot erase the disc's contents. Most CD-ROM drives can read a CD-R.

Figure 21
CD-ROM drives allow the user to access tremendous amounts of pre-recorded information — more than 600 MB of data can be stored on one CD-ROM.

A **CD-RW** (**compact disc-rewritable**) is an erasable disc you can write on multiple times. Originally called an erasable CD (CD-E), a CD-RW overcomes the major disadvantage of CD-R discs, which is that you can write on them only once. With CD-RWs, the disc acts like a floppy or hard disk, allowing you to write and rewrite data, instructions, and information onto it multiple times.

DVD-ROMs

Although CD-ROMs have huge storage capacities, even a CD-ROM is not large enough for many of today's complex programs. Some software, for example, is sold on five or more CD-ROMs. To meet these tremendous storage requirements, some software companies have moved from CD-ROMs to the larger DVD-ROM format — a technology that can be used to store large amounts of text and even videos (Figure 22). A **DVD-ROM** (**digital video disc-ROM**) is a very high capacity compact disc capable of storing from 4.7 GB to 17 GB — more than enough to hold a telephone book containing every resident in the United States.

Web Link
For more information on DVD-ROMs, visit the Introduction to Computers WEB LINK page (**scsite.com/ic4/weblink.htm**) and click **DVD-ROMs**.

Figure 22
A DVD-ROM is an extremely high-capacity disc capable of storing 4.7 GB to 17 GB.

Web Link

For more information on operating systems, visit the Introduction to Computers WEB LINK page (scsite.com/ic4/weblink.htm) and click **Operating Systems**.

COMPUTER SOFTWARE

Computer software is the key to productive use of computers. With the correct software, a computer can become a valuable tool. Software can be categorized into two types: system software and application software.

System Software

System software consists of programs to control the operations of computer equipment. An important part of system software is a set of programs called the operating system. Instructions in the **operating system** tell the computer how to perform the functions of loading, storing, and executing an application program and how to transfer data. For a computer to operate, an operating system must be stored in the computer's memory. When a computer is turned on, the operating system is loaded into the computer's memory from auxiliary storage. This process is called **booting**.

Today, most computers use an operating system that has a **graphical user interface (GUI)** that provides visual cues such as icon symbols to help the user. Each icon represents an application such as word processing, or a file or document where data is stored. Microsoft Windows (Figure 23) is a widely used graphical operating system. Apple Macintosh computers also have a graphical user interface operating system.

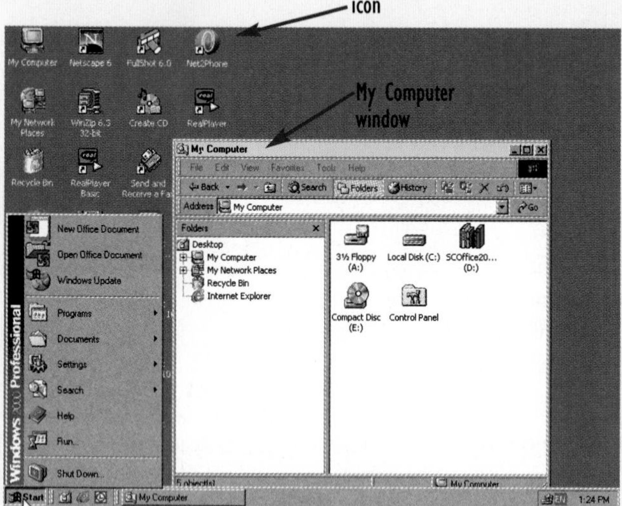

Figure 23
A graphical user interface such as Microsoft Windows makes the computer easier to use. The small pictures, or symbols, on the screen are called icons. Icons represent a program or data the user can choose. A window is a rectangular area of the screen that is used to display a program, data, and/or information.

Application Software

Application software consists of programs that tell a computer how to produce information. The different ways people use computers in their careers or in their personal lives are examples of types of application software. Business, scientific, and educational programs are all examples of application software.

Personal computer users often use application software. Some of the more commonly used applications are word processing, electronic spreadsheet, presentation graphics, database, communications, and electronic mail software. Some software packages, such as Microsoft Office, also include access to the World Wide Web as an integral part of the application.

Web Link

For more information on word processing software, visit the Introduction to Computers WEB LINK page (scsite.com/ic4/weblink.htm) and click **Word Processing Software**.

Word Processing

Word processing software (Figure 24) is used to create, edit, format, and print documents. A key advantage of word processing software is that users easily can make changes in documents, such as correcting spelling, changing margins, and adding, deleting, or relocating entire paragraphs. These changes would be difficult and time consuming to make using manual methods such as a typewriter. With a word processor, documents can be printed quickly and accurately and easily stored on a disk for future use. Word processing software is oriented toward working with text, but most word processing packages also can include numeric and graphic information.

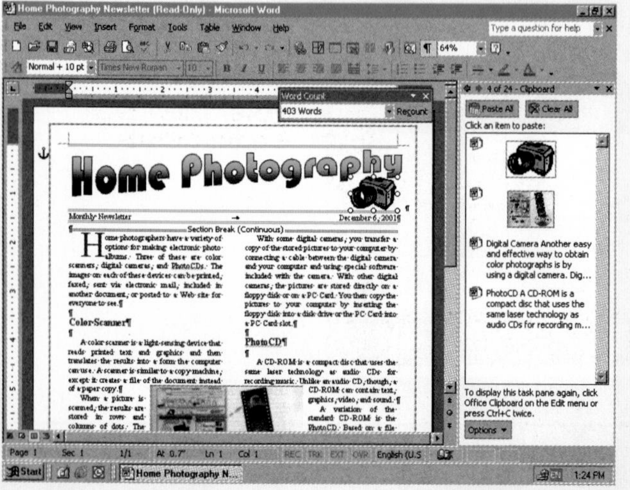

Figure 24
Word processing software is used to create letters, memos, and other documents.

Spreadsheet

Electronic spreadsheet software (Figure 25) allows the user to add, subtract, and perform user-defined calculations on rows and columns of numbers. These numbers can be changed, and the spreadsheet quickly recalculates the new results. Electronic spreadsheet software eliminates the tedious recalculations required with manual methods. Spreadsheet information frequently is converted into a graphic form, such as charts. Graphics capabilities now are included in most spreadsheet packages.

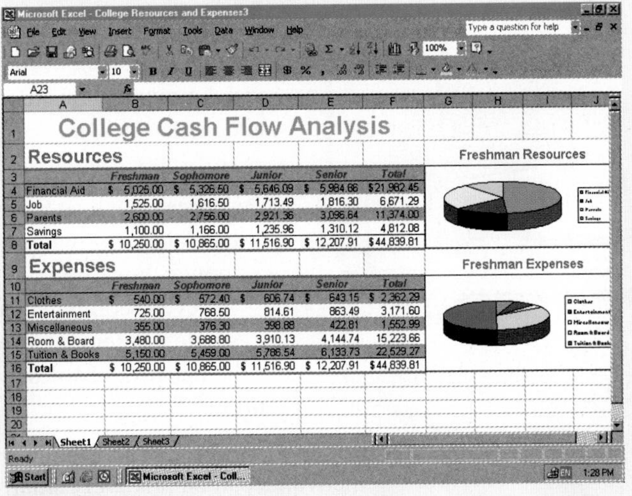

Figure 25
Electronic Spreadsheet software frequently is used by people who work with numbers. The user enters the data and the formulas to be used on the data, and the computer calculates the results.

Web Link
For more information on spreadsheet software, visit the Introduction to Computers WEB LINK page (scsite.com/ic4/weblink.htm) and click **Spreadsheet Software.**

Database

Database software (Figure 26) allows the user to enter, retrieve, and update data in an organized and efficient manner. These software packages have flexible inquiry and reporting capabilities that let users access the data in different ways and create custom reports that include some or all of the information in the database.

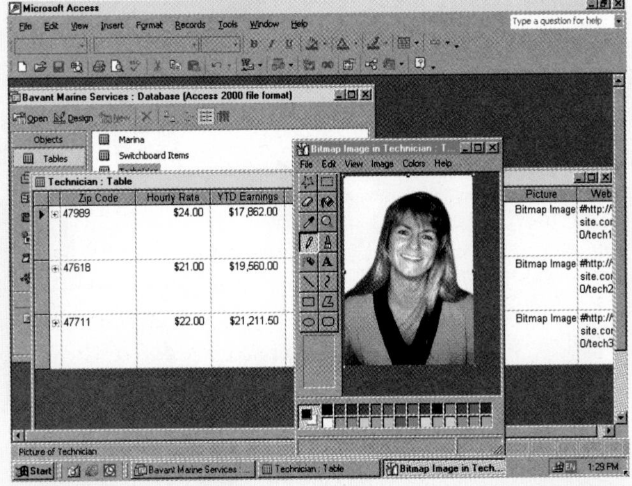

Figure 26
Database software allows the user to enter, retrieve, and update data in an organized and efficient manner.

Web Link
For more information on database software, visit the Introduction to Computers WEB LINK page (scsite.com/ic4/weblink.htm) and click **Database Software.**

Presentation Graphics

Presentation graphics software (Figure 27) allows the user to create documents called slides to be used in making presentations. Using special projection devices, the slides are projected directly from the computer.

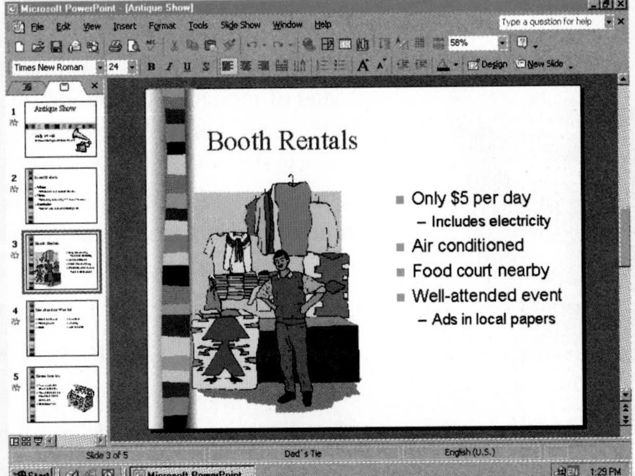

Figure 27
Presentation graphics software allows the user to create documents called slides for use in presentations.

Web Link
For more information on presentation graphics software, visit the Introduction to Computers WEB LINK page (scsite.com/ic4/weblink.htm) and click **Presentation Graphics Software.**

Networks and the Internet

A **network** is a collection of computers and devices connected via communications media and devices such as cables, telephone lines, modems, or other means.

Computers are networked together so users can share resources, such as hardware devices, software programs, data, and information. Sharing resources saves time and money. For example, instead of purchasing one printer for every computer in a company, the firm can connect a single printer and all computers via a network (Figure 28); the network enables all of the computers to access the same printer.

Most business computers are networked together. These networks can be relatively small or quite extensive. A network that connects computers in a limited geographic area, such as a school computer laboratory, office, or group of buildings, is called a **local area network (LAN)**. A network that covers a large geographical area, such as one that connects the district offices of a national corporation, is called a **wide area network (WAN)** (Figure 29).

Figure 28
This local area network (LAN) enables two separate computers to share the same printer.

Figure 29
A network can be quite large and complex, connecting users in district offices around the country (WAN).

Figure 30
Users access the Internet for a variety of reasons: to send messages to other connected users, to access a wealth of information, to shop for goods and services, to meet or converse with people around the world, and for entertainment.

The Internet

The world's largest network is the **Internet**, which is a worldwide collection of networks that links together millions of computers by means of modems, telephone lines, cables, and other communications devices and media. With an abundance of resources and data accessible via the Internet, more than 360 million users around the world are making use of the Internet for a variety of reasons (Figure 30). Some of these reasons include the following:

- Sending messages to other connected users (e-mail)
- Accessing a wealth of information, such as news, maps, airline schedules, and stock market data
- Shopping for goods and services
- Meeting or conversing with people around the world
- Accessing sources of entertainment and leisure, such as online games, magazines, and vacation planning guides

Most users connect to the Internet in one of two ways: through an Internet service provider or through an online service. An **Internet service provider** (**ISP**) is an organization that supplies connections to the Internet for a monthly fee. Like an ISP, an **online service** provides access to the Internet, but it also provides a variety of other specialized content and services such as financial data, hardware and software guides, news, weather, legal information, and other similar commodities. For this reason, the fees for using an online service usually are slightly higher than fees for using an ISP. Two popular online services are America Online and The Microsoft Network.

Web Link

For more information on the Internet, visit the Introduction to Computers WEB LINK page (scsite.com/ic4/weblink.htm) and click **Internet**.

The World Wide Web

One of the more popular segments of the Internet is the **World Wide Web**, also called the **Web**, which contains billions of documents called Web pages. A **Web page** is a document that contains text, graphics, sound, and/or video, and has built-in connections, or hyperlinks, to other Web documents. Web pages are stored on computers throughout the world. A **Web site** is a related collection of Web pages. You access and view Web pages using a software program called a **Web browser**. A Web page has a unique address, called a **Uniform Resource Locator (URL)**.

Web Link

For more information on the World Wide Web, visit the Introduction to Computers WEB LINK page (scsite.com/ic4/weblink.htm) and click **World Wide Web**.

As shown in Figure 31, a URL consists of a protocol, domain name, and sometimes the path to a specific Web page or location in a Web page. Most Web page URLs begin with **http://**, which stands for hypertext transfer protocol, the communications standard used to transfer pages on the Web. The domain name identifies the Web site, which is stored on a Web server. A **Web server** is a computer that delivers (serves) requested Web pages.

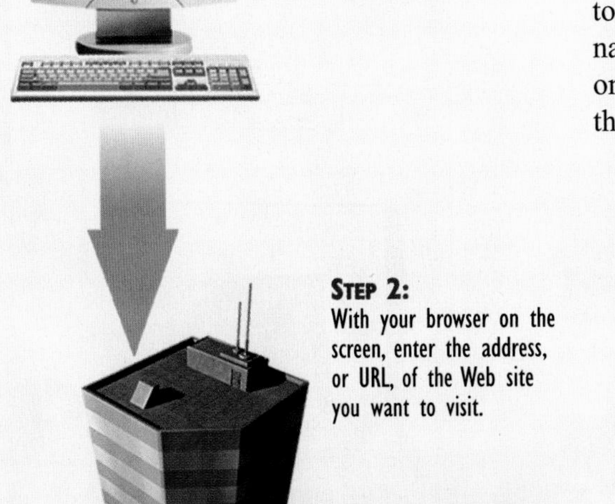

STEP 1:
Use your computer and modem to make a local telephone call to an internet service provider.
STEP 2:
With your browser on the screen, enter the address, or URL, of the Web site you want to visit.

The Web browser locates the Web site for the entered address and displays a Web page on your screen.

Figure 31
One method of connecting to the Web and displaying a Web page.

Electronic Commerce

When you conduct business activities online, you are participating in **electronic commerce**, also known as **e-commerce**. These commercial activities include shopping, investing, and any other venture that represents a business transaction. Today, three types of e-commerce exist: business to consumer, consumer to consumer, and business to business. **Business to consumer** (**B2C**) involves the sale of goods to the general public. **Consumer to consumer** (C2C) involves one consumer selling directly to another. **Business to business** (B2B) provides goods and services to other businesses.

Web Link

For more information on e-commerce, visit the Introduction to Computers WEB LINK page (scsite.com/ic4/weblink.htm) and click **E-Commerce**.

HOW TO PURCHASE, INSTALL, AND MAINTAIN A PERSONAL COMPUTER

The decision to buy a personal computer is an important one — and finding and purchasing a personal computer suited to your needs will require an investment of both time and money. As with many buyers, you may have little computer experience and find yourself unsure of how to proceed. The following guidelines are presented to help you purchase, install, and maintain a desktop computer. These guidelines also apply to the purchase of a notebook computer or handheld computer. Purchasing a notebook computer or handheld computer also involves some additional considerations, which are addressed later.

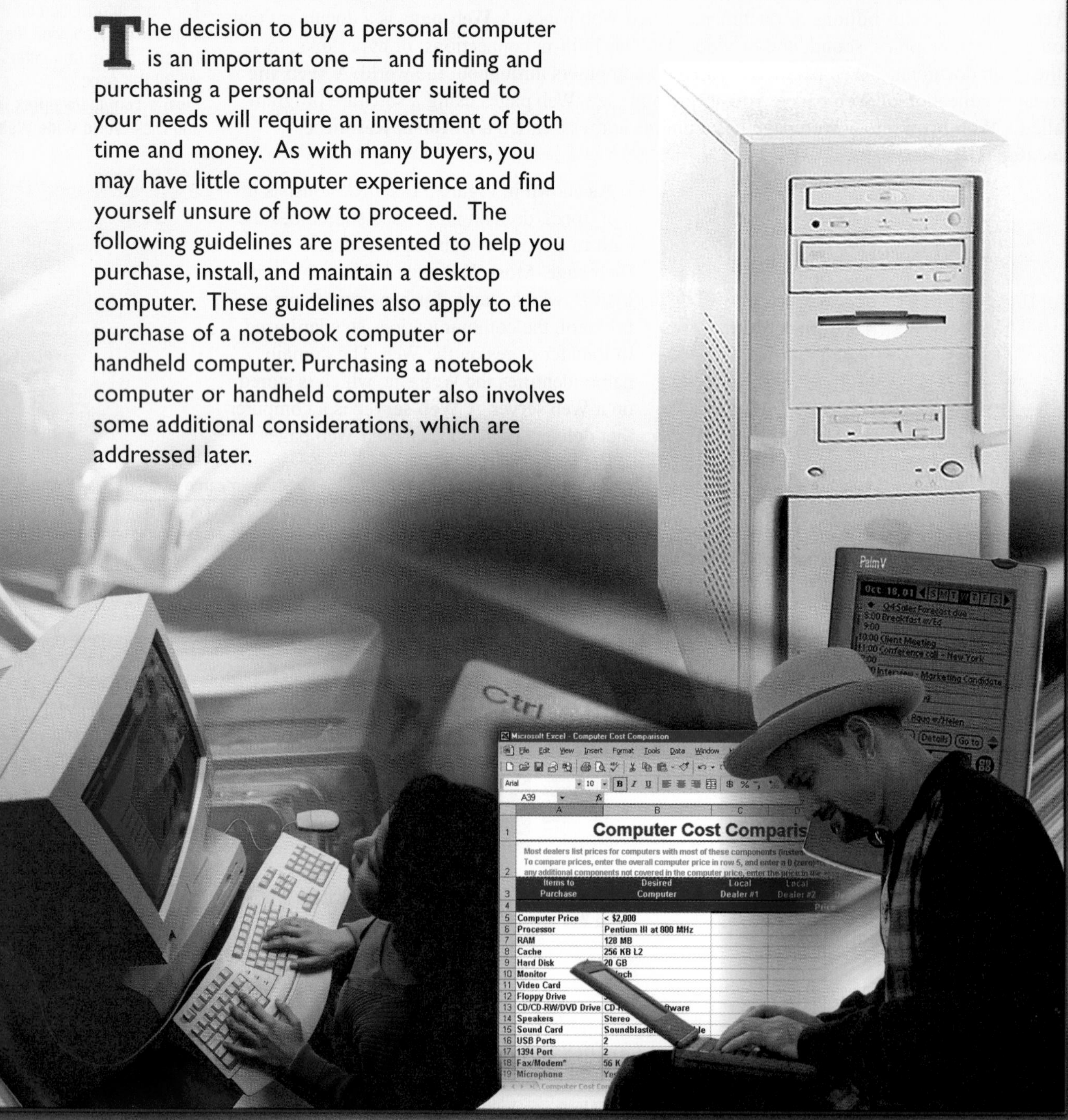

How to Purchase a Desktop Computer

Web Link

For more information on desktop computers, visit the Introduction to Computers WEB LINK page (scsite.com/ic4/weblink.htm) and click **Desktop Computers**.

1 **Determine what application products you will use on your computer.** Knowing what application products you plan to use will help you decide on the type of computer to buy, as well as to define the memory, storage, and other requirements. Certain application products, for example, can run only on Macintosh computers, while others run only on a personal computer with the Windows operating system. Further, some application products require more memory and disk space than others, as well as additional input/output and storage devices. For example, if you want to efficiently create copies of CDs with your computer, then you will need to include two CD drives: one that reads from a CD, and one that reads from and writes to a CD.

When you purchase a computer, it may come bundled with several software products. At the very least, you probably will want software for word processing and a browser to access the World Wide Web. If you need additional applications, such as a spreadsheet, a database, or presentation graphics, consider purchasing a software suite that offers reduced pricing on several applications, such as Microsoft Works or Microsoft Office.

Before selecting a specific package, be sure the software contains the features necessary for the tasks you want to perform. Many Web sites and magazines, such as those listed in Figure 32, provide reviews of software products. These Web sites frequently have articles that rate computers and software on cost, performance, and support.

2 **Before buying a computer, do some research.** Talk to friends, coworkers, and instructors about prospective computers. What type of computers did they buy? Why? Would they recommend their computer and the company from which they bought it? You also should visit the Web sites or read reviews in the magazines listed in Figure 32. As you conduct your research, consider the following important criteria:

- Speed of the processor
- Size and types of memory (RAM) and storage (hard disk, floppy disk, CD-ROM, CD-RW, DVD-ROM, Zip® drive)
- Input/output devices included with the computer (e.g., mouse, keyboard, monitor, printer, sound card, video card)
- Communications devices included with the computer (modem, network interface card)
- Any software included with the computer

Type of Computer	Web Site	URL
PC	Computer Shopper	zdnet.com/computershopper/edit/howtobuy
	PC World Magazine	pcworld.com
	Byte Magazine	byte.com
	Smart Business for New Economy	zdnet.com/smartbusinessmag/
	PC Magazine	zdnet.com/pcmag
	Yahoo! Computers	computers.yahoo.com
	FamilyPC Magazine	familypc.zdnet.com
	Microsoft Network	eshop.msn.com
	Dave's Guide to Buying a PC	css.msu.edu/pc-guide.html
Macintosh	TechWeb News	www.techweb.com/wire/apple
	ZDNet News	zdnet.com/mac
	Macworld Magazine	macworld.zdnet.com
	Apple	apple.com

For an updated list of hardware and software reviews and their Web sites, visit scsite.com/dc2002/ch8/buyers.htm.

Figure 32
Hardware and software reviews.

Figure 33
Some mail-order companies, like Gateway, sell computers online.

3 **Look for free software.** Many computer vendors include free software with their systems. Some sellers even let you choose which software you want. Remember, however, that free software has value only if you would have purchased the software even if it had not come with the computer.

4 **If you are buying a new computer, you have several purchasing options: buying from your school bookstore, a local computer dealer, a local large retail store, or ordering by mail via telephone or the World Wide Web.** Each purchasing option has certain advantages. Many college bookstores, for example, sign exclusive pricing agreements with computer manufacturers and, thus, can offer student discounts. Local dealers and local large retail stores, however, more easily can provide hands-on support. Mail-order companies that sell computers by telephone or online via the Web (Figure 33) often provide the lowest prices but extend less personal service. Some major mail-order companies, however, have started to provide next-business-day, onsite services. A credit card usually is required to buy from a mail-order company. Figure 34 lists some of the more popular mail-order companies and their Web site addresses.

5 **If you are buying a used computer, stick with name brands.** Although brand-name equipment can cost more, most brand-name computers have longer, more comprehensive warranties, are better supported, and have more authorized centers for repair services. As with new computers, you can purchase a used computer from local computer dealers, local large retail stores, or mail order via the telephone or the Web. Classified ads and used computer brokers offer additional outlets for purchasing used computers. Figure 35 lists several major used computer brokers and their Web site addresses.

Type of Computer	Company	URL	Telephone Number
PC	Computer Shopper	computershopper.com	Not Available
	Compaq	compaq.com	1-800-888-0220
	CompUSA	compusa.com	1-800-266-7872
	dartek.com	dartek.com	1-800-531-4622
	Dell	dell.com	1-800-678-1626
	Gateway	gateway.com	1-800-846-4208
	Micron	micron.com	1-800-964-2766
Macintosh	Apple Computer	store.apple.com	1-800-795-1000
	Club Mac	www.clubmac.com	1-800-258-2622
	MacConnection	macconnection.com	1-888-213-0260
	MacExchange	macx.com	1-888-650-4488

For an updated list of new computer mail-order companies and their Web sites, visit scsite.com/dc2002/ch8/buyers.htm.

Figure 34
New computer mail-order companies.

Company	URL	Telephone Number
American Computer Exchange	www.amcoex.com	1-800-786-0717
Custom Edge, Inc.	bocoex.com	1-617-625-7722
U.S. Computer Exchange, Inc.	www.uscomputerexchange.com	1-800-711-9000
eBay	ebay.com	Not Available

For an updated list of used computer mail-order companies and their Web sites, visit *scsite.com/dc2002/ch8/buyers.htm.*

Figure 35
Used computer mail-order companies.

6 **Use a worksheet to compare computers, services, and other considerations.** You can use a separate sheet of paper to take notes on each vendor's computer and then summarize the information on a spreadsheet, such as the one shown in Figure 36. Most companies advertise a price for a base computer that includes components housed in the system unit (processor, RAM, sound card, video card), disk drives (floppy disk, hard disk, CD-ROM, CD-RW, and DVD-ROM), a keyboard, mouse, monitor, printer, speakers, and modem. Be aware, however, that some advertisements list prices for computers with only some of these components. Monitors, printers, and modems, for example, often are not included in a base computers price. Depending on how you plan to use the computers, you may want to invest in additional or more powerful components. When you are comparing the prices of computers, make sure you are comparing identical or similar configurations.

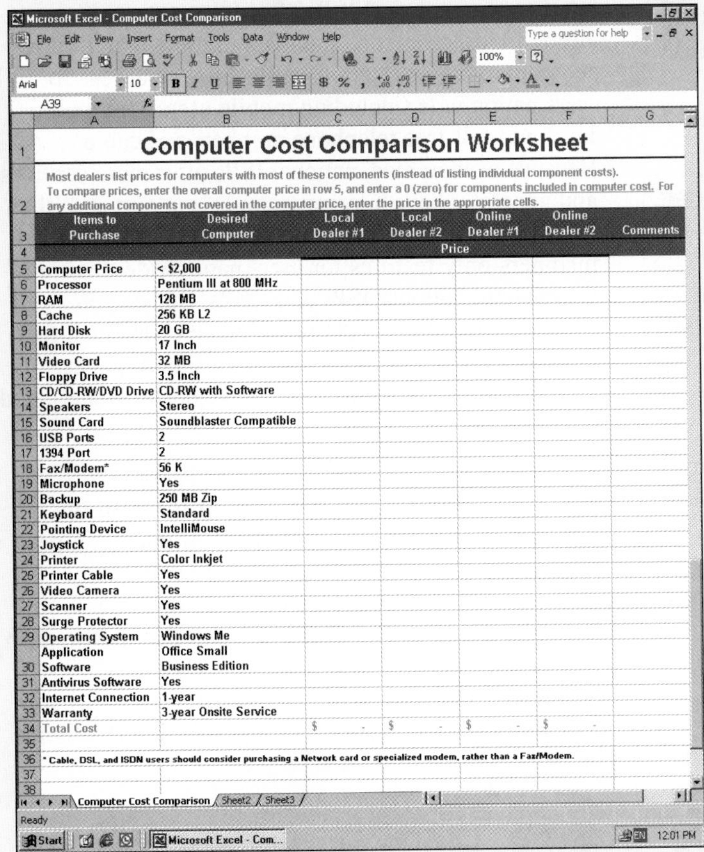

Computer Cost Comparison Worksheet

Most dealers list prices for computers with most of these components (instead of listing individual component costs). To compare prices, enter the overall computer price in row 5, and enter a 0 (zero) for components included in computer cost. For any additional components not covered in the computer price, enter the price in the appropriate cells.

Items to Purchase	Desired Computer	Local Dealer #1	Local Dealer #2	Online Dealer #1	Online Dealer #2	Comments
		Price				
Computer Price	< $2,000					
Processor	Pentium III at 800 MHz					
RAM	128 MB					
Cache	256 KB L2					
Hard Disk	20 GB					
Monitor	17 Inch					
Video Card	32 MB					
Floppy Drive	3.5 Inch					
CD/CD-RW/DVD Drive	CD-RW with Software					
Speakers	Stereo					
Sound Card	Soundblaster Compatible					
USB Ports	2					
1394 Port	2					
Fax/Modem*	56 K					
Microphone	Yes					
Backup	250 MB Zip					
Keyboard	Standard					
Pointing Device	IntelliMouse					
Joystick	Yes					
Printer	Color Inkjet					
Printer Cable	Yes					
Video Camera	Yes					
Scanner	Yes					
Surge Protector	Yes					
Operating System	Windows Me					
Application Software	Office Small Business Edition					
Antivirus Software	Yes					
Internet Connection	1-year					
Warranty	3-year Onsite Service					
Total Cost		$ -	$ -	$ -	$ -	

* Cable, DSL, and ISDN users should consider purchasing a Network card or specialized modem, rather than a Fax/Modem.

Figure 36
A spreadsheet is an effective tool for summarizing and comparing the prices and components of different computer vendors. A copy of the Computer Cost Comparison Worksheet is available via the Web Link on this page. You must use Microsoft Internet Explorer 5 (IE5) or greater to view it.

Web Link
For more information on computer cost comparisons, visit the Introduction to Computers WEB LINK page (scsite.com/ic4/weblink.htm) and click **Computer Cost Comparisons**.

7 **Be aware of hidden costs.** Before purchasing, be sure to consider any additional costs associated with buying a computer, such as an additional telephone line, an uninterruptible power supply (UPS), computer furniture, floppy disks and paper, or computer training classes you may want to take. Depending on where you buy your computer, the seller may be willing to include some or all of these in the computer purchase price.

8 **Consider more than just price.** The lowest cost computer may not be the best buy. Consider such intangibles as the vendor's time in business, the vendor's regard for quality, and the vendor's reputation for support. If you need to upgrade your computer often, you may want to consider a leasing arrangement, in which you pay monthly lease fees but upgrade or add on to your computer as your equipment needs change. If you are a replacement buyer, ask if the vendor will buy your old computer; an increasing number of companies are taking trade-ins. No matter what type of buyer you are, insist on a 30-day, no-questions-asked return policy on your computer.

Company	Service	URL	Telephone Number
America Online	OSP	aol.com	1-800-827-6364
AT&T Data and IP Services	ISP	att.com/wss	1-800-288-3199
CompuServe	OSP	compuserve.com	1-800-848-8990
Earthlink Network	ISP	www.earthlink.com	1-800-395-8425
Juno	Free OSP	juno.com	1-888-829-5866
MCI	ISP	mciworldcom.com	1-800-888-0800
Microsoft Network	OSP	msn.com	1-800-386-5550
NetZero	Free OSP	netzero.com	Not Available
Prodigy	ISP/OSP	prodigy.com	1-800-776-3449

For information on local ISPs or to learn more on any ISPs and OSPs listed here, visit The List™ at thelist.internet.com. The List™ — the most comprehensive and accurate directory of ISPs and OSPs on the Web — compares dial-up services, access hours, and fees for over 9,000 access providers.

For an updated list of ISPs and OSPs, visit scsite.com/dc2002/ ch8/buyers.htm.

Figure 37
National ISPs and OSPs.

9 **Avoid restocking fees.** Some companies charge a restocking fee of 10 to 20 percent as part of their money-back return policy. In some cases, there is no restocking fee for hardware, but there is for software. Ask about the existence and terms of any restocking policies before you buy.

10 **Select an Internet service provider (ISP) or online service provider (OSP).** You can access the Internet in one of two ways: via an ISP or an OSP. Both provide Internet access for a monthly fee that ranges from $5 to $20. Some OSPs offer free Internet access. Local ISPs offer Internet access through local telephone numbers to users in a limited geographic region. National ISPs provide access for users nationwide (including mobile users), through local and toll-free telephone numbers and cable. Because of their size, national ISPs offer more services and generally have a larger technical support staff than local ISPs. OSPs furnish Internet access as well as members-only features for users nationwide. Figure 37 lists several national ISPs and OSPs. Before you choose an Internet access provider, compare such features as the number of access hours, monthly fees, available services (e-mail, Web page hosting, chat), and reliability.

11 **Buy a computer compatible with the ones you use elsewhere.** If you use a personal computer at work or in some other capacity, make sure the computer you buy is compatible. For example, if you use a PC at work, you may not want to purchase a Macintosh for home use. Having a computer compatible with the ones at work or school will allow you to transfer files and spend time at home on work- or school-related projects.

12 **Consider purchasing an onsite service agreement.** If you use your computer for business or are unable to be without your computer, consider purchasing an onsite service agreement through a local dealer or third-party company. Most onsite service agreements state that a technician will come to your home, work, or school within 24 hours. If your computer includes onsite service only for the first year, think about extending the service for two or three years when you buy the computer.

13 **Use a credit card to purchase your new computer.** Many credit cards now offer purchase protection and extended warranty benefits that cover you in case of loss of or damage to purchased goods. Paying by credit card also gives you time to install and use the computer before you have to pay for it. Finally, if you are dissatisfied with the computer and are unable to reach an agreement with the seller, paying by credit card gives you certain rights regarding withholding payment until the dispute is resolved. Check your credit card for specific details.

14 **Avoid buying the smallest computer available.** Computer technology changes rapidly, meaning a computer that seems powerful enough today may not serve your computing needs in a few years. In fact, studies show that many users regret they did not buy a more powerful computer. Plan to buy a computer that will last you for two to three years. You can help delay obsolescence by purchasing the fastest processor, most memory, and largest hard drive you can afford. If you must buy a smaller computer, be sure you can upgrade it with additional memory and auxiliary devices as your computer requirements grow. Figure 38 includes minimum recommendations for each category of user discussed in this book: Home User, Small Business User, Mobile User, Large Business User, and Power User. The Home User category is divided into two groups: Application Home User and Game Home User.

Web Link

For more information on base components, visit the Introduction to Computers WEB LINK page (scsite.com/ic4/weblink.htm) and click **Base Components**.

BASE COMPONENTS						
	Application Home User	Game Home User	Small Business User	Mobile User	Large Business User	Power User
HARDWARE						
Processor	Celeron at 600 MHz	Pentium 4 at 1.4 GHZ	Pentium III at 1 GHZ	Pentium III at 700 MHZ	Pentium 4 at 1.4 GHZ	Pentium 4 at 1.4 GHZ
RAM	96 MB	128 MB	128 MB	128 MB	384 MB	512 MB
Cache	256 KB L2	512 KB L2	512 KB L2	512 KB L2	512 KB L2	2 MB L2
Hard Drive	10 GB	20 GB	20 GB	10 GB	80 GB	80 GB
Video Graphics Card	32 MB	64 MB	32 MB	16 MB	64 MB	64 MB
Monitor	17"	19"	17"	15" active matrix	19"	21"
DVD/CD-ROM Drive	48X CD-ROM	12X DVD with Decoder Card	48X CD-ROM	6X DVD	48X CD-ROM	12X DVD with Decoder Card
CD-RW 2nd Bay	Yes	Yes	Yes	Not Applicable	Yes	Yes
Floppy Drive	3.5"	3.5"	3.5"	3.5"	3.5"	3.5"
Printer	Color inkjet	Color inkjet	8 ppm laser	Portable inkjet	24 ppm laser	8 ppm laser
Fax/Modem or Network Card	Yes	Yes	Yes	Yes	Yes	Yes
Sound Card	Soundblaster Compatible	Soundblaster Compatible	Soundblaster Compatible	Built-In	Soundblaster Compatible	Soundblaster Compatible
Speakers	Stereo	Full-Dolby surround	Stereo	Stereo	Stereo	Full-Dolby surround
TV-Out Connector	Yes	Yes	Yes	Yes	Yes	Yes
USB Port	Yes	Yes	Yes	Yes	Yes	Yes
1394 Port	No	Yes	No	No	Yes	Yes
Pointing Device	IntelliMouse or Optical Mouse	Optical mouse and Joystick	IntelliMouse or Optical Mouse	Touchpad or Pointing Stick and Optical Mouse	IntelliMouse or Optical Mouse	IntelliMouse or Optical Mouse and Joystick
Keyboard	Yes	Yes	Yes	Built-In	Yes	Yes
Backup Disk/Tape Drive	250 MB Zip	1 GB Jaz	1 GB Jaz and Tape	250 MB Zip	2 GB Jaz and Tape	2 GB Jaz and Tape
SOFTWARE						
Operating System	Windows ME	Windows ME	Windows 2000 Professional	Windows 2000 Professional	Windows 2000 Professional	Windows 2000 Professional
Application Software Suite	Office Standard	Office Standard	OfficeSmall Business Edition	Office Small Business Edition	Office Premium	Office Premium
Internet Access	Cable, Online Service, or ISP	Cable, Online Service, or ISP	Cable	Online Service or ISP	LAN/WAN (T1/T3)	LAN
OTHER						
Surge Protector	Yes	Yes	Yes	Portable	Yes	Yes
Warranty	3-Year Limited, 1-Year Next Business Day On-Site Service	3-Year Limited, 1-Year Next Business Day On-Site Service	3-year on-site service	3-Year Limited, 1-Year Next Business Day On-Site Service	3-year on-site service	3-year on-site service
Other		Headset		Docking Station		
				Carrying case		
Optional Components for all Categories						
digital camera						
multifunction device (MFD)						
scanner						
uninterruptable power supply						
ergonomic keyboard						
network interface card						
TV/FM tuner						
video camera						
IrDa port						
mouse pad/wrist rest						

Figure 38
Base computer components and optional computer components. A copy of the Base Components Comparison Worksheet is available via the Web Link on this page. You must use Microsoft Internet Explorer 5 (IE5) or greater to view it.

How to Purchase a Notebook Computer

If you need computing capability when you travel, you may find a notebook computer to be an appropriate choice. The guidelines mentioned in the previous section also apply to the purchase of a notebook computer (Figure 39). The following are additional considerations unique to notebook computers.

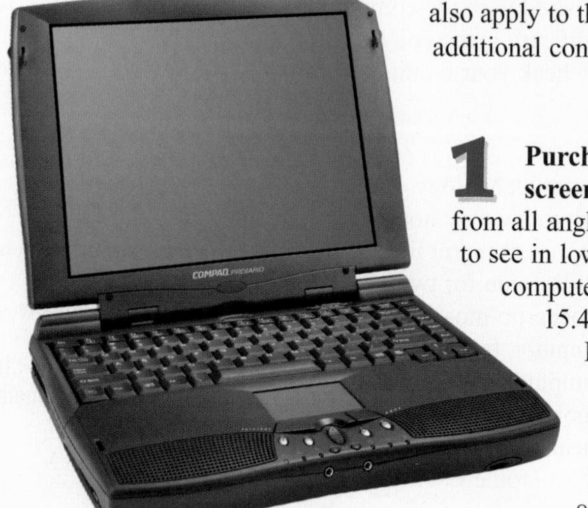

Figure 39
A notebook computer.

1 Purchase a notebook computer with a sufficiently large active-matrix screen. Active-matrix screens display high-quality color that is viewable from all angles. Less expensive, passive-matrix screens sometimes are difficult to see in low-light conditions and cannot be viewed from an angle. Notebook computers typically come with a 12.1-inch, 13.3-inch, 14.1-inch, or 15.4-inch display. For most users, a 14.1-inch display is satisfactory. If you intend to use your notebook computer as a desktop replacement, however, you may opt for a 15.4-inch display. If you travel a lot and portability is essential, consider that most of the lightest machines are equipped with a 13.3-inch display. Regardless of size, the resolution of the display should be at least 800 x 600 pixels.

2 Experiment with different pointing devices and keyboards. Notebook computer keyboards are far less standardized than those for desktop computers. Some notebook computers, for example, have wide wrist rests, while others have none. Notebook computers also use a range of pointing devices, including pointing sticks, touchpads, and trackballs. Before you purchase a notebook computer, try various types of keyboard and pointing devices to determine which is easiest for you to use. Regardless of the pointing device you select, you also may want to purchase a regular mouse unit to use when you are working at a desk or other large surface.

Web Link

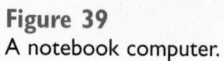

For more information on notebook computers, visit the Introduction to Computers WEB LINK page (scsite.com/ic4/weblink.htm) and click **Notebook Computers**.

3 Make sure the notebook computer you purchase has a CD-ROM or DVD-ROM drive. Loading software, especially large software suites, is much faster if done from a CD-ROM, CD-RW, or DVD-ROM. Today, most notebook computers come with an internal CD-ROM drive. Some notebook computers even come with a CD-ROM drive and a CD-RW drive or both a DVD-ROM drive and a CD-RW drive. Some users prefer a DVD-ROM drive to a CD-ROM drive. Although DVD-ROM drives are more expensive, they allow you to read CD-ROMs and to play movies using your notebook computer.

4 If necessary, upgrade memory and disk storage at the time of purchase. As with a desktop computer, upgrading your notebook computer's memory and disk storage usually is less expensive at the time of initial purchase. Some disk storage is custom designed for notebook computer manufacturers, meaning an upgrade might not be available a year or two after you purchase your notebook computer.

5 If you are going to use your notebook computer on an airplane, purchase a second battery. Two batteries should provide enough power to last through most airplane flights. If you anticipate running your notebook computer on batteries frequently, choose a computer that uses lithium-ion batteries (they last longer than nickel cadmium or nickel hydride batteries).

6 Purchase a well-padded and well-designed carrying case. An amply padded carrying case will protect your notebook computer from the bumps it will receive while traveling. A well-designed carrying case will have room for accessories such as spare floppy disks, CD-ROMs, a user manual, pens, and paperwork (Figure 40).

Figure 40
Well-designed carrying case.

7 If you travel overseas, obtain a set of electrical and telephone adapters. Different countries use different outlets for electrical and telephone connections. Several manufacturers sell sets of adapters that will work in most countries (Figure 41).

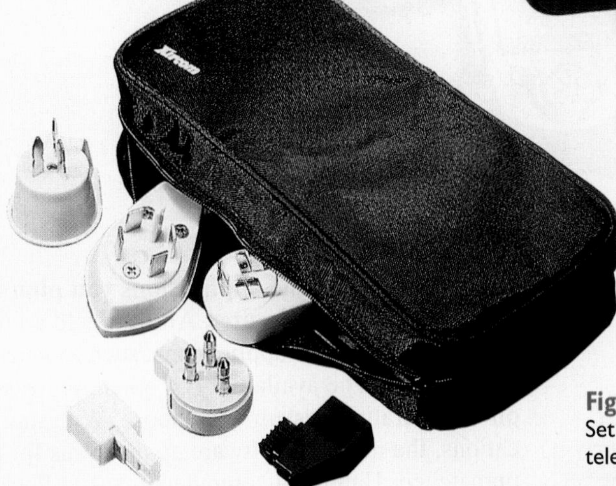

Figure 41
Set of electrical and telephone adapters.

8 If you plan to connect your notebook computer to a video projector, make sure the notebook computer is compatible with the video projector. Some notebook computers will not allow you to display an image on the notebook computer and projection device at the same time (Figure 42). Either of these factors can affect your presentation negatively.

Figure 42
Video projector.

Web Link

For more information on handheld computers, visit the Introduction to Computers WEB LINK page (scsite.com/ic4/weblink.htm) and click **Handheld Computers**.

How to Purchase a Handheld Computer

If you need to stay organized when you are on the go, then a lightweight, palm-size or pocketsize computer, called a handheld computer, may be the right choice. Handheld computers typically are categorized by the operating system they run. Although several are available, the two primary operating systems are Palm OS (Figure 43) and Pocket PC (Figure 44). Listed in this section are a few points you will want to consider when purchasing a handheld computer. You also should visit the Web sites listed in Figure 45.

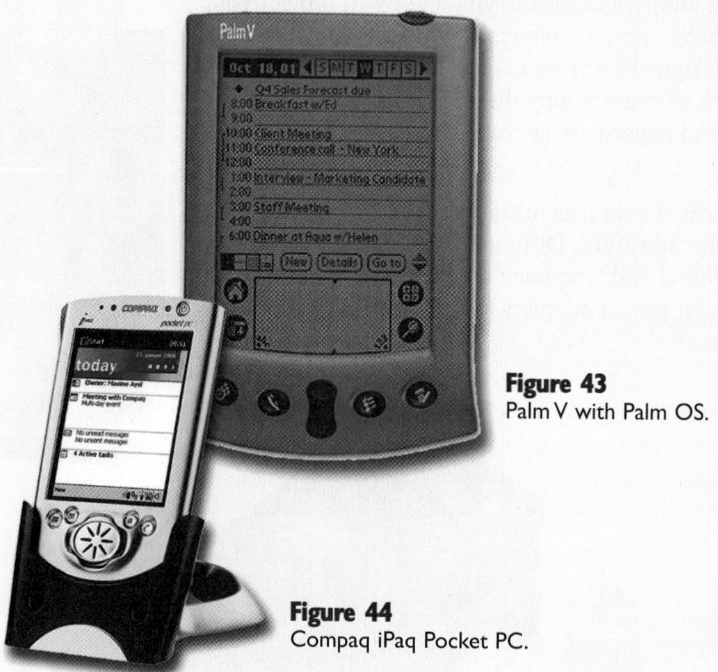

Figure 43
Palm V with Palm OS.

Figure 44
Compaq iPaq Pocket PC.

1 Determine the applications you plan to run on your handheld computer. All handheld computers can handle basic organizer-type applications, such as calendar, address book, and notepad. The availability of other applications is dependent on the operating system you choose. With more than 5,000 applications, the depth of software applications for the Palm OS is unmatched. Handheld computers that run Pocket PC have fewer applications available, but they do run a Windows-like operating system and applications you probably are familiar with, such as Word and Excel.

2 What do you want to pay? The price of handheld computers runs from $100 to $1,000, depending on their capabilities. In general, Palm OS devices are at the lower end of the cost spectrum and Pocket PC devices are at the higher end. The average selling price for handheld computers is in the $300 to $500 range. For the latest handheld computer prices, capabilities, and accessories, visit the Web sites listed in Figure 45.

Web Site	URL
Compaq	compaq.com/products/handhelds
Computer Shopper	computershopper.com
Handspring	handspring.com
Microsoft	pocketpc.com
Mobile Computing	mobilecomputing.com
Palm	palm.com
PDA Buyers Guide	pdabuyersguide.com
smaller.com	smaller.com
Wireless Developer Network	wirelessdevnet.com

For an updated list of handheld computer Web sites, visit *scsite.com/dc2002/ch8/buyers.htm*.

Figure 45
Reviews and information on handheld computers.

3 **Practice with the touch screen and handwriting recognition before deciding on a model.** You use a pen-like stylus to handwrite on the screen. The handheld computer then translates the handwriting into a computerized font. You also can use the stylus as a pointing device to select items on the screen and enter data using a transparent onscreen keyboard. Some handheld computers are easier to use than others. You can buy third-party software to improve a handheld computer's handwriting recognition.

4 **Decide if you want a color screen.** Pocket PC devices have color screens (as many as 65,536 colors), while most Palm OS devices have monochrome screens (4 to 16 shades of gray). More colors result in greater detail. Resolution also influences the quality of the display.

5 **Compare battery life.** Any mobile device is good only if it has the power to run. Palm OS devices with black-and-white screens tend to have a much longer battery life than Pocket PC devices with color screens. To help alleviate this problem, both Palm OS and Pocket PC devices have incorporated rechargeable batteries, but this only works if you are near a recharger.

6 **Check out the accessories.** You need to consider what accessories you want for your handheld computer. Handheld computer accessories include carrying cases, portable keyboards, removable storage, car chargers, GPS systems, dashboard mounts, replacement styli, synchronization cradles and cables, and more.

7 **Decide if you want additional functionality.** You will find that off-the-shelf Pocket PC devices have broader functionality than Palm OS devices. For example, voice-recording capability, e-book player, MP3 (music) player, and video player are standard on most Pocket PC devices. If you are leaning towards a Palm OS device and still want these additional functions, they can be added later if you find you really need them.

8 **Is synchronization of data with other handheld computers, personal computers, or printers important?** Most handheld computers come with a cradle that connects to the USB or serial port on your computer so that you can synchronize data. An infrared port, however, allows you to synchronize data with any device, including other handheld computers that have a similar infrared port.

9 **If you travel often, then consider e-mail and Web access from your handheld computer.** Some handheld computers come with a modem that can send and receive data across telephone. Other handheld computers allow you to connect to your cellular telephone and use it as a modem. More expensive handheld computers have wireless capabilities built in. In either case, for a monthly network connection fee you can access your e-mail, company Web sites, and any other information on the World Wide Web from anywhere.

Web Link

For more information on handheld computer accessories, visit the Introduction to Computers WEB LINK page (scsite.com/ic4/weblink.htm) and click **Handheld Computer Accessories**.

Web Link

For more information on installing computers, visit the Introduction to Computers WEB LINK page (scsite.com/ic4/weblink.htm) and click **Install Computers**.

How to Install a Personal Computer

It is important that you spend time planning for the installation of your computer. Follow these steps to ensure your installation experience will be a pleasant one and that your work area is safe, healthy, and efficient.

1 **Read the installation manuals before you start to install your equipment.** Many manufacturers include separate installation instructions with their equipment that contain important information. You can save a great deal of time and frustration if you make an effort to read the manuals.

2 **Do some research.** To locate additional instructions on installing your computer, review the computer magazines or Web sites listed in Figure 46 to search for articles on installing a computer.

WEB SITE	URL
Getting Started/Installation	
Computers 101	newsday.com/plugin/c101main.htm
HelpTalk Online	helptalk.com
Ergonomics	
Ergonomic Computing	cobweb.creighton.edu/training/ergo.htm
Healthy Choices for Computer Users	www-ehs.ucsd.edu/ergo/ergobk/vdt.htm
Video Display Terminal Health and Safety Guidelines	uhs.berkeley.edu/Facstaff/Ergonomics

For an updated list of reference materials, visit *scsite.com/dc2002/ch8/buyers.htm*.

Figure 46
Web references on setting up and using your computer.

3 **Set up your computer in a well-designed work area, with adequate workspace around the computer.** Ergonomics is an applied science devoted to making the equipment and its surrounding work area safer and more efficient. Ergonomic studies have shown that using the correct type and configuration of chair, keyboard, monitor, and work surface will help you work comfortably and efficiently, and help protect your health. For your computer workspace, experts recommend an area of at least two feet by four feet. Figure 47 illustrates additional guidelines for setting up your work area.

Web Link

For more information on ergonomics, visit the Introduction to Computers WEB LINK page (scsite.com/ic4/weblink.htm) and click **Ergonomics**.

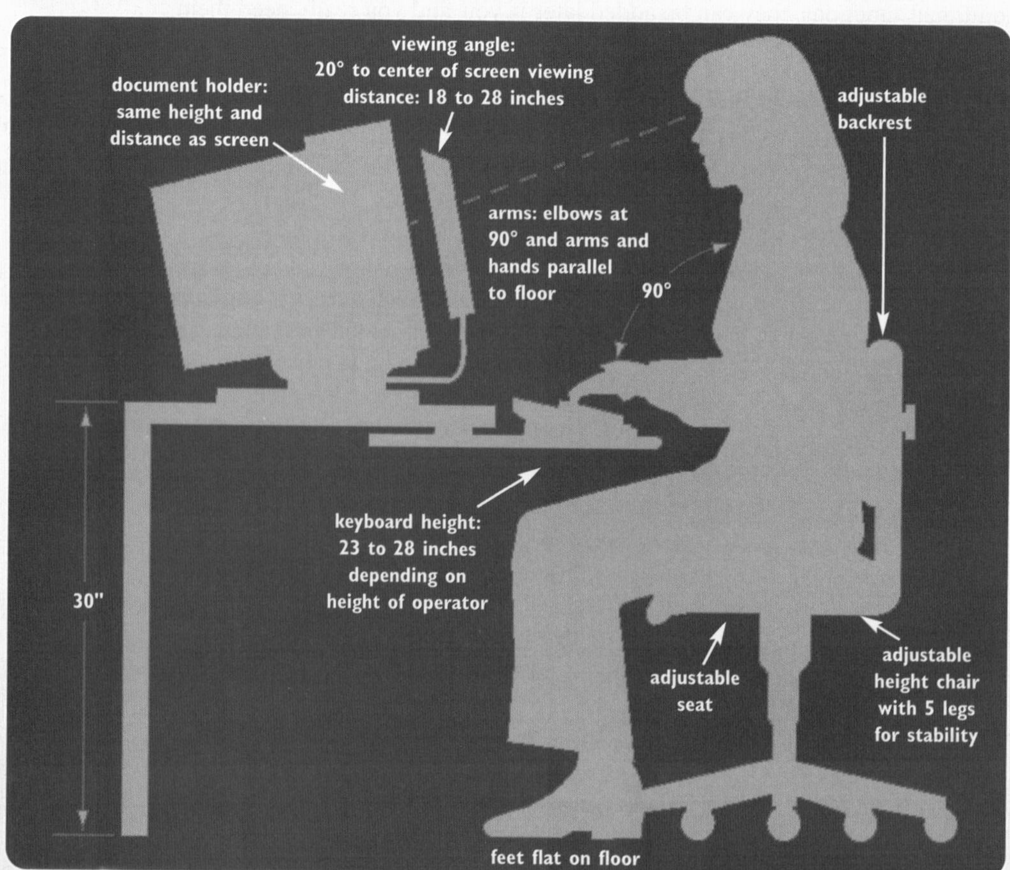

Figure 47
A well-designed work area should be flexible to allow adjustments to the height and build of different individuals. Good lighting and air quality also are important considerations.

4 Install bookshelves. Bookshelves above and/or to the side of your computer area are useful for keeping manuals and other reference materials handy.

5 Have a telephone outlet and telephone or cable connection near your workspace so you can connect your modem and/or place calls while using your computer. To plug in your modem to dial up and access the World Wide Web, you will need a telephone outlet or cable connection close to your computer. Having a telephone nearby also helps if you need to place business or technical support calls while you are working on your computer. Often, if you call a vendor about a hardware or software problem, the support person can talk you through a correction while you are on the telephone. To avoid data loss, however, do not place floppy disks on the telephone or near any other electrical or electronic equipment.

6 While working at your computer, be aware of health issues. Working safely at your computer requires that you consider several health issues. To minimize neck and eye discomfort, for instance, obtain a document holder that keeps documents at the same height and distance as your computer screen. To provide adequate lighting that reduces eye strain, use non-glare light bulbs that illuminate your entire work area. Figure 48 lists additional computer user health guidelines.

7 Obtain a computer tool set. Computer tool sets include any screwdrivers and other tools you might need to work on your computer. Computer dealers, office supply stores, and mail-order companies sell these tool sets. To keep all the tools together, get a tool set that comes in a zippered carrying case.

8 Save all the paperwork that comes with your computer. Keep the documents that come with your computer in an accessible place, along with the paperwork from your other computer-related purchases. To keep different-sized documents together, consider putting them in a manila file folder, large envelope, or sealable plastic bag.

Computer User Health Guidelines

1. Work in a well-designed work area. See Figure 16 on the previous page.
2. Alternate work activities to prevent physical and mental fatigue. If possible, change the order of your work to provide some variety.
3. Take frequent breaks. Every fifteen minutes, look away from the screen to give your eyes a break. At least once per hour, get out of your chair and move around. Every two hours, take at least a fifteen-minute break.
4. Incorporate hand, arm, and body stretching exercises into your breaks. At lunch, try to get outside and walk.
5. Make sure your computer monitor is designed to minimize electromagnetic radiation (EMR). If it is an older model, consider adding EMR reducing accessories.
6. Try to eliminate or minimize surrounding noise. Noisy environments contribute to stress and tension.
7. If you frequently use the telephone and the computer at the same time, consider using a telephone headset. Cradling the telephone between your head and shoulder can cause muscle strain.
8. Be aware of symptoms of repetitive strain injuries: soreness, pain, numbness, or weakness in neck, shoulders, arms, wrists, and hands. Do not ignore early signs; seek medical advice.

Figure 48
Following these health guidelines will help computer users maintain their health.

Web Link

For more information oncomputer health issues, visit the Introduction to Computers WEB LINK page (scsite.com/ic4/weblink.htm) and click **Computer Health Issues**.

9 **Record the serial numbers of all your equipment and software.** Write the serial numbers of your equipment and software on the outside of the manuals packaged with these items. As noted in Figure 49, you also should create a single, comprehensive list that contains the serial numbers of all your equipment and software.

10 **Complete and send in your equipment and software registration cards.** When you register your equipment and software, the vendor usually enters you in its user database. Being a registered user not only can save you time when you call with a support question, it also makes you eligible for special pricing on software upgrades.

11 **Keep the shipping containers and packing materials for all your equipment.** Shipping containers and packing materials will come in handy if you have to return your equipment for servicing or must move it to another location.

12 **Identify device connectors.** At the back of your computer, you will find a number of connectors for your printer, monitor, mouse, telephone line, and so forth (Figure 49). If the manufacturer has not identified them for you, use a marking pen to write the purpose of each connector on the back of the computer case.

13 **Install your computer in an area where you can maintain the temperature and humidity.** You should keep the computer in an area with a constant temperature between 60°F and 80°F. High temperatures and humidity can damage electronic components. Be careful when using space heaters, for example, as the hot, dry air they generate can cause disk problems.

14 **Keep your computer area clean.** Avoid eating and drinking around your computer. Also, avoid smoking. Cigarette smoke can damage the floppy disk drives and floppy disk surfaces.

15 **Check your home or renter's insurance policy.** Some renter's insurance policies have limits on the amount of computer equipment they cover. Other policies do not cover computer equipment at all if it is used for business. In this instance, you may want to obtain a separate insurance policy.

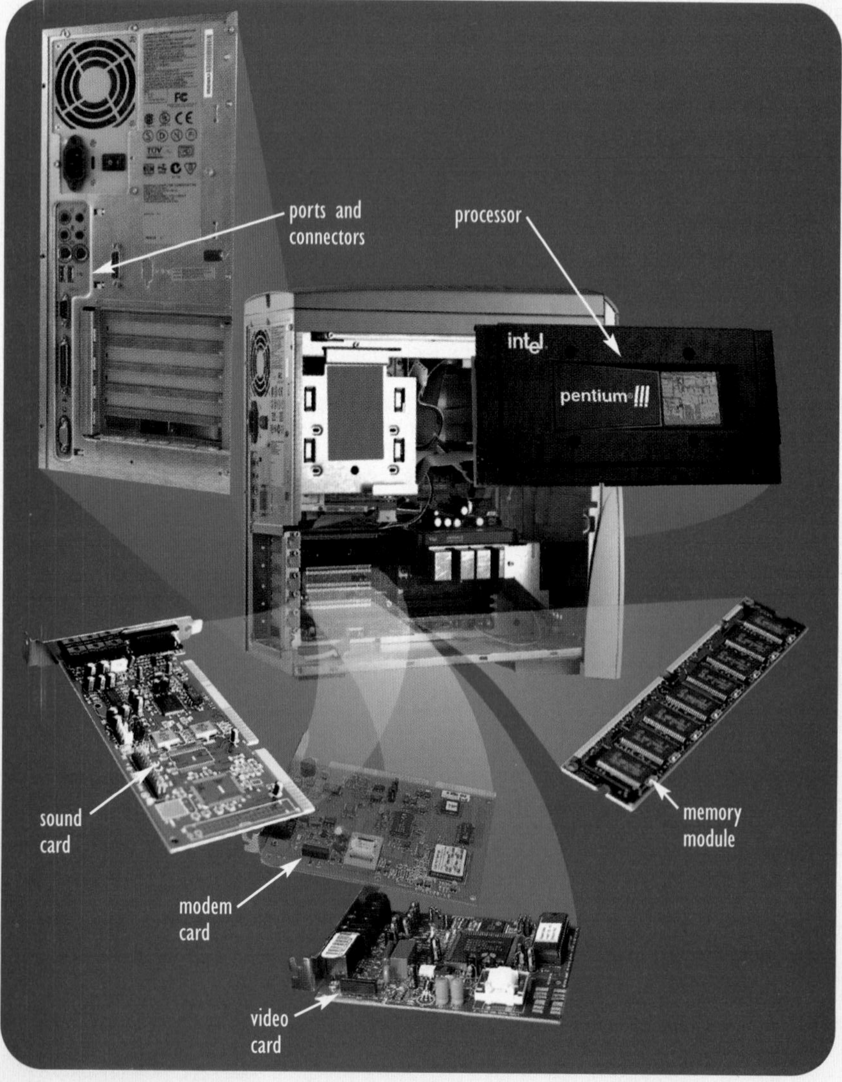

Figure 49
Inside the system unit and the connectors at the back.

How to Maintain a Personal Computer

Even with the most sophisticated hardware and software, you will need to do some type of maintenance to keep everything working properly. You can simplify and minimize the maintenance by following the steps listed below.

Web Link

For more information on maintaining computers, visit the Introduction to Computers WEB LINK page (scsite.com/ic4/weblink.htm) and click **Maintain Computers**.

1 **Start a notebook that includes information on your computer.** Keep a notebook that provides a single source of information about your entire computer, both hardware and software. Each time you make a change to your computer, such as adding or removing hardware or software or altering computer parameters, record the change in your notebook. Include the following items in your notebook:

- Vendor support numbers from your user manuals
- Serial numbers of all equipment and software
- User IDs, passwords, and nicknames for your ISP or OSP, network access, Web sites, and so on
- Vendor and date of purchase for all software and equipment
- Trouble log that provides a chronological history of equipment or software problems
- Notes on any discussions with vendor support personnel

Web Link

For more information on passwords, visit the Introduction to Computers WEB LINK page (scsite.com/ic4/weblink.htm) and click **Passwords**.

Figure 50 provides a suggested outline for the contents of your notebook.

PC OWNER'S NOTEBOOK OUTLINE

1. Vendors
   Vendor
   City/State
   Product
   Telephone #
   URL
2. Internet and online services information
   Service provider name
   Logon telephone number
   Alternate logon telephone number
   Technical support telephone number
   User ID
   Password
3. Web site information
   Web site name
   URL
   User ID
   Password
   Nickname
4. Serial numbers
   Product
   Manufacturer
   Serial #
5. Purchase history
   Date
   Product
   Manufacturer
   Vendor
   Cost
6. Software log
   Date installed/uninstalled
7. Trouble log
   Date
   Time
   Problem
   Resolution
8. Support calls
   Date
   Time
   Company
   Contact
   Problem
   Comments
9. Vendor paperwork

Figure 50
To keep important information about your computer on hand and organized, use an outline such as this sample outline.

2 **Before you work inside your computer, turn off the power and disconnect the equipment from the power source.** Working inside your computer with the power on can affect both you and the computer adversely. Thus, you should turn off the power and disconnect the equipment from the power source before you open a computer to work inside. In addition, before you touch anything inside the computer, you should touch an unpainted metal surface such as the power supply. Doing so will help discharge any static electricity that could damage internal components.

3 **Keep the area surrounding your computer dirt and dust free.** Reducing the dirt and dust around your computer will reduce the need to clean the inside of your computer. If dust builds up inside the computer, remove it carefully with compressed air and a small vacuum. Do not touch the components with the vacuum.

4 **Back up important files and data.** Use the operating system or utility program to create an emergency or rescue disk to help you restart your computer if it crashes. You also regularly should copy important data files to disks, tape, or another computer.

Web Link

For more information on viruses, visit the Introduction to Computers WEB LINK page (scsite.com/ic4/weblink.htm) and click **Viruses**.

5 **Protect your computer from viruses.** A computer virus is a potentially damaging computer program designed to infect other software or files by attaching itself to the software or files with which it comes in contact. Virus programs are dangerous because often they destroy or corrupt data stored on the infected computer. You can protect your computer from viruses by installing an antivirus program.

6 **Keep your computer tuned.** Most operating systems include several computer tools that provide basic maintenance functions. One important tool is the disk defragmenter. Defragmenting your hard disk reorganizes files so they are in contiguous (adjacent) clusters, making disk operations faster. Some programs allow you to schedule maintenance tasks for times when you are not using your computer. If necessary, leave your computer on at night so it can run the required maintenance programs. If your operating system does not provide the tools, you can purchase a stand-alone utility program to perform basic maintenance functions.

Web Link

For more information on diagnostic tools, visit the Introduction to Computers WEB LINK page (scsite.com/ic4/weblink.htm) and click **Diagnostic Tools**.

7 **Learn to use diagnostic tools.** Diagnostic tools help you identify and resolve problems, thereby helping to reduce your need for technical assistance. Diagnostic tools help you test components, monitor resources such as memory and processing power, undo changes made to files, and more. As with basic maintenance tools, most operating systems include diagnostic tools; you also can purchase or download many stand-alone diagnostic tools.

LEARN IT ONLINE

INSTRUCTIONS

To complete these exercises, start your browser, click the Address box, and then enter `scsite.com/off2002/exs.htm`. When the Introduction to Computers Web page displays, follow the instructions in the exercises below.

1. Project Reinforcement - True/False, Multiple Choice, and Short Answer

Click Project Reinforcement. Print the quiz by clicking Print on the File menu. Answer each question. Write your first and last name at the top of each page, and then hand in the printout to your instructor.

2. Practice Test

Click Practice Test. Answer each question, enter your first and last name at the bottom of the page, and then click the Grade Test button. When the graded practice test displays on your screen, click Print on the File menu to print a hard copy. Continue to take practice tests until you score 80% or better. Hand in a printout of the final practice test to your instructor.

3. Who Wants to Be a Computer Genius?

Click Computer Genius. Read the instructions, enter your first and last name at the bottom of the page, and then click the PLAY button. Submit your score to your instructor.

4. Wheel of Terms

Click Wheel of Terms. Read the instructions, and then enter your first and last name and your school name. Click the VERY HIGH SCORES link to see other student scores. Close the HIGH SCORES window. Click the PLAY button. Submit your score to your instructor.

5. Crossword Puzzle Challenge

Click Crossword Puzzle Challenge. Read the instructions, and then enter your first and last name. Click the PLAY button. Work the crossword puzzle. When you are finished, click the Submit button. When the crossword puzzle re-displays, click the Print button. Hand in the printout to your instructor.

6. Using the Web Guide

Click Web Guide. Click the Computers and Computing link, and then take a tour of the Virtual Museum of Computing. When you are finished, close the window, and then use your word processing program to prepare a brief report on your tour. Visit four other Web sites listed in the Web Guide and print the main page of each. Hand in the printouts to your instructor.

7. Visiting Web Link Sites

Click the Web Link link. Visit 10 of the 33 Web Link sites. Print the main Web page for each of the 10 Web sites you visit and hand them in to your instructor.

8. Scavenger Hunt

Click Scavenger Hunt. Print a copy of the Scavenger Hunt page; use this page to write down your answers as you search the Web. Hand in your completed page to your instructor.

9. Search Sleuth

Click Search Sleuth to learn search techniques that will help make you a research expert. Hand in your completed assignment to your instructor.

INDEX

PHOTO CREDITS

Figure 1-3b Courtesy of Intel Corporation; *Figure 1-3c* Courtesy of Labtec, Inc.; *Figure 1-3d* Courtesy of Gateway, Inc.; *Figure 1-3e* Courtesy of Eastman Kodak Company; *Figure 1-3f* Courtesy of Thomson Multimedia; *Figure 1-3g* Courtesy of Microsoft Corporation; *Figure 1-3h* Courtesy of Labtec, Inc.; *Figure 2* Scott Goodwin Photography; *Figure 5* Courtesy of Microsoft; *Figure 6a* Courtesy of Compaq Computer Corporation; *Figure 6b* Courtesy of International Business Machines; *Figure 8* Courtesy of Intel and Amd, Inc.; *Figure 9* Scott Goodwin Photography; *Figure 10* Courtesy of Eastman Kodak Company; *Figure 14* Courtesy of Toshiba America Information Systems, Inc.; *Figure 15* Courtesy of ViewSonics Corporation; *Figure 16* Courtesy of Palm, Inc.; *Figure 17* Scott Goodwin Photography; *Figure 18* Scott Goodwin Photography; *Figure 20* Courtesy of Seagate Technology; *Figure 22* Courtesy of Pioneer Electronics; *Figure 39* Courtesy of Compaq Computer Corporation; *Figure 40* Courtesy of Toshiba America Information Systems, Inc.; *Figure 41* Courtesy of Xirom Corporation; *Figure 42* Courtesy of InFocus Corporation; *Figure 43* Courtesy of Palm, Inc.; *Figure 44* Courtesy of Compaq Computer Corporation; *Figure 49* Courtesy of Compaq Computer Corporation and PhotoDisc, Inc.

Microsoft Windows 2000 and Office XP

PROJECT

An Introduction to Windows 2000 Professional and Office XP

OBJECTIVES

You will have mastered the material in this project when you can:

- Describe the Microsoft Windows 2000 user interface
- Identify the objects on the Microsoft Windows 2000 desktop
- Perform the basic mouse operations: point, click, right-click, double-click, drag, and right-drag
- Open, minimize, maximize, restore, scroll, and close a Windows 2000 window
- Move and resize a window on the desktop
- Understand keyboard shortcut notation
- Launch and quit an application program
- Identify the elements of the Exploring window
- Create, expand, and collapse a folder
- Select and copy one file or a group of files
- Rename and delete a folder or file
- Quit Windows Explorer
- Use Windows 2000 Help
- Shut down Windows XP
- Identify each application in Microsoft Office XP
- Define the Internet, the World Wide Web, and an intranet
- Explain how each Microsoft Office XP application uses the Internet
- Understand the Microsoft Office XP Help system

Windows 2000

Reliability, Manageability, and Internet Ready

The Microsoft Windows 2000 operating system continues to lead the way with its superior software technology. Easy to use, Windows 2000 is helping businesses and individual users boost productivity while enjoying the benefits of increased computing power. Microsoft Corporation under the direction of Bill Gates, chairman and chief software architect, is a constant source of great ideas and innovation in the development of software, services, and Internet technology.

Bill Gates's computing efforts began when he was in grade school, when he and classmate, Paul Allen, learned the BASIC programming language from a manual and programmed a mainframe computer using a Teletype terminal they purchased with the proceeds from a rummage sale. In high school, Gates and Allen had a thirst for more computing power. They wrote custom programs for local businesses during the summer and split their $5,000 salaries between cash and computer time. They also debugged software problems at local businesses in return for computer use.

In Gates's sophomore year, one of his teachers asked him to teach his computer skills to his classmates. In 1972, Gates and Allen read an article in *Electronics* magazine about Intel's first microprocessor chip. They requested a manual from Intel, developed a device that experimented with pushing the chip to its limits, and formed the Traf-O-Data company; an endeavor that ultimately would lead to the formation of something much larger.

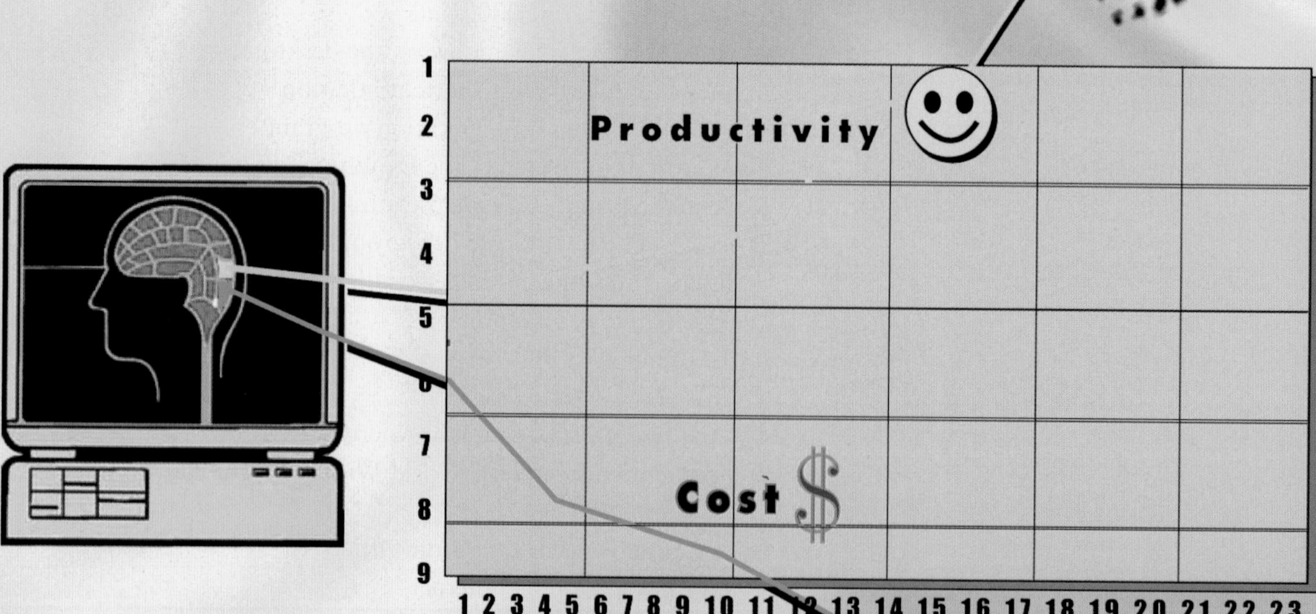

In 1973, Gates entered Harvard and Allen landed a programming job with Honeywell.

They continued to communicate and scheme about the power of computers when, in 1975, the Altair 8800 computer showed up on the cover of *Popular Electronics*. This computer was about the size of the Traf-O-Data device and contained a new Intel computer chip. At that point, they knew they were going into business. Gates left Harvard and Allen left Honeywell.

When they formed Microsoft in 1975, the company had three programmers, one product, and revenues of $16,000. The founders had no business plan, no capital, and no financial backing, but they did have a product — a form of the BASIC programming language tailored for the first microcomputer.

In 1980, IBM approached Microsoft and asked the company to provide an operating system for its new IBM personal computer. The deadline? Three months. Gates purchased the core of a suitable operating system, dubbed Q-DOS (Quick and Dirty Operating System). Microsoft's version, MS-DOS, would become the international standard for IBM and IBM-compatible personal computers. Riding the meteoric rise in sales of IBM-compatible computers and attendant sales of MS-DOS, Microsoft continued to improve its software stream of revisions. At a significant branch of the family tree, Windows made its debut, providing an intuitive graphical user interface (GUI). Similarly, Windows 95, Windows 98, and Windows NT provided further advances.

The Microsoft Windows 2000 operating system family expands the possibilities even further with the Windows 2000 Server, Windows 2000 Advanced Server, and Windows 2000 Data Center designed for use on a server in a computer network.

With the same basic user interface and more reliability, Windows 2000 Professional requires no additional training. To complete the project in this book, you will utilize the same functionality of the desktop, Windows Explorer for file and folder management, and communications with other users on a network. Clearly, Windows 2000 leads the way.

Microsoft Windows 2000 and Office XP

An Introduction to Windows 2000 Professional and Office XP

PROJECT

CASE PERSPECTIVE

After weeks of planning, your organization finally switched from Microsoft Windows 98 to Microsoft Windows 2000 Professional and installed Microsoft Office XP on all computers. As the computer trainer for the upcoming in-house seminar, you realize you should know more about Windows 2000 Professional and Office XP. Since installing Windows 2000 Professional and Office XP, many employees have come to you with questions. You have taken the time to answer their questions by sitting down with them at their computers and searching for the answers using the Microsoft Help system.

From their questions, you determine the seminar should cover the basics of Windows 2000 Professional, including basic mouse operations, working within a window, launching an application, performing file maintenance using Windows Explorer, and searching for answers to employees' questions using Windows 2000 Help. In addition, the seminar should familiarize the participants with each of the Office XP applications. Your goal in this project is to become familiar with Windows 2000 Professional and the Office XP applications in order to teach the seminar.

Introduction

Microsoft Windows 2000 Professional is a widely used version of the Microsoft Windows operating system designed for use on computer workstations and portable computers. A **workstation** is a computer connected to a network. Microsoft Windows 2000 Professional is an easy-to-use program that allows you to control your computer and communicate with other computers on a network.

In this project, you will learn about Microsoft Windows 2000 Professional and how to use the Windows 2000 graphical user interface to organize the manner in which you interact with your computer, simplify the process of working with documents and applications, and use your computer to access information on both the Internet and on an intranet.

In the first part of this project, you will work with the desktop and the windows available on the desktop, learn the basic mouse operations, and launch an application program. Using Windows 2000 Explorer, you will learn to create and view the contents of folders, select and copy a file or group of files, rename and delete files and folders, and use Microsoft Windows 2000 Help.

Microsoft Office XP, the latest edition of the world's best-selling office suite, is a collection of the more popular Microsoft application software products that work similarly and together as if they were a single program. Microsoft Office XP integrates these applications and combines them with the power of the Internet so you can move quickly among applications, transfer text and graphics easily, and interact seamlessly with the World Wide Web. An explanation of each of the application software programs in Microsoft Office XP is given at the end of this project.

What Is Microsoft Windows 2000 Professional?

An **operating system** is the set of computer instructions, called a computer program, that controls the allocation of computer hardware, such as memory, disk devices, printers, and CD-ROM and DVD drives, and provides you with the capability of communicating with your computer. The most powerful Microsoft operating system is the **Microsoft Windows 2000 family of operating systems** consisting of the Microsoft Windows 2000 Server, Microsoft Windows 2000 Advanced Server, Microsoft Windows 2000 Data Center, and Microsoft Windows 2000 Professional. The operating system of choice for computer workstations and portable computers is **Microsoft Windows 2000 Professional** (called **Windows 2000** for the rest of this book).

Windows 2000 is an operating system that performs every function necessary to enable you to communicate with and use your computer. Windows 2000 is called a **32-bit operating system** because it uses 32 bits for addressing and other purposes, which means the operating system can address more than four gigabytes of RAM (random-access memory) and perform tasks faster than older operating systems. Windows 2000 includes **Microsoft Internet Explorer** (**IE**), a browser software program developed by Microsoft Corporation that integrates the Windows 2000 desktop and the Internet. Internet Explorer and allows you to work with programs and files in a similar fashion, whether they are located on your computer, a local network, or the Internet.

Windows 2000 is designed to be compatible with all existing **application programs**, which are the programs that perform an application-related function such as word processing. To use the application programs that can be launched under Windows 2000, you must know about the Windows 2000 user interface.

More About

Microsoft Windows 2000

Microsoft Windows 2000 combines the best business features of Windows 98 with the strengths of Windows NT 4.0. Windows 98, designed for use on personal computers, is the most popular operating system for personal computers. Windows NT 4.0, designed for use on a computer network, is the most widely used version of Windows NT.

What Is a User Interface?

A **user interface** is the combination of hardware and software that you use to communicate with and control your computer. Through the user interface, you are able to make selections on your computer, request information from your computer, and respond to messages displayed by your computer. Thus, a user interface provides the means for dialogue between you and a computer.

Hardware and software together form the user interface. Among the hardware devices associated with a user interface are the monitor, keyboard, and mouse (Figure 1-1). The **monitor** displays messages and provides information.

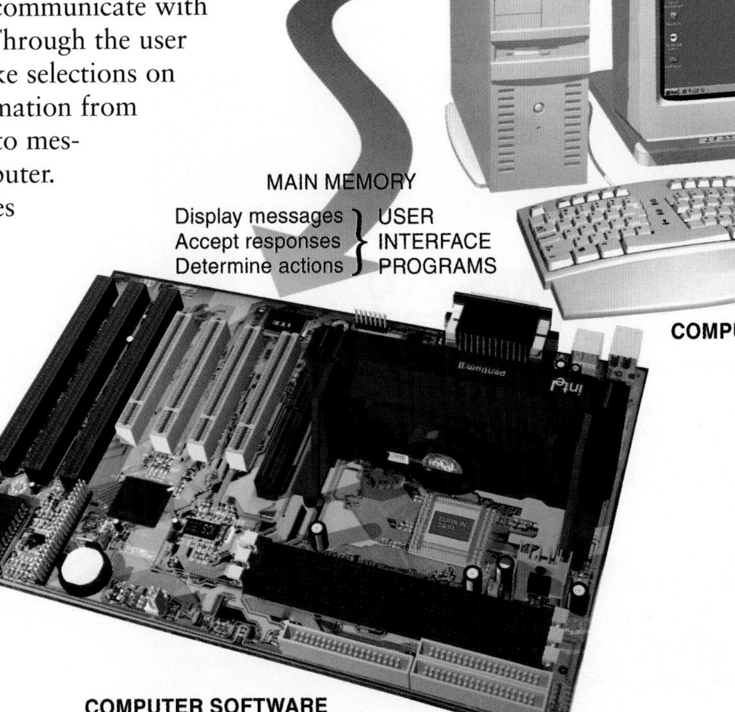

FIGURE 1-1

More About

Windows 2000

For additional information about the Windows 2000 operating system, visit the Office XP More About Web page (scsite.com/offxp/more.htm) and then click Windows 2000.

The Windows 2000 Interface

Some older interfaces, called command-line interfaces, required that you type keywords (special words, phrases, or codes the computer understands) or press special keys on the keyboard to communicate with the interface. Today, graphical user interfaces incorporate colorful graphics, use of the mouse, and Web browser-like features, making today's interfaces user friendly.

You respond by entering data in the form of a command or other response using the **keyboard** or **mouse**. Among the responses available are responses that specify which application program to run, which document to open, when to print, and where to store data for future use.

The computer software associated with the user interface consists of the programs that engage you in dialogue (Figure 1-1 on the previous page). The computer software determines the messages you receive, the manner in which you should respond, and the actions that occur based on your responses.

The goal of an effective user interface is to be **user friendly**, meaning that the software can be used easily by individuals with limited training. Research studies have indicated that the use of graphics can play an important role in aiding users to interact effectively with a computer. A **graphical user interface**, or **GUI** (pronounced gooey), is a user interface that displays graphics in addition to text when it communicates with the user.

The Windows 2000 graphical user interface was designed carefully to be easier to set up, simpler to learn, faster and more powerful, and better integrated with the Internet than previous versions of Microsoft Windows.

Launching Microsoft Windows 2000 Professional

When you turn on the computer, an introductory screen containing the words, Microsoft Windows 2000 Professional, and the Please Wait... screen display momentarily followed by the Welcome to Windows dialog box (Figure 1-2). A **dialog box** displays whenever Windows 2000 needs to supply information to you or wants you to enter information or select an option. The **title bar**, which is at the top of the dialog box and blue in color, identifies the name of the dialog box (Welcome to Windows). The Welcome to Windows dialog box displays on a green background and contains the Windows logo, title (Microsoft Windows 2000 Professional Built on NT Technology), keyboard icon, instructions (Press Ctrl-Alt-Delete to begin.), a message, and the Help link.

Holding down the CTRL key and pressing the ALT and DELETE keys simultaneously will remove the Welcome to Windows dialog box and display the Log On to Windows dialog box (Figure 1-3). The Log On to Windows dialog box contains the User name and Password text boxes, Log on to box, Log on using dial-up connection check box, and four command buttons (OK, Cancel, Shutdown, and Options). A **text box** is a rectangular area in which you can enter text. Currently, the user name (Brad Wilson) displays in the User name text box, a series of asterisks (*****) displays in the Password text box to hide the password entered by the user, and the computer name, BRADWILSON (this computer), displays in the Log on to box. The **check box** represents an option to log on using an established dial-up Internet connection. The **command buttons** allow you to perform different operations, such

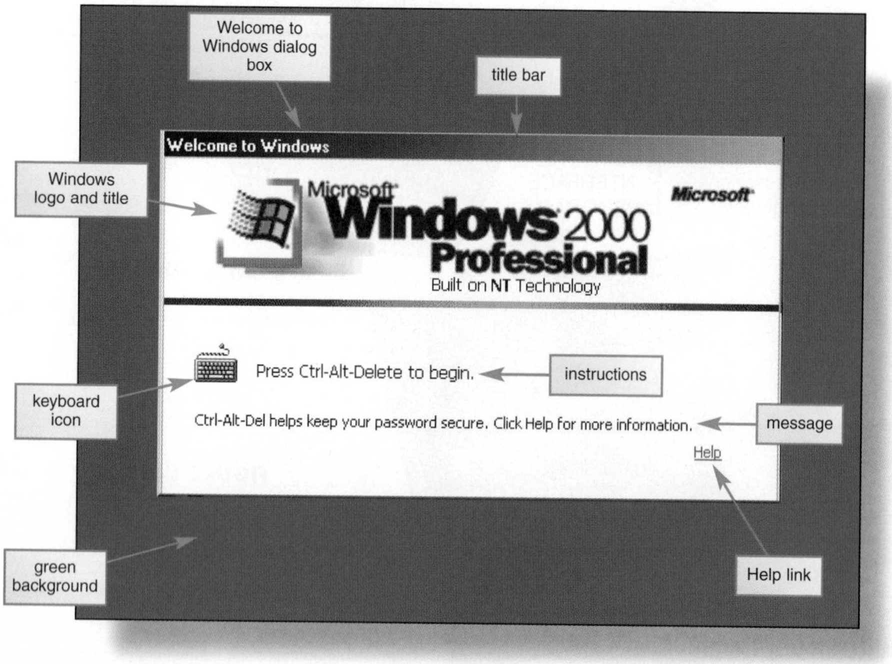

Welcome to Windows dialog box | title bar | Welcome to Windows | Windows logo and title | Microsoft Windows 2000 Professional Built on NT Technology | Microsoft | Press Ctrl-Alt-Delete to begin. | instructions | keyboard icon | Ctrl-Alt-Del helps keep your password secure. Click Help for more information. | message | Help | green background | Help link

FIGURE 1-2

as accepting the user name and password or displaying additional options. If you do not know your user name or password, ask your instructor.

Entering your user name in the User name text box and your password in the Password text box and then clicking the OK button will clear the screen and allow several items to display on a background called the **desktop**. The default color of the desktop background is green, but your computer may display a different color.

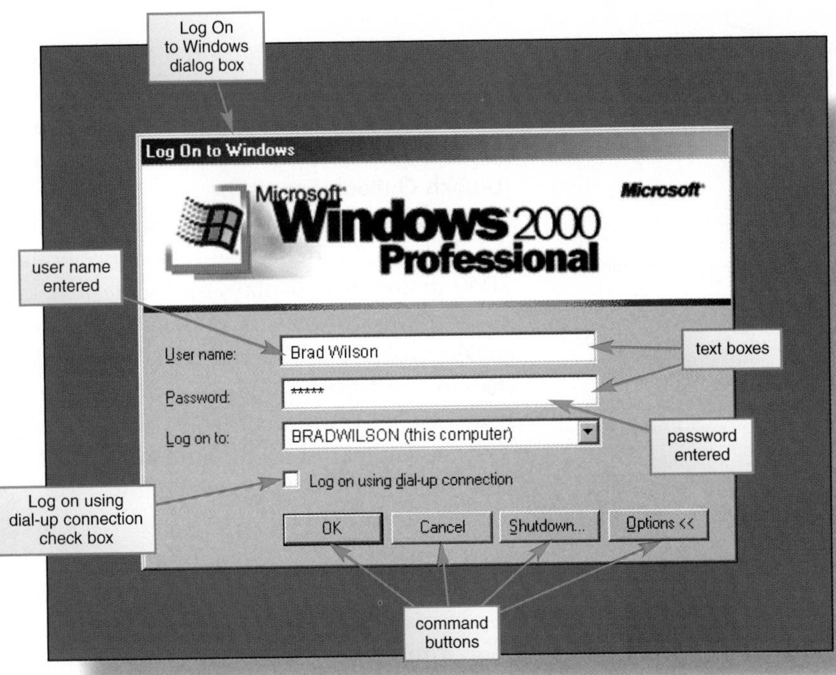

FIGURE 1-3

The items on the desktop in Figure 1-4 include five icons and their names on the left side of the desktop and the taskbar at the bottom of the desktop. Using the five **icons**, you can store documents in one location (**My Documents**), view the contents of the computer (**My Computer**), work with other computers connected to the computer (**My Network Places**), discard unneeded objects (**Recycle Bin**), and browse Web pages on the Internet (**Internet Explorer**). Your computer's desktop may contain more, fewer, or different icons because you can customize the desktop of the computer.

The **taskbar** shown at the bottom of the screen in Figure 1-4 contains the Start button, Quick Launch toolbar, taskbar button area, and tray status area. The **Start button** allows you to launch a program quickly, find or open a document, change the

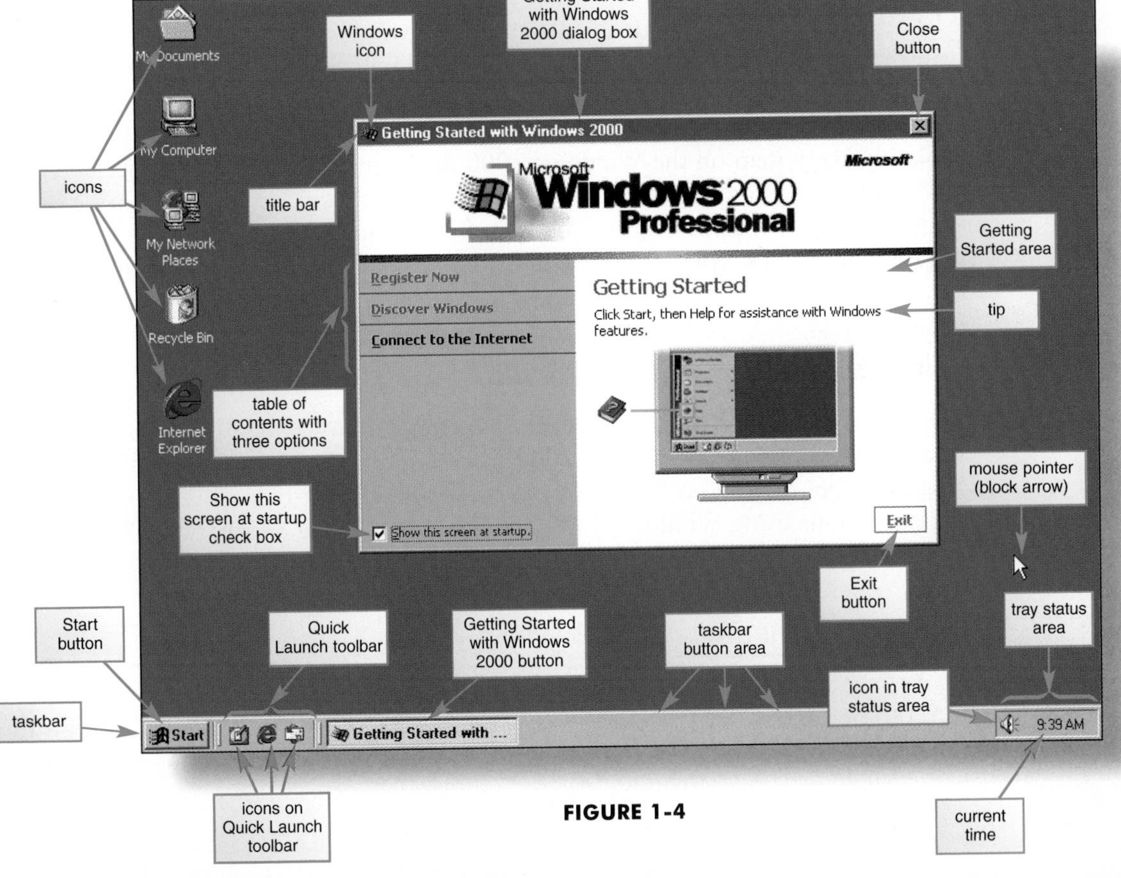

FIGURE 1-4

computer's settings, shut down the computer, and perform many other tasks. The **Quick Launch toolbar** contains three icons. The first icon allows you to view an uncluttered desktop at anytime (**Show Desktop**). The second icon launches Internet Explorer (**Launch Internet Explorer Browser**). The third icon launches Outlook Express (**Launch Outlook Express**).

The **taskbar button area** contains buttons to indicate which windows are open on the desktop. In Figure 1-4 on the previous page, the Getting Started with Windows 2000 dialog box displays on the desktop and the Getting Started with Windows 2000 button displays in the taskbar button area. The **tray status area** contains a speaker icon to adjust the computer's volume level. The tray status area also displays the current time (9:39 AM). The tray status area on your desktop may contain more, fewer, or some different icons because the contents of the tray status area change.

The Getting Started with Windows 2000 dialog box that may display on your desktop when you launch Windows 2000 is shown in Figure 1-4. The **title bar** at the top of the dialog box, which is dark blue in color, contains the Windows icon, identifies the name of the dialog box (Getting Started with Windows 2000), and contains the Close button to close the Getting Started with Windows 2000 dialog box.

In the Getting Started with Windows 2000 dialog box, a table of contents containing three options (Register Now, Discover Windows, and Connect to the Internet) and the Getting Started area containing constantly changing helpful tips about Windows 2000 display. The options in the table of contents allow you to perform different tasks such as registering the Windows 2000 operating system, learning Windows 2000 using the Discover Windows 2000 tour, and connecting to the Internet.

Pointing to an option in the table of contents replaces the contents of the Getting Started area with an explanation of the option. Clicking an option starts the task associated with the option.

A check box containing a check mark displays below the table of contents. The check mark in the check box represents an option to display the Getting Started with Windows 2000 dialog box each time you launch Windows 2000. The **Exit button** at the bottom of the Getting Started area closes the window.

In the lower-right corner of the desktop is the mouse pointer. The **mouse pointer** is the shape of a block arrow. The mouse pointer allows you to point to objects on the desktop and may change shape as it points to different objects.

Nearly every item on the Windows 2000 desktop is considered an object. Even the desktop itself is an object. Every **object** has properties. The **properties** of an object are unique to that specific object and may affect what can be done to the object or what the object does. For example, one of the properties of an object may be its color, such as the color of the desktop.

More About

The Windows 2000 Desktop

Because Windows 2000 is easily customized, the desktop on your computer may not resemble the desktop in Figure 1-4 on page INT 1.07. For example, the icon titles on the desktop may be underlined or objects not shown in Figure 1-4 may display on your desktop. If this is the case, contact your instructor for instructions for selecting the default desktop settings.

More About

Windows 2000 Tips and Tricks

For Windows 2000 tips and tricks, visit the Office XP More About Web page (scsite.com/offxp/more.htm) and then click Windows 2000 Tips and Tricks.

More About

Windows 2000 Performance

To improve Windows 2000 performance, visit the Office XP More About Web page (scsite.com/offxp/more.htm) and then click Windows 2000 Performance.

More About

The Mouse

The mouse, though invented in the 1960s, was not used widely until the Apple Macintosh computer became available in 1984. Even then, some highbrows called mouse users "wimps". Today, the mouse is an indispensable tool for every computer user.

Closing the Getting Started with Windows 2000 Dialog Box

As previously noted, the Getting Started with Windows 2000 dialog box may display when you launch Windows 2000. If the Getting Started with Windows 2000 dialog box does display on the desktop, you should close it before beginning any other operations using Windows 2000. To close the Getting Started with Windows 2000 dialog box, complete the following step.

TO CLOSE THE GETTING STARTED WITH WINDOWS 2000 DIALOG BOX

1. Press and hold the ALT key on the keyboard, press the F4 key on the keyboard, and then release the ALT key.

The Getting Started with Windows 2000 dialog box closes.

The Desktop as a Work Area

The Windows 2000 desktop and the objects on the desktop were designed to emulate a work area in an office or at home. You may think of the Windows desktop as an electronic version of the top of your desk. You can move objects around on the desktop, look at them and then put them aside, and so on. In this project, you will learn how to interact with the Windows 2000 desktop.

Communicating with Microsoft Windows 2000

The Windows 2000 interface provides the means for dialogue between you and your computer. Part of this dialogue involves your requesting information from your computer and responding to messages displayed by your computer. You can request information and respond to messages using either a mouse or a keyboard.

FIGURE 1-5

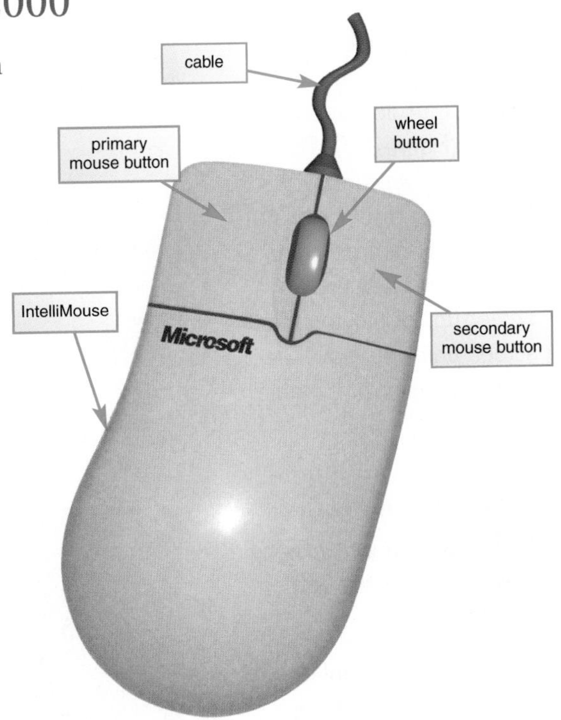

Mouse Operations

A **mouse** is a pointing device that is attached to the computer by a cable. Although not required when using Windows 2000, Windows supports the use of the **Microsoft IntelliMouse** (Figure 1-5). The IntelliMouse contains three buttons: the primary mouse button, the secondary mouse button, and the wheel button between the primary and secondary mouse buttons. Typically, the **primary mouse button** is the left mouse button and the **secondary mouse button** is the right mouse button, although Windows 2000 allows you to switch them. In this book, the left mouse button is the primary mouse button and the right mouse button is the secondary mouse button. The functions the **wheel button** and wheel perform depend on the software application being used. If the mouse connected to your computer is not an IntelliMouse, it will not have a wheel button between the primary and secondary mouse buttons.

Using the mouse, you can perform the following operations: (1) point; (2) click; (3) right-click; (4) double-click; (5) drag; and (6) right-drag. These operations are demonstrated on the following pages.

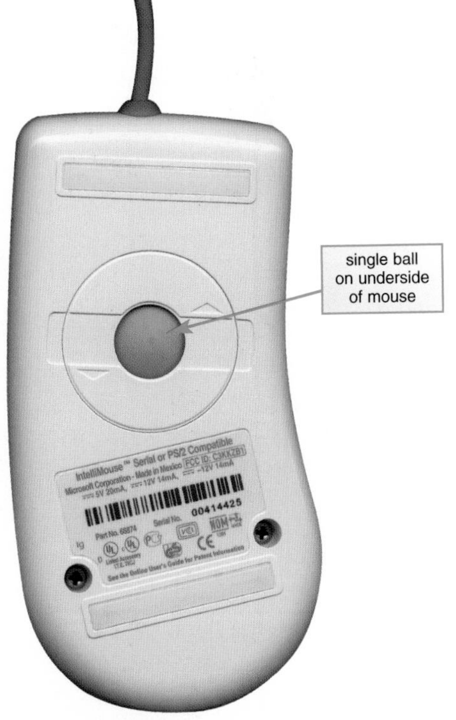

FIGURE 1-6

Point and Click

Point means you move the mouse across a flat surface until the mouse pointer rests on the item of choice on the desktop. As you move the mouse across a flat surface, the movement of a ball on the underside of the mouse (Figure 1-6) is sensed electronically, and the mouse pointer moves across the desktop in the same direction.

Click means you press and release the primary mouse button, which in this book is the left mouse button. In most cases, you must point to an item before you can click it. To become acquainted with the use of the mouse, perform the following steps to point to and click various objects on the desktop.

Steps To Point and Click

1 Point to the Start button on the taskbar by moving the mouse across a flat surface until the mouse pointer rests on the Start button.

The mouse pointer on the Start button displays a ScreenTip (Click here to begin) (Figure 1-7). The ***ScreenTip****, which provides instructions, displays on the desktop for approximately five seconds. Other ScreenTips display on the screen until you move the mouse pointer off the object.*

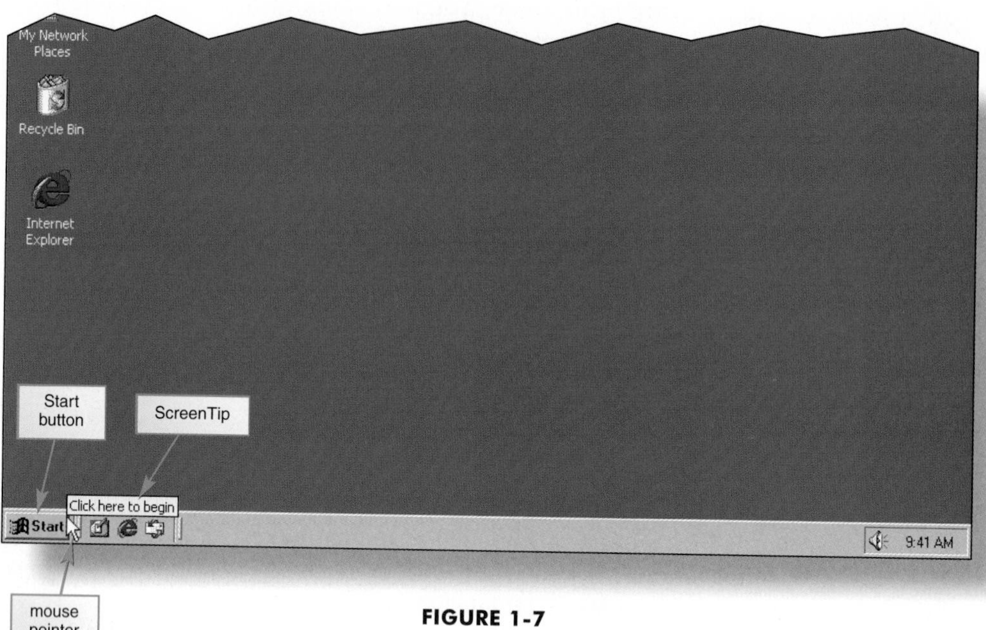

FIGURE 1-7

2 Click the Start button by pressing and releasing the left mouse button.

The Start menu displays and the Start button is recessed on the taskbar (Figure 1-8). A ***menu*** *is a list of related commands. A* ***command*** *directs Windows 2000 to perform a specific action such as shutting down the operating system. Each command on the Start menu consists of an icon and a command name. A* ***right arrow*** *follows some commands to indicate pointing to the command will open a submenu. Two commands (Run and Shut Down) are followed by an* ***ellipsis*** *(...) to indicate more information is required to execute these commands.*

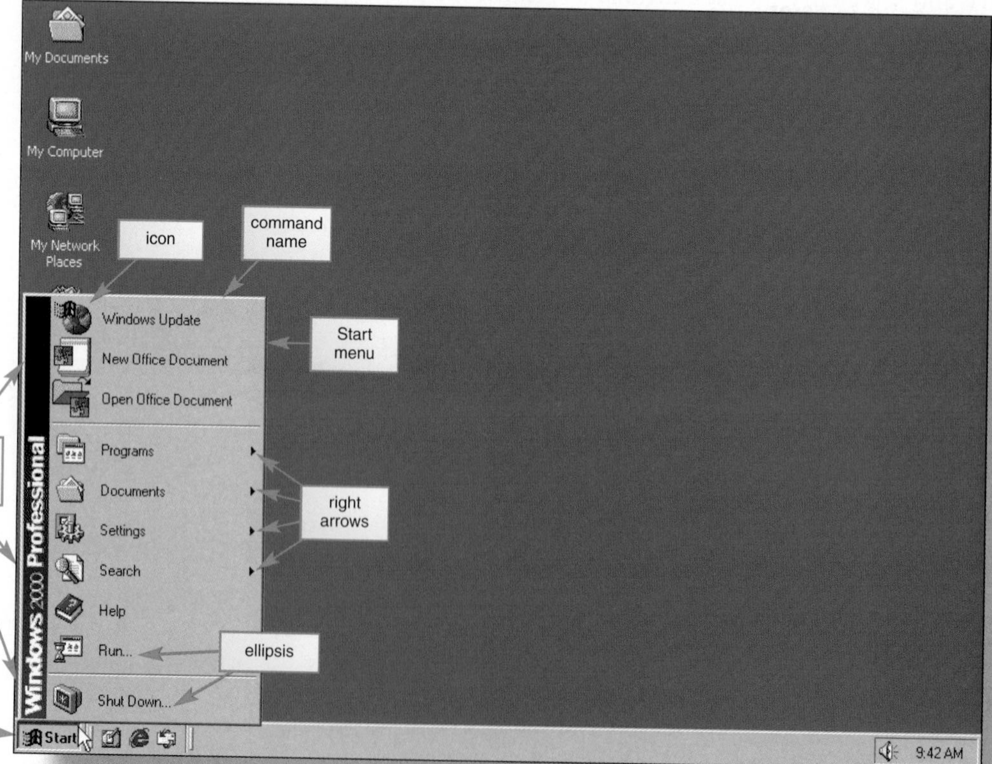

FIGURE 1-8

3 **Point to Programs on the Start menu.**

When you point to Programs, Windows 2000 highlights the Programs command on the Start menu and the Programs submenu displays (Figure 1-9). A ***submenu****, or* ***cascading menu****, is a menu that displays when you point to a command that is followed by a right arrow. Whenever you point to a command on a menu, the command is highlighted.*

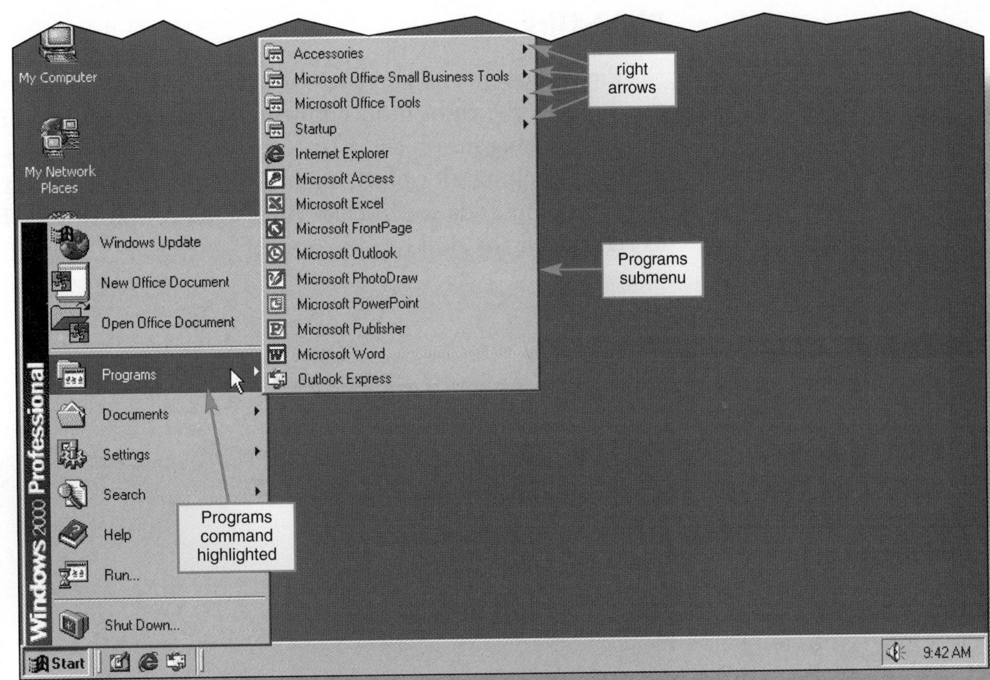

FIGURE 1-9

4 **Point to an open area of the desktop and then click the open area.**

The Start menu and Programs submenu close (Figure 1-10). The mouse pointer points to the desktop. To close a menu anytime, click any open area of the desktop except on the menu itself. The Start button is no longer recessed.

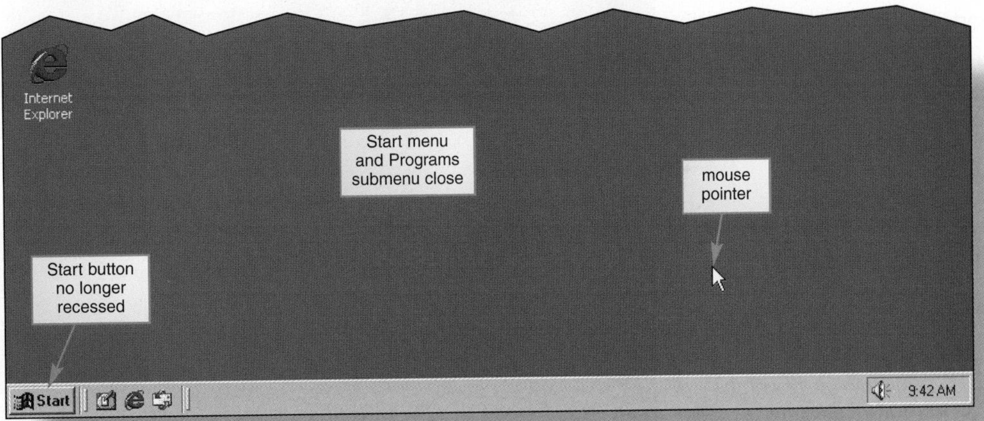

FIGURE 1-10

The Start menu shown in Figure 1-8 is divided into three sections. The top section contains commands to launch the Windows Update application (Windows Update) and create a new or open an existing Microsoft Office document (New Office Document and Open Office Document); the middle section contains commands to launch an application, work with documents or Web sites, customize options, search for files, obtain Help, or run a program from an auxiliary drive (Programs, Documents, Settings, Search, Help, and Run); and the bottom section contains a basic operating task (Shut Down).

When you click an object, such as the Start button, you must point to the object before you click. In the steps on the next page, the instruction that directs you to point to a particular item and then click is, Click the particular item. For example, Click the Start button means point to the Start button and then click.

Buttons

Buttons on the desktop and in programs are an integral part of Windows 2000. When you point to them, their function displays in a ToolTip. When you click them, they appear to indent on the screen to mimic what would happen if you pushed an actual button. All buttons in Windows 2000 behave in the same manner.

Right-Click

Right-click means you press and release the secondary mouse button, which in this book is the right mouse button. As directed when using the primary mouse button for clicking an object, normally you will point to an object before you right-click it. Right-clicking an object, such as the desktop, opens a **shortcut menu** that contains a set of commands specifically for use with that object. Perform the following steps to right-click the desktop.

To Right-Click

1 Point to an open area of the desktop and then press and release the right mouse button.

A shortcut menu displays (Figure 1-11). This shortcut menu consists of eight commands. When a command on a menu appears dimmed, such as the Paste and Paste Shortcut commands, that command is unavailable.

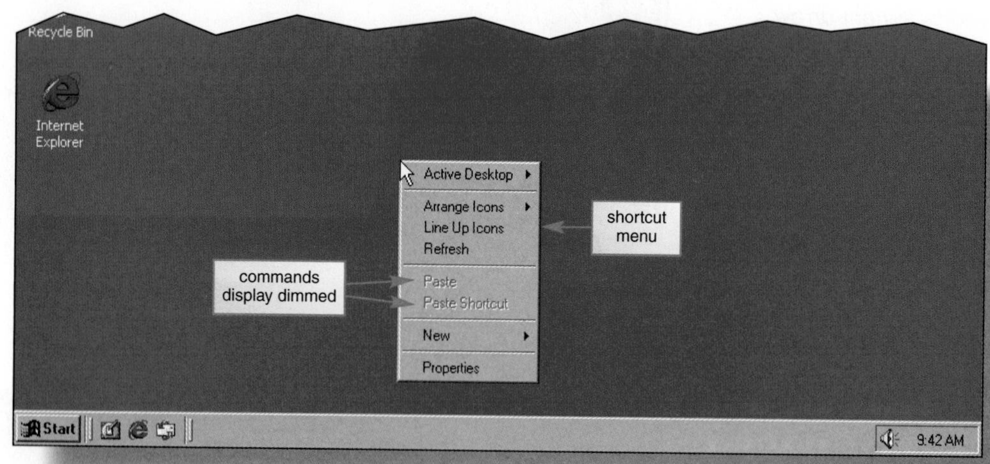

FIGURE 1-11

2 Point to New on the shortcut menu.

When you move the mouse pointer to the New command, Windows 2000 highlights the New command and opens the New submenu (Figure 1-12). The ***New submenu*** *contains a variety of commands. The number of commands and the actual commands that display on your computer may be different.*

3 Point to an open area of the desktop and then click the open area to close the shortcut menu and the New submenu.

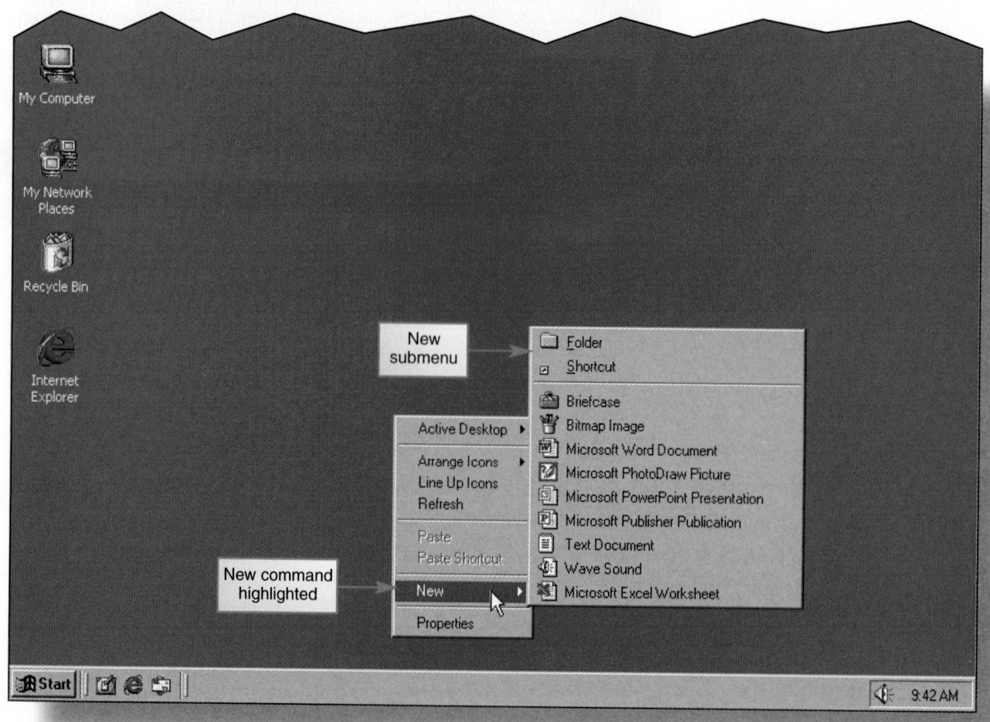

FIGURE 1-12

Whenever you right-click an object, a shortcut menu (also referred to as an **object menu**) will display. As you will see, the use of shortcut menus speeds up your work and adds flexibility to your interface with the computer.

More About

Right-Clicking

Right-clicking an object other than the desktop will display a different shortcut menu with commands useful to that object. Right-clicking an object is thought to be the fastest method of performing an operation on an object.

Double-Click

To double-click, you quickly press and release the left mouse button twice without moving the mouse. In most cases, you must point to an item before you double-click. Perform the following step to open the My Computer window on the desktop by double-clicking the My Computer icon.

To Open a Window by Double-Clicking

1 Point to the My Computer icon on the desktop and then double-click by quickly pressing and releasing the left mouse button twice without moving the mouse.

The My Computer window opens (Figure 1-13). The recessed My Computer button is added to the taskbar button area.

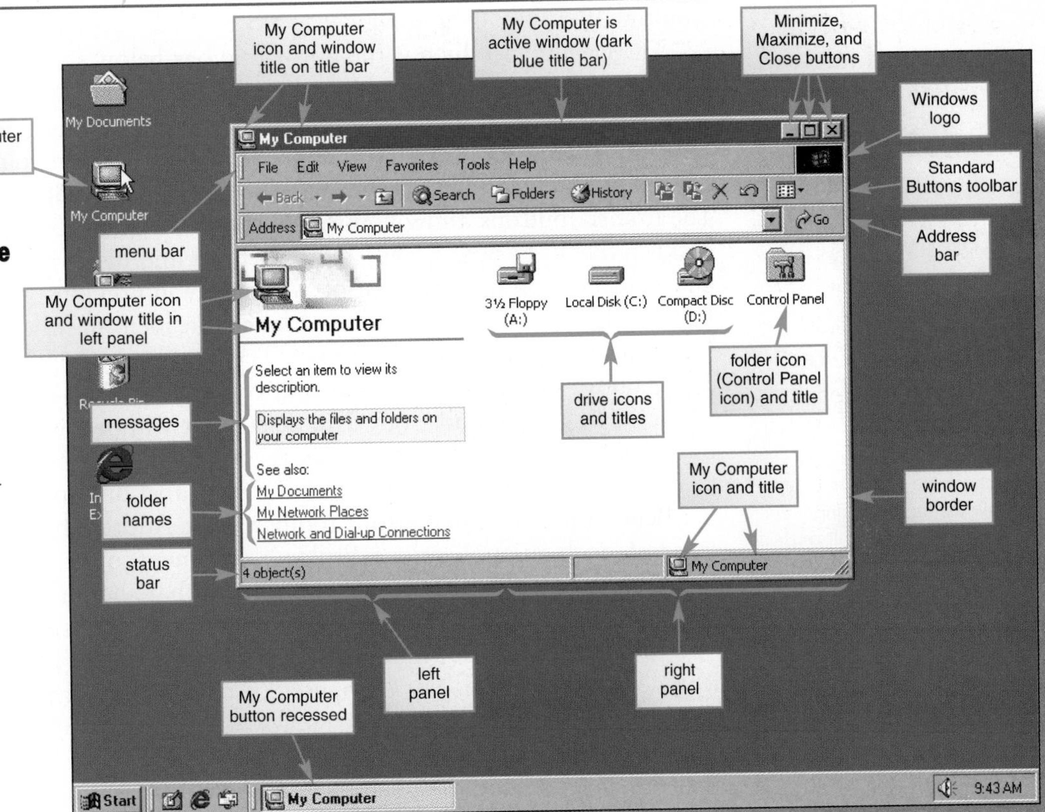

FIGURE 1-13

The My Computer window, the only open window, is the active window. The **active window** is the window currently being used. Whenever you click an object that can be opened, such as the My Computer icon, Windows 2000 will open the object; and the open object will be identified by a recessed button in the taskbar button area. The recessed button identifies the active window.

The contents of the My Computer window on your computer may be different from the contents of the My Computer window illustrated in Figure 1-13.

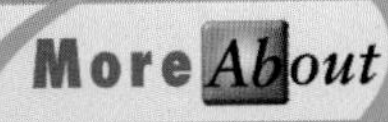

Double-Clicking

Double-clicking is the most difficult mouse skill to learn. Many people have a tendency to move the mouse before they click a second time, even when they do not want to move the mouse. You should find, however, that with a little practice, double-clicking becomes quite natural.

More About

My Computer

The trade press and media have poked fun at the icon name, My Computer. One wag said no one should use Windows 2000 for more than five minutes without changing the name (which is easily done). Microsoft responds that in their usability labs, beginning computer users found the name, My Computer, easier to understand.

More About

My Computer Window

Because Windows 2000 is easily customized, the My Computer window on your computer may not resemble the window in Figure 1-13 on page INT 1.13. If this is the case, check the commands on the View menu by clicking View on the menu bar. If a check mark precedes the as Web Page command, click the as Web Page command. If a large dot does not precede the Large Icons command, click the Large Icons command.

My Computer Window

The thin line, or **window border**, surrounding the My Computer window shown in Figure 1-13 on the previous page determines the window shape and size. The **title bar** at the top of the window contains a small icon that is the same as the icon on the desktop and the **window title** (My Computer) that identifies the window. The color of the title bar (dark blue) and the recessed My Computer button in the taskbar button area indicate the My Computer window is the active window. The color of the active window on your computer may be different from the dark blue color shown in Figure 1-13 on the previous page.

Clicking the icon at the left on the title bar will display the **System menu**, which contains commands to carry out the actions associated with the My Computer window. At the right on the title bar are three buttons, the Minimize button, the Maximize button, and the Close button, that can be used to specify the size of the window or close the window.

The **menu bar**, which is the horizontal bar below the title bar of a window (Figure 1-13 on the previous page), contains a list of menu names for the My Computer window: File, Edit, View, Favorites, Tools, and Help. At the right end of the menu bar is a button containing the Windows logo.

Below the menu bar, eleven buttons display on the **Standard Buttons toolbar.** The first six buttons allow you to navigate through an open window on the desktop (Back, Forward, and Up); search for and display files or folders (Search and Folders); and display a list of Web sites you previously have visited (History). Four of these buttons contain a **text label** that identifies the function of the button (Back, Search, Folders, and History). The last five buttons do not contain text labels. These buttons allow you to move and copy text within a window or between windows (Move To and Copy To); delete text within a window (Delete); undo a previous action (Undo); and display the icons in the window in different formats (Views). Pointing to a button without a text label displays the button name.

Below the Standard Buttons toolbar is the Address bar. The **Address bar** allows you to launch an application, display a document, open another window, and search for information on the Internet. The Address bar shown in Figure 1-13 on the previous page contains the My Computer icon and window title (My Computer).

The area below the Address bar is divided into two panels. The My Computer icon and window title, My Computer, display in the left panel. Several messages and three folder names (My Documents, My Network Places, and Network and Dial-Up Connections) display below the icon and title in the left panel. The three folder names are underlined and display in blue font. Underlined text, such as the folder names, is referred to as a **hyperlink**, or simply a **link**. Pointing to a hyperlink changes the mouse pointer to a hand icon, and clicking a hyperlink displays the contents of the associated folder in the window.

The right panel of the My Computer window contains four icons. A title below each icon identifies the icon. The first three icons, called **drive icons**, represent a 3½ Floppy (A:) drive, a Local Disk (C:) drive, and a Compact Disc (D:) drive. The fourth icon is the Control Panel folder. A **folder** is an object created to contain related documents, applications, and other folders. A folder in Windows 2000 contains items in much the same way a folder on your desk contains items. The **Control Panel folder** allows you to personalize the computer, such as specifying how you want the desktop to look.

Clicking a drive or folder icon selects the icon in the right panel and displays information about the drive or folder in the left panel. Double-clicking a drive or folder icon displays the contents of the drive or folder in the right panel and information about the drive or folder in the left panel. You may find more, fewer, or different drive and folder icons in the My Computer window on your computer.

A message at the left on the **status bar** located at the bottom of the window indicates the right panel contains four objects (Figure 1-13 on page INT 1.13). The My Computer icon and title display to the right of the message on the status bar.

Minimizing Windows

Windows management on the Windows 2000 desktop is important in order to keep the desktop uncluttered. You will find yourself frequently minimizing windows and then later reopening them with a click of a button in the taskbar button area.

Minimize Button

Two buttons on the title bar of a window, the Minimize button and the Maximize button, allow you to control the way a window displays or does not display on the desktop. When you click the **Minimize button** (Figure 1-13 on page INT 1.13), the My Computer window no longer displays on the desktop and the recessed My Computer button in the taskbar button area changes to a non-recessed button. A minimized window still is open but it does not display on the screen. To minimize and then redisplay the My Computer window, complete these steps.

Steps To Minimize and Redisplay a Window

1 Point to the Minimize button on the title bar of the My Computer window.

The mouse pointer points to the Minimize button on the My Computer window title bar (Figure 1-14). A ScreenTip displays below the Minimize button and the My Computer button in the taskbar button area is recessed.

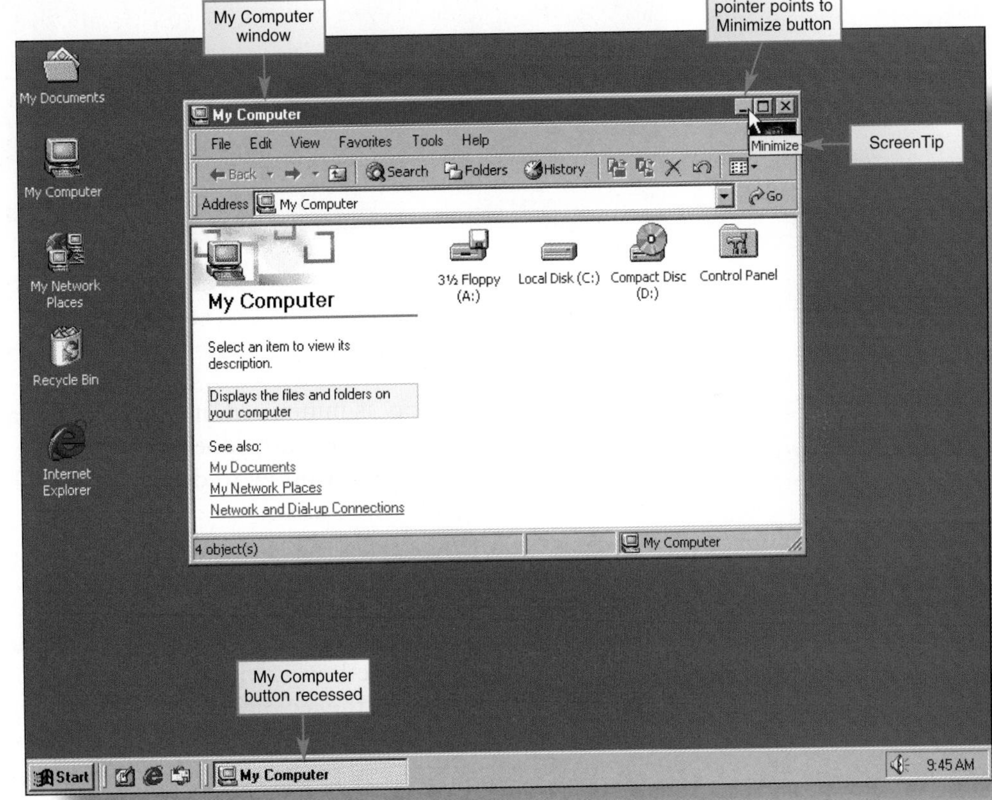

FIGURE 1-14

2 Click the Minimize button.

When you minimize the My Computer window, Windows removes the My Computer window from the desktop and the My Computer button changes to a non-recessed button (Figure 1-15).

FIGURE 1-15

3 Click the My Computer button in the taskbar button area.

The My Computer window displays on the desktop in the same place and size as it was before being minimized (Figure 1-16). In addition, the My Computer window is the active window because it contains the dark blue title bar, and the My Computer button in the taskbar button area is recessed.

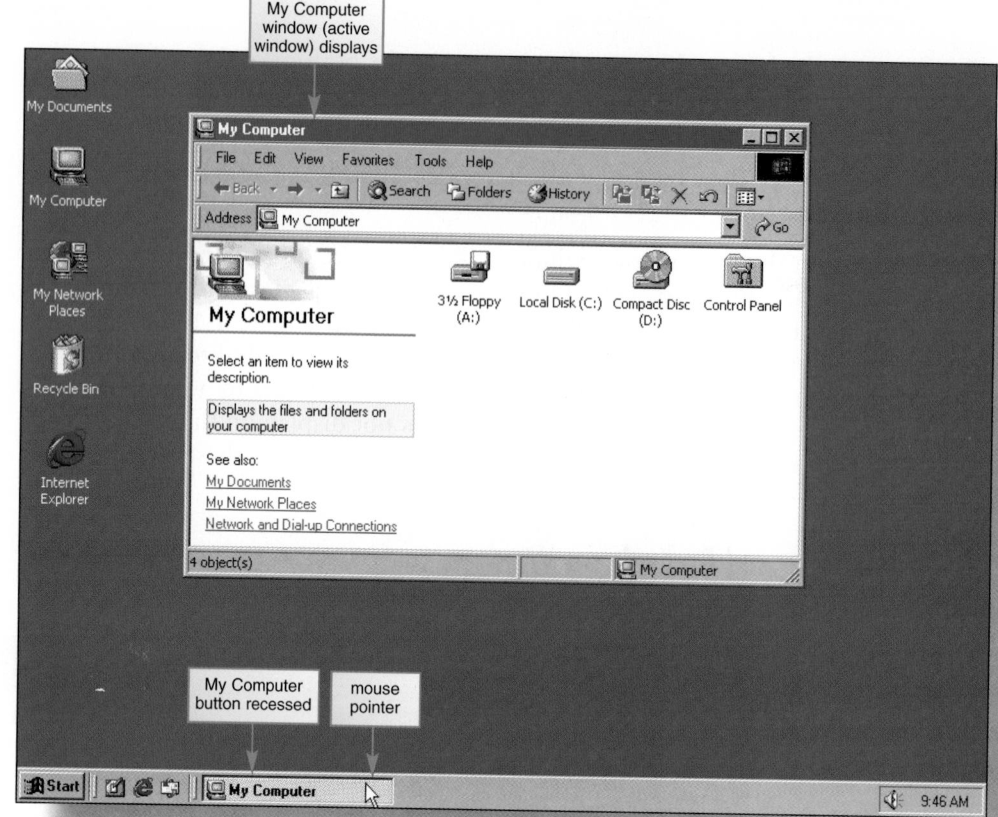

FIGURE 1-16

Maximizing Windows

Many application programs run in a maximized window by default. Often you will find that you want to work with maximized windows.

Minimizing and Maximizing Windows

Many users believe it is easier to double-click the title bar to minimize or maximize a window instead of clicking the Minimize and Maximize button on the title bar.

Whenever a window is minimized, it does not display on the desktop but a non-recessed button for the window does display in the taskbar button area. Whenever you want a minimized window to display and be the active window, click its button in the taskbar button area.

Maximize and Restore Down Buttons

Sometimes when information is displayed in a window, the information is not completely visible. One method of displaying the entire contents of a window is to enlarge the window using the **Maximize button**. The Maximize button maximizes a window so that it fills the entire screen, making it easier to see the contents of the window. When a window is maximized, the **Restore Down button** replaces the Maximize button on the title bar. Clicking the Restore Down button will return the window to its size before maximizing. To maximize and restore the My Computer window, complete the following steps.

To Maximize and Restore a Window

1 Point to the Maximize button on the title bar of the My Computer window (Figure 1-17).

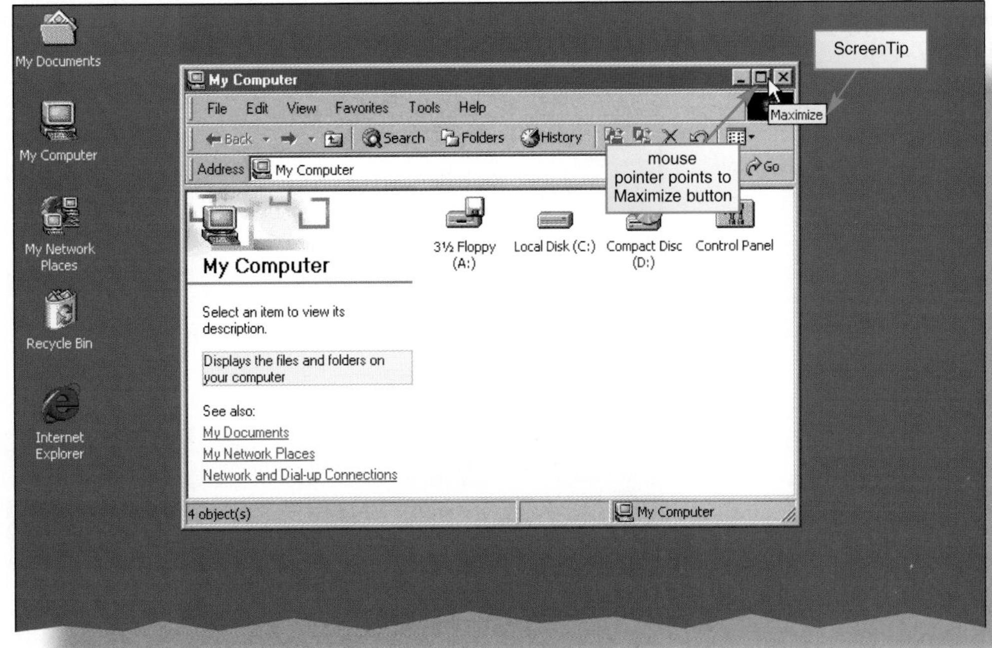

FIGURE 1-17

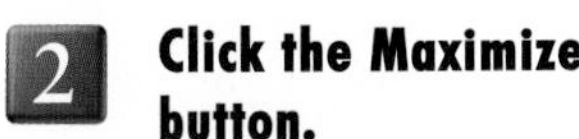

2 Click the Maximize button.

The My Computer window expands so it and the taskbar fill the entire screen (Figure 1-18). The Restore Down button replaces the Maximize button and the My Computer button in the taskbar button area remains recessed. The My Computer window still is the active window.

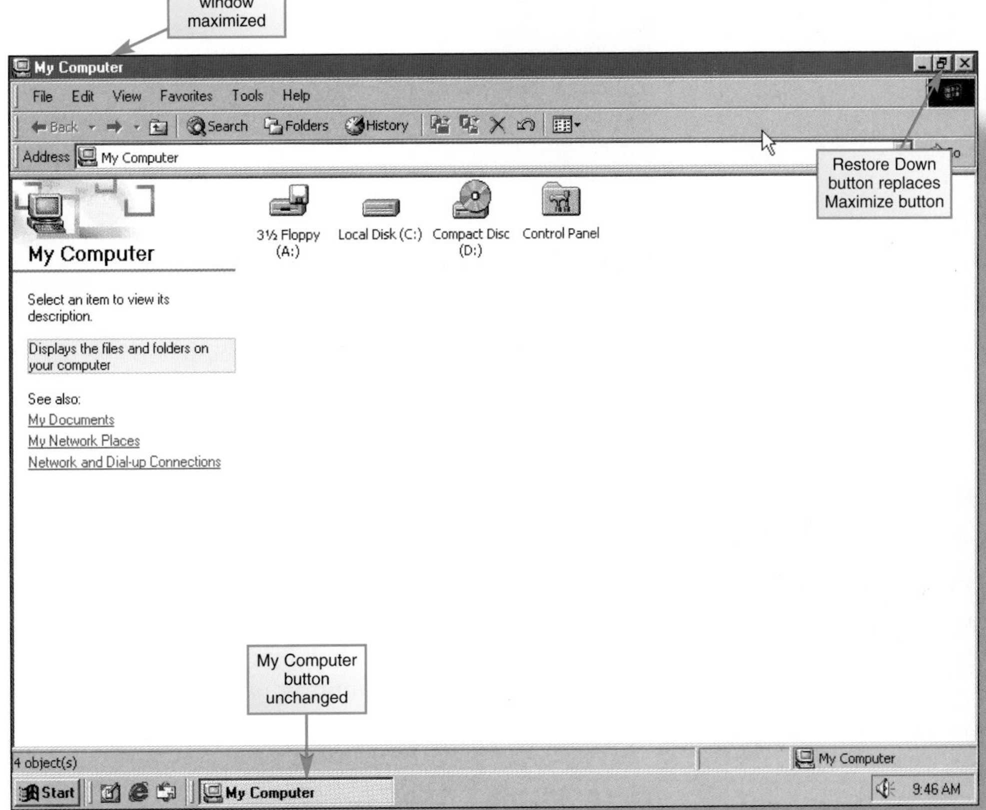

FIGURE 1-18

3 **Point to the Restore Down button on the title bar of the My Computer window (Figure 1-19).**

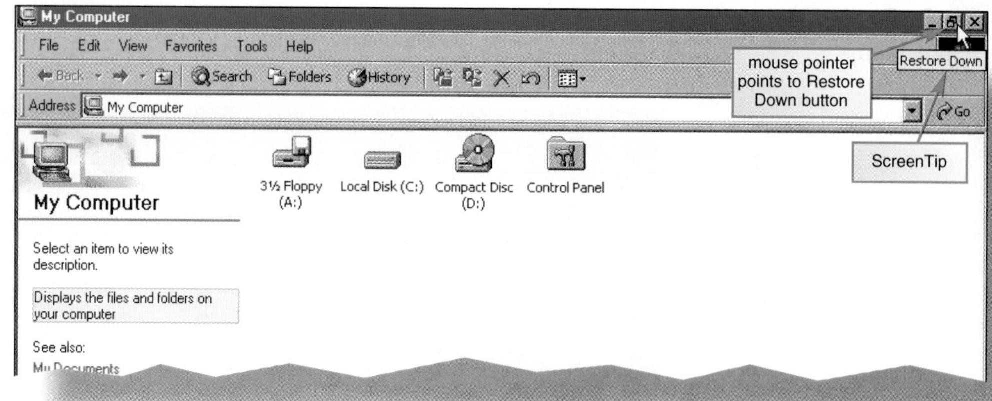

FIGURE 1-19

4 **Click the Restore Down button.**

The My Computer window returns to the size and position it occupied before being maximized (Figure 1-20). The My Computer button does not change. The Maximize button replaces the Restore Down button.

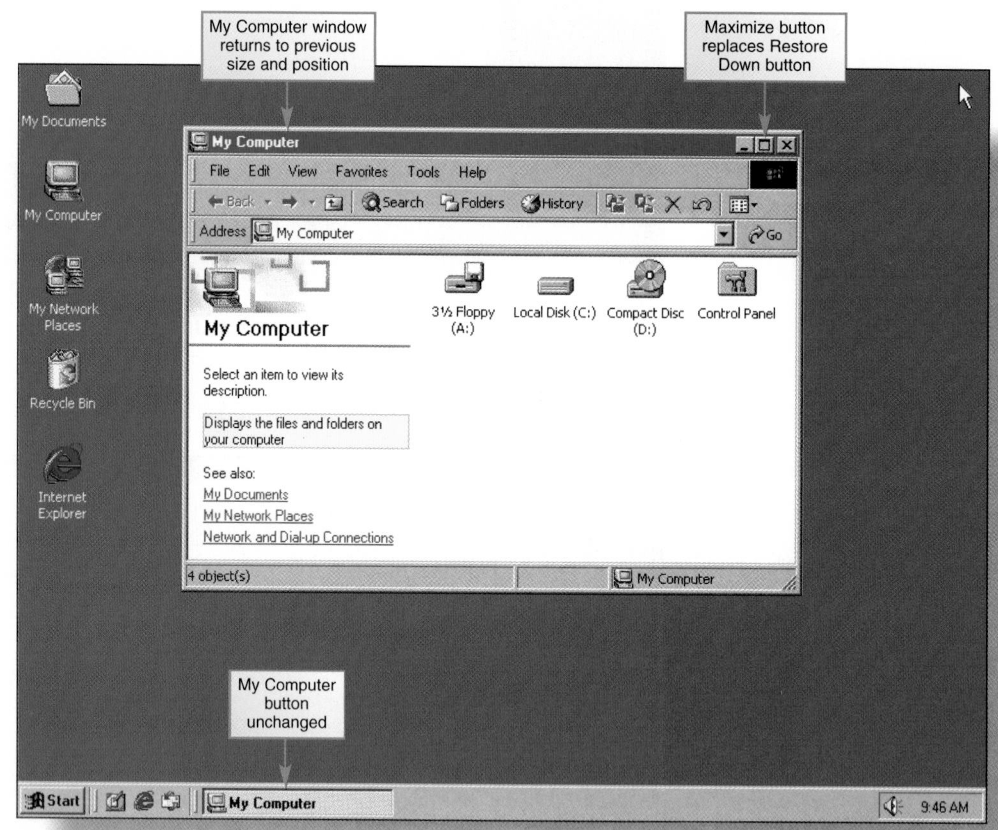

FIGURE 1-20

More About

The Close Button

The Close button was a new innovation in Windows 95. Before Windows 95, the user had to double-click a button or click a command on a menu to close the window. As always, the choice of how to perform an operation such as closing a window is a matter of personal preference. In most cases, you will want to choose the easiest method.

When a window is maximized, as shown in Figure 1-18 on the previous page, you can minimize the window by clicking the Minimize button. If, after minimizing the window, you click its button in the taskbar button area, the window will return to its maximized size.

Close Button

The Close button on the title bar of a window closes the window and removes the window button from the taskbar. To close and then reopen the My Computer window, complete the following steps.

Steps To Close a Window and Reopen a Window

1 Point to the Close button on the title bar of the My Computer window (Figure 1-21).

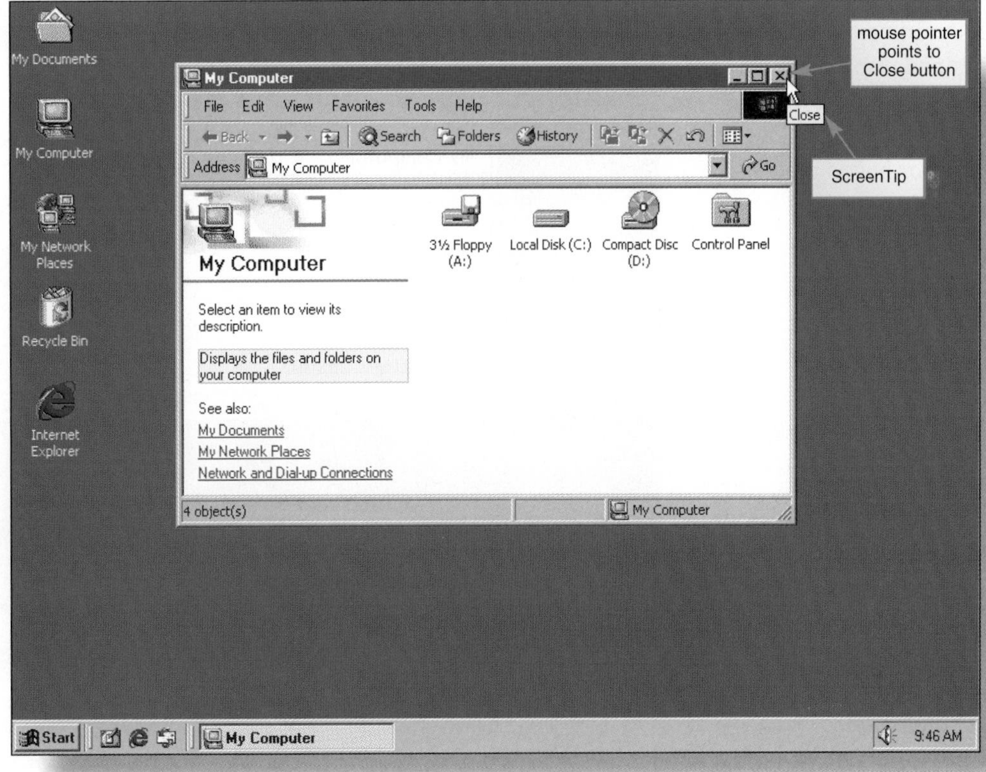

FIGURE 1-21

2 Click the Close button.

The My Computer window closes and the My Computer button no longer displays in the taskbar button area (Figure 1-22).

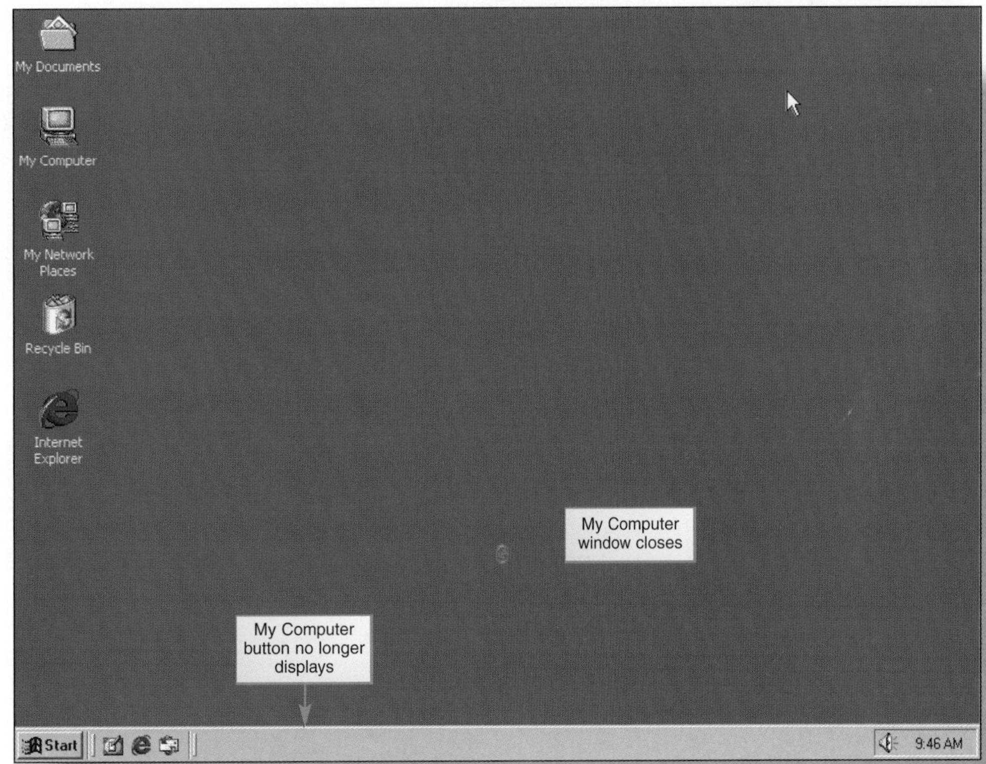

FIGURE 1-22

3 Double-click the My Computer icon on the desktop.

The My Computer window opens and displays on the screen (Figure 1-23). The My Computer button displays in the taskbar button area.

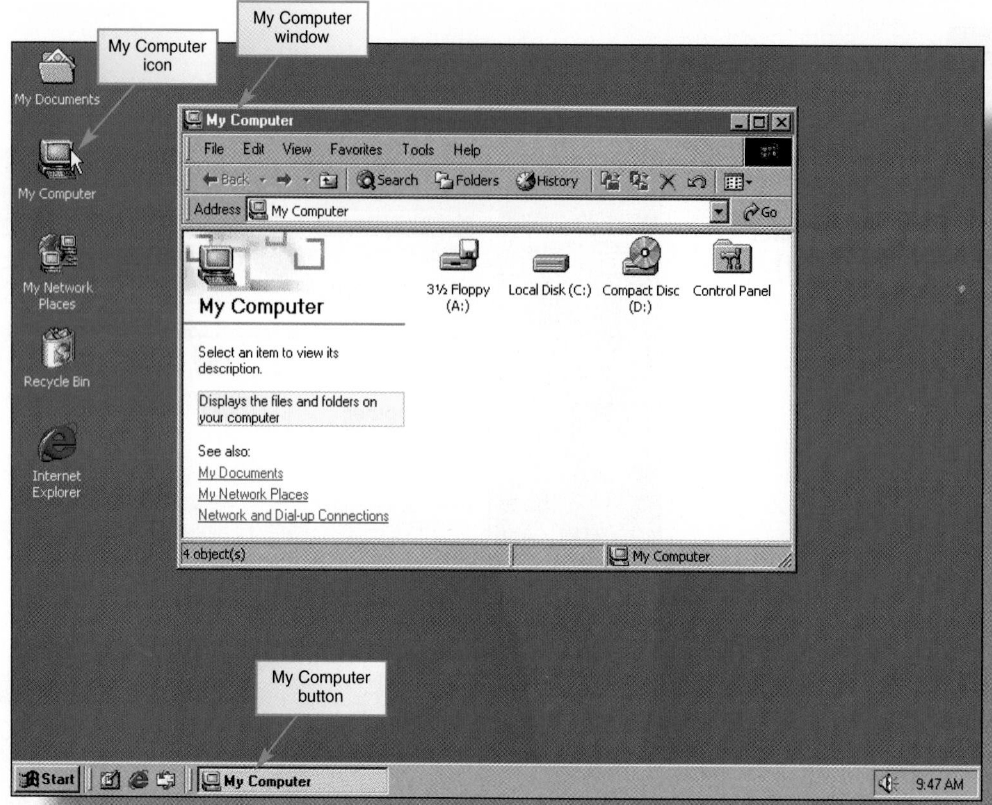

FIGURE 1-23

Dragging

Dragging is the second-most difficult skill to learn with a mouse. You may want to practice dragging a few times so you are comfortable with it.

Drag

Drag means you point to an item, hold down the left mouse button, move the item to the desired location, and then release the left mouse button. You can move any open window to another location on the desktop by pointing to the title bar of the window and dragging the window. To drag the My Computer window to another location on the desktop, perform the following steps.

Steps To Move an Object by Dragging

1 Point to the My Computer window title bar (Figure 1-24).

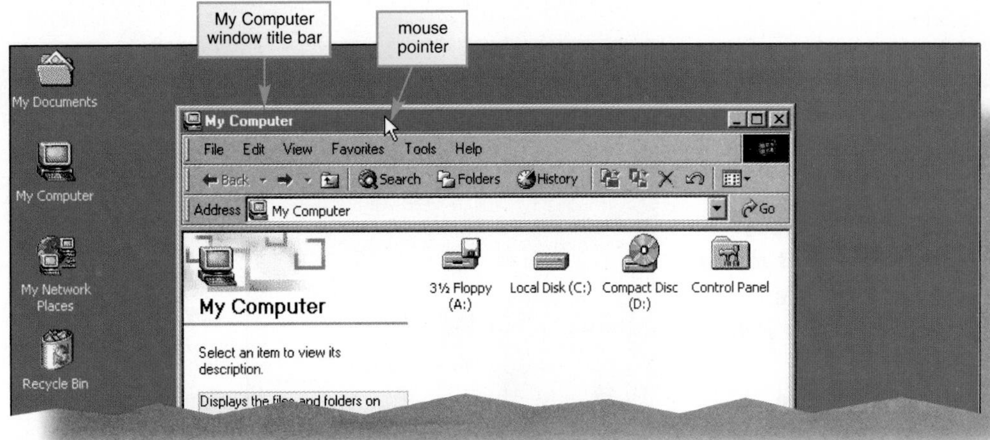

FIGURE 1-24

2 Hold down the left mouse button, move the mouse so the window moves to the center of the desktop, and then release the left mouse button.

As you drag the mouse, the My Computer window moves across the desktop. When you release the left mouse button, the window displays in its new location (Figure 1-25).

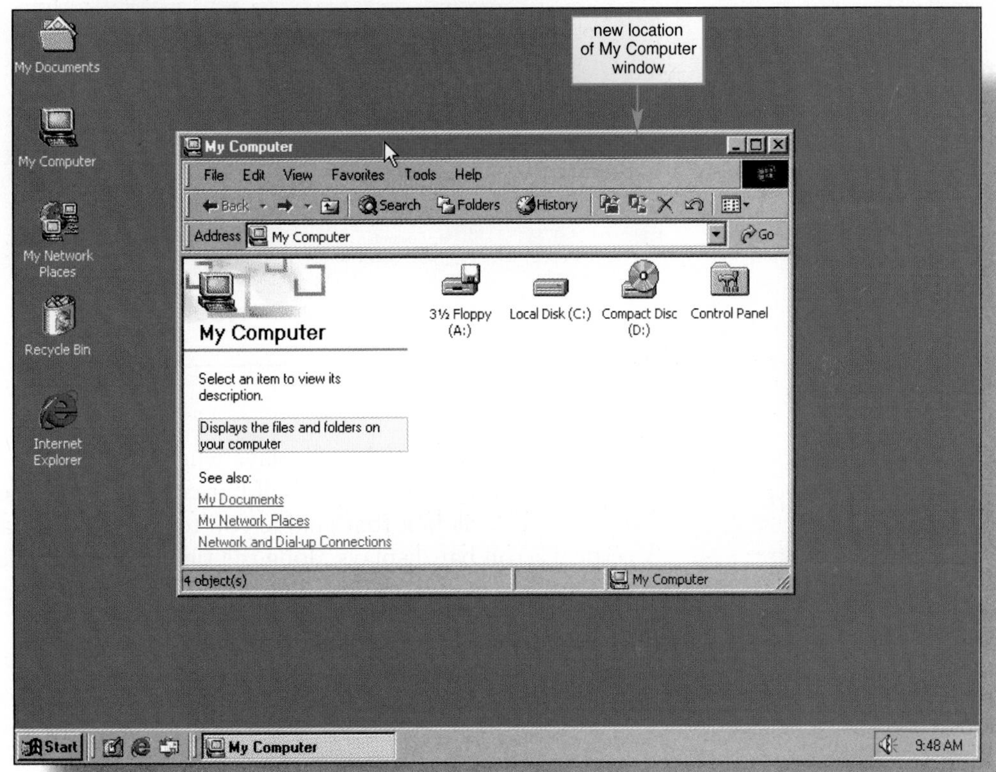

FIGURE 1-25

Sizing a Window by Dragging

You can use dragging for more than just moving an object. For example, you can drag the border of a window to change the size of the window. To change the size of the My Computer window, perform the step on the next page.

To Size a Window by Dragging

1 Position the mouse pointer over the lower-right corner of the My Computer window until the mouse pointer changes to a two-headed arrow. Drag the lower-right corner upward and to the left until the window on your desktop resembles the window shown in Figure 1-26.

As you drag the lower-right corner, the My Computer window changes size, the icons in the right panel display in two rows, a vertical scroll bar displays in the left panel, and a portion of the text in the left panel is not visible (Figure 1-26).

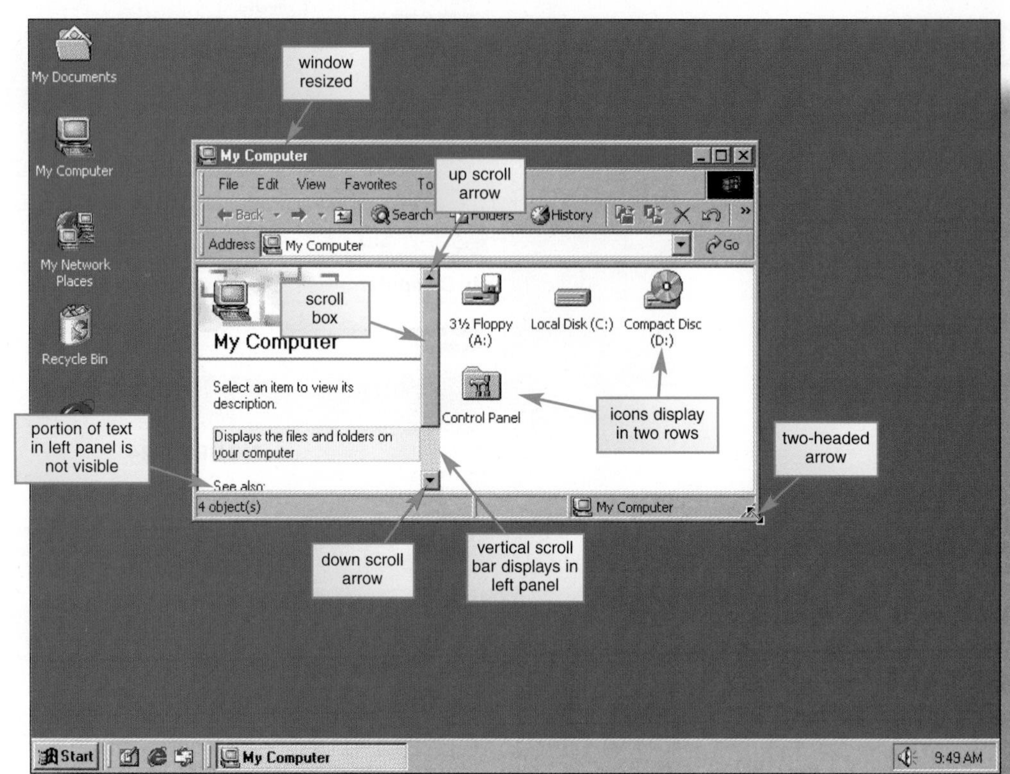

FIGURE 1-26

Window Sizing

Windows 2000 remembers the size of the window when you close the window. When you reopen the window, it will display in the same size as when you closed it.

A **scroll bar** is a bar that displays when the contents of a window are not completely visible. A vertical scroll bar contains an **up scroll arrow**, a **down scroll arrow**, and a **scroll box** that enable you to view areas that currently are not visible. A vertical scroll bar displays along the right edge of the left panel of the My Computer window shown in Figure 1-26. In some cases, vertical scroll bar also may display along the right edge of the right panel of a window.

The size of the scroll box is dependent on the amount of the panel that is visible. The larger the scroll box, the more of the panel that is visible. In Figure 1-26, the scroll box occupies approximately three-fourths of the scroll bar. This indicates that approximately three-fourths of the contents of the left panel are visible. If the scroll box were a tiny rectangle, a large portion of the panel would not be visible.

In addition to dragging a corner of a window, you also can drag any of the borders of a window. If you drag a vertical border, such as the right border, you can move the border left or right. If you drag a horizontal border, such as the bottom border, you can move the border of the window up or down.

As mentioned earlier, maximizing a window is one method of enlarging a window and displaying more information. Dragging a window to enlarge the window is a second method of displaying information in a window that is not visible.

Scrolling

Most people will either maximize a window or size it so all the objects in the window are visible to avoid scrolling because scrolling takes time. It is more efficient not to have to scroll in a window.

Scrolling in a Window

Previously, two methods were shown to display information that was not completely visible in the My Computer window. These methods were maximizing the My Computer window and changing the size of the My Computer window. A third method uses a scroll bar.

Scrolling can be accomplished in three ways: (1) click the scroll arrows; (2) click the scroll bar; and (3) drag the scroll box. Perform the following steps to scroll the left panel of the My Computer window using the scroll arrows.

To Scroll a Window Using Scroll Arrows

1 Point to the down scroll arrow on the vertical scroll bar (Figure 1-27).

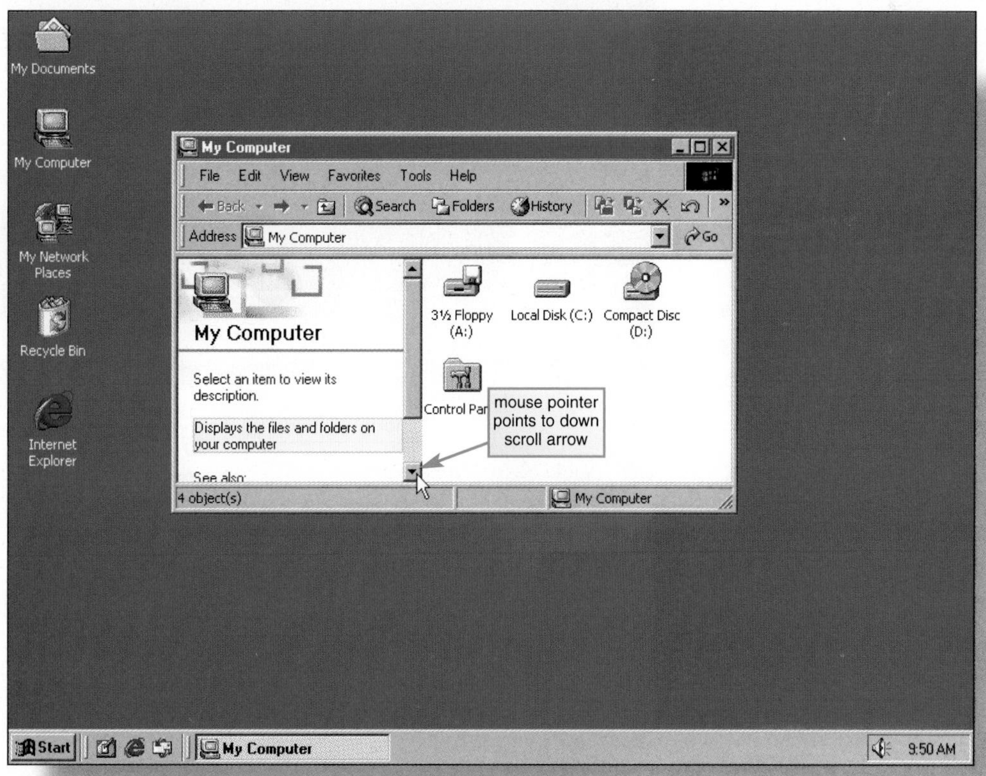

FIGURE 1-27

2 Click the down scroll arrow one time.

The left panel scrolls down (the contents in the left panel move up) and displays text at the bottom of the left panel that previously was not visible (Figure 1-28). Because the size of the left panel does not change when you scroll, the contents in the left panel will change.

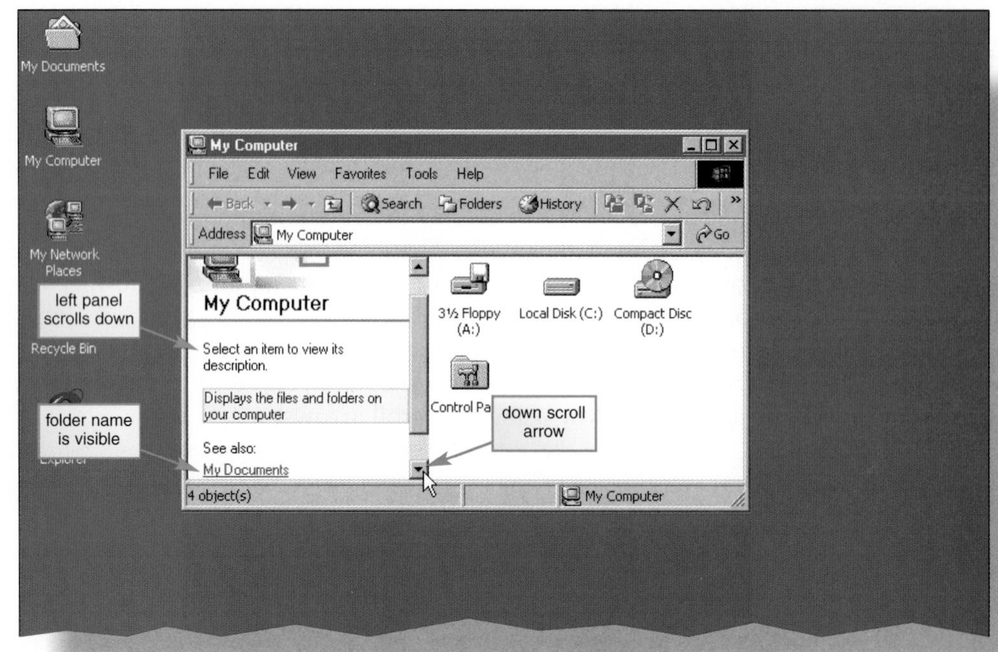

FIGURE 1-28

3 Click the down scroll arrow two more times.

The scroll box moves to the bottom of the scroll bar and the remaining folder names in the left panel display (Figure 1-29).

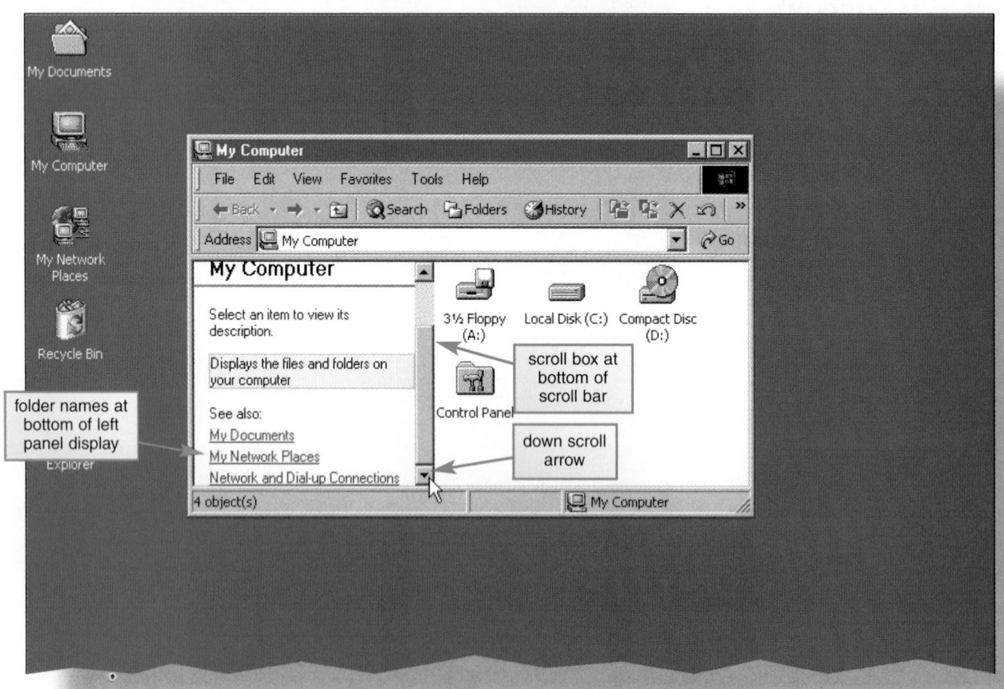

FIGURE 1-29

You can scroll continuously using scroll arrows by pointing to the up or down scroll arrow and holding down the left mouse button. The area being scrolled continues to scroll until you release the left mouse button or you reach the top or bottom of the area. You also can scroll by clicking the scroll bar itself. When you click the scroll bar, the area being scrolled moves up or down a greater distance than when you click the scroll arrows.

The third way in which you can scroll is by dragging the scroll box. When you drag the scroll box, the area being scrolled moves up or down as you drag.

Being able to view the contents of a panel by scrolling is an important Windows 2000 skill because in many cases, the entire contents of a panel are not visible.

Resizing a Window

After moving and resizing a window, you may wish to return the window to approximately its original size. To return the My Computer window to about its original size, complete the following steps.

TO RESIZE A WINDOW

1. Position the mouse pointer over the lower-right corner of the My Computer window border until the mouse pointer changes to a two-headed arrow.
2. Drag the lower-right corner of the My Computer window until the window is the same size as shown in Figure 1-25 on page INT 1.21, and then release the mouse button.

The My Computer window is approximately the same size as it was before you made it smaller.

Closing a Window

After you have completed your work in a window, normally you will close the window. To close the My Computer window, complete the following steps.

TO CLOSE A WINDOW

1. Point to the Close button on the right of the title bar in the My Computer window.
2. Click the Close button.

The My Computer window closes and the desktop does not contain any open windows.

Right-Drag

Right-drag means you point to an item, hold down the right mouse button, move the item to the desired location, and then release the right mouse button. When you right-drag an object, a shortcut menu displays. The shortcut menu contains commands specifically for use with the object being dragged. To right-drag the Launch Outlook Express icon on the Quick Launch toolbar below the icons on the desktop, perform the steps on the next page. If the Launch Outlook Express icon does not display on the Quick Launch toolbar, choose another icon and follow the procedure in the steps.

More About

The Scroll Bar

In many application programs, clicking the scroll bar will move the window a full screen's worth of information up or down. You can step through a word processing document screen by screen, for example, by clicking the scroll bar.

More About

The Scroll Box

Dragging the scroll box is the most efficient technique to scroll long distances. In many application programs, such as Microsoft Word, as you scroll using the scroll box, the page number of the document displays next to the scroll box.

More About

Scrolling Guidelines

General scrolling guidelines: (1) To scroll short distances (line by line), click the scroll arrows; (2) To scroll one screen at a time, click the scroll bar; and (3) To scroll long distances, drag the scroll box.

More About

Right-Dragging

Right-dragging was not available on some earlier versions of Windows, so you might find people familiar with Windows not even considering right-dragging. Because it always produces a shortcut menu, however, right-dragging is the safest way to drag.

Steps To Right-Drag

1 Point to the Launch Outlook Express icon on the Quick Launch toolbar, hold down the right mouse button, drag the icon below the other icons on the desktop, and then release the right mouse button.

The dimmed Launch Outlook Express icon and a shortcut menu display on the desktop (Figure 1-30). A dimmed Launch Outlook Express icon remains at its original location. The shortcut menu contains four commands: Copy Here, Move Here, Create Shortcut(s) Here, and Cancel. The Move Here command in bold (dark) type identifies what would happen if you were to drag the Launch Outlook Express icon with the left mouse button.

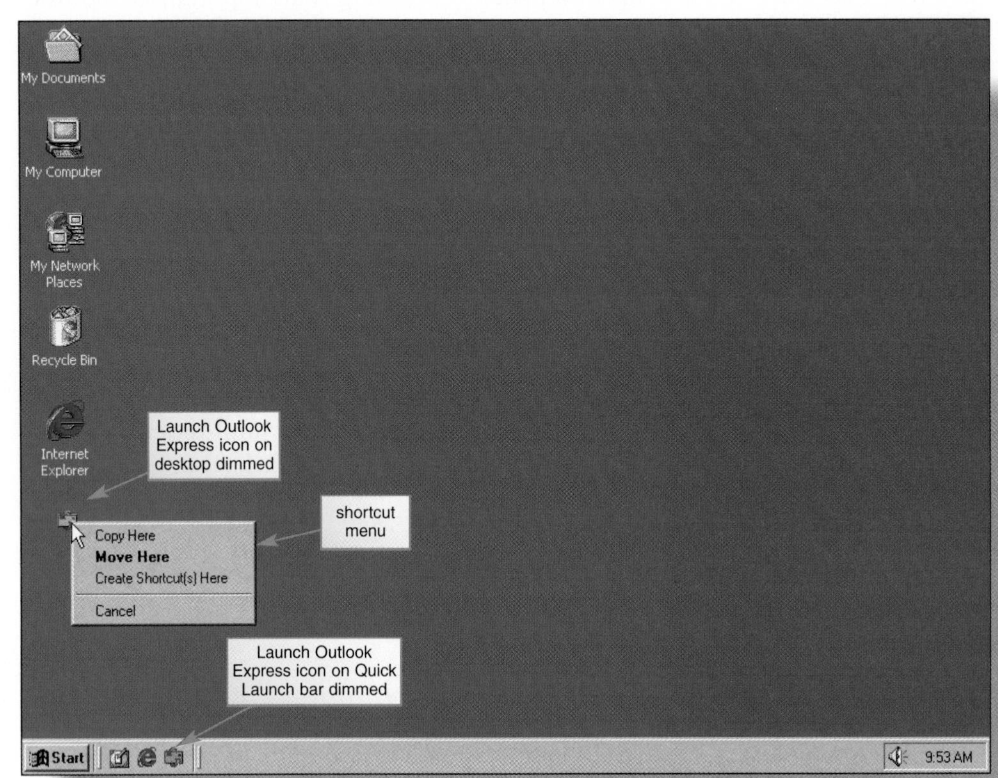

FIGURE 1-30

2 Point to Cancel on the shortcut menu.

The Cancel command is highlighted (Figure 1-31).

3 Click Cancel.

The shortcut menu and the dragged Launch Outlook Express icon disappear from the desktop.

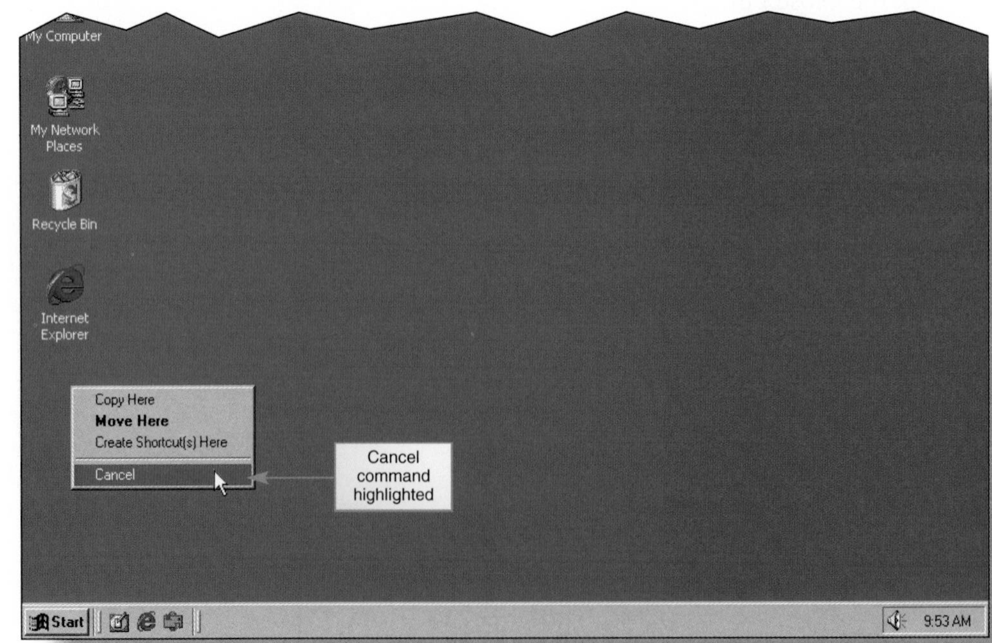

FIGURE 1-31

Whenever you begin an operation but do not want to complete it, you can click Cancel on a shortcut menu or click the Cancel button in a dialog box. The **Cancel** command will reset anything you have done in the operation.

If you click **Move Here** on the shortcut menu shown in Figure 1-30, Windows 2000 will move the icon from its current location to the new location. If you click **Copy Here**, a special object called a shortcut will be created on the desktop and the original icon will display on the Quick Launch toolbar. If you click **Create Shortcut(s) Here**, a shortcut also will be created on the desktop.

Although you can move icons by dragging with the primary (left) mouse button and by right-dragging with the secondary (right) mouse button, it is strongly suggested you right-drag because a menu displays and you can specify the exact operation you want to occur. When you drag using the left mouse button, a default operation takes place and the result may not be what you want.

The Microsoft Natural Keyboard

The Microsoft Natural Keyboard in Figure 1-32b not only has special keys for Windows 2000, but also is designed ergonomically so you type with your hands apart. It takes a little time to get used to, but several authors on the Shelly Cashman Series writing team report they type faster with more accuracy and less fatigue when using the keyboard.

Summary of Mouse and Windows Operations

You have seen how to use the mouse to point, click, right-click, double-click, drag, and right-drag in order to accomplish certain tasks on the desktop. The use of a mouse is an important skill when using Windows 2000. In addition, you have learned how to move around and display windows on the Windows 2000 desktop.

The Keyboard and Keyboard Shortcuts

The **keyboard** is an input device on which you manually key, or type, data. Figure 1-32a shows the enhanced IBM 101-key keyboard, and Figure 1-32b shows a Microsoft Natural keyboard designed specifically for use with Windows. Many tasks you accomplish with a mouse also can be accomplished using a keyboard.

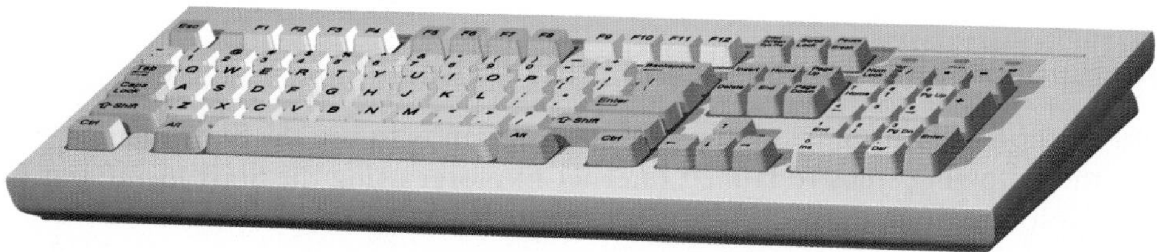

(a) Enhanced IBM 101-Key Keyboard

(b) Microsoft Natural Keyboard

FIGURE 1-32

To perform tasks using the keyboard, you must understand the notation used to identify which keys to press. This notation is used throughout Windows 2000 to identify **keyboard shortcuts**.

Keyboard shortcuts consist of: (1) pressing a single key (press the F1 key); or (2) pressing and holding down one key and then pressing a second key, as shown by two key names separated by a plus sign (CTRL+ESC). For example, to obtain Help about Windows 2000, you can press the F1 key; to open the Start menu, hold down the CTRL key and then press the ESC key (press CTRL+ESC).

Often, computer users will use keyboard shortcuts for operations they perform frequently. For example, many users find pressing the F1 key to launch Windows 2000 Help easier than using the Start menu as shown later in this project. As a user, you probably will find the combination of keyboard and mouse operations that particularly suit you, but it is strongly recommended that generally you use the mouse.

More About

Application Programs

Some application programs, such as Internet Explorer, are part of Windows 2000. Most application programs, however, such as Microsoft Office, Lotus SmartSuite, and others must be purchased separately from Windows 2000.

Launching an Application Program

One of the basic tasks you can perform using Windows 2000 is to launch an application program. A **program** is a set of computer instructions that carries out a task on your computer. An **application program** is a program that allows you to accomplish the specific task, or tasks, for which that program is designed. For example, a **word processing program** is an application program that allows you to create written documents; a **presentation graphics program** is an application program that allows you to create graphic presentations for display on a computer; and a **Web browser program** is an application program that allows you to search for and display Web pages.

The most common activity on a computer is to launch an application program to accomplish tasks using the computer. You can launch an application program in a variety of ways. When several methods are available to accomplish a task, a computer user has the opportunity to try various methods and select the method that best fits his or her needs.

Launching an Application Using the Start Button

One method of launching an application program is to use the Start menu. Perform the following steps to launch Internet Explorer using the Start menu and Internet Explorer command.

Steps To Launch a Program Using the Start Menu

1 **Click the Start button on the taskbar, point to Programs on the Start menu, and then point to Internet Explorer on the Programs submenu.**

The Start menu and Programs submenu display (Figure 1-33). The Programs submenu contains the ***Internet Explorer command*** *to launch the Internet Explorer program. You might find more, fewer, or different commands on the Start menu and Programs submenu on your computer.*

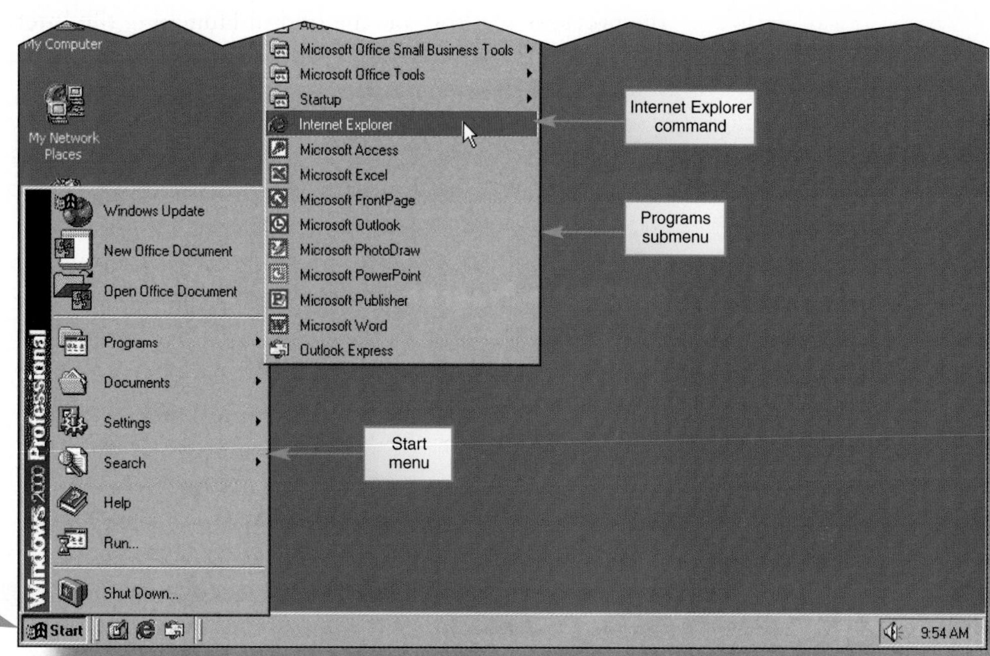

FIGURE 1-33

2 **Click Internet Explorer.**

Windows 2000 launches the Internet Explorer program by opening the Welcome to MSN.com window on the desktop, displaying the MSN Web page in the window, and adding a recessed button to the taskbar button area (Figure 1-34). The URL for the Web page displays on the Address bar. Because Web pages change frequently, the Web page that displays on your desktop may be different.

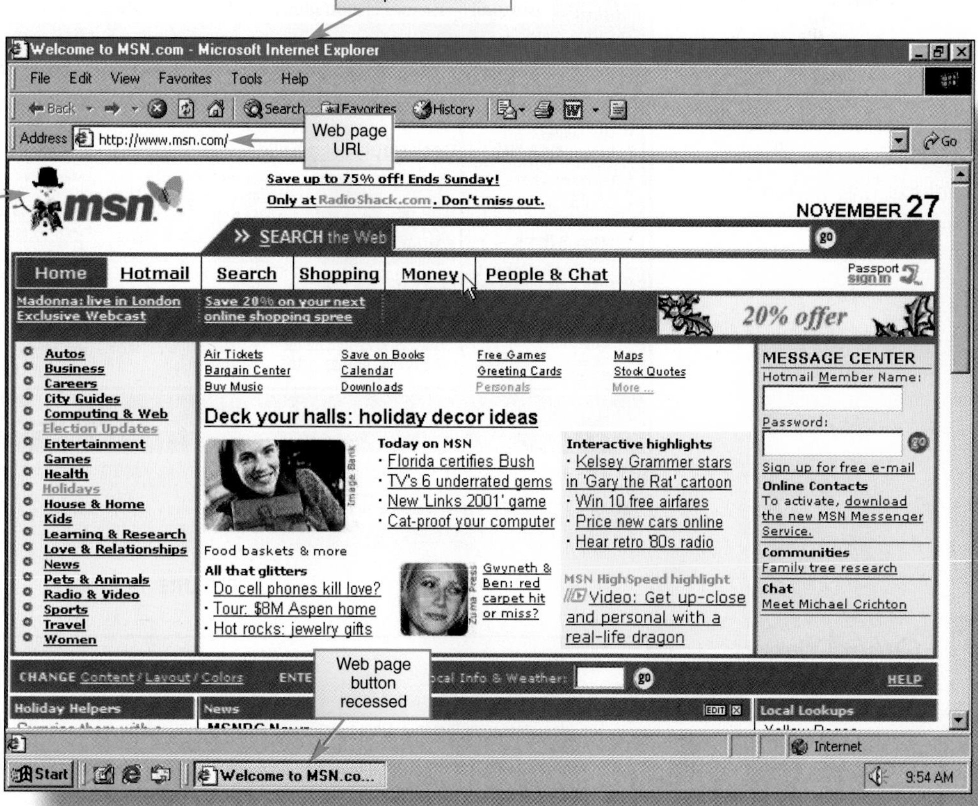

FIGURE 1-34

Other Ways

1. Click Launch Internet Explorer Browser icon on Quick Launch toolbar
2. Double-click Internet Explorer icon on desktop
3. Press CTRL+ESC, press P, press I

After you have launched Internet Explorer, you can use the program to search for and display different Web pages.

Windows 2000 provides a number of ways to accomplish a particular task. In the previous section, one method of launching the Internet Explorer program was illustrated, and then alternate methods were listed in the Other Ways box. The remainder of this book will use the same format: a single set of steps will illustrate how to accomplish a task; and if you can perform the same task using other methods, the Other Ways box will specify the other methods. In each case, the method shown in the steps is the preferred method, but it is important for you to be aware of all the techniques you can use.

Quitting a Program

When you have completed your work using a program, you should quit the program. Perform the following steps to quit the Internet Explorer program.

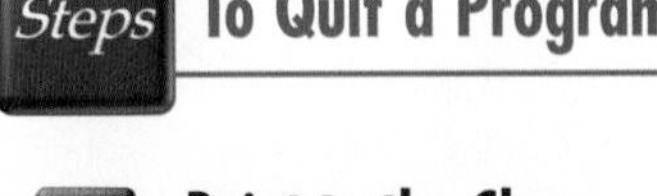

Steps To Quit a Program

1 Point to the Close button in the Internet Explorer window (Figure 1-35).

2 Click the Close button.

Windows 2000 quits Internet Explorer, closes the Microsoft Internet Explorer window, and removes the Microsoft Internet Explorer button from the taskbar.

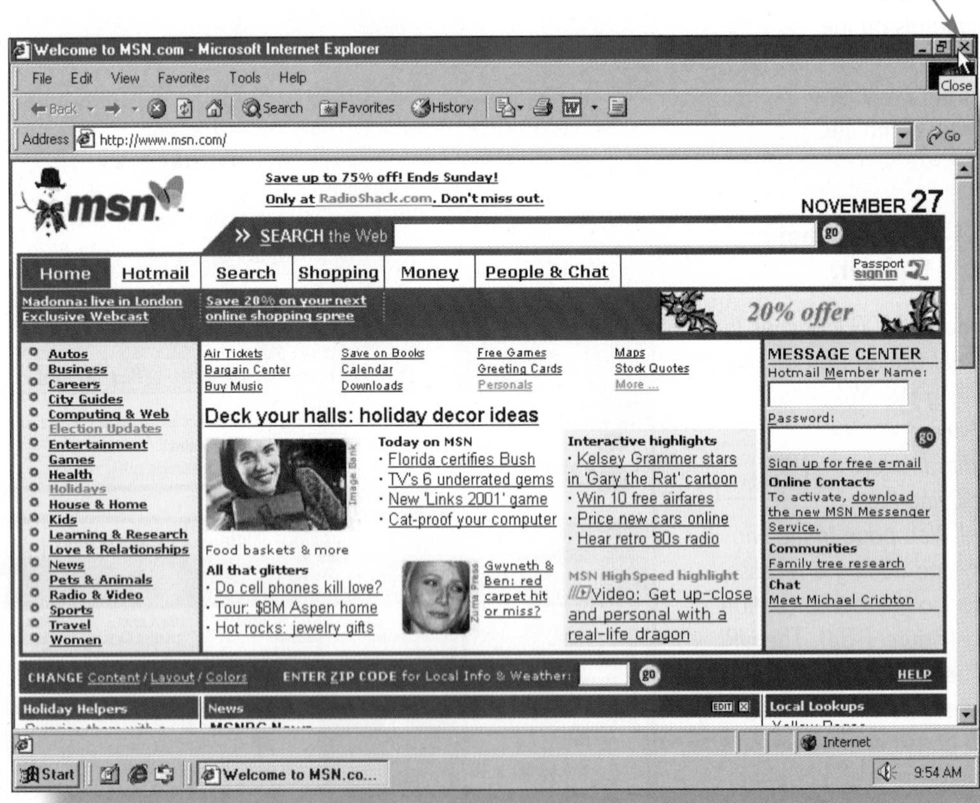

FIGURE 1-35

Other Ways

1. Double-click Internet Explorer logo at left on title bar
2. On File menu click Close
3. Press ALT+F4

In the preceding sections, you launched Internet Explorer and then quit the Internet Explorer program. In the next section, you will launch the Windows Explorer application program.

Windows Explorer

Windows Explorer is an application program included with Windows 2000 that allows you to view the contents of the computer, the hierarchy of folders on the computer, and the files and folders in each folder.

Windows Explorer also allows you to organize the files and folders on the computer by copying, moving, and deleting the files and folders. In this project, you will use Windows Explorer to (1) work with the files and folders on your computer; (2) select and copy a group of files between the hard drive and a floppy disk; (3) create, name, and delete a folder on a floppy disk; and (4) rename and delete a file on a floppy disk. These are common operations that you should understand how to perform.

Starting Windows Explorer and Maximizing Its Window

To explore the files and folders on the computer, launch Windows Explorer and maximize its window by performing the following steps.

To Start Windows Explorer and Maximize Its Window

1 **Right-click the My Computer icon on the desktop and then point to Explore on the shortcut menu.**

A shortcut menu displays (Figure 1-36). The Explore command will launch Windows Explorer.

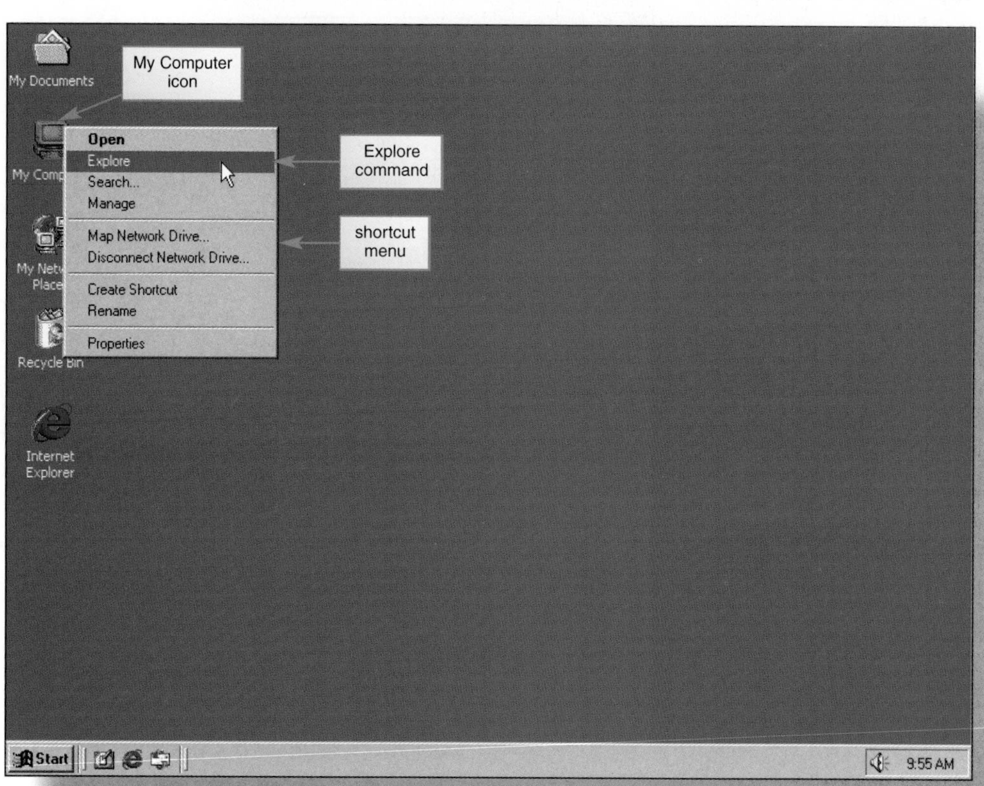

FIGURE 1-36

2 Click Explore and then click the Maximize button on the My Computer title bar.

The My Computer window opens and is maximized. The recessed My Computer button is added to the taskbar button area (Figure 1-37).

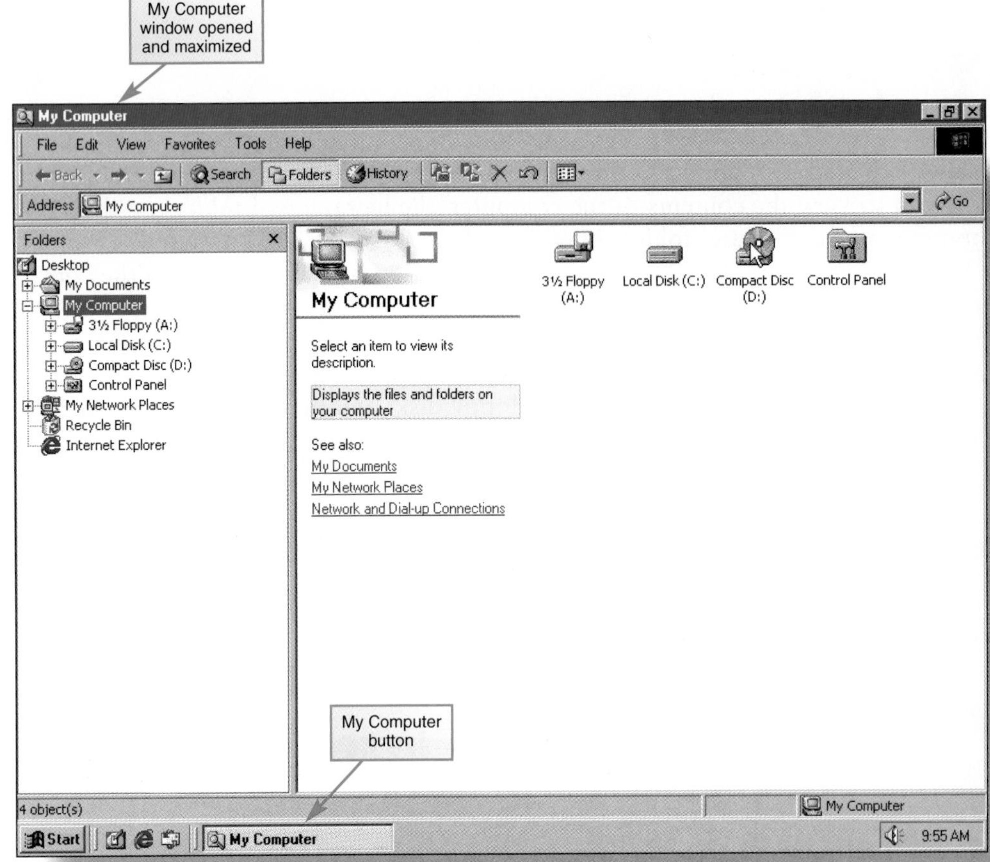

FIGURE 1-37

Other Ways

1. Right-click Start button or any icon on desktop (except Internet Explorer), click Explore on shortcut menu
2. Click Start button, point to Programs, point to Accessories, click Windows Explorer
3. Double-click My Computer icon, click Folders button on Standard Buttons toolbar

The Exploring Window

When you launch Windows Explorer by right-clicking the My Computer icon and then clicking the Explore command on the shortcut menu, Windows 2000 opens the Exploring window (My Computer window) shown in Figure 1-38. The title bar in the window is the same as seen in other windows, and the menu bar contains the File, Edit, View, Favorites, Tools, and Help menu names. These menus contain commands to organize and work with the drives on the computer and the files and folders on those drives. The Standard Buttons toolbar and Address bar display respectively below the menu bar.

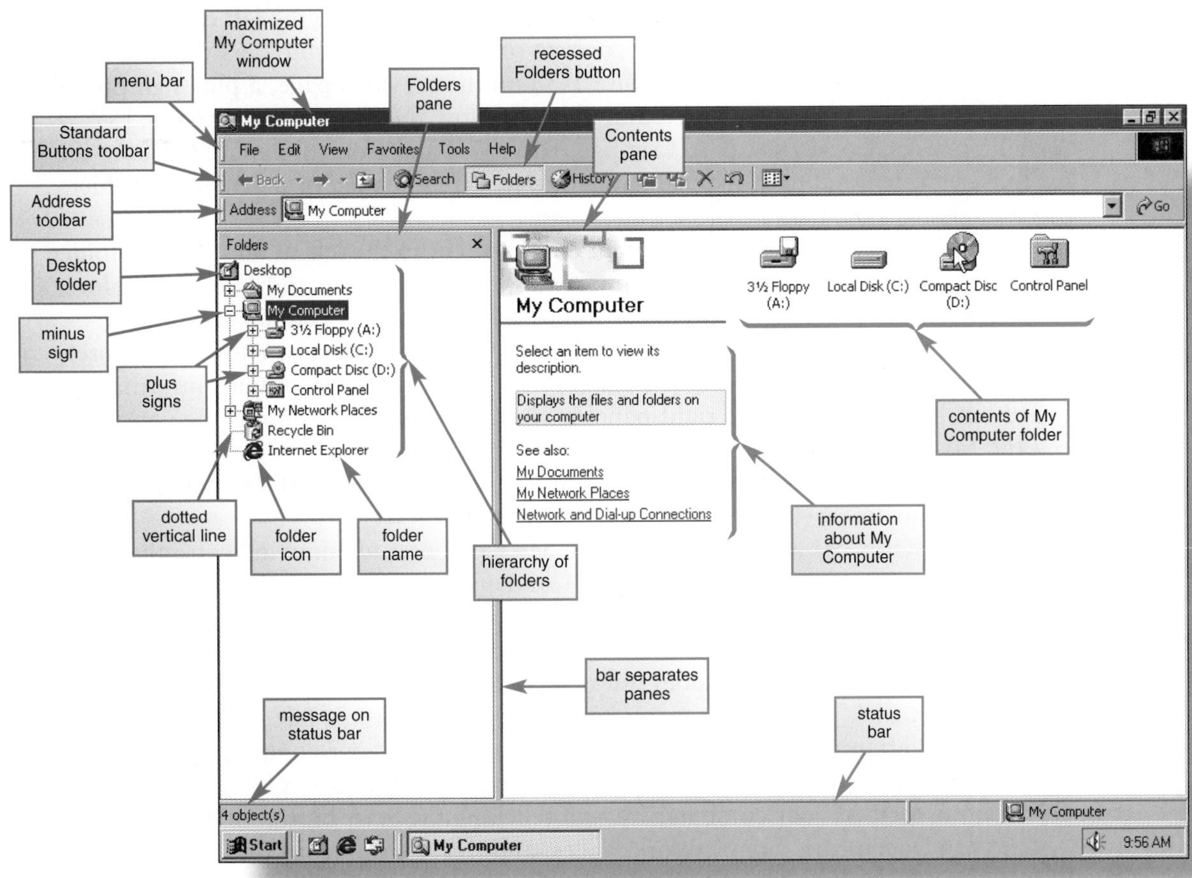

FIGURE 1-38

The main window consists of two panes — the Folders pane on the left and the Contents pane on the right. A bar separates the panes. You can change the size of the Folders and Contents panes by dragging the bar that separates the two panes.

In the **Folders pane**, Explorer displays in **hierarchical structure**, the icons and folder names on the computer. The top level in the hierarchy is the Desktop. Connected by a dotted vertical line below the Desktop are the icons that display on the desktop (My Documents, My Computer, My Network Places, Recycle Bin and Internet Explorer). Your computer may have other icons. Clicking the recessed Folders button on the Standard Buttons toolbar removes the Folders pane from the window, making the My Computer window identical to the My Computer window shown in Figure 1-18 on page INT 1.17.

Windows 2000 displays a **minus sign** (–) in a small box to the left of an icon in the Folders pane to indicate the corresponding folder contains one or more folders that are visible in the Folders pane. These folders, called **subfolders**, are indented and aligned below the folder name. In Figure 1-38, a minus sign (–) precedes the My Computer icon, and four subfolders are indented and display below the My Computer folder name. The four subfolders (3½ Floppy (A:), Local Disk (C:), Compact Disc (D:), and Control Panel) are the four subfolders in the My Computer folder and correspond to the four folders in the Contents pane. Clicking the minus sign, referred to as **collapsing the folder**, removes the indented subfolders from the hierarchy of folders in the Folders pane and changes the minus sign to a plus sign.

More About

A Hierarchy

One definition of hierarchy in *Merriam Webster's Collegiate Dictionary Tenth Edition* is a division of angels. While no one would argue angels have anything to do with Windows 2000, some preach that working with a hierarchical structure as presented by Explorer is less secular (of or relating to the worldly) and more spiritual (of or relating to supernatural phenomena) than the straightforward showing of files in windows. What do you think?

Windows 2000 displays a **plus sign** (+) in a small box to the left of an icon to indicate the corresponding folder consists of one or more subfolders that are not visible in the Folders pane. In Figure 1-38 on the previous page, a plus sign precedes each of the four icons indented and aligned below the My Computer name [3½ Floppy (A:), Local Disk (C:), Compact Disc (D:), and Control Panel]. Clicking the plus sign, referred to as **expanding the folder**, displays a list of indented subfolders and changes the plus sign to a minus sign.

If neither a plus sign nor a minus sign displays to the left of an icon, the folder does not contain subfolders. In Figure 1-38, the Recycle Bin and Internet Explorer icons are not preceded by a plus or minus sign and do not contain subfolders.

The **Contents pane** is identical to the My Computer window shown in Figure 1-18 on page INT 1.17. The left panel in the Contents pane contains information about My Computer. The right panel in the Contents pane contains the contents of the My Computer folder [3½ Floppy (A:), Local Disk (C:), Compact Disc (D:), and Control Panel]. These icons may be different and display in a different format on your computer.

The status bar at the bottom of the My Computer window indicates the number of folders, or objects, displayed in the Contents pane of the window, 4 object(s). Depending on the objects displayed in the Contents pane, the amount of disk space the objects occupy and the amount of unused disk space also may display on the status bar. If the status bar does not display in the My Computer window on your computer, click View on the menu bar and then click Status Bar.

In addition to using Windows Explorer to explore your computer by right-clicking the My Computer icon, you also can use Windows Explorer to explore different aspects of your computer by right-clicking the Start button on the taskbar or the My Documents, My Network Places, and Recycle Bin icons on the desktop.

Displaying the Contents of a Folder

In Figure 1-38, the right panel of the Contents pane contains the contents of the My Computer folder. In addition to displaying the contents of the My Computer folder, the contents of any folder in the Folders pane can be displayed in the Contents pane. Perform the following steps to display the contents of the Local Disk (C:) folder.

To Display the Contents of a Folder

1 Point to the Local Disk (C:) folder name in the Folders pane of the My Computer window (Figure 1-39).

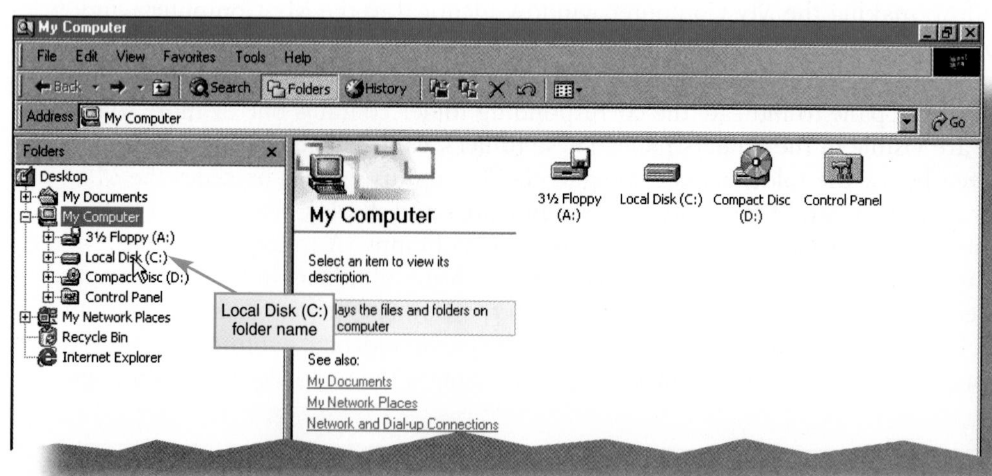

FIGURE 1-39

2 Click the Local Disk (C:) folder name.

The Local Disk (C:) folder name displays highlighted in the Folders pane, the window title and button in the taskbar button area change to reflect the folder name, and the messages on the status bar change (Figure 1-40). The left panel of the Contents pane contains information about Local Disk (C:) and the right panel contains the contents of the Local Disk (C:) folder. Notice that all the folder icons display first and then the file icons display.

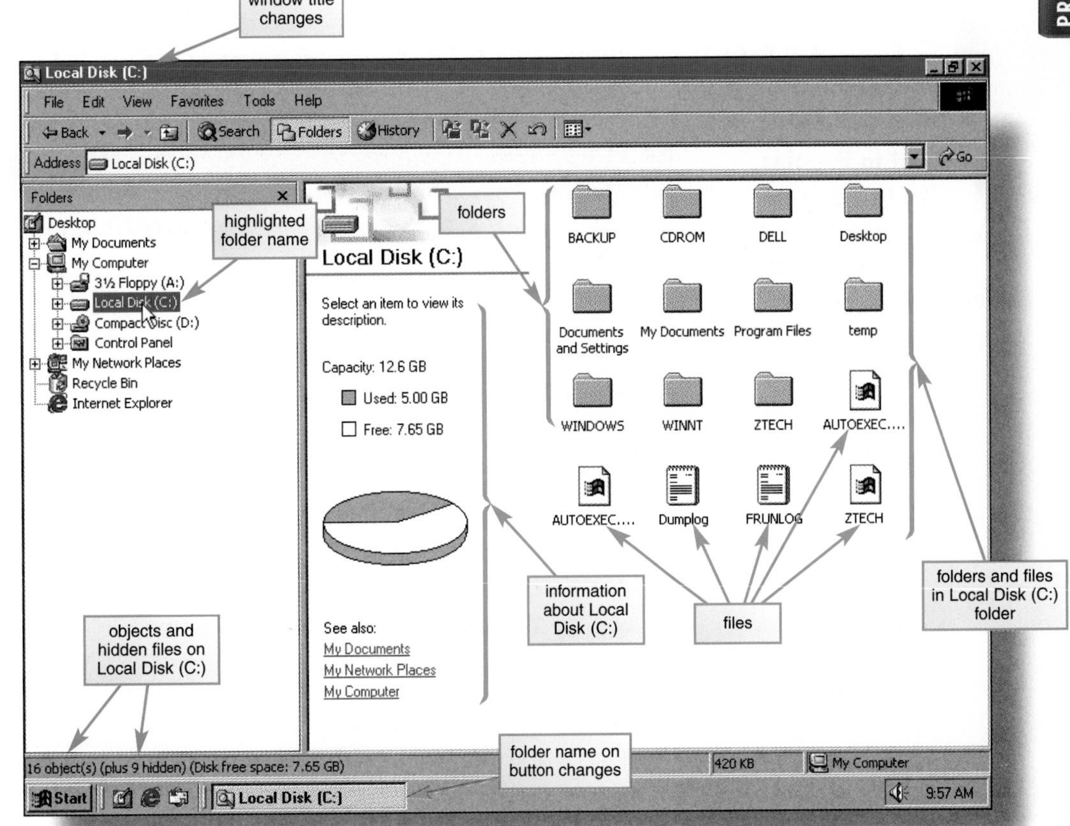

FIGURE 1-40

Other Ways

1. Double-click Local Disk (C:) icon in Contents pane
2. Press TAB to select any icon in Folders pane, press DOWN ARROW or UP ARROW to select Local Disk (C:) icon in Folders pane
3. Press TAB to select any drive icon in Contents pane, press LEFT ARROW or RIGHT ARROW to select Local Disk (C:) icon in Contents pane, press ENTER

The status bar in Figure 1-40 contains information about the folders and files displaying in the right panel of the Contents pane. Sixteen objects display in the panel plus nine hidden files that do not display in the panel. The contents of the Local Disk (C:) folder may be different on your computer.

In addition to displaying the contents of the Local Disk (C:) folder, you can display the contents of the other folders by clicking the corresponding icon or folder name in the Folders pane. Information about the folder and the contents of the folder you click then will display in the Contents pane of the window.

Expanding a Folder

Currently, the Local Disk (C:) folder is highlighted in the Folders pane of the My Computer window, and the contents of the Local Disk (C:) folder display in the right panel of the Contents pane. Windows 2000 displays a plus sign (+) to the left of the Local Disk (C:) icon to indicate the folder contains subfolders that are not visible in the hierarchy of folders in the Folders pane. To expand the Local Disk (C:) folder and display its subfolders, perform the steps on the next page.

More About

Hidden Files

The status bar may or may not indicate that a folder contains a hidden file. Hidden files usually are placed on your hard disk by software vendors such as Microsoft and often are critical to the operation of the software. Rarely will you designate a file as hidden. You should almost never delete a hidden file.

Steps To Expand a Folder

1 Point to the plus sign to the left of the Local Disk (C:) icon in the Folders pane (Figure 1-41).

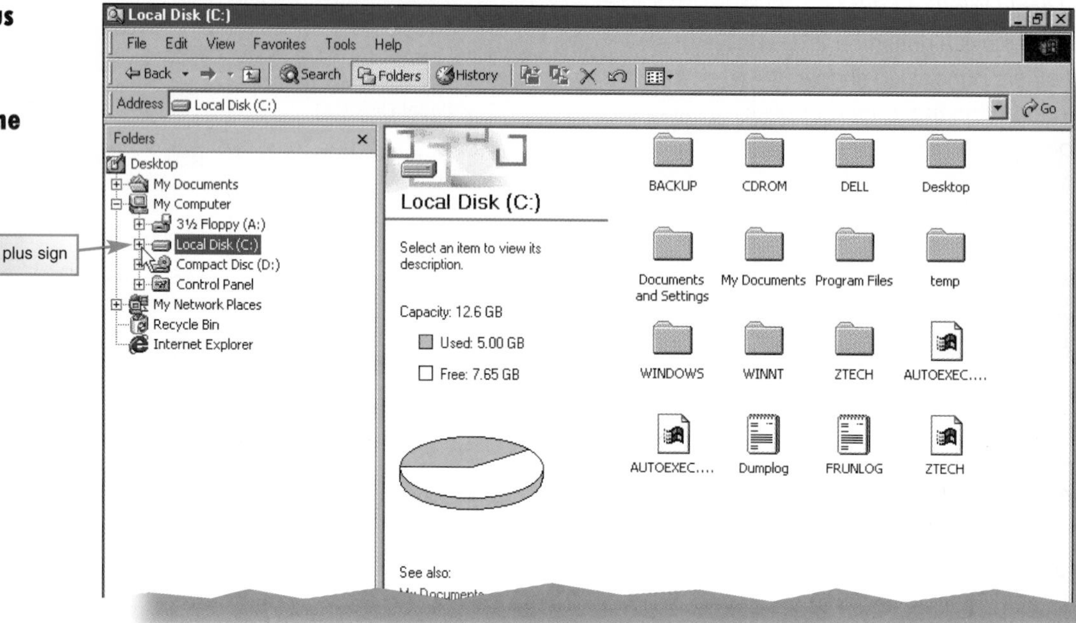

FIGURE 1-41

2 Click the plus sign to display the subfolders in the Local Disk (C:) folder.

The hierarchy below the Local Disk (C:) icon expands to display the folders contained in the Local Disk (C:) folder and a minus sign replaces the plus sign preceding the Local Disk (C:) icon (Figure 1-42).

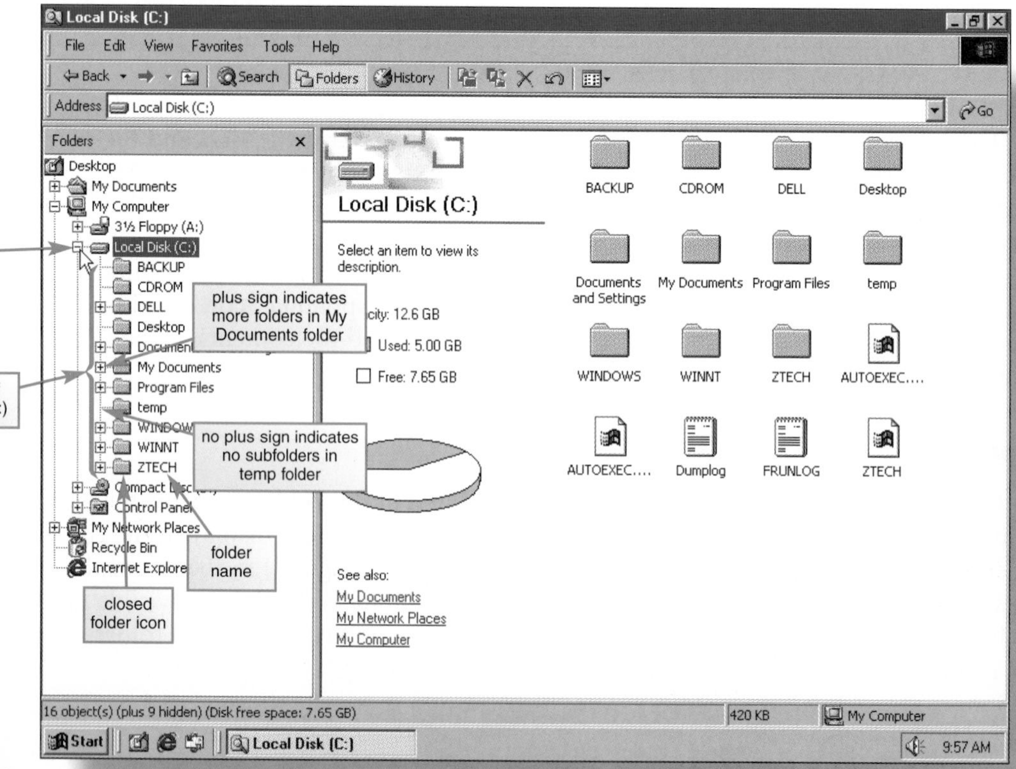

FIGURE 1-42

Other Ways

1. Double-click folder icon
2. Select folder icon, press PLUS SIGN on numeric keypad (or RIGHT ARROW)

The subfolders in the expanded Local Disk (C:) folder shown in Figure 1-42 are indented and aligned below the Local Disk (C:) folder name. A closed folder icon and folder name identify each folder in the Local Disk (C:) folder. A subfolder with a plus sign to the left of it contains more folders. A subfolder without a plus sign contains no more folders. The window title and the files and folders in the Contents pane remain unchanged.

Collapsing a Folder

Currently, the subfolders in the Local Disk (C:) folder display indented and aligned below the Local Disk (C:) folder name (see Figure 1-42). Windows 2000 displays a minus sign (–) to the left of the Local Disk (C:) icon to indicate the folder is expanded. To collapse the Local Disk (C:) folder and remove its subfolders from the hierarchy of folders in the Folders pane, perform the following steps.

To Collapse a Folder

1 Point to the minus sign to the left of the Local Disk (C:) icon in the Folders pane (Figure 1-43).

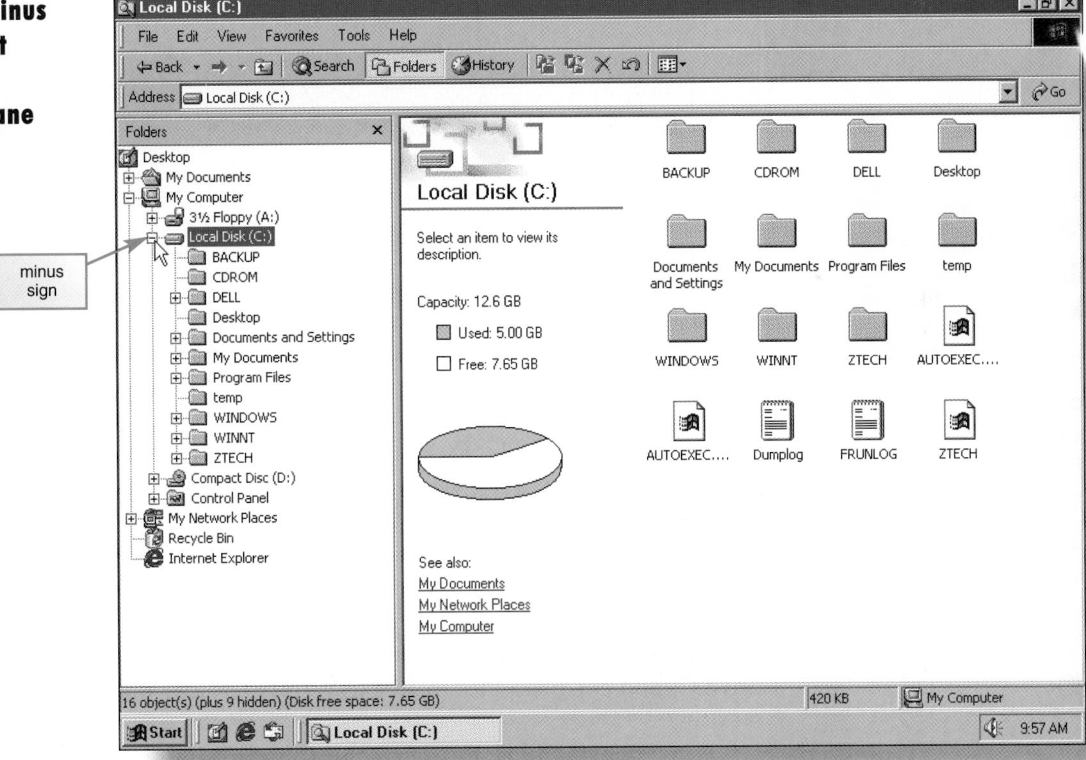

FIGURE 1-43

2 Click the minus sign to display the Local Disk (C:) folder without its subfolders.

A plus sign replaces the minus sign to the left of the Local Disk (C:) icon and the subfolders in the Local Disk (C:) folder are removed from the hierarchy of folders (Figure 1-44).

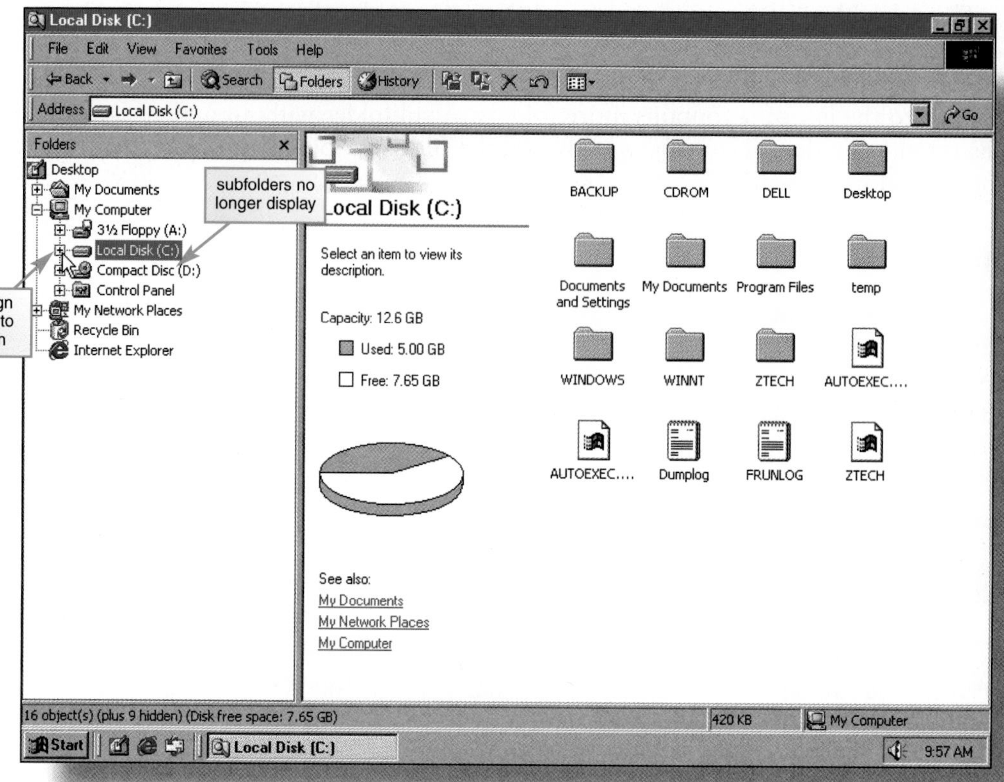

FIGURE 1-44

Other Ways

1. Double-click folder icon
2. Select folder icon, press MINUS SIGN on numeric keypad (or LEFT ARROW)

Moving through the Folders and Contents panes is an important skill because you will find that you use Windows Explorer to perform a significant amount of file maintenance on the computer.

Copying Files to a Folder on a Floppy Disk

One common operation that every student should understand how to perform is copying a file or group of files from one disk to another disk or from one folder to another folder. On the following pages, you will create a new folder, named My Files, on the floppy disk in drive A, select a group of files in the WINNT folder on drive C, and copy the files from the WINNT folder on drive C to the My Files folder on drive A.

When copying files, the drive and folder containing the files to be copied are called the **source drive** and **source folder**, respectively. The drive and folder to which the files are copied are called the **destination drive** and **destination folder**, respectively. Thus, the WINNT folder is the source folder, drive C is the source drive, the My Files folder is the destination folder, and drive A is the destination drive.

Creating a New Folder

In preparation for selecting and copying files from a folder on the hard drive to a folder on the floppy disk in drive A, a new folder with the name of My Files will be created on the floppy disk. Perform the following steps to create the new folder.

Steps To Create a New Folder

1 Insert a formatted floppy disk into drive A on your computer.

2 Click the 3½ Floppy (A:) folder name in the Folders pane and then point to an open area of the Contents pane.

The 3½ Floppy (A:) folder name is highlighted, information about and the contents of the 3½ Floppy (A:) folder display in the Contents pane, and the messages on the status bar change (Figure 1-45). The 3½ Floppy (A:) folder name displays in the window title and on the button in the taskbar button area. Currently, no files or folders display in the Contents pane. The files and folders may be different on your computer.

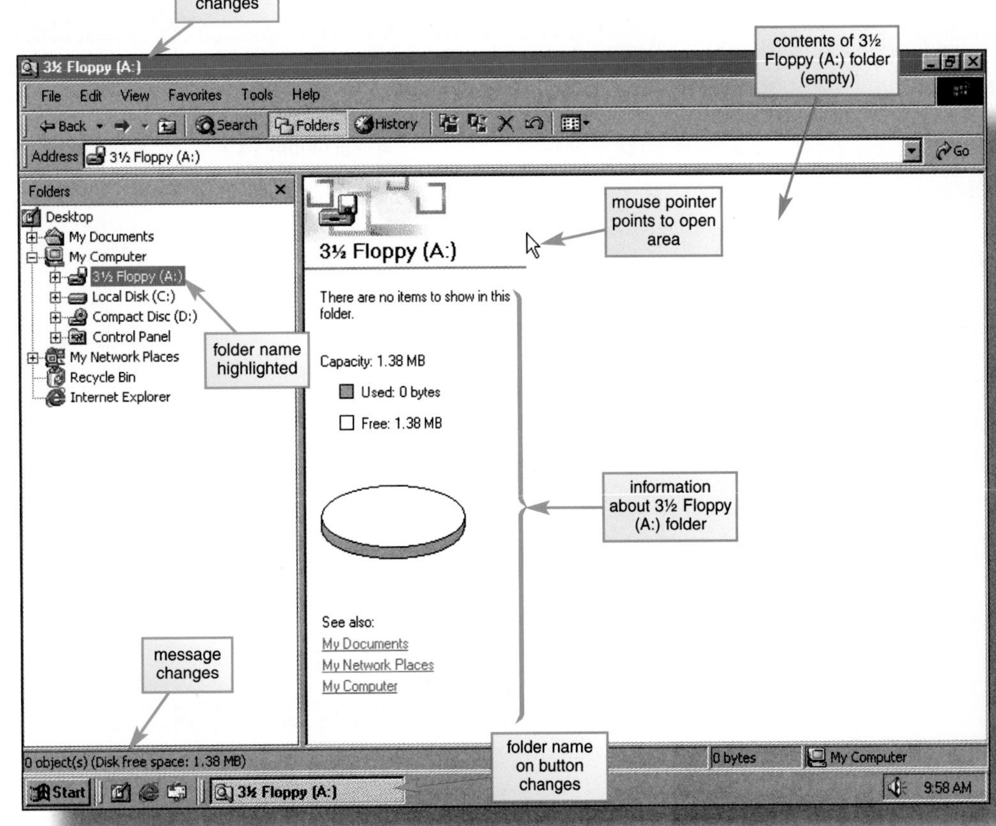

FIGURE 1-45

3 Right-click the open area and then point to New on the shortcut menu.

A shortcut menu and the New submenu display and the New command is highlighted on the shortcut menu (Figure 1-46). Although no subfolders display in the right panel of the Contents pane, a plus sign precedes the 3½ Floppy (A:) icon.

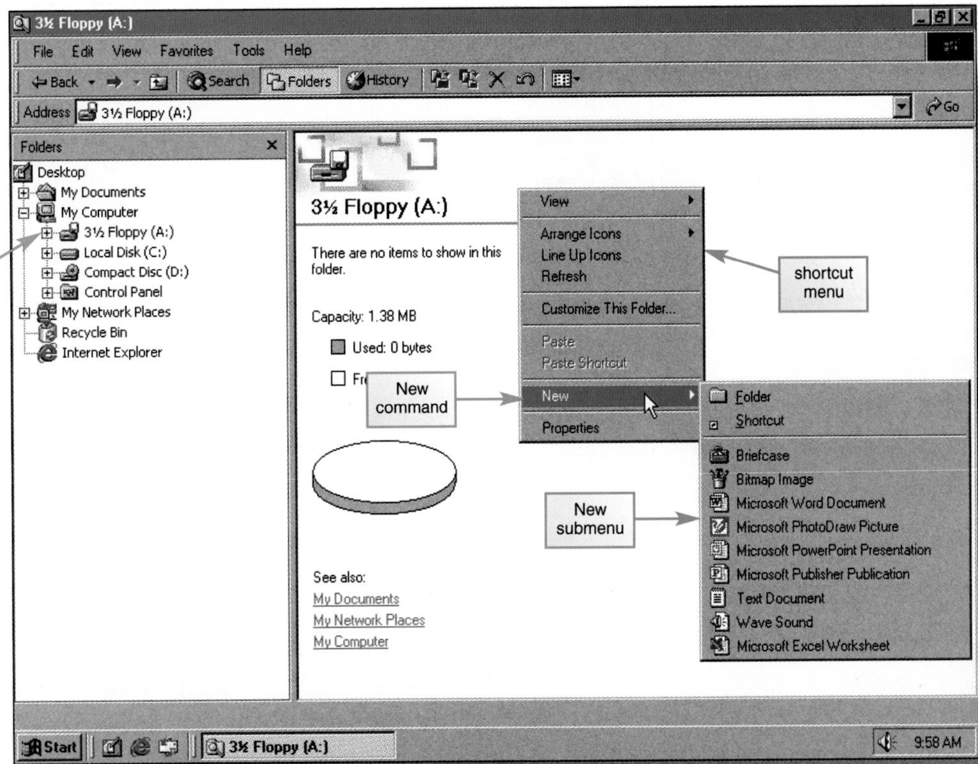

FIGURE 1-46

4 Point to Folder on the New submenu.

The Folder command is highlighted on the New submenu (Figure 1-47). Clicking the Folder command will create a folder in the right panel of the Contents pane using the default folder name, New Folder.

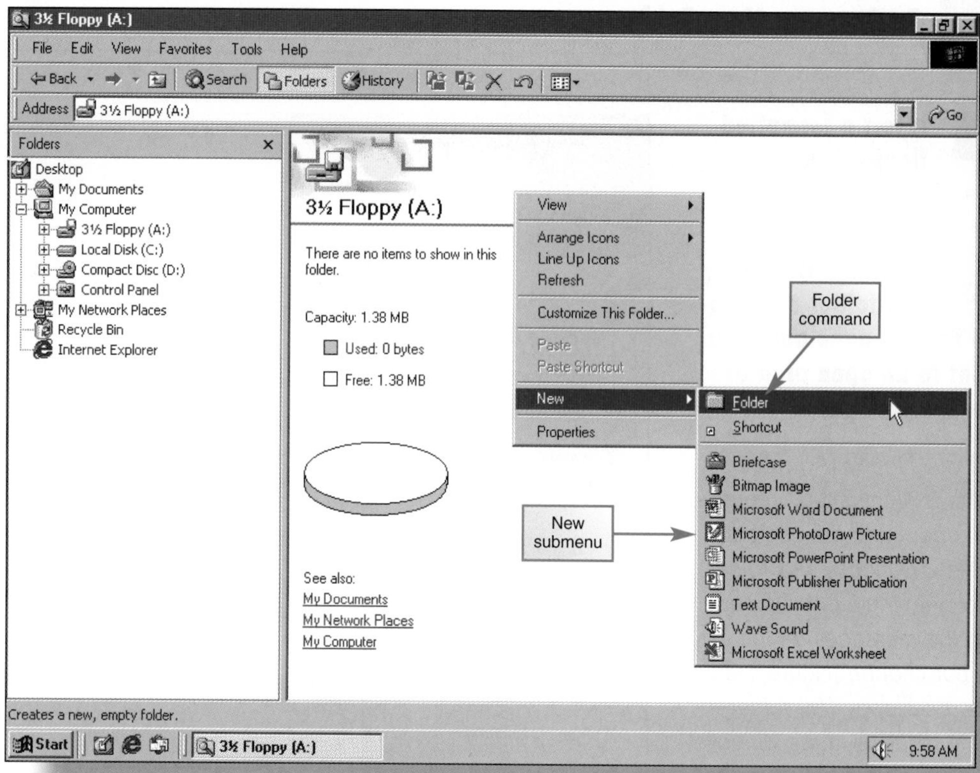

FIGURE 1-47

5 Click Folder.

The New Folder icon displays in the right panel of the Contents pane (Figure 1-48). The text box below the icon contains the highlighted default folder name, New Folder, and an insertion point. A plus sign continues to display to the left of the 3½ Floppy (A:) icon in the Folders pane to indicate the 3½ Floppy (A:) folder contains the New Folder subfolder. The message on the status bar indicates one object is selected in the Contents pane.

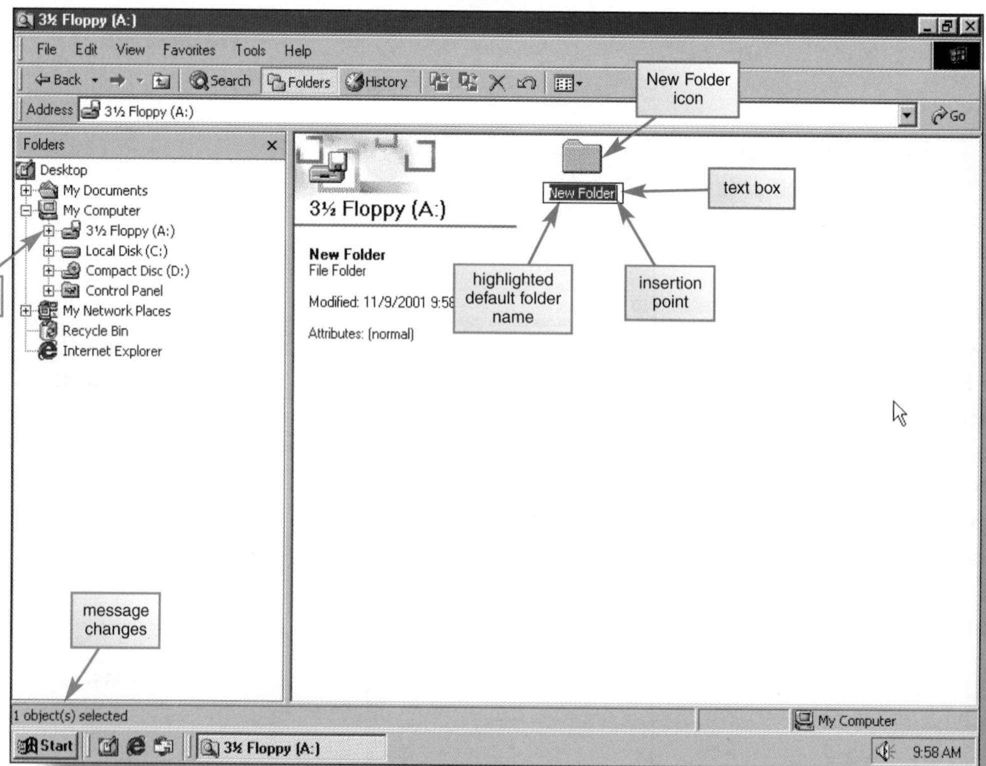

FIGURE 1-48

6 **Type** `My Files` **in the text box and then press the ENTER key.**

The new folder name, My Files, is entered and the text box is removed (Figure 1-49).

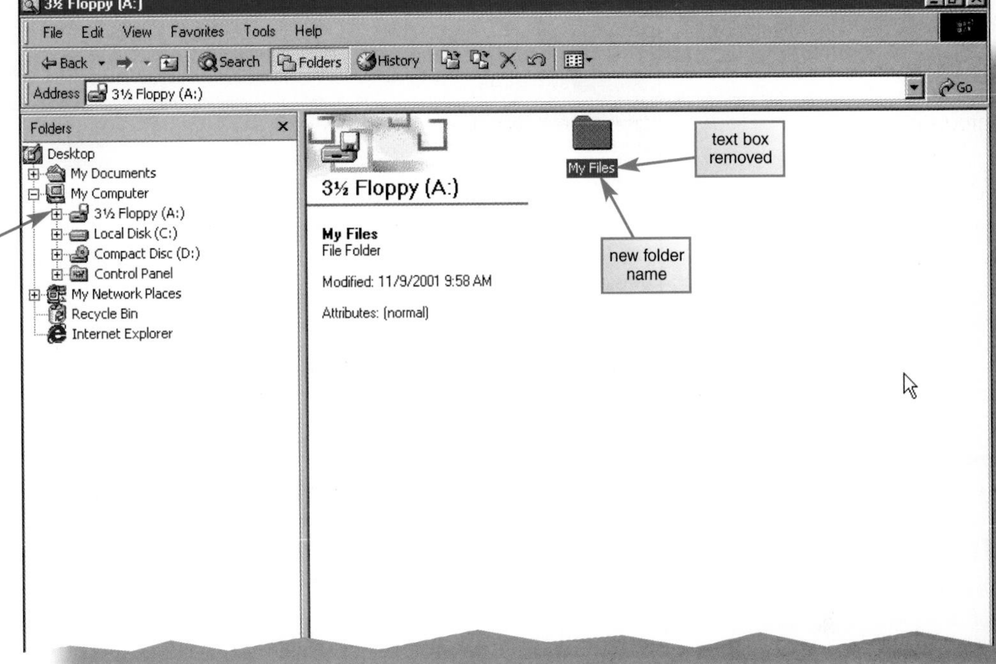

FIGURE 1-49

Other Ways

1. Select drive in Folders pane, on File menu point to New, click Folder on New submenu

After creating the My Files folder on the floppy disk in drive A, you can save files in the folder or copy files from other folders to the folder. On the following pages, you will copy a group of files consisting of the Prairie Wind, Rhododendron, and Santa Fe Stucco files from the WINNT folder on drive C to the My Files folder on drive A.

Displaying the Destination Folder

To copy the three files from the WINNT folder on drive C to the My Files folder on drive A, the files to be copied will be selected in the right panel of the Contents pane and right-dragged to the My Files folder in the Folders pane. Prior to selecting and right-dragging the files, the destination folder (My Files folder on drive A) must be visible in the Folders pane, and the three files to be copied must be visible in the Contents pane.

Currently, the plus sign (+) to the left of the 3½ Floppy (A:) icon indicates the folder contains one or more subfolders that are not visible in the Folders pane (Figure 1-49). Perform the following steps to expand the 3½ Floppy (A:) folder to display the My Files subfolder.

TO EXPAND A FOLDER

1. Point to the plus sign to the left of the 3½ Floppy (A:) icon in the Folders pane.
2. Click the plus sign to display the subfolders in the 3½ Floppy (A:) folder.

A minus sign replaces the plus sign to the left of the 3½ Floppy (A:) folder, the folder name is highlighted, and the My Files subfolder displays in the 3½ Floppy (A:) folder, aligned below the 3½ Floppy (A:) folder name (Figure 1-50 on the next page).

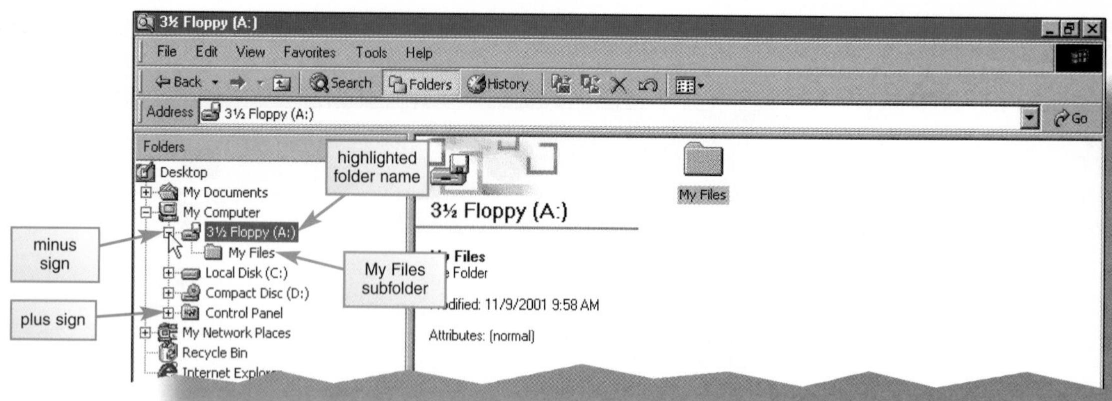

FIGURE 1-50

The WINNT Folder

WINNT is an abbreviation for Windows NT, an older operating system designed for businesses with networks. Because Windows NT used the WINNT folder and Windows 2000 contains many of the features of Windows NT, Microsoft decided to use the WINNT folder name. Some think Microsoft should have used Windows 2000.

Displaying the Contents of the WINNT Folder

Currently, the My Files folder displays in the right panel of the Contents pane of the 3½ Floppy (A:) window. To copy files from the source folder (WINNT folder on drive C) to the My Files folder, the WINNT folder must be visible in the Folders pane and the contents of the WINNT folder must display in the Contents pane. To accomplish this, you must expand the Local Disk (C:) folder in the Folders pane and then click the WINNT folder name in the Folder pane to display the contents of the WINNT folder in the right panel of the Contents pane.

The WINNT folder contains programs and files necessary for the operation of the Windows 2000 operating system. As such, you should exercise caution when working with the contents of the WINNT folder because changing the contents of the folder may cause the programs to stop working correctly. Perform the following steps to display the contents of the WINNT folder.

To Display the Contents of a Folder

1 Click the plus sign to the left of the Local Disk (C:) icon in the Folders pane and then point to the WINNT folder name.

*A minus sign replaces the plus sign to the left of the Local Disk (C:) icon and the subfolders in the Local Disk (C:) folder display (Figure 1-51). In addition to folders and other files, the WINNT folder contains a series of predefined graphics, called **clip art files**, that can be used with application programs.*

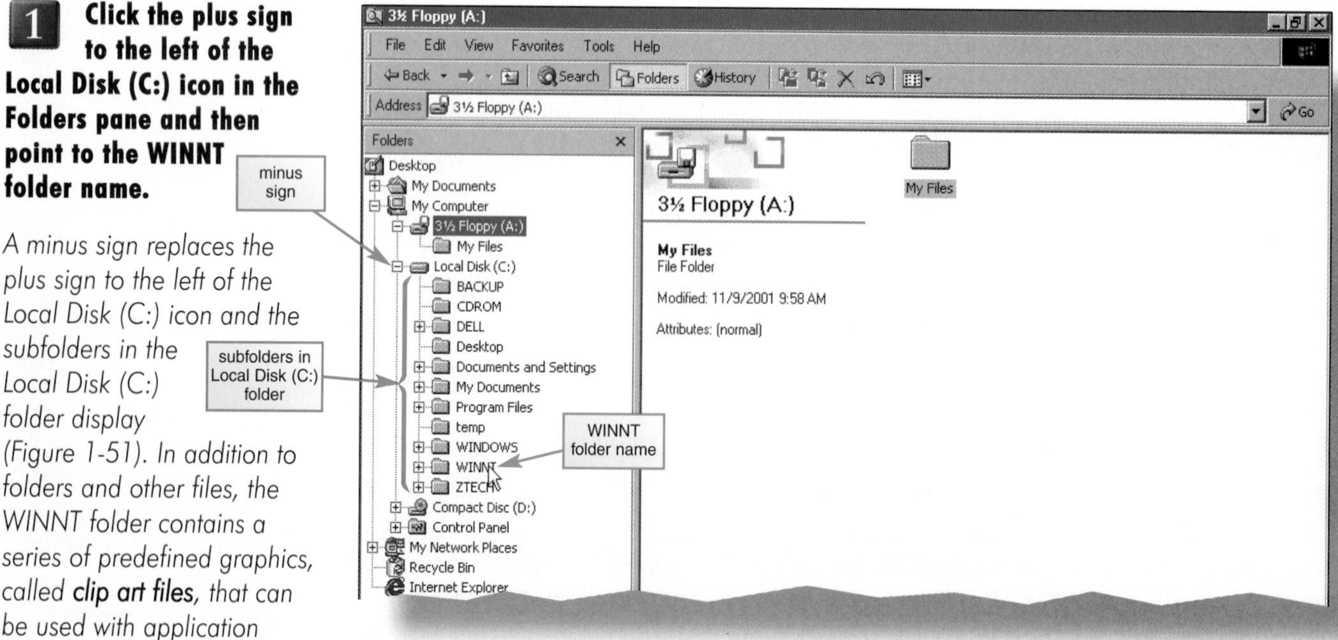

FIGURE 1-51

2 Click the WINNT folder name and then point to the Show Files link.

The WINNT folder name is highlighted in the Folders pane, the closed folder icon preceding the WINNT folder name changes to an open folder icon, and the WINNT button replaces the 3½ Floppy (A:) button. Information about the WINNT folder and the Show Files link display in the left panel of the Contents pane and a graphics image displays in the right panel (Figure 1-52). The mouse pointer changes to a hand and the message in the status area changes.

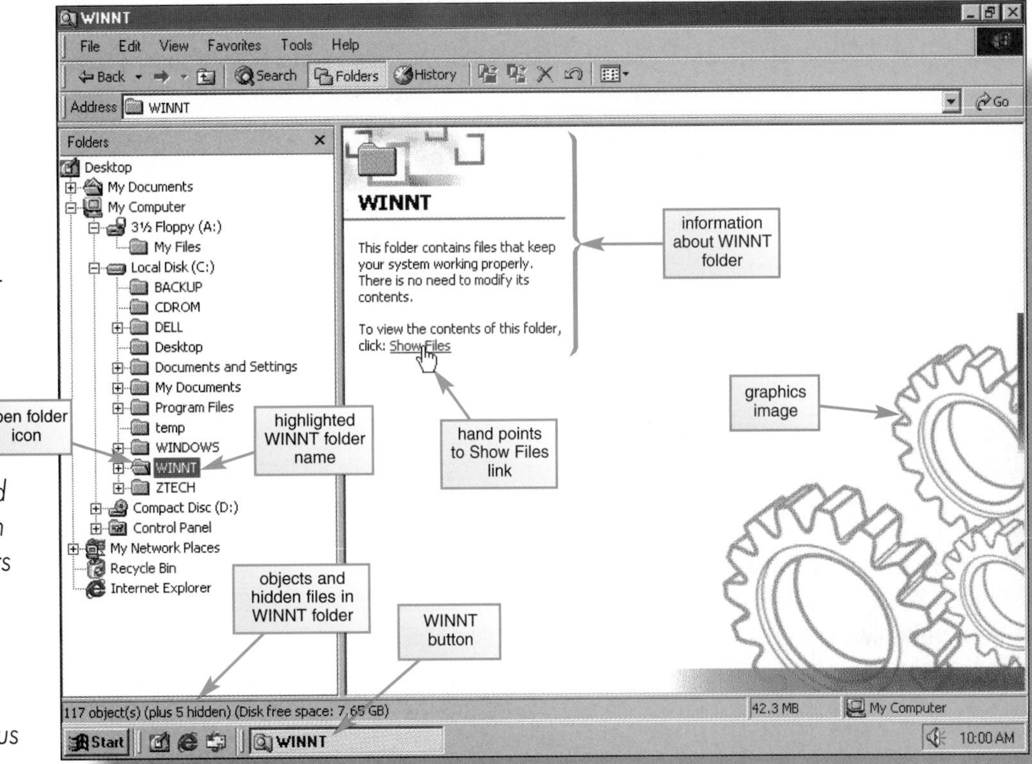

FIGURE 1-52

3 Click Show Files. Scroll the Contents pane to make the Prairie Wind, Rhododendron, and Santa Fe Stucco files in the WINNT folder visible.

The files and folders in the WINNT folder display in the right panel of the Contents pane and the right panel scrolls to display the Prairie Wind, Rhododendron, and Santa Fe Stucco files (Figure 1-53). The files and folders in the WINNT folder may be different and file extensions may display as part of the file names on your computer.

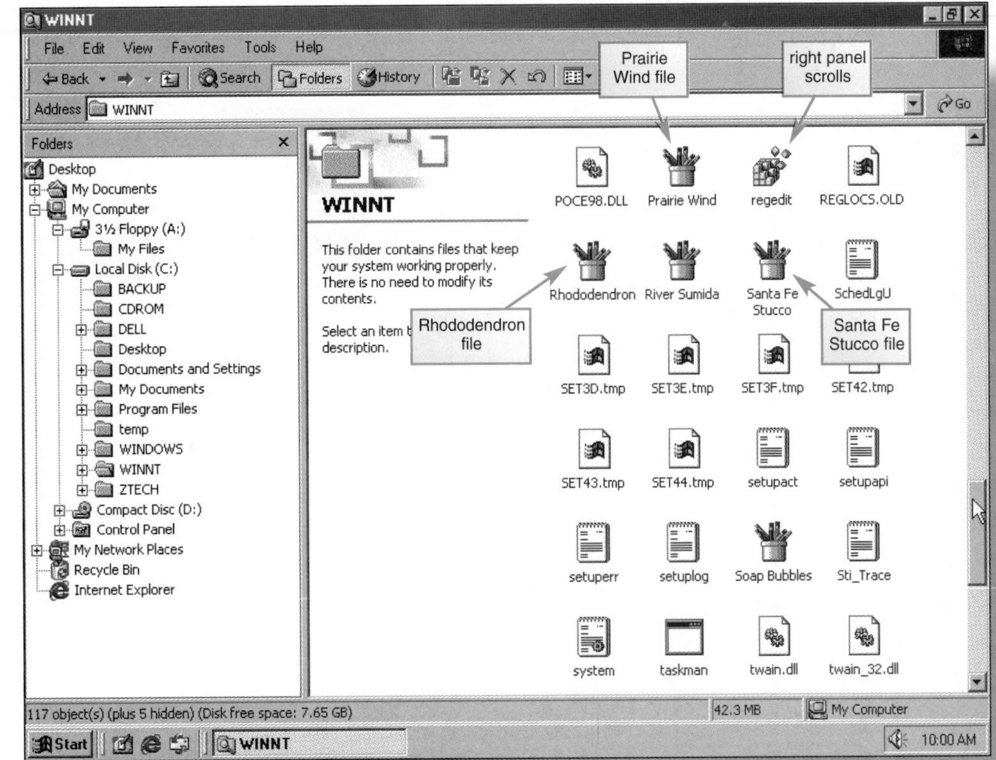

FIGURE 1-53

Selecting a Group of Files

You easily can copy a single file or group of files from one folder to another folder using Windows Explorer. To copy a single file, select the file in the right panel of the Contents pane and right-drag the highlighted file to the folder in the Folders pane where the file is to be copied. Group files are copied in a similar manner by clicking the icon or file name of the first file in a group of files to select it. You select the remaining files in the group by pointing to each file icon or file name, holding down the CTRL key, and then clicking the file icon or file name. Perform the following steps to select the group of files consisting of the Prairie Wind, Rhododendron, and Santa Fe Stucco files.

Steps To Select a Group of Files

1 Select the Prairie Wind file by clicking the Prairie Wind file name, and then point to the Rhododendron file name.

The Prairie Wind file is highlighted in the right panel of the Contents pane, information about and a graphic image of the file displays in the left panel, and two messages display on the status bar (Figure 1-54). The messages indicate the type of file selected (Bitmap Image) and the size of the file (64.4 KB).

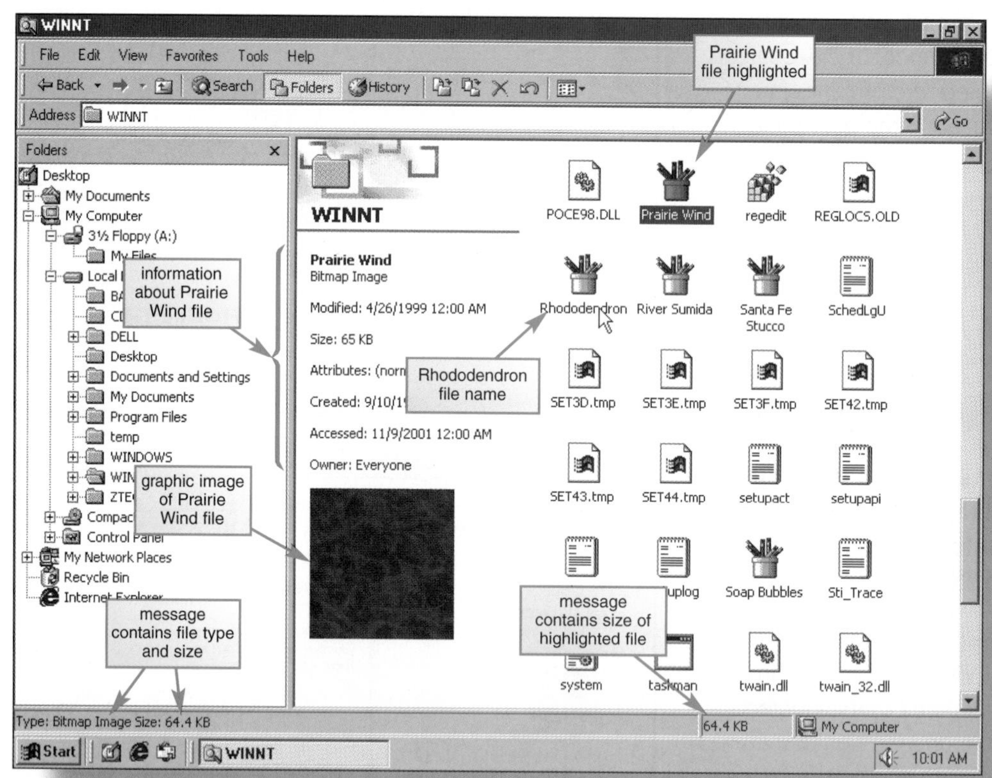

FIGURE 1-54

2 Hold down the CTRL key, click the Rhododendron file name, release the CTRL key, and then point to the Santa Fe Stucco file name.

The Prairie Wind and Rhododendron files are highlighted, information about the two files displays in the left panel of the Contents pane, and the two messages on the status bar change to reflect the additional file selected (Figure 1-55). The messages indicate two files are selected, 2 object(s) selected and the size of the two files, 81.3 KB.

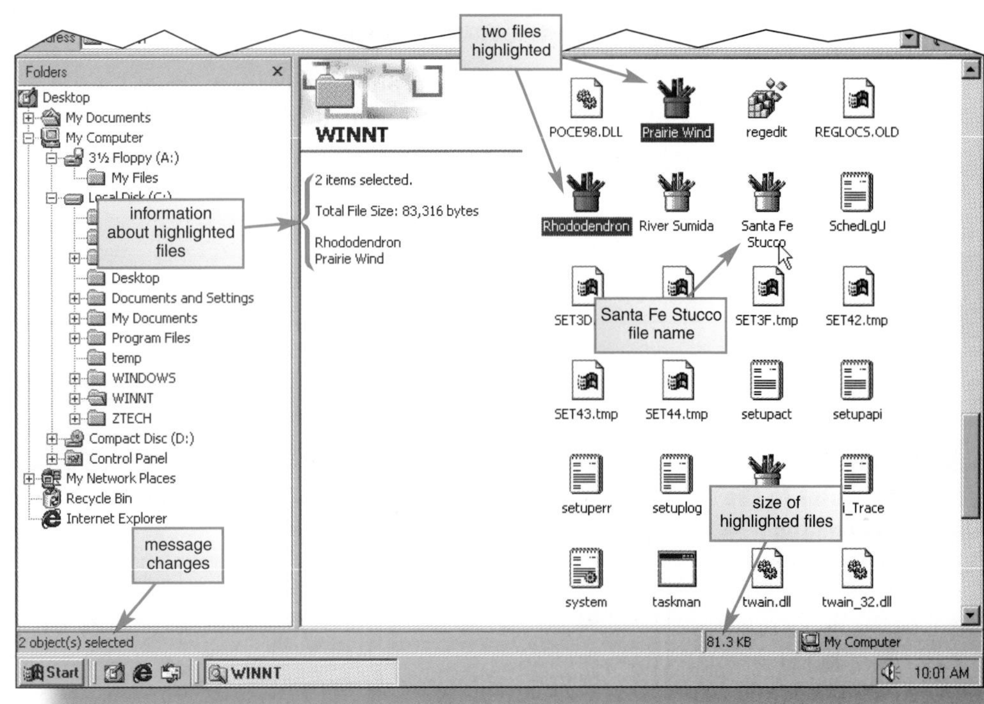

FIGURE 1-55

3 Hold down the CTRL key, click the Santa Fe Stucco file name, and then release the CTRL key.

The group of files consisting of the Prairie Wind, Rhododendron, and Santa Fe Stucco files is highlighted, information about the three files displays in the left panel of the Contents pane, and the messages on the status bar change to reflect the selection of a third file (Figure 1-56). The messages indicate three files are selected, 3 object(s) selected and the size of the three files, 145 KB.

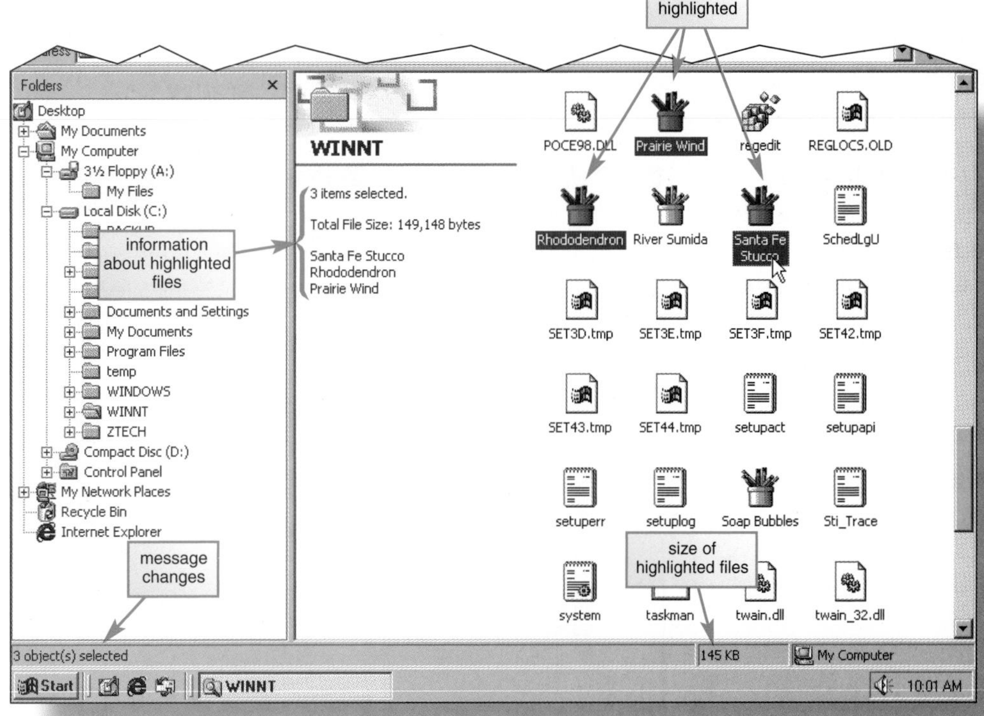

FIGURE 1-56

Other Ways

1. To select contiguous files, select first file name in Contents pane, hold down SHIFT key, click last file name
2. To select all files, on Edit menu click Select All, click OK button

Copying a Group of Files

After selecting a group of files, copy the files to the My Files folder on drive A by pointing to any highlighted file name in the right panel of the Contents pane and right-dragging the file name to the My Files folder in the Folders pane. Perform the following steps to copy a group of files.

Steps To Copy a Group of Files

1 If necessary, scroll the Folders pane to make the My Files folder visible. Point to the highlighted Rhododendron file name in the Contents pane.

The pointer points to the highlighted Rhododendron file name in the Contents pane and the My Files folder is visible in the Folders pane (Figure 1-57).

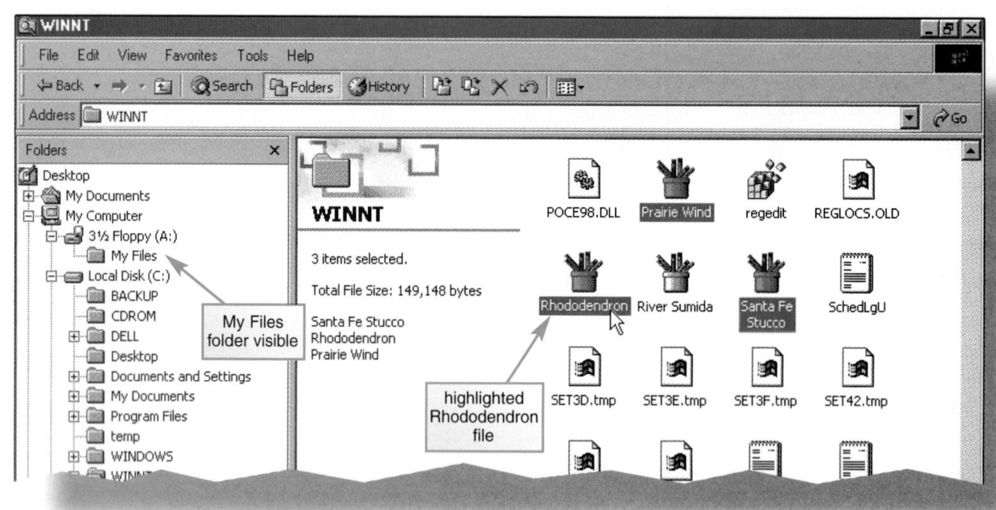

FIGURE 1-57

2 Right-drag the Rhododendron file over the My Files folder name in the Folders pane.

As you drag the file, an outline of three dimmed icons displays and the My Files folder name is highlighted (Figure 1-58). The mouse pointer contains a plus sign to indicate the group of files is being copied, not moved.

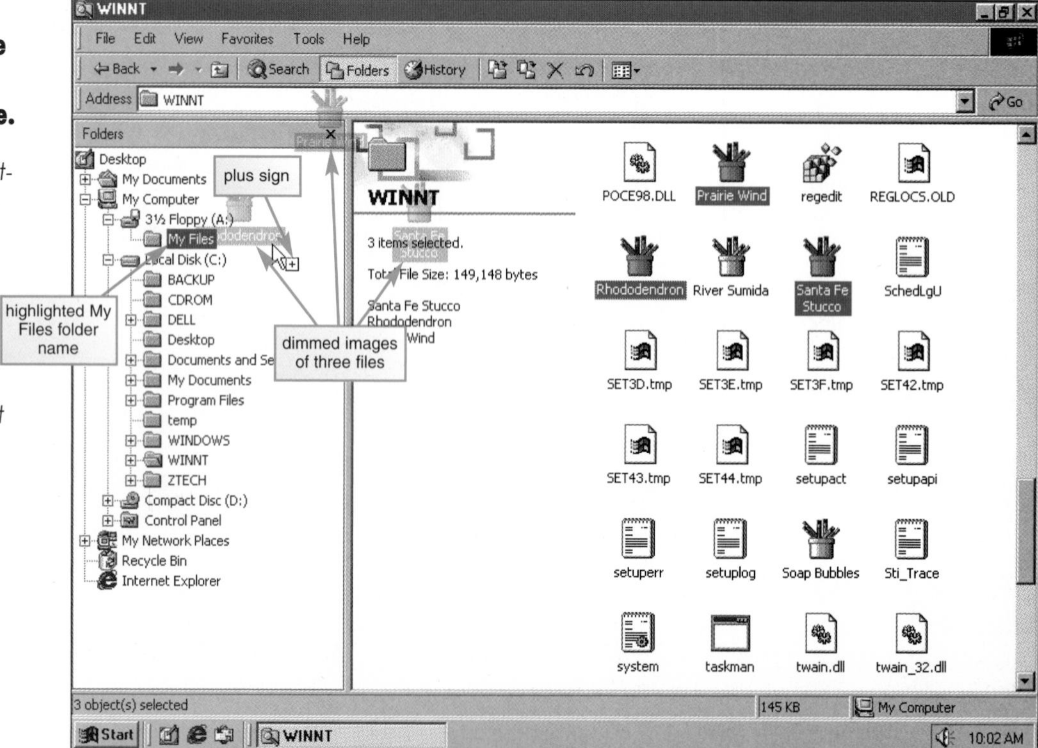

FIGURE 1-58

3 **Release the right mouse button and then point to Copy Here on the shortcut menu.**

A shortcut menu displays and the Copy Here command is highlighted (Figure 1-59).

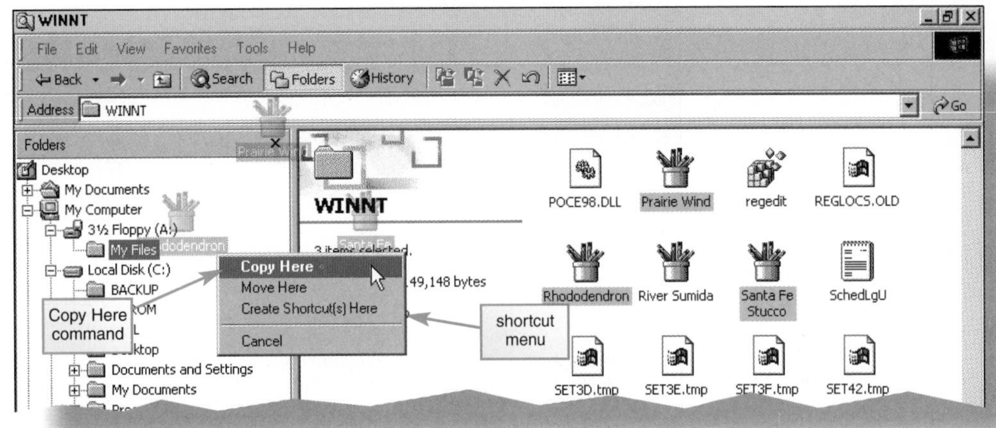

FIGURE 1-59

4 **Click Copy Here.**

The Copying dialog box displays and remains on the screen while each file is copied to the My Files folder (Figure 1-60). The Copying dialog box indicates the Santa Fe Stucco.bmp file is being copied from the WINNT folder to the My Files folder and ten seconds remain in the copy process.

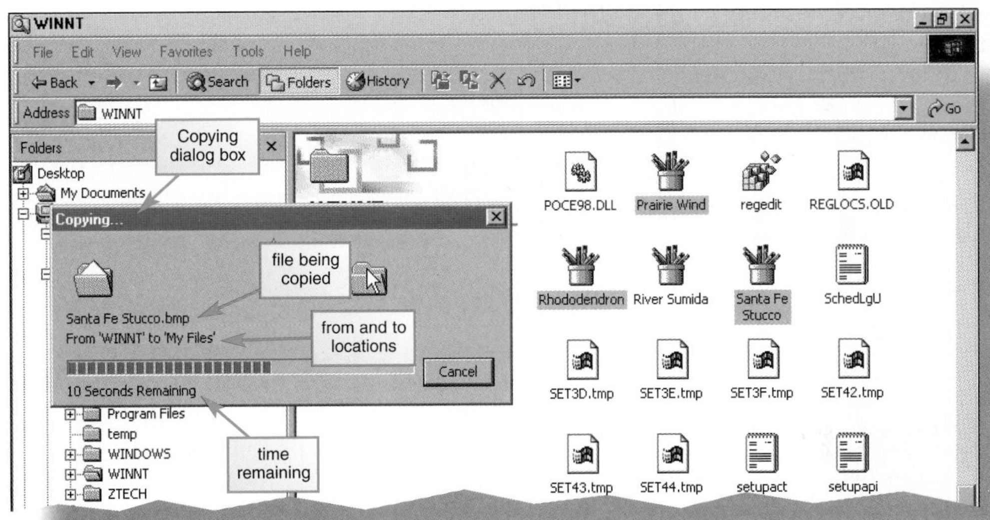

FIGURE 1-60

Displaying the Contents of the My Files Folder

After copying a group of files, you should verify the files were copied into the correct folder. To view the files that were copied to the My Files folder, perform the following steps.

TO DISPLAY THE CONTENTS OF A FOLDER

1 Point to the My Files folder name in the Folders pane.

2 Click the My Files folder name.

The highlighted My Files folder name displays in the Folders pane, the open folder icon replaces the closed folder icon to the left of the My Files folder name, the contents of the My Files folder display in the right panel of the Contents pane, and the message on the status bar changes (Figure 1-61 on the next page). The message on the status bar indicates the amount of free disk space on the floppy disk in drive A, Disk free space: 1.24 MB.

Other Ways

1. Select file to copy in Contents pane, click Copy To button on Standard Buttons toolbar, select folder icon in Browse For Folder dialog box, click OK button
2. Select file to copy in Contents pane, on Edit menu click Copy, select folder icon in Folders pane to receive copy, on Edit menu click Paste
3. Select file to copy in Contents pane, press CTRL+C, select folder icon to receive copy, press CTRL+V

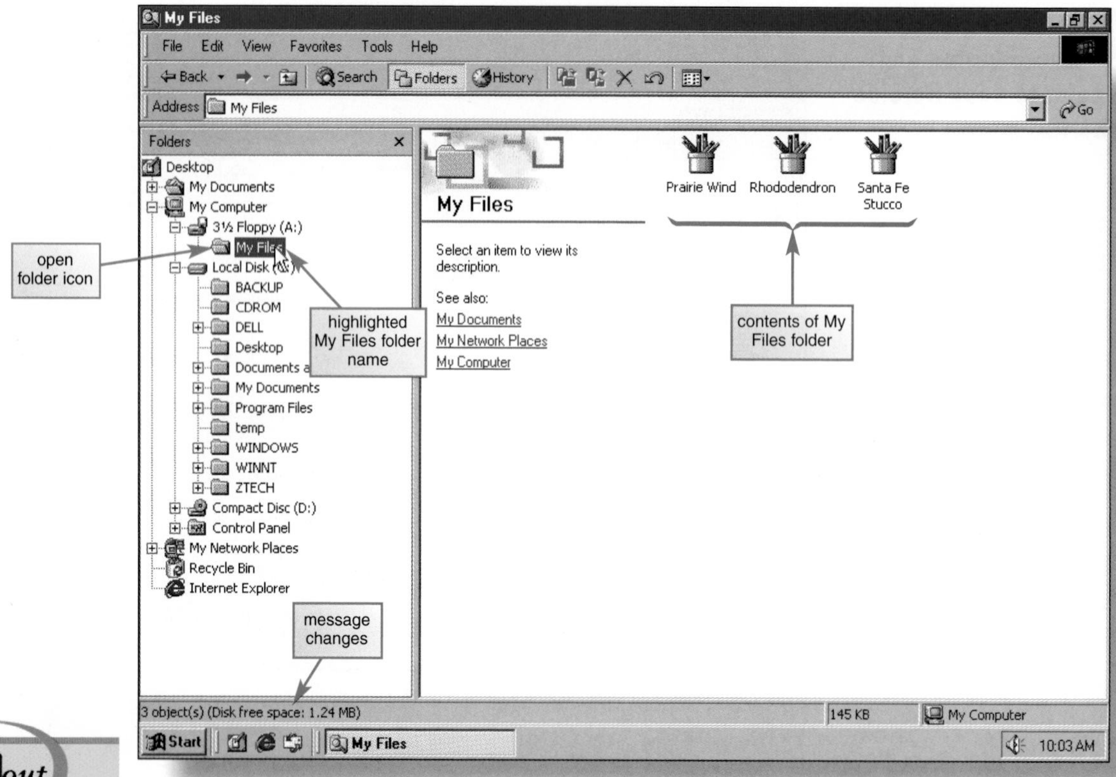

FIGURE 1-61

More About

Renaming a File or Folder

A file or folder name can contain up to 255 characters, including spaces. But, they cannot contain any of the following characters: \/:*?"<>|.

Renaming a File or Folder

For various reasons, you may wish to change the name of a file or folder on a disk. Perform the following steps to change the name of the Santa Fe Stucco file on drive A to Arizona Stucco.

To Rename a File

1 Point to the Santa Fe Stucco file name in the Contents pane (Figure 1-62).

The mouse pointer points to the Santa Fe Stucco file name.

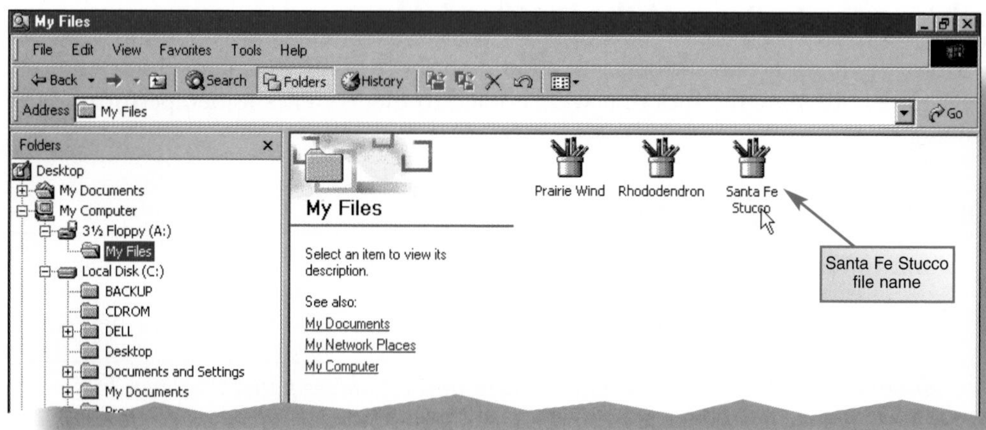

FIGURE 1-62

2 Click the Santa Fe Stucco file name twice (do not double-click the file name).

A text box containing the highlighted Santa Fe Stucco file name and insertion point displays (Figure 1-63).

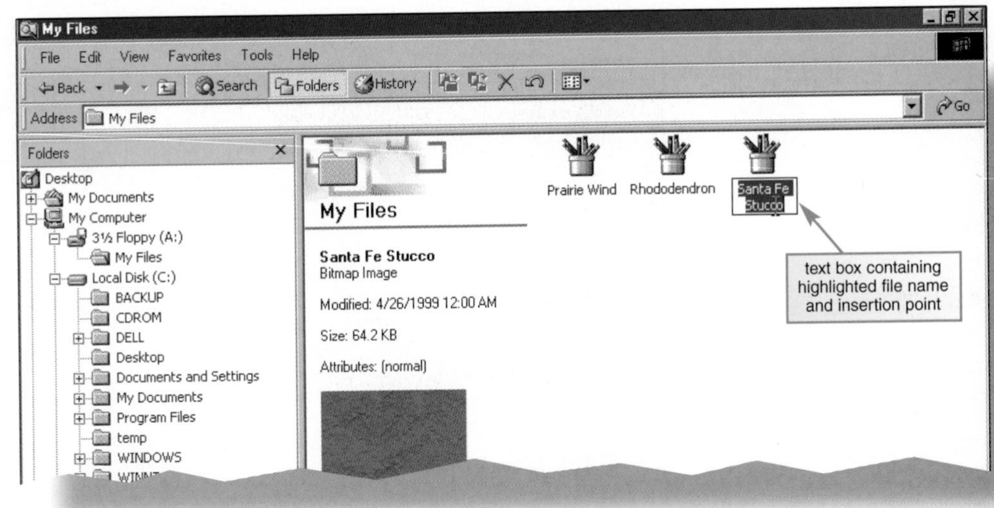

FIGURE 1-63

3 Type `Arizona Stucco` **and then press the ENTER key.**

The file name changes to Arizona Stucco and the text box surrounding the file name is removed (Figure 1-64).

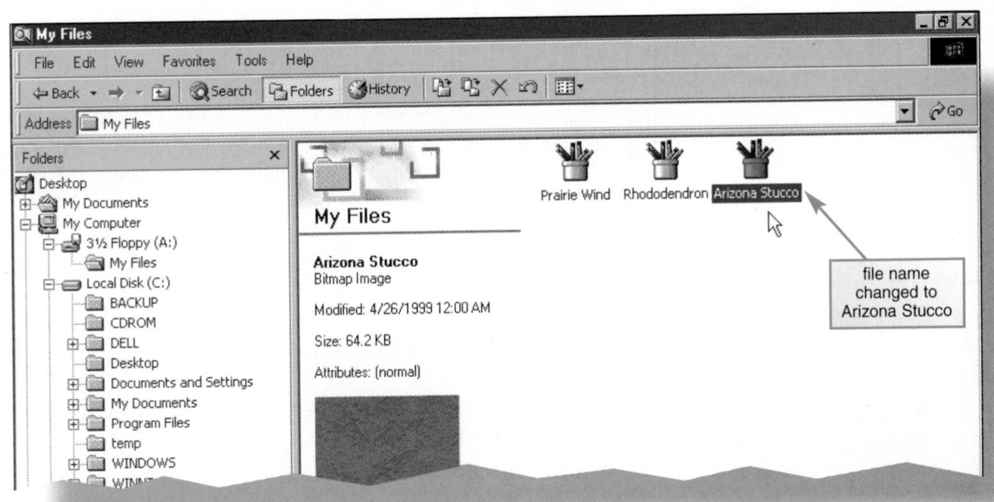

FIGURE 1-64

Other Ways

1. Right-click file name, click Rename on shortcut menu, type new name, press ENTER
2. Select file name, on File menu click Rename, type new name, press ENTER
3. Select file name, press F2, type new name, press ENTER
4. Select file name, press ALT+F, press M, type new name, press ENTER

Follow the same procedure to change a folder name. The following steps change the name of the My Files folder to Clip Art Files.

TO RENAME A FOLDER

1. Point to the My Files folder name in the Folders pane.
2. Click the My Files folder name twice (do not double-click the folder name).
3. Type `Clip Art Files` and then press the ENTER key.

The folder name changes to Clip Art Files and the text box surrounding the folder name is removed (Figure 1-65 on the next page). The new folder name replaces the old folder name in both the window title in the left panel of the Contents pane and on the button in the taskbar button area.

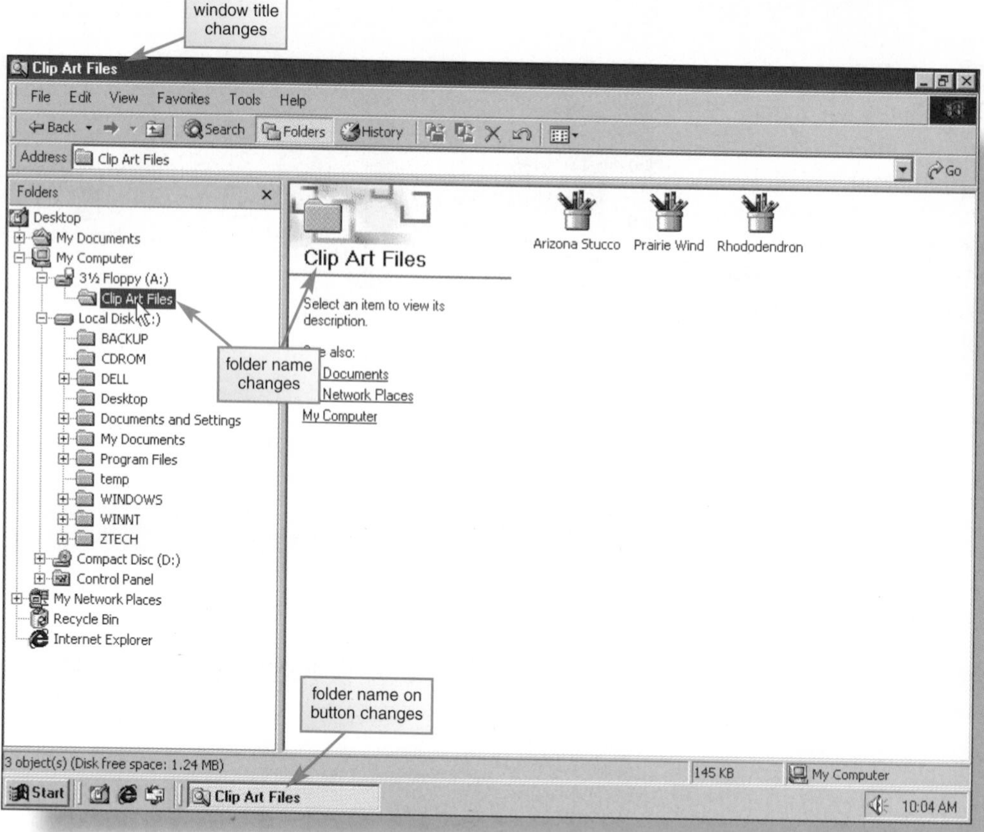

FIGURE 1-65

> **More About**
>
> **Deleting Files**
>
> A few years ago, someone proposed that the Delete command be removed from operating systems. It seems an entire database was deleted by an employee who thought he knew what he was doing, resulting in a company that could not function for more than a week while the database was rebuilt. Millions of dollars in revenue were lost. The Delete command is still around, but it should be considered a dangerous weapon.

Deleting a File or Folder

When you no longer need a file or folder, you can delete it. When you delete a file or folder on the hard drive using the Recycle Bin, Windows 2000 temporarily stores the deleted file or folder in the Recycle Bin until you permanently discard the contents of the Recycle Bin by emptying the Recycle Bin. Until the Recycle Bin is emptied, you can retrieve the files and folders you have deleted previously by mistake or other reasons. Unlike deleting files or folders on the hard drive, when you delete a file or folder located on a floppy disk, the file or folder is deleted immediately and not stored in the Recycle Bin.

Deleting a File by Right-Clicking Its File Name

Right-clicking a file name produces a shortcut menu that contains the Delete command. To illustrate how to delete a file by right-clicking, perform the following steps to delete the Rhododendron file.

Steps To Delete a File by Right-Clicking

1 Right-click the Rhododendron file name in the right panel of the Contents pane and then point to the Delete command on the shortcut menu.

The Rhododendron file name is highlighted in the Contents pane and a shortcut menu displays (Figure 1-66). The Delete command is highlighted on the shortcut menu.

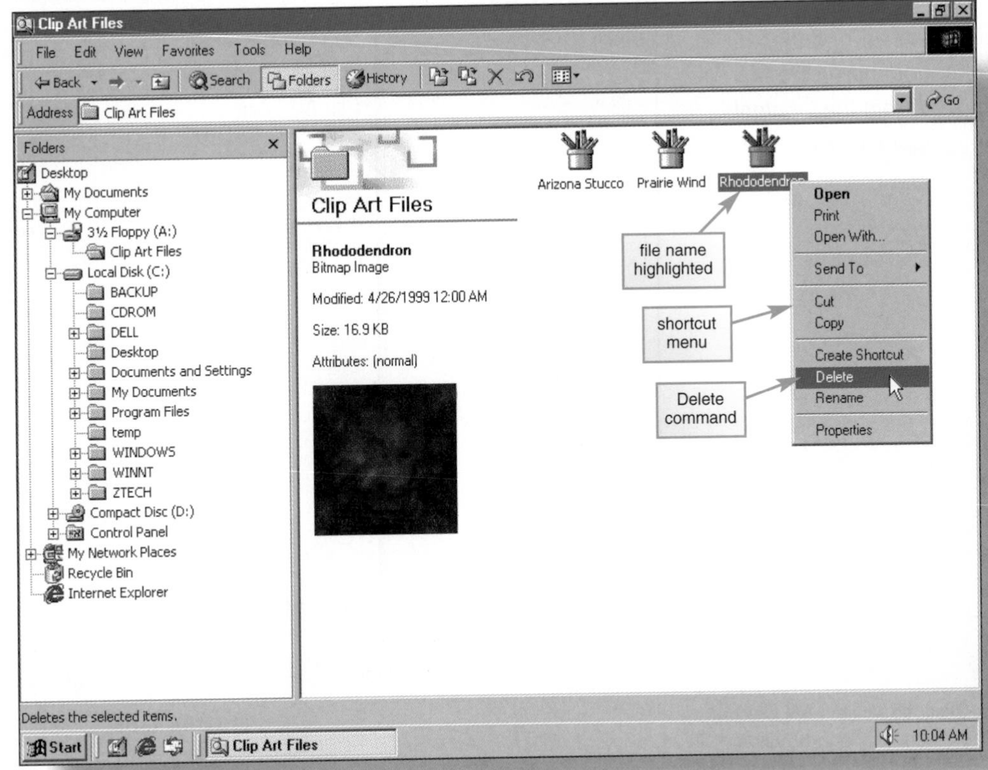

FIGURE 1-66

2 Click Delete. When the Confirm File Delete dialog box displays, point to the Yes button.

The Confirm File Delete dialog box displays (Figure 1-67). The dialog box contains a confirmation message, Are you sure you want to delete 'Rhododendron'?, and the Yes and No command buttons.

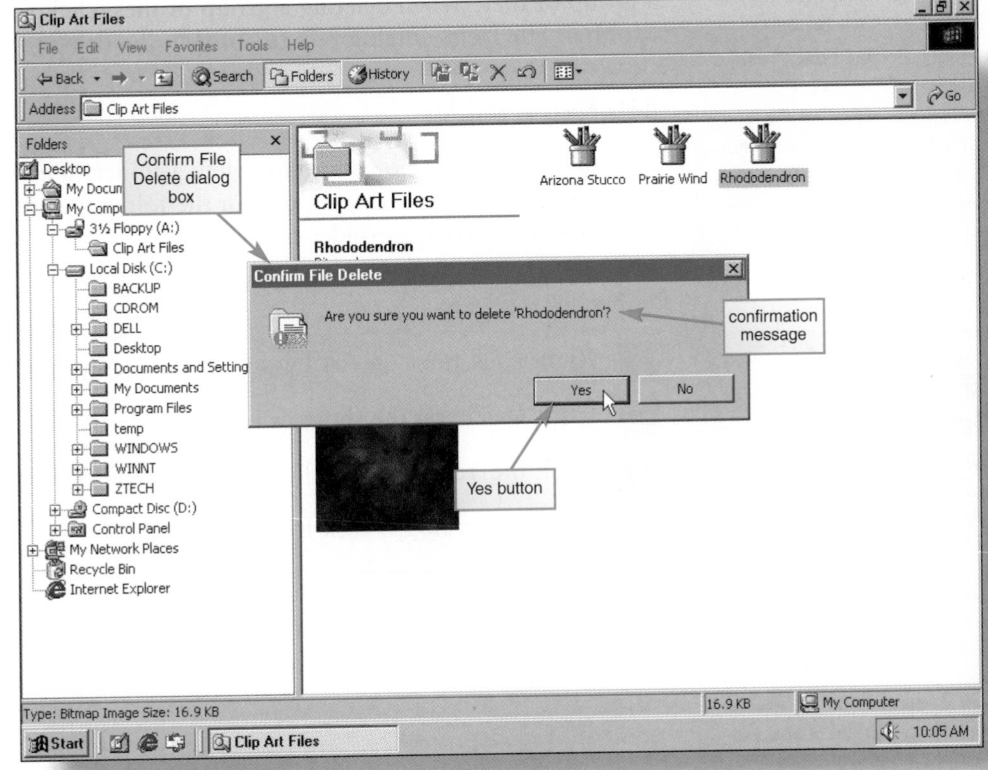

FIGURE 1-67

3 **Click the Yes button.**

A Deleting dialog box displays while the file is being deleted, and then the Rhododendron file is removed from the Contents pane (Figure 1-68).

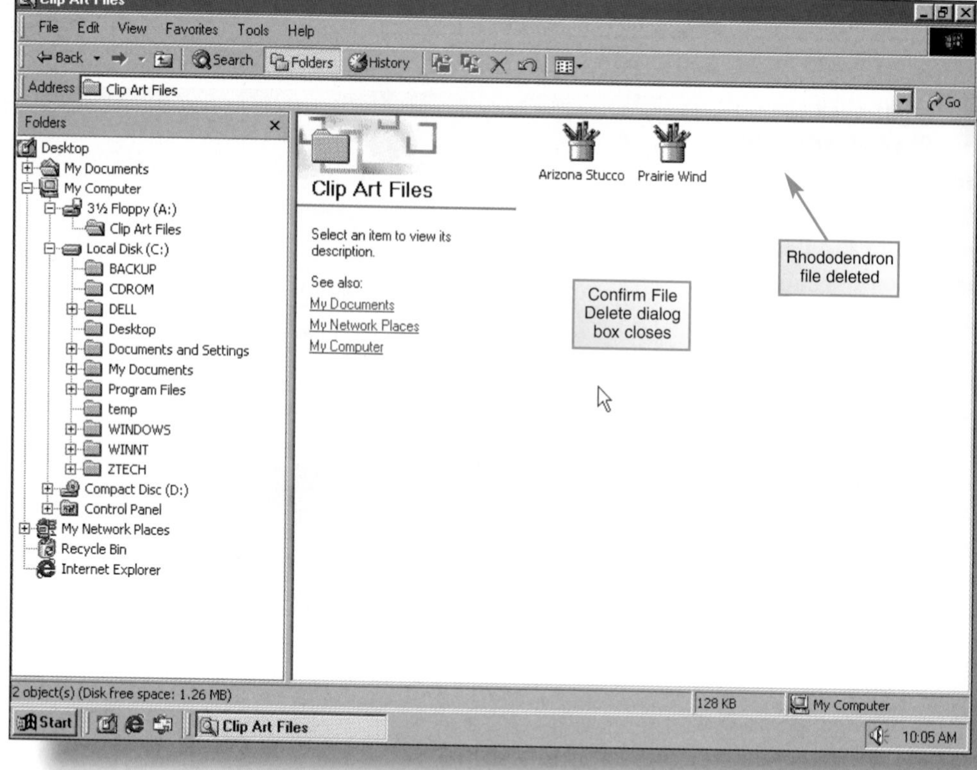

FIGURE 1-68

Other Ways

1. Click file name, click Delete button on Standard Buttons toolbar, click Yes button
2. Right-drag file name over Recycle Bin icon, click Move Here, click Yes button
3. Drag file name over Recycle Bin icon, click Yes button
4. Right-click file name, click Delete, click Yes button
5. Click file name, on File menu click Delete, click Yes button
6. Select file name, press ALT+F, press D, press Y

You can use the file selection techniques illustrated earlier in this project to delete a group of files. When deleting a group of files, click the Yes button in the Confirm Multiple File Delete dialog box to confirm the deletion of the group of files.

Deleting a Folder

Follow the same procedure to delete a folder. When you delete a folder, Windows 2000 deletes any files or subfolders in the folder. Perform the following steps to delete the Clip Art Files folder on drive A.

TO DELETE A FOLDER

1. Right-click the Clip Art Files folder name in the Folders pane.
2. Click Delete on the shortcut menu.
3. Click the Yes button in the Confirm Folder Delete dialog box.
4. Remove the floppy disk from drive A.

A Deleting dialog box displays while the folder is being deleted, the Clip Art Files folder is removed from the Folders pane, and a plus sign replaces the minus sign preceding the 3½ Floppy (A:) icon (Figure 1-69).

More About

Deleting Files

Warning! This is your last warning! Be EXTREMELY careful when deleting files. Hours and weeks of hard work can be lost with one click of a button. If you are going to delete files or folders from your hard disk, consider making a backup of those files to ensure that if you accidentally delete something you need, you will be able to recover.

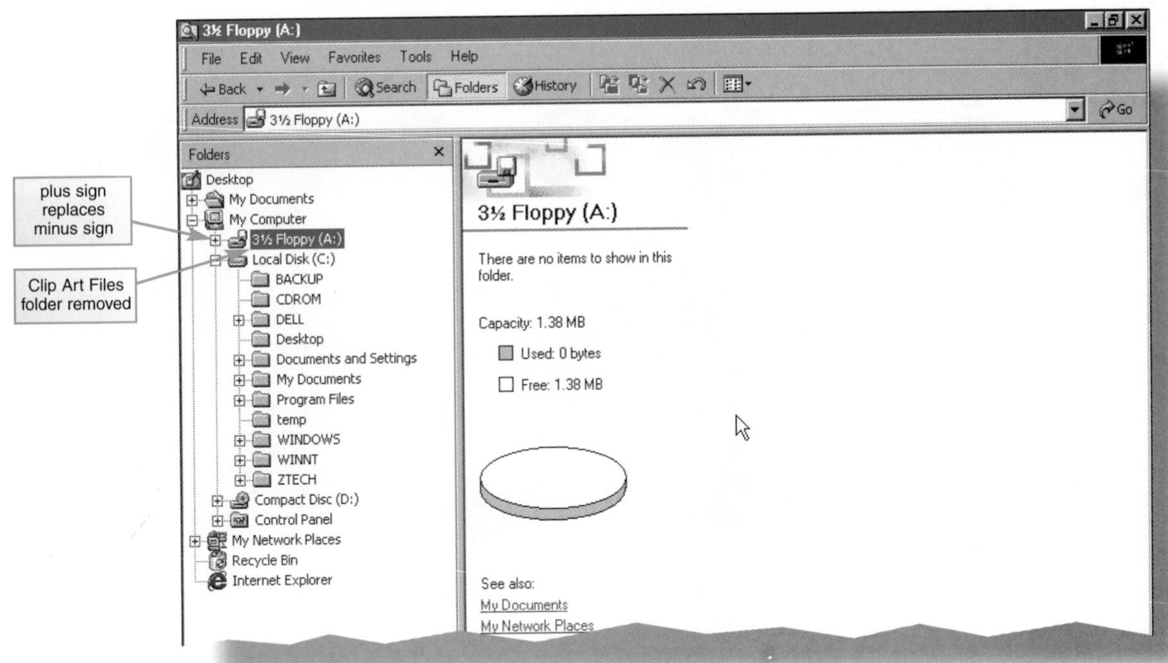

FIGURE 1-69

Quitting Windows Explorer

After completing your work with Windows Explorer, you should quit Windows Explorer. Perform the following steps to quit Windows Explorer.

TO QUIT A PROGRAM

1. Point to the Close button on the Exploring window title bar.
2. Click the Close button.

Windows 2000 closes the Explorer window and quits Windows Explorer.

> **More About**
>
> **Windows 2000 Help**
>
> If you purchased an operating system or application program five years ago, you received at least one, and more often several, thick and heavy technical manuals that explained the software. With Windows 2000, you receive a skinny manual less than 100 pages in length. The Windows 2000 Help system replaces reams and reams of printed pages in hard-to-understand technical manuals.

Using Windows Help

One of the more powerful features in Windows 2000 is Windows Help. **Windows Help** is available when using Windows 2000, or when using any application program running under Windows 2000, to assist you in using Windows 2000 and the various application programs. It contains answers to many questions you may ask with respect to Windows 2000.

Contents Sheet

Windows Help provides a variety of ways in which to obtain information. One method of finding a Help topic involves using the **Contents sheet** to browse through Help topics by category. To illustrate this method, you will use Windows Help to determine how to find a topic in Help. To launch Help, complete the steps on the next page.

Steps To Launch Windows Help

1 Click the Start button on the taskbar. Point to Help on the Start menu (Figure 1-70).

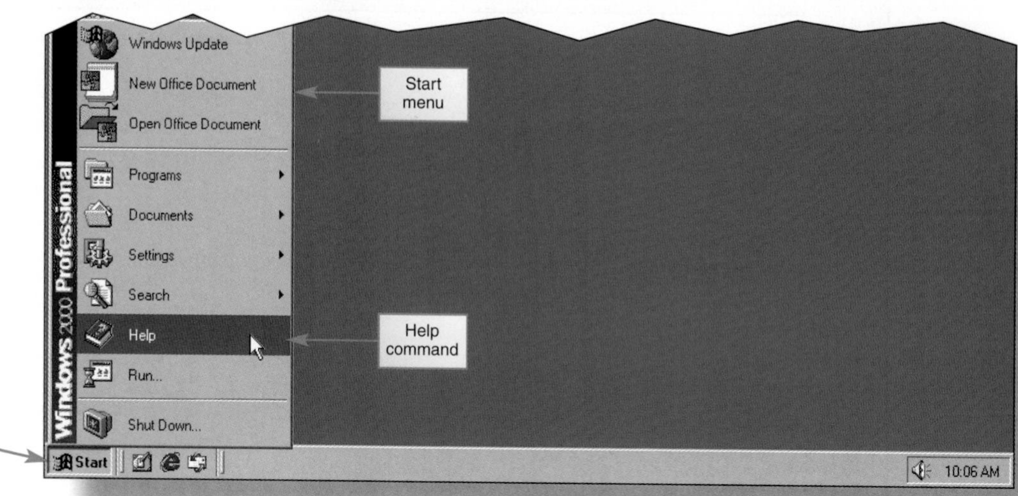

FIGURE 1-70

2 Click Help. Click the Maximize button on the Windows 2000 title bar. If the Contents sheet does not display, click the Contents tab.

The Windows 2000 window opens and maximizes (Figure 1-71). The window contains the Help toolbar and two panes. The left pane, called the ***navigation pane****, contains four tabs. Clicking the Contents tab displays the Contents sheet. The right pane, called the* ***topic pane****, contains the Start Here screen, containing the Microsoft 2000 Professional title and Start Here table of contents.*

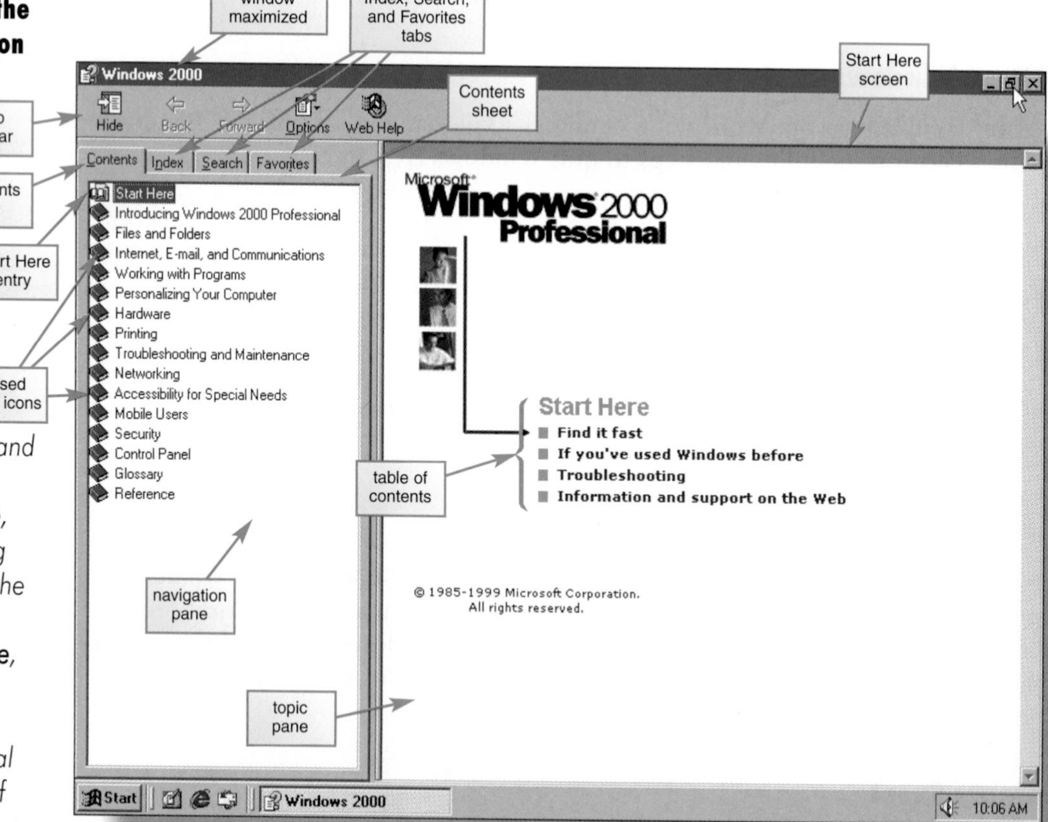

FIGURE 1-71

Other Ways

1. Click open area of desktop, press F1
2. Press WINDOWS+F1 (WINDOWS key on Microsoft Natural keyboard)

The Contents sheet in the navigation pane contains 16 entries. The first entry is identified by an open book and document icon, and the highlighted Start Here name. The **open book and document icon** indicates additional information or an overview is available for the entry. The Start Here entry is highlighted to indicate additional information about the entry displays in the topic pane. The topic pane contains the **Start Here screen**. The Start Here screen contains a table of contents consisting of four items (Find it fast, If you've used Windows before, Troubleshooting, and Information and support on the Web).

A closed book icon precedes each of the remaining 15 entries in the Contents sheet. The **closed book icon** indicates that Help topics or more books are contained in a book but do not display in the Contents sheet. Clicking the Index tab, Search tab, or Favorites tab in the navigation pane displays the Index, Search, or Favorites sheet, respectively.

In addition to launching Help by using the Start button, you also can launch Help by clicking an open area of the desktop and pressing the F1 key.

After launching Help, the next step is to find the topic in which you are interested. Assume you want to find information about locating a Help topic. Perform the following steps to find the topic that describes how to find a topic in Help.

To Use Help to Find a Topic in Help

1 Point to the Introducing Windows 2000 Professional closed book icon.

The mouse pointer changes to a hand when positioned on the icon and the Introducing Windows 2000 book name displays in blue font and underlined (Figure 1-72).

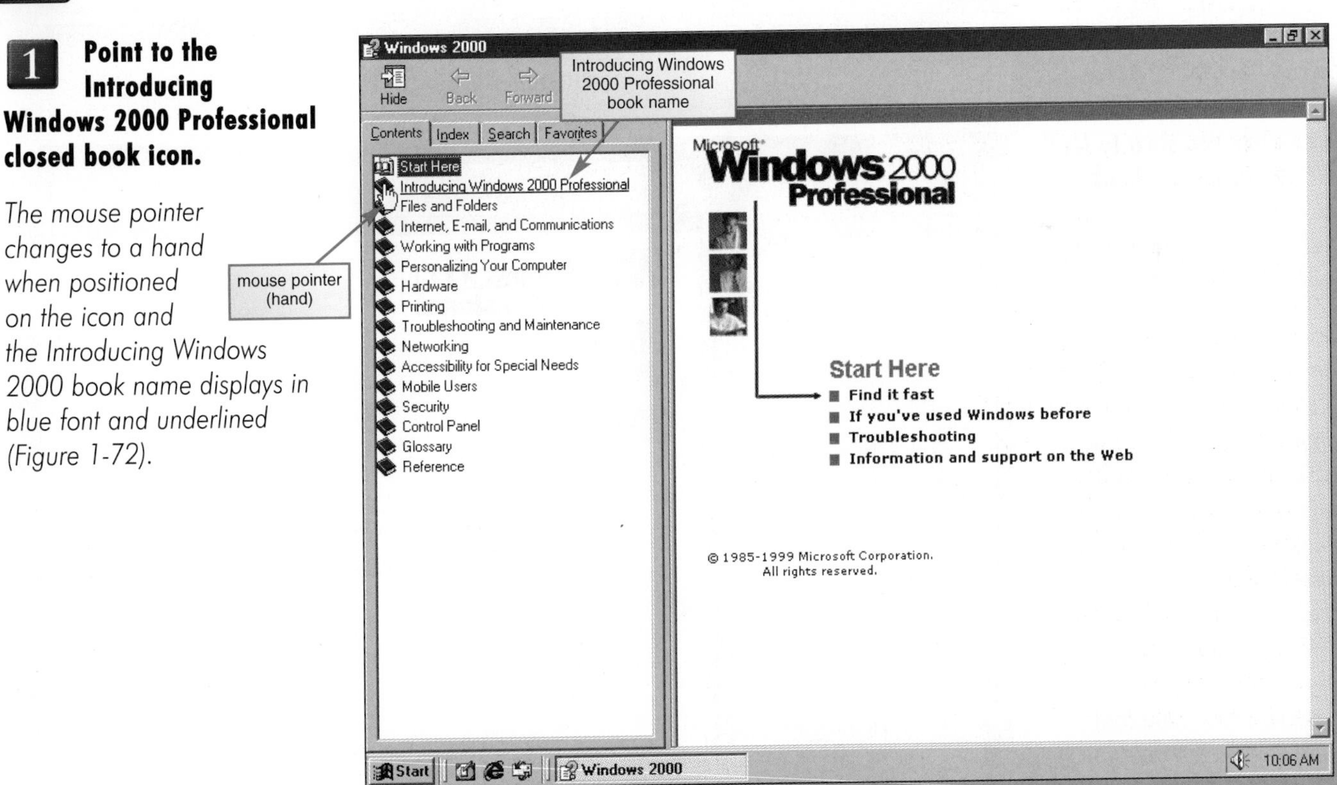

FIGURE 1-72

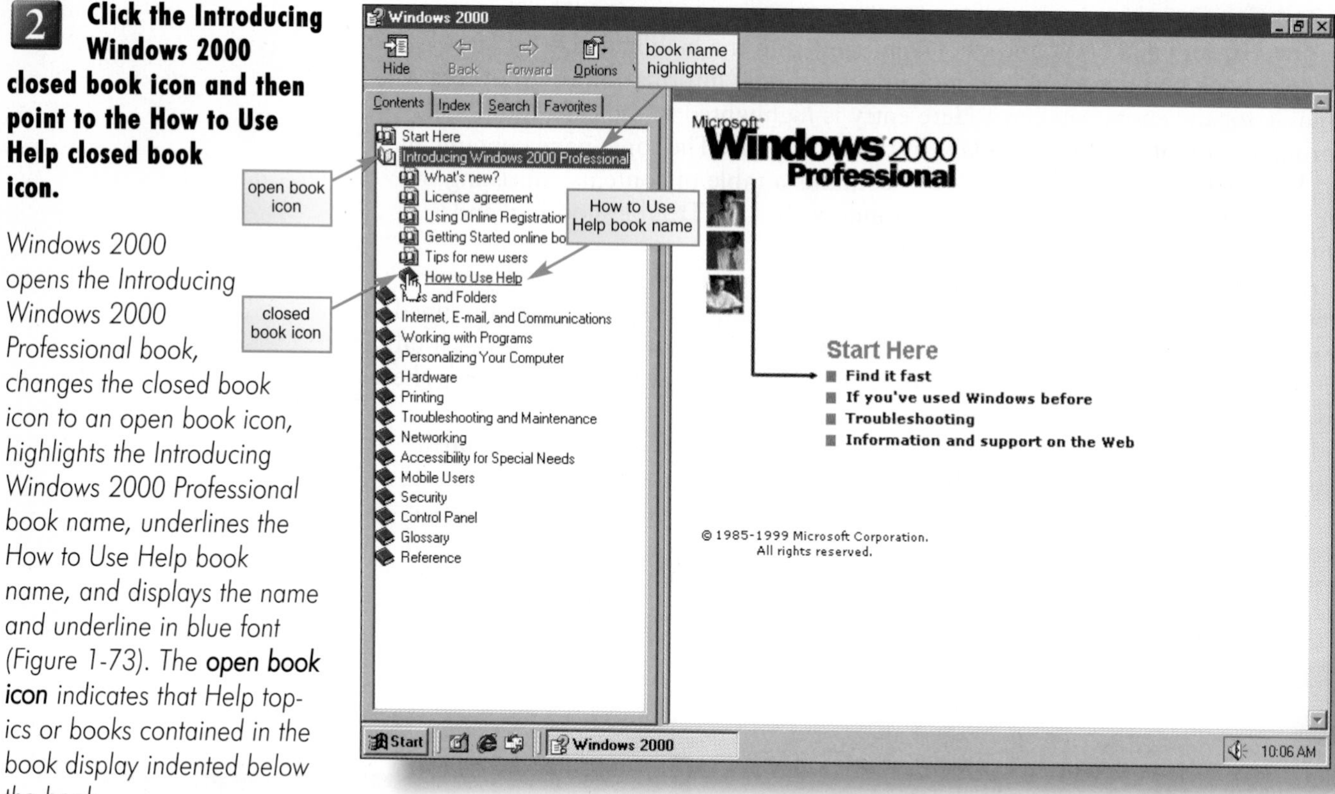

2 Click the Introducing Windows 2000 closed book icon and then point to the How to Use Help closed book icon.

Windows 2000 opens the Introducing Windows 2000 Professional book, changes the closed book icon to an open book icon, highlights the Introducing Windows 2000 Professional book name, underlines the How to Use Help book name, and displays the name and underline in blue font (Figure 1-73). The ***open book icon*** *indicates that Help topics or books contained in the book display indented below the book.*

FIGURE 1-73

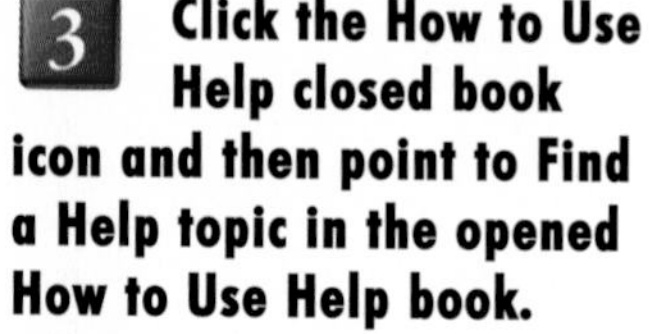

3 Click the How to Use Help closed book icon and then point to Find a Help topic in the opened How to Use Help book.

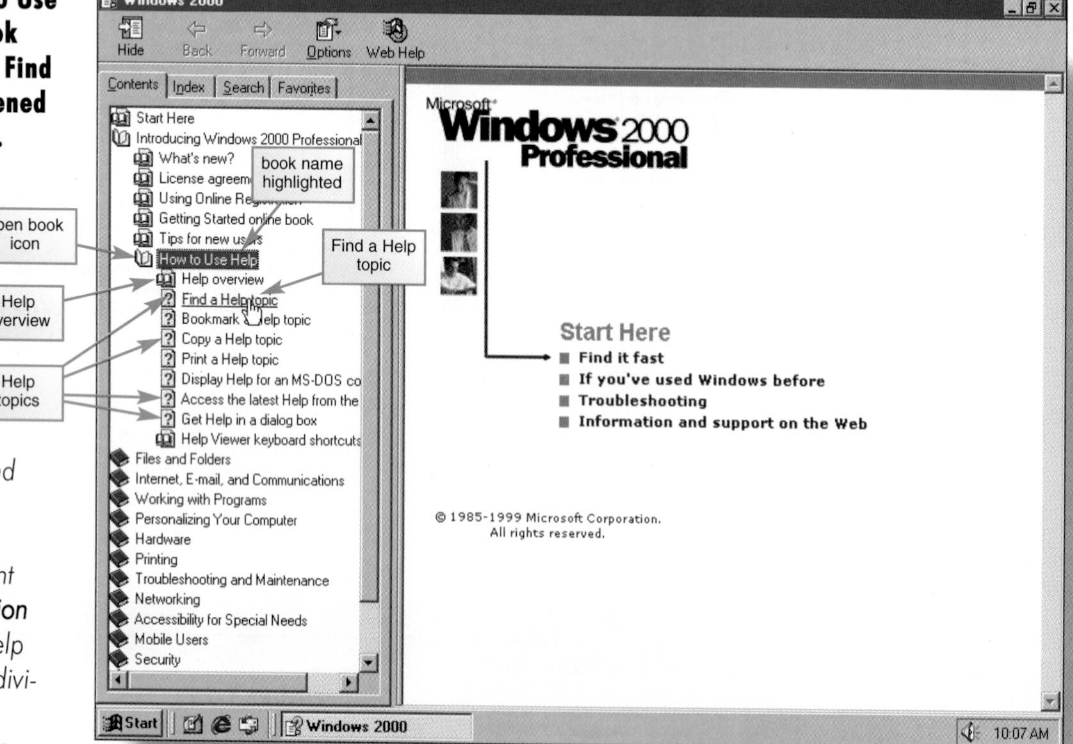

Windows 2000 opens the How to Use Help book, changes the closed book icon to an open book icon, highlights the How to Use Help book name, underlines the Find a Help topic name, and displays the topic name and underline in blue font (Figure 1-74). The ***question mark icon*** *indicates a Help topic without further subdivisions. Clicking the* ***Help overview*** *icon displays an overview of the Help system.*

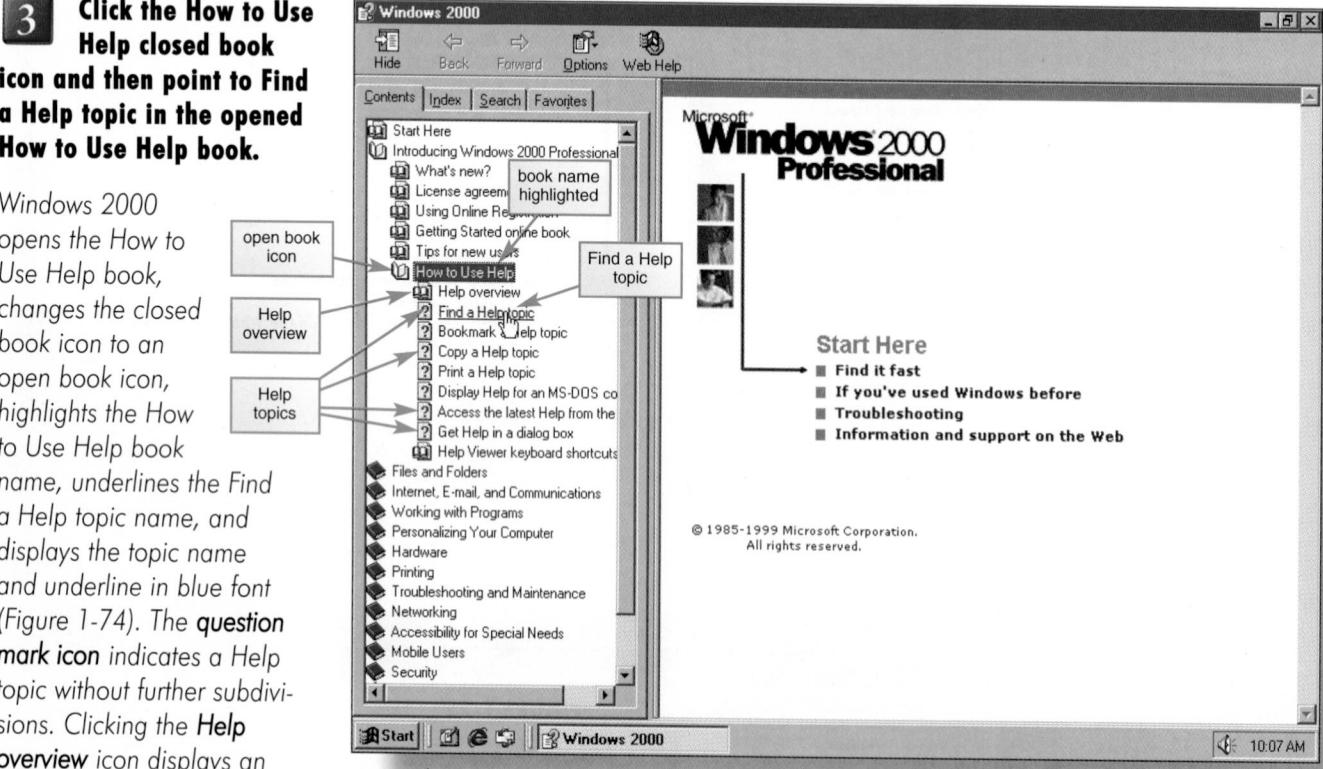

FIGURE 1-74

4 Click Find a Help topic. Read the information about finding a Help topic in the topic pane.

Windows 2000 highlights the Find a Help topic name and displays information about finding a Help topic in the topic pane (Figure 1-75). Clicking the plus sign in the small box to the left of the Contents tab, Index tab, Search tab, or Favorites tab entries in the topic pane displays additional information about the entry.

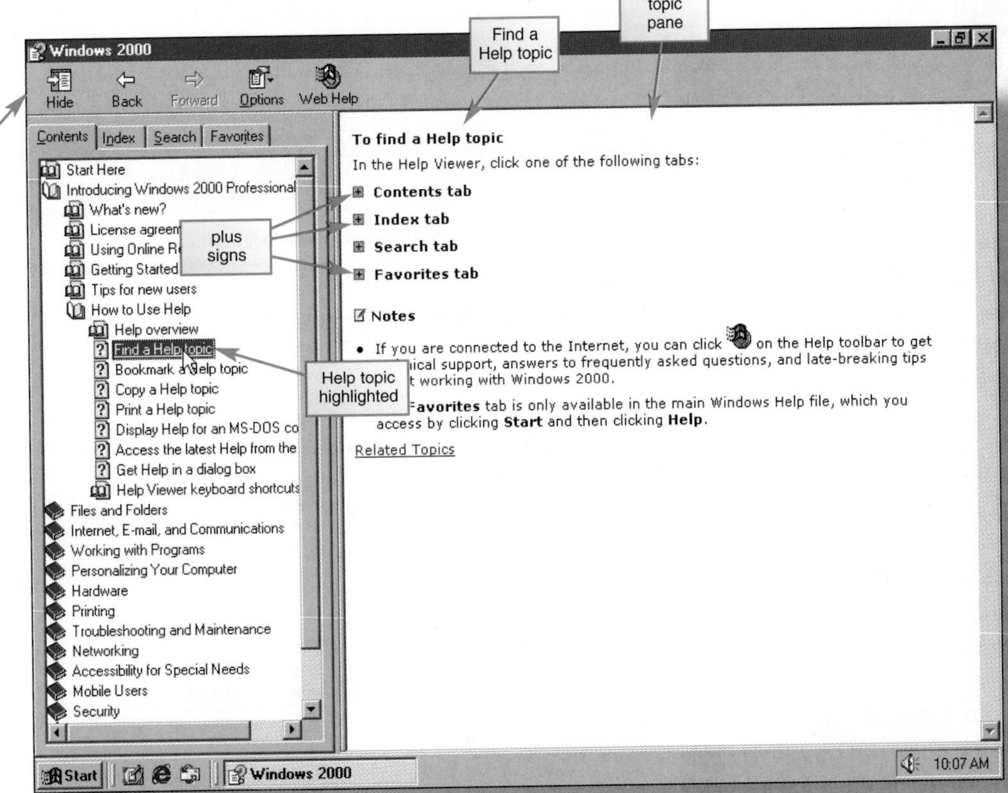

FIGURE 1-75

In Figure 1-75, the Help toolbar contains five icons. If you click the **Hide button** on the Help toolbar, Windows 2000 hides the tabs in the navigation pane and displays only the topic pane in the Windows 2000 window. Clicking the **Back button** or **Forward button** displays a previously displayed Help topic in the topic pane. Clicking the **Options button** allows you to hide or display the tabs in the navigation pane, display previously displayed Help topics in the topic pane, stop the display of a Help topic, refresh the currently displayed Help topic, access the Internet options, access Web Help, and print a Help topic. The **Web Help command** on the Options menu and the **Web Help button** on the Help toolbar allow you to use the Internet to obtain technical support, answers to frequently asked questions, and tips about working with Windows 2000.

Notice also in Figure 1-75 that the Windows 2000 title bar contains a Minimize button, Restore Down button, and Close button. You can minimize or restore the Windows 2000 window as needed and also close the Windows 2000 window.

Index Sheet

A second method of finding answers to your questions about Windows 2000 or application programs running under Windows 2000 is to use the Index sheet. The **Index sheet** contains a list of index entries, each of which references one or more Help screens. Assume you want more information about the desktop and the objects on the desktop. Perform the steps on the next page to learn more about the desktop and the objects on the desktop.

Other Ways

1. Press DOWN ARROW key until book name is highlighted, press RIGHT ARROW (or ENTER), continue until Help topic displays, press ENTER, read Help topic

More About

The Index Sheet

The Index sheet probably is the best source of information in Windows Help because you can enter the subject you are interested in. Sometimes, however, you will have to be creative to discover the index entry that answers your question because the most obvious entry will not always lead to your answer.

Steps To Use the Help Index Sheet

1 Click the Index tab, type desktop **in the Type in the keyword to find text box, and then point to overview in the list.**

The Index sheet, containing the Type in the keyword to find text box, a list box, and Display button, displays (Figure 1-76). When you type an entry in the text box, the list of index entries in the list box automatically scrolls and the entry you type (desktop) is highlighted in the list. Several entries display indented below the desktop entry. The indentation indicates they pertain to the highlighted entry.

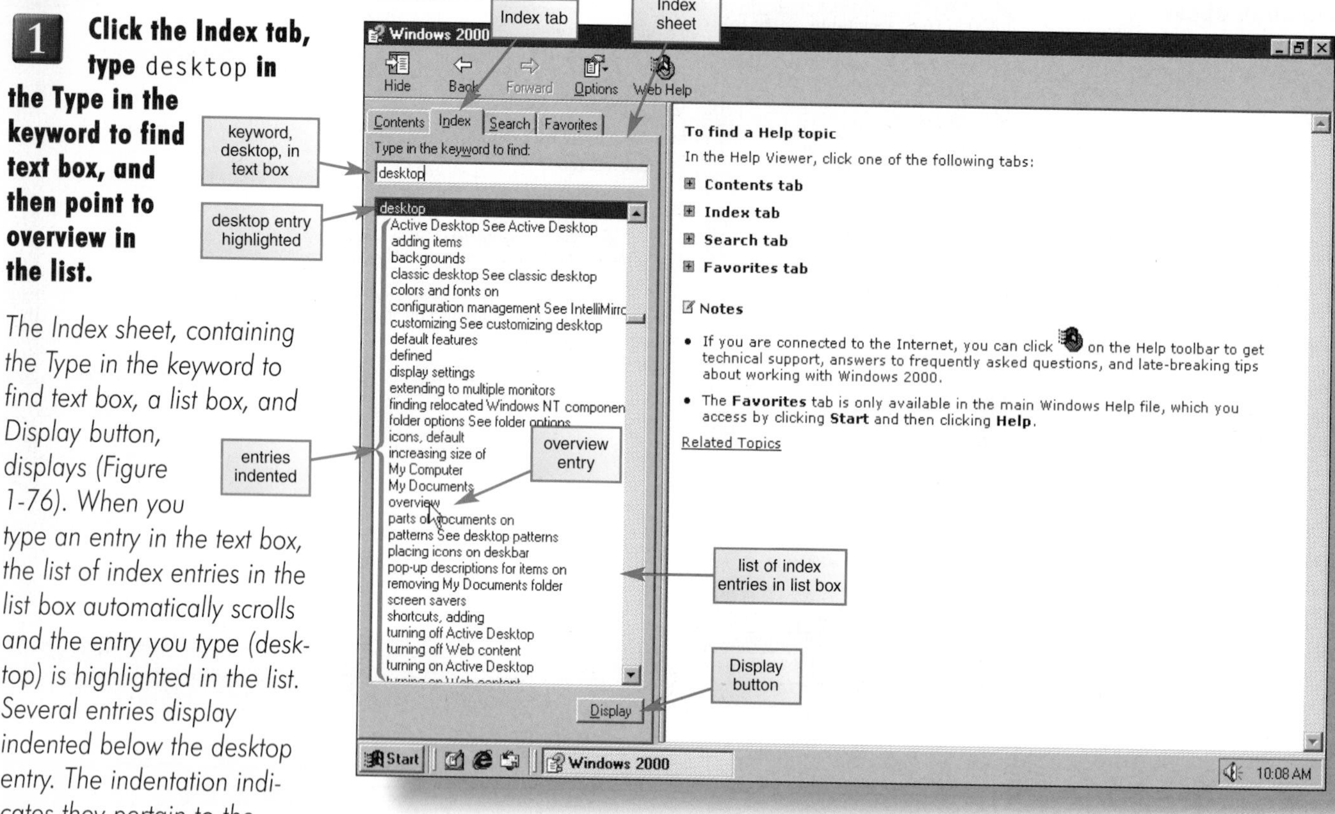

FIGURE 1-76

2 Click overview and then point to the Display button at the bottom of the Index sheet.

Windows 2000 displays the desktop, overview entry in the text box and highlights the overview entry in the list (Figure 1-77).

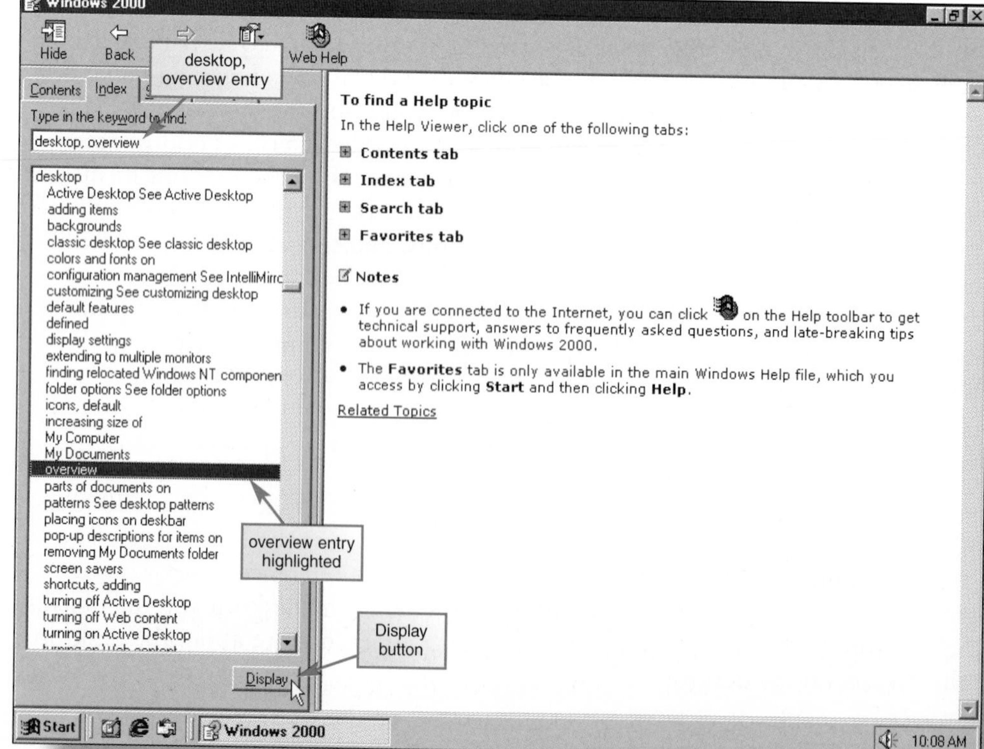

FIGURE 1-77

3 **Click the Display button.**

The Desktop overview topic displays in the topic pane (Figure 1-78). The topic contains an overview of the desktop, a list of desktop features, and several links (shortcuts, programs, active content, channel, Windows 2000 Professional Getting Started, and Related Topics). Clicking the plus sign in the small box to the left of a desktop feature displays additional information about that feature.

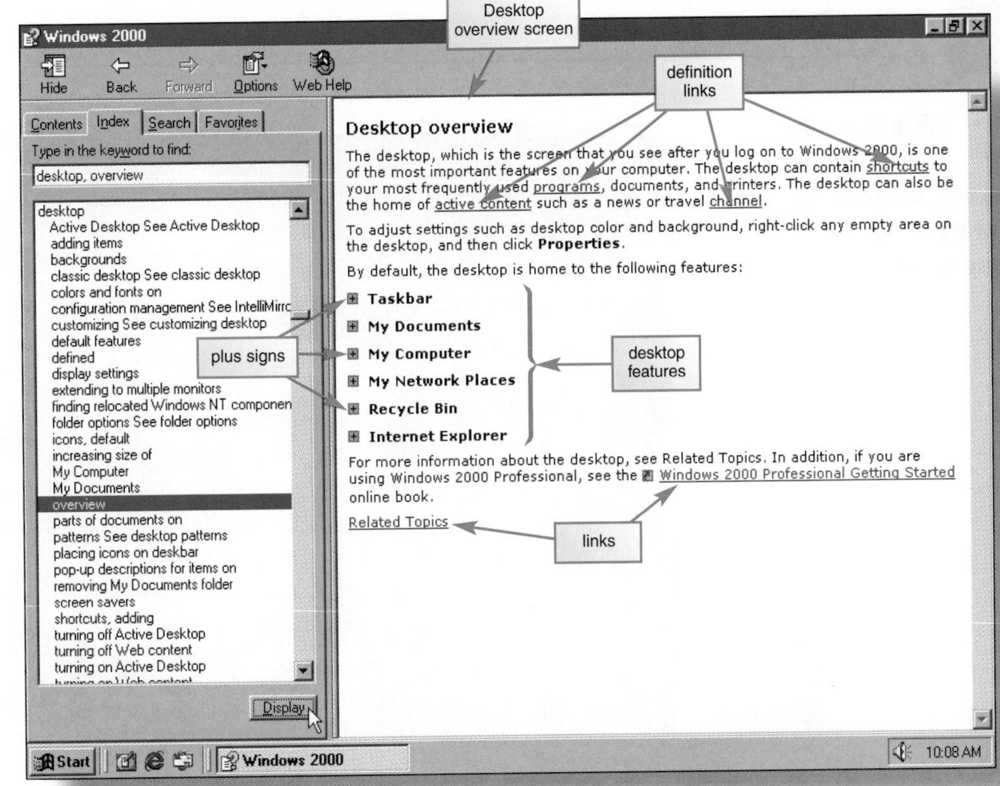

FIGURE 1-78

Other Ways

1. Press ALT+N, type keyword, press DOWN ARROW until topic is highlighted, press ALT+D (or ENTER)

In Figure 1-78, the shortcuts, programs, active content, and channel links are underlined and display in green font to indicate that clicking a link will display its definition. Clicking anywhere off the definition removes the definition.

The Windows 2000 Professional Getting Started and Related Topics links are underlined and display in blue font. Clicking the Windows 2000 Professional Getting Started link displays the Getting Started online book that helps you install Windows 2000, use the desktop, learn about new features, connect to a network, and find answers to commonly asked questions. Clicking the Related Topics link displays a pop-up window that contains topics related to the desktop overview topic.

After viewing the index entries and selecting those you need, normally you will close Windows Help. To close Windows Help, complete the following step.

TO CLOSE WINDOWS HELP

 Click the Close button on the title bar of the Windows 2000 window.

Windows 2000 closes the Windows 2000 window.

Shutting Down Windows 2000

After completing your work with Windows 2000, you may want to shut down Windows 2000 using the Shut Down command on the Start menu. If you are sure you want to shut down Windows 2000, perform the steps on the next page. If you are not sure about shutting down Windows 2000, read the steps without actually performing them.

More About

Shut Down Procedures

Some users of Windows 2000 have turned off their computers without following the shut down procedure only to find data they thought they had stored on disk was lost. Because of the way Windows 2000 writes data on the disk, it is important you shut down Windows properly so you do not lose your work.

To Shut Down Windows 2000

1 Click the Start button on the taskbar and then point to Shut Down on the Start menu (Figure 1-79).

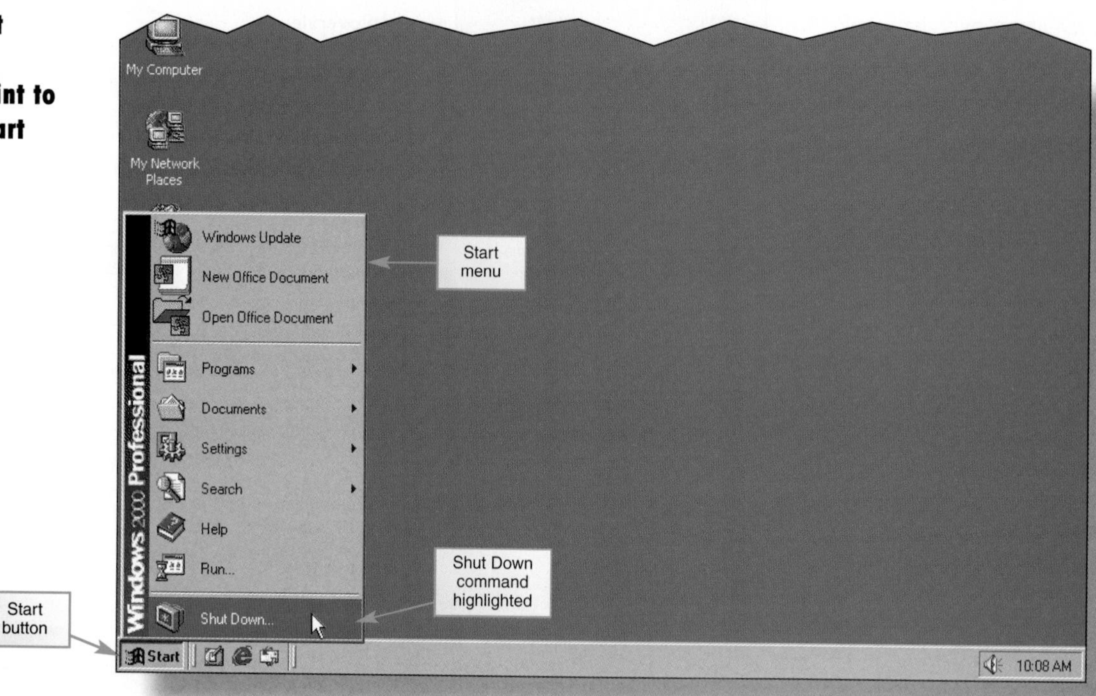

FIGURE 1-79

2 Click Shut Down. Point to the OK button in the Shut Down Windows dialog box.

The desktop darkens and the Shut Down Windows dialog box displays (Figure 1-80). The dialog box contains the What do you want the computer to do? box and three command buttons. The highlighted command, Shut down, displays in the box.

3 Click the OK button.

Windows 2000 is shut down.

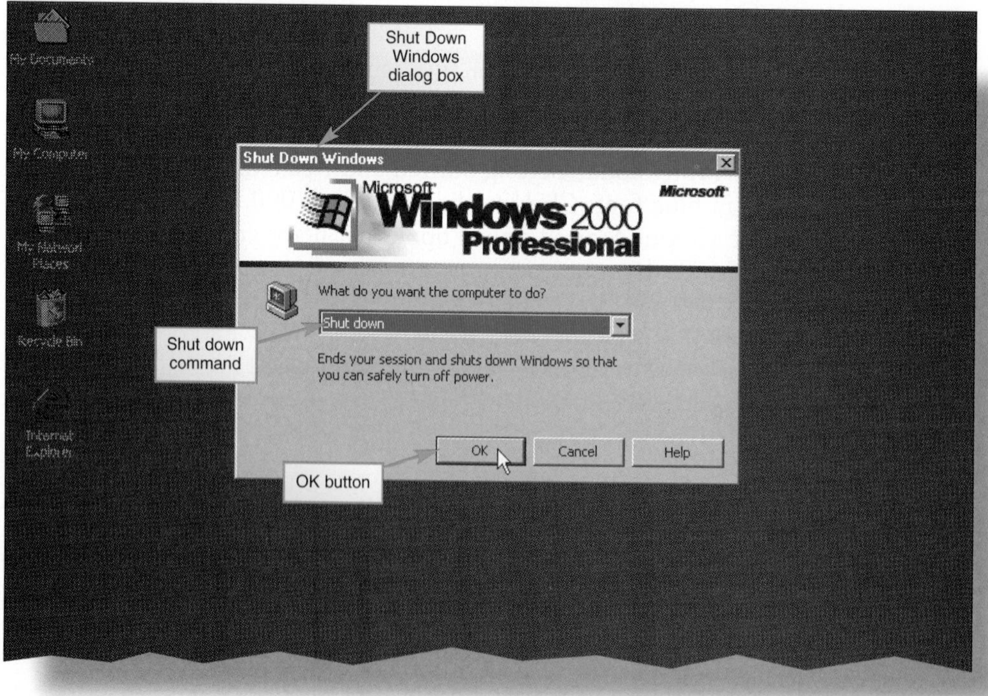

FIGURE 1-80

Other Ways

1. Press CTRL+ESC, press U, press ARROW keys to select Shut down, press ENTER
2. Press ALT+F1, press ARROW keys to select Shut down, press ENTER

While Windows 2000 is shutting down, two dialog boxes display momentarily on a blue background. First, the Please Wait dialog box containing the Windows 2000 logo, Windows 2000 name, and the text, saving your settings, displays momentarily. Then, the Shutdown in Progress dialog box, containing the text, Please wait while the system writes unsaved data to disk, displays. At this point you can turn off the computer. Some computers are programmed to turn off automatically at this point. When shutting down Windows 2000, you should never turn off the computer before these two dialog boxes display.

If you accidentally click Shut Down on the Start menu and you do not want to shut down Windows 2000, click the Cancel button in the Shut Down Windows dialog box to return to normal Windows 2000 operation.

What Is Microsoft Office XP?

Microsoft Office XP (**eXPerience**), the latest edition of the world's best-selling office suite, is a collection of the more popular Microsoft application software products. Microsoft Office XP is available in Standard, Professional, and Developer editions. The **Microsoft Office XP Professional Edition** includes Microsoft Word 2002, Microsoft Excel 2002, Microsoft Access 2002, Microsoft PowerPoint 2002, and Microsoft Outlook 2002. Microsoft Office XP allows you to work more efficiently, communicate more effectively, and improve the appearance of each document you create.

Microsoft Office contains a collection of media files (art, sound, animation, and movies) that you can use to enhance documents. **Microsoft Clip Organizer** allows you to organize the media files on your computer and search for specific files, as well as search for and organize media files located on the Internet. **Microsoft Design Gallery Live** is accessible from the Microsoft Web site and contains thousands of additional media files.

With the Office Speech Recognition software installed and a microphone, you can speak the names of toolbar buttons, menus, and menu commands, and list items, screen alerts, and dialog box controls, such as OK and Cancel. You also can dictate text and numbers to insert as well as delete. If you have speakers, you can instruct the computer to speak a document or worksheet to you. In addition, you can translate a word, phrase, or an entire document from English into Japanese, Chinese, French, Spanish, or German.

Menus and toolbars adjust to the way in which you work. As Microsoft Office detects which commands you use more frequently, these commands display at the top of the menu, and the infrequently used commands are placed in reserve. A button at the bottom of the menu allows you to expand the menu in order to view all its commands. More frequently used buttons on a toolbar display on the toolbar, while less frequently used buttons are not displayed.

In addition, Microsoft Office integrates its applications with the power of the Internet so you can share information, communicate and collaborate on projects over long distances, and conduct online meetings.

More About

Office XP

For more information about any Microsoft Office XP application, click Help on the menu bar of any Office XP application window, and click Office on the Web. Explore a Web page by clicking a hyperlink. After clicking a hyperlink, click the Back button to display the last Web page.

The Internet, World Wide Web, and Intranets

Microsoft Office XP allows you to take advantage of the Internet, the World Wide Web, and intranets. The **Internet** is a worldwide network of thousands of computer networks and millions of commercial, educational, government, and personal computers. The **World Wide Web** is an easy-to-use graphical interface for exploring the Internet. The World Wide Web consists of many individual Web sites. A **Web site** consists of a single **Web page** or multiple Web pages linked together. The first Web page in the Web site is called the **home page** and a unique address, called a **Uniform Resource Locator** (**URL**), identifies each Web page. Web sites are located on computers called Web servers.

A software tool, called a **browser**, allows you to locate and view a Web page. One method of viewing a Web page is to use the browser to enter the URL for the Web page. A widely used browser, called **Microsoft Internet Explorer**, is included with Microsoft Office XP. Another method of viewing a Web page is clicking a hyperlink. A **hyperlink** is colored or underlined text or a graphic that, when clicked, connects to another Web page.

An **intranet** is a special type of Web that is available only to the users of a particular type of computer network, such as a network used within a company or organization for internal communication. Like the Internet, hyperlinks are used within an intranet to access documents, pages, and other destinations on the intranet.

More About

Microsoft Office XP

To subscribe to a free Office XP weekly newsletter delivered via e-mail, visit the Office XP More About Web page (scsite.com/offxp/more.htm) and then click Office XP Newsletter.

Microsoft Office XP and the Internet

Microsoft Office XP was designed in response to customer requests to streamline the process of information sharing and collaboration within their organizations. Organizations that, in the past, made important information available only to a select few, now want their information accessible to a wider range of individuals who are using tools such as Microsoft Office and Microsoft Internet Explorer. Microsoft Office XP allows users to utilize the Internet or an intranet as a central location to view documents, manage files, and work together.

Each of the Microsoft Office XP applications makes publishing documents on a Web server as simple as saving a file on a hard disk. Once the file is placed on the Web server, users can view and edit the documents, and conduct Web discussions and live online meetings.

An explanation of each Microsoft Office XP application software program along with how it is used to access an intranet or the Internet is given on the following pages.

More About

Microsoft Word 2002

For more information about Microsoft Word 2002, click Help on the menu bar of the Microsoft Word window, and click Office on the Web. Explore a Web page by clicking a hyperlink. After clicking a hyperlink, click the Back button to display the last Web page.

Microsoft Word 2002

Microsoft Word 2002 is a full-featured word processing program that allows you to create many types of personal and business communications, including announcements, letters, resumes, business documents, and academic reports, as well as other forms of written documents. Figure 1-81 illustrates the top portion of the announcement that students create in one of the exercises in Project 1 of the Microsoft Word section of this book. The steps to create a similar announcement are shown in Project 1 of Microsoft Word 2002.

The Microsoft Word AutoCorrect, Spelling, and Grammar features allow you to proofread documents for errors in spelling and grammar by identifying the errors and offering corrections as you type. As you create a specific document, such as a business letter or resume, Word provides wizards, which ask questions and then use your answers to format the document before you type the text of the document.

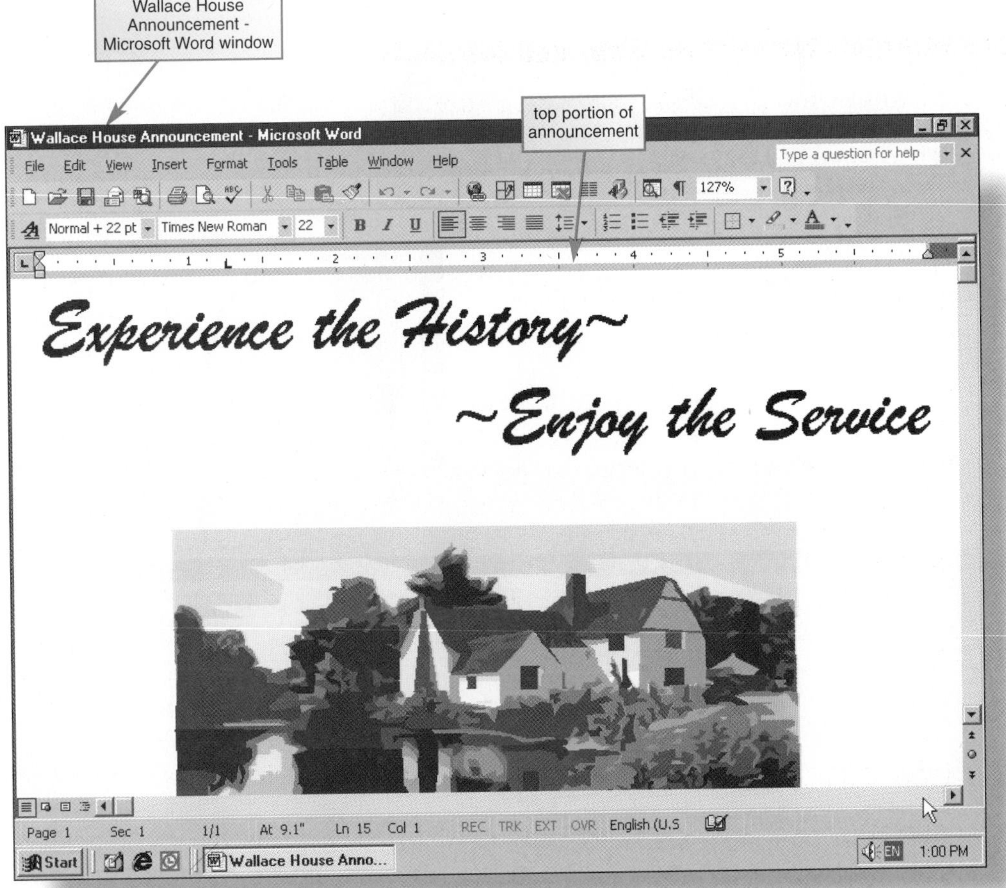

FIGURE 1-81

Microsoft Word automates many often-used tasks and provides you with powerful desktop publishing tools to use as you create professional-looking brochures, advertisements, and newsletters. The drawing tools allow you to design impressive 3-D effects by including shadows, textures, and curves.

Microsoft Word makes it easier for you to share documents in order to collaborate on a document. The Send for Review and Markup features allow you to send a document for review and easily track the changes made to the document.

Microsoft Word 2002 and the Internet

Microsoft Word makes it possible to design and publish Web pages on an intranet or the Internet, insert a hyperlink to a Web page in a word processing document, as well as access other Web pages and search for and retrieve information and pictures from them. Figure 1-82 on the next page illustrates the top portion of a cover letter that contains a hyperlink (e-mail address) that allows you to send an e-mail message to the sender.

Clicking the hyperlink starts the Microsoft Outlook mail program, through which you can send an e-mail message to the author of the cover letter. In Figure 1-83 on the next page, the Resume and Cover Letter – Message – Microsoft Word window that allows you to compose a new e-mail message contains the recipient's e-mail address (carter@worldnet.com), subject of the e-mail message (Resume and Cover Letter), and a brief message.

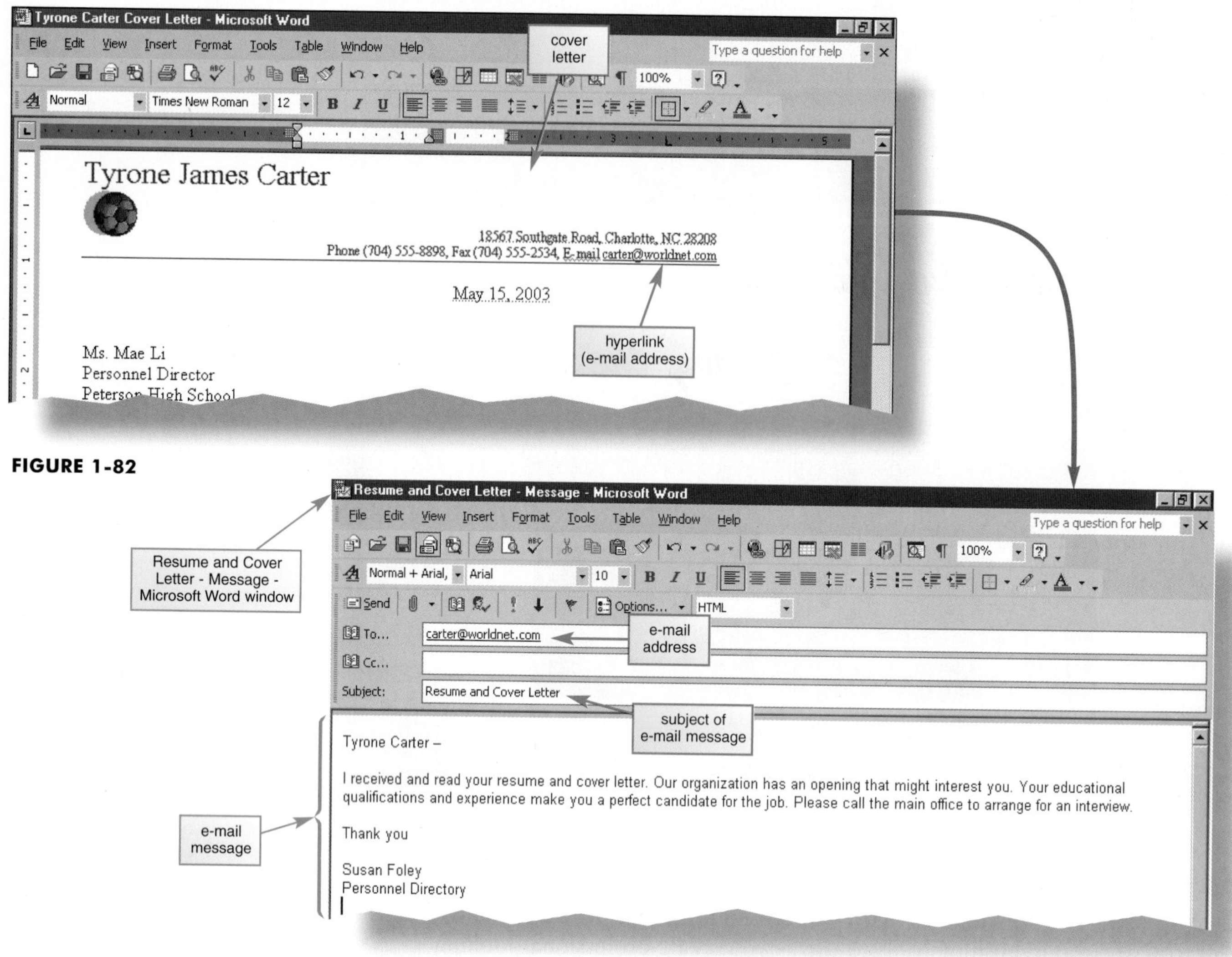

FIGURE 1-82

FIGURE 1-83

> **More About**
>
> **Microsoft Excel 2002**
>
> For more information about Microsoft Excel 2002, click Help on the menu bar of the Microsoft Excel window, and click Office on the Web. Explore a Web page by clicking a hyperlink. After clicking a hyperlink, click the Back button to display the last Web page.

Microsoft Excel 2002

Microsoft Excel 2002 is a spreadsheet program that allows you to organize data, complete calculations, graph data, develop professional-looking reports, publish organized data to the Web, access real-time data from Web sites, and make decisions. Figure 1-84 illustrates the Microsoft Excel window that contains the worksheet and 3-D column chart created in one of the exercises in Project 1 of the Microsoft Excel section of this book.

Microsoft Excel 2002 and the Internet

Using Microsoft Excel, you can create hyperlinks within a worksheet to access other Office XP documents on the network, an organization's intranet, or the Internet. You also can save worksheets as static and dynamic Web pages that can be viewed using a browser. Static Web pages cannot be changed by the person viewing them. Dynamic Web pages give the person viewing them in their browser many capabilities using Excel. In addition, you can create and run queries to retrieve information from a Web page directly into a worksheet.

Figure 1-85 illustrates a worksheet created by running a Web query to retrieve stock market information for two stocks (Network Appliance, Inc. and Cisco

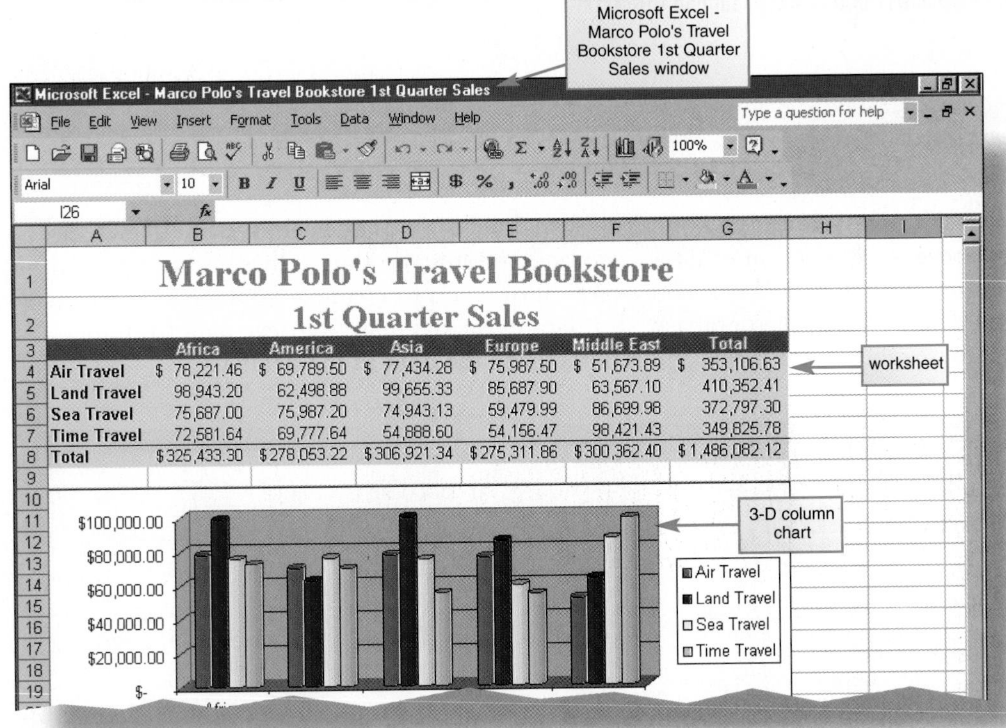

	Africa	America	Asia	Europe	Middle East	Total
Air Travel	$ 78,221.46	$ 69,789.50	$ 77,434.28	$ 75,987.50	$ 51,673.89	$ 353,106.63
Land Travel	98,943.20	62,498.88	99,655.33	85,687.90	63,567.10	410,352.41
Sea Travel	75,687.00	75,987.20	74,943.13	59,479.99	86,699.98	372,797.30
Time Travel	72,581.64	69,777.64	54,888.60	54,156.47	98,421.43	349,825.78
Total	$325,433.30	$278,053.22	$306,921.34	$275,311.86	$300,362.40	$1,486,082.12

FIGURE 1-84

Systems, Inc.). The two hyperlinks were created using the Insert Hyperlink button on the Standard toolbar, and the information in the worksheet was obtained from the MSN MoneyCentral Investor Web site. The Refresh All button on the External Data toolbar allows you to update the last price of the stocks (Last).

Clicking the Refresh All button locates the MSN MoneyCentral Investor Web site, retrieves current information for the stocks listed in the worksheet, and displays the updated information in the worksheet (Figure 1-86). Notice that the stock prices and information in this worksheet differ from what was displayed in the worksheet shown in Figure 1-85.

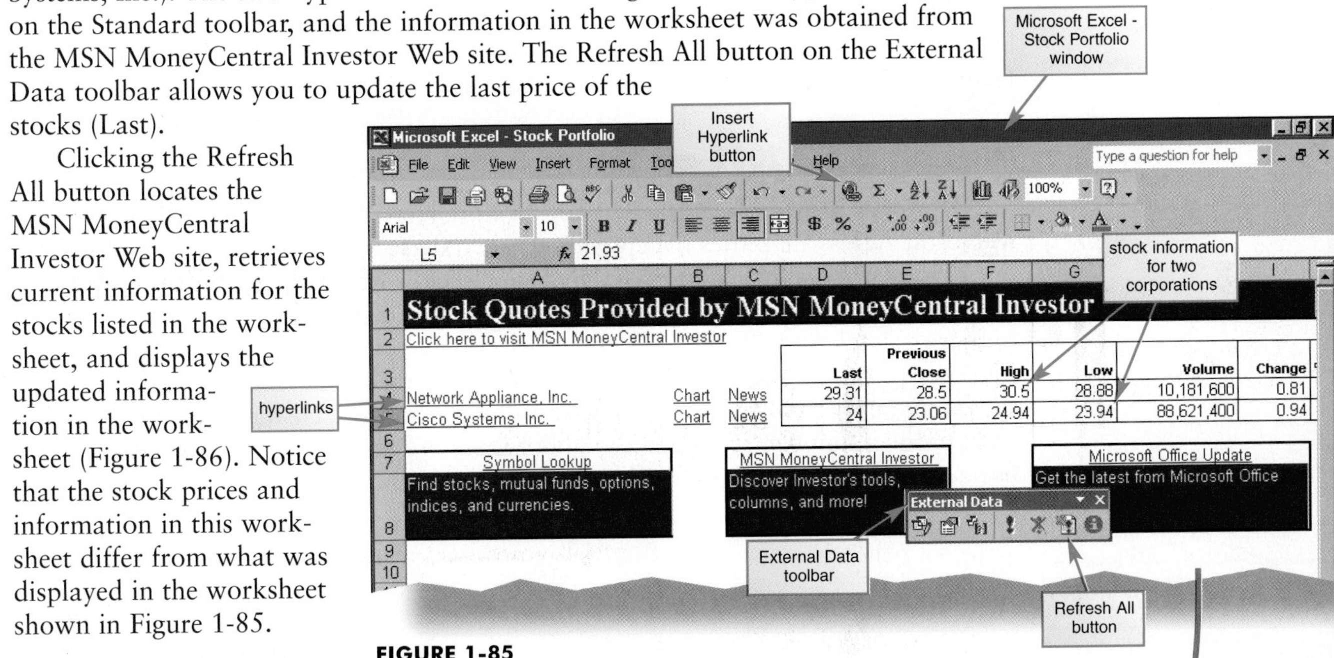

			Last	Previous Close	High	Low	Volume	Change
Network Appliance, Inc.	Chart	News	29.31	28.5	30.5	28.88	10,181,600	0.81
Cisco Systems, Inc.	Chart	News	24	23.06	24.94	23.94	88,621,400	0.94

FIGURE 1-85

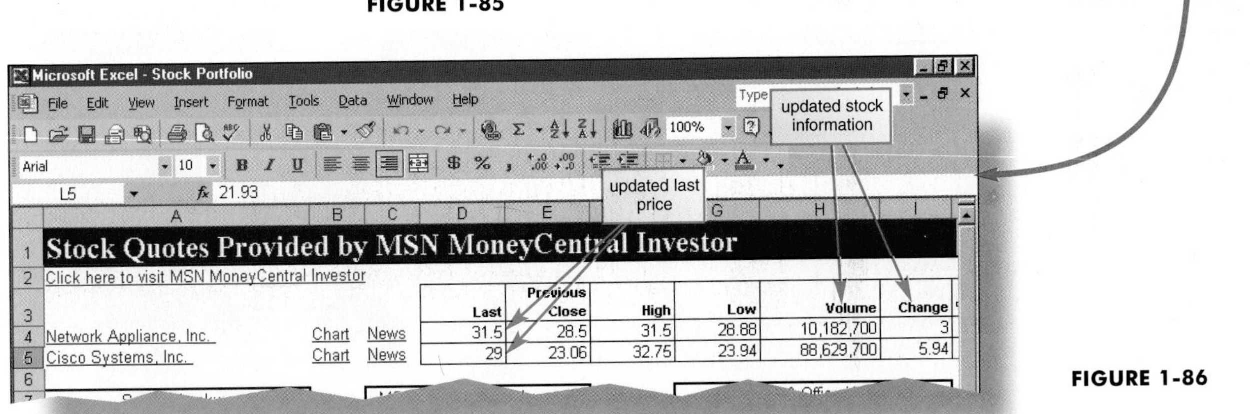

			Last	Previous Close	High	Low	Volume	Change
Network Appliance, Inc.	Chart	News	31.5	28.5	31.5	28.88	10,182,700	3
Cisco Systems, Inc.	Chart	News	29	23.06	32.75	23.94	88,629,700	5.94

FIGURE 1-86

Microsoft Access 2002

Microsoft Access 2002 is a comprehensive **database management system** (**DBMS**). A **database** is a collection of data organized in a manner that allows access, retrieval, and use of that data. Microsoft Access allows you to create a database; add, change, and delete data in the database; sort data in the database; retrieve data from the database; and create forms and reports using the data in the database.

Customer Numb	Name	Address	City	State	Zip Code	Amount Paid	Current Due
BA95	Bayside Hotel	287 Riley	Hansen	FL	38513	$21,876.00	$892.50
BR46	Baldwin-Reed	267 Howard	Fernwood	FL	37023	$26,512.00	$2,672.00
CN21	Century North	1562 Butler	Hansen	FL	38513	$8,725.00	$0.00
FR28	Friend's Movies	871 Adams	Westport	FL	37070	$4,256.00	$1,202.00
GN62	Grand Nelson	7821 Oak	Wood Key	FL	36828	$8,287.50	$925.50
GS29	Great Screens	572 Lee	Hansen	FL	38513	$21,625.00	$0.00
LM22	Lenger Mason	274 Johnson	Westport	FL	37070	$0.00	$0.00
ME93	Merks College	561 Fairhill	Bayville	FL	38734	$24,761.00	$1,572.00

FIGURE 1-87

The database created in Project 1 of the Microsoft Access section of this book displays in the Microsoft Access - [Customer : Table] window illustrated in Figure 1-87. The steps to create this database are shown in Project 1 of Access.

Microsoft Access 2002 and the Internet

Databases provide a central location to store related pieces of information. Microsoft Access simplifies the creation of a database with a wizard that can build one of more than a dozen types of databases quickly. You also can transform lists or worksheets into databases using Access wizards. Data access pages permit you to share a database with other computer users on a network, intranet, or over the Internet, as well as allowing the users to view and edit the database. The database shown in Figure 1-88 contains information (order number, customer number, order date, product number, and quantity) about three orders entered over the Internet using the Microsoft Internet Explorer browser.

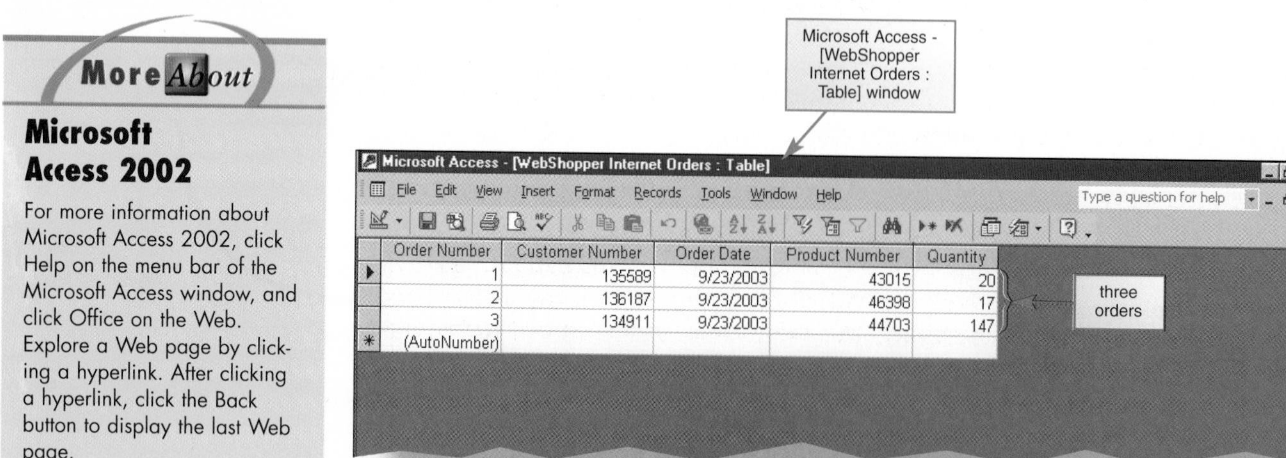

More About

Microsoft Access 2002

For more information about Microsoft Access 2002, click Help on the menu bar of the Microsoft Access window, and click Office on the Web. Explore a Web page by clicking a hyperlink. After clicking a hyperlink, click the Back button to display the last Web page.

FIGURE 1-88

Figure 1-89 illustrates a simple online order form created to enter order information into the database shown in Figure 1-88. The order form, containing information about order number 4, displays in the WebShopper Internet Orders - Microsoft Internet Explorer window.

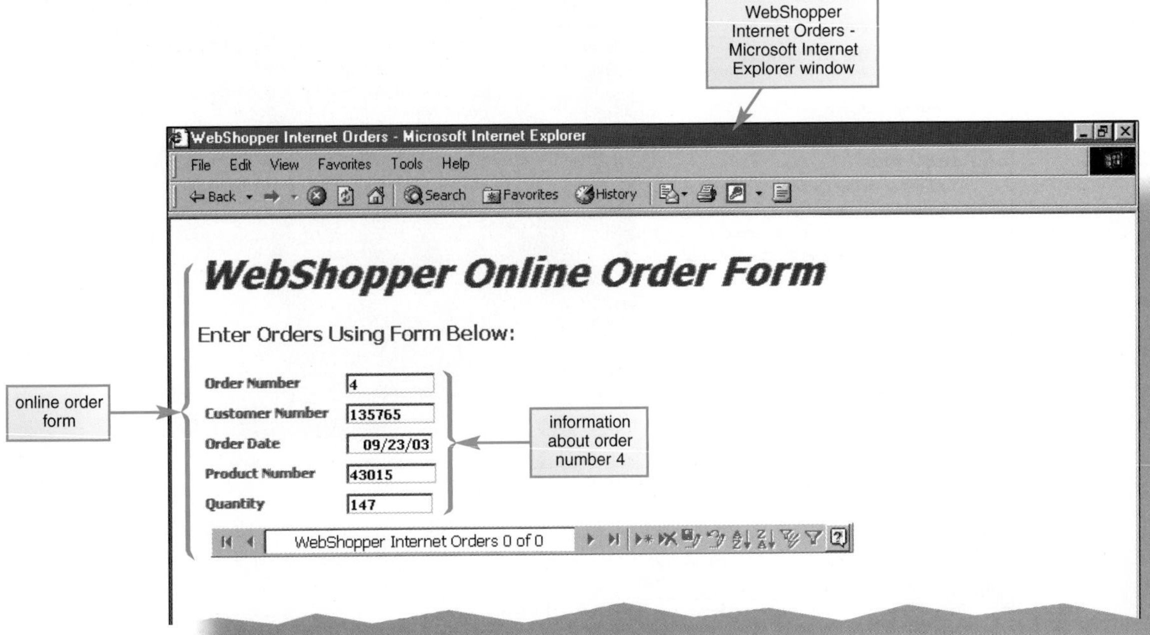

FIGURE 1-89

Microsoft PowerPoint 2002

Microsoft PowerPoint 2002 is a complete **presentation graphics program** that allows you to produce professional-looking presentations. PowerPoint provides the flexibility that lets you make informal presentations using overhead transparencies, make electronic presentations using a projection device attached to a personal computer, make formal presentations using 35mm slides, or run virtual presentations on the Internet.

In PowerPoint 2002, you create a presentation in normal view. **Normal view** allows you to view the tabs pane, slide pane, and notes pane at the same time. The first slide in the presentation created in one of the exercises in Project 1 of the Microsoft PowerPoint section of this book displays in the Microsoft PowerPoint – [Decades of Eating] window illustrated in Figure 1-90 on the next page. The full window contains the Outline tab with the presentation outline, the slide pane displaying the first slide in the presentation, and the notes pane showing a note about the presentation.

Microsoft PowerPoint allows you to create dynamic presentations easily that include multimedia features such as sounds, movies, and pictures. PowerPoint comes with templates that assist you in designing a presentation that you can use to create a slide show. PowerPoint also contains formatting for tables, so that you do not have to create the tables using Excel or Word. The Table Draw tool used in Word to draw tables also is available in PowerPoint.

Microsoft PowerPoint makes it easier for you to share presentations and collaborate on those presentations. The Send for Review feature and Compare and Merge feature allow you to send a presentation for review and easily merge comments and revisions from multiple reviewers.

More About

Microsoft PowerPoint 2002

For more information about Microsoft PowerPoint 2002, click Help on the menu bar of the Microsoft PowerPoint window, and click Office on the Web. Explore a Web page by clicking a hyperlink. After clicking a hyperlink, click the Back button to display the last Web page.

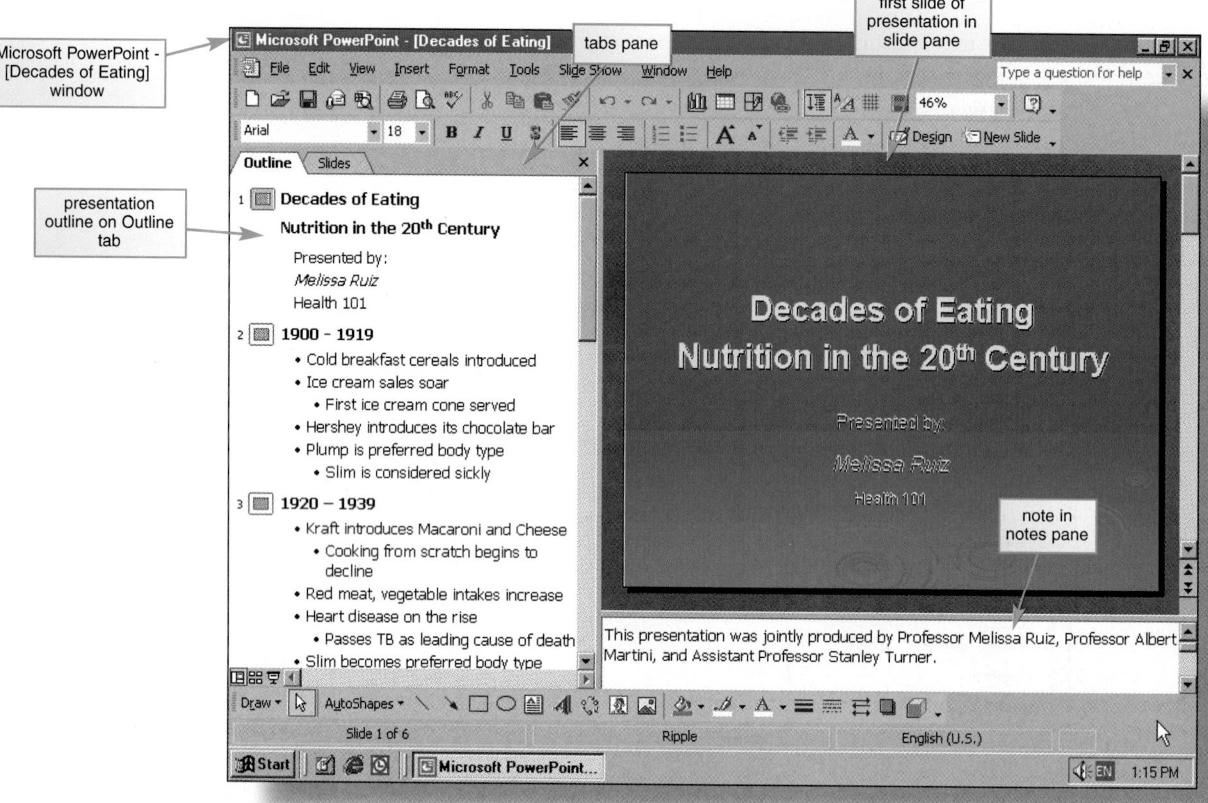

FIGURE 1-90

Microsoft PowerPoint 2002 and the Internet

PowerPoint allows you to publish presentations on the Internet or an intranet. Figure 1-91 illustrates the first slide in a presentation to be published on the Internet. The slide displays in slide view and contains a title (Electronics Explosion) and a presenter message (Presented by Select Electric). The additional slides in this presentation do not display in Figure 1-91.

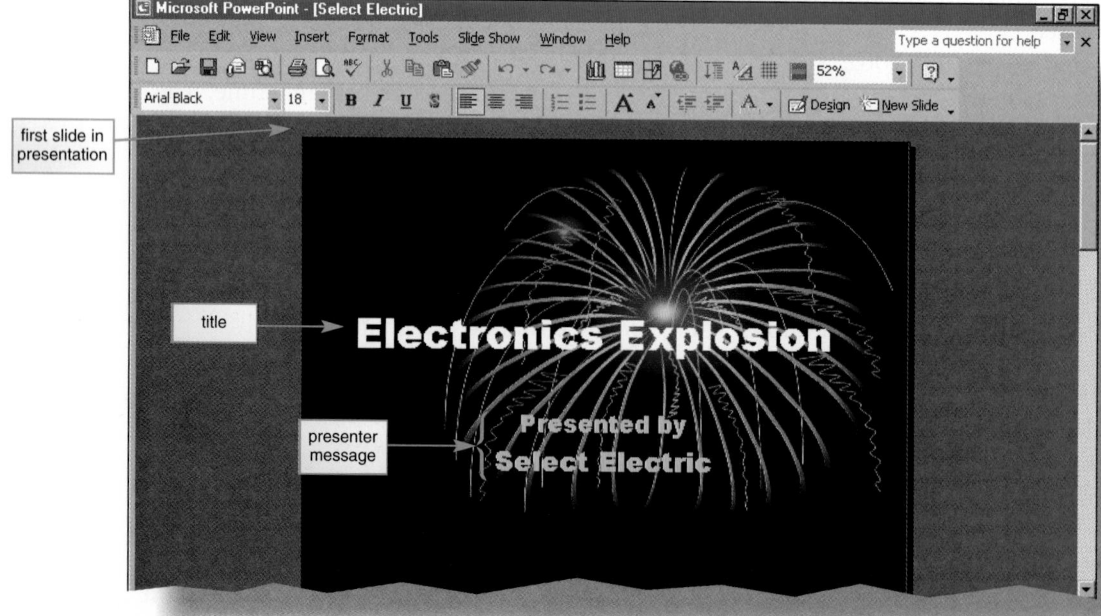

FIGURE 1-91

Figure 1-92 shows the first Web page in a series of Web pages created from the presentation illustrated in Figure 1-91. The Web page displays in the PowerPoint Presentation - Microsoft Internet Explorer window. Navigation buttons below the Web page allow you to view additional Web pages in the presentation.

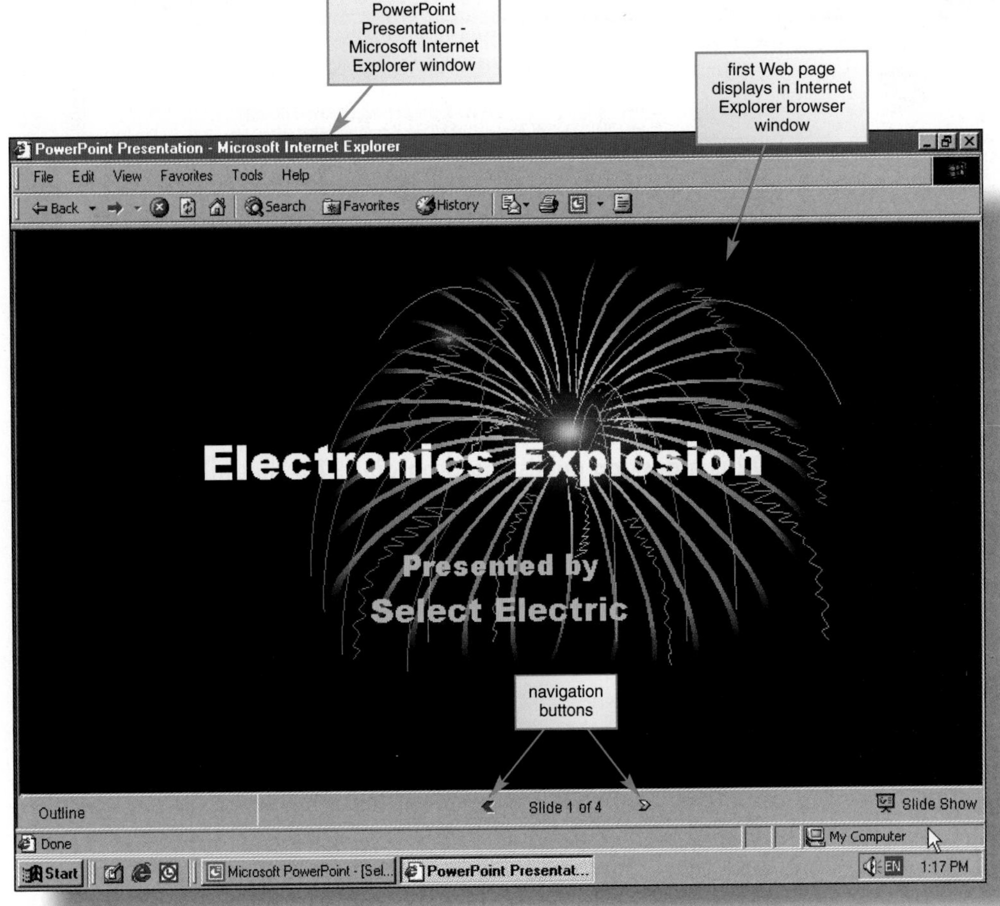

FIGURE 1-92

The Web Toolbar

The easiest method of navigating an intranet or the Internet is to use the Web toolbar. The Web toolbar allows you to search for and open Microsoft Office XP documents that you have placed on an intranet or the Internet. The Web toolbar in the Tyrone Carter Cover Letter - Microsoft Word window shown in Figure 1-93 on the next page is available in all Microsoft Office XP applications except Microsoft FrontPage. Currently, a Word document (cover letter) displays in the window, and the path and file name of the document display in the text box on the Web toolbar.

The buttons and text box on the Web toolbar allow you to jump to Web pages you have viewed previously, cancel a jump to a Web page, update the contents of the current Web page, or replace all other toolbars with the Web toolbar. In addition, you can view the first Web page displayed, search the Web for new Web sites, and add any Web pages you select to the Favorites folder, so you can return to them quickly in the future.

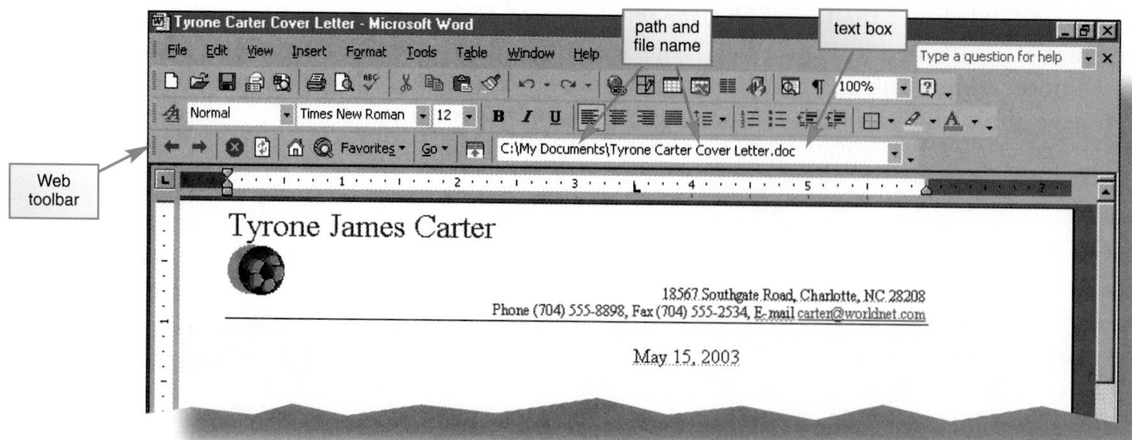

FIGURE 1-93

Microsoft Publisher 2002

Microsoft Publisher 2002 is a **desktop publishing program** (**DTP**) that allows you to design and produce professional-quality documents (newsletters, flyers, brochures, business cards, Web sites, and so on) that combine text, graphics, and photographs. Desktop publishing software provides a variety of tools, including design templates, graphic manipulation tools, color schemes or libraries, and various page wizards and templates. For large jobs, businesses use desktop publishing software to design publications that are **camera ready**, which means the files are suitable for production by outside commercial printers. Publisher also allows you to locate commercial printers, service bureaus, and copy shops willing to accept customer files created in Publisher.

Publisher allows you to design a unique image, or logo, using one of more than 1,600 professional-looking design sets. This, in turn, permits you to use the same design for all your printed documents (letters, business cards, brochures, and advertisements) and Web pages. Microsoft Publisher includes 60 coordinated color schemes, more than 10,000 high-quality clip art images, 1,500 photographs, 1,000 Web-art graphics, 175 fonts, 340 animated graphics, and hundreds of unique Design Gallery elements (quotations, sidebars, and so on). If you wish, you can also download additional images from Microsoft Media Gallery on the Microsoft Web site.

In the Business Card – Hank Landers – Microsoft Publisher window illustrated in Figure 1-94, a business card that was created using the Business Card wizard and the Arcs design set displays.

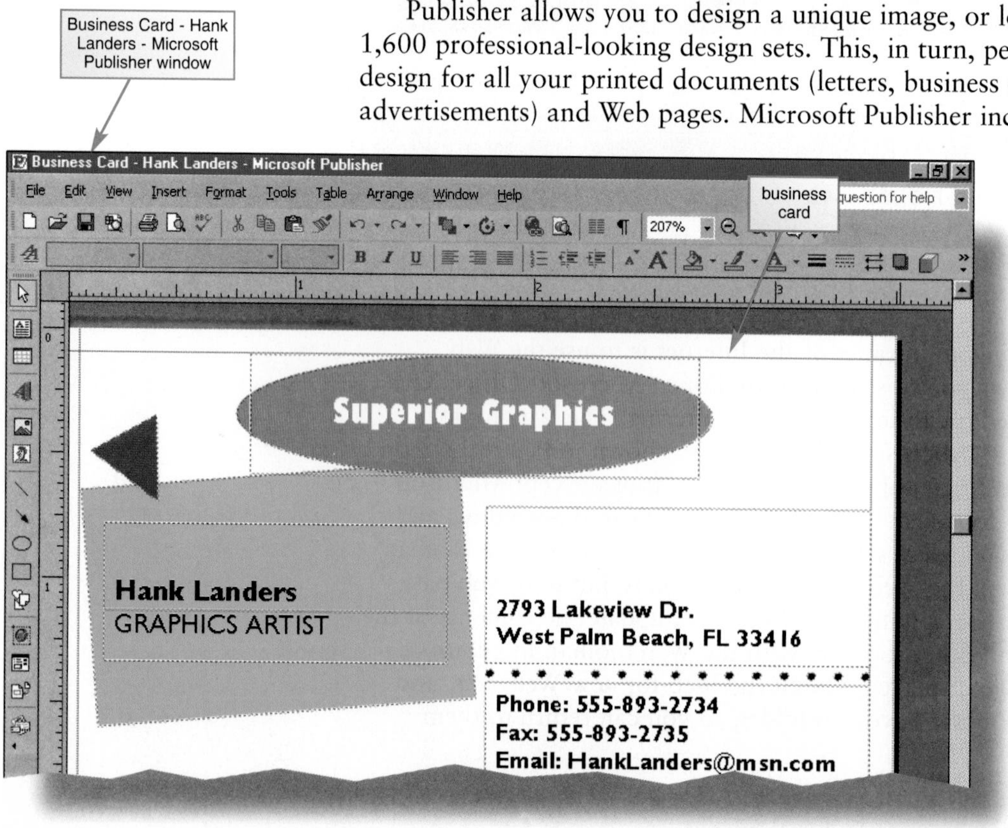

FIGURE 1-94

Microsoft Publisher and the Internet

Microsoft Publisher allows you to create a multi-page Web site with custom color schemes, photo images, animated images, and sounds easily. Figure 1-95 illustrates the Superior Graphics - Microsoft Internet Explorer window displaying the top portion of the home page in a Web site created using the Web page wizard and Arcs design set.

The home page in the Superior Graphics Web site contains text, graphic images, animated graphic images, and displays using the same design set (Arcs) as the business card illustrated in Figure 1-94.

More About

Microsoft Publisher 2002

For more information about Microsoft Publisher 2002, click Help on the menu bar of the Microsoft Publisher window, and click Office on the Web. Explore a Web page by clicking a hyperlink. After clicking a hyperlink, click the Back button to display the last Web page.

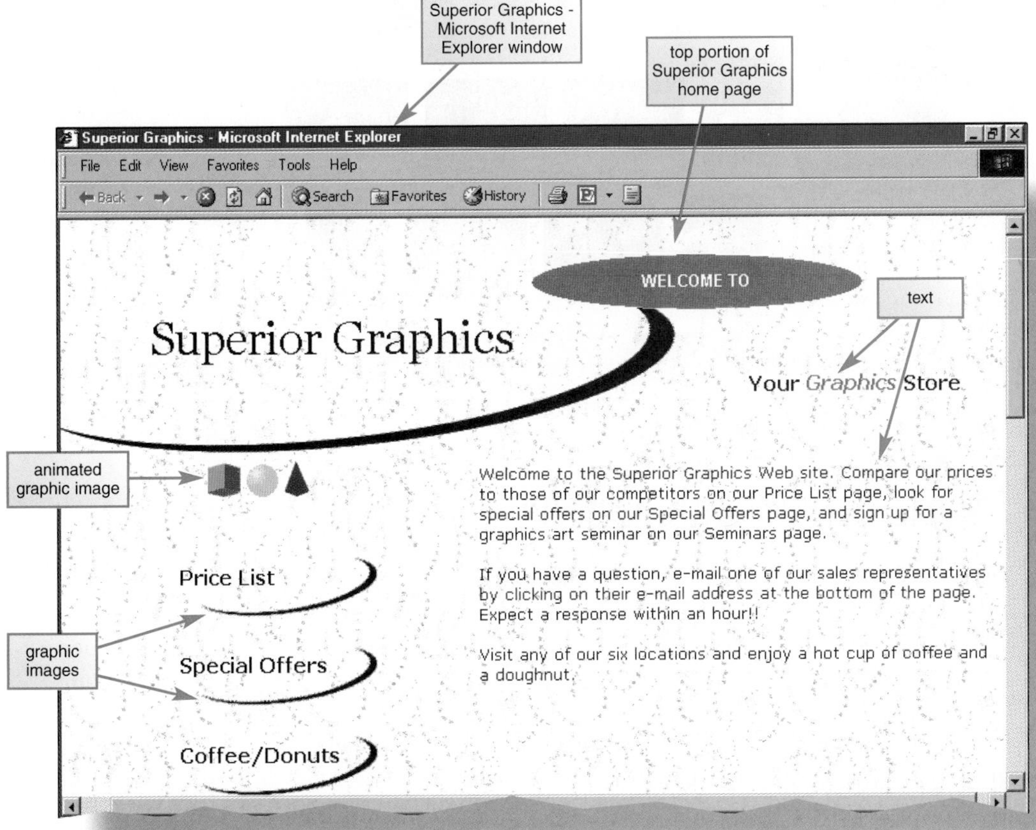

FIGURE 1-95

Microsoft FrontPage 2002

Microsoft FrontPage 2002 is a Web page authoring and site management program that lets you create and manage professional-looking Web sites on the Internet or an intranet. You can create and edit Web pages without knowing HyperText Markup Language (HTML), view the pages and files in the Web site and control their organization, manage existing Web sites, import and export files, and diagnose and fix problems. A variety of templates, including the Workgroup Web template that allows you to set up and maintain the basic structure of a workgroup Web, are available to facilitate managing the Web site.

Figure 1-96 on the next page illustrates the top portion of a Web page created using Microsoft FrontPage 2002 that contains images of friends and family. It displays in the Photos - Microsoft Internet Explorer window.

More About

Microsoft FrontPage 2002

For more information about Microsoft FrontPage 2002, click Help on the menu bar of the Microsoft FrontPage window, and click Office on the Web. Explore a Web page by clicking a hyperlink. After clicking a hyperlink, click the Back button to display the last Web page.

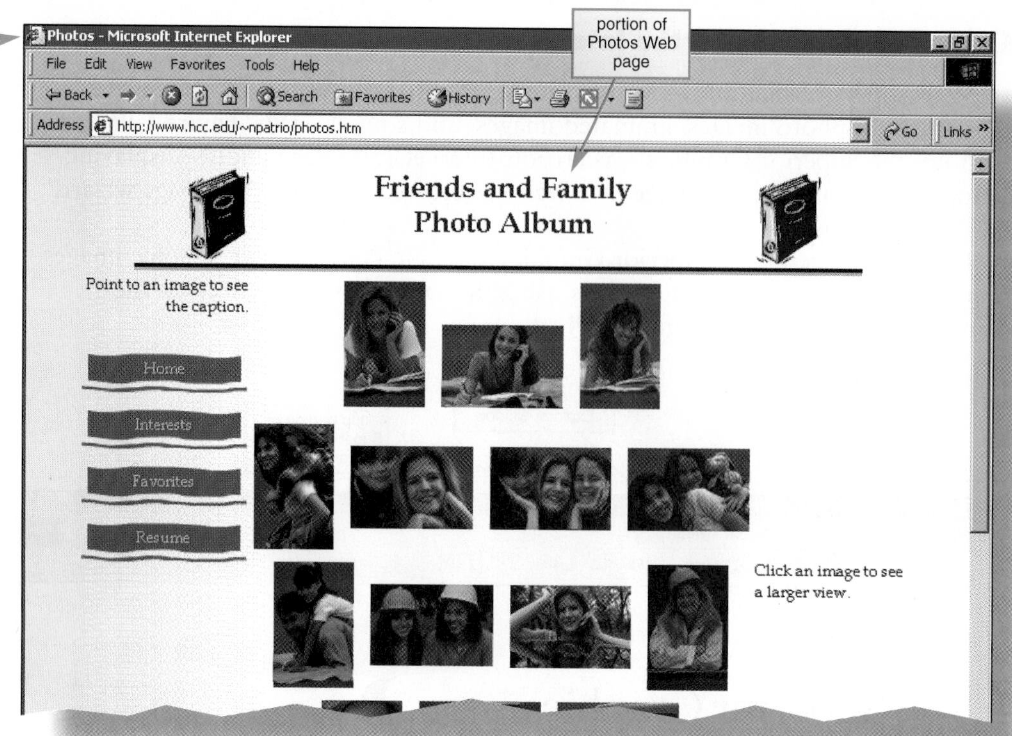

FIGURE 1-96

Microsoft Outlook 2002

For more information about Microsoft Outlook 2002, click Help on the menu bar of the Microsoft Outlook window, and click Office on the Web. Explore a Web page by clicking a hyperlink. After clicking a hyperlink, click the Back button to display the last Web page.

Microsoft Outlook 2002

Microsoft Outlook 2002 is an effective **personal information management** (**PIM**) program that helps you organize information and share information with others. Microsoft Outlook allows you to manage personal and business information such as e-mail, appointments, contacts, tasks, and documents, and keep a journal of your activities. Outlook organizes and stores this information in folders on your computer.

When you start Microsoft Outlook, the Outlook Today - Microsoft Outlook window may display (Figure 1-97). The **information viewer** on the right side of the window contains the current date (Monday, March 10, 2003); a list of scheduled events, appointments, and meetings for the week; a list of tasks to perform; and a summary of your e-mail messages.

The **Outlook Bar** on the left side of the window contains the Outlook Today, Inbox, Calendar, Contacts, Tasks, and Notes shortcuts. Clicking a shortcut on the Outlook Bar displays the contents of the associated folder in the information viewer.

Microsoft Outlook allows you to click the Inbox shortcut on the Outlook Bar to view e-mail messages, click the Calendar shortcut to schedule activities (events, appointments, and meetings), click the Contacts shortcut to maintain a list of contacts and e-mail addresses, click the Tasks shortcut to view a detailed list of tasks, and click the Notes shortcut to make and review electronic reminders, or notes. In addition, you can click the Deleted Items shortcut to view deleted items and click the Journal shortcut to view a log of your Outlook activities.

When you click the Inbox shortcut on the Outlook Bar, the Inbox - Microsoft Outlook window displays and the contents of the Inbox folder (your e-mail messages) display in the window (Figure 1-98).

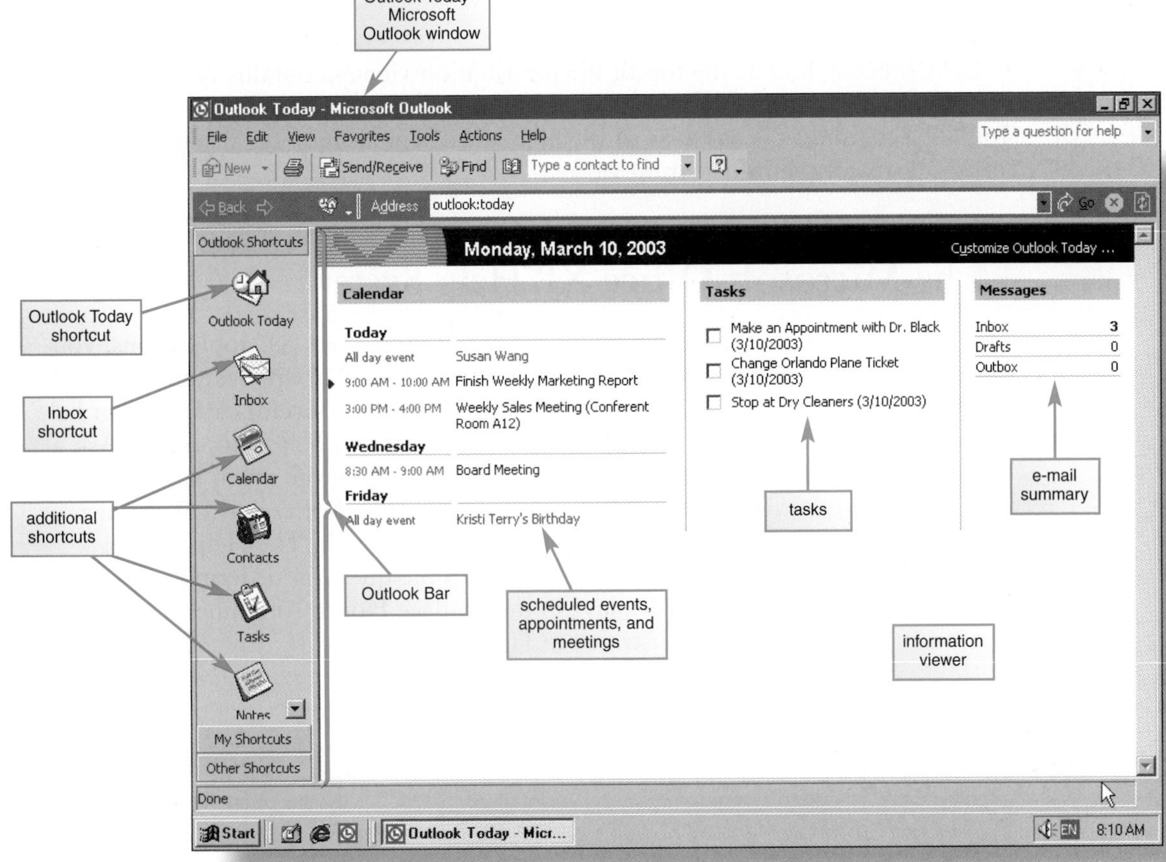

FIGURE 1-97

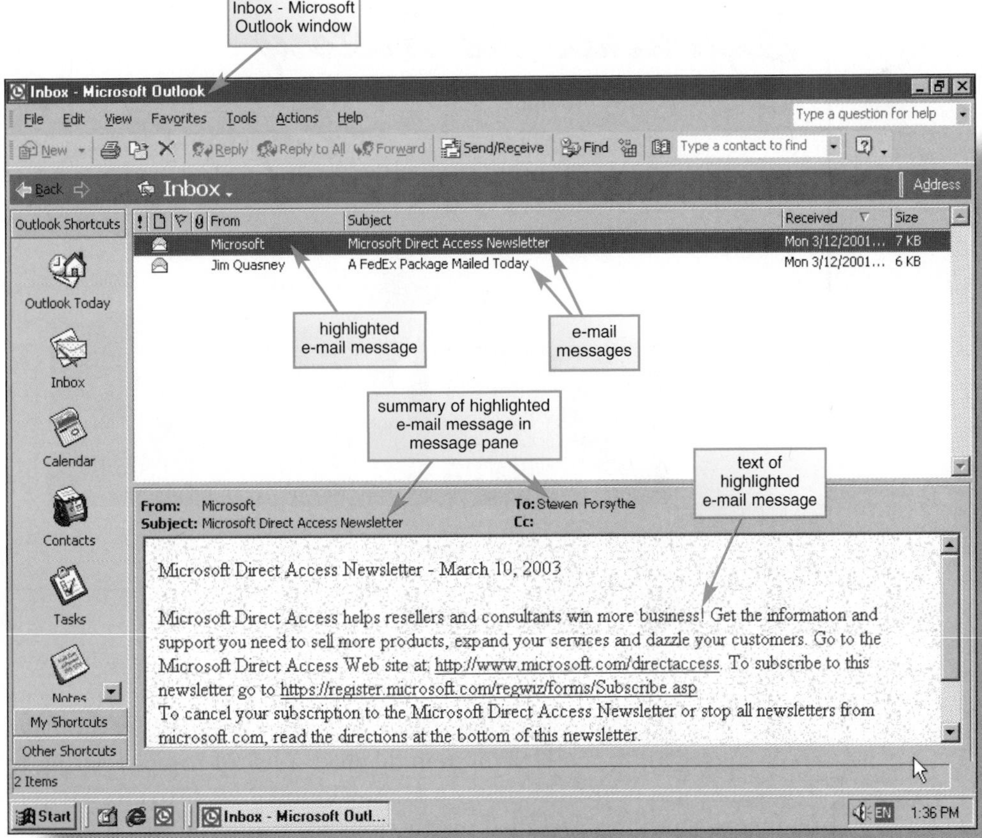

FIGURE 1-98

The Inbox folder at the top of the information viewer contains two e-mail messages. The first e-mail message is highlighted. The summary information (From:, To:, Subject:, and Cc:) and text of the highlighted e-mail message display in the message pane of the information viewer.

The Microsoft Office XP Help System

At any time while you are using one of the Microsoft Office XP applications, you can interact with the **Microsoft Office XP Help system** for that application and display information on any topic associated with the application. Several categories of help are available to you. One of the easiest methods to obtain help is to use the Ask a Question box. The **Ask a Question box** on the right side of the menu bar lets you type free-form questions, such as *how do I save* or *how do I create a Web page,* or you can type terms, such as template, smart tags, or speech. The Help System responds by displaying a list of topics relating to the question or term you entered. The Ask a Question box that displays in the Wallace House Announcement - Microsoft Word window is illustrated in Figure 1-99.

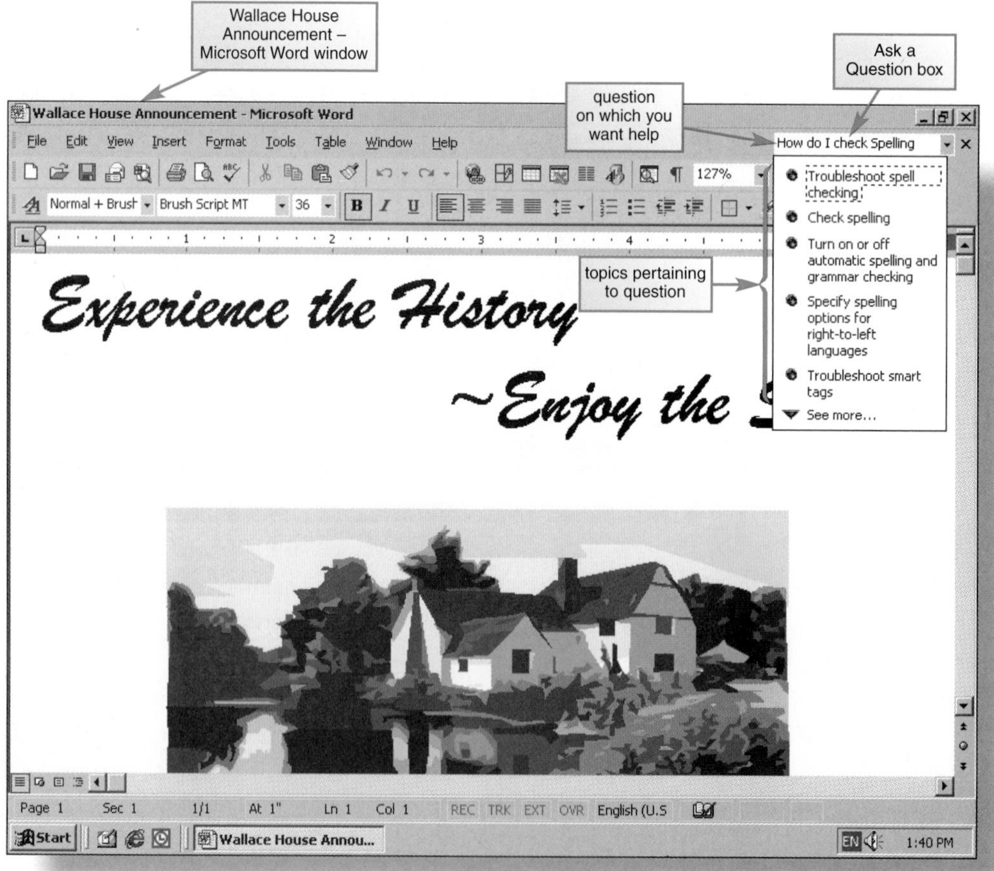

FIGURE 1-99

When you type the question, *How do I check spelling*, in the Ask a Question box in Figure 1-99, the Help system displays a list of topics relating to the question. Clicking a topic in the list opens a Help window that provides Help information about spell checking. Detailed instructions for using the Ask a Question box and the other categories of Help are explained in Appendix A of this book.

CASE PERSPECTIVE SUMMARY

While continuing to answer questions about Windows 2000 Professional and Office XP in the workplace, you spent nearly every free moment in the next two weeks learning about the newly installed operating system and application software. Then, the daily training sessions kept you busy for the following three months. You taught 33 workshops and trained all of the 451 employees in the company. Your supervisor, who attended the Windows 2000 Professional and Word 2002 seminars, complimented your success by giving you a sizeable pay raise and time off to attend the Shelly Cashman Institute at Purdue University.

Project Summary

Project 1 illustrated the Microsoft Windows 2000 graphical user interface and the Microsoft Office XP applications. You started Windows 2000, learned the components of the desktop and the six mouse operations. You opened, closed, moved, resized, minimized, maximized, and scrolled a window. You used Windows Explorer to select and copy a group of files, display the contents of a folder, create a folder, expand and collapse a folder, and rename and delete a file and a folder. You obtained help about using Microsoft Windows 2000 and shut down Windows 2000.

Brief explanations of the Microsoft Word, Microsoft Excel, Microsoft Access, Microsoft PowerPoint, Microsoft Publisher, Microsoft FrontPage, and Microsoft Outlook applications, and examples of how these applications interact with the Internet were given. With this introduction, you are ready to begin a more in-depth study of each of the Microsoft Office XP applications explained in this book.

What You Should Know

Having completed this project, you now should be able to perform the following tasks:

- Close a Window *(INT 1.25)*
- Close a Window and Reopen a Window *(INT 1.19)*
- Close the Getting Started with Windows 2000 Dialog Box *(INT 1.08)*
- Close Windows Help *(INT 1.59)*
- Collapse a Folder *(INT 1.37)*
- Copy a Group of Files *(INT 1.46)*
- Create a New Folder *(INT 1.39)*
- Delete a File by Right-Clicking *(INT 1.51)*
- Delete a Folder *(INT 1.52)*
- Display the Contents of a Folder *(INT 1.34, INT 1.42, INT 1.47)*
- Expand a Folder *(INT 1.36, INT 1.41)*
- Launch a Program Using the Start Menu *(INT 1.29)*
- Launch Windows Help *(INT 1.54)*
- Maximize and Restore a Window *(INT 1.17)*
- Minimize and Redisplay a Window *(INT 1.15)*
- Move an Object by Dragging *(INT 1.21)*
- Open a Window by Double-Clicking *(INT 1.13)*
- Point and Click *(INT 1.10)*
- Quit a Program *(INT 1.30, INT 1.53)*
- Rename a File *(INT 1.48)*
- Rename a Folder *(INT 1.49)*
- Resize a Window *(INT 1.25)*
- Right-Click *(INT 1.12)*
- Right-Drag *(INT 1.26)*
- Scroll a Window Using Scroll Arrows *(INT 1.23)*
- Select a Group of Files *(INT 1.44)*
- Shut Down Windows 2000 *(INT 1.60)*
- Size a Window by Dragging *(INT 1.22)*
- Start Windows Explorer and Maximize Its Window *(INT 1.31)*
- Use Help to Find a Topic in Help *(INT 1.55)*
- Use the Help Index Sheet *(INT 1.58)*

Learn It Online

Instructions: To complete the Learn It Online exercises, start your browser, click the Address bar, and then enter `scsite.com/offxp/exs.htm`. When the Office XP Learn It Online page displays, follow the instructions in the exercises below.

1 Project Reinforcement TF, MC, and SA

Below Windows Project 1, click the Project Reinforcement link. Print the quiz by clicking Print on the File menu. Answer each question. Write your first and last name at the top of each page, and then hand in the printout to your instructor.

2 Flash Cards

Below Windows Project 1, click the Flash Cards link. When Flash Cards displays, read the instructions. Type 20 (or a number specified by your instructor) in the Number of Playing Cards text box, type your name in the Name text box, and then click the Flip Card button. When the flash card displays, read the question and then click the Answer box arrow to select an answer. Flip through Flash Cards. Click Print on the File menu to print the last flash card if your score is 15 (75%) correct or greater and then hand it in to your instructor. If your score is less than 15 (75%) correct, then redo this exercise by clicking the Replay button.

3 Practice Test

Below Windows Project 1, click the Practice Test link. Answer each question, enter your first and last name at the bottom of the page, and then click the Grade Test button. When the graded practice test displays on your screen, click Print on the File menu to print a hard copy. Continue to take practice tests until you score 80% or better. Hand in a printout of the final practice test to your instructor.

4 Who Wants to Be a Computer Genius?

Below Windows Project 1, click the Computer Genius link. Read the instructions, enter your first and last name at the bottom of the page, and then click the Play button. Hand in your score to your instructor.

5 Wheel of Terms

Below Windows Project 1, click the Wheel of Terms link. Read the instructions, and then enter your first and last name and your school name. Click the Play button. Hand in your score to your instructor.

6 Crossword Puzzle Challenge

Below Windows Project 1, click the Crossword Puzzle Challenge link. Read the instructions, and then enter your first and last name. Click the Play button. Work the crossword puzzle. When you are finished, click the Submit button. When the crossword puzzle redisplays, click the Print button. Hand in the printout.

7 Tips and Tricks

Below Windows Project 1, click the Tips and Tricks link. Click a topic that pertains to Project 1. Right-click the information and then click Print on the shortcut menu. Construct a brief example of what the information relates to in Windows to confirm you understand how to use the tip or trick. Hand in the example and printed information.

8 Newsgroups

Below Windows Project 1, click the Newsgroups link. Click a topic that pertains to Project 1. Print three comments. Hand in the comments to your instructor.

9 Expanding Your Horizons

Below Windows Project 1, click the Articles for Microsoft Windows link. Click a topic that pertains to Project 1. Print the information. Construct a brief example of what the information relates to in Windows to confirm you understand the contents of the article. Hand in the example and printed information to your instructor.

10 Search Sleuth

Below Windows Project 1, click the Search Sleuth link. To search for a term that pertains to this project, select a term below the Project 1 title and then use the Google search engine at google.com (or any major search engine) to display and print two Web pages that present information on the term. Hand in the printouts to your instructor.

In the Lab

1 Using the Discover Windows 2000 Professional Tour

Instructions: To use the Discover Windows 2000 tutorial, you will need a copy of the Windows 2000 Professional CD-ROM. If this CD-ROM is not available, skip this lab assignment. Otherwise, use a computer and the CD-ROM to perform the following tasks.

1. If necessary, start Microsoft Windows 2000.
2. Insert the Windows 2000 Professional CD-ROM in your CD-ROM drive. If the Microsoft Windows 2000 CD window displays, click the Close button on the title bar to close the window.
3. Click the Start button on the taskbar, point to Programs on the Start menu, point to Accessories on the Programs submenu, point to System Tools on the Accessories submenu, and then click Getting Started on the System Tools submenu.
4. Click Discover Windows in the Getting Started with Windows 2000 dialog box to display the Discover screen (Figure 1-100). The word, Discover, at the top of the screen identifies the Discover screen. The left side of the Discover screen contains a message to click a category on the right side of the screen. The right side of the screen contains the four categories in the Discover tour (Easier to Use, Easier to Manage, More Compatible, and More Powerful).

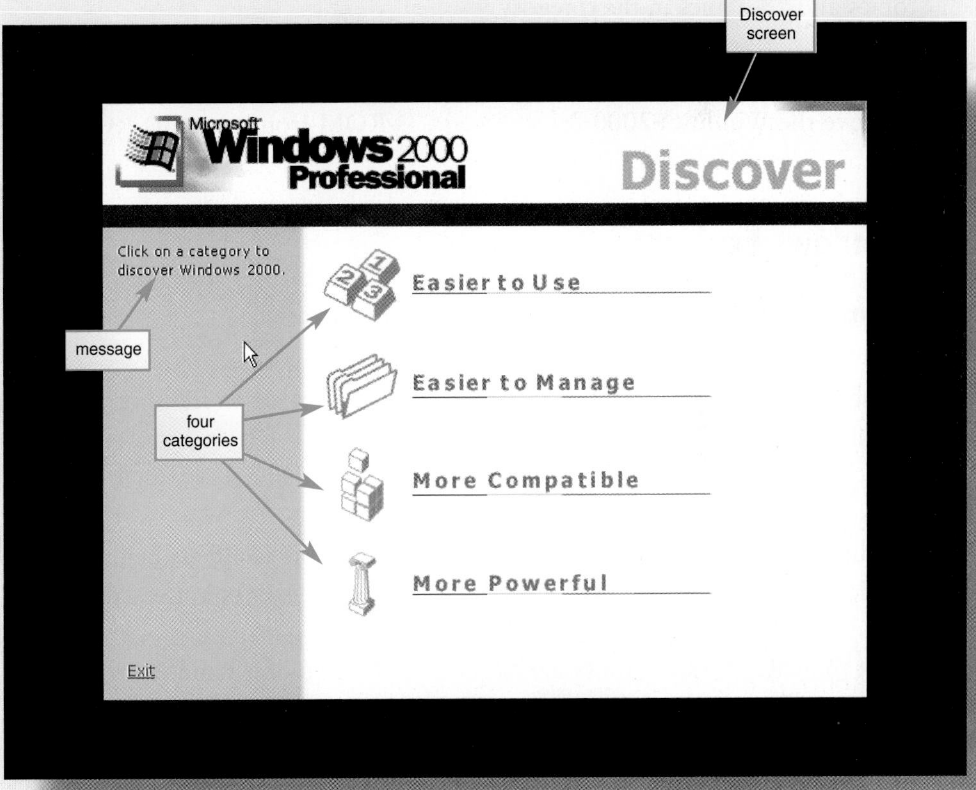

FIGURE 1-100

5. Click Easier to Use on the right side of the Discover screen. The five topics in the Easier to Use category display on the left side of the screen, a summary of the Easier to Use category displays on the right side, and a bar containing the four categories in the Discover tour display above the topics and summary. The Easier to Use category is highlighted on the bar.
6. Click Work with Files on the left side of the Discover screen to display the subtopics in the Work with Files topic.

(continued)

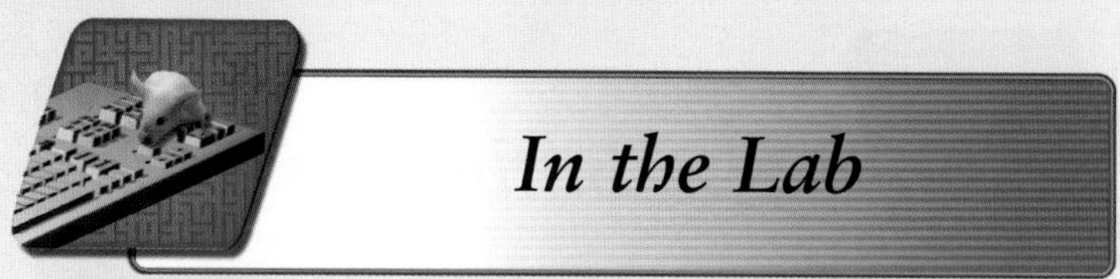

Using the Discover Windows 2000 Professional Tour *(continued)*

7. Click and read each subtopic in the Work with Files topic. When available, click the Play Animation button to view an animation of the topic. When the animation stops, click the Back button.
8. Click each of the remaining four topics in the Easier to Use category and then click and read each subtopic in each topic.
9. Click Easier to Manage on the bar at the top of the Discover screen. Click and read each of the topics and subtopics in the category.
10. Click the More Compatible category on the bar at the top of the Discover screen. Click and read each of the topics and subtopics in the category.
11. Click the More Powerful category on the bar at the top of the Discover screen. Click and read each of the topics and subtopics in the category.
12. When you have finished, click the Exit link in the lower-left corner of the Discover screen.
13. Click the Exit link in the lower-right corner of the Getting Started with Windows 2000 dialog box.
14. Remove the Windows 2000 Professional CD-ROM from your CD-ROM drive.

2 Windows Explorer

Instructions: Use a computer to perform the following tasks.

1. Start Microsoft Windows 2000 and connect to the Internet.
2. Right-click the Start button on the taskbar, click Explore on the shortcut menu, and then maximize the Start Menu window.
3. If necessary, scroll to the left in the Folders pane so the Start Menu and Programs icons are visible.
4. Click the Programs icon in the Start Menu folder.
5. Double-click the Internet Explorer shortcut icon in the Contents pane to launch the Internet Explorer application. What is the URL of the Web page that displays in the Address bar in the Microsoft Internet Explorer window? ______________________________
6. Click the URL in the Address bar in the Internet Explorer window to select it. Type `scsite.com` and then press the ENTER key.
7. Scroll the Web page to display the Browse by Subject area containing the subject categories. Clicking a subject category displays the book titles in that category.
8. Click Operating Systems in the Browse by Subject area.
9. Click the Microsoft Windows 2000 Complete Concepts and Techniques link.
10. Right-click the Microsoft Windows 2000 textbook cover image on the Web page, click Save Picture As on the shortcut menu, type `Windows 2000 Cover` in the File name box, and then click the Save button in the Save Picture dialog box to save the image in the My Pictures folder.
11. Click the Close button in the Microsoft Internet Explorer window.
12. Scroll to the top of the Folders pane to make the drive C icon visible.
13. Click the minus sign in the box to the left of the drive C icon. The 3½ Floppy (A:) and My Documents icons should be visible in the Folders pane.
14. Click the plus sign in the box to the left of the My Documents icon.

In the Lab

15. Click the My Pictures folder name in the Folders pane.
16. Right-click the Windows 2000 Cover icon and then click Properties on the shortcut menu.
    a. What type of file is the Windows 2000 Cover file? ____________________
    b. When was the file last modified? ____________________
    c. With what application does this file open? ____________________
17. Click the Cancel button in the Windows 2000 Cover Properties dialog box.
18. Insert a formatted floppy disk in drive A of your computer.
19. Right-drag the Windows 2000 Cover icon over the 3½ Floppy (A:) icon in the Folders pane. Click Move Here on the shortcut menu. Click the 3½ Floppy (A:) icon in the Folders pane.
    a. Is the Windows 2000 Cover file stored on drive A? ____________________
20. Click the Close button in the 3½ Floppy (A:) window.

3 Using Windows Help

Instructions: Use Windows Help and a computer to perform the following tasks.

Part 1: Using the Question Mark Button

1. If necessary, start Microsoft Windows 2000.
2. Click the Start button on the taskbar, point to Settings on the Start menu, and then click Control Panel on the Settings submenu.
3. Double-click the Folder Options icon in the Control Panel window.
4. If the General sheet does not display, click the General tab in the Folder Options dialog box.
5. Click the Question Mark button on the title bar. The mouse pointer changes to a block arrow with a question mark.
6. Click the icon in the Active Desktop area in the Folder Options dialog box. A pop-up window displays explaining the Active Desktop area. Read the information in the pop-up window.
7. Click an open area of the General sheet to remove the pop-up window.
8. Click the Question Mark button on the title bar and then click the Enable Web content on my desktop option button. A pop-up window displays explaining what happens when you select this option. Read the information in the pop-up window. Click an open area on the General sheet to remove the pop-up window.
9. Click the Question Mark button on the title bar and then click the Use Windows Classic desktop option button. A pop-up window displays explaining what happens when you select this option. Read the information in the pop-up window. Click an open area on the General sheet to remove the pop-up window.
10. Click the Question Mark button on the title bar and then click the Restore Defaults button. A pop-up window displays explaining the function of the button. Read the information in the pop-up window. Click an open area on the General sheet to remove the pop-up window.
11. Summarize the function of the Question Mark button. ____________________
    ____
12. Click the Close button in the Folder Options dialog box.
13. Click the Close button in the Control Panel window.

(continued)

Using Windows Help *(continued)*

Part 2: ***Finding What's New in Windows 2000 Professional***

1. Click the Start button and then click Help on the Start menu.
2. Click the Maximize button on the Windows 2000 title bar.
3. If the Contents sheet does not display, click the Contents tab. Click the Introducing Windows 2000 Professional closed book icon.
4. Click Tips for new users in the Introducing Windows 2000 Professional open book.
5. Click Find a file or folder in the topic pane of the Windows 2000 window.
6. Click the Step-by-step procedure link and read the steps to search for a file or folder.
7. Click the Options button on the Help toolbar to display the Options menu and then click Print.
8. Click the OK button in the Print Topics dialog box to print the steps.

Part 3: ***Reading About the Online Getting Started Manual***

1. Click the Getting Started online book icon in the navigation pane.
2. Click the Windows 2000 Professional Getting Started link in the topic pane to open the Windows 2000 Professional Getting Started window. The Contents sheet containing the Getting Started entry and eight closed book icons displays in the navigation pane of the window. Five links display in the topics pane of the window.
3. If the Contents sheet does not display, click the Contents tab.
4. Click the Preface closed book icon.
5. Click the How to Use Getting Started topic.
6. Click the Options button on the Help toolbar, click Print, and then click the OK button to print the information about the How to Use Getting Started topic.
7. Click the Ch. 1 – Welcome closed book icon. Three Help topics and two closed book icons display beneath the entry when the book is opened. Click and read the Windows 2000 Professional at a Glance and If You're New to Windows topics.
8. Click the Where to Find Information closed book icon.
9. Click the Resources Included with Windows 2000 closed book icon.
10. Click the Troubleshooters topic. Read the information about the topic.
11. Click the Options button on the Help toolbar, click Print, and then click the OK button to print the topic.
12. Click the Introducing Windows 2000 Professional closed book icon. Click and read the nine topics in the open book.
13. Click the Close button in the Windows 2000 Professional Getting Started window.
14. Click the Close button in the Windows 2000 window.

Microsoft WORD 2002

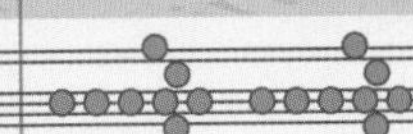

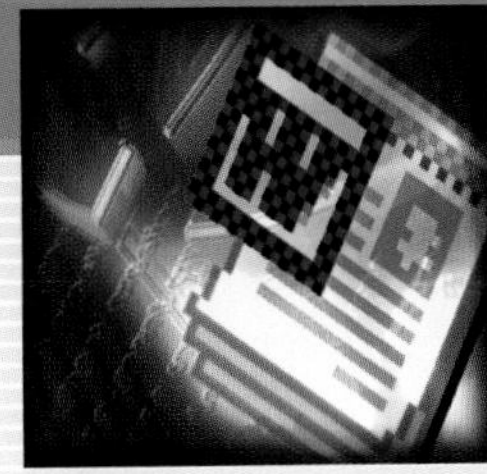

Microsoft Word 2002

PROJECT

Creating and Editing a Word Document

OBJECTIVES

You will have mastered the material in this project when you can:

- Start Word
- Describe the Word window
- Describe the speech and handwriting recognition capabilities of Word
- Zoom page width
- Change the default font size of all text
- Enter text into a document
- Scroll through a document
- Check spelling as you type
- Save a document
- Select text
- Change the font size of selected text
- Change the font of selected text
- Right-align a paragraph
- Center a paragraph
- Undo commands or actions
- Italicize selected text
- Underline selected text
- Bold selected text
- Insert clip art into a document
- Resize a graphic
- Print a document
- Open a document
- Correct errors in a document
- Use Word Help
- Quit Word

Mind Tools and Spell Check

Help for Writers Everywhere

"Learning is a treasure that will follow its owner everywhere."

Chinese Proverb

Good spelling comes naturally to some people, but most people have difficulty remembering how to spell at least some words. For others, spelling is an arduous task. Because the sounds of words and their spellings differ so greatly, for most, spelling simply requires memorization through effort and repetition.

One study reports that 20 percent of writers do not spell well because they cannot visualize words. Even remembering simple spelling rules, such as, i before e, except after c, does not offer much assistance because of all the exceptions!

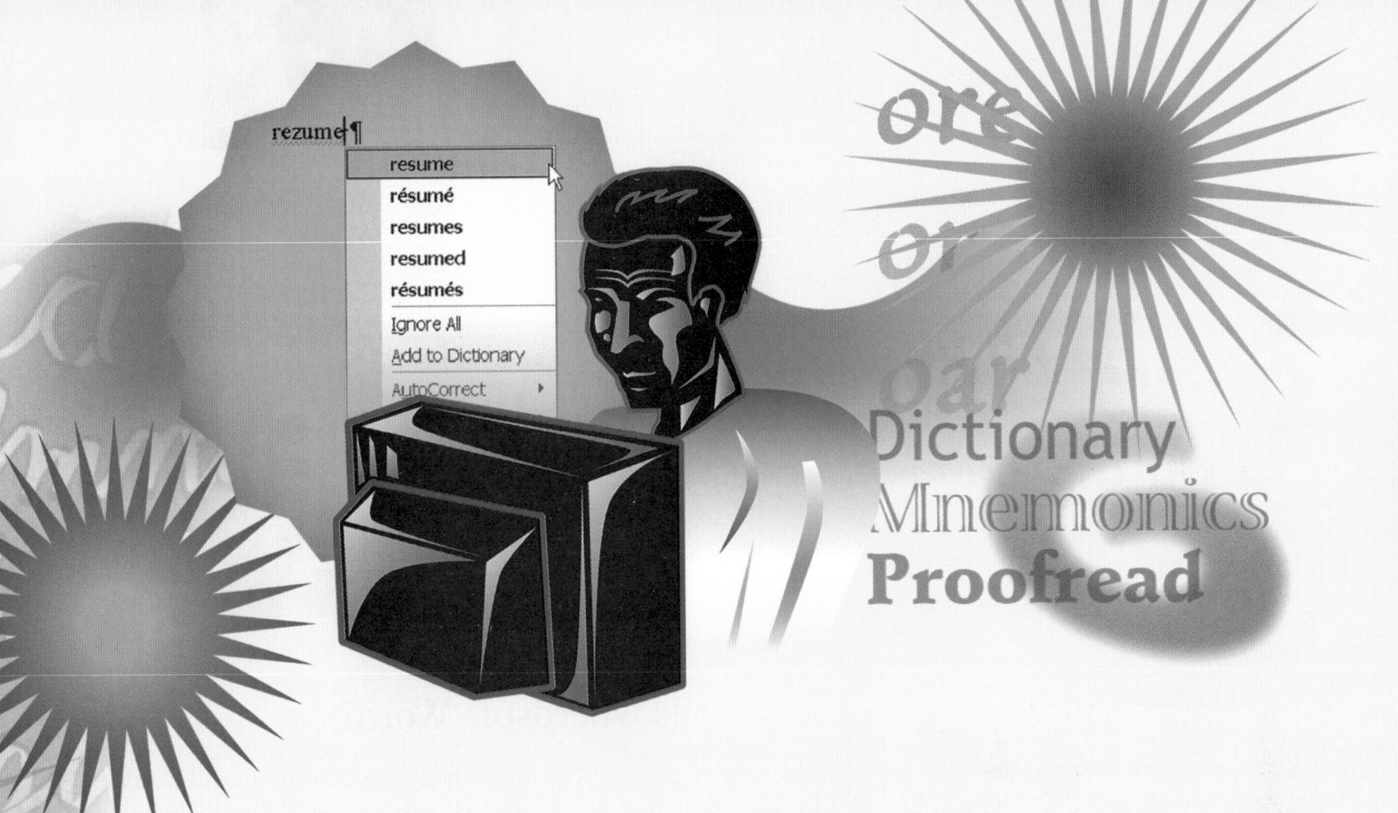

Dictionary
Mnemonics
Proofread

A spelling error in a flyer distributed on campus, a resume sent to a potential employer, or an e-mail message forwarded to an associate could lessen your credibility, cause a reader to doubt the accuracy of your statements, and leave a negative impression. In this project, Microsoft Word checks your typing for possible spelling errors in the Student Government Association announcement of a 30 percent student discount on sailboat rentals at Hidden Lake State Park.

If you type a word that does not appear in Word's dictionary, Word will flag the possible error with a wavy red underline. If the spelling is correct, you can instruct Word to ignore the flagged word. If it is misspelled, the spelling feature will offer a list of suggested corrections. Despite this assistance from the spelling checker, one study indicates college students repeatedly ignore or override the flagged words.

Word's spelling checker is a useful alternative to a dictionary, but you must not rely on it 100 percent. It will not flag commonly misused homophones, which are words that are pronounced alike but are spelled differently. For example, it is easy to confuse the homophones in the sentence, The Web site contains an incorrect cite to the reference material discussing regaining sight after experiencing blindness.

English teachers emphasize that you can learn to spell better, but not by strictly memorizing long lists or having someone mark all the errors in a paper. Instead, you need to try some strategies to improve awareness of spelling difficulties.

First, identify error patterns. For example, do you misspell the same words repeatedly? If so, write them in a list and have a friend dictate them to you. Then write the words again. If you involve your senses, hear the words spelled correctly, and then visualize the words, you increase your awareness of the problem.

Next, always consult a dictionary when you are uncertain of a word's spelling. Note the word's etymology — its origin and history. For example, the word, science, originated from the Latin word, scientia, a form of the verb to know.

Then, try a mnemonic, which is a device or code, such as an image or story that has meaning to you. Mnemonics can assist the memory and help you spell more effectively. To make a mnemonic more helpful, use positive, pleasant images that clearly relate to the word you want to remember, and are vivid enough to recall every time you see a word.

As you proofread, read from right to left. Use a pencil to point at each word as you say it aloud.

Using Microsoft Word's spelling checker, a good dictionary, and other tried-and-true approaches can enhance your spelling ability and help your writing skills.

Microsoft Word 2002

Creating and Editing a Word Document

PROJECT

CASE PERSPECTIVE

Tara Stellenbach is the Activities chairperson for the Student Government Association (SGA) at Green Valley Community College (GVCC). One of her responsibilities is to coordinate student discount programs with local businesses. She then prepares fliers announcing the discount programs.

Tara's favorite pastime is sailing on beautiful Hidden Lake. The large lake has crystal clear water and is located in a mountainous area just 15 miles from campus. Because no motors are allowed on Hidden Lake, it is peaceful and often scattered with sailboats. Tara decides to contact Hidden Lake State Park to inquire about student discounts for sailboat rentals. After meeting with the marketing director, Tara is elated. The marketing director agrees to give all GVCC students a 30 percent discount on sailboat rentals!

As a marketing major, Tara has learned the guidelines for designing announcements. She will use large, bold characters for the headline and title. To attract attention to the announcement, she will include a large graphic of a sailboat. When complete, she will recruit you and other members of the SGA to distribute the flier.

What Is Microsoft Word?

Microsoft Word is a full-featured word processing program that allows you to create and revise professional looking documents such as announcements, letters, resumes, and reports. You can use Word's desktop publishing features to create high-quality brochures, advertisements, and newsletters. Word also provides many tools that enable you to create Web pages with ease. From within Word, you even can place these Web pages directly on a Web server.

Word has many features designed to simplify the production of documents. With Word, you easily can include borders, shading, tables, graphics, pictures, and Web addresses in your documents. You can instruct Word to create a template, which is a form you can use and customize to meet your needs. With proper hardware, you can dictate or handwrite text instead of typing it into Word. You also can speak instructions to Word.

While you are typing, Word can perform tasks automatically. For example, Word can detect and correct spelling and grammar errors in a variety of languages. Word's thesaurus allows you to add variety and precision to your writing. Word also can format text such as headings, lists, fractions, borders, and Web addresses as you type them. Within Word, you also can e-mail a copy of your Word document to an e-mail address.

Project One — Hidden Lake Announcement

To illustrate the features of Word, this book presents a series of projects that use Word to create documents similar to those you will encounter in academic and business environments. Project 1 uses Word to produce the announcement shown in Figure 1-1.

> **More About**
>
> **Word 2002**
>
> For more information on the features of Microsoft Word 2002, visit the Word 2002 More About Web page (scsite.com/wd2002/more.htm) and then click Microsoft Word 2002 Features.

The announcement informs students about student discounts on sailboat rentals at Hidden Lake State Park. The announcement begins with a headline that is followed by a graphic of a sailboat. Below the graphic of the sailboat is the body title, HIDDEN LAKE STATE PARK, followed by the body copy that consists of a brief paragraph about the park and another paragraph about the discount. Finally, the last line of the announcement lists the park's telephone number.

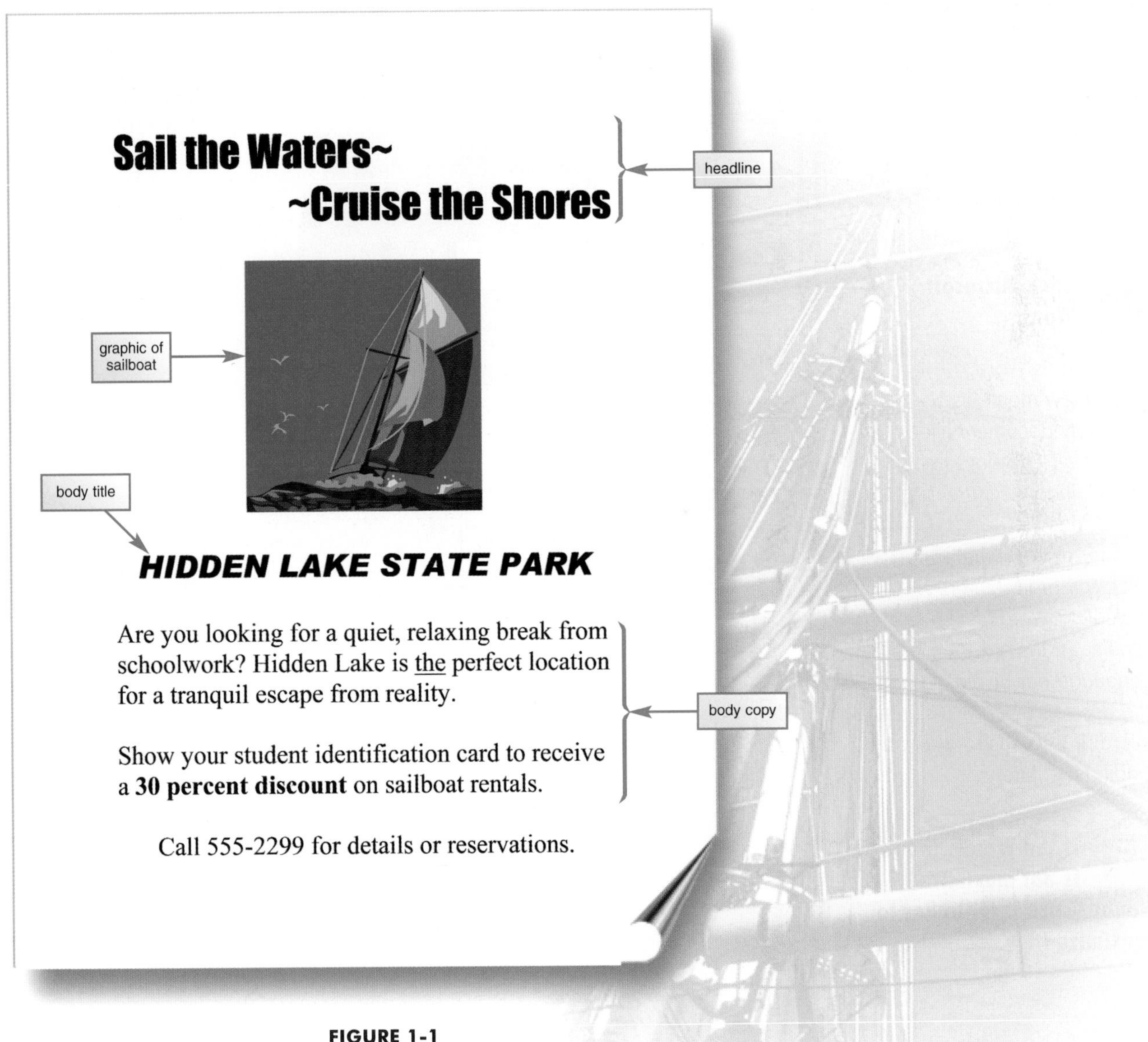

Sail the Waters~
~Cruise the Shores
headline
graphic of sailboat
body title
HIDDEN LAKE STATE PARK
Are you looking for a quiet, relaxing break from schoolwork? Hidden Lake is the perfect location for a tranquil escape from reality.
body copy
Show your student identification card to receive a 30 percent discount on sailboat rentals.
Call 555-2299 for details or reservations.

FIGURE 1-1

Starting and Customizing Word

To start Word, Windows must be running. Perform the steps on the next page to start Word, or ask your instructor how to start Word for your system.

Steps To Start Word

1 Click the Start button on the Windows taskbar, point to Programs on the Start menu, and then point to Microsoft Word on the Programs submenu.

The commands on the Start menu display above the Start button and the Programs submenu displays (Figure 1-2). If the Office Speech Recognition software is installed on your computer, the Language bar may display somewhere on the desktop.

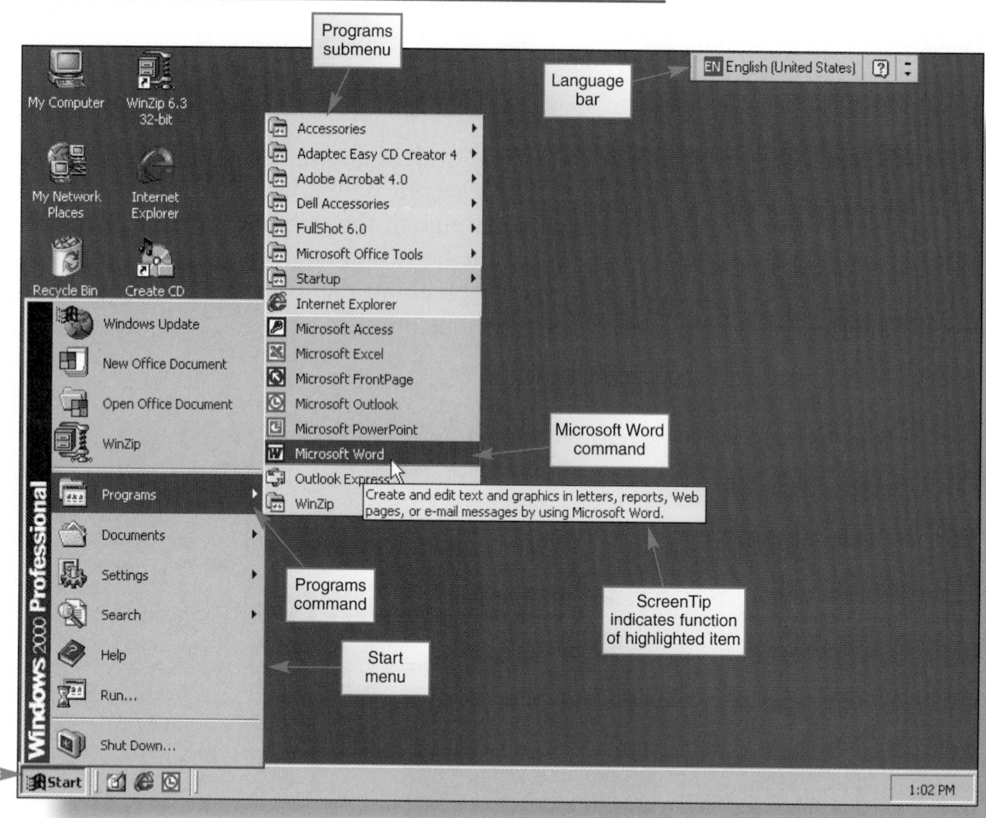

FIGURE 1-2

2 Click Microsoft Word.

Office starts Word. After a few moments, an empty document titled Document1 displays in the Word window (Figure 1-3). The Windows taskbar displays the Word program button, indicating Word is running. If the Language bar displayed on the desktop when you started Word, it expands to display additional buttons.

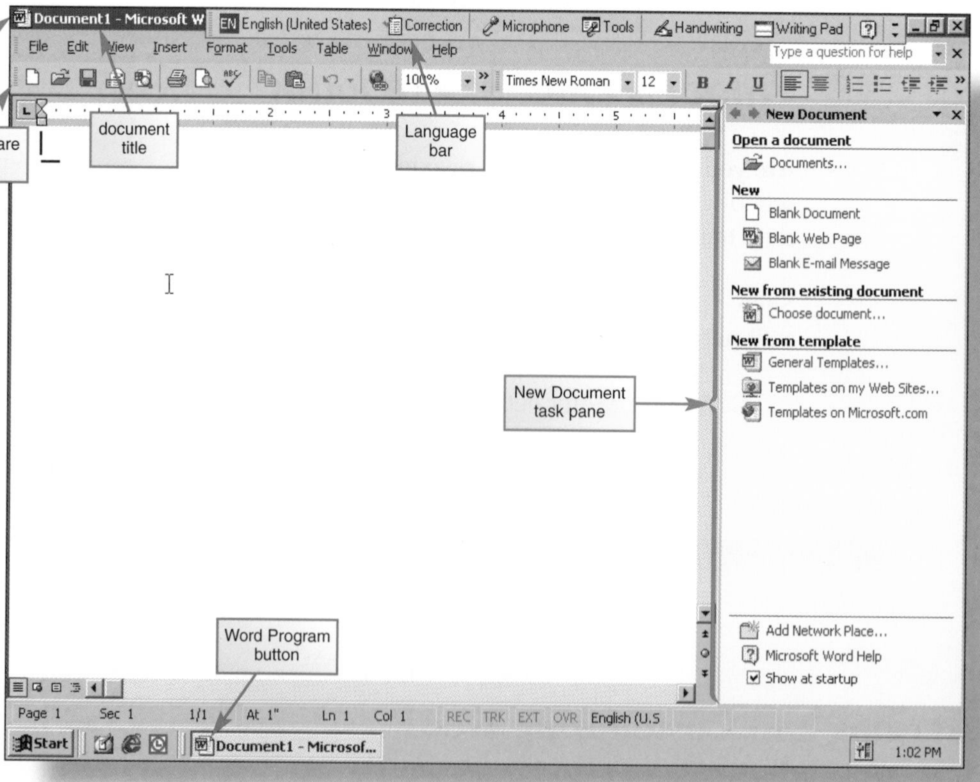

FIGURE 1-3

3 If the Word window is not maximized, double-click its title bar to maximize it.

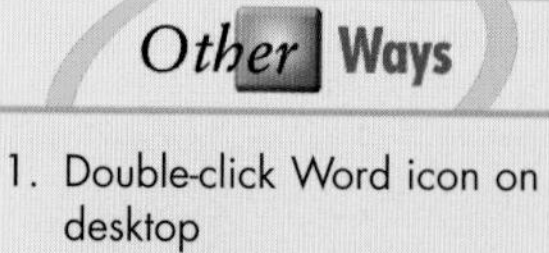

1. Double-click Word icon on desktop
2. Click Start button, click New Office Document, click General tab, double-click Blank Document icon

The screen in Figure 1-3 shows how the Word window looks the first time you start Word after installation on most computers. If the Office Speech Recognition software is installed on your computer, then when you start Word either the Language bar displays somewhere on the desktop (shown at the top of Figure 1-3) or the Language Indicator button displays on the right side of the Windows taskbar (Figure 1-5 on the next page). In this book, the Language bar will be kept minimized until it is used. For additional information about the Language bar, see page WD 1.17 and Appendix B.

Notice also that the New Document task pane displays on the screen, and that the buttons on the toolbars display on a single row. A **task pane** is a separate window that enables users to carry out some Word tasks more efficiently. In this book, to allow the maximum typing area in Word, a task pane should not display when you start Word. For more efficient use of the buttons on the toolbars, they should display on two separate rows instead of sharing a single row.

Perform the following steps to minimize the Language bar, close the New Document task pane, and display the toolbars on two separate rows.

More About

Task Panes

When you first start Word, a small window called a task pane may display docked on the right side of the screen. You can drag a task pane title bar to float the pane in your work area or dock it on either the left or right side of a screen, depending on your personal preference.

Steps To Customize the Word Window

1 If the Language bar displays, point to its Minimize button (Figure 1-4).

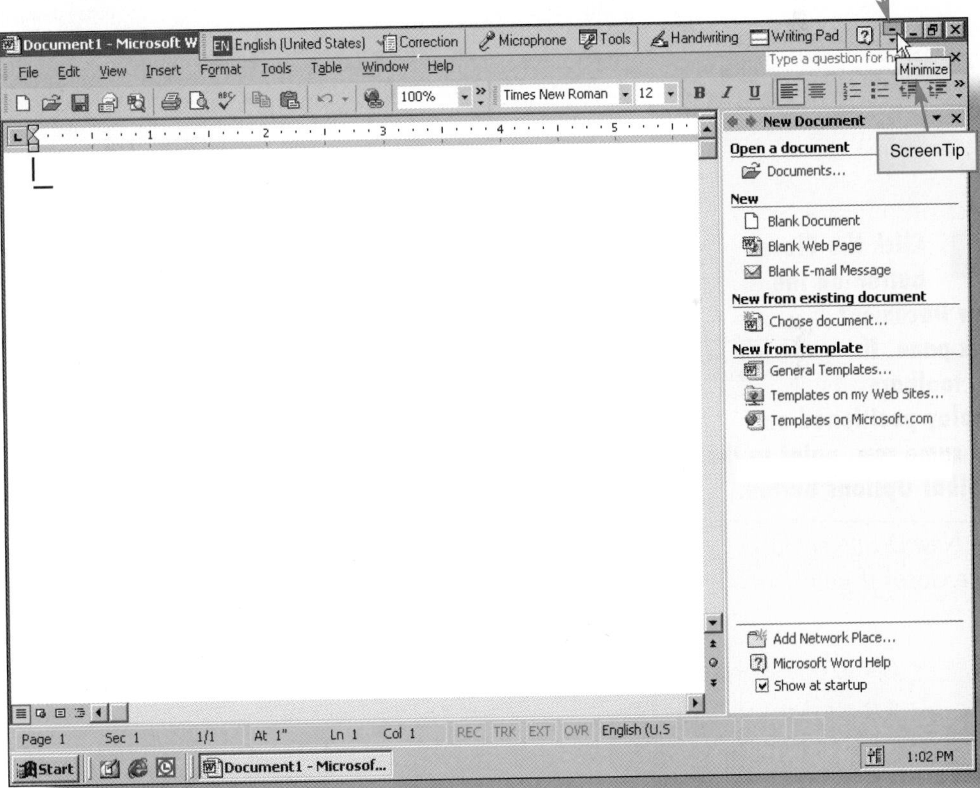

FIGURE 1-4

2 **Click the Minimize button on the Language bar. If the New Document task pane displays, click the Show at startup check box to remove the check mark and then point to the Close button in the upper-right corner of the task pane title bar.**

Word minimizes the Language bar (Figure 1-5). With the check mark removed from the Show at startup check box, Word will not display the New Document task pane the next time Word starts.

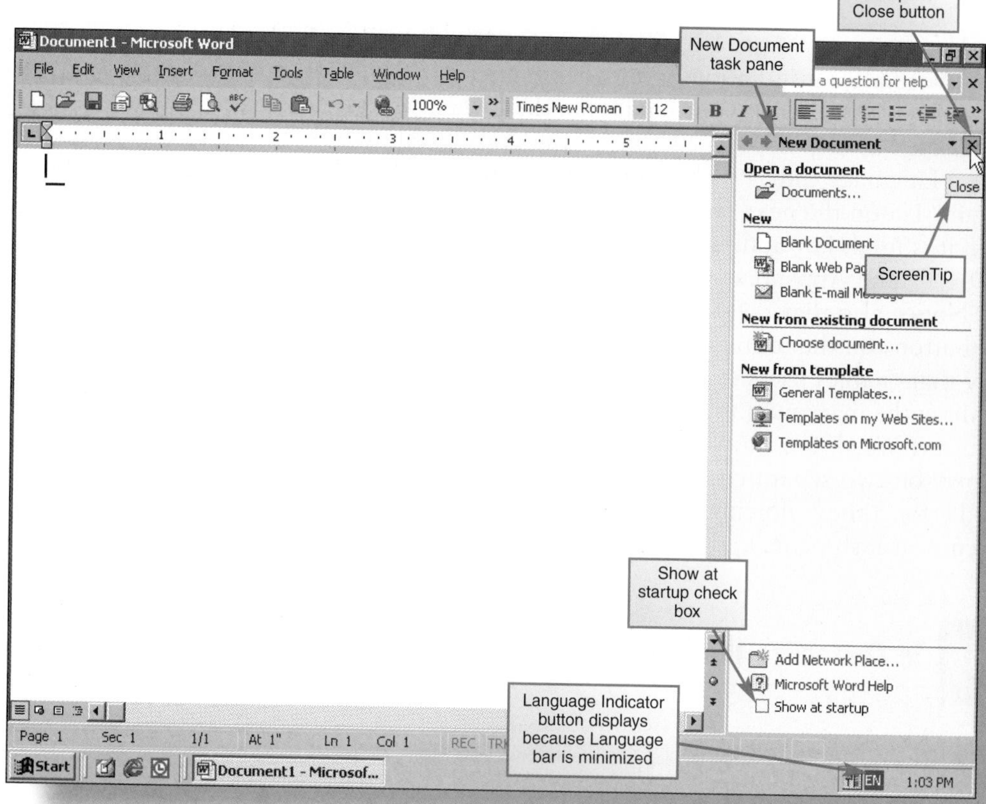

FIGURE 1-5

3 **Click the Close button on the New Document task pane. If the toolbars display positioned on the same row, point to the Toolbar Options button.**

The New Document task pane closes (Figure 1-6).

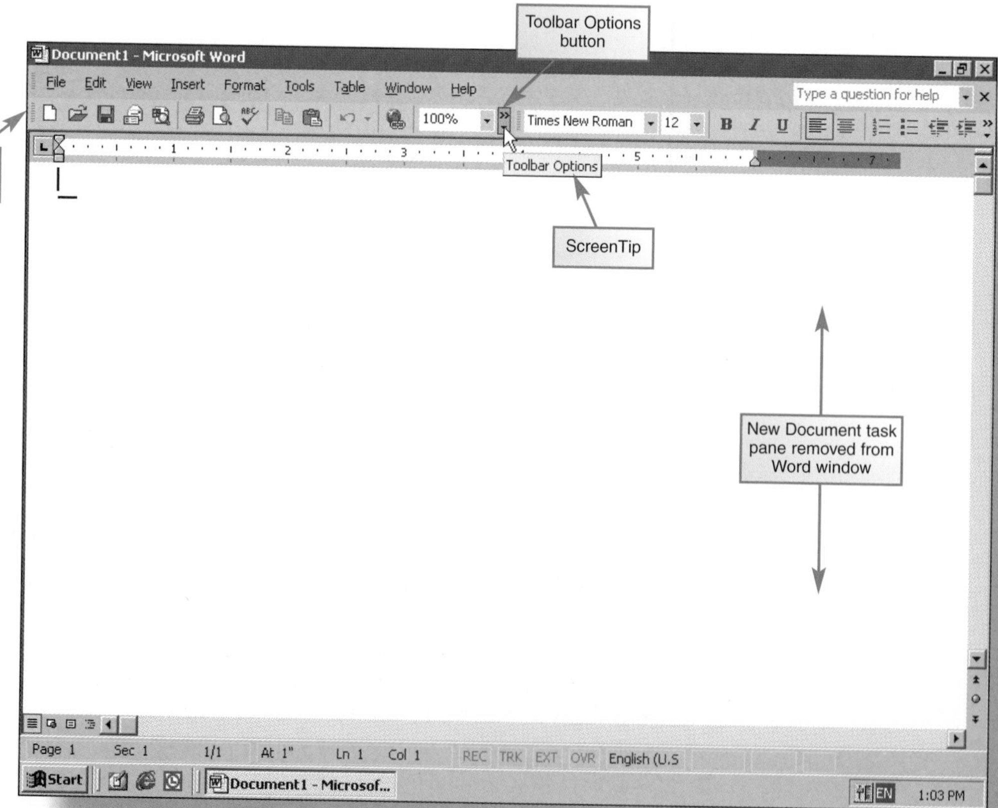

FIGURE 1-6

4 Click the Toolbar Options button and then point to Show Buttons on Two Rows.

Word displays the Toolbar Options list (Figure 1-7). The Toolbar Options list contains buttons that do not fit on the toolbars when the toolbars display on one row.

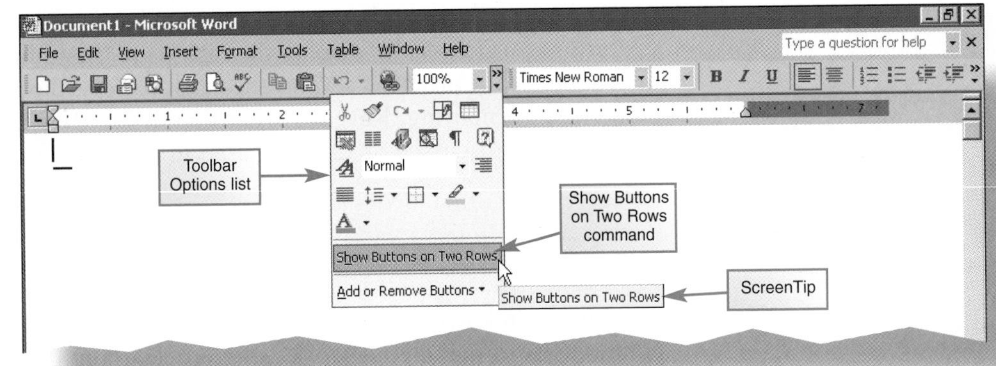

FIGURE 1-7

5 Click Show Buttons on Two Rows. If your screen differs from Figure 1-8, click View on the menu bar and then click Normal.

Word displays the toolbars on two separate rows (Figure 1-8). The Toolbar Options list is empty because all of the buttons fit on the toolbars when they display on two rows.

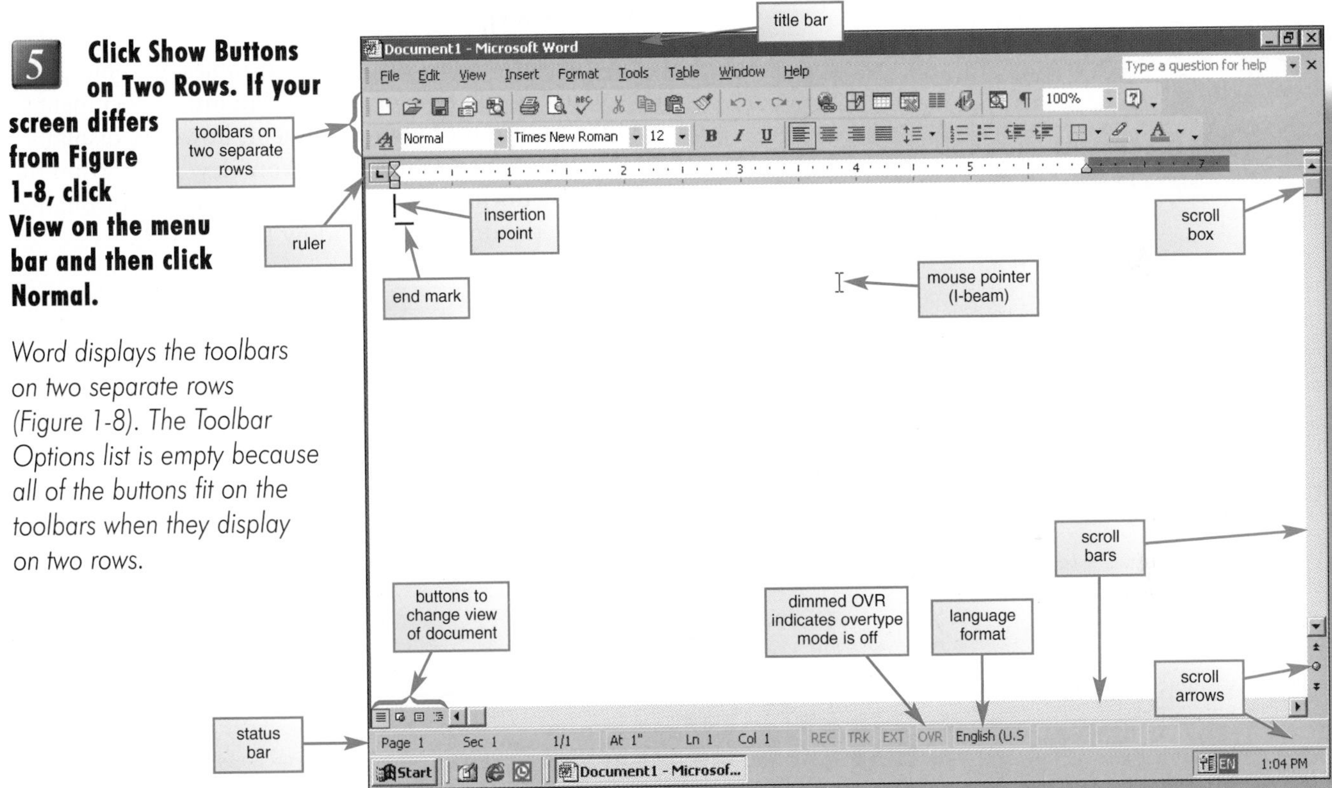

FIGURE 1-8

As an alternative to Steps 4 and 5 above, you can point to the left edge of the Formatting toolbar, and when the mouse pointer changes to a four-headed arrow, drag the toolbar down below the Standard toolbar to create two rows.

When you point to many objects in the Word window, such as a button or command, Word displays a ScreenTip. A **ScreenTip** is a short on-screen note associated with the object to which you are pointing. Examples of ScreenTips are shown in Figures 1-2, 1-4, 1-5, 1-6, and 1-7 on this and the previous pages.

Each time you start Word, the Word window displays the same way it did the last time you used Word. If the toolbars displayed on one row, then they will display on one row the next time you start Word. Similarly, if the Show at startup check box in the New Document task pane contains a check mark, then this task pane will display the next time you start Word.

More About

The Office Assistant

The Office Assistant is an animated object that can answer questions for you. On some installations, the Office Assistant may display when Word starts. If the Office Assistant displays on your screen, right-click it and then click Hide on the shortcut menu.

As you work through creating a document, you will find that certain Word operations automatically display the task pane. In addition to the New Document task pane, Word provides seven other task panes: Clipboard, Search, Insert Clip Art, Styles and Formatting, Reveal Formatting, Mail Merge, and Translate. These task panes will be discussed as they are used in the projects.

The Word Window

The **Word window** (Figure 1-8 on the previous page) consists of a variety of components to make your work more efficient and documents more professional. The following sections discuss these components.

Document Window

The **document window** displays text, tables, graphics, and other items as you type or insert them into a document. Only a portion of your document, however, displays on the screen at one time. You view the portion of the document displayed on the screen through the document window (Figure 1-9).

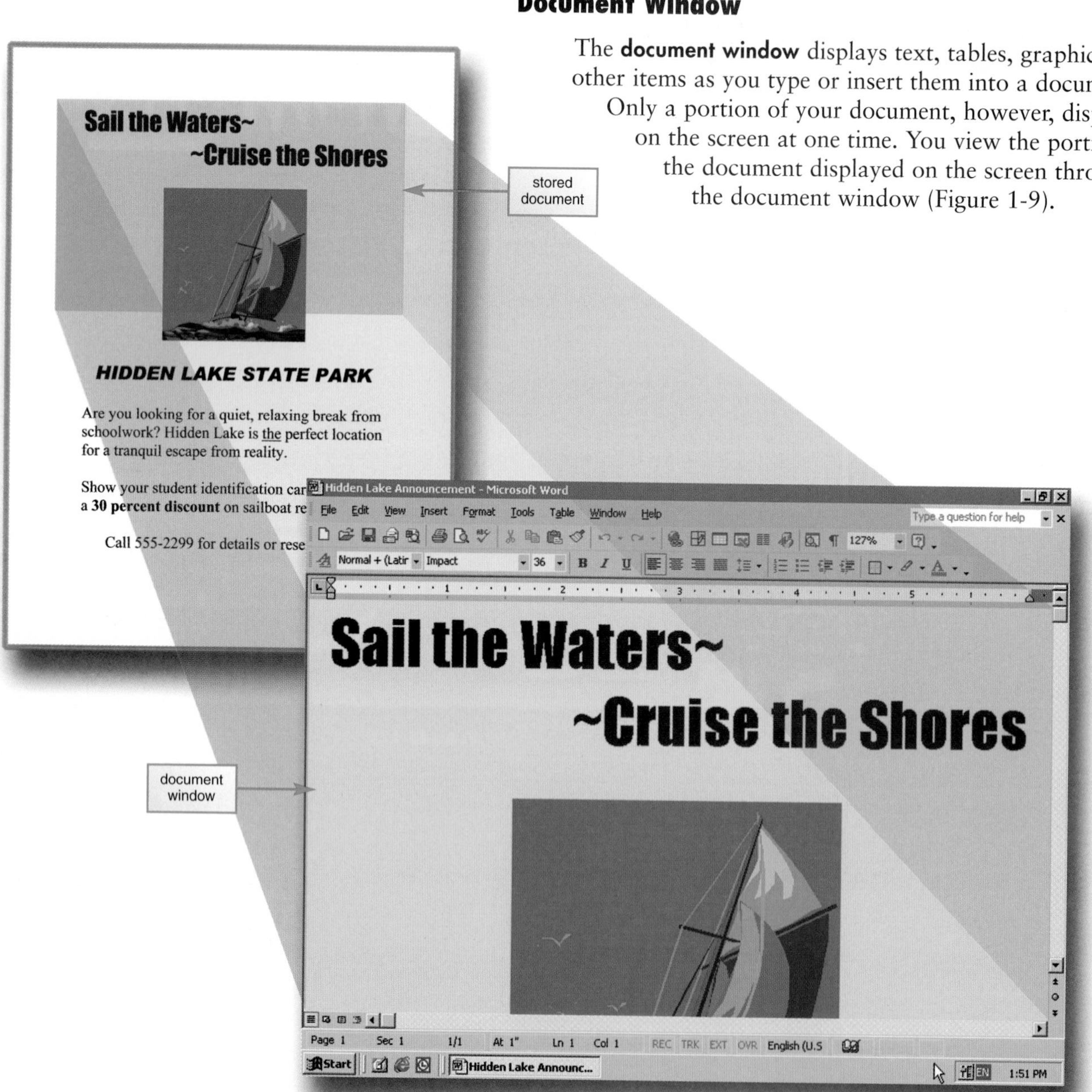

FIGURE 1-9

The document window contains several elements commonly found in other applications, as well as some elements unique to Word. The main elements of the Word document window are the insertion point, end mark, mouse pointer, rulers, scroll bars, and status bar (Figure 1-8 on page WD 1.11).

INSERTION POINT The **insertion point** is a blinking vertical bar that indicates where text will be inserted as you type. As you type, the insertion point moves to the right and, when you reach the end of a line, it moves downward to the beginning of the next line. You also can insert graphics, tables, and other items at the location of the insertion point.

END MARK The **end mark** is a short horizontal line that indicates the end of your document. Each time you begin a new line, the end mark moves downward.

MOUSE POINTER The **mouse pointer** becomes different shapes depending on the task you are performing in Word and the pointer's location on the screen. The mouse pointer in Figure 1-8 has the shape of an I-beam. Other mouse pointer shapes are described as they appear on the screen during this and subsequent projects.

RULERS At the top edge of the document window is the **horizontal ruler.** You use the horizontal ruler, usually simply called the ruler, to set tab stops, indent paragraphs, adjust column widths, and change page margins.

An additional ruler, called the vertical ruler, sometimes displays at the left edge of the Word window when you perform certain tasks. The purpose of the vertical ruler is discussed as it displays on the screen in a later project. If your screen displays a vertical ruler, click View on the menu bar and then click Normal.

SCROLL BARS By using the **scroll bars**, you can display different portions of your document in the document window. At the right edge of the document window is a vertical scroll bar. At the bottom of the document window is a horizontal scroll bar. On both the vertical and horizontal scroll bars, the position of the **scroll box** reflects the location of the portion of the document displaying in the document window.

On the left edge of the horizontal scroll bar are four buttons you can use to change the view of a document. On the bottom of the vertical scroll bar are three buttons you can use to scroll through a document. These buttons are discussed as they are used in later projects.

STATUS BAR The status bar displays at the bottom of the document window, above the Windows taskbar. The **status bar** presents information about the location of the insertion point and the progress of current tasks, as well as the status of certain commands, keys, and buttons.

From left to right, the following information displays on the status bar in Figure 1-9: the page number, the section number, the page containing the insertion point followed by the total number of pages in the document, the position of the insertion point in inches from the top of the page, the line number and column number of the insertion point, followed by several status indicators.

You use the **status indicators** to turn certain keys or modes on or off. The first four status indicators (REC, TRK, EXT, and OVR) display darkened when on and dimmed when off. For example, the dimmed OVR indicates overtype mode is off. To turn these four status indicators on or off, double-click the status indicator. These status indicators are discussed as they are used in the projects.

More About

The Horizontal Ruler

If the horizontal ruler does not display on your screen, click View on the menu bar and then click Ruler. To hide the ruler, also click View on the menu bar and then click Ruler.

More About

Scroll Bars

You can use the vertical scroll bar to scroll through multi-page documents. As you drag the scroll box up or down the scroll bar, Word displays a page indicator to the left of the scroll box. When you release the mouse button, the document window displays the page shown in the page indicator.

More About

Languages

If support for multiple languages was installed on your computer, the status bar also displays the language format, which shows the name of the language you are using to create the document. You add languages through the Control Panel. Double-click the Text Services icon in the Control Panel. Click the Add button in the Installed Services area in the Text Services dialog box. Select the desired language in the Add Input Language dialog box and then click the OK button in each open dialog box.

The next status indicator displays the name of the language that appears at the location of the insertion point. In Figure 1-9 on page WD 1.12, the indicated language is English (U.S.). Word automatically detects the language as you type. Most installations of Word can detect more than 60 languages, including Chinese, Dutch, English, French, German, Italian, Japanese, and Russian. This means Word can check the spelling, grammar, and punctuation in each of these languages.

The remaining status indicators display icons as you perform certain tasks. When you begin typing in the document window, a Spelling and Grammar Status icon displays. When Word is saving your document, a Background Save icon displays. When you print a document, a Background Print icon displays. If you perform a task that requires several seconds (such as saving a document), the status bar displays a message informing you of the progress of the task.

Menu Bar and Toolbars

The menu bar and toolbars display at the top of the screen just below the title bar (Figure 1-10).

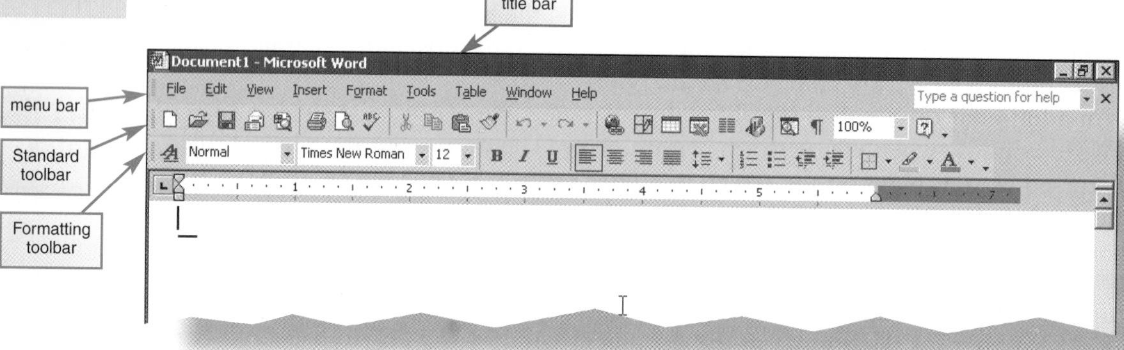

FIGURE 1-10

Menus

Right-clicking an object displays a shortcut menu (also called a context-sensitive or object menu). Depending on the object, the commands in the shortcut menu vary.

MENU BAR The **menu bar** is a special toolbar that displays the Word menu names. Each **menu** contains a list of commands you can use to perform tasks such as retrieving, storing, printing, and formatting data in your document. When you point to a menu name on the menu bar, the area of the menu bar containing the name changes to a button. To display a menu, such as the Edit menu, click the Edit menu name on the menu bar. If you point to a command on a menu that has an arrow to its right edge, a **submenu** displays another list of commands.

When you click a menu name on the menu bar, a **short menu** displays that lists your most recently used commands, as shown in Figure 1-11a.

If you wait a few seconds or click the arrows at the bottom of the short menu, it expands into a full menu. A **full menu** lists all the commands associated with a menu, as shown in Figure 1-11b. You immediately can display a full menu by double-clicking the menu name on the menu bar. In this book, when you display a menu, always display the full menu using one of these techniques:

1. Click the menu name on the menu bar and then wait a few seconds.
2. Click the menu name on the menu bar and then click the arrows at the bottom of the short menu.
3. Click the menu name on the menu bar and then point to the arrows at the bottom of the short menu.
4. Double-click the menu name on the menu bar.

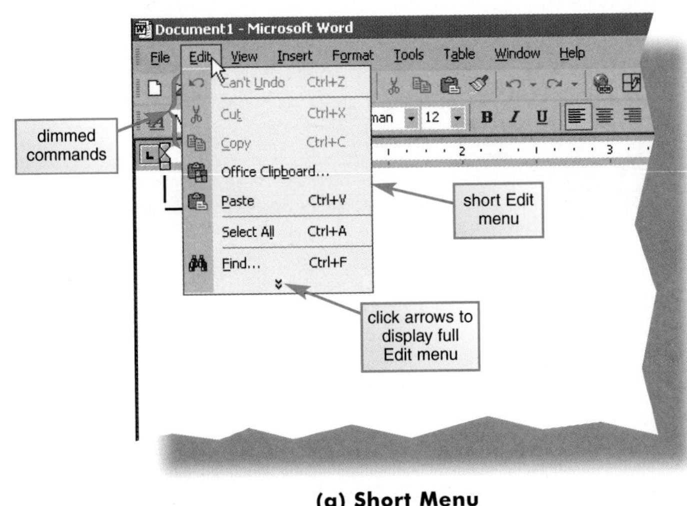

(a) Short Menu

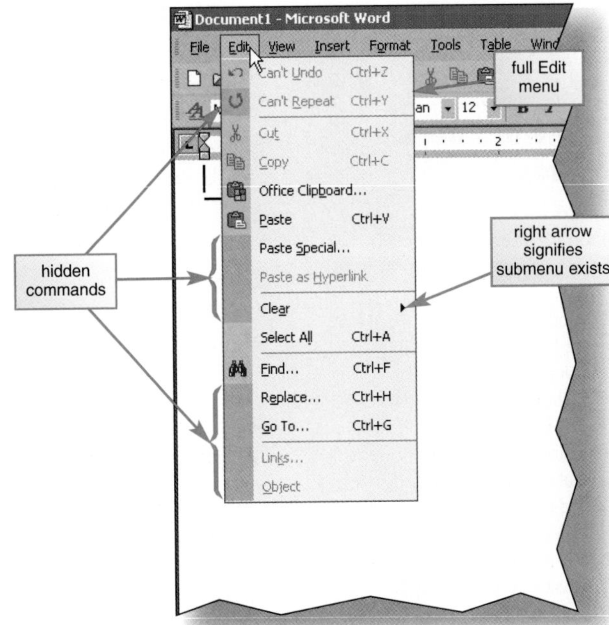

(b) Full Menu

FIGURE 1-11

Both short and full menus display some **dimmed commands** that appear gray, or dimmed, instead of black, which indicates they are not available for the current selection. A command with a dark gray shading in the rectangle to the left of it on a full menu is called a **hidden command** because it does not display on a short menu. As you use Word, it automatically personalizes the short menus for you based on how often you use commands. That is, as you use hidden commands on the full menu, Word *unhides* them and places them on the short menu.

TOOLBARS Word has many pre-defined, or built-in, toolbars. A **toolbar** contains buttons, boxes, and menus that allow you to perform tasks more quickly than using the menu bar and related menus. For example, to print a document, you click the Print button on a toolbar. Each button on a toolbar displays an image to help you remember its function. Also, when you point to a button or box on a toolbar, a ScreenTip displays below the mouse pointer (Figure 1-6 on page WD 1.10).

Two built-in toolbars are the Standard toolbar and the Formatting toolbar. Figure 1-12a illustrates the **Standard toolbar** and identifies its buttons and boxes. Figure 1-12b on the next page illustrates the **Formatting toolbar**. Each button and box is explained in detail as it is used in the projects throughout the book.

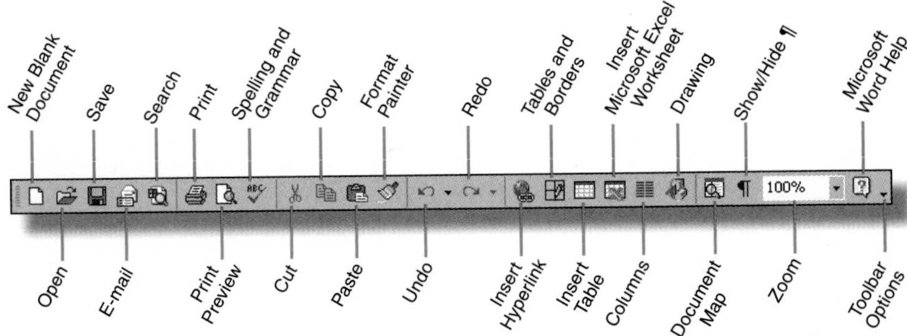

FIGURE 1-12a Standard Toolbar

The Word Help System

Need Help? It is no further than the Ask a Question box in the upper-right corner of the window. Click the box that contains the text, Type a question for help (Figure 1-13a), type `help`, and then press the ENTER key. Word will respond with a list of items you can click to learn about obtaining help on any Word-related topic. To find out what is new in Word 2002, type `what's new in Word` in the Ask a Question box.

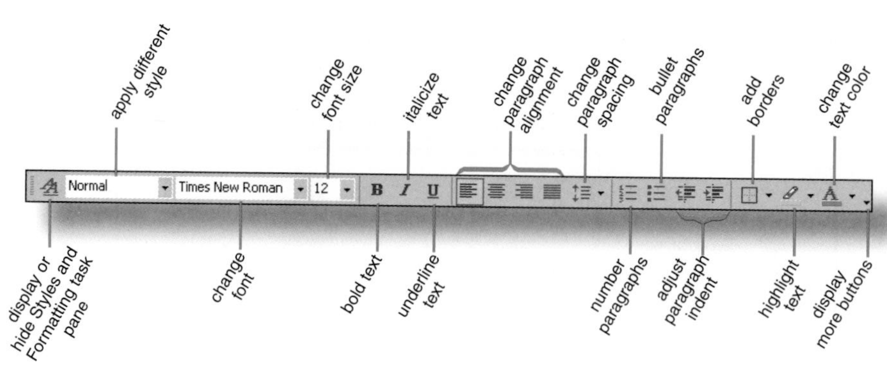

FIGURE 1-12b Formatting Toolbar

When you first install Word, the Standard and Formatting toolbars are preset to display on the same row immediately below the menu bar (Figure 1-13a). Unless the resolution of your display device is greater than 800 × 600, many of the buttons that belong to these toolbars do not display when the two toolbars share one row. The buttons that display on the toolbar are the more frequently used buttons. Hidden buttons display in the Toolbar Options list. When you click the Toolbar Options button on a toolbar, Word displays a Toolbar Options list that contains the toolbar's hidden buttons (Figure 1-13b). In this mode, you also can display all the buttons on either toolbar by double-clicking the **move handle** on the left of each toolbar.

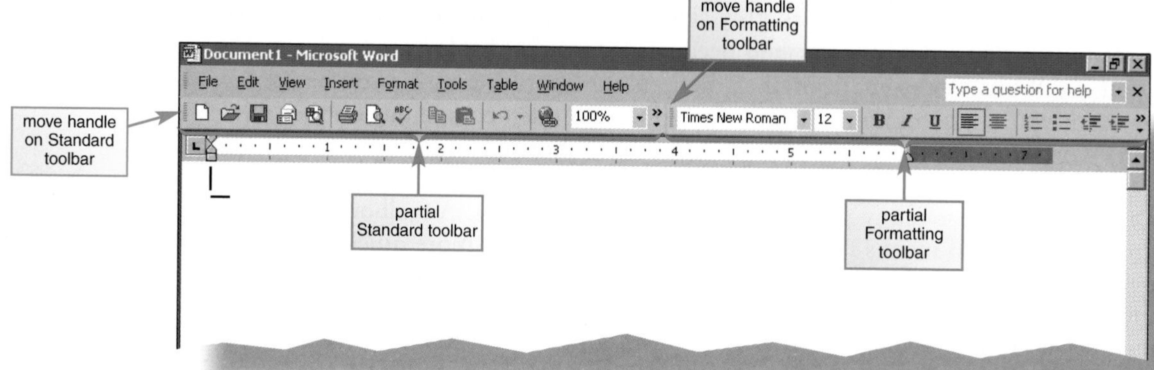

FIGURE 1-13a

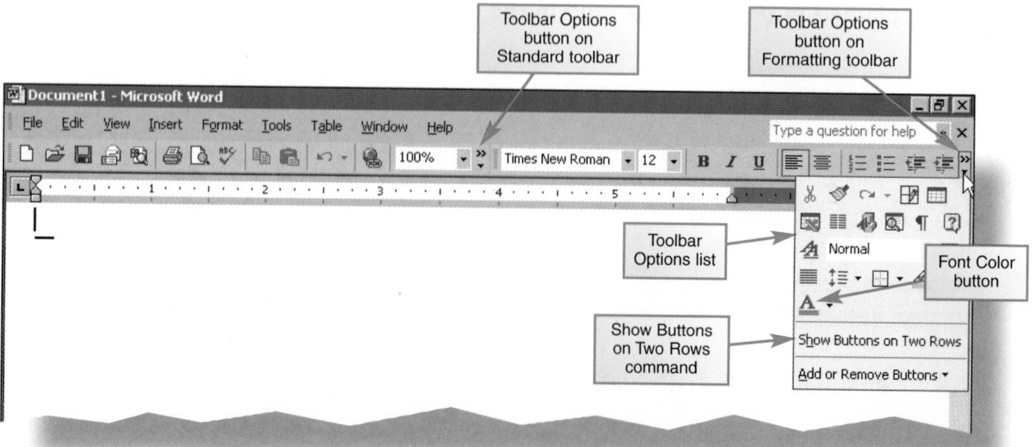

FIGURE 1-13b

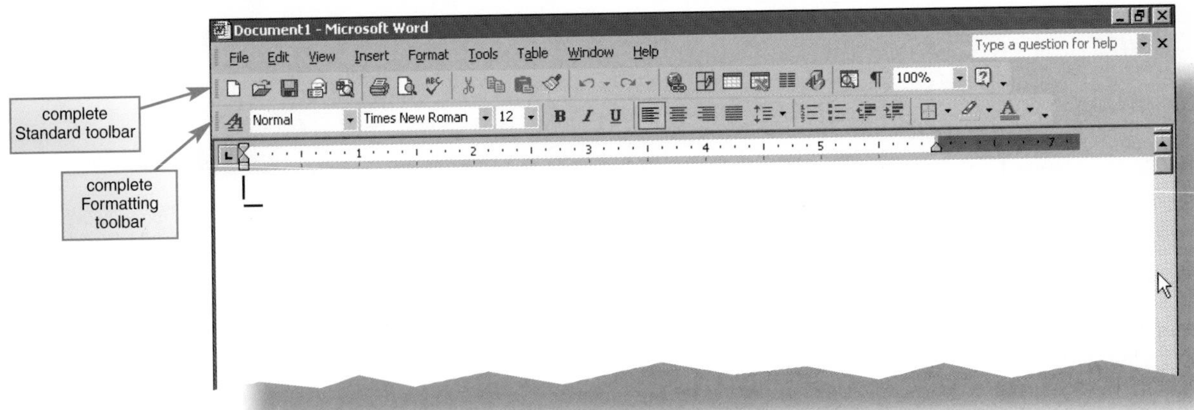

FIGURE 1-13c

In this book, the Standard and Formatting toolbars are shown on separate rows, one below the other so that all buttons display (Figure 1-13c). You show the two toolbars on two rows by clicking the Show Buttons on Two Rows command in the Toolbar Options list (Figure 1-13b).

In the previous figures, the Standard and Formatting toolbars are docked. A **docked toolbar** is one that is attached to the edge of the Word window. Depending on the task you are performing, additional toolbars may display on the Word screen. These additional toolbars display either docked or floating in the Word window. A **floating toolbar** is not attached to an edge of the Word window; that is, it displays in the middle of the Word window. You can rearrange the order of docked toolbars and can move floating toolbars anywhere in the Word window. Later in this book, steps are presented that show you how to float a docked toolbar or dock a floating toolbar.

Resetting Menus and Toolbars

Each project in this book begins with the menus and toolbars appearing as they did at the initial installation of the software. To reset your menus and toolbars so they appear exactly as shown in this book, follow the steps in Appendix D.

Speech Recognition and Handwriting Recognition

With the **Office Speech Recognition software** installed and a microphone, you can speak the names of toolbar buttons, menus, menu commands, list items, alerts, and dialog box controls, such as OK and Cancel. You also can dictate text, such as words and sentences.

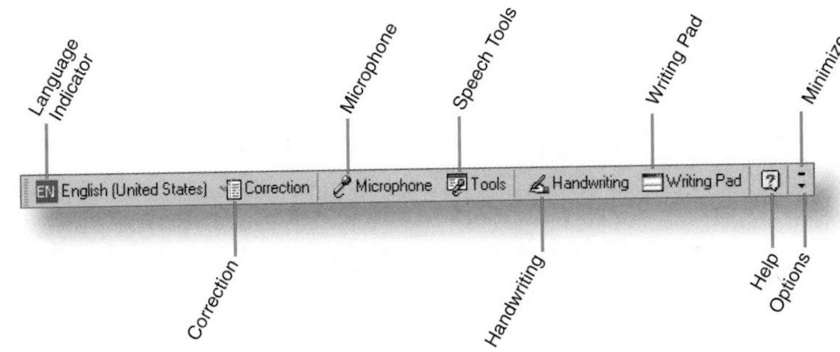

FIGURE 1-14a Language Bar

To indicate whether you want to speak commands or dictate text, you use the **Language bar** (Figure 1-14a). You can display the Language bar in two ways: (1) click the Language Indicator button in the taskbar tray status area by the clock and then click Show the Language bar on the menu (Figure 1-14b on the next page), or (2) click Tools on the menu bar and then click Speech.

More About

Speech Recognition

If Office Speech Recognition software is installed on your computer, you can speak instructions to Word including toolbar button names, menu names and commands, and items in dialog boxes and task panes. You also can dictate so Word writes exactly what you say. The microphone picks up others' voices and background sounds, so speech recognition is most effective when used in a quiet environment.

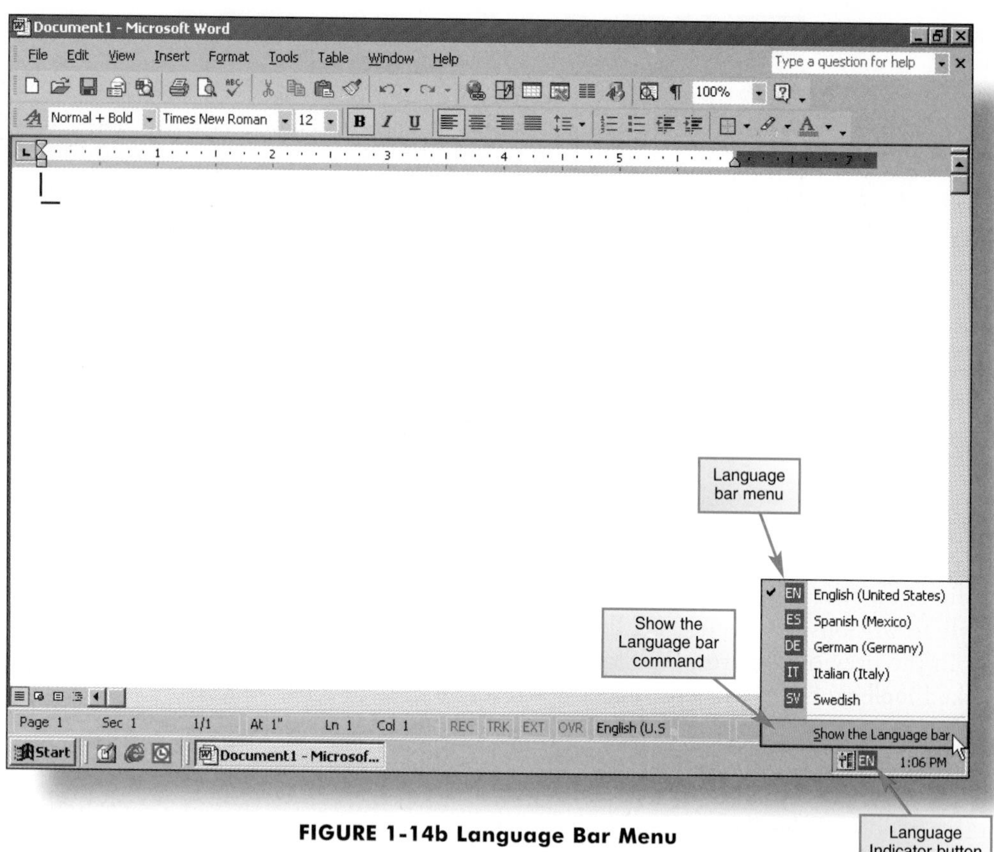

FIGURE 1-14b Language Bar Menu

If the Language Indicator button does not display in the taskbar tray status area, the Office Speech Recognition software may not be installed. To install the software, you first must start Word and then click Speech on the Tools menu.

You can use the speech recognition and handwriting recognition capabilities of Office XP to enter text into Word by speaking or writing, instead of typing. Additional information on the Office Speech Recognition, Handwriting Recognition, and other text services is available in Appendix B.

More About

Handwriting Recognition

If Handwriting Recognition software is installed on your computer, Word can recognize text as you write it on a handwriting input device, such as graphics tablet, or with the mouse. To use the mouse, you drag the mouse to form the cursive characters. If you have a handheld computer, or PDA, you also can convert the handheld computer's handwritten notes into text in Word.

Zooming Page Width

Depending on your Windows and Word settings, the horizontal ruler at the top of the document window may show more inches or fewer inches than the ruler shown in Figure 1-15. The more inches of ruler that display, the smaller the text will be on the screen. The fewer inches of ruler that display, the larger the text will be on the screen. To minimize eyestrain, the projects in this book display the text as large as possible without extending the right margin beyond the right edge of the document window.

Two factors that affect how much of the ruler displays in the document window are the Windows screen resolution and the Word zoom percentage. The screens in this book use a resolution of 800 × 600. With this resolution, you can increase the preset zoom percentage beyond 100% so that the right margin extends to the edge of the document window. To increase or decrease the size of the displayed characters to a point where both the left and right margins are at the edges of the document window, use the **zoom page width** command as shown in the following steps.

Steps To Zoom Page Width

1 **Click the Zoom box arrow on the Standard toolbar and then point to Page Width.**

Word displays a list of available zoom percentages and the Page Width option in the Zoom list (Figure 1-15).

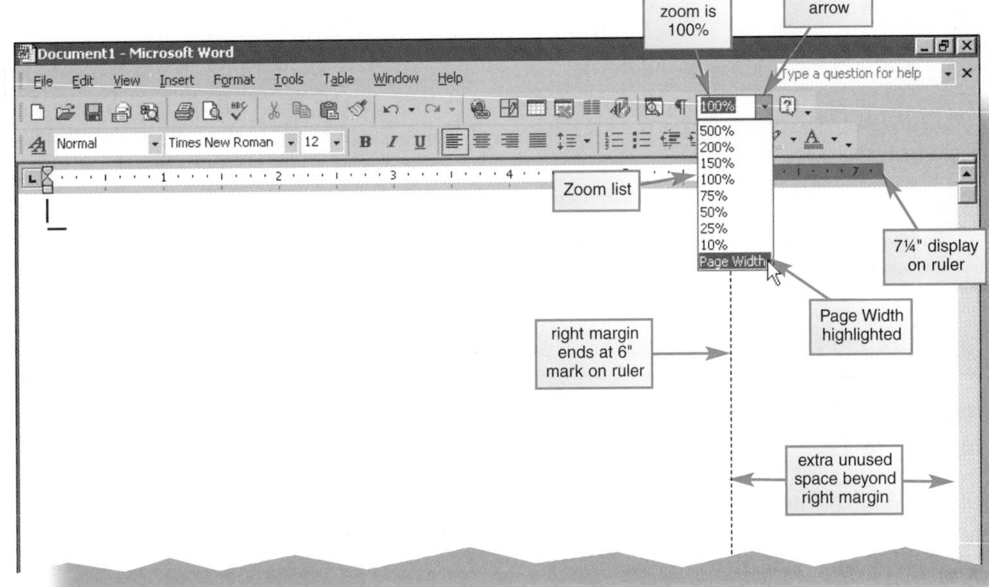

FIGURE 1-15

2 **Click Page Width.**

Word extends the right margin to the right edge of the document window (Figure 1-16).

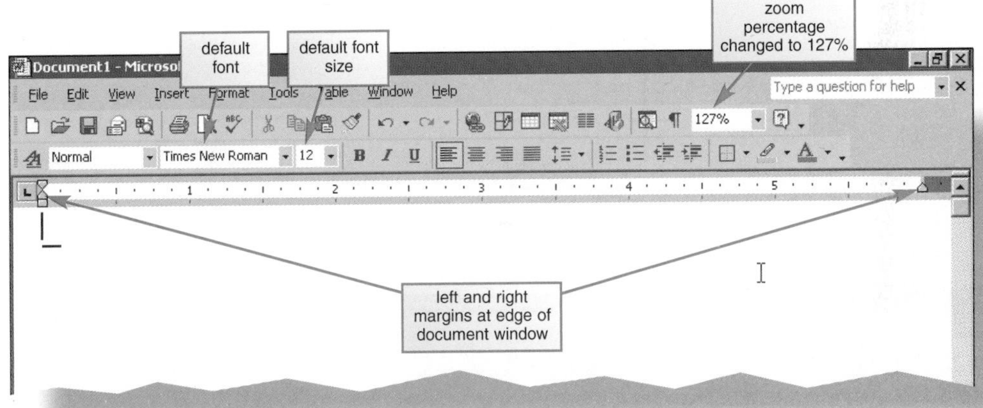

FIGURE 1-16

Other Ways

1. On View menu click Zoom, select Page width, click OK button
2. In Voice Command mode, say "Zoom, Page Width"

If your Zoom list (Figure 1-15) displayed additional options, click View on the menu bar and then click Normal.

The Zoom box in Figure 1-16 displays 127%, which Word computes based on a variety of settings. Your percentage may be different depending on your computer configuration.

Changing the Default Font Size

Characters that display on the screen are a specific shape, size, and style. The **font**, or typeface, defines the appearance and shape of the letters, numbers, and special characters. The preset, or **default**, font is Times New Roman (Figure 1-16). **Font size** specifies the size of the characters and is determined by a measurement system called

More About

Zooming

If you want to zoom to a percentage not in the Zoom list, click the Zoom box on the Standard toolbar, type the desired percentage, and then press the ENTER key.

More About

Font Size

An announcement usually is posted on a wall. Thus, its font size should be as large as possible so that all potential readers easily can see it.

points. A single **point** is about 1/72 of one inch in height. Thus, a character with a font size of 12 is about 12/72 or 1/6 of one inch in height. On most computers, the default font size in Word is 12.

If more of the characters in your document require a larger font size than the default, you easily can change the default font size before you type. In Project 1, many of the characters in the body of the announcement are a font size of 22. Perform the following steps to increase the font size before you begin entering text.

Steps To Increase the Default Font Size Before Typing

1 Click the Font Size box arrow on the Formatting toolbar and then point to 22.

A list of available font sizes displays in the Font Size list (Figure 1-17). The available font sizes depend on the current font, which is Times New Roman.

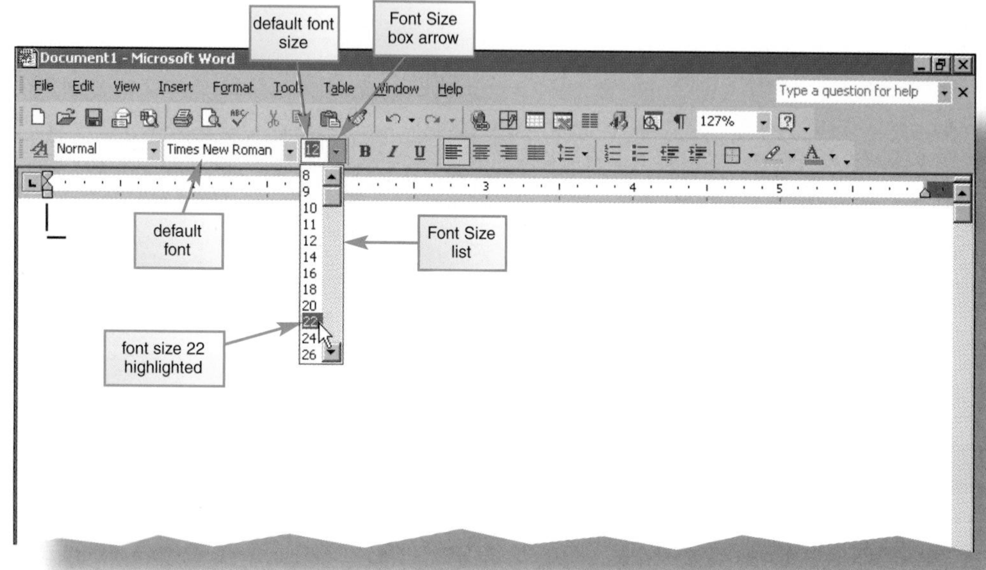

FIGURE 1-17

2 Click 22.

The font size for characters entered in this document changes to 22 (Figure 1-18). The size of the insertion point increases to reflect the new font size.

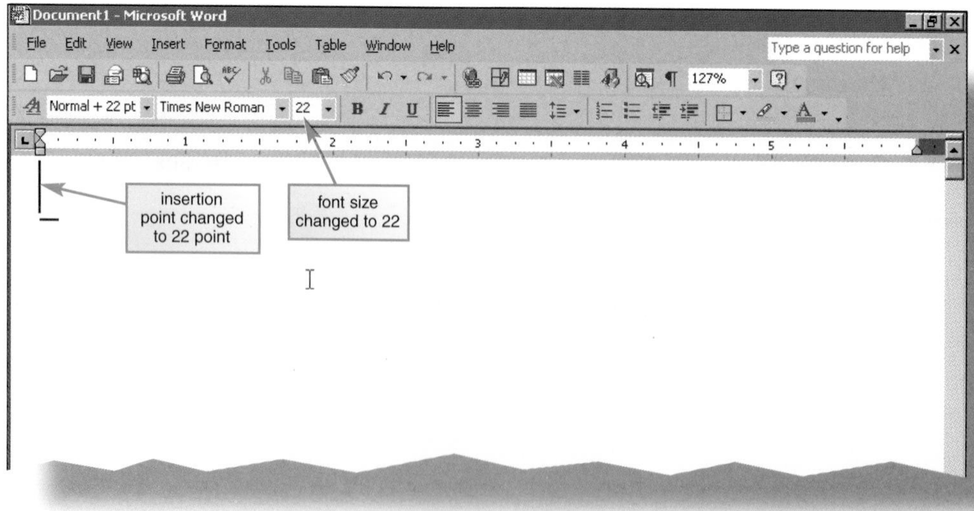

FIGURE 1-18

Other Ways

1. Right-click paragraph mark above end mark, click Font on shortcut menu, click Font tab, select desired font size in Size list, click OK button
2. On Format menu click Font, click Font tab, select desired font size in Size list, click OK button
3. Press CTRL+SHIFT+P, type desired font size, press ENTER
4. In Voice Command mode, say "Font Size, [select font size]"

The new font size takes effect immediately in your document. Word uses this font size for characters you type into this announcement.

Entering Text

To enter text into a document, you type on the keyboard or speak into the microphone. The following example illustrates the steps required to type both lines in the headline of the announcement. These lines will be positioned at the left margin. Later in this project, you will format the headline so that both lines are bold and enlarged and the second line is positioned at the right margin.

Perform the following steps to begin entering the document text.

The Tilde Key

On most keyboards, the TILDE (~) key is located just below the ESCAPE key and just above the TAB key. The tilde is the top character on the key. Thus, to display the tilde character on the screen, press the SHIFT key while pressing the TILDE key.

To Enter Text

1 **Type** `Sail the Waters` **and then press the TILDE (~) key. If you make an error while typing, press the BACKSPACE key until you have deleted the text in error and then retype the text correctly.**

As you type, the insertion point moves to the right (Figure 1-19). On most keyboards, the TILDE (~) key is immediately below the ESCAPE key.

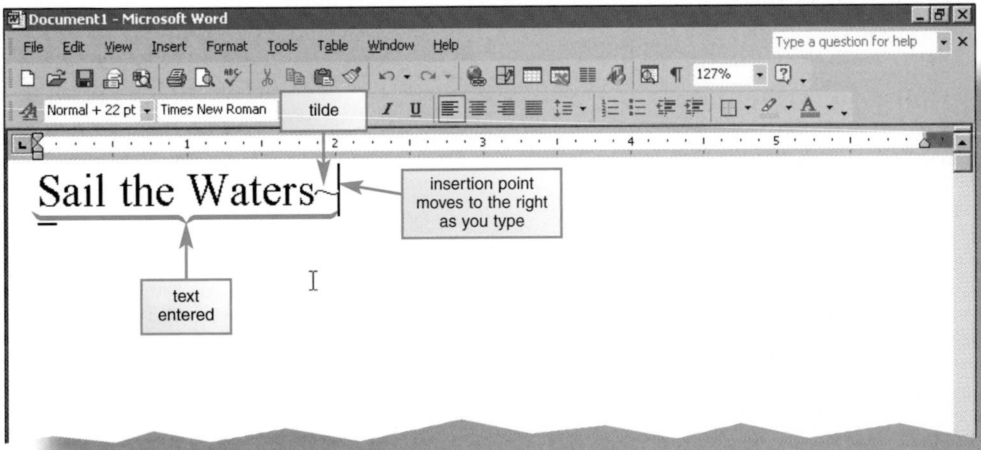

FIGURE 1-19

2 **Press the ENTER key.**

Word moves the insertion point to the beginning of the next line (Figure 1-20). Notice the status bar indicates the current position of the insertion point. That is, the insertion point currently is on line 2 column 1.

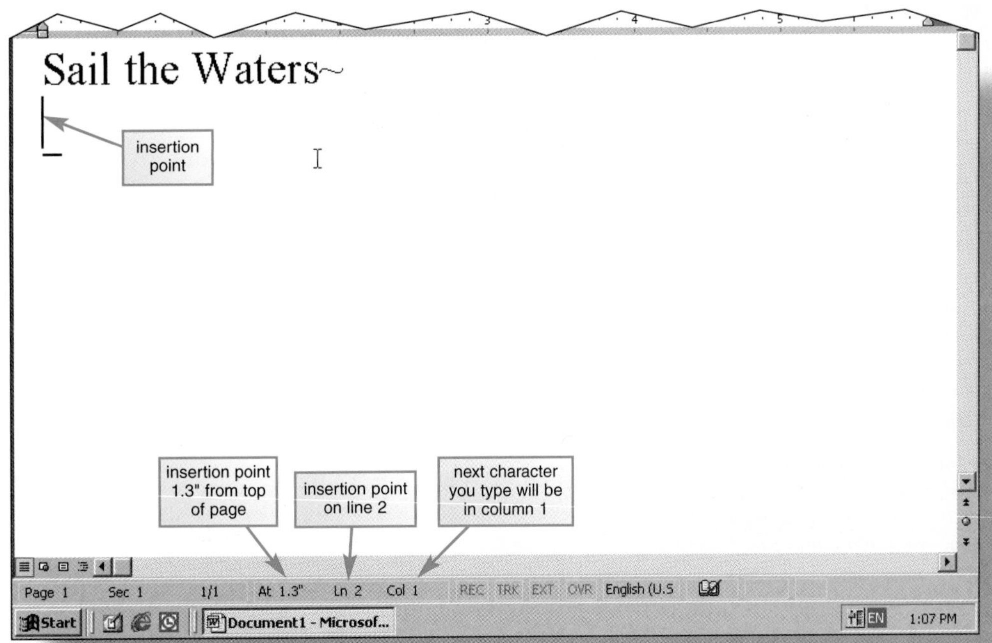

FIGURE 1-20

3 **Press the TILDE (~) key. Type** `Cruise the Shores` **and then press the ENTER key.**

The headline is complete (Figure 1-21). The insertion point is on line 3.

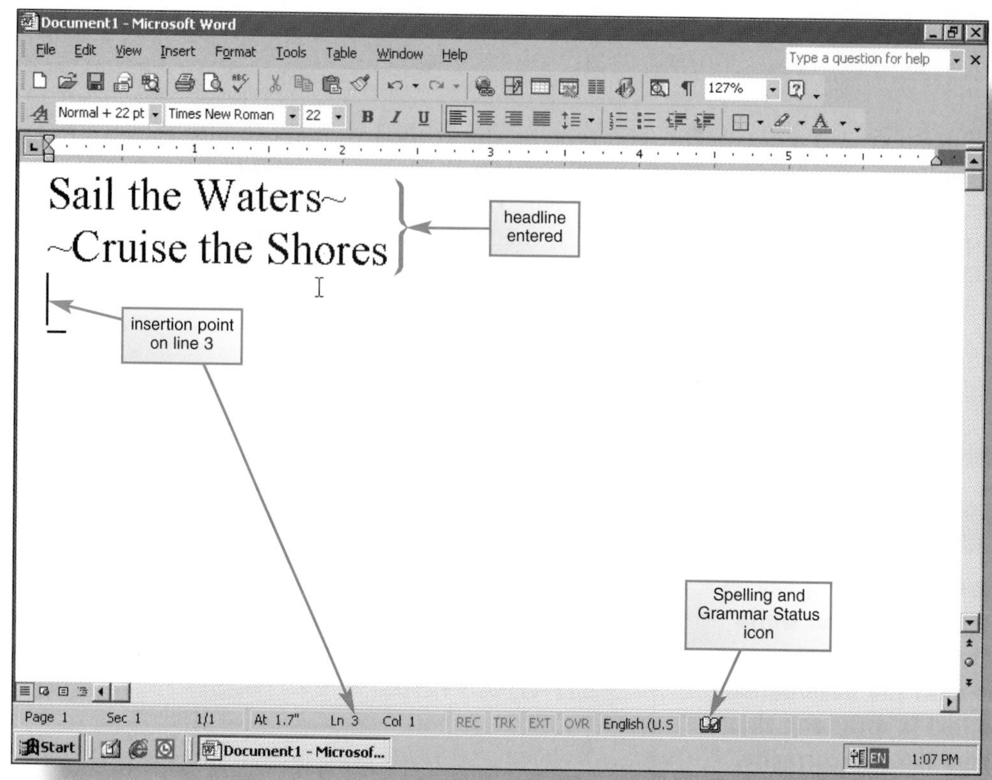

FIGURE 1-21

Other Ways

1. In Dictation mode, say "Sail the Waters, Tilde, New Line, Tilde, Cruise the Shores, New Line"

When you begin entering text into a document, the **Spelling and Grammar Status icon** displays at the right of the status bar (Figure 1-21). As you type, the Spelling and Grammar Status icon shows an animated pencil writing on paper, which indicates Word is checking for possible errors. When you stop typing, the pencil changes to either a red check mark or a red X. In Figure 1-21, the Spelling and Grammar Status icon displays a red check mark.

In general, if all of the words you have typed are in Word's dictionary and your grammar is correct, a red check mark displays on the Spelling and Grammar Status icon. If you type a word not in the dictionary (because it is a proper name or misspelled), a red wavy underline displays below the word. If you type text that may be incorrect grammatically, a green wavy underline displays below the text. When Word flags a possible spelling or grammar error, it also changes the red check mark on the Spelling and Grammar Status icon to a red X. As you enter text into the announcement, your Spelling and Grammar Status icon may show a red X instead of a red check mark. Later in this project, you will check the spelling of these words. At that time, the red X will return to a red check mark.

More About

Entering Text

In the days of typewriters, the letter l was used for both the letter l and the numeral one. Keyboards, however, have both a numeral one and the letter l. Keyboards also have both a numeral zero and the letter o. Be careful to press the correct keyboard character when creating a word processing document.

Entering Blank Lines into a Document

To enter a blank line into a document, press the ENTER key without typing any text on the line. The following example explains how to enter three blank lines below the headline.

To Enter Blank Lines into a Document

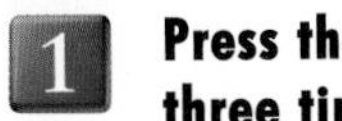

1 Press the ENTER key three times.

Word inserts three blank lines into your document below the headline (Figure 1-22).

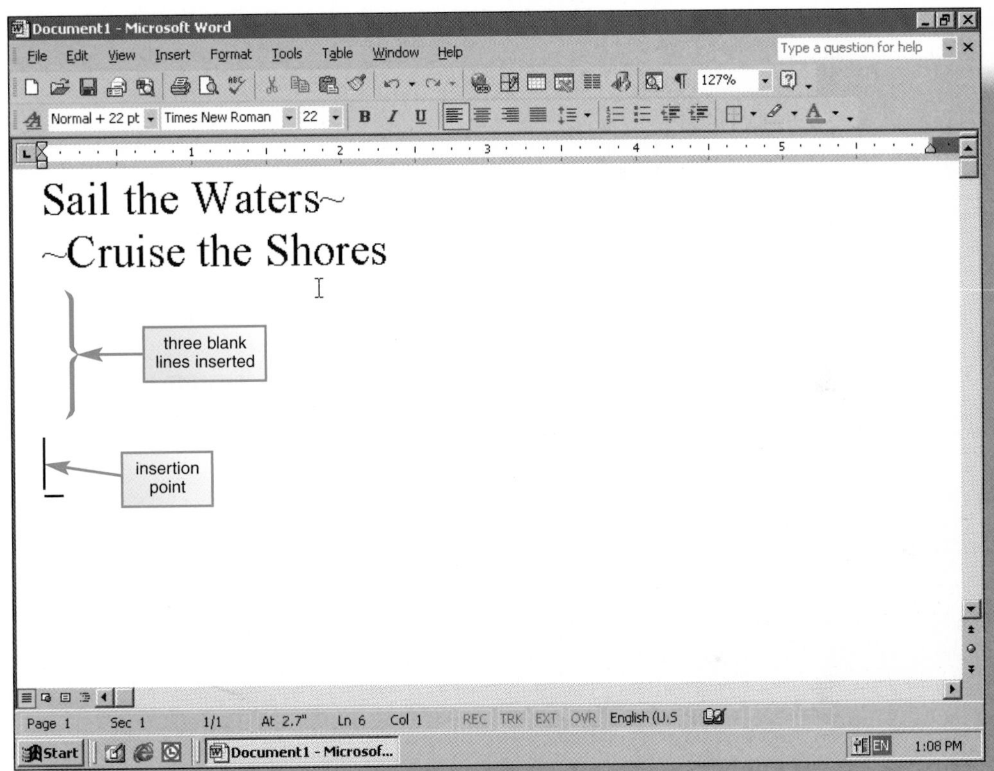

FIGURE 1-22

Other Ways

1. In Dictation mode, say "New Line, New Line, New Line"

Displaying Formatting Marks

To indicate where in the document you press the ENTER key or SPACEBAR, you may find it helpful to display formatting marks. A **formatting mark**, sometimes called a **nonprinting character**, is a character that displays on the screen but is not visible on a printed document. For example, the paragraph mark (¶) is a formatting mark that indicates where you pressed the ENTER key. A raised dot (•) shows where you pressed the SPACEBAR. Other formatting marks are discussed as they display on the screen.

Depending on settings made during previous Word sessions, your screen already may display formatting marks (Figure 1-23 on the next page). If the formatting marks do not display already on your screen, follow the step on the next page to display them.

Steps To Display Formatting Marks

1 If it is not already selected, click the Show/Hide ¶ button on the Standard toolbar.

Word displays formatting marks on the screen (Figure 1-23). The Show/Hide ¶ button is selected. Selected toolbar buttons are shaded light blue and surrounded with a blue outline.

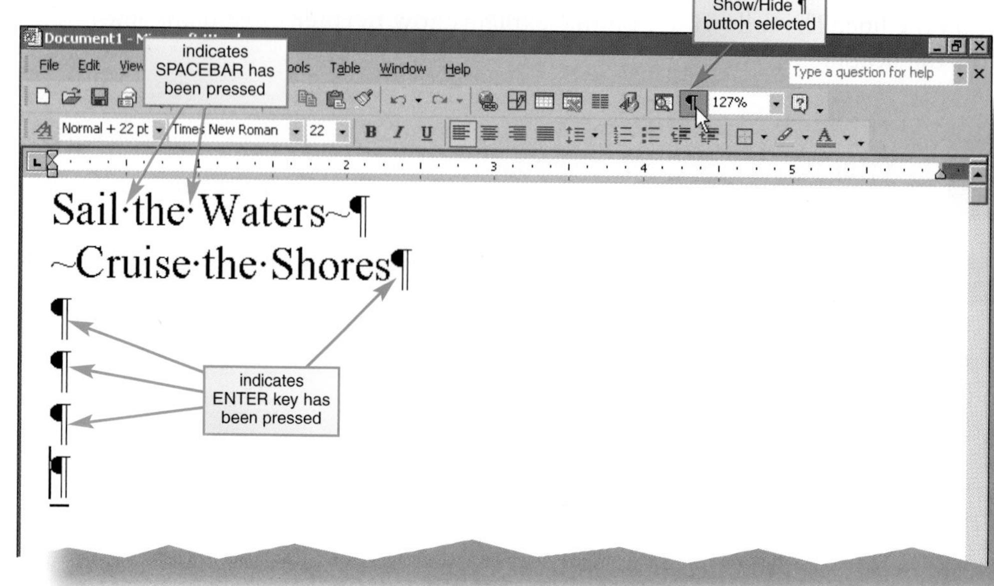

FIGURE 1-23

Other Ways

1. On Tools menu click Options, click View tab, click All, click OK button
2. Press CTRL+SHIFT+ASTERISK (*)
3. In Voice Command mode, say "Show Hide Paragraph"

Notice several changes to the Word document window (Figure 1-23). A paragraph mark displays at the end of each line to indicate you pressed the ENTER key. Each time you press the ENTER key, Word creates a new paragraph. Because you changed the font size, the paragraph marks are 22 point. Notice Word places a paragraph mark above the end mark; you cannot delete this paragraph mark. Between each word, a raised dot appears, indicating you pressed the SPACEBAR. Finally, the Show/Hide ¶ button is shaded light blue and surrounded with a blue outline to indicate it is selected.

If you feel the formatting marks clutter the screen, you can hide them by clicking the Show/Hide ¶ button again. It is recommended that you display formatting marks; therefore, the document windows presented in this book show the formatting marks.

Entering More Text

Every character of the body title (HIDDEN LAKE STATE PARK) in the announcement is capitalized. The next step is to enter this body title in all capital letters into the document window as explained below.

More About

Caps Lock

If you leave the CAPS LOCK key on and begin typing a new sentence, Word automatically may correct the problem for you, depending on its AutoCorrect settings. That is, Word may disengage the CAPS LOCK key and capitalize only the first letter of the first word in the next sentence.

TO ENTER MORE TEXT

1. Press the CAPS LOCK key on the keyboard to turn on capital letters. Verify the CAPS LOCK indicator is lit on your keyboard.
2. Type `HIDDEN LAKE STATE PARK` and then press the CAPS LOCK key to turn off capital letters.
3. Press the ENTER key twice.

The body title displays on line 6 as shown in Figure 1-24.

Using Wordwrap

Wordwrap allows you to type words in a paragraph continually without pressing the ENTER key at the end of each line. When the insertion point reaches the right margin, Word automatically positions it at the beginning of the next line. As you type, if a word extends beyond the right margin, Word also positions that word automatically on the next line with the insertion point.

As you enter text using Word, do not press the ENTER key when the insertion point reaches the right margin. Word creates a new paragraph each time you press the ENTER key. Thus, press the ENTER key only in these circumstances:

1. To insert blank lines into a document
2. To begin a new paragraph
3. To terminate a short line of text and advance to the next line
4. In response to certain Word commands

Perform the following step to familiarize yourself with wordwrap.

Wordwrap

Your printer controls where wordwrap occurs for each line in your document. For this reason, it is possible that the same document could wordwrap differently if printed on different printers.

Steps To Wordwrap Text as You Type

1 **Type** `Are you looking for a quiet, relaxing break from schoolwork?`

Word wraps the word, schoolwork, to the beginning of line 9 because it is too long to fit on line 8 (Figure 1-24). Your document may wordwrap differently depending on the type of printer you are using.

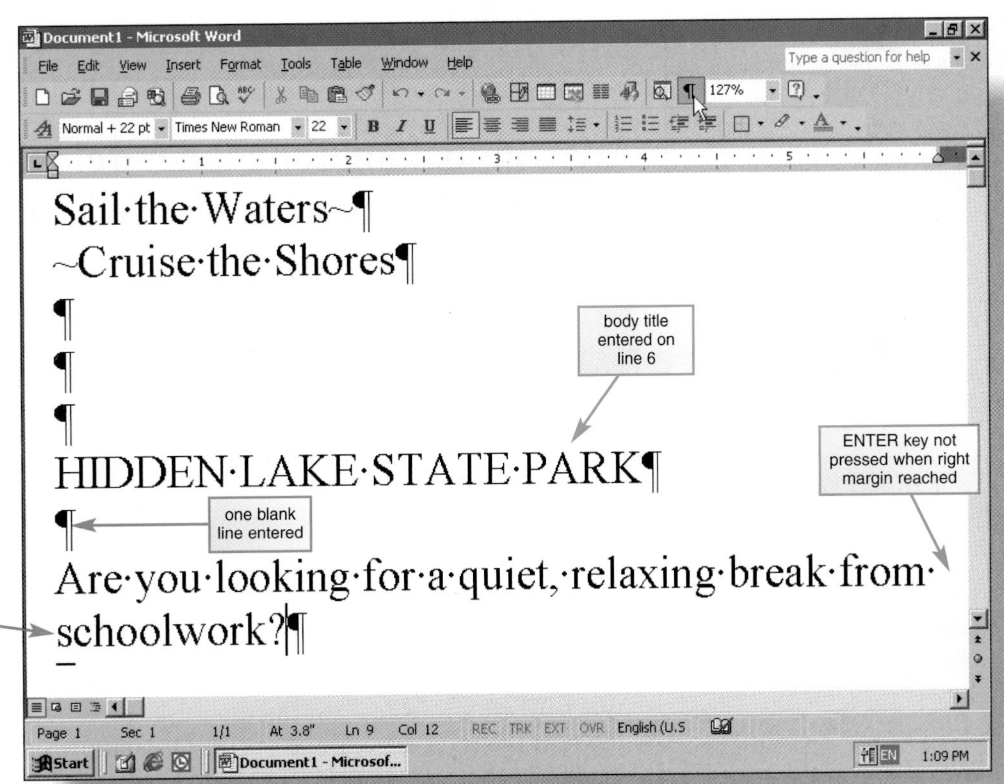

FIGURE 1-24

Other Ways

1. In Dictation mode, say "Are you looking for a quiet Comma relaxing break from schoolwork Question Mark"

Entering Text that Scrolls the Document Window

As you type more lines of text than Word can display in the document window, Word **scrolls** the top portion of the document upward off the screen. Although you cannot see the text once it scrolls off the screen, it remains in the document. As previously discussed, the document window allows you to view only a portion of your document at one time (Figure 1-9 on page WD 1.12).

Perform the following step to enter text that scrolls the document window.

To Enter Text that Scrolls the Document Window

1 **Press the SPACEBAR. Type** Hidden Lake is the perfect location for a tranquil escape from reality. **Press the ENTER key twice.**

Word scrolls the headline off the top of the screen (Figure 1-25). Your screen may scroll differently depending on the type of monitor you are using.

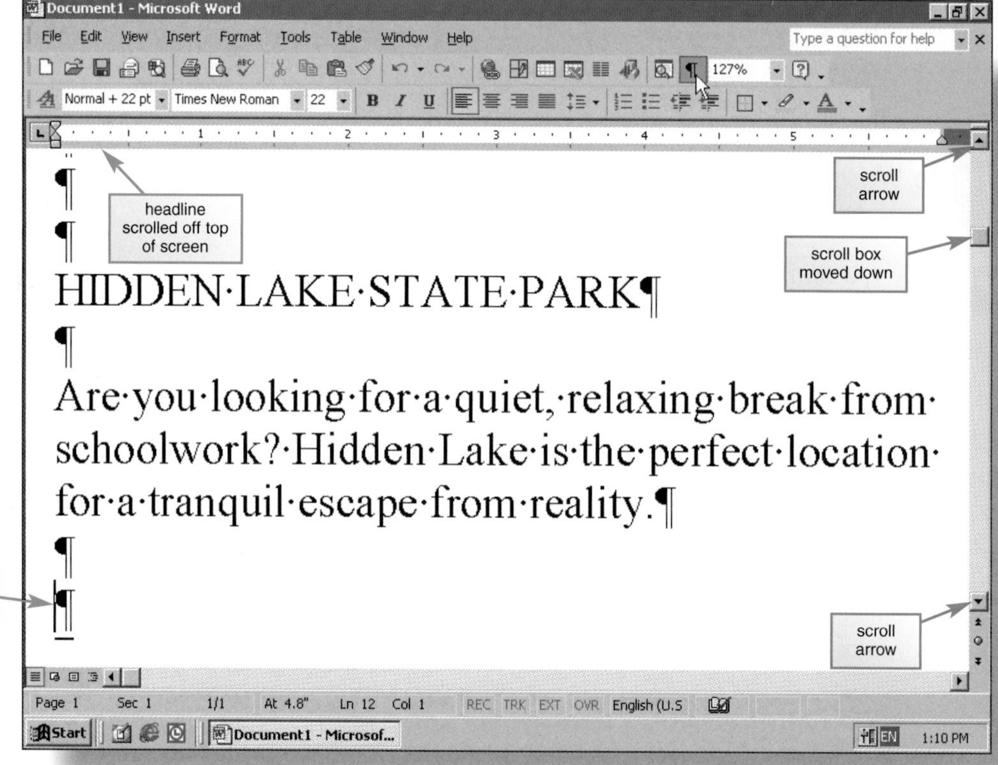

FIGURE 1-25

Other Ways

1. In Dictation mode, say "Hidden Lake is the perfect location for a tranquil escape from reality Period, New Line, New Line"

When Word scrolls text off the top of the screen, the scroll box on the vertical scroll bar at the right edge of the document window moves downward (Figure 1-25). The **scroll box** indicates the current relative location of the insertion point in the document. You may use either the mouse or the keyboard to move the insertion point to a different location in a document.

With the mouse, you use the scroll arrows or the scroll box to display a different portion of the document in the document window, and then click the mouse to move the insertion point to that location. Table 1-1 explains various techniques for scrolling vertically with the mouse.

More About

Microsoft IntelliMouse®

For more information on scrolling with the Microsoft IntelliMouse®, visit the Word 2002 More About Web page (scsite.com/wd2002/more.htm) and then click Microsoft IntelliMouse®.

Table 1-1 Techniques for Scrolling with the Mouse

SCROLL DIRECTION	MOUSE ACTION
Up	Drag the scroll box upward.
Down	Drag the scroll box downward.
Up one screen	Click anywhere above the scroll box on the vertical scroll bar.
Down one screen	Click anywhere below the scroll box on the vertical scroll bar.
Up one line	Click the scroll arrow at the top of the vertical scroll bar.
Down one line	Click the scroll arrow at the bottom of the vertical scroll bar.

More About

Scrolling

Computer users frequently switch between the keyboard and the mouse during a word processing session, which strains the wrist. To help prevent wrist injury, minimize switching. If your fingers are already on the keyboard, use keyboard keys to scroll. If your hand is already on the mouse, use the mouse to scroll.

When you use the keyboard to scroll, the insertion point automatically moves when you press the appropriate keys. Table 1-2 outlines various techniques to scroll through a document using the keyboard.

Table 1-2 Techniques for Scrolling with the Keyboard

SCROLL DIRECTION	KEY(S) TO PRESS	SCROLL DIRECTION	KEY(S) TO PRESS
Left one character	LEFT ARROW	Down one paragraph	CTRL+DOWN ARROW
Right one character	RIGHT ARROW	Up one screen	PAGE UP
Left one word	CTRL+LEFT ARROW	Down one screen	PAGE DOWN
Right one word	CTRL+RIGHT ARROW	To top of document window	ALT+CTRL+PAGE UP
Up one line	UP ARROW	To bottom of document window	ALT+CTRL+PAGE DOWN
Down one line	DOWN ARROW	Previous page	CTRL+PAGE UP
To end of a line	END	Next page	CTRL+PAGE DOWN
To beginning of a line	HOME	To the beginning of a document	CTRL+HOME
Up one paragraph	CTRL+UP ARROW	To the end of a document	CTRL+END

Checking Spelling as You Type

As you type text into the document window, Word checks your typing for possible spelling and grammar errors. If a word you type is not in the dictionary, a red wavy underline displays below it. Similarly, if text you type contains possible grammar errors, a green wavy underline displays below the text. In both cases, the Spelling and Grammar Status icon on the status bar displays a red X, instead of a check mark. Although you can check the entire document for spelling and grammar errors at once, you also can check these errors immediately.

To verify that the check spelling as you type feature is enabled, right-click the Spelling and Grammar Status icon on the status bar and then click Options on the shortcut menu. When the Spelling & Grammar dialog box displays, be sure Check spelling as you type has a check mark and Hide spelling errors in this document does not have a check mark.

When a word is flagged with a red wavy underline, it is not in Word's dictionary. To display a list of suggested corrections for a flagged word, you right-click it. A flagged word, however, is not necessarily misspelled. For example, many names, abbreviations, and specialized terms are not in Word's main dictionary. In these cases, you tell Word to ignore the flagged word. As you type, Word also detects duplicate words. For example, if your document contains the phrase, to the the store, Word places a red wavy underline below the second occurrence of the word, the.

Correcting Spelling

As you type, Word corrects some misspelled words automatically. For example, if you type recieve, Word automatically fixes the misspelling and displays the word, receive, when you press the SPACEBAR or type a punctuation mark. To see a complete list of automatically corrected words, click Tools on the menu bar, click AutoCorrect Options on the Tools menu, click the AutoCorrect tab, and then scroll through the list of words near the bottom of the dialog box.

In the following example, the word, identification, has been misspelled intentionally as indentification to illustrate Word's check spelling as you type feature. If you are doing this project on a personal computer, your announcement may contain different misspelled words, depending on the accuracy of your typing.

Steps To Check Spelling as You Type

1 Type `Show your student indentification` **and then press the SPACEBAR. Position the mouse pointer in the flagged word (indentification, in this case).**

Word flags the misspelled word, indentification, by placing a red wavy underline below it (Figure 1-26). The Spelling and Grammar Status icon on the status bar now displays a red X, indicating Word has detected a possible spelling or grammar error.

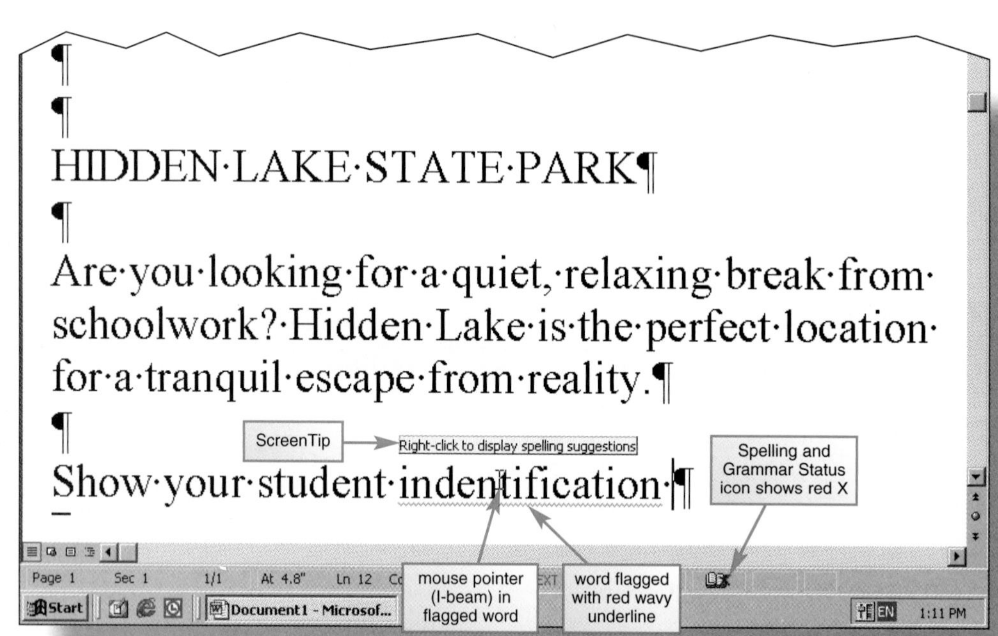

FIGURE 1-26

2 Right-click the flagged word, indentification. When the shortcut menu displays, point to identification.

Word displays a shortcut menu that lists suggested spelling corrections for the flagged word (Figure 1-27).

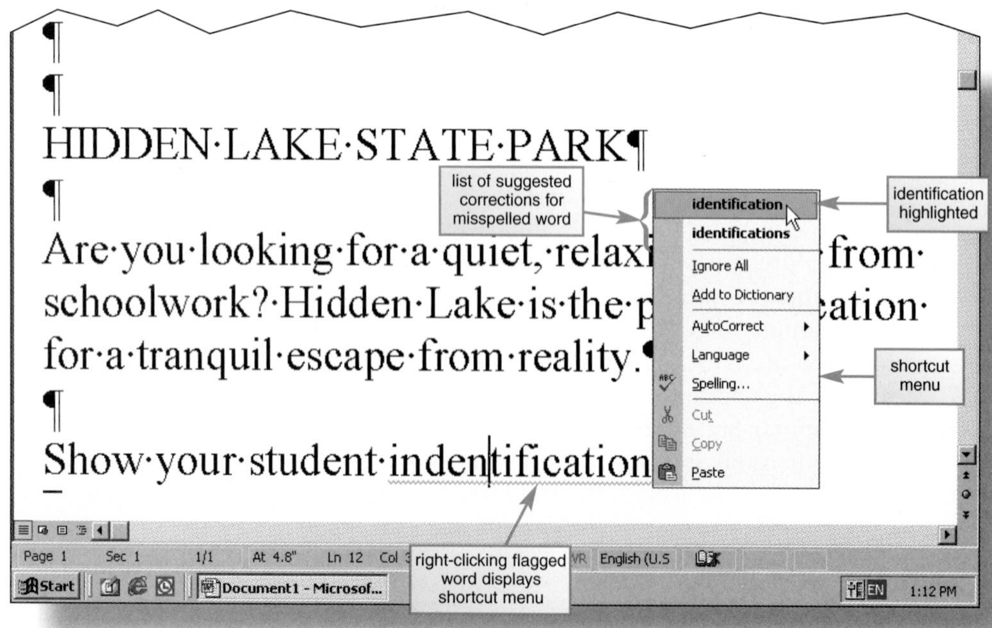

FIGURE 1-27

3 Click identification.

Word replaces the misspelled word with the selected word on the shortcut menu. The Spelling and Grammar Status icon once again displays a red check mark.

4 Press the END key to move the insertion point to the end of the line and then type `card to receive a 30 percent discount on sailboat rentals.` **Press the ENTER key twice. Type** `Call 555-2299 for details or reservations.`

The text of the announcement is complete (Figure 1-28).

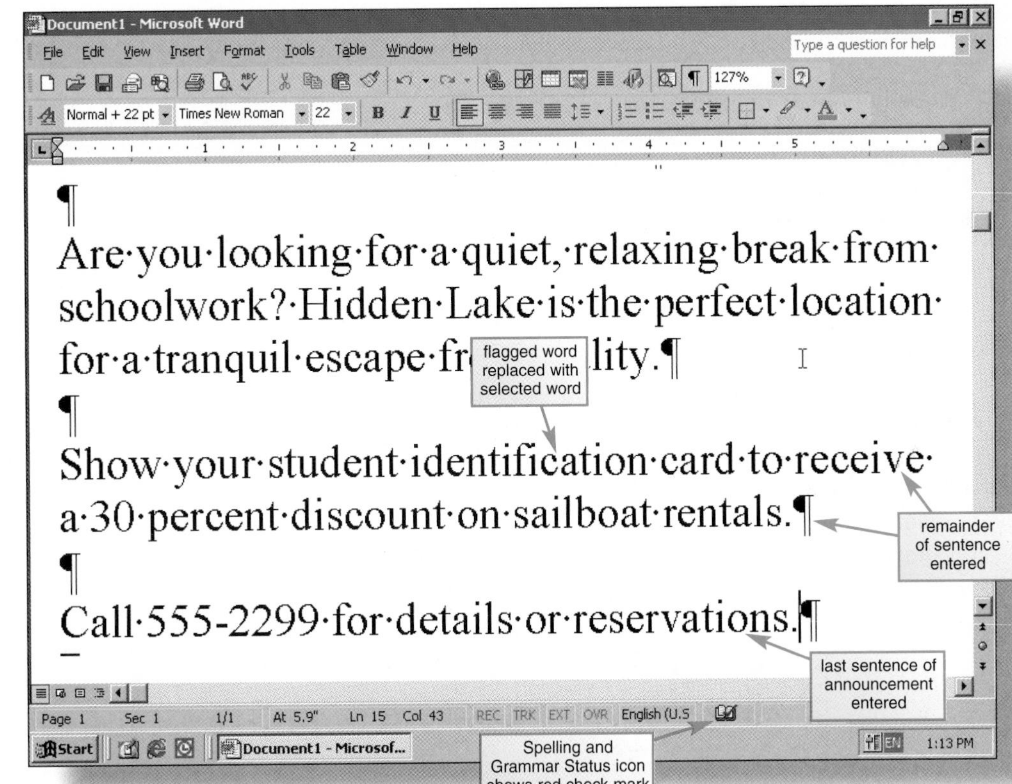
Document1 - Microsoft Word
Are·you·looking·for·a·quiet,·relaxing·break·from·schoolwork?·Hidden·Lake·is·the·perfect·location·for·a·tranquil·escape·fr lity.¶
Show·your·student·identification·card·to·receive·a·30·percent·discount·on·sailboat·rentals.¶
Call·555-2299·for·details·or·reservations.¶
flagged word replaced with selected word
remainder of sentence entered
last sentence of announcement entered
Spelling and Grammar Status icon shows red check mark

FIGURE 1-28

Other Ways

1. Double-click Spelling and Grammar Status icon on status bar, click correct word on shortcut menu
2. In Voice Command mode, say "Spelling and Grammar"

If a flagged word actually is spelled correctly and, for example, is a proper name, you can right-click it and then click Ignore All on the shortcut menu (Figure 1-27). If, when you right-click the misspelled word, your desired correction is not in the list on the shortcut menu, you can click outside the shortcut menu to make the menu disappear and then retype the correct word, or you can click Spelling on the shortcut menu to display the Spelling dialog box. Project 2 discusses the Spelling dialog box.

If you feel the wavy underlines clutter your document window, you can hide them temporarily until you are ready to check for spelling errors. To hide spelling errors, right-click the Spelling and Grammar Status icon on the status bar and then click Hide Spelling Errors on the shortcut menu. To hide grammar errors, right-click the Spelling and Grammar Status icon on the status bar and then click Hide Grammatical Errors on the shortcut menu.

More About

Saving

When you save a document, use meaningful file names. A file name can be up to 255 characters, including spaces. The only invalid characters are the backslash (\), slash (/), colon (:), asterisk (*), question mark (?), quotation mark ("), less than symbol (<), greater than symbol (>), and vertical bar (|).

Saving a Document

As you create a document in Word, the computer stores it in memory. If you turn off the computer or if you lose electrical power, the document in memory is lost. Hence, it is mandatory to save on disk any document that you will use later. The steps on the following pages illustrate how to save a document on a floppy disk inserted in drive A using the Save button on the Standard toolbar.

You will save the document using the file name, Hidden Lake Announcement. Depending on your Windows settings, the file type .doc may display immediately after the file name. The file type .doc indicates the file is a Word document.

Steps To Save a New Document

1 Insert a formatted floppy disk into drive A. Click the Save button on the Standard toolbar.

Word displays the Save As dialog box (Figure 1-29). The first line from the document (Sail the Waters) displays selected in the File name text box as the default file name. With this file name selected, you can change it by immediately typing the new name.

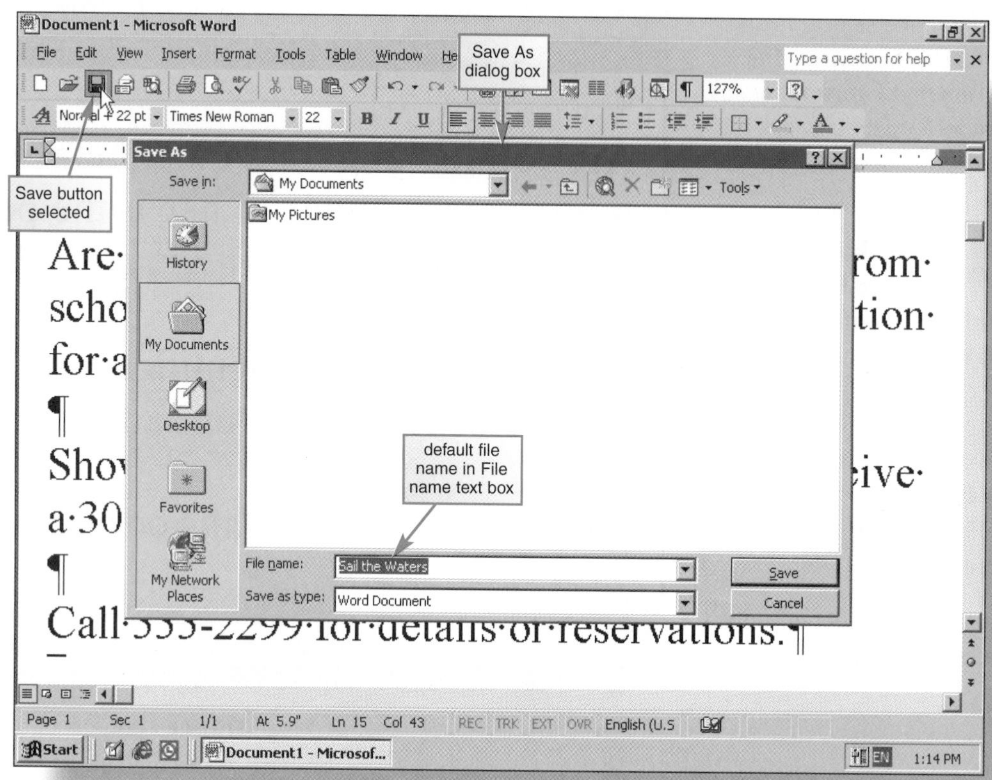

FIGURE 1-29

2 Type `Hidden Lake Announcement` **in the File name text box. Do not press the ENTER key after typing the file name.**

The file name, Hidden Lake Announcement, displays in the File name text box (Figure 1-30). Notice that the current save location is the My Documents folder. A **folder** *is a specific location on a disk. To change to a different save location, use the Save in box.*

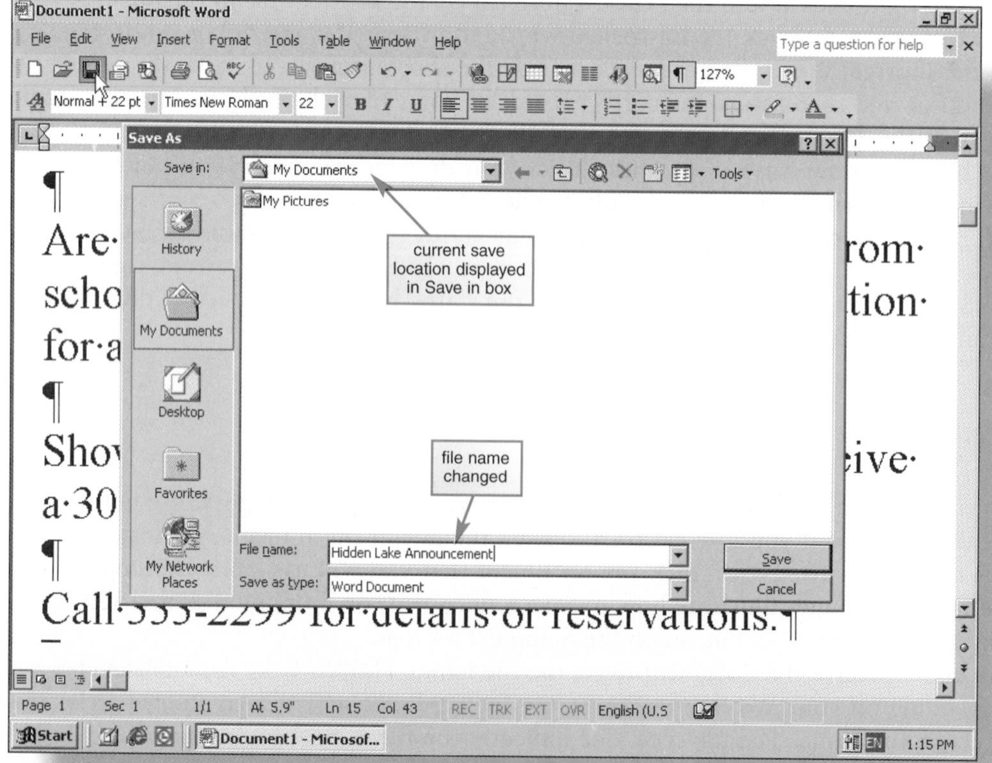

FIGURE 1-30

3 Click the Save in box arrow and then point to 3½ Floppy (A:).

A list of the available save locations displays (Figure 1-31). Your list may differ depending on your system configuration.

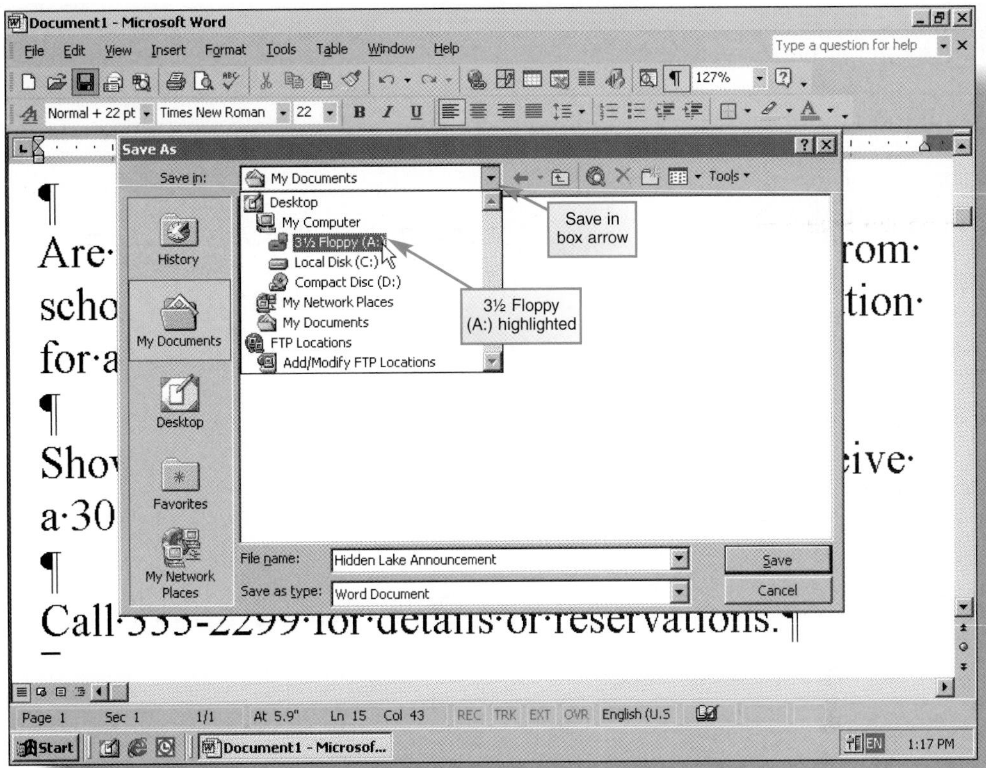

FIGURE 1-31

4 Click 3½ Floppy (A:) and then point to the Save button in the Save As dialog box.

The 3½ Floppy (A:) drive becomes the save location (Figure 1-32). The names of existing files stored on the floppy disk in drive A display. In Figure 1-32, the list is empty because no Word files currently are stored on the floppy disk in drive A.

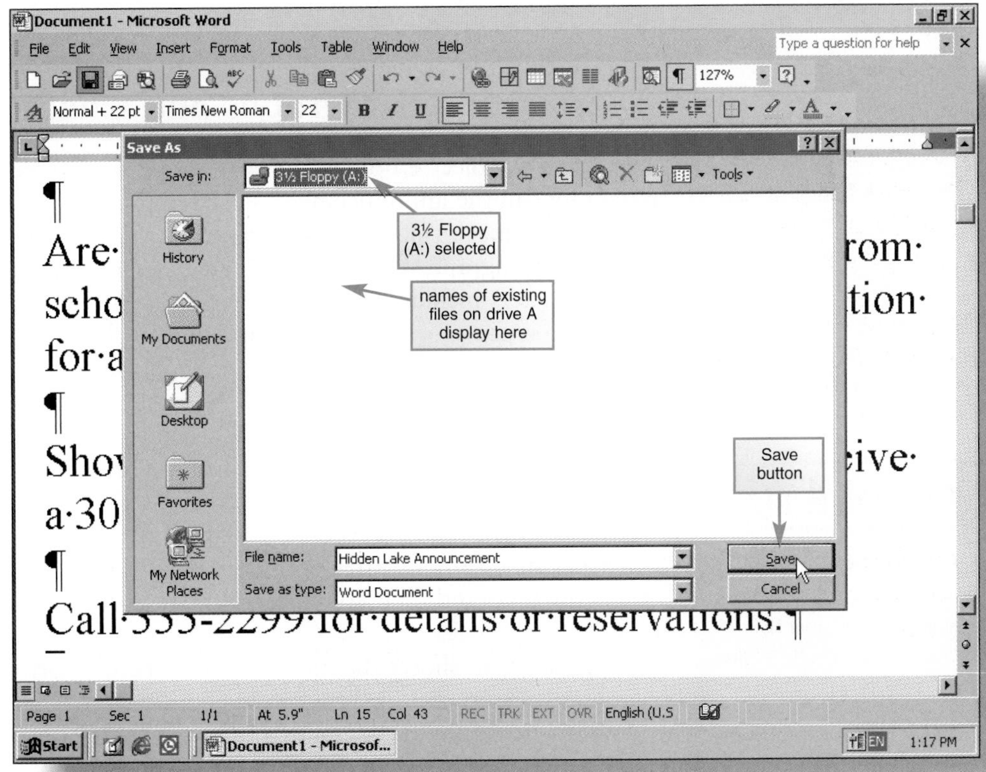

FIGURE 1-32

5 Click the Save button in the Save As dialog box.

Word saves the document on the floppy disk in drive A with the file name Hidden Lake Announcement (Figure 1-33). Although the announcement is saved on a floppy disk, it also remains in main memory and displays on the screen.

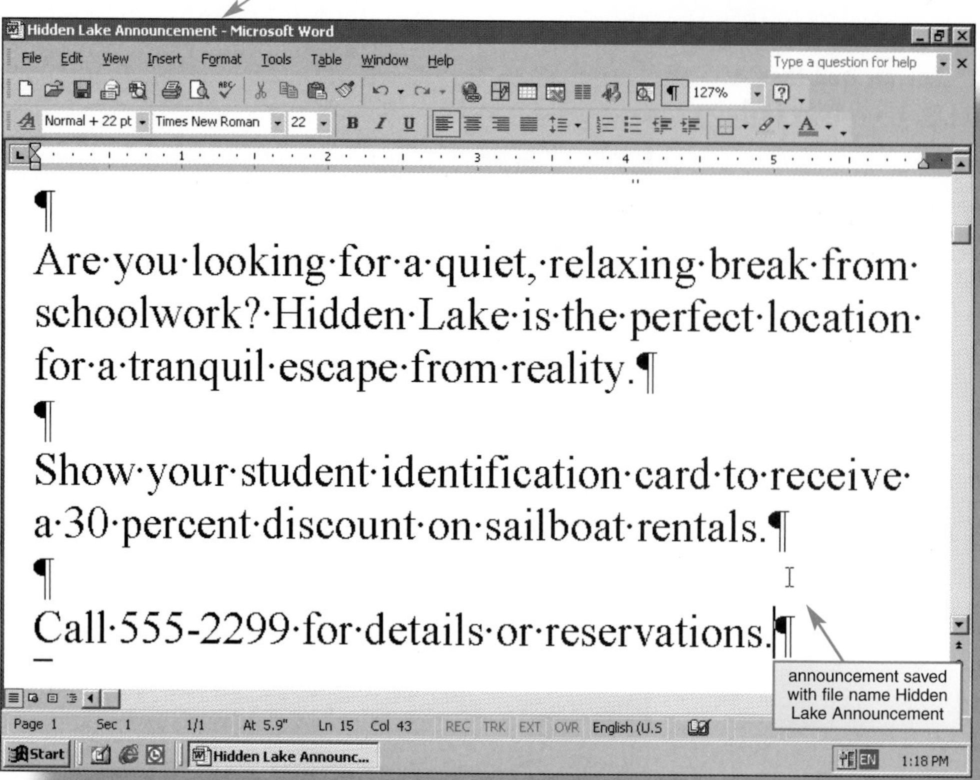

FIGURE 1-33

Other Ways

1. On File menu click Save As, type file name, select location in Save in list, click Save button in dialog box
2. Press CTRL+S, type file name, select location in Save in list, click Save button in dialog box
3. In Voice Command mode, say "File, Save As, [type file name], Save In, [select folder], Save"

Formatting Paragraphs and Characters in a Document

The text for Project 1 now is complete. The next step is to format the characters and paragraphs in the announcement. Paragraphs encompass the text up to and including a paragraph mark (¶). **Paragraph formatting** is the process of changing the appearance of a paragraph. For example, you can center or indent a paragraph.

Characters include letters, numbers, punctuation marks, and symbols. **Character formatting** is the process of changing the way characters appear on the screen and in print. You use character formatting to emphasize certain words and improve readability of a document. For example, you can italicize or underline characters.

Very often, you apply both paragraph and character formatting to the same text. For example, you may center a paragraph (paragraph formatting) and bold the characters in a paragraph (character formatting).

With Word, you can format paragraphs and characters before you type, or you can apply new formats after you type. Earlier, you changed the font size before you typed any text, and then you entered the text. In this section, you format existing text.

Figure 1-34a shows the announcement before formatting the paragraphs and characters. Figure 1-34b shows the announcement after formatting. As you can see from the two figures, a document that is formatted not only is easier to read, but it looks more professional.

More About

Formatting

Character formatting includes changing the font, font style, font size; adding an underline, color, strikethrough, or shadow; embossing; engraving; making a superscript or subscript; and changing the case of the letters. Paragraph formatting includes alignment; indentation; and spacing above, below, and between lines.

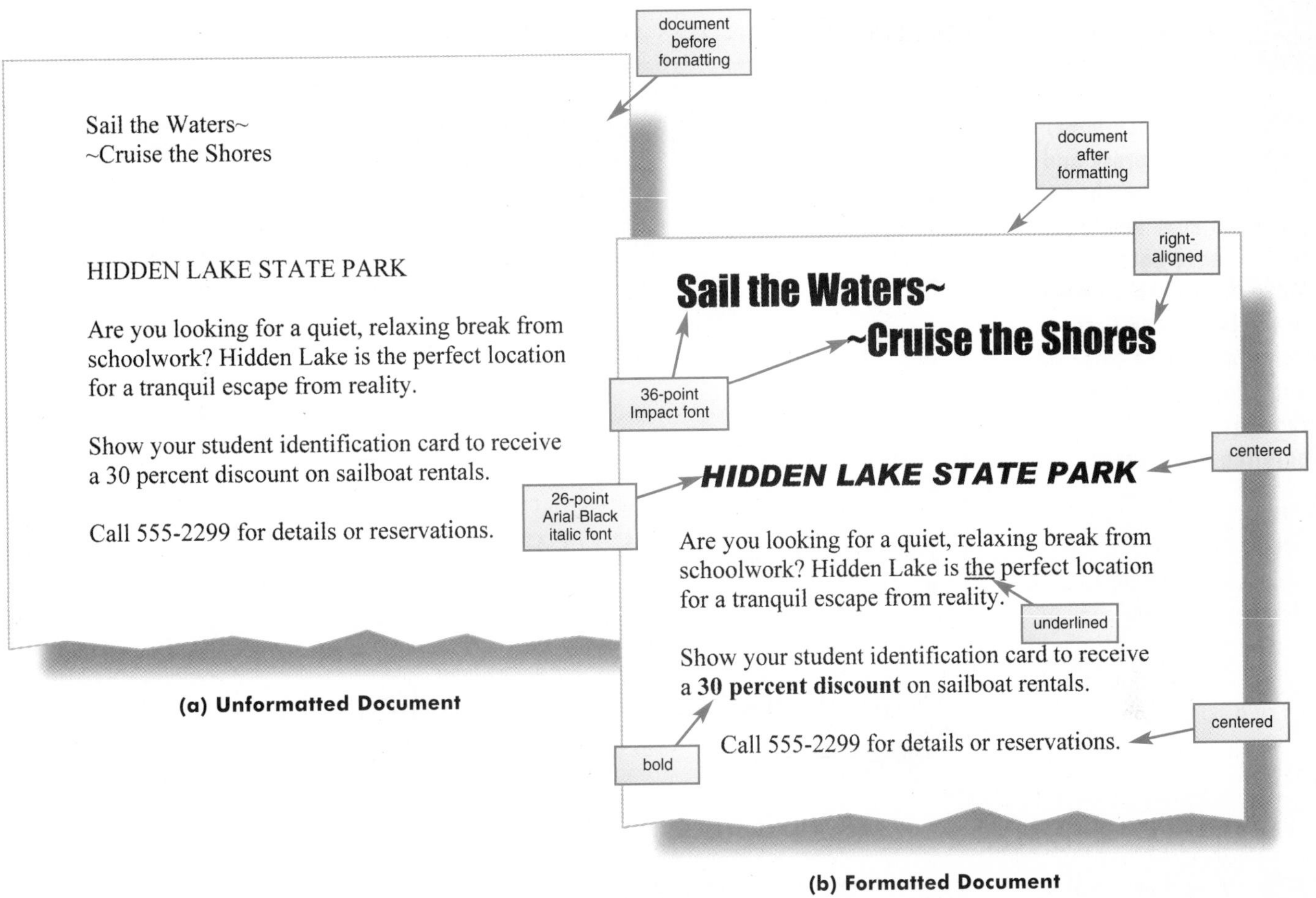

document before formatting
Sail the Waters~
~Cruise the Shores
HIDDEN LAKE STATE PARK
Are you looking for a quiet, relaxing break from schoolwork? Hidden Lake is the perfect location for a tranquil escape from reality.
Show your student identification card to receive a 30 percent discount on sailboat rentals.
Call 555-2299 for details or reservations.
(a) Unformatted Document
document after formatting
right-aligned
Sail the Waters~
~Cruise the Shores
36-point Impact font
centered
HIDDEN LAKE STATE PARK
26-point Arial Black italic font
Are you looking for a quiet, relaxing break from schoolwork? Hidden Lake is the perfect location for a tranquil escape from reality.
underlined
Show your student identification card to receive a 30 percent discount on sailboat rentals.
centered
Call 555-2299 for details or reservations.
bold
(b) Formatted Document

FIGURE 1-34

Selecting and Formatting Paragraphs and Characters

To format a single paragraph, move the insertion point into the paragraph and then format the paragraph. Thus, you do not need to select a paragraph to format it. To format *multiple* paragraphs, however, you must first select the paragraphs you want to format and then format them. In the same manner, to format characters, a word, or words, you first must select the characters, word, or words to be formatted and then format your selection.

Selected text is highlighted text. That is, if your screen normally displays dark letters on a light background, then selected text displays light letters on a dark background.

> **More About**
>
> **Spacing**
>
> Word processing documents use variable character fonts; for example, the letter w takes up more space than the letter i. With these fonts, it often is difficult to determine how many times someone has pressed the SPACEBAR between sentences. Thus, the rule is to press the SPACEBAR only once after periods, colons, and other punctuation marks. Notice in Figure 1-34b that only one space exists between the ? and the H in Hidden.

Selecting Multiple Paragraphs

The first formatting step in this project is to change the font size of the characters in the headline. The headline consists of two separate lines, each ending with a paragraph mark. As previously discussed, Word creates a new paragraph each time you press the ENTER key. Thus, the headline actually is two separate paragraphs.

To change the font size of the characters in the headline, you must first **select**, or highlight, both paragraphs in the headline as shown in the steps on the next page.

Steps To Select Multiple Paragraphs

1 Press CTRL+HOME; that is, press and hold the CTRL key, then press the HOME key, and then release both keys. Move the mouse pointer to the left of the first paragraph to be selected until the mouse pointer changes to a right-pointing block arrow.

CTRL+HOME positions the insertion point at the top of the document (Figure 1-35). The mouse pointer changes to a right-pointing block arrow when positioned to the left of a paragraph.

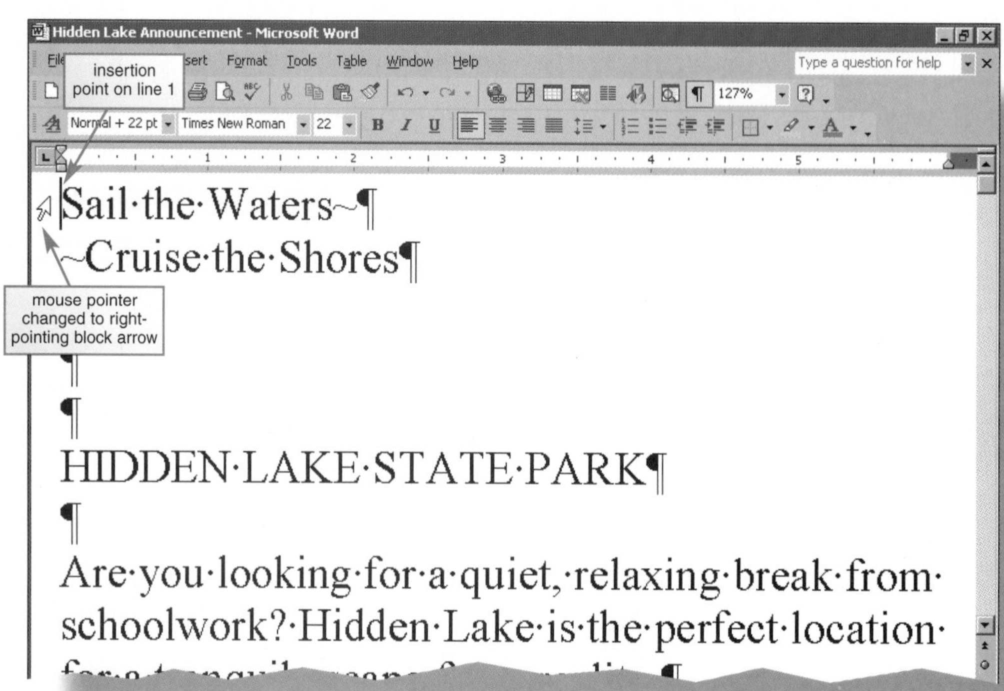

FIGURE 1-35

2 Drag downward until both paragraphs are selected.

Word selects (highlights) both of the paragraphs (Figure 1-36). Recall that dragging is the process of holding down the mouse button while moving the mouse and then releasing the mouse button.

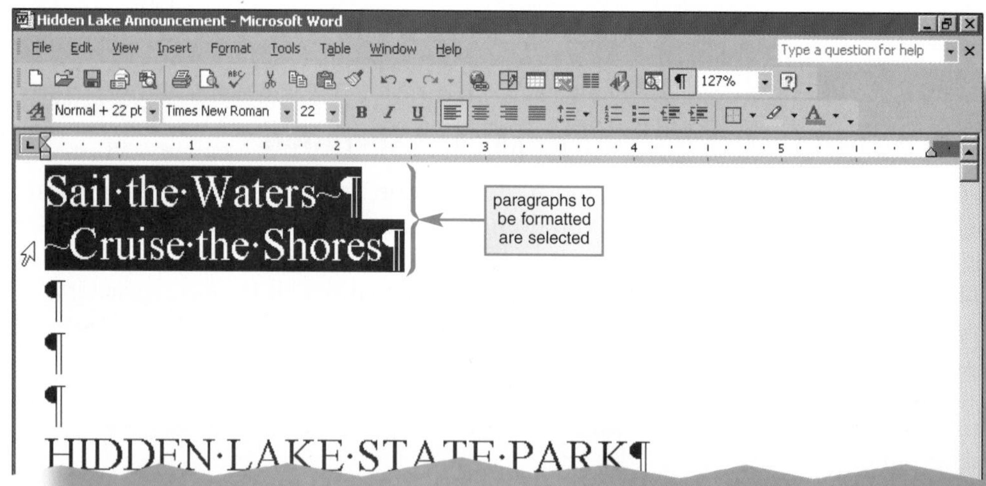

FIGURE 1-36

Other Ways

1. With insertion point at beginning of first paragraph, press CTRL+SHIFT+DOWN ARROW
2. In Voice Command mode, say "Select Paragraph"

Changing the Font Size of Selected Text

The next step is to increase the font size of the characters in the selected headline. Recall that the font size specifies the size of the characters. Earlier in this project, you changed the font size for characters in the entire announcement to 22. To give the headline more impact, it has a font size larger than the body copy. Perform the following steps to increase the font size of the headline from 22 to 36 point.

Steps To Change the Font Size of Selected Text

1 While the text is selected, click the Font Size box arrow on the Formatting toolbar and then point to the down scroll arrow on the Font Size scroll bar.

Word displays a list of the available font sizes (Figure 1-37). Available font sizes vary depending on the font and printer driver.

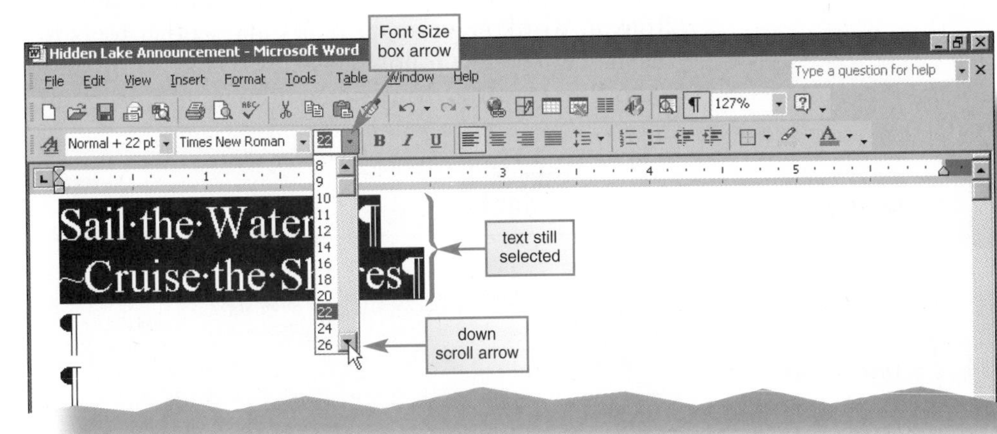

FIGURE 1-37

2 Click the down scroll arrow on the Font Size scroll bar until 36 displays in the list and then point to 36.

Word selects 36 in the list (Figure 1-38).

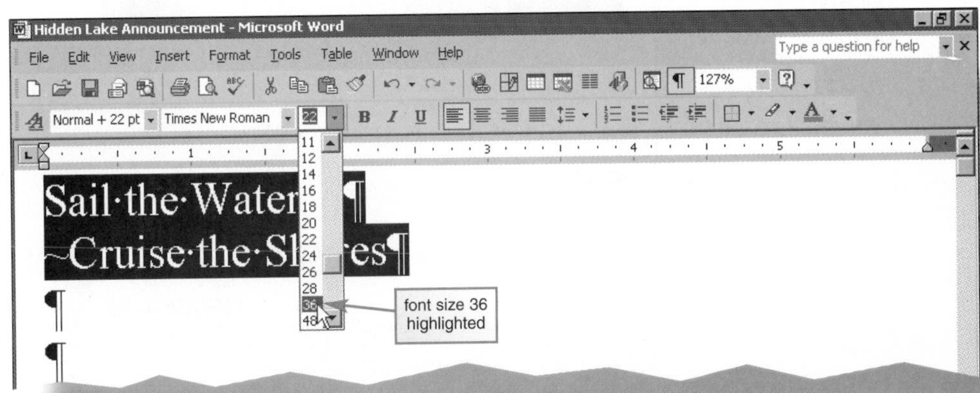

FIGURE 1-38

3 Click 36.

Word increases the font size of the headline to 36 (Figure 1-39). The Font Size box on the Formatting toolbar displays 36, indicating the selected text has a font size of 36.

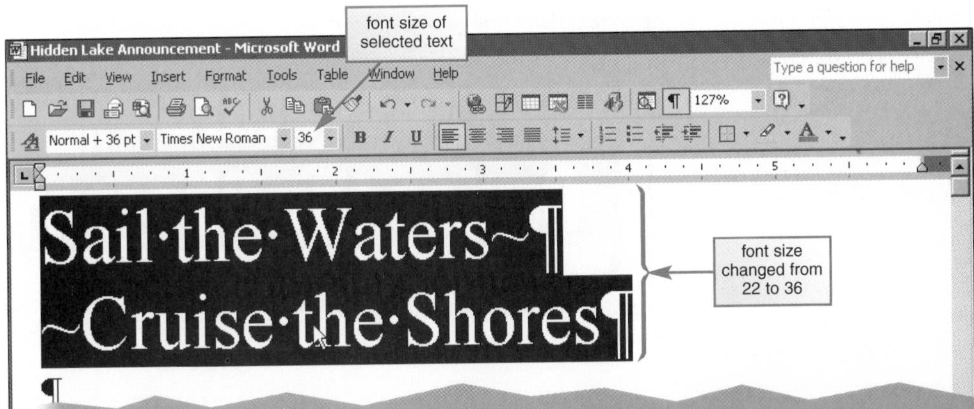

FIGURE 1-39

Other Ways

1. Right-click selected text, click Font on shortcut menu, click Font tab, select font size in Size list, click OK button
2. See Other Ways 2 through 4 on page WD 1.20.

Changing the Font of Selected Text

As mentioned earlier in this project, the default font in Word is Times New Roman. Word, however, provides many other fonts to add variety to your documents. Perform the following steps to change the font of the headline in the announcement from Times New Roman to Impact (or a similar font).

Steps To Change the Font of Selected Text

1 While the text is selected, click the Font box arrow on the Formatting toolbar, scroll through the list until Impact displays, and then point to Impact (or a similar font).

Word displays a list of available fonts (Figure 1-40). Your list of available fonts may differ, depending on the type of printer you are using.

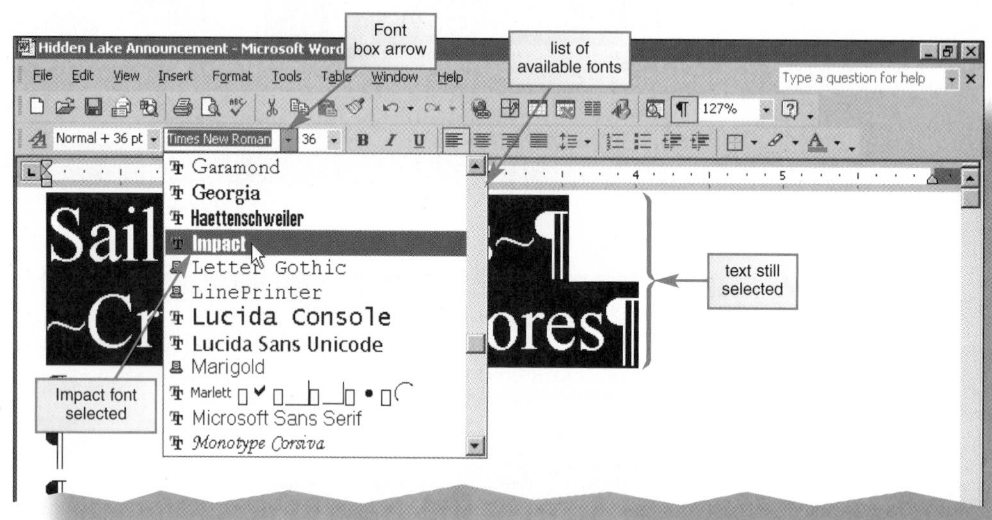

FIGURE 1-40

2 Click Impact (or a similar font).

Word changes the font of the selected text to Impact (Figure 1-41).

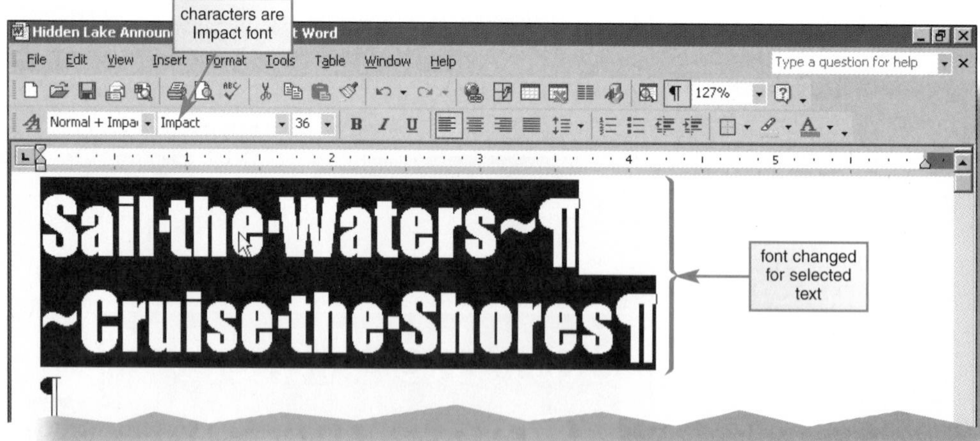

FIGURE 1-41

Other Ways

1. On Format menu click Font, click Font tab, click font name in font list, click OK button
2. Press CTRL+SHIFT+F, press DOWN ARROW to font name, press ENTER
3. In Voice Command mode, say "Font, [select font name]"

Right-Align a Paragraph

The default alignment for paragraphs is **left-aligned**, that is, flush at the left margin of the document with uneven right edges. In Figure 1-42, the Align Left button is selected to indicate the current paragraph is left-aligned.

The second line of the headline, however, is to be **right-aligned**, that is, flush at the right margin of the document with uneven left edges. Recall that the second line of the headline is a paragraph, and paragraph formatting does not require you to select the paragraph prior to formatting. Just position the insertion point in the paragraph to be formatted and then format it accordingly.

Perform the following steps to right-align the second line of the headline.

Steps To Right-Align a Paragraph

1 Click somewhere in the paragraph to be right-aligned. Point to the Align Right button on the Formatting toolbar.

Word positions the insertion point at the location you clicked (Figure 1-42).

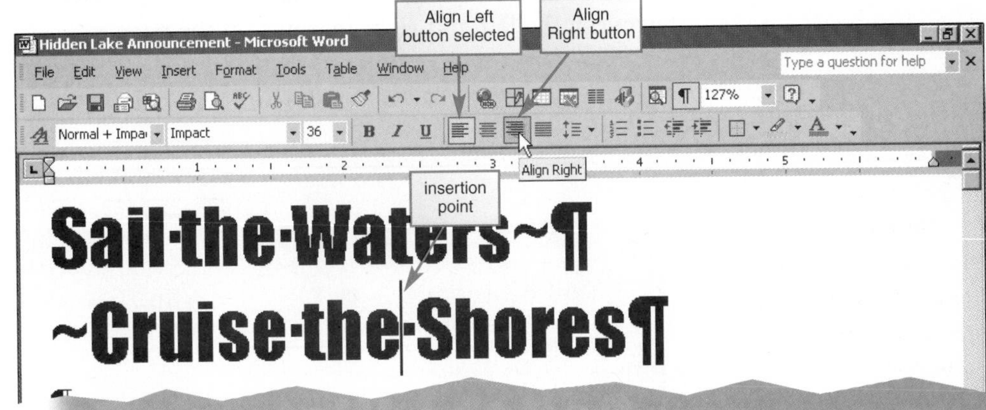

FIGURE 1-42

2 Click the Align Right button.

The second line of the headline is right-aligned (Figure 1-43). Notice that you did not have to select the paragraph before right-aligning it. Paragraph formatting requires only that the insertion point be positioned somewhere in the paragraph.

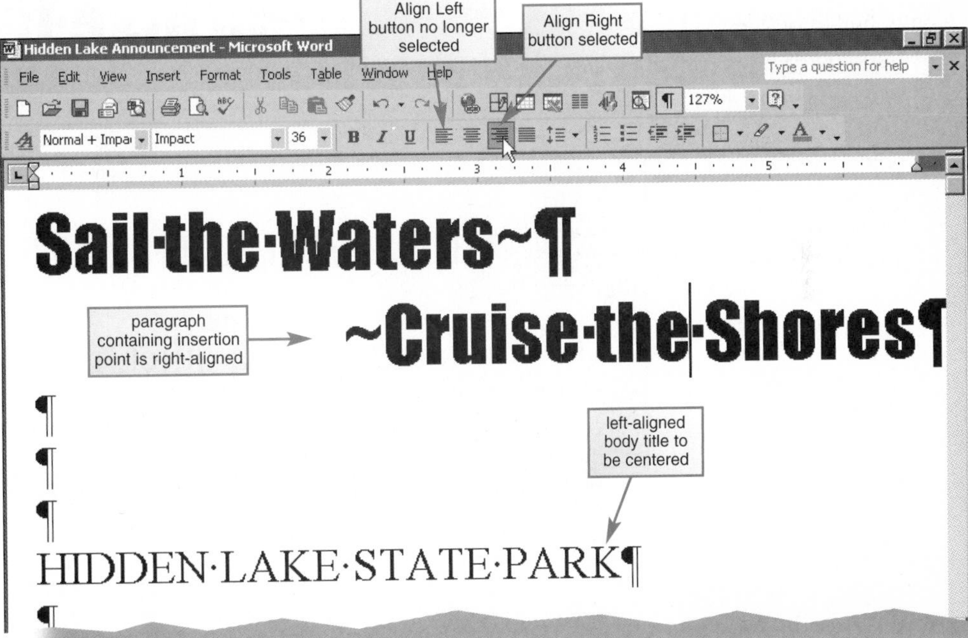

FIGURE 1-43

Other Ways

1. On Format menu click Paragraph, click Indents and Spacing tab, click Alignment box arrow, click Right, click OK button
2. Press CTRL+R
3. In Voice Command mode, say "Align Right"

When a paragraph is right-aligned, the Align Right button on the Formatting toolbar is selected. If, for some reason, you wanted to return the paragraph to left-aligned, you would click the Align Left button on the Formatting toolbar.

Center a Paragraph

The body title currently is left-aligned (Figure 1-43 on the previous page). Perform the following step to **center** it; that is, position the body title horizontally between the left and right margins on the page.

Steps To Center a Paragraph

1 Click somewhere in the paragraph to be centered. Click the Center button on the Formatting toolbar.

Word centers the body title between the left and right margins (Figure 1-44). The Center button on the Formatting toolbar is selected, which indicates the paragraph containing the insertion point is centered.

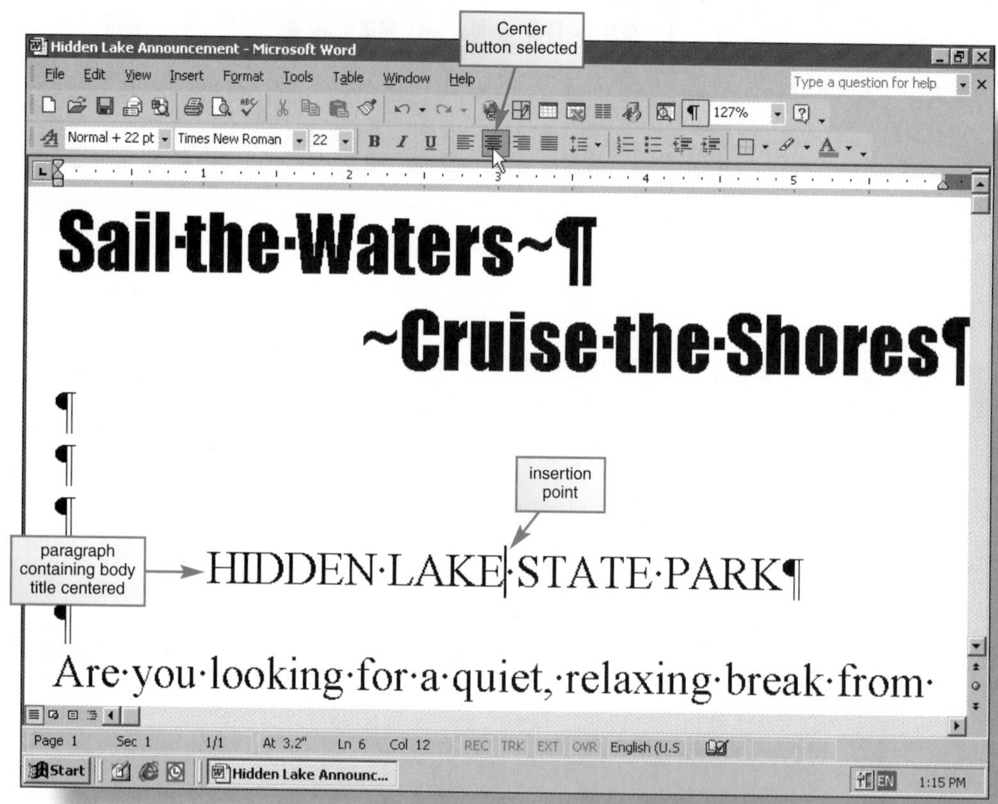

FIGURE 1-44

Other Ways

1. On Format menu click Paragraph, click Indents and Spacing tab, click Alignment box arrow, click Centered, click OK button
2. Right-click paragraph, click Paragraph on shortcut menu, click Indents and Spacing tab, click Alignment box arrow, click Centered, click OK button
3. Press CTRL+E
4. In Voice Command mode, say "Center"

When a paragraph is centered, the Center button on the Formatting toolbar is selected. If, for some reason, you wanted to return the paragraph to left-aligned, you would click the Align Left button on the Formatting toolbar.

Undoing Commands or Actions

Word provides an **Undo button** on the Standard toolbar that you can use to cancel your recent command(s) or action(s). For example, if you format text incorrectly, you can undo the format and try it again. If, after you undo an action, you decide you did not want to perform the undo, you can use the **Redo button** to undo the undo. Word prevents you from undoing or redoing some actions, such as saving or printing a document.

Perform the following steps to undo the center format to the body title using the Undo button and then re-center it using the Redo button.

Steps To Undo an Action

1 Click the Undo button on the Standard toolbar.

Word returns the body title to its formatting before you issued the center command (Figure 1-45). That is, Word left-aligns the body title.

2 Click the Redo button on the Standard toolbar.

Word reapplies the center format to the body title (shown in Figure 1-44).

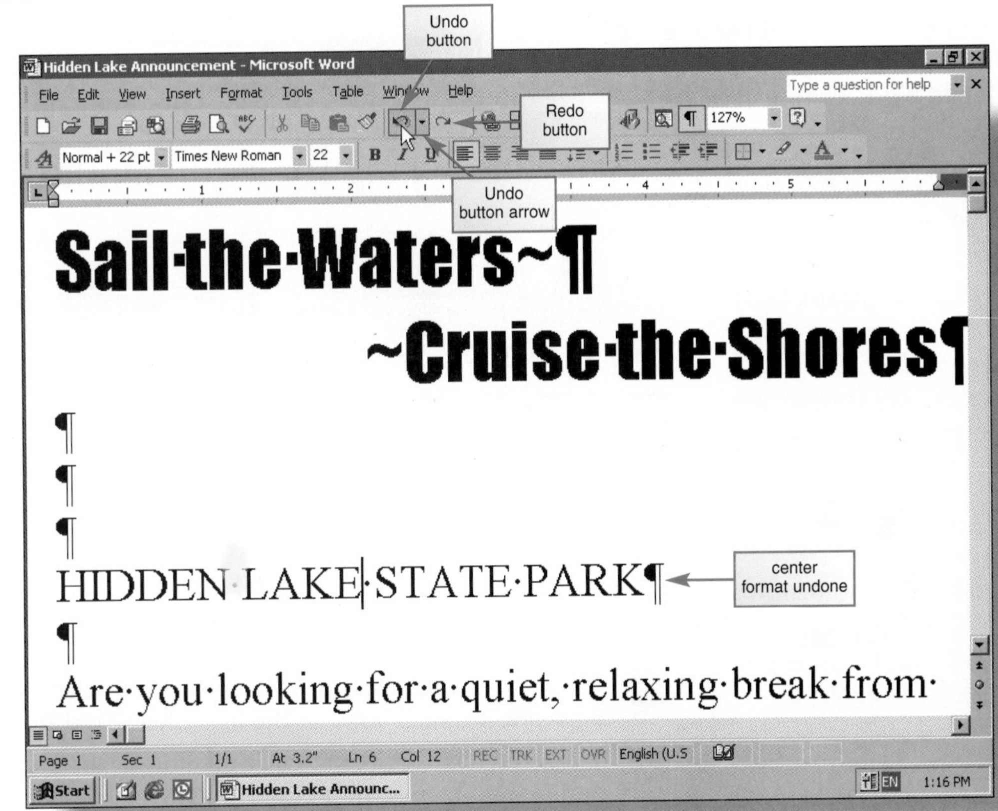

FIGURE 1-45

Other Ways

1. On Edit menu click Undo
2. Press CTRL+Z
3. In Voice Command mode, say "Undo"

You also can cancel a series of prior actions by clicking the Undo button arrow (Figure 1-45) to display the list of undo actions and then dragging through the actions you wish to undo.

Whereas the Undo command cancels an action you did not want to perform, Word also provides a **Repeat command**, which duplicates your last command so you can perform it again. The word(s) listed after Repeat vary, depending on your most recent command. For example, if you centered a paragraph and wish to format another paragraph the exact same way, you could click in the second paragraph to format and then click Repeat Paragraph Alignment on the Edit menu.

Selecting a Line and Formatting It

The characters in the body title, HIDDEN LAKE STATE PARK, are to be a different font, larger font size, and italicized. To make these changes, you must select the line of text containing the body title. Perform the step on the next page to select the body title.

More About

Centering

The Center button on the Formatting toolbar centers text horizontally. You also can center text vertically between the top and bottom margins. To do this, click File on the menu bar, click Page Setup, click the Layout tab, click the Vertical alignment box arrow, click Center in the list, and then click the OK button.

Steps To Select a Line

1 Move the mouse pointer to the left of the line to be selected (HIDDEN LAKE STATE PARK) until it changes to a right-pointing block arrow and then click.

The entire line to the right of the mouse pointer is selected (Figure 1-46).

FIGURE 1-46

Other Ways

1. Drag through the line
2. With insertion point at beginning of desired line, press SHIFT+DOWN ARROW
3. In Voice Command, say "Select Line"

The next step is to change the font of the selected characters from Times New Roman to Arial Black and increase the font size of the selected characters from 22 to 26 point, as explained below.

TO FORMAT A LINE OF TEXT

1. While the text is selected, click the Font box arrow and then scroll to Arial Black, or a similar font, in the list. Click Arial Black, or a similar font.
2. While the text is selected, click the Font Size box arrow on the Formatting toolbar and then scroll to 26 in the list. Click 26.

The characters in the body title are 26-point Arial Black (Figure 1-47).

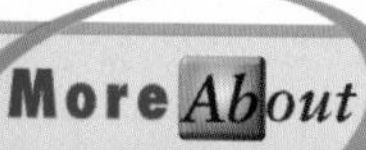

More About

The Font Dialog Box

The Font dialog box has more character formatting options than the Formatting toolbar. For example, you can strikethrough, superscript, subscript, outline, emboss, engrave, and shadow characters using the Font dialog box. To display the Font dialog box, click Format on the menu bar and then click Font.

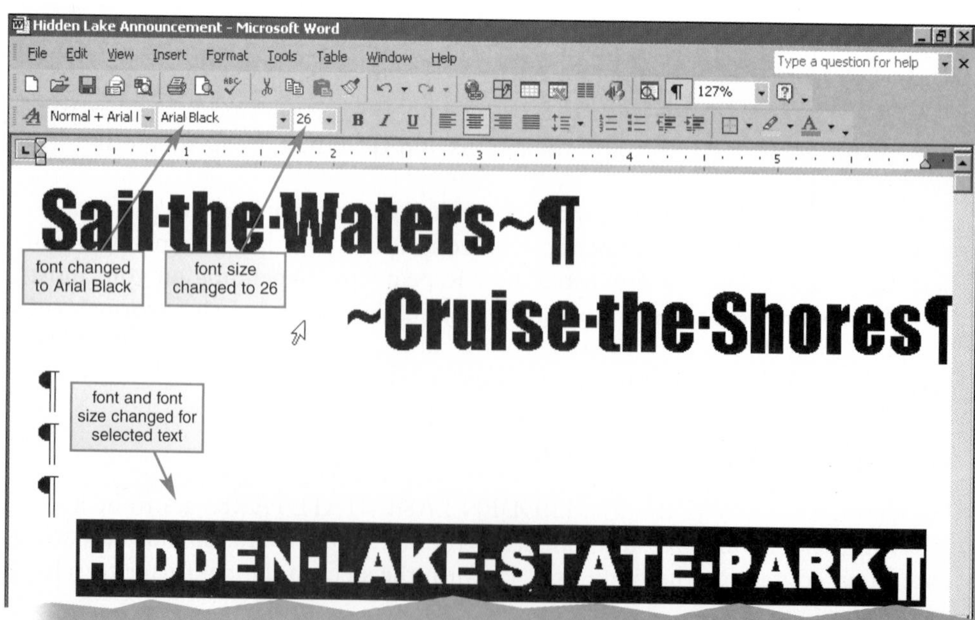

FIGURE 1-47

Italicize Selected Text

Italicized text has a slanted appearance. Perform the following step to italicize the selected characters in the body title.

To Italicize Selected Text

1 With the text still selected, click the Italic button on the Formatting toolbar.

Word italicizes the text (Figure 1-48). The Italic button on the Formatting toolbar is selected.

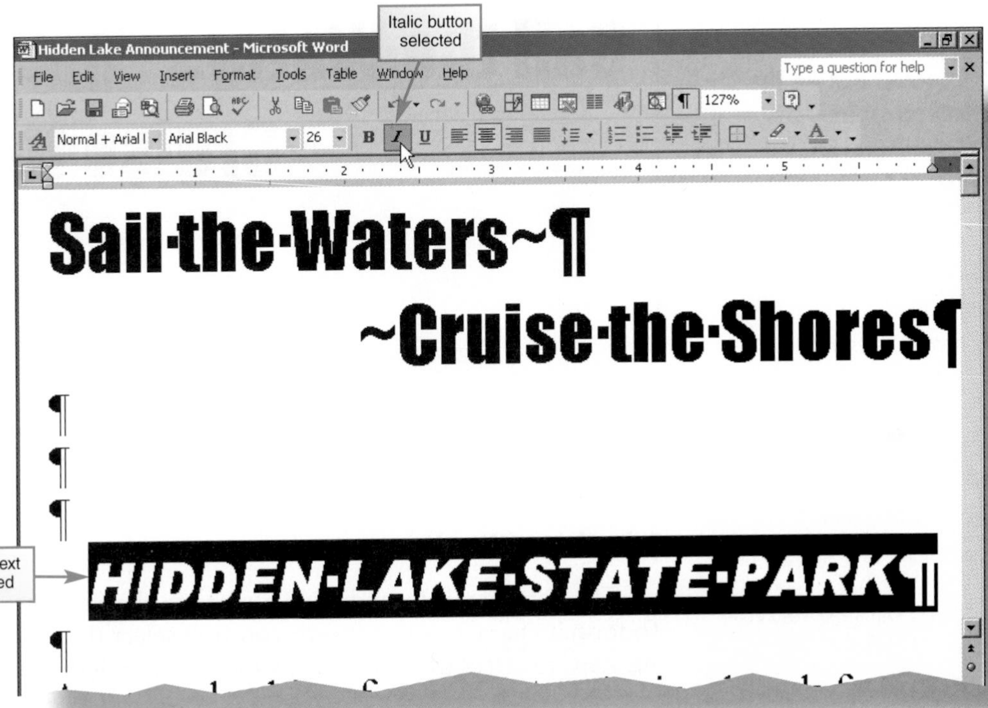

FIGURE 1-48

When the selected text is italicized, the Italic button on the Formatting toolbar is selected. If, for some reason, you wanted to remove the italics from the selected text, you would click the Italic button a second time, or you immediately could click the Undo button on the Standard toolbar.

Scrolling

The next text to format is in the lower portion of the announcement, which does not display in the document window. To continue formatting the document, perform the steps on the next page to scroll down one screen so the lower portion of the announcement displays in the document window.

Other Ways

1. On Format menu click Font, click Font tab, click Italic in Font style list, click OK button
2. Right-click selected text, click Font on shortcut menu, click Font tab, click Italic in Font style list, click OK button
3. Press CTRL+I
4. In Voice Command mode, say "Italic"

More About

Toolbar Buttons

Many of the buttons on the toolbars are toggles; that is, click them once to format the selected text; and click them again to remove the format from the selected text.

Steps To Scroll through the Document

1 Position the mouse pointer below the scroll box on the vertical scroll bar (Figure 1-49).

2 Click below the scroll box on the vertical scroll bar.

Word scrolls down one screen in the document (shown in Figure 1-50 below). Depending on your monitor type, your screen may scroll differently.

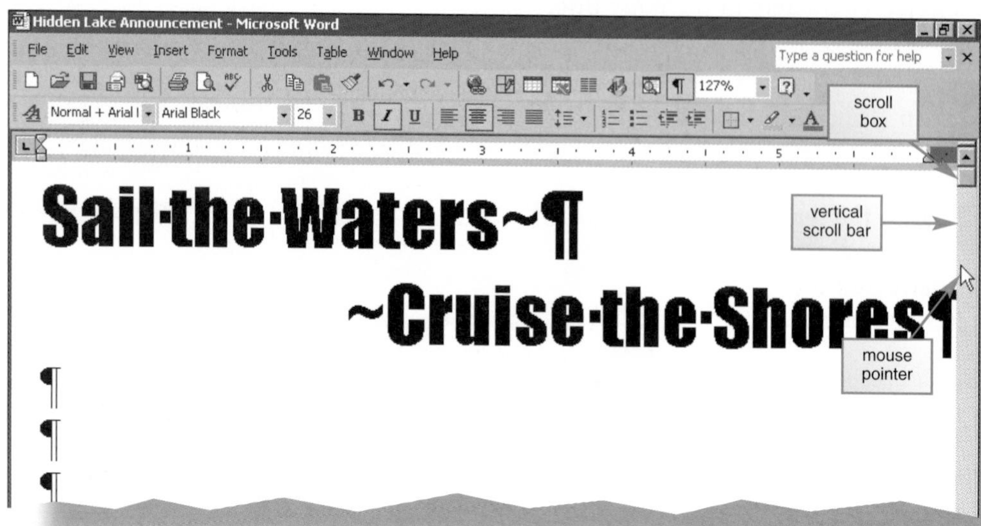
Hidden Lake Announcement - Microsoft Word
scroll box
vertical scroll bar
Sail·the·Waters~¶
~Cruise·the·Shores¶
mouse pointer

FIGURE 1-49

Other Ways

1. Press PAGE DOWN or PAGE UP
2. See Tables 1-1 and 1-2 on page WD 1.27
3. In Dictation mode, say key name(s) in Table 1-2

Selecting a Word

The next step is to underline a word in the first paragraph below the body title. To format characters in a word, you first select the entire word. Perform the following steps to select the word, the, so you can underline it.

Steps To Select a Word

1 Position the mouse pointer somewhere in the word to be formatted (the, in this case).

The mouse pointer's shape is an I-beam when you position it in unselected text in the document window (Figure 1-50).

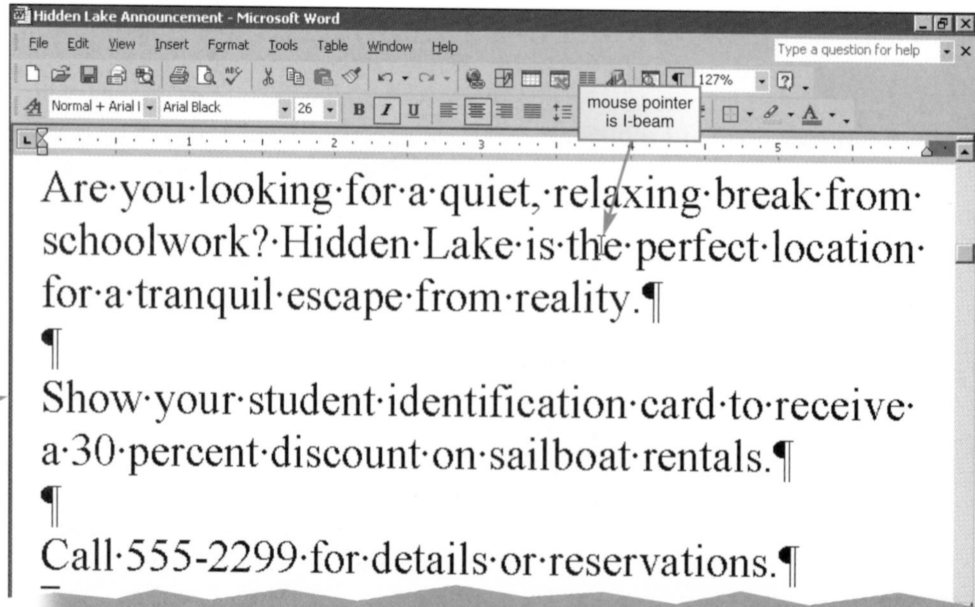
Hidden Lake Announcement - Microsoft Word
mouse pointer is I-beam
next screen of document displays in document window
Are·you·looking·for·a·quiet,·relaxing·break·from·schoolwork?·Hidden·Lake·is·the·perfect·location·for·a·tranquil·escape·from·reality.¶
¶
Show·your·student·identification·card·to·receive·a·30·percent·discount·on·sailboat·rentals.¶
¶
Call·555-2299·for·details·or·reservations.¶

FIGURE 1-50

2 Double-click the word to be selected.

The word, the, is selected (Figure 1-51). Notice that when the mouse pointer is positioned in a selected word, its shape is a left-pointing block arrow.

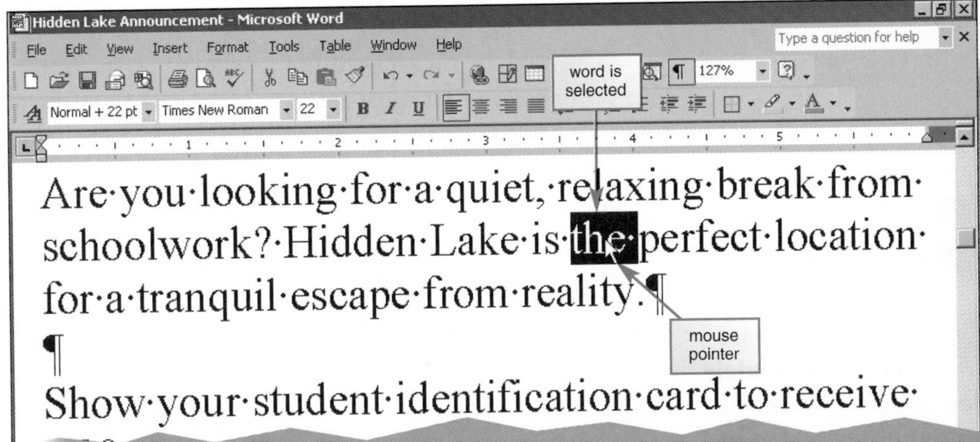
Hidden Lake Announcement - Microsoft Word
word is selected
Are·you·looking·for·a·quiet,·relaxing·break·from·
schoolwork?·Hidden·Lake·is·the·perfect·location·
for·a·tranquil·escape·from·reality.¶
¶
Show·your·student·identification·card·to·receive·
mouse pointer

FIGURE 1-51

Other Ways

1. Drag through the word
2. With insertion point at beginning of desired word, press CTRL+SHIFT+RIGHT ARROW
3. With insertion point at beginning of desired word, in Voice Command mode, say "Select Word"

Underlining Selected Text

Underlined text prints with an underscore (_) below each character. Underlining is used to emphasize or draw attention to specific text. Follow the step below to underline the selected word.

Steps To Underline Selected Text

1 With the text still selected, click the Underline button on the Formatting toolbar.

Word underlines the text (Figure 1-52). The Underline button on the Formatting toolbar is selected.

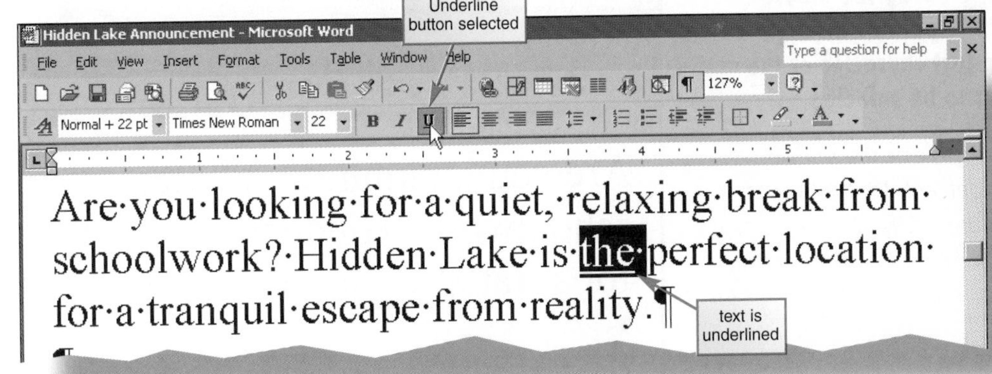
Underline button selected
Hidden Lake Announcement - Microsoft Word
Are·you·looking·for·a·quiet,·relaxing·break·from·
schoolwork?·Hidden·Lake·is·the·perfect·location·
for·a·tranquil·escape·from·reality.¶
text is underlined

FIGURE 1-52

Other Ways

1. On Format menu click Font, click Font tab, click Underline style box arrow, click desired underline style, click OK button
2. Press CTRL+U
3. In Voice Command mode, say "Underline"

When the selected text is underlined, the Underline button on the Formatting toolbar is selected. If, for some reason, you wanted to remove the underline from the selected text, you would click the Underline button a second time, or you immediately could click the Undo button on the Standard toolbar.

In addition to the basic underline shown in Figure 1-52, Word has many decorative underlines that are available in the Font dialog box. For example, you can use double underlines, dotted underlines, and wavy underlines. In the Font dialog box, you also can change the color of an underline and instruct Word to underline only the words and not the spaces between the words. To display the Font dialog box, click Format on the menu bar and then click Font.

Selecting a Group of Words

The next step is to bold the words, 30 percent discount, in the announcement. To do this, you first must select this group of words. Perform the following steps to select a group of words.

Steps To Select a Group of Words

1 Position the mouse pointer immediately to the left of the first character of the text to be selected.

The mouse pointer, an I-beam, is to the left of the 3 in 30 (Figure 1-53).

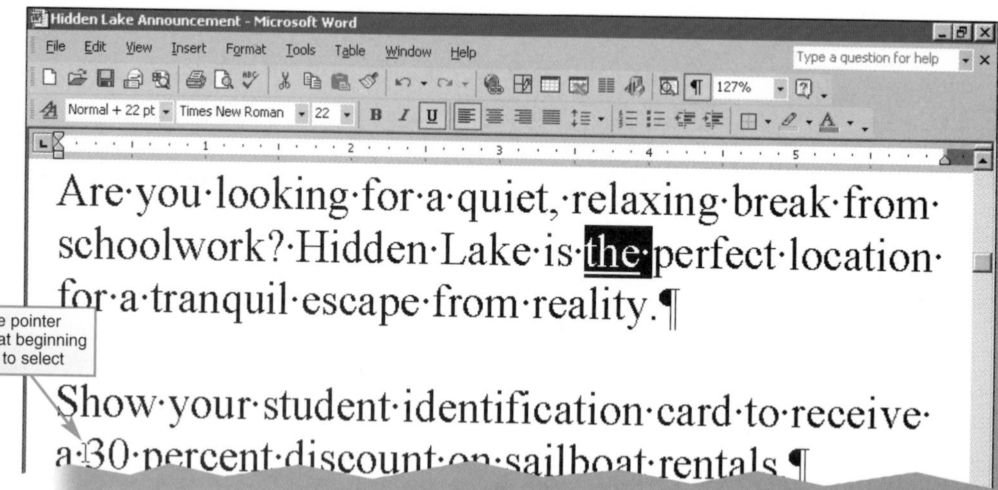
Hidden Lake Announcement - Microsoft Word
Are·you·looking·for·a·quiet,·relaxing·break·from·
schoolwork?·Hidden·Lake·is·the·perfect·location·
for·a·tranquil·escape·from·reality.¶
mouse pointer (I-beam) at beginning of text to select
Show·your·student·identification·card·to·receive·
a·30·percent·discount·on·sailboat·rentals.¶

FIGURE 1-53

2 Drag the mouse pointer through the last character of the text to be selected.

Word selects the phrase, 30 percent discount (Figure 1-54).

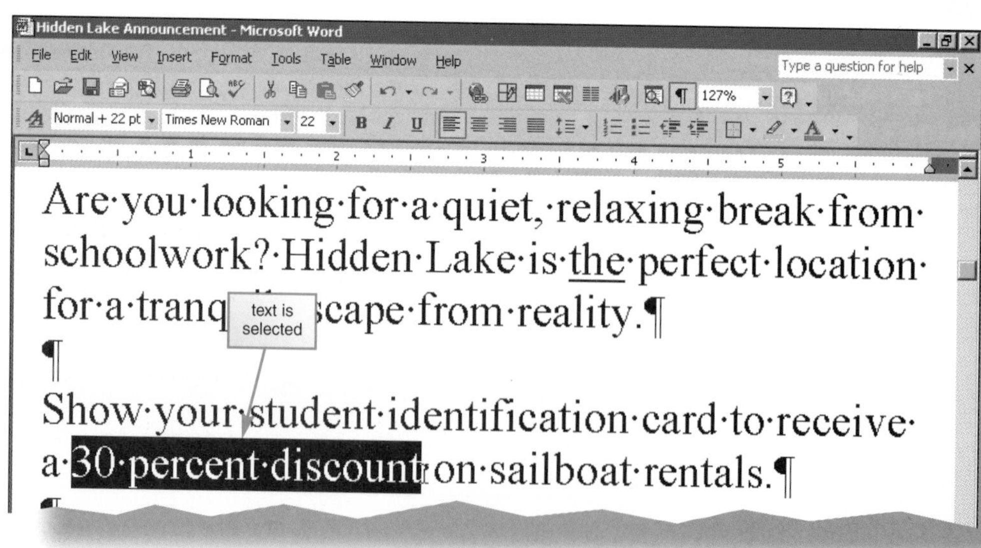
Hidden Lake Announcement - Microsoft Word
Are·you·looking·for·a·quiet,·relaxing·break·from·
schoolwork?·Hidden·Lake·is·the·perfect·location·
for·a·tranq
text is selected
scape·from·reality.¶
¶
Show·your·student·identification·card·to·receive·
a·30·percent·discount·on·sailboat·rentals.¶

FIGURE 1-54

Other Ways

1. With insertion point at beginning of first word in the group, press CTRL+SHIFT+RIGHT ARROW until words are selected
2. In Voice Command mode, repeatedly say "Select Word"

Bold Selected Text

Bold characters display somewhat thicker and darker than those that are not bold. Perform the following step to bold the phrase, 30 percent discount.

Steps To Bold Selected Text

1 While the text is selected, click the Bold button on the Formatting toolbar. Click inside the selected text, which removes the selection (highlight) and positions the insertion point in the bold text.

Word formats the selected text in bold and positions the insertion point inside the bold text (Figure 1-55). The Bold button is selected.

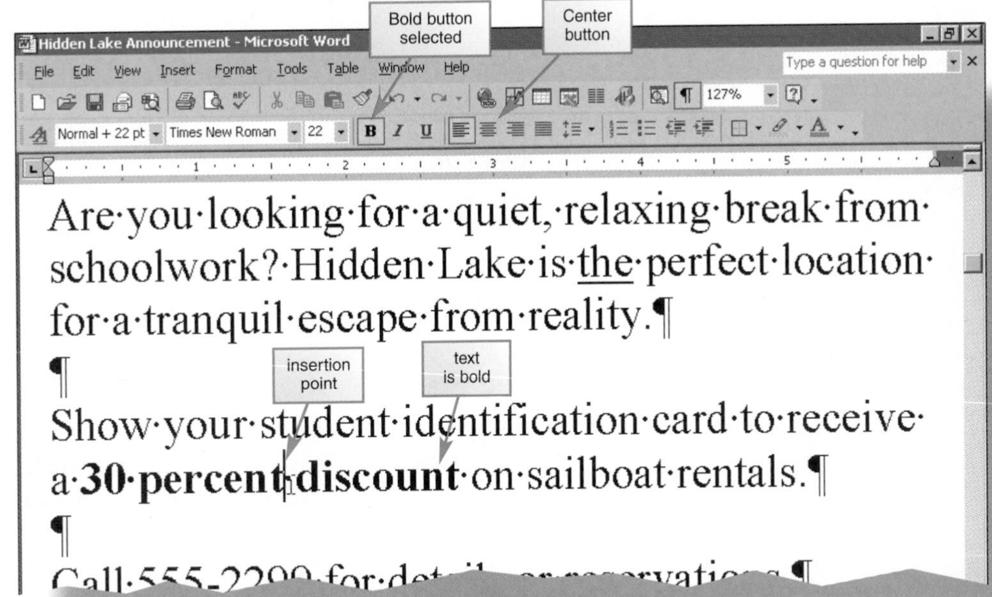

FIGURE 1-55

Other Ways

1. On Format menu click Font, click Font tab, click Bold in Font style list, click OK button
2. Right-click selected text, click Font on shortcut menu, click Font tab, click Bold in Font style list, click OK button
3. Press CTRL+B
4. In Voice Command mode, say "Bold"

To remove a selection (highlight), click the mouse. If you click inside the selection, the Formatting toolbar displays the formatting characteristics of the characters and paragraphs containing the insertion point. For example, at the location of the insertion point, the characters are a 22-point Times New Roman bold font. The paragraph is left-aligned.

When the selected text is bold, the Bold button on the Formatting toolbar is selected. If, for some reason, you wanted to remove the bold format of the selected text, you would click the Bold button a second time.

The next step is to center the last line of the announcement, as described in the following steps.

TO CENTER A PARAGRAPH

1. Click somewhere in the paragraph to be centered.
2. Click the Center button on the Formatting toolbar (shown in Figure 1-55).

Word centers the last line of the announcement (Figure 1-56).

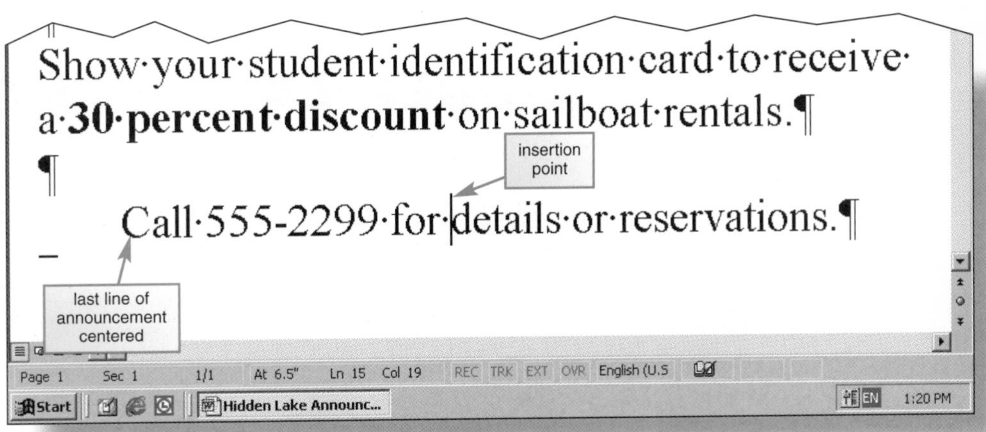

FIGURE 1-56

More About

Clip Art

If Word displays a dialog box when you issue the command to display clip art, click the Now button to catalog all media files. If you are not connected to the Web, Word displays clip art from your hard disk. If you are connected to the Web, Word displays clip art from your hard disk and also from Microsoft's Web site. When clip art images display in the Insert Clip Art task pane, Web clips are identified by a small globe displayed in their lower-left corner.

The formatting for the announcement now is complete. The next step is to insert a graphical image into the document and then resize the image.

Inserting Clip Art into a Word Document

Files containing graphical images, also called **graphics**, are available from a variety of sources. Word 2002 includes a series of predefined graphics called **clip art** that you can insert into a Word document. Clip art is located in the **Clip Organizer**, which contains a collection of clips, including clip art, as well as photographs, sounds, and video clips. The Clip Organizer contains its own Help system to assist you in locating clips suited to your application.

Inserting Clip Art

The next step in the project is to insert a clip art image of a sailboat into the announcement between the headline and the body title. Perform the following steps to use the Insert Clip Art task pane to insert clip art into the document.

Steps To Insert Clip Art into a Document

1 To position the insertion point where you want the clip art to be located, press CTRL+HOME and then press the DOWN ARROW key three times. Click Insert on the menu bar.

The insertion point is positioned on the second paragraph mark below the headline, and the Insert menu displays (Figure 1-57). Remember that a short menu initially displays, which expands into a full menu after a few seconds.

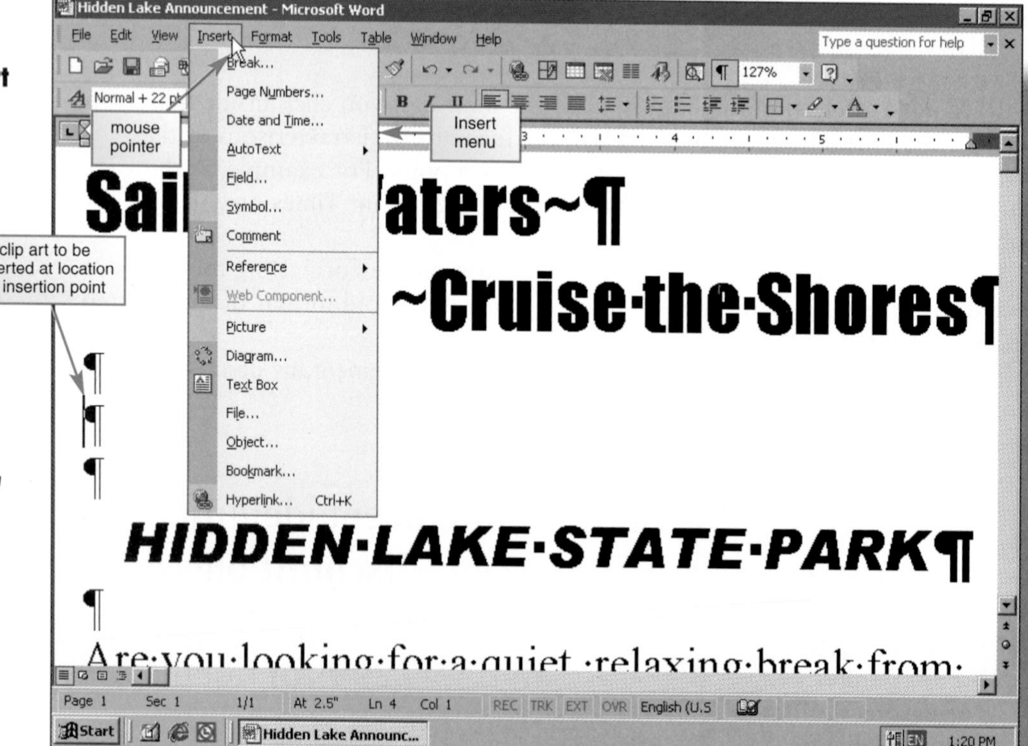

FIGURE 1-57

2 Point to Picture and then point to Clip Art.

The Picture submenu displays (Figure 1-58). As discussed earlier, when you point to a command that has a small arrow to its right, Word displays a submenu associated with that command.

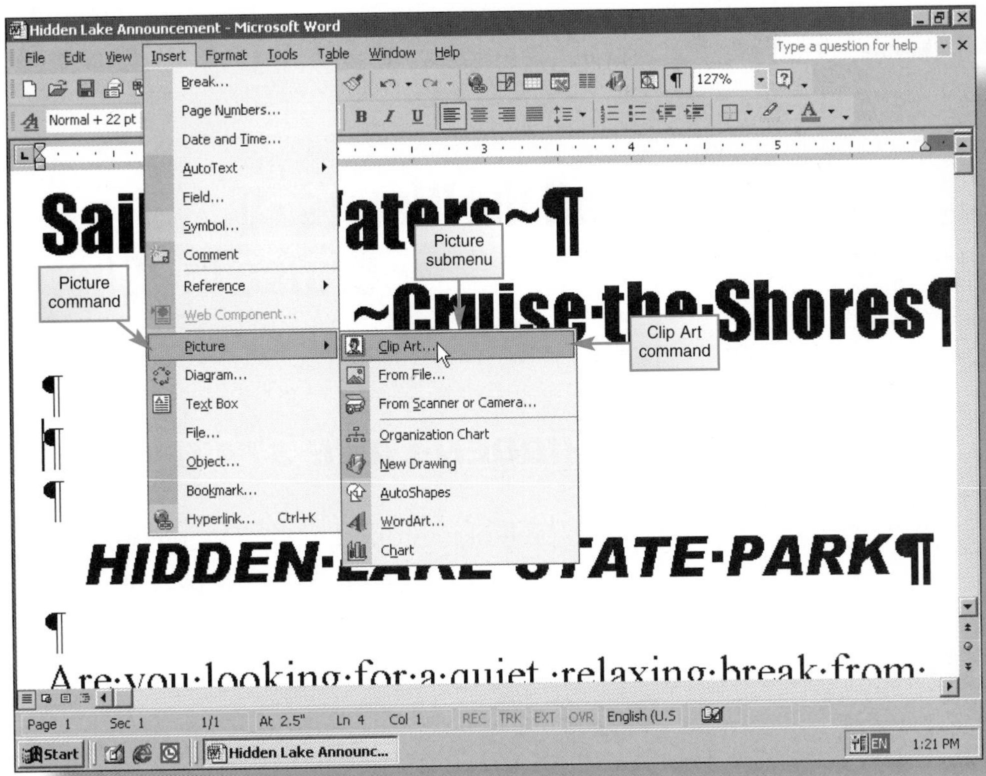

FIGURE 1-58

3 Click Clip Art. If the Search text text box contains text, drag through the text to select it. Type `sailboat` **and then point to the Search button.**

Word displays the Insert Clip Art task pane at the right edge of the Word window (Figure 1-59). Recall that a task pane is a separate window that enables you to carry out some Word tasks more efficiently. When you enter a description of the desired graphic in the Search text text box, Word searches the Clip Organizer for clips that match the description.

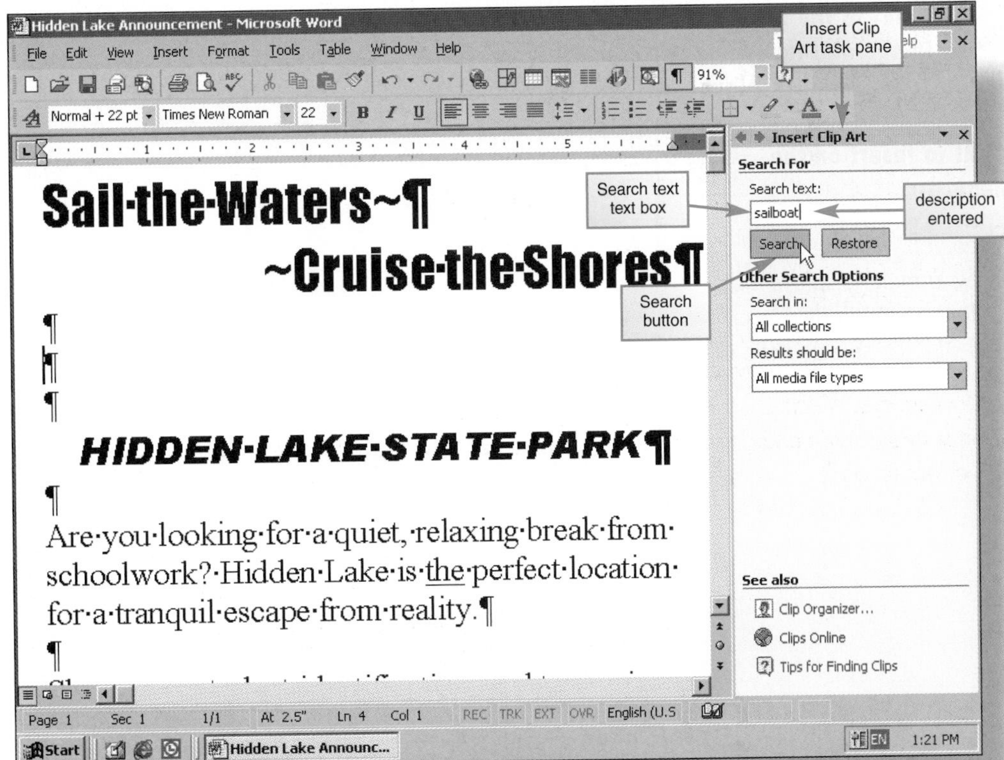

FIGURE 1-59

4 Click the Search button.

A list of clips that match the description, sailboat, displays (Figure 1-60). If you are connected to the Web, the Insert Clip Art task pane will display clips from the Web, as well as those installed on your hard disk.

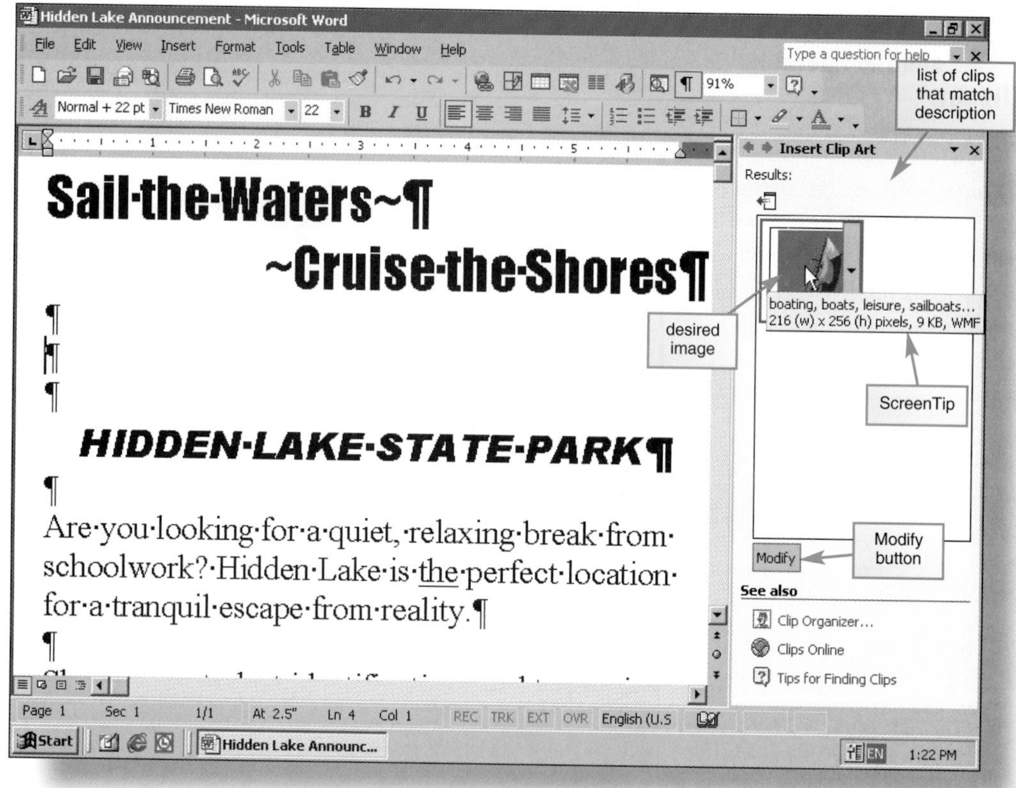

FIGURE 1-60

5 Point to the desired image and then click the box arrow that displays to the right of the image. Point to Insert on the menu.

When you click the box arrow, a menu displays that contains commands associated with the selected clip art image (Figure 1-61).

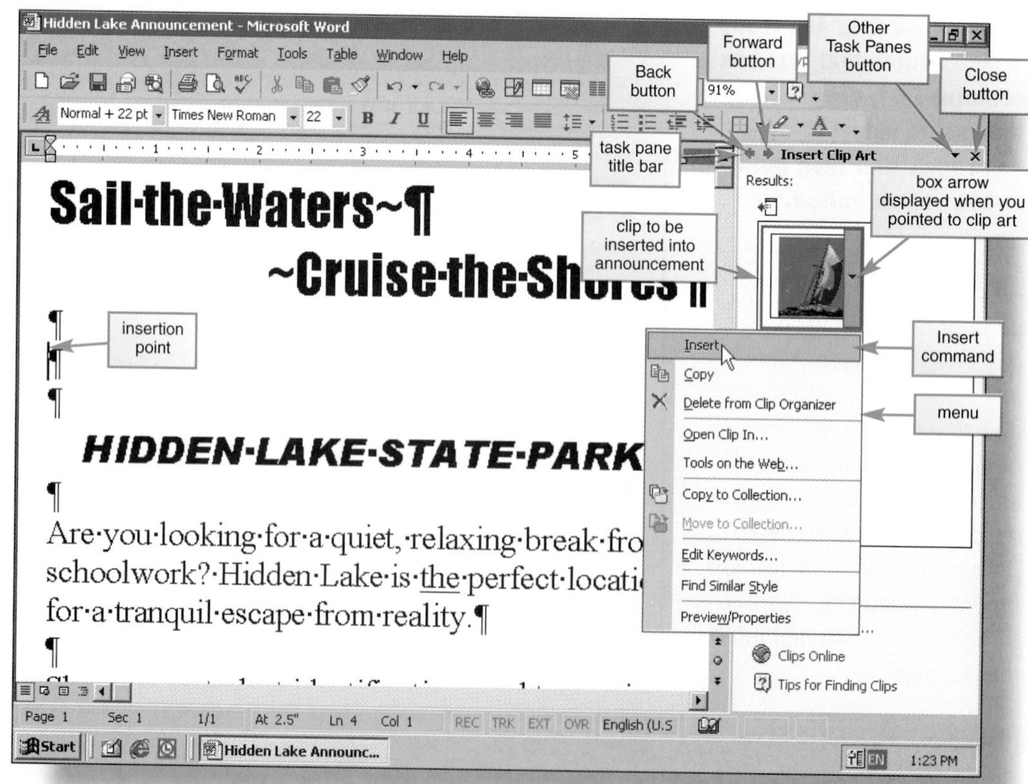

FIGURE 1-61

6 **Click Insert. Click the Close button on the Insert Clip Art task pane title bar.**

Word inserts the clip art into the document at the location of the insertion point (Figure 1-62). The image of the sailboat displays below the headline in the announcement.

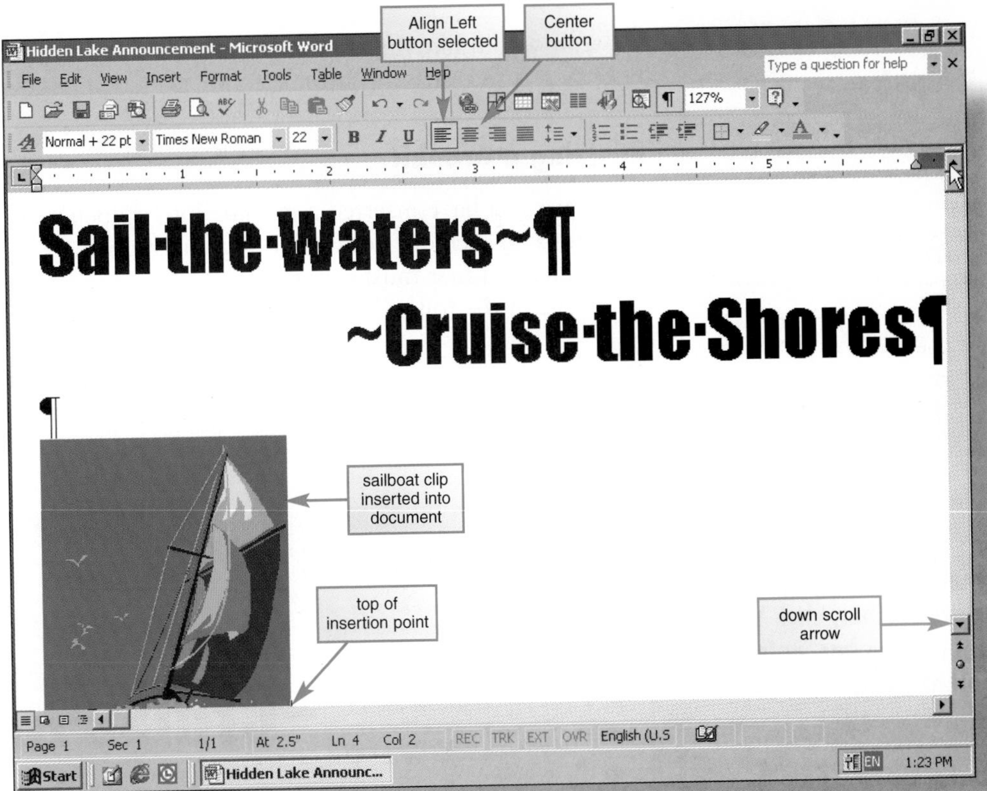

FIGURE 1-62

Other Ways

1. In Voice Command mode, say "Insert, Picture, Clip Art"

After you enter a description of a desired image in the Search text text box, you may want to enter a different description to locate additional or different clip art. To redisplay the Search text text box in the Insert Clip Art task pane, click the Modify button in the task pane (Figure 1-60). This will redisplay the screen shown in Figure 1-59 on page WD 1.47.

Recall that Word has eight task panes that automatically display as you perform certain operations. You also can display a task pane by clicking View on the menu bar and then clicking Task Pane. When you do this, the task pane you most recently used displays in the Word window. To display a different task pane, click the Other Task Panes button (Figure 1-61) to the left of the Close button on the task pane title bar. If you have displayed multiple task panes during a Word session, you can click the Back and Forward buttons at the left edge of the task pane title bar to scroll through the various task panes.

The clip art in the announcement is part of a paragraph. Because that paragraph is left-aligned, the clip art also is left-aligned. Notice the Align Left button on the Formatting toolbar is selected (Figure 1-62). You can use any of the paragraph alignment buttons on the Formatting toolbar to reposition the clip art. Perform the following step to center a graphic that is part of a paragraph.

More About

Clip Art Packages

For more information on the clip art available for purchase, visit the Word 2002 More About Web page (scsite.com/wd2002/more.htm) and then click Clip Art.

More About

Positioning Graphics

Emphasize a graphic by placing it at the optical center of the page. To determine optical center, divide the page in half horizontally and vertically. The optical center is located one third of the way up the vertical line from the point of intersection of the two lines.

TO CENTER A PARAGRAPH CONTAINING A GRAPHIC

1 If necessary, click the down scroll arrow on the scroll bar to display the entire graphic in the document window. With the insertion point on the paragraph mark containing the image, click the Center button on the Formatting toolbar.

Word centers the paragraph, which also centers the graphic in the paragraph (Figure 1-63 on the next page).

Graphics

If you have a scanner or digital camera attached to your computer, Word can insert a graphic directly from these devices. You also can scan a graphic into a file and then insert the scanned file into the Word document.

You would like the clip art in this announcement to be a little larger. Thus, the next step is to resize the graphic.

Resizing a Graphic

Once you have inserted a graphic into a document, you easily can change its size. **Resizing** includes both enlarging and reducing the size of a graphic. To resize a graphic, you first must select it.

Perform the following step to select a graphic.

Steps To Select a Graphic

1 Click anywhere in the graphic. If your screen does not display the Picture toolbar, click View on the menu bar, point to Toolbars, and then click Picture.

Word selects the graphic (Figure 1-63). A selected graphic displays surrounded by a **selection rectangle** *that has small squares, called* **sizing handles**, *at each corner and middle location. You use the sizing handles to change the size of the graphic. When a graphic is selected, the Picture toolbar automatically displays on the screen.*

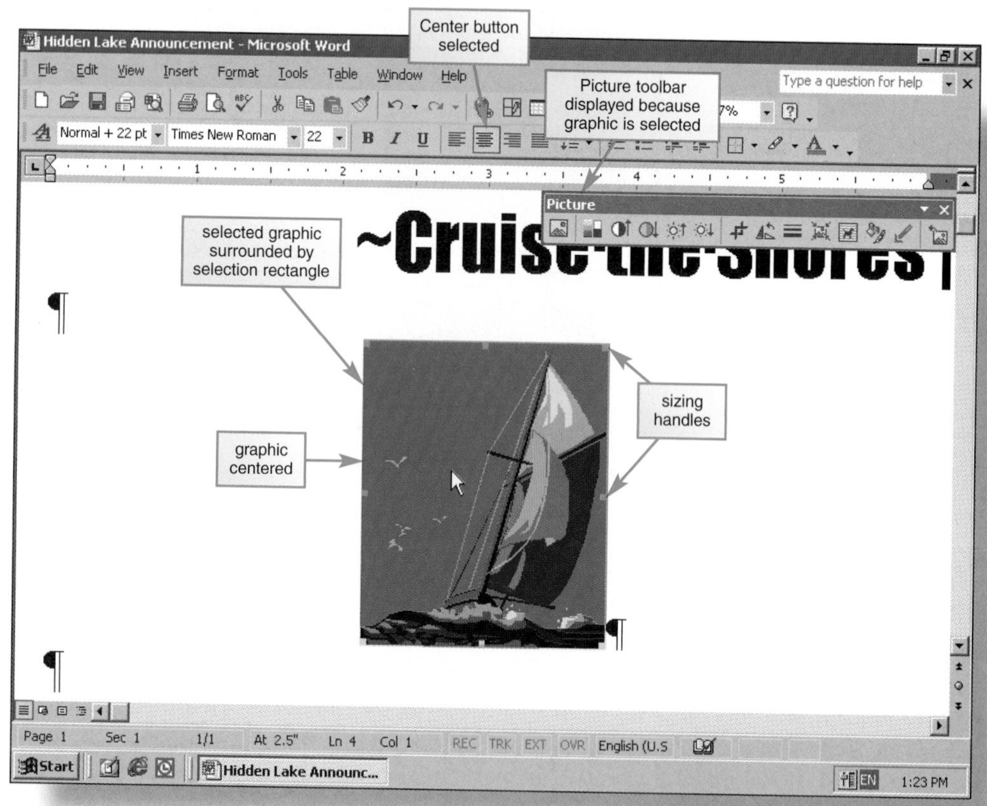

FIGURE 1-63

The Picture Toolbar

The Picture toolbar is a floating toolbar. Thus, you can drag its title bar to move the toolbar to a different location on the screen. You also can double-click the toolbar's title bar to dock the toolbar at the top of the screen.

The following steps show how to resize the graphic you just inserted and selected.

Steps To Resize a Graphic

1 With the graphic still selected, point to the upper-left corner sizing handle.

The mouse pointer shape changes to a two-headed arrow when it is on a sizing handle (Figure 1-64). To resize a graphic, you drag the sizing handle(s) until the graphic is the desired size.

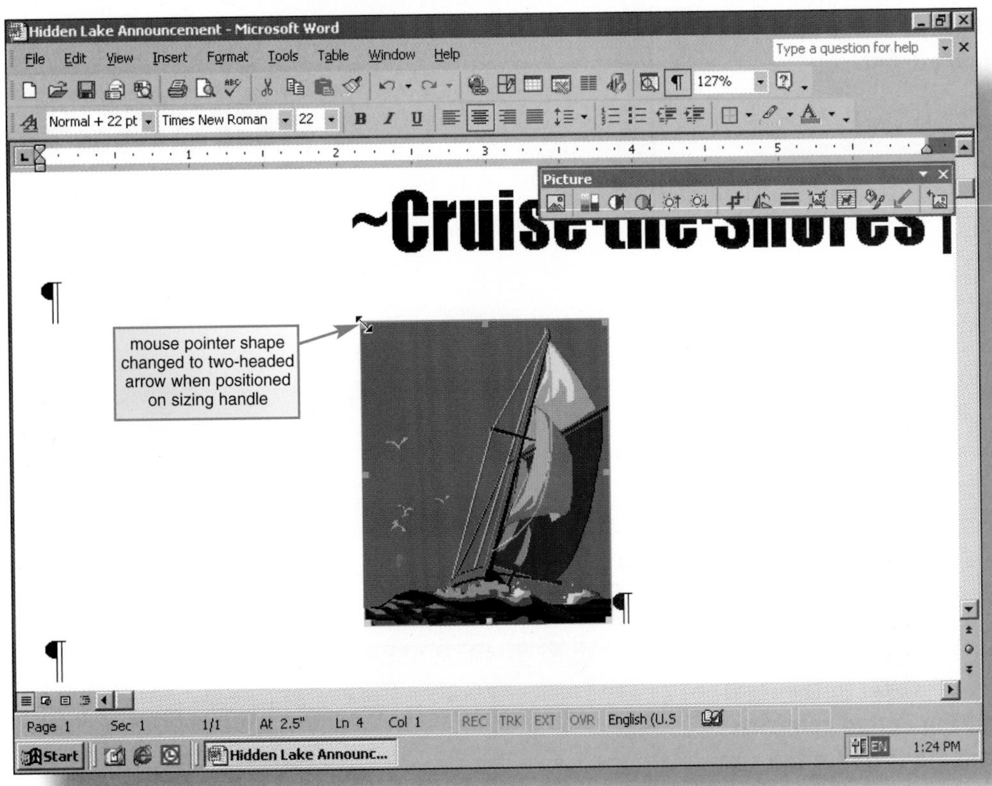

FIGURE 1-64

2 Drag the sizing handle diagonally outward until the dotted selection rectangle is positioned approximately as shown in Figure 1-65.

The graphic has a rectangular shape. When you drag a corner sizing handle, this shape remains intact. In this announcement, the graphic is to have a square shape.

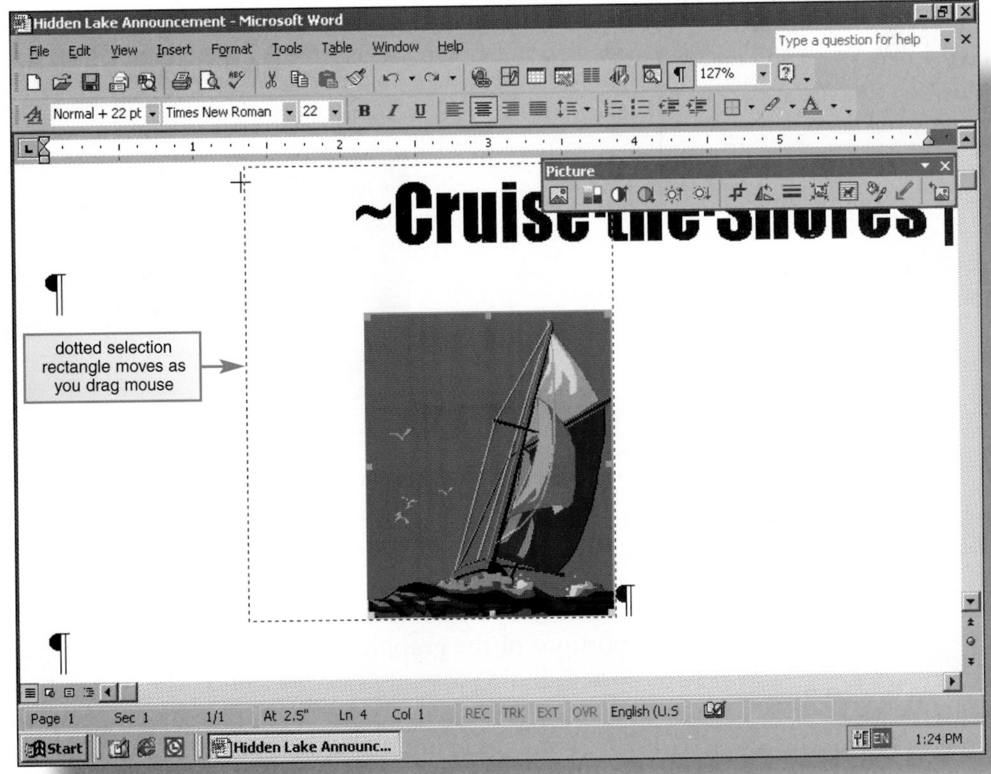

FIGURE 1-65

3 **Release the mouse button. Point to the right-middle sizing handle on the graphic (Figure 1-66).**

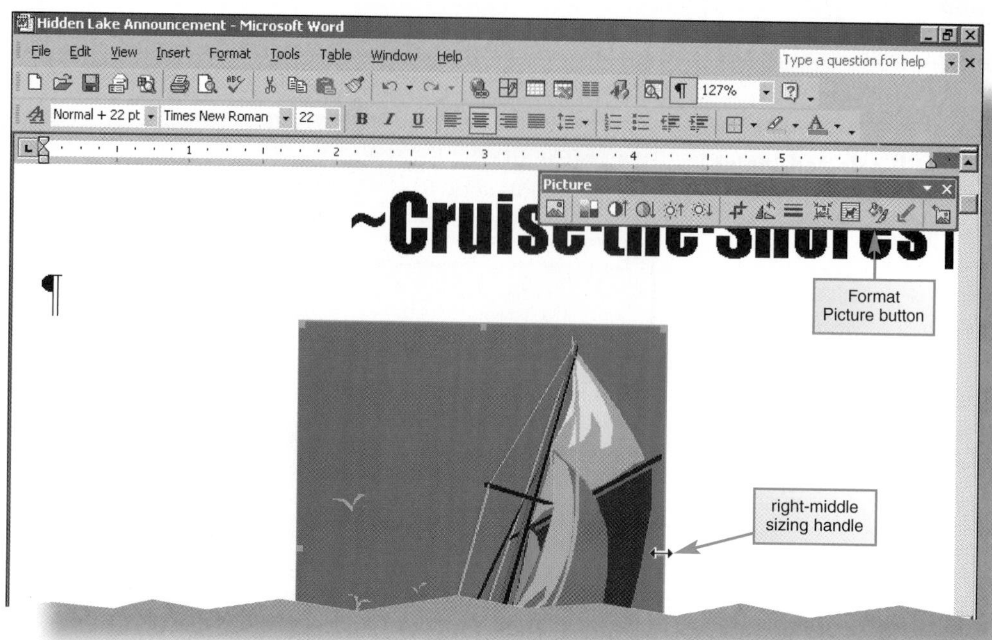

FIGURE 1-66

4 **Drag the sizing handle to the right until the dotted selection rectangle is about the size of a square. Release the mouse button. Press CTRL+HOME.**

Word resizes the graphic (Figure 1-67). When you click outside of a graphic or press a key to scroll through a document, Word deselects the graphic. The Picture toolbar disappears from the screen when you deselect the graphic.

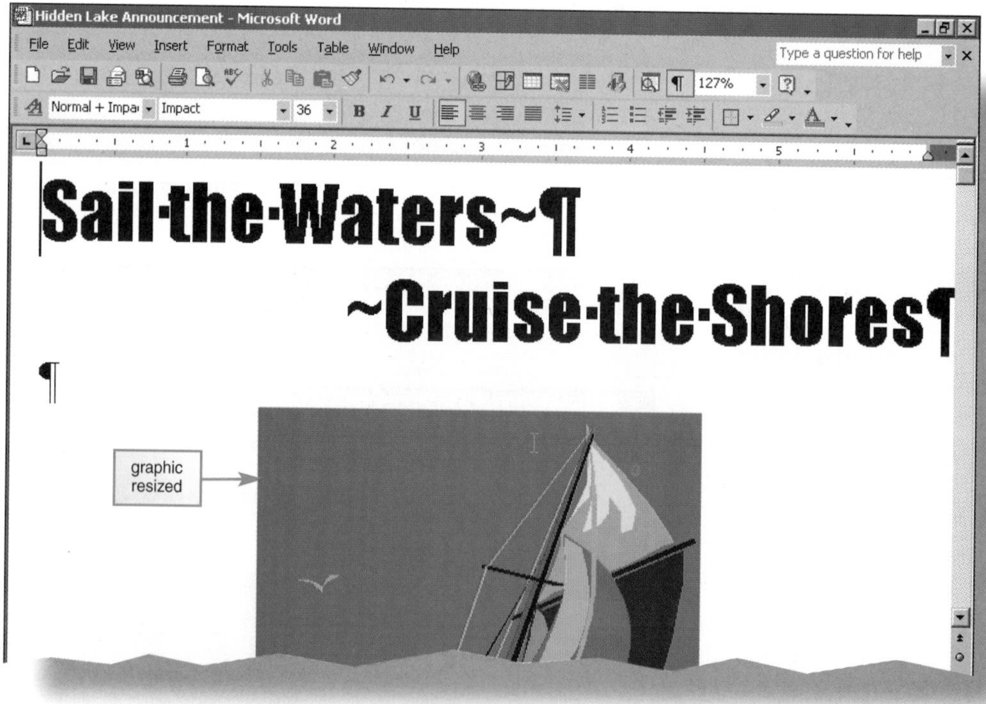

FIGURE 1-67

Other Ways

1. Click Format Picture button on Picture toolbar, click Size tab, enter desired height and width, click OK button
2. On Format menu click Picture, click Size tab, enter desired height and width, click OK button
3. In Voice Command mode, say "Format, Picture"

When you drag a middle sizing handle instead of a corner sizing handle, the proportions of the graphic change, which sometimes causes the graphic to look distorted. In this case, it gives the sail on the sailboat a windblown effect.

Instead of resizing a selected graphic by dragging with the mouse, you also can use the Format Picture dialog box to resize a graphic by clicking the Format Picture button (Figure 1-66) on the Picture toolbar and then clicking the Size tab. Using the

Size sheet, you can enter exact height and width measurements. If you have a precise measurement for a graphic, use the Format Picture dialog box; otherwise, drag the sizing handles to resize a graphic.

Sometimes, you might resize a graphic and realize it is the wrong size. In these cases, you may want to return the graphic to its original size and start again. You could drag the sizing handle until the graphic resembles its original size. To restore a resized graphic to its exact original size, click the graphic to select it and then click the Format Picture button on the Picture toolbar to display the Format Picture dialog box. Click the Size tab and then click the Reset button. Finally, click the OK button.

Resizing Graphics

To maintain the proportions of a graphic, press the SHIFT key while you drag a corner sizing handle.

Saving an Existing Document with the Same File Name

The announcement for Project 1 now is complete. To transfer the modified document with the formatting changes and graphic to your floppy disk in drive A, you must save the document again. When you saved the document the first time, you assigned a file name to it (Hidden Lake Announcement). If you use the following procedure, Word automatically assigns the same file name to the document each time you subsequently save it.

Steps To Save an Existing Document with the Same File Name

1 Click the Save button on the Standard toolbar.

Word saves the document on a floppy disk inserted in drive A using the currently assigned file name, Hidden Lake Announcement (Figure 1-68).

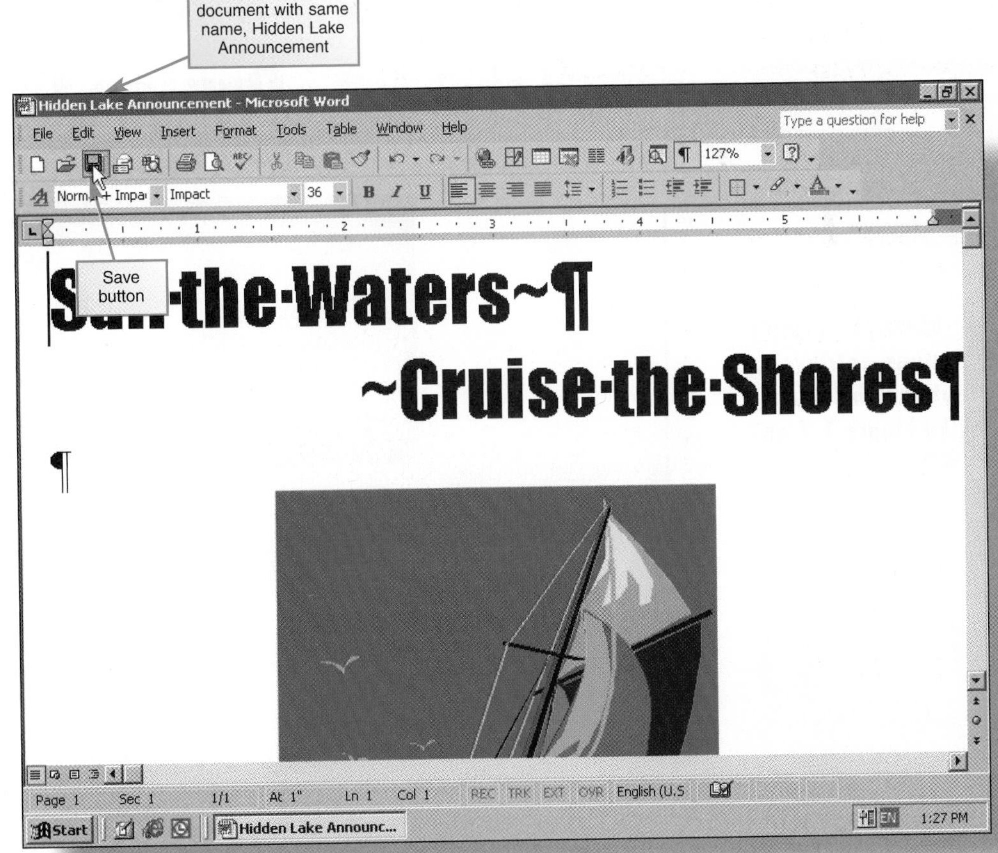

FIGURE 1-68

1. On File menu click Save
2. Press CTRL+S
3. In Voice Command mode, say "Save"

More About

Printing

If you want to save ink, print faster, or decease printer overrun errors, print a draft. Click File on the menu bar and then click Print. Click the Options button, place a check mark in the Draft output check box, and then click the OK button in each dialog box.

While Word is saving the document, the Background Save icon displays near the right edge of the status bar. When the save is complete, the document remains in memory and on the screen.

If, for some reason, you want to save an existing document with a different file name, click Save As on the File menu to display the Save As dialog box. Then, fill in the Save As dialog box as discussed in Steps 2 through 5 on pages WD 1.30 through WD 1.32.

Printing a Document

The next step is to print the document you created. A printed version of the document is called a **hard copy** or **printout**. Perform the following steps to print the announcement created in Project 1.

Steps To Print a Document

1. **Ready the printer according to the printer instructions. Click the Print button on the Standard toolbar.**

   The mouse pointer briefly changes to an hourglass shape as Word prepares to print the document. While the document is printing, a printer icon displays in the tray status area on the taskbar (Figure 1-69).

2. **When the printer stops, retrieve the printout, which should look like Figure 1-1 on page WD 1.07.**

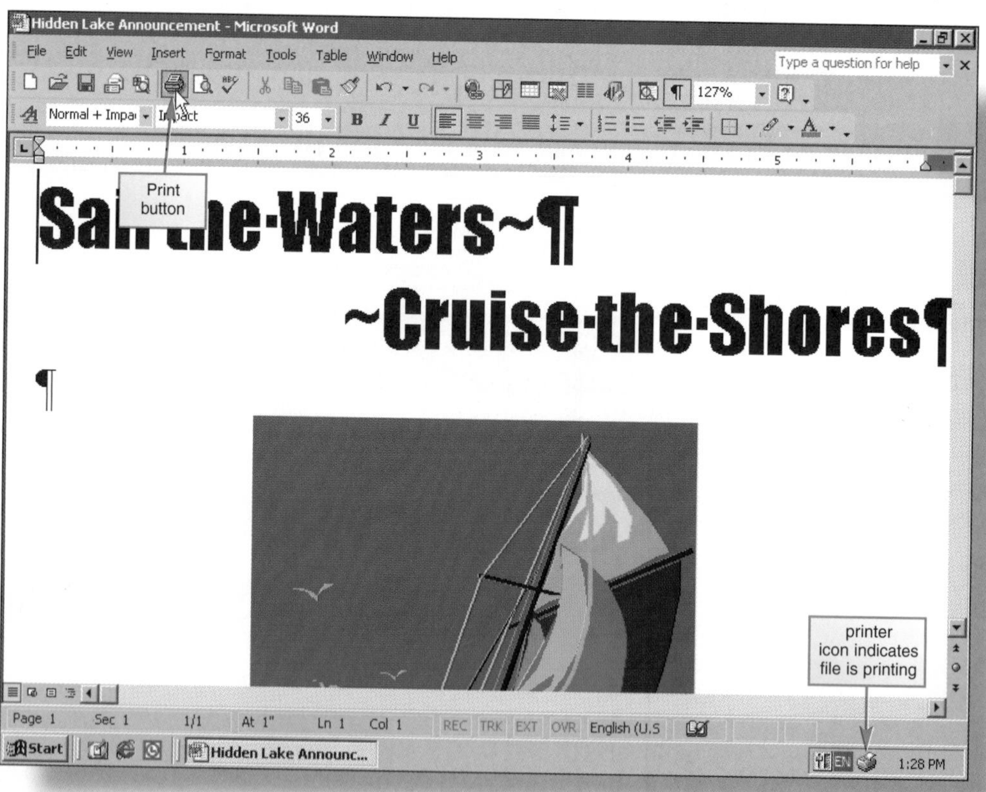

FIGURE 1-69

Other Ways

1. On File menu click Print, click OK button
2. Press CTRL+P, press ENTER
3. In Voice Command mode, say "Print"

When you use the Print button to print a document, Word prints the entire document automatically. You then may distribute the hard copy or keep it as a permanent record of the document.

If you wanted to print multiple copies of the document, click File on the menu bar and then click Print to display the Print dialog box. This dialog box has several printing options, including specifying the number of copies to print.

If you wanted to cancel your job that is printing or one you have waiting to be printed, double-click the printer icon on the taskbar (Figure 1-69). In the printer window, click the job to be canceled and then click Cancel on the Document menu.

Print Preview

To view a document before you print it, click the Print Preview button on the Standard toolbar. To return to the document window, click the Close Preview button on the Print Preview toolbar.

Quitting Word

After you create, save, and print the announcement, Project 1 is complete. To quit Word and return control to Windows, perform the following steps.

To Quit Word

1 Point to the Close button in the upper-right corner of the title bar (Figure 1-70).

2 Click the Close button.

The Word window closes.

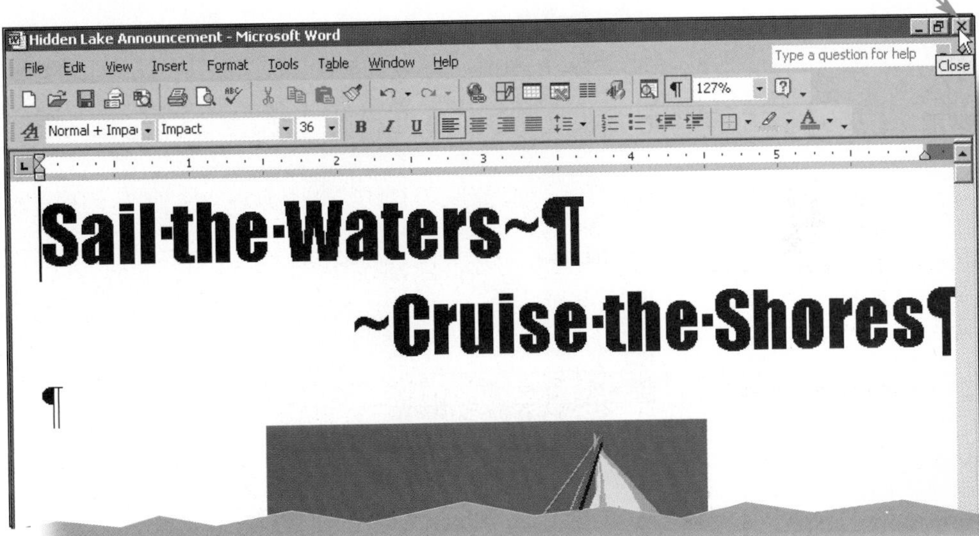

FIGURE 1-70

Other Ways

1. On File menu click Exit
2. Press ALT+F4
3. In Voice Command mode, say "File, Exit"

When you quit Word, a dialog box may display that asks if you want to save the changes. This occurs if you made changes to the document since the last save. Clicking the Yes button in the dialog box saves the changes; clicking the No button ignores the changes; and clicking the Cancel button returns to the document. If you did not make any changes since you saved the document, this dialog box usually does not display.

More About

Opening Files

In Word, you can open a recently used file by clicking File on the menu bar and then clicking the file name on the File menu. To instruct Word to show the recently used documents on the File menu, click Tools on the menu bar, click Options, click the General tab, click Recently used file list to place a check mark in the check box, and then click the OK button.

Opening a Document

Once you have created and saved a document, you often will have reason to retrieve it from disk. For example, you might want to revise the document or print it again. Earlier, you saved the Word document created in Project 1 on a floppy disk using the file name Hidden Lake Announcement.

The steps on the next page illustrate how to open the file Hidden Lake Announcement from a floppy disk in drive A.

To Open a Document

1 **Click the Start button on the taskbar and then point to Open Office Document (Figure 1-71).**

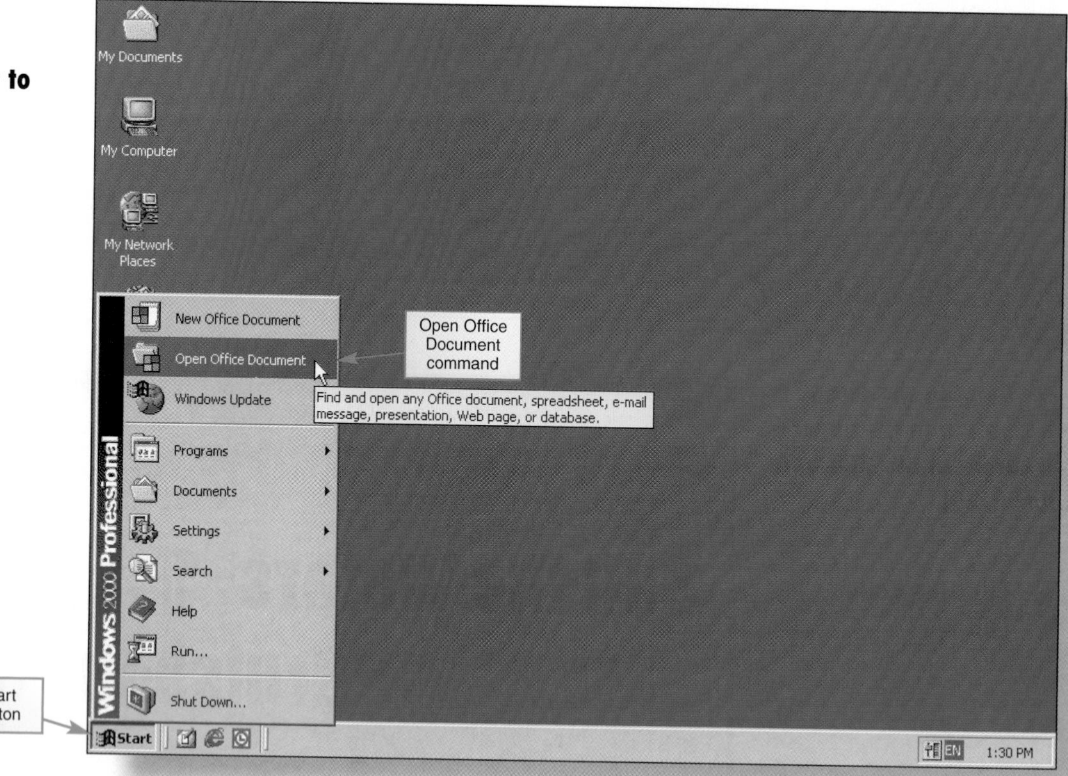

FIGURE 1-71

2 **Click Open Office Document. If necessary, click the Look in box arrow and then click 3½ Floppy (A:). If it is not selected already, click the file name Hidden Lake Announcement. Point to the Open button.**

Office displays the Open Office Document dialog box (Figure 1-72). The names of files on the floppy disk in drive A display in the dialog box.

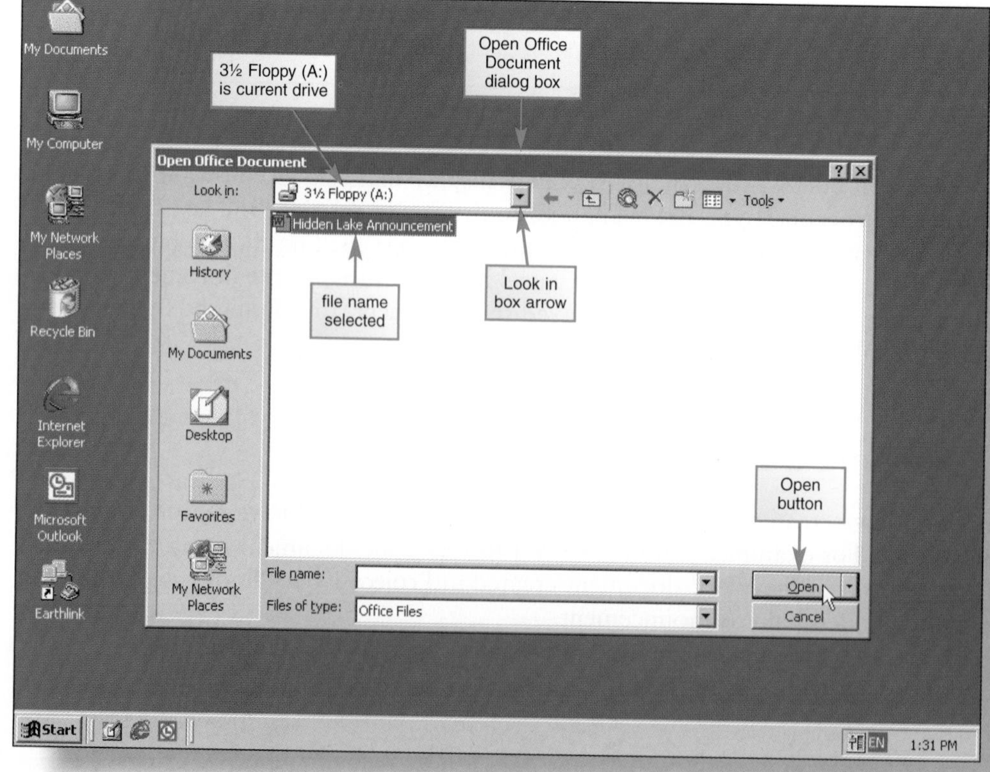

FIGURE 1-72

3 Click the Open button.

Office starts Word, and then Word opens the document, Hidden Lake Announcement, from the floppy disk in drive A. The document displays in the Word window (Figure 1-73).

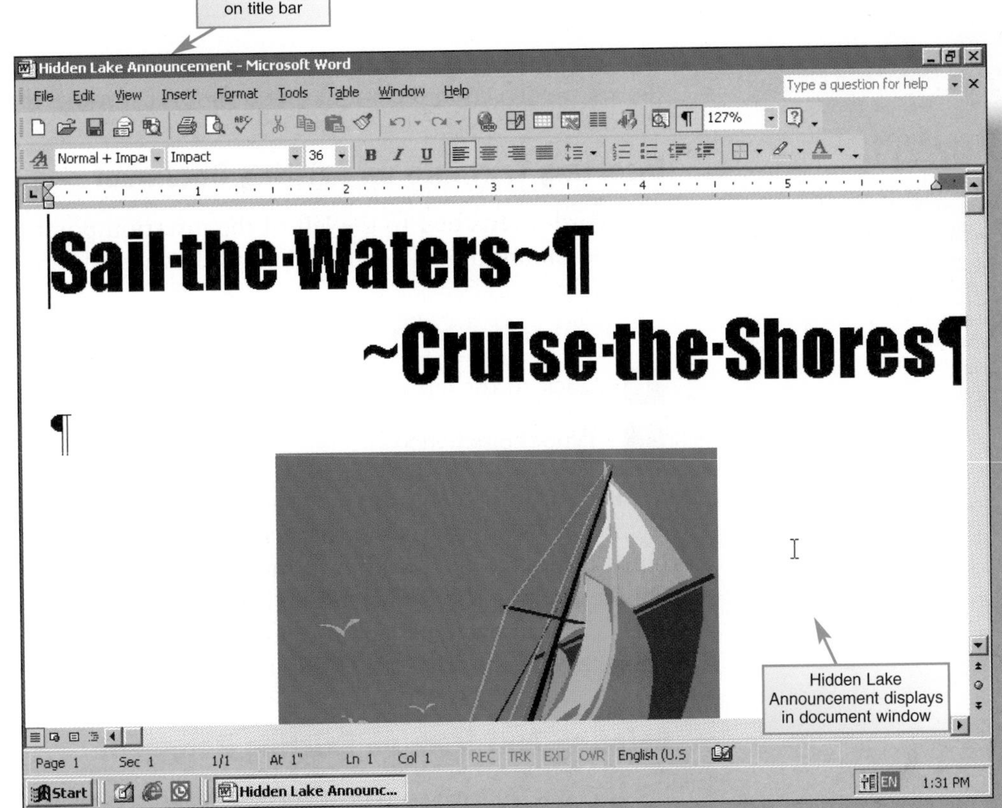

FIGURE 1-73

Other Ways

1. Right-click Start button, click Open All Users, double-click Open Office Document, select file name, click Open button in dialog box
2. Click Open button on Standard toolbar, select file name, click Open button in dialog box
3. On File menu click Open, select file name, click Open button in dialog box
4. In Voice Command mode, say "Open, [select file name], Open"

Correcting Errors

After creating a document, you often will find you must make changes to it. Changes can be required because the document contains an error or because of new circumstances.

Types of Changes Made to Documents

The types of changes made to documents normally fall into one of the three following categories: additions, deletions, or modifications.

ADDITIONS Additional words, sentences, or paragraphs may be required in a document. Additions occur when you omit text from a document and want to insert it later. For example, you may want to insert the word, all, in front of sailboat rentals in the Hidden Lake Announcement.

DELETIONS Sometimes, text in a document is incorrect or is no longer needed. For example, the state park may stop taking reservations. In this case, you would delete the words, or reservations, from the last line of the announcement.

MODIFICATIONS If an error is made in a document or changes take place that affect the document, you might have to revise the word(s) in the text. For example, the state park might change the discount from 30 to 35 percent; thus, you would change the number from 30 to 35.

More About

Overtype

As you type, if existing text is overwritten with new text, you probably are in overtype mode. Double-click the OVR status indicator to turn overtype mode off. You also can press the INSERT key on the keyboard to turn off overtype mode.

Word provides several methods for correcting errors in a document. For each of the error correction techniques, you first must move the insertion point to the error.

Inserting Text into an Existing Document

Word inserts text to the left of the insertion point. The text to the right of the insertion point moves to the right and downward to fit the new text.

TO INSERT TEXT INTO AN EXISTING DOCUMENT

1. Click to the left of the location of text to be inserted.
2. Type the new text.

In Word, the default typing mode is insert mode. In **insert mode**, as you type a character, Word inserts the character and moves all the characters to the right of the typed character one position to the right. You can change to overtype mode by double-clicking the **OVR status indicator** on the status bar (Figure 1-8 on page WD 1.11). In **overtype mode**, Word replaces characters to the right of the insertion point. Double-clicking the OVR status indicator again returns you to insert mode.

Deleting Text from an Existing Document

It is not unusual to type incorrect characters or words in a document. As discussed earlier in this project, you can click the Undo button on the Standard toolbar to immediately undo a command or action — this includes typing. Word also provides other methods of correcting typing errors.

The Clipboard Task Pane

If you click the Cut button (or Copy button) twice in a row, Word displays the Clipboard task pane. You use the Clipboard task pane to copy and paste items within a document or from one Office document to another. To close the Clipboard task pane, click the Close button on the task pane title bar.

TO DELETE AN INCORRECT CHARACTER IN A DOCUMENT

1. Click next to the incorrect character.
2. Press the BACKSPACE key to erase to the left of the insertion point; or press the DELETE key to erase to the right of the insertion point.

TO DELETE (CUT) AN INCORRECT WORD OR PHRASE IN A DOCUMENT

1. Select the word or phrase you want to erase.
2. Right-click the selected word or phrase, and then click Cut on the shortcut menu; or click the Cut button on the Standard toolbar (Figure 1-12a on page WD 1.15); or press the DELETE key.

Closing the Entire Document

Sometimes, everything goes wrong. If this happens, you may want to close the document entirely and start over. You also may want to close a document when you are finished with it so you can begin your next document.

TO CLOSE THE ENTIRE DOCUMENT AND START OVER

1. Click File on the menu bar and then click Close. If Word displays a dialog box, click the No button to ignore the changes since the last time you saved the document.
2. Click the New Blank Document button (Figure 1-12a on page WD 1.15) on the Standard toolbar.

You also can close the document by clicking the Close button at the right edge of the menu bar.

Word Help System

At anytime while you are using Word, you can get answers to questions by using the **Word Help system**. Used properly, this form of online assistance can increase your productivity and reduce your frustrations by minimizing the time you spend learning how to use Word.

The following section shows how to obtain answers to your questions using the Ask a Question box. For additional information on using help, see Appendix A and Table 1-3 on page WD 1.61.

> **More About**
>
> **The Word Help System**
>
> The best way to become familiar with the Word Help system is to use it. Appendix A includes detailed information on the Word Help system as well as exercises that will help you gain confidence in using it.

Obtaining Help Using the Ask a Question Box on the Menu Bar

The **Ask a Question box** on the right side of the menu bar lets you type free-form questions, such as *how do I save* or *how do I create a Web page*, or you can type terms, such as *copy*, *save*, or *format*. Word responds by displaying a list of topics related to the word or phrase you entered. The following steps show how to use the Ask a Question box to obtain information on handwriting recognition.

Steps To Obtain Help Using the Ask a Question Box

1 Click the Ask a Question box on the right side of the menu bar and then type `handwriting recognition` **(Figure 1-74).**

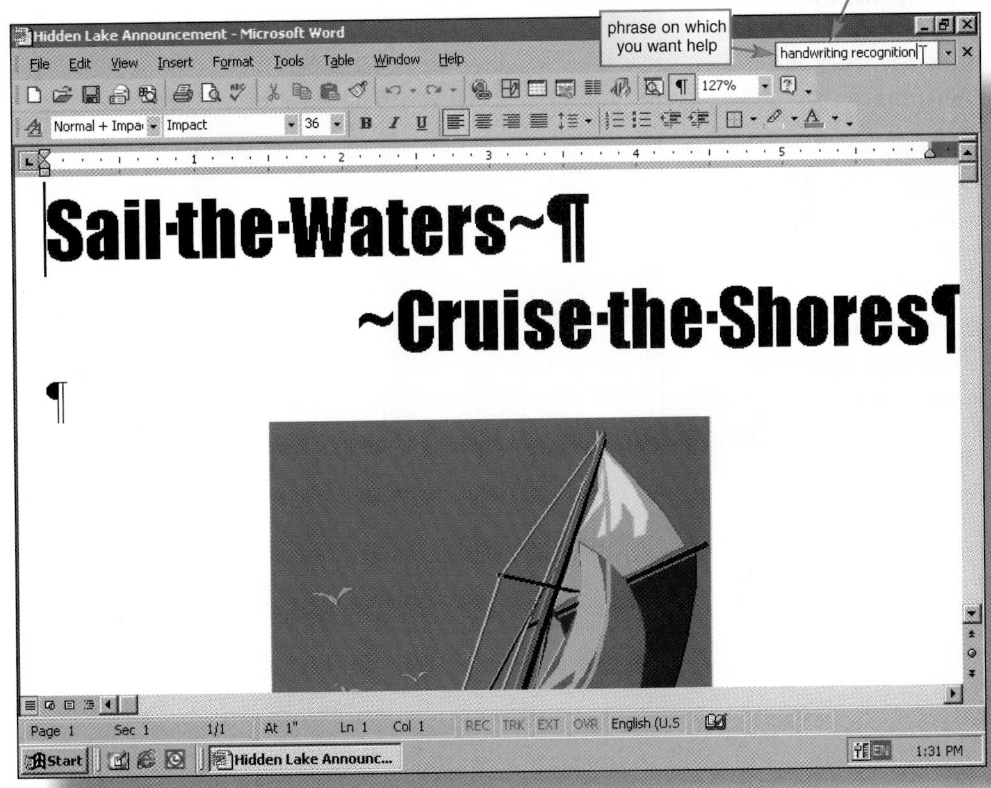

FIGURE 1-74

2 Press the ENTER key. When the list of topics displays below the Ask a Question box, point to the topic, About handwriting recognition.

A list of topics displays relating to the phrase, handwriting recognition. The shape of the mouse pointer changes to a hand, which indicates it is pointing to a link (Figure 1-75).

mouse pointer shape changed to pointing hand
Hidden Lake Announcement - Microsoft Word
handwriting recognition
About handwriting recognition
Change handwriting recognition options
Use handwriting recognition
Troubleshoot handwriting recognition
Handwriting recognition toolbars in East Asian languages
See more...
topics pertaining to phrase, handwriting recognition
Sail the Waters~
~Cruise the Sh
more topics display when you click here

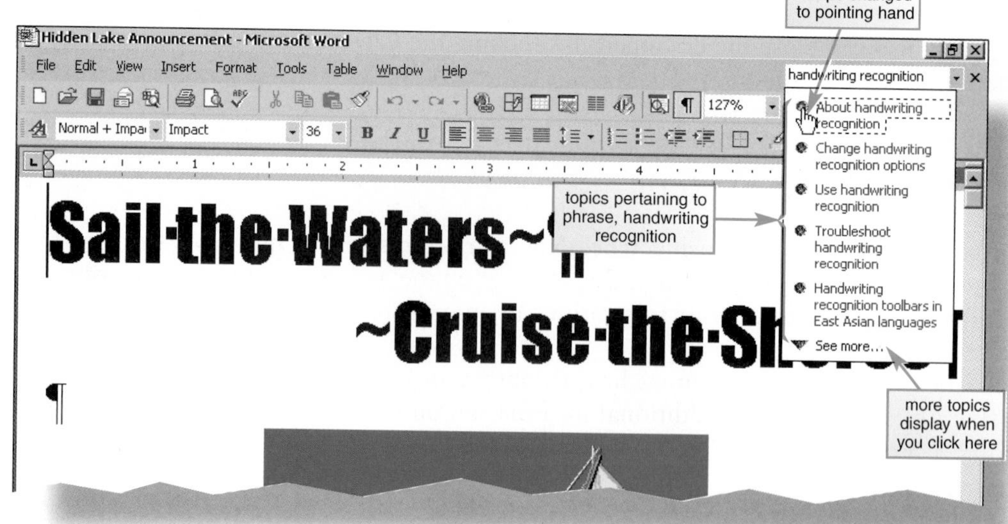

FIGURE 1-75

3 Click About handwriting recognition. When the Word Help window opens, double-click its title bar to maximize it. If necessary, click the Contents tab.

A Word Help window opens that provides Help information about handwriting recognition (Figure 1-76).

4 Click the Close button on the Word Help window title bar.

The Word Help window closes and the Word document window again is active.

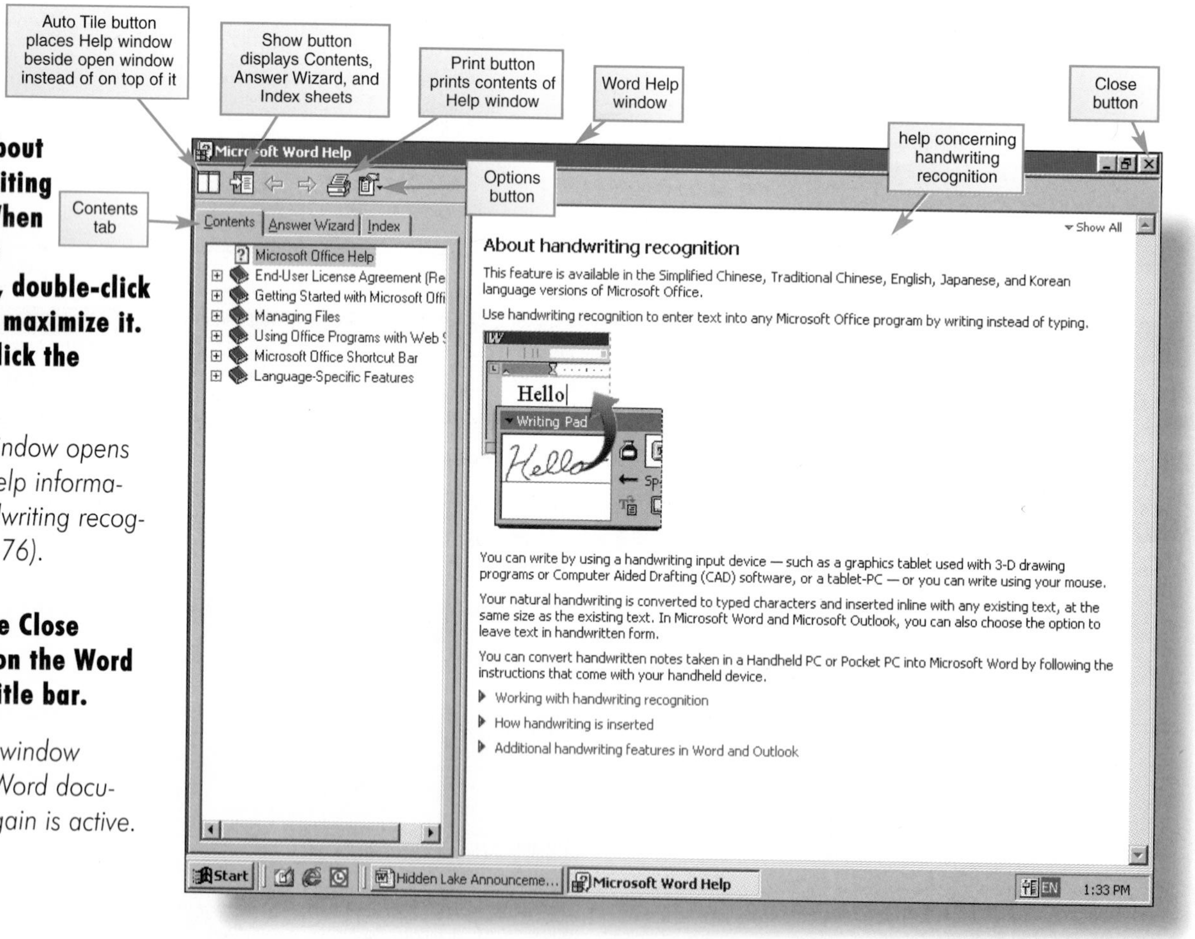

Auto Tile button places Help window beside open window instead of on top of it
Show button displays Contents, Answer Wizard, and Index sheets
Print button prints contents of Help window
Word Help window
Close button
Contents tab
Options button
help concerning handwriting recognition
Microsoft Word Help
Contents
Answer Wizard
Index
Microsoft Office Help
End-User License Agreement (Re
Getting Started with Microsoft Offi
Managing Files
Using Office Programs with Web
Microsoft Office Shortcut Bar
Language-Specific Features
Show All
About handwriting recognition
This feature is available in the Simplified Chinese, Traditional Chinese, English, Japanese, and Korean language versions of Microsoft Office.
Use handwriting recognition to enter text into any Microsoft Office program by writing instead of typing.
Hello
Writing Pad
You can write by using a handwriting input device — such as a graphics tablet used with 3-D drawing programs or Computer Aided Drafting (CAD) software, or a tablet-PC — or you can write using your mouse.
Your natural handwriting is converted to typed characters and inserted inline with any existing text, at the same size as the existing text. In Microsoft Word and Microsoft Outlook, you can also choose the option to leave text in handwritten form.
You can convert handwritten notes taken in a Handheld PC or Pocket PC into Microsoft Word by following the instructions that come with your handheld device.
Working with handwriting recognition
How handwriting is inserted
Additional handwriting features in Word and Outlook
Start
Hidden Lake Announceme...
Microsoft Word Help
1:33 PM

FIGURE 1-76

Use the buttons in the upper-left corner of the Word Help window (Figure 1-76) to navigate through the Help system, change the display, or print the contents of the window.

You can use the Ask a Question box to search for Help on any topic concerning Word. As you enter questions and terms in the Ask a Question box, Word adds them to the Ask a Question list. Thus, if you click the Ask a Question box arrow, a list of previously asked questions and terms will display.

Table 1-3 summarizes the eleven categories of help available to you. This table assumes the Office Assistant is off. See Appendix A for more information.

Table 1-3 Word Help System

TYPE	DESCRIPTION	HOW TO ACTIVATE
Answer Wizard	Answers questions or searches for terms that you type in your own words.	Click the Microsoft Word Help button on the Standard toolbar. Click the Answer Wizard tab.
Ask a Question box	Answers questions or searches for terms that you type in your own words.	Type a question or term in the Ask a Question box on the menu bar and then press the ENTER key.
Contents sheet	Groups Help topics by general categories. Use when you know only the general category of the topic in question. Similar to a table of contents in a book.	Click the Microsoft Word Help button on the Standard toolbar. Click the Contents tab.
Detect and Repair	Automatically finds and fixes errors in the application.	Click Detect and Repair on the Help menu.
Hardware and Software Information	Shows product ID and allows access to system information and technical support information.	Click About Microsoft Word on the Help menu and then click the appropriate button.
Index sheet	Similar to an index in a book. Use when you know exactly what you want.	Click the Microsoft Word Help button on the Standard toolbar. Click the Index tab.
Office Assistant	Similar to the Ask a Question box in that the Office Assistant answers questions that you type in your own words, offers tips, and provides help for a variety of Word features.	Click the Office Assistant icon. If the Office Assistant does not display, click Show the Office Assistant on the Help menu.
Office on the Web	Provides access to technical resources on the Web and allows you to download free product enhancements from the Web.	Click Office on the Web on the Help menu.
Question Mark button	Identifies unfamiliar items in a dialog box.	Click the Question Mark button on the title bar of a dialog box and then click an item in the dialog box.
What's This? command	Identifies unfamiliar items on the screen.	Click What's This? on the Help menu, and then click an item on the screen.
WordPerfect Help	Assists WordPerfect users who are learning Microsoft Word.	Click WordPerfect Help on the Help menu.

The final step in this project is to quit Word.

TO QUIT WORD

1. Click the Close button in the Word window.

The Word window closes.

CASE PERSPECTIVE SUMMARY

Tara is thrilled with the completed announcement. The characters in the headline and body title are large enough so students can read them from a distance, and the image of the sailboat is quite eye-catching. She takes the announcement to the school's Promotions Department and receives approval to post it in several locations around campus, mail it to each student's home, print it in the school newspaper, and publish it on the Web. As a member of the SGA, you assist Tara with these activities.

Project Summary

Project 1 introduced you to starting Word and creating a document. Before entering any text in the document, you learned how to change the font size. You also learned how to save and print a document. You used Word's check spelling as you type feature. Once you saved the document, you learned how to format its paragraphs and characters. Then, you inserted and resized a clip art image. You learned how to insert, delete, and modify text. Finally, you learned one way to use the Word Help system.

What You Should Know

Having completed this project, you now should be able to perform the following tasks:

- Bold Selected Text *(WD 1.45)*
- Center a Paragraph *(WD 1.38, WD 1.45)*
- Center a Paragraph Graphic Containing a Graphic *(WD 1.49)*
- Change the Font of Selected Text *(WD 1.36)*
- Change the Font Size of Selected Text *(WD 1.35)*
- Check Spelling as You Type *(WD 1.28)*
- Close the Entire Document and Start Over *(WD 1.58)*
- Customize the Word Window *(WD 1.9)*
- Delete an Incorrect Character in a Document *(WD 1.58)*
- Delete (Cut) an Incorrect Word or Phrase in a Document *(WD 1.58)*
- Display Formatting Marks *(WD 1.24)*
- Enter Blank Lines into a Document *(WD 1.23)*
- Enter More Text *(WD 1.24)*
- Enter Text *(WD 1.21)*
- Enter Text that Scrolls the Document Window *(WD 1.26)*
- Format a Line of Text *(WD 1.40)*
- Increase the Default Font Size Before Typing *(WD 1.20)*
- Insert Clip Art into a Document *(WD 1.46)*
- Insert Text into an Existing Document *(WD 1.58)*
- Italicize Selected Text *(WD 1.41)*
- Obtain Help Using the Ask a Question Box *(WD 1.59)*
- Open a Document *(WD 1.56)*
- Print a Document *(WD 1.54)*
- Quit Word *(WD 1.55, WD 1.61)*
- Resize a Graphic *(WD 1.51)*
- Right-Align a Paragraph *(WD 1.37)*
- Save a New Document *(WD 1.30)*
- Save an Existing Document with the Same File Name *(WD 1.53)*
- Scroll through the Document *(WD 1.42)*
- Select a Graphic *(WD 1.50)*
- Select a Group of Words *(WD 1.44)*
- Select a Line *(WD 1.40)*
- Select a Word *(WD 1.42)*
- Select Multiple Paragraphs *(WD 1.34)*
- Start Word *(WD 1.08)*
- Underline Selected Text *(WD 1.43)*
- Undo an Action *(WD 1.39)*
- Wordwrap Text as You Type *(WD 1.25)*
- Zoom Page Width *(WD 1.19)*

More About

Microsoft Certification

The Microsoft Office User Specialist (MOUS) Certification program provides an opportunity for you to obtain a valuable industry credential — proof that you have the Word 2002 skills required by employers. For more information, see Appendix E or visit the Shelly Cashman Series MOUS Web page at scsite.com/offxp/cert.htm.

More About

Quick Reference

For a table that lists how to complete tasks covered in this book using the mouse, menu, shortcut menu, and keyboard, see the Quick Reference Summary at the back of this book or visit the Shelly Cashman Series Office XP Web page (scsite.com/offxp/qr.htm) and then click Microsoft Word 2002.

Learn It Online

Instructions: To complete the Learn It Online exercises, start your browser, click the Address bar, and then enter `scsite.com/offxp/exs.htm`. When the Office XP Learn It Online page displays, follow the instructions in the exercises below.

1 Project Reinforcement – TF, MC, and SA

Below Word Project 1, click the Project Reinforcement link. Print the quiz by clicking Print on the File menu. Answer each question. Write your first and last name at the top of each page, and then hand in the printout to your instructor.

2 Flash Cards

Below Word Project 1, click the Flash Cards link. When Flash Cards displays, read the instructions. Type 20 (or a number specified by your instructor) in the Number of Playing Cards text box, type your name in the Name text box, and then click the Flip Card button. When the flash card displays, read the question and then click the Answer box arrow to select an answer. Flip through Flash Cards. Click Print on the File menu to print the last Flash Card if your score is 15 (75%) correct or greater and then hand it in to your instructor. If your score is less than 15 (75%) correct, then redo this exercise by clicking the Replay button.

3 Practice Test

Below Word Project 1, click the Practice Test link. Answer each question, enter your first and last name at the bottom of the page, and then click the Grade Test button. When the graded practice test displays on your screen, click Print on the File menu to print a hard copy. Continue to take practice tests until you score 80% or better. Hand in a printout of the final practice test to your instructor.

4 Who Wants to Be a Computer Genius?

Below Word Project 1, click the Computer Genius link. Read the instructions, enter your first and last name at the bottom of the page, and then click the Play button. Hand in your score to your instructor.

5 Wheel of Terms

Below Word Project 1, click the Wheel of Terms link. Read the instructions, and then enter your first and last name and your school name. Click the Play button. Hand in your score to your instructor.

6 Crossword Puzzle Challenge

Below Word Project 1, click the Crossword Puzzle Challenge link. Read the instructions, and then enter your first and last name. Click the Play button. Work the crossword puzzle. When you are finished, click the Submit button. When the crossword puzzle redisplays, click the Print button. Hand in the printout.

7 Tips and Tricks

Below Word Project 1, click the Tips and Tricks link. Click a topic that pertains to Project 1. Right-click the information and then click Print on the shortcut menu. Construct a brief example of what the information relates to in Word to confirm you understand how to use the tip or trick. Hand in the example and printed information.

8 Newsgroups

Below Word Project 1, click the Newsgroups link. Click a topic that pertains to Project 1. Print three comments. Hand in the comments to your instructor.

9 Expanding Your Horizons

Below Word Project 1, click the Articles for Microsoft Word link. Click a topic that pertains to Project 1. Print the information. Construct a brief example of what the information relates to in Word to confirm you understand the contents of the article. Hand in the example and printed information to your instructor.

10 Search Sleuth

Below Word Project 1, click the Search Sleuth link. To search for a term that pertains to this project, select a term below the Project 1 title and then use the Google search engine at google.com (or any major search engine) to display and print two Web pages that present information on the term. Hand in the printouts to your instructor.

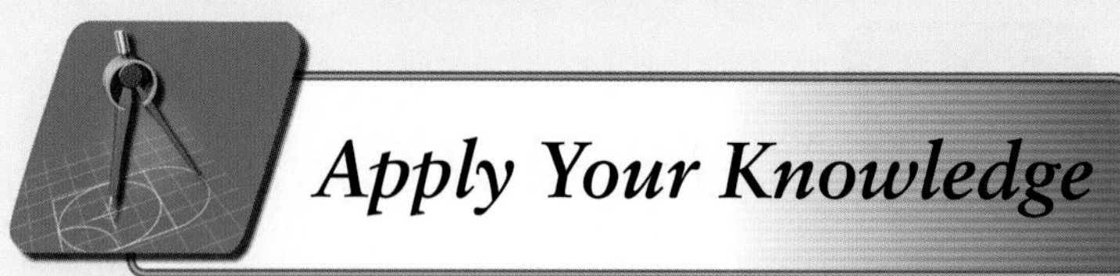

Apply Your Knowledge

1 Checking Spelling and Grammar and Modifying a Document

Instructions: Start Word. Open the document, Volleyball Tournament, on the Data Disk. See the inside back cover of this book for instructions for downloading the Data Disk or see your instructor for information on accessing files in this book.

As shown in Figure 1-77, the document is a volleyball tournament announcement that contains many spelling and grammar errors. You are to right-click each of the errors and then click the appropriate correction on the shortcut menu. You also modify some formats in the announcement.

spelling and grammar errors are flagged on printout to help you identify them

Bring a Freind~
~Bring a Team

Sand Volleyball Tournament

Join us at Central Field on on Saturday, June 21, and Sunday, June 22, for a coed sand volleyball tournament. Teams is limited to 10 plyers.

Games begin at 9:00 a.m. and end st dusk. Complimentary refreshments served aal day.

cash prize for first place! Trophies will be given to the second and third place team's.

Call 555-5583 for entry information.

FIGURE 1-77

Apply Your Knowledge

As discussed in this project, Word flags potential spelling errors with a red wavy underline. A green wavy underline indicates that Word detected a possible grammar error. ***Hint:*** If your screen does not display the grammar errors, use the Word Help system to determine how to enable the check grammar feature. Perform the following tasks:

1. Position the insertion point at the beginning of the document. Right-click the flagged word, Freind. Change the flagged word to the word, Friend, by clicking Friend on the shortcut menu.
2. Right-click the flagged word, on. Click Delete Repeated Word on the shortcut menu to remove the duplicate occurrence of the word, on.
3. Right-click the flagged words, Teams is. Change the flagged words to the words, Teams are, by clicking Teams are on the shortcut menu.
4. Right-click the flagged word, plyers. Change the flagged word to the word, players, by clicking players on the shortcut menu.
5. Right-click the flagged word, st. Because the shortcut menu does not display the correct word, at, click outside the shortcut menu to remove it from the screen. Correct the misspelled word, st, to the correct word, at, by removing the letter s and replacing it with the letter a.
6. Right-click the flagged word, aal. Change the flagged word to the word, all, by clicking all on the shortcut menu.
7. Right-click the flagged word, cash. Capitalize the word, cash, by clicking Cash on the shortcut menu.
8. Right-click the flagged word, team's. Change the flagged word to its correct plural by clicking teams on the shortcut menu.
9. Scroll to the top of the document. Position the insertion point after the word Team in the second line of the headline and then press the EXCLAMATION POINT (!) key. The second line of the headline now should read: Bring a Team!
10. Select the body title line below the graphic by pointing to the left of the line (Sand Volleyball Tournament) then clicking.
11. With the body text selected, click the Font Size box arrow on the Formatting toolbar and then click 24 to change the font size from 28 to 24 point.
12. With the body text selected, click the Font box arrow in the Formatting toolbar and then click Verdana to change the font to Verdana.
13. Double-click the word entry in the last line of the announcement. Click Edit on the menu bar and then click Cut to delete the word, entry.
14. Position the insertion point immediately to the left of the telephone number in the last line of the announcement. Type (708) and then press the SPACEBAR. The last line of the announcement now should read: Call (708) 555-5583 for information.
15. Click File on the menu bar and then click Save As. Save the document using Corrected Volleyball Tournament as the file name.
16. Print the revised document.

In the Lab

1 Creating an Announcement with Clip Art

Problem: Your neighbor is a member of the Prestwick Heights Garden Club. She has asked you to assist her in preparing an announcement for the upcoming club-sponsored garden walk. You prepare the announcement shown in Figure 1-78. ***Hint***: Remember, if you make a mistake while formatting the announcement, you can click the Undo button on the Standard toolbar to undo your last action.

Instructions:

1. Change the font size from 12 to 20 by clicking the Font Size box arrow on the Formatting toolbar and then clicking 20.
2. If necessary, click the Show/Hide ¶ button on the Standard toolbar to display formatting marks.
3. Create the announcement shown in Figure 1-78. Enter the document first without clip art and unformatted; that is without any bold, underlined, italicized, right-aligned, or centered text. If Word flags any misspelled words as you type, check the spelling of these words and correct them.
4. Save the document on a floppy disk with Garden Club Announcement as the file name.
5. Select the two lines of the headline. Change their font to Albertus Extra Bold, or a similar font. Change their font size from 20 to 36.
6. Click somewhere in the second line of the headline. Right-align it.
7. Click somewhere in the body title line. Center it.
8. Select the body title line. Increase its font size from 20 to 28. Bold it.
9. In the second paragraph of the body copy, select the restaurant name: The Botanic Cafeteria. Italicize the name.

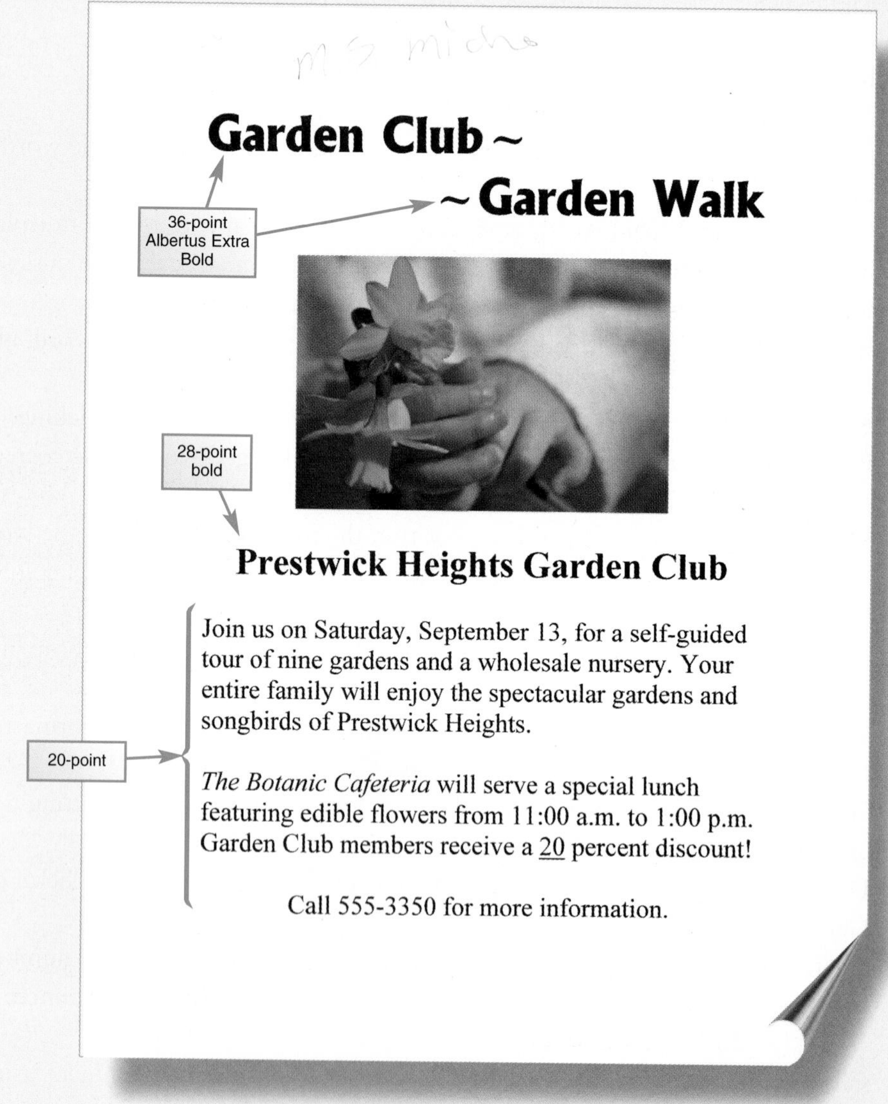

FIGURE 1-78

In the Lab

10. In the same paragraph, select the number 20. Underline it.
11. Click somewhere in the last line of the announcement. Center it.
12. Insert the graphic of the child holding daffodils between the headline and the body title line. Search for the text, daffodils, in the Insert Clip Art task pane to locate the graphic.
13. Center the selected graphic by centering the paragraph.
14. Save the announcement again with the same file name.
15. Print the announcement.

2 Creating an Announcement with Resized Clip Art

Problem: The owner of Wallace House Bed & Breakfast has requested that each student in your class prepare an announcement advertising the inn. The student that creates the winning announcement will receive a complimentary dinner. You prepare the announcement shown in Figure 1-79. ***Hint:*** Remember, if you make a mistake while formatting the announcement, you can click the Undo button on the Standard toolbar to undo your last action.

Instructions:

1. Change the font size from 12 to 22 by clicking the Font Size box arrow on the Formatting toolbar and then clicking 22.
2. If it is not already selected, click the Show/Hide ¶ button on the Standard toolbar to display formatting marks.

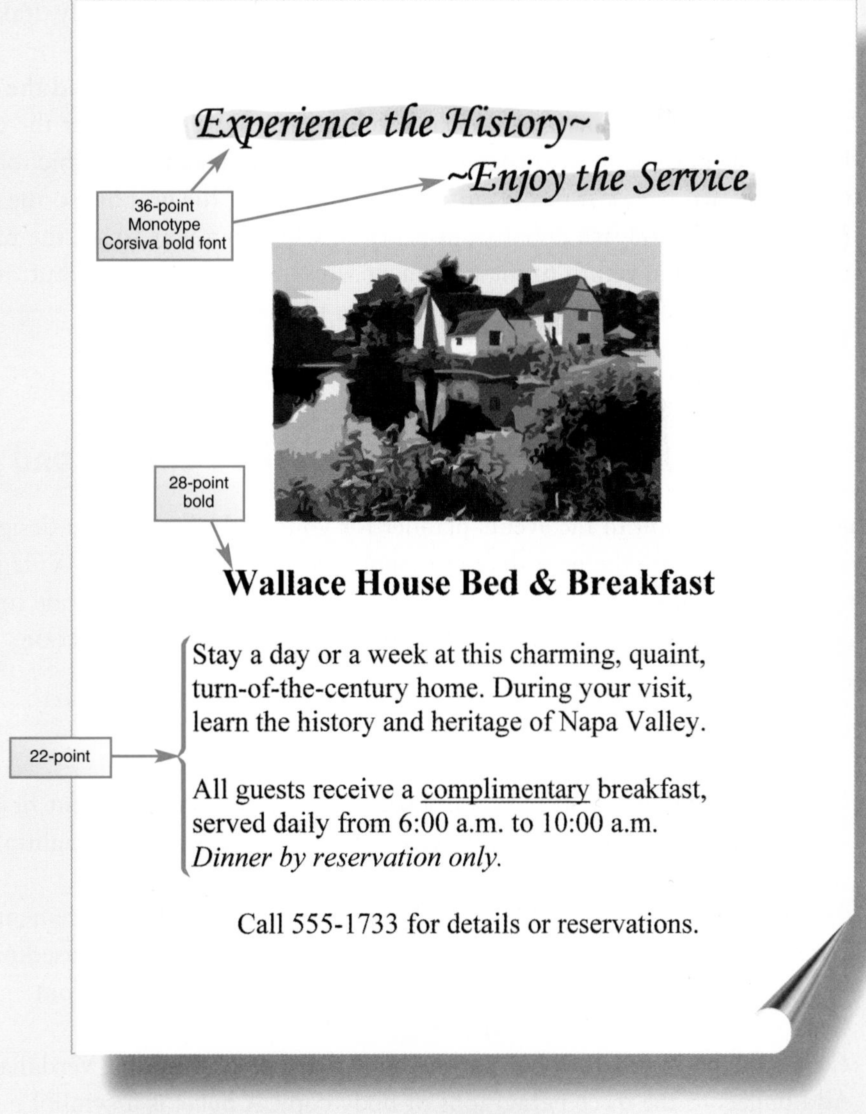

FIGURE 1-79

(continued)

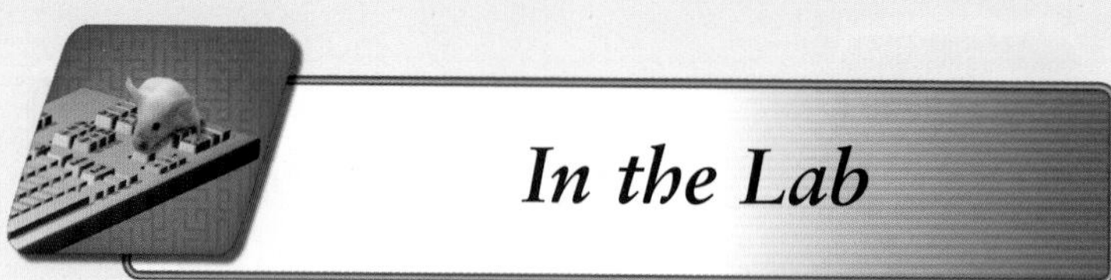

Creating an Announcement with Resized Clip Art *(continued)*

3. Create the announcement shown in Figure 1-79 on the previous page. Enter the document first without the clip art and unformatted; that is, without any bold, underlined, italicized, right-aligned, or centered text. If Word flags any misspelled words as you type, check the spelling of these words and correct them.
4. Save the document on a floppy disk with Wallace House Announcement as the file name.
5. Select the two lines of the headline. Change their font to Monotype Corsiva, or a similar font. Change their font size from 20 to 36. Bold both lines.
6. Click somewhere in the second line of the headline. Right-align it.
7. Click somewhere in the body title line. Center it.
8. Select the body title line. Increase its font size from 22 to 28. Bold it.
9. Select the word, complimentary, in the second paragraph of the body copy. Underline it.
10. In the same paragraph, select the words, Dinner by reservation only. Italicize the words.
11. Click somewhere in the last line of the announcement. Center it.
12. Insert the graphic of the house by the lake between the headline and the body title line. Search for the text, house, in the Insert Clip Art task pane to locate the graphic. Center the graphic.
13. Enlarge the graphic of the house by the lake. If you make the graphic too large, the announcement may flow onto two pages. If this occurs, reduce the size of the graphic so the announcement fits on a single page. *Hint:* Use Help to learn about print preview, which is a way to see the page before you print it. To exit print preview and return to the document window, click the Close button on the Print Preview toolbar.
14. Save the announcement again with the same file name.
15. Print the announcement.

3 Creating an Announcement with Resized Clip Art and a Bulleted List

Problem: As assistant to the events planner for your park district, you design announcements of community activities. Next month, the park district is sponsoring a trip to Hannah Village Zoo. You prepare the announcement shown in Figure 1-80. *Hint:* Remember, if you make a mistake while formatting the announcement, you can click the Undo button on the Standard toolbar to undo your last action.

Instructions:

1. Change the font size from 12 to 18.
2. If they are not already showing, display formatting marks.
3. Create the announcement shown in Figure 1-80. Enter the document first without the clip art and unformatted; that is, without any bulleted, bold, underlined, italicized, right-aligned, or centered text. Check spelling as you type.
4. Save the document on a floppy disk with Hannah Village Announcement as the file name.
5. Format the first line of the headline to 36-point Clarendon Condensed or a similar font. Format the second line of the headline to 36-point Comic Sans MS bold or a similar font.
6. Center both lines of the headline.
7. Center the body title line. Format the body title line to 36-point Verdana bold, or a similar font.
8. Add bullets to the three paragraphs of body copy. A **bullet** is a symbol positioned at the beginning of a paragraph. In Word, the default bullet symbol is a small darkened circle. A list of paragraphs with bullets is called a **bulleted list**. *Hint:* Use Help to learn how to add bullets to a list of paragraphs.

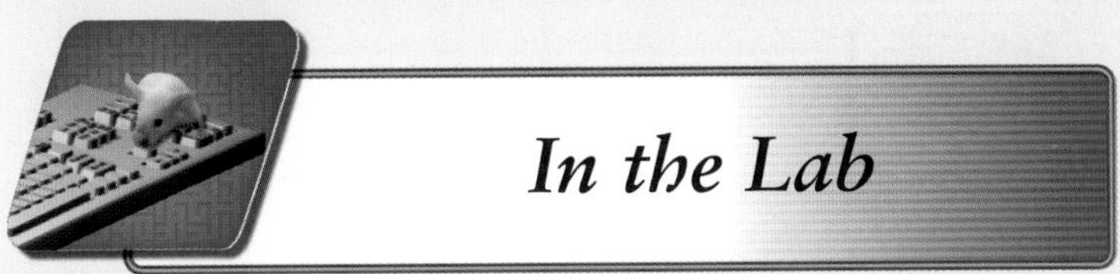

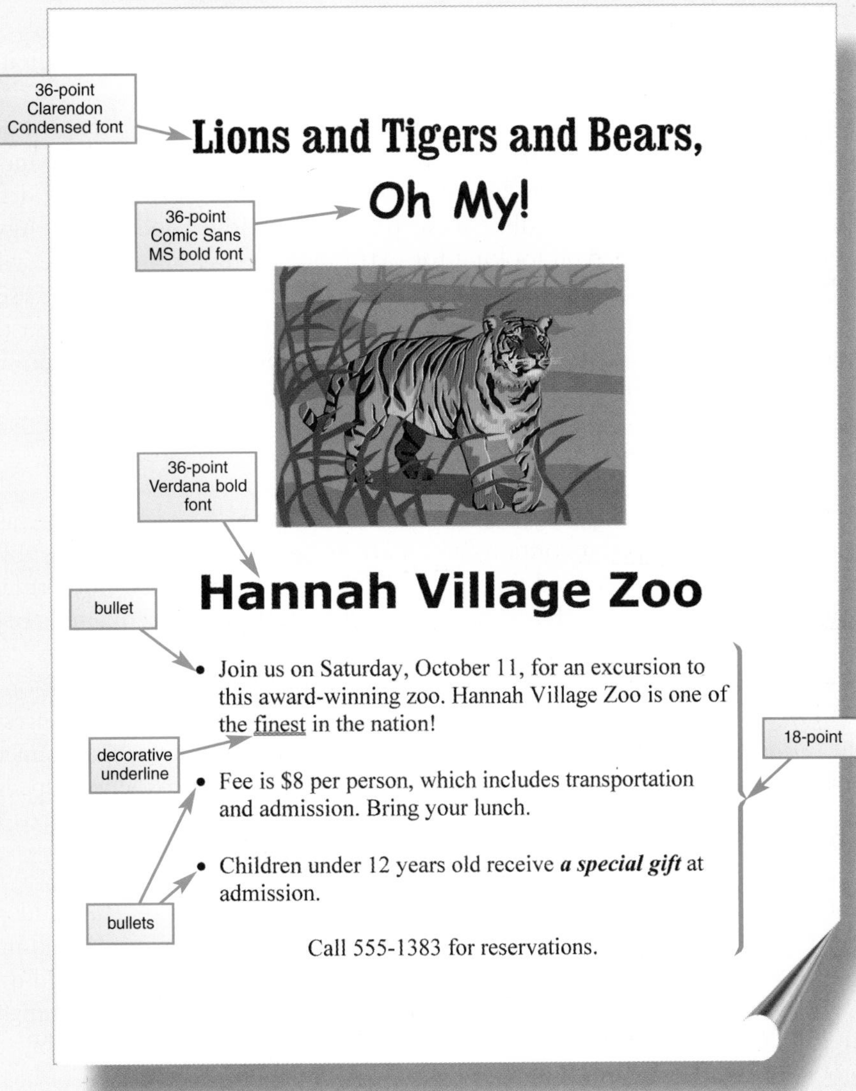

FIGURE 1-80

9. Underline the word, finest, in the first paragraph of the body copy using a decorative underline. ***Hint:*** Use Help to learn how to add a decorative underline to text.
10. Bold and italicize the phrase, a special gift, in the third paragraph of the body copy.
11. Center the last line of the announcement.
12. Insert the graphic of the tiger between the headline and the body title line. Search for the text, tiger, in the Insert Clip Art task pane to locate the graphic. Center the graphic.
13. Enlarge the graphic of the tiger. If you make the graphic too large, the announcement may flow onto two pages. If this occurs, reduce the size of the graphic so the announcement fits on a single page. ***Hint:*** Use Help to learn about print preview, which is a way to see the page before you print it. To exit print preview and return to the document window, click the Close button on the Print Preview toolbar.
14. Save the announcement again with the same file name.
15. Print the announcement.

Cases and Places

The difficulty of these case studies varies:
▸ are the least difficult; ▸▸ are more difficult; and ▸▸▸ are the most difficult.

1 ▸ You have been assigned the task of preparing an announcement for Agway Foods, Inc. The announcement is to contain a clip art image of farm equipment. Use the following text: first line of headline – Need Some $$?; second line of headline – Need a Summer Job?; body title – Agway Foods, Inc.; first paragraph of body copy – Are you looking for extra income this summer? We will show you how to work the fields. No experience necessary for this full-time seasonal employment.; second paragraph of body copy – Work to be performed at various locations in Herndon county. Must have own transportation.; last line – For details, call 555-9000. Use the concepts and techniques presented in this project to create and format this announcement. Ask your instructor if you should bullet the paragraphs of the body copy. Be sure to check spelling in the announcement.

2 ▸ You have been assigned the task of preparing an announcement for a new welding class at the College of Westerville. The announcement contains a clip art image of a welder. Use the following text: first line of headline – Welding Class~; second line of headline – ~Sign up Today; body title – College of Westerville; first paragraph of body copy – For fun or for credit, learn the fundamentals of welding. Our certified welding instructors use a hands-on technique to teach the fine art of welding.; second paragraph of body copy – Class will be taught in the automotive shop at the North Campus on Route 64.; last line – Call 555-3350 for a schedule or to register. Use the concepts and techniques presented in this project to create and format this announcement. Use a decorative underline in the announcement. Ask your instructor if you should bullet the paragraphs of the body copy. Be sure to check spelling in the announcement.

3 ▸▸ Your school district is looking for bus drivers. As an assistant in the transportation department, you have been asked to prepare an announcement that will be sent home with each child in the district. You are to include a graphic of a school bus. The school district's name is Allegheny and number is 314. Bus drivers are needed for the 2003-2004 school year. No experience is necessary. Training will be provided on Friday, August 22, in the transportation lot on Keswick Road. Point out that bus drivers enjoy flexible hours and good pay. More information can be obtained by calling John Stevens at 555-8850. Use the concepts and techniques presented in this project to create the announcement. Use a decorative underline in the announcement. Ask your instructor if you should bullet the paragraphs of the body copy. Be sure to check spelling and grammar in the announcement.

Cases and Places

4 ▶▶ Your neighbor has asked you to prepare an announcement that recruits employees for his business. He provides you with these details. The job openings are for telephone sales representatives. Employees have flexible work hours, day or night. Employees also can earn money while working from home or from the office. The only requirements are a telephone and a pleasant personality. It is a great employment opportunity and has an excellent salary. This job allows you to earn extra cash and unlock the secret to entrepreneurial freedom. Call 555-6879 for more information. Use the concepts and techniques presented in this project to create the announcement. Include a clip art image from the Web by connecting to the Web before searching for clip art in the Insert Clip Art task pane. Use a decorative underline in the announcement. Ask your instructor if you should bullet the list of paragraphs of the body copy. Be sure to check spelling and grammar in the announcement.

5 ▶▶ The owner of your apartment building has asked you to prepare an announcement about an apartment she has for rent. The name of the apartment complex is Country Walker Apartments. The available apartment is a one-bedroom unit with an eat-in kitchen. Air conditioning, heat, and water are included in the rent, which is $600 per month. Pets are allowed. The unit has a one-car garage. The complex has laundry facilities on site. The apartment is located near a large shopping mall, community college, and train station. For more information, call 555-9878. Use the concepts and techniques presented in this project to create the announcement. Include a clip art image from the Web by connecting to the Web before searching for clip art in the Insert Clip Art task pane. Use a decorative underline in the announcement. Ask your instructor if you should bullet the list of paragraphs of the body copy. Be sure to check spelling and grammar in the announcement.

6 ▶▶▶ Schools, churches, libraries, grocery stores, and other public places have bulletin boards for announcements and other postings. Often, these bulletin boards have so many announcements that some go unnoticed. At one of the above-mentioned organizations, find a posted announcement that you think might be overlooked. Copy the text from the announcement. Using this text, together with the techniques presented in this project, create an announcement that would be more likely to catch a reader's eye. Format the announcement effectively and include a bulleted list and suitable clip art image. Use a decorative underline in the announcement. Change the color of the characters. ***Hint:*** Use Help to learn about changing the color of text. Be sure to check spelling and grammar in the announcement.

7 ▶▶▶ Advertisements are a company's way of announcing products or services to the public. You can find advertisements in printed media such as newspapers and magazines. Many companies also advertise on the World Wide Web. Find a printed advertisement or one on the Web that you feel lacks luster. Copy the text from the announcement. Using this text, together with the techniques presented in this project, create an announcement that would be more likely to catch a reader's eye. Format the announcement effectively and include a bulleted list and suitable clip art image. Change the color of the characters. ***Hint:*** Use Help to learn about changing the color of text. Be sure to check spelling and grammar in the announcement.

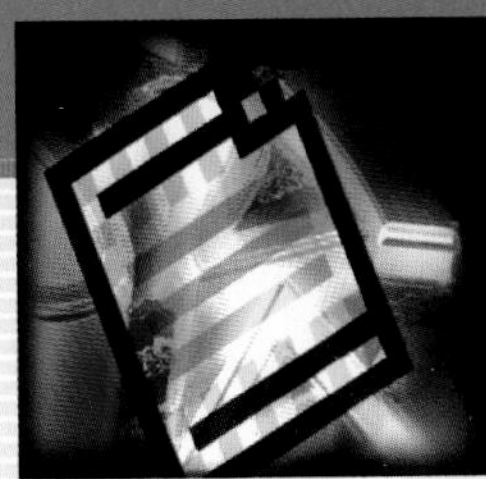

Microsoft Word 2002

PROJECT 2

Creating a Research Paper

OBJECTIVES

You will have mastered the material in this project when you can:

- Describe the MLA documentation style for research papers
- Change the margin settings in a document
- Adjust line spacing in a document
- Use a header to number pages of a document
- Enter text using Click and Type
- Apply formatting using shortcut keys
- Indent paragraphs
- Use Word's AutoCorrect feature
- Add a footnote to a research paper
- Modify a style
- Count the words in a document
- Insert a manual page break
- Create a hanging indent
- Insert a symbol automatically
- Create a hyperlink
- Sort selected paragraphs
- Go to a specific location in a document
- Move text
- Find and replace text
- Use the Paste Options button
- Understand how smart tags work
- Find a synonym for a word
- Check spelling and grammar at once
- Display the Web page associated with a hyperlink
- E-mail a copy of a document

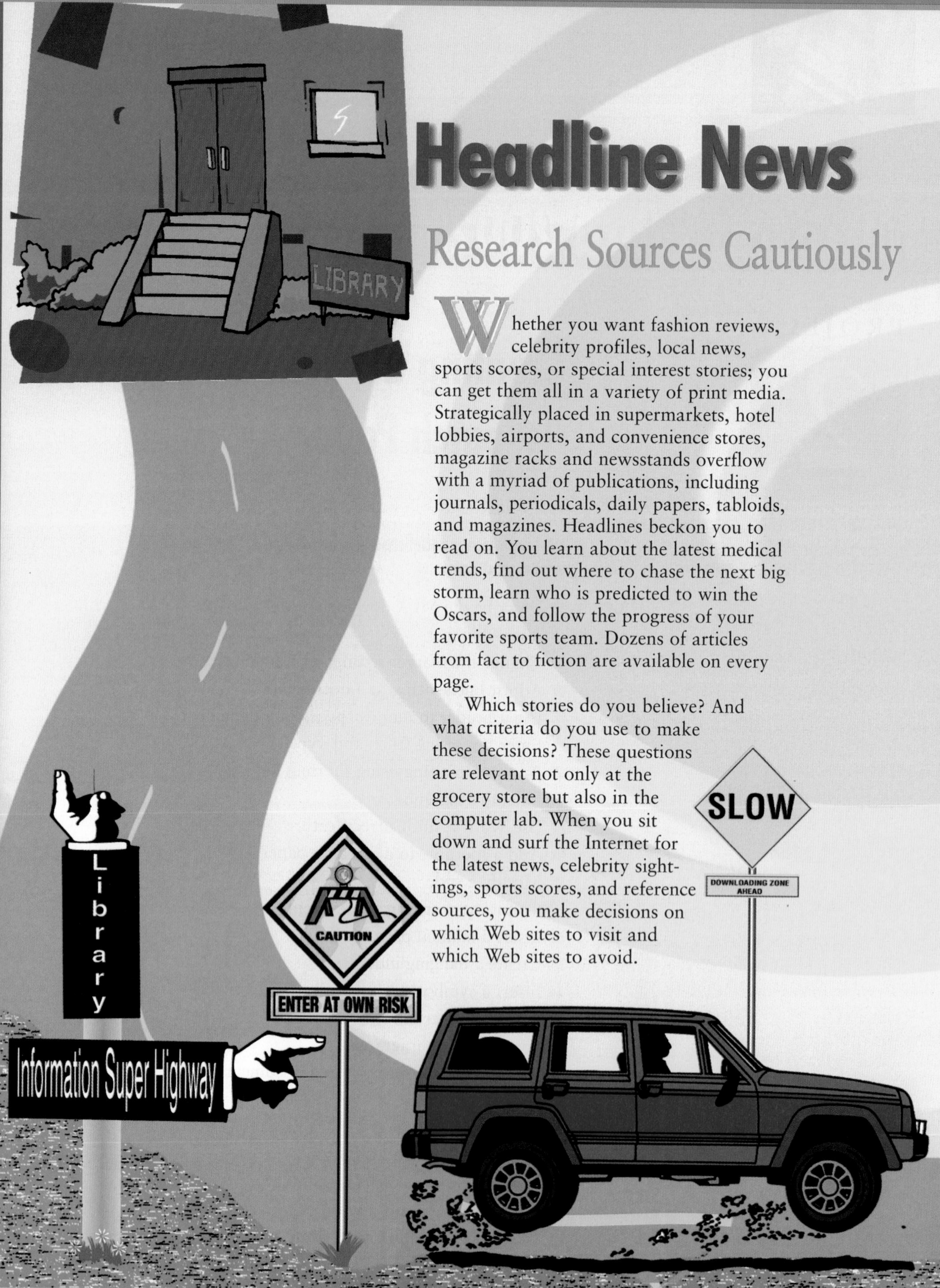

Headline News

Research Sources Cautiously

Whether you want fashion reviews, celebrity profiles, local news, sports scores, or special interest stories; you can get them all in a variety of print media. Strategically placed in supermarkets, hotel lobbies, airports, and convenience stores, magazine racks and newsstands overflow with a myriad of publications, including journals, periodicals, daily papers, tabloids, and magazines. Headlines beckon you to read on. You learn about the latest medical trends, find out where to chase the next big storm, learn who is predicted to win the Oscars, and follow the progress of your favorite sports team. Dozens of articles from fact to fiction are available on every page.

Which stories do you believe? And what criteria do you use to make these decisions? These questions are relevant not only at the grocery store but also in the computer lab. When you sit down and surf the Internet for the latest news, celebrity sightings, sports scores, and reference sources, you make decisions on which Web sites to visit and which Web sites to avoid.

Not so long ago, students relied on only books and magazines in the library for the bulk of their research material. These permanent sources were professionally evaluated and edited. Not so with the Internet, where you will find everything from reliable research to fictitious opinions. No one performs quality control checks to verify accuracy and reliability. Anyone can build a Web site and fill it with any content imaginable. And this content can be updated before your eyes.

In this project, you will create a research paper on the topic of electronic retailing (e-retailing), which is the process of selling products and services using the Web. You will create a hyperlink in the document that allows navigation to a specific Web page when the research paper displays on the screen and the computer is connected to the Internet. The Works Cited page lists the sources used to obtain information for the research report. The sources include material from a book, a report in a periodical, and an article available on the Shelly Cashman Series Web site (scsite.com). How can you judge the reliability of these materials, particularly the article posted on the Web? Just remember the three S's: structure, source, and style.

Structure — Does the information seem objective or biased? Are authorities used as sources? When was the Web site created or updated? Is a contact person listed so you can verify information? Are working hyperlinks provided that refer you to additional sources?

Source — Examine the Web address to find out the Web site's sponsor. Is it a nonprofit organization (.org), a school (.edu), the government (.gov), or a commercial business (.com)? Is the purpose of the Web site to provide information or to make a profit?

Style — Does the Web site look organized and professional? Can you navigate easily with a minimum of mouse clicks? Does it contain an index and the capability of searching for specific information?

William Miller, a former president of the Association of College and Research Libraries, says that on the Web, "Much of what purports to be serious information is simply junk — not current, objective, or trustworthy." By following the three S's, you will be able to determine when you have valuable information.

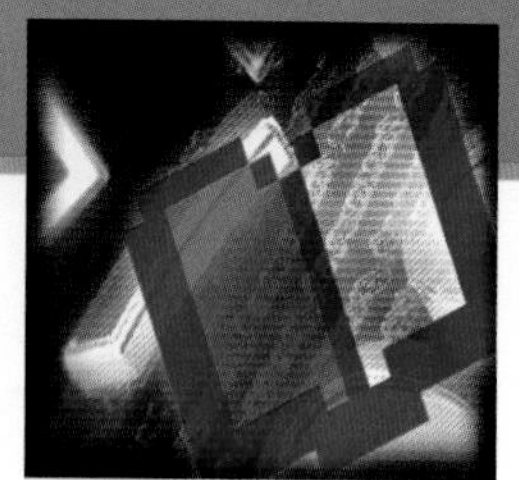

Microsoft Word 2002

Creating a Research Paper

PROJECT

CASE PERSPECTIVE

Jordan Marcott is a full-time college student, majoring in Marketing. Ms. Blythe, the instructor in her introductory computer class, has assigned a short research paper that requires a minimum of 375 words. The paper must discuss some aspect of computers and be written according to the MLA documentation style, which specifies guidelines for report preparation. The paper is to contain one footnote and three references — one of which must be obtained from the World Wide Web. Finally, all students are to submit their papers electronically via e-mail to Ms. Blythe.

When Jordan graduates from college, she plans to work in retail management. She is very interested in retailing on the Web, so she decides to write the research paper on electronic retailing (e-retailing). Jordan intends to review computer magazines at the school's library, surf the Internet, and e-mail a couple of e-retailers for information on their businesses. She also plans to use the Internet to obtain the guidelines for the MLA style of documentation. Jordan has asked you to assist her with the Web searches because you are very familiar with the Internet.

Introduction

In both academic and business environments, you will be asked to write reports. Business reports range from proposals to cost justifications to five-year plans to research findings. Academic reports focus mostly on research findings. Whether you are writing a business report or an academic report, you should follow a standard style when preparing it.

Many different styles of documentation exist for report preparation, depending on the nature of the report. Each style requires the same basic information; the differences among styles appear in the manner of presenting the information. For example, one documentation style may use the term bibliography, whereas another uses references, and yet a third prefers works cited. Two popular documentation styles for research papers are the **MLA** (**Modern Language Association of America**) and **APA** (**American Psychological Association**) styles. This project uses the MLA documentation style.

Project Two — E-Retailing Research Paper

Project 2 illustrates the creation of a short research paper describing e-retailing. As shown in Figure 2-1, the paper follows the MLA documentation style. The first two pages present the research paper and the third page alphabetically lists the works cited.

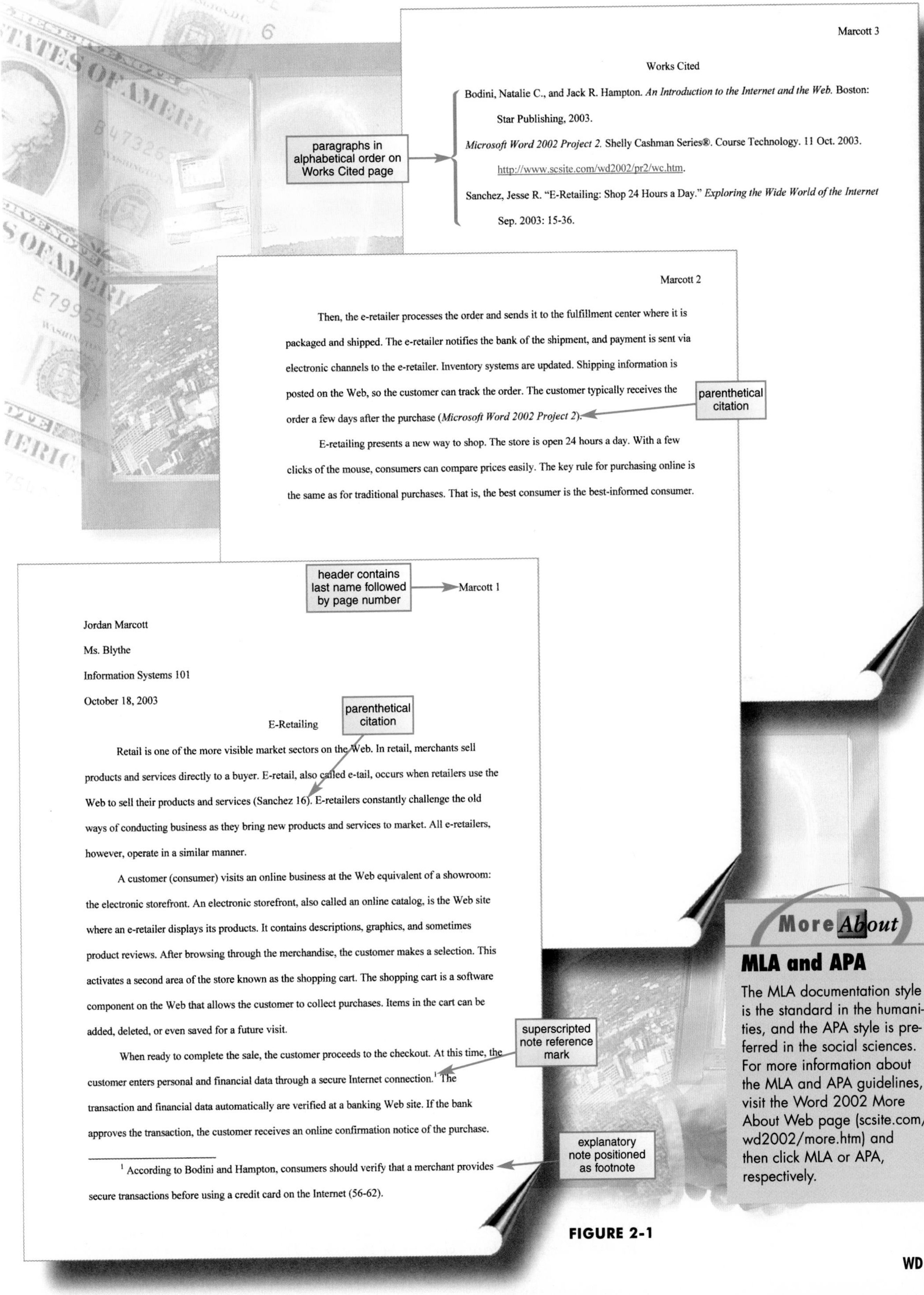

Marcott 3

Works Cited

Bodini, Natalie C., and Jack R. Hampton. *An Introduction to the Internet and the Web.* Boston: Star Publishing, 2003.

Microsoft Word 2002 Project 2. Shelly Cashman Series®. Course Technology. 11 Oct. 2003. http://www.scsite.com/wd2002/pr2/wc.htm.

Sanchez, Jesse R. "E-Retailing: Shop 24 Hours a Day." *Exploring the Wide World of the Internet* Sep. 2003: 15-36.

paragraphs in alphabetical order on Works Cited page

Marcott 2

Then, the e-retailer processes the order and sends it to the fulfillment center where it is packaged and shipped. The e-retailer notifies the bank of the shipment, and payment is sent via electronic channels to the e-retailer. Inventory systems are updated. Shipping information is posted on the Web, so the customer can track the order. The customer typically receives the order a few days after the purchase (*Microsoft Word 2002 Project 2*).

parenthetical citation

E-retailing presents a new way to shop. The store is open 24 hours a day. With a few clicks of the mouse, consumers can compare prices easily. The key rule for purchasing online is the same as for traditional purchases. That is, the best consumer is the best-informed consumer.

header contains last name followed by page number

Marcott 1

Jordan Marcott

Ms. Blythe

Information Systems 101

October 18, 2003

E-Retailing

parenthetical citation

Retail is one of the more visible market sectors on the Web. In retail, merchants sell products and services directly to a buyer. E-retail, also called e-tail, occurs when retailers use the Web to sell their products and services (Sanchez 16). E-retailers constantly challenge the old ways of conducting business as they bring new products and services to market. All e-retailers, however, operate in a similar manner.

A customer (consumer) visits an online business at the Web equivalent of a showroom: the electronic storefront. An electronic storefront, also called an online catalog, is the Web site where an e-retailer displays its products. It contains descriptions, graphics, and sometimes product reviews. After browsing through the merchandise, the customer makes a selection. This activates a second area of the store known as the shopping cart. The shopping cart is a software component on the Web that allows the customer to collect purchases. Items in the cart can be added, deleted, or even saved for a future visit.

When ready to complete the sale, the customer proceeds to the checkout. At this time, the customer enters personal and financial data through a secure Internet connection.[1] The transaction and financial data automatically are verified at a banking Web site. If the bank approves the transaction, the customer receives an online confirmation notice of the purchase.

superscripted note reference mark

[1] According to Bodini and Hampton, consumers should verify that a merchant provides secure transactions before using a credit card on the Internet (56-62).

explanatory note positioned as footnote

FIGURE 2-1

More About

MLA and APA

The MLA documentation style is the standard in the humanities, and the APA style is preferred in the social sciences. For more information about the MLA and APA guidelines, visit the Word 2002 More About Web page (scsite.com/wd2002/more.htm) and then click MLA or APA, respectively.

More About

Citing Sources

Information that commonly is known or accessible to the audience constitutes common knowledge and does not need to be listed as a parenthetical citation or in a bibliography. If, however, you question whether certain information is common knowledge, you should document it — just to be safe.

More About

Titles of Works

Titles of books, periodicals, and Web sites typically are underlined when a research paper is submitted in printed form. Some instructors require that Web addresses be hyperlinks for online access. Word formats hyperlinks with an underline. To distinguish hyperlinks from titles, the MLA allows titles to be italicized, if approved by the instructor.

More About

APA Style

In the APA style, double-space all pages of the paper with 1.5" top, bottom, left, and right margins. Indent the first word of each paragraph .5" from the left margin. In the upper-right margin of each page, place a running head that consists of the page number double-spaced below a summary of the paper title.

MLA Documentation Style

When writing papers, you should adhere to some style of documentation. The research paper in this project follows the guidelines presented by the MLA. To follow the MLA style, double-space text on all pages of the paper with one-inch top, bottom, left, and right margins. Indent the first word of each paragraph one-half inch from the left margin. At the right margin of each page, place a page number one-half inch from the top margin. On each page, precede the page number by your last name.

The MLA style does not require a title page. Instead, place your name and course information in a block at the left margin beginning one inch from the top of the page. Center the title one double-space below your name and course information.

In the body of the paper, place author references in parentheses with the page number(s) of the referenced information. The MLA style uses in-text **parenthetical citations** instead of noting each source at the bottom of the page or at the end of the paper. In the MLA style, notes are used only for optional explanatory notes.

If used, explanatory notes elaborate on points discussed in the body of the paper. Use superscripts (raised numbers) for **note reference marks**, which signal that an explanatory note exists, and also sequence the notes. Position explanatory notes either at the bottom of the page as footnotes or at the end of the paper as endnotes. Indent the first line of each explanatory note one-half inch from the left margin. Place one space following the note reference mark before beginning the note text. Double-space the note text. At the end of the note text, you may list bibliographic information for further reference.

The MLA style uses the term **works cited** for the bibliographical references. The works cited page alphabetically lists works that are referenced directly in the paper. List works by each author's last name, or, if the author's name is not available, by the title of the work. Italicize or underline the title of the work. Place the works cited on a separate numbered page. Center the title, Works Cited, one inch from the top margin. Double-space all lines. Begin the first line of each entry at the left margin, indenting subsequent lines of the same entry one-half inch from the left margin.

Starting Word

Perform the following steps to start Word, or ask your instructor how to start Word for your system.

TO START AND CUSTOMIZE WORD

1. Click the Start button on the Windows taskbar, point to Programs on the Start menu, and then click Microsoft Word on the Programs submenu.
2. If the Word window is not maximized, double-click its title bar to maximize it.
3. If the Language bar displays on the screen, click its Minimize button.
4. If the New Document task pane displays in the Word window, click the Show at startup check box to remove the check mark and then click the Close button in the upper-right corner of the task pane title bar.
5. If the toolbars display positioned on the same row, click the Toolbar Options button and then click Show Buttons on Two Rows.
6. If your screen differs from Figure 2-2 on page WD 2.08, click View on the menu bar and then click Normal.

Word starts. After a few moments, an empty document titled Document1 displays in the Word window (shown in Figure 2-2).

Resetting Menus and Toolbars

To set the menus and toolbars so they appear exactly as shown in this book, you should reset your menus and toolbars as outlined in Appendix D or follow these steps.

TO RESET MENUS AND TOOLBARS

1. Click the Toolbar Options button on the Standard toolbar and then point to Add or Remove Buttons. Point to Standard on the Add or Remove Buttons submenu. Scroll to and then click Reset Toolbar on the Standard submenu.
2. Click the Toolbar Options button on the Formatting toolbar and then point to Add or Remove Buttons. Point to Formatting on the Add or Remove Buttons submenu. Scroll to and then click Reset Toolbar on the Formatting submenu.
3. Click the Toolbar Options button on the Standard toolbar and then point to Add or Remove Buttons. Click Customize on the Add or Remove Buttons submenu.
4. When the Customize dialog box displays, if necessary, click the Options tab. Click the Reset my usage data button. When the Microsoft Word dialog box displays, click the Yes button. Click the Close button in the Customize dialog box.

Word resets the menus and toolbars.

More About

Writing Papers

The Web contains numerous sites with information, tips, and suggestions on writing research papers. College professors and fellow students develop many of these Web sites. For a list of links to Web sites on writing research papers, visit the Word 2002 More About Web page (scsite.com/wd2002/more.htm) and then click Links to Sites on Writing Research Papers.

Displaying Formatting Marks

As discussed in Project 1, it is helpful to display formatting marks that indicate where in the document you pressed the ENTER key, SPACEBAR, and other keys. Perform the following step to display formatting marks.

TO DISPLAY FORMATTING MARKS

1. If the Show/Hide ¶ button on the Standard toolbar is not already selected, click it.

Word displays formatting marks in the document window, and the Show/Hide ¶ button on the Standard toolbar is selected (shown in Figure 2-2 on the next page).

Changing the Margins

Word is preset to use standard 8.5-by-11-inch paper, with 1.25-inch left and right margins and 1-inch top and bottom margins. These margin settings affect every page in the document. Often, you may want to change these default margin settings. For example, the MLA documentation style requires one-inch top, bottom, left, and right margins throughout the paper. Thus, the steps on the next page illustrate how to change the margin settings for a document when the window is in normal view. To verify the document window is in normal view, click View on the menu bar and then click Normal.

More About

Changing Margins

In print layout view, you can change margin settings using the horizontal and vertical rulers. Current margin settings are shaded in gray. The margin boundary is located where the gray meets the white. To change a margin setting, drag the margin boundary on the ruler. To see the numeric margin settings, hold down the ALT key while dragging the margin boundary on the ruler.

Steps To Change the Margin Settings

1 Click File on the menu bar and then point to Page Setup (Figure 2-2).

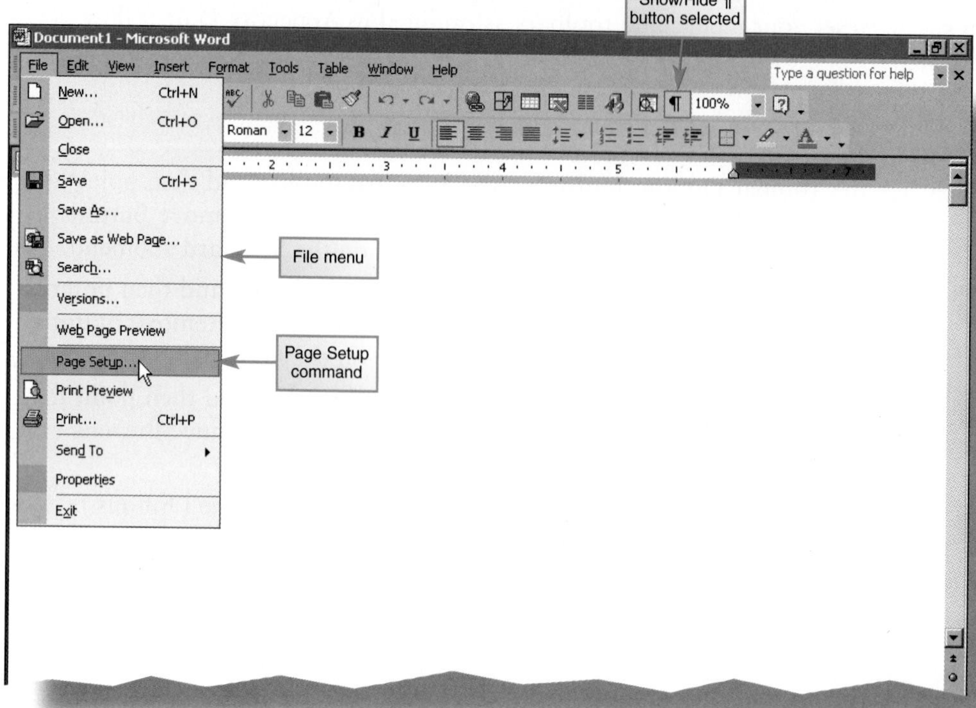

FIGURE 2-2

2 Click Page Setup. If necessary, click the Margins tab when the Page Setup dialog box displays.

Word displays the Page Setup dialog box (Figure 2-3). The current margin settings display in the text boxes.

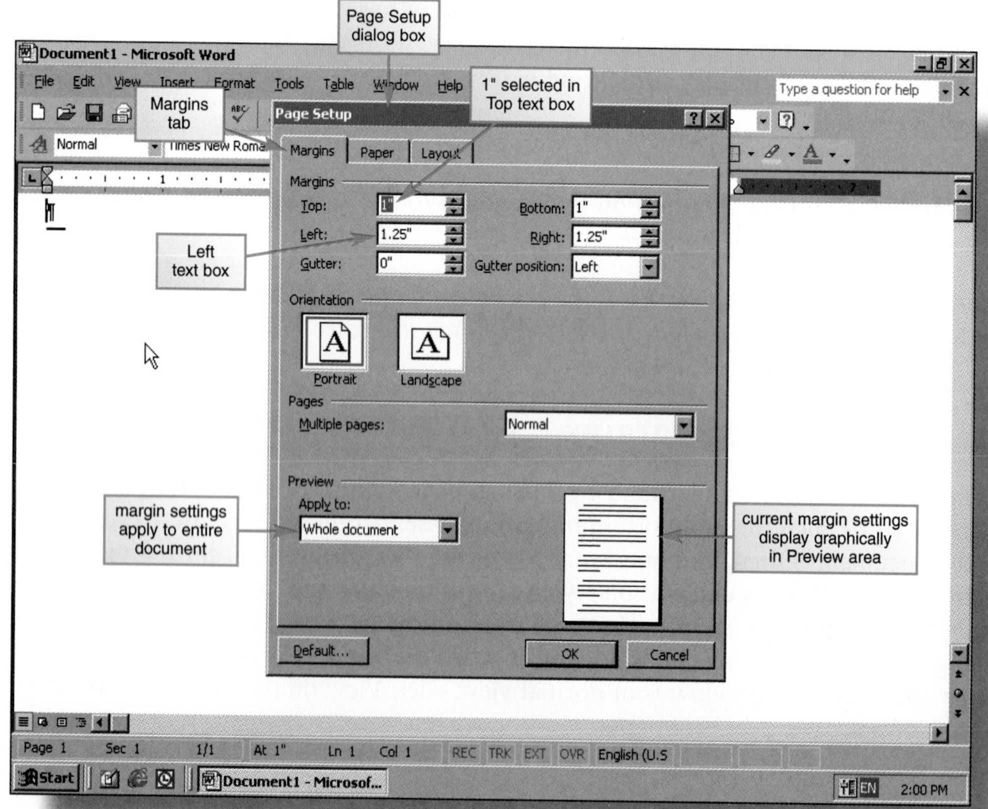

FIGURE 2-3

3 With 1" selected in the Top text box, press the TAB key twice to select 1.25" in the Left text box. Type 1 and then press the TAB key. Type 1 and then point to the OK button.

The new left and right margin settings are 1 inch (Figure 2-4). Instead of typing margin values, you can click the text box arrows to increment or decrement the number in the text box.

Click the OK button.

Word changes the left and right margins.

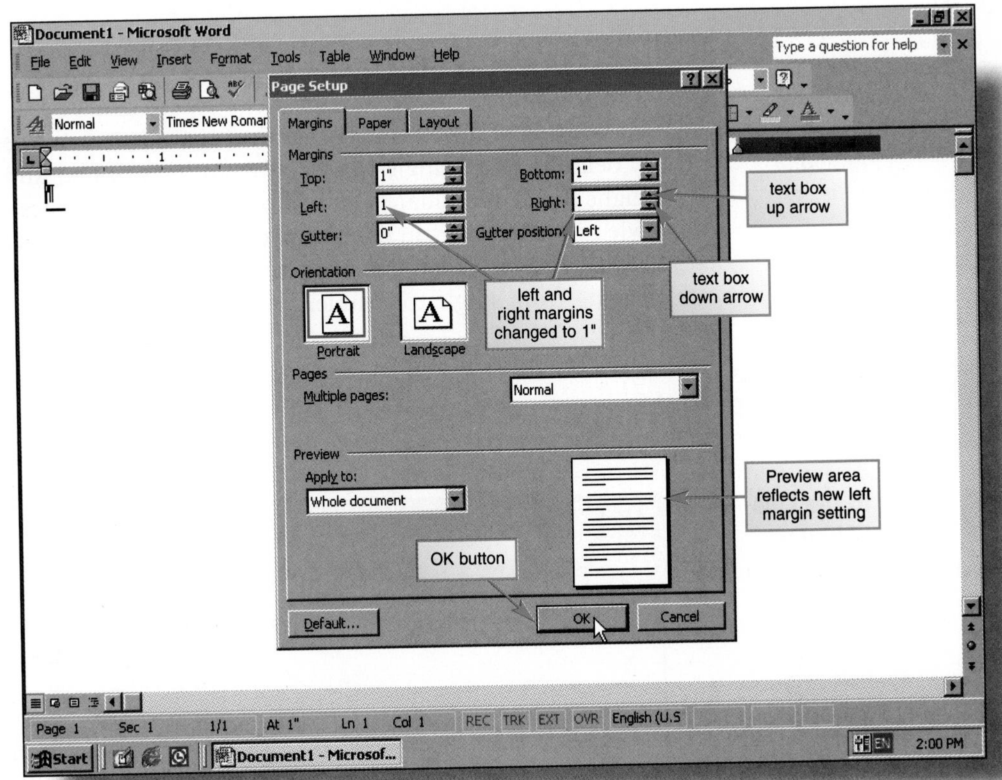

FIGURE 2-4

The new margin settings take effect in the document immediately. Word uses these margins for the entire document.

When you change the margin settings in the text boxes in the Page Setup dialog box, the Preview area (Figure 2-4) does not adjust to reflect a changed margin setting until the insertion point leaves the respective text box. That is, you must press the TAB or ENTER key or click another text box if you want to view a changed margin setting in the Preview area.

Other Ways

1. In print layout view, drag margin boundary(s) on ruler
2. In Voice Command mode, say "File, Page Setup, Margins, Left, [type left margin setting], Right, [type right margin setting], OK"

Zooming Page Width

As discussed in Project 1, when you **zoom page width**, Word displays text on the screen as large as possible without extending the right margin beyond the right edge of the document window. Perform the following steps to zoom page width.

TO ZOOM PAGE WIDTH

1. Click the Zoom box arrow on the Standard toolbar.
2. Click Page Width in the Zoom list.

Word extends the right margin to the right edge of the document window (shown in Figure 2-5 on the next page). Word computes the zoom percentage based on a variety of settings. Your percentage may be different depending on your computer configuration.

More About

The Page Setup Dialog Box

A document printed in portrait orientation is taller than it is wide. A document printed in landscape orientation is wider than it is tall. If you want to change the orientation of a printout from portrait to landscape, click the Landscape box in the Orientation area in the Page Setup dialog box (Figure 2-4).

Adjusting Line Spacing

Line spacing is the amount of vertical space between lines of text in a document. By default, Word single-spaces between lines of text and automatically adjusts line height to accommodate various font sizes and graphics. The MLA documentation style requires that you **double-space** the entire paper; that is, one blank line should display between each line of text. Perform the following steps to adjust the line spacing from single to double.

Steps To Double-Space Text

1 Point to the Line Spacing button arrow on the Formatting toolbar (Figure 2-5).

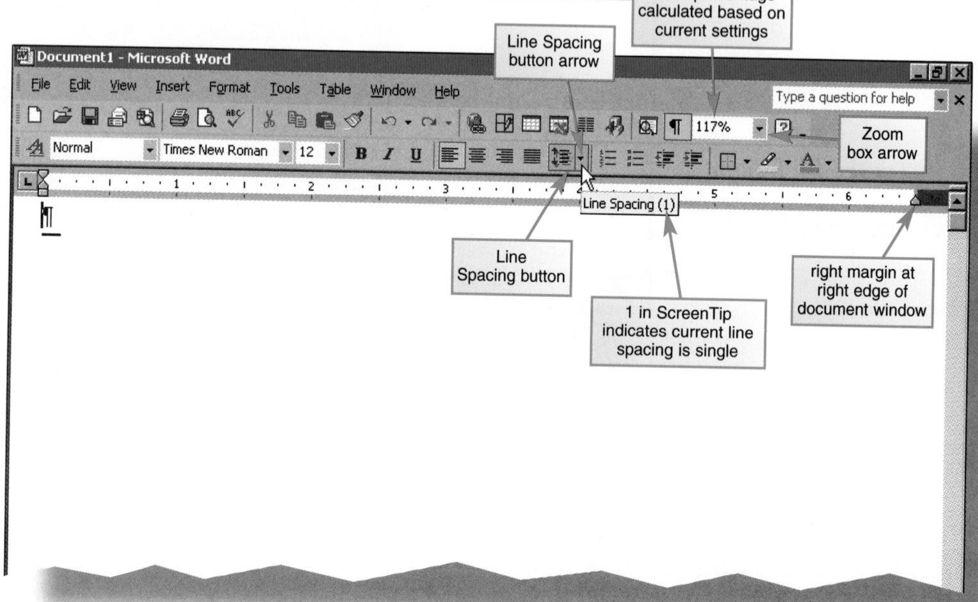

FIGURE 2-5

2 Click the Line Spacing button arrow and then point to 2.0.

Word displays a list of line spacing options (Figure 2-6).

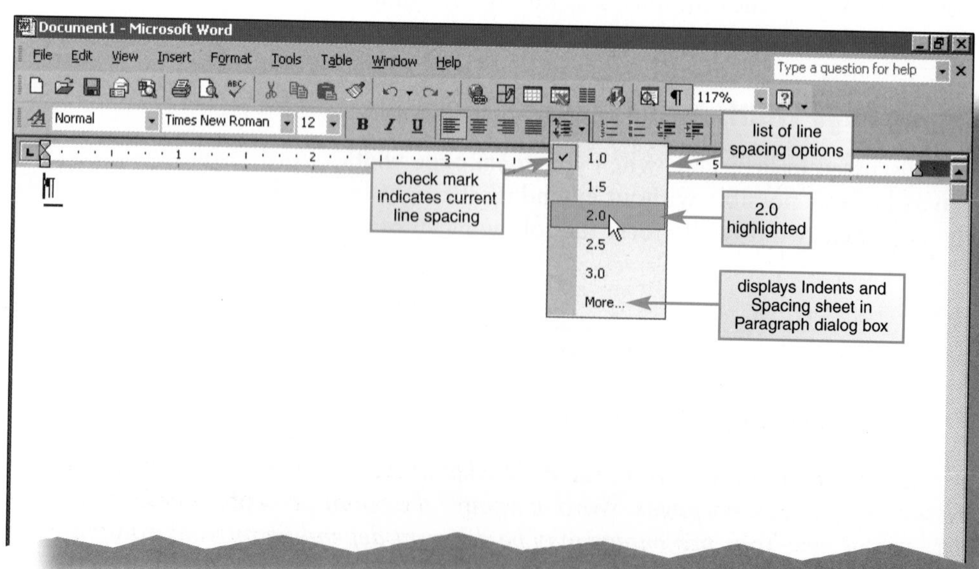

FIGURE 2-6

3 Click 2.0.

Word changes the line spacing to double at the location of the insertion point (Figure 2-7).

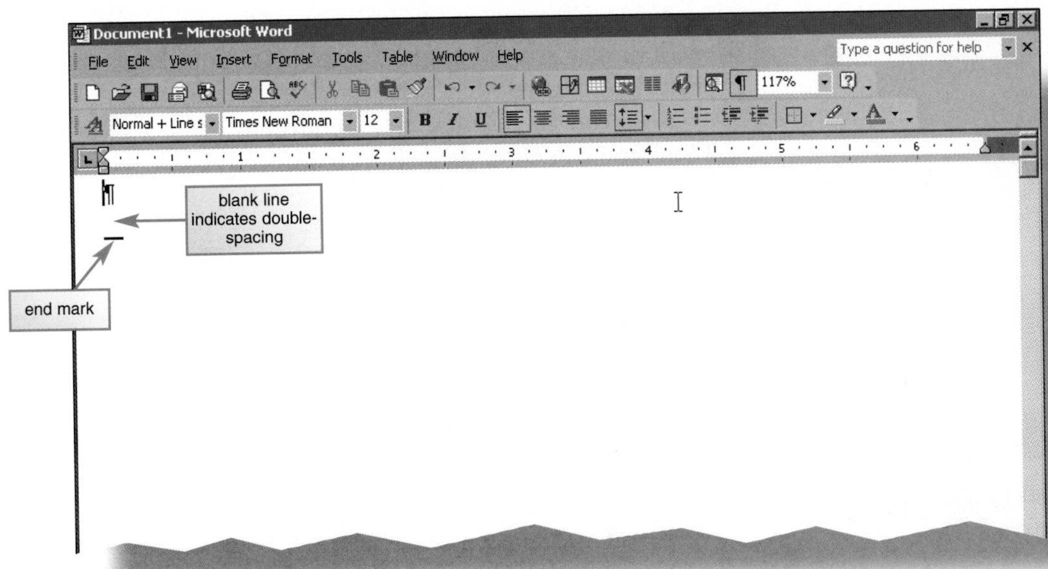

FIGURE 2-7

Notice when line spacing is double (Figure 2-7), the end mark displays one blank line below the insertion point.

The Line Spacing list (Figure 2-6) contains a variety of settings for the line spacing. The default, 1 (for single), and the options 1.5, 2 (for double), 2.5, and 3 (for triple) instruct Word to adjust line spacing automatically to accommodate the largest font or graphic on a line. For additional line spacing options, click More in the Line Spacing list and then click the Line Spacing box arrow in the Indents and Spacing sheet in the Paragraph dialog box.

If you wanted to apply the most recently set line spacing to the current or selected paragraphs, you would click the Line Spacing button instead of the Line Spacing button arrow.

Other Ways

1. On Format menu click Paragraph, click Indents and Spacing tab, click Line spacing box arrow, click Double, click OK button
2. Right-click paragraph, click Paragraph on shortcut menu, click Indents and Spacing tab, click Line Spacing box arrow, click Double, click OK button
3. Press CTRL+2
4. In Voice Command mode, say "Line Spacing, [select 2]"

Using a Header to Number Pages

In Word, you easily can number pages by clicking Insert on the menu bar and then clicking Page Numbers. Using the Page Numbers command, you can specify the location (top or bottom of page) and alignment (right, left, or centered) of the page numbers.

The MLA style requires that your last name display to the left of the page number on each page. The Page Numbers command does not allow you to enter text along with the page number. Thus, to place your name to the left of the page number, you must create a header that contains the page number.

More About

Line Spacing

If the top of characters or a graphic is chopped off, then line spacing probably was set to Exactly in the Paragraph dialog box. To remedy the problem, change the line spacing to Single (1.0), 1.5, Double (2.0), 2.5, 3.0, or At least, all of which accommodate the largest font or graphic. To display the Paragraph dialog box, click Format on the menu bar and then click Paragraph.

Headers and Footers

A **header** is text you want printed at the top of each page in the document. A **footer** is text you want printed at the bottom of every page. In Word, headers print in the top margin one-half inch from the top of every page, and footers print in the bottom margin one-half inch from the bottom of each page, which meets the MLA style. Headers and footers can include text and graphics, as well as the page number, total number of pages, current date, and current time.

In this project, you are to precede the page number with your last name placed one-half inch from the top of each page. Your last name and the page number should print **right-aligned**; that is, at the right margin.

To create the header, first you display the header area in the document window. Then, you can enter the header text into the header area. Use the procedures on the following pages to create the header with page numbers according to the MLA documentation style.

Steps To Display the Header Area

1 Click View on the menu bar and then point to Header and Footer (Figure 2-8).

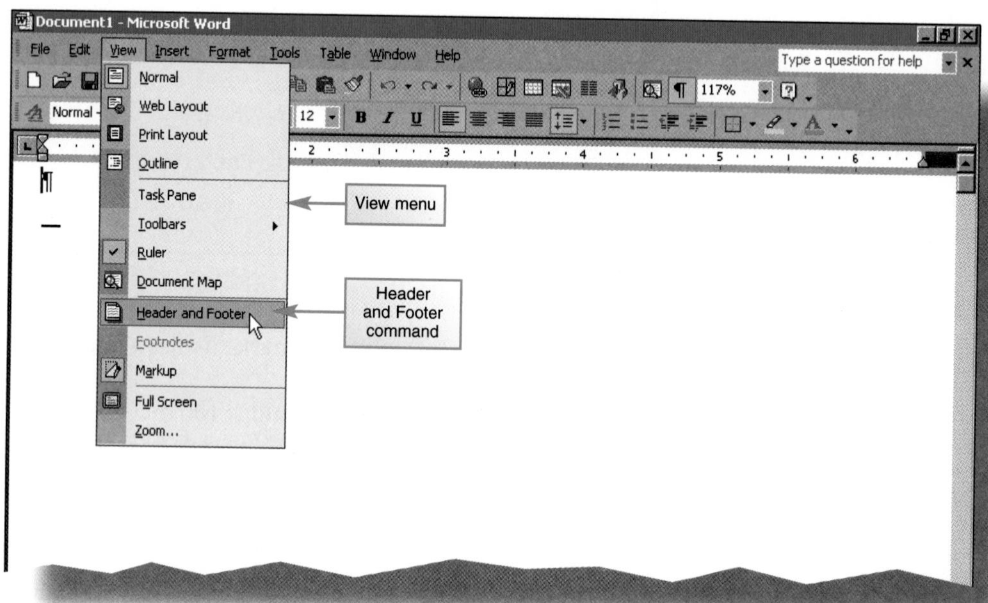

FIGURE 2-8

2 Click Header and Footer.

Word switches from normal view to print layout view and displays the Header and Footer toolbar (Figure 2-9). You type header text in the header area.

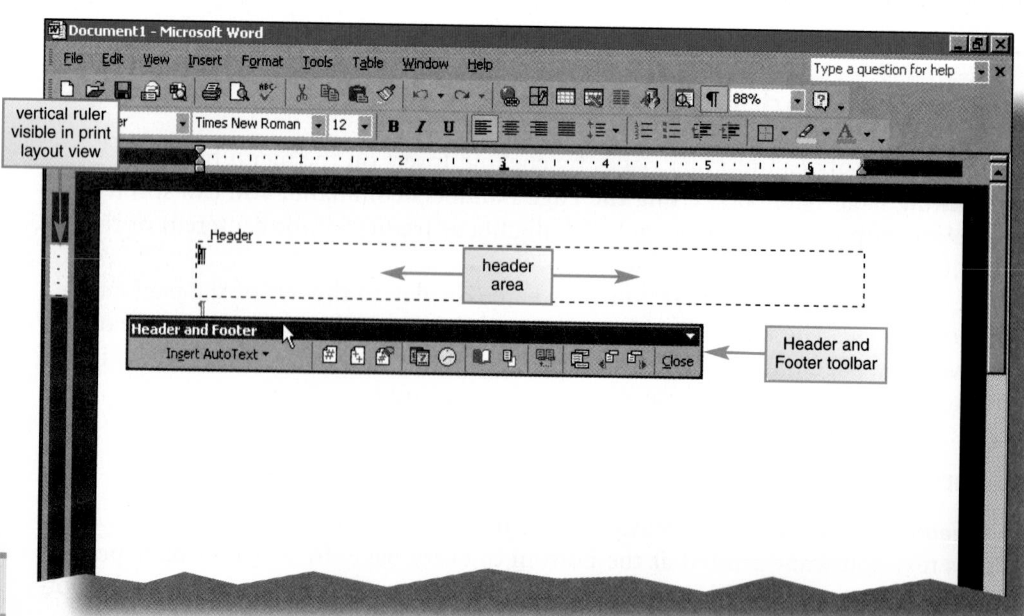

FIGURE 2-9

Other Ways

1. In Voice Command mode, say "View, Header and Footer"

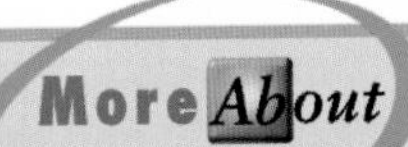

The Header and Footer toolbar initially floats in the document window. To move a floating toolbar, drag its title bar. You can **dock**, or attach, a floating toolbar above or below the Standard and Formatting toolbars by double-clicking the floating toolbar's title bar. To move a docked toolbar, drag its move handle. Recall that the move handle is the vertical bar to the left of the first button on a docked toolbar. If you drag a floating toolbar to an edge of the window, the toolbar snaps to the edge of the window. If you drag a docked toolbar to the middle of the window, the toolbar floats in the Word window. If you double-click between two buttons or boxes on a docked toolbar, it returns to its original floating position.

The header area does not display on the screen when the document window is in normal view because it tends to clutter the screen. To see the header in the document window with the rest of the text, you must display the document in print preview, which is discussed in a later project, or switch to print layout view. When you click the Header and Footer command on the View menu, Word automatically switches to **print layout view**, which displays the document exactly as it will print. In print layout view, the Print Layout View button on the horizontal scroll bar is selected (Figure 2-10 below).

More About

Print Layout View

You also can click the Print Layout View button on the horizontal scroll bar to switch to print layout view, which shows the positioning of headers, footers, and footnotes. In print layout view, click the Select Browse Object button on the vertical scroll bar and then click Browse by Page on the Select Browse Object menu. With this setting, you can click the double arrows on the bottom of the vertical scroll bar to move forward or backward an entire page.

Entering Text Using Click and Type

When in print layout view, you can use **Click and Type** to format and enter text, graphics, and other items. To use Click and Type, you double-click a blank area of the document window. Word automatically formats the item you enter according to the location where you double-click. Perform the following steps to use Click and Type to right-align and then enter the last name into the header area.

More About

Click and Type

Click and Type is not available in normal view, in a bulleted or numbered list, or in a document formatted into multiple columns.

Steps To Click and Type

1 Point to the right edge of the header area to display a right-align icon next to the I-beam.

As you move the Click and Type pointer around the window, the icon changes to represent formatting that will be applied if you double-click at that location (Figure 2-10).

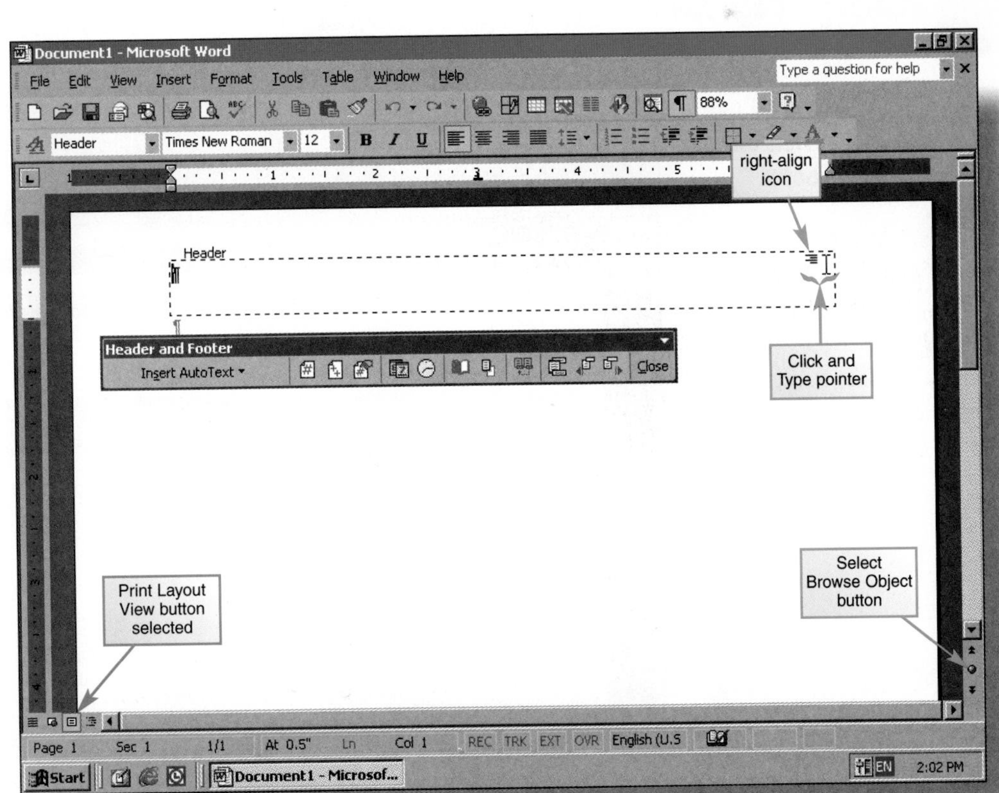

FIGURE 2-10

2 **Double-click. Type** `Marcott` **and then press the SPACEBAR.**

Word displays the last name, Marcott, right-aligned in the header area (Figure 2-11).

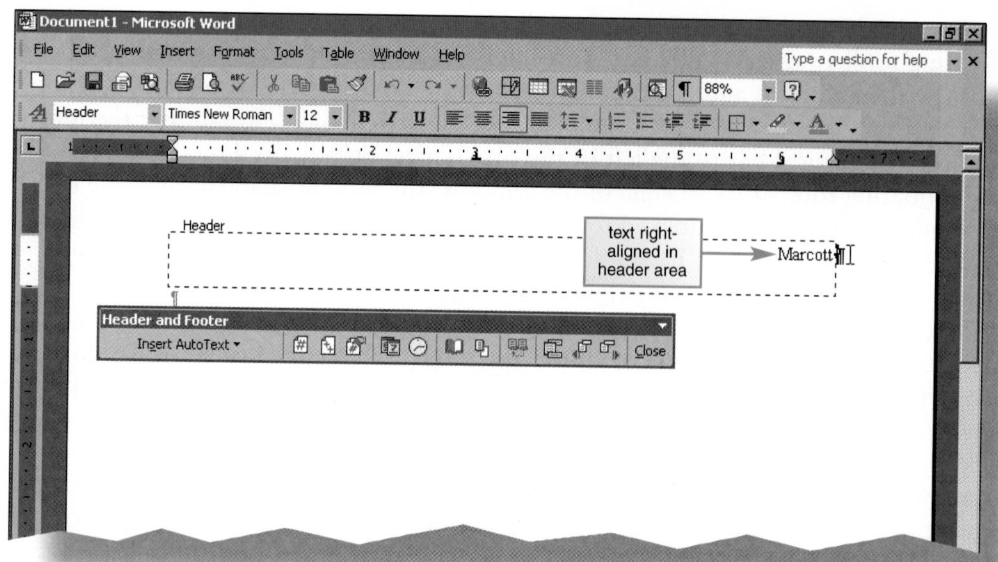

FIGURE 2-11

The next step is to enter the page number into the header area.

Entering a Page Number into the Header

Perform the following steps to enter a page number into the header area.

Steps To Enter a Page Number

1 **Click the Insert Page Number button on the Header and Footer toolbar.**

Word displays the page number 1 in the header area (Figure 2-12).

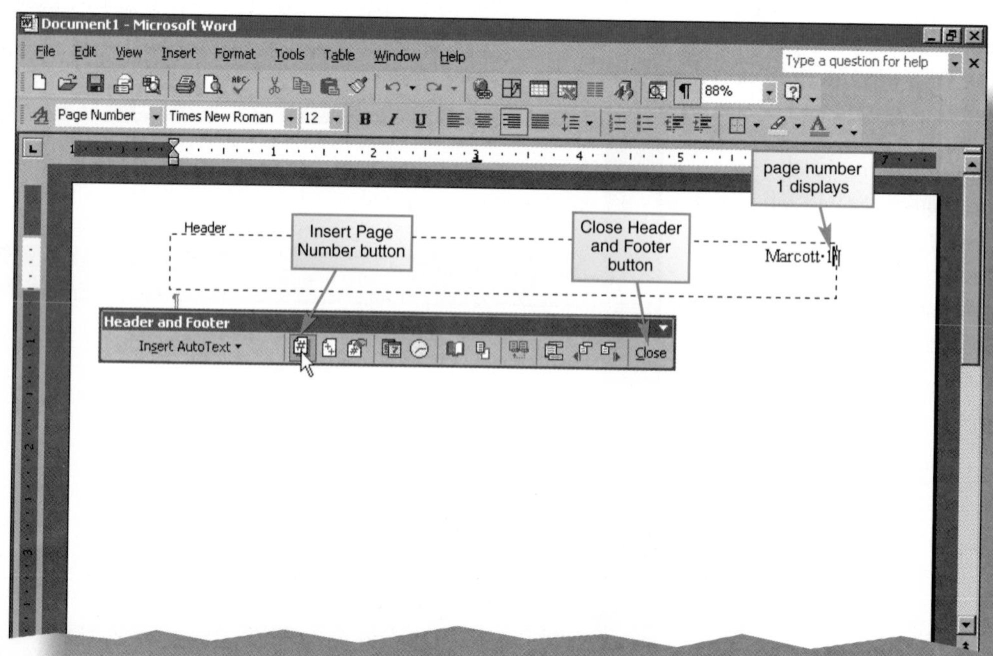

FIGURE 2-12

2 **Click the Close Header and Footer button on the Header and Footer toolbar.**

Word closes the Header and Footer toolbar and returns the screen to normal view (Figure 2-13).

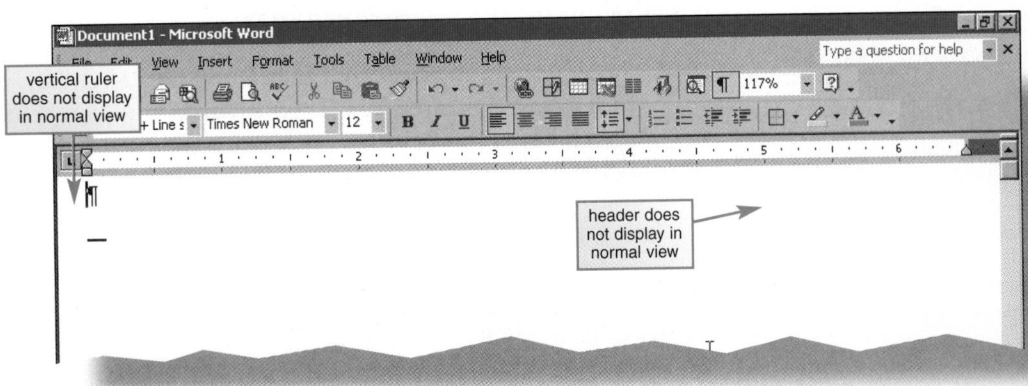

FIGURE 2-13

Other Ways

1. On Insert menu click Page Numbers, click OK button
2. In Voice Command mode, say "Insert Page Number"

The header does not display on the screen in normal view. Although it disappears from the screen, the header still is part of the document. To view the header, you can click View on the menu bar and then click Header and Footer; you can switch to print layout view; or you can display the document in print preview. Project 3 discusses print layout view and print preview in more depth.

Figure 2-14 illustrates the buttons on the Header and Footer toolbar. Just as the Insert Page Number button on the Header and Footer toolbar inserts the page number into the document, three other buttons on the Header and Footer toolbar insert items into the document. The Insert Number of Pages button inserts the total number of pages in the document; the Insert Date button inserts the current date; and the Insert Time button inserts the current time.

To edit an existing header, you can follow the same procedure that you use to create a new header. That is, you can click View on the menu bar and then click Header and Footer to display the header area. If you have multiple headers, click the Show Next button on the Header and Footer toolbar until the appropriate header displays in the header area. Edit the header as you would any Word text and then click the Close Header and Footer button on the Header and Footer toolbar.

To create a footer, click View on the menu bar, click Header and Footer, click the Switch Between Header and Footer button on the Header and Footer toolbar, and then follow the same procedure as you would to create a header.

Other buttons on the Header and Footer toolbar are explained as they are used in later projects.

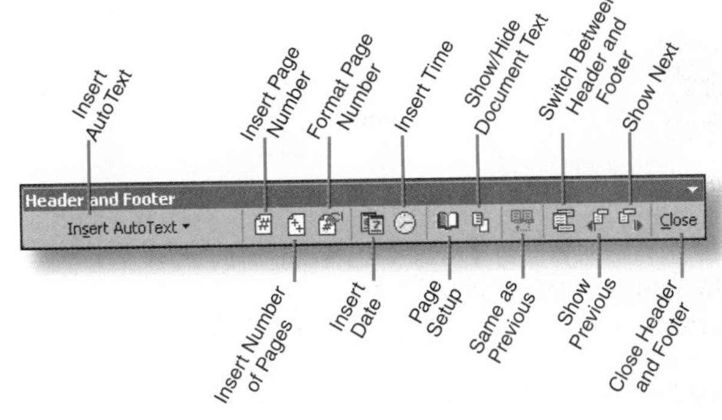

FIGURE 2-14

Typing the Body of the Research Paper

The body of the research paper encompasses the first two pages of the research paper. You will enter the paper and then modify it later in the project so it matches Figure 2-1 on page WD 2.05. The steps on the following pages illustrate how to type the body of the research paper.

As discussed earlier in this project, the MLA style does not require a separate title page for research papers. Instead, place your name and course information in a block at the top of the page at the left margin. Perform the step on the next page to begin typing the body of the research paper.

More About

Writing Papers

When preparing to write a paper, many students take notes to keep track of information. One method is to summarize the information. Another is to paraphrase, or rewrite the information in your own words. A third method is to quote the exact words of the original. Be sure to use quotation marks when directly quoting a source.

More About

APA Title Page

APA guidelines require a title page as a separate page of a research paper, instead of placing name and course information on the paper's first page. The running head (header), which contains a brief summary of the title and the page number, also is on the title page.

TO ENTER NAME AND COURSE INFORMATION

Type `Jordan Marcott` and then press the ENTER key. Type `Ms. Blythe` and then press the ENTER key. Type `Information Systems 101` and then press the ENTER key. Type `October 18, 2003` and then press the ENTER key.

The student name displays on line 1, the instructor name on line 2, the course name on line 3, and the paper due date on line 4 (Figure 2-15).

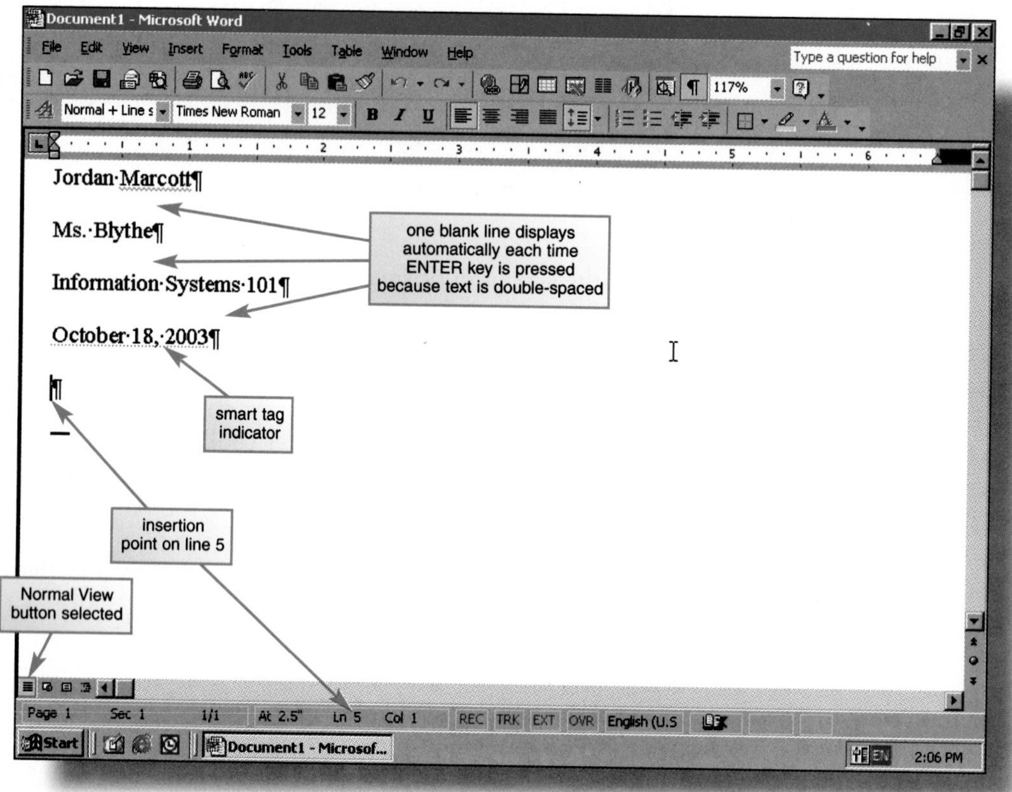

FIGURE 2-15

More About

Smart Tags

Word notifies you of a smart tag by displaying a smart tag indicator, such as the purple dotted underline shown in Figure 2-15. You can use smart tags to perform certain actions. For example, you can schedule an appointment on the underlined date in Outlook Calendar. If your screen does not display smart tag indicators, click Tools on the menu bar, click AutoCorrect Options, click the Smart Tags tab, place a check mark in the Label text with smart tags check box, be sure a check mark is in the Dates check box, and then click the OK button.

Notice in Figure 2-15 that the insertion point currently is on line 5. Each time you press the ENTER key, Word advances two lines on the screen. The line counter on the status bar is incremented by only one, however, because earlier you set line spacing to double.

If you watch the screen as you type, you may have noticed that as you typed the first few characters in the month, Octo, Word displayed the **AutoComplete tip**, October, above the characters. To save typing, you could press the ENTER key while the AutoComplete tip displays, which instructs Word to place the text of the AutoComplete tip at the location of your typing.

More About

Shortcut Keys

To print a complete list of shortcut keys in Word, search for keyboard shortcuts in Help. In the upper-right corner of the Help window, click Show All. Click the Print button and then click the Print button in the dialog box.

Applying Formatting Using Shortcut Keys

The next step is to enter the title of the research paper centered between the page margins. As you type text, you may want to format paragraphs and characters as you type them, instead of entering them and then formatting them later. In Project 1, you typed the characters in the document and then selected the ones to be formatted and applied the desired formatting using toolbar buttons. When your fingers are already on the keyboard, it sometimes is more efficient to use **shortcut keys**, or keyboard key combinations, to format text as you type it.

Perform the following steps to center a paragraph with the shortcut keys CTRL+E and then left-align a paragraph with the shortcut keys CTRL+L. (Recall from Project 1 that a notation such as CTRL+E means to press the letter e while holding the CTRL key.)

Steps To Use Shortcut Keys to Format Text

1 Press CTRL+E. Type `E-Retailing` **and then press the ENTER key.**

Word centers the title between the left and right margins (Figure 2-16). The paragraph mark and insertion point are centered because the formatting specified in the previous paragraph is carried forward to the next paragraph.

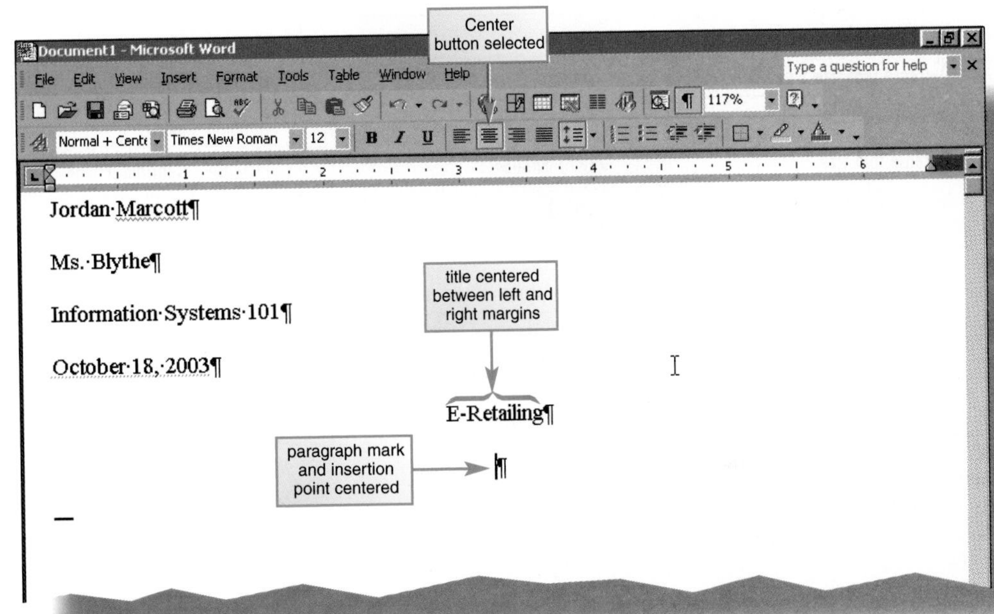

FIGURE 2-16

2 Press CTRL+L.

Word positions the paragraph mark and the insertion point at the left margin (Figure 2-17). The next text you type will be left-aligned.

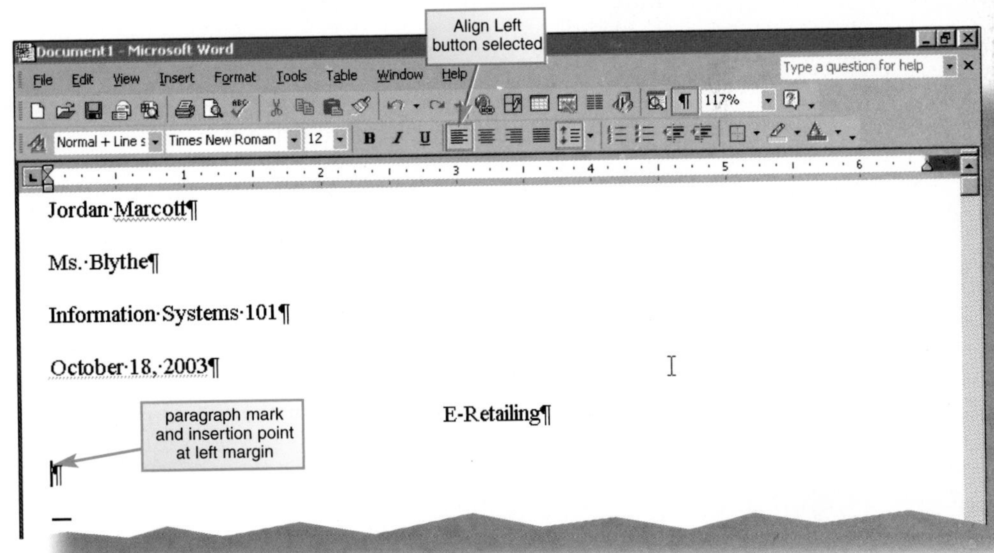

FIGURE 2-17

Word has many shortcut keys for your convenience while typing. Table 2-1 on the next page lists the common shortcut keys for formatting characters. Table 2-2 on the next page lists common shortcut keys for formatting paragraphs.

Table 2-1 Shortcut Keys for Formatting Characters

CHARACTER FORMATTING TASK	SHORTCUT KEYS
All capital letters	CTRL+SHIFT+A
Bold	CTRL+B
Case of letters	SHIFT+F3
Decrease font size	CTRL+SHIFT+<
Decrease font size 1 point	CTRL+[
Double-underline	CTRL+SHIFT+D
Increase font size	CTRL+SHIFT+>
Increase font size 1 point	CTRL+]
Italic	CTRL+I
Remove character formatting (plain text)	CTRL+SPACEBAR
Small uppercase letters	CTRL+SHIFT+K
Subscript	CTRL+=
Superscript	CTRL+SHIFT+PLUS SIGN
Underline	CTRL+U
Underline words, not spaces	CTRL+SHIFT+W

Table 2-2 Shortcut Keys for Formatting Paragraphs

PARAGRAPH FORMATTING TASK	SHORTCUT KEYS
1.5 line spacing	CTRL+5
Add/remove one line above	CTRL+0
Center paragraph	CTRL+E
Decrease paragraph indent	CTRL+SHIFT+M
Double-space lines	CTRL+2
Hanging indent	CTRL+T
Increase paragraph indent	CTRL+M
Justify paragraph	CTRL+J
Left-align paragraph	CTRL+L
Remove hanging indent	CTRL+SHIFT+T
Remove paragraph formatting	CTRL+Q
Right-align paragraph	CTRL+R
Single-space lines	CTRL+1

Saving the Research Paper

You now should save your research paper. For a detailed example of the procedure summarized below, refer to pages WD 1.30 through WD 1.32 in Project 1.

TO SAVE A DOCUMENT

1. Insert a floppy disk into drive A.
2. Click the Save button on the Standard toolbar.
3. Type `E-Retailing Paper` in the File name text box.
4. Click the Save in box arrow and then click 3½ Floppy (A:).
5. Click the Save button in the Save As dialog box.

Word saves your document with the file name, E-Retailing Paper (shown in Figure 2-18).

More About

The Ruler

If the horizontal ruler does not display on your screen, click View on the menu bar and then click Ruler.

Indenting Paragraphs

According to the MLA style, the first line of each paragraph in the research paper is to be indented one-half inch from the left margin. This procedure, called **first-line indent**, can be accomplished using the horizontal ruler. The **First Line Indent marker** is the top triangle at the 0" mark on the ruler (Figure 2-18). The small square at the 0" mark is the **Left Indent marker**. The Left Indent marker is used to change the entire left margin, whereas the First Line Indent marker affects only the first line of the paragraph.

Perform the following steps to first-line indent the paragraphs in the research paper.

Steps To First-Line Indent Paragraphs

1 With the insertion point on the paragraph mark in line 6, point to the First Line Indent marker on the ruler (Figure 2-18).

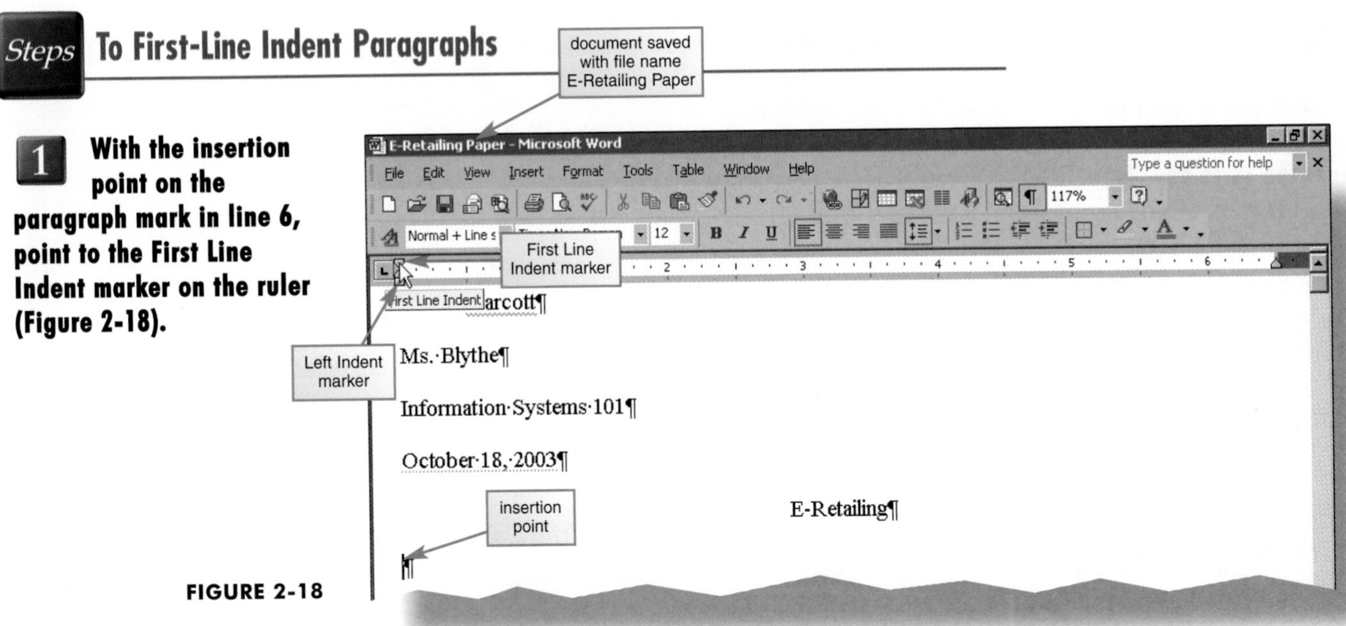

FIGURE 2-18

2 Drag the First Line Indent marker to the .5" mark on the ruler.

As you drag the mouse, a vertical dotted line displays in the document window, indicating the proposed location of the first line of the paragraph (Figure 2-19).

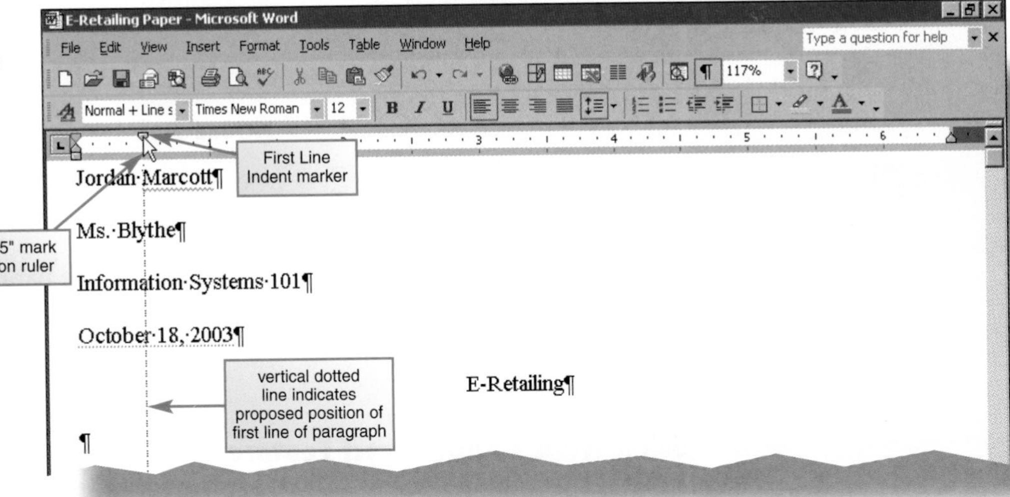

FIGURE 2-19

3 Release the mouse button.

The First Line Indent marker displays at the .5" mark on the ruler, or one-half inch from the left margin (Figure 2-20). The paragraph mark containing the insertion point in the document window also moves one-half inch to the right.

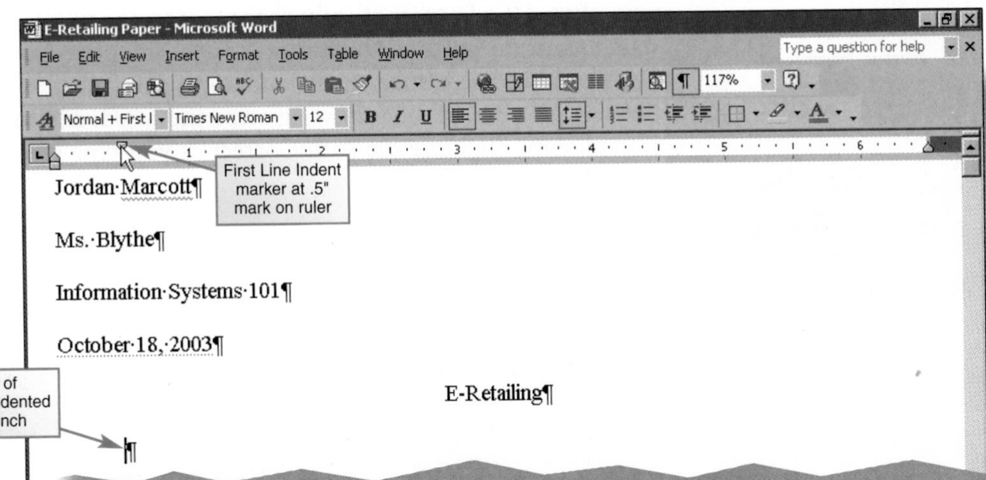

FIGURE 2-20

4 Type the first paragraph of the research paper body as shown in Figure 2-21. Press the ENTER key. Type `A customer (consumer) visits an online business at the Web equivalent of a showroom: the electronic storefront.`

Word automatically indents the first line of the second paragraph by one-half inch (Figure 2-21).

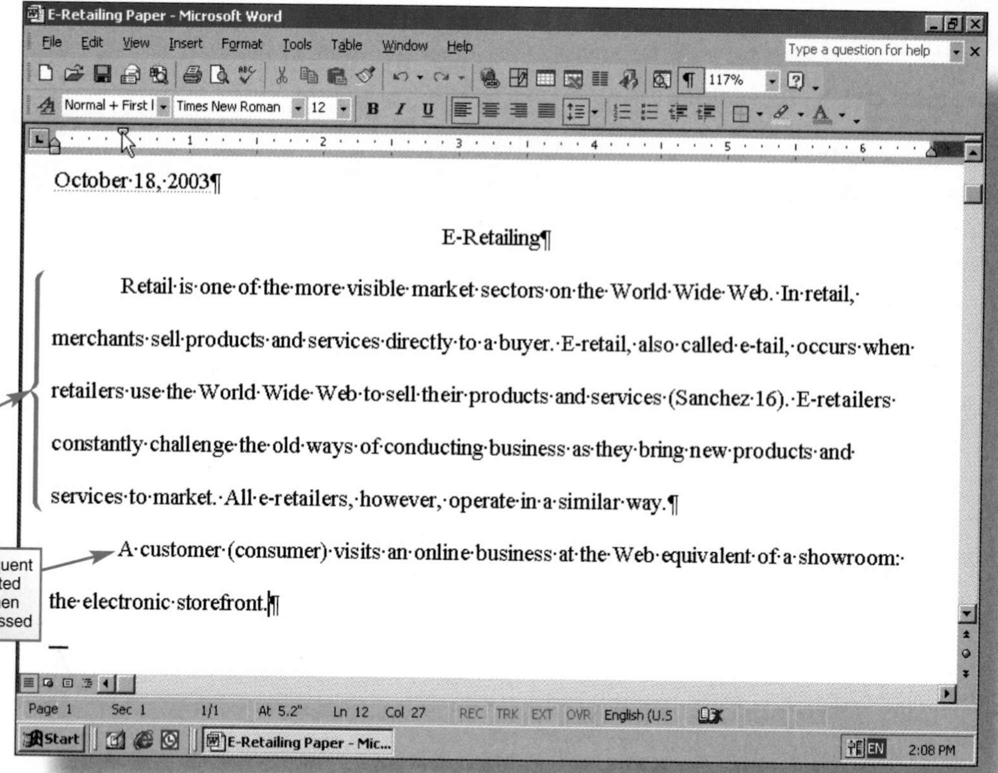
E-Retailing Paper - Microsoft Word
October 18, 2003¶
E-Retailing¶
Retail is one of the more visible market sectors on the World Wide Web. In retail, merchants sell products and services directly to a buyer. E-retail, also called e-tail, occurs when retailers use the World Wide Web to sell their products and services (Sanchez 16). E-retailers constantly challenge the old ways of conducting business as they bring new products and services to market. All e-retailers, however, operate in a similar way.¶
A customer (consumer) visits an online business at the Web equivalent of a showroom: the electronic storefront.¶
first paragraph
first line of subsequent paragraph indented automatically when ENTER key is pressed
Page 1 Sec 1 1/1 At 5.2" Ln 12 Col 27
2:08 PM

FIGURE 2-21

Other Ways

1. On Format menu click Paragraph, click Indents and Spacing tab, click Special box arrow, click First line, click OK button
2. Right-click paragraph, click Paragraph on shortcut menu, click Indents and Spacing tab, click Special box arrow, click First line, click OK button
3. Press TAB key at beginning of paragraph
4. In Voice Command mode, say "Format, Paragraph, Indents and Spacing, Special, First line, OK"

Recall that each time you press the ENTER key, the paragraph formatting in the previous paragraph is carried forward to the next paragraph. Thus, once you set the first-line indent, its format carries forward automatically to each subsequent paragraph you type.

Using Word's AutoCorrect Feature

As you type, you may make typing, spelling, capitalization, or grammar errors. For this reason, Word provides an **AutoCorrect** feature that automatically corrects these kinds of errors as you type them in the document. For example, if you type the text, ahve, Word automatically changes it to the word, have, when you press the SPACEBAR or a punctuation mark key such as a period or comma.

Word has predefined many commonly misspelled words, which it automatically corrects for you. In the following steps the word, catalog, is misspelled intentionally as catelog to illustrate the AutoCorrect as you type feature.

More About

AutoCorrect

You can add entries to the AutoCorrect list while checking spelling. Right-click the word flagged with the red wavy underline. Point to AutoCorrect on the shortcut menu and then click the correction you want added to the AutoCorrect list.

To AutoCorrect as You Type

1 Press the SPACEBAR. Type the beginning of the next sentence and misspell the word, catalog, as follows: `An electronic storefront, also called an online catelog` **as shown in Figure 2-22.**

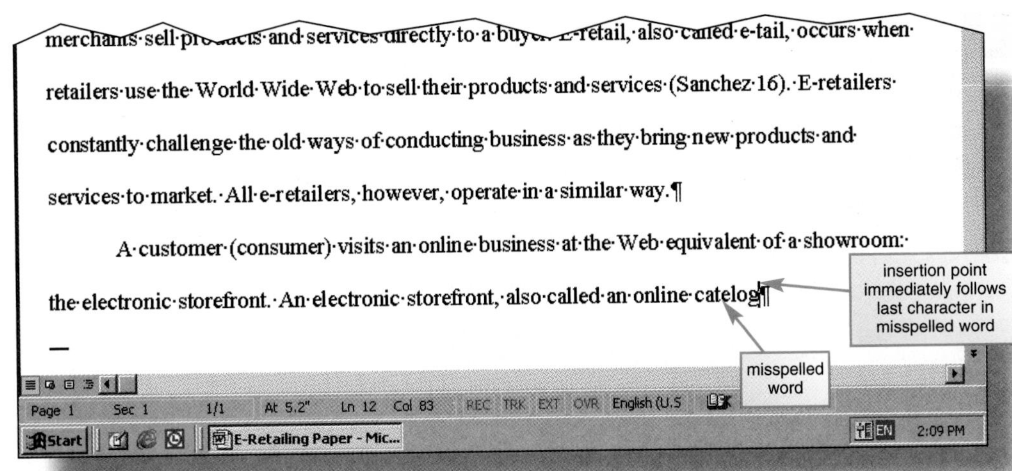
merchants sell products and services directly to a buyer. E-retail, also called e-tail, occurs when retailers use the World Wide Web to sell their products and services (Sanchez 16). E-retailers constantly challenge the old ways of conducting business as they bring new products and services to market. All e-retailers, however, operate in a similar way.¶
A customer (consumer) visits an online business at the Web equivalent of a showroom: the electronic storefront. An electronic storefront, also called an online catelog¶
insertion point immediately follows last character in misspelled word
misspelled word
Page 1 Sec 1 1/1 At 5.2" Ln 12 Col 83 REC TRK EXT OVR English (U.S
Start
E-Retailing Paper - Mic...
2:09 PM

FIGURE 2-22

2 Press the COMMA key. Press the SPACEBAR. Type the rest of the sentence: `is the Web site where an e-retailer displays its products.`

As soon as you press the COMMA key, Word's AutoCorrect feature detects the misspelling and corrects the misspelled word (Figure 2-23).

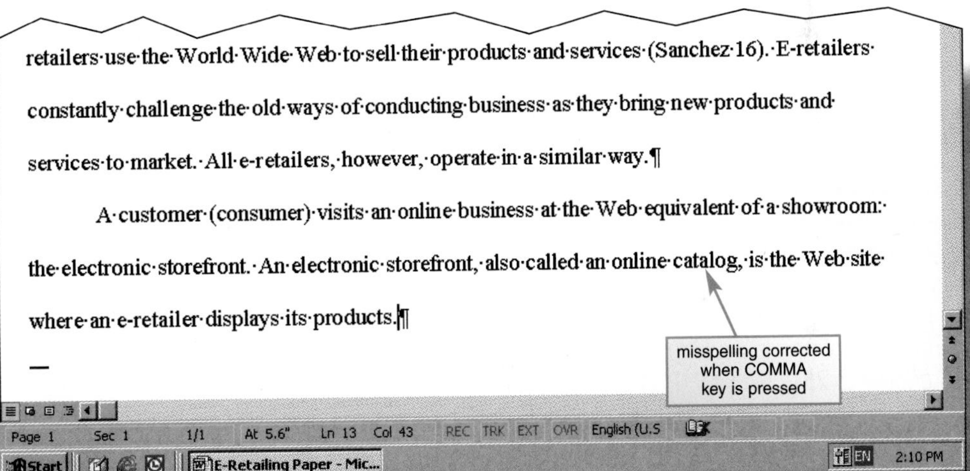
retailers use the World Wide Web to sell their products and services (Sanchez 16). E-retailers constantly challenge the old ways of conducting business as they bring new products and services to market. All e-retailers, however, operate in a similar way.¶
A customer (consumer) visits an online business at the Web equivalent of a showroom: the electronic storefront. An electronic storefront, also called an online catalog, is the Web site where an e-retailer displays its products.¶
misspelling corrected when COMMA key is pressed
Page 1 Sec 1 1/1 At 5.6" Ln 13 Col 43 REC TRK EXT OVR English (U.S
Start
E-Retailing Paper - Mic...
2:10 PM

FIGURE 2-23

Word has a list of predefined typing, spelling, capitalization, and grammar errors that AutoCorrect can detect and correct. If you do not like a change that Word automatically makes in a document and you immediately notice the automatic correction, you can undo the change by clicking the Undo button on the Standard toolbar; clicking Edit on the menu bar and then clicking Undo; or pressing CTRL+Z.

If you do not immediately notice the change, you still can undo a correction automatically made by Word through the AutoCorrect Options button. When you point near text that automatically was corrected, Word displays a small blue box below the text. If you click the small blue box, Word displays the AutoCorrect Options button. When you click the **AutoCorrect Options button**, a menu displays that allows you to undo a correction or change how Word handles future automatic corrections of this type. The steps on the next page show how to use the AutoCorrect Options button and menu.

More About

AutoCorrect Options

The AutoCorrect Options is a type of smart tag. The small blue box that displays below the automatically corrected text (Figure 2-24 on the next page) is one type of smart tag indicator. If the smart tag indicator or AutoCorrect Options button do not display on your screen, click Tools on the menu bar, click AutoCorrect Options, click the AutoCorrect tab, place a check mark in the Show AutoCorrect Options buttons check box, and then click the OK button.

Steps To Use the AutoCorrect Options Button

1 Position the mouse pointer at the beginning of the text automatically corrected by Word (in this case, the c in catalog).

Word displays a small blue box below the automatically corrected text (Figure 2-24).

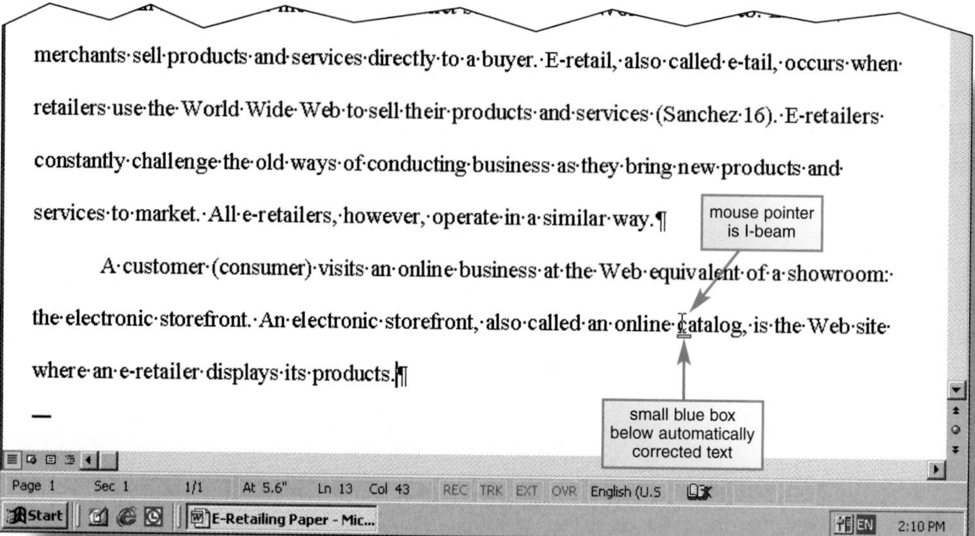
merchants·sell·products·and·services·directly·to·a·buyer.·E-retail,·also·called·e-tail,·occurs·when·
retailers·use·the·World·Wide·Web·to·sell·their·products·and·services·(Sanchez·16).·E-retailers·
constantly·challenge·the·old·ways·of·conducting·business·as·they·bring·new·products·and·
services·to·market.·All·e-retailers,·however,·operate·in·a·similar·way.¶
A·customer·(consumer)·visits·an·online·business·at·the·Web·equivalent·of·a·showroom:·
the·electronic·storefront.·An·electronic·storefront,·also·called·an·online·catalog,·is·the·Web·site·
where·an·e-retailer·displays·its·products.¶
mouse pointer is I-beam
small blue box below automatically corrected text
Page 1 Sec 1 1/1 At 5.6" Ln 13 Col 43 REC TRK EXT OVR English (U.S
Start
E-Retailing Paper - Mic...
2:10 PM

FIGURE 2-24

2 Point to the small blue box to display the AutoCorrect Options button and then click the AutoCorrect Options button.

Word displays the AutoCorrect Options menu (Figure 2-25).

3 Press the ESCAPE key to remove the AutoCorrect Options menu from the window.

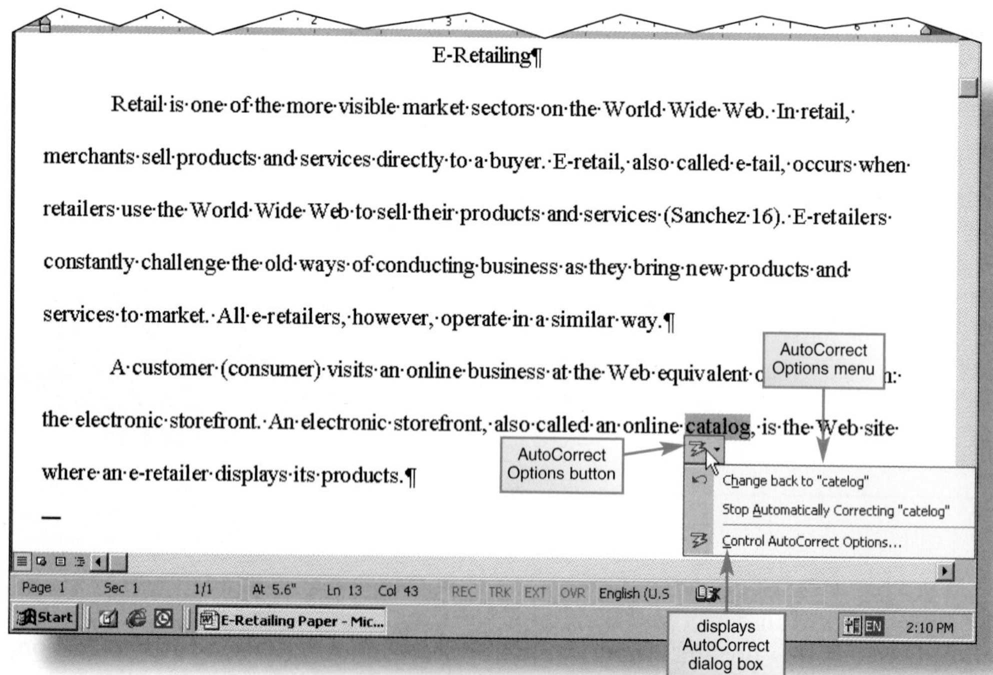
E-Retailing¶
Retail·is·one·of·the·more·visible·market·sectors·on·the·World·Wide·Web.·In·retail,·
merchants·sell·products·and·services·directly·to·a·buyer.·E-retail,·also·called·e-tail,·occurs·when·
retailers·use·the·World·Wide·Web·to·sell·their·products·and·services·(Sanchez·16).·E-retailers·
constantly·challenge·the·old·ways·of·conducting·business·as·they·bring·new·products·and·
services·to·market.·All·e-retailers,·however,·operate·in·a·similar·way.¶
A·customer·(consumer)·visits·an·online·business·at·the·Web·equivalent·
the·electronic·storefront.·An·electronic·storefront,·also·called·an·online·catalog,·is·the·Web·site·
where·an·e-retailer·displays·its·products.¶
AutoCorrect Options menu
AutoCorrect Options button
Change back to "catelog"
Stop Automatically Correcting "catelog"
Control AutoCorrect Options...
displays AutoCorrect dialog box
Page 1 Sec 1 1/1 At 5.6" Ln 13 Col 43 REC TRK EXT OVR English (U.S
Start
E-Retailing Paper - Mic...
2:10 PM

FIGURE 2-25

When you move the mouse pointer, the AutoCorrect Options button disappears from the screen.

In addition to the predefined list of AutoCorrect spelling, capitalization, and grammar errors, you can create your own AutoCorrect entries to add to the list. For example, if you often misspell the word, software, as softare, you should create an AutoCorrect entry for it as shown in these steps.

Steps To Create an AutoCorrect Entry

1 Click Tools on the menu bar and then point to AutoCorrect Options (Figure 2-26).

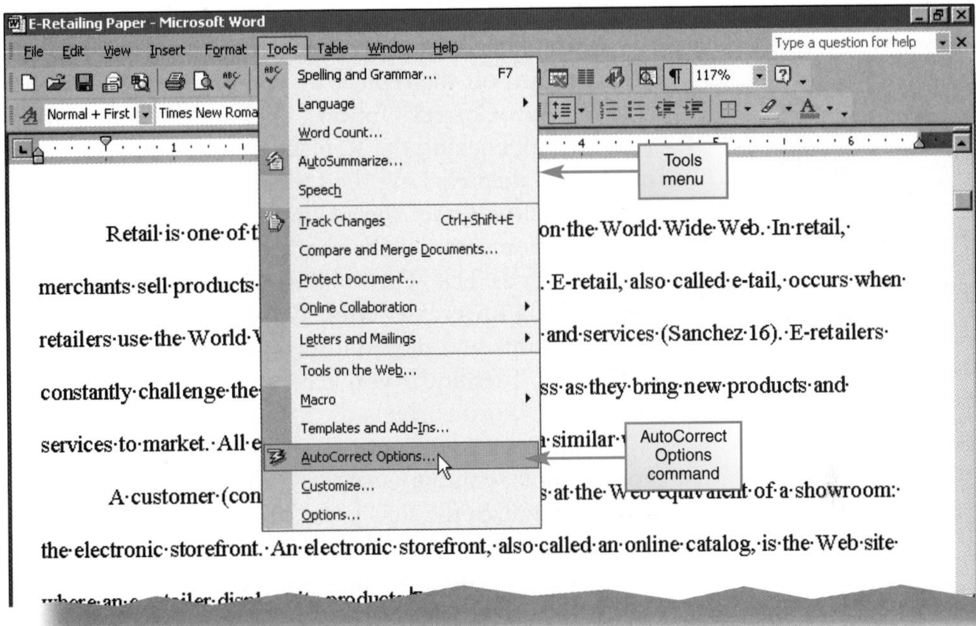

FIGURE 2-26

2 Click AutoCorrect Options. When the AutoCorrect dialog box displays, type `softare` **in the Replace text box. Press the TAB key and then type** `software` **in the With text box. Point to the Add button.**

Word displays the AutoCorrect dialog box. The Replace text box contains the misspelled word, and the With text box contains its correct spelling (Figure 2-27).

3 Click the Add button. (If your dialog box displays a Replace button instead, click it and then click the Yes button in the Microsoft Word dialog box.) Click the OK button.

Word adds the entry alphabetically to the list of words to correct automatically as you type.

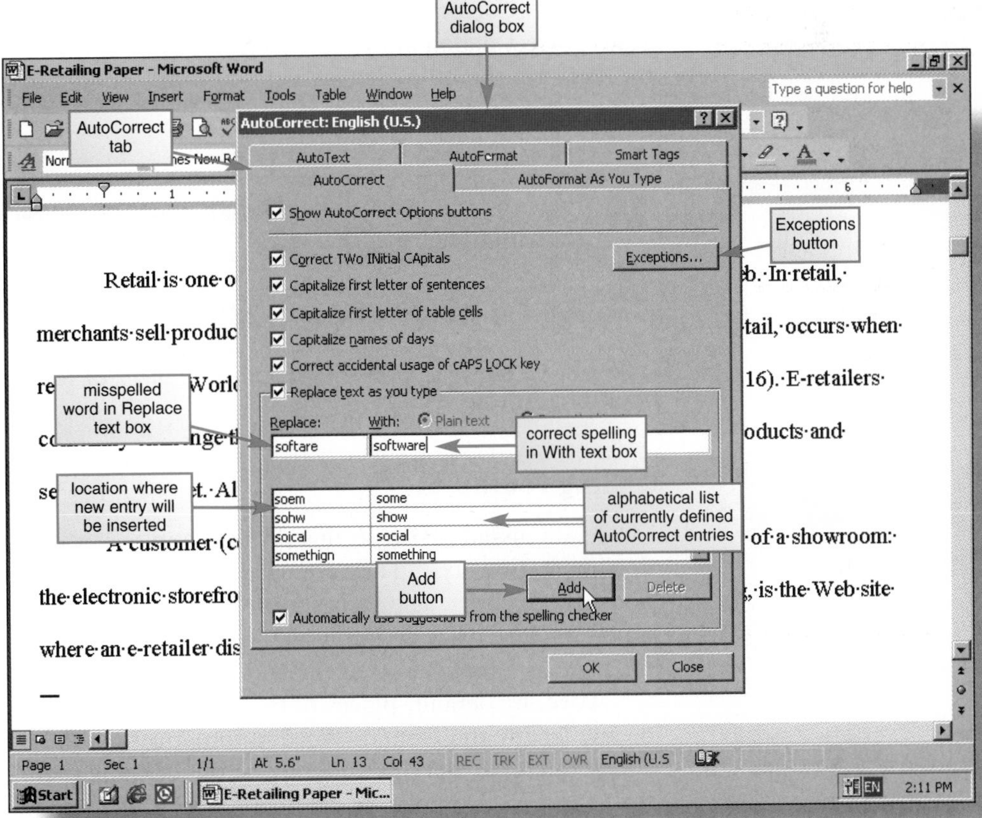

FIGURE 2-27

Quick Reference

For a table that lists how to complete tasks covered in this book using the mouse, menu, shortcut menu, and keyboard, see the Quick Reference Summary at the back of this book or visit the Shelly Cashman Series Office XP Web page (scsite.com/offxp/qr.htm) and then click Microsoft Word 2002.

In addition to creating AutoCorrect entries for words you commonly misspell, you can create entries for abbreviations, codes, and so on. For example, you could create an AutoCorrect entry for asap, indicating that Word should replace this text with the phrase, as soon as possible.

If, for some reason, you do not want Word to correct automatically as you type, you can turn off the replace as you type feature by clicking Tools on the menu bar, clicking AutoCorrect Options, clicking the AutoCorrect tab (Figure 2-27 on the previous page), clicking the Replace text as you type check box to remove the check mark, and then clicking the OK button.

The AutoCorrect sheet (Figure 2-27) contains other check boxes that correct capitalization errors if the check boxes are selected. If you type two capital letters in a row, such as TH, Word makes the second letter lowercase, Th. If you begin a sentence with a lowercase letter, Word capitalizes the first letter of the sentence. If you type the name of a day in lowercase, such as tuesday, Word capitalizes the first letter of the day, Tuesday. If you leave the CAPS LOCK key on and begin a new sentence such as aFTER, Word corrects the typing, After, and turns off the CAPS LOCK key.

Sometimes you do not want Word to AutoCorrect a particular word or phrase. For example, you may use the code WD. in your documents. Because Word automatically capitalizes the first letter of a sentence, the character you enter following the period will be capitalized (in the previous sentence, it would capitalize the letter i in the word, in). To allow the code WD. to be entered into a document and still leave the AutoCorrect feature turned on, you need to set an exception. To set an exception to an AutoCorrect rule, click Tools on the menu bar, click AutoCorrect Options, click the AutoCorrect tab, click the Exceptions button in the AutoCorrect sheet (Figure 2-27), click the appropriate tab in the AutoCorrect Exceptions dialog box, type the exception entry in the text box, click the Add button, click the Close button in the AutoCorrect Exceptions dialog box, and then click the OK button in the AutoCorrect dialog box.

Perform the following steps to continue adding text to the body of the paper.

TO ENTER MORE TEXT

1. Press the SPACEBAR. Type the remainder of the second paragraph of the paper as shown in Figure 2-28.
2. Press the ENTER key. Type the first two sentences of the third paragraph of the paper as shown in Figure 2-28.

The second paragraph and first two sentences of the third paragraph are entered (Figure 2-28).

More About

Citing Sources

Both the MLA and APA guidelines suggest the use of in-text parenthetical citations, as opposed to footnoting each source of material in a paper. These parenthetical acknowledgments guide the reader to the end of the paper for complete information on the source.

Adding Footnotes

As discussed earlier in this project, explanatory notes are optional in the MLA documentation style. They are used primarily to elaborate on points discussed in the body of the paper. The style specifies that a **superscript** (raised number) be used for a note reference mark to signal that an explanatory note exists either at the bottom of the page as a **footnote** or at the end of the document as an **endnote**.

Word, by default, places notes at the bottom of each page. In Word, **note text** can be any length and format. Word automatically numbers notes sequentially by placing a **note reference mark** in the body of the document and also in front of the note text. If you insert, rearrange, or remove notes, Word renumbers any subsequent note reference marks according to their new sequence in the document.

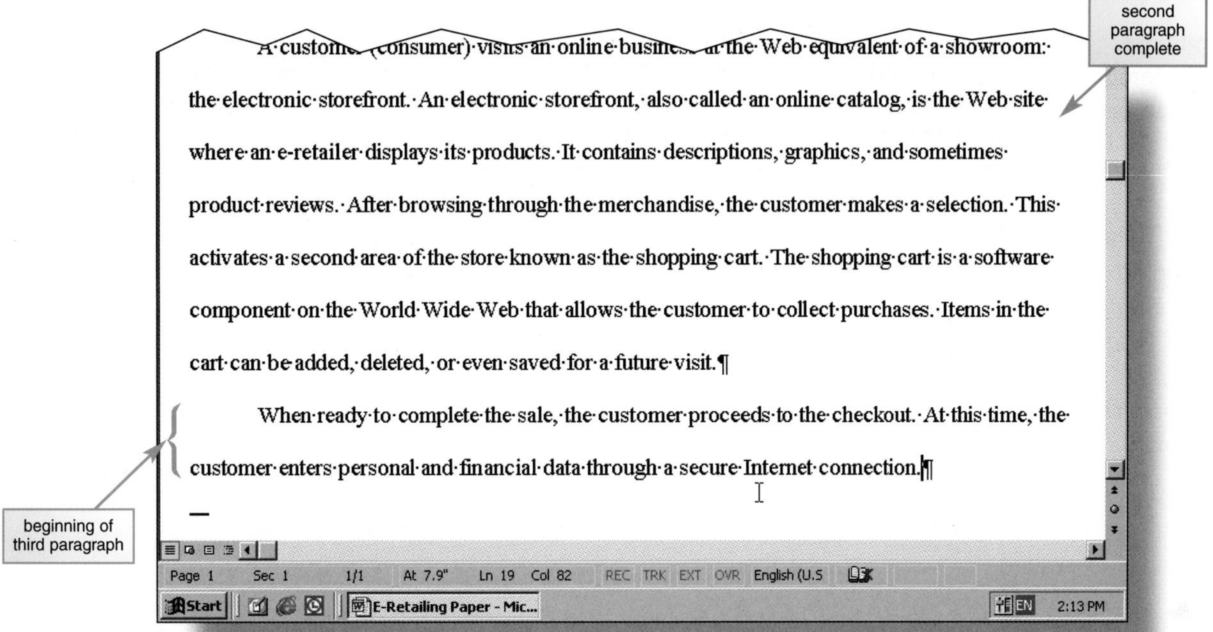
second paragraph complete
A customer (consumer) visits an online business at the Web equivalent of a showroom: the electronic storefront. An electronic storefront, also called an online catalog, is the Web site where an e-retailer displays its products. It contains descriptions, graphics, and sometimes product reviews. After browsing through the merchandise, the customer makes a selection. This activates a second area of the store known as the shopping cart. The shopping cart is a software component on the World Wide Web that allows the customer to collect purchases. Items in the cart can be added, deleted, or even saved for a future visit.
When ready to complete the sale, the customer proceeds to the checkout. At this time, the customer enters personal and financial data through a secure Internet connection.
beginning of third paragraph

FIGURE 2-28

Perform the following steps to add a footnote to the research paper.

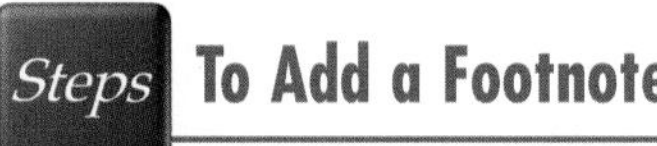

To Add a Footnote

1 Click Insert on the menu bar, point to Reference, and then point to Footnote.

The insertion point is positioned immediately after the period following the end of the second sentence in the third paragraph of the research paper (Figure 2-29).

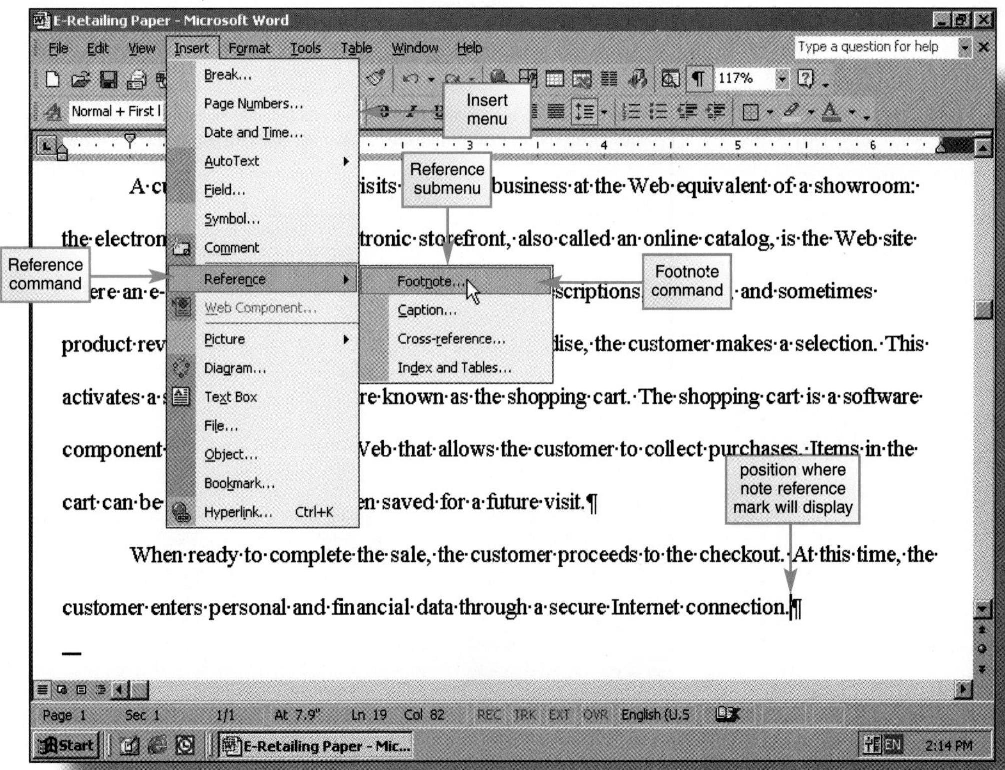
E-Retailing Paper - Microsoft Word
Insert menu
Reference submenu
Reference command
Footnote command
Break...
Page Numbers...
Date and Time...
AutoText
Field...
Symbol...
Comment
Reference
Web Component...
Picture
Diagram...
Text Box
File...
Object...
Bookmark...
Hyperlink... Ctrl+K
Footnote...
Caption...
Cross-reference...
Index and Tables...
position where note reference mark will display

FIGURE 2-29

2 Click Footnote. When the Footnote and Endnote dialog box displays, point to the Insert button.

Word displays the Footnote and Endnote dialog box (Figure 2-30). If you wanted to create endnotes instead of footnotes, you would click Endnotes in the Footnote and Endnote dialog box.

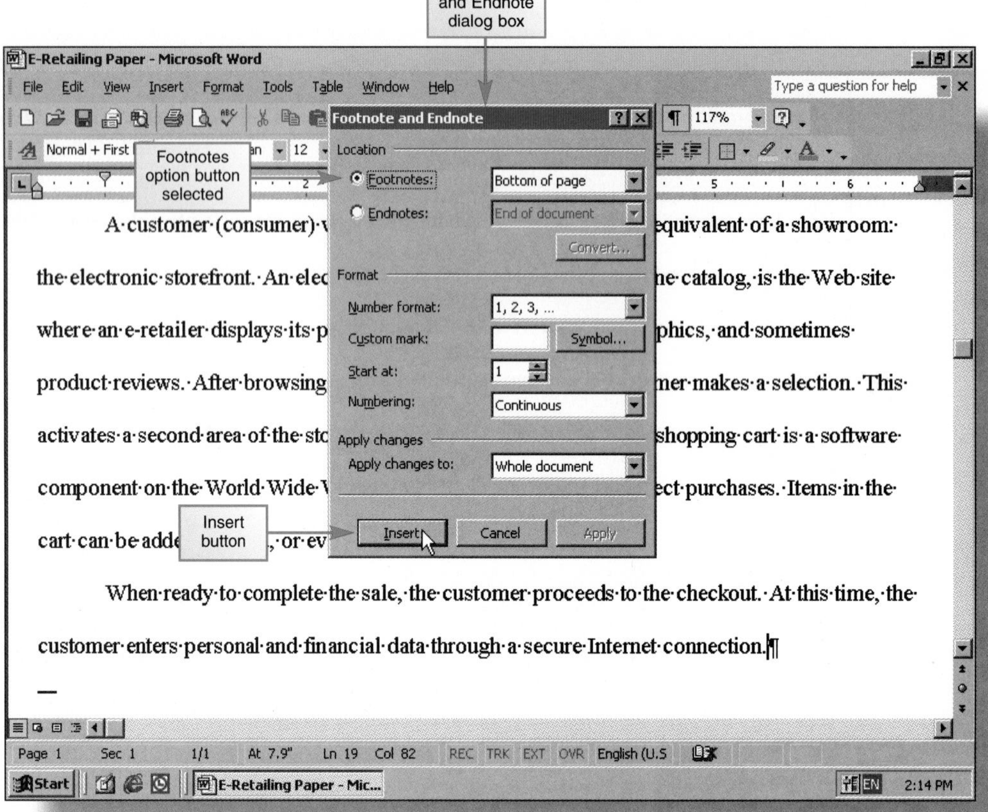

FIGURE 2-30

3 Click the Insert button.

Word opens a ***note pane*** *in the lower portion of the Word window with the note reference mark (a superscripted 1) positioned at the left margin of the note pane (Figure 2-31). The note reference mark also displays in the document window at the location of the insertion point. Note reference marks are, by default, superscripted; that is, raised above other letters.*

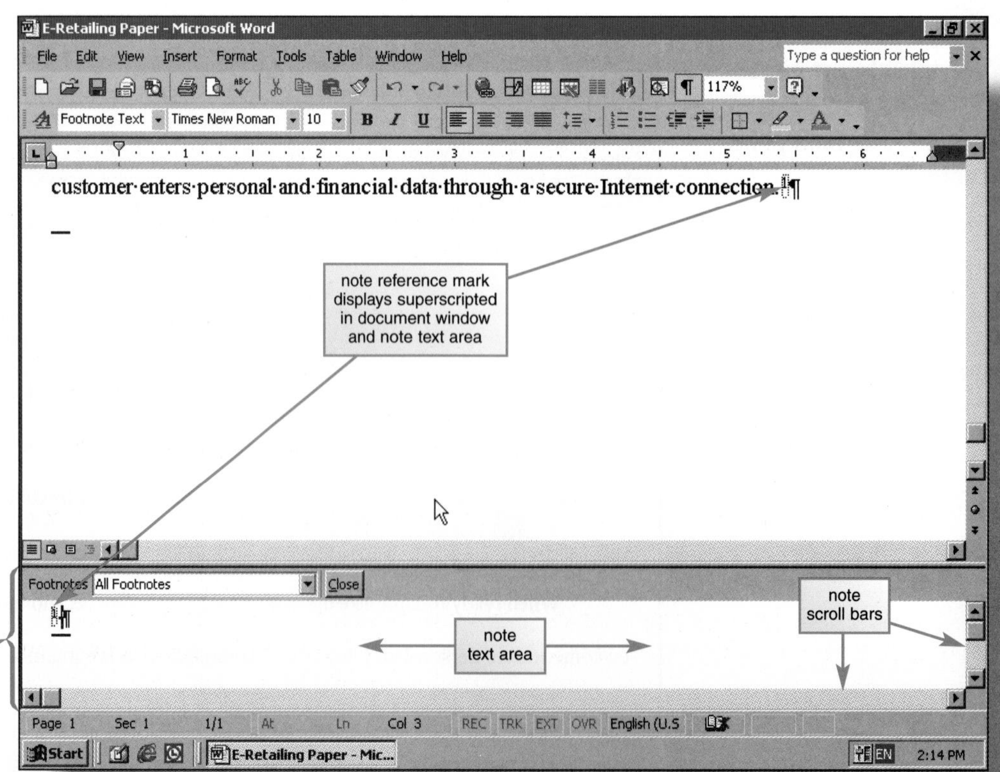

FIGURE 2-31

4 **Type** `According to Bodini and Hampton, consumers should verify that a merchant provides secure transactions before using a credit card on the Internet (56-62).`

The note text displays in the note pane (Figure 2-32).

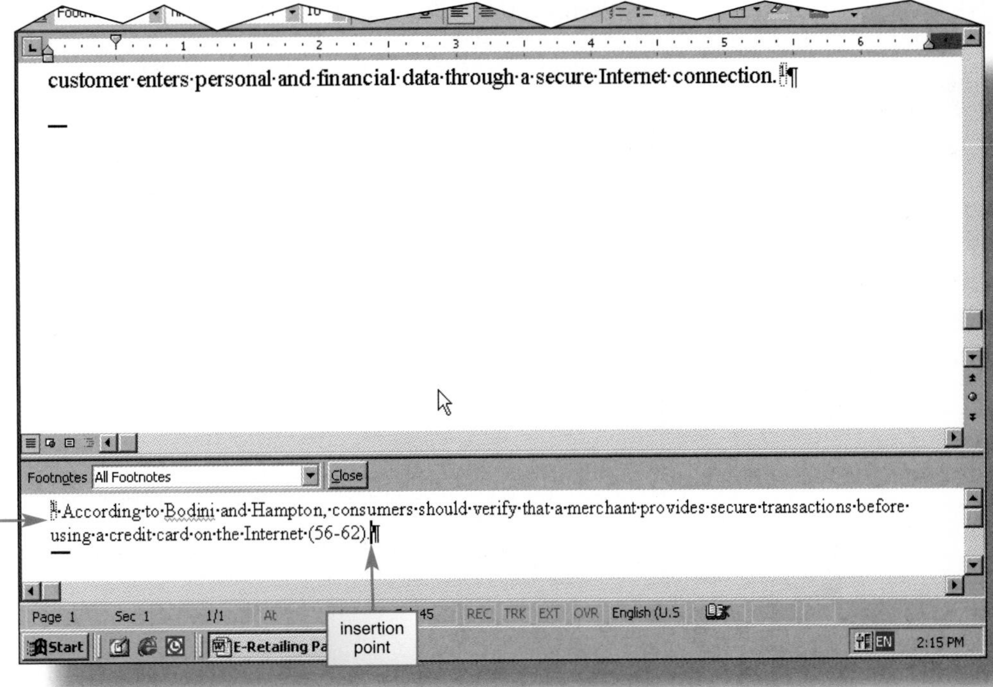
customer·enters·personal·and·financial·data·through·a·secure·Internet·connection.¶
Footnotes All Footnotes
Close
note text entered
According·to·Bodini·and·Hampton,·consumers·should·verify·that·a·merchant·provides·secure·transactions·before·using·a·credit·card·on·the·Internet·(56-62).¶
insertion point
Page 1 Sec 1 1/1
REC TRK EXT OVR English (U.S
Start
E-Retailing Pa
2:15 PM

FIGURE 2-32

Other Ways

1. In Voice Command mode, say "Insert, Reference, Footnote, Insert, Dictation, [note text]"

The footnote is not formatted according to the MLA requirements. Thus, the next step is to modify the style of the footnote.

Modifying a Style

A **style** is a named group of formatting characteristics that you can apply to text. Word has many built-in, or predefined, styles that you may use to format text. The formats defined by these styles include character formatting, such as the font and font size; paragraph formatting, such as line spacing and text alignment; table formatting; and list formatting.

Whenever you create a document, Word formats the text using a particular style. The base style for a new Word document is the **Normal style**, which for a new installation of Word 2002 most likely uses 12-point Times New Roman font for characters and single-spaced, left-aligned paragraphs. As you type, you can apply different styles to the text. You also can create your own styles. A later project discusses applying and creating styles.

When the insertion point is in the note text area, the entered note text is formatted using the Footnote Text style. The Footnote Text style defines characters as 10-point Times New Roman and paragraphs as single-spaced and left-aligned.

You could change the paragraph formatting of the footnote text to first-line indent and double-spacing as you did for the text in the body of the document. Then, you would change the font size from 10 to 12 point. If you use this technique, however, you will need to change the format of the footnote text for each footnote you enter into the document. A more efficient technique is to modify the format of the Footnote Text style to first-line indent and double-spaced paragraphs and a 12-point font size. By changing the formatting of the Footnote Text style, every footnote you enter will use the formats defined in this style.

More About

Styles

The Style box on the Formatting toolbar displays the name of the style applied to the location of the insertion point. To view the list of styles associated with the current document, click the Style box arrow on the Formatting toolbar or display the Styles and Formatting task pane by clicking the Styles and Formatting button on the Formatting toolbar. To apply a style, select the text to format, click the Style box arrow on the Formatting toolbar, and then click the desired style name; or select the desired style name in the Styles and Formatting task pane.

Perform the following steps to modify the Footnote Text style.

To Modify a Style

1 Right-click the note text in the note pane and then point to Style on the shortcut menu (Figure 2-33).

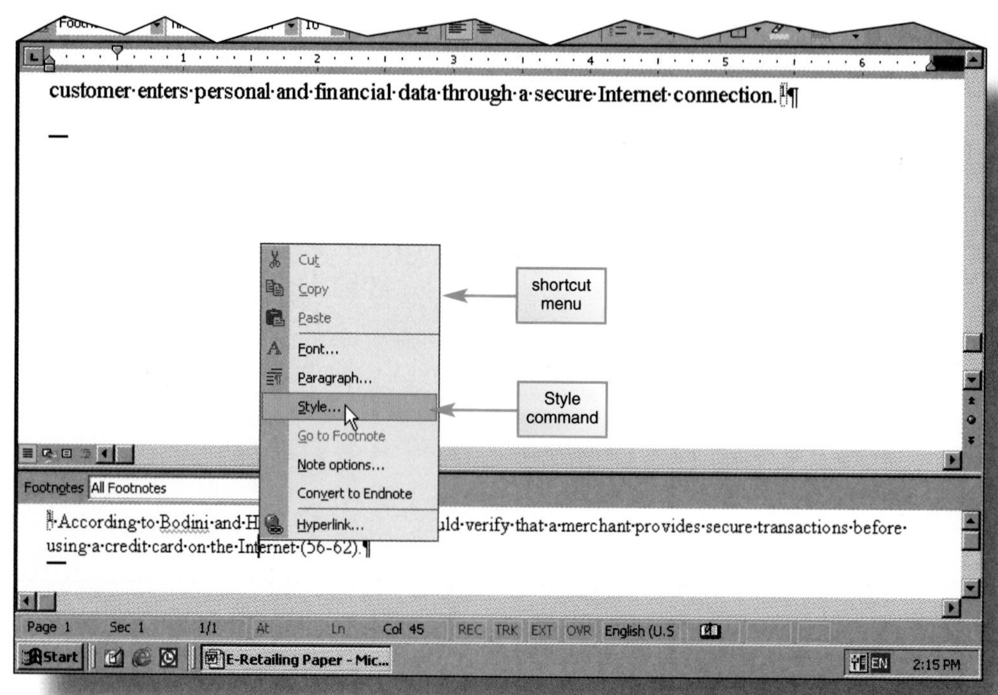

FIGURE 2-33

2 Click Style. When the Style dialog box displays, if necessary, click Footnote Text in the Styles list. Point to the Modify button.

Word displays the Style dialog box (Figure 2-34). Footnote Text is selected in the Styles list. The Preview area shows the formatting associated with the selected style.

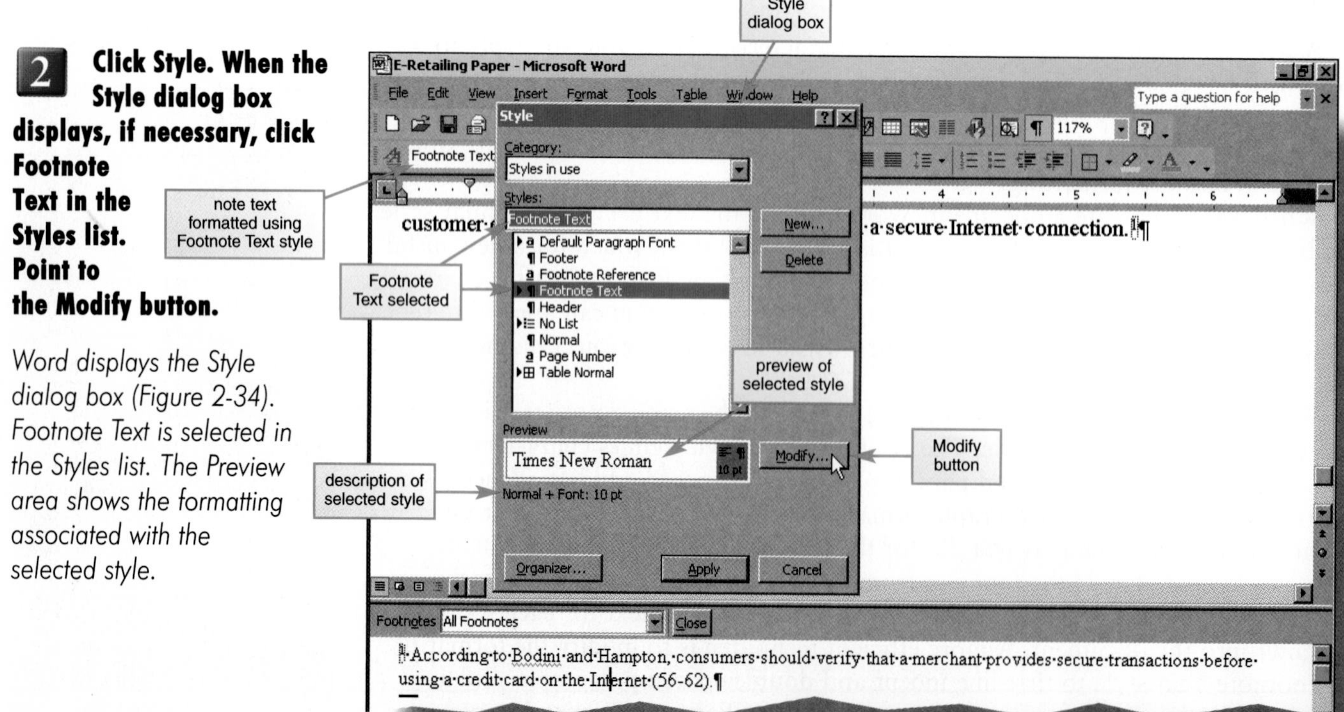

FIGURE 2-34

3 Click the Modify button. When the Modify Style dialog box displays, click the Font Size box arrow in the Formatting area and then click 12 in the Font Size list. Click the Double Space button.

Word displays the Modify Style dialog box (Figure 2-35). The font size for the Footnote Text style is changed to 12, and paragraph spacing is changed to double. The first-line indent still must be set.

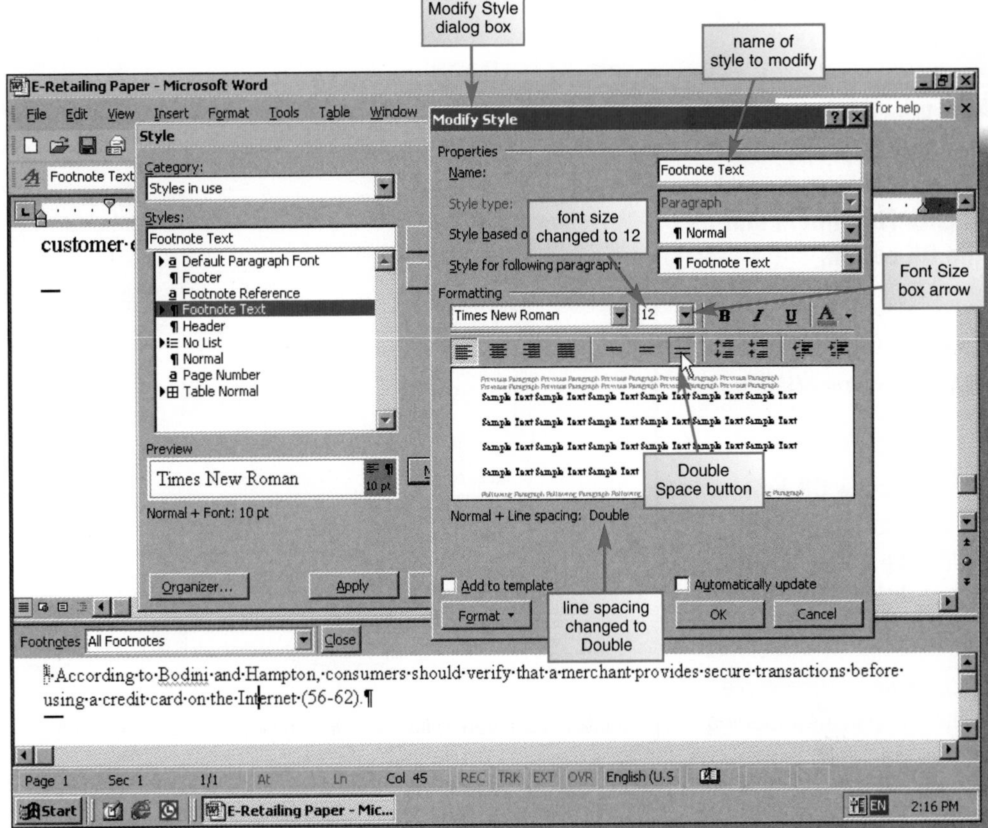

FIGURE 2-35

4 Click the Format button and then point to Paragraph.

A menu of formatting commands displays above the Format button (Figure 2-36).

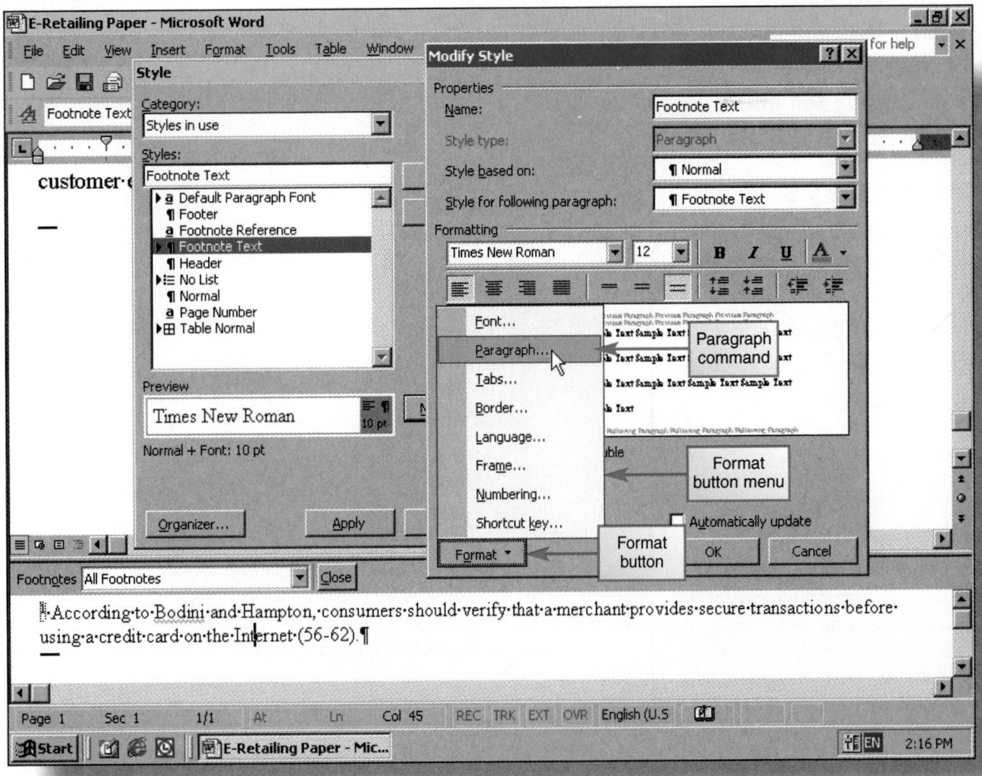

FIGURE 2-36

5 Click Paragraph. When the Paragraph dialog box displays, click the Special box arrow and then click First line. Point to the OK button.

Word displays First line in the Special box (Figure 2-37). Notice the default first-line indent is 0.5".

6 Click the OK button. When the Modify Style dialog box is visible again, point to the OK button.

Word modifies the Footnote Text style to first-line indented paragraphs (Figure 2-38).

7 Click the OK button. When the Style dialog box is visible again, click the Apply button. If necessary, click the up scroll arrow in the note pane to display the entire note text.

Word indents the first line of the note by one-half inch, sets the line spacing for the note to double, and changes the font size of the note text to 12 (shown in Figure 2-39).

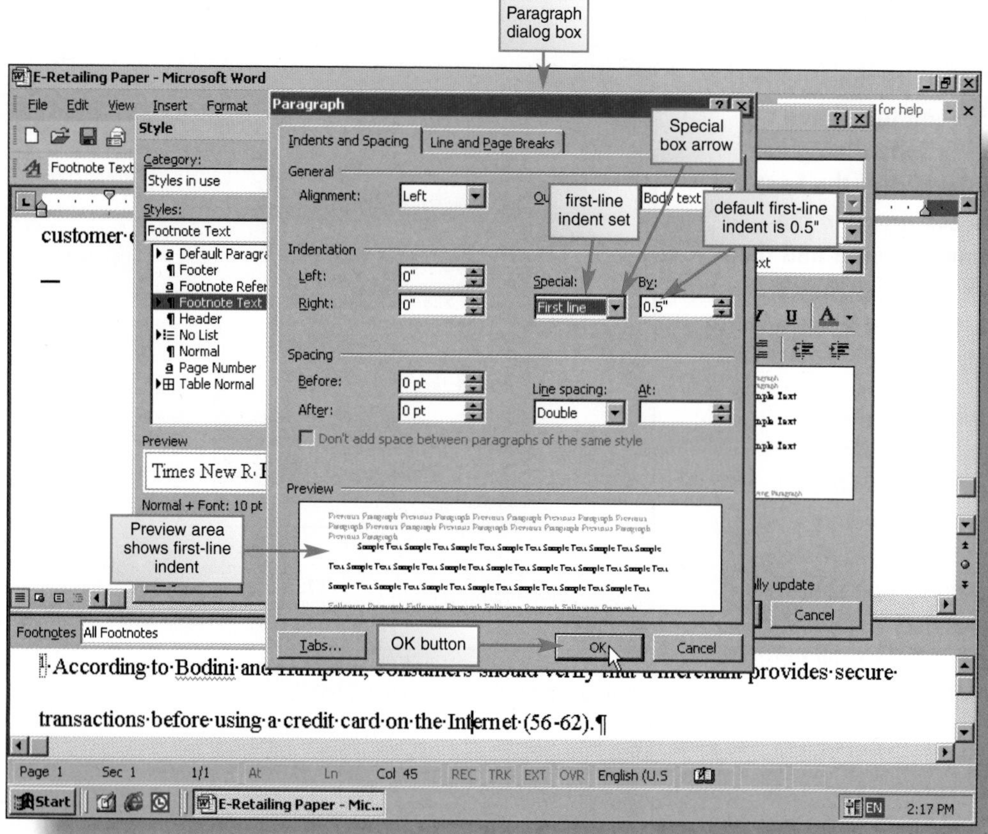

FIGURE 2-37

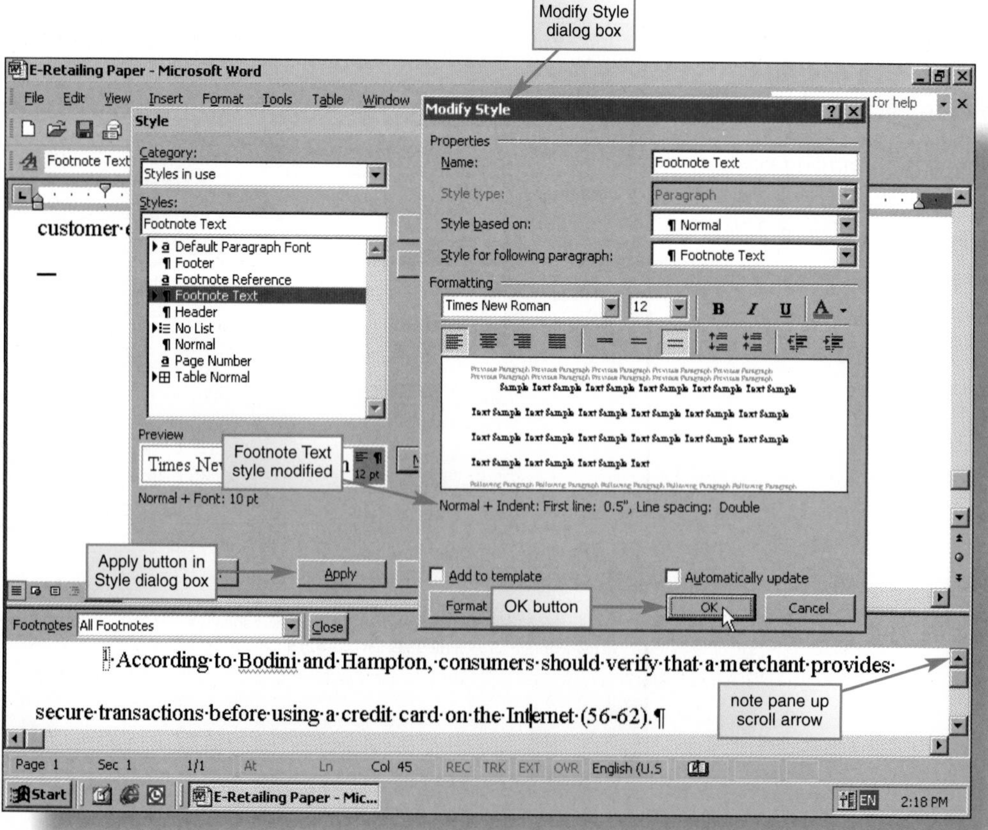

FIGURE 2-38

Other Ways

1. Click Styles and Formatting button on Formatting toolbar, point to style name in Pick formatting to apply list and click style name box arrow, click Modify
2. In Voice Command mode, say "Context menu, Style, Modify, Font Size, [select font size], Double Space, Format, Paragraph, Special, First line, OK, OK, Apply"

Any future footnotes entered into the document will use a 12-point font with the paragraphs first-line indented and double-spaced. The footnote is complete. The next step is to close the note pane.

To Close the Note Pane

1 Point to the Close button in the note pane (Figure 2-39).

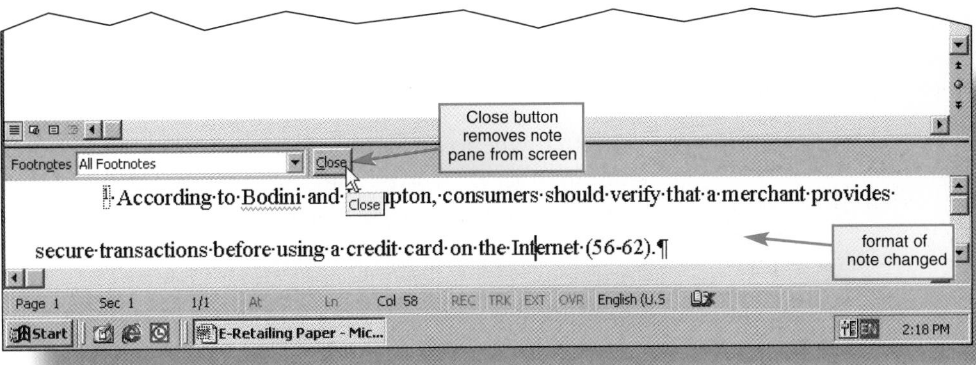
Close button removes note pane from screen
Footnotes
All Footnotes
Close
According to Bodini and Hampton, consumers should verify that a merchant provides secure transactions before using a credit card on the Internet (56-62).¶
format of note changed
Page 1
Sec 1
1/1
Col 58
English (U.S
Start
E-Retailing Paper - Mic...
2:18 PM

FIGURE 2-39

2 Click the Close button. If you want to see the note text while in normal view, point to the note reference mark in the document window.

Word closes the note pane (Figure 2-40).

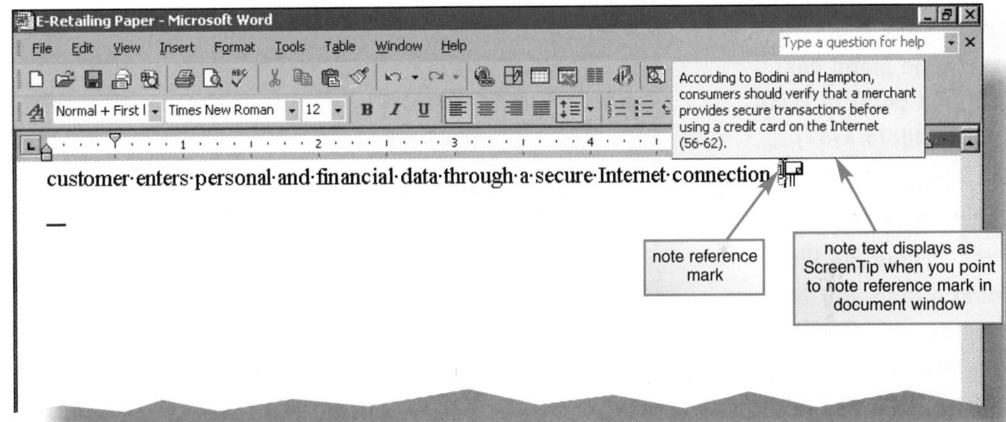
E-Retailing Paper - Microsoft Word
File Edit View Insert Format Tools Table Window Help
Type a question for help
Normal + First l
Times New Roman
12
According to Bodini and Hampton, consumers should verify that a merchant provides secure transactions before using a credit card on the Internet (56-62).
customer enters personal and financial data through a secure Internet connection.
note reference mark
note text displays as ScreenTip when you point to note reference mark in document window

FIGURE 2-40

Other Ways

1. Press ALT+C
2. In Voice Command mode, say "Close"

When Word closes the note pane and returns to the document window, the note text disappears from the screen. Although the note text still exists, it usually is not visible as a footnote in normal view. If, however, you point to the note reference mark, the note text displays above the note reference mark as a ScreenTip (Figure 2-40). To remove the ScreenTip, move the mouse pointer.

If you want to verify that the note text is positioned correctly on the page, you must switch to print layout view or display the document in print preview. Project 3 discusses print preview and print layout view.

To delete a note, you select the note reference mark in the document window (not in the note pane) by dragging through the note reference mark and then clicking the Cut button on the Standard toolbar. Another way to delete a note is to click immediately to the right of the note reference mark in the document window and then press the BACKSPACE key twice, or click immediately to the left of the note reference mark in the document window and then press the DELETE key twice.

More About

Note Numbering

To change the number format of footnotes or endnotes (e.g., from 1, 2, 3, to i, ii, iii), click the Number format box arrow in the Footnote and Endnote dialog box (Figure 2-30 on page WD 2.26) and then click the desired format.

Notes

To convert current footnotes to endnotes, click Insert on the menu bar, point to Reference, and then click Footnote. Click the Convert button in the Footnote and Endnote dialog box. Click Convert all footnotes to endnotes and then click the OK button. Click the Close button in the Footnote and Endnote dialog box.

To move a note to a different location in a document, select the note reference mark in the document window (not in the note pane), click the Cut button on the Standard toolbar, click the location where you want to move the note, and then click the Paste button on the Standard toolbar. When you move or delete notes, Word automatically renumbers any remaining notes in the correct sequence.

You edit note text using the note pane at the bottom of the Word window. To display the note text in the note pane, double-click the note reference mark in the document window or click View on the menu bar and then click Footnotes. Edit the note as you would any Word text and then click the Close button in the note pane.

Using Word Count

Often when you write papers, you are required to compose a paper with a minimum number of words. The requirement for the research paper in this project was a minimum of 375 words. Word provides a command that displays the number of words, as well as the number of pages, characters, paragraphs, and lines in your document. The following steps show how to use word count and display the Word Count toolbar, which allows you easily to recount words as you type more text.

To Count Words

1 Click Tools on the menu bar and then point to Word Count (Figure 2-41).

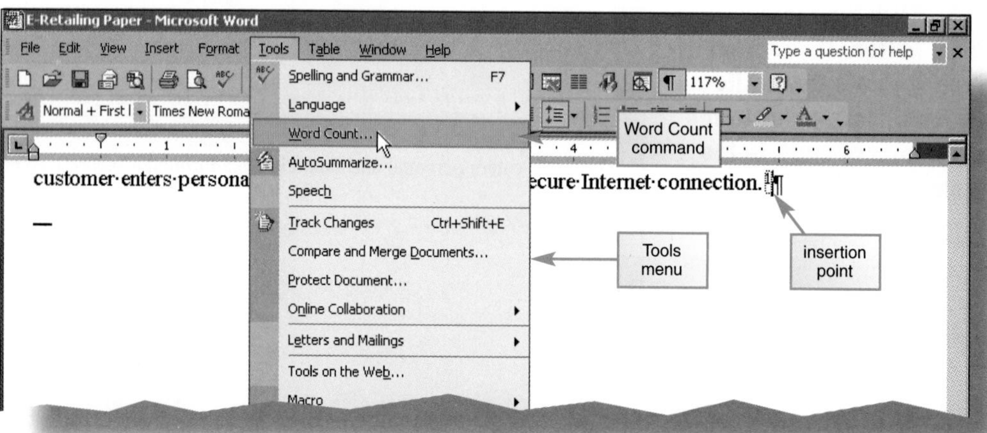

FIGURE 2-41

2 Click Word Count. When the Word Count dialog box displays, if necessary, click Include footnotes and endnotes to place a check mark in the check box. Click the Show Toolbar button.

Word displays the Word Count dialog box (Figure 2-42). The Word Count toolbar displays floating in the Word window.

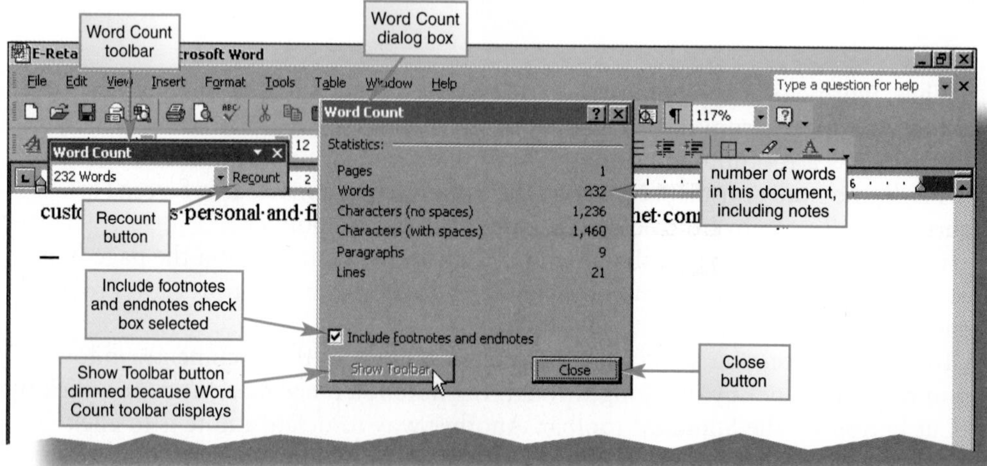

FIGURE 2-42

3 Click the Close button in the Word Count dialog box.

Word removes the Word Count dialog box from the screen, but the Word Count toolbar remains on the screen (shown in Figure 2-43).

The Word Count dialog box presents a variety of statistics about the current document, including number of pages, words, characters, paragraphs, and lines (Figure 2-42). You can choose to have note text included or not included in these statistics. If you want statistics on only a section of the document, select the section and then issue the Word Count command.

At anytime, you can recount the number of words in a document by clicking the Recount button on the Word Count toolbar. The Word Count toolbar floats on the screen. As discussed earlier in this project, you can move a floating toolbar by dragging its title bar.

More About

Word Count

You also can display statistics about a document by clicking File on the menu bar, clicking Properties, and then clicking the Statistics tab. The information in this tabbed sheet, however, does not include words and characters in the footnotes or endnotes.

Automatic Page Breaks

As you type documents that exceed one page, Word automatically inserts page breaks, called **automatic page breaks** or **soft page breaks**, when it determines the text has filled one page according to paper size, margin settings, line spacing, and other settings. If you add text, delete text, or modify text on a page, Word recomputes the position of automatic page breaks and adjusts them accordingly.

Word performs page recomputation between the keystrokes, that is, in between the pauses in your typing. Thus, Word refers to the automatic page break task as **background repagination**. In normal view, automatic page breaks display on the Word screen as a single dotted horizontal line. The following step illustrates Word's automatic page break feature.

Steps To Page Break Automatically

1 With the insertion point positioned as shown in Figure 2-41, press the SPACEBAR and then type the last two sentences of the third paragraph of the paper. Press the ENTER key and then type the fourth paragraph. Italicize the text in the parenthetical citation.

As you type, Word places an automatic page break between the third and fourth paragraphs in the paper (Figure 2-43). The status bar now displays Page 2 as the current page.

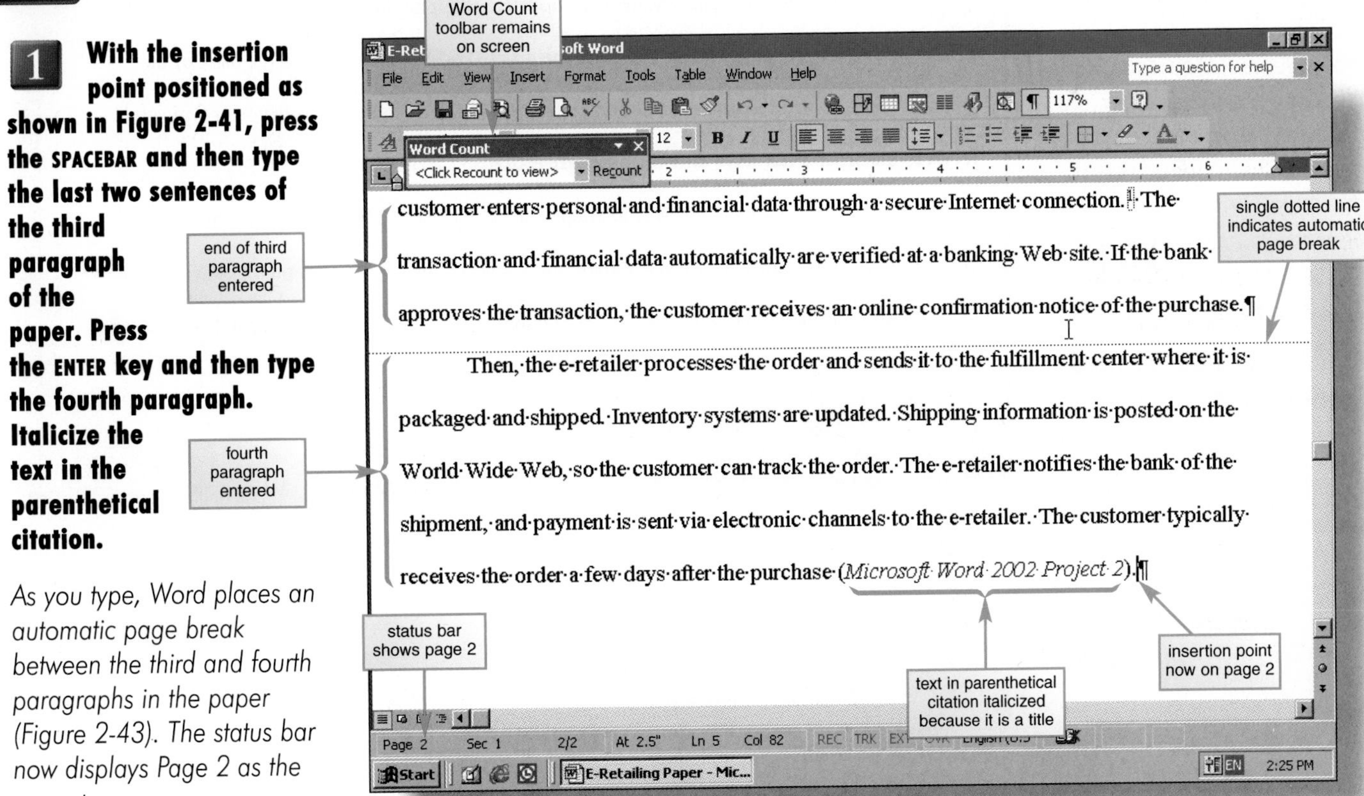
Word Count toolbar remains on screen
end of third paragraph entered
fourth paragraph entered
single dotted line indicates automatic page break
status bar shows page 2
text in parenthetical citation italicized because it is a title
insertion point now on page 2
Word Count
<Click Recount to view>
Recount
customer enters personal and financial data through a secure Internet connection. The transaction and financial data automatically are verified at a banking Web site. If the bank approves the transaction, the customer receives an online confirmation notice of the purchase.
Then, the e-retailer processes the order and sends it to the fulfillment center where it is packaged and shipped. Inventory systems are updated. Shipping information is posted on the World Wide Web, so the customer can track the order. The e-retailer notifies the bank of the shipment, and payment is sent via electronic channels to the e-retailer. The customer typically receives the order a few days after the purchase (Microsoft Word 2002 Project 2).
Page 2 Sec 1 2/2 At 2.5" Ln 5 Col 82
E-Retailing Paper - Mic...
2:25 PM

FIGURE 2-43

Your page break may occur at a different location, depending on the type of printer connected to the computer.

The header, although not shown in normal view, contains the name Marcott and the page number 2. If you wanted to view the header, click View on the menu bar and then click Header and Footer. Then, click the Close Header and Footer button on the Header and Footer toolbar to return to normal view.

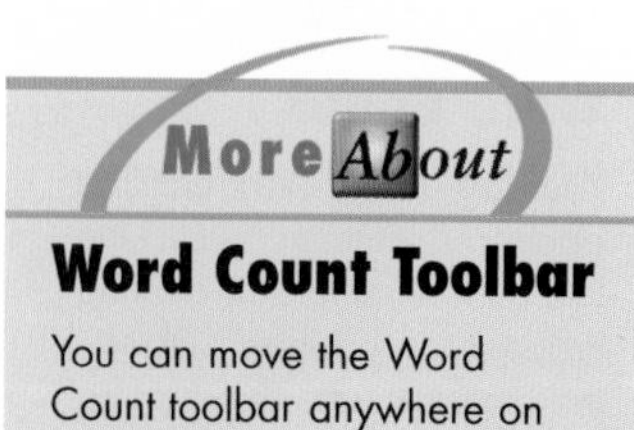

Word Count Toolbar

You can move the Word Count toolbar anywhere on the screen by dragging its title bar.

Recounting Words in a Document

As soon as you type the last paragraph of the body of the paper, you want to recount the number of words to see if you have met the minimum number of words requirement. Perform the following steps to use the Word Count toolbar to recount words in a document.

To Recount Words

1 Press the ENTER key. Type the last paragraph of the research paper as shown in Figure 2-44. Click the Recount button on the Word Count toolbar.

The Word Count toolbar displays the number of words in the document. You can close the Word Count toolbar because the research paper contains the required minimum number of words.

2 Click the Close button on the Word Count toolbar.

Word removes the Word Count toolbar from the screen.

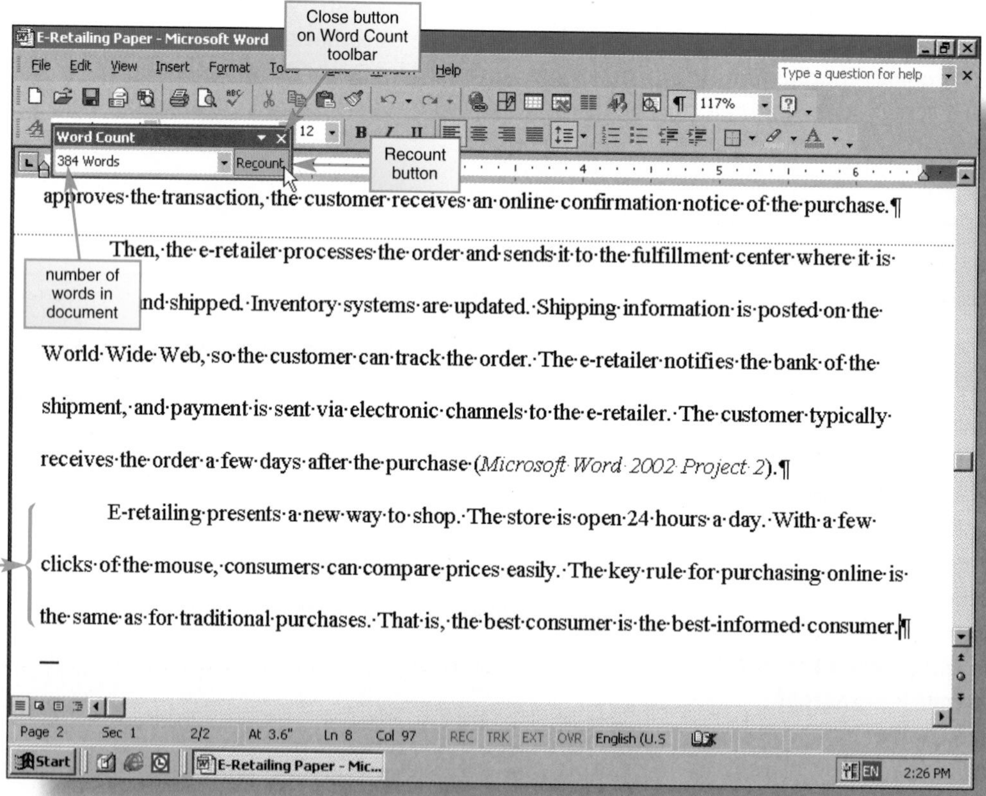
E-Retailing Paper - Microsoft Word
Close button on Word Count toolbar
Word Count
384 Words
Recount
Recount button
number of words in document
last paragraph entered
approves·the·transaction,·the·customer·receives·an·online·confirmation·notice·of·the·purchase.¶
Then,·the·e-retailer·processes·the·order·and·sends·it·to·the·fulfillment·center·where·it·is·
nd·shipped.·Inventory·systems·are·updated.·Shipping·information·is·posted·on·the·
World·Wide·Web,·so·the·customer·can·track·the·order.·The·e-retailer·notifies·the·bank·of·the·
shipment,·and·payment·is·sent·via·electronic·channels·to·the·e-retailer.·The·customer·typically·
receives·the·order·a·few·days·after·the·purchase·(Microsoft·Word·2002·Project·2).¶
E-retailing·presents·a·new·way·to·shop.·The·store·is·open·24·hours·a·day.·With·a·few·
clicks·of·the·mouse,·consumers·can·compare·prices·easily.·The·key·rule·for·purchasing·online·is·
the·same·as·for·traditional·purchases.·That·is,·the·best·consumer·is·the·best-informed·consumer.¶
Page 2 Sec 1 2/2 At 3.6" Ln 8 Col 97 REC TRK EXT OVR English (U.S
Start
E-Retailing Paper - Mic...
2:26 PM

FIGURE 2-44

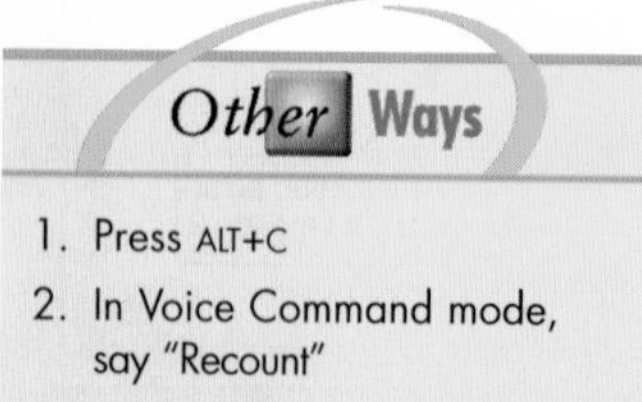

1. Press ALT+C
2. In Voice Command mode, say "Recount"

Creating an Alphabetical Works Cited Page

According to the MLA style, the **works cited page** is a bibliographical list of works that are referenced directly in the research paper. Place the list on a separate numbered page with the title, Works Cited, centered one inch from the top margin.

The works are to be alphabetized by the author's last name or, if the work has no author, by the work's title. The first line of each entry begins at the left margin. Indent subsequent lines of the same entry one-half inch from the left margin.

The first step in creating the works cited page is to force a page break so the works cited display on a separate page.

More About

Bibliographical References

The MLA documentation style uses the title, Works Cited, for the page containing bibliographical references, whereas the APA style uses the title, References. APA guidelines for preparing the reference list entries differ significantly from the MLA style. Refer to an APA handbook or the Web for specifics.

Manual Page Breaks

The works cited are to display on a separate numbered page. Thus, you must insert a manual page break following the body of the research paper. A **manual page break**, or **hard page break**, is one that you force into the document at a specific location. Manual page breaks display on the screen as a horizontal dotted line, separated by the words, Page Break. Word never moves or adjusts manual page breaks; however, Word does adjust any automatic page breaks that follow a manual page break. Word inserts manual page breaks just before the location of the insertion point.

Perform the following step to insert a manual page break after the body of the research paper.

Steps To Page Break Manually

1 With the insertion point at the end of the research paper, press the ENTER key. Then, press CTRL+ENTER.

The shortcut keys, CTRL+ENTER, instruct Word to insert a manual page break immediately above the insertion point and position the insertion point immediately below the manual page break (Figure 2-45). The status bar indicates the insertion point now is located on page 3.

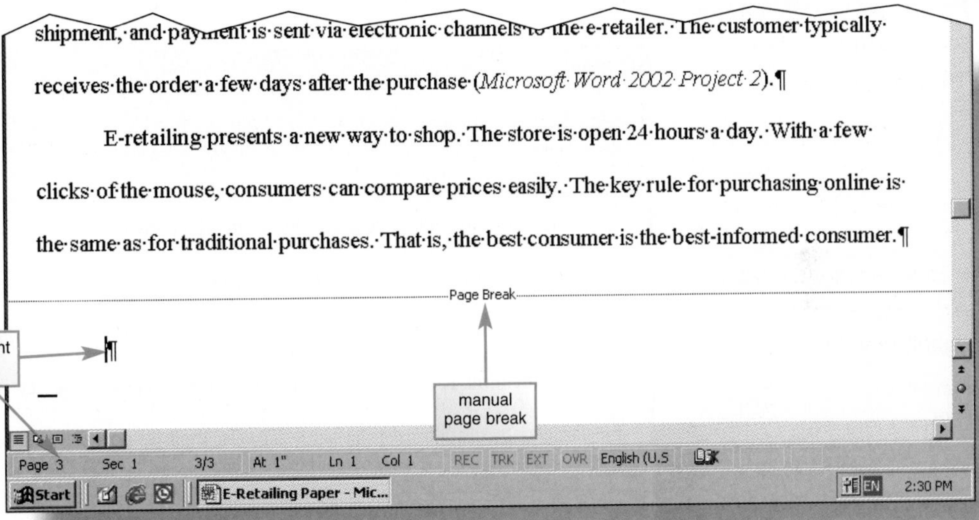
shipment, and payment is sent via electronic channels to the e-retailer. The customer typically
receives the order a few days after the purchase (Microsoft Word 2002 Project 2).¶
E-retailing presents a new way to shop. The store is open 24 hours a day. With a few
clicks of the mouse, consumers can compare prices easily. The key rule for purchasing online is
the same as for traditional purchases. That is, the best consumer is the best-informed consumer.¶
Page Break
insertion point on page 3
manual page break
Page 3 Sec 1 3/3 At 1" Ln 1 Col 1 REC TRK EXT OVR English (U.S
Start
E-Retailing Paper - Mic...
2:30 PM

FIGURE 2-45

Other Ways

1. On Insert menu click Break, click Page break, click OK button
2. In Voice Command mode, say "Insert, Break, OK"

The manual page break displays as a horizontal dotted line with the words, Page Break, in the middle of the line. The header, although not shown in normal view, contains the name Marcott and the page number 3. If you wanted to view the header, click View on the menu bar and then click Header and Footer. Then, click the Close Header and Footer button on the Header and Footer toolbar to return to normal view.

If, for some reason, you wanted to remove a manual page break from your document, you must first select it by double-clicking it. Then, press the DELETE key; or click the Cut button on the Standard toolbar; or right-click the selection and then click Cut on the shortcut menu.

Centering the Title of the Works Cited Page

The works cited title is to be centered between the margins. If you simply click the Center button on the Formatting toolbar, the title will not be centered properly. Instead, it will be one-half inch to the right of the center point because earlier you set first-line indent at one-half inch. That is, Word indents the first line of every paragraph one-half inch. To properly center the title of the works cited page, you must move the First Line Indent marker back to the left margin before clicking the Center button as described in the following steps.

More About

Reveal Formatting

To see a list of formatting that has been applied to text in a document, select the text, click Format on the menu bar, and then click Reveal Formatting to display the Reveal Formatting task pane. To change a format applied to the selected text, click the blue link in the Reveal Formatting task pane and then change the format in the dialog box that displays.

TO CENTER THE TITLE OF THE WORKS CITED PAGE

1. Drag the First Line Indent marker to the 0" mark on the ruler.
2. Click the Center button on the Formatting toolbar.
3. Type `Works Cited` as the title.
4. Press the ENTER key.
5. Because your fingers already are on the keyboard, press CTRL+L to left-align the paragraph mark.

The title displays centered properly, and the insertion point is left-aligned (Figure 2-46).

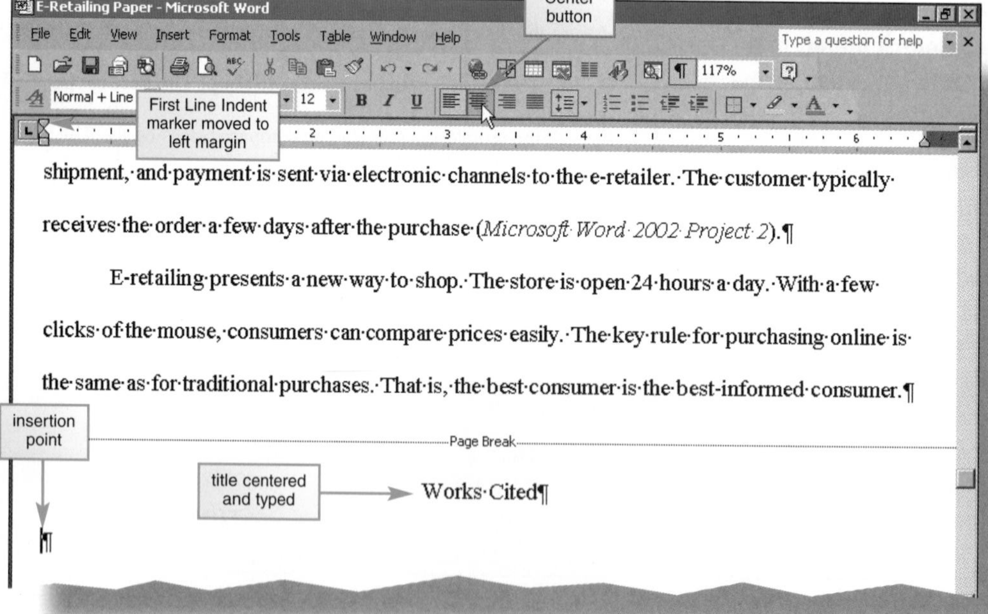

FIGURE 2-46

More About

Crediting Sources

When writing a research paper, you must acknowledge sources of information. Citing sources is a matter of ethics and honesty. Use caution when summarizing or paraphrasing a source. Do not plagiarize, which includes using someone else's words or ideas and claiming them as your own.

Creating a Hanging Indent

On the works cited page, the first line of each entry begins at the left margin. Subsequent lines in the same paragraph are indented one-half inch from the left margin. In essence, the first line hangs to the left of the rest of the paragraph; thus, this type of paragraph formatting is called a **hanging indent.**

One method of creating a hanging indent is to use the horizontal ruler. The **Hanging Indent marker** is the bottom triangle at the 0" mark on the ruler (Figure 2-47). As discussed earlier in this project, the small square at the 0" mark is called the Left Indent marker. Perform the following steps to create a hanging indent.

To Create a Hanging Indent

1 With the insertion point in the paragraph to format (Figure 2-46), point to the Hanging Indent marker on the ruler (Figure 2-47).

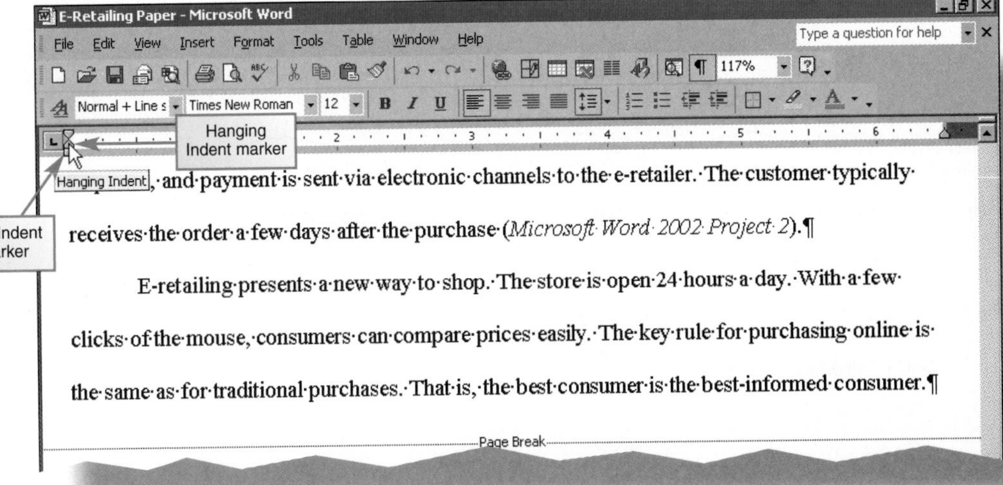

FIGURE 2-47

2 Drag the Hanging Indent marker to the .5" mark on the ruler.

The Hanging Indent marker and Left Indent marker display one-half inch from the left margin (Figure 2-48). When you drag the Hanging Indent marker, the Left Indent marker moves with it. The insertion point in the document window remains at the left margin because only subsequent lines in the paragraph are to be indented.

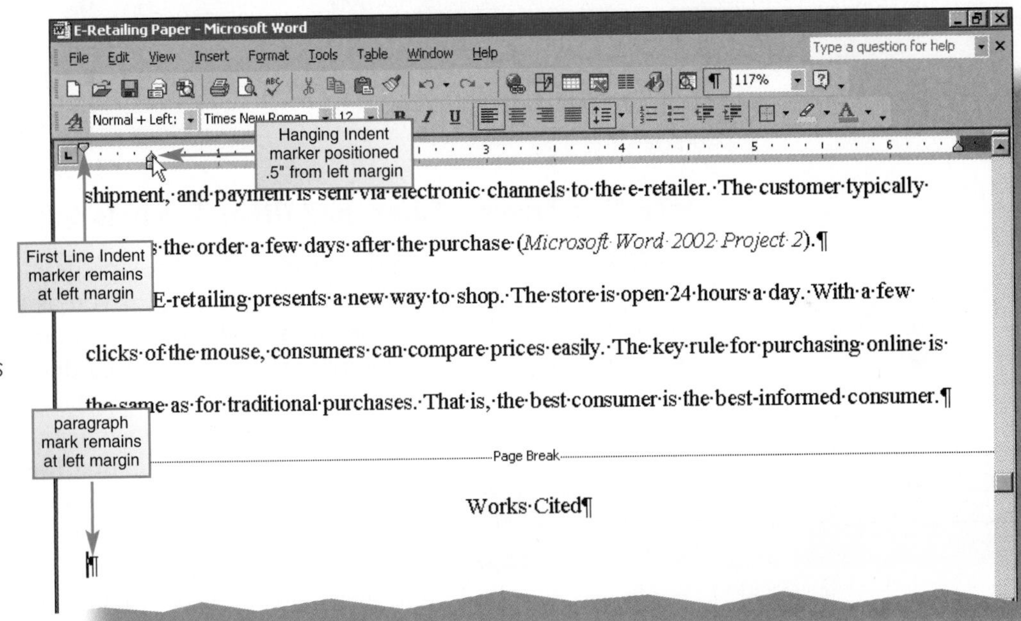

FIGURE 2-48

Other Ways

1. On Format menu click Paragraph, click Indents and Spacing tab, click Special box arrow, click Hanging, click OK button
2. Press CTRL+T
3. In Voice Command mode, say "Format, Paragraph, Indents and Spacing, Special, Hanging, OK"

To drag both the First Line Indent and Hanging Indent markers at the same time, you drag the Left Indent marker on the ruler.

Enter two of the works in the works cited as explained in the following steps.

TO ENTER WORKS CITED PARAGRAPHS

1. Type `Sanchez, Jesse R. "E-Retailing: Shop 24 Hours a Day."` Press the SPACEBAR. Press CTRL+I to turn on italics. Type `Exploring the Wide World of the Internet` and then press CTRL+I to turn off italics. Press the SPACEBAR. Type `Sep. 2003: 15-36.` Press the ENTER key.

2 Type `Bodini, Natalie C., and Jack R. Hampton.` Press the SPACEBAR. Press CTRL+I to turn on italics. Type `An Introduction to the Internet and the Web.` Press CTRL+I to turn off italics. Press the SPACEBAR. Type `Boston: Star Publishing, 2003.` Press the ENTER key.

Two of the works cited paragraphs are entered (Figure 2-49).

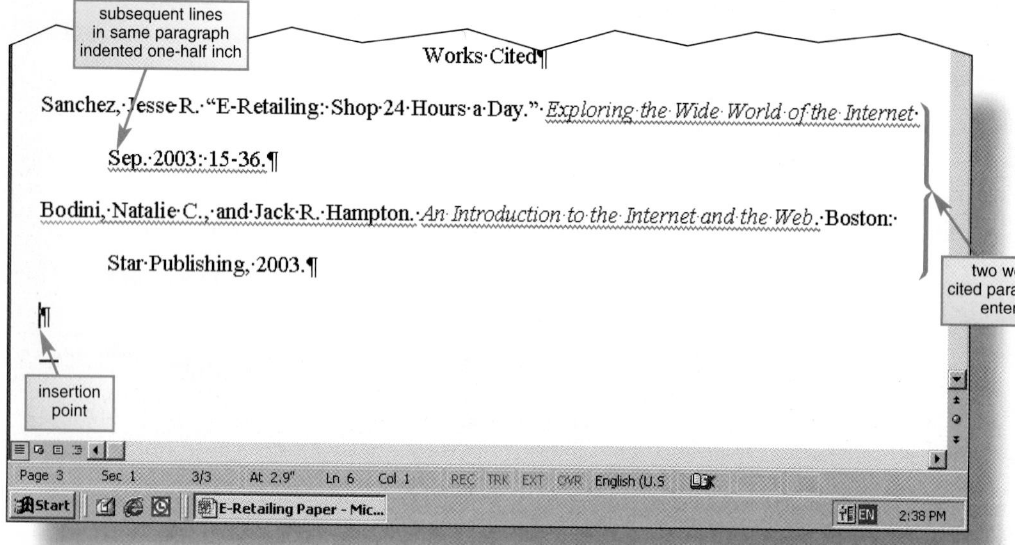

FIGURE 2-49

When Word wraps the text in each works cited paragraph, it automatically indents the second line of the paragraph by one-half inch. When you press the ENTER key at the end of the first paragraph of text, the insertion point returns automatically to the left margin for the next paragraph. Recall that each time you press the ENTER key, Word carries forward the paragraph formatting from the previous paragraph to the next paragraph.

Inserting Arrows, Faces, and Other Symbols Automatically

As discussed earlier in this project, Word has predefined many commonly misspelled words, which it automatically corrects for you as you type. In addition to words, this built-in list of **AutoCorrect entries** also contains some commonly used symbols. For example, to insert a smiling face into a document, you type :) and Word automatically changes it to ☺. Table 2-3 lists the characters you type to insert arrows, faces, and other symbols into a Word document.

Table 2-3 Word's Automatic Symbols

TO DISPLAY	DESCRIPTION	TYPE
©	copyright symbol	(c)
®	registered trademark symbol	(r)
™	trademark symbol	(tm)
…	ellipsis	...
☺	smiling face	:) or :-)
😐	indifferent face	:| or :-|
☹	frowning face	:(or :-(
→	thin right arrow	-->
←	thin left arrow	<--
➔	thick right arrow	==>
⇐	thick left arrow	<==
⇔	double arrow	<=>

You also can enter the first four symbols in Table 2-3 and other symbols by clicking Insert on the menu bar, clicking Symbol, clicking the Special Characters tab, clicking the desired symbol in the Character list, clicking the Insert button, and then clicking the Close button in the Symbol dialog box.

As discussed earlier in this project, if you do not like a change that Word automatically makes in a document and you immediately notice the automatic correction, you can undo the change by clicking the Undo button on the Standard toolbar; clicking Edit on the menu bar and then clicking Undo; or pressing CTRL+Z.

If you do not immediately notice the change, you can undo a correction automatically made by Word through the AutoCorrect Options button. Figures 2-24 and 2-25 on page WD 2.22 illustrated how to display and use the AutoCorrect Options button.

The next step in the research paper is to enter text that uses the registered trademark symbol. Perform the following steps to insert automatically the registered trademark symbol into the research paper.

To Insert a Symbol Automatically

1 **With the insertion point positioned as shown in Figure 2-49, press CTRL+I to turn on italics. Type** `Microsoft Word 2002 Project 2`. **Press CTRL+I to turn off italics. Press the SPACEBAR. Type** `Shelly Cashman Series(r` **as shown in Figure 2-50.**

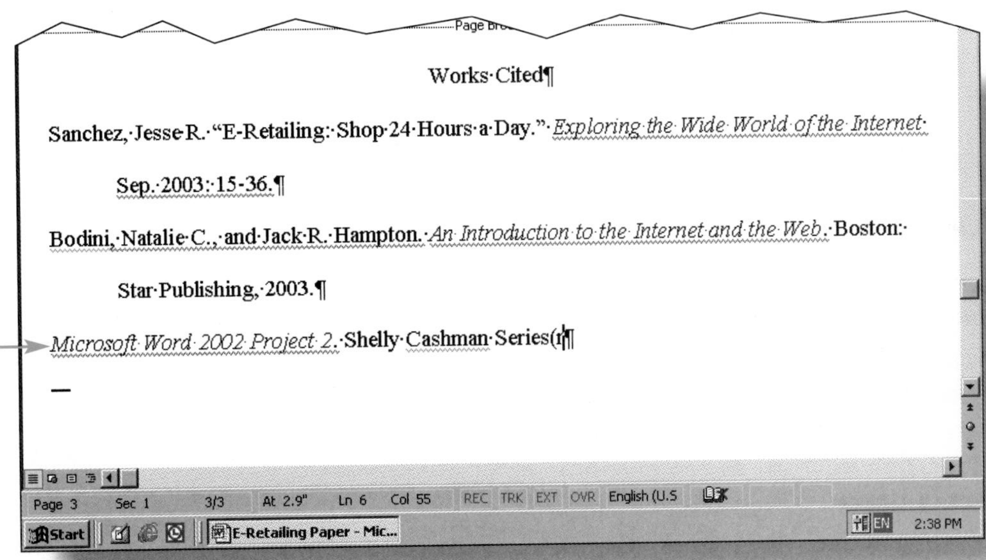
Works Cited¶
Sanchez, Jesse R. "E-Retailing: Shop 24 Hours a Day." Exploring the Wide World of the Internet
Sep. 2003: 15-36.¶
Bodini, Natalie C., and Jack R. Hampton. An Introduction to the Internet and the Web. Boston:
Star Publishing, 2003.¶
Microsoft Word 2002 Project 2. Shelly Cashman Series(r¶
text entered
Page 3 Sec 1 3/3 At 2.9" Ln 6 Col 55 REC TRK EXT OVR English (U.S
Start
E-Retailing Paper - Mic...
2:38 PM

FIGURE 2-50

2 **Press the RIGHT PARENTHESIS key.**

Word automatically converts the (r) to ®, the registered trademark symbol (Figure 2-51).

3 **Press the PERIOD key. Press the SPACEBAR. Type** `Course Technology. 11 Oct. 2003.` **Press the SPACEBAR.**

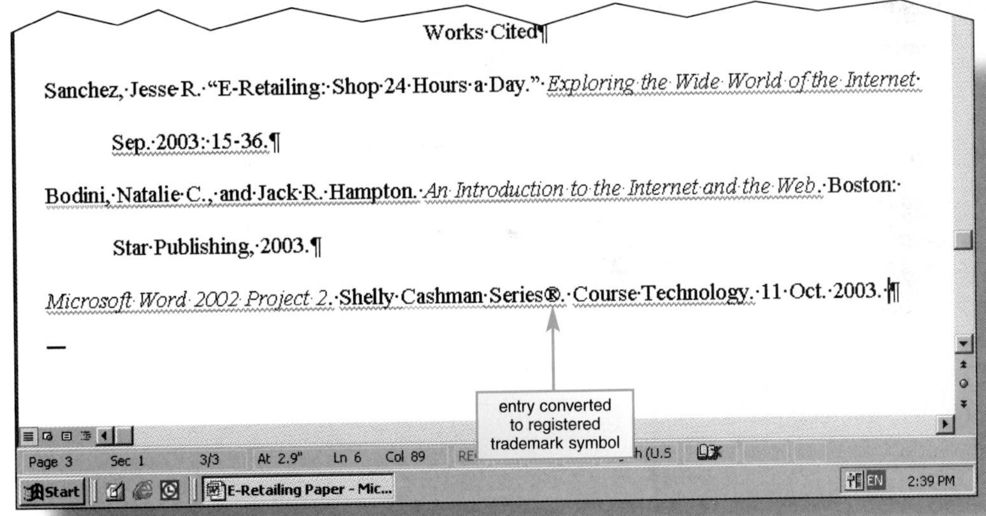
Works Cited¶
Sanchez, Jesse R. "E-Retailing: Shop 24 Hours a Day." Exploring the Wide World of the Internet
Sep. 2003: 15-36.¶
Bodini, Natalie C., and Jack R. Hampton. An Introduction to the Internet and the Web. Boston:
Star Publishing, 2003.¶
Microsoft Word 2002 Project 2. Shelly Cashman Series®. Course Technology. 11 Oct. 2003. ¶
entry converted to registered trademark symbol
Page 3 Sec 1 3/3 At 2.9" Ln 6 Col 89
Start
E-Retailing Paper - Mic...
2:39 PM

FIGURE 2-51

Creating a Hyperlink

In Word, you can create a hyperlink simply by typing the address of the file or Web page to which you want to link and then pressing the SPACEBAR or the ENTER key. A **hyperlink** is a shortcut that allows a user to jump easily and quickly to another location in the same document or to other documents or Web pages. **Jumping** is the process of following a hyperlink to its destination. For example, by clicking a hyperlink in the document window while pressing the CTRL key (called CTRL+clicking), you jump to another document on your computer, on your network, or on the World Wide Web. When you close the hyperlink destination page or document, you return to the original location in your Word document.

More About

Hyperlinks

If Word does not automatically convert your Web addresses to hyperlinks, click Tools on the menu bar, click AutoCorrect Options, click the AutoFormat As You Type tab, place a check mark in the Internet and network paths with hyperlinks check box, and then click the OK button.

In this project, one of the works cited is from a Web page on the Internet. When someone displays your research paper on the screen, you want him or her to be able to CTRL+click the Web address in the work and jump to the associated Web page for more information. If you wish to create a hyperlink to a Web page from a Word document, you do not have to be connected to the Internet. Perform the following steps to create a hyperlink as you type.

To Create a Hyperlink as You Type

1 With the insertion point positioned as shown in Figure 2-51 on the previous page, type `http://www.scsite.com/wd2002/pr2/wc.htm.` **as shown in Figure 2-52.**

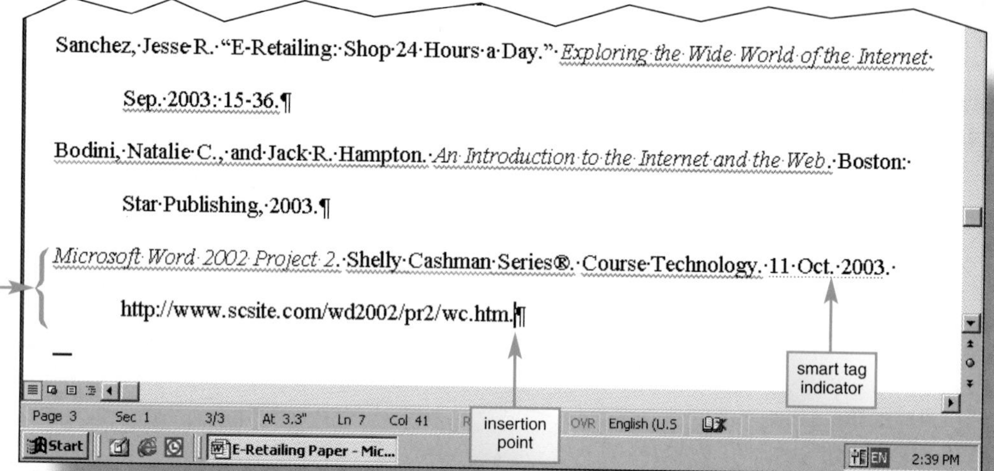
Sanchez, Jesse R. "E-Retailing: Shop 24 Hours a Day." Exploring the Wide World of the Internet Sep. 2003: 15-36.
Bodini, Natalie C., and Jack R. Hampton. An Introduction to the Internet and the Web. Boston: Star Publishing, 2003.
Microsoft Word 2002 Project 2. Shelly Cashman Series®. Course Technology. 11 Oct. 2003. http://www.scsite.com/wd2002/pr2/wc.htm.
last works cited paragraph
insertion point
smart tag indicator
Page 3 Sec 1 3/3 At 3.3" Ln 7 Col 41
OVR English (U.S
Start
E-Retailing Paper - Mic...
2:39 PM

FIGURE 2-52

2 Press the ENTER key.

As soon as you press the ENTER key after typing the Web address, Word formats it as a hyperlink (Figure 2-53). That is, the Web address is underlined and colored blue.

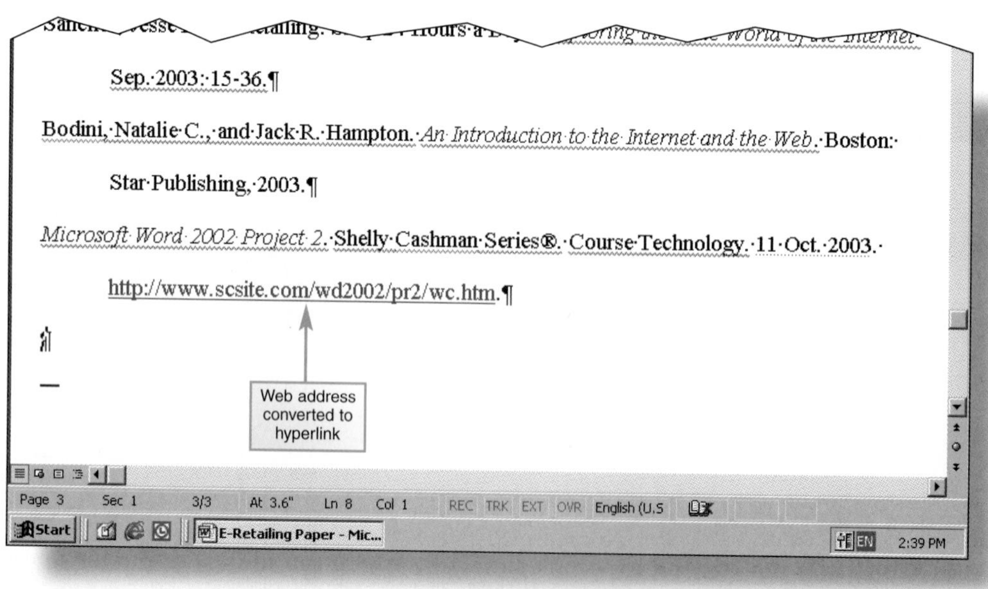
Sep. 2003: 15-36.
Bodini, Natalie C., and Jack R. Hampton. An Introduction to the Internet and the Web. Boston: Star Publishing, 2003.
Microsoft Word 2002 Project 2. Shelly Cashman Series®. Course Technology. 11 Oct. 2003. http://www.scsite.com/wd2002/pr2/wc.htm.
Web address converted to hyperlink
Page 3 Sec 1 3/3 At 3.6" Ln 8 Col 1
REC TRK EXT OVR English (U.S
Start
E-Retailing Paper - Mic...
2:39 PM

FIGURE 2-53

Other Ways

1. Select text, click Insert Hyperlink button on Standard toolbar, click Existing File or Web Page in the Link to bar, type Web address in Address text box, click OK button
2. Right-click selected text, click Hyperlink on shortcut menu, click Existing File or Web Page in the Link to bar, type Web address in Address text box, click OK button

Later in this project, you will jump to the hyperlink just created.

Sorting Paragraphs

The MLA style requires that the works cited be listed in alphabetical order by the first character in each work. In Word, you can arrange paragraphs in alphabetic, numeric, or date order based on the first character in each paragraph. Ordering characters in this manner is called **sorting**. Perform the following steps to sort the works cited paragraphs.

Steps To Sort Paragraphs

1 Select all the works cited paragraphs by pointing to the left of the first paragraph and dragging down. Click Table on the menu bar and then point to Sort.

Word displays the Table menu (Figure 2-54). All of the paragraphs to be sorted are selected.

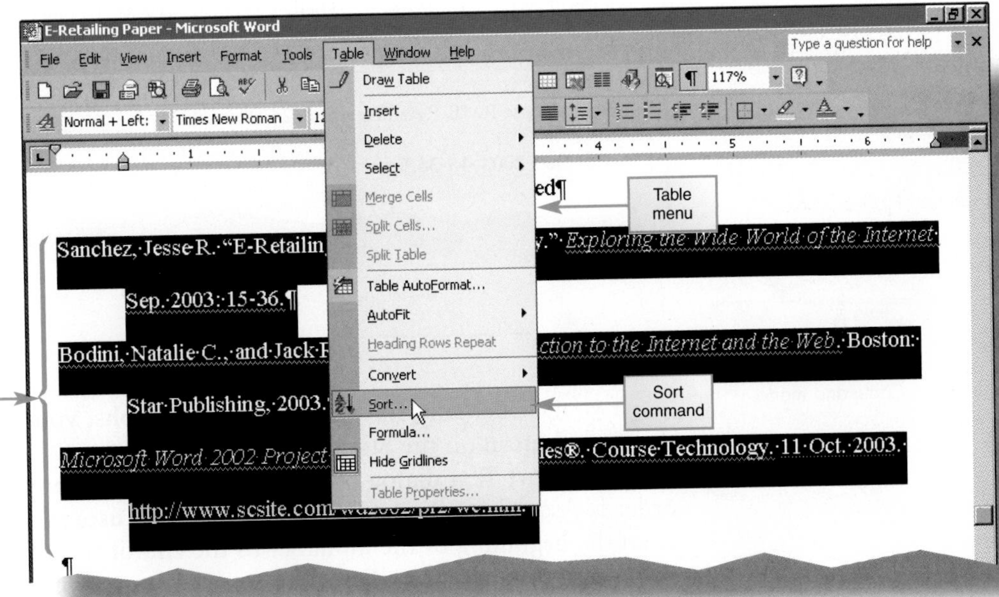

FIGURE 2-54

2 Click Sort. When the Sort Text dialog box displays, point to the OK button.

Word displays the Sort Text dialog box (Figure 2-55). In the Sort by area, Ascending, the default, is selected. Ascending sorts in alphabetic, numeric, or earliest to latest date order.

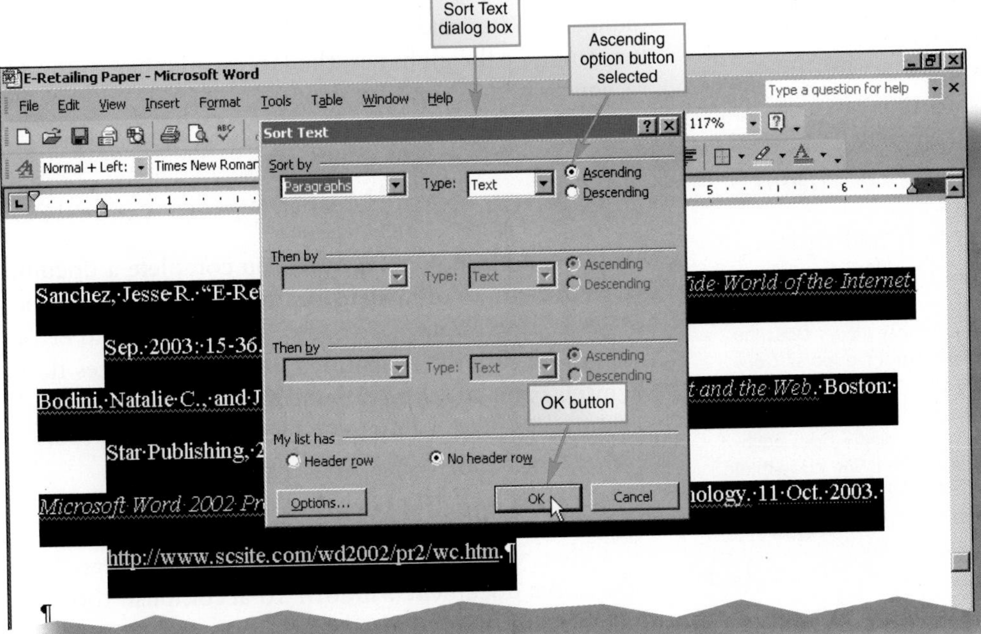

FIGURE 2-55

3 **Click the OK button. Click inside the selected text to remove the selection.**

Word sorts the works cited paragraphs alphabetically (Figure 2-56).

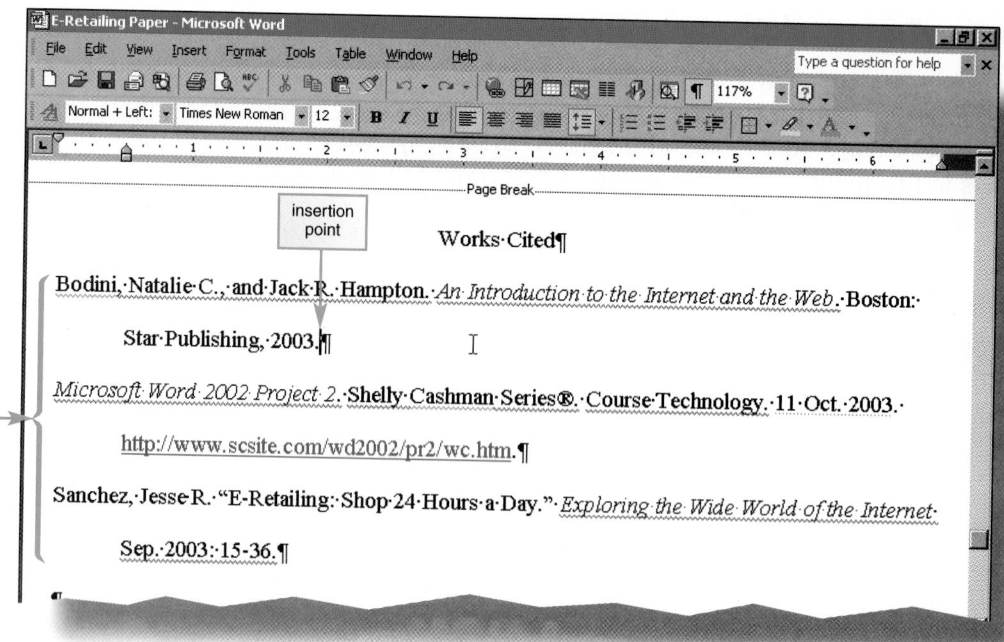
E-Retailing Paper - Microsoft Word
Type a question for help
Normal + Left:
Times New Roman
12
117%
Page Break
insertion point
Works·Cited¶
Bodini,·Natalie·C.,·and·Jack·R.·Hampton.·An·Introduction·to·the·Internet·and·the·Web.·Boston:·
Star·Publishing,·2003.¶
paragraphs sorted alphabetically
Microsoft·Word·2002·Project·2.·Shelly·Cashman·Series®.·Course·Technology.·11·Oct.·2003.·
http://www.scsite.com/wd2002/pr2/wc.htm.¶
Sanchez,·Jesse·R.·"E-Retailing:·Shop·24·Hours·a·Day."·Exploring·the·Wide·World·of·the·Internet·
Sep.·2003:·15-36.¶

FIGURE 2-56

Other Ways

1. In Voice Command mode, say "Table, Sort, OK"

If you accidentally sort the wrong paragraphs, you can undo a sort by clicking the Undo button on the Standard toolbar.

In the Sort Text dialog box (Figure 2-55 on the previous page), the default sort order is Ascending. By default, Word orders in **ascending sort order**, which means from the beginning of the alphabet to the end of the alphabet, smallest number to the largest number, or earliest date to the most recent date. For example, if the first character of each paragraph to be sorted is a letter, Word sorts the selected paragraphs alphabetically.

You also can sort in descending order by clicking Descending in the Sort Text dialog box. **Descending sort order** means sorting from the end of the alphabet to the beginning of the alphabet, the largest number to the smallest number, or the most recent date to the earliest date.

More About

Proofreading

When proofreading a paper, ask yourself these questions: Is the purpose clear? Does the title suggest the topic? Does the paper have an introduction, body, and conclusion? Is the thesis clear? Does each paragraph in the body relate to the thesis? Is the conclusion effective? Are all sources acknowledged?

Proofing and Revising the Research Paper

As discussed in Project 1, once you complete a document, you might find it necessary to make changes to it. Before submitting a paper to be graded, you should proofread it. While **proofreading**, you look for grammatical errors and spelling errors. You want to be sure the transitions between sentences flow smoothly and the sentences themselves make sense. To assist you in this proofreading effort, Word provides several tools. The following pages discuss these tools.

Going to a Specific Location in a Document

Often, you would like to bring a certain page, footnote, or other object into view in the document window. To accomplish this, you could scroll through the document to find a desired page, footnote, or item. Instead of scrolling through the document, Word provides an easier method of going to a specific location via the Select Browse Object menu. Perform the following steps to go to the top of page two in the research paper.

To Browse by Page

1 Click the Select Browse Object button on the vertical scroll bar. When the Select Browse Object menu displays, point to Browse by Page.

Word displays the Select Browse Object menu (Figure 2-57). As you point to various commands on the Select Browse Object menu, Word displays the command name at the bottom of the menu.

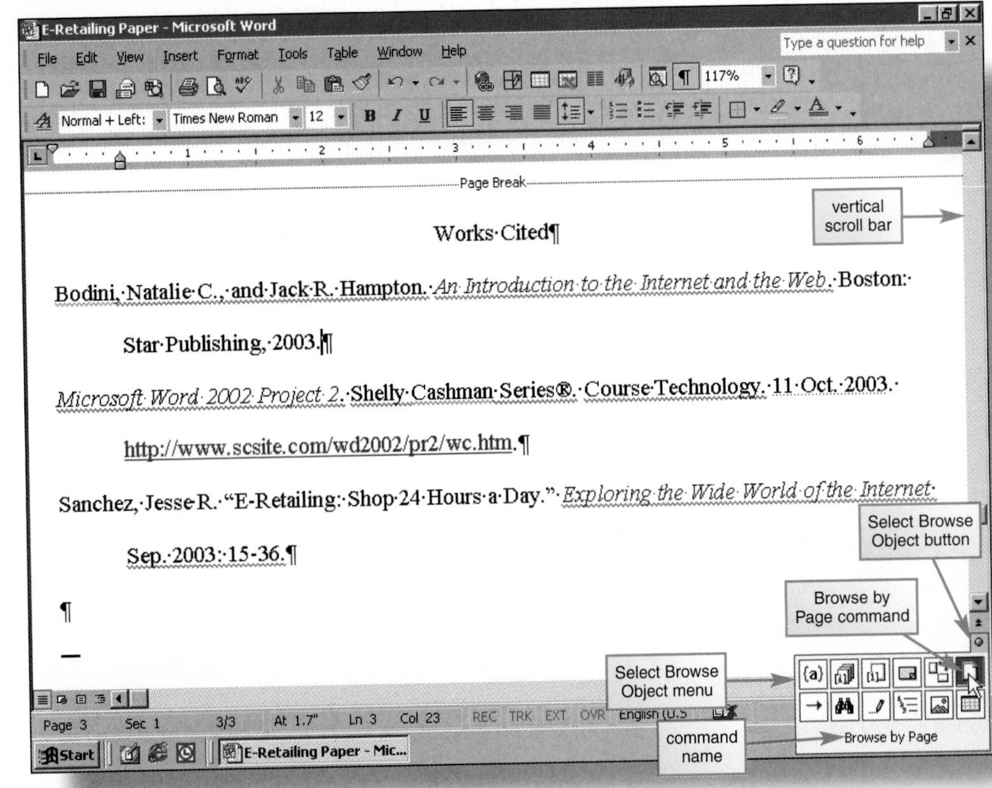
E-Retailing Paper - Microsoft Word
Page Break
vertical scroll bar
Works Cited¶
Bodini, Natalie C., and Jack R. Hampton. An Introduction to the Internet and the Web. Boston:
Star Publishing, 2003.¶
Microsoft Word 2002 Project 2. Shelly Cashman Series®. Course Technology. 11 Oct. 2003.
http://www.scsite.com/wd2002/pr2/wc.htm.¶
Sanchez, Jesse R. "E-Retailing: Shop 24 Hours a Day." Exploring the Wide World of the Internet
Sep. 2003: 15-36.¶
Select Browse Object button
Browse by Page command
Select Browse Object menu
command name
Browse by Page

FIGURE 2-57

2 Click Browse by Page. Point to the Previous Page button on the vertical scroll bar.

Word closes the Select Browse Object menu and displays the top of page 3 at the top of the document window (Figure 2-58).

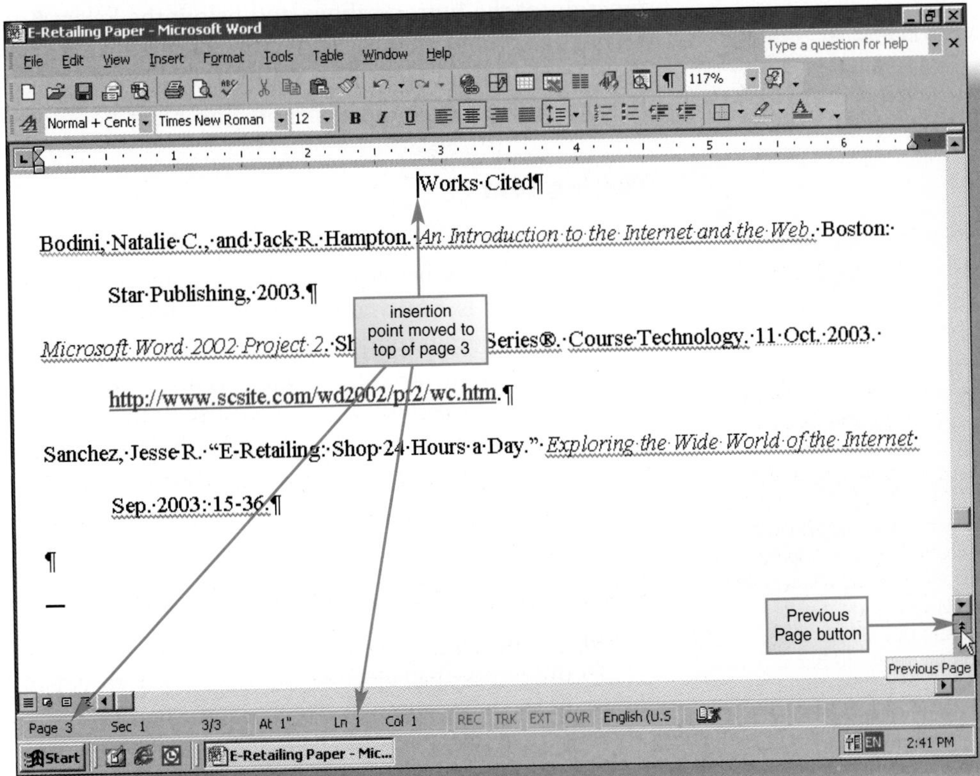
E-Retailing Paper - Microsoft Word
Works Cited¶
Bodini, Natalie C., and Jack R. Hampton. An Introduction to the Internet and the Web. Boston:
Star Publishing, 2003.¶
insertion point moved to top of page 3
Microsoft Word 2002 Project 2. Shelly Cashman Series®. Course Technology. 11 Oct. 2003.
http://www.scsite.com/wd2002/pr2/wc.htm.¶
Sanchez, Jesse R. "E-Retailing: Shop 24 Hours a Day." Exploring the Wide World of the Internet
Sep. 2003: 15-36.¶
Previous Page button
Previous Page

FIGURE 2-58

3 Click the Previous Page button.

Word places the top of page 2 (the previous page) at the top of the document window (Figure 2-59).

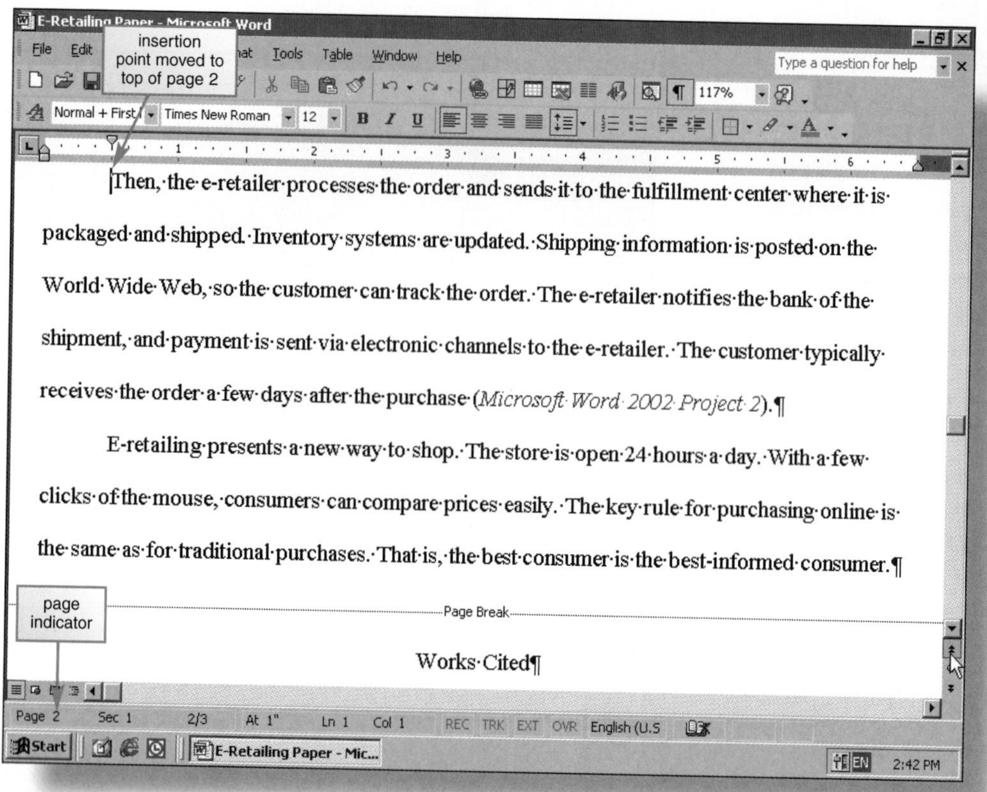

insertion point moved to top of page 2
Then, the e-retailer processes the order and sends it to the fulfillment center where it is packaged and shipped. Inventory systems are updated. Shipping information is posted on the World Wide Web, so the customer can track the order. The e-retailer notifies the bank of the shipment, and payment is sent via electronic channels to the e-retailer. The customer typically receives the order a few days after the purchase (Microsoft Word 2002 Project 2).¶
E-retailing presents a new way to shop. The store is open 24 hours a day. With a few clicks of the mouse, consumers can compare prices easily. The key rule for purchasing online is the same as for traditional purchases. That is, the best consumer is the best-informed consumer.¶
page indicator
Page Break
Works Cited¶
Page 2 Sec 1 2/3 At 1" Ln 1 Col 1

FIGURE 2-59

Other Ways

1. Double-click page indicator on status bar (Figure 2-59), click Page in Go to what list, type page number in Enter page number text box, click Go To button, click Close button
2. On Edit menu click Go To, and then proceed as described in 1 above starting with click Page in Go to what list
3. Press CTRL+G, and then proceed as described in 1 above starting with click Page in Go to what list
4. In Voice Command mode, click "Select Browse Object, Go To, Page, [type page number], Go To, Close"

Depending on the command you click in the Select Browse Object menu, the function of the buttons above and below the Select Browse Object button on the vertical scroll bar changes. When you select Browse by Page, the buttons become Previous Page and Next Page buttons; when you select Browse by Footnote, the buttons become Previous Footnote and Next Footnote buttons, and so on.

Moving Text

While proofreading the research paper, you realize that text in the fourth paragraph would flow better if the fourth sentence was moved so it followed the first sentence. That is, you want to move the fourth sentence so it is the second sentence in the fourth paragraph.

To move text, such as words, characters, sentences, or paragraphs, you first select the text to be moved and then use drag-and-drop editing or the cut-and-paste technique to move the selected text. With **drag-and-drop editing**, you drag the selected item to the new location and then insert, or *drop*, it there. **Cutting** involves removing the selected item from the document and then placing it on the **Clipboard**, which is a temporary Windows storage area. **Pasting** is the process of copying an item from the Clipboard into the document at the location of the insertion point. Project 3 demonstrates cutting and pasting. This project demonstrates using drag-and-drop editing.

To drag-and-drop a sentence in the research paper, first select a sentence as shown in the next step.

More About

Moving Text

When moving text a long distance or between applications, use the Clipboard task pane to cut and paste. (To display the Clipboard task pane, click Edit on the menu bar and then click Office Clipboard.) When moving text a short distance, the drag-and-drop technique is more efficient.

Steps To Select a Sentence

1 Position the mouse pointer (an I-beam) in the sentence to be moved. Press and hold the CTRL key. While holding the CTRL key, click the sentence. Release the CTRL key.

Word selects the entire sentence (Figure 2-60). Notice that Word includes the space following the period in the selection.

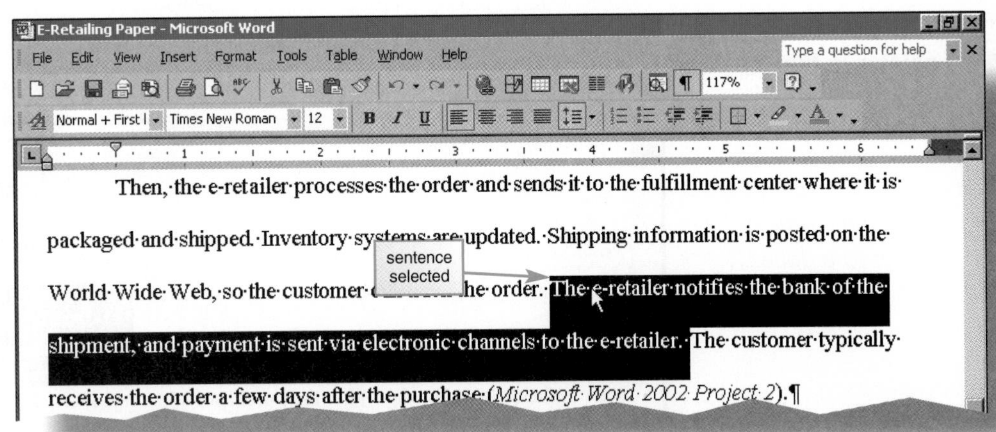
E-Retailing Paper - Microsoft Word
File Edit View Insert Format Tools Table Window Help
Type a question for help
Then, the e-retailer processes the order and sends it to the fulfillment center where it is packaged and shipped. Inventory systems are updated. Shipping information is posted on the World Wide Web, so the customer can track the order. The e-retailer notifies the bank of the shipment, and payment is sent via electronic channels to the e-retailer. The customer typically receives the order a few days after the purchase (Microsoft Word 2002 Project 2).¶
sentence selected

FIGURE 2-60

Other Ways

1. Drag through the sentence
2. With insertion point at beginning of sentence, press CTRL+SHIFT+RIGHT ARROW until sentence is selected
3. In Voice Command mode, say "Select sentence"

In the previous steps and throughout Projects 1 and 2, you have selected text and then formatted it. Table 2-4 summarizes the techniques used to select various items with the mouse.

Table 2-4 Techniques for Selecting Items with the Mouse

ITEM TO SELECT	MOUSE ACTION
Block of text	Click at beginning of selection, scroll to end of selection, position mouse pointer at end of selection, hold down SHIFT key and then click; or drag through the text
Character(s)	Drag through character(s)
Document	Move mouse to left of text until mouse pointer changes to a right-pointing block arrow and then triple-click
Graphic	Click the graphic
Line	Move mouse to left of line until mouse pointer changes to a right-pointing block arrow and then click
Lines	Move mouse to left of first line until mouse pointer changes to a right-pointing block arrow and then drag up or down
Paragraph	Triple-click paragraph; or move mouse to left of paragraph until mouse pointer changes to a right-pointing block arrow and then double-click
Paragraphs	Move mouse to left of paragraph until mouse pointer changes to a right-pointing block arrow, double-click and then drag up or down
Sentence	Press and hold CTRL key and then click sentence
Word	Double-click the word
Words	Drag through words

More About

Selecting Text

In Word, you can select nonadjacent text. This is helpful if you want to format multiple items the same way. To select items that are not next to each other (nonadjacent), do the following. Select the first item, such as a word or paragraph, as usual. Press and hold down the CTRL key. While holding down the CTRL key, select any additional items. All selected items display highlighted on the screen.

With the sentence to be moved selected, you can use drag-and-drop editing to move it. You should be sure that drag-and-drop editing is enabled by clicking Tools on the menu bar, clicking Options, clicking the Edit tab, verifying a check mark is next to Drag-and-drop text editing, and then clicking the OK button.

Perform the steps on the next page to move the selected sentence so it becomes the second sentence in the paragraph.

Steps To Move Text

1 With the mouse pointer in the selected text, press and hold the mouse button.

When you begin to drag the selected text, the insertion point changes to a dotted insertion point (Figure 2-61).

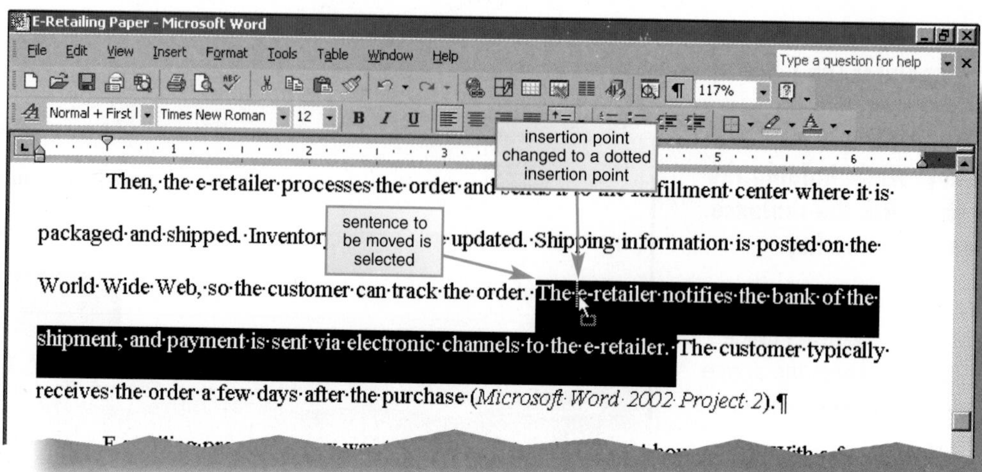
E-Retailing Paper - Microsoft Word
insertion point changed to a dotted insertion point
sentence to be moved is selected
Then, the e-retailer processes the order and sends it to the fulfillment center where it is packaged and shipped. Inventory systems are updated. Shipping information is posted on the World Wide Web, so the customer can track the order. The e-retailer notifies the bank of the shipment, and payment is sent via electronic channels to the e-retailer. The customer typically receives the order a few days after the purchase (Microsoft Word 2002 Project 2).¶

FIGURE 2-61

2 Drag the dotted insertion point to the location where the selected text is to be moved.

The dotted insertion point follows the space after the first sentence in the paragraph (Figure 2-62).

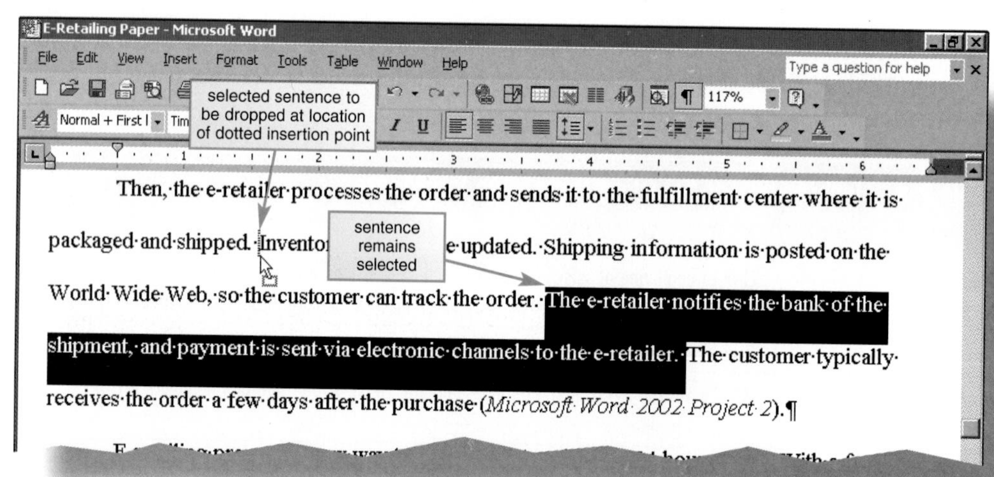
E-Retailing Paper - Microsoft Word
selected sentence to be dropped at location of dotted insertion point
sentence remains selected

FIGURE 2-62

3 Release the mouse button. Click outside the selected text to remove the selection.

Word moves the selected text to the location of the dotted insertion point (Figure 2-63).

Other Ways

1. Click Cut button on Standard toolbar, click where text is to be pasted, click Paste button on Standard toolbar

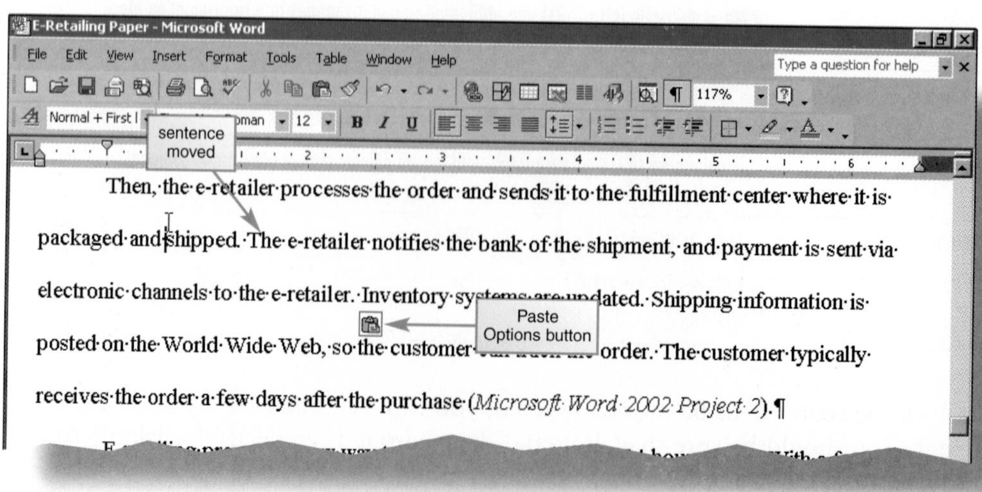
E-Retailing Paper - Microsoft Word
sentence moved
Paste Options button
Then, the e-retailer processes the order and sends it to the fulfillment center where it is packaged and shipped. The e-retailer notifies the bank of the shipment, and payment is sent via electronic channels to the e-retailer. Inventory systems are updated. Shipping information is posted on the World Wide Web, so the customer can track the order. The customer typically receives the order a few days after the purchase (Microsoft Word 2002 Project 2).¶

FIGURE 2-63

If you accidentally drag text to the wrong location, you can click the Undo button on the Standard toolbar.

You can use drag-and-drop editing to move any selected item. That is, you can select words, sentences, phrases, and graphics and then use drag-and-drop editing to move them.

When you drag-and-drop text, Word automatically displays a Paste Options button near the location of the dropped text (Figure 2-63). If you click the **Paste Options button**, a menu displays that allows you to change the format of the text that was moved. The following steps show how to display the Paste Options menu.

More About

Drag-and-Drop

If you hold down the CTRL key while dragging a selected item, Word copies the item instead of moving it.

Steps To Display the Paste Options Menu

1 Click the Paste Options button.

Word displays the Paste Options menu (Figure 2-64).

2 Press the ESCAPE key to remove the Paste Options menu from the window.

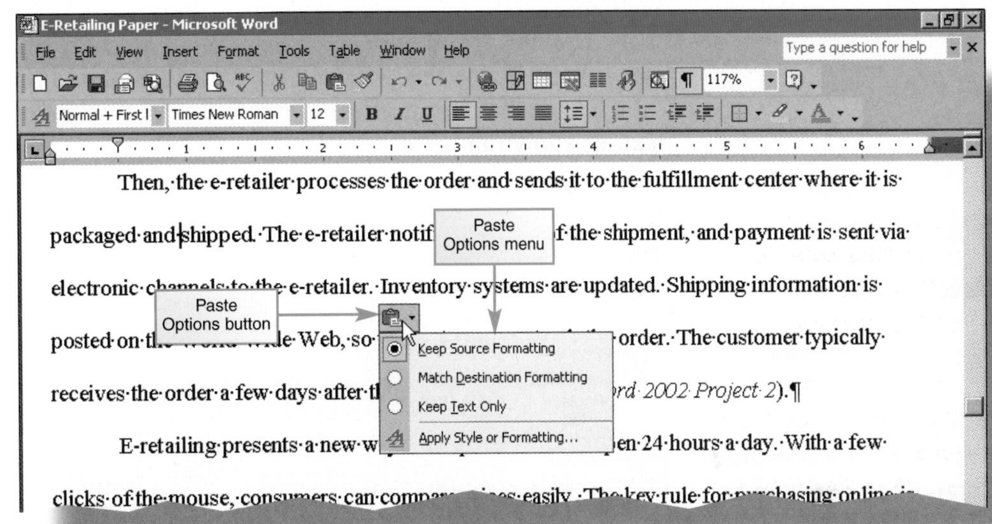

FIGURE 2-64

Smart Tags

A **smart tag** is a button that automatically appears on the screen when Word performs a certain action. In this project, you used two smart tags: AutoCorrect Options (Figures 2-24 and 2-25 on page WD 2.22) and Paste Options (Figure 2-64). In addition to AutoCorrect Options and Paste Options, Word provides other smart tags. Table 2-5 summarizes the smart tags available in Word.

With the AutoCorrect Options and Smart Tag Actions, Word notifies you that the smart tag is available by displaying a **smart tag indicator** on the screen. The smart tag indicator for AutoCorrect Options smart tag is a small blue box. The smart tag

Table 2-5 Smart Tags in Word

BUTTON	NAME	MENU FUNCTION
	AutoCorrect Options	Undoes an automatic correction, stops future automatic corrections of this type, or displays the AutoCorrect Options dialog box
	Paste Options	Specifies how moved or pasted items should display, e.g., with original formatting, without formatting, or with different formatting
	Smart Tag Actions	
	• Person name	Adds this name to Outlook Contacts folder, sends an e-mail, or schedules a meeting in Outlook Calendar with this person
	• Date or time	Schedules a meeting in Outlook Calendar at this date or time or displays your calendar
	• Address	Adds this address to Outlook Contacts folder or displays a a map or driving directions
	• Place	Adds this place to Outlook Contacts folder or schedules a meeting in Outlook Calendar at this location

Smart Tag Actions

The commands in the Smart Tag Actions menu vary depending on the smart tag. For example, the Smart Tag Actions menu for a date includes commands that allow you to schedule a meeting in Outlook Calendar or display your Outlook Calendar. The Smart Tag Actions menu for an address includes commands for displaying a map of the address or driving directions to or from the address.

indicator for Smart Tag Actions is a purple dotted line, as shown in Figure 2-15 on page WD 2.16. If you want to display a smart tag button, point to the smart tag indicator.

Clicking a smart tag button displays a menu that contains commands relative to the action performed at the location of the smart tag. For example, if you want to add a name in your Word document to the Outlook Contacts folder, point to the purple dotted line below the name to display the Smart Tag Actions button, click the Smart Tag Actions button to display the Smart Tag Actions menu, and then click Add to Contacts on the Smart Tag Actions menu to display the Contacts dialog box in Outlook.

Finding and Replacing Text

While proofreading the paper, you notice that it contains the phrase, World Wide Web, more than once in the document (Figure 2-65). You prefer to use the word, Web. Therefore, you wish to change all occurrences of World Wide Web to just the word, Web. To do this, you can use Word's find and replace feature, which automatically locates each occurrence of a word or phrase and then replaces it with specified text, as shown in these steps.

Steps To Find and Replace Text

1 **Press CTRL+HOME to position the insertion point at the top of the document. Double-click the status bar anywhere to the left of the status indicators. When the Find and Replace dialog box displays, click the Replace tab. Type** `World Wide Web` **in the Find what text box. Press the TAB key. Type** `Web` **in the Replace with text box. Point to the Replace All button.**

Word displays the Find and Replace dialog box (Figure 2-65). The Replace All button replaces all occurrences of the Find what text with the Replace with text.

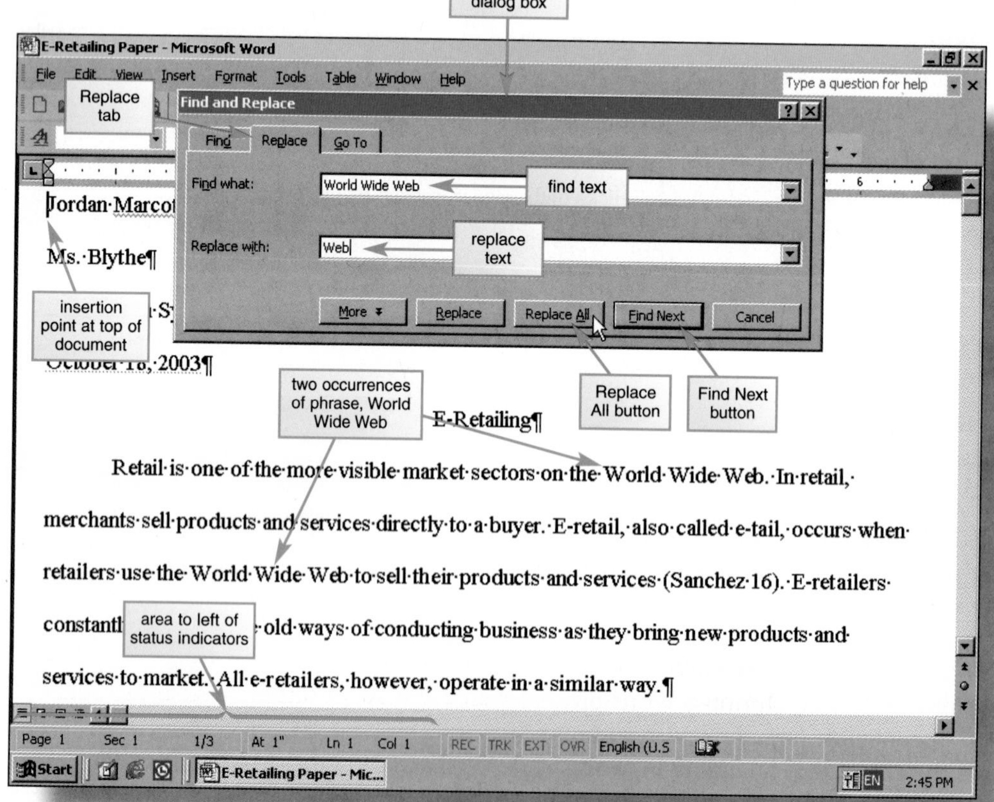

FIGURE 2-65

2 Click the Replace All button.

A Microsoft Word dialog box displays indicating the total number of replacements made (Figure 2-66). The word, Web, displays in the document instead of the phrase, World Wide Web.

3 Click the OK button. Click the Close button in the Find and Replace dialog box.

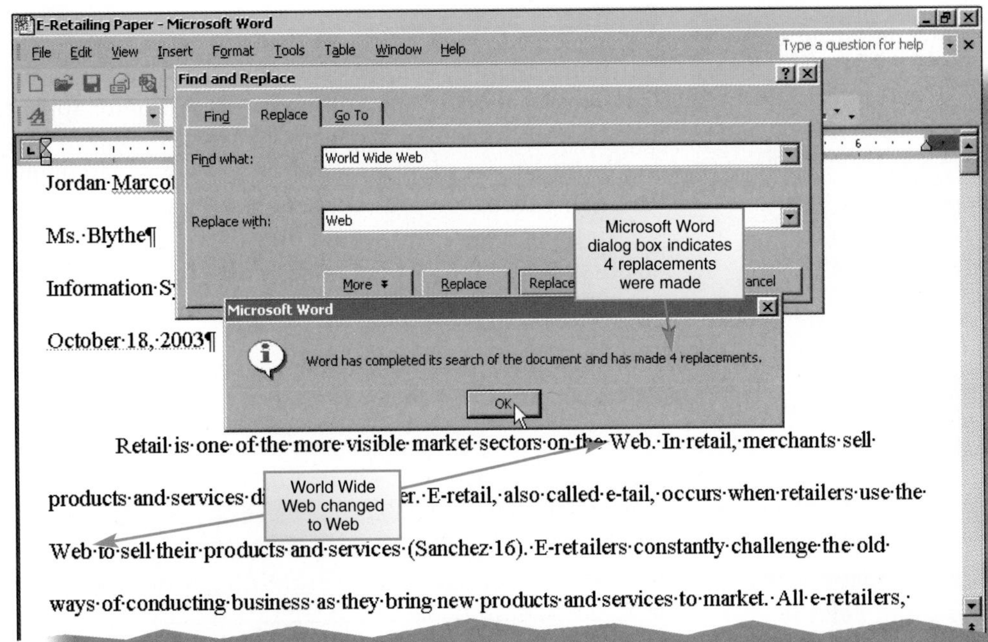

FIGURE 2-66

In some cases, you may want to replace only certain occurrences of the text, not all of them. To instruct Word to confirm each change, click the Find Next button in the Find and Replace dialog box (Figure 2-65), instead of the Replace All button. When Word locates an occurrence of the text, it pauses and waits for you to click either the Replace button or the Find Next button. Clicking the Replace button changes the text; clicking the Find Next button instructs Word to disregard the replacement and look for the next occurrence of the Find what text.

If you accidentally replace the wrong text, you can undo a replacement by clicking the Undo button on the Standard toolbar. If you used the Replace All button, Word undoes all replacements. If you used the Replace button, Word undoes only the most recent replacement.

Other Ways

1. Click Select Browse Object button on vertical scroll bar, click Find, click Replace tab, type Find what text, type Replace with text, click Replace All button, click Close button
2. On Edit menu click Replace, and then proceed as described in 1 above starting with type Find what text
3. Press CTRL+H, and then proceed as described in 1 above starting with type Find what text
4. In Voice Command mode, say "Select Browse Object, Find, Replace, [type text to find], Tab, [type text to replace], OK, OK, Close"

Finding Text

Sometimes, you may want only to find text, instead of finding *and* replacing text. To search for just a single occurrence of text, you would follow these steps.

TO FIND TEXT

1. Click the Select Browse Object button on the vertical scroll bar and then click Find on the Select Browse Object menu.
2. Type the text to locate in the Find what text box and then click the Find Next button. To edit the text, click the Cancel button in the Find and Replace dialog box; to find the next occurrence of the text, click the Find Next button.

More About

Finding

To search for formatting or special characters, click the More button in the Find dialog box. To find formatting, use the Format button in the Find dialog box. To find a special character, use the Special button.

Synonyms

For access to an online thesaurus, visit the Word 2002 More About Web page (scsite.com/wd2002/more.htm) and then click Online Thesaurus.

Finding a Synonym

When writing, you may discover that you used the same word in multiple locations or that a word you used was not quite appropriate. In these instances, you will want to look up a **synonym**, or word similar in meaning, to the duplicate or inappropriate word. A **thesaurus** is a book of synonyms. Word provides synonyms and a thesaurus for your convenience.

In this project, you would like a synonym for the word, way, at the end of the first paragraph of the research paper. Perform the following steps to find an appropriate synonym.

Steps To Find a Synonym

1. **Right-click the word for which you want to find a synonym (way, in this case). Point to Synonyms on the shortcut menu and then point to the appropriate synonym (manner) on the Synonyms submenu.**

Word displays a list of synonyms for the word containing the insertion point (Figure 2-67).

2. **Click the synonym you want (manner).**

Word replaces the word, way, in the document with the selected word, manner (shown in Figure 2-68).

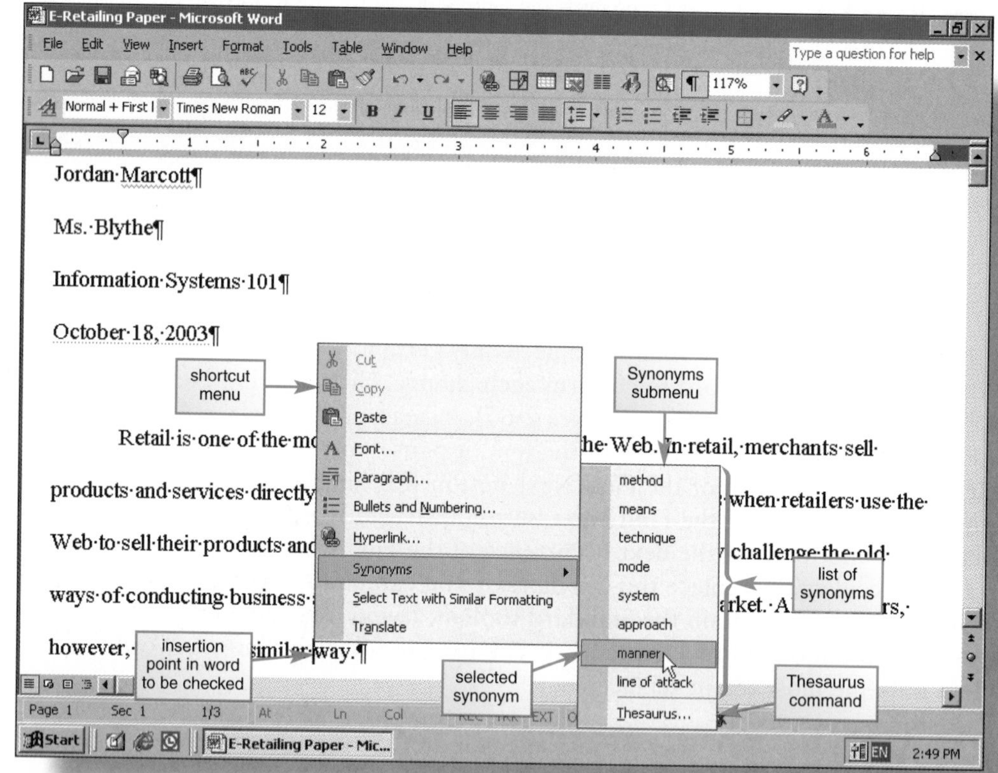

FIGURE 2-67

Other Ways

1. Click word, press SHIFT+F7, click appropriate meaning in Meanings list, click desired synonym in Replace with Synonym list, click Replace button
2. In Voice Command mode, with insertion point in word, say "Right Click, Synonyms, [select synonym]"

If the synonyms list does not display an appropriate word, you can display the Thesaurus dialog box by clicking Thesaurus on the Synonyms submenu (Figure 2-67). In the Thesaurus dialog box, you can look up synonyms for a different meaning of the word. You also can look up an **antonym**, or word with an opposite meaning.

Checking Spelling and Grammar At Once

As discussed in Project 1, Word checks your spelling and grammar as you type and places a wavy underline below possible spelling or grammar errors. Project 1 illustrated how to check these flagged words immediately. As an alternative, you can wait and check the entire document for spelling and grammar errors at once.

The following steps illustrate how to check spelling and grammar in the E-Retailing Paper at once. In the following example the word, constantly, has been misspelled intentionally as constently to illustrate the use of Word's check spelling and grammar at once feature. If you are completing this project on a personal computer, your research paper may contain different misspelled words, depending on the accuracy of your typing.

More About

Flagged Words

If you right-click a word, a shortcut menu displays. Commands in a shortcut menu vary depending on the object you right-click. If you right-click a word flagged with a red or green wavy underline, the shortcut menu displays spelling or grammar corrections for the flagged word.

Steps To Check Spelling and Grammar At Once

1 Press CTRL+HOME to move the insertion point to the beginning of the document. Point to the Spelling and Grammar button on the Standard toolbar.

When you click the Spelling and Grammar button, Word will begin the spelling and grammar check at the location of the insertion point, which is at the beginning of the document (Figure 2-68).

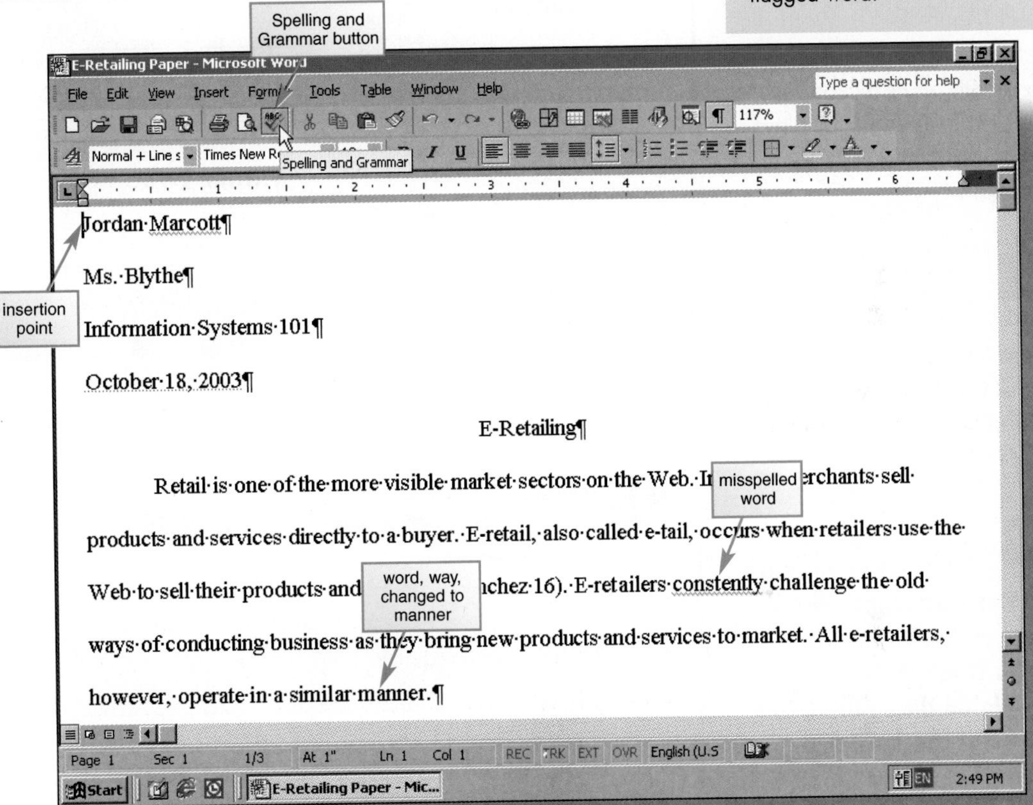

FIGURE 2-68

2 Click the Spelling and Grammar button. When the Spelling and Grammar dialog box displays, point to the Ignore All button.

Word displays the Spelling and Grammar dialog box (Figure 2-69). Word did not find Marcott in its dictionary because Marcott is a proper name. Marcott is spelled correctly.

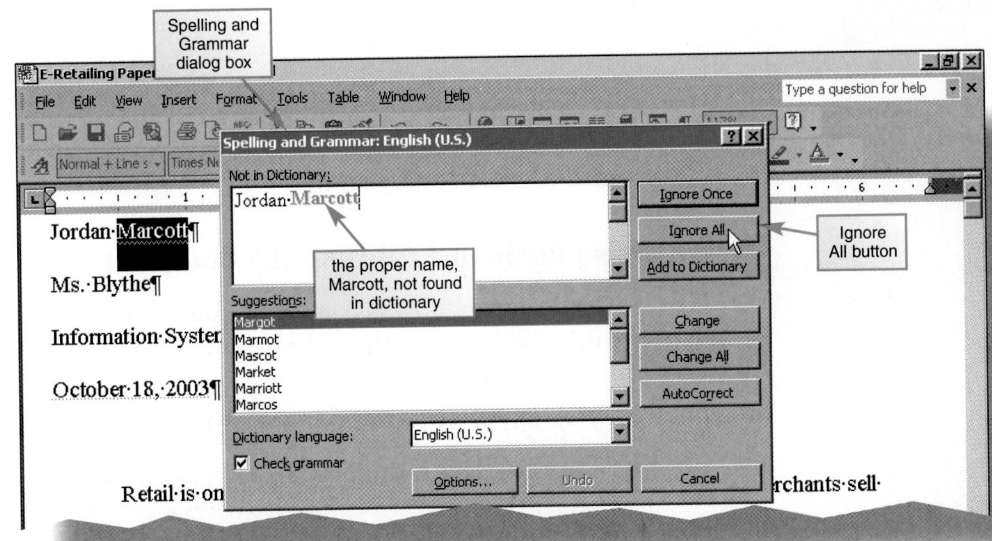

FIGURE 2-69

3 Click the Ignore All button. When Word flags the misspelled word, constently, point to the Change button.

Word continues the spelling and grammar check until it finds the next error or reaches the end of the document (Figure 2-70). Word did not find the misspelled word, constently, in its dictionary. The Suggestions list displays suggested corrections for the flagged word.

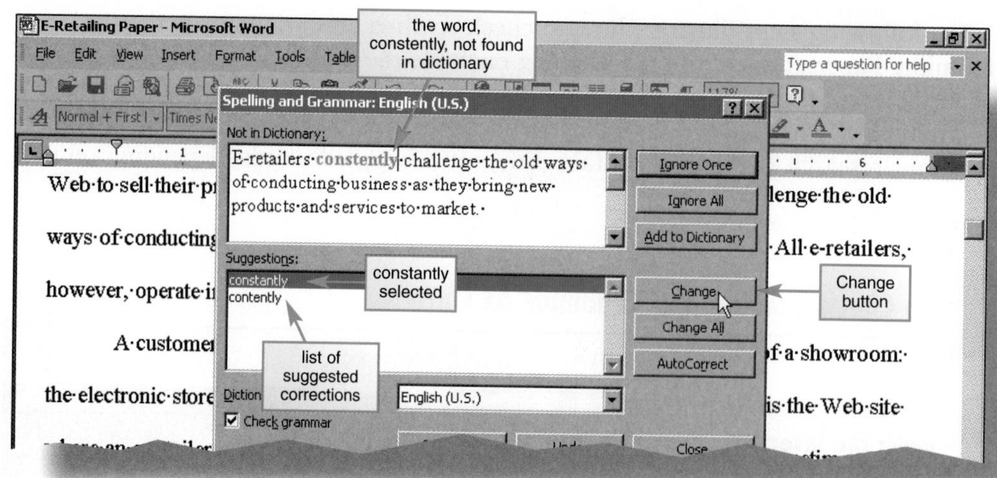

FIGURE 2-70

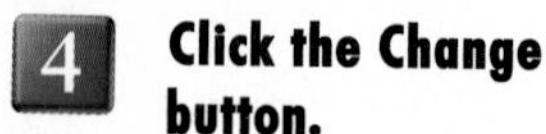

4 Click the Change button.

Word corrects the misspelled word and then flags an error on the Works Cited page (Figure 2-71).

5 Click the Ignore Once button for each grammar error that Word flags on the Works Cited page. When Word has completed the spelling and grammar check, click the OK button to close the dialog box.

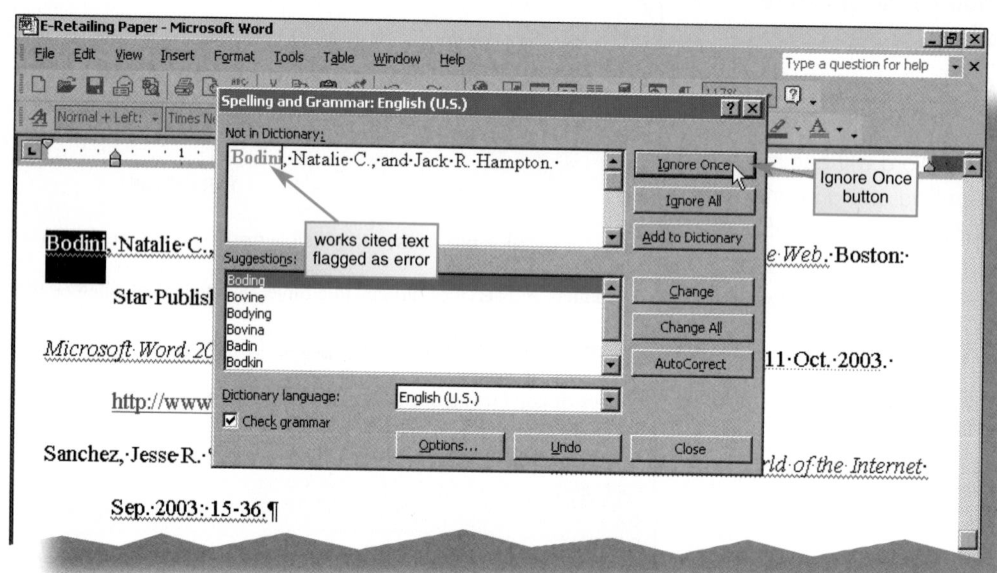

FIGURE 2-71

Other Ways

1. On Tools menu click Spelling and Grammar
2. Right-click flagged word, click Spelling on shortcut menu
3. Press F7
4. In Voice Command mode, say "Spelling and Grammar"

Your document no longer displays red and green wavy underlines below words and phrases. In addition, the red X on the Spelling and Grammar Status icon has returned to a red check mark.

Saving Again and Printing the Document

The document now is complete. You should save the research paper again and print it, as described in the following steps.

TO SAVE A DOCUMENT AGAIN AND PRINT IT

1. Click the Save button on the Standard toolbar and then click the Print button.

Word saves the research paper with the same file name, E-Retailing Paper. The completed research paper prints as shown in Figure 2-1 on page WD 2.05.

Navigating to a Hyperlink

Recall that a requirement of this research paper is that one of the works be a Web page and be formatted as a hyperlink. Perform the following steps to check your hyperlink.

Steps To Navigate to a Hyperlink

1 Display the third page of the research paper in the document window and then point to the hyperlink.

When you point to a hyperlink in a Word document, a ScreenTip displays above the hyperlink (Figure 2-72).

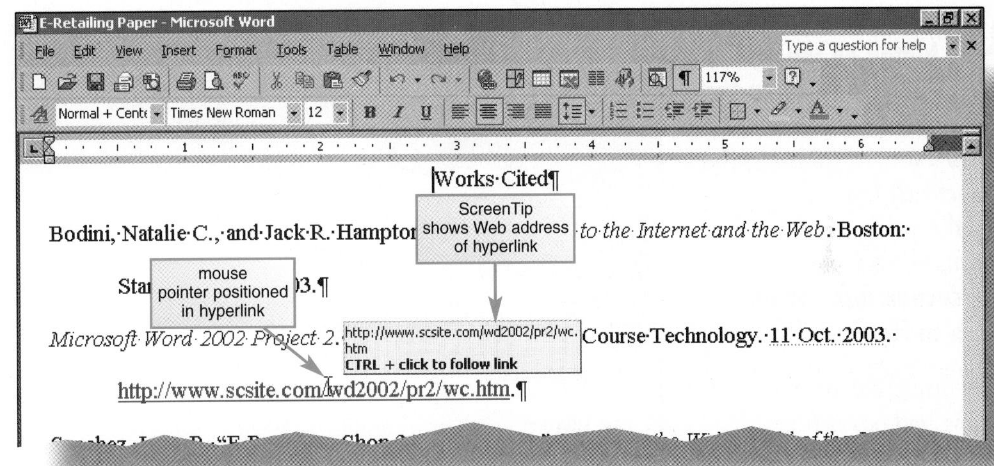

FIGURE 2-72

2 While holding the CTRL key, click the hyperlink. Release the CTRL key.

If you currently are not connected to the Web, Word connects you using your default browser. The www.scsite.com/wd2002/pr2/wc.htm Web page displays (Figure 2-73).

3 Close the browser window. If necessary, click the Microsoft Word program button on the taskbar to redisplay the Word window. Press CTRL+HOME.

The first page of the research paper displays in the Word window.

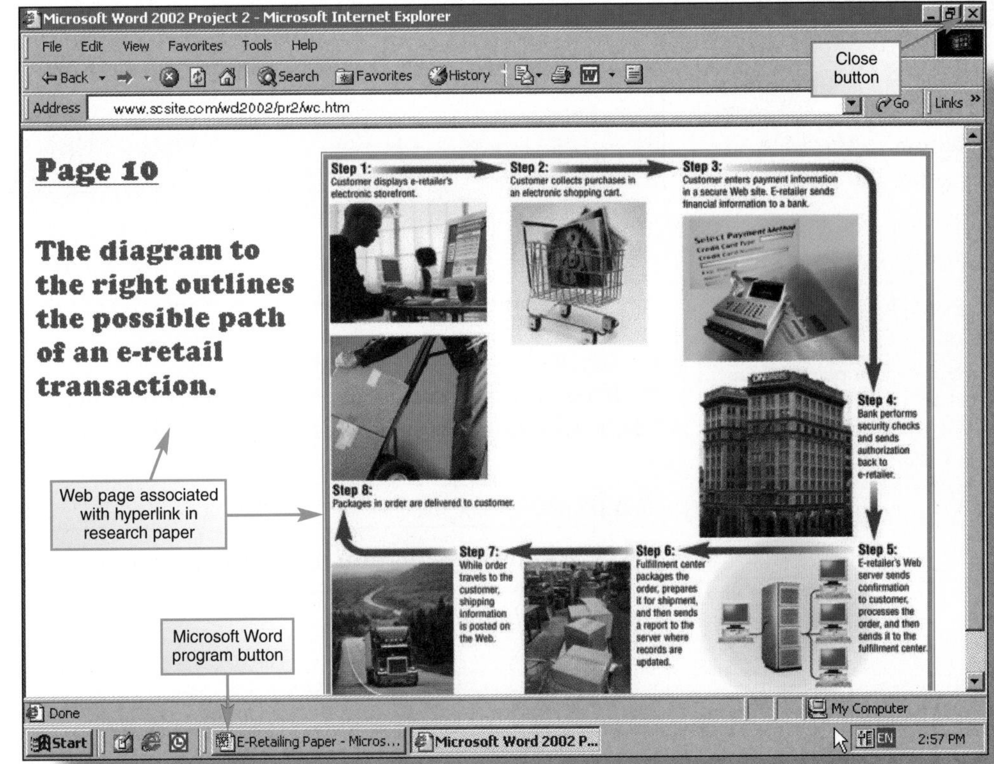

FIGURE 2-73

E-Mailing

To e-mail a document as an attachment, click File on the menu bar, point to Send To, and then click Mail Recipient (as Attachment).

E-Mailing a Copy of the Research Paper

Your instructor, Ms. Blythe, has requested you e-mail her a copy of your research paper so she can verify your hyperlink. Perform the following step to e-mail the document from within Word.

Steps To E-Mail a Document

1 Click the E-mail button on the Standard toolbar. Fill in the To text box with Ms. Blythe's e-mail address, the Subject text box with the name of the paper, and the Introduction text box as shown in Figure 2-74.

Word displays certain buttons and boxes from your e-mail editor inside the Word window.

2 Click the Send a Copy button.

The document is e-mailed to the recipient named in the To text box.

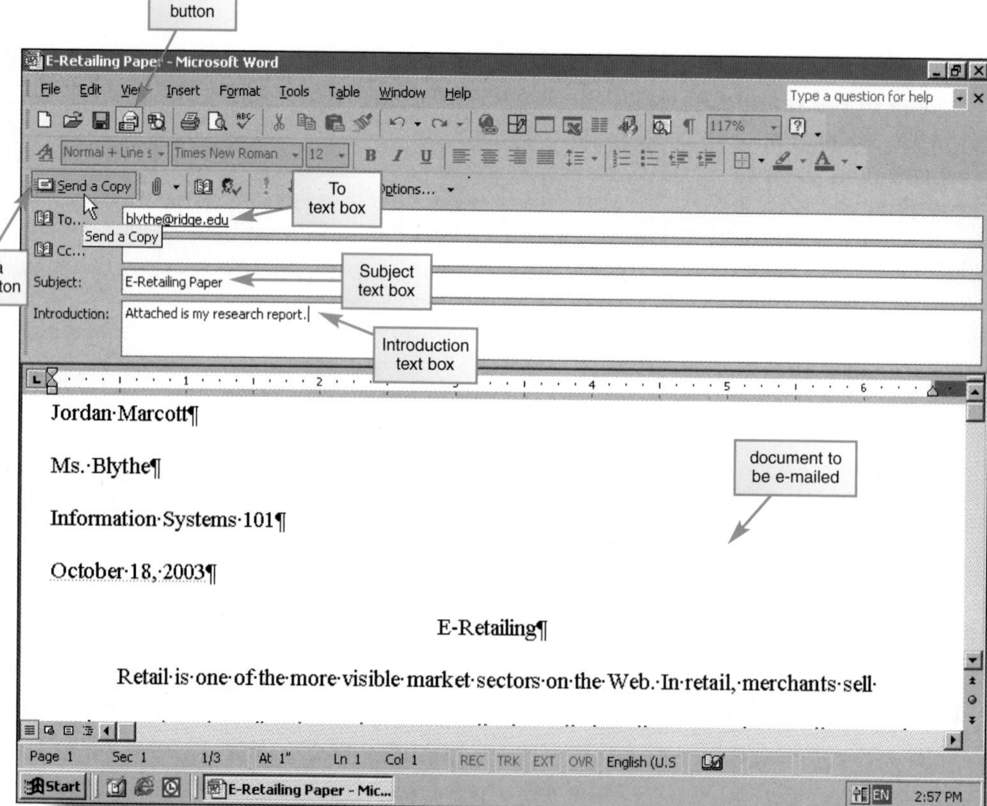

FIGURE 2-74

Other Ways

1. On File menu point to Send To, on Send To submenu click Mail Recipient
2. In Voice Command mode, say "E-mail"

If you want to cancel the e-mail operation, click the E-mail button again. The final step in this project is to quit Word, as described in the following step.

TO QUIT WORD

1 Click the Close button in the Word window.

The Word window closes.

CASE PERSPECTIVE SUMMARY

Jordan accomplished her goal — learning about e-retailing while completing Ms. Blythe's research paper assignment. Based on her findings, she has decided to pursue a career in retail management for a Web-based merchant. She decides to create a resume, listing this goal as the objective on her resume. Jordan decides to use Word's Resume Wizard to create her resume. She also contacts the Office of Career Development at her school to assist her with wording on the resume. After finishing the resume, she shows Ms. Blythe. Jordan cannot wait to begin her new career!

Project Summary

Project 2 introduced you to creating a research paper using the MLA documentation style. You learned how to change margin settings, adjust line spacing, create headers with page numbers, and indent paragraphs. You learned how to use Word's AutoCorrect feature. Then, you added a footnote in the research paper. You alphabetized the works cited page by sorting its paragraphs and included a hyperlink to a Web page in one of the works. You learned how to count words, browse through a Word document, move text, and find and replace text. You looked up a synonym and checked spelling and grammar in the entire document. Finally, you navigated to a hyperlink and e-mailed a copy of a document.

What You Should Know

Having completed this project, you now should be able to perform the following tasks:

- Add a Footnote *(WD 2.25)*
- AutoCorrect as You Type *(WD 2.21)*
- Browse by Page *(WD 2.43)*
- Center the Title of the Works Cited Page *(WD 2.36)*
- Change the Margin Settings *(WD 2.08)*
- Check Spelling and Grammar At Once *(WD 2.51)*
- Click and Type *(WD 2.13)*
- Close the Note Pane *(WD 2.31)*
- Count Words *(WD 2.32)*
- Create a Hanging Indent *(WD 2.37)*
- Create a Hyperlink as You Type *(WD 2.40)*
- Create an AutoCorrect Entry *(WD 2.23)*
- Display Formatting Marks *(WD 2.07)*
- Display the Header Area *(WD 2.12)*
- Display the Paste Options Menu *(WD 2.47)*
- Double-Space Text *(WD 2.10)*
- E-Mail a Document *(WD 2.54)*
- Enter a Page Number *(WD 2.14)*
- Enter More Text *(WD 2.24)*
- Enter Name and Course Information *(WD 2.16)*
- Enter Works Cited Paragraphs *(WD 2.37)*
- Find a Synonym *(WD 2.50)*
- Find and Replace Text *(WD 2.48)*
- Find Text *(WD 2.49)*
- First-Line Indent Paragraphs *(WD 2.19)*
- Insert a Symbol Automatically *(WD 2.39)*
- Modify a Style *(WD 2.28)*
- Move Text *(WD 2.46)*
- Navigate to a Hyperlink *(WD 2.53)*
- Page Break Automatically *(WD 2.33)*
- Page Break Manually *(WD 2.35)*
- Quit Word *(WD 2.54)*
- Recount Words *(WD 2.34)*
- Reset Menus and Toolbars *(WD 2.07)*
- Save a Document *(WD 2.18)*
- Save a Document Again and Print It *(WD 2.52)*
- Select a Sentence *(WD 2.45)*
- Sort Paragraphs *(WD 2.41)*
- Start and Customize Word *(WD 2.06)*
- Use Shortcut Keys to Format Text *(WD 2.17)*
- Use the AutoCorrect Options Button *(WD 2.22)*
- Zoom Page Width *(WD 2.09)*

More About

Microsoft Certification

The Microsoft Office User Specialist (MOUS) Certification program provides an opportunity for you to obtain a valuable industry credential - proof that you have the Word 2002 skills required by employers. For more information, see Appendix E or visit the Shelly Cashman Series MOUS Web page at scsite.com/offxp/cert.htm.

Learn It Online

Instructions: To complete the Learn It Online exercises, start your browser, click the Address bar, and then enter `scsite.com/offxp/exs.htm`. When the Office XP Learn It Online page displays, follow the instructions in the exercises below.

1 Project Reinforcement TF, MC, and SA

Below Word Project 2, click the Project Reinforcement link. Print the quiz by clicking Print on the File menu. Answer each question. Write your first and last name at the top of each page, and then hand in the printout to your instructor.

2 Flash Cards

Below Word Project 2, click the Flash Cards link. When Flash Cards displays, read the instructions. Type `20` (or a number specified by your instructor) in the Number of Playing Cards text box, type your name in the Name text box, and then click the Flip Card button. When the flash card displays, read the question and then click the Answer box arrow to select an answer. Flip through Flash Cards. Click Print on the File menu to print the last flash card if your score is 15 (75%) correct or greater and then hand it in to your instructor. If your score is less than 15 (75%) correct, then redo this exercise by clicking the Replay button.

3 Practice Test

Below Word Project 2, click the Practice Test link. Answer each question, enter your first and last name at the bottom of the page, and then click the Grade Test button. When the graded practice test displays on your screen, click Print on the File menu to print a hard copy. Continue to take practice tests until you score 80% or better. Hand in a printout of the final practice test to your instructor.

4 Who Wants to Be a Computer Genius?

Below Word Project 2, click the Computer Genius link. Read the instructions, enter your first and last name at the bottom of the page, and then click the Play button. Hand in your score to your instructor.

5 Wheel of Terms

Below Word Project 2, click the Wheel of Terms link. Read the instructions, and then enter your first and last name and your school name. Click the Play button. Hand in your score to your instructor.

6 Crossword Puzzle Challenge

Below Word Project 2, click the Crossword Puzzle Challenge link. Read the instructions, and then enter your first and last name. Click the Play button. Work the crossword puzzle. When you are finished, click the Submit button. When the crossword puzzle redisplays, click the Print button. Hand in the printout.

7 Tips and Tricks

Below Word Project 2, click the Tips and Tricks link. Click a topic that pertains to Project 2. Right-click the information and then click Print on the shortcut menu. Construct a brief example of what the information relates to in Word to confirm you understand how to use the tip or trick. Hand in the example and printed information.

8 Newsgroups

Below Word Project 2, click the Newsgroups link. Click a topic that pertains to Project 2. Print three comments. Hand in the comments to your instructor.

9 Expanding Your Horizons

Below Word Project 2, click the Articles for Microsoft Word link. Click a topic that pertains to Project 2. Print the information. Construct a brief example of what the information relates to in Word to confirm you understand the contents of the article. Hand in the example and printed information to your instructor.

10 Search Sleuth

Below Word Project 2, click the Search Sleuth link. To search for a term that pertains to this project, select a term below the Project 2 title and then use the Google search engine at google.com (or any major search engine) to display and print two Web pages that present information on the term. Hand in the printouts to your instructor.

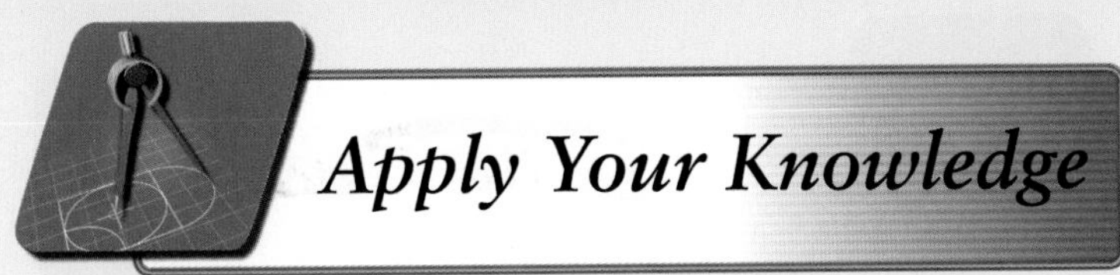

Apply Your Knowledge

1 Revising a Document

Instructions: Start Word. Open the document, Picture CD Paragraph, on the Data Disk. See the inside back cover of this book for instructions for downloading the Data Disk or see your instructor for information on accessing the files in this book.

The document is a paragraph of text. You are to revise the paragraph as follows: move a sentence; change the format of the moved sentence; replace all occurrences of the word, electronic, with the word, digital; and remove an automatic hyperlink format. The revised paragraph is shown in Figure 2-75.

Perform the following tasks:

1. Press and hold the CTRL key. While holding the CTRL key, click in the sentence that is italicized to select the sentence. Release the CTRL key.
2. Press and hold down the left mouse button. Drag the dotted insertion point to the end of the paragraph and then release the mouse button to move the sentence. Click outside the selection to remove the highlight.
3. Click the Paste Options button that displays to the right of the moved sentence. To remove the italic format from the moved sentence, click Keep Text Only on the shortcut menu.
4. Press CTRL+HOME to position the insertion point at the top of the document. Double-click the status bar anywhere to the left of the status indicators. When the Find and Replace dialog box displays, click the Replace tab.
5. Type `electronic` in the Find what text box, press the TAB key, and then type `digital` in the Replace with text box. Click the Replace All button. Click the OK button in the Microsoft Word dialog box. Click the Close button in the Find and Replace dialog box.
6. At the end of the paragraph, press the SPACEBAR and then type this sentence: `For more information on Picture CDs, enter the Web address of www.scsite.com/dc2002/ch7/weblink.htm and click Picture CDs.`
7. To remove the hyperlink automatic format from the Web address, point to the beginning of the Web address (that is, the w in www). Click the small blue box below the w and then click the AutoCorrect Options button. Click Undo Hyperlink on the shortcut menu.
8. Click File on the menu bar and then click Save As. Use the file name, Revised Picture CD Paragraph, and then save the document on your floppy disk.
9. Print the revised paragraph.

Internet evangelists have predicted the move to digital and online photograph storage. These predictions now are becoming reality. Picture CD is a new film digitation service from Kodak. This technology bridges the film to digital gap by providing a solution that gives people the benefit of both film and digital pictures. Picture CDs allow you to view pictures on the computer. With a Picture CD, you can print, modify, improve, and enhance photographs, and send e-mail postcards. To purchase a Picture CD, just check the box for Kodak Picture CD on your processing envelope when you drop off film for processing. For more information on Picture CDs, enter the Web address of www.scsite.com/dc2002/ch7/weblink.htm and click Picture CDs.

FIGURE 2-75

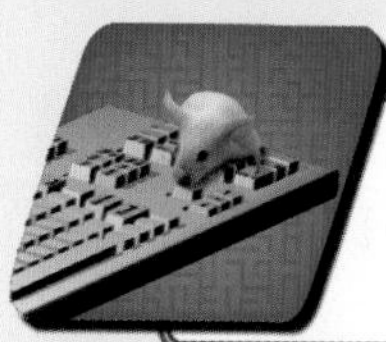

In the Lab

1 Preparing a Research Paper

Problem: You are a college student currently enrolled in a business data systems class. Your assignment is to prepare a short research paper (400-425 words) about a global positioning system (GPS). The requirements are that the paper be presented according to the MLA documentation style and have three references (Figures 2-76a through 2-76c). One of the three references must be from the Web and formatted as a hyperlink on the Works Cited page.

Hazelwood 1

Terry Hazelwood

Mr. Winkler

Business Data Systems 110

November 11, 2003

Global Positioning System

A global positioning system (GPS) consists of one or more earth-based receivers that accept and analyze signals sent by satellites in order to determine the receiver's geographic location. A GPS receiver is a handheld or mountable device, which can be secured to an automobile, boat, airplane, farm and construction equipment, or a computer. Some GPS receivers send location information to a base station, where humans can give you personal directions.

GPS has a variety of uses: to locate a person or object; ascertain the best route between two points; monitor the movement of a person or object; or create a map (Slifka 16-19). GPSs help scientists, farmers, pilots, dispatchers, and rescue workers operate more productively and safely. A rescue worker, for example, might use a GPS to locate a motorist stranded in a blizzard. A surveyor might use a GPS to create design maps for construction projects.

GPSs also are popular in consumer products for travel and recreational activities (*Microsoft Word 2002 Project 2*). Many cars use GPSs to provide drivers with directions or other information, automatically call for help if the airbag deploys, dispatch roadside assistance, unlock the driver's side door if keys are locked in the car, and track the vehicle if it is stolen. For cars not equipped with a GPS, drivers can mount or place one in the glove compartment. Hikers and remote campers also carry GPS receivers in case they need emergency help or directions.

A new use of GPS places the device on a computer chip. The chip, called Digital Angel™, is worn as a bracelet or chain or woven into fabric and has an antenna that

FIGURE 2-76a

In the Lab

Hazelwood 2

communicates with a GPS satellite (Dugan and Rosen 42-50). The chip measures and sends biological information to the GPS satellite. If information relayed indicates a person needs medical attention, dispatchers can send emergency medical help immediately. Other possible uses of Digital Angel™ include locating a missing person or pet, tracking parolees, and protecting valuables. Retailers take advantage of this technology, too. For example, a coffee shop could send a coupon into a handheld computer as the people walk by their store.

FIGURE 2-76b

Hazelwood 3

Works Cited

Dugan, Richard D., and Betty Ann Rosen. *Digital Concepts for the New Age*. San Francisco: Webster Clark Publishing, 2003.

Microsoft Word 2002 Project 2. Shelly Cashman Series® Course Technology. 6 Nov. 2003. http://www.scsite.com/wd2002/pr2/wc1.htm.

Slifka, Henry R. "An Introduction to GPS." *Modern Computing* Oct. 2003: 10-35.

FIGURE 2-76c

Instructions:

1. If necessary, click the Show/Hide ¶ button on the Standard toolbar. Change all margins to one inch. Adjust line spacing to double. Create a header to number pages. Type the name and course information at the left margin. Center and type the title. First-line indent all paragraphs in the paper.
2. Type the body of the paper as shown in Figure 2-76a and Figure 2-76b. To enter the trademark symbol (™), type (tm). At the end of the body of the research paper, press the ENTER key and then insert a manual page break.
3. Create the works cited page (Figure 2-76c).
4. Check the spelling of the paper at once.
5. Save the document on a floppy disk using GPS Paper as the file name.
6. If you have access to the Web, CTRL+click the hyperlink to test it.
7. Print the research paper. Handwrite the number of words in the research paper above the title of your printed research paper.

In the Lab

2 Preparing a Research Report with Footnotes

Problem: You are a college student currently enrolled in a data communications class. Your assignment is to prepare a short research paper in any area of interest to you. The requirements are that the paper be presented according to the MLA documentation style and have three references. One of the three references must be from the Internet and formatted as a hyperlink on the works cited page. You decide to prepare a paper on computers and entertainment (Figures 2-77a and 2-77b).

Frey 1

Holly Frey

Ms. Robinson

Data Communications 100

November 5, 2003

Computers and Entertainment

In the past, you played board games with friends and family members, viewed fine art in an art gallery, listened to music on your stereo, watched a movie at a theater or on television, and inserted pictures into sleeves of photo albums. Today, you can have a much more fulfilling experience in each of these areas of entertainment.

In addition to playing exciting, action-packed, 3-D multiplayer games, you can find hours of entertainment on the computer. For example, you can make a family tree, read a book or magazine online, listen to music on the computer, compose a video, edit pictures, or plan a vacation. These forms of entertainment are available on CD-ROM, DVD-ROM, and also on the Web. On the Web, you can view images of fine art in online museums, galleries, and centers.[1] Some artists sell their works online. Others display them for your viewing pleasure.

You have several options if you wish to listen to music while working on the computer. Insert your favorite music CD into the CD or DVD drive on your computer and listen while you work. Visit an online radio station to hear music, news, and sporting events (Peyton 25). At some of these sites, you even can watch videos of artists as they sing or play their songs.

Instead of driving to the music store or video store to purchase music or movies, you can buy them on the Web. After paying for the music or movie online, you download it to your hard

[1] Simms and Foster list many Web addresses of fine art galleries, such as the Louvre, that display works online for your enjoyment (78-93).

FIGURE 2-77a

In the Lab

Frey 2

disk. Once on your hard disk, you listen to the music or watch the movie on the computer. Or, you can transfer it to a CD using a CD-RW and play the music on any audio CD player or the movie on a DVD player (*Microsoft Word 2002 Project 2*).

Some people prefer to create their own music or movies. You can compose music and other sound effects using external devices such as an electric piano keyboard or synthesizer. You also can transfer or create movies by connecting a video camera to the computer. Once on the computer, the music or movies are ready for editing, e-mailing, or posting to a Web page.

FIGURE 2-77b

Part 1 Instructions: Perform the following tasks to create the research paper:

1. If necessary, click the Show/Hide ¶ button on the Standard toolbar. Change all margin settings to one inch. Adjust line spacing to double. Create a header to number pages. Type the name and course information at the left margin. Center and type the title. First-line indent all paragraphs in the paper.
2. Type the body of the paper as shown in Figure 2-77a and Figure 2-77b. At the end of the body of the research paper, press the ENTER key once and insert a manual page break.
3. Create the works cited page. Enter the works cited shown below as separate paragraphs. Format the works properly and then sort the paragraphs.
   (a) Simms, Jeffrey K., and Laura C. Foster. Technological Entertainment. Chicago: Clark Davidson Press, 2003.
   (b) Peyton, Bonnie R. "World Music: A Multitude of Radio Waves Now Online." Technology April 2003: 25-29.
   (c) Microsoft Word 2002 Project 2. Shelly Cashman Series®. Course Technology. 30 Oct. 2003. http://www.scsite.com/wd2002/pr2/wc2.htm.
4. Check the spelling of the paper.
5. Save the document on a floppy disk using Computers and Entertainment Paper as the file name.
6. If you have access to the Web, CTRL+click the hyperlink to test it.
7. Print the research paper. Handwrite the number of words, including the footnotes, in the research paper above the title of your printed research paper.

Part 2 Instructions: Perform the following tasks to modify the research paper:

1. Use Word to find a synonym of your choice for the word, find, in the first sentence of the second paragraph.
2. Change all occurrences of the word, pictures, to the word, photographs.
3. Insert a second footnote at the end of the third sentence in the last paragraph of the research paper. Use the following footnote text: Many digital video cameras allow you also to take digital still photographs.

(continued)

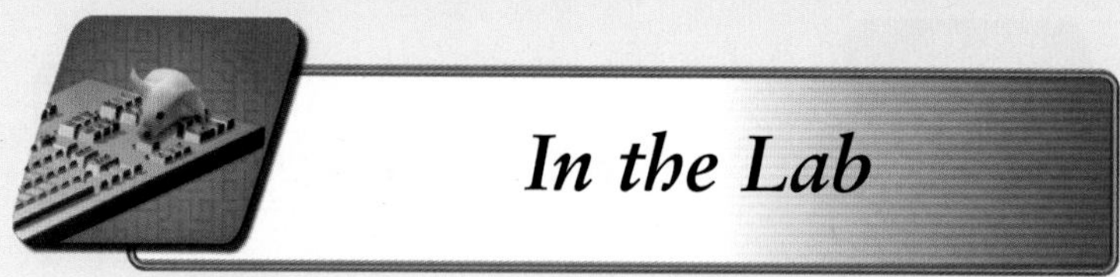

Preparing a Research Report with Footnotes *(continued)*

4. In the first footnote, find the word, display, and change it to the word, exhibit.
5. Save the document on a floppy disk using Computers and Entertainment Paper - Part 2a as the file name.
6. Print the revised research paper with the notes positioned as footnotes.
7. Convert the footnotes to endnotes. Recall that endnotes display at the end of a document. (***Hint***: Use Help to learn about converting footnotes to endnotes.)
8. Modify the Endnote text style to 12-point font, double-spaced text with a first-line indent. Insert a page break so the endnotes are placed on a separate, numbered page. Center the title, Endnotes, double-spaced above the notes.
9. Change the format of the note reference marks to capital letters (A, B, etc.). ***Hint***: Use Help to learn about changing the number format of note reference marks.
10. Save the document on a floppy disk using Computers and Entertainment Paper - Part 2b as the file name.
11. Print the revised research paper with notes positioned as endnotes. Handwrite the number of words, including the footnotes, in the research paper above the title of the printed research paper.

3 Composing a Research Paper from Notes

Problem: You have drafted the notes shown in Figure 2-78. Your assignment is to prepare a short research paper from these notes. Review the notes and then rearrange and reword them. Embellish the paper as you deem necessary. Add a footnote that refers the reader to the Web for more information. Present the paper according to the MLA documentation style.

Instructions: Perform the following tasks:

1. Change all margin settings to one inch. Adjust line spacing to double. Create a header to number pages. Type the name and course information at the left margin. Center and type the title. First-line indent all paragraphs in the paper.
2. Create an AutoCorrect entry that automatically corrects the spelling of the misspelled word, moniters, to the correct spelling, monitors.
3. Compose the body of the paper from the notes in Figure 2-78. Be sure to include a footnote as specified. At the end of the body of the research paper, press the ENTER key once and insert a manual page break. Create the works cited page from the listed sources. Be sure to sort the works.
4. Check the spelling and grammar of the paper. Save the document on a floppy disk using Green Computing Research Paper as the file name. Print the research paper. Handwrite the number of words, including the footnotes, in the research paper above the title of the printed research paper.
5. E-mail the research paper to your instructor, if your instructor gives you permission to do so.

In the Lab

Green computing involves reducing the electricity and environmental waste while using a computer. Computers use, and often waste, resources such as electricity and paper. Society has become aware of this waste and is taking measures to combat it.

ENERGY STAR program (source: "What's New in Computing Today," an article on pages 9-24 in the September 2003 issue of High Tech, author Roger R. Mobley):

- ENERGY STAR program encourages manufacturers to create energy-efficient devices that require little power when they are not in use. For example, many devices switch to standby mode after a specified number of inactive minutes.
- Computers and devices that meet ENERGY STAR guidelines display an ENERGY STAR® label.
- Personal computers, monitors, and printers should comply with the ENERGY STAR program, which was developed by the United States Department of Energy (DOE) and the United States Environmental Protection Agency (EPA).

Obsolete computers and devices (source: Computer Learning for the New Professional, a book published by Gulf Publishing Company in Houston, Texas, 2003, pages 56-64, authors James D. Holmes and Katie A. Marsden.):

- Do not store obsolete computers and devices in your basement, storage room, attic, warehouse, or any other location.
- Computers, monitors, and other equipment contain toxic materials and potentially dangerous elements including lead, mercury, and flame retardants. In a landfill, these materials release into the environment.
- Experts recommend refurbishing or recycling the equipment. For this reason, local governments are working on methods to make it easy for the consumer to recycle this type of equipment. Manufacturers can use the millions of pounds of recycled raw material in products such as outdoor furniture and automotive parts.

To reduce further the environmental impact of computing, simply alter a few habits (source: a Web site titled Microsoft Word 2002 Project 2 sponsored by the Shelly Cashman Series® at Course Technology; site visited on 1 Oct. 2003; Web address is http://www.scsite.com/wd2002/pr2/wc3.htm.):

- Use computers and devices that comply with the ENERGY STAR program.
- Recycle toner cartridges. Recycle old computers and printers.
- Telecommute (saves gas).
- Do not leave the computer and devices running overnight.
- Use paperless methods to communicate.
- Recycle paper. Buy recycled paper.
- Turn off your monitor, printer, and other devices when not in use.
- Shop online (saves gas).

FIGURE 2-78

Cases and Places

The difficulty of these case studies varies:
▶ are the least difficult; ▶▶ are more difficult; and ▶▶▶ are the most difficult.

1 ▶ Project 1 of this book discussed the components of the Word window (pages WD 1.12 through WD 1.17). Using the material presented on these pages, write a short research paper (350-400 words) that describes the purpose and functionality of one or more of these components: the document window, insertion point, end mark, mouse pointer, rulers, scroll bars, status bar, menu bar, or toolbars. Use your textbook, Word Help, and any other resources available. Include at least two references and one explanatory note. Use the concepts and techniques presented in this project to format the paper.

2 ▶▶ A smart card, which is similar in size to a credit card or ATM card, stores data on a thin microprocessor embedded in the card. Using the school library, other textbooks, magazines, the Internet, or other resources, research the types of smart cards, popular uses of smart cards, or the role of e-money with smart cards. Then, prepare a brief research paper (400-450 words) that discusses your findings. Include at least one explanatory note and two references, one of which must be a Web site on the Internet. Use the concepts and techniques presented in this project to format the paper.

3 ▶▶ A handheld computer, sometimes called a PDA, is a lightweight, palm-sized or pocket-sized computer. Using the school library, other textbooks, the Internet, magazines, or other resources, research the points to consider when purchasing a handheld computer. Then, prepare a brief research paper (400-450 words) that discusses features, applications, price, and accessories of current handheld computers. Include at least one explanatory note and two references, one of which must be a Web site on the Internet. Use the concepts and techniques presented in this project to format the paper.

4 ▶▶ An electronic book is a digital text that gives a user access to information through links, which often are bold or underlined words. Using the school library, other textbooks, the Internet, magazines, or other resources, research electronic books on the market today. Then, prepare a brief research paper (400-450 words) that discusses the features of these books and the methods publishers use to distribute these electronic books. Include at least one explanatory note and two references, one of which must be a Web site on the Internet. Use the concepts and techniques presented in this project to format the paper.

5 ▶▶▶ The options available for obtaining software have grown considerably in the past few years. You can shop in-person at a bricks-and-mortar retail store or purchase online through a retailer on the Web. On the Web, you can subscribe to software, download software, or have it delivered to your doorstep. Select a software application, such as word processing, spreadsheets, accounting, or graphics. Investigate the various means available for obtaining this software. Visit or call a bricks-and-mortar computer store. Look through newspapers or magazines for retailers. Search the Web for an online store. Then, prepare a brief research paper (500-550 words) on the various options for the software application and recommend the one you believe is the best choice. Include at least two explanatory notes and three references, one of which must be a Web site on the Internet. Use the concepts and techniques presented in this project to format the paper.

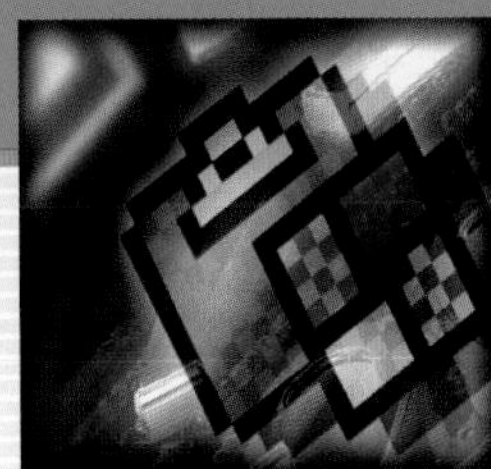

Microsoft Word 2002

PROJECT

Creating a Resume Using a Wizard and a Cover Letter with a Table

OBJECTIVES

You will have mastered the material in this project when you can:

- Create a resume using Word's Resume Wizard
- Identify the Word screen in print layout view
- Zoom text width
- Identify styles in a document
- Replace selected text with new text
- Insert a line break
- AutoFormat text as you type
- Use print preview to view and print a document
- Open a new document window
- Add color to characters
- Set and use tab stops
- Switch from one open Word document to another
- Collect and paste using the Clipboard task pane
- Add a bottom border to a paragraph
- Clear formatting
- Convert a hyperlink to regular text
- Identify the components of a business letter
- Insert the current date
- Create an AutoText entry
- Insert a nonbreaking space
- Insert an AutoText entry
- Insert a Word table
- Enter data into a Word table
- Format a Word table
- Create a bulleted list as you type
- Address and print an envelope

Allow me to introduce myself, my name is
Albert Einstein and I am seeking an associate
professor teaching position in the Physics
department. I believe my qualifications below
will speak for themselves and I look forward
to meeting with you about the teaching position
in the near future.
1902. Temporary teaching job
the Swiss Patent Office
the Swiss Patent Office in Bern.
Discovered the principle of equivalence
Appointment as lecturer at Bern University

Present Your Image

A Great Resume Makes Your Words Count

In 1905, a young physicist sought a teaching position at the university level. His handwritten resume included his educational background, his qualifications, and his personal interests. At that time, he had submitted his Ph.D thesis, which was awaiting acceptance. His works included papers on particle theory, quantum theory, and the special theory of relativity. He played the violin and sailed, and was a family man. Who was this young physicist?

Yes, he was Albert Einstein, who wrote by hand literally dozens of letters seeking employment as a teacher while he labored in relative obscurity at the Swiss patent office. The same year, he published three studies that set the world of science on its ear. Fame eventually helped, but persistence in his search paid off when he finally landed a teaching appointment at the University of Zurich after years as a patent clerk.

No one can tell whether Einstein might have met his goals more quickly if he would have had the benefit of modern word processing software, but certainly Microsoft Word would have made his life easier.

As you embark on your professional life, you have the advantage of using Word to prepare a resume and a personalized cover letter. In this project, you will learn these skills. Resume writing is important in directing the image you present to a potential employer. The stronger the skill and experience descriptions in your resume, the more likely you are to obtain interviews and salary offers. With employers receiving hundreds of resumes, it is vital to capture their attention quickly with a well-written document that matches your skills with the job you seek. Providing a personalized cover letter with each resume enables you to elaborate on positive points in your resume and gives you an opportunity to show a potential employer your written communications skills.

Using the Résumé Wizard creates a resume that is tailored to your preferences. The Wizard provides the style, formats the resume with appropriate headings and spacing, and makes it easy for you to present your best qualities.

If good guidelines exist for doing something, then why not use them? This same practicality is built into the Résumé Wizard. Word provides the tools that eliminate the need to start from scratch every time, while you provide responses and supply the substance.

To understand the importance of using these guidelines, consider the meaning of the word represent: to bring clearly before the mind. When creating letters and resumes, which are two elements of business life that are fundamental to success, it is critical to bring a favorable image to mind. These documents must be crisp, to the point, and good-looking, because usually they are the first glimpse a prospective employer gets of a job-seeker.

As you contemplate a career or a career move, present your image by identifying and promoting your top skills, and use a design that gets attention and content that sells. Then, think about the words of Oliver Wendell Holmes: "Every calling is great when greatly pursued."

Microsoft Word 2002

Creating a Resume Using a Wizard and a Cover Letter with a Table

PROJECT

CASE PERSPECTIVE

Tyrone James Carter recently graduated from North Carolina State with a bachelor's degree in social studies teaching. He plans to continue toward a master's degree in education and also obtain his North Carolina teaching certificate, so he can teach social studies at the high-school level. While continuing his education, he wants to work as a teacher's assistant. In the classified section of the *Herald Times*, Tyrone locates a social studies teacher's assistant position at Peterson High School. The ad requests a resume and an accompanying cover letter from all applicants. Tyrone has neither. Because you work in the school's Office of Career Development, Tyrone has asked you to help him create a professional resume and cover letter.

Based on your suggestion, Tyrone will use Word's Resume Wizard to create his resume. He will address the cover letter to Ms. Mae Li, personnel director at Peterson High School and include all essential business letter components. With Tyrone's solid background and your resume writing expertise, you create an effective package that should ensure his success in obtaining the position.

Introduction

At some time in your professional life, you will prepare a resume along with a personalized cover letter to send to a prospective employer(s). In addition to some personal information, a **resume** usually contains the applicant's educational background and job experience. Employers review many resumes for each vacant position. Thus, you should design your resume carefully so it presents you as the best candidate for the job. You also should attach a personalized cover letter to each resume you send. A **cover letter** enables you to elaborate on positive points in your resume; it also provides you with an opportunity to show a potential employer your written communication skills. Accordingly, it is important that your cover letter is written well and follows proper business letter rules.

Composing documents from scratch can be a difficult process for many people. To assist with this task, Word provides wizards and templates. A **wizard** asks you several basic questions and then uses a template to prepare and format a document for you based on your responses. A **template** is similar to a form with prewritten text; that is, Word prepares the requested document with text and/or formatting common to all documents of this nature. Once Word creates a document from a template, you then fill in the blanks or replace prewritten words in the document. In addition to wizards using templates, Word also provides many templates you can use to create documents. This project discusses how to use a wizard. Project 5 discusses creating a document directly from a template.

Project Three — Resume and Cover Letter

Tyrone James Carter, a recent college graduate, is seeking a full-time position as a teacher's assistant at a high school. Project 3 uses Word to produce his resume, shown in Figure 3-1, and a personalized cover letter and envelope, shown in Figure 3-2 on the next page.

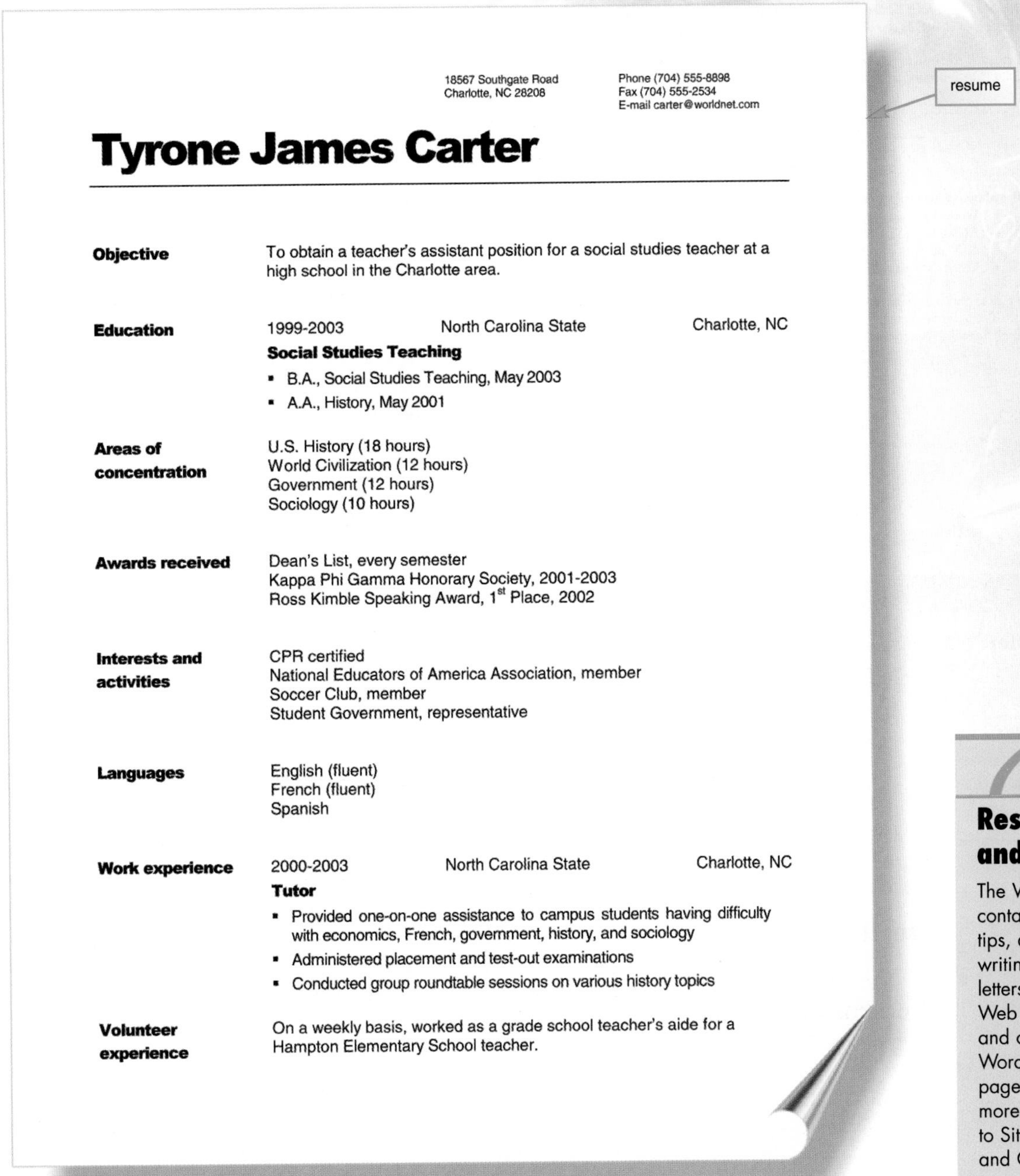

18567 Southgate Road
Charlotte, NC 28208

Phone (704) 555-8898
Fax (704) 555-2534
E-mail carter@worldnet.com

resume

Tyrone James Carter

Objective — To obtain a teacher's assistant position for a social studies teacher at a high school in the Charlotte area.

Education — 1999-2003 North Carolina State Charlotte, NC

Social Studies Teaching

- B.A., Social Studies Teaching, May 2003
- A.A., History, May 2001

Areas of concentration

U.S. History (18 hours)
World Civilization (12 hours)
Government (12 hours)
Sociology (10 hours)

Awards received

Dean's List, every semester
Kappa Phi Gamma Honorary Society, 2001-2003
Ross Kimble Speaking Award, 1st Place, 2002

Interests and activities

CPR certified
National Educators of America Association, member
Soccer Club, member
Student Government, representative

Languages

English (fluent)
French (fluent)
Spanish

Work experience — 2000-2003 North Carolina State Charlotte, NC

Tutor

- Provided one-on-one assistance to campus students having difficulty with economics, French, government, history, and sociology
- Administered placement and test-out examinations
- Conducted group roundtable sessions on various history topics

Volunteer experience — On a weekly basis, worked as a grade school teacher's aide for a Hampton Elementary School teacher.

FIGURE 3-1

More About

Resumes and Cover Letters

The World Wide Web contains a host of information, tips, and suggestions on writing resumes and cover letters. For a list of links to Web sites on writing resumes and cover letters, visit the Word 2002 More About Web page (scsite.com/wd2002/more.htm) and then click Links to Sites on Writing Resumes and Cover Letters.

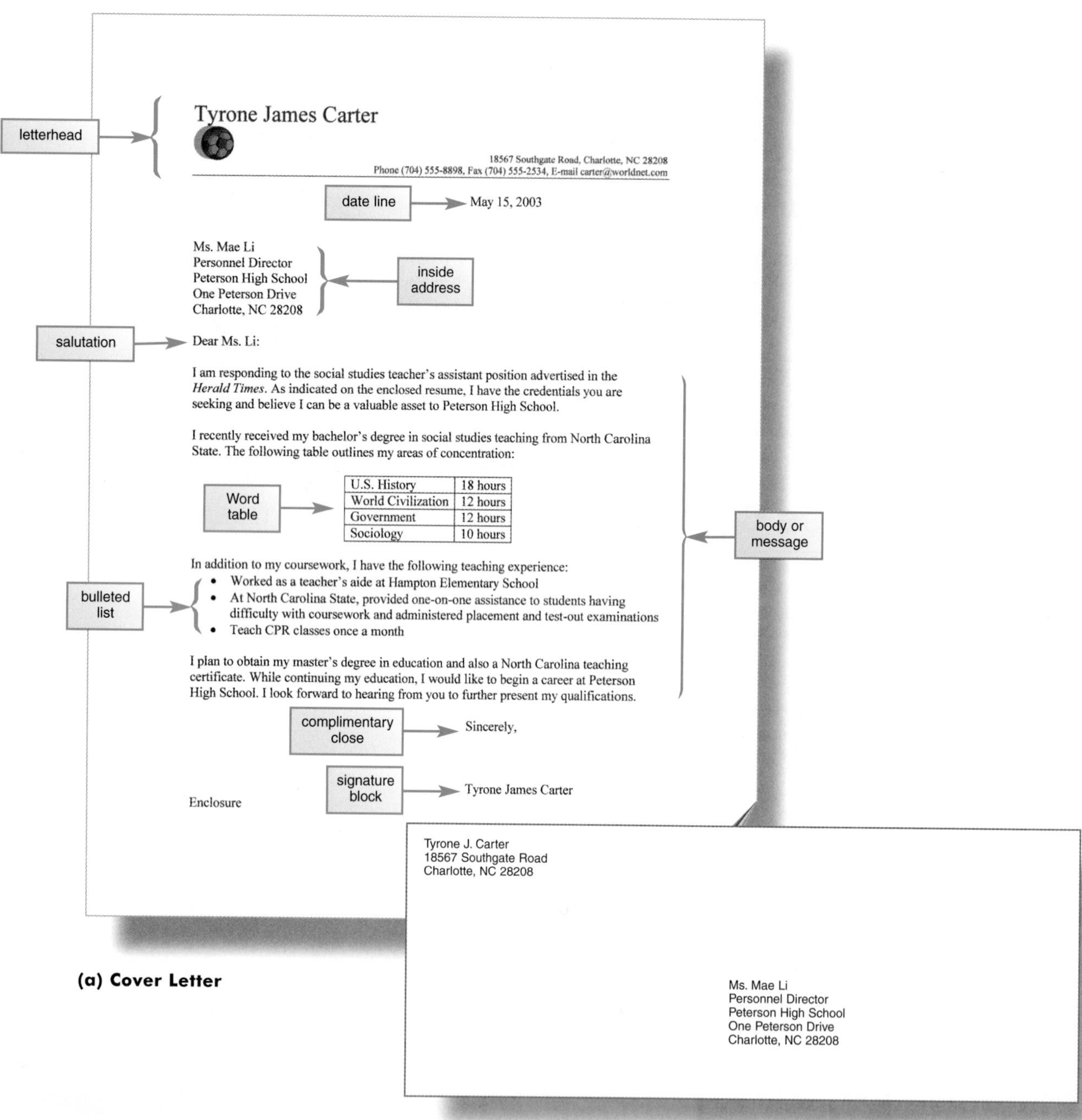
Tyrone James Carter

18567 Southgate Road, Charlotte, NC 28208
Phone (704) 555-8898, Fax (704) 555-2534, E-mail carter@worldnet.com

May 15, 2003

Ms. Mae Li
Personnel Director
Peterson High School
One Peterson Drive
Charlotte, NC 28208

Dear Ms. Li:

I am responding to the social studies teacher's assistant position advertised in the *Herald Times*. As indicated on the enclosed resume, I have the credentials you are seeking and believe I can be a valuable asset to Peterson High School.

I recently received my bachelor's degree in social studies teaching from North Carolina State. The following table outlines my areas of concentration:

U.S. History	18 hours
World Civilization	12 hours
Government	12 hours
Sociology	10 hours

In addition to my coursework, I have the following teaching experience:

- Worked as a teacher's aide at Hampton Elementary School
- At North Carolina State, provided one-on-one assistance to students having difficulty with coursework and administered placement and test-out examinations
- Teach CPR classes once a month

I plan to obtain my master's degree in education and also a North Carolina teaching certificate. While continuing my education, I would like to begin a career at Peterson High School. I look forward to hearing from you to further present my qualifications.

Sincerely,

Tyrone James Carter

Enclosure

Tyrone J. Carter
18567 Southgate Road
Charlotte, NC 28208

Ms. Mae Li
Personnel Director
Peterson High School
One Peterson Drive
Charlotte, NC 28208

(a) Cover Letter

(b) Envelope

FIGURE 3-2

More About

Business Letters

A finished business letter should look like a symmetrically framed picture with evenly-spaced margins, all balanced below an attractive letterhead. In addition, the contents of the letter should contain proper grammar, correct spelling, logically constructed sentences, flowing paragraphs, and sound ideas.

Starting Word

Perform the following steps to start Word, or ask your instructor how to start Word for your system.

TO START AND CUSTOMIZE WORD

1. Click the Start button on the Windows taskbar, point to Programs on the Start menu, and then click Microsoft Word on the Programs submenu.
2. If the Word window is not maximized, double-click its title bar to maximize it.
3. If the Language bar displays on the screen, click its Minimize button.
4. If the New Document task pane displays in the Word window, click the Show at startup check box to remove the check mark and then click the Close button in the upper-right corner of the task pane title bar.
5. If the toolbars display positioned on the same row, click the Toolbar Options button and then click Show Buttons on Two Rows.
6. If your screen differs from Figure 3-3 on the next page, click View on the menu bar and then click Normal.

Office starts Word. After a few moments, an empty document displays in the Word window (shown in Figure 3-3 on the next page).

More About

Job Searches

The World Wide Web has several sites that assist you in locating a job. For a list of links to Web sites on job searches, visit the Word 2002 More About Web page (scsite.com/wd2002/more.htm) and then click Links to Sites on Job Searches.

Resetting Menus and Toolbars

To set the menus and toolbars so they appear exactly as shown in this book, you should reset your menus and toolbars as outlined in Appendix D or follow these steps.

TO RESET MENUS AND TOOLBARS

1. Click the Toolbar Options button on the Standard toolbar and then point to Add or Remove Buttons. Point to Standard on the Add or Remove Buttons submenu. Scroll to and then click Reset Toolbar on the Standard submenu.
2. Click the Toolbar Options button on the Formatting toolbar and then point to Add or Remove Buttons. Point to Formatting on the Add or Remove Buttons submenu. Scroll to and then click Reset Toolbar on the Formatting submenu.
3. Click the Toolbar Options button on the Standard toolbar and then point to Add or Remove Buttons. Click Customize on the Add or Remove Buttons submenu.
4. When the Customize dialog box displays, if necessary, click the Options tab and then click the Reset my usage data button. When the Microsoft Word dialog box displays, click the Yes button. Click the Close button in the Customize dialog box.

Word resets the menus and toolbars.

Displaying Formatting Marks

As discussed in Project 1, it is helpful to display formatting marks that indicate where in the document you pressed the ENTER key, SPACEBAR, and other keys. Perform the following step to display formatting marks.

TO DISPLAY FORMATTING MARKS

1. If the Show/Hide ¶ button on the Standard toolbar is not already selected, click it.

Word displays formatting marks in the document window, and the Show/Hide ¶ button on the Standard toolbar is selected (shown in Figure 3-3 on the next page).

More About

Wizards and Templates

Once you have created a document using a wizard or template, Word displays the wizard or template name in the New from template area in the New Document task pane. Thus, your Figure 3-4 may differ from the one shown below. In addition to those installed on your hard disk, Microsoft has more wizards and templates available on the Web that you can download. To do this, click Templates on Microsoft.com in the New from template area in the New Document task pane.

Using Word's Resume Wizard to Create a Resume

You can type a resume from scratch into a blank document window, or you can use the **Resume Wizard** and let Word format the resume with appropriate headings and spacing. Then, you can customize the resulting resume by filling in the blanks or selecting and replacing text.

When you use a wizard, Word displays a dialog box with the wizard's name on its title bar. A wizard's dialog box displays a list of **panel names** along its left side with the currently selected panel displaying on the right side of the dialog box (Figure 3-6). Each panel presents a different set of options, in which you select preferences or enter text. To move from one panel to the next within the wizard's dialog box, you click the Next button or click the panel name on the left side of the dialog box.

Perform the following steps to create a resume using the Resume Wizard. A wizard retains the settings selected by the last person who used the wizard. Thus, some selections on your screen initially may display differently from the figures shown here. Be sure to verify that your settings match the screens shown in the following steps before clicking the Next button in each dialog box.

Steps To Create a Resume Using Word's Resume Wizard

1 Click File on the menu bar and then point to New (Figure 3-3).

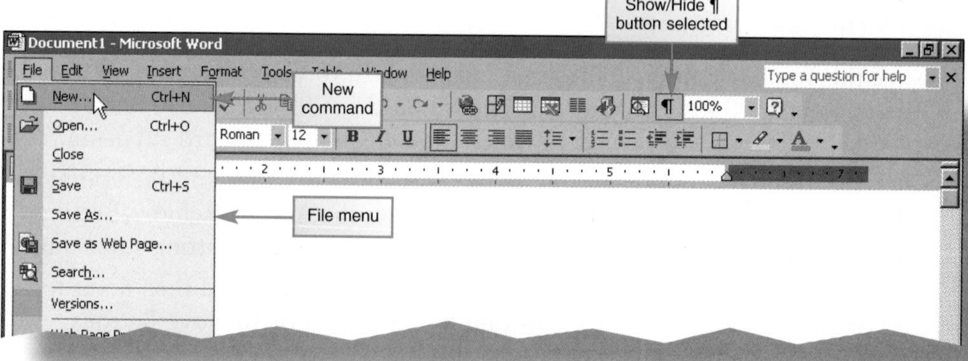

FIGURE 3-3

2 Click New. When the New Document task pane displays, point to General Templates in the New from template area.

Word displays the New Document task pane (Figure 3-4). You access wizards through the General Templates dialog box.

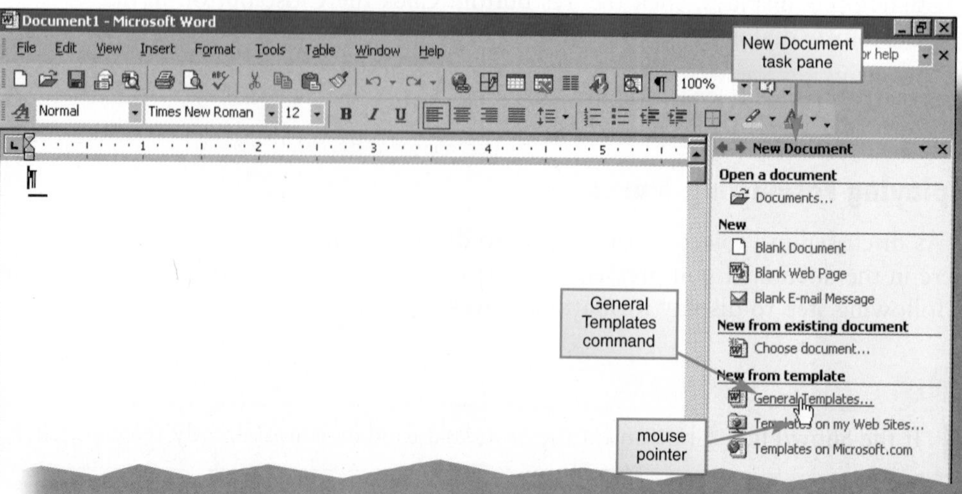

FIGURE 3-4

3 Click General Templates. If necessary, click the Other Documents tab when the Templates dialog box displays. Click the Resume Wizard icon.

Office displays several wizard and template icons in the Other Documents sheet in the Templates dialog box (Figure 3-5). Icons without the word, wizard, are templates. If you click an icon, a sample of the resulting document displays in the Preview area.

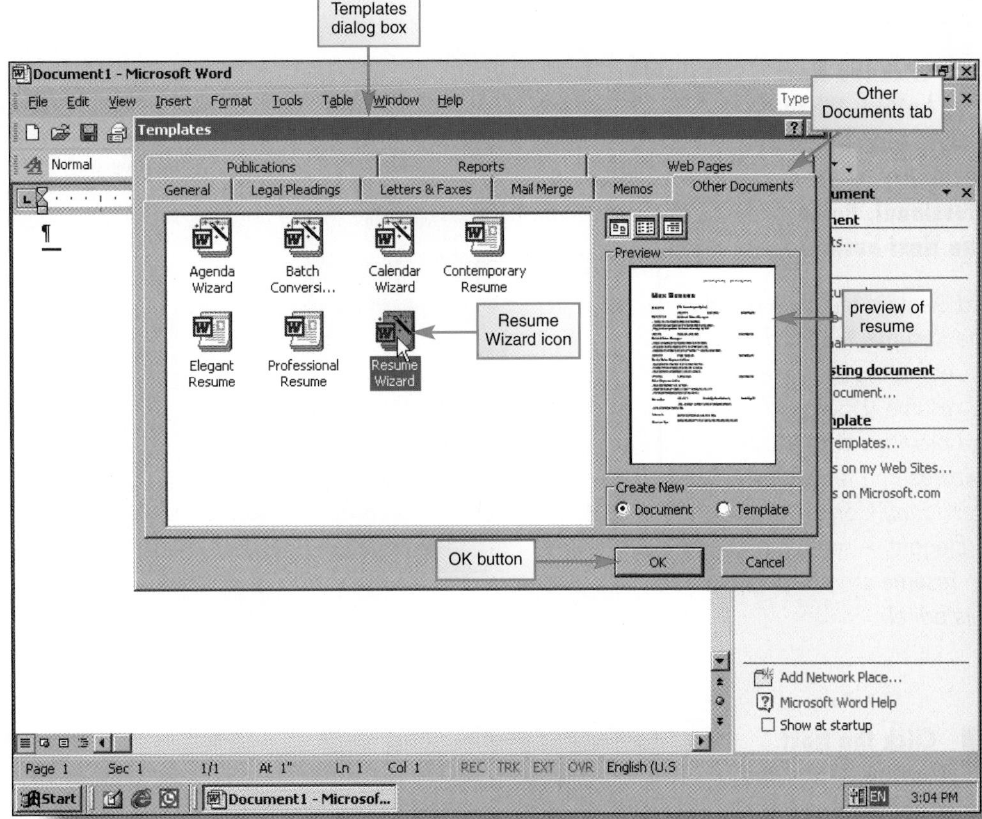

FIGURE 3-5

4 Click the OK button. When the Resume Wizard dialog box displays, point to the Next button.

After a few seconds, Word displays the Start panel *of the Resume Wizard dialog box, informing you the Resume Wizard has started (Figure 3-6). This dialog box has a* Microsoft Word Help button *you can click to obtain help while using this wizard. When you create a document based on a wizard, Word creates a new document window, which is called Document2 in this figure.*

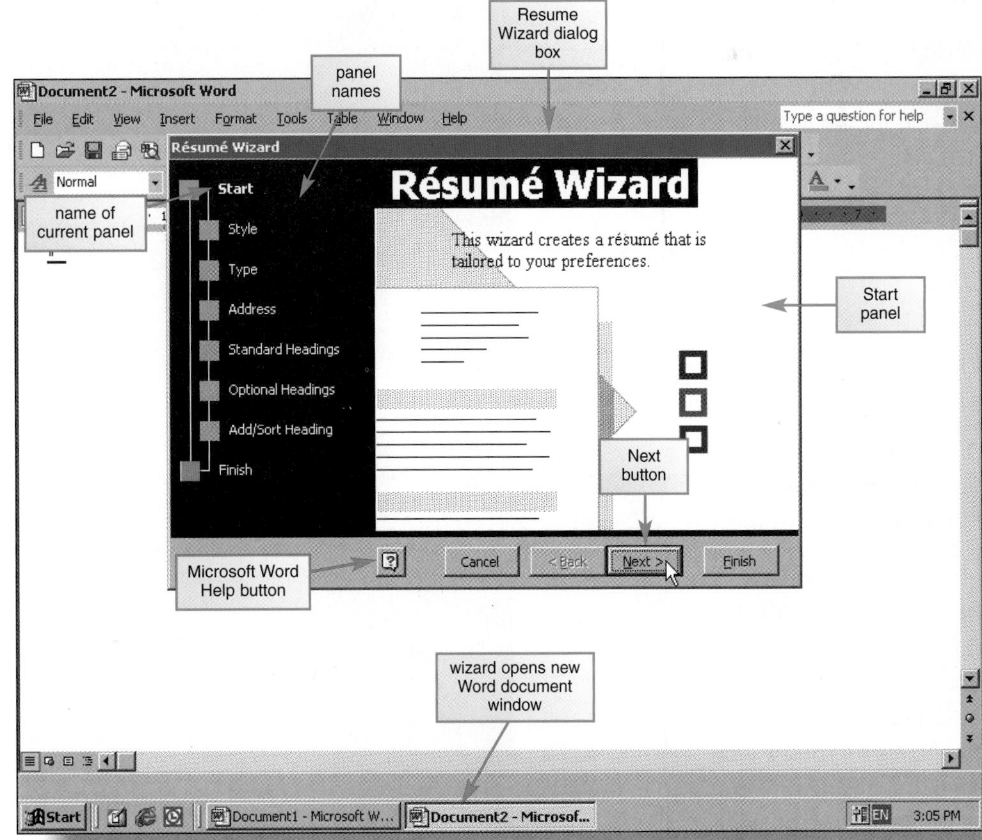

FIGURE 3-6

5 Click the Next button. When the Style panel displays, if necessary, click Professional. Point to the Next button.

*Word displays the **Style panel** in the Resume Wizard dialog box, requesting the style of your resume (Figure 3-7). Word provides three styles of wizards and templates: Professional, Contemporary, and Elegant. A sample of each resume style displays in this panel.*

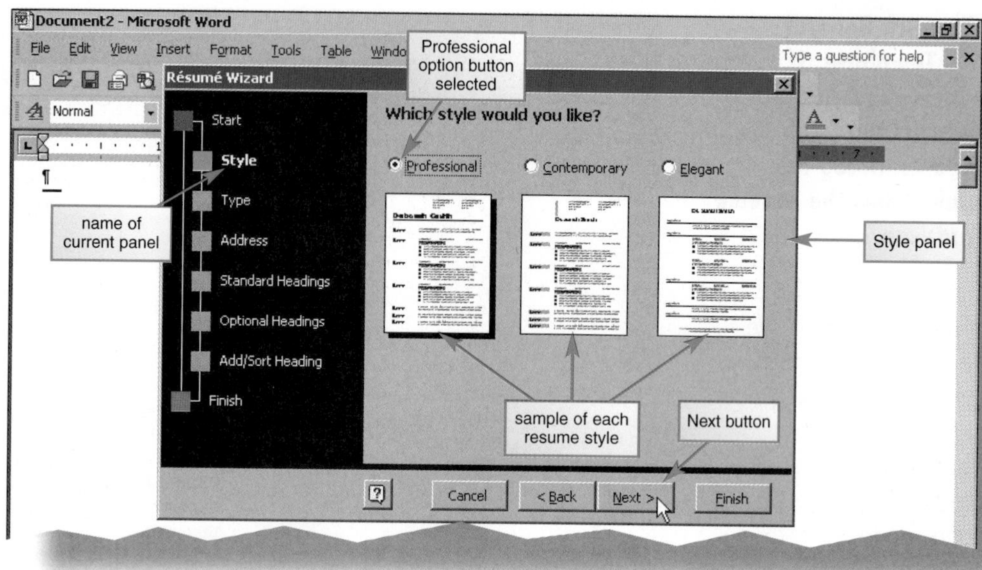

FIGURE 3-7

6 Click the Next button. When the Type panel displays, if necessary, click Entry-level resume. Point to the Next button.

*Word displays the **Type panel** in the Resume Wizard dialog box, asking for the type of resume that you want to create (Figure 3-8).*

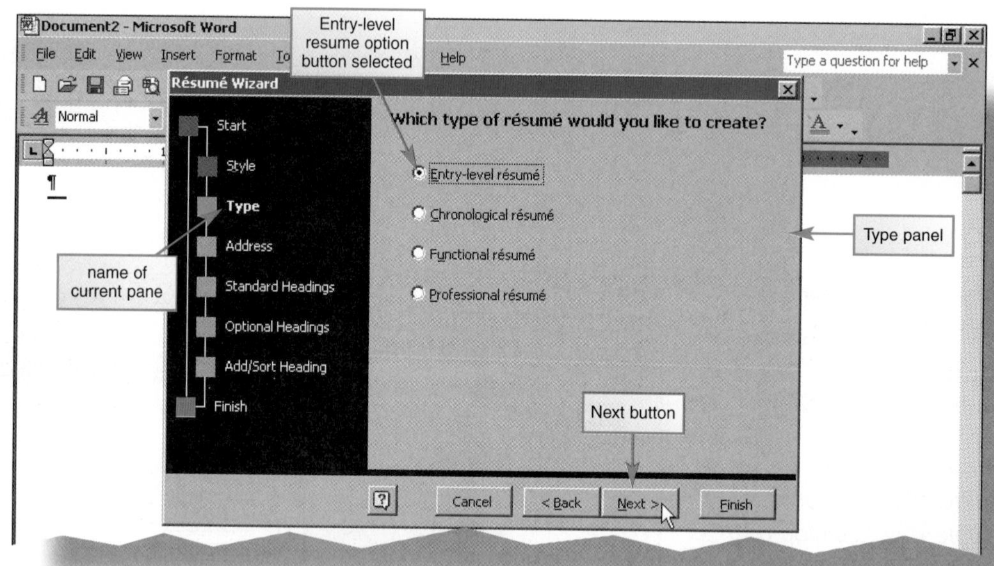

FIGURE 3-8

7 Click the Next button.

*Word displays the **Address panel** in the Resume Wizard dialog box, with the name selected (Figure 3-9). The name displayed and selected in your Name text box will be different, depending on the name of the last person who used the Resume Wizard.*

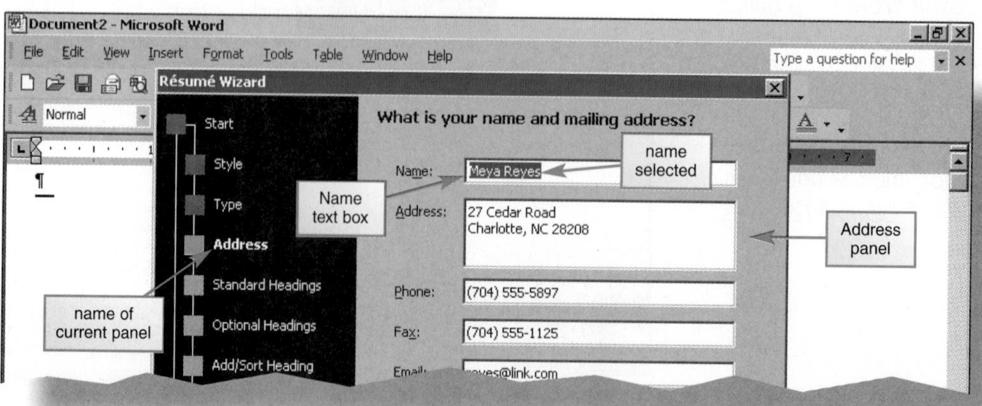

FIGURE 3-9

8 **With the name in the Name text box selected, type** `Tyrone James Carter` **and then press the TAB key. Type** `18567 Southgate Road` **and then press the ENTER key. Type** `Charlotte, NC 28208` **and then press the TAB key. Type** `(704) 555-8898` **and then press the TAB key. Type** `(704) 555-2534` **and then press the TAB key. Type** `carter@worldnet.com` **and then point to the Next button.**

As you type the new text, it automatically replaces the selected text (Figure 3-10).

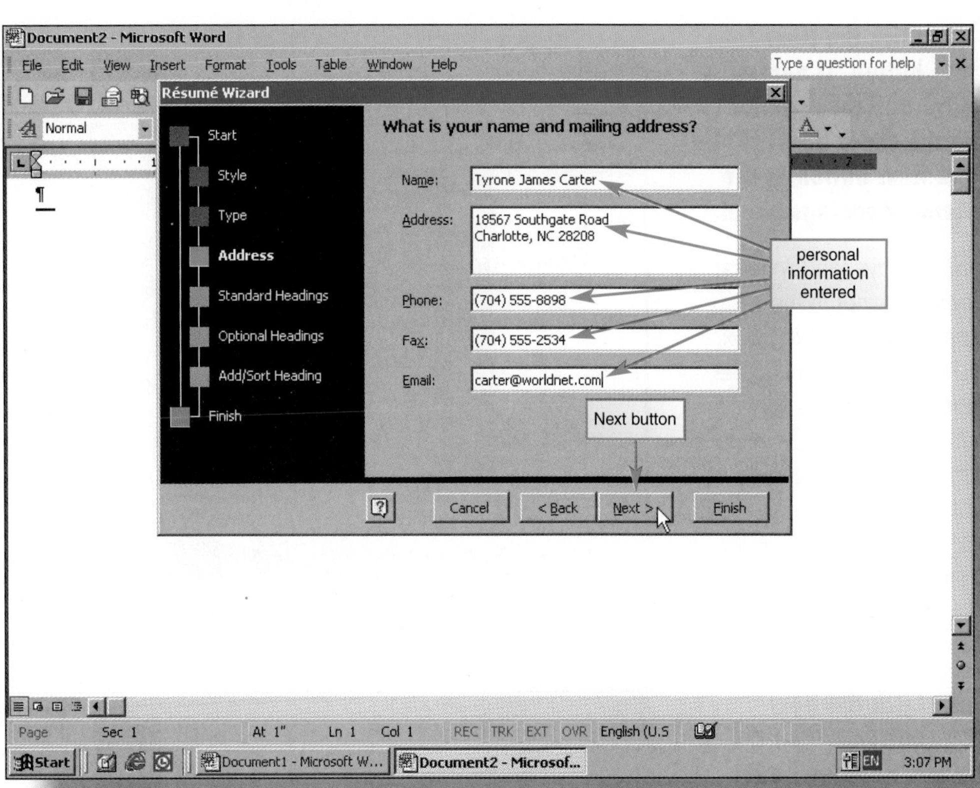

FIGURE 3-10

9 **Click the Next button. When the Standard Headings panel displays, if necessary, click Hobbies and References to remove the check marks. All other check boxes should have check marks. If any do not, place a check mark in the check box by clicking it. Point to the Next button.**

Word displays the ***Standard Headings panel*** *in the Resume Wizard dialog box, which requests the headings you want on your resume (Figure 3-11). You want all headings, except for these two: Hobbies and References.*

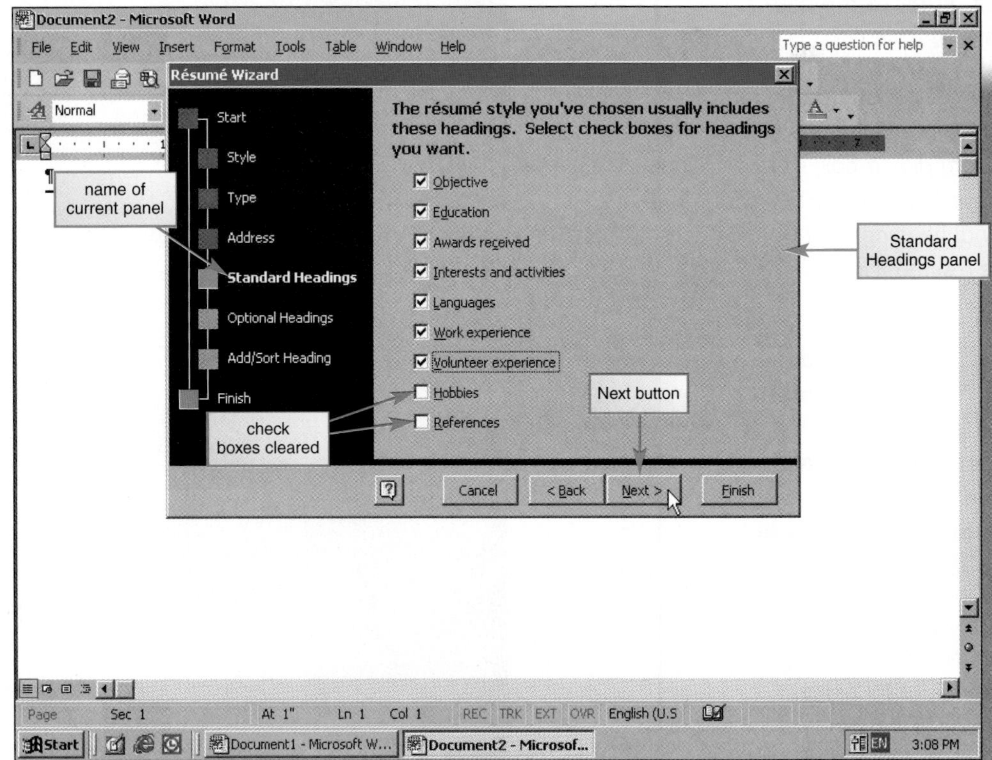

FIGURE 3-11

10 **Click the Next button. If necessary, remove any check marks from the check boxes. Point to the Next button in the Optional Headings panel.**

Word displays the Optional Headings panel in the Resume Wizard dialog box, which allows you to choose additional headings for your resume (Figure 3-12). All of these check boxes should be empty because none of these headings is required on the resume.

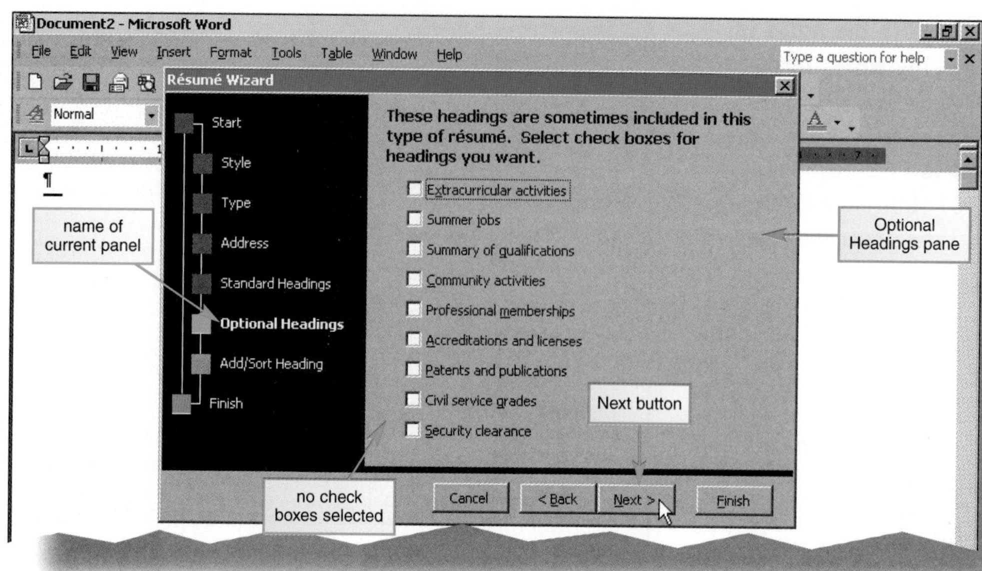

FIGURE 3-12

11 **Click the Next button. When the Add/Sort Heading panel displays, type** `Areas of concentration` **in the additional headings text box. Point to the Add button.**

Word displays the Add/Sort Heading panel in the Resume Wizard dialog box, which allows you to enter any additional headings you want on the resume (Figure 3-13).

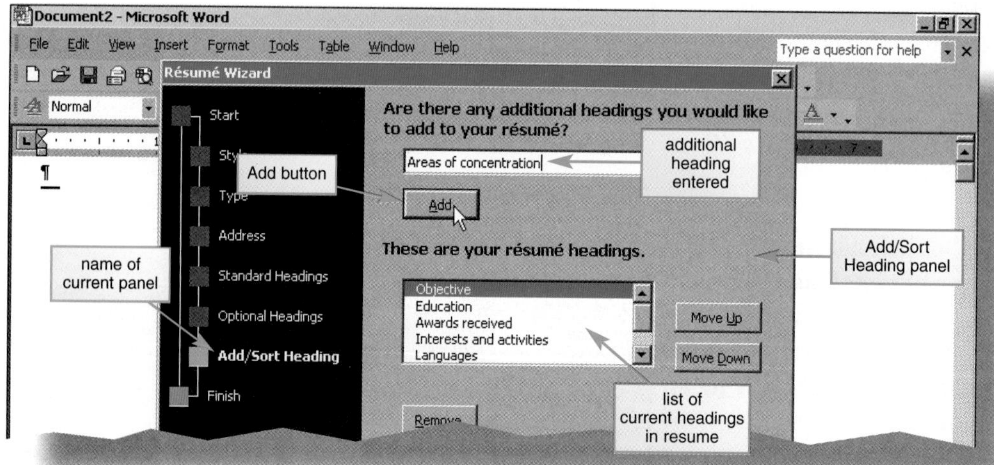

FIGURE 3-13

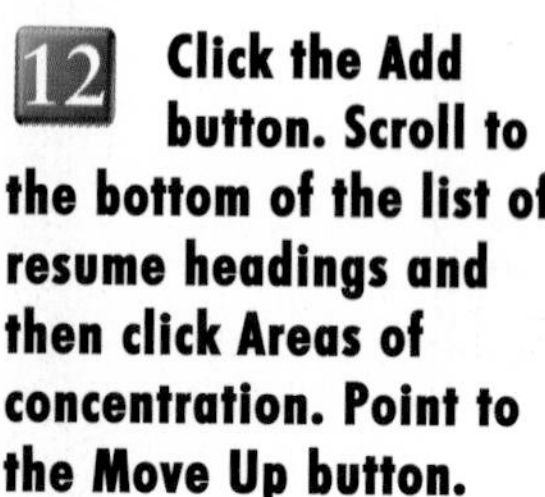

12 **Click the Add button. Scroll to the bottom of the list of resume headings and then click Areas of concentration. Point to the Move Up button.**

Word selects the Areas of concentration heading (Figure 3-14). You can rearrange the order of the headings on your resume by selecting a heading and then clicking the appropriate button (Move Up button or Move Down button).

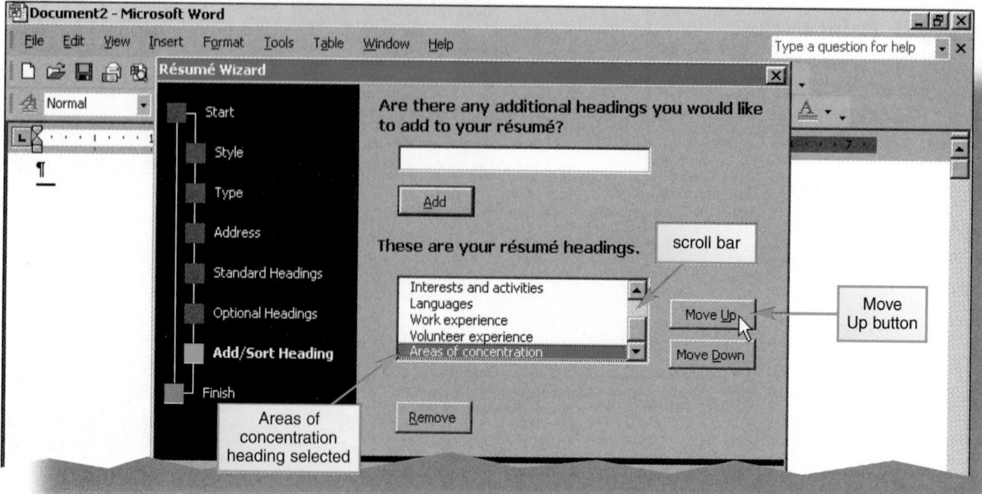

FIGURE 3-14

13 Click the Move Up button five times.

Word moves the heading, Areas of concentration, above the Awards received heading (Figure 3-15).

14 If the last person using the Resume Wizard included additional headings, you may have some unwanted headings. Your heading list should be as follows: Objective, Education, Areas of concentration, Awards received, Interests and activities, Languages, Work experience, and Volunteer experience. If you have an additional heading(s), click the unwanted heading and then click the Remove button.

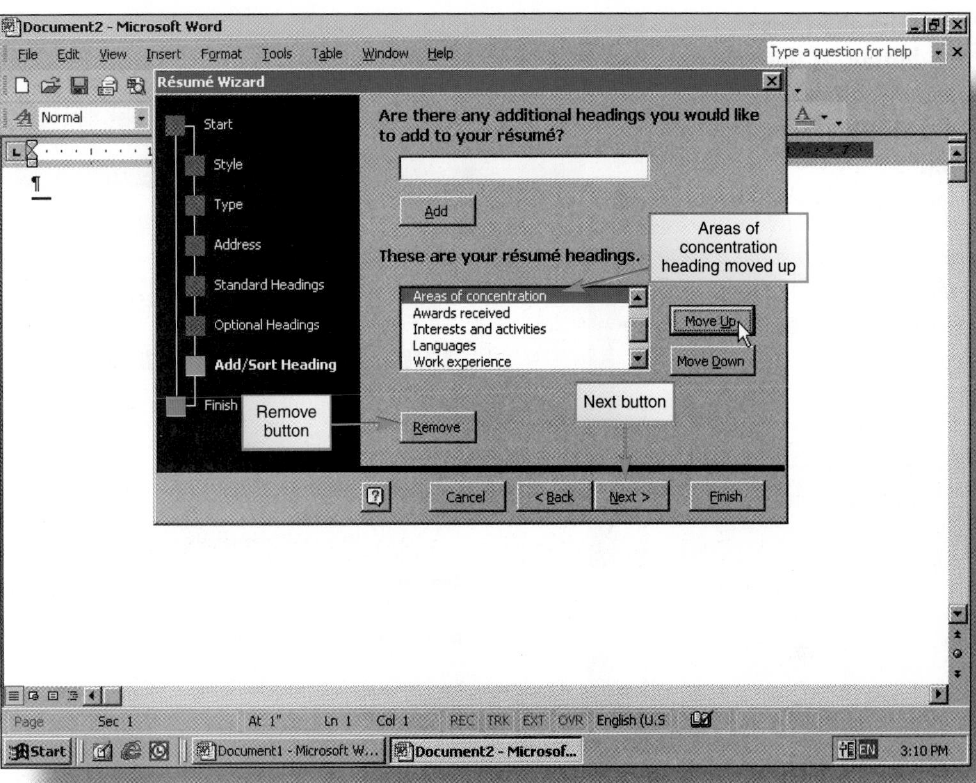

FIGURE 3-15

15 Click the Next button. When the Finish panel displays, point to the Finish button.

Word displays the Finish panel *in the Resume Wizard dialog box, which indicates the wizard is ready to create your document (Figure 3-16).*

FIGURE 3-16

16 Click the Finish button. If the Office Assistant displays on the screen, click its Cancel button.

Word creates an entry-level professional style resume layout (Figure 3-17). You are to personalize the resume as indicated.

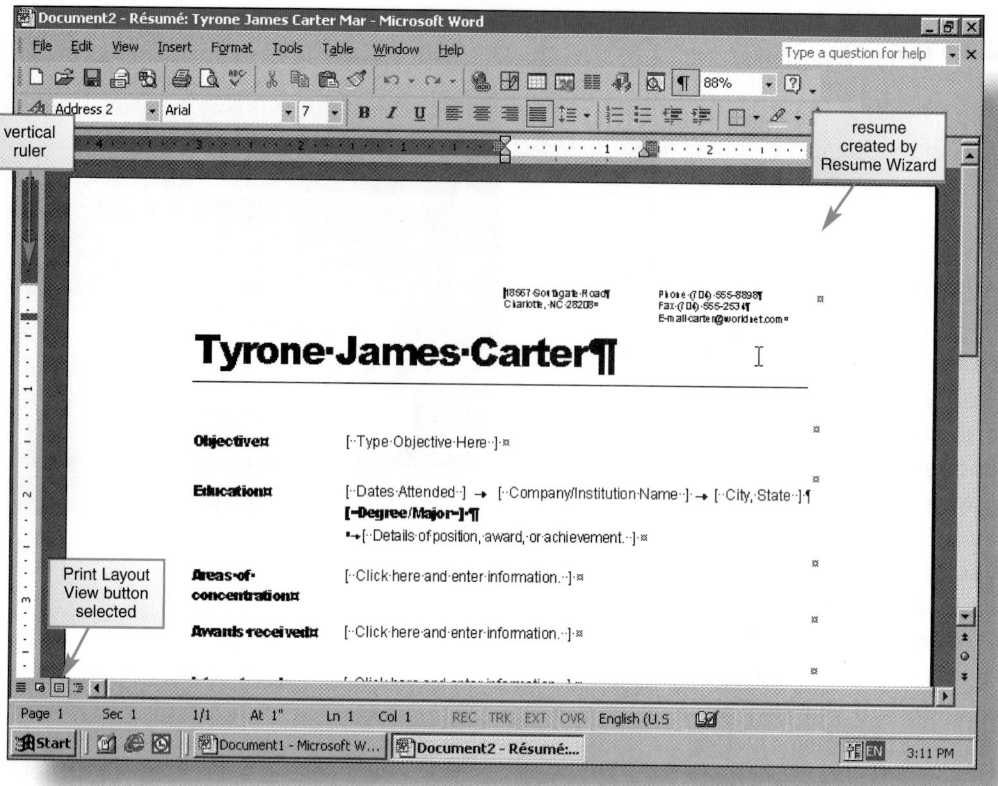

FIGURE 3-17

Other Ways

1. On View menu click Task Pane, click Other Task Panes button on task pane title bar and then click New Document, click General Templates, click Other Documents tab, double-click Resume Wizard icon
2. Click Start button on Windows taskbar, click New Office Document, click Other Documents tab, double-click Resume Wizard icon
3. Right-click Start button on Windows taskbar, click Open All Users, double-click New Office Document, click Other Documents tab, double-click Resume Wizard icon
4. With task pane displaying, in Voice Command mode, say "General Templates, Other Documents, [select Resume Wizard], OK"

Program Buttons

If the Windows taskbar does not display a separate program button for each open Word document, click Tools on the menu bar, click Options, click the View tab, place a check mark in the Windows in Taskbar check box, and then click the OK button.

When you create a resume using the Resume Wizard (Figure 3-16 on the previous page), you can click the panel name or the Back button in any panel of the Resume Wizard dialog box to change the previous options you selected. To exit from the Resume Wizard and return to the document window without creating the resume, click the Cancel button in any panel of the Resume Wizard dialog box.

In addition to the Resume Wizard, Word provides many other wizards to assist you in creating documents: agenda for a meeting, calendar, envelope, fax cover sheet, legal pleading, letter, mailing label, memorandum, and Web page.

Word displays the resume in the document window in print layout view. You can tell that the document window is in print layout view by looking at the screen (Figure 3-17 above). In print layout view, the **Print Layout View button** on the horizontal scroll bar is selected. Also, a **vertical ruler** displays at the left edge of the document window, in addition to the horizontal ruler at the top of the window.

Your screen was in normal view when you created documents in Project 1 and for most of Project 2. In Project 2, when you created the header, the window switched to print layout view. In both normal view and print layout view, you can type and edit text. The difference is that **print layout view** shows you an exact view of the printed page. That is, in print layout view, Word places the entire piece of paper in the document window, showing precisely the positioning of the text, margins, headers, footers, and footnotes.

To display more of the document on the screen in print layout view, you can hide the white space at the top and bottom of the pages and the gray space between pages. Perform the following steps to hide the white space, if your screen displays it.

Steps To Hide White Space

1 **Point to the top of the page in the document window until the Hide White Space button displays.**

The mouse pointer changes to the Hide White Space button when positioned at the top of the page (Figure 3-18).

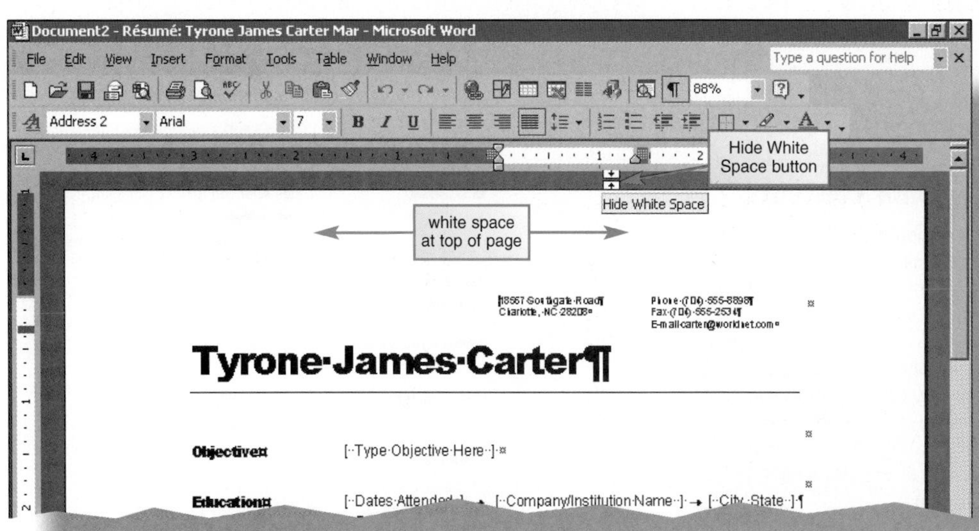

FIGURE 3-18

2 **Click the Hide White Space button.**

Word moves the page up in the document window (Figure 3-19).

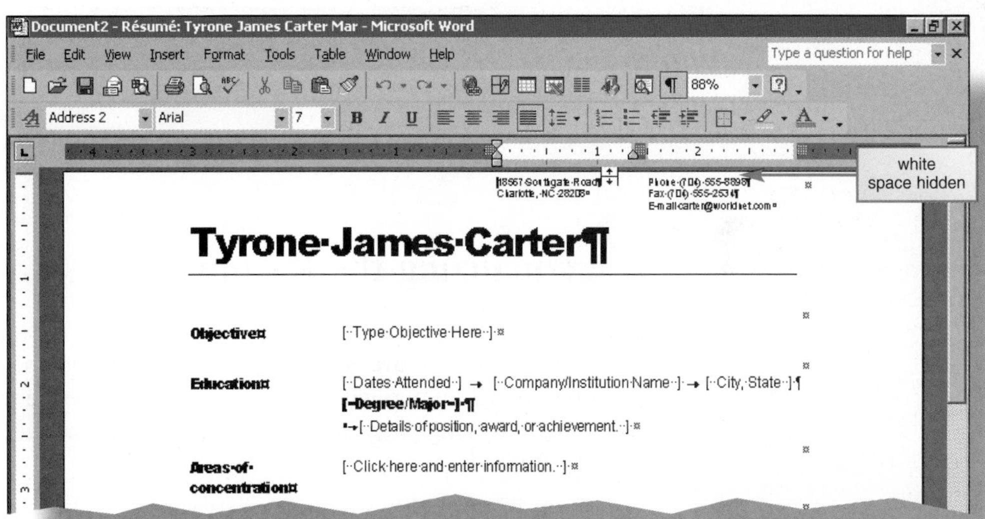

FIGURE 3-19

To see the entire resume created by the Resume Wizard, you should print the document that displays in the Word window, as described in the following steps.

TO PRINT THE RESUME CREATED BY THE RESUME WIZARD

1 Ready the printer and then click the Print button on the Standard toolbar.

2 When the printer stops, retrieve the hard copy resume from the printer.

The printed resume is shown in Figure 3-20 on the next page.

More About

Hiding White Space

If you want Word always to hide white space, click Tools on the menu bar, click Options, click the View tab, remove the check mark from the White space between pages check box, and then click the OK button. This command is available only when the Word screen is in print layout view.

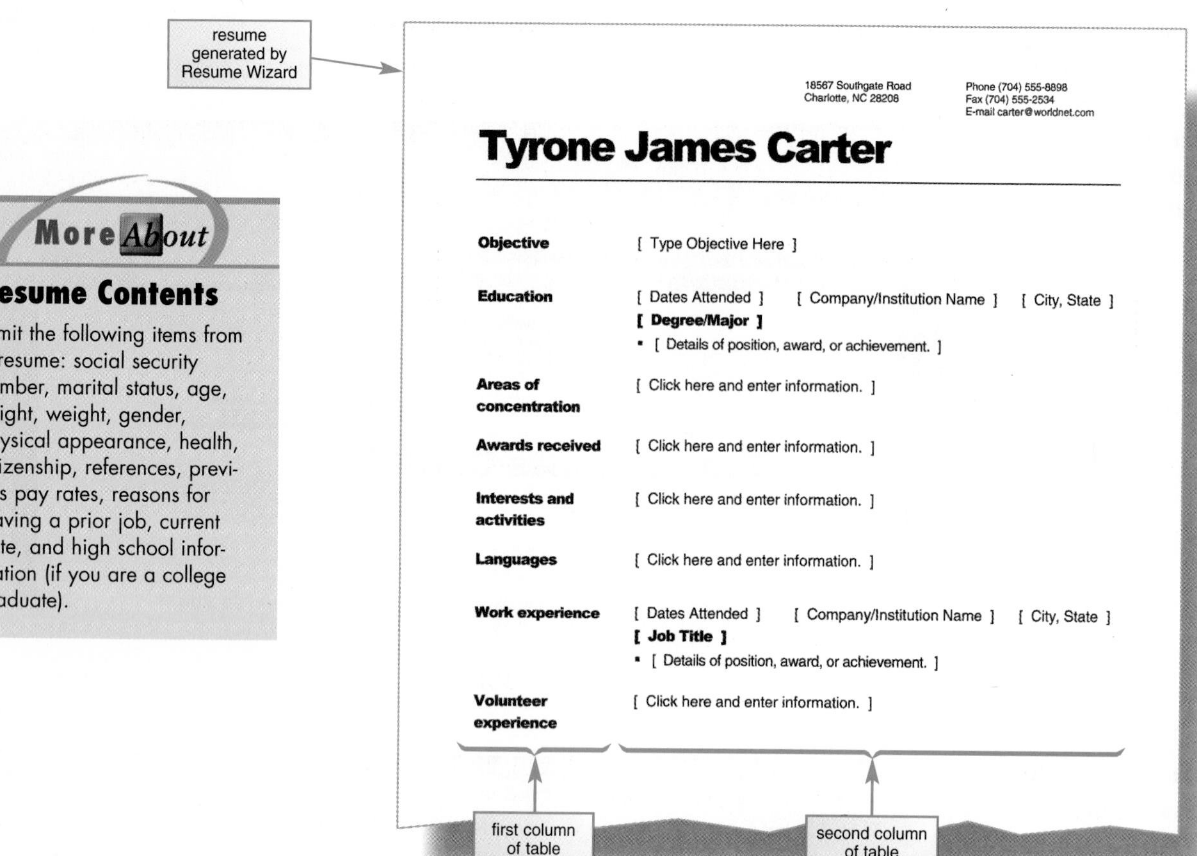

FIGURE 3-20

More About

Resume Contents

Omit the following items from a resume: social security number, marital status, age, height, weight, gender, physical appearance, health, citizenship, references, previous pay rates, reasons for leaving a prior job, current date, and high school information (if you are a college graduate).

Personalizing the Resume

The next step is to personalize the resume. Where Word has indicated, you type the objective, education, areas of concentration, awards received, interests and activities, languages, work experience, and volunteer experience next to the respective headings. The following pages show how to personalize the resume generated by the Resume Wizard.

Tables

When the Resume Wizard prepares a resume, it arranges the body of the resume as a table. A Word **table** is a collection of rows and columns. As shown in Figure 3-21, the first column of the table in the resume contains the section headings (Objective, Education, Areas of concentration, Awards received, Interests and activities, Languages, Work experience, and Volunteer experience). The second column of the table contains the details for each of these sections. Thus, this table contains two columns. It also contains eight rows — one row for each section of the resume.

The intersection of a row and a column is called a **cell**, and cells are filled with text. Each cell has an **end-of-cell mark**, which is a formatting mark that assists you with selecting and formatting cells. Recall that formatting marks do not print on a hard copy.

More About

Tables

To select a single cell in a table, click to the left of the cell. To select an entire row, click to the left of the row. To select an entire column, click the column's top border. To add a row or column to the middle of a table, click where you want to insert the row or column, click Table on the menu bar, point to Insert, and then click the appropriate command.

To see clearly the rows, columns, and cells in a Word table, some users prefer to show gridlines. As illustrated in Figure 3-21, **gridlines** help identify the rows and columns in a table. If you want to display gridlines in a table, position the insertion point somewhere in the table, click Table on the menu bar, and then click **Show Gridlines.** If you want to hide the gridlines, click somewhere in the table, click Table on the menu bar, and then click **Hide Gridlines.**

More About

The Ruler

When the insertion point is in a table, the ruler shows the boundaries of each column in the table. For example, in Figure 3-21, the address information at the top of the resume is a separate table of one row and two columns. The ruler shows the width of each column.

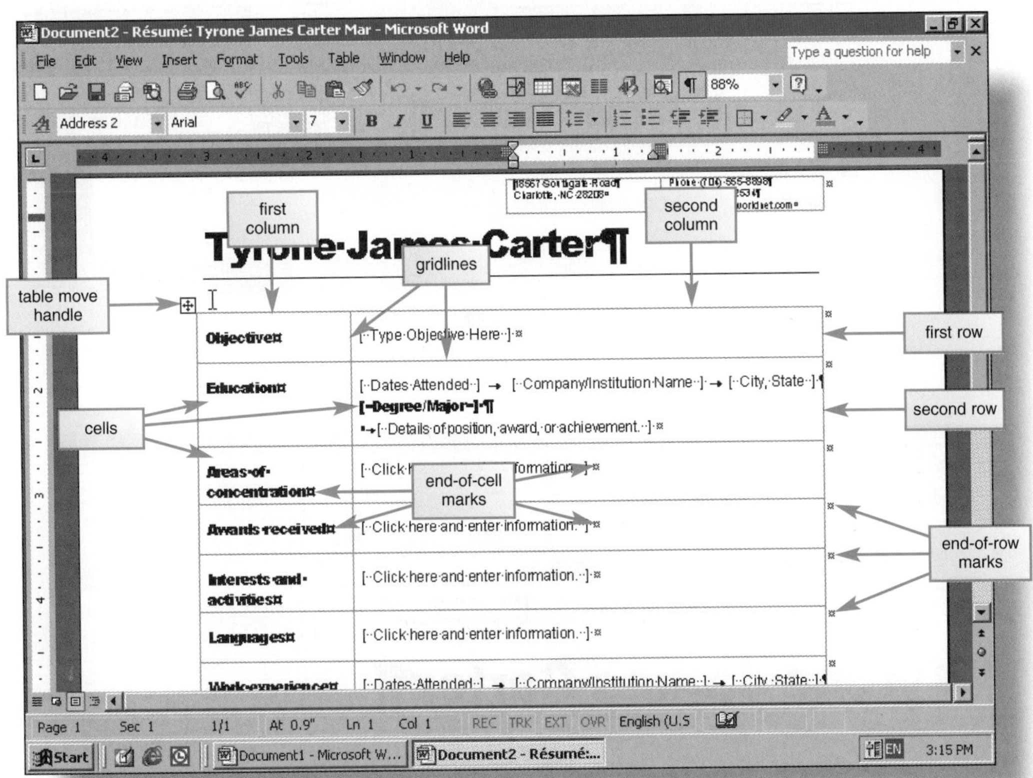

FIGURE 3-21

When you point to the upper-left corner of the table, the table move handle displays. You drag the **table move handle** to move the table to a new location. You also can resize a table, add or delete rows or columns in a table, and format a table. These and other features of tables are discussed in more depth when you create the cover letter later in this project.

Zooming Text Width

In Projects 1 and 2, your screen was in normal view and you used the zoom page width command to display text on the screen as large as possible without extending the right margin beyond the right edge of the document window. In print layout view, the zoom page width command places the edges of the paper at the margins — making the text smaller on the screen. To make the text as large as possible on the screen in print layout view, you should **zoom text width** as shown in the steps on the next page.

Zooming

If you have a Microsoft IntelliMouse®, you can zoom in and out of a document by holding the CTRL key while rotating the wheel forward or backward. To learn other features of the IntelliMouse®, click the Start button on the taskbar, point to Programs, point to Microsoft Hardware, point to Mouse, and then click Online User's Guide.

Steps To Zoom Text Width

1 Click the Zoom box arrow on the Standard toolbar and then point to Text Width in the Zoom list (Figure 3-22).

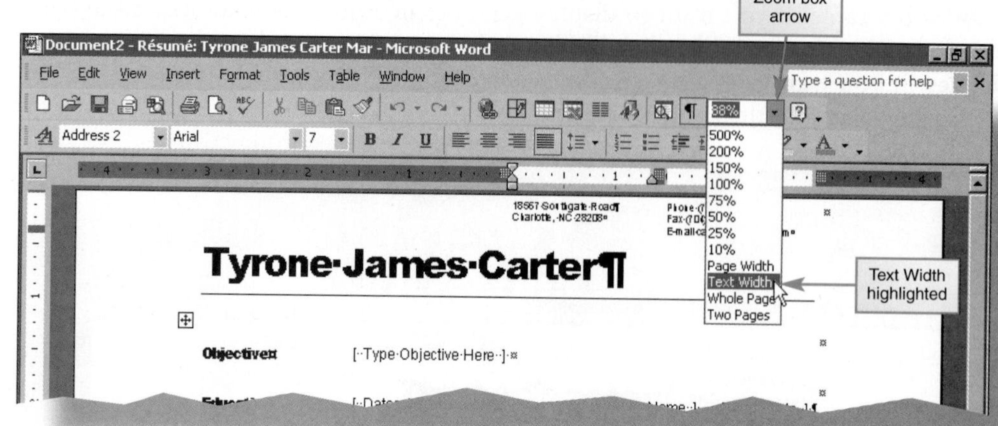

FIGURE 3-22

2 Click Text Width.

Word extends the text to the edges of the document window (Figure 3-23).

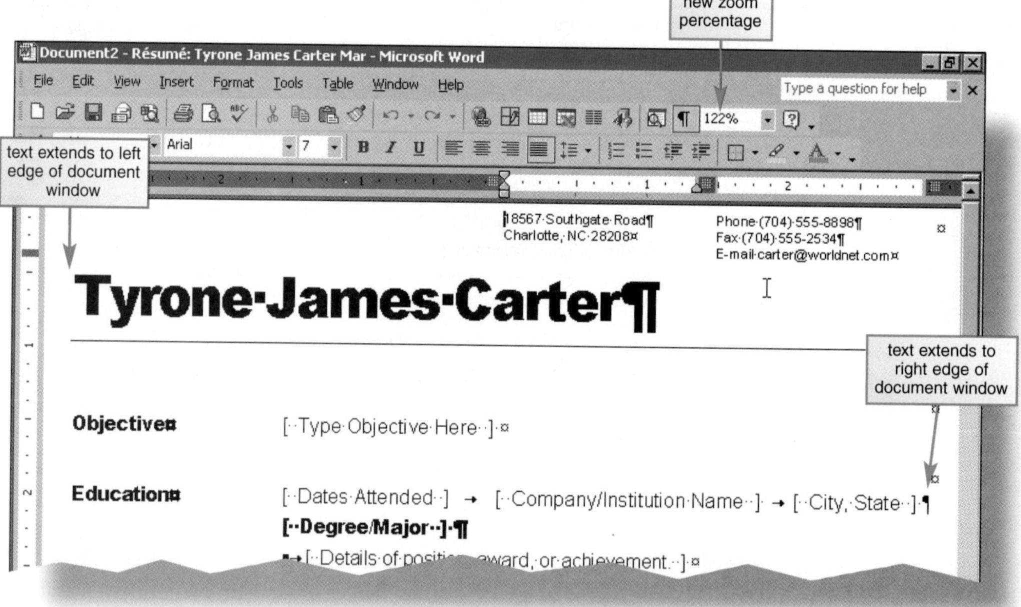

FIGURE 3-23

Other Ways

1. On View menu click Zoom, select Text Width, click OK button
2. In Voice Command mode, say "Zoom, Text Width"

Word computes a zoom percentage based on a variety of settings. The percentage that displays in your Zoom box may be different, depending on your system configuration. Notice in Figure 3-22 above that the Zoom list contains more options when the document window is in print layout view than when it is in normal view.

Styles

When you use a wizard to create a document, Word formats the document using styles. As discussed in Project 2, a **style** is a named group of formatting characteristics that you can apply to text. Recall that the formats defined by a style include character formatting, such as the font and font size; paragraph formatting, such as line spacing and text alignment; table formatting; and list formatting. In Project 2, you changed the formats assigned to the Footnote Text style.

The Style box on the Formatting toolbar displays the name of the style associated with the location of the insertion point or selection. You can identify many of the characteristics assigned to a style by looking at the Formatting toolbar. For example, in Figure 3-24 below, the characters in the selected paragraph are formatted with the Objective style, which uses 10-point Arial font.

If you click the Style box arrow on the Formatting toolbar, the list of styles associated with the current document displays. You also may select the appropriate style from the Style list before typing the text so that the text you type will be formatted according to the selected style.

Another way to work with styles is by clicking the Styles and Formatting button on the Formatting toolbar, which displays the Styles and Formatting task pane. Through the **Styles and Formatting task pane** you can view, create, and apply styles. The Styles and Formatting task pane is shown later when it is used.

In Word, four basic styles exist: paragraph styles, character styles, list styles, and table styles. **Paragraph styles** affect formatting of an entire paragraph, whereas **character styles** affect formats of only selected characters. **List styles** affect alignment and fonts in a numbered or bulleted list, and **table styles** affect the borders, shading, alignment, and fonts in a Word table. In the Style list and Styles and Formatting task pane, paragraph style names usually are followed by a proofreader's paragraph mark (¶); character style names usually are followed by an underlined letter a (a); list styles usually are followed by a bulleted list icon (☰); and table styles usually are followed by a table icon (⊞).

> **More About**
>
> **Styles**
>
> Another way to see the formatting is to display the Styles and Formatting task pane by clicking the Styles and Formatting button on the Formatting toolbar. This task pane displays the formats applied to text at the location of the insertion point. To apply a different style, click the desired style in the Pick formatting to apply list in the Styles and Formatting task pane. Or, click the Style box arrow on the Formatting toolbar and then click the desired style.

Selecting and Replacing Text

The next step in personalizing the resume is to select text that the Resume Wizard inserted into the resume and replace it with personal information. The first heading on the resume is the objective. You enter the objective where the Resume Wizard inserted the words, Type Objective Here, which is called **placeholder text.**

To replace text in Word, select the text to be removed and then type the desired text. To select the placeholder text, Type Objective Here, you click it. Then, type the objective. As soon as you begin typing, Word deletes the selected placeholder text. Thus, you do not need to delete the selection before you begin typing.

Perform the following steps to enter the objective into the resume.

Steps To Select and Replace Placeholder Text

1 Click the placeholder text, Type Objective Here.

Word selects the placeholder text in the resume (Figure 3-24). Notice the style is Objective in the Style box on the Formatting toolbar.

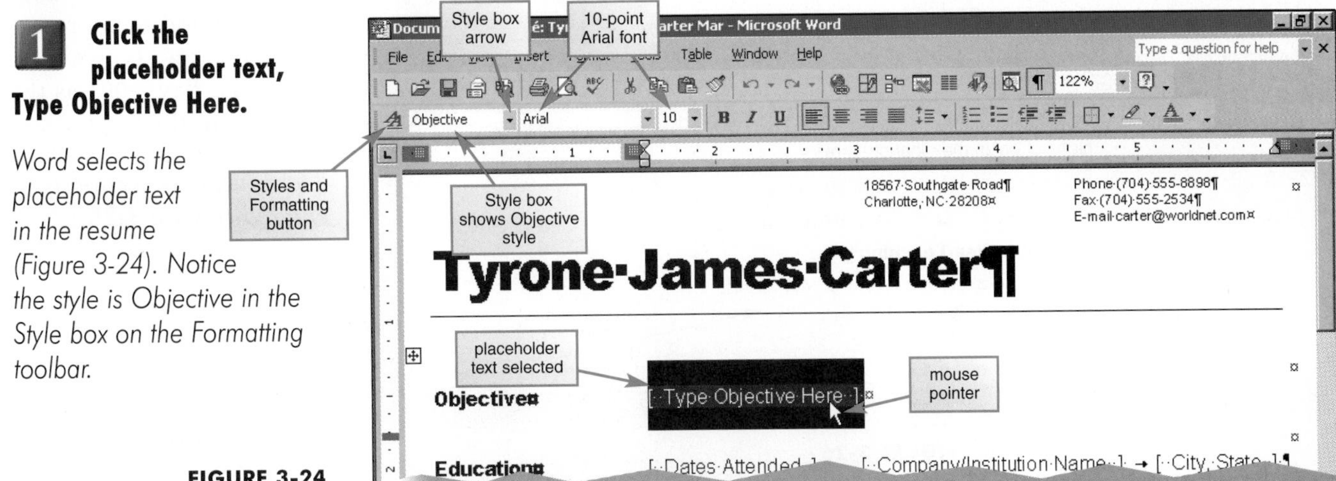

FIGURE 3-24

2 **Type** `To obtain a teacher's assistant position for a social studies teacher at a high school in the Charlotte area.`

Word replaces the selected placeholder text, Type Objective Here, with the objective you type (Figure 3-25). Your document may wordwrap on a different word depending on the type of printer you are using.

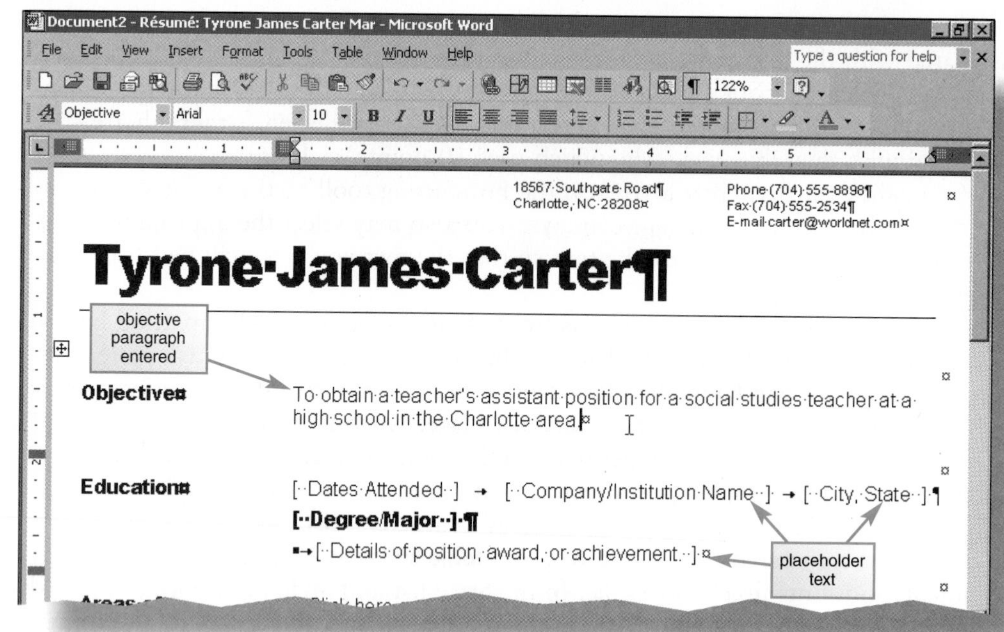

FIGURE 3-25

The next step in personalizing the resume is to replace the placeholder text in the education section of the resume with your own words and phrases as described in the following steps.

TO SELECT AND REPLACE MORE PLACEHOLDER TEXT

1 If necessary, scroll down to display the entire education section of the resume. Click, or if necessary drag through, the placeholder text, Dates Attended. Type `1999-2003` and then click the placeholder text, Company/Institution Name.

2 Type `North Carolina State` and then click the placeholder text, City, State. Type `Charlotte, NC` and then click the placeholder text, Degree/Major. Type `Social Studies Teaching` and then click the placeholder text, Details of position, award, or achievement.

3 Type `B.A., Social Studies Teaching, May 2003` and then press the ENTER key. Type `A.A., History, May 2001` as the last item in the list.

The education section is entered (Figure 3-26).

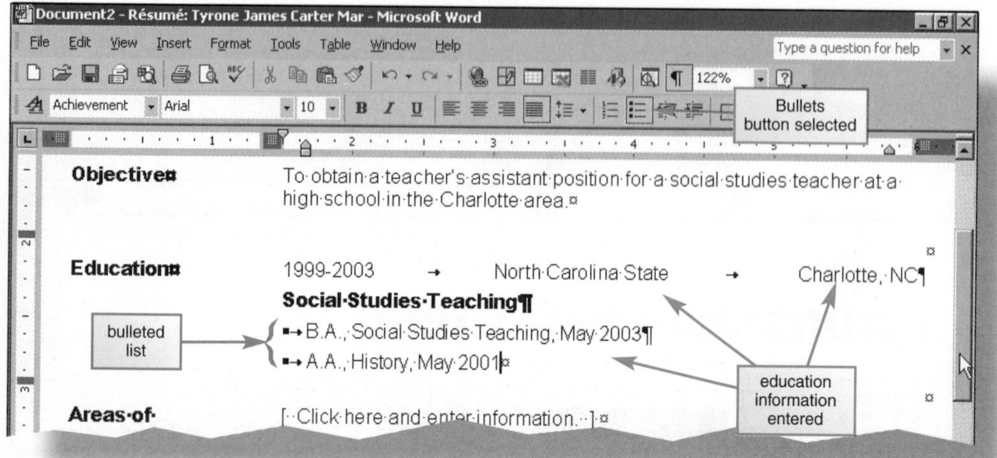

FIGURE 3-26

A **bullet** is a dot or other symbol positioned at the beginning of a paragraph. A **bulleted list** is a list of paragraphs that each begin with a bullet character. For example, the list of degrees in the education section of the resume is a bulleted list (Figure 3-26). When the insertion point is in a paragraph containing a bullet, the Bullets button on the Formatting toolbar is selected. In a bulleted list, each time you press the ENTER key, a bullet displays at the beginning of the new paragraph. This is because Word carries forward paragraph formatting when you press the ENTER key.

More About

Bullets

To apply a different bullet character to selected paragraphs, click Format on the menu bar, click Bullets and Numbering, click the desired bullet style, and then click the OK button. For additional bullet styles, click the Customize button in the Bullets and Numbering dialog box.

Entering a Line Break

The next step in personalizing the resume is to enter text in the areas of concentration section. The style used for the characters in the areas of concentration section of the resume is the Objective style. A paragraph formatting characteristic of the Objective style is that when you press the ENTER key, the insertion point advances downward at least 11 points, which leaves nearly an entire blank line between each paragraph.

You want the lines within the areas of concentration section to be close to each other (Figure 3-1 on page WD 3.05). Thus, you will not press the ENTER key between each area of concentration. Instead, you press SHIFT+ENTER to create a **line break**, which advances the insertion point to the beginning of the next physical line — ignoring any paragraph formatting instructions.

Perform the following steps to enter text in the areas of concentration section using a line break, instead of a paragraph break, between each line.

Steps To Enter a Line Break

1 If necessary, scroll down to display the areas of concentration section of the resume. In the areas of concentration section, click the placeholder text, Click here and enter information. Type `U.S. History (18 hours)` **and then press SHIFT+ENTER.**

Word inserts a ***line break character****, which is a formatting mark, at the end of the line and moves the insertion point to the beginning of the next physical line (Figure 3-27).*

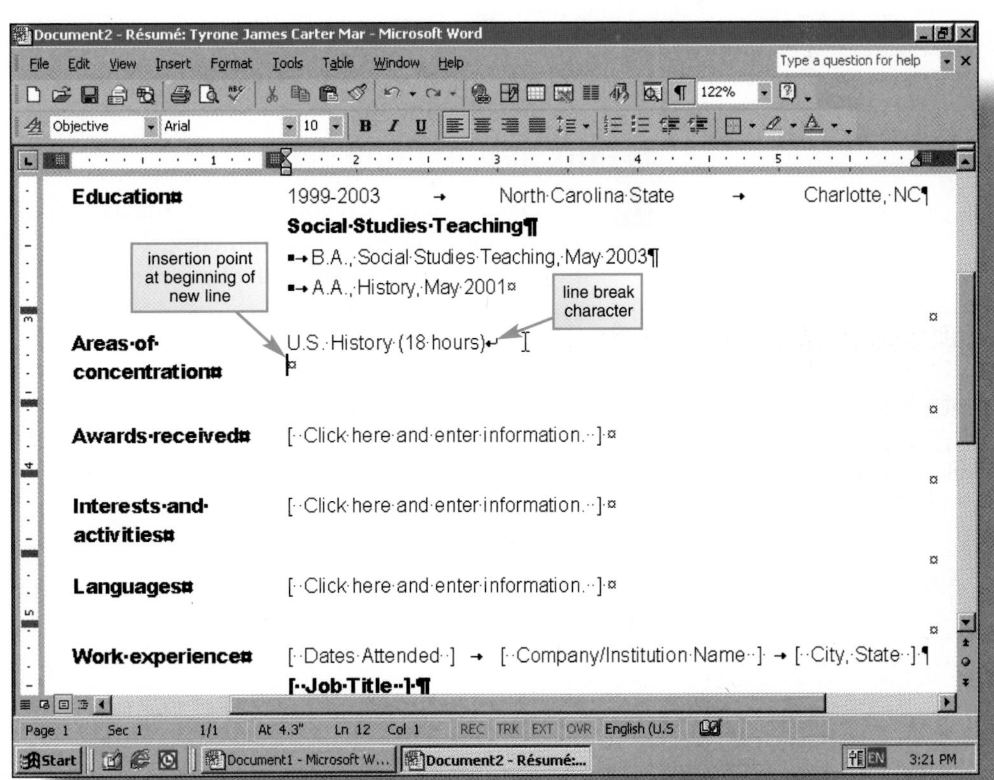

FIGURE 3-27

2 **Type** World Civilization (12 hours) **and then press SHIFT+ENTER. Type** Government (12 hours) **and then press SHIFT+ENTER. Type** Sociology (10 hours) **as the last entry. Do not press SHIFT+ENTER at the end of this line.**

The areas of concentration section is entered (Figure 3-28).

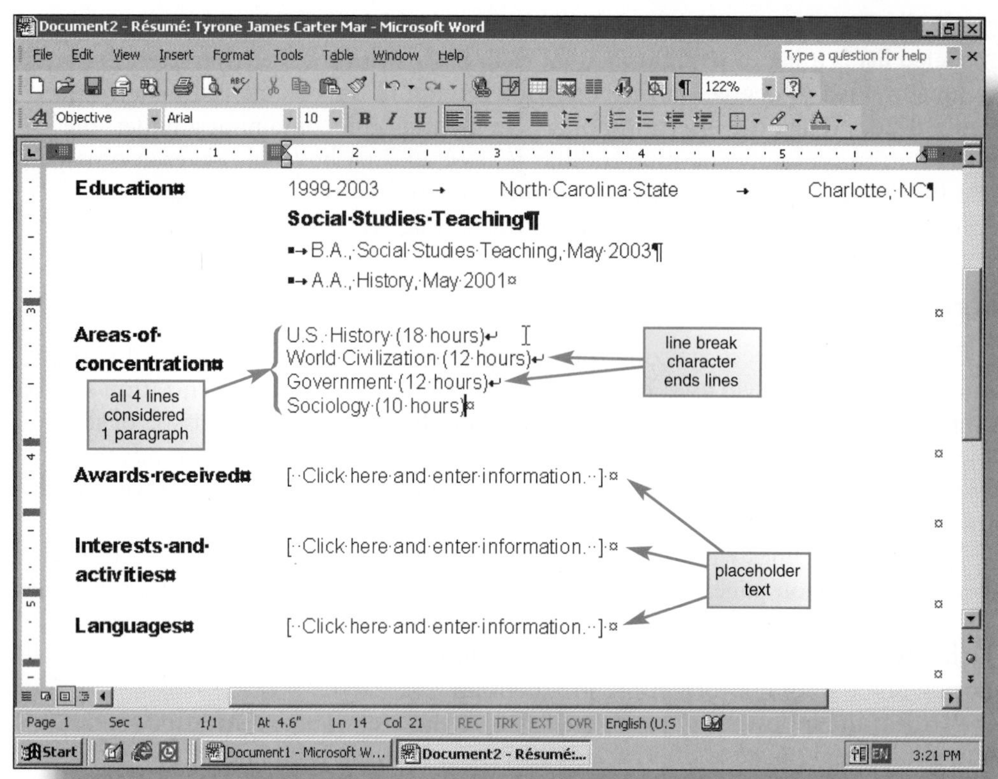

FIGURE 3-28

The next step is to enter the first two awards in the awards received section of the resume.

TO ENTER MORE TEXT WITH LINE BREAKS

1. If necessary, scroll down to display the awards received section of the resume. In the awards received section, click the placeholder text, Click here and enter information. Type `Dean's List, every semester` and then press SHIFT+ENTER.
2. Type `Kappa Phi Gamma Honorary Society, 2001-2003` and then press SHIFT+ENTER.

The first two awards are entered in the awards received section (shown in Figure 3-29).

AutoFormat

For an AutoFormat option to work as expected, it must be turned on. To check if an AutoFormat option is enabled, click Tools on the menu bar, click AutoCorrect Options, click the AutoFormat As You Type tab, select the appropriate check boxes, and then click the OK button. For example, Format beginning of list item like the one before it and Automatic bulleted lists both should contain check marks if you want Word to add bullets automatically as you type.

AutoFormat As You Type

As you type text into a document, Word automatically formats it for you. Table 3-1 outlines commonly used AutoFormat As You Type options and their results.

Table 3-1 Commonly Used AutoFormat As You Type Options

TYPED TEXT	AUTOFORMAT FEATURE	EXAMPLE
Quotation marks or apostrophes	Changes straight quotation marks or apostrophes to curly ones	"the" becomes “the”
Text, a space, one hyphen, one or no spaces, text, space	Changes the hyphen to an en dash	ages 20 - 45 becomes ages 20 – 45
Text, two hyphens, text, space	Changes the two hyphens to an em dash	Two types--yellow and red becomes Two types—yellow and red
Web or e-mail address followed by space or ENTER key	Formats Web or e-mail address as a hyperlink	www.scsite.com becomes www.scsite.com
Three hyphens, underscores, equal signs, asterisks, tildes, or number signs and then ENTER key	Places a border above a paragraph	--- This line becomes ______ This line
Number followed by a period, hyphen, right parenthesis, or greater than sign and then a space or tab followed by text	Creates a numbered list when you press the ENTER key	1. Word 2. Excel becomes 1. Word 2. Excel
Asterisk, hyphen, or greater than sign and then a space or tab followed by text	Creates a bulleted list when you press the ENTER key	* Standard toolbar * Formatting toolbar becomes • Standard toolbar • Formatting toolbar
Fraction and then a space or hyphen	Converts the entry to a fraction-like notation	1/2 becomes ½
Ordinal and then a space or hyphen	Makes the original a superscript	3rd becomes 3rd

Steps To AutoFormat as You Type

1 **Type** Ross Kimble Speaking Award, 1st **(Figure 3-29).**

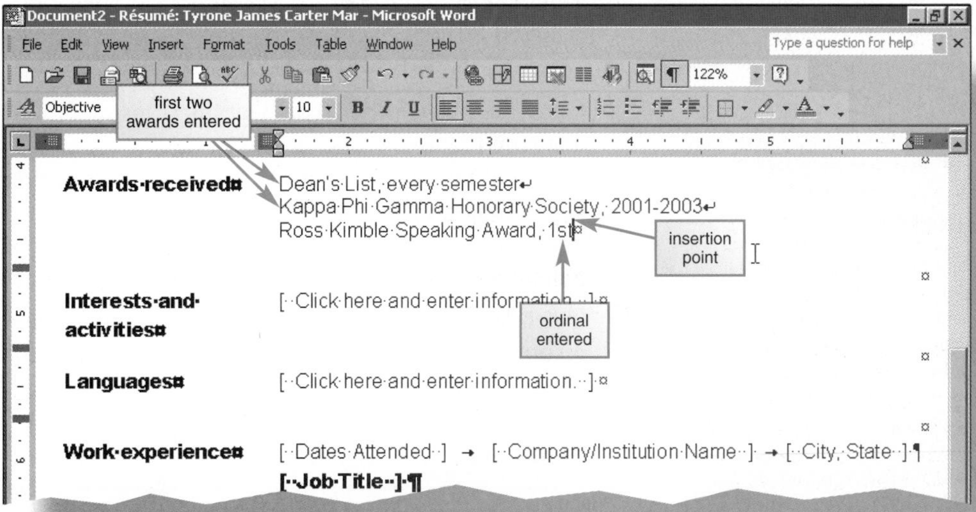

FIGURE 3-29

2 **Press the SPACEBAR. Type** `Place, 2002` **as the end of the award.**

Word automatically converts the st in 1st to a superscript (Figure 3-30).

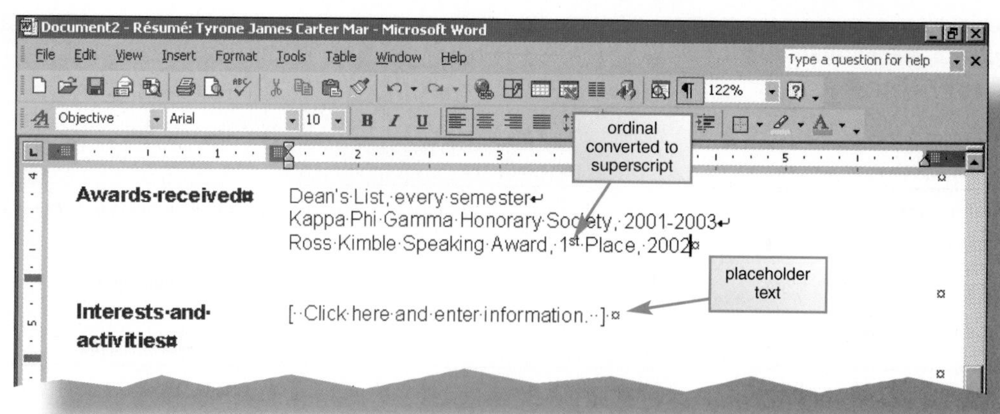

FIGURE 3-30

Enter the remaining text for the resume as described in the following steps.

TO ENTER THE REMAINING SECTIONS OF THE RESUME

1. If necessary, scroll down to display the interests and activities section of the resume. Click the placeholder text, Click here and enter information. Type `CPR certified` and then press SHIFT+ENTER.
2. Type `National Educators of America Association, member` and then press SHIFT+ENTER. Type `Soccer Club, member` and then press SHIFT+ENTER. Type `Student Government, representative` as the last activity. Do not press SHIFT+ENTER at the end of this line.
3. If necessary, scroll down to display the languages section of the resume. Click the placeholder text, Click here and enter information. Type `English (fluent)` and then press SHIFT+ENTER. Type `French (fluent)` and then press SHIFT+ENTER. Type `Spanish` as the last language. Do not press SHIFT+ENTER at the end of this line.
4. If necessary, scroll down to display the work experience section of the resume. Click, or if necessary drag through, the placeholder text, Dates Attended. Type `2000-2003` as the years. Click the placeholder text, Company/Institution Name. Type `North Carolina State` and then click the placeholder text, City, State. Type `Charlotte, NC` and then click the placeholder text, Job Title. Type `Tutor` as the title.
5. Click the placeholder text, Details of position, award, or achievement. Type `Provided one-on-one assistance to campus students having difficulty with economics, French, government, history, and sociology` and then press the ENTER key. Type `Administered placement and test-out examinations` and then press the ENTER key. Type `Conducted group roundtable sessions on various history topics` as the last item in the list.
6. If necessary, scroll down to display the volunteer experience section of the resume. Click the placeholder text, Click here and enter information. Type `On a weekly basis, worked as a grade school teacher's aide for a Hampton Elementary School teacher.` Do not press the ENTER key at the end of this line.

The interests and activities, languages, work experience, and volunteer experience sections of the resume are complete (Figure 3-31).

More About

References

Do not list references on your resume, and do not state "References Available Upon Request." Employers assume you will give references, if asked, and this information simply clutters a resume. Often you are asked to list references on your application. Be sure to give your references a copy of your resume.

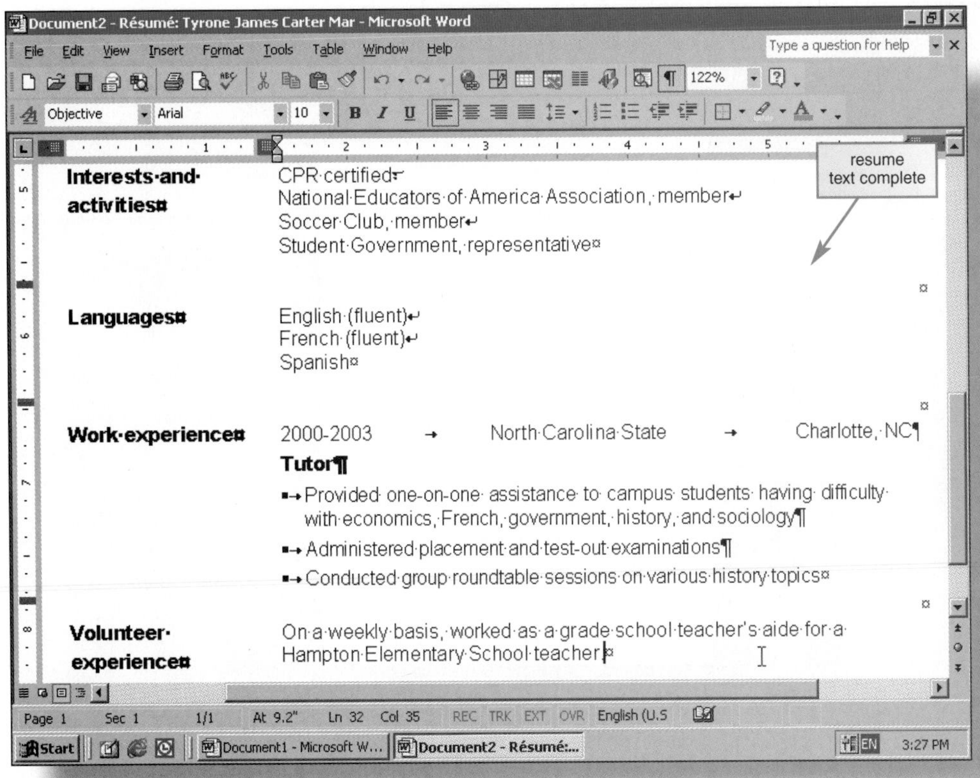

FIGURE 3-31

Viewing and Printing the Resume in Print Preview

To see exactly how a document will look when you print it, you should display it in **print preview**. Print preview displays the entire document in reduced size on the Word screen. In print preview, you can edit and format text, adjust margins, view multiple pages, reduce the document to fit on a single page, and print the document.

Perform the following steps to view and print the resume in print preview.

Printing

If you want to save ink, print faster, or decrease printer overrun errors, print a draft. Click File on the menu bar, click Print, click the Options button, place a check mark in the Draft output check box, and then click the OK button in both dialog boxes.

To Print Preview a Document

1 Point to the Print Preview button on the Standard toolbar (Figure 3-32).

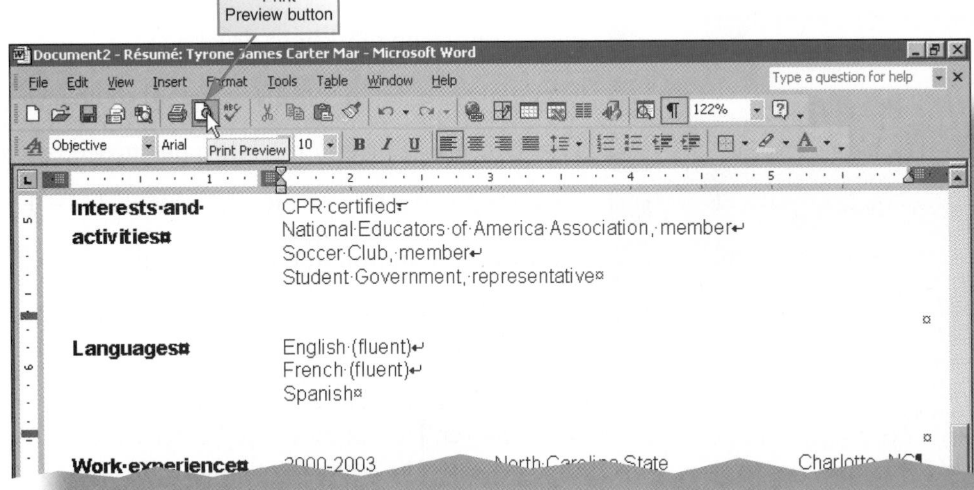

FIGURE 3-32

2 Click the Print Preview button. Point to the Print button on the Print Preview toolbar.

Word displays the document in print preview (Figure 3-33). The Print Preview toolbar displays below the menu bar; the Standard and Formatting toolbars disappear from the screen.

3 Click the Print button on the Print Preview toolbar. When the printer stops, retrieve the printout (shown in Figure 3-1 on page WD 3.05). Click the Close Preview button on the Print Preview toolbar.

Word returns to the document window, displaying the resume (shown in Figure 3-34).

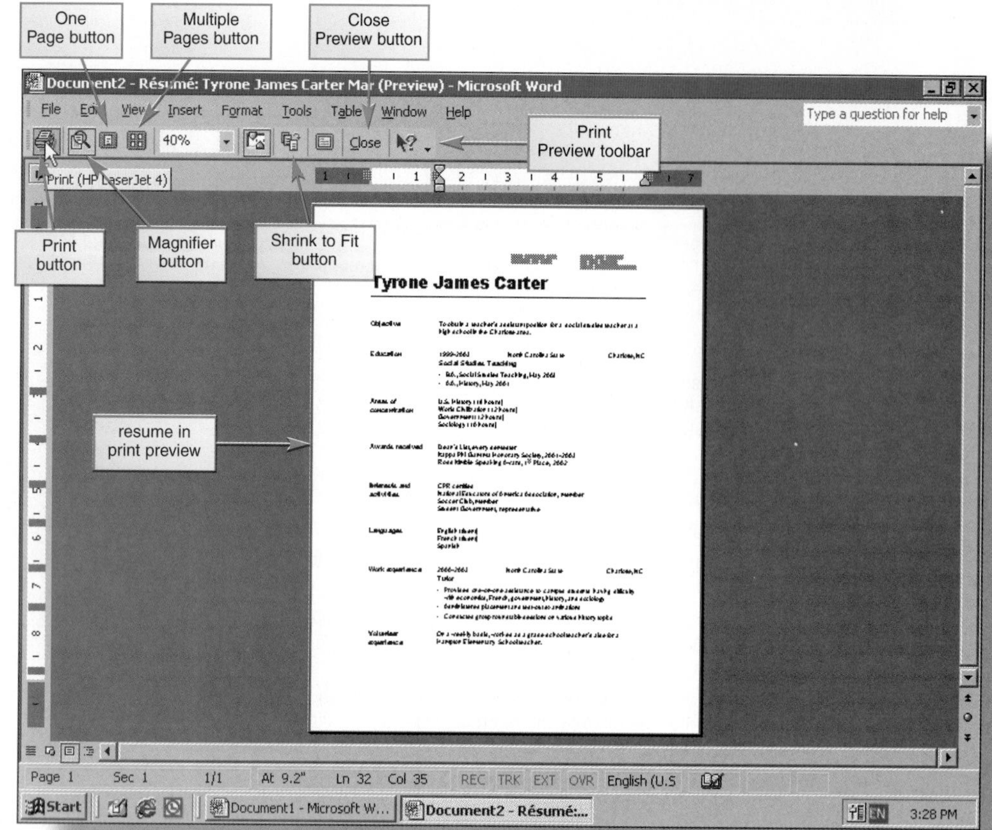

FIGURE 3-33

Other Ways

1. On File menu click Print Preview
2. Press CTRL+F2
3. In Voice Command mode, say "Print Preview"

More About

Print Preview

If the page is not centered in the Print Preview window, click the One Page button. With the Magnifier button on the Print Preview toolbar selected, you can click in the document to zoom in or out. Magnifying a page does not affect the printed document. To edit a document, click the Magnifier button to deselect it and then edit the text. If a document spills onto a second page by a line or two, click the Shrink to Fit button and Word will try to fit it all on a single page.

Saving the Resume

The resume now is complete. Thus, you should save it. For a detailed example of the procedure summarized below, refer to pages WD 1.30 through WD 1.32 in Project 1.

TO SAVE A DOCUMENT

1. Insert your floppy disk into drive A.
2. Click the Save button on the Standard toolbar.
3. Type `Carter Resume` in the File name text box. Do not press the ENTER key.
4. Click the Save in box arrow and then click 3½ Floppy (A:).
5. Click the Save button in the Save As dialog box.

Word saves the document on a floppy disk in drive A with the file name, Carter Resume (shown in Figure 3-34).

The next step in Project 3 is to create a cover letter to send with the resume to a potential employer. Do not close the Carter Resume. You will use it again later in this project to copy the address, telephone, fax, and e-mail information.

Creating a Letterhead

You have created a resume to send to prospective employers. Along with the resume, you will enclose a personalized cover letter. You would like the cover letter to have a professional looking letterhead (Figure 3-2a on page WD 3.06). The following pages describe how to use Word to create a letterhead.

In many businesses, letterhead is preprinted on stationery that everyone in a company uses for correspondence. For personal letters, the expense of preprinted letterhead can be costly. Thus, you can create your own letterhead and save it in a file. When you want to create a letter with the letterhead, you simply open the letterhead file and then save the file with a new name, preserving the original letterhead file.

The steps on the following pages illustrate how to create a personal letterhead file.

More About

Letterhead Design

Letterhead designs vary. Some are centered at the top of the page, while others have text or graphics aligned with the left and right margins. Another style places the company's name and logo at the top of the page with the address and other information at the bottom. A well-designed letterhead adds professionalism to correspondence.

Opening a New Document Window

The resume currently displays in the document window. You want the resume document to remain open because you intend to use it again during this Word session. That is, you will be working with two documents at the same time: the resume and the letterhead. Word will display each of these documents in a separate document window.

Perform the following steps to open a new document window for the letterhead file.

Steps To Open a New Document Window

1 **Point to the New Blank Document button on the Standard toolbar (Figure 3-34).**

2 **Click the New Blank Document button.**

Word opens a new document window (shown in Figure 3-35 on the next page).

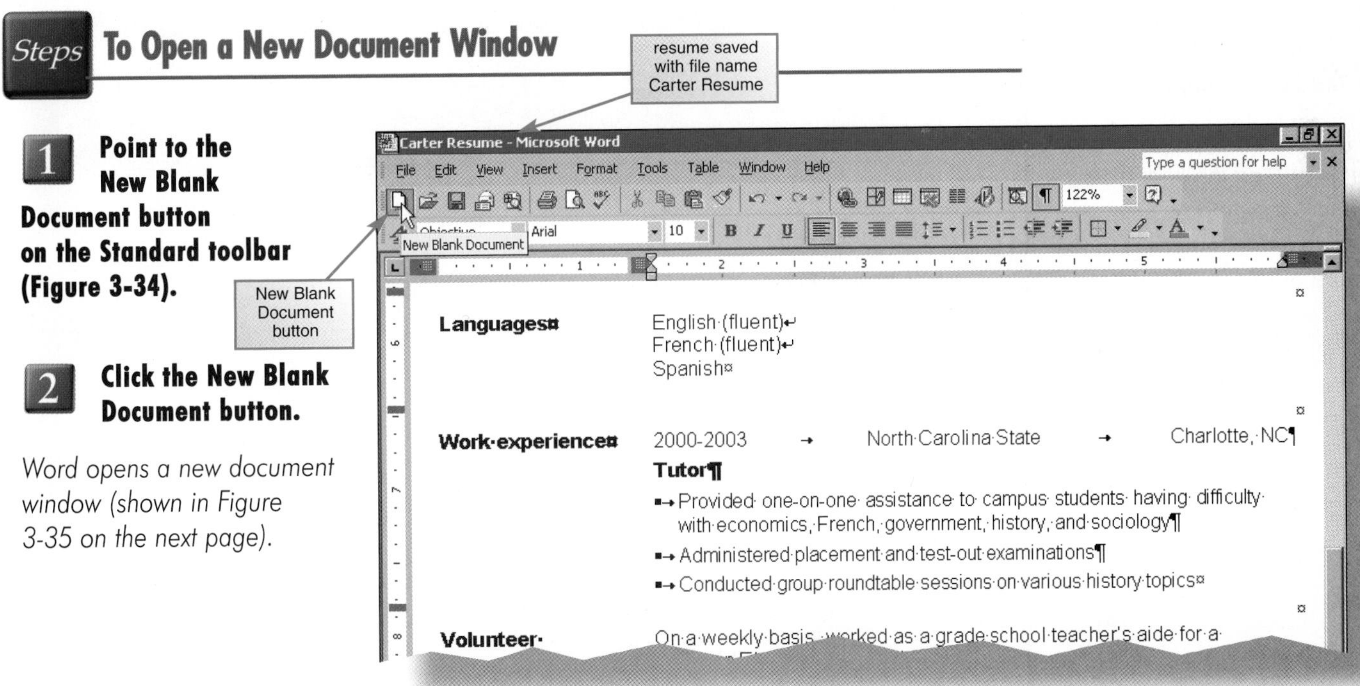

FIGURE 3-34

Other Ways

1. On File menu click New, click Blank Document in New area in New Document task pane
2. Press CTRL+N
3. In Voice Command mode, say "New Blank Document"

Program Buttons

If the Windows taskbar does not display a separate program button for each open Word document, click Tools on the menu bar, click Options, click the View tab, place a check mark in the Windows in Taskbar check box, and then click the OK button.

The Carter Resume document still is open. The program buttons on the taskbar display the names of the open Word document windows. The Document3 button on the taskbar is recessed, indicating that it is the active document currently displaying in the Word document window.

The name in the letterhead is to be a font size of 20. Perform the following steps to change the font size.

TO CHANGE THE FONT SIZE

1. Click the Font Size box arrow on the Formatting toolbar.
2. Click 20 in the Font Size list.

Word changes the displayed font size to 20 (shown in Figure 3-35 below).

Adding Color to Characters

The characters in the letterhead are to be dark red. Perform the following steps to change the color of the characters before you type them.

Steps To Color Characters

1 Point to the Font Color button arrow on the Formatting toolbar.

The color that displays below the letter A on the Font Color button is the most recently used color for characters (Figure 3-35). The color on your button may differ from this figure.

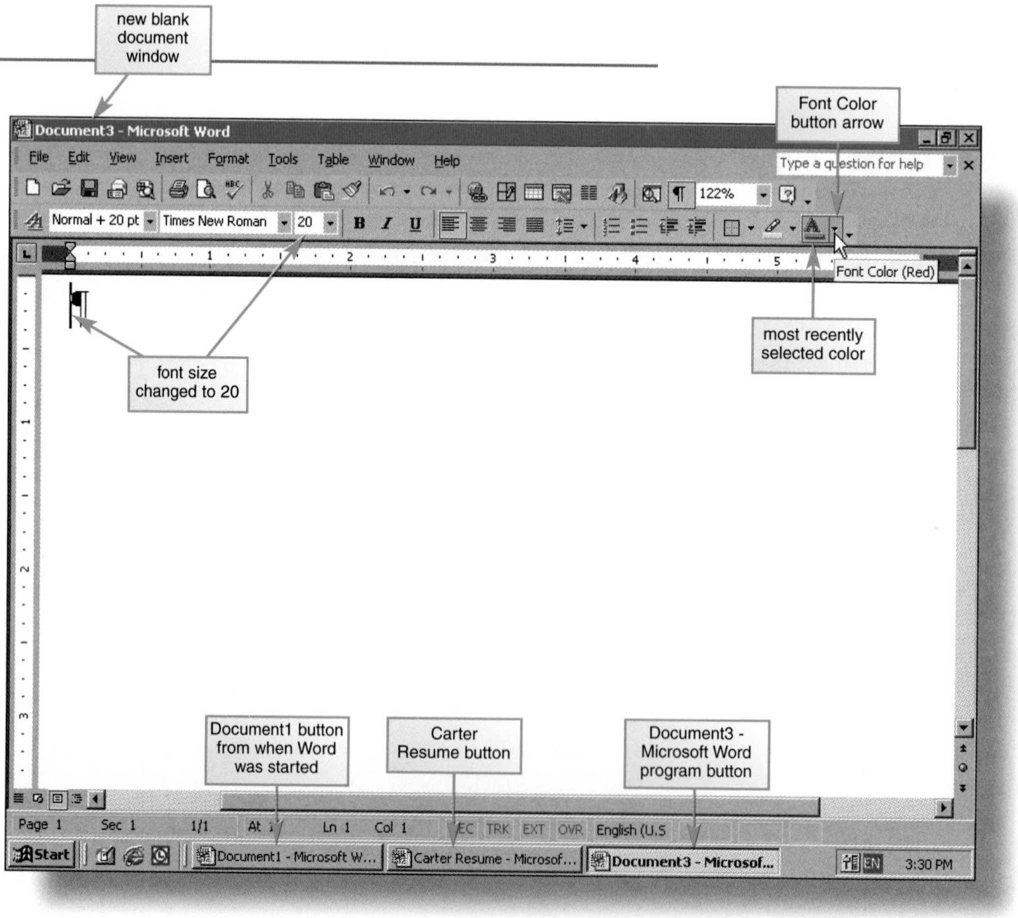

FIGURE 3-35

2 Click the Font Color button arrow. Point to Dark Red, which is the first color on the second row on the color palette.

Word displays a list of available colors on the color palette (Figure 3-36). Automatic is the default color, which usually is black.

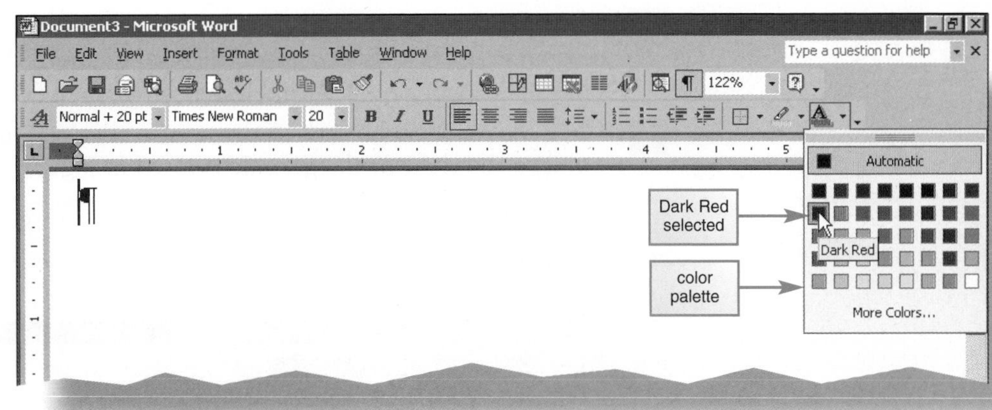

FIGURE 3-36

3 Click Dark Red. Type `Tyrone James Carter` **and then press the ENTER key.**

Word displays the first line of the letterhead in dark red (Figure 3-37).

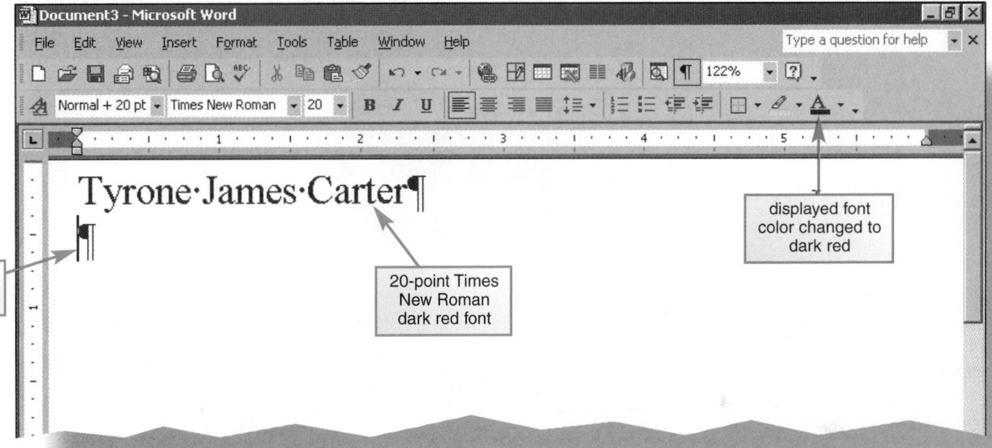

FIGURE 3-37

Other Ways

1. On Format menu click Font, click Font tab, click Font color box arrow, click desired color, click OK button
2. Right-click paragraph mark or selected text, click Font on shortcut menu, click Font tab, click Font color box arrow, click desired color, click OK button
3. In Voice Command mode, say "Font Color, Dark Red"

Notice the paragraph mark on line 2 is dark red. Recall that each time you press the ENTER key, Word carries forward formatting to the next paragraph. If, for some reason, you wanted to change the text back to black at this point, you would click the Font Color button arrow on the Formatting toolbar and then click Automatic on the color palette.

The next step is to insert a graphic of a soccer ball and resize it as described in the following steps.

TO INSERT AND RESIZE A GRAPHIC

1. With the insertion point below the name as shown in Figure 3-37, click Insert on the menu bar, point to Picture, and then click Clip Art on the Picture submenu.
2. When the Insert Clip Art task pane displays, if necessary, drag through any text in the Search text text box to select the text. Type `soccer` and then press the ENTER key.
3. Point to the clip of the soccer ball that matches the one shown in Figure 3-38 on the next page. Click the button arrow that displays to the right of the clip and then click Insert on the menu. Click the Close button on the Insert Clip Art task pane title bar.

4 Click the graphic to select it. Drag the upper-right corner sizing handle diagonally toward the center of the graphic until the selection rectangle is positioned approximately as shown in Figure 3-38.

5 Click the paragraph mark to the right of the graphic to position the insertion point to the right of the graphic (shown in Figure 3-39).

Word inserts the graphic of the soccer ball (Figure 3-38). You resize the graphic to approximately one-eighth of its original size (shown in Figure 3-39).

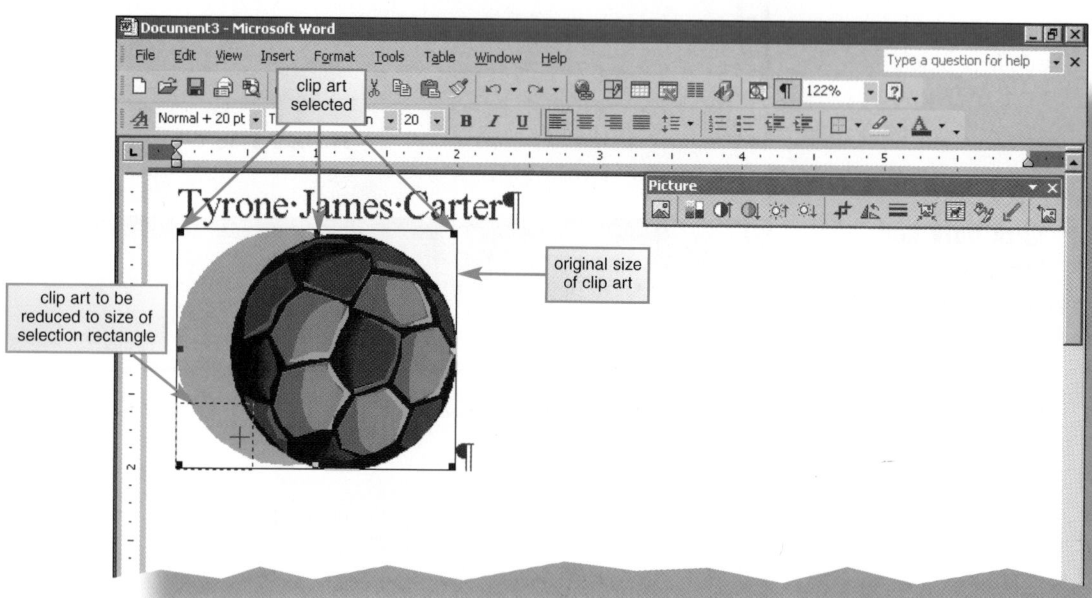

FIGURE 3-38

Setting Tab Stops Using the Tabs Dialog Box

The graphic of the soccer ball is left-aligned (Figure 3-38). The address is to be positioned at the right margin of the same line. If you click the Align Right button, the graphic will be right-aligned. In Word, a paragraph cannot be both left-aligned and right-aligned. To place text at the right margin of a left-aligned paragraph, you set a tab stop at the right margin.

A **tab stop** is a location on the horizontal ruler that tells Word where to position the insertion point when you press the TAB key on the keyboard. A tab stop is useful for indenting text or aligning columns.

Word, by default, places a tab stop at every .5" mark on the ruler (Figure 3-40). These default tabs are indicated on the horizontal ruler by small **tick marks**. You also can set your own custom tab stops. When you set a **custom tab stop**, Word clears all default tab stops to the left of the custom tab stop. You can specify how the text will align at a tab stop: left, centered, right, or decimal. Word stores tab settings in the paragraph mark at the end of each paragraph. Thus, each time you press the ENTER key, any custom tab stops are carried forward to the next paragraph.

In the letterhead for this project, you want the tab stop to be right-aligned with the right margin, that is, at the 6" mark on the ruler. One method of setting custom tab stops is to click the ruler at the desired location of the tab stop. You cannot click, however, at the right margin location. Thus, use the Tabs dialog box to set a custom tab stop at the 6" mark, as shown in the following steps.

More About

The Tabs Dialog Box

You can use the Tabs dialog box to change an existing tab stop's alignment or position. You also can place leader characters in the empty space occupied by the tab. Leader characters, such as a series of dots, often are used in a table of contents to precede the page number. Simply click the desired type of leader in the Leader area in the Tabs dialog box.

To Set Custom Tab Stops Using the Tabs Dialog Box

1 With the insertion point positioned between the paragraph mark and the graphic, click Format on the menu bar and then point to Tabs (Figure 3-39).

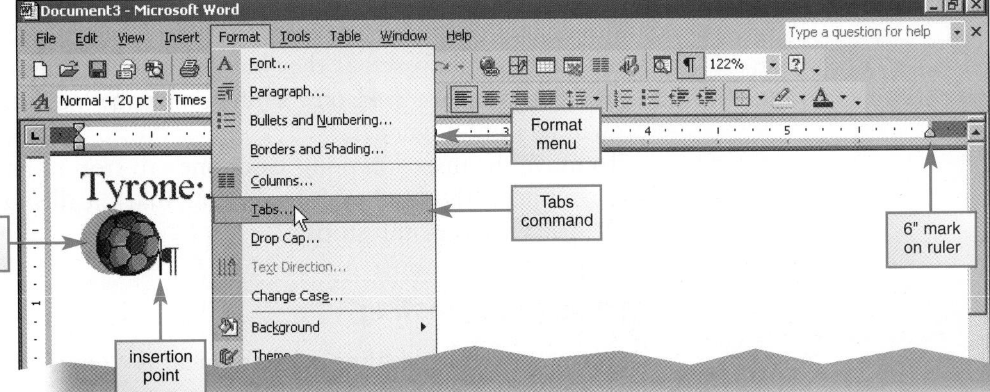

FIGURE 3-39

2 Click Tabs. When the Tabs dialog box displays, type 6 **in the Tab stop position text box and then click Right in the Alignment area. Point to the Set button.**

Word displays the Tabs dialog box (Figure 3-40).

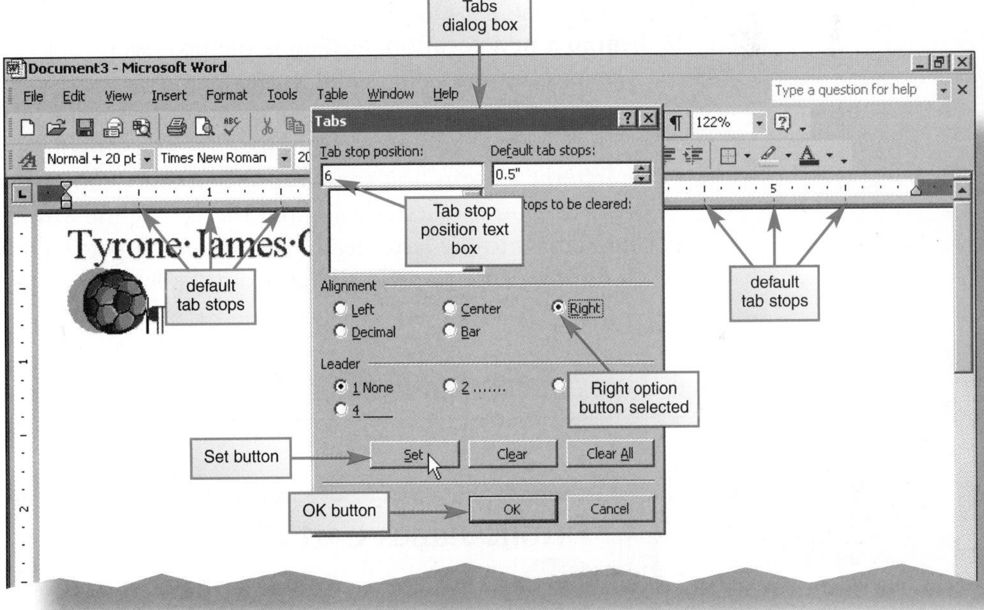

FIGURE 3-40

3 Click the Set button and then click the OK button.

Word places a right tab marker at the 6" mark on the ruler and removes all default tab stops that display to the left of the tab marker (Figure 3-41).

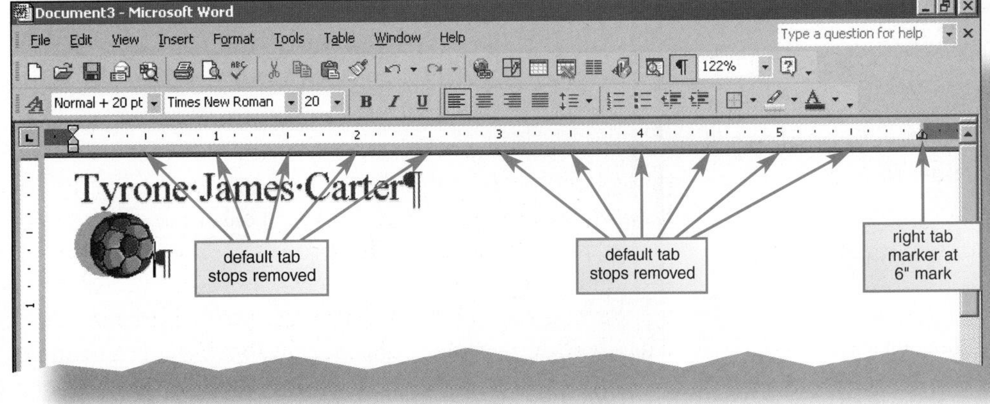

FIGURE 3-41

Other Ways

1. Click button on left of ruler until desired tab stop alignment displays and then click ruler
2. In Voice Command mode, say "Format, Tabs"

Tab Alignment

If you have a series of numbers that you want aligned on the decimal point, such as dollar amounts, use a decimal-aligned tab stop for the data.

When you set a custom tab stop, the tab marker on the ruler reflects the alignment of the characters at the location of the tab stop. A capital letter L ( ) indicates a left-aligned tab stop. A mirror image of a capital letter L ( ) indicates a right-aligned tab stop. An upside down T ( ) indicates a centered tab stop. An upside down T with a dot next to it ( ) indicates a decimal-aligned tab stop. The tab markers are discussed as they are presented in these projects. The tab marker on the ruler in Figure 3-41 on the previous page indicates text entered at that tab stop will be right-aligned.

To move the insertion point from one tab stop to another, you press the TAB key. When you press the TAB key, a formatting mark, called a **tab character**, displays in the empty space between tab stops.

More About

Clipboards

The Windows Clipboard, which can hold only one item at a time, is separate from the Office Clipboard. When you collect multiple items on the Office Clipboard, the last copied item also is copied to the Windows Clipboard. When you clear the Office Clipboard, the Windows Clipboard also is cleared.

Collecting and Pasting

The next step in creating the letterhead is to copy the address, telephone, fax, and e-mail information from the resume to the letterhead. To copy multiple items from one Office document to another, you use the Office Clipboard. The **Office Clipboard** is a temporary storage area that can hold up to 24 items (text or graphics) copied from any Office application. You copy, or **collect**, items and then paste them in a new location. **Pasting** is the process of copying an item from the Office Clipboard into the document at the location of the insertion point. When you paste an item into a document, the contents of the Office Clipboard are not erased.

To copy the address, telephone, fax, and e-mail information from the resume to the letterhead, you first switch to the resume, copy the items to the Office Clipboard, switch back to the letterhead, and then paste the information from the Office Clipboard into the letterhead. The following pages illustrate this process.

Follow these steps to switch from the letterhead to the resume.

Steps To Switch from One Open Document to Another

1 Point to the Carter Resume - Microsoft Word button on the Windows taskbar (Figure 3-42).

2 Click the Carter Resume - Microsoft Word button.

Word switches from the cover letter to the resume (shown in Figure 3-43).

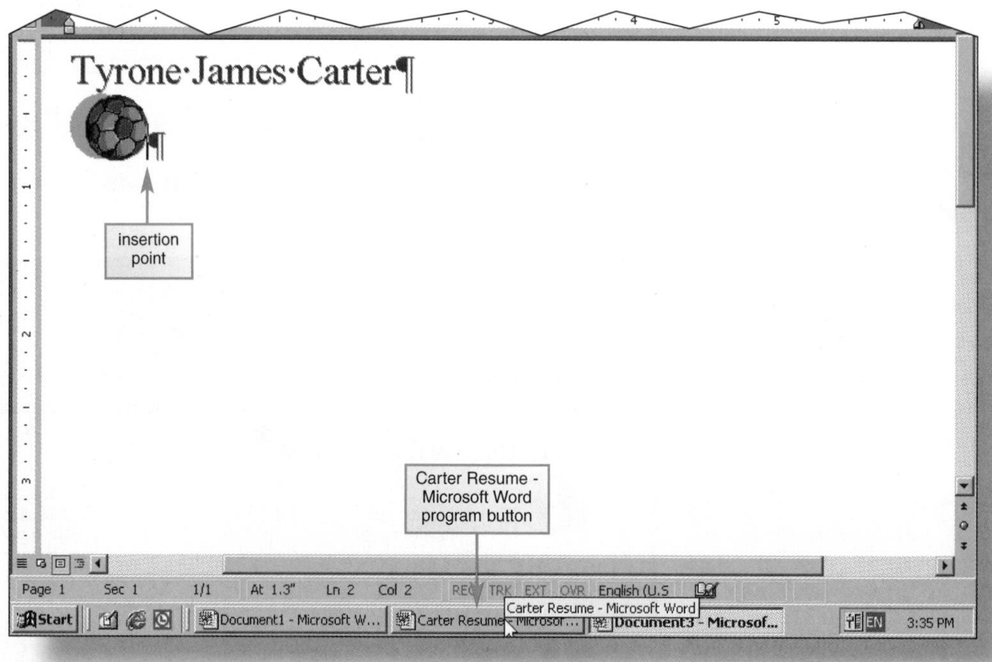

FIGURE 3-42

Other Ways

1. On Window menu click document name
2. Press ALT+TAB
3. In Voice Command mode, say "Window [document number]"

You can copy multiple items to the Office Clipboard and then can paste them later. Each copied item displays as an entry in the Office Clipboard gallery of the Clipboard task pane. The entry displays an icon that indicates the Office program from which the item was copied. The entry also displays a portion of text that was copied or a thumbnail of a graphic that was copied. The most recently copied item displays at the top of the gallery.

Perform the following steps to copy five items to the Office Clipboard.

> **More About**
>
> **The Office Clipboard**
>
> The Office Clipboard may display automatically on the Word screen if you click the Copy button or the Cut button on the Standard toolbar twice in succession, or if you copy and paste an item and then copy another item.

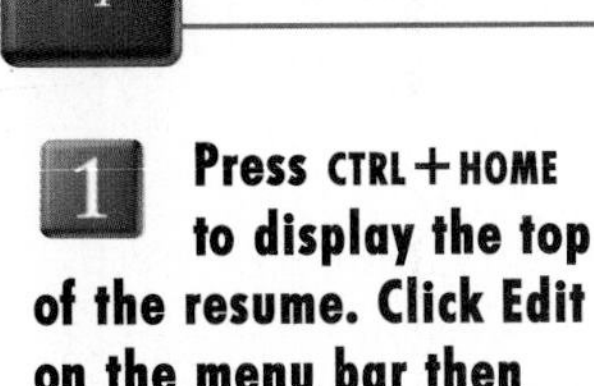

To Collect Items

1 Press CTRL+HOME to display the top of the resume. Click Edit on the menu bar then point to Office Clipboard (Figure 3-43).

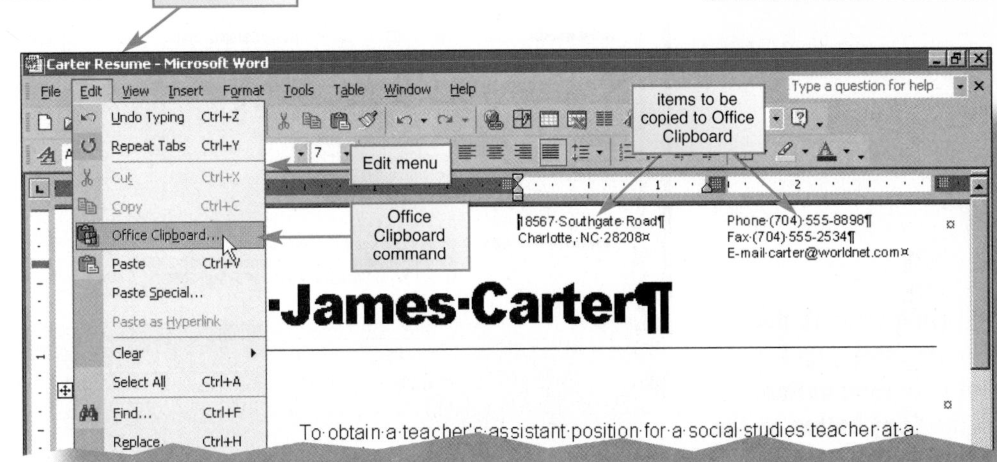

FIGURE 3-43

2 Click Office Clipboard. If the Office Clipboard gallery in the Clipboard task pane is not empty, click the Clear All button in the Clipboard task pane. In the resume, drag through the street address, 18567 Southgate Road (do not select the paragraph mark after the address). Point to the Copy button on the Standard toolbar.

The Clipboard task pane displays on the screen (Figure 3-44). The Office Clipboard icon displays in the tray status area of the Windows taskbar, indicating the Office Clipboard displays in at least one open Office program.

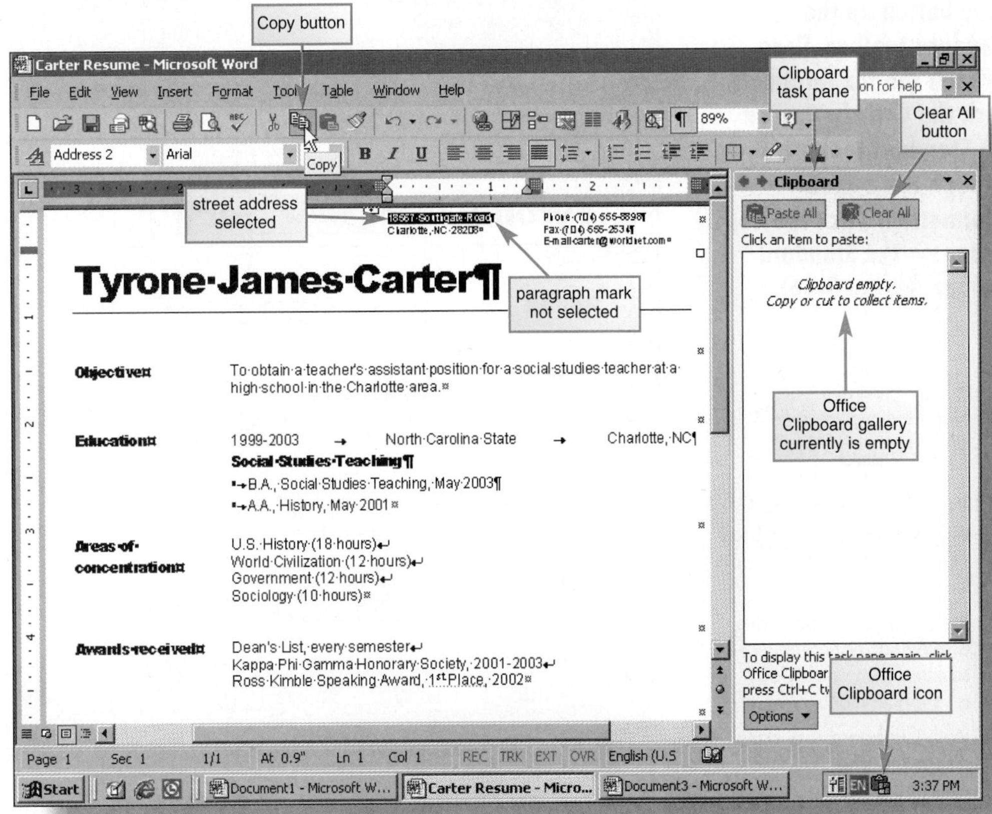

FIGURE 3-44

3 Click the Copy button.

Word copies the selection to the Office Clipboard and places an entry in the Office Clipboard gallery in the Clipboard task pane (Figure 3-45).

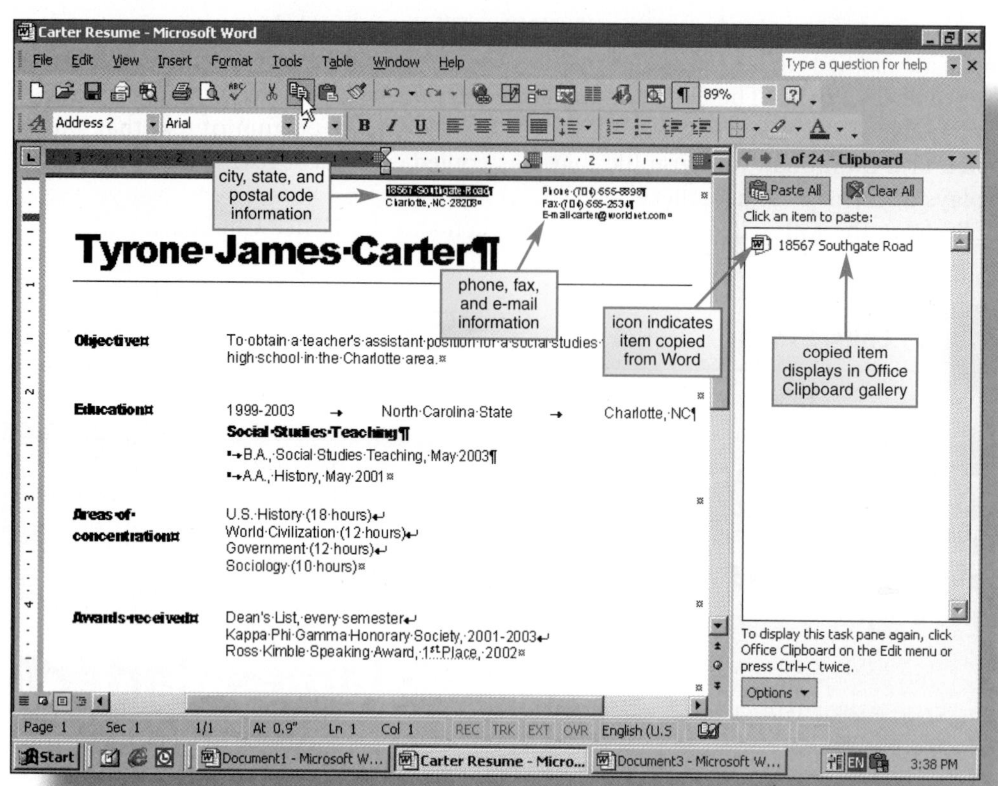

FIGURE 3-45

4 Drag through the city, state, and postal code information. Click the Copy button on the Standard toolbar. Drag through the telephone information. Click the Copy button on the Standard toolbar. Drag through the fax information. Click the Copy button on the Standard toolbar. Drag through the e-mail information. Click the Copy button on the Standard toolbar (Figure 3-46).

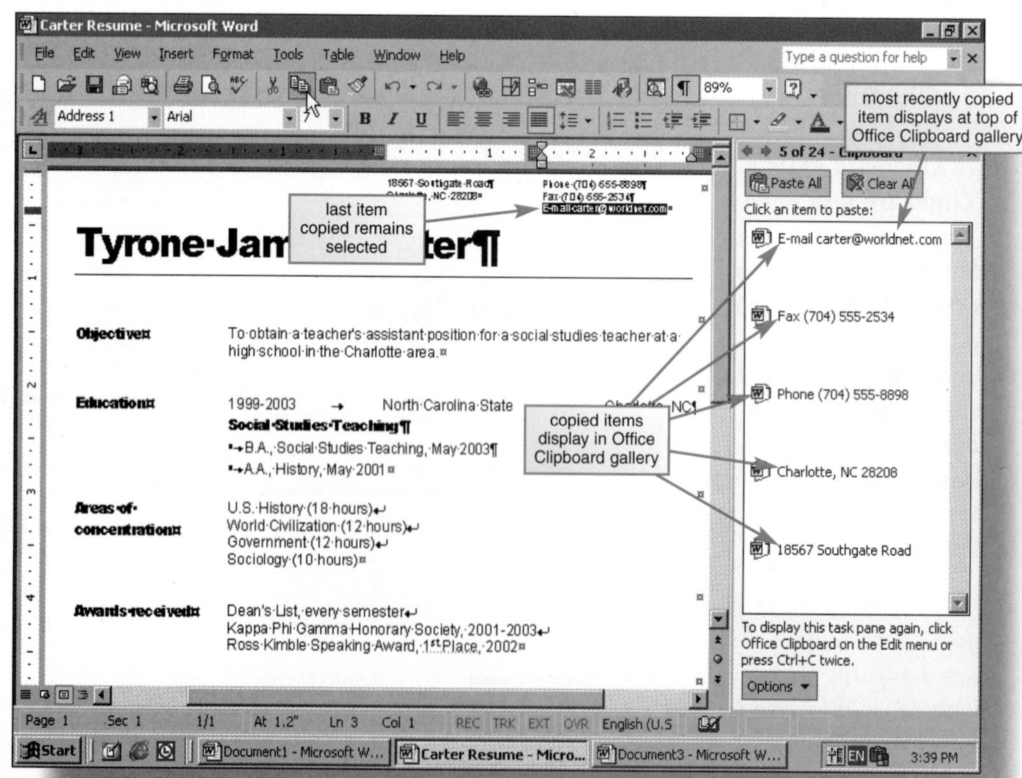

FIGURE 3-46

Other Ways

1. With Clipboard task pane displaying and item to copy selected, on Edit menu click Copy
2. With Clipboard task pane displaying, right-click selected item, click Copy on shortcut menu
3. With Clipboard task pane displaying and item to copy selected, press CTRL+C
4. With Clipboard task pane displaying, in Voice Command mode, say "Copy"

Each time you copy an item to the Office Clipboard, a ScreenTip displays above the Office Clipboard icon in the tray status area of the Windows taskbar, indicating the number of entries currently in the Office Clipboard. The Office Clipboard can store up to 24 items at one time. When you copy a 25th item, Word deletes the first item to make room for the new item. When you point to a text entry in the Office Clipboard gallery of the Office task pane, the first several characters of text in the item display as a ScreenTip.

The next step is to paste the copied items into the letterhead. When you switch to another document, the Clipboard task pane might not display on the screen. You could display it by clicking Edit on the menu bar and then clicking Office Clipboard. If the Office Clipboard icon displays in the tray status area, however, you can double-click the icon to display the Clipboard task pane.

Perform the following steps to paste the items from the Office Clipboard into the letterhead.

The Office Clipboard Icon

If the Office Clipboard icon does not display on the Windows taskbar (Figure 3-47), click the Options button at the bottom of the Clipboard task pane and then click Show Office Clipboard icon on Taskbar.

Steps To Paste from the Office Clipboard

1 Click the Document3 - Microsoft Word button on the Windows taskbar to display the letterhead document window. Double-click the Office Clipboard icon in the tray status area of the Windows task bar to display the Clipboard task pane.

2 With the insertion point between the paragraph mark and the soccer ball graphic (shown in Figure 3-42 on page WD 3.32), press the TAB key.

The insertion point is positioned at the 6" mark on the ruler, the location of the right-aligned tab stop (Figure 3-47). The right-pointing arrow is a formatting mark that displays each time you press the TAB key.

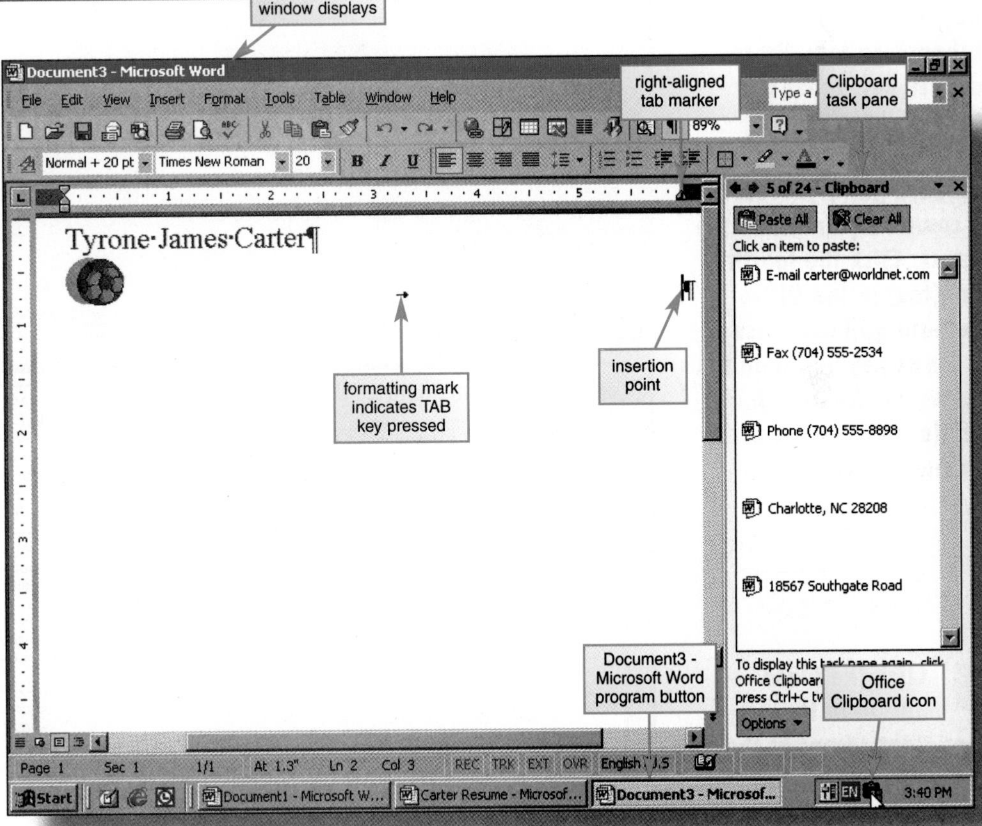

FIGURE 3-47

3 Point to the bottom (first) entry in the Office Clipboard gallery to select it and then click.

Word pastes the contents of the clicked item at the location of the insertion point (Figure 3-48). Notice the text is aligned with the right margin because the tab stop is right-aligned.

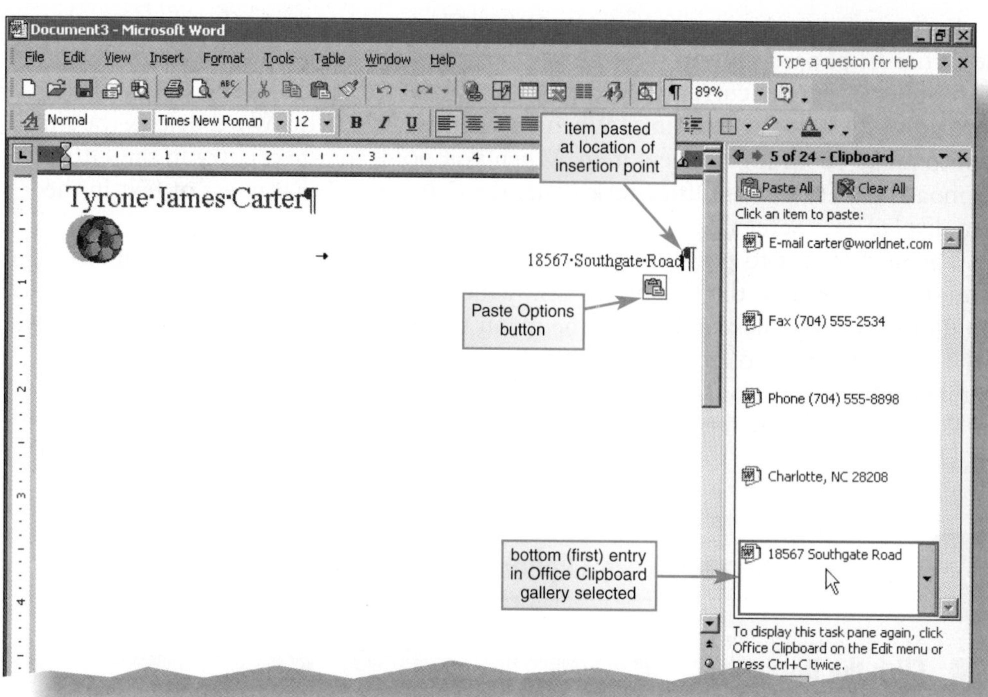

FIGURE 3-48

4 Press the COMMA key and then the SPACEBAR. Click the second entry (city, state, postal code) in the Office Clipboard gallery. Press the ENTER key. Press the TAB key. Click the third entry (phone) in the Office Clipboard gallery. Press the COMMA key and then the SPACEBAR. Click the fourth entry (fax) in the Office Clipboard gallery. Press the COMMA key and then the SPACEBAR. Click the fifth entry (e-mail) in the Office Clipboard gallery.

Items from the Office Clipboard are pasted into the letterhead (Figure 3-49).

5 Click the Close button in the upper-right corner of the Clipboard task pane title bar to close the task pane.

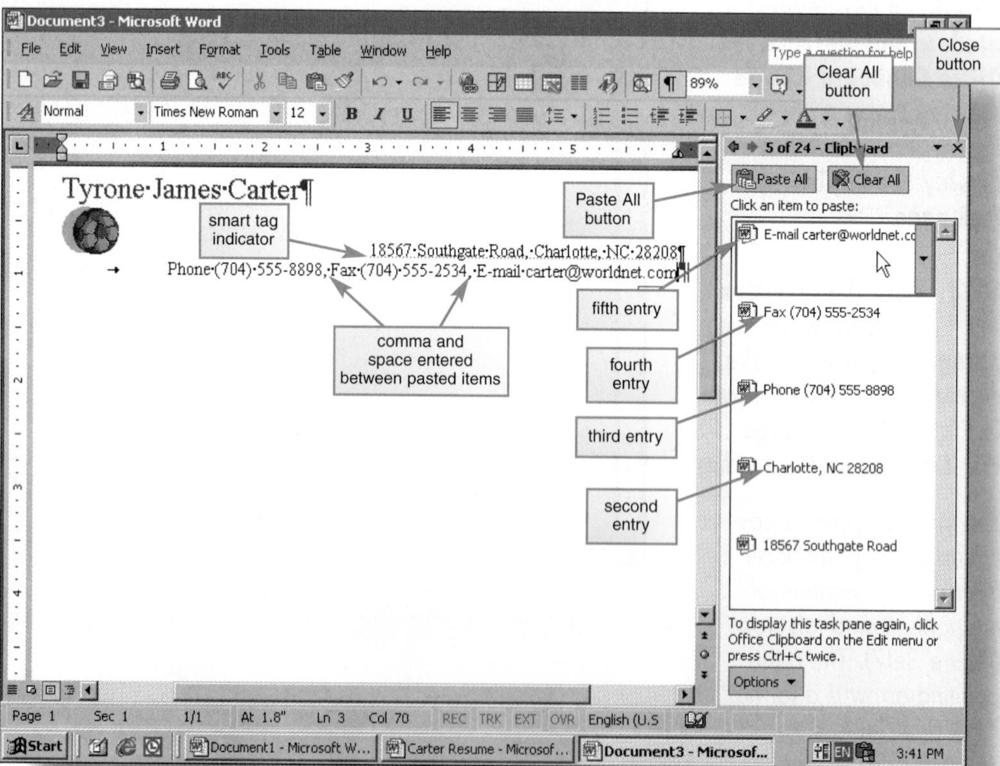

FIGURE 3-49

Other Ways

1. With Clipboard task pane displaying, on Edit menu click Paste
2. With Clipboard task pane displaying, press CTRL+V
3. With Clipboard task pane displaying, in Voice Command mode, say "Paste"

If you wanted to paste all items in a row without any characters in between them, you would click the Paste All button in the Clipboard task pane. If you wanted to erase all items on the Office Clipboard, you would click the Clear All button in the Clipboard task pane.

The next step is to change the font size to 9 and the color of the characters to dark red in the address, telephone, fax, and e-mail information in the letterhead.

More About

Paste Options

To change the format of a pasted item, click the Paste Options button (Figure 3-48) and then click the desired format. For example, to remove all formats such as extra paragraph marks, click Keep Text Only on the Paste Options menu.

TO CHANGE THE FONT SIZE

1. Drag through the address, telephone, fax, and e-mail information in the letterhead, including both paragraph marks at the end of the lines.
2. Click the Font Size box arrow on the Formatting toolbar and then click 9 in the Font Size list.

Word changes the font size to 9 (shown in Figure 3-50 below).

Recall that the Font Color button displays the most recently used color, which is dark red, in this case. When the color you want to use displays on the Font Color button, you simply click the button as shown in the following steps.

More About

The Clipboard Gallery

To delete an item from the Office Clipboard gallery, point to the item in the gallery, click the box arrow to the right of the item, and then click Delete.

Steps To Color Characters the Same Color

1 With the address, telephone, fax, and e-mail information still selected, point to the Font Color button on the Formatting toolbar (Figure 3-50).

2 Click the Font Color button. Click inside the selected text to remove the highlight.

Word changes the color of the selected characters to dark red (shown in Figure 3-51 on the next page).

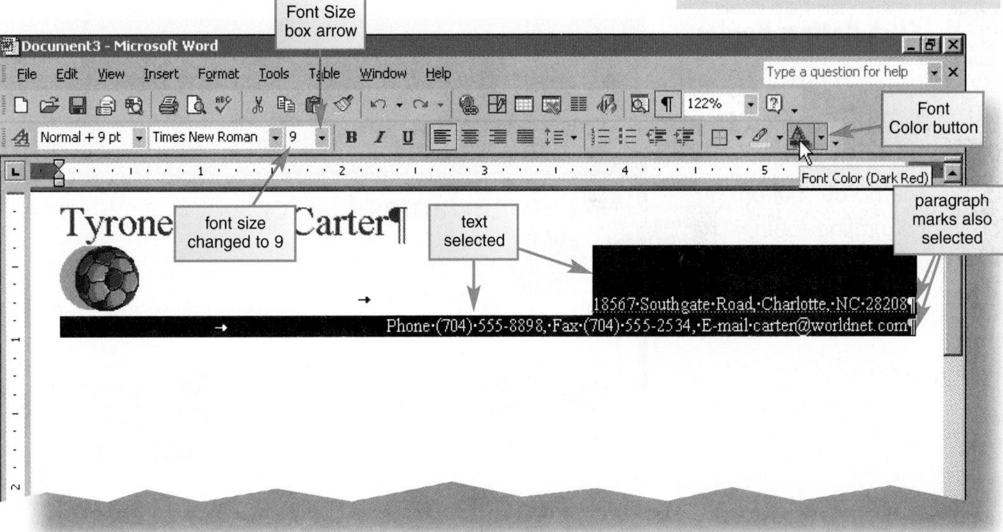

FIGURE 3-50

Other Ways

1. On Format menu click Font, click Font tab, click Font color box arrow, click desired color, click OK button
2. Right-click paragraph mark or selected text, click Font on shortcut menu, click Font tab, click Font color box arrow, click desired color, click OK button
3. In Voice Command mode, say "Font Color, Dark Red"

Adding a Bottom Border to a Paragraph

To add professionalism to the letterhead, you would like to draw a horizontal line from the left margin to the right margin immediately below the telephone, fax, and e-mail information. In Word, you can draw a solid line, called a **border**, at any edge of a paragraph. That is, borders may be added above or below a paragraph, to the left or right of a paragraph, or any combination of these sides.

Perform the steps on the next page to add a bottom border to the paragraph containing telephone, fax, and e-mail information.

Steps To Bottom Border a Paragraph

1 Position the insertion point in the paragraph to border, click the Border button arrow on the Formatting toolbar, and then point to Bottom Border on the border palette.

Word displays the border palette either horizontally or vertically below the Border button (Figure 3-51). Using the border palette, you can add a border to any edge of a paragraph.

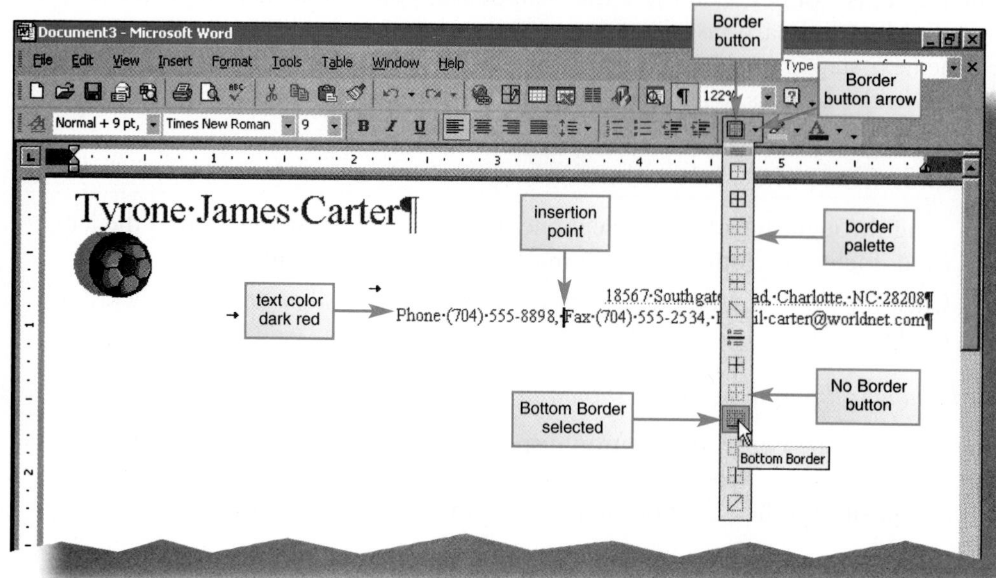

FIGURE 3-51

2 Click Bottom Border.

Word places a bottom border below the paragraph containing the insertion point (Figure 3-52). The Border button on the Formatting toolbar now displays the icon for a bottom border.

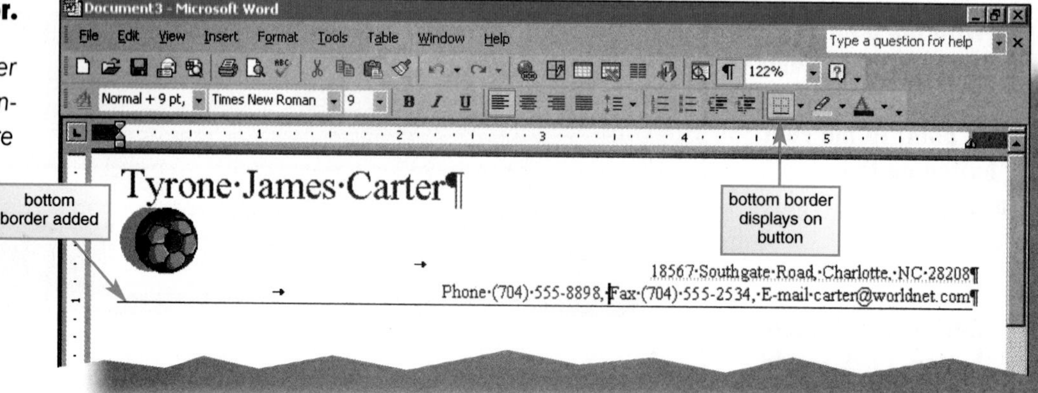

FIGURE 3-52

Other Ways

1. Click Border button arrow on Tables and Borders toolbar, click Bottom Border
2. On Format menu click Borders and Shading, click Borders tab, click Bottom button in Preview area, click OK button
3. In Voice Command mode, say "Borders, Outside Border"

If, for some reason, you wanted to remove a border from a paragraph, you would position the insertion point in the paragraph, click the Border button arrow on the Formatting toolbar, and then click the No Border button (Figure 3-51) on the border palette.

Clearing Formatting

The next step is to position the insertion point below the letterhead, so that you can type the content of the letter. When you press the ENTER key at the end of a paragraph containing a border, Word moves the border forward to the next paragraph. It also retains all current settings. That is, the paragraph will be a dark red font with a bottom border. Instead, you want the paragraph and characters on the new line to use the Normal style: black font with no border. In Word the term, **clear formatting**, refers to returning the formatting to the Normal style.

Perform the following steps to clear formatting at the location of the insertion point.

Steps To Clear Formatting

1 Press the END key to position the insertion point at the end of line 3 and then press the ENTER key. Click the Styles and Formatting button on the Formatting toolbar.

Word displays the Styles and Formatting task pane (Figure 3-53). The insertion point is on line 4. Formatting at the insertion point consists of a bottom border and a dark red font. You want to clear this formatting.

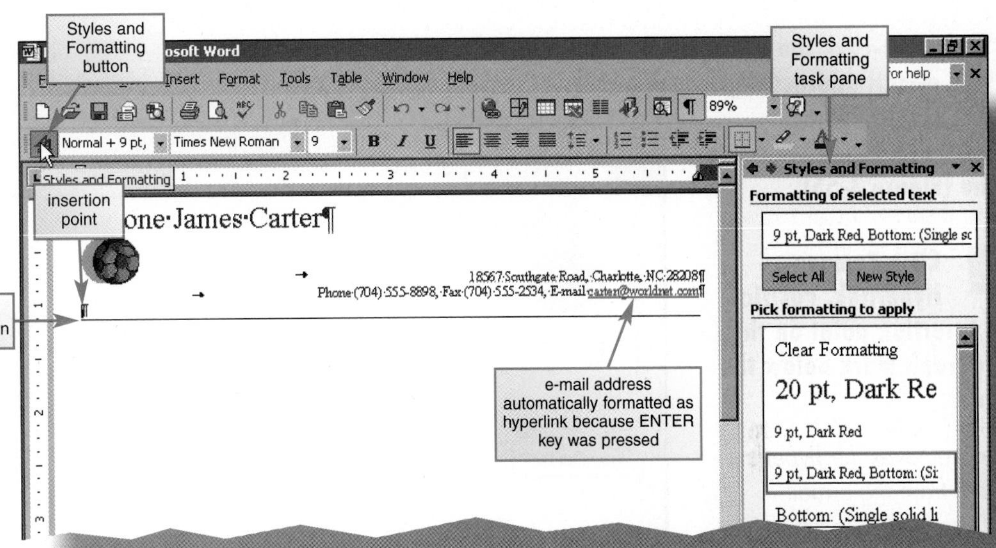

FIGURE 3-53

2 Click Clear Formatting in the Pick formatting to apply area in the Styles and Formatting task pane.

Word applies the Normal style to the location of the insertion point (Figure 3-54).

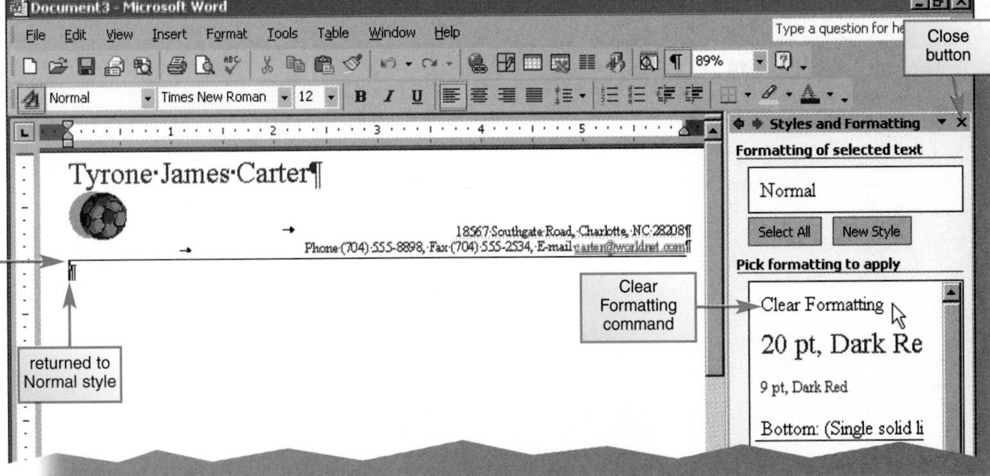

FIGURE 3-54

3 Click the Close button in the upper-right corner of the task pane title bar to close the task pane.

Other Ways

1. Click Style box arrow on Formatting toolbar, scroll to and click Clear Formatting
2. Press CTRL+SPACEBAR, press CTRL+Q
3. In Voice Command mode, say "Styles and Formatting, Clear Formatting, Styles and Formatting"

The next step is to remove the hyperlink autoformat from the e-mail address in the letterhead. As discussed earlier in this project, Word automatically formats text as you type. When you press the ENTER key or SPACEBAR after entering an e-mail address or Web address, Word automatically formats the address as a hyperlink, that is, colored blue and underlined (shown in Figure 3-53). You do not want this format applied to the e-mail address.

Perform the following steps to convert the e-mail address from a hyperlink to regular text.

Steps To Convert a Hyperlink to Regular Text

1 Right-click the e-mail address and then point to Remove Hyperlink on the shortcut menu (Figure 3-55).

2 Click Remove Hyperlink. Position the insertion point on the paragraph mark below the border.

Word removes the hyperlink format from the e-mail address (shown in Figure 3-56 on page WD 3.42).

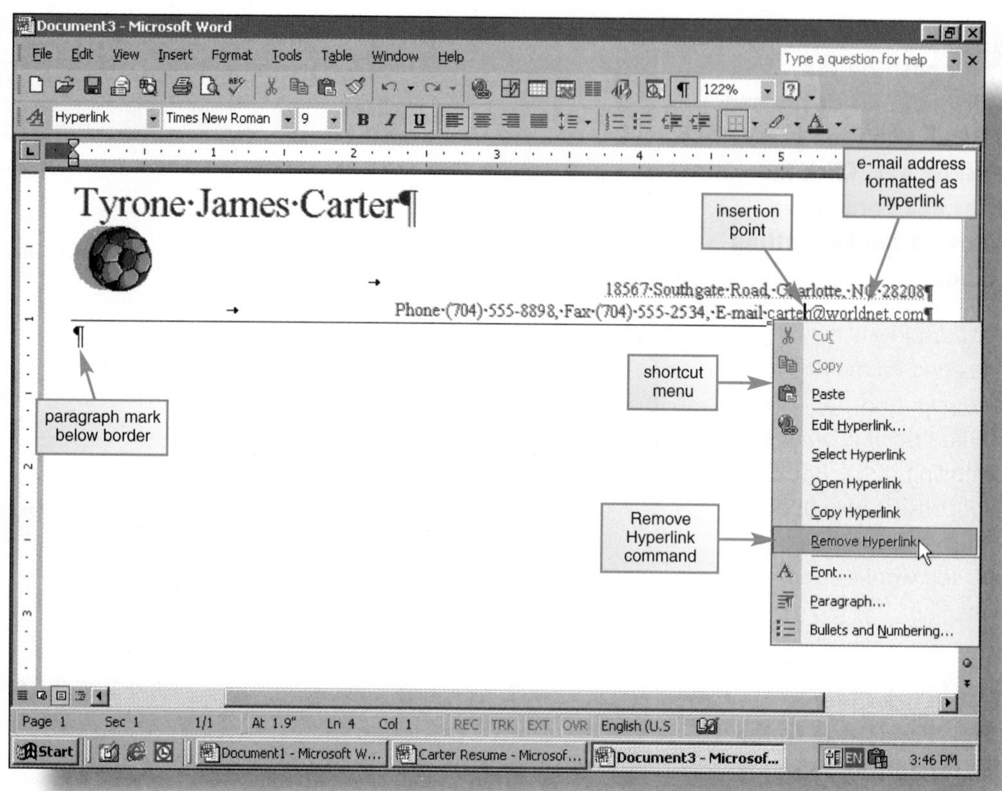

FIGURE 3-55

Other Ways

1. With insertion point in hyperlink, click Insert Hyperlink button on Standard toolbar, click Remove Link button
2. With insertion point in hyperlink, on Insert menu click Hyperlink, click Remove Link button
3. With insertion point in hyperlink, press CTRL+K, press ALT+R
4. With insertion point in hyperlink, in Voice Command mode, say "Right Click, Remove Hyperlink"

Letterhead

Letterhead should contain the complete legal name of the company, group, or individual; full street address including building, room, suite number, or post office box; city; state; and postal code. Some also include a logo, telephone and fax number, Web and e-mail address.

Now that you have created your letterhead, you should save it in a file.

TO SAVE THE LETTERHEAD

1. Insert your floppy disk into drive A.
2. Click the Save button on the Standard toolbar.
3. Type the file name `Carter Letterhead` in the File name text box.
4. If necessary, click the Save in box arrow and then click 3½ Floppy (A:).
5. Click the Save button in the Save As dialog box.

Word saves the document on a floppy disk in drive A with the file name, Carter Letterhead.

Each time you wish to create a letter, you would open your letterhead file (Carter Letterhead) and then immediately save it with a new file name. By doing this, your letterhead file will remain unchanged for future use.

Creating a Cover Letter

You have created a letterhead for the cover letter. The next step is to compose the cover letter. The following pages outline how to use Word to compose a cover letter that contains a table and a bulleted list.

More About

Cover Letters

You always should send a personalized cover letter with a resume. The cover letter should highlight aspects of your background relevant to the position. To help you recall past achievements and activities, keep a personal file containing documents that outline your accomplishments.

Components of a Business Letter

During your professional career, you most likely will create many business letters. A **cover letter** is one type of business letter. All business letters contain the same basic components.

When preparing business letters, you should include all essential elements. **Essential business letter elements** include the date line, inside address, message, and signature block (Figure 3-2a on the page WD 3.06). The **date line**, which consists of the month, day, and year, is positioned two to six lines below the letterhead. The **inside address**, placed three to eight lines below the date line, usually contains the addressee's courtesy title plus full name, business affiliation, and full geographical address. The **salutation**, if present, begins two lines below the last line of the inside address. The body of the letter, the message, begins two lines below the salutation. Within the **message**, paragraphs are single-spaced with double-spacing between paragraphs. Two lines below the last line of the message, the **complimentary close** displays. Capitalize only the first word in a complimentary close. Type the **signature block** at least four lines below the complimentary close, allowing room for the author to sign his or her name.

You can follow many different styles when you create business letters. The cover letter in this project follows the **modified block style**. Table 3-2 outlines the differences between three common styles of business letters.

Table 3-2 Common Business Styles

LETTER STYLES	*FEATURES*
Block	All components of the letter begin flush with the left margin.
Modified Block	The date, complimentary close, and signature block are centered, positioned approximately ½" to the right of center, or at the right margin. All other components of the letter begin flush with the left margin.
Modified Semi-Block	The date, complimentary close, and signature block are centered, positioned approximately ½" to the right of center, or at the right margin. The first line of each paragraph in the body of the letter is indented ½" to 1" from the left margin. All other components of the letter begin flush with the left margin.

Saving the Cover Letter with a New File Name

The document in the document window currently has the name Carter Letterhead, the name of the personal letterhead. You want the letterhead to remain intact. Thus, you should save the document with a new file name, as described in these steps.

Saving

As an alternative to saving the letterhead as a Word document, you could save it as a template by clicking the Save as type box arrow in the Save As dialog box and then clicking Document Template. To use the template, click File on the menu bar, click New, click General Templates in the New Document task pane, and then double-click the template icon or name.

TO SAVE THE DOCUMENT WITH A NEW FILE NAME

1. If necessary, insert your floppy disk into drive A.
2. Click File on the menu bar and then click Save As.
3. Type the file name `Carter Cover Letter` in the File name text box.
4. If necessary, click the Save in box arrow and then click 3½ Floppy (A:).
5. Click the Save button in the Save As dialog box.

Word saves the document on a floppy disk in drive A with the file name, Carter Cover Letter (shown in Figure 3-56 on the next page).

Tabs

To insert a vertical line at a tab stop, click the button at the left edge of the horizontal ruler until its icon changes to a Bar Tab icon (a vertical bar) and then click the location on the ruler.

Setting Tab Stops Using the Ruler

The first required element of the cover letter is the date line, which in this letter is to be positioned two lines below the letterhead. The date line, which contains the month, day, and year, begins 3.5 inches from the left margin, or one-half inch to the right of center. Thus, you should set a custom tab stop at the 3.5" mark on the ruler.

Earlier you used the Tabs dialog box to set a tab stop because you could not use the ruler to set a tab stop at the right margin. In the following steps, you set a left-aligned tab stop using the ruler.

Steps To Set Custom Tab Stops Using the Ruler

1 With the insertion point on the paragraph mark below the border, press the ENTER key. If necessary, click the button at the left edge of the horizontal ruler until it displays the Left Tab icon. Point to the 3.5" mark on the ruler.

Each time you click the button at the left of the horizontal ruler, its icon changes (Figure 3-56). The left tab icon looks like a capital letter L (L).

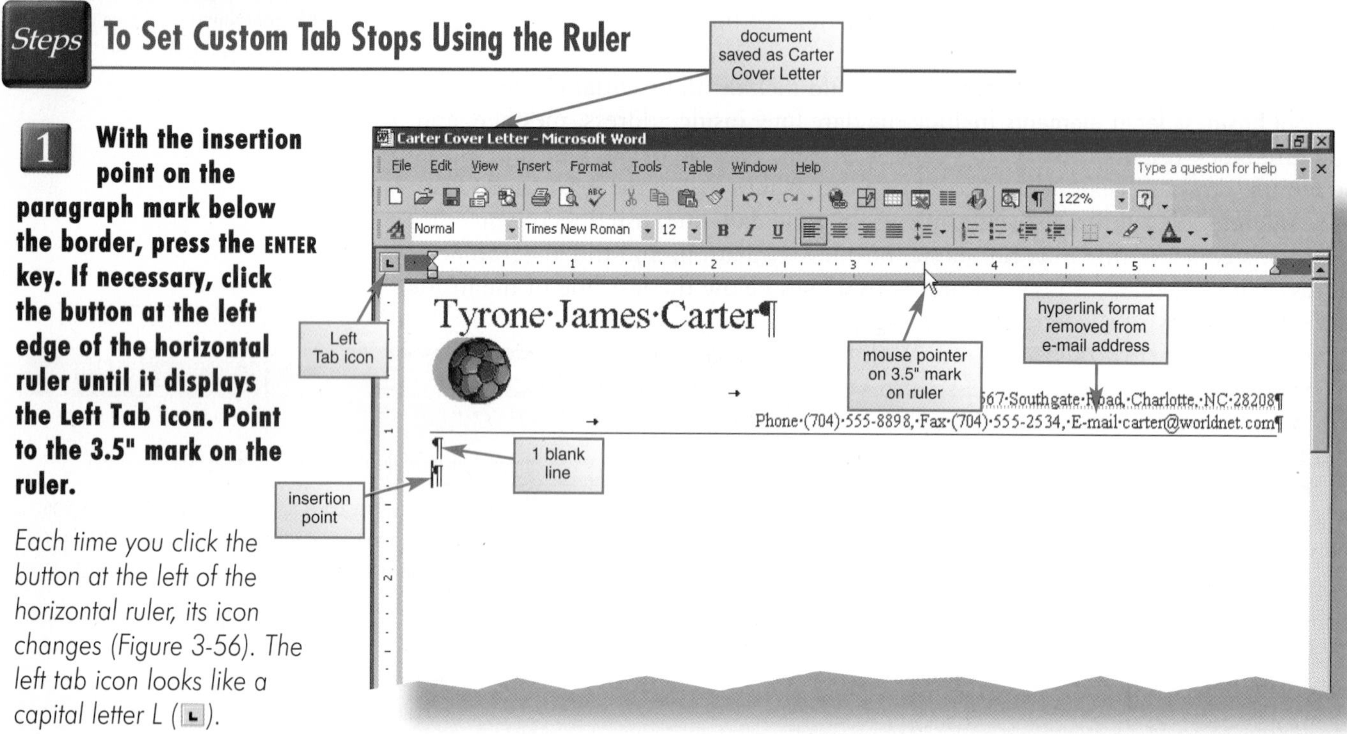

FIGURE 3-56

2 Click the 3.5" mark on the ruler.

Word places a left tab marker at the 3.5" mark on the ruler (Figure 3-57). The text you type at this tab stop will be left-aligned.

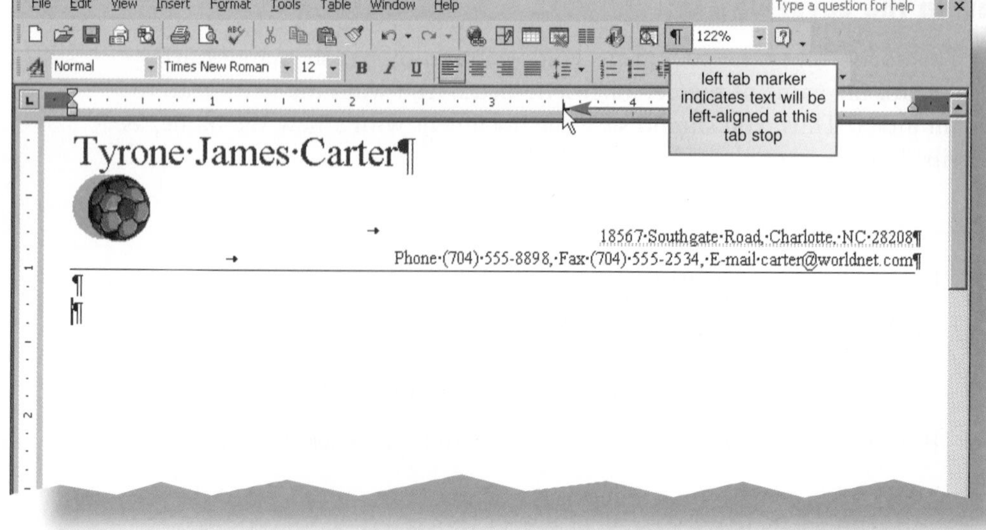

FIGURE 3-57

Other Ways

1. On Format menu click Tabs, enter tab stop position, click appropriate alignment, click OK button
2. In Voice Command mode, say "Format, Tabs"

If, for some reason, you wanted to move a custom tab stop, drag the tab marker to the desired location on the ruler.

If you wanted to change the alignment of a custom tab stop, you could remove the existing tab stop and then insert a new one as described in the steps above. To remove a custom tab stop, point to the tab marker on the ruler and then drag the tab marker down and out of the ruler. You also could use the Tabs dialog box to change an existing tab stop's alignment or position. As discussed earlier in this project, you click Format on the menu bar and then click Tabs to display the Tabs dialog box.

More About

Dates

A field is a set of codes that instructs Word to perform a certain action. If you want Word to display the current date or time when you print a document, make it a field. That is, place a check mark in the Update automatically check box in the Date and Time dialog box (Figure 3-59 on the next page) when you insert the current date or time.

Inserting the Current Date into a Document

The next step is to enter the current date at the 3.5" tab stop in the document. Word provides a method of inserting a computer's system date into a document. Perform the following steps to insert the current date into the cover letter.

Steps To Insert the Current Date into a Document

1 Press the TAB key. Click Insert on the menu bar and then point to Date and Time (Figure 3-58).

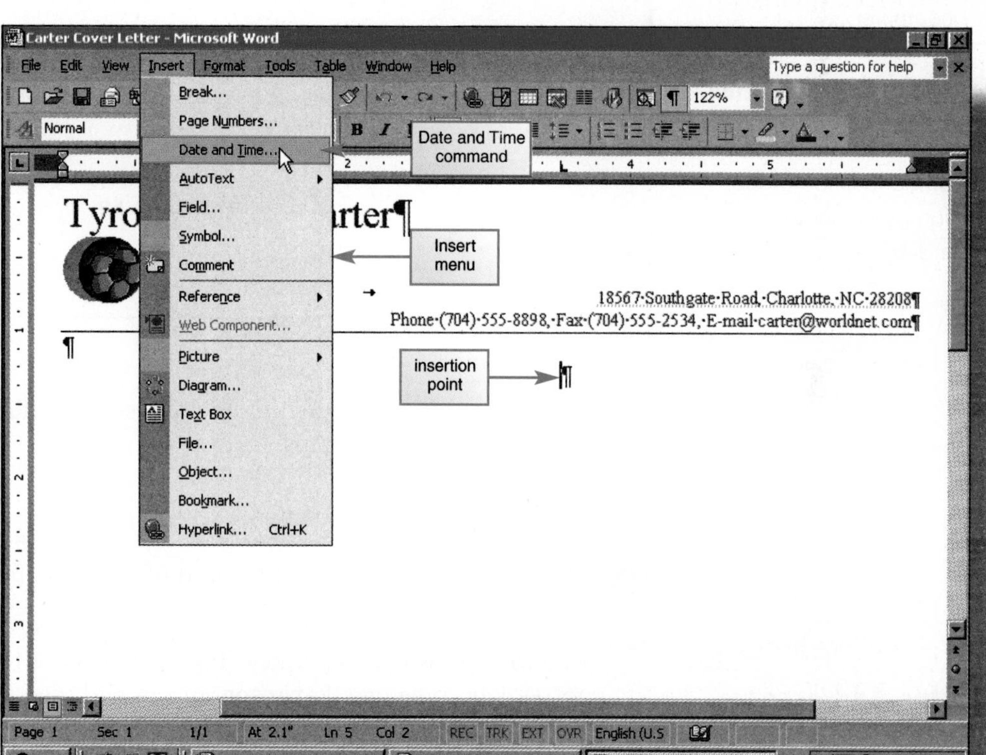

FIGURE 3-58

2 Click Date and Time. When the Date and Time dialog box displays, click the desired format (in this case, May 15, 2003). If a check mark displays in the Update automatically check box, click the check box to remove the check mark. Point to the OK button.

Word displays a list of available dates and times in the Date and Time dialog box (Figure 3-59). Your dialog box will differ, showing the current system date stored in your computer.

Click the OK button.

Word displays the current date at the location of the insertion point (shown in Figure 3-60).

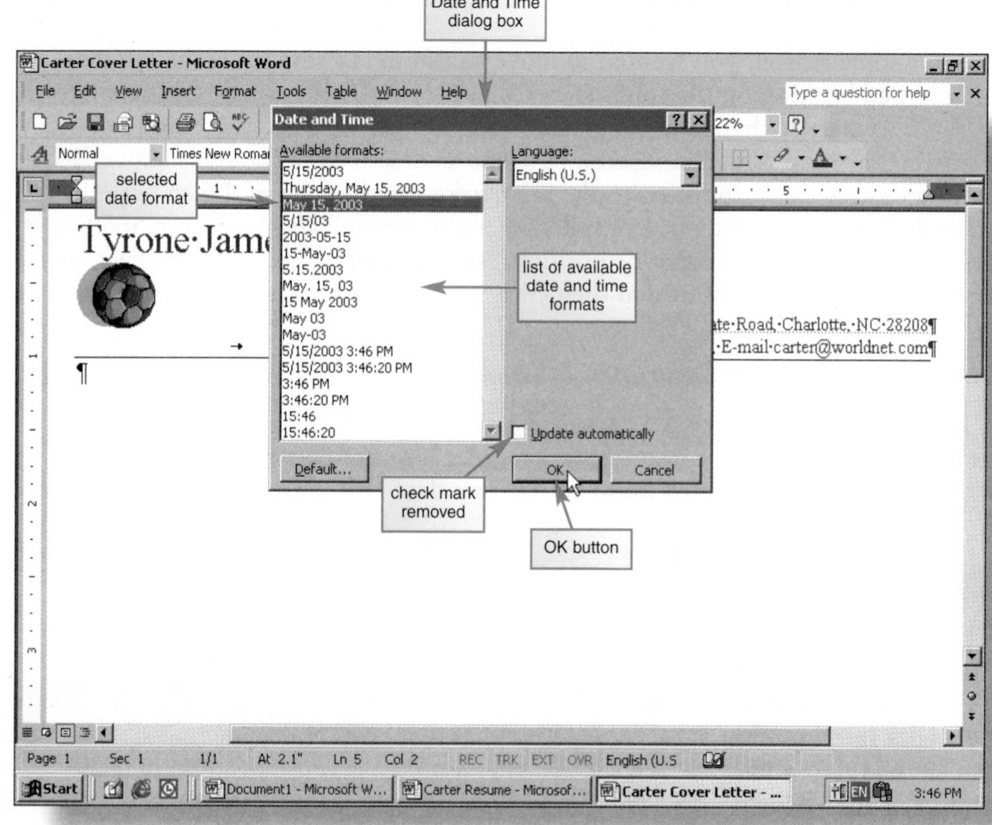

FIGURE 3-59

1. In Voice Command mode, say "Insert, Date and Time, [select format], OK"

Inside Addresses

Pay close attention to the spelling, punctuation, and official abbreviations of company names. For example, does the company name spell out the word, and, or does it use the ampersand character (&)? Is the word, Company, spelled out or abbreviated?

The next step is to type the inside address and salutation in the cover letter as described in the following steps.

TO ENTER THE INSIDE ADDRESS AND SALUTATION

1. With the insertion point at the end of the date, press the ENTER key three times.
2. Type `Ms. Mae Li` and then press the ENTER key. Type `Personnel Director` and then press the ENTER key. Type `Peterson High School` and then press the ENTER key. Type `One Peterson Drive` and then press the ENTER key. Type `Charlotte, NC 28208` and then press the ENTER key twice.
3. Type `Dear Ms. Li` and then press the COLON key (:).

The inside address and salutation are entered (Figure 3-60).

Creating an AutoText Entry

If you use the same text frequently, you can store the text in an **AutoText entry** and then use the stored entry throughout the open document, as well as future documents. That is, you type the entry only once, and for all future occurrences of the text, you access the stored entry as you need it. In this way, you avoid entering the text inconsistently or incorrectly in different locations throughout the same document.

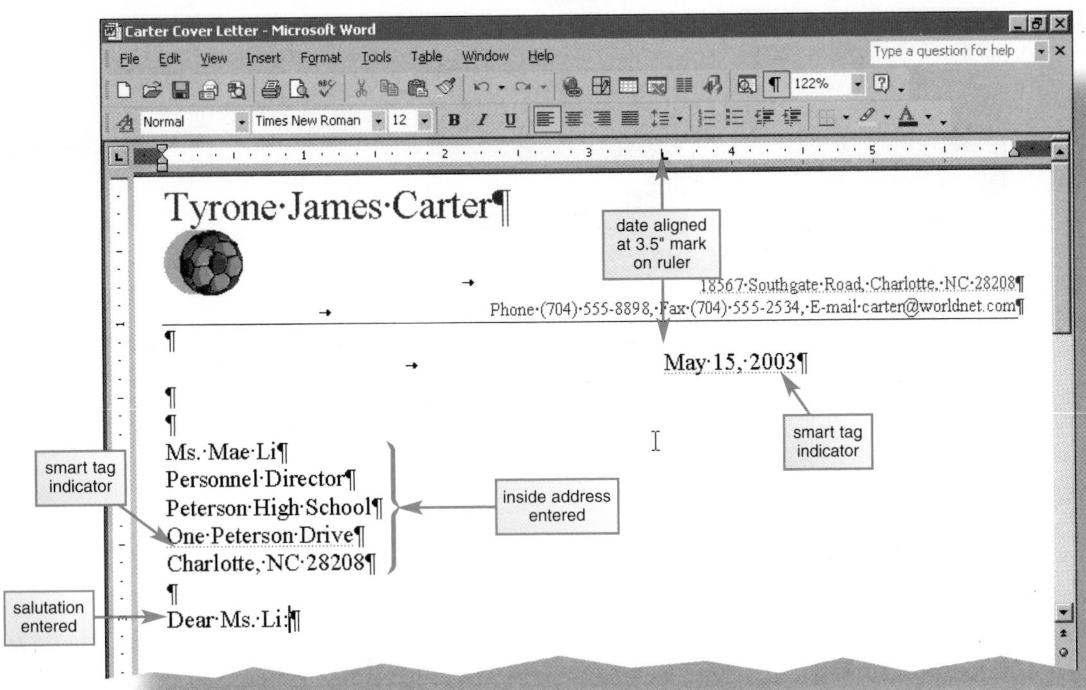

FIGURE 3-60

Perform the following steps to create an AutoText entry for the prospective employer's name.

Steps To Create an AutoText Entry

1 Drag through the text to be stored, in this case, Peterson High School. If the Smart Tag Actions button displays when you try to drag, move the mouse pointer up and then try dragging again. Be sure not to select the paragraph mark at the end of the text. Click Insert on the menu bar and then point to AutoText. Point to New on the AutoText submenu.

The employer name, Peterson High School, in the inside address is selected (Figure 3-61). Notice the paragraph mark is not part of the selection.

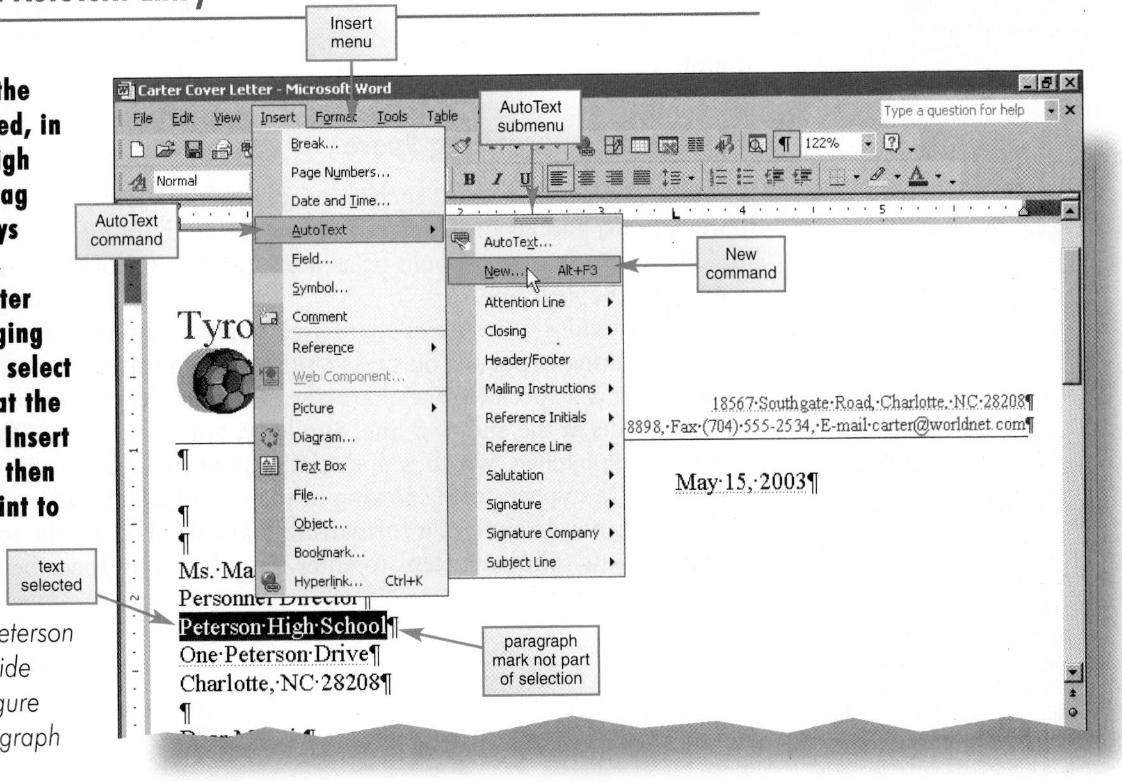

FIGURE 3-61

2 **Click New. When the Create AutoText dialog box displays, type** phs **and then point to the OK button.**

Word displays the Create AutoText dialog box (Figure 3-62). In this dialog box, Word proposes a name for the AutoText entry. You change it to a shorter name, phs.

3 **Click the OK button. If Word displays a dialog box, click the Yes button.**

Word stores the AutoText entry and closes the AutoText dialog box.

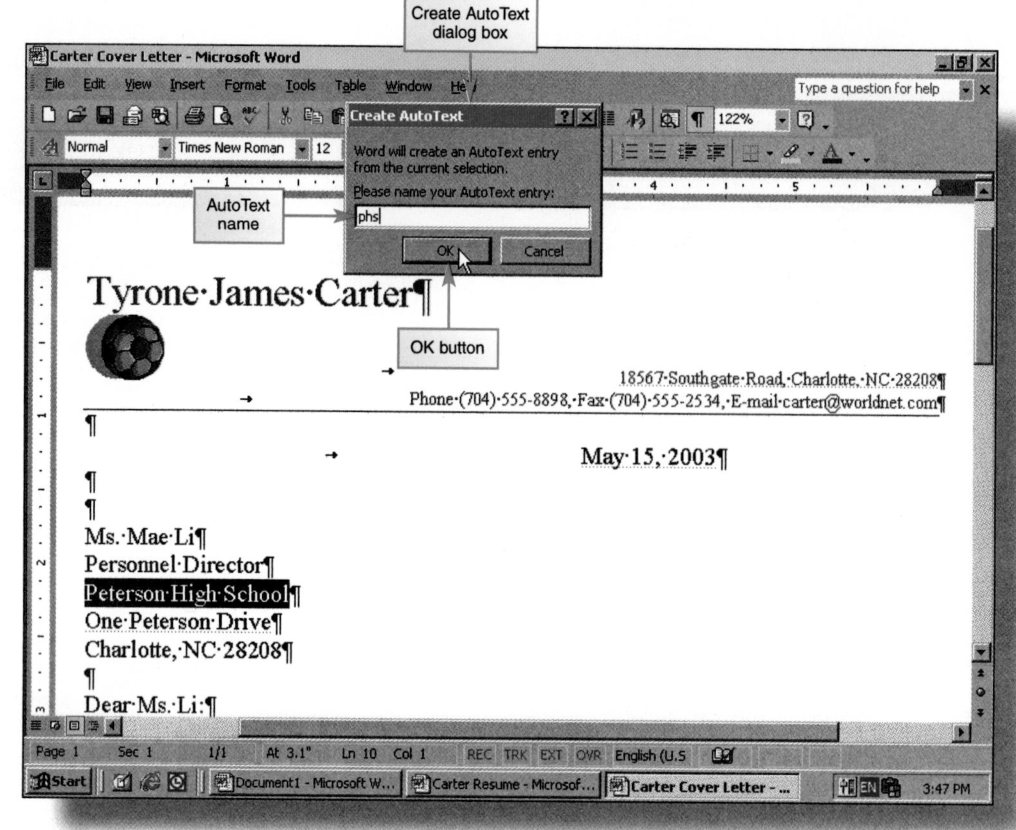

FIGURE 3-62

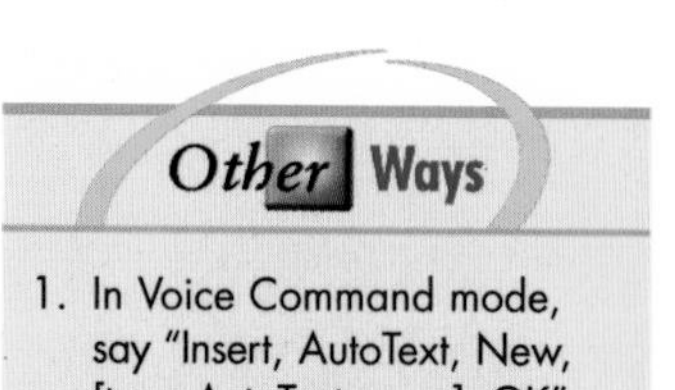

1. In Voice Command mode, say "Insert, AutoText, New, [type AutoText name], OK"

The name, phs, has been stored as an AutoText entry. Later in the project, you will use the AutoText entry, phs, instead of typing the employer name, Peterson High School.

Entering a Nonbreaking Space

Some compound words, such as proper names, dates, units of time and measure, abbreviations, and geographic destinations, should not be divided at the end of a line. These words either should fit as a unit at the end of a line or be wrapped together to the next line.

Word provides two special characters to assist with this task: nonbreaking space and nonbreaking hyphen. You press CTRL+SHIFT+SPACEBAR to enter a **nonbreaking space**, which is a special space character that prevents two words from splitting if the first word falls at the end of a line. Similarly, you press CTRL+SHIFT+HYPHEN to enter a **nonbreaking hyphen**, which is a special type of hyphen that prevents two words separated by a hyphen from splitting at the end of a line. When you enter these characters into a document, a formatting mark displays on the screen.

Perform the following steps to enter a nonbreaking space between the words in the newspaper name.

Salutations

The salutation "To whom it may concern" should be avoided — it is extremely impersonal. If you cannot obtain the name and gender of the company officer to whom you are addressing the letter, then use the recipient's title in the salutation, e.g., Dear Personnel Supervisor.

Steps To Insert a Nonbreaking Space

1 Scroll the salutation to the top of the document window. Click after the colon in the salutation and then press the ENTER key twice. If the Office Assistant displays, click Just type the letter without help. Type `I am responding to the social studies teacher's assistant position advertised in the` **and then press the SPACEBAR. Press CTRL+I to turn on italics. Type** `Herald` **and then press CTRL+SHIFT+SPACEBAR.**

Word enters a nonbreaking space after the word, Herald (Figure 3-63).

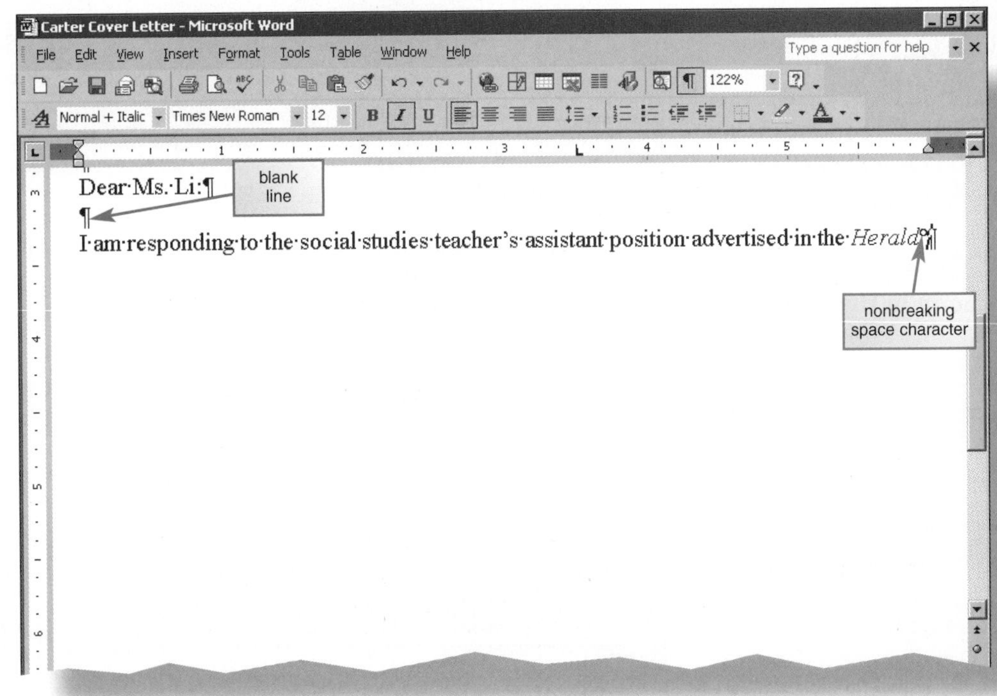

FIGURE 3-63

2 Type `Times` **and then press CTRL+I to turn off italics. Press the PERIOD key.**

Word wraps the two words in the newspaper title, Herald Times, to the next line (Figure 3-64).

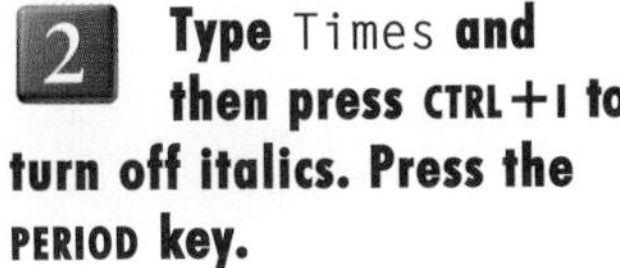

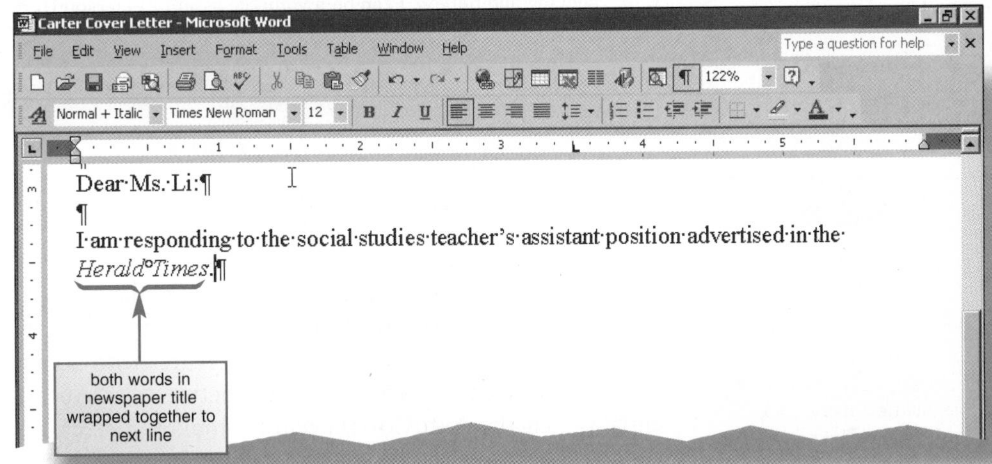

FIGURE 3-64

Other Ways

1. On Insert menu click Symbol, click Special Characters tab, click Nonbreaking Space in Character list, click Insert button, click Close button
2. In Dictation mode, say "Control Shift Spacebar"

Inserting an AutoText Entry

At the end of the next sentence in the body of the cover letter, you want to put the prospective employer name, Peterson High School. Recall that earlier in this project, you stored an AutoText entry name of phs for Peterson High School. Thus, you will type the AutoText entry's name and then instruct Word to replace the AutoText entry's name with the stored entry of Peterson High School.

Perform the steps on the next page to insert an AutoText entry.

Steps To Insert an AutoText Entry

1 **Press the SPACEBAR. Type** As indicated on the enclosed resume, I have the credentials you are seeking and believe I can be a valuable asset to phs **as shown in Figure 3-65.**

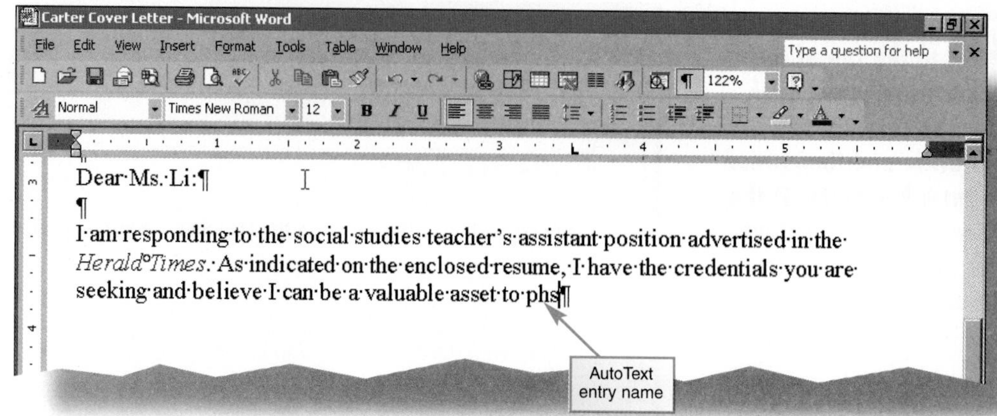

FIGURE 3-65

2 **Press the F3 key. Press the PERIOD key.**

Word replaces the characters, phs, with the stored AutoText entry, Peterson High School, when you press the F3 key (Figure 3-66).

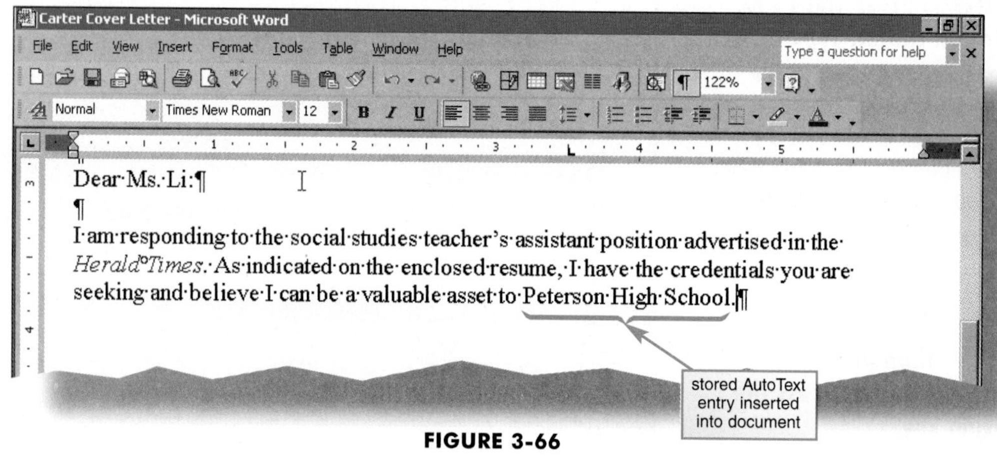

FIGURE 3-66

Other Ways

1. Type first few characters to display AutoComplete tip, press ENTER
2. On Insert menu point to AutoText, point to appropriate AutoText entry, click desired AutoText entry on submenu
3. On Insert menu point to AutoText, click AutoText, select desired AutoText entry name, click OK button

Pressing the F3 key instructs Word to replace the AutoText entry name with the stored AutoText entry. In Project 2, you learned how to use the AutoCorrect feature, which enables you to insert and also create AutoCorrect entries (just as you did for this AutoText entry). The difference between an AutoCorrect entry and an AutoText entry is that the AutoCorrect feature makes corrections for you automatically as soon as you press the SPACEBAR or a punctuation mark key, whereas you must press the F3 key or click the AutoText command to instruct Word to make an AutoText correction.

If you watch the screen as you type, you may discover that AutoComplete tips display on the screen. As you type, Word searches the list of AutoText entry names and if one matches your typing, Word displays its complete name above your typing as an **AutoComplete tip**. In addition to AutoText entries, Word proposes AutoComplete tips for the current date, a day of the week, a month, and so on. If your screen does not display AutoComplete tips, click Tools on the menu bar, click AutoCorrect Options, click the AutoText tab, click Show AutoComplete suggestions, and then click the OK button. To view the complete list of entries, click Tools on the menu bar, click AutoCorrect, click the AutoText tab, and then scroll through the list of entries. To ignore an AutoComplete tip proposed by Word, simply continue typing to remove the AutoComplete tip from the screen.

Perform the following steps to enter the next paragraph into the cover letter.

TO ENTER A PARAGRAPH

1. Press the ENTER key twice.
2. Type I recently received my bachelor's degree in social studies teaching from North Carolina State. The following table outlines my areas of concentration and then press the COLON key.
3. Press the ENTER key twice.

The paragraph is entered (shown in Figure 3-67 below).

The next step is to enter a table into the cover letter.

Creating a Table with the Insert Table Button

The next step in composing the cover letter is to place a table listing your areas of concentration (Figure 3-2a on page WD 3.06). You create this table using Word's table feature. As discussed earlier in this project, a Word table is a collection of rows and columns, and the intersection of a row and a column is called a cell.

Within a Word table, you easily can rearrange rows and columns, change column widths, sort rows and columns, and sum the contents of rows and columns. You also can format and chart table data.

The first step in creating a table is to insert an empty table into the document. When inserting a table, you must specify the total number of rows and columns required, which is called the **dimension** of the table. The table in this project has two columns. You often do not know the total number of rows in a table. Thus, many Word users create one row initially and then add rows as they need them. The first number in a dimension is the number of rows, and the second is the number of columns.

Perform the following steps to insert a 1 × 2 table; that is, a table with one row and two columns.

Word Tables

Although you can use the TAB key to create a table, many Word users prefer to use the table feature. With a Word table, you can arrange numbers and text in columns. For emphasis, tables can be shaded and have borders. The contents of Word tables can be sorted, and you can have Word sum the contents of an entire row or column.

Steps To Insert an Empty Table

1. **Click the Insert Table button on the Standard toolbar. Point to the cell in the first row and second column of the grid to select the first two cells in the first row of the grid.**

Word displays a grid to define the dimension of the desired table (Figure 3-67). Word will insert the table immediately above the insertion point.

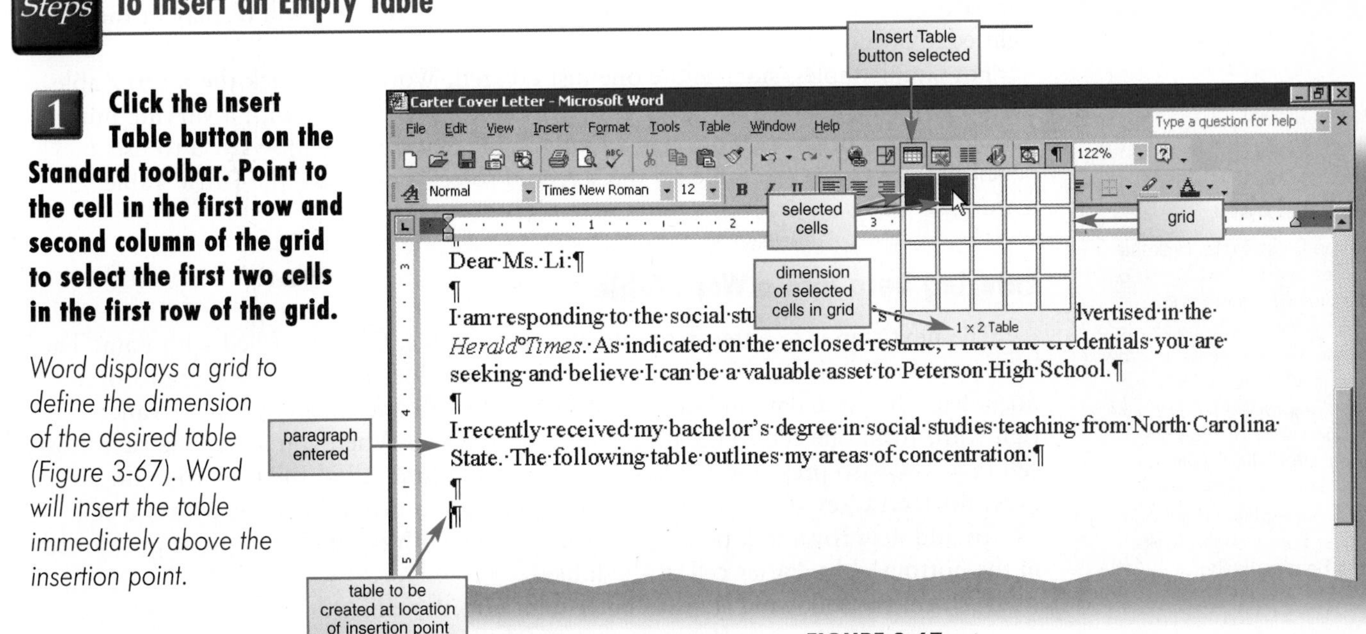

FIGURE 3-67

2 **Click the cell in the first row and second column of the grid.**

Word inserts an empty 1 × 2 table into the document (Figure 3-68). The insertion point is in the first cell (row 1 and column 1) of the table.

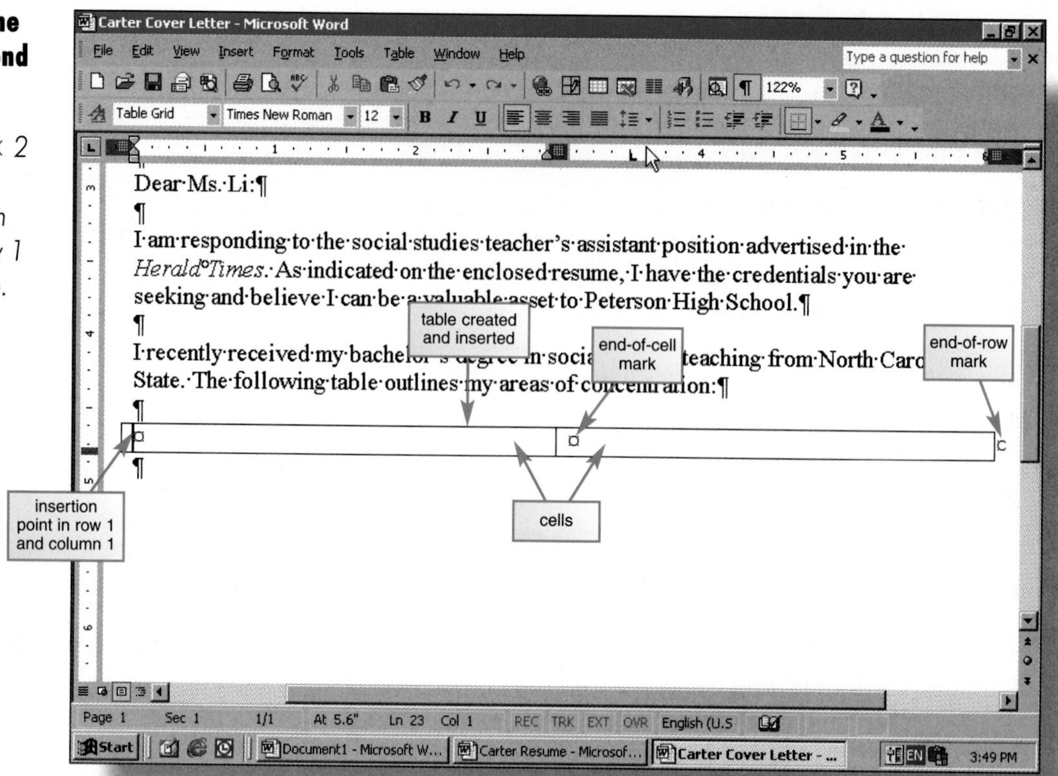

FIGURE 3-68

Other Ways

1. On Table menu point to Insert, click Table on Insert submenu, enter number of columns, enter number of rows, click OK button
2. In Voice Command mode, say "Insert Table, [select table dimension]"

More About

Draw Table

To use Draw Table, click the Tables and Borders button on the Standard toolbar to change the mouse pointer to a pencil. Use the pencil to draw from one corner to the opposite diagonal corner to define the perimeter of the table. Then, draw the column and row lines inside the perimeter. To remove a line, use the Eraser button on the Tables and Borders toolbar.

As discussed earlier in this project, each row of a table has an end-of-row mark, which you can use to add columns to the right of a table. Each cell has an end-of-cell mark, which you can use to select a cell. The end-of-cell mark currently is left-aligned; thus it is positioned at the left edge of each cell. You can use any of the paragraph formatting buttons on the Formatting toolbar to change the alignment of the text within the cells. For example, if you click the Align Right button on the Formatting toolbar, the end-of-cell mark and any entered text will display at the right edge of the cell.

For simple tables, such as the one just created, Word users click the Insert Table button to create a table. For more complex tables, such as one with a varying number of columns per row, Word has a Draw Table feature that allows you to use a pencil pointer to draw a table on the screen. Project 4 discusses the Draw Table feature.

Entering Data into a Word Table

The next step is to enter data into the empty table. Cells are filled with data. The data you enter within a cell wordwraps just as text does between the margins of a document. To place data into a cell, you click the cell and then type. To advance rightward from one cell to the next, press the TAB key. When you are at the rightmost cell in a row, also press the TAB key to move to the first cell in the next row; do not press the ENTER key. The ENTER key is used to begin a new paragraph within a cell.

To add new rows to a table, press the TAB key with the insertion point positioned in the bottom right corner cell of the table.

Perform the following steps to enter data into the table.

To Enter Data into a Table

1 If necessary, scroll the table up in the document window. With the insertion point in the left cell of the table, type U.S. History **and then press the TAB key. Type** 18 hours **and then press the TAB key.**

Word enters the table data into the first row of the table and adds a second row to the table (Figure 3-69). The insertion point is positioned in the first cell of the second row.

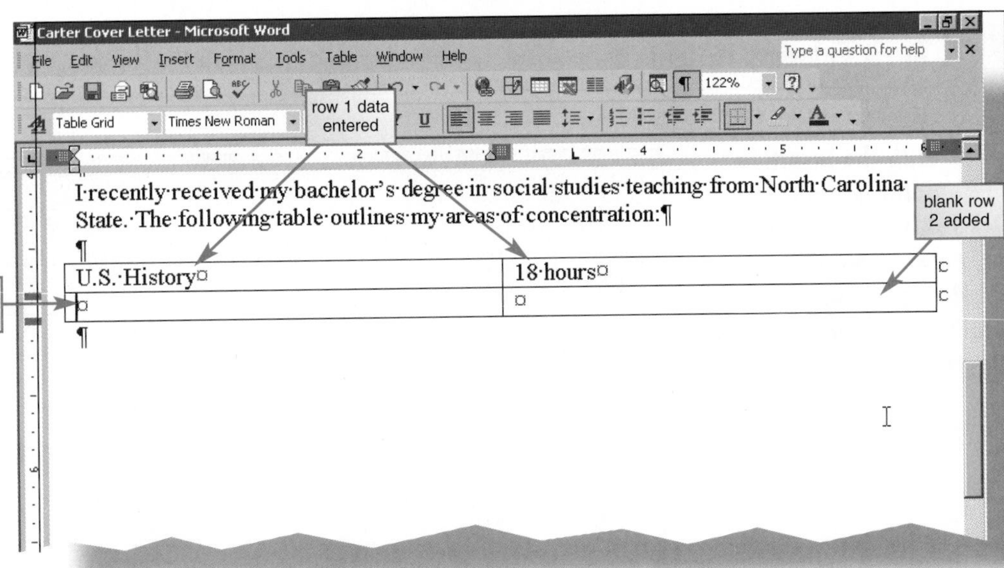

FIGURE 3-69

2 Type World Civilization **and then press the TAB key. Type** 12 hours **and then press the TAB key. Type** Government **and then press the TAB key. Type** 12 hours **and then press the TAB key. Type** Sociology **and then press the TAB key. Type** 10 hours **as shown in Figure 3-70.**

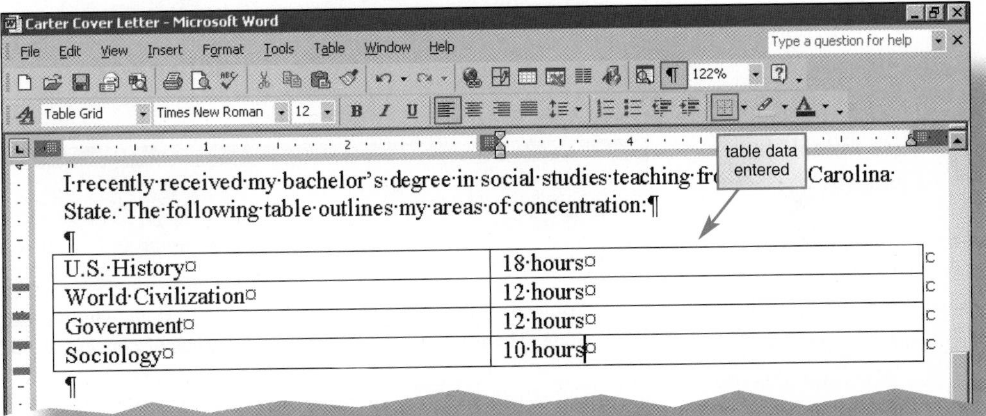

FIGURE 3-70

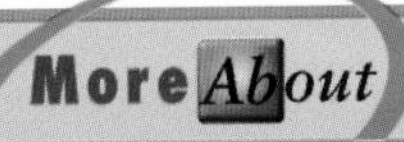

1. In Dictation mode, say "U.S. History, Tab, 18 hours, Tab"

You modify the contents of cells just as you modify text in a document. To delete the contents of a cell, select the cell contents by pointing to the left edge of a cell and clicking when the mouse pointer changes direction, and then press the DELETE key. To modify text in a cell, click in the cell and then correct the entry. You can double-click the OVR indicator on the status bar to toggle between insert and overtype modes. You also can drag and drop or cut and paste the contents of cells.

More About

Table Commands

If a Table command is dimmed on the Table menu, the insertion point might not be in the table.

Resizing Table Columns

The table in this project currently extends from the left margin to the right margin of the document. You want each column only to be as wide as the longest entry in the table. That is, the first column must be wide enough to accommodate the words, World Civilization; and the second column must be wide enough for the phrase, 18 hours.

Perform the following steps to instruct Word to fit automatically the width of the columns to the contents of the table.

Steps To Fit Columns to Table Contents

1 With the insertion point in the table, click Table on the menu bar, point to AutoFit, and then point to AutoFit to Contents (Figure 3-71).

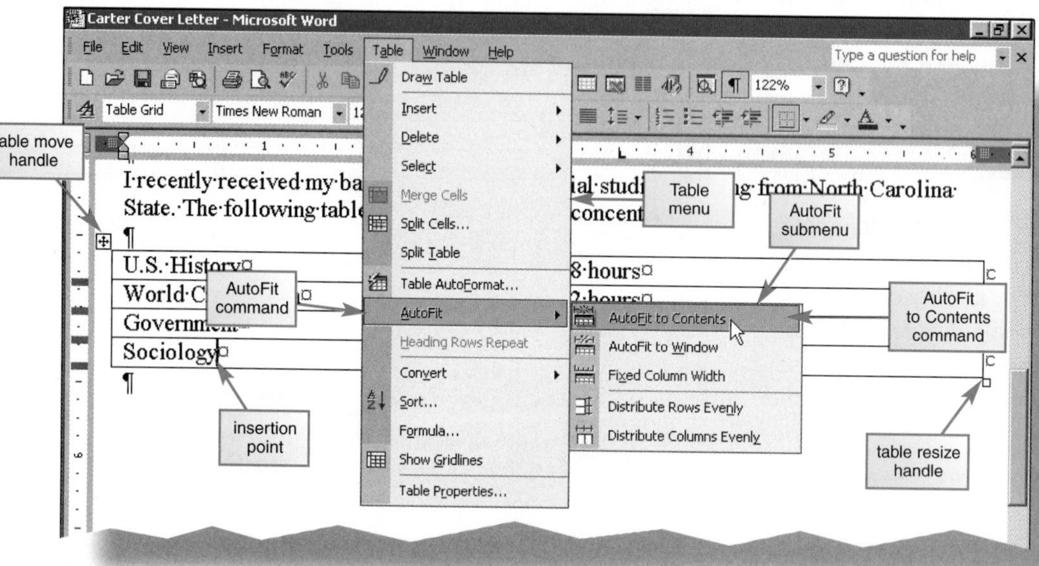

FIGURE 3-71

2 Click AutoFit to Contents.

Word automatically adjusts the widths of the columns based on the amount of text in the table (Figure 3-72). In this case, Word reduces the widths of the columns.

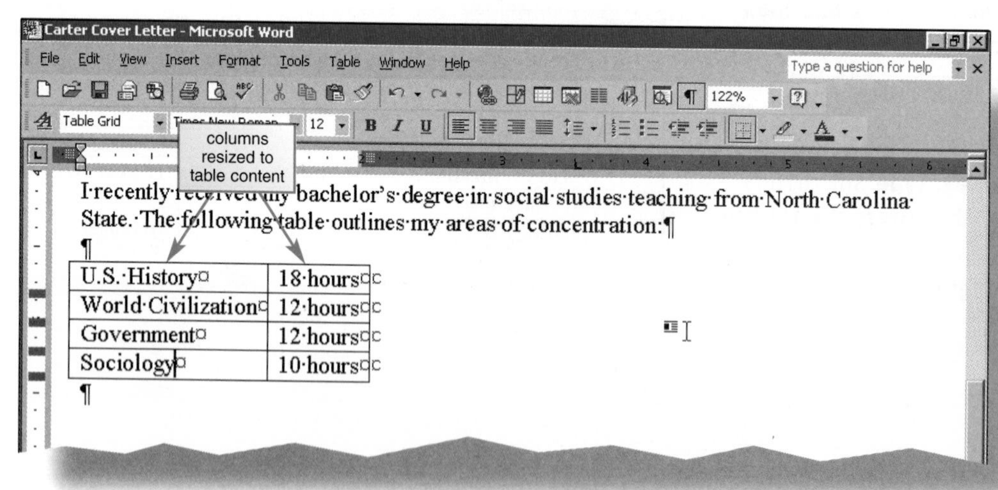

FIGURE 3-72

Other Ways

1. Double-click column boundary
2. Right-click table, point to AutoFit on shortcut menu, click AutoFit to Contents
3. In Voice Command mode, say "Table, AutoFit, AutoFit to Contents"

If you do not want to resize the columns to the table widths, Word provides other options. You can drag a **column boundary**, the border to the right of a column, until the column is the desired width. Similarly, you can resize a row by dragging the **row boundary**, the border at the top of a row, until the row is the desired height. You also can resize the entire table by dragging the **table resize handle**, which is a small square that will display when you point to the bottom right corner of the table (Figure 3-71).

Changing the Table Alignment

When you first create a table, it is left-aligned; that is, flush with the left margin. In this cover letter, the table should be centered. To center a table, you first must select the entire table and then center it using the Center button on the Formatting toolbar, as shown in the following series of steps.

More About

AutoFormat

Word has many predefined table formats that you can apply to tables. With the insertion point in the table, click Table on the menu bar, click Table AutoFormat (Figure 3-71), click the desired format, and then click the OK button.

To Select a Table

1 Position the mouse pointer in the table so the table move handle displays. Position the mouse pointer on the table move handle and then click.

Word selects the entire table (Figure 3-73).

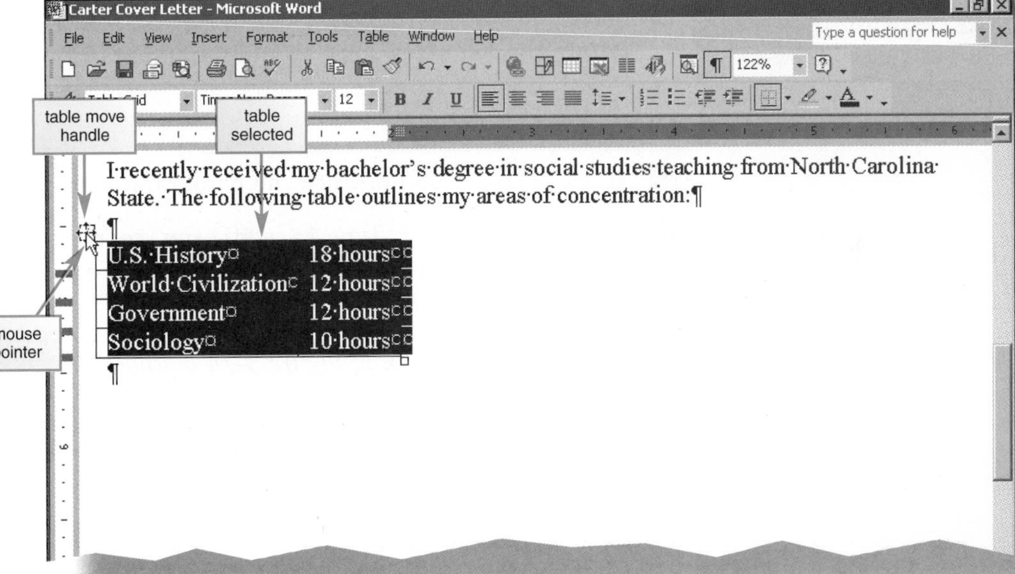

FIGURE 3-73

Other Ways

1. On Table menu point to Select, click Table
2. With insertion point in table, press ALT+5 (using the 5 on the numeric keypad with NUM LOCK off)
3. In Voice Command mode, say "Table, Select, Table"

When working with tables, you may need to select the contents of cells, rows, columns, or the entire table. Table 3-3 identifies how to select various items in a table.

Table 3-3 Selecting Items in a Table

ITEM TO SELECT	ACTION
Cell	Click left edge of cell
Column	Click border at top of column
Multiple cells, rows, or columns adjacent to one another	Drag through cells, rows, or columns
Multiple cells, rows, or columns not adjacent to one another	Select first cell, row, or column and then hold down CTRL key while selecting next cell, row, or column
Next cell	Press TAB key
Previous cell	Press SHIFT+TAB
Row	Click to left of row
Table	Click table move handle

More About

Tabs

The TAB key advances the insertion point from one cell to the next in a table. Thus, press CTRL+TAB to insert a tab character into a cell.

Table Formats

You can change the width of a column to an exact measurement. Hold down the ALT key while dragging markers on the ruler. Or, click Table on the menu bar, click Table Properties, click the Column tab, enter desired measurements, and then click the OK button. Similarly, to change the row height to an exact measurement, click the Row tab in the Table Properties dialog box, enter desired measurements, and then click the OK button.

Perform the following step to center the selected table between the margins.

TO CENTER A SELECTED TABLE

1 Click the Center button on the Formatting toolbar.

Word centers the selected table between the left and right margins (shown in Figure 3-73 on the previous page).

When an entire table is selected and you click the Center button on the Formatting toolbar, Word centers the entire table. If you wanted to center the contents of the cells, you would select the cells by dragging through them and then click the Center button.

Perform the following steps to add more text below the table.

TO ADD MORE TEXT

1 If necessary, scroll up. Click the paragraph mark below the table.

2 Press the ENTER key. Type `In addition to my coursework, I have the following teaching experience` and then press the COLON key. Press the ENTER key.

The text is entered (shown in Figure 3-74 below).

The next step is to enter a bulleted list into the cover letter.

Bulleting a List

You can type a list and then place the bullets on the paragraphs at a later time, or you can use Word's AutoFormat As You Type feature to bullet the paragraphs as you type them (Table 3-1 on page WD 3.23).

Perform the following steps to add bullets automatically to a list as you type.

Steps To Bullet a List as You Type

1 **Press the ASTERISK key (*). Press the SPACEBAR. Type** `Worked as a teacher's aide at Hampton Elementary School` **as the first list item (Figure 3-74).**

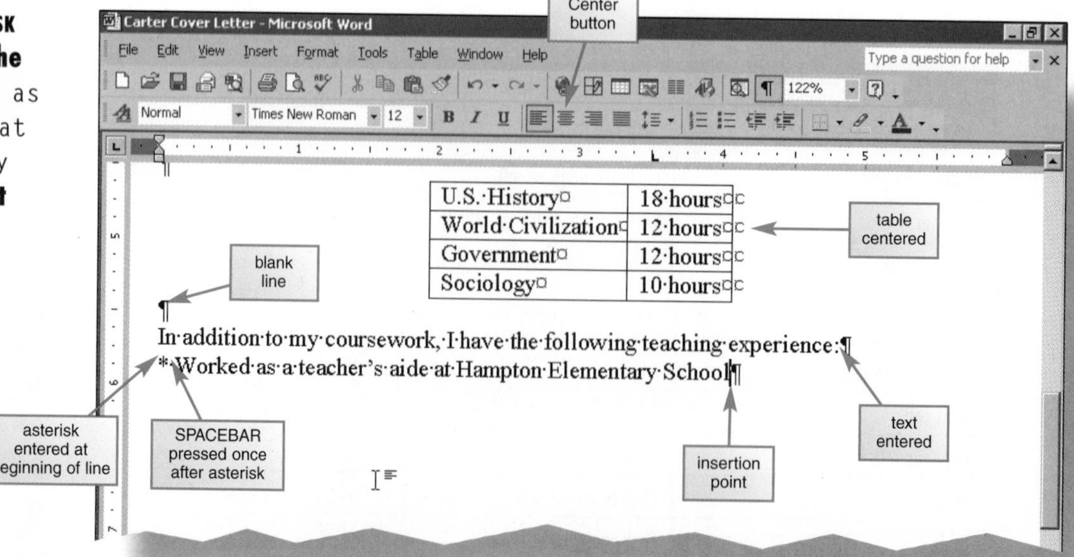

FIGURE 3-74

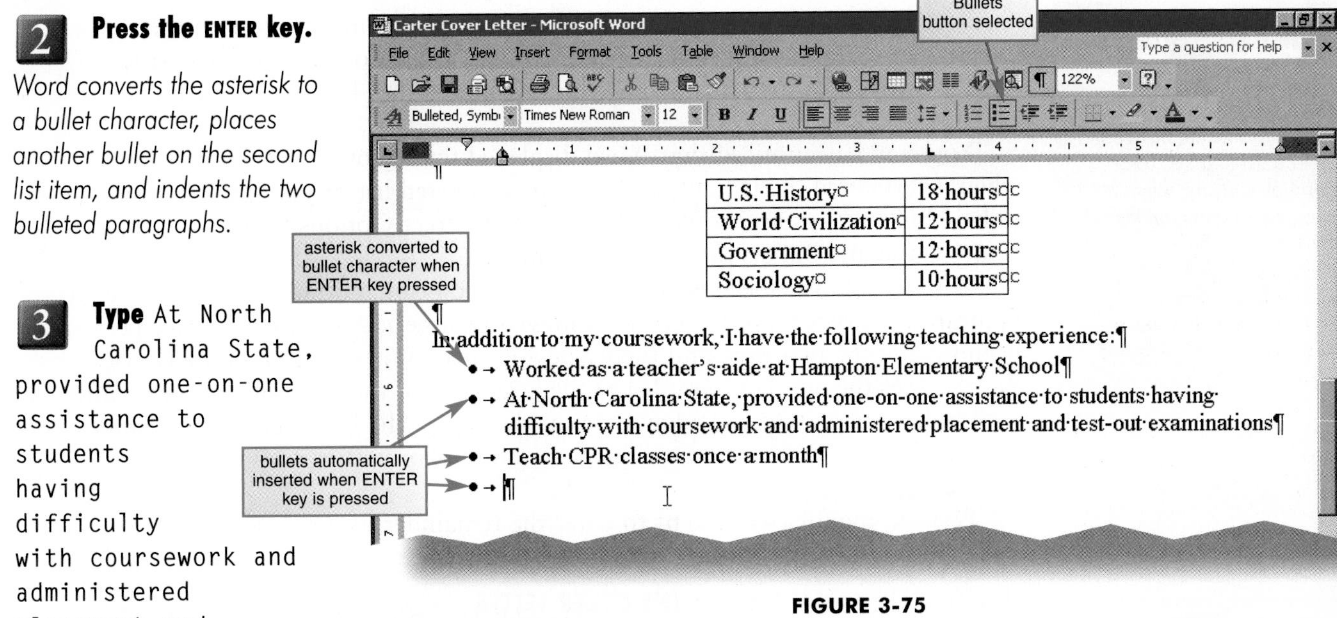

2 Press the ENTER key.

Word converts the asterisk to a bullet character, places another bullet on the second list item, and indents the two bulleted paragraphs.

3 Type `At North Carolina State, provided one-on-one assistance to students having difficulty with coursework and administered placement and test-out examinations` **and then press the ENTER key. Type** `Teach CPR classes once a month` **and then press the ENTER key.**

Word places a bullet on the next line (Figure 3-75).

FIGURE 3-75

4 Press the ENTER key.

Word removes the lone bullet because you pressed the ENTER key twice (Figure 3-76). The Bullets button no longer is selected.

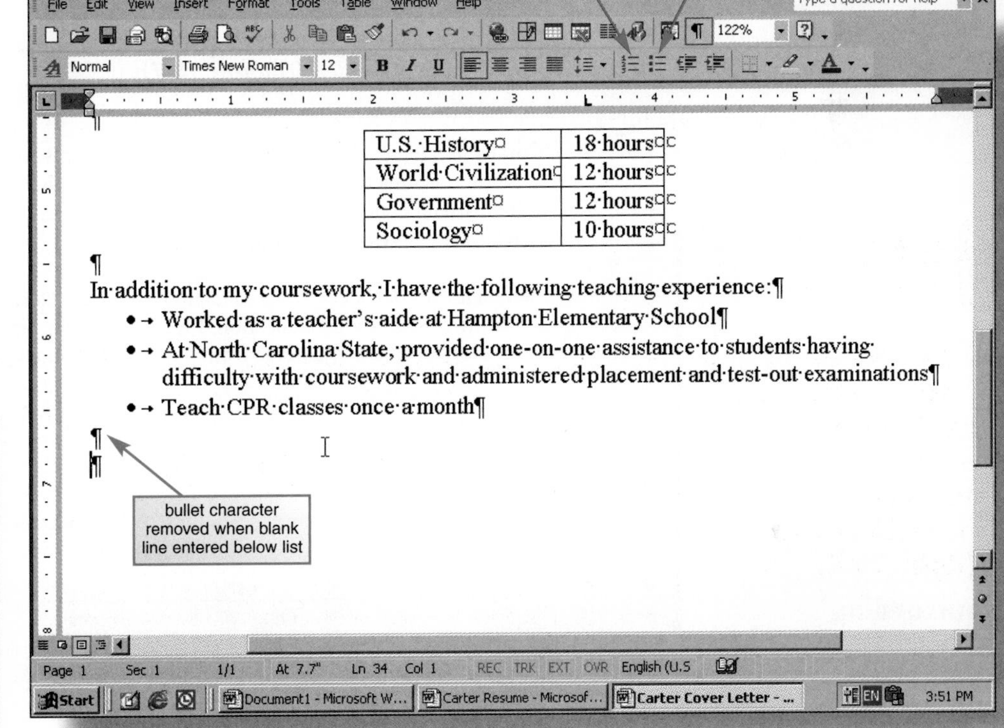

FIGURE 3-76

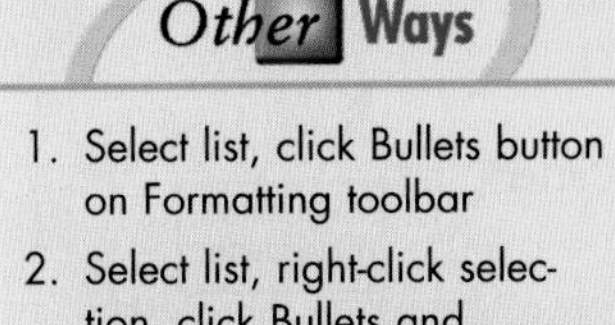

1. Select list, click Bullets button on Formatting toolbar
2. Select list, right-click selection, click Bullets and Numbering on shortcut menu, click Bulleted tab, click desired bullet type, click OK button
3. Select list, on Format menu click Bullets and Numbering, click Bulleted tab, click desired bullet type, click OK button
4. With list selected, in Voice Command mode, say "Bullets"

More About

Numbered Lists

To apply a different numbering style to a list (e.g., a, b, c, instead of 1, 2, 3), select the list, click Format on the menu bar, click Bullets and Numbering, click the Numbered tab, click the desired numbering scheme, and then click the OK button.

When the insertion point is in a bulleted list, the Bullets button on the Formatting toolbar is selected (Figure 3-75 on the previous page). To instruct Word to stop bulleting paragraphs, you press the ENTER key twice or click the Bullets button.

You may have noticed that Word displayed the AutoCorrect Options button when it formatted the list automatically to a bulleted list. If you did not want the list to be a bulleted list, you could click the AutoCorrect Options button and then click Undo Automatic Bullets on the shortcut menu.

You can add numbers as you type, just as you can add bullets as you type. To number a list, type the number one followed by a period and then a space (1.) at the beginning of the first item and then type your text. When you press the ENTER key, Word places the number two (2.) at the beginning of the next line automatically. As with bullets, press the ENTER key twice at the end of the list or click the Numbering button (Figure 3-76 on the previous page) on the Formatting toolbar to stop numbering.

Perform the following steps to enter the remainder of the cover letter.

More About

AutoText

Word provides many AutoText categories of entries for business letters. Categories include attention line, closing, mailing instructions, salutation, and subject line. To insert an AutoText entry, click Insert on the menu bar, point to AutoText, point to the desired category, and then click the desired entry. Or, click the All Entries button on the AutoText toolbar, point to the desired category, and then click the desired entry.

TO ENTER THE REMAINDER OF THE COVER LETTER

1. Type the paragraph shown in Figure 3-77, making certain you use the AutoText entry, phs, to insert the school name.
2. Press the ENTER key twice. Press the TAB key. Type `Sincerely` and then press the COMMA key.
3. Press the ENTER key four times. Press the TAB key. Type `Tyrone James Carter` and then press the ENTER key.
4. Type `Enclosure` as the final text.

The cover letter text is complete (Figure 3-77).

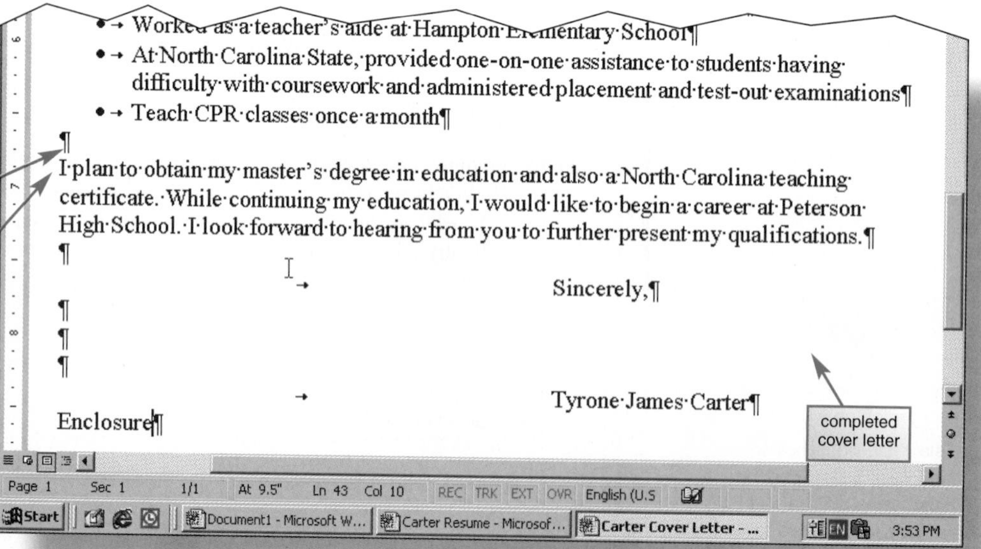

FIGURE 3-77

More About

Proofreading

You should be absolutely certain that your resume and accompanying cover letter are error free. Check spelling and grammar using Word. Proofread for errors. Set the resume and cover letter aside for a couple of days, and then proofread them again. Ask others, such as a friend or teacher, to proofread them also.

Saving Again and Printing the Cover Letter

The cover letter for the resume now is complete. You should save the cover letter again and then print it as described in the following steps.

TO SAVE A DOCUMENT AGAIN

1. Click the Save button on the Standard toolbar.

Word saves the cover letter with the same file name, Carter Cover Letter.

TO PRINT A DOCUMENT

1. Click the Print button on the Standard toolbar.

The completed cover letter prints as shown in Figure 3-2a on page WD 3.06.

Printing

Use a laser printer to print the resume and cover letter on standard letter-size white or ivory paper. Be sure to print a copy for yourself, and read it — especially before the interview. Most likely, the interviewer will have copies in hand, ready to ask you questions about the contents of both the resume and cover letter.

Addressing and Printing Envelopes and Mailing Labels

The final step in this project is to address and print an envelope, as shown in the following steps.

Steps To Address and Print an Envelope

1 Scroll through the cover letter to display the inside address in the document window. Drag through the inside address to select it. Click Tools on the menu bar, point to Letters and Mailings, and then point to Envelopes and Labels on the Letters and Mailings submenu (Figure 3-78).

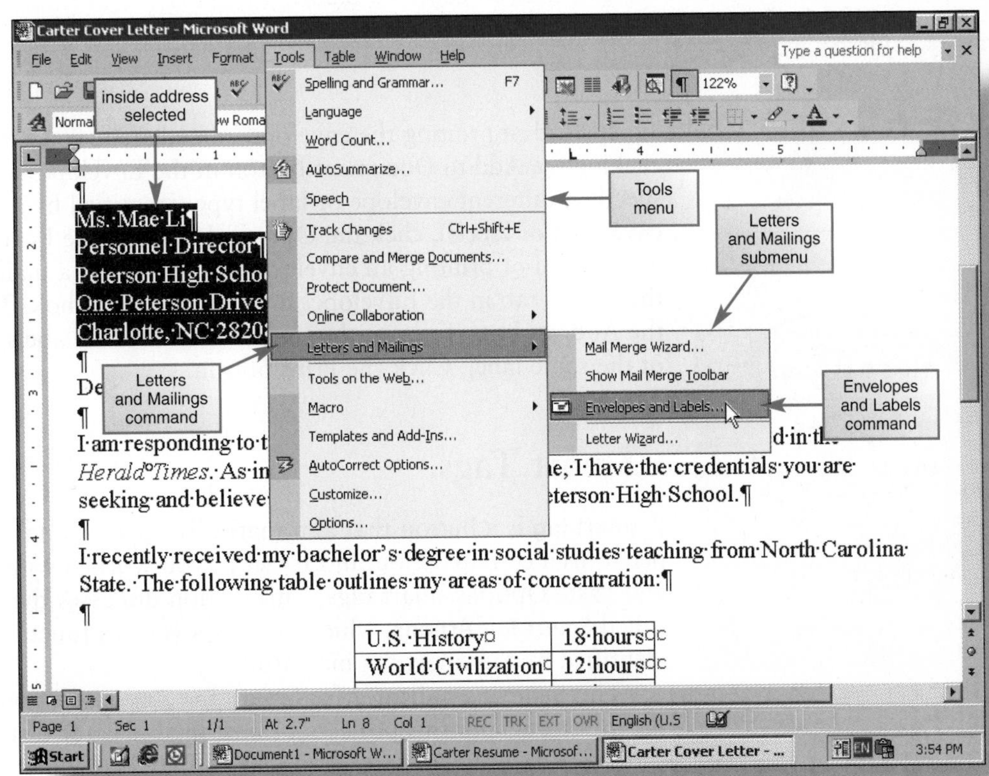

FIGURE 3-78

2 **Click Envelopes and Labels. When the Envelopes and Labels dialog box displays, if necessary, click the Envelopes tab. Click the Return address text box. Type** `Tyrone J. Carter` **and then press the ENTER key. Type** `18567 Southgate Road` **and then press the ENTER key. Type** `Charlotte, NC 28208` **and then point to the Print button in the Envelopes and Labels dialog box.**

Word displays the Envelopes and Labels dialog box (Figure 3-79).

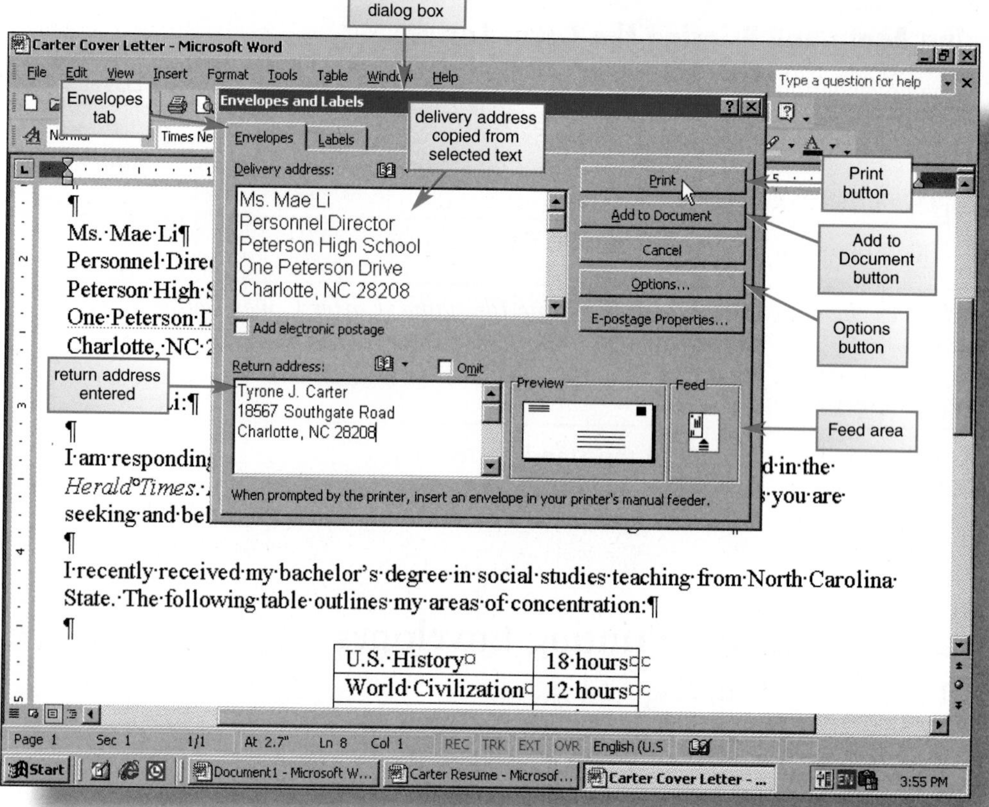

FIGURE 3-79

3 **Insert an envelope into your printer, as shown in the Feed area of the dialog box. Click the Print button in the dialog box. If a Microsoft Word dialog box displays, click the No button.**

Word prints the envelope (shown in Figure 3-2b on page WD 3.06).

Instead of printing the envelope immediately, you can add it to the document by clicking the Add to Document button in the Envelopes and Labels dialog box. To specify a different envelope or label type (identified by a number on the box of envelopes or labels), click the Options button in the Envelopes and Labels dialog box.

Instead of printing an envelope, you can print a mailing label. To do this, click the Labels tab in the Envelopes and Labels dialog box. Type the delivery address in the Address box. To print the same address on all labels on the page, click Full page of the same label. Click the Print button.

> **More About**
>
> **Office Supplies**
>
> For more information on where to obtain supplies for printing documents, visit the Word 2002 More About Web page (scsite.com/wd2002/more.htm) and then click Online Office Supplies.

Smart Tags

A **smart tag** is a button that automatically appears on the screen when Word performs a certain action. In Project 2, you worked with the AutoCorrect Options and Paste Options smart tags. This section discusses the third type of smart tag, called **Smart Tag Actions**, which performs various functions depending on the object identified by the smart tag indicator.

The smart tag indicator for Smart Tag Actions is a purple dotted underline. As shown throughout this project, a smart tag indicator displays below addresses and dates. A smart tag indicator also may display below names, places, times, and financial symbols. To view or change the list of objects recognized as smart tags, click Tools on the menu bar, click AutoCorrect Options, and then click the Smart Tags tab.

When you point to a smart tag indicator, the Smart Tag Actions button displays on the screen. Clicking the Smart Tag Actions button displays a Smart Tag Actions menu. The commands in the Smart Tag Actions menu vary depending on the smart tag. For example, the Smart Tag Actions menu for a date includes commands that allow you to schedule a meeting in Outlook Calendar or display your Outlook Calendar. The Smart Tag Actions menu for an address includes commands for displaying a map of the address or driving directions to or from the address.

Perform the following steps to use a smart tag to display a map showing the location of the employer's address in the cover letter. In order for the following steps to work properly, your computer must have an Internet connection.

> **More About**
>
> **Quick Reference**
>
> For a table that lists how to complete tasks covered in this book using the mouse, menu, shortcut menu, and keyboard, see the Quick Reference Summary at the back of this book or visit the Shelly Cashman Series Office XP Web page (scsite.com/offxp/qr.htm) and then click Microsoft Word 2002.

Steps To Use the Smart Tag Actions Button

1 Click anywhere to remove the highlight. Position the mouse pointer on the smart tag indicator below the street address, One Peterson Drive, in the inside address of the cover letter.

Word displays the Smart Tag Actions button (Figure 3-80).

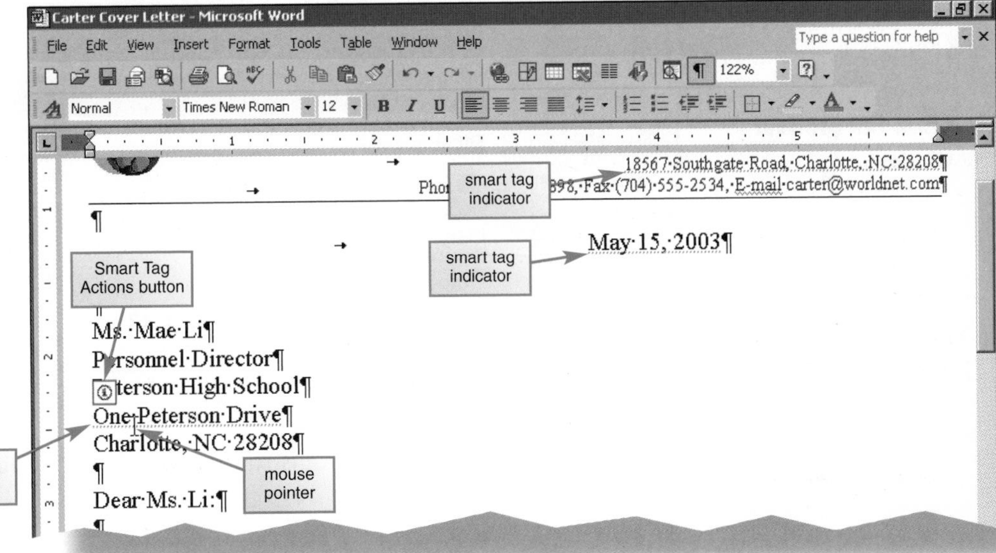

FIGURE 3-80

2 Click the Smart Tag Actions button. Point to Display Map on the Smart Tag Actions menu (Figure 3-81).

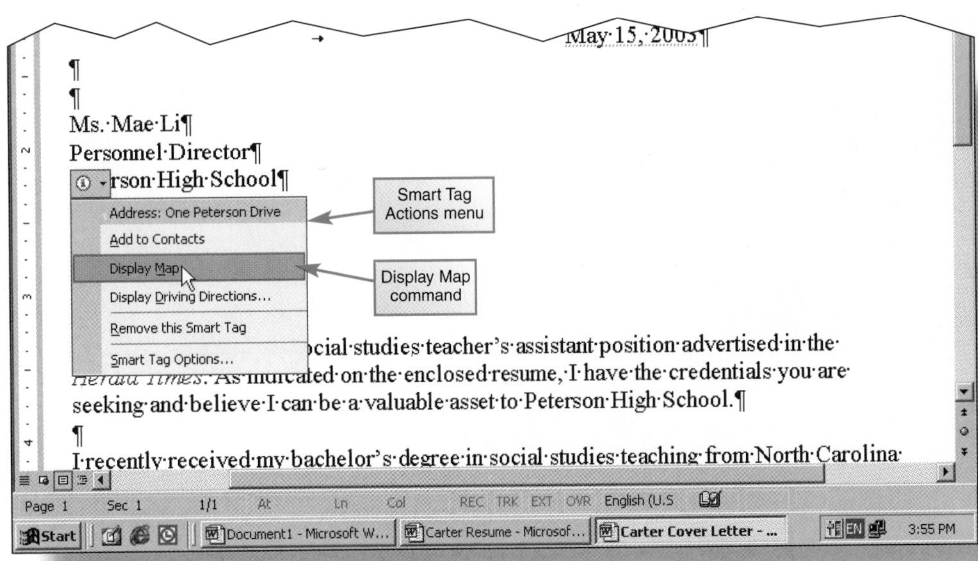

FIGURE 3-81

3 Click Display Map. If the browser asks you to select a specific address from a list, do so and then click Find a map at the bottom of the window.

Word starts your browser program. If necessary, your computer connects to the Web. The browser window displays a map of the address in the Word document (Figure 3-82). You can print, save, or e-mail the map.

4 Close the browser window.

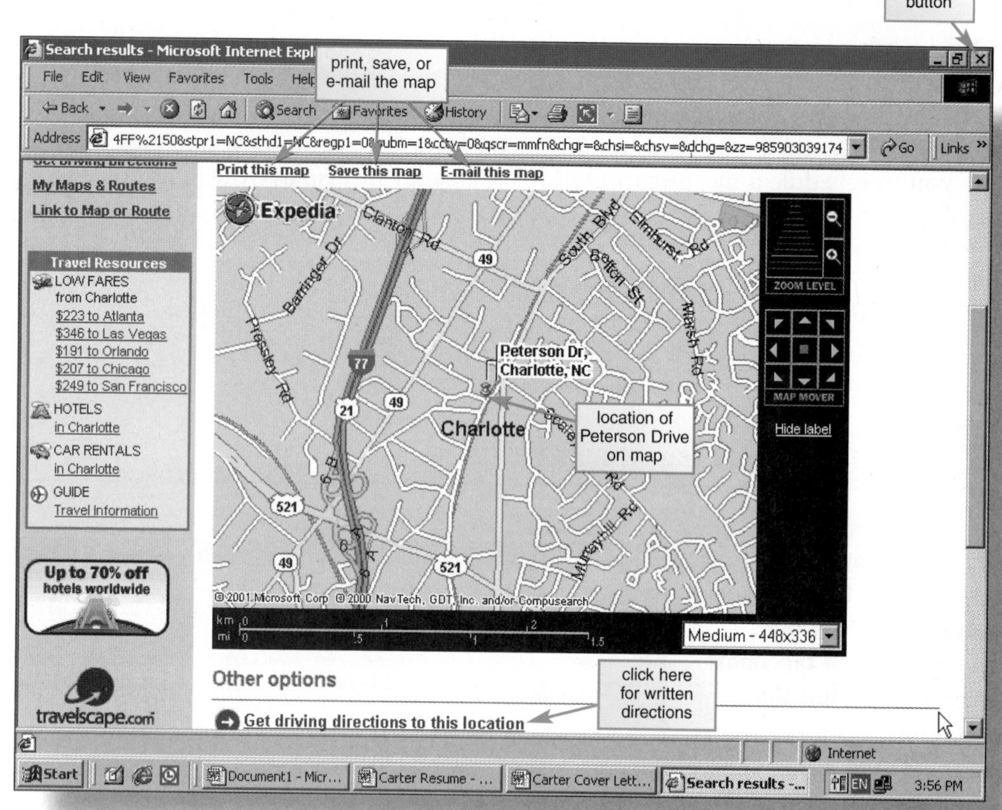

FIGURE 3-82

The final step in this project is to quit Word as described in the step below.

TO QUIT WORD

 Click the Close button in the Word window.

The Word window closes.

CASE PERSPECTIVE SUMMARY

With your resume writing expertise and Tyrone's solid background, you have created an effective resume and cover letter. Tyrone immediately staples the two documents together, places them in the envelope, adds necessary postage, and delivers the envelope to the post office. As he places his cover letter and resume in the mail, Tyrone dreams about starting a career at Peterson High School. He plans to wait one week to hear from Ms. Li, the personnel director at Peterson High School. If she has not contacted him in that time, Tyrone plans to follow up with a telephone call to her.

Project Summary

Project 3 introduced you to creating a resume using a wizard and creating a cover letter with a letterhead, a bulleted list, and a table. You used the Resume Wizard to create a resume and then used several formatting techniques to personalize the resume. You viewed and printed the resume in print preview. You created a letterhead and then the cover letter. While creating the letterhead, you learned how to add color to characters, set custom tab stops, collect and paste between documents, and add a border to a paragraph. You created an AutoText entry, which you used when you personalized the cover letter. Finally, you addressed and printed an envelope.

What You Should Know

Having completed this project, you now should be able to perform the following tasks:

- Add More Text *(WD 3.54)*
- Address and Print an Envelope *(WD 3.57)*
- AutoFormat as You Type *(WD 3.23)*
- Bottom Border a Paragraph *(WD 3.38)*
- Bullet a List as You Type *(WD 3.54)*
- Center a Selected Table *(WD 3.54)*
- Change the Font Size *(WD 3.28, WD 3.37)*
- Clear Formatting *(WD 3.39)*
- Collect Items *(WD 3.33)*
- Color Characters *(WD 3.28)*
- Color Characters the Same Color *(WD 3.37)*
- Convert a Hyperlink to Regular Text *(WD 3.40)*
- Create a Resume Using Word's Resume Wizard *(WD 3.08)*
- Create an AutoText Entry *(WD 3.45)*
- Display Formatting Marks *(WD 3.07)*
- Enter a Line Break *(WD 3.21)*
- Enter a Paragraph *(WD 3.49)*
- Enter Data into a Table *(WD 3.51)*
- Enter More Text with Line Breaks *(WD 3.22)*
- Enter the Inside Address and Salutation *(WD 3.44)*
- Enter the Remainder of the Cover Letter *(WD 3.56)*
- Enter the Remaining Sections of the Resume *(WD 3.24)*
- Fit Columns to Table Contents *(WD 3.52)*
- Hide White Space *(WD 3.15)*
- Insert a Nonbreaking Space *(WD 3.47)*
- Insert an AutoText Entry *(WD 3.48)*
- Insert an Empty Table *(WD 3.49)*
- Insert and Resize a Graphic *(WD 3.29)*
- Insert the Current Date into a Document *(WD 3.43)*
- Open a New Document Window *(WD 3.27)*
- Paste from the Office Clipboard *(WD 3.35)*
- Print a Document *(WD 3.57)*
- Print Preview a Document *(WD 3.25)*
- Print the Resume Created by the Resume Wizard *(WD 3.15)*
- Quit Word *(WD 3.60)*
- Reset Menus and Toolbars *(WD 3.07)*
- Save a Document *(WD 3.26)*
- Save a Document Again *(WD 3.57)*
- Save the Document with a New File Name *(WD 3.41)*
- Save the Letterhead *(WD 3.40)*
- Select a Table *(WD 3.53)*
- Select and Replace Placeholder Text *(WD 3.19)*
- Select and Replace More Placeholder Text *(WD 3.20)*
- Set Custom Tab Stops Using the Ruler *(WD 3.42)*
- Set Custom Tab Stops Using the Tabs Dialog Box *(WD 3.31)*
- Start and Customize Word *(WD 3.07)*
- Switch From One Open Document to Another *(WD 3.32)*
- Use the Smart Tags Actions Button *(WD 3.59)*
- Zoom Text Width *(WD 3.18)*

More About

Microsoft Certification

The Microsoft Office User Specialist (MOUS) Certification program provides an opportunity for you to obtain a valuable industry credential — proof that you have the Word 2002 skills required by employers. For more information, see Appendix E or visit the Shelly Cashman Series MOUS Web page at scsite.com/offxp/cert.htm.

Learn It Online

Instructions: To complete the Learn It Online exercises, start your browser, click the Address bar, and then enter `scsite.com/offxp/exs.htm`. When the Office XP Learn It Online page displays, follow the instructions in the exercises below.

1 Project Reinforcement TF, MC, and SA

Below Word Project 3, click the Project Reinforcement link. Print the quiz by clicking Print on the File menu. Answer each question. Write your first and last name at the top of each page, and then hand in the printout to your instructor.

2 Flash Cards

Below Word Project 3, click the Flash Cards link. When Flash Cards displays, read the instructions. Type 20 (or a number specified by your instructor) in the Number of Playing Cards text box, type your name in the Name text box, and then click the Flip Card button. When the flash card displays, read the question and then click the Answer box arrow to select an answer. Flip through Flash Cards. Click Print on the File menu to print the last flash card if your score is 15 (75%) correct or greater and then hand it in to your instructor. If your score is less than 15 (75%) correct, then redo this exercise by clicking the Replay button.

3 Practice Test

Below Word Project 3, click the Practice Test link. Answer each question, enter your first and last name at the bottom of the page, and then click the Grade Test button. When the graded practice test displays on your screen, click Print on the File menu to print a hard copy. Continue to take practice tests until you score 80% or better. Hand in a printout of the final practice test to your instructor.

4 Who Wants to Be a Computer Genius?

Below Word Project 3, click the Computer Genius link. Read the instructions, enter your first and last name at the bottom of the page, and then click the Play button. Hand in your score to your instructor.

5 Wheel of Terms

Below Word Project 3, click the Wheel of Terms link. Read the instructions, and then enter your first and last name and your school name. Click the Play button. Hand in your score to your instructor.

6 Crossword Puzzle Challenge

Below Word Project 3, click the Crossword Puzzle Challenge link. Read the instructions, and then enter your first and last name. Click the Play button. Work the crossword puzzle. When you are finished, click the Submit button. When the crossword puzzle redisplays, click the Print button. Hand in the printout.

7 Tips and Tricks

Below Word Project 3, click the Tips and Tricks link. Click a topic that pertains to Project 3. Right-click the information and then click Print on the shortcut menu. Construct a brief example of what the information relates to in Word to confirm you understand how to use the tip or trick. Hand in the example and printed information.

8 Newsgroups

Below Word Project 3, click the Newsgroups link. Click a topic that pertains to Project 3. Print three comments. Hand in the comments to your instructor.

9 Expanding Your Horizons

Below Word Project 3, click the Articles for Microsoft Word link. Click a topic that pertains to Project 3. Print the information. Construct a brief example of what the information relates to in Word to confirm you understand the contents of the article. Hand in the example and printed information to your instructor.

10 Search Sleuth

Below Word Project 3, click the Search Sleuth link. To search for a term that pertains to this project, select a term below the Project 3 title and then use the Google search engine at google.com (or any major search engine) to display and print two Web pages that present information on the term. Hand in the printouts to your instructor.

Apply Your Knowledge

1 Working with a Table

Instructions: Start Word. Open the document, College Expenses Table, on the Data Disk. See the inside back cover of this book for instructions for downloading the Data Disk or see your instructor for information on accessing the files in this book.

The document is a Word table that you are to edit and format. The revised table is shown in Figure 3-83. Perform the following tasks:

College Expenses

	Freshman	Sophomore	Junior	Senior
Room & Board	$3,290.00	$3,454.50	$3,627.58	$3,818.52
Tuition & Books	4,850.25	5,092.48	5,347.99	5,347.30
Clothing	490.00	514.65	540.23	567.22
Entertainment	635.29	666.82	700.05	735.09
Miscellaneous	325.34	341.20	358.38	276.34
Total	$9,590.88	$10,069.65	$10,574.23	$10,744.47

FIGURE 3-83

1. Select the Phone row by pointing to the left of the row until the mouse pointer changes to a right pointing arrow and then clicking. Right-click in the selected row and then click Delete Rows on the shortcut menu to delete the Phone row.
2. Add a new row to the bottom of the table. In the first cell of the new row, type `Total` as the entry.
3. Point to the top of the Senior column until the mouse pointer changes to a downward pointing arrow and then click to select the column. Right-click the selected column and then click Insert Columns on the shortcut menu to insert a column. Fill in the column as follows: Column Title – Junior; Room & Board - $3,627.58; Tuition & Books – 5,347.99; Clothing – 540.23; Entertainment – 700.05; Miscellaneous – 358.38.
4. Click the Tables and Borders button on the Standard toolbar to display the Tables and Borders toolbar. If necessary, click the Draw Table button on the Tables and Borders toolbar to deselect the button. Position the insertion point in the Freshman Total cell (second column, last row). Click the AutoSum button on the Tables and Borders toolbar to sum the contents of the column. Repeat for Sophomore, Junior, and Senior totals. Click the Close button on the Tables and Borders toolbar to remove the toolbar from the screen. Leave the screen in print layout view.
5. Select all cells containing numbers and then click the Align Right button on the Formatting toolbar.
6. Click somewhere in the table. Click Table on the menu bar and then click Table AutoFormat. In the Table AutoFormat dialog box, scroll to and then click Table Elegant in the Table styles list. If necessary, remove the check mark from the Heading rows check box. Click the Apply button.
7. Point to the upper-left corner of the table to display the table move handle. Click the table move handle to select the table. Click the Center button on the Formatting toolbar to center the table. Click anywhere to remove the selection.
8. Point to the column border between the first and second columns and then double-click to increase the width of the first column.
9. Click File on the menu bar and then click Save As. Use the file name, Revised College Expenses Table, to save the document on your floppy disk.
10. Print the revised table.

In the Lab

1 Using Word's Resume Wizard to Create a Resume

Problem: You are a student at Wooster State College expecting to receive your Bachelor of Science degree in Mechanical Engineering this May. As the semester end is approaching quickly, you are beginning a search for full-time employment upon graduation. You prepare the resume shown in Figure 3-84 using Word's Resume Wizard.

2007 Pine Hill Road
Troy, Ohio 45373

Phone (937) 555-7137
Fax (937) 555-7138
E-mail jduke@globe.com

Jessica Clare Duke

Objective	To obtain a position as a Maintenance Engineer in the Seattle, Washington, area.
Education	1999-2003 Wooster State College Wooster, Ohio **Mechanical Engineering** ▪ B.S., Mechanical Engineering, May 2003 ▪ A.A.S., Electrical Engineering, December 2001 ▪ A.A.S., Construction Technology, May 2001
Awards received	Dean's List, every quarter Mechanical Engineering Senior of the Year, 2003 Alpha Beta Gamma Honorary Society, 2002-2003 Electronic Journeyman Award, 2002 John Kraniotes Scholarship, 1999-2003
Certificates	Electronic Mechanic Journeyman card Safety, First Aid, and CPR certificates
Languages	English (fluent) Italian (working knowledge) Portuguese (fluent) Spanish (fluent)
Work experience	2000-2003 Bloomfield Trade School Troy, Ohio **Technician** ▪ Worked as a trainee engineering technician for the Operations department ▪ Assisted instructors in the Engineering department during laboratory experiments
Volunteer experience	Participant in American Cancer Society fund-raisers
Extracurricular activities	Wooster Golf Team Intramural Soccer Softball Teams

FIGURE 3-84

Instructions:

1. Use the Resume Wizard to create a resume. Select the Professional style for the resume. Use the name and address information in Figure 3-84 when the Resume Wizard requests it.
2. Personalize the resume as shown in Figure 3-84. When entering multiple lines in the Awards received, Certificates, Languages, and Extracurricular activities sections, be sure to enter a line break at the end of each line, instead of a paragraph break.
3. Check the spelling of the resume.
4. Save the resume on a floppy disk with Duke Resume as the file name.
5. View and print the resume from within print preview.

In the Lab

2 Creating a Cover Letter with a Table

Problem: You prepared the resume shown in Figure 3-84 and now are ready to create a cover letter to send to a prospective employer (Figure 3-85).

Instructions:

1. Create the letterhead shown at the top of Figure 3-85. If you completed In the Lab 1, use the Office Clipboard to copy and paste the address information from the resume to the letterhead. Save the letterhead with the file name, Duke Letterhead.
2. Create the letter shown in Figure 3-85 using the modified block style. Set a tab stop at the 3.5" mark on the ruler for the date line, complimentary close, and signature block. Insert the current date. After entering the inside address, create an AutoText entry for Thermal Power Plant #424, and insert the AutoText entry whenever you have to enter the company name. Remove the hyperlink format from the e-mail address. Center the table.
3. Save the letter on a floppy disk with Duke Cover Letter as the file name.
4. Check the spelling of the cover letter. Save the cover letter again with the same file name.
5. View and print the cover letter from within print preview.
6. Address and print an envelope and a mailing label using the inside and return addresses in the cover letter.

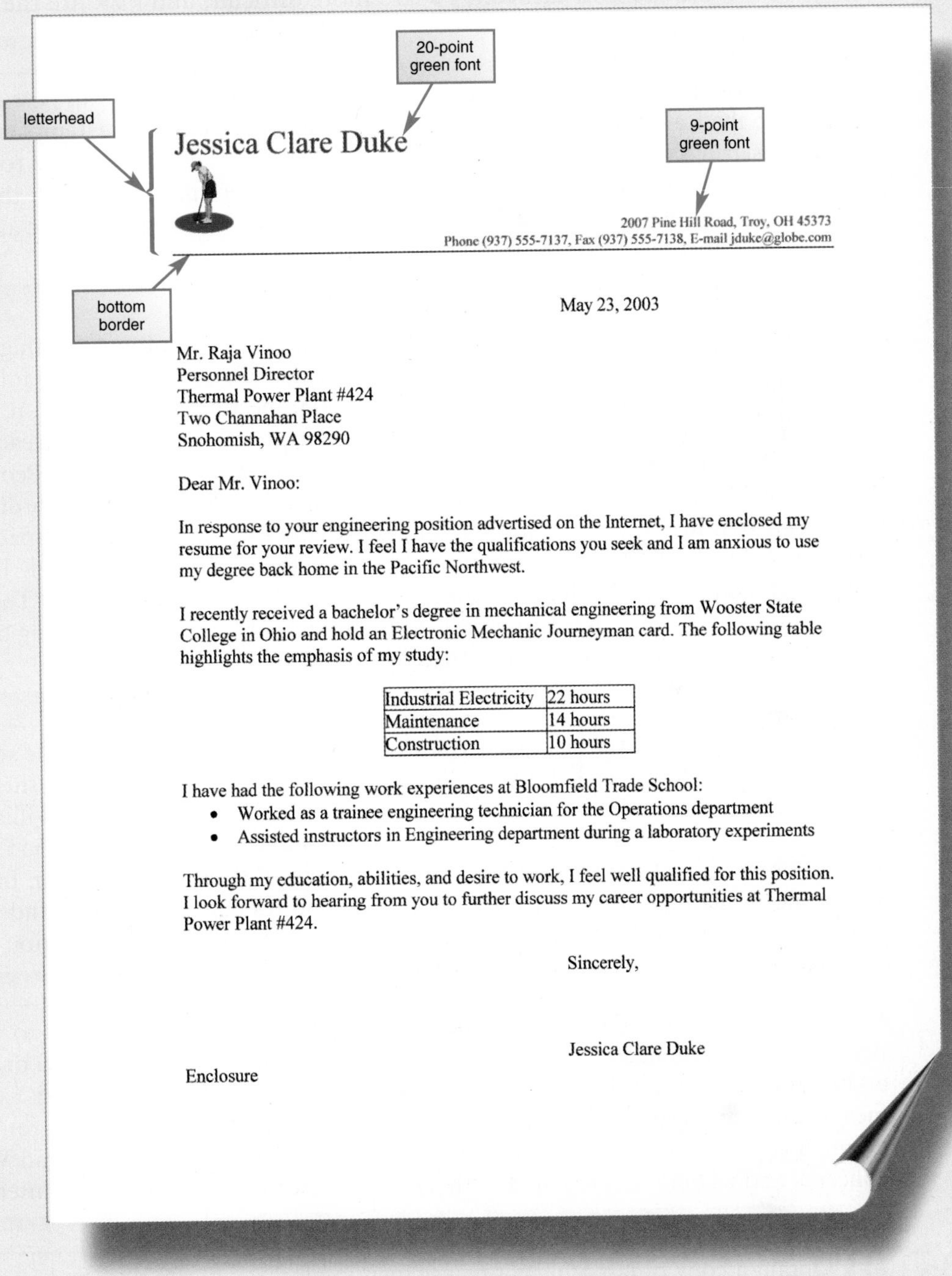

Jessica Clare Duke

2007 Pine Hill Road, Troy, OH 45373
Phone (937) 555-7137, Fax (937) 555-7138, E-mail jduke@globe.com

May 23, 2003

Mr. Raja Vinoo
Personnel Director
Thermal Power Plant #424
Two Channahan Place
Snohomish, WA 98290

Dear Mr. Vinoo:

In response to your engineering position advertised on the Internet, I have enclosed my resume for your review. I feel I have the qualifications you seek and I am anxious to use my degree back home in the Pacific Northwest.

I recently received a bachelor's degree in mechanical engineering from Wooster State College in Ohio and hold an Electronic Mechanic Journeyman card. The following table highlights the emphasis of my study:

Industrial Electricity	22 hours
Maintenance	14 hours
Construction	10 hours

I have had the following work experiences at Bloomfield Trade School:

- Worked as a trainee engineering technician for the Operations department
- Assisted instructors in Engineering department during a laboratory experiments

Through my education, abilities, and desire to work, I feel well qualified for this position. I look forward to hearing from you to further discuss my career opportunities at Thermal Power Plant #424.

Sincerely,

Jessica Clare Duke

Enclosure

FIGURE 3-85

Cases and Places

The difficulty of these case studies varies:
◗ are the least difficult; ◗◗ are more difficult; and ◗◗◗ are the most difficult.

1 ◗ Your boss has asked you to create a calendar for January so he can post it on the office bulletin board. Use the Calendar Wizard in the Other Documents sheet in the Templates dialog box. Use the following settings in the wizard: banner style, portrait print direction, leave room for a picture, January 2003 for both the start and end date. With the calendar on the screen, click the current graphic and delete it. Insert a clip art image of a snowflake or a similar seasonal graphic and then resize the image so it fits in the entire space for the graphic.

2 ◗ You have been asked to prepare the agenda for the next morning meeting. Use the Agenda Wizard in the Other Documents sheet in the Templates dialog box. Use the following settings in the wizard: style – standard; meeting date – 10/21/2003; meeting time – 8:00 a.m. to 8:45 a.m.; title – Morning Meeting; meeting location – Oak Room; include all headings in Headings panel; names on agenda – Meeting called by, Facilitator, Note taker, and Attendees; Topics, People, and Minutes – Monthly goals, Jim Johnson, 30; Safety, Bob Ayala, 15; add a form for recording the minutes. On the agenda created by the wizard, add the following names in the appropriate spaces: G. Esteban called the meeting and is the facilitator, R. Wasilowski will be the note taker; all people listed in this assignment will be attending – along with T. Brooks, D. Lopez, M. Cartright, and you. The meeting is an informational meeting. Also, attendees should read the minutes from the last meeting and bring their own coffee. As a special note, remind the attendees to please be on time.

3 ◗◗ A potential employer has asked you to fax your cover letter and resume so she may review it immediately. Use the Fax Wizard and the following settings: create the fax cover sheet with a note and print the fax so you can send it on a separate fax machine. It must be faxed to William O'Brien at Linkland Materials (1972 Elwood Drive, Snohomish, Washington 98290; telephone 555-2346; fax 555-2347). Each is one page in length. Fax a copy to Craig Ziemba at the same number. In the fax, write a message informing William O'Brien that your cover letter and resume are attached and that he can contact you if he has any questions. Use your own name, address, and telephone information in the fax.

4 ◗◗ As chairperson of the annual company outing, you look for volunteers to assist with various activities. You have compiled a list of jobs for the picnic: publicity, plan meal and order food, activities, setup, and cleanup. A tent has been reserved on the grounds of the Hannah Nature Center. You prepare a memorandum that informs fellow employees of the event location and asks for their assistance with the event. A copy of the memo should be sent to Barbara Lindahl. Use the Memo Wizard, together with the concepts and techniques presented in this project, to create and format the interoffice memorandum.

5 ◗◗◗ Obtain a copy of last Sunday's newspaper. Look through the classified section and cut out a want ad in an area of interest. Assume you are in the market for the position being advertised. Use the Resume Wizard to create a resume. Include a table and a numbered list in the cover letter. After setting tabs at the 3.5" mark, change them to the 3" mark. Use the want ad for the inside address and your personal information for the return address. Try to be as accurate as possible when personalizing the resume and cover letter. Submit the want ad with your cover letter and resume. Address and print an envelope. Then, print an entire page of mailing labels using your home address.

Microsoft Word 2002

Creating Web Pages Using Word

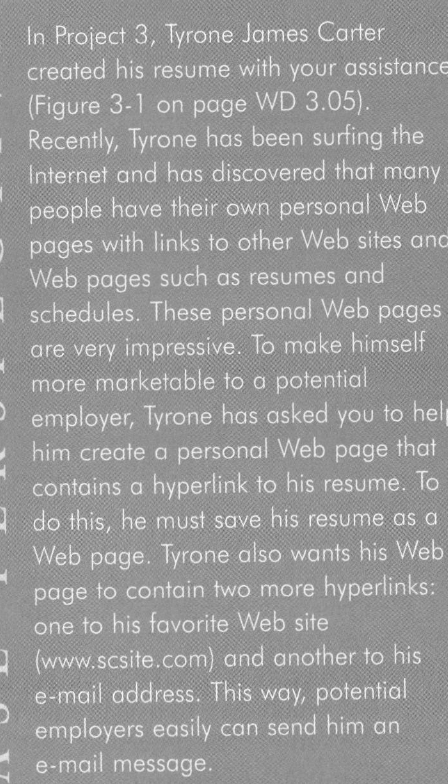

CASE PERSPECTIVE

In Project 3, Tyrone James Carter created his resume with your assistance (Figure 3-1 on page WD 3.05). Recently, Tyrone has been surfing the Internet and has discovered that many people have their own personal Web pages with links to other Web sites and Web pages such as resumes and schedules. These personal Web pages are very impressive. To make himself more marketable to a potential employer, Tyrone has asked you to help him create a personal Web page that contains a hyperlink to his resume. To do this, he must save his resume as a Web page. Tyrone also wants his Web page to contain two more hyperlinks: one to his favorite Web site (www.scsite.com) and another to his e-mail address. This way, potential employers easily can send him an e-mail message.

To complete this Web Feature, you will need the resume created in Project 3 so you can save it as a Web page and then use the resulting Web page as a hyperlink destination. (If you did not create the resume, see your instructor for a copy of it.)

Introduction

Word provides three techniques for creating Web pages. If you have an existing Word document, you can save it as a Web page. If you do not have an existing Word document, you can create a Web page by using a Web page template or the Web Page Wizard, which provides customized templates you can modify easily. In addition to these Web tools, Word has many other **Web page authoring** features. For example, you can include frames, hyperlinks, sounds, videos, pictures, scrolling text, bullets, horizontal lines, check boxes, option buttons, list boxes, text boxes, and scripts on Web pages.

In this Web Feature, you save the resume created in Project 3 as a Web page. Then, you use Word's Web Page Wizard to create another Web page that contains two frames (Figure 1a on the next page). A **frame** is a rectangular section of a Web page that can display another separate Web page. Thus, a Web page that contains multiple frames can display multiple Web pages simultaneously. Word stores all frames associated with a Web page in a single file called the **frames page**. The frames page is not visible on the screen; it simply is a container for all frames associated with a Web page. When you open the frames page in Word or a Web browser, all frames associated with the Web page display on the screen.

In this Web Feature, the file name of the frames page is Carter Personal Web Page. When you initially open this frames page, the left frame contains the title Tyrone James Carter and two hyperlinks — My Resume and My Favorite Site; the right frame displays Tyrone's resume (Figure 1a). As discussed in Project 3, a hyperlink is a shortcut that allows a user to jump easily and quickly to another location in the same document or to other documents or Web pages. In the left frame, the My Resume hyperlink is a link to the resume Web page, and the My Favorite Site hyperlink is a link to www.scsite.com.

When you click the My Favorite Site hyperlink in the left frame, the www.scsite.com Web site displays in the right frame (Figure 1b). When you click the My Resume hyperlink in the left frame, the resume Web page displays in the right frame. The resume itself contains a hyperlink to an e-mail address. When you click the e-mail address, Word opens your e-mail program automatically with the recipient's address (carter@worldnet.com) already filled in (Figure 1c). You simply type a message and then click the Send button, which places the message in the Outbox or sends it if you are connected to an e-mail server.

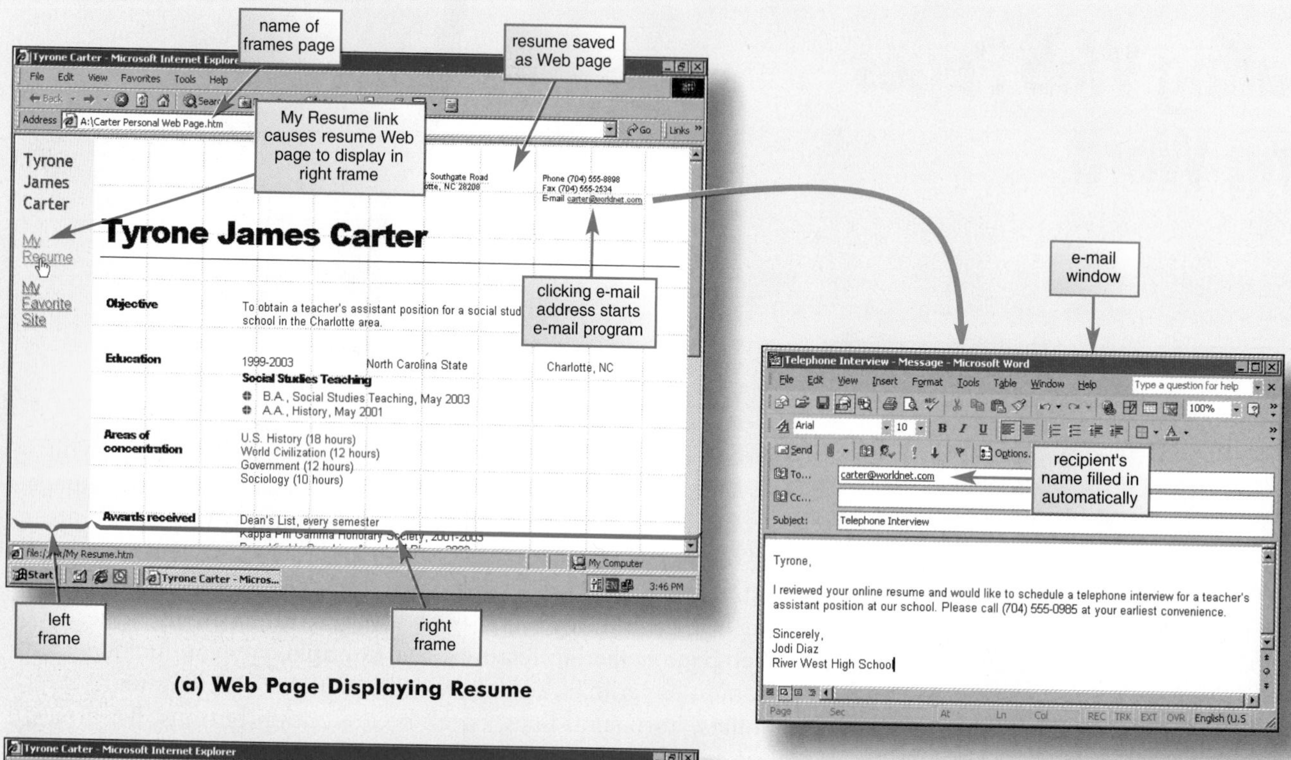

(a) Web Page Displaying Resume

(c) E-mail Program

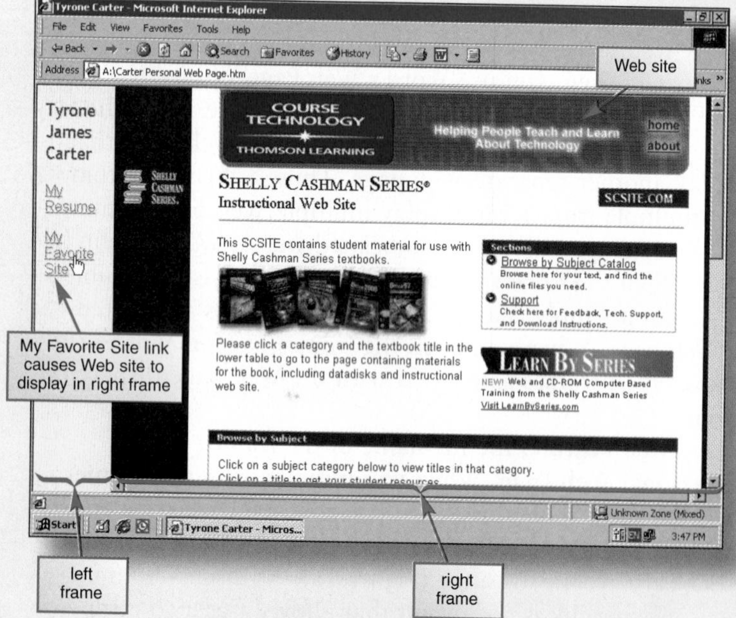

(b) Web Page Displaying Web Site

FIGURE 1

Once you have created Web pages, you can publish them. **Publishing** is the process of making Web pages available to others, for example on the World Wide Web or on a company's intranet. In Word, you can publish Web pages by saving them to a Web folder or to an FTP location. The procedures for publishing Web pages in Microsoft Office are discussed in Appendix C.

This Web Feature is for instructional purposes. Thus, you create and save your frames page and associated Web pages on a floppy disk rather than to the Web. Saving these pages to the floppy disk may be a slow process because writing to a floppy disk takes more time than writing to a hard disk — please be patient.

Saving a Word Document as a Web Page

Once you have created a Word document, you can save it as a Web page so that it can be published and then viewed by a Web browser, such as Internet Explorer. Perform the following steps to save the resume created in Project 3 as a Web page.

More About

Web Page Titles

To change the title that displays on the title bar of a Web page, click the Change Title button in the Save As dialog box (see Figure 3).

Steps To Save a Word Document as a Web Page

1 Start Word and then open the file named Carter Resume created in Project 3. Click File on the menu bar and then point to Save as Web Page (Figure 2).

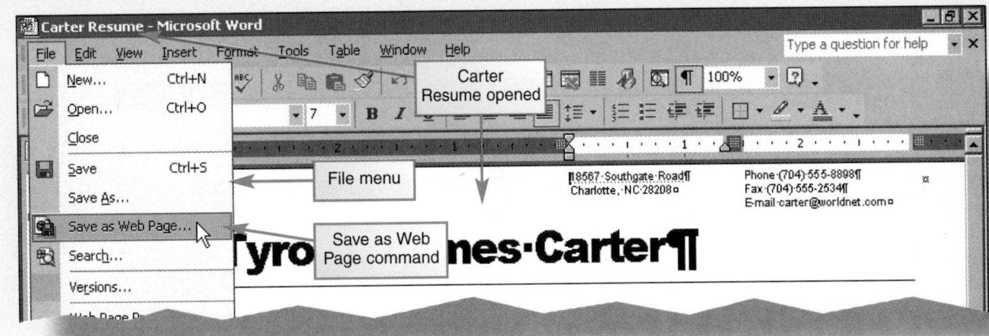

FIGURE 2

2 Click Save as Web Page. When the Save As dialog box displays, type `Carter Resume Web Page` **in the File name text box and then, if necessary, change the Save in location to 3½ Floppy (A:) as shown in Figure 3. Point to the Save button in the Save As dialog box.**

3 Click the Save button in the Save As dialog box.

Word saves the resume as a Web page and displays it in the Word window (shown in Figure 4 on the next page).

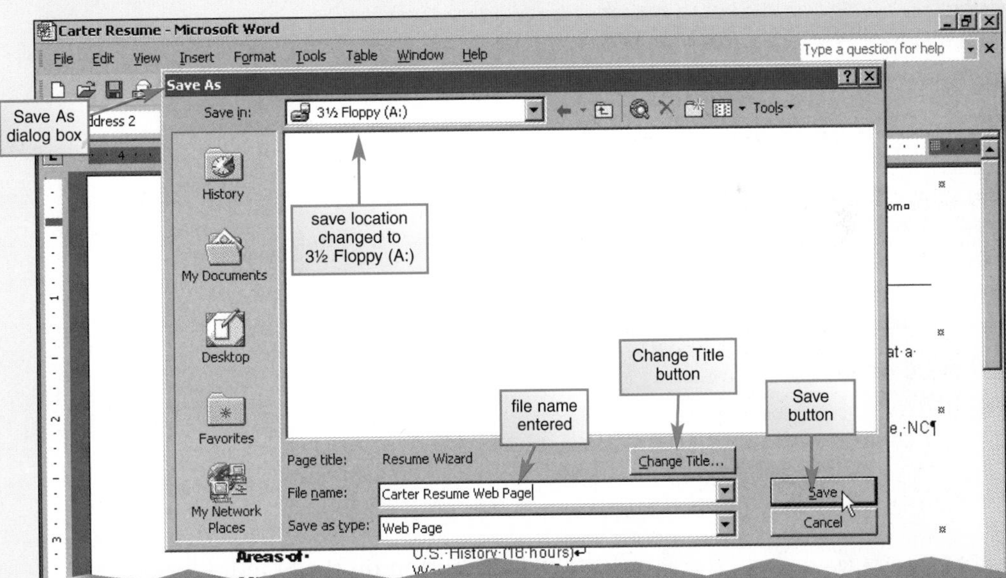

FIGURE 3

More About

Web Page Design

For information on guidelines for designing Web pages, visit the Word 2002 More About Web page (scsite.com/wd2002/more.htm) and then click Web Page Design.

Word switches to Web layout view and also changes some of the toolbar buttons and menu commands to provide Web page authoring features. For example, the Standard toolbar now displays a New Web Page button (Figure 4). The Web Layout View button on the horizontal scroll bar is selected.

The resume displays in the Word window much like it will display in a Web browser. Some of Word's formatting features are not supported by Web pages. Thus, your Web page may display slightly different from the original Word document.

Formatting the E-Mail Address as a Hyperlink

You want the e-mail address in your resume to be formatted as a hyperlink so that when someone clicks the e-mail address on the Web page, his or her e-mail program starts automatically and displays an e-mail window with your e-mail address already filled in.

As described in Project 3, when you press the SPACEBAR or ENTER key after a Web or e-mail address, Word automatically formats it as a hyperlink. Perform the following steps to format the e-mail address as a hyperlink.

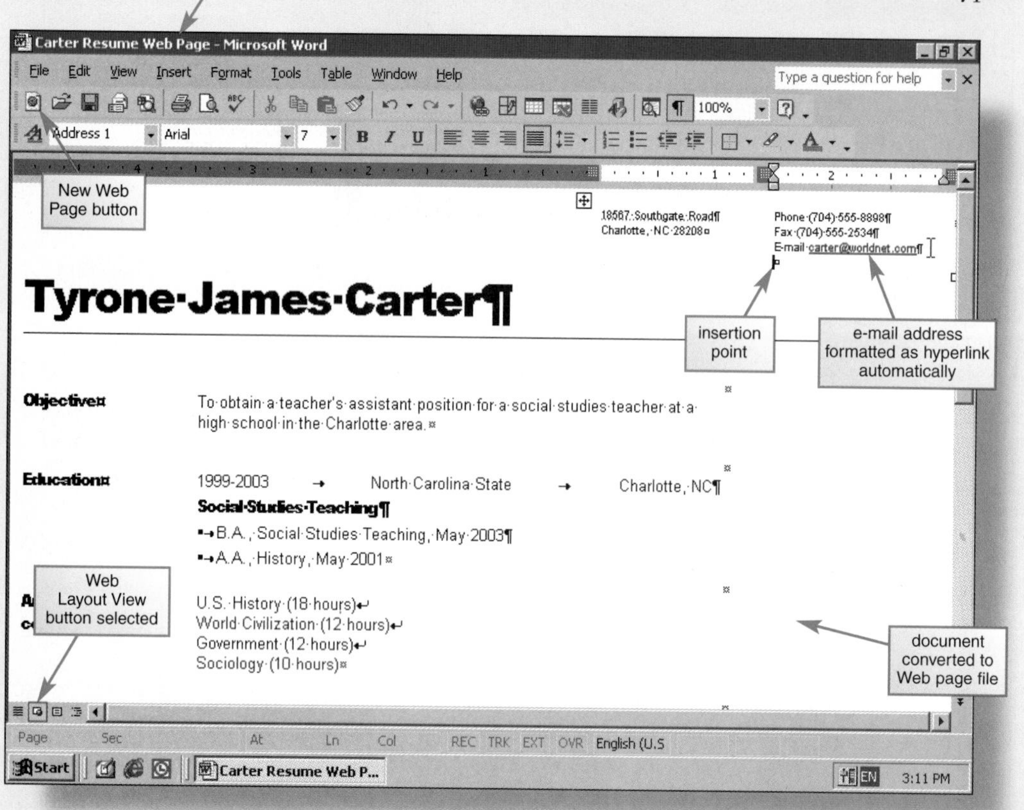

FIGURE 4

TO FORMAT A HYPERLINK AUTOMATICALLY

1 Position the insertion point immediately after the e-mail address; that is, after the m in com.

2 Press the ENTER key. If Word displays a dialog box about installing an AutoCorrections feature, click the No button.

Word automatically formats the e-mail address as a hyperlink; that is, it is colored blue and underlined (Figure 4).

You now are finished modifying the Carter Resume Web Page file. Perform the following steps to save the file again and then close it.

TO SAVE AND CLOSE A WEB PAGE

1 Click the Save button on the Standard toolbar.

2 Click File on the menu bar and then click Close.

Word saves the file and closes it. The Word window is empty.

> **More About**
>
> **AutoFormat**
>
> If Word does not automatically convert an e-mail or Web address to a hyperlink as you type, click Tools on the menu bar, click AutoCorrect Options, click the AutoFormat As You Type tab, place a check mark in the Internet and network paths with hyperlinks check box, and then click the OK button.

Using Word's Web Page Wizard to Create a Web Page

In the previous section, you saved an existing Word document as a Web page. Next, you want to create a Web page that contains a link to the Web page just created. You can create a Web page from scratch using a Web page template or you can use the **Web Page Wizard**. Because this is your first experience creating a new Web page with frames, you should use the Web Page Wizard as shown in the following steps.

Steps To Create a Web Page Using the Web Page Wizard

1 Click File on the menu bar and then click New. When the New Document task pane displays, click General Templates. When the Templates dialog box displays, if necessary, click the Web Pages tab. Point to the Web Page Wizard icon.

Word displays several Web page template icons and the Web Page Wizard icon in the Web Pages sheet of the Templates dialog box (Figure 5).

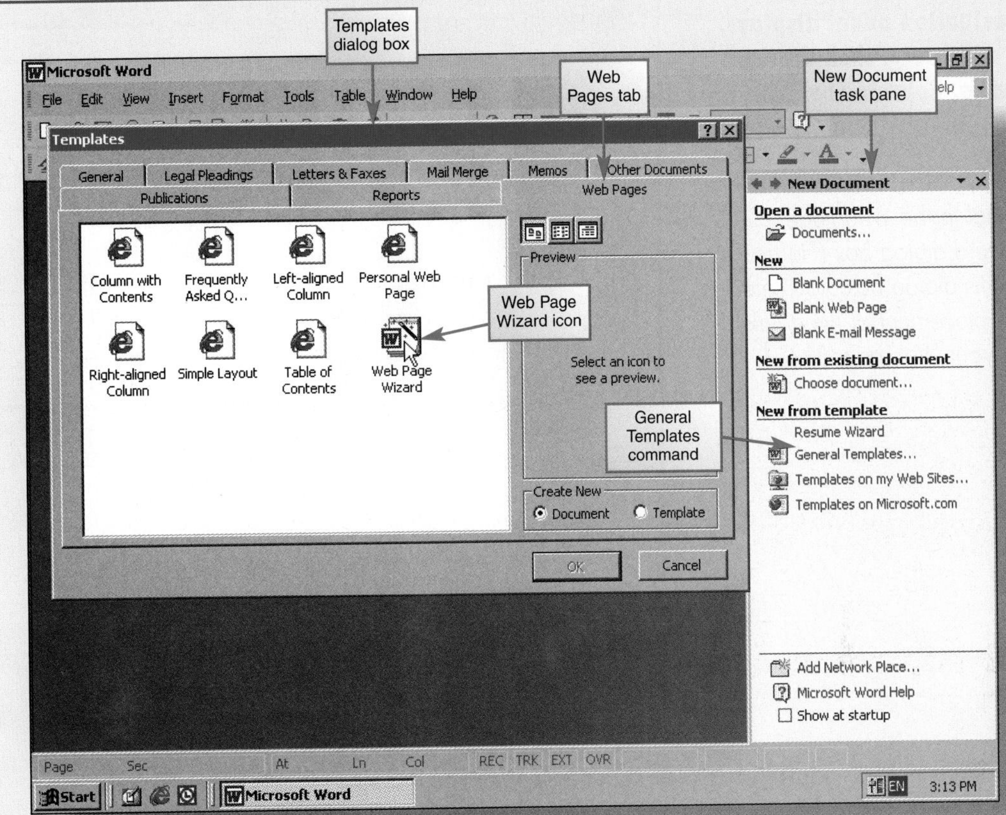

FIGURE 5

2 Double-click the Web Page Wizard icon. When the Start panel displays in the Web Page Wizard dialog box, click the Next button. When the Title and Location panel displays, type `Tyrone Carter` **in the Web site title text box. Press the TAB key and then type** `a:` **in the Web site location text box. Point to the Next button.**

Word displays the Title and Location panel in the Web Page Wizard dialog box (Figure 6). The title you enter in this dialog box displays in the Web browser's title bar.

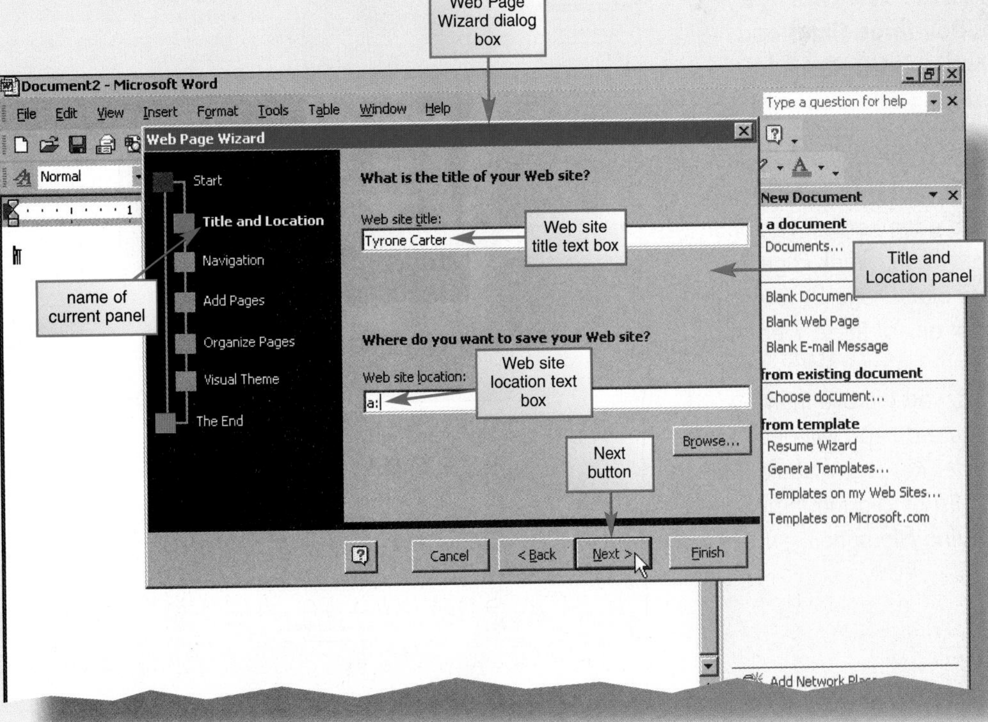

FIGURE 6

3 Click the Next button. When the Navigation panel displays, if necessary, click Vertical frame. Point to the Next button.

Word displays the **Navigation panel** *in the Web Page Wizard dialog box (Figure 7). In this dialog box, you select the placement of hyperlinks on your Web page(s).*

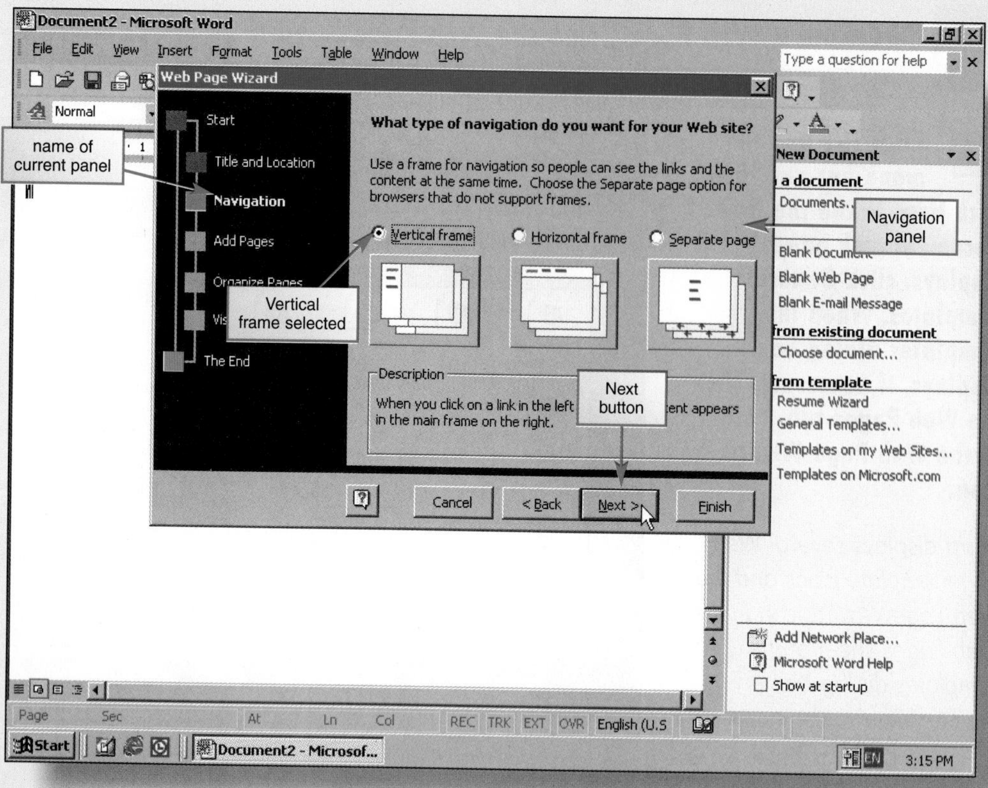

FIGURE 7

4 Click the Next button. When the Add Pages panel displays, click the Remove Page button three times and then point to the Add Existing File button.

Word displays the **Add Pages panel** *that initially lists three Web page names: Personal Web Page, Blank Page 1, and Blank Page 2. You do not want any of these Web page names on your Web page; thus, you remove them (Figure 8). You will add Carter Resume Web Page to the list by clicking the Add Existing File button.*

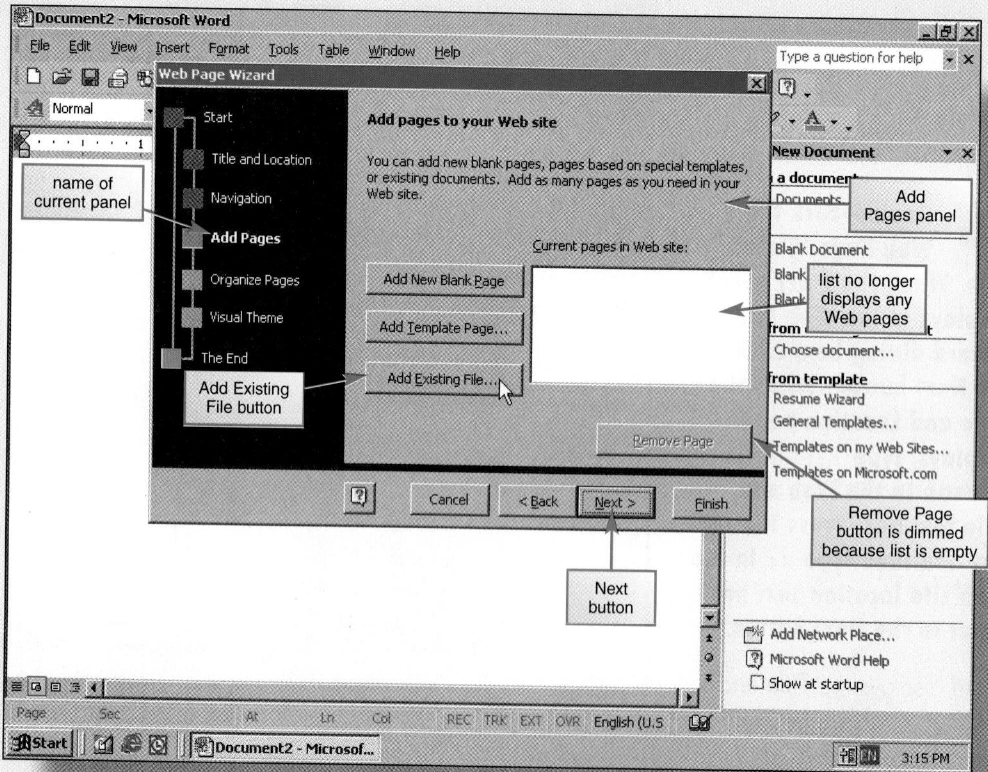

FIGURE 8

5 Click the Add Existing File button to display the Open dialog box. If necessary, change the Look in location to 3½ Floppy (A:). Click Carter Resume Web Page and then point to the Open button in the Open dialog box (Figure 9).

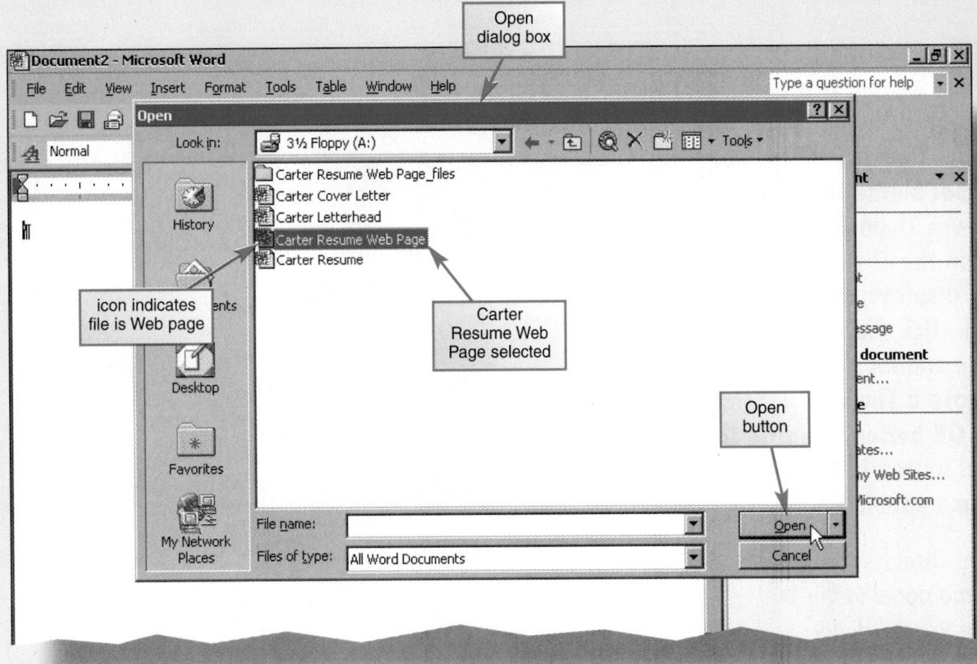

FIGURE 9

6 Click the Open button in the Open dialog box. When the Add Pages panel is visible again, click the Next button.

The wizard adds Carter Resume Web Page to the list in the Add Pages panel.

7 When the Organize Pages panel displays, click the Rename button. When the Rename Hyperlink dialog box displays, type My Resume **in the text box. Point to the OK button.**

In the Organize Pages panel in the Web Page Wizard, you specify the sequence and names of the hyperlinks that will display in the left frame of the Web page (Figure 10).

8 Click the OK button.

Word renames the hyperlink to My Resume.

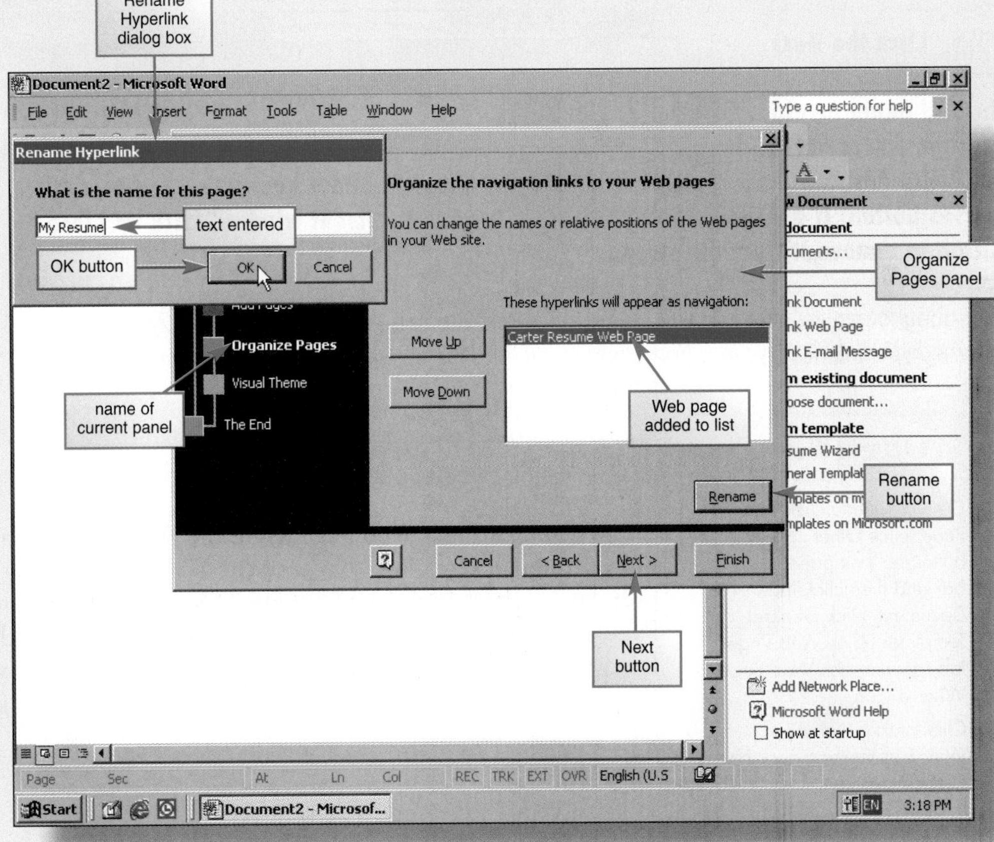

FIGURE 10

9 **Click the Next button. If the displayed theme in the Visual Theme panel is not Global Marketing, click the Browse Themes button. When the Theme dialog box displays, scroll to and then click Global Marketing (or a similar theme) in the Choose a Theme list. Click the OK button. Point to the Next button in the Visual Theme panel.**

Word displays the Visual Theme panel in the Web Page Wizard dialog box (Figure 11). A theme is a collection of defined design elements and color schemes.

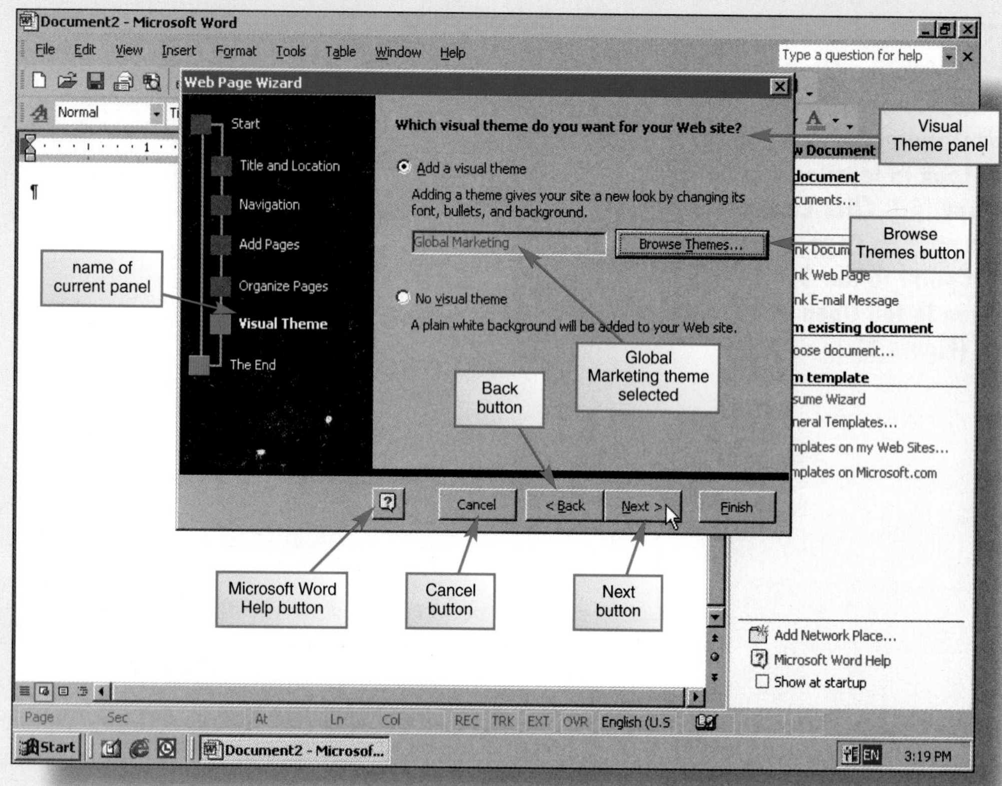

FIGURE 11

10 **Click the Next button. When the The End panel displays, click the Finish button. If the Office Assistant or a dialog box displays a message about navigation features, click the Yes button. If a Frames toolbar displays in your document window, click its Close button to remove it from the screen.**

After about a minute, Word displays a layout of the Web pages (shown in Figure 12). The My Resume hyperlink displays in a frame on the left, and the resume displays in a frame on the right.

Other Ways

1. On View menu click Task Pane, click Other Task Panes button on task pane title bar and then click New Document, click General Templates, click Web Pages tab, double-click Web Page Wizard icon
2. Click Start button on Windows taskbar, click New Office Document, click Web Pages tab, double-click Web Page Wizard icon
3. With task pane displaying, in Voice Command mode, say "General Templates, Other Documents, [select Web Page Wizard], OK"

When creating a Web page using the Web Page Wizard, you can click the Back button (Figure 11) in any panel of the Web Page Wizard dialog box to change any previously entered information. For help with entering information into the Web Page Wizard, click the Microsoft Word Help button in the appropriate panel. To exit from the Web Page Wizard and return to the document window without creating the Web page, click the Cancel button in any of the Web Page Wizard dialog boxes.

Modifying a Web Page

The next step is to modify the Web pages. First, you make the left frame smaller, and then you add the My Favorite Site hyperlink to the left frame.

The Web page is divided into two frames, one on the left and one on the right. A **frame border** separates the frames. When you point to the frame border, the mouse pointer shape changes to a double-headed arrow.

You want to make the left frame narrower. To do this, you drag the frame border as illustrated in the following steps.

Steps To Resize a Web Page Frame

1 Point to the frame border.

The mouse pointer shape changes to a double-headed arrow, and Word displays the ScreenTip, Resize (Figure 12).

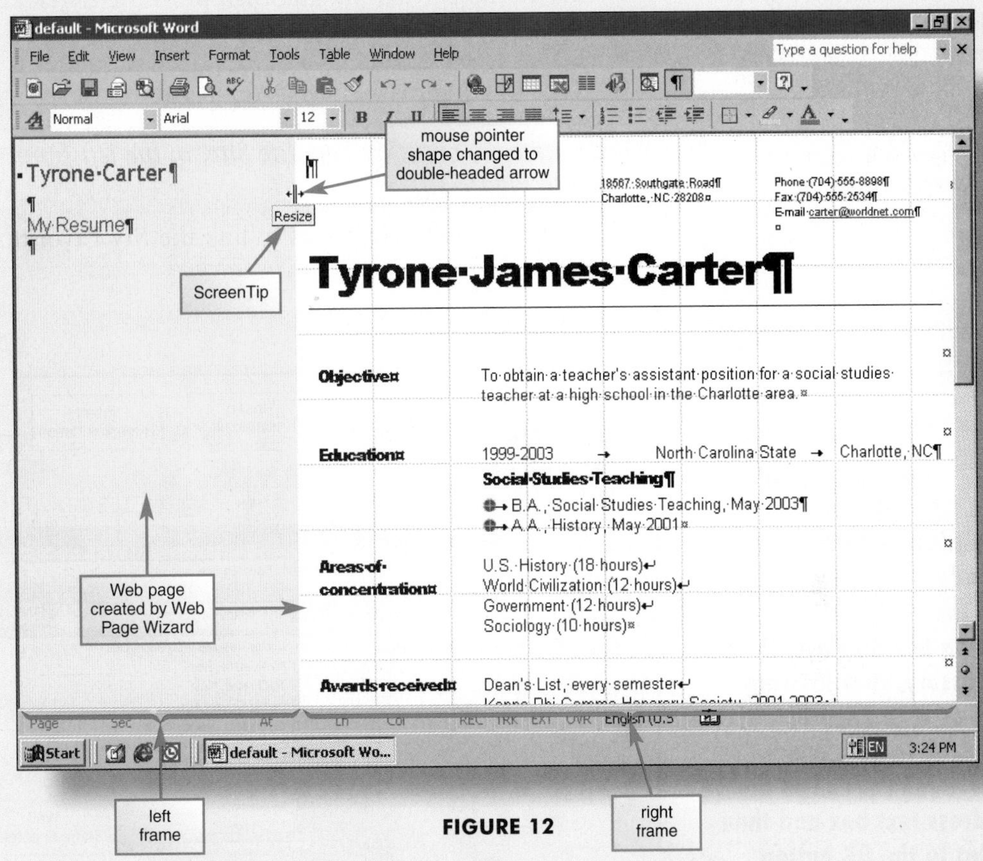

FIGURE 12

2 Drag the frame border to the left until it is positioned on the letter a in Carter (Figure 13).

Word narrows the left frame and widens the right frame (shown in Figure 14 on the next page).

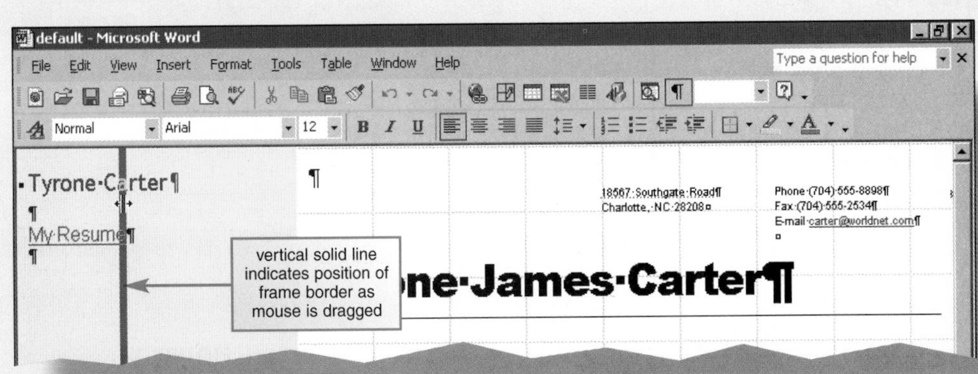

FIGURE 13

In the left frame, you want to add a My Favorite Site hyperlink. You used the Web Page Wizard to link the My Resume hyperlink to the Web page file called Carter Resume Web Page, which means when you click the My Resume link in the left frame, the Carter Resume Web Page file displays in the right frame. Similarly, when you click the My Favorite Site hyperlink, you want a Web site to display in the right frame.

The first step is to enter the hyperlink text, My Favorite Site, into the left frame as described in the steps on the next page.

More About

Highlights

Highlighting alerts the reader to the text's importance, much like a highlight marker does on a printed document. To highlight text, select it, click the Highlight button arrow on the Formatting toolbar, and then click the desired highlight color.

More About

Linking

Instead of linking to a file, you can link to objects in a document, such as bookmarks. To link text to an object, click Place in This Document in the Link to area in the Insert Hyperlink dialog box and then click the object name in the Look in area.

TO ENTER AND FORMAT TEXT

1. Click in the left frame of the Web page. Click the paragraph mark below the My Resume hyperlink and then press the ENTER key.
2. Click the Font Size box arrow and then click 12.
3. Type `My Favorite Site` as the text.

Word enters the text, My Favorite Site, in the left frame using a font size of 12 (shown in Figure 14).

Perform the following steps to link the My Favorite Site text to a Web site.

Steps To Add a Hyperlink

1 Drag through the text, My Favorite Site. Click the Insert Hyperlink button on the Standard toolbar. When the Insert Hyperlink dialog box displays, if necessary, click Existing File or Web Page in the Link to bar. Type `www.scsite.com` in the Address text box and then point to the OK button (Figure 14).

2 Click the OK button.

Word formats the text, My Favorite Site, as a hyperlink that when clicked displays the associated Web site in the right frame (shown in Figure 1b on page WDW 1.02).

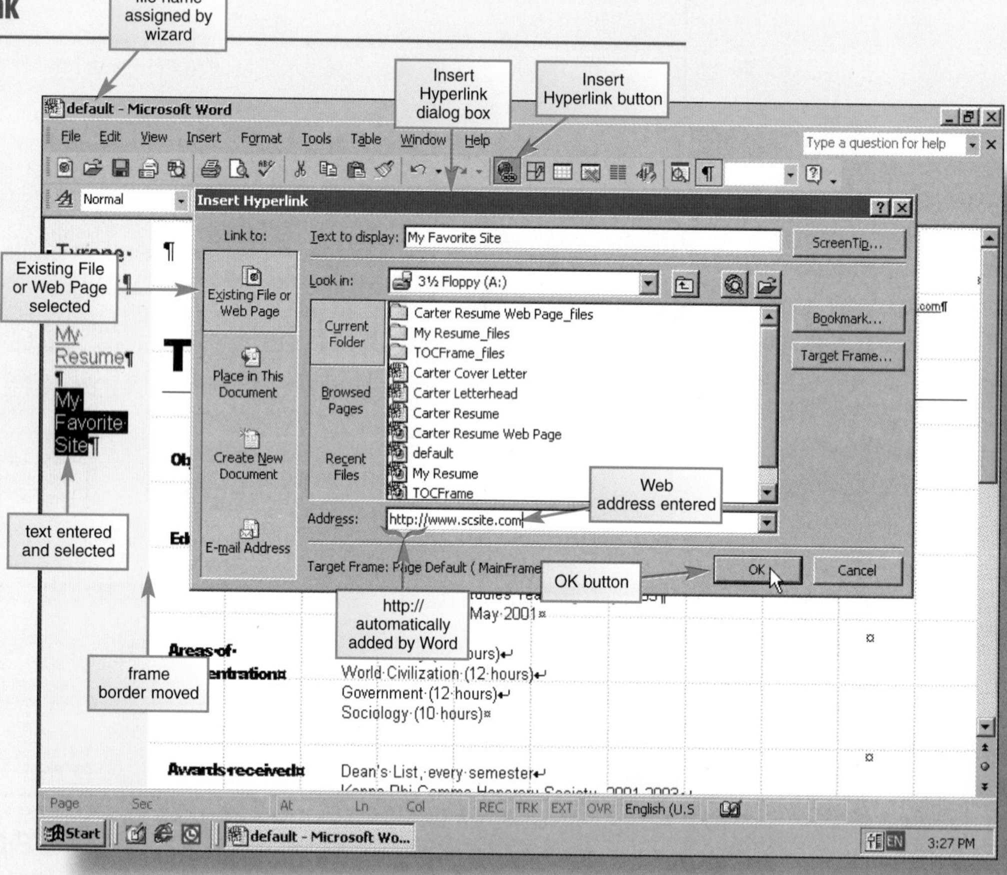

FIGURE 14

More About

Quick Reference

For a table that lists how to complete tasks covered in this book using the mouse, menu, shortcut menu, and keyboard, see the Quick Reference Summary at the back of this book or visit the Shelly Cashman Series Office XP Web page (scsite.com/offxp/qr.htm) and then click Microsoft Word 2002.

If you wanted to edit an existing hyperlink, you right-click the hyperlink text and then click Edit Hyperlink on the shortcut menu. Word will display the Edit Hyperlink dialog box instead of the Insert Hyperlink dialog box. Other than the title bar, these two dialog boxes are the same.

The Resume Wizard assigned the file name, default, to this frames page (Figure 14). The next step is to save the frames page with a new file name, as described in the following steps.

TO SAVE THE FRAMES PAGE WITH A NEW FILE NAME

1. Insert your floppy disk into drive A. Click File on the menu bar and then click Save As.
2. Type the file name `Carter Personal Web Page` in the File name text box. Do not press the ENTER key.
3. If necessary, click the Save in box arrow and then click 3½ Floppy (A:). Click the Save button in the Save As dialog box.

Word saves the frames page and associated frames on a floppy disk in drive A with the file name, Carter Personal Web Page.

HTML

If you wish to view the HTML source code associated with the Web page you have created, click View on the menu bar and then click HTML Source, which starts the Script Editor. To quit the Script Editor, click File on the menu bar and then click Exit.

Viewing the Web Page in Your Default Browser

To see how the Web page looks in your default browser without actually connecting to the Internet, use the **Web Page Preview command**, which displays on the File menu when Word is in Web layout view, as shown in these steps.

Steps To View a Web Page in the Browser Window

1. **Click File on the menu bar and then point to Web Page Preview (Figure 15).**

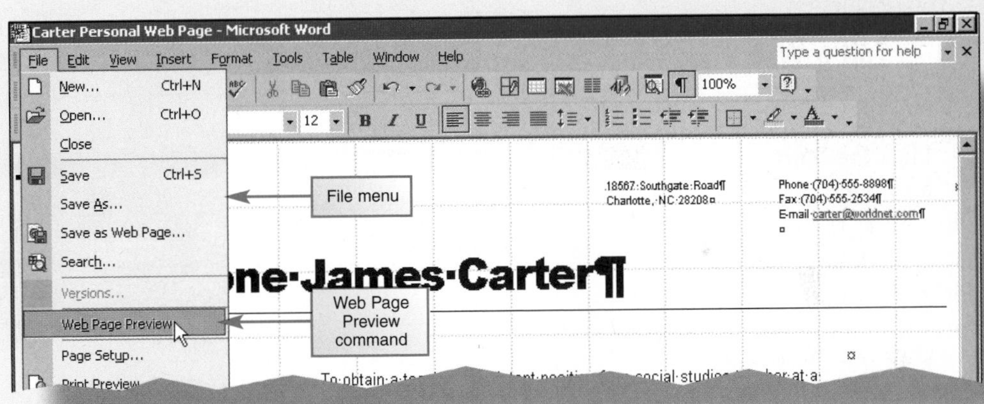

FIGURE 15

2. **Click Web Page Preview. If necessary, maximize the browser window.**

Word opens the Web browser in a separate window and displays the open Web page file in the browser window (Figure 16).

3. **Click the Close button on the browser title bar to close the browser window.**

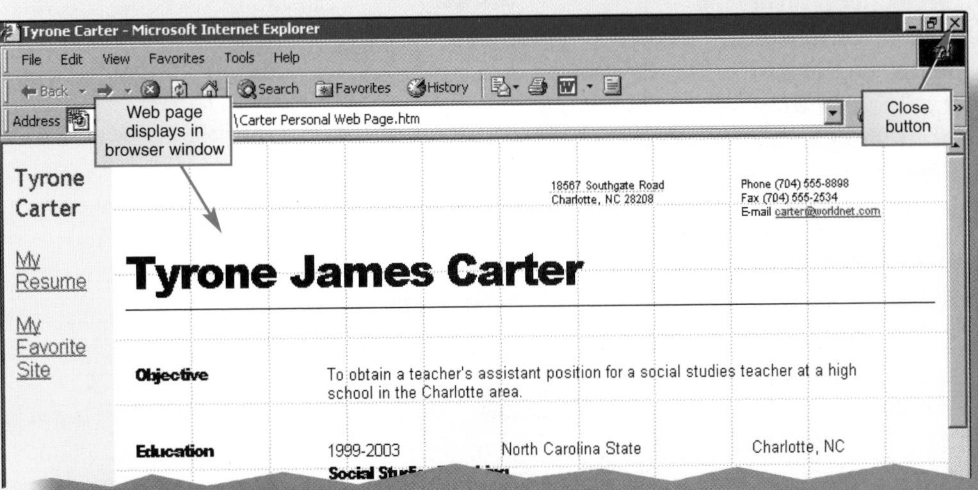

FIGURE 16

From the browser window (Figure 16 on the previous page), you can test your hyperlinks to be sure they work — before you publish them to the Web. For example, in the left frame, click the My Favorite Site link to display the Web site www.scsite.com in the right frame. (If you are not connected to the Internet, your browser will connect you and then display the Web site.) Click the My Resume link to display the Carter Resume Web Page in the right frame. Click the e-mail address to open your e-mail program with the address, carter@worldnet.com, entered in the recipient's address box.

The next step is to quit Word.

Opening Web Pages

To open the Web page directly from Word, click the Open button on the Standard toolbar. If necessary, click the Files of type box arrow and then click Web Pages (or All Files). Click the file name of the Web page (which has an extension of .htm or .html) and then click the Open button in the dialog box.

TO QUIT WORD

1 Click the Close button on the Word title bar.

The Word window closes.

Editing a Web Page from Your Browser

One of the powerful features of Office XP is the ability to edit a Web page directly from Internet Explorer. The following steps illustrate how to open your Web page in Internet Explorer and then edit it from Internet Explorer.

Steps To Edit a Web Page from Your Browser

1 Click the Start button on the taskbar, point to Programs, and then click Internet Explorer. When the Internet Explorer window opens, click the Address box. Type a: and then press the ENTER key. Double-click Carter Personal Web Page in the list. When the resume Web page displays, if necessary, maximize the window. Point to the Edit with Microsoft Word button on the toolbar.

Internet Explorer opens the Carter Personal Web Page and displays it in the browser window (Figure 17). Internet Explorer determines the Office program you used to create the Web page and associates that program with the Edit button.

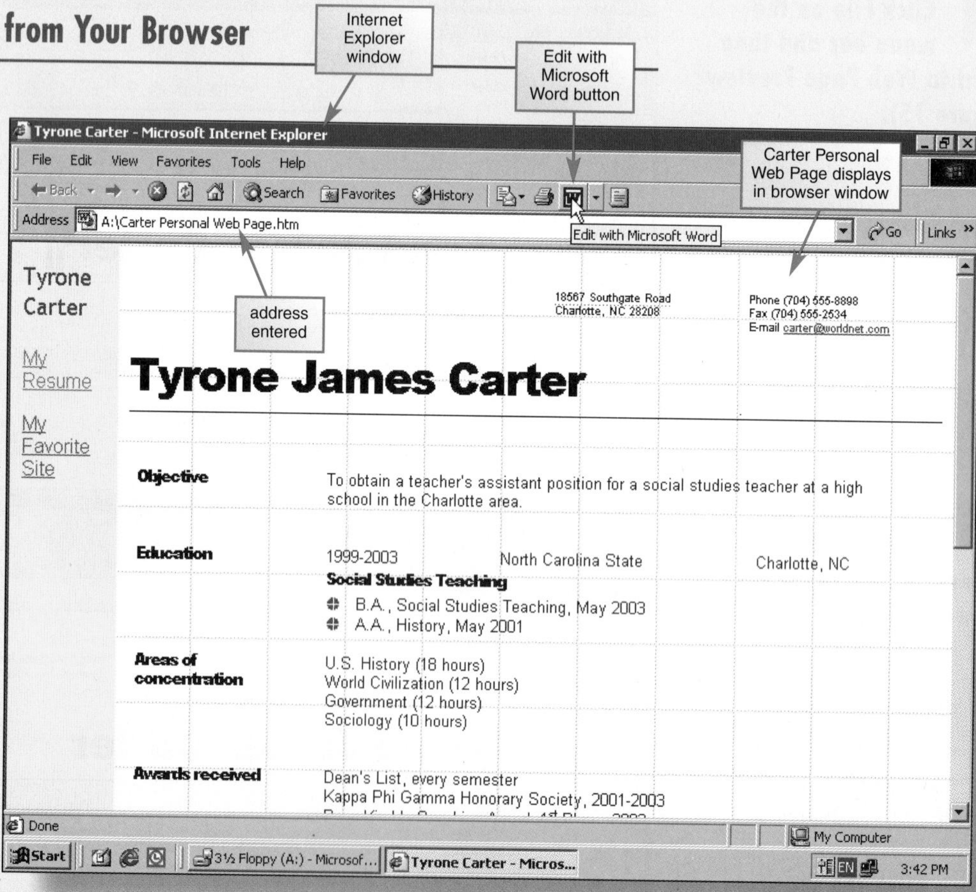

FIGURE 17

2 Click the Edit with Microsoft Word button.

Internet Explorer starts Microsoft Word and displays the Carter Personal Web Page in the Word window.

3 In the left frame, click to the left of the C in Carter. Type James **and then press the SPACEBAR.**

Tyrone's middle name displays in the left frame of the Web page (Figure 18).

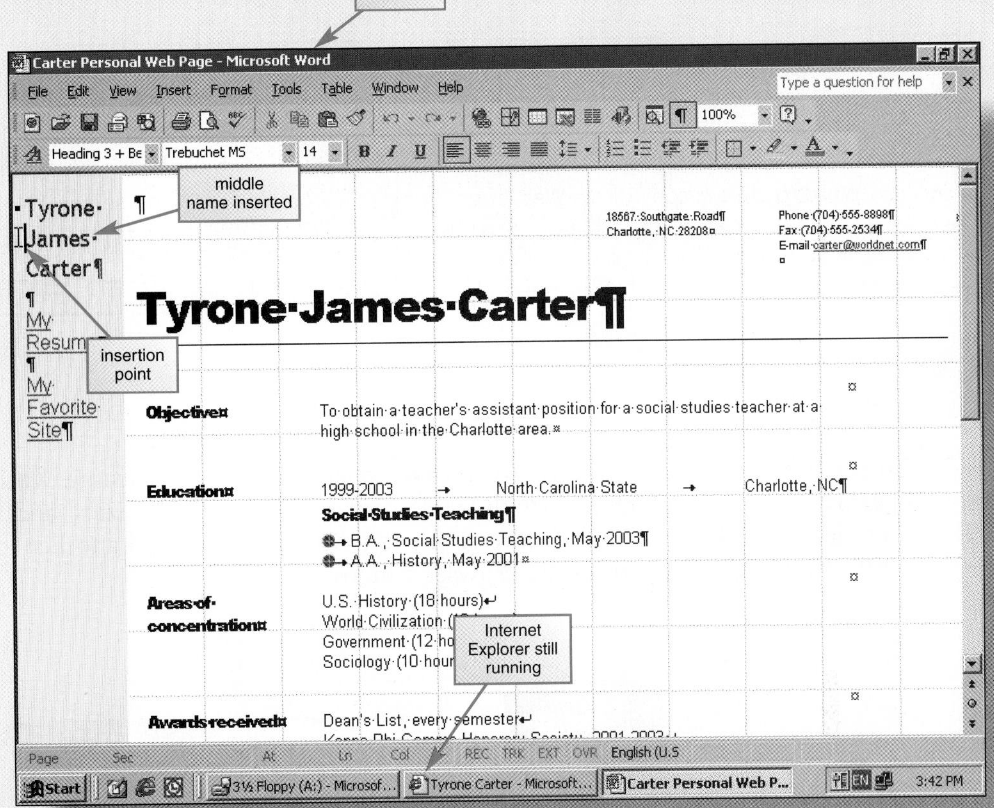

FIGURE 18

4 Click the Save button on the Standard toolbar. Click the Close button on the Word title bar to close the Word window. When the Internet Explorer window redisplays, click the Refresh button on the toolbar.

Internet Explorer displays the revised Web page (Figure 19).

5 Click the Close button on the Internet Explorer window title bar to close the browser window.

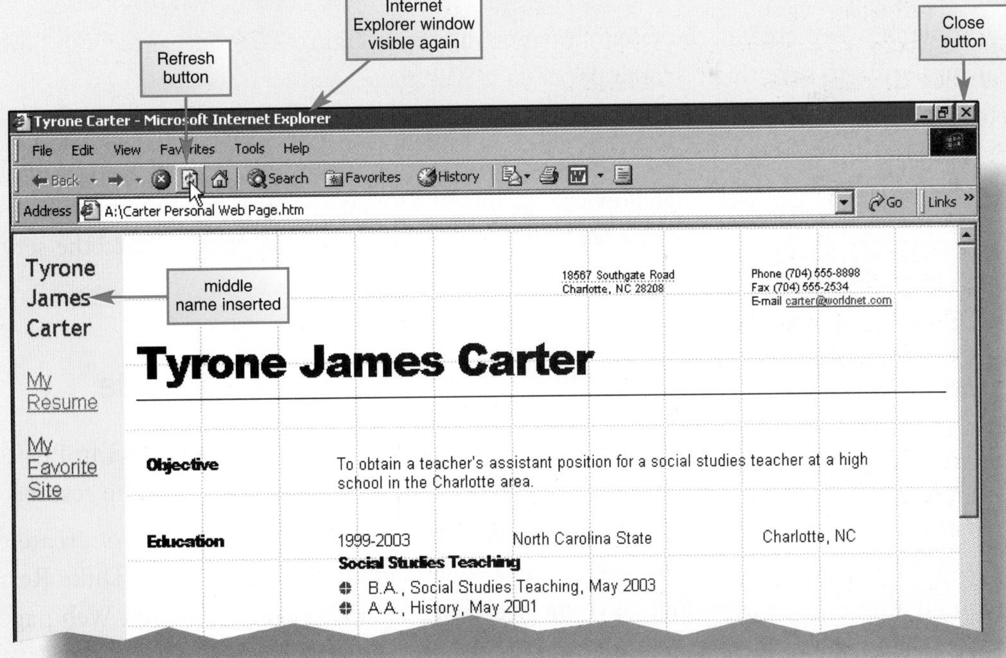

FIGURE 19

The final step is to make your Web pages and associated files available to others on a network, on an intranet, or on the World Wide Web. See Appendix C and then talk to your instructor about how you should do this for your system.

CASE PERSPECTIVE SUMMARY

Tyrone is thrilled with his personal Web pages. They look so professional! Tyrone now is ready to publish the Web pages and associated files to the World Wide Web. After talking with his ISP's technical support staff, he learns he can use Word to save a copy of his Web page files directly on his ISP's Web server. You are familiar with this feature of Word and assist Tyrone with this task. Next, he connects to the Web and displays his personal Web pages from his browser. Tyrone is quite impressed with himself!

Web Feature Summary

This Web Feature introduced you to creating a Web page by saving an existing Word document as a Web page file. You also created a new Web page with frames using the Web Page Wizard and then modified this Web page. You created a hyperlink to an e-mail address, one to a Web page file, and another to a Web site. Finally, you viewed and edited a Web page from the browser window.

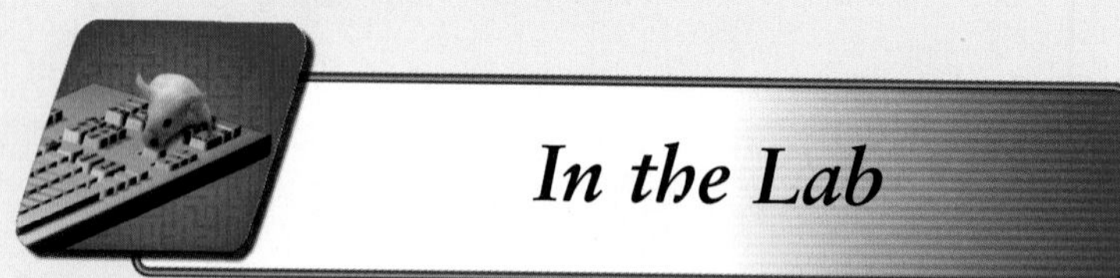

1 Saving a Word Document as a Web Page

Problem: You created the research paper shown in Figure 2-76 on pages WD 2.58 and WD 2.59 in Project 2. You decide to save this research paper as a Web page.

Instructions: Open the GPS Paper shown in Figure 2-76. (If you did not create the research paper, see your instructor for a copy.) Then, save the paper as a Web page using the file name, GPS Paper Web Page. Print the Web page. Use the Web Page Preview command to view the Web page in your browser. Close the browser window. If you have access to a Web server or ftp site, save the Web page to the server or site (see Appendix C for instructions).

2 Creating a Web Page with a Hyperlink to a Web Site

Problem: You created the resume shown in Figure 3-84 on page WD 3.63 in Project 3. You decide to create a personal Web page with a link to this resume. Thus, you also must save the resume as a Web page.

Instructions: Open the Duke Resume shown in Figure 3-84. (If you did not create the resume, see your instructor for a copy.) Then, save the resume as a Web page using the file name, Duke Resume Web Page. Convert the e-mail address to a hyperlink. Save the Web page again. Create a personal Web page with frames using the Web Page Wizard. Use the following settings as the wizard requests them: apply vertical frame navigation; create a hyperlink to the Duke Resume Web Page; change the name of the hyperlink to My Resume; and select a visual theme you like best. Insert a hyperlink called My Favorite Site and link it to your favorite Web address. Resize the left frame. Save the Web page. Test your Web page links. Print the Web page. Use the Web Page Preview command to view the Web page in your browser. Close the browser window. Quit Word. Start Internet Explorer and display the Web page in the browser window. Click the Edit with Microsoft Word button. In Word, change the name on the resume to your name. Save the change and quit Word. Refresh the Internet Explorer window.

2002

Microsoft

Excel

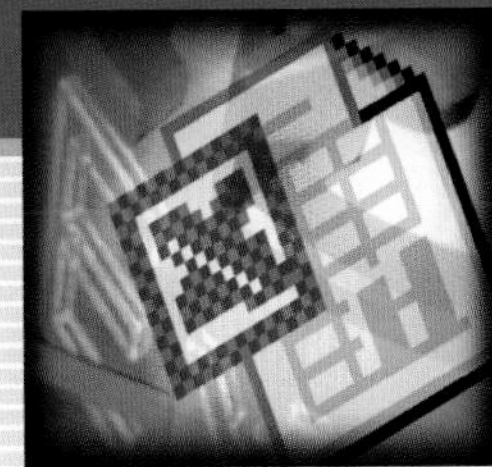

Microsoft Excel 2002

PROJECT

Creating a Worksheet and Embedded Chart

OBJECTIVES

You will have mastered the material in this project when you can:

- Start Excel
- Describe the Excel worksheet
- Describe the speech recognition capabilities of Excel
- Select a cell or range of cells
- Enter text and numbers
- Use the AutoSum button to sum a range of cells
- Copy a cell to a range of cells using the fill handle
- Bold font, change font size, and change font color
- Center cell contents across a series of columns
- Apply the AutoFormat command to format a range
- Use the Name box to select a cell
- Create a Column chart using the Chart Wizard
- Save a workbook
- Print a worksheet
- Quit Excel
- Open a workbook
- Use the AutoCalculate area to determine totals
- Correct errors on a worksheet
- Use the Excel Help system to answer your questions

Smaller Is Smarter

Smart Card Technology in Your Wallet

It withdraws funds from your bank, opens your dorm room door, pays for telephone calls, and much more. You carry it in a pocket, purse, or wallet. What is it? It is a smart card.

It looks like an ordinary credit-card-sized piece of plastic, but instead of a magnetic strip on the back, it has an embedded microprocessor chip in it. For both individuals and businesses, smart cards provide convenience and security.

Students are familiar with the card. An increasing number of colleges and universities across the United States participate in smart card programs for campus IDs, as well as many foreign colleges and universities in Canada, Europe, Australia, and Israel. Close to one million smart cards are estimated to be in use in the college market, representing one in seventeen students.

Central Michigan University (CMU) uses the Chip Card for student, faculty, and staff identification and access to many of the university resources including computer labs and the campus library. In addition, if individuals opt for certain plans, they can use their cards to store a dollar amount for convenient use on campus, at selected businesses, and for ATM and debit cards.

In January 2001, the Smart Card Industry Association (SCIA) and the Smart Card Forum (SCF) combined their two organizations to form the Smart Card Alliance (the Alliance). The Alliance is the largest smart card-oriented, nonprofit group in the world with more than 225 member organizations, serving the smart card industry in the

United States (smartcardalliance.org). Members represent a cross-section of technology experts and smart card users in the government, private, and education sectors. Applications include telephony, financial, IT, government, identification, transportation, and health care.

Some visionaries predict 3.75 billion smart cards will be issued by 2005, with owners using them to make 25 billion transactions yearly. The cost to manufacture one card ranges from 80 cents to 15 dollars depending on the application and complexity.

Two types of smart cards are available. One is a memory card. The memory card contains a stored value that the owner can spend on transactions such as paying bus fare or making a call from a public telephone. When the value is depleted, the card is useless.

The second is an intelligent smart card. The intelligent card contains a processor that can store data and make decisions. Owners begin with a set monetary value, such as $100, and then they can make a purchase that does not exceed this figure. If the amount is insufficient, they can add money to the balance. These functions are similar to the activities you will perform using Microsoft Excel in this project for the Dynamite Music company, where you will enter numbers in predefined storage areas, or cells, and then calculate a sum.

The smart card originated in 1974 when Roland Moreno, a reporter and self-taught inventor, secured a chip on an epoxy card. His vision was for merchants to accept electronic payments by inserting three cards in his Take the Money and Run (TMR) machine. One card identified the merchant, the second contained the customer's electronic money, and the third had a list of deadbeat accounts that could not be used to make a transaction. Pictures and descriptions of Moreno's invention and other smart card developments are found in the Smart Card Museum (cardshow.com).

Today, chips for the cards are manufactured by such industry leaders as Motorola, Gemplus, and Schlumberger. These companies are working to meet the demand for the cards, which is increasing at a rate of 30 percent annually. With an ever-growing global marketplace, smart cards are smarter.

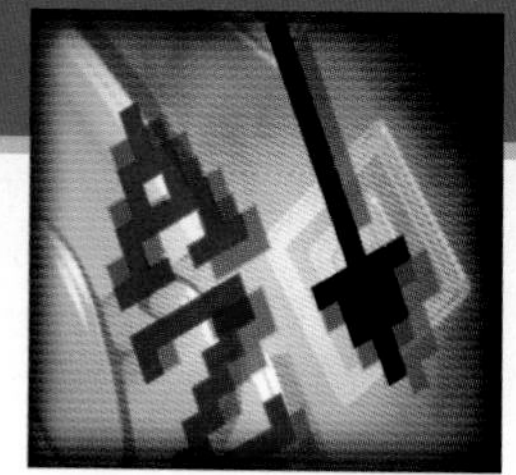

Microsoft Excel 2002

Creating a Worksheet and Embedded Chart

PROJECT

CASE PERSPECTIVE

Three years ago while in college, Nadine Mitchell and four of her friends came up with the idea of starting a company that sold music to young adults through store outlets in malls. After graduation, they invested $5,000 each and started their dream company, Dynamite Music.

The friends opened their first music store in Boston. Initially, they sold compact discs, cassettes, and rare records (vintage vinyls). As sales grew, they opened additional outlets in Chicago, Denver, and Phoenix. Last year, they started selling their products on the Web. Rather than use a central Web site for Web sales, they decided to maintain Web sites for each store. This year they began to sell music by allowing customers to download music to their personal computers.

As sales continue to grow, the management at Dynamite Music has realized it needs a better tracking system for sales by quarter. As a result, the company has asked you to prepare a fourth quarter sales worksheet that shows the sales for the fourth quarter.

In addition, Nadine has asked you to create a graphical representation of the fourth quarter sales because she finds it easier to work with than lists of numbers.

What Is Microsoft Excel?

Microsoft Excel is a powerful spreadsheet program that allows you to organize data, complete calculations, make decisions, graph data, develop professional looking reports, publish organized data to the Web, and access real-time data from Web sites. The four major parts of Excel are:

- **Worksheets** Worksheets allow you to enter, calculate, manipulate, and analyze data such as numbers and text. The term worksheet means the same as spreadsheet.
- **Charts** Charts pictorially represent data. Excel can draw a variety of two-dimensional and three-dimensional charts.
- **Databases** Databases manage data. For example, once you enter data onto a worksheet, Excel can sort the data, search for specific data, and select data that satisfy a criteria.
- **Web Support** Web support allows Excel to save workbooks or parts of a workbook in HTML format so they can be viewed and manipulated using a browser. You also can access real-time data using Web queries.

Project One — Dynamite Music Fourth Quarter Sales

From your meeting with Dynamite Music's management, you have determined the following: needs, source of data, calculations, and chart requirements.

Needs: An easy-to-read worksheet (Figure 1-1) that shows Dynamite Music's fourth quarter sales for each of the product groups (Cassettes, Compact Discs, Vintage Vinyls, and Web Downloads) by store (Boston, Chicago, Denver, and Phoenix). The worksheet also should include total sales for each product group, each store, and total company sales for the fourth quarter.

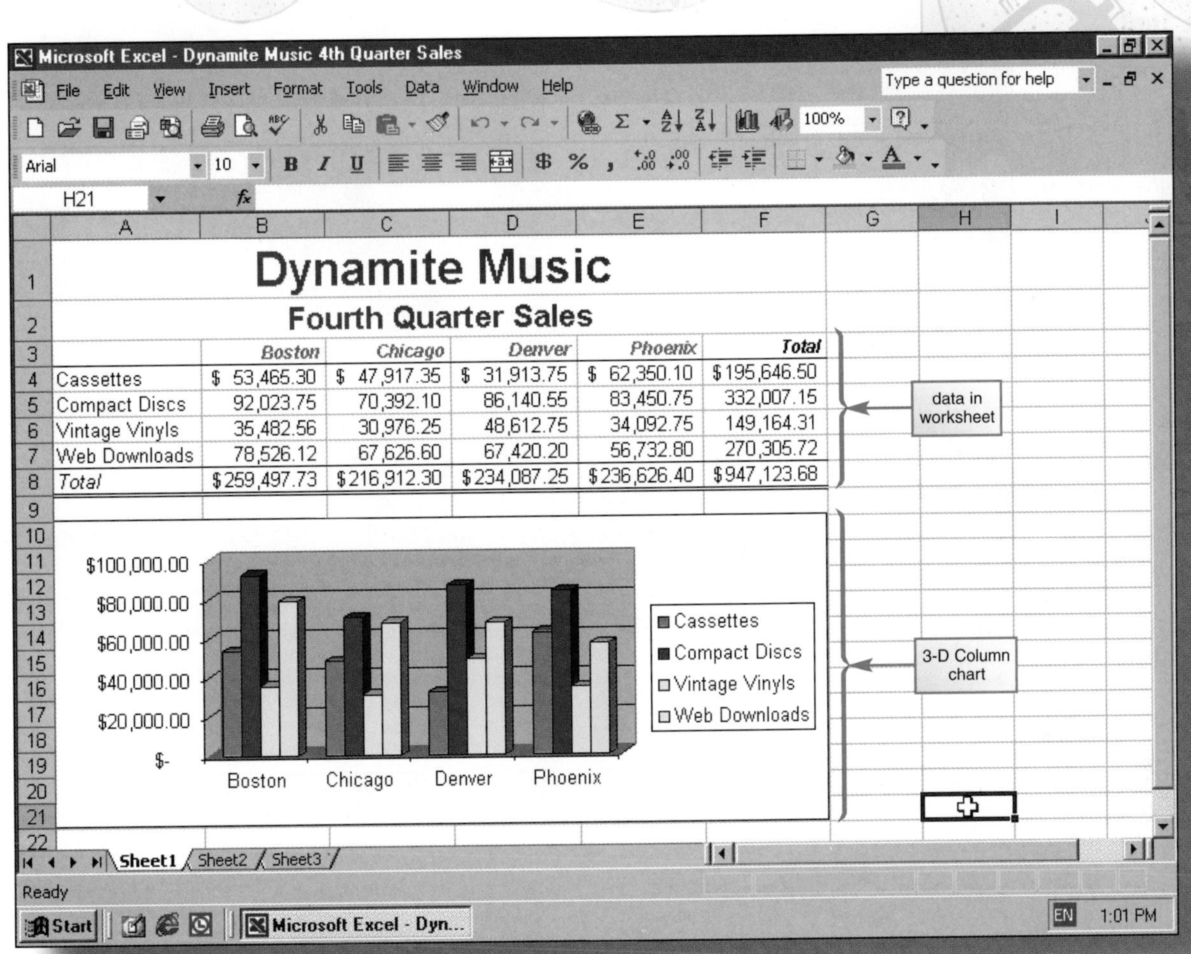

FIGURE 1-1

Source of Data: The data for the worksheet is available at the end of the fourth quarter from the chief financial officer (CFO) of Dynamite Music.

Calculations: You have determined that the following calculations must be made for the worksheet: (a) total fourth quarter sales for each of the four product groups; (b) total fourth quarter sales for each of the four stores; and (c) fourth quarter sales for the company.

Chart Requirements: Below the worksheet, construct a 3-D Column chart that compares the amount of sales for each product group within each store.

Starting and Customizing Excel

To start Excel, Windows must be running. Perform the steps on the next page to start Excel, or ask your instructor how to start Excel for your system.

More About

Excel 2002

With its smart tags, speech recognition, shortcut menus, toolbars, what-if analysis tools, Web capabilities, hundreds of functions, and speech playback, Excel 2002 is one of the easiest, and yet most powerful, worksheet packages available. Its powerful analytical features make it possible to answer complicated what-if questions. Its Web capabilities allow you to create, publish, view, and analyze data on an intranet or the World Wide Web.

Steps To Start Excel

1 Click the Start button on the Windows taskbar, point to Programs on the Start menu, and then point to Microsoft Excel on the Programs submenu.

The commands on the Start menu display above the Start button and the Programs submenu displays (Figure 1-2). If the Office Speech Recognition software is installed on your computer, then the Language bar may display somewhere on the desktop.

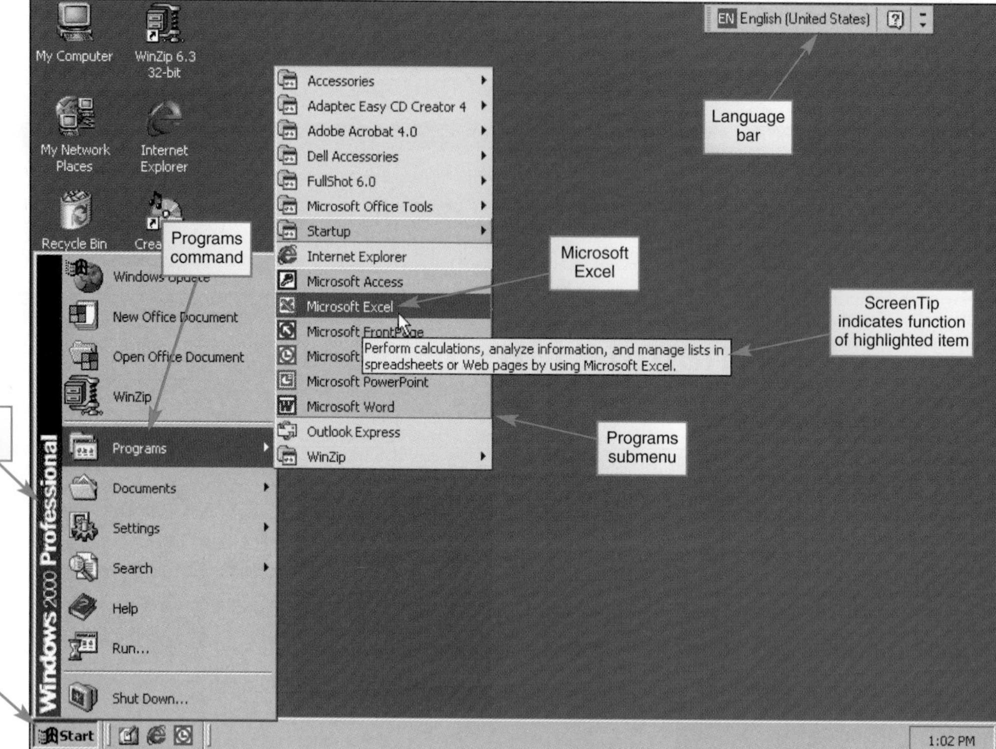

FIGURE 1-2

2 Click Microsoft Excel.

Excel starts. After several seconds, a blank workbook titled Book1 displays in the Excel window (Figure 1-3).

3 If the Excel window is not maximized, double-click its title bar to maximize it.

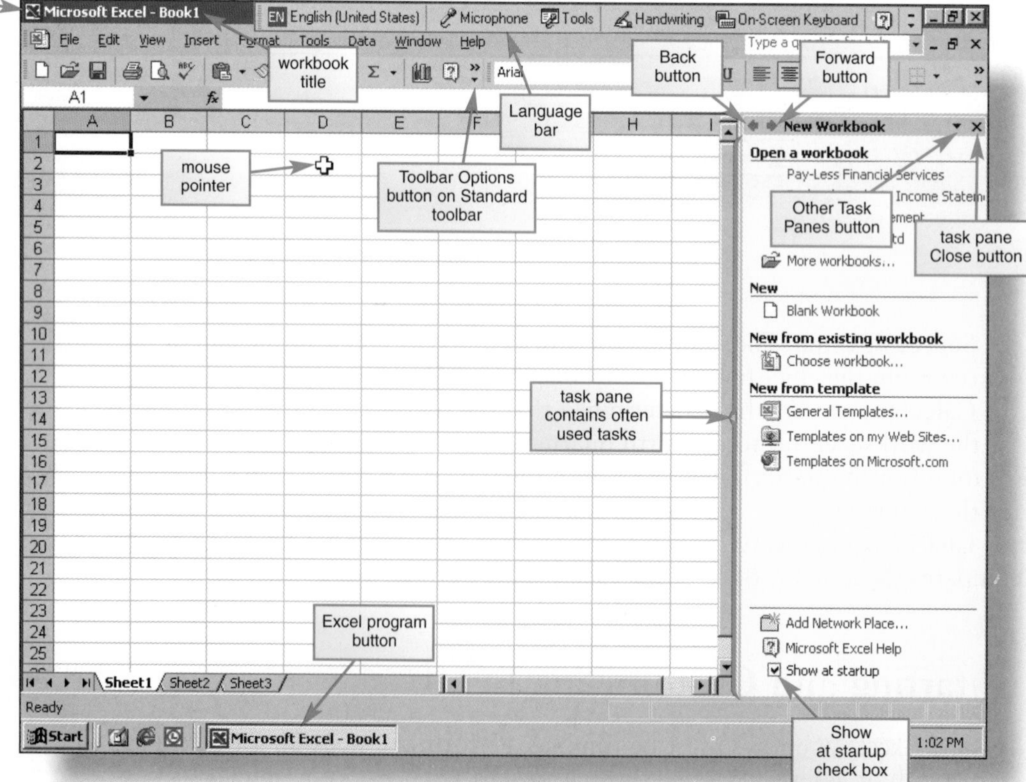

FIGURE 1-3

Other Ways

1. Double-click Excel icon on desktop
2. Right-click Start button, click Open All Users, double-click New Office Document, click General tab, double-click Blank Workbook icon
3. Click Start button, click New Office Document, click General tab, double-click Blank Workbook icon

The screen in Figure 1-3 shows how the Excel window looks the first time you start Excel after installation on most computers. If the Office Speech Recognition software is installed on your system, then when you start Excel either the Language bar expands to include the functions available in Excel (shown at the top of Figure 1-3) or the language indicator displays on the right side of the Windows taskbar (Figure 1-7 on page E 1.11). In this book, the Language bar will be kept minimized until it is used. For additional information about the Language bar, see page E 1.16 and Appendix B.

Notice also that a task pane displays on the screen, and that the buttons on the toolbar display on a single row. A **task pane** is a separate window that enables users to carry out some Excel tasks more efficiently. In this book, to allow the maximum number of columns to display in Excel, a task pane should not display. For more efficient use of the buttons, they should display on two separate rows instead of sharing a single row. Perform the following steps to close the New Workbook task pane, minimize the Language bar, and display the buttons on two separate rows.

Task Panes

You can drag a task pane title bar (Figure 1-3) to float the pane in your work area or dock it on either the left or right side of a screen, depending on your personal preference.

The Excel Help System

Need Help? It is no further away than the Ask a Question box in the upper-right corner of the window. Click the box that contains the text, Type a question for help (Figure 1-4), type `help`, and then press the ENTER key. Excel will respond with a list of items you can click to learn about obtaining help on any Excel-related topic. To find out what is new in Excel 2002, type `what's new in Excel` in the Ask a Question box.

Steps To Customize the Excel Window

1 If the New Workbook task pane displays in your Excel window, click the Show at startup check box to remove the check mark and then click the Close button in the upper-right corner of the task pane (Figure 1-3). If the Language bar displays, point to its Minimize button.

Excel removes the check mark from the Show at startup check box. With the check mark removed, Excel will not display the New Workbook task pane the next time Excel starts. The New Workbook task pane closes resulting in additional columns displaying (Figure 1-4).

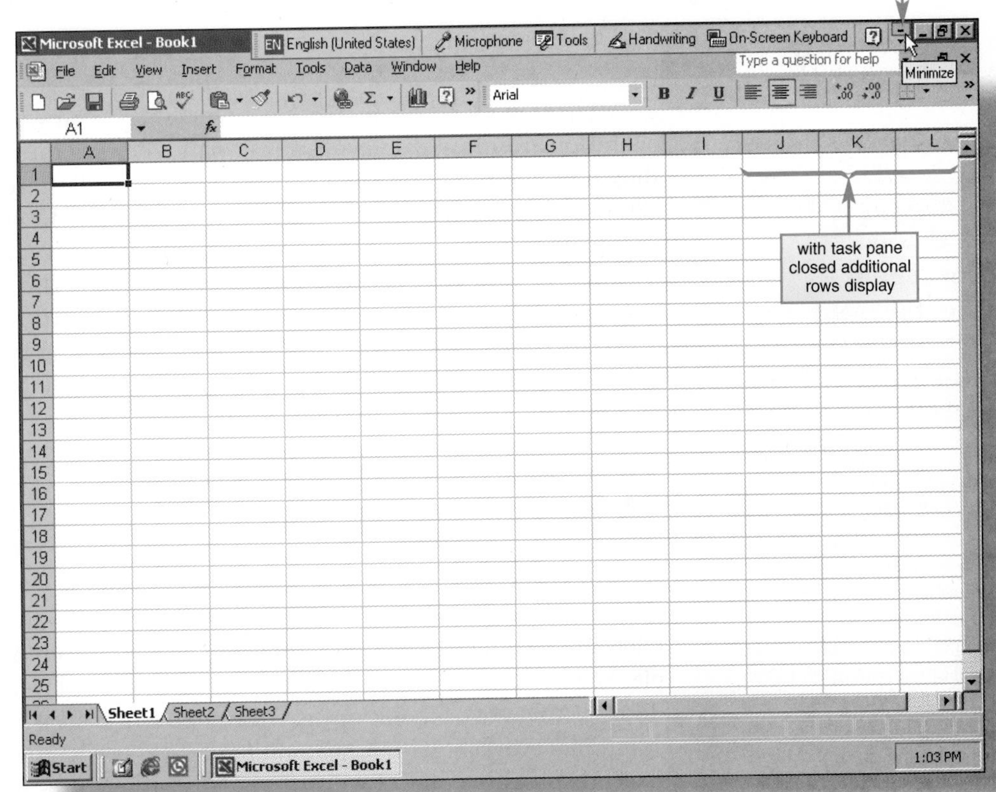

FIGURE 1-4

2 Click the Minimize button on the Language bar. If the toolbars display positioned on the same row, click the Toolbar Options button and then point to Show Buttons on Two Rows.

The Toolbar Options list displays showing the buttons that do not fit on the toolbars when buttons display on one row (Figure 1-5).

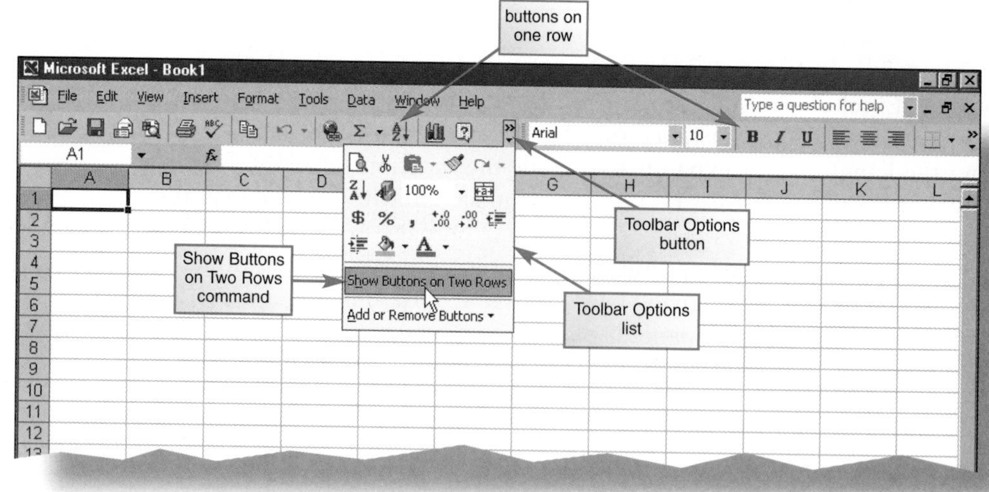

FIGURE 1-5

3 Click Show Buttons on Two Rows.

Excel displays the buttons on two separate rows (Figure 1-6). The Toolbar Options list shown in Figure 1-5 is empty because all of the buttons display on two rows.

FIGURE 1-6

Worksheet Development

The key to developing a useful worksheet is careful planning. Careful planning can reduce your effort significantly and result in a worksheet that is accurate, easy to read, flexible, and useful. When analyzing a problem and designing a worksheet solution, you should follow these steps: (1) define the problem, including need, source of data, calculations, charting and Web or special requirements; (2) design the worksheet; (3) enter the data and formulas; and (4) test the worksheet.

As you work through creating a worksheet, you will find that certain Excel operations result in displaying a task pane. Besides the New Workbook task pane shown in Figure 1-3 on page E 1.08, Excel provides three additional task panes: the Clipboard task pane, the Search task pane, and the Insert Clip Art task pane. These task panes are discussed when they are used. You can display or hide a task pane by clicking the **Task Pane command** on the **View menu**. You can activate additional task panes by clicking the down arrow to the left of the Close button on the task pane title bar (Figure 1-3) and then selecting a task pane in the list. Using the Back and Forward buttons on the left side of the task pane title bar, you can switch between task panes.

The Excel Worksheet

When Excel starts, it creates a new blank workbook, called Book1. The **workbook** (Figure 1-7) is like a notebook. Inside the workbook are sheets, called **worksheets.** Each sheet name displays on a **sheet tab** at the bottom of the workbook. For example, Sheet1 is the name of the active worksheet displayed in the workbook called Book1. A new workbook opens with three worksheets. If necessary, you can add additional worksheets to a maximum of 255. If you click the tab labeled Sheet2, Excel displays the Sheet2 worksheet. This project uses only the Sheet1 worksheet.

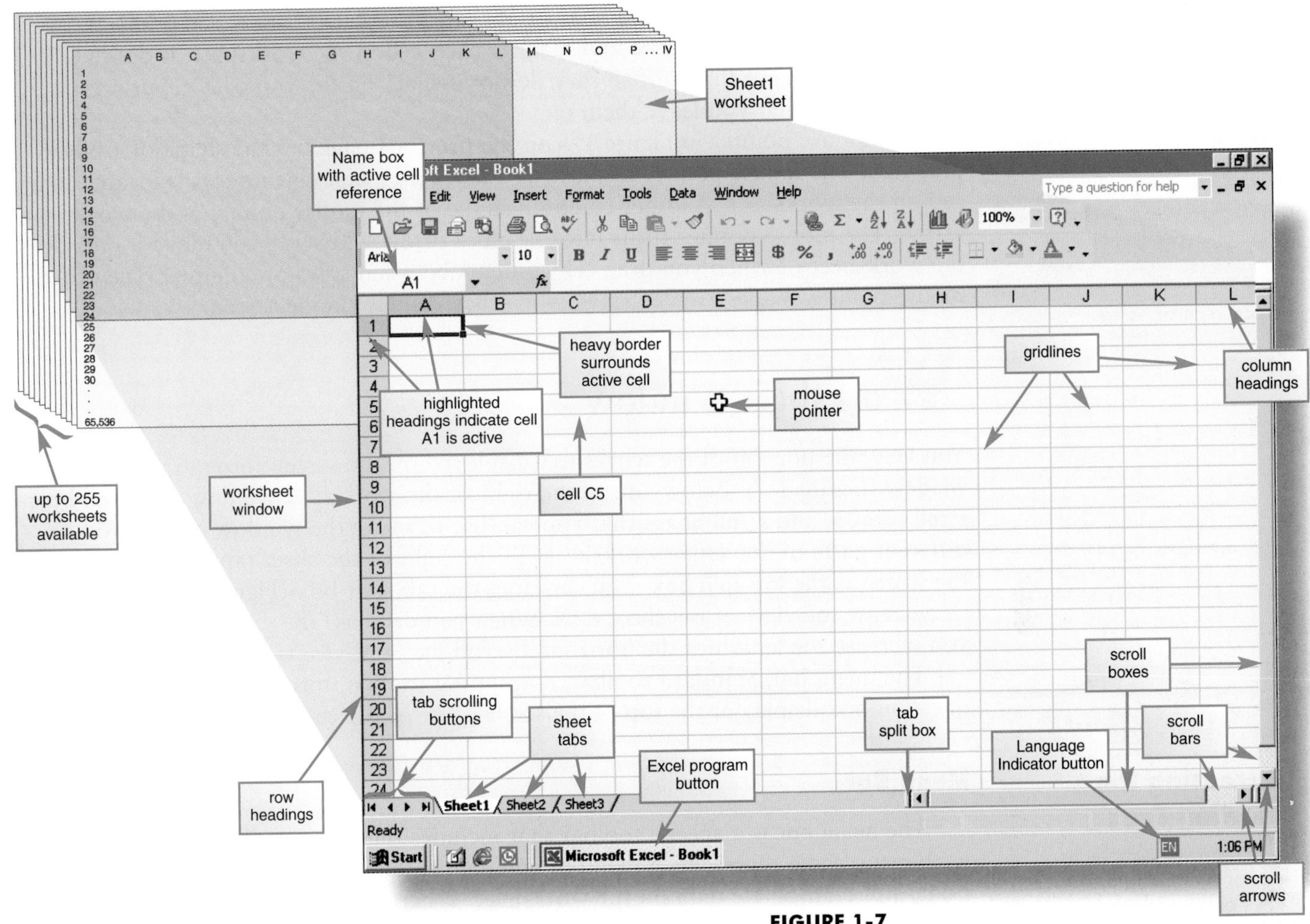

FIGURE 1-7

The Worksheet

The worksheet is organized into a rectangular grid containing columns (vertical) and rows (horizontal). A column letter above the grid, also called the **column heading**, identifies each column. A row number on the left side of the grid, also called the **row heading**, identifies each row. With the screen resolution set to 800 × 600, 12 columns (A through L) and 24 rows (1 through 24) of the worksheet display on the screen when the worksheet is maximized as shown in Figure 1-7.

The intersection of each column and row is a cell. A **cell** is the basic unit of a worksheet into which you enter data. Each worksheet in a workbook has 256 columns and 65,536 rows for a total of 16,777,216 cells. The column headings begin with A and end with IV. The row headings begin with 1 and end with 65,536. Only a small fraction of the active worksheet displays on the screen at one time.

A cell is referred to by its unique address, or **cell reference**, which is the coordinates of the intersection of a column and a row. To identify a cell, specify the column letter first, followed by the row number. For example, cell reference C5 refers to the cell located at the intersection of column C and row 5 (Figure 1-7).

One cell on the worksheet, designated the **active cell**, is the one into which you can enter data. The active cell in Figure 1-7 is A1. The active cell is identified in three ways. First, a heavy border surrounds the cell; second, the active cell reference displays immediately above column A in the **Name box**; and third, the column heading A and row heading 1 are highlighted so it is easy to see which cell is active (Figure 1-7).

More About

The Worksheet Size and Window

256 columns and 65,536 rows make for a huge worksheet that you might imagine takes up the entire wall of a large room. Your computer screen, by comparison, is a small window that allows you to view only a minute area of the worksheet at one time. While you can't see the entire worksheet, you can move the window over the worksheet to view any part of it. To display the last row in a blank worksheet, press the END key and then press the DOWN ARROW key. Press CTRL+HOME to return to the top of the worksheet.

The Mouse Pointer

The mouse pointer can change to one of more than fifteen different shapes, such as an arrow, cross hair, or chart symbol, depending on the task you are performing in Excel and the mouse pointer's location on the screen.

The horizontal and vertical lines on the worksheet itself are called **gridlines.** Gridlines make it easier to see and identify each cell in the worksheet. If desired, you can turn the gridlines off so they do not display on the worksheet, but it is recommended that you leave them on.

The mouse pointer in Figure 1-7 on the previous page has the shape of a block plus sign. The mouse pointer displays as a **block plus sign** whenever it is located in a cell on the worksheet. Another common shape of the mouse pointer is the block arrow. The mouse pointer turns into the **block arrow** whenever you move it outside the worksheet or when you drag cell contents between rows or columns. The other mouse pointer shapes are described when they display on the screen.

Worksheet Window

You view the portion of the worksheet displayed on the screen through a **worksheet window** (Figure 1-7). Below and to the right of the worksheet window are **scroll bars, scroll arrows**, and **scroll boxes** that you can use to move the window around to view different parts of the active worksheet. To the right of the sheet tabs at the bottom of the screen is the **tab split box**. You can drag the tab split box (Figure 1-7) to increase or decrease the view of the sheet tabs. When you decrease the view of the sheet tabs, you increase the length of the horizontal scroll bar, and vice versa.

The menu bar, Standard toolbar, Formatting toolbar, formula bar, and Ask a question box display at the top of the screen, just below the title bar (Figure 1-8a).

More About

Increasing the Viewing Area

If you want to increase the size of the viewing area to see more of the worksheet, click Full Screen on the View menu. You can also increase the viewing area by changing to a higher resolution. You change to a higher resolution by right-clicking the Windows desktop, clicking Properties, clicking the Settings tab, and increasing the Screen area.

Menu Bar

The **menu bar** is a special toolbar that includes the menu names (Figure 1-8a). Each **menu name** represents a menu of commands that you can use to retrieve, store, print, and manipulate data on the worksheet. When you point to a menu name on the menu bar, the area of the menu bar containing the name changes to a button. To display a menu, such as the Edit menu, click the Edit menu name on the menu bar (Figures 1-8b and 1-8c). A **menu** is a list of commands. If you point to a command on the menu with an arrow to its right, a **submenu** displays from which you can choose a command.

When you click a menu name on the menu bar, a **short menu** displays listing the most recently used commands (Figure 1-8b). If you wait a few seconds or click the arrows at the bottom of the short menu, the full menu displays. The **full menu** lists all the commands associated with a menu (Figure 1-8c). You also can display a full menu immediately by double-clicking the menu name on the menu bar. In this book, when you display a menu, always display the full menu using one of the following techniques.

1. Click the menu name on the menu bar and then wait a few seconds.
2. Click the menu name and then click the arrows at the bottom of the short menu.
3. Click the menu name and then point to the arrows at the bottom of the short menu.
4. Double-click the menu name.

Both short and full menus display some **dimmed commands** that appear gray, or dimmed, instead of black, which indicates they are not available for the current selection. A command with a dark gray shading to the left of it on a full menu is called a **hidden command** because it does not display on a short menu. As you use Excel, it automatically personalizes the short menus for you based on how often you use commands. That is, as you use hidden commands, Excel *unhides* them and places them on the short menu.

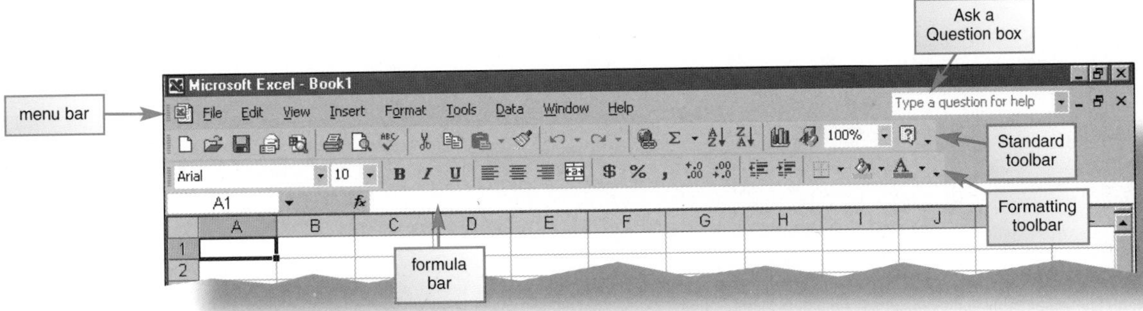

(a) Menu bar and Toolbars

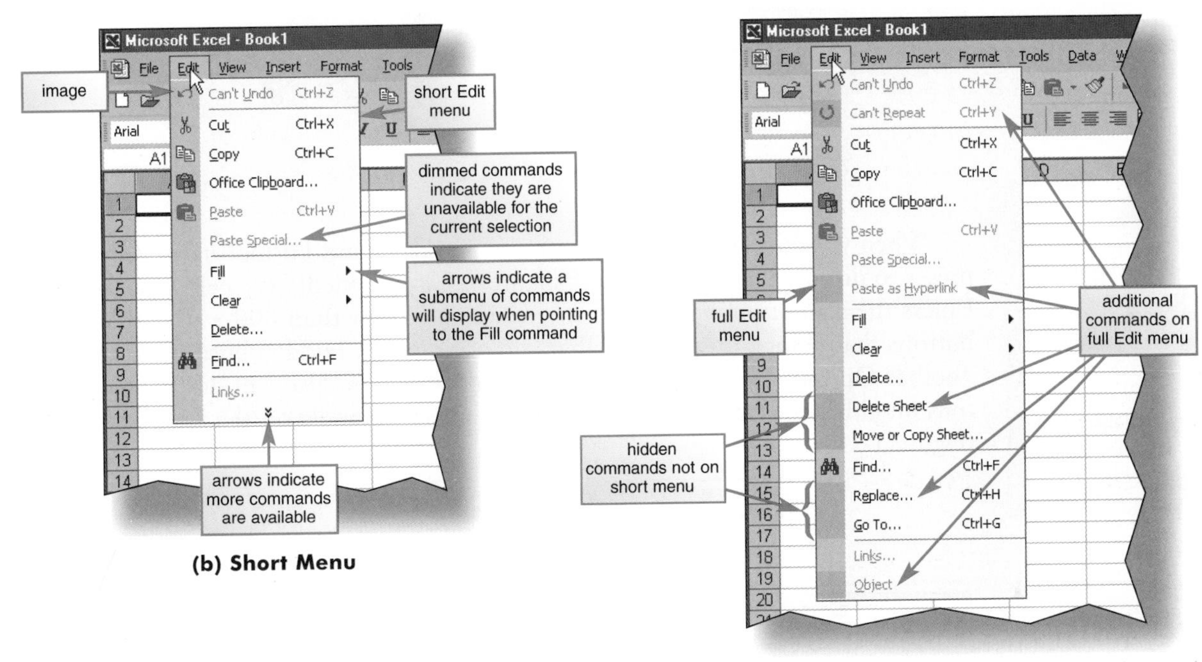

(b) Short Menu

(c) Full Menu

FIGURE 1-8

The menu bar can change to include other menu names depending on the type of work you are doing in Excel. For example, if you are working with a chart sheet rather than a worksheet, the Chart menu bar displays with menu names that reflect charting commands.

Standard Toolbar and Formatting Toolbar

The **Standard toolbar** and the **Formatting toolbar** (Figure 1-8a) contain buttons and list boxes that allow you to perform frequent tasks more quickly than when using the menu bar. For example, to print a worksheet, you click the Print button on the Standard toolbar. Each button has a picture on the button face that helps you remember the button's function. Also, when you move the mouse pointer over a button or box, the name of the button or box displays below it in a **ScreenTip**.

Figures 1-9a and 1-9b on the next page illustrate the Standard and Formatting toolbars and describe the functions of the buttons. Each of the buttons and boxes will be explained in detail when they are used.

More About

Toolbars

You can move a toolbar to any location on the screen. Drag the move handle (Figure 1-10a on page E 1.14) to the desired location. Once the toolbar is in the window area, drag the title bar to move it. Each side of the screen is called a dock. You can drag a toolbar to a dock so it does not clutter the window.

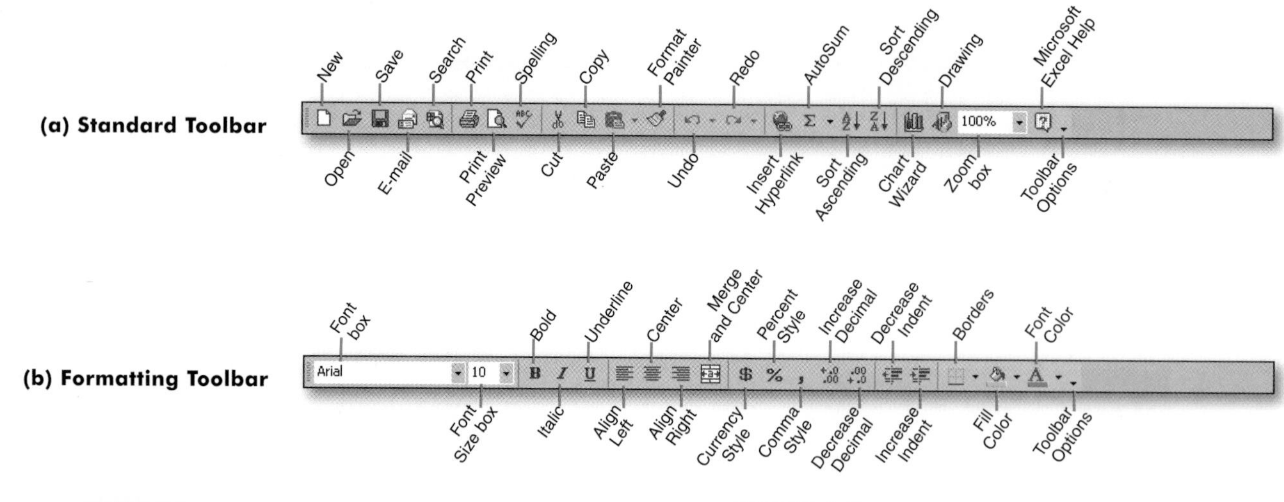

FIGURE 1-9

More About

Resetting Toolbars

If your toolbars have a different set of buttons than shown in Figure 1-10c, it probably means that a previous user added or deleted buttons. To reset the toolbars to their default, see Appendix D.

When you first install Excel, both the Standard and Formatting toolbars are preset to display on the same row (Figure 1-10a), immediately below the menu bar. Unless the resolution of your display device is greater than 800 × 600, many of the buttons that belong on these toolbars do not display. Hidden buttons display in the Toolbar Options list (Figure 1-10b). In this mode, you also can display all the buttons on either toolbar by double-clicking the **move handle** on the left of each toolbar (Figure 1-10a).

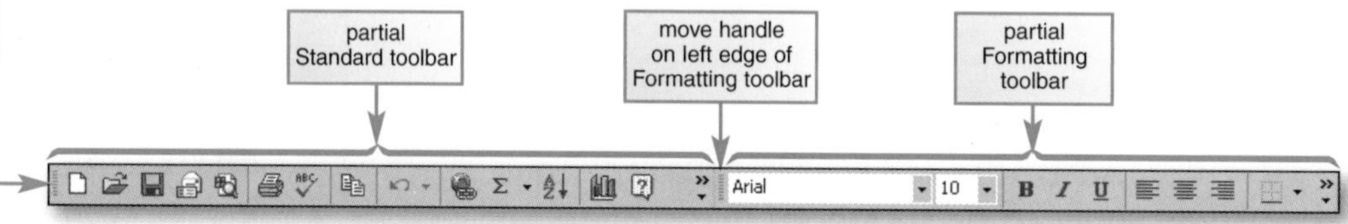

(a) Standard and Formatting Toolbars on One Row

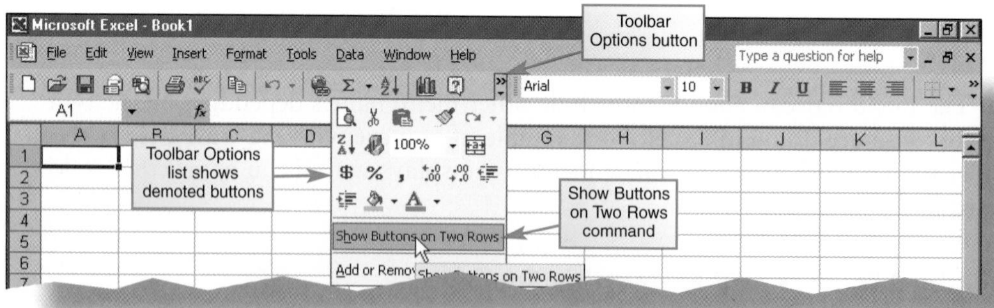

(b) Toolbar Options List

(c) Standard and Formatting Toolbars on Two Rows

FIGURE 1-10

In this book, the Standard and Formatting toolbars are shown on two rows, one under the other so that all buttons display (Figure 1-10c). You show the two toolbars on two rows by clicking the **Show Buttons on Two Rows command** in the Toolbar Options list (Figure 1-10b).

Formula Bar

Below the Standard and Formatting toolbars is the formula bar (Figure 1-11). As you type, the data displays in the **formula bar**. Excel also displays the active cell reference on the left side of the formula bar in the Name box.

Sizing Toolbar Buttons

If you have difficulty seeing the small buttons on the toolbars, you can increase their size by clicking View on the menu bar, pointing to Toolbars, clicking Customize on the Toolbars submenu, clicking the Options tab, clicking the Large icons checkbox, and clicking the Close button.

Status Bar

Immediately above the Windows taskbar at the bottom of the screen is the status bar. The **status bar** displays a brief description of the command selected (highlighted) in a menu, the function of the button the mouse pointer is pointing to, or the mode of Excel. **Mode indicators**, such as Enter and Ready, display on the status bar and specify the current mode of Excel. When the mode is Ready, Excel is ready to accept the next command or data entry. When the mode indicator reads Enter, Excel is in the process of accepting data through the keyboard into the active cell.

In the middle of the status bar is the AutoCalculate area. The **AutoCalculate area** can be used in place of a calculator to view the sum, average, or other types of totals of a group of numbers on the worksheet. The AutoCalculate area is discussed in detail later in this project.

Keyboard indicators, such as CAPS (Caps Lock), NUM (Num Lock), and SCRL (Scroll) show which keys are engaged. Keyboard indicators display on the right side of the status bar within the small rectangular boxes (Figure 1-11).

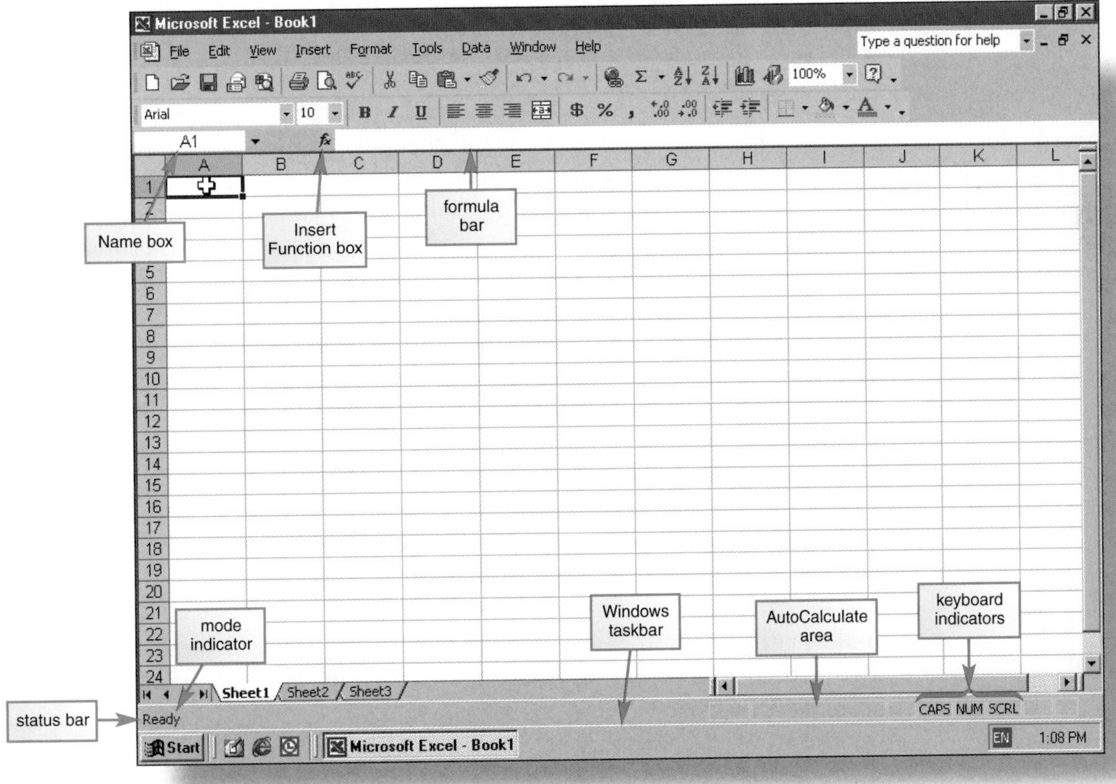

FIGURE 1-11

Speech Recognition and Speech Playback

With the **Office Speech Recognition software** installed and a microphone, you can speak the names of toolbar buttons, menus, menu commands, list items, alerts, and dialog box controls, such as OK and Cancel. You also can dictate cell entries, such as text and numbers. To indicate whether you want to speak commands or dictate cell entries, you use the **Language bar** (Figure 1-12a). You can display the Language bar in two ways: (1) click the Language Indicator button in the taskbar tray status area by the clock, and then click Show the Language bar on the menu (Figure 1-12b); or (2) point to the **Speech command** on the **Tools menu** and then click the **Speech Recognition command** on the **Speech submenu**.

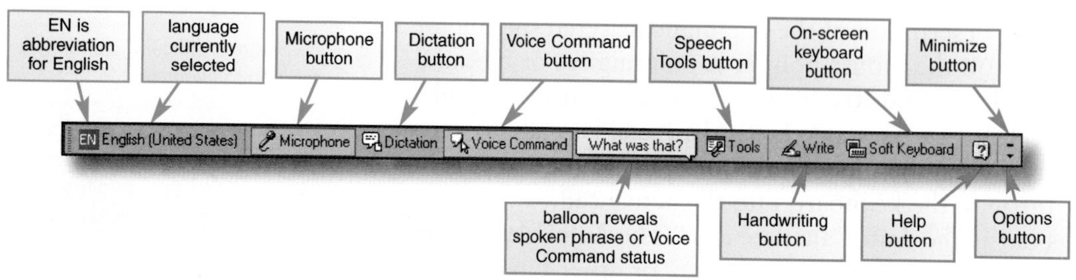

(a) Language Bar

Language bar menu

English (United States)

English (Zimbabwe)

French (Canada)

French (France)

German (Germany)

Swahili

Show the Language bar

Show the Language bar command

Language Indicator button in tray status area on Windows taskbar

1:08 PM

(b) Language Bar Menu

FIGURE 1-12

If the Language Indicator button does not display in the tray status area, and if the Speech command is dimmed on the Tools menu, the Office Speech Recognition software is not installed. To install the software, you first must start Word and then click Speech on the Tools menu.

If you have speakers, you can instruct the computer to read a worksheet to you. By selecting the appropriate option, you can have the worksheet read in a male or female voice.

Additional information on the speech recognition and speech playback capabilities in Excel is available in Appendix B.

Selecting a Cell

To enter data into a cell, you first must select it. The easiest way to **select a cell** (make it active) is to use the mouse to move the block plus sign to the cell and then click.

An alternative method is to use the **arrow keys** that are located just to the right of the typewriter keys on the keyboard. An arrow key selects the cell adjacent to the active cell in the direction of the arrow on the key.

You know a cell is selected (active) when a heavy border surrounds the cell (cell A1 in Figure 1-11 on the previous page) and the active cell reference displays in the Name box on the left side of the formula bar.

Selecting a Cell

You can select any cell by entering the cell reference, such as b4, in the Name box on the left side of the formula bar.

Entering Text

In Excel, any set of characters containing a letter, hyphen (as in a telephone number), or space is considered **text**. Text is used to place titles on the worksheet, such as worksheet titles, column titles, and row titles. In Project 1 (Figure 1-13), the worksheet title, Dynamite Music, identifies the worksheet. The worksheet subtitle, Fourth Quarter Sales, identifies the type of report. The column titles in row 3 (Boston, Chicago, Denver, Phoenix, and Total) identify the numbers in each column. The row titles in column A (Cassettes, Compact Discs, Vintage Vinyls, Web Downloads, and Total) identify the numbers in each row.

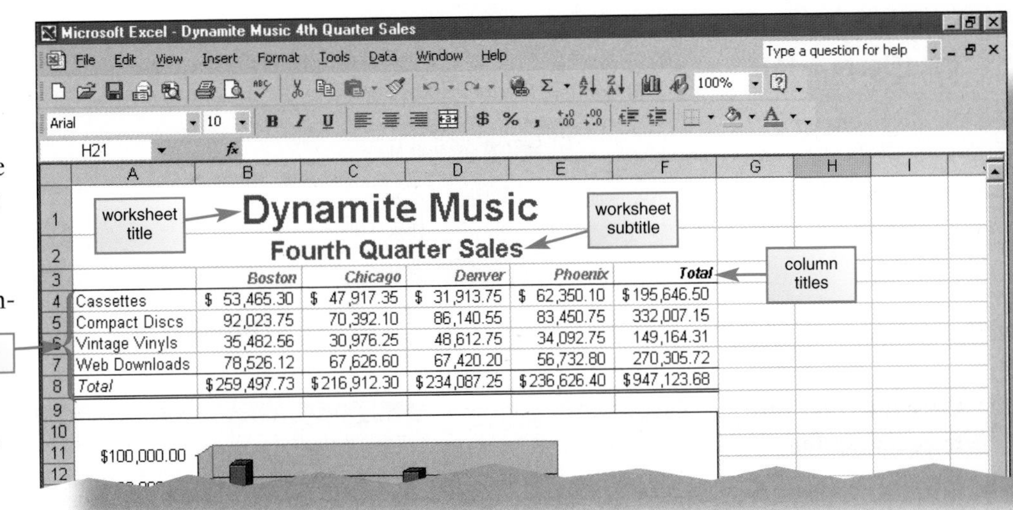

FIGURE 1-13

More About

Text

A text entry in a cell can contain from 1 to 32,767 characters. Although text entries are primarily used to identify parts of the worksheet, there are applications in which text entries are data that you dissect, string together, and manipulate using text functions.

Entering the Worksheet Titles

The following steps show how to enter the worksheet titles in cells A1 and A2. Later in this project, the worksheet titles will be formatted so it displays as shown in Figure 1-13. Perform the following steps to enter the worksheet tiles.

Steps To Enter the Worksheet Titles

1 Click cell A1.

Cell A1 becomes the active cell and a heavy border surrounds it (Figure 1-14).

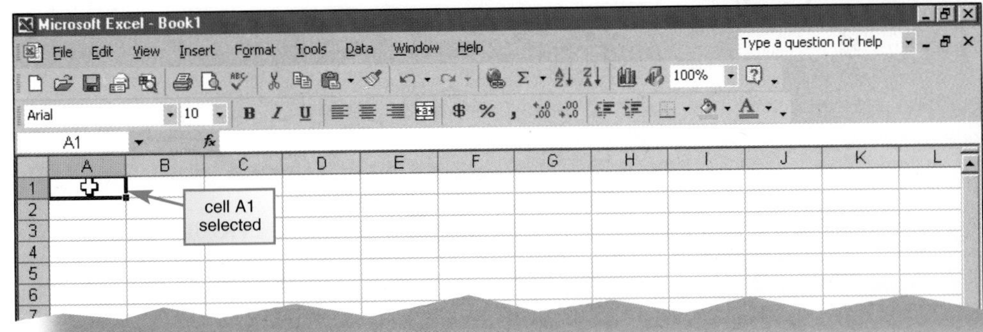

FIGURE 1-14

2 Type `Dynamite Music` **in cell A1.**

The title displays in the formula bar and in cell A1. The text in cell A1 is followed by the insertion point (Figure 1-15). The insertion point is a blinking vertical line that indicates where the next typed character will display.

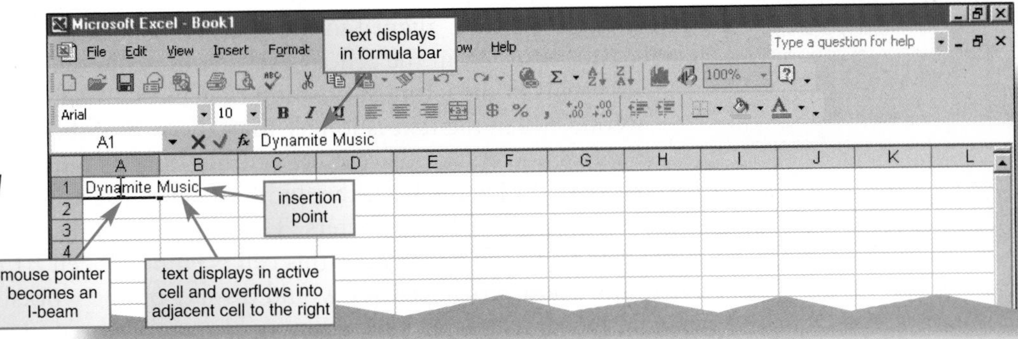

FIGURE 1-15

3 Point to the Enter box (Figure 1-16).

When you begin typing a cell entry, Excel displays two additional boxes in the formula bar: the Cancel box and the Enter box.

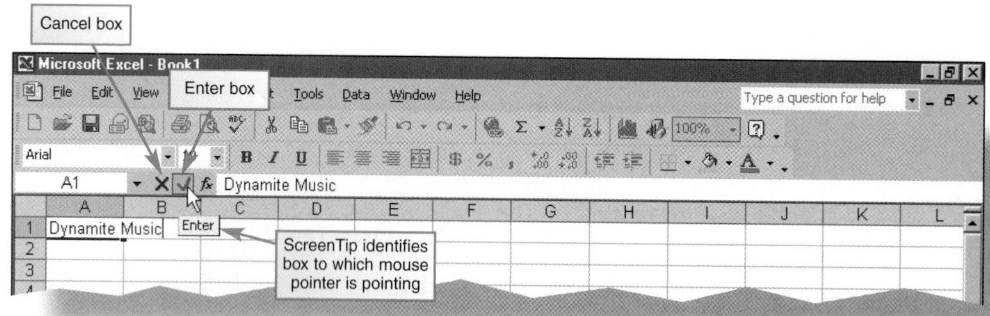

FIGURE 1-16

4 Click the Enter box to complete the entry.

Excel enters the worksheet title in cell A1 (Figure 1-17).

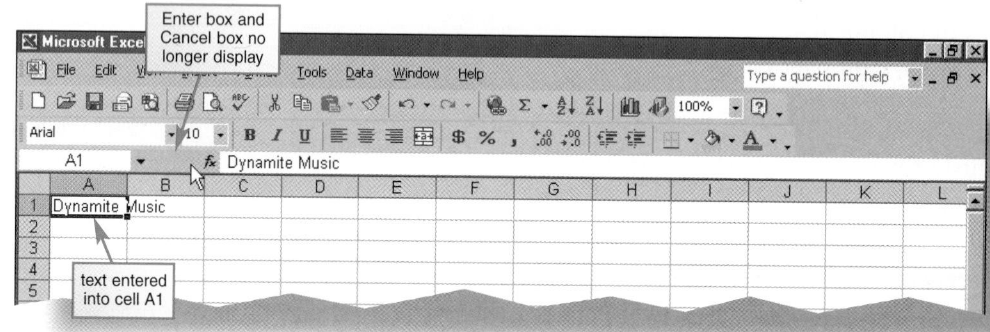

FIGURE 1-17

5 Click cell A2 to select it. Type `Fourth Quarter Sales` **as the cell entry. Click the Enter box to complete the entry.**

Excel enters the worksheet subtitle in cell A2 (Figure 1-18).

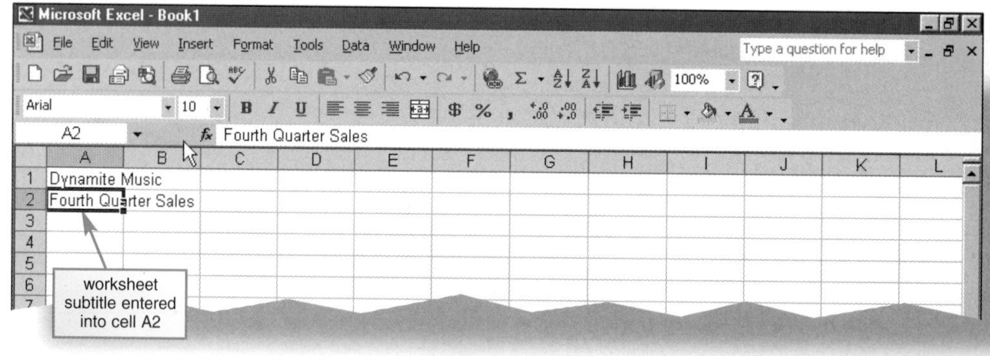

FIGURE 1-18

Other Ways

1. To complete entry, click any cell other than active cell
2. To complete entry, press ENTER key
3. To complete entry, press HOME, PAGE UP, PAGE DOWN, or END key
4. In Voice Command mode say, "Enter" to complete entry

In Steps 3 and 4, clicking the **Enter box** completes the entry. Clicking the **Cancel box** cancels the entry.

When you complete a text entry into a cell, a series of events occurs. First, Excel positions the text left-aligned in the cell. **Left-aligned** means the cell entry is positioned at the far left in the cell. Therefore, the D in the worksheet title, Dynamite Music, begins in the leftmost position of cell A1.

Second, when the text is longer than the width of a column, Excel displays the overflow characters in adjacent cells to the right as long as these adjacent cells contain no data. In Figure 1-17, the width of cell A1 is approximately nine characters. The text consists of 14 characters. Therefore, Excel displays the overflow characters from cell A1 in cell B1 because this cell is empty. If cell B1 contained data, only the first nine characters in cell A1 would display on the worksheet. Excel would hide the overflow characters, but they still would remain stored in cell A1 and display in the formula bar whenever cell A1 is the active cell.

Third, when you complete an entry by clicking the Enter box, the cell in which the text is entered remains the active cell.

Correcting a Mistake While Typing

If you type the wrong letter and notice the error before clicking the Enter box or pressing the ENTER key, use the BACKSPACE key to erase all the characters back to and including the one that is wrong. To cancel the entire entry before entering it into the cell, click the Cancel box in the formula bar or press the ESC key. If you see an error in a cell, select the cell and retype the entry. Later in this project, additional error-correction techniques are discussed.

AutoCorrect

The **AutoCorrect feature** of Excel works behind the scenes, correcting common mistakes when you complete a text entry in a cell. AutoCorrect makes three types of corrections for you:

1. Corrects two initial capital letters by changing the second letter to lowercase.
2. Capitalizes the first letter in the names of days.
3. Replaces commonly misspelled words with their correct spelling. For example, it will change the misspelled word *recieve* to *receive* when you complete the entry. AutoCorrect will correct the spelling automatically of more than 400 commonly misspelled words.

Entering Column Titles

To enter the column titles in row 3, select the appropriate cell and then enter the text, as described in the following steps.

More About

The ENTER Key

When you first install Excel, the ENTER key not only completes the entry but moves the selection to an adjacent cell. You can instruct Excel not to move the selection after pressing the ENTER key by clicking Options on the Tools menu, clicking the Edit tab, removing the check mark from the Move Selection after Enter check box, and then clicking the OK button.

More About

The IntelliSense™ Technology

Office XP's IntelliSense™ Technology tries to understand what you are doing and helps you do it. The adoptive menus, Ask a Question box, AutoCorrect, AutoComplete, smart tags, and formula error checker are part of the IntelliSense™ Technology. For more information on these features, type them one at a time in the Ask a Question box.

To Enter Column Titles

Click cell B3.

Cell B3 becomes the active cell. The active cell reference in the Name box changes from A2 to B3 (Figure 1-19).

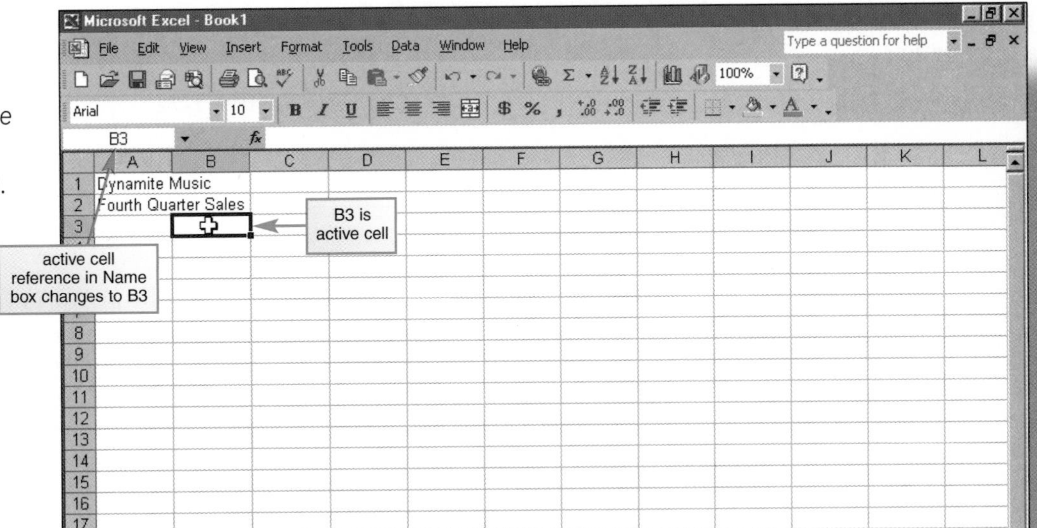

FIGURE 1-19

2 **Type** Boston **in cell B3.**

Excel displays Boston in the formula bar and in cell B3 (Figure 1-20).

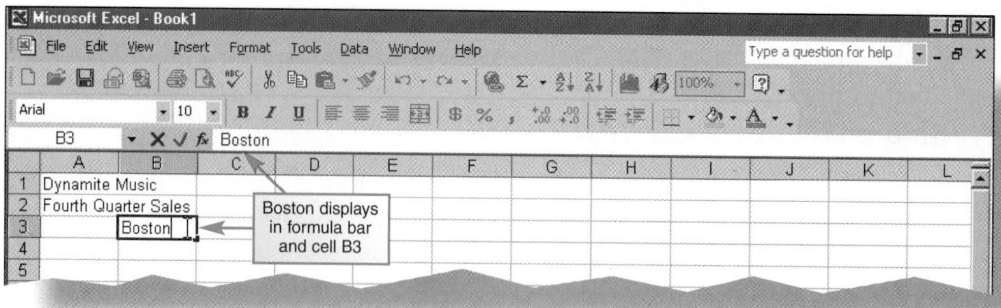

FIGURE 1-20

3 **Press the RIGHT ARROW key.**

Excel enters the column title, Boston, in cell B3 and makes cell C3 the active cell (Figure 1-21).

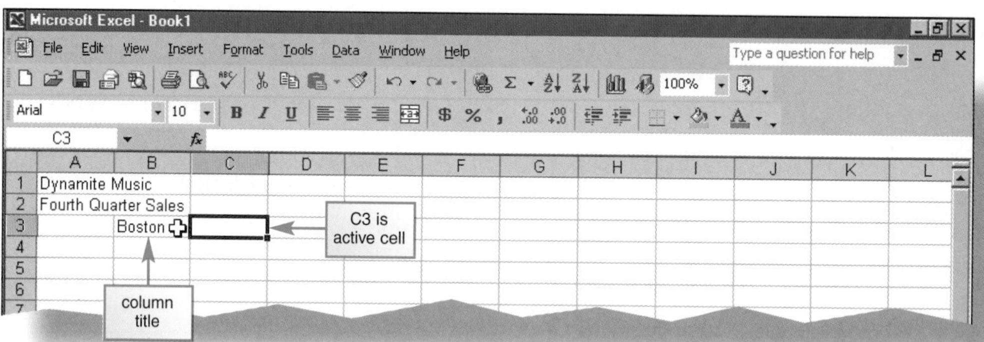

FIGURE 1-21

4 **Repeat Steps 2 and 3 for the remaining column titles in row 2. That is, enter** Chicago **in cell C3,** Denver **in cell D3,** Phoenix **in cell E3, and** Total **in cell F3. Complete the last entry in cell F3 by clicking the Enter box in the formula bar.**

The column titles display left-aligned as shown in Figure 1-22.

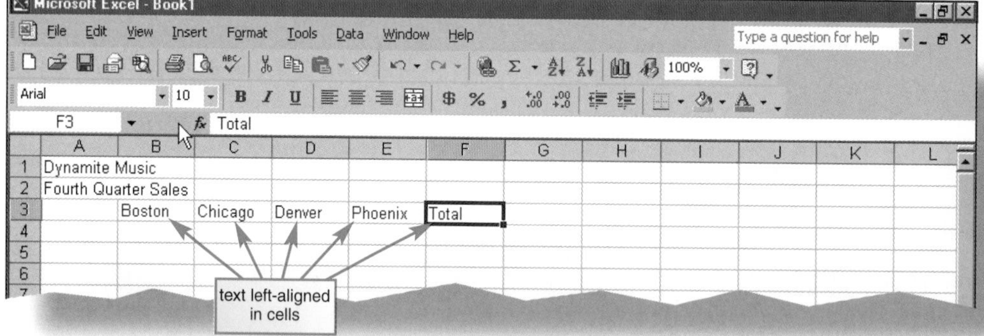

FIGURE 1-22

If the next entry is in an adjacent cell, use the arrow keys to complete the entry in a cell. When you press an arrow key to complete an entry, the adjacent cell in the direction of the arrow (up, down, left, or right) becomes the active cell. If the next entry is in a non-adjacent cell, click the next cell in which you plan to enter data, or click the Enter box or press the ENTER key and then click the appropriate cell for the next entry.

Entering Row Titles

The next step in developing the worksheet in Project 1 is to enter the row titles in column A. This process is similar to entering the column titles and is described in the following steps.

Steps To Enter Row Titles

1 **Click cell A4. Type** `Cassettes` **and then press the DOWN ARROW key.**

Excel enters the row title, Cassettes, in cell A4, and cell A5 becomes the active cell (Figure 1-23).

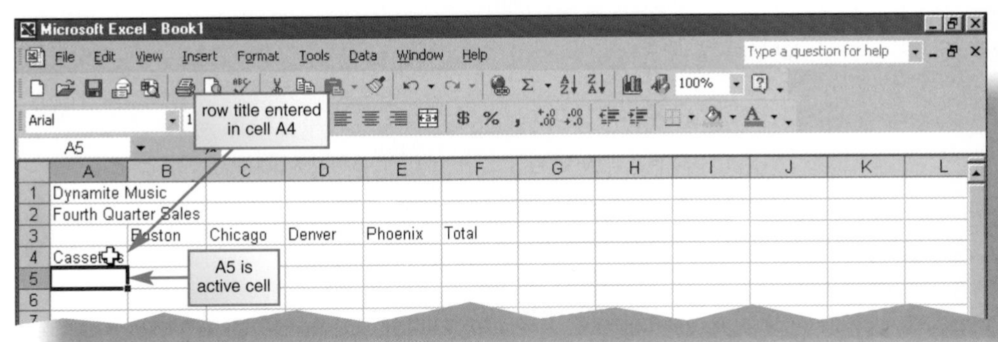

FIGURE 1-23

2 **Repeat Step 1 for the remaining row titles in column A. Enter** `Compact Discs` **in cell A5,** `Vintage Vinyls` **in cell A6,** `Web Downloads` **in cell A7, and** `Total` **in cell A8.**

The row titles display as shown in Figure 1-24.

FIGURE 1-24

In Excel, text is left-aligned in a cell unless you change it by realigning it. Excel treats any combination of numbers, spaces, and nonnumeric characters as text. For example, the following entries are text:

401AX21, 921-231, 619 321, 883XTY

Entering Numbers

In Excel, you can enter numbers into cells to represent amounts. Numbers can contain only the following characters:

0 1 2 3 4 5 6 7 8 9 + - ( ) , / . $ % E e

If a cell entry contains any other keyboard character (including spaces), Excel interprets the entry as text and treats it accordingly. The use of the special characters is explained when they are used in the project.

In Project 1, the Dynamite Music Fourth Quarter numbers are summarized to the right in Table 1-1. These numbers, which represent fourth quarter sales for each of the stores and product groups, must be entered in rows 4, 5, 6, and 7. Perform the steps on the next page to enter these values one row at a time.

Table 1-1 Dynamite Music Fourth Quarter Data

	BOSTON	CHICAGO	DENVER	PHOENIX
Cassettes	53465.30	47917.35	31913.75	62350.10
Compact Discs	92023.75	70392.10	86140.55	83450.75
Vintage Vinyls	35482.56	30976.25	48612.75	34092.75
Web Downloads	78526.12	67626.60	67420.20	56732.80

Steps To Enter Numeric Data

1 **Click cell B4. Type** 53465.30 **and then press the RIGHT ARROW key.**

Excel enters the number 53465.30 in cell B4 and changes the active cell to cell C4 (Figure 1-25). Excel does not display the insignificant zero. The zero will reappear when the numbers are formatted with dollar signs and commas later in this project.

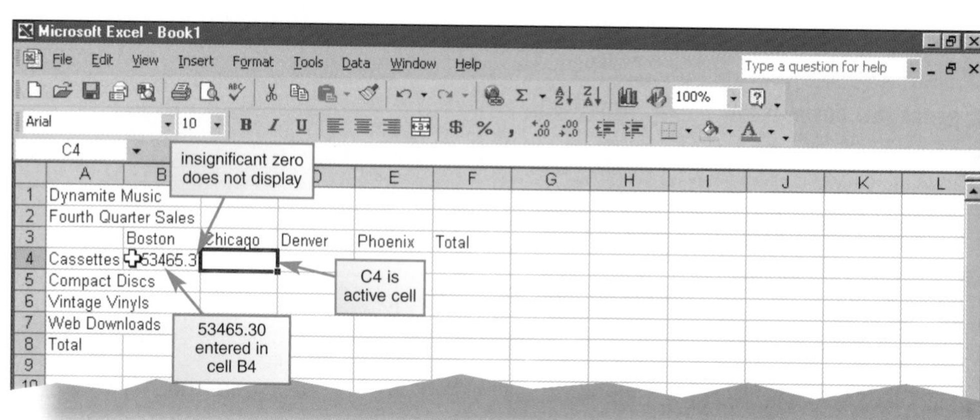

FIGURE 1-25

2 **Enter** 47917.35 **in cell C4,** 31913.75 **in cell D4, and** 62350.10 **in cell E4.**

Row 4 now contains the fourth quarter sales by store for the product group Cassettes (Figure 1-26). The numbers in row 4 are ***right-aligned****, which means Excel displays the cell entry to the far right in the cell.*

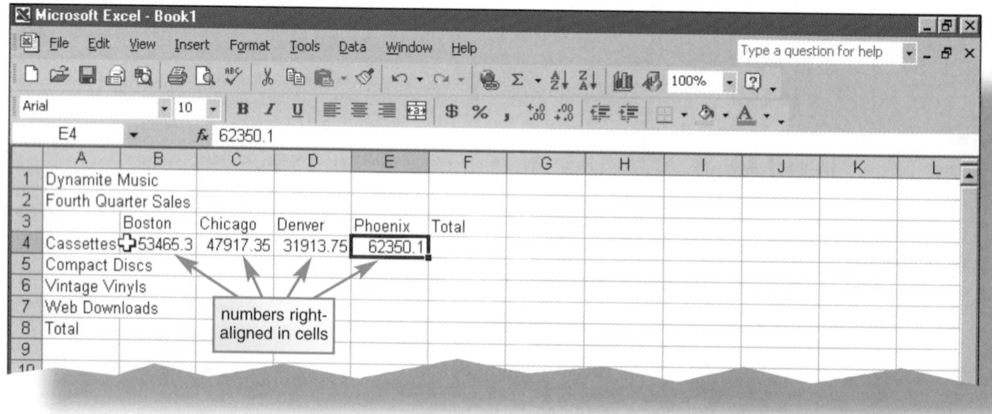

FIGURE 1-26

3 **Click cell B5. Enter the remaining fourth quarter sales provided in Table 1-1 on the previous page for each of the three remaining product groups in rows 5, 6, and 7.**

The fourth quarter sales display as shown in Figure 1-27.

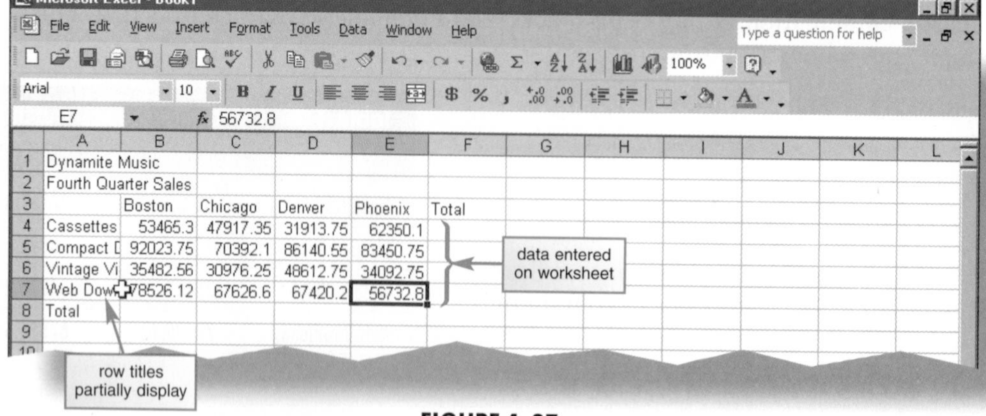

FIGURE 1-27

More About

Entering Numbers as Text

There are times when you will want Excel to treat numbers, such as zip codes and telephone numbers, as text. To enter a number as text, start the entry with an apostrophe (').

As you can see in Figure 1-27, when you enter data into the cell in column B, the row titles in column A partially display. Later when the worksheet is formatted, the row titles will display in their entirety.

Steps 1 through 3 complete the numeric entries. You are not required to type dollar signs, commas, or trailing zeros. As shown in Figure 1-27, trailing zeros do not display. When you enter a number that has cents, however, you must add the decimal point and the numbers representing the cents when you enter the number. Later in this project, dollar signs, commas, and trailing zeros will be added to improve the appearance and readability of the numbers.

More About

Number Limits

In Excel, a number can be between approximately -1×10^{308} and 1×10^{308}. That's a negative 1 followed by 308 zeros or a positive 1 followed by 308 zeros. To enter a number such as 7,500,000,000,000 you can type it as shown or you can type 7.5E12, which stands for 7.5×10^{12}.

Calculating a Sum

The next step in creating the worksheet is to determine the total fourth quarter sales for the Boston store in column B. To calculate this value in cell B8, Excel must add the numbers in cells B4, B5, B6, and B7. Excel's **SUM function** provides a convenient means to accomplish this task.

To use the SUM function, first you must identify the cell in which the sum will be stored after it is calculated. Then, you can use the **AutoSum button** on the Standard toolbar to enter the SUM function as shown in the following steps.

Steps To Sum a Column of Numbers

1 **Click cell B8 and then point to the AutoSum button on the Standard toolbar.**

Cell B8 becomes the active cell (Figure 1-28).

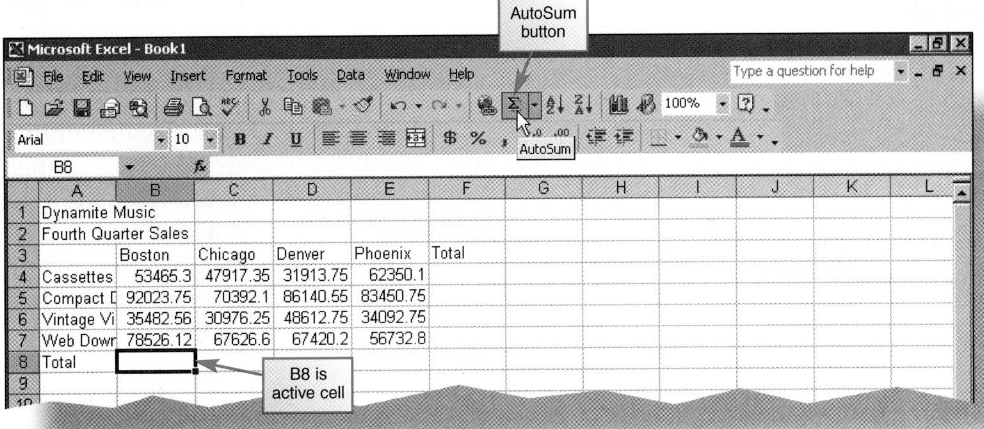

FIGURE 1-28

2 **Click the AutoSum button.**

Excel responds by displaying =SUM(B4:B7) in the formula bar and in the active cell B8 (Figure 1-29). A ScreenTip displays below the active cell. The B4:B7 within parentheses following the function name SUM is Excel's way of identifying the cells B4 through B7. Excel also surrounds the proposed cells to sum with a moving border, called a ***marquee****.*

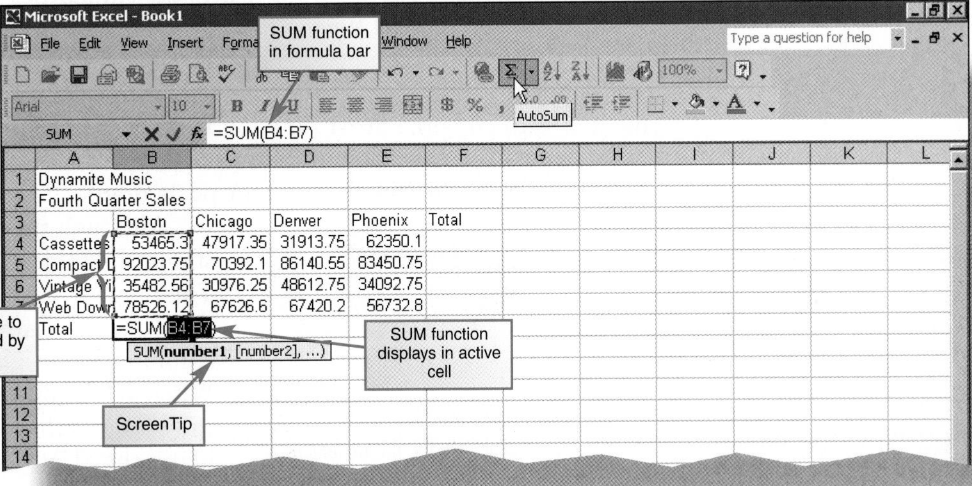

FIGURE 1-29

3 Click the AutoSum button a second time.

Excel enters the sum of the fourth quarter sales in cell B8 (Figure 1-30). The SUM function assigned to cell B8 displays in the formula bar when cell B8 is the active cell.

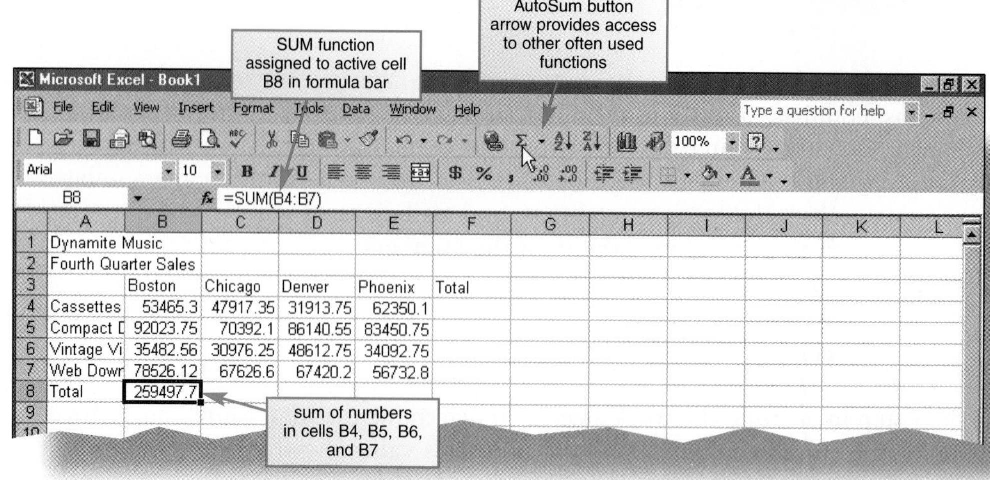

FIGURE 1-30

Other Ways

1. Click Insert Function button in formula bar, select SUM in Select a function list, click OK button, select range, click OK button
2. On Insert menu click Function, select SUM in Select a function list, click OK button, select range, click OK button
3. Press ALT+EQUAL SIGN (=) twice
4. In Voice Command mode say, "AutoSum, Sum, Enter"

When you enter the SUM function using the AutoSum button, Excel automatically selects what it considers to be your choice of the group of cells to sum. The group of adjacent cells B4, B5, B6, and B7 is called a **range**. A range is a series of two or more adjacent cells in a column or row or a rectangular group of cells. Many Excel operations, such as summing numbers, take place on a range of cells.

When proposing the range to sum, Excel first looks for a range of cells with numbers above the active cell and then to the left. If Excel proposes the wrong range, you can drag through the correct range anytime prior to clicking the AutoSum button a second time. You also can enter the correct range by typing the beginning cell reference, a colon (:), and the ending cell reference.

If you click the AutoSum button arrow on the right side of the AutoSum button, Excel displays a list of often used functions from which you can choose. The list includes functions that allow you to determine the average, the minimum value, and the maximum value of a range of numbers.

Using the Fill Handle to Copy a Cell to Adjacent Cells

Excel also must calculate the totals for Chicago in cell C8, Denver in cell D8, and for Phoenix in cell E8. Table 1-2 illustrates the similarities between the entry in cell B8 and the entries required for the totals in cells C8, D8, and E8.

To place the SUM functions in cells C8, D8, and E8, you can follow the same steps shown previously in Figures 1-28 through 1-30. A second, more efficient method is to copy the SUM function from cell B8 to the range C8:E8. The cell being copied is called the **source area** or **copy area**. The range of cells receiving the copy is called the **destination area** or **paste area**.

Table 1-2 Function Entries in Row 8

CELL	SUM FUNCTION ENTRIES	REMARK
B8	=SUM(B4:B7)	Sums cells B4, B5, B6, and B7
C8	=SUM(C4:C7)	Sums cells C4, C5, C6, and C7
D8	=SUM(D4:D7)	Sums cells D4, D5, D6, and D7
E8	=SUM(E4:E7)	Sums cells E4, E5, E6, and E7

Although the SUM function entries are similar in Table 1-2, they are not exact copies. The range in each SUM function entry to the right of cell B8 uses cell references that are one column to the right of the previous column. When you copy cell references, Excel automatically adjusts them for each new position, resulting in the SUM function entries illustrated in Table 1-2. Each adjusted cell reference is called a **relative reference**.

The easiest way to copy the SUM formula from cell B8 to cells C8, D8, and E8 is to use the fill handle. The **fill handle** is the small black square located in the lower-right corner of the heavy border around the active cell. Perform the following steps to use the fill handle to copy cell B8 to the adjacent cells C8:E8.

Steps To Copy a Cell to Adjacent Cells in a Row

1 With cell B8 active, point to the fill handle.

The mouse pointer changes to a cross hair (Figure 1-31).

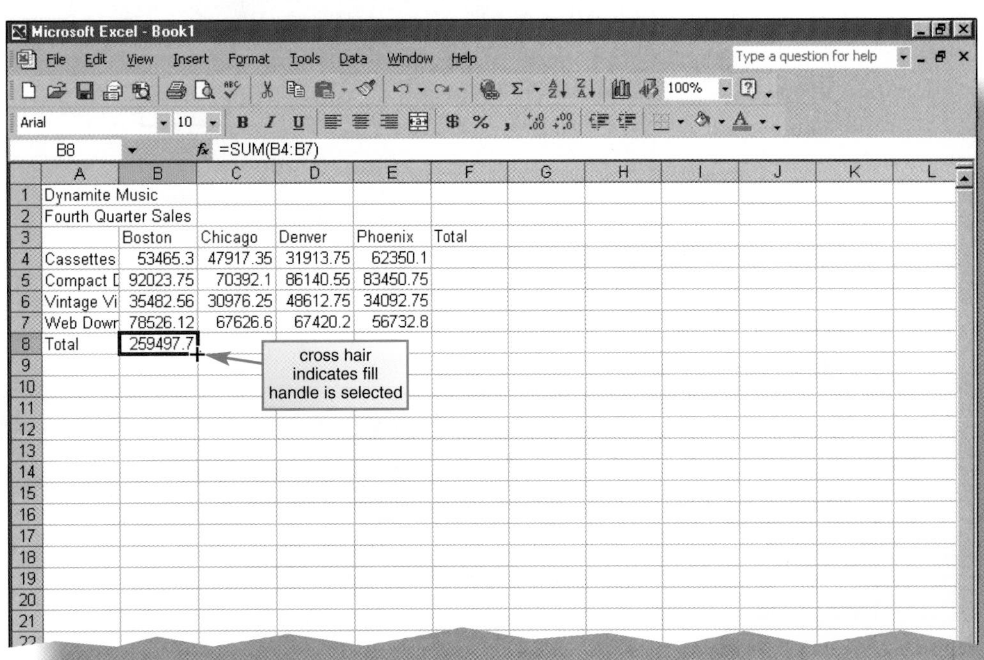

FIGURE 1-31

2 Drag the fill handle to select the destination area, range C8:E8.

Excel displays a shaded border around the destination area, range C8:E8, and the source area, cell B8 (Figure 1-32).

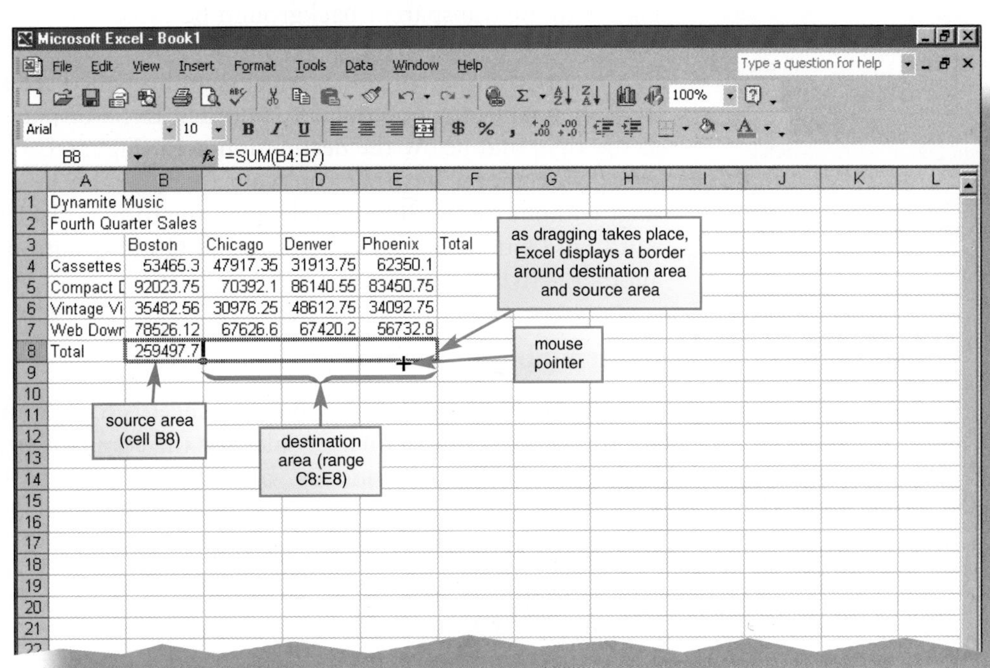

FIGURE 1-32

3 **Release the mouse button.**

Excel copies the SUM function in cell B8 to the range C8:E8 (Figure 1-33). In addition, Excel calculates the sums and enters the results in cells C8, D8, and E8. The Auto Fill Options button displays to the right and below the destination area.

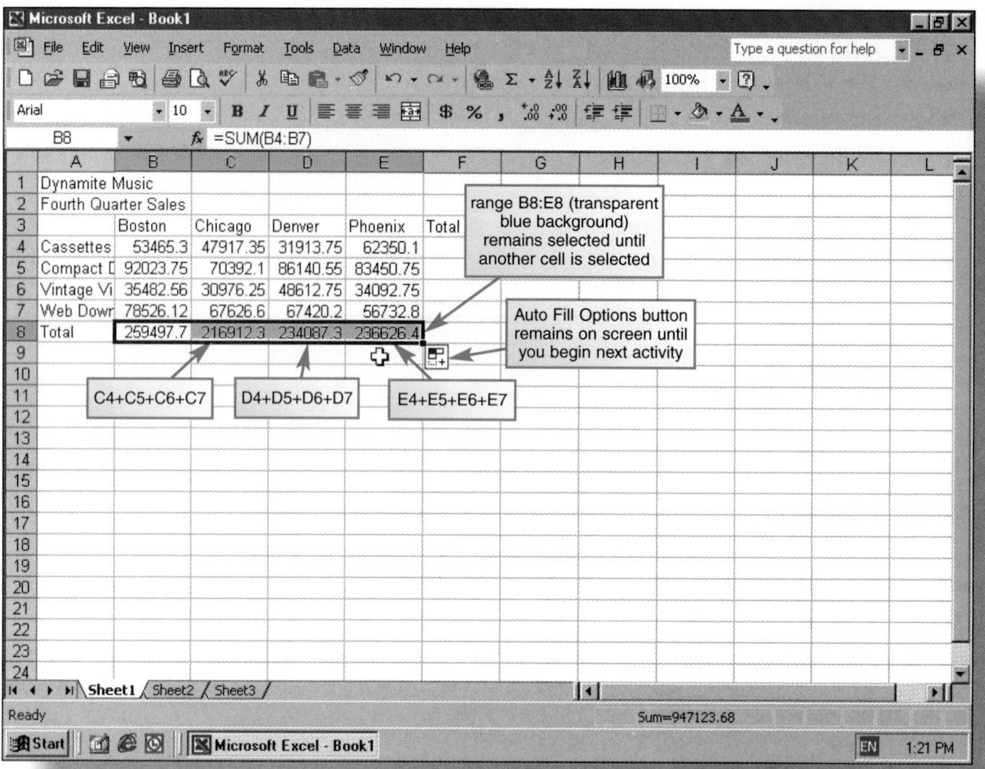

FIGURE 1-33

Other Ways

1. Select source area, on Edit menu click Copy, select destination area, on Edit menu click Paste
2. Right-click source area, click Copy on shortcut menu, right-click destination area, click Paste on shortcut menu
3. Select source area and point to border of range; while holding down the CTRL key, drag source area to destination area
4. Select source area, press CTRL+C, select destination area, press CTRL+V
5. Select source area, in Voice Command mode say, "Copy, [select destination area], Paste"

Once the copy is complete, Excel continues to display a heavy border and transparent (blue) background around cells B8:E8. The heavy border and transparent background indicate a selected range. Cell B8, the first cell in the range, does not display with the transparent background be cause it is the active cell. If you click any cell, Excel will remove the heavy border and transparent background. The heavy border and transparent (blue) background is called **see-through view**.

When you copy one range to another, Excel displays an Auto Fill Options button to the right and below the destination area (Figure 1-33). The **Auto Fill Options button** allows you choose whether you want to copy the value in the price area with formatting, without formatting, or only copy the format. To list the selections, click the Auto Fill Options button. The Auto Fill Options button disappears when you begin another activity.

Determining Row Totals

The next step in building the worksheet is to determine totals for each product group and total fourth quarter sales for the company in column F. Use the SUM function in the same manner as you did when the sales by store were totaled in row 8. In this example, however, all the rows will be totaled at the same time. The following steps illustrate this process.

Steps To Determine Multiple Totals at the Same Time

1 Click cell F4.

Cell F4 becomes the active cell (Figure 1-34).

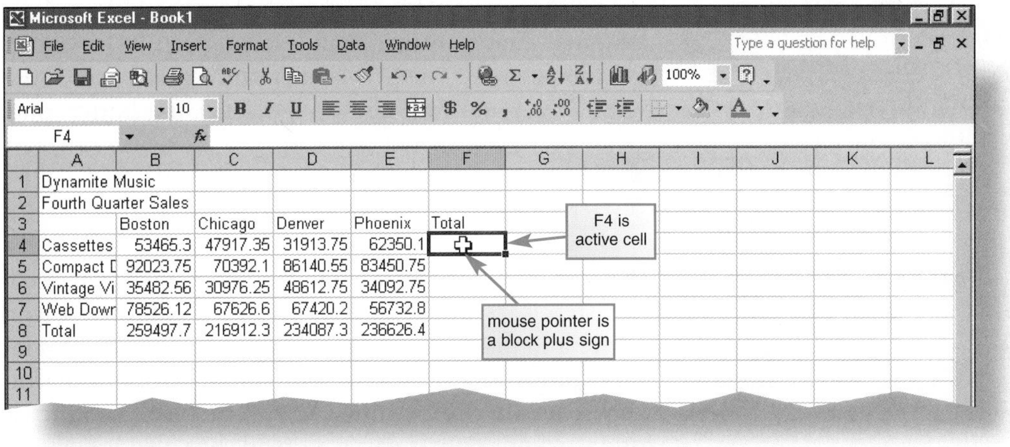

F4 is active cell

mouse pointer is a block plus sign

FIGURE 1-34

2 With the mouse pointer in cell F4 and in the shape of a block plus sign, drag the mouse pointer down to cell F8.

Excel highlights the range F4:F8 (Figure 1-35).

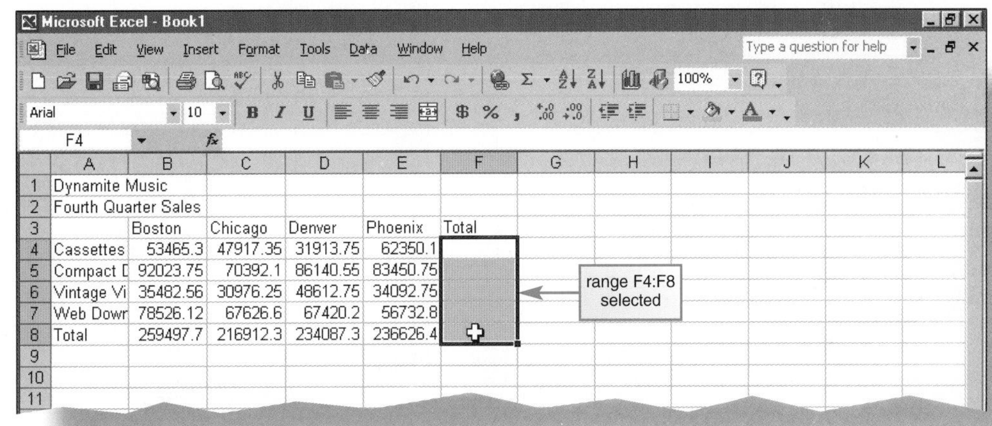

FIGURE 1-35

3 Click the AutoSum button on the Standard toolbar.

Excel assigns the appropriate SUM functions to cell F4, F5, F6, F7, and F8, and then calculates and displays the sums in the respective cells (Figure 1-36).

4 Select cell A9 to deselect the range F4:F8.

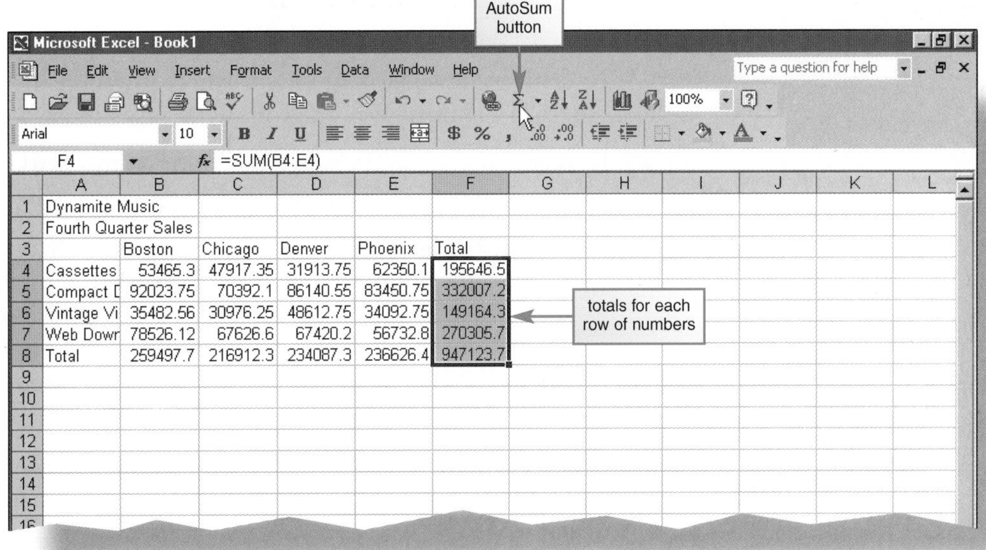

FIGURE 1-36

Summing Columns and Rows

A more efficient way to determine the totals in row 8 and column F in Figure 1-36 is to select the range (B4:F8) and then click the AutoSum button. The range B4:F8 includes the numbers to sum plus an additional row (row 8) and an additional column (column F), in which the totals will display.

If each cell in the selected range is next to a row of numbers, Excel assigns the SUM function to each cell in the selected range when you click the AutoSum button. Thus, five SUM functions with different ranges were assigned to the selected range, one for each row. This same procedure could have been used earlier to sum the columns. That is, rather than selecting cell B8, clicking the AutoSum button twice, and then copying the SUM function to the range C8:E8, you could have selected the range B8:E8 and then clicked the AutoSum button once.

Formatting the Worksheet

The text, numeric entries, and functions for the worksheet now are complete. The next step is to format the worksheet. You **format** a worksheet to emphasize certain entries and make the worksheet easier to read and understand.

Figure 1-37a shows the worksheet before formatting. Figure 1-37b shows the worksheet after formatting. As you can see from the two figures, a worksheet that is formatted not only is easier to read, but also looks more professional.

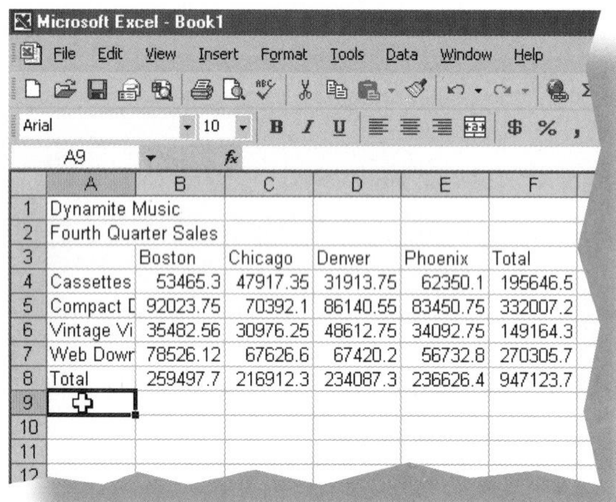

(a) Before Formatting

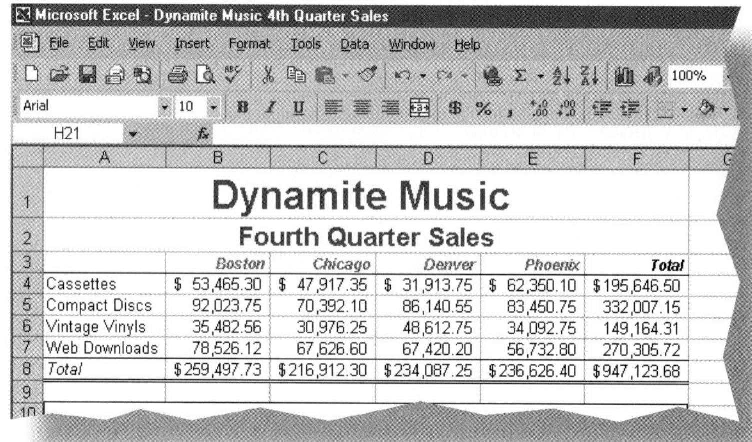

(b) After Formatting

FIGURE 1-37

To change the unformatted worksheet in Figure 1-37a to the formatted worksheet in Figure 1-37b, the following tasks must be completed:

1. Bold, enlarge, and change the color of the worksheet titles in cells A1 and A2.
2. Center the worksheet titles in cells A1 and A2 across columns A through F.
3. Format the body of the worksheet. The body of the worksheet, range A3:F8, includes the column titles, row titles, and numbers. Formatting the body of the worksheet results in numbers represented in a dollars-and-cents format, dollar signs in the first row of numbers and the total row, underlining that emphasizes portions of the worksheet, and modified column widths.

The process required to format the worksheet is explained in the remainder of this section. Although the format procedures will be carried out in the order described above, you should be aware that you can make these format changes in any order.

Fonts, Font Color, Font Size, and Font Style

Characters that display on the screen are a specific shape, size, color, and style. The **font type** defines the appearance and shape of the letters, numbers, and special characters. The **font size** specifies the size of the characters on the screen. Font size is gauged by a measurement system called points. A single point is about 1/72 of one inch in height. Thus, a character with a **point size** of 10 is about 10/72 of one inch in height.

Font style indicates how the characters are formatted. Common font styles include regular, bold, underlined, or italicized. The font also can display in a variety of colors.

When Excel begins, the preset font type for the entire workbook is Arial with a size and style of 10-point regular black. Excel allows you to change the font characteristics in a single cell, a range of cells, the entire worksheet, or the entire workbook.

More About

Changing Fonts

In general, use no more than two font types and font styles in a worksheet.

Bolding a Cell

You **bold** an entry in a cell to emphasize it or make it stand out from the rest of the worksheet. Perform the following steps to bold the worksheet title in cell A1.

Steps To Bold a Cell

1 Click cell A1 and then point to the Bold button on the Formatting toolbar.

The ScreenTip displays immediately below the Bold button to identify the function of the button (Figure 1-38).

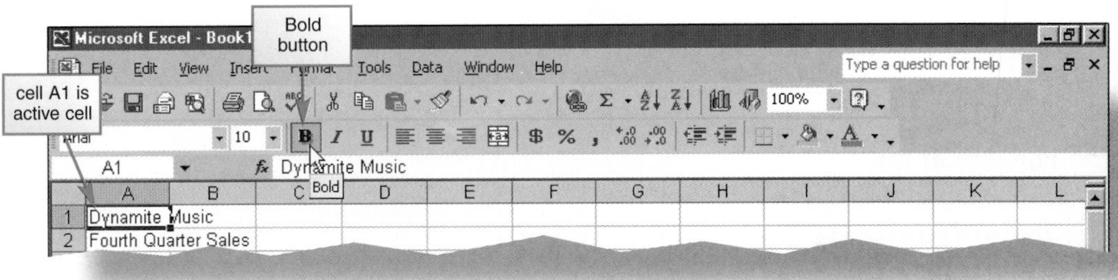

FIGURE 1-38

2 Click the Bold button.

Excel applies a bold format to the worksheet title, Dynamite Music (Figure 1-39).

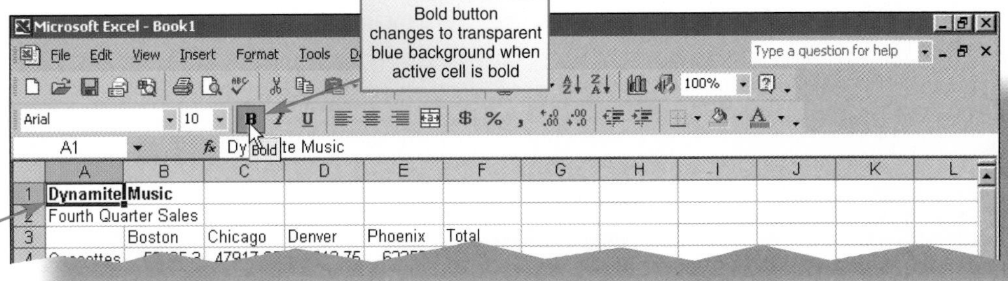

FIGURE 1-39

Other Ways

1. On Format menu click Cells, click Font tab, click Bold, click OK button
2. Right-click cell, click Format Cells on shortcut menu, click Font tab, click Bold, click OK button
3. Press CTRL+B
4. In Voice Command mode say, "Bold"

When the active cell is bold, the Bold button on the Formatting toolbar displays with a transparent blue background (Figure 1-39). Clicking the Bold button a second time removes the bold format.

Increasing the Font Size

Increasing the font size is the next step in formatting the worksheet title. You increase the font size of a cell so the entry stands out and is easier to read. Perform the steps on the next page to increase the font size of the worksheet title in cell A1.

To Increase the Font Size of a Cell Entry

1 With cell A1 selected, click the Font Size box arrow on the Formatting toolbar and then point to 24 in the Font Size list.

The Font Size list displays as shown in Figure 1-40.

FIGURE 1-40

2 Click 24. The font size of the characters in the worksheet title in cell A1 increase from 10 point to 24 point (Figure 1-41).

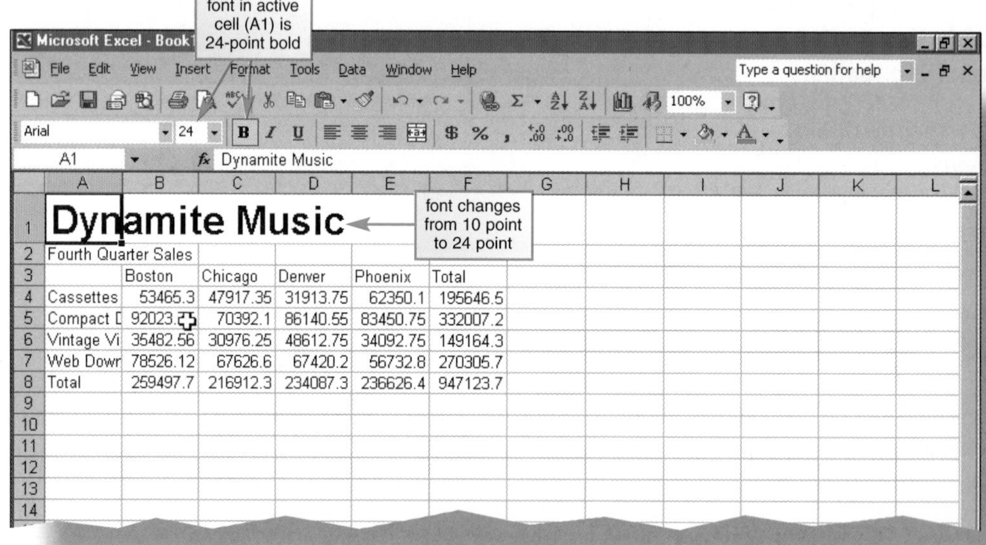

FIGURE 1-41

Other Ways

1. On Format menu click Cells, click Font tab, select font size in Size box, click OK button
2. Right-click cell, click Format Cells on shortcut menu, click Font tab, select font size in Size box, click OK button
3. In Voice Command mode say, "Font Size, [desired font size]"

An alternative to clicking a font size in the Font Size list is to click the Font Size box, type the font size, and then press the ENTER key. With cell A1 selected (Figure 1-41), the Font Size box shows the new font size 24 and the transparent blue Bold button shows the active cell is bold.

Changing the Font Color of a Cell

The next step is to change the color of the font in cell A1 from black to violet. Perform the following steps to change the color of the font.

Steps To Change the Font Color of a Cell

1 With cell A1 selected, click the Font Color button arrow on the Formatting toolbar. Point to the color Violet (column 7, row 3) on the Font Color palette.

The Font Color palette displays (Figure 1-42).

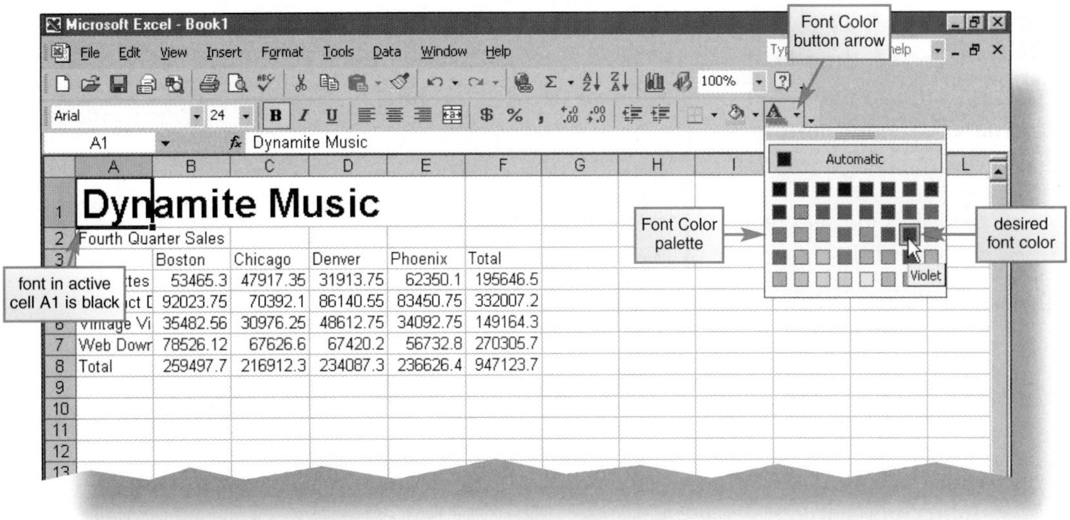

FIGURE 1-42

2 Click Violet.

The font in the worksheet title in cell A1 changes from black to violet (Figure 1-43).

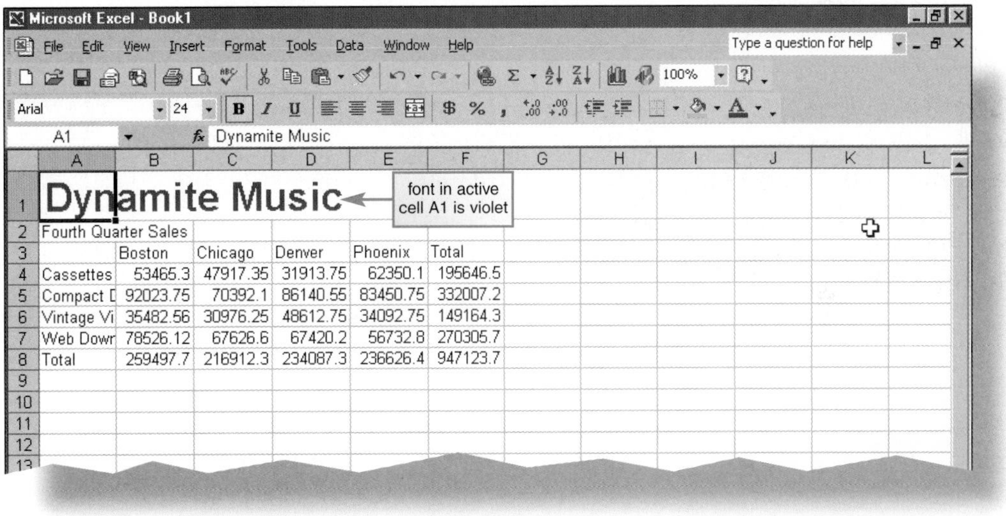

FIGURE 1-43

Other Ways

1. On Format menu, click Cells, click Font tab, click Color button, select color, click OK button
2. Right-click cell, click Format Cells on shortcut menu, click Font tab, click Color button, select color, click OK button
3. In Voice Command mode say, "Font Color, [desired color]"

You can choose from 40 different font colors in the Font Color palette in Figure 1-42. Your Font Color palette may have more or fewer colors, depending on color settings of your operating system. When you choose a color, Excel changes the Font Color button on the Formatting toolbar to the chosen color. Thus, to change the font color of the text in another cell to the same color, you need only select the cell and click the Font Color button.

Centering the Worksheet Title across Columns

The final step in formatting the worksheet title is to center it across columns A through F. Centering a worksheet title across the columns used in the body of the worksheet improves the worksheet's appearance. Perform the steps on the next page to center the worksheet title.

Steps To Center a Cell's Contents across Columns

1 With cell A1 selected, drag to cell F1. Point to the Merge and Center button on the Formatting toolbar.

Excel highlights the selected cells (Figure 1-44).

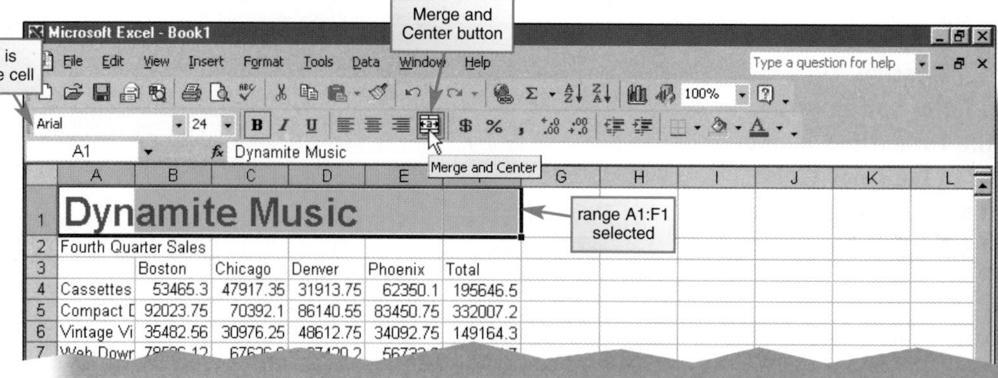

FIGURE 1-44

2 Click the Merge and Center button.

Excel merges the cells A1 through F1 to create a new cell A1 and centers the contents of cell A1 across columns A through F (Figure 1-45). After the merge, cells B1 through F1 no longer exist on the worksheet.

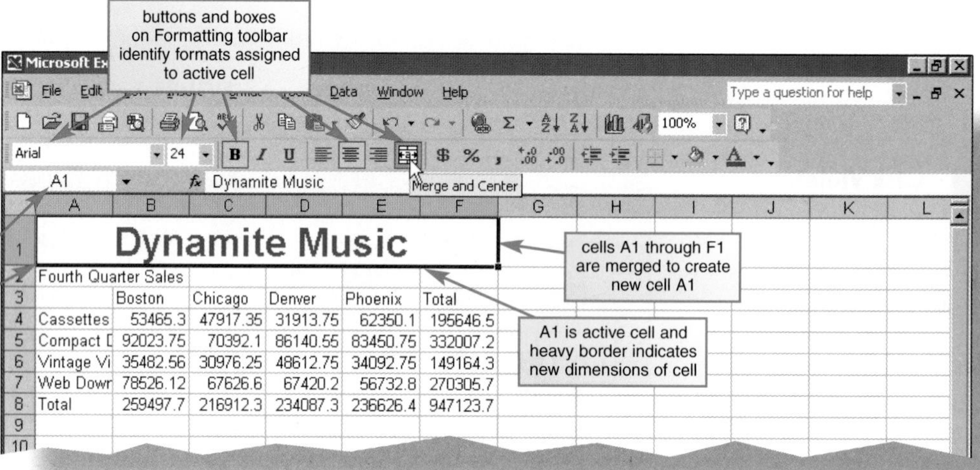

FIGURE 1-45

Other Ways

1. On Format menu click Cells, click Alignment tab, select Center Across Selection in Horizontal list, click OK button
2. Right-click cell, click Format Cells on shortcut menu, click Alignment tab, select Center Across Selection in Horizontal list, click OK button
3. In Voice Command mode say, "Merge and Center"

Excel not only centers the worksheet title across the range A1:F1, but it also merges cells A1 through F1 into one cell, cell A1. The alternative to merging cells is **splitting a cell**. You split a merged cell by selecting it and clicking the Merge and Center button. For example, if you click the Merge and Center button a second time in Step 2, it will change cell A1 to cells A1, B1, C1, D1, E1, and F1. For the Merge and Center button to work properly, all the cells except the leftmost cell in the range of cells must be empty.

Most formats assigned to a cell will display on the Formatting toolbar when the cell is selected. For example, with cell A1 selected in Figure 1-45 the font type and font size display in their appropriate boxes. Transparent blue buttons indicate an assigned format. To determine if less frequently used formats are assigned to a cell, point to the cell and right-click. Next, click Format Cells, and then click each of the tabs in the Format Cells dialog box.

Formatting the Worksheet Subtitle

The worksheet subtitle in cell A2 is to be formatted the same as the worksheet title in cell A1, except that the font size should be 16 rather than 24. Perform the following steps to format the worksheet subtitle in cell A2.

TO FORMAT THE WORKSHEET SUBTITLE

1. Select cell A2.
2. Click the Bold button on the Formatting toolbar.
3. Click the Font Size arrow on the Formatting toolbar and click 16.
4. Click the Font Color button.
5. Select the range A2:F2 and then click the Merge and Center button on the Formatting toolbar.

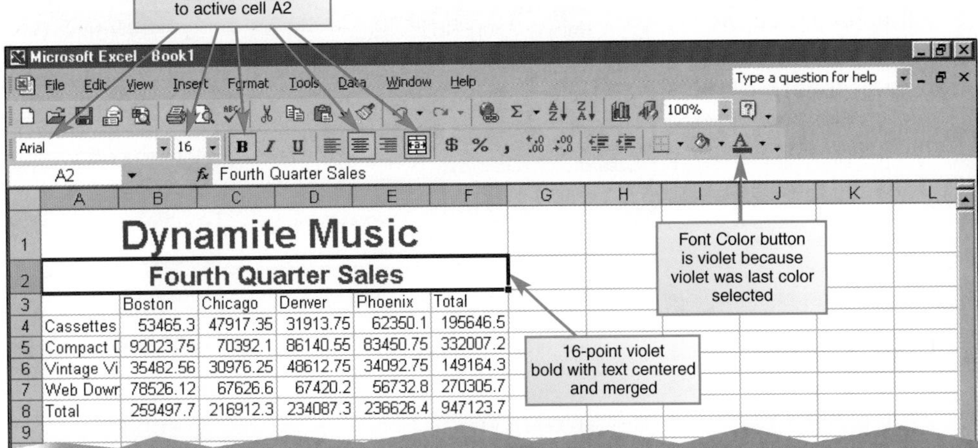

FIGURE 1-46

The worksheet subtitle in cell A2 display as shown in Figure 1-46.

With cell A2 selected, the buttons and boxes on the Formatting toolbar describe the primary formats assigned to cell A2. The steps used to format the worksheet subtitle in cell A2 were the same as the steps used to assign the formats to the worksheet title in cell A1, except for assigning the font color. To color the worksheet title font in cell A1 violet, the Font Color arrow and Font Color palette were used. To color the worksheet subtitle in cell A2 violet, the Font Color button was used. Recall that the Font Color button is assigned the last font color used, which was violet.

Using AutoFormat to Format the Body of a Worksheet

Excel has several customized format styles called **table formats** that allow you to format the body of the worksheet. Using table formats can give your worksheet a professional appearance. Follow these steps to format the range A3:F8 automatically using the **AutoFormat command** on the **Format menu**.

Steps To Use AutoFormat to Format the Body of a Worksheet

1. **Select cell A3, the upper-left corner cell of the rectangular range to format. Drag the mouse pointer to cell F8, the lower-right corner cell of the range to format.**

Excel highlights the range to format with a heavy border and transparent blue background (Figure 1-47).

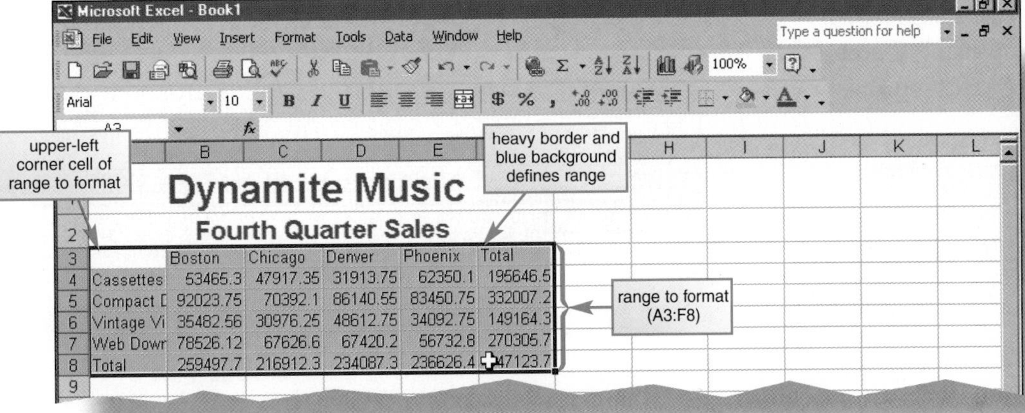

FIGURE 1-47

2 **Click Format on the menu bar and then point to AutoFormat.**

The Format menu displays (Figure 1-48).

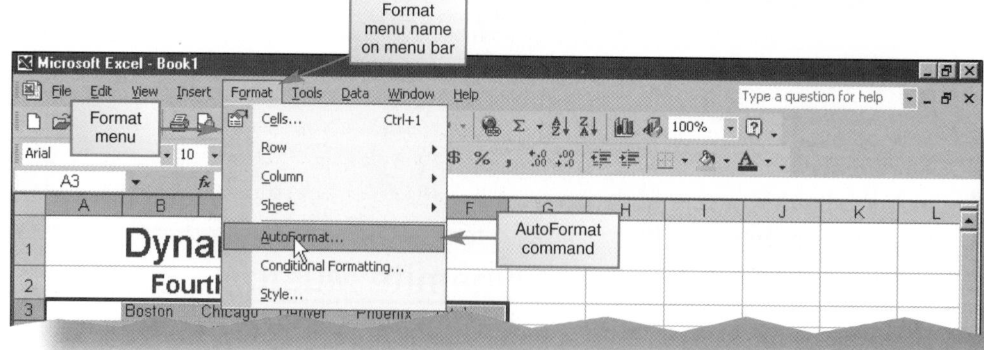

FIGURE 1-48

3 **Click AutoFormat. Click the Accounting 1 format in the AutoFormat dialog box. Point to the OK button.**

The AutoFormat dialog box displays with a list of customized formats (Figure 1-49). Each format illustrates how the body of the worksheet will display if it is chosen.

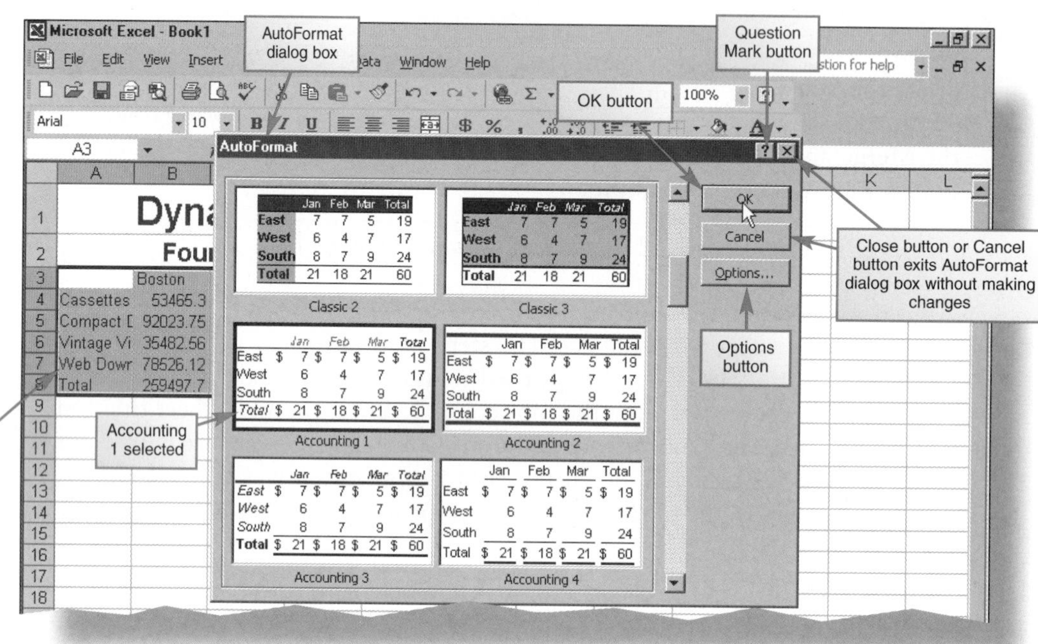

FIGURE 1-49

4 **Click the OK button. Select cell A10 to deselect the range A3:F8.**

Excel displays the worksheet with the range A3:F8 using the customized format, Accounting 1 (Figure 1-50).

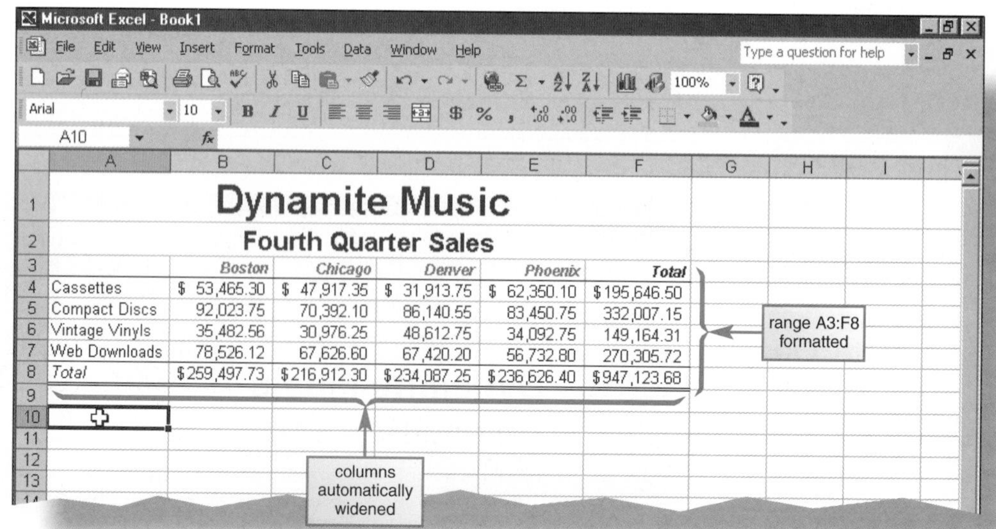

FIGURE 1-50

Other Ways

1. Press ALT+O, A
2. In Voice Command mode say, "Format, AutoFormat, [desired AutoFormat], OK"

The formats associated with Accounting 1 include bold, italic, right-aligned column titles; numbers displayed as dollars and cents with comma separators; numbers aligned on the decimal point; dollar signs in the first row of numbers and in the total row; and top and bottom rows display with borders. The width of column A also has been increased so the longest row title in cell A7, Web Downloads, just fits in the column. The widths of columns B through F have been increased so that the formatted numbers will fit in the cells.

The AutoFormat dialog box shown in Figure 1-49 includes 17 table formats and five buttons. Use the vertical scroll bar in the dialog box to view the 11 table formats that do not display. Each one of these table formats offers a different look. The one you choose depends on the worksheet you are creating. The last table format in the list, called None, removes all formats.

The five buttons in the dialog box allow you to cancel, complete the entries, get Help, and adjust a customized format. The **Close button** terminates current activity without making changes. You also can use the **Cancel button**, immediately below the **OK button**, for this purpose. Use the **Question Mark button**, to obtain Help on any box or button located in the dialog box. The **Options button** allows you to select additional formats to assign as part of the selected customized format.

The worksheet now is complete. The next step is to chart the fourth quarter sales for the four product groups by store. To create the chart, you must select the cell in the upper-left corner of the range to chart (cell A3). Rather than clicking cell A3 to select it, the next section describes how to use the Name box to select the cell.

More About

Merging Table Formats

It is not uncommon to apply two or more of the table formats in Figure 1-49 to the same range. If you assign two table formats to a range, Excel does not remove the original format from the range; it simply adds the second table format to the first. Thus, if you decide to change a table format to another, select the table format None from the bottom of the list to clear the first table format.

Using the Name Box to Select a Cell

The Name box is located on the left side of the formula bar. To select any cell, click the Name box and enter the cell reference of the cell you want to select. Perform the following steps to select cell A3.

To Use the Name Box to Select a Cell

1 **Click the Name box in the formula bar. Type** a3 **in the Name box.**

Even though cell A10 is the active cell, the Name box displays the typed cell reference a3 (Figure 1-51).

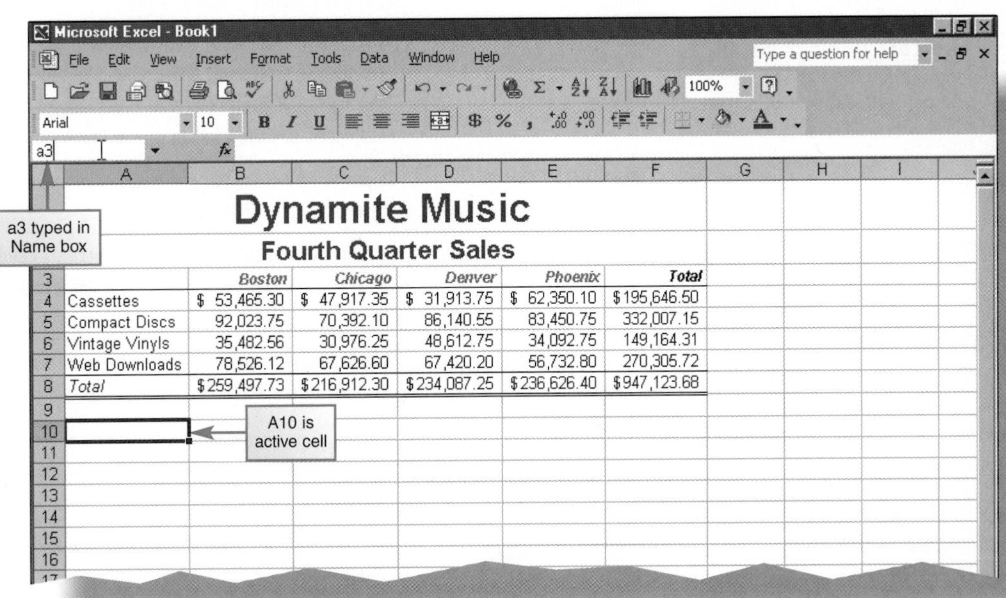

FIGURE 1-51

2 Press the ENTER key.

Excel changes the active cell from cell A10 to cell A3 (Figure 1-52).

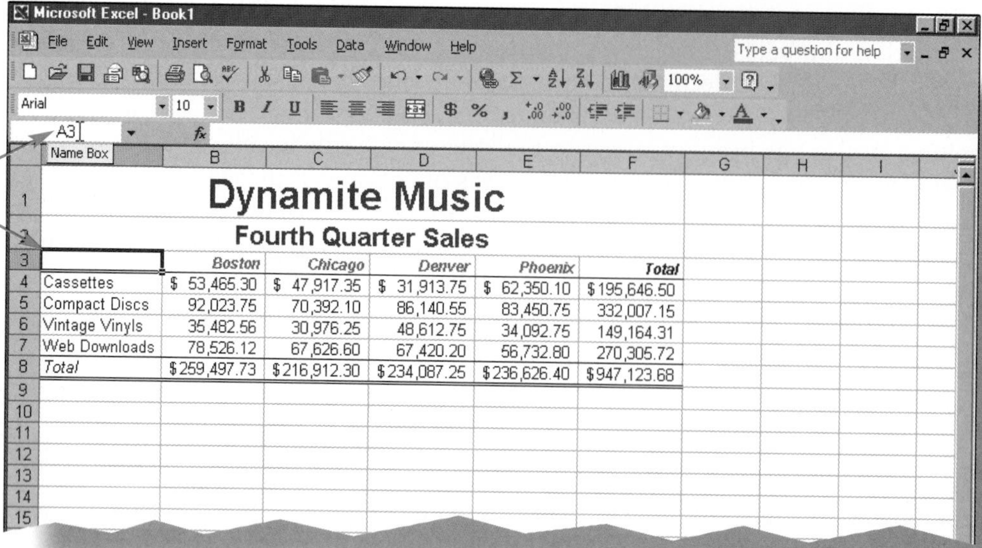

FIGURE 1-52

Naming Cells and Ranges

If you repeatedly select certain cells in a worksheet, consider naming the cells in the Name box. Select the cells one at a time and then type in a name in the Name box for each, such as Company Total for cell F8 in Figure 1-52. Then, when you want to select one of the named cells, click the Name box arrow and then click the cell name in the Name box list. You can also name ranges the same way.

Navigation

For more information on selecting cells that contain certain entries, such as constants or formulas, visit the Excel 2002 More About Web page (scsite.com/ex2002/more.htm) and click Using Go To Special.

As you will see in later projects, besides using the Name box to select any cell in a worksheet, you also can use it to assign names to a cell or range of cells.

Excel supports several additional ways to select a cell, as summarized in Table 1-3.

Table 1-3 Selecting Cells in Excel

KEY, BOX, OR COMMAND	FUNCTION
ALT+PAGE DOWN	Selects the cell one window to the right and moves the window accordingly.
ALT+PAGE UP	Selects the cell one window to the left and moves the window accordingly.
ARROW	Selects the adjacent cell in the direction of the arrow on the key.
CTRL+ARROW	Selects the border cell of the worksheet in combination with the arrow keys and moves the window accordingly. For example, to select the rightmost cell in the row that contains the active cell, press CTRL+RIGHT ARROW. You also can press the END key, release it, and then press the arrow key to accomplish the same task.
CTRL+HOME	Selects cell A1 or the cell one column and one row below and to the right of frozen titles and moves the window accordingly.
Find command on Edit menu	Finds and selects a cell that contains specific contents that you enter in the Find dialog box. If necessary, Excel moves the window to display the cell. You can press SHIFT+F5 or CTRL+F to display the Find dialog box.
F5 or Go To command on Edit menu	Selects the cell that corresponds to the cell reference you enter in the Go To dialog box and moves the window accordingly. You can press CTRL+G to display the Go To dialog box.
HOME	Selects the cell at the beginning of the row that contains the active cell and moves the window accordingly.
Name box	Selects the cell in the workbook that corresponds to the cell reference you enter in the Name box.
PAGE DOWN	Selects the cell down one window from the active cell and moves the window accordingly.
PAGE UP	Selects the cell up one window from the active cell and moves the window accordingly.

Adding a 3-D Column Chart to the Worksheet

The 3-D Column chart in Figure 1-53 is called an **embedded chart** because it is drawn on the same worksheet as the data.

For the Boston store, the light blue column represents the fourth quarter sales for the Cassettes product group ($53,465.30); the purple column represents the fourth quarter sales for Compact Discs ($92,023.75); the light yellow column represents the fourth quarter sales for Vintage Vinyls ($35,482.56); and the turquoise column represents the fourth quarter sales for Web Downloads ($78,526.12). For the stores Chicago, Denver, and Phoenix, the columns follow the same color scheme to represent the comparable fourth quarter sales. The totals from the worksheet are not represented because the totals were not in the range specified for charting.

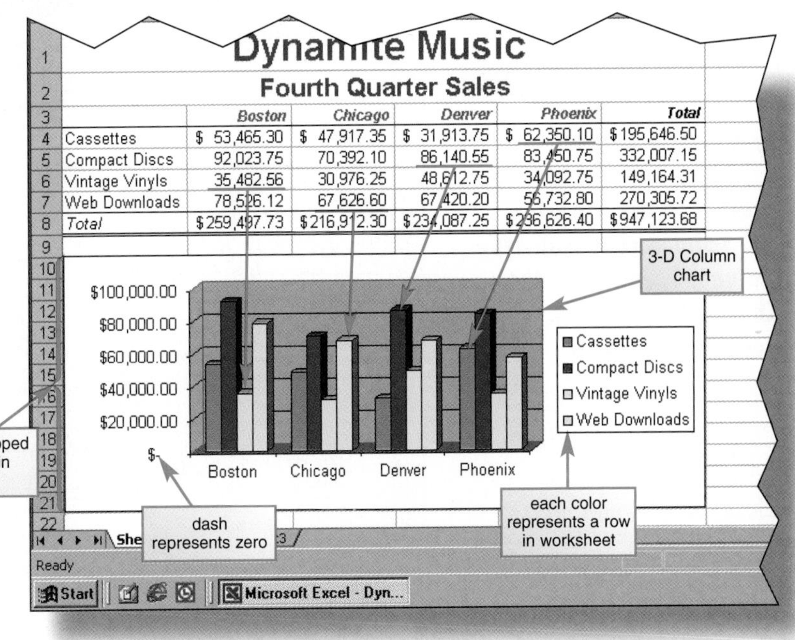

FIGURE 1-53

Excel derives the scale along the vertical axis (also called the **y-axis** or **value axis**) of the chart on the basis of the values in the worksheet. For example, no value in the range B4:E7 is less than zero or greater than $100,000.00. Excel also determines the $20,000.00 increments along the y-axis automatically. The format used by Excel for the numbers along the y-axis includes representing zero (0) with a dash (Figure 1-53).

With the range to chart selected, you click the **Chart Wizard button** on the Standard toolbar to initiate drawing the chart. The area on the worksheet where the chart displays is called the **chart location**. The chart location is the range A10:F20, immediately below the worksheet data.

Follow the steps below to draw a 3-D Column chart that compares the fourth quarter sales by product group for the four stores.

Steps To Add a 3-D Column Chart to the Worksheet

1 With cell A3 selected, position the block plus sign mouse pointer within the cell's border and drag the mouse pointer to the lower-right corner cell (cell E7) of the range to chart (A3:E7). Point to the Chart Wizard button on the Standard toolbar.

Excel highlights the range to chart (Figure 1-54).

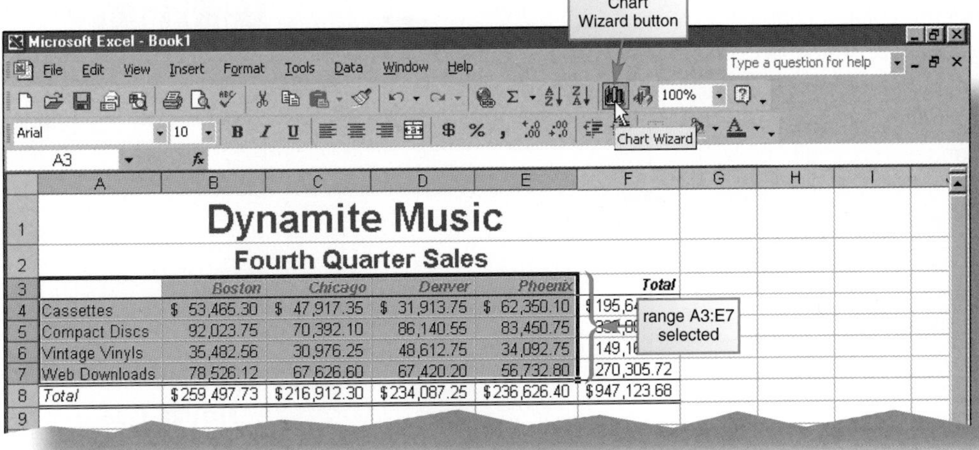

FIGURE 1-54

2 Click the Chart Wizard button.

The Chart Wizard - Step 1 of 4 - Chart Type dialog box displays.

3 With Column selected in the Chart type list, click the 3-D Column chart sub-type (column 1, row 2) in the Chart sub-type area. Point to the Finish button.

Column is highlighted in the Chart type list and Clustered column with a 3-D visual effect is highlighted in the Chart sub-type area (Figure 1-55).

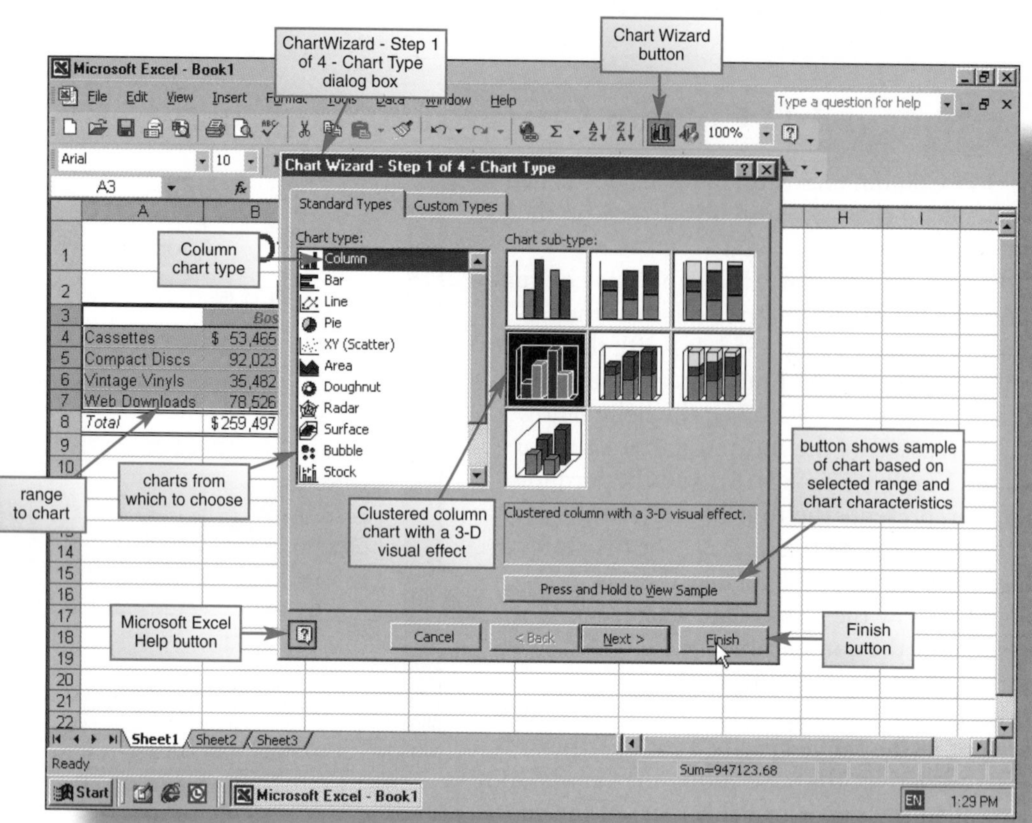

FIGURE 1-55

4 Click the Finish button. If the chart toolbar displays, click its Close button. When the chart displays, point to an open area in the lower-right section of the Chart Area so the ScreenTip, Chart Area, displays.

Excel draws the 3-D Clustered column chart (Figure 1-56). The chart displays in the middle of the window in a selection rectangle. The small ***sizing handles*** *at the corners and along the sides of the selection rectangle indicate the chart is selected.*

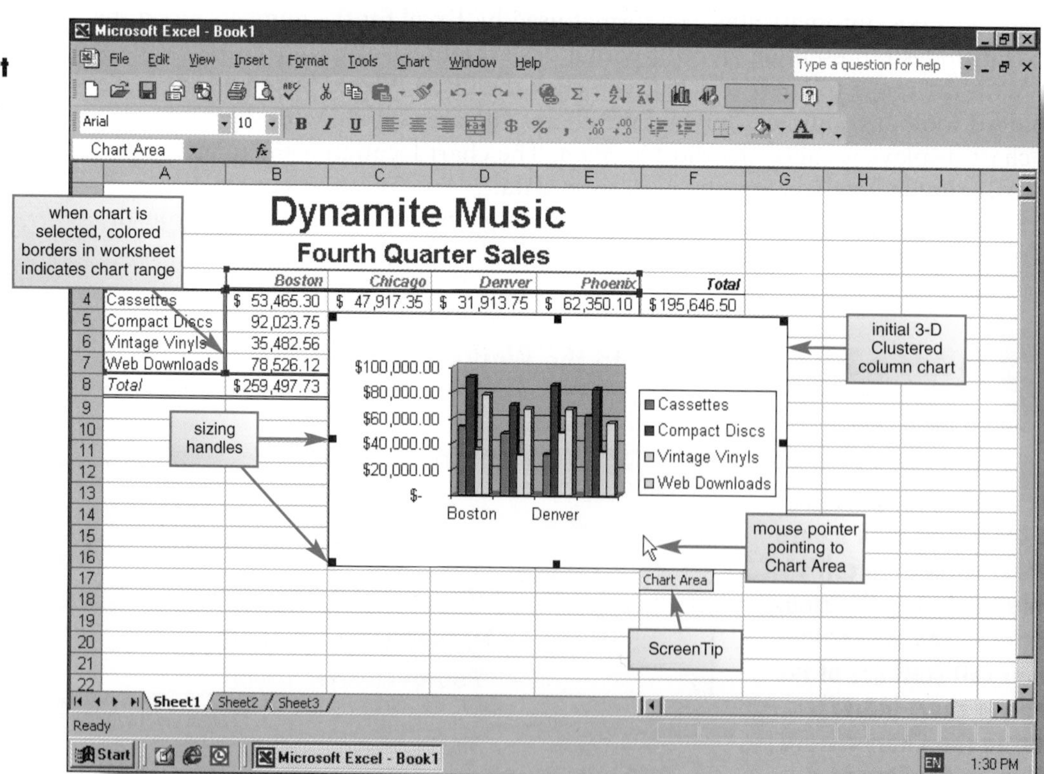

FIGURE 1-56

5 Drag the chart down and to the left to position the upper-left corner of the dotted line rectangle over the upper-left corner of cell A10 (Figure 1-57).

Excel displays a dotted line rectangle showing the new chart location. As you drag the selected chart, the mouse pointer changes to a cross hair with four arrowheads.

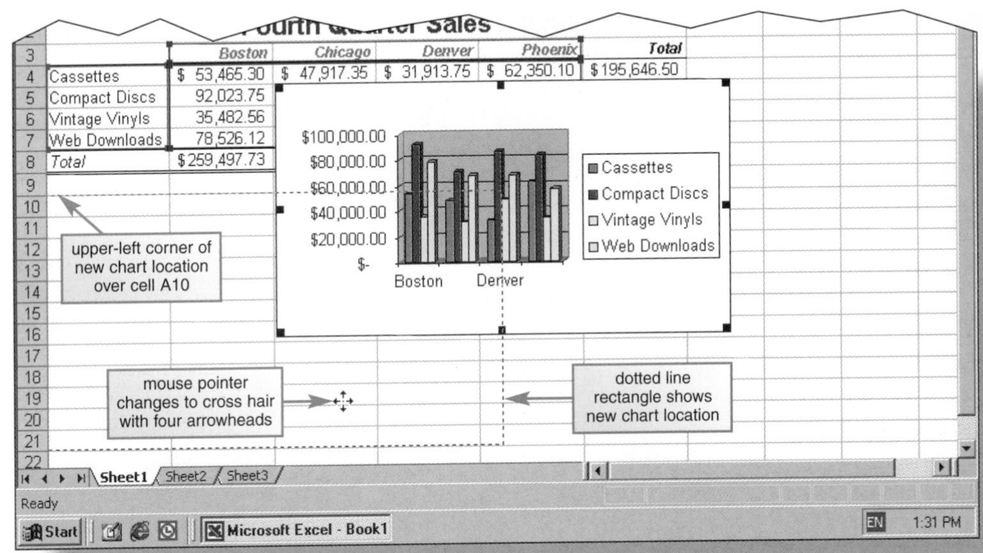

FIGURE 1-57

6 Release the mouse button. Point to the middle sizing handle on the right edge of the selection rectangle.

The chart displays in a new location (Figure 1-58). The mouse pointer changes to a horizontal line with two arrowheads when it points to a sizing handle.

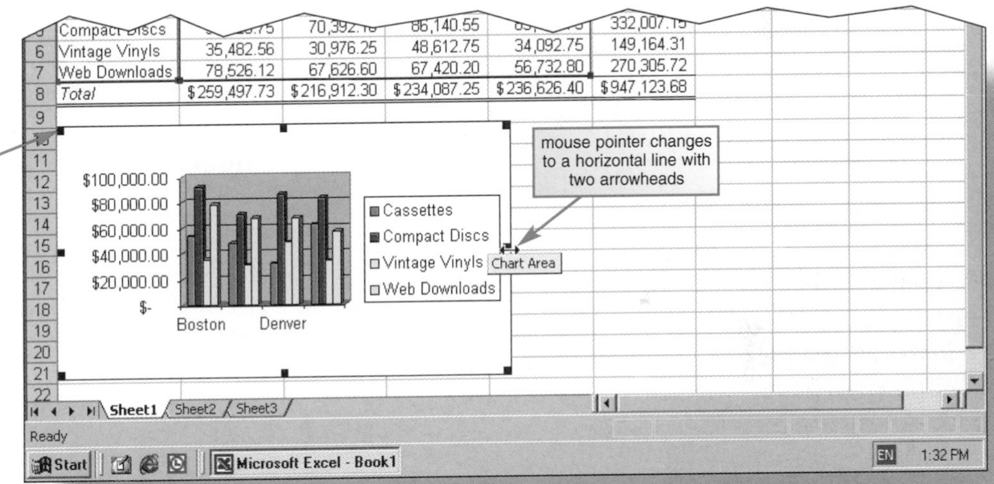

FIGURE 1-58

7 While holding down the ALT key, drag the sizing handle to the right edge of column F. Release the mouse button.

While you drag, the dotted line rectangle shows the new chart location (Figure 1-59). Holding down the ALT key while you drag a chart snaps (aligns) the new border to the worksheet gridlines.

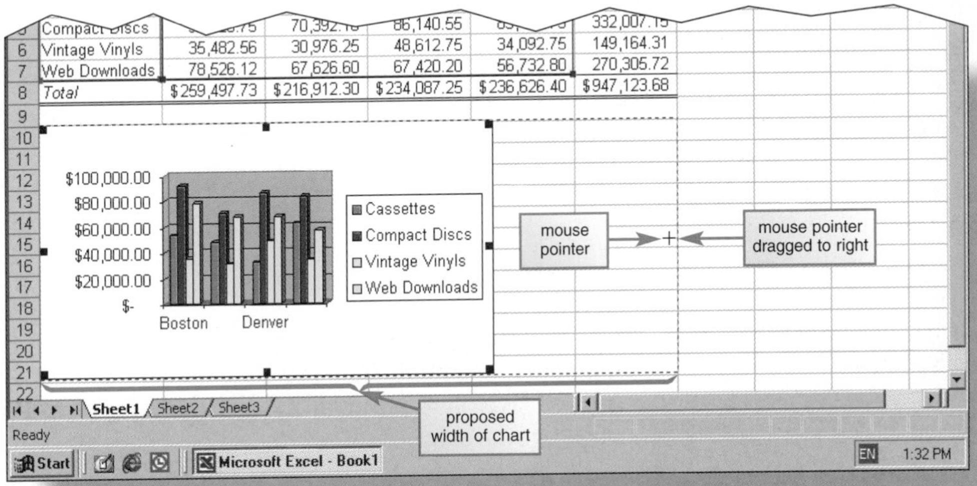

FIGURE 1-59

8 **If necessary, hold down the ALT key and drag the lower-middle sizing handle down to the bottom border of row 21. Click cell H21 to deselect the chart.**

The new chart location extends from the top of cell A10 to the bottom of cell F21 (Figure 1-60).

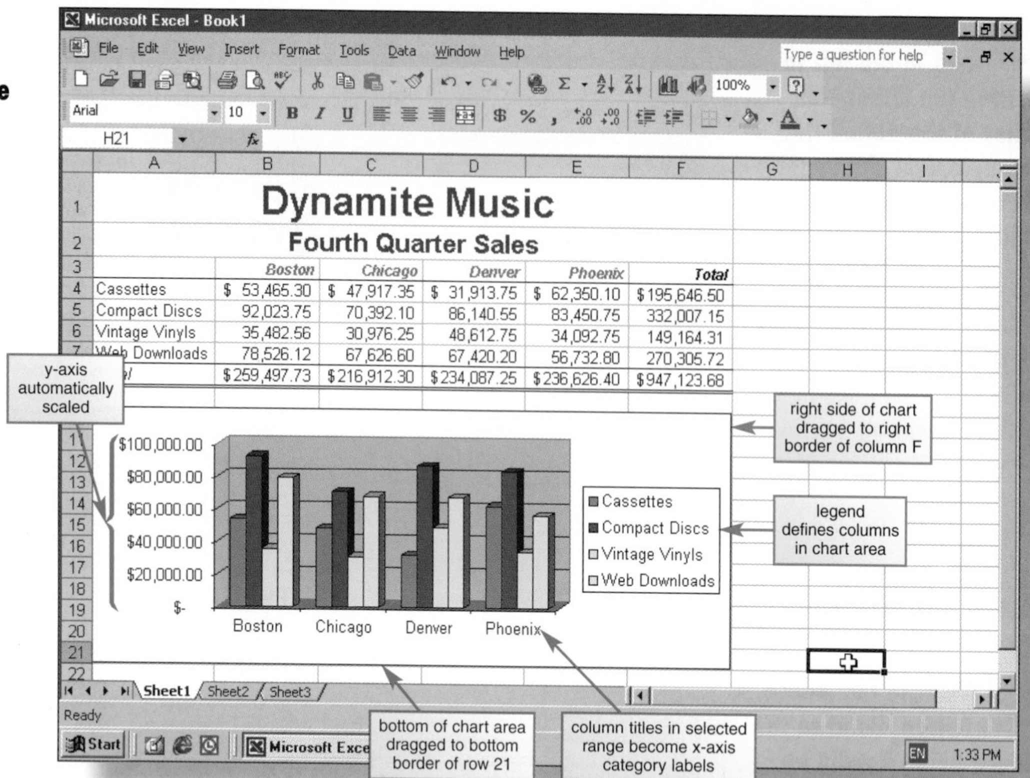

FIGURE 1-60

Other Ways

1. On Insert menu click Chart
2. Press F11
3. In Voice Command mode say, "Chart Wizard"

More About

Chart Types

You can change the embedded 3-D Column chart to another type by clicking the chart location and clicking the Chart Type button arrow on the Chart toolbar. You also can use the Chart toolbar to format the chart to make it look more professional. If the Chart toolbar does not display when you click the chart, right-click any toolbar and click Chart.

The embedded 3-D Column chart in Figure 1-60 compares the fourth quarter sales for the four product groups within each store. It also allows you to compare fourth quarter sales among the stores.

Excel automatically selects the entries in the topmost row of the range (row 3) as the titles for the horizontal axis (also called the **x-axis** or **category axis**) and draws a column for each of the 16 cells in the range containing numbers. The small box to the right of the column chart in Figure 1-55 on page E 1.38 contains the legend. The **legend** identifies each bar in the chart. Excel automatically selects the leftmost column of the range (column A) as titles within the legend. As indicated earlier, it also automatically scales the y-axis on the basis of the magnitude of the numbers in the chart range.

Excel offers 14 different chart types (Figure 1-55 on page E 1.38). The **default chart type** is the chart Excel draws if you click the Finish button in the first Chart Wizard dialog box. When you install Excel on a computer, the default chart type is the 2-D (two-dimensional) Column chart.

Saving a Workbook

While you are building a workbook, the computer stores it in memory. If the computer is turned off or if you lose electrical power, the workbook is lost. Hence, you must save on a floppy disk or hard disk any workbook that you will use later. A saved workbook is referred to as a **file**. The following steps illustrate how to save a workbook on a floppy disk in drive A using the Save button on the Standard toolbar.

Steps To Save a Workbook

1 With a floppy disk in drive A, click the Save button on the Standard toolbar.

The Save As dialog box displays (Figure 1-61). The preset Save in folder is Documents and Settings (your Save in folder may be different), the preset file name is Book1, and the file type is Microsoft Excel Workbook. The buttons on the top and on the side are used to select folders and change the display of file names and other information.

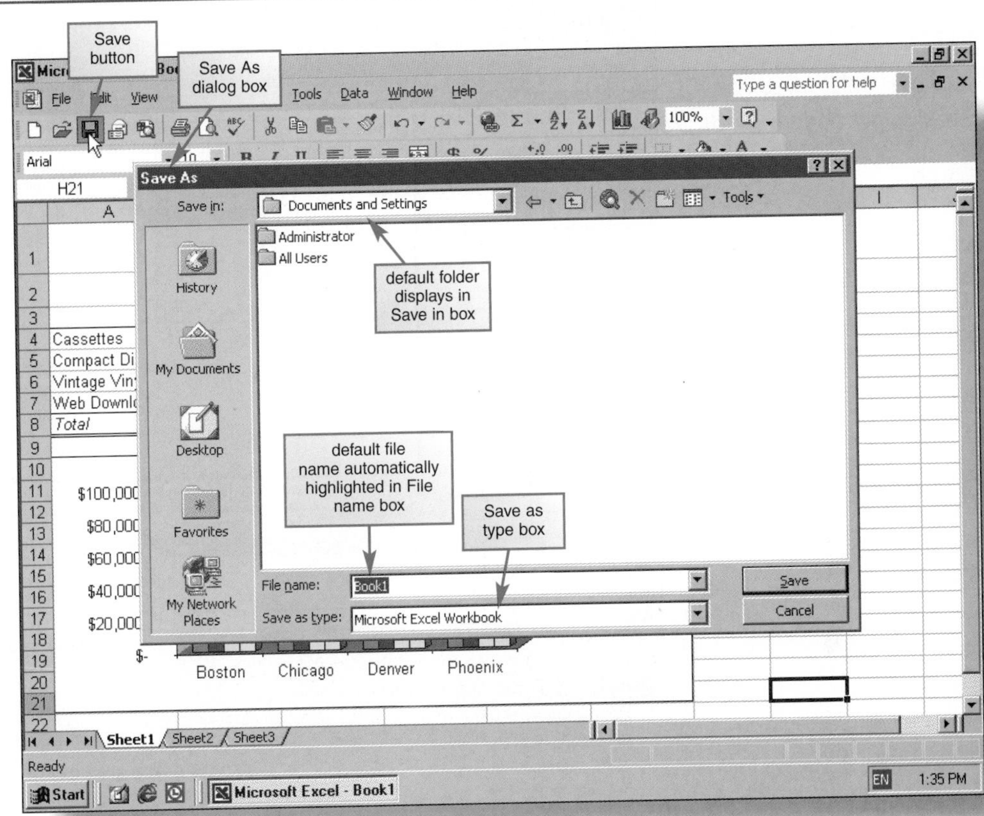

FIGURE 1-61

2 Type `Dynamite Music 4th Quarter Sales` **in the File name box. Point to the Save in box arrow.**

The new file name replaces Book1 in the File name text box (Figure 1-62). A file name can be up to 255 characters and can include spaces.

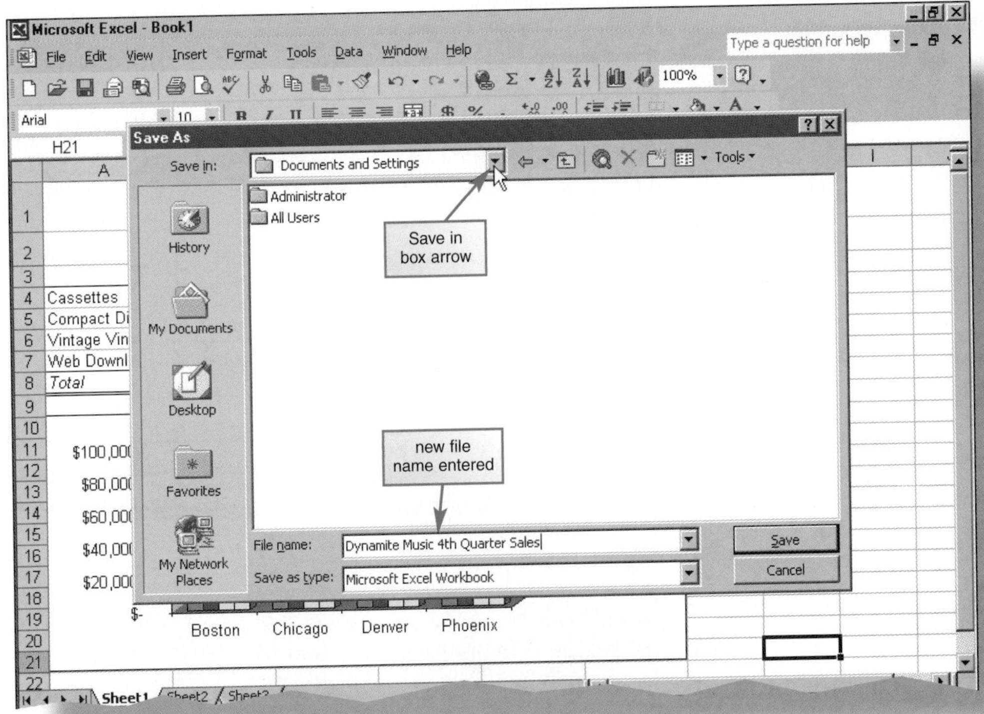

FIGURE 1-62

3 **Click the Save in box arrow and then point to 3½ Floppy (A:).**

A list of available drives and folders displays (Figure 1-63).

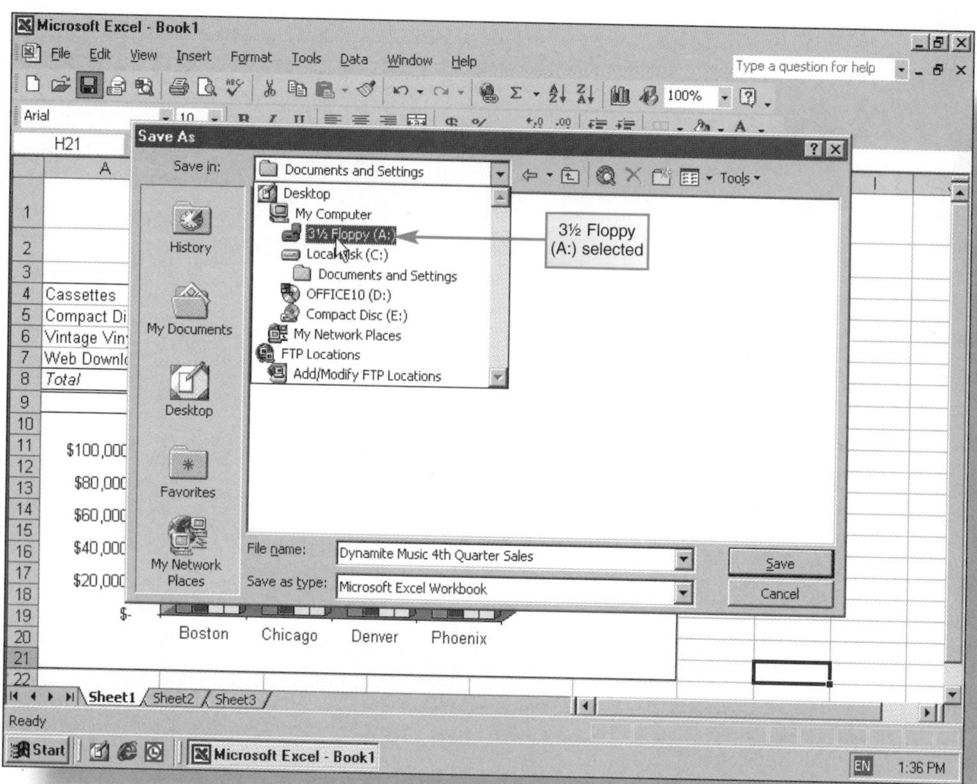

FIGURE 1-63

4 **Click 3½ Floppy (A:) and then point to the Save button in the Save As dialog box.**

Drive A becomes the selected drive (Figure 1-64).

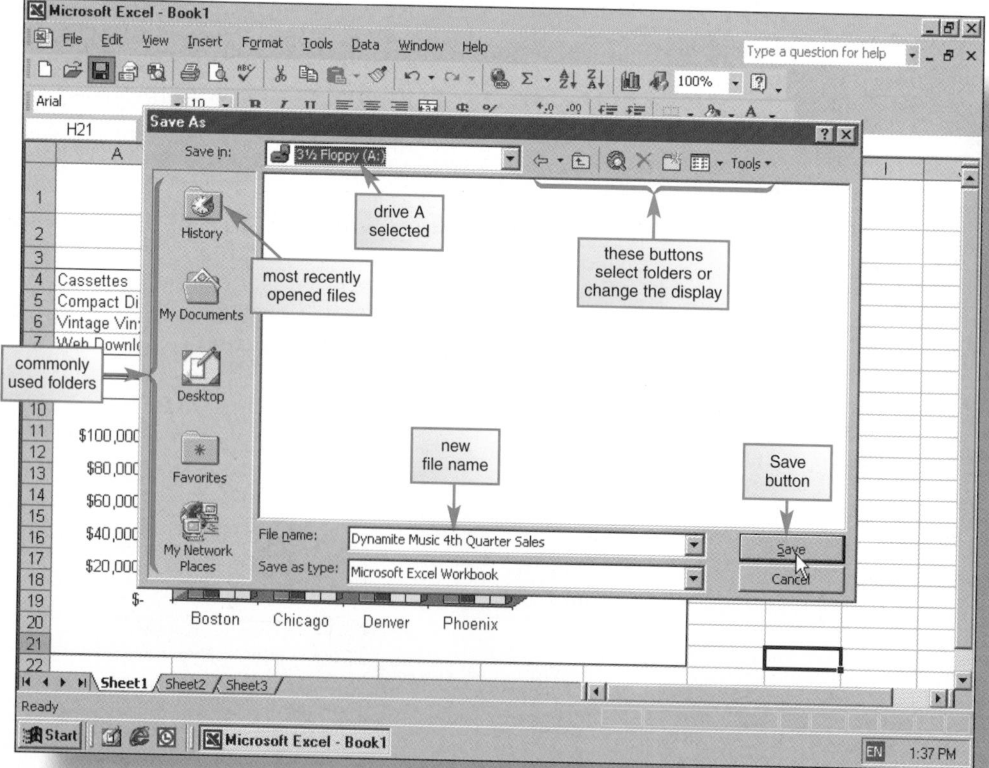

FIGURE 1-64

5 Click the Save button.

Excel saves the workbook on the floppy disk in drive A using the file name, Dynamite Music 4th Quarter Sales. Excel automatically appends the extension .xls to the file name you entered in Step 2, which stands for Excel workbook. Although the workbook is saved on a floppy disk, it also remains in memory and displays on the screen (Figure 1-65). The new file name displays on the title bar.

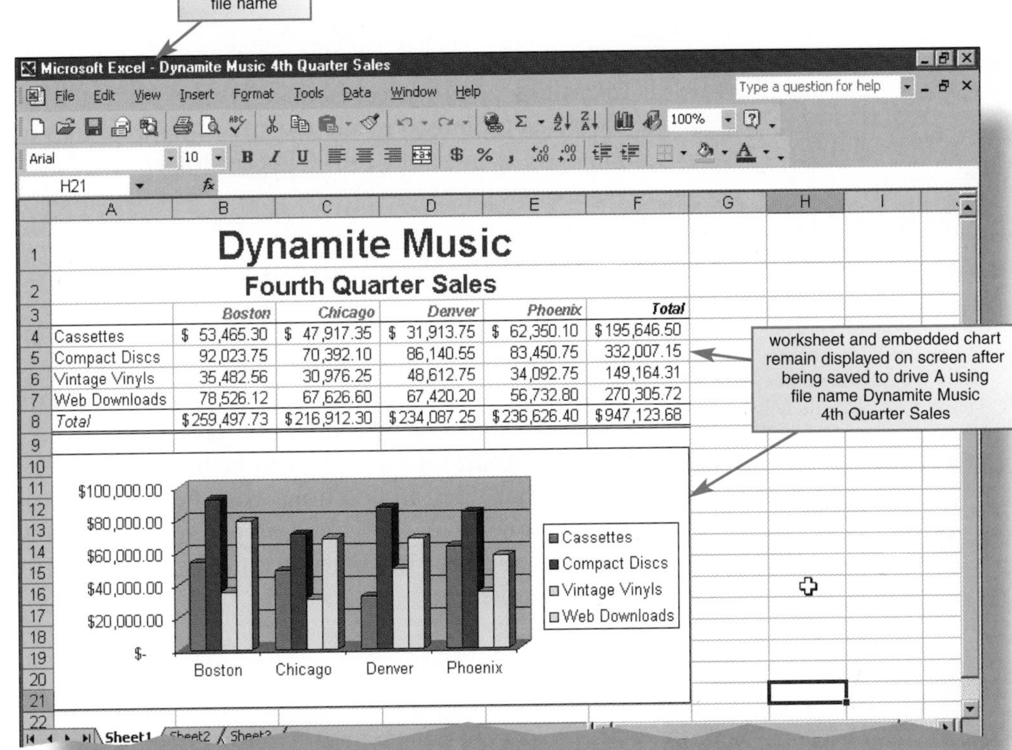
title bar displays new workbook file name
Microsoft Excel - Dynamite Music 4th Quarter Sales
Dynamite Music
Fourth Quarter Sales
worksheet and embedded chart remain displayed on screen after being saved to drive A using file name Dynamite Music 4th Quarter Sales

FIGURE 1-65

Other Ways

1. On File menu click Save As, type file name, select drive or folder, click OK button
2. Press CTRL+S, type file name, select drive or folder, click OK button
3. In Voice Command mode say, "File, Save As, [type desired file name], Save"

While Excel is saving the workbook, it momentarily changes the word Ready on the status bar to Saving. It also displays a horizontal bar on the status bar indicating the amount of the workbook saved. After the save operation is complete, Excel changes the name of the workbook in the title bar from Book1 to Dynamite Music 4th Quarter Sales (Figure 1-65).

The seven buttons at the top and to the right in the Save As dialog box in Figure 1-64 and their functions are summarized in Table 1-4.

When you click the **Tools button** in the Save As dialog box, a list displays. The **General Options command** in the list allows you to save a backup copy of the workbook, create a password to limit access to the workbook, and carry out other functions that are discussed later. Saving a backup workbook means that each time you save a workbook, Excel copies the current version of the workbook on disk to a file with the same name, but with the words, Backup of, appended to the front of the file name. In the case of a power failure or some other problem, use the backup version to restore your work.

You also can use the General Options command on the Tools list to assign a password to a workbook so others cannot open it. A password is case-sensitive and can be up to 15 characters long. **Case-sensitive** means Excel can differentiate between uppercase and lowercase letters. If you assign a password and forget the password, you cannot access the workbook.

Table 1-4 Save As Dialog Box Toolbar Buttons

BUTTON	BUTTON NAME	FUNCTION
	Default File Location	Displays contents of default file location
	Up One Level	Displays contents of next level up folder
	Search the Web	Starts browser and displays search engine
	Delete	Deletes selected file or folder
	Create	New Folder Creates new folder
	Views	Changes view of files and folders
Tools	Tools	Lists commands to print or modify file names and folders

Saving Workbooks

Excel allows you to save a workbook in over 30 different file formats. You choose the file format by clicking the Save as type box arrow at the bottom of the Save As dialog box (Figure 1-64 on page E 1.42). Microsoft Excel Workbook is the default file format. But you can, for example, save a workbook in Web Page format so you can publish it to the World Wide Web.

The five buttons on the left of the Save As dialog box in Figure 1-64 on page E 1.42 allow you to select frequently used folders. The **History button** displays a list of shortcuts (pointers) to the most recently used files in a folder titled Recent. You cannot save workbooks to the Recent folder.

Printing a Worksheet

Once you have created the worksheet, you might want to print it. A printed version of the worksheet is called a **hard copy** or **printout**.

You might want a printout for several reasons. First, to present the worksheet and chart to someone who does not have access to a computer, it must be in printed form. A printout, for example, can be handed out in a management meeting about fourth quarter sales. In addition, worksheets and charts often are kept for reference by people other than those who prepare them. In many cases, worksheets and charts are printed and kept in binders for use by others. Perform the following steps to print the worksheet.

Steps To Print a Worksheet

1 Ready the printer according to the printer instructions. Point to the Print button on the Standard toolbar (Figure 1-66).

FIGURE 1-66

2 Click the Print button. When the printer stops printing the worksheet and the chart, retrieve the printout.

Excel sends the worksheet to the printer, which prints it (Figure 1-67).

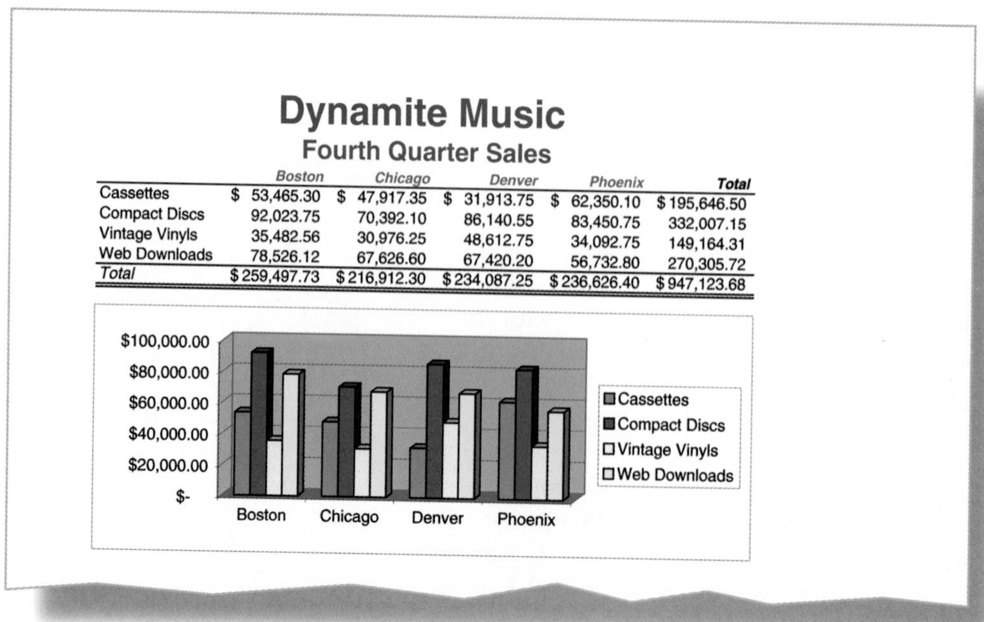

Dynamite Music

Fourth Quarter Sales

	Boston	Chicago	Denver	Phoenix	Total
Cassettes	$ 53,465.30	$ 47,917.35	$ 31,913.75	$ 62,350.10	$ 195,646.50
Compact Discs	92,023.75	70,392.10	86,140.55	83,450.75	332,007.15
Vintage Vinyls	35,482.56	30,976.25	48,612.75	34,092.75	149,164.31
Web Downloads	78,526.12	67,626.60	67,420.20	56,732.80	270,305.72
Total	$ 259,497.73	$ 216,912.30	$ 234,087.25	$ 236,626.40	$ 947,123.68

FIGURE 1-67

Other Ways

1. On File menu click Print, click OK button
2. Right-click workbook Control-menu icon on menu bar, click Print on shortcut menu, click OK button
3. Press CTRL+P, click OK button
4. In Voice Command mode say, "Print"

Prior to clicking the Print button, you can select which columns and rows in the 44worksheet to print. The range of cells you choose to print is called the **print area**. If you do not select a print area, as was the case in the previous set of steps, Excel automatically selects a print area on the basis of used cells. As you will see in future projects, Excel has many different print options, such as allowing you to preview the printout on the screen to see if the printout is satisfactory before sending it to the printer.

More About

Saving Paper

If you are concerned with saving paper, you can preview the printout on your screen, make adjustments to the worksheet, and then print it only when it appears exactly as you want. The Print Preview button is immediately to the right of the Print button on the Standard toolbar. Each time you preview rather than print, you save paper destined for the wastepaper basket, which, in turn, saves trees.

Quitting Excel

After you build, save, and print the worksheet and chart, Project 1 is complete. To quit Excel, complete the following steps.

Steps To Quit Excel

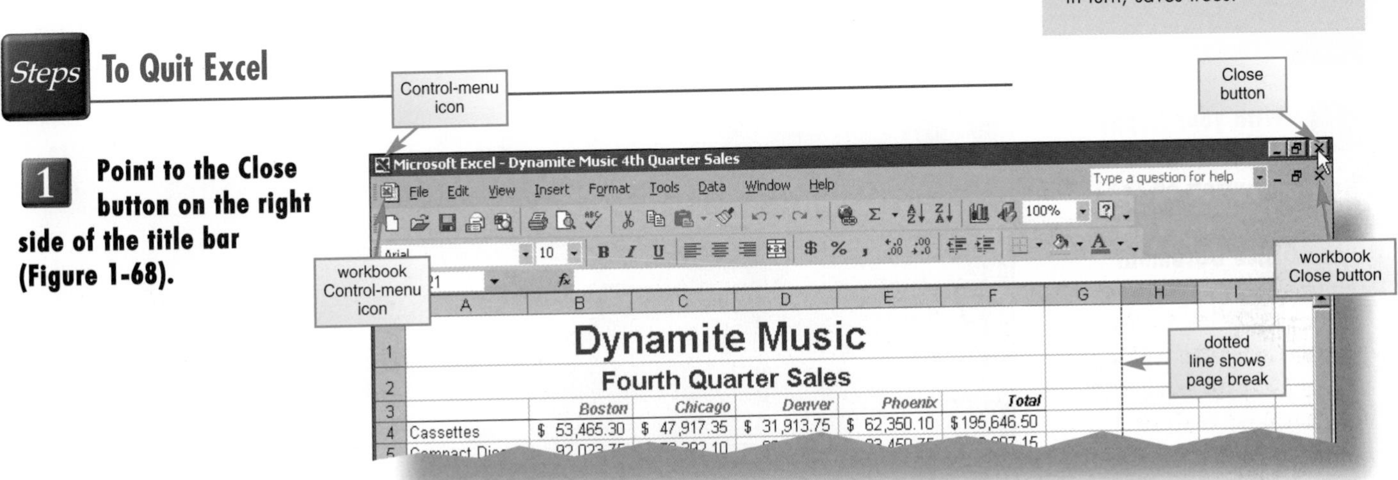

1 **Point to the Close button on the right side of the title bar (Figure 1-68).**

FIGURE 1-68

2 **Click the Close button.**

If you made changes to the workbook, the Microsoft Excel dialog box displays the question, Do you want to save the changes you made to 'Dynamite Music 4th Quarter Sales.xls'? (Figure 1-69). Clicking the Yes button saves the changes before quitting Excel. Clicking the No button quits Excel without saving the changes. Clicking the Cancel button cancels the exit and returns control to the worksheet.

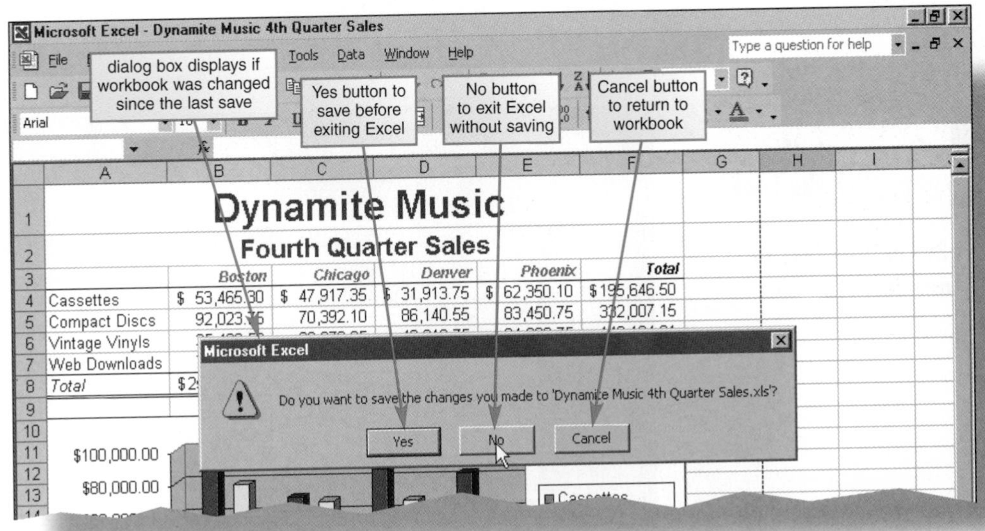

FIGURE 1-69

3 **Click the No button.**

1. On File menu click Exit
2. In Voice Command mode say, "File, Exit"

In Figure 1-68 on the previous page, you can see that two Close buttons and two Control-menu icons display. The Close button and Control-menu icon on the title bar close Excel. The Close button and Control-menu icon on the menu bar close the workbook, but not Excel.

Starting Excel and Opening a Workbook

Once you have created and saved a workbook, you often will have reason to retrieve it from a floppy disk. For example, you might want to review the calculations on the worksheet and enter additional or revised data on it. The following steps assume Excel is not running.

Steps To Start Excel and Open a Workbook

1 With your floppy disk in drive A, click the Start button on the taskbar and then point to Open Office Document (Figure 1-70).

FIGURE 1-70

2 Click Open Office Document. If necessary, click the Look in box arrow and then click 3½ Floppy (A:) in the Look in list.

The Open Office Document dialog box displays (Figure 1-71).

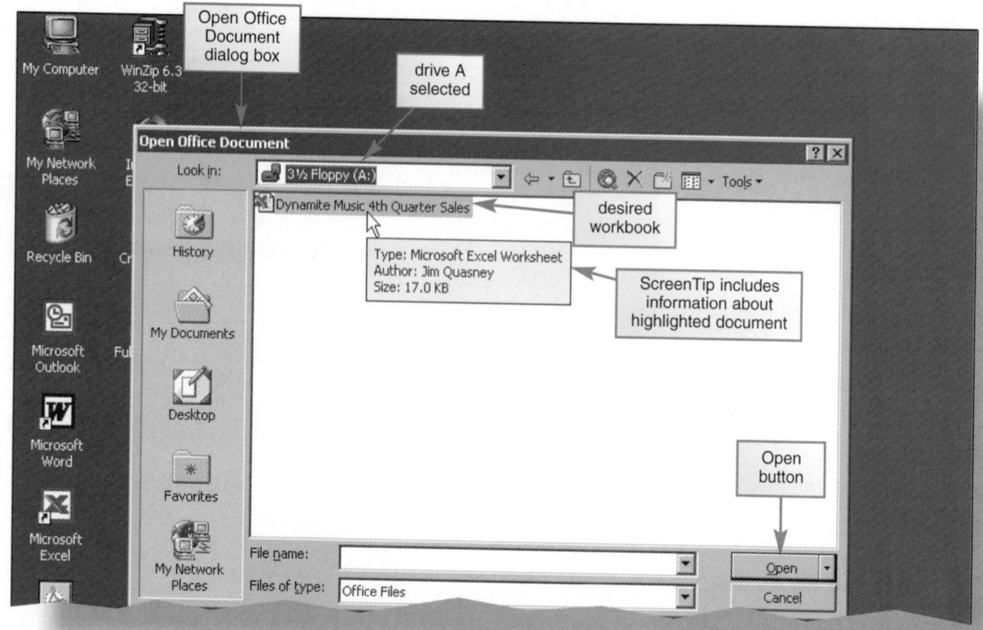

FIGURE 1-71

3 Double-click the file name Dynamite Music 4th Quarter Sales.

Excel starts, opens the workbook Dynamite Music 4th Quarter Sales.xls from drive A, and displays it on the screen (Figure 1-72). An alternative to double-clicking the file name is to click it and then click the Open button in the Open Office Document dialog box.

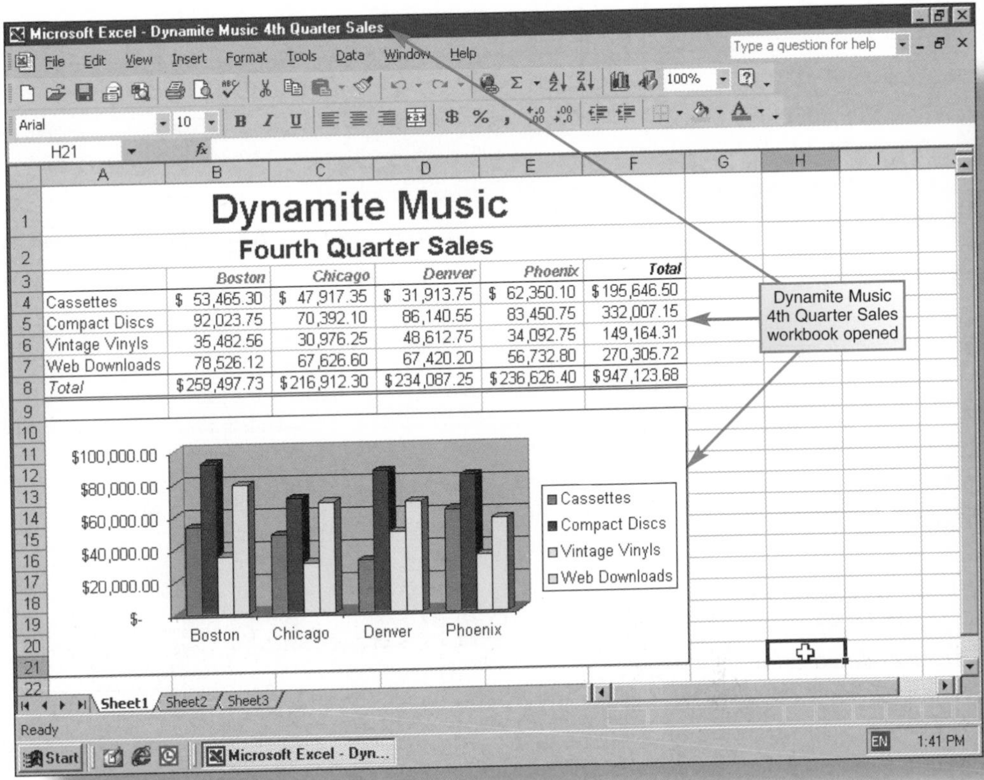

FIGURE 1-72

Other Ways

1. Right-click Start button, click Explore, display contents of drive A, double-click file name
2. In Microsoft Excel, in Voice Command mode say, "Open, [select file name], Open"

AutoCalculate

You easily can obtain a total, an average, or other information about the numbers in a range by using the AutoCalculate area on the status bar. All you need do is select the range of cells containing the numbers you want to check. Next, right-click the AutoCalculate area to display the shortcut menu (Figure 1-73 on the next page). The check mark to the left of the active function (Sum) indicates that the sum of the selected range displays. The function commands on the AutoCalculate shortcut menu are described in Table 1-5.

Table 1-5 AutoCalculate Shortcut Menu Commands

COMMAND	FUNCTION
None	No value displays in the AutoCalculate area
Average	Displays the average of the numbers in the selected range
Count	Displays the number of nonblank cells in the selected range
Count Nums	Displays the number of cells containing numbers in the selected range
Max	Displays the highest value in the selected range
Min	Displays the lowest value in the selected range
Sum	Displays the sum of the numbers in the selected range

The steps on the next page show how to display the average fourth quarter sales by store for the Cassettes product group.

To Use the AutoCalculate Area to Determine an Average

1 Select the range B4:E4. Right-click the AutoCalculate area on the status bar.

The sum of the numbers in the range B4:E4 displays ($195,646.50) as shown in Figure 1-73 because Sum is active in the AutoCalculate area. You may see a total other than the sum in your AutoCalculate area. The shortcut menu listing the various types of functions displays above the AutoCalculate area.

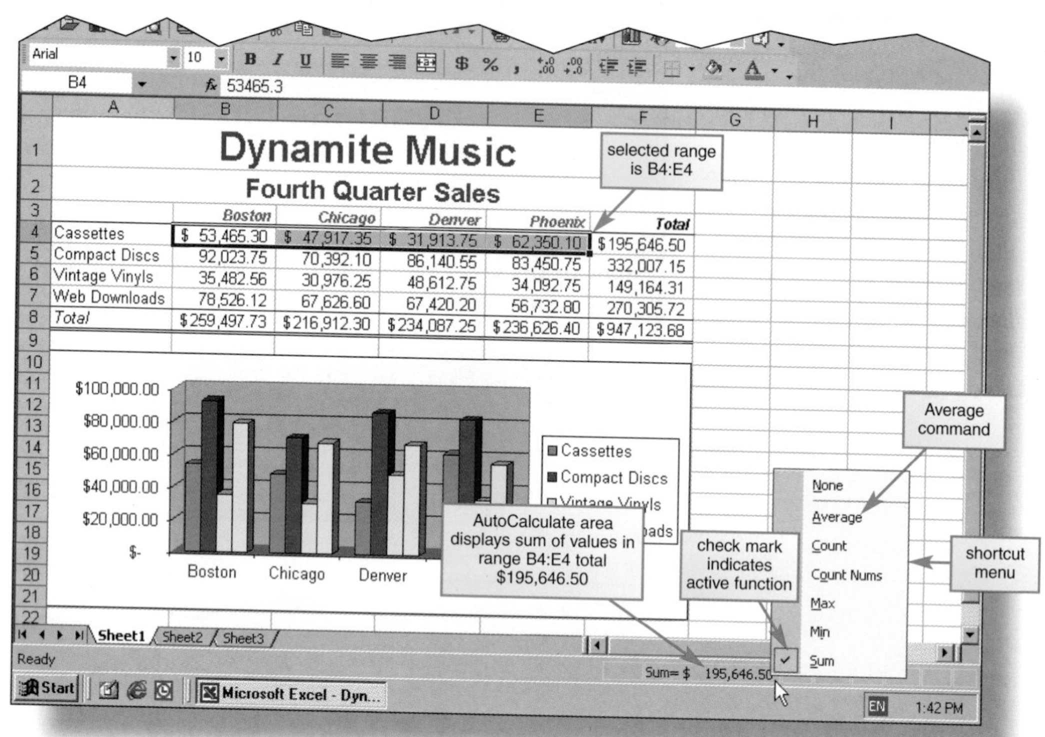

FIGURE 1-73

2 Click Average on the shortcut menu.

The average of the numbers in the range B4:E4 displays in the AutoCalculate area (Figure 1-74).

3 Right-click the AutoCalculate area and then click Sum on the shortcut menu.

The AutoCalculate area displays the sum as shown earlier in Figure 1-73.

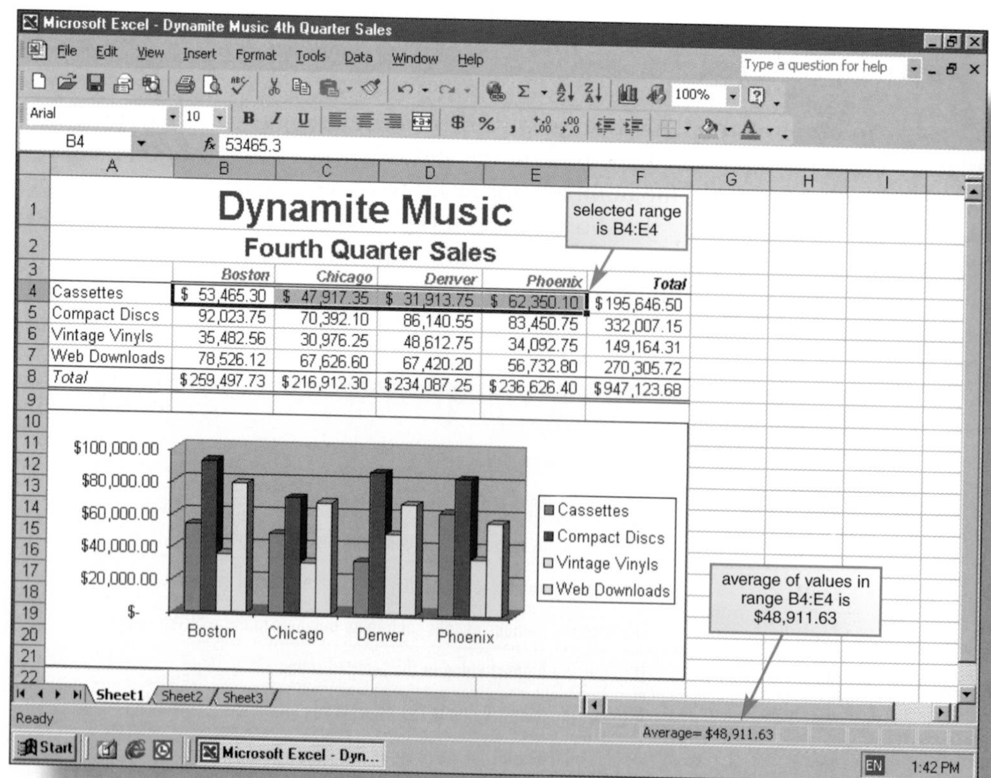

FIGURE 1-74

To change to any one of the other five functions for the range B4:E4, right-click the AutoCalculate area, then click the desired function.

The selection None at the top of the AutoCalculate shortcut menu in Figure 1-73 turns off the AutoCalculate area. Thus, if you select None, then no value will show in the AutoCalculate area when you select a range.

Shortcut Menus

Shortcut menus display the most frequently used commands that relate to the object to which the mouse pointer is pointing. To display a shortcut menu, right-click the object as shown in Step 1. To hide a shortcut menu, click outside the shortcut menu or press the ESC key.

Correcting Errors

You can correct errors on a worksheet using one of several methods. The method you choose will depend on the extent of the error and whether you notice it while typing the data or after you have entered the incorrect data into the cell.

Correcting Errors While You Are Typing Data into a Cell

If you notice an error while you are typing data into a cell, press the BACKSPACE key to erase the portion in error and then type the correct characters. If the error is a major one, click the Cancel box in the formula bar or press the ESC key to erase the entire entry and then reenter the data from the beginning.

In-Cell Editing

If you find an error in the worksheet after entering the data, you can correct the error in one of two ways:

1. If the entry is short, select the cell, retype the entry correctly, and click the Enter box or press the ENTER key. The new entry will replace the old entry.
2. If the entry in the cell is long and the errors are minor, the **Edit mode** may be a better choice. Use the Edit mode as described below.
   a. Double-click the cell containing the error. Excel switches to Edit mode, the active cell contents display in the formula bar, and a flashing insertion point displays in the active cell (Figure 1-75). This editing procedure is called **in-cell editing** because you can edit the contents directly in the cell. The active cell contents also display in the formula bar.
   b. Make your changes, as indicated below.
      (1) To insert between two characters, place the insertion point between the two characters and begin typing. Excel inserts the new characters at the location of the insertion point.
      (2) To delete a character in the cell, move the insertion point to the left of the character you want to delete and then press the DELETE key, or place the insertion point to the right of the character you want to delete and then press the BACKSPACE key. You also can use the mouse to drag through the character or adjacent characters you want to delete and then press the DELETE key or click the **Cut button** on the Standard toolbar.
      (3) When you are finished editing an entry, click the Enter box or press the ENTER key.

In-Cell Editing

An alternative to double-clicking the cell to edit is to select the cell and press F2.

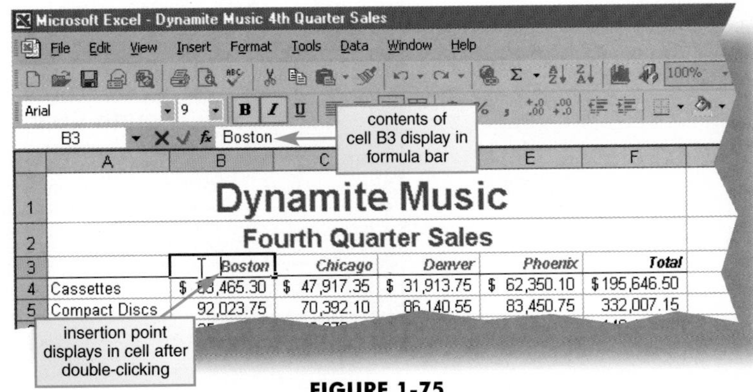

FIGURE 1-75

Editing the Contents of a Cell

Rather than using in-cell editing, you can select the cell and then click the formula bar to edit the contents.

When Excel enters the Edit mode, the keyboard usually is in Insert mode. In **Insert mode**, as you type a character, Excel inserts the character and moves all characters to the right of the typed character one position to the right. You can change to Overtype mode by pressing the INSERT key. In **Overtype mode**, Excel overtypes, or replaces, the character to the right of the insertion point. The INSERT key toggles the keyboard between Insert mode and Overtype mode.

While in Edit mode, you may have reason to move the insertion point to various points in the cell, select portions of the data in the cell, or switch from inserting characters to overtyping characters. Table 1-6 summarizes the more common tasks used during in-cell editing.

Table 1-6 Summary of In-Cell Editing Tasks

TASK	*MOUSE*	*KEYBOARD*
Move the insertion point to the beginning of data in a cell	Point to the left of the first character and click	Press HOME
Move the insertion point to the end of data in a cell	Point to the right of the last character and click	Press END
Move the insertion point anywhere in a cell	Point to the appropriate position and click the character	Press RIGHT ARROW or LEFT ARROW
Highlight one or more adjacent characters	Drag the mouse pointer through adjacent characters	Press SHIFT+RIGHT ARROW or SHIFT+LEFT ARROW
Select all data in a cell	Double-click the cell with the insertion point in the cell	
Delete selected characters	Click the Cut button on the Standard toolbar	Press DELETE
Delete characters to the left of insertion point		Press BACKSPACE
Toggle between Insert and Overtype modes		Press INSERT

Escaping an Activity

When it comes to canceling the current activity, the most important key on the keyboard is the ESC (Escape) key. Whether you are entering data into a cell or responding to a dialog box, pressing the ESC key cancels the current activity.

Undoing the Last Entry

Excel provides the **Undo command** on the **Edit menu** and the **Undo button** on the Standard toolbar (Figure 1-76) that you can use to erase the most recent worksheet entries. Thus, if you enter incorrect data in a cell and notice it immediately, click the Undo command or Undo button and Excel changes the cell contents to what they were prior to entering the incorrect data.

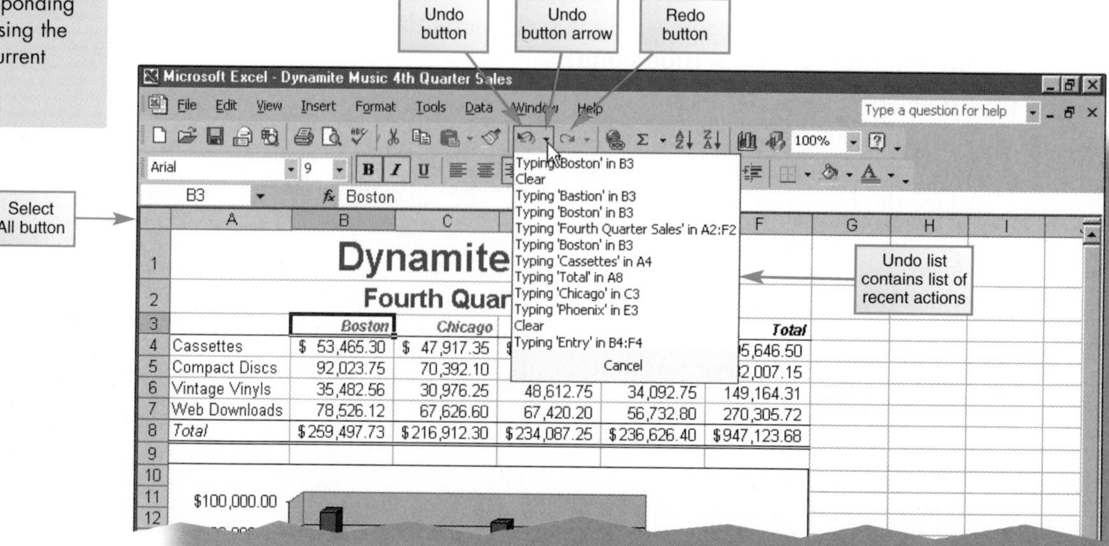

FIGURE 1-76

If Excel cannot undo an action, then the Undo button is inoperative. Excel remembers the last 16 actions you have completed. Thus, you can undo up to 16 previous actions by clicking the Undo button arrow to display the Undo list and clicking the action to be undone (Figure 1-76). You can drag through several actions in the Undo list to undo all of them at once.

Next to the Undo button on the Standard toolbar is the Redo button. The **Redo button** allows you to repeat previous actions. You also can click Redo on the Edit menu rather than using the Redo button.

More About

The Undo Button

The Undo button can undo far more complicated worksheet activities than just removing the latest entry from a cell. In fact, most commands can be undone if you click the Undo button before you make another entry or issue another command. You cannot undo a save or print, but, as a general rule, the Undo button can restore the worksheet data and settings to what they were the last time Excel was in Ready mode. With Excel 2002, you have multiple-level undo and redo capabilities.

Clearing a Cell or Range of Cells

If you enter data into the wrong cell or range of cells, you can erase, or clear, the data using one of several methods. ***Never press the SPACEBAR to clear a cell.*** Pressing the SPACEBAR enters a blank character. A blank character is text and is different from an empty cell, even though the cell may appear empty.

Excel provides four methods to clear the contents of a cell or a range of cells, which are discussed below.

TO CLEAR CELL CONTENTS USING THE FILL HANDLE

1. Select the cell or range of cells and point to the fill handle so the mouse pointer changes to a cross hair.
2. Drag the fill handle back into the selected cell or range until a shadow covers the cell or cells you want to erase. Release the mouse button.

TO CLEAR CELL CONTENTS USING THE SHORTCUT MENU

1. Select the cell or range of cells to be cleared.
2. Right-click the selection.
3. Click Clear Contents on the shortcut menu.

TO CLEAR CELL CONTENTS USING THE DELETE KEY

1. Select the cell or range of cells to be cleared.
2. Press the DELETE key.

TO CLEAR CELL CONTENTS USING THE CLEAR COMMAND

1. Select the cell or range of cells to be cleared.
2. Click Edit on the menu bar and then point to Clear.
3. Click All on the Clear submenu.

You also can select a range of cells and click the Cut button on the Standard toolbar or click Cut on the Edit menu. Be aware, however, that the Cut button or Cut command not only deletes the contents from the range, but also copies the contents of the range to the Office Clipboard.

More About

Getting Back to Normal

If you accidentally assign unwanted formats to a range of cells, you can use the Clear command on the Edit menu to delete the formats of a selected range. Doing so changes the format to Normal style. To view the characteristics of the Normal style, click Style on the Format menu or press ALT+APOSTROPHE (').

Clearing the Entire Worksheet

Sometimes, everything goes wrong. If this happens, you may want to clear the worksheet entirely and start over. To clear the worksheet, follow the steps on the next page.

TO CLEAR THE ENTIRE WORKSHEET

1. Click the Select All button on the worksheet (Figure 1-76 on page E 1.50).
2. Press the DELETE key or click Edit on the menu bar, point to Clear and then click All on the Clear submenu.

The **Select All button** selects the entire worksheet. Instead of clicking the Select All button, you also can press CTRL+A. You also can clear an unsaved workbook by clicking the workbook's Close button or by clicking the **Close command** on the File menu. If you close the workbook, click the **New button** on the Standard toolbar or click the **New command** on the File menu to begin working on the next workbook.

To delete an embedded chart, complete the following steps.

TO DELETE AN EMBEDDED CHART

1. Click the chart to select it.
2. Press the DELETE key.

> **More About**
>
> **Quick Reference**
>
> For a table that lists how to complete the tasks covered in this book using the mouse, menu, shortcut menu, and keyboard, see the Quick Reference Summary at the back of this book or visit the Shelly Cashman Series Office XP Web page (scsite.com/offxp/qr.htm) and then click Microsoft Excel 2002.

Excel Help System

At any time while you are using Excel, you can get answers to questions using the Excel Help system. You can activate the Excel Help system by using the Ask a Question box on the menu bar, the Microsoft Excel Help button on the Standard toolbar, or the Help menu (Figure 1-77). Used properly, this form of online assistance can increase your productivity and reduce your frustrations by minimizing the time you spend learning how to use Excel.

The following section shows how to get answers to your questions using the Ask a Question box. Additional information on using the Excel Help system is available in Appendix A and Table 1-7 on page E1.54.

> **More About**
>
> **The Excel Help System**
>
> The best way to become familiar with the Excel Help system is to use it. Appendix A includes detailed information on the Excel Help system and exercises that will help you gain confidence in using it.

Obtaining Help Using the Ask a Question Box on the Menu Bar

The **Ask a Question box** on the right side of the menu bar lets you type free-form questions such as. *how do I save* or *how do I create a Web page*, or you can type in terms such as, *copy*, *save*, or *formatting*. Excel responds by displaying a list of topics related to what you entered. The following steps show how to use the Ask a Question box to obtain information on formatting a worksheet.

Steps To Obtain Help Using the Ask a Question Box

1. **Type** `formatting` **in the Ask a Question box on the right side of the menu bar (Figure 1-77).**

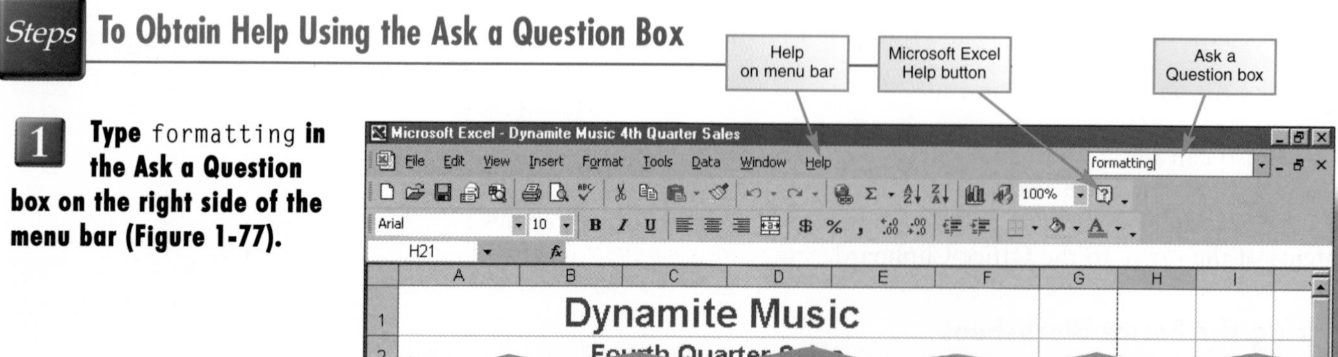

FIGURE 1-77

2 Press the ENTER key. When the list of topics displays below the Ask a Question box, point to the topic, About formatting worksheets and data.

A list of topics displays relating to the term, formatting. The mouse pointer changes to a hand indicating it is pointing to a link (Figure 1-78).

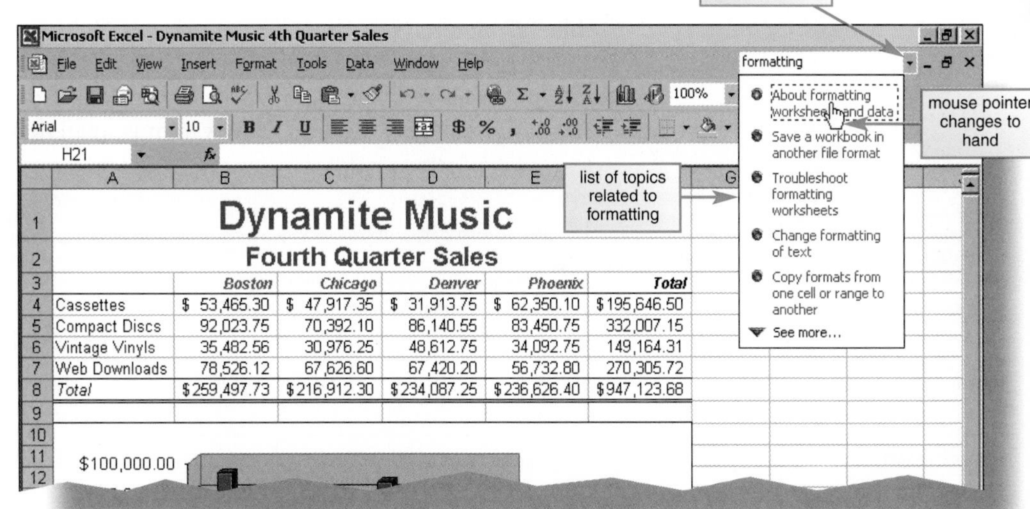

FIGURE 1-78

3 Click About formatting worksheets and data. When the Microsoft Excel Help window displays, double-click its title bar to maximize it.

Excel opens a Microsoft Excel Help window that provides Help information about worksheet formatting (Figure 1-79).

4 Click the Close button on the Microsoft Excel Help window title bar.

The Microsoft Excel Help window closes and the worksheet is active.

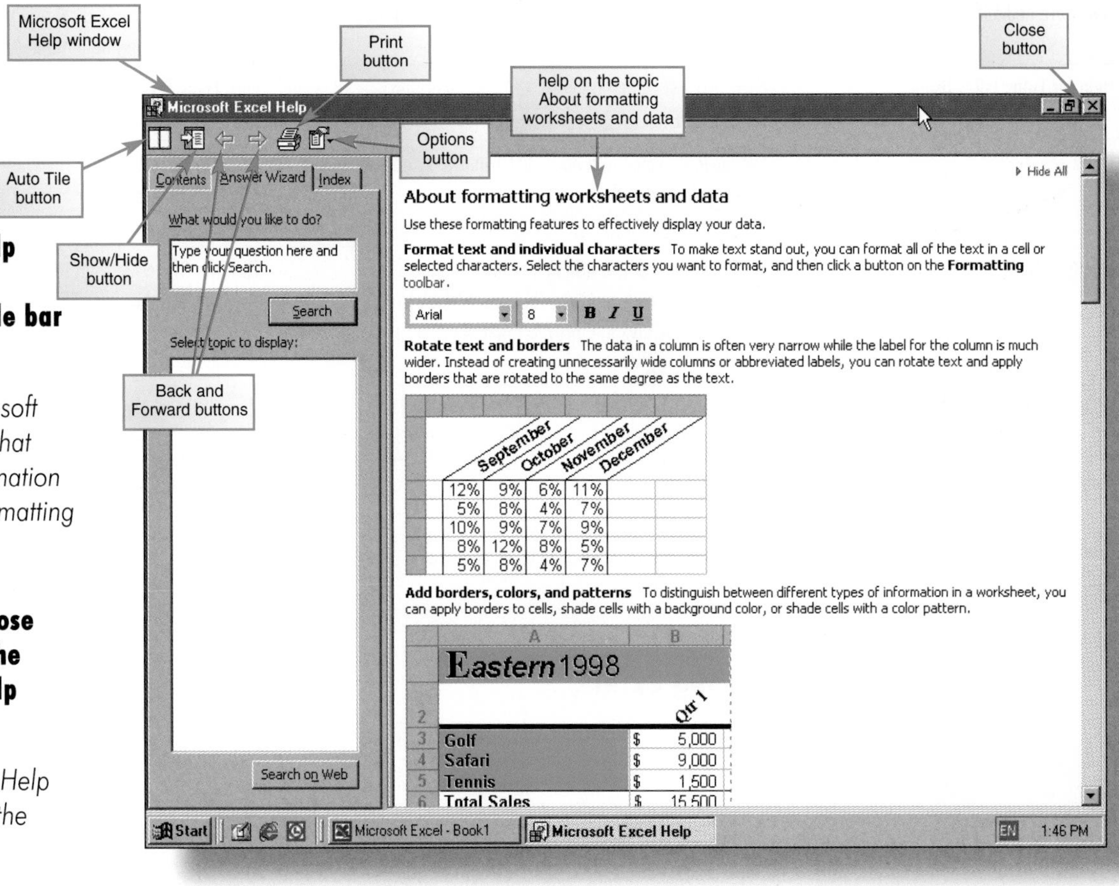

FIGURE 1-79

Use the buttons in the upper-left corner of the Microsoft Excel Help window (Figure 1-79) to navigate through the Help system, change the display, and print the contents of the window.

As you enter questions and terms in the Ask a Question box, Excel adds them to its list. Thus, if you click the Ask a Question box arrow (Figure 1-78), a list of previously asked questions and terms will display.

Excel Tips

To receive a newsletter titled ExcelTips regularly via e-mail at no charge, visit the Excel 2002 More About Web page (scsite.com/ex2002/more.htm) and click ExcelTips.

Table 1-7 summarizes the 11 categories of Help available to you. Because of the way the Excel Help system works, be sure to review the rightmost column of Table 1-7 if you have difficulties activating the desired category of Help. Additional information on using the Excel Help system is available in Appendix A.

Table 1-7 Excel Help System

TYPE	DESCRIPTION	HOW TO ACTIVATE
Answer Wizard	Answers questions or searches for terms that you type in your own words.	Click the Microsoft Excel Help button on the Standard toolbar. Click the Answer Wizard tab.
Ask a Question box	Answers questions or searches for terms that you type in your own words.	Type a question or term in the Ask a Question box on the menu bar and then press the ENTER key.
Contents sheet	Groups Help topics by general categories. Use when you know only the general category of the topic in question.	Click the Microsoft Excel Help button on the Standard toolbar. Click the Contents tab.
Detect and Repair	Automatically finds and fixes errors in the application.	Click Detect and Repair on the Help menu.
Hardware and Software Information	Shows Product ID and allows access to system information and technical support information.	Click About Microsoft Excel on the Help menu and then click the appropriate button.
Help for Lotus 1-2-3 Users	Used to assist Lotus 1-2-3 users who are learning Microsoft Excel.	Click Lotus 1-2-3 Help on the Help menu.
Index sheet	Similar to an index in a book. Use when you know exactly what you want.	Click the Microsoft Excel Help button on the Standard toolbar. If necessary, maximize the Help window by double-clicking its title bar. Click the Index tab.
Office Assistant	Similar to the Ask a Question box in that the Office Assistant answers questions that you type in your own words, offers tips, and provides help for a variety of Excel features.	Click the Office Assistant icon. If the Office Assistant does not display, click Show the Office Assistant on the Help menu.
Office on the Web	Used to access technical resources and download free product enhancements on the Web.	Click Office on the Web on the Help menu.
Question Mark button	Used to identify unfamiliar items in a dialog box.	Click the Question Mark button in the title bar of a dialog box and then click an item in the dialog box.
What's This? command	Used to identify unfamiliar items on the screen.	Click What's This? on the Help menu, and then click an item on the screen.

Quitting Excel

To quit Excel, complete the following steps.

More About

Quitting Excel

Do not forget to remove your floppy disk from drive A after quitting Excel, especially if you are working in a laboratory environment. Nothing can be more frustrating than leaving all of your hard work behind on a floppy disk for the next user.

TO QUIT EXCEL

1. Click the Close button on the right side of the title bar (see Figure 1-68 on page E 1.45).
2. If the Microsoft Excel dialog box displays, click the No button.

CASE PERSPECTIVE SUMMARY

The worksheet created in this project allows the management of Dynamite Music to examine fourth quarter sales for the four key product groups. Furthermore, the 3-D Column chart should meet the needs of Nadine Mitchell, who as you recall, would rather view the numbers graphically.

Project Summary

In creating the Dynamite Music Fourth Quarter Sales worksheet and chart in this project, you gained a broad knowledge of Excel. First, you were introduced to starting Excel. You learned about the Excel window and how to enter text and numbers to create a worksheet. You learned how to select a range and how to use the AutoSum button to sum numbers in a column or row. Using the fill handle, you learned how to copy a cell to adjacent cells.

Once the worksheet was built, you learned how to change the font size of the title, bold the title, and center the title across a range using buttons on the Formatting toolbar. Using the steps and techniques presented in the project, you formatted the body of the worksheet using the AutoFormat command, and you used the Chart Wizard to add a 3-D Column chart. After completing the worksheet, you saved the workbook on disk, printed the worksheet and chart, and then quit Excel. You learned how to start Excel by opening an Excel document, use the AutoCalculate area, and edit data in cells. Finally, you learned how to use the Excel Help system to answer your questions.

What You Should Know

Having completed this project, you now should be able to perform the following tasks:

- Add a 3-D Column Chart to the Worksheet *(E 1.37)*
- Bold a Cell *(E 1.29)*
- Center a Cell's Contents across Columns *(E 1.32)*
- Change the Font Color of a Cell *(E 1.31)*
- Clear Cell Contents Using the Clear Command *(E 1.51)*
- Clear Cell Contents Using the DELETE Key *(E 1.51)*
- Clear Cell Contents Using the Fill Handle *(E 1.51)*
- Clear Cell Contents Using the Shortcut Menu *(E 1.51)*
- Clear the Entire Worksheet *(E 1.52)*
- Copy a Cell to Adjacent Cells in a Row *(E 1.25)*
- Customize the Excel Window *(E 1.09)*
- Delete an Embedded Chart *(E 1.52)*
- Determine Multiple Totals at the Same Time *(E 1.27)*
- Enter Column Titles *(E 1.19)*
- Enter Numeric Data *(E 1.22)*
- Enter Row Titles *(E 1.21)*
- Enter the Worksheet Titles *(E 1.17)*
- Format the Worksheet Subtitle *(E 1.33)*
- Increase the Font Size of a Cell Entry *(E 1.30)*
- Obtain Help Using the Ask a Question Box *(E 1.52)*
- Print a Worksheet *(E 1.44)*
- Quit Excel *(E 1.45, E 1.54)*
- Save a Workbook *(E 1.41)*
- Start Excel *(E 1.08)*
- Start Excel and Open a Workbook *(E 1.46)*
- Sum a Column of Numbers *(E 1.23)*
- Use AutoFormat to Format the Body of a Worksheet *(E 1.33)*
- Use the AutoCalculate Area to Determine an Average *(E 1.48)*
- Use the Name Box to Select a Cell *(E 1.35)*

More About

Microsoft Certification

The Microsoft Office User Specialist (MOUS) Certification program provides an opportunity for you to obtain a valuable industry credential — proof that you have the Excel 2002 skills required by employers. For more information, see Appendix E or visit the Shelly Cashman Series MOUS Web page at scsite.com/offxp/cert.htm.

Learn It Online

Instructions: To complete the Learn It Online exercises, start your browser, click the Address bar, and then enter `scsite.com/offxp/exs.htm`. When the Office XP Learn It Online page displays, follow the instructions in the exercises below.

1 Project Reinforcement TF, MC, and SA

Below Excel Project 1, click the Project Reinforcement link. Print the quiz by clicking Print on the File menu. Answer each question. Write your first and last name at the top of each page, and then hand in the printout to your instructor.

2 Flash Cards

Below Excel Project 1, click the Flash Cards link. When Flash Cards displays, read the instructions. Type 20 (or a number specified by your instructor) in the Number of Playing Cards text box, type your name in the Name text box, and then click the Flip Card button. When the flash card displays, read the question and then click the Answer box arrow to select an answer. Flip through Flash Cards. Click Print on the File menu to print the last flash card if your score is 15 (75%) correct or greater and then hand it in to your instructor. If your score is less than 15 (75%) correct, then redo this exercise by clicking the Replay button.

3 Practice Test

Below Excel Project 1, click the Practice Test link. Answer each question, enter your first and last name at the bottom of the page, and then click the Grade Test button. When the graded practice test displays on your screen, click Print on the File menu to print a hard copy. Continue to take practice tests until you score 80% or better. Hand in a printout of the final practice test to your instructor.

4 Who Wants to Be a Computer Genius?

Below Excel Project 1, click the Computer Genius link. Read the instructions, enter your first and last name at the bottom of the page, and then click the Play button. Hand in your score to your instructor.

5 Wheel of Terms

Below Excel Project 1, click the Wheel of Terms link. Read the instructions, and then enter your first and last name and your school name. Click the Play button. Hand in your score to your instructor.

6 Crossword Puzzle Challenge

Below Excel Project 1, click the Crossword Puzzle Challenge link. Read the instructions, and then enter your first and last name. Click the Play button. Work the crossword puzzle. When you are finished, click the Submit button. When the crossword puzzle redisplays, click the Print button. Hand in the printout.

7 Tips and Tricks

Below Excel Project 1, click the Tips and Tricks link. Click a topic that pertains to Project 1. Right-click the information and then click Print on the shortcut menu. Construct a brief example of what the information relates to in Excel to confirm you understand how to use the tip or trick. Hand in the example and printed information.

8 Newsgroups

Below Excel Project 1, click the Newsgroups link. Click a topic that pertains to Project 1. Print three comments. Hand in the comments to your instructor.

9 Expanding Your Horizons

Below Excel Project 1, click the Articles for Microsoft Excel link. Click a topic that pertains to Project 1. Print the information. Construct a brief example of what the information relates to in Excel to confirm you understand the contents of the article. Hand in the example and printed information to your instructor.

10 Search Sleuth

Below Excel Project 1, click the Search Sleuth link. To search for a term that pertains to this project, select a term below the Project 1 title and then use the Google search engine at google.com (or any major search engine) to display and print two Web pages that present information on the term. Hand in the printouts to your instructor.

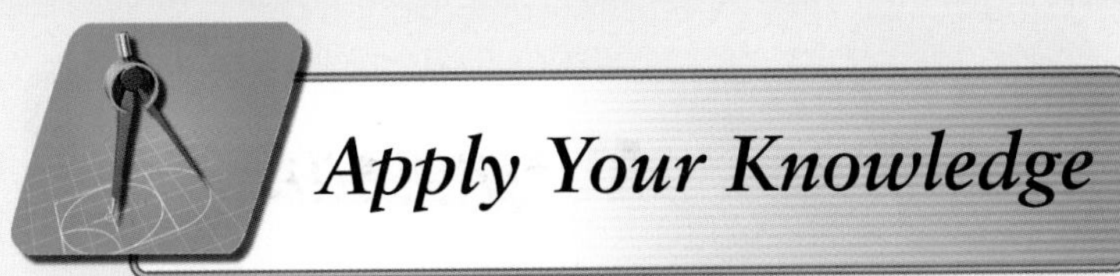

1 Marco Polo's Travel Bookstore 1st Quarter Sales Worksheet

Instructions: Start Excel. Open the workbook Magellan's Travel Bookstore 1st Quarter Sales from the Data Disk. See the inside back cover of this book for instructions for downloading the Data Disk or see your instructor for information on accessing the files required in this book.

Make the changes to the worksheet described in Table 1-8 so it appears as shown in Figure 1-80. As you edit the values in the cells containing numeric data, watch in the totals in row 8, the totals in column G, and the chart change. When you enter a new value, Excel automatically recalculates the formulas. After you have successfully made the changes listed in the table, the total sales in cell G8 should be $1,486,082.12.

Table 1-8 New Worksheet Data

CELL	*CHANGE CELL CONTENTS TO*
A1	Marco Polo's Travel Bookstore
B4	78,221.46
C4	69,789.50
D6	74,943.13
F6	86,699.98
F7	98,421.43

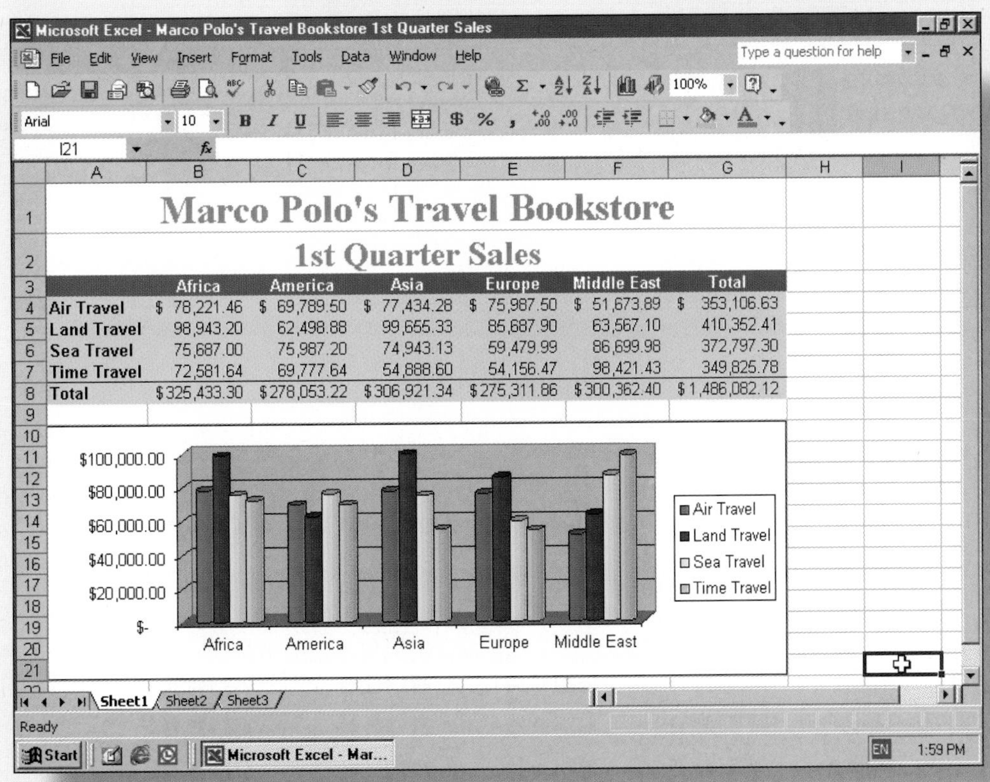

	Africa	America	Asia	Europe	Middle East	Total
Air Travel	$ 78,221.46	$ 69,789.50	$ 77,434.28	$ 75,987.50	$ 51,673.89	$ 353,106.63
Land Travel	98,943.20	62,498.88	99,655.33	85,687.90	63,567.10	410,352.41
Sea Travel	75,687.00	75,987.20	74,943.13	59,479.99	86,699.98	372,797.30
Time Travel	72,581.64	69,777.64	54,888.60	54,156.47	98,421.43	349,825.78
Total	$325,433.30	$278,053.22	$306,921.34	$275,311.86	$300,362.40	$1,486,082.12

FIGURE 1-80

To learn how to split cells, click cell A1 and then click the Merge and Center button to split cell A1 into cells A1, B1, C1, D1, E1, F1, and G1. To re-merge the cells into one, select the range A1:G1 and click the Merge and Center button.

Enter your name, course, laboratory assignment number, date, and instructor name in cells A24 through A28. Save the workbook. Use the file name, Marco Polo's Travel Bookstore 1st Quarter Sales. Print the revised worksheet and hand in the printout to your instructor.

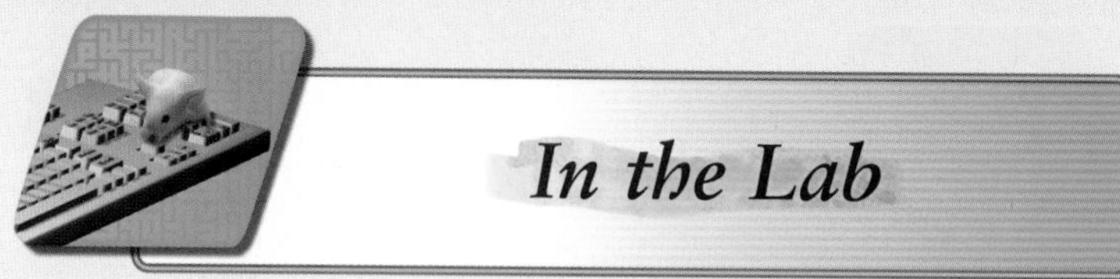

1 Madonna's Virtual Sojourn Annual Sales Analysis Worksheet

Problem: The president of Madonna's Virtual Sojourn, a travel agency that courts college age students, needs a sales analysis worksheet similar to the one shown in Figure 1-81. Your task is to develop the worksheet.

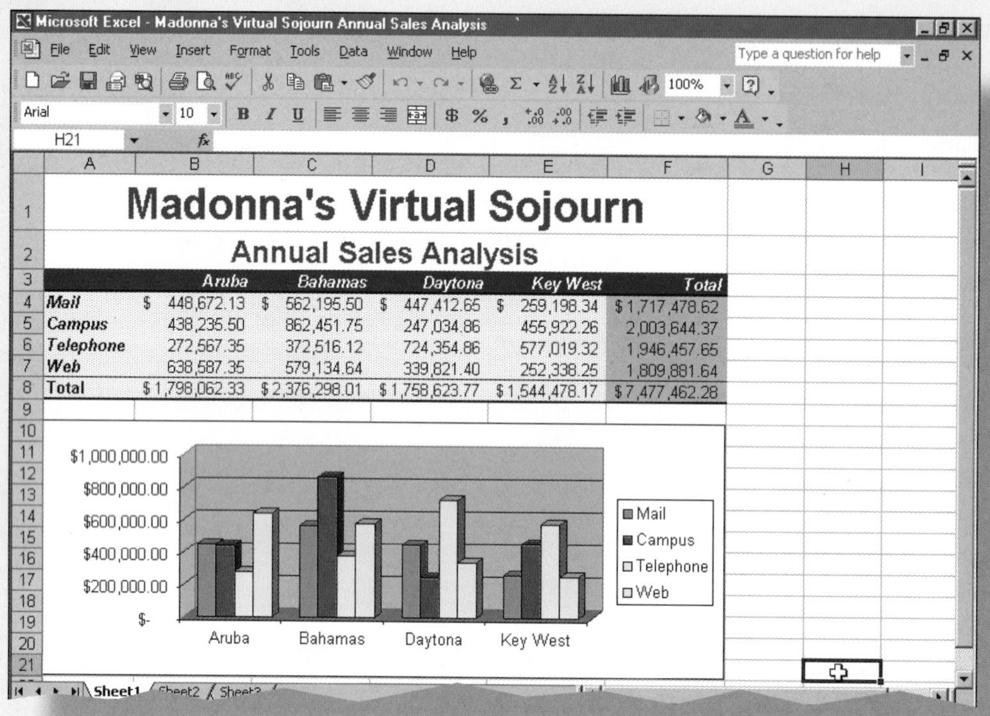

FIGURE 1-81

Instructions: Perform the following tasks.

1. Create the worksheet shown in Figure 1-81 using the sales amounts and categories in Table 1-9.

Table 1-9 Madonna's Virtual Sojourn Annual Sales Data				
	ARUBA	BAHAMAS	DAYTONA	KEY WEST
Mail	448,672.13	562,195.50	447,412.65	259,198.34
Campus	438,235.50	862,451.75	247,034.86	455,922.26
Telephone	272,567.35	372,516.12	724,354.86	577,019.32
Web	638,587.35	579,134.64	339,821.40	252,338.25

2. Determine the totals for the types of sales channels, travel destinations, and company totals.
3. Format the worksheet title, Madonna's Virtual Sojourn, to 26-point Arial, bold brown font, centered across columns A through F. Do not be concerned if the edges of the worksheet title do not display.
4. Format the worksheet subtitle, Annual Sales Analysis, to 18-point Arial, bold brown font, centered across columns A through F.

In the Lab

5. Format the range A3:F8 using the AutoFormat command on the Format menu as follows: (a) Select the range A3:F8 and then apply the table format Accounting 1; and (b) with the range A3:F8 still selected, apply the table format Colorful 2. Excel appends the formats of Colorful 2 to the formats of Accounting 1.
6. Select the range A3:E7 and then use the Chart Wizard button on the Standard toolbar to draw a Clustered column with a 3-D visual effect chart (column 1, row 2 in Chart sub-type list). Move the chart to the upper-left corner of cell A10 and then drag the lower-right corner of the chart location to cell F21. If all the labels along the horizontal axis do not display as shown in Figure 1-81, select a cell in column F, click Format on the menu bar, point to Column on the Format menu, click Width on the Column submenu, increase the column width by two or more units, and then click the OK button.
7. Enter your name, course, laboratory assignment number, date, and instructor name in cells A24 through A28.
8. Save the workbook using the file name Madonna's Virtual Sojourn Annual Sales Analysis.
9. Print the worksheet.
10. Make the following two corrections to the sales amounts: $596,321.75 for Bahamas sales by telephone (cell C6), $157,390.58 for Key West sales by mail (cell E4). After you enter the corrections, the company totals should equal $7,599,460.15 in cell F8.
11. Print the revised worksheet. Close the workbook without saving the changes.

2 Razor Sharp Scooter 3rd Quarter Expenses Worksheet

Problem: As the chief accountant for Razor Sharp Scooter, Inc., the vice president has asked you to create a worksheet to analyze the 3rd quarter expenses for the company by department and expense category (Figure 1-82). The expenses for the 3rd quarter are shown in Table 1-10.

Table 1-10 Razor Sharp Scooter 3rd Quarter Expenses

	FINANCE	*HELP DESK*	*MARKETING*	*SALES*	*SYSTEMS*
Benefits	12378.23	11934.21	15823.10	10301.60	4123.89
Travel	23761.45	15300.89	6710.35	18430.15	6510.25
Wages	18001.27	13235.50	17730.58	12000.45	20931.53
Other	6145.20	3897.21	4910.45	8914.34	1201.56

Instructions: Perform the following tasks.

1. Create the worksheet shown in Figure 1-82 on the next page using the data in Table 1-10.
2. Direct Excel to determine totals expenses for the five departments, the totals for each expense category, and the company total.
3. Format the worksheet title, Razor Sharp Scooter, in 24-point Arial bold violet font, and center it across columns A through G.
4. Format the worksheet subtitle, 3rd Quarter Expenses, in 18-point Arial bold violet font, and center it across columns A through G.

(continued)

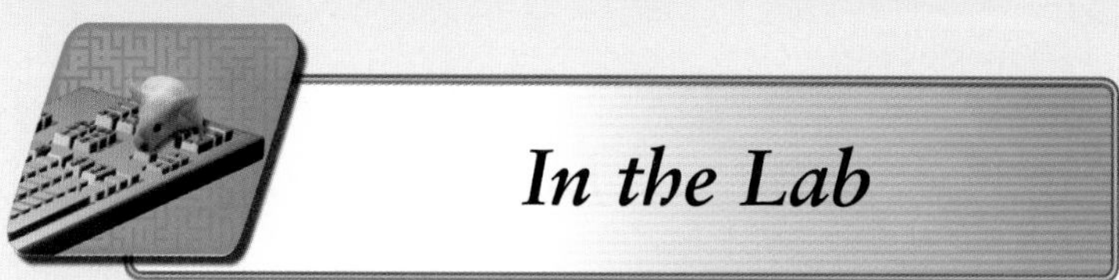

Razor Sharp Scooter 3rd Quarter Expenses Worksheet *(continued)*

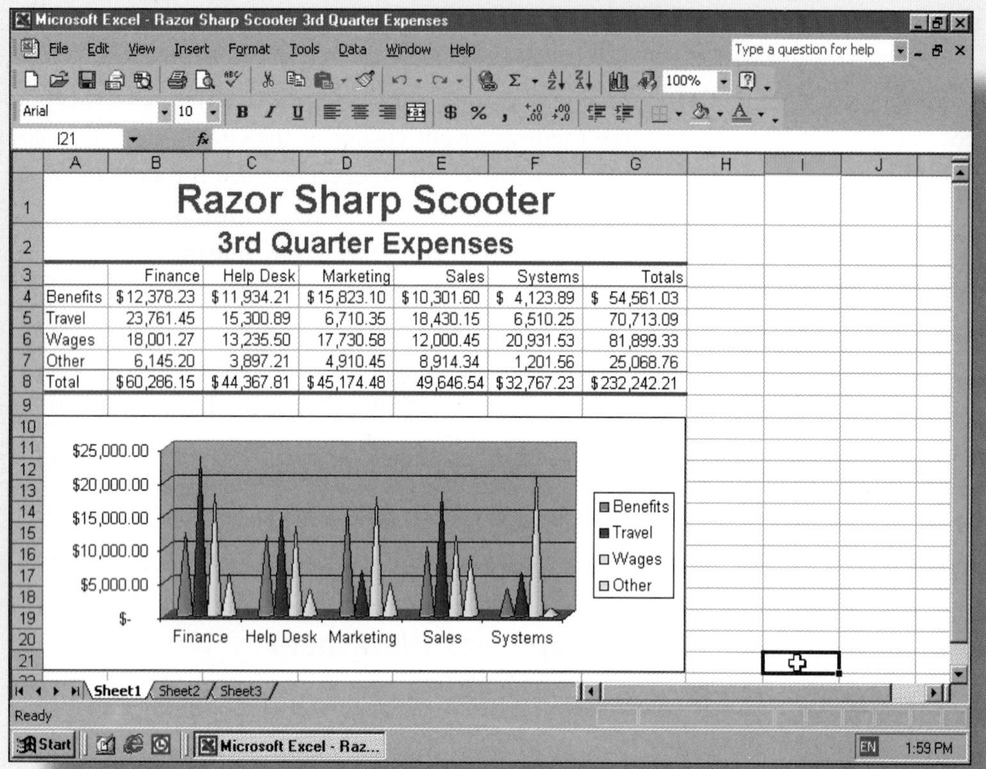

FIGURE 1-82

5. Use the AutoFormat command on the Format menu to format the range A3:G8. Use the table format Accounting 2.
6. Use the ChartWizard button on the Standard toolbar to draw the 3-D Cone chart (column 1, row 1 in the Chart sub-type list), as shown in Figure 1-82. Chart the range A3:F7 and use the chart location A10:G21. If all the labels along the horizontal axis do not display as shown in Figure 1-82, select a cell in column G, click Format on the menu bar, point to Column on the Format menu, click Width on the Column submenu, increase the column width by two or more units, and then click the OK button.
7. Enter your name, course, laboratory assignment number, date, and instructor name in cells A24 through A28.
8. Save the workbook using the file name, Razor Sharp Scooter 3rd Quarter Expenses. Print the worksheet.
9. Two corrections to the expenses were sent in from the accounting department. The correct expenses are $22,537.43 for wages in the Finance department and $21,962.75 for travel in the Sales department. After you enter the two corrections, the company total should equal $240,310.97 in cell G8. Print the revised worksheet.
10. Use the Undo button to change the worksheet back to the original numbers in Table 1-10. Use the Redo button to change the worksheet back to the revised state.
11. Hand in all printouts to your instructor. Close the workbook without saving the changes.

In the Lab

3 College Cash Flow Analysis Worksheet

Problem: Attending college is an expensive proposition and your resources are limited. To plan for your four-year college career, you have decided to organize your anticipated resources and expenses in a worksheet. The data required to prepare your worksheet is shown in Table 1-11.

Table 1-11 College Cash Flow Analysis

RESOURCES	*FRESHMAN*	*SOPHOMORE*	*JUNIOR*	*SENIOR*
Financial Aid	5,025.00	5326.50	5646.09	5984.86
Job	1,525.00	1616.50	1713.49	1816.30
Parents	2,600.00	2756.00	2921.36	3096.64
Savings	1,100.00	1166.00	1235.96	1310.12
EXPENSES	*FRESHMAN*	*SOPHOMORE*	*JUNIOR*	*SENIOR*
Clothes	540.00	572.40	606.74	643.15
Entertainment	725.00	768.50	814.61	863.49
Miscellaneous	355.00	376.30	398.88	422.81
Room & Board	3480.00	3688.80	3910.13	4144.74
Tuition & Books	5150.00	5459.00	5786.54	6133.73

Part 1 Instructions: Using the numbers in Table 1-11, follow the steps below to create the worksheet shown in columns A through F in Figure 1-83 on the next page.

1. Enter the worksheet title in cell A1 and the section titles, Resources and Expenses, in cells A2 and A9, respectively.
2. Use the AutoSum button to calculate the totals in rows 8 and 16 and column F.
3. Increase the font in the worksheet title to 24 and change its color to red. Center the worksheet title in cell A1 across columns A through F. Increase the font size in the table titles in cells A2 and A9 to 18 and change their color to green.
4. Format the range A3:F8 using the AutoFormat command on the Format menu as follows: (a) Select the range A3:F8 and then apply the table format Accounting 1; and (b) with the range A3:F8 still selected, apply the table format List 1. Format the range A10:F16 using the AutoFormat command on the Format menu as follows: (a) Select the range A10:F16 and then apply the table format Accounting 1; and (b) with the range A3:F8 still selected, apply the table format List 1.
5. Enter your name in cell A19 and your course, laboratory assignment number, date, and instructor name in cells A20 through A23. Save the workbook using the file name, College Resources and Expenses.
6. Print the worksheet in landscape orientation. You print in landscape orientation by clicking Landscape on the Page tab in the Page Setup dialog box. Click Page Setup on the File menu to display the Page Setup dialog box. Click the Save button on the Standard toolbar to save the workbook with the new print settings.
7. All Junior-year expenses in column D increased by $500. Re-enter the new Junior-year expenses. Change the financial aid for the Junior year by the amount required to cover the increase in expenses. The totals in cells F8 and F16 should equal $47,339.82. Print the worksheet. Close the workbook without saving changes. Hand in the two printouts to your instructor.

(continued)

In the Lab

College Cash Flow Analysis Worksheet *(continued)*

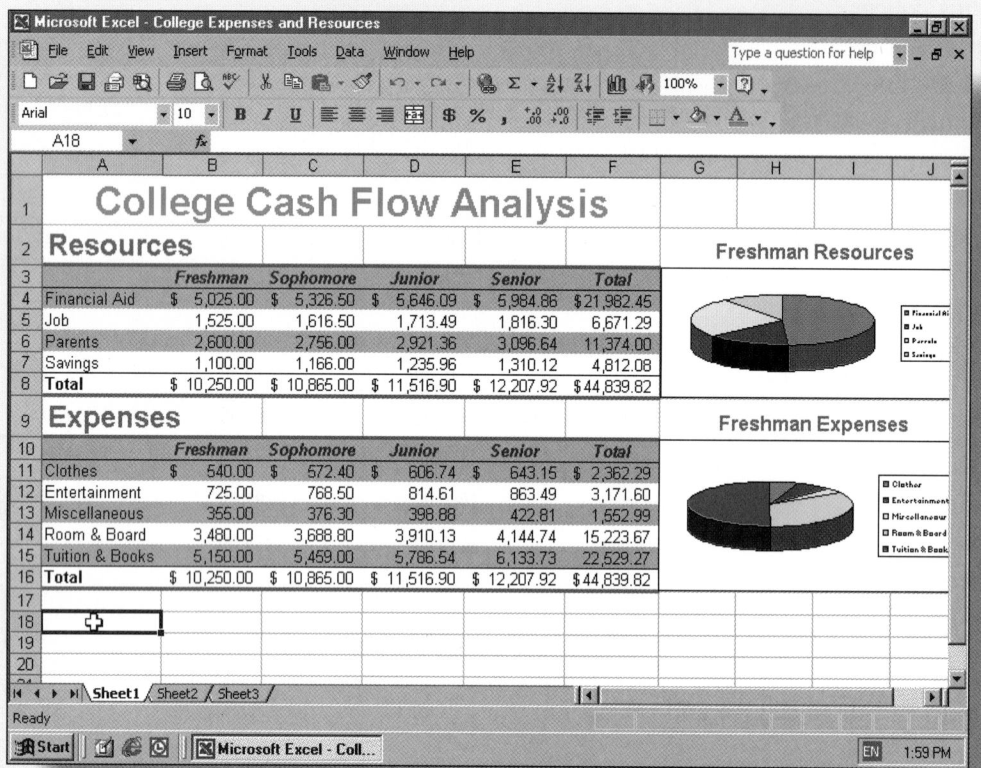

	A	B	C	D	E	F
1	College Cash Flow Analysis					
2	Resources					
3		Freshman	Sophomore	Junior	Senior	Total
4	Financial Aid	$ 5,025.00	$ 5,326.50	$ 5,646.09	$ 5,984.86	$21,982.45
5	Job	1,525.00	1,616.50	1,713.49	1,816.30	6,671.29
6	Parents	2,600.00	2,756.00	2,921.36	3,096.64	11,374.00
7	Savings	1,100.00	1,166.00	1,235.96	1,310.12	4,812.08
8	Total	$ 10,250.00	$ 10,865.00	$ 11,516.90	$ 12,207.92	$44,839.82
9	Expenses					
10		Freshman	Sophomore	Junior	Senior	Total
11	Clothes	$ 540.00	$ 572.40	$ 606.74	$ 643.15	$ 2,362.29
12	Entertainment	725.00	768.50	814.61	863.49	3,171.60
13	Miscellaneous	355.00	376.30	398.88	422.81	1,552.99
14	Room & Board	3,480.00	3,688.80	3,910.13	4,144.74	15,223.67
15	Tuition & Books	5,150.00	5,459.00	5,786.54	6,133.73	22,529.27
16	Total	$ 10,250.00	$ 10,865.00	$ 11,516.90	$ 12,207.92	$44,839.82

FIGURE 1-83

Part 2 Instructions: Open the workbook College Resources and Expenses created in Part 1. Draw a 3-D Pie chart in the range G3:J8 that shows the contribution of each category of resource for the freshman year. Chart the range A4:B7. Add the Pie chart title shown in cell G2 in Figure 1-83. Change the Pie chart title's font to 12-point, bold green. Center the Pie chart title over the range G2:J2. Draw a 3-D Pie chart in the range G10:J16 that shows the contribution of each category of expense for the Freshman year. Chart the range A11:B15. Add the Pie chart title shown in cell G9 in Figure 1-83. Change the Pie chart title's font to 12-point, bold green. Center the Pie chart title over the range G9:J9. Save the workbook using the file name, College Resources and Expenses 2. Print the worksheet. Hand in the printout to your instructor.

Part 3 Instructions: Open the workbook College Resources and Expenses 2 created in Part 2. A close inspection of Table 1-11 on the previous page shows a 6% increase each year over the previous year. Use the Ask a Question box on the menu bar to learn how to enter the data for the last three years using a formula and the Copy command. For example, the formula to enter in cell C4 is =B4 * 1.06. Enter formulas to replace all the numbers in the range C4:E7 and C11:E15. If necessary, reformat the tables as described in Part 1. The worksheet should appear as shown in Figure 1-83, except that some of the totals will be off by 0.01 due to round-off errors. Save the worksheet using the file name, College Resources and Expenses 3. Print the worksheet. Press CTRL+ACCENT (`) to display the formulas. Print the formulas version. Hand in both printouts to your instructor.

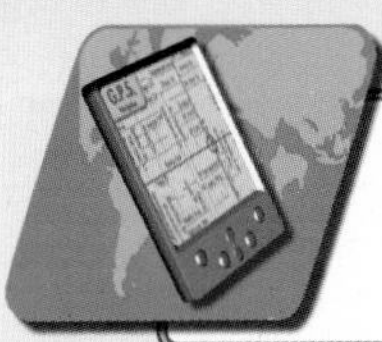

Cases and Places

The difficulty of these case studies varies:
▶ are the least difficult; ▶▶ are more difficult; and ▶▶▶ are the most difficult.

1 ▶ You work part time for Kylie's Pet Shop. Your primary responsibilities include caring for the pets. Your manager, Elma Presley, recently learned that you are enrolled in a computer class. She has asked you to prepare a worksheet and chart to help her analyze the 3rd quarter sales by store and by pet (Table 1-12). Use the concepts and techniques presented in this project to create the worksheet and chart.

Table 1-12 Kylie's Pet Shop 3rd Quarter Sales

	BOSTON	*CLEVELAND*	*SAN DIEGO*	*DALLAS*
Birds	16734	17821	24123	17989
Cats	15423	12134	16574	33401
Dogs	13495	26291	17345	27098
Fish	25462	22923	28034	25135

2 ▶ Computer Discount Sales sells computers throughout the state of Indiana. The number of servers, desktop computers, notebook computers, and handheld computers sold has increased each year from 1998 through 2002, as indicated in Table 1-13. Create a worksheet and 3-D Column chart that illustrates these increases. Use the concepts and techniques presented in this project to create the worksheet and chart.

Table 1-13 Computer Discount Sales 1998-2002

	SERVERS	*DESKTOPS*	*NOTEBOOKS*	*HANDHELDS*
1998	7323	22231	6125	225
1999	7498	32356	26315	1257
2000	7615	38489	36727	13313
2001	7734	42501	46501	24407
2002	7944	52578	56623	26761

3 ▶ As a newspaper reporter, you are preparing an article on the coming election based on a recent survey of the electorate, arranged by age of those polled (Table 1-14). You have been asked to produce a worksheet to accompany your article. Use the concepts and techniques presented in this project to create the worksheet and an embedded Column chart.

Table 1-14 Valley Heights Mayoral Race Election Poll Results

	18-29	*30-41*	*42-53*	*54-65*	*66+*
Groen	625	301	512	440	205
Sabol	235	279	357	213	410
Walker	462	732	433	176	399
Webb	724	521	321	835	276

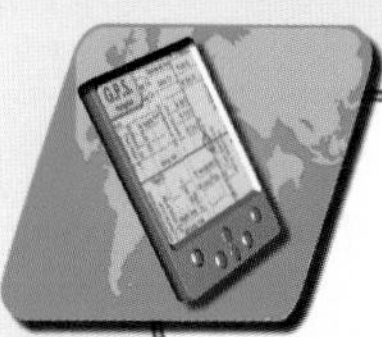

Cases and Places

4 ▶ Alyssa's Boutique on 5th Avenue in New York sells costume jewelry to an exclusive clientele. The company is trying to decide whether it is feasible to open another boutique in the Boston area. You have been asked to develop a worksheet totaling all the revenue received last year from customers living in the Boston area. The revenue from customers living in the Boston area by quarter is: Quarter 1, $104,561.38; Quarter 2, $91,602.55; Quarter 3, $258,220.10; and Quarter 4, $333,725.25. Create a 3-D Pie chart to illustrate Boston-area revenue contribution by quarter. Use the AutoCalculate area to find the average quarterly revenue.

5 ▶▶ The Virtual Reality Theater is a movie house that shows virtual reality movies at weekday evening, weekend matinee, and weekend evening screenings. Three types of tickets are sold at each presentation: general admission, senior citizen, and children. The theater management has asked you to prepare a worksheet, based on the revenue from a typical week, that can be used in reevaluating its ticket structure. During an average week, weekday evening shows generate $9,835 from general admission ticket sales, $5,630 from senior citizen ticket sales, and $1,675 from children ticket sales. Weekend matinee shows make $7,250 from general admission ticket sales, $2,345 from senior citizen ticket sales, and $3,300 from children ticket sales. Weekend evening shows earn $9,230 from general admission ticket sales, $8,125 from senior citizen ticket sales, and $1,600 from children ticket sales. Use the concepts and techniques presented in this project to prepare a worksheet that includes total revenues for each type of ticket and for each presentation time, and a Bar chart illustrating ticket revenues.

6 ▶▶▶ Athletic footwear stores must track carefully the sales of their different shoe brands so they can restock their inventory promptly. Visit an athletic shoe store and make a list of the top five brands of running shoes. Find out how many of each brand was sold each of the last three months. Using this information, create a worksheet showing the number of each brand sold each month, the total number of running shoes sold each month, the total number of each brand sold over three months, and a total number of all running shoes sold over three months. Include a 3-D Column chart to illustrate the data.

7 ▶▶▶ Visit the Registrar's office at your school and obtain the ages of students majoring in at least five different academic departments this semester. Separate the ages of the students in the departments by four different age groups. Using this information, create a worksheet showing the number of attending students by age group in each department. Include totals and a 3-D Column chart.

Microsoft Excel 2002

PROJECT 2

Formulas, Functions, Formatting, and Web Queries

OBJECTIVES

You will have mastered the material in this project when you can:

- Enter multiple lines of text in the same cell
- Enter a formula using the keyboard
- Enter formulas using Point mode
- Identify the arithmetic operators +, –, *, /, %, and ^
- Recognize smart tags
- Apply the AVERAGE, MAX, and MIN functions
- Determine a percentage
- Verify a formula using Range Finder
- Change the font of a cell
- Color the characters and background of a cell
- Add borders to a range
- Format numbers using the Format Cells dialog box
- Add conditional formatting to a range of cells
- Align text in cells
- Change the width of a column and height of a row
- Check the spelling of a worksheet
- Preview how a printed copy of the worksheet will look
- Distinguish between portrait and landscape orientation
- Print a partial or complete worksheet
- Display and print the formulas version of a worksheet
- Print to fit
- Use a Web query to get real-time data from a Web site
- Rename sheets
- E-mail the active workbook from within Excel

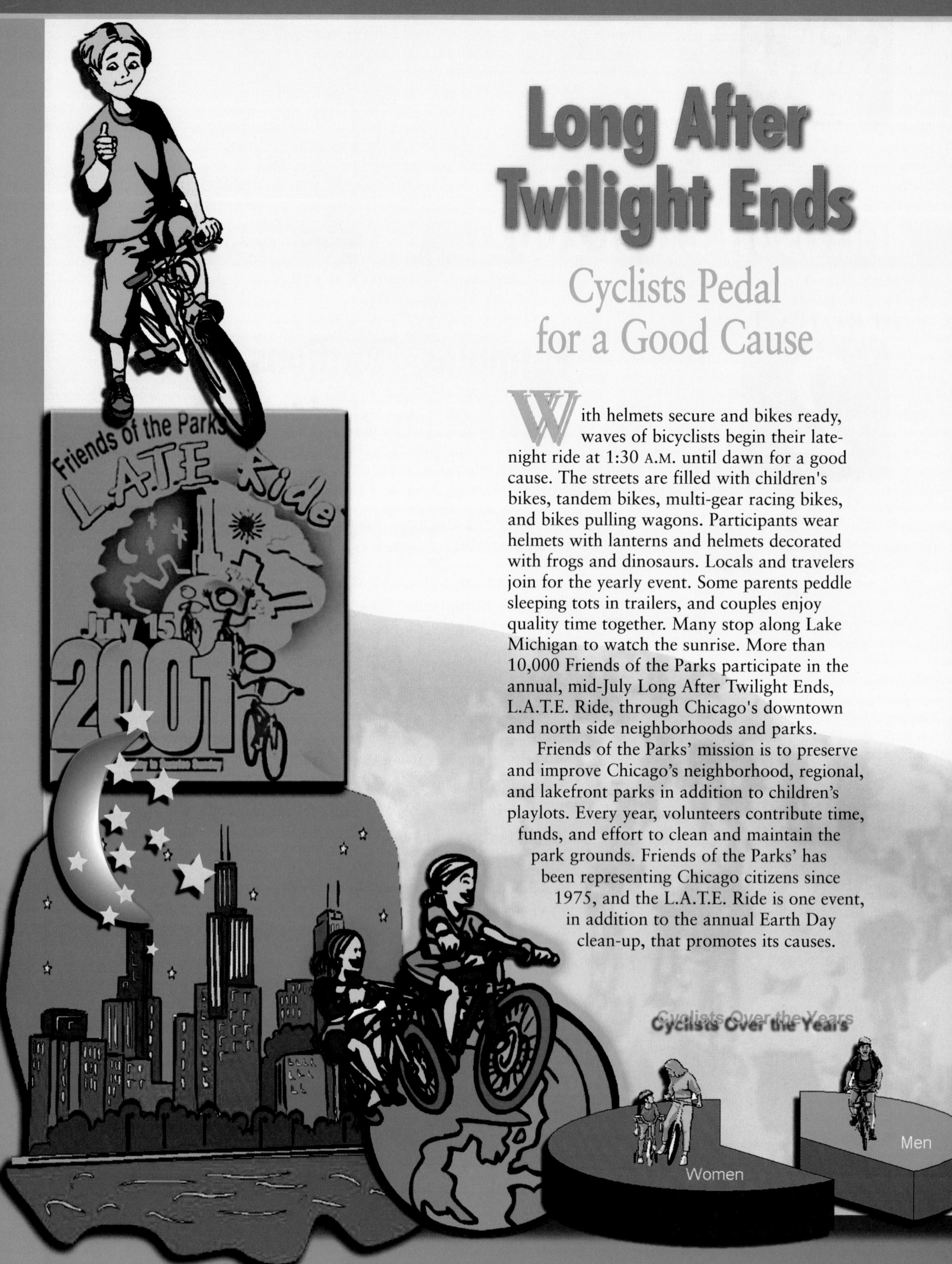

Long After Twilight Ends

Cyclists Pedal for a Good Cause

With helmets secure and bikes ready, waves of bicyclists begin their late-night ride at 1:30 A.M. until dawn for a good cause. The streets are filled with children's bikes, tandem bikes, multi-gear racing bikes, and bikes pulling wagons. Participants wear helmets with lanterns and helmets decorated with frogs and dinosaurs. Locals and travelers join for the yearly event. Some parents peddle sleeping tots in trailers, and couples enjoy quality time together. Many stop along Lake Michigan to watch the sunrise. More than 10,000 Friends of the Parks participate in the annual, mid-July Long After Twilight Ends, L.A.T.E. Ride, through Chicago's downtown and north side neighborhoods and parks.

Friends of the Parks' mission is to preserve and improve Chicago's neighborhood, regional, and lakefront parks in addition to children's playlots. Every year, volunteers contribute time, funds, and effort to clean and maintain the park grounds. Friends of the Parks' has been representing Chicago citizens since 1975, and the L.A.T.E. Ride is one event, in addition to the annual Earth Day clean-up, that promotes its causes.

So how does the Friends of the Parks' organization attempt to manage and organize information about the more than 10,000 participants who take part in the L.A.T.E. Ride event each year? Staff, many of whom volunteer their time and expertise, use worksheets to organize, chart, and present all types of data with relative ease. They analyze and manipulate data; specifically, they input numbers and enter formulas to determine averages and percentages, as well as find the minimum and maximum numbers in a series. In addition, they create traditional Pie charts, Column charts, and other chart forms to represent the data visually.

If they want to determine the demographics of the L.A.T.E. bike riders, they input participants' ages taken from a Friends of the Parks' survey and let the worksheet generate Pie charts depicting the age breakdowns. Moreover, they can create a Column chart showing the number of participants from year to year. The Friends of the Parks' also can track how many participants live in Chicago, the suburbs, or other states and the number of male and female cyclists.

You will perform similar tasks in this project when you create a worksheet for the Greenback Stock Club. You will enter formulas, use the AVERAGE, MAX, and MIN functions, and then verify the formulas for accuracy.

The L.A.T.E. Ride was established in 1989 with 350 cyclists; today more than 10,000 bike riders have participated. It is not by sheer coincidence that the numbers have escalated dramatically. Once the staff at the Friends of the Parks' collects survey data, they then input the numbers into worksheets using ranges of numbers, enter formulas, and apply formats for appropriate charts. Such data is important to determine marketing strategies or finalize the total number of glow-in-the-dark T-shirts and number tags needed for the participants to don for the ride.

Join the people of the Windy City who pedal for the parks in Chicago's only 25-mile nocturnal bicycling event by visiting The L.A.T.E. Ride Web site at lateride.org

Microsoft Excel 2002

Formulas, Functions, Formatting, and Web Queries

CASE PERSPECTIVE

Several years ago, while in college, Abby Lane and five of her friends started Greenback Stock Club. The friends decided to focus on researching and investing in well established companies. Every month, they invested $25 each, researched an assigned company, and came to the meeting with their buy and sell recommendations.

All have graduated from college, are married, and are living in different parts of the country. They still invest in the stock market and have increased their monthly contributions to $100 each.

The value of the club's portfolio, or group of investments, recently surpassed the $300,000.00 mark. As a result, the members voted unanimously to purchase a new computer and a copy of Microsoft Office XP for Abby, the club's permanent treasurer. With Excel, she plans to create a worksheet summarizing the club's stock activities that she can e-mail to the club members. She wants to use its Web query capabilities to access real-time stock quotes. Abby has asked you to show her how to create the workbook and access real-time stock quotes over the Internet using Excel.

Introduction

In Project 1, you learned how to enter data, sum values, make the worksheet easier to read, and draw a chart. You also learned about online Help and saving, printing, and opening a workbook from a floppy disk. This project continues to emphasize these topics and presents some new ones.

The new topics include formulas, smart tags, verifying formulas, changing fonts, adding borders, formatting numbers and text, conditional formatting, changing the widths of columns and heights of rows, spell checking, e-mailing from within an application, and alternative types of worksheet displays and printouts. One alternative display and printout shows the formulas rather than the values in the worksheet. When you display the formulas in the worksheet, you see exactly what text, data, formulas, and functions you have entered into it. Finally, this project covers Web queries to obtain real-time data from a Web site.

Project Two — Greenback Stock Club

The summary notes from your meeting with Abby include the following: need, source of data, calculations, and Web requirements.

Need: An easy-to-read worksheet that summarizes the club's investments (Figure 2-1a). For each stock, the worksheet is to include the stock name, stock symbol, date acquired, number of shares, initial price per share, initial cost, current price per share, current value, gain/loss, and percent gain/loss. Abby also has requested that the worksheet include totals and the average, highest value, and lowest value for each column of numbers. Finally, Abby wants to use Excel to access real-time stock quotes using Web queries (Figure 2-1b).

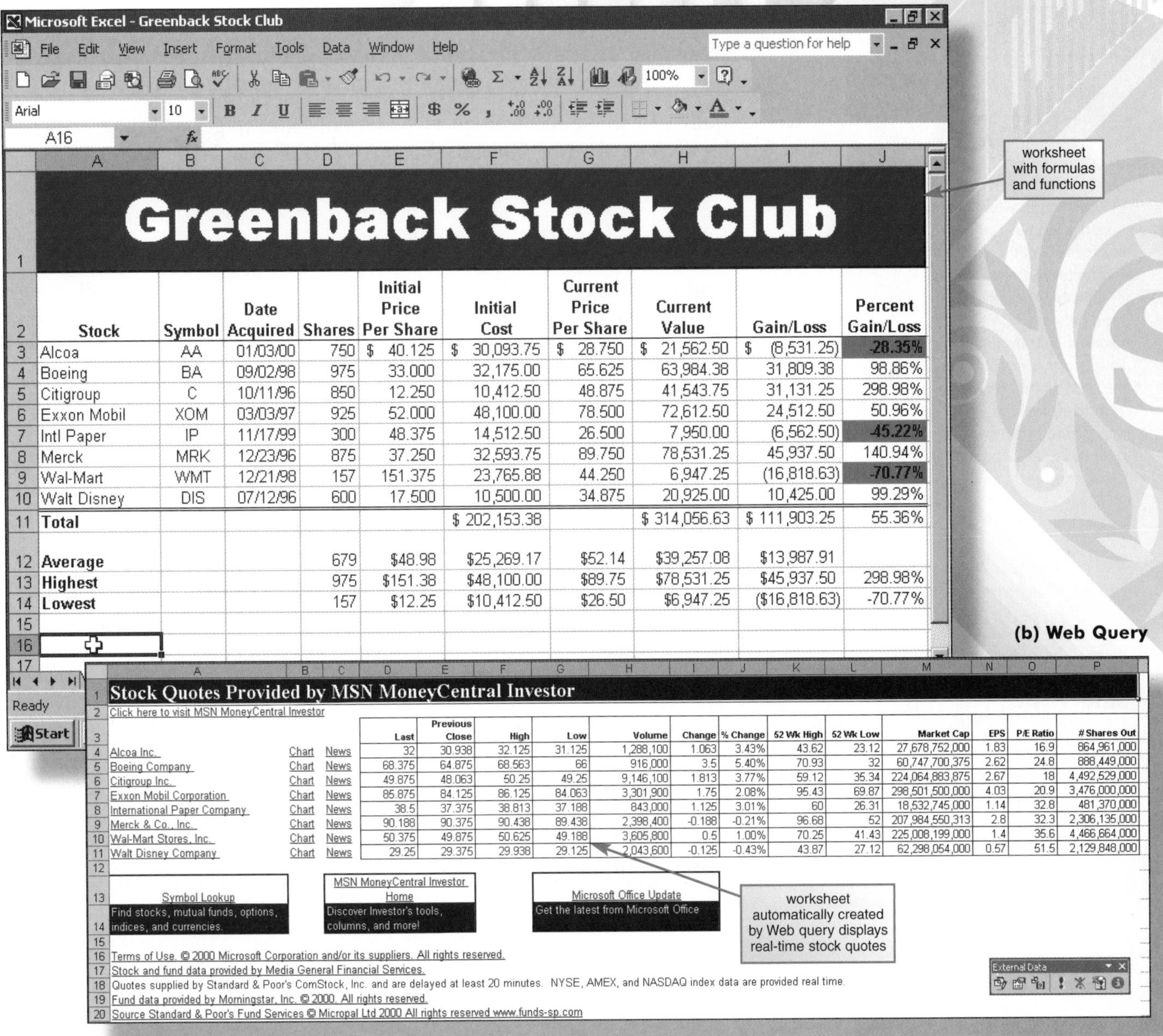

Greenback Stock Club

	Stock	Symbol	Date Acquired	Shares	Initial Price Per Share	Initial Cost	Current Price Per Share	Current Value	Gain/Loss	Percent Gain/Loss
3	Alcoa	AA	01/03/00	750	$ 40.125	$ 30,093.75	$ 28.750	$ 21,562.50	$ (8,531.25)	-28.35%
4	Boeing	BA	09/02/98	975	33.000	32,175.00	65.625	63,984.38	31,809.38	98.86%
5	Citigroup	C	10/11/96	850	12.250	10,412.50	48.875	41,543.75	31,131.25	298.98%
6	Exxon Mobil	XOM	03/03/97	925	52.000	48,100.00	78.500	72,612.50	24,512.50	50.96%
7	Intl Paper	IP	11/17/99	300	48.375	14,512.50	26.500	7,950.00	(6,562.50)	-45.22%
8	Merck	MRK	12/23/96	875	37.250	32,593.75	89.750	78,531.25	45,937.50	140.94%
9	Wal-Mart	WMT	12/21/98	157	151.375	23,765.88	44.250	6,947.25	(16,818.63)	-70.77%
10	Walt Disney	DIS	07/12/96	600	17.500	10,500.00	34.875	20,925.00	10,425.00	99.29%
11	Total					$ 202,153.38		$ 314,056.63	$ 111,903.25	55.36%
12	Average			679	$48.98	$25,269.17	$52.14	$39,257.08	$13,987.91	
13	Highest			975	$151.38	$48,100.00	$89.75	$78,531.25	$45,937.50	298.98%
14	Lowest			157	$12.25	$10,412.50	$26.50	$6,947.25	($16,818.63)	-70.77%

Stock Quotes Provided by MSN MoneyCentral Investor

Click here to visit MSN MoneyCentral Investor

			Last	Previous Close	High	Low	Volume	Change	% Change	52 Wk High	52 Wk Low	Market Cap	EPS	P/E Ratio	# Shares Out
Alcoa Inc.	Chart	News	32	30.938	32.125	31.125	1,288,100	1.063	3.43%	43.62	23.12	27,678,752,000	1.83	16.9	864,961,000
Boeing Company	Chart	News	68.375	64.875	68.563	66	916,000	3.5	5.40%	70.93	32	60,747,700,375	2.62	24.8	888,449,000
Citigroup Inc.	Chart	News	49.875	48.063	50.25	49.25	9,146,100	1.813	3.77%	59.12	35.34	224,064,883,875	2.67	18	4,492,529,000
Exxon Mobil Corporation	Chart	News	85.875	84.125	86.125	84.063	3,301,900	1.75	2.08%	95.43	69.87	298,501,500,000	4.03	20.9	3,476,000,000
International Paper Company	Chart	News	38.5	37.375	38.813	37.188	843,000	1.125	3.01%	60	26.31	18,532,745,000	1.14	32.8	481,370,000
Merck & Co., Inc.	Chart	News	90.188	90.375	90.438	89.438	2,398,400	-0.188	-0.21%	96.68	52	207,984,550,313	2.8	32.3	2,306,135,000
Wal-Mart Stores, Inc.	Chart	News	50.375	49.875	50.625	49.188	3,605,800	0.5	1.00%	70.25	41.43	225,008,199,000	1.4	35.6	4,466,664,000
Walt Disney Company	Chart	News	29.25	29.375	29.938	29.125	2,043,600	-0.125	-0.43%	43.87	27.12	62,298,054,000	0.57	51.5	2,129,848,000

Symbol Lookup
Find stocks, mutual funds, options, indices, and currencies.

MSN MoneyCentral Investor Home
Discover Investor's tools, columns, and more!

Microsoft Office Update
Get the latest from Microsoft Office

Terms of Use. © 2000 Microsoft Corporation and/or its suppliers. All rights reserved.
Stock and fund data provided by Media General Financial Services.
Quotes supplied by Standard & Poor's ComStock, Inc. and are delayed at least 20 minutes. NYSE, AMEX, and NASDAQ index data are provided real time.
Fund data provided by Morningstar, Inc. © 2000. All rights reserved.
Source Standard & Poor's Fund Services © Micropal Ltd 2000 All rights reserved www.funds-sp.com

FIGURE 2-1

Source of Data: The data supplied by Abby includes the stock names, symbols, dates acquired, number of shares, initial price per share, and current price per share. This data is shown in Table 2-1.

Calculations: The following calculations must be made for each of the stocks:

1. Initial Cost = Shares × Initial Price Per Share
2. Current Value = Shares × Current Price Per Share
3. Gain/Loss = Current Value – Initial Cost
4. Percent Gain/Loss = $\frac{\text{Gain/Loss}}{\text{Initial Cost}}$
5. Compute the totals for initial cost, current value, and gain/loss.
6. Use the AVERAGE function to determine the average for the number of shares, initial price per share, initial cost per share, current price per share, current value, and gain/loss.
7. Use the MAX and MIN functions to determine the highest and lowest values for the number of shares, initial price per share, initial cost per share, current price per share, current value, gain/loss, and percent gain/loss.

Web Requirements: Use the Web query feature of Excel to get real-time stock quotes for the stocks owned by Greenback Stock Club (Figure 2-1b on the previous page).

Starting Excel

When you launch Excel, you can alter its behavior using a command-line switch. For example, /e opens Excel without opening a new workbook; /l starts Excel with a maximized window; /p "folder" sets the active path to folder–ignoring the default folder; /r "filename" opens filename in read-only mode; /s starts Excel in safe mode. To set a temporary command line, click the Start button on the Windows Taskbar and click Run. Then, enter the complete path to Excel's application file, Excel.exe, and the switch.

Web Queries and Smart Tags

Thinking about dabbling in the stock market? If so, you will find Excel's Web Queries and smart tags to be an invaluable tool. Both features can return near real-time stock quotes and links to breaking news. For example, smart tags recognize a stock symbol, such as MSFT, in a cell if you have the Smart Tag technology enabled (see page E 2.77).

Starting and Customizing Excel

To start and customize Excel, Windows must be running. Perform the following steps to start Excel. Once the Excel window opens, steps 3 through 5 close the task pane, minimize the Language bar, and ensure that the Standard and Formatting toolbars display on two rows.

TO START AND CUSTOMIZE EXCEL

1. Click the Start button on the Windows taskbar, point to Programs on the Start menu, and then click Microsoft Excel on the Programs submenu.
2. If the Excel window is not maximized, double-click its title bar to maximize it.
3. If the New Workbook task pane displays, click the Show at startup check box at the bottom of the task pane to remove the check mark and then click the Close button in the upper-right corner to close the task pane.
4. If the Language bar displays, click its Minimize button.
5. If the Standard and Formatting toolbars display on one row, click the Toolbar Options button on the right side of either toolbar and then click Show Buttons on Two Rows on the Toolbar Options menu.

The Excel window with the Standard and Formatting toolbars on two rows displays as shown in Figure 2-1a on the previous page.

Entering the Titles and Numbers into the Worksheet

The worksheet title in Figure 2-1a on the previous page is centered across columns A through J in row 1. Because the centered text first must be entered into the leftmost column of the area across which it is centered, it will be entered into cell A1, as shown in the following steps.

TO ENTER THE WORKSHEET TITLE

1. Select cell A1. Type `Greenback Stock Club` in the cell.
2. Press the DOWN ARROW key.

The worksheet title displays in cell A1 as shown in Figure 2-2 on page E 2.09.

The column titles in row 2 begin in cell A2 and extend through cell J2. As shown in Figure 2-1a, the column titles in row 2 include multiple lines of text. To start a new line in a cell, press ALT+ENTER after each line, except for the last line, which is completed by clicking the Enter box, pressing the ENTER key, or pressing one of the arrow keys. When you see ALT+ENTER in a step, while holding down the ALT key, press the ENTER key and then release both keys.

The stock names and the row titles Total, Average, Highest, and Lowest in column A begin in cell A3 and continue down to cell A14.

The stock club's investments are summarized in Table 2-1. These numbers are entered into rows 3 through 10. The steps required to enter the column titles, stock names and symbols, total row titles, and numbers as shown in Figure 2-2 on page E 2.09 are explained in the remainder of this section.

Table 2-1 Greenback Stock Club Portfolio

STOCK	SYMBOL	DATE ACQUIRED	SHARES	INITIAL PRICE PER SHARE	CURRENT PRICE PER SHARE
Alcoa	AA	01/03/2000	750	40.125	28.75
Boeing	BA	09/02/1998	975	33.00	65.625
Citigroup	C	10/11/1996	850	12.25	48.875
Exxon Mobil	XOM	03/03/1997	925	52.00	78.5
Intl Paper	IP	11/17/1999	300	48.375	26.5
Merck	MRK	12/23/1996	875	37.25	89.75
Wal-Mart	WMT	12/21/1998	157	151.375	44.25
Walt Disney	DIS	07/12/1996	600	17.50	34.875

TO ENTER THE COLUMN TITLES

1. With cell A2 selected, type `Stock` and then press the RIGHT ARROW key.
2. Type `Symbol` and then press the RIGHT ARROW key.
3. Type `Date` and then press ALT+ENTER. Type `Acquired` and then press the RIGHT ARROW key.
4. Type `Shares` and then press the RIGHT ARROW key.

More About

Wrapping Text

If you have a long text entry, such as a paragraph, you can instruct Excel to wrap the text in a cell, rather than pressing ALT+ENTER to end a line. To wrap text, click Format Cells on the shortcut menu, click the Alignment tab, and click the Wrap Text check box. Excel will automatically increase the height of the cell so the additional lines will fit. However, if you want to control the contents of a line in a cell, rather than letting Excel wrap based on the width of a cell, then you must end a line with ALT+ENTER.

More About

Formatting a Worksheet

With early worksheet packages, users often skipped rows to improve the appearance of the worksheet. With Excel it is not necessary to skip rows because you can increase the height of rows to add white space between information.

5. Type `Initial` and then press ALT+ENTER. Type `Price` and then press ALT+ENTER. Type `Per Share` and then press the RIGHT ARROW key.
6. Type `Initial` and then press ALT+ENTER. Type `Cost` and then press the RIGHT ARROW key.
7. Type `Current` and then press ALT+ENTER. Type `Price` and then press ALT+ENTER. Type `Per Share` and then press the RIGHT ARROW key.
8. Type `Current` and then press ALT+ENTER. Type `Value` and then press the RIGHT ARROW key.
9. Type `Gain/Loss` and press the RIGHT ARROW key.
10. Type `Percent` and then press ALT+ENTER. Type `Gain/Loss` and then click cell A3.

The column titles display as shown in row 2 of Figure 2-2. When you press ALT+ENTER to add more lines to a cell, Excel automatically increases the height of the entire row.

Two-Digit Years

When you enter a two-digit year value, and the Short date format under Regional Options in Control Panel is set to M/dd/yyyy, Excel changes a two-digit year prior to 30 to 20xx and a two-digit year of 30 and greater to 19xx. Use four-digit years to ensure that Excel interprets year values the way you intend.

The stock data in Table 2-1 on the previous page includes a date on which each stock was acquired. Excel considers a date to be a number and, therefore, displays it right-aligned in the cell.

The following steps describe how to enter the stock data shown in Table 2-1 on the previous page, which includes dates. The dates in column C will be formatted later in this project to a two-digit year.

TO ENTER THE STOCK DATA

1. With cell A3 selected, type `Alcoa` and then press the RIGHT ARROW key. Type `AA` and then press the RIGHT ARROW key.
2. With cell C3 selected, type `01/03/2000` and then press the RIGHT ARROW key. Type `750` and then press the RIGHT ARROW key.
3. With cell E3 selected, type `40.125` and then press the RIGHT ARROW key twice. Type `28.75` and then press the ENTER key.
4. Click cell A4. Enter the data in Table 2-1 for the seven remaining stocks in rows 4 through 10.

The stock data displays in rows 3 through 10 as shown in Figure 2-2.

Entering Numbers into a Range

An efficient way to enter data into a range of cells, is first to select a range. Enter the number that you want to assign to the upper-left cell of the range. Excel responds by entering the value and moving the active cell selection down one cell. When you enter the last value in the first column, Excel moves to the top of the next column.

TO ENTER THE TOTAL ROW TITLES

1. Click cell A11. Type `Total` and then press the DOWN ARROW key. With cell A12 selected, type `Average` and then press the DOWN ARROW key.
2. With cell A13 selected, type `Highest` and then press the DOWN ARROW key. With cell A14 selected, type `Lowest` and then press the ENTER key. Click cell F3.

The total row titles display as shown in Figure 2-2.

FIGURE 2-2

Entering Formulas

The initial cost for each stock, which displays in column F, is equal to the number of shares in column D times the initial price per share in column E. Thus, the initial cost for Alcoa in cell F3 is obtained by multiplying 750 (cell D3) times 40.125 (cell E3).

One of the reasons Excel is such a valuable tool is that you can assign a **formula** to a cell and Excel will calculate the result. Consider, for example, what would happen if you had to multiply 750 × 40.125 and then manually enter the result, 30093.75, in cell F3. Every time the values in cells D3 and E3 changed, you would have to recalculate the product and enter the new value in cell F3. By contrast, if you enter a formula in cell F3 to multiply the values in cells D3 and E3, Excel recalculates the product whenever new values are entered into those cells and displays the result in cell F3. Complete the following steps to enter the initial cost formula in cell F3 using the keyboard.

Automatic Recalculation

Every time you enter a value into a cell in the worksheet, Excel recalculates all formulas. You can change to manual recalculation by clicking Options on the Tools menu and then clicking Manual on the Calculation sheet. In manual calculation mode, press F9 to recalculate.

Steps To Enter a Formula Using the Keyboard

1 **With cell F3 selected, type** =d3*e3 **in the cell.**

The formula displays in the formula bar and in cell F3 (Figure 2-3). Excel displays colored borders around the cells referenced in the formula.

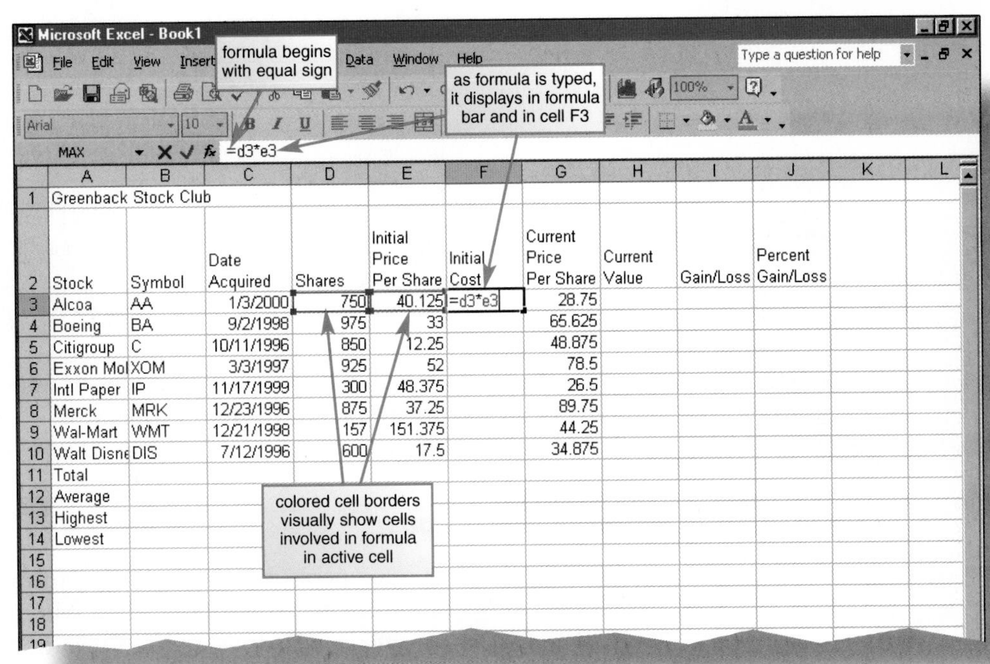

FIGURE 2-3

2 Press the RIGHT ARROW key twice to select cell H3.

Instead of displaying the formula in cell F3, Excel completes the arithmetic operation indicated by th e formula and displays the result, 30093.75 (Figure 2-4).

FIGURE 2-4

Initiating Formulas

Besides the equal sign (=), you can start a formula with a plus sign (+) or a minus sign (-). If you do not begin with one of these three characters, Excel interprets the formula as text.

The equal sign (=) preceding d3*e3 is an important part of the formula: it alerts Excel that you are entering a formula or function and not text. Because the most common error is to mistakenly reference the wrong cell in a formula, Excel colors the borders of the cells selected to visually show which cells you are referencing. The coloring helps in the reviewing process to ensure the cell references are correct.

The asterisk (*) following d3 is the arithmetic operator that directs Excel to perform the multiplication operation. The valid Excel arithmetic operators are described in Table 2-2.

Table 2-2 Summary of Arithmetic Operators

ARITHMETIC OPERATOR	MEANING	EXAMPLE OF USAGE	MEANING
–	Negation	–95	Negative 95
%	Percentage	=65%	Multiplies 65 by 0.01
^	Exponentiation	=3 ^ 4	Raises 3 to the fourth power, which in this example is equal to 81
*	Multiplication	=12.4 * D5	Multiplies the contents of cell D5 by 12.4
/	Division	=J2 / J4	Divides the contents of cell J2 by the contents of cell J4
+	Addition	=2 + 6	Adds 2 and 6
–	Subtraction	=H12 – 29	Subtracts 29 from the contents of cell H12

More About

Troubling Formulas

If Excel does not accept a formula, remove the equal sign from the left side and complete the entry as text. Later, after entering additional data or once you have determined the error, reinsert the equal sign to change the text to a formula.

You can enter the cell references in formulas in uppercase or lowercase, and you can add spaces before and after arithmetic operators to make the formulas easier to read. That is, =d3*e3 is the same as =d3 * e3, =D3 * e3, or =D3 * E3.

Order of Operations

When more than one operator is involved in a formula, Excel follows the same basic order of operations that you use in algebra. Moving from left to right in a formula, the **order of operations** is as follows: first negation (–), then all percentages (%), then all exponentiations (^), then all multiplications (*) and divisions (/), and finally, all additions (+) and subtractions (–).

You can use **parentheses** to override the order of operations. For example, if Excel follows the order of operations, 5 * 6 – 2 equals 28. If you use parentheses, however, to change the formula to 5 * (6 – 2), the result is 20, because the parentheses instruct Excel to subtract 2 from 6 before multiplying by 5. Table 2-3 illustrates several examples of valid formulas and explains the order of operations.

The first formula (=d3*e3) in the worksheet was entered into cell F3 using the keyboard. The next section shows you how to enter the formulas in cells H3 and I3 using the mouse to select cell references in a formula.

Table 2-3 Examples of Excel Formulas

FORMULA	REMARK
=K3	Assigns the value in cell K3 to the active cell.
=24 + – 4^2	Assigns the sum of 24 + 16 (or 40) to the active cell.
=4 * D4 or =D4 * 4 or =(4 * D4)	Assigns four times the contents of cell D4 to the active cell.
=25% * 8	Assigns the product of 0.25 times 8 (or 2) to the active cell.
= – (Q5 * Z17)	Assigns the negative value of the product of the values contained in cells Q5 and Z17 to the active cell.
=3 * (M3 – P2)	Assigns the product of three times the difference between the values contained in cells M3 and P2 to the active cell.
=K5 / Y7 – D6 * L9 + W4 ^ V10	From left to right: first exponentiation (W4 ^ V10), then division (K5 / Y7), then multiplication (D6 * L9), then subtraction (K5 / Y7) – (D6 * L9), and finally addition (K5 / Y7 – D6 * L9) + (W4 ^ V10). If cells K5 = 10, D6 = 6, L9 = 2, W4 = 5, V10 = 2, and Y7 = 2, then Excel assigns the active cell the value 18; that is, 10 / 2 - 6 * 2 + 5 ^ 2 = 18.

Entering Formulas Using Point Mode

In the worksheet shown in Figure 2-1a on page E 2.05, the current value of each stock displays in column H. The current value for Alcoa in cell H3 is equal to the number of shares in cell D3 times the current price per share in cell G3. The gain/loss for Alcoa in cell I3 is equal to the current value in cell H3 minus the initial cost in cell F3. The percent gain/loss for Alcoa in cell J3 is equal to the gain/loss in cell I3 divided by the initial cost in cell F3.

Instead of using the keyboard to enter the formulas =D3*G3 in cell H3, =H3 – F3 in cell I3, and =I3/F3 in cell J3, you can use the mouse and Point mode to enter these three formulas. **Point mode** allows you to select cells for use in a formula by using the mouse. Perform the following steps to enter formulas using Point mode.

More About

Using Point Mode

Point mode allows you to create formulas using the mouse. You can use the on-screen keyboard and mouse to enter the arithmetic operators. The on-screen keyboard is available through the Language bar (see Appendix B). Thus, with Excel you can enter entire formulas without ever touching the keyboard.

To Enter Formulas Using Point Mode

1 With cell H3 selected, type = (equal sign) to begin the formula and then click cell D3.

Excel surrounds cell D3 with a marquee and appends D3 to the equal sign (=) in cell H3 (Figure 2-5).

marquee surrounds selected cell D3

cell reference D3 appended to formula

FIGURE 2-5

2 **Type * (asterisk) and then click cell G3.**

Excel surrounds cell G3 with a marquee and appends G3 to the asterisk (*) in cell H3 (Figure 2-6).

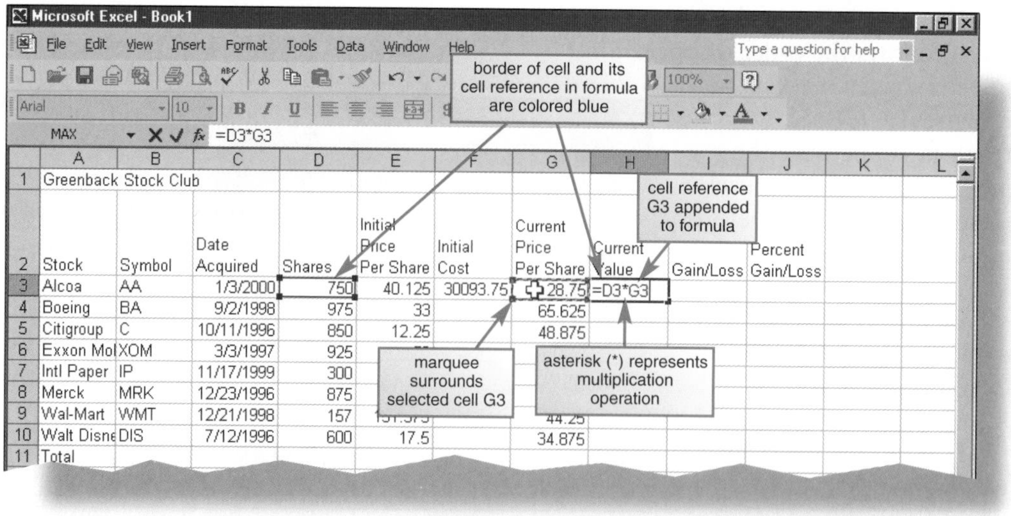

border of cell and its cell reference in formula are colored blue

cell reference G3 appended to formula

marquee surrounds selected cell G3

asterisk (*) represents multiplication operation

FIGURE 2-6

3 **Click the Enter box. Click cell I3. Type = (equal sign) and then click cell H3. Type – (minus sign) and then click cell F3.**

*Excel determines the product of =D3*G3 and displays the result, 21562.5, in cell H3. The formula =H3 – F3 displays in cell I3 and in the formula bar (Figure 2-7).*

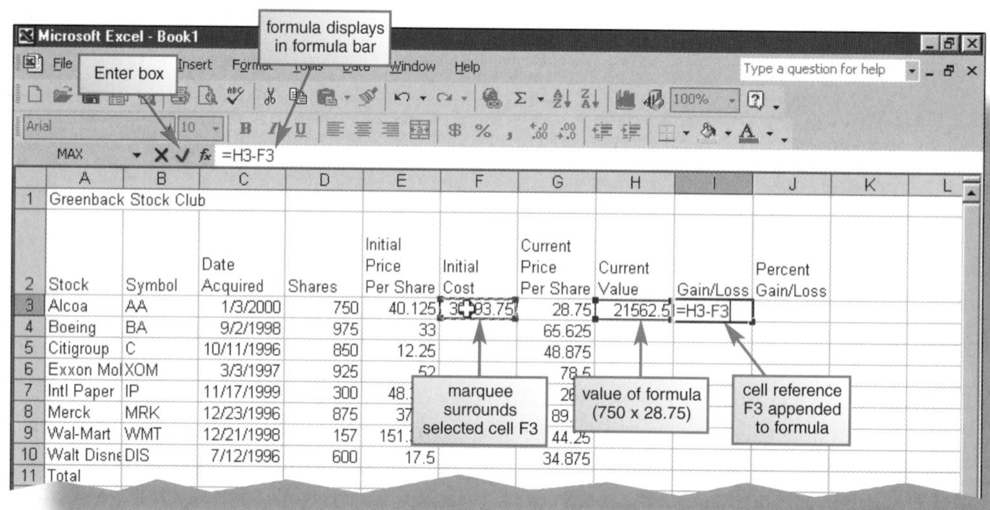

FIGURE 2-7

4 **Click the Enter box. Click cell J3. Type = (equal sign) and then click cell I3. Type / (division sign) and then click cell F3. Click the Enter box.**

The Gain/Loss for Alcoa, -8531.25, displays in cell I3 and the Percent Gain/Loss for Alcoa, -0.28349, displays in cell J3 (Figure 2-8). The -0.28349 represents approximately -28.35%.

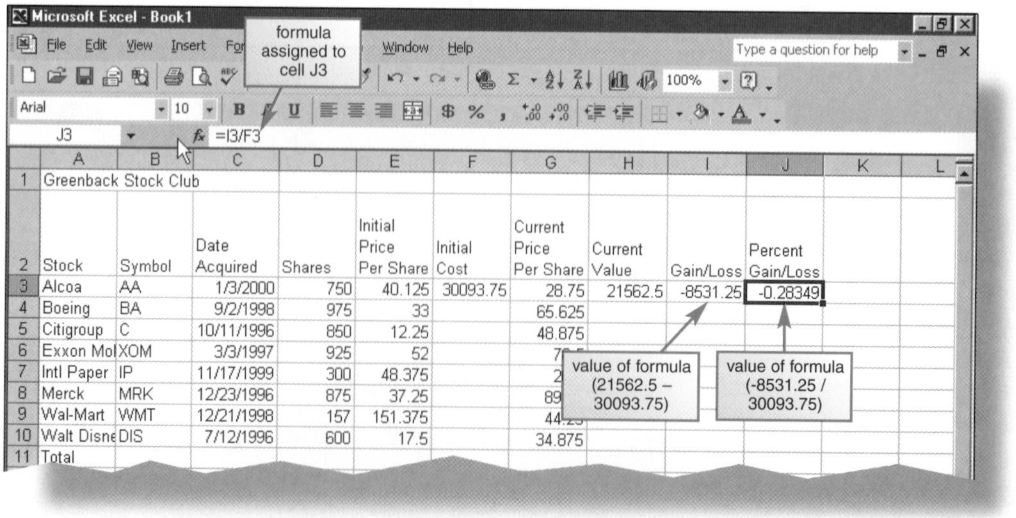

formula assigned to cell J3

value of formula (21562.5 – 30093.75)

value of formula (-8531.25 / 30093.75)

FIGURE 2-8

Depending on the length and complexity of the formula, using Point mode to enter formulas often is faster and more accurate than using the keyboard. In some instances, you may want to combine the keyboard and mouse when entering a formula in a cell. You can use the keyboard to begin the formula, for example, and then use the mouse to select a range of cells.

The true value assigned by Excel to cell J3 from the division operation in Step 4 is -0.283489097. While all the decimal places do not display in Figure 2-8, Excel maintains all of them for computational purposes. Thus, if cell J3 is referenced in a formula, the value used for computational purposes is -0.283489097, not -0.28349. Excel displays the value in cell J3 as -0.28349 because the width of the cell will hold only 7 digits, the minus sign, and the decimal point. If you increase the width of column J, then the true value -0.283489097 displays. It is important to recognize this difference between the displayed value and the actual value to better understand why in some cases the sum of a column is a penny off from the expected value.

Formulas

To change a formula to a number (constant), select the cell, click the Copy button on the Standard toolbar, click the Past button arrow on the Standard toolbar, click Paste Special, click Values, and click the OK button.

Copying the Formulas Using the Fill Handle

The four formulas for Alcoa in cells F3, H3, I3, and J3 now are complete. You could enter the same four formulas one at a time for the seven remaining stocks, Boeing, Citigroup, Exxon Mobil, International Paper, Merck, Wal-Mart, and Walt Disney. A much easier method of entering the formulas, however, is to select the formulas in row 3 and then use the fill handle to copy them through row 10. Recall from Project 1 that the fill handle is a small rectangle in the lower-right corner of the active cell. Perform the following steps to copy the formulas.

Steps To Copy Formulas Using the Fill Handle

1 Click cell F3 and then point to the fill handle. Drag the fill handle down through cell F10 and continue to hold down the mouse button.

A border surrounds the source and destination areas (range F3:F10) and the mouse pointer changes to a cross hair (Figure 2-9).

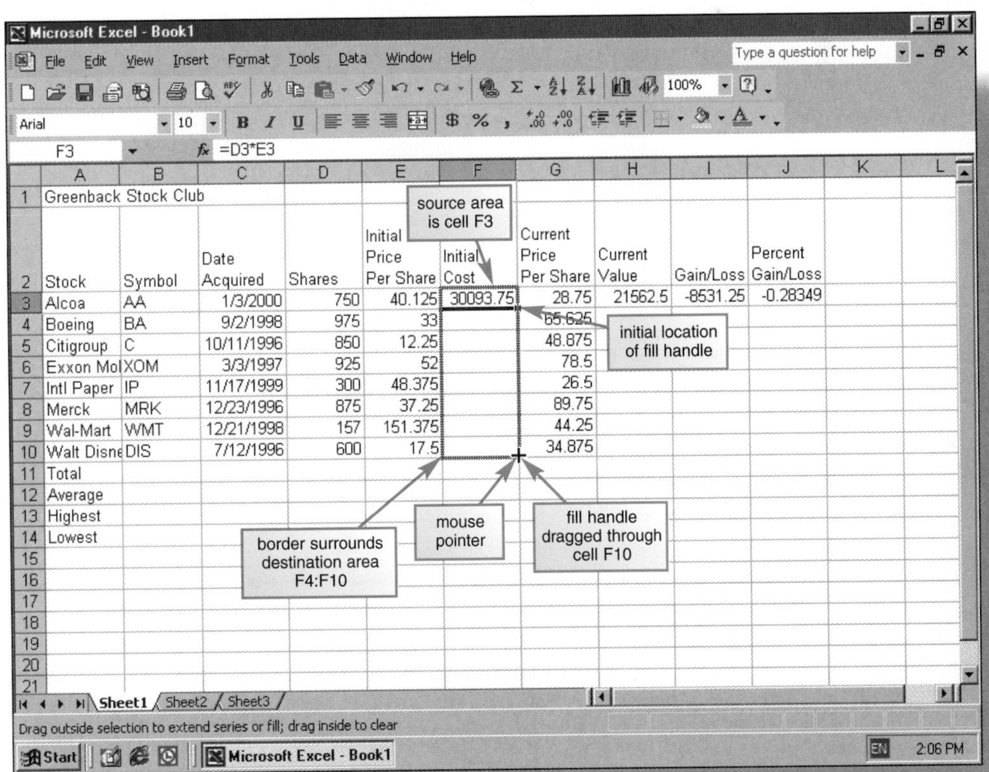

FIGURE 2-9

2 **Release the mouse button. Select the range H3:J3 and then point to the fill handle.**

*Excel copies the formula =D3*E3 to the range F4:F10 and displays the initial costs for the remaining seven stocks. The range H3:J3 is selected (Figure 2-10). The Auto Fill Options button displays, which allows you to refine the copy.*

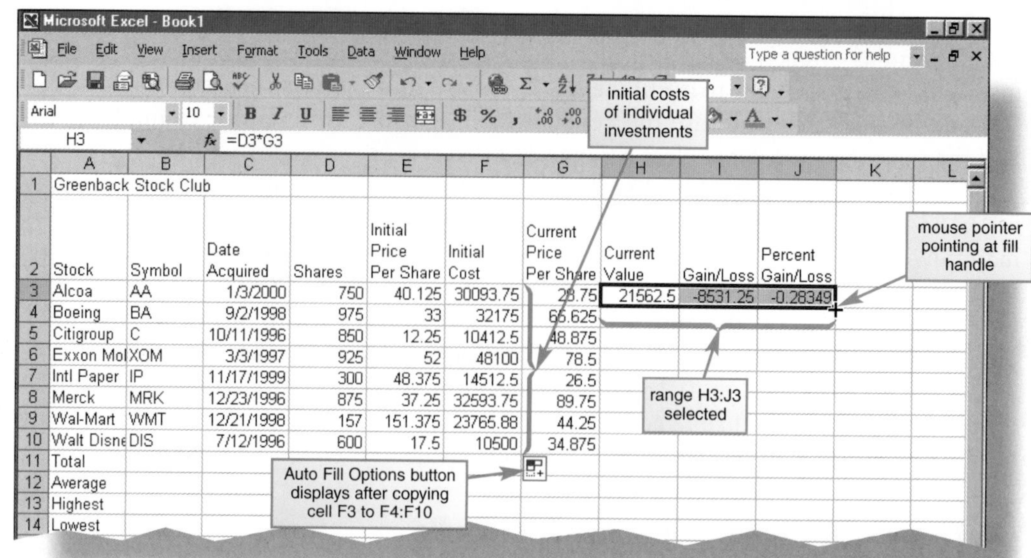

FIGURE 2-10

3 **Drag the fill handle down through the range H4:J10.**

*Excel copies the three formulas =D3*G3 in cell H3, =H3-F3 in cell I3, and =I3/F3 in cell J3 to the range H4:J10 and displays the current value, gain/loss, and percent gain/loss for the remaining seven stocks (Figure 2-11).*

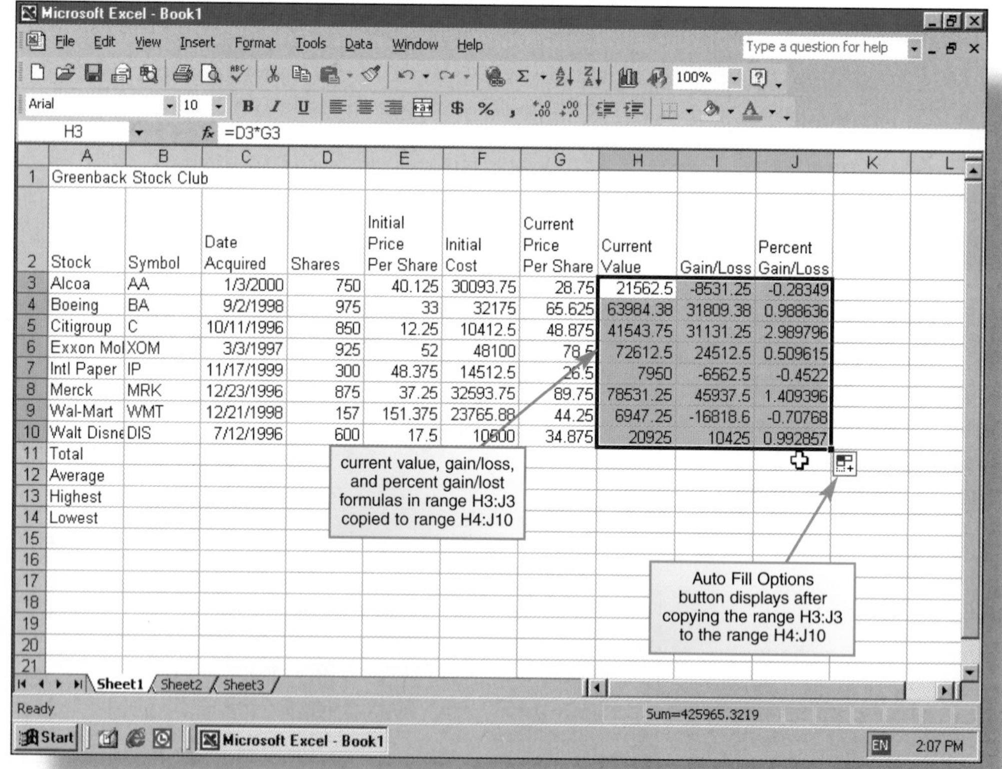

FIGURE 2-11

Other Ways

1. Select source area, click Copy button on Standard toolbar, select destination area, click Paste button on Standard toolbar
2. Select source area, on Edit menu click Copy, select destination area, on Edit menu click Paste
3. Select source area, right-click source area, click Copy on shortcut menu, select destination area, right-click destination area, click Paste on shortcut menu
4. Select source area, in Voice Command mode say, "Copy," select destination area, in Voice Command mode say, "Paste"

Recall that when you copy a formula, Excel adjusts the cell references so the new formulas contain references corresponding to the new location and performs calculations using the appropriate values. Thus, if you copy downward, Excel adjusts the row portion of cell references. If you copy across, then Excel adjusts the column portion of cell references. These cell references are called **relative references**.

Smart Tags

A **smart tag** is a button that automatically appears on the screen, such as the Auto Fill Options button in Figures 2-10 and 2-11. Table 2-4 summarizes the smart tags available in Excel. When you see a smart tag, click it to display a menu of options that you can choose from to modify the previous operation or obtain additional information.

With some of the smart tags, such as the Trace Error and Smart Tag Actions, Excel notifies you that it is available by displaying a smart tag indicator in a cell. A smart tag indicator is a small triangle located in one of the corners of the cell. If you select a cell with a smart tag indicator, the smart tag button displays.

Table 2-4 Smart Tags in Excel

BUTTON	NAME	MENU FUNCTION
	Auto Fill Options	Gives options for how to fill cells following a fill operation, such as dragging the fill handle
	AutoCorrect Options	Undoes an automatic correction, stops future automatic corrections of this type, or displays the AutoCorrect Options dialog box
	Insert Options	Lists formatting options following an insert of cells, rows, or columns
	Paste Options	Specifies how moved or pasted items should display, e.g., with original formatting, without formatting, or with different formatting
	Smart Tag Actions	Lists information options for a cell containing data recognized by Excel, such as a stock symbol (see In the Lab 3, Part 4 on Page E 2.77)
	Trace Error	Lists error checking options following the assignment of an invalid formula to a cell

Determining the Totals Using the AutoSum Button

The next step is to determine the totals in row 11 for the initial cost in column F, current value in column H, and gain/loss in column I. To determine the total initial cost in column F, you must sum cells F3 through F10. To do so, you can enter the function =sum(f3:f10) in cell F11, or you can select cell F11 and then click the AutoSum button on the Standard toolbar twice. Similar SUM functions or the AutoSum button can be used in cells H11 and I11 to determine total current value and total gain/loss, respectively. Recall from Project 1 that when you select one cell and use the AutoSum button, you must click the button twice. If you select a range, then you need only click the AutoSum button once.

TO DETERMINE TOTALS USING THE AUTOSUM BUTTON

1. Select cell F11. Click the AutoSum button twice. (Do not double-click.)
2. Select the range H11:I11. Click the AutoSum button.

The three totals display in row 11 as shown in Figure 2-12.

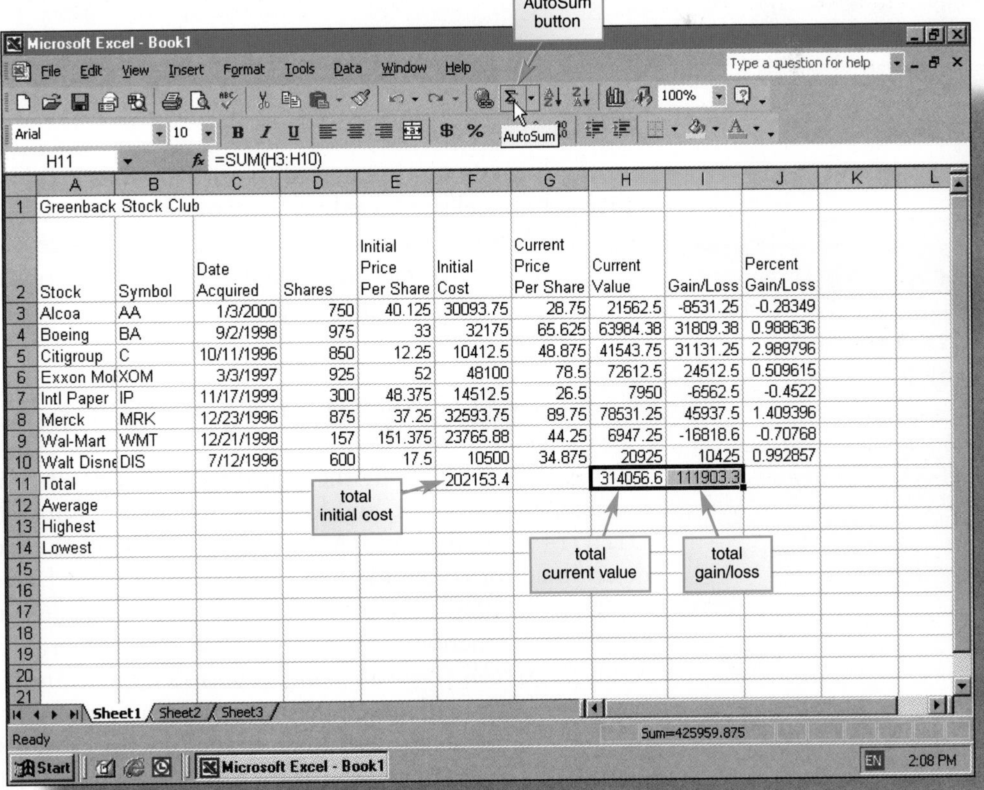

FIGURE 2-12

More About

Selecting a Range

If you dislike dragging to select a range, press F8 and use the arrow keys to select one corner of the range and then the cell diagonally opposite it in the proposed range. Make sure you press F8 to turn selection off after you are finished with the range or you will continue to select ranges.

Rather than using the AutoSum button to calculate column totals individually, you can select all three cells before clicking the AutoSum button to calculate all three column totals at one time. To select the nonadjacent range F11, H11, and I11, select cell F11, and then, while holding down the CTRL key, drag through the range H11:I11. Next, click the AutoSum button.

Determining the Total Percent Gain/Loss

With the totals in row 11 determined, you can copy the percentage gain/loss formula in cell J10 to cell J11 as shown in the following steps.

Microsoft Excel - Book1

J10 =I10/F10

	A	B	C	D	E	F	G	H	I	J
1	Greenback Stock Club									
2	Stock	Symbol	Date Acquired	Shares	Initial Price Per Share	Initial Cost	Current Price Per Share	Current Value	Gain/Loss	Percent Gain/Loss
3	Alcoa	AA	1/3/2000	750	40.125	30093.75	28.75	21562.5	-8531.25	-0.28349
4	Boeing	BA	9/2/1998	975	33	32175	65.625	63984.38	31809.38	0.988636
5	Citigroup	C	10/11/1996	850	12.25	10412.5	48.875	41543.75	31131.25	2.989796
6	Exxon Mol	XOM	3/3/1997	925	52	48100	78.5	72612.5	24512.5	0.509615
7	Intl Paper	IP	11/17/1999	300	48.375	14512.5	26.5	7950	-6562.5	-0.4522
8	Merck	MRK	12/23/1996	875	37.25	32593.75	89.75	78531.25	45937.5	1.409396
9	Wal-Mart	WMT	12/21/1998	157	151.375	23765.88	44.25	6947.25	-16818.6	-0.70768
10	Walt Disne	DIS	7/12/1996	600	17.5	10500	34.875	20925	10425	0.992857
11	Total					202153.4		314056.6	111903.3	0.553556
12	Average									
13	Highest									
14	Lowest									

formula is =I10/F10

formula is =I11/F11

Auto Fill Options button displays after copying cell J10 to cell J11

FIGURE 2-13

TO DETERMINE THE TOTAL PERCENT GAIN/LOSS

1. Select cell J10 and then point to the fill handle.
2. Drag the fill handle down through cell J11.

The formula, =I10/F10, in cell J10 is copied to cell J11. The resultant formula in cell J11 is =I11/F11, which shows a total club gain on the club's holdings of 0.553556 or 55.3556% (Figure 2-13).

The formula was not copied to cell J11 when cell J3 was copied to the range J4:J10 because both cells involved in the computation (I11 and F11) were blank, or zero, at the time. A **blank cell** in Excel has a numerical value of zero, which would have resulted in an error message in cell J11. Once the totals were determined, both cells I11 and F11 (especially F11, because it is the divisor) had non-zero numerical values.

More About

Formulas and Functions

For more information on entering formulas and functions, visit the Excel 2002 More About Web page (scsite.com/ex2002/more.htm) and click using Formulas and Functions.

Using the AVERAGE, MAX, and MIN Functions

The next step in creating the Greenback Stock Club worksheet is to compute the average, highest value, and lowest value for the number of shares in the range D12:D14 using the AVERAGE, MAX, and MIN functions. Once the values are determined for column D, the entries can be copied across to the other columns.

Excel includes prewritten formulas called **functions** to help you compute these statistics. A function takes a value or values, performs an operation, and returns a result to the cell. The values that you use with a function are called **arguments**. All functions begin with an equal sign and include the arguments in parentheses after the function name. For example, in the function =AVERAGE(D3:D10), the function name is AVERAGE, and the argument is the range D3:D10.

With Excel, you can enter functions using one of six methods: (1) the keyboard or mouse; (2) the Insert Function box on the formula bar; (3) the AutoSum menu; (4) the Function command on the Insert menu; (5) type equal sign in cell and then select function from Name box area in formula bar (Figure 2-14); and (6) Voice Command mode. The method you choose will depend on your typing skills and whether you can recall the function name and required arguments. In the following pages, each of the first three methods will be used. The keyboard and mouse will be used to determine the average number of shares (cell D12). The AutoSum menu will be used to determine the highest number of shares (cell D13). The Insert Function button on the formula bar will be used to determine the lowest number of shares (cell D14).

Statistical Functions

A blank cell usually is considered to be equal to zero. The statistical functions, however, ignore blank cells. Thus, in Excel, the average of three cells with values of 7, blank, and 5 is 6 or (7 + 5) / 2 and not 4 or (7 + 0 + 5) /3.

Determining the Average of a Range of Numbers

The AVERAGE function sums the numbers in the specified range and then divides the sum by the number of non-zero cells in the range. To determine the average of the numbers in the range D3:D10, use the AVERAGE function, as shown in the following steps.

Steps: To Determine the Average of a Range of Numbers Using the Keyboard and Mouse

1 **Select cell D12. Type** =average(**in the cell. Click cell D3, the first endpoint of the range to average. Drag through cell D10, the second endpoint of the range to average.**

A marquee surrounds the range D3:D10. When you click cell D3, Excel appends cell D3 to the left parenthesis in the formula bar and surrounds cell D3 with a marquee. When you begin dragging, Excel appends to the argument a colon (:) and the cell reference of the cell where the mouse pointer is located (Figure 2-14).

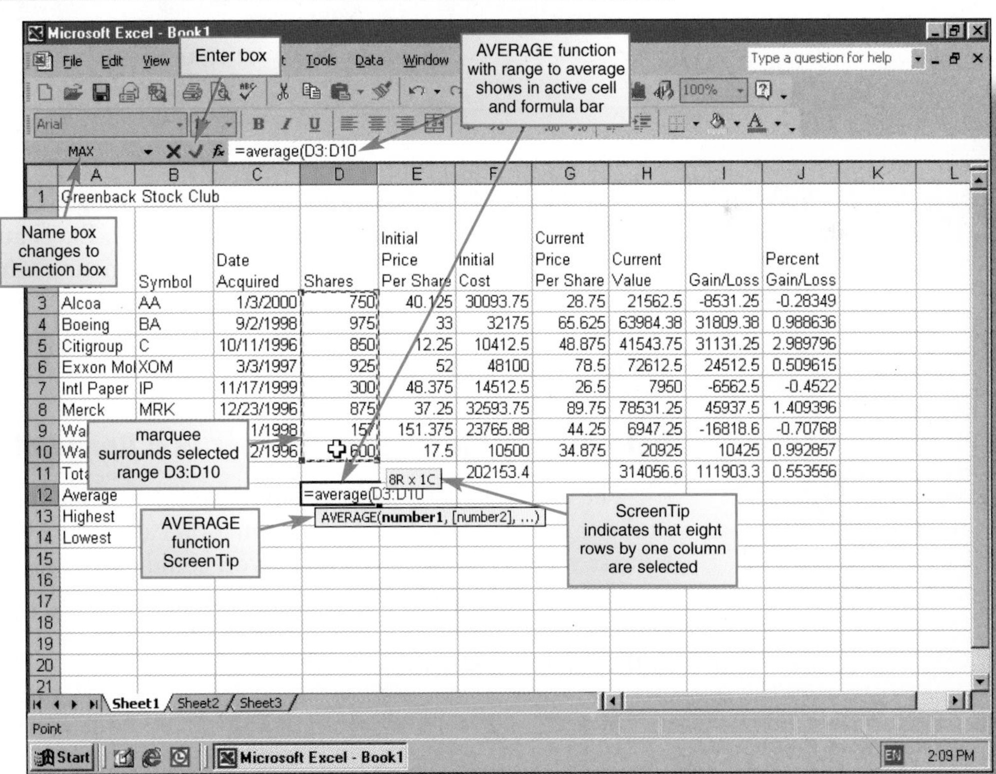

FIGURE 2-14

2 **Click the Enter box.**

Excel computes the average of the eight numbers in the range D3:D10 and displays the result, 679, in cell D12 (Figure 2-15). Thus, the average number of shares owned in the eight companies is 679.

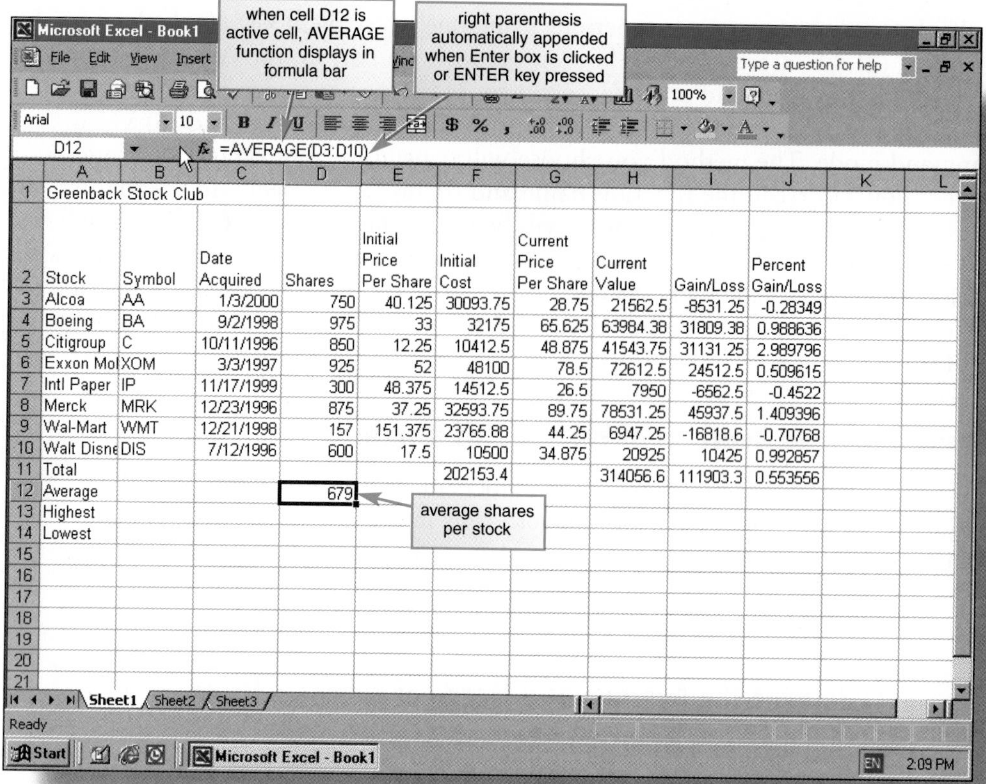
when cell D12 is active cell, AVERAGE function displays in formula bar
right parenthesis automatically appended when Enter box is clicked or ENTER key pressed
=AVERAGE(D3:D10)
average shares per stock

FIGURE 2-15

Other Ways

1. Click Insert Function box in formula bar, click AVERAGE function
2. Click AutoSum button arrow on Standard toolbar, click AVERAGE function
3. On Insert menu click Function, click AVERAGE function
4. In Voice Command mode say, "Insert, Function," [select Statistical category], in Voice Command mode say, "AVERAGE, OK"

The AVERAGE function requires that the range (the argument) be included within parentheses following the function name. Excel automatically appends the right parenthesis to complete the AVERAGE function when you click the Enter box or press the ENTER key. When you use Point mode, as in the previous steps, you cannot use the arrow keys to complete the entry. While in Point mode, the arrow keys change the selected cell reference in the range you are selecting.

Determining the Highest Number in a Range of Numbers

The next step is to select cell D13 and determine the highest (maximum) number in the range D3:D10. Excel has a function called the **MAX function** that displays the highest value in a range. Although you could enter the MAX function using the keyboard and Point mode as described in the previous steps, an alternative method to entering the function is to use the Insert Function box on the formula bar, as shown in the following steps.

Steps To Determine the Highest Number in a Range of Numbers Using the Insert Function Box

1 Select cell D13. Click the Insert Function box on the formula bar. When the Insert Function dialog box displays, click MAX in the Select a function box. Point to the OK button.

The Insert Function dialog box displays (Figure 2-16).

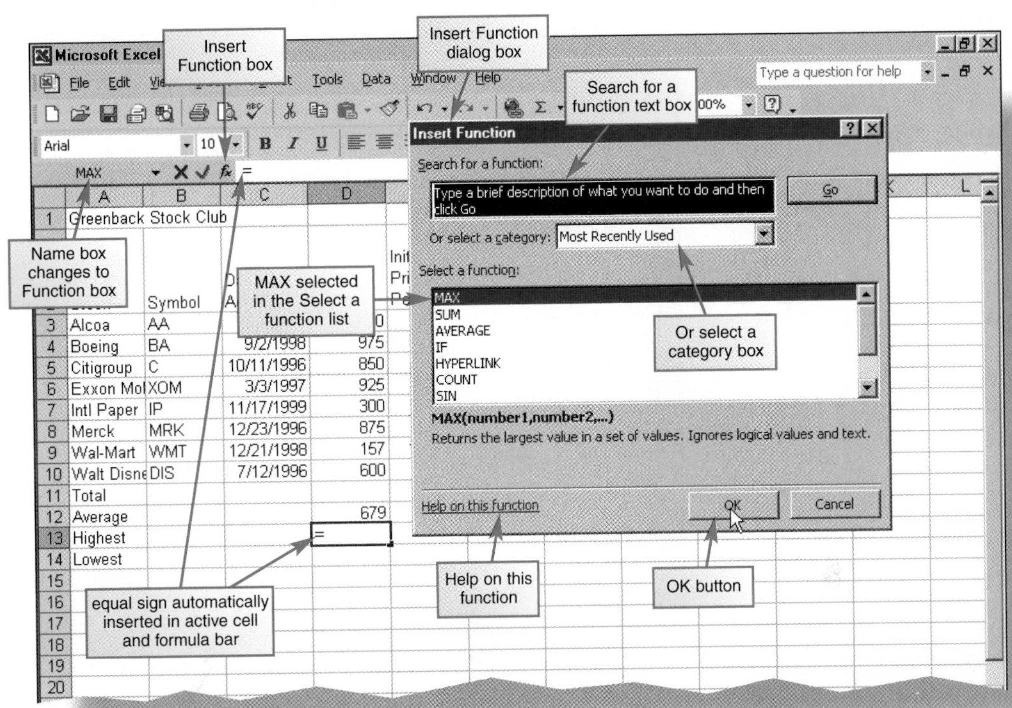

FIGURE 2-16

2 Click the OK button. When the Function Arguments dialog box displays, type `d3:d10` **in the Number 1 box. Point to the OK button.**

The Function Arguments dialog box displays with the range d3:d10 entered in the Number 1 box (Figure 2-17). The completed MAX function displays in the formula bar, and the end of the function displays in the active cell, D13.

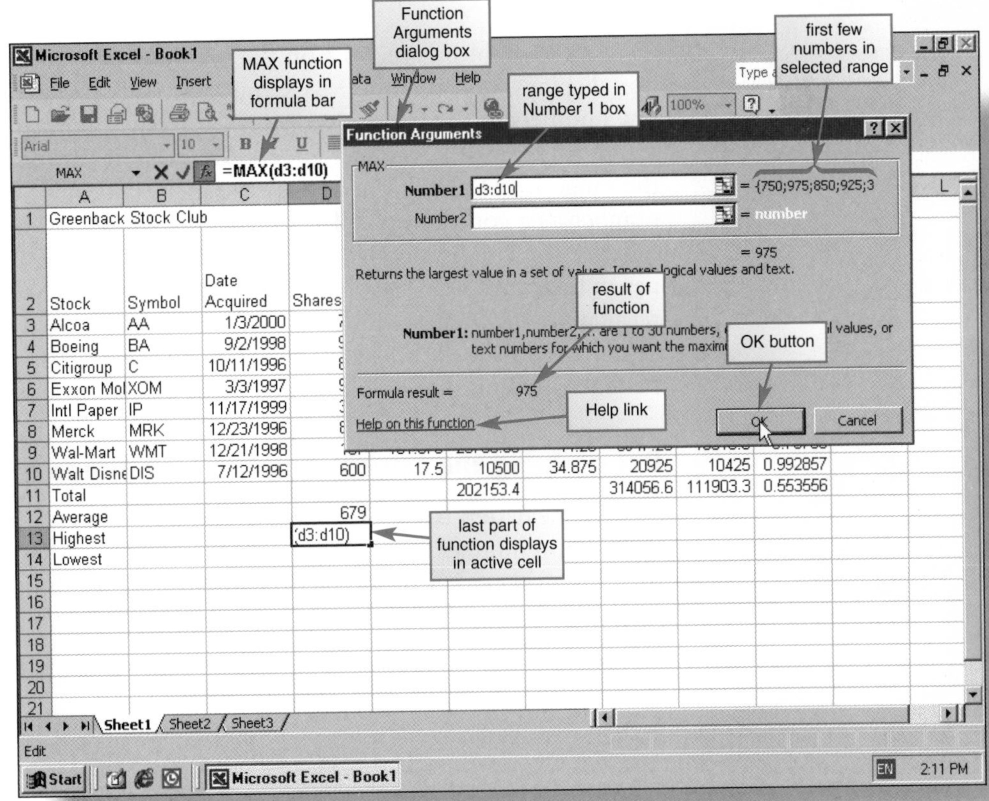

FIGURE 2-17

3 Click the OK button.

Excel determines that the highest value in the range D3:D10 is 975 (value in cell D4) and displays it in cell D13 (Figure 2-18).

	A	B	C	D	E	F	G	H	I	J
1	Greenback Stock Club									
2	Stock	Symbol	Date Acquired	Shares	Initial Price Per Share	Initial Cost	Current Price Per Share	Current Value	Gain/Loss	Percent Gain/Loss
3	Alcoa	AA	1/3/2000	750	40.125	30093.75	28.75	21562.5	-8531.25	-0.28349
4	Boeing	BA	9/2/1998	975	33	32175	65.625	63984.38	31809.38	0.988636
5	Citigroup	C	10/11/1996	850	12.25	10412.5	48.875	41543.75	31131.25	2.989796
6	Exxon Mol	XOM	3/3/1997	925	52	48100	78.5	72612.5	24512.5	0.509615
7	Intl Paper	IP	11/17/1999	300	48.375	14512.5	26.5	7950	-6562.5	-0.4522
8	Merck	MRK	12/23/1996	875	37.25	32593.75	89.75	78531.25	45937.5	1.409396
9	Wal-Mart	WMT	12/21/1998	157	151.375	23765.88	44.25	6947.25	-16818.6	-0.70768
10	Walt Disne	DIS	7/12/1996	600	17.5	10500	34.875	20925	10425	0.992857
11	Total					202153.4		314056.6	111903.3	0.553556
12	Average			679						
13	Highest			975						
14	Lowest									

FIGURE 2-18

Other Ways

1. Click Insert Function box in formula bar, click MAX function
2. On Insert menu click Function, click MAX function
3. Type MAX function in cell
4. In Voice Command mode say, "Insert, Function," [select Statistical category], in Voice Command mode say, "MAX, OK"

As shown in Figure 2-17 on the previous page, the Function Arguments dialog box displays the value the MAX function will return to cell D13. It also lists the first few numbers in the selected range, next to the Number 1 box.

In this example, rather than entering the MAX function, you easily could scan the range D3:D10, determine that the highest number of shares is 975, and enter the number as a constant in cell D13. The display would be the same as Figure 2-18. Because it contains a constant, cell D13 will continue to display 975, even if the values in the range D3:D10 change. If you use the MAX function, however, Excel will recalculate the highest value in the range D3:D10 each time a new value is entered into the worksheet. Manually determining the highest value in the range also would be more difficult if the club owned more stocks.

The Formula Palette

In Figure 2-17 on the previous page, you can drag the Function Arguments dialog box out of the way and drag through the desired range. You can also click the Collapse Dialog button to the right of the Number 1 box to hide the Formula Palette. After selecting the range, click the Collapse Dialog button a second time to display the Formula Palette.

Determining the Lowest Number in a Range of Numbers

The next step is to enter the MIN function in cell D14 to determine the lowest (minimum) number in the range D3:D10. Although you can enter the MIN function using either of the methods used to enter the AVERAGE and MAX functions, the following steps show an alternative using the AutoSum menu on the Standard toolbar.

Steps To Determine the Lowest Number in a Range of Numbers Using the AutoSum Menu

1 Select cell D14. Click the AutoSum button arrow on the Standard toolbar. When the AutoSum menu displays, point to Min.

The AutoSum menu displays (Figure 2-19).

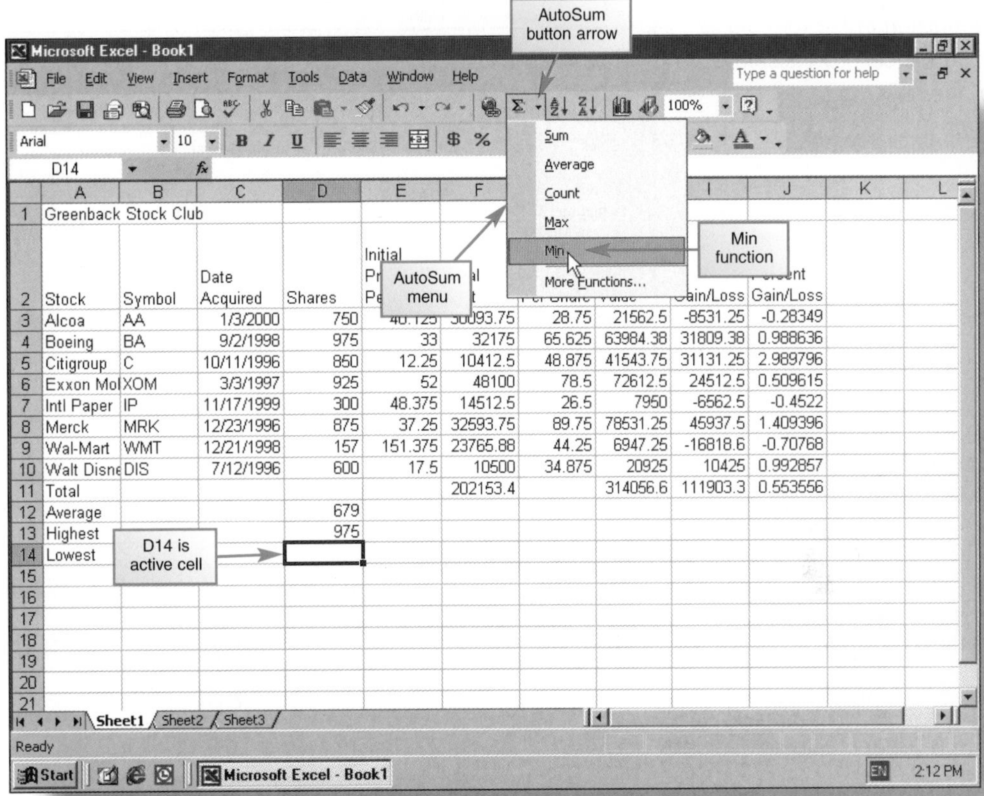

FIGURE 2-19

2 Click Min.

The function =MIN (D12:D13) displays in the formula bar and in cell D14. A marquee surrounds the range D12:D13 (Figure 2-20). The range D12:D13 automatically selected by Excel is not correct.

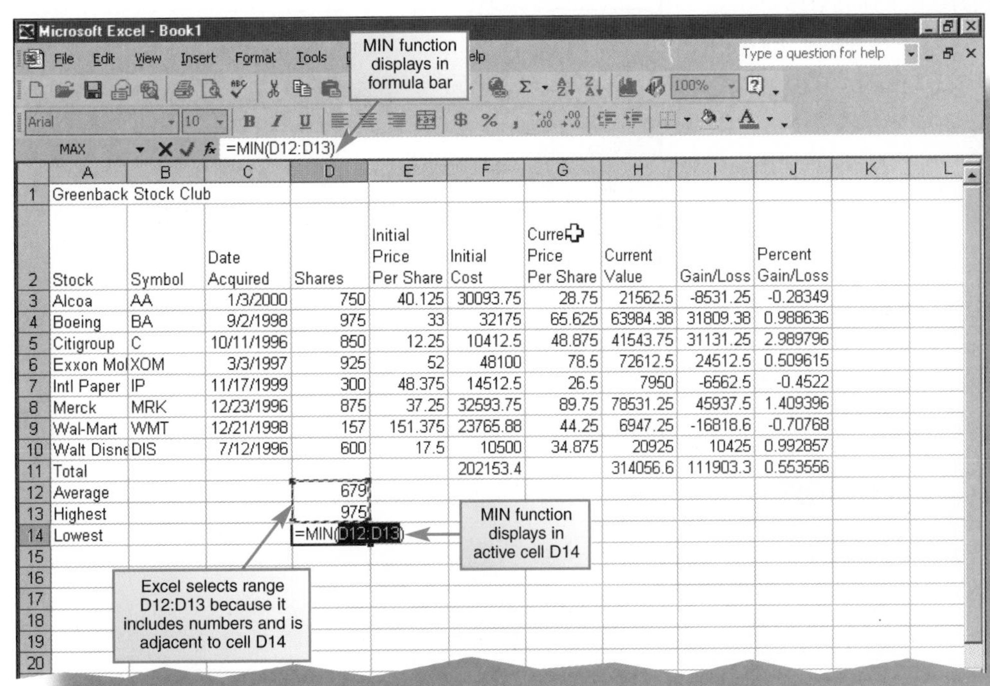

FIGURE 2-20

3 Click cell D3 and then drag through cell D10.

The function in the formula bar and in cell D14 displays with the new range D3:D10 (Figure 2-21).

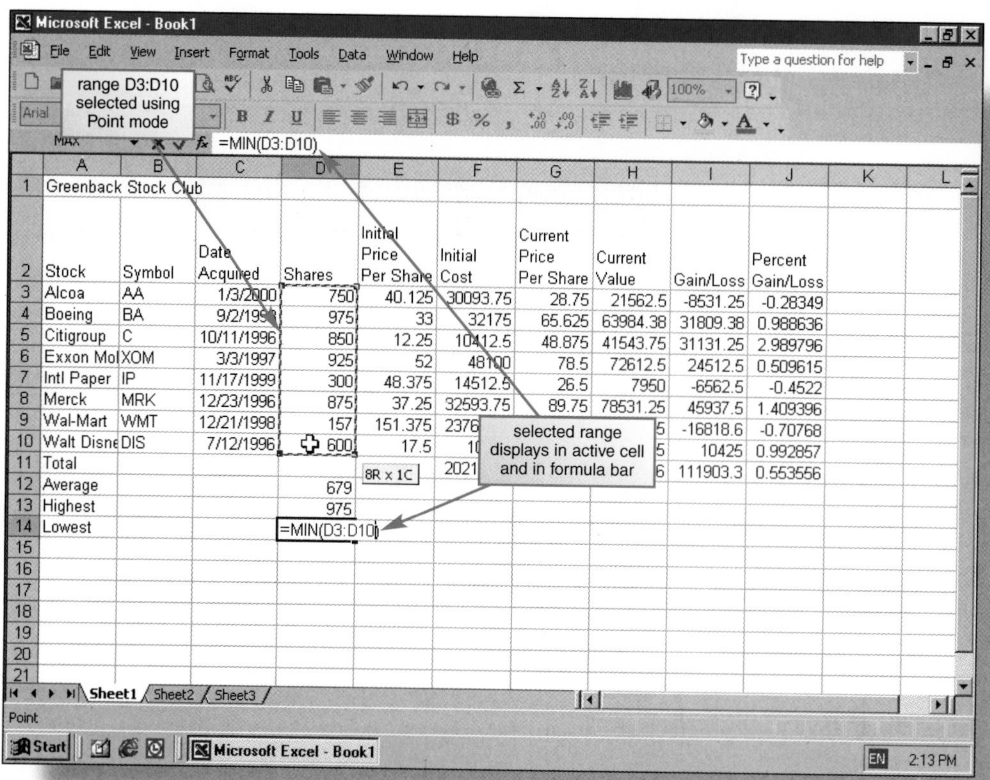

FIGURE 2-21

4 Click the Enter box.

Excel determines that the lowest value in the range D3:D10 is 157 and displays it in cell D14 (Figure 2-22).

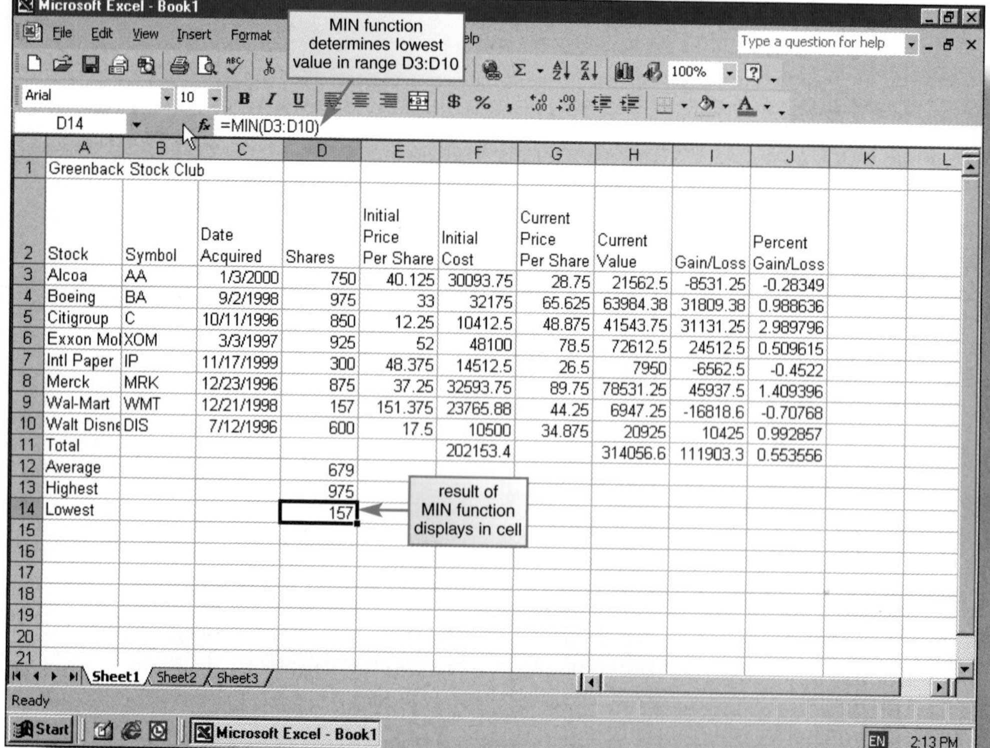

FIGURE 2-22

Other Ways

1. Click Insert Function box in formula bar, click MIN function
2. On Insert menu click Function, click MIN function
3. Type MIN function in cell
4. In Voice Command mode say, "Insert, Function," [select Statistical category], in Voice Command mode say, "MIN, OK"

You can see from the previous example that using the AutoSum menu allows you to enter one of the often-used functions into a cell easily without requiring you to memorize its name or the required arguments. If you need to use a function not available in the AutoSum menu and can not remember its name, then click More Functions in the list or click the Insert Function box on the formula bar.

Thus far, you have learned to use the SUM, AVERAGE, MAX, and MIN functions. In addition to these four functions, Excel has more than 400 additional functions that perform just about every type of calculation you can imagine. These functions are categorized in the Insert Function dialog box in Figure 2-16 on page E 2.19. To view the categories, click the Or select a category box arrow. To obtain a description of a selected function, select its name in the Insert Function dialog box. The description displays below the Select a function list in the dialog box.

Functions

To obtain a summary list of all the functions available by category in Excel, click the Help button on the Standard toolbar, click the Index tab on the left side of the window, type `function` in the Type keywords text box, click the Search button, click Worksheet functions listed by category in the Choose a topic list. Click each category on the right side of the window. Click the Print button for a printed copy.

Copying the AVERAGE, MAX, and MIN Functions

The next step is to copy the AVERAGE, MAX, and MIN functions in the range D12:D14 to the range E12:J14. The fill handle again will be used to complete the copy. The following steps illustrate this procedure.

To Copy a Range of Cells across Columns to an Adjacent Range Using the Fill Handle

1 Select the range D12:D14. Drag the fill handle in the lower-right corner of the selected range through cell J14 and continue to hold down the mouse button.

Excel displays an outline around the source and destination areas (range D12:J14) as shown in Figure 2-23.

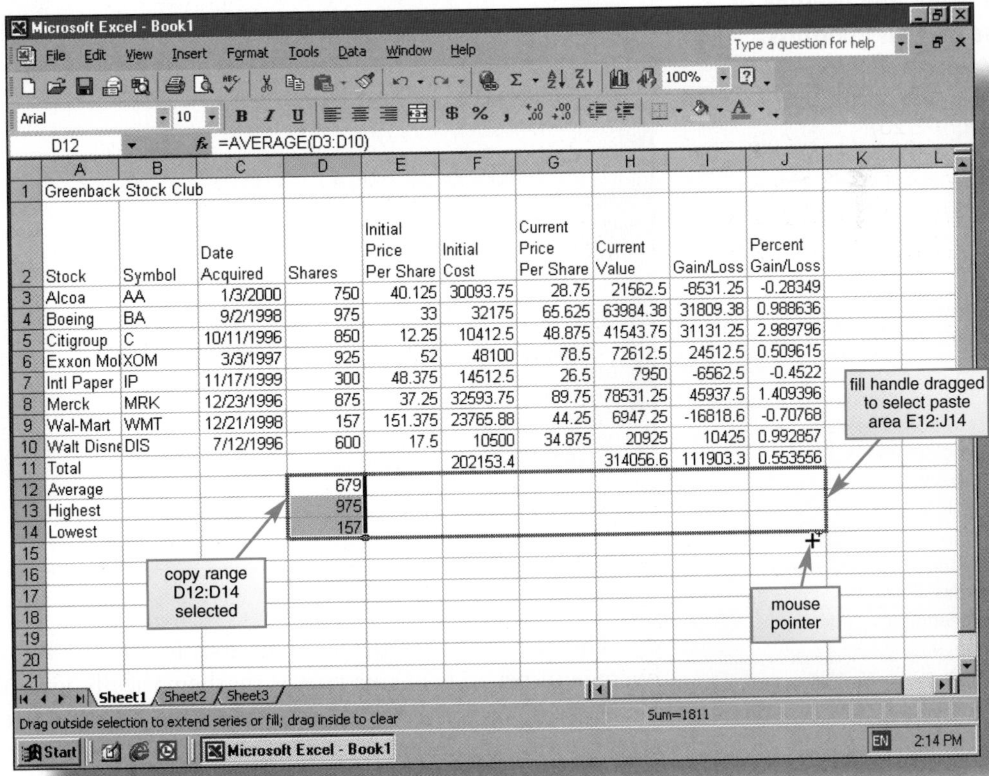

FIGURE 2-23

2 Release the mouse button.

Excel copies the three functions to the range E12:J14 (Figure 2-24). The Auto Fill Options button displays, which allows you to refine the copy.

Microsoft Excel - Book1

D12 =AVERAGE(D3:D10)

	A	B	C	D	E	F	G	H	I	J
1	Greenback Stock Club									
2	Stock	Symbol	Date Acquired	Shares	Initial Price Per Share	Initial Cost	Current Price Per Share	Current Value	Gain/Loss	Percent Gain/Loss
3	Alcoa	AA	1/3/2000	750	40.125	30093.75	28.75	21562.5	-8531.25	-0.28349
4	Boeing	BA	9/2/1998	975	33	32175	65.625	63984.38	31809.38	0.988636
5	Citigroup	C	10/11/1996	850	12.25	10412.5	48.875	41543.75	31131.25	2.989796
6	Exxon Mol	XOM	3/3/1997	925	52	48100	78.5	72612.5	24512.5	0.509615
7	Intl Paper	IP	11/17/1999	300	48.375	14512.5	26.5	7950	-6562.5	-0.4522
8	Merck	MRK	12/23/1996	875	37.25	32593.75	89.75	78531.25	45937.5	1.409396
9	Wal-Mart	WMT	12/21/1998	157	151.375	23765.88	44.25	6947.25	-16818.6	-0.70768
10	Walt Disne	DIS	7/12/1996	600	17.5	10500	34.875	20925	10425	0.992857
11	Total					202153.4		314056.6	111903.3	0.553556
12	Average			679	48.98438	25269.17	52.14063	39257.08	13987.91	0.680867
13	Highest			975	151.375	48100	89.75	78531.25	45937.5	2.989796
14	Lowest			157	12.25	10412.5	26.5	6947.25	-16818.6	-0.70768

AVERAGE, MAX, and MIN functions in range D12:D14 copied to range E12:J14

Auto Fill Options button

FIGURE 2-24

3 Select cell J12 and press the DELETE key to delete the average of the percent gain/loss.

Cell J12 is blank (Figure 2-25).

Save button

J12

	A	B	C	D	E	F	G	H	I	J
1	Greenback Stock Club									
2	Stock	Symbol	Date Acquired	Shares	Initial Price Per Share	Initial Cost	Current Price Per Share	Current Value	Gain/Loss	Percent Gain/Loss
3	Alcoa	AA	1/3/2000	750	40.125	30093.75	28.75	21562.5	-8531.25	-0.28349
4	Boeing	BA	9/2/1998	975	33	32175	65.625	63984.38	31809.38	0.988636
5	Citigroup	C	10/11/1996	850	12.25	10412.5	48.875	41543.75	31131.25	2.989796
6	Exxon Mol	XOM	3/3/1997	925	52	48100	78.5	72612.5	24512.5	0.509615
7	Intl Paper	IP	11/17/1999	300	48.375	14512.5	26.5	7950	-6562.5	-0.4522
8	Merck	MRK	12/23/1996	875	37.25	32593.75	89.75	78531.25	45937.5	1.409396
9	Wal-Mart	WMT	12/21/1998	157	151.375	23765.88	44.25	6947.25	-16818.6	-0.70768
10	Walt Disne	DIS	7/12/1996	600	17.5	10500	34.875	20925	10425	0.992857
11	Total					202153.4		314056.6	111903.3	0.553556
12	Average			679	48.98438	25269.17	52.14063	39257.08	13987.91	
13	Highest			975	151.375	48100	89.75	78531.25	45937.5	2.989796
14	Lowest			157	[illegible]	[illegible]	26.5	6947.25	-16818.6	-0.70768

percents in range J3:J10 cannot be averaged

FIGURE 2-25

Other Ways

1. Select source area and point to border of range, while holding down CTRL key, drag copy area to destination area
2. Select source area, on Edit menu click Copy, select destination area, on Edit menu click Paste
3. Right-click source area, click Copy on shortcut menu, right-click destination area, click Paste
4. Select source area, press CTRL+C, select destination area, press CTRL+V
5. Select source area, in Voice Command mode say, "Copy," [select destination area], in Voice Command mode say, "Paste"

The average of the percent gain/loss in cell J12 was deleted in Step 3 because an average of percents of this type is mathematically invalid.

Remember that Excel adjusts the ranges in the copied functions so each function refers to the column of numbers above it. Review the numbers in rows 12 through 14 in Figure 2-24. You should see that the functions in each column return the appropriate values, based on the numbers in rows 3 through 10 of that column.

Saving the Workbook

With the data and formulas entered into the workbook, the next step is to save the workbook using the file name Greenback Stock Club.

TO SAVE THE WORKBOOK

1. Click the Save button on the Standard toolbar.
2. When the Save As dialog box displays, type `Greenback Stock Club` in the File name text box.
3. If necessary, click 3½ Floppy (A:) in the Save in list. Click the Save button in the Save As dialog box.

Excel saves the workbook on the floppy disk in drive A using the file name Greenback Stock Club.

This concludes entering the data and formulas into the worksheet. After saving the file, the worksheet remains on the screen with the file name, Greenback Stock Club, on the title bar.

File Types

Excel lets you save a workbook in over 30 different file formats, such as Microsoft Excel Workbook, text, Web page, XML Spreadsheet, Unicode Text, Lotus 1-2-3 format, dBASE format, Text (Macintosh), and many more. You choose the file format from the Save as type list at the bottom of the Save As dialog box. The different formats come in handy when you need to transfer the data in a workbook to another application package or to non-PC hardware.

Verifying Formulas Using Range Finder

One of the more common mistakes made with Excel is to include a wrong cell reference in a formula. An easy way to verify that a formula references the cells you want it to reference is to use Excel's Range Finder. **Range Finder** can be used to check which cells are being referenced in the formula assigned to the active cell. Range Finder allows you to make immediate changes to the cells referenced in a formula.

To use Range Finder to verify that a formula contains the intended cell references, double-click the cell with the formula you want to check. Excel responds by highlighting the cells referenced in the formula so you can check that the correct cells are being used. The following steps use Range Finder to check the formula in cell J3.

To Verify a Formula Using Range Finder

1 Double-click cell J3.

Excel responds by displaying the cells in the worksheet referenced by the formula in cell J3 using different color borders (Figure 2-26). The different colors allow you to see easily which cells are being referenced by the formula in cell J3.

2 Press the ESC key to quit Range Finder. Select cell A16.

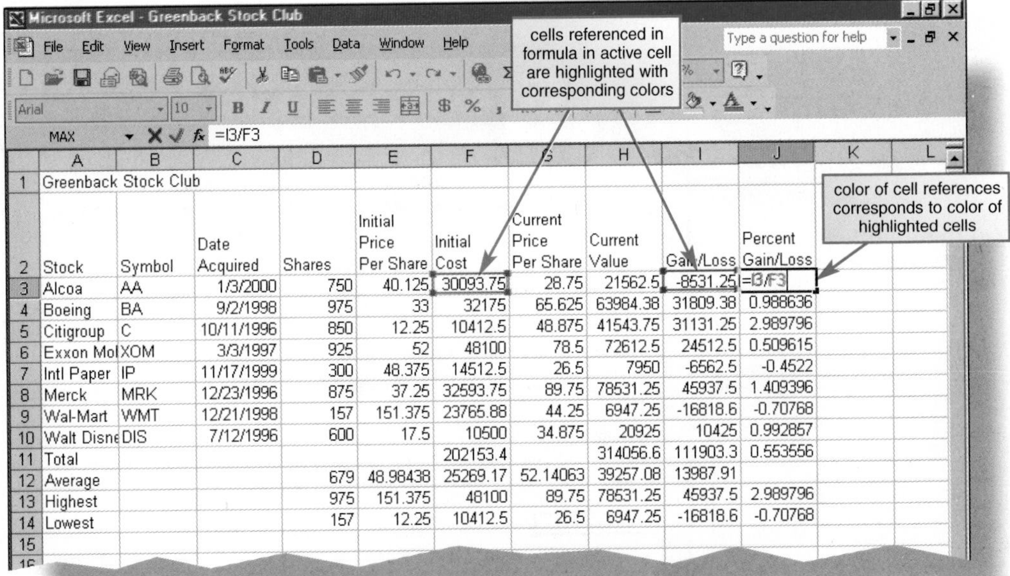

	A	B	C	D	E	F	G	H	I	J
1	Greenback Stock Club									
2	Stock	Symbol	Date Acquired	Shares	Initial Price Per Share	Initial Cost	Current Price Per Share	Current Value	Gain/Loss	Percent Gain/Loss
3	Alcoa	AA	1/3/2000	750	40.125	30093.75	28.75	21562.5	-8531.25	=I3/F3
4	Boeing	BA	9/2/1998	975	33	32175	65.625	63984.38	31809.38	0.988636
5	Citigroup	C	10/11/1996	850	12.25	10412.5	48.875	41543.75	31131.25	2.989796
6	Exxon Mol	XOM	3/3/1997	925	52	48100	78.5	72612.5	24512.5	0.509615
7	Intl Paper	IP	11/17/1999	300	48.375	14512.5	26.5	7950	-6562.5	-0.4522
8	Merck	MRK	12/23/1996	875	37.25	32593.75	89.75	78531.25	45937.5	1.409396
9	Wal-Mart	WMT	12/21/1998	157	151.375	23765.88	44.25	6947.25	-16818.6	-0.70768
10	Walt Disne	DIS	7/12/1996	600	17.5	10500	34.875	20925	10425	0.992857
11	Total					202153.4		314056.6	111903.3	0.553556
12	Average			679	48.98438	25269.17	52.14063	39257.08	13987.91	
13	Highest			975	151.375	48100	89.75	78531.25	45937.5	2.989796
14	Lowest			157	12.25	10412.5	26.5	6947.25	-16818.6	-0.70768
15										

FIGURE 2-26

More About

Auditing Formulas

An alternative to using the Range Finder is to use the Formula Auditing command on the Tools menu. The Formula Auditing command displays a menu of auditing commands that give a more detailed analysis of formulas and offer different ways to view formulas. Another useful command on the Tools menu is the Error Checking command, which checks all formulas in a workbook to ensure they are referencing valid data.

Not only does Range Finder show you the cells referenced in the formula in cell J3, but you can drag the colored borders to other cells and Excel will change the cell references in the formula to the newly selected cells. If you use Range Finder to change cells referenced in a formula, press the ENTER key to complete the edit.

Formatting the Worksheet

Although the worksheet contains the appropriate data, formulas, and functions, the text and numbers need to be formatted to improve their appearance and readability.

In Project 1, you used the AutoFormat command to format the majority of the worksheet. This section describes how to change the unformatted worksheet in Figure 2-27a to the formatted worksheet in Figure 2-27b using the Formatting toolbar and Format Cells command.

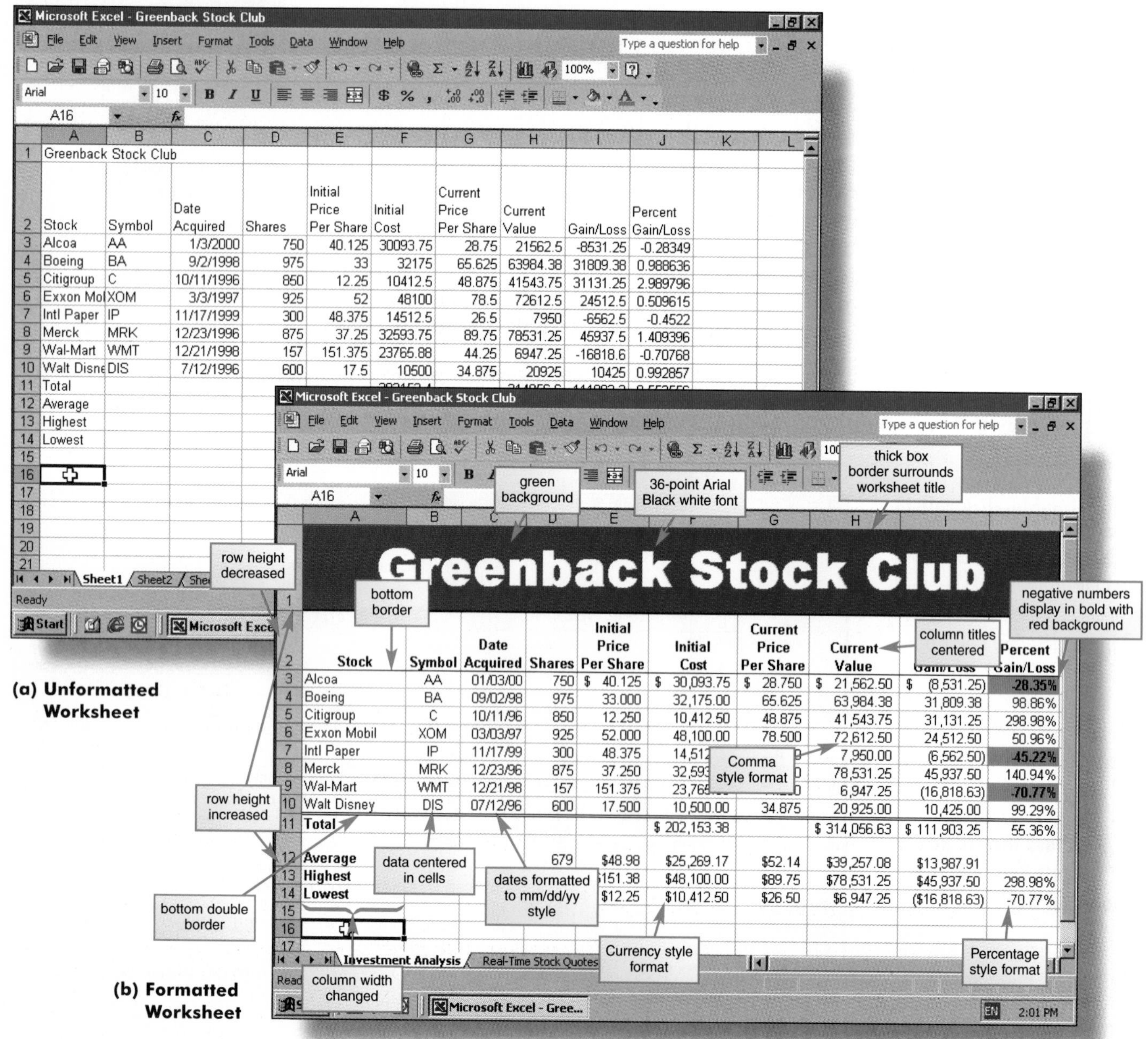

(a) Unformatted Worksheet

(b) Formatted Worksheet

FIGURE 2-27

The following outlines the type of formatting that is required in Project 2:

1. Worksheet title
   a. Font type — bold Arial Black
   b. Font size — 36
   c. Font style — bold
   d. Alignment — center across columns A through J and center vertically
   e. Background color (range A1:J1) — green
   f. Font color — white
   g. Border — thick box border around range A1:J1
2. Column titles
   a. Font style — bold
   b. Alignment — center
   c. Border — bottom border on row 2
3. Data
   a. Alignment — center data in column B
   b. Format dates in column C to the mm/dd/yy format
   c. Numbers in top row (columns E through I in row 3) — Currency style
   d. Numbers below top row (rows 4 through 10) — Comma style
   e. Border — bottom double border on row 10
4. Total line
   a. Row title in cell A11 font Style — bold
   b. Numbers — Currency style with floating dollar sign
5. Function lines
   a. Row titles in range A12:A14 font style — bold
   b. Numbers — Currency style with floating dollar sign in columns E through I
6. Percentages in column J
   a. Numbers — Percentage style with two decimal places; if a cell in range J3:J10 is less than zero, then bold font and color background of cell red
7. Column widths
   a. Column A — 14.00 characters
   b. Columns B through E — best fit
   c. Columns F, H, and I — 12.00 characters
   d. Column G and J — 9.43
8. Row heights
   a. Row 1 — 61.50 points
   b. Rows 2 — 42.00 points
   c. Row 12 — 24.00 points
   d. Remaining rows — default

Except for vertically centering the worksheet title in row 1, the Date format assigned to the dates in column C, the Currency style assigned to the functions in rows 12 through 14, and the conditional formatting in column J, all of the listed formats can be assigned to cells using the Formatting toolbar and mouse.

Changing the Font and Centering the Worksheet Title

When developing presentation-quality worksheets, different fonts often are used in the same worksheet. Excel allows you to change the font of individual characters in a cell or all the characters in a cell, in a range of cells, or in the entire worksheet. To emphasize the worksheet title in cell A1, the font type, size, and style are changed and the worksheet title is centered as described in the steps on the next page.

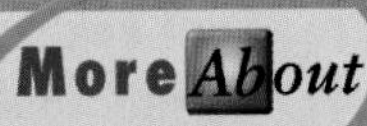

Choosing Colors

Knowing how people perceive colors helps you emphasize parts of your worksheet. Warmer colors (red and orange) tend to reach toward the reader. Cooler colors (blue, green, and violet) tend to pull away from the reader. Bright colors jump out of a dark background and are easiest to see. White or yellow text on a dark blue, green, purple, or black background is ideal.

Toolbars

You can remove a button from a toolbar by holding down the ALT key and dragging it off the toolbar. See Appendix D to reset a toolbar to its default settings.

More About

Font Colors

Excel has the Cycle Font Color button that cycles through the font colors in the selected cell. Click the button and the color of the font changes in the active cell. Keep clicking, and eventually the font colors repeat. To add the Cycle Font Color button to a toolbar, right-click a toolbar, click Customize, click the Commands tab, click Format in the Categories list, scroll down to the Cycle Font Color button in the Commands list, and drag it to a toolbar.

Steps To Change the Font and Center the Worksheet Title

1 Click cell A1. Click the Font box arrow on the Formatting toolbar. Point to Arial Black (or Impact if your system does not have Arial Black).

The Font list displays with Arial Black highlighted (Figure 2-28).

current font of cell A1
Font box arrow
desired font
Font list
font names show font style

FIGURE 2-28

2 Click Arial Black (or Impact). Click the Font Size box arrow on the Formatting toolbar and click 36 on the Font Size list. Click the Bold button.

The text in cell A1 displays in 36-point Arial Black bold font. Excel automatically increases the height of row 1 so that the larger characters fit in the cells (Figure 2-29).

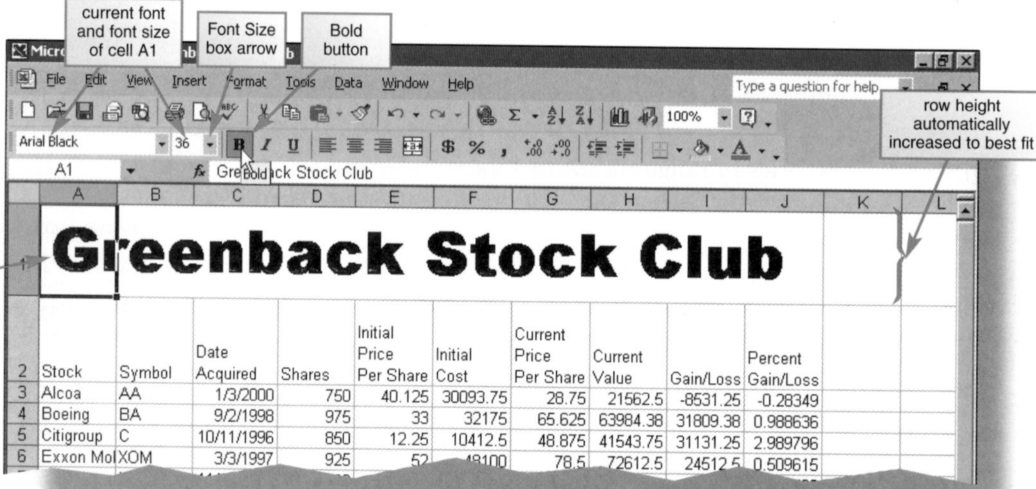

FIGURE 2-29

3 Select the range A1:J1. Right-click the selection. Point to Format Cells on the shortcut menu.

The shortcut menu displays (Figure 2-30).

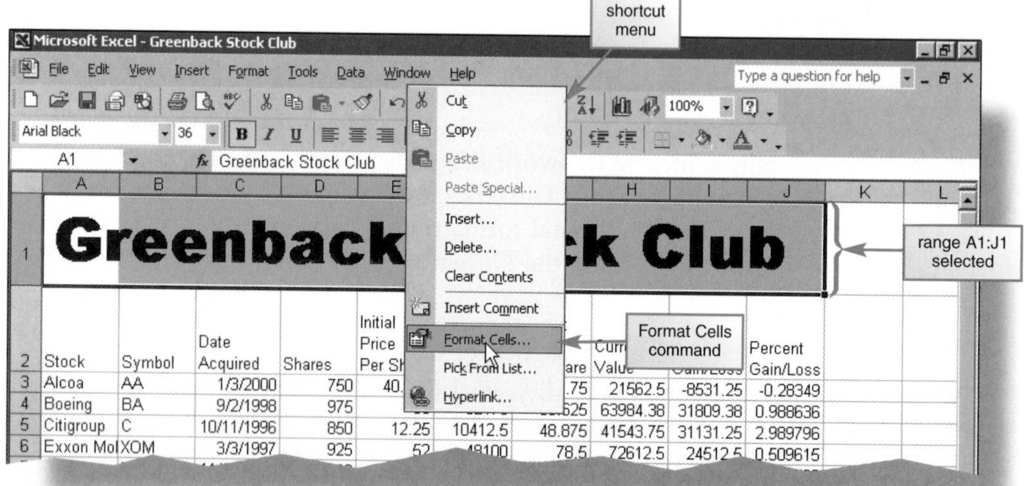

FIGURE 2-30

4 Click Format Cells on the shortcut menu. When the Format Cells dialog box displays, click the Alignment tab. Click the Horizontal box arrow and select Center in the Horizontal list. Click the Vertical box arrow and select Center in the Vertical list. Click the Merge cells check box in the Text control area. Point to the OK button.

The Format Cells dialog box displays as shown in Figure 2-31.

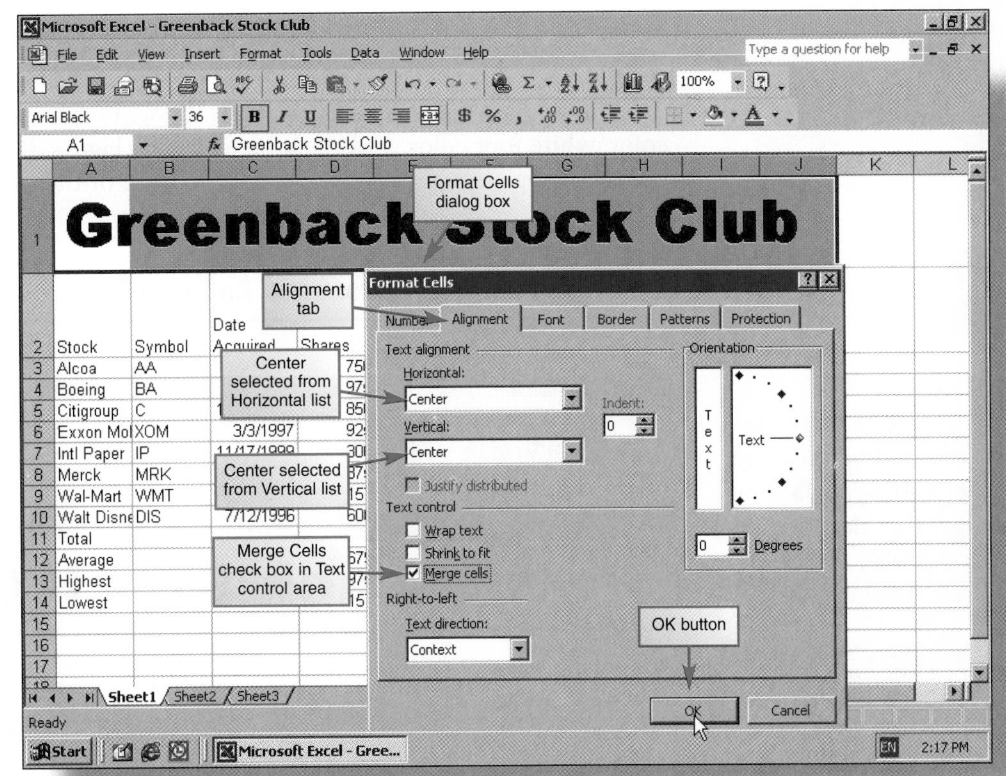

FIGURE 2-31

5 Click the OK button.

Excel merges the cells A1 through J1 to create a new cell A1 and centers the worksheet title across columns A through J and centers it vertically in row 1 (Figure 2-32).

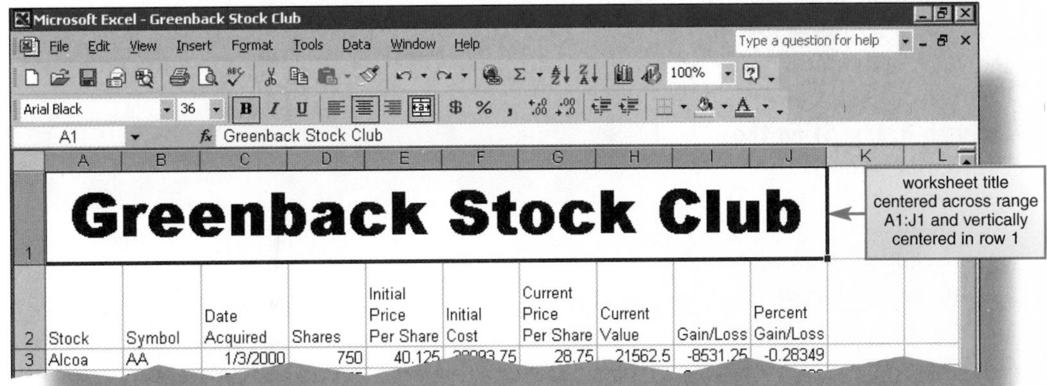

FIGURE 2-32

You can change a font type, size, or style at any time while the worksheet is active. Some Excel users prefer to change fonts before they enter any data. Others change the font while they are building the worksheet or after they have entered all the data.

In Project 1, the Merge and Center button on the Formatting toolbar was used to center the worksheet title across columns. Instead, Step 4 used the Alignment tab in the Format Cells dialog box, because the project also called for vertically centering the worksheet title in row 1.

Other Ways

1. On Format menu click Cells, click appropriate tab, select formats, click OK button
2. Right-click cell, click Format Cells on shortcut menu, click appropriate tab, select formats, click OK button
3. Press CTRL+1, click appropriate tab, select formats, click OK button
4. In Voice Command mode say, "Format, Cells, [desired tab], [desired format], OK"

Changing the Worksheet Title Background and Font Colors and Applying an Outline Border

The final formats to be assigned to the worksheet title are the green background color, white font color, and thick box border (Figure 2-27b on page E 2.26). Perform the following steps to complete the formatting of the worksheet title.

Steps To Change the Title Background and Font Colors and Apply an Outline Border

1 **With cell A1 selected, click the Fill Color button arrow on the Formatting toolbar and then point to the color Green (column 4, row 2) on the Fill Color palette.**

The Fill Color palette displays (Figure 2-33).

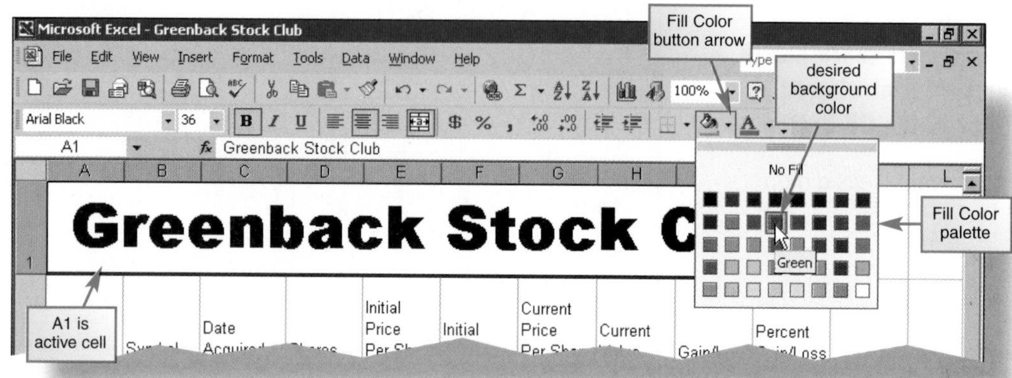

FIGURE 2-33

2 **Click the color Green. Click the Font Color button arrow on the Formatting toolbar. Point to the color White (column 8, row 5) on the Font Color palette.**

The background color of cell A1 changes from white to green, and the Font Color palette displays (Figure 2-34).

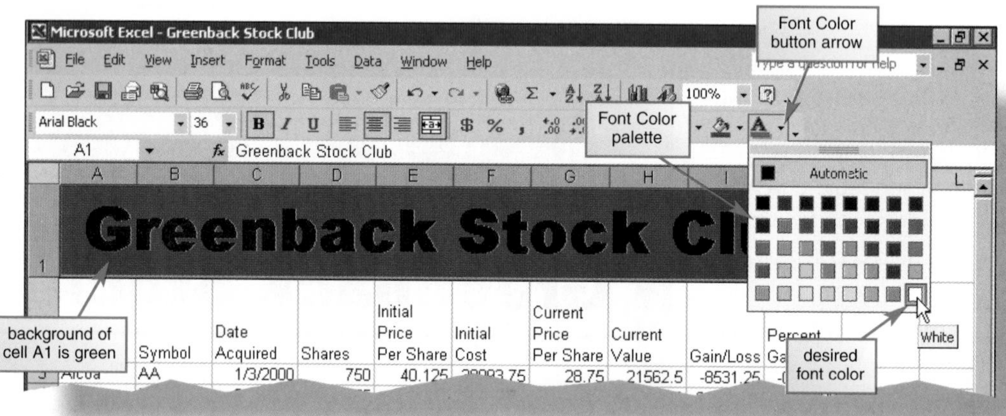

FIGURE 2-34

3 **Click the color White. Click the Borders button arrow on the Formatting toolbar and then point to the Thick Box Border button (column 4, row 3) on the Borders palette.**

The font in the worksheet title changes from black to white, and the Borders palette displays (Figure 2-35).

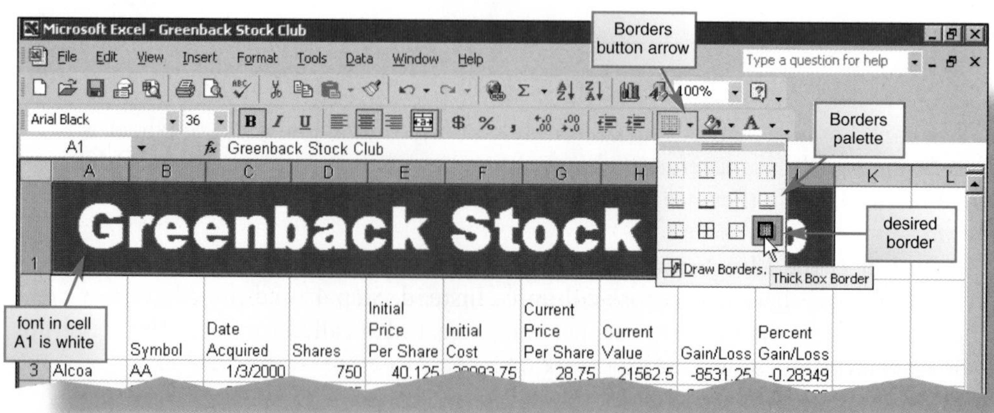

FIGURE 2-35

4 Click the Thick Box Border button. Click cell A2 to deselect cell A1.

Excel displays a thick box border around cell A1 (Figure 2-36).

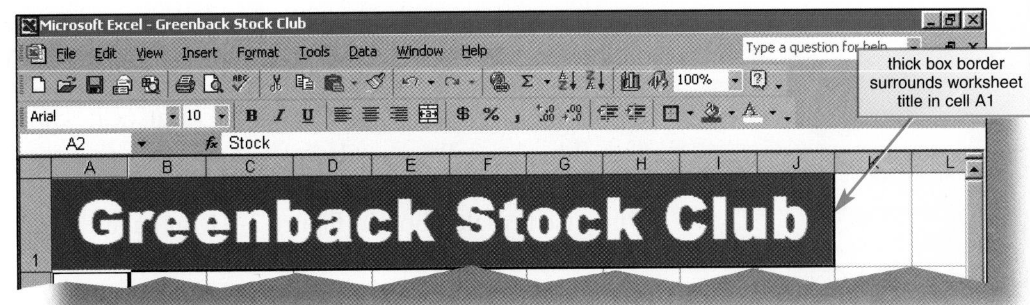

FIGURE 2-36

Other Ways

1. On Format menu click Cells, click appropriate tab, click desired format, click OK button
2. Right-click range, click Format Cells on shortcut menu, click appropriate tab, click desired format, click OK button
3. Press CTRL+1, click appropriate tab, click desired format, click OK button
4. In Voice Command mode say, "Format, Cells, [desired tab], [desired format], OK"

You can remove borders, such as the thick box border around cell A1, by selecting the range and clicking the No Border button on the Borders palette. You can remove a background color by selecting the range, clicking the Fill Color button arrow on the Formatting toolbar, and clicking No Fill on the Fill Color palette. The same technique allows you to change the font color back to Excel's default, except you use the Font Color button arrow and click Automatic.

Applying Formats to the Column Titles

According to Figure 2-27b on page E 2.26, the column titles are bold, centered, and have a bottom border (underline). The following steps assign these formats to the column titles.

Steps To Bold, Center, and Underline the Column Titles

1 Select the range A2:J2. Click the Bold button on the Formatting toolbar. Click the Center button on the Formatting toolbar. Click the Borders button arrow on the Formatting toolbar and then point to the Bottom Border button (column 2, row 1) on the Borders palette.

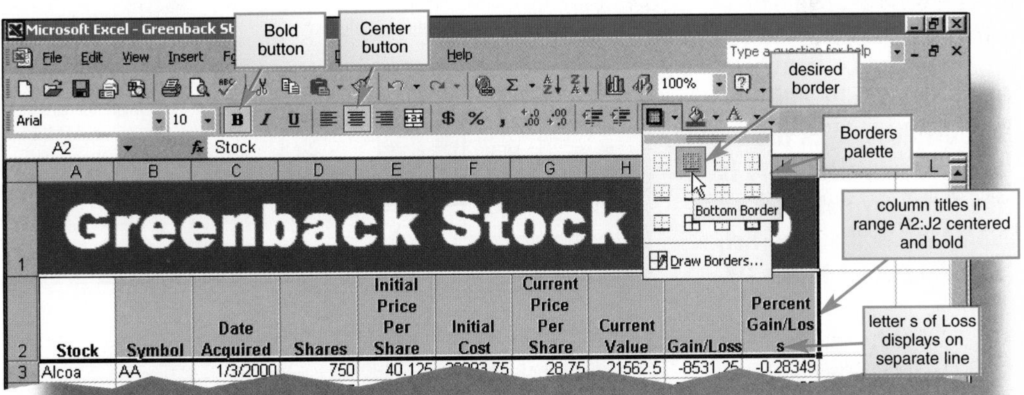

FIGURE 2-37

The column titles in row 2 are bold and centered (Figure 2-37). The Borders palette displays. The column titles in columns E and G display on four lines and the column title in J2 displays with the letter s from the word Loss on a line by itself. These column titles will be fixed later by increasing the column widths.

2 Click the Bottom Border button (column 2 row 1) on the Borders palette.

Excel adds a bottom border to the range A2:J2.

Other Ways

1. Same as 1 to 3 in the above Other Ways box
2. In Voice Command mode say, "Bold, Center, Borders, Bottom Border"

You can align the contents of cells in several different ways. Left alignment, center alignment, and right alignment are the more frequently used alignments. In fact, these three alignments are used so often that Excel has Align Left, Center, and Align Right buttons on the Formatting toolbar. In addition to aligning the contents of a cell horizontally, you also can align the contents of a cell vertically as shown earlier. In addition, you can rotate the contents of a cell to various angles (see the Format Cells dialog box in Figure 2-31 on page E 2.29).

Adding Colors and Borders

Colors and borders can change a boring worksheet into an interesting and easy-to-read worksheet. Colors and borders can also be used to make important information stand out.

Centering the Stock Symbols and Formatting the Dates and Numbers in the Worksheet

With the column titles formatted, the next step is to center the stock symbols in column B and format the dates in column C. If a cell entry is short, such as the stock symbols in column B, centering the entries within their respective columns improves the appearance of the worksheet. The following steps center the data in cells B3 to B10 and formats the dates in cells C3 to C10.

To Center Data in Cells and Format Dates

1 Select the range B3:B10. Click the Center button on the Formatting toolbar.

The stock symbols in column B are centered.

2 Select the range C3:C10. Right-click the selected range and click Format Cells. When the Format Cells dialog box displays, click the Number tab, click Date in the Category list, click 03/14/01 in the Type list, and then point to the OK button.

The Format Cells dialog box displays as shown in Figure 2-38.

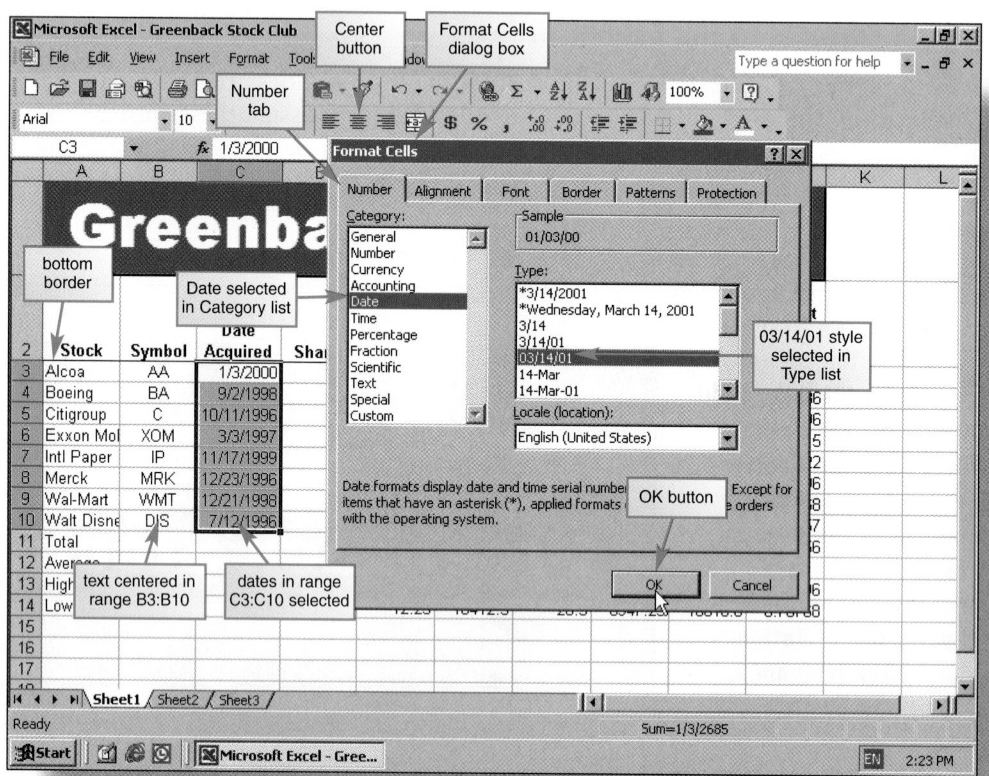

FIGURE 2-38

3 Click the OK button. Select cell E3 to deselect the range C3:C10.

The dates in column C display using the date format style mm/dd/yy (Figure 2-39).

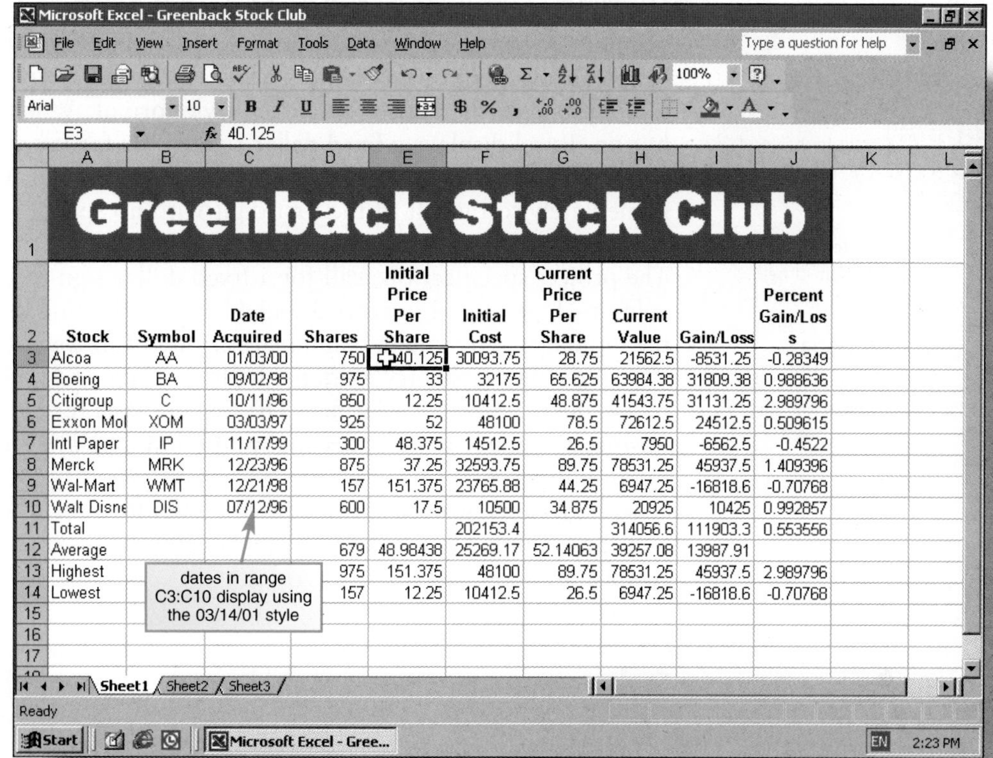

FIGURE 2-39

Other Ways

1. On Format menu click Cells, click appropriate tab, click desired format, click OK button
2. Right-click range, click Format Cells on shortcut menu, click appropriate tab, click desired format, click OK button
3. Press CTRL+1, click appropriate tab, click desired format, click OK button
4. In Voice Command mode say, "Format, Cells, [desired tab], [desired format], OK"

Rather than selecting the range B3:B10 in Step 1, you could have clicked the column B heading immediately above cell B1, and then clicked the Center button on the Formatting toolbar. In this case, all cells in column B down to cell B65536 would have been assigned center alignment. This same procedure could have been used to format the dates in column C.

Formatting Numbers Using the Formatting Toolbar

You can use the buttons on the Formatting toolbar to format numbers as dollar amounts, whole numbers with comma placement, and percentages. Customized numeric formats also can be assigned using the **Cells command** on the Format menu or the Format Cells command on the shortcut menu.

As shown in Figure 2-27(b) on page E 2.26, the worksheet is formatted to resemble an accounting report. For example, in columns E through I, the first row of numbers (row 3), the totals (row 11), and the rows below the totals (rows 13 and 14) display with dollar signs, while the remaining numbers (rows 4 through 10) in these columns do not. To display a dollar sign in a number, you should use the Currency style format.

Rotating and Fitting Text in Cells

Besides aligning text horizontally and vertically in a cell, you can rotate text and shrink text to fit in a cell. To rotate text or shrink text to fit in a cell, click Format Cells on the shortcut menu, click the Alignment tab, and then select the type of text control you want.

The **Currency style format** displays a dollar sign to the left of the number, inserts a comma every three positions to the left of the decimal point, and displays numbers to the nearest cent (hundredths place). The **Currency Style button** on the Formatting toolbar assigns the desired Currency style format. When you use the Currency Style button, Excel displays a **fixed dollar sign** to the far left in the cell, often with spaces between it and the first digit. To assign a **floating dollar sign** that displays immediately to the left of the first digit with no spaces, you must use the Cells command on the Format menu or the Format Cells command on the shortcut menu. The project specifications call for a fixed dollar sign to be assigned to the numbers in columns E through I in rows 3 and 11, and a floating dollar sign to be assigned to the monetary amounts in columns E through I in rows 12 through 14.

To display monetary amounts with commas and no dollar signs, you will want to use the Comma style format. The **Comma style format** inserts a comma every three positions to the left of the decimal point and displays numbers to the nearest hundredths (cents).

The following steps show how to assign formats using the Currency Style button and the Comma Style button on the Formatting toolbar. These steps also underline row 10 and bold the total row titles.

To Apply a Currency Style Format and Comma Style Format Using the Formatting Toolbar

1 Select the range E3:I3. While holding down the CTRL key, select the nonadjacent range F11:I11. Point to the Currency Style button on the Formatting toolbar.

The nonadjacent ranges display as shown in Figure 2-40.

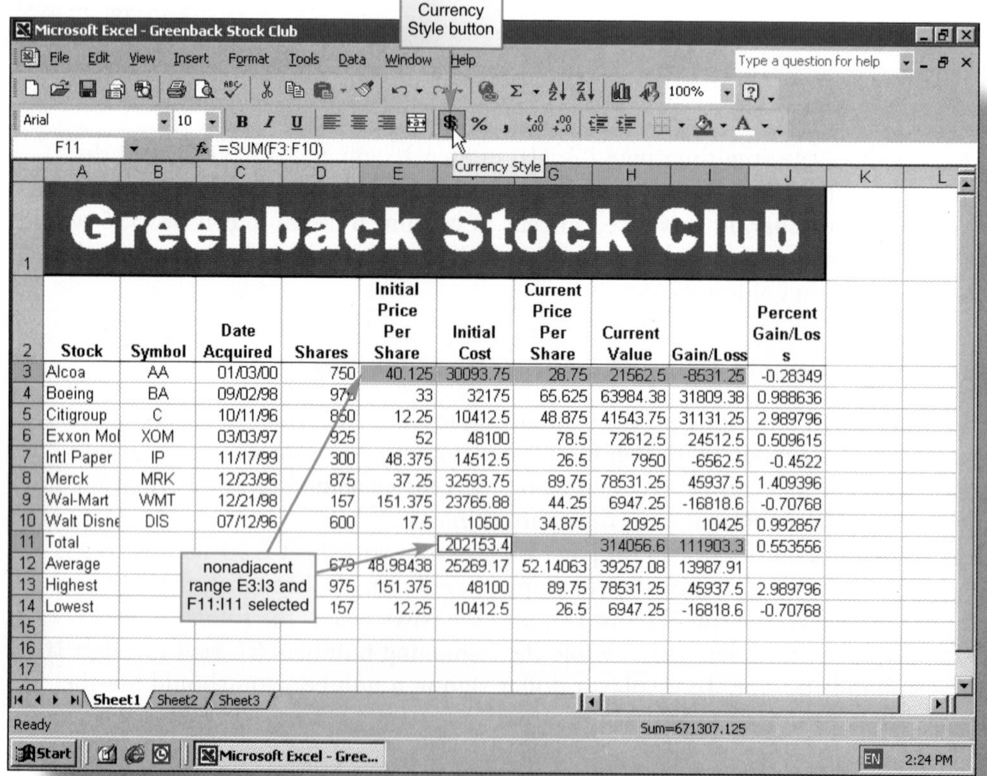

FIGURE 2-40

2 **Click the Currency Style button. Select the range E4:I10 and then point to the Comma Style button on the Formatting toolbar.**

Excel automatically increases the width of columns F, H, and I to best fit, so the numbers assigned the Currency style format will fit in the cells (Figure 2-41). The range E4:I10 is selected.

Microsoft Excel - Greenback Stock Club

Comma Style button

Comma Style

E4 33

Greenback Stock Club

	Stock	Symbol	Date Acquired	Shares	Initial Price Per Share	Initial Cost	Current Price Per Share	Current Value	Gain/Loss	Perc Gain/ s
3	Alcoa	AA	01/03/00	750	$ 40.13	$ 30,093.75	$ 28.75	$ 21,562.50	$ (8,531.25)	-0.28349
4	Boeing	BA	09/02/98	975	33	32175	65.625	63984.375	31809.375	0.988636
5	Citigroup	C	10/11/96	850	12.25	10412.5	48.875	41543.75	31131.25	2.989796
6	Exxon Mol	XOM	03/03/97	925	52	48100	78.5	72612.5	24512.5	0.50961
7	Intl Paper	IP	11/17/99	300	48.375	14512.5	26.5	7950	-6562.5	-0.452
8	Merck	MRK	12/23/96	875	37.25	32593.75	89.75	78531.25	45937.5	1.409396
9	Wal-Mart	WMT	12/21/98	157	151.375	23765.875	44.25	6947.25	-16818.625	-0.70768
10	Walt Disne	DIS	07/12/96	600	17.5	10500	34.875	20925	10425	0.992857
11	Total					$202,153.38		$314,056.63	$111,903.25	0.553556
12	Average			679	48.98438	25269.17188	52.14063	39257.07813	13987.90625	
13	Highest			975	151.375	48100	89.75	78531.25	45937.5	2.989796
14	Lowest			157	12.25	10412.5	26.5	6947.25	-16818.625	-0.70768

parentheses indicate number is negative

range E4:I10 selected

Currency style format with fixed dollar signs

width of columns automatically increased due to formatting

FIGURE 2-41

3 **Click the Comma Style button.**

Excel assigns the Comma style format to the range E4:I10.

4 **Click cell E3. Click the Increase Decimal button on the Formatting toolbar. Do the same to cell G3. Select the range E4:E10. Click the Increase Decimal button on the Formatting toolbar. Do the same to the range G4:G10. Click cell A10 to deselect the range G4:G10.**

The initial prices and current prices display with three decimal positions (Figure 2-42).

Microsoft Excel - Greenback Stock Club

Increase Decimal button

Decrease Decimal button

A10 Walt Disney

Greenback Stock Club

	Stock	Symbol	Date Acquired	Shares	Initial Price Per Share	Initial Cost	Current Price Per Share	Current Value	Gain/Loss	Percent Gain/Los s
3	Alcoa	AA	01/03/00	750	$ 40.125	$ 30,093.75	$ 28.750	$ 21,562.50	$ (8,531.25)	-0.28349
4	Boeing	BA	09/02/98	975	33.000	32,175.00	65.625	63,984.38	31,809.38	0.988636
5	Citigroup	C	10/11/96	850	12.250	10,412.50	48.875	41,543.75	31,131.25	2.989796
6	Exxon Mol	XOM	03/03/97	925	52.000	48,100.00	78.500	72,612.50	24,512.50	0.509615
7	Intl Paper	IP	11/17/99	300	48.375	14,512.50	26.500	7,950.00	(6,562.50)	-0.4522
8	Merck	MRK	12/23/96	875	37.250	32,593.75	89.750	78,531.25	45,937.50	1.409396
9	Wal-Mart	WMT		157	151.375	23,765.88	44.250	6,947.25	(16,818.63)	-0.70768
10	Walt Disne	DIS		600	17.500	10,500.00	34.875	20,925.00	10,425.00	0.992857
11	Total					$202,153.38		$314,056.63	$111,903.25	0.553556
12	Average			679	48.98438	25269.17188	52.14063	39257.07813	13987.90625	
13	Highest			975	151.375	48100	89.75	78531.25	45937.5	2.989796
14	Lowest			157	12.25	10412.5	26.5	6947.25	-16818.625	-0.70768

Comma style format with three decimal places

FIGURE 2-42

The **Increase Decimal button** on the Formatting toolbar is used to display additional decimal places in a cell. Each time you click the Increase Decimal button, Excel adds a decimal place to the selected cell. The **Decrease Decimal button** removes a decimal place from the selected cell each time it is clicked.

Formatting Numbers as You Enter Them

You can format numbers when you enter them by entering a dollar sign ($), comma (,), or percent sign (%) as part of the number. For example, if you enter 1500, Excel displays 1500. However, if you enter $1500, Excel displays $1,500.

The Currency Style button assigns a fixed dollar sign to the numbers in the ranges E3:I3 and F11:I11. In each cell in these ranges, the dollar sign displays to the far left with spaces between it and the first digit in the cell. Excel automatically rounds a number to fit the selected format.

Underlining the Row above the Title Row and Bolding the Total Row Titles

The following steps add a bottom double border to row 10 and bolds the total row titles.

TO UNDERLINE THE ROW ABOVE THE TITLE ROW AND BOLD THE TOTAL ROW TITLES

1. Select the range A10:J10, click the Borders button arrow on the Formatting toolbar, and then click the Bottom Double Border (column 1, row 2) on the Borders palette.
2. Select the range A11:A14, click the Bold button on the Formatting toolbar. Select cell E12.

The row immediately above the total row has a double underline, signifying the last stock in the worksheet. The row titles in the range A11:A14 are bold (Figure 2-43).

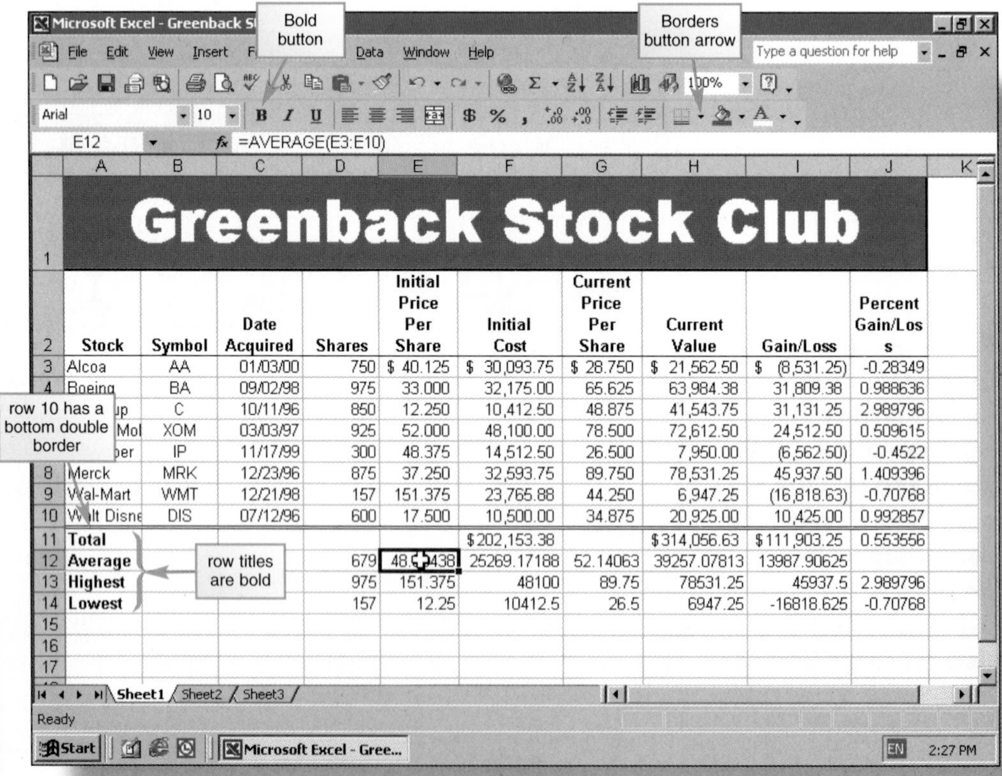

	Stock	Symbol	Date Acquired	Shares	Initial Price Per Share	Initial Cost	Current Price Per Share	Current Value	Gain/Loss	Percent Gain/Los s
3	Alcoa	AA	01/03/00	750	$ 40.125	$ 30,093.75	$ 28.750	$ 21,562.50	$ (8,531.25)	-0.28349
4	Boeing	BA	09/02/98	975	33.000	32,175.00	65.625	63,984.38	31,809.38	0.988636
5	...up	C	10/11/96	850	12.250	10,412.50	48.875	41,543.75	31,131.25	2.989796
6	...Mol	XOM	03/03/97	925	52.000	48,100.00	78.500	72,612.50	24,512.50	0.509615
7	...per	IP	11/17/99	300	48.375	14,512.50	26.500	7,950.00	(6,562.50)	-0.4522
8	Merck	MRK	12/23/96	875	37.250	32,593.75	89.750	78,531.25	45,937.50	1.409396
9	Wal-Mart	WMT	12/21/98	157	151.375	23,765.88	44.250	6,947.25	(16,818.63)	-0.70768
10	Walt Disne	DIS	07/12/96	600	17.500	10,500.00	34.875	20,925.00	10,425.00	0.992857
11	**Total**					$202,153.38		$314,056.63	$111,903.25	0.553556
12	**Average**			679	48.4438	25269.17188	52.14063	39257.07813	13987.90625	
13	**Highest**			975	151.375	48100	89.75	78531.25	45937.5	2.989796
14	**Lowest**			157	12.25	10412.5	26.5	6947.25	-16818.625	-0.70768

FIGURE 2-43

Formatted Numbers in Calculations

The numbers you see on your screen may not be the same ones used in calculations. When a number has more decimal places than are showing on the screen because you formatted it, the actual number and not the displayed number is used in the computation.

Formatting Numbers Using the Format Cells Command on the Shortcut Menu

The following steps show you how to use the Format Cells command on the shortcut menu to apply the Currency style format with a floating dollar sign to the totals in the range E12:I14.

Steps To Apply a Currency Style Format with a Floating Dollar Sign Using the Format Cells Command

1 Select the range E12:I14. Right-click the selected range. Point to Format Cells on the shortcut menu.

The shortcut menu displays (Figure 2-44).

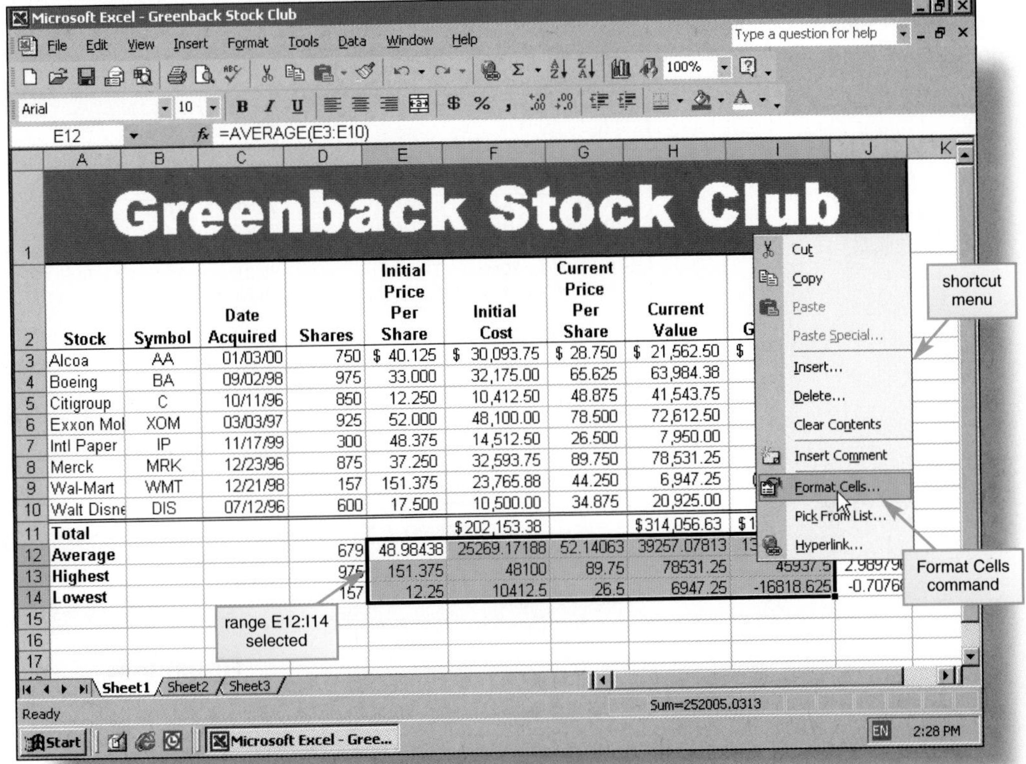

FIGURE 2-44

2 Click Format Cells. Click the Number tab in the Format Cells dialog box. Click Currency in the Category list, click the third style ($1,234.10) in the Negative numbers list, and then point to the OK button.

The Format Cells dialog box displays (Figure 2-45).

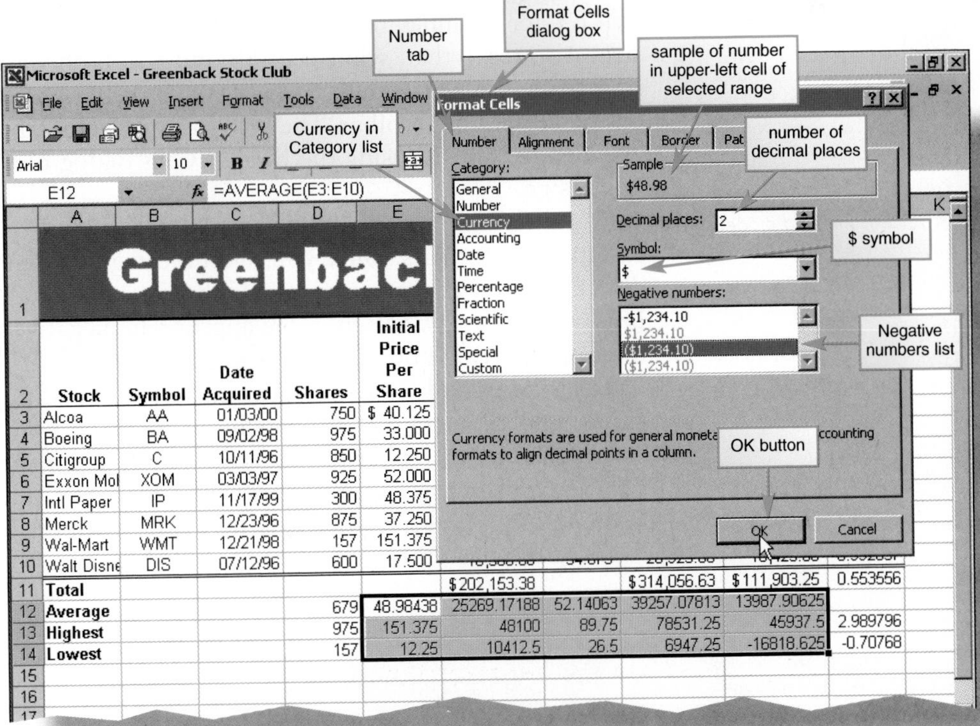

FIGURE 2-45

3 **Click the OK button.**

The worksheet displays with the totals in rows 12 through 14 assigned the Currency style format with a floating dollar sign (Figure 2-46).

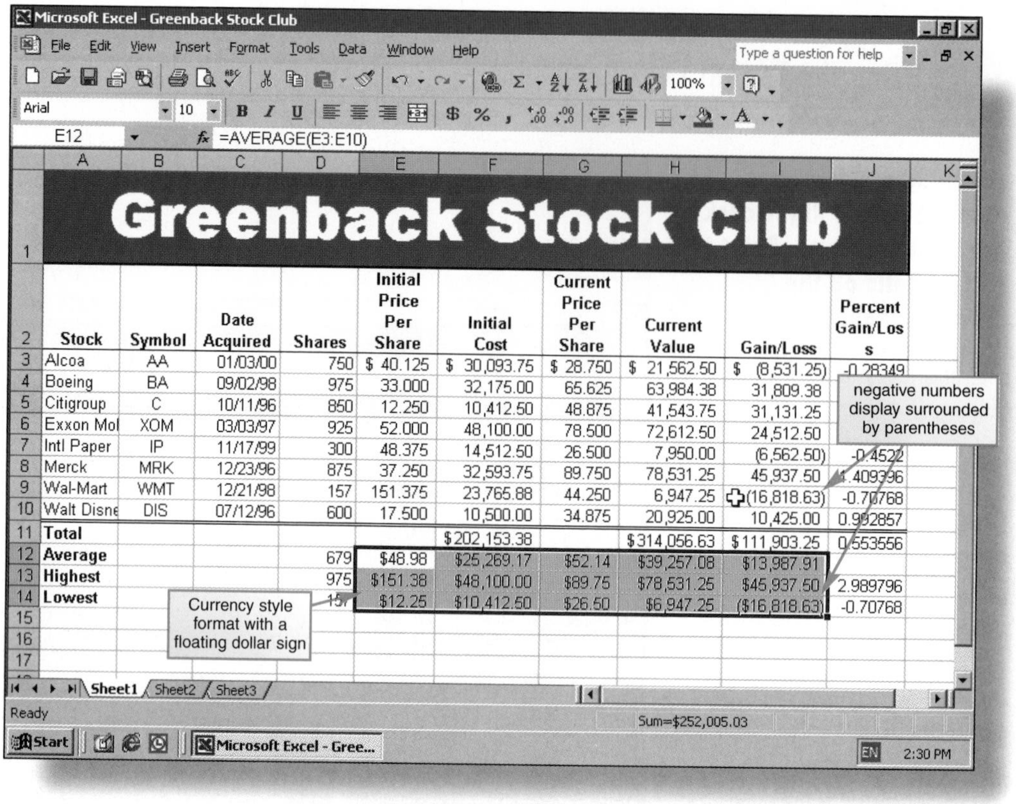

Microsoft Excel - Greenback Stock Club

E12 =AVERAGE(E3:E10)

	A	B	C	D	E	F	G	H	I	J
1	**Greenback Stock Club**									
2	**Stock**	**Symbol**	**Date Acquired**	**Shares**	**Initial Price Per Share**	**Initial Cost**	**Current Price Per Share**	**Current Value**	**Gain/Loss**	**Percent Gain/Los s**
3	Alcoa	AA	01/03/00	750	$ 40.125	$ 30,093.75	$ 28.750	$ 21,562.50	$ (8,531.25)	-0.28349
4	Boeing	BA	09/02/98	975	33.000	32,175.00	65.625	63,984.38	31,809.38	
5	Citigroup	C	10/11/96	850	12.250	10,412.50	48.875	41,543.75	31,131.25	
6	Exxon Mol	XOM	03/03/97	925	52.000	48,100.00	78.500	72,612.50	24,512.50	
7	Intl Paper	IP	11/17/99	300	48.375	14,512.50	26.500	7,950.00	(6,562.50)	-0.4522
8	Merck	MRK	12/23/96	875	37.250	32,593.75	89.750	78,531.25	45,937.50	1.409396
9	Wal-Mart	WMT	12/21/98	157	151.375	23,765.88	44.250	6,947.25	(16,818.63)	-0.70768
10	Walt Disne	DIS	07/12/96	600	17.500	10,500.00	34.875	20,925.00	10,425.00	0.992857
11	**Total**					$202,153.38		$314,056.63	$111,903.25	0.553556
12	**Average**			679	$48.98	$25,269.17	$52.14	$39,257.08	$13,987.91	
13	**Highest**			975	$151.38	$48,100.00	$89.75	$78,531.25	$45,937.50	2.989796
14	**Lowest**			15	$12.25	$10,412.50	$26.50	$6,947.25	($16,818.63)	-0.70768

negative numbers display surrounded by parentheses

Currency style format with a floating dollar sign

Sheet1 / Sheet2 / Sheet3

Ready Sum=$252,005.03

FIGURE 2-46

Other Ways

1. On Format menu click Cells, click Number tab, click Currency in Category list, select format, click OK button
2. Press CTRL+1, click Number tab, click Currency in Category list, select format, click OK button
3. Press CTRL+SHIFT+DOLLAR SIGN
4. In Voice Command mode say, "Format, Cells, Number, Currency, OK"

Recall that a floating dollar sign always displays immediately to the left of the first digit, and the fixed dollar sign always displays on the left side of the cell. Cell E3, for example, has a fixed dollar sign, while cell E12 has a floating dollar sign. Also recall that, while cells E3 and E12 both were assigned a Currency style format, the Currency style was assigned to cell E3 using the Currency Style button on the Formatting toolbar. The result is a fixed dollar sign. The Currency style was assigned to cell E12 using the Format Cells dialog box and the result is a floating dollar sign.

As shown in Figure 2-45 on the previous page, you can choose from 12 categories of formats. Once you select a category, you can select the number of decimal places, whether or not a dollar sign should display, and how negative numbers should display. Selecting the appropriate negative numbers format in Step 2 is important, because doing so adds a space to the right of the number (as do the Currency Style and Comma Style buttons). Some of the available negative number formats do not align the numbers in the worksheet on the decimal points.

The negative number format selected in the previous set of steps displays in cell I14, which has a negative entry. The third selection in the Negative numbers list (Figure 2-45) purposely was chosen to agree with the negative number format assigned to cell I9 using the Comma Style button.

Formatting Numbers Using the Percent Style Button and Increase Decimal Button

The last entry in the worksheet that needs to be formatted is the percent gain/loss in column J. Currently, the numbers in column J display as a decimal fraction (-0.28349 in cell J3). Follow these steps to change to the Percent style format with two decimal places.

Steps To Apply a Percent Style Format

1 Select the range J3:J14. Click the Percent Style button on the Formatting toolbar.

The numbers in column J display as a rounded whole percent.

2 Click the Increase Decimal button on the Formatting toolbar twice.

The numbers in column J display with two decimal places (Figure 2-47).

Microsoft Excel - Greenback Stock Club

Percent Style button

Increase Decimal button

Decrease Decimal button

Increase Decimal

J3 =I3/F3

Greenback Stock Club

Percent style format with two decimal places

	Stock	Symbol	Date Acquired	Shares	Initial Price Per Share	Initial Cost	Current Price Per Share	Current Value	Gain/Loss	Percent Gain/Los s
3	Alcoa	AA	01/03/00	750	$ 40.125	$ 30,093.75	$ 28.750	$ 21,562.50	$ (8,531.25)	-28.35%
4	Boeing	BA	09/02/98	975	33.000	32,175.00	65.625	63,984.38	31,809.38	98.86%
5	Citigroup	C	10/11/96	850	12.250	10,412.50	48.875	41,543.75	31,131.25	298.98%
6	Exxon Mol	XOM	03/03/97	925	52.000	48,100.00	78.500	72,612.50	24,512.50	50.96%
7	Intl Paper	IP	11/17/99	300	48.375	14,512.50	26.500	7,950.00	(6,562.50)	-45.22%
8	Merck	MRK	12/23/96	875	37.250	32,593.75	89.750	78,531.25	45,937.50	140.94%
9	Wal-Mart	WMT	12/21/98	157	151.375	23,765.88	44.250	6,947.25	(16,818.63)	-70.77%
10	Walt Disne	DIS	07/12/96	600	17.500	10,500.00	34.875	20,925.00	10,425.00	99.29%
11	Total					$202,153.38		$314,056.63	$111,903.25	55.36%
12	Average			679	$48.98	$25,269.17	$52.14	$39,257.08	$13,987.91	
13	Highest			975	$151.38	$48,100.00	$89.75	$78,531.25	$45,937.50	298.98%
14	Lowest			157	$12.25	$10,412.50	$26.50	$6,947.25	($16,818.63)	-70.77%

FIGURE 2-47

The **Percent Style button** on the Formatting toolbar is used to display a value determined by multiplying the cell entry by 100, rounding the result to the nearest percent, and adding a percent sign. For example, when cell J3 is formatted using the Percent Style and Increase Decimal buttons, the actual value -0.283489097 displays as -28.35%.

Other Ways

1. On Format menu click Cells, click Number tab, click Percentage in Category list, select format, click OK button
2. Right-click range, click Format Cells on shortcut menu, click Number tab, click Percentage in Category list, select format, click OK button
3. Press CTRL+1, click Number tab, click Percentage in Category list, select format, click OK button
4. Press CTRL+SHIFT+PERCENT SIGN (%)
5. In Voice Command mode say, "Format, Cells, Number, Percentage, OK"

Conditional Formatting

The last formatting requirement is to emphasize the negative percents in column J by formatting them in bold with a red background. The **Conditional Formatting command** on the Format menu will be used to complete this task.

Excel lets you apply formatting that appears only when the value in a cell meets conditions that you specify. This type of formatting is called **conditional formatting**. You can apply conditional formatting to a cell, a range of cells, the entire worksheet, or the entire workbook. Usually, you apply it to a range of cells that contains values you want to highlight if conditions warrant. For example, you can instruct Excel to bold and change the color of the background of a cell if the value in the cell meets a condition, such as being less than zero. Assume you assign the range J3:J10 the following condition:

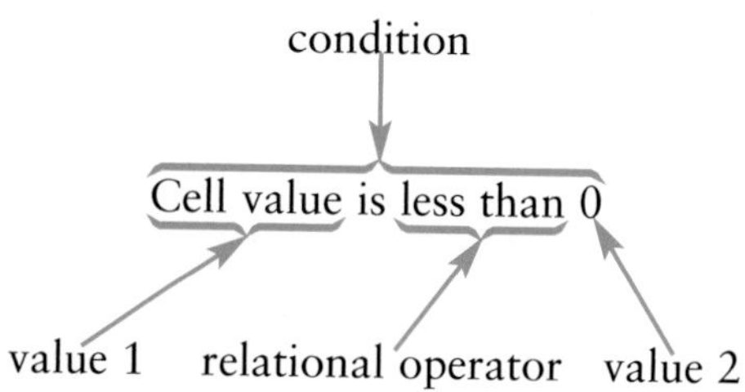

Conditional Formatting

You can conditionally assign any format to a cell, a range of cells, the worksheet, or an entire workbook. If the value of the cell changes and no longer meets the specified condition, Excel temporarily suppresses the formats that highlight that condition.

A **condition**, which is made up of two values and a relational operator, is true or false for each cell in the range. If the condition is true, then Excel applies the formatting. If the condition is false, then Excel suppresses the formatting. What makes conditional formatting so powerful is that the cell's appearance can change as you enter new values in the worksheet.

The following steps show how to assign conditional formatting to the range J3:J10. In this case, any cell value less than zero will cause the number in the cell to display in bold with a red background.

Steps To Apply Conditional Formatting

1 Select the range J3:J10. Click Format on the menu bar and then point to Conditional Formatting.

The Format menu displays (Figure 2-48).

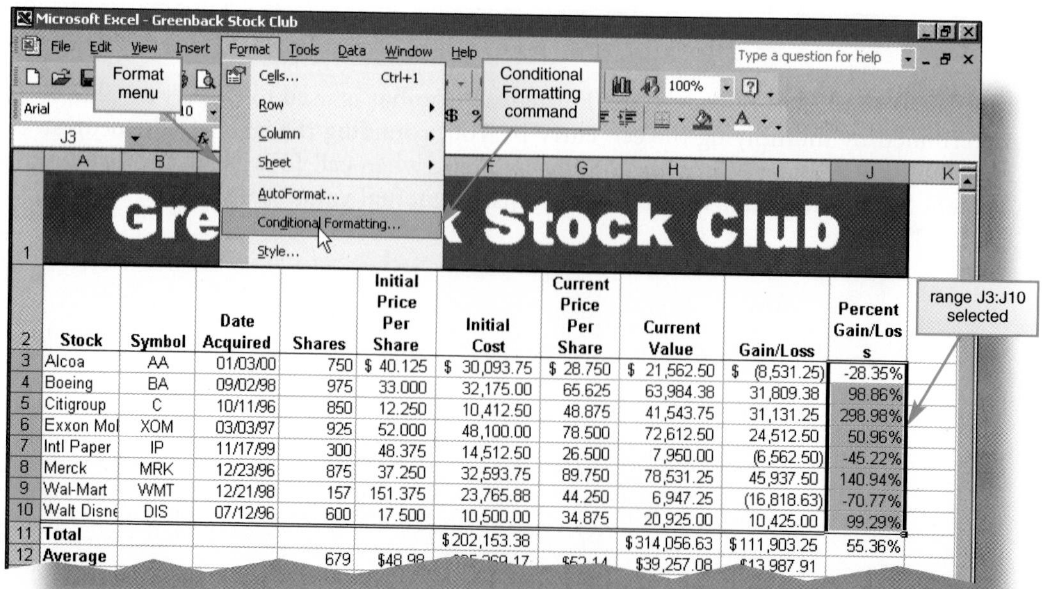

FIGURE 2-48

2 Click Conditional Formatting. When the Conditional Formatting dialog box displays, if necessary, click the leftmost text box arrow and then click Cell Value Is. Click the middle text box arrow and then click less than. Type 0 in the rightmost text box. Point to the Format button.

The Conditional Formatting dialog box displays as shown in Figure 2-49.

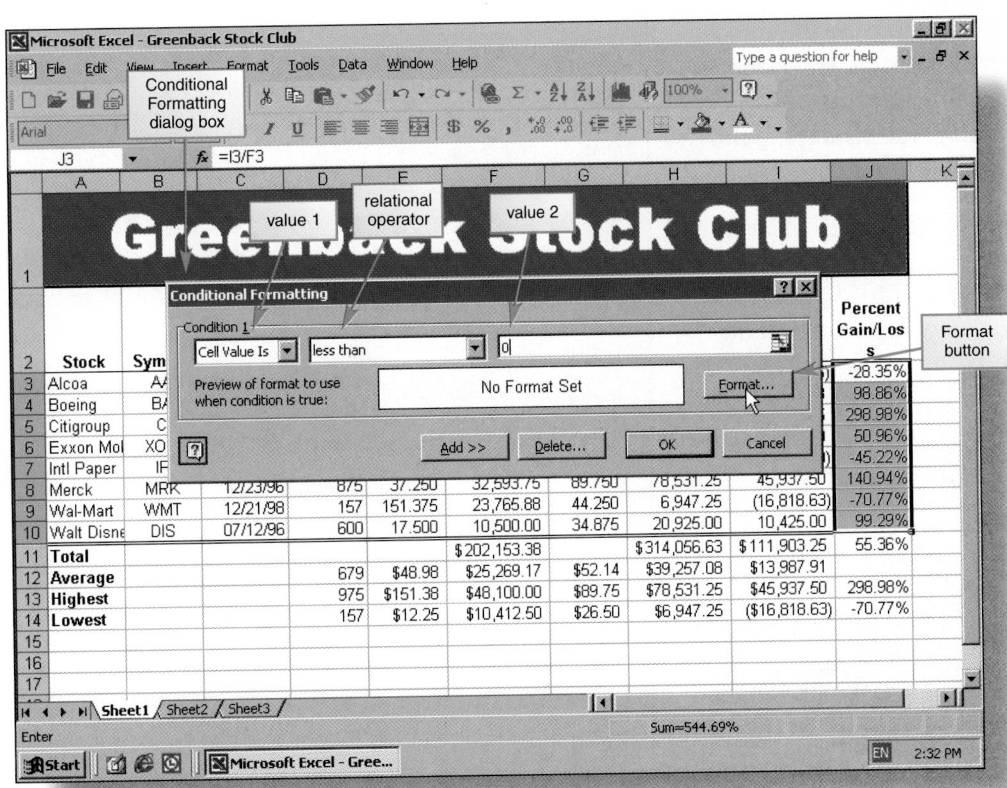

FIGURE 2-49

3 Click the Format button. When the Format Cells dialog box displays, click the Font tab and then click Bold in the Font style list. Click the Patterns tab. Click the color Red (column 1, row 3). Point to the OK button.

The Patterns sheet in the Format Cells dialog box displays as shown in Figure 2-50.

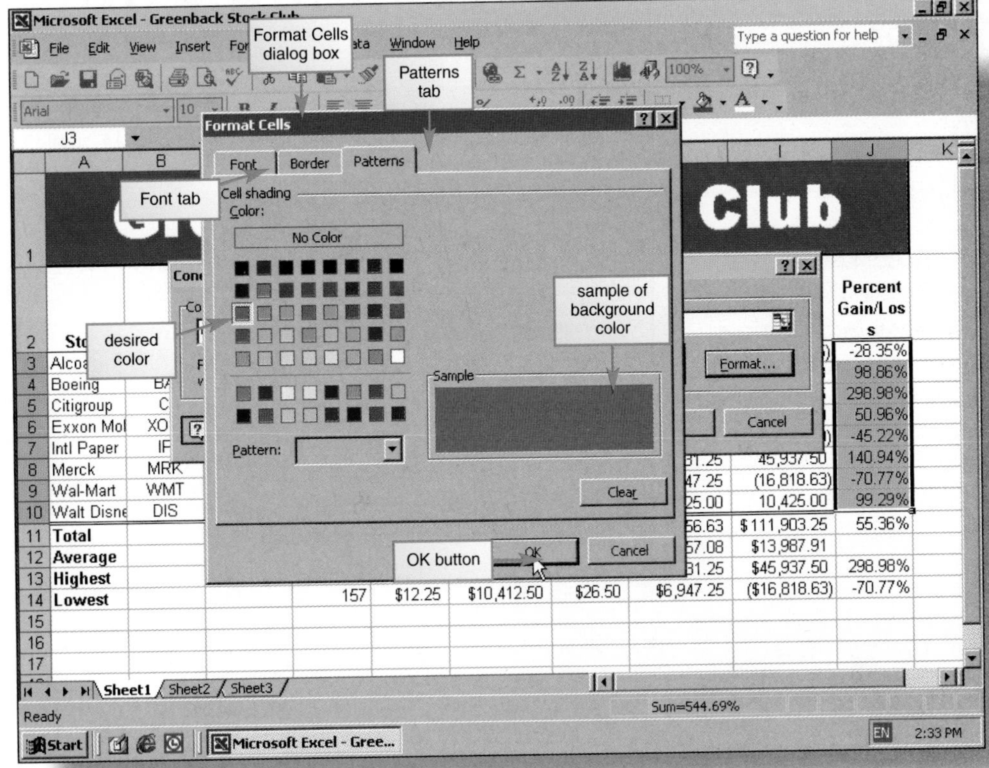

FIGURE 2-50

4 Click the OK button. When the Conditional Formatting dialog box displays, point to the OK button.

The Conditional Formatting dialog box displays as shown in Figure 2-51. In the middle of the dialog box, Excel displays a preview of the format to use when the condition is true.

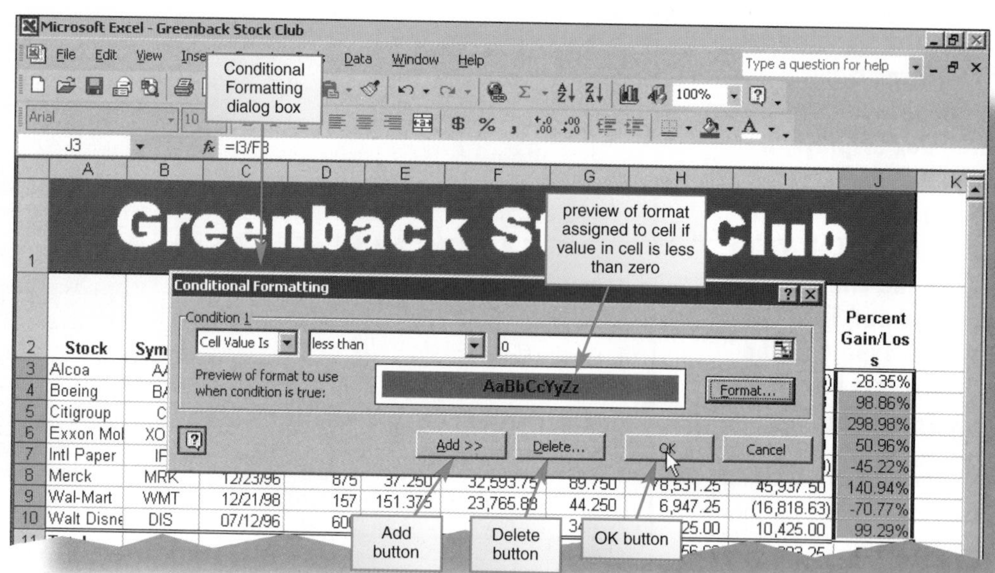

FIGURE 2-51

5 Click the OK button. Click cell A16 to deselect the range J3:J10.

Excel assigns the conditional format to the range J3:J10. Any negative value in this range displays in bold with a red background (Figure 2-52).

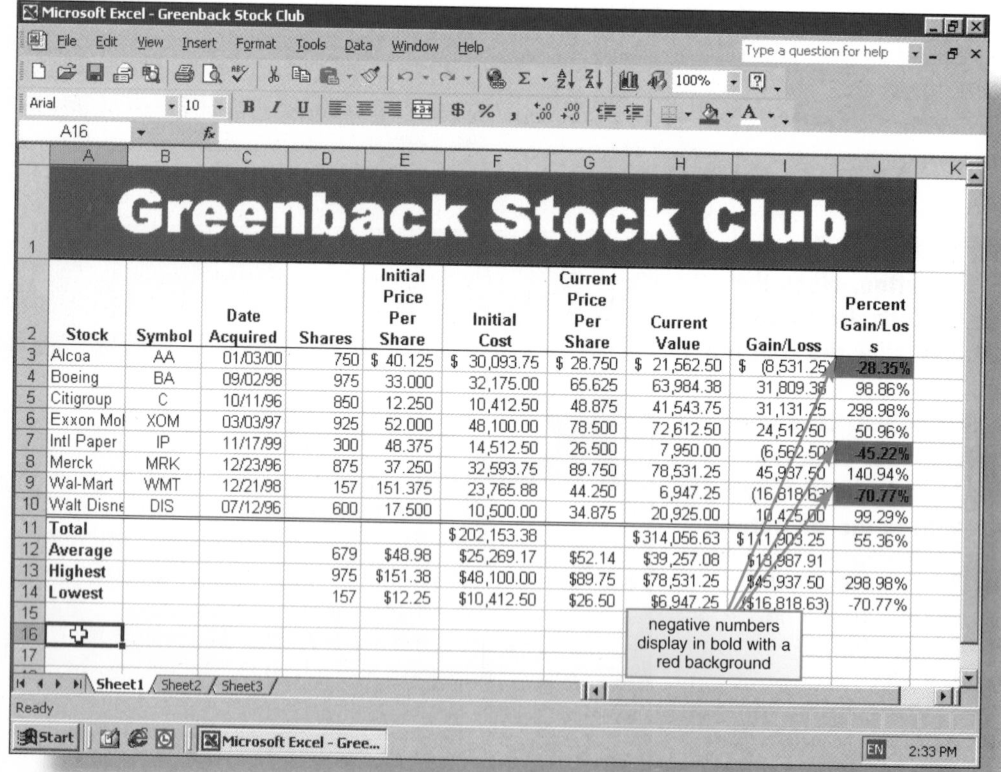

FIGURE 2-52

Other Ways

1. Press ALT+O, D
2. In Voice Command mode say, "Format, Conditional Formatting"

In Figure 2-51, the **preview box** in the Conditional Formatting dialog box shows the format that will be assigned to all cells in the range J3:J10 that have a value less than zero. This preview allows you to modify the format before you click the OK button. The **Add button** in the Conditional Formatting dialog box allows you to add up to two additional conditions. The **Delete button** allows you to delete one or more active conditions.

The middle text box in the Conditional Formatting dialog box contains the relational operator. The eight different relational operators from which you can choose are summarized in Table 2-5.

With the number formatting complete, the next step is to change the column widths and row heights to make the worksheet easier to read.

Table 2-5 Summary of Conditional Formatting Relational Operators

RELATIONAL OPERATOR	DESCRIPTION
Between	Cell value is between two numbers
Not between	Cell value is not between two numbers
Equal to	Cell value is equal to a number
Not equal to	Cell value is not equal to a number
Greater than	Cell value is greater than a number
Less than	Cell value is less than a number
Greater than or equal to	Cell value is greater than or equal to a number
Less than or equal to	Cell value is less than or equal to a number

Changing the Widths of Columns and Heights of Rows

When Excel starts and the blank worksheet displays on the screen, all of the columns have a default width of 8.43 characters, or 64 pixels. A **character** is defined as a letter, number, symbol, or punctuation mark in 10-point Arial font, the default font used by Excel. An average of 8.43 characters in this font will fit in a cell. Another measure is pixels, which is short for picture element. A **pixel** is a dot on the screen that contains a color. The size of the dot is based on your screen's resolution. At a common resolution of 800 × 600, 800 pixels display across the screen and 600 pixels display down the screen for a total of 480,000 pixels. It is these 480,000 pixels that form the font and other items you see on the screen.

The default row height in a blank worksheet is 12.75 points (or 17 pixels). Recall from Project 1 that a point is equal to 1/72 of an inch. Thus, 12.75 points is equal to about one-sixth of an inch. You can change the width of the columns or height of the rows at any time to make the worksheet easier to read or to ensure that an entry displays properly in a cell.

More About

Painting Formats

Painting is not an envious chore. In Excel, however, if you know how to paint you can save yourself time and effort when formatting a worksheet. For example, if you see a cell that has the format you want to assign to another cell or range of cells, click the cell with the desired format, click the Format Painter button on the Standard toolbar, and then click the cell or drag through the cells you want to paint the format with.

Changing the Widths of Columns

When changing the column width, you can set the width manually or you can instruct Excel to size the column to best fit. **Best fit** means that the width of the column will be increased or decreased so the widest entry will fit in the column. Sometimes, you may prefer more or less white space in a column than best fit provides. Excel thus allows you to change column widths manually.

When the format you assign to a cell causes the entry to exceed the width of a column, Excel automatically changes the column width to best fit. This happened earlier when the Currency style format was used (Figure 2-41 on page E 2.35). If you do not assign a cell in a column a format, the width will remain 8.43 characters, as is the case in columns A and B. To set a column width to best fit, double-click the right boundary of the column heading above row 1.

The following changes will be made to the column widths: column A to 14.00 characters; B through D to best fit; columns E, G and J to 9.43 characters columns; and F, H, and I to 12.00 characters. Perform the steps on the next page to change the column widths.

More About

Best Fit

Although Excel automatically increases the width of a column or the height of a row when you assign a format to a cell, it will not increase the column width or row height when a cell contains a formula and you change the value of a cell that is referenced in the formula. For example, if you change the number of shares in cell D3 from 750 to 100,000, Excel will recalculate the formulas and display number signs (#) for the initial cost, gain/lost, and current value because the results of the formulas have more digits than can fit in the cell. You can fix the problem by double-clicking the right boundary of the column heading to change to best fit.

To Change the Widths of Columns

1 **Point to the boundary on the right side of the column A heading above row 1. When the mouse pointer changes to a split double arrow, drag to the right until the ScreenTip, Width: 14.00 (103 pixels), displays.**

A dotted line shows the proposed right border of column A (Figure 2-53).

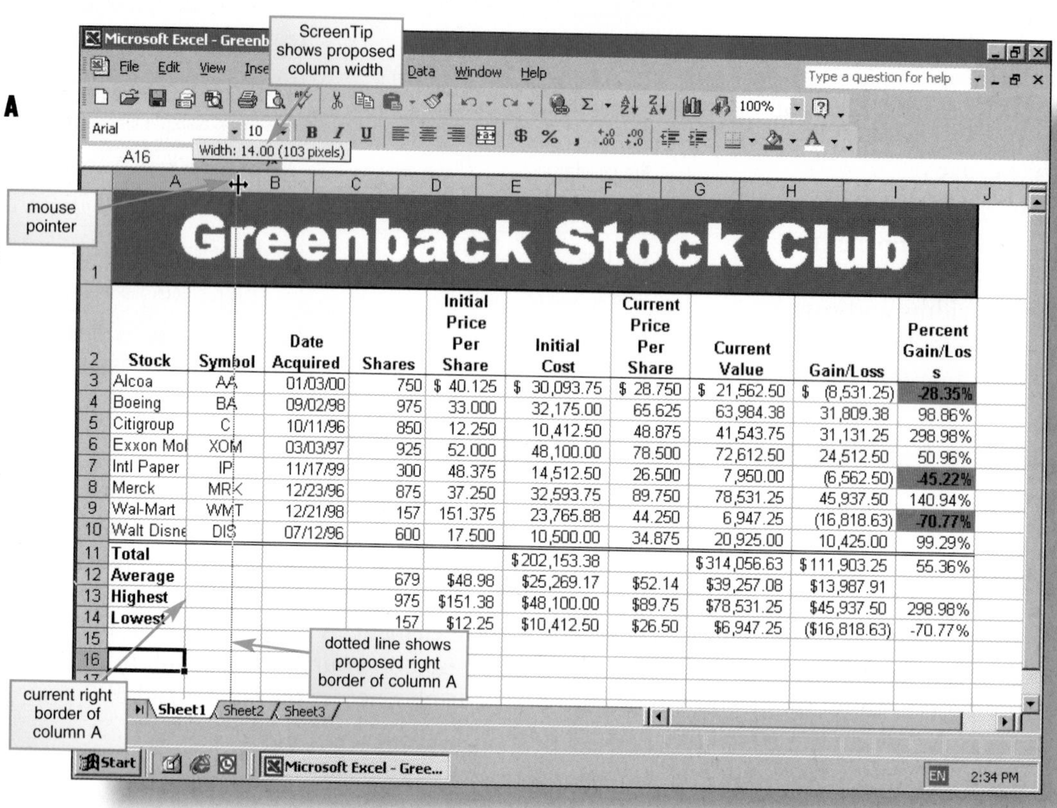

FIGURE 2-53

2 **Release the mouse button. Drag through column headings B through D above row 1. Point to the boundary on the right side of column heading D.**

The mouse pointer becomes a split double arrow (Figure 2-54).

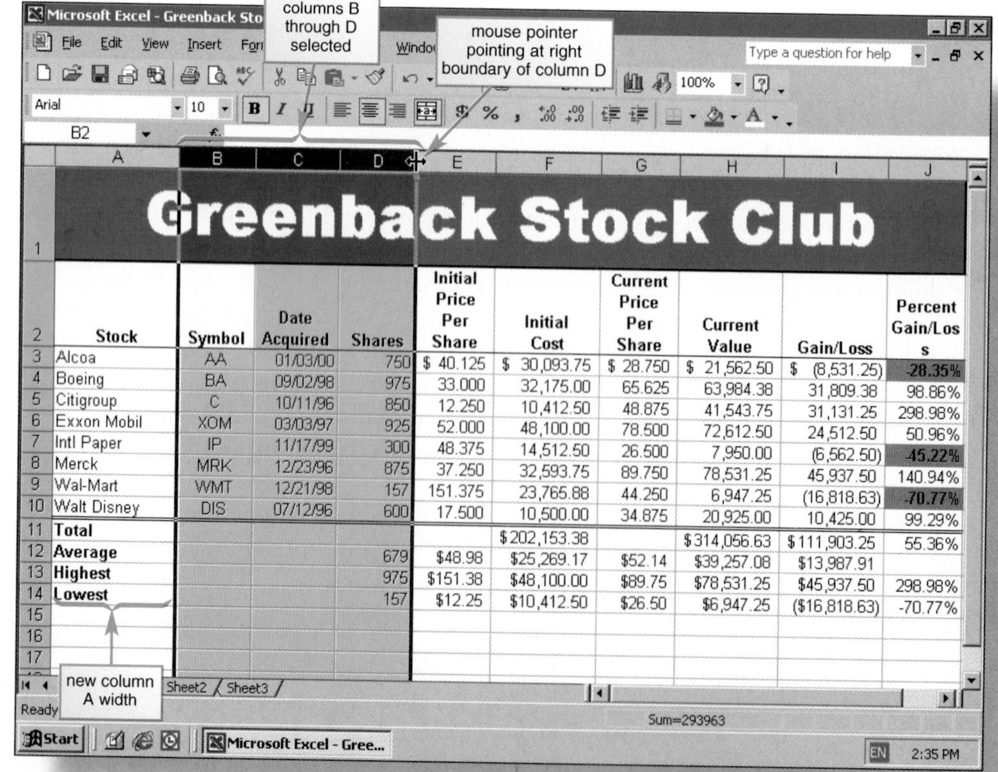

FIGURE 2-54

3 **Double-click the right boundary of column heading D to change the width of columns B, C, and D to best fit. Click the column E heading above row 1. While holding down the CTRL key, click the column G heading and then the column J heading above row 1 so that columns E, G, and J are selected. Point to the boundary on the right side of the column J heading above row 1. Drag to the right until the ScreenTip, Width: 9.43 (71 pixels), displays.**

A dotted line shows the proposed right border of column J (Figure 2-55).

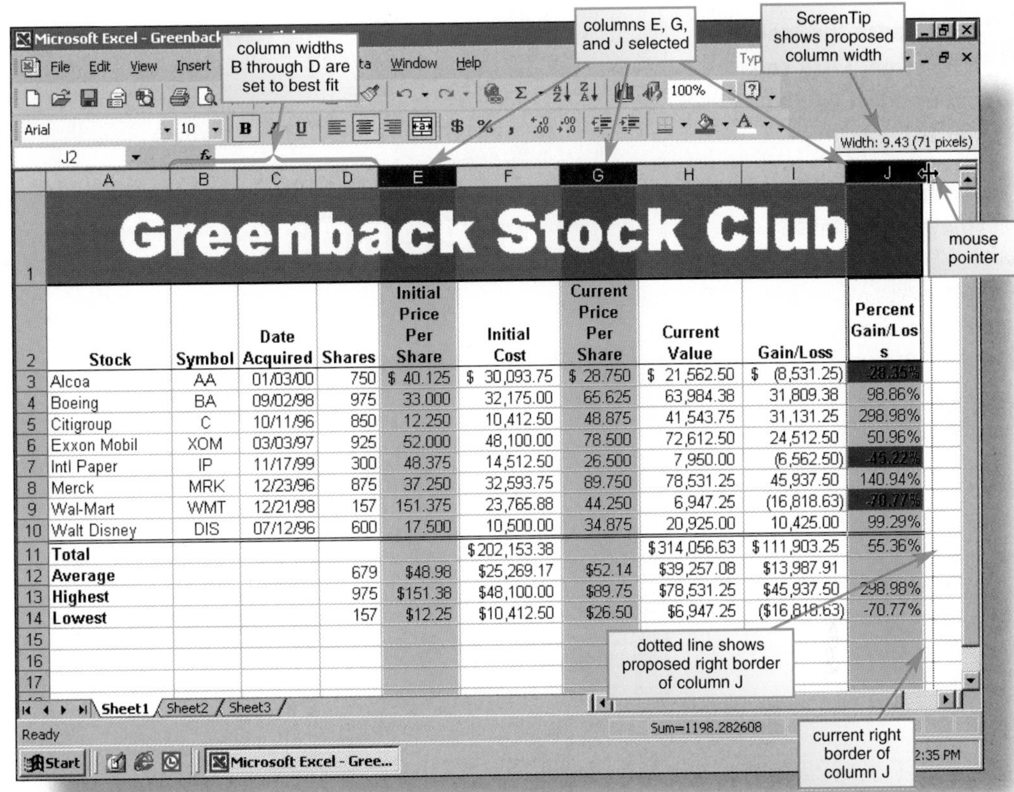

FIGURE 2-55

4 **Release the mouse button. Click the column F heading above row 1 to select column F. While holding down the CTRL key, click the column H and I headings above row 1 so that columns F, H, and I are selected. Point to the boundary on the right side of the column I heading above row 1. Drag to the right until the ScreenTip, Width: 12.00 (89 pixels), displays.**

A dotted line shows the proposed right border of column I (Figure 2-56).

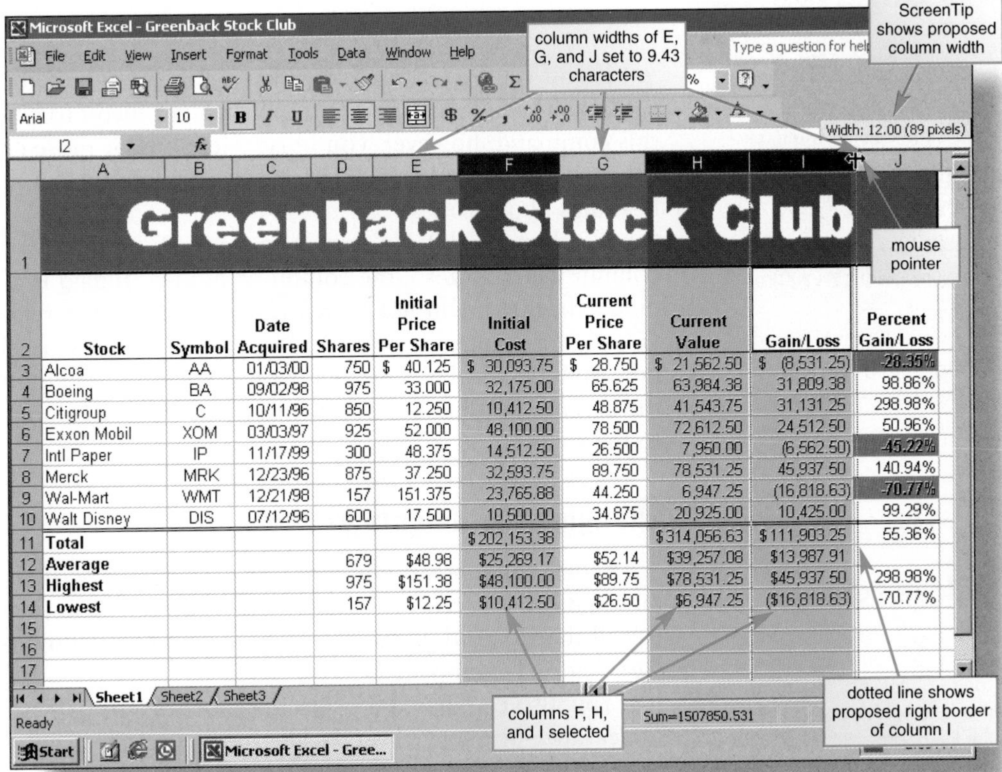

FIGURE 2-56

5 **Release the mouse button. Click cell A16 to deselect columns F, H, and I.**

The worksheet displays with the new columns widths (Figure 2-57).

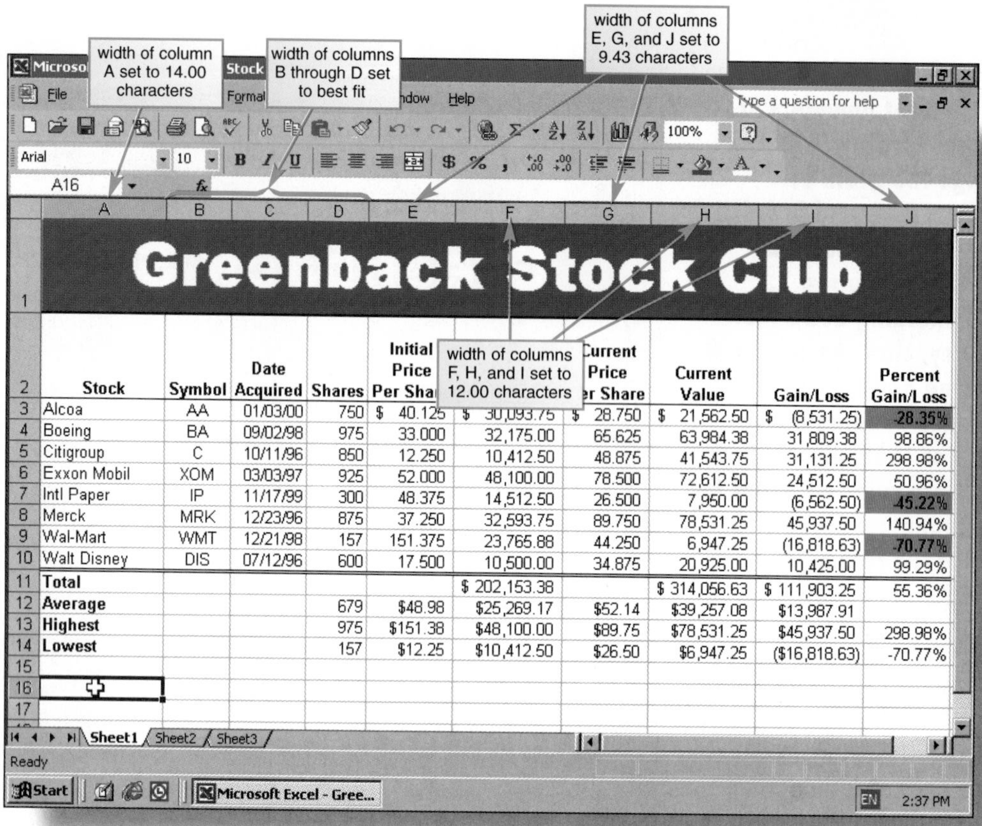

width of column A set to 14.00 characters

width of columns B through D set to best fit

width of columns E, G, and J set to 9.43 characters

width of columns F, H, and I set to 12.00 characters

Greenback Stock Club

Stock	Symbol	Date Acquired	Shares	Initial Price Per Share		Current Price Per Share	Current Value	Gain/Loss	Percent Gain/Loss
Alcoa	AA	01/03/00	750	$ 40.125	$ 30,093.75	$ 28.750	$ 21,562.50	$ (8,531.25)	-28.35%
Boeing	BA	09/02/98	975	33.000	32,175.00	65.625	63,984.38	31,809.38	98.86%
Citigroup	C	10/11/96	850	12.250	10,412.50	48.875	41,543.75	31,131.25	298.98%
Exxon Mobil	XOM	03/03/97	925	52.000	48,100.00	78.500	72,612.50	24,512.50	50.96%
Intl Paper	IP	11/17/99	300	48.375	14,512.50	26.500	7,950.00	(6,562.50)	-45.22%
Merck	MRK	12/23/96	875	37.250	32,593.75	89.750	78,531.25	45,937.50	140.94%
Wal-Mart	WMT	12/21/98	157	151.375	23,765.88	44.250	6,947.25	(16,818.63)	-70.77%
Walt Disney	DIS	07/12/96	600	17.500	10,500.00	34.875	20,925.00	10,425.00	99.29%
Total					$ 202,153.38		$ 314,056.63	$ 111,903.25	55.36%
Average			679	$48.98	$25,269.17	$52.14	$39,257.08	$13,987.91	
Highest			975	$151.38	$48,100.00	$89.75	$78,531.25	$45,937.50	298.98%
Lowest			157	$12.25	$10,412.50	$26.50	$6,947.25	($16,818.63)	-70.77%

FIGURE 2-57

Other Ways

1. Select cell or range of cells, on Format menu click Column, click Width, enter desired column width, click OK button
2. Right-click column heading, click Column Width on shortcut menu, enter desired column width, click OK button
3. In Voice Command mode say, "Format, Column, Width, [enter width], OK"

If you want to increase or decrease the column width significantly, you can use the **Column Width command** on the shortcut menu to change a column's width. To use this command, however, you must select one or more entire columns. As shown in the previous set of steps, you select entire columns by dragging through the column headings above row 1.

A column width can vary from zero (0) to 255 characters. If you decrease the column width to zero, the column is hidden. **Hiding** is a technique you can use to hide data that might not be relevant to a particular report or sensitive data that you do not want others to see. When you print a worksheet, hidden columns do not print. To display a hidden column, position the mouse pointer to the right of the column heading boundary where the hidden column is located and then drag to the right.

More About

Hidden Columns

It often gets frustrating trying to use the mouse to unhide a range of columns. An alternative is to unhide columns using the keyboard. First select the columns to the right and left of the hidden ones and then press CTRL+SHIFT+RIGHT PARENTHESIS. To use the keyboard to hide a range of columns, press CTRL+0.

Changing the Heights of Rows

When you increase the font size of a cell entry, such as the title in cell A1, Excel automatically increases the row height to best fit so the characters display properly. Recall that Excel did this earlier when you entered multiple lines in a cell in row 2 (see Figure 2-2 on page E 2.09).

You also can increase or decrease the height of a row manually to improve the appearance of the worksheet. The following steps show how to improve the appearance of the worksheet by increasing the height of row 1 to 61.50 points, decreasing the height of row 2 to 42.00 points, and increasing the height of row 12 to 24.00 points. Perform the following steps to change the heights of these three rows.

Steps To Change the Height of a Row by Dragging

1 Point to the boundary below row heading 1. Drag down until the ScreenTip, Height: 61.50 (82 pixels), displays.

The mouse pointer changes to a split double arrow (Figure 2-58). The distance between the dotted line and the top of row 1 indicates the proposed row height for row 1.

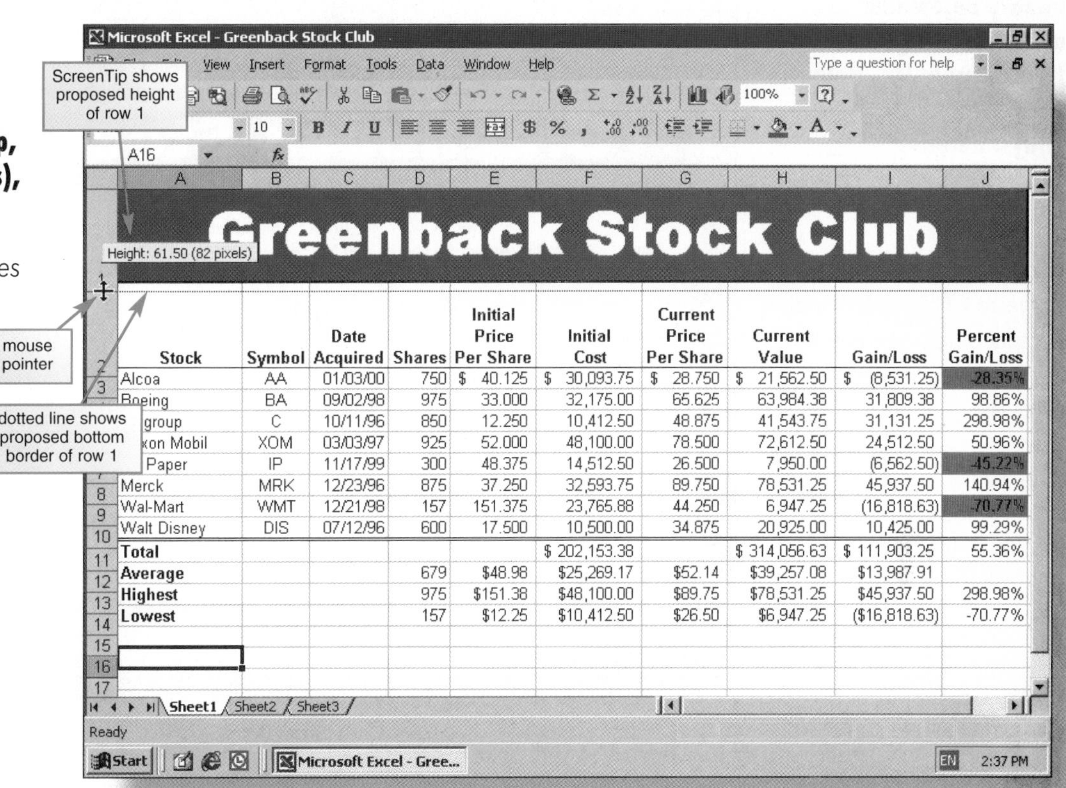

FIGURE 2-58

2 Release the mouse button. Point to the boundary below row heading 2. Drag up until the ScreenTip, Height: 42.00 (56 pixels), displays.

Excel displays a horizontal dotted line (Figure 2-59). The distance between the dotted line and the top of row 2 indicates the proposed height for row 2.

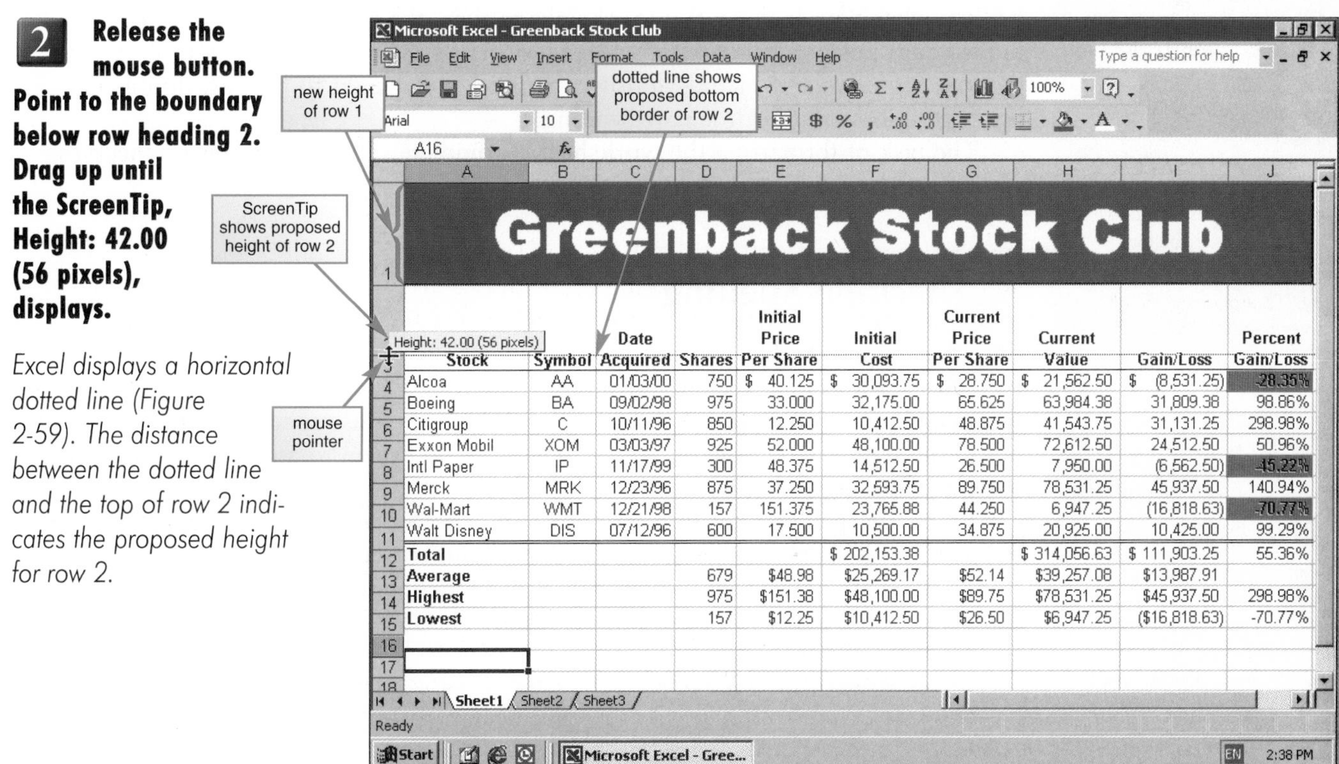

FIGURE 2-59

3 Release the mouse button. Point to the boundary below row heading 12. Drag down until the ScreenTip, Height: 24.00 (32 pixels), displays. Release the mouse button. Click cell A16.

The Total row and the Average row have additional white space between them, which improves the appearance of the worksheet (Figure 2-60). The formatting of the worksheet is complete.

	Stock	Symbol	Date Acquired	Shares	Initial Price Per Share	Initial Cost	Current Price Per Share	Current Value	Gain/Loss	Percent Gain/Loss
3	Alcoa	AA	01/03/00	750	$ 40.125	$ 30,093.75	$ 28.750	$ 21,562.50	$ (8,531.25)	-28.35%
4	Boeing	BA	09/02/98	975	33.000	32,175.00	65.625	63,984.38	31,809.38	98.86%
5	Citigroup	C	10/11/96	850	12.250	10,412.50	48.875	41,543.75	31,131.25	298.98%
6	Exxon Mobil	XOM	03/03/97	925	52.000	48,100.00	78.500	72,612.50	24,512.50	50.96%
7	Intl Paper	IP	11/17/99	300	48.375	14,512.50	26.500	7,950.00	(6,562.50)	-45.22%
8	Merck	MRK	12/23/96	875	37.250	32,593.75	89.750	78,531.25	45,937.50	140.94%
9	Wal-Mart	WMT	12/21/98	157	151.375	23,765.88	44.250	6,947.25	(16,818.63)	-70.77%
10	Walt Disney	DIS	07/12/96	600	17.500	10,500.00	34.875	20,925.00	10,425.00	99.29%
11	Total					$ 202,153.38		$ 314,056.63	$ 111,903.25	55.36%
12	Average			679	$48.98	$25,269.17	$52.14	$39,257.08	$13,987.91	
13	Highest			975	$151.38	$48,100.00	$89.75	$78,531.25	$45,937.50	298.98%
14	Lowest			157	$12.25	$10,412.50	$26.50	$6,947.25	($16,818.63)	-70.77%

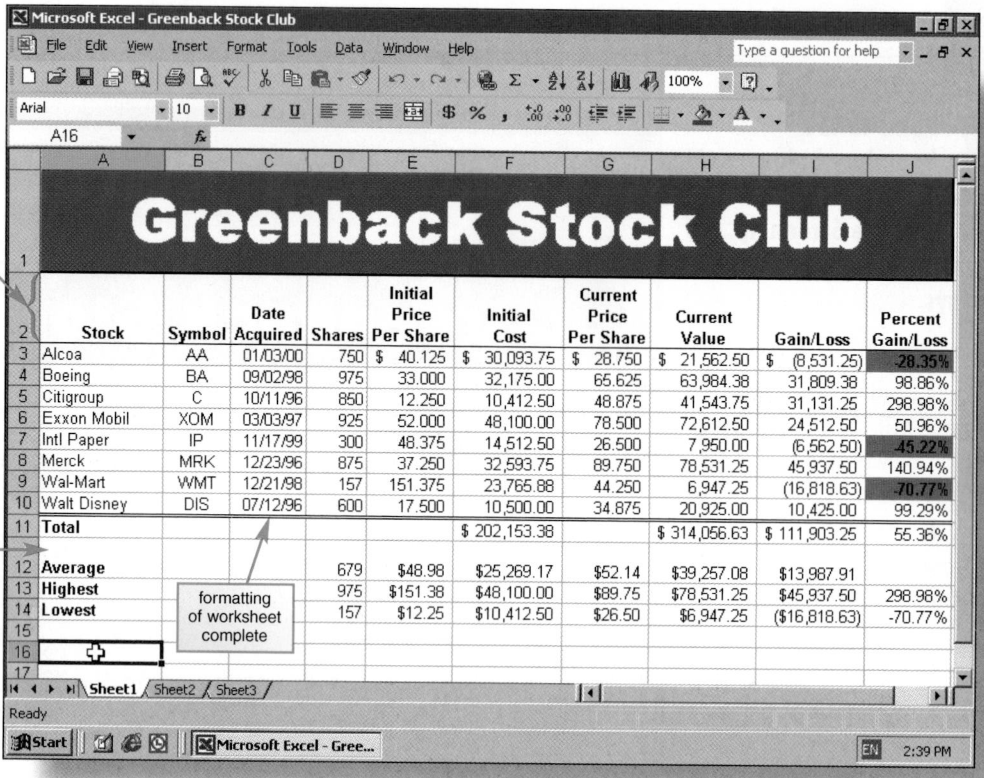

FIGURE 2-60

Other Ways

1. Select cell or range of cells in column, on Format menu click Row, click Height, enter desired row height, click OK button
2. Right-click row heading or drag through multiple row headings and right-click, click Row Height on shortcut menu, enter desired row height, click OK button
3. In Voice Command mode say, "Format, Row, Height, [enter height], OK"

More About

Hidden Rows

You can use the keyboard to unhide a range of rows. First select the rows immediately above and below the hidden ones and press CTRL+SHIFT+LEFT PARENTHESIS. To use the keyboard to hide a range of rows, press CTRL+9.

The row height can vary between zero (0) and 409 points. As with column widths, when you decrease the row height to zero, the row is hidden. To display a hidden row, position the mouse pointer just below the row heading boundary where the row is hidden and then drag down. To set a row height to best fit, double-click the bottom boundary of the row heading.

The task of formatting the worksheet is complete. The next step is to check the spelling of the worksheet.

Checking Spelling

Excel has a **spell checker** you can use to check the worksheet for spelling errors. The spell checker looks for spelling errors by comparing words on the worksheet against words contained in its standard dictionary. If you often use specialized terms that are not in the standard dictionary, you may want to add them to a custom dictionary using the **Spelling dialog box.**

When the spell checker finds a word that is not in either dictionary, it displays the word in the Spelling dialog box. You then can correct it if it is misspelled.

To illustrate how Excel responds to a misspelled word, the word, Symbol, in cell B2 is misspelled purposely as the word, Simbol, as shown in Figure 2-61.

Steps To Check Spelling on the Worksheet

1 Select cell B2 and enter `Simbol` **to misspell the word Symbol. Select cell A1. Click the Spelling button on the Standard toolbar. When the spell checker stops on cell B2 and with the word, Symbol, highlighted in the Suggestions list, point to the Change button.**

When the spell checker identifies the misspelled word, Simbol, the Spelling dialog box displays (Figure 2-61).

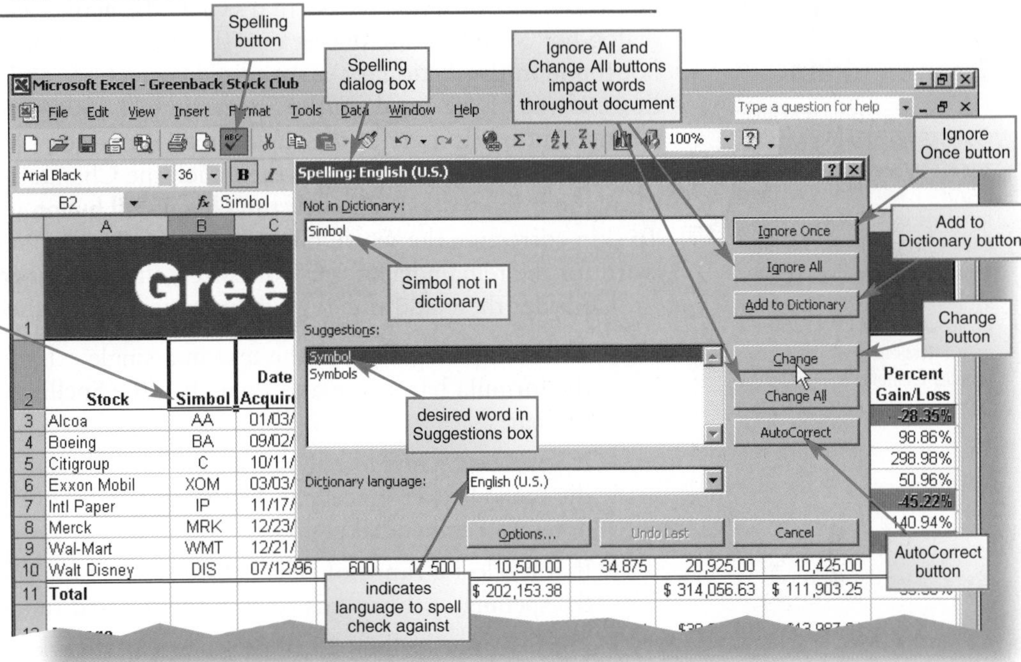

FIGURE 2-61

2 Click the Change button. As the spell checker checks the remainder of the worksheet, click the Ignore All and Change buttons as needed.

The spell checker changes the misspelled word, Simbol, to the correct word, Symbol, and continues spell checking the worksheet. When the spell checker is finished, it displays the Microsoft Excel dialog box with a message indicating that the spell check is complete (Figure 2-62).

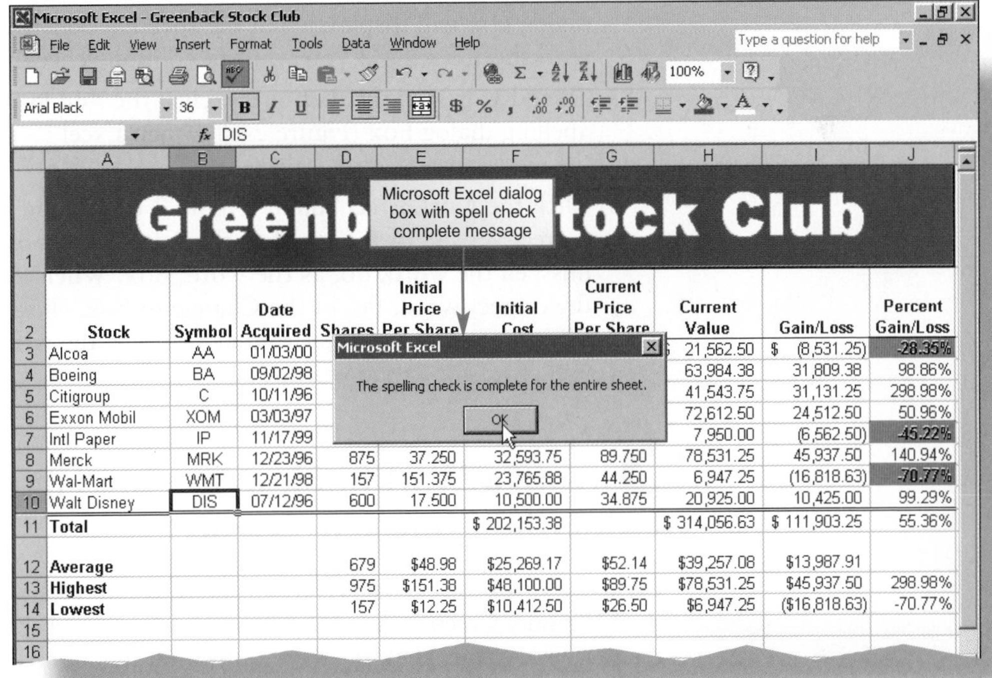

FIGURE 2-62

3 Click the OK button.

Other Ways

1. On Tools menu click Spelling
2. Press F7
3. In Voice Command mode say, "Spelling"

Error Checking

Always take the time to check the spelling and formulas of a worksheet before submitting it to your supervisor. You check formulas by invoking the Error Checking command on the Tools menu. Nothing deflates an impression more than a professional-looking report with misspelled words and invalid formulas.

When the spell checker identifies that a cell contains a word not in its standard or custom dictionary, it selects that cell as the active cell and displays the Spelling dialog box. The Spelling dialog box (Figure 2-61 on the previous page) lists the word not found in the dictionary, a suggested correction, and a list of alternative suggestions. If one of the words in the Suggestions list is correct, click it and then click the Change button. If none of the suggestions is correct, type the correct word in the Not in Dictionary text box and then click the Change button. To change the word throughout the worksheet, click the **Change All button** instead of the Change button. To skip correcting the word, click the **Ignore Once button**. To have Excel ignore the word for the remainder of the worksheet, click the **Ignore All button**.

Consider these additional guidelines when using the spell checker:

- To check the spelling of the text in a single cell, double-click the cell to make the formula bar active and then click the Spelling button on the Standard toolbar.
- If you select a single cell so that the formula bar is not active and then start the spell checker, Excel checks the remainder of the worksheet, including notes and embedded charts.
- If you select a range of cells before starting the spell checker, Excel checks the spelling of the words only in the selected range.
- To check the spelling of all the sheets in a workbook, click Select All Sheets on the sheet tab shortcut menu and then start the spell checker. To display the sheet tab shortcut menu, right-click the sheet tab.
- If you select a cell other than cell A1 before you start the spell checker, a dialog box will display when the spell checker reaches the end of the worksheet, asking if you want to continue checking at the beginning.
- To add words to the dictionary, click the **Add to Dictionary button** in the Spelling dialog box (Figure 2-61) when Excel identifies the word as not in the dictionary.
- Click the **AutoCorrect button** (Figure 2-61) to add the misspelled word and the correct version of the word to the AutoCorrect list. For example, suppose you misspell the word, do, as the word, dox. When the Spelling dialog box displays the correct word, do, in the Change to box, click the AutoCorrect button. Then, anytime in the future that you type the word, dox, Excel automatically will change it to the word, do.

Saving a Workbook a Second Time Using the Same File Name

Earlier in this project, you saved an intermediate version of the workbook using the file name, Greenback Stock Club. To save the workbook a second time using the same file name, click the Save button on the Standard toolbar as shown in the following step.

More About

Saving a Workbook

You should save your workbooks every 5 to 10 minutes so that if the system fails you can retrieve a copy without a major loss of work.

TO SAVE A WORKBOOK A SECOND TIME USING THE SAME FILE NAME

 Click the Save button on the Standard toolbar.

Excel saves the workbook on the floppy disk in drive A using the file name Greenback Stock Club.

Excel automatically stores the latest version of the workbook using the same file name, Greenback Stock Club. When you save a workbook a second time using the same file name, Excel will not display the Save As dialog box as it does the first time you save the workbook. You also can click **Save** on the File menu or press SHIFT+F12 or CTRL+S to save a workbook again.

If you want to save the workbook using a new name or on a different drive, click Save As on the File menu. Some Excel users, for example, use the Save button to save the latest version of the workbook on the default drive. Then, they use the Save As command to save a copy on another drive.

Previewing and Printing the Worksheet

In Project 1, you printed the worksheet without first previewing it on the screen. By previewing the worksheet, however, you see exactly how it will look without generating a printout. Previewing allows you to see if the worksheet will print on one page in portrait orientation. **Portrait orientation** means the printout is printed across the width of the page. **Landscape orientation** means the printout is printed across the length of the page. Previewing a worksheet using the **Print Preview command** on the File menu or **Print Preview button** on the Standard toolbar can save time, paper, and the frustration of waiting for a printout only to discover it is not what you want.

Perform the following steps to preview and then print the worksheet.

Print Preview

A popular button in the preview window (Figure 2-64 on the next page) is the Margins button. The Margins button allows you to drag the top, bottom, left, and right margins to center a worksheet or add room to fit a wide or long worksheet on a page. You can even change the column widths.

Steps To Preview and Print a Worksheet

1 Point to the Print Preview button on the Standard toolbar (Figure 2-63).

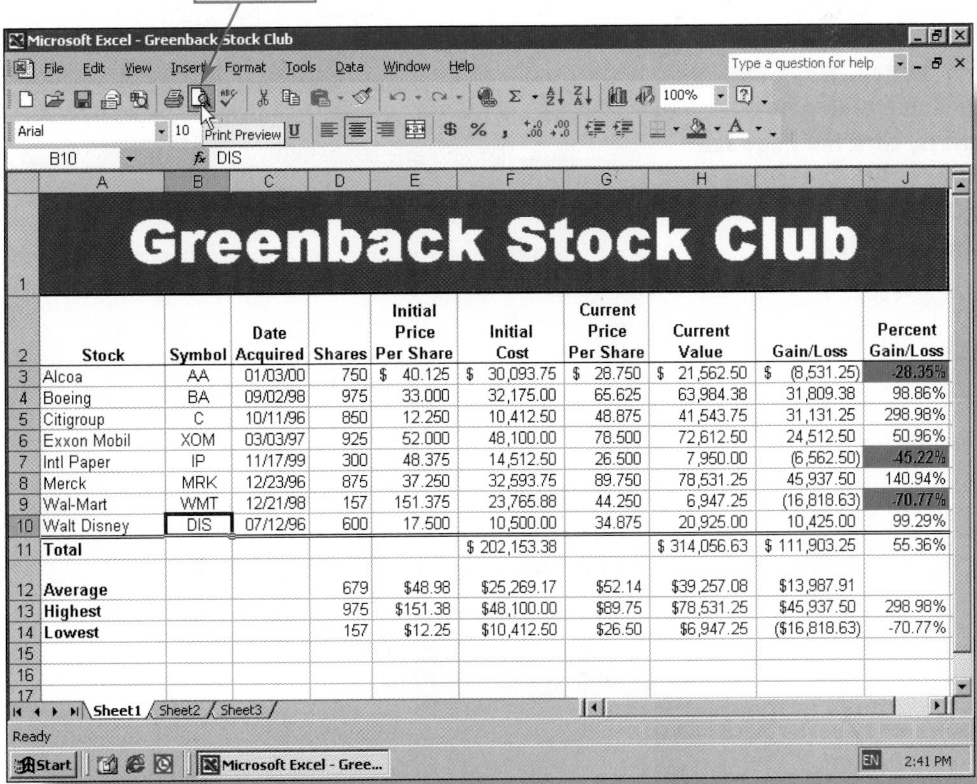

FIGURE 2-63

2 Click the Print Preview button. When the Preview window opens, point to the Setup button.

Excel displays a preview of the worksheet in portrait orientation, because portrait is the default orientation. In portrait orientation, the worksheet does not fit on one page (Figure 2-64).

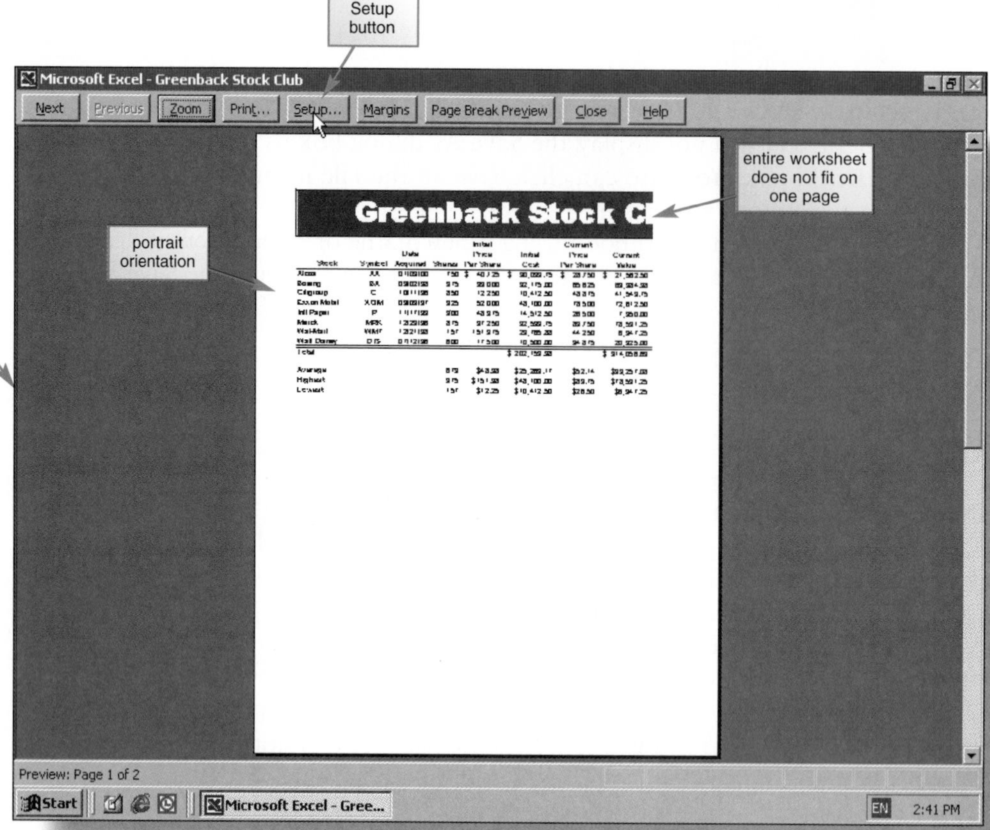

FIGURE 2-64

3 Click the Setup button. When the Page Setup dialog box displays, click the Page tab and then click Landscape in the Orientation area. Point to the OK button.

The Page Setup dialog box displays. The Orientation area contains two option buttons, Portrait and Landscape (Figure 2-65).

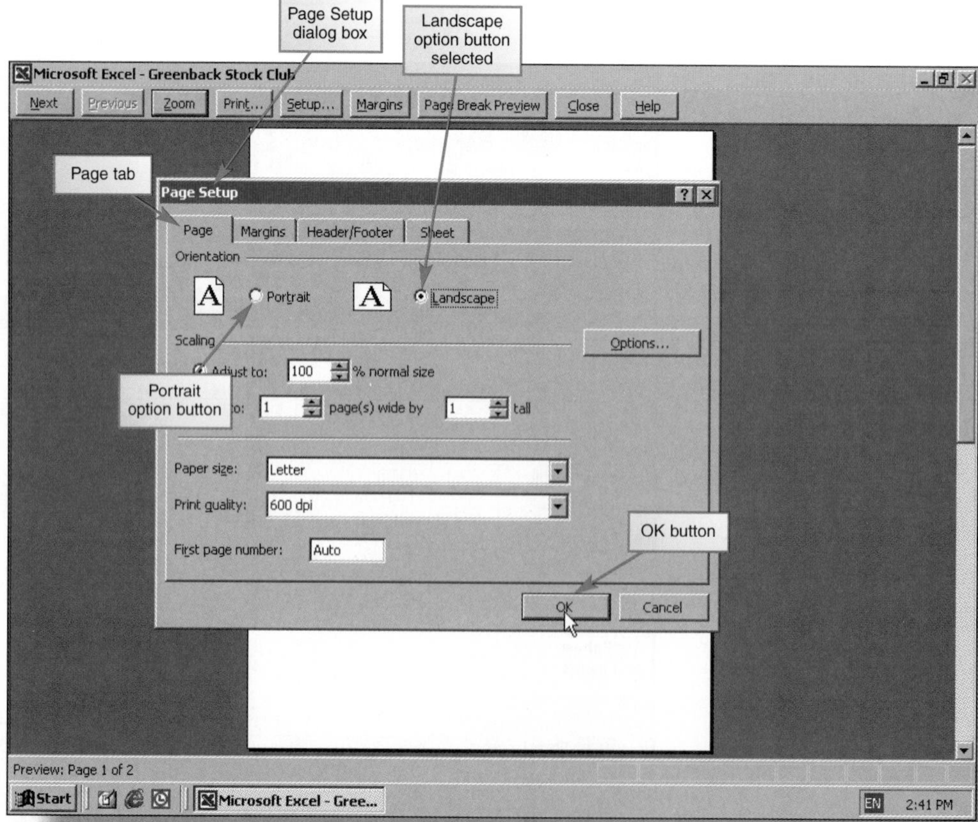

FIGURE 2-65

4 Click the OK button. Point to the Print button at the top of the Preview window.

The worksheet displays in the Preview window in its entirety in landscape orientation (Figure 2-66).

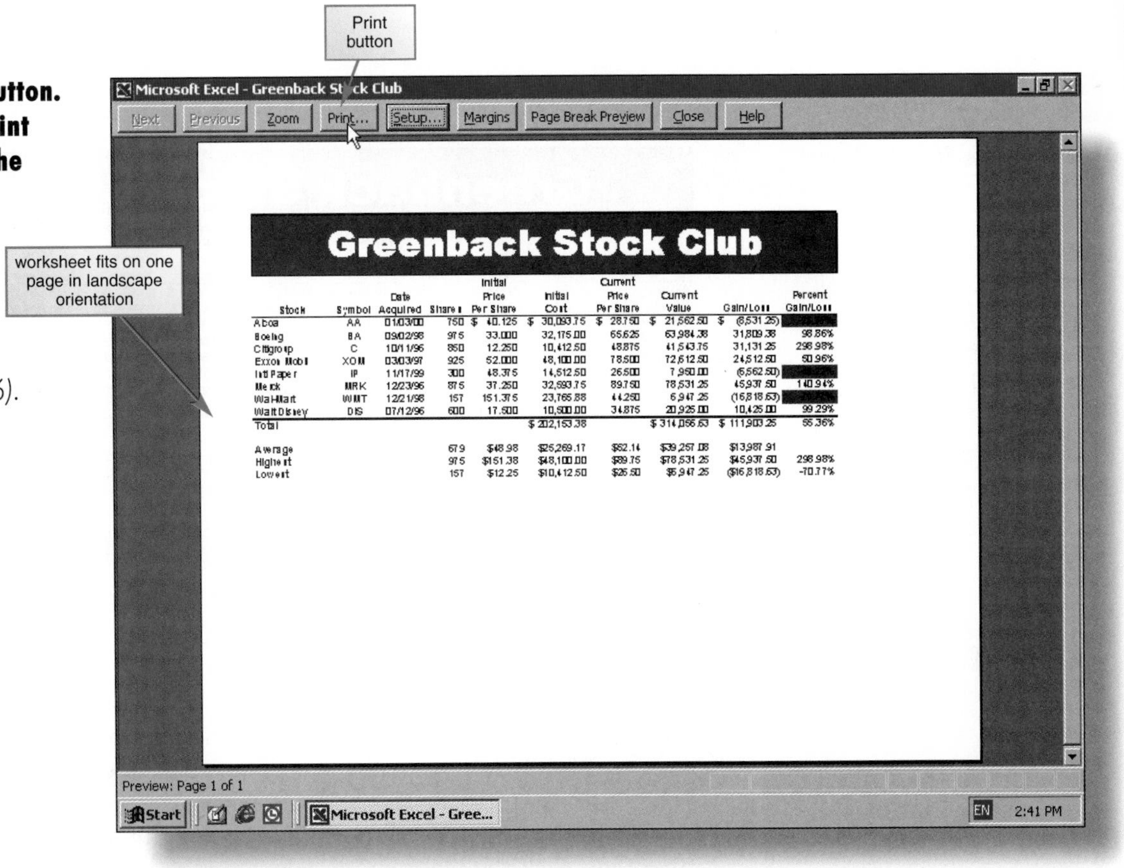

Stock	Symbol	Date Acquired	Shares	Initial Price Per Share	Initial Cost	Current Price Per Share	Current Value	Gain/Loss	Percent Gain/Loss
Alcoa	AA	01/03/00	750	$ 40.125	$ 30,093.75	$ 28.750	$ 21,562.50	$ (8,531.25)	
Boeing	BA	09/02/98	975	33.000	32,175.00	65.625	63,984.38	31,809.38	98.86%
Citigroup	C	10/11/96	850	12.250	10,412.50	48.875	41,543.75	31,131.25	298.98%
Exxon Mobil	XOM	03/03/97	925	52.000	48,100.00	78.500	72,612.50	24,512.50	50.96%
Intl Paper	IP	11/17/99	300	48.375	14,512.50	26.500	7,950.00	(6,562.50)	
Merck	MRK	12/23/96	875	37.250	32,593.75	89.750	78,531.25	45,937.50	140.94%
Wal-Mart	WMT	12/21/98	157	151.375	23,765.88	44.250	6,947.25	(16,818.63)	
Walt Disney	DIS	07/12/96	600	17.500	10,500.00	34.875	20,925.00	10,425.00	99.29%
Total					$ 202,153.38		$ 314,056.63	$ 111,903.25	55.36%
Average			679	$48.98	$25,269.17	$52.14	$39,257.08	$13,987.91	
Highest			975	$151.38	$48,100.00	$89.75	$78,531.25	$45,937.50	298.98%
Lowest			157	$12.25	$10,412.50	$26.50	$6,947.25	($16,818.63)	-70.77%

FIGURE 2-66

5 Click the Print button. When the Print dialog box displays, point to the OK button.

The Print dialog box displays as shown in Figure 2-67.

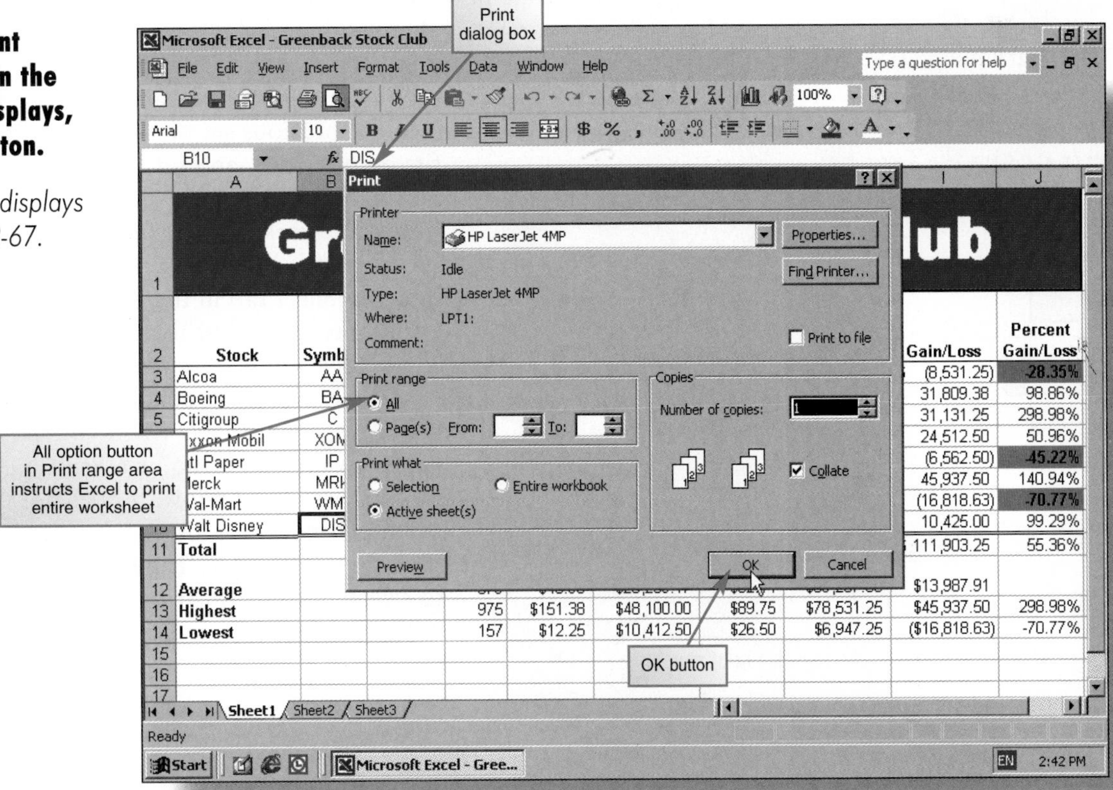

FIGURE 2-67

6 **Click the OK button. Click the Save button on the Standard toolbar.**

Excel prints the worksheet (Figure 2-68). The workbook is saved with the landscape orientation.

landscape orientation

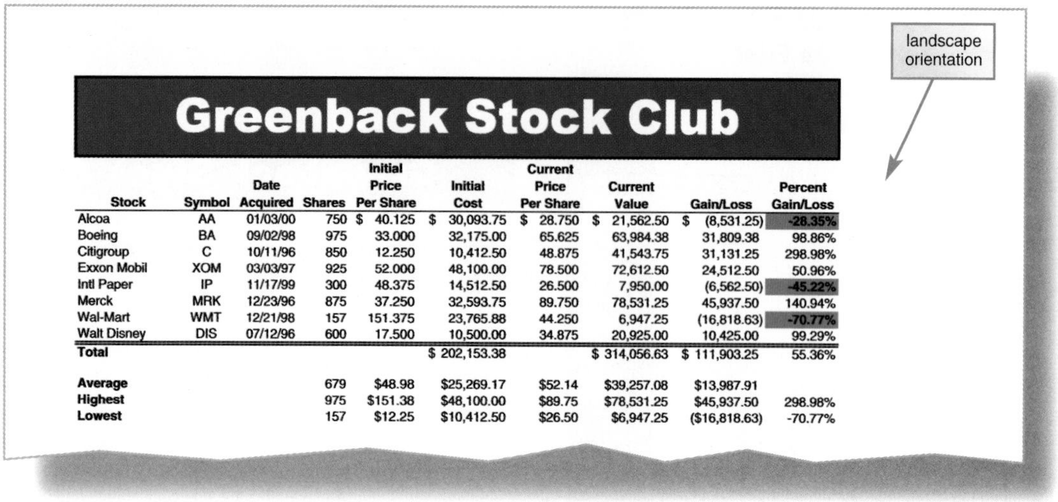

Greenback Stock Club

Stock	Symbol	Date Acquired	Shares	Initial Price Per Share	Initial Cost	Current Price Per Share	Current Value	Gain/Loss	Percent Gain/Loss
Alcoa	AA	01/03/00	750	$ 40.125	$ 30,093.75	$ 28.750	$ 21,562.50	$ (8,531.25)	-28.35%
Boeing	BA	09/02/98	975	33.000	32,175.00	65.625	63,984.38	31,809.38	98.86%
Citigroup	C	10/11/96	850	12.250	10,412.50	48.875	41,543.75	31,131.25	298.98%
Exxon Mobil	XOM	03/03/97	925	52.000	48,100.00	78.500	72,612.50	24,512.50	50.96%
Intl Paper	IP	11/17/99	300	48.375	14,512.50	26.500	7,950.00	(6,562.50)	-45.22%
Merck	MRK	12/23/96	875	37.250	32,593.75	89.750	78,531.25	45,937.50	140.94%
Wal-Mart	WMT	12/21/98	157	151.375	23,765.88	44.250	6,947.25	(16,818.63)	-70.77%
Walt Disney	DIS	07/12/96	600	17.500	10,500.00	34.875	20,925.00	10,425.00	99.29%
Total					$ 202,153.38		$ 314,056.63	$ 111,903.25	55.36%
Average			679	$48.98	$25,269.17	$52.14	$39,257.08	$13,987.91	
Highest			975	$151.38	$48,100.00	$89.75	$78,531.25	$45,937.50	298.98%
Lowest			157	$12.25	$10,412.50	$26.50	$6,947.25	($16,818.63)	-70.77%

FIGURE 2-68

Other **Ways**

1. On File menu click Print Preview
2. On File menu click Page Setup, click Print Preview button
3. On File menu click Print, click Entire Workbook, click Preview button
4. In Voice Command mode say, "Print Preview"

Once you change the orientation and save the workbook, it will remain until you change it. When you open a new workbook, Excel sets the orientation to portrait.

Several buttons are at the top of the Preview window (see Figure 2-66 on the previous page). The functions of these buttons are summarized in Table 2-6.

Rather than click the Next and Previous buttons to move from page to page as described in Table 2-6, you can press the PAGE UP and PAGE DOWN keys. You also can click the previewed page in the Preview window when the mouse pointer shape is a magnifying glass to carry out the function of the Zoom button.

The Page Setup dialog box in Figure 2-65 on page E 2.52 allows you to make changes to the default settings for a printout. For example, on the Page tab, you can set the orientation as was done in the previous set of steps, scale the printout so it fits on one page, and set the page size and print quality. Scaling is an alternative to changing the orientation to fit a wide worksheet on one page. This technique will be discussed shortly. The Margins tab, Header/Footer tab, and Sheet tab in the Page Setup dialog box allow even more control of the way the printout will appear. These tabs will be discussed when they are used.

Table 2-6 Print Preview Buttons

BUTTON	FUNCTION
Next	Previews the next page
Previous	Previews the previous page
Zoom	Magnifies or reduces the print preview
Print...	Prints the worksheet
Setup...	Displays the Print Setup dialog box
Margins	Changes the print margins
Page Break Preview	Previews page breaks
Close	Closes the Preview window
Help	Displays Help about the Preview window

The Print dialog box shown in Figure 2-67 on the previous page displays when you use the Print command on the File menu or a Print button in a dialog box or Preview window. It does not display when you use the Print button on the Standard toolbar, as was the case in Project 1. The Print dialog box allows you to select a printer, instruct Excel what to print, and indicate how many copies of the printout you want.

Printing a Section of the Worksheet

You might not always want to print the entire worksheet. You can print portions of the worksheet by selecting the range of cells to print and then clicking the Selection option button in the Print what area in the Print dialog box. The following steps show how to print the range A2:F14.

Steps To Print a Section of the Worksheet

1 Select the range A2:F14. Click File on the menu bar and then click Print. Click Selection in the Print what area. Point to the OK button.

The Print dialog box displays (Figure 2-69). Because the Selection option button is selected, Excel will print only the selected range.

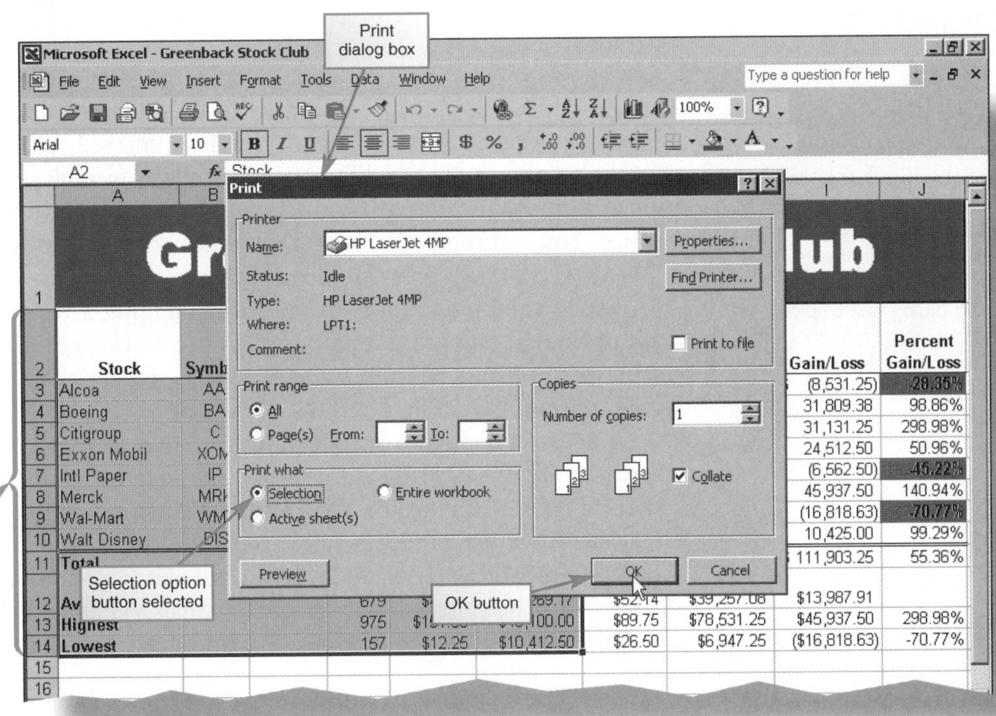

FIGURE 2-69

2 Click the OK button. Click cell A16 to deselect the range A2:F14.

Excel prints the selected range of the worksheet on the printer (Figure 2-70).

only selected range prints

Stock	Symbol	Date Acquired	Shares	Initial Price Per Share	Initial Cost
Alcoa	AA	01/03/00	750	$ 40.125	$ 30,093.75
Boeing	BA	09/02/98	975	33.000	32,175.00
Citigroup	C	10/11/96	850	12.250	10,412.50
Exxon Mobil	XOM	03/03/97	925	52.000	48,100.00
Intl Paper	IP	11/17/99	300	48.375	14,512.50
Merck	MRK	12/23/96	875	37.250	32,593.75
Wal-Mart	WMT	12/21/98	157	151.375	23,765.88
Walt Disney	DIS	07/12/96	600	17.500	10,500.00
Total					$ 202,153.38
Average			679	$48.98	$25,269.17
Highest			975	$151.38	$48,100.00
Lowest			157	$12.25	$10,412.50

FIGURE 2-70

Other Ways

1. Select range to print, on File menu click Print Area, click Set Print Area, click Print button on the Standard toolbar; on File menu click Print Area, click Clear Print Area
2. Select range to print, in Voice Command mode say, "File, Print Area, Set Print Area"

Three option buttons display in the Print what area in the Print dialog box (Figure 2-69). As shown in the previous steps, the **Selection option button** instructs Excel to print the selected range. The **Active sheet(s) option button** instructs Excel to print the active sheet (the one displaying on the screen) or the selected sheets. Finally, the **Entire workbook option button** instructs Excel to print all the sheets with content in the workbook.

Printing

To avoid wasting ink, print worksheets with color in black and white. You print in black and white by clicking Page Setup on the File menu prior to printing. When the Page Setup dialog box displays, click the Sheet tab, click Black and White in the Print area, and click the OK button. Then, click the Print button.

Displaying and Printing the Formulas Version of the Worksheet

Thus far, you have been working with the **values version** of the worksheet, which shows the results of the formulas you have entered, rather than the actual formulas. Excel also allows you to display and print the **formulas version** of the worksheet, which displays the actual formulas you have entered, rather than the resulting values. You can toggle between the values version and formulas version by pressing CTR+ACCENT MARK (`) to the left of the number 1 key.

The formulas version is useful for debugging a worksheet. **Debugging** is the process of finding and correcting errors in the worksheet. Because the formula version displays and prints formulas and functions, rather than the results, it is easier to see if any mistakes were made in the formulas.

When you change from the values version to the formulas version, Excel increases the width of the columns so the formulas and text do not overflow into adjacent cells on the right. The formulas version of the worksheet thus usually is significantly wider than the values version. To fit the wide printout on one page, you can use landscape orientation and the **Fit to option** on the Page tab in the Page Setup dialog box. To change from the values version to the formulas version of the worksheet and print the formulas on one page, perform the following steps.

To Display the Formulas in the Worksheet and Fit the Printout on One Page

1 Press CTRL+ACCENT MARK (`). Click the right horizontal scroll arrow until column J displays.

Excel changes the display of the worksheet from values to formulas (Figure 2-71). The formulas in the worksheet display showing unformatted numbers, formulas, and functions that were assigned to the cells. Excel automatically increases the column widths.

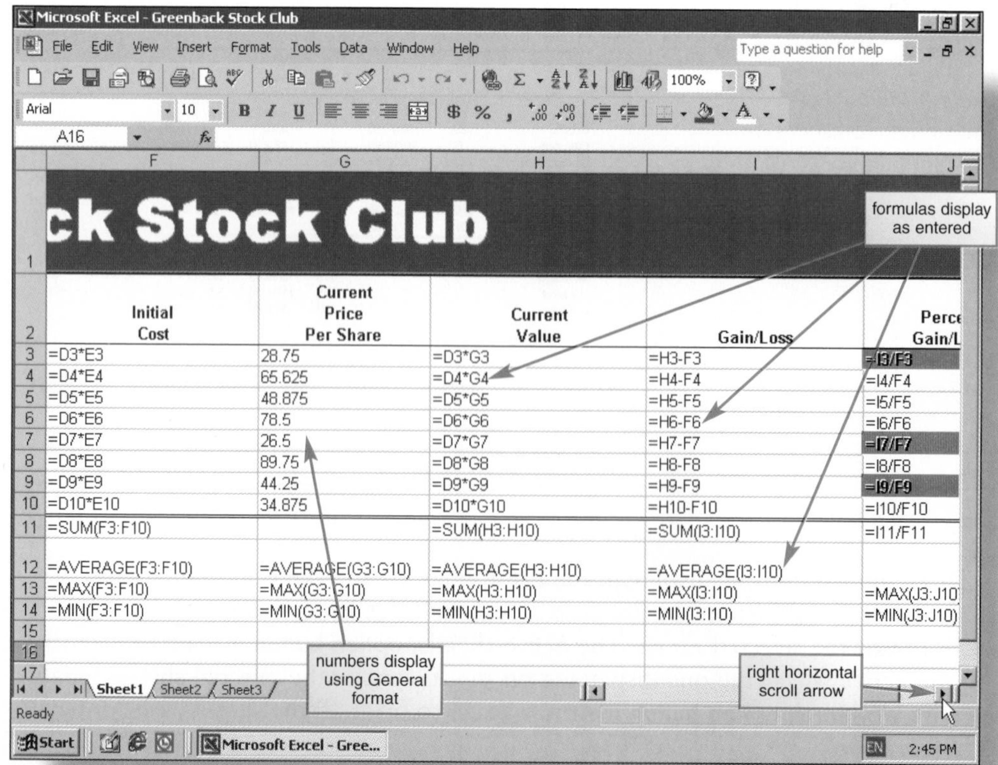

FIGURE 2-71

2 Click File on the menu bar and then click Page Setup. When the Page Setup dialog box displays, click the Page tab. If necessary, click Landscape to select it, and then click Fit to in the Scaling area. Point to the Print button in the Page Setup dialog box.

Excel displays the Page Setup dialog box with the Landscape and Fit to option buttons selected (Figure 2-72.

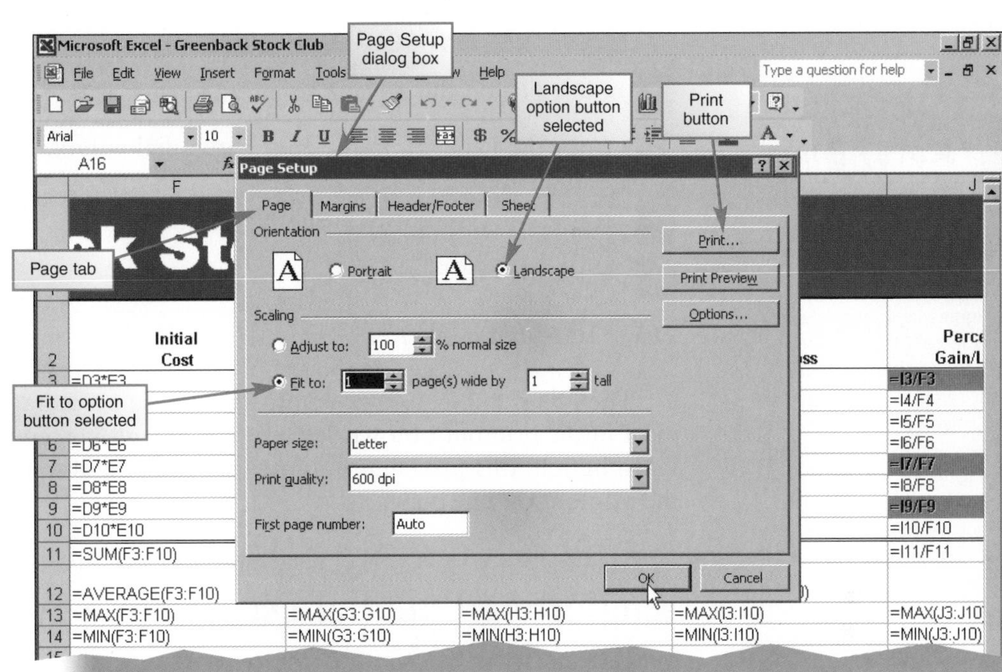

FIGURE 2-72

3 Click the Print button. When the Print dialog box displays, click the OK button. When you are done viewing and printing the formulas version, press CTRL+ACCENT MARK (`) to display the values version.

Excel prints the formulas in the worksheet on one page in landscape orientation (Figure 2-73). Excel displays the values version of the worksheet.

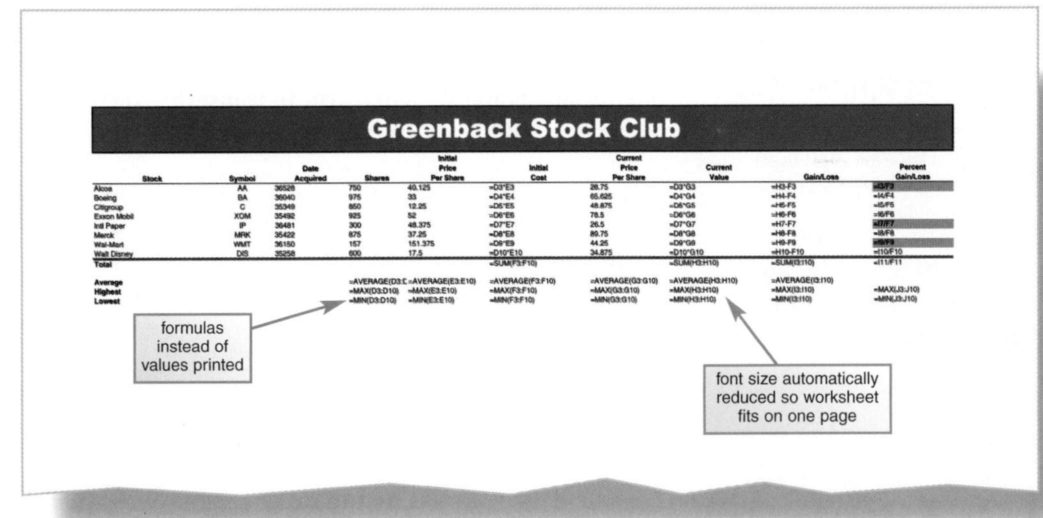

FIGURE 2-73

Other Ways

1. On Tools menu click Options, click View tab, click Formulas check box, click OK button
2. In Voice Command mode say, "Tools, Options, View, Formulas, OK"

Although the formulas version of the worksheet was printed in the previous example, you can see from Figure 2-71 that the display on the screen also can be used for debugging the worksheet.

Changing the Print Scaling Option Back to 100%

Depending on your printer driver, you may have to change the Print Scaling option back to 100% after using the Fit to option. Complete the steps on the next page to reset the Print Scaling option so future worksheets print at 100%, instead of being squeezed on one page.

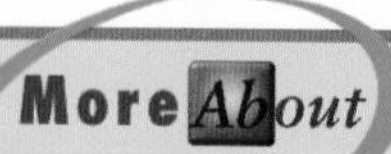

Values versus Formulas

When completing class assignments, don't enter numbers in cells that require formulas. Most instructors require their students to hand in both the values version and formulas version of the worksheet. The formulas version verifies that you entered formulas, rather than numbers in formula-based cells.

TO CHANGE THE PRINT SCALING OPTION BACK TO 100%

1. Click File on the menu bar and then click Page Setup.
2. Click the Page tab in the Page Setup dialog box. Click Adjust to in the Scaling area.
3. If necessary, type 100 in the Adjust to box.
4. Click the OK button.

The print scaling is set to normal.

The **Adjust to box** allows you to specify the percentage of reduction or enlargement in the printout of a worksheet. The default percentage is 100%. When click the Fit to option, this percentage automatically changes to the percentage required to fit the printout on one page.

The Fit To Option

Don't take the Fit To option lightly. Most applications involve worksheets that extend well beyond the 8 ½" by 11" page. However, most users want the information on one page, at least with respect to the width of the worksheet. Thus, the Fit To option is a common choice among Excel users.

Importing External Data from a Web Source Using a Web Query

One of the major features of Excel is its capability of importing external data from sites on the World Wide Web. To import external data from a World Wide Web site, you must have access to the Internet. You then can import data stored on a World Wide Web site using a **Web query**. When you run a Web query, Excel imports the external data in the form of a worksheet. As described in Table 2-7, three Web queries are available when you first install Excel. All three Web queries relate to investment and stock market activities.

Table 2-7 Excel Web Queries

QUERY	EXTERNAL DATA RETURNED
MSN MoneyCentral Investor Currency Rates	Currency rates
MSN MoneyCentral Investor Major Indices	Major indices
MSN MoneyCentral Investor Stock Quotes	Up to 20 stocks of your choice

Web Queries

Most Excel specialists that do Web queries use the worksheet returned from the Web query as an engine that supplies data to another worksheet in the workbook. With 3-D cell references, you can create a worksheet similar to the Greenback Stock Club worksheet which feeds the Web query stock symbols and gets refreshed stock prices in return.

The data returned by the stock-related Web queries is real-time in the sense that it is no more than 20 minutes old during the business day. The steps below show how to get the most recent stock quotes for the eight stocks owned by the Greenback Stock Club — Alcoa, Boeing, Citigroup, Exxon Mobil, International Paper, Merck, Wal-Mart, and Walt Disney. Although you can have a Web query return data to a blank workbook, the following steps have the data returned to a blank worksheet in the Greenback Stock Club workbook.

Steps To Import Data from a Web Source Using a Web Query

1 With the Greenback Stock Club workbook open, click the Sheet2 tab at the bottom of the window. Click cell A1. Click Data on the menu bar, point to Import External Data and then point to Import Data on the Import External Data submenu.

The Import External Data submenu displays as shown in Figure 2-74.

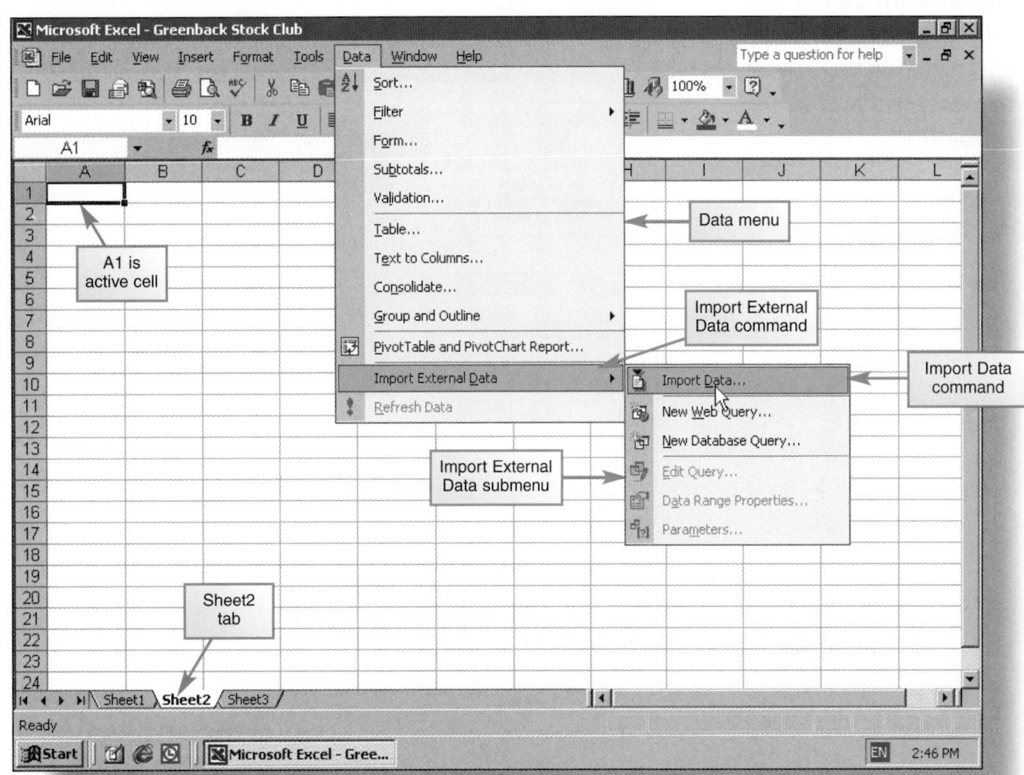

FIGURE 2-74

2 Click Import Data. When the Select Data Source dialog box displays, click MSN MoneyCentral Investor Stock Quotes. Point to the Open button.

The Select Data Source dialog box displays (Figure 2-75). If your display is different, ask your instructor for the folder location of the Web queries.

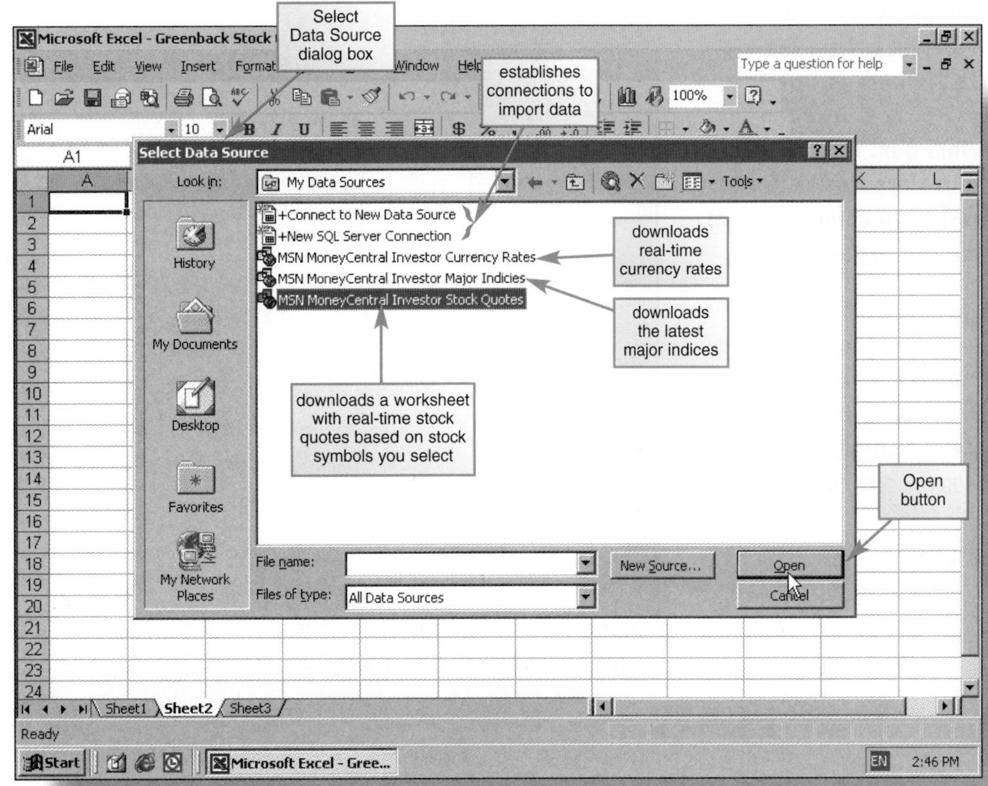

FIGURE 2-75

3 Click the Open button. When the Import Data dialog box displays, if necessary, click Existing worksheet to select it. Point to the OK button.

The Import Data dialog box displays (Figure 2-76).

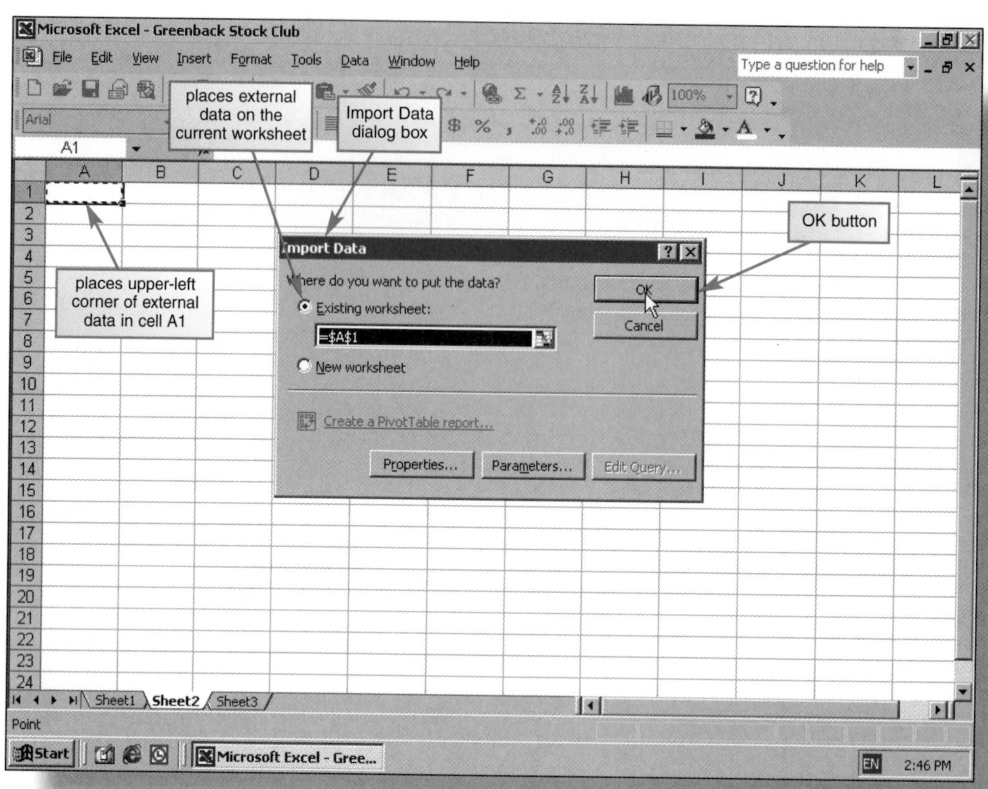

FIGURE 2-76

4 Click the OK button. When the Enter Parameter Value dialog box displays, type the eight stock symbols `aa ba c xom ip mrk wmt dis` **in the text box. Click Use this value/reference for future refreshes to select it. Point to the OK button.**

The Enter Parameter Value dialog box displays (Figure 2-77). You can enter up to 20 stock symbols separated by spaces (or commas).

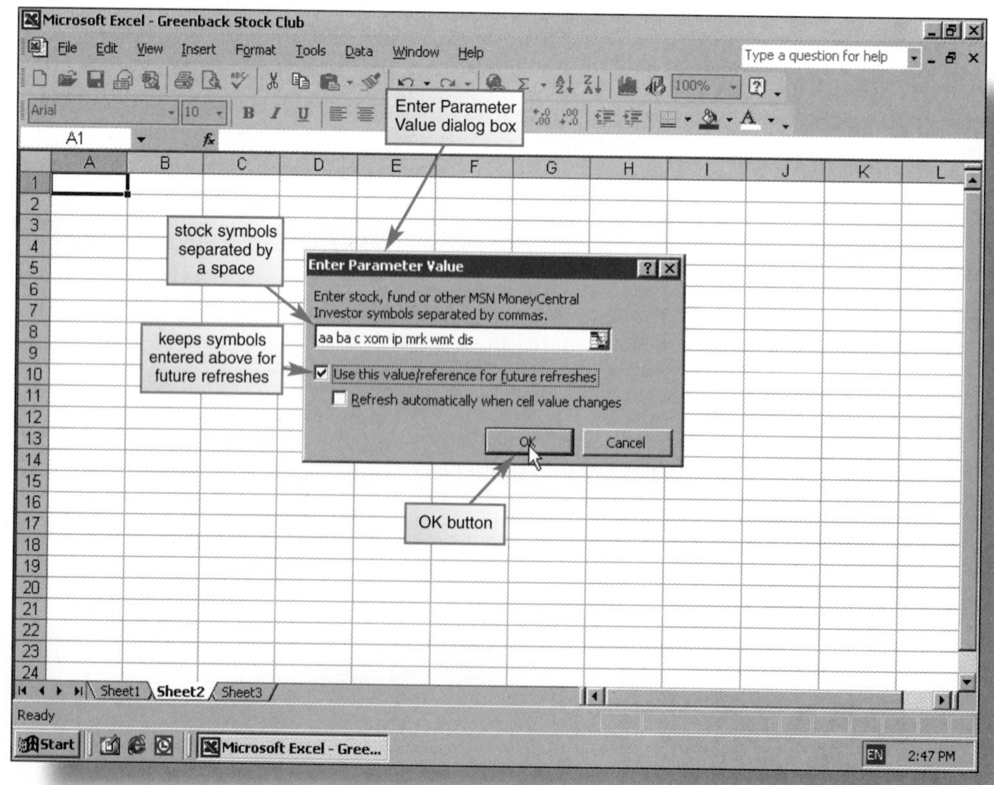

FIGURE 2-77

5 Click the OK button.

Once your computer connects to the Internet, a message displays to inform you that Excel is getting external data. After a short period, Excel displays a new worksheet with the desired data (Figure 2-78). A complete display of the worksheet is shown in Figure 2-1b on page E 2.05.

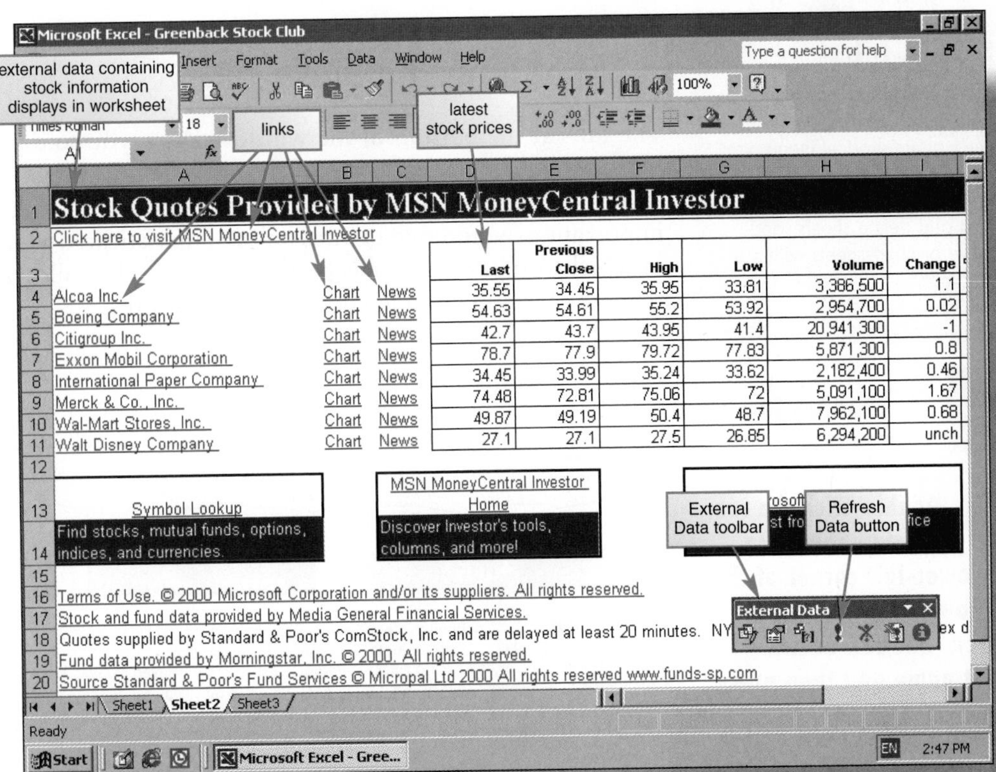

FIGURE 2-78

Other Ways

1. Press ALT+D, D, D
2. In Voice Command mode say, "Data, Import External Data, Import Data"

As shown in Figure 2-78, Excel displays the data returned from the Web query in an organized, formatted worksheet, which has a worksheet title, column titles, and a row of data for each stock symbol entered. Other than the first column, which contains the stock name and stock symbol, you have no control over the remaining columns of data returned. The latest price of each stock displays in column D.

Once the worksheet displays, you can refresh the data as often as you want. To refresh the data for all the stocks, click the **Refresh All button** on the **External Data toolbar** (Figure 2-79). Because the Use this value/reference for future refreshes check box was selected (Figure 2-77), Excel will continue to use the same stock symbols each time it refreshes. You can change the symbols by clicking the **Query Parameters button** on the External Data toolbar.

If the External Data toolbar does not display, right-click any toolbar and then click External Data. Rather than use the External Data toolbar, you also can invoke any Web query command by right-clicking the returned worksheet to display a shortcut menu.

This section gives you an idea of the potential of Web queries by having you use just one of Excel's Web queries. To reinforce the topics covered here, work through In the Lab 3 on page E 2.74.

The workbook is nearly complete. The final step is to change the names of the sheets located on the sheet tabs at the bottom of the Excel window.

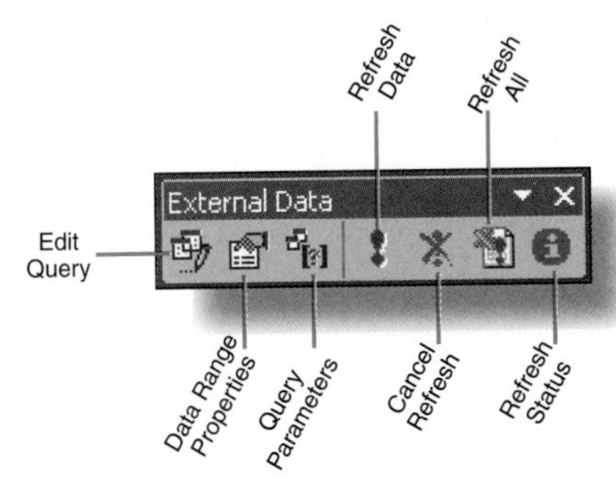

FIGURE 2-79

Sheets Tabs

The name of the active sheet is bold on a white background. Through its shortcut menu, you can rename the sheets, color the tab, reorder the sheets, add and delete sheets, and move or copy sheets within a workbook or to another workbook.

Changing the Sheet Names

The tabs at the bottom of the window allow you to display any sheet in the workbook. You click the tab of the sheet you want to display. The names of the sheets are preset to Sheet1, Sheet2, and so on. These names become increasingly important as you move towards more sophisticated workbooks, especially those in which you reference cells between sheets. The following steps show how to rename sheets by double-clicking the sheet tabs.

Steps To Rename the Sheets

1 Double-click the tab labeled Sheet2 in the lower-left corner of the window. Type `Real-Time Stock Quotes` **as the sheet name and then press the ENTER key.**

The new sheet name displays on the tab (Figure 2-80).

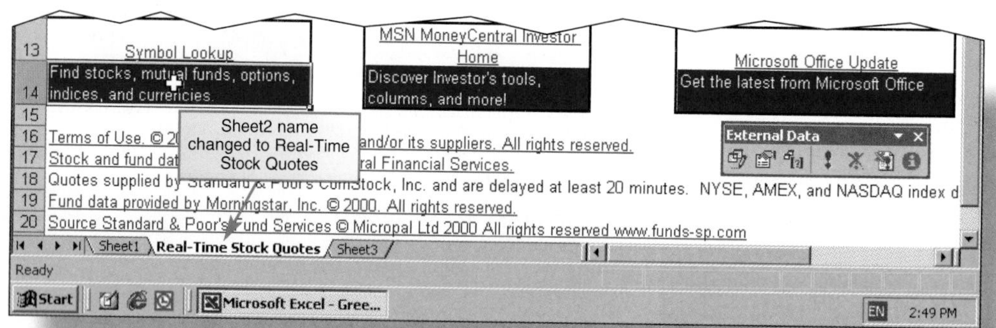

FIGURE 2-80

2 Double-click the tab labeled Sheet1 in the lower-left corner of the window. Type `Investment Analysis` **as the sheet name and then press the ENTER key.**

The sheet name changes from Sheet1 to Investment Analysis (Figure 2-81).

	Stock	Symbol	Date Acquired	Shares	Initial Price Per Share	Initial Cost	Current Price Per Share	Current Value	Gain/Loss	Percent Gain/Loss
3	Alcoa	AA	01/03/00	750	$ 40.125	$ 30,093.75	$ 28.750	$ 21,562.50	$ (8,531.25)	-28.35%
4	Boeing	BA	09/02/98	975	33.000	32,175.00	65.625	63,984.38	31,809.38	98.86%
5	Citigroup	C	10/11/96	850	12.250	10,412.50	48.875	41,543.75	31,131.25	298.98%
6	Exxon Mobil	XOM	03/03/97	925	52.000	48,100.00	78.500	72,612.50	24,512.50	50.96%
7	Intl Paper	IP	11/17/99	300	48.375	14,512.50	26.500	7,950.00	(6,562.50)	-45.22%
8	Merck	MRK	12/23/96	875	37.250	32,593.75	89.750	78,531.25	45,937.50	140.94%
9	Wal-Mart	WMT	12/21/98	157	151.375	23,765.88	44.250	6,947.25	(16,818.63)	-70.77%
10	Walt Disney	DIS	07/12/96	600	17.500	10,500.00	34.875	20,925.00	10,425.00	99.29%
11	**Total**					$ 202,153.38		$ 314,056.63	$ 111,903.25	55.36%
12	**Average**			9	$48.98	$25,269.17	$52.14	$39,257.08	$13,987.91	
13	**Highest**			5	$151.38	$48,100.00		$78,531.25	$45,937.50	298.98%
14	**Lowest**			7	$12.25	$10,412.50		$6,947.25	($16,818.63)	-70.77%

FIGURE 2-81

Sheet names can be up to 31 characters (including spaces) in length. Longer sheet names, however, mean that fewer tabs will display. To display more sheet tabs, you can drag the tab split box (Figure 2-81) to the right. This will reduce the size of the scroll bar at the bottom of the screen. Double-click the tab split box to reset it to its normal position.

You also can use the tab scrolling buttons to the left of the sheet tabs (Figure 2-81) to move between sheets. The leftmost and rightmost scroll buttons move to the first or last sheet in the workbook. The two middle scroll buttons move one sheet to the left or right.

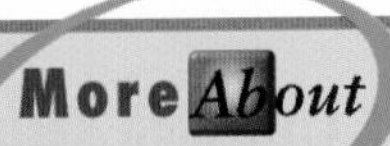

E-Mail

Several Web sites are available that allow you to sign up for free e-mail. For more information on signing up for free e-mail, visit the Excel 2002 More About Web page (scsite.com/ex2002/more.htm) and click Signing Up for E-mail.

E-Mailing a Workbook from within Excel

The most popular service on the Internet is electronic mail, or e-mail. Using **e-mail**, you can converse with friends across the room or on another continent. One of the features of e-mail is the ability to attach Office files, such as Word documents or Excel workbooks, to an e-mail and send it to a co-worker. In the past, if you wanted to send a workbook you saved it, closed the file, launched your e-mail program, and then attached the workbook to the e-mail before sending it. With Excel you have the capability of e-mailing the worksheet or workbook directly from within Excel. For these steps to work properly, you must have an e-mail address and one of the following as your e-mail program: Outlook, Outlook Express, Microsoft Exchange Client, or another 32-bit e-mail program compatible with Messaging Application Programming Interface. The following steps show how to e-mail the workbook from within Excel to Abby Lane. Assume her e-mail address is lane_abby@hotmail.com.

More About

Quick Reference

For a table that lists how to complete the tasks covered in this book using the mouse, menu, shortcut menu, and keyboard, see the Quick Reference Summary at the back of this book or visit the Shelly Cashman Series Office XP Web page site (scsite.com/offxp/qr.htm) and then click Excel 2002.

Steps To E-Mail a Workbook from within Excel

1 With the Greenback Stock Club workbook open, click File on the menu bar, point to Send To, and then point to Mail Recipient (as Attachment) on the Send To submenu.

The File menu and Send To submenu display as shown in Figure 2-82.

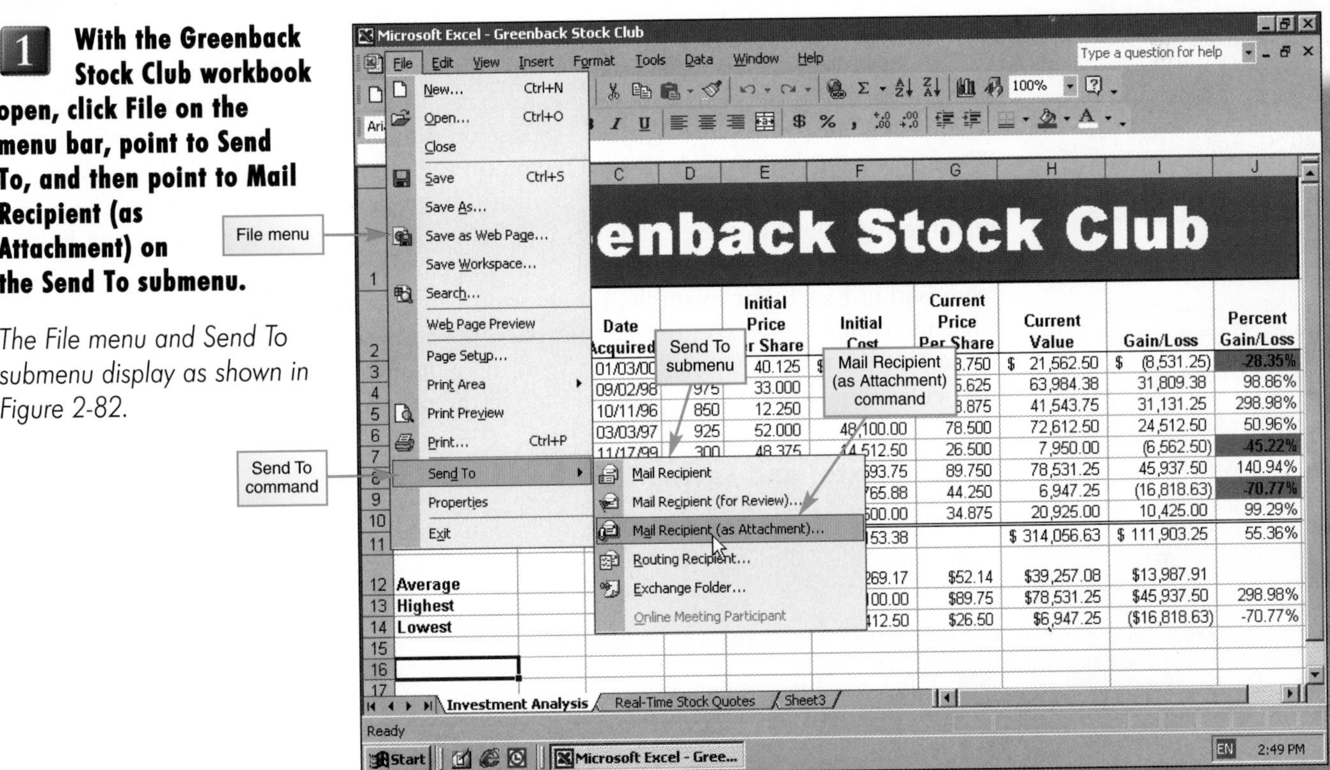

FIGURE 2-82

2 **Click Mail Recipient (as Attachment). When the e-mail Message window opens, type** `lane_abby@hotmail.com` **in the To text box. Type the message shown in the message area in Figure 2-83. Point to the Send button.**

Excel displays the e-mail Message window (Figure 2-83).

3 **Click the Send button.**

The e-mail with the attached workbook is sent to lane_abby@hotmail.com.

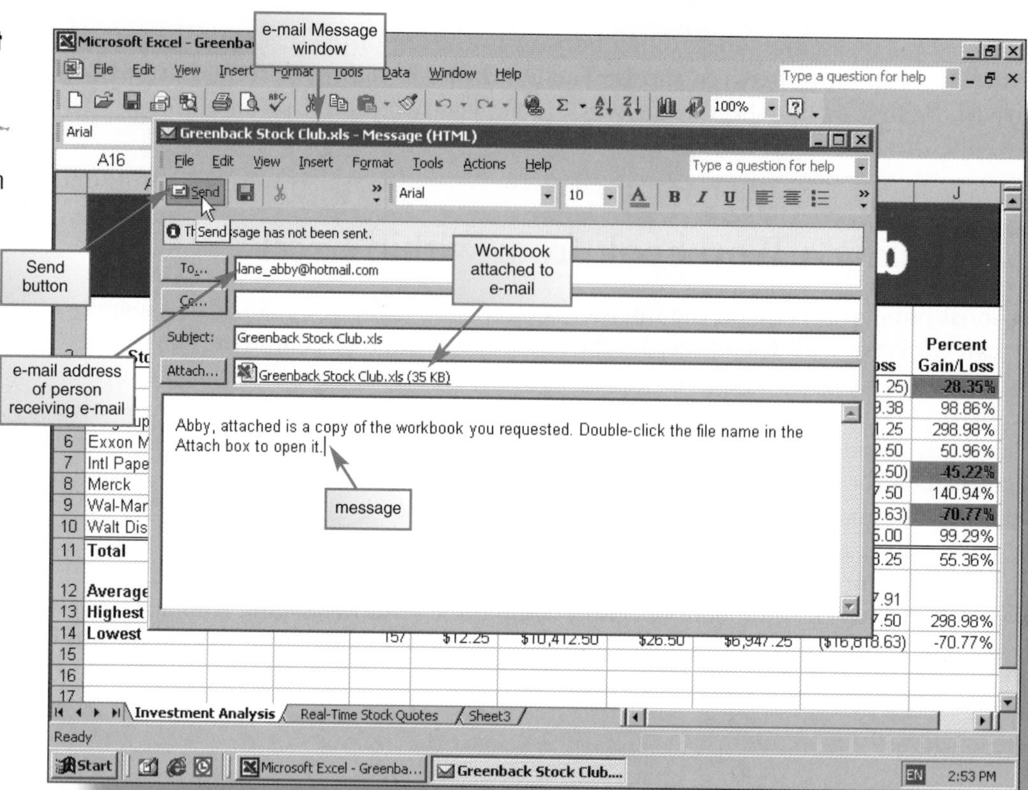

FIGURE 2-83

Other Ways

1. Click E-mail button on Standard toolbar
2. On File menu point to Send To, click Mail Recipient
3. In Voice Command mode say, "File, Send To, Mail Recipient as Attachment"

More About

Microsoft Certification

The Microsoft Office User Specialist (MOUS) Certification program provides an opportunity for you to obtain a valuable industry credential - proof that you have the Excel 2002 skills required by employers. For more information, see Appendix E or visit the Shelly Cashman Series MOUS Web page at scsite.com/offxp/cert.htm.

Because the workbook was sent as an attachment, Abby Lane can double-click the attachment in the e-mail to open it in Excel, or she can save it to disk and then open it at a later time. The worksheet also could have been sent as part of the Word document by using the **E-mail button** on the Standard toolbar or by clicking the **Mail Recipient command** on the File menu. In this case, Abby would be able to read the worksheet in the e-mail message, but would not be able to open it in Excel.

Many more options are available that you can choose when you send an e-mail from within Excel. For example, the Bcc and From buttons on the toolbar in the Message window give you the same capabilities as an e-mail program. The Options button on the toolbar allows you to send the e-mail to a group of people in a particular sequence and get responses along the route.

Quitting Excel and Saving the Workbook

After completing the workbook and related activities, you can quit Excel by performing the following steps.

TO QUIT EXCEL AND SAVE THE WORKBOOK

1. Click the Investment Analysis tab.
2. Click the Close button on the upper-right corner of the title bar.
3. When the Microsoft Excel dialog box displays, click the Yes button to quit Excel and save the changes to the workbook on disk.

CASE PERSPECTIVE SUMMARY

The Worksheet and Web query (Figure 2-1 on page E 2.05) you created for Abby Lane will serve her purpose well. The worksheet, which she plans to e-mail to club members, contains valuable information in an easy-to-read format. Finally, the Web query allows Abby to obtain the latest stock prices to keep the workbook as up to date as possible.

Project Summary

In creating the Greenback Stock Club workbook, you learned how to enter formulas, calculate an average, find the highest and lowest numbers in a range, verify formulas using Range Finder, change fonts, draw borders, format numbers, change column widths and row heights, and add conditional formatting to a range of numbers. You learned how to spell check a worksheet, preview a worksheet, print a worksheet, print a section of a worksheet, and display and print the formulas in the worksheet using the Fit to option. You also learned how to complete a Web query to generate a worksheet using external data obtained from the World Wide Web and rename sheet tabs. Finally, you learned how to send an e-mail directly from within Excel with the opened workbook attached.

What You Should Know

Having completed this project, you now should be able to perform the following tasks:

- Apply a Currency Style Format and Comma Style Format Using the Formatting Toolbar *(E 2.34)*
- Apply a Currency Style Format with a Floating Dollar Sign Using the Format Cells Command *(E 2.37)*
- Apply a Percent Style Format *(E 2.39)*
- Apply Conditional Formatting *(E 2.40)*
- Bold, Center, and Underline the Column Titles *(E 2.31)*
- Center Data in Cells and Format Dates *(E 2.32)*
- Change the Font and Center the Worksheet Title *(E 2.28)*
- Change the Height of a Row by Dragging *(E 2.47)*
- Change the Print Scaling Option Back to 100% *(E 2.58)*
- Change the Title Background and Font Colors and Apply an Outline Border *(E 2.30)*
- Change the Widths of Columns *(E 2.44)*
- Check Spelling on the Worksheet *(E 2.49)*
- Copy a Range of Cells across Columns to an Adjacent Range Using the Fill Handle *(E 2.23)*
- Copy Formulas Using the Fill Handle *(E 2.13)*
- Determine the Average of a Range of Numbers Using the Keyboard and Mouse *(E 2.17)*
- Determine the Highest Number in a Range of Numbers Using the Insert Function Box *(E 2.19)*
- Determine the Lowest Number in a Range of Numbers Using the AutoSum Menu *(E 2.21)*
- Determine the Total Percent Gain/Loss *(E 2.16)*
- Determine Totals Using the AutoSum Button *(E 2.15)*
- Display the Formulas in the Worksheet and Fit the Printout on One Page *(E 2.56)*
- E-Mail a Workbook from within Excel *(E 2.63)*
- Enter a Formula Using the Keyboard *(E 2.09)*
- Enter Formulas Using Point Mode *(E 2.11)*
- Enter the Column Titles *(E 2.07)*
- Enter the Stock Data *(E 2.08)*
- Enter the Total Row Titles *(E 2.08)*
- Enter the Worksheet Title *(E 2.07)*
- Import Data from a Web Source Using a Web Query *(E 2.59)*
- Preview and Print a Worksheet *(E 2.51)*
- Print a Section of the Worksheet *(E 2.55)*
- Quit Excel and Save the Workbook *(E 2.64)*
- Rename the Sheets *(E 2.62)*
- Save a Workbook a Second Time Using the Same File Name *(E 2.50)*
- Save the Workbook *(E 2.25)*
- Start and Customize Excel *(E 2.06)*
- Underline the Row above the Title Row and Bold the Total Row Titles *(E 2.36)*
- Verify a Formula Using Range Finder *(E 2.25)*

Learn It Online

Instructions: To complete the Learn It Online exercises, start your browser, click the Address bar, and then enter `scsite.com/offxp/exs.htm`. When the Office XP Learn It Online page displays, follow the instructions in the exercises below.

1 Project Reinforcement TF, MC, and SA

Below Excel Project 2, click the Project Reinforcement link. Print the quiz by clicking Print on the File menu. Answer each question. Write your first and last name at the top of each page, and then hand in the printout to your instructor.

2 Flash Cards

Below Excel Project 2, click the Flash Cards link. When Flash Cards displays, read the instructions. Type `20` (or a number specified by your instructor) in the Number of Playing Cards text box, type your name in the Name text box, and then click the Flip Card button. When the flash card displays, read the question and then click the Answer box arrow to select an answer. Flip through Flash Cards. Click Print on the File menu to print the last flash card if your score is 15 (75%) correct or greater and then hand it in to your instructor. If your score is less than 15 (75%) correct, then redo this exercise by clicking the Replay button.

3 Practice Test

Below Excel Project 2, click the Practice Test link. Answer each question, enter your first and last name at the bottom of the page, and then click the Grade Test button. When the graded practice test displays on your screen, click Print on the File menu to print a hard copy. Continue to take practice tests until you score 80% or better. Hand in a printout of the final practice test to your instructor.

4 Who Wants to Be a Computer Genius?

Below Excel Project 2, click the Computer Genius link. Read the instructions, enter your first and last name at the bottom of the page, and then click the Play button. Hand in your score to your instructor.

5 Wheel of Terms

Below Excel Project 2, click the Wheel of Terms link. Read the instructions, and then enter your first and last name and your school name. Click the Play button. Hand in your score to your instructor.

6 Crossword Puzzle Challenge

Below Excel Project 2, click the Crossword Puzzle Challenge link. Read the instructions, and then enter your first and last name. Click the Play button. Work the crossword puzzle. When you are finished, click the Submit button. When the crossword puzzle redisplays, click the Print button. Hand in the printout.

7 Tips and Tricks

Below Excel Project 2, click the Tips and Tricks link. Click a topic that pertains to Project 2. Right-click the information and then click Print on the shortcut menu. Construct a brief example of what the information relates to in Excel to confirm you understand how to use the tip or trick. Hand in the example and printed information.

8 Newsgroups

Below Excel Project 2, click the Newsgroups link. Click a topic that pertains to Project 2. Print three comments. Hand in the comments to your instructor.

9 Expanding Your Horizons

Below Excel Project 2, click the Articles for Microsoft Excel link. Click a topic that pertains to Project 2. Print the information. Construct a brief example of what the information relates to in Excel to confirm you understand the contents of the article. Hand in the example and printed information to your instructor.

10 Search Sleuth

Below Excel Project 2, click the Search Sleuth link. To search for a term that pertains to this project, select a term below the Project 2 title and then use the Google search engine at google.com (or any major search engine) to display and print two Web pages that present information on the term. Hand in the printouts to your instructor.

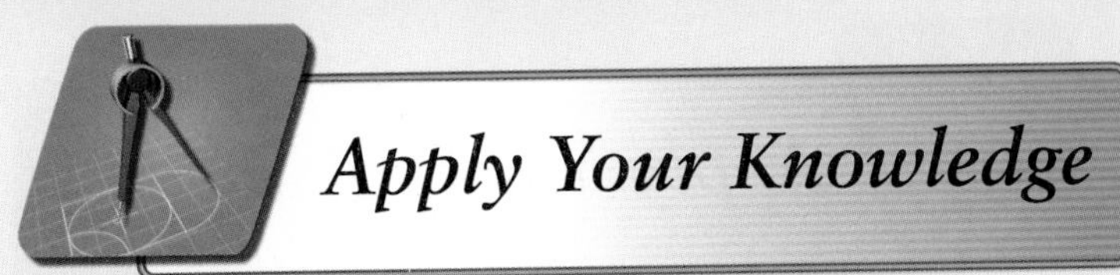

1 Buy It Online Profit Analysis Worksheet

Instructions: Start Excel. Open the workbook Buy It Online from the Data Disk. See the inside back cover of this book for instructions for downloading the Data Disk or see your instructor for information on accessing the files required in this book. The purpose of this exercise is to open a partially completed workbook, enter formulas and functions, copy the formulas and functions, and then format the numbers. As shown in Figure 2-84, the completed worksheet analyzes profits by product.

Microsoft Excel - Buy It Online 2

Buy It Online
Profit Analysis

Product	Description	Unit Cost	Unit Profit	Units Sold	Total Sales	Total Profit	% Total Profit
1H34	Hard Disk	$ 92.95	$ 19.75	32,435	$ 3,655,424.50	$ 640,591.25	17.524%
1J76	Monitor	175.99	45.65	16,534	3,664,595.76	754,777.10	20.596%
2L98	Printer	110.60	62.50	32,102	5,556,856.20	2,006,375.00	36.106%
2Q78	Scanner	160.50	55.25	43,910	9,473,582.50	2,426,027.50	25.608%
3K03	Stereo Speakers	121.35	38.75	34,391	5,505,999.10	1,332,651.25	24.204%
3A04	System Unit	200.23	95.15	23,910	7,062,535.80	2,275,036.50	32.213%
4P01	PDA	50.65	12.85	45,219	2,871,406.50	581,064.15	20.236%
4T43	Tax Software	34.20	14.35	63,213	3,068,991.15	907,106.55	29.557%
5W34	FTP Software	43.00	12.75	52,109	2,905,076.75	664,389.75	22.870%
9C31	Game Software	38.25	13.00	76,145	3,902,431.25	989,885.00	25.366%
Totals				419,968	$ 47,666,899.51	$ 12,577,904.05	
Lowest		$34.20	$12.75	16,534	$2,871,406.50	$581,064.15	17.524%
Highest		$200.23	$95.15	76,145	$9,473,582.50	$2,426,027.50	36.106%
Average		$102.77	$37.00	41,997	$4,766,689.95	$1,257,790.41	

Report / Sheet2 / Sheet3

FIGURE 2-84

Perform the following tasks.

1. Complete the following entries in row 3:
   a. Total Sales (cell F3) = Units Sold * (Unit Cost + Unit Profit) or =E3 * (C3+D3)
   b. Total Profit (cell G3) = Unit Profit * Units Sold or = D3 * E3
   c. % Total Profit (cell H3) = Total Profit / Total Sales or = G3 / F3
2. Use the fill handle to copy the three formulas in the range F3:H3 to the range F4:H12. After the copy is complete, click the Fill Options button and click the Fill Without Formatting option to maintain the bottom double border in the range F12:H12.
3. Determine totals for the Units Sold, Total Sales, and Total Profit in row 13.
4. In the range C14:C16, determine the lowest value, highest value, and average value, respectively for the range C3:C12. Use the fill handle to copy the three functions to the range D14:H16. Delete the average from cell H16, because you cannot average percents.

(continued)

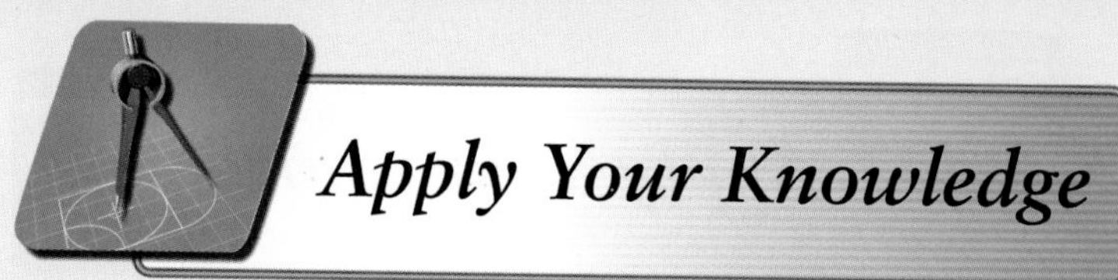

Buy It Online Profit Analysis Worksheet *(continued)*

5. Use the Currency Style button on the Formatting toolbar to format the numbers in the ranges C3:D3, F3:G3, and F13:G13. Use the Comma Style button on the Formatting toolbar to format the numbers in cell E3, the range C4:G12, and the range E13:E16. Use the Decrease Decimal button on the Formatting toolbar to display the numbers in the range E3:E16 as whole numbers. Use the Percent Style and the Increase Decimal buttons on the Formatting toolbar to format the range H3:H15. Increase the decimal positions in this range to 3. Use the Format Cells command on the shortcut menu to format the numbers in the ranges C14:D16 and F14:G16 to a floating dollar sign.
6. Use Range Finder to verify the formula in cell G3.
7. Enter your name, course, laboratory assignment number (Apply 2-1), date, and instructor name in the range A20:A24.
8. Preview and print the worksheet in landscape orientation. Save the workbook. Use the file name, Buy It Online 2.
9. Print the range A1:H13. Print the formulas version (press CTRL+ACCENT MARK (`) to display the formulas version of the worksheet in landscape orientation on one page (Figure 2-85) using the Fit to option in the Page sheet in the Page Setup dialog box. Press CTRL+ACCENT MARK (`) to display the values version.
10. In column D, use the keyboard to add manually \$2.00 to the profit of each product with a Unit Profit less than \$30.00; else add \$3.00. You should end up with \$13,568,687.05 in cell G13. Print the worksheet. Do not save the workbook.
11. Hand in the four printouts to your instructor.

Report

Buy It Online
Profit Analysis

Product	Description	Unit Cost	Unit Profit	Units Sold	Total Sales	Total Profit	% Total Profit
1H34	Hard Disk	92.95	19.75	32435	=E3*(C3+D3)	=E3*D3	=G3/F3
1J76	Monitor	175.99	45.65	16534	=E4*(C4+D4)	=E4*D4	=G4/F4
2L98	Printer	110.6	62.5	32102	=E5*(C5+D5)	=E5*D5	=G5/F5
2Q78	Scanner	160.5	55.25	43910	=E6*(C6+D6)	=E6*D6	=G6/F6
3K03	Stereo Speakers	121.35	38.75	34391	=E7*(C7+D7)	=E7*D7	=G7/F7
3A04	System Unit	200.23	95.15	23910	=E8*(C8+D8)	=E8*D8	=G8/F8
4P01	PDA	50.65	12.85	45219	=E9*(C9+D9)	=E9*D9	=G9/F9
4T43	Tax Software	34.2	14.35	63213	=E10*(C10+D10)	=E10*D10	=G10/F10
5W34	FTP Software	43	12.75	52109	=E11*(C11+D11)	=E11*D11	=G11/F11
9C31	Game Software	38.25	13	76145	=E12*(C12+D12)	=E12*D12	=G12/F12
Totals				=SUM(E3:E12)	=SUM(F3:F12)	=SUM(G3:G12)	
Lowest		=MIN(C3:C12)	=MIN(D3:D12)	=MIN(E3:E12)	=MIN(F3:F12)	=MIN(G3:G12)	=MIN(H3:H12)
Highest		=MAX(C3:C12)	=MAX(D3:D12)	=MAX(E3:E12)	=MAX(F3:F12)	=MAX(G3:G12)	=MAX(H3:H12)
Average		=AVERAGE(C3:C12)	=AVERAGE(D3:D12)	=AVERAGE(E3:E12)	=AVERAGE(F3:F12)	=AVERAGE(G3:G12)	

FIGURE 2-85

In the Lab

1 Ray's Ready Mix Concrete Weekly Payroll Worksheet

Problem: Ray's Ready Mix Concrete has hired you as an intern in its software applications department. Because you took an Excel course last semester, the assistant manager has asked you to prepare a weekly payroll report for the six employees listed in Table 2-8.

Table 2-8 Ray's Ready Mix Concrete Weekly Payroll Data

EMPLOYEE	*RATE*	*HOURS*	*DEPENDENTS*
Sanchez, Edgar	32.25	49.50	6
Wright, Felix	23.50	28.00	1
Wreath, Christy	22.40	70.00	4
Elamain, Al	29.75	18.00	5
Pedal, Rose	21.35	36.00	4
Space, Si	16.25	42.00	2

Microsoft Excel - Ray's Ready Mix Concrete

Ray's Ready Mix Concrete

Employee	Rate	Hours	Dep.	Gross Pay	Fed. Tax	State Tax	Net Pay
Sanchez, Edgar	32.25	49.50	6.00	1,596.38	273.12	51.08	1,272.17
Wright, Felix	23.50	28.00	1.00	658.00	123.91	21.06	513.04
Wreath, Christy	22.40	70.00	4.00	1,568.00	282.83	50.18	1,234.99
Elamain, Al	29.75	18.00	5.00	535.50	68.64	17.14	449.72
Pedal, Rose	21.35	36.00	4.00	768.60	122.95	24.60	621.05
Space, Si	16.25	42.00	2.00	682.50	121.12	21.84	539.54
Totals		243.50		5,808.98	992.57	185.89	4,630.52
Average	24.25	40.58	3.67	968.16	165.43	30.98	771.75
Highest	32.25	70.00	6.00	1,596.38	282.83	51.08	1,272.17
Lowest	16.25	18.00	1.00	535.50	68.64	17.14	449.72

FIGURE 2-86

Instructions: Perform the following tasks to create a worksheet similar to the one shown in Figure 2-86.

1. Enter the worksheet title Ray's Ready Mix Concrete in cell A1. Enter the column titles in row 2, the data from Table 2-8 in columns A through D, and the row titles in the range A9:A12.

(continued)

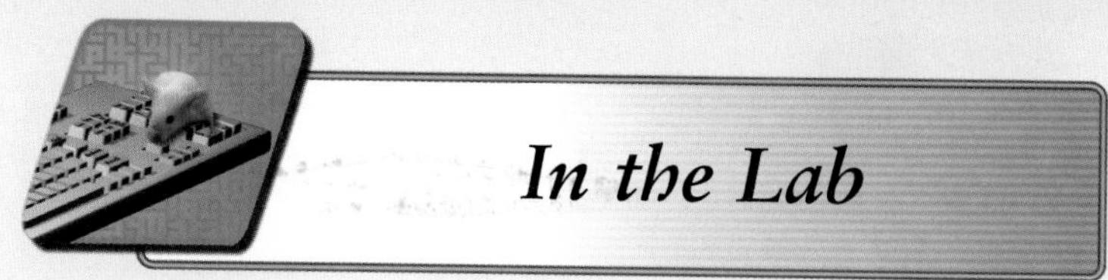

Ray's Ready Mix Concrete Weekly Payroll Worksheet *(continued)*

2. Use the following formulas to determine the gross pay, federal tax, state tax, and net pay for the first employee:
   a. Gross Pay (cell E3) = Rate*Hours or =B3*C3.
   b. Federal Tax (cell F3) = 20% * (Gross Pay – Dependents * 38.46) or =20% *(E3 – D3 * 38.46)
   c. State Tax (cell G3) = 3.2% * Gross Pay or =3.2% * E3
   d. Net Pay (cell H3) = Gross Pay – (Federal Tax + State Tax) or =E3 – (F3 + G3)
   Copy the formulas for the first employee to the remaining employees.
3. Calculate totals for hours, gross pay, federal tax, state tax, and net pay in row 9.
4. Use the appropriate functions to determine the average, highest, and lowest values of each column in rows 10 through 12.
5. Use Range Finder to verify each of the formulas entered in row 3.
6. Change the worksheet title to 26-point Arial Black bold orange font (or a font of your choice). Center the worksheet title across columns A through H. Vertically center the worksheet title. Use buttons on the Formatting toolbar to assign the Comma style with two decimal places to the range B3:H12. Bold, italicize, and assign a bottom border (column 2, row 1 on the Borders palette) to the range A2:H2. Align right the column titles in the range B2:H2. Bold and italicize the range A9:A12. Assign a top and thick bottom border (column 1, row 3 on the Borders palette) to the range A9:H9.
7. Change the width of column A to 18.00 characters. If necessary, change the widths of columns B through H to best fit. Change the heights of row 1 to 39.75 points and rows 2 and 10 to 30.00 points.
8. Use the Conditional Formatting command on the Format menu to display bold white font on an orange background for any net pay less than $550.00 in the range H3:H8.
9. Enter your name, course, laboratory assignment number (Lab 2-1), date, and instructor name in the range A14:A18.
10. Spell check the worksheet. Save the workbook using the file name Ray's Ready Mix Concrete.
11. Preview and then print the worksheet.
12. Press CTRL+ACCENT MARK (`) to change the display from the values version to the formulas version. Print the formulas version of the worksheet in landscape orientation using the Fit to option on the Page tab in the Page Setup dialog box. After the printer is finished, press CTRL+ACCENT MARK (`) to reset the worksheet to display the values version. Reset the Scaling option to 100% by clicking the Adjust to option button in the Page sheet in the Page Setup dialog box and then setting the percent value to 100%.
13. Use the keyboard to increase manually the number of hours worked for each employee by 16 hours. The total net pay in cell H9 should equal $6,418.42. If necessary, increase the width of column F to best fit to view the new federal tax total. Preview and print the worksheet with the new values. Hand in the printouts to your instructor.
14. Click cell A1. Try to click cells B1 through H1. You can't because cells B1 through H1 were merged into cell A1 in Step 6. With cell A1 selected, click the Merge and Center button to split cell A1 into cells A1, B1, C1, D1, E1, F1, G1, and H1. Now click cells B1 through H1. Close the workbook without saving changes.

In the Lab

2 Emelyne's Secret Emporium Monthly Accounts Receivable Balance Sheet

Problem: You are a consultant to the Accounting department of Emelyne's Secret Emporium, a popular Manhattan-based merchandise company with several outlets along the East coast. You have been asked to use Excel to generate a report (Figure 2-87) that summarizes the monthly accounts receivable balance. A graphic breakdown of the data also is desired. The customer accounts receivable data in Table 2-9 is available for test purposes.

Table 2-9 Emelyne's Secret Emporium Accounts Receivable Data

CUSTOMER ID	CUSTOMER NAME	BEGINNING BALANCE	PURCHASES	PAYMENTS	CREDITS
C3451110	Stone, Emerald	16548.30	2691.70	4012.00	435.10
G2343865	Skiles, L'Triece	8340.10	5000.80	6000.00	0.00
G9147655	Juarez, Louis	3401.65	750.30	1050.00	25.00
K3433390	Wong, Ho-Young	18761.60	5560.00	2200.00	35.25
M6104458	Patel, Radjika	2098.20	1596.10	1200.00	189.95
S3918744	Penn, Shem	8231.80	200.20	1375.00	67.00
T6501934	Jasmine, Zo	2090.00	1080.00	500.00	35.00

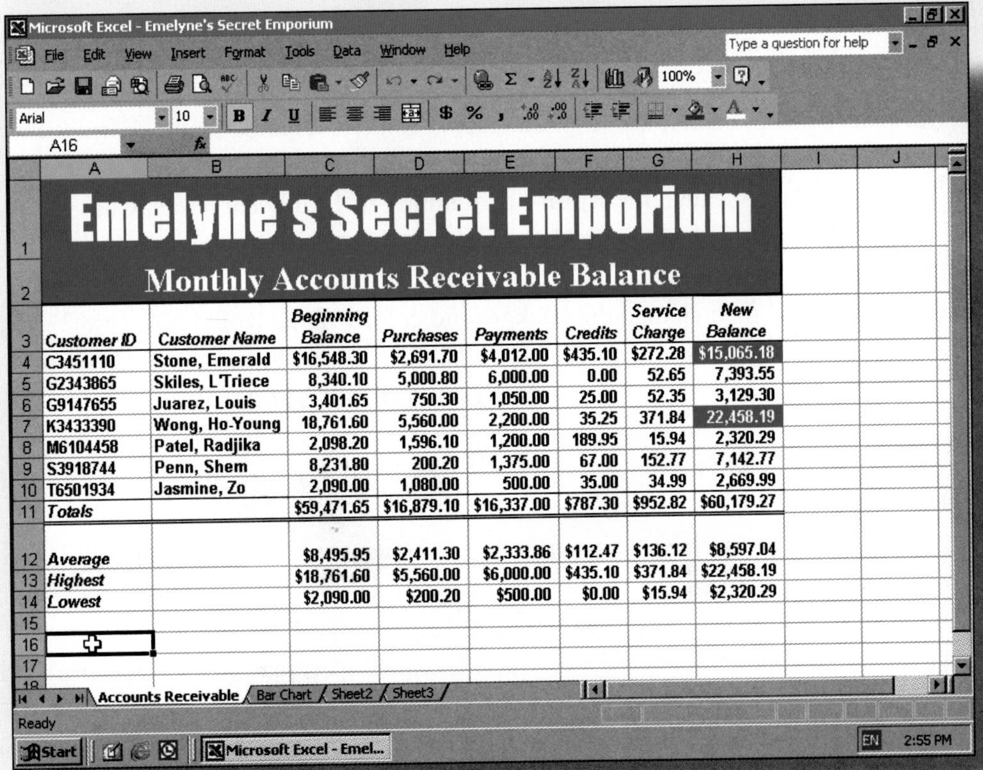

Emelyne's Secret Emporium

Monthly Accounts Receivable Balance

Customer ID	Customer Name	Beginning Balance	Purchases	Payments	Credits	Service Charge	New Balance
C3451110	Stone, Emerald	$16,548.30	$2,691.70	$4,012.00	$435.10	$272.28	$15,065.18
G2343865	Skiles, L'Triece	8,340.10	5,000.80	6,000.00	0.00	52.65	7,393.55
G9147655	Juarez, Louis	3,401.65	750.30	1,050.00	25.00	52.35	3,129.30
K3433390	Wong, Ho-Young	18,761.60	5,560.00	2,200.00	35.25	371.84	22,458.19
M6104458	Patel, Radjika	2,098.20	1,596.10	1,200.00	189.95	15.94	2,320.29
S3918744	Penn, Shem	8,231.80	200.20	1,375.00	67.00	152.77	7,142.77
T6501934	Jasmine, Zo	2,090.00	1,080.00	500.00	35.00	34.99	2,669.99
Totals		$59,471.65	$16,879.10	$16,337.00	$787.30	$952.82	$60,179.27
Average		$8,495.95	$2,411.30	$2,333.86	$112.47	$136.12	$8,597.04
Highest		$18,761.60	$5,560.00	$6,000.00	$435.10	$371.84	$22,458.19
Lowest		$2,090.00	$200.20	$500.00	$0.00	$15.94	$2,320.29

FIGURE 2-87

(continued)

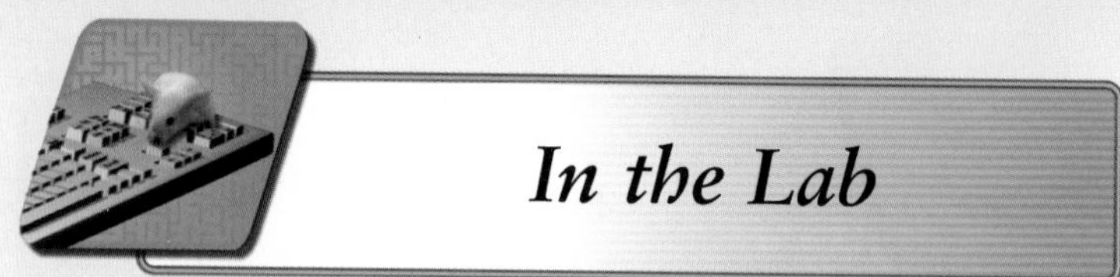

Emelyne's Secret Emporium Monthly Accounts Receivable Balance Sheet *(continued)*

Instructions Part 1: Create a worksheet similar to the one shown in Figure 2-87 on the previous page. Include all seven customers in Table 2-9 on the previous page in the report, plus a service charge and a new balance for each customer. Assume no negative unpaid monthly balances. Perform the following tasks.

1. Click the Select All button (to the left of column heading A) and then click the Bold button on the Standard toolbar to bold the entire worksheet.
2. Assign the worksheet title, Emelyne's Secret Emporium, to cell A1. Assign the worksheet subtitle, Monthly Accounts Receivable Balance, to cell A2.
3. Enter the column titles in the range A3:H3 as shown in Figure 2-87.
4. Enter the customer numbers and row titles in column A. Enter the remaining data in Table 2-9.
5. Use the following formulas to determine the monthly service charge in column G and the new balance in column H for customer C3451110. Copy the two formulas down through the remaining customers.
   a. Service Charge = 2.25% * (Beginning Balance – Payments – Credits)
   b. New Balance = Beginning Balance + Purchases – Payments – Credits + Service Charge
6. Calculate totals for beginning balance, purchases, payments, credits, service charge, and new balance in row 11.
7. Assign cell C12 the appropriate function to calculate the average value in the range C4:C10. Copy cell C12 to the range D12:H12.
8. Assign cell C13 the appropriate function to calculate the maximum value in the range C4:C10. Copy cell C13 to the range D13:H13.
9. Assign cell C14 the appropriate function to calculate the minimum value in the range C4:C10. Copy cell C14 to the range D14:H14.
10. Change the worksheet title in cell A1 to 36-point Impact font (or a similar font). Format the worksheet subtitle in cell A2 to 20-point CG Times font. Center the worksheet titles in cells A1 and A2 vertically and across column A through H. Change the width of column A to 12.00 characters. Change the widths of columns B through H to best fit. Change the height of row 1 to 53.25 points. Change the heights of rows 2, 3, and row 12 to 27.75 points.
11. Select the range A1:H2 and then change the background color to Blue (column 6, row 2) on the Fill Color palette. Change the font color in the range A1:H2 to White (column 8, row 5) on the Font Color palette.
12. Italicize the column titles in row 3. Use the Borders button to add a bottom border to the column titles in row 3. Center the column titles in the range B3:H3. Italicize the titles in the range A11:A14. Use the Borders button to add a top and double bottom border (column 4, row 2 on the Borders palette) to the range A11:H11.
13. Use the Format Cells command on the shortcut menu to assign the Currency style with a floating dollar sign to the cells containing numeric data in row 4 and rows 11 through 14. Use the same command to assign the Comma style (currency with no dollar sign) to the range C5:H10. The Format Cells command is preferred over the Comma Style button because the worksheet specifications call for displaying zero as 0.00 rather than as a dash (-), as shown in Figure 2-87.
14. Use the Conditional Formatting command on the Format menu to change the font to white bold on a blue background in any cell in the range H4:H10 that contains a value greater than or equal to 10000.
15. Change the widths of columns C through H to best fit again, if necessary.

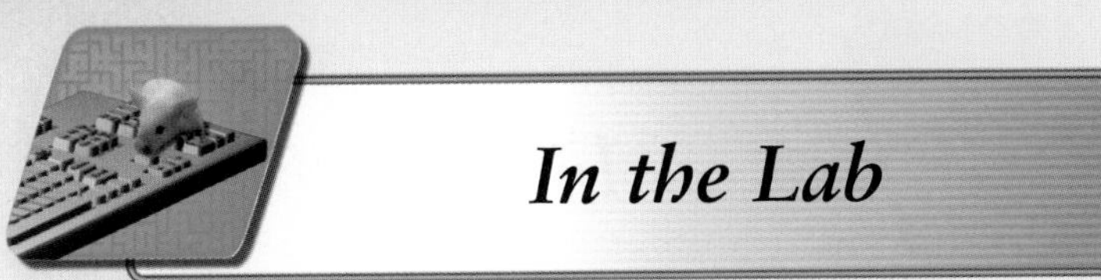

16. Rename the sheet Accounts Receivable.
17. Enter your name, course, laboratory assignment number (Lab 2-2), date, and instructor name in the range A16:A20.
18. Spell check the worksheet. Save the workbook using the file name Emelyne's Secret Emporium.
19. Preview and then print the worksheet. Print the range A3:C14. Press CTRL+ACCENT MARK (`) to change the display from the values version to the formulas version and then print the worksheet to fit on one page in landscape orientation. After the printer is finished, press CTRL+ACCENT MARK (`) to reset the worksheet to display the values version. Reset the Scaling option to 100% by clicking the Adjust to option button on the Page tab in the Page Setup dialog box and then setting the percent value to 100%. Hand in the three printouts to your instructor.

Instructions Part 2: This part requires that you use the Chart Wizard button on the Standard toolbar to draw a 3-D Bar chart. If necessary, use the Ask a Question box on the menu bar to obtain information on drawing a Bar chart.

Draw the 3-D Bar chart showing each customer's total new balance as shown in Figure 2-88. Select the nonadjacent chart ranges B4:B10 and H4:H10. That is, select the range B4:B10 and then hold down the CTRL key and select the range H4:H10. The category names in the range B4:B10 will identify the bars, while the data series in the range H4:H10 will determine the length of the bars. Click the Chart Wizard button on the Standard toolbar. Draw the 3-D Bar chart on a new chart sheet. Use the Bar chart sub-type Clustered Bar with 3-D visual effect (column 1, row 2). Click the Next button to display the next dialog box. Add the chart title Accounts Receivable.

Rename the Chart1 sheet Bar Chart. Drag the Accounts Receivable tab to the left of the Bar Chart tab. Save the workbook using the same file name as in Part 1. Preview and print the chart. Hand in the printout to your instructor.

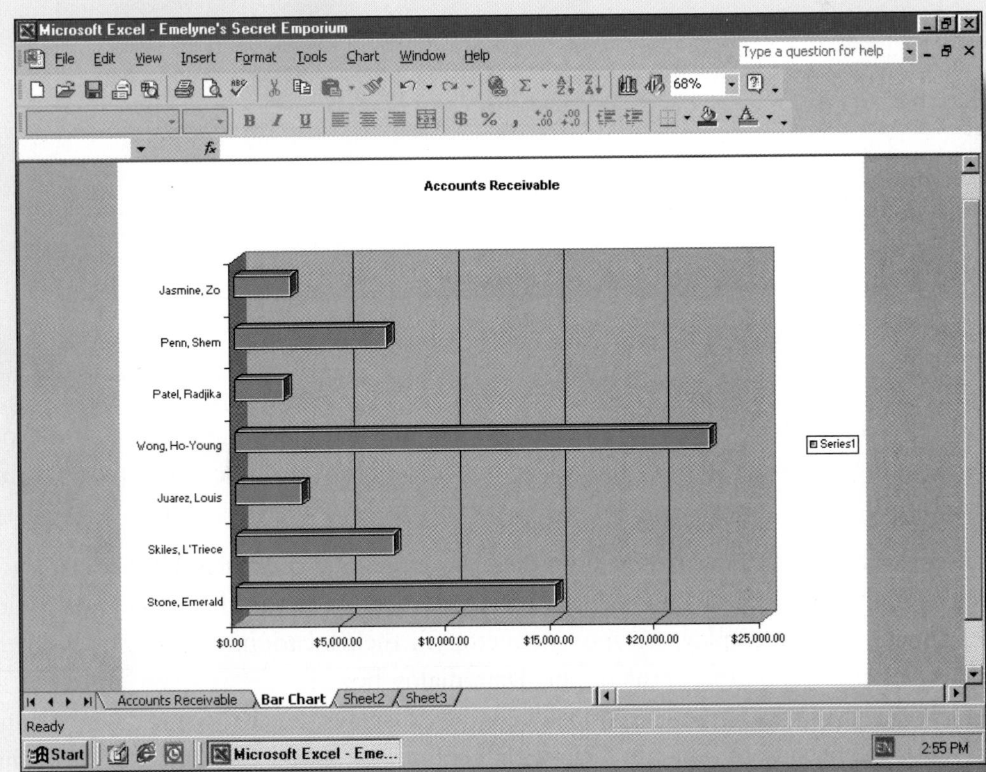

FIGURE 2-88

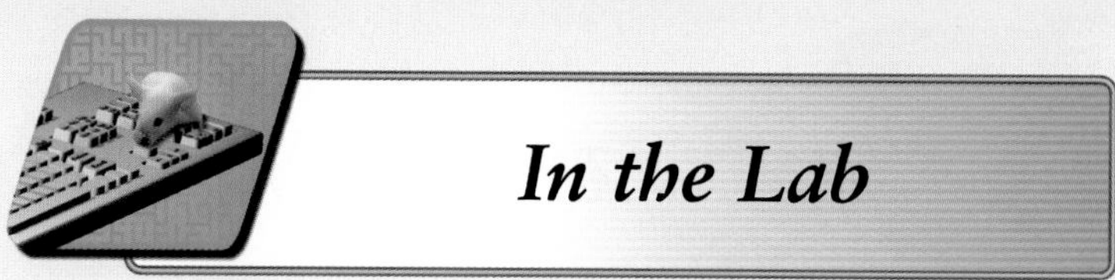

Emelyne's Secret Emporium Monthly Accounts Receivable Balance Sheet *(continued)*

Instructions Part 3: Change the following purchases: account number G9147655 to $5000.00; account number T6501934 to $2500.00. The total new balance in cell H11 should equal $65,848.97. Select both sheets by holding down the SHIFT key and clicking the Bar Chart tab. Preview and print the selected sheets. Hand in the printouts to your instructor.

Instructions Part 4: With your instructor's permission, e-mail the workbook with the changes indicated in Part 3 as an attachment to your instructor. Close the workbook without saving the changes.

3 Equity Web Queries

Problem: Francis Florida, president of Live Snakes and Gators, Inc., recently attended a Microsoft Office seminar at the local community college and learned that Excel can connect to the World Wide Web, download real-time stock data into a worksheet, and then refresh the data as often as needed. Because you have had courses in Excel and the Internet, he has hired you as a consultant to develop a stock analysis workbook. His portfolio is listed in Table 2-10.

Table 2-10 Francis Florida's Stock Portfolio

COMPANY	STOCK SYMBOL
Caterpillar	CAT
General Electric	GE
Microsoft	MSFT
Pfizer	PFE
Sun Microsystems	SUNW
Wal-Mart	WMT

Instructions Part 1: If necessary, connect to the Internet. Open a new Excel workbook and select cell A1. Perform the following steps to run a Web query to obtain multiple stock quotes, using the stock symbols in Table 2-10.

1. Point to Import External Data on the Data menu and then click Import Data.
2. Double-click MSN MoneyCentral Investor Stock Quotes in the Select Data Source dialog box. If the Web queries do not display, see your instructor for their location.
3. Click the OK button in the Import Data dialog box.
4. When the Enter Parameter Value dialog box displays, enter the stock symbols in Table 2-10 into the text box, being sure to separate them with a comma or space. Click the Use this value/reference for future refreshes check box, click the Refresh automatically when cell value changes, and then click the OK button. After several seconds, the stock data returned by the Web query displays in a worksheet as shown in Figure 2-89. Because the stock data returned is real-time, the numbers on your worksheet may be different.

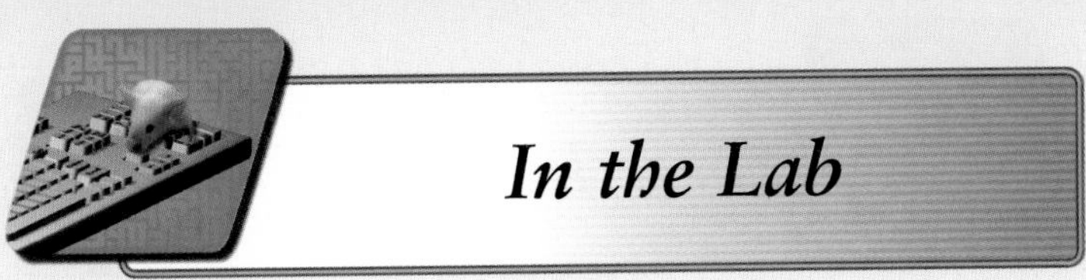

5. Enter your name, course, laboratory assignment number (Lab 2-3a), date, and instructor name in the range A22:A26.
6. Rename the sheet Multiple Quotes. Save the workbook using the file name Francis Florida's Equities Online. Preview and then print the worksheet in landscape orientation using the Fit to option.
7. Click the following links and print each: Click here to visit MSN MoneyCentral Investor; Pfizer Inc; and Pfizer Inc News. Also, print the latest news item regarding Pfizer from the Pfizer Inc News page. After printing each Web page, close the browser. If necessary, click the Microsoft Excel button on the taskbar to activate Excel. Hand in the printouts to your instructor.

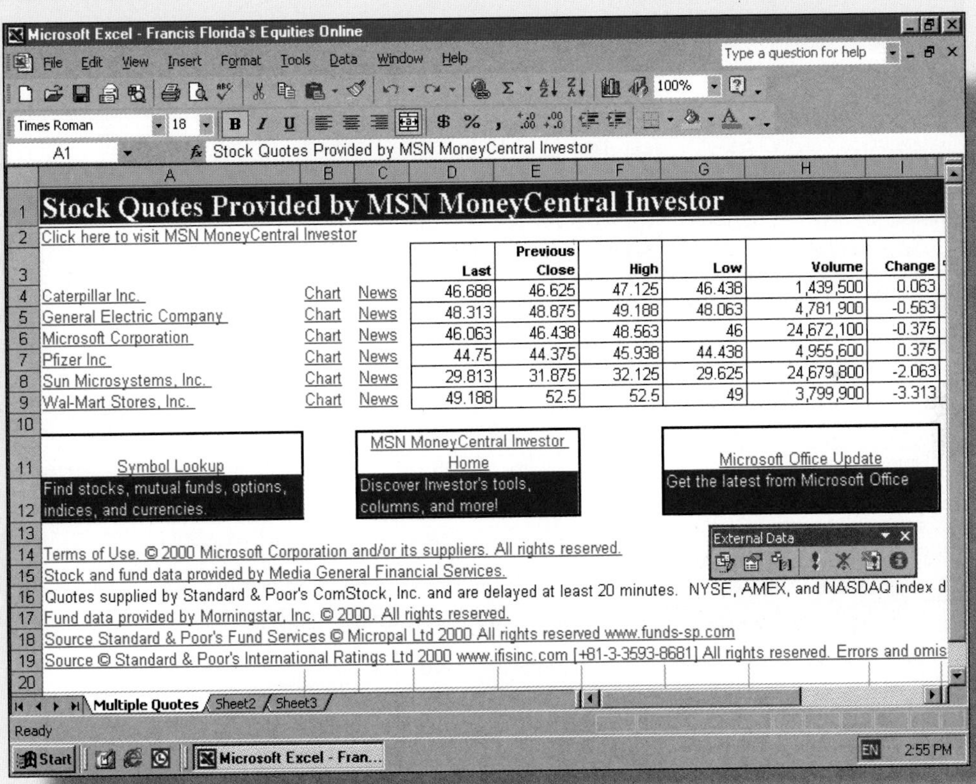

FIGURE 2-89

Instructions Part 2: Perform the following tasks to create a worksheet listing the major indices and their current values as shown in Figure 2-90 on the next page.

1. With the workbook created in Part 1 open, click the Sheet2 tab. Point to Import External Data on the Data menu and then click Import Data.
2. Double-click MSN MoneyCentral Investor Major Indices in the Select Data Source dialog box.
3. Click the OK button in the Import Data dialog box, starting the data in cell A1 of the existing worksheet.
4. The Web query returns the worksheet shown in Figure 2-90 on the next page. Your results may differ.
5. Enter your name, course, laboratory assignment number (Lab 2-3b), date, and instructor name in the range A26:A30.

(continued)

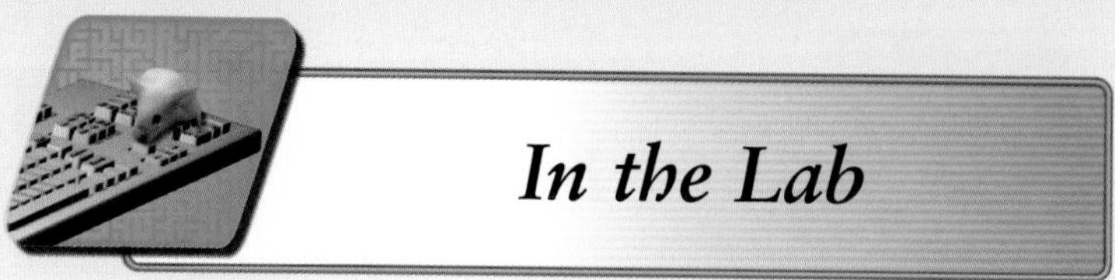

Equity Web Queries *(continued)*

6. Rename the sheet Major Indices. Save the workbook using the same file as in Part 1. Preview and then print the worksheet in landscape orientation using the Fit to option. Hand in the printout to your instructor.

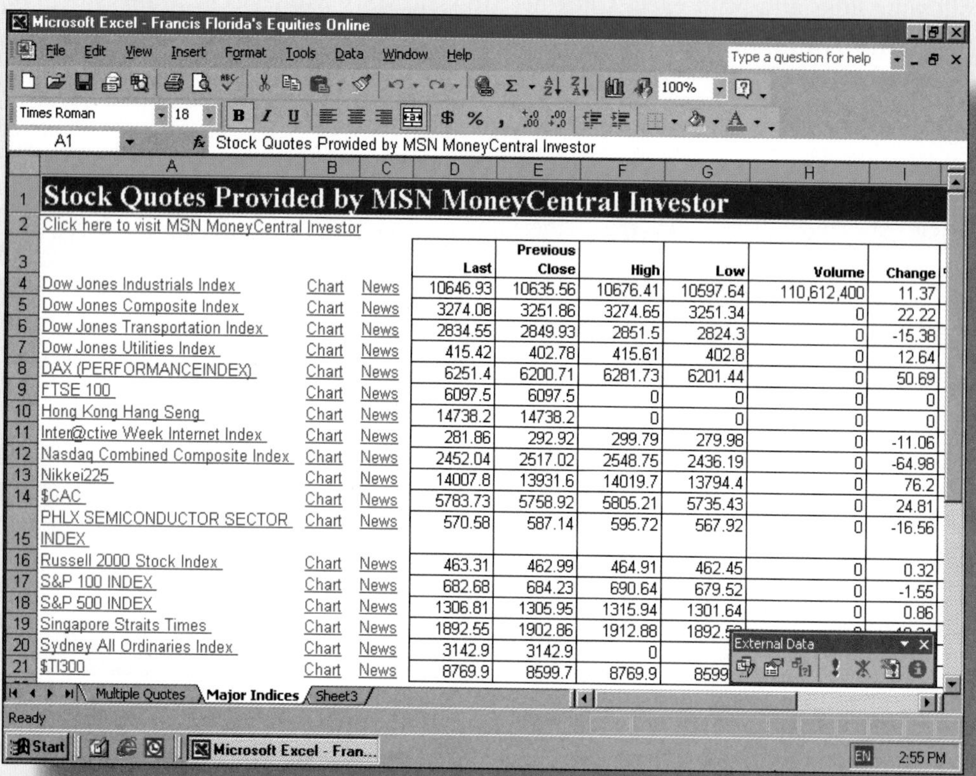

			Last	Previous Close	High	Low	Volume	Change
Dow Jones Industrials Index	Chart	News	10646.93	10635.56	10676.41	10597.64	110,612,400	11.37
Dow Jones Composite Index	Chart	News	3274.08	3251.86	3274.65	3251.34	0	22.22
Dow Jones Transportation Index	Chart	News	2834.55	2849.93	2851.5	2824.3	0	-15.38
Dow Jones Utilities Index	Chart	News	415.42	402.78	415.61	402.8	0	12.64
DAX (PERFORMANCEINDEX)	Chart	News	6251.4	6200.71	6281.73	6201.44	0	50.69
FTSE 100	Chart	News	6097.5	6097.5	0	0	0	0
Hong Kong Hang Seng	Chart	News	14738.2	14738.2	0	0	0	0
Inter@ctive Week Internet Index	Chart	News	281.86	292.92	299.79	279.98	0	-11.06
Nasdaq Combined Composite Index	Chart	News	2452.04	2517.02	2548.75	2436.19	0	-64.98
Nikkei225	Chart	News	14007.8	13931.6	14019.7	13794.4	0	76.2
$CAC	Chart	News	5783.73	5758.92	5805.21	5735.43	0	24.81
PHLX SEMICONDUCTOR SECTOR INDEX	Chart	News	570.58	587.14	595.72	567.92	0	-16.56
Russell 2000 Stock Index	Chart	News	463.31	462.99	464.91	462.45	0	0.32
S&P 100 INDEX	Chart	News	682.68	684.23	690.64	679.52	0	-1.55
S&P 500 INDEX	Chart	News	1306.81	1305.95	1315.94	1301.64	0	0.86
Singapore Straits Times	Chart	News	1892.55	1902.86	1912.88	1892.5[illegible]		
Sydney All Ordinaries Index	Chart	News	3142.9	3142.9	0			
$TI300	Chart	News	8769.9	8599.7	8769.9	8599		

FIGURE 2-90

Instructions Part 3: Create a worksheet showing the latest currency rates (Figure 2-91).

1. With the workbook created in Part 1 open, click the Sheet3 tab. Point to Import External Data on the Data menu and then click Import Data.
2. Double-click MSN MoneyCentral Investor Currency Rates in the Select Data Source dialog box.
3. Click the OK button in the Import Data dialog box, starting the data in cell A1 of the existing worksheet.
4. The Web query returns the worksheet shown in Figure 2-91. Your results may differ.
5. Enter your name, course, laboratory assignment number (Lab 2-3c), date, and instructor name in the range A68:A72.
6. Rename the sheet Currency Rates. Save the workbook using the same file as in Part 1. Preview and then print the worksheet in portrait orientation using the Fit to option. Hand in the printout to your instructor.

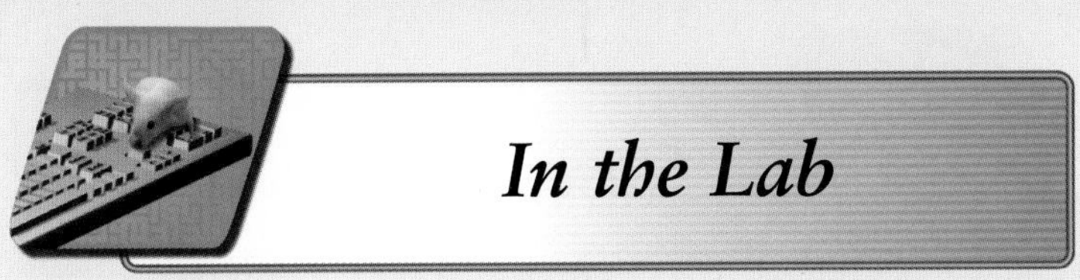

In the Lab

Microsoft Excel - Francis Florida's Equities Online

A1 — Currency Rates Provided by MSN MoneyCentral Investor

	A	B	C
1	Currency Rates Provided by MSN MoneyCentral Investor		
2	Click here to visit MSN MoneyCentral Investor		
3			
4	Name	In US$	Per US$
5	Argentinian Peso	1.001	0.999
6	Australian Dollar	0.559	1.789
7	Austrian Schilling	0.06754	14.805
8	Belgian Franc	0.02305	43.39
9	Baharain Dinar	2.6529	0.377
10	Bolivian Bolivano	0.15723	6.36

FIGURE 2-91

Instructions Part 4: Excel recognizes certain types of data in a cell, such as stock symbols, that it labels with **smart tags.** Excel inserts a **smart tag indicator** (a small purple triangle) in the lower right corner of any cell to indicate that it recognizes the data. If you click the cell with the smart tag indicator, Excel displays the Smart Tag Actions button. If you click the Smart Tag Actions button, Excel displays a menu (Figure 2-92) that can be used to gain instant access to information about the data.

Do the following:

1. Click the New button on the Standard toolbar to display a new workbook. To ensure smart tags is enabled, click AutoCorrect Options on the Tools menu and when the AutoCorrect dialog box displays, click the Smart Tags tab. If necessary, add check marks to the Label data with smart tags, Smart tags list, and Embed smart tags in this workbook check boxes. Click the OK button.
2. Enter the column title `Stock Symbols` in cell A1. Enter the three stock symbols `AMD` (Advanced Micro Device), `CSCO` (Cisco Systems), and `INTC` (Intel) in the range A2:A4 (Figure 2-92). Save the workbook using the file name Smart Tags.
3. Click cell A4. When the Smart Tag Actions button displays, click it to display the Smart Tag Action list (Figure 2-92). One at a time, click the first four commands under Financial Symbol. Insert the refreshable stock price on a new worksheet. Print the new worksheet and the Web pages that display when you invoke the other three commands. Hand the printouts in to your instructor.
4. Repeat Step 3 for the stock symbols in cells A2 and A3.

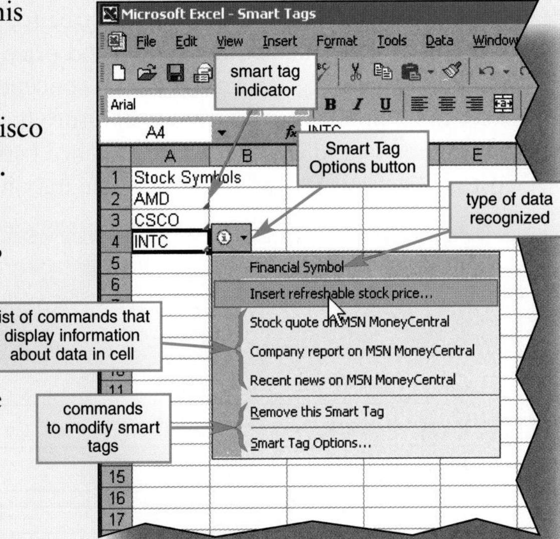

FIGURE 2-92

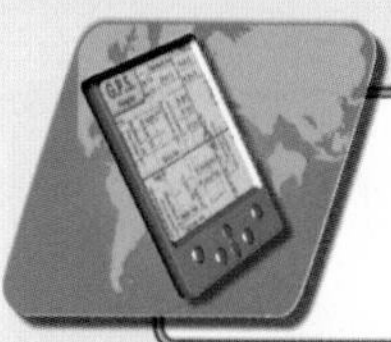

Cases and Places

The difficulty of these case studies varies:
◗ are the least difficult; ◗◗ are more difficult; and ◗◗◗ are the most difficult.

1 ◗ You are the chairman of the fund-raising committee for the computer club. You want to compare various fund-raising ideas to determine which will give you the best profit. You obtain information from six businesses about their products (Table 2-11). Using this data, produce a worksheet to share the information with your committee. Write formulas for the percent profit and the profit per 100 sales. Show the minimum and maximum values for the four numeric columns in Table 2-11. Use the concepts and techniques presented in this project to create and format the worksheet.

Table 2-11 Fund-Raising Data

COMPANY	PRODUCT	SELLING PRICE	PROFIT	PERCENT PROFIT	PROFIT PER 100 SALES
Stickum	Stickers	$2.50	$0.75		
Granny's Best	Cookies	2.00	1.00		
Write Stuff	Stationary	1.75	0.40		
Best Candy	Candy Bars	1.60	0.35		
Gum-It	Gum	1.75	0.50		
Dip-N-Donuts	Donuts	2.60	0.45		

2 ◗ Occasionally, you buy magazines for you and your family members. In an effort to save money, you are considering subscribing to some of these magazines, even though every issue will not be read. To help you decide which magazines to subscribe to, you make the list shown in Table 2-12 showing the magazines you purchase frequently, the newsstand price, how many times you purchase the magazine each year, and the annual subscription cost. Use the concepts and techniques presented in this project to prepare a worksheet to compare your yearly expenditure for each magazine to the cost of an annual subscription. Include annual newsstand cost and the difference between the annual subscription cost and the annual newsstand cost for each magazine. Determine the maximum, minimum, and average for each numeric column.

Table 2-12 Magazine Subscription Data

MAGAZINE NAME	NEWSSTAND PRICE	ISSUES PURCHASED EACH YEAR	ANNUAL SUBSCRIPTION PRICE	ANNUAL NEWSTAND PRICE	SUBSCRIPTION LESS NEWSSTAND
Country Living Gardner	$3.95	4	$12.00		
Disney Adventures	2.99	3	11.85		
Fitness	2.75	4	13.75		
Fortune	5.95	10	35.00		
Newsweek	3.75	25	28.50		
Parenting	2.85	4	12.97		
Sports Illustrated	2.99	30	42.00		
T.V. Guide	1.95	28	49.50		

Cases and Places

3 ▸ In order to determine the effectiveness of their endangered species recovery plan, the Fish and Wildlife Department traps and releases red wolves in selected areas and records how many are pregnant. To obtain a representative sample, the department tries to trap approximately 20% of the population. The sample for five sections is shown in Table 2-13.

Use the following formula to determine the total red wolf population for each section:

Table 2-13 Red Wolf Catch Data

SECTION	WOLVES CAUGHT	WOLVES PREGNANT	ANNUAL DEATH RATE
1	5	2	51%
2	6	1	67%
3	7	2	54%
4	4	2	13%
5	2	1	51%

Wolves in a Section = 5 * (Total Catch + Pregnant Wolves) – 5 * Death Rate * (Total Catch + Pregnant Wolves)

Use the concepts and techniques presented in this project to create the worksheet. Determine appropriate totals. Finally, estimate the total state red wolf population if 898 sections are in the state.

4 ▸ You and your three roommates have just received the monthly electric bill for $545, and they have accused you of driving up the total by burning the midnight oil. You are convinced your late-night studying has little effect on the total amount due. You obtain a brochure from the electric company that lists the typical operating costs of appliance s based on average sizes and local electricity rates (Table 2-14). With this data, you produce a worksheet to share with your roommates. Use the concepts and techniques presented in this project to create and format the worksheet.

Table 2-14 Typical Electrical Operating Costs of Appliances

APPLIANCE	COST PER HOUR	HOURS USED DAILY	TOTAL COST PER DAY	TOTAL COST PER MONTH (30 DAYS)
Clothes dryer	$0.9222	3		
Iron	$0.2157	2.5		
Light bulb (150 watt)	$0.0420	6		
Personal computer	$0.0524	4		
Radio	$0.0095	3		
Stereo	$0.0101	6.5		
Television	$0.0267	4		
VCR	$0.0065	1		

5 ▸▸ Mortimer's Furniture uses a formula to determine the selling price of an item based on that item's wholesale cost. The formula is Selling Price = Wholesale Cost / (1 – Margin). Use this formula to determine the selling price for margins of 60%, 65%, and 70% for the following items and their costs: Sofa, $350; Lamp, $125; End Table, $225; Chair, $215; Rug, $425; Picture, $100. Prepare a professional-looking worksheet showing each item's wholesale cost, selling price for the three margins, and the retailer's profit for each of the three margins. Show totals, averages, maximums, and minimums. Include a chart illustrating what part of the profit is represented by each item when all six items are sold.

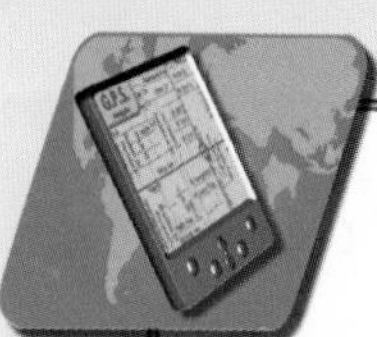

Cases and Places

6 ▶▶ Use the concepts and techniques described in this project to run the Web queries titled MSN MoneyCentral Investor Major Indices and Microsoft MoneyCentral Investor Currency Rates on separate worksheets shortly after the stock market opens. Print each worksheet to fit on one page in landscape orientation. Refresh the worksheets later in the day near the stock market close. Print the worksheets and compare them.

7 ▶▶▶ Computer Discount Sales has decided to pay a 2.5% commission to its salespeople to stimulate sales. The company currently pays each employee a base salary. The management has projected each employee's sales for the next quarter. This information — employee name, employee base salary, and projected sales — follows: Balast, Jack, $8,000.00, $325,557.00; Franks, Ed, $9,500.00, $464,188.00; Hass, Tim, $7,000.00, $199,250.00; Moore, Renee, $5,320.00, $398,450.00; Lister, Bob, $9,250.00, $832,897.00.

With this data, you have been asked to develop a worksheet calculating the amount of commission and the projected quarterly salary for each employee. The following formulas can be used to obtain this information:

Commission Amount = 2.5% x Projected Sales

Quarterly Salary = Employee Base Salary + Commission Amount

Include a total, average value, highest value, and lowest value for employee base salary, commission amount, and quarterly salary. Create a 3-D Pie chart illustrating the portion each employee's quarterly salary contributes to the total quarterly salary. Use the concepts and techniques presented in this project to create and format the worksheet. Use the Excel Help system to create a professional-looking 3-D Pie chart with title and data labels.

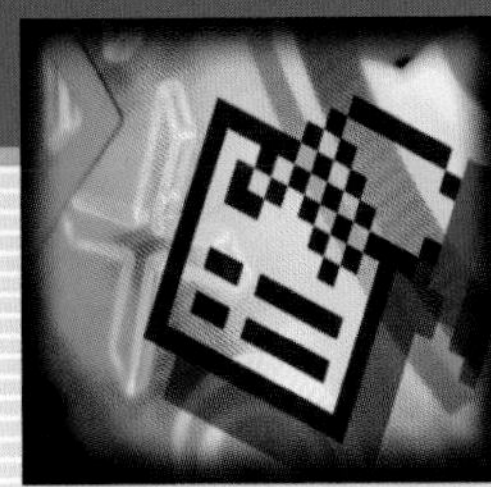

Microsoft Excel 2002

PROJECT

What-If Analysis, Charting, and Working with Large Worksheets

OBJECTIVES

You will have mastered the material in this project when you can:

- Rotate text in a cell
- Create a series of month names
- Use the Format Painter button to format cells
- Copy and paste
- Insert and delete cells
- Use smart tags
- Format numbers using format symbols
- Freeze titles
- Display and format the system date
- Use absolute cell references in a formula
- Use the IF function to perform a logical test
- Copy absolute cell references
- Display and dock toolbars
- Add a drop shadow to a range of cells
- Create a 3-D Pie chart on a separate chart sheet
- Color worksheet tabs
- Rearrange sheets in a workbook
- Preview and print multiple sheets
- Use the Zoom box to change the worksheet view
- View different parts of the worksheet through window panes
- Use Excel to answer what-if questions
- Goal seek

Cash in on Financial Advice

Make Money Management Count

Coinage in America dates back to the eighteenth century when Congress created the United States Mint on April 2, 1792. To ensure that the Nation could conduct its trade and commerce, the U.S. Mint produced a sufficient quantity of circulating coinage. Traditionally, between 14 and 20 billion coins are circulated annually. Recently, the introduction of the 50 States Commemorative Quarter and the Golden Dollar has increased annual Mint production to more than 27 billion coins.

In a single room in the basement of the main United States Treasury building, two men and four women separated and sealed by hand $1 and $2 United States Notes, which had been printed by private bank note companies. This event led to the establishment of the Bureau of Engraving and Printing on August 29, 1862, with the first currency being printed by the Bureau in the fall of 1863.

Counting currency today is an automated process, but imagine if you were asked to count one trillion Golden Dollar coins. At a rate of one per second, twenty-four hours a day, it would require 32,000 years; an impossible feat.

The current U.S. national debt exceeds five trillion dollars ($5,000,000,000,000) with projected annual interest payments of more than $235 billion. Italy, Japan, and Australia also face debts in trillions of dollars. It is no wonder that financial counselors encourage sound fiscal control and budgeting to avoid deficit spending or debt. People who borrow are

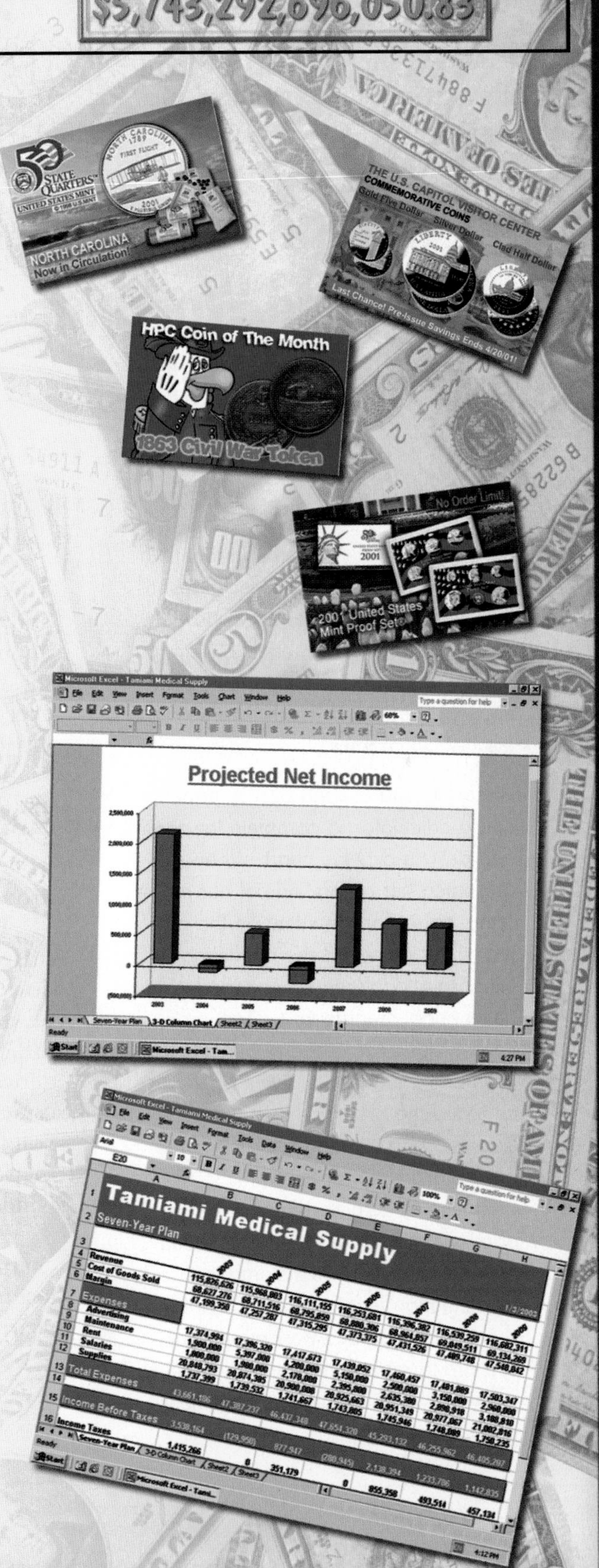

expected both to be able and willing to pay back what they owe along with an appropriate amount of interest.

When working with any sum of money — whether an individual's thousands, the more than 125 American billionaires' billions, or even the nation's trillions — creating a realistic budget indeed can be difficult. Budgets provide a sense of perspective that makes it possible to keep debt at a minimum. Although you are not responsible for preparing a national $1.64 trillion budget, knowing where your money goes is the first step in planning a sound personal budget.

Budgeting using worksheets helps reconcile income and expenses. For example, based on a loan calculation and a budget, you can determine a reasonable monthly car payment. Your living expenses may include rent, food, utilities, car and loan payments, credit card payments, and entertainment. Developing a solid budget for these expenses can help you determine if you will be able to buy a future home. Budgets track your income, expenses, net worth, and cash flow, while organizing your financial data in a logical format. Using electronic spreadsheet software makes it easy to show exactly how you spend money.

In this project, you will use Excel's automatic recalculation feature to complete what-if analysis. It is a powerful tool used to analyze worksheet data. It allows you to scrutinize the impact of changing values in cells that are referenced by a formula in another cell. What if you need to know how much money to put down on a home loan in order to find a manageable monthly payment? What if your income changes or you add a new expense or pay a final payment? These questions and more can be answered easily with Excel's what-if capabilities. Excel not only recalculates all the formulas in a worksheet when new data is entered, it also redraws any associated charts.

Although seemingly restrictive at times, a personal financial plan allows you to examine line by line how your money is spent. Because monetary problems can happen to anyone, regardless of income, sensible use of credit cards, budgeting, and family money management are key components for maintaining an average debt-to-asset ratio of 30 percent. When a situation looks bleak, cash in on financial advice: use credit-counseling services to help with credit repair and education.

Microsoft Excel 2002

What-If Analysis, Charting, and Working with Large Worksheets

PROJECT

CASE PERSPECTIVE

Maria Cianti is the chief executive officer (CEO) of Awesome Intranets, a computer company that specializes in the installation of intranets worldwide. Twice a year, Maria submits a plan to her senior staff to show projected revenues, expenses, and net income for the next six months.

Last June, Maria used pencil, paper, and a calculator to complete the report and draw a 3-D Pie chart. When she presented her report, one of her managers asked for the effect on the projected net income if the marketing expense allocation was changed. While her management team waited impatiently, Maria took several minutes to calculate the answers. Once she changed the projected expenses, the 3-D Pie chart no longer matched the projections. Maria now wants to use a computer and spreadsheet software to address what-if questions so she can take advantage of its instantaneous recalculation feature. As lead spreadsheet specialist for Awesome Intranets, you are to meet with Maria, determine her needs, and create the worksheet and chart.

Introduction

This project introduces you to techniques that will enhance your abilities to create worksheets and draw charts. You will learn about other methods for entering values in cells and formatting these values. You also will learn how to use absolute cell references and how to use the IF function to assign a value to a cell based on a logical test.

In the previous projects, you learned how to use the Standard and Formatting toolbars. Excel has several other toolbars that can make your work easier. One such toolbar is the **Drawing toolbar**, which allows you to draw shapes and arrows and add drop shadows to cells you want to emphasize.

Worksheets normally are much larger than those created in the previous projects, often extending beyond the size of the window (Figure 3-1a). Because you cannot see the entire worksheet on the screen at one time, working with a large worksheet can be difficult. For this reason, Excel provides several commands that allow you to change the display on the screen so you can view critical parts of a large worksheet at one time. One command lets you freeze the row and column titles so they always display on the screen. Another command splits the worksheet into separate window panes so you can view different parts of a worksheet.

From your work in Project 1, you are aware of how easily charts can be created. This project covers additional charting techniques that allow you to convey your message in a dramatic pictorial fashion (Figure 3-1b).

When you set up a worksheet, you should use as many cell references in formulas as possible, rather than constant values. The cell references in a formula are called assumptions. **Assumptions** are values in cells you can change to determine new values for formulas. This project emphasizes the use of assumptions and introduces you to answering what-if questions such as, what if you decrease the marketing expenses assumption (cell B21 in Figure 3-1a) by 5% — how would the decrease affect the projected six-month net income (cell H14 in Figure 3-1a)? Being able to quickly analyze the effect of changing values in a worksheet is an important skill in making business decisions.

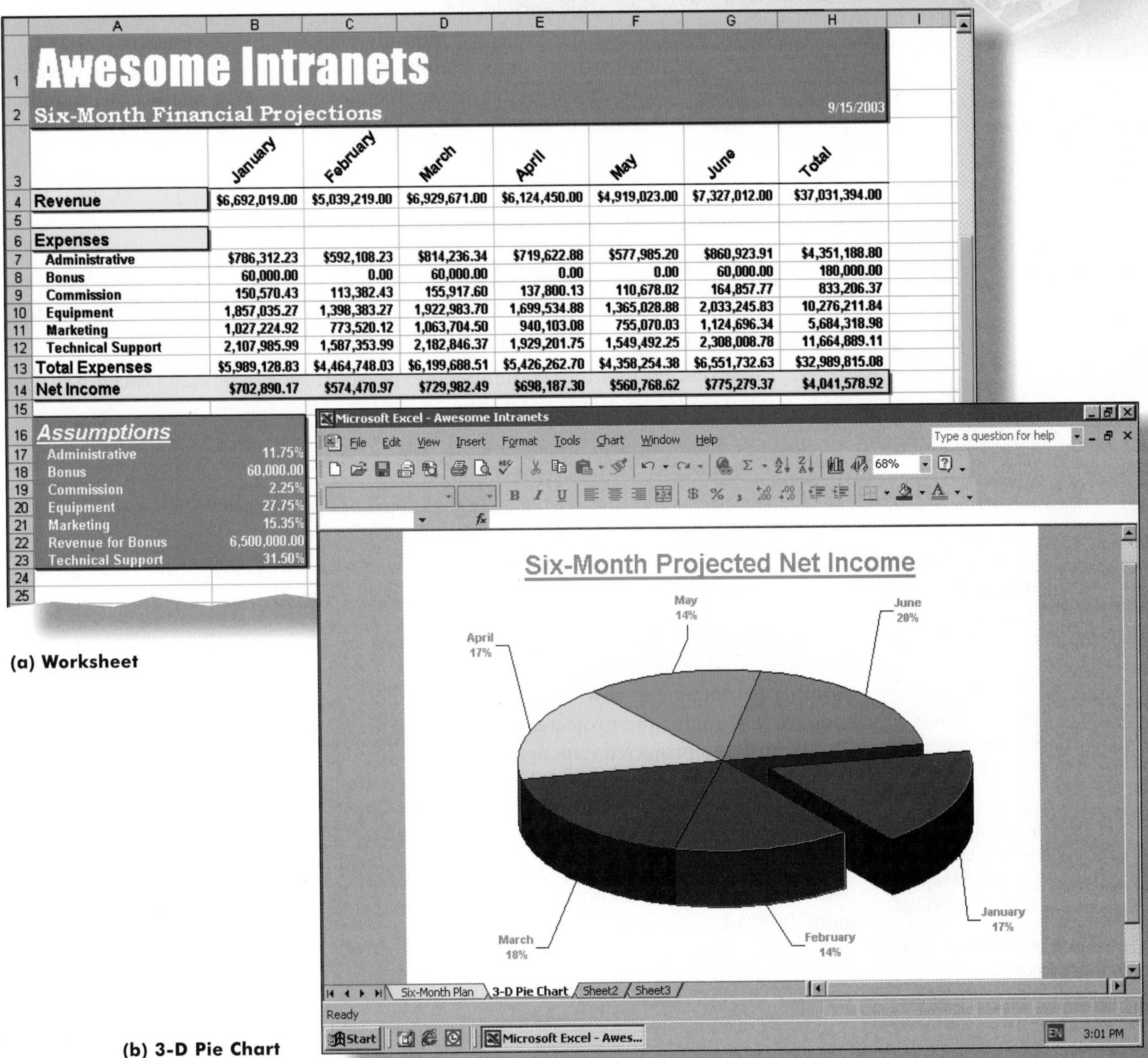

Awesome Intranets

Six-Month Financial Projections — 9/15/2003

	January	February	March	April	May	June	Total
Revenue	$6,692,019.00	$5,039,219.00	$6,929,671.00	$6,124,450.00	$4,919,023.00	$7,327,012.00	$37,031,394.00
Expenses							
Administrative	$786,312.23	$592,108.23	$814,236.34	$719,622.88	$577,985.20	$860,923.91	$4,351,188.80
Bonus	60,000.00	0.00	60,000.00	0.00	0.00	60,000.00	180,000.00
Commission	150,570.43	113,382.43	155,917.60	137,800.13	110,678.02	164,857.77	833,206.37
Equipment	1,857,035.27	1,398,383.27	1,922,983.70	1,699,534.88	1,365,028.88	2,033,245.83	10,276,211.84
Marketing	1,027,224.92	773,520.12	1,063,704.50	940,103.08	755,070.03	1,124,696.34	5,684,318.98
Technical Support	2,107,985.99	1,587,353.99	2,182,846.37	1,929,201.75	1,549,492.25	2,308,008.78	11,664,889.11
Total Expenses	$5,989,128.83	$4,464,748.03	$6,199,688.51	$5,426,262.70	$4,358,254.38	$6,551,732.63	$32,989,815.08
Net Income	$702,890.17	$574,470.97	$729,982.49	$698,187.30	$560,768.62	$775,279.37	$4,041,578.92

Assumptions	
Administrative	11.75%
Bonus	60,000.00
Commission	2.25%
Equipment	27.75%
Marketing	15.35%
Revenue for Bonus	6,500,000.00
Technical Support	31.50%

(a) Worksheet

(b) 3-D Pie Chart

FIGURE 3-1

Project Three — Awesome Intranets' Six-Month Financial Projections

You took the following notes about the required worksheet and chart in your meeting with the CEO, Maria Cianti.

Need: A worksheet (Figure 3-1a on the previous page) and 3-D Pie chart (Figure 3-1b on the previous page) are required. The worksheet is to show Awesome Intranets' projected monthly revenue, expenses, and net income for a six-month period. The 3-D Pie chart is to show the contribution of each projected month's net income to the projected six-month total net income.

Source of Data: The six projected monthly revenues (row 4 of Figure 3-1a) and the seven assumptions (range B17:B23) that are used to determine the projected monthly expenses are based on the company's historical data. All the remaining numbers in Figure 3-1a are determined from these 13 numbers using formulas.

Calculations: Each of the projected monthly expenses in the range B7:G12 of Figure 3-1a — administrative, bonus, commission, equipment, marketing, and technical support — is determined by taking an assumed percentage of the corresponding projected monthly revenue in row 4. The assumptions in the range B17:B23 are as follows:

1. The projected monthly administrative expenses (row 7) are 11.75% (cell B17) of the projected monthly revenue (row 4).
2. The projected monthly bonus (row 8) is $60,000.00 (cell B18) if the projected monthly revenue (row 4) exceeds the revenue for bonus (cell B22) to be awarded; otherwise, the projected monthly bonus is zero. The revenue for bonus value is in cell B22 ($6,500,000.00).
3. The projected monthly commission expenses (row 9) are 2.25% (cell B19) of the projected monthly revenue (row 4).
4. The projected monthly equipment expenses (row 10) are 27.75% (cell B20) of the projected monthly revenue (row 4).
5. The projected monthly marketing expenses (row 11) are 15.35% (cell B21) of the projected monthly revenue (row 4).
6. The projected monthly technical support expenses (row 12) are 31.50% (cell B23) of the projected monthly revenue (row 4).

The projected total monthly expenses in row 13 of Figure 3-1a are the sum of the corresponding projected monthly expenses in rows 7 through 12. The projected monthly net income in row 14 is equal to the corresponding projected monthly revenue (row 4) minus the projected monthly total expenses (row 13).

Because the projected expenses in rows 7 through 12 are dependent on the assumptions in the range B17:B23, you can use the what-if capability of Excel to determine the impact of changing these assumptions on the projected monthly total expenses in row 13 and the projected monthly net income in row 14.

Chart Requirements: A 3-D Pie chart is required on a separate sheet (Figure 3-1b) that shows the contribution of each month to the projected net income for the six-month period.

> **More About**
>
> **Correctness**
>
> Studies have shown that over 25% of all business worksheets have errors. If you are not careful entering data and formulas, then your worksheet is prone to errors. You can ensure correctness in your formulas by carefully checking them using Range Finder and the Error Checking command on the Tools menu. The Auditing command on the Tools menu can also be helpful when verifying formulas.

> **More About**
>
> **Large Worksheets**
>
> The automatic recalculation feature of Excel can become annoying when working with large worksheets with many formulas. You can easily grow impatient waiting for the recalculation to take place each time you complete an entry. You can switch Excel to manual recalculation by clicking Tools on the menu bar, clicking Options, clicking the Calculation tab, and then clicking the Manual option button. You then press F9 to recalculate when you are done entering all the values.

Starting and Customizing Excel

To start Excel, Windows must be running. Perform the following steps to start and customize Excel. Once the Excel window opens, steps 4 and 5 close the task pane and ensure that the Standard and Formatting toolbars display on two rows.

TO START AND CUSTOMIZE EXCEL

1. Click the Start button on the Windows taskbar, point to Programs on the Start menu, and then click Microsoft Excel on the Programs submenu.
2. If the Excel window is not maximized, double-click its title bar to maximize it.
3. If the New Workbook task pane displays, click the Show at startup check box at the bottom of the task pane to remove the check mark and then click the Close button in the upper-right corner to close the task pane.
4. If the Language bar displays, click its Minimize button.
5. If the Standard and Formatting toolbars display on one row, click the Toolbar Options button on the right side of either toolbar and then click Show Buttons on Two Rows in the Toolbar Options list.

The Excel window with the Standard and Formatting toolbars on two rows displays as shown in Figure 3-2 on the next page.

If your toolbars display differently than those shown in Figure 3-2, see Appendix D for additional information on resetting the toolbars and menus.

More About

The Startup Submenu

Any application on the Startup submenu starts automatically when you turn your computer on. To add Excel to the Startup submenu, do the following: 1) Click Start on the Windows taskbar, point to Programs, and then point to Startup on the Programs submenu; 2) Right drag Microsoft Excel from the Programs submenu to the Startup submenu; 3) When the shortcut menu displays, click Copy. The next time you turn your computer on, Excel will automatically start.

Changing the Font of the Entire Worksheet to Bold

After starting Excel, the next step is to change the font of the entire worksheet to bold so all entries will be emphasized.

TO BOLD THE FONT OF THE ENTIRE WORKSHEET

1. Click the Select All button immediately above row heading 1 and to the left of column heading A.
2. Click the Bold button on the Formatting toolbar.

No immediate change takes place on the screen. As you enter text and numbers into the worksheet, however, Excel will display them in bold.

More About

Eliminating Eyestrain

Bolding the entire worksheet makes it easier for users to read the worksheet. An alternative is to increase the font size of the entire worksheet to 12- or 14-point or increase the percentage in the Zoom box, especially if users have less than average eyesight.

Entering the Worksheet Titles

The worksheet contains two titles, one in cell A1, and another in cell A2. In the previous projects, titles were centered across the worksheet. With large worksheets that extend beyond the size of a window, it is best to enter titles in the upper-left corner as shown in Figure 3-1a on page E 3.05. Perform the following steps to enter the worksheet titles.

TO ENTER THE WORKSHEET TITLES

1. Select cell A1 and then enter `Awesome Intranets` as the worksheet title.
2. Select cell A2 and then enter `Six-Month Financial Projections` as the worksheet subtitle.

Excel responds by displaying the worksheet titles in cells A1 and A2 in bold as shown in Figure 3-2 on the next page.

More About

Positioning Data in a Cell

In Excel, you use the Alignment sheet shown in Figure 3-3 to position data in a cell by centering, left-aligning, right-aligning, indenting, aligning at the top, bottom, or center, and rotating. If you enter 90° in the Degrees box, the text will display vertically and read from bottom to top in the cell.

Rotating Text and Using the Fill Handle to Create a Series

When you first enter text, its angle is zero degrees (0°), and it reads from left to right in a cell. You can **rotate text** counterclockwise by entering a number between 1° and 90° on the Alignment sheet in the Format Cells dialog box.

In Projects 1 and 2, you used the fill handle to copy a cell or a range of cells to adjacent cells. You also can use the fill handle to create a series of numbers, dates, or month names automatically. Perform the following steps to enter the month name, January, in cell B3, format cell B3 (including rotating the text), and then enter the remaining month names in the range C3:G3 using the fill handle.

Steps To Rotate Text and Use the Fill Handle to Create a Series of Month Names

1 **Select cell B3. Type** January **as the cell entry and then click the Enter box. Click the Font Size box arrow on the Formatting toolbar and then click 11 in the Font Size list. Click the Borders button arrow and then click the Bottom Border button on the Borders palette. Right-click cell B3 and then point to Format Cells on the shortcut menu.**

The text, January, displays in cell B3 using the assigned formats (Figure 3-2). The shortcut menu displays.

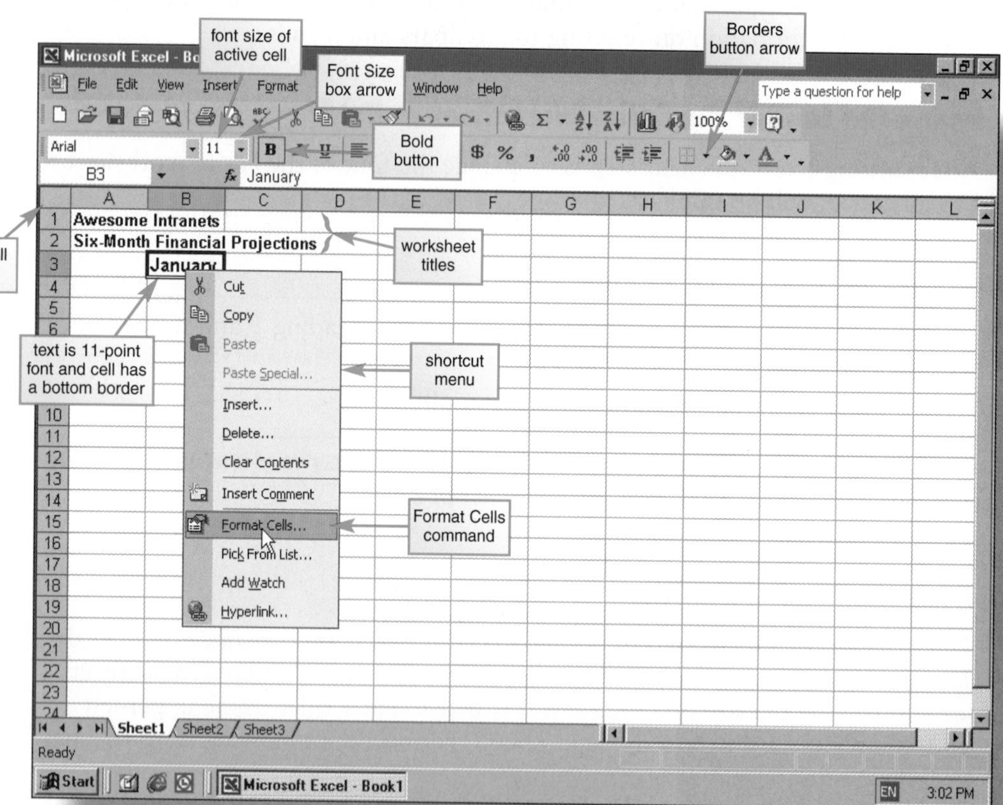

FIGURE 3-2

2 Click Format Cells. When the Format Cells dialog box displays, click the Alignment tab. Click the 45° point in the Orientation area and point to the OK button.

The Alignment sheet in the Format Cells dialog box displays. The Text hand in the Orientation area points to the 45° point and 45 displays in the Degrees box (Figure 3-3).

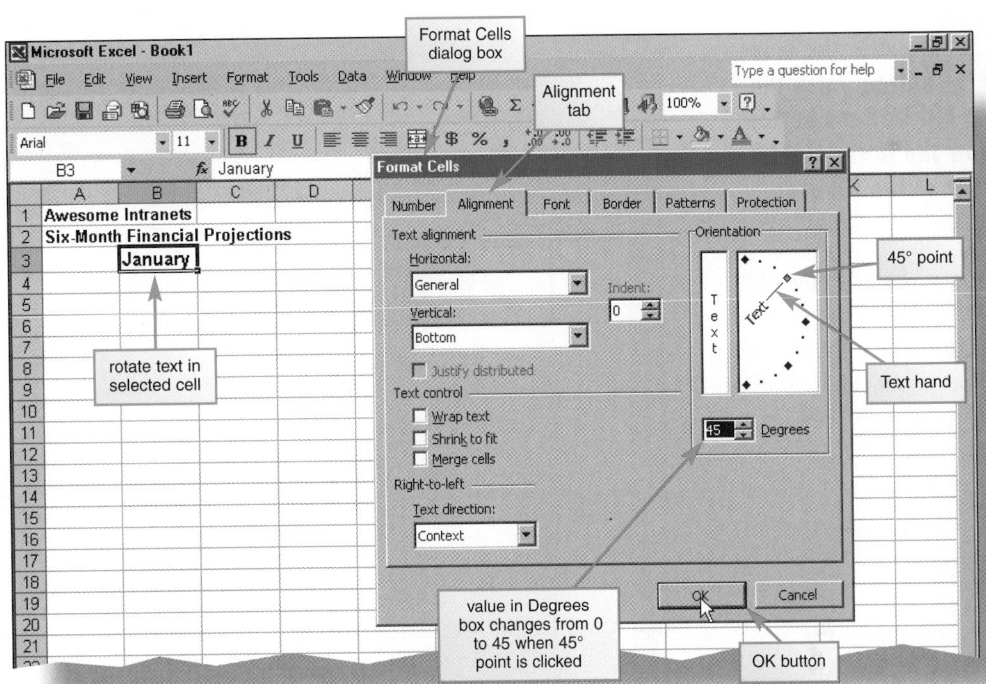

FIGURE 3-3

3 Click the OK button. Point to the fill handle on the lower-right corner of cell B3.

The text, January, in cell B3 displays at a 45° angle (Figure 3-4). Excel automatically increases the height of row 3 to best fit to display the rotated text. The mouse pointer changes to a cross hair.

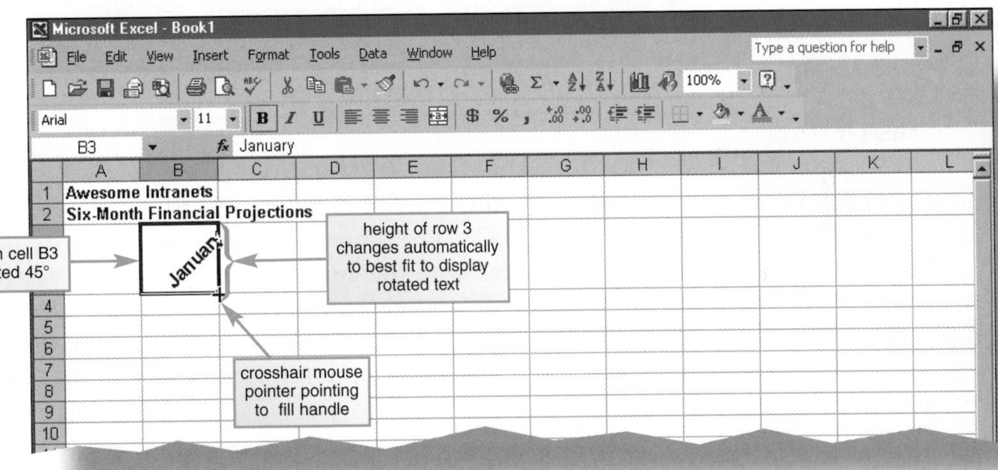

FIGURE 3-4

4 Drag the fill handle to the right to select the range C3:G3.

Excel displays a light border that surrounds the selected range (Figure 3-5). A ScreenTip displays indicating the month of the last cell in the selected range.

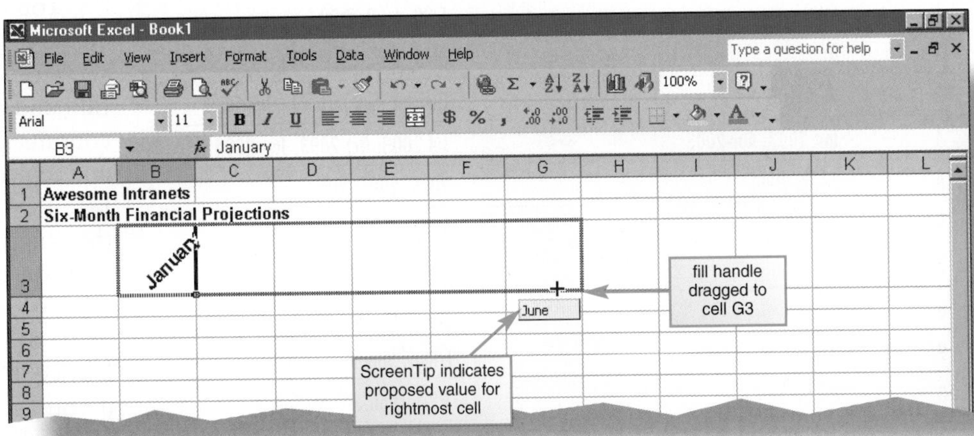

FIGURE 3-5

5 Release the mouse button. Click the Auto Fill Options button below the lower-right corner of the fill area.

Using January in cell B3 as the basis, Excel creates the month name series February through June in the range C3:G3 (Figure 3-6). The formats assigned to cell B3 earlier in Step 1 (11-point font, bottom border, text rotated 45°) also are copied to the range C3:G3. The Auto Fill Options menu displays the fill options available.

6 Click the Auto Fill Options button to hide the Fill Options list.

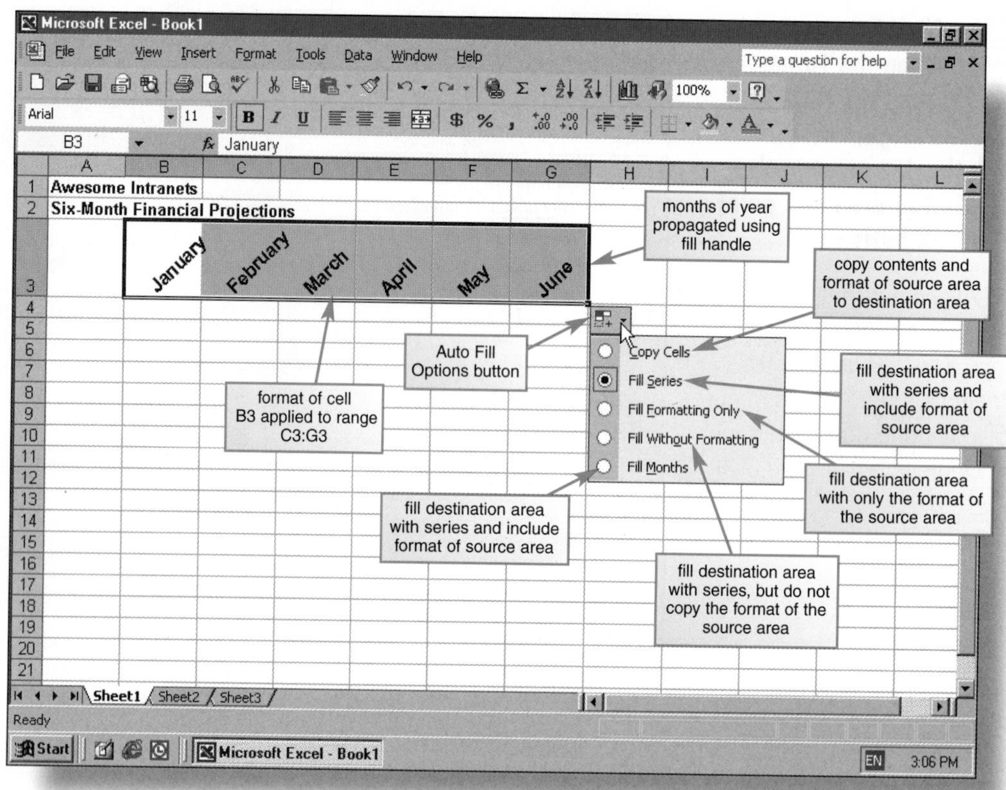

FIGURE 3-6

Other Ways

1. Enter start month in cell, right-drag fill handle in direction to fill, click Fill Months on shortcut menu
2. Select range to fill, in Voice Command mode say, "Edit, Fill, Series, Auto Fill"

Besides creating a series of values, the fill handle also copies the format of cell B3 to the range C3:G3. With some fill operations, you may not want to duplicate the formats of the cell with the initial value. If this is the case, then after the range fills, click the Auto Fill Options button (Figure 3-6) and select the option you desire from the Auto Fill Options menu. As shown in Figure 3-6, the Fill Series option is the default. That is, this is the option Excel uses to fill the area. If you choose another option in the Auto Fill Options menu, then Excel immediately changes the contents of the fill area. The Auto Fill Options button remains active until you begin the next Excel operation.

You can use the fill handle to create longer series than the one shown in Figure 3-6. If you drag the fill handle past cell G3 in Step 4, Excel continues to increment the months and logically will repeat January, February, and so on, if you extend the range far enough to the right.

You can create several different types of series using the fill handle. Table 3-1 illustrates several examples. Notice in examples 4 through 7 that, if you use the fill handle to create a series of numbers or non-sequential

Table 3-1 Examples of Series Using the Fill Handle

EXAMPLE	CONTENTS OF CELL(S) COPIED USING THE FILL HANDLE	NEXT THREE VALUES OF EXTENDED SERIES
1	4:00	5:00, 6:00, 7:00
2	Qtr2	Qtr3, Qtr4, Qtr1
3	Quarter 3	Quarter 4, Quarter 1, Quarter 2
4	Jan-2003, Apr-2003	Jul-2003, Oct-2003, Jan-2004
5	2003, 2004	2005, 2006, 2007
6	1, 2	3, 4, 5
7	780, 760	740, 720, 700
8	Mon	Tue, Wed, Thr
9	Monday, Wednesday	Friday, Sunday, Tuesday
10	2nd Section	3rd Section, 4th Section, 5th Section
11	-101, -103	-105, -107, -109

months, you must enter the first item in the series in one cell and the second item in the series in an adjacent cell. Next, select both cells and drag the fill handle through the destination area.

Copying a Cell's Format Using the Format Painter Button

Because Total, the last column title, is not part of the series, it must be entered separately in cell H3 and formatted to match the other column titles. Imagine how many steps it would take, however, to assign the formatting of the other column titles to this cell — first, you have to change the font to 11 point, then add a bottom border, and finally, rotate the text 45°. Using the **Format Painter button** on the Standard toolbar, however, you can format a cell quickly by copying a cell's format to another cell. The following steps enter the column title, Total, in cell H3 and format the cell using the Format Painter button.

More About

The Mighty Fill Handle

If you drag the fill handle to the left or up, Excel will decrement the series rather than increment the series. To use the fill handle to copy a potential series initiator, like the word January, to a destination area, hold down the CTRL key while you drag. If you drag the fill handle back into the middle of a cell, Excel erases the contents.

Steps To Copy a Cell's Format Using the Format Painter Button

1 Click cell H3. Type `Total` **and then press the LEFT ARROW key. With cell G3 selected, click the Format Painter button on the Standard toolbar. Point to cell H3.**

The mouse pointer changes to a block plus sign with a paint brush (Figure 3-7).

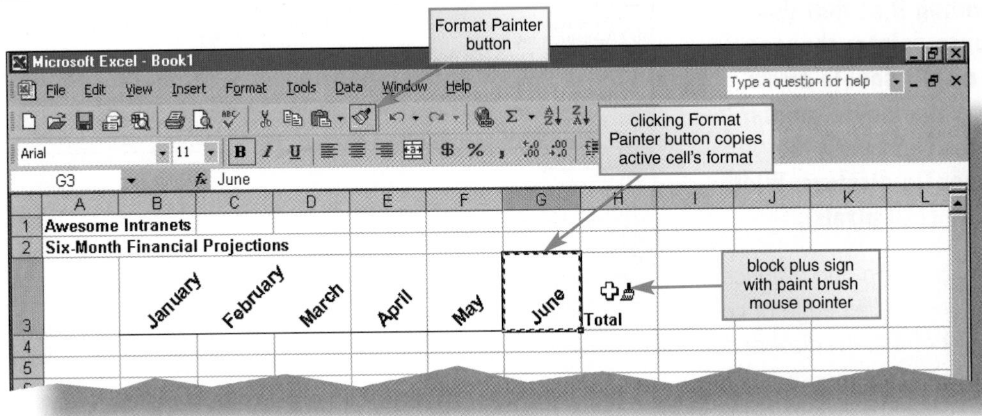

FIGURE 3-7

2 Click cell H3 to assign the format of cell G3 to cell H3. Click cell A4.

Excel copies the format of cell G3 (11-point font, bottom border, text rotated 45°) to cell H3 (Figure 3-8). Cell A4 is now the active cell.

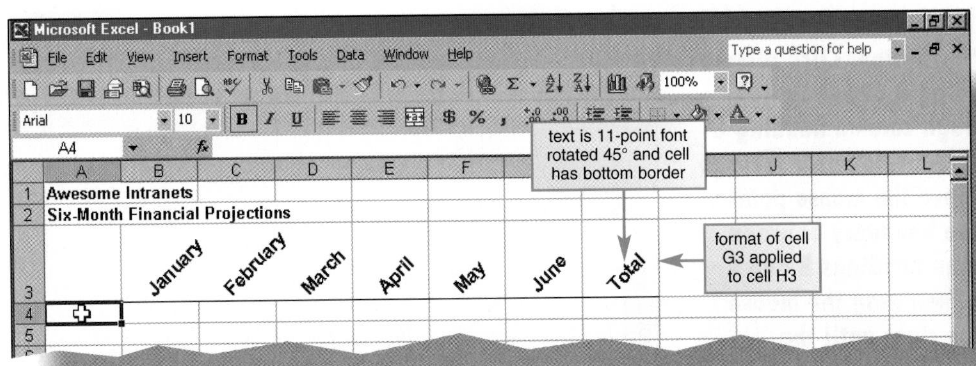

FIGURE 3-8

Other Ways

1. Select cell with desired format, in Voice Command mode say, "Format Painter," select cell or range of cells

Painting a Format

Double-click the Format Painter button to copy the formats to non-adjacent ranges and then drag through the ranges. Click the Format Painter button to deactivate it.

The Format Painter button also can be used to copy the formats of a cell to a range of cells. To copy formats to a range of cells, select the cell or range with the desired format, click the Format Painter button on the Standard toolbar, and then drag through the range to which you want to paste the formats.

Increasing the Column Widths and Entering Row Titles

In Project 2, the column widths were increased after the values were entered into the worksheet. Sometimes, you may want to increase the column widths before you enter the values and, if necessary, adjust them later. The following steps increase the column widths and add the row titles in column A down to Assumptions in cell A16.

To Increase Column Widths and Enter Row Titles

1 Move the mouse pointer to the boundary between column heading A and column heading B so that the mouse pointer changes to a split double arrow. Drag the mouse pointer to the right until the ScreenTip displays, Width: 25.00 (180 pixels).

The ScreenTip and distance between the left edge of column A and the vertical dotted line below the mouse pointer shows the proposed column width (Figure 3-9).

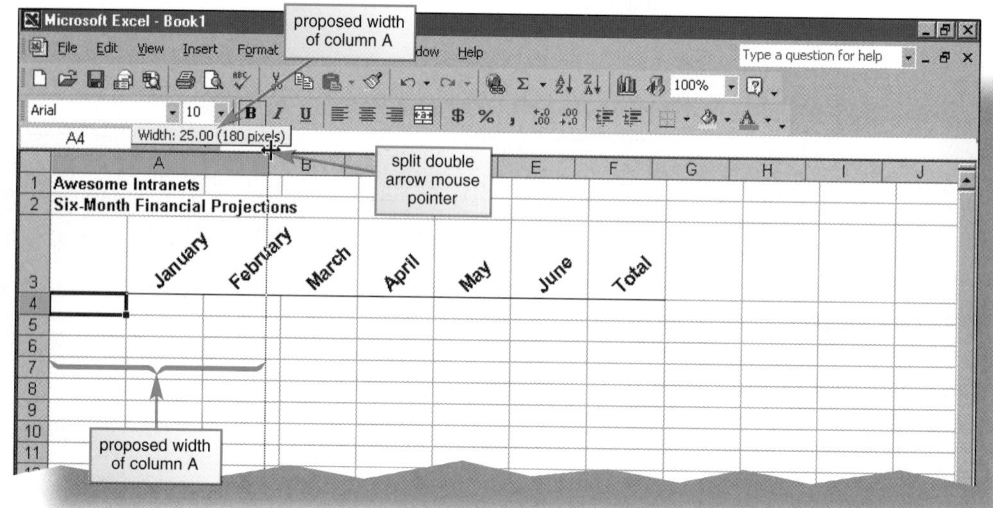

FIGURE 3-9

2 Release the mouse button. Click column heading B and drag through column heading G to select columns B through G. Move the mouse pointer to the boundary between column headings B and C and then drag the mouse to the right until the ScreenTip displays, Width: 13.00 (96 pixels).

The distance between the left edge of column B and the vertical line below the mouse pointer shows the proposed width of columns B through G (Figure 3-10).

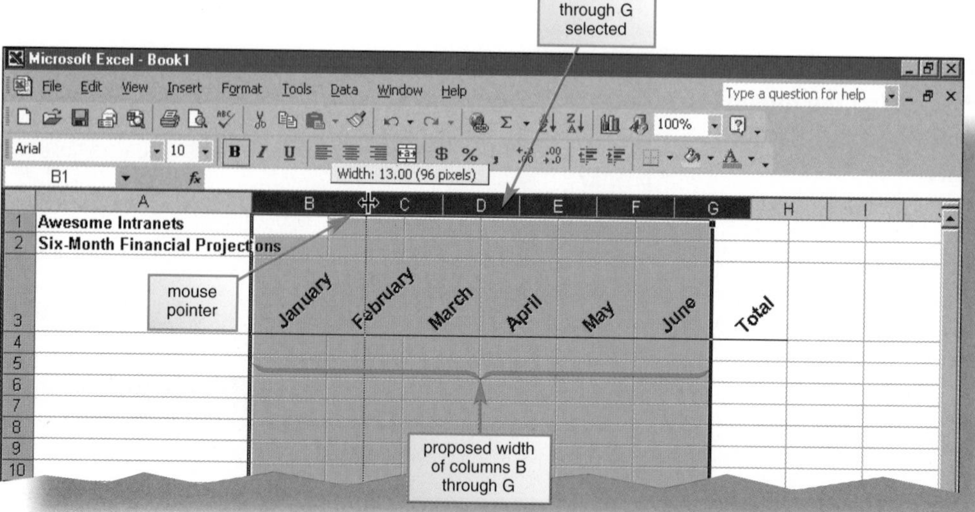

FIGURE 3-10

3 **Release the mouse button. Use the technique described in Step 1 to increase the width of column H to 15.00. Enter** Revenue **in cell A4,** Expenses **in cell A6,** Administrative **in cell A7,** Bonus **in cell A8,** Commission **in cell A9,** Equipment **in cell A10. Enter** Marketing **in cell A11,** Technical Support **in cell A12,** Total Expenses **in cell A13,** Net Income **in cell A14, and** Assumptions **in cell A16. Select the range A7:A12. Click the Increase Indent button on the Formatting toolbar. Click cell A17.**

The row titles display as shown in Figure 3-11.

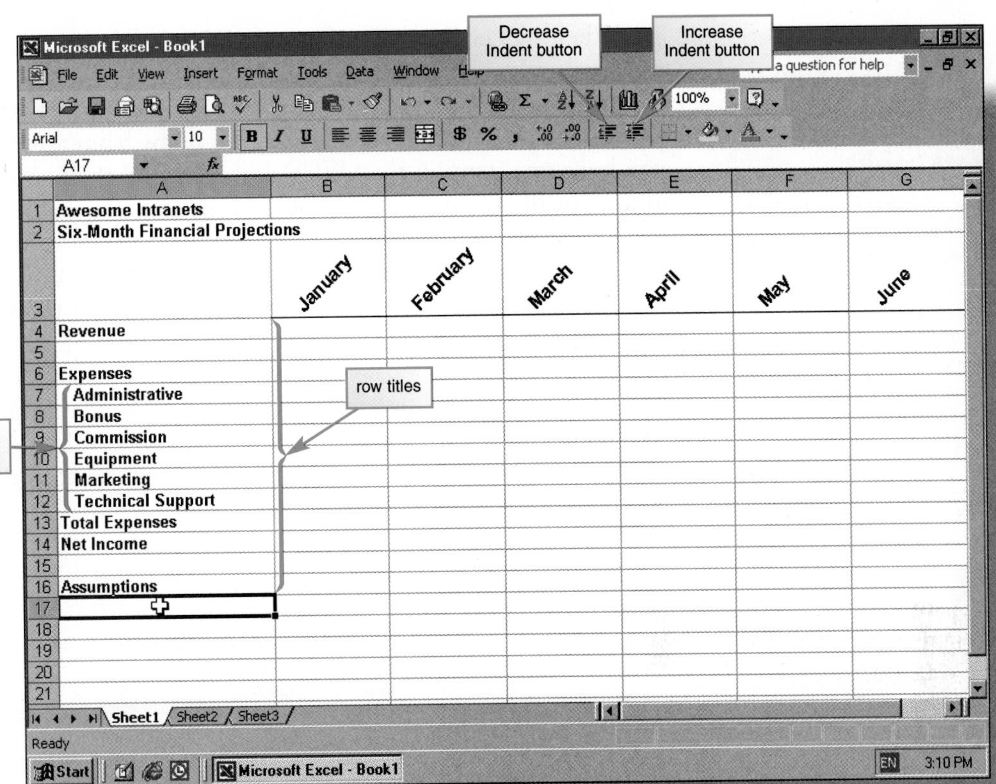

FIGURE 3-11

The **Increase Indent button** indents the contents of a cell to the right by three spaces each time you click it. The **Decrease Indent button** decreases the indent by three spaces each time you click it.

Other Ways

1. To indent, right-click range, click Format Cells, click Alignment tab, click Left (Indent) in Horizontal list, type number of spaces to indent in Indent text box, click OK button
2. To indent, in Voice Command mode say, "Increase Indent"

Copying a Range of Cells to a Nonadjacent Destination Area

As shown in Figure 3-1a on page E 3.05, the row titles in the Assumptions table in the range A17:A23 are the same as the row titles in the range A7:A12, with the exception of the additional entry in cell A22. Hence, you can create the Assumptions table row titles by copying the range A7:A12 to the range A17:A22 and inserting a row for the additional entry in cell A22. The range to copy (range A7:A12) is not adjacent to the destination area (range A17:A22). In the first two projects, you used the fill handle to copy a range of cells to an adjacent destination area. To copy a range of cells to a nonadjacent destination area, however, you cannot use the fill handle.

A more versatile method of copying a cell or range of cells is to use the Copy button and Paste button on the Standard toolbar. You can use these two buttons to copy a range of cells to an adjacent or nonadjacent destination area.

More About

Shrink to Fit

An alternative to increasing the column widths is to shrink the characters in the cell to fit the current width of the column. To shrink to fit, click Format on the menu bar, click Cells, click the Alignment tab, and click the Shrink to fit check box in the Text control area.

Copying Across Workbooks

You can copy a range of cells in one workbook to another by opening the source workbook, selecting the range, clicking the Copy button to place the range of cells on the Office Clipboard, activating the destination workbook, selecting the destination area, and clicking the Paste button.

When you click the **Copy button**, it copies the contents and format of the selected range and places the copy on the Office Clipboard. The **Copy command** on the Edit menu or shortcut menu works the same as the Copy button. The **Office Clipboard** allows you to collect up to 24 different items from any Office application. When you have one item on the Office clipboard and then copy a second item, Excel automatically displays the **Clipboard task pane** on the left side of the screen showing its contents. You can display the Clipboard task pane at anytime by clicking the **Task Pane command** on the **View menu**. If the Workbook or Search task pane displays, click the **Other Task Panes arrow** on the Task Pane title bar and click Clipboard.

The **Paste button** copies the newest item on the Office Clipboard to the destination area. The **Paste command** on the Edit menu or shortcut menu works the same as the Paste button. If you want to copy an older item on the Office Clipboard, click the icon representing the item on the Clipboard task pane. The following steps use the Copy and Paste buttons to copy a range of cells to a nonadjacent destination area.

To Copy a Range of Cells to a Nonadjacent Destination Area

1 Select the range A7:A12 and then click the Copy button on the Standard toolbar. Click cell A17, the top cell in the destination area. Point to the Paste button.

Excel surrounds the range A7:A12 with a marquee when you click the Copy button (Figure 3-12). Excel also copies the values and formats of the range A7:A12 onto the Office Clipboard.

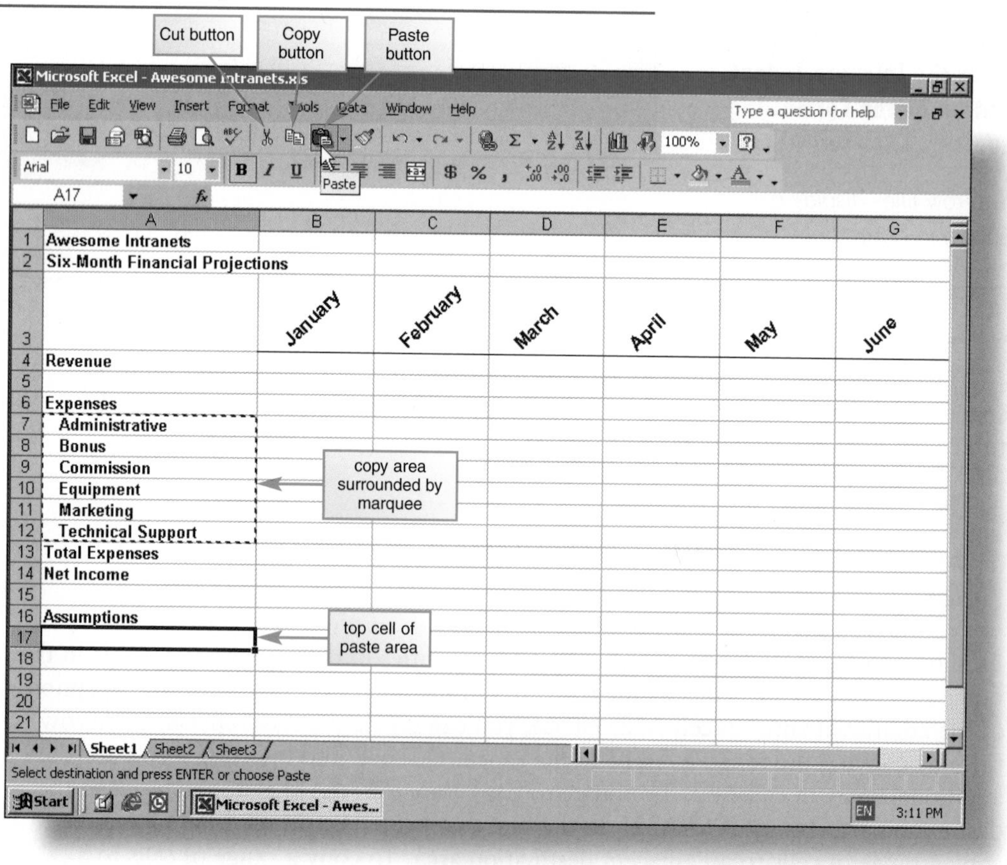

FIGURE 3-12

2 Click the Paste button on the Standard toolbar. Click the Paste Options button to the right of the destination area to view the paste options available.

Excel copies the values and formats of the last item placed on the Office Clipboard (range A7:A12) to the destination area A17:A22 (Figure 3-13). The Paste Options menu displays showing the available paste options. The default option is Keep Source Formatting, which means both the contents and format are copied.

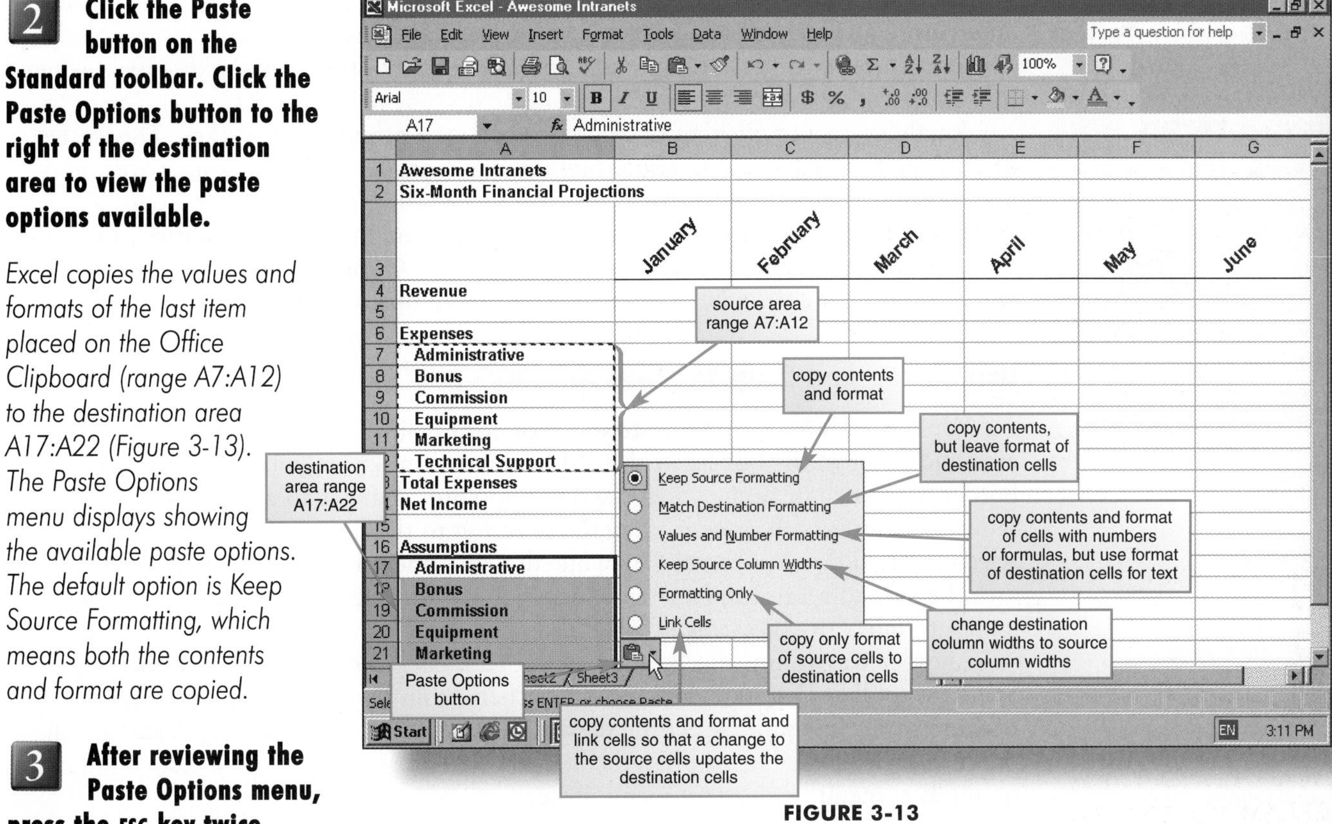

FIGURE 3-13

3 After reviewing the Paste Options menu, press the ESC key twice.

The first time you press the ESC key, Excel hides the Paste Options menu. The second time you press the ESC key, it removes the marquee from the source area and disables the Paste button on the Standard toolbar.

Other Ways

1. Select source area, on Edit menu click Copy, select destination area, on Edit menu click Paste
2. Right-click source area, click Copy on shortcut menu, right-click destination area, click Paste on shortcut menu
3. Select source area and point to border of range; while holding down the CTRL key, drag source area to destination area
4. Select source area, press CTRL+C, select destination area, press CTRL+V
5. Select source area, in Voice Command mode say, "Copy," select destination area, in Voice Command mode say, "Paste"

In Step 1 and Figure 3-12, you can see that you are not required to select the entire destination area (range A17:A22) before clicking the Paste button. Because the destination area is exactly the same size as the source area, you have to select only the upper-left cell of the destination area. In the case of a single column range such as A17:A22, the top cell of the destination area (cell A17) also is the upper-left cell of the destination area.

When you complete a copy, the values and formats in the destination area are replaced with the values and formats of the latest item placed on the Office Clipboard. Any data contained in the destination area prior to the copy and paste is lost. If you accidentally delete valuable data, immediately click the Undo button on the Standard toolbar or click the **Undo Paste command** on the Edit menu to undo the paste.

The Paste Options menu in Figure 3-13 shows the paste options available immediately after clicking the Paste button. If you select an option, Excel modifies the most recent paste operation to agree with your selection. The default is to copy the contents and formats of the cells. In the previous set of steps, it was not necessary to click the Paste Options button. It was clicked in Step 2 to show the paste options available following a copy and paste operation.

Copying versus Moving

You may hear someone say, "move it or copy it , its all the same." No, it's not the same! When you move cells, the original location is blanked and the format is reset to the default. When you copy cells, the copy area remains intact. In short, copy cells to duplicate and move cells to rearrange.

The Cut Command

When you cut a cell or range of cells using the Cut command or Cut button, it is copied to the Office Clipboard but it is not removed from the worksheet until you paste it in the destination area by clicking the Paste button or pressing the ENTER key. When you complete the paste, the entry and its formats are removed from the source area.

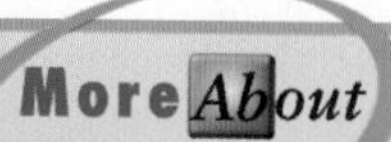

Inserting Multiple Rows

If you want to insert multiple rows, you have two choices. First, you can insert a single row by using the Insert command on the shortcut menu and then press F4 repeatedly to keep inserting rows. The second method involves selecting rows before inserting. For instance, if you want to insert five rows, select five existing rows in the worksheet and then click Insert on the shortcut menu.

The Paste button on the Standard toolbar (Figure 3-12 on page E 3.14) includes an arrow, which displays a list of advanced paste options (Formulas, Values, No Borders, Transpose, Paste Link, Paste Special). These options will be discussed when they are used.

An alternative to clicking the Paste button is to press the ENTER key. The ENTER key completes the paste operation, removes the marquee from the source area, and disables the Paste button so that you cannot paste to other destination areas. The ENTER key was not used in the previous set of steps so that the capabilities of the Paste Options button could be discussed. The Paste Options button does not display when you use the ENTER key to complete the paste operation.

Using Drag and Drop to Move or Copy Cells

You also can use the mouse to move or copy cells. First, you select the source area and point to the border of the cell or range. You know you are pointing to the border of the cell or range when the mouse pointer changes to a **block arrow**. To move the selected cell or cells, drag the selection to the destination area. To copy a selection, hold down the CTRL key while dragging the selection to the destination area. Be sure to release the mouse button before you release the CTRL key. Using the mouse to move or copy cells is called **drag and drop**.

Another way to move cells is to select them, click the Cut button on the Standard toolbar (Figure 3-12) to remove them from the worksheet and copy them to the Office Clipboard, select the destination area, and then click the Paste button on the Standard toolbar or press the ENTER key. You also can use the Cut command on the Edit menu or shortcut menu, instead of the Cut button.

Inserting and Deleting Cells in a Worksheet

At anytime while the worksheet is on the screen, you can insert cells to enter new data or delete cells to remove unwanted data. You can insert or delete individual cells, a range of cells, entire rows, entire columns, or entire worksheets.

Inserting Rows

The **Rows command** on the Insert menu or the **Insert command** on the shortcut menu allows you to insert rows between rows that already contain data. In the Assumptions table at the bottom of the worksheet, a row must be inserted between rows 21 and 22 so the Revenue for Bonus assumption can be added (shown in Figure 3-1a on page E 3.05). The following steps show how to accomplish the task of inserting a new row into the worksheet.

Steps To Insert a Row

1 Right-click row heading 22 and then point to Insert on the shortcut menu.

Row 22 is selected, and the shortcut menu displays (Figure 3-14).

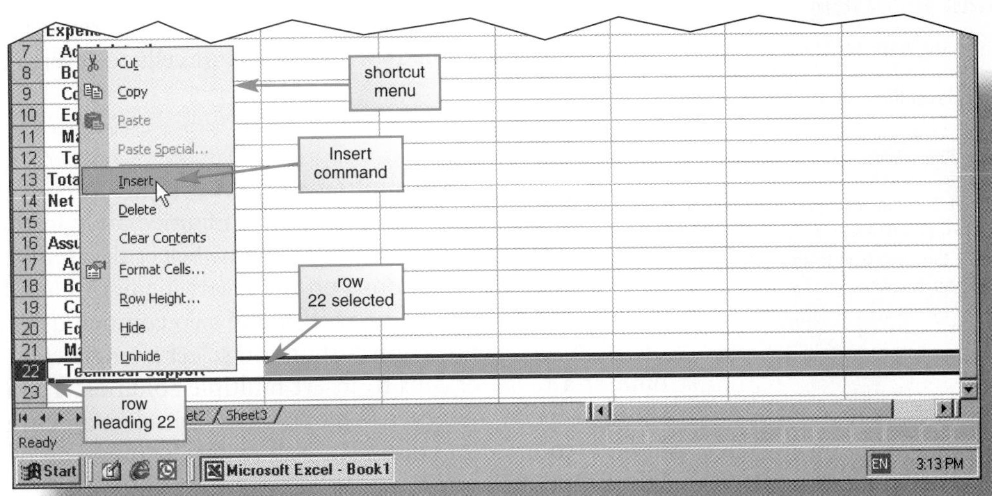

FIGURE 3-14

2 Click Insert.

Excel inserts a new row in the worksheet by shifting down the selected row 22 and all rows below it (Figure 3-15). Excel selects the new row. The Insert Options button displays just above the row inserted.

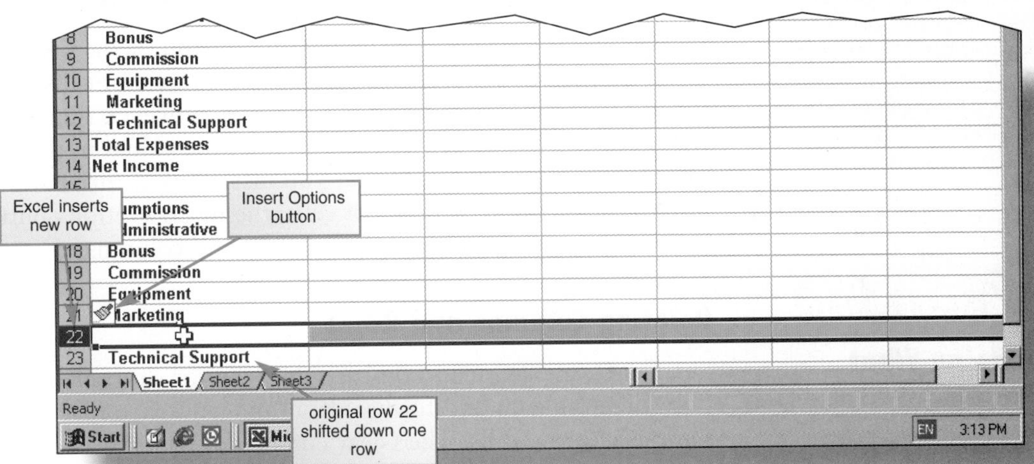

FIGURE 3-15

Other Ways

1. On Insert menu, click Rows
2. Click row heading, press CTRL+SHIFT+PLUS SIGN
3. Select number of rows to insert, in Voice Command mode say, "Insert, Rows"

To insert adjacent rows, select as many rows as you want by dragging through the row headings immediately below where you want the new rows inserted, and then right-click the selected rows.

When you insert a row, Excel automatically copies the format from the row above the inserted row. You can change this by clicking the **Insert Options button** that displays immediately above the inserted row (Figure 3-15). Following the insertion of a row, the Insert Options button lets you select from the following: (1) Format Same As Above; (2) Format Same As Below; and (3) Clear Formatting. The Format Same as Above option is the default. The Insert Options button remains active until you begin the next Excel operation.

If the rows that are shifted down include any formulas, Excel adjusts the cell references to the new locations. Thus, if a formula in the worksheet references a cell in row 22 before the insert, then the cell reference in the formula is adjusted to row 23 after the insert.

More About

Moving, Copying, and Inserting

You can move and insert between existing cells by holding down the SHIFT key while you drag the selection to the gridline where you want to insert. You can also copy and insert by holding down the CTRL and SHIFT keys while you drag the selection to the desired gridline.

The primary difference between the Insert command on the shortcut menu and the Rows command on the Insert menu is that the Insert command on the shortcut menu requires that you select an entire row (or rows) in order to insert a row (or rows). The Rows command on the Insert menu requires that you select a single cell in a row to insert one row or a range of cells to insert multiple rows.

Inserting Columns

You insert columns into a worksheet in the same way you insert rows. To insert columns, begin your column selection immediately to the right of where you want Excel to insert the new blank columns. Select the number of columns you want to insert. Next, click Columns on the Insert menu or click Insert on the shortcut menu. The primary difference between these two commands is this: The **Columns command** on the Insert menu requires that you select a single cell in a column to insert one column or a range of cells to insert multiple columns. The Insert command on the shortcut menu, however, requires that you select an entire column (or columns) to insert a column (or columns). Following the insertion of a column, Excel displays the Insert Options button, which allows you to modify the insertion in a fashion similar to that discussed earlier when inserting rows.

The Insert Options Button

When inserting columns or rows, the Insert Options button only displays if there are formats assigned to the leftmost column or top row of the selection.

Inserting Individual Cells or a Range of Cells

The Insert command on the shortcut menu or the **Cells command** on the Insert menu allows you to insert a single cell or a range of cells. You should be aware that if you shift a single cell or a range of cells, however, they no longer may be lined up with their associated cells. To ensure that the values in the worksheet do not get out of order, it is recommended that you insert only entire rows or entire columns. If you insert a single cell or a range of cells, the Insert Options button allows you to modify the insert the same as for inserting rows and columns.

Undoing What You Did

Copying, deleting, inserting, and moving have the potential to render a worksheet useless. Carefully review these actions before continuing on to the next task. If your not sure the action is correct, click the Undo button on the Standard toolbar.

Deleting Columns and Rows

The Delete command on the Edit menu or shortcut menu removes cells (including the data and format) from the worksheet. Deleting cells is not the same as clearing cells. The Clear command, which was described earlier in Project 1 on page E 1.51, clears the data from the cells, but the cells remain in the worksheet. The **Delete command** removes the cells from the worksheet and shifts the remaining rows up (when you delete rows) or shifts the remaining columns to the left (when you delete columns). If formulas located in other cells reference cells in the deleted row or column, Excel does not adjust these cell references. Excel displays the error message **#REF!** in those cells to indicate a cell reference error. For example, if cell A7 contains the formula =A4+A5 and you delete row 5, Excel assigns the formula =A4+#REF! to cell A6 (originally cell A7) and displays the error message #REF! in cell A6. It also displays an Error Options button when you select the cell containing the value #REF!, which allows you to select options to determine the nature of the problem.

Deleting Individual Cells or a Range of Cells

Although Excel allows you to delete an individual cell or range of cells, you should be aware that if you shift a cell or range of cells on the worksheet, they no longer may be lined up with their associated cells. For this reason, it is recommended that you delete only entire rows or entire columns.

Entering Numbers with a Format Symbol

The next step in creating the Six-Month Financial Projections worksheet is to enter the row title, Revenue for Bonus, in cell A22 and enter the assumption values in the range B17:B23. You can enter the assumption numbers and then format them later, as you did in Projects 1 and 2, or you can enter them with format symbols. When you enter a number with a **format symbol**, Excel immediately displays the number with the assigned format. Valid format symbols include the dollar sign ($), comma (,), and percent sign (%).

If you enter a whole number, it displays without any decimal places. If you enter a number with one or more decimal places and a format symbol, Excel displays the number with two decimal places. Table 3-2 illustrates several examples of numbers entered with format symbols. The number in parentheses in column 4 indicates the number of decimal places.

The following steps describe how to complete the entries in the Assumptions table.

Table 3-2 Numbers Entered with Format Symbols

FORMAT SYMBOL	TYPED IN FORMULA BAR	DISPLAYS IN CELL	COMPARABLE FORMAT
,	5,435	5,435	Comma (0)
	2,164.7	2,164.70	Comma (2)
$	$812	$812	Currency (0)
	$7723.82	$7,723.82	Currency (2)
	$96,291.4	$96,291.40	Currency (2)
%	78%	78%	Percent (0)
	38.5%	38.50%	Percent (1)
	29.83%	29.83%	Percent (2)

Steps To Enter a Number with a Format Symbol

1 **Click cell A22 and enter the row title** `Revenue for Bonus` **in the cell.**

2 **Enter** `11.75%` **in cell B17,** `60,000.00` **in cell B18,** `2.25%` **in cell B19,** `27.75%` **in cell B20,** `15.35%` **in cell B21,** `6,500,000.00` **in cell B22, and** `31.5%` **in cell B23.**

The entries display in a format based on the format symbols entered with the numbers (Figure 3-16).

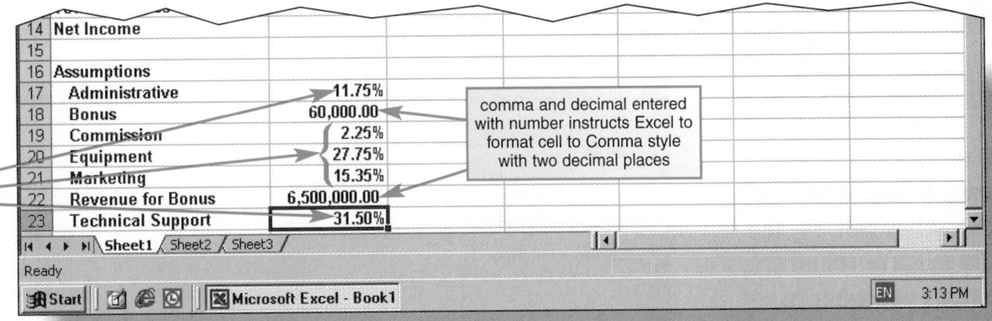

FIGURE 3-16

Other Ways

1. Right-click range, click Format Cells on shortcut menu, click Number tab, click desired category in Category list, [select desired format], click OK button
2. Press CTRL+1, click Number tab, click category in Category list, [desired format], click OK button
3. In Voice Command mode say, "Format, Cells, Number, [desired category and format], OK"

Saving the Workbook

The next step is to save the workbook using the file name, Awesome Intranets.

Freezing Titles

If you only want to freeze column headings, select the appropriate cell in column A before you click Freeze Panes on the Window menu. If you only want to freeze row titles, then select the appropriate cell in row 1. To freeze both column and row titles, select the cell that is the intersection of the column and row titles.

TO SAVE THE WORKBOOK

1. Click the Save button on the Standard toolbar.
2. When the Save As dialog box displays, type `Awesome Intranets` in the File name text box.
3. If necessary, click 3½ Floppy (A:) in the Save in list. Click the Save button in the Save As dialog box.

Excel saves the workbook on the floppy disk in drive A using the file name, Awesome Intranets.

Freezing Worksheet Titles

Freezing worksheet titles is a useful technique for viewing large worksheets that extend beyond the window. For example, when you scroll down or to the right, the column titles in row 3 and the row titles in column A that define the numbers no longer display on the screen. This makes it difficult to remember what the numbers represent. To alleviate this problem, Excel allows you to freeze the titles so they display on the screen no matter how far down or to the right you scroll.

Complete the following steps to freeze the worksheet title and column titles in rows 1, 2, and 3, and the row titles in column A using the **Freeze Panes command** on the **Window menu**.

To Freeze Column and Row Titles

1. **Press CTRL+HOME to select cell A1 and ensure that row 1 and column 1 display on the screen. Click cell B4, the cell below the column headings you want to freeze and to the right of the row titles you want to freeze. Click Window on the menu bar and then point to Freeze Panes.**

The Window menu displays (Figure 3-17).

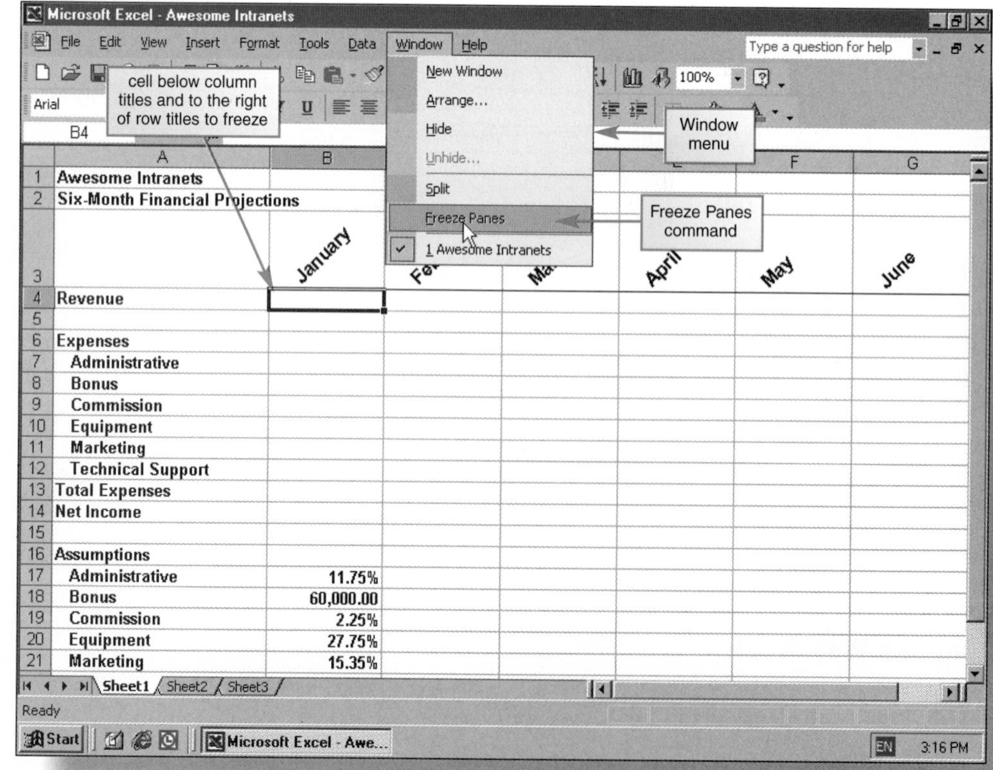

FIGURE 3-17

2 Click Freeze Panes on the Window menu.

Excel displays a thin black border on the right side of column A indicating the split between the frozen row titles in column A and the rest of the worksheet. It also displays a thin black line below row 3 indicating the split between the frozen column titles in rows 1 through 3 and the rest of the worksheet (Figure 3-18).

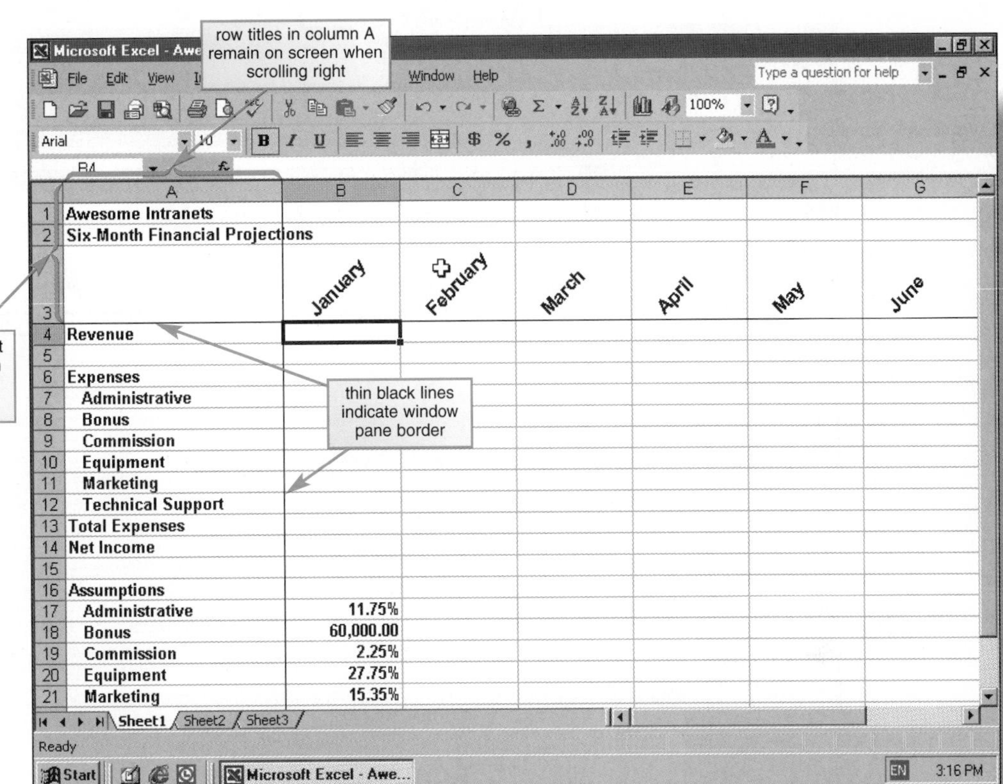

FIGURE 3-18

Other Ways

1. Press ALT+W, F
2. In Voice Command mode say, "Window, Freeze Panes"

Once frozen, the row titles in column A will remain on the screen even when you scroll to the right to display column H. The titles remain frozen until you unfreeze them. You unfreeze the titles by clicking the **Unfreeze Panes command** on the Window menu. Later steps in this project show you how to use the Unfreeze Panes command.

It is important that you display the upper-left corner of the screen before you freeze the titles. For example, if in Step 1, cell B4 was selected without first selecting cell A1 to ensure the upper-left corner of the screen displayed, then Excel would have frozen the titles and also hidden rows 1 and 2. That is, you would not be able to display rows 1 and 2 until you unfreeze the titles.

More About

Freezing Titles

If any columns to the left or rows at the top of the worksheet are scrolled off the screen when you freeze titles, then you will not be able to view these columns or rows until you unfreeze titles.

Entering the Projected Revenue

The next step is to enter the projected monthly revenue in row 4 and compute the projected six-month total revenue in cell H4. Enter these numbers without any format symbols as shown in the following steps.

TO ENTER THE PROJECTED REVENUE

1. Enter 6692019 in cell B4, 5039219 in cell C4, 6929671 in cell D4, 6124450 in cell E4, 4919023 in cell F4, and 7327012 in cell G4.
2. Click cell H4 and then click the AutoSum button on the Standard toolbar twice.

The projected six-month total revenue (37031394) displays in cell H4 (Figure 3-19 on the next page). Columns B and C have scrolled off the screen, but column A remains because it was frozen earlier.

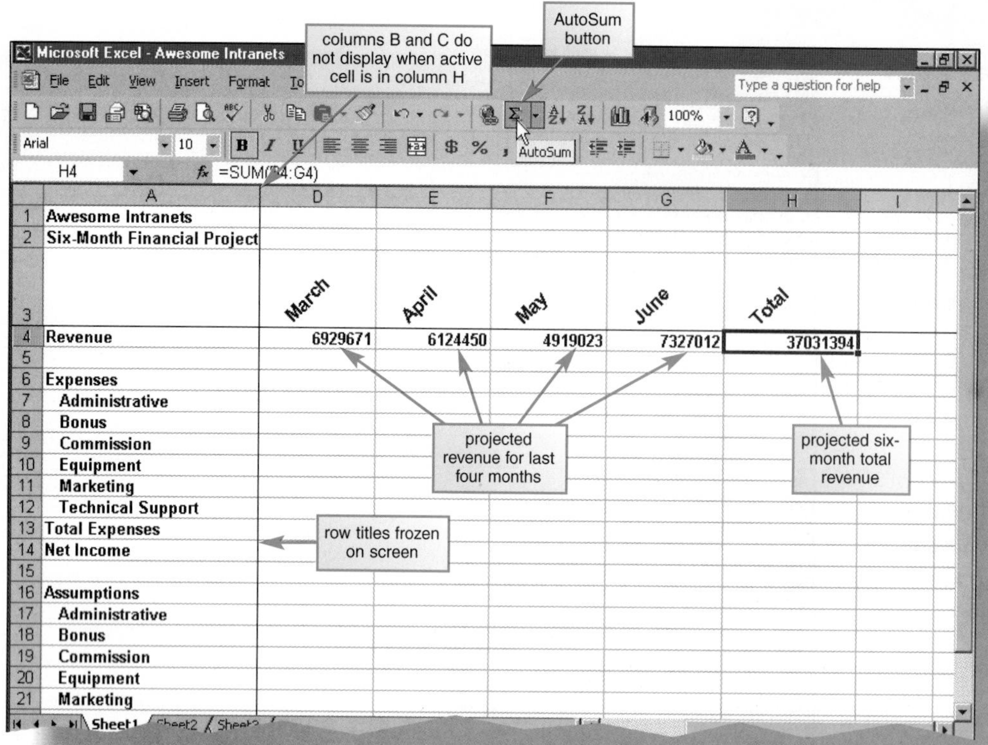

FIGURE 3-19

Recall from Projects 1 and 2 that if you select a single cell below or to the right of a range of numbers, you must click the AutoSum button twice to display the sum. If you select a range of cells below or to the right of a range of numbers, you need to click the AutoSum button only once to display the sums.

> **More About**
>
> **The Number of Days**
>
> How many days have you been alive? Enter today's date (i.e., 12/5/2003) in cell A1. Next, enter your birth date (i.e., 6/22/1986) in cell A2. Select cell A3 and enter the formula =A1 - A2. Format cell A3 to the General style using the Cells command on the Format menu. Cell A3 will display the number of days you have been alive.

Displaying the System Date

The worksheet in Figure 3-1a on page E 3.05 includes a date stamp in cell H2. A **date stamp** shows the system date of which your computer keeps track. If the computer's system date is set to the current date, which normally it is, then the date stamp is equivalent to the current date.

In information processing, a report often is meaningless without a date stamp. For example, if a printout of the worksheet in this project were distributed to the company's analysts, the date stamp would show when the six-month projections were made.

To enter the system date in a cell in the worksheet, use the **NOW function**. The NOW function is one of 14 date and time functions available in Excel. When assigned to a cell, the NOW function returns a number that corresponds to the date and time beginning with December 31, 1899. For example, January 1, 1900 equals 1, January 2, 1900 equals 2, and so on. Noon equals .5. Thus, noon on January 1, 1900 equals 1.5 and 6 P.M. on January 1, 1900 equals 1.75.

Excel automatically formats the date stamp to the date and time format, mm/dd/yy hh:mm, where the first mm is the month, dd is the day of the month, yy is the last two digits of the year, hh is the hour of the day, and mm is the minutes past the hour.

The following steps show how to enter the NOW function and change the format from mm/dd/yy hh:mm to mm/dd/yyyy. With the recent turn of the century, it is recommended that you display all dates with a four-digit year.

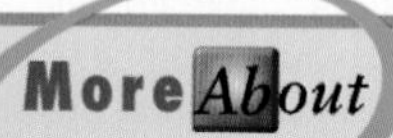

> **More About**
>
> **Updating the Date and Time**
>
> If the system date displays in a cell and changes while the workbook is active, then the date and time in the cell will not change until an entry is made into another cell or you complete some other activity, such as undoing a previous activity or pressing function key F9.

Steps To Enter and Format the System Date

1 Click cell H2 and then click the Insert Function box on the formula bar. When the Insert Function dialog box displays, click the Or select a category box arrow, and select Date & Time in the list. Scroll down in the Select a function list and then click NOW. Point to the OK button.

Excel displays an equal sign in the active cell and in the formula bar. The Insert Function dialog box displays as shown in Figure 3-20.

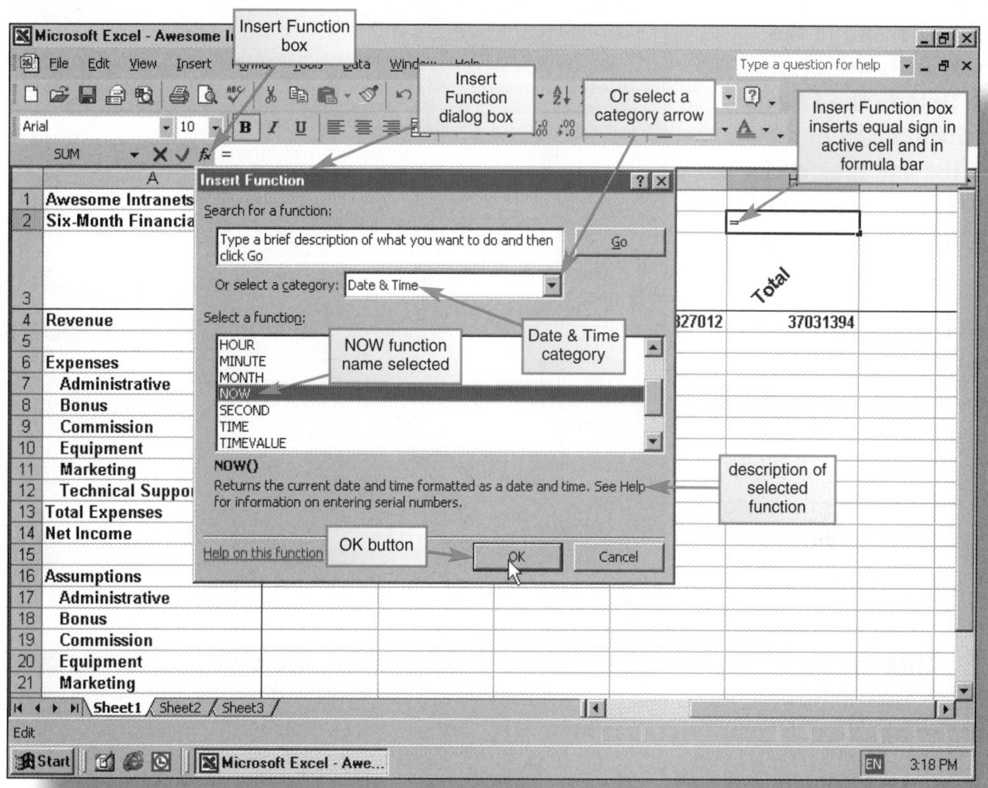

FIGURE 3-20

2 Click the OK button. When the Function Arguments dialog box displays, click the OK button. Right-click cell H2 and point to Format Cells.

Excel displays the system date and time in cell H2 using the default date and time format m/d/yy hh:mm. The system date on your computer may be different. The shortcut menu displays (Figure 3-21).

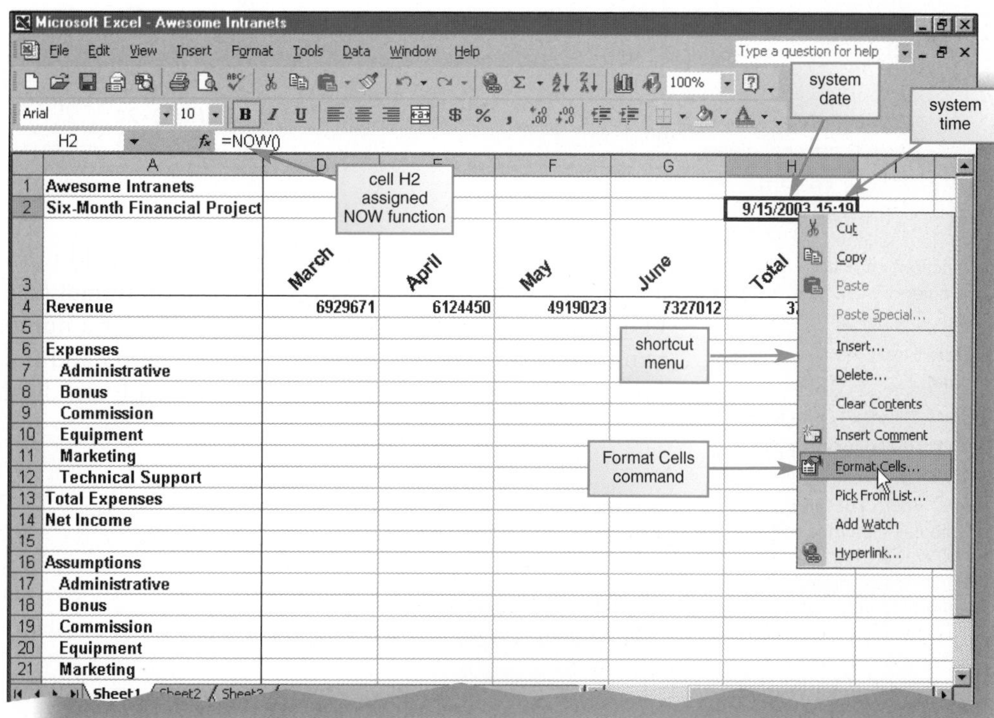

FIGURE 3-21

Click Format Cells on the shortcut menu. If necessary, click the Number tab in the Format Cells dialog box. Click Date in the Category list. Scroll down in the Type list and then click 3/14/2001. Point to the OK button.

Excel displays the Format Cells dialog box with Date selected in the Category list and 3/14/2001 (mm/dd/yyyy) selected in the Type list (Figure 3-22). A sample of the format using the data in the active cell (H2) displays in the Sample area.

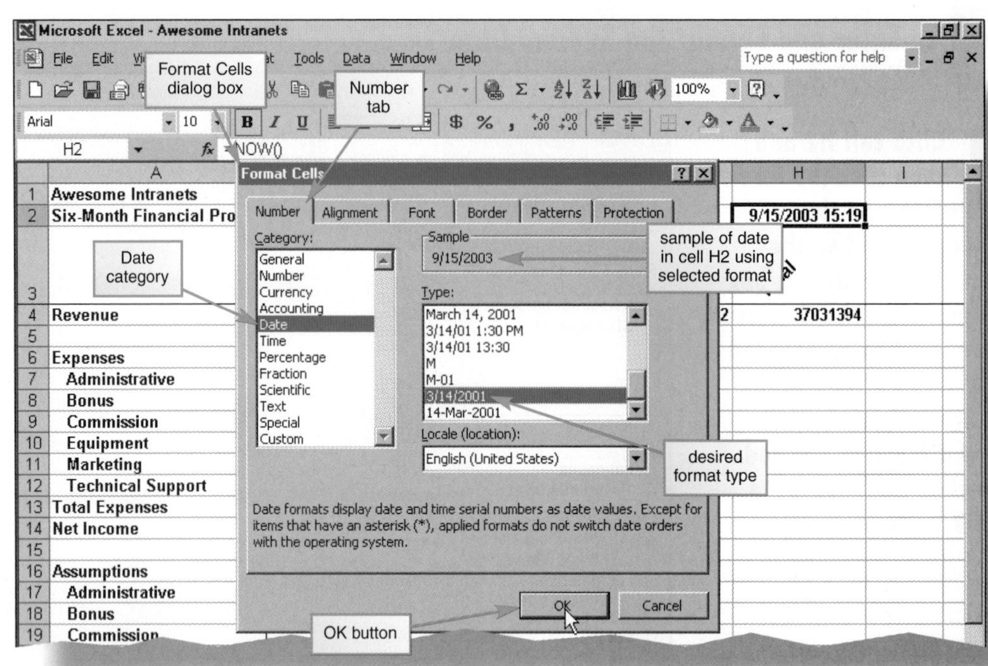

FIGURE 3-22

4 Click the OK button.

Excel displays the system date in the form m/d/yyyy (Figure 3-23).

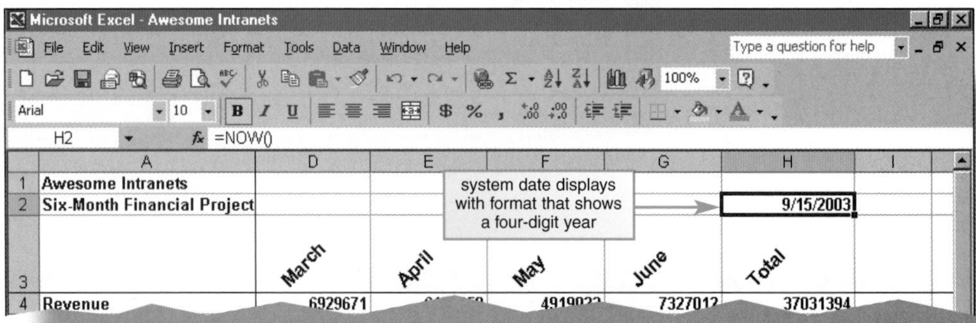

FIGURE 3-23

Other Ways

1. On Insert menu click Function, click Date & Time in category list, click NOW, click OK button
2. Press CTRL+; (not a volatile date)
3. Press CTRL+SHIFT+# to format date to day-month-year
4. In Voice Command mode say, "Insert, Function, [select Date & Time category], NOW, OK"

In Figure 3-23, the date displays right-aligned in the cell because Excel treats a date as a number. If you assign the **General format** (Excel's default format for numbers) to a date in a cell, the date displays as a number. For example, if the system time and date is 6:00 P.M. on June 29, 2003 and the cell containing the NOW function is assigned the General format, then Excel displays the following number in the cell:

37801.75

number of days since December 31, 1899 — time of day is 6:00 P.M. (¾ of day complete)

The whole number portion of the number (37801) represents the number of days since December 31, 1899. The decimal portion .75 represents the time of day (6:00 P.M.). To assign the General format to a cell, click General in the Category list in the Format Cells dialog box (Figure 3-22).

Absolute Versus Relative Addressing

The next step is to enter the formulas that calculate the projected monthly expenses in the range B7:G13 and the net incomes in row 14 (Figure 3-1a on page E 3.05). The projected monthly expenses are based on the projected monthly revenue in row 4 and the assumptions in the range B17:B23. The formulas for each column (month) are the same, except for the reference to the projected monthly revenues in row 4, which varies according to the month (B4 for January, C4 for February, and so on). Thus, the formulas can be entered for January in column B and copied to columns C through G. The formulas for determining the projected January expenses and net income in column B are shown in Table 3-3.

If you enter the formulas shown in the third column in Table 3-3 in column B for January and then copy them to columns C through G (February through June) in the worksheet, Excel will adjust the cell references for each column automatically. Thus, after the copy, the February administrative expense in cell C7 would be =C17*C4. While the cell reference C4 (February Revenue) is correct, the cell reference C17 references an empty cell. The formula for cell C7 should read =B17*C4 rather than =C17*C4. In this instance, you need a way to keep a cell reference in a formula the same when it is copied.

Table 3-3 Formulas for Determining January Expenses and Net Income

CELL	EXPENSE/INCOME	FORMULA	COMMENT
B7	Administrative	=B17 * B4	Administrative % times January revenue
B8	Bonus	=IF(B4 >= B22, B18, 0)	Bonus equals value in B18 or zero
B9	Commission	=B19 * B4	Commission % times January revenue
B10	Equipment	=B20 * B4	Equipment % times January revenue
B11	Marketing	=B21 * B4	Marketing % times January revenue
B12	Technical Support	=B23 * B4	Technical Support % times January revenue
B13	Total Expenses	=SUM(B7:B12)	Sum of January expenses
B14	Net Income	=B4 - B13	January Revenue minus January Expenses

To keep a cell reference constant when it copies a formula or function, Excel uses a technique called **absolute referencing**. To specify an absolute reference in a formula, enter a dollar sign ($) before any column letters or row numbers you want to keep constant in formulas you plan to copy. For example, $B$17 is an absolute reference, while B17 is a relative reference. Both reference the same cell. The difference becomes apparent when they are pasted into a destination area. A formula using the absolute reference $B$17 instructs Excel to keep the cell reference B17 constant (absolute) as it is pastes the formula to a new location. A formula using the relative cell reference B17 instructs Excel to adjust the cell reference as it pastes. Table 3-4 gives some additional examples of absolute references. A cell reference with only one dollar sign before either the column or the row is called a **mixed cell reference**.

Table 3-4 Additional Examples of Absolute References

CELL REFERENCE	TYPE OF REFERENCE	MEANING
$B$17	Absolute reference	Both column and row references remain the same when you copy this cell reference because they are absolute.
B$17	Mixed reference	This cell reference is mixed. The column reference changes when you copy this cell reference to another column because it is relative. The row reference does not change because it is absolute.
$B17	Mixed reference	This cell reference is mixed. The row reference changes when you copy this cell reference to another row because it is relative. The column reference does not change because it is absolute.
B17	Relative reference	Both column and row references are relative. When copied to another row and column, both the row and column in the cell reference are adjusted to reflect the new location.

More About

Absolute Referencing

Absolute referencing is one of the most difficult worksheet concepts to understand. One point to keep in mind is that the paste operation is the only one affected by an absolute cell reference. An absolute cell reference instructs the paste operation to keep the same cell reference as it copies a formula from one cell to another.

Entering a Formula Containing Absolute Cell References

The following steps show how to enter the Administrative formula (=$B$17*B4) in cell B7 using Point mode. To enter an absolute reference, you can type the dollar sign ($) as part of the cell reference or with the insertion point in or to the right of the cell reference you want to change to absolute, press F4.

To Enter a Formula Containing Absolute Cell References

1 Press CTRL+HOME and then click cell B7. Type = (equal sign) and then click cell B17. Press F4 to change B17 to an absolute reference in the formula. Type * (asterisk) and then click cell B4.

*The formula =$B$17*B4 displays in cell B7 and in the formula bar (Figure 3-24). A marquee surrounds cell B4.*

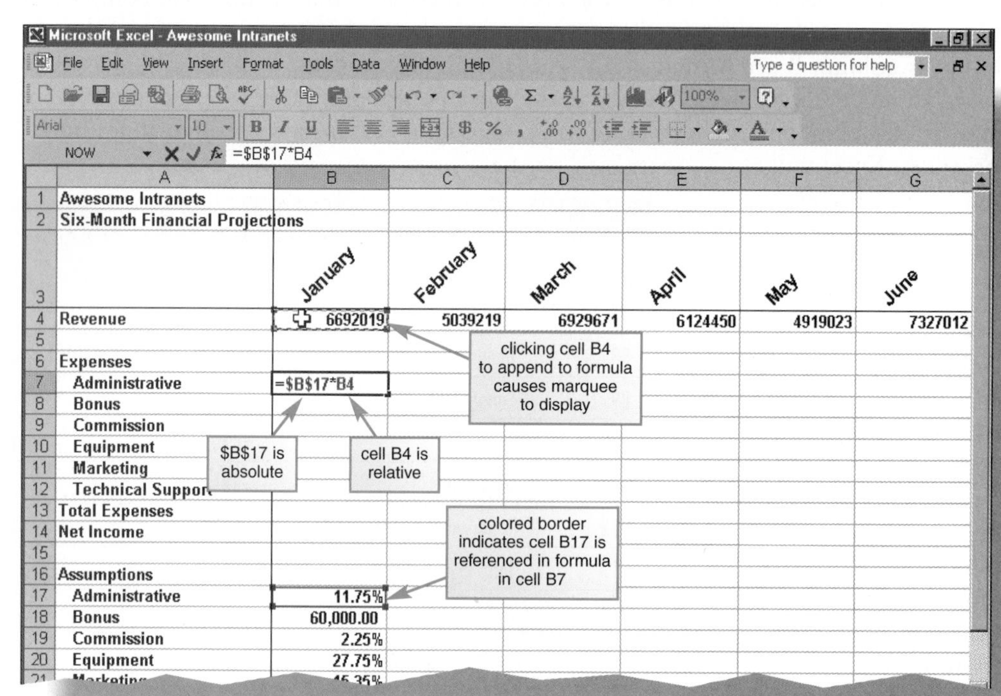

FIGURE 3-24

2 Click the Enter box on the formula bar.

Excel displays the result, 786312.2325, of the formula in cell B7 (Figure 3-25). With cell B7 selected, the formula assigned to it displays in the formula bar.

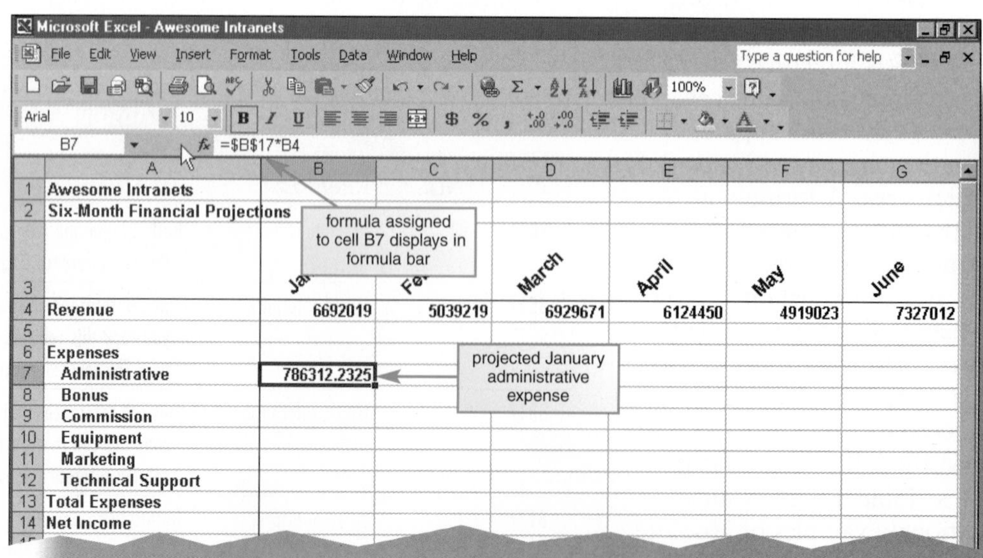

FIGURE 3-25

Making Decisions — The IF Function

If the projected January revenue in cell B4 is greater than or equal to the revenue for bonus in cell B22 (6,500,000.00), then the projected January bonus in cell B8 is equal to the amount in cell B18 (60,000.00); otherwise, cell B8 is equal to zero. One way to assign the projected monthly bonus in row 8 is to check each month individually to see if the projected revenue in row 4 equals or exceeds the revenue for bonus amount in cell B22 and, if so, then to enter 60,000.00 in row 8 for the corresponding month. Because the data in the worksheet changes each time you prepare the report or adjust the figures, however, you will find it preferable to have Excel assign the projected monthly bonus to the entries in the appropriate cells automatically. To do so, you need a formula or function in cell B8 that displays 60,000.00 or 0.00 (zero), depending on whether the projected January revenue in cell B4 is greater than or equal to or less than the number in cell B22.

The Excel **IF function** is useful when the value you want to assign to a cell is dependent on a logical test. For example, assume you assign cell B8 the IF function:

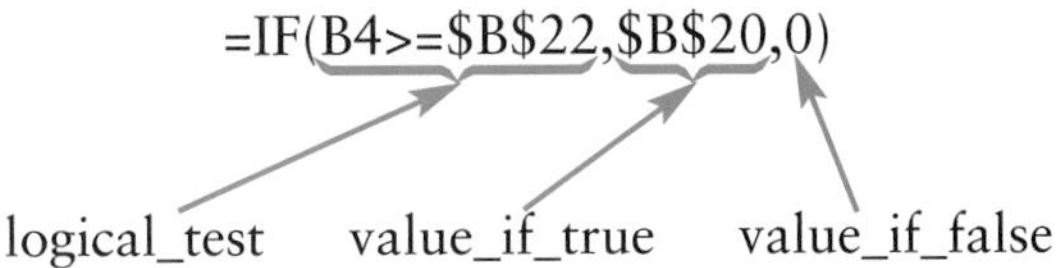

If the projected January revenue in cell B4 is greater than or equal to the value in cell B22, then the value in cell B18, 60000, displays in cell B8. If the projected January revenue in cell B4 is less than the value in cell B22, then cell B8 displays 0 (zero).

The general form of the IF function is:

=IF(logical_test, value_if_true, value_if_false)

The argument, value_if_true, is the value you want displayed in the cell when the logical test is true. The argument, value_if_false, is the value you want displayed in the cell when the logical test is false.

The leftmost entry in the general form of the IF function, **logical_test**, is made up of two expressions and a comparison operator. Each expression can be a cell reference, a number, text, a function, or a formula. Valid **comparison operators**, their meaning, and examples of their use in IF functions are shown in Table 3-5.

The steps on the next page assign the IF function =IF(B4>=$B$22,$B$18,0) to cell B8. This IF function will determine whether or not the worksheet assigns a bonus for January.

Table 3-5 Comparison Operators

COMPARISON OPERATOR	*MEANING*	*EXAMPLE*
=	Equal to	=IF(D4 = K6, T15 ^ $4, K7 + K3)
<	Less than	=IF(D29 * G2 < 398, $F$3, U23 - 3)
>	Greater than	=IF(MAX(F3:F5) > 90, 0, 1)
>=	Greater than or equal to	=IF(L9 >= $H$6, A8 * X4, 5)
<=	Less than or equal to	=IF(Z6 + W2 <= 43, $B10, 25 * V17)
<>	Not equal to	=IF(R3 <> B$4, "Yes","No")

More About

Nested IF functions

Nested IF functions include one or more IF functions in the value_if_true or value_if_false arguments. Assume you want to set cell A10 to the value 100 if cell B1 is equal to 1, 200 if cell B1 is equal to 2, and 300 if cell B1 is equal to any other value. The following IF function assigned to cell A10 would solve the problem: =IF(B1 = 1, 100, IF(B1 = 2, 200, 300)).

Steps To Enter an IF Function

1 Click cell B8. Type =if(b4>=b22,b18,0 **in the cell. Click the Insert Function box on the formula bar to display the Function Arguments dialog box to view the function arguments. Point to the OK button.**

The IF function displays in the formula bar and in the active cell B8. The Function Arguments dialog box displays showing the logical_test, value_if_true, value_if_false, results of each part of the IF function, and the value that will be assigned to the cell based on the logical test (Figure 3-26).

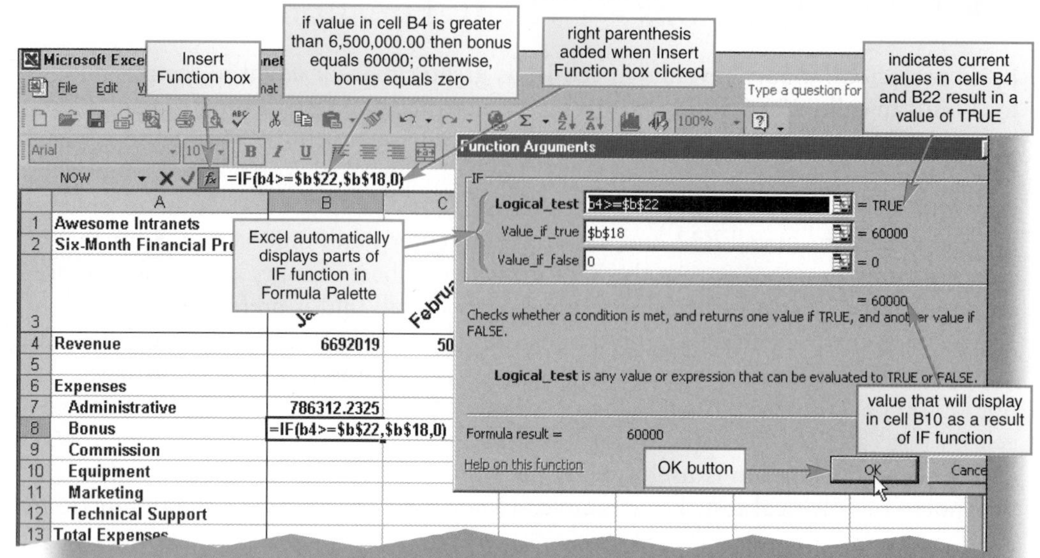

FIGURE 3-26

2 Click the OK button.

Excel displays 60000 in cell B8 because the value in cell B4 (6692019) is greater than or equal to the value in cell B22 (6,500,000.00) (Figure 3-27).

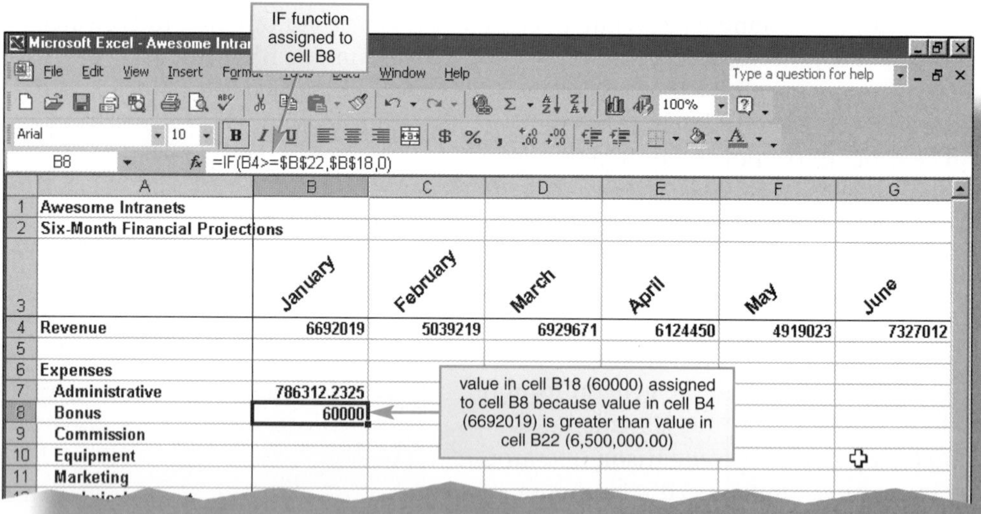

FIGURE 3-27

Other Ways

1. On Insert menu click Function, click Logical category, click IF, click OK button
2. Click Insert Function button on formula bar, click Logical category, click IF, click OK button
3. In Voice Command mode say, "Insert, Function," [select Logical category], in Voice Command mode say, "If, OK"

In Step 1, you could have clicked the Enter box or pressed the ENTER key to complete the entry rather than clicking the Edit Formula box. The Edit Formula box was clicked so you could see the IF function arguments in the Function Arguments dialog box before assigning the function to cell B8.

The value that Excel displays in cell B8 depends on the values assigned to cells B4, B18, and B22. For example, if the projected revenue in cell B4 is reduced below 6,500,000.00, then the IF function in cell B8 will change the display to zero. If you change the bonus in cell B18 and the revenue is large enough, it will change the results in cell B8. Finally, increasing the revenue for bonus in cell B22 so that it exceeds the projected monthly revenue will change the results in cell B8.

Entering the Remaining Projected Expense and Net Income Formulas for January

The projected January commission expense in cell B9 is equal to the commission assumption in cell B19 (2.25%) times the projected January revenue in cell B4. The projected January equipment expense in cell B10 is equal to the equipment assumption in cell B20 (27.75%) times the projected January revenue in cell B4. Similar formulas determine the projected January marketing expense in cell B11 and the January technical support expense in cell B12.

The projected total expenses for January in cell B13 is equal to the sum of the January expenses in the range B7:B12. The projected January net income in cell B14 is equal to the projected January revenue in cell B4 minus the projected January expenses in cell B13. The formulas are short, and therefore they are typed in the following steps, rather than entered using Point mode.

More About

Replacing a Formula with a Constant

You can replace a formula with its result so it remains constant. Do the following: (1) click the cell with the formula; (2) press F2 or click in the formula bar; (3) press F9 to display the value in the formula bar; (4) press the ENTER key.

TO ENTER THE REMAINING PROJECTED JANUARY EXPENSE AND NET INCOME FORMULAS

1. Click cell B9. Type =b19*b4 and then press the down arrow key. Type =b20*b4 and then press the down arrow key. Type =b21*b4 and then press the down arrow key. Type =b23*b4 and then press the down arrow key. With cell B13 selected, click the AutoSum button on the Standard toolbar twice. Click cell B14. Type =b4-b13 and then press the ENTER key.
2. Press CTRL+ACCENT MARK(`).
3. When you are finished viewing the formulas version, press CTRL+ACCENT MARK(`) to display the values version.

The projected January expenses, total expenses, and net income display (Figure 3-28a). Excel displays the formulas version of the worksheet (Figure 3-28b).

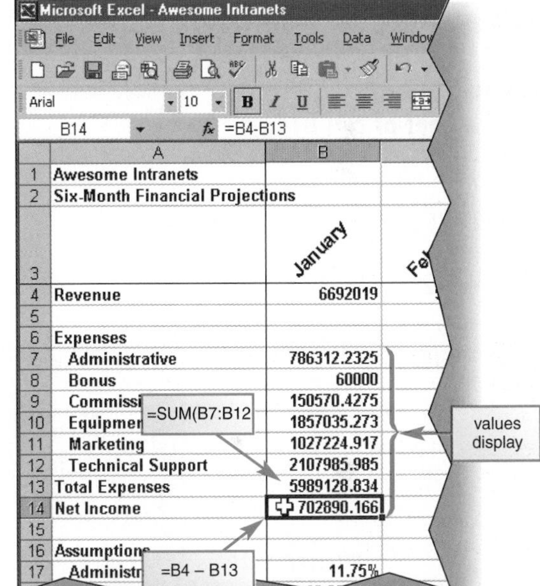

(a) Values Version

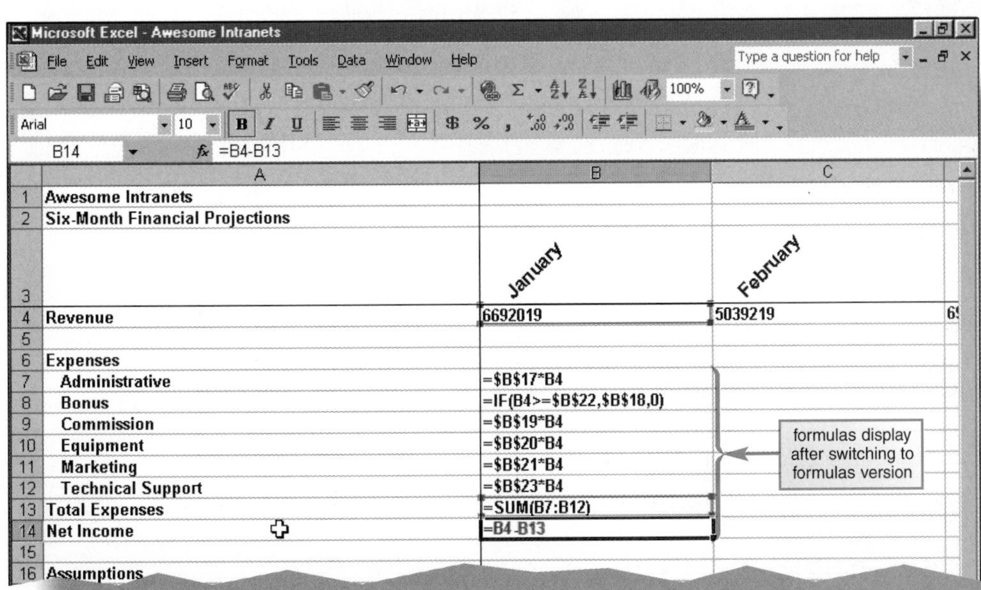

(b) Formulas Version

FIGURE 3-28

Viewing the formulas version (Figure 3-28b on the previous page) of the worksheet allows you to check the formulas assigned to the range B7 through B14. You can see that Excel converts all the formulas to uppercase.

Copying the Projected January Expenses and Net Income Formulas to the Other Months

To copy the projected expenses and totals for January to the other five months, complete the following steps using the fill handle.

Steps To Copy the Projected January Expenses and Net Income Using the Fill Handle

1 Select the range B7:B14. Point to the fill handle in the lower-right corner of cell B14.

The range B7:B14 is selected and the mouse pointer changes to a cross hair (Figure 3-29).

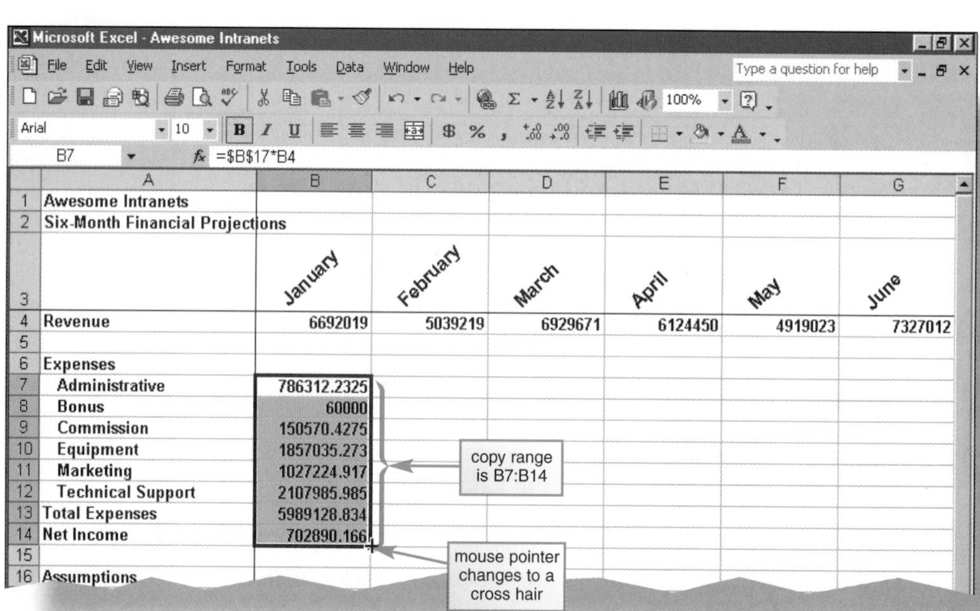

FIGURE 3-29

2 Drag the fill handle to select the destination area C7:G14. Release the mouse button.

Excel copies the formulas in the range B7:B14 to the destination area C7:G14 and displays the calculated amounts (Figure 3-30). The Auto Fill Options button displays below the fill area.

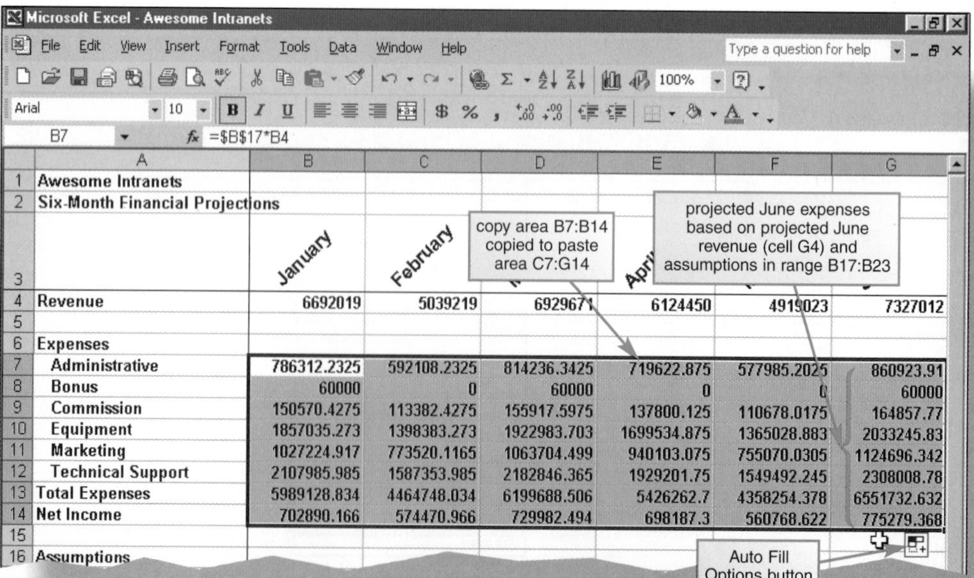

FIGURE 3-30

Determining the Projected Total Expenses by Category and Total Net Income

Follow the steps below to determine the total projected expenses by category and net income in the range H7:H14.

TO DETERMINE THE PROJECTED TOTAL EXPENSES BY CATEGORY AND TOTAL NET INCOME

1. Select the range H7:H14.
2. Click the AutoSum button on the Standard toolbar.

The projected total expenses by category and total net income display in the range H7:H14 (Figure 3-31).

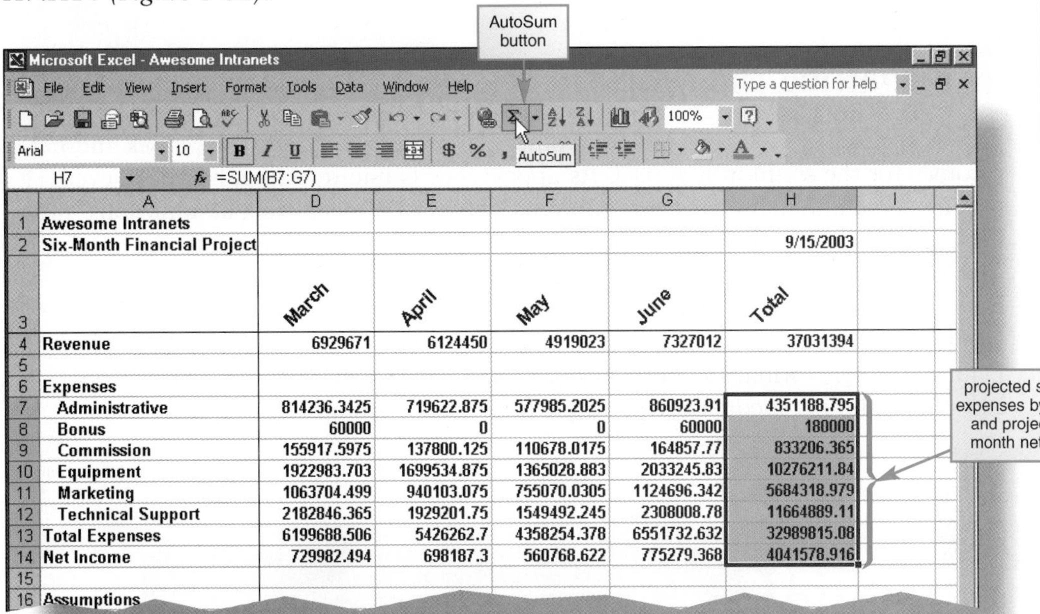

FIGURE 3-31

More About

Error Values

Excel displays an error value in a cell when it cannot calculate the formula. Error values always begin with a number sign #. The more common occurring error values are: #DIV/0! (trying to divide by zero); #NAME? (use of a name Excel does not recognize); #N/A (refers to a value not available); #NULL! (specifies an invalid intersection of two areas; #NUM! (uses a number incorrectly); #REF (refers to a cell that is not valid); #VALUE! (uses an incorrect argument or operand); and ##### (cell not wide enough).

Unfreezing Worksheet Titles and Saving the Workbook

All the text, data, and formulas have been entered into the worksheet. The next step is to improve the appearance of the worksheet. Before modifying the worksheet's appearance, complete the following steps to unfreeze the titles and save the workbook using its current file name, Awesome Intranets.

TO UNFREEZE THE WORKSHEET TITLES AND SAVE THE WORKBOOK

1. Click cell B4 to clear the range selection from the previous steps.
2. Click Window on the menu bar and then point to Unfreeze Panes (Figure 3-32 on the next page).
3. Click Unfreeze Panes.
4. Click the Save button on the Standard toolbar.

Excel unfreezes the titles so that column A scrolls off the screen when you scroll to the right and the first three rows scroll off the screen when you scroll down. The latest changes to the workbook are saved on disk using the file name, Awesome Intranets.

Toggle Commands

Many of the commands on menus and shortcut keys function as a toggle. For example, if you invoke the Freeze Panes command, the command changes to Unfreeze Panes the next time you display the Windows menu. These types of commands work like an On-Off switch or toggle.

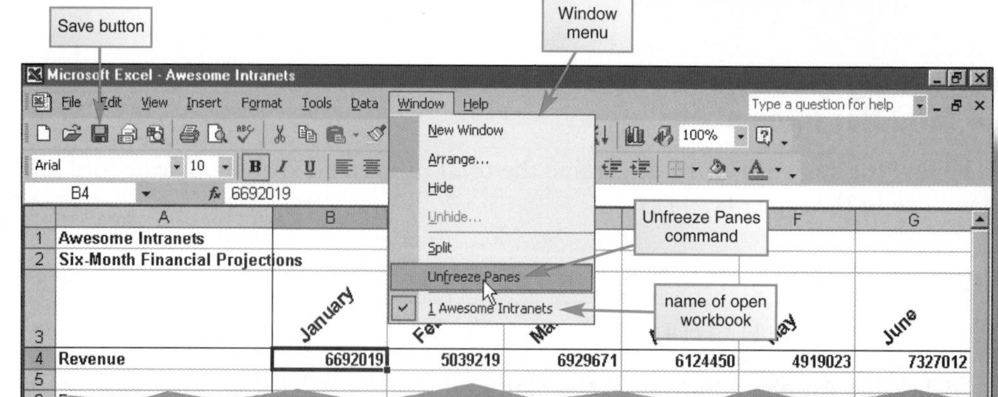

FIGURE 3-32

> **More About**
>
> **Work Days**
>
> Assume that you have two dates: one in F3 and the other in F4. The date in F3 is your starting date and the date in F4 is the ending date. To calculate the work days between the two dates (excludes weekends), use the following formula: =NETWORKDAYS(F3, F4). For this function to work, make sure the Analysis ToolPak add-in is installed. You can install it by clicking Add-In on the Tools menu.

Formatting the Worksheet

The worksheet created thus far determines the projected monthly expenses and net incomes for the six-month period. Its appearance is uninteresting, however, even though some minimal formatting (bolding worksheet, formatting assumptions' numbers, changing the column widths, and formatting the date) was performed earlier. This section will complete the formatting of the worksheet to make the numbers easier to read and to emphasize the titles, assumptions, categories, and totals. The worksheet will be formatted in the following manner so it appears as shown in Figure 3-33: (1) format the numbers; (2) format the worksheet title, column title, row titles, and net income row; and (3) format the assumptions table.

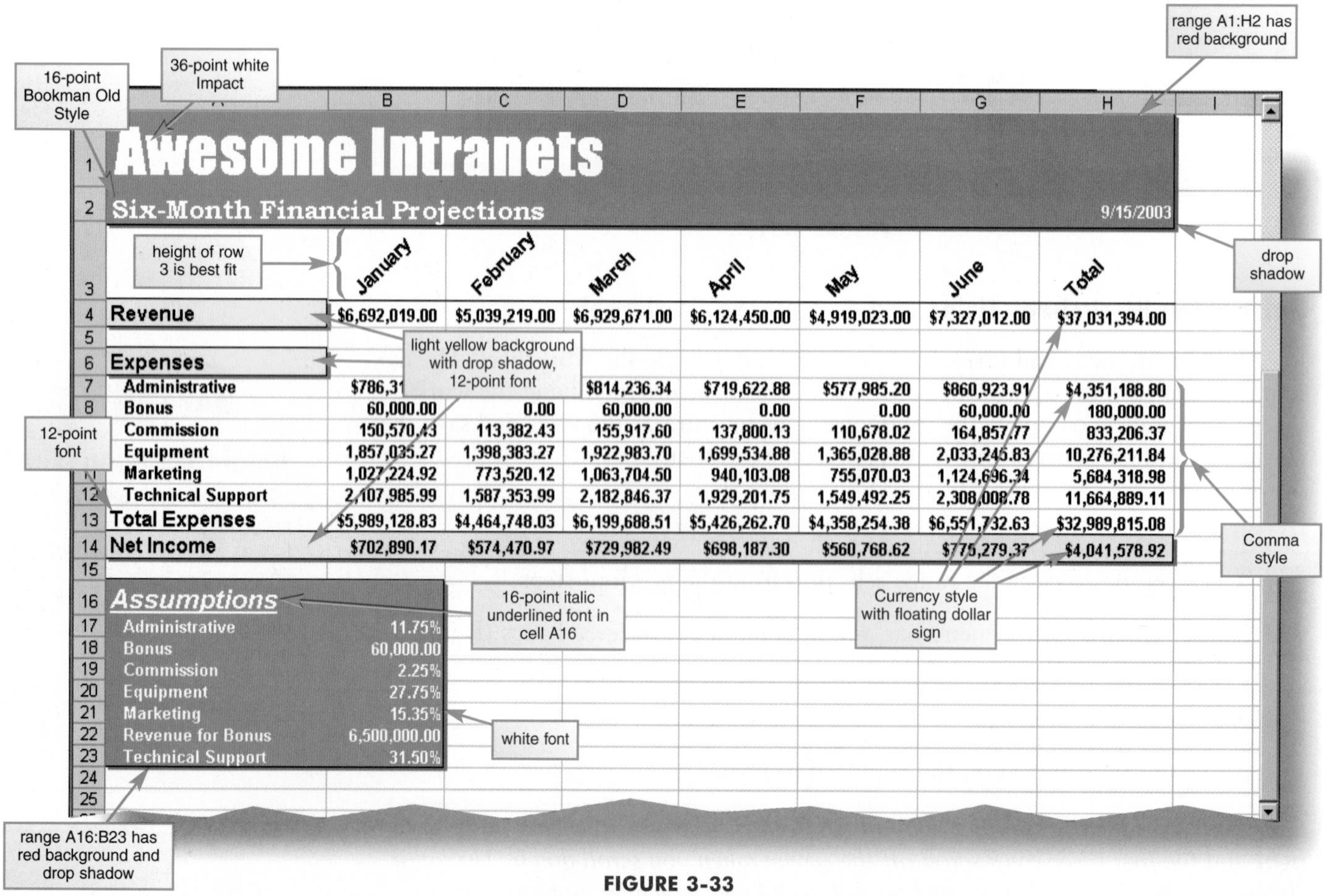

	A	B	C	D	E	F	G	H
1	Awesome Intranets							
2	Six-Month Financial Projections							9/15/2003
3		January	February	March	April	May	June	Total
4	Revenue	$6,692,019.00	$5,039,219.00	$6,929,671.00	$6,124,450.00	$4,919,023.00	$7,327,012.00	$37,031,394.00
5								
6	Expenses							
7	Administrative	$786,31		$814,236.34	$719,622.88	$577,985.20	$860,923.91	$4,351,188.80
8	Bonus	60,000.00	0.00	60,000.00	0.00	0.00	60,000.00	180,000.00
9	Commission	150,570.43	113,382.43	155,917.60	137,800.13	110,678.02	164,857.77	833,206.37
10	Equipment	1,857,035.27	1,398,383.27	1,922,983.70	1,699,534.88	1,365,028.88	2,033,245.83	10,276,211.84
11	Marketing	1,027,224.92	773,520.12	1,063,704.50	940,103.08	755,070.03	1,124,696.34	5,684,318.98
12	Technical Support	2,107,985.99	1,587,353.99	2,182,846.37	1,929,201.75	1,549,492.25	2,308,008.78	11,664,889.11
13	Total Expenses	$5,989,128.83	$4,464,748.03	$6,199,688.51	$5,426,262.70	$4,358,254.38	$6,551,732.63	$32,989,815.08
14	Net Income	$702,890.17	$574,470.97	$729,982.49	$698,187.30	$560,768.62	$775,279.37	$4,041,578.92
15								
16	Assumptions							
17	Administrative	11.75%						
18	Bonus	60,000.00						
19	Commission	2.25%						
20	Equipment	27.75%						
21	Marketing	15.35%						
22	Revenue for Bonus	6,500,000.00						
23	Technical Support	31.50%						

FIGURE 3-33

Formatting the Numbers

The projected monthly revenue and expenses in the range B4:H13 are to be formatted as follows:

1. Assign the Currency style with a floating dollar sign to rows 4, 7, 13, and 14.
2. Assign a customized Comma style to rows 8 through 12.

To assign a Currency style with a floating dollar sign, you must use the Format Cells command rather than the Currency Style button on the Formatting toolbar, which assigns a fixed dollar sign. The Comma style also must be assigned using the Format Cells command, because the Comma Style button on the Formatting toolbar displays a dash (-) when a cell has a value of zero. The specifications for this worksheet call for displaying a value of zero as 0.00 (see cell C8 in Figure 3-33), rather than as a dash. To create a Comma style using the Format Cells command, you can assign a Currency style with no dollar sign. The following steps format the numbers in rows 4 and 7 through 14.

More About

Nonadjacent Ranges

One of the more difficult tasks to learn is selecting nonadjacent ranges. To complete this task, do not hold down the CTRL key when you select the first range because Excel will consider the current active cell to be the first selection. Once the first range is selected, hold down the CTRL key and drag through the ranges. If a desired range is not in the window, use the scroll arrows to move the window over the range. It is not necessary to hold down the CTRL key while you scroll.

To Assign Formats to Nonadjacent Ranges

1 Select the range B4:H4. While holding down the CTRL key, select the nonadjacent ranges B7:H7 and B13:H14. Use the horizontal scroll button to display cells to select, if necessary. Release the CTRL key. Right-click the selected range and then point to Format Cells on the shortcut menu.

Excel highlights the selected nonadjacent ranges, and the shortcut menu displays as shown in Figure 3-34.

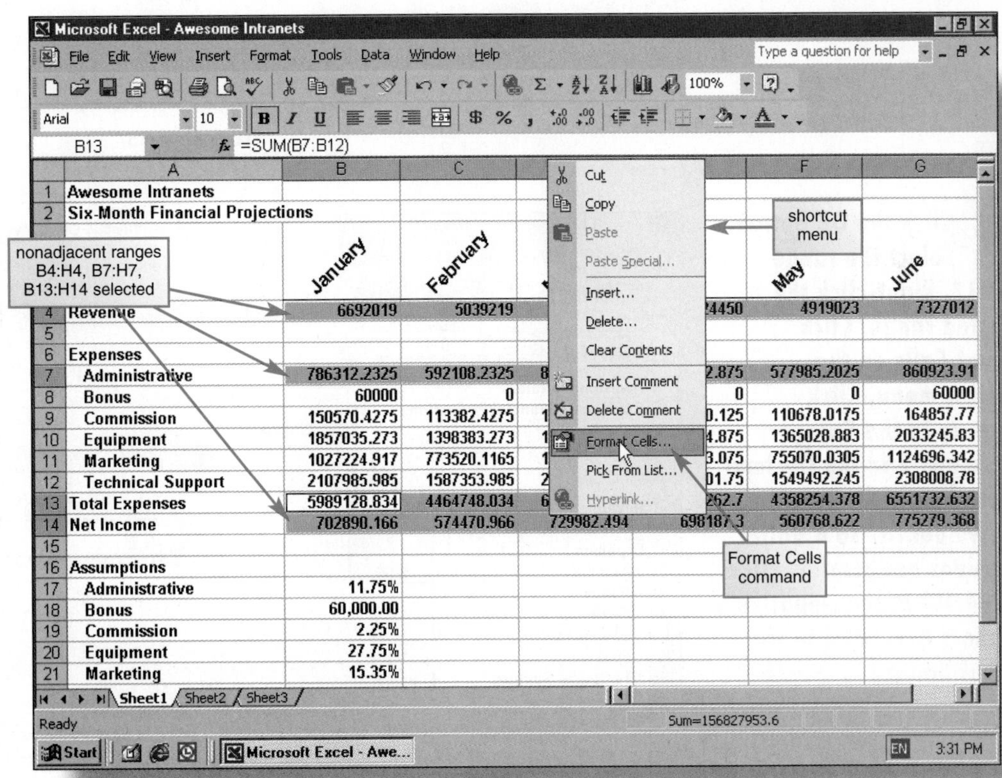

FIGURE 3-34

2 Click Format Cells. When the Format Cells dialog box displays, click the Number tab, click Currency in the Category list, select 2 in the Decimal places box, click $ in the Symbol list to ensure a dollar sign displays, and click ($1,234.10) in the Negative numbers list. Point to the OK button.

The cell format settings display in the Number sheet of the Format Cells dialog box (Figure 3-35).

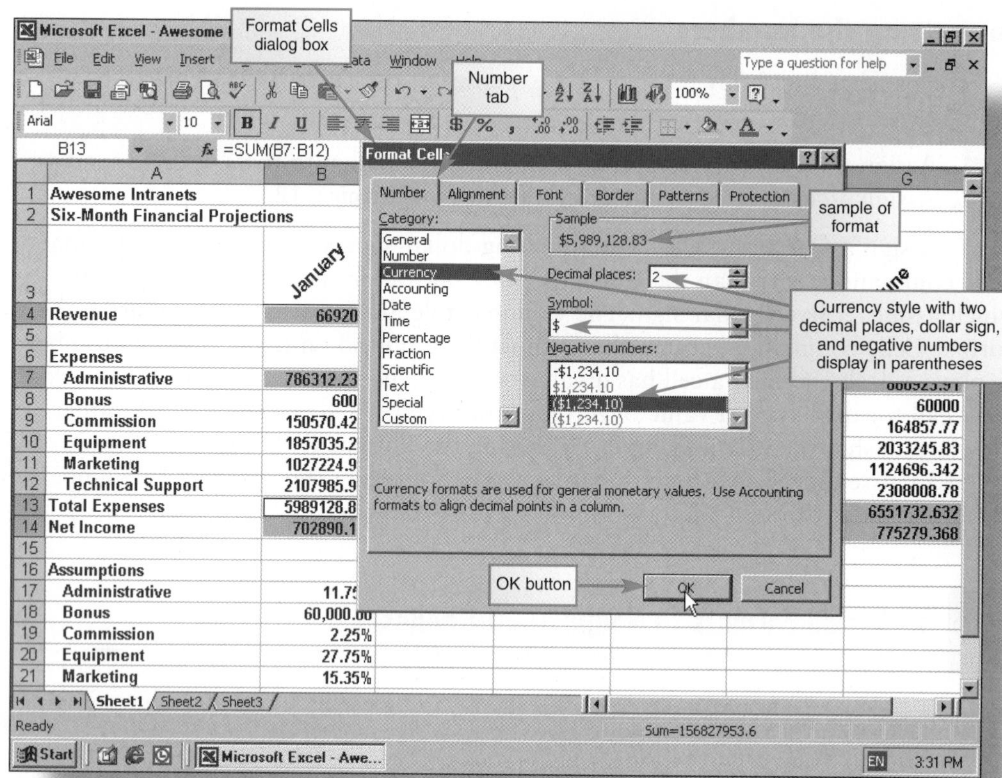

FIGURE 3-35

3 Click the OK button. Select the range B8:H12. Right-click the selected range. Click Format Cells on the shortcut menu. Click Currency in the Category list, select 2 in the Decimal places box, click None in the Symbol list so a dollar sign does not display, click (1,234.10) in the Negative numbers list. Point to the OK button.

The format settings display in the Format Cells dialog box as shown in Figure 3-36.

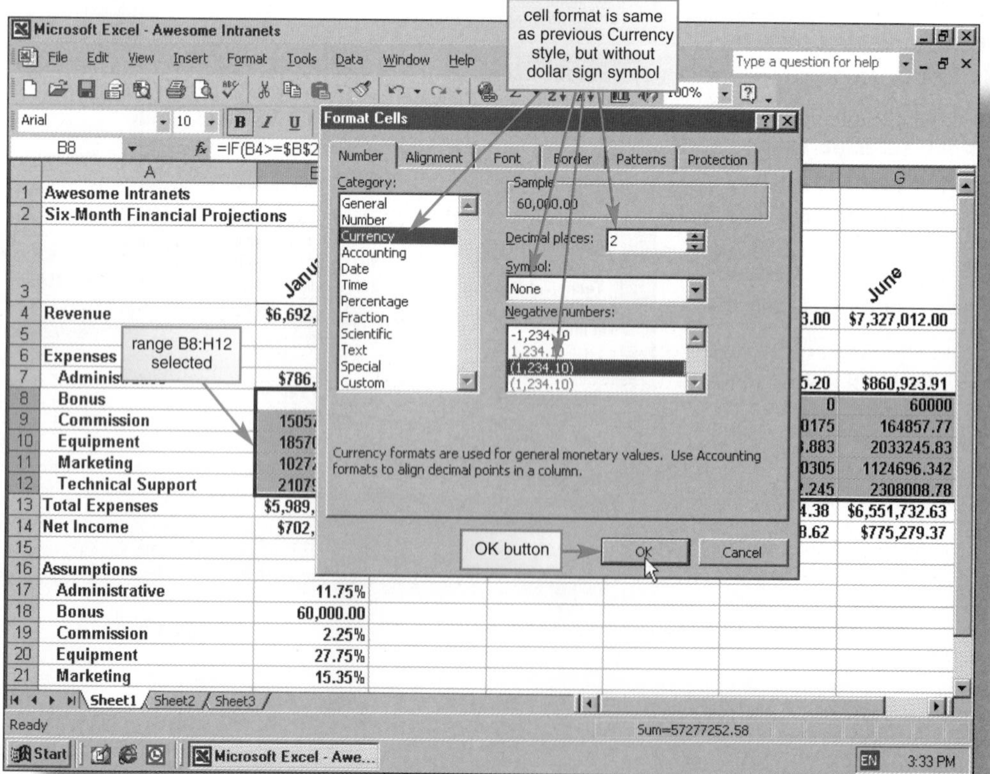

FIGURE 3-36

4 Click the OK button. Select cell A1 to deselect the range B8:H12.

The cell formats display as shown in Figure 3-37.

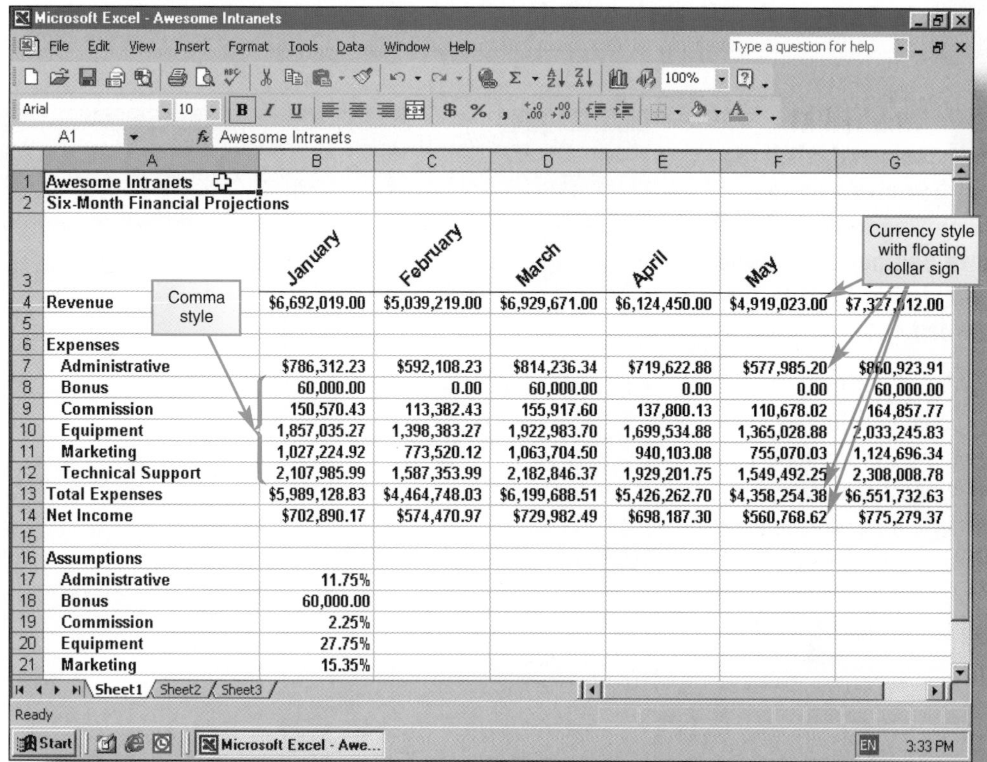

FIGURE 3-37

In accounting, negative numbers often are displayed with parentheses surrounding the value rather than with a negative sign preceding the value. Thus, in Step 3 the format (1,234.10) in the Negative numbers list was clicked. The data being used in this project contains no negative numbers. You must, however, select a format for negative numbers, and you must be consistent if you are choosing different formats in a column, otherwise the decimal points may not line up.

Instead of selecting Currency in the Category list in Step 3 (Figure 3-36), you could have selected Accounting to generate the same format. You should review the formats available below each category title. Thousands of combinations of format styles can be created using the options in the Format Cells dialog box.

Other Ways

1. On Format menu click Cells, click Number tab, click category in Category list, select format, click OK button
2. Right-click range, click Format Cells on shortcut menu, click Number tab, click category in Category list, select format, click OK button
3. Press CTRL+1, click Number tab, click category in Category list, select format, click OK button
4. In Voice Command mode say, "Format, Cells, Number, [desired category], OK"

Formatting the Worksheet Titles

To emphasize the worksheet titles in cells A1 and A2, the font type, size, and color are changed as described in the steps on the next page.

Steps To Format the Worksheet Titles

1 With cell A1 selected, click the Font box arrow on the Formatting toolbar. Scroll down and point to Impact (or a similar font) in the Font list.

The Font list displays as shown in Figure 3-38. The names of the fonts in the Font list display in the font style they represent, allowing you to view the style before you assign it to a cell or range of cells.

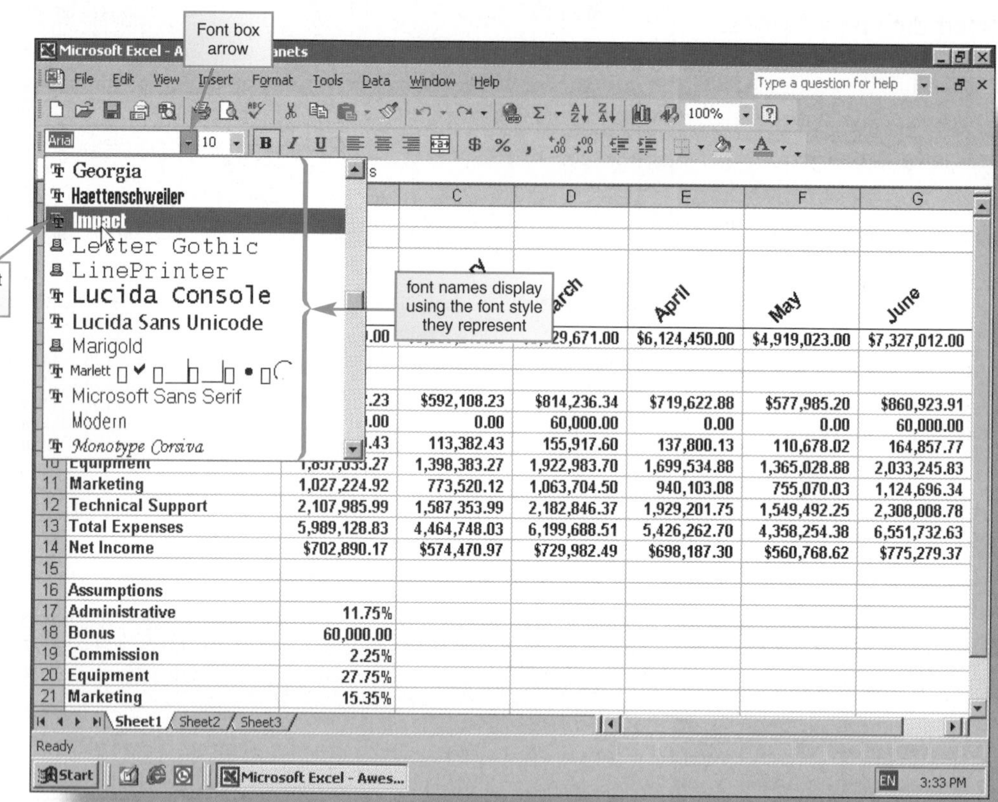

FIGURE 3-38

2 Click Impact. Click the Font Size box arrow on the Formatting toolbar and then click 36.

3 Click cell A2. Click the Font box arrow. Click Bookman Old Style (or a similar font) in the Font list. Click the Font Size box arrow and then click 16 in the Font Size list.

The worksheet titles in cells A1 and A2 display as shown in Figure 3-39.

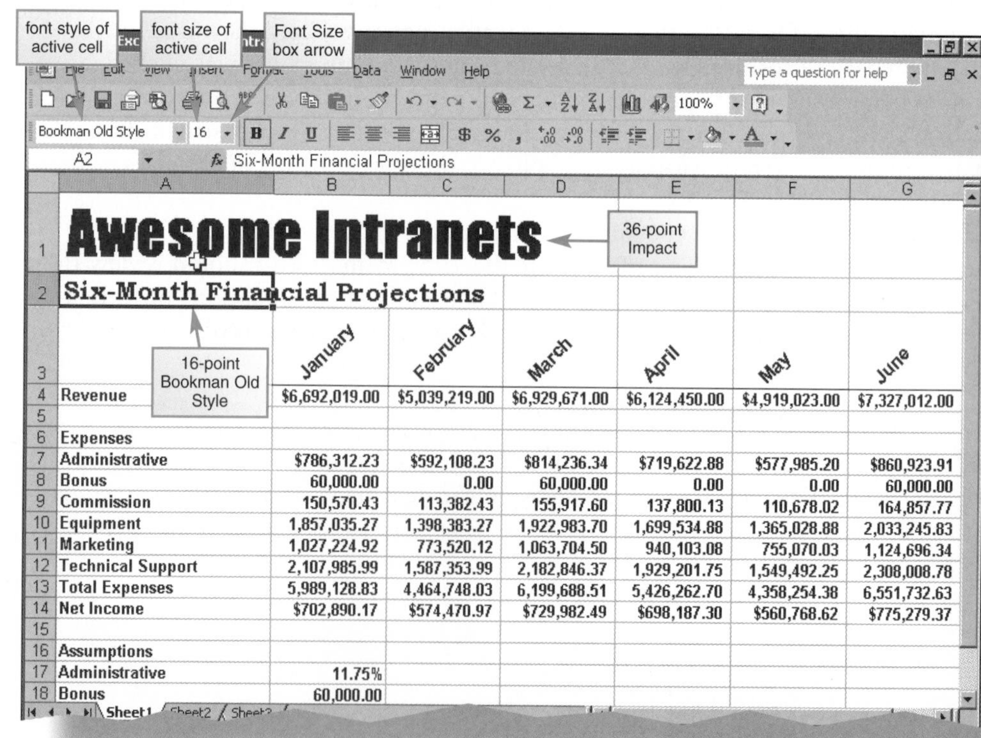

FIGURE 3-39

4 Select the range A1:H2. Click the Fill Color button arrow on the Formatting toolbar. Click Red (column 1, row 3) on the Fill Color palette. Click the Font Color button arrow on the Formatting toolbar. Point to White (column 8, row 5) on the Font Color palette.

Excel assigns a red background to the selected range and the Font Color palette displays (Figure 3-40).

5 Click White.

Excel changes the color of the font in the range A1:H2 from black to white (see Figure 3-33 on page E 3.32).

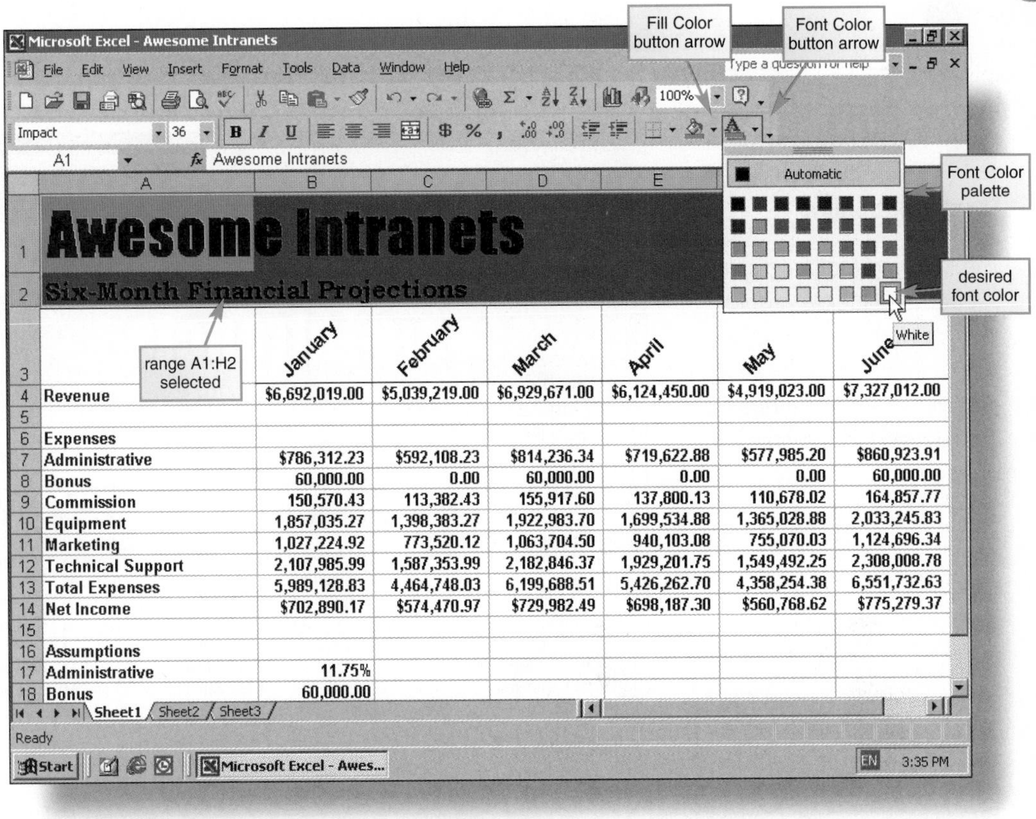

Fill Color button arrow

Font Color button arrow

Font Color palette

desired font color

range A1:H2 selected

FIGURE 3-40

Other Ways

1. On Format menu click Cells, click Patterns tab to color background (or click Font tab to color font), click OK button
2. Right-click range, click Format Cells on shortcut menu, click Patterns tab to color background (or click Font tab to color font), click OK button
3. Press CTRL+1, click Patterns tab to color background (or click Font tab to color font), click OK button
4. In Voice Command mode say, "Format, Cells, Patterns (or Font), [desired color], OK"

The next step is to add a drop shadow to the selected range A1:H2 using the Shadow button on the Drawing toolbar. First, the Drawing toolbar must display on the screen. The following section describes how to display an inactive (hidden) toolbar and then dock it.

Displaying the Drawing Toolbar

Excel has hundreds of toolbar buttons, most of which display on 19 built-in toolbars. Two of these 19 built-in toolbars are the Standard toolbar and Formatting toolbar, which usually display at the top of the screen. Another built-in toolbar is the Drawing toolbar. The **Drawing toolbar** provides tools that can simplify adding lines, boxes, and other geometric figures to a worksheet. You also can create customized toolbars containing the buttons that you use often.

You can use the shortcut menu that displays when you right-click a toolbar or the **Toolbars command** on the View menu to display or hide any Excel toolbar. The Drawing toolbar also can be displayed or hidden by clicking the Drawing button on the Standard toolbar. Perform the step on the next page to display the Drawing toolbar.

To Display the Drawing Toolbar

1 Click the Drawing button on the Standard toolbar.

The Drawing toolbar displays (Figure 3-41). Excel displays the Drawing toolbar on the screen in the same location and with the same shape as it displayed the last time it was used.

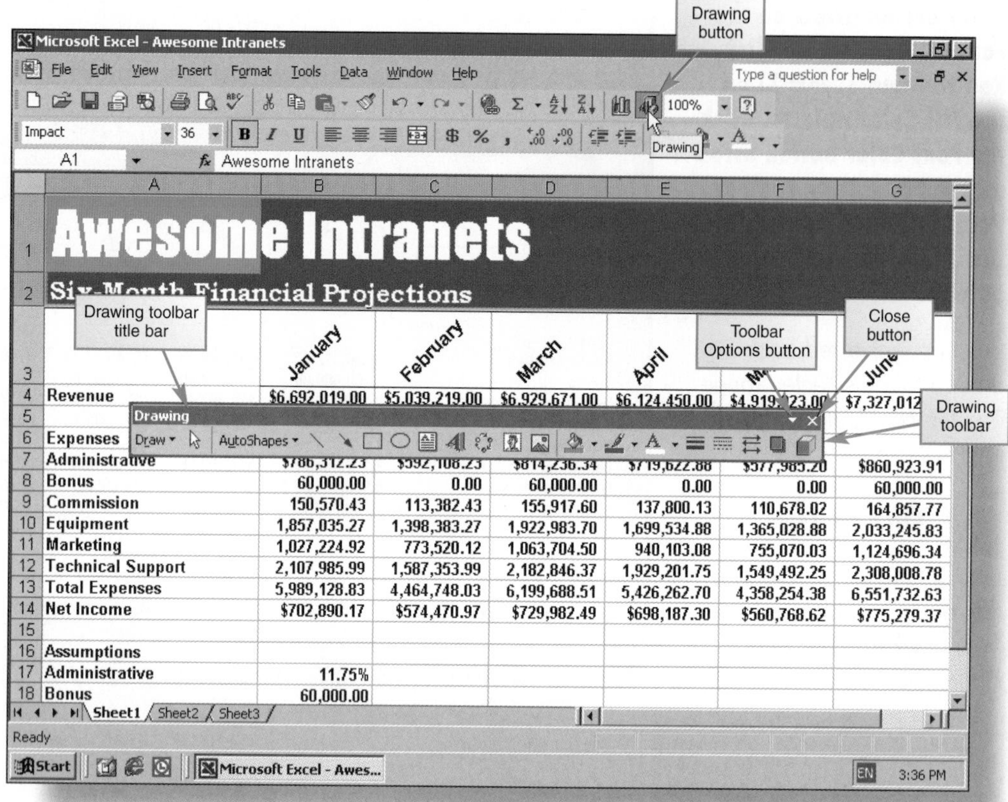

FIGURE 3-41

1. On View menu point to Toolbars, click Drawing
2. Right-click Standard or Formatting toolbar, click Drawing on shortcut menu
3. In Voice Command mode say, "View, Toolbars, Drawing"

When a toolbar displays in the middle of the screen as shown in Figure 3-41, the toolbar includes a title bar. The Toolbar Options button and Close button display on the right side of the title bar.

Moving and Docking a Toolbar

The Drawing toolbar in Figure 3-41 is called a **floating toolbar** because it displays in its own window and can be moved anywhere in the Excel window. You move the toolbar by pointing to the toolbar title bar or to a blank area within the toolbar window (not a button) and then dragging the toolbar to its new location. As with any window, you also can resize the toolbar by dragging the toolbar window borders. To hide a floating toolbar, click the Close button on the toolbar title bar. Sometimes a floating toolbar gets in the way no matter where you move it or how you resize it. Hiding the toolbar is one solution. At times, however, you will want to keep the toolbar available for use. For this reason, Excel allows you to position toolbars on the edge of its window. If you drag the toolbar close to the edge of the window, Excel positions the toolbar in a **toolbar dock**.

Excel has four toolbar docks, one on each of the four sides of the window. You can add as many toolbars to a dock as you want. Each time you dock a toolbar, however, the Excel window slightly decreases in size to compensate for the room occupied by the toolbar. The following steps show how to dock the Drawing toolbar at the bottom of the screen below the scroll bar.

More About

Color Palettes

If your Color palette contains more or less colors than shown on the Color palette in Figure 3-40 on the previous page, then your computer is using a different Color palette setting. The figures in this book were created using High Color (16 bit). To check your Color palette setting, return to the desktop, right-click the desktop, click Properties on the shortcut menu, click the Settings tab, and locate the Color palette box.

To Dock a Toolbar at the Bottom of the Screen

1 Point to the Drawing toolbar title bar or to a blank area in the Drawing toolbar.

2 Drag the Drawing toolbar over the status bar at the bottom of the screen.

Excel docks the Drawing toolbar at the bottom of the screen (Figure 3-42).

Drawing toolbar docked horizontally across bottom of window

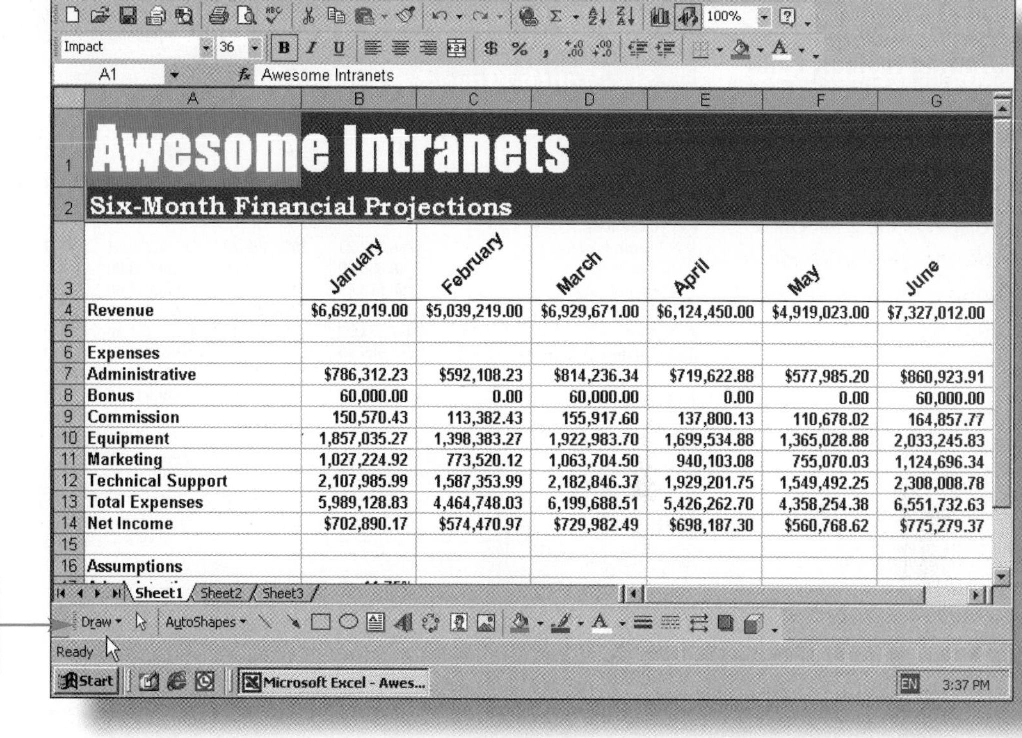

	A	B	C	D	E	F	G
1	Awesome Intranets						
2	Six-Month Financial Projections						
3		January	February	March	April	May	June
4	Revenue	$6,692,019.00	$5,039,219.00	$6,929,671.00	$6,124,450.00	$4,919,023.00	$7,327,012.00
5							
6	Expenses						
7	Administrative	$786,312.23	$592,108.23	$814,236.34	$719,622.88	$577,985.20	$860,923.91
8	Bonus	60,000.00	0.00	60,000.00	0.00	0.00	60,000.00
9	Commission	150,570.43	113,382.43	155,917.60	137,800.13	110,678.02	164,857.77
10	Equipment	1,857,035.27	1,398,383.27	1,922,983.70	1,699,534.88	1,365,028.88	2,033,245.83
11	Marketing	1,027,224.92	773,520.12	1,063,704.50	940,103.08	755,070.03	1,124,696.34
12	Technical Support	2,107,985.99	1,587,353.99	2,182,846.37	1,929,201.75	1,549,492.25	2,308,008.78
13	Total Expenses	5,989,128.83	4,464,748.03	6,199,688.51	5,426,262.70	4,358,254.38	6,551,732.63
14	Net Income	$702,890.17	$574,470.97	$729,982.49	$698,187.30	$560,768.62	$775,279.37
15							
16	Assumptions						

FIGURE 3-42

Compare Figure 3-42 with Figure 3-41. Excel automatically resizes the Drawing toolbar to fit across the window and between the scroll bar and status bar. Also notice that the heavy window border that surrounded the floating toolbar has changed to a light border. To move a toolbar to any of the other three docks, drag the toolbar from its current position to the desired side of the window. To move a docked toolbar, it is easiest to point to the move handle and when the mouse pointer changes to a cross with four arrowheads, drag it to the desired locator.

Adding a Drop Shadow to the Title Area

With the Drawing toolbar docked at the bottom of the screen, the next step is to add the drop shadow to the range A1:H2, as shown in the steps on the next page.

More About

Docking Toolbars

If you dock a toolbar on the left or right edge of the window that includes a box or a button with a list, the list will not be available.

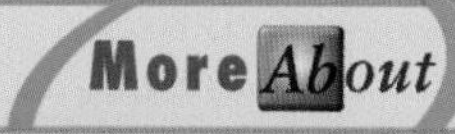

Toolbars

You can create your own toolbar and assemble the buttons you want on it by using the Customize command on the shortcut menu that displays when you right-click a toolbar. When the Customize dialog box displays, click the Toolbars tab, click the New button, name the toolbar, click the Commands tab, drag buttons to the new toolbar.

Steps To Add a Drop Shadow

1 With the range A1:H2 selected, click the Shadow Style button on the Drawing toolbar. Point to Shadow Style 14 (column 2, row 4) on the Shadow Style palette.

Excel displays the Shadow Style palette of drop shadows with varying shadow depths (Figure 3-43).

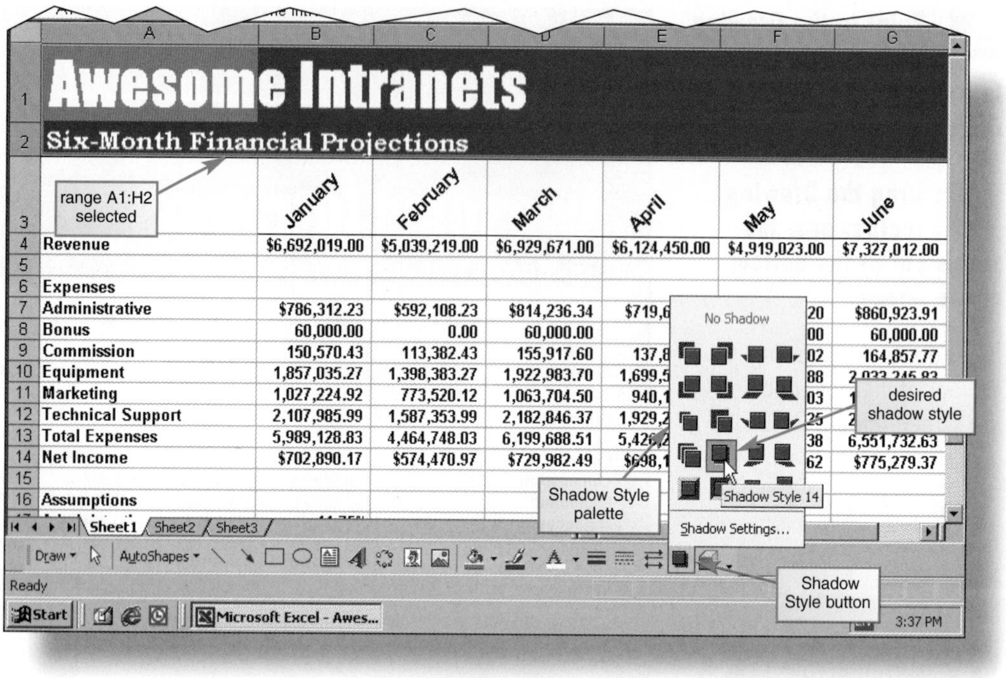

FIGURE 3-43

2 Click Shadow Style 14. Click cell A4 to deselect the drop shadow.

Excel adds a drop shadow to the range A1:H2 (Figure 3-44).

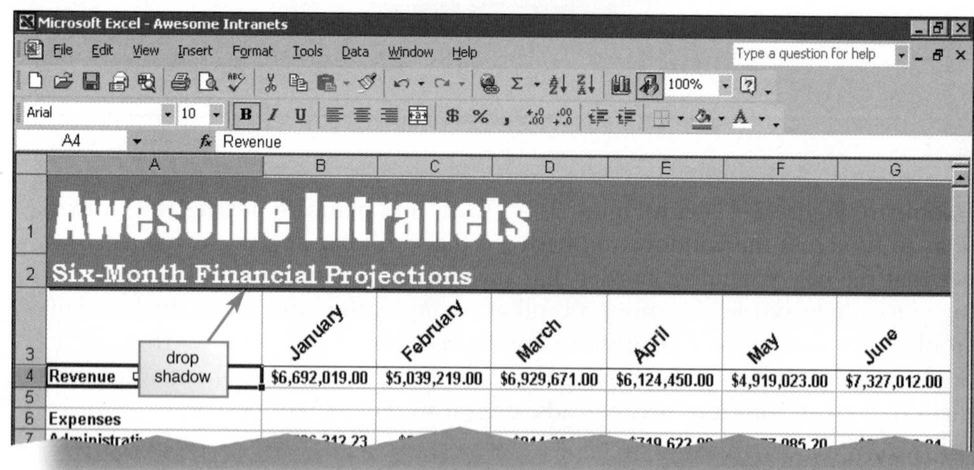

FIGURE 3-44

Other Ways

1. In Voice Command mode say, "Drawing, Shadow Style, Shadow Style 14"

When you add a drop shadow to a range of cells, Excel selects the drop shadow and surrounds it with handles. To deselect the drop shadow, select any cell, as described in Step 2 above.

Formatting the Category Row Titles and Net Income Row

The following steps change the font size in cells A4, A6, A13, and A14 to 12 point; and then adds the light yellow background color and drop shadows to cells A4, A6, and the range A14:H14.

Steps To Change Font Size, Add Background Colors, and Add Drop Shadows to Nonadjacent Selections

1 **With cell A4 selected, hold down the CTRL key, click cells A6, A13, and A14. Click the Font Size box arrow on the Formatting toolbar and then click 12 in the Font Size list.**

The font size in cells A4, A6, A13, and A14 changes to 12 point.

2 **Click cell A4. While holding down the CTRL key, click cell A6 and then select the range A14:H14. Click the Fill Color button arrow on the Formatting toolbar. Click Light Yellow (column 3, row 5) on the Fill Color palette. Click the Shadow Style button on the Drawing toolbar and point to Shadow Style 14 (column 2, row 4) on the Shadow palette.**

The nonadjacent ranges are selected and the background color is changed to yellow (Figure 3-45). The Shadow Style palette displays.

3 **Click Shadow Style 14.**

Excel adds a drop shadow to cells A4, A6, and the range A14:H14 (Figure 3-46).

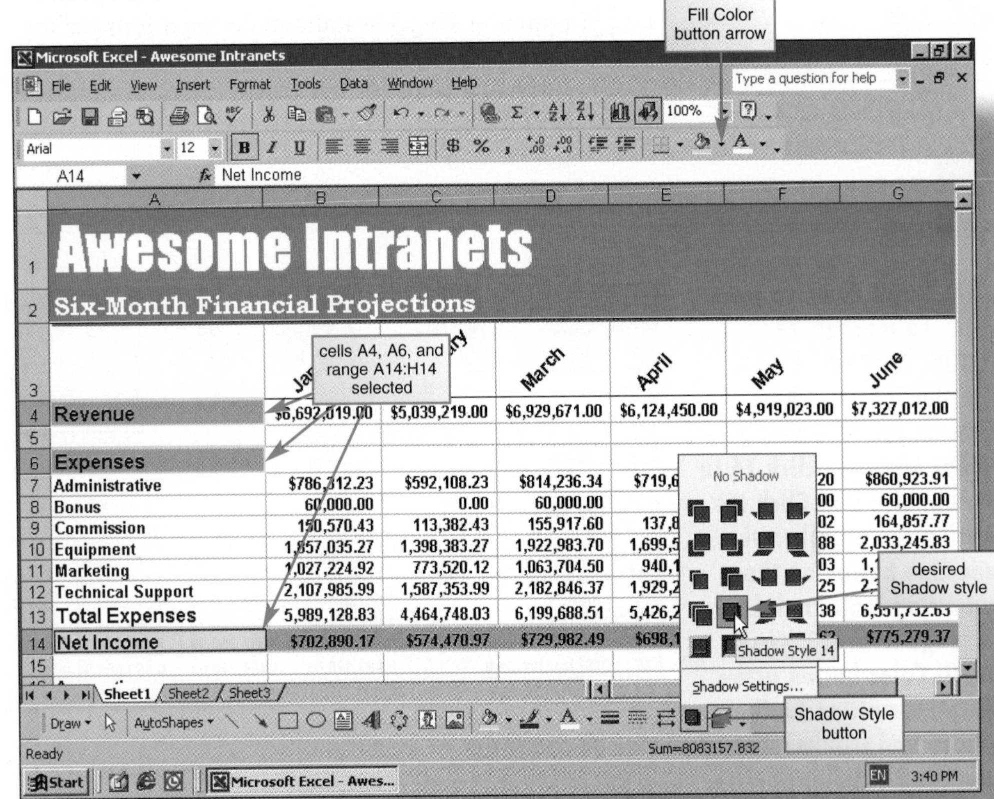

FIGURE 3-45

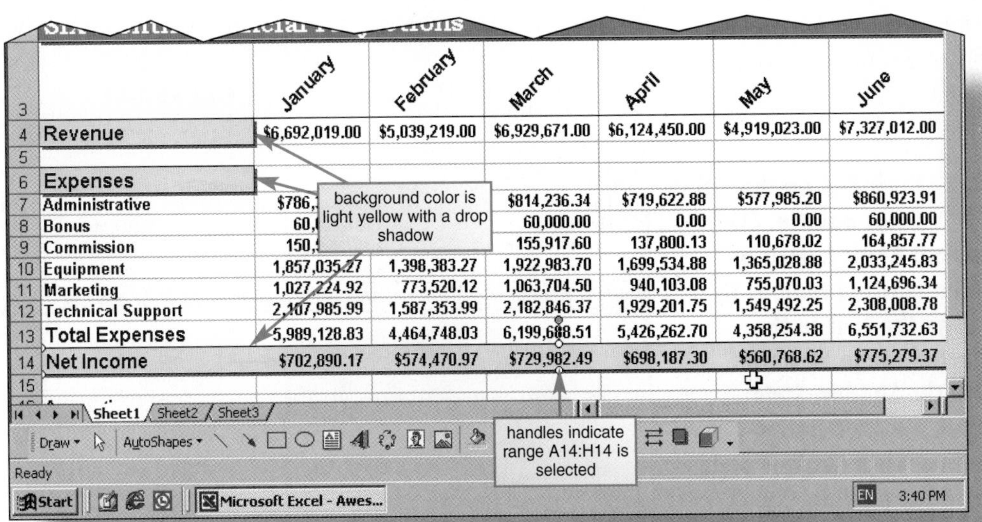

FIGURE 3-46

An alternative to formatting all three areas (cell A4, cell A6, and the range A14:H14) at once is to select each one separately and apply the formats.

Formatting the Assumptions Table

The last step to improving the appearance of the worksheet is to format the Assumptions table in the range A16:B23. The specifications in Figure 3-33 on page E 3.32 require a 16-point italic underlined font for the title in cell A16. The range A16:B23 has a red background color, white font, and a drop shadow that surrounds it. The following steps format the Assumptions table.

Steps To Format the Assumptions Table

1 Scroll down so rows 16 through 23 display. Click cell A16. Click the Font Size box arrow on the Formatting toolbar and then click 16 in the Font Size list. Click the Italic button and then the Underline button on the Formatting toolbar. Select the range A16:B23. Click the Fill Color button arrow on the Formatting toolbar. Point to Red (column 1, row 3) on the Fill Color palette.

The Assumptions table heading displays with the new formats. The range A16:B23 is selected and the Fill Color palette displays (Figure 3-47).

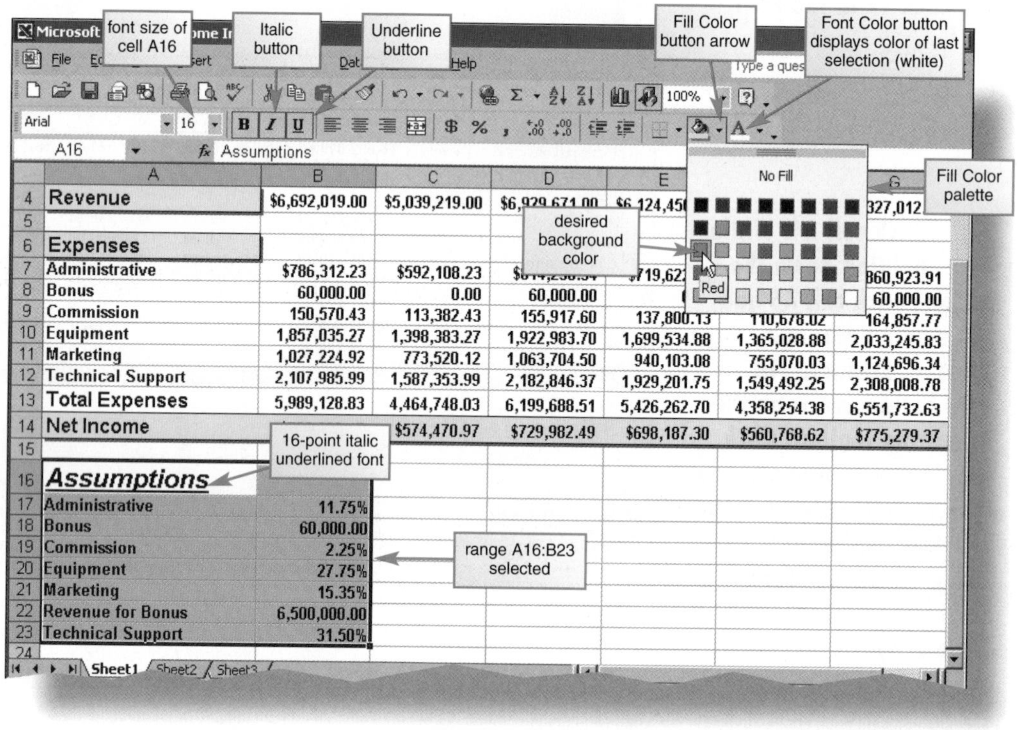

font size of cell A16
Italic button
Underline button
Fill Color button arrow
Font Color button displays color of last selection (white)
Fill Color palette
desired background color
16-point italic underlined font
range A16:B23 selected

FIGURE 3-47

2 Click Red on the Fill Color palette. Click the Font Color button on the Formatting toolbar to change the font in the selected range to white. Click the Shadow Style button on the Drawing toolbar. Click Shadow Style 14 on the Shadow Style palette. Select cell D23 to deselect the range A16:B23.

The Assumptions table displays as shown in Figure 3-48.

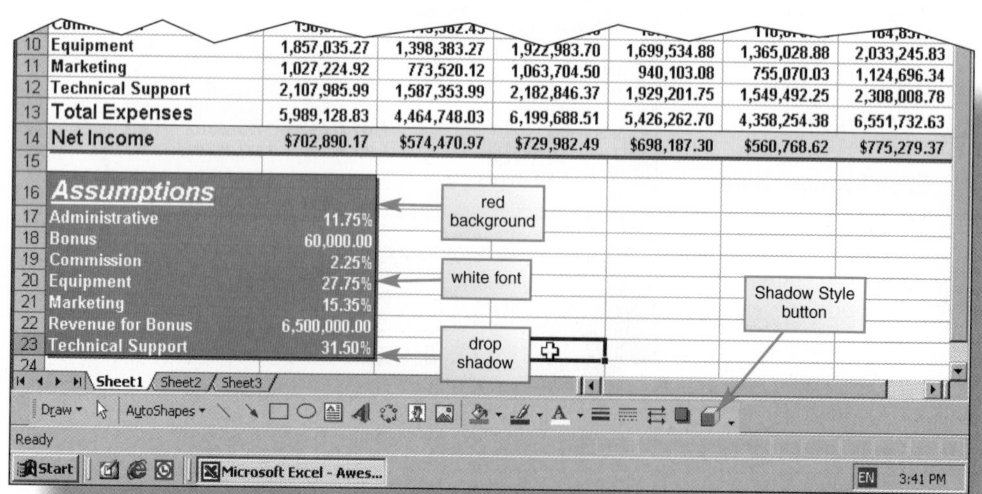

FIGURE 3-48

The previous steps introduced you to two new formats, italic and underline. When you assign the **italic** font style to a cell, Excel slants the characters slightly to the right as shown in cell A16 in Figure 3-47. The **underline** format underlines only the characters in the cell rather than the entire cell as is the case when you assign a cell a bottom border.

More About

Drop Shadows

To remove an unwanted drop shadow, click it so the handles appear on the drop shadow, and then press the DELETE key. A drop shadow is a shape and not a format. Thus, if you used the Format Painter button to apply formats from a range with a drop shadow, then the drop shadow will not be copied.

Hiding the Drawing Toolbar and Saving the Workbook

The formatting of the worksheet is complete. The following steps hide the Drawing toolbar and save the workbook.

TO HIDE THE DRAWING TOOLBAR AND SAVE THE WORKBOOK

1. Click the Drawing button on the Standard toolbar.
2. Click the Save button on the Standard toolbar

Excel hides the Drawing toolbar (Figure 3-49) and saves the workbook using the file name Awesome Intranets.

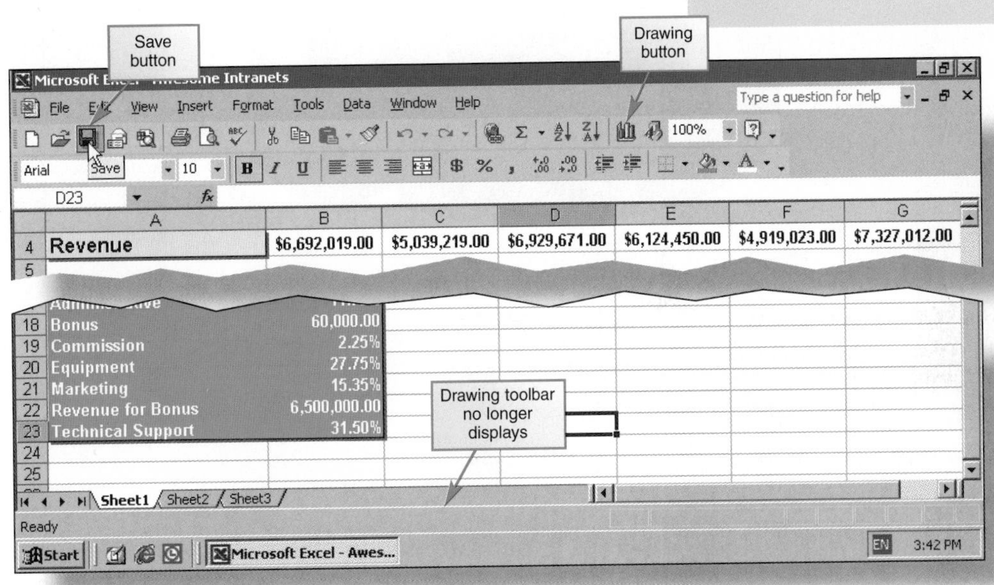

FIGURE 3-49

Adding a 3-D Pie Chart to the Workbook

The next step in the project is to draw the 3-D Pie chart on a separate sheet in the workbook Awesome Intranets, as shown in Figure 3-50 on the next page. A **Pie chart** is used to show the relationship or proportion of parts to a whole. Each slice (or wedge) of the pie shows what percent that slice contributes to the total (100%). The 3-D Pie chart in Figure 3-50 shows the contribution of each projected month's net income to the projected six-month net income. The Pie chart makes it easy to evaluate January's contribution to the projected six-month net income in comparison to the other months.

Unlike the 3-D Column chart in Project 1, the 3-D Pie chart in Figure 3-50 is not embedded in the worksheet. This Pie chart resides on a separate sheet called a **chart sheet**.

The ranges in the worksheet to chart are the nonadjacent ranges B3:G3 (month names) and B14:G14 (monthly net incomes). The month names in the range B3:G3 will identify the slices; these entries are called **category names**. The range B14:G14 contains the data that determines the size of the slices in the pie; these entries are called the **data series**. Because there are six months, the 3-D Pie chart contains six slices.

This project also calls for emphasizing the January contribution to the projected total net income by offsetting its slice from the main portion. A Pie chart with one or more slices offset is called an **exploded Pie chart**.

More About

Chart Selection

Line chart, bar chart, pie chart — which chart will best describe your worksheet data? For answers, click the Contents tab in the Microsoft Excel Help window. Double click the Charts book. If necessary, double-click the Creating Charts book. Click WEB: Gallery of chart examples. You must have access to the Web to display the Web page result.

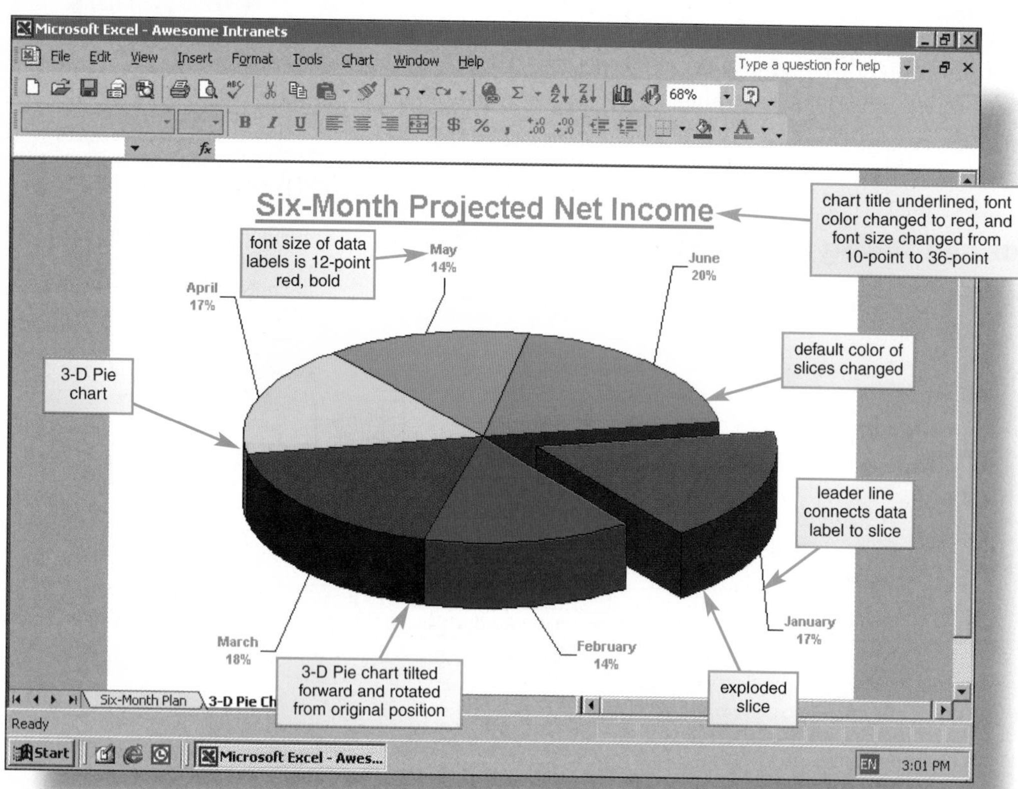

FIGURE 3-50

As shown in Figure 3-50, the default 3-D Pie chart also has been enhanced by rotating and tilting the pie forward, changing the colors of the slices, and modifying the chart title and labels that identify the slices.

Drawing a 3-D Pie Chart on a Separate Chart Sheet

The following steps show how to draw the 3-D Pie chart on a separate chart sheet using the Chart Wizard button on the Standard toolbar.

Steps To Draw a 3-D Pie Chart on a Separate Chart Sheet

1 Select the range B3:G3. While holding down the CTRL key, select the range B14:G14. Point to the Chart Wizard button on the Standard toolbar.

The nonadjacent ranges are selected (Figure 3-51).

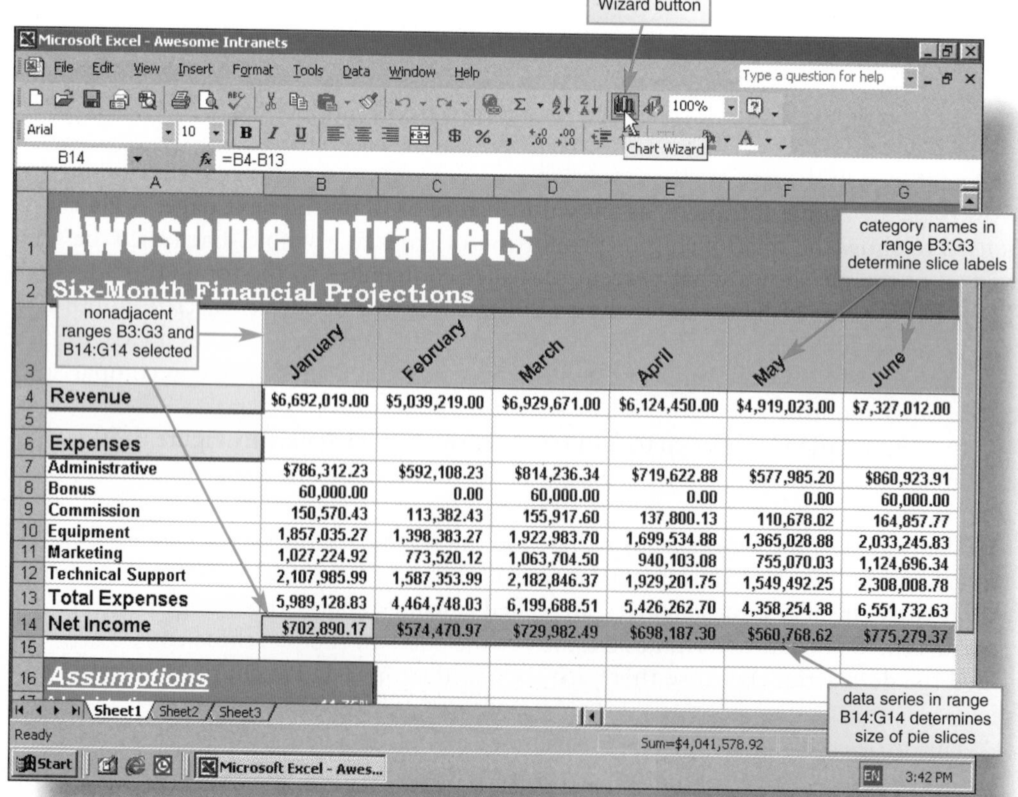

FIGURE 3-51

2 Click the Chart Wizard button on the Standard toolbar. When the Chart Wizard - Step 1 of 4 - Chart Type dialog box displays, click Pie in the Chart type list and then click the 3-D Pie chart (column 2, row 1) in the Chart sub-type box. Point to the Next button.

The Chart Wizard - Step 1 of 4 - Chart Type dialog box displays, which allows you to select one of the 14 types of charts available in Excel (Figure 3-52).

FIGURE 3-52

3 Click the Next button.

The Chart Wizard - Step 2 of 4 - Chart Source Data dialog box displays showing a sample of the 3-D Pie chart and the chart data range. A marquee surrounds the nonadjacent ranges on the worksheet (Figure 3-53).

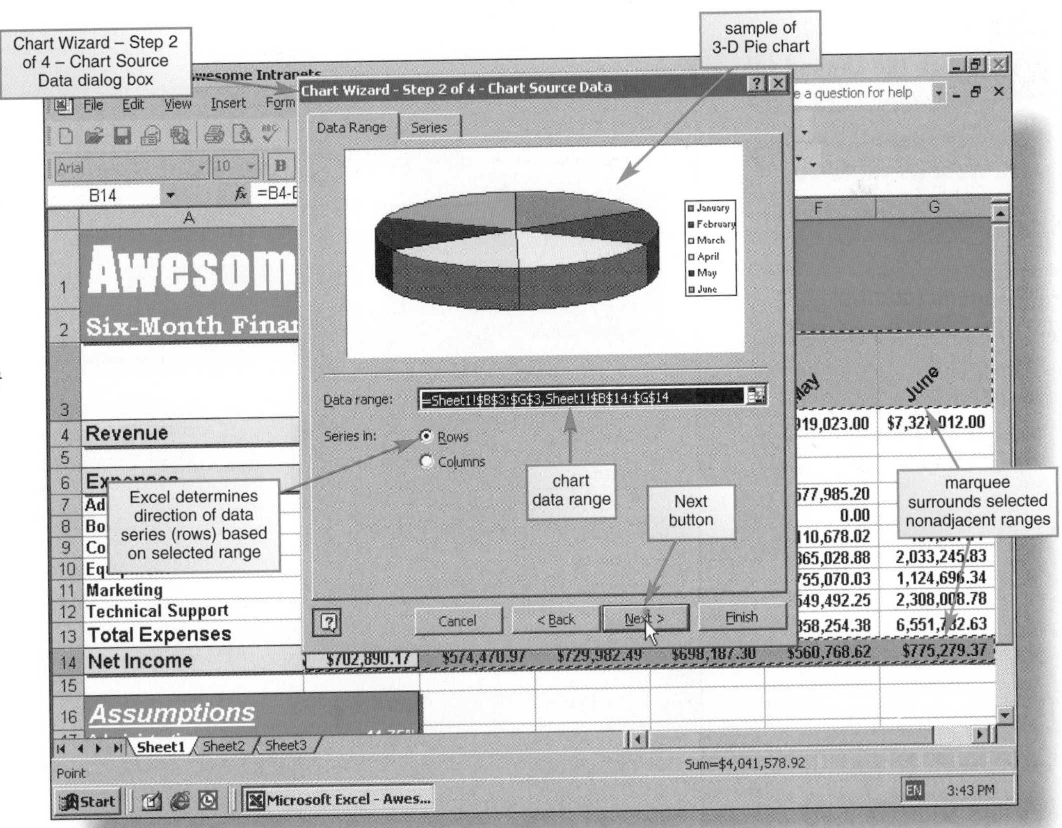

FIGURE 3-53

4 Click the Next button. When the Chart Wizard - Step 3 of 4 - Chart Options dialog box displays, type `Six-Month Projected Net Income` **in the Chart title text box. Point to the Legend tab.**

Excel redraws the sample 3-D Pie chart with the chart title, Six-Month Projected Net Income (Figure 3-54). Excel automatically bolds the chart title.

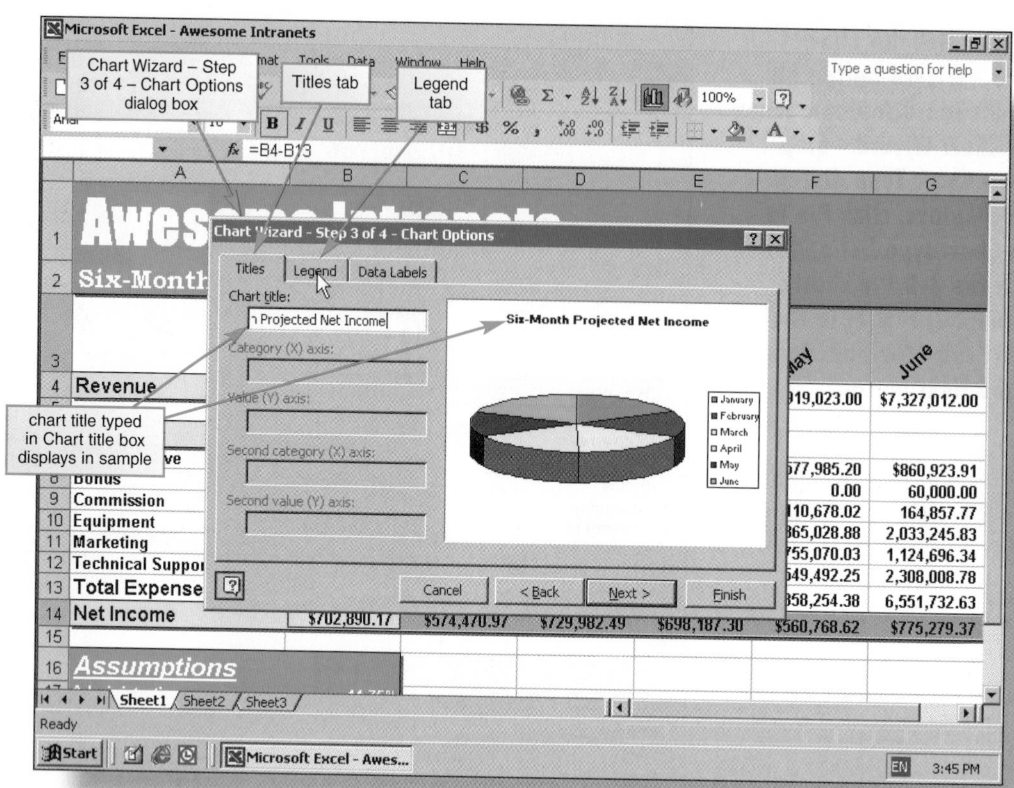

FIGURE 3-54

5 Click the Legend tab and then click Show legend to remove the check mark from its check box. Point to the Data Labels tab.

The Legend tab displays. Excel redraws the sample 3-D Pie chart without the legend. (Figure 3-55).

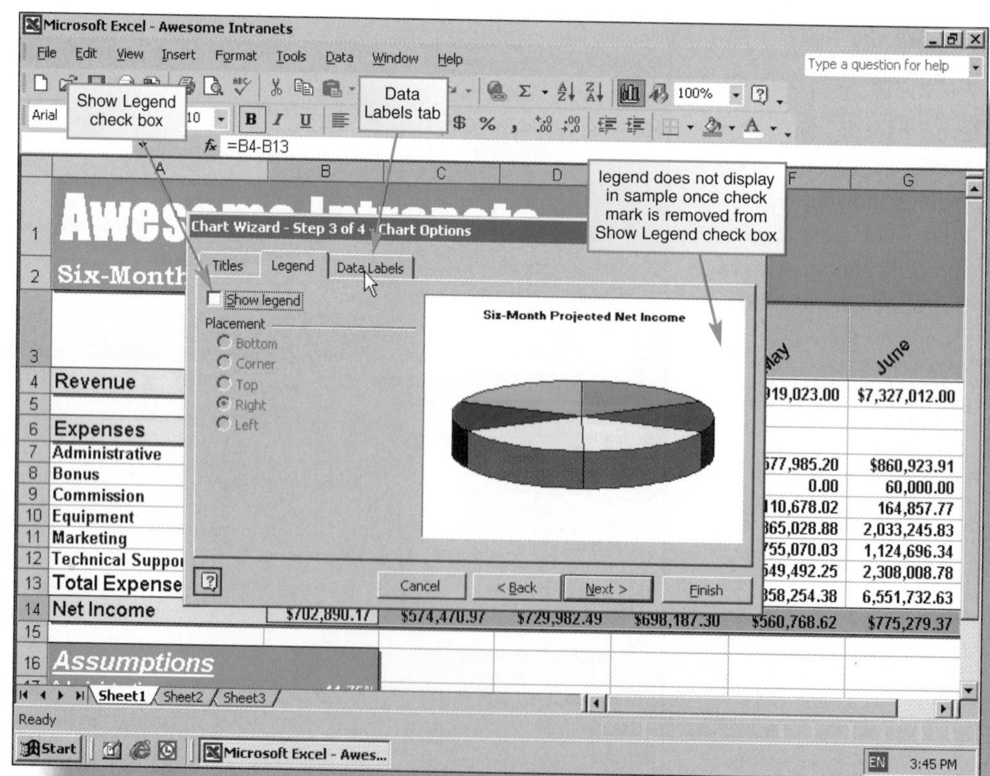

FIGURE 3-55

6 Click the Data Labels tab. In the Label Contains area, click Category name and click Percentage to add check marks to their respective check boxes. Click Show leader lines to add a check mark to its check box. Point to the Next button.

The Data Labels sheet displays. Excel redraws the sample 3-D Pie chart with data labels and percentages (Figure 3-56).

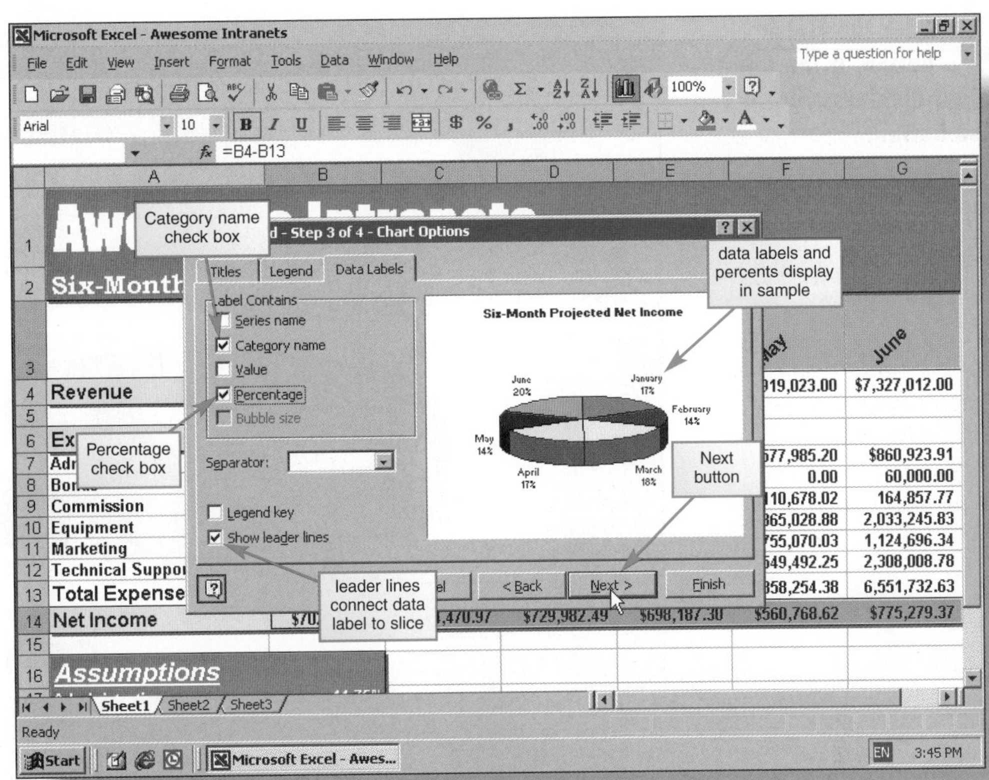

FIGURE 3-56

7 Click the Next button. When the Chart Wizard - Step 4 of 4 - Chart Location dialog box displays, click As new sheet. Point to the Finish button.

The Chart Wizard - Step 4 of 4 - Chart Location dialog box gives you two chart location options: to draw the chart on a new sheet in the workbook or to draw it as an object in a worksheet (Figure 3-57).

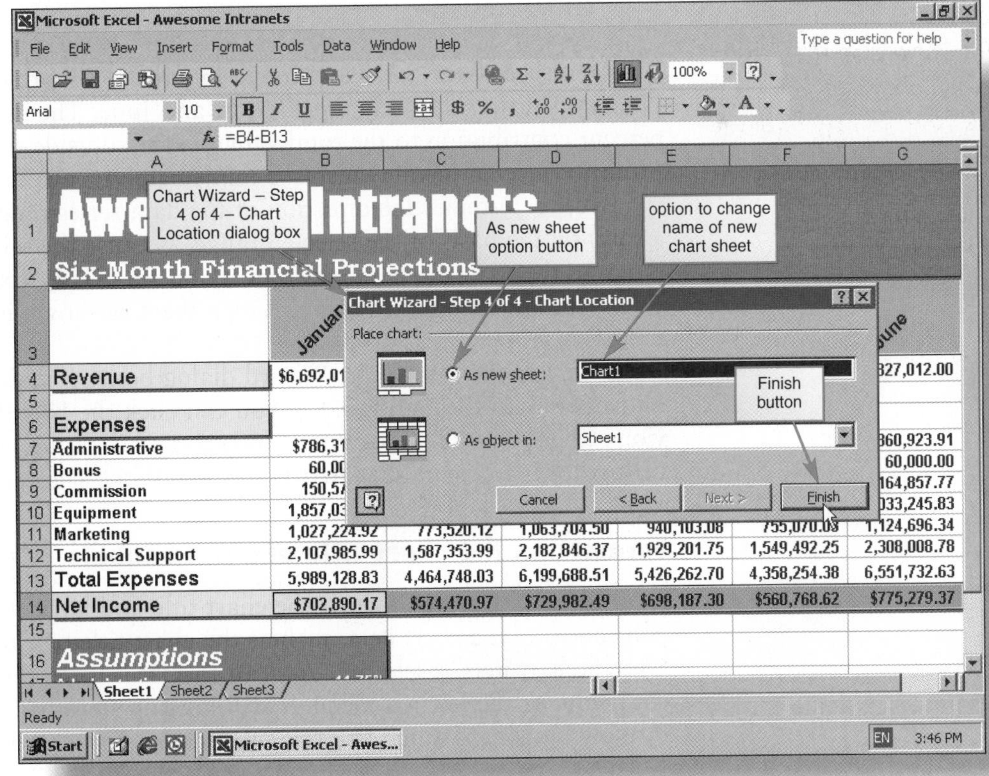

FIGURE 3-57

8 **Click the Finish button. If the Chart toolbar displays, click it's Close button.**

Excel draws the 3-D Pie chart on a separate chart sheet (Chart1) in the Awesome Intranets workbook (Figure 3-58).

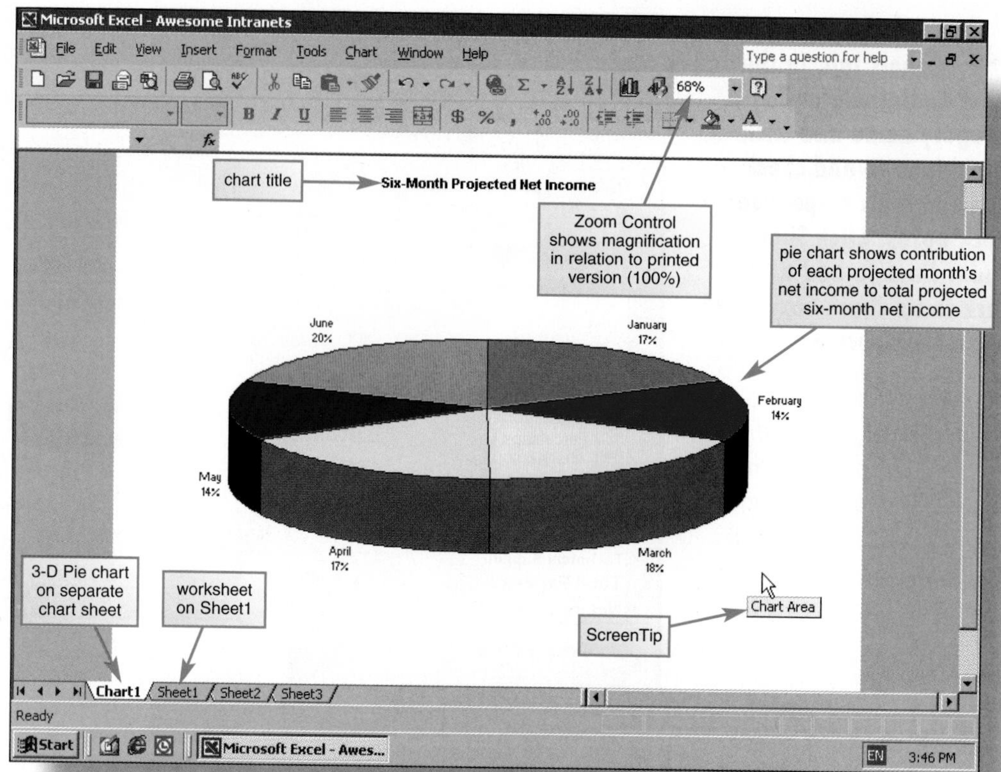

FIGURE 3-58

Other Ways

1. Select range to chart, press F11
2. Select range to chart, press ALT+I, H
3. Select range to chart, in Voice Command mode say, "Chart Wizard, [desired chart type]"

Each slice of the 3-D Pie chart in Figure 3-58 represents one of the six months – January, February, March, April, May, and June. The names of the months and the percent contribution to the total value display outside the slices. The chart title, Six-Month Projected Income, displays immediately above the 3-D Pie chart.

Excel determines the direction of the data series range (down a column or across a row) on the basis of the selected range. Because the selection for the 3-D Pie chart is across the worksheet (ranges B3:G3 and B14:G14), Excel automatically selects the Rows option button in the Data Range sheet as shown in Figure 3-53 on page E 3.45.

In any of the four Chart Wizard dialog boxes (Figure 3-52 through Figure 3-57 on page E 3.45 through E 3.47), you can click the Back button to return to the previous Chart Wizard dialog box. You also can click the Finish button in any of the dialog boxes to create the chart with the options selected up to that point.

Formatting the Chart Title and Data Labels

The next step is to format the chart title and labels that identify the slices. Before you can format a **chart item**, such as the chart title or data labels, you must select it. Once a chart item is selected, you can format it using the Formatting toolbar, shortcut menu, or the Format menu. The following steps use the Formatting toolbar to format chart items much like cell entries were formatted earlier.

Steps To Format the Chart Title and Data Labels

1 **Click the chart title. On the Formatting toolbar, click the Font Size box arrow, click 28 in the Font Size list, click the Underline button, click the Font Color button arrow, and then point to Red (column 1, row 3) on the Font Color palette.**

Excel displays a selection rectangle around the chart title, increases the font size of the chart title, and underlines the chart title (Figure 3-59). The Font Color palette displays.

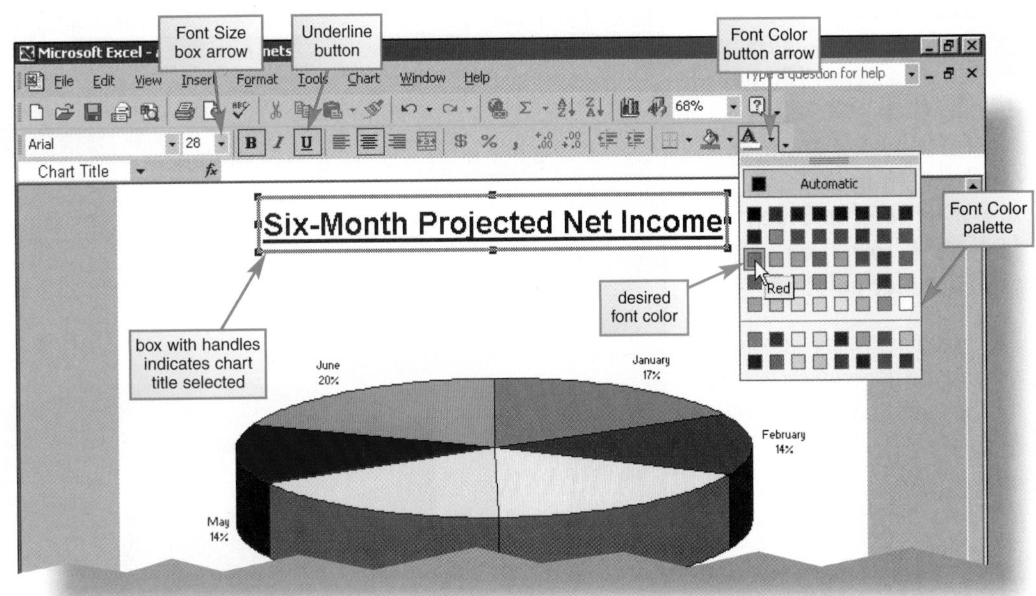

FIGURE 3-59

2 **Click Red. Click one of the five data labels that identify the slices. On the Formatting toolbar, click the Font Size box arrow, click 12 in the Font Size list, click the Bold button, and then click the Font Color button to change the font to the color red.**

The chart title and data labels display in red as shown in Figure 3-60. The data labels are selected.

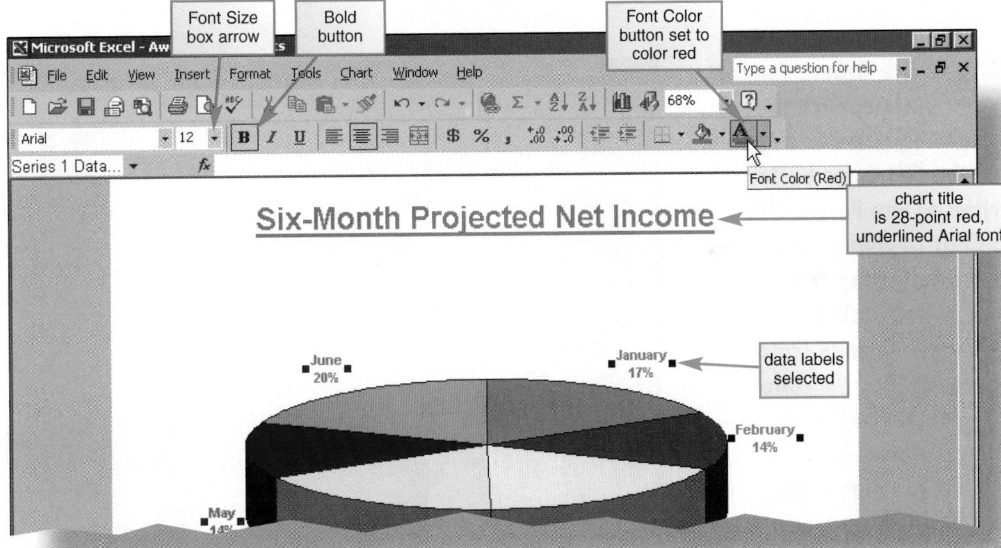

FIGURE 3-60

Other Ways

1. Right-click title or labels, click Format Chart Title or click Format Data Labels on shortcut menu
2. Press CTRL+B to bold
3. Press CTRL+U to underline
4. In Voice Command mode say, "Bold" or say, "Underline"

If you compare Figure 3-60 with Figure 3-58, you can see that the labels and chart title are easier to read and make the chart sheet look more professional.

Changing the Colors of the Slices

The next step is to change the colors of the slices of the pie. The colors shown in Figure 3-60 are the default colors Excel uses when you first create a 3-D Pie chart. Project 3 requires that the colors be changed to those shown in Figure 3-50 on page E 3.44. To change the colors of the slices, select them one at a time and use the Fill Color button arrow on the Formatting Toolbar as shown in the steps on the next page.

Steps To Change the Colors of the Pie Slices

1 Click the January slice twice. (Do not double-click.) Click the Fill Color button arrow on the Formatting toolbar and then point to Green (column 4, row 2) on the Fill Color palette.

Excel displays sizing handles around the January slice, and the Fill Color palette displays (Figure 3-61).

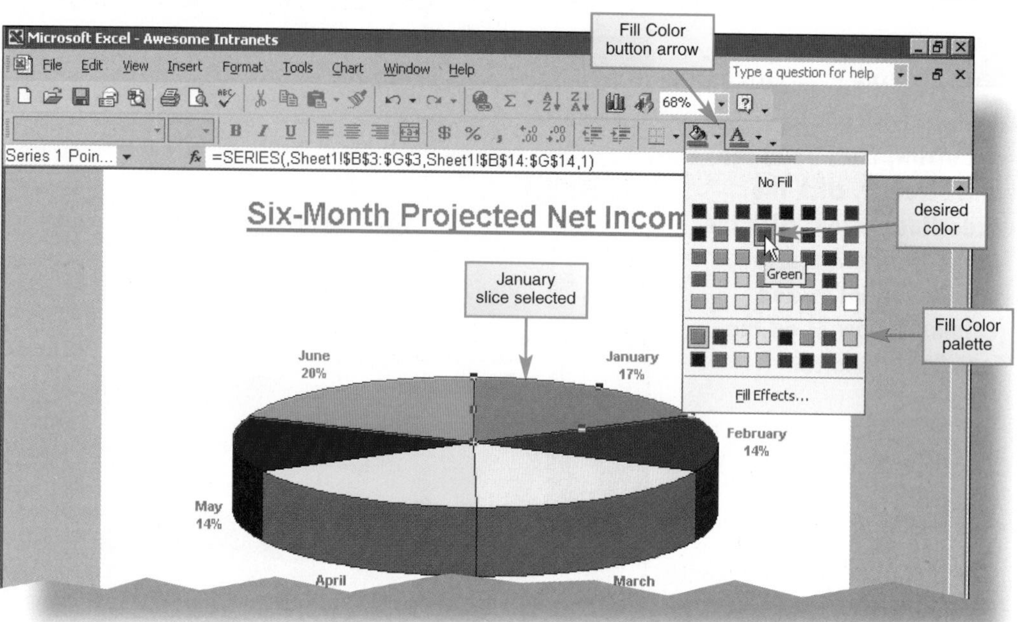

FIGURE 3-61

2 Click Green. One at a time, click the remaining slices and then use the Fill Color button arrow on the Formatting toolbar to change each slice to the following colors: June – Red (column 1, row 3); May – Orange (column 2, row 2); April – Yellow (column 3, row 4); March – Plum (column 7, row 4); and February – Blue (column 6, row 2). Click outside the Chart Area.

The chart displays with colors assigned to the slices as shown in Figure 3-62.

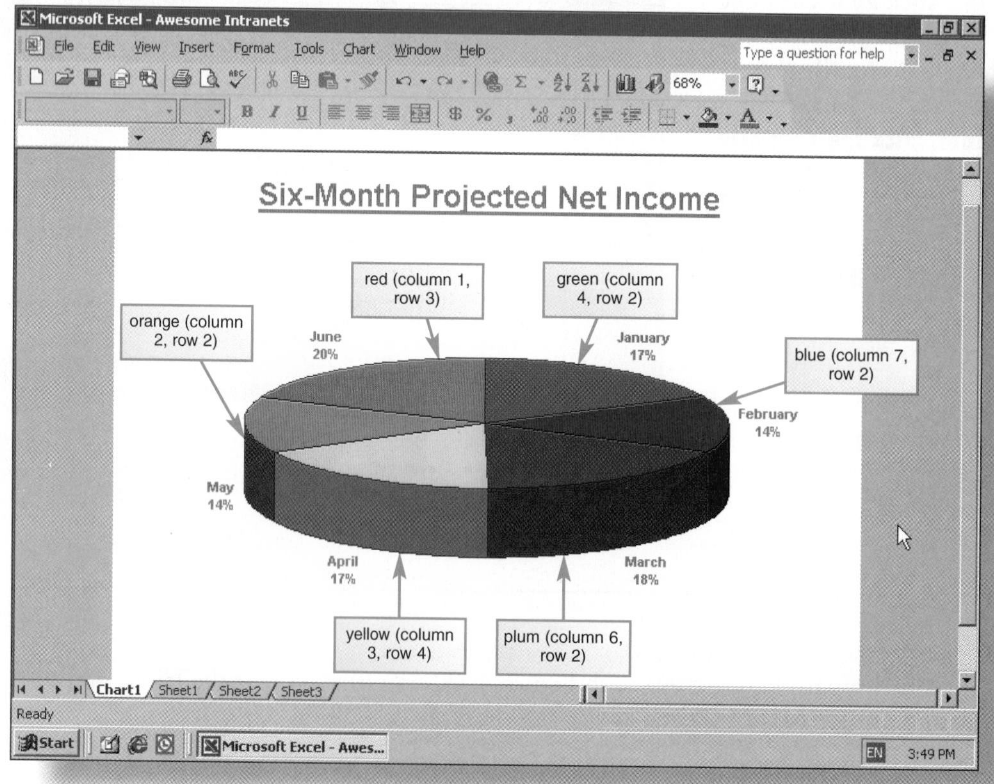

FIGURE 3-62

Other Ways

1. Click slice twice, right-click selected slice, click Format Data Point on shortcut menu, click Patterns tab, click color, click OK button
2. Click slice twice, in Voice Command mode say, "Format, Selected Data Point, Patterns, [desired color], OK"

Exploding the 3-D Pie Chart

The next step is to emphasize the slice representing January by offsetting, or exploding, it from the rest of the slices so that it stands out. Perform the following steps to explode a slice of the 3-D Pie chart.

Steps To Explode the 3-D Pie Chart

1 Click the slice labeled January twice. (Do not double-click.)

Excel displays sizing handles around the January slice.

2 Drag the slice to the desired position and then release the mouse button.

Excel redraws the 3-D Pie chart with the January slice offset from the rest of the slices (Figure 3-63).

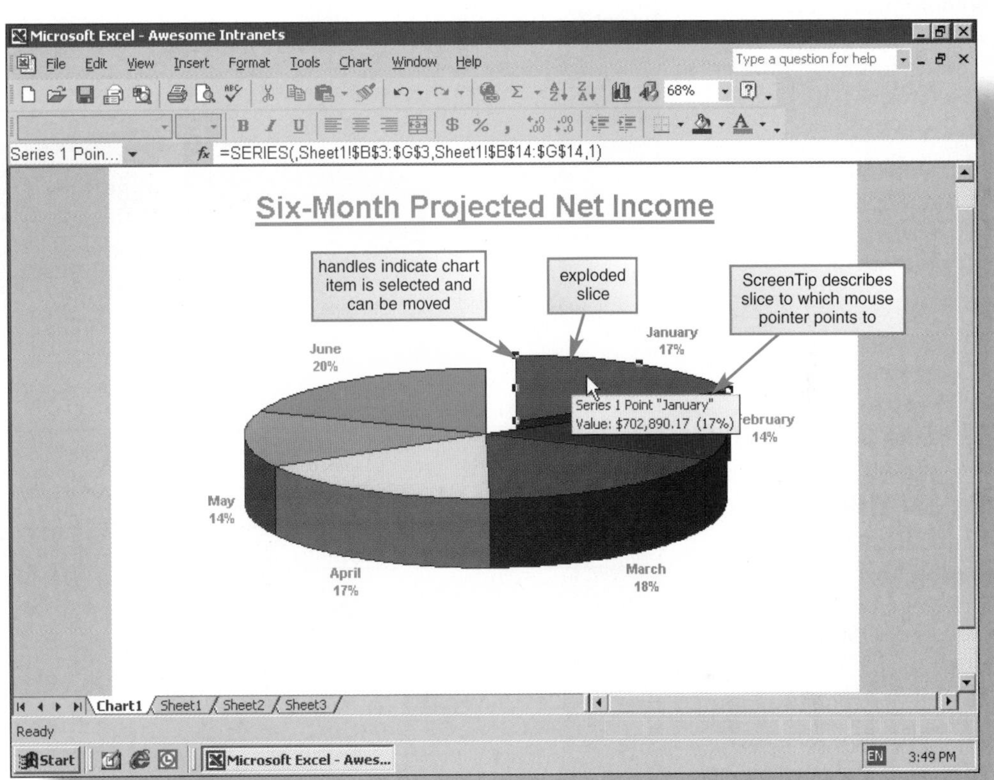

FIGURE 3-63

You can offset as many slices as you want, but remember that the reason for offsetting a slice is to emphasize it. Offsetting multiple slices tends to reduce the impact on the reader and reduces the overall size of the pie chart.

Exploding a 3-D Pie Chart

If you click the 3-D Pie Chart so that all the slices are selected, you can drag one of the slices to explode all of the slices.

Rotating and Tilting the 3-D Pie Chart

With a three-dimensional chart, you can change the view to better display the section of the chart you are trying to emphasize. Excel allows you to control the rotation angle, elevation, perspective, height, and angle of the axes by using the **3-D View command** on the Chart menu.

To obtain a better view of the offset January slice, you can rotate the 3-D Pie chart 80° to the left. The rotation angle of the 3-D Pie chart is defined by the line that divides the January and June slices. When Excel initially draws a pie chart, it always points one of the dividing lines between two slices to 12 o'clock (or zero degrees). Besides rotating the 3-D Pie chart, the steps on the next page also change, or tilt, the elevation so the 3-D Pie chart is at less of an angle to the viewer.

Steps To Rotate and Tilt the 3-D Pie Chart

1 With the January slice selected, click Chart on the menu bar and then point to 3-D View.

The Chart menu displays (Figure 3-64).

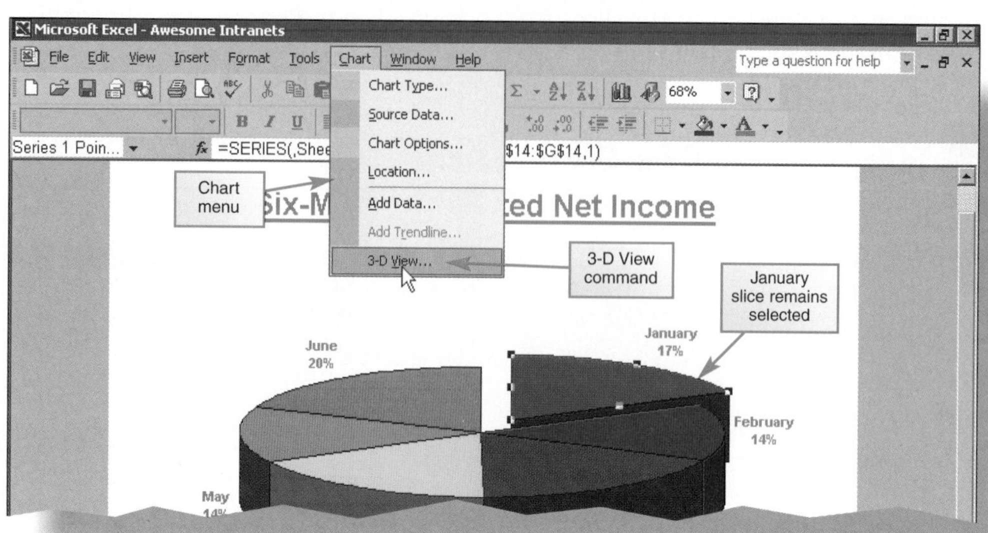

FIGURE 3-64

2 Click 3-D View. Click the up arrow button in the 3-D View dialog box until 25 displays in the Elevation box.

The 3-D View dialog box displays (Figure 3-65). A sample of the 3-D Pie chart displays in the dialog box. The result of increasing the elevation of the 3-D Pie chart is to tilt it forward.

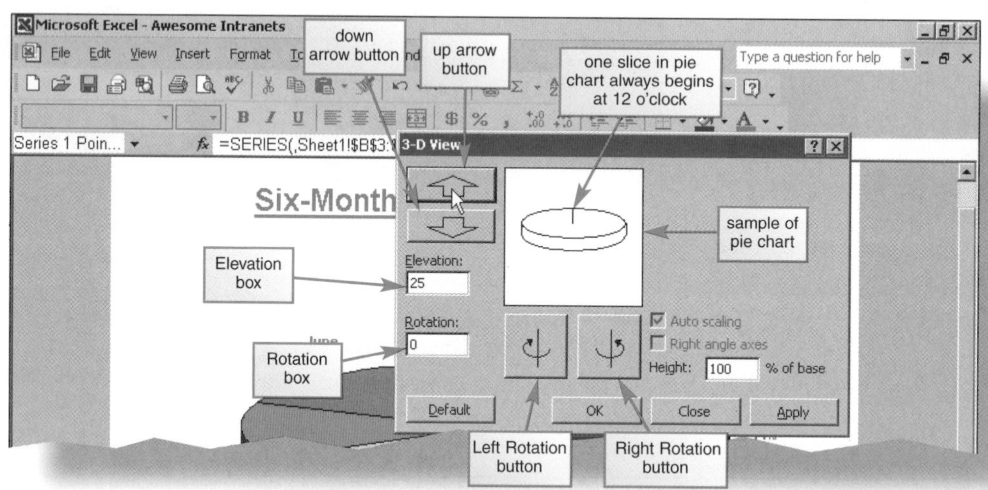

FIGURE 3-65

3 Rotate the Pie chart by clicking the Left Rotation button until the Rotation box displays 80. Point to the OK button.

The new rotation setting (80) displays in the ***Rotation box*** *as shown in Figure 3-66. A sample of the rotated pie chart displays in the dialog box.*

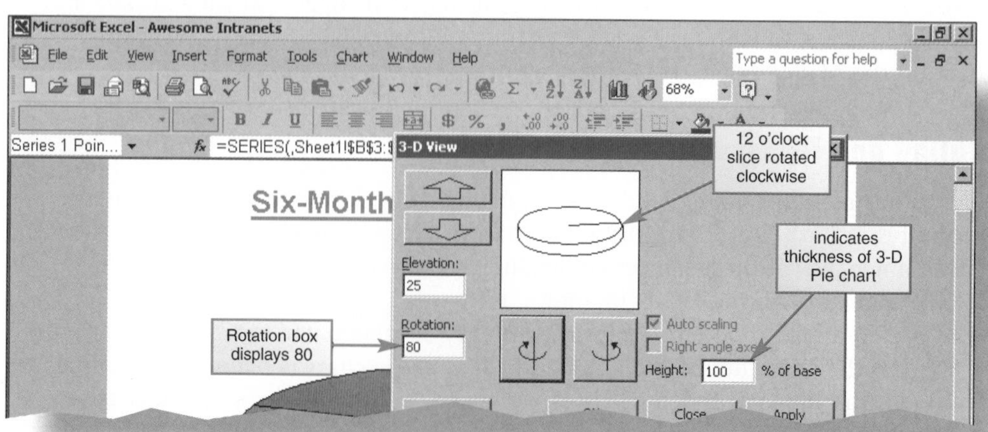

FIGURE 3-66

4 Click the OK button. Click outside the chart area.

Excel displays the 3-D Pie chart tilted forward and rotated to the left, which makes the space between the January slice and the main portion of the pie more prominent (Figure 3-67).

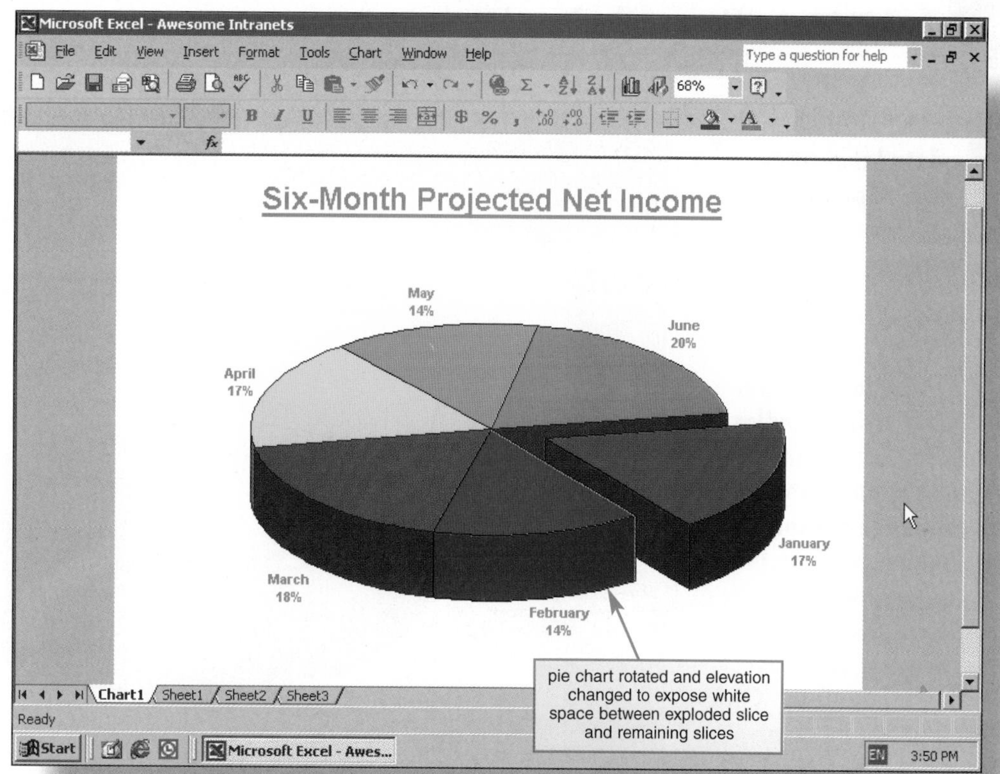

FIGURE 3-67

Compare Figure 3-67 with Figure 3-64. The offset of the January slice is more noticeable in Figure 3-67 because the pie chart has been tilted and rotated to expose the white space between the January slice and the main portion of the 3-D Pie chart.

In addition to controlling the rotation angle and elevation, you also can control the thickness of the 3-D Pie chart by entering a percent smaller or larger than the default 100% in the **Height text box** (Figure 3-66).

Changing a Pie Chart's Perspective

You can increase or decrease the base height (thickness) of the Pie chart by changing the height to base ratio in the Format 3-D View dialog box.

Adding Leader Lines to the Data Labels

If you drag the data labels away from each slice, Excel draws thin **leader lines** that connect each data label to its corresponding slice. If the leader lines do not display, click Chart Options on the Chart menu, click the Data Labels tab, and click the Show leader lines option button (Figure 3-56 on page E 3.47). Perform the steps on the next page to add leader lines to the data labels.

To Add Leader Lines to the Data Labels

1 Click the January data label twice. (Do not double-click.)

Excel displays a box with handles around the January data label.

2 Point to the upper-left sizing handles on the box border and drag the January data label away from the January slice. Select and drag the remaining data labels away from their corresponding slices as shown in Figure 3-68. Click outside the chart area.

The data labels display with leader lines as shown in Figure 3-68.

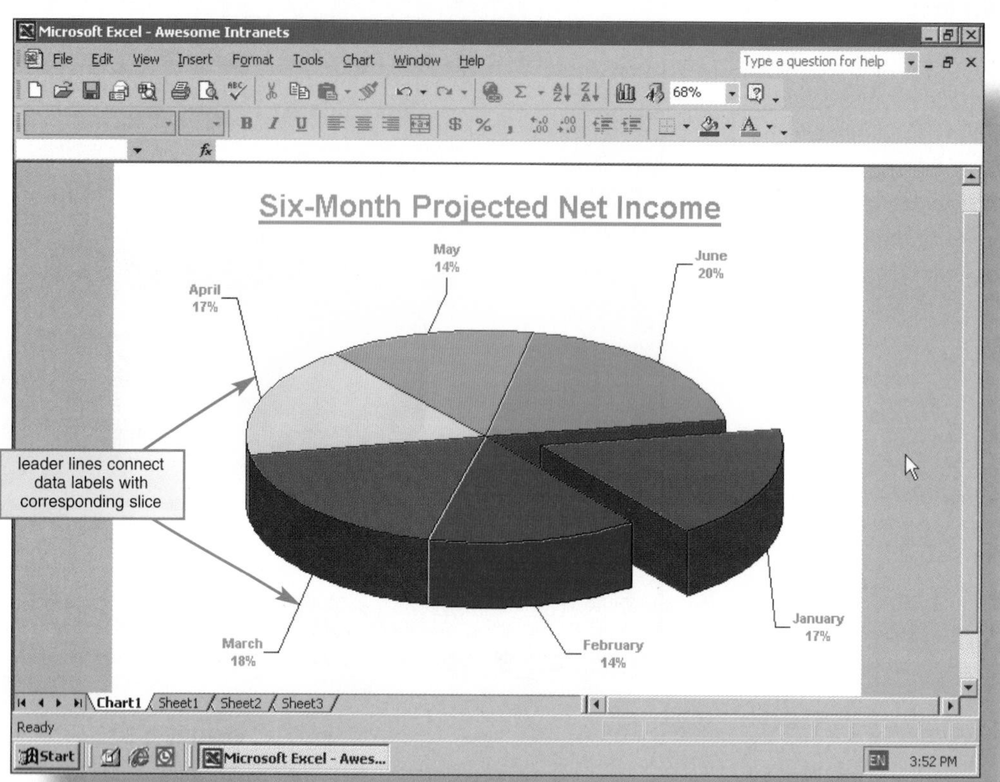

FIGURE 3-68

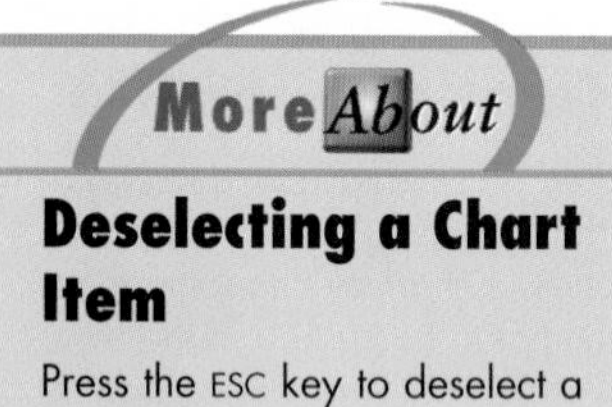

Deselecting a Chart Item

Press the ESC key to deselect a chart item.

You also can select and format individual labels by clicking a specific data label after all the data labels have been selected. Making an individual data label larger or a different color, for example, helps you emphasize a small or large slice in a pie chart.

Renaming and Reordering the Sheets and Coloring Their Tabs

The final step in creating the workbook is to adjust the tabs at the bottom of the screen. The following steps show you how to rename the sheets, color the tabs, and reorder the sheets so the worksheet precedes the chart sheet.

Steps To Rename and Reorder the Sheets, and Color Their Tabs

1 **Double-click the tab labeled Chart1 at the bottom of the screen. Type** `3-D Pie Chart` **as the new tab label. Press the ENTER key. Right-click the tab and point to Tab Color on the shortcut menu.**

The label on the Chart1 tab changes to 3-D Pie Chart (Figure 3-69). The shortcut menu displays.

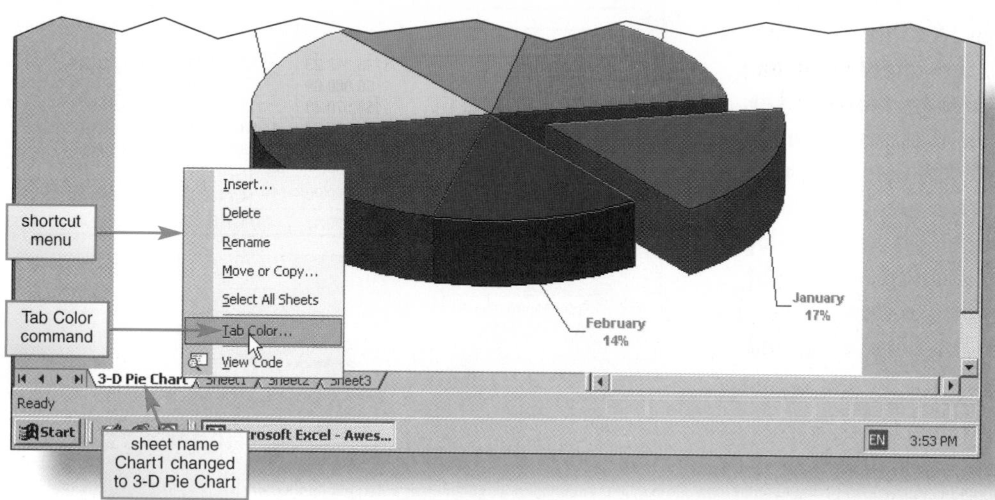

FIGURE 3-69

2 **Click Tab Color. When the Format Tab Color dialog box displays, click Red (column 1, row 3) in the Tab Color area. Point to the OK button.**

The Format Tab Color dialog box displays as shown in Figure 3-70.

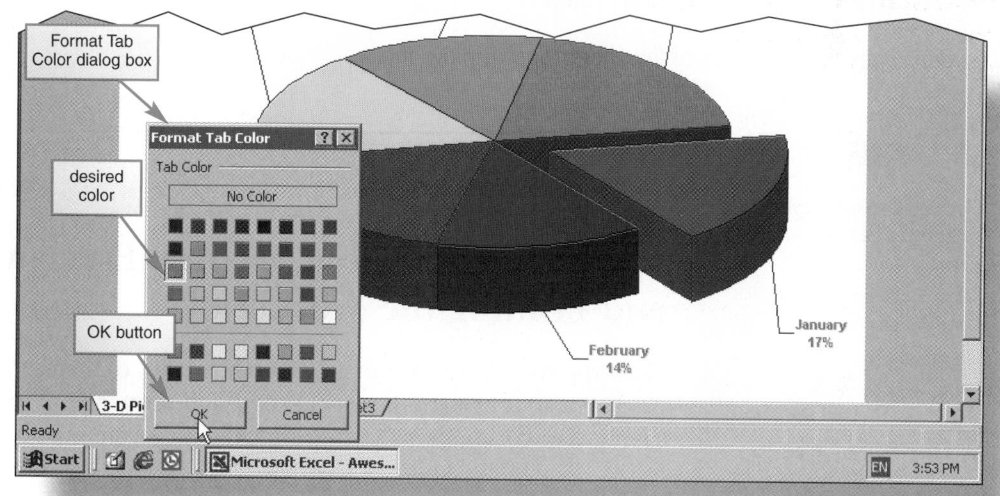

FIGURE 3-70

3 **Click the OK button.**

Excel displays the name on the tab with a red underline (Figure 3-71). The red underline indicates the sheet is active. When the sheet is inactive, the tab will display with a red background.

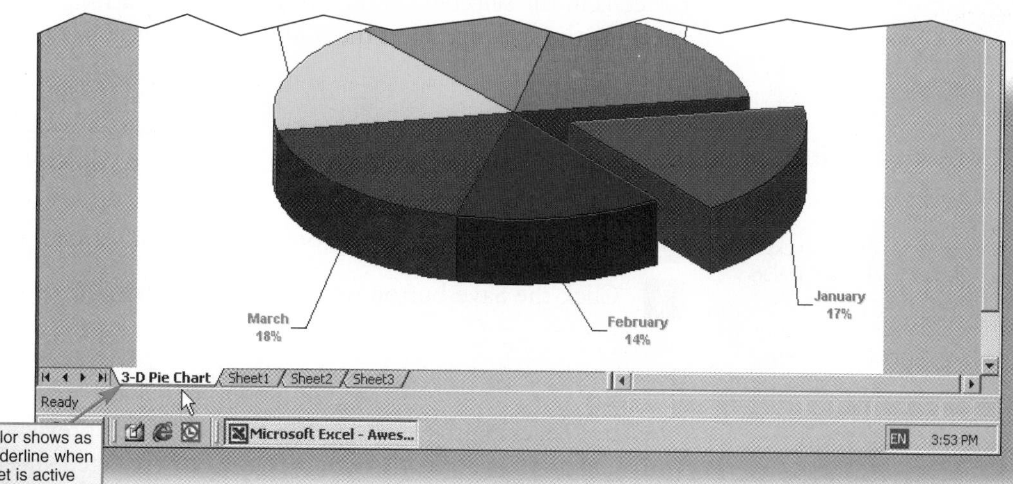

FIGURE 3-71

4 **Double-click the tab labeled Sheet1 at the bottom of the screen. Type** `Six-Month Plan` **as the new sheet name and then press the ENTER key. Right-click the tab and click Tab Color on the shortcut menu. When the Format Tab Color dialog box displays, click Light Yellow (column 3, row 5) in the Tab Color area, and then click the OK button.**

Excel displays the name on the tab with a yellow underline.

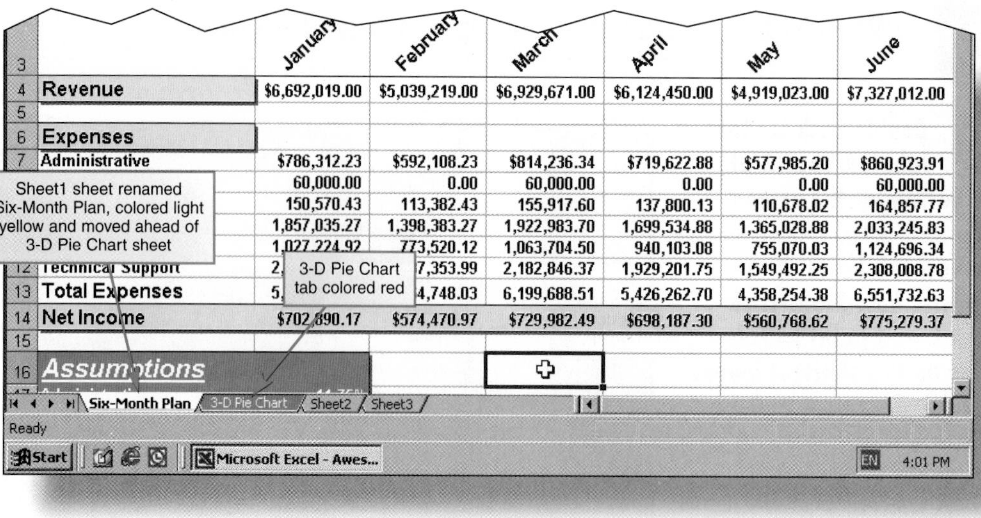

FIGURE 3-72

5 **Drag the Six-Month Plan tab to the left in front of the 3-D Pie Chart tab. Click cell D16 to deselect the chart ranges.**

Excel rearranges the sequence of the sheets and displays the worksheet (Figure 3-72).

Other Ways

1. To rename sheet, right-click sheet tab, click Rename on shortcut menu
2. To move sheet, on Edit menu click Move or Copy
3. To move sheet, right-click sheet tab, click Move or Copy on shortcut menu
4. To move sheet, in Voice Command mode say, "Edit, Move" or "Edit, Copy"

Checking Spelling, Saving, Previewing, and Printing the Workbook

With the workbook complete, the next series of steps checks spelling, saves, previews, and prints the workbook. Each sequence of steps concludes with saving the workbook to ensure that the latest changes are saved on disks.

Checking Spelling in Multiple Sheets

The spell checker checks the spelling only in the selected sheets. It will check all the cells in the selected sheets unless you select a range of two or more cells. Before checking the spelling, select the 3-D Pie Chart sheet as described in the following steps.

More About

Checking Spelling

Unless a range of cells or an object is selected when you check spelling, Excel checks the selected worksheet, including all cell values, cell comments, embedded charts, text boxes, buttons, and headers and footers.

TO CHECK SPELLING IN MULTIPLE SHEETS

1. With the Six-Month Plan sheet active, hold down the CTRL key and then click the 3-D Pie Chart tab.
2. Click the Spelling button on the Standard toolbar. Correct any errors.
3. Click the Save button on the Standard toolbar.

Previewing and Printing the Workbook

After checking the spelling, the next step is to preview and print the sheets. As with spelling, Excel previews and prints only selected sheets. Also, because the worksheet is too wide to print in portrait orientation, the orientation must be changed to landscape. Perform the following steps to preview and print the workbook.

TO PREVIEW AND PRINT THE WORKBOOK IN LANDSCAPE ORIENTATION

1. Ready the printer. If both sheets are not selected, hold down the CTRL key and then click the tab of the inactive sheet.
2. Click File on the menu bar and then click Page Setup. Click the Page tab and then click Landscape.
3. Click the Print Preview button in the Page Setup dialog box. When the preview of the first of the selected sheets displays, click the Next button to view the next sheet. Click the Previous button to redisplay the first sheet.
4. Click the Print button at the top of the Print Preview window. When the Print dialog box displays, click the OK button.
5. Right-click the Six-Month Plan tab. Click Ungroup Sheets on the shortcut menu to deselect the 3-D Pie Chart tab.
6. Click the Save button on the Standard toolbar.

The worksheet and 3-D Pie chart print as shown in Figures 3-73(a) and 3-73(b).

More About

Printing in Black and White

You can speed up the printing process and save ink if you do the following before printing: click File on the menu bar, click Page Setup, click the Sheet tab, click the Black and white check box.

Awesome Intranets

Six-Month Financial Projections 9/15/2003

	January	February	March	April	May	June	Total
Revenue	$6,692,019.00	$5,039,219.00	$6,929,671.00	$6,124,450.00	$4,919,023.00	$7,327,012.00	$37,031,394.00
Expenses							
Administrative	$786,312.23	$592,108.23	$814,236.34	$719,622.88	$577,985.20	$860,923.91	$4,351,188.80
Bonus	60,000.00	0.00	60,000.00	0.00	0.00	60,000.00	180,000.00
Commission	150,570.43	113,382.43	155,917.60	137,800.13	110,678.02	164,857.77	833,206.37
Equipment	1,857,035.27	1,398,383.27	1,922,983.70	1,699,534.88	1,365,028.88	2,033,245.83	10,276,211.84
Marketing	1,027,224.92	773,520.12	1,063,704.50	940,103.08	755,070.03	1,124,696.34	5,684,318.98
Technical Support	2,107,985.99	1,587,353.99	2,182,846.37	1,929,201.75	1,549,492.25	2,308,008.78	11,664,889.11
Total Expenses	5,989,128.83	4,464,748.03	6,199,688.51	5,426,262.70	4,358,254.38	6,551,732.63	32,989,815.08
Net Income	$702,890.17	$574,470.97	$729,982.49	$698,187.30	$560,768.62	$775,279.37	$4,041,578.92

Assumptions	
Administrative	11.75%
Bonus	60,000.00
Commission	2.25%
Equipment	27.75%
Marketing	15.35%
Revenue for Bonus	6,500,000.00
Technical Support	31.50%

(a) Worksheet

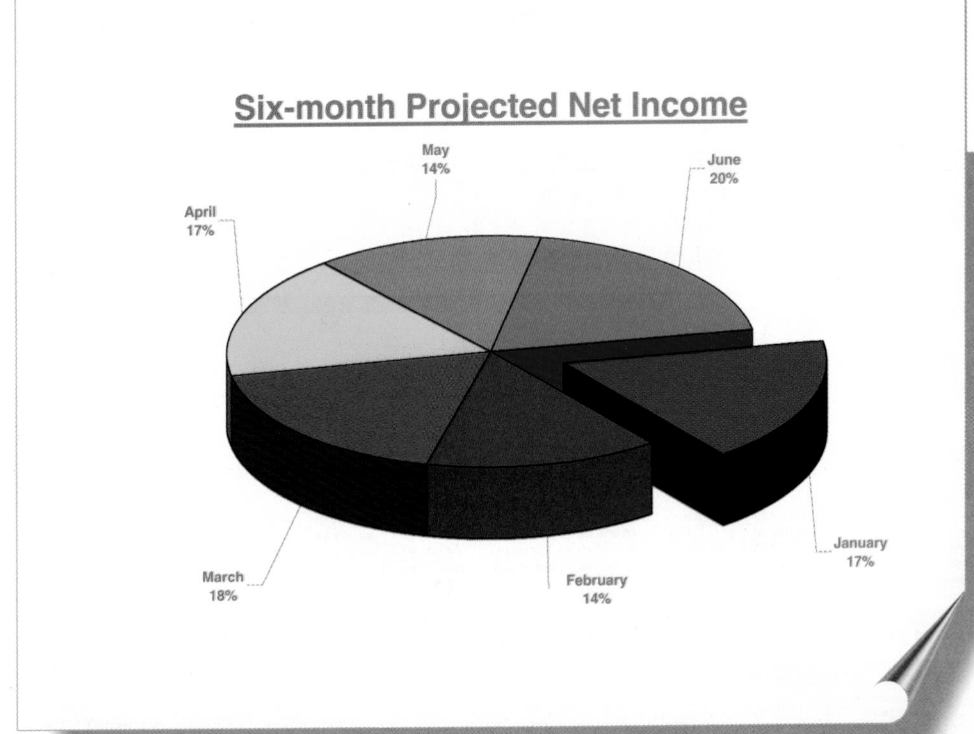

(b) 3-D Pie Chart

FIGURE 3-73

Zooming

You can type any number between 10 and 400 in the Zoom box on the Standard toolbar to reduce or enlarge the display of the worksheet.

Changing the View of the Worksheet

With Excel, you easily can change the view of the worksheet. For example, you can magnify or shrink the worksheet on the screen. You also can view different parts of the worksheet through **window panes**.

Shrinking and Magnifying the View of a Worksheet or Chart

You can magnify (zoom in) or shrink (zoom out) the display of a worksheet or chart by using the **Zoom box** on the Standard toolbar. When you magnify a worksheet, the characters on the screen become larger, and fewer columns and rows display. Alternatively, when you shrink a worksheet, more columns and rows display. Magnifying or shrinking a worksheet affects only the view; it does not change the window size or printout of the worksheet or chart. Perform the following steps to shrink and magnify the view of the worksheet.

Steps To Shrink and Magnify the View of a Worksheet or Chart

1 Click the Zoom box arrow on the Standard toolbar. Point to 75% in the Zoom list.

A list of percentages displays (Figure 3-74).

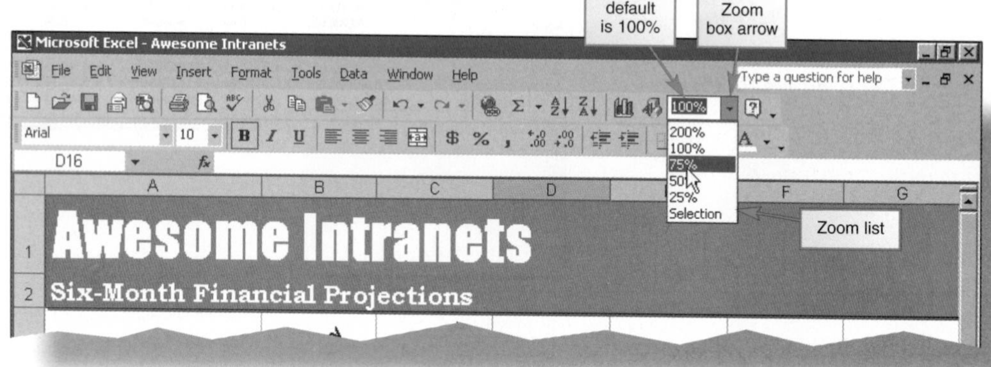

FIGURE 3-74

2 Click 75%.

Excel shrinks the display of the worksheet to 75% of its normal display (Figure 3-75). With the worksheet zoomed out to 75%, you can see more rows and columns than you did at 100% magnification. Many of the numbers, however, display as a series of number signs (#) because the columns are not wide enough to display the formatted numbers.

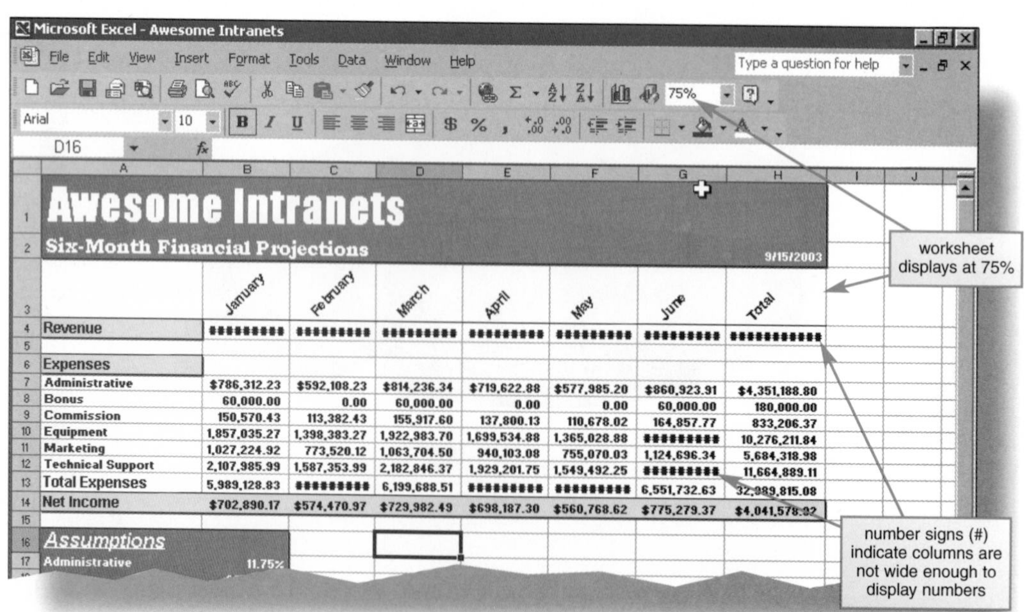

FIGURE 3-75

3 Click the Zoom box arrow on the Standard toolbar and then click 100%.

Excel returns to the default display of 100%.

4 Click the 3-D Pie Chart tab at the bottom of the screen. Click the Zoom box arrow on the Standard toolbar and then click 100%.

Excel changes the magnification of the chart from 68% (shown in Figure 3-68 on page E 3.54) to 100% (Figure 3-76). The chart displays at the same size as the printout of the chart.

5 Enter 68 in the Zoom box to return the chart to its original magnification.

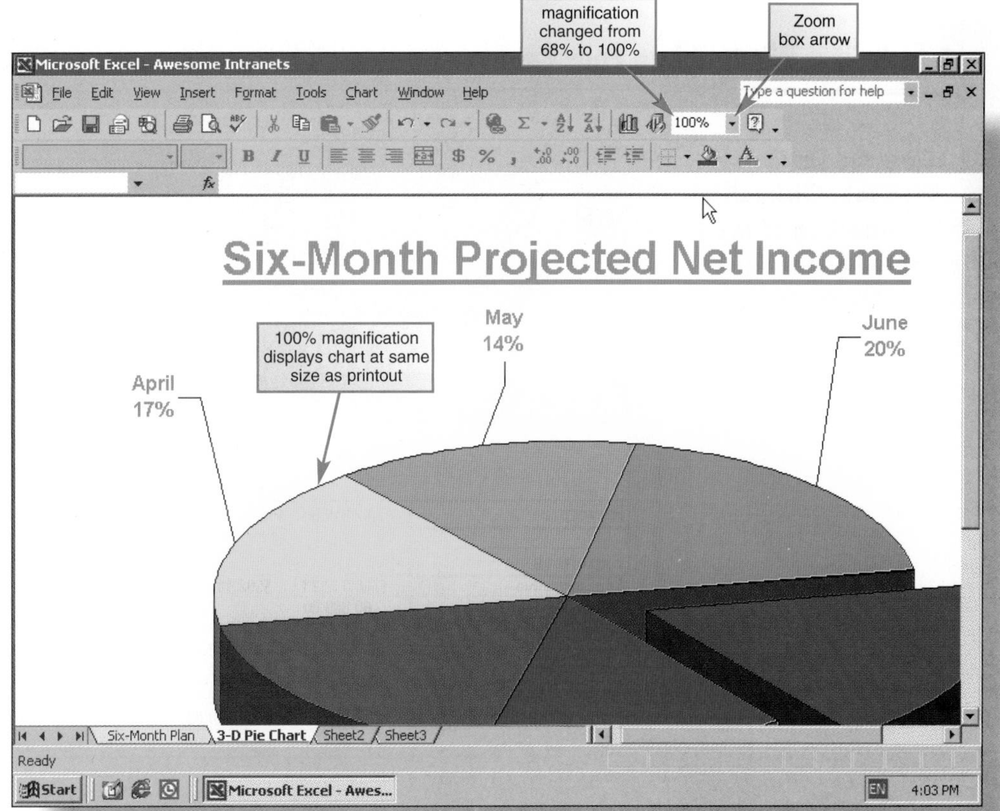

FIGURE 3-76

Other Ways

1. On View menu click Zoom, click desired percent magnification, click OK button
2. Type desired percent magnification in Zoom box on Standard toolbar
3. Press ALT+V, Z
4. In Voice Command mode say, "Zoom [desired percent magnification]"

Excel normally displays a chart at approximately 70% magnification at 800 × 600 resolution so that the entire chart displays on the screen. By changing the magnification to 100%, you can see only a part of the chart, but at a magnification that corresponds with the chart's size on a printout. Excel allows you to enter a percent magnification in the Zoom box between 10 and 400 for worksheets and chart sheets.

Splitting the Window into Panes

Previously in this project, you used the Freeze Panes command to freeze worksheet titles on a large worksheet so they always would display on the screen. When working with a large worksheet, you also can split the window into two or four window panes to view different parts of the worksheet at the same time. To split the window into four panes, select the cell where you want the four panes to intersect. Next, click the Split command on the Window menu. Follow the steps on the next page to split the window into four panes.

Steps To Split a Window into Four Panes

1 Click the Six-Month Plan tab. Click cell D5, the intersection of the four proposed panes. Click Window on the menu bar and then point to Split.

The Window menu displays (Figure 3-77).

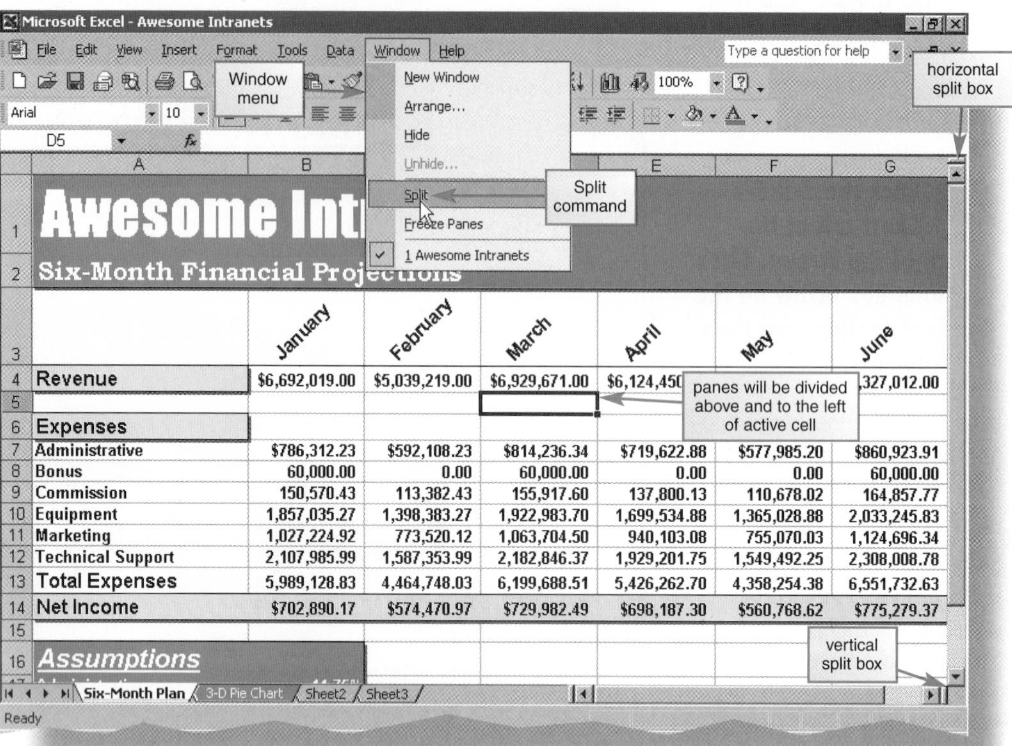

FIGURE 3-77

2 Click Split. Use the scroll arrows to display the four corners of the worksheet.

Excel divides the window into four panes, and the four corners of the worksheet display (Figure 3-78).

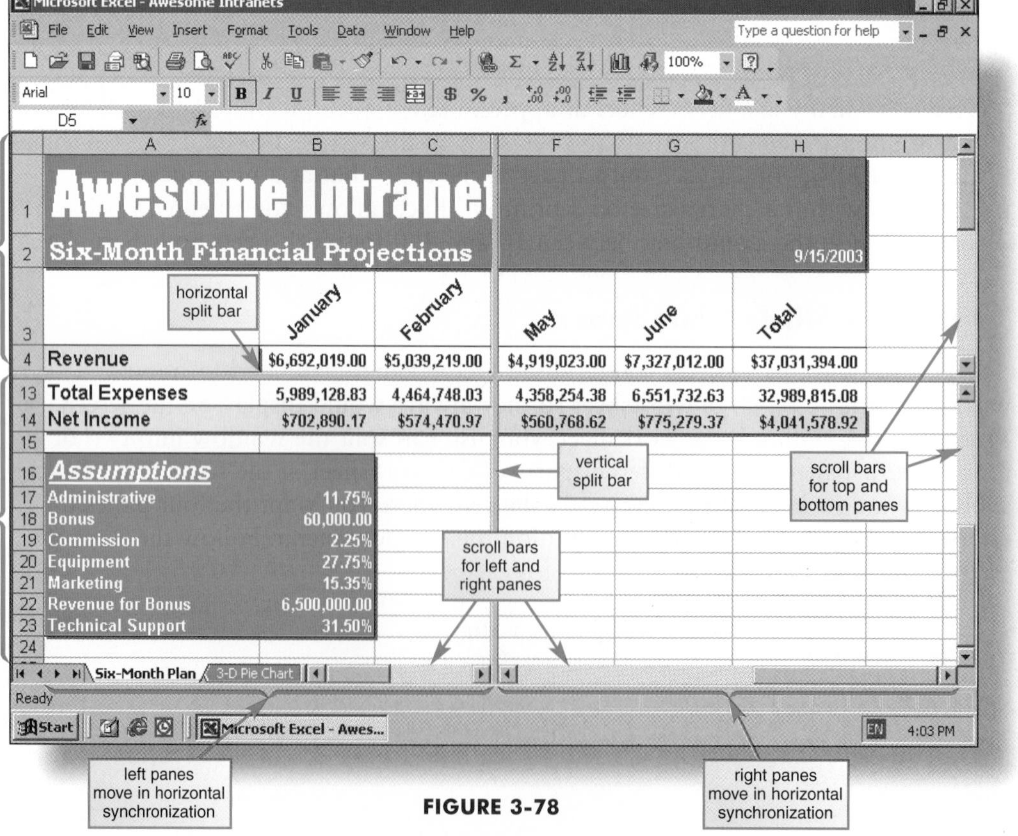

FIGURE 3-78

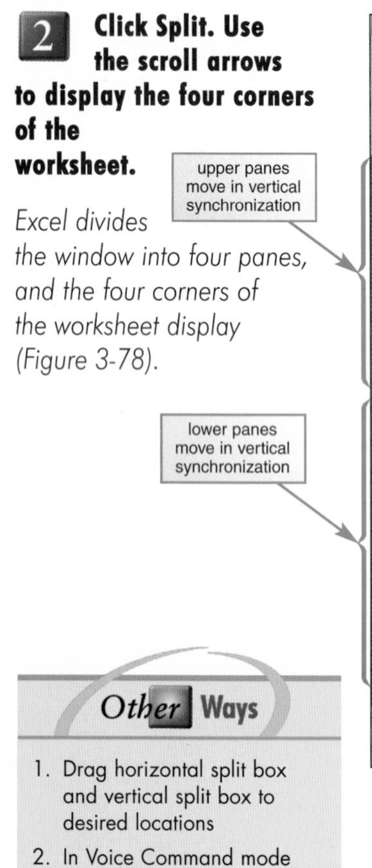

Other Ways

1. Drag horizontal split box and vertical split box to desired locations
2. In Voice Command mode say, "Window, Split"

The four panes in Figure 3-78 are used to display the following: (1) the upper-left pane displays the range A1:C4; (2) the upper-right pane displays the range F1:I4; (3) the lower-left pane displays the range A13:C24; and (4) the lower-right pane displays the range F13:I24.

The vertical bar going up and down the middle of the window is called the **vertical split bar.** The horizontal bar going across the middle of the window is called the **horizontal split bar.** If you use the scroll bars below the window and to the right of the window to scroll the window, you will see that the panes split by the horizontal split bar scroll together vertically. The panes split by the vertical split bar scroll together horizontally. To resize the panes, drag either split bar to the desired location in the window.

You can change the values of cells in any of the four panes. Any change you make in one pane also takes effect in the other panes. To remove one of the split bars from the window, drag the split box to the edge of the window or double-click the split bar. Follow these steps to remove both split bars.

More About

Window Panes

If you want to split the window into two panes, rather than four, drag the vertical split box or horizontal split box (Figure 3-77) to the desired location. You can also drag the center of the four panes in any direction to change the size of the panes.

TO REMOVE THE FOUR PANES FROM THE WINDOW

1. Position the mouse pointer at the intersection of the horizontal and vertical split bars.
2. Double-click the split four-headed arrow.

Excel removes the four panes from the window.

What-If Analysis

The automatic recalculation feature of Excel is a powerful tool that can be used to analyze worksheet data. Using Excel to scrutinize the impact of changing values in cells that are referenced by a formula in another cell is called **what-if analysis** or **sensitivity analysis.** Excel not only recalculates all formulas in a worksheet when new data is entered, but also redraws any associated charts.

In Project 3, the projected monthly expenses and net incomes in the range B7:G14 are dependent on the assumptions in the range B17:B23. Thus, if you change any of the assumption values, Excel immediately recalculates the projected monthly expenses in rows 7 through 12, and the projected monthly expenses and net incomes in rows 13 and 14. Finally, because the projected monthly net incomes in row 14 change, Excel redraws the 3-D Pie chart, which is based on these numbers.

A what-if question for the worksheet in Project 3 might be, what if the Bonus, Equipment, and Marketing assumptions in the Assumptions table are changed as follows: Bonus $60,000.00 to $40,000.00; Equipment 27.75% to 15.50%; Marketing 15.35% to 10.00% — how would these changes affect the projected six-month total net income in cell H14? To answer a question like this, you need to change only the second, fourth, and fifth values in the Assumptions table. Excel instantaneously recalculates the worksheet and redraws the 3-D Pie chart to answer the question regarding the projected six-month total net income in cell H14.

The steps on the next page change the three assumptions as indicated in the previous paragraph and determine the new projected six-month total net income in cell H14. To ensure that the Assumptions table and the projected six-month total net income in cell H14 display on the screen at the same time, the steps also divide the window into two vertical panes.

More About

What-If Analysis

Besides manually changing assumptions in a worksheet, Excel has additional methods for answering what-if questions, including Goal Seeking, Solver, Pivot Tables, Scenario Manager, and the Analysis ToolPak. For more information, enter each of these what-if tools in the Ask a Question box on the menu bar.

Steps To Analyze Data in a Worksheet by Changing Values

1 Use the vertical scroll bar to move the window so cell A4 is in the upper-left corner of the screen.

2 Drag the vertical split box (see Figure 3-77 on page E 3.60) from the lower-right corner of the screen to the left so that the vertical split bar is positioned in the middle of column F. Use the right scroll arrow to display the totals in column H in the right pane. Click cell B18 in the left pane.

Excel divides the window into two vertical panes and shows the totals in column H in the pane on the right side of the window (Figure 3-79).

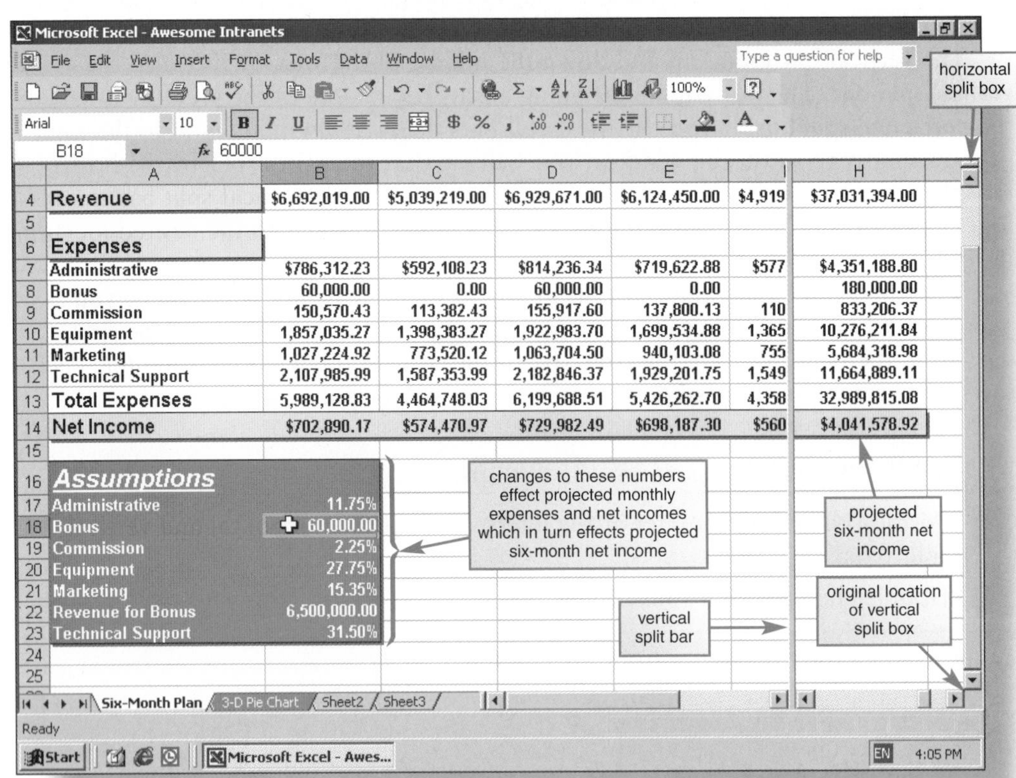

FIGURE 3-79

3 Enter 40000 **in cell B18,** 15.5 **in cell B20, and** 10 **in cell B21.**

Excel immediately recalculates all the formulas in the worksheet, including the projected six-month total net income in cell H14 (Figure 3-80).

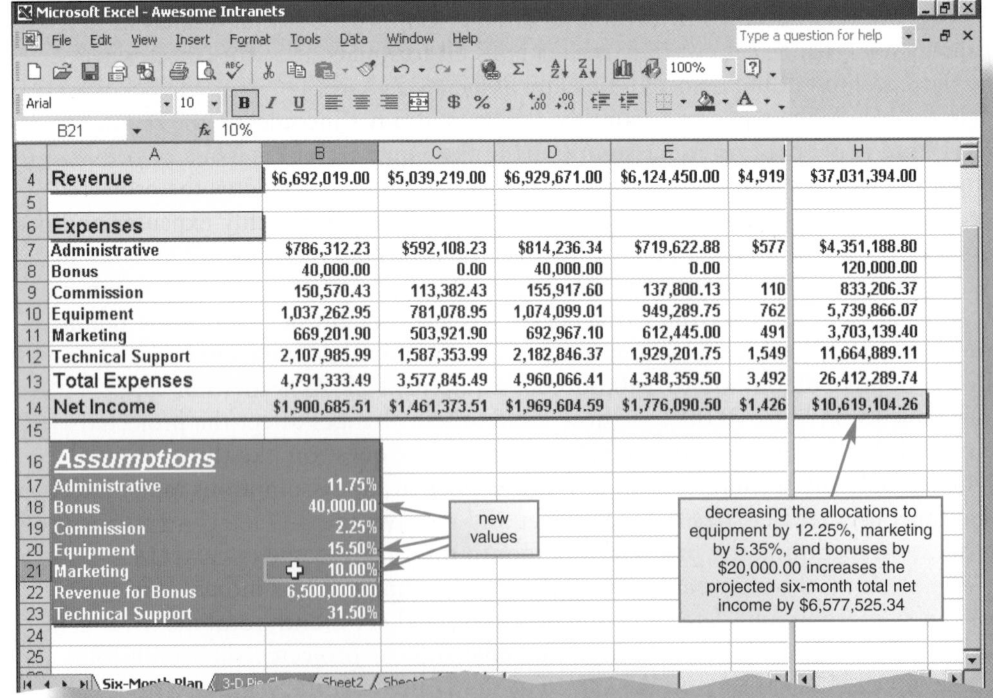

FIGURE 3-80

Each time you enter a new assumption, Excel recalculates the worksheet and redraws the 3-D Pie chart. This process usually takes less than one second, depending on how many calculations must be performed and the speed of your computer. Compare the projected six-month total net incomes in cell H14 in Figures 3-79 and 3-80. By changing the values of the three assumptions (Figure 3-80), the projected six-month total net income in cell H14 increases from $4,041,578.92 to $10,619,104.26. This translates into an increase of $6,577,525.34 for the projected six-month total net income.

Undo

The Undo button is ideal for returning the worksheet to its original state after you have changed the values in a worksheet to answer a what-if question. To display the original worksheet after answering a what-if question, click the Undo button for each value you changed.

Goal Seeking

If you know the result you want a formula to produce, you can use **goal seeking** to determine the value of a cell on which the formula depends. The following steps close and reopen the Awesome Intranets workbook and use the **Goal Seek command** on the Tools menu to determine what projected technical support percentage in cell B23 will yield a projected six-month total net income of $6,000,000.00 in cell H14, rather than $4,041,578.92.

To Goal Seek

1 Close the Awesome Intranets workbook without saving changes. Click the Open button on the Standard toolbar and then reopen Awesome Intranets.

2 Drag the vertical split box to the middle of column F. Scroll down so row 4 is at the top of the screen. Display column H in the right pane. Click cell H14, the cell that contains the projected six-month total net income. Click Tools on the menu bar and then point to Goal Seek.

The vertical split bar displays in the middle of column F, and the Tools menu displays (Figure 3-81).

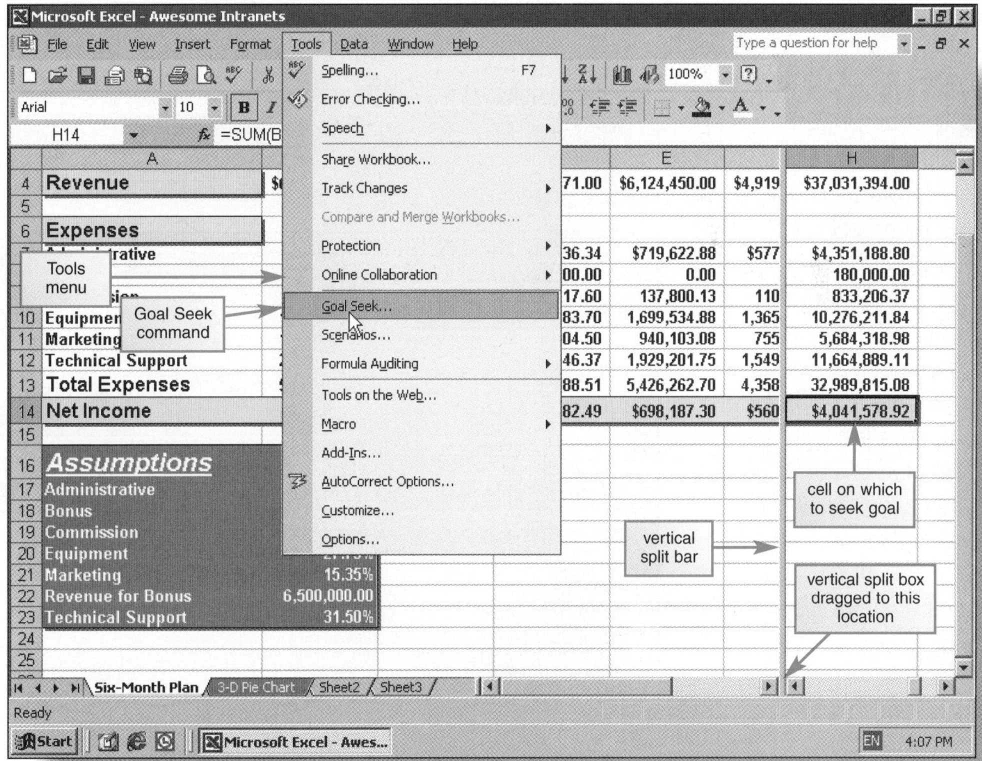

FIGURE 3-81

3 Click Goal Seek.

The Goal Seek dialog box displays. The Set cell box is assigned the cell reference of the active cell in the worksheet (cell H14) automatically.

4 Click the To value text box. Type 6,000,000 **and then click the By changing cell box. Click cell B23 on the worksheet and then point to the OK button.**

The Goal Seek dialog box displays as shown in Figure 3-82. A marquee displays around cell B23.

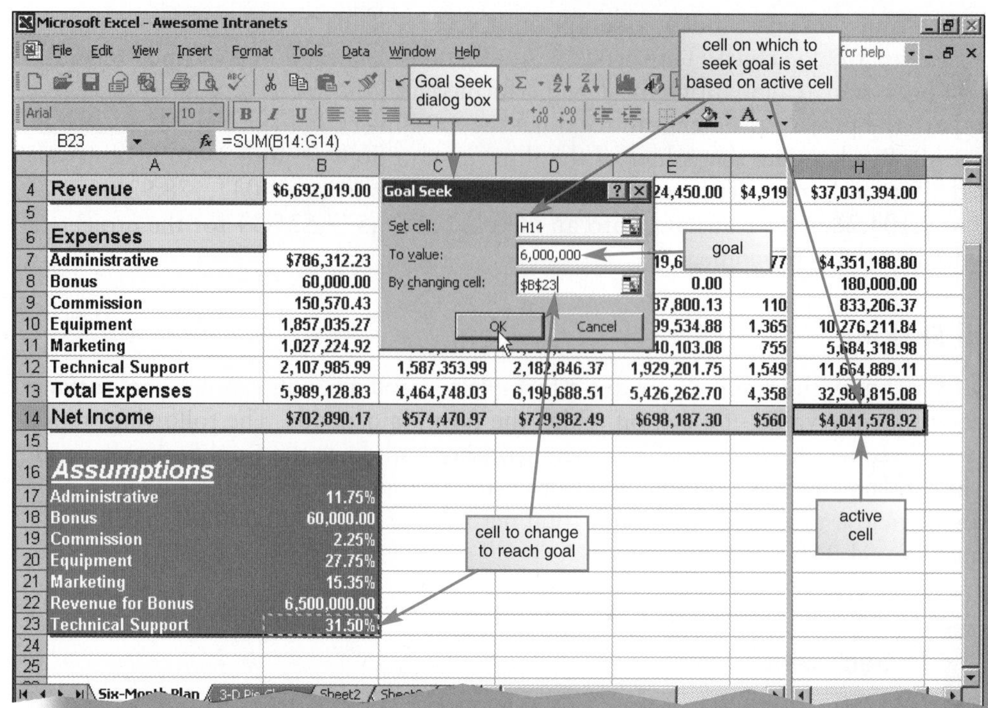

FIGURE 3-82

5 Click the OK button.

Excel immediately changes cell H14 from $4,041,578.92 to the desired value of $6,000,000.00. More importantly, Excel changes the technical support assumption in cell B23 from 31.50% to 26.21% (Figure 3-83). Excel also displays the Goal Seek Status dialog box. If you click the OK button, Excel keeps the new values in the worksheet. If you click the Cancel button, Excel redisplays the original values.

6 Click the Cancel button in the Goal Seek Status dialog box.

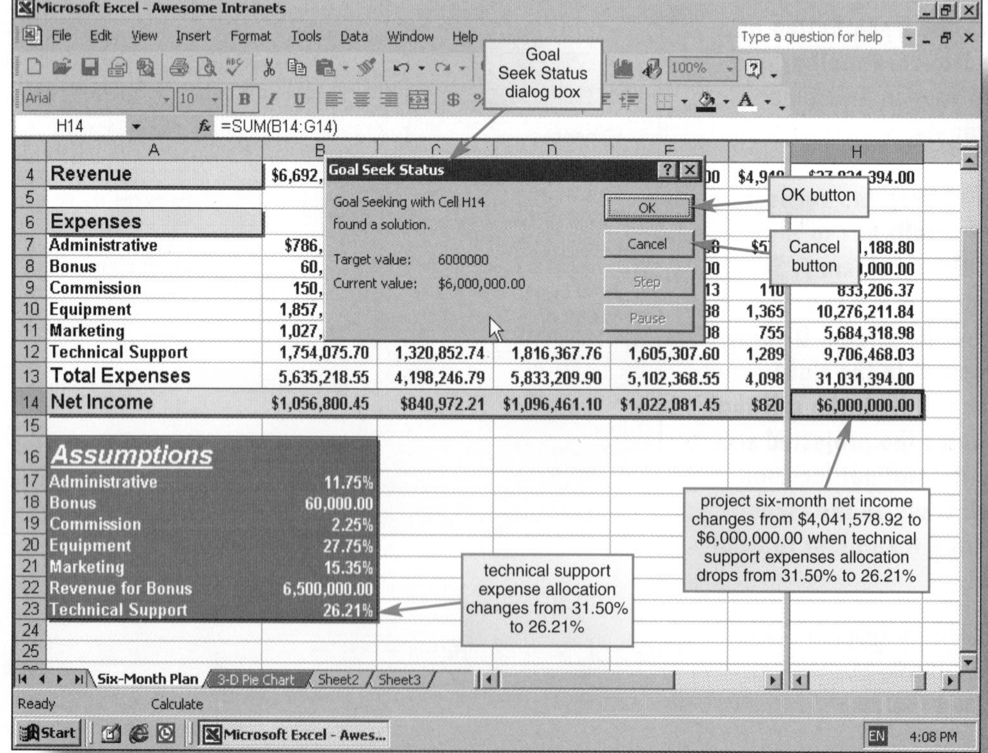

FIGURE 3-83

Other Ways

1. Press ALT+T, G
2. In Voice Command mode say, "Tools, Goal Seek," enter desired values, in Voice Command mode say, "OK"

Goal seeking assumes you can change the value of only one cell referenced directly or indirectly. In this example, to change the projected six-month total net income in cell H14 to $6,000,000.00, the technical support percentage in cell B23 must decrease by 5.29% from 31.50% to 26.21%.

You can see from this goal seeking example that the cell to change (cell B23) does not have to be referenced directly in the formula or function. For example, the projected six-month total net income in cell H14 is calculated by the function =SUM(B14:G14). Cell B23 is not referenced in the function. Instead, cell B23 is referenced in the formulas in rows 7 through 12, on which the projected monthly net incomes in row 14 are based. Excel is capable of goal seeking on the projected six-month total net income by varying the technical support assumption.

More About

Goal Seeking

Goal seeking is a methodology in which you know what answer you want a formula in a cell to be, but you do not know the value to place in a cell that is involved in the formula. You can goal seek by changing the value in a cell that is indirectly used in the formula as illustrated in Figures 3-82 and 3-83.

Quitting Excel

To quit Excel, complete the following steps.

TO QUIT EXCEL

1. Click the Close button on the title bar.
2. If the Microsoft Excel dialog box displays, click the No button.

CASE PERSPECTIVE SUMMARY

With the worksheet and chart developed in this project, the CEO of Awesome Intranets, Maria Cianti, easily can respond to any what-if questions brought up by her senior management team the next time she presents her semi-annual plan. Questions that took several minutes to answer with paper and pencil now can be answered in a few seconds. Furthermore, computational errors are less likely to occur.

Project Summary

In creating the Awesome Intranets workbook, you learned how to work with large worksheets that extend beyond the window and how to use the fill handle to create a series. You learned to display hidden toolbars, dock a toolbar at the bottom of the screen, and hide an active toolbar. You learned about the difference between absolute cell references and relative cell references and how to use the IF function. You also learned how to rotate text in a cell, generate a series, freeze titles, change the magnification of the worksheet, display different parts of the worksheet through panes, create a 3-D Pie chart, and improve the appearance of a 3-D Pie chart. Finally, this project introduced you to using Excel to do what-if analysis by changing values in cells and goal seeking.

More About

The Quick Reference

For a table that lists how to complete the tasks covered in this book using the mouse, menu, shortcut menu, and keyboard, see the Quick Reference Summary at the back of this book or visit the Shelly Cashman Series Office site (scsite.com/offxp/qr.htm) and click the application name.

What You Should Know

Having completed this project, you now should be able to perform the following tasks:

- Add a Drop Shadow *(E 3.40)*
- Add Leader Lines to the Data Labels *(E 3.54)*
- Analyze Data in a Worksheet by Changing Values *(E 3.62)*
- Assign Formats to Nonadjacent Ranges *(E 3.33)*
- Bold the Font of the Entire Worksheet *(E 3.07)*
- Change Font Size, Add Background Colors, and Add Drop Shadows to Nonadjacent Selections *(E 3.41)*
- Change the Colors of the Pie Slices *(E 3.50)*
- Check Spelling in Multiple Sheets *(E 3.56)*
- Copy a Cell's Format Using the Format Painter Button *(E 3.11)*
- Copy a Range of Cells to a Nonadjacent Destination Area *(E 3.14)*
- Copy the Projected January Expenses and Net Income Using the Fill Handle *(E 3.30)*
- Determine the Projected Total Expenses by Category and Total Net Income *(E 3.31)*
- Display the Drawing Toolbar *(E 3.38)*
- Dock a Toolbar at the Bottom of the Screen *(E 3.39)*
- Draw a 3-D Pie Chart on a Separate Chart Sheet *(E 3.44)*
- Enter a Formula Containing Absolute Cell References *(E 3.26)*
- Enter a Number with a Format Symbol *(E 3.19)*
- Enter an IF Function *(E 3.28)*
- Enter and Format the System Date *(E 3.23)*
- Enter the Projected Revenue *(E 3.21)*
- Enter the Remaining Projected January Expense and Net Income Formulas *(E 3.29)*
- Enter the Worksheet Titles *(E 3.07)*
- Explode the 3-D Pie Chart *(E 3.51)*
- Format the Assumptions Table *(E 3.42)*
- Format the Chart Title and Data Labels *(E 3.49)*
- Format the Worksheet Titles *(E 3.36)*
- Freeze Column and Row Titles *(E 3.20)*
- Goal Seek *(E 3.53)*
- Hide the Drawing Toolbar and Save the Workbook *(E 3.43)*
- Increase Column Widths and Enter Row Titles *(E 3.12)*
- Insert a Row *(E 3.17)*
- Preview and Print the Workbook in Landscape Orientation *(E 3.57)*
- Quit Excel *(E 3.65)*
- Remove the Four Panes from the Window *(E 3.61)*
- Rename and Reorder the Sheets, and Color Their Tabs *(E 3.55)*
- Rotate and Tilt the 3-D Pie Chart *(E 3.52)*
- Rotate Text and Use the Fill Handle to Create a Series of Month Names *(E 3.08)*
- Save the Workbook *(E 3.20)*
- Shrink and Magnify the View of a Worksheet or Chart *(E 3.58)*
- Split a Window into Four Panes *(E 3.60)*
- Start and Customize Excel *(E 3.07)*
- Unfreeze the Worksheet Titles and Save the Workbook *(E 3.31)*

More About

Microsoft Certification

The Microsoft Office User Specialist (MOUS) Certification program provides an opportunity for you to obtain a valuable industry credential - proof that you have the Excel 2002 skills required by employers. For more information, see Appendix E or visit the Shelly Cashman Series MOUS Web page at scsite.com/offxp/cert.htm.

Learn It Online

Instructions: To complete the Learn It Online exercises, start your browser, click the Address bar, and then enter `scsite.com/offxp/exs.htm`. When the Office XP Learn It Online page displays, follow the instructions in the exercises below.

1 Project Reinforcement TF, MC, and SA

Below Excel Project 3, click the Project Reinforcement link. Print the quiz by clicking Print on the File menu. Answer each question. Write your first and last name at the top of each page, and then hand in the printout to your instructor.

2 Flash Cards

Below Excel Project 3, click the Flash Cards link. When Flash Cards displays, read the instructions. Type `20` (or a number specified by your instructor) in the Number of Playing Cards text box, type your name in the Name text box, and then click the Flip Card button. When the flash card displays, read the question and then click the Answer box arrow to select an answer. Flip through Flash Cards. Click Print on the File menu to print the last flash card if your score is 15 (75%) correct or greater and then hand it in to your instructor. If your score is less than 15 (75%) correct, then redo this exercise by clicking the Replay button.

3 Practice Test

Below Excel Project 3, click the Practice Test link. Answer each question, enter your first and last name at the bottom of the page, and then click the Grade Test button. When the graded practice test displays on your screen, click Print on the File menu to print a hard copy. Continue to take practice tests until you score 80% or better. Hand in a printout of the final practice test to your instructor.

4 Who Wants to Be a Computer Genius?

Below Excel Project 3, click the Computer Genius link. Read the instructions, enter your first and last name at the bottom of the page, and then click the Play button. Hand in your score to your instructor.

5 Wheel of Terms

Below Excel Project 3, click the Wheel of Terms link. Read the instructions, and then enter your first and last name and your school name. Click the Play button. Hand in your score to your instructor.

6 Crossword Puzzle Challenge

Below Excel Project 3, click the Crossword Puzzle Challenge link. Read the instructions, and then enter your first and last name. Click the Play button. Work the crossword puzzle. When you are finished, click the Submit button. When the crossword puzzle redisplays, click the Print button. Hand in the printout.

7 Tips and Tricks

Below Excel Project 3, click the Tips and Tricks link. Click a topic that pertains to Project 3. Right-click the information and then click Print on the shortcut menu. Construct a brief example of what the information relates to in Excel to confirm you understand how to use the tip or trick. Hand in the example and printed information.

8 Newsgroups

Below Excel Project 3, click the Newsgroups link. Click a topic that pertains to Project 3. Print three comments. Hand in the comments to your instructor.

9 Expanding Your Horizons

Below Excel Project 3, click the Articles for Microsoft Excel link. Click a topic that pertains to Project 3. Print the information. Construct a brief example of what the information relates to in Excel to confirm you understand the contents of the article. Hand in the example and printed information to your instructor.

10 Search Sleuth

Below Excel Project 3, click the Search Sleuth link. To search for a term that pertains to this project, select a term below the Project 3 title and then use the Google search engine at google.com (or any major search engine) to display and print two Web pages that present information on the term. Hand in the printouts to your instructor.

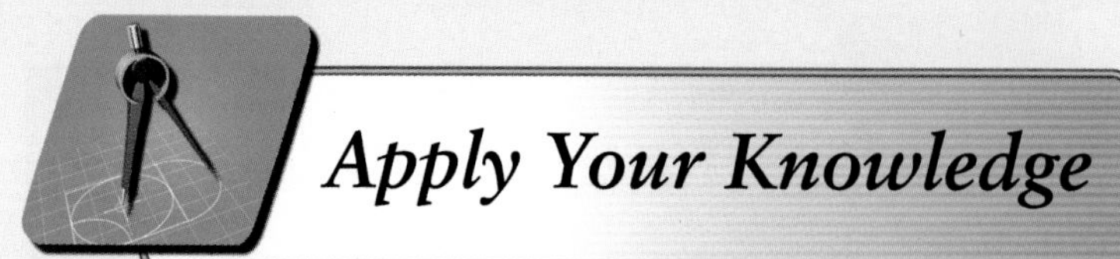

1 Understanding the IF Function and Absolute Referencing

Instructions: Fill in the correct answers.

1. Determine the truth value (true or false) of the following logical tests, given the following cell values: X4 = 40; Y3 = 49; K7 = 120; Z2 = 10; and Q9 = 25. Enter true or false.
   a. Y3 < X4 Truth value: ____________
   b. Q9 = K7 Truth value: ____________
   c. X4 + 15 * Z2 / 5 <> K7 Truth value: ____________
   d. K7 / Z2 > X4 – Y3 Truth value: ____________
   e. Q9 * 2 – 42 < (X4 + Y3 - 8) / 9 Truth value: ____________
   f. K7 + 300 <= X4 * Z2 + 10 Truth value: ____________
   g. Q9 + K7 > 2 * (Q9 + 25) Truth value: ____________
   h. X4 + Z2 <> 2 * (Q9 / 5) Truth value: ____________
2. Write an IF function for cell G7 that assigns the value of cell B7 to cell G7 if the value in cell K6 is greater than the value in cell H7; otherwise, have the IF function assign zero (0) to cell G7.
   Function: ____________
3. Write an IF function for cell J8 that assigns the text "OK" if the value in cell L9 is three times greater than the value in cell M6; otherwise, have the IF function assign the text "Not OK" to cell J8.
   Function: ____________
4. A nested IF function is an IF function that contains another IF function in the value_if_true or value_if_false arguments. For example, =IF(A1 = "NY","Region 1", IF(A1 = "MI", "Region 2", "Not Applicable")) is a valid nested IF function. Start Excel and enter this IF function in cell B1 and then use the fill handle to copy the function down through cell B7. Enter the following data in the cells in the range A1:A7 and then write down the results that display in cells B1 through B7 for each set. Set 1: A1 = IL; A2 = NY; A3 = NY; A4 = MI; A5 = NY; A6 = MI; A7 = NY. Set 2: A1= WI; A2 = KY; A3 = NY; A4 = IL; A5 = NY; A6 = NY; A7 = IL.
   Set 1 Results: ____________
   Set 2 Results: ____________
5. Write cell X49 as a relative reference, absolute reference, mixed reference with the row varying, and mixed reference with the column varying.
   ____________ ____________ ____________ ____________
6. Write the formula for cell J8 that divides cell K4 by the sum of cells M7 through M10. Write the formula so that when it is copied to cells K8 and L8, cell K4 remains absolute.
   Formula: ____________
7. Write the formula for cell T5 that divides cell V5 by the sum of cells C4, D4, and E4. Write the formula so that when it is copied to cells T6, T7, and T8, cell V5 remains absolute.
   Formula: ____________
8. Write the formula for cell A2 that multiplies cell U4 by the sum of cells M7 through M12. Write the formula so that when it is copied to cells A2 and A3, Excel adjusts all the cell references according to the new location.
   Formula: ____________

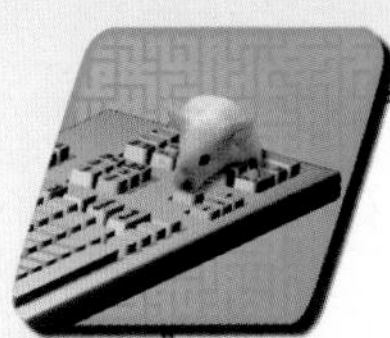

In the Lab

1 Tamiami Medical Supply Seven-Year Financial Plan

Problem: As the spreadsheet specialist at Tamiami Medical Supply, you have been asked to create a worksheet that will project the revenue, expenses, taxes, and income for the next seven years based on the assumptions in Table 3-6. The desired worksheet is shown in Figure 3-84.

Table 3-6 Data for Assumptions	
Units Sold in Year 2002	9,492,016
Unit Cost	7.23
Annual Sales Growth	5.95%
Annual Price Decrease	5.50%
Margin	40.75%

Tamiami Medical Supply

Seven-Year Plan — 1/3/2003

	2003	2004	2005	2006	2007	2008	2009
Revenue	115,826,626	115,968,803	116,111,155	116,253,681	116,396,382	116,539,259	116,682,311
Cost of Goods Sold	68,627,276	68,711,516	68,795,859	68,880,306	68,964,857	69,049,511	69,134,269
Margin	47,199,350	47,257,287	47,315,295	47,373,375	47,431,526	47,489,748	47,548,042
Expenses							
Advertising	17,374,994	17,396,320	17,417,673	17,439,052	17,460,457	17,481,889	17,503,347
Maintenance	1,900,000	5,397,000	4,200,000	5,150,000	2,500,000	3,150,000	2,960,000
Rent	1,800,000	1,980,000	2,178,000	2,395,800	2,635,380	2,898,918	3,188,810
Salaries	20,848,793	20,874,385	20,900,008	20,925,663	20,951,349	20,977,067	21,002,816
Supplies	1,737,399	1,739,532	1,741,667	1,743,805	1,745,946	1,748,089	1,750,235
Total Expenses	43,661,186	47,387,237	46,437,348	47,654,320	45,293,132	46,255,962	46,405,207
Income Before Taxes	3,538,164	(129,950)	877,947	(280,945)	2,138,394	1,233,786	1,142,835
Income Taxes	1,415,266	0	351,179	0	855,358	493,514	457,134
Net Income	2,122,898	(129,950)	526,768	(280,945)	1,283,036	740,271	685,701

Assumptions	
Units Sold in Year 2002	9,492,016
Unit Cost	$7.23
Annual Sales Growth	5.95%
Annual Price Decrease	5.50%
Margin	40.75%

FIGURE 3-84

Instructions Part 1: Complete the following steps to create the worksheet shown in Figure 3-84.

1. Use the Select All button and Bold button to bold the entire worksheet. Enter the worksheet titles in cells A1 and A2. Enter the system date in cell H2 using the NOW function. Format the date to the 3/14/2001 style.

(continued)

In the Lab

Tamiami Medical Supply Seven-Year Financial Plan *(continued)*

2. Enter the seven column titles 2003 through 2009 in the range B3:H3 by entering 2003 in cell B3, formatting it, and using the fill handle. Format cell B3 as follows: a) change the number in cell B3 to text by assigning it the format Text in the Format Cells dialog box; b) center and italicize cell B3; c) rotate its contents 45°. Use the Format Painter button to copy the format assigned to cell B3 to the range C3:H3.
3. Enter the row titles in the range A4:A24. Change the font size in cells A7, A13, A15, and A17 to 12 point. Change the font size in cell A19 to 14 point and underline the characters in the cell. Add a heavy bottom border to the range A3:H3.
4. Change the following column widths: A = 23.43; B through H = 11.00. Change the heights of rows 7, 13, 15, 16, and 17 to 24.00.
5. Enter the assumptions values in Table 3-6 in the range B20:B24. Use format symbols.
6. Assign the Comma style format with no decimal places to the range B4:H17.
7. Complete the following entries:
   a. 2003 Revenue (cell B4) = Units Sold 2002 * (Unit Cost / (1 – Margin)) or =B20 * (B21 / (1 – B24))
   b. 2004 Revenue (cell C4) = 2003 Revenue * (1 + Annual Sales Growth) * (1 – Annual Price Decrease) or =B4 * (1 + $B$22) * (1 – $B$23)
   c. Copy cell C4 to the range D4:H4.
   d. 2003 Cost of Goods Sold (cell B5) = 2003 Revenue – (2003 Revenue * Margin) or =B4 * (1 - $B$24)
   e. Copy cell B5 to the range C5:H5.
   f. 2003 Margin (cell B6) = 2003 Revenue – 2003 Cost of Goods Sold or =B4 – B5
   g. Copy cell B6 to the range C6:H6.
   h. 2003 Advertising (cell B8) = 1000 + 15% * 2003 Revenue or =1000 + 15% * B4
   i. Copy cell B8 to the range C8:H8.
   j. Maintenance (row 9): 2003 = 1,900,000; 2004 = 5,397,000; 2005 = 4,200,000; 2006 = 5,150,000; 2007 = 2,500,000; 2008 = 3,150,000; 2009 = 2,960,000
   k. 2003 Rent (cell B10) = 1,800,000
   l. 2004 Rent (cell C10) = 2003 Rent + 10% * 2003 Rent or =B10 + (10% * B10)
   m. Copy cell C10 to the range D10:H10.
   n. 2003 Salaries (cell B11) = 18% * 2003 Revenue or =18% * B4
   o. Copy cell B11 to the range C11:H11.
   p. 2003 Supplies (cell B12) = 1.5% * 2003 Revenue or =1.5% * B4
   q. Copy cell B12 to the range C12:H12.
   r. 2003 Total Expenses (cell B13) = SUM(B8:B12)
   s. Copy cell B13 to the range C13:H13.
   t. 2003 Income Before Taxes (cell B15) = 2003 Margin – 2003 Total Expenses or =B6 – B13
   u. Copy cell B15 to the range C15:H15.
   v. 2003 Income Taxes (cell B16): If 2003 Income Before Taxes is less than zero, then 2003 Income Taxes equal zero; otherwise 2003 Income Taxes equal 40% * 2003 Income Before Taxes or =IF(B15 < 0, 0, 40% * B15)
   w. Copy cell B16 to the range C16:H16.
   x. 2003 Net Income (cell B17) = 2003 Income Before Taxes – 2003 Income Taxes or =B15 – B16
   y. Copy cell B17 to the range C17:H17.

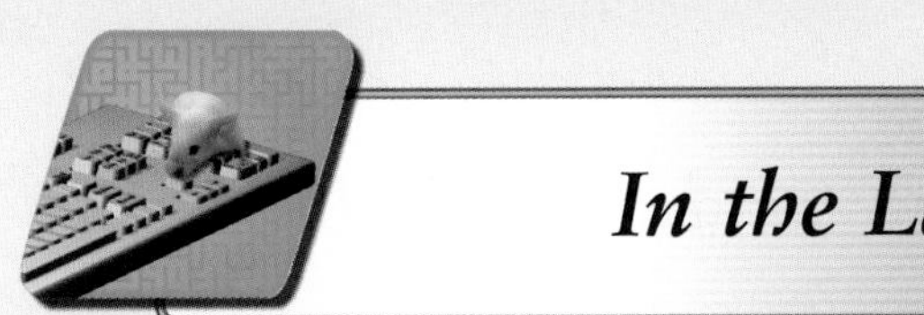

8. Change the font in cell A1 to 26-point Arial Black (or a similar font). Change the font in cell A2 to 16-point Arial Narrow (or a similar font). Change the font in cell H2 to 10-point Century Gothic (or a similar font). Change the background and font colors and add drop shadows as shown in Figure 3-84 on page E 3.69.
9. Enter your name, course, laboratory assignment (Lab 3-1), date, and instructor name in the range A27:A31. Save the workbook using the file name, Tamiami Medical Supply.
10. Use the Page Setup command on the File menu to fit the printout on one page in portrait orientation. Preview and print the worksheet. Preview and print the formulas version (CTRL+ACCENT MARK) of the worksheet in landscape orientation using the Fit to option button in the Page Setup dialog box. After printing the formulas version, reset the print scaling to 100%. Press CTRL+ACCENT MARK to display the values version of the worksheet. Save the workbook again.
11. Zoom to: (a) 200%; (b) 75%; (c) 25%; (d) 100%.

Instructions Part 2: Draw a 3-D Column chart (Figure 3-85) that compares the projected net incomes for the years 2003 through 2009. Use the nonadjacent ranges B3:H3 and B17:H17. Add the chart title and format it as shown in Figure 3-85. To change the color of the columns, right-click a column and then click Format Data Series. To change the color of the walls behind and to the left of the columns, right-click a wall and then click Format Walls. Rename and rearrange the sheets, and color their tabs as shown in Figure 3-85. Save the workbook using the same file name (Tamiami Medical Supply) as defined in Part 1. Print both sheets.

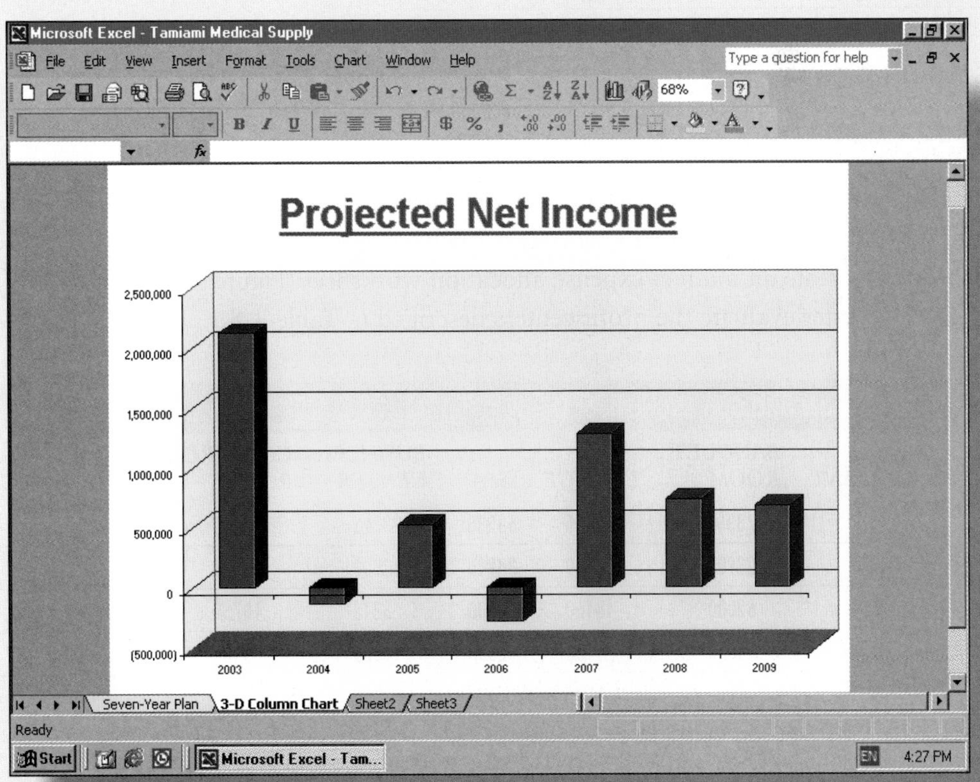

FIGURE 3-85

(continued)

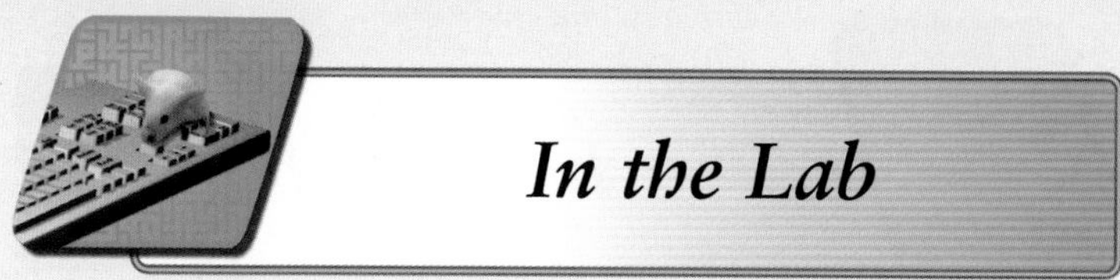

Tamiami Medical Supply Seven-Year Financial Plan *(continued)*

Instructions Part 3: If the 3-D Column chart is on the screen, click the Seven-Year Plan tab to display the worksheet. Divide the window into two panes by dragging the horizontal split bar between rows 6 and 7. Use the scroll bars to display both the top and bottom of the worksheet.

Using the numbers in columns 2 and 3 of Table 3-7, analyze the effect of changing the annual sales growth (cell B22) and annual price decrease (cell B23) on the annual net incomes in row 17. The resulting answers are in column 4 of Table 3-7. Print both the worksheet and chart for each case.

Close the workbook without saving it, and then reopen it. Use the Goal Seek command to determine a margin (cell B24) that would result in a net income in 2009 of $5,000,000 (cell H17). You should end up with a margin of 45.85% in cell B24. After you complete the goal seeking, print only the worksheet. Do not save the workbook with the latest changes.

Table 3-7 Data to Analyze and Results

CASE	ANNUAL SALES GROWTH	ANNUAL PRICE DECREASE	2009 RESULTING NET INCOME
1	16.50%	3.50%	$5,079,297
2	19.75%	-3.75%	$12,284,399
3	32.15%	11.65%	$7,312,377

2 Sun-N-Fun Resort and Spa Indirect Expense Allocation

Problem: You are a summer intern at the elegant five-star Sun-N-Fun Resort and Spa. Your work-study advisor at school and your supervisor at Sun-N-Fun Resort and Spa have agreed on a challenging Excel project for you to do. They want you to create an indirect expense allocation worksheet (Figure 3-86) that will help the resort and spa administration better evaluate the profit centers described in Table 3-8.

Table 3-8 Sun-N-Fun Resort and Spa Worksheet Data

	RESTAURANT	BANQUET ROOM	LOUNGE	SPA	BUSINESS CENTER	CONFERENCE ROOMS	GIFT SHOP	CHILDREN'S GAME ROOM
Revenue	625900	478350	392775	53230	133125	78450	85350	17435
Cost of Sales	213450	123900	105630	34945	12600	42500	34000	8550
Direct Expenses	145750	62000	48460	12500	6345	18750	30200	6200
Square Footage	2250	4650	1400	2350	600	5500	500	600

In the Lab

	Restaurant	Banquet Room	Lounge	Spa	Business Center	Conference Rooms	Gift Shop	Children's Game Room	Total
Sun-N-Fun Resort and Spa									
Indirect Expenses of Profit Centers									12/8/2003
Revenue	$625,900.00	$478,350.00	$392,775.00	$53,230.00	$133,125.00	$78,450.00	$85,350.00	$17,435.00	$1,864,615.00
Cost of Sales	213,450.00	123,900.00	105,630.00	34,945.00	12,600.00	42,500.00	34,000.00	8,550.00	575,575.00
Direct Expenses	145,750.00	62,000.00	48,460.00	12,500.00	6,345.00	18,750.00	30,200.00	6,200.00	330,205.00
Indirect Expenses									
Administrative	$24,336.26	$18,599.21	$15,271.89	$2,069.69	$5,176.17	$3,050.29	$3,318.58	$677.91	$72,500.00
Depreciation	7,720.59	15,955.88	4,803.92	8,063.73	2,058.82	18,872.55	1,715.69	2,058.82	61,250.00
Energy	15,440.94	11,800.88	9,689.75	1,313.18	3,284.19	1,935.36	2,105.58	430.12	46,000.00
Insurance	1,575.63	3,256.30	980.39	1,645.66	420.17	3,851.54	350.14	420.17	12,500.00
Maintenance	3,277.31	6,773.11	2,039.22	3,422.97	873.95	8,011.20	728.29	873.95	26,000.00
Marketing	17,538.89	13,404.26	11,006.29	1,491.60	3,730.41	2,198.32	2,391.67	488.56	52,250.00
Total Indirect Expenses	$69,889.61	$69,789.65	$43,791.45	$18,006.83	$15,543.71	$37,919.26	$10,609.95	$4,949.53	$270,500.00
Net Income	$196,810.39	$222,660.35	$194,893.55	($12,221.83)	$98,636.29	($20,719.26)	$10,540.05	($2,264.53)	$688,335.00
Square Footage	2,250	4,650	1,400	2,350	600	5,500	500	600	17,850
Planned Indirect Expenses									
Administrative	$72,500.00								
Depreciation	$61,250.00								
Energy	$46,000.00								
Insurance	$12,500.00								
Maintenance	$26,000.00								
Marketing	$52,250.00								

FIGURE 3-86

Instructions Part 1: Do the following to create the worksheet shown in Figure 3-86.

1. Use the Select All button and Bold button to bold the entire worksheet. Enter the worksheet titles `Sun-N-Fun Resort and Spa` in cell A1 and `Indirect Expenses of Profit Centers` in cell A2. Enter the system date in cell J2 using the NOW function. Format the date to the 3/14/2001 format style.
2. Enter the first four rows of data in Table 3-8 in rows 3 through 6. In row 3, use ALT+ENTER to display the column titles on two lines in a cell. Select the range J4:J6 and click the AutoSum button. Add a bottom border to the range B3:J3. Center the column headings in the range B3:J3.
3. Enter the Square Footage row in Table 3-8 in row 16 using the Comma format symbol. Select cell J16 and use the AutoSum button to determine the sum of the values in the range B16:I16. Vertically center the range A16:J16.
4. Change the following column widths: A = 26.00; B through I = 12.00, and J = 13.00. Change the height of row 16 to 39.00.
5. Enter the remaining row titles in the range A7:A17 as shown in Figure 3-86. Use the Indent button on the Formatting toolbar to indent the row titles in the range A8:A13. Increase the font size to 12 in cells A7, A14, and A15.
6. Copy the range A8:A13 to the range A18:A23. Enter the numbers shown in the range B18:B23 of Figure 3-86 with format symbols.

(continued)

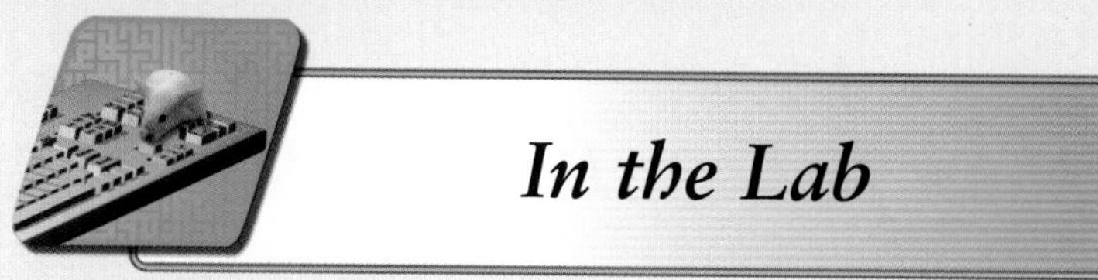

Sun-N-Fun Resort and Spa Indirect Expense Allocation *(continued)*

7. The planned indirect expenses in the range B18:B23 are to be prorated across the profit center as follows: Administrative (row 8), Energy (row 10), and Marketing (row 13) on the basis of revenue volume; Depreciation (row 92), Insurance (row 11), and Maintenance (row 12) on the basis of square feet. Use the following formulas to accomplish the prorating:
   a. Restaurant Administrative (cell B8) = Administrative Expenses * Restaurant Revenue / Total Revenue or =$B$18 * B4 / $J$4
   b. Restaurant Depreciation (cell B9) = Depreciation Expenses * Restaurant Square Feet / Total Square Feet or =$B$19 * B16 / $J$16
   c. Restaurant Energy (cell B10) = Energy Expenses * Restaurant Revenue / Total Revenue or =$B$20 * B4 / $J$4
   d. Restaurant Insurance (cell B11) = Insurance Expenses * Restaurant Square Feet / Total Square Feet or =$B$21 * B16 / $J$16
   e. Restaurant Maintenance (cell B12) = Maintenance Expenses * Restaurant Square Feet / Total Square Feet or =$B$22 * B16 / $J$16
   f. Restaurant Marketing (cell B13) = Marketing Expenses * Restaurant Revenue / Total Revenue or =$B$23 * B4 / $J$4
   g. Restaurant Total Indirect Expenses (cell B14) = SUM(B8:B13)
   h. Restaurant Net Income (cell B15) = Revenue – (Cost of Sales + Direct Expenses + Indirect Expenses) or =B4 – (B5 + B6 + B14)
   i. Use the fill handle to copy the range B8:B15 to the range C8:I15.
   j. Select the range J8:J15 and click the AutoSum button on the Standard toolbar.
8. Add a bottom border to the range B13:J13. Use the Format Cells dialog box to assign the Currency style with two decimal places and display negative numbers in parentheses to the following ranges: B4:J4; B8:J8; and B14:J15. Assign the format Comma style with two decimal places and display negative numbers in parentheses to the following ranges: B5:J6 and B9:J13.
9. Change the font in cell A1 to 48-point Arial Black (or a similar font). Change the font in cell A2 to 26-point Arial Black (or a similar font). Change the font in cell A17 to 14-point italic and underlined.
10. Use the background color Blue (column 6, row 2) on the Fill Color palette, the font color White (column 8, row 5) on the Font Color palette, and a drop shadow (Shadow Style 14) for the following ranges: A1:J2; A7; A15:J15; and A17:B23. The Shadow Style button is on the Drawing toolbar.
11. Rename the Sheet1 sheet, Indirect Expenses, and color its tab blue.
12. Enter your name, course, laboratory assignment (Lab 3-2), date, and instructor name in the range A27:A31. Save the workbook using the file name, Sun-N-Fun Resort and Spa.
13. Use the Page Setup command on the File menu to change the orientation to landscape. Preview and print the worksheet. Preview and print the formulas version (CTRL+ACCENT MARK) of the worksheet in landscape orientation using the Fit to option button in the Page Setup dialog box. After printing the formulas version, reset the print scaling to 100%. Press CTRL+ACCENT MARK to display the values version of the worksheet. Save the workbook again.
14. Divide the window into four panes and display the four corners of the worksheet. Remove the four panes.

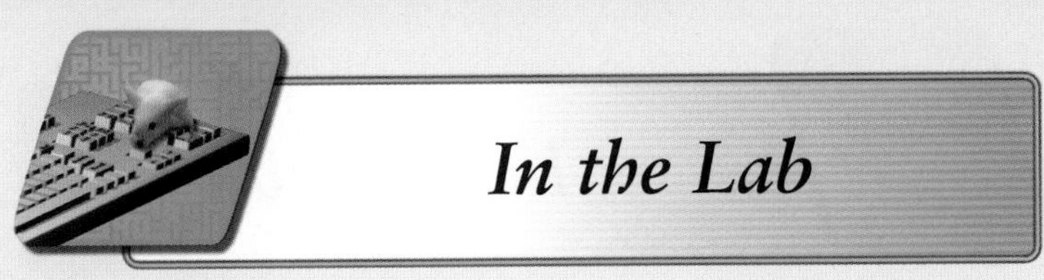

Instructions Part 2: Draw a 3-D Pie chart (Figure 3-87) that shows the contribution of each category of indirect expense to the total indirect expenses. That is, chart the nonadjacent ranges A8:A13 (category names) and J8:J13 (data series). Show labels and percents. Do not show the legend. Make the following changes to the 3-D Pie chart:

1. Add the chart title and format it to 36-point Arial blue underlined font.
2. Explode the Administrative slice.
3. Select a slice and use the 3-D View command on the shortcut menu to change the elevation to 35° and the rotation to 80°.
4. Change the color of the slices as shown in Figure 3-87. Change the data labels to bold 12 point. Color the data labels the same as the slice they represent.
5. Drag the data labels away from the 3-D Pie chart so the leader lines from the data labels to the corresponding slices display.
6. Rename the Chart1 sheet 3-D Pie Chart and color its tab red. Rearrange the sheets so the Indirect Expenses sheet is to the left of the 3-D Pie Chart sheet. Click the Indirect Expenses tab.
7. Save the workbook using the file name Sun-N-Fun Resort and Spa. Preview and print both sheets.

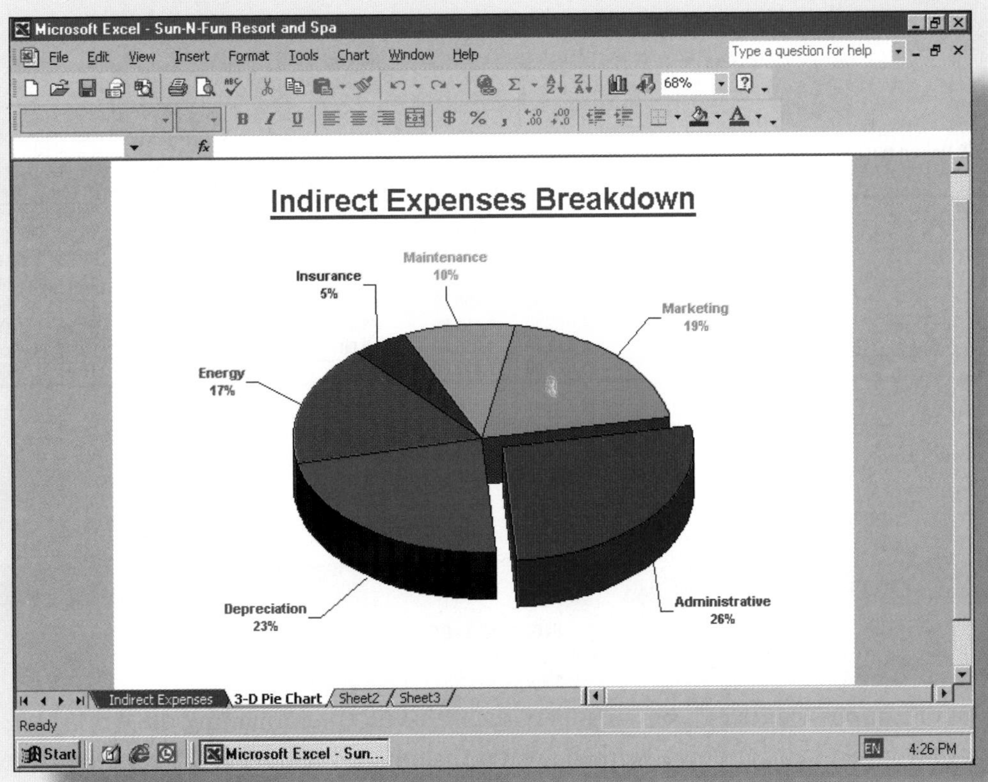

FIGURE 3-87

(continued)

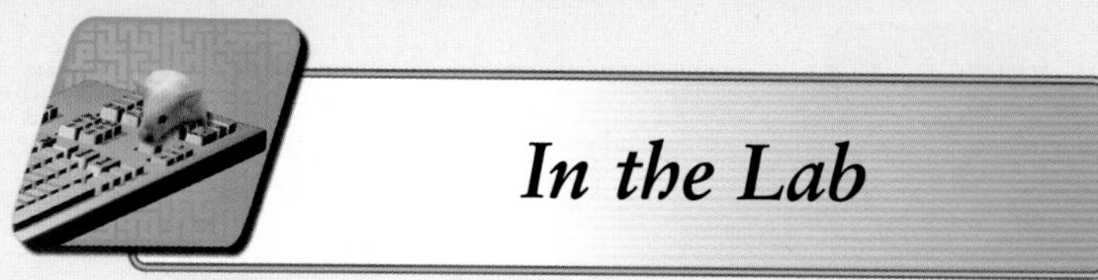

Sun-N-Fun Resort and Spa Indirect Expense Allocation *(continued)*

Instructions Part 3: Using the numbers in Table 3-9, analyze the effect of changing the planned indirect expenses in the range B18:B23 on the net incomes for each profit center. Print the worksheet for each case. You should end with the following totals in cell J15: Case 1 = $611,835.00 and Case 2 = $724,585.00

Table 3-9 What-IF Data

	CASE 1	CASE 2
Administrative	95,000.00	63,500.00
Depreciation	76,500.00	61,000.00
Energy	52,000.00	29,500.00
Insurance	22,500.00	12,250.00
Maintenance	39,000.00	18,000.00
Marketing	62,000.00	50,000.00

3 Modifying Ray's Ready Mix Concrete Weekly Payroll Worksheet

Problem: Your supervisor in the Payroll department has asked you to modify the payroll workbook developed in Exercise 1 of the Project 2 In the Lab section on page E 2.69, so that it displays as shown in Figure 3-88. If you did not complete Exercise 1 in Project 2, ask your instructor for a copy of the Ray's Ready Mix Concrete workbook or complete that exercise before you begin this one.

	A	B	C	D	E	F	G	H	I	J	K	L
1	Ray's Ready Mix Concrete											
2	Weekly Payroll Report for	9/15/2003										
3	Employee	Rate	Hours	Dep.	YTD Soc. Sec.	Gross Pay	Soc. Sec.	Medicare	Fed. Tax	State Tax	Net Pay	
4	Sanchez, Edgar	32.25	49.50	6	4,974.00	1,749.56	108.47	25.37	303.76	55.99	1,255.97	
5	Wright, Felix	12.00	28.00	10	5,540.20	336.00	13.70	4.87	0.00	10.75	306.68	
6	Wreath, Christy	22.40	70.00	4	4,254.00	1,904.00	118.05	27.61	350.03	60.93	1,347.38	
7	Elamain, Al	29.75	18.00	5	5,553.90	535.50	0.00	7.76	68.64	17.14	441.96	
8	Space, Si	16.25	42.00	2	4,825.50	698.75	43.32	10.13	124.37	22.36	498.57	
9	Tuf, Chang	22.15	48.00	6	4,825.50	1,151.80	71.41	16.70	184.21	36.86	842.62	
10	Knob, Doris	29.15	36.25	4	5,553.90	1,056.69	0.00	15.32	180.57	33.81	826.98	
11	Totals		291.75		35,527.00	7,432.30	354.95	107.77	1,211.58	237.83	5,520.17	
12												
13	Social Security Tax	6.20%										
14	Medicare Tax	1.45%										
15	Maximum Social Security	$5,553.90										
16												
17												
18												
19												

FIGURE 3-88

The major modifications requested by your supervisor include: (1) reformatting the worksheet; (2) adding computations of time-and-a-half for hours worked greater than 40; (3) removing the conditional formatting assigned to the range E3:E8; (4) charging no federal tax in certain situations; (5) adding Social Security and Medicare deductions; (6) adding and deleting employees; and (7) changing employee information.

In the Lab

Instructions Part 1: Open the workbook, Ray's Ready Mix Concrete, created in Project 2. Perform the following tasks.

1. Select the range A2:H12. Point to Clear on the Edit menu and use the Format command on the Clear submenu to clear all formats. Change the worksheet title font to the color red.
2. Delete rows 10 through 12. Select rows 2 through 15 by dragging through the row headings and click the Bold button. Insert a row above row 2, click the Insert Options button that displays immediately below the new row 2, and select the Format Same As Below option. Enter the worksheet subtitle `Weekly Payroll Report for` in cell A2.
3. Insert a new column between columns D and E by right-clicking the column E heading and inserting a column. Enter the new column E title, `YTD Soc. Sec`, in cell E3. Insert two new columns between columns F and G. Enter the new column G title `Soc. Sec.` in cell G3. Enter the new column H title `Medicare` in cell H3. Freeze the panes (titles) in column A and rows 1 through 3.
4. Change the column widths and row heights as follows: A = 25.00; B = 9.43; C = 6.43; D = 6.00; E = 13.14; F through K = 9.71; and row 3 = 18.00. Right-align the column titles in the range B3:K3. Assign the NOW function to cell B2 and format it to the 3/14/2001 style.
5. Delete row 8 (Pedal, Rose). Change Felix Wright's rate of pay to 12 and number of dependents to 10.
6. In column E, enter the YTD Social Security values listed in Table 3-10.
7. Insert two new rows immediately above the Totals row. Add the new employee data as listed in Table 3-11.
8. Use the Format Cells dialog box to assign a Comma style and two decimal places to the ranges B4:C11 and E4:K11. Center the range D4:D10.
9. Enter the Social Security and Medicare tax information headings in the range A13:A15. Enter the values in the range B13:B15. Use format symbols to format the numbers as shown in Figure 3-88.
10. Change the formulas to determine the gross pay in column F and the federal tax in column I.
    a. In cell F4, enter an IF function that applies the following logic:

    If Hours <= 40, then Gross Pay = Rate * Hours, otherwise Gross Pay = Rate * Hours + 0.5 * Rate * (Hours – 40)

    b. Copy the IF function in cell F4 to the range F5:F10.
    c. In cell I4, enter the IF function that applies the following logic:

    If (Gross Pay – Dependents * 38.46) > 0, then Federal Tax = 20% * (Gross Pay – Dependents * 38.46), otherwise Federal Tax = 0

    d. Copy the IF function in cell I4 to the range I5:I10.

Table 3-10 YTD Social Security Values

NAME	YTD SOC. SEC.
Sanchez, Edgar	4,974.00
Wright, Felix	5,540.20
Wreath, Christy	4,254.00
Elamain, Al	5,553.90
Space, Si	4,825.50

Table 3-11 New Employee Data

EMPLOYEE	RATE	HOURS	DEPENDENTS	YTD SOC. SEC.
Tuf, Chang	22.15	48	6	4,825.50
Knob, Doris	29.15	36.25	4	5,553.90

(continued)

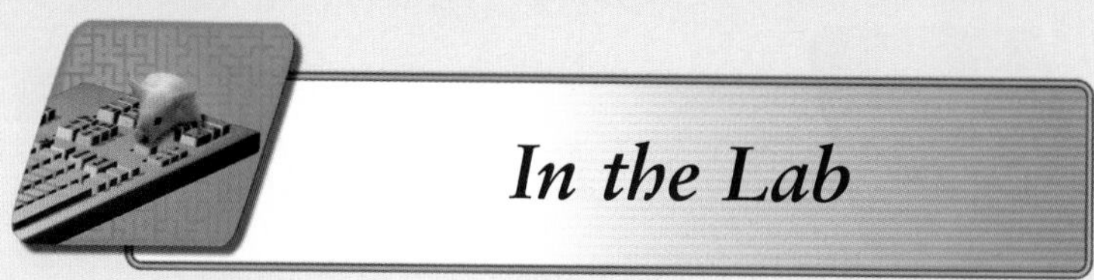

In the Lab

Modifying Ray's Ready Mix Concrete Weekly Payroll Worksheet *(continued)*

11. An employee pays Social Security tax only if his or her YTD Social Security is less than the maximum Social Security in column E. Use the following logic to determine the Social Security tax for Edgar Sanchez in cell G4:

    If Soc. Sec. Tax * Gross Pay + YTD Soc. Sec. > Maximum Soc. Sec., then Maximum Soc. Sec. – YTD Soc. Sec., otherwise Soc. Sec. Tax * Gross Pay

12. Make sure references to the values in the social security tax table (B13:B15) are absolute, and then copy the IF function to the range G5:G10.
13. In cell H4, enter the following formula and then copy it to the range H5:H10:

    Medicare = Medicare Tax * Gross Pay

14. Copy the state tax in cell J4 to the range J5:J10.
15. In cell K4, enter the following formula and copy it to the range K5:K10:

    Gross Pay – (Soc. Sec. + Medicare + Fed. Tax + State Tax)

16. Determine any new totals as shown in row 11 of Figure 3-88.
17. Enter your name, course, laboratory assignment (Lab 3-3), date, and instructor name in the range A18:A22.
18. Unfreeze the panes (titles). Save the workbook using the file name Ray's Ready Mix Concrete 2.
19. Use the Zoom box on the Standard toolbar to change the view of the worksheet. One by one, select all the percents in the Zoom list. When you are done, return the worksheet to 100% magnification.
20. Use the Page Setup command on the File menu to change the orientation to landscape. Preview the worksheet. If number signs display in place of numbers in any columns, adjust the column widths. Print the worksheet. Save the worksheet using the same file name.
21. Preview and print the formulas version (CTRL+ACCENT MARK) in landscape orientation using the Fit to option button in the Page Setup dialog box. Close the worksheet without saving the latest changes.

Instructions Part 2: Using the numbers in Table 3-12, analyze the effect of changing the Social Security tax in cell B13 and the Medicare tax in cell B14. Print the worksheet for each case. The first case should result in a total Social Security tax in cell G11 of $509.07. The second case should result in a total Social Security tax of $632.91.

Table 3-12 Social Security and Medicare Taxes

CASE	SOCIAL SECURITY TAX	MEDICARE TAX
1	9%	3.25%
2	11.25%	2.75%

Instructions Part 3: Hand in your handwritten results for this exercise to your instructor. Start Excel and open Ray's Ready Mix Concrete 2.

1. Select cell F4. Write down the formula that displays in the formula bar. Select the range C4:C10. Point to the border surrounding the range and drag the selection to the range D13:D19. Click cell F4, and write down the formula that displays in the formula bar below the one you wrote down earlier. Compare the two formulas. What can you conclude about Excel when you move cells involved in a formula? Click the Undo button on the Standard toolbar.
2. Right-click the range C4:C10 and click Delete. When the Delete dialog box displays, click Shift cells left. What displays in cell F4? Use the Excel Help system to find a definition of the display in cell F4. Write the definition down. Click the Undo button on the Standard toolbar.
3. Right-click the range C4:C10 and click Insert. When the Delete dialog box displays, click Shift cell right. What displays in the formula bar when you click cell F4? What displays in the formula bar when you click cell G4? What can you conclude about inserting cells? Close the workbook without saving the changes.

Cases and Places

The difficulty of these case studies varies:
▶ are the least difficult; ▶▶ are more difficult; and ▶▶▶ are the most difficult.

1 ▶ Rose's floral shop is open all year, but most of the shop's production revolves around four holidays: Valentine's Day (14,500 flowers), Sweetest Day (8,250 flowers), Mother's Day (11,500 flowers), and Memorial Day (5,975 flowers). On these days 42% of the store's output is roses, 18% is carnations, 31% is mums, and the remaining 9% is tulips. The roses sell for $5.00 each, the carnations for $1.95 each, the mums for $3.50 each, and the tulips for $2.50 each. Rose's management is considering revising its production figures. They have asked you to create a worksheet they can use in making this decision. The worksheet should show the total number of each flower ordered for each holiday, total flowers ordered for the four holidays, potential sales for each type of flower, total potential sales for each holiday, and total potential sales from each type of flower. Include an appropriate chart illustrating total potential sales for each flower type. Use the concepts and techniques presented in this project to create and format the worksheet.

2 ▶ You are the product manager for Class Publishers, a company that produces textbooks for the college market. One of your responsibilities is to submit income projections to your publisher for the books you plan to sign. The projected first year net sales for the books you plan to do are shown in Table 3-13. Also included in the table are the percent of net sales for payment of royalties and manufacturing costs. Use the concepts and techniques presented in this project to create and format a worksheet that shows the projected royalties, projected manufacturing cost, net income for each book, and totals for the four numeric columns in Table 3-13. The net income for a book is equal to the net sales minus the royalty and manufacturing costs.

Table 3-13 Projected 1st Year Net Sales

BOOK	NET SALES	ROYALTY	MANU. COSTS	NET INCOME
A	2,453,345.75	—	—	—
B	1,372,915.50	—	—	—
C	945,238.25	—	—	—
TOTAL	—	—	—	—
ASSUMPTIONS				
ROYALTIES	16.25%			
MANU. COSTS	23.5%			

Your publisher reviewed your plan and returned it, requesting printouts of the worksheet for the following set of values: Set 1 – Royalty 12.5%; Manufacturing Costs 30.5%; Set 2 – Royalty 18.5%; Manufacturing Costs 32%.

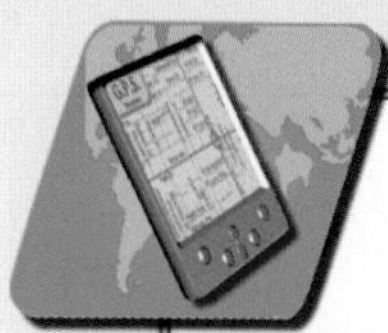

Cases and Places

3 ▸ Nivo Power Company is the largest utility company in the Northeast. The company generates revenue from the sale of natural gas and electricity. A fixed percentage of this revenue is spent on marketing, payroll, equipment, production costs, and administrative expenses. Nivo Power's president has summarized the company's receipts and expenditures over the past year on a quarterly basis as shown in Table 3-14.

Table 3-14 Projected Revenue and Expenses

REVENUES	*QUARTER 1*	*QUARTER 2*	*QUARTER 3*	*QUARTER 4*
NATURAL GAS	87,345,450	78,415,823	82,245,111	67,712,810
ELECTRICITY	72,631,781	61,712,992	75,312,643	61,324,912
EXPENDITURES				
MARKETING	15.25%			
PAYROLL	25.35%			
EQUIPMENT	19.25%			
PRODUCTION	9.75%			
ADMINISTRATIVE	12.25%			

With this data, you have been asked to prepare a worksheet similar to Figure 3-1a on page E 3.05 for the next shareholders' meeting. The worksheet should show total revenues, total expenditures, and net income for each quarterly period. Include a chart that illustrates quarterly net income. Use the concepts and techniques presented in this project to create and format the worksheet and chart. During the meeting, one shareholder lobbied to reduce marketing expenditures by 1.75% and payroll costs by 7.5%. Perform a what-if analysis reflecting the proposed changes in expenditures.

4 ▸▸ Your neighbors want to save enough money to send their son to a private school. They have job orders at their cabinet shop for the next six months: $1,200 in July, $975 in August, $1,900 in September, $1,175 in October, $675 in November, and $955 in December. Each month, they spend 37.25% of the job order income on material, 2.25% on patterns, 4.55% on their retirement account, and 43% on food and clothing. The remaining profits (orders – expenses) will be put aside for the boy's education. The husband's parents have agreed to provide an additional $25 whenever their monthly profit exceeds $150. Your neighbors have asked you to create a worksheet that shows orders, expenses, profits, bonuses, and savings for the next six months, and totals for each category. They would like you to (a) goal seek to determine what percentage of profits to spend on food and clothing if $800 is needed for the school, and (b) perform a what-if analysis to determine the effect of reducing the percentage spent on material to 25%. Use the concepts and techniques presented in this project to create and format the worksheet.

5 ▸▸▸ Balancing a budget is a significant challenge for many students attending college. Whether you work part-time or simply draw on a sum of money while going to school, you must equalize income and expenditures to maintain your budget. Use the concepts and techniques presented in this project to create and format a worksheet that reflects your monthly budget throughout the school year. Indicate the amount of money you have available each month. Hypothesize percentages for monthly expenditures (tuition, books, entertainment, and so on). On the basis of these assumptions, determine expenditures for each month. Include a row for occasional miscellaneous expenses (such as travel). Ascertain the amount of money remaining at the end of each month; this amount will become part or all of the money available for the subsequent month. Perform at least one what-if analysis to examine the effect of changing one or more of the values in the worksheet, and goal seek to determine how an expenditure must be modified to have an additional $500 available at the end of the school year.

Microsoft Excel 2002

Creating Static and Dynamic Web Pages Using Excel

CASE PERSPECTIVE

Quick Lube, an auto oil and lubrication commerce, has experienced explosive growth since its beginning three years ago. Thanks to the popularity of their guaranteed 15-minute turnaround, complimentary coffee and rolls, and overall service, the company has grown faster than anyone could have imagined.

John French is the national sales manager for Quick Lube. He has a workbook that he and his group use to analyze weekly sales. In the past, John printed the worksheet and chart, sent it out to duplicate it, and mailed it to his distribution list. He also made his computer available to members of his workgroup who did not have Excel, so they could analyze sales using the workbook.

John would like to save the Excel workbook (Figure 1a) on the company's intranet as a Web page (Figure 1b) so members on the distribution list could display it using their browser. He also suggested publishing the same workbook on the company's intranet as a dynamic (interactive) Web page (Figure 1c) so his workgroup could use its browser to manipulate the formulas and Bar chart without requiring Excel 2002.

Introduction

Excel provides fast, easy methods for saving workbooks as Web pages that can be stored on the World Wide Web, a company's intranet, or a local hard drive. A user then can display the workbook using a browser, rather than Excel.

You can save a workbook, or a portion of a workbook, as a static Web page or a dynamic Web page. A **static Web page**, also called a **noninteractive Web page** or **view-only Web page** is a snapshot of the workbook. It is similar to a printed report in that you can view it through your browser, but you cannot modify it. A **dynamic Web page**, also called an **interactive Web Page**, includes the interactivity and functionality of the workbook. For example, with a dynamic Web page you can enter formulas, re-format cells, and change values in the worksheet to do what-if analysis while displaying a copy of the worksheet in your browser. A user does not even need Excel on their computer to complete these tasks.

As shown in Figure 1 on the next page, this Web Feature shows you how to save a workbook (Figure 1a) as a static Web page (Figure 1b) and view it using your browser. Then it shows you how to take the same workbook and save it as a dynamic Web page (Figure 1c) and view it using your browser. After displaying the dynamic Web page in your browser, this Web Feature shows you how to change values to test the Web page's interactivity and functionality.

The Save as Web Page command on the File menu allows you to **publish** workbooks, which is the process of making them available to others; for example, on the World Wide Web or on a company's intranet. If you have access to a Web server, you can publish Web pages by saving them to a Web folder or to an FTP location. The procedures for publishing Web pages to a Web folder or FTP location using Microsoft Office applications are discussed in Appendix C.

This Web Feature shows you how to create and save the Web pages and associated folders on a floppy disk rather than to a Web server. Before creating the Web pages, this feature also shows you how to preview a workbook as a Web page and how to create a new folder through the Save As dialog box.

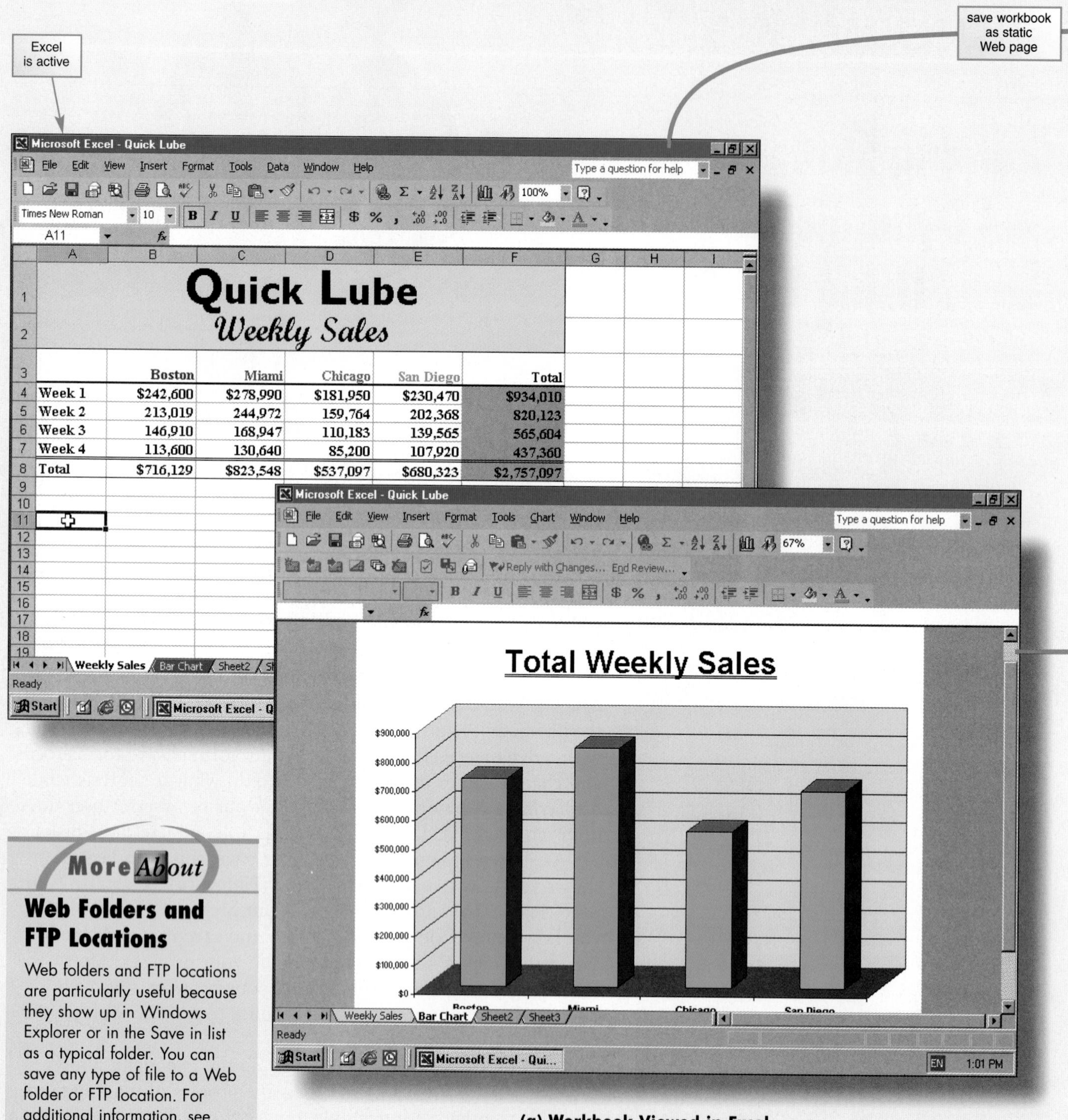

(a) Workbook Viewed in Excel

FIGURE 1

More About

Web Folders and FTP Locations

Web folders and FTP locations are particularly useful because they show up in Windows Explorer or in the Save in list as a typical folder. You can save any type of file to a Web folder or FTP location. For additional information, see Appendix C.

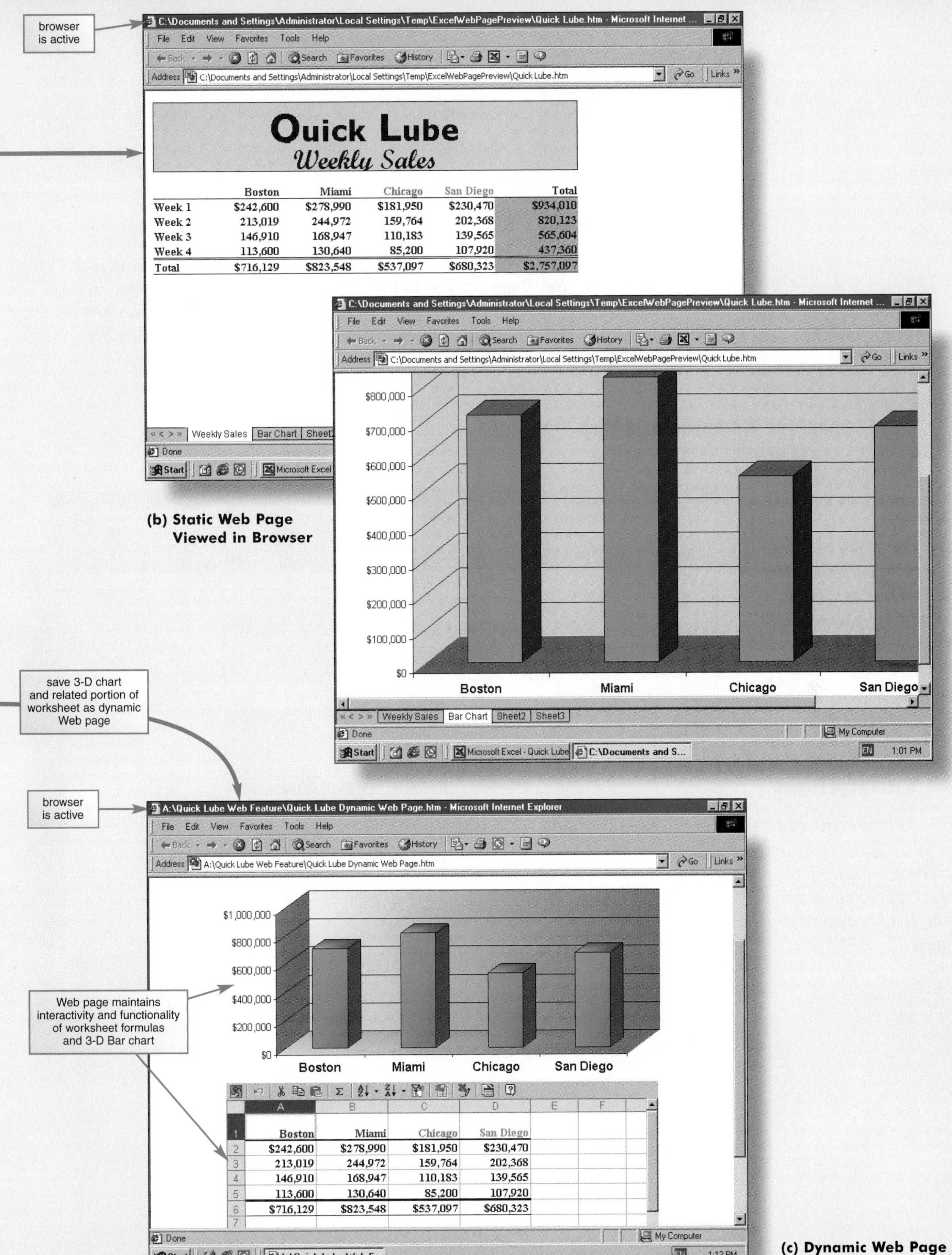

(b) Static Web Page Viewed in Browser

(c) Dynamic Web Page Viewed in Browser

Using Web Page Preview and Saving an Excel Workbook as a Static Web Page

Once you have created an Excel workbook, you can preview it as a Web page. If the preview is acceptable, then you can save the workbook as a Web page.

Web Page Preview

At anytime during the construction of a workbook, you can preview it as a Web page by using the **Web Page Preview command** on the File menu. When you invoke the Web Page Preview command, it starts your browser and displays the active sheet in the workbook as a Web page. The following steps show how to use the Web Page Preview command.

Steps To Preview the Workbook as a Web Page

1 Insert the Data Disk in drive A. See the inside back cover of this book for instructions for downloading the Data Disk or see your instructor for information on accessing the files required in this book. Start Excel and then open the workbook, Quick Lube, on drive A. Click File on the menu bar and then point to Web Page Preview.

Excel starts and opens the workbook Quick Lube. The workbook is made up of two sheets, the worksheet and a chart. The File menu displays (Figure 2).

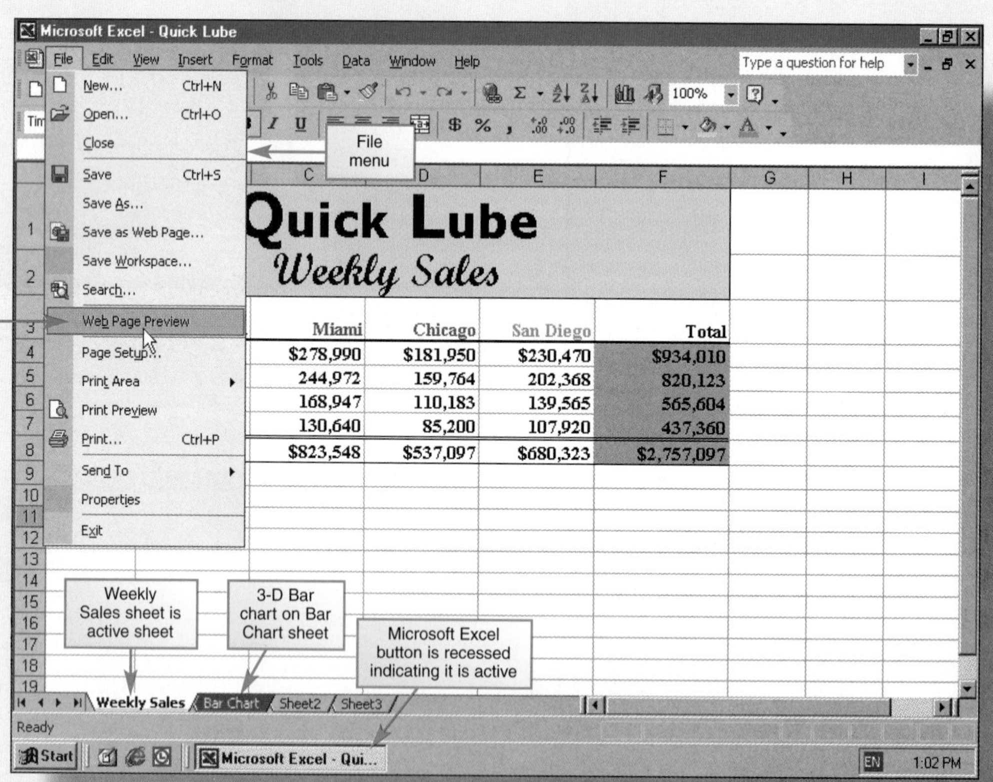

FIGURE 2

2 Click Web Page Preview.

Excel starts your browser and displays a Web page preview of the Weekly Sales sheet in the Quick Lube workbook (Figure 3). The Excel button on the taskbar is no longer recessed. A recessed browser button displays on the taskbar indicating it is active. A preview of the chart is available by clicking the Bar Chart tab at the bottom of the Web page. The Web page preview in the browser is nearly identical to the display of the worksheet in Excel.

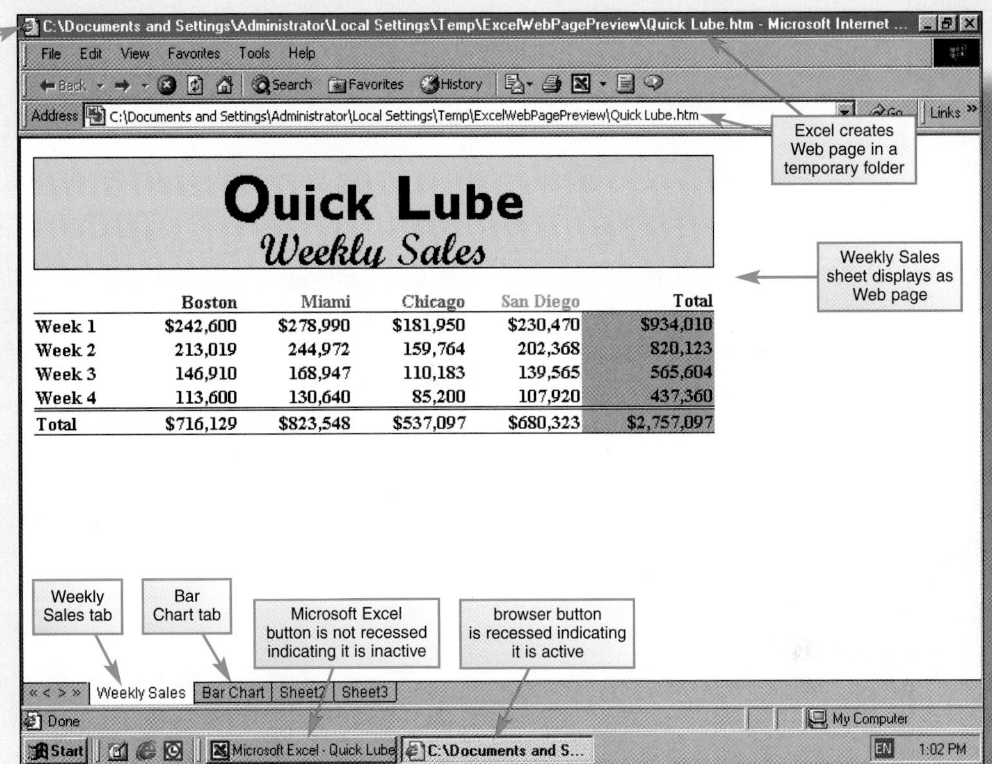

FIGURE 3

3 Click the Bar Chart tab at the bottom of the Web page.

The 3-D Bar chart displays in the browser (Figure 4).

4 When you are finished viewing the Web page preview of the Quick Lube workbook, click the Close button on the right side of the browser title bar.

The browser closes, Excel becomes active, and the worksheet displays.

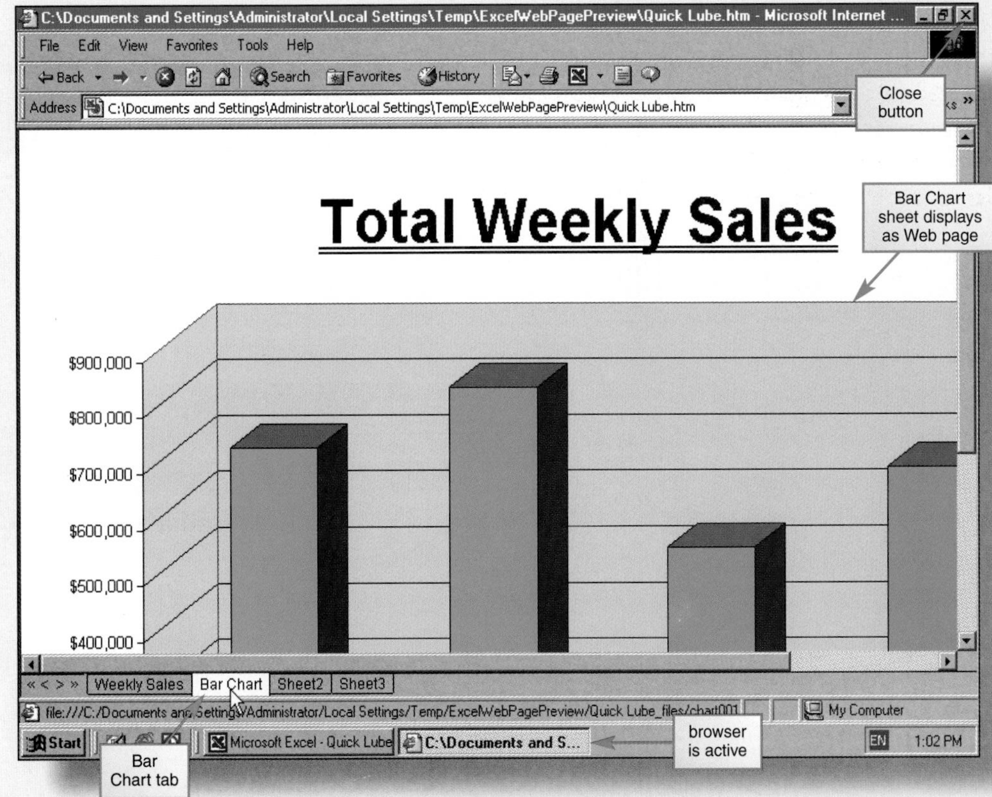

FIGURE 4

The Web Page preview shows that Excel has the capability to produce professional-looking Web pages from workbooks.

Publishing Web Pages

For more information on publishing Web pages using Excel, visit the Excel 2002 More About Web page (scsite.com/ex2002/more.htm) and click Publishing Web Pages using Excel.

Saving a Workbook as a Static Web Page to a New Folder

Once the preview of the workbook as a Web page is acceptable, you can save it as a Web page so it can be viewed by others using a Web browser, such as Internet Explorer or Netscape. The file format that Excel saves the workbook in is called **HTML** (**hypertext markup language**), which is a language browsers can interpret.

Experienced users organize their storage devices by creating folders. They then save related files to a common folder. Excel allows you to create folders in the Save As dialog box before saving a file. Perform the following steps to create a new folder on drive A and save the workbook as a static Web page to the new folder.

To Save an Excel Workbook as a Static Web Page to a Newly Created Folder

1 With the workbook Quick Lube open, click File on the menu bar and then point to Save as Web Page.

The File menu displays (Figure 5).

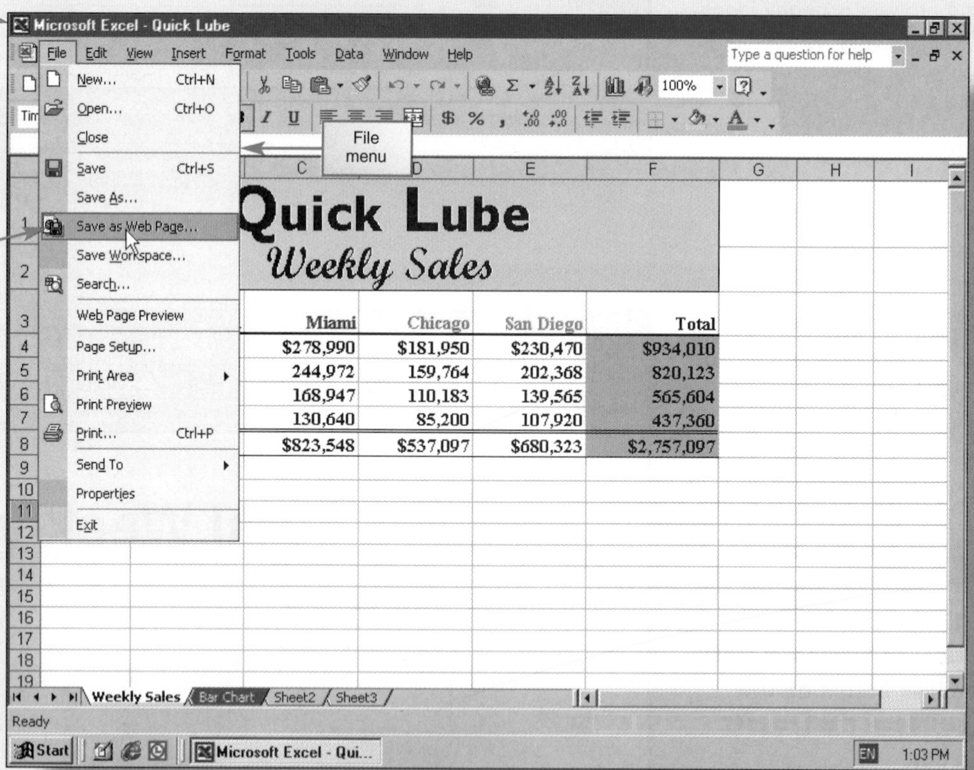

FIGURE 5

2 **Click Save as Web Page. When the Save As dialog box displays, type** `Quick Lube Static Web Page` **in the File name text box. Click the Save in box arrow and select 3½ Floppy (A:). Click the Create New Folder button. When the New Folder dialog box displays, type** `Quick Lube Web Feature` **in the Name box. Point to the OK button.**

The Save As dialog box and the New Folder dialog box display as shown in Figure 6.

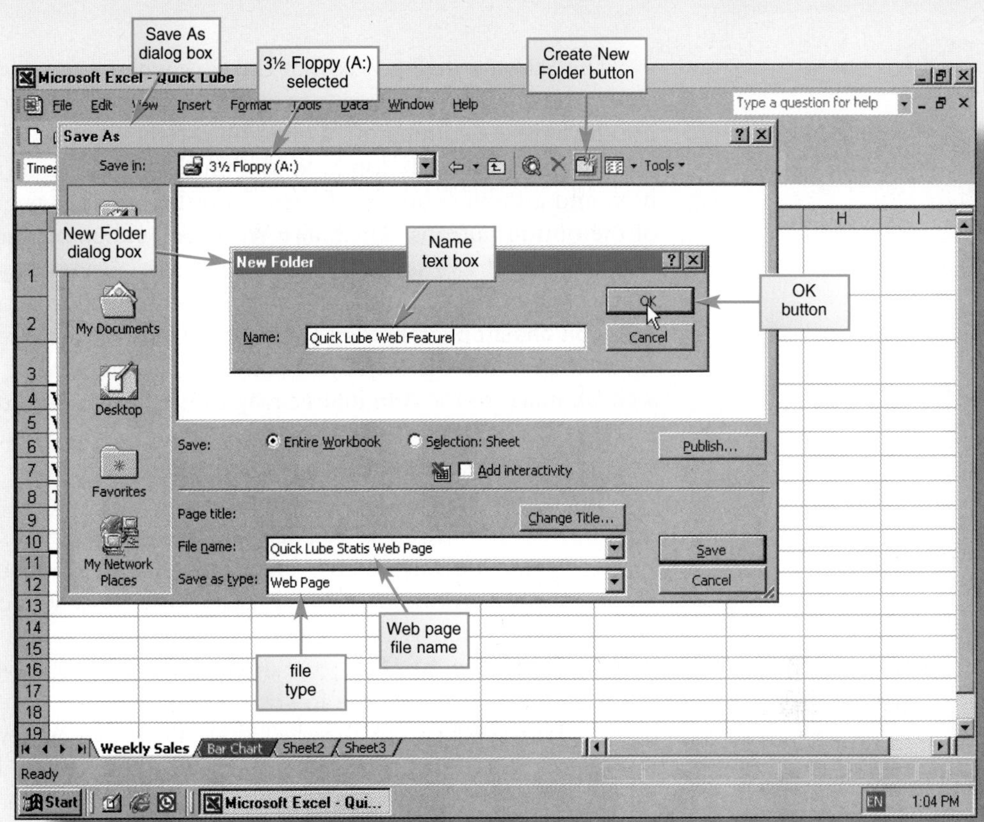

FIGURE 6

3 **Click the OK button. Point to the Save button in the Save As dialog box.**

The Save As dialog box displays as shown in Figure 7.

4 **Click the Save button. Click the Close button on the right side of the title bar to close Excel.**

Excel saves the workbook in HTML format on drive A in the folder Quick Lube Web Feature using the file name Quick Lube Static Web Page.htm. Excel shuts down.

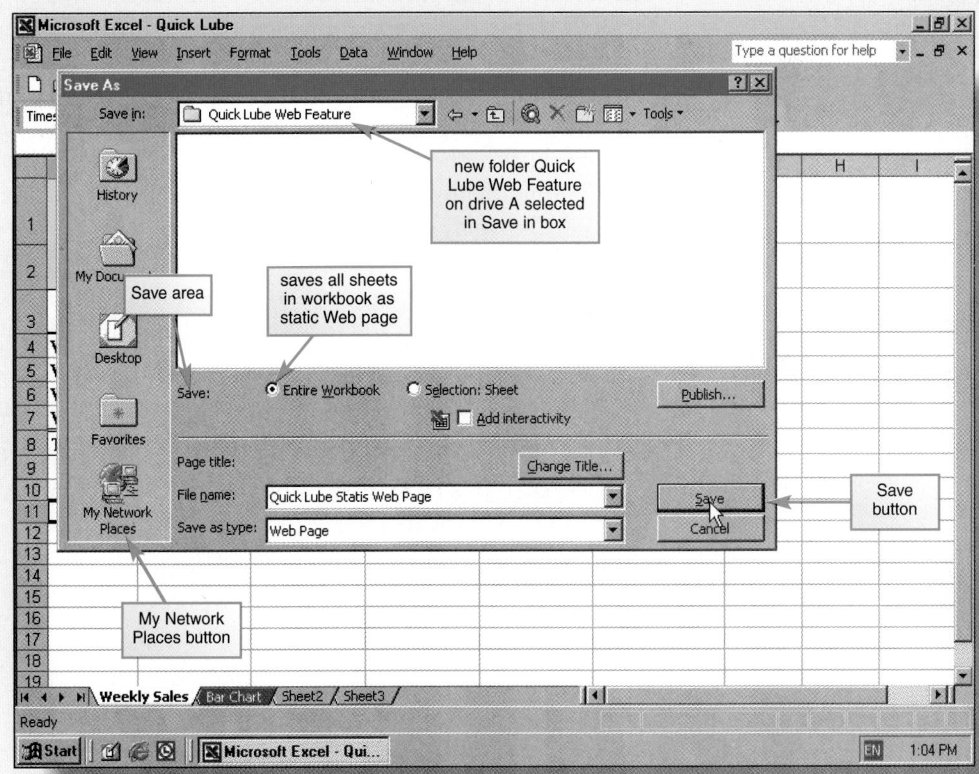

FIGURE 7

The Favorites Folder

To add a workbook to your Favorites folder, click Save As on the File menu, right-click the file in its original folder and choose Create Shortcut. Next, select the newly created shortcut in the same folder and choose Add To Favorites from the Tools menu (click the Tools arrow on the far right side in the Save As dialog box). To open the file at a later date, simply click the Favorites folder on the Places bar. If you prefer to store the shortcut in your default folder, just cut and paste the shortcut from one folder to another.

The Save As dialog box that displays when you use the Save as Web Page command is slightly different from the Save As dialog box that displays when you use the Save As command. When you use the Save as Web Page command, a **Save area** displays in the dialog box. Within the Save area are two option buttons, a check box, and a Publish button (Figure 7 on the previous page). You can select only one of the option buttons. The **Entire Workbook option button** is selected by default. This indicates Excel will save all the active sheets (Weekly Sales and Bar Chart) in the workbook as a static Web page if you click the Save button. The alternative is the **Selection Sheet option button**. If you select this option, Excel will save only the active sheet (the one that is displaying in the Excel window) in the workbook. If you add a check mark to the **Add interactivity check box**, then Excel saves the sheet as a dynamic Web page. If you leave the Add interactivity check box unchecked, Excel saves the active sheet as a static Web page.

The **Publish button** in the Save As dialog box in Figure 7 is an alternative to the Save button. It allows you to customize the Web page further. In the previous set of steps, the Save button was used to complete the save. Later in this feature, the Publish button will be used to explain further how you can customize a Web page.

If you have access to a Web server and it allows you to save files to a Web folder, then you can save the Web page directly to the Web server by clicking the **My Network Places button** in the lower left corner of the Save As dialog box (Figure 7). If you have access to a Web server that allows you to save to an FTP site, then you can select the FTP site under **FTP locations** in the Save in box just as you select any folder to save a file to. To save a workbook to a Web server, see Appendix C.

After Excel saves the workbook in Step 4, the HTML file (not the workbook) displays in the Excel window. Excel can continue to display the workbook in HTML format because within the HTML file that it created, it also saved the Excel formats that allow it to display the HTML file in Excel. This is referred to as **round tripping** the HTML file back to the application in which it was created.

It was not necessary to create a new folder in the previous set of steps. The Web page could have been saved to drive A in the same manner files were saved to drive A in the previous projects. Creating a new folder, however, allows you to organize your work. Whether you save the Web page to the drive A or to a folder on drive A, Excel automatically creates an additional folder which it uses to store the graphics required to display the Web page.

Another point concerning the new folder created in the previous set of steps is that Excel automatically inserts the new folder name in the Save in box when you click the OK button in the New Folder dialog box (Figure 7).

More About

Viewing Web Pages Created in Excel

To view static (noninteractive) Web pages created in Excel, you can use any browser. To view dynamic (interactive) Web pages created in Excel, viewers must have the Microsoft Office Web Components and Microsoft Internet Explorer 4.01 or later installed on your computer. The Microsoft Office Web Components come with Microsoft Office XP.

Viewing the Static Web Page Using Your Browser

With the static Web page saved to the folder Quick Lube Web Feature on drive A, the next step is to view it using your browser as shown in the following steps. You can use Microsoft Internet Explorer or Netscape to view a static Web page.

Steps To View and Manipulate the Static Web Page Using Your Browser

1 If necessary, insert the Data Disk in drive A. Click the Start button on the taskbar, point to Programs, and then click Internet Explorer. When the Internet Explorer window displays, type `a:\quick lube web feature\quick lube static web page.htm` **in the Address bar and then press the ENTER key.**

The Web page, Quick Lube Static Web Page.htm, displays with the Weekly Sales sheet active (Figure 8).

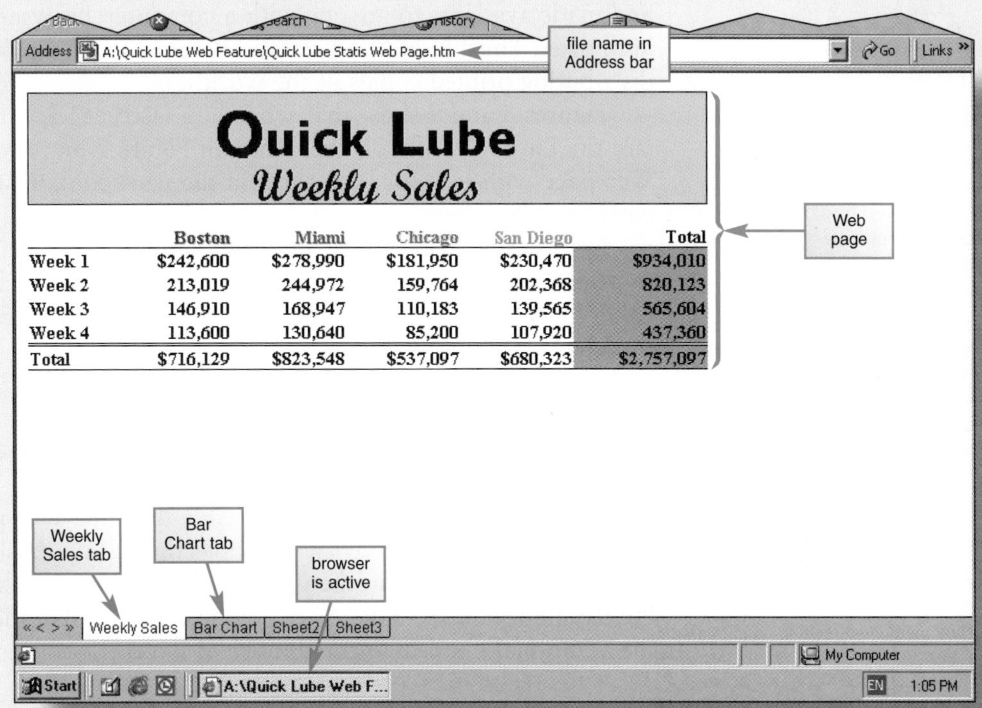

FIGURE 8

2 Click the Bar Chart tab at the bottom of the window. Use the scroll arrows to display the lower portion of the chart.

The 3-D Bar chart displays as shown in Figure 9.

3 Click the Close button at the right side of the Internet Explorer title bar.

The Internet Explorer window closes.

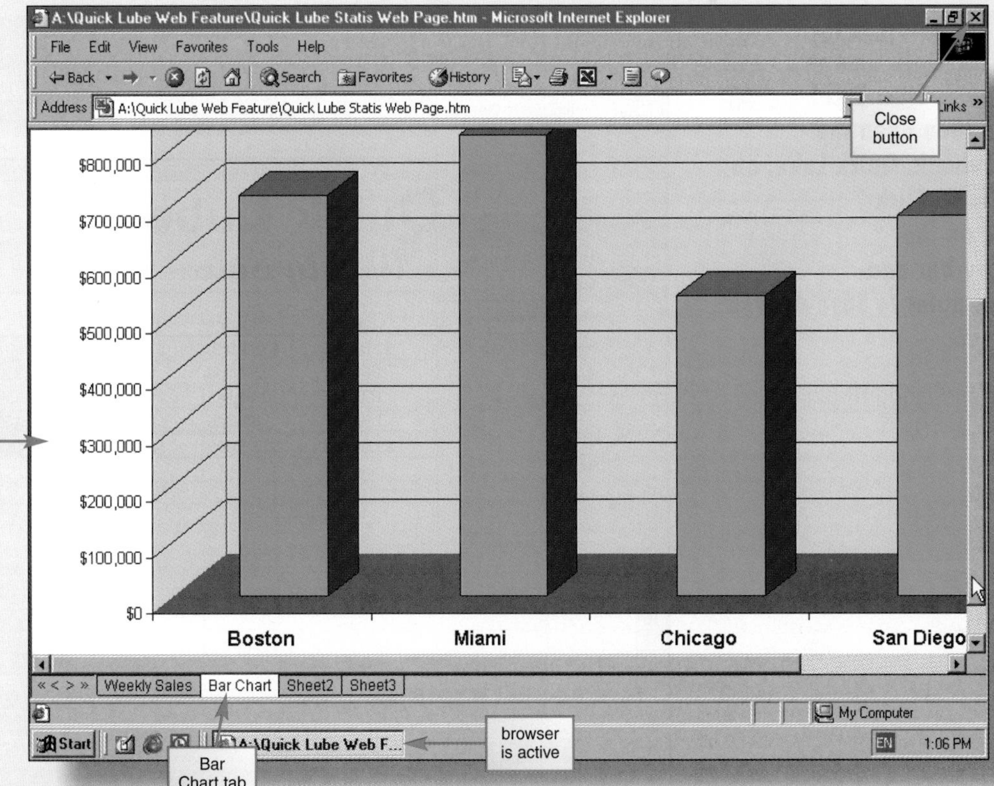

FIGURE 9

Viewing the Source Code

To view the HTML source code for the static Web page created in Excel, display the Web page in your browser, click View menu on the menu bar, and then click Source in Microsoft Internet Explorer or Page Source in Netscape Navigator. If you are familiar with HTML, you will notice additional XML (Extensible Markup Language) code. The XML code contains the Excel formats so you can open the HTML file in Excel.

You can see from Figures 8 and 9 on the previous page that the static Web page is an ideal media for distributing information to a large group of people. For example, the static Web page could be published to a Web server connected to the Internet and made available to anyone with a computer, browser, and the address of the Web page. Thus, publishing a static Web page of a workbook is an alternative to distributing printed copies of the workbook.

Figures 8 and 9 show that when you instruct Excel to save the entire workbook (see the Entire Workbook check box in Figure 7 on page EW 1.07), it creates a Web page with tabs for each sheet in the workbook. Clicking a tab displays the corresponding sheet.

If you want, you can use the Print command on the File menu in your browser to print the sheets one at a time. You can also view the HTML source created by Excel by clicking Source on the View menu in Internet Explorer or Page Source on the View menu in Netscape.

Saving an Excel Chart as a Dynamic Web Page

This section shows you how to publish a dynamic Web page that includes Excel functionality and interactivity. The objective is to publish the 3-D Bar chart that is on the Bar Chart sheet in the Quick Lube workbook. The following steps use the Publish button in the Save As dialog box, rather than the Save button, to illustrate the additional publishing capabilities of Excel.

Steps To Save an Excel Chart as a Dynamic Web Page

1 Insert the Data Disk in drive A. Start Excel and then open the workbook, Quick Lube, on drive A. Click File on the menu bar and then point to Save as Web Page.

The File menu displays (Figure 10).

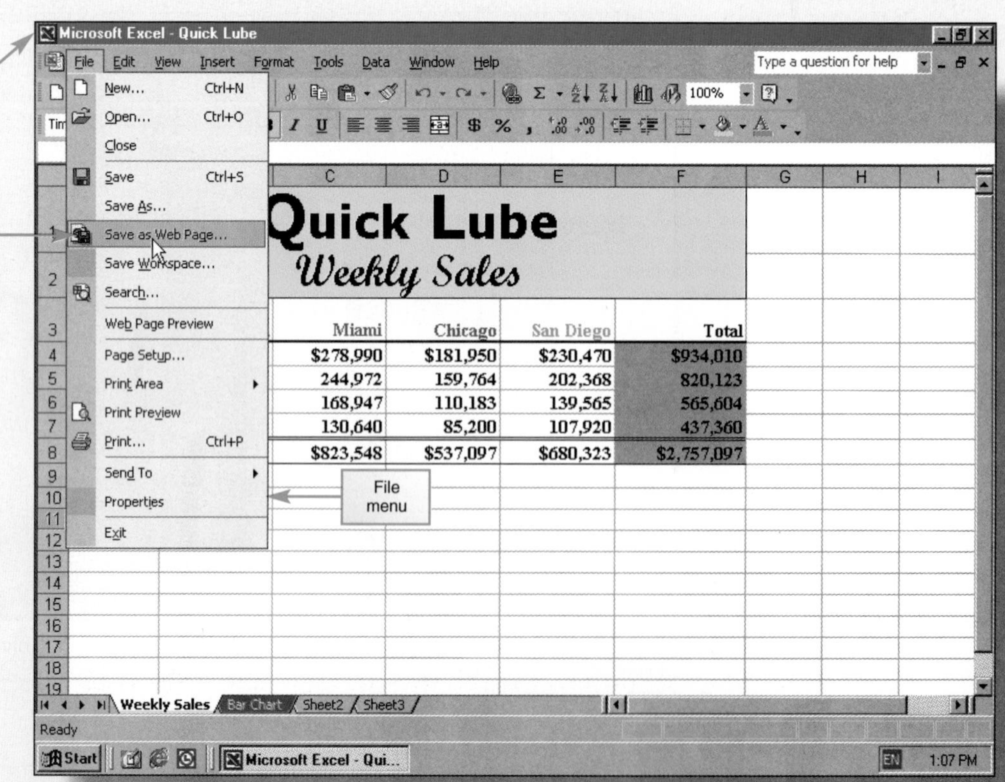

FIGURE 10

2 Click Save as Web Page. When the Save As dialog box displays, type `Quick Lube Dynamic Web Page` **in the File name text box. If necessary, click the Save in box arrow, select 3½ Floppy (A:) in the Save in list, and then select the folder Quick Lube Web Feature. Point to the Publish button.**

The Save As dialog box displays (Figure 11). When you use the Publish button, you do not have to concern yourself with the option buttons and check box in the Save area.

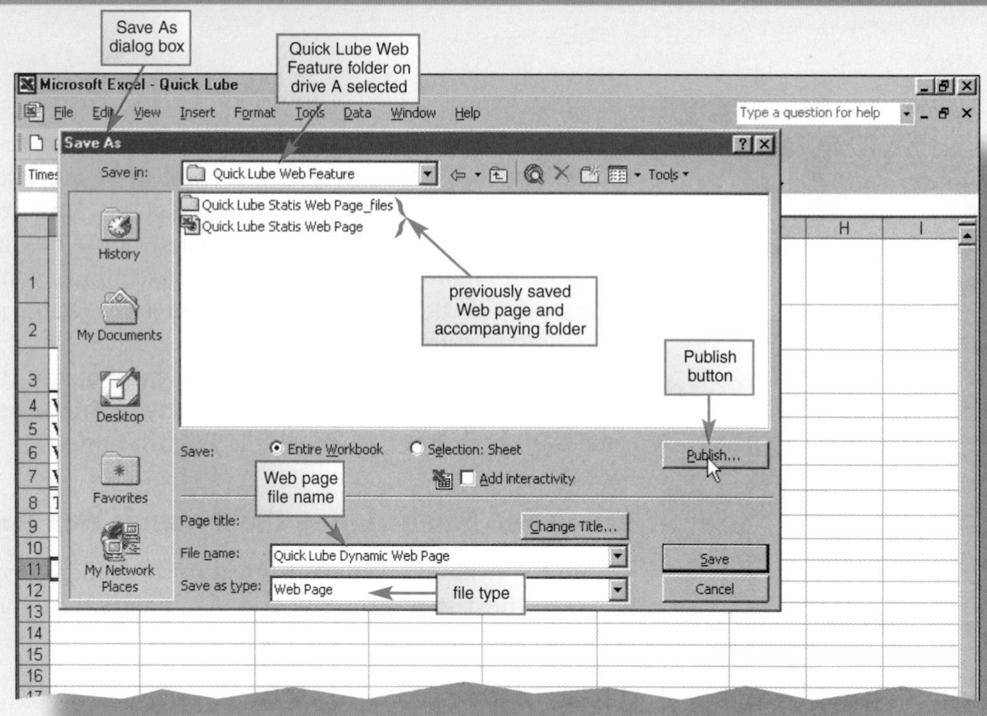

FIGURE 11

3 Click the Publish button. When the Publish as Web Page dialog box displays, click the Choose box arrow and then click Items on Bar Chart. Click the Add interactivity with check box in the Viewing options area. If necessary, select Chart functionality in the list box in the Viewing options area. Point to the Publish button.

The Publish as Web page dialog box displays (Figure 12). When you select Items on the Bar Chart, Excel immediately displays the Bar Chart sheet in the Excel window.

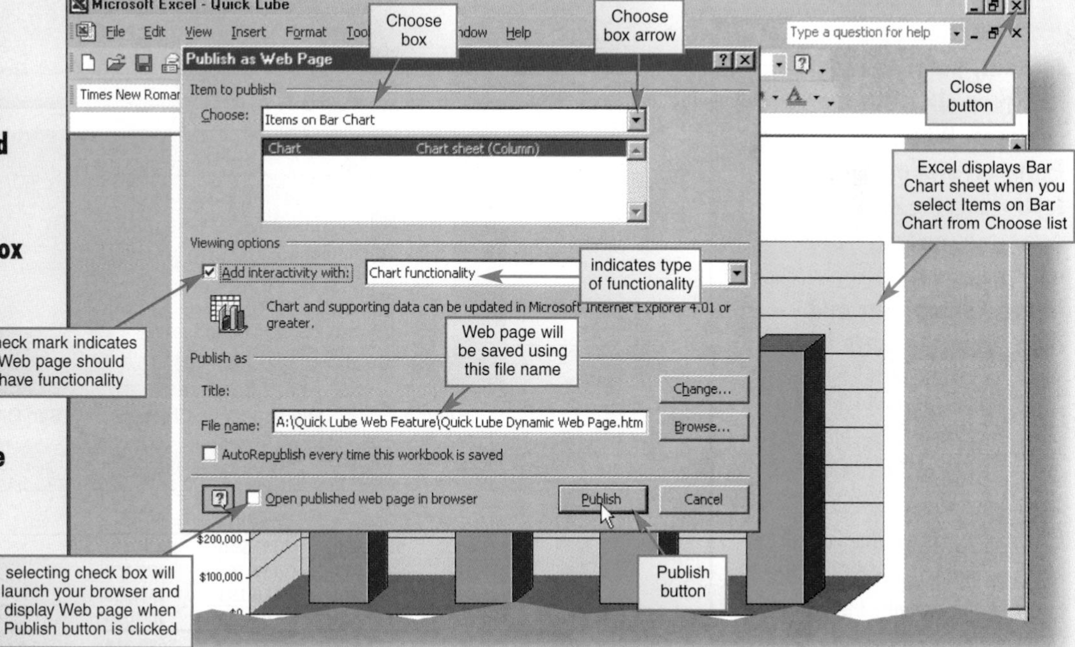

FIGURE 12

Click the Publish button. Click the Close button on the right side of the Excel title bar to close Excel.

Excel saves the dynamic Web page to the folder Quick Lube Web Feature on the Data Disk in drive A using the file name, Quick Lube Dynamic Web Page.htm. Excel shuts down.

Excel allows you to save an entire workbook, a sheet in the workbook, or a range on a sheet as a Web page. In Figure 11 on the pervious page, you have the option in the Save area to save the entire workbook or a sheet. These option buttons are used with the Save button. If you want to be more selective in what you save, then you can disregard the option buttons in the Save area in Figure 11 and click the Publish button as described in Step 3. The Choose box in the Publish as Web Page dialog box in Figure 12 on the previous page allows you more options in what to include on the Web page. You also may save the Web page as a dynamic Web page (interactive) or a static Web page (noninteractive) by selecting the appropriate options in the Viewing options area. The check box at the bottom of the dialog box gives you the opportunity to start your browser automatically and display the newly created Web page when you click the Publish button.

How Excel Saves Web Pages

A saved static Web page includes an HTML file and an additional folder to hold the graphics that display as part of the Web page. All the components of a dynamic Web page are saved in a single HTML file.

Viewing and Manipulating the Dynamic Web Page Using Your Browser

With the dynamic Web page saved to the folder Quick Lube Web Feature on drive A, the next step is to view and manipulate the dynamic Web page using your browser as shown in the following steps.

To View and Manipulate the Dynamic Web Page Using Your Browser

1 Click the Start button on the taskbar, point to Programs, and then click Internet Explorer. When the Internet Explorer window displays, type `a:\quick lube web feature\quick lube dynamic web page.htm` **in the Address bar and then press the ENTER key.**

The Web page, Quick Lube Dynamic Web Page.htm, displays as shown in Figure 13. This Web page contains information from the Quick Lube workbook. The 3-D Bar chart displays with the rows and columns of the worksheet that determine the heights of the bars in the chart immediately below it.

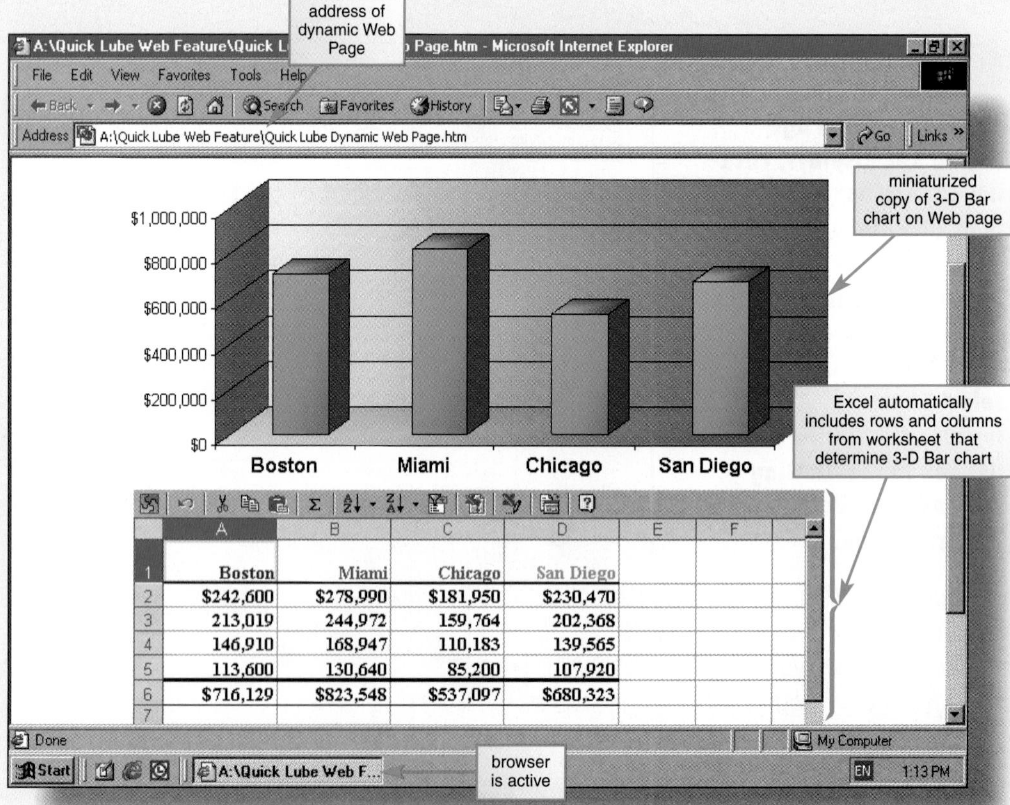

	A	B	C	D	E	F
1	Boston	Miami	Chicago	San Diego		
2	$242,600	$278,990	$181,950	$230,470		
3	213,019	244,972	159,764	202,368		
4	146,910	168,947	110,183	139,565		
5	113,600	130,640	85,200	107,920		
6	$716,129	$823,548	$537,097	$680,323		
7						

FIGURE 13

2 Click cell B4 and then enter 600000.

The 600,000 replaces the 168,947. The formulas in the worksheet portion are recalculated and the heights of the bars in the 3-D Bar chart and the scaling factor along the y-axis change to agree with the new totals in row 6 (Figure 14).

3 Click the Close button at the right side of the Internet Explorer title bar.

The Internet Explorer window closes.

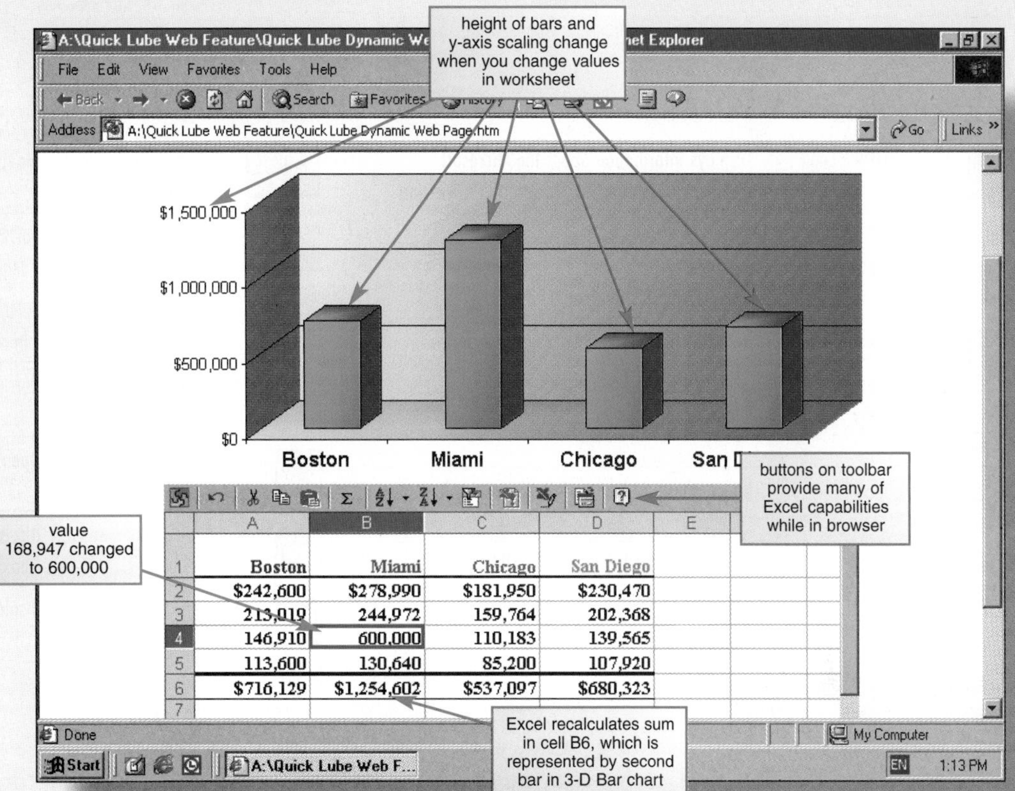

FIGURE 14

Figure 13 shows the result of saving the 3-D Bar chart as a dynamic Web page. Excel displays a miniature version of the 3-D Bar chart and automatically adds the columns and rows from the worksheet below the chart that affect the numbers charted. As shown in Figure 14, you can change the numbers in the worksheet that determine the heights of the bars in the chart and the Web page instantaneously recalculates all formulas and redraws the chart with a new scaling factor along the y-axis. When cell B4 is changed from 168,947 to 600,000, the Web page recalculates the totals in row 6. The bar representing Miami is based on the number in cell B6. Thus, when the number in cell B6 changes from 823,548 to 1,254,602 because of the change made to cell B4, the bar representing Miami changes to a much taller one in relation to the other bars. The interteractivity and functionality allow you to share a workbook's formulas and charts with others who may not have access to Excel, but do have access to a browser.

More About

The Quick Reference

For a table that lists how to complete the tasks covered in this book using the mouse, menu, shortcut menu, and keyboard, see the Quick Reference Summary at the back of this book or visit the Shelly Cashman Series Office XP Web page (scsite.com/offxp/qr.htm), and then click Microsoft Excel 2002.

Modifying the Worksheet on a Dynamic Web Page

Immediately above the rows and columns in the worksheet in Figure 14 is a toolbar. The toolbar allows you to invoke the most commonly used worksheet commands. For example, you can select a cell immediately below a column of numbers and click the AutoSum button to sum the numbers in the column. Cut, copy, and paste capabilities also are available. The functions of the buttons on the toolbar in Figure 14 are summarized in Table 1 on the next page.

More About

Dynamic Web Pages

When you change a value in a dynamic Web page, it does not affect the saved workbook or the saved HTML file. If you save a modified Web page using the Save As command on the browser's File menu, it will save the original version and not the modified one you see on the screen.

Table 1 Toolbar Options

BUTTON	NAME OF BUTTON	FUNCTION
	Office Logo	Displays information about the Microsoft Office Web component, including the version number installed
	Undo	Reverses the last command or action, or deletes the last entry typed
	Cut	Removes the selection and places it on the Office Clipboard
	Copy	Copy the selection to the Office Clipboard
	Paste	Inserts the most recent item placed on the Clipboard
	AutoSum	Inserts the SUM function in a cell and selects a range to sum
	Sort Ascending	Sorts the selected items in ascending sequence
	Sort Descending	Sorts the selected items in descending sequence
	AutoFilter	Selects specific items you want to display in a list
	Refresh All	Refreshes data when connected to the Web
	Export to Excel	Opens the Web page as a workbook in Excel
	Commands and Options	Displays the Commands and Options dialog box
	Help	Displays Microsoft Spreadsheet Help

More About

Creating Links

You can add hyperlinks to an Excel workbook before you save it as a Web page. You can add hyperlinks that link to a Web page, a location in a Web page, or to an e-mail address that automatically starts the viewer's e-mail program.

In general, you can add formulas, format, sort, and export the Web page to Excel. Many additional Excel capabilities are available through the **Commands and Options dialog box** (Figure 15). You display the Commands and Options dialog box by clicking the **Commands and Options button** on the toolbar. When the Command and Options dialog box displays, click the Format tab. You can see in Figure 15, that many of the common formats, such as bold, italic, underline, font color, font style, and font size, are available through your browser for the purpose of formatting cells in the worksheet below the 3-D Bar chart on the Web page.

Modifying the dynamic Web page does not change the makeup of the original workbook or the Web page stored on disk, even if you use the Save As command on the browser's File menu. If you do use the Save As command in your browser, it will save the original htm file without any changes you might have made. You can, however, use the **Export to Excel button** on the Spreadsheet toolbar to create a workbook that will include any changes you made in your browser. The Export to Excel button only saves the worksheet and not the chart.

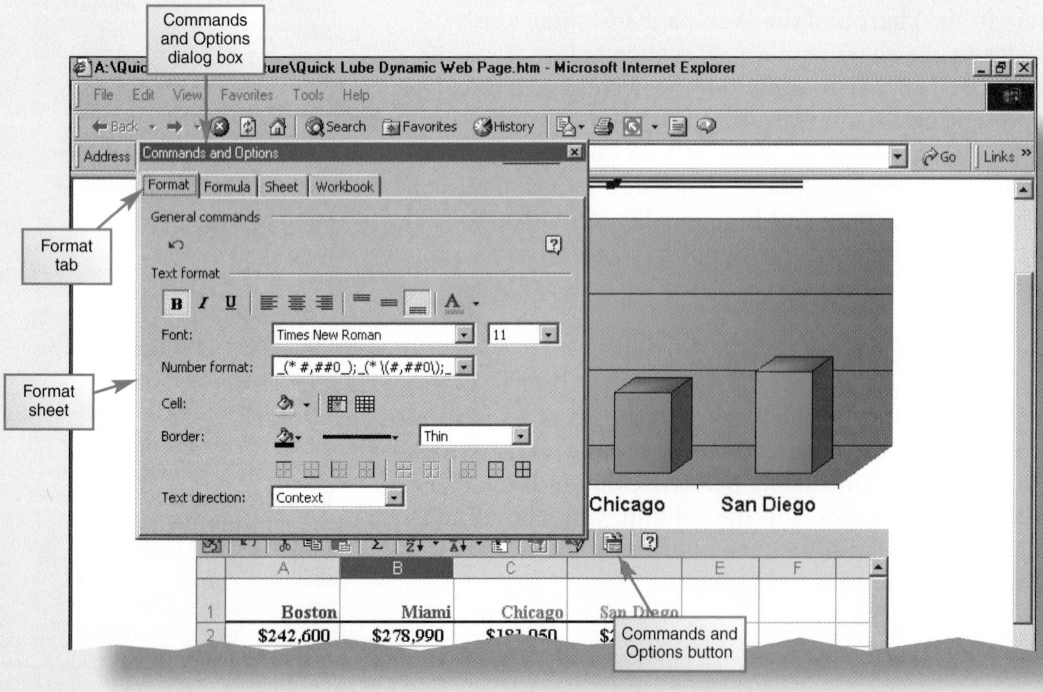

FIGURE 15

CASE PERSPECTIVE SUMMARY

John is excited with the two Web pages you created. By publishing the static Web page on the company's intranet, he no longer has to mail printouts of the Workbook to his distribution list. Furthermore, because he can make the worksheet and chart available as a dynamic Web page, members of his group no longer need to use his computer.

Web Feature Summary

This Web Feature introduced you to previewing a Web page, creating a new folder on disk, and publishing and viewing two types of Web pages: static and dynamic. Whereas the static Web page is a snapshot of the workbook, a dynamic Web page adds functionality and interactivity to the Web page. Besides changing the data and generating new results with a dynamic Web page, you also can add formulas and change the formats in your browser to improve the appearance of the Web page.

What You Should Know

Having completed this project, you now should be able to perform the following tasks:

- Preview the Workbook as a Web Page (EW 1.04)
- Save an Excel Chart as a Dynamic Web Page *(EW 1.10)*
- Save an Excel Workbook as a Static Web Page to a Newly Created Folder *(EW 1.06)*
- View and Manipulate the Dynamic Web Page Using Your Browser *(EW 1.12)*
- View and Manipulate the Static Web Page Using Your Browser *(EW 1.09)*

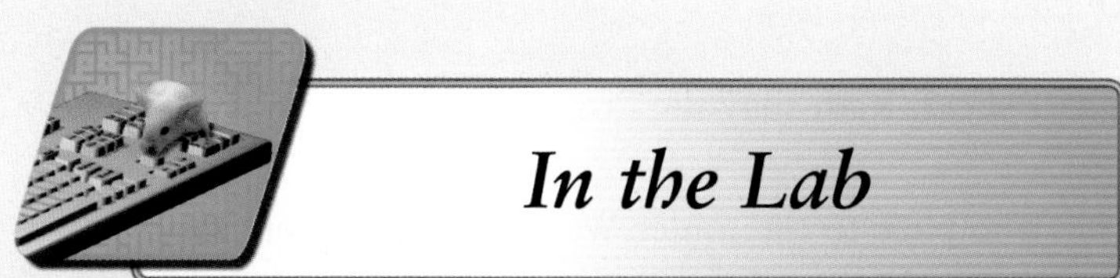

1 Web CD Club Web Page

Problem: You are a student employed part-time as a spreadsheet specialist by Web CD Club. Your supervisor has asked you to create a static Web page and dynamic Web page from the company's annual sales workbook.

Instructions Part 1: Start Excel and open the Web CD Club workbook from the Data Disk. Perform the following tasks:

1. Review the worksheet and chart so you have an idea of what the workbook contains. Preview the workbook as a Web page.
2. Save the workbook as a Web page to a new folder titled Web Feature 1 Exercises on drive A using the file name, Web CD Club Static Web Page. Make sure you select Entire Workbook in the Save area before you click the Save button. Close Excel.
3. Start your browser. Type `a:\web feature 1 exercises\web cd club static web page.htm` in the Address bar. When the Web page displays, click the tabs at the bottom of the window to view the sheets. As you view each sheet, print it in landscape orientation. Close your browser window.

(continued)

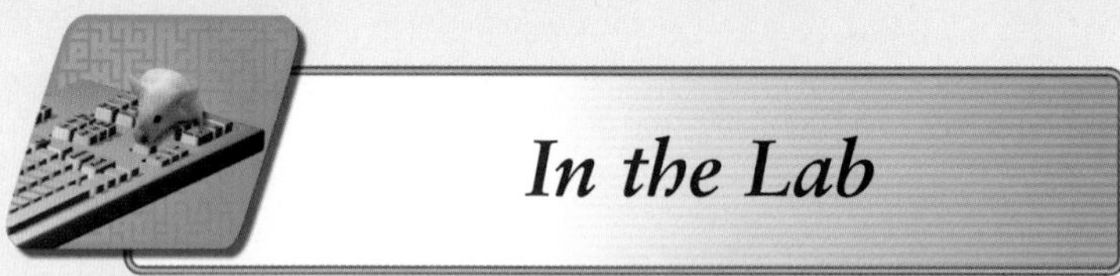

Web CD Club Web Page *(continued)*

Instructions Part 2: Start Excel and open the Web CD Club workbook from the Data Disk. Perform the following tasks:

1. Click File on the menu bar and then click Save as Web Page. Use the Publish button to save the workbook as a Web page to the folder Web Feature 1 Exercises on drive A using the file name, Web CD Club Dynamic Web Page. In the Publish as Web Page dialog box, select Items on Bar Chart in the Choose box, click the Add Interactivity with check box and add chart functionality. Click the Publish button. Quit Excel.
2. Start your browser. Type `a:\web feature 1 exercises\web cd club dynamic web page.htm` in the Address bar. When the Web page displays, click cell B6 and then click the AutoSum button on the toolbar twice. Cell B6 should equal $2,806,007. Print the Web page.
3. Enter the following gross sales: East = 235,000; North = 542,500; South = 300,500; West = 200,000; and International = 1,500,000. Cell B6 should equal $2,778,000. Print the Web page. Close the browser window.

2 Refurbished Computers Plus Web Page

Problem: You are the spreadsheet analyst for Refurbished Computers Plus. You have been asked to create a static Web page and dynamic Web page from the workbook that the company uses to project sales and payroll expenses.

Instructions Part 1: Start Excel and open the Refurbished Computers Plus workbook from the Data Disk. Perform the following tasks:

1. Display the 3-D Pie Chart sheet. Redisplay the Projected Expenses sheet. Preview the workbook as a Web page.
2. Save the workbook as a Web page to the folder Web Feature 1 Exercises on drive A using the file name, Refurbished Computers Plus Static Web Page. Make sure you select Entire Workbook in the Save area before you click the Save button. Quit Excel.
3. Start your browser. Type `a:\web feature 1 exercises\refurbished computers plus static web page.htm` in the Address bar. When the Web page displays, click the tabs at the bottom of the window to view the sheets. Print each sheet in landscape orientation. Quit your browser.

Instructions Part 2: Start Excel and open the Refurbished Computers Plus workbook from the Data Disk. Perform the following tasks:

1. Click File on the menu bar and then click Save as Web Page. Use the Publish button to save the workbook as a Web page to the folder Web Feature 1 Exercises on drive A using the file name, Refurbished Computers Plus Dynamic Web Page. In the Publish as Web Page dialog box, select Items on 3-D Pie Chart in the Choose box, click the Add Interactivity with check box and add chart functionality. Click the Publish button. Quit Excel.
2. Start your browser. Type `a:\web feature 1 exercises\refurbished computers plus dynamic web page.htm` in the Address bar. When the Web page displays, print it in landscape orientation.
3. Scroll down and change the values of the following cells: cell B15 = 28%; cell B16 = 4.5%; cell B17 = 25,000; cell B19 = 20.25%; and cell B20 = 7.75%. Cell H12 should equal $1,782,939.49. The 3-D Pie chart should change to display the new contributions to the projected payroll expenses.

2002

Microsoft

ACCESS

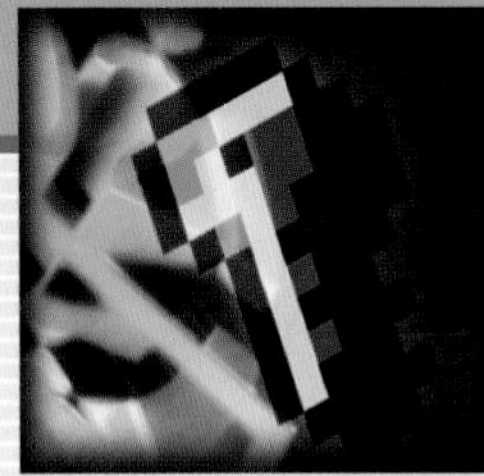

Microsoft Access 2002

PROJECT 1

Creating a Database Using Design and Datasheet Views

OBJECTIVES

You will have mastered the material in this project when you can:

- Describe databases and database management systems
- Describe the speech recognition capabilities of Access
- Start Access
- Describe the features of the Access desktop
- Create a database
- Create a table and define the fields in a table
- Open a table
- Add records to a table
- Close a table
- Close a database and quit Access
- Open a database
- Print the contents of a table
- Use a form to view data
- Create a custom report
- Use the Access Help system to answer your questions
- Design a database to eliminate redundancy

Education and Mentoring

Enriching the Learning Experience

Advocates of educational reform are making a difference in the learning experience. They work in partnership with educators, students, community members, and financial supporters. Their goal is to enhance student learning, deliver a common message to the education system, align priorities, encourage collaboration at every level, document successful outcomes from a variety of programs, and work toward long-term systemic change. They strive to improve the quality of education, reduce classroom sizes, integrate technology, and strengthen relationships among the partners.

One effective way of enriching the learning process is to involve various groups in education. College students, for example, who qualify for the Federal Work-Study Community Service Program work off campus helping students in kindergarten through ninth grade in the America Reads Program, whose goal is to ensure that every child can read well and independently by the end of the third grade and the America Counts Program, whose purpose is to help students through the ninth grade in developing and building strong mathematical skills.

More than 6,600 schools serving 1,600 communities have received grants and participate in the 21st Century Community Learning Centers program, which is a key component in the U.S. Department of Education Administration's efforts to keep children safe and provide academic development and other recreational and enrichment opportunities.

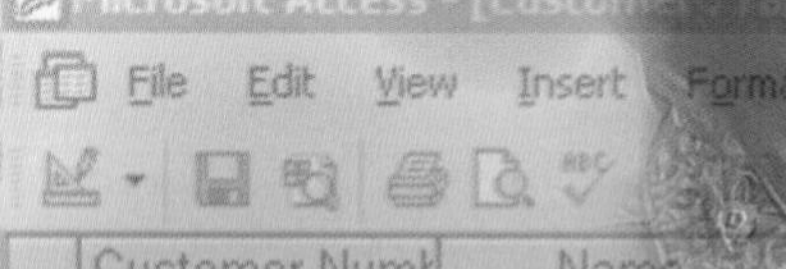

Building Databases

The International Telementor Center, hosted by the Center for Science, Mathematics & Technology Education (CSMATE) at Colorado State University, assists telementoring relationships between professional adults and students worldwide. The goal of telementoring, which combines mentoring with electronic communication, is to help students in the important subject areas of math, science, engineering, communications, and career and education planning.

In mythology, Mentor advised Odysseus, who led the Greeks in the Trojan War. Today, mentors instruct and lead others in need of guidance and direction. Common partnerships in the computer field bring together network experts with culturally diverse school districts to network classrooms within the region; technology buffs to develop distance education programs for students in remote areas; and software experts to install programs in computer labs and then train teachers.

Building these partnerships requires superb technological and organizational skills, strong marketing, and dedicated staff members. The nation's largest nonprofit computerization assistance center, CompuMentor, is one of these successful partnering organizations. CompuMentor has linked its staff with more than 23,000 schools and other nonprofit organizations since 1987.

The heart of its success is matching computer experts with the appropriate school or organization. Some mentors volunteer long term, while others agree to work intensively for a few days, particularly in telecommunications areas. Potential mentors complete an application at CompuMentor's Web site (www.compumentor.org) by entering specific information in boxes, called fields, pertaining to their knowledge of operating systems, networking, and hardware repair. They give additional information about their available working hours, training experience, and special skills in office and accounting applications, databases, and desktop publishing.

This information structures records in the CompuMentor database. The staff then can search these records to find a volunteer whose skills match the school's or organization's needs. Similarly in Project 1, you will use the Access database management system to enter records in the Alisa Vending Services database so the staff can match drivers with vendors whose machines require replenishing, maintenance, and repairs.

Uniting schools with appropriate experts increases awareness of educational issues and ultimately improves the learning process. For more information on building mentoring relationships, visit the U.S. Department of Education Web site (www.ed.gov) or call 1-800-USA-LEARN.

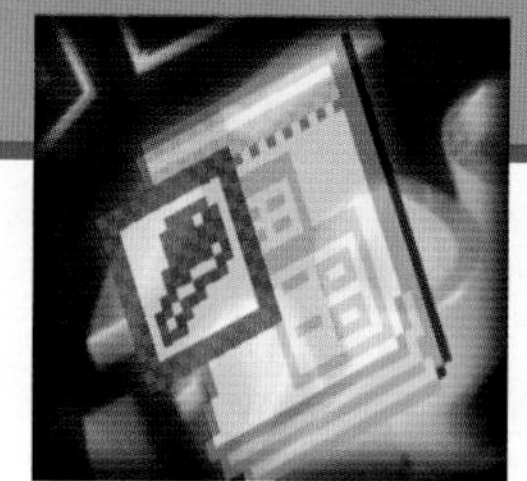

Microsoft Access 2002

Creating a Database Using Design and Datasheet Views

PROJECT

CASE PERSPECTIVE

Alisa Vending Services is a company that places vending machines in its customers' facilities. In return for the privilege of placing the vending machine, Alisa pays each customer a share of the profits from the machine. Payments are made quarterly. Alisa must track the amount already paid to each customer this year. It also must track the amount due to each customer for the current quarter.

Alisa employs drivers to service its customers. Each customer is assigned to a specific driver. The driver replenishes the food and beverage items in the machine, collects the money, and performs routine maintenance and simple repairs.

To ensure operations run smoothly, Alisa Vending Services needs to maintain data on its drivers and their assigned customers. Rather than using a manual system, Alisa wants to organize the data in a database, managed by a database management system such as Access. In this way, Alisa can keep its data current and accurate while management can analyze the data for trends and produce a variety of useful reports. Your task is to help Alisa Vending Services in creating and using their database.

What Is Microsoft Access?

Microsoft Access is a powerful database management system (DBMS) that functions in the Windows environment and allows you to create and process data in a database. Some of the key features are:

- **Data entry and update** Access provides easy mechanisms for adding, changing, and deleting data, including the ability to make mass changes in a single operation.
- **Queries (questions)** Using Access, it is easy to ask complex questions concerning the data in the database and receive instant answers.
- **Forms** In Access, you can produce attractive and useful forms for viewing and updating data.
- **Reports** Access contains a feature to create sophisticated reports easily for presenting your data.
- **Web Support** Access allows you to save objects, reports, and tables in HTML format so they can be viewed using a browser. You also can create data access pages to allow real-time access to data in the database via the Internet.

Project One — Alisa Vending Services

Creating, storing, sorting, and retrieving data are important tasks. In their personal lives, many people keep a variety of records such as names, addresses, and telephone numbers of friends and business associates, records of investments, records of expenses for tax purposes, and so on. These records must be arranged for quick access. Businesses also must be able to store and access information quickly and easily. Personnel and inventory records, payroll information, client records, order data, and accounts receivable information all are crucial and must be available readily.

The term **database** describes a collection of data organized in a manner that allows access, retrieval, and use of that data. A database management system, such as Access, allows you to use a computer to create a database; add, change, and delete data in the database; sort the data in the database; retrieve data in the database; and create forms and reports using the data in the database.

In Access, a database consists of a collection of tables. Figure 1-1 shows a sample database for Alisa Vending Services, which consists of two tables. The Customer table contains information about the customers to whom Alisa Vending Services provides services. Each customer is assigned to a specific driver. The Driver table contains information about the drivers to whom these customers are assigned.

The rows in the tables are called **records.** A record contains information about a given person, product, or event. A row in the Customer table, for example, contains information about a specific customer.

The columns in the tables are called fields. A **field** contains a specific piece of information within a record. In the Customer table, for example, the fourth field, City, contains the city where the customer is located.

More About

Databases in Access

In some DBMSs, every table, query, form, or report is stored in a separate file. This is not the case in Access, in which a database is stored in a single file on disk. The file contains all the tables, queries, forms, reports, and programs that you create for this database.

fields

customers of driver Larissa Tuttle

records

Customer table

CUSTOMER NUMBER	NAME	ADDRESS	CITY	STATE	ZIP CODE	AMOUNT PAID	CURRENT DUE	DRIVER NUMBER
BA95	Bayside Hotel	287 Riley	Hansen	FL	38513	$21,876.00	$892.50	30
BR46	Baldwin-Reed	267 Howard	Fernwood	FL	37023	$26,512.00	$2,672.00	60
CN21	Century North	1562 Butler	Hansen	FL	38513	$8,725.00	$0.00	60
FR28	Friend's Movies	871 Adams	Westport	FL	37070	$4,256.00	$1,202.00	75
GN62	Grand Nelson	7821 Oak	Wood Key	FL	36828	$8,287.50	$925.50	30
GS29	Great Screens	572 Lee	Hansen	FL	38513	$21,625.00	$0.00	60
LM22	Lenger Mason	274 Johnson	Westport	FL	37070	$0.00	$0.00	60
ME93	Merks College	561 Fairhill	Bayville	FL	38734	$24,761.00	$1,572.00	30
RI78	Riter University	26 Grove	Fernwood	FL	37023	$11,682.25	$2,827.50	75
TU20	Turner Hotel	8672 Quincy	Palmview	FL	36114	$8,521.50	$0.00	60

driver Larissa Tuttle

Driver table

DRIVER NUMBER	LAST NAME	FIRST NAME	ADDRESS	CITY	STATE	ZIP CODE	HOURLY RATE	YTD EARNINGS
30	Tuttle	Larissa	7562 Hickory	Laton Springs	FL	37891	$16.00	$21,145.25
60	Powers	Frank	57 Ravenwood	Gillmore	FL	37572	$15.00	$19,893.50
75	Ortiz	Jose	341 Pierce	Douglas	FL	37613	$17.00	$23,417.00

FIGURE 1-1

The first field in the Customer table is the Customer Number. This is a code assigned by Alisa Vending Services to each customer. Similar to many organizations, Alisa Vending Services calls it a *number* although it actually contains letters. The customer numbers have a special format. They consist of two uppercase letters followed by a two-digit number.

These numbers are unique; that is, no two customers will be assigned the same number. Such a field can be used as a **unique identifier**. This simply means that a given customer number will display only in a single record in the table. Only one record exists, for example, in which the customer number is CN21. A unique identifier also is called a **primary key**. Thus, the Customer Number field is the primary key for the Customer table.

The next seven fields in the Customer table are Name, Address, City, State, Zip Code, Amount Paid, and Current Due. The Amount Paid field contains the amount that Alisa has paid already to the customer this year. The Current Due field contains the amount due from Alisa to the customer for the current period, but not yet paid.

For example, customer BA95 is Bayside Hotel. It is located at 287 Riley in Hansen, Florida. The zip code is 38513. The customer has been paid $21,876.00 so far this year and is due to be paid $892.50 for the current period.

Each customer is assigned to a single driver. The last field in the Customer table, Driver Number, gives the number of the customer's driver.

The first field in the Driver table, Driver Number, is the number assigned by Alisa Vending Services to the driver. These numbers are unique, so Driver Number is the primary key of the Driver table.

The other fields in the Driver table are Last Name, First Name, Address, City, State, Zip Code, Hourly Rate, and YTD Earnings. The Hourly Rate field gives the driver's hourly billing rate, and the YTD Earnings field contains the total amount that has been paid to the driver for services so far this year.

For example, driver 30 is Larissa Tuttle. She lives at 7562 Hickory in Laton Springs, Florida. Her zip code is 37891. Her hourly billing rate is $16.00 and her YTD earnings are $21,145.25.

The driver number displays in both the Customer table and the Driver table. It is used to relate customers and drivers. For example, in the Customer table, you see that the driver number for customer BA95 is 30. To find the name of this driver, look for the row in the Driver table that contains 30 in the Driver Number field. Once you have found it, you know the customer is assigned to Larissa Tuttle. To find all the customers assigned to Larissa Tuttle, on the other hand, look through the Customer table for all the customers that contain 30 in the Driver Number field. Her customers are BA95 (Bayside Hotel), GN62 (Grand Nelson), and ME93 (Merks College).

The Access Help System

Need Help? It is no further than the Ask a Question box in the upper-right corner of the window. Click the box that contains the text Type a question for help (Figure 1-3), type `help` and then press the ENTER key. Access will respond with a list of items you can click to learn about obtaining help on any Access-related topic. To find out what is new in Access 2002, type `what's new in Access` in the Ask a Question box.

Together with the management of Alisa Vending Services, you have determined the data that must be maintained in the database is that shown in Figure 1-1 on the previous page. You first must create the database and the tables it contains. In the process, you must define the fields included in the two tables, as well as the type of data each field will contain. You then must add the appropriate records to the tables. You also must print the contents of the tables. Finally, you must create a report with the Customer Number, Name, Amount Paid, and Current Due fields for each customer served by Alisa Vending Services. Other reports and requirements for the database at Alisa Vending Services will be addressed with the Alisa Vending Services management in the future.

Starting Access

To start Access, Windows must be running. Perform the following steps to start Access.

Steps To Start Access

1 Click the Start button on the Windows taskbar, point to Programs on the Start menu, and then point to Microsoft Access on the Programs submenu.

The commands on the Start menu display above the Start button and the Programs submenu displays (Figure 1-2). If the Office Voice Recognition software is installed on your computer, then the Language bar may display somewhere on the desktop.

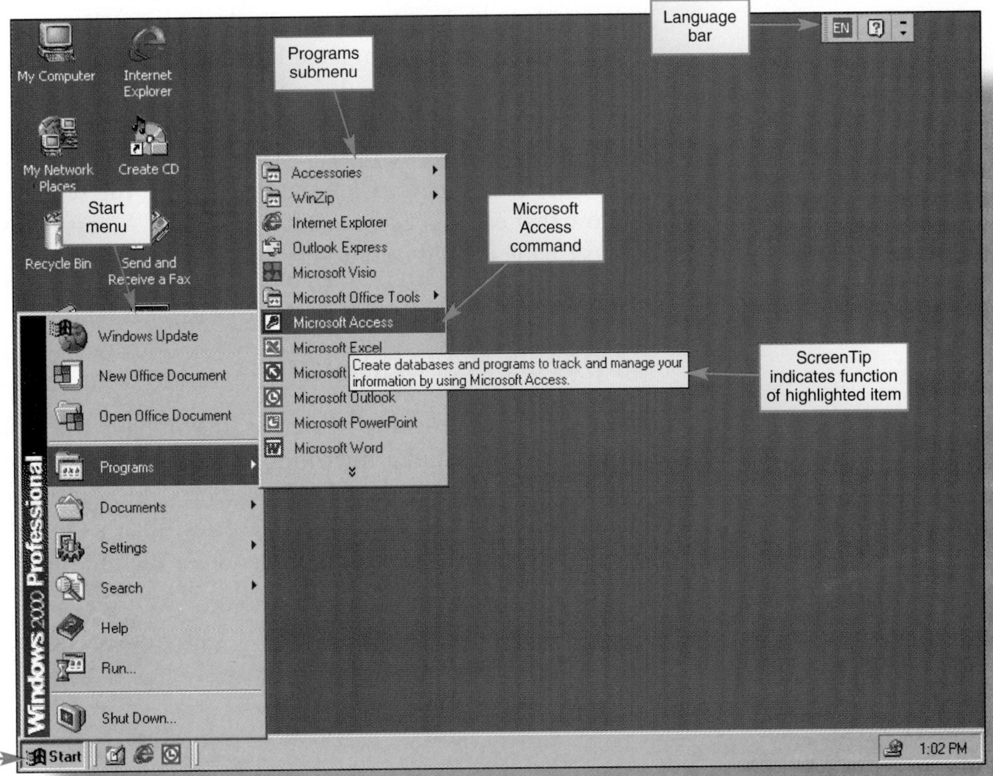

FIGURE 1-2

2 Click Microsoft Access.

Access starts. After several seconds, the Access window displays (Figure 1-3). If the Language bar displayed on the desktop when you started Access, then it expands to display additional buttons.

3 If the Access window is not maximized, double-click its title bar to maximize it.

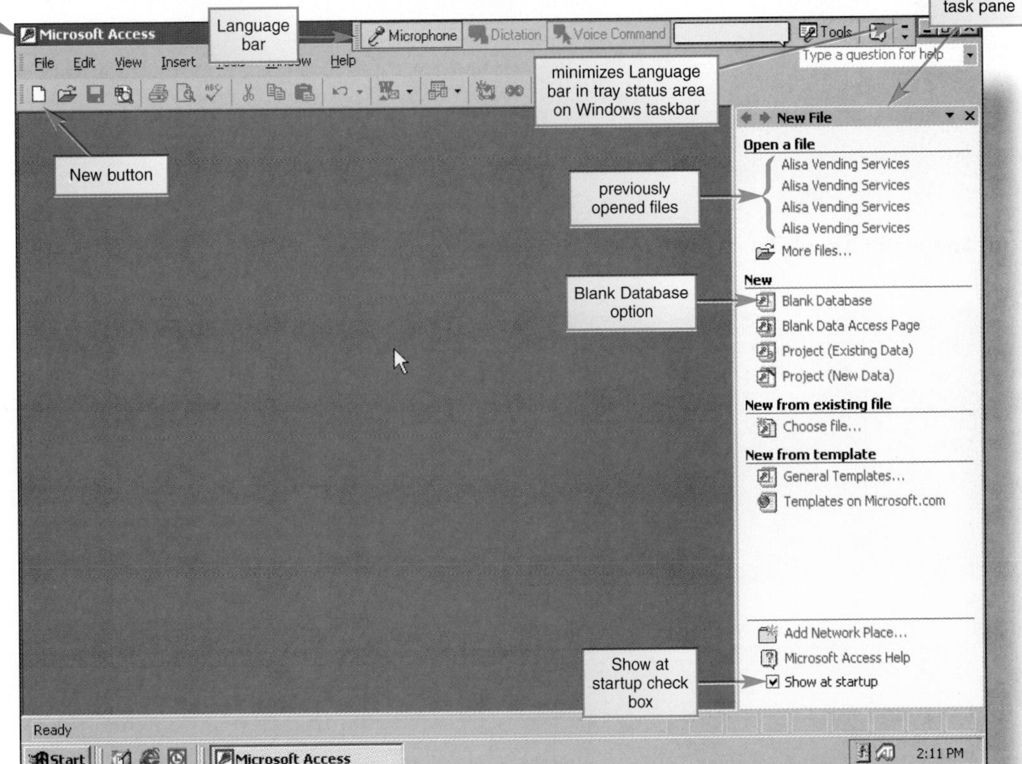

FIGURE 1-3

Task Panes

When you first start Access, a small window called a task pane may display docked on the right side of the screen. You can drag a task pane title bar to float the pane in your work area or dock it on either the left or right side of a screen, depending on your personal preference.

The screen in Figure 1-3 on the previous page shows how the Access window looks the first time you start Access after installation on most computers. If the Office Speech Recognition software is installed on your system, then when you start Access either the Language bar displays somewhere on the desktop (shown at the top of Figure 1-3) or the Language Indicator button displays on the right side of the Windows taskbar (Figure 1-5). In this book, the Language bar will be kept minimized until it is used. For additional information about the Language bar, see Appendix B on page A B.01.

Notice also that a task pane displays on the screen. A **task pane** is a separate window that enables users to carry out some Access tasks more efficiently. In this book, the task pane is used only to create a new database and then it should not display.

Speech Recognition

When you begin working in Access, if you have the **Office Speech Recognition software** installed and a microphone, you can speak the names of toolbar buttons, menus, menu commands, list items, alerts, and dialog box controls, such as OK and Cancel. You also can dictate field entries, such as text and numbers. To indicate whether you want to speak commands or dictate field entries, you use the **Language bar** (Figure 1-4a). You can display the Language bar in two ways: (1) click the Language Indicator button in the tray status area on the Windows taskbar by the clock, and then click Show the Language bar on the menu (Figure 1-4b), or (2) point to the **Speech command** on the **Tools menu** and then click the **Speech Recognition command** on the **Speech submenu.**

If the Language Indicator button does not display in the tray status area, and if the Speech command is unavailable (dimmed) on the Tools menu, the Office Speech Recognition software is not installed. To install the software, you first must start Word and then click Speech on the Tools menu.

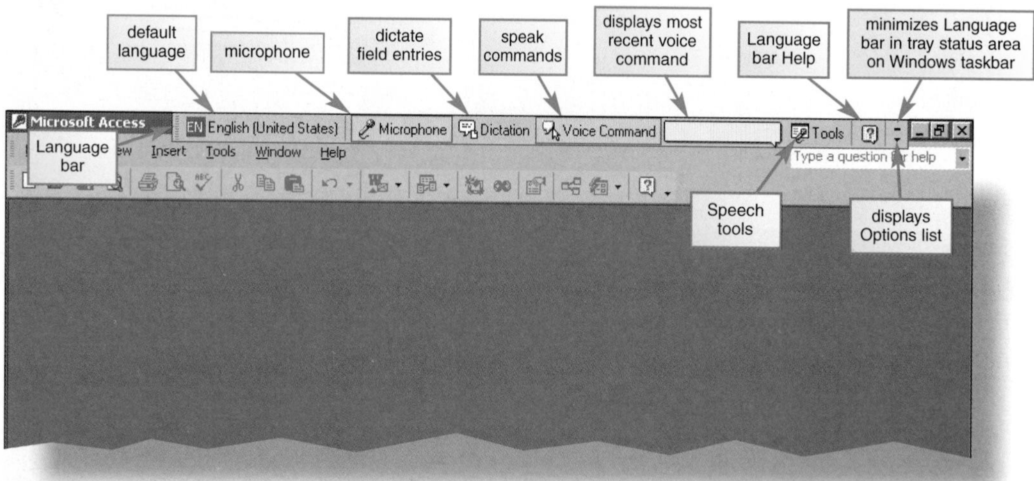

(a) Language Bar

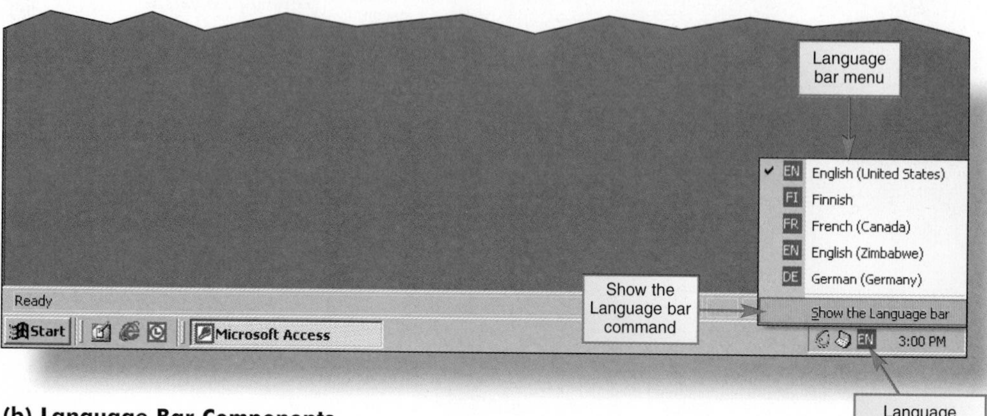

(b) Language Bar Components

FIGURE 1-4

If you have speakers, you can instruct the computer to read a document to you. By selecting the appropriate option, you can have the document read in a male or female voice.

Additional information on the Office speech and handwriting recognition capabilities is available in Appendix B.

More About

Creating a Database: The Database Wizard

Access includes a Database Wizard that can guide you by suggesting some commonly used databases. To use the Database Wizard, click New on the Database toolbar, and then click General Templates in the New File task pane. When the Templates dialog box displays, click the Databases tab, and then click the database that is most appropriate for your needs. Follow the instructions in the Database Wizard dialog boxes to create the database.

Creating a New Database

In Access, all the tables, reports, forms, and queries that you create are stored in a single file called a database. Thus, before creating any of these objects, you first must create the database that will hold them. You use the Blank Database option in the task pane to create a new database. To allow the full Access window to display when you work with a database, you should close the task pane after creating a new database. Perform the following steps to create a new database and save the database on a floppy disk in drive A.

Steps To Create a New Database

1 If the Language bar displays, click its Minimize button. If a dialog box displays, click the OK button. If necessary, click the New button on the Database toolbar to display the task pane. Click the Blank Database option in the task pane (see Figure 1-3 on page A 1.09), and then click the Save in box arrow. Point to 3½ Floppy (A:).

The Save in List displays in the File New Database dialog box (Figure 1-5). Your file name text box may display db1.mdb.

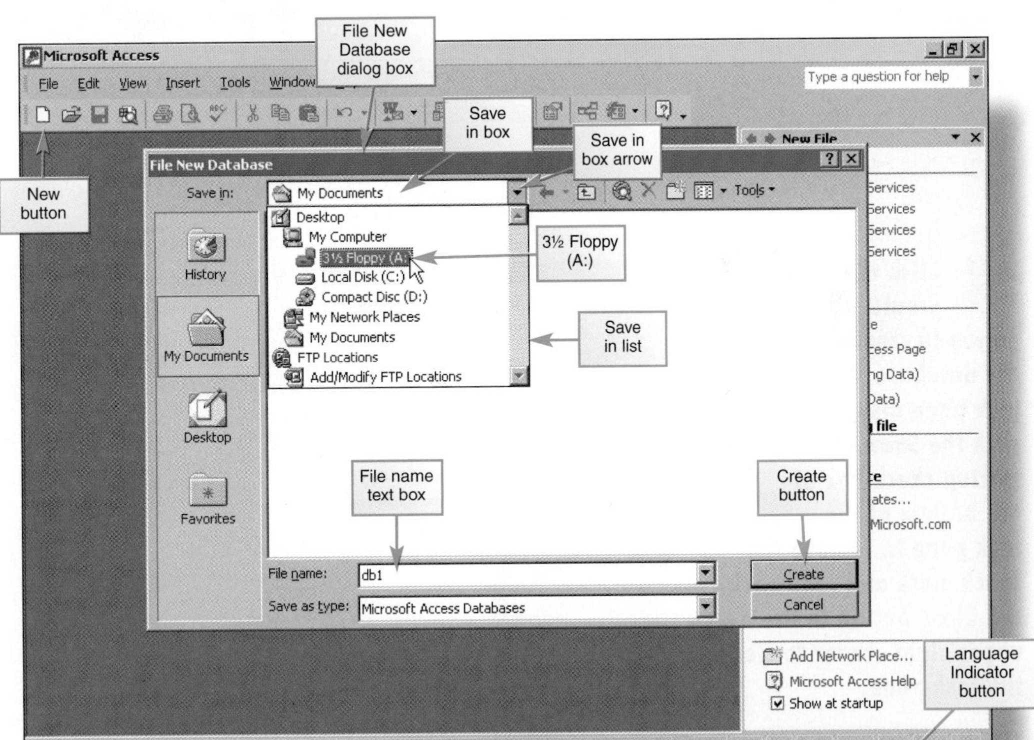

FIGURE 1-5

2 Click 3½ Floppy (A:). Click the File name text box. Repeatedly press the BACKSPACE key to delete db1 and then type `Alisa Vending Services` **as the file name. Point to the Create button.**

The file name is changed to Alisa Vending Services (Figure 1-6).

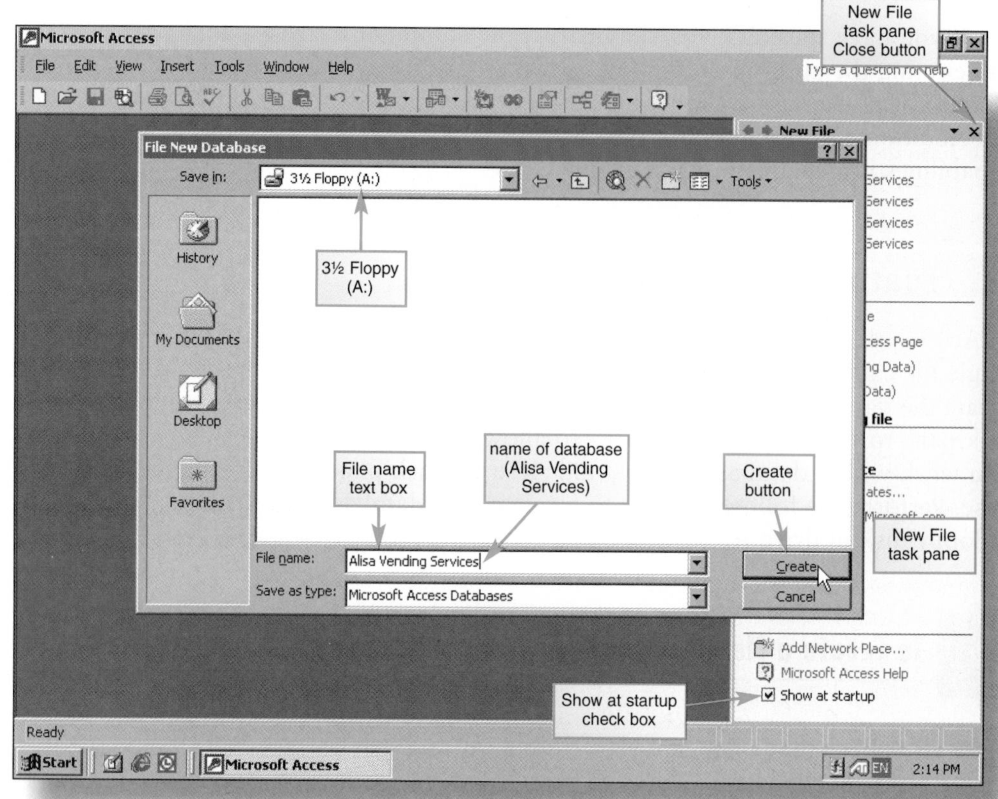

FIGURE 1-6

3 Click the Create button to create the database. If the task pane displays, click the Show at startup check box at the bottom of the task pane to remove the check mark and then click the Close button in the upper-right corner to close the task pane.

The Alisa Vending Services database is created. The Alisa Vending Services : Database window displays on the desktop (Figure 1-7). The New File task pane does not display.

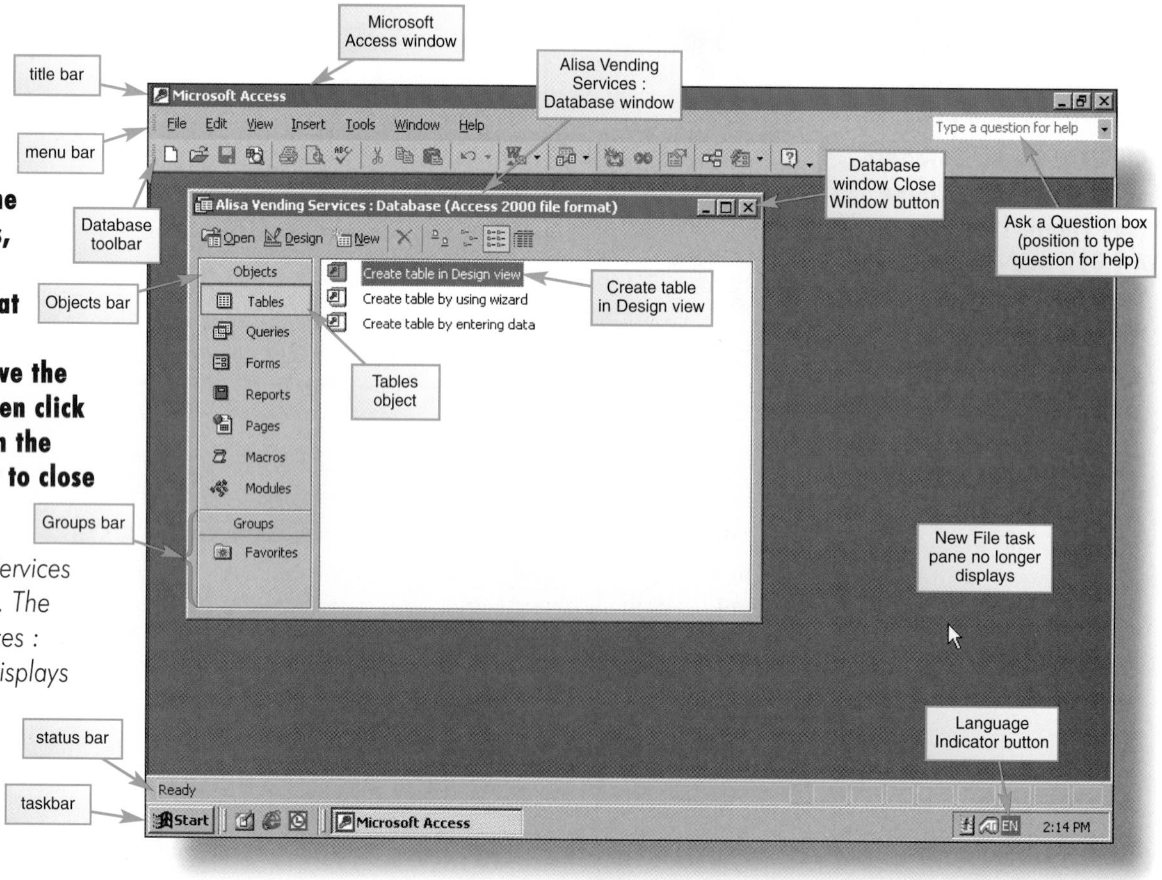

Microsoft Access window
title bar
menu bar
Alisa Vending Services : Database window
Database toolbar
Database window Close Window button
Ask a Question box (position to type question for help)
Objects bar
Create table in Design view
Tables object
Groups bar
New File task pane no longer displays
Language Indicator button
status bar
taskbar

FIGURE 1-7

The Access Desktop and the Database Window

The first bar on the desktop (Figure 1-7) is the **title bar**. It displays the title of the product, Microsoft Access. The button on the right is the **Close button**. Clicking the Close button closes the window.

The second bar is the **menu bar**. It contains a list of menu names. To open a menu from the menu bar, click the menu name. Initially a personalized version of the menu, a short menu that consists of commands you have selected most recently, displays. After a few seconds, the full menu displays. If the command you wish to select is on the short menu, you can select it immediately. If not, wait a few seconds to view the full menu. (The menus shown throughout this book are the full menus, the ones that display after a few seconds.)

The third bar is the **Database toolbar**. The Database toolbar contains buttons that allow you to perform certain tasks more quickly than using the menu bar. Each button contains a picture, or **icon**, depicting its function. The specific toolbar or toolbars that display will vary, depending on the task on which you are working.

The **taskbar** at the bottom of the screen displays the Start button, any active windows, and the current time.

Immediately above the Windows taskbar is the **status bar** (Figure 1-7). It contains special information that is appropriate for the task on which you are working. Currently, it contains the word, Ready, which means Access is ready to accept commands.

The **Database window**, referred to in Figure 1-7 as the Alisa Vending Services : Database window, is a special window that allows you to access easily and rapidly a variety of objects such as tables, queries, forms, and reports. To do so, you will use the various components of the window.

Creating a Table

An Access database consists of a collection of tables. Once you have created the database, you must create each of the tables within it. In this project, for example, you must create both the Customer and Driver tables shown in Figure 1-1 on page A 1.07.

To create a table, you describe the **structure** of the table to Access by describing the fields within the table. For each field, you indicate the following:

1. **Field name** — Each field in the table must have a unique name. In the Customer table (Figure 1-8 on the next page), for example, the field names are Customer Number, Name, Address, City, State, Zip Code, Amount Paid, Current Due, and Driver Number.
2. **Data type** — Data type indicates to Access the type of data the field will contain. Some fields can contain only numbers. Others, such as Amount Paid and Current Due, can contain numbers and dollar signs. Still others, such as Name and Address, can contain letters.
3. **Description** — Access allows you to enter a detailed description of the field.

You also can assign field widths to text fields (fields whose data type is Text). This indicates the maximum number of characters that can be stored in the field. If you do not assign a width to such a field, Access assumes the width is 50.

More About

Toolbars

Normally, the correct Access toolbar automatically will display. If it does not, click View on the menu bar, and then click Toolbars. Click the toolbar for the activity in which you are engaged and then click the Close button. See Appendix D for additional details.

More About

Access File Formats

By default, Access creates a new database in Access 2000 format. A file in Access 2000 file format can be opened in both Access 2000 and Access 2002. This allows you to share your database with users who do not have Access 2002. You can open a file in Access 2002 format only in Access 2002. Certain features of Access 2002 are not available if the database is in Access 2000 file format.

More About

Creating a Table: The Table Wizard

Access includes a Table Wizard that guides you by suggesting some commonly used tables and fields. To use the Table Wizard, click the Tables object in the Database window. Right-click Create table by using wizard and then click Open on the shortcut menu. Follow the directions in the Table Wizard dialog boxes. After you create the table, you can modify it at any time by opening the table in Design view.

Structure of Customer table

FIELD NAME	DATA TYPE	FIELD SIZE	PRIMARY KEY?	DESCRIPTION
Customer Number	Text	4	Yes	Customer Number (Primary Key)
Name	Text	20		Customer Name
Address	Text	15		Street Address
City	Text	15		City
State	Text	2		State (Two-Character Abbreviation)
Zip Code	Text	5		Zip Code (Five-Character Version)
Amount Paid	Currency			Amount Paid to Customer This Year
Current Due	Currency			Amount Due to Customer This Period
Driver Number	Text	2		Number of Customer's Driver

Data for Customer table

CUSTOMER NUMBER	NAME	ADDRESS	CITY	STATE	ZIP CODE	AMOUNT PAID	CURRENT DUE	DRIVER NUMBER
BA95	Bayside Hotel	287 Riley	Hansen	FL	38513	$21,876.00	$892.50	30
BR46	Baldwin-Reed	267 Howard	Fernwood	FL	37023	$26,512.00	$2,672.00	60
CN21	Century North	1562 Butler	Hansen	FL	38513	$8,725.00	$0.00	60
FR28	Friend's Movies	871 Adams	Westport	FL	37070	$4,256.00	$1,202.00	75
GN62	Grand Nelson	7821 Oak	Wood Key	FL	36828	$8,287.50	$925.50	30
GS29	Great Screens	572 Lee	Hansen	FL	38513	$21,625.00	$0.00	60
LM22	Lenger Mason	274 Johnson	Westport	FL	37070	$0.00	$0.00	60
ME93	Merks College	561 Fairhill	Bayville	FL	38734	$24,761.00	$1,572.00	30
RI78	Riter University	26 Grove	Fernwood	FL	37023	$11,682.25	$2,827.50	75
TU20	Turner Hotel	8672 Quincy	Palmview	FL	36114	$8,521.50	$0.00	60

FIGURE 1-8

You also must indicate which field or fields make up the **primary key**; that is, the unique identifier, for the table. In the sample database, the Customer Number field is the primary key of the Customer table and the Driver Number field is the primary key of the Driver table.

The rules for field names are:

1. Names can be up to 64 characters in length.
2. Names can contain letters, digits, and spaces, as well as most of the punctuation symbols.
3. Names cannot contain periods, exclamation points (!), accent graves (`), or square brackets ([ ]).
4. The same name cannot be used for two different fields in the same table.

Data Types (General)

Different database management systems have different available data types. Even data types that are essentially the same can have different names. The Access Text data type, for example, is referred to as Character in some systems and Alpha in others.

Each field has a **data type**. This indicates the type of data that can be stored in the field. The data types you will use in this project are:

1. **Text** — The field can contain any characters.
2. **Number** — The field can contain only numbers. The numbers either can be positive or negative. Fields are assigned this type so they can be used in arithmetic operations. Fields that contain numbers but will not be used for arithmetic operations usually are assigned a data type of Text. The Driver Number field, for example, is a text field because the driver numbers will not be involved in any arithmetic.
3. **Currency** — The field can contain only dollar amounts. The values will be displayed with dollar signs, commas, decimal points, and with two digits following the decimal point. Like numeric fields, you can use currency fields in arithmetic operations. Access assigns a size to currency fields automatically.

The field names, data types, field widths, primary key information, and descriptions for the Customer table are shown in Figure 1-8. With this information, you are ready to begin creating the table. To create the table, use the following steps.

Data Types (Access)

Access offers a wide variety of data types, some of which have special options associated with them. For more information on data types, visit the Access 2002 More About Web page (scsite.com/ac2002/more.htm) and then click Data Types.

Steps To Create a Table

1 Right-click Create table in Design view and then point to Open on the shortcut menu.

The shortcut menu for creating a table in Design view displays (Figure 1-9).

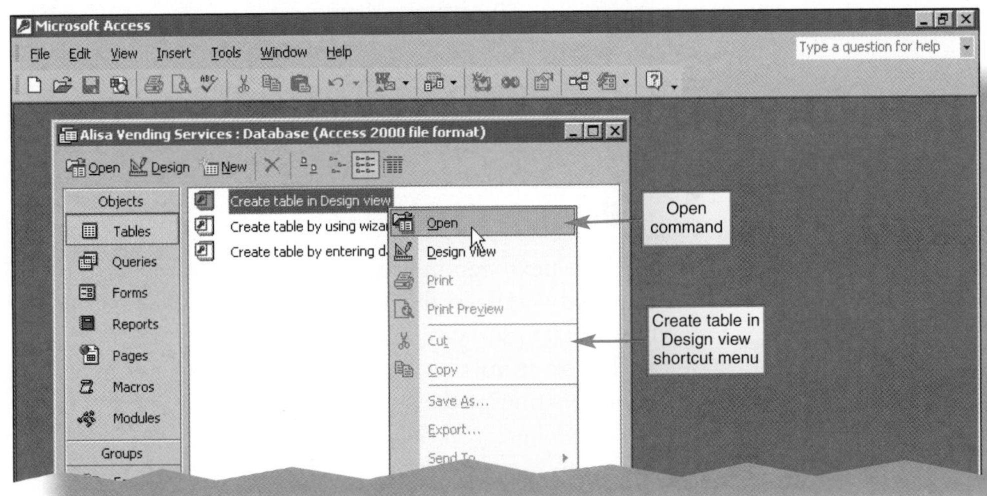

FIGURE 1-9

2 Click Open and then point to the Maximize button for the Table1 : Table window.

The Table1 : Table window displays (Figure 1-10).

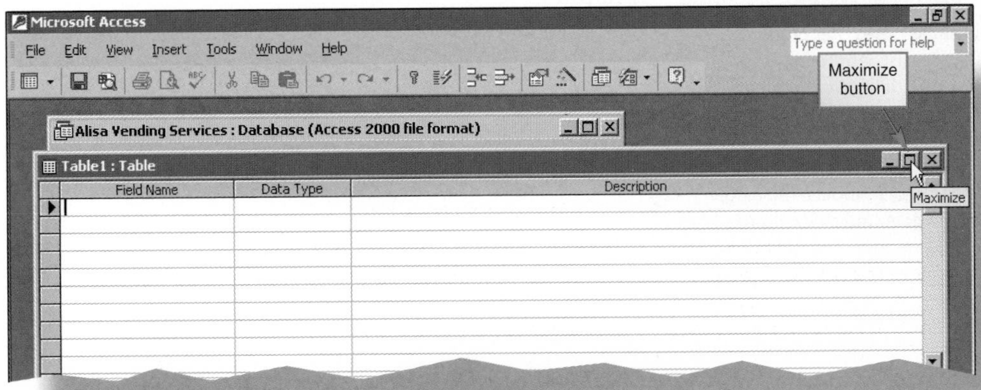

FIGURE 1-10

3 Click the Maximize button for the Table1 : Table window.

A maximized Table1 : Table window displays (Figure 1-11).

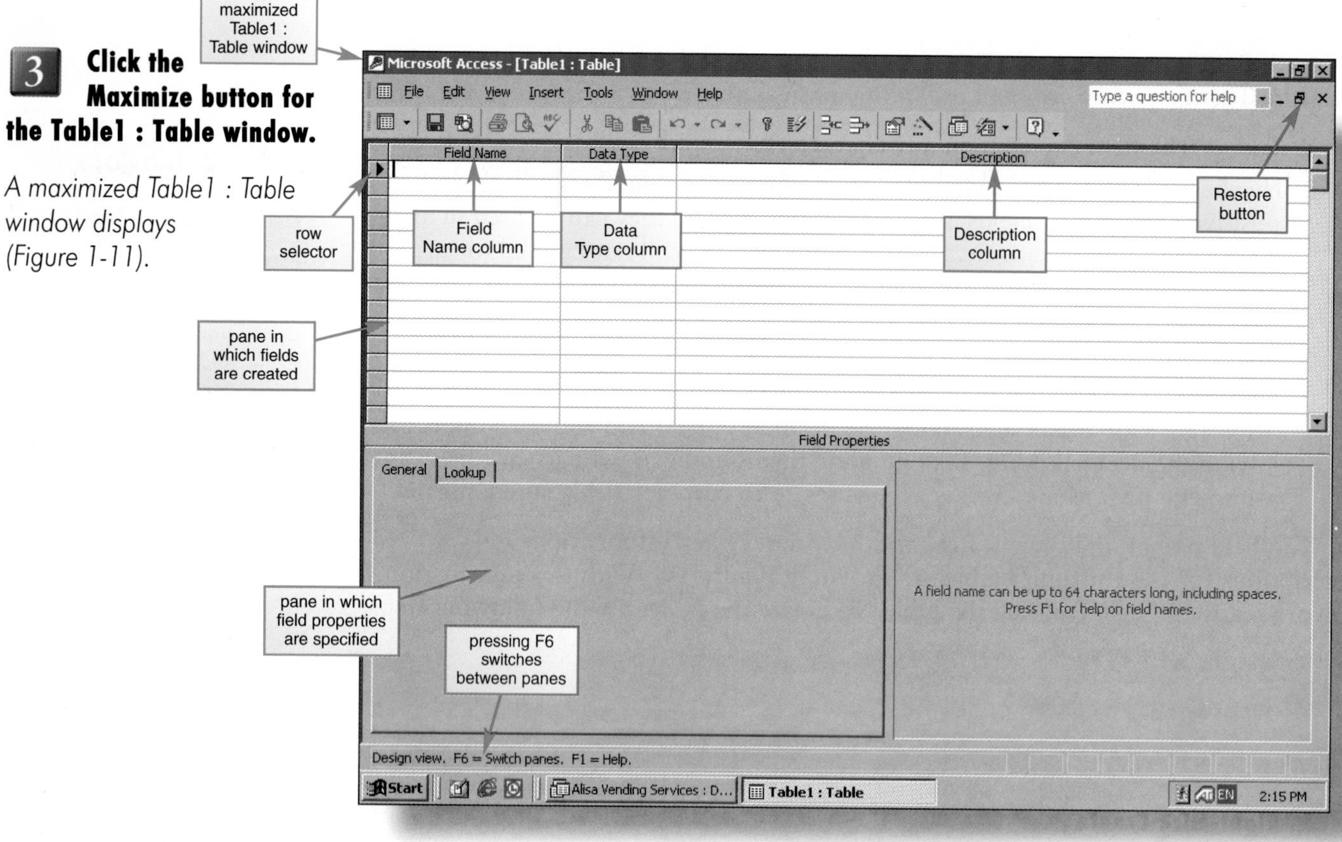

FIGURE 1-11

Other Ways

1. Click New button on Database window toolbar
2. On Insert menu click Table
3. Press ALT+N
4. In Voice Command mode, say "Insert, Table"

Defining the Fields

The next step in creating the table is to define the fields by specifying the required details in the Table window. Make entries in the Field Name, Data Type, and Description columns. Enter additional information in the Field Properties box in the lower portion of the Table window. Press the F6 key to move from the upper **pane** (portion of the screen), the one where you define the fields, to the lower pane, the one where you define field properties. Enter the appropriate field size and then press the F6 key to return to the upper pane. As you define the fields, the **row selector** (Figure 1-11), the small box or bar that, when clicked, selects the entire row, indicates the field you currently are describing. It is positioned on the first field, indicating Access is ready for you to enter the name of the first field in the Field Name column.

Perform the following steps to define the fields in the table.

More About

Primary Keys

In some cases, the primary key consists of a combination of fields rather than a single field. For more information on determining primary keys in such situations, visit the Access 2002 More About Web page (scsite.com/ac2002/more.htm) and then click Primary Key.

Steps To Define the Fields in a Table

1 **Type** `Customer Number` **(the name of the first field) in the Field Name column and then press the TAB key.**

The words, Customer Number, display in the Field Name column and the insertion point advances to the Data Type column, indicating you can enter the data type (Figure 1-12). The word, Text, one of the possible data types, currently displays. The arrow indicates a list of data types is available by clicking the arrow. The field properties for the Customer Number field display in the lower pane.

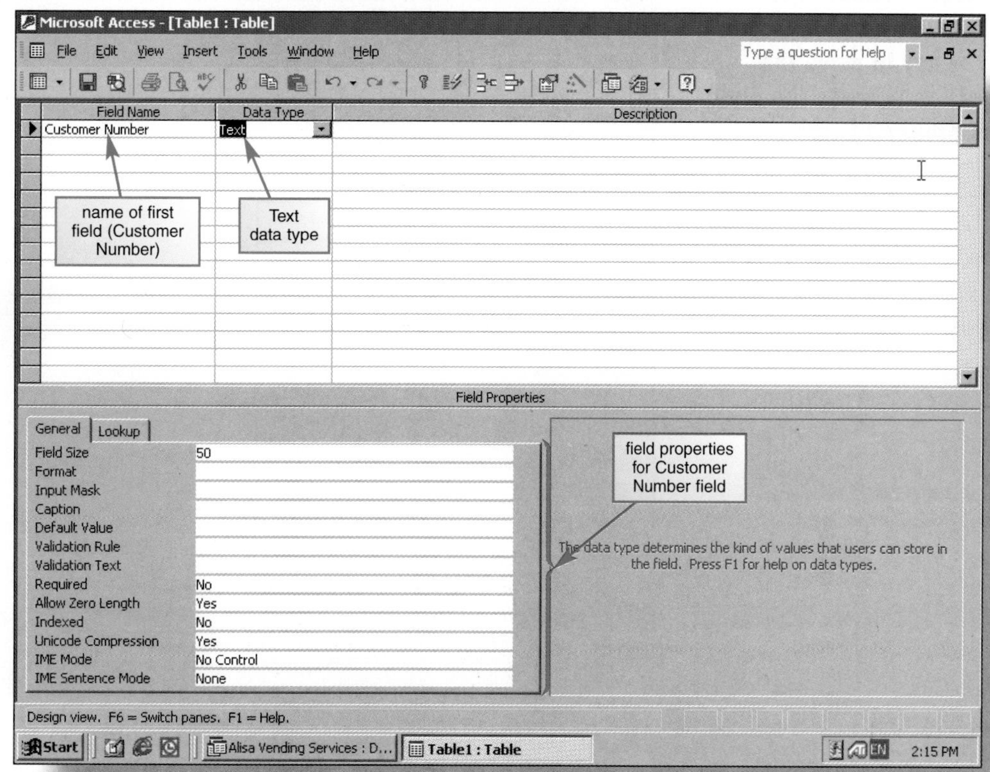

FIGURE 1-12

2 **Because Text is the correct data type, press the TAB key to move the insertion point to the Description column, type** `Customer Number (Primary Key)` **as the description and then point to the Primary Key button on the Table Design toolbar.**

A ***ScreenTip****, which is a description of the button, displays partially obscuring the description of the first field (Figure 1-13).*

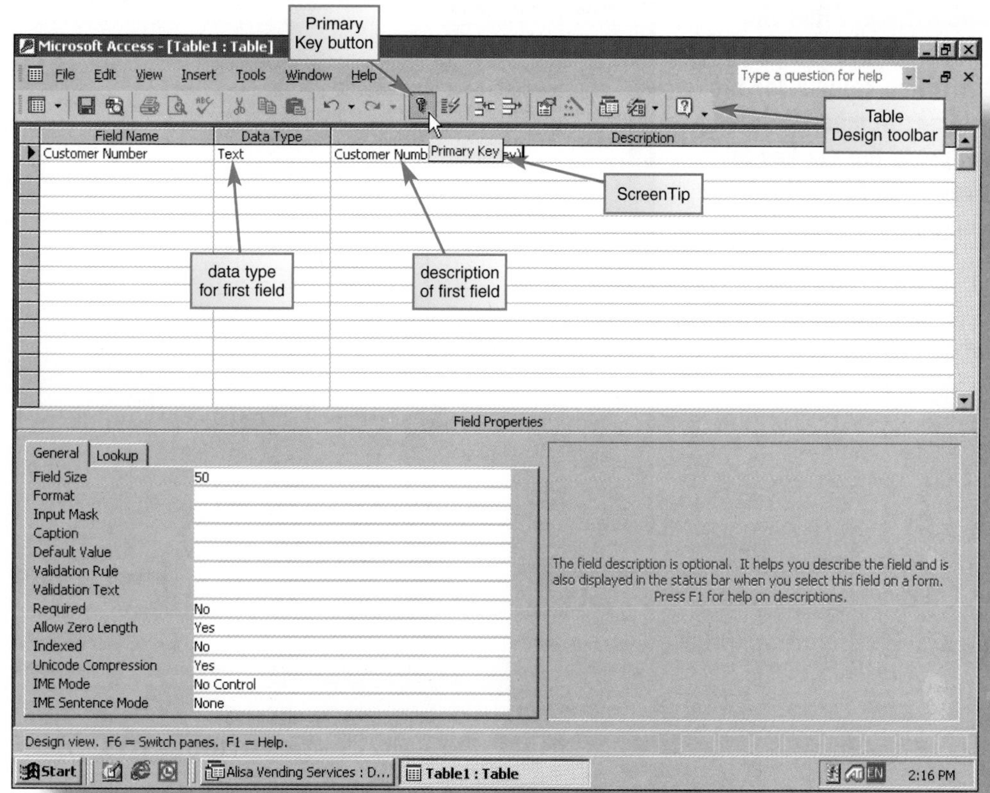

FIGURE 1-13

3 **Click the Primary Key button to make Customer Number the primary key and then press the F6 key to move the insertion point to the Field Size property box.**

The Customer Number field is the primary key as indicated by the key symbol that displays in the row selector (Figure 1-14). The current entry in the Field Size property box (50) is selected.

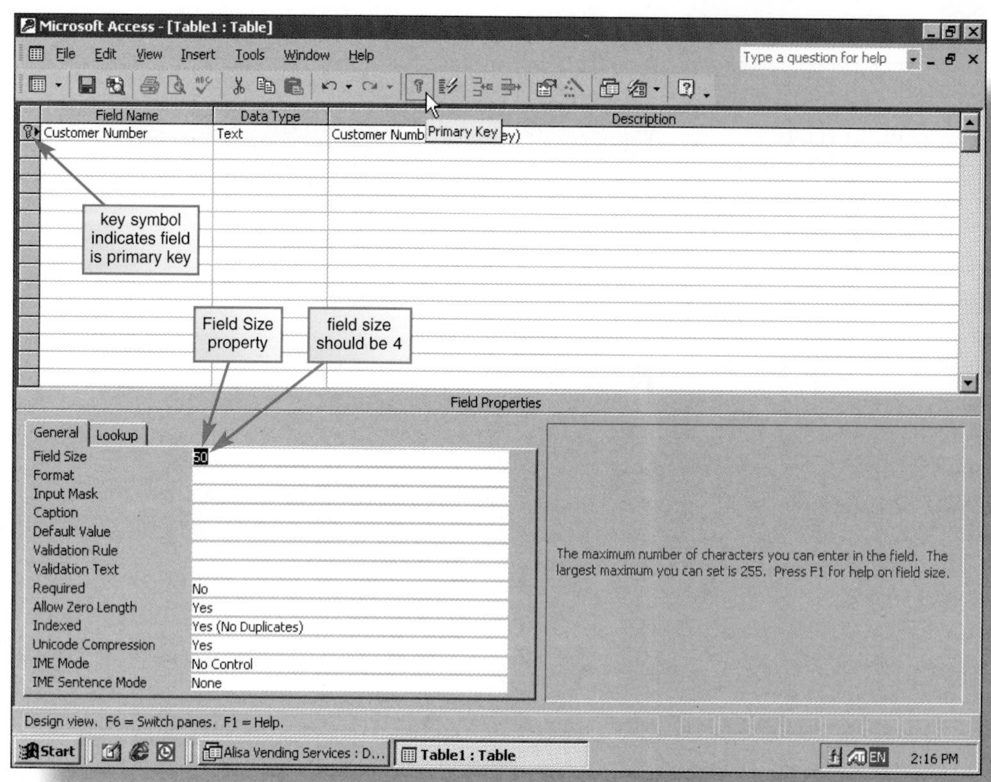

FIGURE 1-14

4 **Type** 4 **as the size of the Customer Number field. Press the F6 key to return to the Description column for the Customer Number field and then press the TAB key to move to the Field Name column in the second row.**

The insertion point moves to the second row just below the field name Customer Number (Figure 1-15).

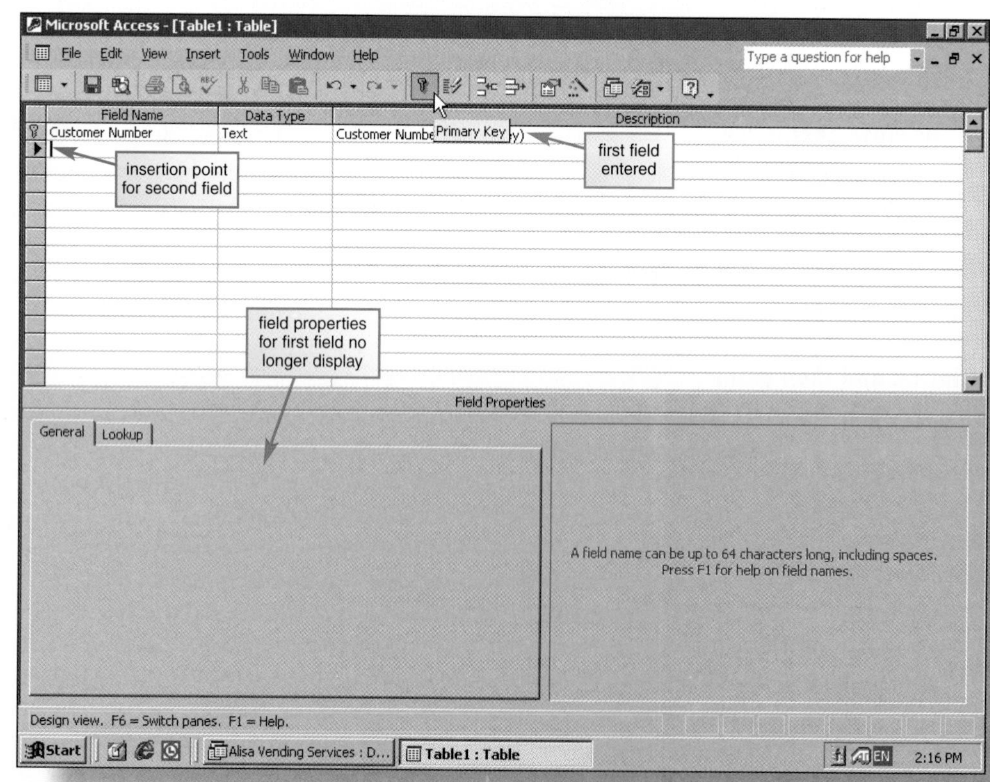

FIGURE 1-15

5 **Use the techniques illustrated in Steps 1 through 4 to make the entries from the Customer table structure shown in Figure 1-8 on page A 1.14 up through and including the name of the Amount Paid field. Click the Data Type box arrow and then point to Currency.**

The additional fields are entered (Figure 1-16). A list of available data types displays in the Data Type column for the Amount Paid field.

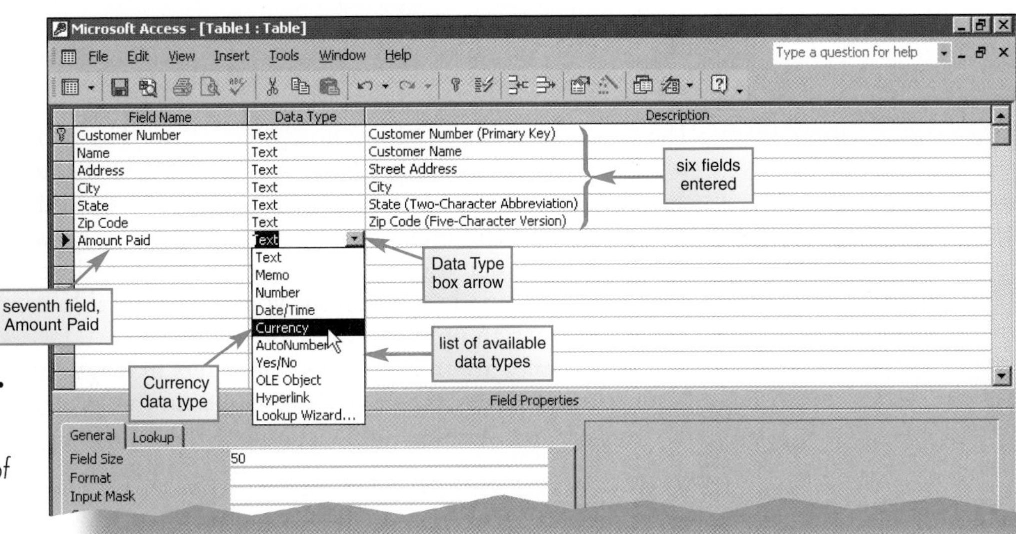

FIGURE 1-16

6 **Click Currency and then press the TAB key. Make the remaining entries from the Customer table structure shown in Figure 1-8.**

The fields are all entered (Figure 1-17).

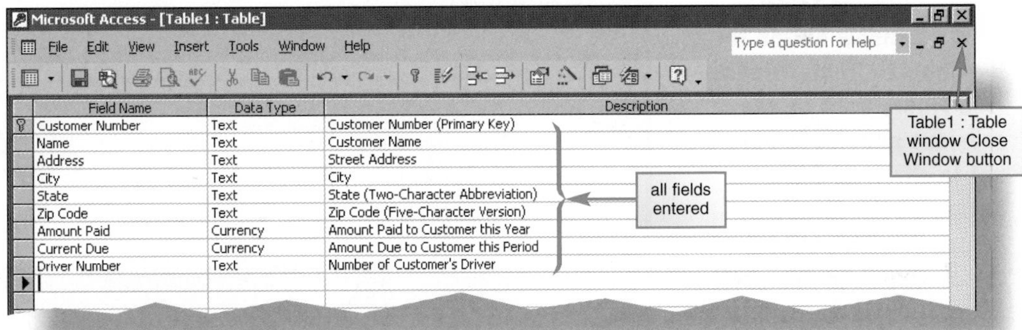

FIGURE 1-17

Correcting Errors in the Structure

When creating a table, check the entries carefully to ensure they are correct. If you make a mistake and discover it before you press the TAB key, you can correct the error by repeatedly pressing the BACKSPACE key until the incorrect characters are removed. Then, type the correct characters. If you do not discover a mistake until later, you can click the entry, type the correct value, and then press the ENTER key.

If you accidentally add an extra field to the structure, select the field by clicking the row selector (the leftmost column on the row that contains the field to be deleted). Once you have selected the field, press the DELETE key. This will remove the field from the structure.

If you forget a field, select the field that will follow the field you wish to add by clicking the row selector, and then press the INSERT key. The remaining fields move down one row, making room for the missing field. Make the entries for the new field in the usual manner.

If you made the wrong field a primary key field, click the correct primary key entry for the field and then click the Primary Key button on the Table Design toolbar.

As an alternative to these steps, you may want to start over. To do so, click the Close Window button for the Table1 : Table window and then click No. The original desktop displays and you can repeat the process you used earlier.

More About

Correcting Errors

Even after you have entered data, it still is possible to correct errors in the structure. Access will make all the necessary adjustments to the structure of the table as well as to the data within it. (It is simplest to make the correction, however, before any data is entered.)

Adding Records

As soon as you have entered or modified a record and moved to another record, the original record is saved. This is different from other tools. The rows entered in a spreadsheet, for example, are not saved until the entire spreadsheet is saved.

Saving and Closing a Table

The Customer table structure now is complete. The final step is to save the table within the database. At this time, you should give the table a name. Once you save the table structure, you can continue working in the Table window or you can close the window. To continue working in the Table Design window, click the Save button on the Table Design toolbar. To save the table and close the Table Design window, click the Close Window button. If you close the Table window without saving first, Access provides an opportunity to do so.

Table names are from 1 to 64 characters in length and can contain letters, numbers, and spaces. The two table names in this project are Customer and Driver.

To save and close the table, complete the following steps.

To Save and Close a Table

1 Click the Close Window button for the Table1 : Table window (see Figure 1-17 on the previous page). (Be sure not to click the Close button on the Microsoft Access title bar, because this would close Microsoft Access.) Point to the Yes button in the Microsoft Access dialog box.

The Microsoft Access dialog box displays (Figure 1-18).

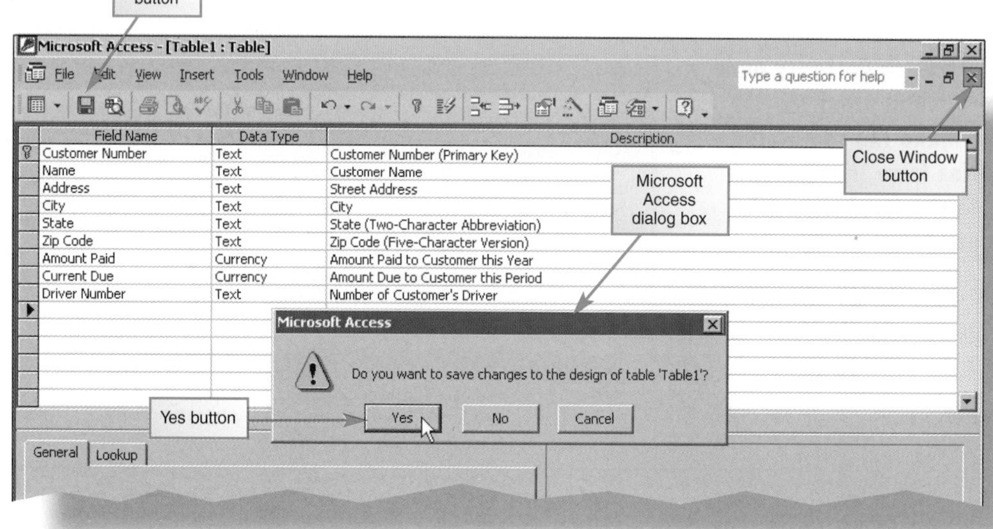

FIGURE 1-18

2 Click the Yes button in the Microsoft Access dialog box and then type `Customer` **as the name of the table. Point to the OK button.**

The Save As dialog box displays (Figure 1-19). The table name is entered.

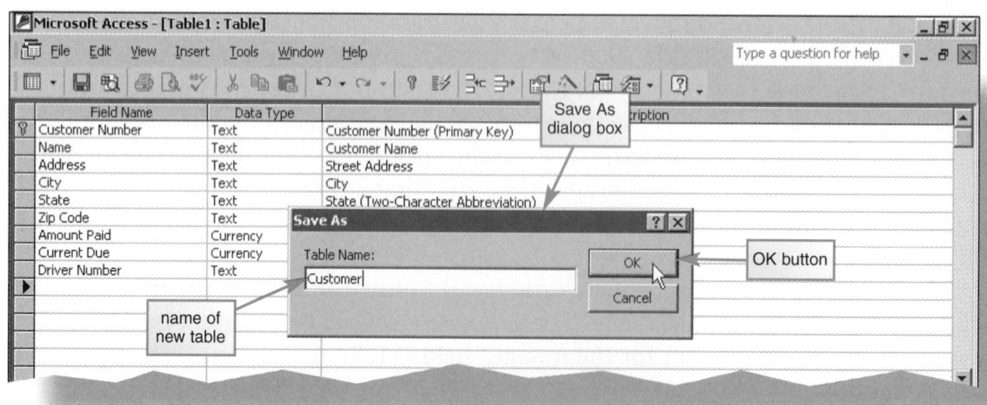

FIGURE 1-19

3 Click the OK button in the Save As dialog box.

The table is saved. The window containing the table design no longer displays.

Other Ways

1. Click Save button on Table Design toolbar
2. In Voice Command mode, say "Save"

Adding Records to a Table

Creating a table by building the structure and saving the table is the first step in a two-step process. The second step is to add records to the table. To add records to a table, the table must be open. To open a table, right-click the table in the Database window and then click Open on the shortcut menu. The table displays in Datasheet view. In **Datasheet view**, the table is represented as a collection of rows and columns called a **datasheet**. It looks very much like the tables shown in Figure 1-1 on page A 1.07.

You often add records in phases. You may, for example, not have enough time to add all the records in one session. To illustrate this process, this project begins by adding the first two records in the Customer table (Figure 1-20). The remaining records are added later.

Customer table (first 2 records)

CUSTOMER NUMBER	NAME	ADDRESS	CITY	STATE	ZIP CODE	AMOUNT PAID	CURRENT DUE	DRIVER NUMBER
BA95	Bayside Hotel	287 Riley	Hansen	FL	38513	$21,876.00	$892.50	30
BR46	Baldwin-Reed	267 Howard	Fernwood	FL	37023	$26,512.00	$2,672.00	60

FIGURE 1-20

To open the Customer table and then add records, perform the following steps.

Steps To Add Records to a Table

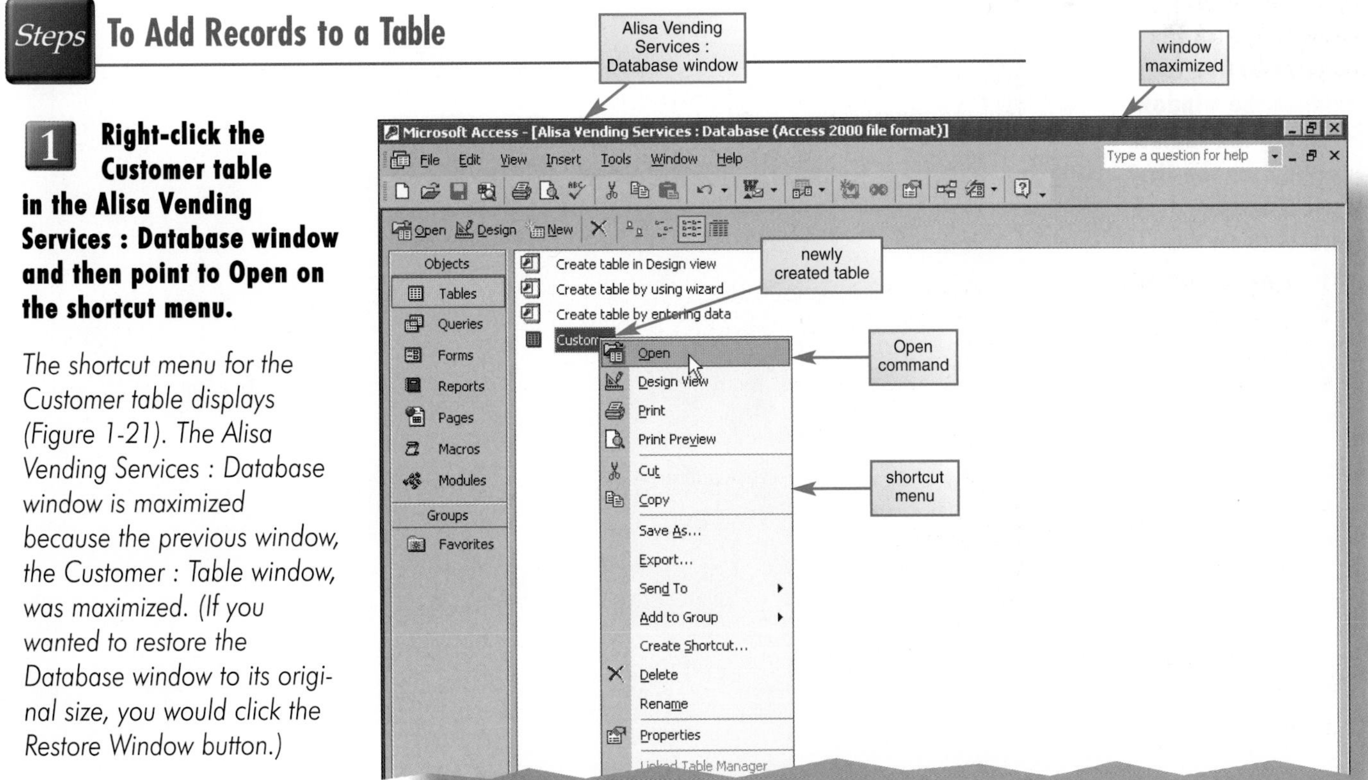

1 **Right-click the Customer table in the Alisa Vending Services : Database window and then point to Open on the shortcut menu.**

The shortcut menu for the Customer table displays (Figure 1-21). The Alisa Vending Services : Database window is maximized because the previous window, the Customer : Table window, was maximized. (If you wanted to restore the Database window to its original size, you would click the Restore Window button.)

FIGURE 1-21

2 Click Open on the shortcut menu.

*The Customer : Table window displays (Figure 1-22). The window contains the Datasheet view for the Customer table. The **record selector**, the small box or bar that, when clicked, selects the entire record, is positioned on the first record. The status bar at the bottom of the window also indicates that the record selector is positioned on record 1.*

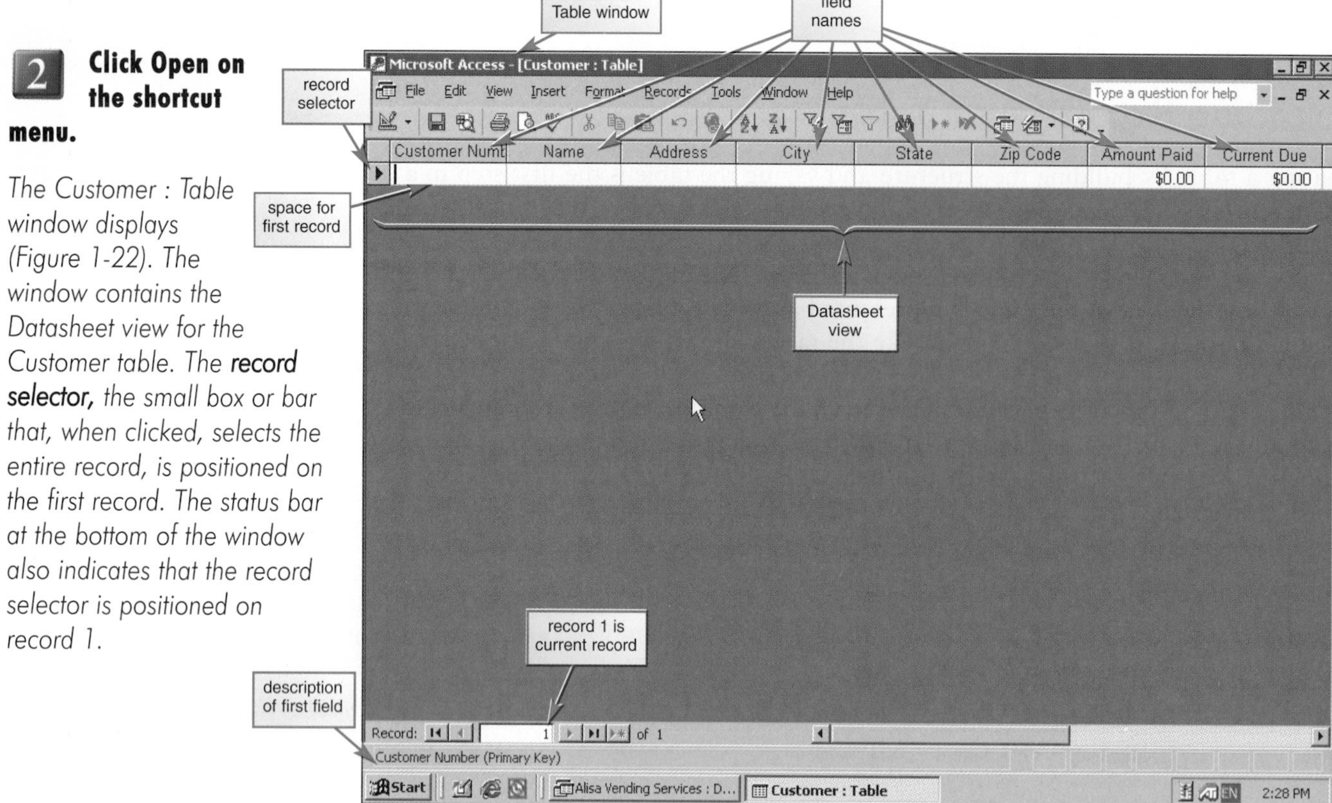

FIGURE 1-22

3 If your window is not already maximized, click the Maximize button to maximize the window containing the table. Type BA95 **as the first customer number (see Figure 1-20 on the previous page). Be sure you type the letters in uppercase, because that is the way they are to be entered in the database.**

The customer number is entered, but the insertion point is still in the Customer Number field (Figure 1-23).

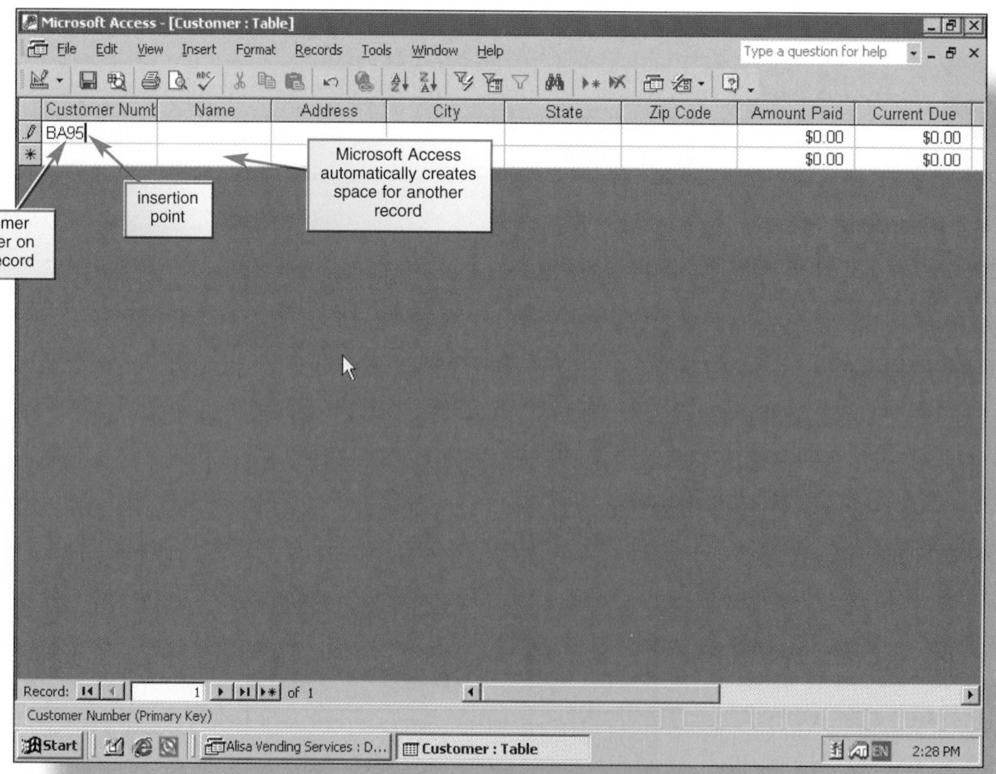

FIGURE 1-23

4 **Press the TAB key to complete the entry for the Customer Number field. Type the following entries, pressing the TAB key after each one:** `Bayside Hotel` **as the name,** `287 Riley` **as the address,** `Hansen` **as the city,** `FL` **as the state, and** `38513` **as the zip code.**

The Name, Address, City, State, and Zip Code fields are entered (Figure 1-24).

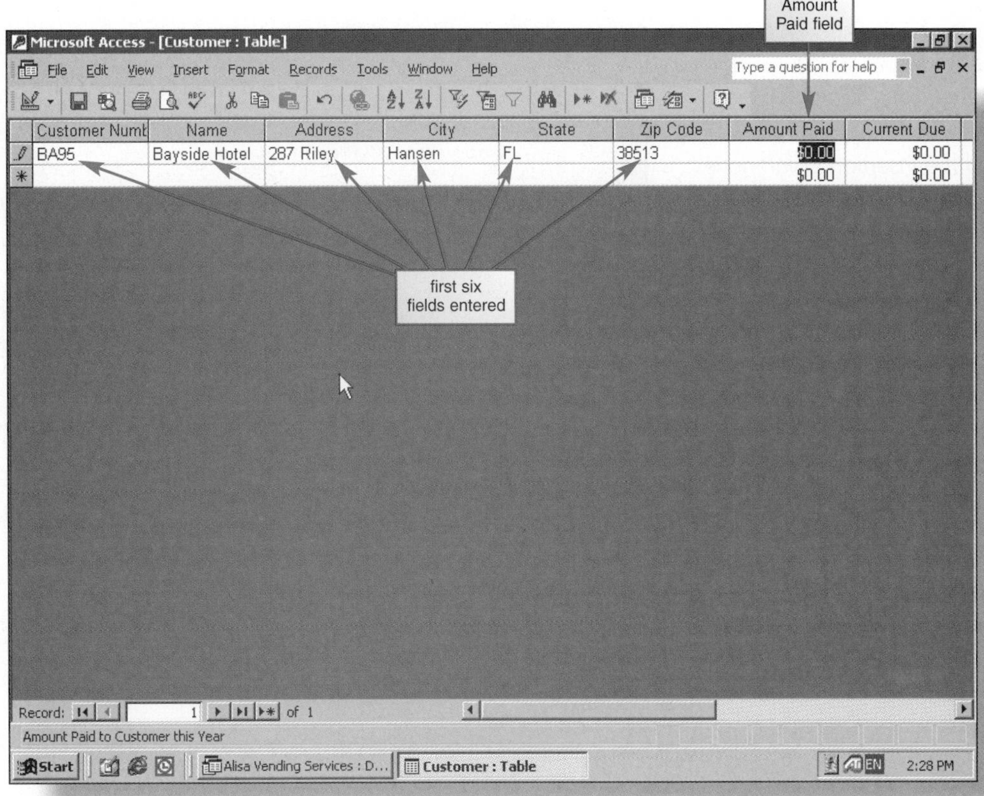

FIGURE 1-24

5 **Type** `21876` **as the amount paid amount and then press the TAB key. (You do not need to type dollar signs or commas. In addition, because the digits to the right of the decimal point were both zeros, you did not need to type either the decimal point or the zeros.) Type** `892.50` **as the current due amount and then press the TAB key. Type** `30` **as the driver number to complete the record.**

The fields have shifted to the left (Figure 1-25). The amount paid and current due values display with dollar signs and decimal points. The insertion point is positioned in the Driver Number field.

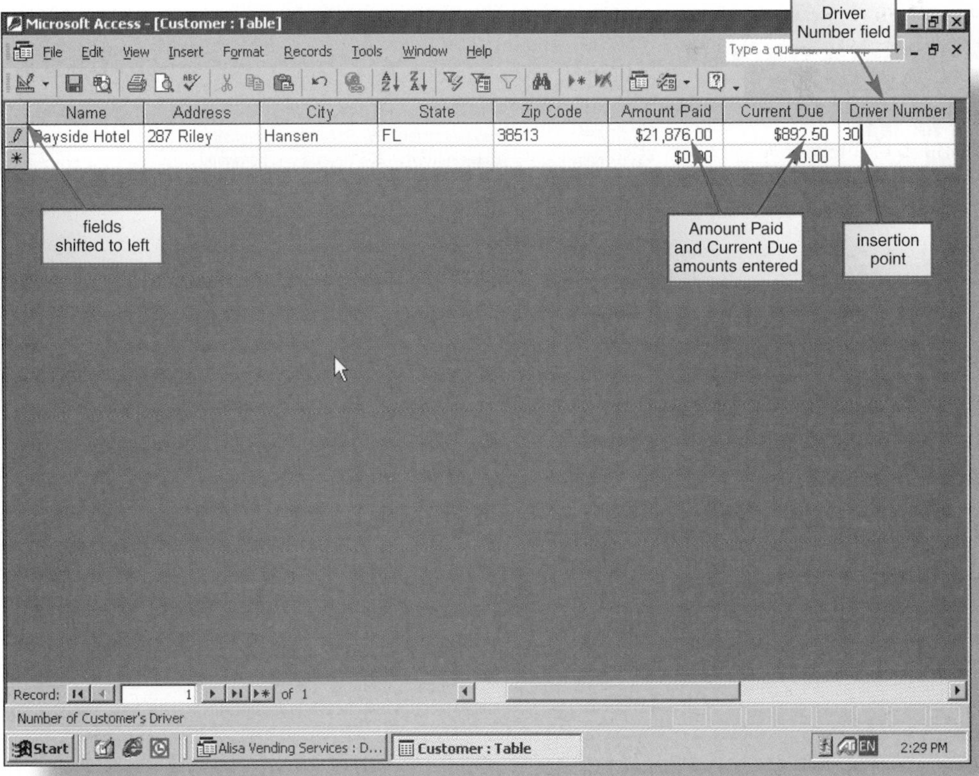

FIGURE 1-25

6 Press the TAB key.

The fields shift back to the right, the record is saved, and the insertion point moves to the customer number on the second row (Figure 1-26).

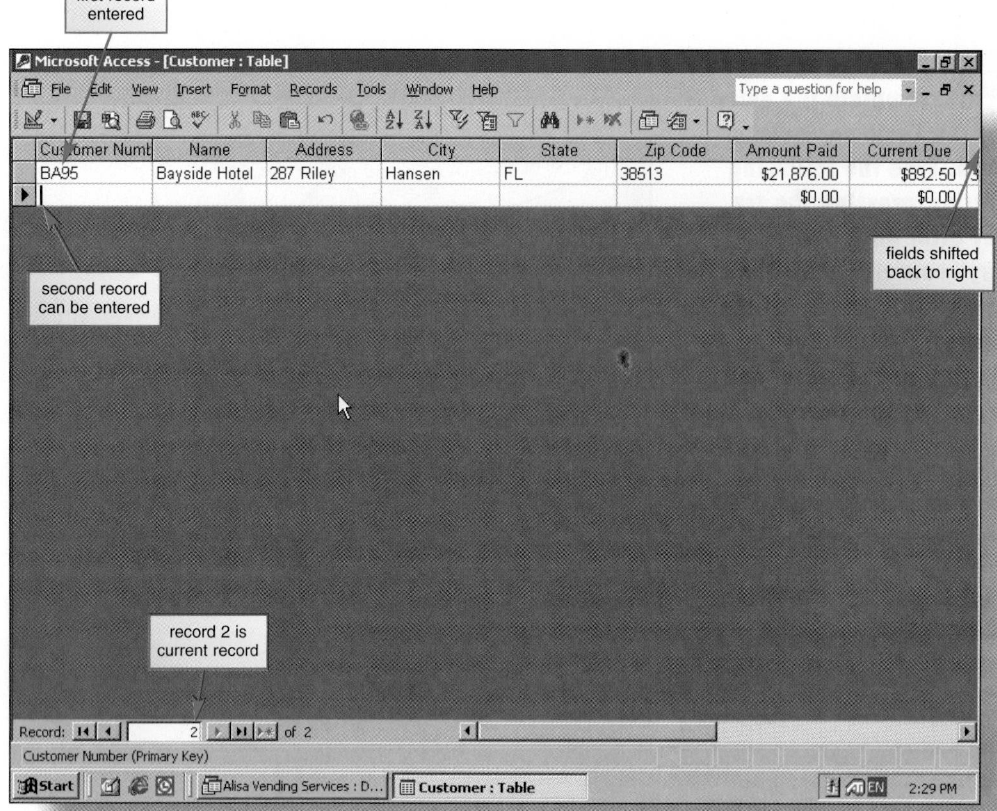

FIGURE 1-26

7 Use the techniques shown in Steps 3 through 6 to add the data for the second record in Figure 1-20 on page A 1.21. Point to the Close Window button.

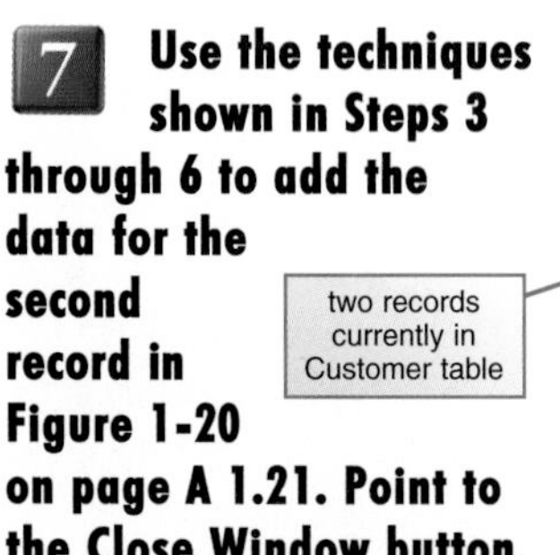

The second record is added and the insertion point moves to the customer number on the third row (Figure 1-27).

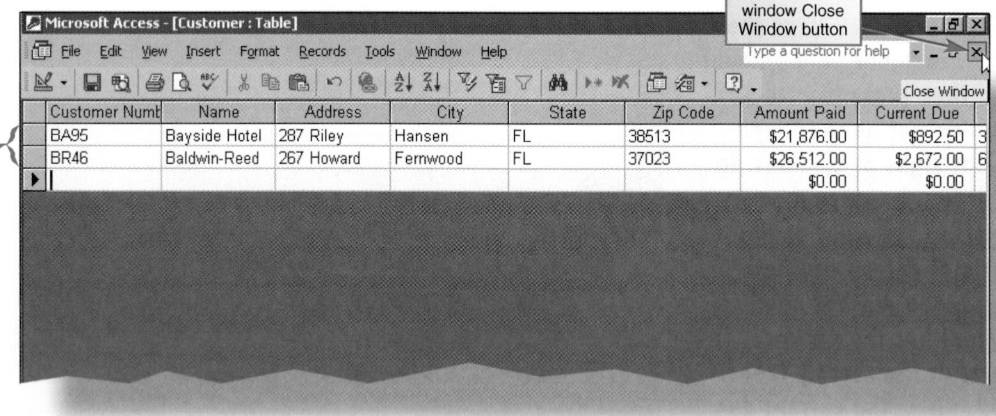

FIGURE 1-27

Closing a Table and Database

It is a good idea to close a table as soon as you have finished working with it. It keeps the screen from getting cluttered and prevents you from making accidental changes to the data in the table. Assuming that these two records are the only records you plan to add during this session, perform the following steps to close the table and the database. If you no longer will work with the database, you should close the database as well.

Steps To Close a Table and Database

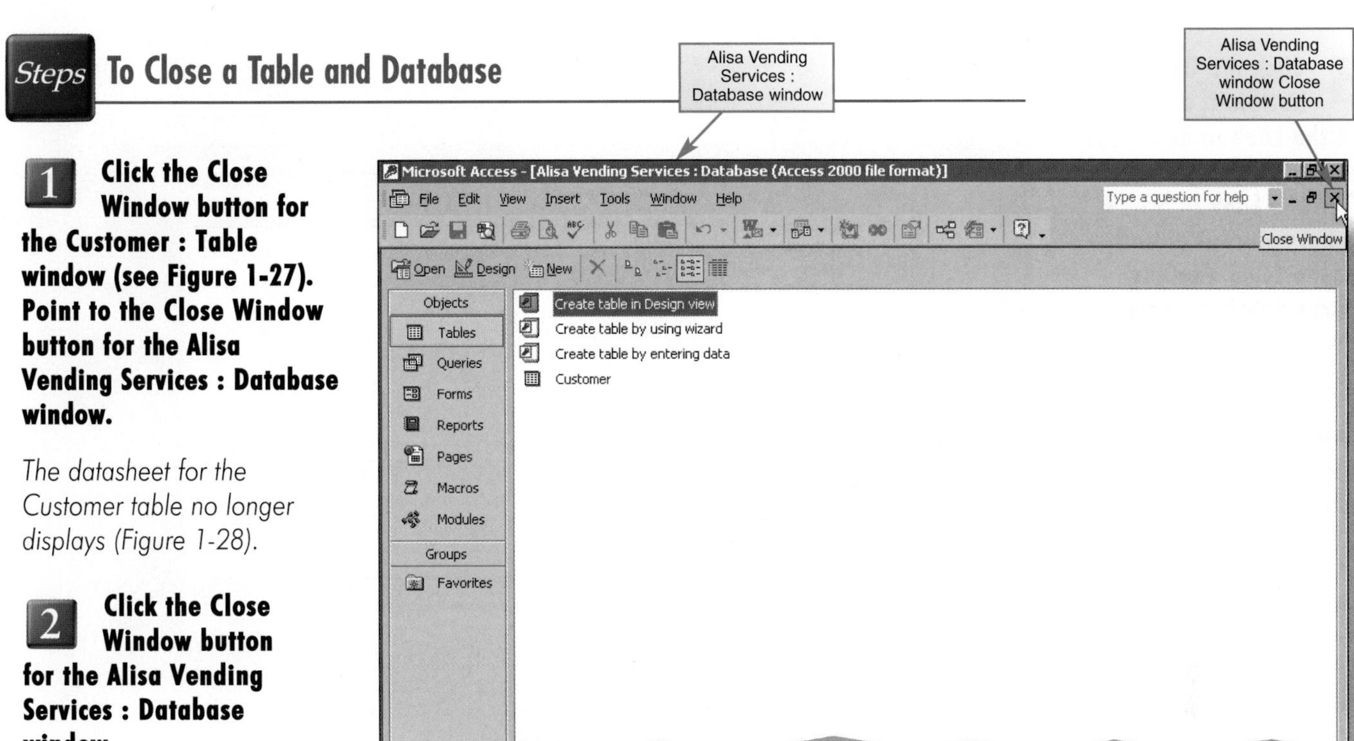

FIGURE 1-28

1 Click the Close Window button for the Customer : Table window (see Figure 1-27). Point to the Close Window button for the Alisa Vending Services : Database window.

The datasheet for the Customer table no longer displays (Figure 1-28).

2 Click the Close Window button for the Alisa Vending Services : Database window.

The Alisa Vending Services : Database window no longer displays.

Opening a Database

To work with any of the tables, reports, or forms in a database, the database must be open. To open a database from within Access, click Open on the Database toolbar. To resume adding records to the Customer table, open the database by performing the following steps.

Steps To Open a Database

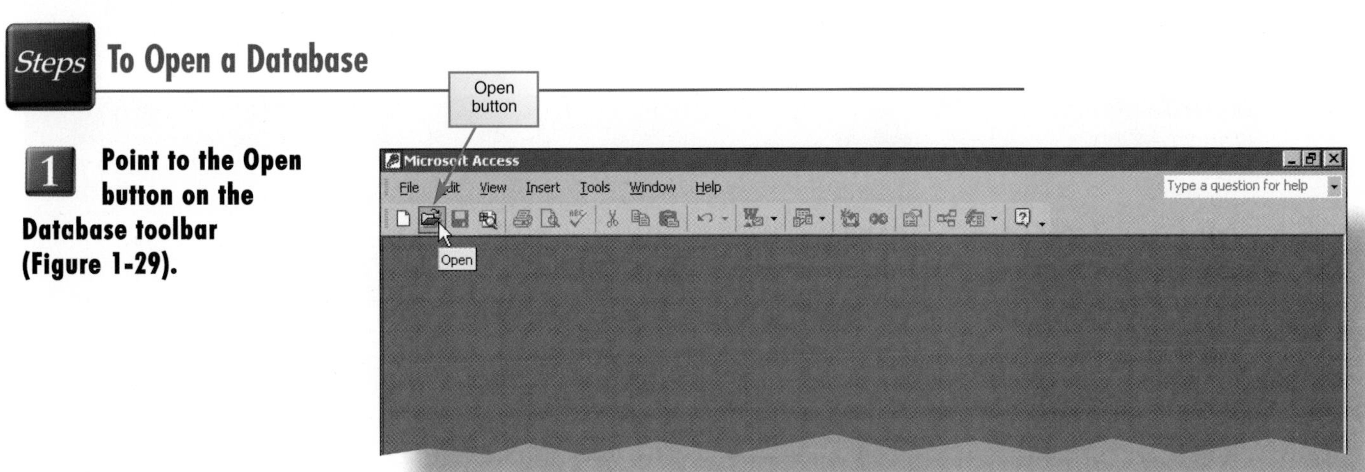

FIGURE 1-29

1 Point to the Open button on the Database toolbar (Figure 1-29).

2 Click the Open button. If necessary, click the Look in box arrow and then click 3½ Floppy (A:) in the Look in box. If it is not selected already, click the Alisa Vending Services database name. Point to the Open button.

The Open dialog box displays (Figure 1-30). The 3½ Floppy (A:) folder displays in the Look in box and the files on the floppy disk in drive A display. (Your list may be different.)

3 Click the Open button.

The database opens and the Alisa Vending Services : Database window displays.

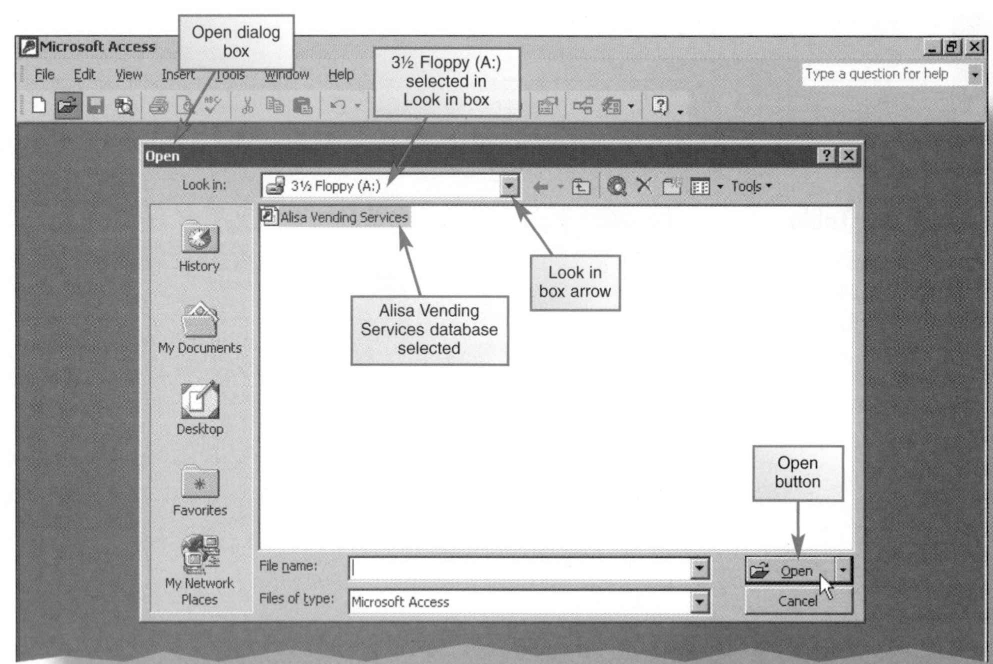

FIGURE 1-30

Table 1-1 Navigation Buttons in Datasheet View	
BUTTON	PURPOSE
First Record	Moves to the first record in the table
Previous Record	Moves to the previous record
Next Record	Moves to the next record
Last Record	Moves to the last record in the table
New Record	Moves to the end of the table to a position for entering a new record

Adding Additional Records

You can add records to a table that already contains data using a process almost identical to that used to add records to an empty table. The only difference is that you place the insertion point after the last data record before you enter the additional data. To do so, use the **Navigation buttons** found near the lower-left corner of the screen. The purpose of each of the Navigation buttons is described in Table 1-1.

Complete the following steps to add the remaining records (Figure 1-31) to the Customer table.

Customer table (last 8 records)

CUSTOMER NUMBER	NAME	ADDRESS	CITY	STATE	ZIP CODE	AMOUNT PAID	CURRENT DUE	DRIVER NUMBER
CN21	Century North	1562 Butler	Hansen	FL	38513	$8,725.00	$0.00	60
FR28	Friend's Movies	871 Adams	Westport	FL	37070	$4,256.00	$1,202.00	75
GN62	Grand Nelson	7821 Oak	Wood Key	FL	36828	$8,287.50	$925.50	30
GS29	Great Screens	572 Lee	Hansen	FL	38513	$21,625.00	$0.00	60
LM22	Lenger Mason	274 Johnson	Westport	FL	37070	$0.00	$0.00	60
ME93	Merks College	561 Fairhill	Bayville	FL	38734	$24,761.00	$1,572.00	30
RI78	Riter University	26 Grove	Fernwood	FL	37023	$11,682.25	$2,827.50	75
TU20	Turner Hotel	8672 Quincy	Palmview	FL	36114	$8,521.50	$0.00	60

FIGURE 1-31

Steps To Add Additional Records to a Table

1 Right-click the Customer table in the Alisa Vending Services : Database window and then click Open on the shortcut menu. When the Customer table displays, maximize the window by clicking the Maximize button. Point to the New Record button.

The datasheet displays (Figure 1-32).

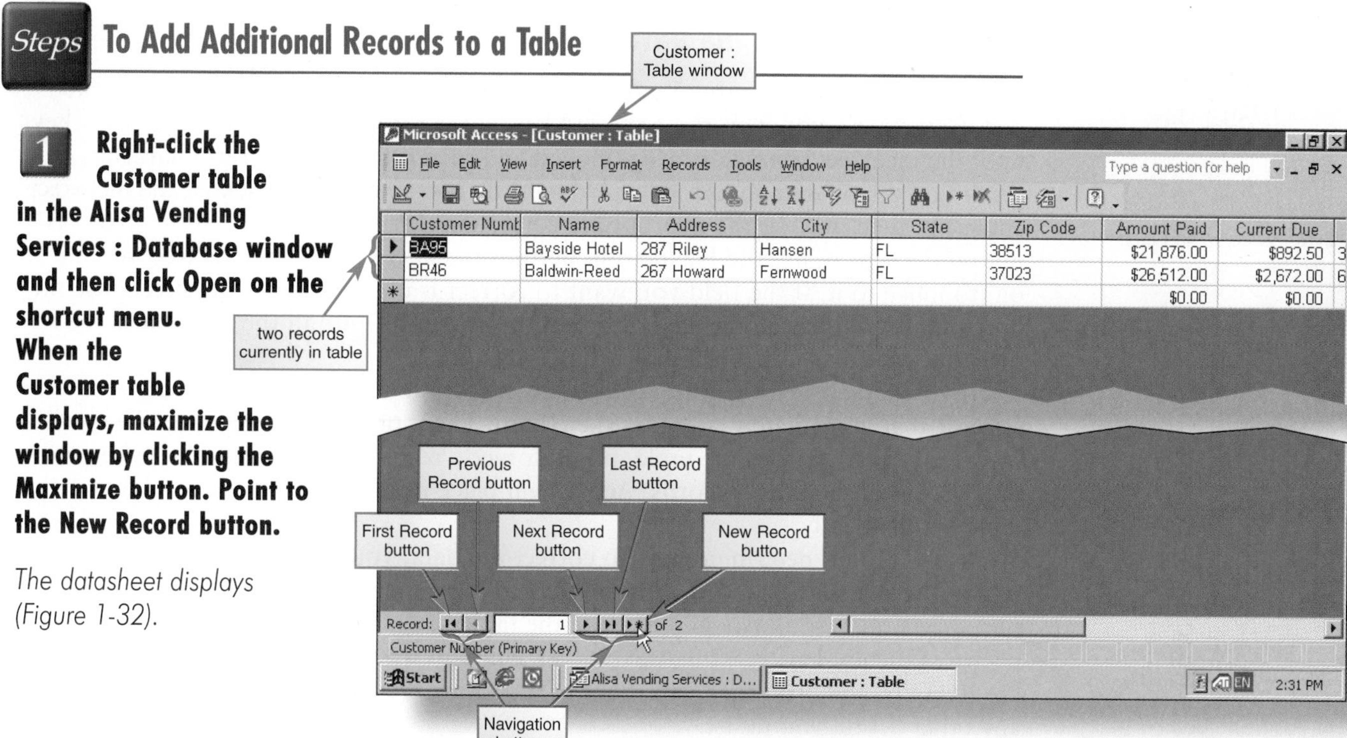

FIGURE 1-32

2 Click the New Record button.

Access places the insertion point in position to enter a new record (Figure 1-33).

insertion point positioned on new record

Microsoft Access - [Customer : Table]

Customer Numb	Name	Address	City	State	Zip Code	Amount Paid	Current Due
BA95	Bayside Hotel	287 Riley	Hansen	FL	38513	$21,876.00	$892.50
BR46	Baldwin-Reed	267 Howard	Fernwood	FL	37023	$26,512.00	$2,672.00
						$0.00	$0.00

FIGURE 1-33

3 Add the remaining records from Figure 1-31 using the same techniques you used to add the first two records. Point to the Close Window button.

The additional records are added (Figure 1-34).

Close Window button

all 10 records entered

Microsoft Access - [Customer : Table]

Customer Numb	Name	Address	City	State	Zip Code	Amount Paid	Current Due
BA95	Bayside Hotel	287 Riley	Hansen	FL	38513	$21,876.00	$892.50
BR46	Baldwin-Reed	267 Howard	Fernwood	FL	37023	$26,512.00	$2,672.00
CN21	Century North	1562 Butler	Hansen	FL	38513	$8,725.00	$0.00
FR28	Friend's Movies	871 Adams	Westport	FL	37070	$4,256.00	$1,202.00
GN62	Grand Nelson	7821 Oak	Wood Key	FL	36828	$8,287.50	$925.50
GS29	Great Screens	572 Lee	Hansen	FL	38513	$21,625.00	$0.00
LM22	Lenger Mason	274 Johnson	Westport	FL	37070	$0.00	$0.00
ME93	Merks College	561 Fairhill	Bayville	FL	38734	$24,761.00	$1,572.00
RI78	Riter University	26 Grove	Fernwood	FL	37023	$11,682.25	$2,827.50
TU20	Turner Hotel	8672 Quincy	Palmview	FL	36114	$8,521.50	$0.00
						$0.00	$0.00

FIGURE 1-34

4 Click the Close Window button.

The window containing the table closes and the Alisa Vending Services : Database window displays.

Correcting Errors in the Data

Check your entries carefully to ensure they are correct. If you make a mistake and discover it before you press the TAB key, correct it by pressing the BACKSPACE key until the incorrect characters are removed and then typing the correct characters.

If you discover an incorrect entry later, correct the error by clicking the incorrect entry and then making the appropriate correction. If the record you must correct is not on the screen, use the Navigation buttons (Next Record, Previous Record, and so on) to move to it. If the field you want to correct is not visible on the screen, use the horizontal scroll bar along the bottom of the screen to shift all the fields until the one you want displays. Then make the correction.

If you add an extra record accidentally, select the record by clicking the record selector that immediately precedes the record. Then, press the DELETE key. This will remove the record from the table. If you forget a record, add it using the same procedure as for all the other records. Access will place it in the correct location in the table automatically.

If you cannot determine how to correct the data, you are, in effect, stuck on the record. Access neither allows you to move to any other record until you have made the correction, nor allows you to close the table. If you encounter this situation, simply press the ESC key. Pressing the ESC key will remove from the screen the record you are trying to add. You then can move to any other record, close the table, or take any other action you desire.

Other Ways

1. Click New Record button on Table Datasheet toolbar
2. In Voice Command mode, say "New Record"

More About

Printing the Contents of a Table

You can change the paper size, paper source, or the printer that will be used to print the report. To change any of these, select the Page sheet in the Page Setup dialog box, click the appropriate down arrow, and then select the desired option. You can change the margins by selecting the Margins sheet in the Page Setup dialog box.

Previewing and Printing the Contents of a Table

When working with a database, you often will need to print a copy of the table contents. Figure 1-35 shows a printed copy of the contents of the Customer table. (Yours may look slightly different, depending on your printer.) Because the Customer table is wider substantially than the screen, it also will be wider than the normal printed page in portrait orientation. **Portrait orientation** means the printout is across the width of the page. **Landscape orientation** means the printout is across the length of the page. Thus, to print the wide database table, use landscape orientation. If you are printing the contents of a table that fits on the screen, you will not need landscape orientation. A convenient way to change to landscape orientation is to **preview** what the printed copy will look like by using Print Preview. This allows you to determine whether landscape orientation is necessary and, if it is, to change easily the orientation to landscape. In addition, you also can use Print Preview to determine whether any adjustments are necessary to the page margins.

Customer 9/8/2003

Customer Num	Name	Address	City	State	Zip Code	Amount Paid	Current Due	Driver Number
BA95	Bayside Hotel	287 Riley	Hansen	FL	38513	$21,876.00	$892.50	30
BR46	Baldwin-Reed	267 Howard	Fernwood	FL	37023	$26,512.00	$2,672.00	60
CN21	Century North	1562 Butler	Hansen	FL	38513	$8,725.00	$0.00	60
FR28	Friend's Movies	871 Adams	Westport	FL	37070	$4,256.00	$1,202.00	75
GN62	Grand Nelson	7821 Oak	Wood Key	FL	36828	$8,287.50	$925.50	30
GS29	Great Screens	572 Lee	Hansen	FL	38513	$21,625.00	$0.00	60
LM22	Lenger Mason	274 Johnson	Westport	FL	37070	$0.00	$0.00	60
ME93	Merks College	561 Fairhill	Bayville	FL	38734	$24,761.00	$1,572.00	30
RI78	Riter University	26 Grove	Fernwood	FL	37023	$11,682.25	$2,827.50	75
TU20	Turner Hotel	8672 Quincy	Palmview	FL	36114	$8,521.50	$0.00	60

FIGURE 1-35

Perform the following steps to use Print Preview to preview and then print the Customer table.

Steps To Preview and Print the Contents of a Table

1 Right-click the Customer table and then point to Print Preview on the shortcut menu.

The shortcut menu for the Customer table displays (Figure 1-36).

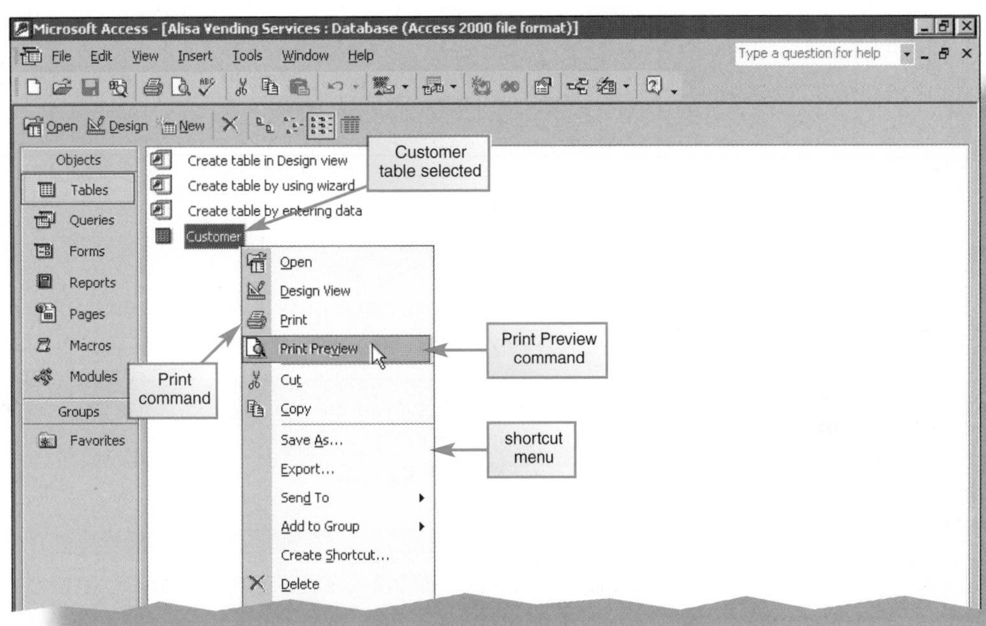

FIGURE 1-36

2 Click Print Preview on the shortcut menu. Point to the approximate position shown in Figure 1-37.

The preview of the report displays. The mouse pointer shape changes to a magnifying glass, indicating you can magnify a portion of the report.

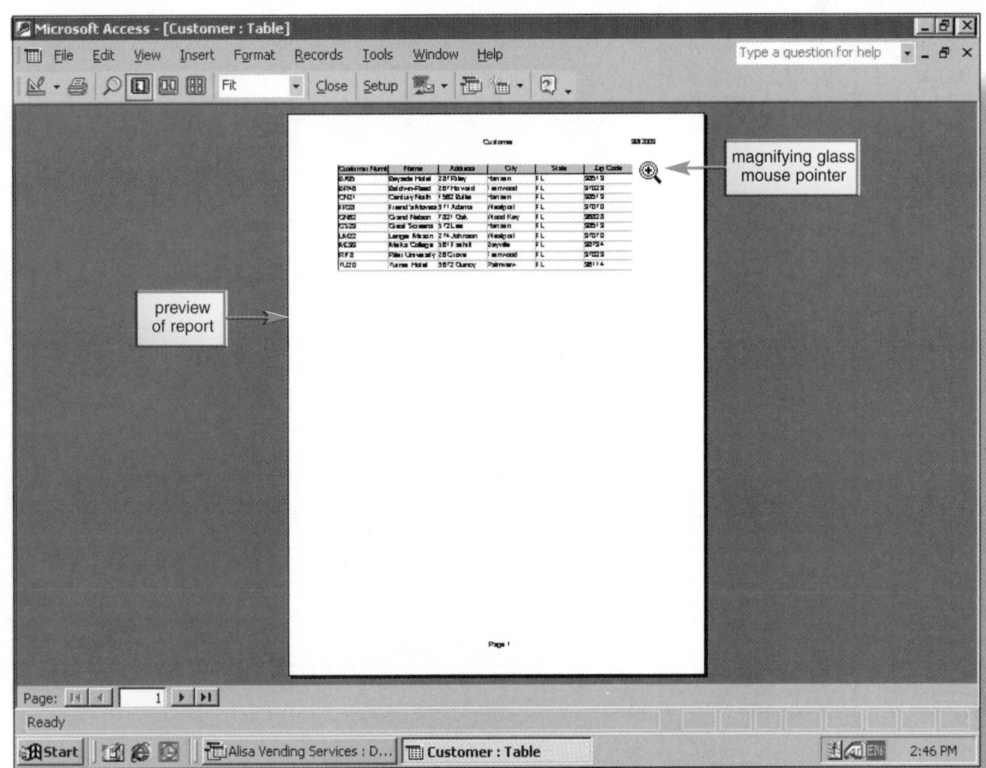

FIGURE 1-37

3 Click the magnifying glass mouse pointer in the approximate position shown in Figure 1-37 on the previous page.

The portion surrounding the mouse pointer is magnified (Figure 1-38). The last field that displays is the Zip Code field. The Amount Paid, Current Due, and Driver Number fields do not display. To display the additional fields, you will need to switch to landscape orientation.

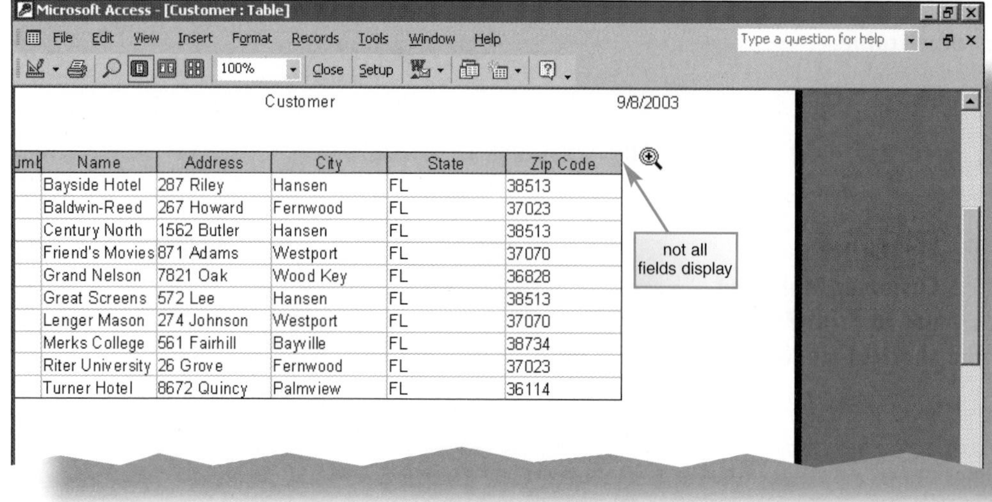

FIGURE 1-38

4 With the mouse pointer in the approximate position shown in Figure 1-38, right-click the report and then point to Page Setup.

The shortcut menu displays (Figure 1-39).

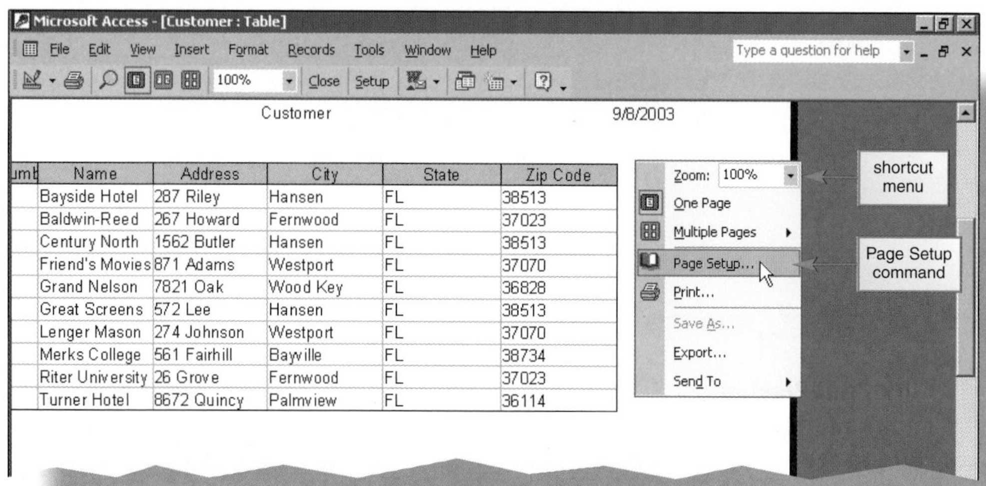

FIGURE 1-39

5 Click Page Setup and then point to the Page tab.

The Page Setup dialog box displays (Figure 1-40).

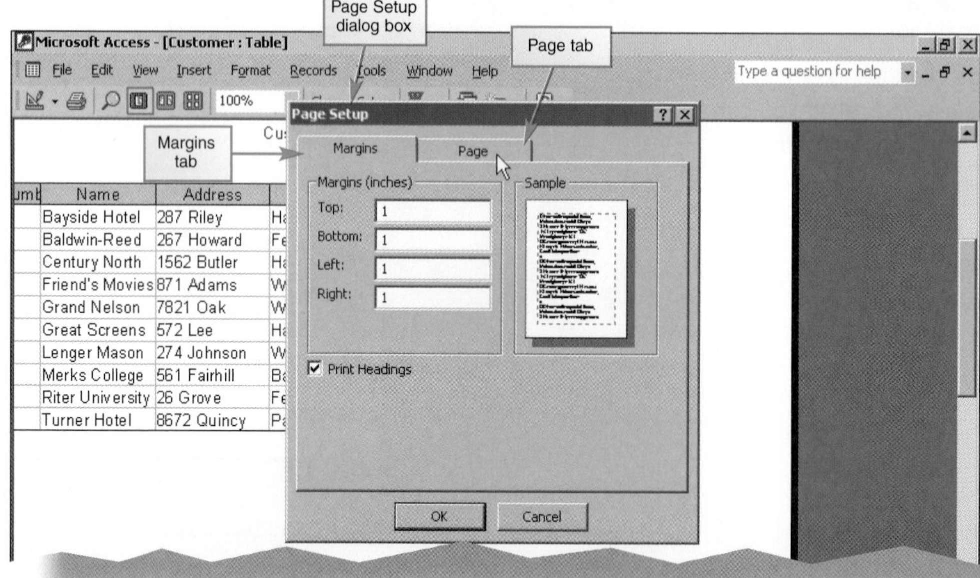

FIGURE 1-40

6 Click the Page tab and then point to the Landscape option button.

*The Page sheet displays (Figure 1-41). The Portrait option button currently is selected. (**Option button** refers to the round button that indicates choice in a dialog box. When the corresponding option is selected, the button contains within it a solid circle. Clicking an option button selects it, and deselects all others.)*

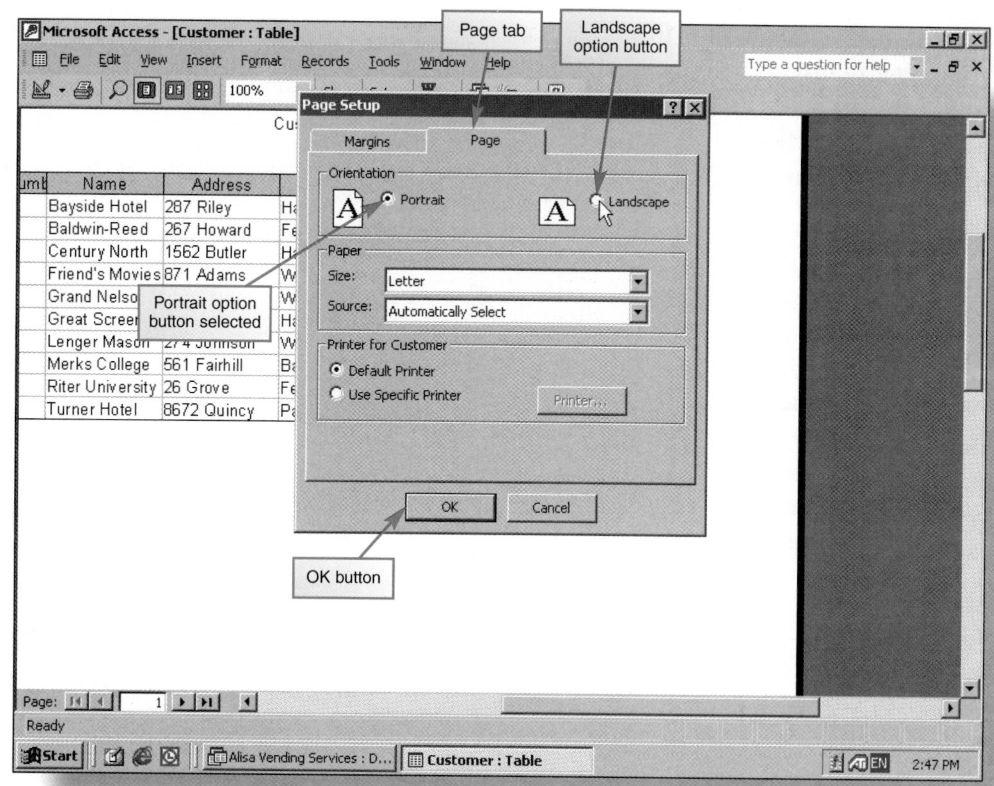

FIGURE 1-41

7 Click Landscape and then click the OK button. Point to the Print button on the Print Preview toolbar.

The orientation is changed to landscape as shown by the report that displays on the screen (Figure 1-42). The last field that displays is the Driver Number field, so all fields currently display. If they did not, you could decrease the left and right margins; that is, the amount of space left by Access on the left and right edges of the report.

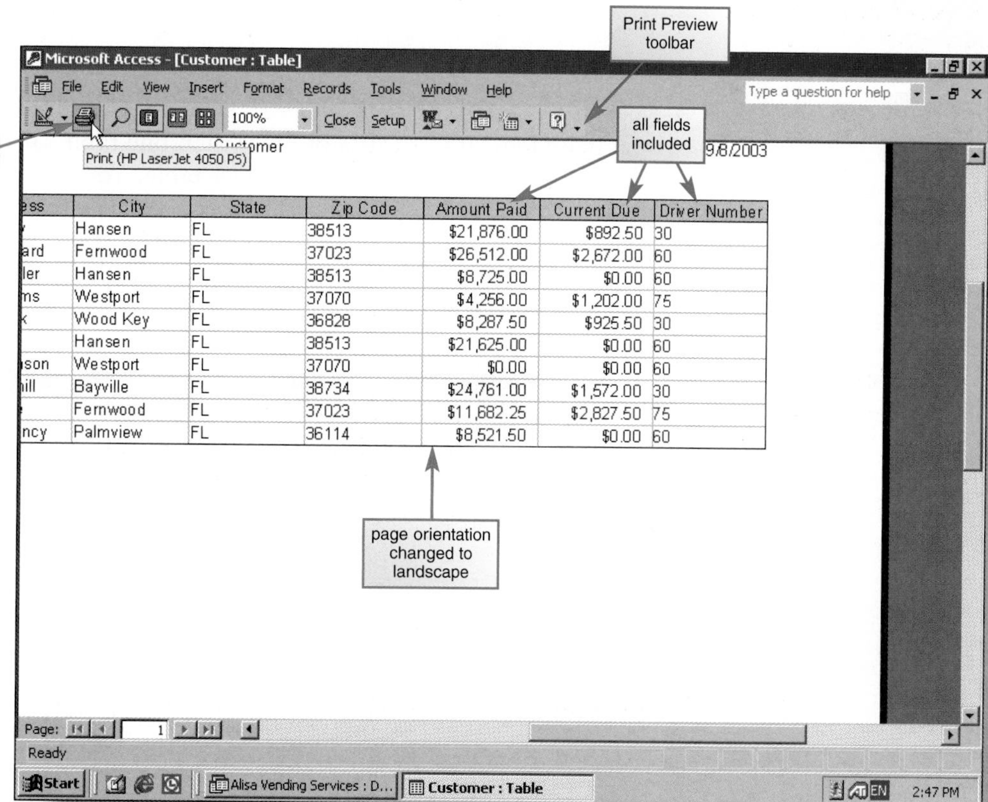

FIGURE 1-42

8 Click the Print button to print the report and then point to the Close button on the Print Preview toolbar (Figure 1-43).

The report prints. It looks like the report shown in Figure 1-35 on page A 1.28.

9 Click the Close button on the Print Preview toolbar when the report has been printed to close the Print Preview window.

The Print Preview window closes and the Alisa Vending Services : Database window displays.

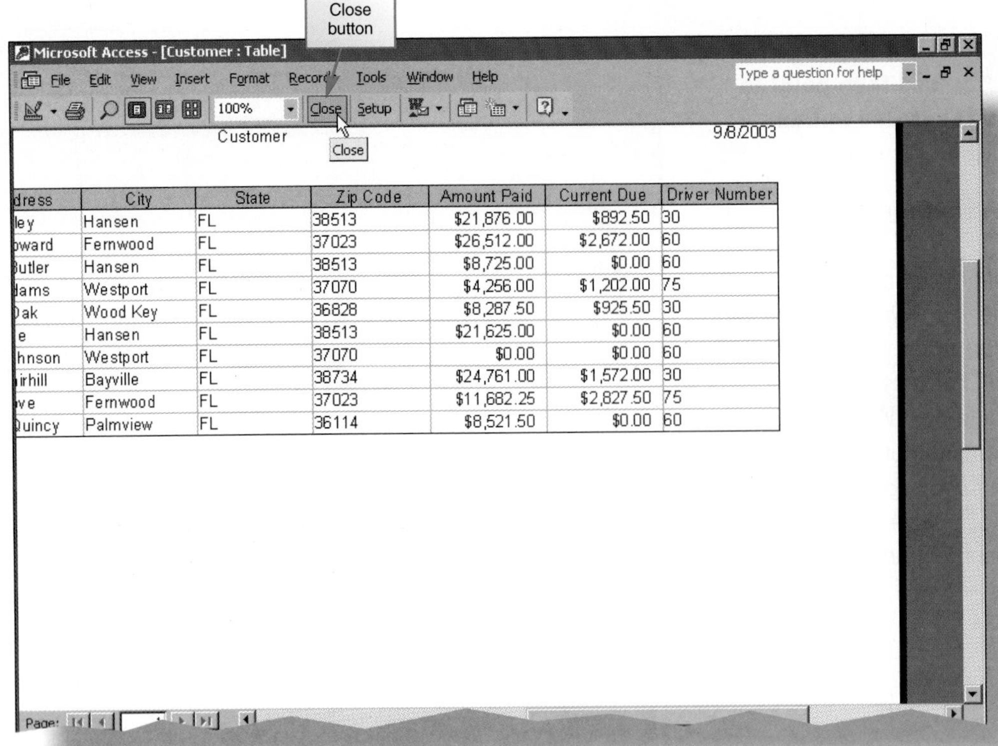

FIGURE 1-43

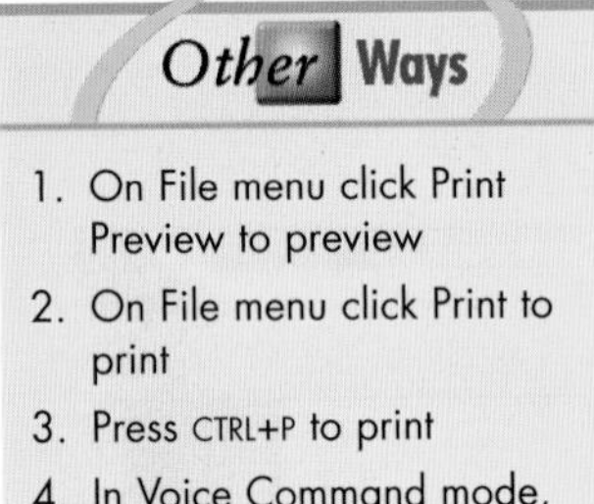

Other Ways

1. On File menu click Print Preview to preview
2. On File menu click Print to print
3. Press CTRL+P to print
4. In Voice Command mode, say "Print Preview" to preview; say "Print" to print

Creating Additional Tables

A database typically consists of more than one table. The sample database contains two, the Customer table and the Driver table. You need to repeat the process of creating a table and adding records for each table in the database. In the sample database, you need to create and add records to the Driver table. The structure for the table is given in Figure 1-44a and the data for the table is given in Figure 1-44b. The steps to create the table follow.

Structure of Driver table

FIELD NAME	DATA TYPE	FIELD SIZE	PRIMARY KEY?	DESCRIPTION
Driver Number	Text	2	Yes	Driver Number (Primary key)
Last Name	Text	10		Last Name of Driver
First Name	Text	8		First Name of Driver
Address	Text	15		Street Address
City	Text	15		City
State	Text	2		State (Two-Character Abbreviation)
Zip Code	Text	5		Zip Code (Five-Character Version)
Hourly Rate	Currency			Hourly Rate of Driver
YTD Earnings	Currency			YTD Earnings of Driver

FIGURE 1-44a

Data for Driver table								
DRIVER NUMBER	*LAST NAME*	*FIRST NAME*	*ADDRESS*	*CITY*	*STATE*	*ZIP CODE*	*HOURLY RATE*	*YTD EARNINGS*
30	Tuttle	Larissa	7562 Hickory	Laton Springs	FL	37891	$16.00	$21,145.25
60	Powers	Frank	57 Ravenwood	Gillmore	FL	37572	$15.00	$19,893.50
75	Ortiz	Jose	341 Pierce	Douglas	FL	37613	$17.00	$23,417.00

FIGURE 1-44b

Steps To Create an Additional Table

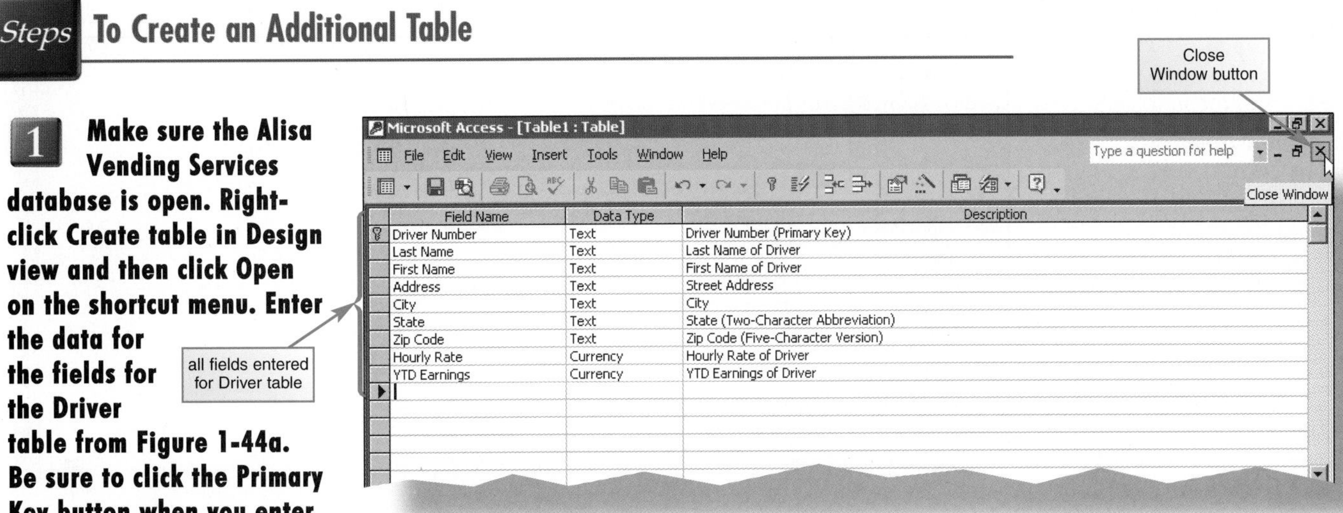

FIGURE 1-45

1 Make sure the Alisa Vending Services database is open. Right-click Create table in Design view and then click Open on the shortcut menu. Enter the data for the fields for the Driver table from Figure 1-44a. Be sure to click the Primary Key button when you enter the Driver Number field. Point to the Close Window button for the Table1 : Table window after you have entered all the fields.

The entries display (Figure 1-45).

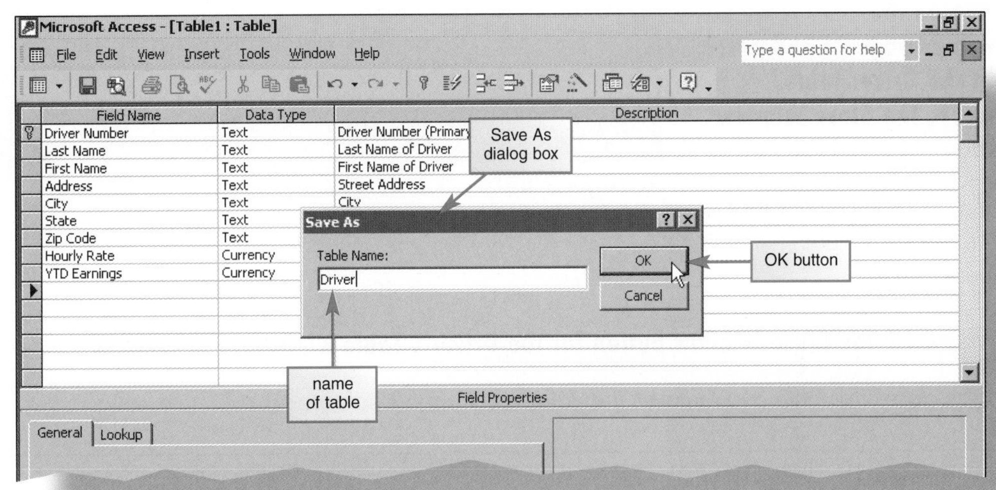

FIGURE 1-46

2 Click the Close Window button, click the Yes button in the Microsoft Access dialog box when asked if you want to save the changes, type `Driver` **as the name of the table, and then point to the OK button in the Save As dialog box.**

The Save As dialog box displays (Figure 1-46). The table name is entered.

3 Click the OK button.

The table is saved in the Alisa Vending Services database. The window containing the table structure no longer displays.

Adding Records to the Additional Table

Now that you have created the Driver table, use the following steps to add records to it.

Steps To Add Records to an Additional Table

1 **Right-click the Driver table and point to Open on the shortcut menu.**

The shortcut menu for the Driver table displays (Figure 1-47).

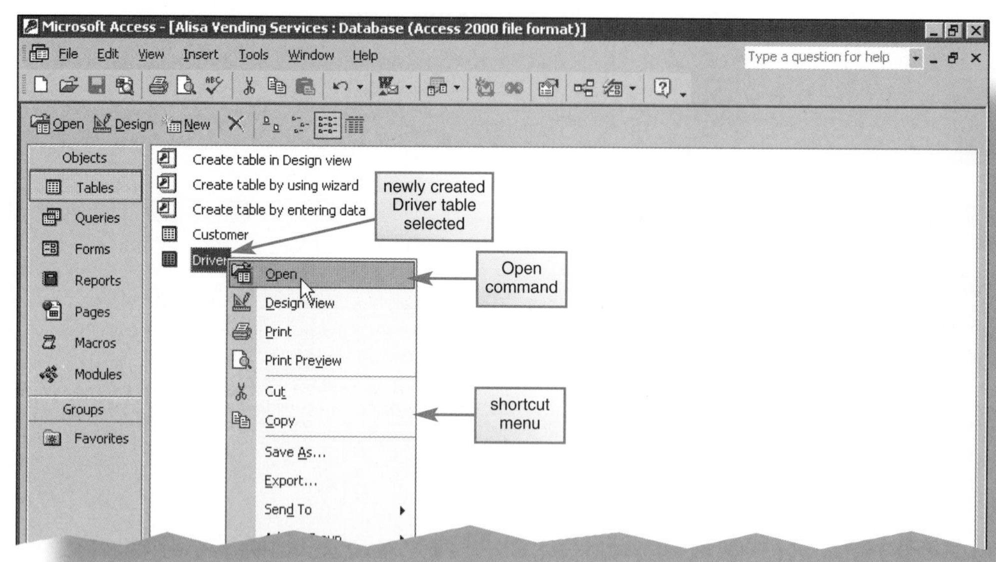

FIGURE 1-47

2 **Click Open on the shortcut menu and then enter the Driver data from Figure 1-44b on the previous page into the Driver table. Point to the Close Window button.**

The datasheet displays with three records entered (Figure 1-48).

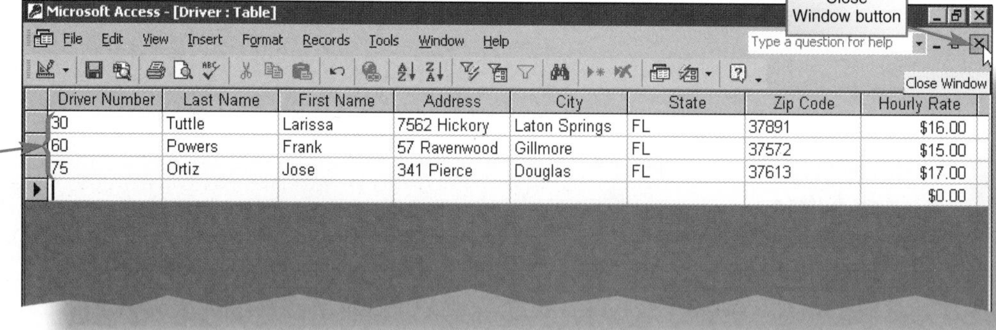

FIGURE 1-48

3 **Click the Close Window button for the Driver : Table window.**

Access closes the table and removes the datasheet from the screen.

Using a Form to View Data

In creating tables, you have used Datasheet view; that is, the data on the screen displayed as a table. You also can use **Form view**, in which you see a single record at a time.

The advantage with Datasheet view is you can see multiple records at once. It has the disadvantage that, unless you have few fields in the table, you cannot see all the fields at the same time. With Form view, you see only a single record, but you can see all the fields in the record. The view you choose is a matter of personal preference.

AutoForms

When you create an AutoForm, you also can specify whether the layout is to be columnar, tabular, or datasheeet. To do so, click Form on the New Object list. When the New Form dialog box displays, choose the appropriate layout for the AutoForm by clicking AutoForm: Columnar, AutoForm: Tabular, or AutoForm: Datasheet.

Creating a Form

To use Form view, you first must create a form. The simplest way to create a form is to use the New Object: AutoForm button on the Database toolbar. To do so, first select the table for which the form is to be created in the Database window and then click the New Object: AutoForm button. A list of available objects displays. Click AutoForm in the list to select it.

Perform the following steps using the New Object: AutoForm button to create a form for the Customer table.

To Use the New Object: AutoForm Button to Create a Form

1 Make sure the Alisa Vending Services database is open, the Database window displays, and the Customer table is selected. Point to the New Object: AutoForm button arrow on the Database toolbar (Figure 1-49).

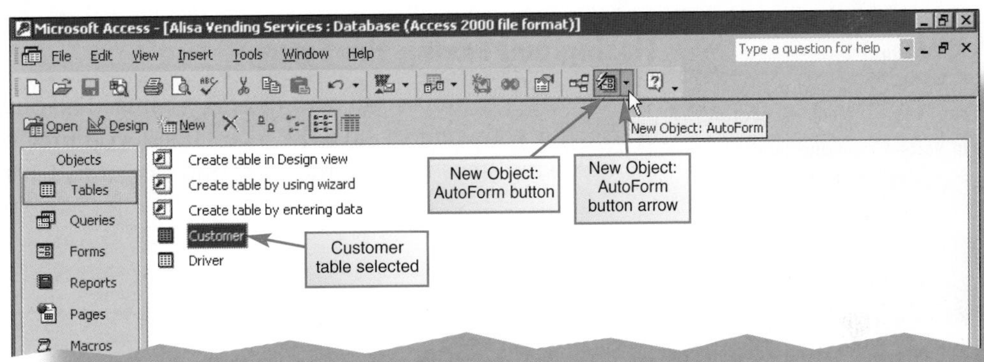

FIGURE 1-49

2 Click the New Object: AutoForm button arrow and then point to AutoForm.

A list of objects that can be created displays (Figure 1-50).

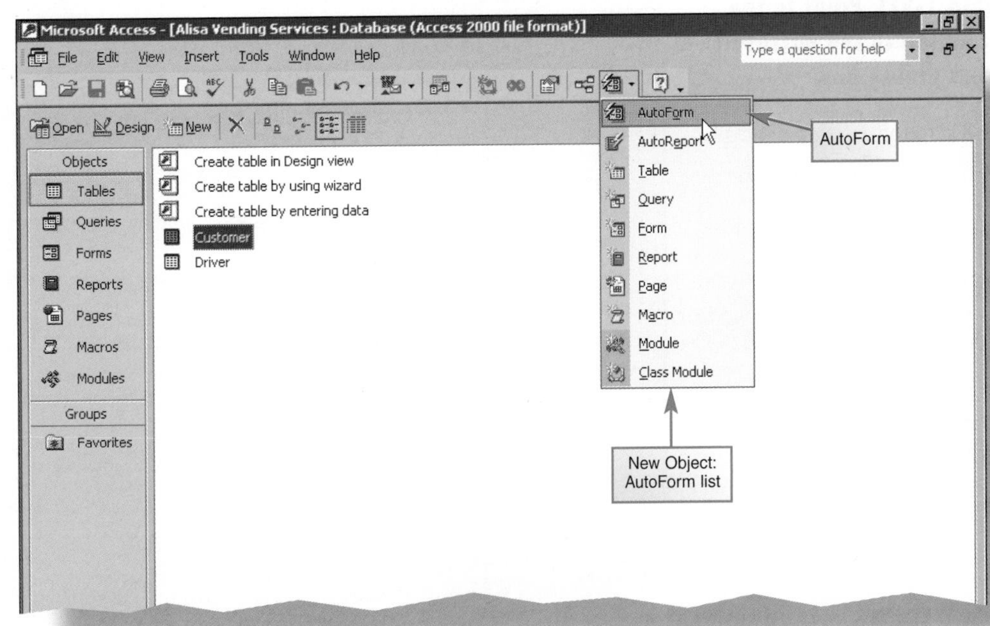

FIGURE 1-50

3 **Click AutoForm in the New Object: AutoForm list.**

After a brief delay, the form displays (Figure 1-51). If you do not move the mouse pointer after clicking AutoForm, the ScreenTip for the Database Window button may display when the form opens. An additional toolbar, the Formatting toolbar, also displays. (When you close the form, this toolbar no longer displays.)

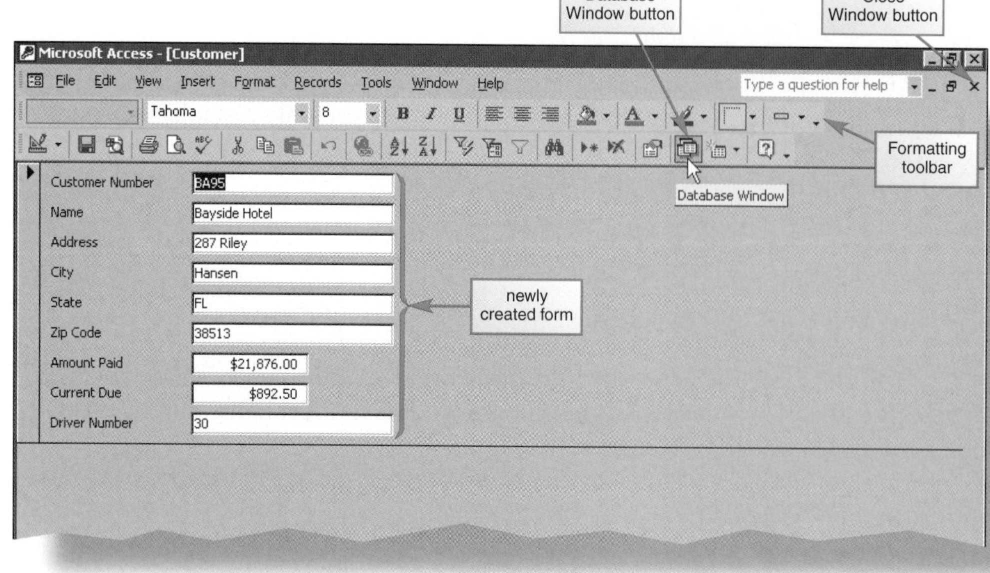

FIGURE 1-51

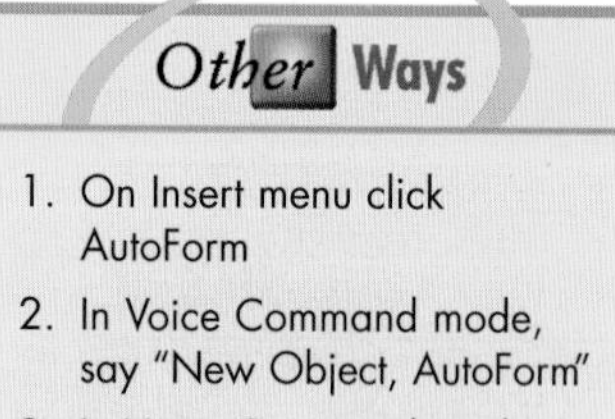

1. On Insert menu click AutoForm
2. In Voice Command mode, say "New Object, AutoForm"
3. In Voice Command mode, say "Insert, AutoForm"

Closing and Saving the Form

Closing a form is similar to closing a table. The only difference is that you will be asked if you want to save the form unless you previously have saved it. Perform the following steps to close the form and save it as Customer.

Steps To Close and Save a Form

1 **Click the Close Window button for the Customer window (see Figure 1-51). Point to the Yes button in the Microsoft Access dialog box.**

The Microsoft Access dialog box displays (Figure 1-52).

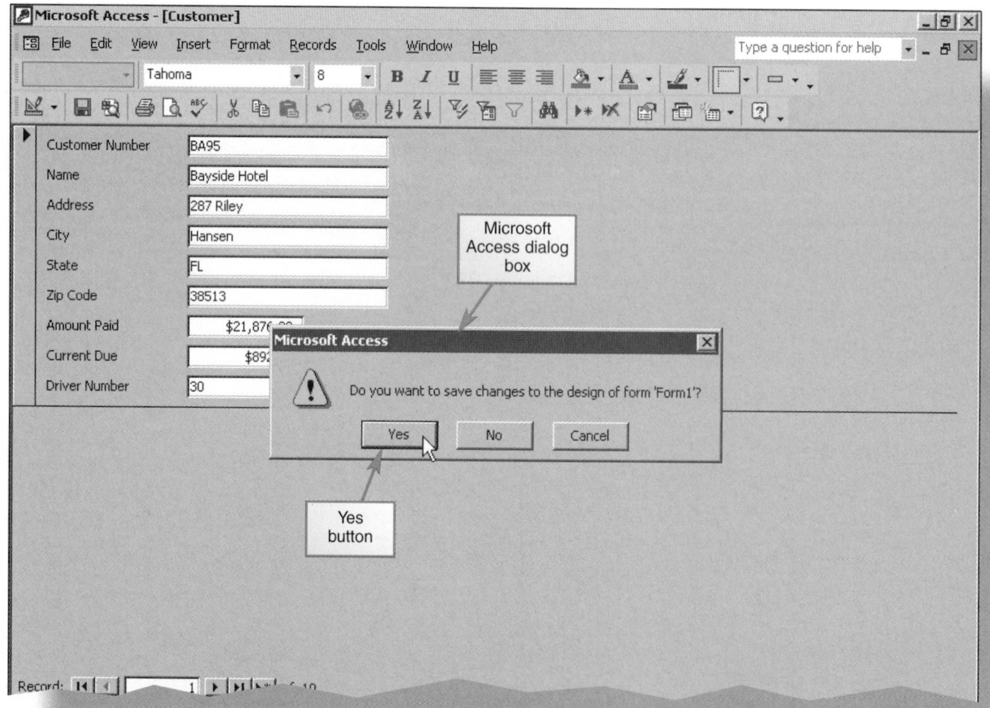

FIGURE 1-52

2 Click the Yes button and then point to the OK button in the Save As dialog box.

The Save As dialog box displays (Figure 1-53). The name of the table (Customer) becomes the name of the form automatically. This name could be changed, if desired.

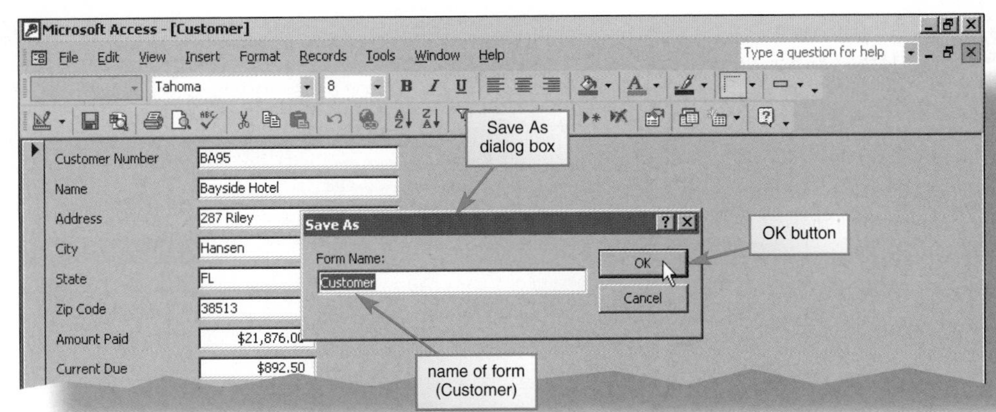

FIGURE 1-53

3 Click the OK button.

The form is saved as part of the database and the form closes. The Alisa Vending Services : Database window again displays.

Other Ways

1. Double-click Control-menu icon on title bar for window
2. On File menu click Close
3. In Voice Command mode, say "File, Close"

Opening the Saved Form

Once you have saved a form, you can use it at any time in the future by opening it. Opening a form is similar to opening a table; that is, make sure the form to be opened is selected, right-click, and then click Open on the shortcut menu. Before opening the form, however, the Forms object, rather than the Tables object, must be selected.

Perform the following steps to open the Customer form.

Steps To Open a Form

1 With the Alisa Vending Services database open and the Database window on the screen, click Forms on the Objects bar.

The Forms object is selected and the list of available forms displays (Figure 1-54). Currently, the Customer form is the only form.

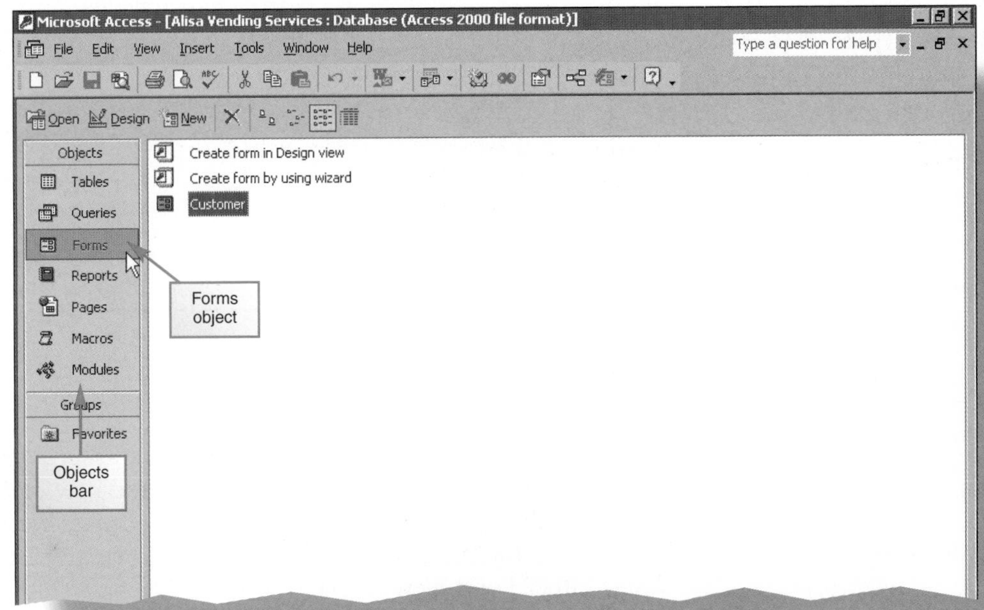

FIGURE 1-54

2 Right-click the Customer form, and then point to Open on the shortcut menu.

The shortcut menu for the Customer form displays (Figure 1-55).

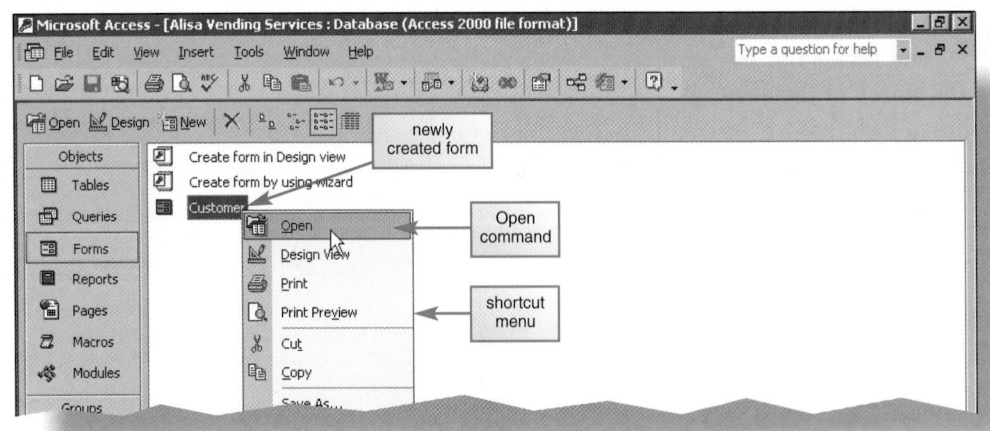

FIGURE 1-55

3 Click Open on the shortcut menu and then point to the Next Record button in preparation for the next task.

The Customer form displays (Figure 1-56).

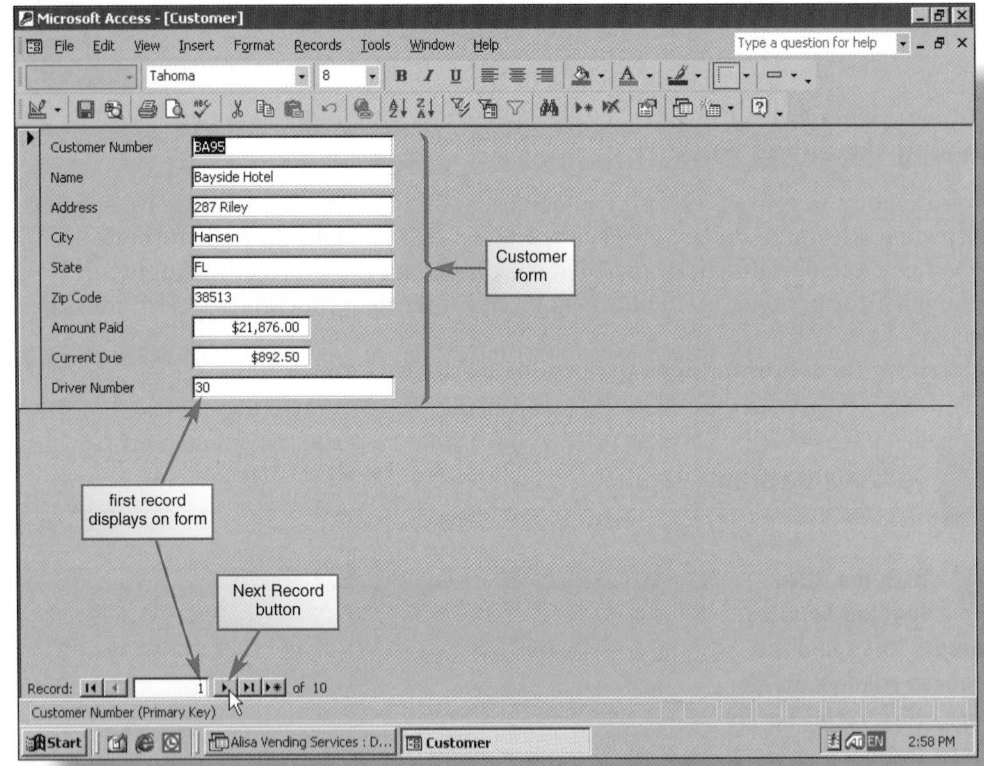

FIGURE 1-56

Other Ways

1. Click Forms object, double-click desired form
2. Click Forms object, click desired form, click Open button
3. Click Forms object, click desired form, press ALT+O
4. In Voice Command mode, say "Forms, [click desired form], Open"

Using the Form

You can use the form just as you used Datasheet view. You use the Navigation buttons to move between records. You can add new records or change existing ones. To delete the record displayed on the screen, after selecting the record by clicking its record selector, press the DELETE key. Thus, you can perform database operations using either Form view or Datasheet view.

Because you can see only one record at a time in Form view, to see a different record, such as the fifth record, use the Navigation buttons to move to it. To move from record to record in Form view, perform the following step.

Steps To Use a Form

1 Click the Next Record button four times.

The fifth record displays on the form (Figure 1-57).

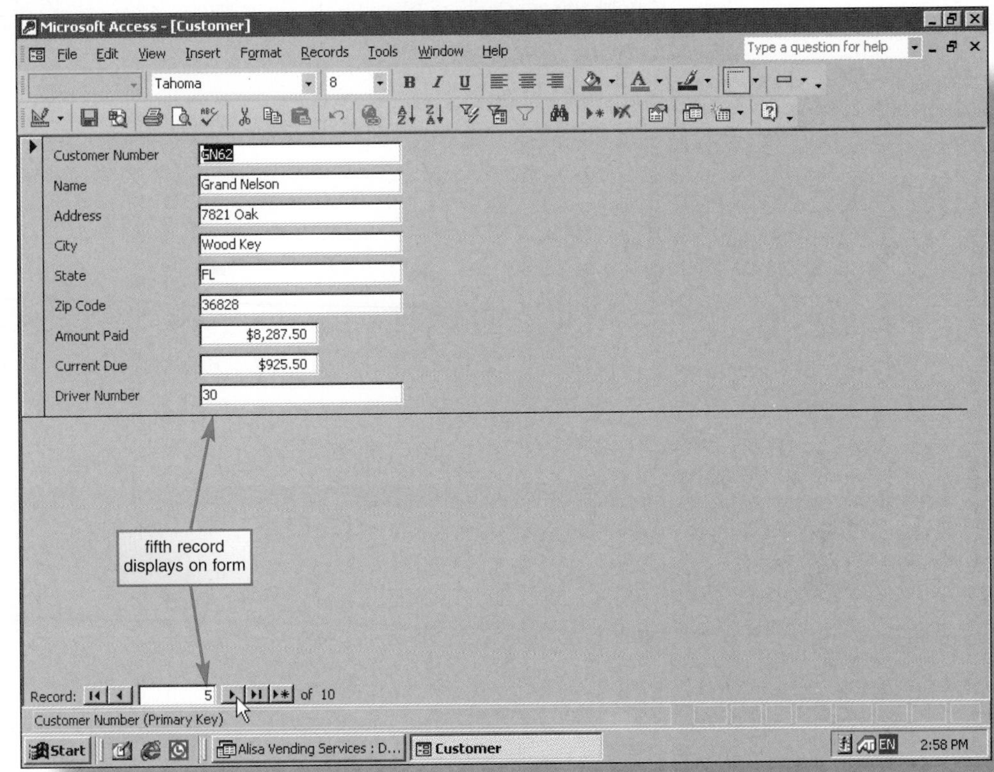

FIGURE 1-57

Switching Between Form View and Datasheet View

In some cases, once you have seen a record in Form view, you will want to move to Datasheet view to again see a collection of records. To do so, click the View button arrow on the Form View toolbar and then click Datasheet View in the list that displays.

Perform the following steps to switch from Form view to Datasheet view.

Steps To Switch from Form View to Datasheet View

1 Point to the View button arrow on the Form View toolbar (Figure 1-58).

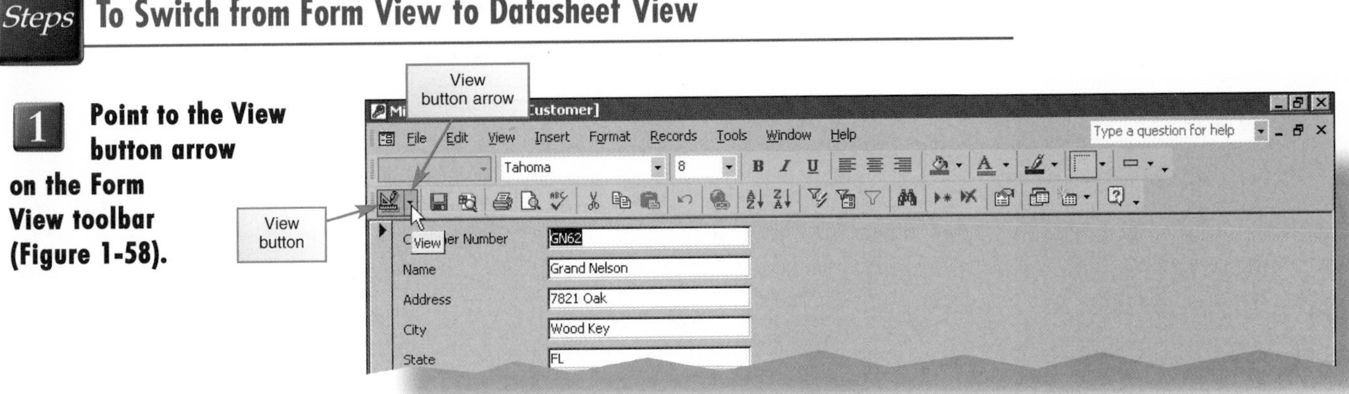

FIGURE 1-58

2 Click the View button arrow and then point to Datasheet View.

The list of available views displays (Figure 1-59).

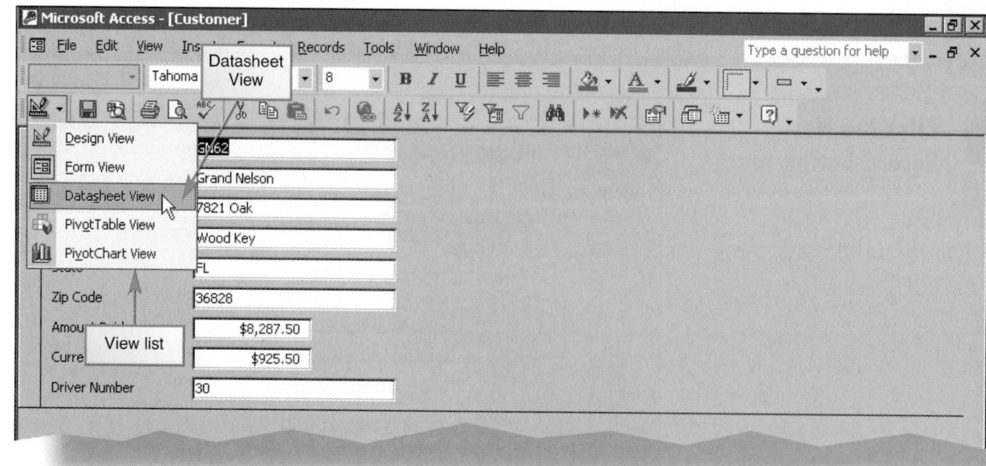

FIGURE 1-59

3 Click Datasheet View.

The table displays in Datasheet view (Figure 1-60). The record selector is positioned on the fifth record.

4 Click the Close Window button.

The Customer window closes and the datasheet no longer displays.

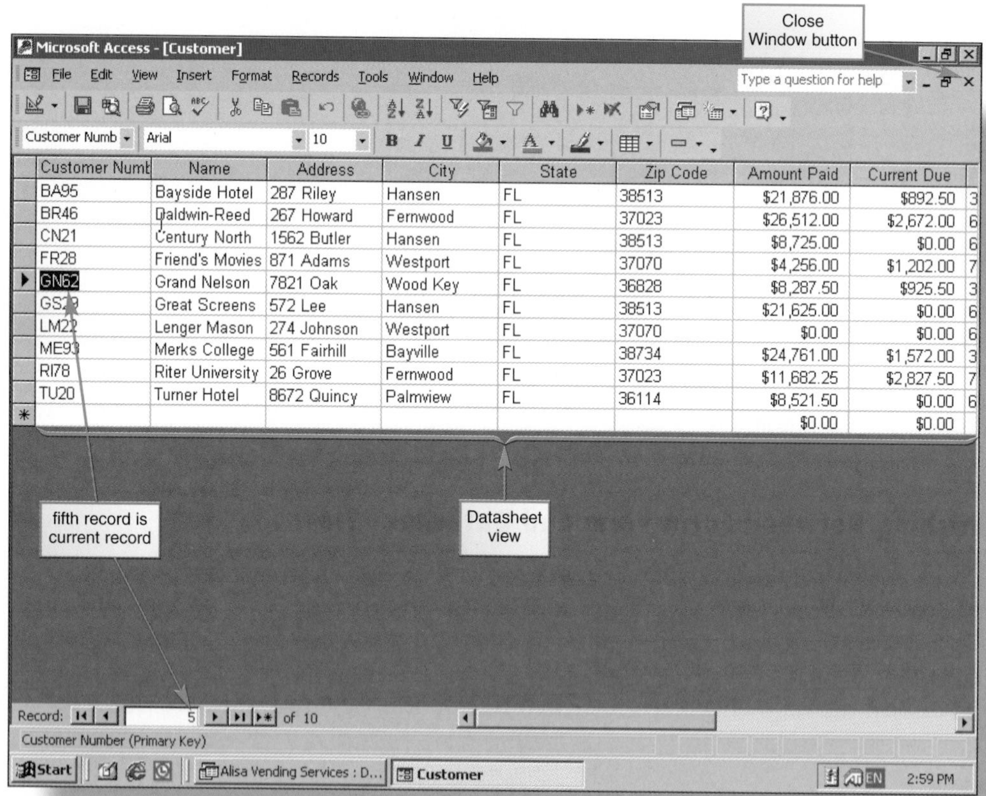

FIGURE 1-60

Other Ways

1. On View menu click Datasheet View
2. In Voice Command mode, say "View, Datasheet View"

Creating a Report

Earlier in this project, you printed a table using the Print button. The report you produced was shown in Figure 1-35 on page A 1.28. While this type of report presented the data in an organized manner, the format is very rigid. You cannot select the fields to display, for example; the report automatically includes all the fields and they display in precisely the same order as in the table. There is no way to change the title, which will automatically be the same as the name of the table.

In this section, you will create the report shown in Figure 1-61. This report features significant differences from the one in Figure 1-35 The portion at the top of the report in Figure 1-61, called a **page header**, contains a custom title. The contents of this page header display at the top of each page. The **detail lines**, which are the lines that are printed for each record, contain only those fields you specify and in the order you specify.

More About

Reports

Custom reports represent one of the most important ways of presenting the data in a database. Reports can incorporate data from multiple tables and can be formatted in a wide variety of ways. The ability to create sophisticated custom reports is one of the major benefits of a DBMS like Access.

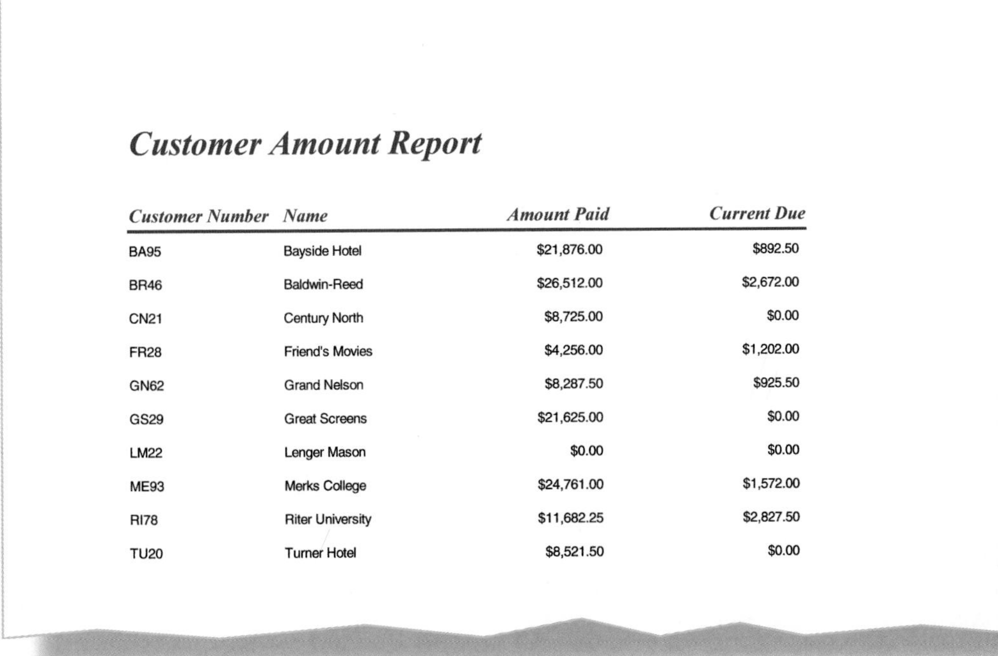

Customer Amount Report

Customer Number	*Name*	*Amount Paid*	*Current Due*
BA95	Bayside Hotel	$21,876.00	$892.50
BR46	Baldwin-Reed	$26,512.00	$2,672.00
CN21	Century North	$8,725.00	$0.00
FR28	Friend's Movies	$4,256.00	$1,202.00
GN62	Grand Nelson	$8,287.50	$925.50
GS29	Great Screens	$21,625.00	$0.00
LM22	Lenger Mason	$0.00	$0.00
ME93	Merks College	$24,761.00	$1,572.00
RI78	Riter University	$11,682.25	$2,827.50
TU20	Turner Hotel	$8,521.50	$0.00

FIGURE 1-61

Perform the following steps to create the report in Figure 1-61.

Steps To Create a Report

1 Click Tables on the Objects bar. Make sure the Customer table is selected. Click the New Object: AutoForm button arrow on the Database toolbar and then point to Report.

The list of available objects displays (Figure 1-62).

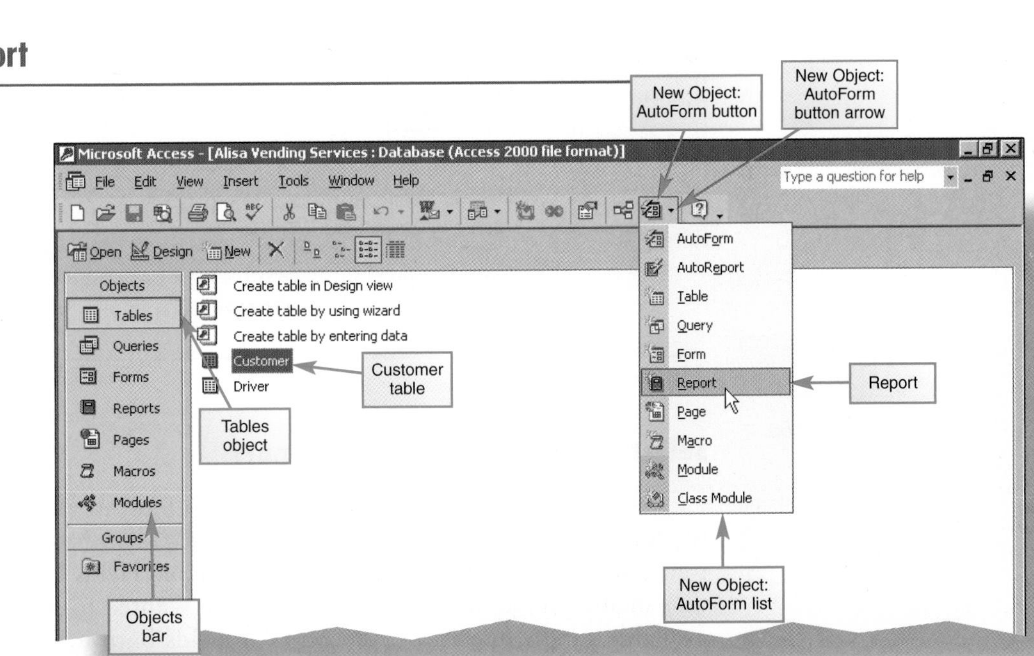

FIGURE 1-62

2 Click Report and then point to Report Wizard.

The New Report dialog box displays (Figure 1-63).

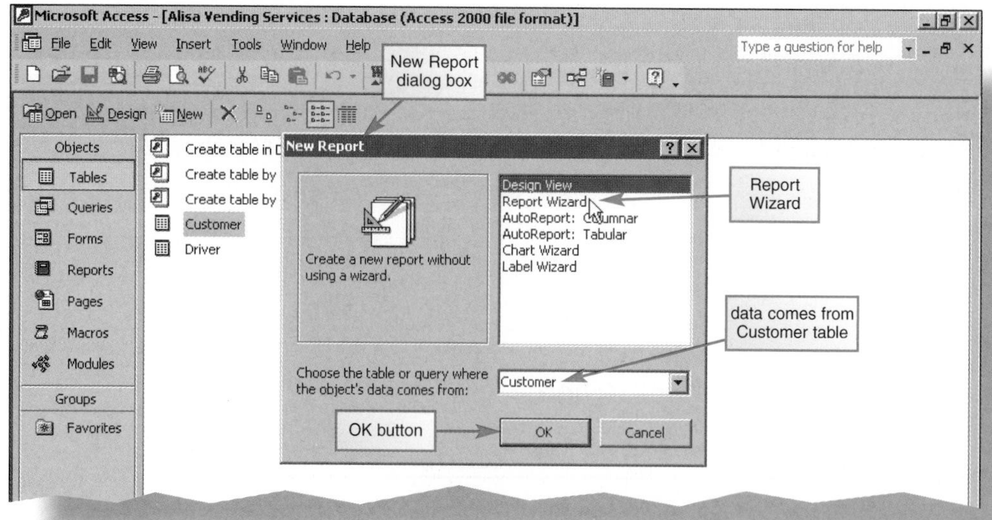

FIGURE 1-63

3 Click Report Wizard and then click the OK button. Point to the Add Field button.

The Report Wizard dialog box displays (Figure 1-64).

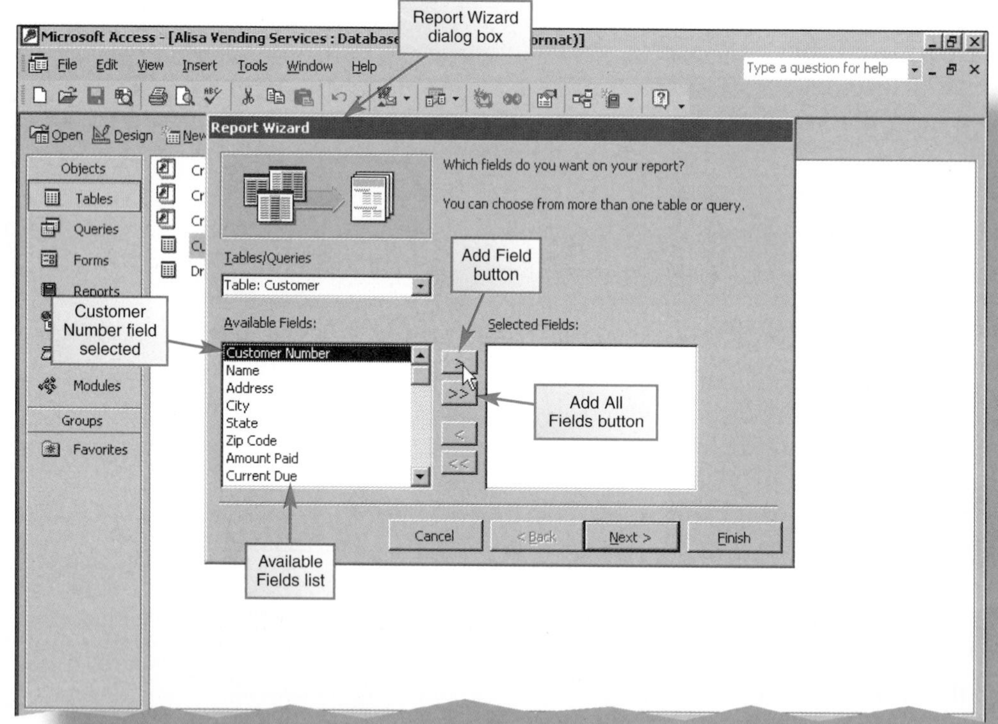

FIGURE 1-64

Other Ways

1. On Insert menu click Report
2. On Objects bar click Reports, click New
3. In Voice Command mode, say "Insert, Report"
4. In Voice Command mode, say "Reports, New"

Selecting the Fields for the Report

To select a field for the report, that is, to indicate the field is to be included in the report, click the field in the Available Fields list. Next, click the Add Field button. This will move the field from the Available Fields box to the Selected Fields box, thus including the field in the report. If you wanted to select all fields, a shortcut is available simply by clicking the Add All Fields button.

To select the Customer Number, Name, Amount Paid, and Current Due fields for the report, perform the following steps.

Steps To Select the Fields for a Report

1 Click the Add Field button to add the Customer Number field. Add the Name field by clicking it and then clicking the Add Field button. Add the Amount Paid and Current Due fields just as you added the Customer Number and Name fields. Point to the Next button.

The fields for the report display in the Selected Fields box (Figure 1-65).

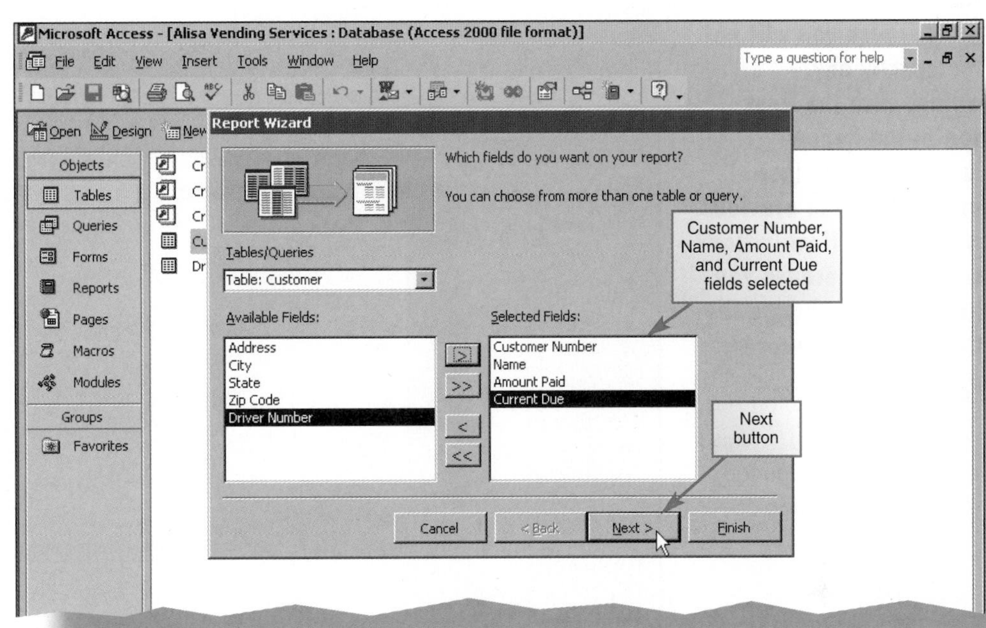

FIGURE 1-65

2 Click the Next button.

The Report Wizard dialog box displays (Figure 1-66).

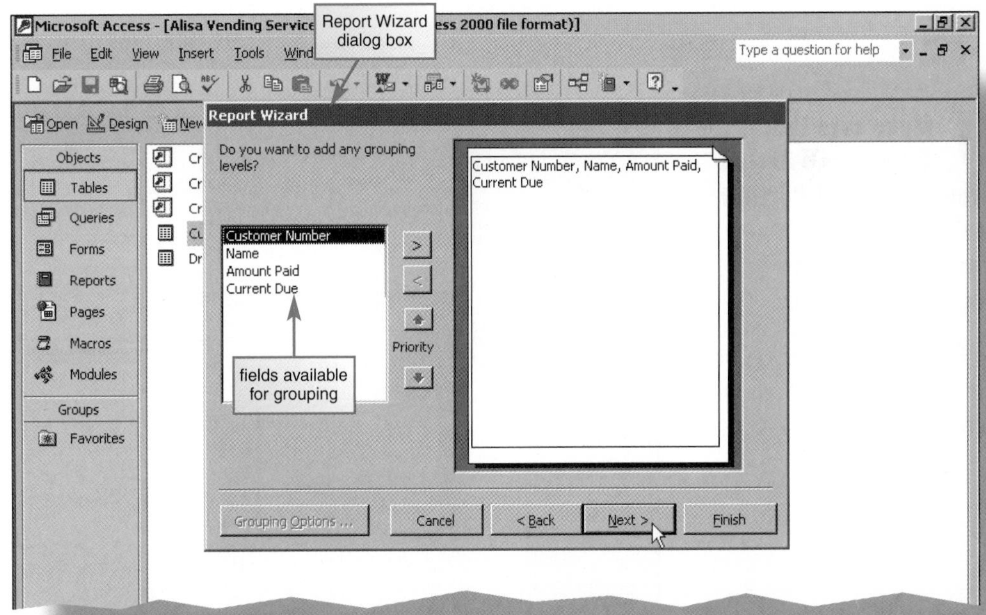

FIGURE 1-66

Other Ways

1. Double-click field

Completing the Report

Several additional steps are involved in completing the report. With the exception of changing the title, the Access selections are acceptable, so you simply will click the Next button.

Perform the steps on the next page to complete the report.

Steps To Complete a Report

1 Because you will not specify any grouping, click the Next button in the Report Wizard dialog box (see Figure 1-66 on the previous page. Click the Next button a second time because you will not need to change the sort order for the records.

The Report Wizard dialog box displays (Figure 1-67). In this dialog box, you can change the layout or orientation of the report.

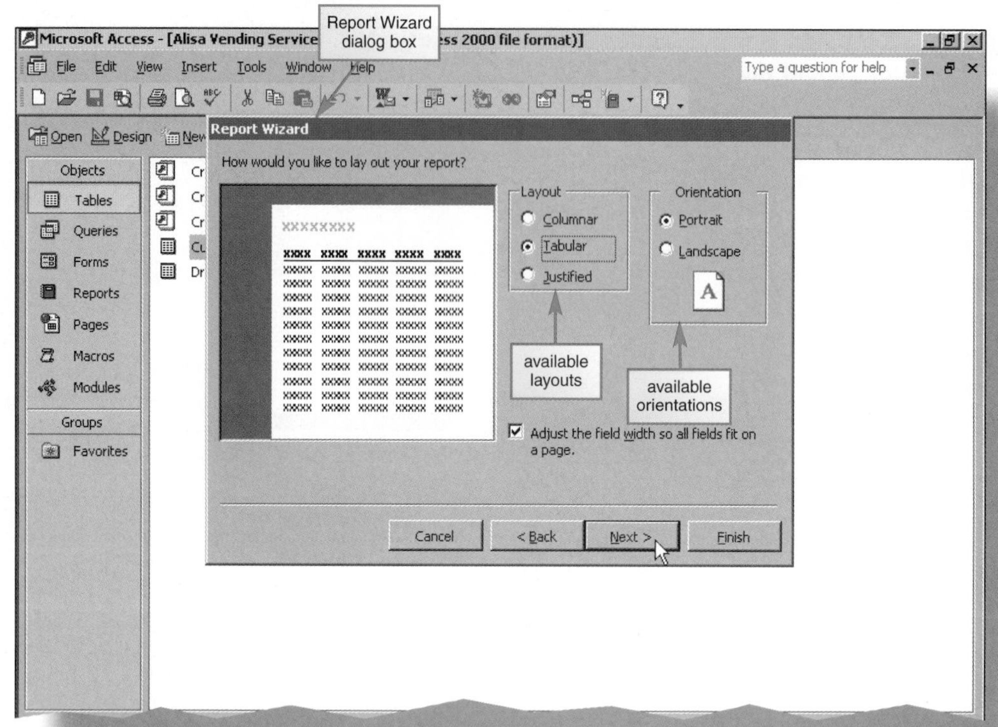

FIGURE 1-67

2 Make sure that Tabular is selected as the layout and Portrait is selected as the orientation and then click the Next button.

The Report Wizard dialog box displays (Figure 1-68). In this dialog box, you can select a style for the report.

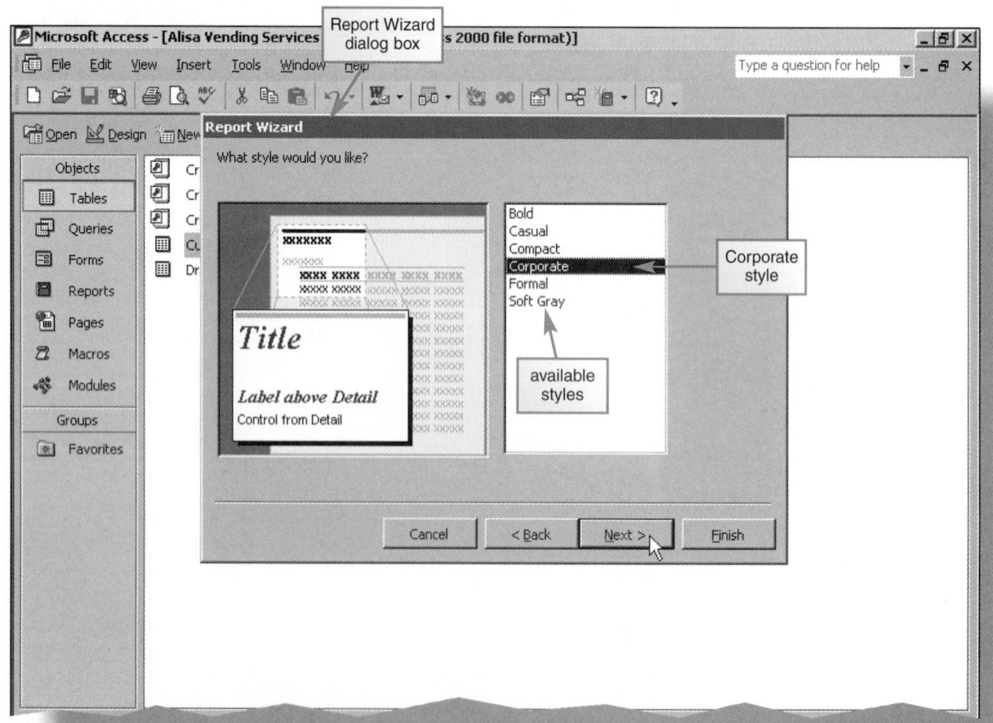

FIGURE 1-68

3 **Be sure that the Corporate style is selected, click the Next button, type** `Customer Amount Report` **as the new title, and then point to the Finish button.**

The Report Wizard dialog box displays (Figure 1-69). The title is typed.

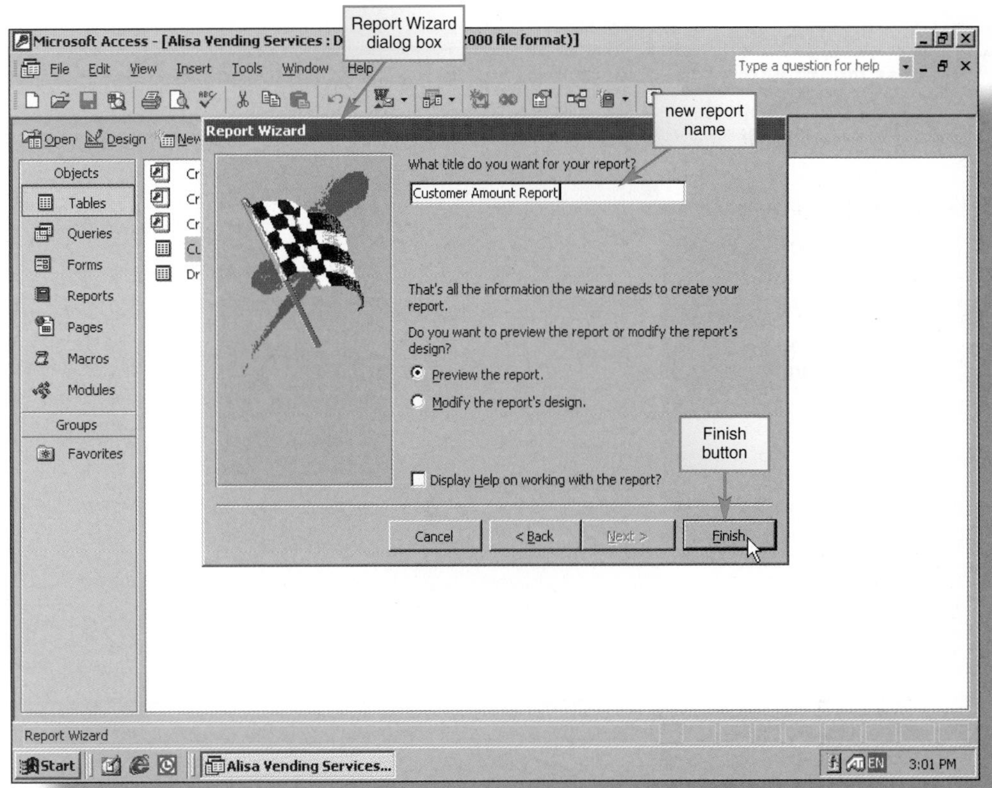

FIGURE 1-69

4 **Click the Finish button.**

A preview of the report displays (Figure 1-70). Yours may look slightly different, depending on your printer.

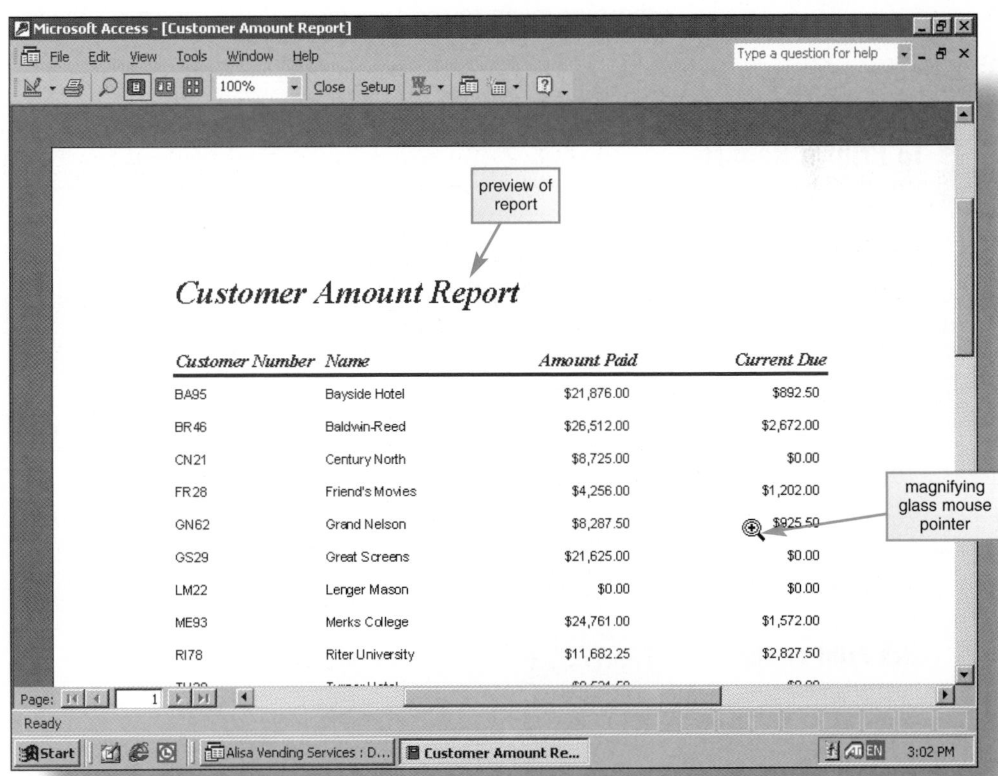

FIGURE 1-70

5 Click the magnifying glass mouse pointer anywhere within the report to see the entire report.

The entire report displays (Figure 1-71).

6 Click the Close Window button in the Customer Amount Report window.

The report no longer displays. It has been saved automatically using the name Customer Amount Report.

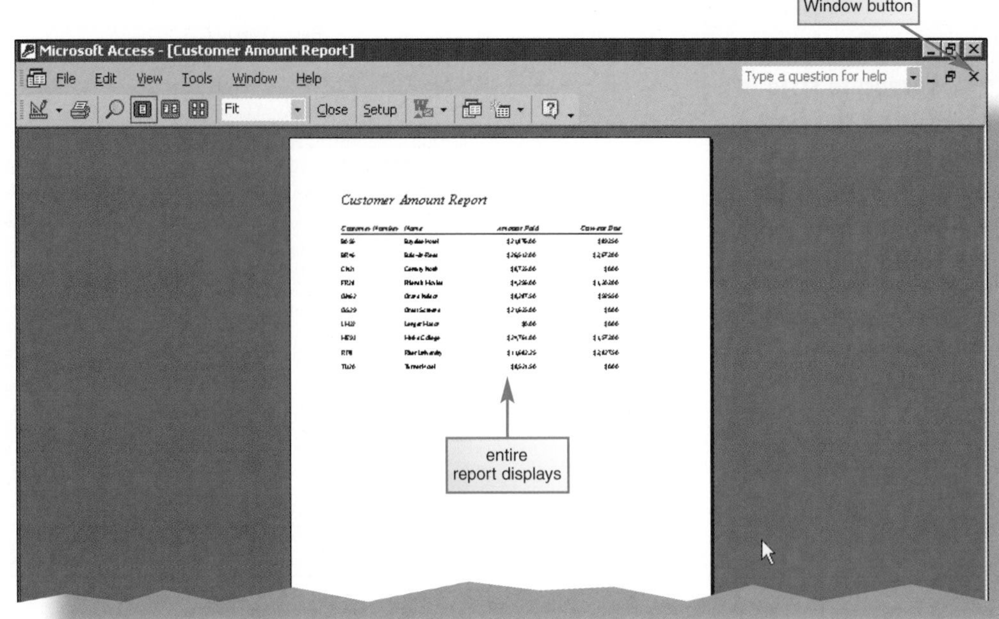

FIGURE 1-71

Printing the Report

To print a report from the Database window, first right-click the report. Then click Print on the shortcut menu to print the report or click Print Preview on the shortcut menu to see a preview of the report on the screen.

Perform the following steps to print the report.

Steps To Print a Report

1 If necessary, click Reports on the Objects bar in the Database window, right-click the Customer Amount Report, and then point to Print on the shortcut menu.

The shortcut menu for the Customer Amount Report displays (Figure 1-72).

2 Click Print on the shortcut menu.

The report prints. It should look similar to the one shown in Figure 1-61 on page A 1.41.

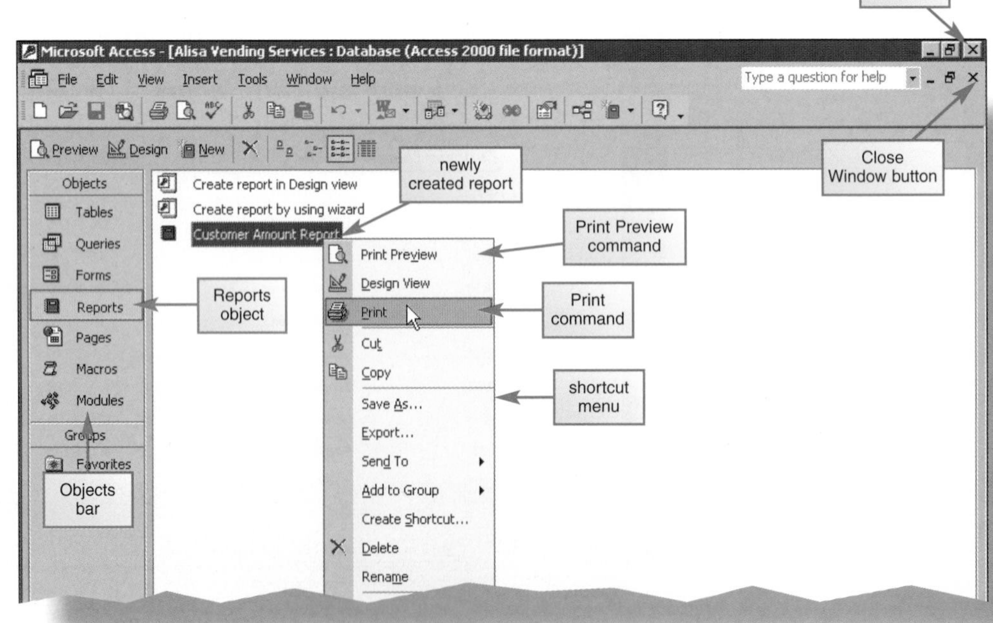

FIGURE 1-72

Closing the Database

Once you have finished working with a database, you should close it. The following step closes the database by closing its Database window.

TO CLOSE A DATABASE

1 Click the Close Window button for the Alisa Vending Services : Database window.

> **More About**
>
> **Quick Reference**
>
> For a table that lists how to complete tasks covered in this book using the mouse, menu, shortcut menu, and keyboard, see the Quick Reference Summary at the back of this book or visit the Shelly Cashman Series Office XP Web page (scsite.com/offxp/qr.htm) and then click Microsoft Access 2002.

Access Help System

At any time while you are using Access, you can get answers to questions by using the Access Help system. Used properly, this form of online assistance can increase your productivity and reduce your frustrations by minimizing the time you spend learning how to use Access.

The following section shows how to get answers to your questions using the Ask a Question box. For additional information on using the Access Help system, see Appendix A on page A A.01 and Table 1-2 on page A 1.49.

> **More About**
>
> **The Access Help System**
>
> The best way to become familiar with the Access Help system is to use it. Appendix A includes detailed information on the Access Help system and exercises that will help you gain confidence in using it.

Obtaining Help Using the Ask a Question Box on the Menu Bar

The **Ask a Question box** on the right side of the menu bar lets you type in free-form questions, such as *how do I save* or *how do I create a Web page*, or you can type in terms, such as *copy*, *save*, or *formatting*. Access responds by displaying a list of topics related to what you entered. The following steps show how to use the Ask a Question box to obtain information on removing a primary key.

Steps To Obtain Help Using the Ask a Question Box

1 **Click the Ask a Question box on the right side of the menu bar. Type** how do I remove a primary key **in the box (Figure 1-73).**

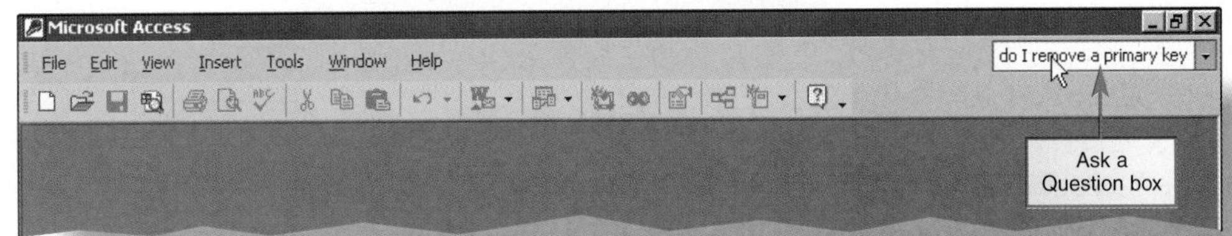

FIGURE 1-73

2 **Press the ENTER key.**

A list of topics displays relating to the question, "how do I remove a primary key" (Figure 1-74).

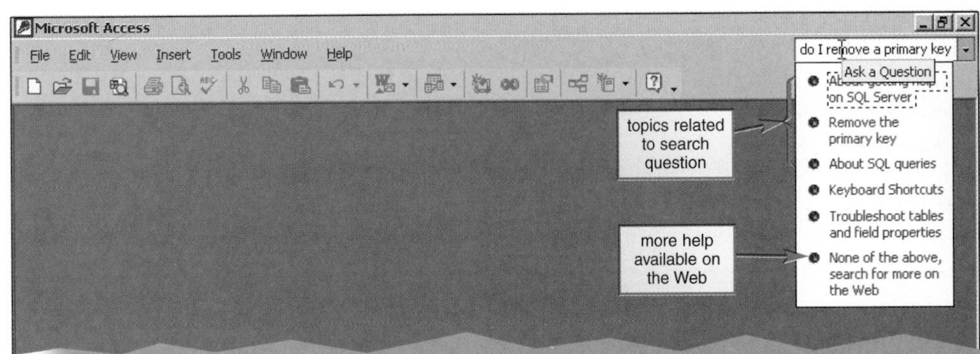

FIGURE 1-74

3 Point to the Remove the primary key topic.

The mouse pointer changes to a hand indicating it is pointing to a link (Figure 1-75).

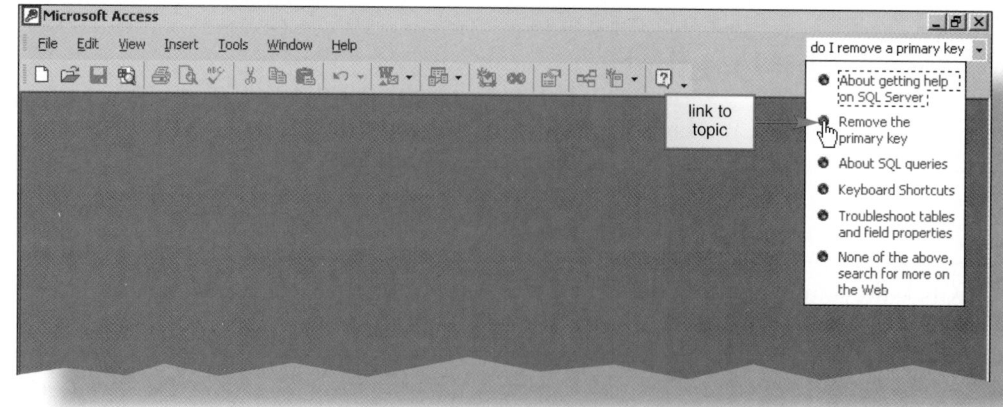

FIGURE 1-75

4 Click Remove the primary key.

Access displays a Microsoft Access Help window that provides Help information about removing the primary key (Figure 1-76).

5 Click the Close button on the Microsoft Access Help window title bar.

The Microsoft Access Help window closes.

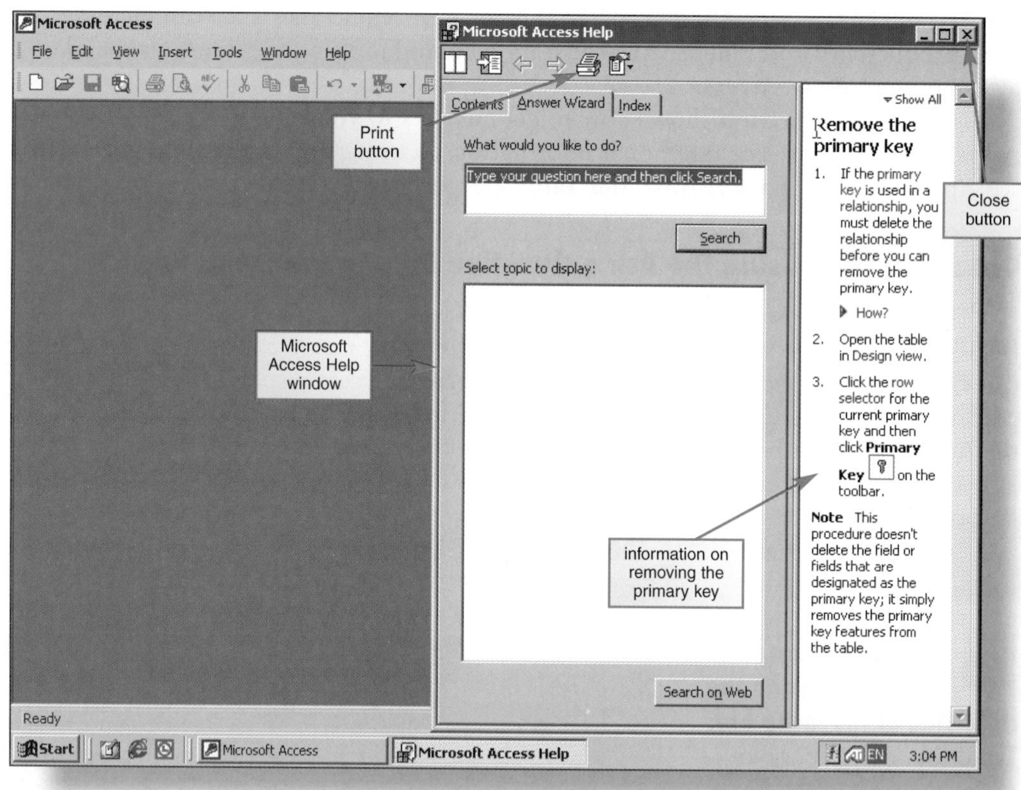

FIGURE 1-76

Other Ways

1. Click Microsoft Access Help button on toolbar
2. On Help menu click Microsoft Access Help
3. In Voice Command mode, say "Help, Microsoft Access Help"

Use the buttons in the upper-left corner of the Microsoft Access Help window (Figure 1-76) to navigate through the Help system, change the display, and print the contents of the window.

As you enter questions and terms in the Ask a Question box, Access adds them to its list. Thus, if you click the Ask a Question box arrow, a list of previously asked questions and terms will display.

Table 1-2 summarizes the 10 categories of Help available to you. Because of the way the Access Help system works, be sure to review the rightmost column of Table 1-2 if you have difficulties activating the desired category of Help. Additional information on using the Access Help system is available in Appendix A.

Table 1-2 Access Help System

TYPE	DESCRIPTION	HOW TO ACTIVATE
Answer Wizard	Answers questions or searches for terms that you type in your own words.	Click the Microsoft Access Help button on the Database window toolbar. Click the Answer Wizard tab.
Ask a Question box	Answers questions or searches for terms that you type in your own words.	Type a question or term in the Ask a Question box on the menu bar and then press the ENTER key.
Contents sheet	Groups Help topics by general categories. Use when you know only the general category of the topic in question.	Click the Microsoft Access Help button on the Database window toolbar. Click the Contents tab.
Detect and Repair	Automatically finds and fixes errors in the application.	Click Detect and Repair on the Help menu.
Hardware and Software Information	Shows Product ID and allows access to system information and technical support information.	Click About Microsoft Access on the Help menu and then click the appropriate button.
Index sheet	Similar to an index in a book. Use when you know exactly what you want.	Click the Microsoft Access Help button on the Database window toolbar. If necessary, maximize the Help window by double-clicking its title bar. Click the Index tab.
Office Assistant	Similar to the Ask a Question box in that the Office Assistant answers questions that you type in your own words, offers tips, and provides help for a variety of Access features.	Click the Office Assistant icon. If the Office Assistant does not display, click Show the Office Assistant on the Help menu.
Office on the Web	Used to access technical resources and download free product enhancements on the Web.	Click Office on the Web on the Help menu.
Question Mark button	Used to identify unfamiliar items in a dialog box.	Click the Question Mark button on the title bar in a dialog box and then click an item in the dialog box.
What's This? command	Used to identify unfamiliar items on the screen.	Click What's This? on the Help menu and then click an item on the screen.

You can use the Office Assistant to search for Help on any topic concerning Access. For additional information on using the Access Help system, see Appendix A.

Quitting Access

After you close a database, you can open another database, create a new database, or simply quit Access and return to the Windows desktop. The following step quits Access.

TO QUIT ACCESS

1. Click the Close button in the Microsoft Access window (see Figure 1-72 on page A 1.46).

Designing a Database

Database design refers to the arrangement of data into tables and fields. In the example in this project, the design is specified, but in many cases, you will have to determine the design based on what you want the system to accomplish.

With large, complex databases, the database design process can be extensive. Major sections of advanced database textbooks are devoted to this topic. Often, however, you should be able to design a database effectively by keeping one simple principle in mind: Design to remove redundancy. **Redundancy** means storing the same fact in more than one place.

To illustrate, you need to maintain the following information shown in Figure 1-77. In the figure, all the data is contained in a single table. Notice that the data for a given driver (number, name, address, and so on) occurs on more than one record.

Customer table

CUSTOMER NUMBER	NAME	ADDRESS	CITY	STATE	ZIP CODE	AMOUNT PAID	CURRENT DUE	DRIVER NUMBER	LAST NAME	FIRST NAME	ADDRESS
BA95	Bayside Hotel	287 Riley	Hansen	FL	38513	$21,876.00	$892.50	30	Tuttle	Larissa	7562 Hickory
BR46	Baldwin-Reed	267 Howard	Fernwood	FL	37023	$26,512.00	$2,672.00	60	Powers	Frank	57 Ravenwood
CN21	Century North	1562 Butler	Hansen	FL	38513	$8,725.00	$0.00	60	Powers	Frank	57 Ravenwood
FR28	Friend's Movies	871 Adams	Westport	FL	37070	$4,256.00	$1,202.00	75	Ortiz	Jose	341 Pierce
GN62	Grand Nelson	7821 Oak	Wood Key	FL	36828	$8,287.50	$925.50	30	Tuttle	Larissa	7562 Hickory
GS29	Great Screens	572 Lee	Hansen	FL	38513	$21,625.00	$0.00	60	Powers	Frank	57 Ravenwood
LM22	Lenger Mason	274 Johnson	Westport	FL	37070	$0.00	$0.00	60	Powers	Frank	57 Ravenwood
ME93	Merks College	561 Fairhill	Bayville	FL	38734	$24,761.00	$1,572.00	30	Tuttle	Larissa	7562 Hickory
RI78	Riter University	26 Grove	Fernwood	FL	37023	$11,682.25	$2,827.50	75	Ortiz	Jose	341 Pierce
TU20	Turner Hotel	8672 Quincy	Palmview	FL	36114	$8,521.50	$0.00	60	Powers	Frank	57 Ravenwood

duplicate driver names

FIGURE 1-77

Database Design (Normalization)

A special technique for identifying and eliminating redundancy is called normalization. For more information on normalization, visit the Access 2002 More About Web page (scsite.com/ac2002/more.htm) and then click Normalization.

Storing this data on multiple records is an example of redundancy, which causes several problems, including:

1. Redundancy wastes space on the disk. The address of driver 30 (Larissa Tuttle), for example, should be stored only once. Storing this fact several times is wasteful.
2. Redundancy makes updating the database more difficult. If, for example, Larissa Tuttle moves, her address would need to be changed in several different places.
3. A possibility of inconsistent data exists. Suppose, for example, that you change the address of Larissa Tuttle on customer GN62's record to 146 Valley, but do not change it on customer BA95's record. In both cases, the driver number is 30, but the addresses are different. In other words, the data is inconsistent.

Database Design (Design Method)

A variety of methods have been developed for designing complex databases given a set of input and output requirements. For more information on database design methods, visit the Access 2002 More About Web page (scsite.com/ac2002/more.htm) and then click Database Design.

The solution to the problem is to place the redundant data in a separate table, one in which the data will no longer be redundant. If, for example, you place the data for drivers in a separate table (Figure 1-78), the data for each driver will display only once.

Notice that you need to have the driver number in both tables. Without it, no way exists to tell which driver is associated with which customer. All the other driver data, however, was removed from the Customer table and placed in the Driver table. This new arrangement corrects the problems of redundancy in the following ways:

1. Because the data for each driver is stored only once, space is not wasted.
2. Changing the address of a driver is easy. You have only to change one row in the Driver table.
3. Because the data for a driver is stored only once, inconsistent data cannot occur.

driver data is in separate table

Driver table

DRIVER NUMBER	LAST NAME	FIRST NAME	ADDRESS	CITY	STATE	ZIP CODE	HOURLY RATE	YTD EARNINGS
30	Tuttle	Larissa	7562 Hickory	Laton Springs	FL	37891	$16.00	$21,145.25
60	Powers	Frank	57 Ravenwood	Gillmore	FL	37572	$15.00	$19,893.50
75	Ortiz	Jose	341 Pierce	Douglas	FL	37613	$17.00	$23,417.00

Customer table

CUSTOMER NUMBER	NAME	ADDRESS	CITY	STATE	ZIP CODE	AMOUNT PAID	CURRENT DUE	DRIVER NUMBER
BA95	Bayside Hotel	287 Riley	Hansen	FL	38513	$21,876.00	$892.50	30
BR46	Baldwin-Reed	267 Howard	Fernwood	FL	37023	$26,512.00	$2,672.00	60
CN21	Century North	1562 Butler	Hansen	FL	38513	$8,725.00	$0.00	60
FR28	Friend's Movies	871 Adams	Westport	FL	37070	$4,256.00	$1,202.00	75
GN62	Grand Nelson	7821 Oak	Wood Key	FL	36828	$8,287.50	$925.50	30
GS29	Great Screens	572 Lee	Hansen	FL	38513	$21,625.00	$0.00	60
LM22	Lenger Mason	274 Johnson	Westport	FL	37070	$0.00	$0.00	60
ME93	Merks College	561 Fairhill	Bayville	FL	38734	$24,761.00	$1,572.00	30
RI78	Riter University	26 Grove	Fernwood	FL	37023	$11,682.25	$2,827.50	75
TU20	Turner Hotel	8672 Quincy	Palmview	FL	36114	$8,521.50	$0.00	60

FIGURE 1-78

Designing to omit redundancy will help you to produce good and valid database designs.

CASE PERSPECTIVE SUMMARY

In Project 1, you assisted Alisa Vending Services in their efforts to place their data in a database. You created the database that Alisa will use. Within the Alisa Vending Services database, you created the Customer and Driver tables by defining the fields within them. You then added records to these tables. Once you created the tables, you printed the contents of the tables. You also used a form to view the data in the table. Finally, you used the Report Wizard to create a report containing the Customer Number, Name, Amount Paid, and Current Due fields for each customer served by Alisa Vending Services.

Project Summary

In Project 1, you learned about databases and database management systems. You learned how to create a database and how to create the tables within a database. You saw how to define the fields in a table by specifying the characteristics of the fields. You learned how to open a table, how to add records to it, and how to close it. You also printed the contents of a table. You created a form to view data on the screen and also created a custom report. You learned how to use Microsoft Access Help. Finally, you learned how to design a database to eliminate redundancy.

What You Should Know

Having completed this project, you now should be able to perform the following tasks:

- Add Additional Records to a Table (*A 1.27*)
- Add Records to a Table (*A 1.21*)
- Add Records to an Additional Table (*A 1.34*)
- Close a Database (*A 1.47*)
- Close a Table and Database (*A 1.25*)
- Close and Save a Form (*A 1.36*)
- Complete a Report (*A 1.44*)
- Create a New Database (A 1.11)
- Create a Report (*A 1.41*)
- Create a Table (*A 1.15*)
- Create an Additional Table (*A 1.33*)
- Define the Fields in a Table (*A 1.17*)
- Obtain Help Using the Ask a Question Box (*A 1.47*)
- Open a Database (*A 1.25*)
- Open a Form (*A 1.37*)
- Preview and Print the Contents of a Table (*A 1.29*)
- Print a Report (*A 1.46*)
- Quit Access (A 1.47)
- Save and Close a Table (A 1.20)
- Select the Fields for a Report (*A 1.43*)
- Start Access (*A 1.09*)
- Switch from Form View to Datasheet View (*A 1.39*)
- Use a Form (*A 1.39*)
- Use the New Object: AutoForm Button to Create a Form (*A 1.35*)

More About

Microsoft Certification

The Microsoft Office User Specialist (MOUS) Certification program provides an opportunity for you to obtain a valuable industry credential — proof that you have the Access 2002 skills required by employers. For more information, see Appendix E or visit the Shelly Cashman Series MOUS Web page at scsite.com/offxp/cert.htm.

Learn It Online

Instructions: To complete the Learn It Online exercises, start your browser, click the Address bar, and then enter scsite.com/offxp/exs.htm. When the Office XP Learn It Online page displays, follow the instructions in the exercises below.

1 Project Reinforcement TF, MC, and SA

Below Access Project 1, click the Project Reinforcement link. Print the quiz by clicking Print on the File menu. Answer each question. Write your first and last name at the top of each page, and then hand in the printout to your instructor.

2 Flash Cards

Below Access Project 1, click the Flash Cards link. When Flash Cards displays, read the instructions. Type 20 (or a number specified by your instructor) in the Number of Playing Cards text box, type your name in the Name text box, and then click the Flip Card button. When the flash card displays, read the question and then click the Answer box arrow to select an answer. Flip through Flash Cards. Click Print on the File menu to print the last flash card if your score is 15 (75%) correct or greater and then hand it in to your instructor. If your score is less than 15 (75%) correct, then redo this exercise by clicking the Replay button.

3 Practice Test

Below Access Project 1, click the Practice Test link. Answer each question, enter your first and last name at the bottom of the page, and then click the Grade Test button. When the graded practice test displays on your screen, click Print on the File menu to print a hard copy. Continue to take practice tests until you score 80% or better. Hand in a printout of the final practice test to your instructor.

4 Who Wants to Be a Computer Genius?

Below Access Project 1, click the Computer Genius link. Read the instructions, enter your first and last name at the bottom of the page, and then click the Play button. Hand in your score to your instructor.

5 Wheel of Terms

Below Access Project 1, click the Wheel of Terms link. Read the instructions, and then enter your first and last name and your school name. Click the Play button. Hand in your score to your instructor.

6 Crossword Puzzle Challenge

Below Access Project 1, click the Crossword Puzzle Challenge link. Read the instructions, and then enter your first and last name. Click the Play button. Work the crossword puzzle. When you are finished, click the Submit button. When the crossword puzzle redisplays, click the Print button. Hand in the printout.

7 Tips and Tricks

Below Access Project 1, click the Tips and Tricks link. Click a topic that pertains to Project 1. Right-click the information and then click Print on the shortcut menu. Construct a brief example of what the information relates to in Access to confirm you understand how to use the tip or trick. Hand in the example and printed information.

8 Newsgroups

Below Access Project 1, click the Newsgroups link. Click a topic that pertains to Project 1. Print three comments. Hand in the comments to your instructor.

9 Expanding Your Horizons

Below Access Project 1, click the Articles for Microsoft Access link. Click a topic that pertains to Project 1. Print the information. Construct a brief example of what the information relates to in Access to confirm you understand the contents of the article. Hand in the example and printed information to your instructor.

10 Search Sleuth

Below Access Project 1, click the Search Sleuth link. To search for a term that pertains to this project, select a term below the Project 1 title and then use the Google search engine at google.com (or any major search engine) to display and print two Web pages that present information on the term. Hand in the printouts to your instructor.

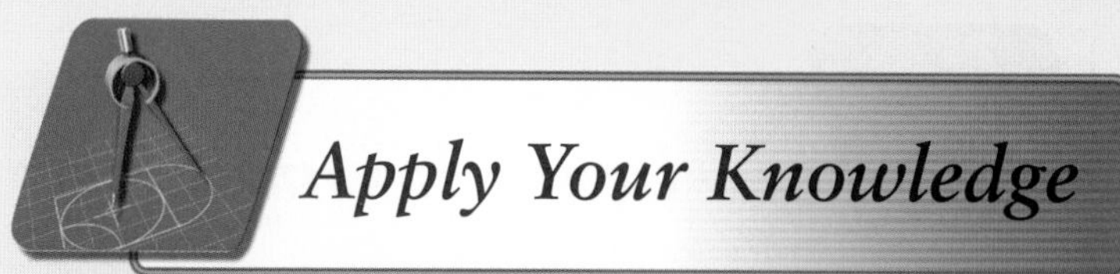

Apply Your Knowledge

1 Changing Data and Creating Reports

Instructions: Start Access. Open the database Beyond Clean from the Data Disk. See the inside back cover of this book for instructions for downloading the Data Disk or see your instructor for information on accessing the files required in this book. Beyond Clean is a company that specializes in cleaning and light custodial work for commercial businesses. Beyond Clean has a database that keeps track of its custodians and clients. The database has two tables. The Client table contains data on the clients who use the services of Beyond Clean. The Custodian table contains data on the individuals employed by Beyond Clean. The structure and data are shown for the Client table in Figure 1-79 and for the Custodian table in Figure 1-80.

Structure of Client table

FIELD NAME	DATA TYPE	FIELD SIZE	PRIMARY KEY?	DESCRIPTION
Client Number	Text	4	Yes	Client Number (Primary Key)
Name	Text	20		Client Name
Address	Text	15		Street Address
City	Text	15		City
State	Text	2		Sate (Two-Character Abbreviation)
Zip Code	Text	5		Zip Code (Five-Character Version)
Telephone Number	Text	12		Telephone Number (999-999-9999 Version)
Balance	Currency			Amount Owed by Client
Custodian Id	Text	3		Id of Client's Custodian

Data for Client table

CLIENT NUMBER	NAME	ADDRESS	CITY	STATE	ZIP CODE	TELEPHONE NUMBER	BALANCE	CUSTODIAN ID
AD23	Adder Cleaners	407 Mallery	Anders	TX	31501	512-555-4070	$105.00	002
AR76	The Artshop	200 Wymberly	Liberty Estates	TX	31499	510-555-0200	$80.00	009
BE29	Beacher's	224 Harbor Oak	Liberty Estates	TX	31499	510-555-2024	$70.00	009
CR67	Cricket Store	506 Mallery	Anders	TX	31501	512-555-6050	$0.00	002
DL61	Del Sol	123 Village	Kingston	TX	31534	513-555-1231	$135.00	013
GR36	Great Foods	1345 Frederic	Kingston	TX	31534	513-555-5431	$104.00	013
HA09	Halyards Mfg	5689 Demerre	Anders	TX	31501	512-555-6895	$145.00	009
ME17	Merry Café	879 Vinca	Kingston	TX	31534	513-555-9780	$168.00	013
RO45	Royal Palms	678 Liatris	Anders	TX	31501	512-555-4567	$0.00	002
ST21	Steed's	809 Lantana	Liberty Estates	TX	31499	510-555-9080	$123.00	009

FIGURE 1-79

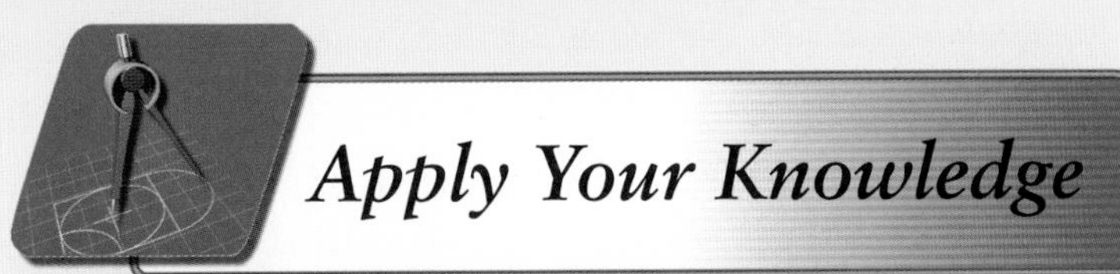

Apply Your Knowledge

Structure of Custodian table

FIELD NAME	DATA TYPE	FIELD SIZE	PRIMARY KEY?	DESCRIPTION
Custodian Id	Text	3	Yes	Custodian Identification Number (Primary Key)
Last Name	Text	12		Last Name of Custodian
First Name	Text	8		First Name of Custodian
Address	Text	15		Street Address
City	Text	15		City
State	Text	2		State (Two-Character Abbreviation)
Zip Code	Text	5		Zip Code (Five-Character Version)
Pay Rate	Currency			Hourly Pay Rate

Data for Custodian table

CUSTODIAN ID	LAST NAME	FIRST NAME	ADDRESS	CITY	STATE	ZIP CODE	PAY RATE
002	Deakle	Terry	764 Hubbard	Anders	TX	31501	$9.50
009	Lee	Michelle	78 Dunlop	Liberty Estates	TX	31499	$9.75
013	Torres	Juan	345 Red Poppy	Anders	TX	31501	$9.65

FIGURE 1-80

Perform the following tasks.

1. Open the Custodian table in Datasheet view and add the following record to the table:

CUSTODIAN ID	LAST NAME	FIRST NAME	ADDRESS	CITY	STATE	ZIP CODE	PAY RATE
011	Meeder	Pat	113 Lantana	Liberty Estates	TX	31499	$9.50

   Close the Custodian table.
2. Open the Custodian table again. Notice that the record you just added has been moved. It is no longer at the end of the table. The records are in order by the primary key, Custodian Id.
3. Print the Custodian table.
4. Open the Client table.
5. Change the Custodian Id for client BE29 to 011.
6. Print the Client table.
7. Create the report shown in Figure 1-81 for the Client table.
8. Print the report.

Balance Due Report

Client Number	Name	Balance
AD23	Adder Cleaners	$105.00
AR76	The Artshop	$80.00
BE29	Beacher's	$70.00
CR67	Cricket Store	$0.00
DL61	Del Sol	$135.00
GR36	Great Foods	$104.00
HA09	Halyards Mfg	$145.00
ME17	Merry Café	$168.00
RO45	Royal Palms	$0.00
ST21	Steed's	$123.00

FIGURE 1-81

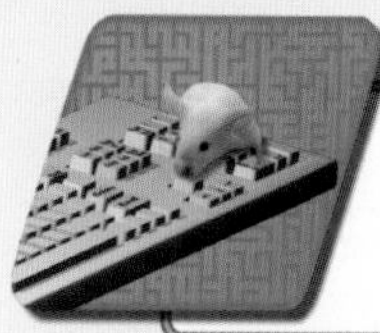

In the Lab

1 Creating the Wooden Crafts Database

Problem: Jan Merchant is an enterprising business person who has a small kiosk in a shopping mall that sells handcrafted wooden items for children, such as trains, tractors, and puzzles. Jan purchases products from individuals that make wooden products by hand. The database consists of two tables. The Product table contains information on products available for sale. The Supplier table contains information on the individuals that supply the products.

Instructions: Perform the following tasks.

1. Create a new database in which to store all the objects related to the merchandise data. Call the database Wooden Crafts.
2. Create the Product table using the structure shown in Figure 1-82. Use the name Product for the table.
3. Add the data shown in Figure 1-82 to the Product table.
4. Print the Product table.
5. Create the Supplier table using the structure shown in Figure 1-83. Use the name Supplier for the table.
6. Add the data shown in Figure 1-83 to the Supplier table.
7. Print the Supplier table.
8. Create a form for the Product table. Use the name Product for the form.

Structure of Product table

FIELD NAME	DATA TYPE	FIELD SIZE	PRIMARY KEY?	DESCRIPTION
Product Id	Text	4	Yes	Product Id Number (Primary Key)
Description	Text	20		Description of Product
On Hand	Number			Number of Units On Hand
Cost	Currency			Cost of Product
Selling Price	Currency			Selling Price of Product
Supplier Code	Text	2		Code of Product Supplier

Data for Product table

PRODUCT ID	DESCRIPTION	ON HAND	COST	SELLING PRICE	SUPPLIER CODE
BF01	Barnyard Friends	3	$54.00	$60.00	PL
BL23	Blocks in Box	5	$29.00	$32.00	AP
CC14	Coal Car	8	$14.00	$18.00	BH
FT05	Fire Truck	7	$9.00	$12.00	AP
LB34	Lacing Bear	4	$12.00	$16.00	AP
MR06	Midget Railroad	3	$31.00	$34.00	BH
PJ12	Pets Jigsaw	10	$8.00	$12.00	PL
RB02	Railway Bridge	1	$17.00	$20.00	BH
SK10	Skyscraper	6	$25.00	$30.00	PL
UM09	USA Map	12	$14.00	$18.00	AP

FIGURE 1-82

In the Lab

Structure for Supplier table

FIELD NAME	DATA TYPE	FIELD SIZE	PRIMARY KEY?	DESCRIPTION
Supplier Code	Text	2	Yes	Supplier Code (Primary Key)
First Name	Text	10		First Name of Supplier
Last Name	Text	15		Last Name of Supplier
Address	Text	20		Street Address
City	Text	20		City
State	Text	2		State (Two-Character Abbreviation)
Zip Code	Text	5		Zip Code (Five-Character Version)
Telephone Number	Text	12		Telephone Number (999-999-9999 Version)

Data for Supplier table

SUPPLIER CODE	FIRST NAME	LAST NAME	ADDRESS	CITY	STATE	ZIP CODE	TELEPHONE NUMBER
AP	Antonio	Patino	34 Fourth	Bastrop	NM	75123	505-555-1111
BH	Bert	Huntington	67 Beafort	Richford	CA	95418	707-555-3334
PL	Ping	Luang	12 Crestview	Mockington	AZ	85165	602-555-9990

FIGURE 1-83

9. Create and print the report shown in Figure 1-84 for the Product table.

Inventory Report

Product Id	*Description*	*On Hand*	*Cost*
BF01	Barnyard Friends	3	$54.00
BL23	Blocks in Box	5	$29.00
CC14	Coal Car	8	$14.00
FT05	Fire Truck	7	$9.00
LB34	Lacing Bear	4	$12.00
MR06	Midget Railroad	3	$31.00
PJ12	Pets Jigsaw	10	$8.00
RB02	Railway Bridge	1	$17.00
SK10	Skyscraper	6	$25.00
UM09	USA Map	12	$14.00

FIGURE 1-84

2 Creating the Restaurant Supply Database

Problem: A distributor supplies local restaurants with non-food supplies such as napkins, paper towels, and cleaning supplies. The distributor employs sales representatives who receive a base salary as well as a commission on sales. The database consists of two tables. The Customer table contains information on the restaurants that buy supplies from the distributor. The Sales Rep table contains information on the sales representative assigned to the restaurant account.

(continued)

In the Lab

Creating the Restaurant Supply Database *(continued)*

Instructions: Perform the following tasks.

1. Create a new database in which to store all the objects related to the restaurant data. Call the database Restaurant Supply.
2. Create the Customer table using the structure shown in Figure 1-85. Use the name Customer for the table.
3. Add the data shown in Figure 1-85 to the Customer table.
4. Print the Customer table.
5. Create the Sales Rep table using the structure shown in Figure 1-86. To change the field size for the Comm Rate field, click the row selector for the field, and then click the Field Size property box. Click the Field Size property box arrow, and then click Double in the list. Use the name Sales Rep for the table.

Structure of Customer table

DATA FIELD NAME	DATA TYPE	FIELD SIZE	PRIMARY KEY?	DESCRIPTION
Customer Number	Text	4	Yes	Customer Number (Primary Key)
Name	Text	20		Name of Customer
Address	Text	15		Street Address
Telephone	Text	8		Telephone (999-9999 Version)
Balance	Currency			Amount Currently Due
Amount Paid	Currency			Amount Paid Year-to-Date
Sales Rep Number	Text	2		Number of Sales Representative

Data for Customer table

CUSTOMER NUMBER	NAME	ADDRESS	TELEPHONE	BALANCE	AMOUNT PAID	SALES REP NUMBER
AM23	American Pie	223 Johnson	555-2150	$95.00	$1,595.00	44
BB34	Bob's Café	1939 Jackson	555-1939	$50.00	$0.00	51
BI15	Bavarian Inn	3294 Devon	555-7510	$445.00	$1,250.00	49
CB12	China Buffet	1632 Clark	555-0804	$45.00	$610.00	49
CM09	Curry and More	3140 Halsted	555-0604	$195.00	$980.00	51
EG07	El Gallo	1805 Broadway	555-1404	$0.00	$1,600.00	44
JS34	Joe's Seafood	2200 Lawrence	555-0313	$260.00	$600.00	49
LV20	Little Venice	13 Devon	555-5161	$100.00	$1,150.00	49
NC25	New Crete	1027 Wells	555-4210	$140.00	$450.00	44
RD03	Reuben's Deli	787 Monroe	555-7657	$0.00	$875.00	51
VG21	Veggie Gourmet	1939 Congress	555-6554	$60.00	$625.00	44

FIGURE 1-85

6. Add the data shown in Figure 1-86 to the Sales Rep table.
7. Print the Sales Rep table.
8. Create a form for the Customer table. Use the name Customer for the form.

In the Lab

Structure of Sales Rep table

FIELD NAME	DATA TYPE	FIELD SIZE	PRIMARY KEY?	DESCRIPTION
Sales Rep Number	Text	2	Yes	Sales Rep Number (Primary Key)
Last Name	Text	15		Last Name of Sales Rep
First Name	Text	10		First Name of Sales Rep
Address	Text	15		Street Address
City	Text	15		City
State	Text	2		State (Two-Character Abbreviation)
Zip Code	Text	5		Zip Code (Five-Character Version)
Salary	Currency			Annual Base Salary
Comm Rate	Number	Double		Commission Rate
Commission	Currency			Year-to-Date Total Commissions

Data for Sales Rep table

SALES REP NUMBER	LAST NAME	FIRST NAME	ADDRESS	CITY	STATE	ZIP CODE	SALARY	COMM RATE	COMMISSION
44	Charles	Pat	43 Fourth	Lawncrest	WA	67845	$19,000.00	0.05	$213.50
49	Gupta	Pinn	678 Hillcrest	Manton	OR	68923	$20,000.00	0.06	$216.60
51	Ortiz	Jose	982 Victoria	Lawncrest	WA	67845	$18,500.00	0.05	$92.75

FIGURE 1-86

9. Open the form you created and change the address for customer number EG07 to 185 Broad.
10. Change to Datasheet view and delete the record for customer number BB34.
11. Print the Customer table.
12. Create and print the report shown in Figure 1-87 for the Customer table.

Customer Status Report

Customer Number	*Name*	*Balance*	*Amount Paid*
AM23	American Pie	$95.00	$1,595.00
BI15	Bavarian Inn	$445.00	$1,250.00
CB12	China Buffet	$45.00	$610.00
CM09	Curry and More	$195.00	$980.00
EG07	El Gallo	$0.00	$1,600.00
JS34	Joe's Seafood	$260.00	$600.00
LV20	Little Venice	$100.00	$1,150.00
NC25	New Crete	$140.00	$450.00
RD03	Reuben's Deli	$0.00	$875.00
VG21	Veggie Gourmet	$60.00	$625.00

FIGURE 1-87

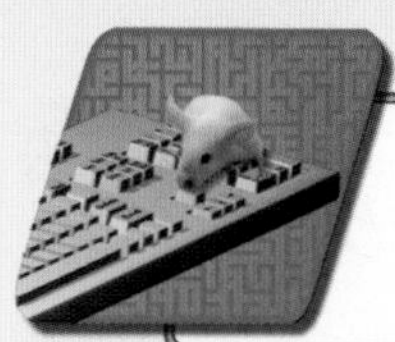

In the Lab

3 Creating the Condo Management Database

Problem: A condo management company located in a ski resort community provides a rental service for condo owners who want to rent their units. The company rents the condos by the week to ski vacationers. The database consists of two tables. The Condo table contains information on the units available for rent. The Owner table contains information on the owners of the rental units.

Instructions: Perform the following tasks.

1. Create a new database in which to store all the objects related to the rental data. Call the database Condo Management.
2. Create the Condo table using the structure shown in Figure 1-88. Use the name Condo for the table. Note that the table uses a new data type, Yes/No for the Powder Room and Linens fields. The Yes/No data type stores data that has one of two values. A Powder Room is a half-bathroom; that is, there is a sink and a toilet but no shower or tub.
3. Add the data shown in Figure 1-88 to the Condo table. To add a Yes value to the Powder Room and Linens fields, click the check box that displays in each field.

Structure of Condo table

FIELD NAME	DATA TYPE	FIELD SIZE	PRIMARY KEY?	DESCRIPTION
Unit Number	Text	3	Yes	Condo Unit Number (Primary Key)
Bedrooms	Number			Number of Bedrooms
Bathrooms	Number			Number of Bathrooms
Sleeps	Number			Maximum Number that can sleep in rental unit
Powder Room	Yes/No			Does the condo have a powder room?
Linens	Yes/No			Are linens (sheets and towels) furnished?
Weekly Rate	Currency			Weekly Rental Rate
Owner Id	Text	4		Id of Condo Unit's Owner

Data for Condo table

UNIT NUMBER	BEDROOMS	BATHROOMS	SLEEPS	POWDER ROOM	LINENS	WEEKLY RATE	OWNER ID
101	1	1	2			$675.00	HJ05
108	2	1	3		Y	$1,050.00	AB10
202	3	2	8	Y	Y	$1,400.00	BR18
204	2	2	6	Y		$1,100.00	BR18
206	2	2	5		Y	$950.00	GM50
308	2	2	6	Y	Y	$950.00	GM50
403	1	1	2			$700.00	HJ05
405	1	1	3			$750.00	AB10
500	3	3	8	Y	Y	$1,100.00	AB10
510	2	1	4	Y	Y	$825.00	BR18

FIGURE 1-88

In the Lab

Structure of Owner table

FIELD NAME	DATA TYPE	FIELD SIZE	PRIMARY KEY?	DESCRIPTION
Owner Id	Text	4	Yes	Owner Id (Primary Key)
Last Name	Text	15		Last Name of Owner
First Name	Text	10		First Name of Owner
Address	Text	15		Street Address
City	Text	15		City
State	Text	2		State (Two-Character Abbreviation)
Zip Code	Text	5		Zip Code (Five-Character Version)
Telephone	Text	12		Telephone Number (999-999-9999 Version)

Data for Owner table

OWNER ID	LAST NAME	FIRST NAME	ADDRESS	CITY	STATE	ZIP CODE	TELEPHONE
AB10	Alonso	Bonita	281 Robin	Whitehall	OK	45241	405-555-6543
BR18	Beerne	Renee	39 Oak	Pearton	WI	48326	715-555-7373
GM50	Graty	Mark	21 West 8th	Greenview	KS	31904	913-555-2225
HJ05	Heulbert	John	314 Central	Munkton	MI	49611	616-555-3333

FIGURE 1-89

4. Use Microsoft Access Help to learn how to resize column widths in Datasheet view and then reduce the size of the Unit Number, Bedrooms, Bathrooms, Sleeps, Powder Room, and Linens columns. Be sure to save the changes to the layout of the table.
5. Print the Condo table.
6. Create the Owner table using the structure shown in Figure 1-89. Use the name Owner for the table.
7. Add the data shown in Figure 1-89 to the Owner table.
8. Print the Owner table.
9. Create a form for the Condo table. Use the name Condo for the form.
10. Open the form you created and change the weekly rate for Unit Number 206 to $925.00.
11. Print the Condo table.
12. Create and print the report shown in Figure 1-90 for the Condo table.

Available Condo Rentals Report

Unit Number	Bedrooms	Bathrooms	Weekly Rate	Owner Id
101	1	1	$675.00	HJ05
108	2	1	$1,050.00	AB10
202	3	2	$1,400.00	BR18
204	2	2	$1,100.00	BR18
206	2	2	$925.00	GM50
308	2	2	$950.00	GM50
403	1	1	$700.00	HJ05
405	1	1	$750.00	AB10
500	3	3	$1,100.00	AB10
510	2	1	$825.00	BR18

FIGURE 1-90

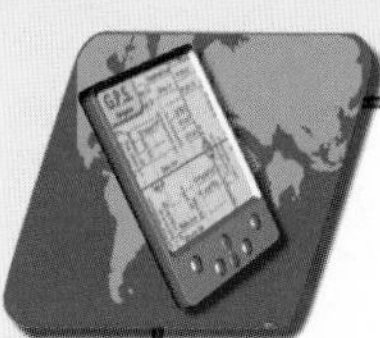

Cases and Places

The difficulty of these case studies varies:
▶ are the least difficult; ▶▶ are more difficult; and ▶▶▶ are the most difficult.

1 ▶ To help finance your college education, you and two of your friends have formed a small business. You provide help to organizations in need of computer expertise. You have established a small clientele and realize that you need to computerize your business. You gather the information shown in Figure 1-91.

Design and create a database to store the data related to your business. Then create the necessary tables, enter the data from Figure 1-91, and print the tables. To personalize this database, replace Jan Smith's name with your own name.

CUSTOMER NUMBER	NAME	ADDRESS	TELEPHONE NUMBER	BALANCE	HELPER ID	HELPER LAST NAME	HELPER FIRST NAME	HOURLY RATE
AL35	Alores Gifts	12 Thistle	555-1222	$145.00	89	Smith	Jan	$12.50
AR43	Arsan Co.	34 Green	555-3434	$180.00	82	Ortega	Javier	$12.45
BK18	Byrd's Kites	56 Pampas	555-5678	$0.00	82	Ortega	Javier	$12.45
CJ78	Cee J's	24 Thistle	555-4242	$170.00	78	Chang	Pinn	$12.35
CL45	Class Act	89 Lime	555-9876	$129.00	89	Smith	Jan	$12.50
LB42	Le Boutique	12 Lemon	555-9012	$160.00	82	Ortega	Javier	$12.45
LK23	Learn n Kids	44 Apple	555-4004	$0.00	78	Chang	Pinn	$12.35
ME30	Meeker Co.	789 Poppy	555-0987	$195.00	89	Smith	Jan	$12.50
RE20	Ready Eats	90 Orange	555-9123	$0.00	78	Chang	Pinn	$12.35
SR34	Shoe Repair	62 Lime	555-4378	$140.00	89	Smith	Jan	$12.50

FIGURE 1-91

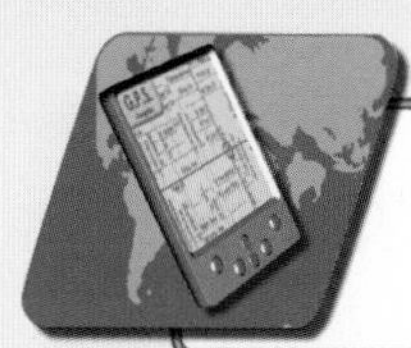

Cases and Places

2 ◗ After lengthy negotiations, your town now has a minor league baseball team. The team owners and the town government are vigorously promoting the benefits of the new team. As part of their marketing strategy, they are selling items with the new team logo. The marketing team has asked you to create and update a database that they can use to keep track of their inventory and suppliers. The current inventory is shown in Figure 1-92.

Design and create a database to store the team's inventory. Then create the necessary tables, enter the data from Figure 1-92, and print the tables.

ITEM ID	DESCRIPTION	UNITS ON HAND	COST	SELLING PRICE	SUPPLIER CODE	SUPPLIER NAME	SUPPLIER TELEPHONE
3663	Baseball Cap	30	$10.15	$18.95	LG	Logo Goods	517-555-3853
3683	Coasters (4)	12	$7.45	$9.00	BH	Beverage Holders	317-555-4747
4563	Coffee Mug	20	$1.85	$4.75	BH	Beverage Holders	317-555-4747
4593	Glasses (4)	8	$8.20	$10.75	BH	Beverage Holders	317-555-4747
5923	Jacket	12	$44.75	$54.95	LG	Logo Goods	517-555-3853
5953	Shorts	10	$14.95	$19.95	AC	Al's Clothes	616-555-9228
6189	Sports Towel	24	$3.25	$6.75	LG	Logo Goods	517-555-3853
6343	Sweatshirt	9	$27.45	$34.95	AC	Al's Clothes	616-555-9228
7810	Tee Shirt	32	$9.50	$14.95	AC	Al's Clothes	616-555-9228
7930	Travel Mug	11	$2.90	$3.25	BH	Beverage Holders	317-555-4747

FIGURE 1-92

3 ◗◗ The tourism director of your town has asked you to create a database of local attractions. She wants to keep track of the type of attraction, for example, museums, historic homes, zoo, botanical gardens, nature trails, hike/bike paths, or public parks. She also needs to know the address of the attraction, days and times it is open, whether or not there is a cost associated with the attraction, and a telephone number for more information.

Design and create a database to meet the tourism director's needs. Create the necessary tables, enter some sample data, and print the tables to show the director. *Note*: Type of attraction is really a category into which the attraction fits. Use the Table Wizard and select the Category table to create this table. If you want, you can rename the fields in the table. (*Hint*: See More About Creating a Table: The Table Wizard on page A 1.13.)

Cases and Places

4 ▶▶ The high school Math club has started a tutoring program. Math club members are tutoring elementary students in basic math concepts. Each math club member is assigned one or more students to tutor. The elementary students who participate can earn points that can be redeemed for prizes donated by local merchants. Club members who participate keep track of the hours they spend tutoring. The state has promised to reward the high school club with the most number of tutoring hours. The club must keep track of the elementary students including each student's name, school the student attends, year in school, identity of the high school student tutor, and hours tutored. The club also must keep track of the high school students recording such information as name, year in school, and total number of hours spent tutoring.

Design and create a database to meet the Math club's needs.

5 ▶▶▶ As a hobby, many people collect items such as baseball cards, ceramic frogs, model trains, and ships in a bottle. Sometimes, they also trade items with other collectors. What do you collect? Create a database that can store data related to a particular hobby collection.

Determine the type of data you will need, then design and create a database to meet those needs. Create the necessary tables, enter some sample data, and print the tables.

6 ▶▶▶ You are getting ready to look for a job and realize you will need to plan your job search carefully. The Database Wizard includes a Contact Management template that can create a database that will help you keep track of your job contacts.

Create the Contact Management database using the Database Wizard. (***Hint***: See More About Creating a Database: The Database Wizard on page A 1.11.) Determine whether or not you need any extra fields, such as home telephone. Use the form that the wizard creates to enter some sample data. Then, print the report that the wizard created with the sample data.

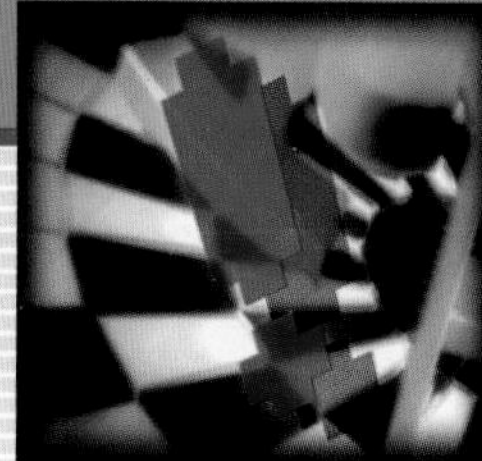

Microsoft Access 2002

PROJECT

Querying a Database Using the Select Query Window

OBJECTIVES

You will have mastered the material in this project when you can:

- State the purpose of queries
- Create a new query
- Use a query to display all records and all fields
- Run a query
- Print the answer to a query
- Close a query
- Clear a query
- Use a query to display selected fields
- Use text data and wildcards in criteria in a query
- Use numeric data and comparison operators in criteria
- Use compound criteria
- Sort the answer to a query
- Join tables in a query and restrict the records in a join
- Use calculated fields in a query
- Calculate statistics in a query
- Save a query and use a saved query

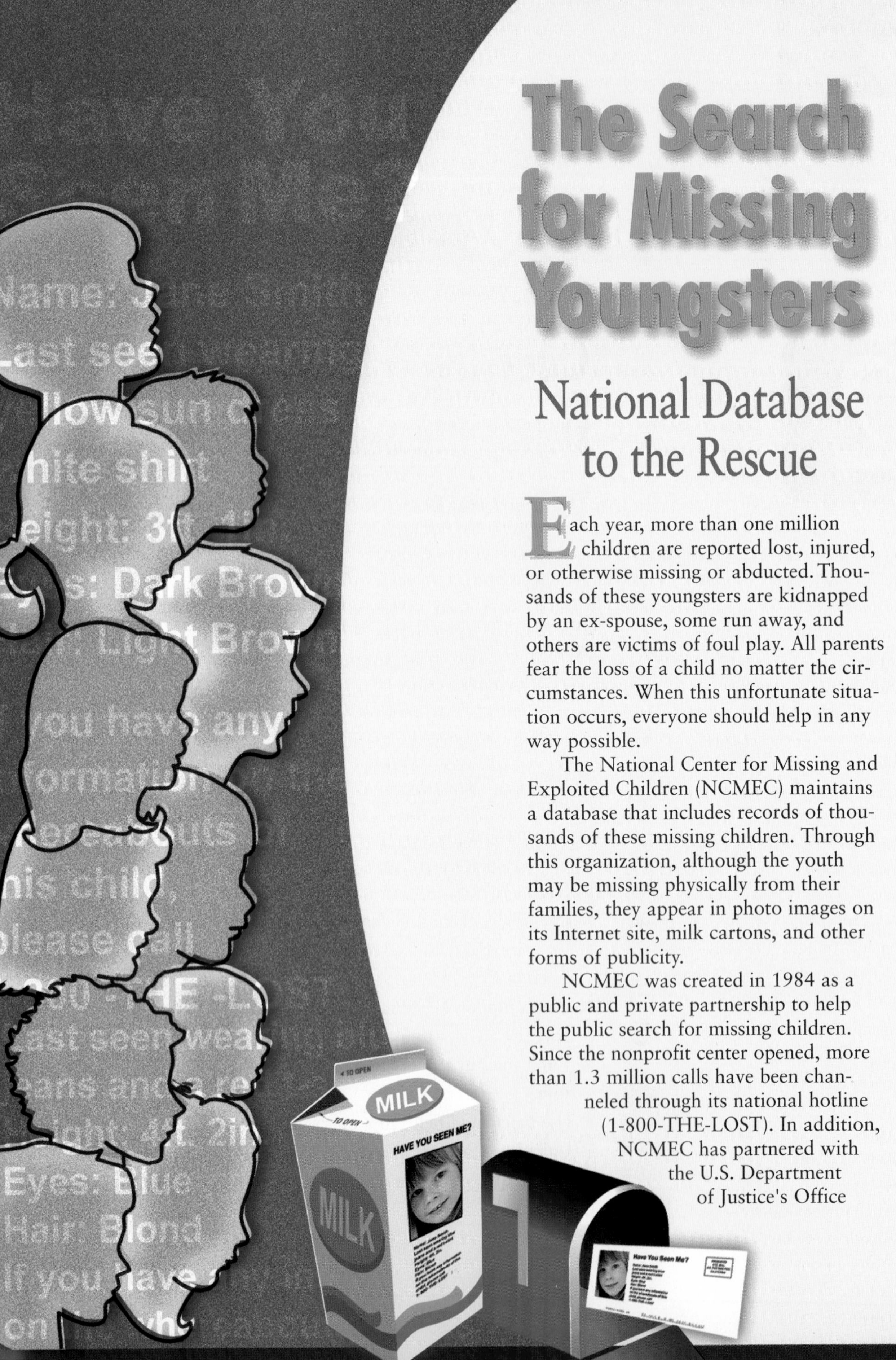

The Search for Missing Youngsters

National Database to the Rescue

Each year, more than one million children are reported lost, injured, or otherwise missing or abducted. Thousands of these youngsters are kidnapped by an ex-spouse, some run away, and others are victims of foul play. All parents fear the loss of a child no matter the circumstances. When this unfortunate situation occurs, everyone should help in any way possible.

The National Center for Missing and Exploited Children (NCMEC) maintains a database that includes records of thousands of these missing children. Through this organization, although the youth may be missing physically from their families, they appear in photo images on its Internet site, milk cartons, and other forms of publicity.

NCMEC was created in 1984 as a public and private partnership to help the public search for missing children. Since the nonprofit center opened, more than 1.3 million calls have been channeled through its national hotline (1-800-THE-LOST). In addition, NCMEC has partnered with the U.S. Department of Justice's Office

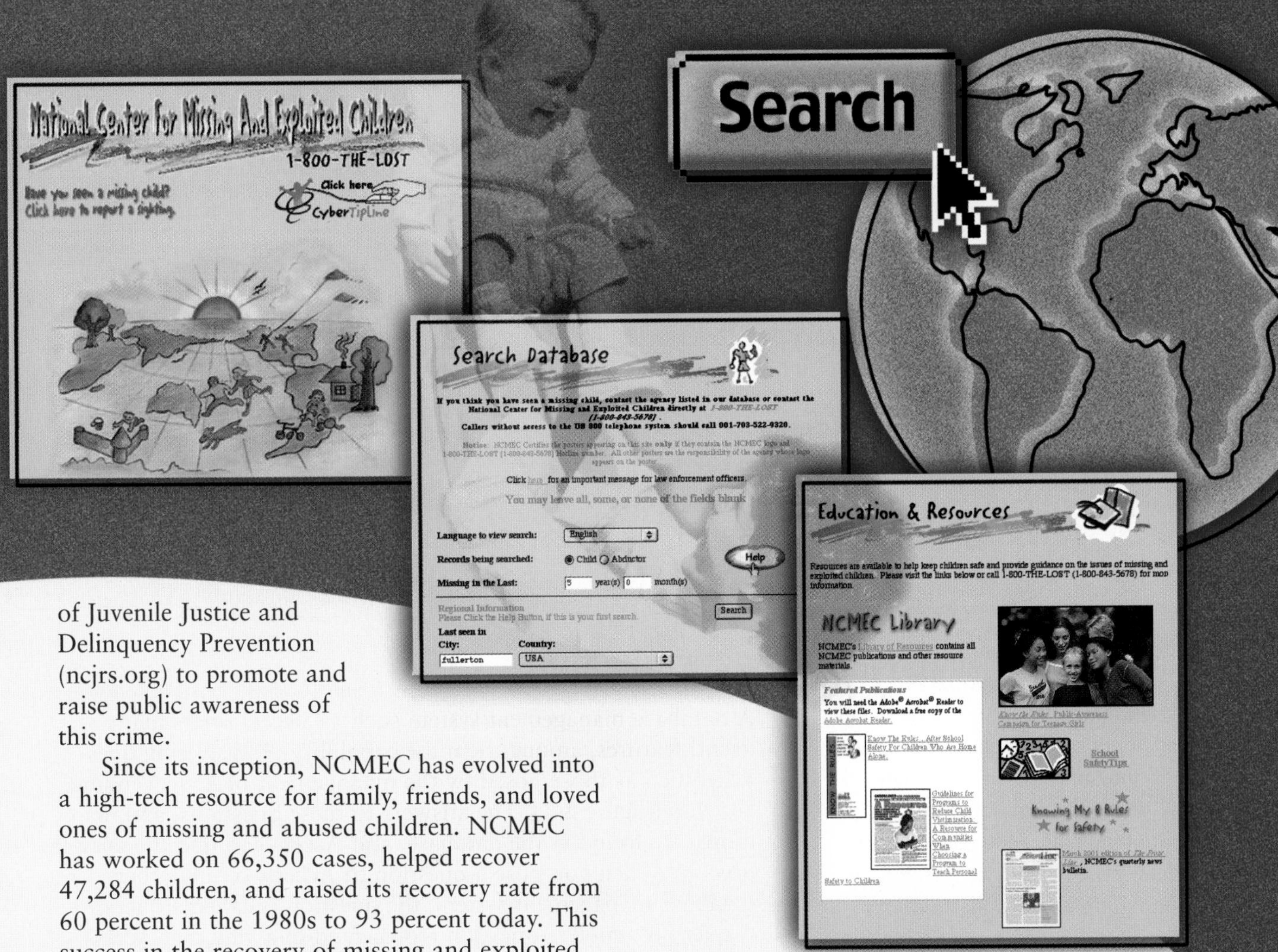

of Juvenile Justice and Delinquency Prevention (ncjrs.org) to promote and raise public awareness of this crime.

Since its inception, NCMEC has evolved into a high-tech resource for family, friends, and loved ones of missing and abused children. NCMEC has worked on 66,350 cases, helped recover 47,284 children, and raised its recovery rate from 60 percent in the 1980s to 93 percent today. This success in the recovery of missing and exploited youth worldwide is attributed to human resources, technological advancements, training workshops, program development, and research and evaluation. Through consistent private, community, and public partnerships, including relationships with Intel, IBM, and Tektronix, NCMEC has grown into a solid force for solving child cases.

One example of the advanced technology utilized by NCMEC is a database that contains photographs of missing children. Investigators and Web users are able to open the database and create a precise query based on such fields as the child's name, age, eye color, and weight. Then they run the query, and within a matter of seconds they have answers to the requested information. You can create queries and view some of these images at the NCMEC Web site (ncmec.org). Similarly, you will query the Alisa Vending Services database in this project to obtain answers to questions regarding customer names and locations, current balances, and driver names.

Moreover, NCMEC's imaging specialists can alter a child's photograph to show how he or she might appear many years after disappearing. Subsequently, these images are stored in corresponding fields in the computerized imaging database. Many children who may not have been located otherwise have been found using this enhancement technology.

The Multimedia Kiosk Program, which IBM donated to NCMEC, placed 50 kiosks in high pedestrian traffic areas such as LaGuardia Airport in New York and in large shopping malls throughout the country. They provide a functional database for the general public to learn about missing children and a means to transfer information quickly to affected friends and family.

Through the efforts of NCMEC, the nation now has a solid weapon and resource for the fight against child endangerment.

Microsoft Access 2002

Querying a Database Using the Select Query Window

PROJECT

CASE PERSPECTIVE

With the database consisting of customer and driver data created, the management and staff of Alisa Vending Services expect to obtain the benefits they anticipated when they set up the database. One of the more important benefits is the capability of easily asking questions concerning the data in the database and rapidly getting the answers. Among the questions they want answered are the following:

1. What are the amount paid and current due amount for customer FR28?
2. Which customers' names begin with Gr?
3. Which customers are located in Hansen?
4. What is the total amount (amount paid plus current due amount) for each customer?
5. Which customers of driver 60 have amounts paid of greater than $20,000?

Your task is to assist the management of Alisa Vending Services in obtaining answers to these questions as well as any other questions they deem important.

Introduction

A database management system such as Access offers many useful features, among them the capability of answering questions such as those posed by the management of Alisa Vending Services (Figure 2-1). The answers to these questions, and many more, are found in the database, and Access can find the answers quickly. When you pose a question to Access, or any other database management system, the question is called a query. A **query** is simply a question represented in a way that Access can understand.

Thus, to find the answer to a question, you first create a corresponding query using the techniques illustrated in this project. Once you have created the query, you instruct Access to run the query; that is, to perform the steps necessary to obtain the answer. Access then will display the answer in Datasheet view.

Project Two — Querying the Alisa Vending Services Database

You must obtain answers to the questions posed by the management of Alisa Vending Services. These include the questions shown in Figure 2-1, as well as any other questions that management deems important.

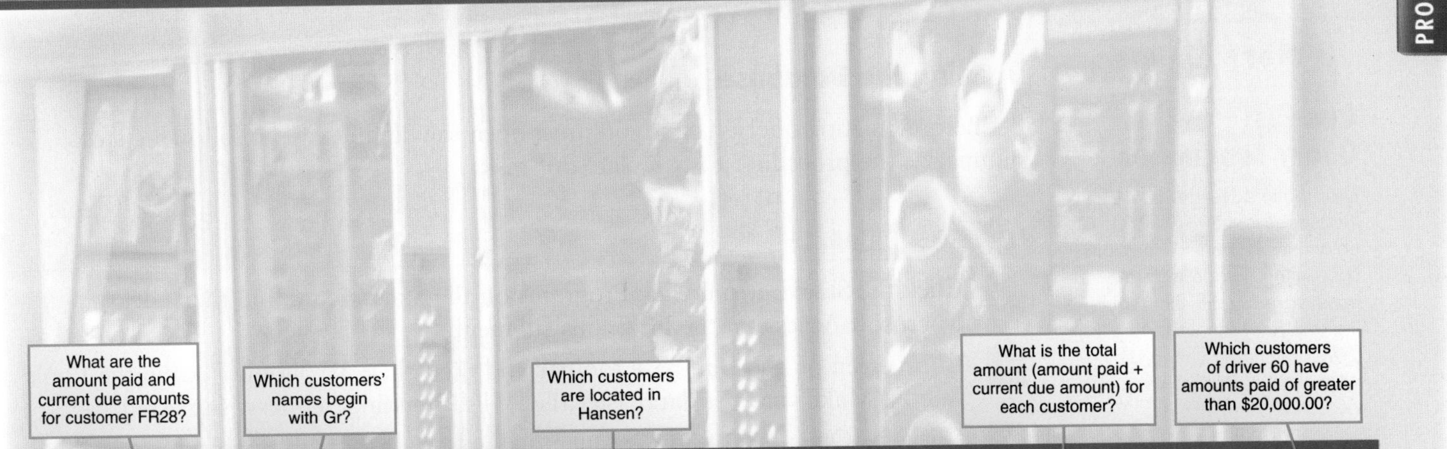

What are the amount paid and current due amounts for customer FR28?

Which customers' names begin with Gr?

Which customers are located in Hansen?

What is the total amount (amount paid + current due amount) for each customer?

Which customers of driver 60 have amounts paid of greater than $20,000.00?

Customer table

CUSTOMER NUMBER	NAME	ADDRESS	CITY	STATE	ZIP CODE	AMOUNT PAID	CURRENT DUE	DRIVER NUMBER
BA95	Bayside Hotel	287 Riley	Hansen	FL	38513	$21,876.00	$892.50	30
BR46	Baldwin-Reed	267 Howard	Fernwood	FL	37023	$26,512.00	$2,672.00	60
CN21	Century North	1562 Butler	Hansen	FL	38513	$8,725.00	$0.00	60
FR28	Friend's Movies	871 Adams	Westport	FL	37070	$4,256.00	$1,202.00	75
GN62	Grand Nelson	7821 Oak	Wood Key	FL	36828	$8,287.50	$925.50	30
GS29	Great Screens	572 Lee	Hansen	FL	38513	$21,625.00	$0.00	60
LM22	Lenger Mason	274 Johnson	Westport	FL	37070	$0.00	$0.00	60
ME93	Merks College	561 Fairhill	Bayville	FL	38734	$24,761.00	$1,572.00	30
RI78	Riter University	26 Grove	Fernwood	FL	37023	$11,682.25	$2,827.50	75
TU20	Turner Hotel	8672 Quincy	Palmview	FL	36114	$8,521.50	$0.00	60

CUSTOMER NUMBER	NAME
GN62	Grand Nelson
GS29	Great Screens

CUSTOMER NUMBER	NAME
BR46	Baldwin-Reed
GS29	Great Screens

CUSTOMER NUMBER	NAME	ADDRESS
BA95	Bayside Hotel	287 Riley
CN21	Century North	1562 Butler
GS29	Great Screens	572 Lee

CUSTOMER NUMBER	NAME	TOTAL AMOUNT
BA95	Bayside Hotel	$22,768.50
BR46	Baldwin-Reed	$29,184.00
CN21	Century North	$8,725.00
FR28	Friend's Movies	$5,458.00
GN62	Grand Nelson	$9,213.00
GS29	Great Screens	$21,625.00
LM22	Lenger Mason	$0.00
ME93	Merks College	$26,333.00
RI78	Riter University	$14,509.75
TU20	Turner Hotel	$8,521.50

CUSTOMER NUMBER	NAME	AMOUNT PAID	CURRENT DUE
FR28	Friend's Movies	$4,256.00	$1,202.00

FIGURE 2-1

More About

Queries: Query Languages

Prior to the advent of query languages in the mid 1970s, obtaining answers to questions concerning data in a database was very difficult, requiring that someone write lengthy (several hundred line) programs in languages like COBOL.

More About

Queries: The Simple Query Wizard

The Simple Query Wizard creates select queries that retrieve data from the fields you specify in one or more tables. To use the Simple Query Wizard, click the New Object: AutoForm button arrow and then click Query on the list that displays. When the New Query dialog box displays, click Simple Query Wizard. Follow the directions in the Simple Query Wizard dialog boxes.

Opening the Database

Before creating queries, first you must open the database. The following steps summarize the procedure to complete this task.

TO OPEN A DATABASE

1. Click the Start button, click Programs on the Start menu, and then click Microsoft Access on the Programs submenu.
2. Click Open on the Database toolbar and then click 3½ Floppy (A:) in the Look in box. Make sure the database called Alisa Vending Services is selected.
3. Click the Open button in the Open dialog box. If the Tables object is not already selected, click Tables on the Objects bar.

The database is open and the Alisa Vending Services : Database window displays.

Creating a New Query

You create a query by making entries in a special window called a **Select Query window**. Once the database is open, the first step in creating a query is to select the table for which you are creating a query in the Database window. Next, using the New Object: AutoForm button, you will design the new query. The Select Query window will display. It typically is easier to work with the Select Query window if it is maximized. Thus, as a standard practice, maximize the Select Query window as soon as you have created it. In addition, it often is useful to resize both panes within the window. This enables you to resize the field list that displays in the upper pane so more fields display.

Perform the following steps to begin creating a query.

Steps To Create a Query

1. **Be sure the Alisa Vending Services database is open, the Tables object is selected, and the Customer table is selected. Click the New Object: AutoForm button arrow on the Database toolbar and point to Query on the list that displays.**

The list of available objects displays (Figure 2-2).

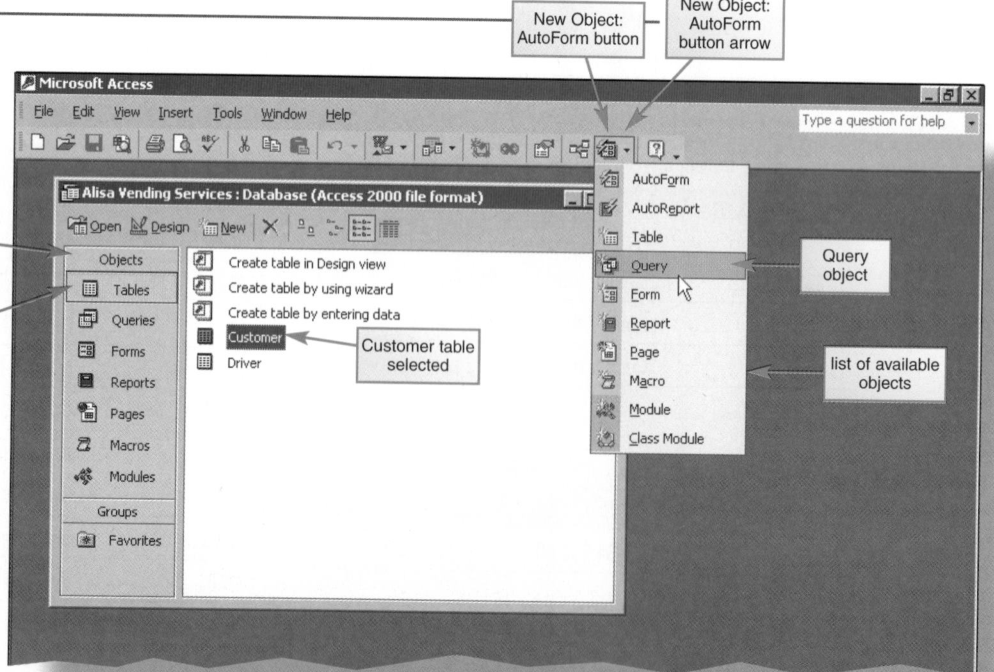

FIGURE 2-2

2 Click Query and point to the OK button.

The New Query dialog box displays (Figure 2-3).

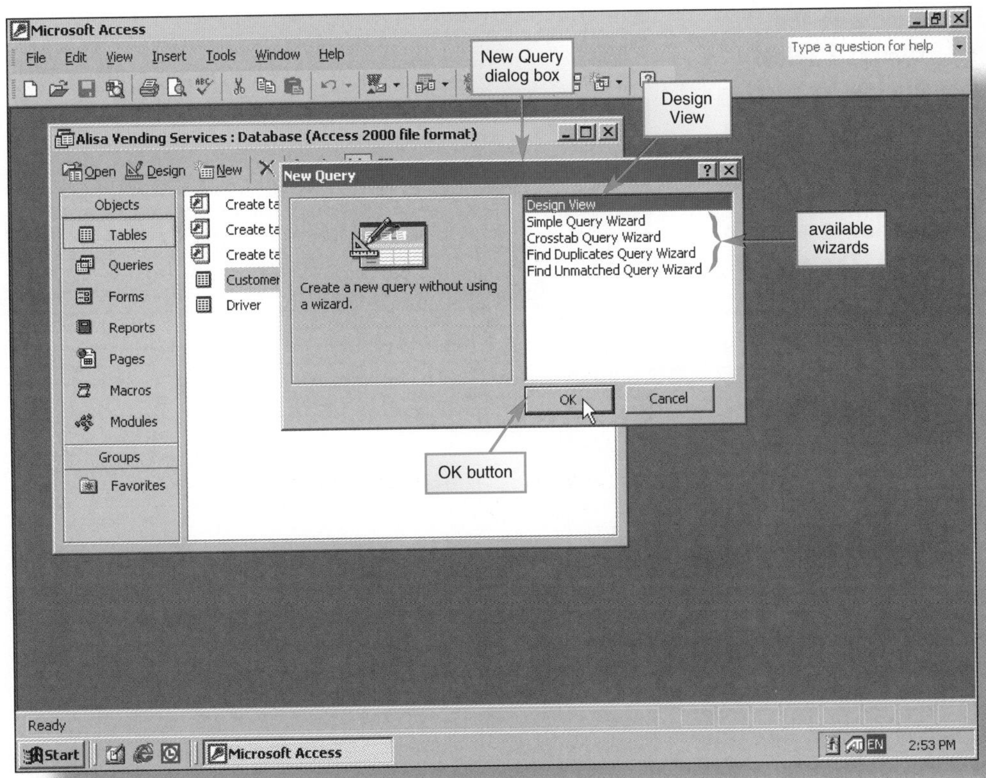

FIGURE 2-3

3 With Design View selected, click the OK button and then point to the Maximize button for the Query1 : Select Query window.

The Query1 : Select Query window displays (Figure 2-4).

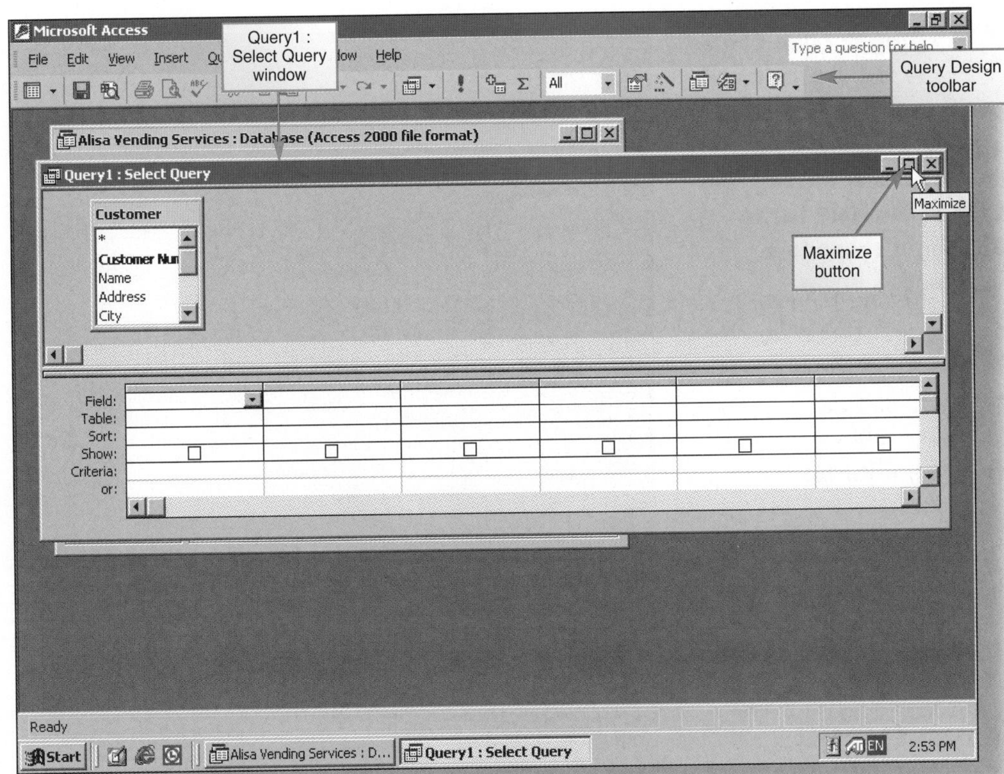

FIGURE 2-4

4 **Maximize the Query1 : Select Query window by clicking its Maximize button, and then point to the dividing line that separates the upper and lower panes of the window. The mouse pointer will change shape to a two-headed arrow with a horizontal bar.**

*The Query1 : Select Query window is maximized (Figure 2-5). The upper pane contains a field list for the Customer table. The lower pane contains the **design grid**, which is the area where you specify fields to be included, sort order, and the criteria the records you are looking for must satisfy.*

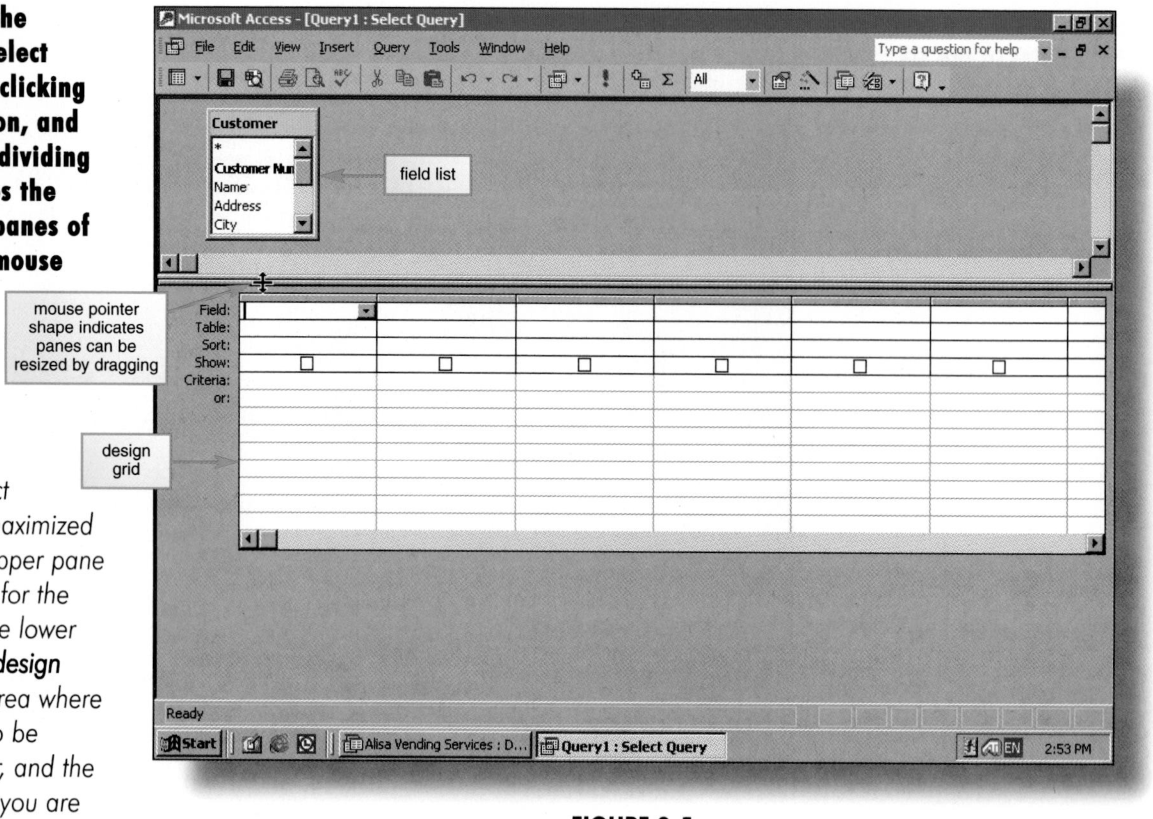

FIGURE 2-5

5 **Drag the line down to the approximate position shown in Figure 2-6 and then move the mouse pointer to the lower edge of the field list so it changes shape to a two-headed arrow.**

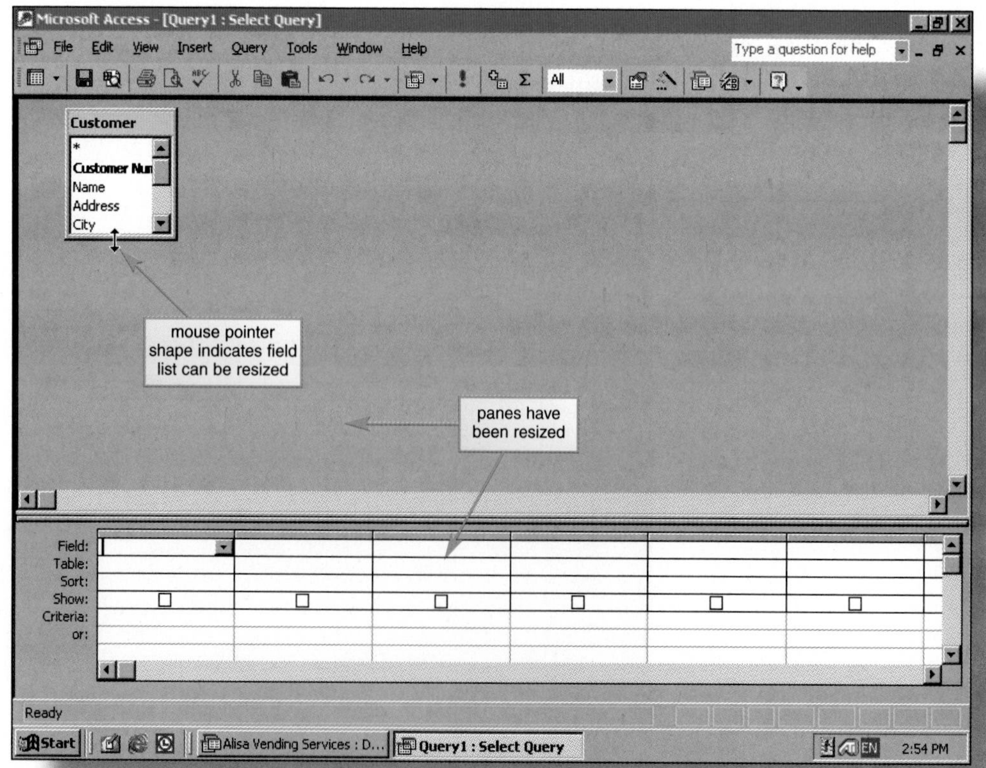

FIGURE 2-6

6 Drag the lower edge of the field list down far enough so all fields in the Customer table are visible.

All fields in the Customer table display (Figure 2-7).

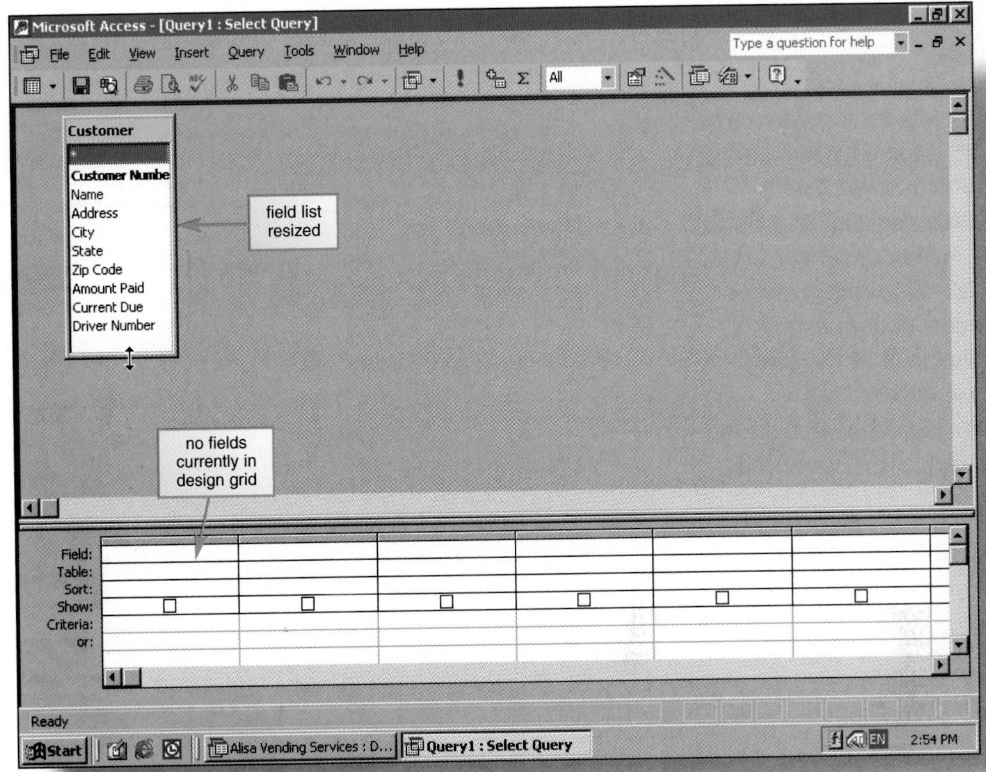

FIGURE 2-7

Other Ways

1. Click Queries object, double-click Create query in Design view
2. On Insert menu click Query
3. In Voice Command mode, say "Insert, Query"

Using the Select Query Window

Once you have created a new Select Query window, you are ready to create the actual query by making entries in the design grid in the lower pane of the window. You enter the names of the fields you want included in the Field row in the grid. You also can enter criteria, such as the fact that the customer number must be FR28, in the Criteria row of the grid. When you do so, only the record or records that match the criterion will be included in the answer.

Displaying Selected Fields in a Query

Only the fields that appear in the design grid will be included in the results of the query. Thus, to display only certain fields, place only these fields in the grid, and no others. If you place the wrong field in the grid inadvertently, click Edit on the menu bar and then click Delete to remove it. Alternatively, you could click Clear Grid on the Edit menu to clear the entire design grid and then start over.

The steps on the next page create a query to show the customer number, name, and driver number for all customers by including only those fields in the design grid.

More About

Queries: Query-by-Example

Query-by-Example, often referred to as QBE, was a query language first proposed in the mid 1970s. In this approach, users asked questions by filling in a table on the screen. The approach to queries taken by several DBMSs is based on Query-by-Example. For more information, visit the Access 2002 More About Web page (scsite.com/ac2002/more.htm) and then click QBE.

Steps To Include Fields in the Design Grid

1 Make sure you have a maximized Query1 : Select Query window containing a field list for the Customer table in the upper pane of the window and an empty design grid in the lower pane. Point to the Customer Number field in the field list (Figure 2-8).

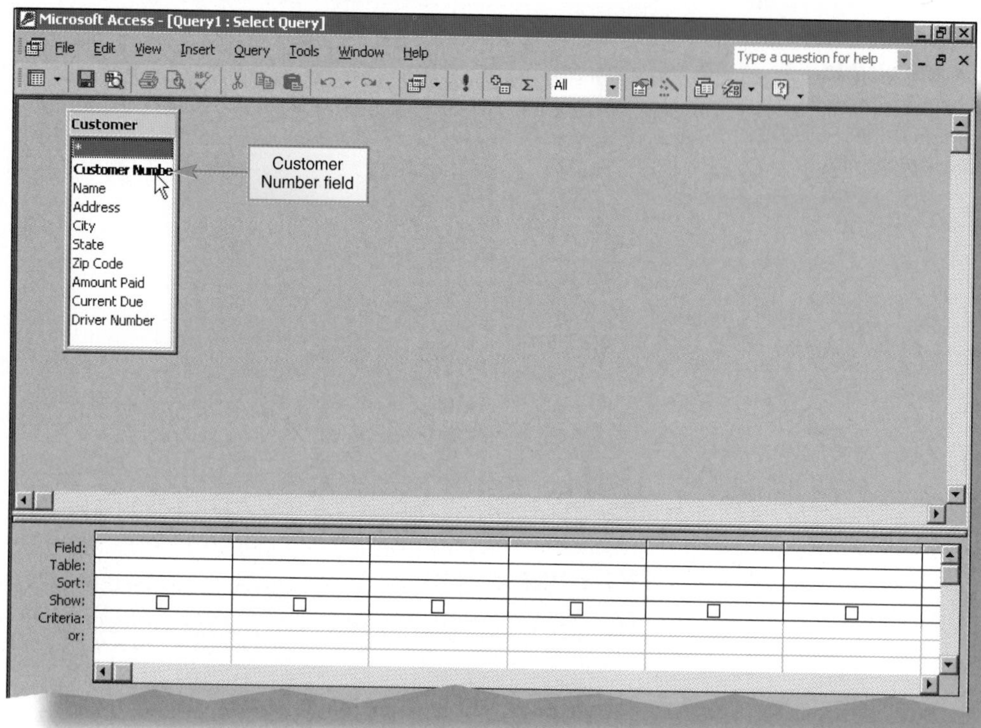

FIGURE 2-8

2 Double-click the Customer Number field to include it in the query. Point to, and then double-click, the Name field to include it in the query. Include the Driver Number field using the same technique. Point to the Run button on the Query Design toolbar.

The Customer Number, Name, and Driver Number fields are included in the query (Figure 2-9).

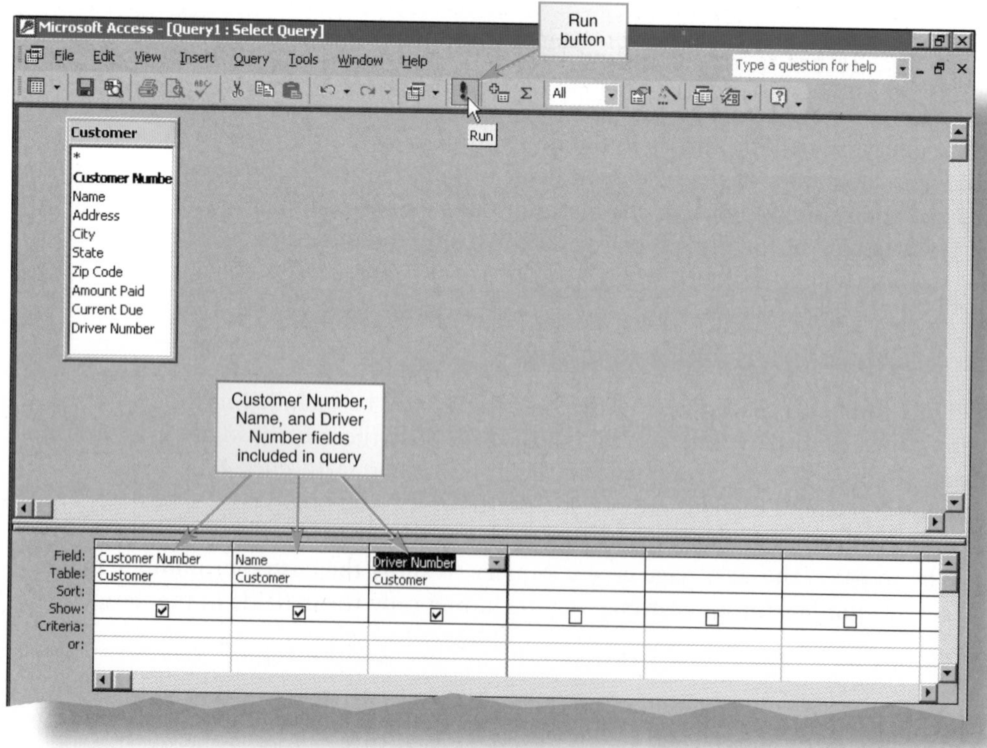

FIGURE 2-9

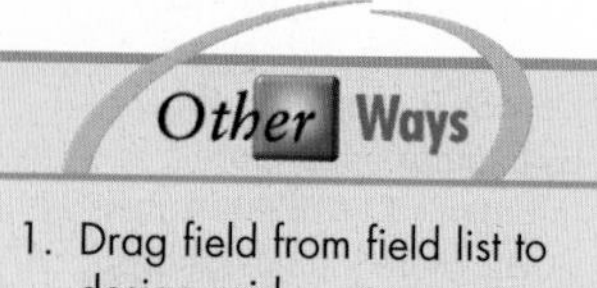

1. Drag field from field list to design grid
2. Click column in grid, click arrow, click field

Queries: SQL

The most widespread of all the query languages is a language called SQL. Many database management systems, including Access, offer SQL as one option for querying databases. For more information, visit the Access 2002 More About Web page (scsite.com/ac2002/more.htm) and then click SQL.

Running a Query

Once you have created the query, you need to run the query to produce the results. To do so, click the Run button. Access then will perform the steps necessary to obtain and display the answer. The set of records that makes up the answer will be displayed in Datasheet view. Although it looks like a table that is stored on your disk, it really is not. The records are constructed from data in the existing Customer table. If you were to change the data in the Customer table and then rerun this same query, the results would reflect the changes. Perform the following step to run the query.

To Run the Query

1 Click the Run button on the Query Design toolbar.

The query is executed and the results display (Figure 2-10).

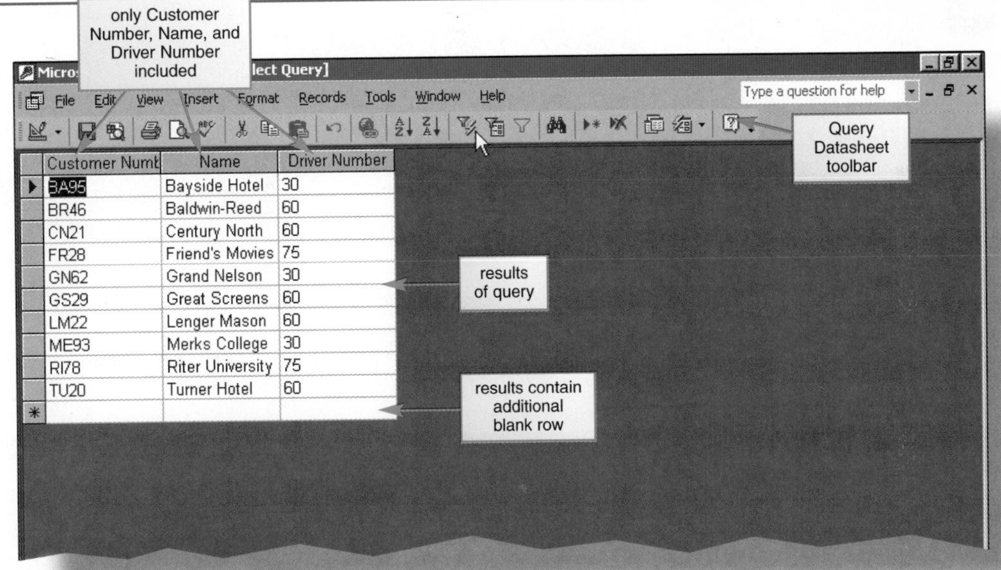

FIGURE 2-10

1. On Query menu click Run
2. In Voice Command mode, say "Run"

Printing the Results of a Query

To print the results of a query, use the same techniques you learned in Project 1 on page A 1.29 to print the data in the table. Complete the following steps to print the query results that currently display on the screen.

TO PRINT THE RESULTS OF A QUERY

1. Point to the Print button on the Query Datasheet toolbar (Figure 2-11).
2. Click the Print button.

The results print.

If the results of a query require landscape orientation, switch to landscape orientation before you click the Print button as indicated in Project 1 on page A 1.29.

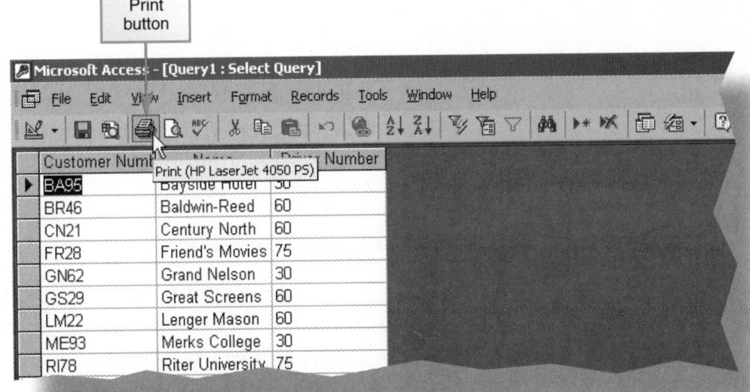

FIGURE 2-11

Returning to the Select Query Window

You can examine the results of a query on your screen to see the answer to your question. You can scroll through the records, if necessary, just as you scroll through the records of any other table. You also can print a copy of the table. In any case, once you are finished working with the results, you can return to the Select Query window to ask another question. To do so, use the View button arrow on the Query Datasheet toolbar as shown in the following steps.

To Return to the Select Query Window

1 Point to the View button arrow on the Query Datasheet toolbar (Figure 2-12).

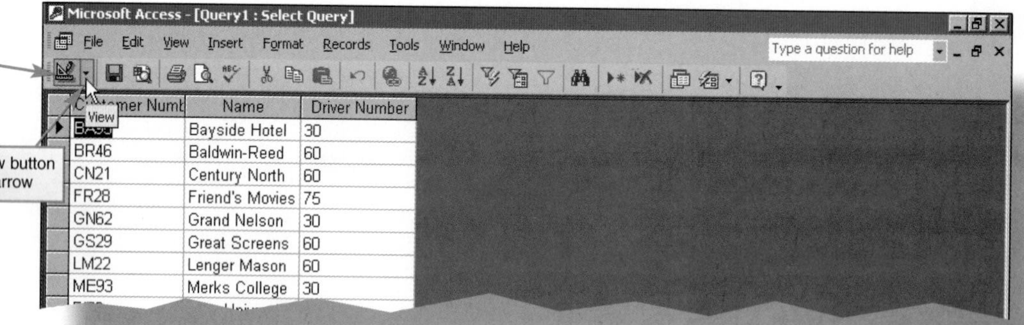

FIGURE 2-12

2 Click the View button arrow and then point to Design View.

The Query View list displays (Figure 2-13).

3 Click Design View.

The Query1 : Select Query window again displays.

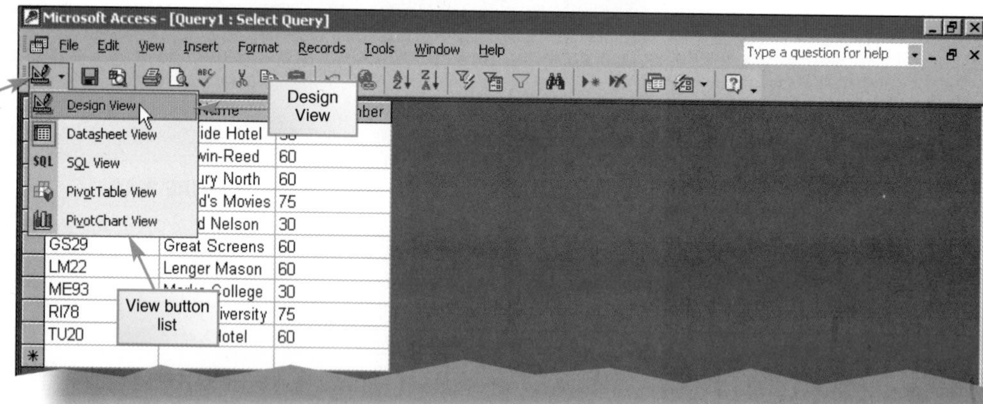

FIGURE 2-13

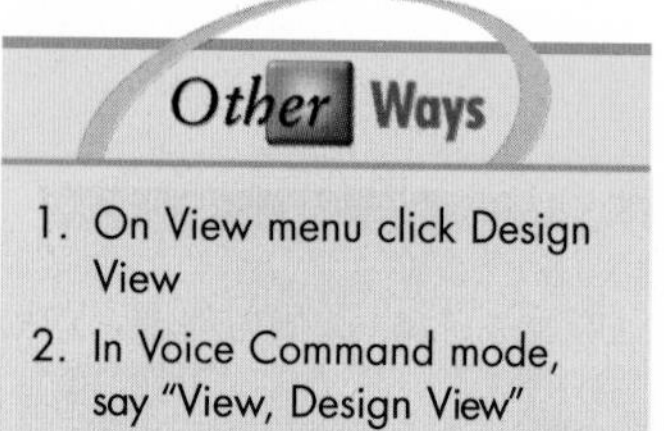

Other Ways

1. On View menu click Design View
2. In Voice Command mode, say "View, Design View"

Because Design View is the first command on the View button list, you do not have to click the View button arrow and then click Design View. You simply can click the View button itself.

Closing a Query

To close a query, close the Select Query window. When you do so, Access displays the Microsoft dialog box asking if you want to save your query for future use. If you think you will need to create the same exact query often, you should save the query. For now, you will not save any queries. You will see how to save them later in the project. The following steps close a query without saving it.

To Close the Query

1 Point to the Close Window button for the Query1 : Select Query window (Figure 2-14).

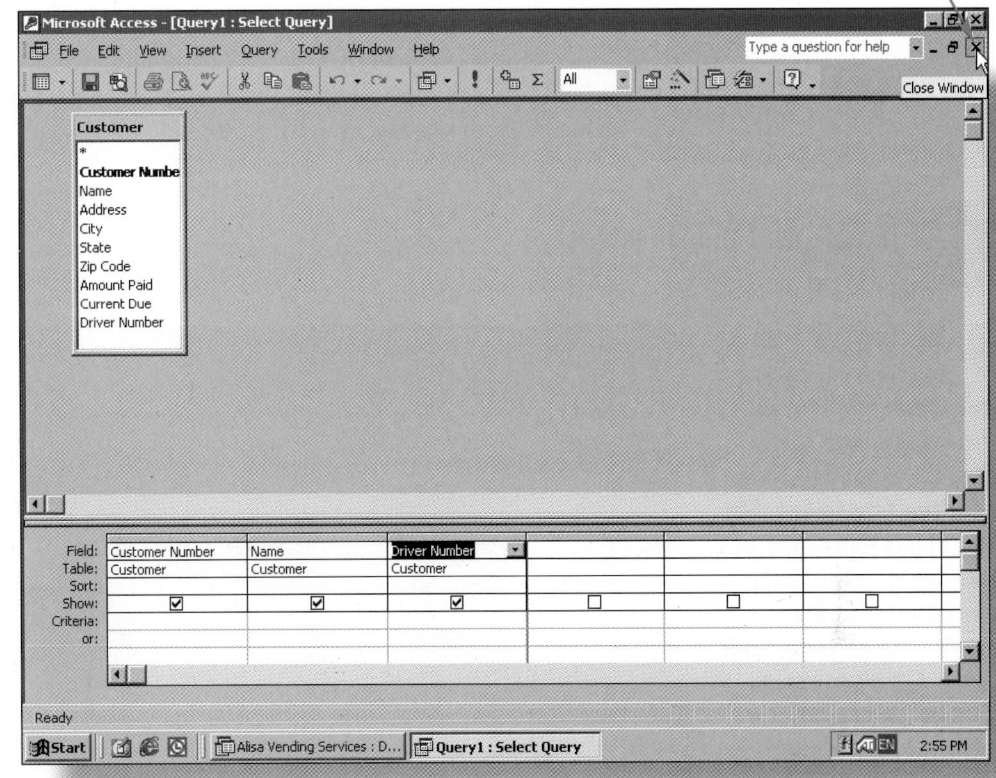

FIGURE 2-14

2 Click the Close Window button for the Query1 : Select Query window and then point to the No button.

The Microsoft Access dialog box displays (Figure 2-15). Clicking the Yes button saves the query and clicking the No button closes the query without saving.

3 Click the No button in the Microsoft Access dialog box.

The Query1 : Select Query window closes and no longer displays. The query is not saved.

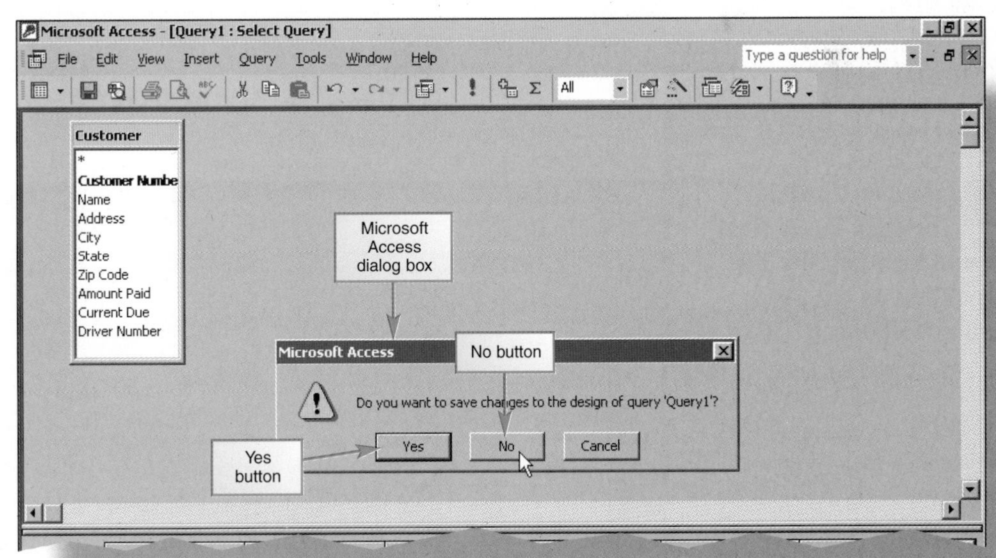

FIGURE 2-15

1. On File menu click Close
2. In Voice Command mode, say "File, Close"

Including All Fields in a Query

If you want to include all fields in a query, you could select each field individually. There is a simpler way to include all fields, however. By selecting the **asterisk** (*) in the field list, you are indicating that all fields are to be included. Complete the following steps to use the asterisk to include all fields.

Steps To Include All Fields in a Query

1 Be sure you have a maximized Query1 : Select Query window with resized upper and lower panes, an expanded field list for the Customer table in the upper pane, and an empty design grid in the lower pane. (See Steps 1 through 6 on pages A 2.06 through A 2.09 to create the query and resize the window.) Point to the asterisk at the top of the field list.

A maximized Query1 : Select Query window displays (Figure 2-16). The two panes have been resized.

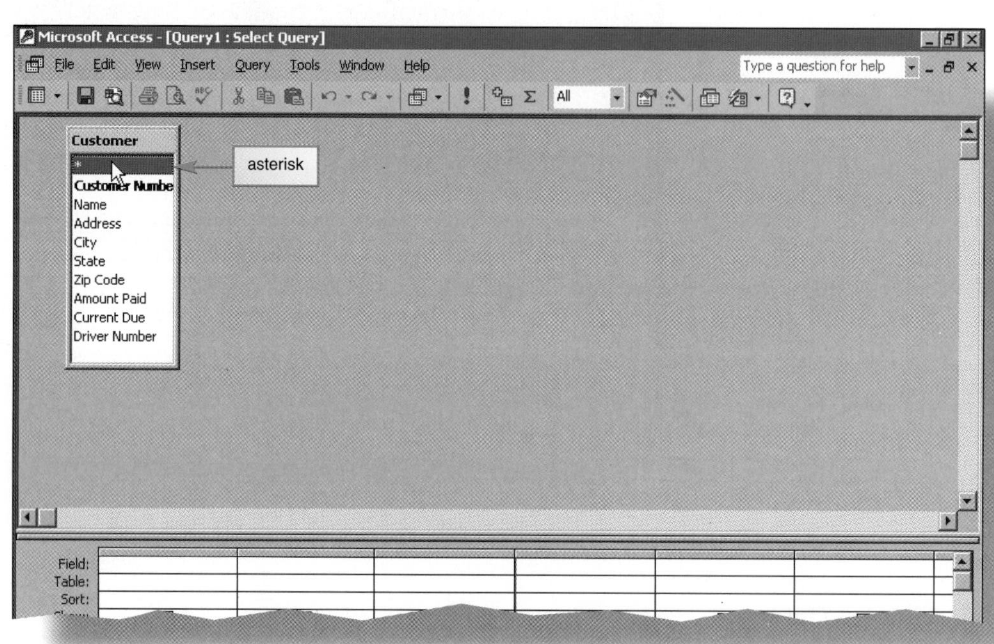

FIGURE 2-16

2 Double-click the asterisk in the field list and then point to the Run button on the Query Design toolbar.

The table name, Customer, followed by a period and an asterisk is added to the design grid (Figure 2-17), indicating all fields are included.

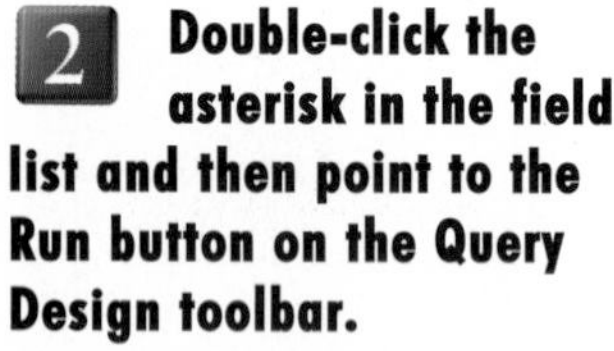

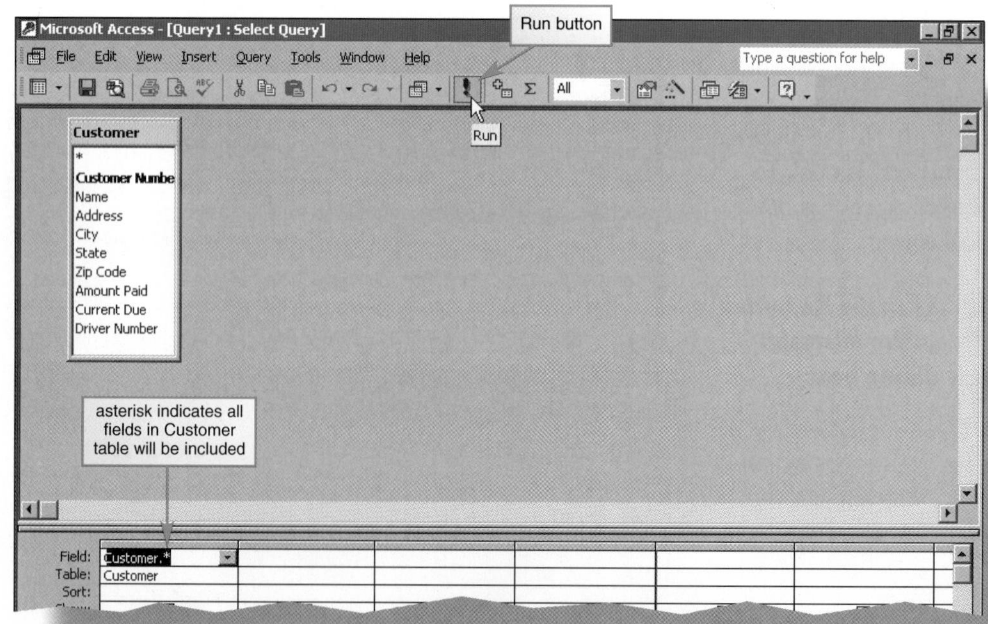

FIGURE 2-17

3 Click the Run button.

The results display and all fields in the Customer table are included (Figure 2-18).

4 Click the View button on the Query Datasheet toolbar to return to the Query1 : Select Query window.

The Query1 : Select Query window replaces the datasheet.

Microsoft Access - [Query1 : Select Query]

Customer Numb	Name	Address	City	State	Zip Code	Amount Paid	Current Due
BA95	Bayside Hotel	287 Riley	Hansen	FL	38513	$21,876.00	$892.50
BR46	Baldwin-Reed	267 Howard	Fernwood	FL	37023	$26,512.00	$2,672.00
CN21	Century North	1562 Butler	Hansen	FL	38513	$8,725.00	$0.00
FR28	Friend's Movies	871 Adams	Westport	FL	37070	$4,256.00	$1,202.00
GN62	Grand Nelson	7821 Oak	Wood Key	FL	36828	$8,287.50	$925.50
GS29	Great Screens	572 Lee	Hansen	FL	38513	$21,625.00	$0.00
LM22	Lenger Mason	274 Johnson	Westport	FL	37070	$0.00	$0.00
ME93	Merks College	561 Fairhill	Bayville	FL	38734	$24,761.00	$1,572.00
RI78	Riter University	26 Grove	Fernwood	FL	37023	$11,682.25	$2,827.50
TU20	Turner Hotel	8672 Quincy	Palmview	FL	36114	$8,521.50	$0.00
						$0.00	$0.00

View button

all fields included

FIGURE 2-18

Other Ways

1. Drag asterisk from field list to design grid
2. Click column in grid, click arrow, click Customer.*

Clearing the Design Grid

If you make mistakes as you are creating a query, you can fix each one individually. Alternatively, you simply may want to **clear the query**; that is, clear out the entries in the design grid and start over. One way to clear out the entries is to close the Select Query window and then start a new query just as you did earlier. A simpler approach, however, is to click Clear Grid on the Edit menu. Perform the following steps to clear a query.

Steps To Clear a Query

1 Click Edit on the menu bar and then point to Clear Grid on the Edit menu.

The Edit menu displays (Figure 2-19). If the Clear Grid command does not display immediately, wait a few seconds for the full menu to display.

2 Click Clear Grid.

Access clears the design grid so you can enter your next query.

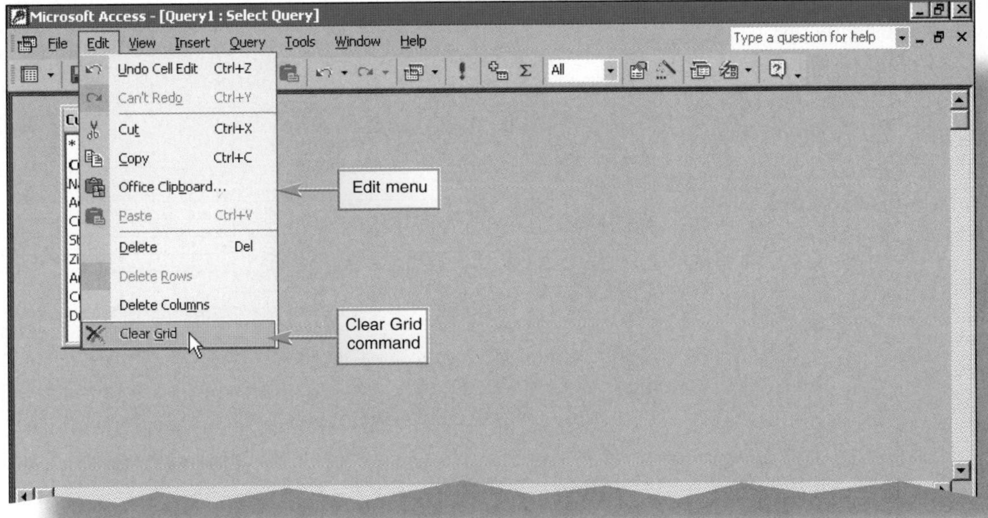

FIGURE 2-19

More About

The Access Help System

Need Help? It is no further than the Ask a Question box in the upper-right corner of the window. Click the box that contains the text, Type a question for help (Figure 2-20), type `help`, and then press the ENTER key. Access will respond with a list of items you can click to learn about obtaining help on any Access-related topic. To find out what is new in Access 2002, type `what's new in Access` in the Ask a Question box.

Entering Criteria

When you use queries, usually you are looking for those records that satisfy some criterion. You might want the name, amount paid, and current due amounts of the customer whose number is FR28, for example, or of those customers whose names start with the letters, Gr. To enter criteria, enter them in the Criteria row in the design grid below the field name to which the criterion applies. For example, to indicate that the customer number must be FR28, you first must add the Customer Number field to the design grid. You then would type FR28 in the Criteria row below the Customer Number field.

The next examples illustrate the types of criteria that are available.

Using Text Data in Criteria

To use **text data** (data in a field whose data type is Text) in criteria, simply type the text in the Criteria row below the corresponding field name. The following steps query the Customer table and display the customer number, name, amount paid, and current due amount of customer FR28.

Steps To Use Text Data in a Criterion

1 One by one, double-click the Customer Number, Name, Amount Paid, and Current Due fields to add them to the query. Point to the Criteria row for the first field in the design grid.

The Customer Number, Name, Amount Paid, and Current Due fields are added to the design grid (Figure 2-20). The mouse pointer on the Criteria entry for the first field (Customer Number) has changed shape to an I-beam.

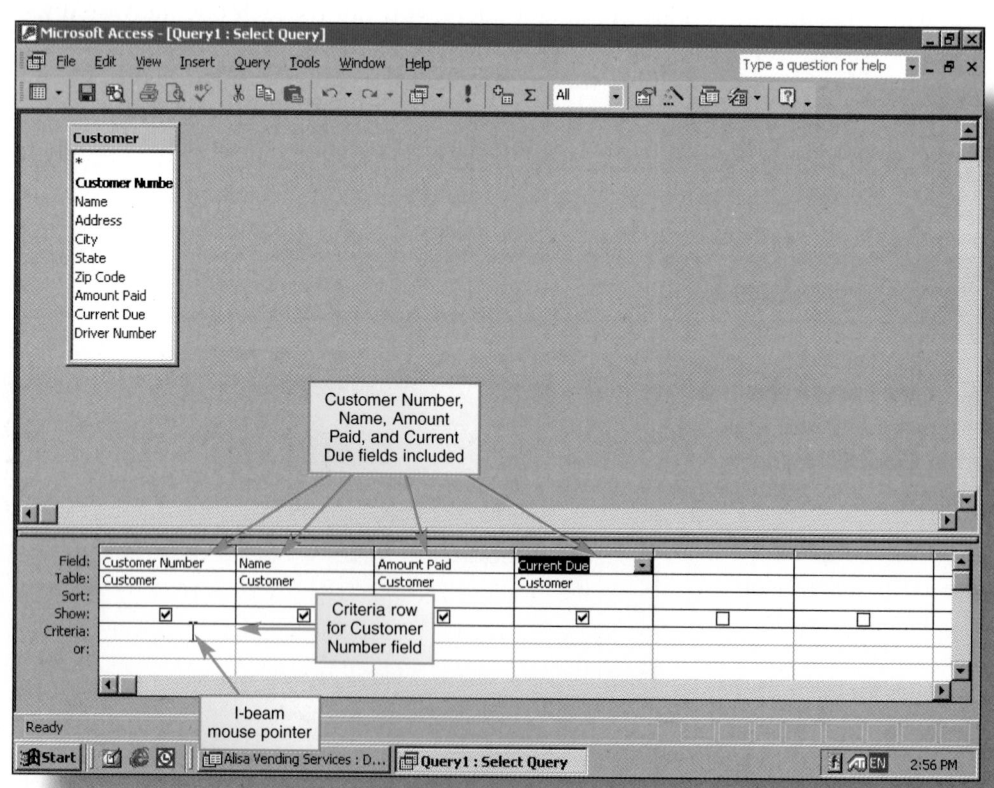

FIGURE 2-20

2 **Click the Criteria row, type** FR28 **as the criterion for the Customer Number field and then point to the Run button on the Query Design toolbar.**

The criterion is entered (Figure 2-21).

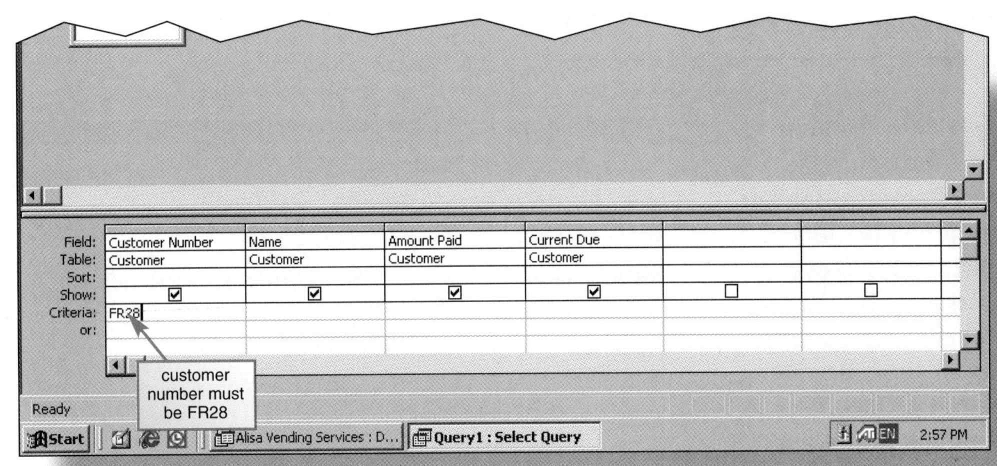

FIGURE 2-21

3 **Click the Run button to run the query.**

The results display (Figure 2-22). Only customer FR28 is included. (The extra blank row contains $0.00 in the Amount Paid and Current Due fields. Unlike text fields, which are left blank, number and currency fields in the extra row contain 0. Because the Amount Paid and Current Due fields are currency fields, the values display as $0.00.)

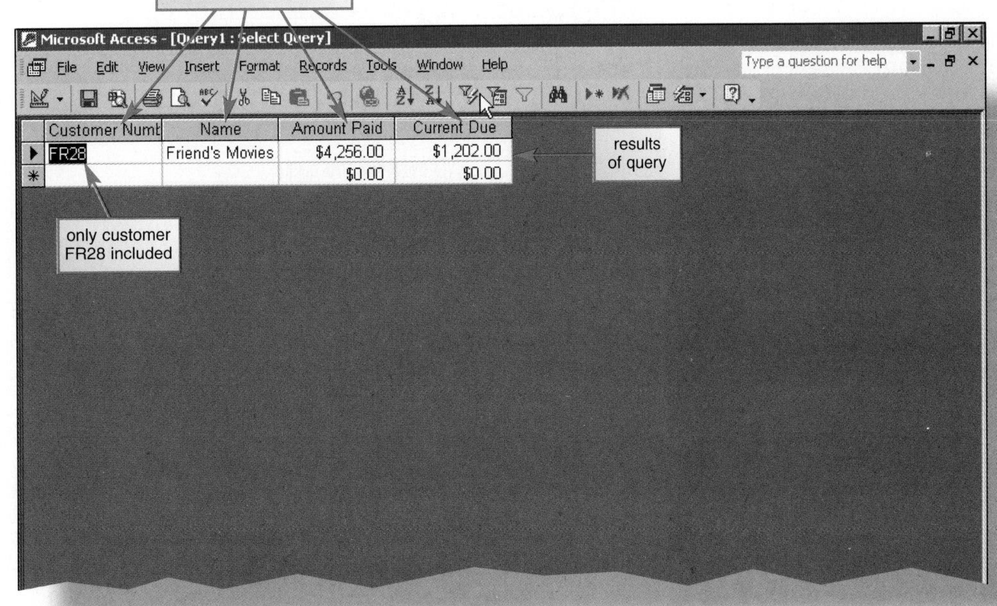

FIGURE 2-22

Using Wildcards

Two special wildcards are available in Microsoft Access. **Wildcards** are symbols that represent any character or combination of characters. The first of the two wildcards, the **asterisk** (*), represents any collection of characters. Thus Gr* represents the letters, Gr, followed by any collection of characters. The other wildcard symbol is the **question mark** (?), which represents any individual character. Thus t?m represents the letter, T, followed by any single character followed by the letter, m, such as Tim or Tom.

The steps on the next page use a wildcard to find the number, name, and address of those customers whose names begin with Gr. Because you do not know how many characters will follow the Gr, the asterisk is appropriate.

Using Text Data in Criteria

Some database systems require that text data must be enclosed in quotation marks. For example, to find customers in Texas, TX would be entered as the criterion for the State field. In Access this is not necessary, because Access will insert the quotation marks automatically.

Steps To Use a Wildcard

1 **Click the View button on the Query Datasheet toolbar to return to the Query1 : Select Query window. If necessary, click the Criteria row under the Customer Number field. Use the DELETE or BACKSPACE key to delete the current entry ("FR28"). Click the Criteria row under the Name field. Type Gr* as the entry and point to the Run button on the Query Design toolbar.**

The criterion is entered (Figure 2-23).

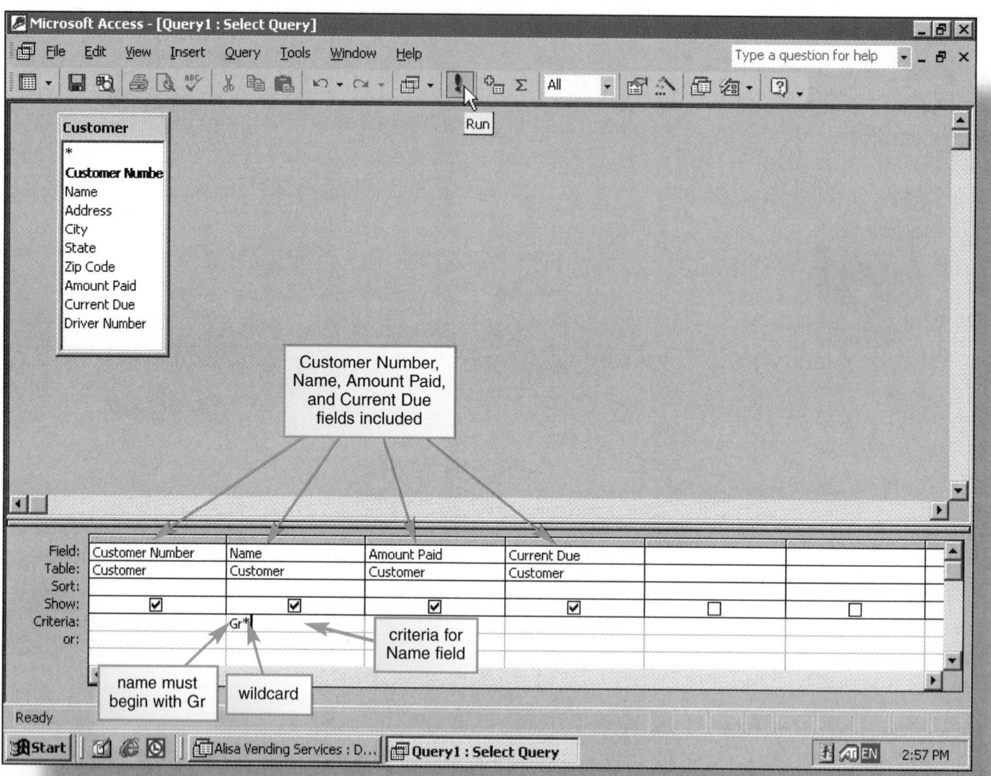

FIGURE 2-23

2 **Click the Run button to run the query.**

The results display (Figure 2-24). Only the customers whose names start with Gr are included.

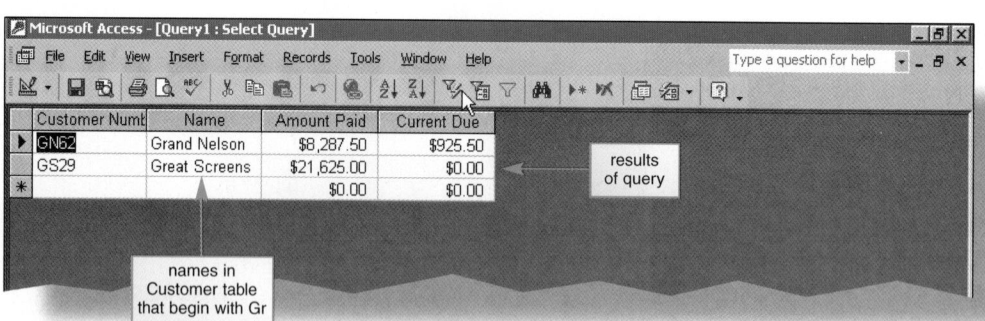

FIGURE 2-24

Criteria for a Field Not in the Result

In some cases, you may have criteria for a particular field that should not appear in the results of the query. For example, you may wish to see the customer number, name, address, and amount paid for all customers located in Hansen. The criterion involves the City field, which is not one of the fields to be included in the results.

To enter a criterion for the City field, it must be included in the design grid. Normally, this also would mean it would appear in the results. To prevent this from happening, remove the check mark from its Show check box in the Show row of the grid. The following steps illustrate the process by displaying the customer number, name, and amount paid for customers located in Hansen.

To Use Criteria for a Field Not Included in the Results

1 Click the View button on the Query Datasheet toolbar to return to the Query1 : Select Query window. On the Edit menu, click Clear Grid.

Access clears the design grid so you can enter the next query.

2 Include the Customer Number, Name, Address, Amount Paid, and City fields in the query. Type Hansen **as the criterion for the City field and then point to the City field's Show check box.**

The fields are included in the grid, and the criterion for the City field is entered (Figure 2-25).

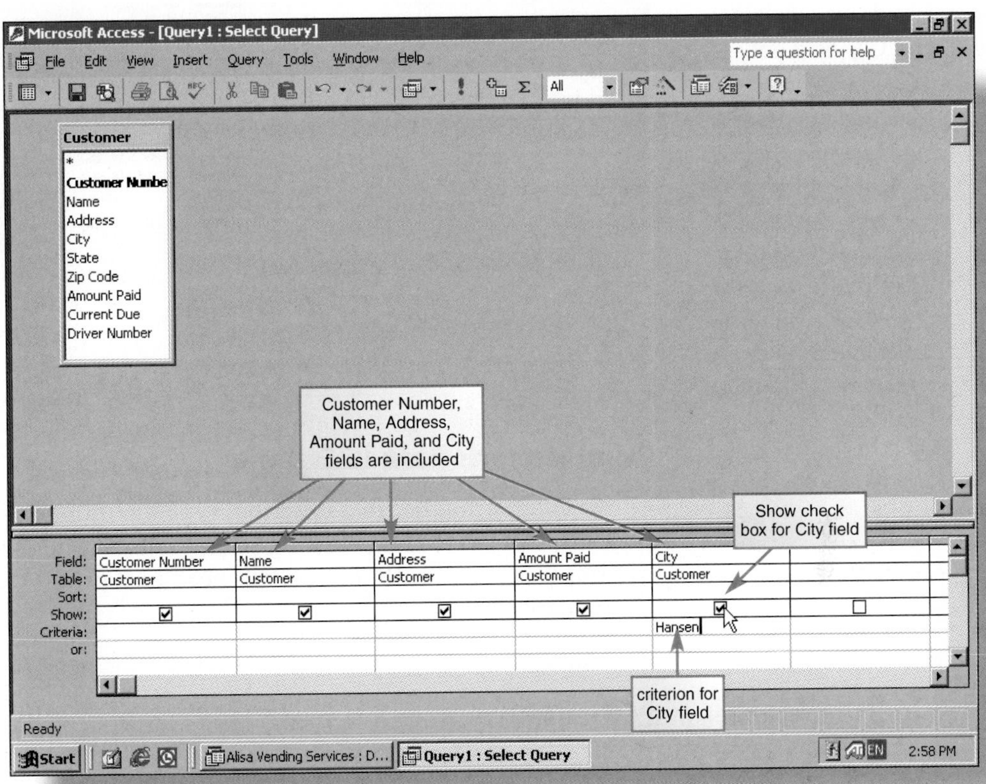

FIGURE 2-25

3 Click the Show check box to remove the check mark and then point to the Run button on the Query Design toolbar.

The check mark is removed from the Show check box for the City field (Figure 2-26), indicating it will not show in the result. Because the City field is a text field, Access has added quotation marks before and after Hansen automatically.

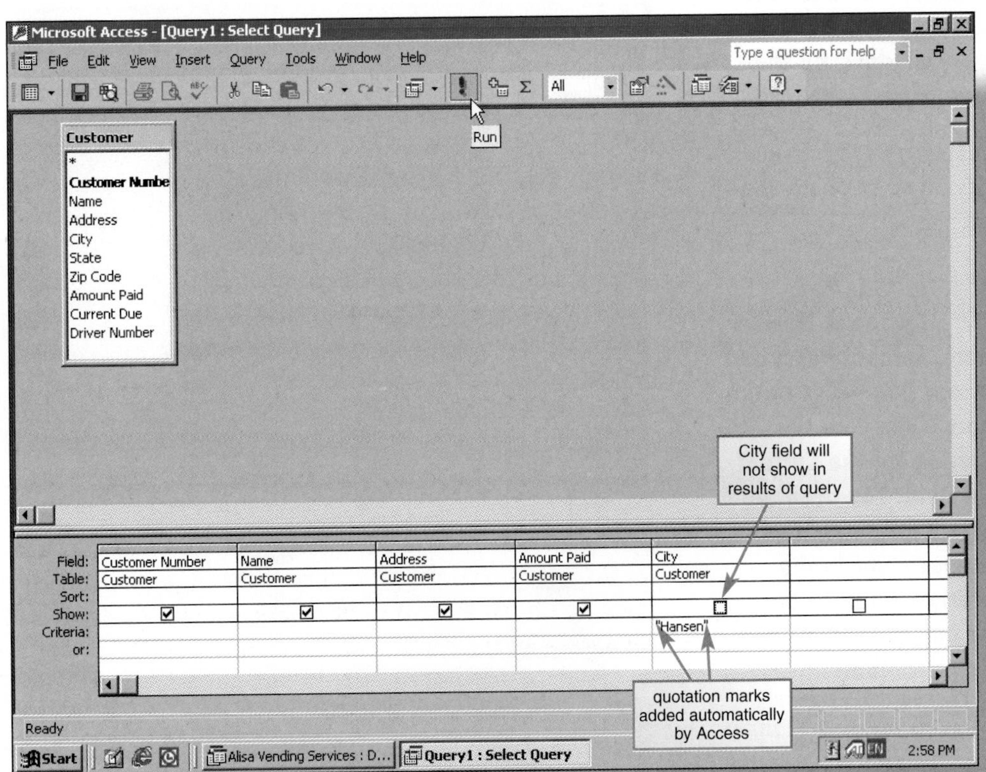

FIGURE 2-26

4 **Click the Run button to run the query.**

The results display (Figure 2-27). The City field does not display. The only customers included are those located in Hansen.

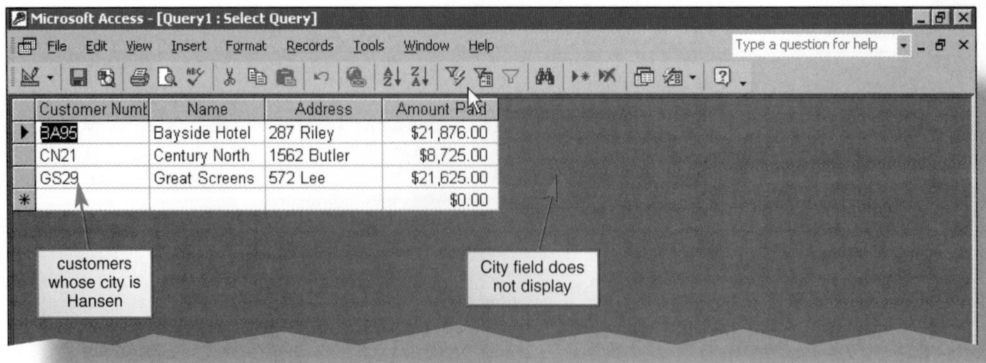

Customer Numb	Name	Address	Amount Paid
BA95	Bayside Hotel	287 Riley	$21,876.00
CN21	Century North	1562 Butler	$8,725.00
GS29	Great Screens	572 Lee	$21,625.00
			$0.00

FIGURE 2-27

Using Numeric Data in Criteria

To enter a number in a criterion, type the number without any dollar signs or commas. Complete the following steps to display all customers whose current due amount is $0.00. To do so, you will need to type a 0 (zero) as the criterion for the Current Due field.

Steps To Use a Number in a Criterion

1 **Click the View button on the Query Datasheet toolbar to return to the Query1 : Select Query window. On the Edit menu, click Clear Grid.**

Access clears the design grid so you can enter the next query.

2 **Include the Customer Number, Name, Amount Paid, and Current Due fields in the query. Type** 0 **as the criterion for the Current Due field. You need not enter a dollar sign or decimal point in the criterion. Point to the Run button on the Query Design toolbar.**

The fields are selected and the criterion is entered (Figure 2-28).

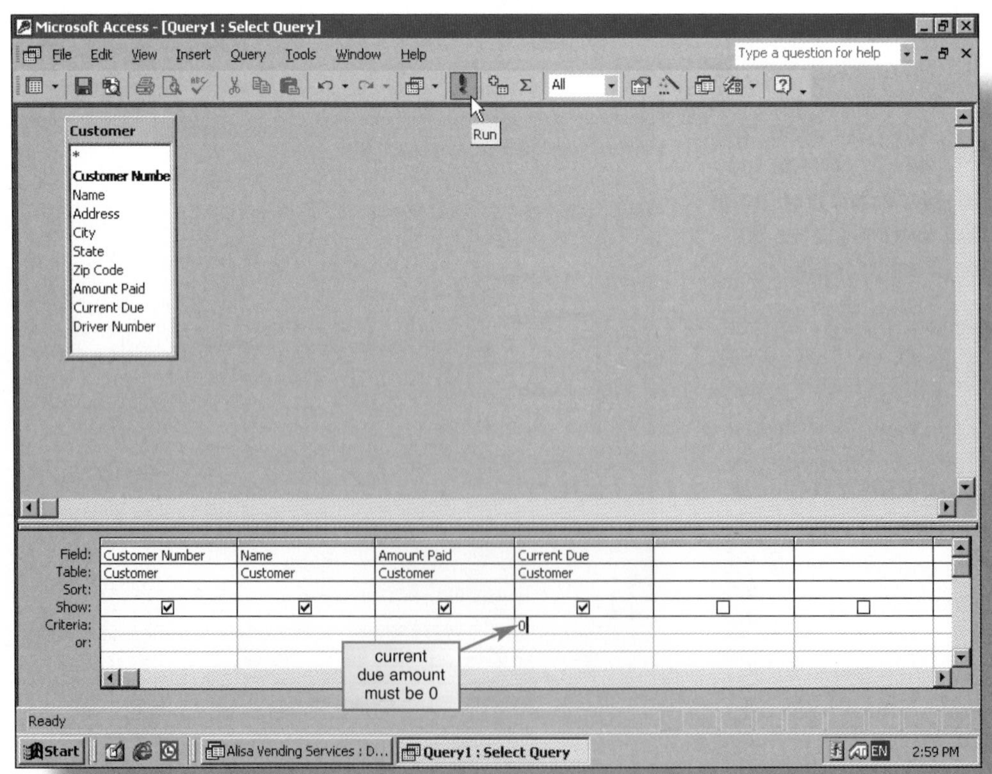

FIGURE 2-28

3 Click the Run button to run the query.

The results display (Figure 2-29). Only those customers that have a current due amount of $0.00 are included.

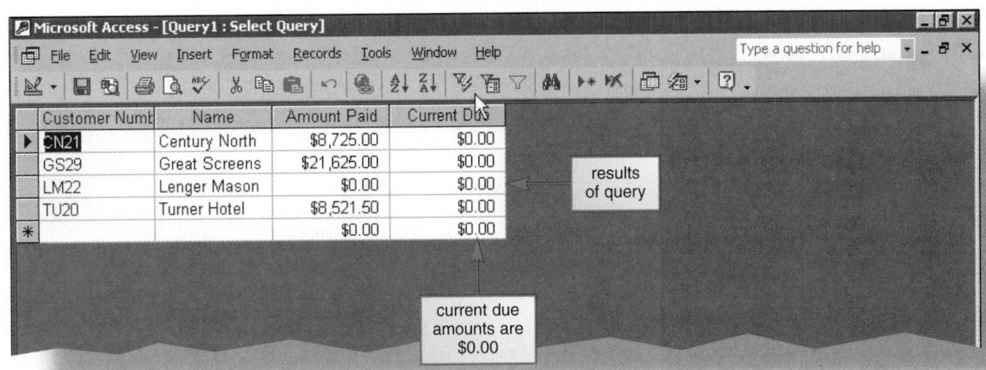

FIGURE 2-29

Using Comparison Operators

Unless you specify otherwise, Access assumes that the criteria you enter involve equality (exact matches). In the last query, for example, you were requesting those customers whose current due amount was equal to 0 (zero). If you want something other than an exact match, you must enter the appropriate **comparison operator**. The comparison operators are > (greater than), < (less than), >= (greater than or equal to), <= (less than or equal to), and NOT (not equal to).

Perform the following steps to use the > operator to find all customers whose amount paid is greater than $20,000.

Steps To Use a Comparison Operator in a Criterion

1 Click the View button on the Query Datasheet toolbar to return to the Query1 : Select Query window. On the Edit menu, click Clear Grid.

Access clears the design grid so you can enter the next query.

2 Include the Customer Number, Name, Amount Paid, and Current Due fields in the query. Type >20000 **as the criterion for the Amount Paid field.**

The fields are selected and the criterion is entered (Figure 2-30).

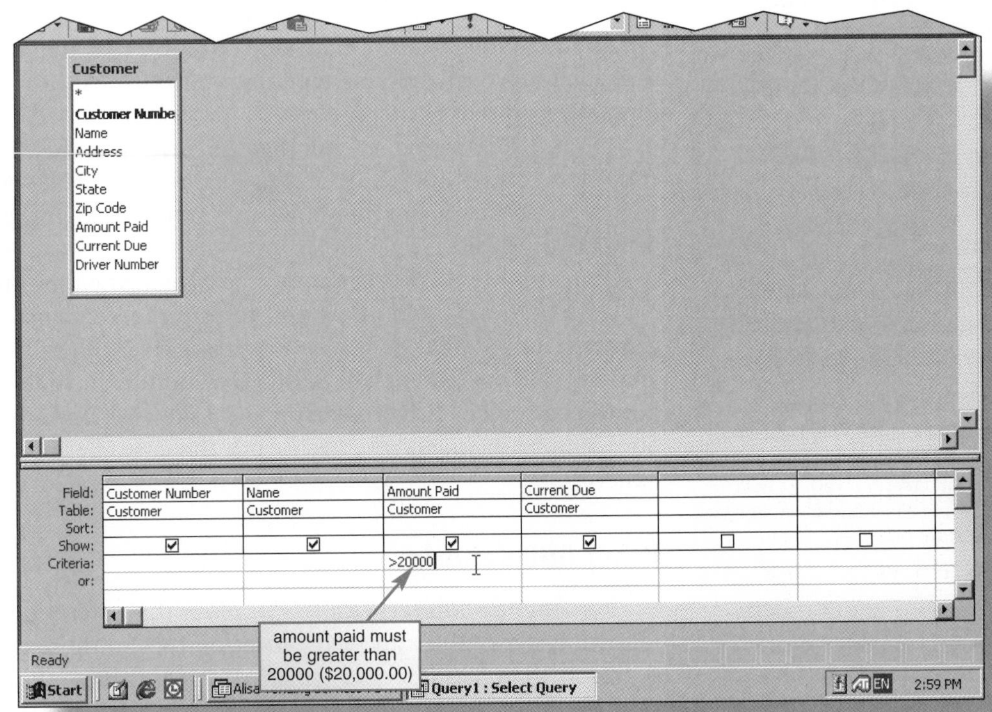

FIGURE 2-30

3 **Click the Run button on the Query Design toolbar to run the query.**

The results display (Figure 2-31). Only those customers who have an amount paid greater than $20,000 are included.

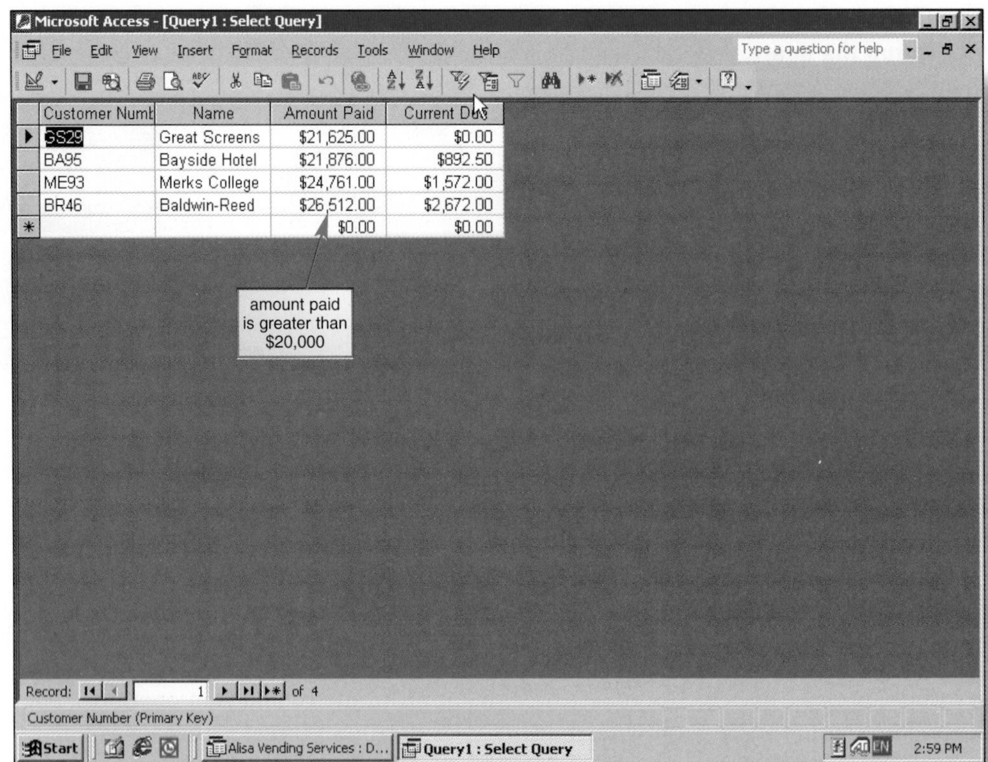

FIGURE 2-31

Using Compound Criteria

Often you will have more than one criterion that the data for which you are searching must satisfy. This type of criterion is called a **compound criterion**. Two types of compound criteria exist.

In an **AND criterion**, each individual criterion must be true in order for the compound criterion to be true. For example, an AND criterion would allow you to find those customers that have an amount paid greater than $20,000 and whose driver is driver 60.

Conversely, an **OR criterion** is true provided either individual criterion is true. An OR criterion would allow you to find those customers that have an amount paid greater than $20,000 or whose driver is driver 60. In this case, any customer whose amount paid is greater than $20,000 would be included in the answer whether or not the customer's driver is driver 60. Likewise, any customer whose driver is driver 60 would be included whether or not the customer had an amount paid greater than $20,000.

Compound Criteria

The BETWEEN operator allows you to search for a range of values in one field. For example, to find all customers whose amount paid amount is between $5,000 and $10,000, you would enter `Between 5000 and 10000` in the Criteria row for the Amount Paid field. It also is possible to create compound criteria involving both OR and AND operators. For more information, visit the Access 2002 More About Web page (scsite.com/ac2002/more.htm) and then click Compound Criteria.

Using AND Criteria

To combine criteria with AND, place the criteria on the same line. Perform the following steps to use an AND criterion to find those customers whose amount paid is greater than $20,000 and whose driver is driver 60.

To Use a Compound Criterion Involving AND

1 Click the View button on the Query Datasheet toolbar to return to the Query1 : Select Query window. Include the Driver Number field in the query. Be sure >20000 **is entered in the Criteria row for the Amount Paid field. Click the Criteria entry for the Driver Number field and then type** 60 **as the criterion for the Driver Number field.**

Criteria have been entered for the Amount Paid and Driver Number fields (Figure 2-32).

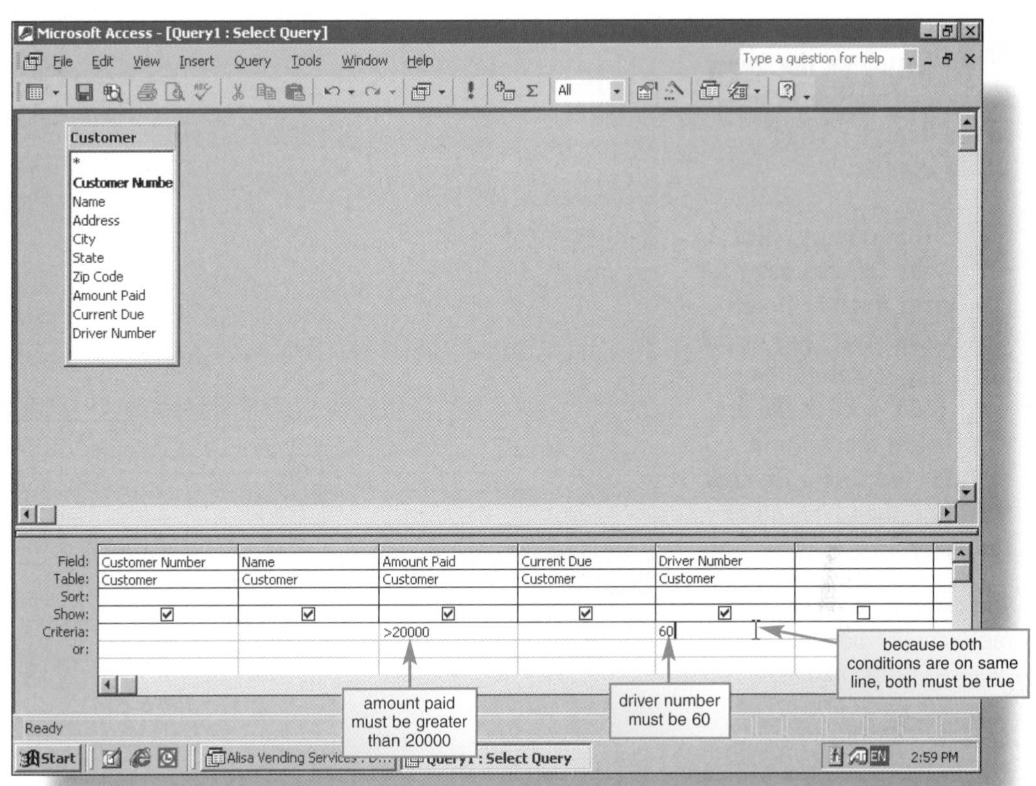

FIGURE 2-32

2 Click the Run button on the Query Design toolbar to run the query.

The results display (Figure 2-33). Only the customers whose amount paid is greater than $20,000 and whose driver number is 60 are included.

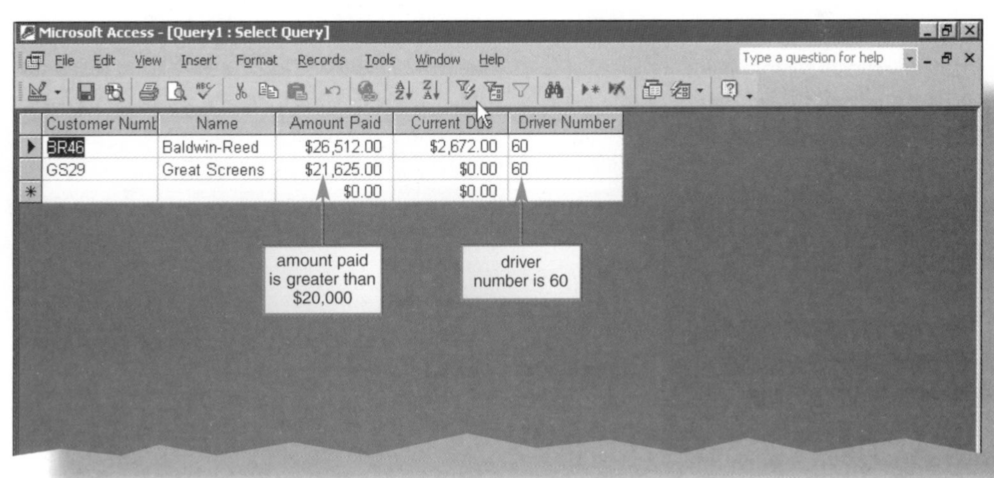

FIGURE 2-33

Using OR Criteria

To combine criteria with OR, the criteria must go on separate lines in the Criteria area of the grid. The steps on the next page use an OR criterion to find those customers whose amount paid is greater than $20,000 or whose driver is driver 60 (or both).

Steps To Use a Compound Criterion Involving OR

1 Click the View button on the Query Datasheet toolbar to return to the Query1 : Select Query window.

2 If necessary, click the Criteria entry for the Driver Number field. Use the BACKSPACE key or the DELETE key to delete the entry ("60"). Click the or: row (below the Criteria row) for the Driver Number field and then type 60 **as the entry.**

The criteria are entered for the Amount Paid and Driver Number fields on different lines (Figure 2-34).

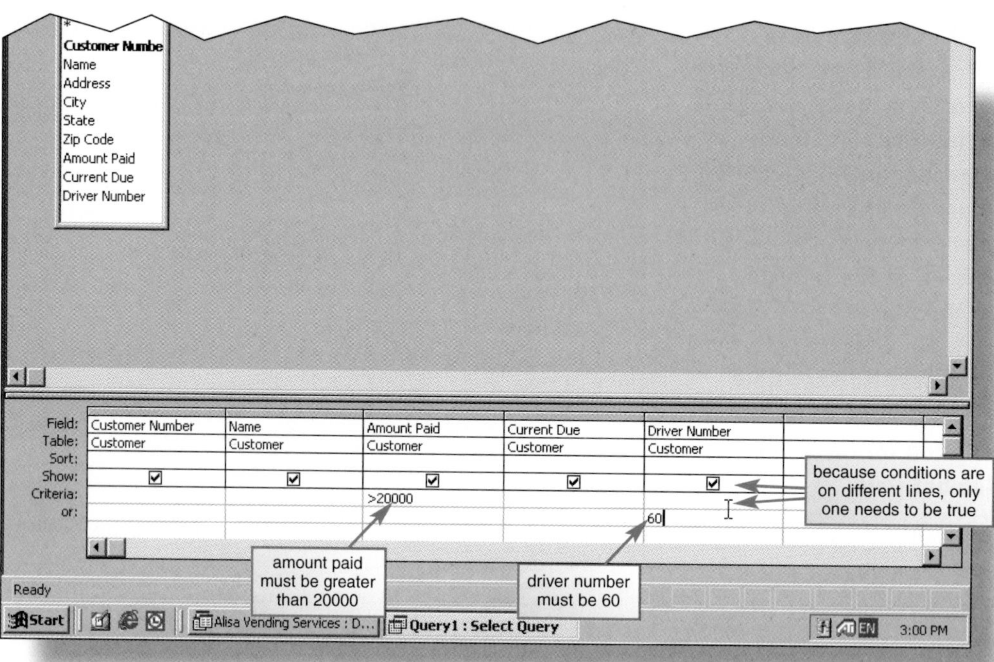

FIGURE 2-34

3 Click the Run button on the Query Design toolbar to run the query.

The results display (Figure 2-35). Only those customers whose amount paid is greater than $20,000 or whose driver number is 60 are included.

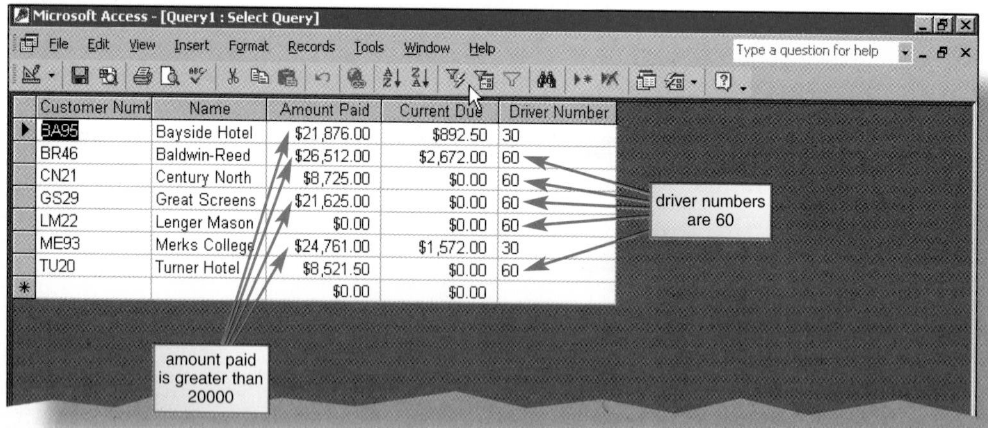

FIGURE 2-35

Sorting Data in a Query

In some queries, the order in which the records are displayed really does not matter. All you need be concerned about are the records that appear in the results. It does not matter which one is first or which one is last.

In other queries, however, the order can be very important. You may want to see the cities in which customers are located and would like them arranged alphabetically. Perhaps you want to see the customers listed by driver number. Further, within all the customers of any given driver, you would like them to be listed by amount paid.

To order the records in the answer to a query in a particular way, you **sort** the records. The field or fields on which the records are sorted is called the **sort key**. If you are sorting on more than one field (such as sorting by amount paid within driver number), the more important field (Driver Number) is called the **major key** (also called the **primary sort key**) and the less important field (Amount Paid) is called the **minor key** (also called the **secondary sort key**).

To sort in Microsoft Access, specify the sort order in the Sort row of the design grid below the field that is the sort key. If you specify more than one sort key, the sort key on the left will be the major sort key and the one on the right will be the minor sort key.

The following steps sort the cities in the Customer table.

More About

Sorting Data in a Query

When sorting data in a query, the records in the underlying tables (the tables on which the query is based) are not actually rearranged. Instead, the DBMS will determine the most efficient method of simply displaying the records in the requested order. The records in the underlying tables remain in their original order.

Steps To Sort Data in a Query

1 **Click the View button on the Query Datasheet toolbar to return to the Query1 : Select Query window. On the Edit menu, click Clear Grid.**

2 **Include the City field in the design grid. Click the Sort row below the City field, and then click the Sort row arrow that displays.**

The City field is included (Figure 2-36). A list of available sort orders displays.

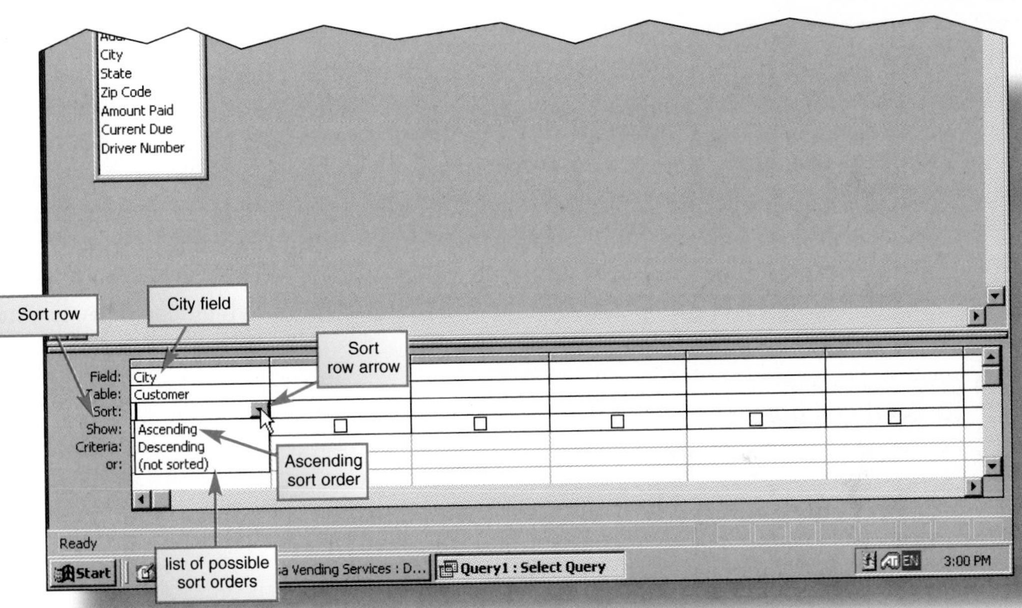

FIGURE 2-36

3 **Click Ascending.**

Ascending is selected as the order (Figure 2-37).

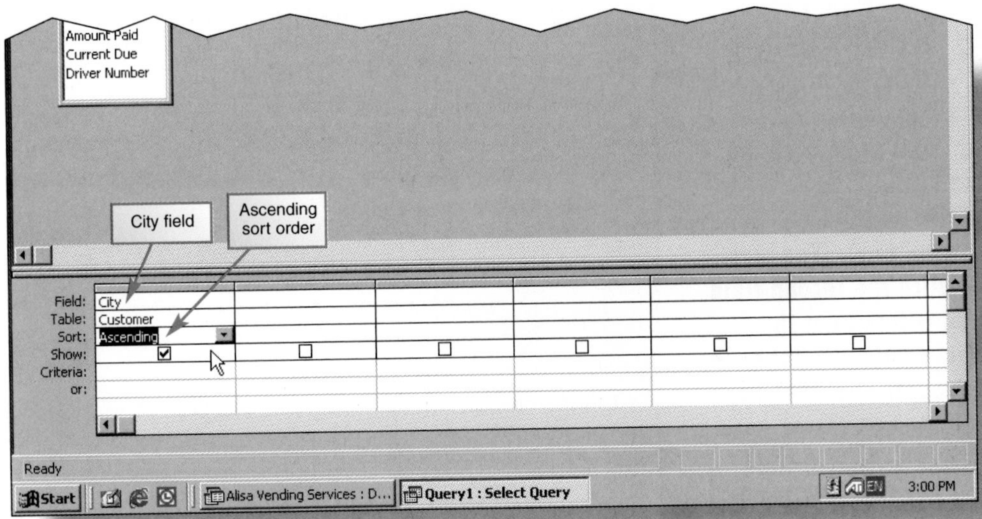

FIGURE 2-37

4 Click the Run button on the Query Design toolbar to run the query.

The results contain the cities from the Customer table (Figure 2-38). The cities display in alphabetical order. Duplicates, also called identical rows, are included.

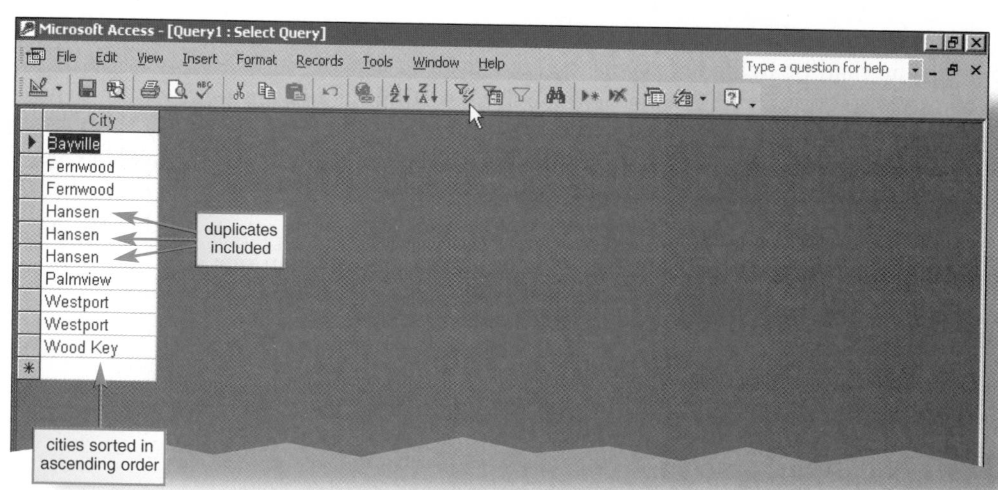

FIGURE 2-38

Omitting Duplicates

When you sort data, duplicates normally are included. In Figure 2-38, for example, Fernwood appeared twice, Hansen appeared three times, and Westport appeared twice. If you do not want duplicates included, use the Properties command and specify Unique Values Only. Perform the following steps to produce a sorted list of the cities in the Customer table in which each city is listed only once.

Steps To Omit Duplicates

1 Click the View button on the Query Datasheet toolbar to return to the Query1 : Select Query window. On the Edit menu, click Clear Grid.

2 Include the City field, click Ascending as the sort order, and right-click the second field in the design grid (the empty field following City). (You must right-click the second field or you will not get the correct results.) Point to the Properties command.

The shortcut menu displays (Figure 2-39).

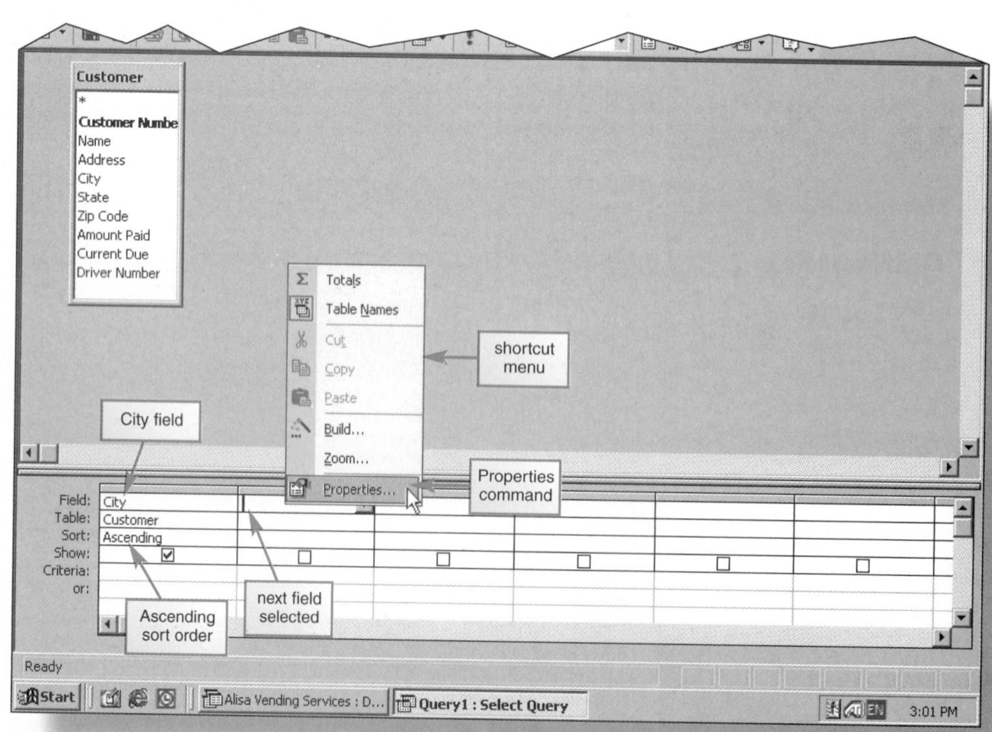

FIGURE 2-39

3 **Click Properties on the shortcut menu and then point to the Unique Values property box.**

The Query Properties sheet displays (Figure 2-40). (If your sheet looks different, you right-clicked the wrong place. Close the sheet that displays and right-click the second field in the grid.)

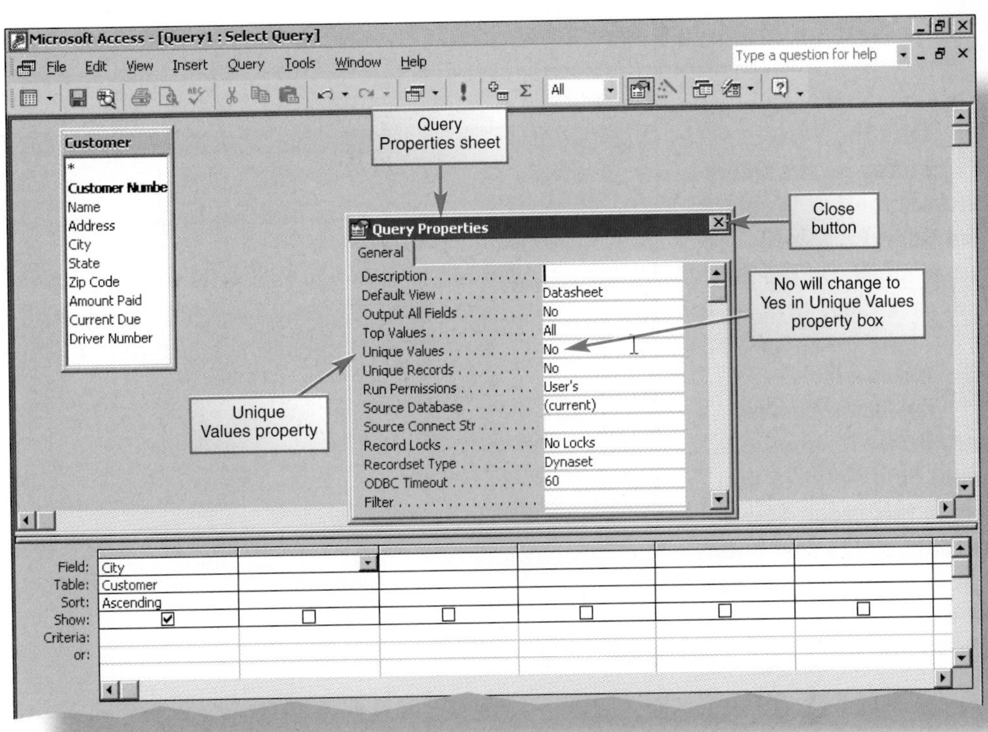

FIGURE 2-40

4 **Click the Unique Values property box, and then click the arrow that displays to produce a list of available choices for Unique Values. Click Yes and then close the Query Properties sheet by clicking its Close button. Click the Run button on the Query Design toolbar to run the query.**

The results display (Figure 2-41). The cities are sorted alphabetically. Each city is included only once.

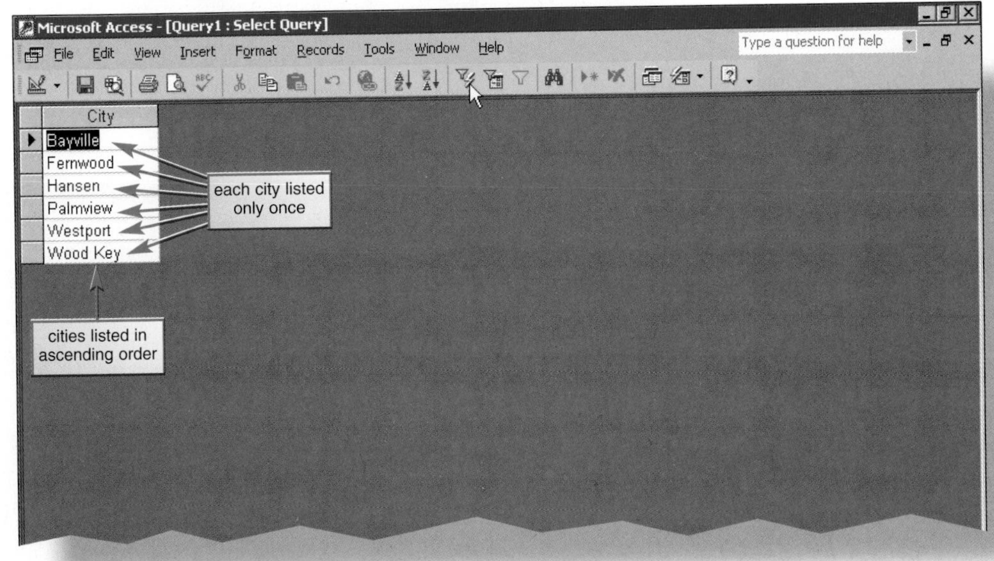

FIGURE 2-41

Other Ways

1. Click Properties button on toolbar
2. On View menu click Properties
3. In Voice Command mode, say "Properties"

Sorting on Multiple Keys

The next example lists the number, name, driver number, and amount paid for all customers. The data is to be sorted by amount paid within driver number, which means that the Driver Number field is the major key and the Amount Paid field is the minor key.

The steps on the next page accomplish this sorting by specifying the Driver Number and Amount Paid fields as sort keys.

Steps To Sort on Multiple Keys

1 **Click the View button on the Query Datasheet toolbar to return to the Query1 : Select Query window. On the Edit menu, click Clear Grid.**

2 **Include the Customer Number, Name, Driver Number, and Amount Paid fields in the query in this order. Select Ascending as the sort order for both the Driver Number field and the Amount Paid field (Figure 2-42).**

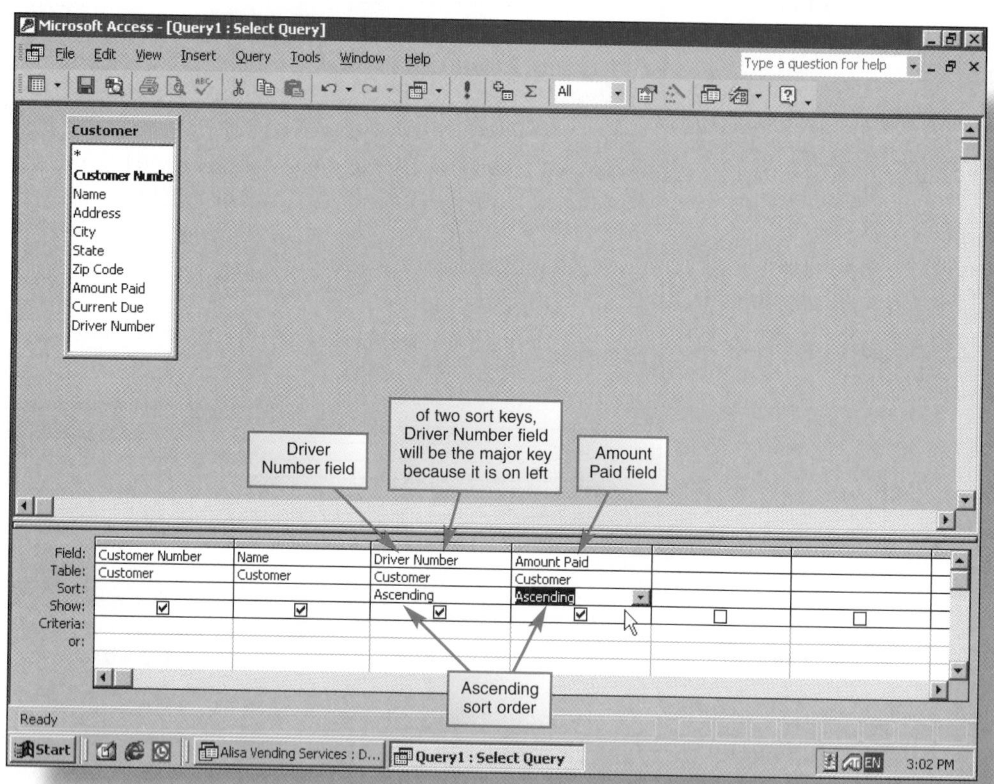

FIGURE 2-42

3 **Click the Run button on the Query Design toolbar to run the query.**

The results display (Figure 2-43). The customers are sorted by driver number. Within the collection of customers having the same driver, the customers are sorted by amount paid.

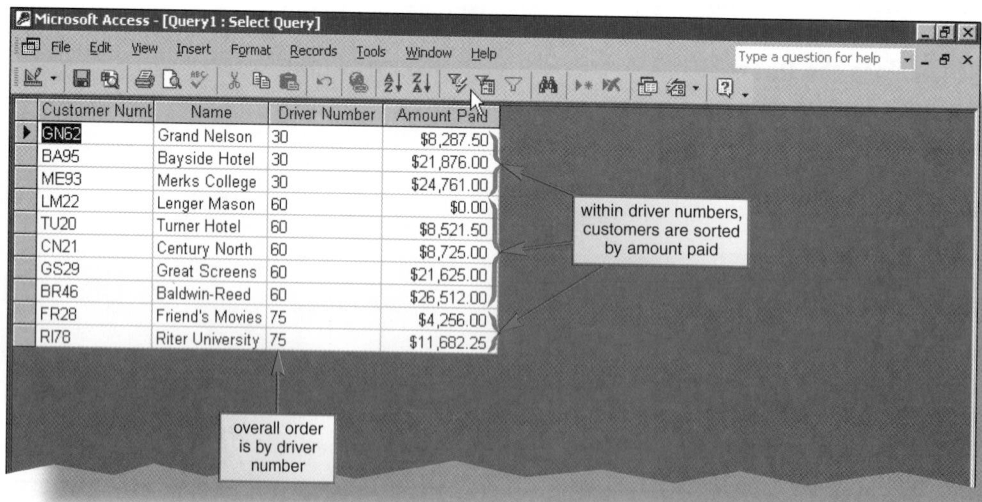

FIGURE 2-43

It is important to remember that the major sort key must appear to the left of the minor sort key in the design grid. If you attempted to sort by amount paid within driver number, but placed the Amount Paid field to the left of the Driver Number field, your results would be incorrect.

Joining Tables

Alisa Vending Services needs to list the number and name of each customer along with the number and name of the customer's driver. The customer's name is in the Customer table, whereas the driver's name is in the Driver table. Thus, this query cannot be satisfied using a single table. You need to **join** the tables; that is, to find records in the two tables that have identical values in matching fields (Figure 2-44). In this example, you need to find records in the Customer table and the Driver table that have the same value in the Driver Number fields.

More About

Joining Tables

One of the key features that distinguishes database management systems from file systems is the ability to join tables, that is, to create queries that draw data from two or more tables. Several types of joins are available. The most common type, the one illustrated in this project formally is called the natural join. For more information, visit the Access 2002 More About Web page (scsite.com/ac2002/more.htm) and then click Join Types.

Give me the number and name of each customer along with the number and name of the customer's driver.

Customer table

CUSTOMER NUMBER	NAME	. . .	DRIVER NUMBER
BA95	Bayside Hotel	...	30
BR46	Baldwin-Reed	...	60
CN21	Century North	...	60
FR28	Friend's Movies	...	75
GN62	Grand Nelson	...	30
GS29	Great Screens	...	60
LM22	Lenger Mason	...	60
ME93	Merks College	...	30
RI78	Riter University	...	75
TU20	Turner Hotel	...	60

Driver table

DRIVER NUMBER	LAST NAME	FIRST NAME	. . .
30	Tuttle	Larissa	...
60	Powers	Frank	...
75	Ortiz	Jose	...

CUSTOMER NUMBER	NAME	. . .	DRIVER NUMBER	LAST NAME	FIRST NAME	. . .
BA95	Bayside Hotel	...	30	Tuttle	Larissa	...
BR46	Baldwin-Reed	...	60	Powers	Frank	...
CN21	Century North	...	60	Powers	Frank	...
FR28	Friend's Movies	...	75	Ortiz	Jose	...
GN62	Grand Nelson	...	30	Tuttle	Larissa	...
GS29	Great Screens	...	60	Powers	Frank	...
LM22	Lenger Mason	...	60	Powers	Frank	...
ME93	Merks College	...	30	Tuttle	Larissa	...
RI78	Riter University	...	75	Ortiz	Jose	...
TU20	Turner Hotel	...	60	Powers	Frank	...

FIGURE 2-44

To join tables in Access, first you bring field lists for both tables to the upper pane of the Select Query window. Access will draw a line, called a **join line**, between matching fields in the two tables indicating that the tables are related. You then can select fields from either table. Access will join the tables automatically.

The first step is to add an additional table, the Driver table, to the query. A join line will display connecting the Driver Number fields in the two field lists. This join line indicates how the tables are related; that is, linked through these matching fields. (If you fail to give the matching fields the same name, Access will not insert the line. You can insert it manually, however, by clicking one of the two matching fields and dragging the mouse pointer to the other matching field.)

The following steps add the Driver table and then select the appropriate fields.

Steps To Join Tables

1 Click the View button on the Query Datasheet toolbar to return to the Query1 : Select Query window. On the Edit menu, click Clear Grid.

2 Right-click any open area in the upper pane of the Query1 : Select Query window and then point to Show Table on the shortcut menu.

The shortcut menu displays (Figure 2-45).

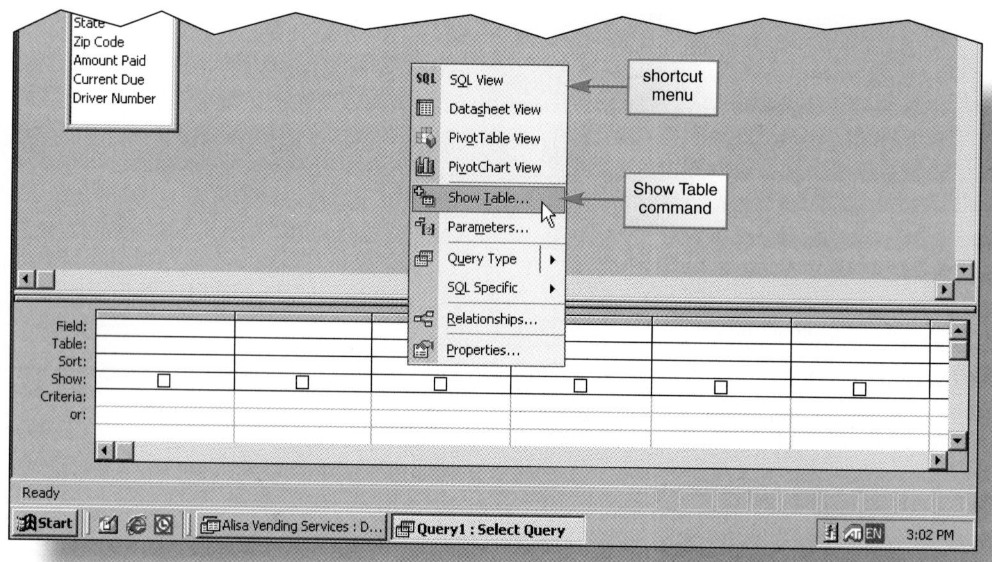

FIGURE 2-45

3 Click Show Table on the shortcut menu and then point to Driver.

The Show Table dialog box displays (Figure 2-46).

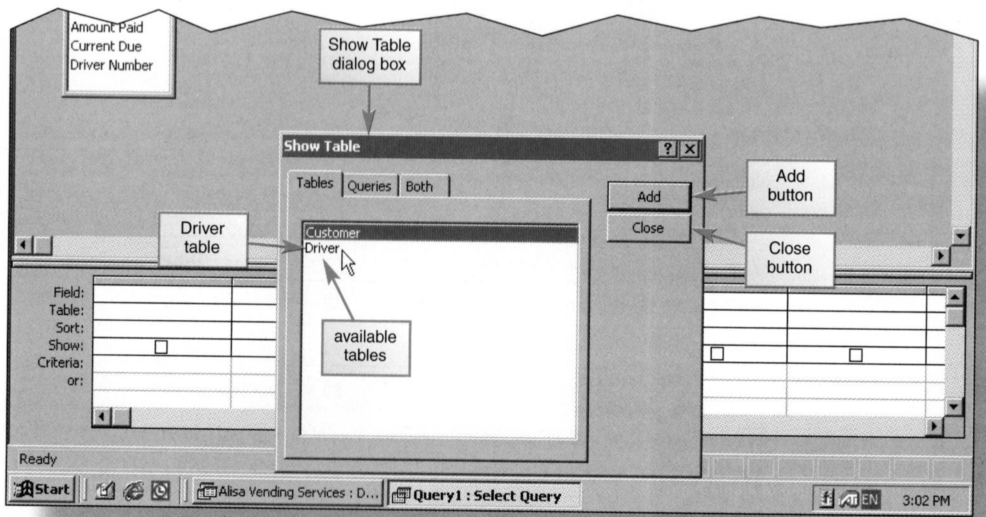

FIGURE 2-46

4 Click Driver to select the Driver table and then click the Add button. Close the Show Table dialog box by clicking the Close button. Expand the size of the field list so all the fields in the Driver table display.

The field lists for both tables display (Figure 2-47). A join line connects the two field lists.

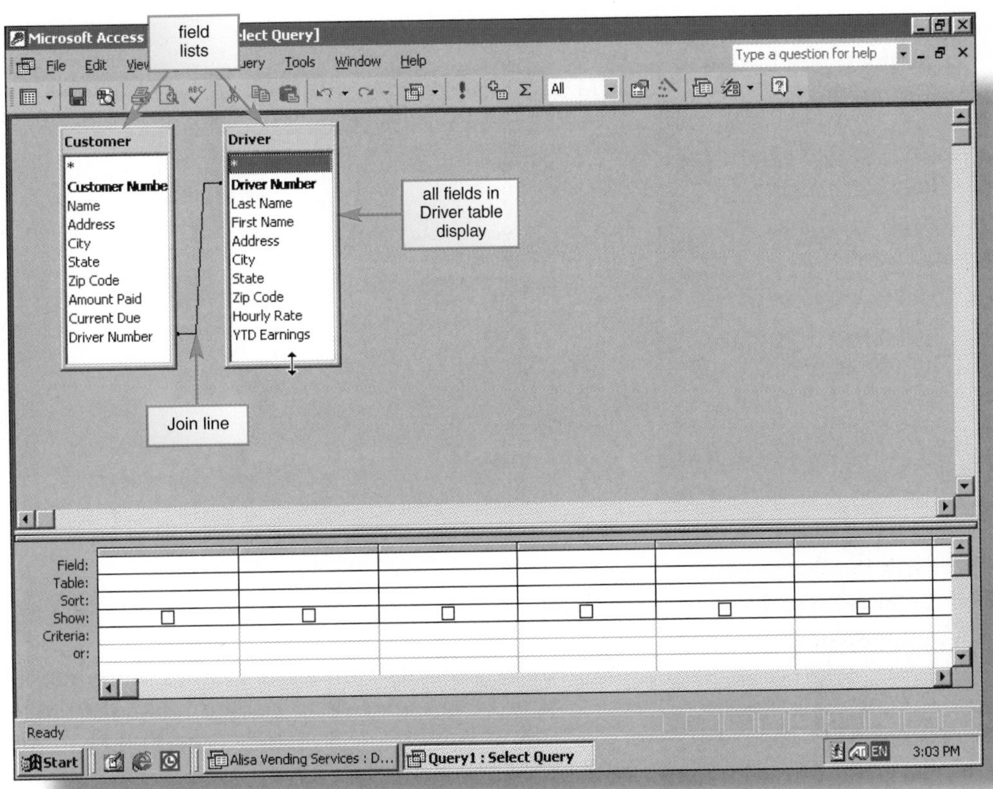

FIGURE 2-47

5 Include the Customer Number, Name, and Driver Number fields from the Customer table and the Last Name and First Name fields from the Driver table.

The fields from both tables are selected (Figure 2-48).

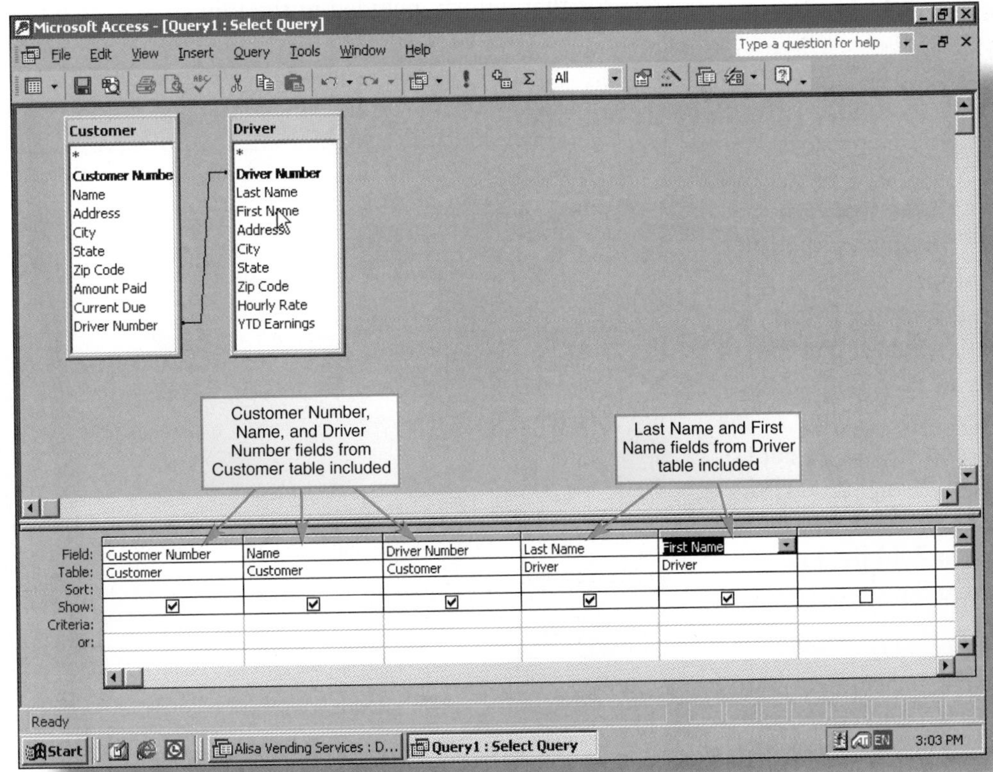

FIGURE 2-48

6 Click the Run button on the Query Design toolbar to run the query.

The results display (Figure 2-49). They contain data from both the Customer and the Driver tables.

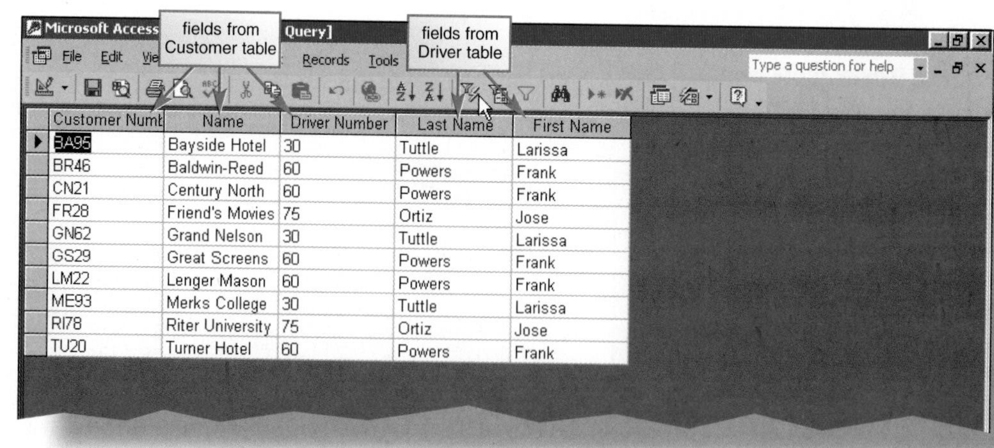

Customer Number	Name	Driver Number	Last Name	First Name
BA95	Bayside Hotel	30	Tuttle	Larissa
BR46	Baldwin-Reed	60	Powers	Frank
CN21	Century North	60	Powers	Frank
FR28	Friend's Movies	75	Ortiz	Jose
GN62	Grand Nelson	30	Tuttle	Larissa
GS29	Great Screens	60	Powers	Frank
LM22	Lenger Mason	60	Powers	Frank
ME93	Merks College	30	Tuttle	Larissa
RI78	Riter University	75	Ortiz	Jose
TU20	Turner Hotel	60	Powers	Frank

FIGURE 2-49

Other Ways

1. Click Show Table button on toolbar
2. On Query menu click Show Table
3. In Voice Command mode, say "Show Table"

Restricting Records in a Join

Sometimes you will want to join tables, but you will not want to include all possible records. In such cases, you will relate the tables and include fields just as you did before. You also will include criteria. For example, to include the same fields as in the previous query, but only those customers whose amount paid is greater than $20,000, you will make the same entries as before and then also type >20000 as a criterion for the Amount Paid field.

The following steps modify the query from the previous example to restrict the records that will be included in the join.

Steps To Restrict the Records in a Join

1 Click the View button on the Query Datasheet toolbar to return to the Query1 : Select Query window. Add the Amount Paid field to the query. Type >20000 as the criterion for the Amount Paid field and then click the Show check box for the Amount Paid field to remove the check mark.

The Amount Paid field displays in the design grid (Figure 2-50). A criterion is entered for the Amount Paid field and the Show check box is empty, indicating that the field will not display in the results of the query.

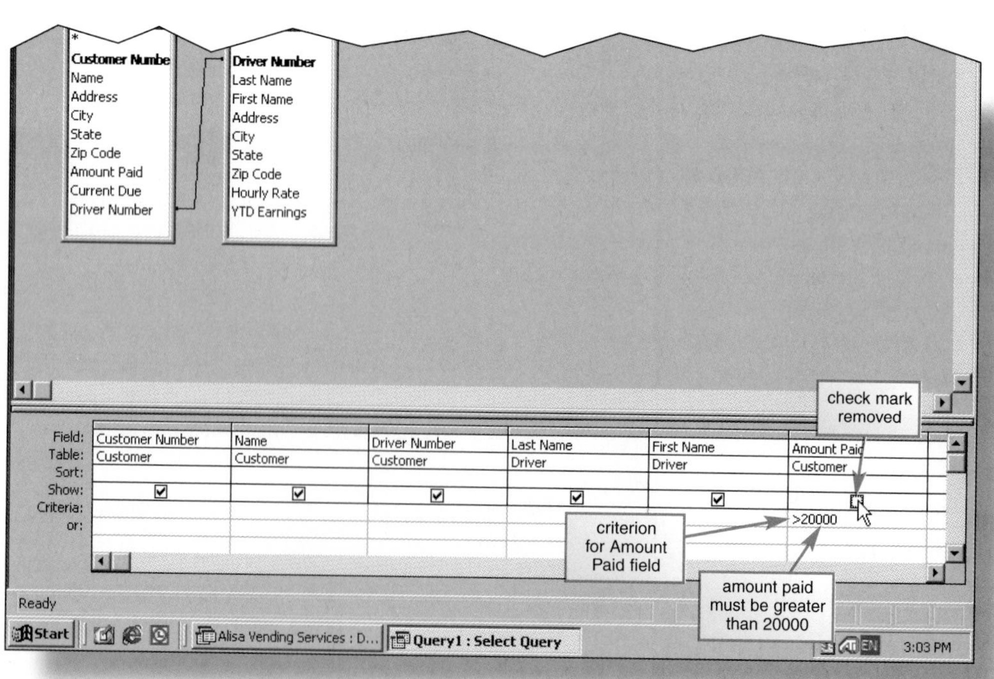

FIGURE 2-50

2 Click the Run button on the Query Design toolbar to run the query.

The results display (Figure 2-51). Only those customers with an amount paid greater than $20,000 display in the result. The Amount Paid field does not display.

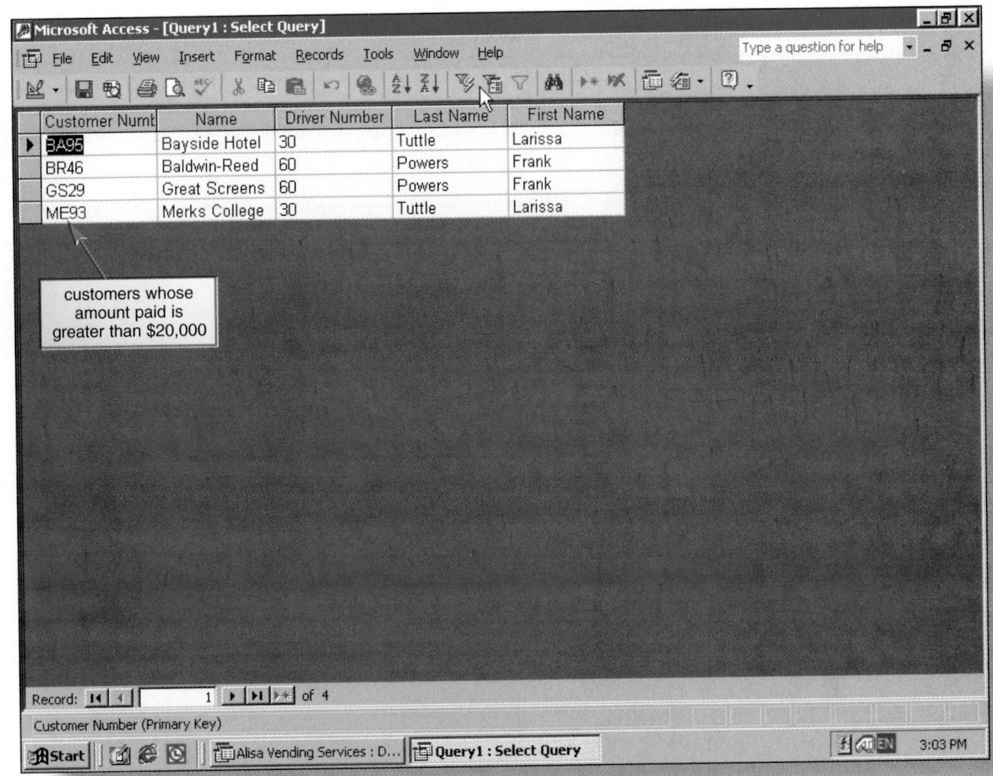

FIGURE 2-51

Using Calculated Fields in a Query

It is important to Alisa Vending Services to know the total amount for each customer; that is, the amount paid plus the current due amount. This poses a problem because the Customer table does not include a field for total amount. You can calculate it, however, because the total amount is equal to the amount paid plus the current due amount. Such a field is called a **calculated field**.

To include calculated fields in queries, you enter a name for the calculated field, a colon, and then the expression in one of the columns in the Field row. Any fields included in the expression must be enclosed in square brackets ([ ]). For the total amount, for example, you will type `Total Amount:[Amount Paid]+[Current Due]` as the expression.

You can type the expression directly into the Field row. You will not be able to see the entire entry, however, because the Field row is not large enough. The preferred way is to select the column in the Field row, right-click to display the shortcut menu, and then click Zoom. The Zoom dialog box displays where you can type the expression.

You are not restricted to addition in calculations. You can use subtraction (-), multiplication (*), or division (/). You also can include parentheses in your calculations to indicate which calculations should be done first.

Perform the steps on the next page to remove the Driver table from the query (it is not needed), and then use a calculated field to display the number, name, and total amount of all customers.

Calculated Fields

Because it is easy to compute values in a query, there is no need to store calculated fields, also called computed fields, in a database.

Formatting Results in a Calculated Field

When you create a calculated field, you may want the results to display in a specific format, for example, currency. To format the results of a calculated field, right-click the calculated field in the design grid. When the property sheet for the field displays, click the Format property box, click the property box arrow, and then select the appropriate format.

Steps To Use a Calculated Field in a Query

1 Click the View button on the Query Datasheet toolbar to return to the Query1 : Select Query window. Right-click any field in the Driver table field list. Point to Remove Table on the shortcut menu.

The shortcut menu displays (Figure 2-52).

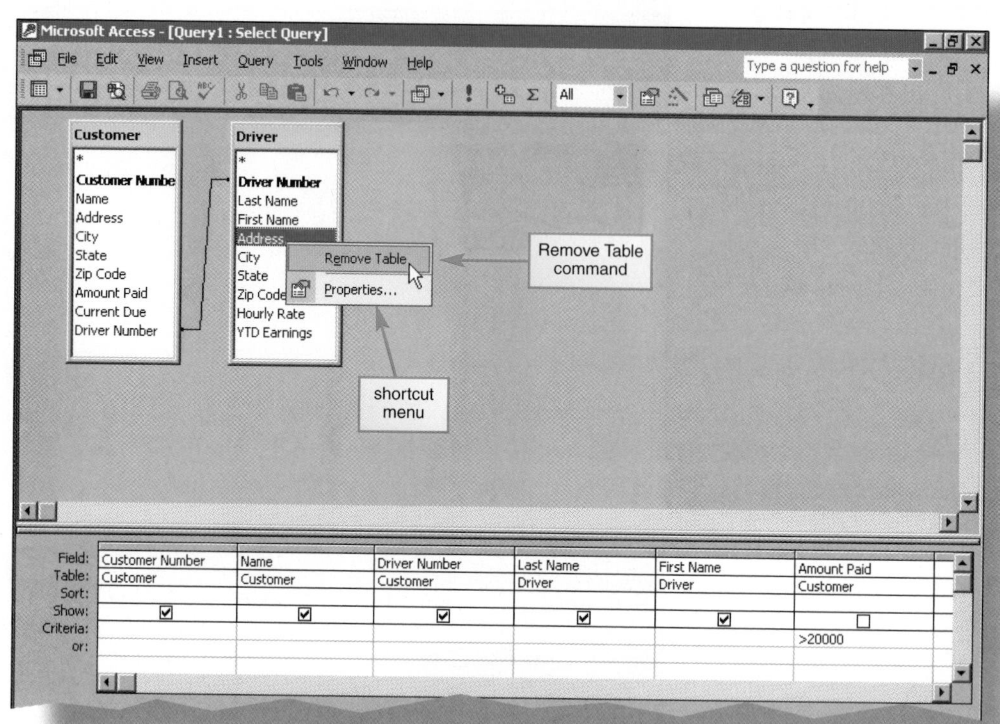

FIGURE 2-52

2 Click Remove Table to remove the Driver table from the Query1 : Select Query window. On the Edit menu, click Clear Grid.

3 Include the Customer Number and Name fields. Right-click the Field row in the first open column in the design grid and then point to Zoom on the shortcut menu.

The shortcut menu displays (Figure 2-53).

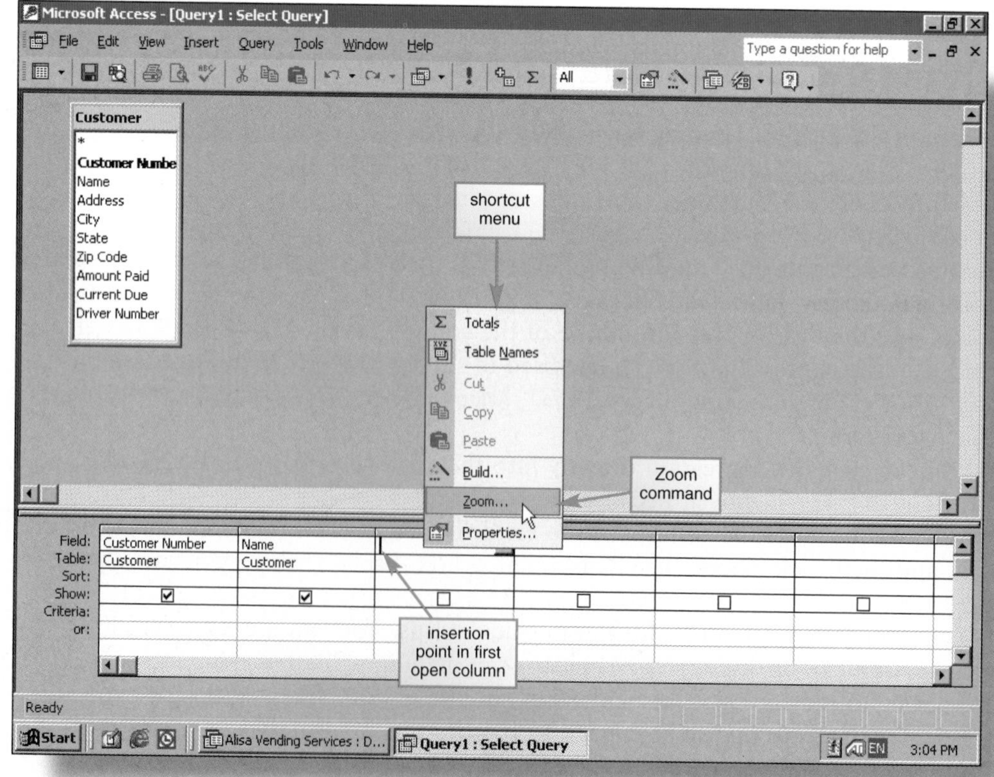

FIGURE 2-53

4 Click Zoom on the shortcut menu. Type `Total Amount:[Amount Paid]+[Current Due]` **in the Zoom dialog box that displays. Point to the OK button.**

The Zoom dialog box displays (Figure 2-54). The expression you typed displays within the dialog box.

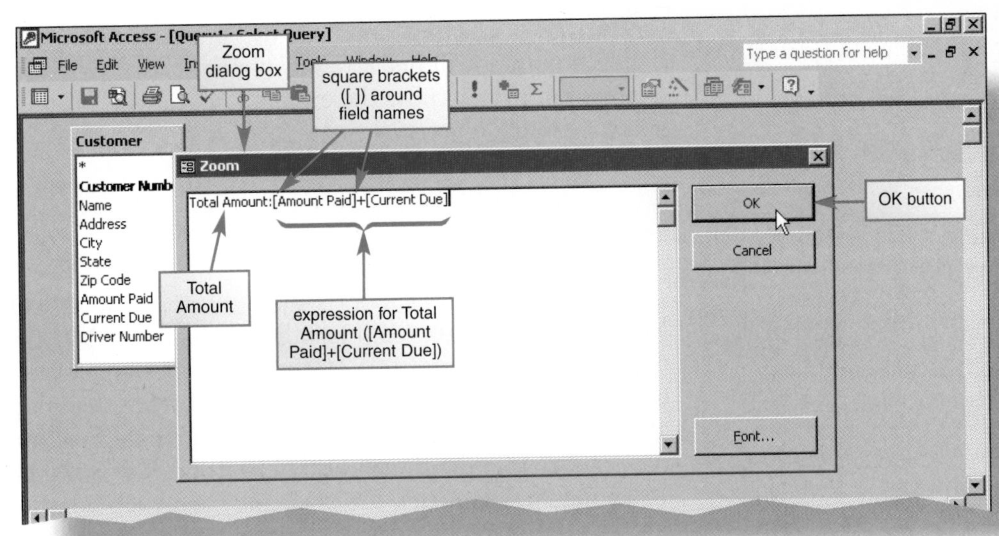

FIGURE 2-54

5 Click the OK button.

The Zoom dialog box no longer displays (Figure 2-55). A portion of the expression you entered displays in the third field in the design grid.

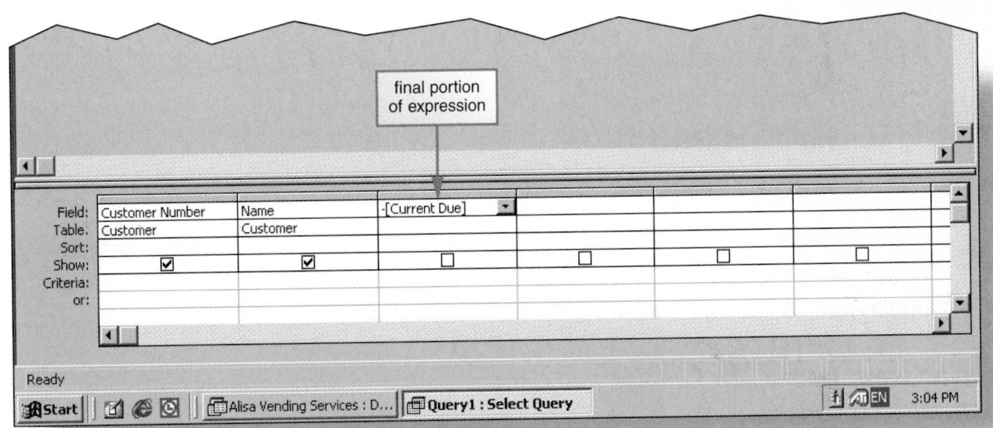

FIGURE 2-55

6 Click the Run button on the Query Design toolbar to run the query.

The results display (Figure 2-56). Microsoft Access has calculated and displayed the total amounts.

Microsoft Access - [Query1 : Select Query]

Customer Numb	Name	Total Amount
BA95	Bayside Hotel	$22,768.50
BR46	Baldwin-Reed	$29,184.00
CN21	Century North	$8,725.00
FR28	Friend's Movies	$5,458.00
GN62	Grand Nelson	$9,213.00
GS29	Great Screens	$21,625.00
LM22	Lenger Mason	$0.00
ME93	Merks College	$26,333.00
RI78	Riter University	$14,509.75
TU20	Turner Hotel	$8,521.50

Total Amount field

FIGURE 2-56

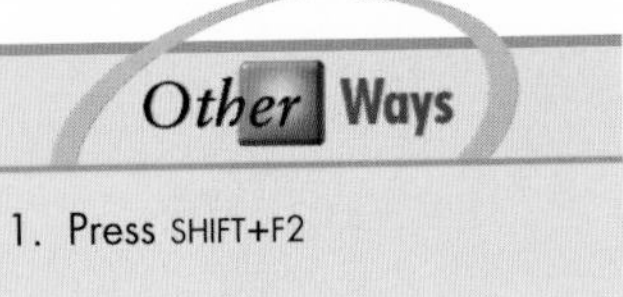

1. Press SHIFT+F2

Renaming Aggregate Results

When you use aggregate functions in a query, Access assigns a default name to the column that displays the result. For example, the column name for the average amount paid is Avgof Amount Paid. You can rename the column by typing the new name directly into the Field row. For example, to change the default column for average amount paid, position the cursor to the left of the field name in the Field row and type Average of Amount Paid: as the new name of the column. Run the query.

Instead of clicking Zoom on the shortcut menu, you can click Build. The Build dialog box then will display. This dialog box provides assistance in creating the expression. If you know the expression you will need, however, it usually is easier to enter it using Zoom.

Calculating Statistics

Microsoft Access supports the built-in statistics: COUNT, SUM, AVG (average), MAX (largest value), MIN (smallest value), STDEV (standard deviation), VAR (variance), FIRST, and LAST. These statistics are called aggregate functions. An **aggregate function** is a function that performs some mathematical function against a group of records. To use any of these aggregate functions in a query, you include it in the Total row in the design grid. The Total row routinely does not appear in the grid. To include it, right-click the grid, and then click Totals on the shortcut menu.

The following example illustrates how you use these functions by calculating the average amount paid for all customers.

To Calculate Statistics

1 **Click the View button on the Query Datasheet toolbar to return to the Query1 : Select Query window. On the Edit menu, click Clear Grid. Right-click the grid and point to Totals on the shortcut menu.**

The shortcut menu displays (Figure 2-57).

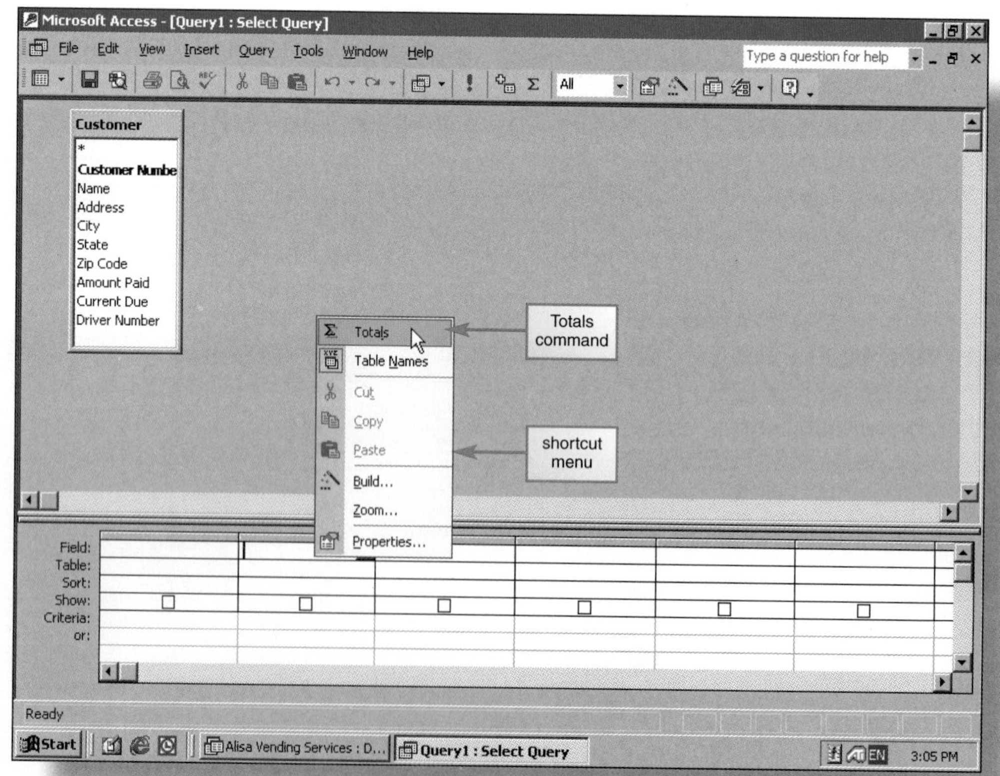

FIGURE 2-57

2 Click Totals on the shortcut menu and then include the Amount Paid field. Point to the Total row in the Amount Paid column.

The Total row now is included in the design grid (Figure 2-58). The Amount Paid field is included, and the entry in the Total row is Group By. The mouse pointer, which has changed shape to an I-beam, is positioned on the Total row under the Amount Paid field.

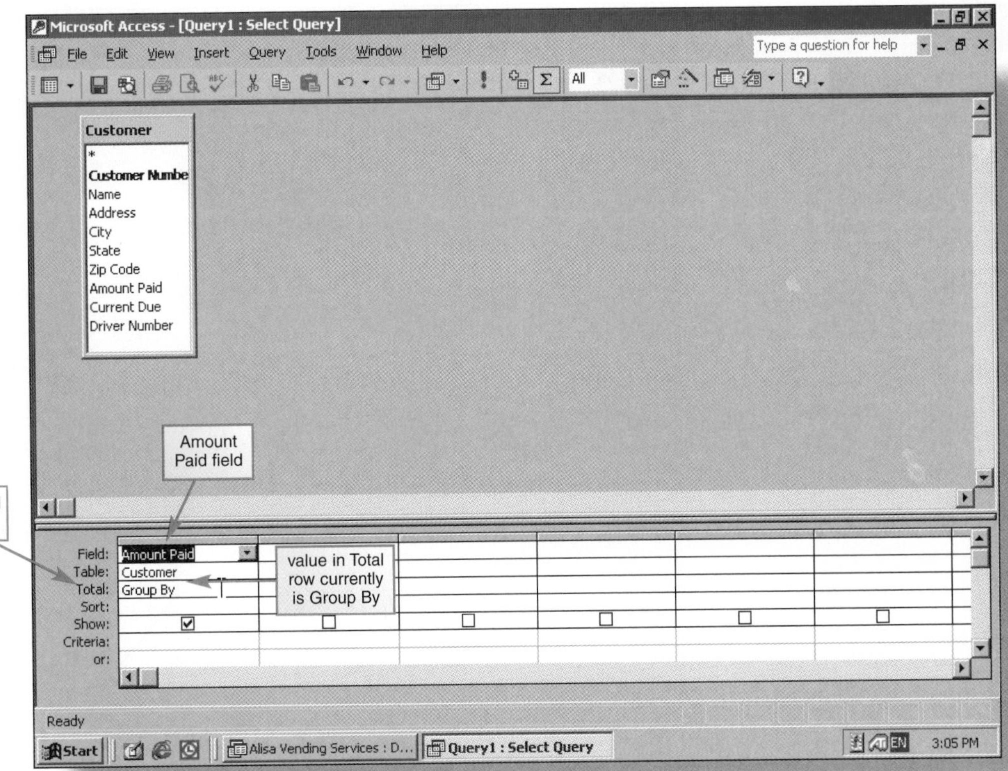

FIGURE 2-58

3 Click the Total row in the Amount Paid column, and then click the row arrow that displays. Point to Avg in the list that displays.

The list of available selections displays (Figure 2-59).

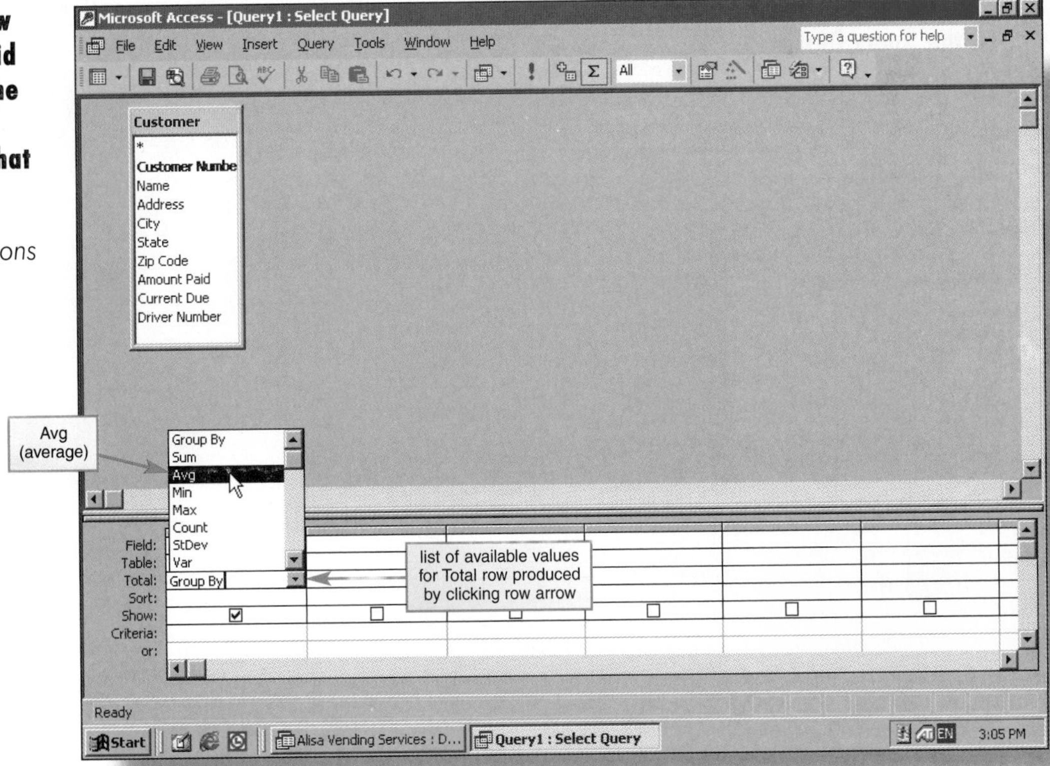

FIGURE 2-59

4 **Click Avg.**

Avg is selected (Figure 2-60).

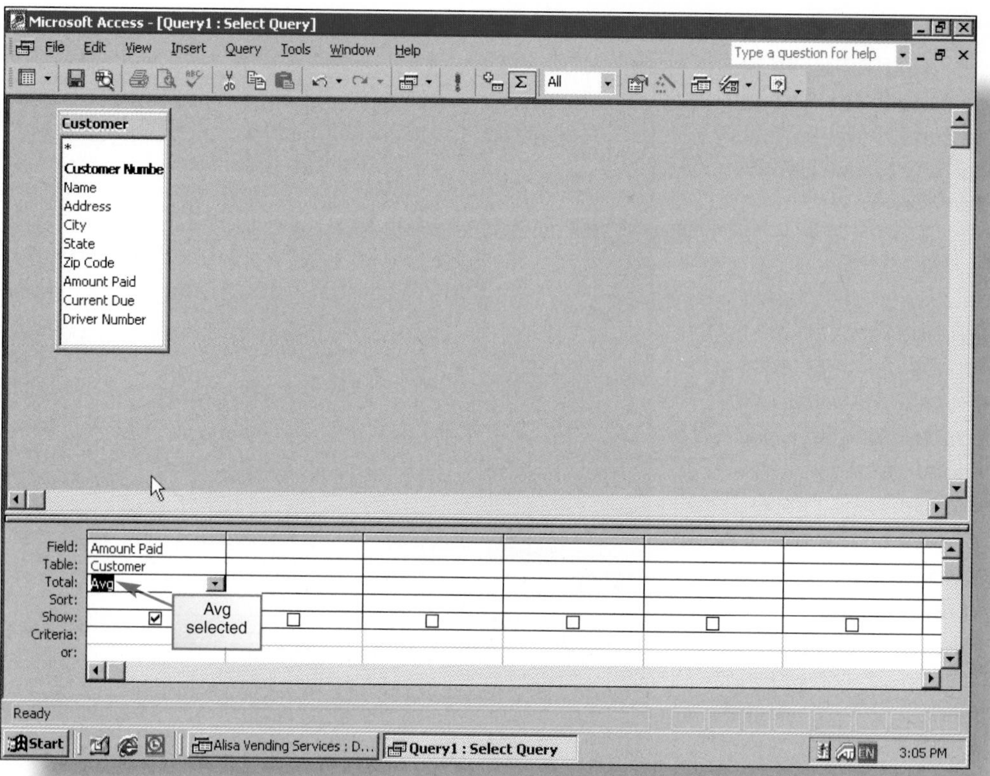

FIGURE 2-60

5 **Click the Run button on the Query Design toolbar to run the query.**

The result displays (Figure 2-61), showing the average amount paid for all customers.

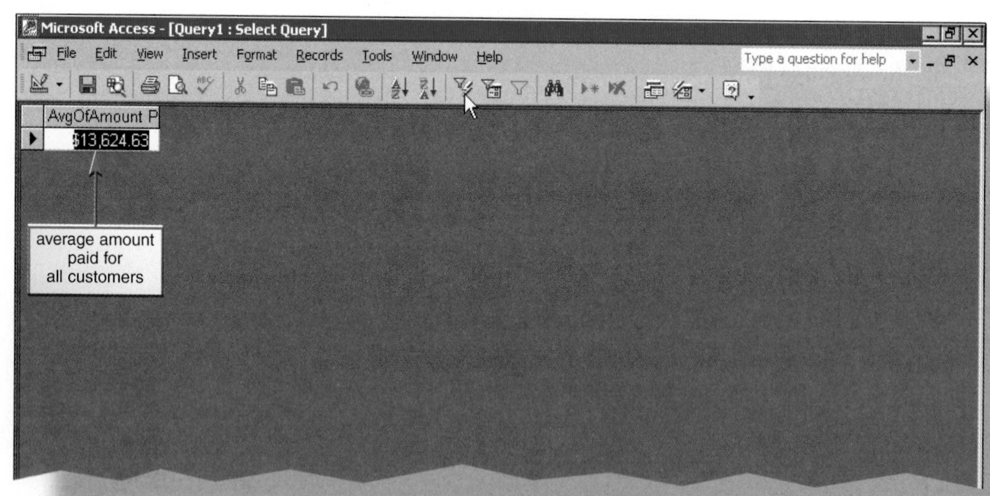

FIGURE 2-61

1. Click Totals button on toolbar
2. On View menu click Totals
3. In Voice Command mode, say "Totals"

Using Criteria in Calculating Statistics

Sometimes calculating statistics for all the records in the table is appropriate. In other cases, however, you will need to calculate the statistics for only those records that satisfy certain criteria. To enter a criterion in a field, first you select Where as the entry in the Total row for the field and then enter the criterion in the Criteria row. The following steps use this technique to calculate the average amount paid for customers of driver 60.

Steps To Use Criteria in Calculating Statistics

1 Click the View button on the Query Datasheet toolbar to return to the Query1 : Select Query window.

2 Include the Driver Number field in the design grid. Produce the list of available options for the Total row entry just as you did when you selected Avg for the Amount Paid field. Use the vertical scroll bar to move through the options until the word, Where, displays. Point to the word, Where, in the list that displays.

The list of available selections displays (Figure 2-62). The Group By entry in the Driver Number field may not be highlighted on your screen depending on where you clicked in the Total row.

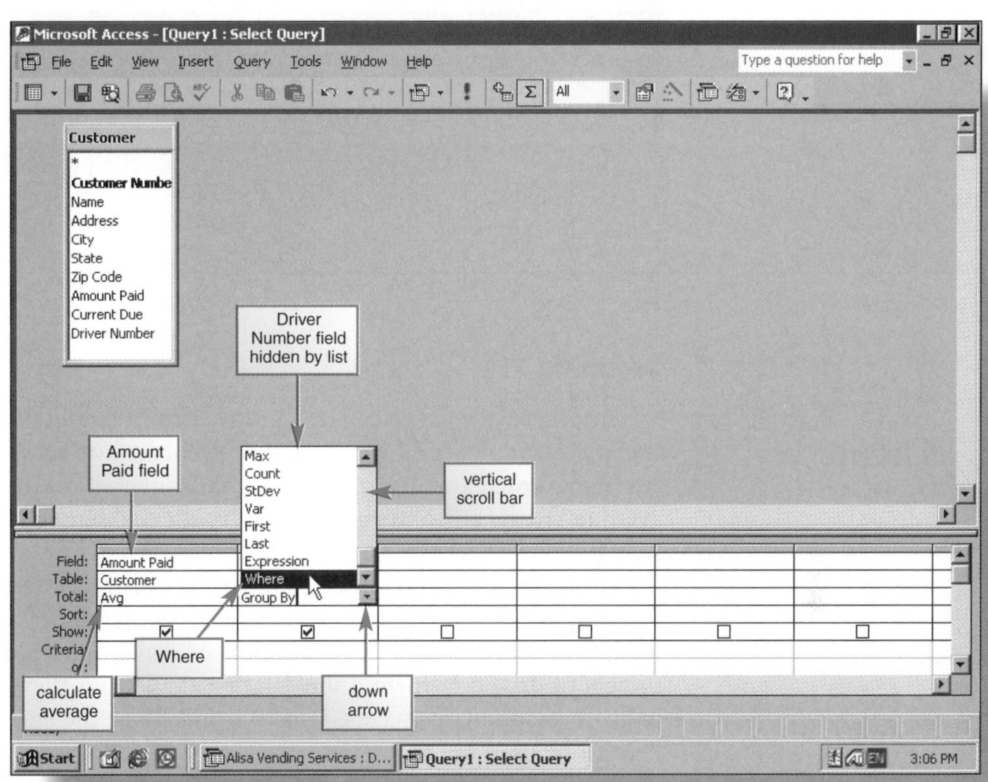

FIGURE 2-62

3 Click Where. Type 60 as the criterion for the Driver Number field.

Where is selected as the entry in the Total row for the Driver Number field (Figure 2-63) and 60 is entered as the Criterion.

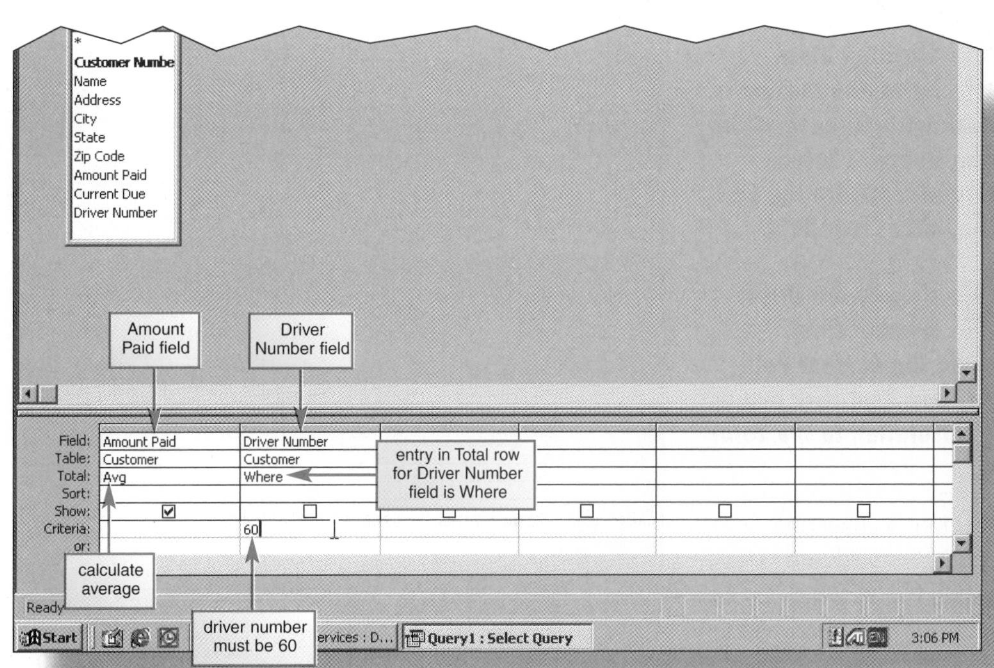

FIGURE 2-63

4 Click the Run button to run the query.

The result displays (Figure 2-64), giving the average amount paid for customers of driver 60.

FIGURE 2-64

Quick Reference

For a table that lists how to complete tasks covered in this book using the mouse, menu, shortcut menu, and keyboard, see the Quick Reference Summary at the back of this book or visit the Shelly Cashman Series Office XP Web page (scsite.com/offxp/qr.htm) and then click Microsoft Access 2002.

Grouping

Another way statistics often are used is in combination with grouping; that is, statistics are calculated for groups of records. You may, for example, need to calculate the average amount paid for the customers of each driver. You will want the average for the customers of driver 30, the average for customers of driver 60, and so on.

Grouping means creating groups of records that share some common characteristic. In grouping by the Driver Number field, for example, the customers of driver 30 would form one group, the customers of driver 60 would be a second, and the customers of driver 75 form a third. The calculations then are made for each group. To indicate grouping in Access, select Group By as the entry in the Total row for the field to be used for grouping.

Perform the following steps to calculate the average amount paid for customers of each driver.

Steps To Use Grouping

1 Click the View button on the Query Datasheet toolbar to return to the Query1 : Select Query window. On the Edit menu, click Clear Grid.

2 Include the Driver Number field. Include the Amount Paid field, and then click Avg as the calculation in the Total row.

The Driver Number and Amount Paid fields are included (Figure 2-65). Group By currently is the entry in the Total row for the Driver Number field, which is correct; thus, it was not changed.

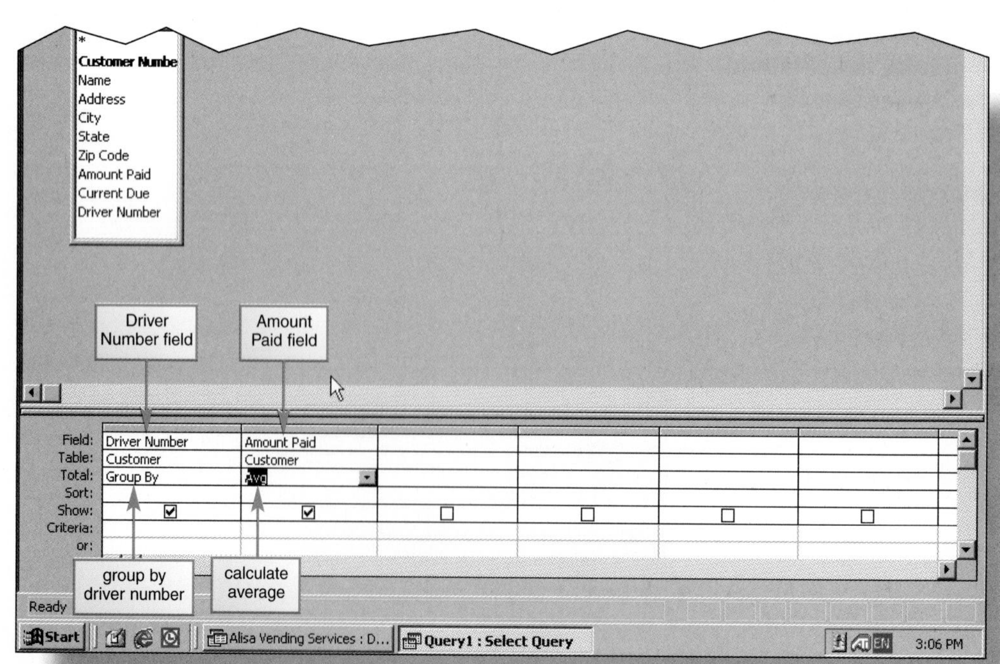

FIGURE 2-65

3 Click the Run button to run the query.

The result displays (Figure 2-66), showing each driver's number along with the average amount paid for the customers of that driver.

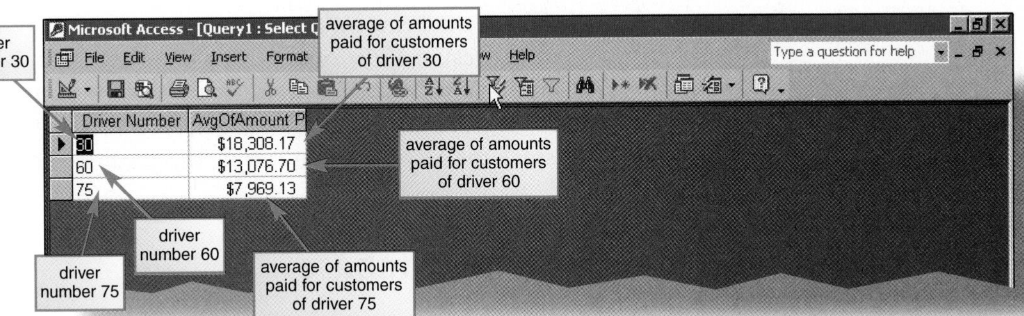

FIGURE 2-66

Saving a Query

In many cases, you will construct a query you will want to use again. By saving the query, you will eliminate the need to repeat all your entries. The following steps illustrate the process by saving the query you just have created and assigning it the name Average Amount Paid by Driver.

More About

Saved Queries

Forms and reports can be based on either tables or saved queries. To create a report or form based on a query, click Queries on the Objects bar, select the query, click the New Object : AutoForm button arrow, and then click the appropriate command (Report or Form). From that point on the process is the same as for a table.

Steps To Save a Query

1 Click the View button on the Query Datasheet toolbar to return to the Query1 : Select Query window. Click the Close Window button to close the window containing the query. Click the Yes button in the Microsoft Access dialog box when asked if you want to save the changes to the design of the query. Type `Average Amount Paid by Driver` **and then point to the OK button.**

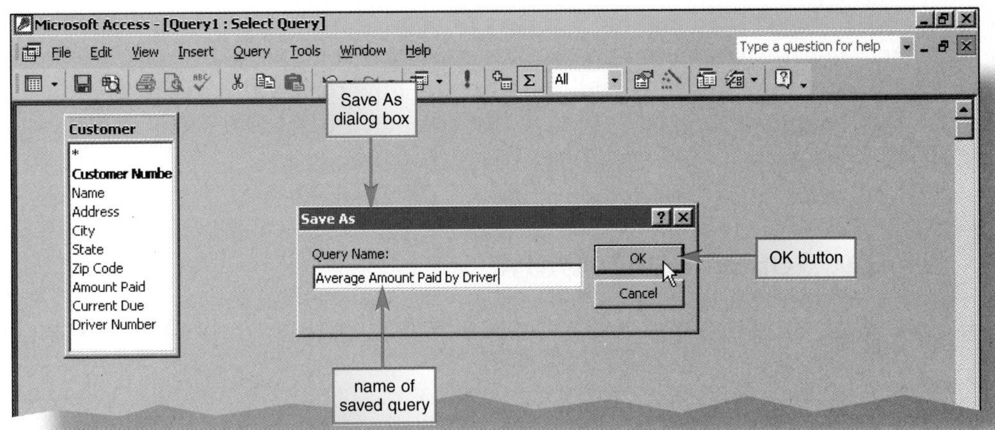

FIGURE 2-67

The Save As dialog box displays with the query name you typed (Figure 2-67).

2 Click the OK button to save the query.

Access saves the query and closes the Query1 : Select Query window.

Other Ways

1. On File menu click Save
2. Press CTRL+S
3. In Voice Command mode, say "Save"

Once you have saved a query, you can use it at any time in the future by opening it. To open a saved query, click the Queries object in the Database window, right-click the query, and then click Open on the shortcut menu. You then could print the

More About

Microsoft Certification

The Microsoft Office User Specialist (MOUS) Certification program provides an opportunity for you to obtain a valuable industry credential — proof that you have the Access 2002 skills required by employers. For more information, see Appendix E or visit the Shelly Cashman Series MOUS Web page at scsite.com/offxp/cert.htm.

results by clicking the Print button. If you wish to change the design of the query, you would click Design View on the shortcut menu instead of Open. If you wanted to print it without first opening it, you would click Print on the shortcut menu.

The query is run against the current database. Thus, if changes have been made to the data since the last time you ran it, the results of the query may be different.

Closing a Database

The following step closes the database by closing its Database window.

TO CLOSE A DATABASE

1 Click the Close Window button for the Alisa Vending Services : Database window.

CASE PERSPECTIVE SUMMARY

In Project 2, you assisted the management of Alisa Vending Services by creating and running queries to obtain answers to important questions. You used various types of criteria in these queries. You joined tables in some of the queries. Some Alisa Vending Services queries used calculated fields and statistics. Finally, you saved one of the queries for future use.

Project Summary

In Project 2, you created and ran a variety of queries. You saw how to select fields in a query. You used text data and wildcards in criteria. You also used comparison operators in criteria involving numeric data. You combined criteria with both AND and OR. You saw how to sort the results of a query, how to join tables, and how to restrict the records in a join. You created computed fields and calculated statistics. You learned how to use grouping as well as how to save a query for future use.

What You Should Know

Having completed this project, you now should be able to perform the following tasks:

- Calculate Statistics *(A 2.36)*
- Clear a Query *(A 2.15)*
- Close a Database *(A 2.42)*
- Close the Query *(A 2.13)*
- Create a Query *(A 2.06)*
- Include All Fields in a Query *(A 2.14)*
- Include Fields in the Design Grid *(A 2.10)*
- Join Tables *(A 2.30)*
- Omit Duplicates *(A 2.26)*
- Open a Database *(A 2.06)*
- Print the Results of a Query *(A 2.11*
- Restrict the Records in a Join *(A 2.32)*
- Return to the Select Query Window *(A 2.12)*
- Run the Query *(A 2.11)*
- Save a Query *(A 2.41)*
- Sort Data in a Query *(A 2.25)*
- Sort on Multiple Keys *(A 2.28)*
- Use a Calculated Field in a Query *(A 2.34)*
- Use a Comparison Operator in a Criterion *(A 2.21)*
- Use a Compound Criterion Involving AND *(A 2.23)*
- Use a Compound Criterion Involving OR *(A 2.24)*
- Use a Number in a Criterion *(A 2.20)*
- Use a Wildcard *(A 2.18)*
- Use Criteria for a Field Not Included in the Results *(A 2.19)*
- Use Criteria in Calculating Statistics *(A 2.39)*
- Use Grouping *(A 2.40)*
- Use Text Data in a Criterion *(A 2.16)*

Learn It Online

Instructions: To complete the Learn It Online exercises, start your browser, click the Address bar, and then enter `scsite.com/offxp/exs.htm`. When the Office XP Learn It Online page displays, follow the instructions in the exercises below

1 Project Reinforcement TF, MC, and SA

Below Access Project 2, click the Project Reinforcement link. Print the quiz by clicking Print on the File menu. Answer each question. Write your first and last name at the top of each page, and then hand in the printout to your instructor.

2 Flash Cards

Below Access Project 2, click the Flash Cards link. When Flash Cards displays, read the instructions. Type `20` (or a number specified by your instructor) in the Number of Playing Cards text box, type your name in the Name text box, and then click the Flip Card button. When the flash card displays, read the question and then click the Answer box arrow to select an answer. Flip through Flash Cards. Click Print on the File menu to print the last flash card if your score is 15 (75%) correct or greater and then hand it in to your instructor. If your score is less than 15 (75%) correct, then redo this exercise by clicking the Replay button.

3 Practice Test

Below Access Project 2, click the Practice Test link. Answer each question, enter your first and last name at the bottom of the page, and then click the Grade Test button. When the graded practice test displays on your screen, click Print on the File menu to print a hard copy. Continue to take practice tests until you score 80% or better. Hand in a printout of the final practice test to your instructor.

4 Who Wants to Be a Computer Genius?

Below Access Project 2, click the Computer Genius link. Read the instructions, enter your first and last name at the bottom of the page, and then click the Play button. Hand in your score to your instructor.

5 Wheel of Terms

Below Access Project 2, click the Wheel of Terms link. Read the instructions, and then enter your first and last name and your school name. Click the Play button. Hand in your score to your instructor.

6 Crossword Puzzle Challenge

Below Access Project 2, click the Crossword Puzzle Challenge link. Read the instructions, and then enter your first and last name. Click the Play button. Work the crossword puzzle. When you are finished, click the Submit button. When the crossword puzzle redisplays, click the Print button. Hand in the printout.

7 Tips and Tricks

Below Access Project 2, click the Tips and Tricks link. Click a topic that pertains to Project 2. Right-click the information and then click Print on the shortcut menu. Construct a brief example of what the information relates to in Access to confirm you understand how to use the tip or trick. Hand in the example and printed information.

8 Newsgroups

Below Access Project 2, click the Newsgroups link. Click a topic that pertains to Project 2. Print three comments. Hand in the comments to your instructor.

9 Expanding Your Horizons

Below Access Project 2, click the Articles for Microsoft Access link. Click a topic that pertains to Project 2. Print the information. Construct a brief example of what the information relates to in Access to confirm you understand the contents of the article. Hand in the example and printed information to your instructor.

10 Search Sleuth

Below Access Project 2, click the Search Sleuth link. To search for a term that pertains to this project, select a term below the Project 2 title and then use the Google search engine at google.com (or any major search engine) to display and print two Web pages that present information on the term. Hand in the printouts to your instructor.

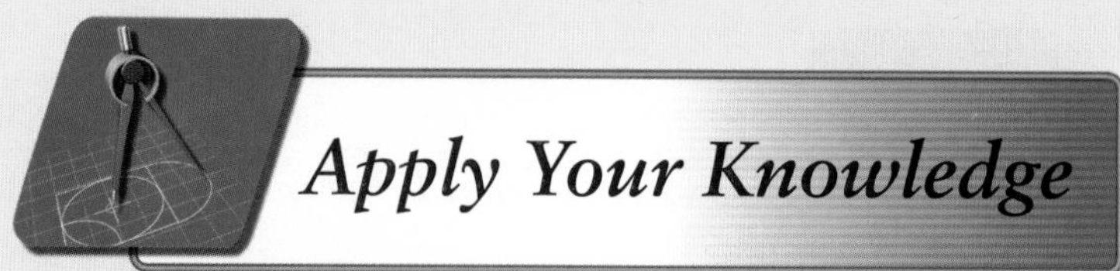

1 Querying the Beyond Clean Database

Instructions: Start Access. Open the database Beyond Clean that you used in Project 1 or see your instructor for information on accessing the files required for this book. Perform the following tasks.

1. Create a new query for the Client table.
2. Add the Client Number, Name, and Address fields to the design grid.
3. Restrict retrieval to only those records where the customer has an address on Mallery.
4. Run the query and print the results.
5. Return to Design view and clear the grid.
6. Add the Client Number, Name, Address, Telephone Number, and Balance fields to the design grid.
7. Restrict retrieval to only those records where the balance is greater than $125.
8. Run the query and print the results.
9. Return to Design view and clear the grid.
10. Add the Client Number, Name, Address, and Custodian Id to the design grid.
11. Restrict retrieval to only those records where the Custodian Id is either 011 or 013.
12. Run the query and print the results.
13. Return to Design view and clear the grid.
14. Display and print the cities in ascending order. Each city should display only once.
15. Run the query and print the results.
16. Return to Design view and clear the grid.
17. Join the Client and Custodian tables. Add the Client Number, Name, and Custodian Id fields from the Client table and the First Name and Last Name fields from the Custodian table.
18. Sort the records in ascending order by Custodian Id.
19. Run the query and print the results.

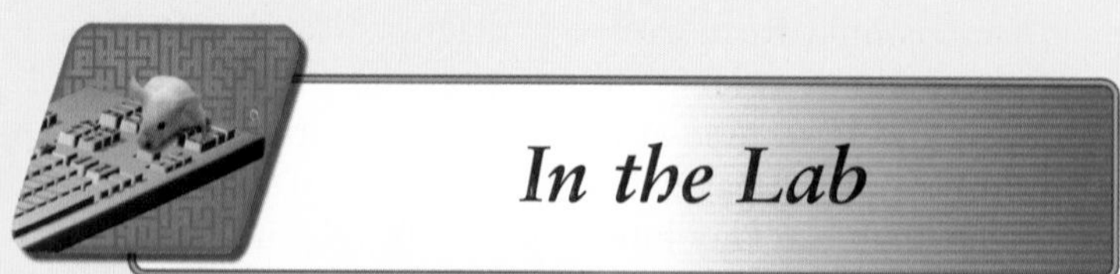

1 Querying the Wooden Crafts Database

Problem: Jan Merchant has determined a number of questions she wants the database management system to answer. You must obtain the answers to the questions posed by Jan.

Instructions: Use the database created in the In the Lab 1 of Project 1 for this assignment or see your instructor for information on accessing the files required for this book. Perform the following tasks.

1. Open the Wooden Crafts database.
2. Use the Simple Query Wizard to create a new query to display and print the Product Id, Description, On Hand, and Selling Price for records in the table as shown in Figure 2-68. (*Hint:* See More About Queries: The Simple Query Wizard on page A 2.06 to solve this problem.)

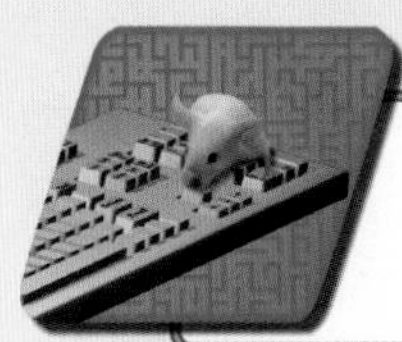

In the Lab

3. Display all fields and print all the records in the table.
4. Display and print the Product Id, Description, Cost, and Supplier Code fields for all products where the Supplier Code is AP.
5. Display and print the Product Id and Description fields for all items where the description includes the letters, rail.
6. Display and print the Product Id, Description, and Supplier Code fields for all items with a cost less than $15.
7. Display and print the Product Id and Description fields for all products that have a selling price greater than $30.
8. Display and print all fields for those items with a selling price greater than $10 and where the number on hand is at least 10.
9. Display and print all fields for those items that have a supplier code of PL or a selling price greater than $30.
10. Join the Product table and the Supplier table. Display the Product Id, Description, Cost, First Name, Last Name, and Telephone Number fields. Run the query and print the results.
11. Restrict the records retrieved in task 10 above to only those products where number on hand is less than 5. Run the query and print the results.
12. Remove the Supplier table and clear the design grid.
13. Include the Product Id and Description fields in the design grid. Calculate the on-hand value (on hand * cost) for all records in the table. Run the query and print the results.

Microsoft Access - [Product Query : Select Query]

File Edit View Insert Format Records Tools Window Help | Type a question for help

Product Id	Description	On Hand	Selling Price
BF01	Barnyard Friend	3	$60.00
BL23	Blocks in Box	5	$32.00
CC14	Coal Car	8	$18.00
FT05	Fire Truck	7	$12.00
LB34	Lacing Bear	4	$16.00
MR06	Midget Railroad	3	$34.00
PJ12	Pets Jigsaw	10	$12.00
RB02	Railway Bridge	1	$20.00
SK10	Skyscraper	6	$30.00
UM09	USA Map	12	$18.00
*		0	$0.00

FIGURE 2-68

14. Display and print the average selling price of all products.
15. Display and print the average selling price of products grouped by supplier code.
16. Join the Product and Supplier tables. Include the Supplier Code, First Name, and Last Name fields from the Supplier table. Include the Product Id, Description, Cost, and On Hand fields from the Product table. Sort the query in ascending order by the Supplier Code field. Run the query and print the results. Save the query as Suppliers and Products.

2 Querying the Restaurant Supply Database

Problem: The restaurant supply company has determined a number of questions that they want the database management system to answer. You must obtain the answers to the questions posed by the company.

(continued)

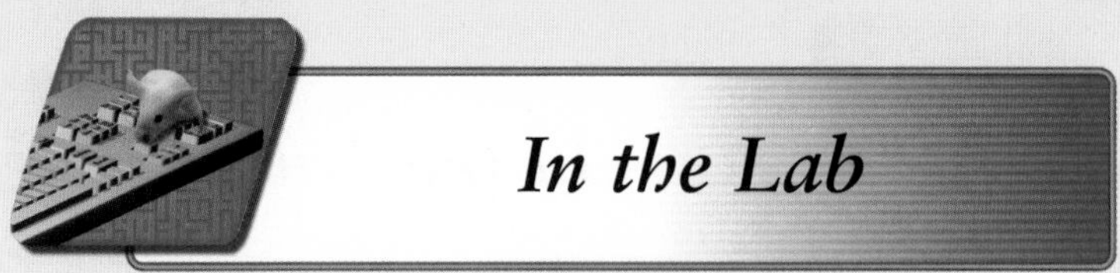

Querying the Restaurant Supply Database *(continued)*

Instructions: Use the database created in the In the Lab 2 of Project 1 for this assignment or see your instructor for information on accessing the files required for this book. Perform the following tasks.

1. Open the Restaurant Supply database and create a new query for the Customer table.
2. Display and print the Customer Number, Name, Balance, and Amount Paid fields for all the records in the table.
3. Display and print the Customer Number, Name, and Balance fields for all customers where the sales rep number is 51.
4. Display and print the Customer Number, Name, and Balance fields for all customers where the balance is greater than $100.
5. Display and print the Customer Number, Name, and Amount Paid fields for all customers where the sales rep number is 49 and the amount paid is greater than $1,000.
6. Display and print the Customer Number, Name, and Address fields for all customers with an address on Devon.
7. Display and print the Customer Number, Name, and Balance fields for all customers where the sales rep number is 49 or the balance is less than $50.
8. Include the Customer Number, Name, and Balance fields in the design grid. Sort the records in descending order by the Balance field. Display and print the results.
9. Display and print the Customer Number, Name, and Amount Paid fields for all customers where the sales rep number is 44 or 49 and the balance is greater than $100. (***Hint:*** See More About Compound Criteria on page A 2.22 to solve this problem.)
10. Display and print the Customer Number, Name, Balance, and Amount Paid fields from the Customer table and the First Name, Last Name, and Comm Rate fields from the Sales Rep table.
11. Restrict the records retrieved in task 10 above to only those customers that have a balance of 0. Display and print the results.
12. Clear the design grid and add the First Name, Last Name, and Comm Rate fields from the Sales Rep table to the grid. Add the Name and Balance fields from the Customer table. Calculate the pending commission (balance * comm rate) for the Sales Rep table. Sort the records in ascending order by last name and format pending commission as currency. (***Hint:*** See More About Formatting Results in a Calculated Field on page A 2.33 to solve this problem.) Run the query and print the results.
13. Display and print the following statistics: the total balance and total amount paid for all customers; the total balance for customers of sales rep 44; and the total amount paid for each sales rep.
14. Create a query that includes the Sales Rep Number, Last Name, First Name, Customer Number, Name, Balance, and Amount Paid fields. Sort the query in ascending order by the Sales Rep Number field. Run the query and then save the query as Sales Reps and Customers.

3 Querying the Condo Management Database

Problem: The condo management company has determined a number of questions that they want the database management system to answer. You must obtain the answers to the questions posed by the company.

In the Lab

Instructions: Use the database created in the In the Lab 3 of Project 1 for this assignment or see your instructor for information on accessing the files required for this book. Perform the following tasks.

1. Open the Condo Management database and create a new query for the Condo table.
2. Display and print the Unit Number, Weekly Rate, and Owner Id fields for all the records in the table as shown in Figure 2-69.

Microsoft Access - [Query1 : Select Query]

File Edit View Insert Format Records Tools Window Help — Type a question for help

Unit Number	Weekly Rate	Owner Id
101	$675.00	HJ05
108	$1,050.00	AB10
202	$1,400.00	BR18
204	$1,100.00	BR18
206	$925.00	GM50
308	$950.00	GM50
403	$700.00	HJ05
405	$750.00	AB10
500	$1,100.00	AB10
510	$825.00	BR18
*	$0.00	

FIGURE 2-69

3. Display and print the Unit Number and Weekly Rate fields for all units that rent for less than $1,000 per week.
4. Display and print the Unit Number, Sleeps, and Weekly Rate for all units that sleep more than four people and have a powder room.
5. Display and print the Unit Number, Bedrooms, and Weekly Rate fields for all units that have 2 bedrooms and a powder room or that have 3 bedrooms. (***Hint:*** See More About Compound Criteria on page A 2.22 to solve this problem.)
6. Display and print the Unit Number and Weekly Rate fields for all units that are on the fifth floor. (***Hint:*** The first digit of the Unit Number field indicates the floor.)
7. Display and print the Unit Number, Bedrooms, and Weekly Rate fields for all units that have more than one bedroom and more than one bathroom and provide linens.
8. Include the Unit Number, Bedrooms, Sleeps, and Weekly Rate fields in the design grid. Sort the records in descending order by bedrooms within sleeps. The Bedrooms field should display in the result to the left of the Sleeps field. (***Hint:*** Use Microsoft Access Help to solve this problem.)
9. Display and print the weekly rates in descending order. Each rate should display only once.
10. Display and print the Unit Number and Weekly Rate fields from the Condo table and First Name, Last Name, and Telephone fields from the Owner table.
11. Restrict the records retrieved in task 10 above to only those units that rent for more than $1,000 per week. Display and print the results.
12. Clear the design grid and remove the Owner table from the query. Owner BR18 offers a 15 percent discount on the weekly rate if renters rent for more than one week at a time. What is the discounted weekly rental rate for her units? Display the unit number, bedrooms, bathrooms, sleeps, and discounted weekly rate in your result. Format the discounted weekly rate as currency. (***Hint:*** See More About Formatting Results in a Calculated Field on page A 2.33 to solve this problem.) Run the query and print the results.
13. Display and print the average weekly rate for each owner.
14. Create a query that includes the Owner Id, First Name, Last Name, Unit Number, and Weekly Rate fields. Sort the query in ascending order by the Owner Id field. Save the query as Owners and Condo Units.

Cases and Places

The difficulty of these case studies varies:
▶ are the least difficult; ▶▶ are more difficult; and ▶▶▶ are the most difficult.

1 ▶ Use the Computer Expertise database you created in Case Study 1 of Project 1 for this assignment. You now want to use the database to find answers to questions that will help you manage your company better. Perform the following: (a) Display and print the customer number, name, and telephone number of all customers whose name begins with the letter L. (b) Display and print the customer number, name, telephone number, and balance for all customers who have a balance greater than $150. (c) Display and print the customer number, name, balance, helper first name, and helper last name for all customers. Sort the records in ascending order by helper last name. (d) Display and print the average balance of all customers. (e) Display and print the average balance of customers grouped by helper. (f) Display and print the total balance of all customers.

2 ▶ Use the Baseball database you created in Case Study 2 of Project 1 for this assignment. The marketing team has put together a list of the most common type of questions they would like to ask the database. They want to know if the database you created can answer these questions. Perform the following: (a) Display and print the description, cost, and units on hand of all items supplied by Beverage Holders. (b) Display and print the item id, description, and on-hand value (units on hand * cost) of all items. (c) Display and print the item id, description, units on hand, and current profit (selling price – cost) of all items that have a selling price greater than $15. (d) Display and print the item id, description, units on hand, supplier name, and supplier telephone number for all items where there are less than 10 items on hand. (e) Display and print the description and selling price sorted in ascending order by selling price. (f) Find the lowest priced item and the highest priced item.

3 ▶▶ Use the local attractions database you created in Case Study 3 of Project 1 for this assignment. The tourism director is pleased with the database you have created. You have asked her to put together a list of questions for which she regularly will need the answers. Perform the following: (a) List the name and telephone number of all attractions. (b) List all attractions by type of attraction. (c) List all attractions that have no cost associated with them. (d) List all attractions that do have a cost associated with them. (e) List all attractions that are open on Sunday. (f) List all attractions that are historic homes.

4 ▶▶ Use the high school Math club database you created in Case Study 4 of Project 1 for this assignment. Display and print the following: (a) A list of all high school students involved in the tutoring program. (b) A list of all elementary students being tutored. (c) A list of all high school students along with the students they are tutoring. Sort the list by high school student. (d) The elementary school student with the highest number of points. (e) The high school student with the highest number of hours tutored. (f) The total number of hours spent tutoring. (g) The total number of hours spent tutoring by high school student. Change the default column headings for those queries that calculate statistics.

5 ▶▶▶ Use the hobby or collection database you created in Case Study 5 of Project 1 for this assignment. Develop a list of questions that you want the database to be able to answer. Query the database using the list you developed and print the results.

Microsoft Access 2002

PROJECT

Maintaining a Database Using the Design and Update Features of Access

OBJECTIVES

You will have mastered the material in this project when you can:

- Add records to a table
- Locate records
- Filter records
- Change the contents of records in a table
- Delete records from a table
- Restructure a table
- Change field characteristics
- Add a field
- Save the changes to the structure
- Update the contents of a single field
- Make changes to groups of records
- Delete groups of records
- Create validation rules
- Update a table with validation rules
- Specify referential integrity
- Use subdatasheets
- Order records
- Create single-field and multiple-field indexes

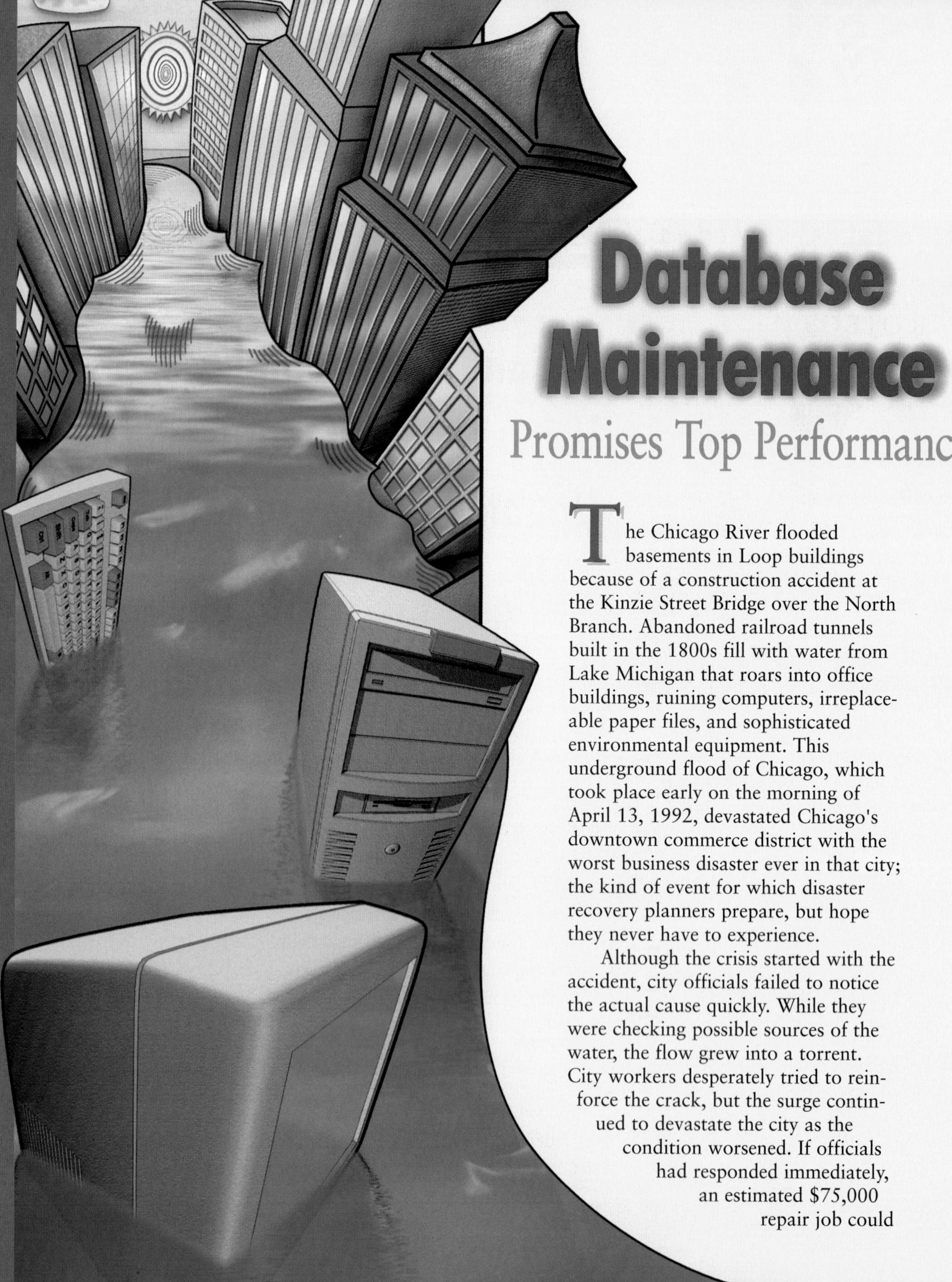

Database Maintenance

Promises Top Performance

The Chicago River flooded basements in Loop buildings because of a construction accident at the Kinzie Street Bridge over the North Branch. Abandoned railroad tunnels built in the 1800s fill with water from Lake Michigan that roars into office buildings, ruining computers, irreplaceable paper files, and sophisticated environmental equipment. This underground flood of Chicago, which took place early on the morning of April 13, 1992, devastated Chicago's downtown commerce district with the worst business disaster ever in that city; the kind of event for which disaster recovery planners prepare, but hope they never have to experience.

Although the crisis started with the accident, city officials failed to notice the actual cause quickly. While they were checking possible sources of the water, the flow grew into a torrent. City workers desperately tried to reinforce the crack, but the surge continued to devastate the city as the condition worsened. If officials had responded immediately, an estimated $75,000 repair job could have saved the city the eventual $1 billion loss. Individuals seldom are faced with problems that have such massive financial impact. Unlike the Maytag repairman, however, people must contend with maintenance issues on a regular basis: cars, homes, dental work, even personal computers. All are issues important to health, safety, and well-being. How a person handles these can make the difference between a happy life and a trying one. Likewise, for many business people, scientific researchers, and self-employed individuals, professional survival depends on maintaining their computer databases.

Information flows in today's world like the waters of all the rivers combined. From telephone lines, customer service terminals, satellite feeds, the mail, and so on, literally billions of pieces of data enter daily into the databases of entities such as insurance companies, banks, mail-order firms, astronomical observatories, medical research labs, doctors' offices, automobile dealerships, home-based businesses, and multitudesof others. Based on the content of this information, decisions are made and actions taken, often triggering a corresponding flow of information to other interested users. The process of handling this data — the lifeblood of today's information-based society — is known as database maintenance.

Microsoft Access 2002 is a powerful tool that facilitates designing the database and then maintaining it with ease. Effective design and update features in Access allow you to add, change, and delete records in a table, change the size of or add new fields to the database, and then quickly update the restructured database. In this project, you will learn the techniques to maintain any type of database with which you might work in your academic or professional life.

During college, you may use a personal database to organize and maintain information such as names, addresses, and telephone numbers of friends, family, and club members, or possessions such as a CD or tape collection, videos, or books. As a club member, you may be asked to design, update, and maintain a database of club members and information.

Your first use for a database may come when you start your search for the right graduate school or as you begin your mailing campaign for future employment opportunities. Once employed, you will be exposed to the use of databases in all facets of business. Learning the important skills associated with database maintenance will pave the way for opportunity in the workplace.

Although a mundane task at best, the effort you expend in database maintenance will assure you are prepared when restoring computer operations in the event of a disaster.

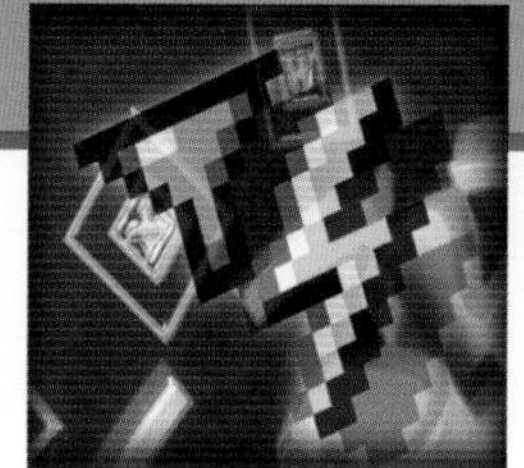

Microsoft Access 2002

Maintaining a Database Using the Design and Update Features of Access

PROJECT

CASE PERSPECTIVE

Alisa Vending Services has created and loaded its database. The management and staff have received many benefits from the database, including the ability to ask a variety of questions concerning the data in the database. They now face the task of keeping the database up to date. They must add new records as they take on new customers and drivers. They must make changes to existing records to reflect additional billings, payments, changes of address, and so on. Alisa Vending Services also found that it needed to change the structure of the database in two specific ways. The management decided they needed to categorize the customers by type, so they need to add a Customer Type field to the Customer table. They also discovered the Name field was too short to contain the name of one of the customers so they need to enlarge the field. In addition, they want to establish rules for the data entered in the database to ensure that users can enter only valid data. Finally, they determined they want to improve the efficiency of certain types of processing, specifically sorting and retrieving data. Your task is to help Alisa Vending Services in all these activities.

Introduction

Once a database has been created and loaded with data, it must be maintained. **Maintaining the database** means modifying the data to keep it up to date, such as adding new records, changing the data for existing records, and deleting records. **Updating** can include **mass updates** or **mass deletions**; that is, updates to, or deletions of, many records at the same time.

In addition to adding, changing, and deleting records, maintenance of a database periodically can involve the need to **restructure** the database; that is, to change the database structure. This can include adding new fields to a table, changing the characteristics of existing fields, and removing existing fields. It also can involve the creation of **indexes**, which are similar to indexes found in the back of books and are used to improve the efficiency of certain operations.

Figure 3-1 summarizes some of the various types of activities involved in maintaining a database.

Project Three — Maintaining the Alisa Vending Services Database

You are to make the changes to the data in the Alisa Vending Services database as requested by the management of Alisa Vending Services. You must restructure the database to meet the current needs of Alisa Vending Services. This includes adding an additional field as well as increasing the width of one of the existing fields. You must modify the structure of the database in a way that prevents users from entering invalid data. Finally, management is concerned that some operations, for example, those involving sorting the data, are taking longer than they would like. You are to create indexes to attempt to address this problem.

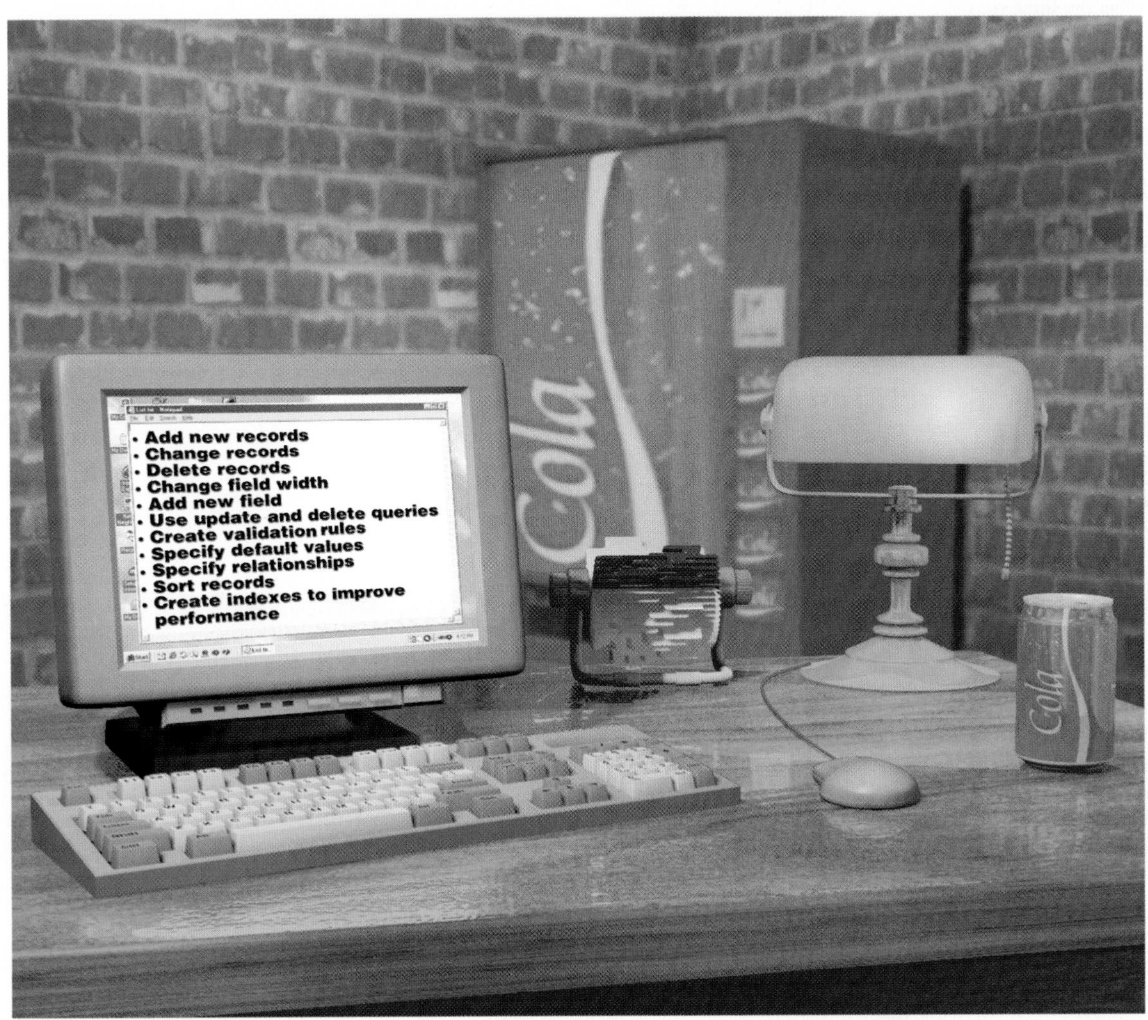
• Add new records
• Change records
• Delete records
• Change field width
• Add new field
• Use update and delete queries
• Create validation rules
• Specify default values
• Specify relationships
• Sort records
• Create indexes to improve performance
Cola
Cola

FIGURE 3-1

Opening the Database

Before carrying out the steps in this project, first you must open the database. To do so, perform the following steps.

TO OPEN A DATABASE

1. Click the Start button, click Programs on the Start menu, and then click Microsoft Access on the Programs submenu.
2. Click Open on the Database toolbar and then click 3½ Floppy (A:) in the Look in box. If necessary, click the Alisa Vending Services database name.
3. Click the Open button.

The database opens and the Alisa Vending Services : Database window displays.

More About

Maintaining a Database: Backup

Before making changes to the database, it is a good idea to make a copy of the database (called a backup or a save copy). To do so, use the copy features in Windows to copy the database to another file with a different name (for example, Alisa Vending Backup).

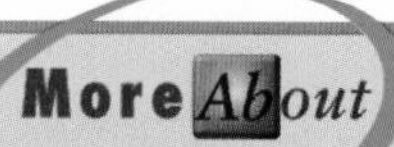

Maintaining a Database: Recovery

If a problem occurs that damages either the data in the database or the structure of the database, the database is recovered by copying the backup copy over it. To do so, use the copy features of Windows to copy the backup version (for example, Alisa Vending Backup) over the actual database (for example, Alisa Vending Services). This will return the database to the state it was in when the backup was made.

Adding, Changing, and Deleting

Keeping the data in a database up to date requires three tasks: adding new records, changing the data in existing records, and deleting existing records.

Adding Records

In Project 1, you added records to a database using Datasheet view; that is, as you were adding records, the records were displayed on the screen in the form of a datasheet, or table. When you need to add additional records, you can use the same techniques.

In Project 1, you used a form to view records. This is called **Form view**. You also can use Form view to update the data in a table. To add new records, change existing records, or delete records, you will use the same techniques you used in Datasheet view. To add a record to the Customer table with a form, for example, use the following steps. These steps use the Customer form you created in Project 1.

Steps To Use a Form to Add Records

1 With the Alisa Vending Services database open, point to Forms on the Objects bar (Figure 3-2).

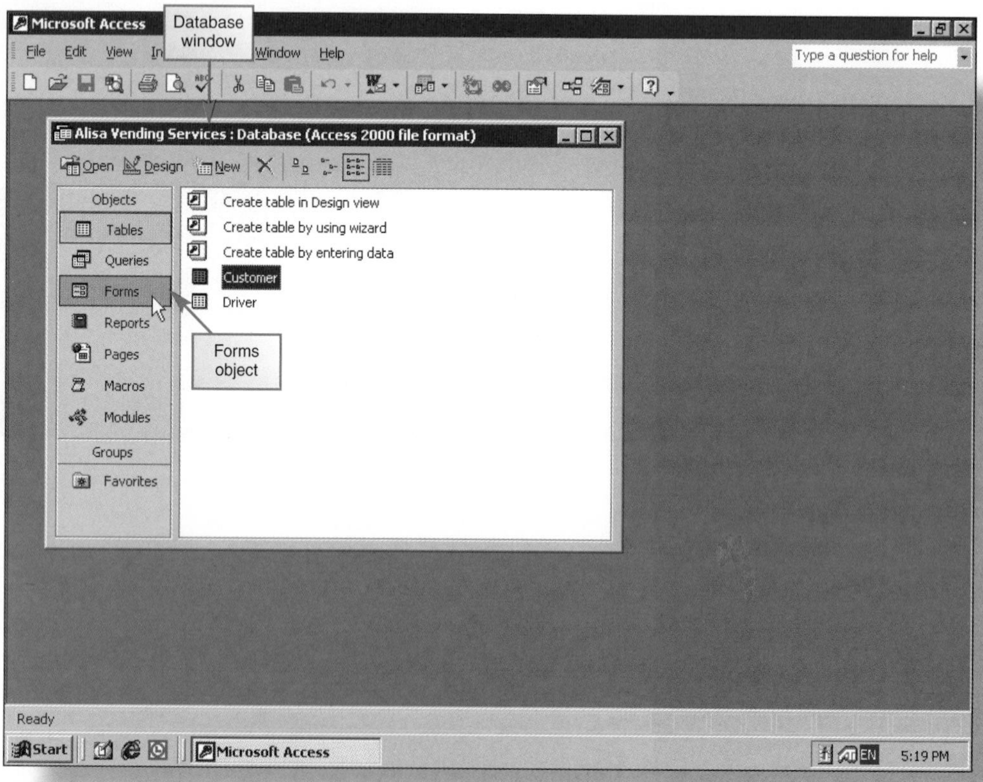

FIGURE 3-2

2 Click Forms. Right-click Customer and then point to Open on the shortcut menu.

The shortcut menu displays (Figure 3-3).

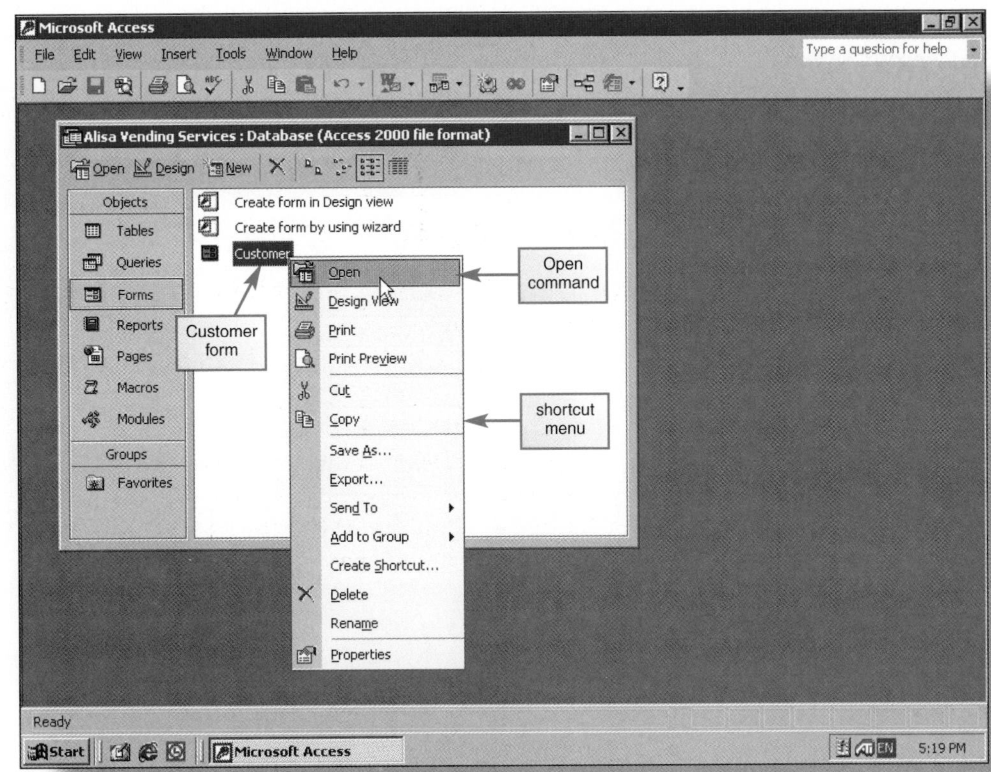

FIGURE 3-3

3 Click Open on the shortcut menu and then point to the New Record button.

The form for the Customer table displays (Figure 3-4).

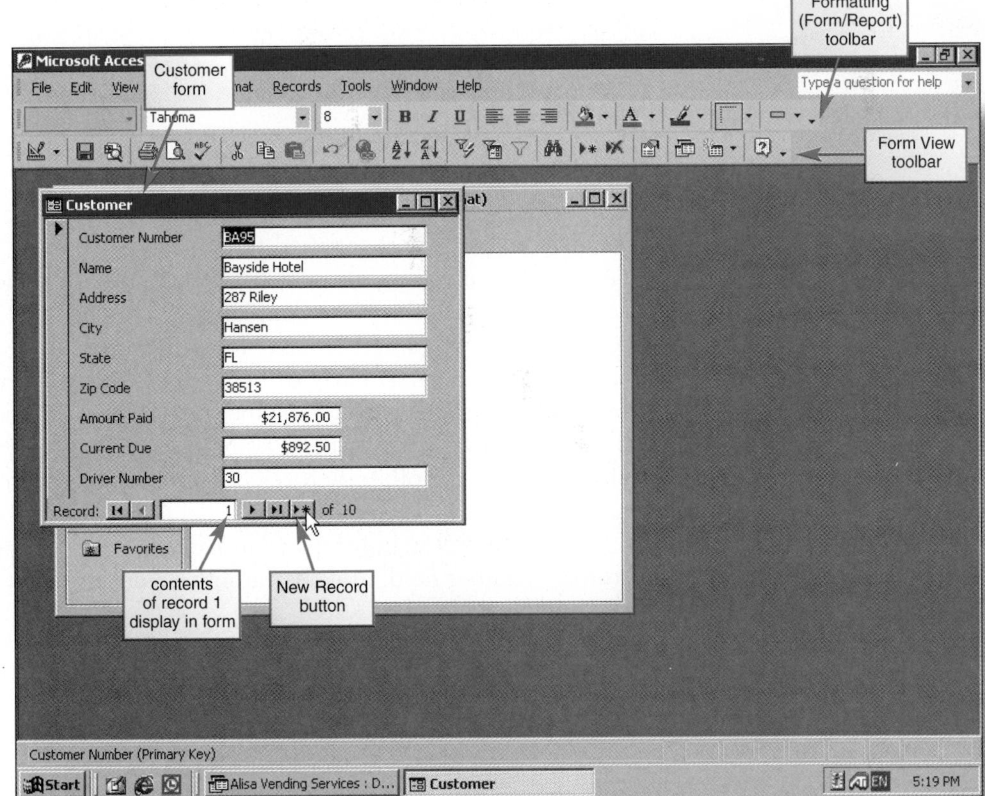

FIGURE 3-4

4 Click the New Record button and then type the data for the new record as shown in Figure 3-5. Press the TAB key after typing the data in each field, except after typing the final field (Driver Number).

The record displays.

5 Press the TAB key.

The record now is added to the Customer table and the contents of the form are erased.

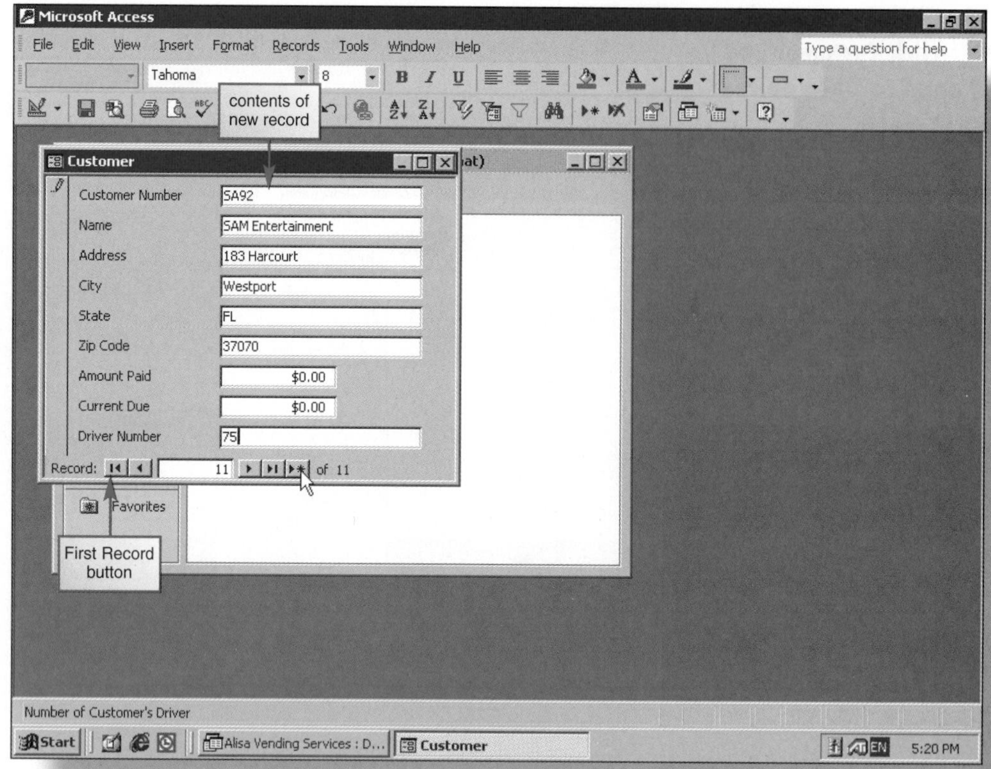

FIGURE 3-5

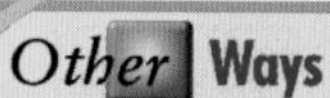

Other Ways

1. Click New Record button on Form View toolbar
2. On Insert menu click New Record
3. In Voice Command mode, say "Insert, New Record"

Searching for a Record

In the database environment, **searching** means looking for records that satisfy some criteria. Looking for the customer whose number is LM22 is an example of searching. The queries in Project 2 also were examples of searching. Access had to locate those records that satisfied the criteria.

A need for searching also exists when using Form view or Datasheet view. To update customer LM22, for example, first you need to find the customer. In a small table, repeatedly pressing the Next Record button until customer LM22 is on the screen may not be particularly difficult. In a large table with many records, however, this would be extremely cumbersome. You need a way to be able to go directly to a record just by giving the value in some field. This is the function of the **Find button** on the Form View toolbar. Before clicking the Find button, select the field for the search.

Perform the following steps to move to the first record in the table, select the Customer Number field, and then use the Find button to search for the customer whose number is LM22.

Steps To Search for a Record

1 Make sure the Customer table is open and the form for the Customer table is on the screen. Click the First Record button (see Figure 3-5) to display the first record. If the Customer Number field currently is not selected, select it by clicking the field name. Point to the Find button on the Form View toolbar.

The first record displays on the form (Figure 3-6).

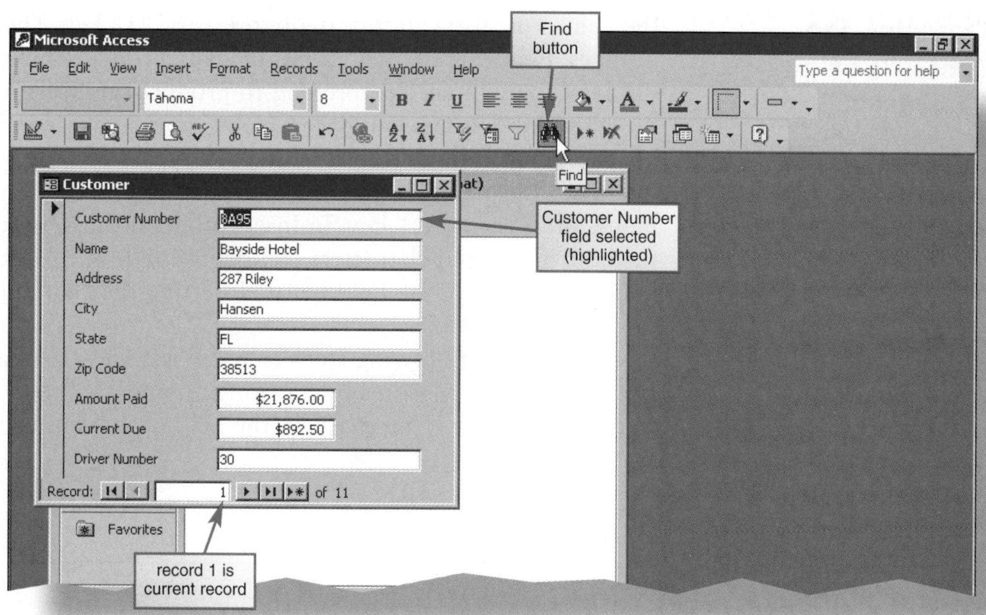

FIGURE 3-6

2 Click the Find button. Type LM22 **in the Find What text box in the Find and Replace dialog box and then click the Find Next button.**

Access locates the record for customer LM22. The Find and Replace dialog box displays and the Find What text box contains the entry, LM22 (Figure 3-7).

3 Click the Close button in the Find and Replace dialog box.

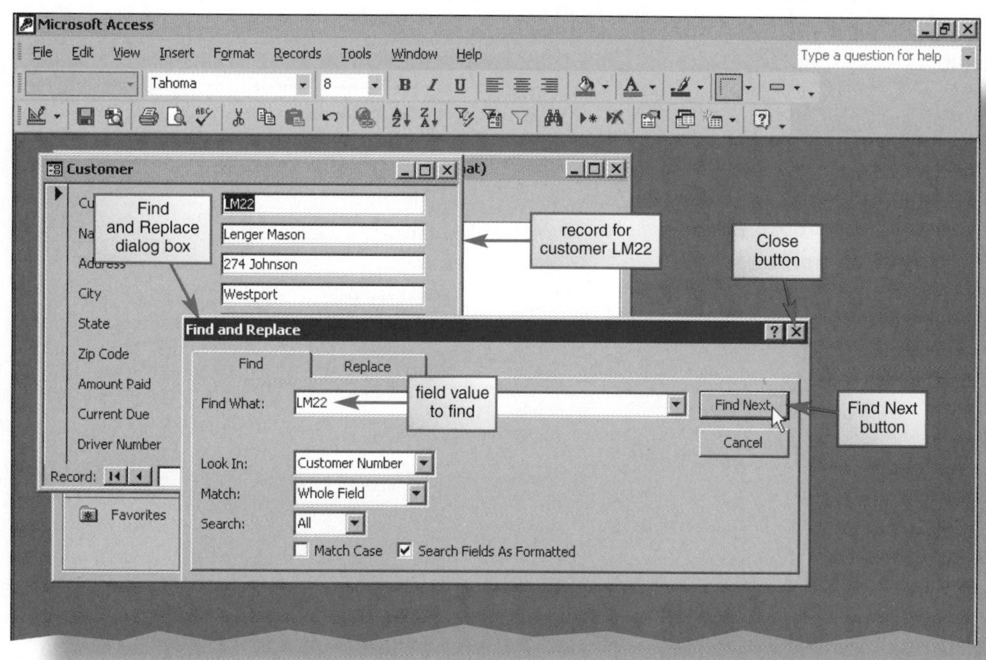

FIGURE 3-7

Other Ways

1. On Edit menu click Find
2. Press CTRL+F
3. In Voice Command mode, say "Find"

In some cases, after locating a record that satisfies a criterion, you might need to find the next record that satisfies the same criterion. For example, if you just found the first customer whose driver number is 30, you then may want to find the second such customer, then the third, and so on. To do so, repeat the same process. You will not need to retype the value, however.

Changing the Contents of a Record

When you are changing the value in a field, clicking within the field will produce an insertion point. Clicking the name of the field will select the entire field. The new entry typed then will replace completely the previous entry.

Changing the Contents of a Record

After locating the record to be changed, select the field to be changed by clicking the field. You also can repeatedly press the TAB key. Then make the appropriate changes. (Clicking the field automatically produces an insertion point. If you use the TAB key, you will need to press F2 to produce an insertion point.)

Normally, Access is in **Insert mode**, so the characters typed will be inserted at the appropriate position. To change to **Overtype mode**, press the INSERT key. The letters, OVR, will display near the bottom right edge of the status bar. To return to Insert mode, press the INSERT key. In Insert mode, if the data in the field completely fills the field, no additional characters can be inserted. In this case, you would need to increase the size of the field before inserting the characters. You will see how to do this later in the project.

Perform the following steps to use Form view to change the name of customer LM22 to Lenger Mason's by inserting an apostrophe (') and the letter, s, after Mason. Sufficient room exists in the field to make this change.

Steps To Update the Contents of a Field

1 Position the mouse pointer in the Name field text box for customer LM22 after the word, Mason.

The mouse pointer shape is an I-beam (Figure 3-8).

2 Click to produce an insertion point and then type 's **to correct the name.**

The name now is Lenger Mason's.

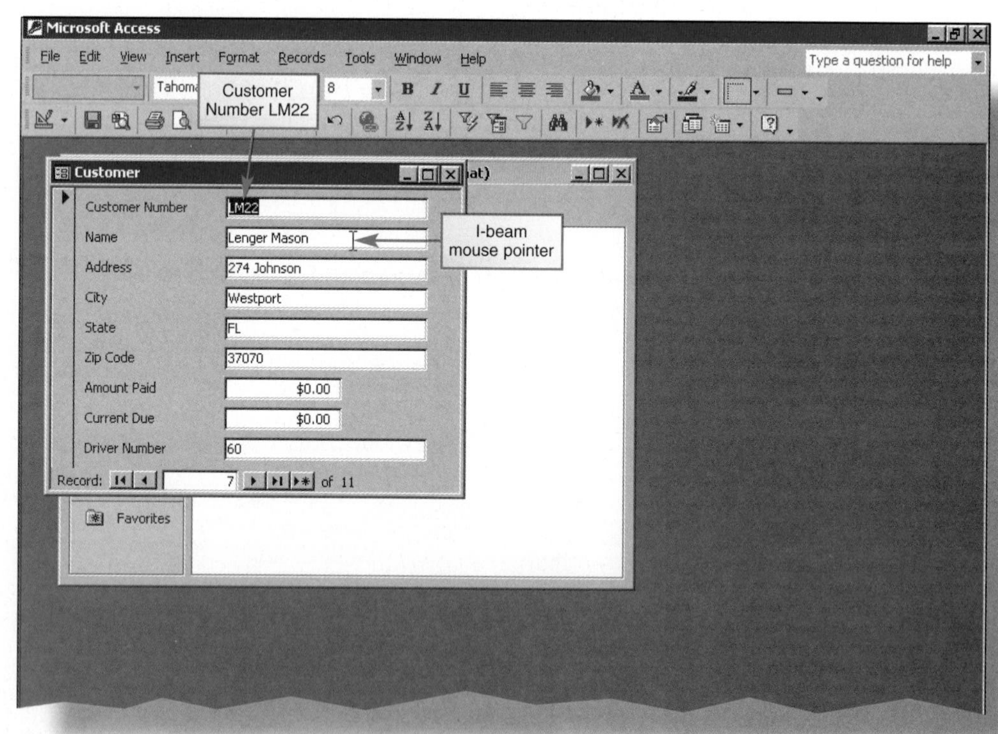

FIGURE 3-8

Switching Between Views

Sometimes, after working in Form view where you can see all fields, but only one record, it would be helpful to see several records at a time. To do so, switch to Datasheet view by clicking the View button arrow and then clicking Datasheet View. Perform the following steps to switch from Form view to Datasheet view.

To Switch from Form View to Datasheet View

1 Point to the View button arrow on the Form View toolbar (Figure 3-9).

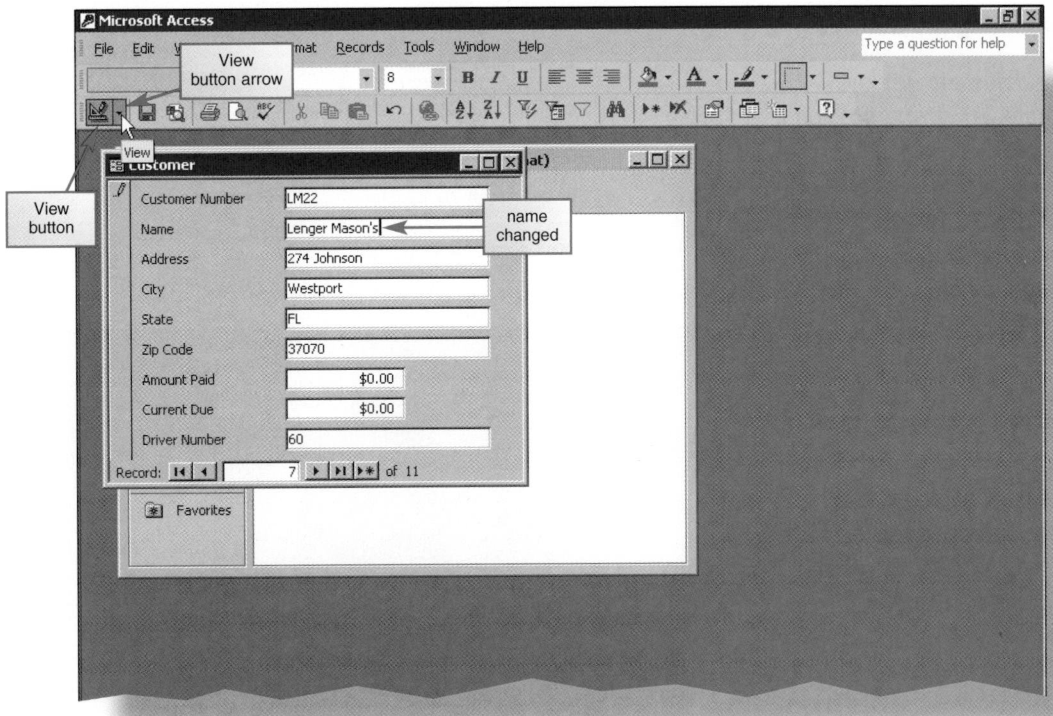

FIGURE 3-9

2 Click the View button arrow and then point to Datasheet View.

The View list displays (Figure 3-10).

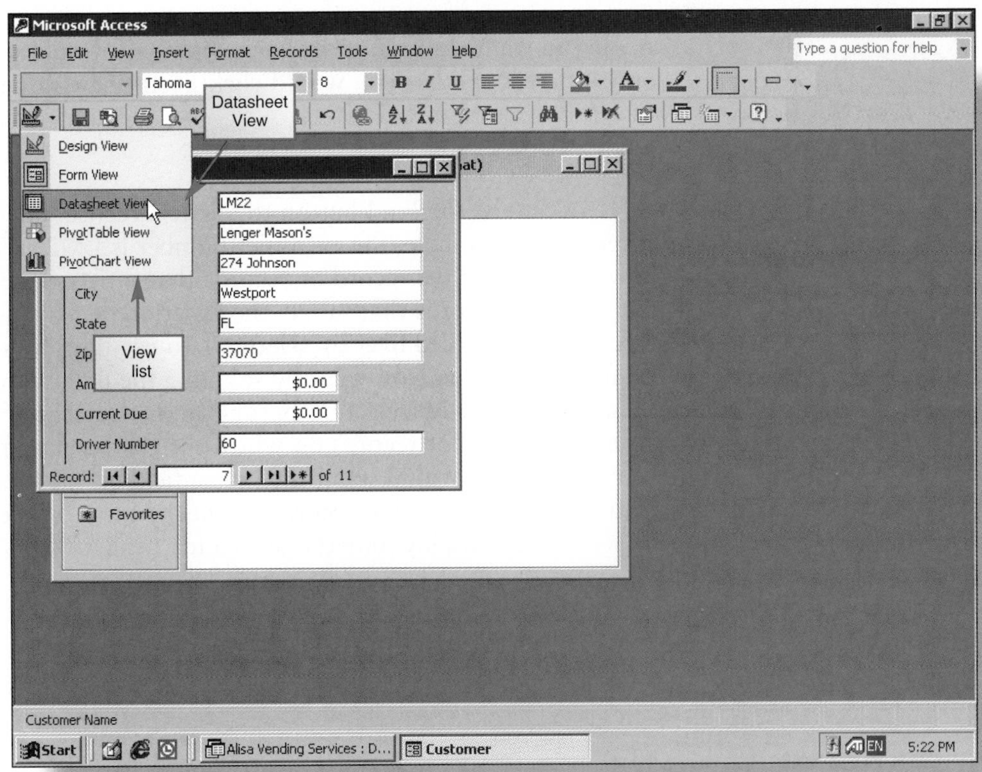

FIGURE 3-10

3 Click Datasheet View and then maximize the window containing the datasheet.

The datasheet displays (Figure 3-11). The position in the table is maintained. The current record selector points to customer LM22, the customer that displayed on the screen in Form view. The Name field, the field in which the insertion point is displayed, is selected. The new record for customer SA92 is currently the last record in the table. When you close the table and open it later, customer SA92 will be in its appropriate location.

Customer Numb	Name	Address	City	State	Zip Code	Amount Paid	Current Due
BA95	Bayside Hotel	287 Riley	Hansen	FL	38513	$21,876.00	$892.50
BR46	Baldwin-R		Fernwood	FL	37023	$26,512.00	$2,672.00
CN21	Century N		Hansen	FL	38513	$8,725.00	$0.00
FR28	Friend's Movies		Westport	FL	37070	$4,256.00	$1,202.00
GN62	Grand Nelson	7821 Oak	Wood Key	FL	36828	$8,287.50	$925.50
GS29	Great Screen	572 Lee	Hansen	FL	38513	$21,625.00	$0.00
LM22	Lenger Mason's	274 Johnson	Westport	FL	37070	$0.00	$0.00
ME93	Merks College	561 Fairhill	Bayville	FL	38734	$24,761.00	$1,572.00
RI78	Riter University	26 Grove	Fernwood	FL	37023	$11,682.25	$2,827.50
TU20	Turner Hotel	8672 Quincy	Palmview	FL	36114	$8,521.50	$0.00
SA92	SAM Entertainn	183 Harcourt	Westport	FL	37070	$0.00	$0.00
						$0.00	$0.00

FIGURE 3-11

1. On View menu click Datasheet View
2. In Voice Command mode, say "View, Datasheet View"

Advanced Filters

To create complex filters, for example, filters that use wildcards, or that require both OR and AND criteria use the Advanced Filter/Sort command. With the table or query results displaying, click Records on the menu bar, click Filter, and then click Advanced Filter/Sort. A Filter/Sort window will display. The window is similar to the Select Query window and displays a field list and a design grid. Use the same techniques you used to create queries to create advanced filters. To apply the filter, click Filter on the menu bar, and then click Apply Filter/Sort.

If you wanted to return to Form view, you would use the same process. The only difference is that you would click Form View rather than Datasheet View.

Filtering Records

You can use the Find button to locate a record quickly that satisfies some criterion (for example, the customer number is LM22). All records display, however, not just the record or records that satisfy the criterion. To have only the record or records that satisfy the criterion display, use a filter. The simplest type of filter is called **filter by selection**. To use filter by selection, give Access an example of the data you want by selecting the data within the table and then clicking the Filter By Selection button on the Datasheet View toolbar. For example, if only the record or records on which the customer name is Lenger Mason's are to be included, you would select the Name field on the record for customer LM22, because the name on that record is Lenger Mason's. The following steps use filter by selection to display only the record for Lenger Mason's.

Steps To Filter Records

1 **Make sure the name for customer LM22 (Lenger Mason's) is selected and then point to the Filter By Selection button on the Datasheet View toolbar (Figure 3-12).**

Filter By Selection button

Name field for Lenger Mason's selected

Customer Numb	Name	Address	City	State	Zip Code	Amount Paid	Current Due
BA95	Bayside Hotel	287 Riley	Hansen	FL	38513	$21,876.00	$892.50
BR46		267 Howard	Fernwood	FL	37023	$26,512.00	$2,672.00
CN21		1562 Butler	Hansen	FL	38513	$8,725.00	$0.00
FR28		871 Adams	Westport	FL	37070	$4,256.00	$1,202.00
GN62	Grand Nelson	7821 Oak	Wood Key	FL	36828	$8,287.50	$925.50
GS29	Great Screens	572 Lee	Hansen	FL	38513	$21,625.00	$0.00
LM22	Lenger Mason's	274 Johnson	Westport	FL	37070	$0.00	$0.00
ME93	Merks College	561 Fairhill	Bayville	FL	38734	$24,761.00	$1,572.00
RI78	Riter University	26 Grove	Fernwood	FL	37023	$11,682.25	$2,827.50
TU20	Turner Hotel	8672 Quincy	Palmview	FL	36114	$8,521.50	$0.00
SA92	SAM Entertainn	183 Harcourt	Westport	FL	37070	$0.00	$0.00
						$0.00	$0.00

FIGURE 3-12

2 **Click the Filter By Selection button.**

Only the customer whose name is Lenger Mason's displays (Figure 3-13).

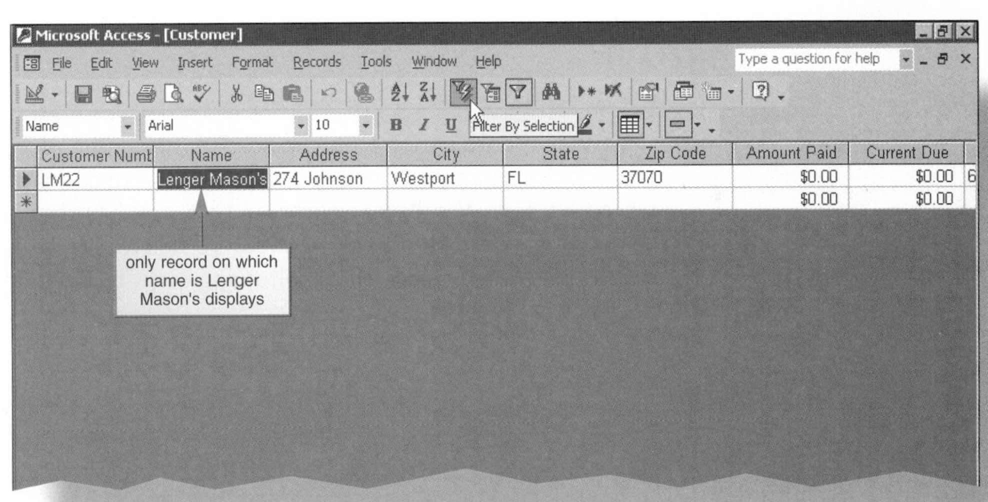

FIGURE 3-13

Because there is only one customer in the database with the name Lenger Mason's, only one customer displays. If you instead had selected the City field on the same record (Hansen) before clicking the Filter By Selection button, three customers would display, because there currently are three customers located in Hansen (customers BA95, CN21, and GS29).

In order to have all records once again display, remove the filter by clicking the Remove Filter button on the Datasheet View toolbar as in the steps on the next page.

Filters: Filter by Form

If you want to filter records based on values in more than one field, click the Filter by Form button instead of the Filter by Selection button. You then will be able to fill in values in as many fields as you want. Once you are finished, click the Apply Filter button. Only those records containing all the values you entered will display.

Steps To Remove a Filter

1 Point to the Remove Filter button on the Datasheet View toolbar (Figure 3-14).

2 Click the Remove Filter button.

All records once again display.

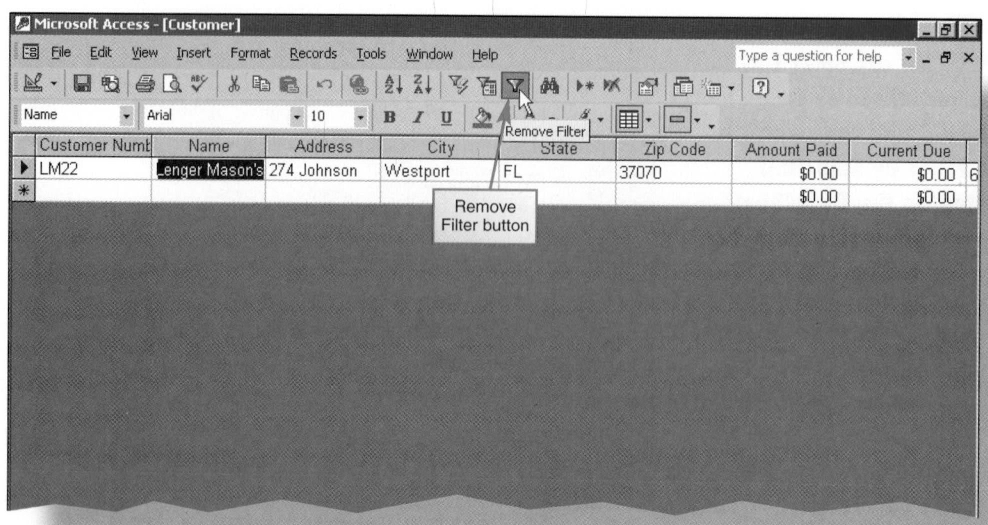

FIGURE 3-14

Other Ways

1. On Records menu click Filter, then click Filter By Selection
2. In Voice Command mode, say "Filter By Selection"

Deleting Records

When records are no longer needed, **delete the records** (remove them) from the table. If, for example, customer GN62 has moved its offices to a city that is not served by Alisa Vending Services and already has received its final payment, that customer's record should be deleted. To delete a record, first locate it and then press the DELETE key. Complete the following steps to delete customer GN62.

Steps To Delete a Record

1 With the datasheet for the Customer table on the screen, position the mouse pointer on the record selector of the record in which the customer number is GN62 (Figure 3-15).

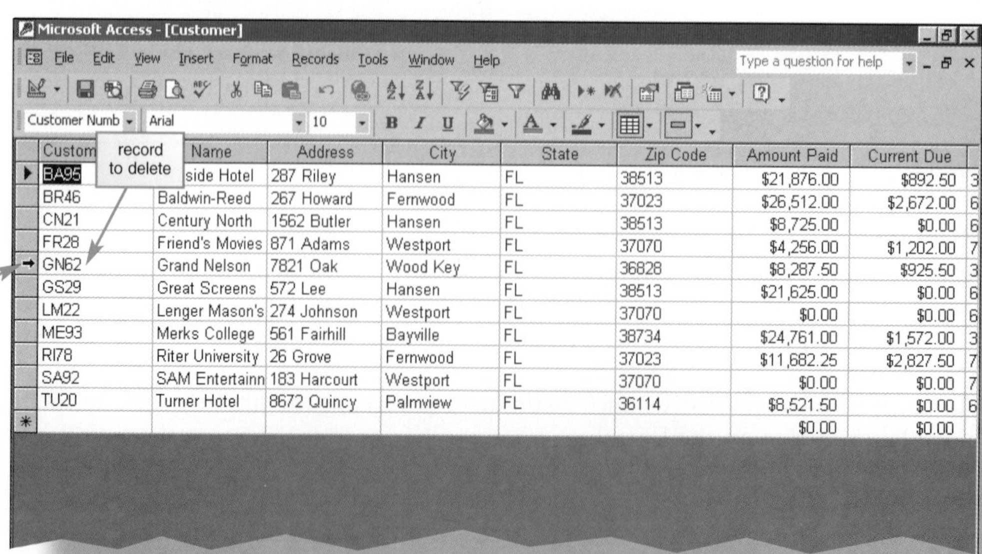

FIGURE 3-15

2 **Click the record selector to select the record, press the DELETE key to delete the record, and then point to the Yes button in the Microsoft Access dialog box.**

The Microsoft Access dialog box displays (Figure 3-16). The message indicates that one record will be deleted.

3 **Click the Yes button to complete the deletion. Close the window containing the table by clicking its Close Window button.**

The record is deleted and the table no longer displays.

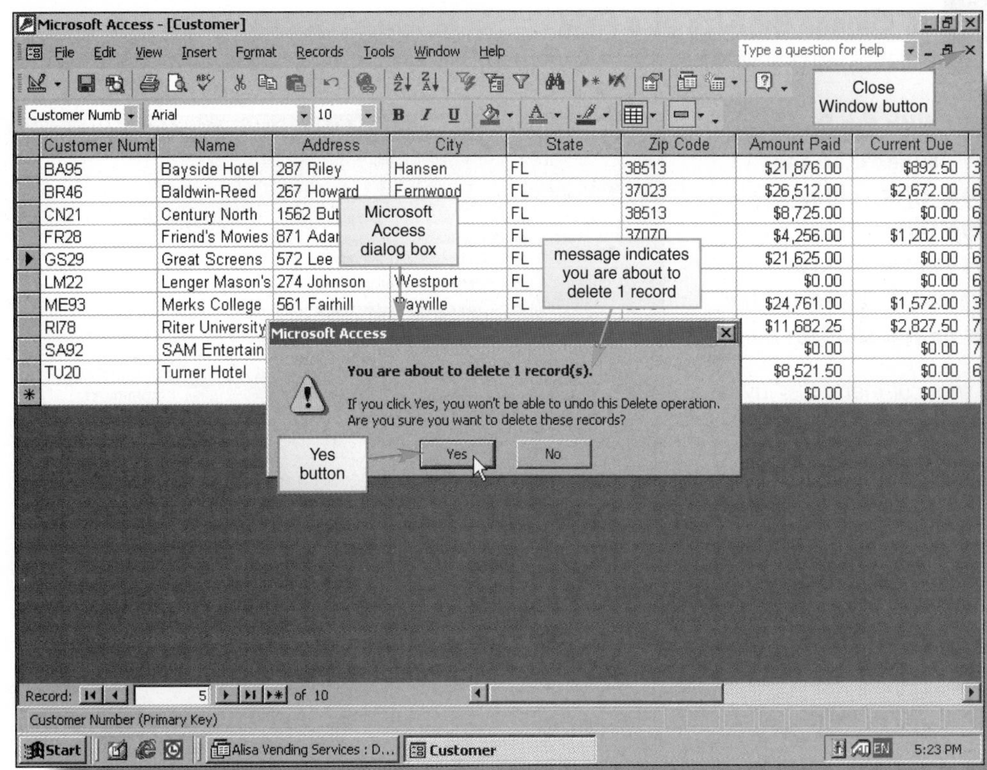

FIGURE 3-16

Changing the Structure

When you initially create a database, you define its **structure**; that is, you indicate the names, types, and sizes of all the fields. In many cases, the structure you first defined will not continue to be appropriate as you use the database. A variety of reasons exist why the structure of a table might need to change. Changes in the needs of users of the database may require additional fields to be added. In the Customer table, for example, if it is important to store a code indicating the customer type of a customer, you need to add such a field.

Characteristics of a given field may need to change. For example, the customer Century North's name is stored incorrectly in the database. It actually should be Century North Industries. The Name field is not large enough, however, to hold the correct name. To accommodate this change, you need to increase the width of the Name field.

It may be that a field currently in the table no longer is necessary. If no one ever uses a particular field, it is not needed in the table. Because it is occupying space and serving no useful purpose, it should be removed from the table. You also would need to delete the field from any forms, reports, or queries that include it.

To make any of these changes, click Design View on the shortcut menu.

Deleting Records Using a Form

You can delete records using a form just as you can delete records using a datasheet. To do so, first navigate to the record to be deleted. For example, you can use the navigation buttons or you can locate the desired record using the Find button. Once you locate the record to be deleted, click the Record Selector (the triangle in front of the record) to select the entire record. Press the Delete key, and then click the Yes button when asked if you want to delete the record.

Changing the Size of a Field

The steps on the next page change the size of the Name field from 20 to 25 to accommodate the change of name from Century North to Century North Industries.

Steps To Change the Size of a Field

1 With the Database window on the screen, click Tables on the Objects bar and then right-click Customer. Point to Design View on the shortcut menu.

The shortcut menu displays (Figure 3-17).

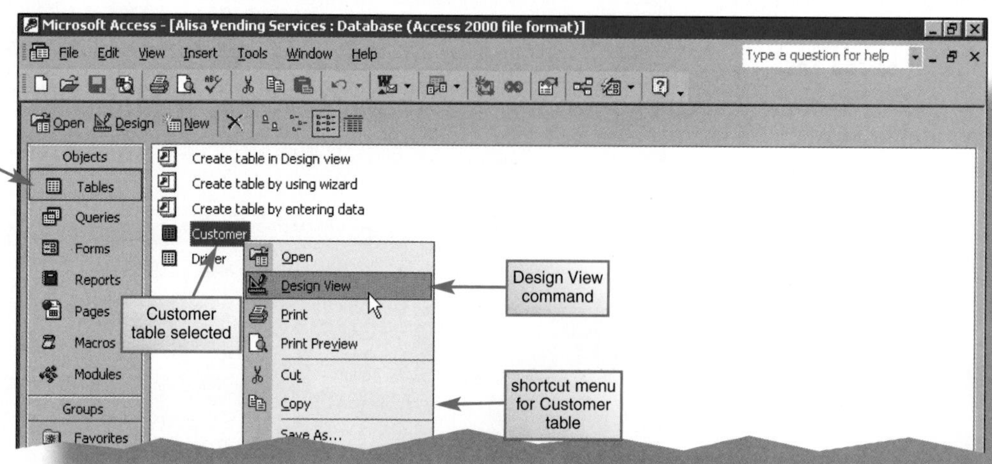

FIGURE 3-17

2 Click Design View on the shortcut menu and then point to the row selector for the Name field.

The Customer : Table window displays (Figure 3-18).

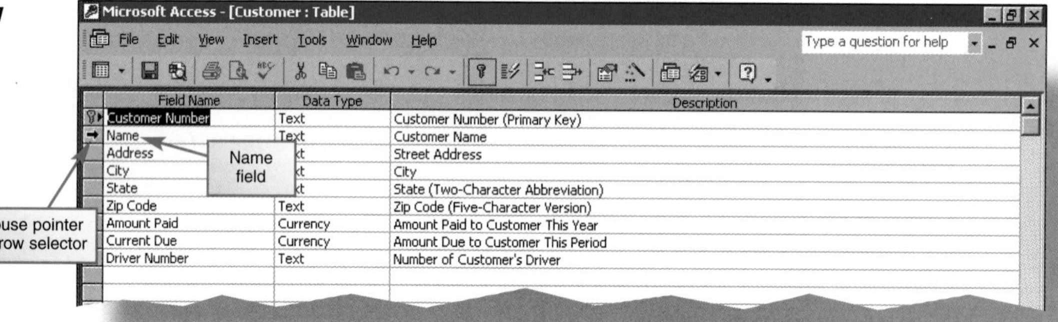

FIGURE 3-18

3 Click the row selector for the Name field.

The Name field is selected (Figure 3-19).

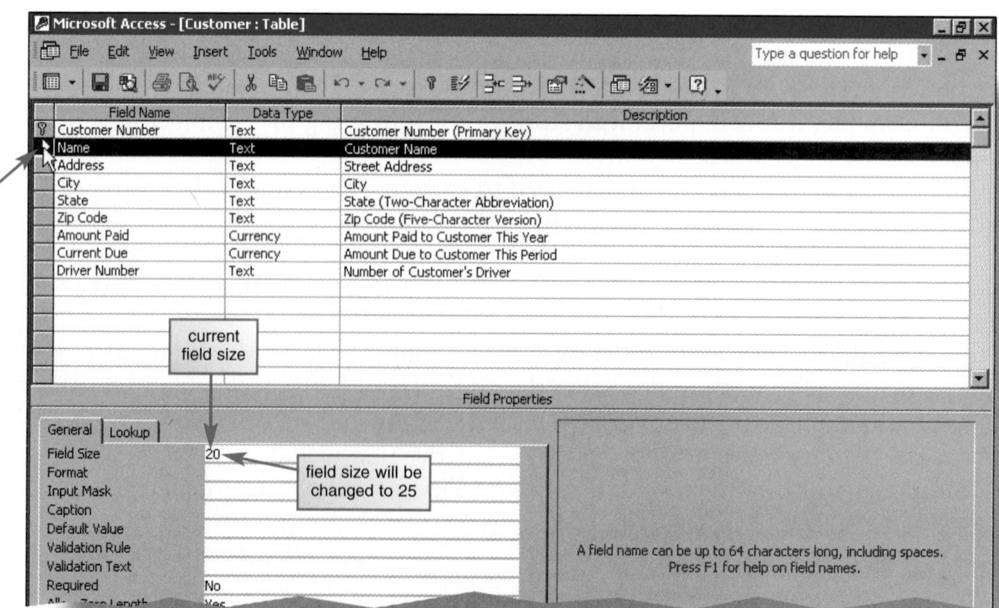

FIGURE 3-19

4 Press F6 to select the field size, type 25 **as the new size, and press F6 again.**

The size is changed (Figure 3-20).

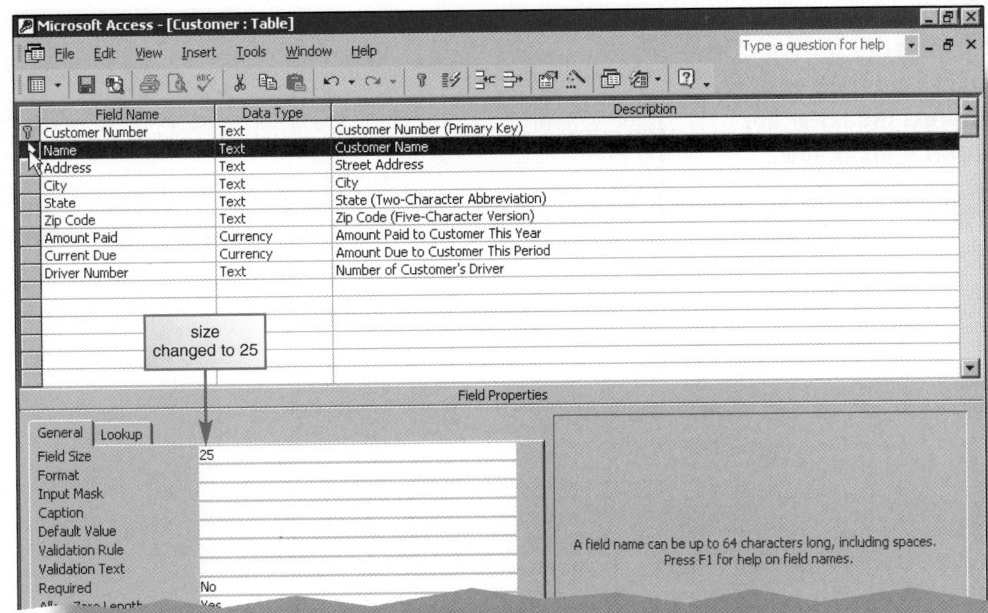

FIGURE 3-20

Adding a New Field

The management of Alisa Vending Services decided they needed to categorize the customers. To do so, they want to add an additional field, Customer Type. The possible values for Customer Type are EDU (which indicates the customer is an educational institution), MAN (which indicates the customer is a manufacturing organization), or SER (which indicates the customer is a service organization).

To be able to store the customer type, the following steps add a new field, called Customer Type, to the table. The possible entries in this field are EDU, MAN, and SER. The new field will follow the Zip Code field in the list of fields; that is, it will be the seventh field in the restructured table. The current seventh field (Amount Paid) will become the eighth field, Current Due will become the ninth field, and so on. Complete the following steps to add the field.

Adding a New Field

Tables frequently need to be expanded to include additional fields for a variety of reasons. Users' needs can change. The field may have been omitted by mistake when the table first was created. Government regulations may change in such a way that the organization needs to maintain additional information.

To Add a Field to a Table

1 Point to the row selector for the Amount Paid field (Figure 3-21).

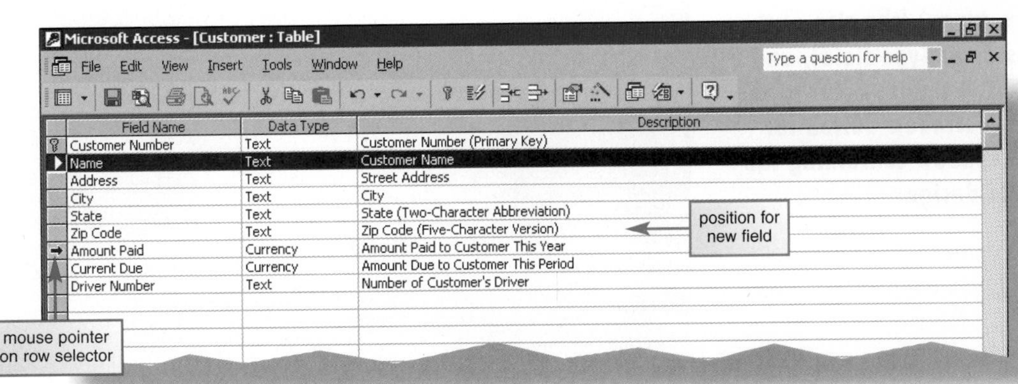

FIGURE 3-21

2 **Click the row selector for the Amount Paid field and then press the INSERT key to insert a blank row.**

A blank row displays in the position for the new field (Figure 3-22).

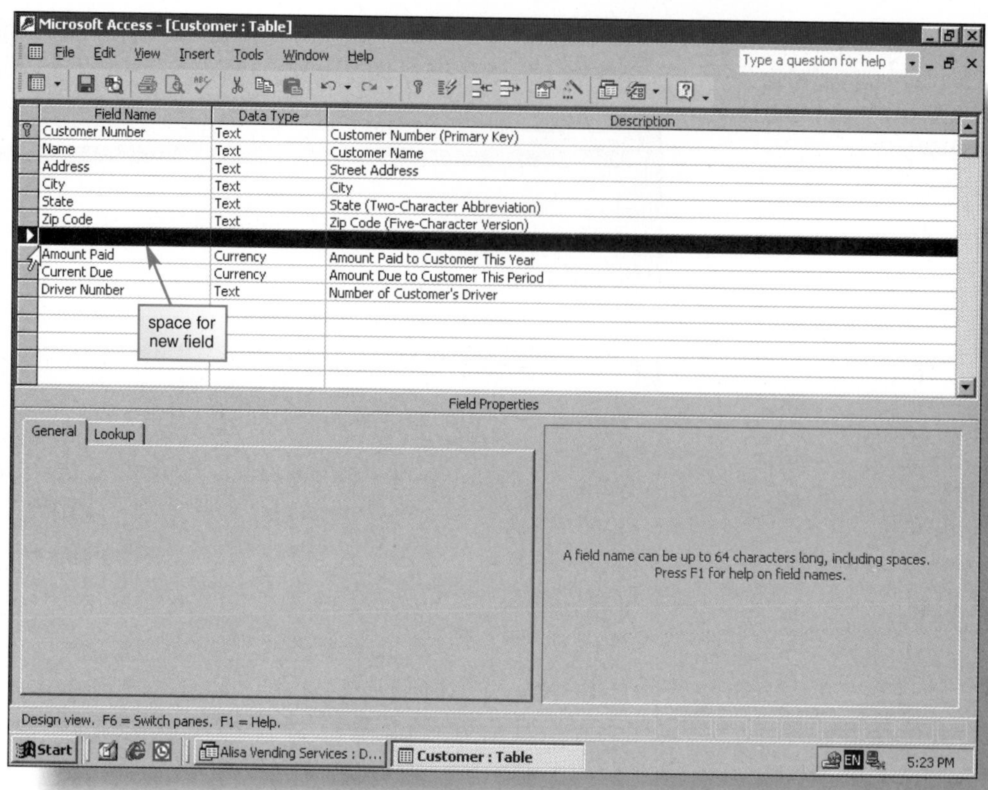

FIGURE 3-22

3 **Click the Field Name column for the new field. Type** `Customer Type` **as the field name and then press the TAB key. Select the Text data type by pressing the TAB key. Type** `Customer Type (EDU - Education, MAN - Manufacturing, or SER - Service)` **as the description. Press F6 to move to the Field Size text box, type** 3 **(the size of the Customer Type field), and press F6 again. Point to the Close Window button for the window containing the table design.**

The entries for the new field are complete (Figure 3-23).

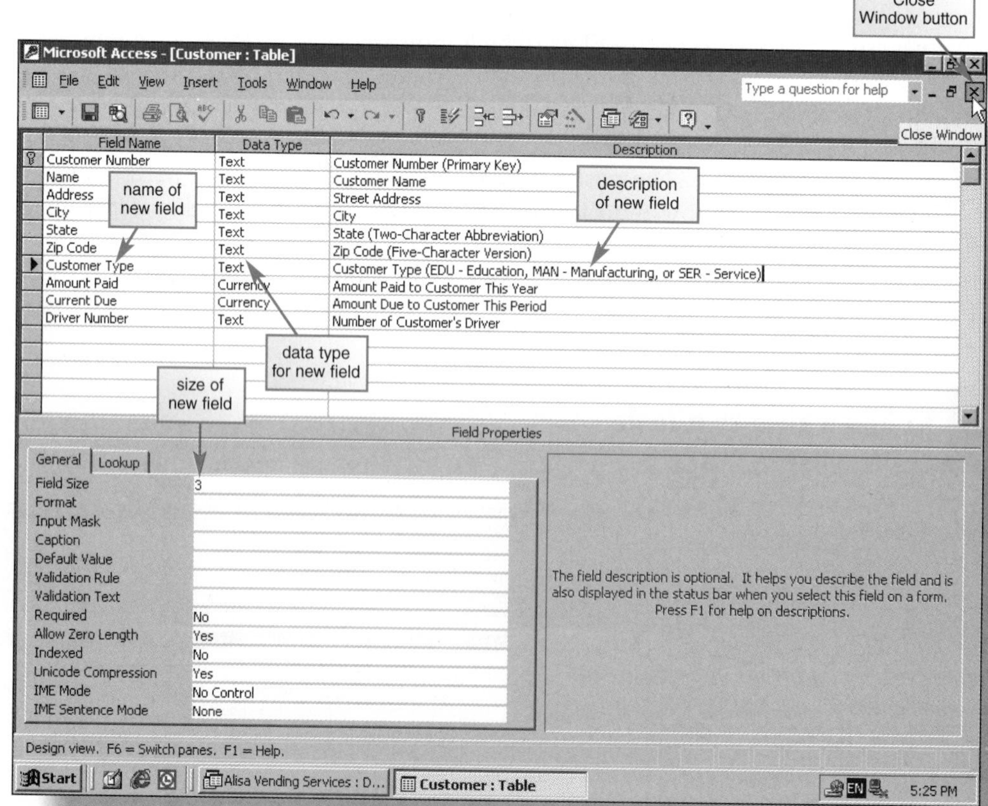

FIGURE 3-23

4 **Close the Customer : Table window by clicking its Close Window button. Point to the Yes button in the Microsoft Access dialog box.**

The Microsoft Access dialog box displays (Figure 3-24).

5 **Click the Yes button to save the changes.**

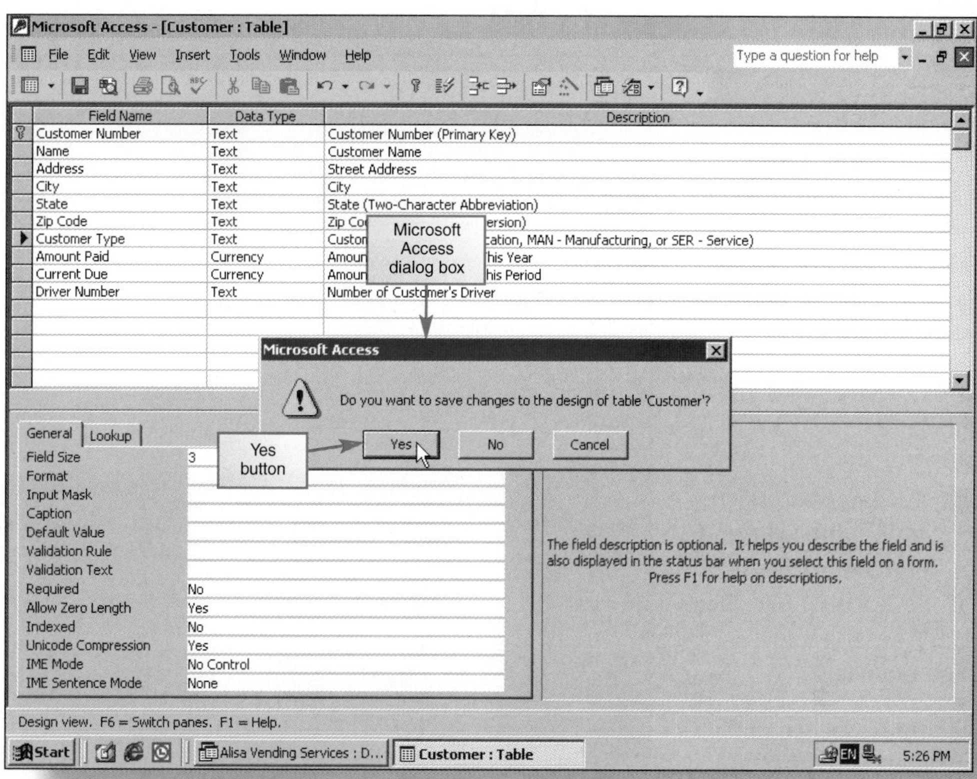

FIGURE 3-24

Deleting a Field

It is possible to find that a field in one of your tables is no longer needed. It may no longer serve a useful purpose or it may have been included by mistake. In such a case, you should delete the field. To do so, you first would open the table in Design view and then click the row selector for the field to select it. You then would press the DELETE key to delete the field. Access would request confirmation that you do indeed wish to delete the field. If you click the Yes button and then save your changes, the field will be removed from the table.

Updating the Restructured Database

Changes to the structure are available immediately. The Name field is longer, although it does not appear that way on the screen, and the new Customer Type field is included.

To make a change to a single field, such as changing the name from Century North to Century North Industries, click the field to be changed, and then make the necessary correction. If the record to be changed is not on the screen, use the Navigation buttons (Next Record, Previous Record) to move to it. If the field to be corrected simply is not visible on the screen, use the horizontal scroll bar along the bottom of the screen to shift all the fields until the correct one displays. Then make the change.

Perform the steps on the next page to change the name of Century North to Century North Industries.

The Access Help System

Need Help? It is no further than the Ask a Question box in the upper-right corner of the window. Click the box that contains the text, Type a question for help (Figure 3-24), type `help`, and then press the ENTER key. Access will respond with a list of items you can click to learn about obtaining help on any Access-related topic. To find out what is new in Access 2002, type `what's new in Access` in the Ask a Question box.

To Update the Contents of a Field

1 **Right-click Customer. Click Open on the shortcut menu. Position the I-beam mouse pointer to the right of the letter h in Century North (customer CN21).**

The datasheet displays (Figure 3-25).

2 **Click immediately to the right of the letter h in Century North, press the SPACEBAR, and then type** `Industries` **to change the name.**

The name is changed from Century North to Century North Industries.

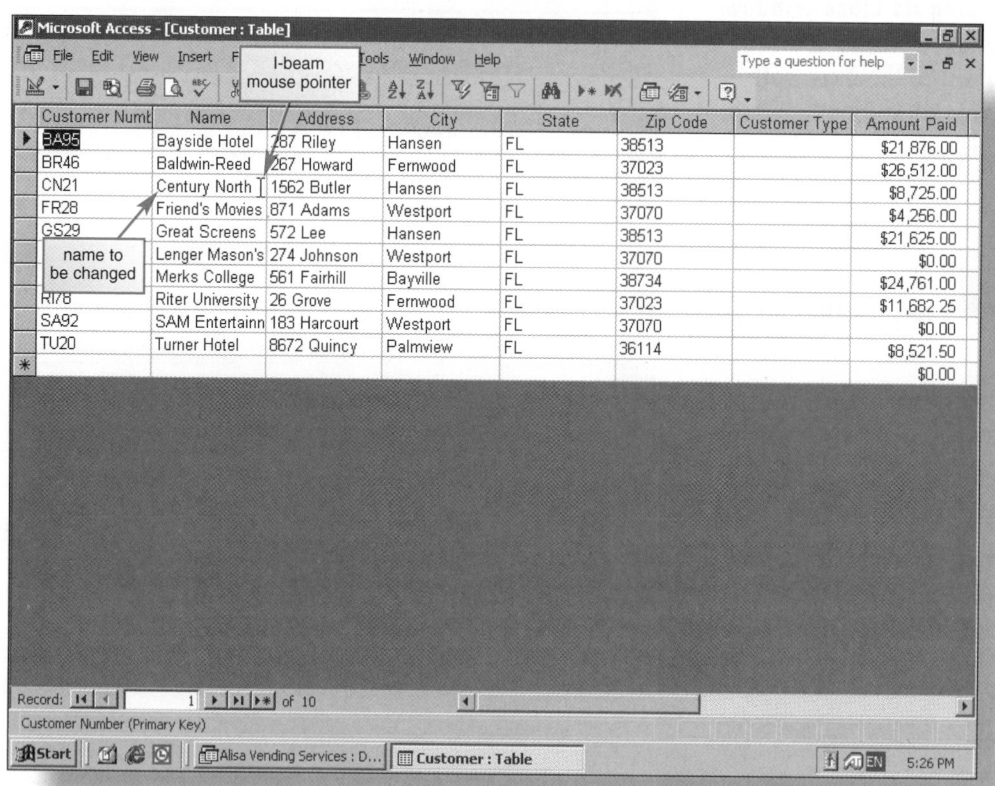

FIGURE 3-25

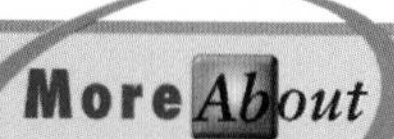

Resizing Columns

After you have changed the size of a field, the forms you have created will not reflect your changes. If you used the AutoForm command, you can change the field sizes by simply recreating the form. To do so, right-click the form, click Delete, and then create the form as you did in Project 1.

Resizing Columns

The default column sizes provided by Access do not always allow all the data in the field to display. You can correct this problem by **resizing the column** (changing its size) in the datasheet. In some instances, you actually may want to reduce the size of a column. The City field, for example, is short enough that it does not require all the space on the screen that is allotted to it.

Both types of changes are made the same way. Position the mouse pointer on the right boundary of the column's **field selector** (the line in the column heading immediately to the right of the name of the column to be resized). The mouse pointer will change to a two-headed arrow with a vertical bar. You then can drag the line to resize the column. In addition, you can double-click in the line, in which case Access will determine the best size for the column.

The following steps illustrate the process for resizing the Name column to the size that best fits the data.

Steps To Resize a Column

1 Point to the right boundary of the field selector for the Name field (Figure 3-26).

field selector for Name field

right boundary of field selector

mouse pointer shape indicates column can be resized

name has been changed

Customer Numb	Name	Address	City	State	Zip Code	Customer Type	Amount Paid
BA95	Bayside Hotel	287 Riley	Hansen	FL	38513		$21,876.00
BR46	Baldwin-Reed	267 Howar			37023		$26,512.00
CN21	North Industries	1562 Butle			38513		$8,725.00
FR28	Friend's Movies	871 Adams			37070		$4,256.00
GS29	Great Screens	572 Lee	Hansen	FL	38513		$21,625.00
LM22	Lenger Mason's	274 Johnson	Westport	FL	37070		$0.00
ME93	ollege	561 Fairhill	Bayville	FL	38734		$24,761.00
RI78	versity	26 Grove	Fernwood	FL	37023		$11,682.25
SA92	SAM Entertainn	183 Harcourt	Westport	FL	37070		$0.00
TU20	Turner Hotel	8672 Quincy	Palmview	FL	36114		$8,521.50
							$0.00

FIGURE 3-26

2 Double-click the right boundary of the field selector for the Name field.

The Name column has been resized (Figure 3-27).

Customer Numb	Name	Address	City	State	Zip Code	Customer Type	Amour
BA95	Bayside Hotel	287 Riley	Hansen	FL	38513		$21,
BR46	Baldwin-Reed	267 Howard	Fernwood	FL	37023		$26,
CN21	Century North Industries	1562 Butler	Hansen	FL	38513		$8,
FR28	Friend's Movies	871 Adams	Westport	FL	37070		$4,
GS29	Great Screens	572 Lee	Hansen	FL	38513		$21,
LM22	Lenger Mason's	274 Johnson	Westport	FL	37070		
ME93	Merks College	561 Fairhill	Bayville	FL	38734		$24,
RI78	Riter University	26 Grove	Fernwood	FL	37023		$11,
SA92	SAM Entertainment	183 Harcourt	Westport	FL	37070		
TU20	Turner Hotel	8672 Quincy	Palmview	FL	36114		$8,

column resized

FIGURE 3-27

3 Use the same technique to resize the Customer Number, Address, City, State, Zip Code, and Amount Paid columns to best fit the data.

The columns have been resized (Figure 3-28).

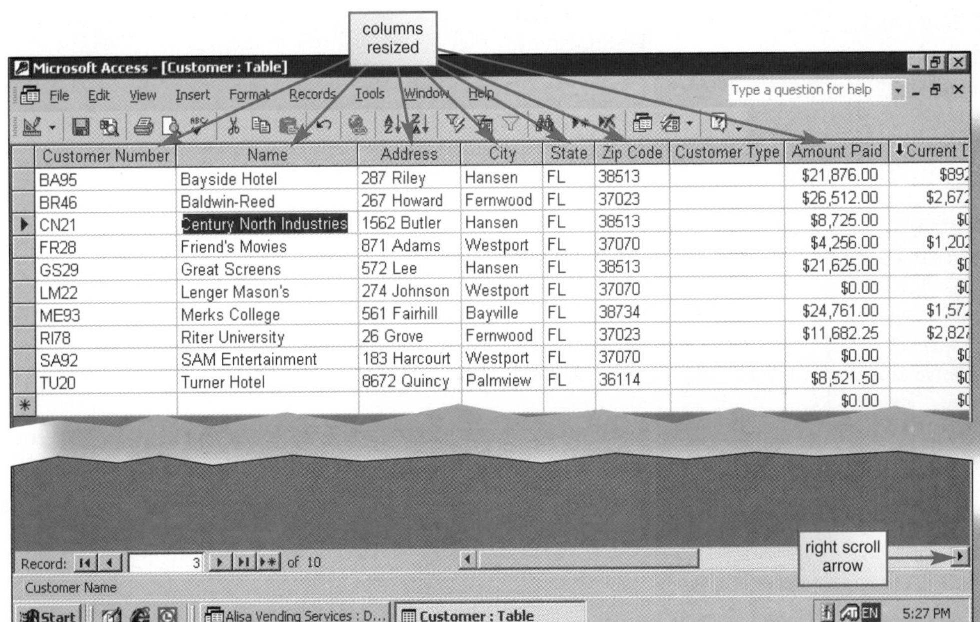

Customer Number	Name	Address	City	State	Zip Code	Customer Type	Amount Paid	Current
BA95	Bayside Hotel	287 Riley	Hansen	FL	38513		$21,876.00	$89
BR46	Baldwin-Reed	267 Howard	Fernwood	FL	37023		$26,512.00	$2,67
CN21	Century North Industries	1562 Butler	Hansen	FL	38513		$8,725.00	$
FR28	Friend's Movies	871 Adams	Westport	FL	37070		$4,256.00	$1,20
GS29	Great Screens	572 Lee	Hansen	FL	38513		$21,625.00	$
LM22	Lenger Mason's	274 Johnson	Westport	FL	37070		$0.00	$
ME93	Merks College	561 Fairhill	Bayville	FL	38734		$24,761.00	$1,57
RI78	Riter University	26 Grove	Fernwood	FL	37023		$11,682.25	$2,82
SA92	SAM Entertainment	183 Harcourt	Westport	FL	37070		$0.00	$
TU20	Turner Hotel	8672 Quincy	Palmview	FL	36114		$8,521.50	$
							$0.00	$

FIGURE 3-28

4 **If necessary, click the right scroll arrow to display the Current Due and Driver Number columns, and then resize the columns to best fit the data. Point to the Close Window button for the Customer : Table window.**

All the columns have been resized (Figure 3-29).

Close Window button

remaining columns resized

Microsoft Access - [Customer : Table]

Name	Address	City	State	Zip Code	Customer Type	Amount Paid	Current Due	Driver Number
Bayside Hotel	287 Riley	Hansen	FL	38513		$21,876.00	$892.50	30
Baldwin-Reed	267 Howard	Fernwood	FL	37023		$26,512.00	$2,672.00	60
Century North Industries	1562 Butler	Hansen	FL	38513		$8,725.00	$0.00	60
Friend's Movies	871 Adams	Westport	FL	37070		$4,256.00	$1,202.00	75
Great Screens	572 Lee	Hansen	FL	38513		$21,625.00	$0.00	60
Lenger Mason's	274 Johnson	Westport	FL	37070		$0.00	$0.00	60
Merks College	561 Fairhill	Bayville	FL	38734		$24,761.00	$1,572.00	30
Riter University	26 Grove	Fernwood	FL	37023		$11,682.25	$2,827.50	75
SAM Entertainment	183 Harcourt	Westport	FL	37070		$0.00	$0.00	75
Turner Hotel	8672 Quincy	Palmview	FL	36114		$8,521.50	$0.00	60
						$0.00	$0.00	

FIGURE 3-29

5 **Close the Customer : Table window by clicking its Close Window button and then point to the Yes button in the Microsoft Access dialog box.**

The Microsoft Access dialog box displays (Figure 3-30). Changing a column width changes the layout or design of a table.

6 **Click the Yes button.**

The change to the layout is saved. The next time the datasheet displays, the columns will have the new widths.

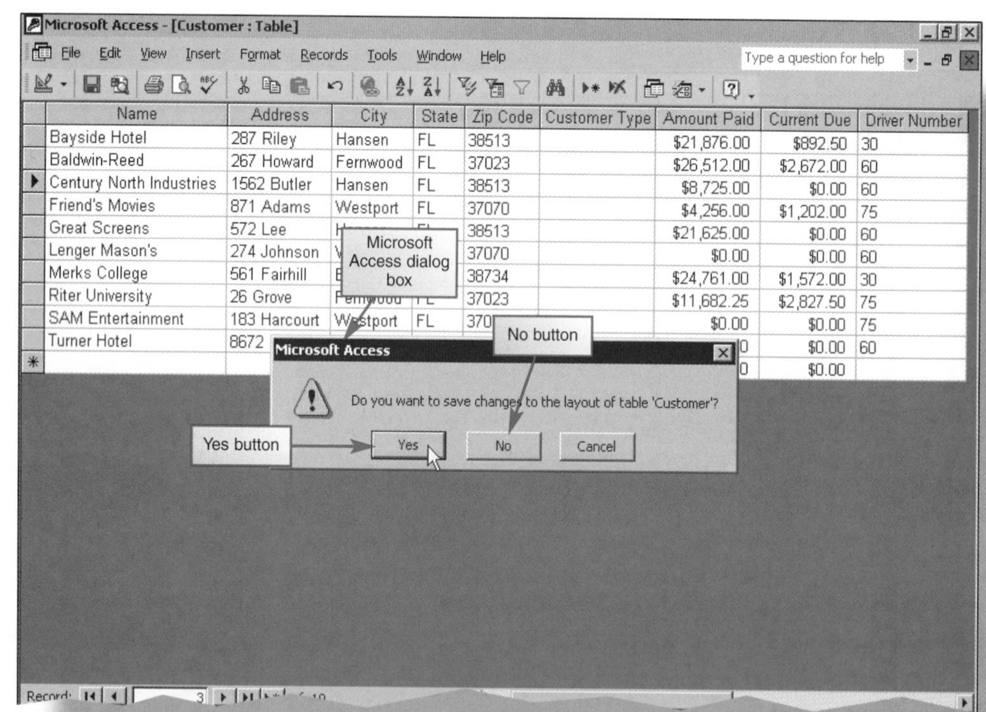

FIGURE 3-30

Other Ways

1. On Format menu click Column Width
2. In Voice Command mode, say "Format, Column Width"

Using an Update Query

The Customer Type field is blank on every record. One approach to entering the information for the field would be to step through the entire table, assigning each record its appropriate value. If most of the customers have the same type, a simpler approach is available.

At Alisa Vending Services, for example, most customers are type SER. Initially, you can set all the values to SER. To accomplish this quickly and easily, you use a special type of query called an **update query**. Later, you can change the type for educational institutions and manufacturing organizations.

The process for creating an update query begins the same as the process for creating the select queries in Project 2. After selecting the table for the query, right-click any open area of the upper pane, click Query Type on the shortcut menu, and then click Update Query on the menu of available query types. An extra row, Update To:, displays in the design grid. Use this additional row to indicate the way the data will be updated. If a criterion is entered, then only those records that satisfy the criterion will be updated.

Perform the following steps to change the value in the Customer Type field to SER for all the records. Because all records are to be updated, no criteria will be entered.

Action Queries

An action query is a query that makes changes to many records in just one operation. There are four types of action queries: delete, update, append, and make-table. In this project you learn how to use update, delete, and append queries.

To Use an Update Query to Update All Records

1 **With the Customer table selected, click the New Object: AutoForm button arrow on the Database toolbar, and then point to Query on the list that displays.**

The New Object: AutoForm list displays (Figure 3-31).

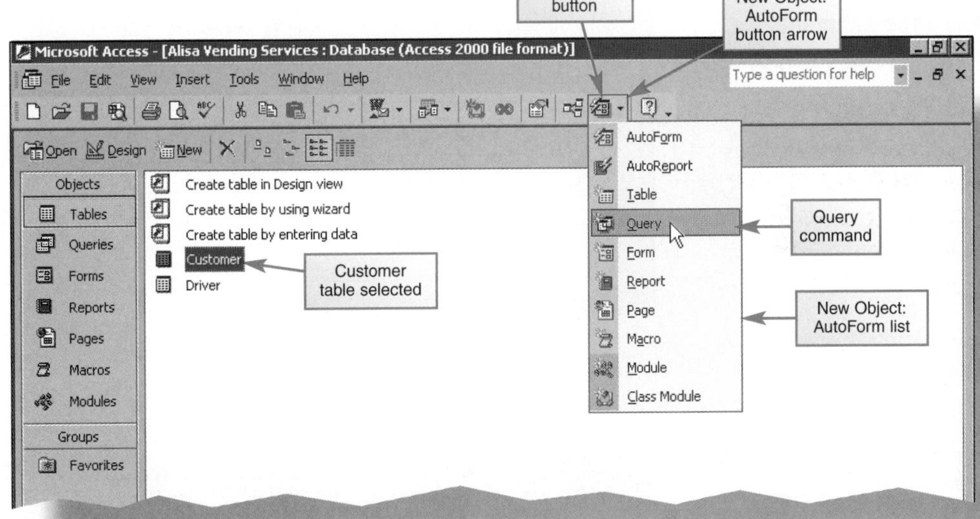

FIGURE 3-31

2 **Click Query and then point to the OK button in the New Query dialog box.**

The New Query dialog box displays (Figure 3-32). Design View is selected.

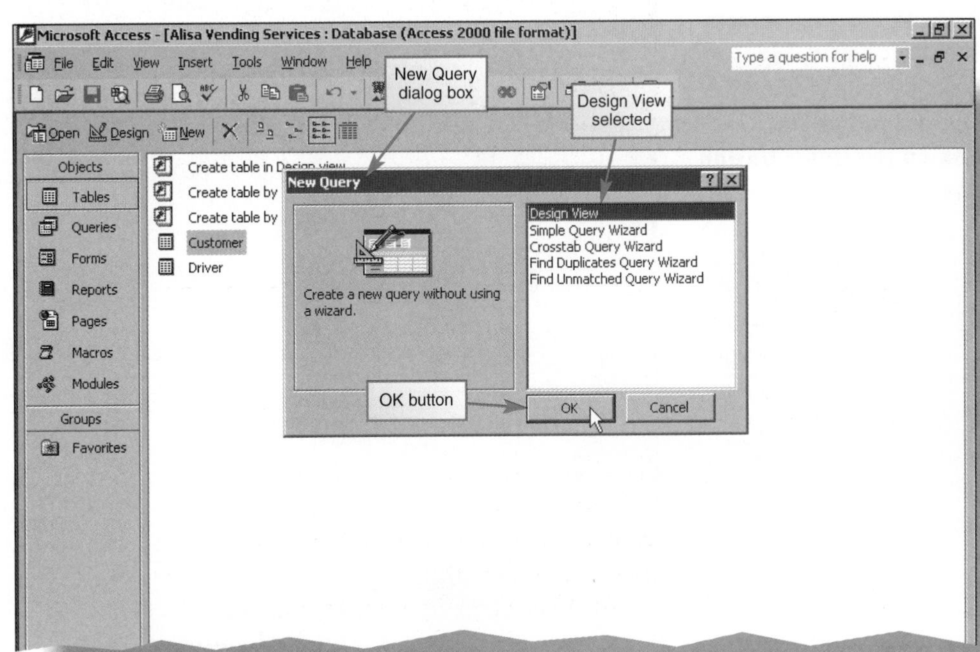

FIGURE 3-32

3 Click the OK button, and then be sure the Query1 : Select Query window is maximized. Resize the upper and lower panes of the window as well as the Customer table field list so all fields in the field list display (see page A 2.08 Project 2). Right-click the upper pane and point to Query Type on the shortcut menu. When the Query Type submenu displays, point to Update Query.

The shortcut menu displays (Figure 3-33). The Query Type submenu displays, showing available query types.

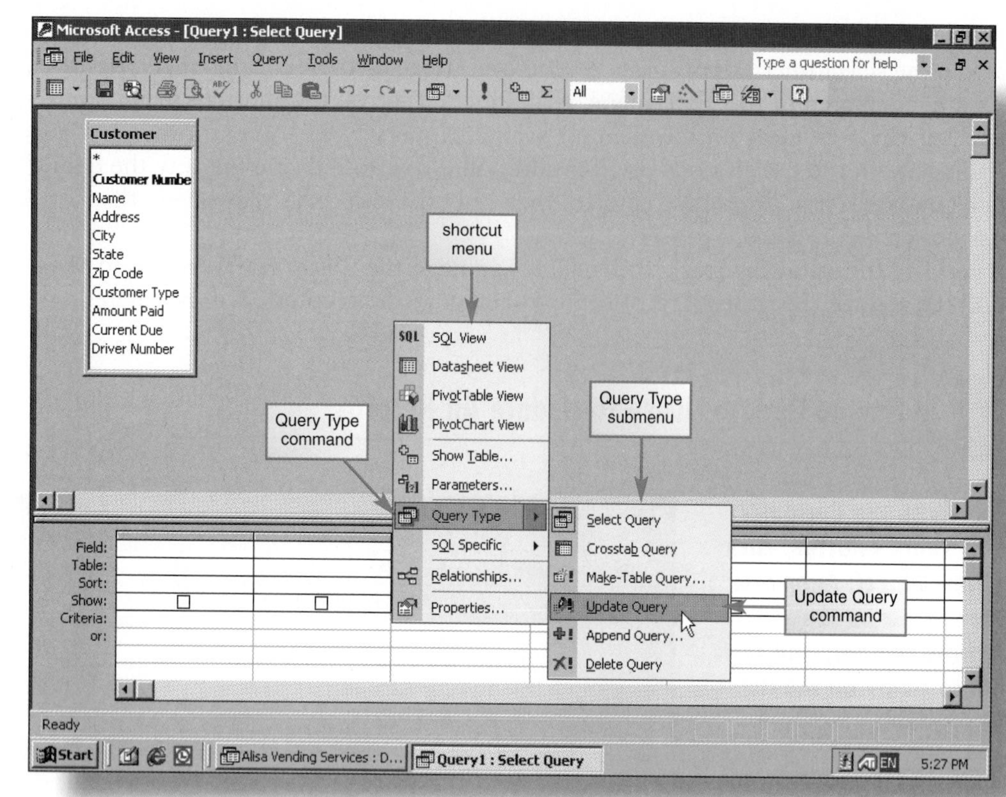

FIGURE 3-33

4 Click Update Query on the submenu, double-click the Customer Type field to select the field, click the Update To text box in the first column of the design grid, type SER **as the new value, and then point to the Run button on the Query Design toolbar.**

The Customer Type field is selected (Figure 3-34). In an Update Query, the Update To row displays in the design grid. The value to which the field is to be changed is entered as SER. Because no criteria are entered, the Customer Type value on every row will be changed to SER.

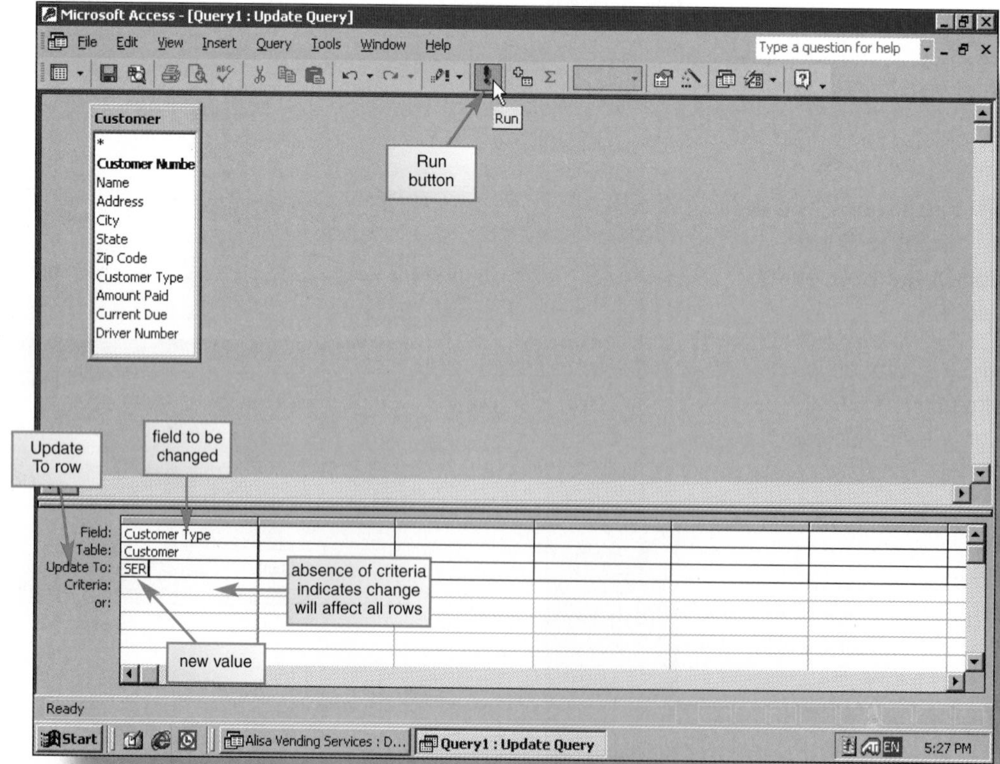

FIGURE 3-34

5 **Click the Run button and then point to the Yes button in the Microsoft Access dialog box.**

The Microsoft Access dialog box displays (Figure 3-35). The message indicates that 10 rows will be updated by the query.

6 **Click the Yes button.**

The changes are made.

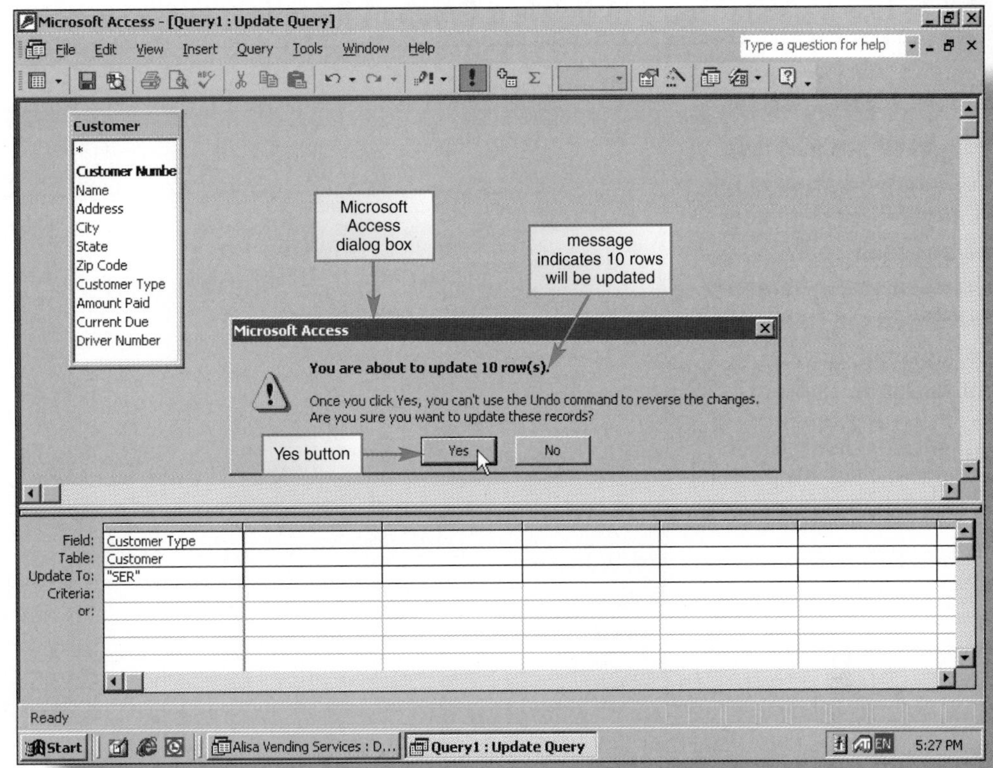

FIGURE 3-35

Other Ways

1. Click Query Type button arrow on Query Design toolbar, click Update Query
2. On Query menu click Update Query
3. In Voice Command mode, say "Query, Update Query"

Using a Delete Query

In some cases, you may need to delete several records at a time. If, for example, all customers in a particular zip code are to be serviced by another firm, the customers with this zip code can be deleted from the Alisa Vending Services database. Instead of deleting these customers individually, which could be very cumbersome, you can delete them in one operation by using a **delete query**, which is a query that will delete all the records satisfying the criterion entered in the query.

You can preview the data to be deleted in a Delete query before actually performing the deletion. To do so, you would click the View button arrow and then click Datasheet view after creating the query, but before running it. The records to be deleted then would display in Datasheet view. To delete the records, you would click the View button arrow, click Design View, and then click the Run button. Click the Yes button when asked if you want to delete the records.

Perform the steps on the next page to use a delete query to delete any customer whose zip code is 36114 without previewing the data. (There happens to be only one such customer currently in the database.)

More About

Action Queries: Append Queries

An append query adds a group of records from one table to the end of another table. For example, suppose that Alisa Vending Services acquires some new customers and a database containing a table on those customers. To avoid entering all this information manually, you can append it to the Customer table in the Alisa Vending Services database.

Steps To Use a Delete Query to Delete a Group of Records

1 Click Edit on the menu bar and then click Clear Grid to clear the grid. Right-click the upper pane and then point to Query Type on the shortcut menu. When the Query Type submenu displays, point to Delete Query.

The shortcut menu displays (Figure 3-36). The Query Type submenu displays the available query types.

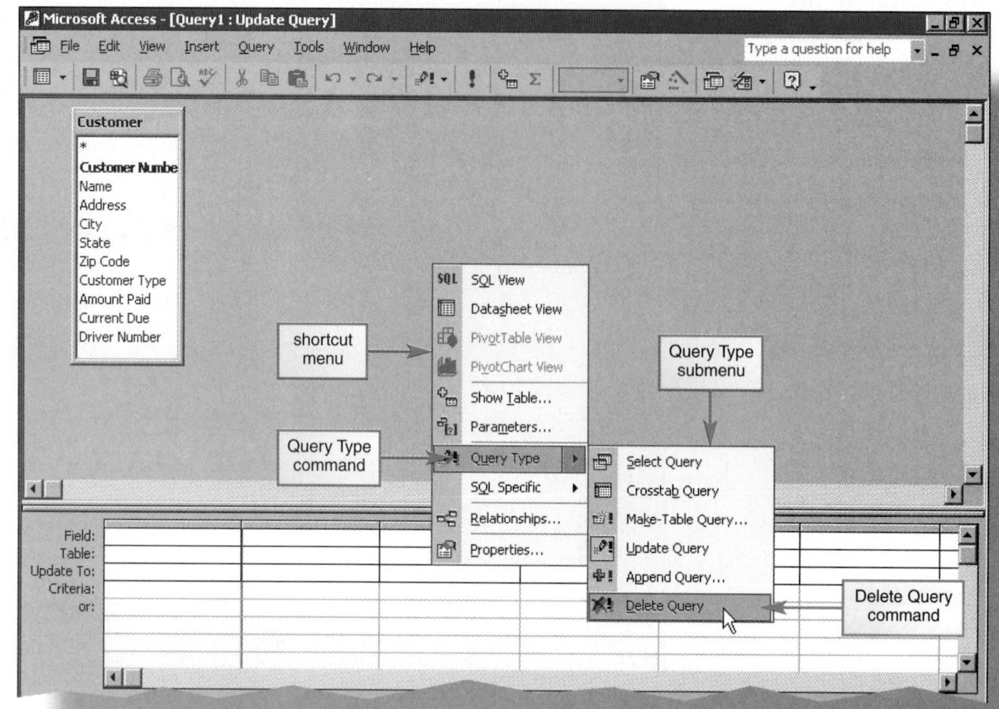

FIGURE 3-36

2 Click Delete Query on the submenu, double-click the Zip Code field to select the field, and then click the Criteria row. Type 36114 **as the criterion and then point to the Run button on the Query Design toolbar.**

The criterion is entered in the Zip Code column (Figure 3-37). In a delete query, the Delete row displays in the design grid.

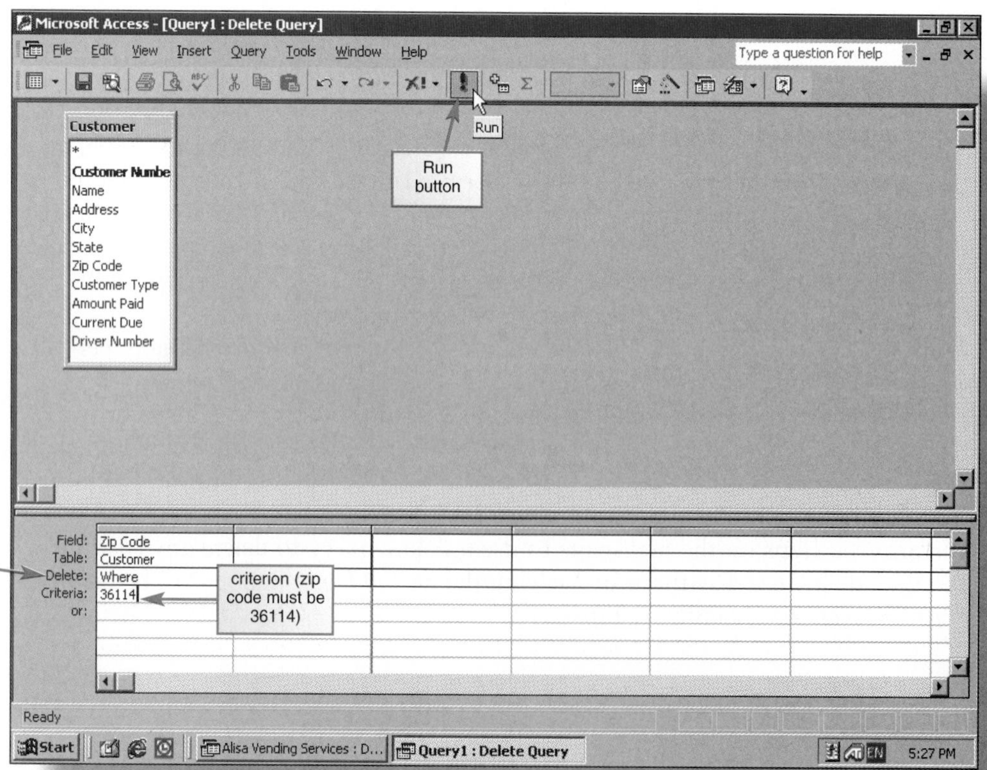

FIGURE 3-37

3 Click the Run button to run the query. Point to the Yes button in the Microsoft Access dialog box.

The Microsoft Access dialog box displays (Figure 3-38). The message indicates the query will delete 1 row (record).

4 Click the Yes button. Close the Query window. Do not save the query.

The customer with zip code 36114 has been removed from the table.

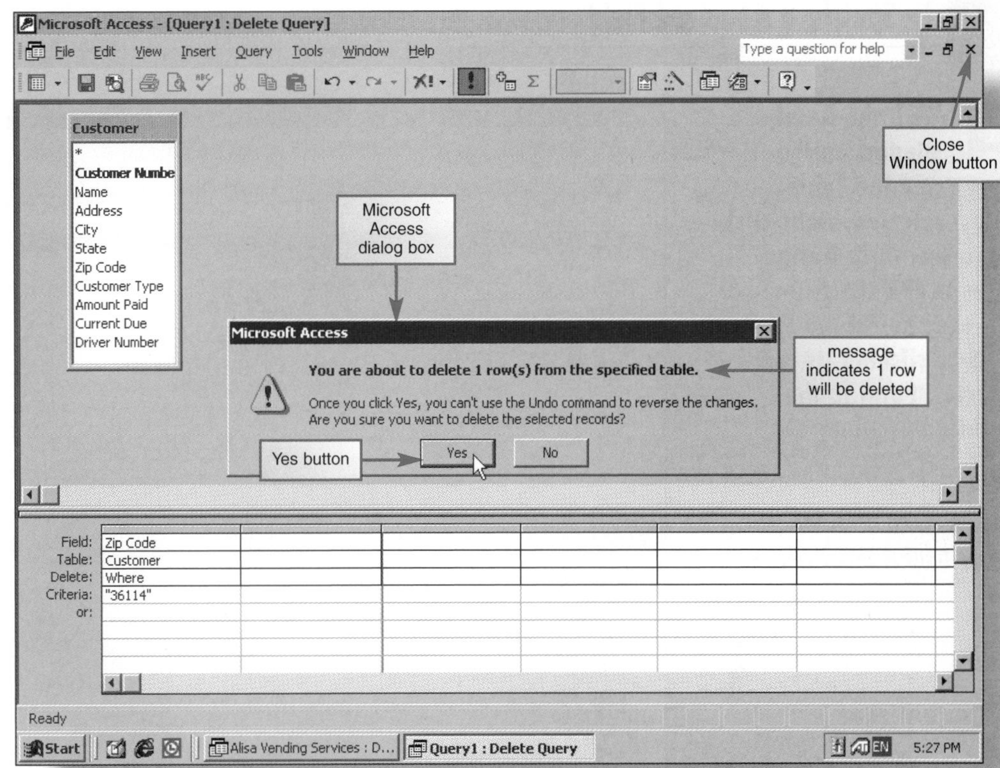

FIGURE 3-38

Other Ways

1. Click Query Type button arrow on Query Design toolbar, click Delete Query
2. On Query menu click Delete Query
3. In Voice Command mode, say "Query, Delete Query"

Creating Validation Rules

You now have created, loaded, queried, and updated a database. Nothing you have done so far, however, ensures that users enter only valid data. To do so, you create **validation rules**; that is, rules that the data entered by a user must follow. As you will see, Access will prevent users from entering data that does not follow the rules. The steps also specify **validation text**, which is the message that will be displayed if a user violates the validation rule.

Validation rules can indicate a **required field**, a field in which the user actually must enter data. For example, by making the Name field a required field, a user actually must enter a name (that is, the field cannot be blank). Validation rules can make sure a user's entry lies within a certain **range of values**; for example, that the values in the Amount Paid field are between $0.00 and $90,000.00. They can specify a **default value**; that is, a value that Access will display on the screen in a particular field before the user begins adding a record. To make data entry of customer numbers more convenient, you also can have lowercase letters displayed automatically as uppercase letters. Finally, validation rules can specify a collection of acceptable values; for example, that the only legitimate entries for the Customer Type field are EDU, MAN, and SER.

More About

Creating Append Queries

To create an append query, create a select query for the table containing the records to append. In the design grid, indicate which fields to include. Then, right-click the upper pane, click Query Type, and then click Append Query on the Query Type submenu. When the Append Query dialog box displays, specify the name of the table to receive the new records, and its location.

Specifying a Required Field

To specify that a field is to be required, change the value in the Required property box from No to Yes. The steps on the next page specify that the Name field is to be a required field.

Steps To Specify a Required Field

1 With the Database window on the screen and the Tables object selected, right-click Customer. Click Design View on the shortcut menu, and then select the Name field by clicking its row selector. Point to the Required property box.

The Customer : Table window displays (Figure 3-39). The Name field is selected.

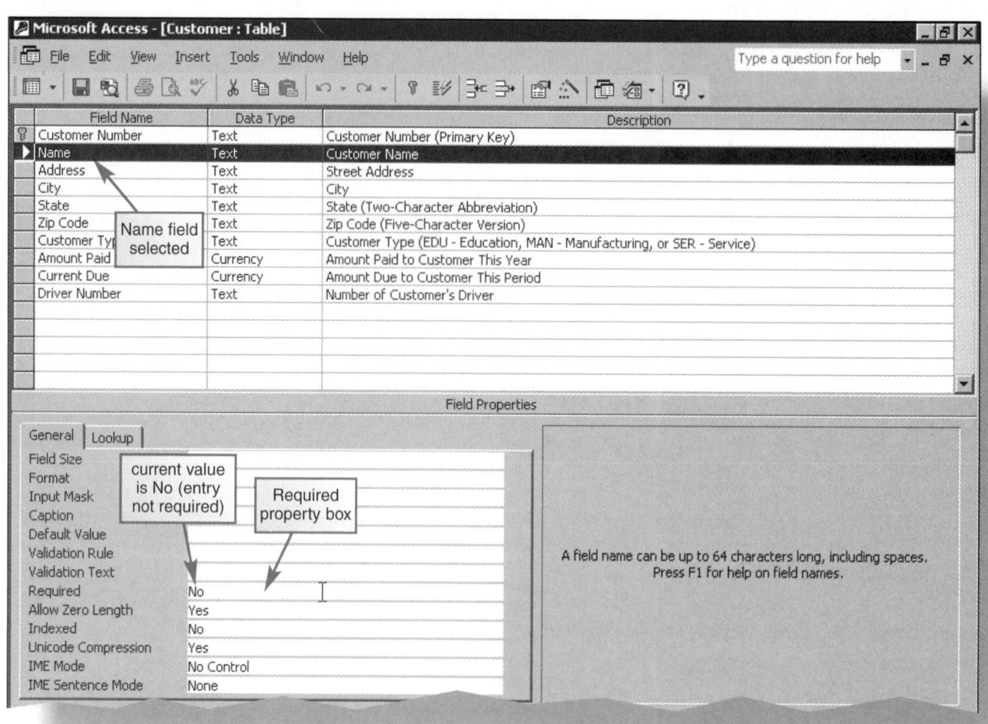

FIGURE 3-39

2 Click the Required property box in the Field Properties pane, and then click the property box arrow that displays. Click Yes in the list.

The value in the Required property box changes to Yes (Figure 3-40). It now is required that the user enter data into the Name field when adding a record.

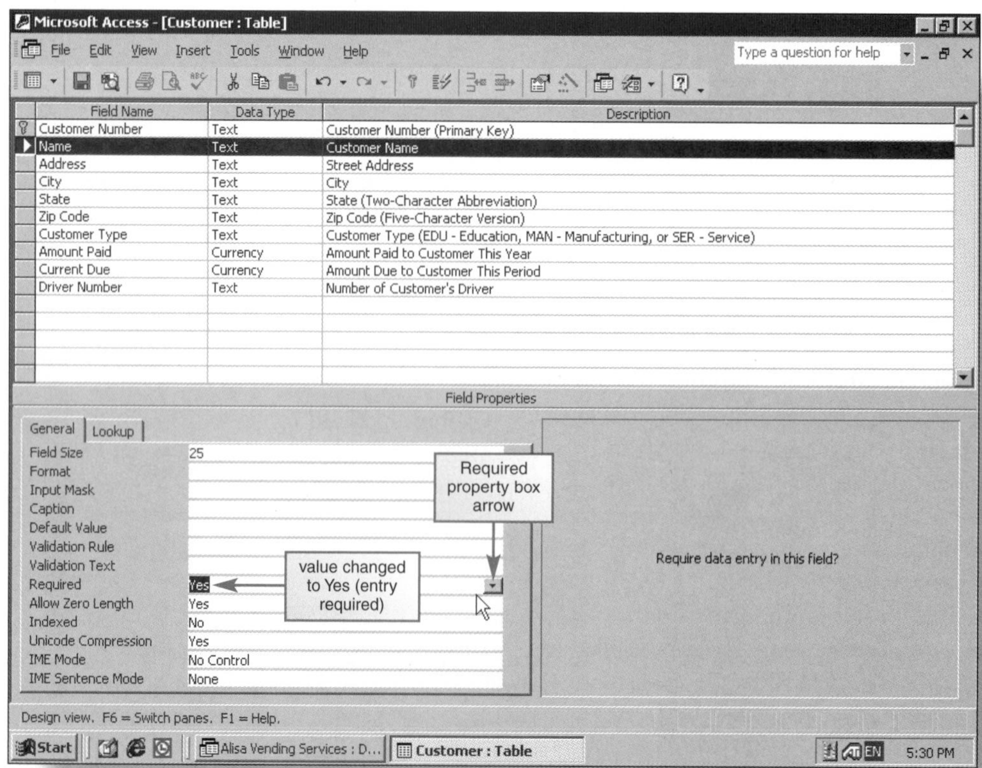

FIGURE 3-40

Specifying a Range

The following step specifies that entries in the Amount Paid field must be between $0.00 and $90,000.00. To indicate this range, you will enter a condition that specifies that the amount paid amount must be both >= 0 (greater than or equal to zero) and <= 90000 (less than or equal to 90000).

To Specify a Range

1 **Select the Amount Paid field by clicking its row selector. Click the Validation Rule property box to produce an insertion point, and then type** `>=0 and <=90000` **as the rule. Click the Validation Text property box to produce an insertion point, and then type** `Must be between $0.00 and $90,000.00` **as the text. In the Validation Text property box, you should type all the text, including the dollar signs and comma.**

The validation rule and text are entered (Figure 3-41). In the Validation Rule property box, Access automatically changed the lowercase letter, a, to uppercase in the word, and.

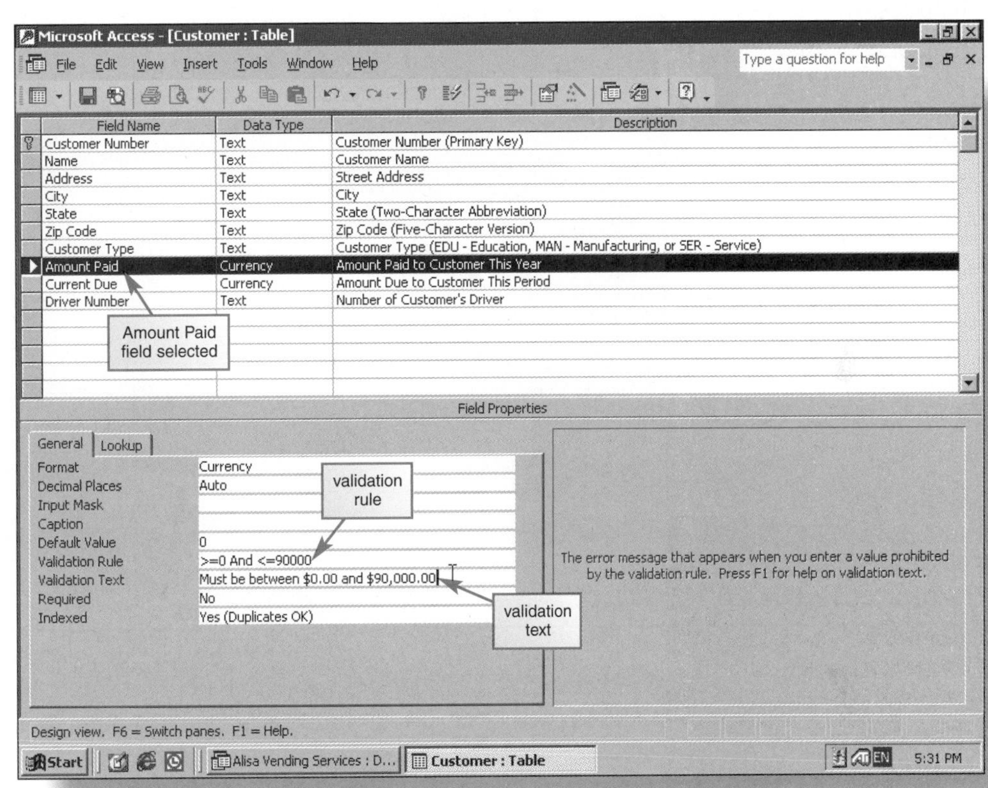

FIGURE 3-41

Users now will be prohibited from entering an amount paid amount that either is less than $0.00 or greater than $90,000.00 when they add records or change the value in the Amount Paid field.

Specifying a Default Value

To specify a default value, enter the value in the Default Value property box. The step on the next page specifies SER as the default value for the Customer Type field. This simply means that if users do not enter a customer type, the type will be SER.

To Specify a Default Value

1 Select the Customer Type field. Click the Default Value property box and then type =SER **as the value.**

The Customer Type field is selected. The default value is entered in the Default Value property box (Figure 3-42).

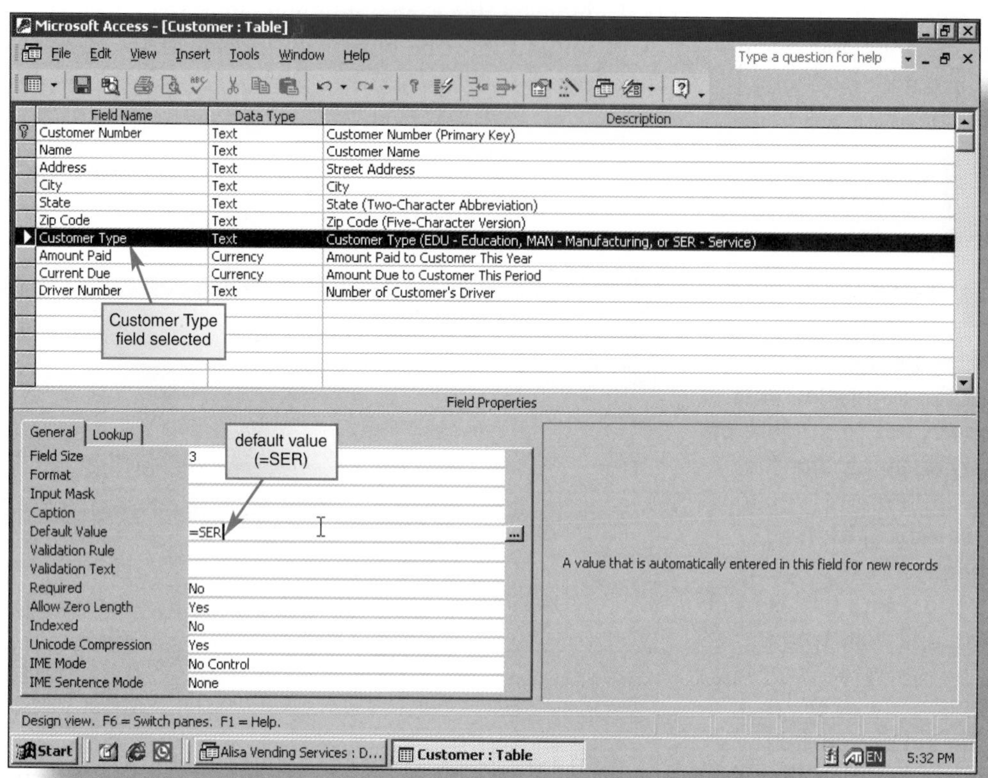

FIGURE 3-42

From this point on, if users do not make an entry in the Customer Type field when adding records, Access will set the value equal to SER.

Validation Rules

You can include the special wildcard symbols in validation rules. For example, to restrict data entry to only those states that start with the letter A, enter A? in the Validation Rule text box.

Specifying a Collection of Legal Values

The only **legal values** for the Customer Type field are EDU, MAN, and SER. An appropriate validation rule for this field can direct Access to reject any entry other than these three possibilities. Perform the following step to specify the legal values for the Customer Type field.

Steps To Specify a Collection of Legal Values

1 Make sure the Customer Type field is selected. Click the Validation Rule property box and then type `=EDU or =MAN or =SER` **as the validation rule. Click the Validation Text property box and then type** `Must be EDU, MAN, or SER` **as the validation text.**

The Customer Type field is selected. The validation rule and text have been entered (Figure 3-43). In the Validation Rule property box, Access automatically inserted quotation marks around the EDU, MAN, and SER values and changed the lowercase letter, o, to uppercase in the word, or.

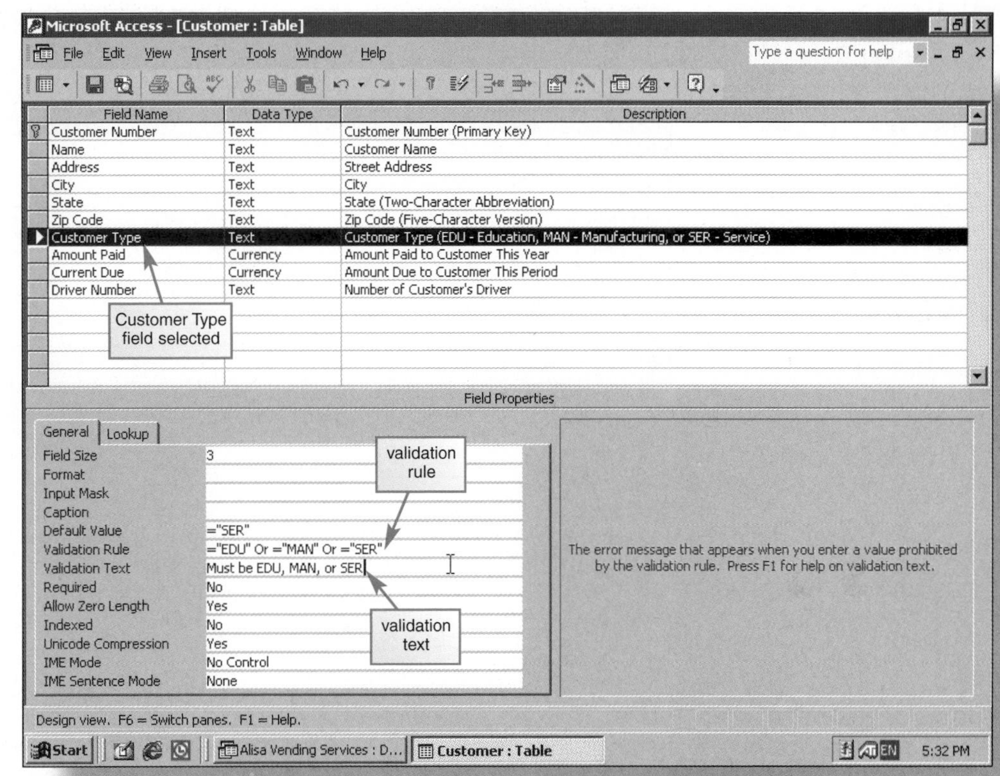

FIGURE 3-43

Users now will be allowed to enter only EDU, MAN, or SER in the Customer Type field when they add records or make changes to this field.

Using a Format

To affect the way data is displayed in a field, you can use a **format**. To use a format, you enter a special symbol, called a **format symbol**, in the field's Format property box. The step on the next page specifies a format for the Customer Number field in the Customer table. The format symbol used in the example is >, which causes Access to display lowercase letters automatically as uppercase. The format symbol < would cause Access to display uppercase letters automatically as lowercase.

More About

Formatting a Datasheet

You also can format the datasheet to display different fonts, cell effects, and gridline colors. To do so, use the Format menu. For example, to change the datasheet font, click Format on the menu bar, click Font, select the desired font, and then click the OK button. To change a cell effect or gridline color, click Format on the menu bar, and then click Datasheet. Click the desired option button to change a cell effect. Click the Gridline Color list box, and then select the desired color to change a gridline color. Click the OK button.

Steps To Specify a Format

1 Select the Customer Number field. Click the Format property box and then type > (Figure 3-44).

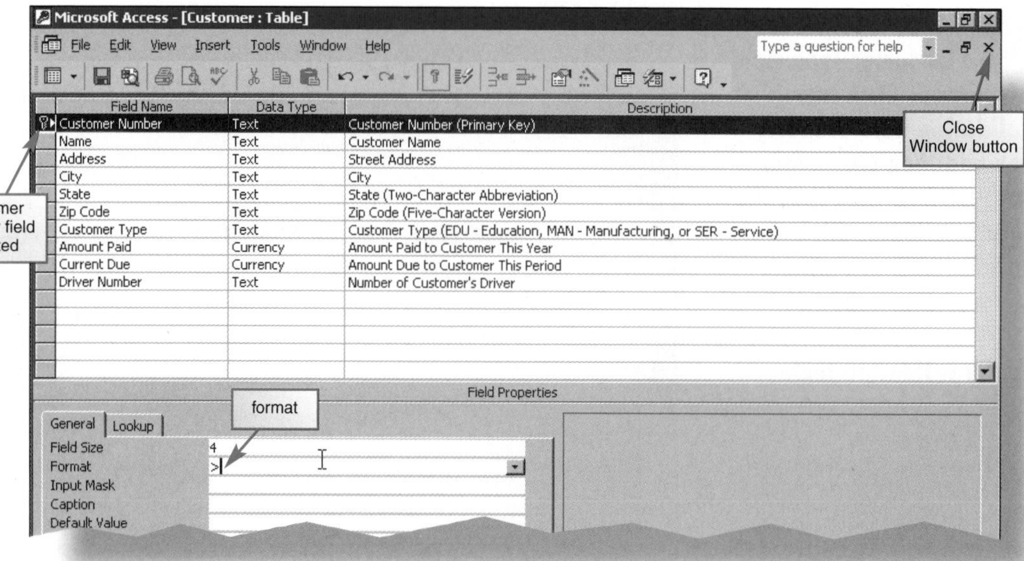

FIGURE 3-44

From this point on, any lowercase letters will be displayed automatically as uppercase when users add records or change the value in the Customer Number field.

Saving Rules, Values, and Formats

To save the validation rules, default values, and formats, perform the following steps.

To Save the Validation Rules, Default Values, and Formats

1 Click the Close Window button for the Customer : Table window to close the window and then point to the Yes button in the Microsoft Access dialog box.

The Microsoft Access dialog box displays, asking if you want to save your changes (Figure 3-45).

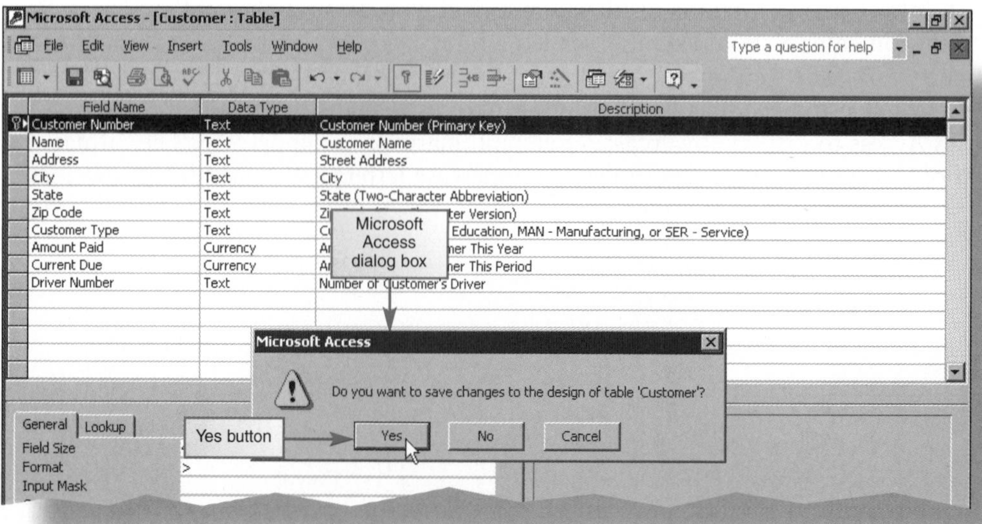

FIGURE 3-45

2 Click the Yes button to save the changes.

The Microsoft Access dialog box displays (Figure 3-46). This message asks if you want the new rules applied to current records. If this were a database used to run a business or to solve some other critical need, you would click Yes. You would want to be sure that the data already in the database does not violate the rules.

3 Click the No button.

The changes are saved.

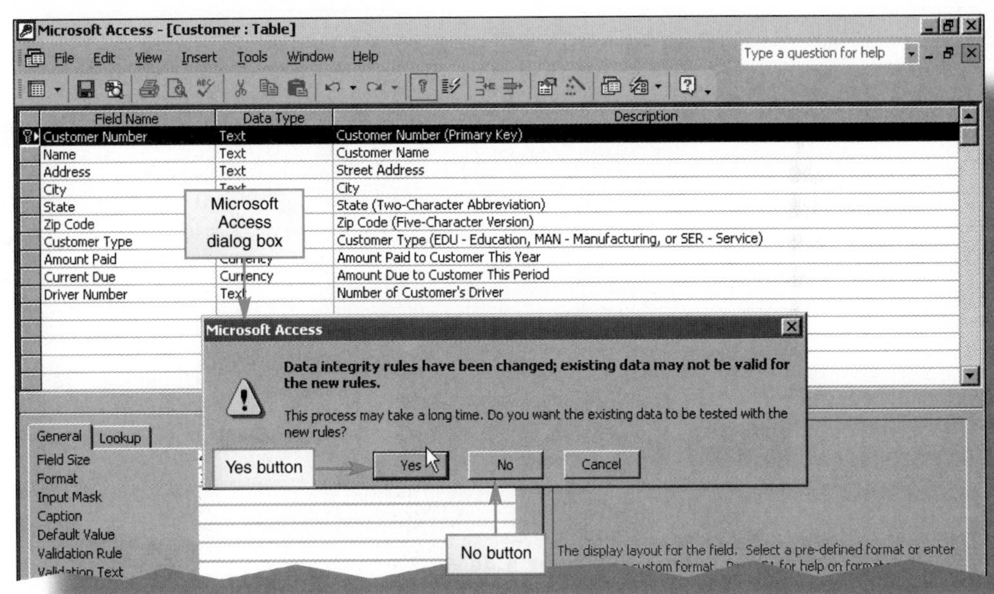

FIGURE 3-46

Updating a Table that Contains Validation Rules

When updating a table that contains validation rules, Access provides assistance in making sure the data entered is valid. It helps in making sure that data is formatted correctly. Access also will not accept invalid data. Entering a number that is out of the required range, for example, or entering a value that is not one of the possible choices, will produce an error message in the form of a dialog box. The database will not be updated until the error is corrected.

If the Customer number entered contains lowercase letters, such as dr22 (Figure 3-47), Access will display the data automatically as DR22 (Figure 3-48).

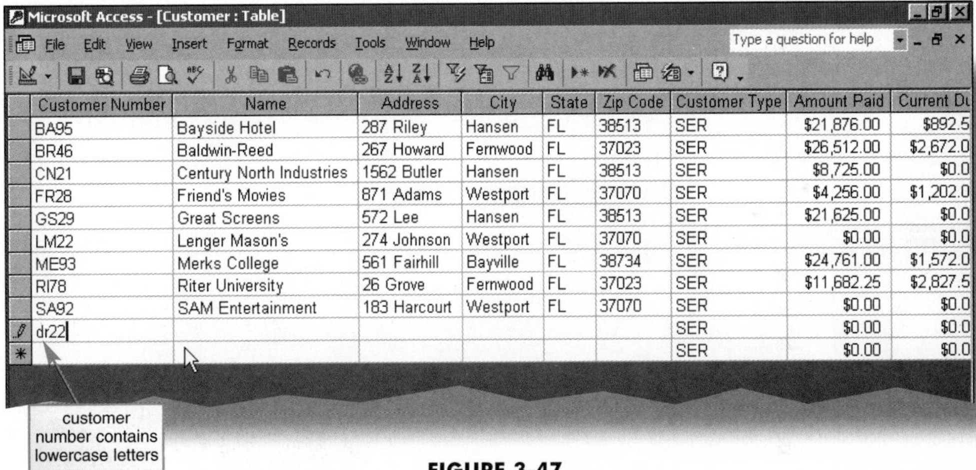

FIGURE 3-47

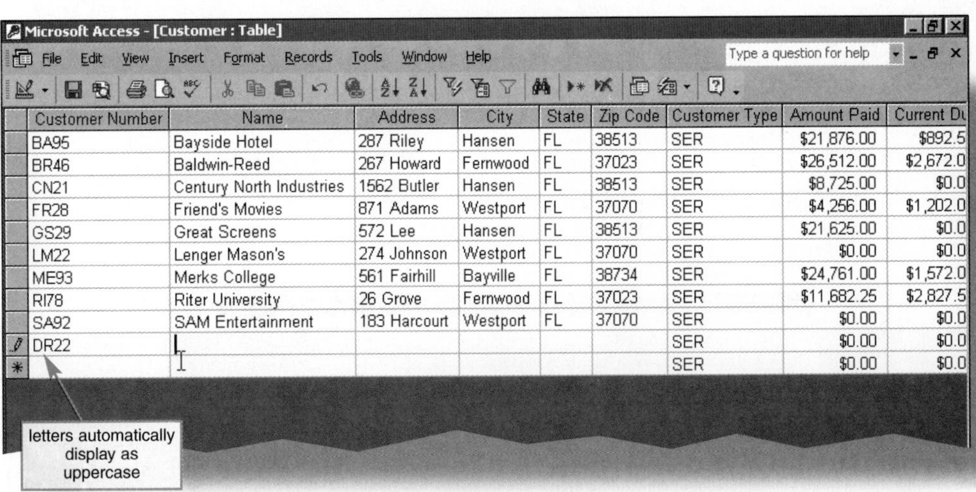

FIGURE 3-48

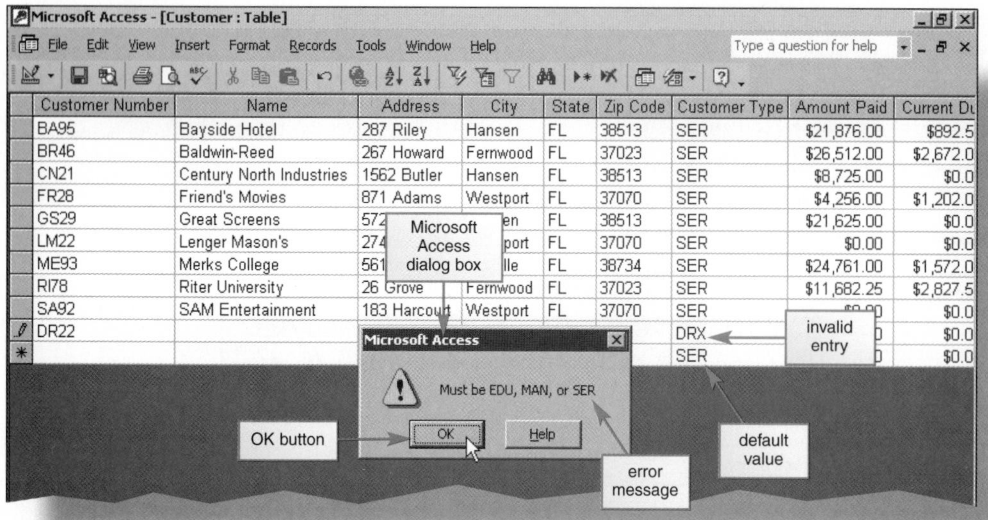

FIGURE 3-49

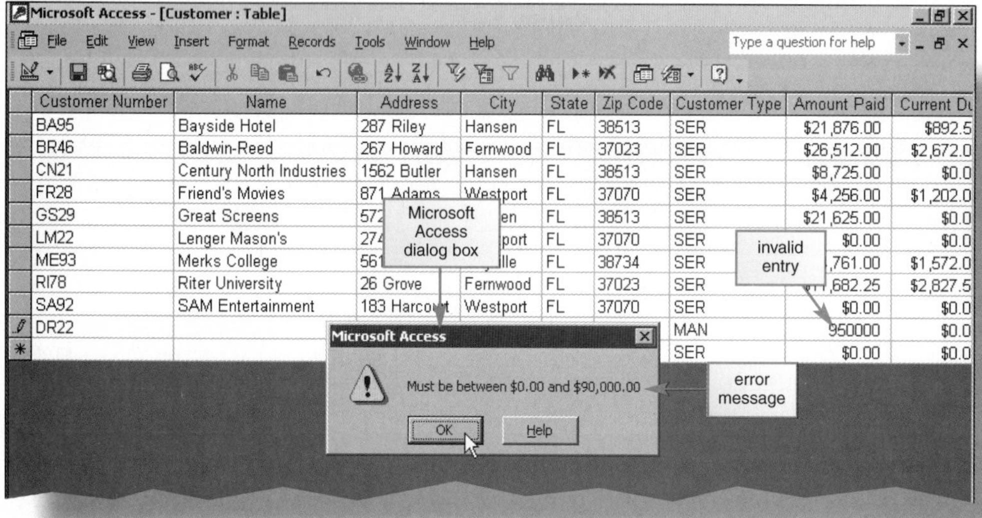

FIGURE 3-50

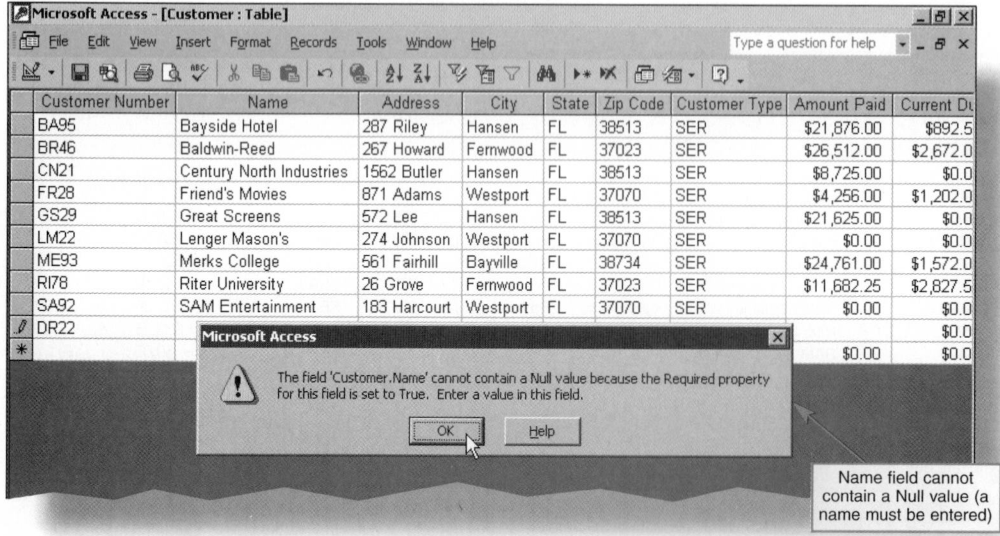

FIGURE 3-51

Instead of the Customer Type field initially being blank, it now contains the value SER, because SER is the default value. Thus, for any customer whose type is SER, it is not necessary to enter the value. By pressing the TAB key, the value SER is accepted.

If the customer type is not valid, such as DRX, Access will display the text message you specified (Figure 3-49) and not allow the data to enter the database.

If the amount paid value is not valid, such as 950000, which is too large, Access also displays the appropriate message (Figure 3-50) and refuses to accept the data.

If a required field contains no data, Access indicates this by displaying an error message as soon as you attempt to leave the record (Figure 3-51). The field must contain a valid entry before Access will move to a different record.

When entering data into a field with a validation rule, you may find that the system displays the error message and you find yourself unable to make the necessary correction. It may be that you cannot remember the validation rule you created or it was created incorrectly. In such a case, you will find that you neither can leave the field nor close the table because you have entered data into a field that violates the validation rule.

If this happens, first try again to type an acceptable entry. If this does not work, repeatedly press the BACKSPACE key to erase the contents of the field and then try to leave the field. If you are unsuccessful using this procedure, press the ESC key until the record is removed from the screen. The record will not be added to the database.

Should the need arise to take this drastic action, you probably have a faulty validation rule. Use the techniques of the previous sections to correct the existing validation rules for the field.

Making Individual Changes to a Field

Earlier, you changed all the entries in the Customer Type field to SER. You now have created a rule that will ensure that only legitimate values (EDU, MAN, or SER) can be entered in the field. To make a change, click the field to be changed to produce an insertion point, use the BACKSPACE or DELETE key to delete the current entry, and then type the new entry.

Complete the following steps to change the Customer Type value on the second and sixth records to MAN and on the seventh and eighth records to SER.

Steps To Make Individual Changes

1 Make sure the Customer table displays in Datasheet view. Click to the right of the SER entry in the Customer Type field on the second record.

An insertion point displays in the Customer Type field on the second record (Figure 3-52).

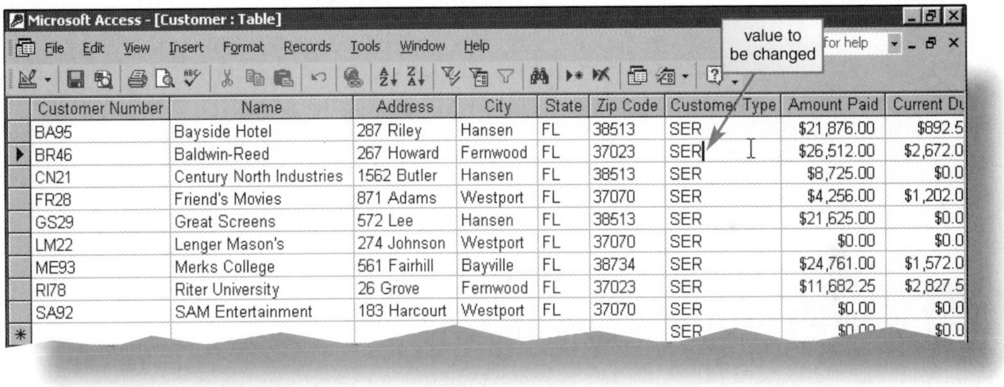

FIGURE 3-52

2 Press the BACKSPACE key three times to delete SER and then type MAN as the new value. In a similar fashion, change the SER on the sixth record to MAN, on the seventh record to EDU, and on the eighth record to EDU (Figure 3-53).

3 Close the Customer : Table window by clicking its Close Window button.

The Customer Type field changes now are complete.

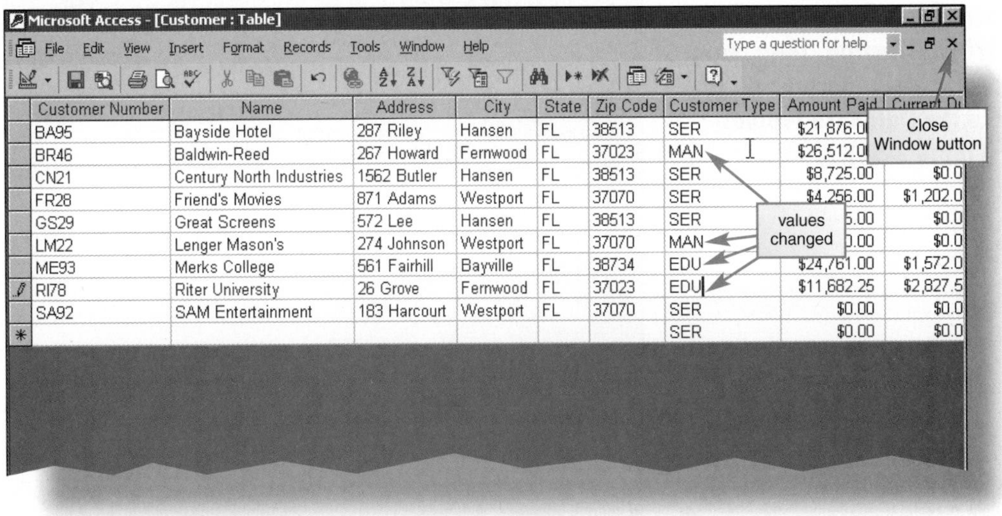

FIGURE 3-53

Specifying Referential Integrity

The property that ensures that the value in a foreign key must match that of another table's primary key is called **referential integrity**. A **foreign key** is a field in one table whose values are required to match the *primary key* of another table. In the Customer table, the Driver Number field is a foreign key that must match the primary key of the Driver table; that is, the driver number for any customer must be a driver currently in the Driver table. A customer whose driver number is 92, for example, should not be stored because there is no such driver.

In Access, to specify referential integrity, you must define a relationship between the tables by using the Relationships command. Access then prohibits any updates to the database that would violate the referential integrity. Access will not allow you to store a customer with a driver number that does not match a driver currently in the Driver table. Access also will prevent you from deleting a driver who currently has customers. Driver 60, for example, currently has customers in the Customer table. If you deleted driver 60, these customers' driver numbers would no longer match anyone in the Driver table.

The type of relationship between two tables specified by the Relationships command is referred to as a **one-to-many relationship**. This means that *one* record in the first table is related to (matches) *many* records in the second table, but each record in the second table is related to only *one* record in the first. In the Alisa Vending Services database, for example, a one-to-many relationship exists between the Driver table and the Customer table. *One* driver is associated with *many* customers, but each customer is associated with only a single driver. In general, the table containing the foreign key will be the *many* part of the relationship.

The following steps use the Relationships command to specify referential integrity by specifying a relationship between the Driver and Customer tables.

Referential Integrity

Referential integrity is an essential property for databases, but providing support for it proved to be one of the most difficult tasks facing the developers of relational database management systems. For more information, visit the Access 2002 More About Web page (scsite.com/ac2002/more.htm) and then click Referential Integrity.

To Specify Referential Integrity

1 **Close any open datasheet on the screen by clicking its Close Window button. Then, point to the Relationships button on the Database toolbar (Figure 3-54).**

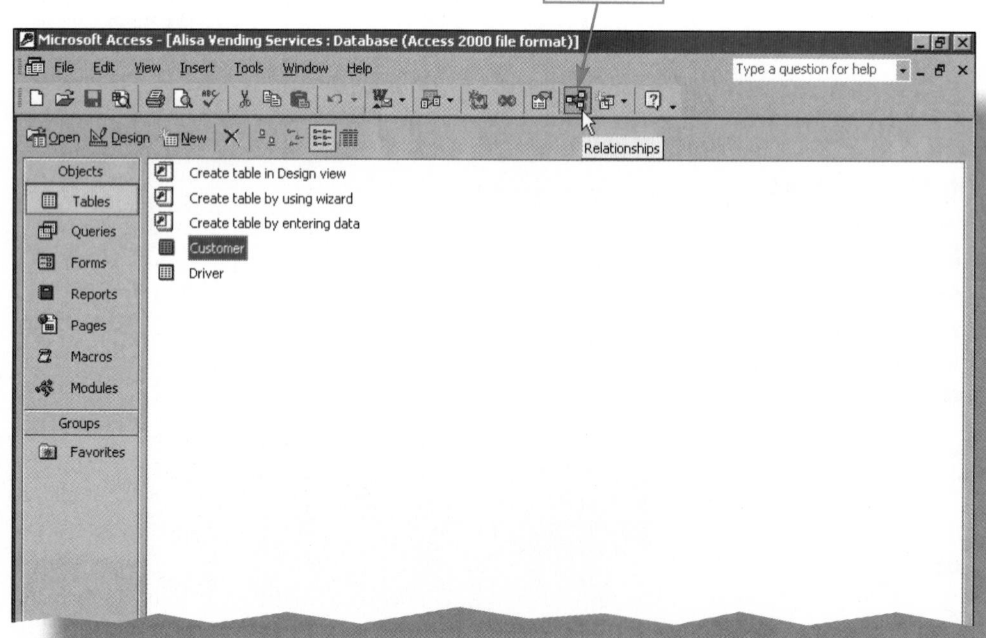

FIGURE 3-54

2 Click the Relationships button, select the Driver table and then point to the Add button in the Show Table dialog box.

The Show Table dialog box displays (Figure 3-55).

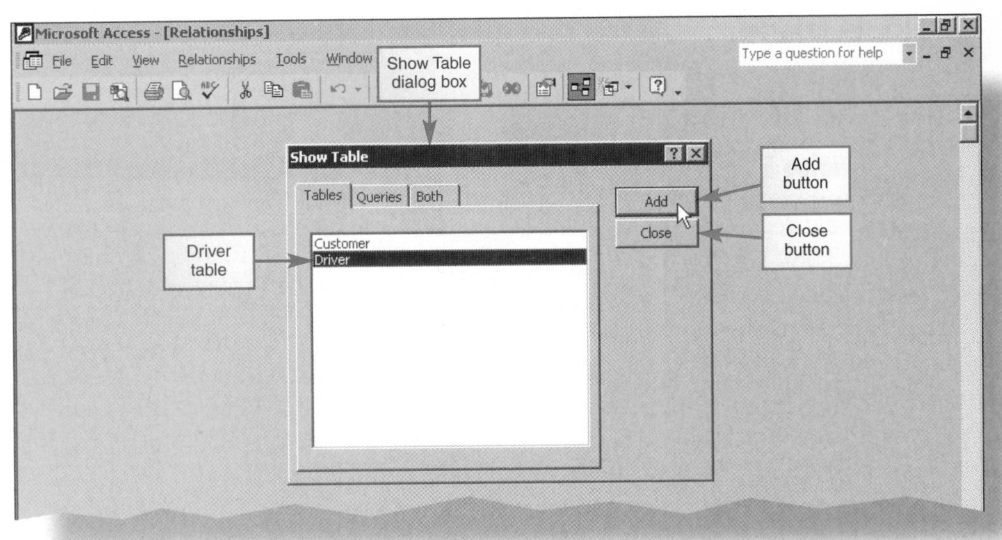

FIGURE 3-55

3 Click the Add button, click the Customer table, click the Add button again, and then click the Close button in the Show Table dialog box. Resize the field lists that display so all fields are visible. Point to the Driver Number field in the field list for the Driver table.

Field lists for the Driver and Customer tables display (Figure 3-56). The lists have been resized so all fields are visible.

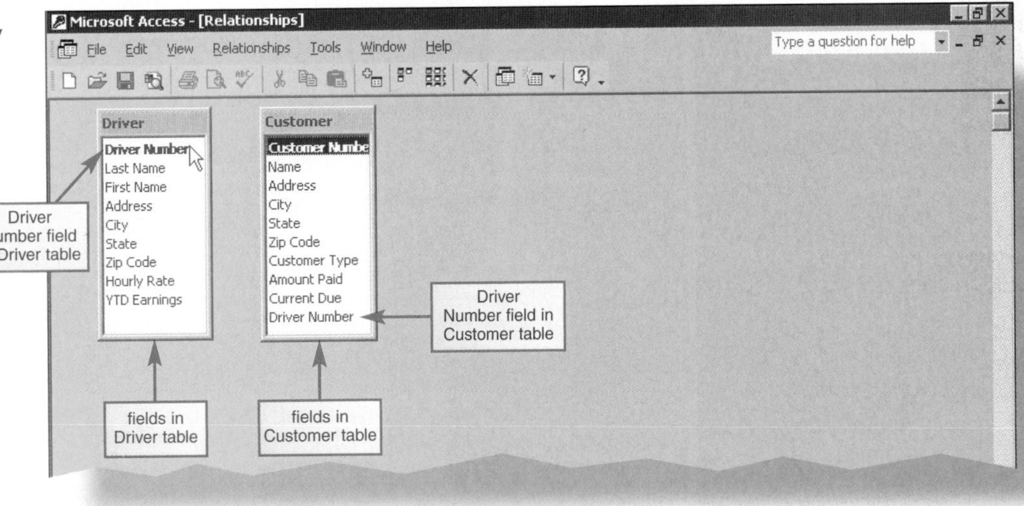

FIGURE 3-56

4 Drag the Driver Number field in the Driver table field list to the Driver Number field in the Customer table field list. Point to the Enforce Referential Integrity check box in the Edit Relationships dialog box.

The Edit Relationships dialog box displays (Figure 3-57). The correct fields (the Driver Number fields) have been identified as the matching fields.

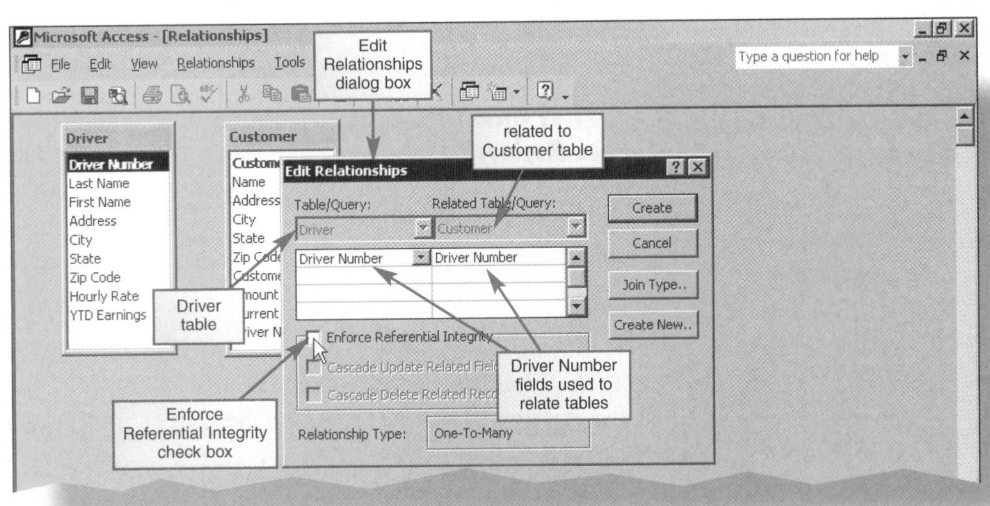

FIGURE 3-57

5 Click the Enforce Referential Integrity check box and point to the Create button in the Edit Relationships dialog box.

Enforce Referential Integrity is selected (Figure 3-58). With Enforce Referential Integrity selected, Access will reject any update that would violate referential integrity.

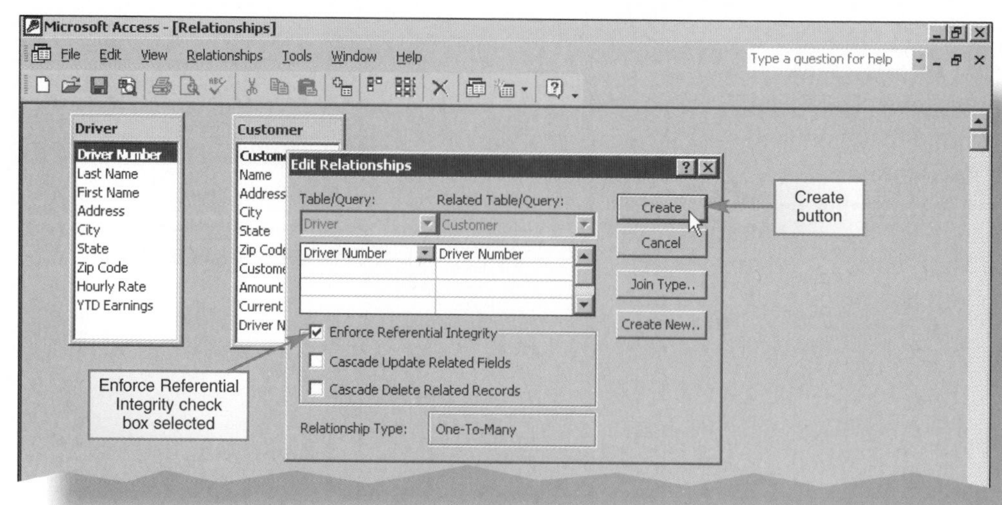

FIGURE 3-58

6 Click the Create button. Point to the Close Window button for the Relationships window.

Access creates the relationship and displays it visually with the **relationship line** *joining the two Driver Number fields (Figure 3-59). The number 1 at the top of the relationship line close to the Driver Number field in the Driver table indicates that the Driver table is the "one" part of the relationship. The infinity symbol at the other end of the relationship line indicates that the Customer table is the "many" part of the relationship.*

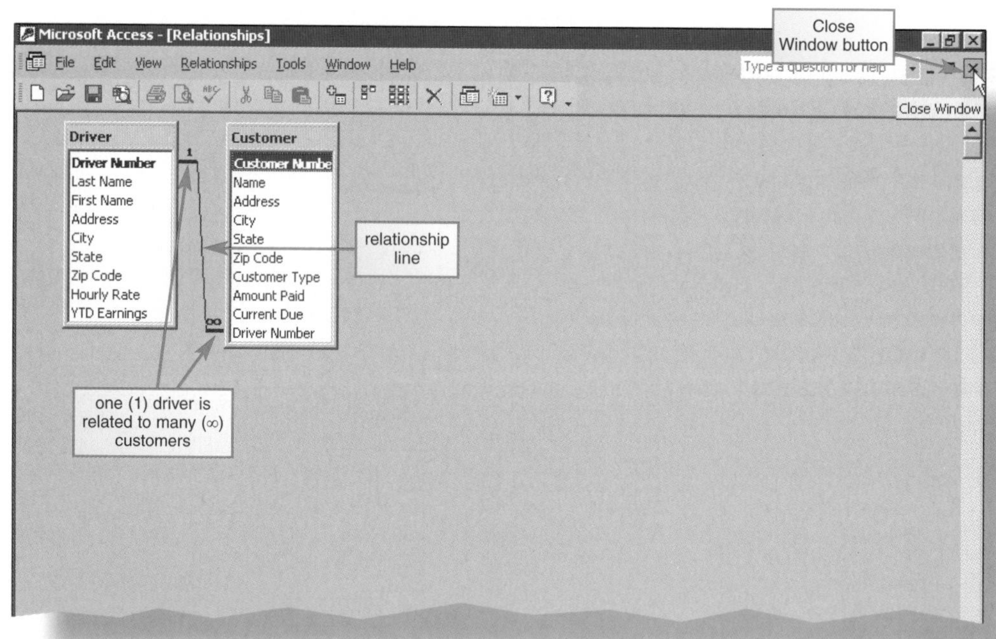

FIGURE 3-59

7 Close the Relationships window by clicking its Close Window button. When the Microsoft Access dialog box displays, click the Yes button to save the relationship you created.

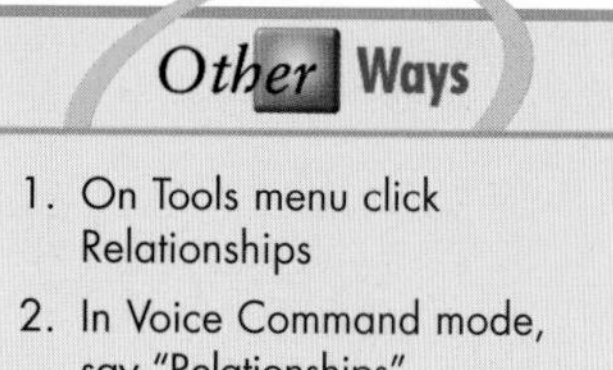

1. On Tools menu click Relationships
2. In Voice Command mode, say "Relationships"

Access now will reject any number in the Driver Number field in the Customer table that does not match a driver number in the Driver table. Attempting to add a customer whose Driver Number field does not match would result in the error message shown in Figure 3-60.

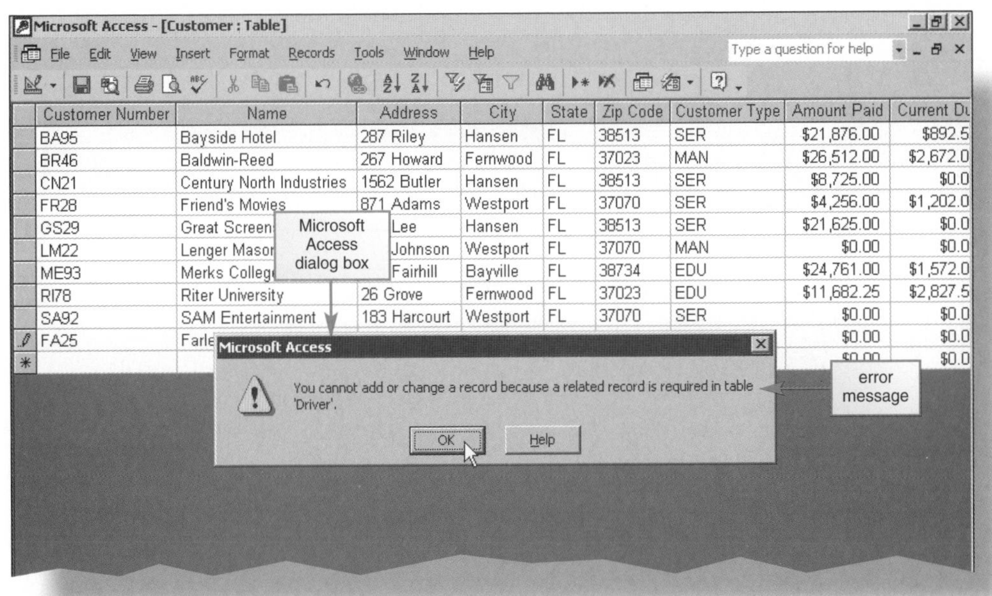

FIGURE 3-60

A deletion of a driver for whom related customers exist also would be rejected. Attempting to delete driver 60 from the Driver table, for example, would result in the message shown in Figure 3-61.

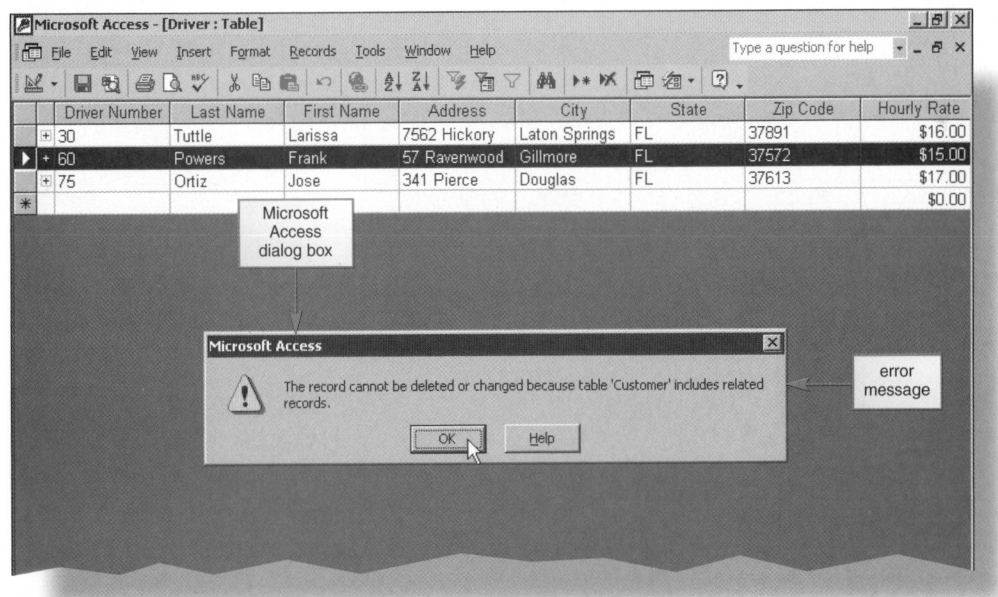

FIGURE 3-61

Using Subdatasheets

Now that the Driver table is related to the Customer table, it is possible to view the customers of a given driver when you are viewing the datasheet for the Driver table. The customers for the driver will display right under the driver in a **subdatasheet**. The fact that such a subdatasheet is available is indicated by a plus sign that displays in front of the rows in the Driver table. To display the subdatasheet, click the plus sign. The steps on the next page display the subdatasheet for driver 60.

More About

Relationships: The Find Unmatched Query Wizard

Occasionally, you may want to find records in one table that have no matching records in another table. For example, suppose the customers of Alisa Vending Services placed orders for vending machine maintenance. You may want to know which customers have no orders. The Find Unmatched Query Wizard allows you to find unmatched records. To use the Find Unmatched Query Wizard, click the New Object: AutoForm button arrow, and then click Query. When the New Query dialog box displays, click the Find Unmatched Query Wizard. Follow the directions in the Find Unmatched Query Wizard dialog boxes.

More About

Relationships: Printing Relationships

You can obtain a printed copy of your relationships once you have created them. To do so, first click the Relationships button to display the relationships. Next, click File on the menu bar and then click Print Relationships.

Steps To Use a Subdatasheet

1 With the Database window on the screen and the Tables object selected, right-click Driver. Click Open on the shortcut menu. Point to the plus sign in front of the row for driver 60 (Figure 3-62).

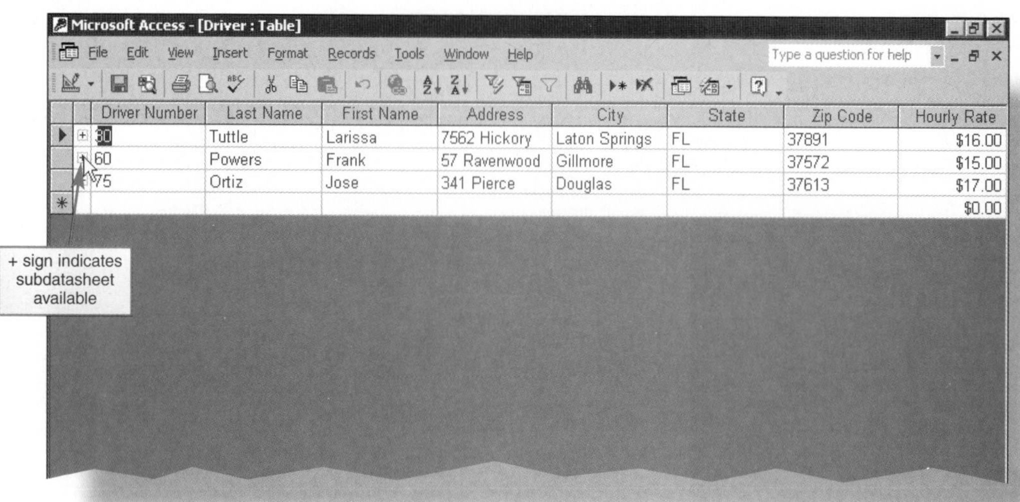

FIGURE 3-62

2 Click the plus sign in front of the row for driver 60.

The subdatasheet displays (Figure 3-63). It contains only those customers that are assigned to driver 60.

3 Click the minus sign to remove the subdatasheet and then close the datasheet for the Driver table by clicking its Close Window button.

The subdatasheet is removed and the datasheet no longer displays.

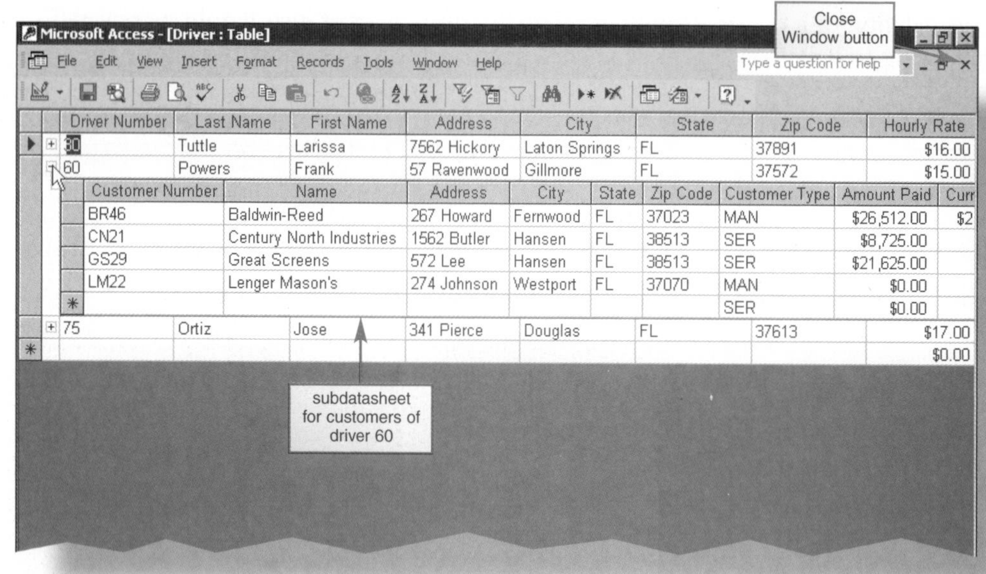

FIGURE 3-63

Ordering Records

Recall from previous discussions that Access sequences the records by customer number whenever listing them because the Customer Number field is the primary key. To change the order in which records display, use the Sort Ascending or Sort Descending buttons on the Table Datasheet toolbar. Either button reorders the records based on the field in which the insertion point is located.

Perform the following steps to order the records by city using the Sort Ascending button.

Steps To Use the Sort Ascending Button to Order Records

1 Open the Customer table in Datasheet view, and then click the City field on the first record (any other record would do as well). Point to the Sort Ascending button on the Table Datasheet toolbar (Figure 3-64).

Customer Number	Name	Address	City	State	Zip Code	Customer Type	Amount Paid	Current Du
BA95	Bayside Hotel	287	sen	FL	38513	SER	$21,876.00	$892.5
BR46	Baldwin-Reed	267 Howard	Fernwo	FL	37023	MAN	$26,512.00	$2,672.0
CN21	Century North Industries	1562 Butler	Hansen	FL	38513	SER	$8,725.00	$0.0
FR28	Friend's Movies	871 Adams	Westport	FL	37070	SER	$4,256.00	$1,202.0
GS29	Great Screens	572 Lee	Hans		38513	SER	$21,625.00	$0.0
LM22	Lenger Mason's	274 Johnson	Wes		37070	MAN	$0.00	$0.0
ME93	Merks College	561 Fairhill	Bayville	FL	38734	EDU	$24,761.00	$1,572.0
RI78	Riter University	26 Grove	Fernwood	FL	37023	EDU	$11,682.25	$2,827.5
SA92	SAM Entertainment	183 Harcourt	Westport	FL	37070	SER	$0.00	$0.0
*						SER	$0.00	$0.0

FIGURE 3-64

2 Click the Sort Ascending button.

The rows now are ordered by city (Figure 3-65).

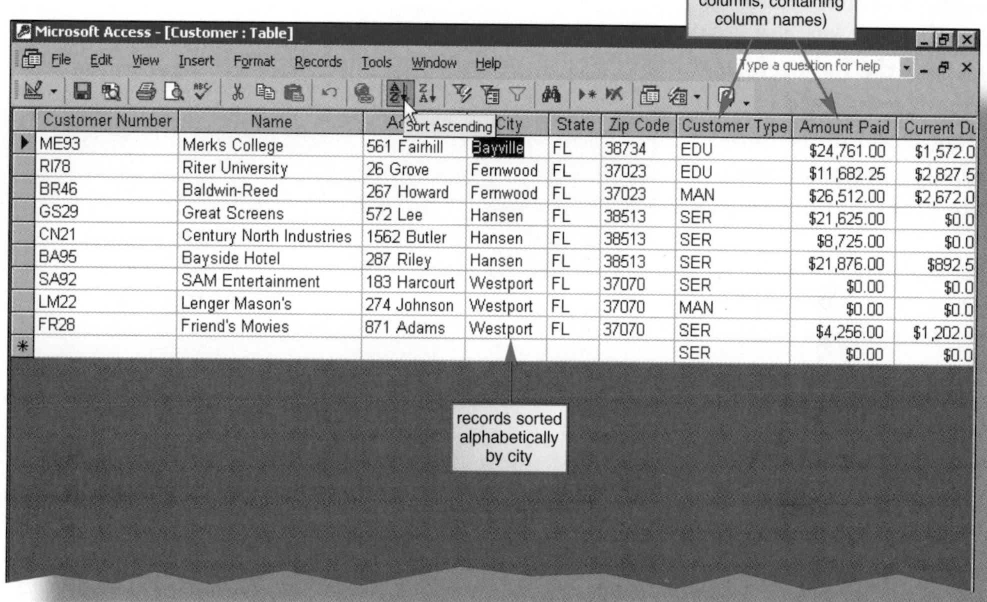

Customer Number	Name	Address	City	State	Zip Code	Customer Type	Amount Paid	Current Du
ME93	Merks College	561 Fairhill	Bayville	FL	38734	EDU	$24,761.00	$1,572.0
RI78	Riter University	26 Grove	Fernwood	FL	37023	EDU	$11,682.25	$2,827.5
BR46	Baldwin-Reed	267 Howard	Fernwood	FL	37023	MAN	$26,512.00	$2,672.0
GS29	Great Screens	572 Lee	Hansen	FL	38513	SER	$21,625.00	$0.0
CN21	Century North Industries	1562 Butler	Hansen	FL	38513	SER	$8,725.00	$0.0
BA95	Bayside Hotel	287 Riley	Hansen	FL	38513	SER	$21,876.00	$892.5
SA92	SAM Entertainment	183 Harcourt	Westport	FL	37070	SER	$0.00	$0.0
LM22	Lenger Mason's	274 Johnson	Westport	FL	37070	MAN	$0.00	$0.0
FR28	Friend's Movies	871 Adams	Westport	FL	37070	SER	$4,256.00	$1,202.0
*						SER	$0.00	$0.0

FIGURE 3-65

Other Ways

1. On Records menu click Sort, then click Sort Ascending
2. In Voice Command mode, say "Sort Ascending"

If you wanted to sort the data in reverse order, you would click the Sort Descending button instead of the Sort Ascending button.

Ordering Records on Multiple Fields

Just as you are able to sort the answer to a query on multiple fields, you also can sort the data that displays in a datasheet on multiple fields. To do so, the major and minor keys must be next to each other in the datasheet with the major key on the left. (If this is not the case, you can drag the columns into the correct position. Instead of dragging, however, usually it will be easier to use a query that has the data sorted in the desired order.)

Given that the major and minor keys are in the correct position, select both fields and then click the Sort Ascending button on the Table Datasheet toolbar. To select the fields, use the **field selector**, the small bar at the top of the column that you click to select an entire field in a datasheet. Click the field selector for the first field (the major key). Next, hold down the SHIFT key and then click the field selector for the second field (the minor key).

Order records on the combination of the Customer Type and Amount Paid fields using the Sort Ascending button by completing the following steps.

Steps To Use the Sort Ascending Button to Order Records on Multiple Fields

1 Click the field selector (see Figure 3-65 on the previous page) at the top of the Customer Type column to select the entire column. Hold down the SHIFT key and then click the field selector for the Amount Paid column. Point to the Sort Ascending button on the Table Datasheet toolbar.

The Customer Type and Amount Paid columns both are selected (Figure 3-66).

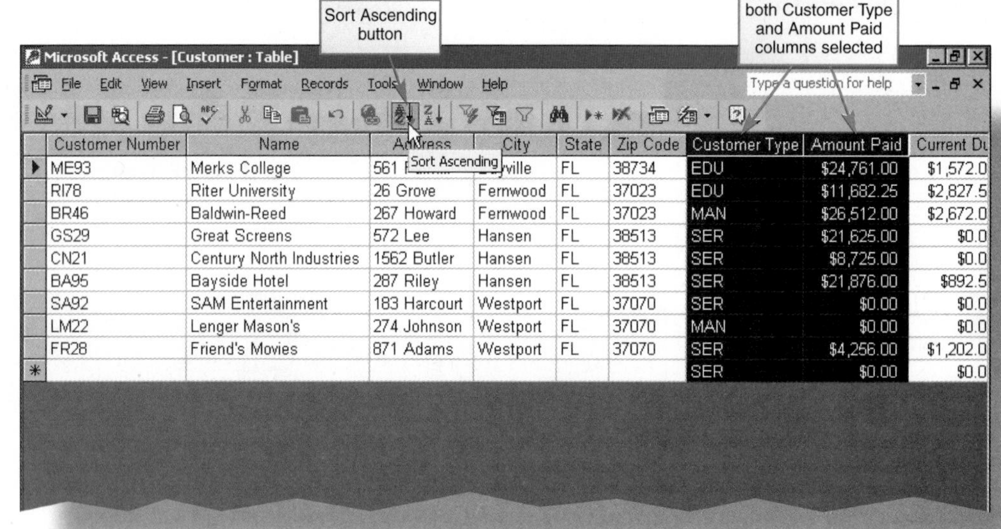

FIGURE 3-66

2 Click the Sort Ascending button.

The rows are ordered by customer type (Figure 3-67). Within each group of customers of the same type, the rows are ordered by the amount paid amount.

3 Close the Customer : Table window by clicking its Close Window button. Click the No button in the Microsoft Access dialog box to abandon the changes.

The next time the table is open, the records will display in their original order.

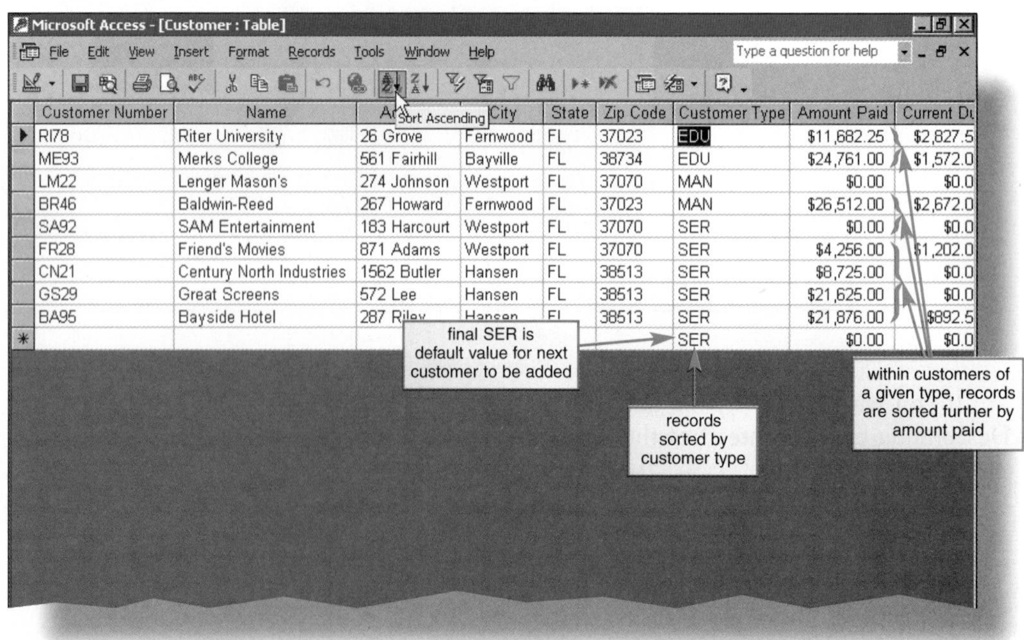

FIGURE 3-67

Creating and Using Indexes

You already are familiar with the concept of an index. The index in the back of a book contains important words or phrases together with a list of pages on which the given words or phrases can be found. An **index** for a table is similar. Figure 3-68, for example, shows the Customer table along with an index built on names. In this case, the items of interest are names instead of keywords or phrases as is the case in the back of this book. The field or fields on which the index is built is called the **index key**. Thus, in Figure 3-68, the Name field is the index key. (The structure of an index actually is a little more complicated than the one shown in the figure and is beyond the scope of this book. The concept is the same, however, and the structure shown in the figure illustrates the important concepts.)

Index on Name

NAME	RECORD NUMBER
Baldwin-Reed	2
Bayside Hotel	1
Century North Industries	3
Friend's Movies	4
Great Screens	5
Lenger Mason's	6
Merks College	7
Riter University	8
SAM Entertainment	9

Customer Table

RECORD NUMBER	CUSTOMER NUMBER	NAME	ADDRESS	CITY	STATE	ZIP CODE	...
1	BA95	Bayside Hotel	287 Riley	Hansen	FL	38513	...
2	BR46	Baldwin-Reed	267 Howard	Fernwood	FL	37023	...
3	CN21	Century North Industries	1562 Butler	Hansen	FL	38513	...
4	FR28	Friend's Movies	871 Adams	Westport	FL	37070	...
5	GS29	Great Screens	572 Lee	Hansen	FL	38513	...
6	LM22	Lenger Mason's	274 Johnson	Westport	FL	37070	...
7	ME93	Merks College	561 Fairhill	Bayville	FL	38734	
8	RI78	Riter University	26 Grove	Fernwood	FL	37023	
9	SA92	SAM Entertainment	183 Harcourt	Westport	FL	37070	...

FIGURE 3-68

Each name occurs in the index along with the number of the record on which the corresponding customer is located. Further, the names appear in the index in alphabetical order. If Access were to use this index to find the record on which the name is Friend's Movies, for example, it could scan rapidly the names in the index to find Friend's Movies. Once it did, it would determine the corresponding record number (4) and then go immediately to record 4 in the Customer table, thus finding this customer more quickly than if it had to look through the entire Customer table one record at a time. Indexes make the process of retrieving records very fast and efficient. (With relatively small tables, the increased efficiency associated with indexes will not be apparent readily. In practice, it is common to encounter tables with thousands, tens of thousands, or even hundreds of thousands, of records. In such cases, the increase in efficiency is dramatic. In fact, without indexes, many operations in such databases would simply not be practical. They would take too long to complete.)

Indexes

The most common structure for high-performance indexes is called a B-tree. It is a highly efficient structure that supports very rapid access to records in the database as well as a rapid alternative to sorting records. Virtually all systems use some version of the B-tree structure. For more information, visit the Access 2002 More About Web page (scsite.com/ac2002/more.htm) and then click B-tree.

Because no two customers happen to have the same name, the Record Number column contains only single values. This may not always be the case. Consider the index on the Zip Code field shown in Figure 3-69. In this index, the Record Number column contains several values, namely all the records on which the corresponding zip code displays. The first row, for example, indicates that zip code 37023 is found on records 2 and 8; the second row indicates that zip code 37070 is found on records 4, 6, and 9. If Access were to use this index to find all customers in zip code 37070, it could scan rapidly the zip codes in the index to find 37070. Once it did, it would determine the corresponding record numbers (4, 6, and 9) and then go immediately to these records. It would not have to examine any other records in the Customer table.

Index on Zip Code

ZIP CODE	RECORD NUMBER
37023	2,8
37070	4,6,9
38513	1,3,5
38734	7

Customer Table

RECORD NUMBER	CUSTOMER NUMBER	NAME	ADDRESS	CITY	STATE	ZIP CODE	. . .
1	BA95	Bayside Hotel	287 Riley	Hansen	FL	38513	...
2	BR46	Baldwin-Reed	267 Howard	Fernwood	FL	37023	...
3	CN21	Century North Industries	1562 Butler	Hansen	FL	38513	
4	FR28	Friend's Movies	871 Adams	Westport	FL	37070	...
5	GS29	Great Screens	572 Lee	Hansen	FL	38513	...
6	LM22	Lenger Mason's	274 Johnson	Westport	FL	37070	...
7	ME93	Merks College	561 Fairhill	Bayville	FL	38734	
8	RI78	Riter University	26 Grove	Fernwood	FL	37023	
9	SA92	SAM Entertainment	183 Harcourt	Westport	FL	37070	...

FIGURE 3-69

Another benefit of indexes is that they provide an efficient way to order records. That is, if the records are to display in a certain order, Access can use an index instead of physically having to rearrange the records in the database. Physically rearranging the records in a different order, which is called **sorting**, can be a very time-consuming process.

To see how indexes can be used for alphabetizing records, look at the record numbers in the index (Figure 3-68 on the previous page). Suppose you used these to list all customers; that is, simply follow down the Record Number column, listing the corresponding customers. In this example, first you would list the customer on record 2 (Baldwin-Reed), then the customer on record 1 (Bayside Hotel), then the customer on record 3 (Century North Industries), and so on. The customers would be listed alphabetically by name without actually sorting the table.

To gain the benefits from an index, you first must create one. Access automatically creates an index on the primary key as well as some other special fields. If, as is the case with both the Customer and Driver tables, a table contains a field called Zip Code, for example, Access will create an index for it automatically. You must create any other indexes you feel you need, indicating the field or fields on which the index is to be built.

Although the index key usually will be a single field, it can be a combination of fields. For example, you might want to sort records by amount paid within customer type. In other words, the records are ordered by a combination of fields: Customer Type and Amount Paid. An index can be used for this purpose by using a combination of fields for the index key. In this case, you must assign a name to the index. It is a good idea to assign a name that represents the combination of fields. For example, an index whose key is the combination of the Customer Type and Amount Paid fields, might be called TypePaid.

How Does Access Use an Index?

Access creates an index whenever you request that it do so. It takes care of all the work in setting up and maintaining the index. In addition, Access will use the index automatically.

If you request that data be sorted in a particular order and Access determines that an index is available that it can use to make the process efficient, it will do so. If no index is available, it still will sort the data in the order you requested; it will just take longer.

Similarly, if you request that Access locate a particular record that has a certain value in a particular field, Access will use an index if an appropriate one exists. If not, it will have to examine each record until it finds the one you want.

In both cases, the added efficiency provided by an index will not be apparent readily in tables that have only a few records. As you add more records to your tables, however, the difference can be dramatic. Even with only 50 to 100 records, you will notice a difference. You can imagine how dramatic the difference would be in a table with 50,000 records.

When Should You Create an Index?

An index improves efficiency for sorting and finding records. On the other hand, indexes occupy space on your disk. They also require Access to do extra work. Access must maintain all the indexes that have been created up to date. Thus, both advantages and disadvantages exist to using indexes. Consequently, the decision as to which indexes to create is an important one. The following guidelines should help you in this process.

Create an index on a field (or combination of fields) if one or more of the following conditions are present:

1. The field is the primary key of the table (Access will create this index automatically).
2. The field is the foreign key in a relationship you have created.
3. You frequently will need your data to be sorted on the field.
4. You frequently will need to locate a record based on a value in this field.

Because Access handles 1 automatically, you need only to concern yourself about 2, 3, and 4. If you think you will need to see customer data arranged in order of amount paid amounts, for example, you should create an index on the Amount Paid field. If you think you will need to see the data arranged by amount paid within driver number, you should create an index on the combination of the Driver Number field and the Amount Paid field. Similarly, if you think you will need to find a customer given the customer's name, you should create an index on the Name field.

More About

More About Quick Reference

For a table that lists how to complete tasks covered in this book using the mouse, menu, shortcut menu, and keyboard, see the Quick Reference Summary at the back of this book, or visit the Shelly Cashman Series Office XP Web page (scsite.com/offxp/qr.htm) and then click Microsoft Access 2002.

More About

Primary Keys: The Find Duplicates Query Wizard

One reason to include a primary key for a table is to eliminate duplicate records. There still is a possibility, however, that duplicate records can get into your database. (Perhaps, a customer's name was misspelled and the data entry person assumed it was a new customer.) The Find Duplicates Query Wizard allows you to find duplicate records. To use the Find Duplicates Query Wizard, click the table that you want to query, click the New Object: AutoForm button arrow, and then click Query. When the New Query dialog box displays, click the Find Duplicates Query Wizard. Follow the directions in the Find Duplicates Query Wizard dialog boxes.

Creating Single-Field Indexes

A **single-field index** is an index whose key is a single field. In this case, the index key is to be the Name field. In creating an index, you need to indicate whether to allow duplicates in the index key; that is, two records that have the same value. For example, in the index for the Name field, if duplicates are not allowed, Access would not allow the addition of a customer whose name is the same as the name of a customer already in the database. In the index for the Name field, duplicates will be allowed. Perform the following steps to create a single-field index.

Steps To Create a Single-Field Index

1 Right-click Customer. Click Design View on the shortcut menu, and then, if necessary, maximize the Customer : Table window. Click the row selector to select the Name field. Click the Indexed property box in the Field Properties pane. Click the property box arrow that displays.

The Indexed list displays (Figure 3-70). The items in the list are No (no index), Yes (Duplicates OK) (create an index and allow duplicates), and Yes (No Duplicates) (create an index but reject (do not allow) duplicates).

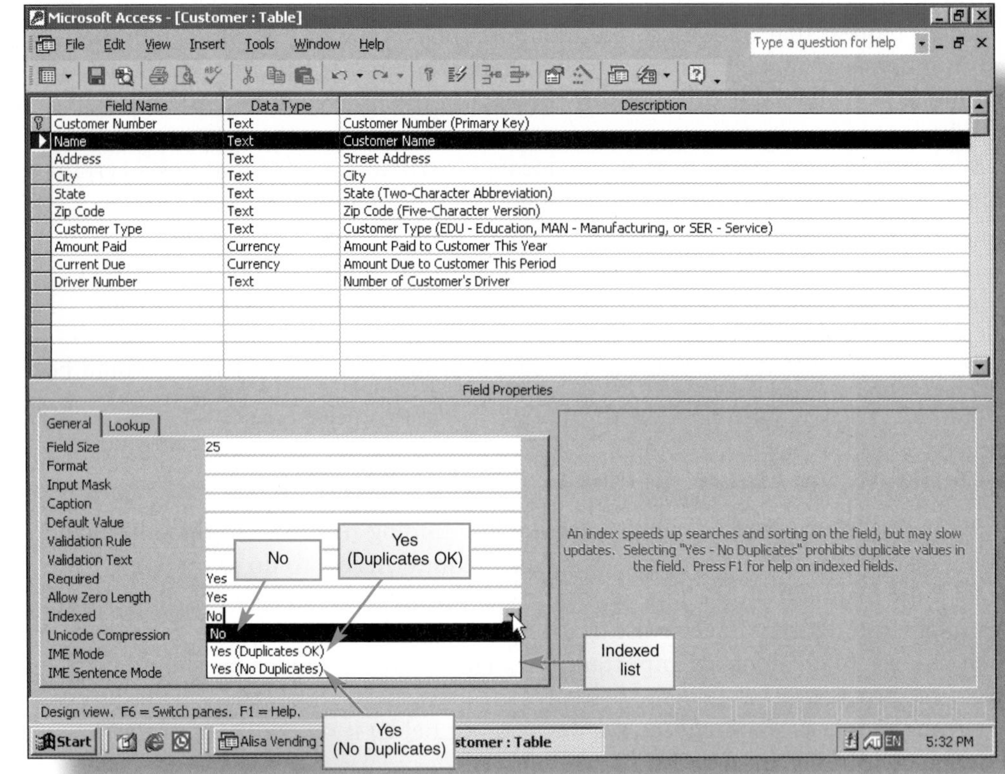

FIGURE 3-70

2 Click the Yes (Duplicates OK) item in the list.

The index on the Name field now will be created and is ready for use as soon as you save your work.

Creating Multiple-Field Indexes

Creating **multiple-field indexes**, that is, indexes whose key is a combination of fields, involves a different process from creating single-field indexes. To create multiple-field indexes, you will use the **Indexes button** on the Table Design toolbar, enter a name for the index, and then enter the combination of fields that make up the index key. The following steps create a multiple-field index with the name TypePaid. The key will be the combination of the Customer Type field and the Amount Paid fields.

Steps To Create a Multiple-Field Index

1 Point to the Indexes button on the Table Design toolbar (Figure 3-71).

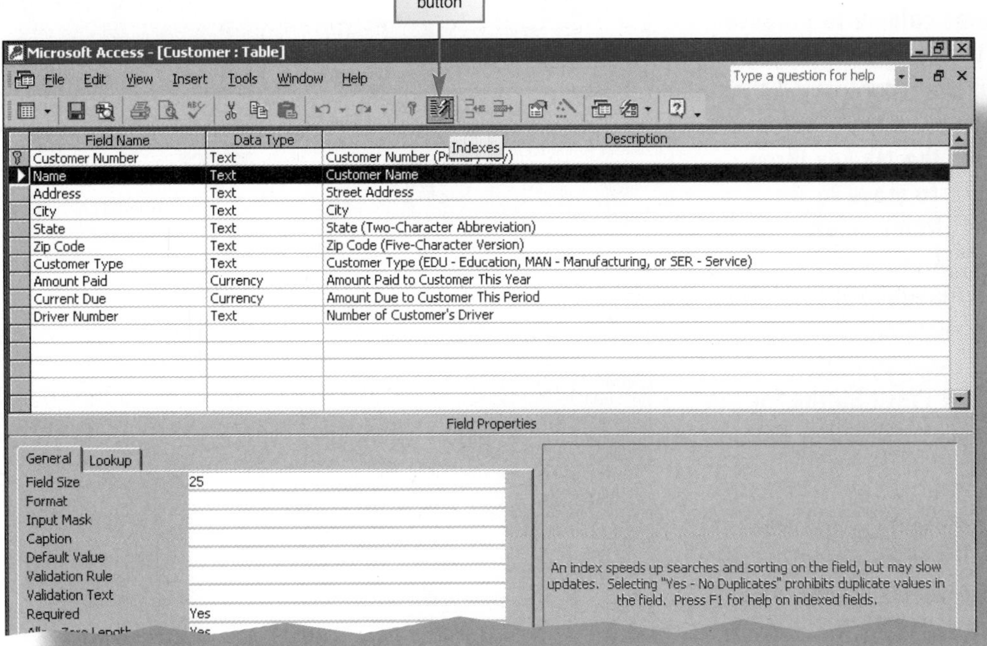

FIGURE 3-71

2 Click the Indexes button. Click the blank row (the row following Name) in the Index Name column in the Indexes: Customer dialog box. Type `TypePaid` **as the index name, and then press the TAB key. Point to the down arrow.**

The Indexes: Customer dialog box displays. It shows the indexes that already have been created and allows you to create additional indexes (Figure 3-72). The index name has been entered as TypePaid. An insertion point displays in the Field Name column. The index on the Customer Number field is the primary index and was created automatically by Access. The index on the Name field is the one just created. Access created other indexes (for example, the Zip Code and Amount Paid fields) automatically. In this dialog box, you can create additional indexes.

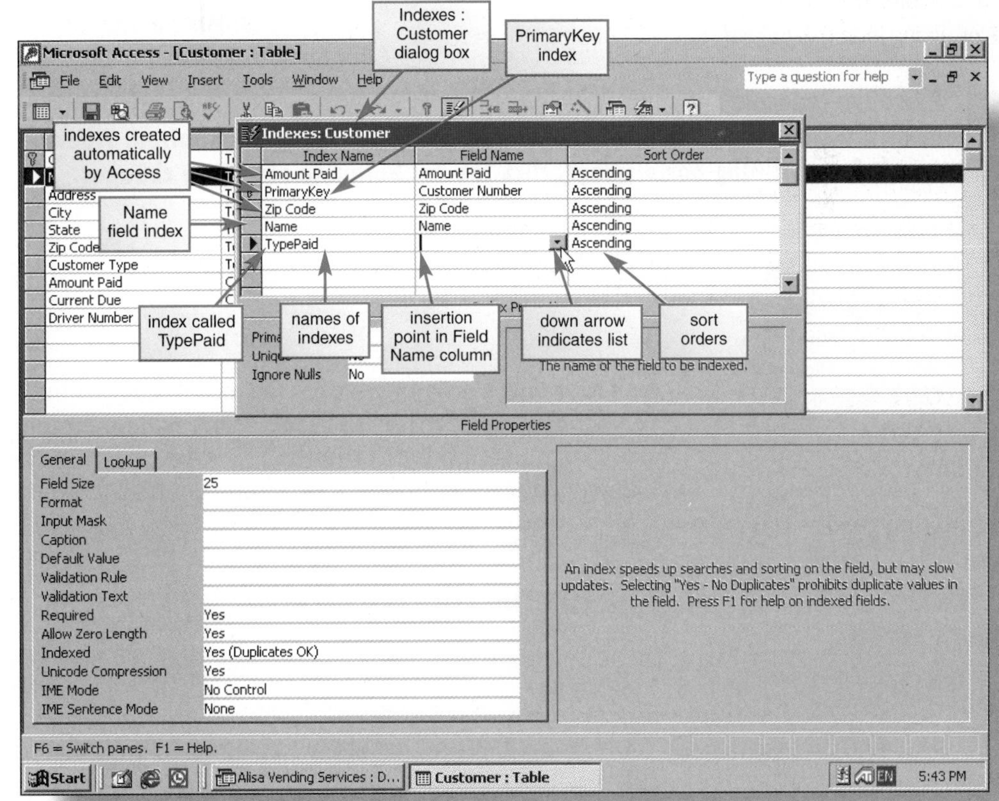

FIGURE 3-72

3 **Click the down arrow in the Field Name column to produce a list of fields in the Customer table, and then select Customer Type. Press the TAB key three times to move to the Field Name column on the following row. Select the Amount Paid field in the same manner as the Customer Type field. Point to the Close button for the Indexes: Customer dialog box.**

Customer Type and Amount Paid are selected as the two fields for the TypePaid index (Figure 3-73). The absence of an index name on the row containing the Amount Paid field indicates that it is part of the previous index, TypePaid.

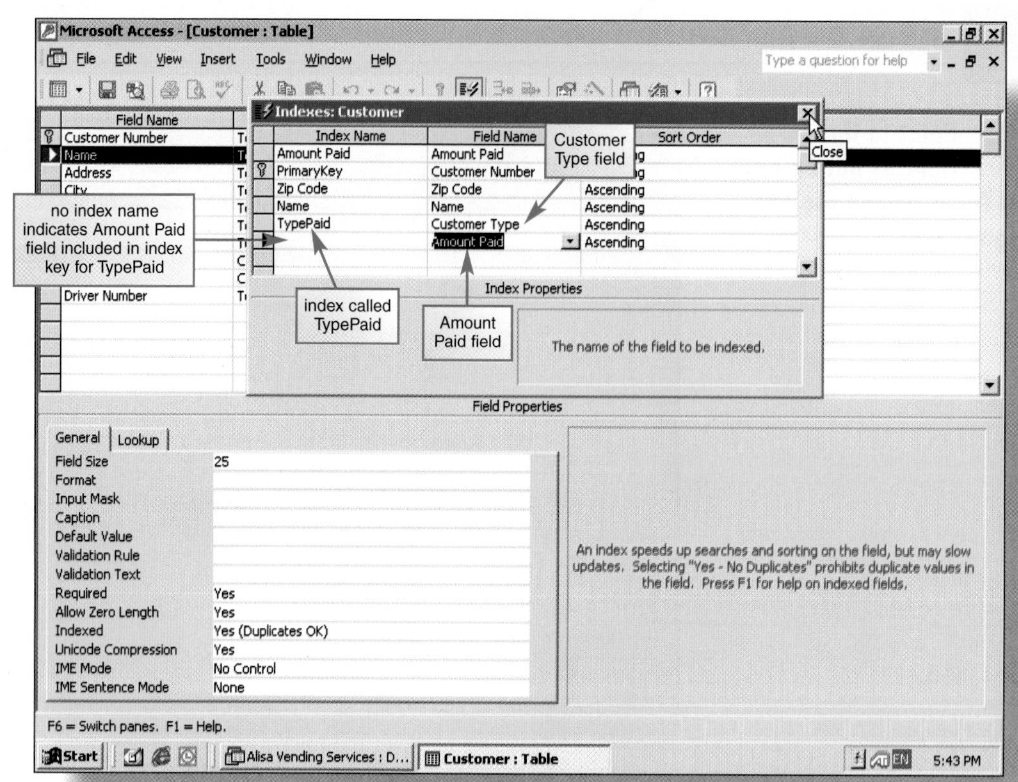

FIGURE 3-73

4 **Close the Indexes: Customer dialog box by clicking its Close button, and then close the Customer : Table window by clicking its Close Window button. When the Microsoft Access dialog box displays, click the Yes button to save your changes.**

The indexes are created and the Database window displays.

Other Ways

1. On View menu click Indexes
2. In Voice Command mode, say "Indexes"

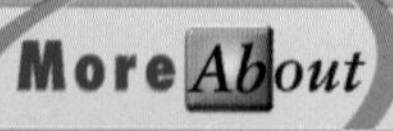

More About

Microsoft Certification

The Microsoft Office User Specialist (MOUS) Certification program provides an opportunity for you to obtain a valuable industry credential — proof that you have the Access 2002 skills required by employers. For more information, see Appendix E or visit the Shelly Cashman Series MOUS Web page at scsite.com/offxp/cert.htm.

The indexes now have been created. Access will use them automatically whenever possible to improve efficiency of ordering or finding records. Access also will maintain them automatically. That is, whenever the data in the Customer table is changed, Access will make appropriate changes in the indexes automatically.

Closing the Database

The following step closes the database by closing its Database window.

TO CLOSE A DATABASE

1. Click the Close button for the Alisa Vending Services : Database window.

The database closes.

CASE PERSPECTIVE SUMMARY

In Project 3, you assisted Alisa Vending Services in the maintenance of the database. You used Form view to add a record to the database and searched for a record satisfying a criterion. You used a filter so you could view only the record you needed. You changed and deleted records. You changed the structure of the Customer table in the Alisa Vending Services database, created validation rules, and specified referential integrity. You used a subdatasheet to view the customers assigned to a driver while viewing driver data. You made mass changes and created indexes to improve performance.

Project Summary

In Project 3, you learned how to maintain a database. You saw how to use Form view to add records to a table. You learned how to locate and filter records. You saw how to change the contents of records in a table and how to delete records from a table. You restructured a table, both by changing field characteristics and by adding a new field. You saw how to make changes to groups of records and how to delete groups of records. You learned how to create a variety of validation rules to specify a required field, specify a range, specify a default value, specify legal values, and specify a format. You examined the issues involved in updating a table with validation rules. You also saw how to specify referential integrity. You learned how to view related data by using subdatasheets. You learned how to order records. Finally, you saw how to improve performance by creating single-field and multiple-field indexes.

What You Should Know

Having completed this project, you now should be able to perform the following tasks:

- Add a Field to a Table (*A 3.17*)
- Change the Size of a Field (*A 3.16*)
- Close a Database (*A 3.48*)
- Create a Multiple-Field Index (*A 3.47*)
- Create a Single-Field Index (*A 3.46*)
- Delete a Record (*A 3.14*)
- Filter Records (*A 3.13*)
- Make Individual Changes (*A 3.35*)
- Open a Database (*A 3.05*)
- Remove a Filter (*A 3.14*)
- Resize a Column (*A 3.21*)
- Save the Validation Rules, Default Values, and Formats (*A 3.32*)
- Search for a Record (*A 3.09*)
- Specify a Collection of Legal Values (*A 3.31*)
- Specify a Default Value (*A 3.30*)
- Specify a Format (*A 3.32*)
- Specify a Range (*A 3.29*)
- Specify a Required Field (*A 3.29*)
- Specify Referential Integrity (*A 3.36*)
- Switch from Form View to Datasheet View (*A 3.11*)
- Update the Contents of a Field (*A 3.10, A 3.20*)
- Use a Delete Query to Delete a Group of Records (*A 3.26*)
- Use a Form to Add Records (*A 3.06*)
- Use a Subdatasheet (*A 3.40*)
- Use an Update Query to Update All Records (*A 3.23*)
- Use the Sort Ascending Button to Order Records (*A 3.41*)
- Use the Sort Ascending Button to Order Records on Multiple Fields (*A 3.42*)

Learn It Online

Instructions: To complete the Learn It Online exercises, start your browser, click the Address bar, and then enter `scsite.com/offxp/exs.htm`. When the Office XP Learn It Online page displays, follow the instructions in the exercises below.

1 Project Reinforcement TF, MC, and SA

Below Access Project 3, click the Project Reinforcement link. Print the quiz by clicking Print on the File menu. Answer each question. Write your first and last name at the top of each page, and then hand in the printout to your instructor.

2 Flash Cards

Below Access Project 3, click the Flash Cards link. When Flash Cards displays, read the instructions. Type 20 (or a number specified by your instructor) in the Number of Playing Cards text box, type your name in the Name text box, and then click the Flip Card button. When the flash card displays, read the question and then click the Answer box arrow to select an answer. Flip through Flash Cards. Click Print on the File menu to print the last flash card if your score is 15 (75%) correct or greater and then hand it in to your instructor. If your score is less than 15 (75%) correct, then redo this exercise by clicking the Replay button.

3 Practice Test

Below Access Project 3, click the Practice Test link. Answer each question, enter your first and last name at the bottom of the page, and then click the Grade Test button. When the graded practice test displays on your screen, click Print on the File menu to print a hard copy. Continue to take practice tests until you score 80% or better. Hand in a printout of the final practice test to your instructor.

4 Who Wants to Be a Computer Genius?

Below Access Project 3, click the Computer Genius link. Read the instructions, enter your first and last name at the bottom of the page, and then click the Play button. Hand in your score to your instructor.

5 Wheel of Terms

Below Access Project 3, click the Wheel of Terms link. Read the instructions, and then enter your first and last name and your school name. Click the Play button. Hand in your score.

6 Crossword Puzzle Challenge

Below Access Project 3, click the Crossword Puzzle Challenge link. Read the instructions, and then enter your first and last name. Click the Play button. Work the crossword puzzle. When you are finished, click the Submit button. When the crossword puzzle redisplays, click the Print button. Hand in the printout.

7 Tips and Tricks

Below Access Project 3, click the Tips and Tricks link. Click a topic that pertains to Project 3. Right-click the information and then click Print on the shortcut menu. Construct a brief example of what the information relates to in Access to confirm you understand how to use the tip or trick. Hand in the example and printed information.

8 Newsgroups

Below Access Project 3, click the Newsgroups link. Click a topic that pertains to Project 3. Print three comments. Hand in the comments.

9 Expanding Your Horizons

Below Access Project 3, click the Articles for Microsoft Access link. Click a topic that pertains to Project 3. Print the information. Construct a brief example of what the information relates to in Access to confirm you understand the contents of the article. Hand in the example and printed information.

10 Search Sleuth

Below Access Project 3, click the Search Sleuth link. To search for a term that pertains to this project, select a term below the Project 3 title and then use the Google search engine at google.com (or any major search engine) to display and print two Web pages that present information on the term. Hand in the printout.

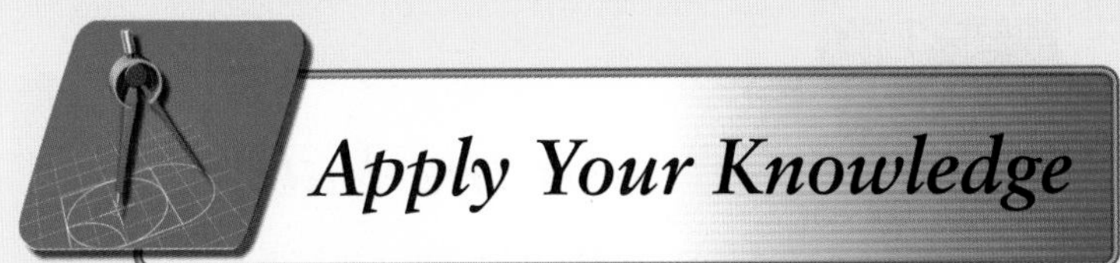

Apply Your Knowledge

1 Maintaining the Beyond Clean Database

Instructions: Start Access. Open the database Beyond Clean that you used in Project 2 or see your instructor for information on accessing the files required for this book. Perform the following tasks.

1. Open the Client table in Design view as shown in Figure 3-74.

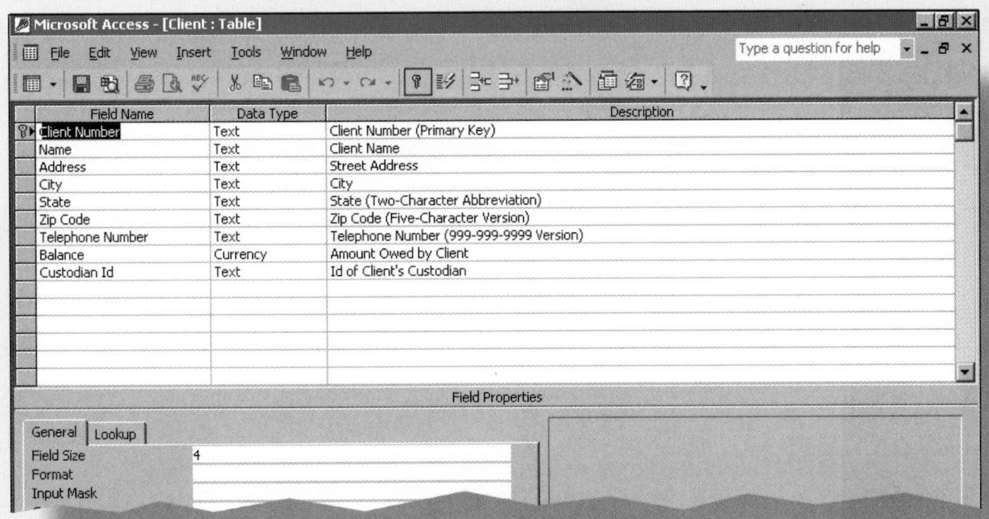

FIGURE 3-74

2. Increase the size of the Name field to 25.
3. Format the Client Number and State fields so any lowercase letters display in uppercase.
4. Make the Name field a required field.
5. Specify that balance amounts must be less than or equal to $200.00. Include validation text.
6. Create an index that allows duplicates for the Name field.
7. Save the changes to the structure.
8. Open the Client table in Datasheet view.
9. Change the name of client HA09 to Halyards Manufacturing.
10. Resize the Name column so the complete name for client HA09 displays. Resize the State, Zip Code, Balance, and Custodian Id columns to the best size.
11. Close the table and click Yes to save the changes to the layout of the table.
12. Print the table. If necessary, change the margins so the table prints on one page in landscape orientation.
13. Open the Client table and use Filter By Selection to find the record for client BE29. Delete the record.
14. Remove the filter and then print the table.
15. Sort the data in ascending order by balance.
16. Print the table. Close the table. If you are asked to save changes to the design of the table, click the No button.
17. Establish referential integrity between the Custodian table (the one table) and the Client table (the many table). Print the Relationships window by making sure the Relationships window is open, clicking File on the menu bar, and then clicking Print Relationships.

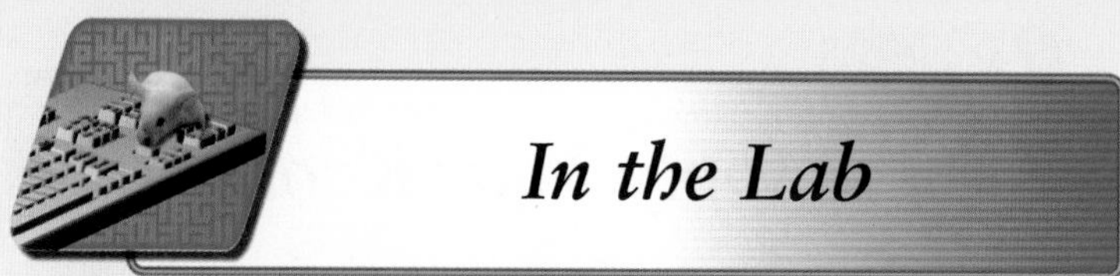

1 Maintaining the Wooden Crafts Database

Problem: Jan Merchant would like to make some changes to the Wooden Crafts database structure. She needs to increase the size of the Description field and add an additional index. She also would like to add some validation rules to the database. Finally, some new products must be added to the database.

Instructions: Use the database created in the In the Lab 1 of Project 1 for this assignment or see your instructor for information on accessing the files required for this book. Perform the following tasks.

1. Open the Wooden Crafts database and open the Product table in Design view as shown in Figure 3-75.

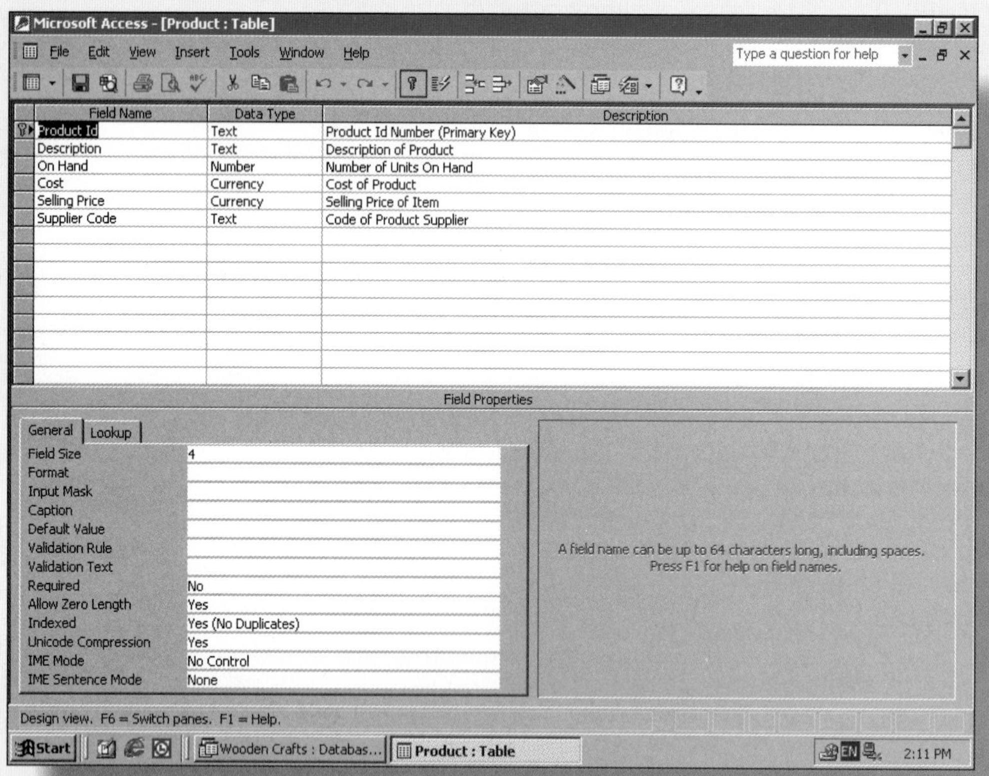

FIGURE 3-75

2. Create an index for the Description field. Be sure to allow duplicates.
3. Create and save the following validation rules for the Product table. List the steps involved on your own paper.
   a. Make the Description field a required field.
   b. Ensure that any lowercase letters entered in the Product Id field are displayed as uppercase.
   c. Specify that the on hand units must be between 0 and 20. Include validation text.
4. Save the changes.

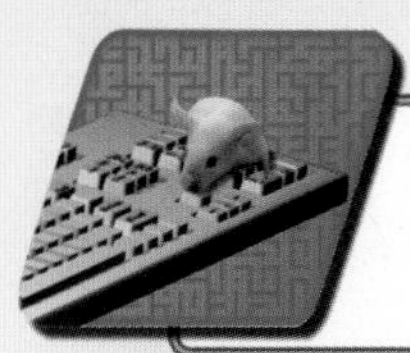

In the Lab

5. Open the Product form you created in Project 1, and then add the following record to the Product table:

PRODUCT ID	DESCRIPTION	ON HAND	COST	SELLING PRICE	SUPPLIER CODE
AD01	Animal Dominoes	5	$18.00	$21.00	BH

6. Switch to Datasheet view and sort the records in descending order on the combination of the On Hand and Cost fields.
7. Print the table. Close the table. If you are asked to save changes to the design of the table, click the No button.
8. Create a new query for the Product table.
9. Using a query, delete all records in the Product table where the description starts with the letter R. (***Hint:*** Use online Help to solve this problem.) Close the query without saving it.
10. Print the Product table.
11. Open the Supplier table in Design view and add a new field to the end of the table. Name the field, Fax Number. This new field has the same data type and length as Telephone Number. Enter the same comment as Telephone Number but replace Telephone with Fax. Save the change to the table design.
12. Open the Supplier table in Datasheet view, and then add the following data to the Fax Number field.

SUPPLIER CODE	FAX NUMBER
AP	505-555-6574
BH	707-555-8967
PL	602-555-9991

13. Resize all columns in the Supplier table to the best size.
14. Print the table. If necessary, change the margins so the table prints on one page in landscape orientation. Save the change to the layout of the table.
15. Specify referential integrity between the Supplier table (the one table) and the Product table (the many table). Print the Relationships window by making sure the Relationships window is open, clicking File on the menu bar, and then clicking Print Relationships.

2 Maintaining the Restaurant Supply Database

Problem: The restaurant supply company has purchased the business of an independent contractor who also serviced restaurants. You now need to merge the customers of the two businesses. Because the business has expanded, you also need to change the database structure and add some validation rules to the database.

Instructions: Use both the Restaurant Supply database created in the In the Lab 2 of Project 1 and the Independent Supply database for this assignment. Be sure both databases are on the same disk before starting In the Lab 2. If you do not know how to do this, see your instructor for assistance. Perform the following tasks.

1. Open the Independent Supply database from the Data Disk. See the preface at the front of this book for instructions for downloading the Data Disk or see your instructor for information on accessing the files required in this book.

(continued)

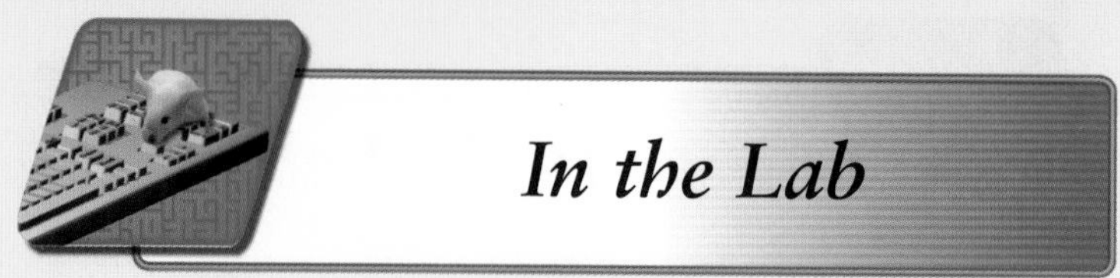

Maintaining the Restaurant Supply Database *(continued)*

2. Create a new query for the Customer table and double-click the asterisk in the field list to add all fields to the query.
3. Change the query type to an Append Query.
4. When the Append dialog box displays, make the entries shown in Figure 3-76 and then click the OK button. If your Restaurant Supply database is not located on the disk in drive A, you will need to enter the appropriate information in the File Name text box.

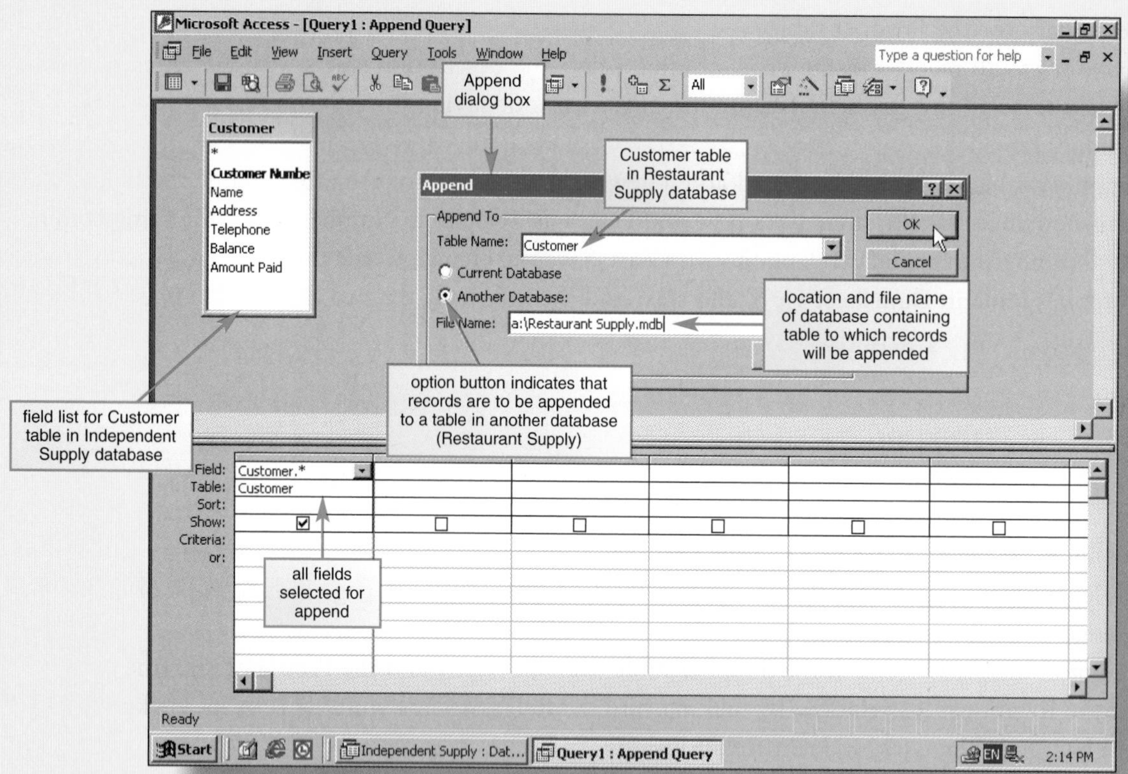

FIGURE 3-76

5. Click the Run button to run the Append query. When the Microsoft Access dialog box displays with the message that you are about to append 3 rows, click Yes.
6. Close the append query without saving it, and then close the Independent Supply database. Open the Restaurant Supply database, and then open the Customer table in Datasheet view. There should be 13 records in the table.
7. The customers added from the Independent Supply database do not have a sales rep assigned to them. Assign customer PP43 to sales rep 44, customer RR15 to sales rep 49, and customer TD01 to sales rep 51. Print the Customer table. If necessary, change the margins so the table prints on one page in landscape orientation. Close the table.
8. Open the Customer table in Design view.

In the Lab

9. Add the field, Dining Type, to the Customer table. Define the field as text with a width of 3. Insert the field after the Telephone field. This field will contain data on the type of restaurant. Restaurants are classified as fine dining (FIN), family (FAM), and fast food/takeout (FFT). Save these changes.
10. Using a query, change all the entries in the Dining Type column to FAM. This will be the type of most restaurants. Do not save the query.
11. Open the Customer table and resize all columns to best fit the data. Print the table. Save the changes to the layout of the table.
12. Create the following validation rules for the Customer table and save the changes to the table. List the steps involved on your own paper.
    a. Make the Name field a required field.
    b. Specify the legal values FIN, FAM, and FFT for the Dining Type field.
    c. Ensure that any letters entered in the Customer Number field are displayed as uppercase.
    d. Specify that balance must be less than or equal to $500.000. Include validation text.
13. You can use either Form view or Datasheet view to change records in a table. To use Form view, you must replace the form you created in Project 1 with a form that includes the new field, Dining Type. With the Customer table selected, click the New Object: AutoForm button arrow on the Database Window toolbar. Click AutoForm. Use this form that contains the new field to change the dining type for the following records:

CUSTOMER NUMBER	DINING TYPE
AM23	FFT
BI15	FIN
EG07	FIN
RD03	FFT
VG21	FFT

14. Close the form. Click the Yes button when asked if you want to save the form. Save the form as Customer. Click the Yes button when asked if you want to replace the Customer form you created in Project 1.
15. Open the table in Datasheet view and print the table.
16. Use Filter By Form to find all records where the customer has a balance of $350.00 and has the Dining Type of FAM. Delete these records. (***Hint***: Read the More About: Filter By Form on page A 3.13 to solve this problem.)
17. Remove the filter and print the Customer table. If you are asked to save changes to the design of the table, click the No button.
18. Specify referential integrity between the Sales Rep table (the one table) and the Customer table (the many table). Print the Relationships window by making sure the Relationships window is open, clicking File on the menu bar, and then clicking Print Relationships.

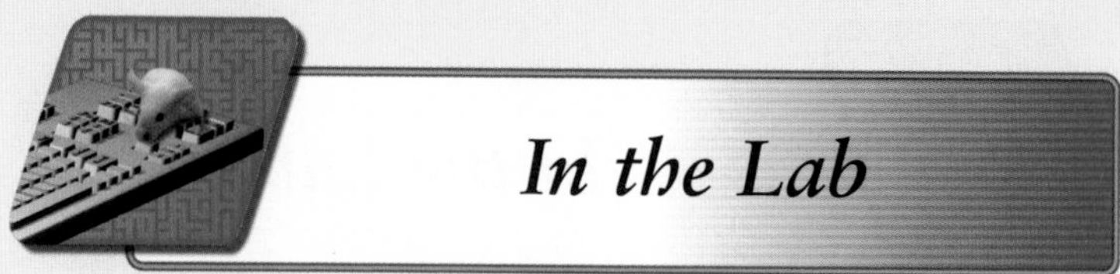

3 Maintaining the Condo Management Database

Problem: The condo management company has determined that some changes must be made to the database structure. Another field must be added. Because several different individuals update the data, the company also would like to add some validation rules to the database. Finally, some additions and deletions are required to the database.

Instructions: Use the database created in the In the Lab 3 of Project 1 for this assignment or see your instructor for information on accessing the files required for this book. Perform the following tasks.

1. Open the Condo Management database and open the Condo table in Design view as shown in Figure 3-77.

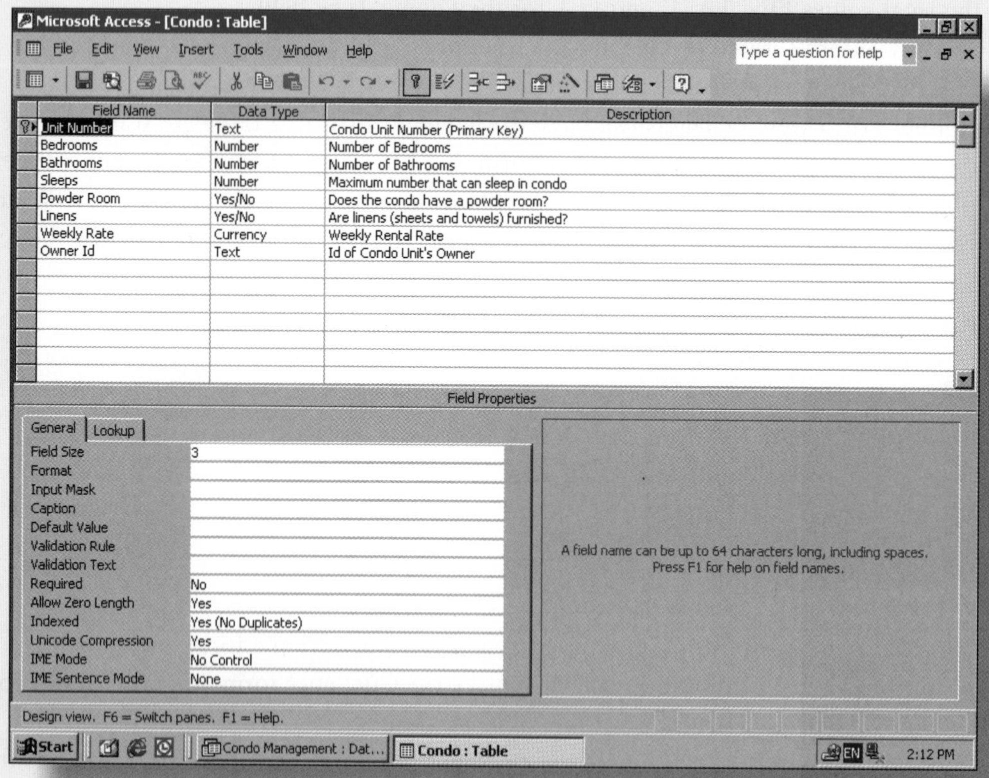

FIGURE 3-77

2. Create an index on the combination of the Bedrooms and Bathrooms fields. Name the index Bedbath. Create an index on the combination of the Sleeps and Bedrooms field. Name the index SleepBed. Save these changes.
3. Display the Condo table in Datasheet view and use the Sort Ascending button to order the records by bathrooms within bedrooms.
4. Print the table and then close the table. If you are asked to save changes to the design of the table, click the No button.

In the Lab

5. Add the field, For Sale, to the Condo table. Define the field as a Yes/No field. Insert the field after the Weekly Rate field. This field will indicate whether or not the condo unit is for sale.
6. Save these changes and display the Condo table in Datasheet view.
7. Units 101, 108, and 403 are for sale. Update the records for these condo units. Decrease the width of the For Sale column.
8. Print the table. If necessary, change the page orientation and margins so the table prints on one page. Close the table. Save the layout changes to the table.
9. Create the following validation rules for the Condo table and save the changes to the table. List the steps involved on your own paper.
   a. Make the Bedrooms, Bathrooms, and Sleeps field required fields.
   b. Assign a default value of 1 to the Bedrooms and Bathrooms fields. Assign a default value of 2 to the Sleeps field.
   c. Specify that the Bedrooms and Bathrooms fields must be at least one and the Sleeps field must be at least two. Include validation text.
   d. Specify that weekly rate must be between $600 and $1,800. Include validation text.
10. The management office has just received a new listing from Mark Graty. It is unit 300. The unit sleeps 10, has 3 bedrooms, 2 bathrooms, a powder room, and linens are provided. The weekly rate is $1,300 and the owner is interested in selling the unit. Add this record to your database. You can use either Form view or Datasheet view to add records to a table. To use Form view, you must replace the form you created in Project 1 with a form that includes the new field, For Sale. With the Condo table selected, click the New Object: AutoForm button arrow on the Database window toolbar. Click , and then use the form to add the record.
11. If necessary, close the form. Click Yes when asked if you want to save the form. Save the form as Condo. Click the Yes button when asked if you want to replace the Condo form you created in Project 1.
12. Change to Datasheet view and print the table.
13. Using a query, delete all records in the table where the condo has 2 bedrooms, 1 bathroom, and no powder room. Preview the deleted records before running the query.
14. Print the Condo table.
15. Specify referential integrity between the Owner table (the one table) and the Condo table (the many table). Print the Relationships window by making sure the Relationships window is open, clicking File on the menu bar, and then clicking Print Relationships.

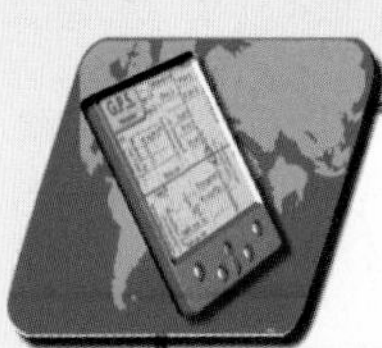

Cases and Places

The difficulty of these case studies varies:
▶ are the least difficult; ▶▶ are more difficult; and ▶▶▶ are the most difficult.

1 ▶ Use the Computer Expertise database you created in Case Study 1 of Project 1 for this assignment. Perform each of the following tasks and then print the results:

(a) The name for customer LK23 should really be Learn n Kids Day Care.
(b) To help manage the business better, it is important to know the type of customer being served. Customer types are RET (retail), SER (service), MFG (manufacturing), and DIN (dining.) No other customer type should be entered in the database. Customers AL35, BK18, and LB42 are retail organizations. Customers CL45, LK23, and SR34 are service organizations. Customers AR43 and ME30 are manufacturing organizations and customers CJ78 and RE20 are dining establishments.
(c) Ready Eats now has a balance of $175.00.
(d) Specify referential integrity between the two tables in the database.

2 ▶ Use the Baseball database you created in Case Study 2 of Project 1 for this assignment. Perform each of these tasks and then print the results:

(a) The description for item 7930 is really Coffee Travel Mug.
(b) Logo Goods has increased the cost of their items by 10 percent. The marketing team has decided to raise the selling price by 5 percent for these items. (***Hint:*** Use an update query to solve this problem.)
(c) The team has sold seven tee shirts and five baseball caps.
(d) Only numbers should be entered as item ids and the supplier codes always should display in uppercase.
(e) Specify referential integrity between the two tables in the database.

3 ▶▶ Use the local attractions database you created in Case Study 3 of Project 1 for this assignment:

(a) Determine and create the appropriate validity check for the type of attraction.
(b) Ensure that data always is entered in the Name, Address, and Telephone Number fields.
(c) Create an index on the combination of attraction type and attraction name.
(d) Add two records to the database.

4 ▶▶ Use the high school Math club database you created in Case Study 4 of Project 1 for this assignment:

(a) Add a field to the database to store the date an elementary student started in the tutoring program. Enter some sample data for this field.
(b) Determine and create appropriate validity checks for the fields in your database.
(c) Add two records to the database.
(d) Determine and create appropriate indexes for your database. Use the indexes to sort the data.
(e) Analyze the database and determine if you have a one-to-many relationship between any tables. If so, specify referential integrity between the one table and the many table.

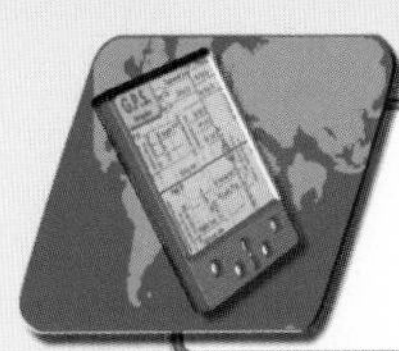

Cases and Places

5 ▶▶▶ Use the hobby or collection database you created in Case Study 5 of Project 1 for this assignment:

(a) Analyze the database and determine if you need any additional fields. Do you have a field for the date you acquired the item in your collection? Do you have a price or cost associated with each item? Add any fields that you now think would be useful to the database. Determine if there are any duplicate records in your database. (***Hint***: See More About Primary Keys: The Find Duplicate Query Wizard on page A 3.45 to solve this problem.)

(b) Determine and create appropriate validity checks for the fields in your database.

(c) Add two records to the database.

(d) Determine and create appropriate indexes for your database. Use the indexes to sort the data.

(e) Analyze the database and determine if you have a one-to-many relationship between any tables. If so, specify referential integrity between the one table and the many table. Determine if there are any records in one table that do not have related records in another table. (***Hint:*** See More About Relationships: The Find Unmatched Query Wizard on page A 3.36 to solve this problem.)

(f) For at least one of the tables in your database, change the format of the datasheet. Adjust column widths. Experiment with different font styles, cell effects, and gridline colors.

Microsoft Access 2002

Publishing to the Internet Using Data Access Pages

CASE PERSPECTIVE

Alisa Vending Services is pleased with all the work you have done for them thus far. They appreciate the database you have designed and created. They also like the ease with which they can query the database. They find the default values, validation rules, validation text, and the relationships you created to be useful in ensuring the database contains only valid data. They also find the report you created in Project 1 to be useful. They are pleased with the form you created for them in Project 1, which they have used to view and update customer data. They would like to use a Web page that would be similar to this form in order to view and/or update customer data over the Internet. They would like you to develop a sample of such a Web page, which they then would review. If they determine that it satisfies their needs, they will instruct the network administrator to make both the database and your Web page accessible on the Internet.

Introduction

Microsoft Access 2002 supports data access pages. A **data access page** is an HTML document that can be bound directly to data in the database. The fact that it is an HTML document implies that it can be run in the Internet Explorer browser. The fact that it is bound directly to the database means that it can access data in the database directly.

Figure 1 on the next page shows a sample data access page run in the Internet Explorer browser. Notice that it is similar to the form created in Project 1 (see Figure 1-56 on page A 1.38). Although running in the browser, the data access page is displaying data in the Alisa Vending Services database. Furthermore, the page can be used to change this data. You can use it to change the contents of existing records, to delete records, and to add new records.

In this project, you will create the data access page shown in Figure 1 on the next page. (This data access page is located on a disk in drive A. The database it is accessing also is located on the disk. In order to use this page on the Internet, both the page and the database would need to be located on some server that would be available to the Internet. The address entered in the browser would be changed to reflect the true location of the page.)

Opening the Database

Before carrying out the steps in this project, you first must open the database. To do so, perform the steps on the next page.

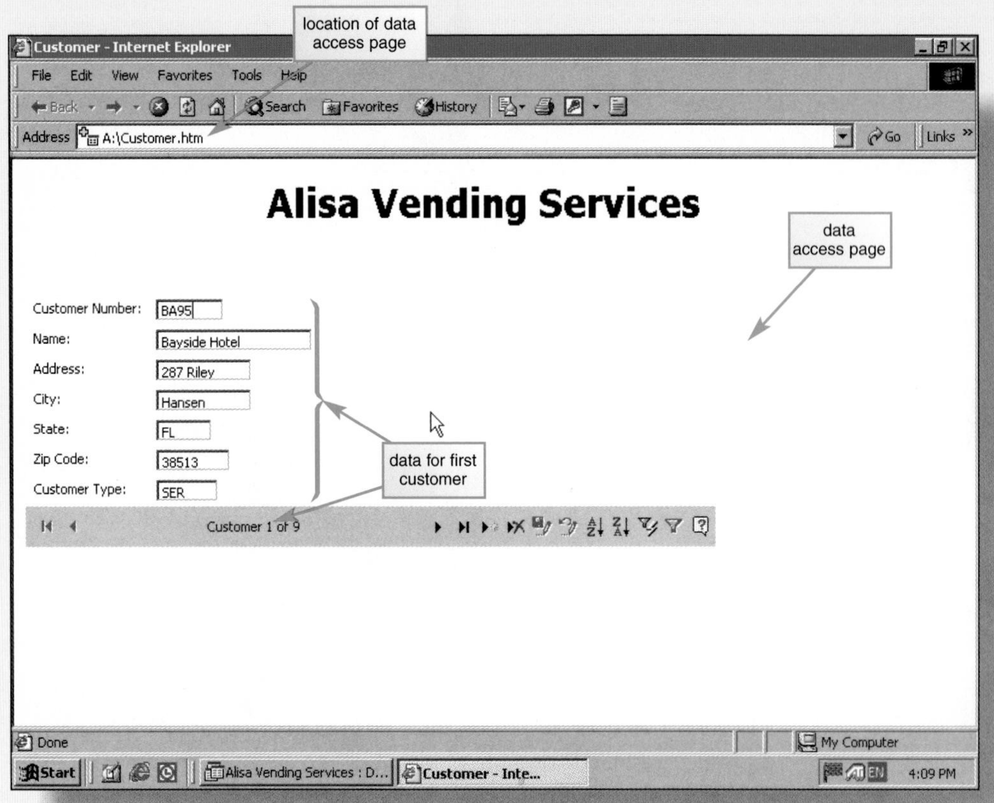

FIGURE 1

TO OPEN A DATABASE

1. Click the Start button, click Programs on the Start menu, and then click Microsoft Access.
2. Click the Open button on the Database toolbar and then click 3½ Floppy (A:) in the Look in box. If necessary, click the Alisa Vending Services database name.
3. Click the Open button.

The database opens and the Alisa Vending Services : Database window displays.

Creating a Data Access Page

To create a data access page, use the Page Wizard as shown in the following steps.

Steps To Create a Data Access Page

1 With the Customer table selected, click the New Object: AutoForm button arrow on the Database toolbar. Point to Page on the New Object: AutoForm button list.

The list of available objects displays (Figure 2).

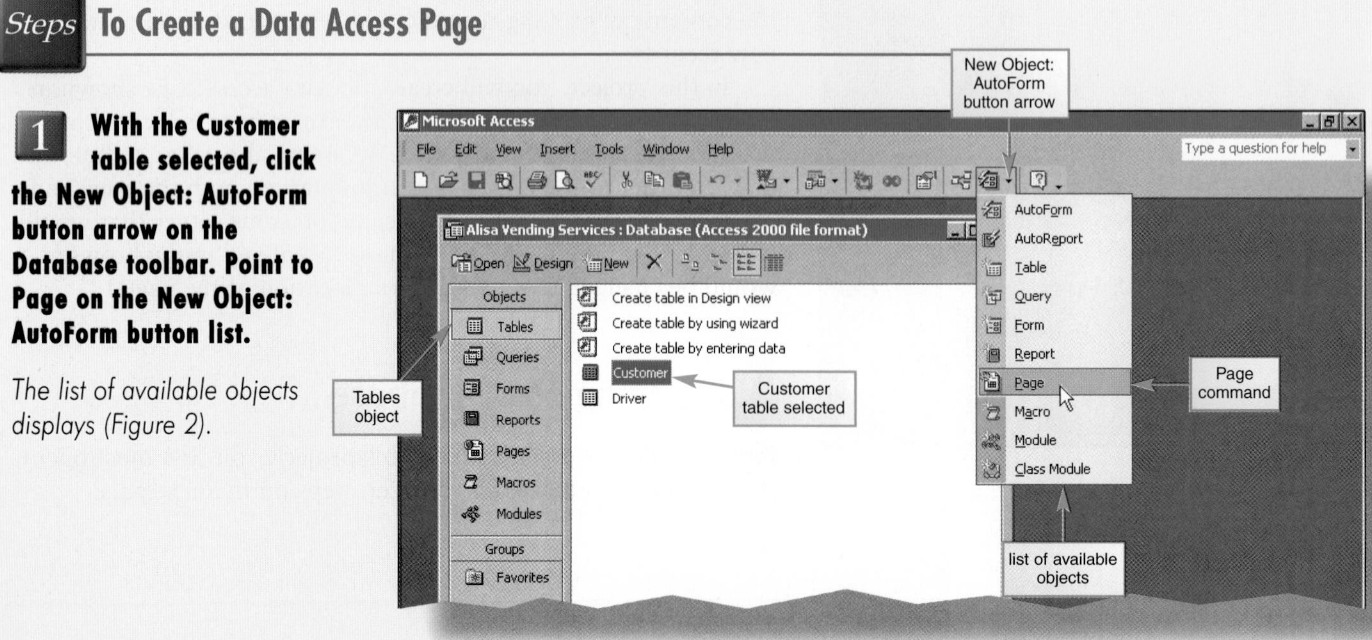

FIGURE 2

2 Click Page, select Page Wizard in the New Data Access Page dialog box, and then point to the OK button.

The New Data Access Page dialog box displays (Figure 3).

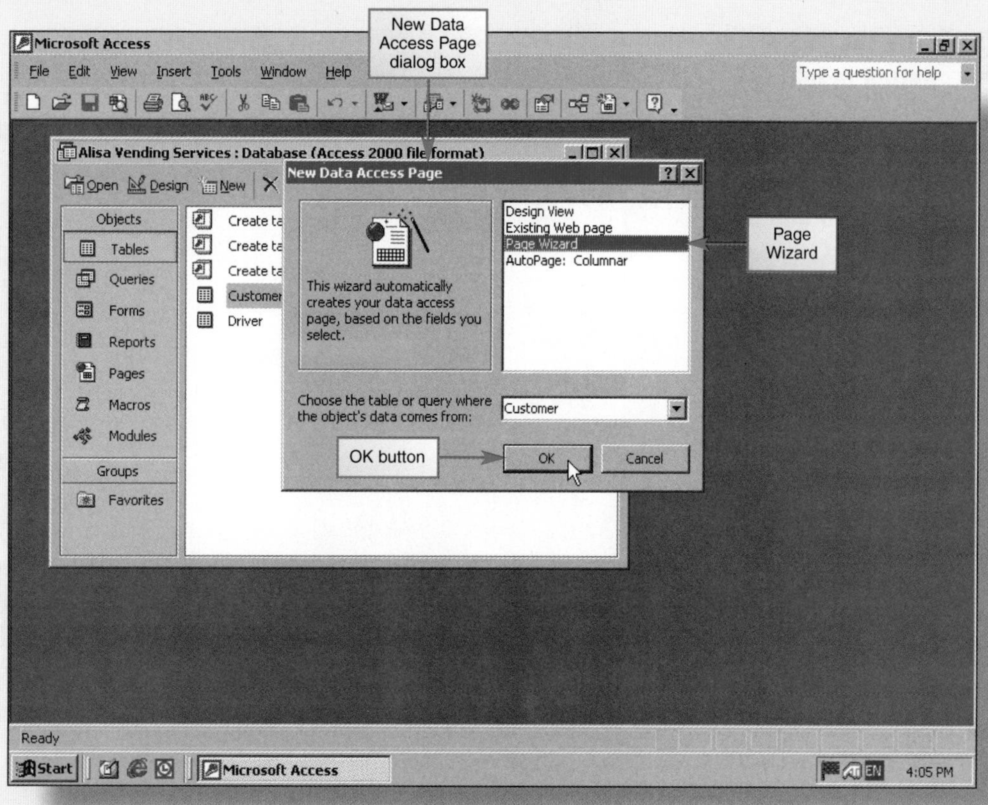

FIGURE 3

3 Click the OK button and then point to the Add Field button.

The Page Wizard dialog box displays (Figure 4). The fields in the Customer table display in the list of available fields. The Customer Number field currently is selected.

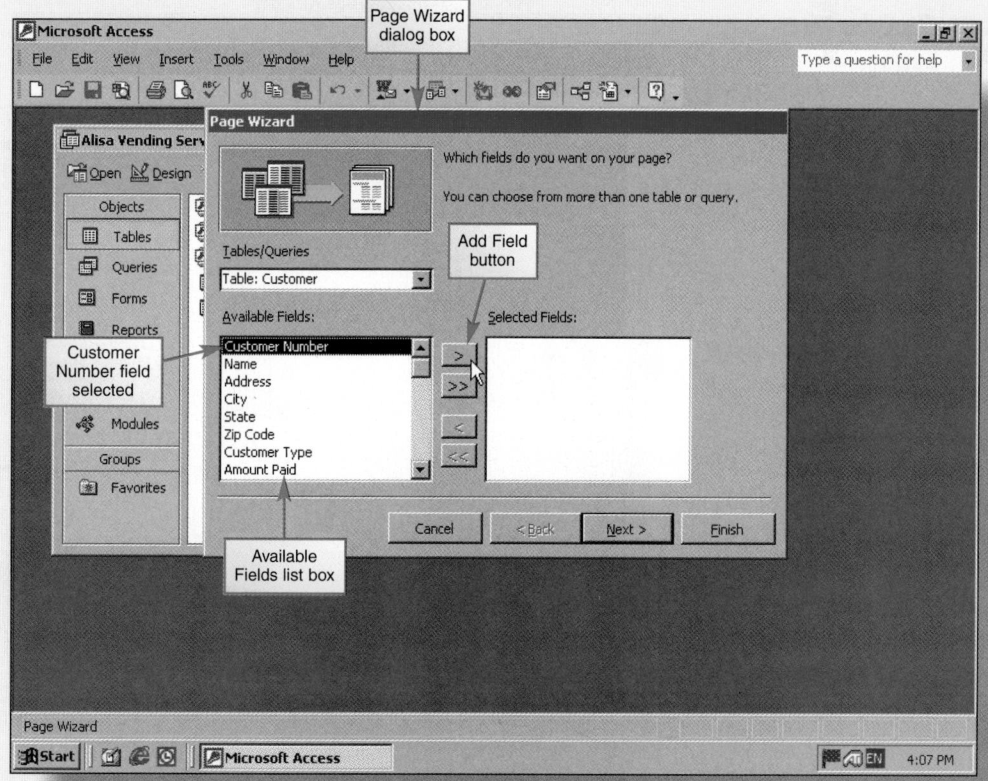

FIGURE 4

4 Click the Add Field button to add the Customer Number field to the list of selected fields. Click the Add Field button six more times to add the Name, Address, City, State, Zip Code, and Customer Type fields. Point to the Next button.

The Customer Number, Name, Address, City, State, Zip Code, and Customer Type fields are selected (Figure 5).

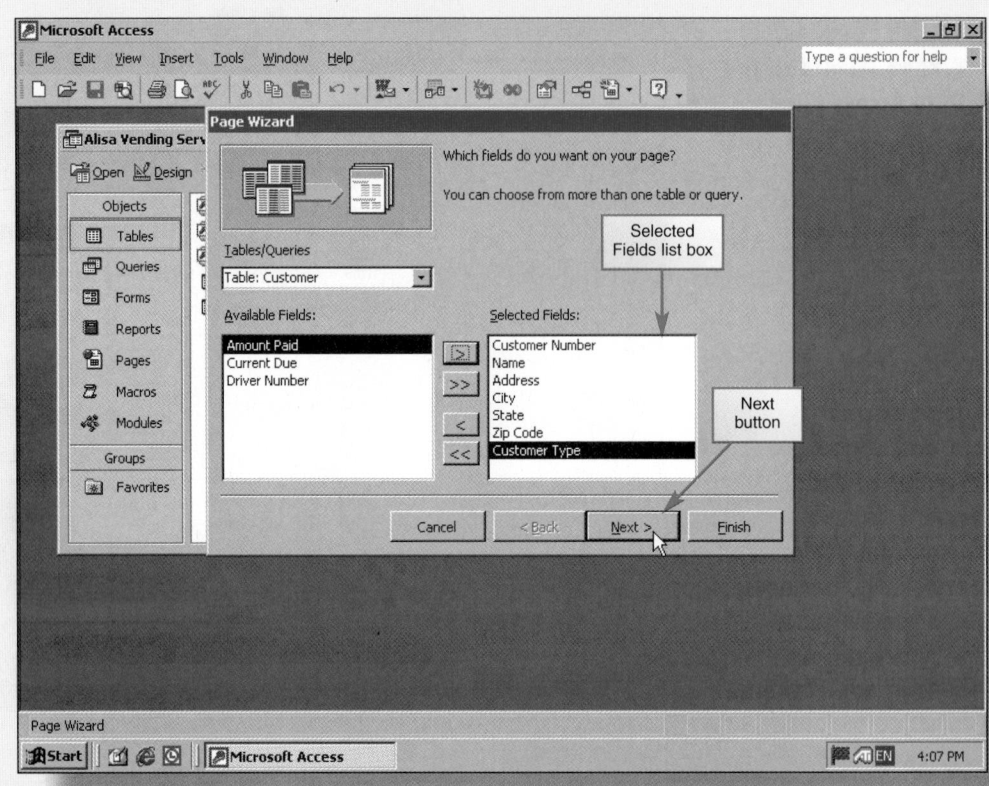

FIGURE 5

5 Click the Next button.

The Page Wizard dialog box displays, asking if you want to add any grouping levels (Figure 6).

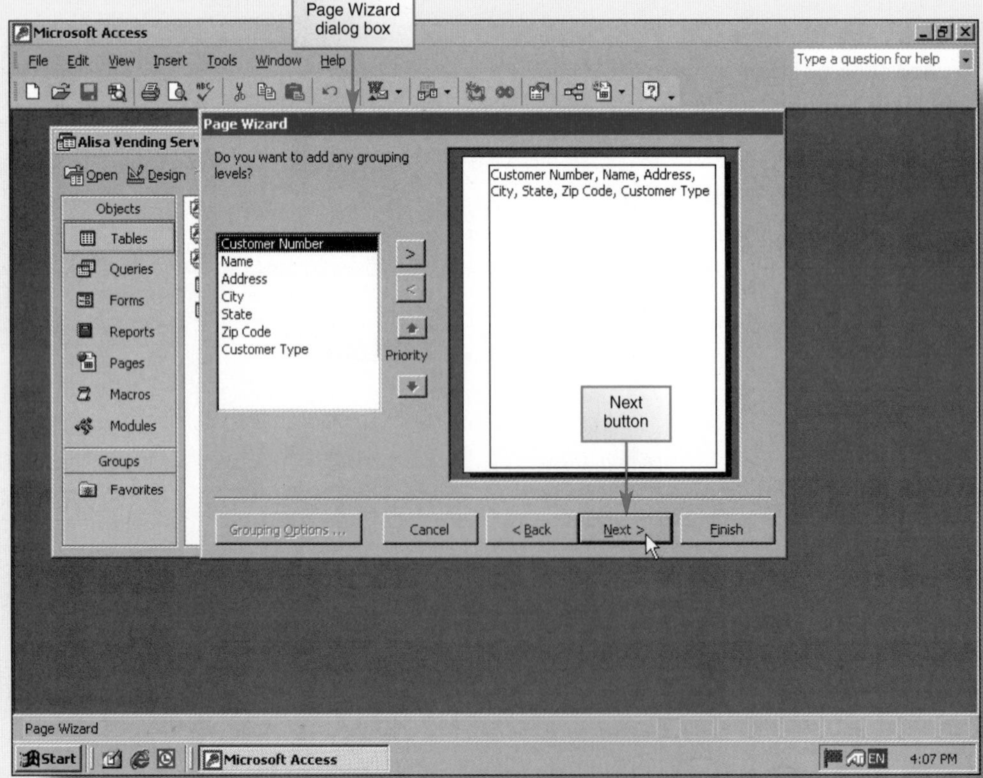

FIGURE 6

6 Click the Next button because you do not need any grouping levels. Click the Next button a second time because you do not need to make any changes on the following screen, which enables you to specify a special sort order. Point to the Finish button.

The Page Wizard dialog box displays (Figure 7).

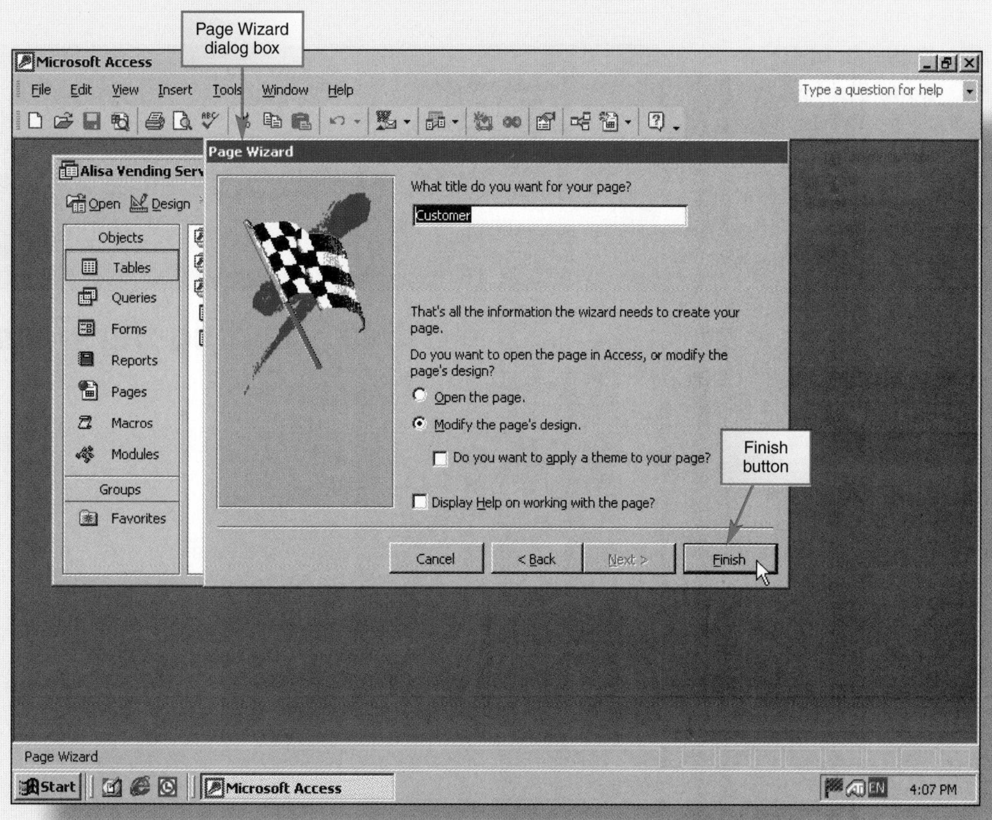

FIGURE 7

7 Click the Finish button. The Field List pane may display. (The contents of your Field List pane may be different.) If the Field List pane does display, point to the Close button for the Field List pane.

The Customer data access page displays (Figure 8).

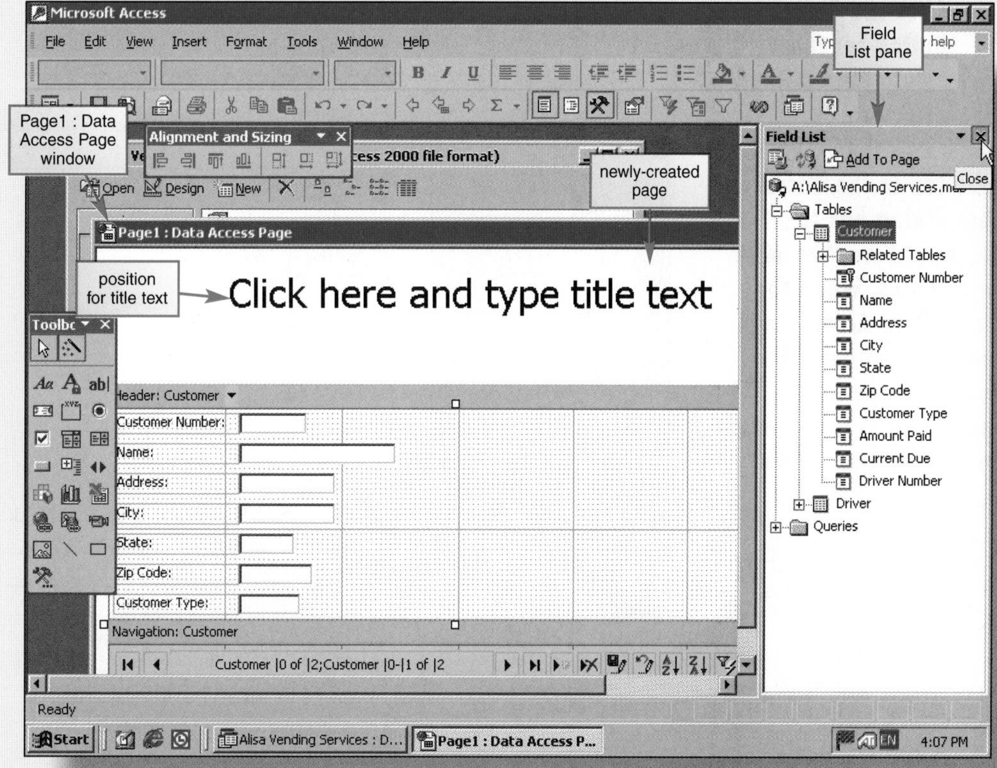

FIGURE 8

8 **If the Field List pane displays, click the Close button for the Field List pane. Click anywhere in the portion of the screen labeled "Click here and type title text" and then type** `Alisa Vending Services` **as the title text. Point to the Close button for the Page1 : Data Access Page window.**

The data access page displays (Figure 9). The title is changed to Alisa Vending Services.

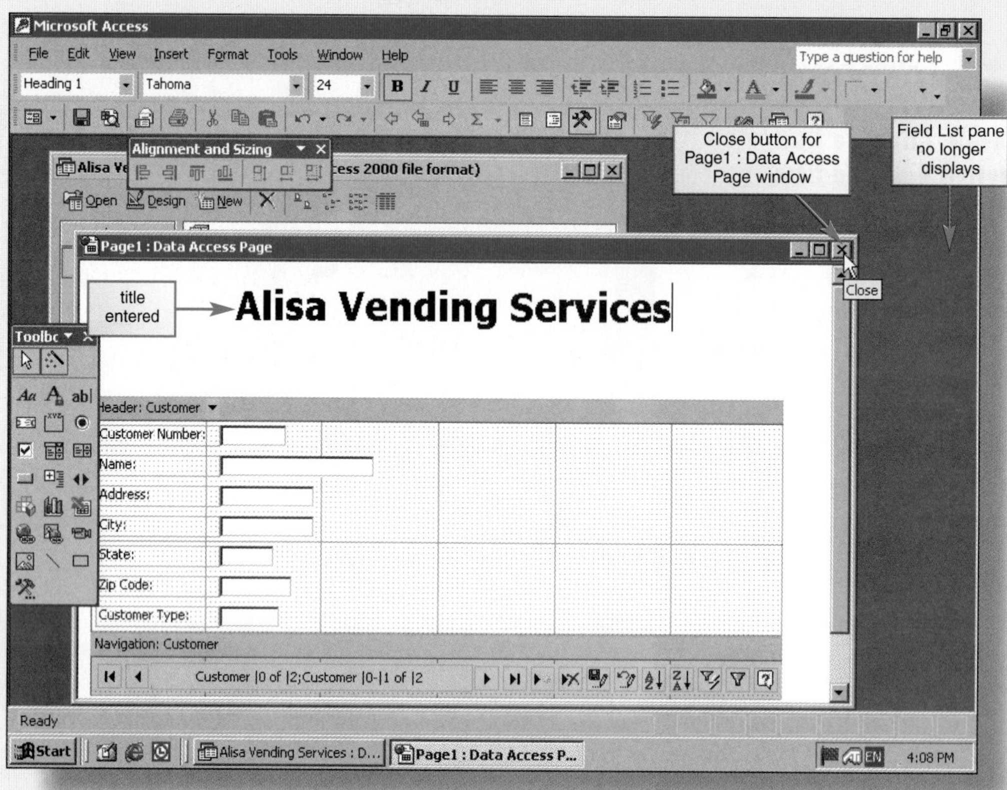

FIGURE 9

9 **Click the Close button for the Page1 : Data Access Page window to close the window and then click the Yes button in the Microsoft Access dialog box to indicate you want to save your changes. When the Save As Data Access Page dialog box displays, be sure 3½ Floppy (A:) is selected and that the file name is Customer. Point to the Save button.**

The Save As Data Access Page dialog box displays (Figure 10).

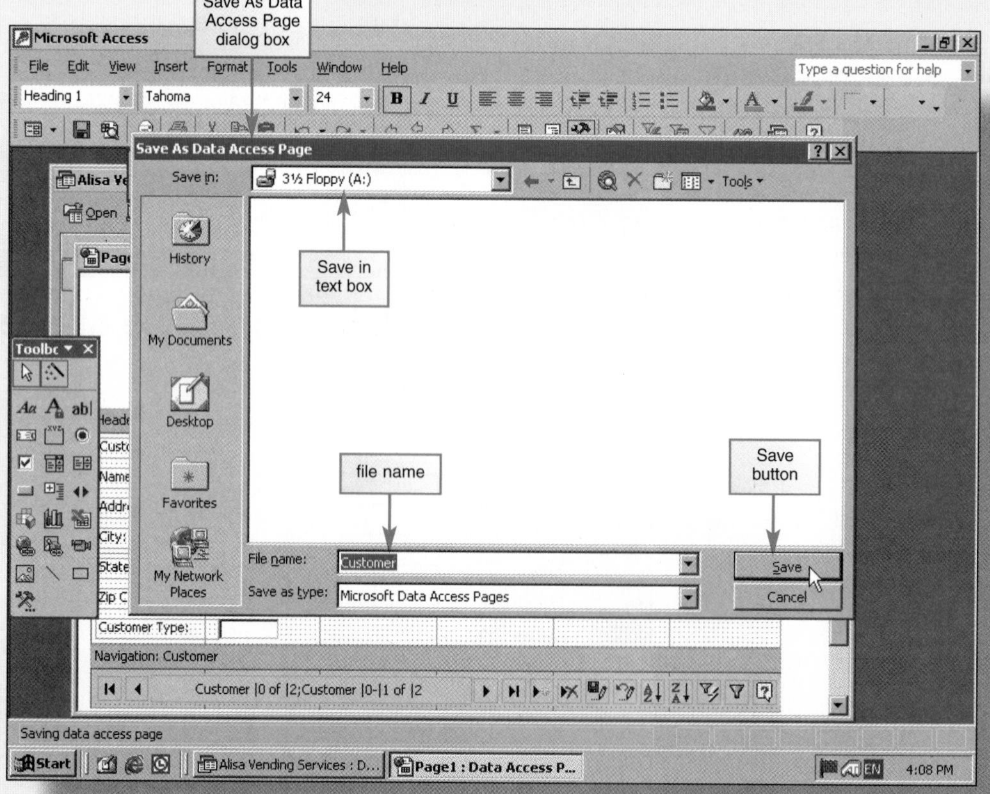

FIGURE 10

10 Click the Save button. If you see a message similar to the one in Figure 11, click the OK button because the file location you specified is acceptable. (This message indicates that you will need to specify a Universal Naming Convention (UNC) address, instead of the file location you have specified if you want the page to be accessible over a network.)

The data access page is created.

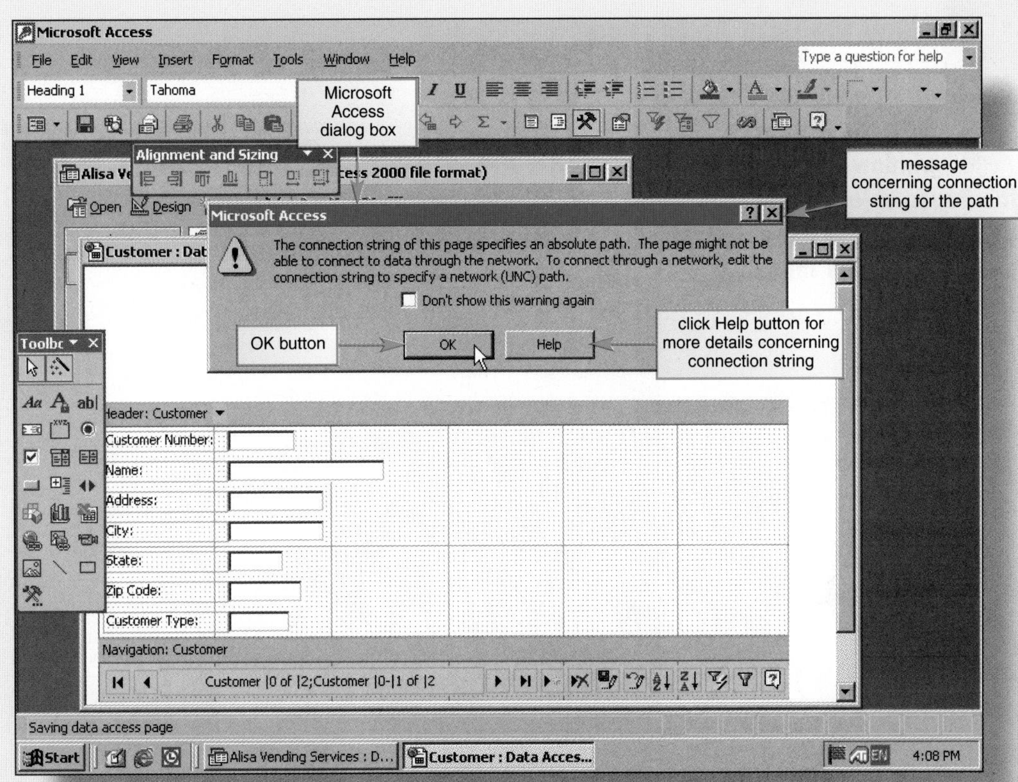

FIGURE 11

Viewing the Data Access Page

If you are connected to the Internet, you can view the data access page in the browser (see Figure 1 on page AW 1.02). To do this you use the Web Page Preview command on the shortcut menu. When not connected to the Internet, you can view the data access page using the Open command on the shortcut menu. The following steps use the Open command to view the data access page that was just created.

More About

Quick Reference

For a table that lists how to complete tasks covered in this book using the mouse, menu, shortcut menu, and keyboard, see the Quick Reference Summary at the back of this book or visit the Shelly Cashman Series Office XP Web page (scsite.com/offxp/qr.htm) and then click Microsoft Access 2002.

View the Data Access Page

1 With the Database window open, click the Pages object. Right-click Customer and then point to Open on the shortcut menu.

The shortcut menu for the Customer data access page displays (Figure 12).

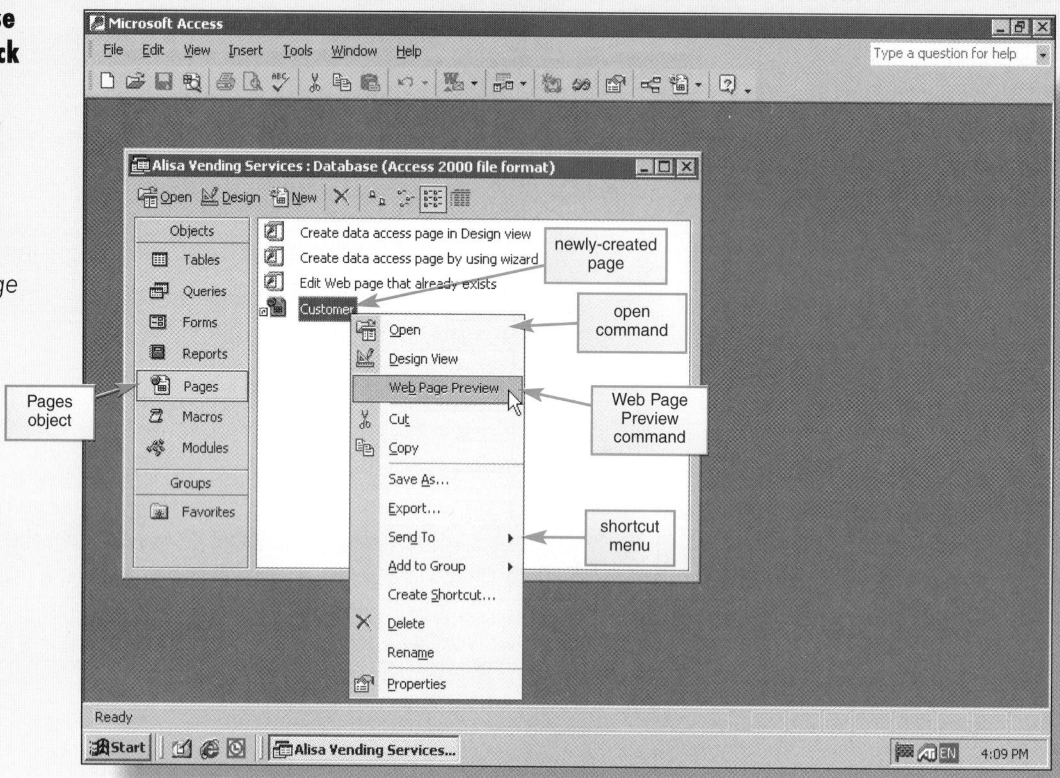

FIGURE 12

2 Click Open on the shortcut menu and then maximize the window.

The page displays (Figure 13).

3 Click the Close Window button to close the data access page. Close the database.

The page no longer displays. The database is closed.

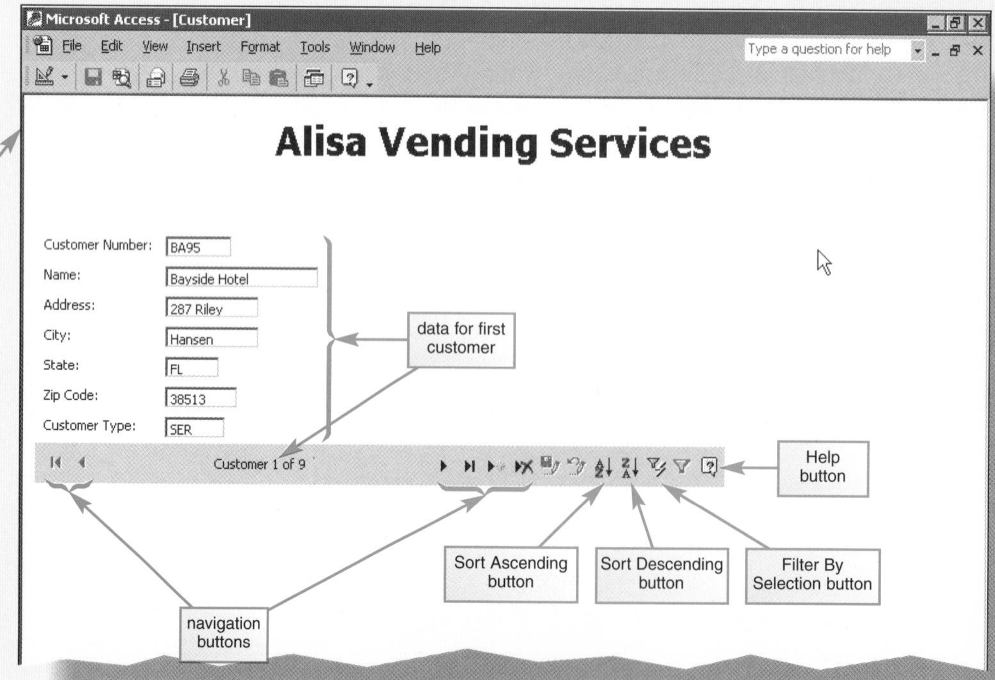

FIGURE 13

Using the Data Access Page

To use the data access page, start Internet Explorer, type the location of the data access page (for example, a:\customer.htm if you created the page on your disk), and then press the ENTER key. The page then will display and look similar to the one in Figure 1 on page AW 1.02.

You can use the navigation buttons, the Sort Ascending and Sort Descending buttons, and the Filter By Selection button just as you do when viewing a datasheet or a form in Access. You can get help on the way you use the page by clicking the Help button (see Figure 13). A book icon indicates subtopics are available. Double-clicking the icon displays the subtopics. A question mark icon indicates that information on the topic will display when you click the question mark. In Figure 14, for example, the subtopics for both Getting Started and Getting Help display. The question mark in front of "Get Help using a data access page" has been clicked so the information on that topic displays. In addition, the window has been maximized, which makes it easier to read the help information.

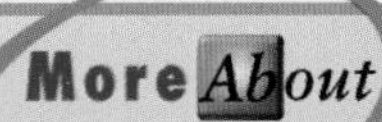

Microsoft Certification

The Microsoft User Specialist (MOUS) Certification program provides an opportunity for you to obtain a valuable industry credential — proof that you have the Access 2002 skills required by employers. For more information, see Appendix E or visit the Shelly Cashman Series MOUS Web page at (scsite.com/offxp/cert.htm).

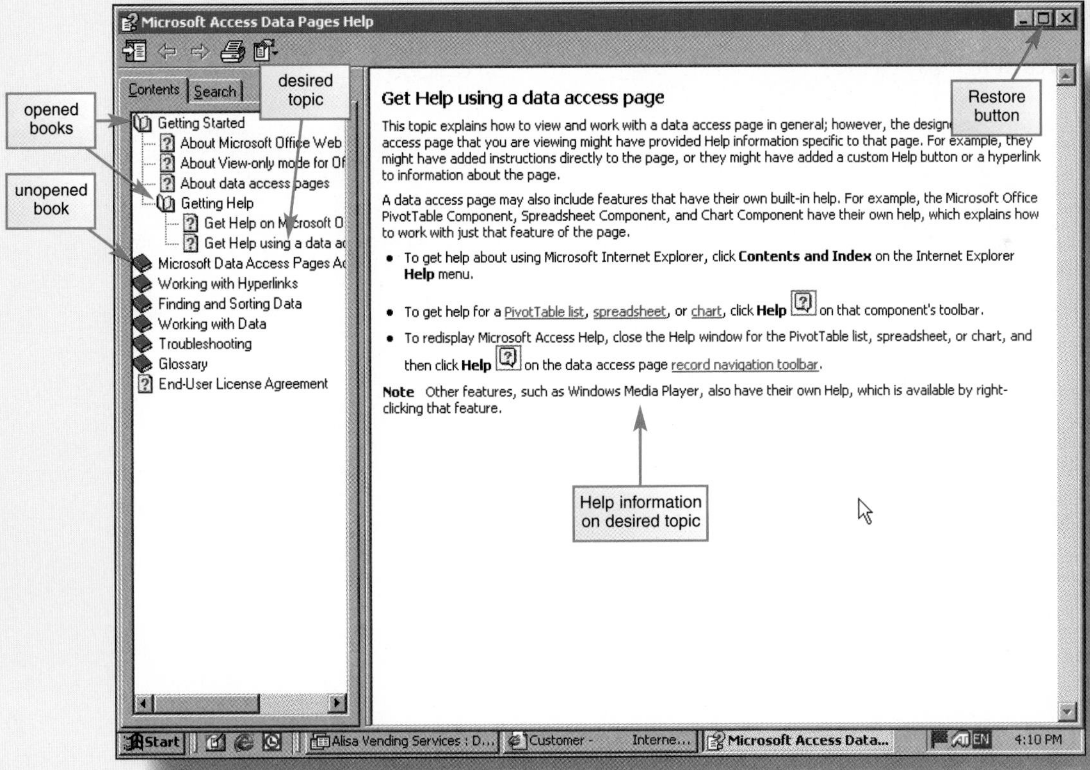

FIGURE 14

CASE PERSPECTIVE SUMMARY

In this Web Feature, you created a data access page for the Customer table in the Alisa Vending Services database. This page will enable Alisa to access their database using the Internet.

Web Feature Summary

In this Web Feature, you created a data access page for the Customer table in the Alisa Vending Services database. To do so, you used the Page Wizard. You then saw how to view the data access page from within Access. Finally, you saw how to use the data access page.

What You Should Know

Having completed this Web Feature, you now should be able to perform the following tasks:

- Create a Data Access Page (*AW 1.02*)
- Open a Database (*AW 1.02*)
- View a Data Access Page (*AW 1.07*)

More About

Publishing to the Internet: Saving Other Objects

You also can publish other objects such as reports and datasheets to the Internet. To publish a datasheet or a report to the Internet, save the object as a Web page in HTML format. To do so, select the name of the object in the Database window, click File on the menu bar, and then click Export. In the Save As Type box, click HTML Documents.

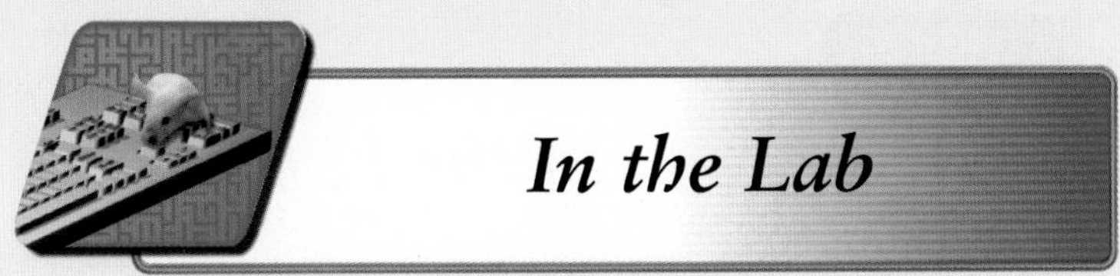

1 Creating a Data Access Page for the Beyond Clean Database

Instructions: Start Access. Open the Beyond Clean database that you used in Project 3 or see your instructor for information on accessing the files required for this book. Perform the following tasks.

1. Use the Page Wizard to create a data access page for the Custodian table (Figure 15). When the Page Wizard dialog box displays that asks what sort order you want for your records, select Custodian Id.

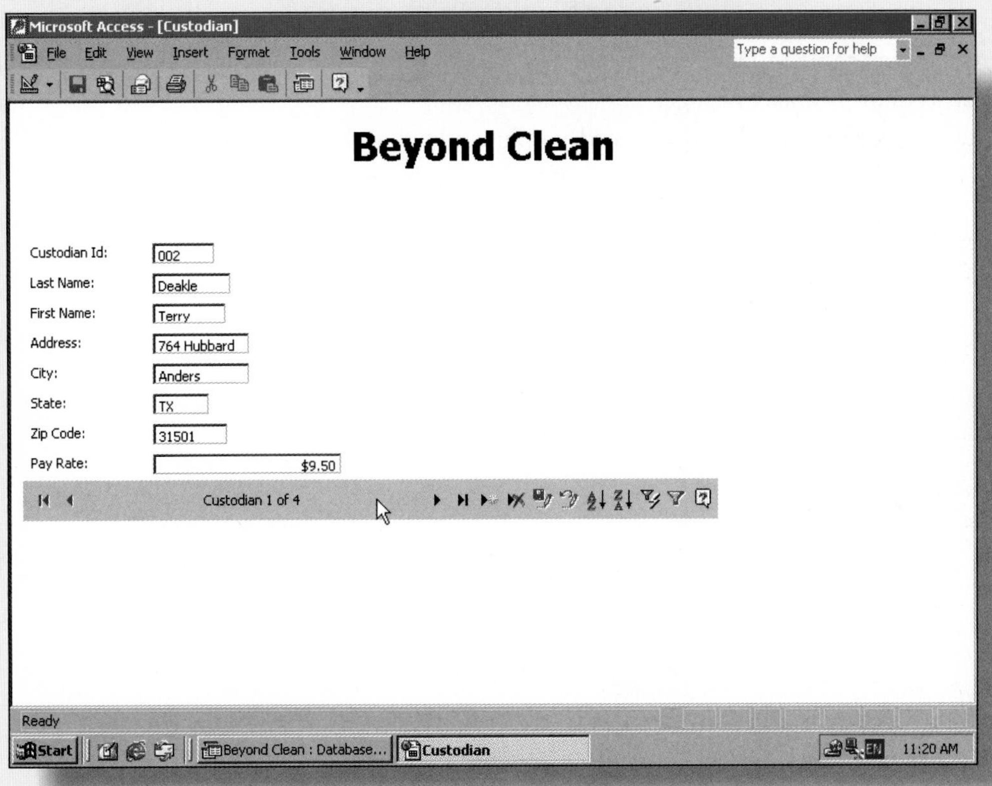

FIGURE 15

2. Print the data access page. To print the page, open the page, click File on the menu bar, and then click Print.

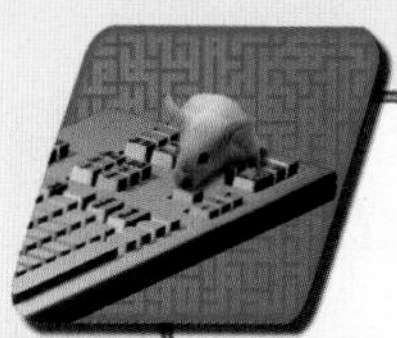

In the Lab

2 Using a Data Access Page

Instructions: Make sure the disk containing the Beyond Clean database and the data access page you created in the In the Lab 1 is in drive A. Perform the following tasks.

1. Start Access and then open the Custodian data access page.
2. Use the data access page to add yourself as a new record to the Custodian table. Use 099 as the custodian id, and $9.25 as the hourly pay rate. Refer to Figure 1-81 on page A 1.55 for the maximum field sizes for the remaining fields. Close the data access page.
3. Open the Custodian table in Datasheet view. You now should have five records. Print the table.
4. Open the Custodian data access page.
5. Use the data access page to delete the record you just added and then close the page.
6. Open the Custodian table in Datasheet view. Print the table and then quit Access.

2002

Microsoft

PowerPoint

Microsoft PowerPoint 2002

PROJECT 1

Using a Design Template and Text Slide Layout to Create a Presentation

OBJECTIVES

You will have mastered the material in this project when you can:

- Start and customize PowerPoint
- Describe the PowerPoint window
- Describe the speech recognition capabilities of PowerPoint
- Select a design template
- Create a title slide
- Change the font size and font style
- Save a presentation
- Add a new slide
- Create a text slide with a single-level bulleted list
- Create a text slide with a multi-level bulleted list
- End a slide show with a black slide
- Move to another slide in normal view
- View a presentation in slide show view
- Quit PowerPoint
- Open a presentation
- Check spelling and consistency, correct errors, and edit a presentation
- Display a presentation in black and white
- Print a presentation in black and white
- Use the PowerPoint Help system to answer your questions

COMDEX Glitz

Presentations Dazzle the Masses

Thousands of the world's computer industry executives attend, including keynote speakers, Bill Gates, Andy Grove, and Michael Dell. They are joined by hundreds of thousands of technology enthusiasts, industry professionals, and curious spectators seeking the latest trends in hardware, software, and the Internet, as well as the hottest new gizmos, gadgets, and games.

They will be attending COMDEX, North America's largest trade show. COMDEX/Fall is held in Las Vegas each November, and COMDEX/Spring is held in Chicago in April. Both shows feature speeches by industry leaders, tutorials on the latest technologies, and thousands of square feet of exhibits showcasing the latest in computer technology.

Information technology (IT) experts headline COMDEX as the premier IT event in the world. Indeed, more than 10,000 new products are unveiled at the Fall show. Since COMDEX's inception in 1979, some of the more notable product launches have been the IBM PC in 1981, COMPAQ's suitcase-sized portable computer, Microsoft's first version of Windows, Apple's original Macintosh computer, and CD-ROM drives, and the promise of wireless technology utilizing the Bluetooth™ standard.

Attendance and industry representation have grown steadily. The first show featured 150 exhibitions seen by 4,000 curious visitors. Six years later, more than 1,000 companies displayed their wares for more than 100,000 techies. Recent shows have produced as many as 2,400 booths visited by 250,000-plus attendees.

Computer companies realize their sales forces need to capture their audiences' attention, so they add sensory cues to their exhibits. They treat the trade show visitors to a multimedia blitz of sound, visuals, and action with the help of presentation software such as Microsoft PowerPoint 2002. This program enhances the presenters' speeches by highlighting keywords in the presentation, displaying graphs, pictures, and diagrams, and playing sound and video clips.

In this project, you will learn to use PowerPoint 2002 to create a presentation (also called a slide show) for a Westview College counselors' orientation using a design template and one of PowerPoint's layouts. Then, you will run the slide show and print audience handouts.

PowerPoint's roots stem from the innovative work performed by a small company called Forethought, Inc. Programmers at this pioneering business coined the phrase, desktop presentation graphics, for formal slide shows and created a complete software package that automated creating slides containing text, charts, and graphics. Microsoft liked the visual appeal of the software and acquired Forethought in 1987. Company executives decided to market the software to Apple Macintosh users because Mac computers were considered clearly superior to IBM-based personal computers for graphics applications.

Microsoft PowerPoint became a favorite among Mac users. Meanwhile, Lotus Freelance Graphics and Software Publishing Harvard Graphics were popular within the PC community. This division ceased, however, when Microsoft released Windows 3.0 in 1990 and subsequently developed a Windows version of PowerPoint to run on PCs.

Since that time, Macintosh and PC users alike have utilized the presentation power of PowerPoint. The package has grown to include animation, audio and video clips, and Internet integration. Certainly the technology gurus at COMDEX have realized PowerPoint's dazzling visual appeal. So will you as you complete the exercises in this textbook.

Microsoft PowerPoint 2002

Using a Design Template and Text Slide Layout to Create a Presentation

CASE PERSPECTIVE

As a receptionist in your college's counseling office, you meet students who are waiting for their scheduled appointments. You have noticed that many of them seem sad. They sit silently and do not make eye contact or speak with their fellow students.

Because of your concern, you mention this observation to Jennifer Williams, the dean of counseling. She tells you that most college students are lonely. In fact, a Carnegie study finds that only 36 percent of college students participate in student activities other than sports. Consequently, they are self-absorbed and miss the joys of college. She says that Intro to Loneliness would be one class that would fill quickly because loneliness is one of college students' worst enemies. Many of these students do not adjust well to the initial move from home, which makes it difficult for them to meet new people and make friends. Therefore, they play it safe and stay by themselves.

You suggest that counselors discuss this loneliness at freshmen orientation, and Jennifer agrees. She knows you are proficient at PowerPoint and asks you to develop a presentation focusing on how to make friends on campus.

What Is Microsoft PowerPoint?

Microsoft PowerPoint is a complete presentation graphics program that allows you to produce professional looking presentations. A PowerPoint **presentation** also is called a **slide show**. PowerPoint gives you the flexibility to make presentations using a projection device attached to a personal computer (Figure 1-1a) and using overhead transparencies (Figure 1-1b). In addition, you can take advantage of the World Wide Web and run virtual presentations on the Internet (Figure 1-1c). PowerPoint also can create paper printouts of the individual slides, outlines, and speaker notes.

PowerPoint contains several features to simplify creating a slide show. For example, you can instruct PowerPoint to create a predesigned presentation, and then you can modify the presentation to fulfill your requirements. You quickly can format a slide show using one of the professionally designed presentation design templates. To make your presentation more impressive, you can add tables, charts, pictures, video, sound, and animation effects. You also can check the spelling or style of your slide show as you type or after you have completed designing the presentation. For example, you can instruct PowerPoint to restrict the number of bulleted items on a slide or limit the number of words in each paragraph. Additional PowerPoint features include the following:

- **Word processing** — create bulleted lists, combine words and images, find and replace text, and use multiple fonts and type sizes.
- **Outlining** — develop your presentation using an outline format. You also can import outlines from Microsoft Word or other word processing programs.
- **Charting** — create and insert charts into your presentations. The two chart types are: standard, which includes bar, line, pie, and xy (scatter) charts; and custom, which displays such objects as floating bars, colored lines, and three-dimensional cones.

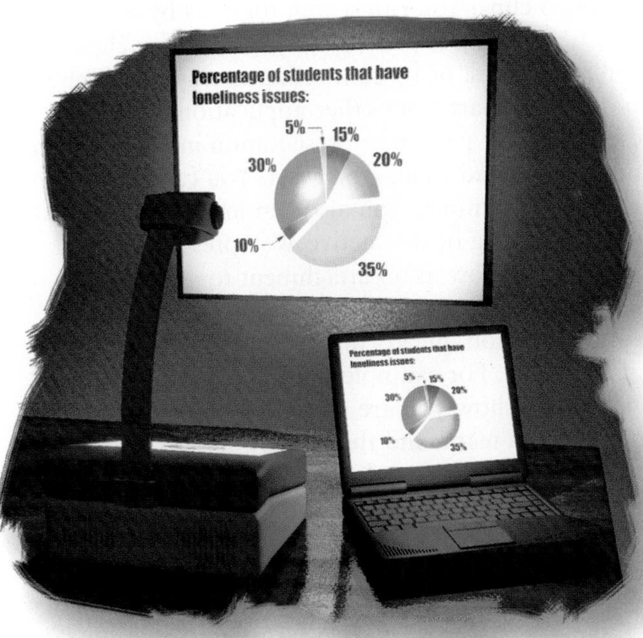

(a) Projection Device Connected to a Personal Computer

(b) Overhead Transparencies

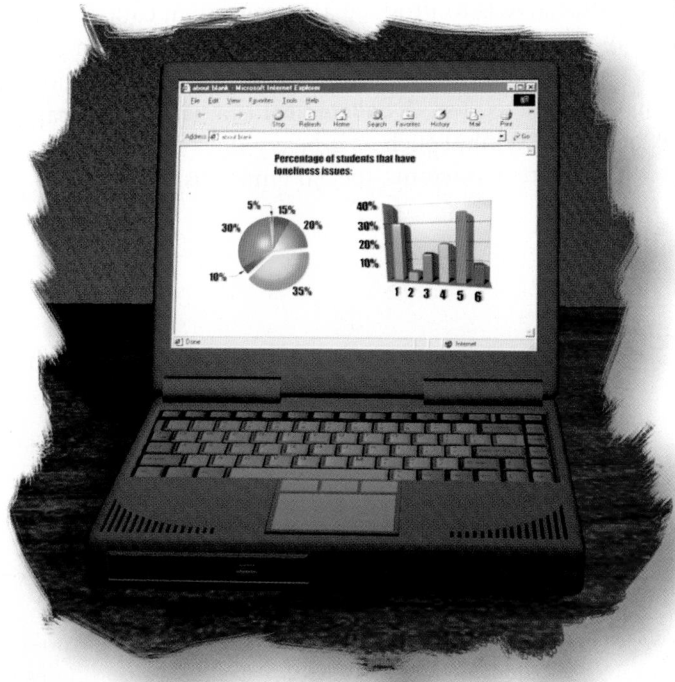

(c) PowerPoint Presentation on the World Wide Web

FIGURE 1-1

More About

Microportable Projectors

Light, sleek multimedia projectors are extremely popular. The newer devices weigh less than three pounds and can be held in one hand. They offer zooms, contrast controls, and HDTV support. For more information, visit the PowerPoint 2002 More About Web page (scsite.com/pp2002/more.htm) and then click Projectors.

- **Drawing** — form and modify diagrams using shapes such as arcs, arrows, cubes, rectangles, stars, and triangles.
- **Inserting multimedia** — insert artwork and multimedia effects into your slide show. The Microsoft Media Gallery contains hundreds of clip art images, pictures, photos, sounds, and video clips. You can search for clips by entering words or phrases that describe the subject you want by looking for clips with similar artistic styles, colors, or shapes, or by connecting to a special Web site just for clip art. You also can import art from other applications.
- **Web support** — save presentations or parts of a presentation in HTML format so they can be viewed and manipulated using a browser. You can publish your slide show to the Internet or to an intranet. You also can insert action buttons and hyperlinks to create a self-running or interactive Web presentation.
- **E-mailing** — send your entire slide show as an attachment to an e-mail message.
- **Using Wizards** — create a presentation quickly and efficiently by answering prompts for specific content criteria. For example, the **AutoContent Wizard** gives prompts for the type of slide show you are planning, such as communicating serious news or motivating a team, and the type of output, such as an on-screen presentation or black and white overheads. If you are planning to run your presentation on another computer, the **Pack and Go Wizard** helps you bundle everything you need, including any objects associated with that presentation. If you cannot confirm that this other computer has PowerPoint installed, you also can include the **PowerPoint Viewer**, a program that allows you to run, but not edit, a PowerPoint slide show.

Project One — Time to Start Making Friends

PowerPoint allows you to produce slides similar to those you would develop in an academic or business environment. In Project 1, you create the presentation shown in Figures 1-2a through 1-2d. The objective is to produce a presentation, called Time to Start Making Friends, to display using a projection device. As an introduction to PowerPoint, this project steps you through the most common type of presentation, which is a **text slide** consisting of a bulleted list. A **bulleted list** is a list of paragraphs, each preceded by a bullet. A **bullet** is a symbol such as a heavy dot (•) or other character that precedes text when the text warrants special emphasis.

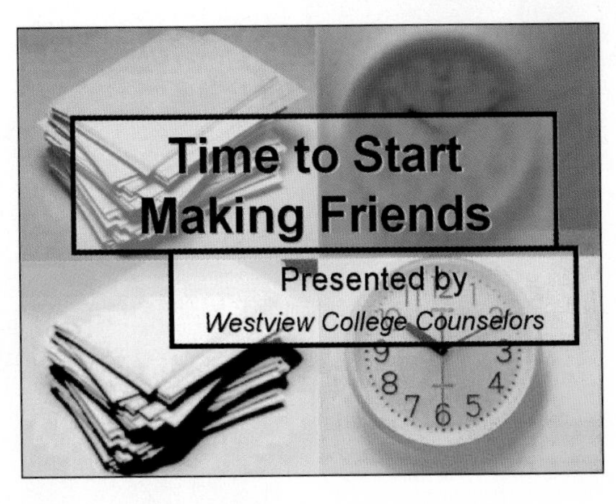

(a) Slide 1

(b) Slide 2

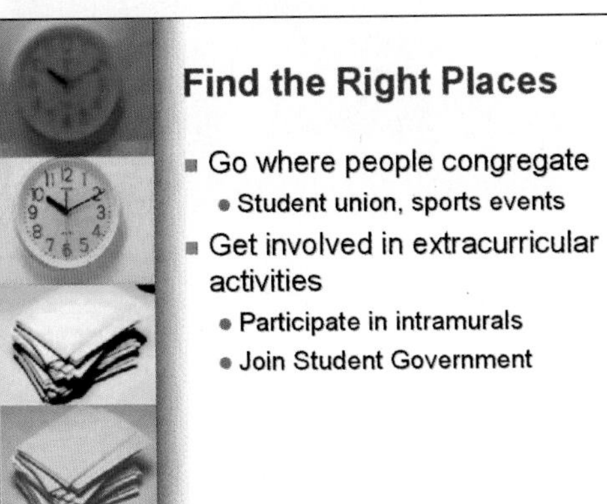

(c) Slide 3

(d) Slide 4

FIGURE 1-2

Starting and Customizing PowerPoint

To start PowerPoint, Windows must be running. The quickest way to begin a new presentation is to use the **Start button** on the **Windows taskbar** at the bottom of the screen. Perform these steps to start PowerPoint and a new presentation, or ask your instructor how to start PowerPoint for your system.

Steps To Start PowerPoint

1 Click the Start button on the Windows taskbar, point to Programs on the Start menu, and then point to Microsoft PowerPoint on the Programs submenu.

The commands on the Start menu display above the Start button and the Programs submenu displays (Figure 1-3). If the Office Speech Recognition software is installed on your computer, then the Language bar may display somewhere on the desktop.

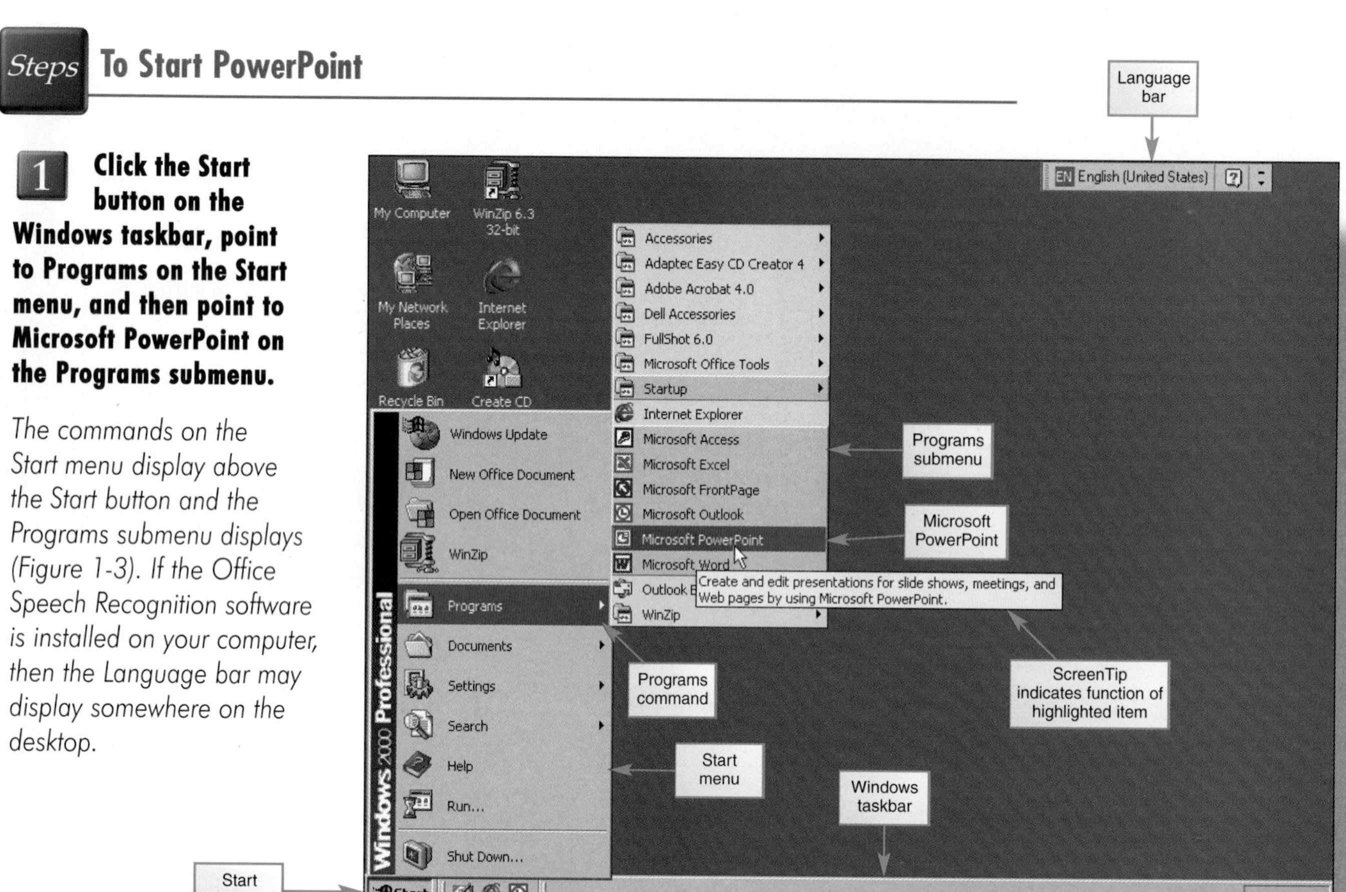

FIGURE 1-3

2 Click PowerPoint.

PowerPoint starts. While PowerPoint is starting, the mouse pointer changes to the shape of an hourglass. After a few moments, a blank presentation titled Presentation1 displays in the PowerPoint window (Figure 1-4).

3 If the PowerPoint window is not maximized, double-click its title bar to maximize it.

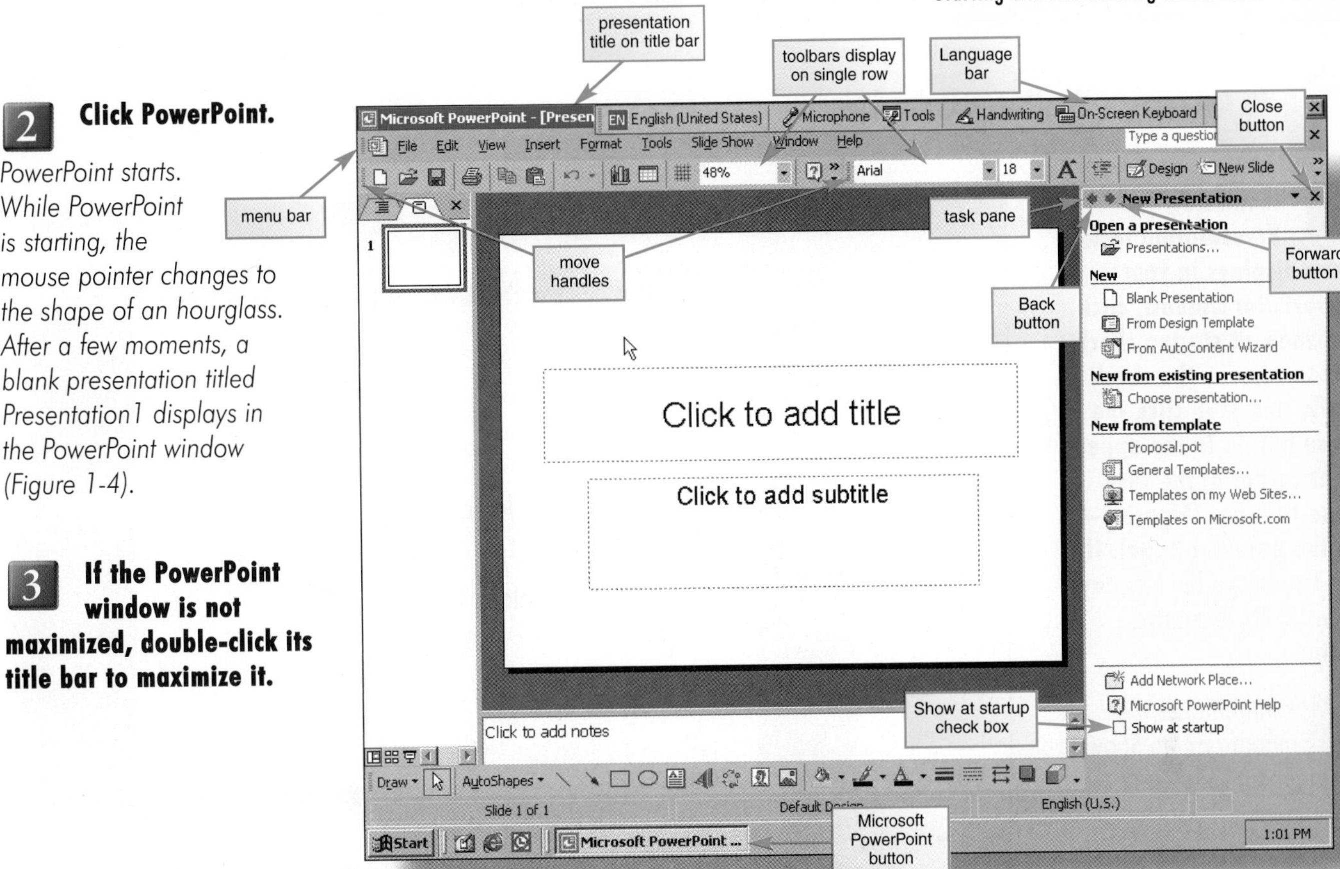

FIGURE 1-4

The screen in Figure 1-4 shows how the PowerPoint window looks the first time you start PowerPoint after installation on most computers. Notice that a task pane displays on the screen and the toolbars display on a single row. A **task pane** is a separate window within the application that provides commonly used commands and enables users to carry out some PowerPoint tasks efficiently. By default, both toolbars display on the same row immediately below the menu bar. Unless the resolution of your display device is greater than 800 × 600, many of the buttons that belong on these toolbars do not display. Hidden buttons display on the **Toolbar Options list**.

In this book, to allow the maximum slide space in the PowerPoint window, the New Presentation task pane that displays at startup is closed. For the most efficient use of the toolbars, the buttons are displayed on two separate rows instead of sharing a single row. You show the toolbar buttons on two rows by clicking the **Show Buttons on Two Rows command** in the Toolbar Options list. You also may display all the buttons on either toolbar by double-clicking the **move handle** on the left side of each toolbar (Figure 1-4). Perform the steps on the next page to customize the PowerPoint window at startup by removing the task pane from the startup instructions and displaying the toolbar buttons on two rows, instead of one.

Other Ways

1. Double-click PowerPoint icon on desktop
2. Right-click Start button, click Open All Users, double-click New Office Document, click General tab, double-click Blank Presentation icon
3. On Start menu click New Office Document, click General tab, click New Presentation icon
4. Click New Office Document button on Microsoft Office Shortcut Bar, click General tab, double-click Blank Presentation icon, point to Programs, click Microsoft PowerPoint

Steps To Customize the PowerPoint Window

1 If the New Presentation task pane displays in your PowerPoint window, click the Show at startup check box to remove the check mark, and then click the Close button in the upper-right corner of the task pane title bar (Figure 1-4 on the previous page). If the Language bar displays, point to its Minimize button.

PowerPoint removes the check mark from the Show at startup check box. PowerPoint will not display the New Presentation task pane the next time PowerPoint starts. The New Presentation task pane closes (Figure 1-5).

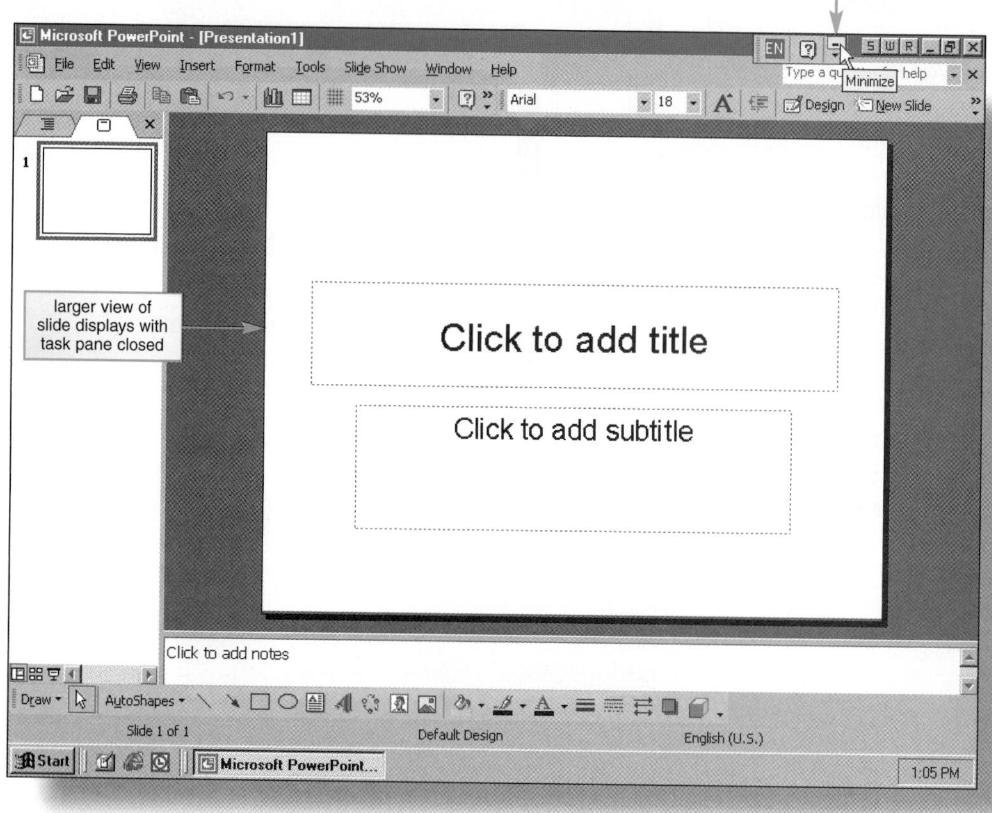

FIGURE 1-5

2 Click the Minimize button on the Language bar. If the toolbars display positioned on the same row, click the Toolbar Options button on the Standard toolbar and then point to Show Buttons on Two Rows.

The Toolbar Options list displays showing the buttons that do not fit on the toolbars when the buttons display on one row (Figure 1-6).

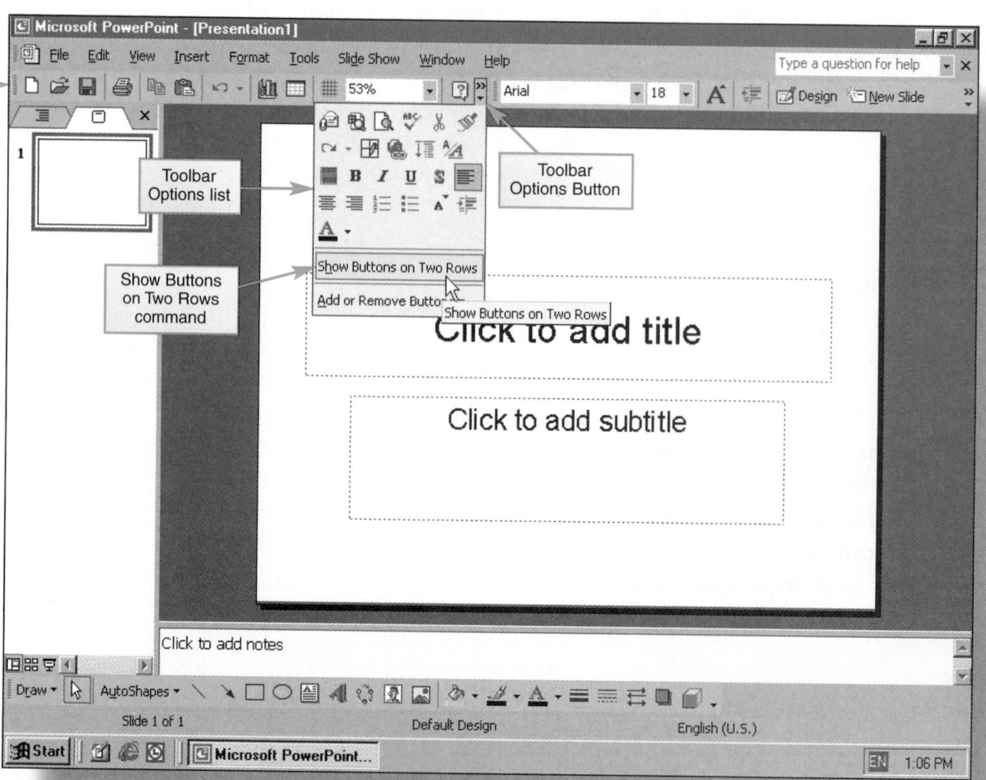

FIGURE 1-6

3 Click Show Buttons on Two Rows.

PowerPoint displays the buttons on the Standard and Formatting toolbars on two separate rows (Figure 1-7). The Toolbar Options list is empty because all the buttons fit on two rows.

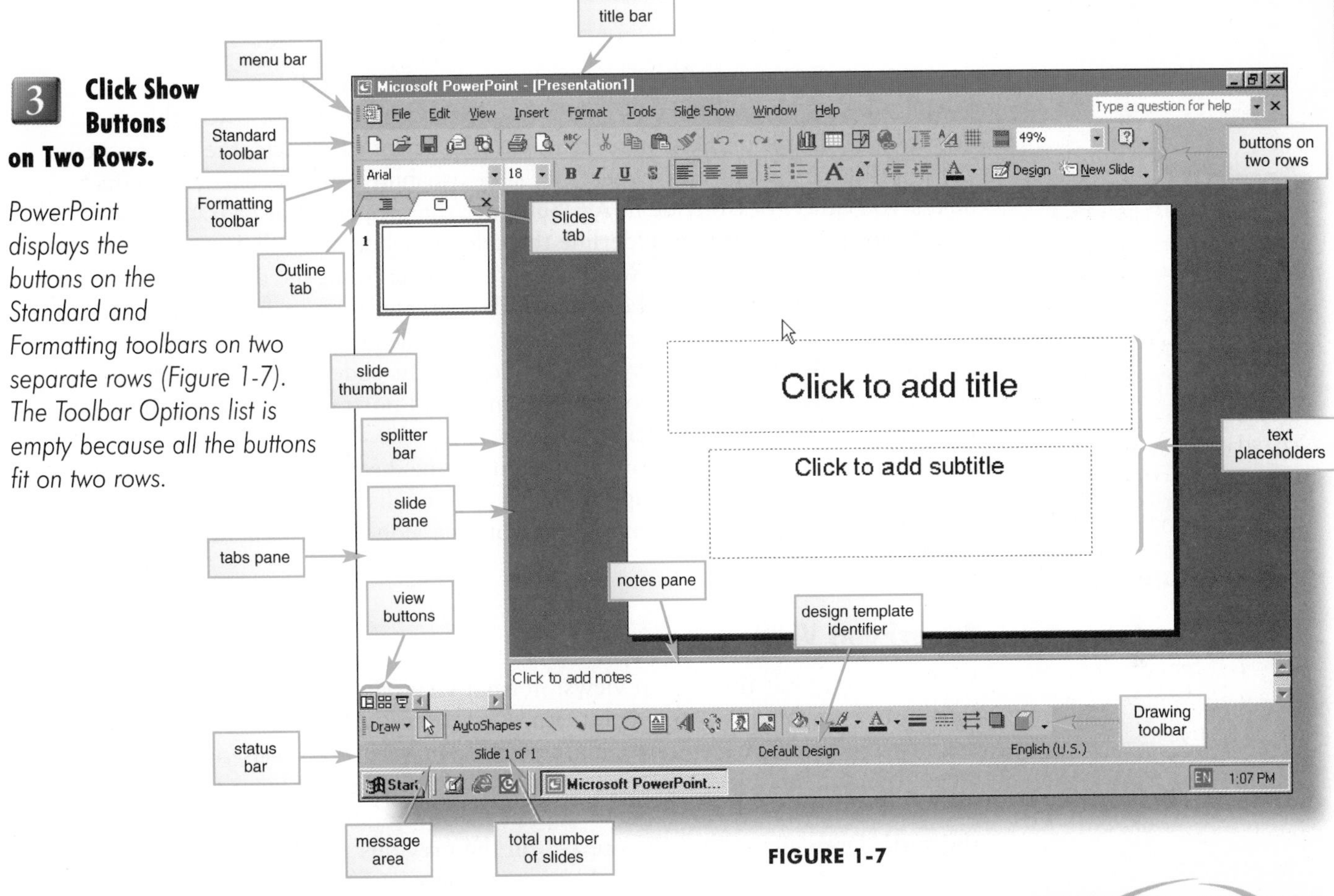

FIGURE 1-7

More About

Task Panes

When you first start PowerPoint, a small window called a task pane may display docked on the right side of the screen. You can drag a task pane title bar to float the pane in your work area or dock it on either the left or right side of a screen, depending on your personal preference.

When you point to a button or other areas on a toolbar, PowerPoint displays a ScreenTip. A **ScreenTip** is a short onscreen note associated with the object to which you are pointing, such as the name of the button. For examples of ScreenTips, see Figure 1-3 on page PP 1.10 and Figure 1-5.

As you work through creating a presentation, you will find that certain PowerPoint operations result in displaying a task pane. Besides the New Presentation task pane shown in Figure 1-4 on page 1.11, PowerPoint provides nine additional task panes: Clipboard, Basic Search, Advanced Search, Slide Layout, Slide Design – Design Templates, Slide Design – Color Schemes, Slide Design – Animation Schemes, Custom Animation, and Slide Transition. These task panes are discussed as they are used. You can display or hide a task pane by clicking the **Task Pane command** on the View menu. You can activate additional task panes by clicking the down arrow to the left of the Close button on the task pane title bar and then selecting a task pane in the list. To switch between task panes, use the Back and Forward buttons on the left side of the task pane title bar.

The PowerPoint Window

The basic unit of a PowerPoint presentation is a **slide**. A slide contains one or many **objects**, such as a title, text, graphics, tables, charts, and drawings. An object is the building block for a PowerPoint slide. PowerPoint assumes the first slide in a new presentation is the **title slide**. The title slide's purpose is to introduce the presentation to the audience.

Resolution

Resolution refers to the number of pixels, or dots, that can fit into one square inch. It is measured, consequently, in dots per inch, which is abbreviated, dpi. PowerPoint's default screen resolution is 72 dpi, and it can be set as high as 1,200 dpi. Use a resolution of 150 dpi if you are going to print handouts of your slides. For more information, visit the PowerPoint 2002 More About Web page (scsite.com/pp2002/more.htm) and then click Resolution.

In PowerPoint, you have the option of using the PowerPoint default settings or establishing your own. A **default setting** is a particular value for a variable that PowerPoint assigns initially. It controls the placement of objects, the color scheme, the transition between slides, and other slide attributes, and it remains in effect unless you cancel or override it. **Attributes** are the properties or characteristics of an object. For example, if you underline the title of a slide, the title is the object, and the underline is the attribute. When you start PowerPoint, the default **slide layout** is **landscape orientation**, where the slide width is greater than its height. In landscape orientation, the slide size is preset to 10 inches wide and 7.5 inches high. You can change the slide layout to **portrait orientation**, so the slide height is greater than its width, by clicking Page Setup on the File menu. In portrait orientation, the slide width is 7.5 inches, and the height is 10 inches.

When a PowerPoint window is open, its name displays in an icon on the Windows taskbar. The **active application** is the one displaying in the foreground of the desktop. That application's corresponding icon on the Windows taskbar displays recessed.

PowerPoint Views

PowerPoint has three main views: normal view, slide sorter view, and slide show view. A **view** is the mode in which the presentation displays on the screen. You may use any or all views when creating a presentation, but you can use only one at a time. You also can select one of these views to be the default view. Change views by clicking one of the view buttons located at the lower-left of the PowerPoint window above the Drawing toolbar (Figure 1-7 on the previous page). The PowerPoint window display varies depending on the view. Some views are graphical while others are textual.

More About

Sizing Panes

The three panes in normal view allow you to work on all aspects of your presentation simultaneously. You can drag the splitter bar and the pane borders to make each area larger or smaller.

You generally will use normal view and slide sorter view when you are creating a presentation. **Normal view** is composed of three working areas that allow you to work on various aspects of a presentation simultaneously (Figure 1-7). The left side of the screen has a tabs pane that consists of an **Outline tab** and a **Slides tab** that alternate between views of the presentation in an outline of the slide text and a thumbnail, or miniature, view of the slides. You can type the text of the presentation on the Outline tab and easily rearrange bulleted lists, paragraphs, and individual slides. As you type, you can view this text in the **slide pane**, which displays a large view of the current slide on the right side of the window. You also can enter text, graphics, animations, and hyperlinks directly in the slide pane. The **notes pane** at the bottom of the window is an area where you can type notes and additional information. This text can consist of notes to yourself or remarks to share with your audience.

In normal view, you can adjust the width of the slide pane by dragging the **splitter bar** and the height of the notes pane by dragging the pane borders. After you have created at least two slides, **scroll bars**, **scroll arrows**, and **scroll boxes** will display below and to the right of the windows, and you can use them to view different parts of the panes.

Slide sorter view is helpful when you want to see all the slides in the presentation simultaneously. A thumbnail version of each slide displays, and you can rearrange their order, add transitions and timings to switch from one slide to the next in a presentation, add and delete slides, and preview animations.

Slide show view fills the entire screen and allows you to see the slide show just as your audience will view it. Transition effects, animation, graphics, movies, and timings display as they will during an actual presentation.

Table 1-1 identifies the view buttons and provides an explanation of each view.

Table 1-1 View Buttons and Functions

BUTTON	*BUTTON NAME*	*FUNCTION*
	Normal View	Displays three panes: the tabs pane with either the Outline tab or the Slides tab, the slide pane, and the notes pane.
	Slide Sorter View	Displays thumbnail versions of all slides in a presentation. You then can copy, cut, paste, or otherwise change the slide position to modify the presentation. Slide sorter view also is used to add timings, to select animated transitions, and to preview animations.
	Slide Show View	Displays the slides as an electronic presentation on the full screen of your computer's monitor. Looking much like a slide projector display, you can see the effect of transitions, build effects, slide timings, and animations.

Placeholders, Text Areas, Mouse Pointer, and Scroll Bars

The PowerPoint window contains elements similar to the document windows in other Microsoft Office applications. Other features are unique to PowerPoint. The main elements are the text placeholders, the mouse pointer, and scroll bars.

PLACEHOLDERS **Placeholders** are boxes that display when you create a new slide. All layouts except the Blank slide layout contain placeholders. Depending on the particular slide layout selected, placeholders display for the slide title, body text, charts, tables, organization charts, media clips, and clip art. You type titles, body text, and bulleted lists in **text placeholders**; you place graphic elements in chart placeholders, table placeholders, organizational chart placeholders, and clip art placeholders. A placeholder is considered an **object**, which is a single element of a slide.

TEXT AREAS **Text areas** are surrounded by a dotted outline. The title slide in Figure 1-7 has two text areas that contain the text placeholders where you will type the main heading, or title, of a new slide and the subtitle, or other object. Other slides in a presentation may use a layout that contains text areas for a title and bulleted lists.

MOUSE POINTER The **mouse pointer** can become one of several different shapes depending on the task you are performing in PowerPoint and the pointer's location on the screen. The different shapes are discussed when they display.

SCROLL BARS When you add a second slide to a presentation, a **vertical scroll bar** displays on the right side of the slide pane. PowerPoint allows you to use the scroll bar to move forward or backward through the presentation.

The **horizontal scroll bar** may display. It is located on the bottom of the slide pane and allows you to display a portion of the slide when the entire slide does not fit on the screen.

Pointing Devices

The Microsoft IntelliMouse® pointing device can help you build presentations efficiently. For example, you can roll the wheel forward or backward instead of clicking a scroll bar. You also can have your document scroll automatically. For more information, visit the PowerPoint 2002 More About Web page (scsite.com/pp2002/ more.htm) and then click IntelliMouse.

Status Bar, Menu Bar, Standard Toolbar, Formatting Toolbar, and Drawing Toolbar

The status bar displays at the bottom of the screen above the Windows taskbar (Figure 1-7). The menu bar, Standard toolbar, and Formatting toolbar display at the top of the screen just below the title bar. The Drawing toolbar displays above the status bar.

The Default Design Template

Some PowerPoint slide show designers create presentations using the Default Design template. This blank design allows them to concentrate on the words being used to convey the message and does not distract them with colors and various text attributes. Once the text is entered, the designers then select an appropriate design template.

STATUS BAR Immediately above the Windows taskbar at the bottom of the screen is the status bar. The **status bar** consists of a message area and a presentation design template identifier (Figure 1-7 on page PP 1.13). Generally, the message area displays the current slide number and the total number of slides in the slide show. For example, in Figure 1-7 the message area displays Slide 1 of 1. Slide 1 is the current slide, and of 1 indicates the slide show contains only 1 slide. The template identifier displays Default Design, which is the template PowerPoint uses initially.

MENU BAR The **menu bar** is a special toolbar that includes the PowerPoint menu names (Figure 1-8a). Each **menu name** represents a menu of commands that you can use to perform tasks such as retrieving, storing, printing, and manipulating objects in a presentation. When you point to a menu name on the menu bar, the area of the menu bar containing the name changes to a button. To display a menu, such as the Edit menu, click the Edit menu name on the menu bar. A **menu** is a list of commands. If you point to a command on a menu that has an arrow to its right edge, a **submenu** displays another list of commands.

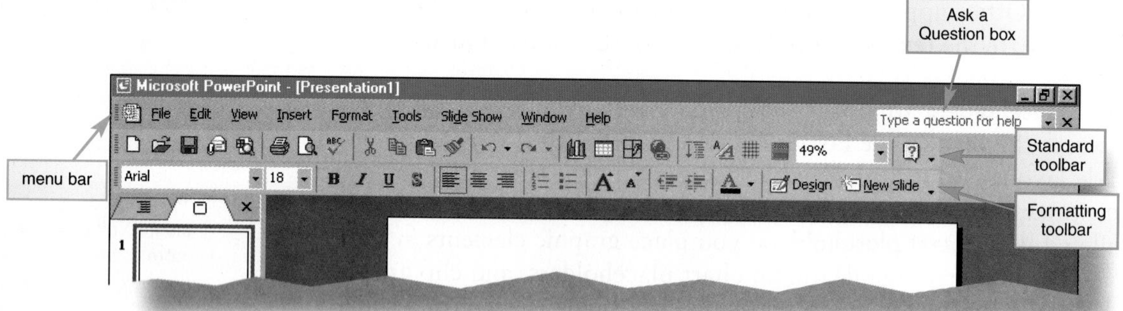

(a) Menu Bar and Toolbars

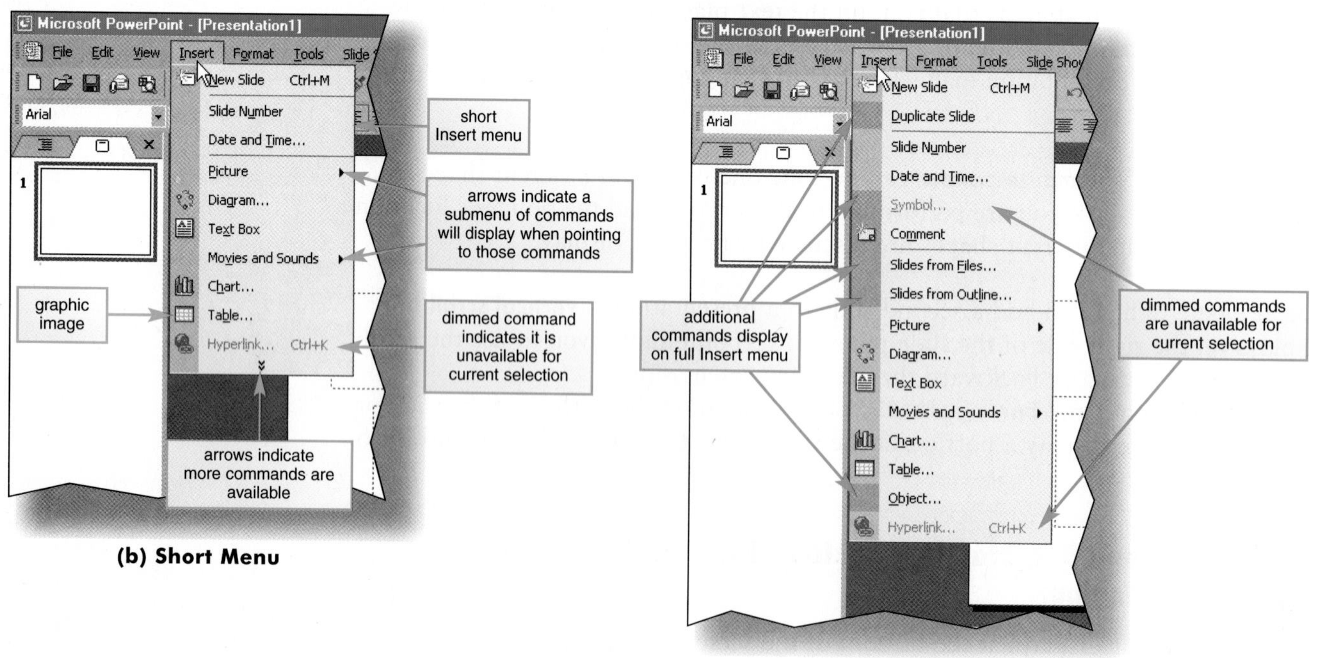

(b) Short Menu

(c) Full Menu

FIGURE 1-8

When you click a menu name on the menu bar, a short menu displays that lists your most recently used commands (Figure 1-8b).

If you wait a few seconds or click the arrows at the bottom of the short menu, it expands into a full menu. A **full menu** lists all the commands associated with a menu (Figure 1-8c). You immediately can display a full menu by double-clicking the menu name on the menu bar. In this book, when you display a menu, always display the full menu using one of these techniques:

1. Click the menu name on the menu bar and then wait a few seconds.
2. Click the menu name on the menu bar and then click the arrows at the bottom of the short menu.
3. Click the menu name on the menu bar and then point to the arrows at the bottom of the short menu.
4. Double-click the menu name on the menu bar.

Hiding Toolbars

To display more of the PowerPoint window, you can hide a toolbar you no longer need. To hide a toolbar, right-click any toolbar and then click the check mark next to the toolbar you want to hide on the shortcut menu.

Both short and full menus display some commands with an image to the left, which associates the command with a graphic image and dimmed commands that appear gray, or dimmed, instead of black, which indicates they are not available for the current selection. A command with a dark gray shading to the left of it on a full menu is called a hidden command because it does not display on a short menu. As you use PowerPoint, it automatically personalizes the short menus for you based on how often you use commands. That is, as you use hidden commands, PowerPoint *unhides* them and places them on the short menu.

The menu bar can change to include other menu names depending on the type of work you are doing in PowerPoint. For example, if you are adding a chart to a slide, Data and Chart menu names are added to the menu bar with commands that reflect charting options.

STANDARD, FORMATTING, AND DRAWING TOOLBARS The Standard toolbar (Figure 1-9a), Formatting toolbar (Figure 1-9b), and Drawing toolbar (Figure 1-9c on the next page) contain buttons and boxes that allow you to perform frequent tasks more quickly than when using the menu bar. For example, to print a slide show, you click the Print button on the Standard toolbar. Each button has an image on the button and a ScreenTip that help you remember the button's function.

Figure 1-9 illustrates the Standard, Formatting, and Drawing toolbars and describes the functions of the buttons. Each of the buttons and boxes are explained in detail when they are used.

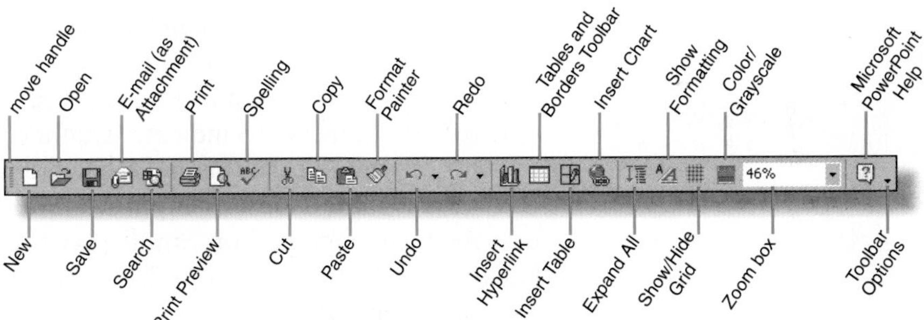

FIGURE 1-9a Standard Toolbar

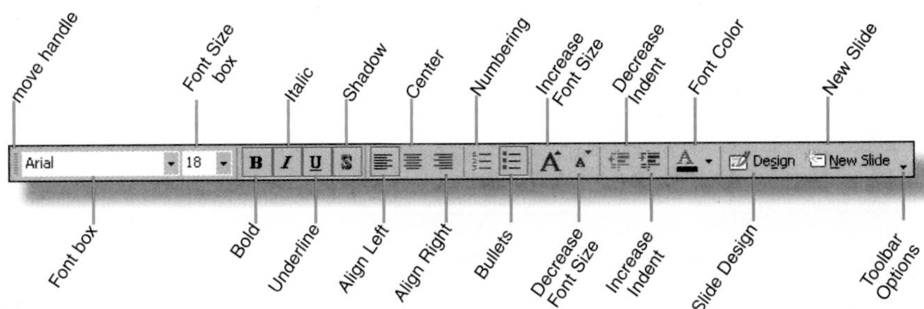

FIGURE 1-9b Formatting Toolbar

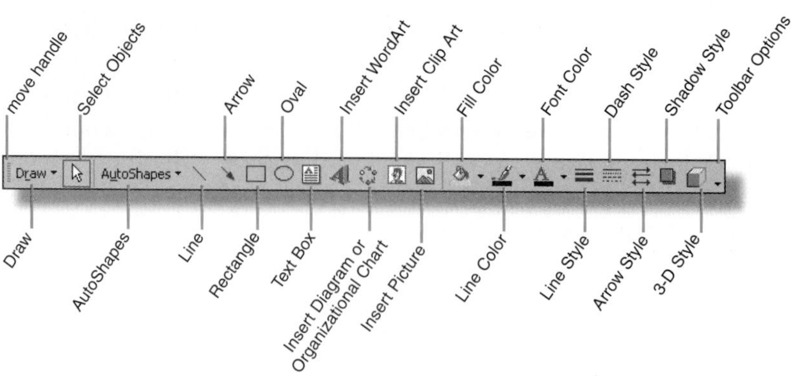

FIGURE 1-9c Drawing Toolbar

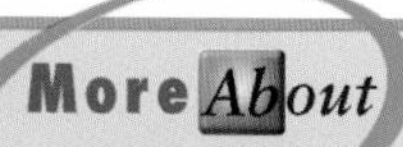

Shortcut Menus

When you point to or select an item and right-click, a shortcut menu usually displays. This special menu contains frequently used commands related to that object. In some cases, you also can display the shortcut menu by selecting an object, such as a paragraph, and then pressing SHIFT+F10. To hide a shortcut menu, click outside the shortcut menu or press the ESC key.

PowerPoint has several additional toolbars you can display by pointing to Toolbars on the View menu and then clicking the respective name on the Toolbars submenu. You also may display a toolbar by pointing to a toolbar and right-clicking to display a shortcut menu, which lists the available toolbars. A **shortcut menu** contains a list of commands or items that relate to the item to which you are pointing when you right-click.

Speech Recognition

With the **Office Speech Recognition software** installed and a microphone, you can speak the names of toolbar buttons, menus, menu commands, list items, alerts, and dialog box controls, such as OK and Cancel. You also can dictate cell entries, such as text and numbers. To indicate whether you want to speak commands or dictate cell entries, you use the **Language bar** (Figure 1-10a), which also is used for handwriting recognition and for Input Method Editors (IME) that convert keystrokes to East Asian characters. You can display the Language bar in two ways: (1) click the Language Indicator button in the Windows taskbar tray status area by the clock, and then click Show the Language bar on the Language bar menu (Figure 1-10b); or (2) click the **Speech command** on the **Tools menu**.

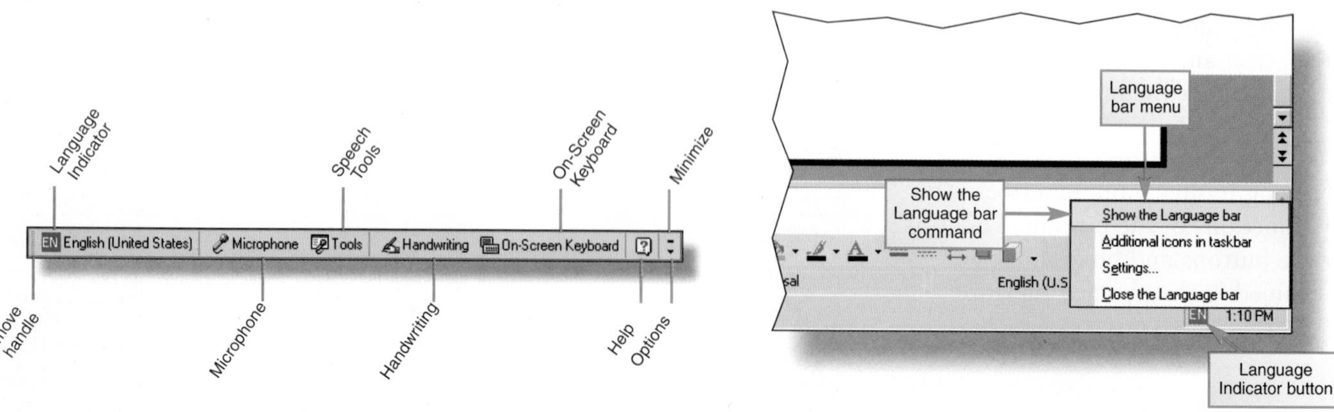

(a) Language Bar

(b) Language Bar Menu

FIGURE 1-10

If the Language Indicator button does not display in the tray status area, and if the Speech command is not displayed or is dimmed on the Tools menu, the Office Speech Recognition software is not installed. To install the software, you first must start Word and then click Speech on the Tools menu.

If you have speakers, you can instruct the computer to read a slide show to you. By selecting the appropriate option, you can have the slides read in a male or female voice.

Additional information on the Office speech and handwriting recognition capabilities is available in Appendix B.

More About

Additional Templates

While the Slide Design task pane displays a wide variety of templates, more are available in the Microsoft Office Template Gallery at the Microsoft Web site. These templates are arranged in various categories according to the type of presentation.

Choosing a Design Template

A **design template** provides consistency in design and color throughout the entire presentation. It determines the color scheme, font and font size, and layout of a presentation. PowerPoint has three Slide Design task panes that allow you to choose and change the appearance of slides in your presentation. The **Slide Design – Design Templates task pane** displays a variety of styles. You can alter the colors used in the design templates by using the **Slide Design – Color Schemes task pane.** In addition, you can animate elements of your presentation by using the **Slide Design – Animation Schemes task pane.**

In this project, you will select a particular design template by using the Slide Design – Design Templates task pane. The top section of the task pane, labeled Used in This Presentation, displays the template currently used in the slide show. PowerPoint uses the **Default Design** template until you select a different style. When you place your mouse over a template, the name of the template displays. The next section of the task pane is the Recently Used templates. This area displays the four templates you have used in your newest slide shows. The Available For Use area shows additional templates. The templates display in alphabetical order in the two columns.

You want to change the template for this presentation from the Default Design to Proposal. Perform the following steps to apply the Proposal design template.

More About

The PowerPoint Help System

Need Help? It is no further than the Ask a Question box in the upper-right corner of the window. Click the box that contains the text, Type a question for help (Figure 1-8a on page PP 1.16), type `help`, and then press the ENTER key. PowerPoint will respond with a list of items you can click to learn about obtaining help on any PowerPoint-related topic. To find out what is new in PowerPoint 2002, type `what's new in PowerPoint` in the Ask a Question box.

Steps To Choose a Design Template

1 **Point to the Slide Design button on the Formatting toolbar (Figure 1-11).**

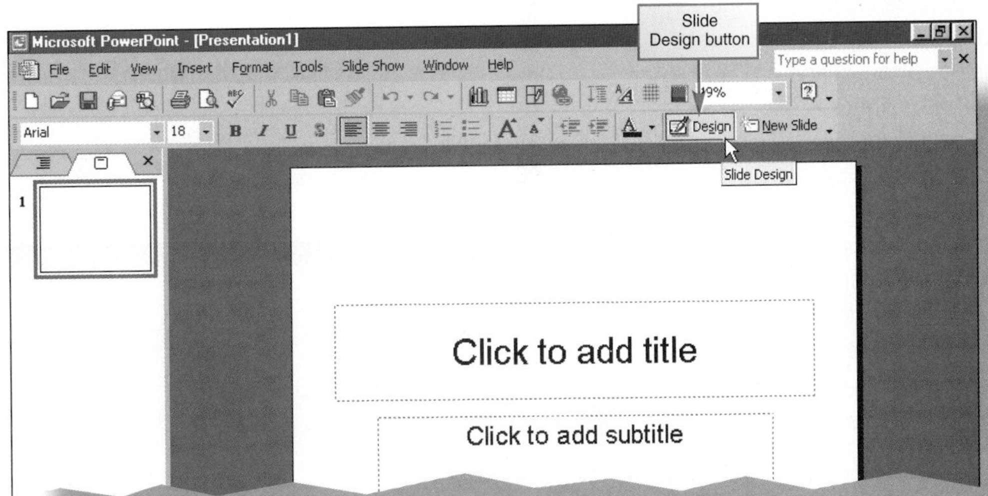

FIGURE 1-11

2 Click the Slide Design button and then point to the down scroll arrow in the Apply a design template list.

The Slide Design task pane displays (Figure 1-12). The Apply a design template list displays thumbnail views of numerous design templates. Your list may look different depending on your computer. The Default Design template is highlighted in the Used in This Presentation area. Other templates display in the Available For Use area and possibly in the Recently Used area. The Close button in the Slide Design task pane can be used to close the task pane if you do not want to apply a new template.

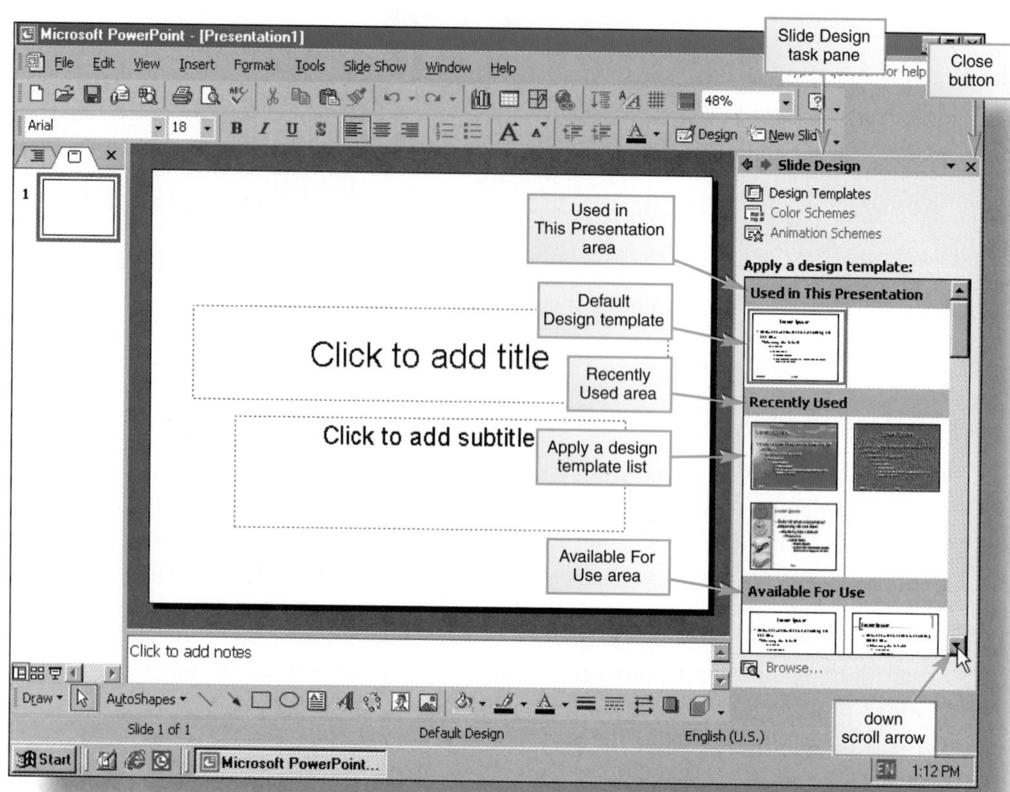

FIGURE 1-12

3 Click the down scroll arrow to scroll through the list of design templates until Proposal displays (row 17, column 1) in the Available For Use area. Point to the Proposal template.

The proposal template is selected, as indicated by the blue box around the template and the arrow button on the right side (Figure 1-13). PowerPoint provides 45 templates in the Available For Use area. Their names are listed in alphabetical order. A ScreenTip displays the template's name. Your system may display the ScreenTip, Proposal.pot, which indicates the design template's file extension (.pot).

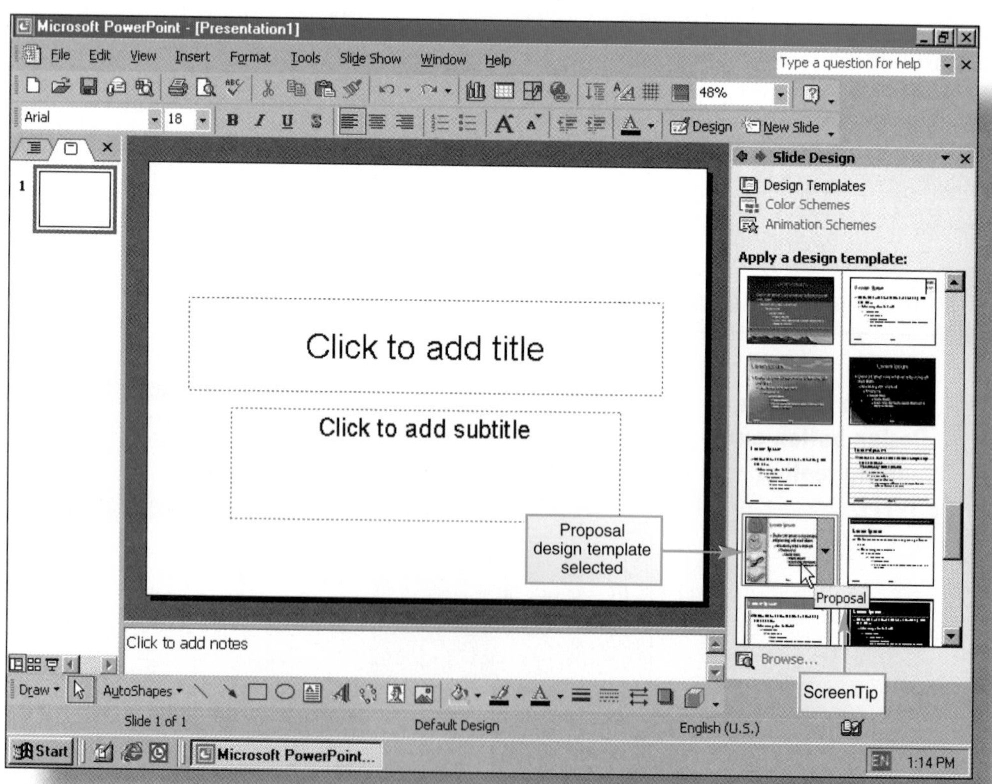

FIGURE 1-13

4 Click Proposal. Point to the Close button in the Slide Design task pane.

The template is applied to Slide 1, as shown in the slide pane and Slides tab (Figure 1-14).

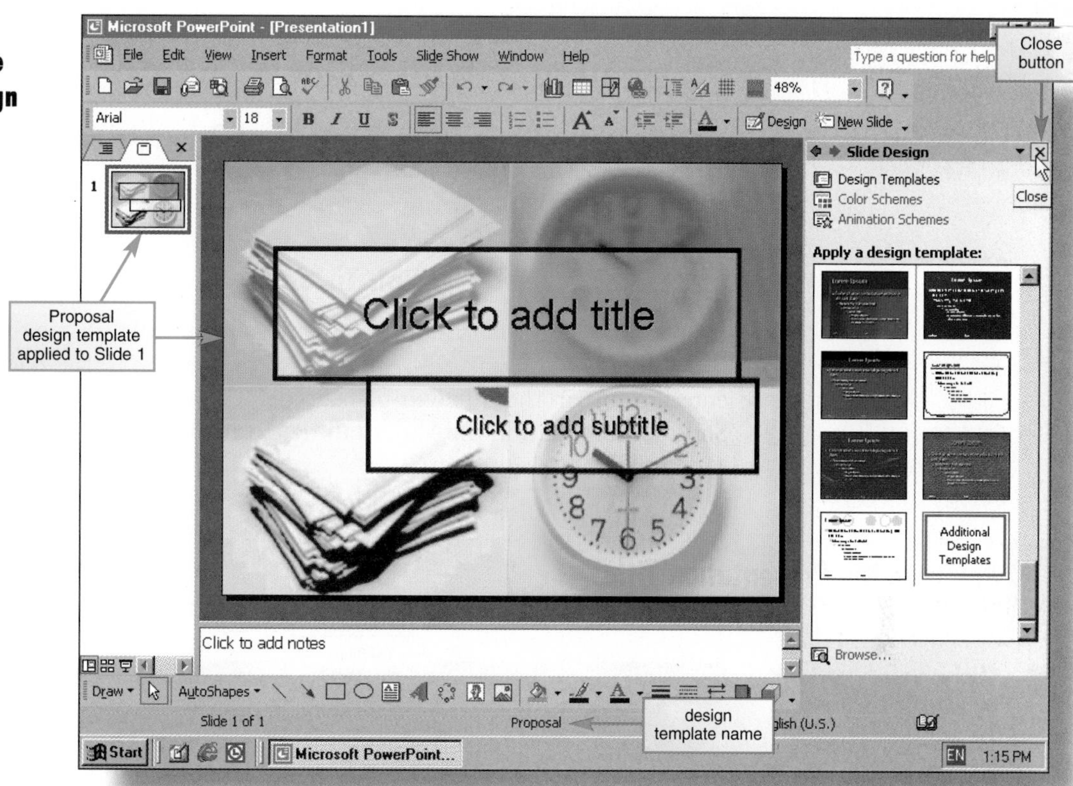

FIGURE 1-14

5 Click the Close button.

Slide 1 displays in normal view with the Proposal design template (Figure 1-15).

FIGURE 1-15

Other Ways

1. Double-click Proposal in list

Creating a Title Slide

With the exception of a blank slide, PowerPoint assumes every new slide has a title. To make creating a presentation easier, any text you type after a new slide displays becomes title text in the title text placeholder.

Entering the Presentation Title

The presentation title for Project 1 is Time to Start Making Friends. To enter text in your slide, you type on the keyboard or speak into the microphone. As you begin entering text in the title text placeholder, the title text displays immediately in the Slide 1 thumbnail in the Slides tab. Perform the following steps to create the title slide for this presentation.

Steps To Enter the Presentation Title

1 Click the label, Click to add title, located inside the title text placeholder.

The insertion point is in the title text placeholder (Figure 1-16). The ***insertion point*** *is a blinking vertical line (|), which indicates where the next character will display. The mouse pointer changes to an I-beam. A* ***selection rectangle*** *displays around the title text placeholder. The placeholder is selected as indicated by the border and sizing handles displaying on the edges.*

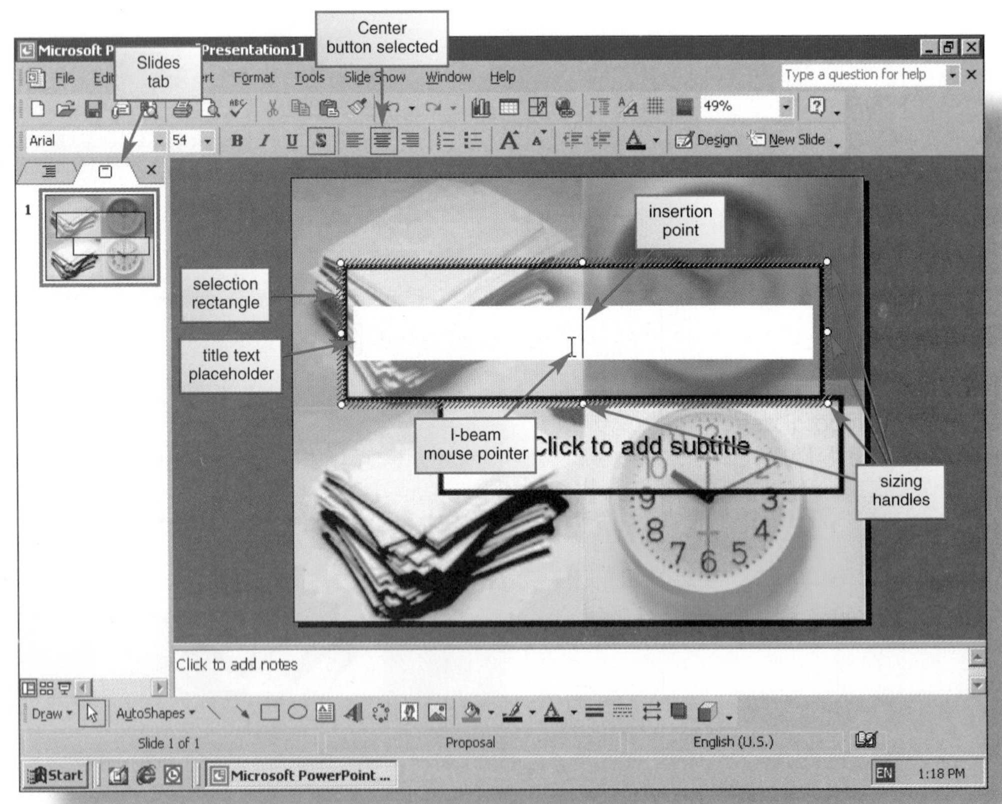

FIGURE 1-16

2 In the title text placeholder type `Time to Start` **and then press the ENTER key. Type** `Making Friends` **but do not press the ENTER key.**

The title text, Time to Start Making Friends, displays on two lines in the title text placeholder and in the Slides tab (Figure 1-17). The insertion point displays after the letter s in Friends. The title text displays centered in the placeholder with the default text attributes: Arial font, font size 54, and shadow effect.

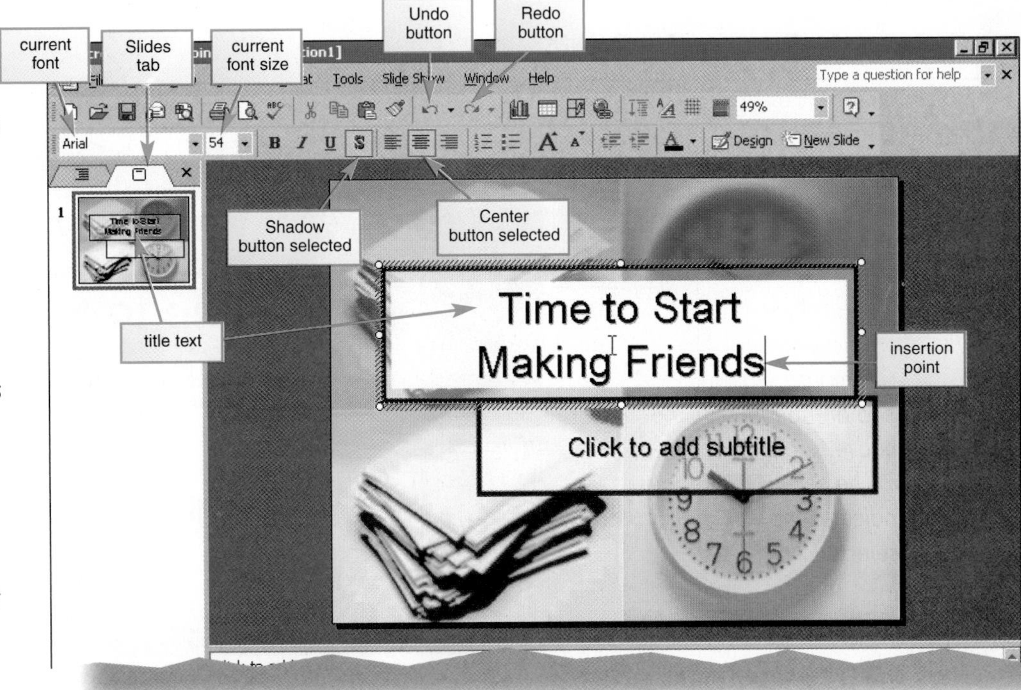

FIGURE 1-17

Other Ways

1. In Dictation mode, say "Time to start, New Line, Making friends"

PowerPoint **line wraps** text that exceeds the width of the placeholder. One of PowerPoint's features is **text AutoFit**. If you are creating a slide and need to squeeze an extra line in the text placeholder, PowerPoint will prompt you to resize the existing text in the placeholder so the spillover text will fit on the slide.

Correcting a Mistake When Typing

If you type the wrong letter, press the BACKSPACE key to erase all the characters back to and including the one that is incorrect. If you mistakenly press the ENTER key after typing the title and the insertion point is on the new line, simply press the BACKSPACE key to return the insertion point to the right of the letter s in the word Friends.

When you install PowerPoint, the default setting allows you to reverse up to the last 20 changes by clicking the **Undo button** on the Standard toolbar. The ScreenTip that displays when you point to the Undo button changes to indicate the type of change just made. For example, if you type text in the title text placeholder and then point to the Undo button, the ScreenTip that displays is Undo Typing. For clarity, when referencing the Undo button in this project, the name displaying in the ScreenTip is referenced. Another way to reverse changes is to click the **Undo command** on the Edit menu. As with the Undo button, the Undo command reflects the last type of change made to the presentation.

You can reapply a change that you reversed with the Undo button by clicking the **Redo button** on the Standard toolbar. Clicking the Redo button reverses the last undo action. The ScreenTip name reflects the type of reversal last preformed.

More About

The 7 × 7 Rule

All slide shows in the projects and exercises in this book follow the 7 × 7 rule. This guideline states that each slide should have a maximum of seven lines, and each of these lines should have a maximum of seven words. This rule requires PowerPoint designers to choose their words carefully and, in turn, helps viewers read the slides easily.

Entering the Presentation Subtitle

The next step in creating the title slide is to enter the subtitle text into the subtitle text placeholder. Complete the steps on the next page to enter the presentation subtitle.

Steps To Enter the Presentation Subtitle

1 Click the label, Click to add subtitle, located inside the subtitle text placeholder.

The insertion point displays in the subtitle text placeholder (Figure 1-18). The mouse pointer changes to an I-beam indicating the mouse is in a text placeholder. The selection rectangle indicates the placeholder is selected.

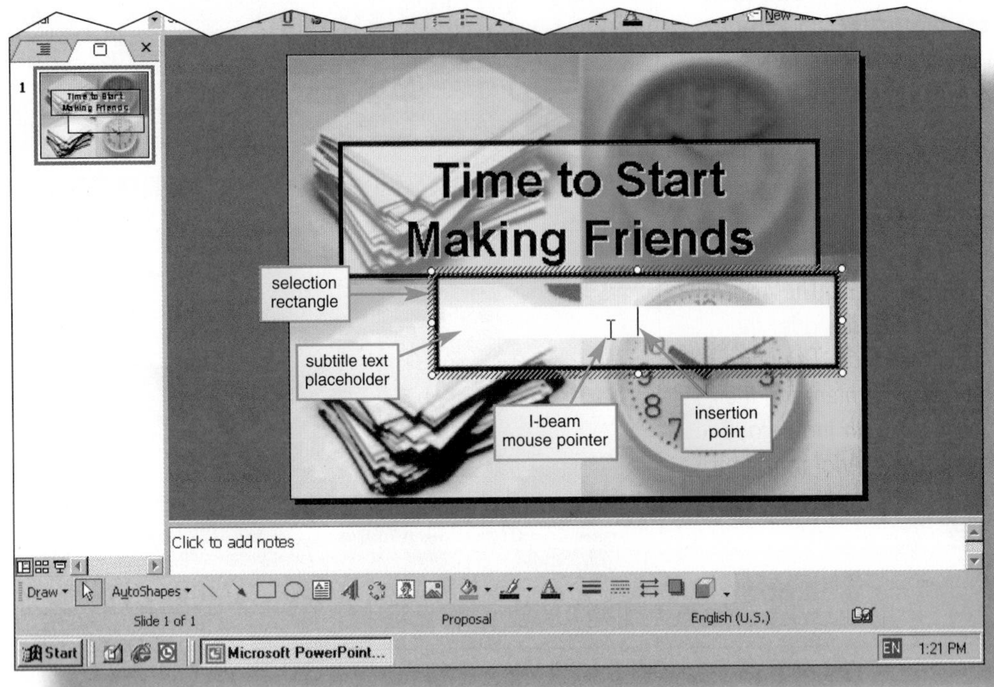

FIGURE 1-18

2 Type `Presented by` **and then press the ENTER key. Type** `Westview College Counselors` **but do not press the ENTER key.**

The subtitle text displays in the subtitle text placeholder and the Slides tab (Figure 1-19). The insertion point displays after the letter s in Counselors. A red wavy line displays below the word, Westview, to indicate a possible spelling error.

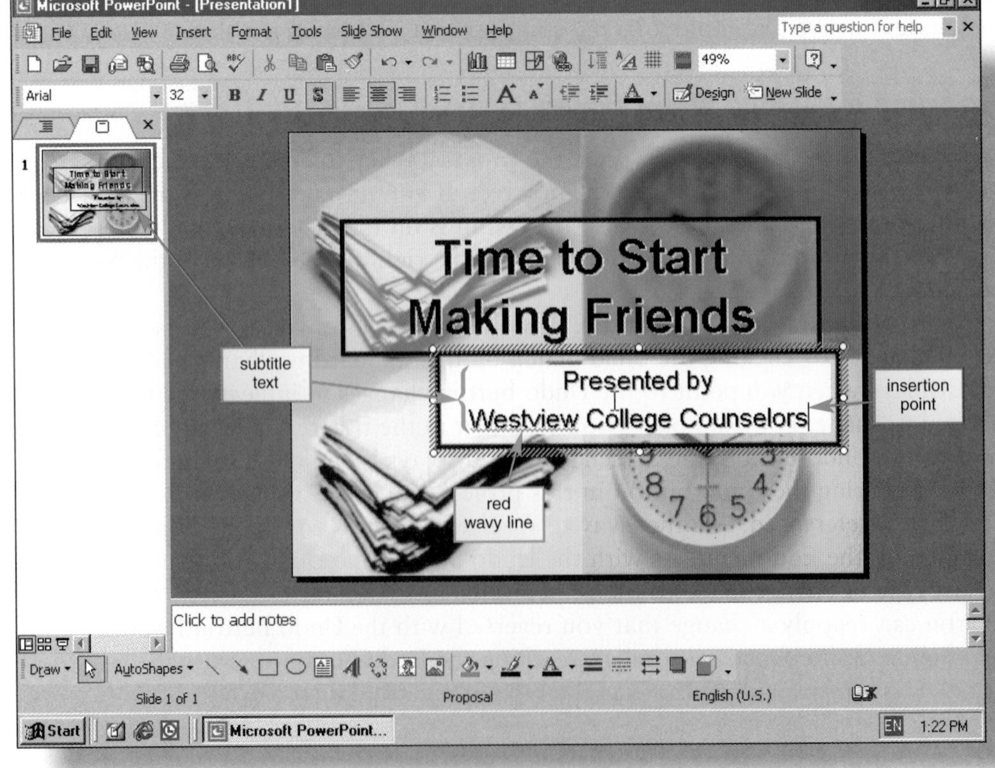

FIGURE 1-19

Other Ways

1. In Dictation mode, say "Presented by, New Line, Westview College Counselors"

After pressing the ENTER key in Step 2, PowerPoint created a new line, which is the second paragraph in the placeholder. A **paragraph** is a segment of text with the same format that begins when you press the ENTER key and ends when you press the ENTER key again.

Text Attributes

This presentation uses the Proposal design template. Each design template has its own text attributes. A **text attribute** is a characteristic of the text, such as font, font size, font style, or text color. You can adjust text attributes any time before, during, or after you type the text. Recall that a design template determines the color scheme, font and font size, and layout of a presentation. Most of the time, you use the design template's text attributes and color scheme. Occasionally, you may want to change the way a presentation looks, however, and still keep a particular design template. PowerPoint gives you that flexibility. You can use the design template and change the font and the font's color, effects, size, and style. Text may have one or more font styles and effects simultaneously. Table 1-2 explains the different text attributes available in PowerPoint.

The next two sections explain how to change the font size and font style attributes.

More About

Modifying Fonts

Designers recommend using a maximum of two fonts and two font styles or effects in a slide show. This design philosophy maintains balance and simplicity.

Table 1-2 Design Template Text Attributes

ATTRIBUTE	*DESCRIPTION*
Color	Defines the color of text. Displaying text in color requires a color monitor. Printing text in color requires a color printer or plotter.
Effects	Effects include underline, shadow, emboss, superscript, and subscript. Effects can be applied to most fonts.
Font	Defines the appearance and shape of letters, numbers, and special characters.
Size	Specifies the height of characters on the screen. Character size is gauged by a measurement system called points. A single point is about 1/72 of an inch in height. Thus, a character with a point size of 18 is about 18/72 (or 1/4) of an inch in height.
Style	Font styles include regular, bold, italic, and bold italic.

Changing the Style of Text to Italic

Text font styles include plain, italic, bold, shadowed, and underlined. PowerPoint allows you to use one or more text font styles in a presentation. Perform the steps on the next page to add emphasis to the first line of the subtitle text by changing regular text to italic text.

Steps To Change the Text Font Style to Italic

1 Triple-click the paragraph, Westview College Counselors, in the subtitle text placeholder, and then point to the Italic button on the Formatting toolbar.

The paragraph, Westview College Counselors, is highlighted (Figure 1-20). The Italic button *is surrounded by a blue box. You select an entire paragraph quickly by triple-clicking any text within the paragraph.*

FIGURE 1-20

2 Click the Italic button.

The text is italicized on the slide and the slide thumbnail (Figure 1-21).

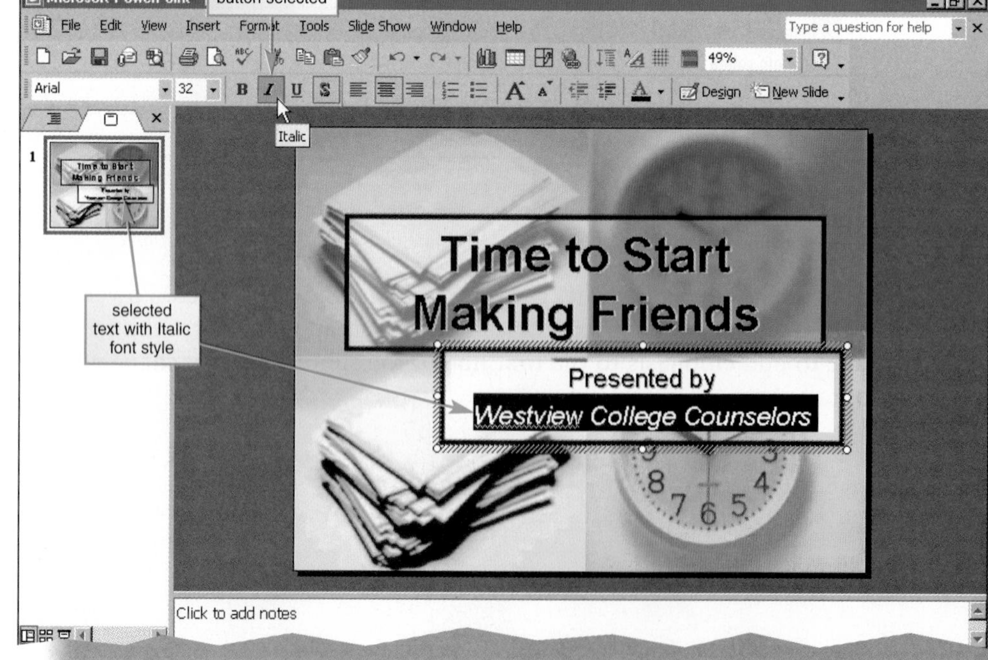

FIGURE 1-21

Other Ways

1. Right-click selected text, click Font on shortcut menu, click Italic in Font style list
2. On Format menu click Font, click Italic in Font style list
3. Press CTRL+I
4. In Voice Command mode, say "Italic"

To remove the italic style from text, select the italicized text and then click the Italic button. As a result, the Italic button is not selected, and the text does not have the italic font style.

Changing the Font Size

The Proposal design template default font size is 54 point for title text and 32 point for body text. A point is 1/72 of an inch in height. Thus, a character with a point size of 54 is 54/72 (or 3/4) of an inch in height. Slide 1 requires you to increase the font size for the paragraph, Presented by. Perform the following steps to increase the font size.

Steps To Increase Font Size

1 Position the mouse pointer in the paragraph, Presented by, and then triple-click.

PowerPoint selects the entire paragraph (Figure 1-22).

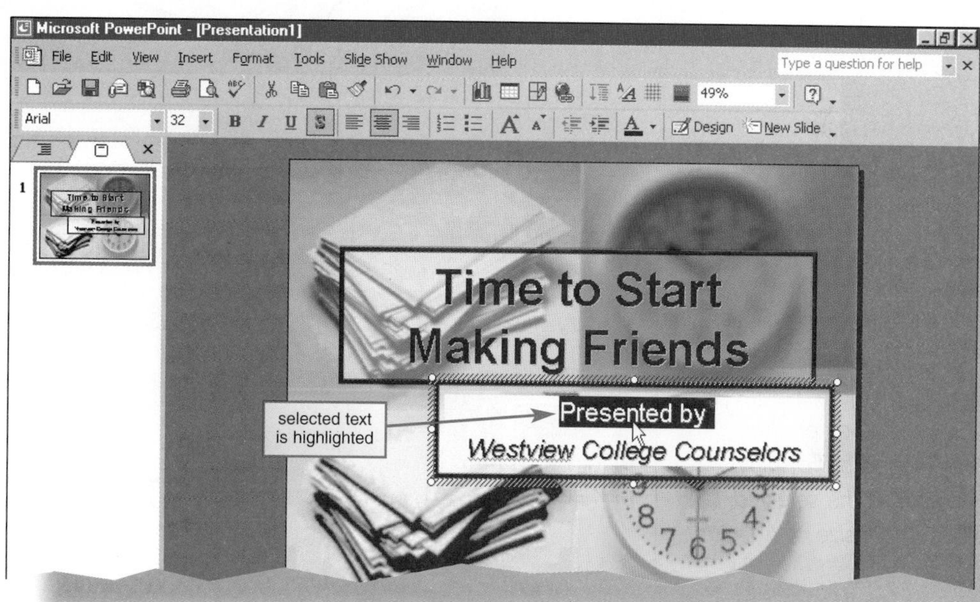

FIGURE 1-22

2 Point to the Font Size box arrow on the Formatting toolbar.

The ScreenTip displays the words, Font Size (Figure 1-23). The **Font Size box** *is surrounded by a blue box and indicates that the subtitle text is 32 point.*

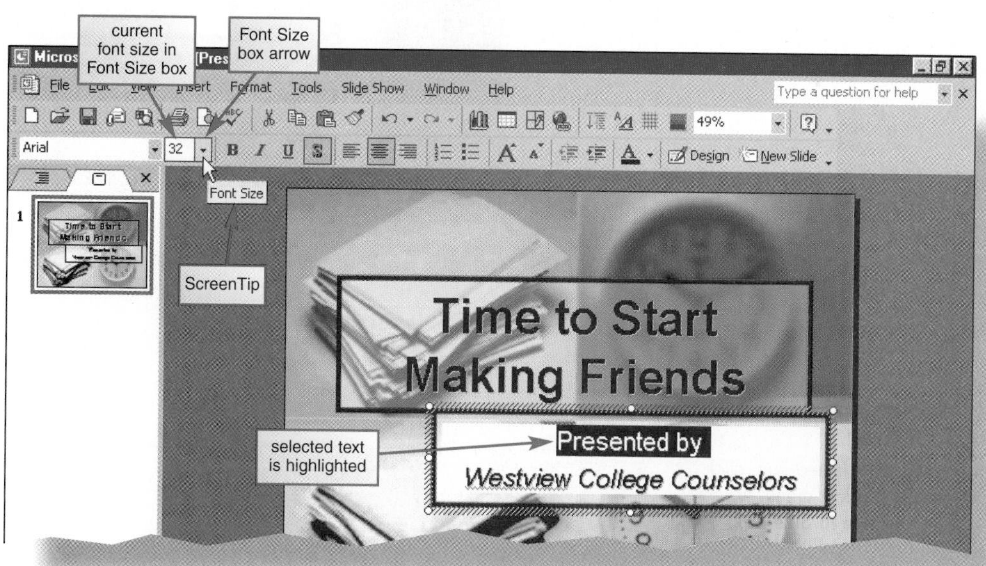

FIGURE 1-23

3 Click the Font Size box arrow, click the Font Size box scroll bar one time, and then point to 40 in the Font Size list.

When you click the **Font Size box arrow,** *a list of available font sizes displays in the Font Size list (Figure 1-24). The font sizes displayed depend on the current font, which is Arial. Font size 40 is highlighted.*

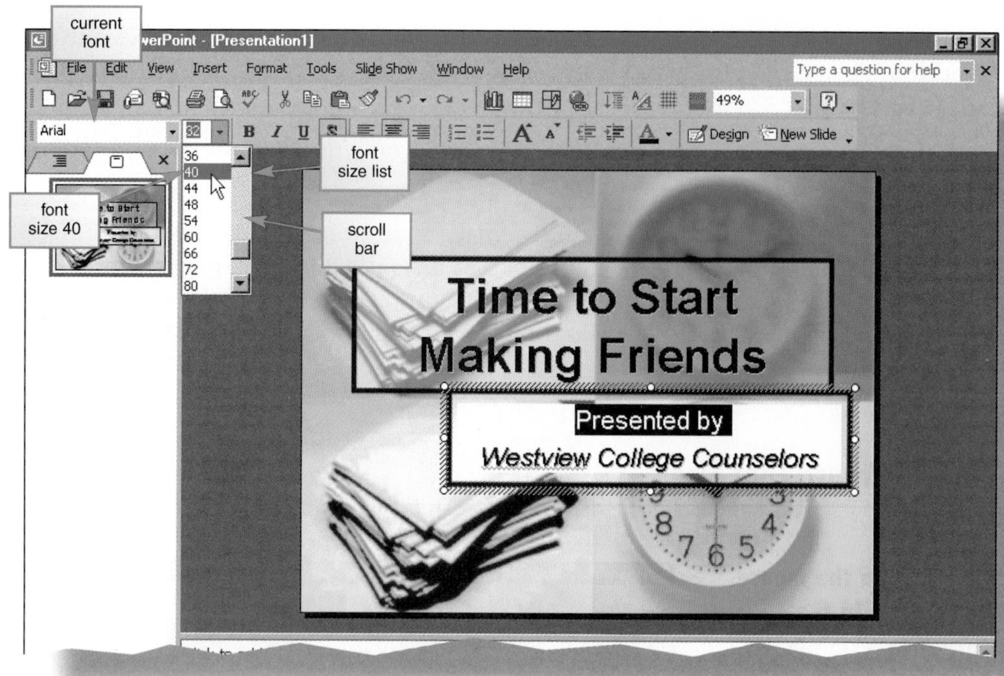

FIGURE 1-24

4 Click 40.

The font size of the subtitle text, Presented by, increases to 40 point (Figure 1-25). The Font Size box on the Formatting toolbar displays 40, indicating the selected text has a font size of 40.

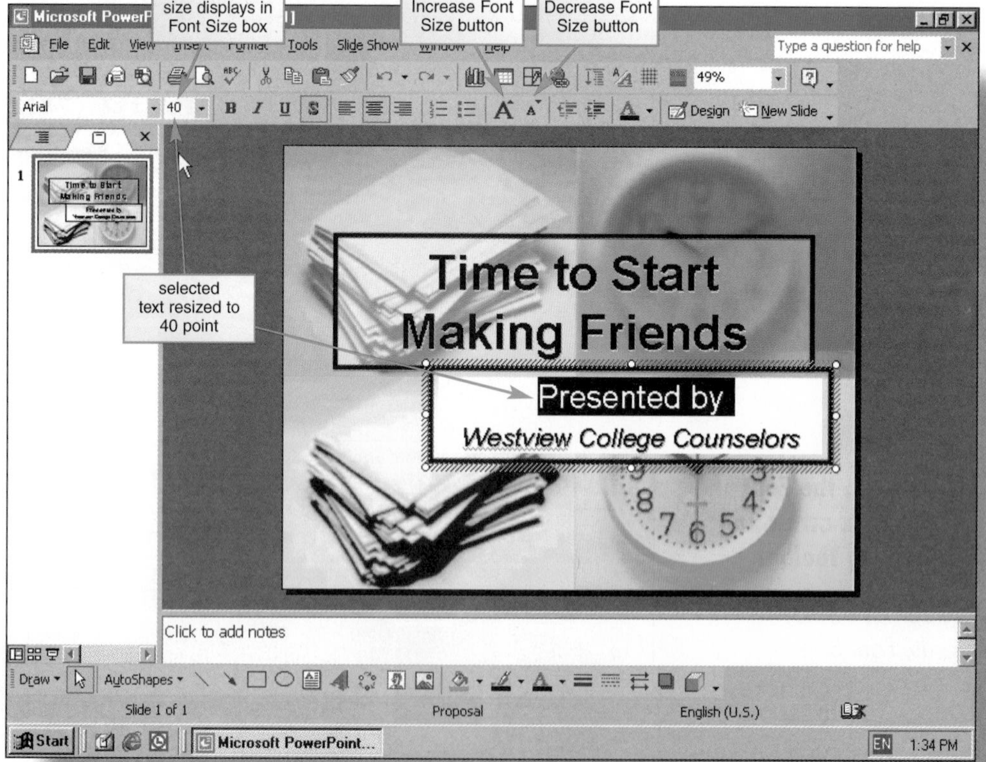

FIGURE 1-25

Other Ways

1. Click Increase Font Size button on Formatting toolbar
2. On Format menu click Font, click new font size in Size box, or type font size between 1 and 4000, click OK button
3. Right-click selected text, click Font on shortcut menu, type new font size in Size box, click OK button
4. In Voice Command mode, say "Font Size, [font size]"

The **Increase Font Size button** on the Formatting toolbar (Figure 1-25) increases the font size in preset increments each time you click the button. If you need to decrease the font size, click the Font Size box arrow and then select a size smaller than 32. The **Decrease Font Size button** on the Formatting toolbar (Figure 1-25) also decreases the font size in preset increments each time you click the button.

Text Attributes

The Microsoft Web site contains a comprehensive glossary of typography terms. The information includes a diagram illustrating text attributes. For more information, visit the PowerPoint 2002 More About Web page (scsite.com/pp2002/more.htm) and then click Attributes.

Saving the Presentation on a Floppy Disk

While you are building a presentation, the computer stores it in memory. It is important to save the presentation frequently because the presentation will be lost if the computer is turned off or you lose electrical power. Another reason to save your work is that if you run out of lab time before completing your project, you may finish the project later without starting over. Therefore, always save any presentation you will use later. Before you continue with Project 1, save the work completed thus far. Perform the following steps to save a presentation on a floppy disk using the Save button on the Standard toolbar.

To Save a Presentation on a Floppy Disk

1 Insert a formatted floppy disk in drive A. Click the Save button on the Standard toolbar.

The Save As dialog box displays (Figure 1-26). The default folder, My Documents, displays in the Save in box. Time to Start Making Friends displays highlighted in the File name text box because PowerPoint uses the words in the title text placeholder as the default file name. Presentation displays in the Save as type box. Clicking the Cancel button closes the Save As dialog box.

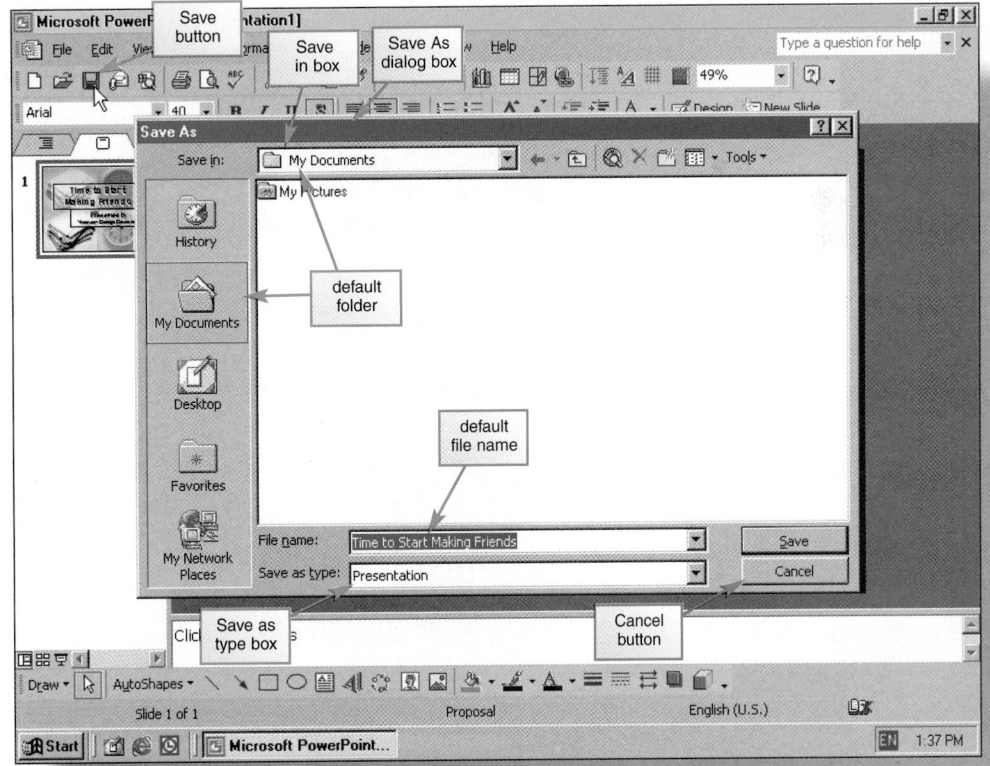

FIGURE 1-26

2 **Type** `Make Friends` **in the File name text box. Do not press the ENTER key after typing the file name. Point to the Save in box arrow.**

The name, Make Friends, displays in the File name text box (Figure 1-27).

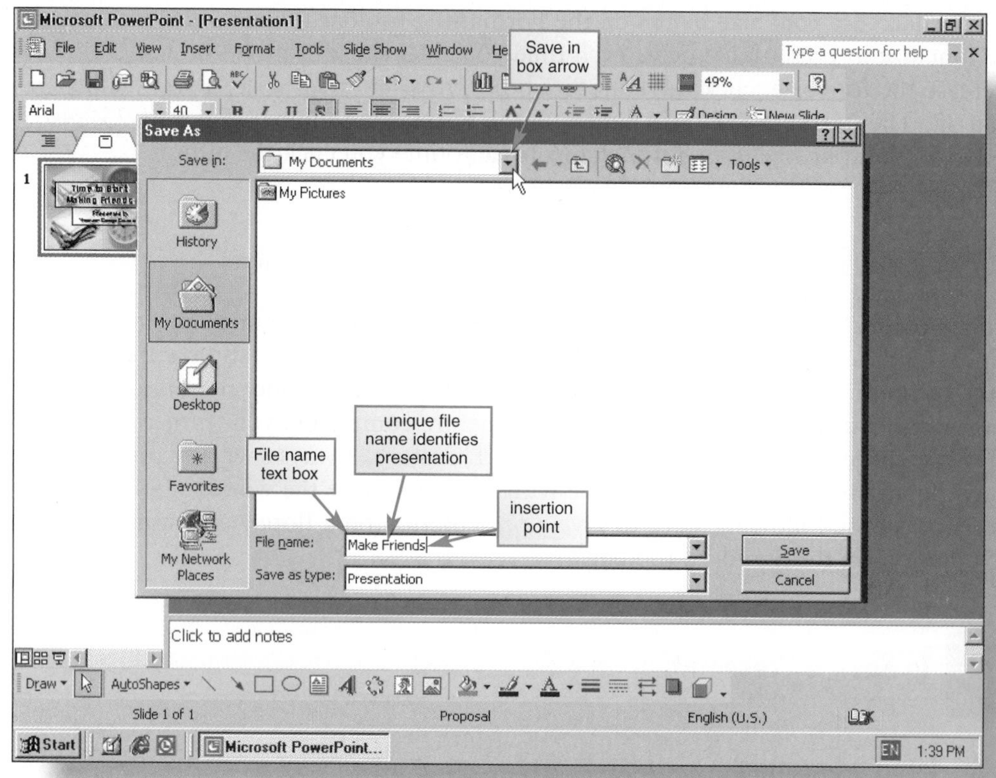

FIGURE 1-27

3 **Click the Save in box arrow. Point to 3½ Floppy (A:) in the Save in list.**

The Save in list displays a list of locations in which to save a presentation; 3½ Floppy (A:) is highlighted (Figure 1-28). Your list may look different depending on the configuration of your system.

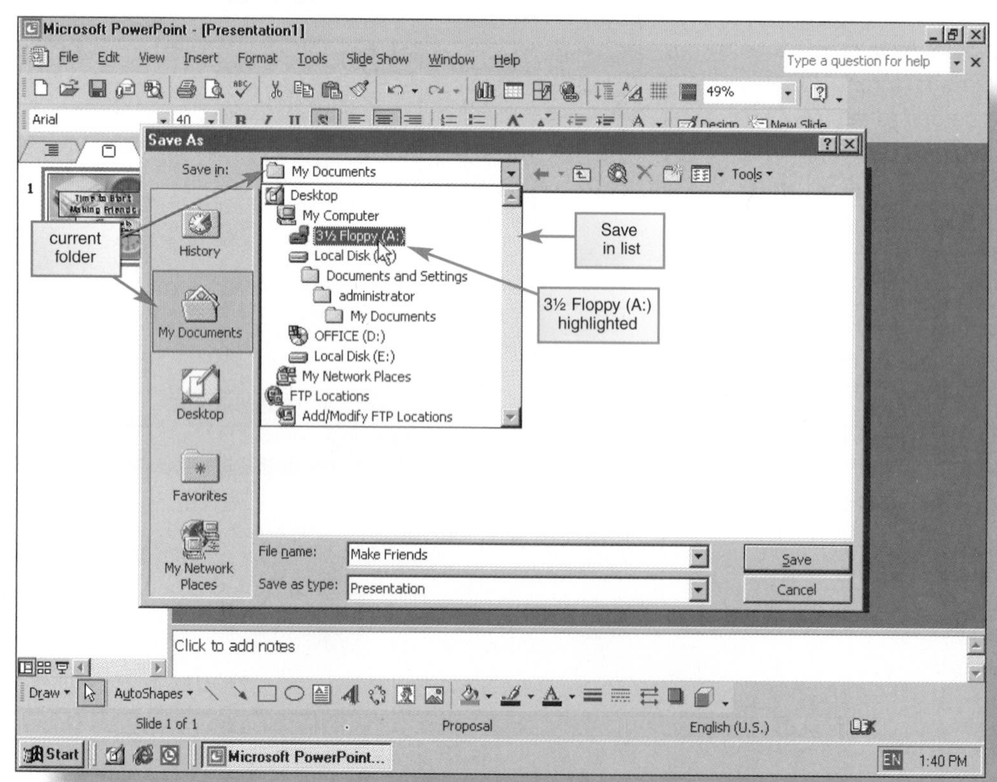

FIGURE 1-28

4 Click 3½ Floppy (A:) and then point to the Save button in the Save As dialog box.

Drive A becomes the current drive (Figure 1-29).

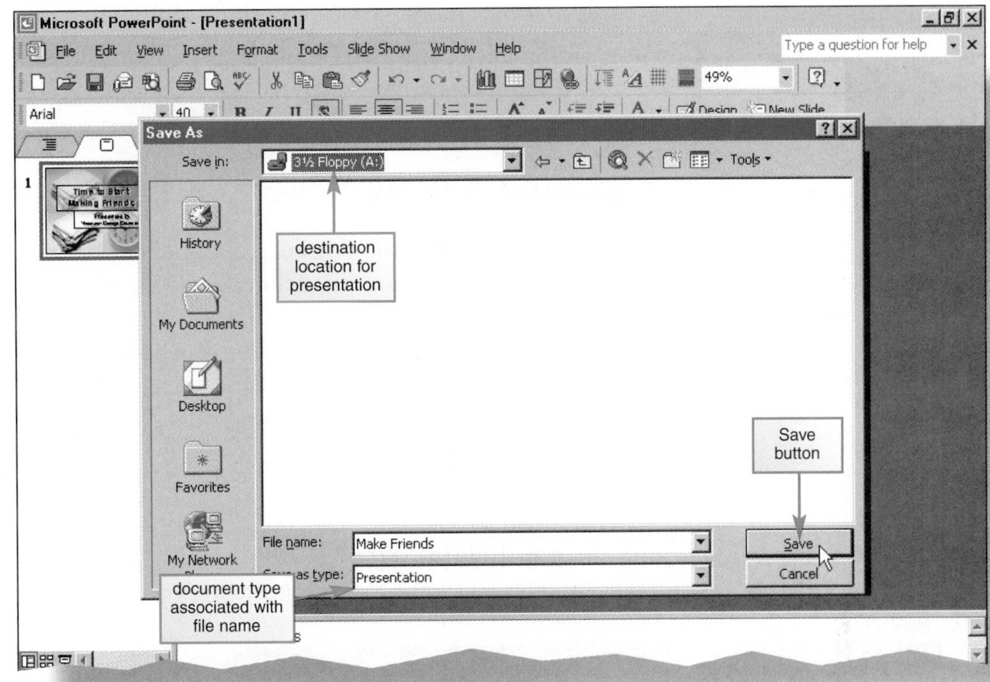

FIGURE 1-29

5 Click the Save button.

PowerPoint saves the presentation on the floppy disk in drive A. The title bar displays the file name used to save the presentation, Make Friends (Figure 1-30).

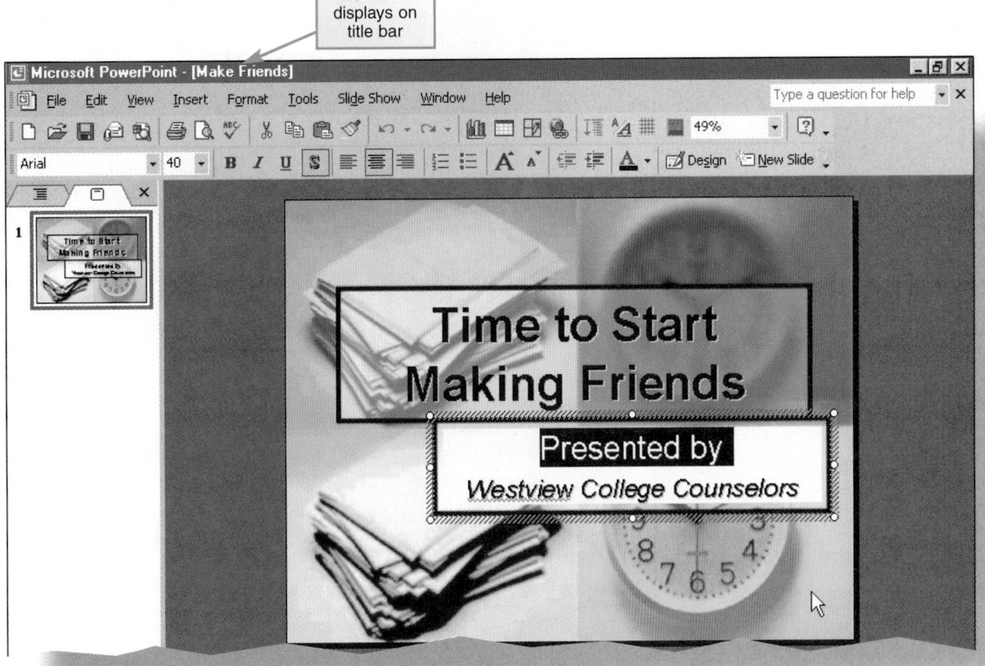

FIGURE 1-30

Other Ways

1. On File menu click Save As
2. Press CTRL+S or press SHIFT+F12
3. In Voice Command mode, say "File, Save As, [type file name], Save"

PowerPoint automatically appends the extension .ppt to the file name, Make Friends. The **.ppt** extension stands for **P**ower**P**oin**t**. Although the slide show, Make Friends, is saved on a floppy disk, it also remains in memory and displays on the screen.

It is a good practice to save periodically while you are working on a project. By doing so, you protect yourself from losing all the work you have done since the last time you saved.

Adding a New Slide to a Presentation

With the title slide for the presentation created, the next step is to add the first text slide immediately after the title slide. Usually, when you create a presentation, you add slides with text, graphics, or charts. When you add a new slide, PowerPoint uses the Title and Text slide layout. Some placeholders allow you to double-click the placeholder and then access other objects, such as media clips, charts, diagrams, and organization charts.

Perform the following steps to add a new Text slide layout with a bulleted list.

To Add a New Text Slide with a Bulleted List

1 Click to the New Slide button on the Formatting toolbar (Figure 1-31).

The Slide Layout task pane opens. The Title and Text slide layout is selected. Slide 2 of 2 displays on the status bar.

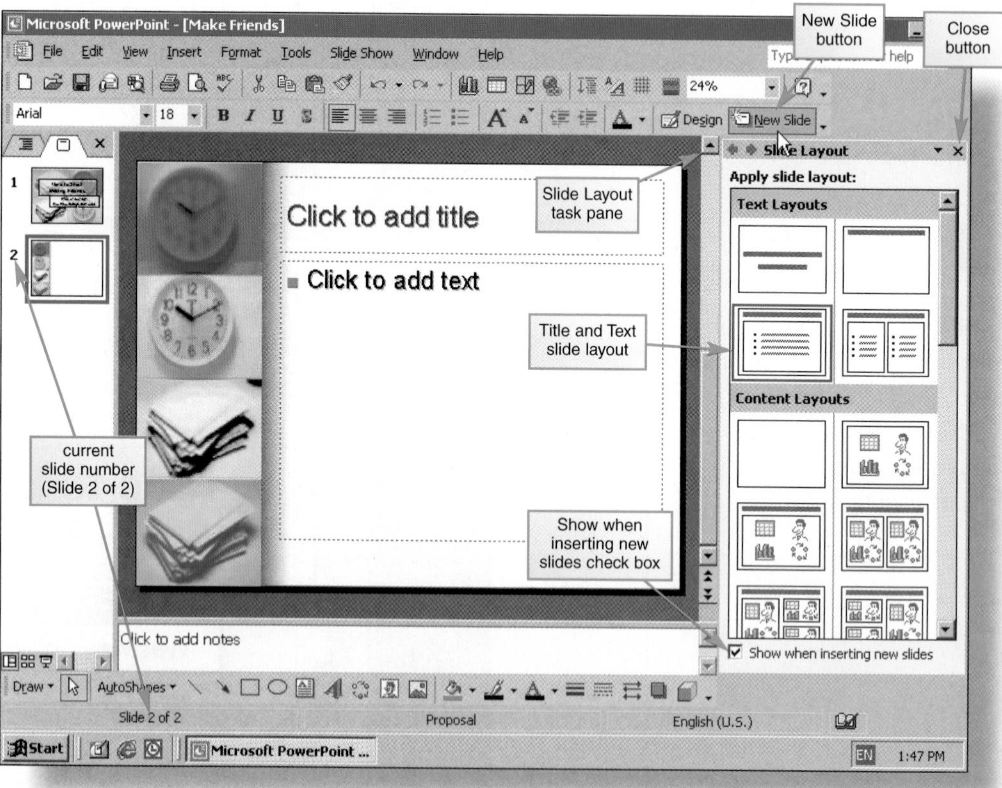

FIGURE 1-31

2 **Click the Show when inserting new slides check box to remove the check mark. Click the Close button on the Slide Layout task pane.**

Slide 2 displays in both the slide pane and Slides tab retaining the attributes of the Proposal design template (Figure 1-32). The vertical scroll bar displays in the slide pane. The bullet displays as a square.

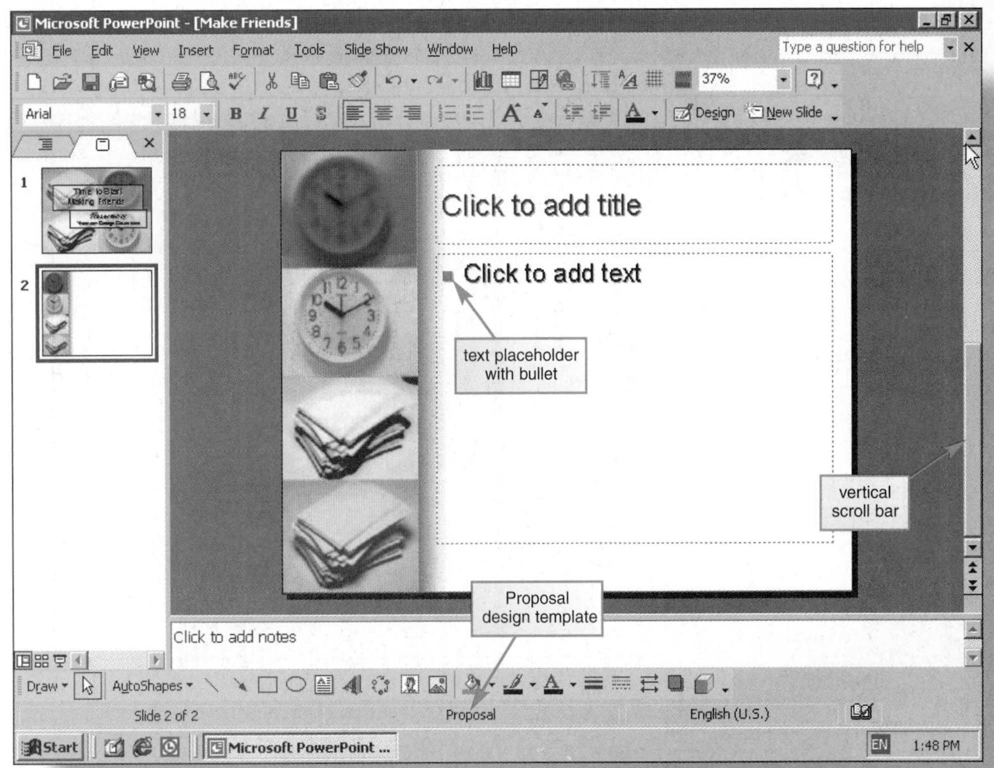

FIGURE 1-32

Slide 2 displays with a title text placeholder and a text placeholder with a bullet. You can change the layout for a slide at any time during the creation of a presentation by clicking Format on the menu bar and then clicking Slide Layout. You also can click View on the menu bar and then click Task Pane. You then can double-click the slide layout of your choice from the Slide Layout task pane.

Other Ways

1. On Insert menu click New Slide
2. Press CTRL+M
3. In Voice Command mode, say "New Slide"

Creating a Text Slide with a Single-Level Bulleted List

The information in the Slide 2 text placeholder is presented in a bulleted list. All the bullets display on one level. A **level** is a position within a structure, such as an outline, that indicates the magnitude of importance. PowerPoint allows for five paragraph levels. Each paragraph level has an associated bullet. The bullet font is dependent on the design template.

Entering a Slide Title

PowerPoint assumes every new slide has a title. The title for Slide 2 is Meet People. Perform the step on the next page to enter this title.

Steps To Enter a Slide Title

1 Type `Meet People` **in the title text placeholder. Do not press the ENTER key.**

The title, Meet People, displays in the title text placeholder and in the Slides tab (Figure 1-33). The insertion point displays after the e in People. The selection rectangle indicates the title text placeholder is selected.

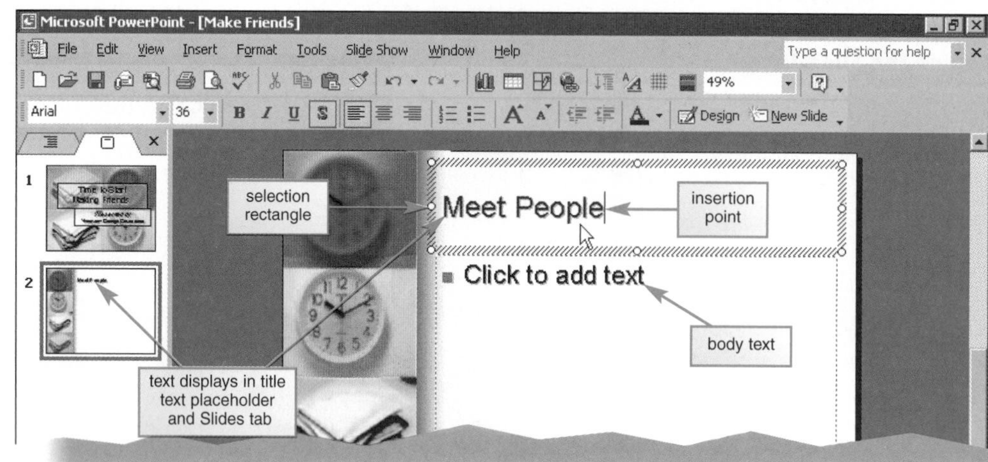

FIGURE 1-33

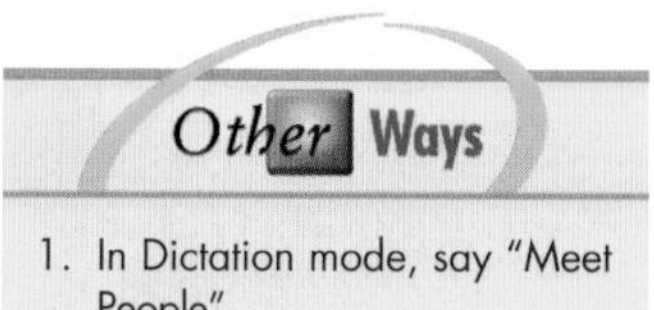

Other Ways

1. In Dictation mode, say "Meet People"

Selecting a Text Placeholder

Before you can type text into the text placeholder, you first must select it. Perform the following step to select the text placeholder on Slide 2.

Steps To Select a Text Placeholder

1 Click the bulleted paragraph labeled, Click to add text.

The insertion point displays immediately to the right of the bullet on Slide 2 (Figure 1-34). The mouse pointer may change shape if you move it away from the bullet. The selection rectangle indicates the text placeholder is selected.

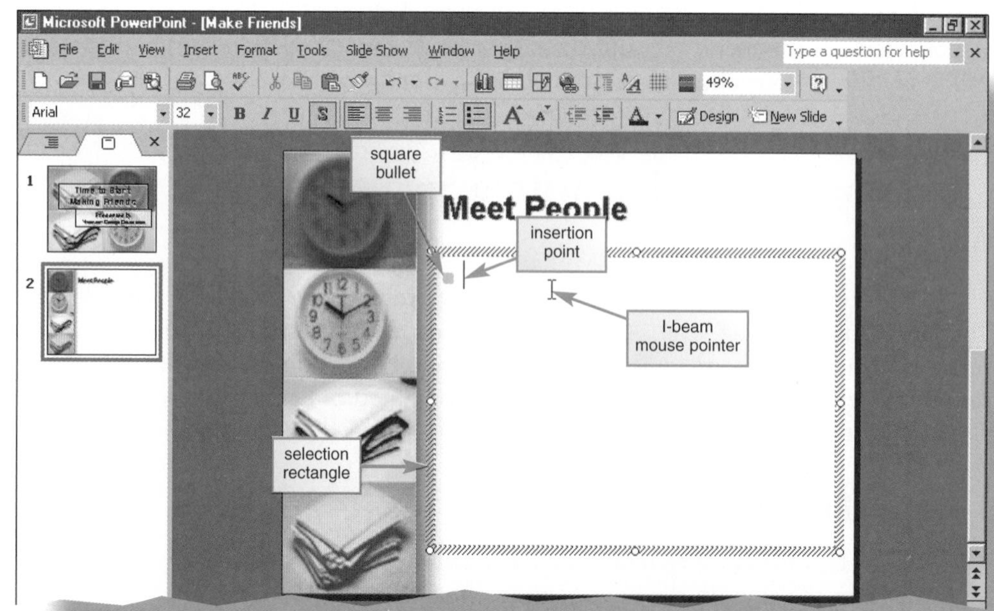

FIGURE 1-34

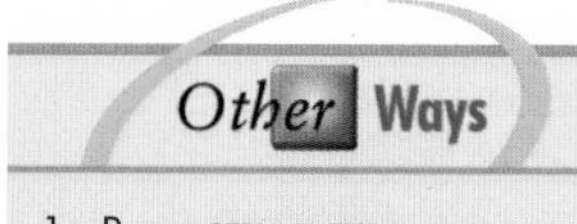

Other Ways

1. Press CTRL+ENTER

Typing a Single-Level Bulleted List

As discussed previously, a bulleted list is a list of paragraphs, each of which is preceded by a bullet. A paragraph is a segment of text ended by pressing the ENTER key. The next step is to type the single-level bulleted list, which consists of four entries (Figure 1-2b on page PP 1.09). Perform the following steps to type a single-level bulleted list.

To Type a Single-Level Bulleted List

1 **Type** `Develop confidence to introduce yourself to others` **and then press the ENTER key.**

The paragraph, Develop confidence to introduce yourself to others, displays (Figure 1-35). The font size is 32. The insertion point displays after the second bullet. When you press the ENTER key, PowerPoint ends one paragraph and begins a new paragraph. With the Text slide layout, PowerPoint places a pink square bullet in front of the new paragraph.

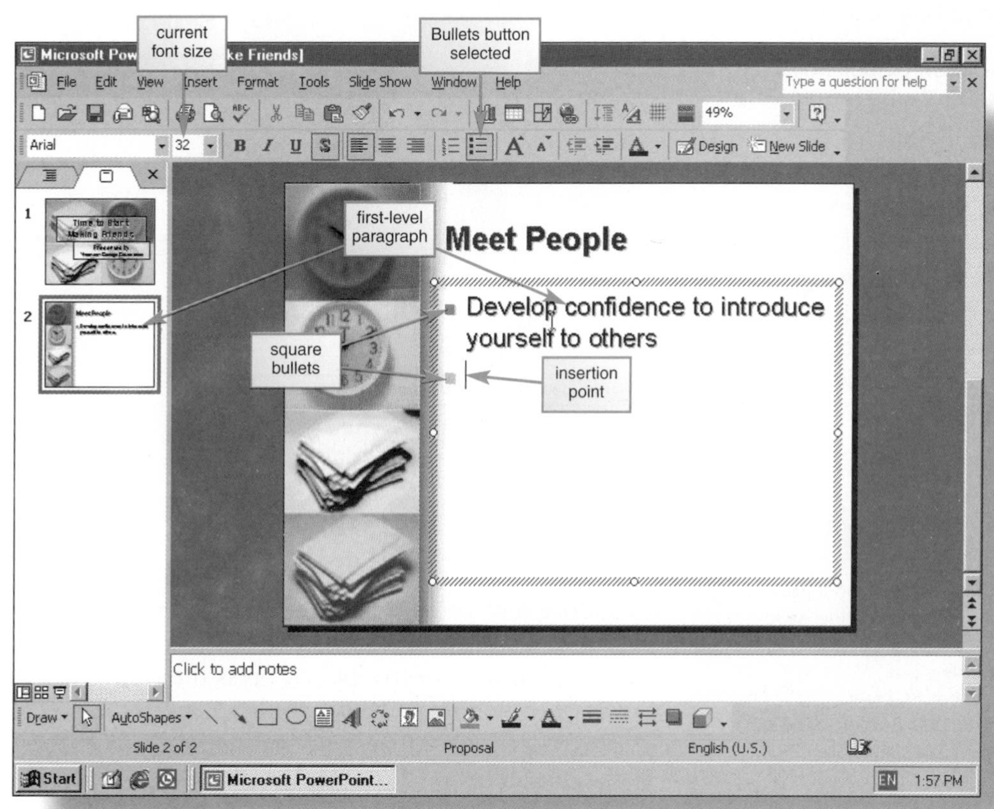

FIGURE 1-35

2 **Type** `Make eye contact` **and then press the ENTER key. Type** `Smile and say, "Hi"` **and then press the ENTER key. Type** `Do not wait; start early in the semester` **but do not press the ENTER key. Point to the New Slide button on the Formatting toolbar.**

The insertion point displays after the r in semester (Figure 1-36). Three new first-level paragraphs display with square bullets in both the text placeholder and the Slides tab. When you press the ENTER *key, PowerPoint adds a new paragraph at the same level as the previous paragraph.*

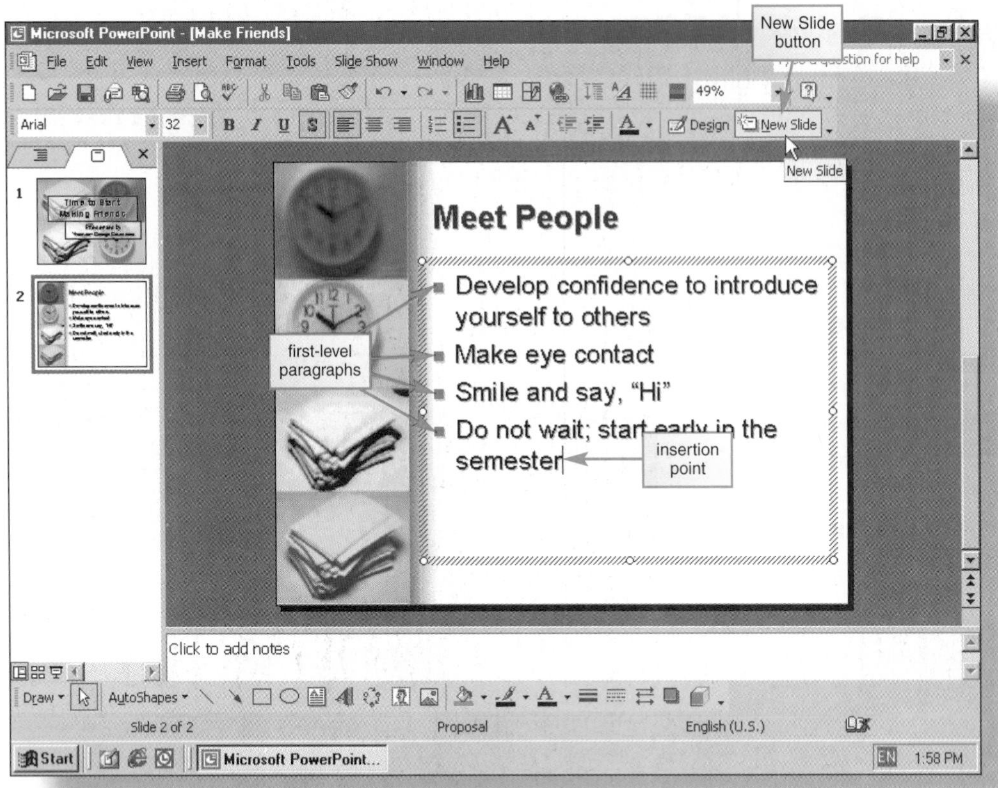

FIGURE 1-36

1. In Dictation mode, say "Develop confidence to introduce yourself to others, New Line, Make eye contact, New Line, Smile and say, Comma, Open Quote, Hi, Close Quote, New Line, Do not wait semicolon start early in the semester"

Notice that you did not press the ENTER key after typing the last paragraph in Step 2. If you press the ENTER key, a new bullet displays after the last entry on this slide. To remove an extra bullet, press the BACKSPACE key.

Creating a Text Slide with a Multi-Level Bulleted List

Slides 3 and 4 in Figure 1-2 on page PP 1.09 contain more than one level of bulleted text. A slide that consists of more than one level of bulleted text is called a **multi-level bulleted list slide**. Beginning with the second level, each paragraph indents to the right of the preceding level and is pushed down to a lower level. For example, if you increase the indent of a first-level paragraph, it becomes a second-level paragraph. This lower-level paragraph is a subset of the higher-level paragraph. It usually contains information that supports the topic in the paragraph immediately above it. You increase the indent of a paragraph by clicking the **Increase Indent button** on the Formatting toolbar.

When you want to raise a paragraph from a lower level to a higher level, you click the **Decrease Indent button** on the Formatting toolbar.

Creating a text slide with a multi-level bulleted list requires several steps. Initially, you enter a slide title in the title text placeholder. Next, you select the body text placeholder. Then, you type the text for the multi-level bulleted list, increasing and decreasing the indents as needed. The next several sections explain how to add a slide with a multi-level bulleted list.

Adding New Slides and Entering Slide Titles

When you add a new slide to a presentation, PowerPoint keeps the same layout used on the previous slide. PowerPoint assumes every new slide has a title. The title for Slide 3 is Find the Right Places. Perform the following steps to add a new slide (Slide 3) and enter a title.

Steps To Add a New Slide and Enter a Slide Title

1 Click the New Slide button.

Slide 3 of 3 displays in the slide pane and Slides tab (Figure 1-37).

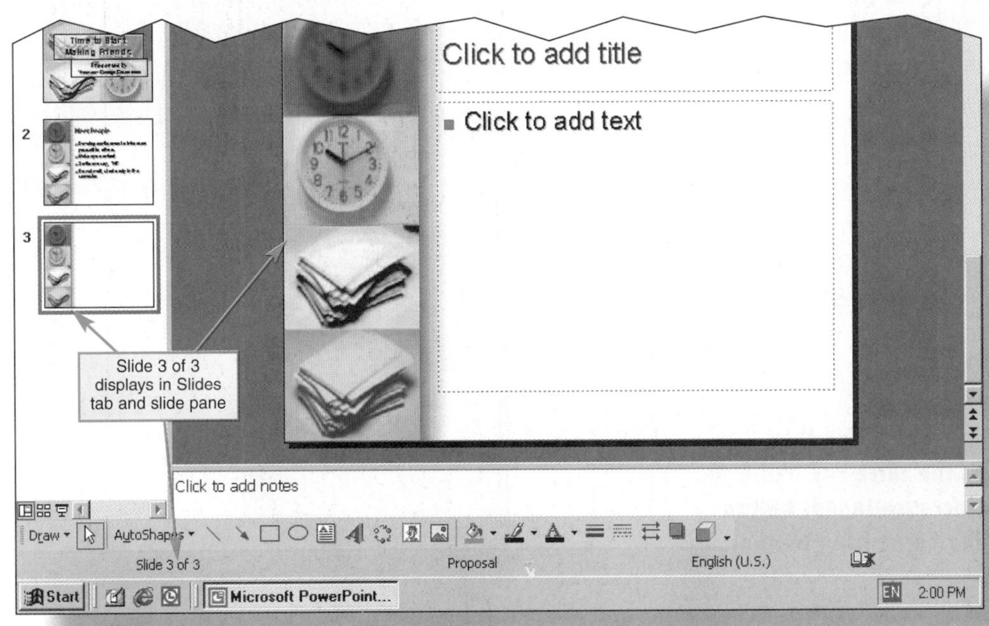

FIGURE 1-37

2 Type `Find the Right Places` **in the title text placeholder. Do not press the ENTER key.**

Slide 3 displays the Text slide layout with the title, Find the Right Places, in the title text placeholder and in the Slides tab (Figure 1-38). The insertion point displays after the s in Places.

FIGURE 1-38

Slide 3 is added to the presentation with the desired title.

1. Press SHIFT+CTRL+M
2. In Dictation mode, say "New Slide, Find the right places"

Typing a Multi-Level Bulleted List

The next step is to select the body text placeholder and then type the multi-level bulleted list, which consists of five entries (Figure 1-2c on page PP 1.09). Perform the following steps to create a list consisting of three levels.

To Type a Multi-Level Bulleted List

1 **Click the bulleted paragraph labeled, Click to add text.**

The insertion point displays immediately to the right of the bullet on Slide 3. The mouse pointer may change shape if you move it away from the bullet.

2 **Type** `Go where people congregate` **and then press the ENTER key. Point to the Increase Indent button on the Formatting toolbar.**

The paragraph, Go where people congregate, displays (Figure 1-39). The font size is 32. The insertion point displays to the right of the second bullet.

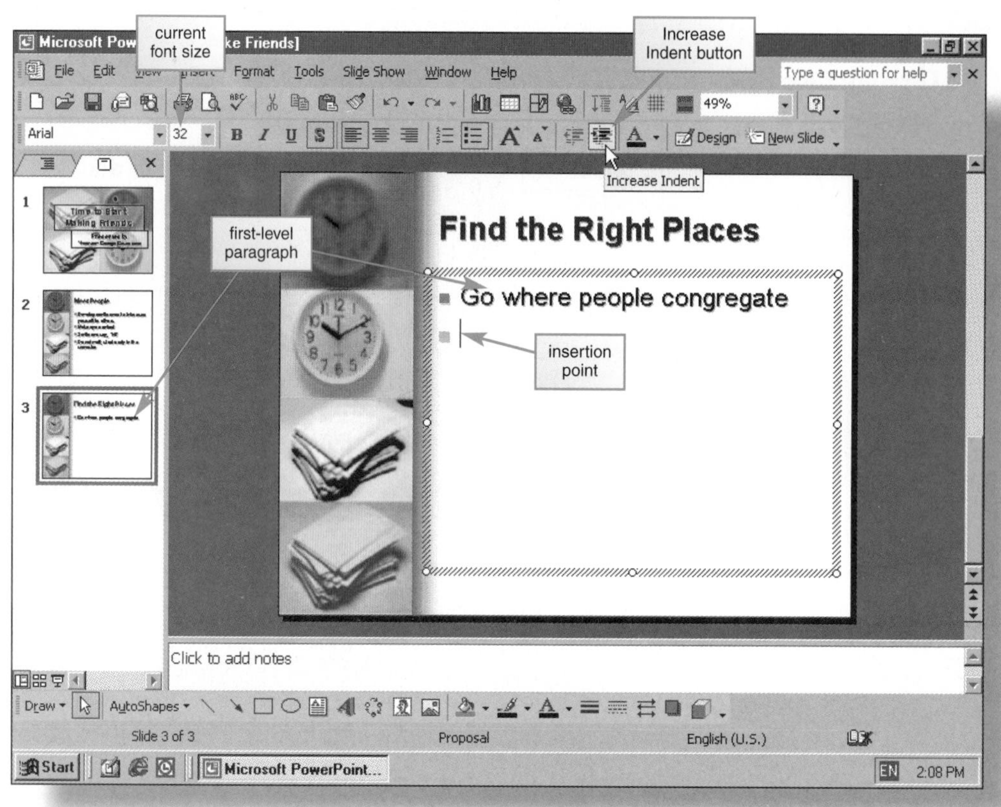

FIGURE 1-39

3 Click the Increase Indent button.

The second paragraph indents below the first and becomes a second-level paragraph (Figure 1-40). The bullet to the left of the second paragraph changes from a square to a circle, and the font size for the paragraph now is 28. The insertion point displays to the right of the circle.

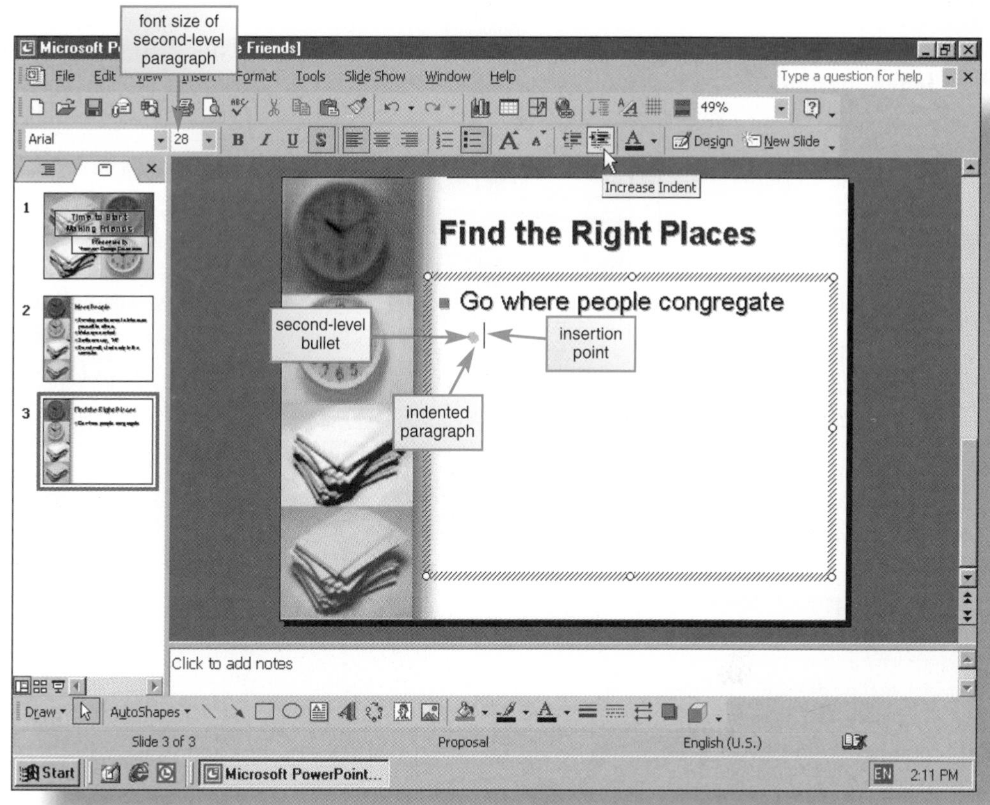

FIGURE 1-40

4 Type `Student union, sports events` **and then press the ENTER key. Point to the Decrease Indent button on the Formatting toolbar.**

The first second-level paragraph displays with a brown circle bullet in both the slide pane and the Slides tab (Figure 1-41). When you press the ENTER key, PowerPoint adds a new paragraph at the same level as the previous paragraph.

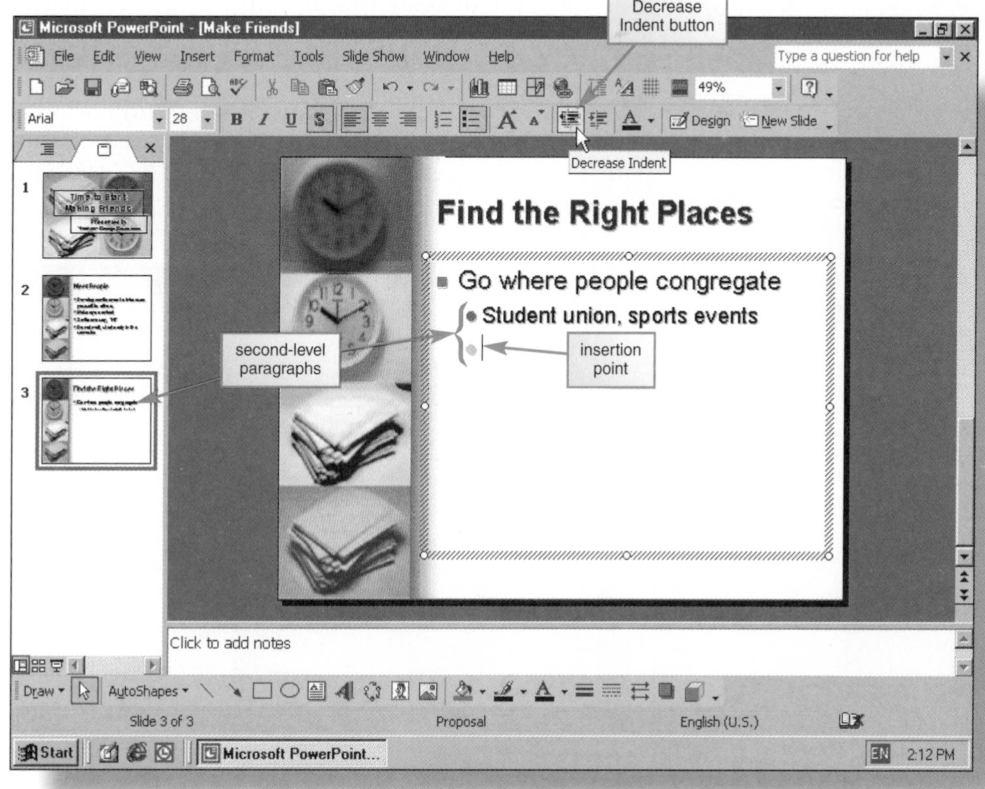

FIGURE 1-41

5 Click the Decrease Indent button.

The second-level paragraph becomes a first-level paragraph (Figure 1-42). The bullet of the new paragraph changes from a circle to a square, and the font size for the paragraph is 32. The insertion point displays to the right of the square bullet.

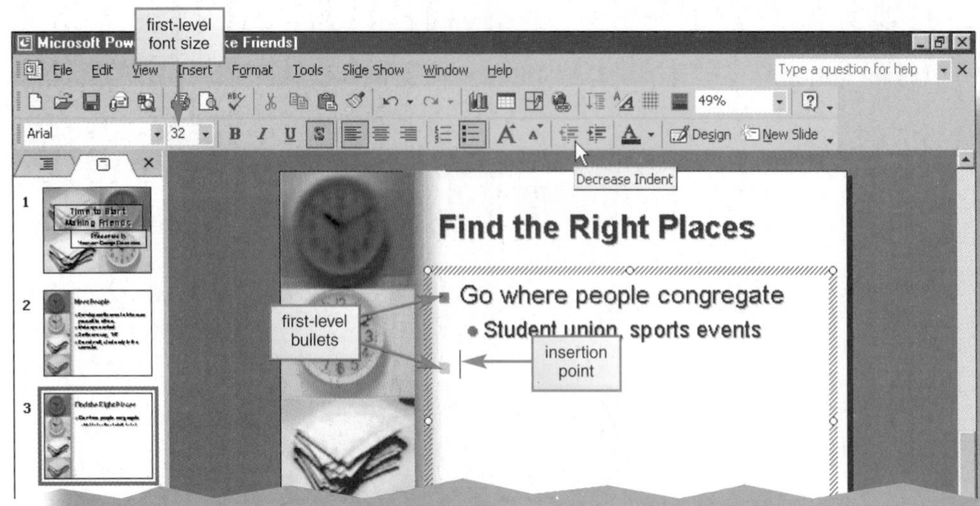

FIGURE 1-42

Other Ways

1. In Dictation mode, say, "Go where people congregate, New Line, Tab, Student union comma sports events, New Line, [type Backspace]"

Perform the following steps to complete the text for Slide 3.

TO TYPE THE REMAINING TEXT FOR SLIDE 3

1. Type `Get involved in extracurricular activities` and then press the ENTER key.
2. Click the Increase Indent button on the Formatting toolbar.
3. Type `Participate in intramurals` and then press the ENTER key.
4. Type `Join Student Government` but do not press the ENTER key.

Slide 3 displays as shown in Figure 1-43. The insertion point displays after the t in Government.

Other Ways

1. In Dictation mode, say "Get involved in extracurricular activities, New Line, Tab, Participate in intramurals, New Line, Join Student Government"

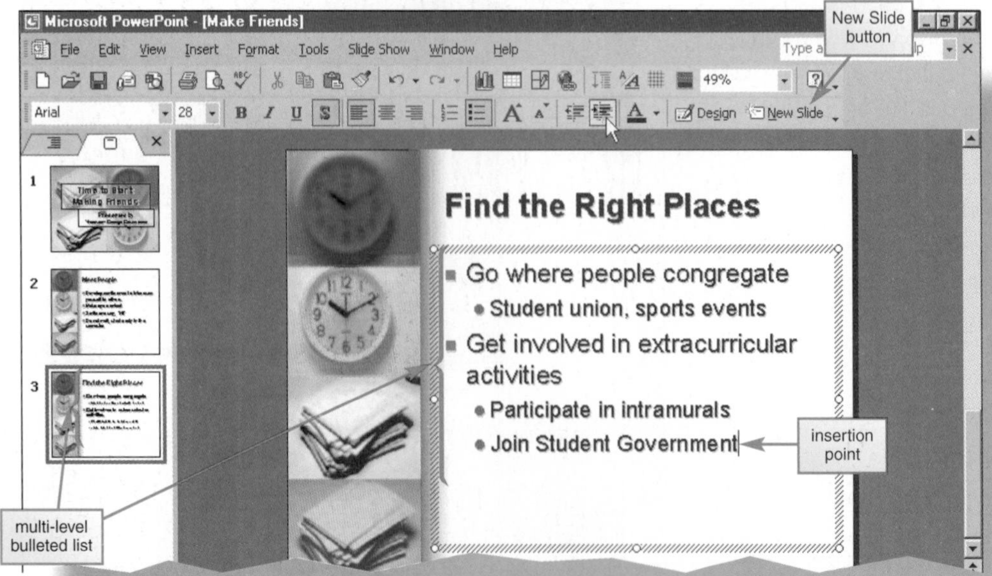

FIGURE 1-43

In Step 4 above, you did not press the ENTER key after typing the last paragraph. If you press the ENTER key, a new bullet displays after the last entry on this slide. To remove an extra bullet, press the BACKSPACE key.

Slide 4 is the last slide in this presentation. It also is a multi-level bulleted list and has three levels. Perform the following steps to create Slide 4.

TO CREATE SLIDE 4

1. Click the New Slide button on the Formatting toolbar.
2. Type `Start a Conversation` in the title text placeholder.
3. Press CTRL+ENTER to move the insertion point to the body text placeholder.
4. Type `Talk about almost anything` and then press the ENTER key.
5. Click the Increase Indent button on the Formatting toolbar. Type `Comment on what is going on` and then press the ENTER key.

The title and first two levels of bullets are added to Slide 4 (Figure 1-44).

Other Ways

1. In Dictation mode, say "New Slide, Start a conversation, New, Talk about almost anything, New Line, Tab, Comment on what is going on"

Creating a Third-Level Paragraph

The next line in Slide 4 is indented an additional level to the third level. Perform the following steps to create an additional level.

Steps To Create a Third-Level Paragraph

1 Click the Increase Indent button on the Formatting toolbar.

The second-level paragraph becomes a third-level paragraph (Figure 1-44). The bullet to the left of the new paragraph changes from a circle to a square, and the font size for the paragraph is 24. The insertion point displays after the square bullet.

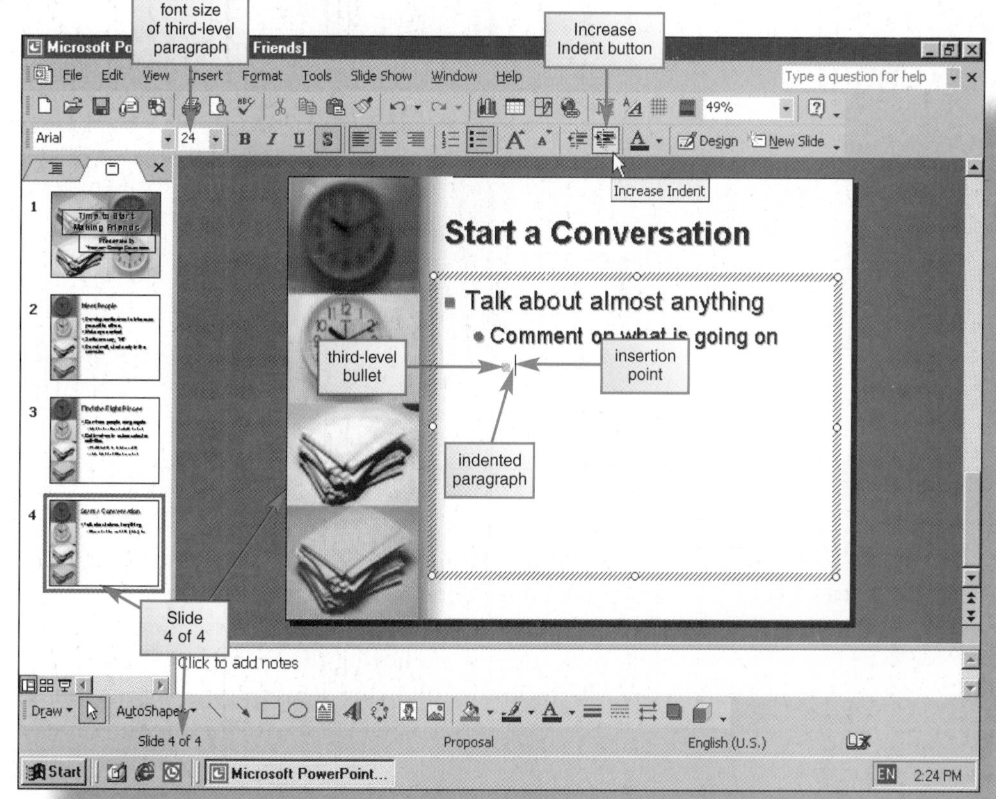

FIGURE 1-44

2 **Type** `Long lines, class assignments` **and then press the ENTER key. Point to the Decrease Indent button on the Formatting toolbar.**

The first third-level paragraph, Long lines, class assignments, displays with the bullet for a second third-level paragraph (Figure 1-45).

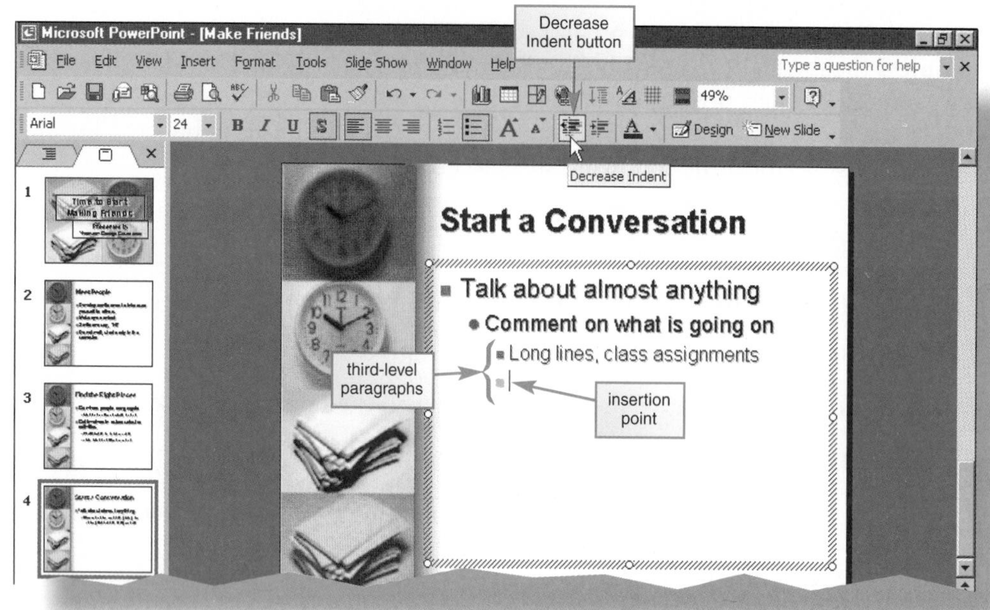

FIGURE 1-45

3 **Click the Decrease Indent button two times.**

The insertion point displays at the first level (Figure 1-46).

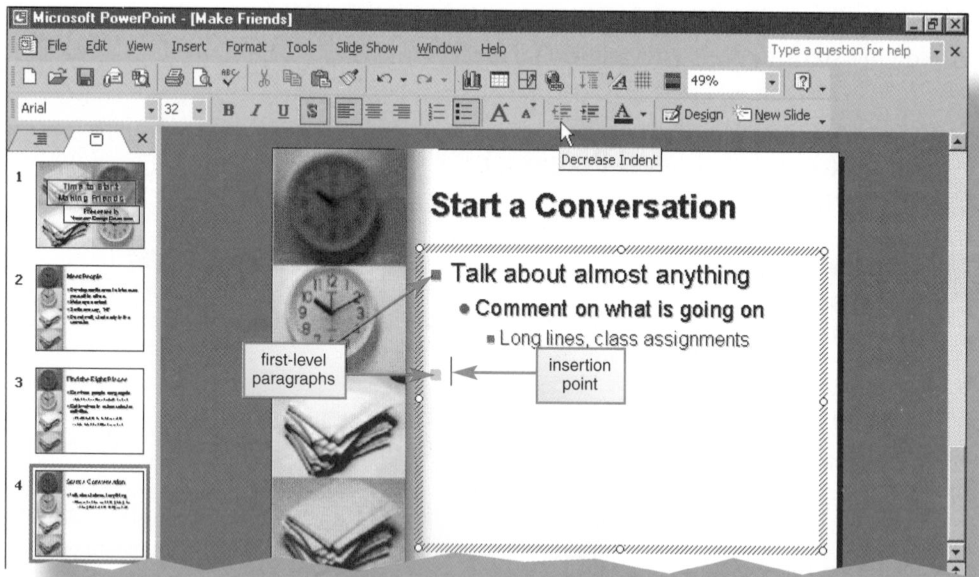

FIGURE 1-46

Other Ways

1. In Dictation mode, say "Tab, Long lines comma class assignments, New Line, [type backspace]"

The title text and three levels of paragraphs discussing conversation topics are complete. The next three paragraphs concern the types of questions to ask. As an alternative to clicking the Increase Indent button, you can press the TAB key. Likewise, instead of clicking the Decrease Indent button, you can press the SHIFT+TAB keys. Perform the following steps to type the remaining text for Slide 4.

TO TYPE THE REMAINING TEXT FOR SLIDE 4

1. Type `Ask questions` and then press the ENTER key.
2. Press the TAB key to increase the indent to the second level.
3. Type `Get people to discuss their lives` and then press the ENTER key.
4. Press the TAB key to increase the indent to the third level.
5. Type `Hobbies, classes, and work` but do not press the ENTER key.

The Slide 4 title text and body text display in the slide pane and Slides tabs (Figure 1-47). The insertion point displays after the k in work.

1. In Dictation mode, say "Ask questions, New Line, Tab, Get people to discuss their lives, New Line, Tab, Hobbies comma classes comma and work"

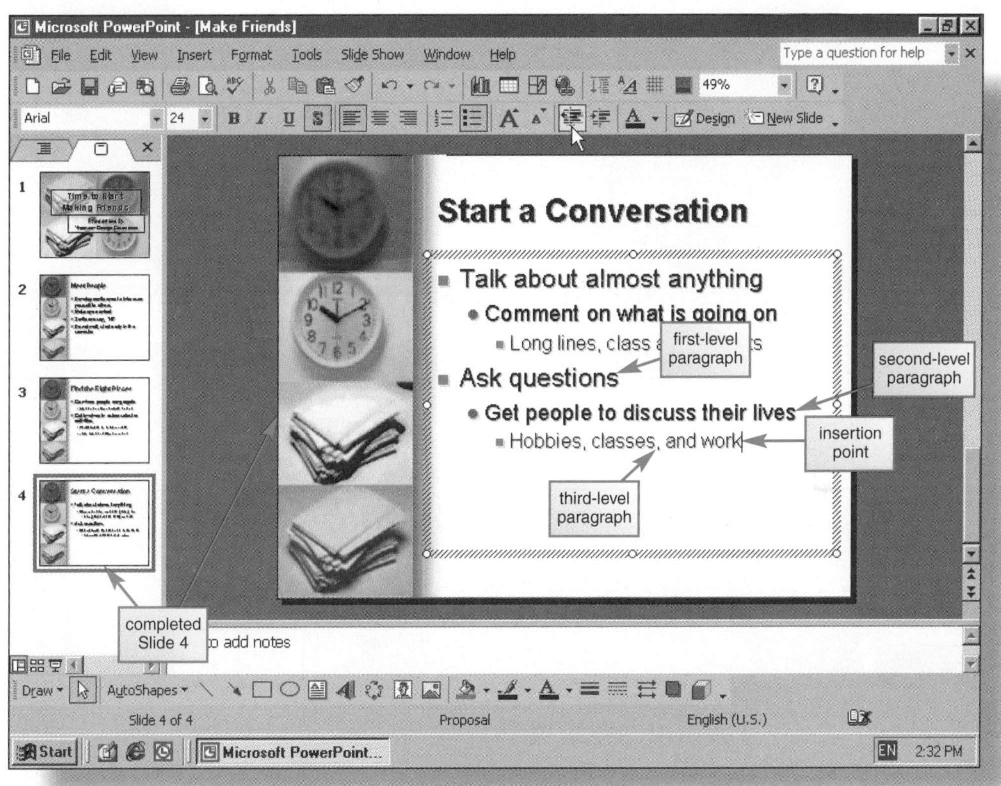

FIGURE 1-47

All the slides are created for the Make Friends slide show. This presentation consists of a title slide and three text slides with a multi-level bulleted list.

Ending a Slide Show with a Black Slide

After the last slide in the slide show displays, the default PowerPoint setting is to end the presentation with a black slide. This black slide displays only when the slide show is running and concludes the slide show gracefully so your audience never sees the PowerPoint window. A **black slide** ends all slide shows unless the option setting is deselected. Perform the steps on the next page to verify the End with black slide option is activated.

More About Black Slides

Black slides can be used effectively to end a presentation, to pause for discussion, or to separate sections of a large presentation. The black slide focuses the audience's attention on you, the speaker, and away from the screen display.

Steps To End a Slide Show with a Black Slide

1 Click Tools on the menu bar and then point to Options (Figure 1-48).

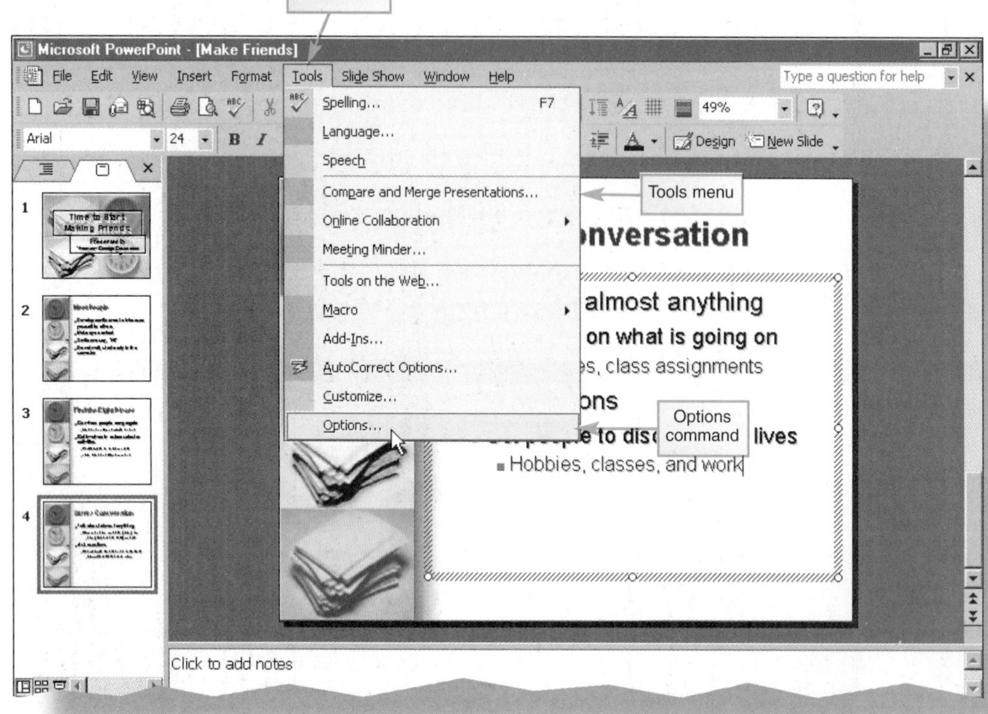

FIGURE 1-48

2 Click Options. If necessary, click the View tab when the Options dialog box displays. Verify that the End with black slide check box is selected. If a check mark does not display, click End with black slide, and then point to the OK button.

The Options dialog box displays (Figure 1-49). The View sheet contains settings for the overall PowerPoint display and for a particular slide show.

3 Click the OK button.

The End with black slide option will cause the slide show to end with a black slide until it is deselected.

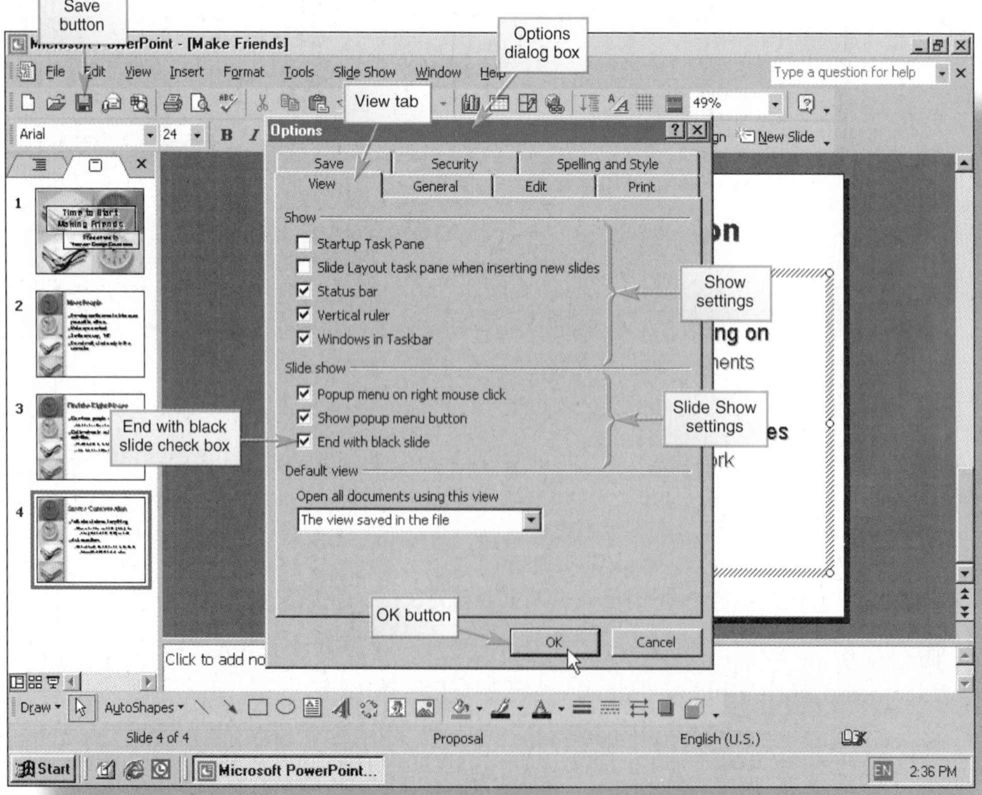

FIGURE 1-49

With all aspects of the presentation complete, it is important to save the additions and changes you have made to the Make Friends presentation.

Saving a Presentation with the Same File Name

Saving frequently cannot be overemphasized. When you first saved the presentation, you clicked the Save button on the Standard toolbar and the Save dialog box displayed. When you want to save the changes made to the presentation after your last save, you again click the Save button. This time, however, the Save dialog box does not display because PowerPoint updates the document called Make Friends.ppt on the floppy disk. Perform the following steps to save the presentation again.

TO SAVE A PRESENTATION WITH THE SAME FILE NAME

1. Be sure your floppy disk is in drive A.
2. Click the Save button on the Standard toolbar.

PowerPoint overwrites the old Make Friends.ppt document on the floppy disk in drive A with the revised presentation document. Slide 4 displays in the PowerPoint window.

Other Ways

1. In Voice Command mode, say "Save"

Moving to Another Slide in Normal View

When creating or editing a presentation in normal view, you often want to display a slide other than the current one. You can move to another slide using several methods. In the Outline tab, you can point to any of the text in a particular slide to display that slide in the slide pane, or you can drag the scroll box on the vertical scroll bar up or down to move through the text in the presentation. In the slide pane, you can click the Previous Slide or Next Slide button on the vertical scroll bar. Clicking the **Next Slide button** advances to the next slide in the presentation. Clicking the **Previous Slide button** backs up to the slide preceding the current slide. You also can drag the scroll box on the vertical scroll bar. When you drag the scroll box, the **slide indicator** displays the number and title of the slide you are about to display. Releasing the mouse button displays the slide.

A slide's **Zoom setting** affects the portion of the slide displaying in the slide pane. PowerPoint defaults to a setting of approximately 50 percent so the entire slide displays. This percentage depends on the size and type of your monitor. If you want to display a small portion of the current slide, you would zoom in by clicking the **Zoom box arrow** and then clicking the desired magnification. You can display the entire slide in the slide pane by clicking **Fit** in the Zoom list. The Zoom setting affects the action of the vertical and horizontal scroll bars. If Zoom is set so the entire slide is not visible in the slide pane, clicking the up scroll arrow on the vertical scroll bar displays the next portion of the slide, not the previous slide.

More About

Zoom Settings

You can increase your Zoom setting as large as 400% when you want to see details on small objects. Likewise, you can decrease your Zoom setting as small as 10%. When you want to redisplay the entire slide, click Fit in the Zoom list.

Using the Scroll Box on the Slide Pane to Move to Another Slide

Before continuing with Project 1, you want to display the title slide. Perform the steps on the next page to move from Slide 4 to Slide 1 using the scroll box on the slide pane vertical scroll bar.

Steps To Use the Scroll Box on the Slide Pane to Move to Another Slide

1 Position the mouse pointer on the scroll box. Press and hold down the mouse button.

Slide: 4 of 4 Start a Conversation displays in the slide indicator (Figure 1-50). When you click the scroll box, the Slide 4 thumbnail is not shaded in the Slides tab.

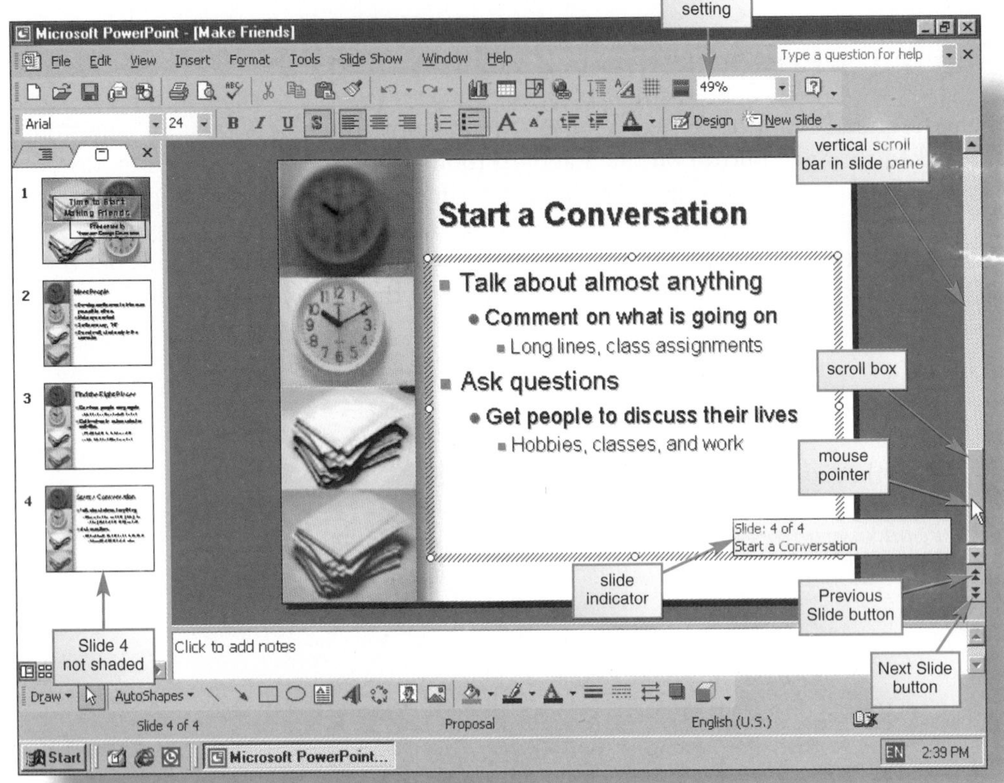

FIGURE 1-50

2 Drag the scroll box up the vertical scroll bar until Slide: 1 of 4 Time to Start Making Friends displays in the slide indicator.

Slide: 1 of 4 Time to Start Making Friends displays in the slide indicator (Figure 1-51). Slide 4 still displays in the PowerPoint window.

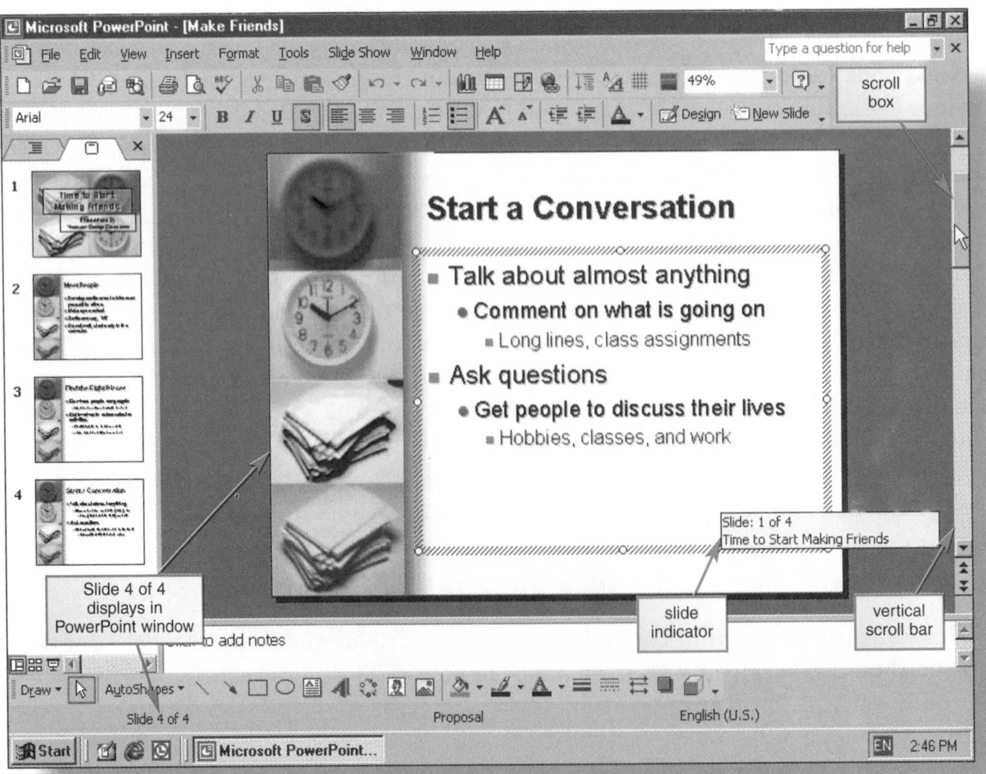

FIGURE 1-51

3 Release the mouse button.

Slide 1, titled Time to Start Making Friends, displays in the PowerPoint window (Figure 1-52). The Slide 1 thumbnail is shaded in the Slides tab indicating it is selected.

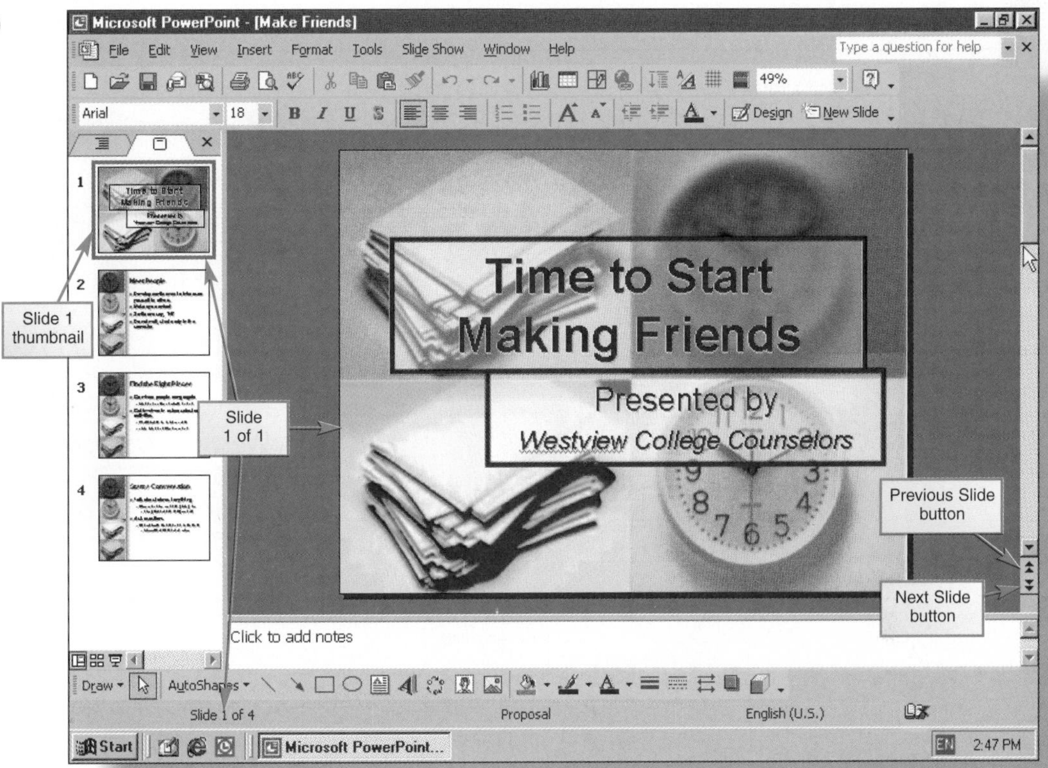

FIGURE 1-52

Other Ways

1. Click Next Slide button or Previous Slide button to move forward or back one slide
2. Press PAGE DOWN or PAGE UP to move forward or back one slide
3. In Voice Command mode, say "Next page" or "Previous page"

Viewing the Presentation in Slide Show View

The **Slide Show button**, located at the lower-left of the PowerPoint window above the status bar, allows you to display a presentation electronically using a computer. The computer acts like a slide projector, displaying each slide on a full screen. The full screen slide hides the toolbars, menus, and other PowerPoint window elements. When making a presentation, you use **slide show view**. You can start slide show view from normal view or slide sorter view.

Starting Slide Show View

Slide show view begins when you click the Slide Show button at the lower-left of the PowerPoint window above the status bar. PowerPoint then displays the current slide on the full screen without any of the PowerPoint window objects, such as the menu bar or toolbars. Perform the steps on the next page to start slide show view.

Steps To Start Slide Show View

1 Point to the Slide Show button in the lower-left corner of the PowerPoint window above the status bar (Figure 1-53).

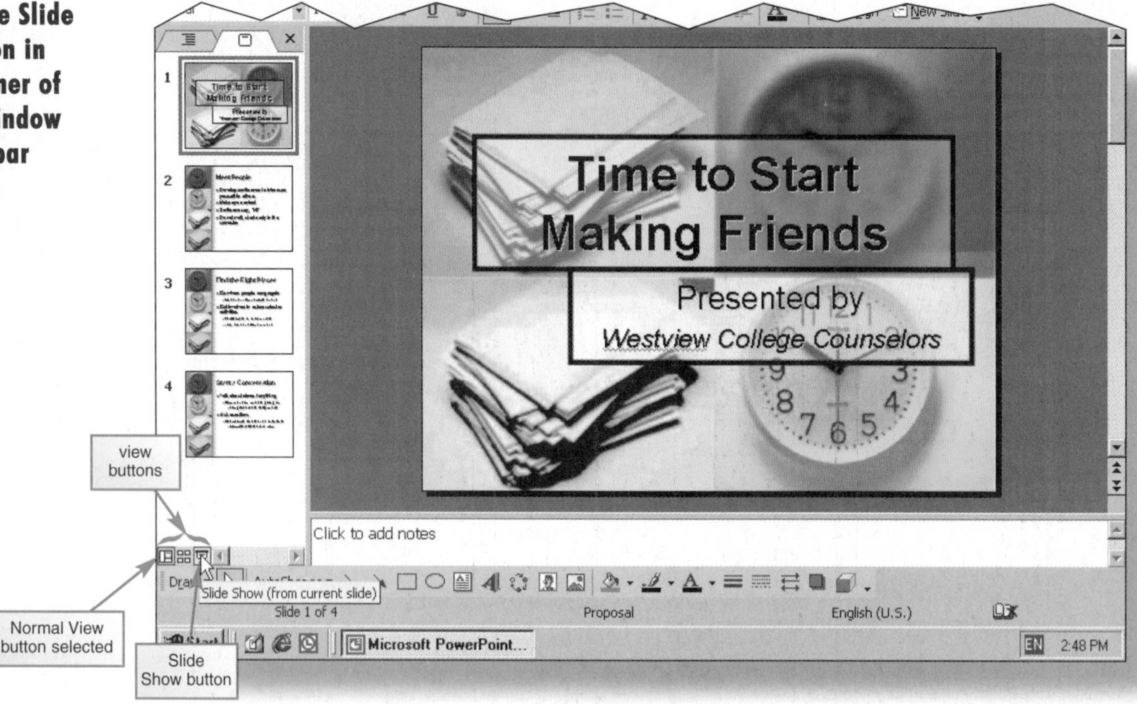

FIGURE 1-53

2 Click the Slide Show button.

A starting slide show message displays momentarily and then the title slide fills the screen (Figure 1-54). The PowerPoint window is hidden.

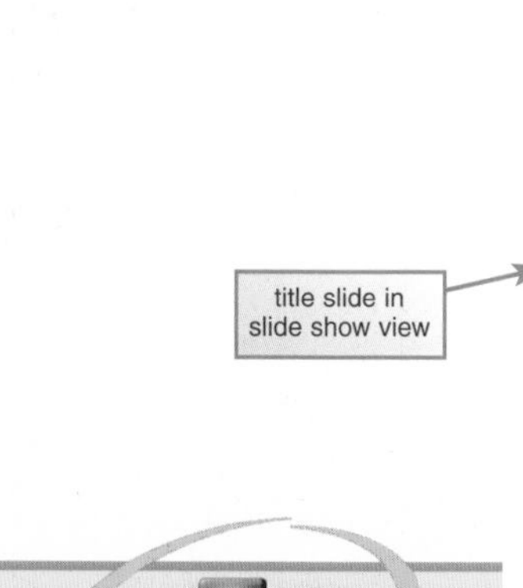

FIGURE 1-54

1. On View menu click Slide Show
2. Press F5
3. In Voice Command mode, say "View show"

Advancing Through a Slide Show Manually

After you begin slide show view, you can move forward or backward through the slides. PowerPoint allows you to advance through the slides manually or automatically. Perform the following steps to move manually through the slides.

To Move Manually Through Slides in a Slide Show

1 Click each slide until the Start a Conversation slide (Slide 4) displays.

Slide 4 displays (Figure 1-55). Each slide in the presentation displays on the screen, one slide at a time. Each time you click the mouse button, the next slide displays.

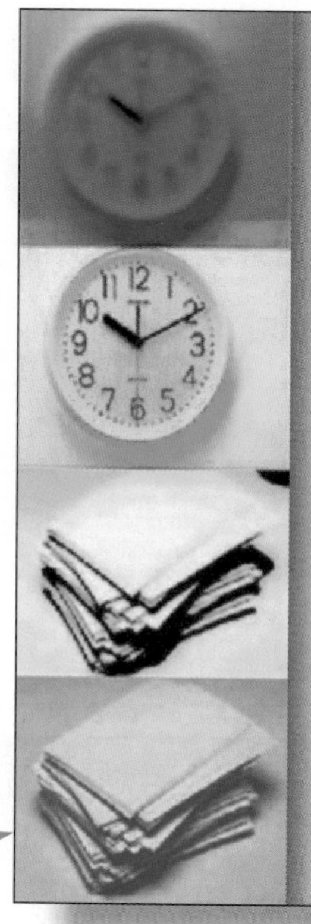

FIGURE 1-55

2 Click Slide 4.

The black slide displays (Figure 1-56). The message at the top of the slide announces the end of the slide show. If you wanted to end the presentation at this point and return to normal view, you would click the black slide.

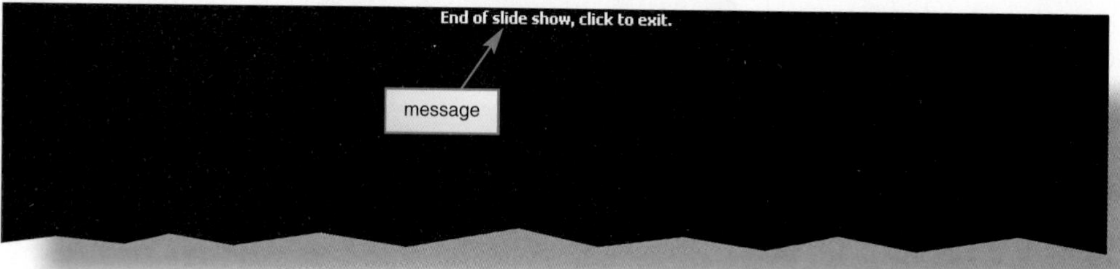

FIGURE 1-56

Other Ways

1. Press PAGE DOWN to advance one slide at a time, or press PAGE UP to go backward one slide at a time
2. Press RIGHT ARROW to advance one slide at a time, or press LEFT ARROW key to go back one slide at a time

Using the Popup Menu to Go to a Specific Slide

Slide show view has a shortcut menu, called the **Popup menu**, that displays when you right-click a slide in slide show view. This menu contains commands to assist you during a slide show. For example, clicking the **Next command** moves to the next slide. Clicking the **Previous command** moves to the previous slide. Pointing to the **Go command** and then clicking Slide Navigator allows you to move to any slide in the presentation. The **Slide Navigator dialog box** contains a list of the slides in the presentation. Go to the requested slide by double-clicking the name of that slide. Perform the following steps to go to the title slide (Slide 1) in the Make Friends presentation.

Steps To Display the Popup Menu and Go to a Specific Slide

1 With the black slide displaying in slide show view, right-click the slide. Point to Go on the Popup menu, and then point to Slide Navigator on the Go submenu.

The Popup menu displays on the black slide, and the Go submenu displays (Figure 1-57). Your screen may look different because the Popup menu displays near the location of the mouse pointer at the time you right-click.

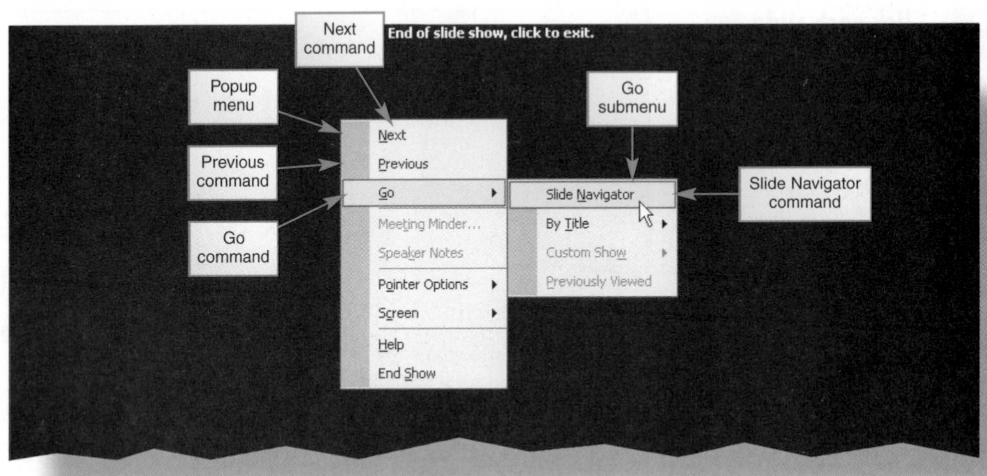

FIGURE 1-57

2 Click Slide Navigator. When the Slide Navigator dialog box displays, point to 1. Time to Start Making Friends in the Slide titles list.

The Slide Navigator dialog box contains a list of the slides in the presentation (Figure 1-58).

FIGURE 1-58

3 Double-click 1. Time to Start Making Friends.

The title slide, Time to Start Making Friends (shown in Figure 1-54 on page PP 1.48), displays.

Other Ways

1. Right-click slide, point to Go on Popup menu, click Slide Navigator, type slide number, press ENTER

Additional Popup menu commands allow you to write meeting minutes or to create a list of action items during a slide show, change the mouse pointer to a pen that draws in various colors, blacken the screen, and end the slide show. Popup menu commands are discussed as they are used.

Using the Popup Menu to End a Slide Show

The **End Show command** on the Popup menu ends slide show view and returns to the same view as when you clicked the Slide Show button. Perform the following steps to end slide show view and return to normal view.

To Use the Popup Menu to End a Slide Show

1 Right-click the title slide and then point to End Show on the Popup menu.

The Popup menu displays on Slide 1 (Figure 1-59).

2 Click End Show. If the Microsoft PowerPoint dialog box displays, click the Yes button.

PowerPoint ends slide show view and returns to normal view (shown in Figure 1-60 on the next page). Slide 1 displays because it is the last slide displayed in slide show view.

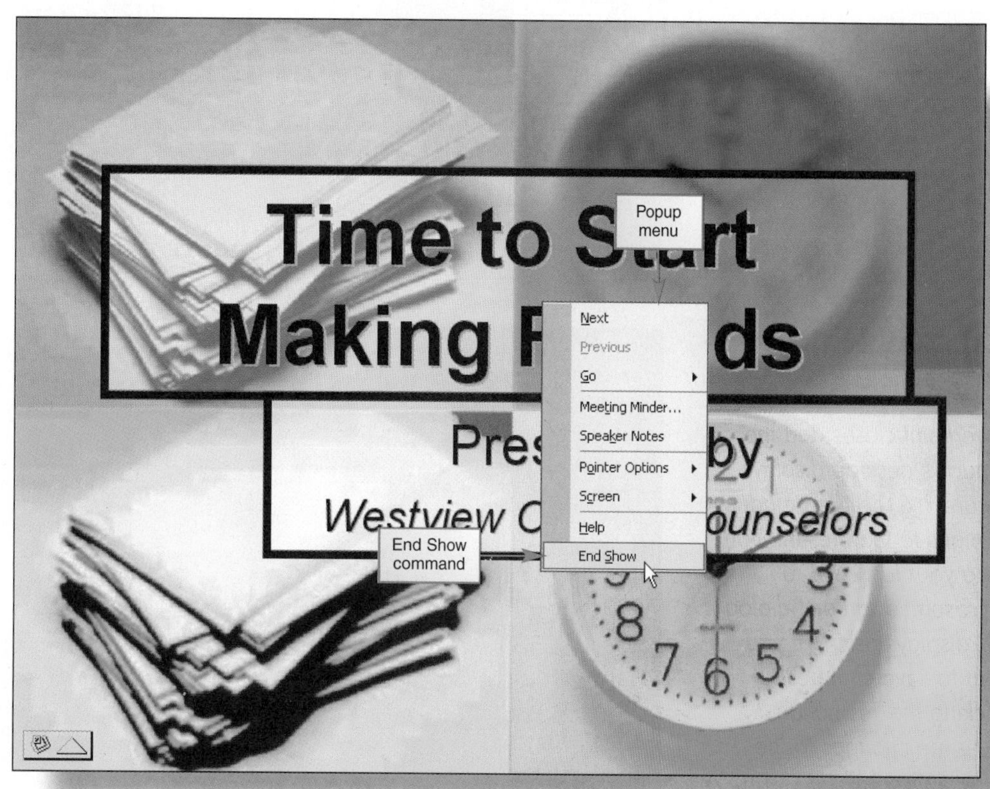

FIGURE 1-59

Other Ways

1. Click last slide in presentation (returns to normal view to slide at which slide show view began)
2. Press ESC (displays slide last viewed in slide show view)
3. In Voice Command mode say "Escape"

Quitting PowerPoint

The Make Friends presentation now is complete. When you quit PowerPoint, PowerPoint prompts you to save any changes made to the presentation since the last save, closes all PowerPoint windows, and then quits PowerPoint. Closing PowerPoint returns control to the desktop. Perform the steps on the next page to quit PowerPoint.

Steps To Quit PowerPoint

1 Point to the Close button on the PowerPoint title bar (Figure 1-60).

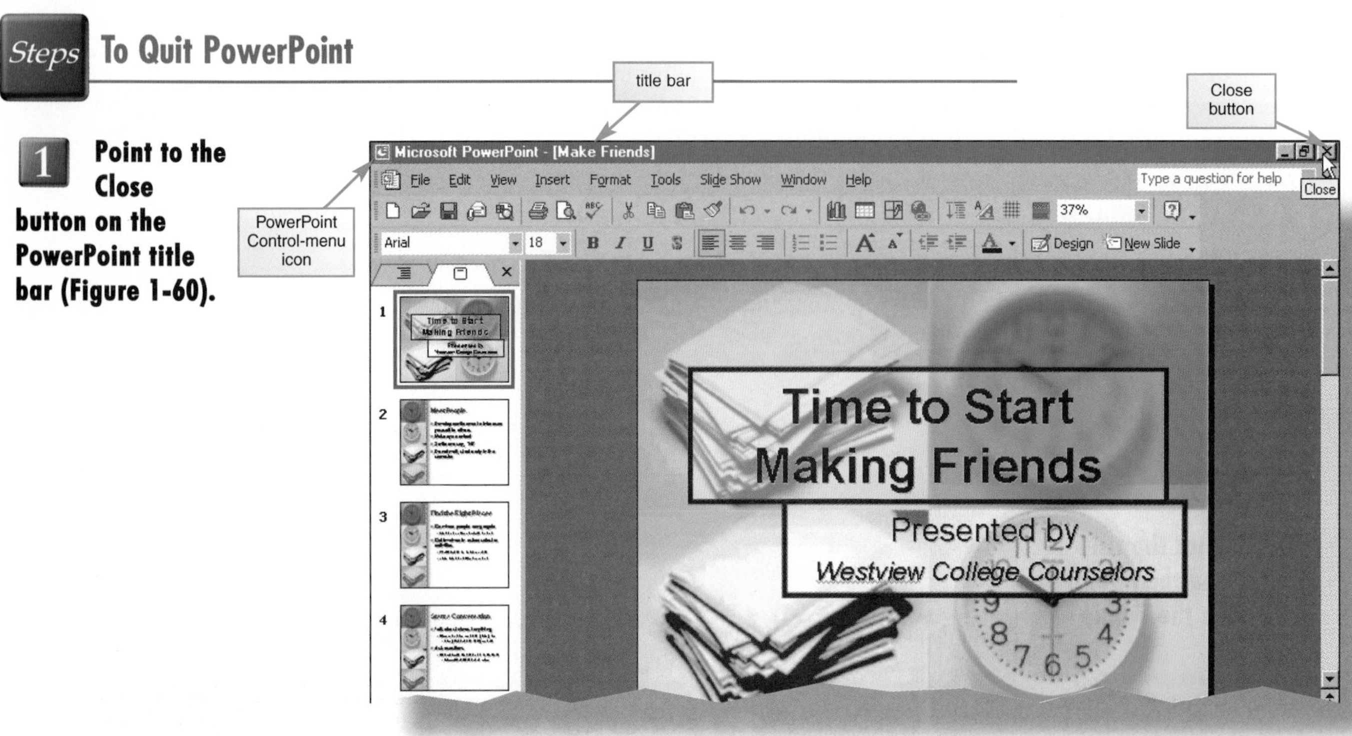

FIGURE 1-60

2 Click the Close button.

PowerPoint closes and the Windows desktop displays (Figure 1-61). If you made changes to the presentation since your last save, a Microsoft PowerPoint dialog box displays asking if you want to save changes. Clicking the Yes button saves the changes to the presentation before closing PowerPoint. Clicking the No button quits PowerPoint without saving the changes. Clicking the Cancel button returns to the presentation.

FIGURE 1-61

Other Ways

1. Double-click PowerPoint Control-menu icon; or click PowerPoint Control-menu icon, on Control menu click Close
2. On File menu click Exit
3. Press CTRL+Q or press ALT+F4

Opening a Presentation

Earlier, you saved the presentation on a floppy disk using the file name, Make Friends. Once you create and save a presentation, you may need to retrieve it from the floppy disk to make changes. For example, you may want to replace the design template or modify some text. Recall that a presentation is a PowerPoint document. Use the **Open Office Document command** to open an existing presentation.

More About

Sound Files

Creating slide shows can be exciting if you add sound cues that play sounds when you scroll, open dialog boxes, and zoom in or out. You can download sound files from the Microsoft Web site. For more information, visit the PowerPoint 2002 More About Web page (scsite.com/pp2002/more.htm) and then click Sound Files.

Opening an Existing Presentation

Be sure that the floppy disk used to save the Make Friends presentation is in drive A. Then, perform the following steps to open the presentation using the Open Office Document command on the Start menu.

To Open an Existing Presentation

1 Click the Start button on the Windows taskbar and then point to Open Office Document.

The Windows Start menu displays and Open Office Document is highlighted (Figure 1-62). The ScreenTip displays the function of the command.

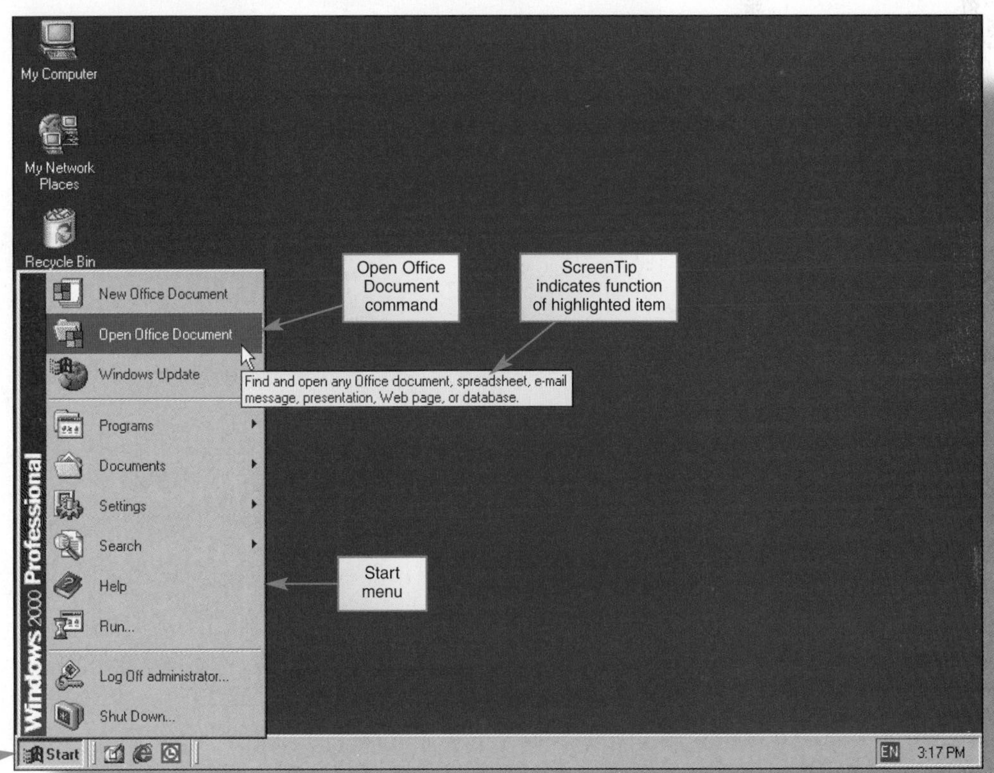

FIGURE 1-62

2 Click Open Office Document. When the Open Office Document dialog box displays, if necessary, click the Look in box arrow and then click 3½ Floppy (A:) in the Look in list.

The Open Office Document dialog box displays (Figure 1-63). A list of existing files displays on drive A. Notice that Office Files displays in the Files of type box. The file, Make Friends, is highlighted. Your list of existing files may be different depending on the files saved on your floppy disk.

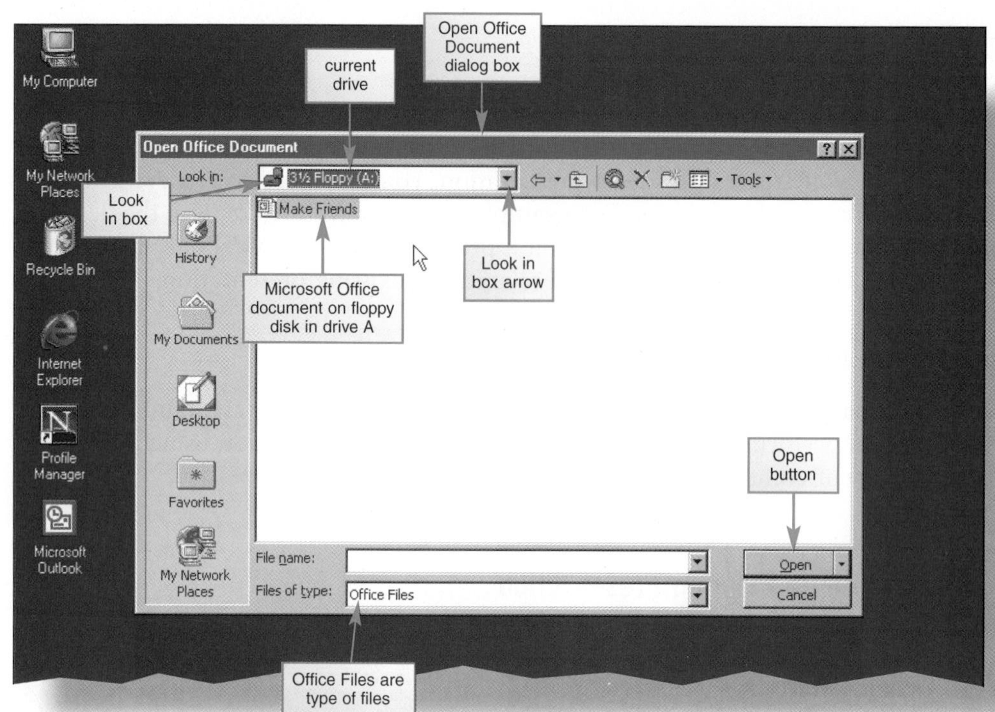

FIGURE 1-63

3 Double-click the file name, Make Friends.

PowerPoint starts, opens Make Friends on drive A, and displays the first slide in the PowerPoint window (Figure 1-64). The presentation displays in normal view because PowerPoint opens a presentation in the same view in which it was saved.

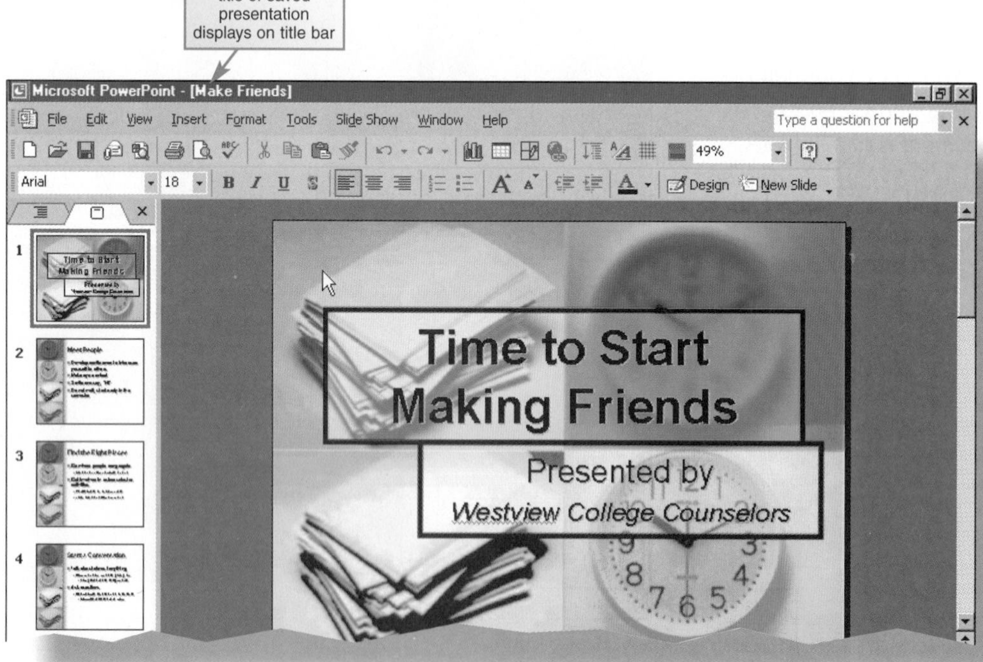

FIGURE 1-64

Other Ways

1. Click Open button on Standard toolbar, select file name, click Open button in Open Office Document dialog box
2. On File menu click Open, select file name, click Open button in Open dialog box
3. From desktop, right-click Start button, click either Open or Open All Users on shortcut menu, double-click Open Office Document, select file name, click Open button in Open Office Document dialog box
4. In Voice Command mode, say "Open file, [type file name], Open"

When you start PowerPoint and open Make Friends, the application name and file name display on a recessed button on the Windows taskbar. When more than one application is open, you can switch between applications by clicking the appropriate application button.

Checking a Presentation for Spelling and Consistency

Spelling Checker

While PowerPoint's Spelling checker is a valuable tool, it is not infallible. You should proofread your presentation carefully by saying each word aloud and pointing to each word as you say it. Be mindful of commonly misused words such as its and it's, their and they're, and you're and your.

After you create a presentation, you should check it visually for spelling errors and style consistency. In addition, you can use PowerPoint's Spelling and Style tools to identify possible misspellings and inconsistencies.

Checking a Presentation for Spelling Errors

PowerPoint checks the entire presentation for spelling mistakes using a standard dictionary contained in the Microsoft Office group. This dictionary is shared with the other Microsoft Office applications such as Word and Excel. A **custom dictionary** is available if you want to add special words such as proper names, cities, and acronyms. When checking a presentation for spelling errors, PowerPoint opens the standard dictionary and the custom dictionary file, if one exists. When a word displays in the Spelling dialog box, you perform one of the actions listed in Table 1-3.

Table 1-3 Summary of Spelling Checker Actions

FEATURE	*DESCRIPTION*
Ignore the word	Click the Ignore button when the word is spelled correctly but not found in the dictionaries. PowerPoint continues checking the rest of the presentation.
Ignore all occurrences of the word	Click the Ignore All button when the word is spelled correctly but not found in the dictionaries. PowerPoint ignores all occurrences of the word and continues checking the rest of the presentation.
Select a different spelling	Click the proper spelling of the word from the list in the Suggestions box. Click the Change button. PowerPoint corrects the word and continues checking the rest of the presentation.
Change all occurrences of the misspelling to a different spelling	Click the proper spelling of the word from the list in the Suggestions box. Click the Change All button. PowerPoint changes all occurrences of the misspelled word and continues checking the rest of the presentation.
Add a word to the custom dictionary	Click the Add button. PowerPoint opens the custom dictionary, adds the word, and continues checking the rest of the presentation.
View alternative spellings	Click the Suggest button. PowerPoint lists suggested spellings. Click the correct word from the Suggestions box or type the proper spelling. Then click the Change button. PowerPoint continues checking the rest of the presentation.
Add spelling error to AutoCorrect list	Click the AutoCorrect button. PowerPoint adds the spelling error and its correction to the AutoCorrect list. Any future misspelling of the word is corrected automatically as you type.
Close	Click the Close button to close the Spelling checker and return to the PowerPoint window.

The standard dictionary contains commonly used English words. It does not, however, contain proper names, abbreviations, technical terms, poetic contractions, or antiquated terms. PowerPoint treats words not found in the dictionaries as misspellings.

Starting the Spelling Checker

Perform the steps on the next page to start the Spelling checker and check the entire presentation.

Steps To Start the Spelling Checker

1 Point to the Spelling button on the Standard toolbar (Figure 1-65).

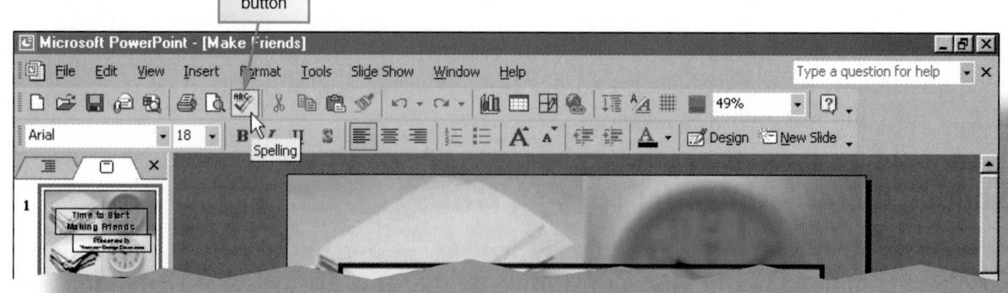

FIGURE 1-65

2 Click the Spelling button. When the Spelling dialog box displays, point to the Ignore button.

PowerPoint starts the Spelling checker and displays the Spelling dialog box (Figure 1-66). The word, Westview, displays in the Not in Dictionary box. Depending on the custom dictionary, Westview may not be recognized as a misspelled word.

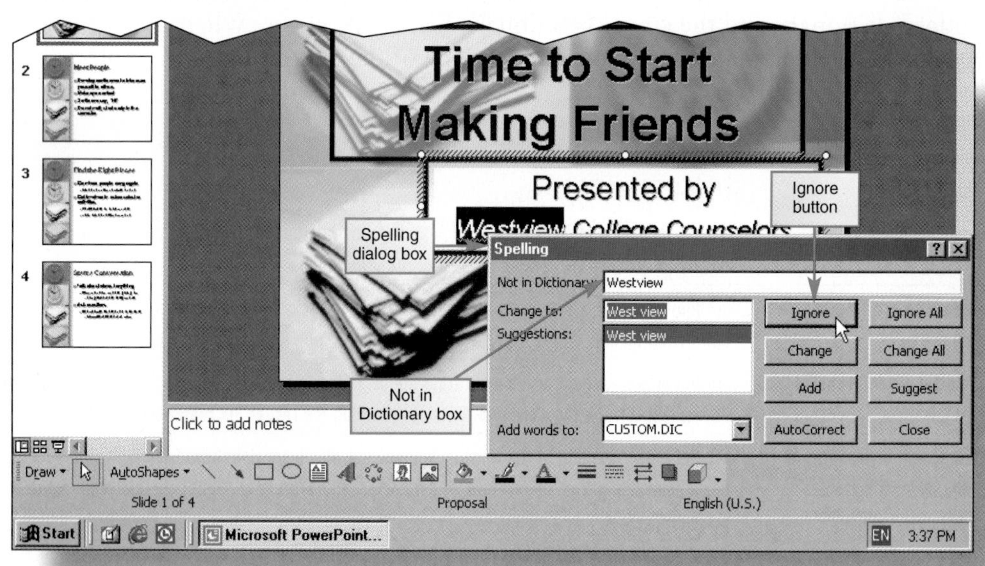

FIGURE 1-66

3 Click the Ignore button. When the Microsoft PowerPoint dialog box displays, point to the OK button.

PowerPoint ignores the word, Westview, and continues searching for additional misspelled words. PowerPoint may stop on additional words depending on your typing accuracy. When PowerPoint has checked all slides for misspellings, it displays the Microsoft PowerPoint dialog box informing you that the spelling check is complete (Figure 1-67).

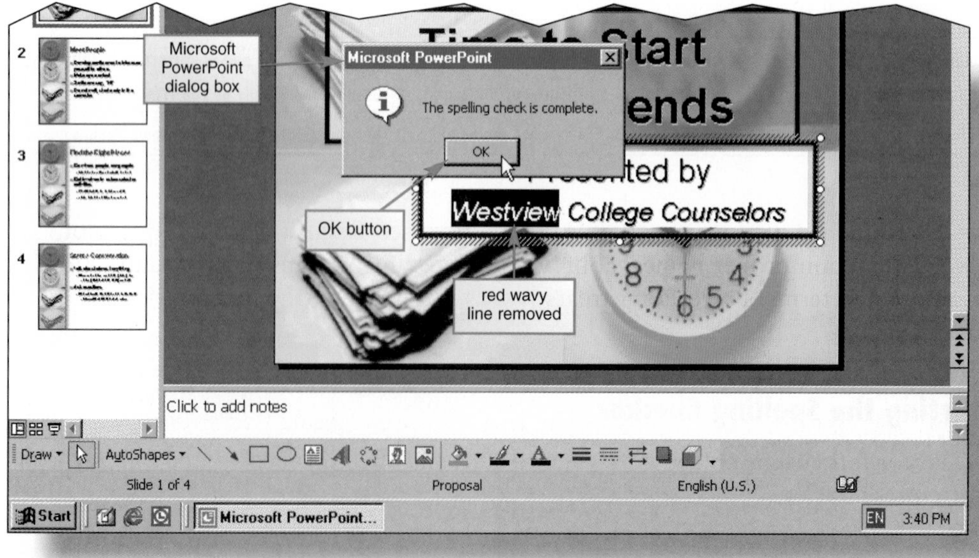

FIGURE 1-67

4 Click the OK button.

PowerPoint closes the Spelling checker and returns to the current slide, Slide 1 (Figure 1-68), or to the slide where a possible misspelled word displayed.

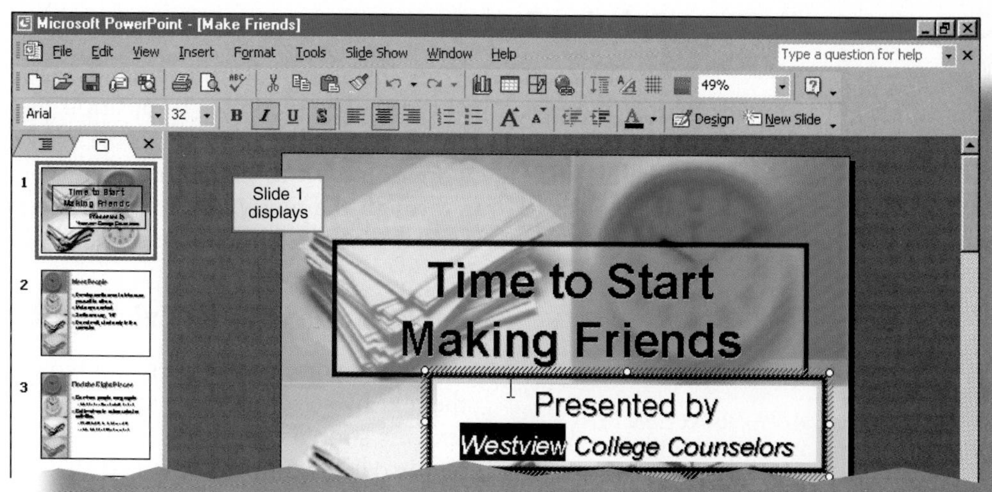

FIGURE 1-68

Other Ways

1. On Tools menu click Spelling
2. Press ALT+T, press S; when finished, press ENTER
3. In Voice Command mode, say "Tools, Spelling"

The red wavy line below the word, Westview, is gone because you instructed PowerPoint to ignore that word, which does not appear in the standard dictionary. You also could have added that word to the dictionary so it would not be flagged as a possible misspelled word in subsequent presentations you create using that word.

Correcting Errors

After creating a presentation and running the Spelling checker, you may find that you must make changes. Changes may be required because a slide contains an error, the scope of the presentation shifts, or the style is inconsistent. This section explains the types of errors that commonly occur when creating a presentation.

Types of Corrections Made to Presentations

You generally make three types of corrections to text in a presentation: additions, deletions, and replacements.

- **Additions** are necessary when you omit text from a slide and need to add it later. You may need to insert text in the form of a sentence, word, or single character. For example, you may want to add the rest of the presenter's first name on the title slide.
- **Deletions** are required when text on a slide is incorrect or no longer is relevant to the presentation. For example, a slide may look cluttered. Therefore, you may want to remove one of the bulleted paragraphs to add more space.
- **Replacements** are needed when you want to revise the text in a presentation. For example, you may want to substitute the word, their, for the word, there.

Editing text in PowerPoint basically is the same as editing text in a word processing package. The following sections illustrate the most common changes made to text in a presentation.

More About

Quick Reference

For a table that lists how to complete tasks covered in this book using the mouse, menu, shortcut menu, and keyboard, see the Quick Reference Summary at the back of this book or visit the Shelly Cashman Series Office XP Web page (scsite.com/offxp/qr.htm) and then click Microsoft PowerPoint 2002.

Deleting Text

You can delete text using one of four methods. One is to use the BACKSPACE key to remove text just typed. The second is to position the insertion point to the left of the text you wish to delete and then press the DELETE key. The third method is to double-click the word you wish to delete and then type the correct text. The fourth method is to drag through the text you wish to delete and then press the DELETE key. (Use the fourth method when deleting large sections of text.)

Table 1-4 Appearance in Black and White View

OBJECT	APPEARANCE IN BLACK AND WHITE VIEW
Bitmaps	Grayscale
Embossing	Hidden
Fills	Grayscale
Frame	Black
Lines	Black
Object shadows	Grayscale
Pattern fills	Grayscale
Slide backgrounds	White
Text	Black
Text shadows	Hidden

Replacing Text in an Existing Slide

When you need to correct a word or phrase, you can replace the text by selecting the text to be replaced and then typing the new text. As soon as you press any key on the keyboard, the highlighted text is deleted and the new text displays.

PowerPoint inserts text to the left of the insertion point. The text to the right of the insertion point moves to the right (and shifts downward if necessary) to accommodate the added text.

Displaying a Presentation in Black and White

Printing handouts of a presentation allows you to use them to make overhead transparencies. The **Color/Grayscale button** on the Standard toolbar displays the presentation in black and white before you print. Table 1-4 identifies how PowerPoint objects display in black and white.

Perform the following steps to display the presentation in black and white.

Steps To Display a Presentation in Black and White

1 Click the Color/Grayscale button on the Standard toolbar and then point to Pure Black and White in the list.

The Color/Grayscale list displays (Figure 1-69). Pure Black and White alters the slides' appearance so that only black lines display on a white background. Grayscale displays varying degrees of gray.

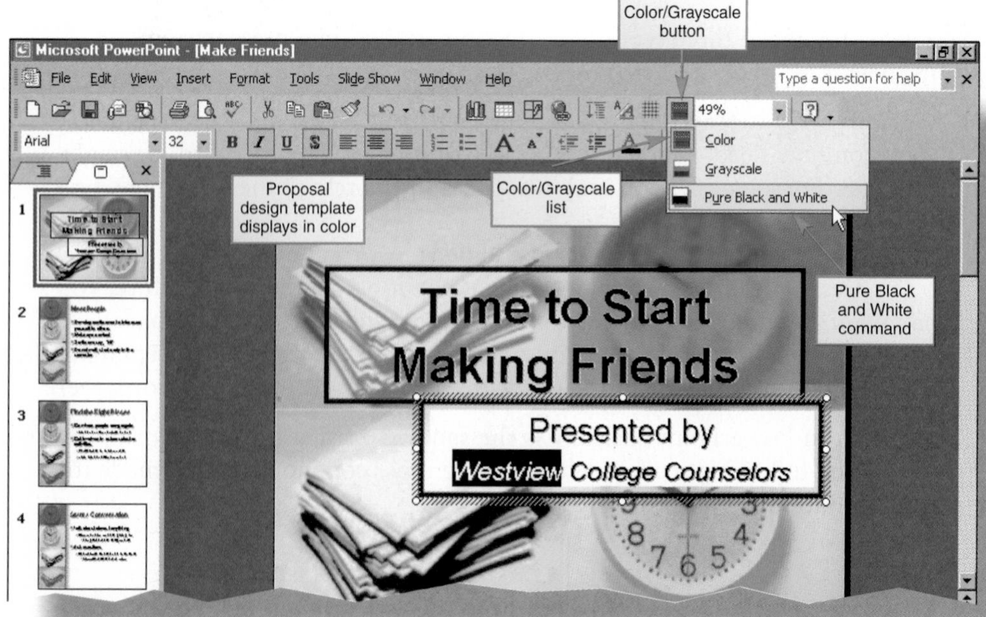

FIGURE 1-69

2 Click Pure Black and White.

Slide 1 displays in black and white in the slide pane (Figure 1-70). The four slide thumbnails display in color in the Slides tab. The Grayscale View toolbar displays. The Color/Grayscale button on the Standard toolbar changes from color bars to black and white.

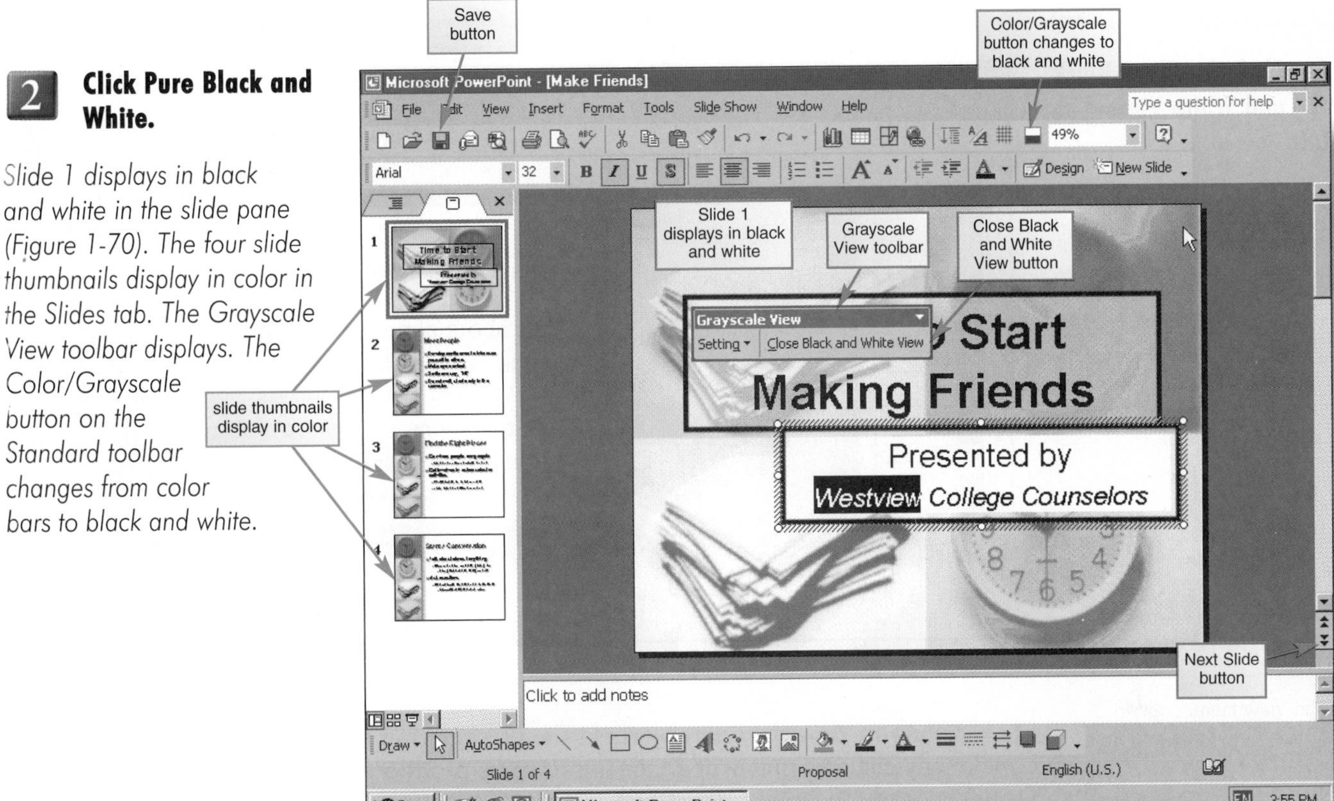

FIGURE 1-70

3 Click the Next Slide button three times to view all slides in the presentation in black and white. Point to the Close Black and White View button on the Grayscale View toolbar (Figure 1-71).

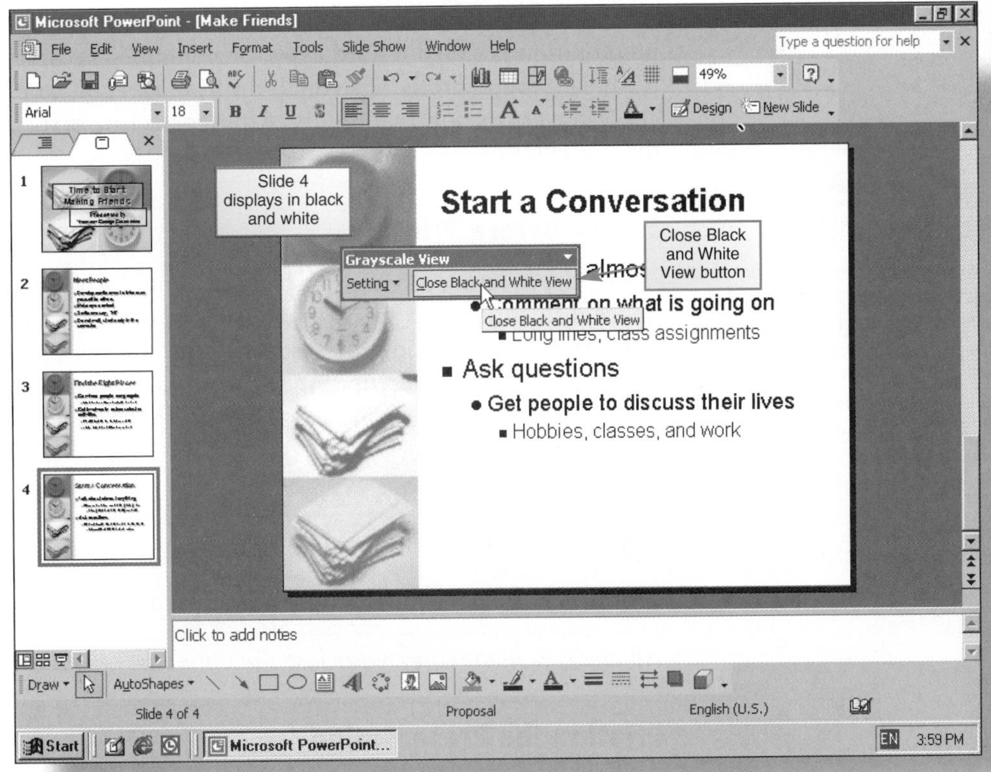

FIGURE 1-71

4 Click the Close Black and White View button.

Slide 4 displays with the default Proposal color scheme (Figure 1-72).

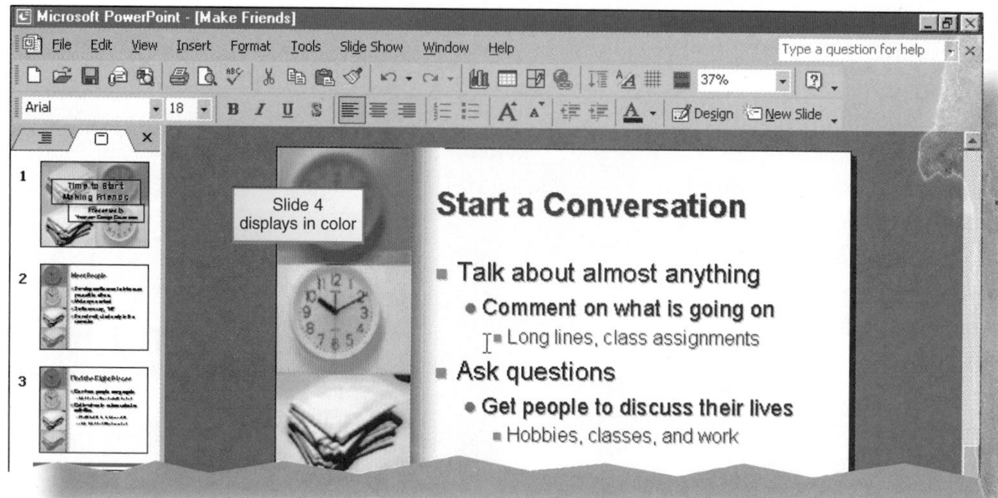

FIGURE 1-72

Other Ways

1. On View menu point to Color/Grayscale and then click Pure Black and White
2. In Voice Command mode, say "View, Color Grayscale, Pure Black and White"

After you view the text objects in the presentation in black and white, you can make any changes that will enhance printouts produced from a black and white printer or photocopier.

Printing a Presentation

After you create a presentation, you often want to print it. A printed version of the presentation is called a **hard copy**, or **printout**. The first printing of the presentation is called a **rough draft**. The rough draft allows you to proofread the presentation to check for errors and readability. After correcting errors, you print the final copy of the presentation.

More About

Printing

If you want to save ink, print faster, or decrease printer overrun errors, print a presentation in black and white. Click File on the menu bar and then click Print. When the Print dialog box displays, click the Color/grayscale box arrow, click Pure Black and White in the list, and then click the OK button.

Saving Before Printing

Before printing a presentation, you should save your work in the event you experience difficulties with the printer. You occasionally may encounter system problems that can be resolved only by restarting the computer. In such an instance, you will need to reopen the presentation. As a precaution, always save the presentation before you print. Perform the following steps to save the presentation before printing.

TO SAVE A PRESENTATION BEFORE PRINTING

1. Verify that the floppy disk is in drive A.
2. Click the Save button on the Standard toolbar.

All changes made after your last save now are saved on a floppy disk.

Printing the Presentation

After saving the presentation, you are ready to print. Clicking the **Print button** on the Standard toolbar causes PowerPoint to print all slides in the presentation. Perform the following steps to print the presentation slides.

Steps To Print a Presentation

1 Ready the printer according to the printer instructions. Then click the Print button on the Standard toolbar.

The printer icon in the tray status area on the Windows taskbar indicates a print job is processing (Figure 1-73). After several moments, the slide show begins printing on the printer. When the presentation is finished printing, the printer icon in the tray status area on the Windows taskbar no longer displays.

2 When the printer stops, retrieve the printouts of the slides.

The presentation, Make Friends, prints on four pages (Figures 1-2a through 1-2d on page PP 1.09).

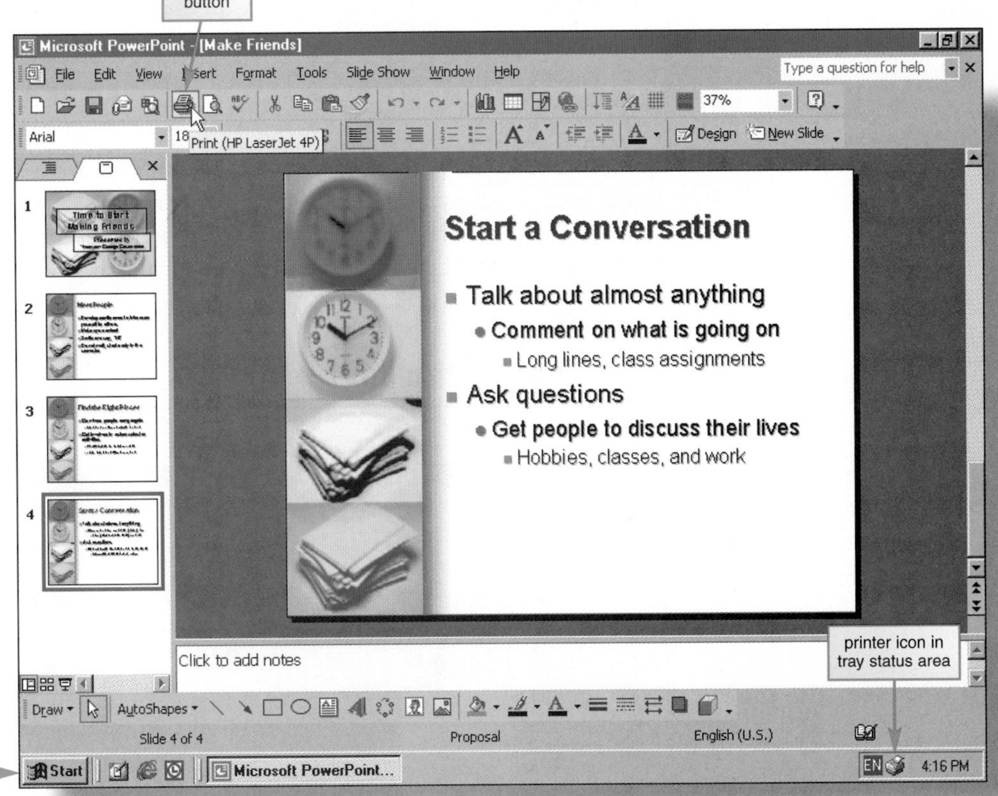

FIGURE 1-73

Other Ways

1. On File menu click Print
2. Press CTRL+P or press CTRL+SHIFT+F12
3. In Voice Command mode, say "Print"

You can click the printer icon next to the clock in the tray status area on the Windows taskbar to obtain information about the presentations printing on your printer and to delete files in the print queue that are waiting to be printed.

Making a Transparency

With the handouts printed, you now can make overhead transparencies using one of several devices. One device is a printer attached to your computer, such as an ink-jet printer or a laser printer. Transparencies produced on a printer may be in black and white or color, depending on the printer. Another device is a photocopier. Because each of these devices requires a special transparency film, check the user's manual for the film requirement of your specific device, or ask your instructor.

More About

The PowerPoint Help System

The best way to become familiar with the PowerPoint Help system is to use it. Appendix A includes detailed information on the PowerPoint Help system and exercises that will help you gain confidence in using it.

PowerPoint Help System

You can get answers to PowerPoint questions at any time by using the **PowerPoint Help system.** Used properly, this form of assistance can increase your productivity and reduce your frustrations by minimizing the time you spend learning how to use PowerPoint.

The following section shows how to get answers to your questions using the Ask a Question box on the menu bar. For additional information on using the PowerPoint Help system, see Appendix A and Table 1-5 on page PP 1.65.

Obtaining Help Using the Ask a Question Box on the Menu Bar

The **Ask a Question box** on the right side of the menu bar lets you type free-form questions such as, how do I save or how do I create a Web page, or you can type terms such as, copy, save, or format. PowerPoint responds by displaying a list of topics related to what you typed. The following steps show how to use the Ask a Question box to obtain information on formatting a presentation.

Steps To Obtain Help Using the Ask a Question Box

1 Click the Ask a Question box on the right side of the menu bar and then type `bullet` **(Figure 1-74).**

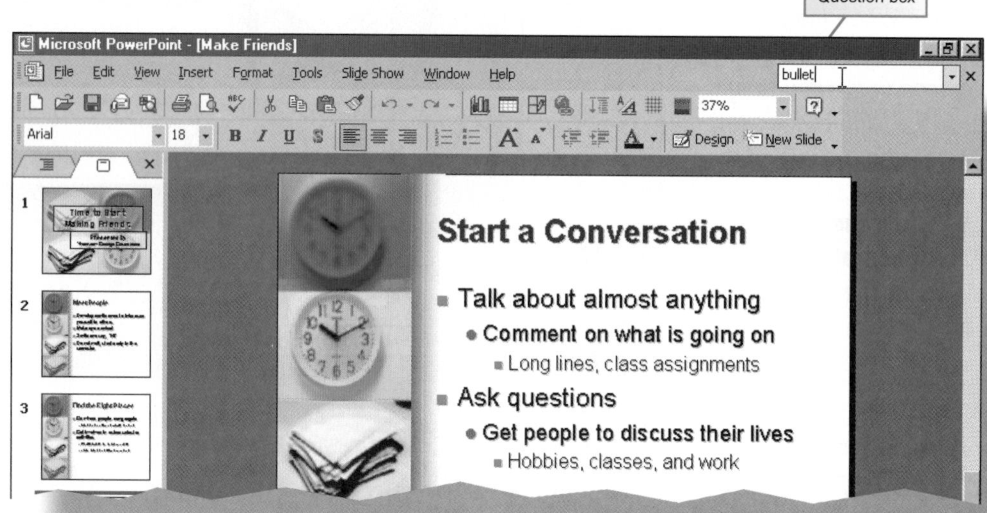

FIGURE 1-74

2 Press the ENTER key. When the list of topics displays below the Ask a Question box, point to the topic, Change the bullet style in a list.

A list of topics displays relating to the phrase, change the bullet style in a list (Figure 1-75). The mouse pointer changes to a hand, which indicates it is pointing to a link.

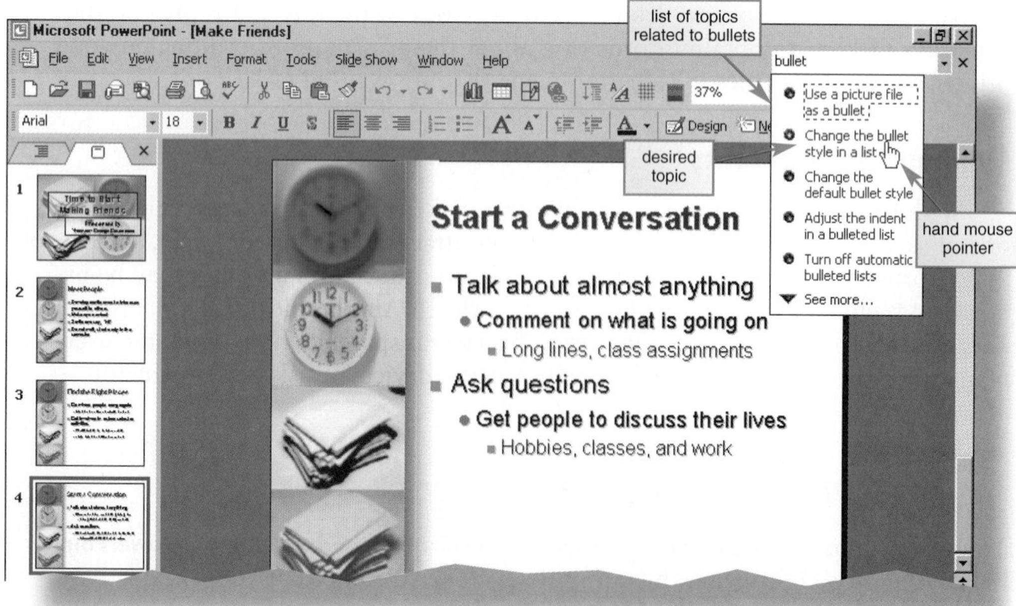

FIGURE 1-75

3 Click Change the bullet style in a list. When the Microsoft PowerPoint Help window displays, double-click its title bar to maximize it. Point to Change the bullet style for a single list.

A Microsoft PowerPoint Help window displays that provides Help information about changing the bullet style for a slide (Figure 1-76). The mouse pointer changes to a hand. The Index, Answer Wizard, or Content sheet is active on the left side of the Microsoft PowerPoint Help window.

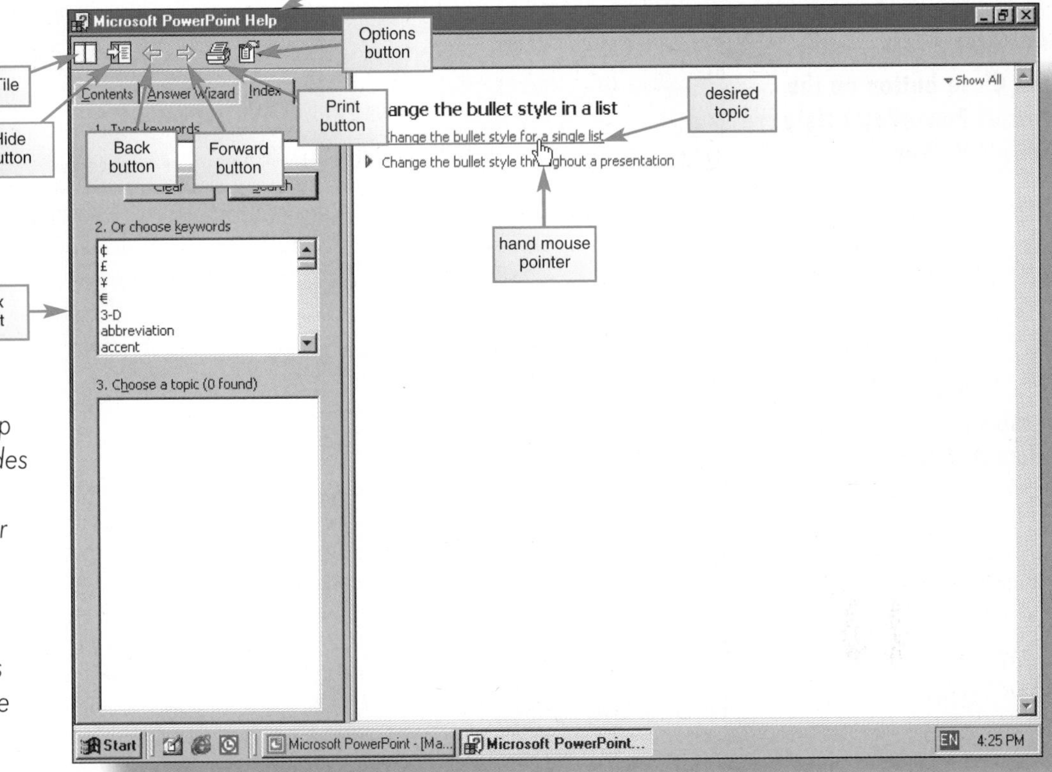

FIGURE 1-76

4 Click Change the bullet style for a single list. Point to Change the bullet color.

Directions for changing a bullet style on a single slide display. Options include changing a bullet character, changing a bullet size, and changing a bullet color (Figure 1-77).

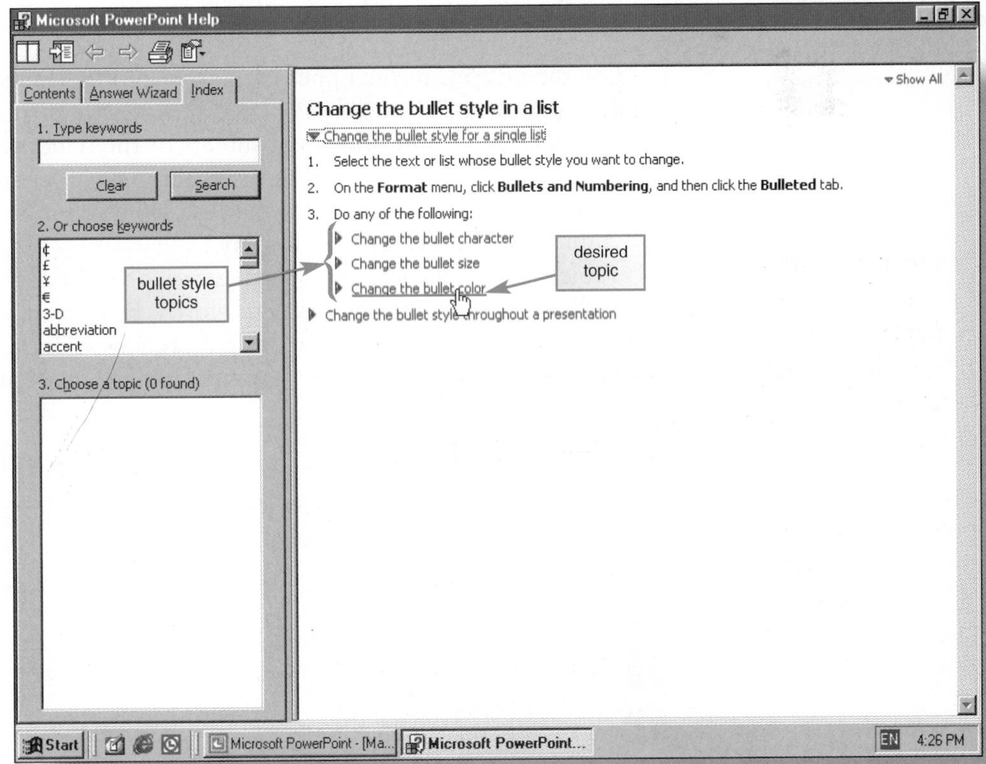

FIGURE 1-77

5 Click Change the bullet color. Point to the Close button on the Microsoft PowerPoint Help window title bar.

Specific details of changing the color of the bullets on a slide display (Figure 1-78).

6 Click the Close button on the Microsoft PowerPoint Help window title bar.

The PowerPoint Help window closes, and the PowerPoint presentation displays.

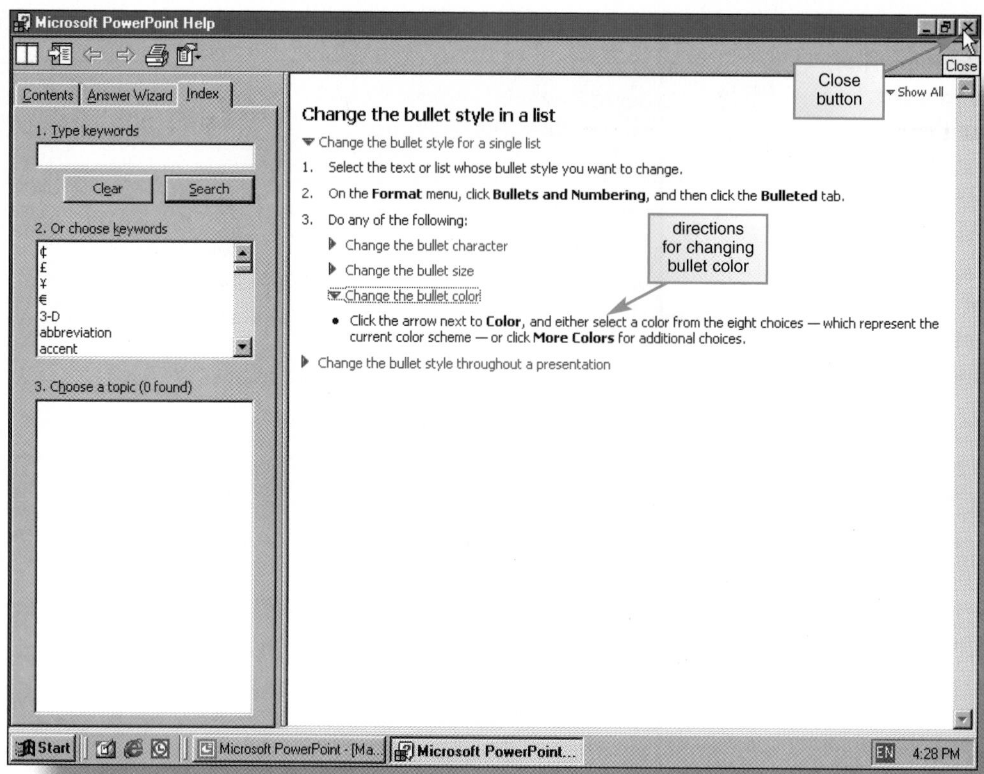

FIGURE 1-78

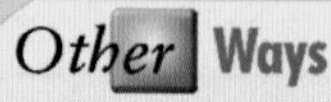

Other Ways

1. Click Microsoft PowerPoint Help button on Standard toolbar; or on Help menu click Microsoft PowerPoint Help
2. Press F1

Use the buttons in the upper-left corner of the Microsoft PowerPoint Help window (Figure 1-76 on page PP 1.63) to navigate through the Help system, change the display, and print the contents of the window.

As you enter questions and terms in the Ask a Question box, PowerPoint adds them to its list. Thus, if you click the Ask a Question box arrow, a list of previously asked questions and terms will display.

Table 1-5 summarizes the 10 categories of Help available to you. Because of the way the PowerPoint Help system works, be certain to review the rightmost column of Table 1-5 if you have difficulties activating the desired category of help. For additional information on using the PowerPoint Help system, see Appendix A.

Quitting PowerPoint

Project 1 is complete. The final task is to close the presentation and quit PowerPoint. Perform the following steps to quit PowerPoint.

TO QUIT POWERPOINT

1. Click the Close button on the title bar.
2. If prompted to save the presentation before quitting PowerPoint, click the Yes button in the Microsoft PowerPoint dialog box.

Table 1-5 PowerPoint Help System

TYPE	DESCRIPTION	HOW TO ACTIVATE
Answer Wizard	Answers questions or searches for terms that you type in your own words.	Click the Microsoft PowerPoint Help button on the Standard toolbar. Click the Answer Wizard tab.
Ask a Question box	Answers questions or searches for terms that you type in your own words.	Type a question or term in the Ask a Question box on the menu bar and then press the ENTER key.
Contents sheet	Groups Help topics by general categories. Use when you know only the general category of the topic in question.	Click the Microsoft PowerPoint Help button on the Standard toolbar. Click the Contents tab.
Detect and Repair	Automatically finds and fixes errors in the application.	Click Detect and Repair on the Help menu.
Hardware and Software Information	Shows Product ID and allows access to system information and technical support information.	Click About Microsoft PowerPoint on the Help menu and then click the appropriate button.
Index sheet	Similar to an index in a book. Use when you know exactly what you want.	Click the Microsoft PowerPoint Help button on the Standard toolbar. If necessary, maximize the Help window by double-clicking its title bar. Click the Index tab.
Office Assistant	Similar to the Ask a Question box in that the Office Assistant answers questions that you type in your own words, offers tips, and provides help for a variety of PowerPoint features.	Click the Office Assistant icon if it is on the screen. If the Office Assistant does not display, click Show the Office Assistant on the Help menu.
Office on the Web	Used to access technical resources and download free product enhancements on the Web.	Click Office on the Web on the Help menu.
Question Mark button	Used to identify unfamiliar items in a dialog box.	Click the Question Mark button on the title bar of a dialog box and then click an item in the dialog box.
What's This? Command	Used to identify unfamiliar items on the screen.	Click What's This? on the Help menu, and then click an item on the screen.

CASE PERSPECTIVE SUMMARY

Jennifer Williams is pleased with the Time to Start Making Friends PowerPoint slide show. The counseling staff will present methods of facing loneliness to incoming freshmen attending orientation sessions at your school. The four slides display a variety of ways students can make friends on campus. The title slide identifies the topic of the presentation, and the next three slides give key pointers regarding going to appropriate places to meet people and start a conversation. The counselors will use your slides to make overhead transparencies to organize their speeches, and the students will keep handouts of your slides for future reference.

Project Summary

Project 1 introduced you to starting PowerPoint and creating a presentation consisting of a title slide and single- and multi-level bulleted lists. You learned about PowerPoint design templates, objects, and attributes. This project illustrated how to create an interesting introduction to a presentation by changing the text font style to italic and increasing font size on the title slide. Completing these tasks, you saved the presentation. Then, you created three text slides with bulleted lists, two with multi-level bullets, to explain how to meet friends in college. Next, you learned how to view the presentation in slide show view. Then, you learned how to quit PowerPoint and how to open an existing presentation. You used the Spelling checker to search for spelling errors. You learned how to display the presentation in black and white. You learned how to print hard copies of the slides in order to make handouts and overhead transparencies. Finally, you learned how to use the PowerPoint Help system.

What You Should Know

Having completed this project, you now should be able to perform the following tasks:

- Add a New Slide and Enter a Slide Title *(PP 1.37)*
- Add a New Text Slide with a Bulleted List *(PP 1.32)*
- Change the Text Font Style to Italic *(PP 1.26)*
- Choose a Design Template *(PP 1.19)*
- Create a Third-Level Paragraph *(PP 1.41)*
- Create Slide 4 *(PP 1.41)*
- Customize the PowerPoint Window *(PP 1.12)*
- Display a Presentation in Black and White *(PP 1.58)*
- Display the Popup Menu and Go to a Specific Slide *(PP 1.50)*
- End a Slide Show with a Black Slide *(PP 1.44)*
- Enter a Slide Title *(PP 1.34)*
- Enter the Presentation Subtitle *(PP 1.24)*
- Enter the Presentation Title *(PP 1.22)*
- Increase Font Size *(PP 1.27)*
- Move Manually Through Slides in a Slide Show *(PP 1.49)*
- Obtain Help Using the Ask a Question Box *(PP 1.62)*
- Open an Existing Presentation *(PP 1.53)*
- Print a Presentation *(PP 1.61)*
- Quit PowerPoint *(PP 1.52, 1.64)*
- Save a Presentation Before Printing *(PP 1.60)*
- Save a Presentation on a Floppy Disk *(PP 1.29)*
- Save a Presentation with the Same File Name *(PP 1.45)*
- Select a Text Placeholder *(PP 1.34)*
- Start PowerPoint *(PP 1.10)*
- Start Slide Show View *(PP 1.48)*
- Start the Spelling Checker *(PP 1.56)*
- Type a Multi-Level Bulleted List *(PP 1.38)*
- Type a Single-Level Bulleted List *(PP 1.35)*
- Type the Remaining Text for Slide 3 *(PP 1.40)*
- Type the Remaining Text for Slide 4 *(PP 1.43)*
- Use the Popup Menu to End a Slide Show *(PP 1.51)*
- Use the Scroll Box on the Slide Pane to Move to Another Slide *(PP 1.46)*

More About

Microsoft Certification

The Microsoft Office User Specialist (MOUS) Certification program provides an opportunity for you to obtain a valuable industry credential — proof that you have the PowerPoint 2002 skills required by employers. For more information, see Appendix E or visit the Shelly Cashman Series MOUS Web page at scsite.com/offxp/cert.htm.

Learn It Online

Instructions: To complete the Learn It Online excercises, start your browser, click the Address bar, and then enter `scsite.com/offxp/exs.htm`. When the Office XP Learn It Online page displays, follow the instructions in the exercises below.

1 Project Reinforcement TF, MC, and SA

Below PowerPoint Project 1, click the Project Reinforcement link. Print the quiz by clicking Print on the File menu. Answer each question. Write your first and last name at the top of each page, and then hand in the printout to your instructor.

2 Flash Cards

Below PowerPoint Project 1, click the Flash Cards link. When Flash Cards displays, read the instructions. Type `20` (or a number specified by your instructor) in the Number of Playing Cards text box, type your name in the Name text box, and then click the Flip Card button. When the flash card displays, read the question and then click the Answer box arrow to select an answer. Flip through Flash Cards. Click Print on the File menu to print the last flash card if your score is 15 (75%) correct or greater and then hand it in to your instructor. If your score is less than 15 (75%) correct, then redo this exercise by clicking the Replay button.

3 Practice Test

Below PowerPoint Project 1, click the Practice Test link. Answer each question, enter your first and last name at the bottom of the page, and then click the Grade Test button. When the graded practice test displays on your screen, click Print on the File menu to print a hard copy. Continue to take practice tests until you score 80% or better. Hand in a printout of the final practice test to your instructor.

4 Who Wants to Be a Computer Genius?

Below PowerPoint Project 1, click the Computer Genius link. Read the instructions, enter your first and last name at the bottom of the page, and then click the Play button. Hand in your score to your instructor.

5 Wheel of Terms

Below PowerPoint Project 1, click the Wheel of Terms link. Read the instructions, and then enter your first and last name and your school name. Click the Play button. Hand in your score.

6 Crossword Puzzle Challenge

Below PowerPoint Project 1, click the Crossword Puzzle Challenge link. Read the instructions, and then enter your first and last name. Click the Play button. Work the crossword puzzle. When you are finished, click the Submit button. When the crossword puzzle redisplays, click the Print button. Hand in the printout.

7 Tips and Tricks

Below PowerPoint Project 1, click the Tips and Tricks link. Click a topic that pertains to Project 1. Right-click the information and then click Print on the shortcut menu. Construct a brief example of what the information relates to in PowerPoint to confirm you understand how to use the tip or trick. Hand in the example and printed information.

8 Newsgroups

Below PowerPoint Project 1, click the Newsgroups link. Click a topic that pertains to Project 1. Print three comments. Hand in the comments.

9 Expanding Your Horizons

Below PowerPoint Project 1, click the Articles for Microsoft PowerPoint link. Click a topic that pertains to Project 1. Print the information. Construct a brief example of what the information relates to in PowerPoint to confirm you understand the contents of the article. Hand in the example and printed information.

10 Search Sleuth

Below PowerPoint Project 1, click the Search Sleuth link. To search for a term that pertains to this project, select a term below the Project 1 title and then use the Google search engine at google.com (or any major search engine) to display and print two Web pages that present information on the term. Hand in the printout.

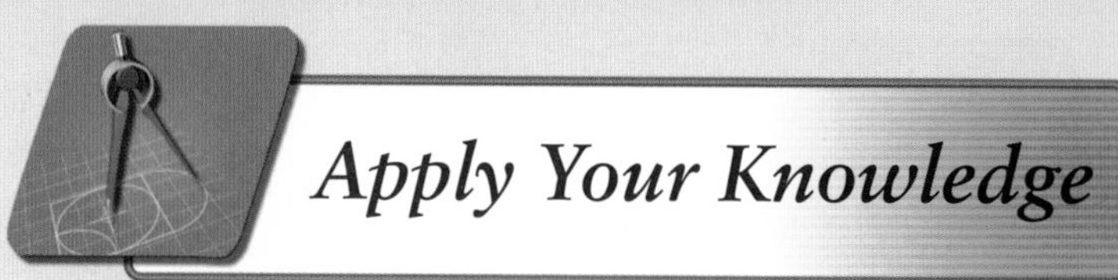

1 Trends in Computer Technology

Instructions: Start PowerPoint. Open the presentation Computer Trends from the Data Disk. See the inside back cover of this book for instructions for downloading the Data Disk or see your instructor for information on accessing the files required for this book. This slide lists hardware and software trends in the computer industry. Perform the following tasks to change the slide so it looks like the one in Figure 1-79.

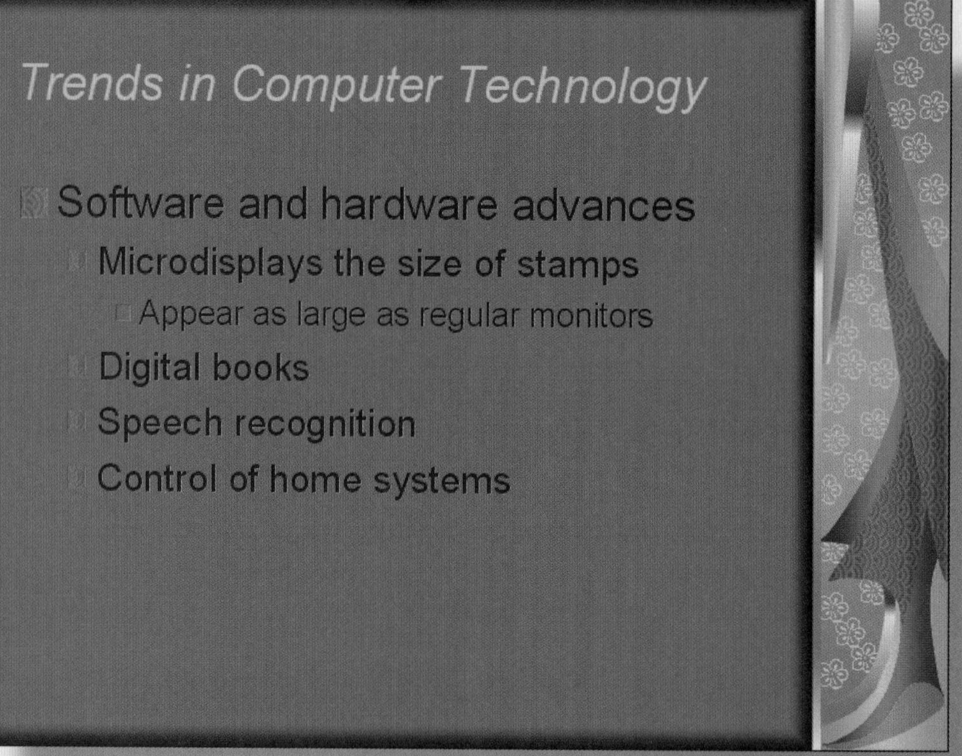

FIGURE 1-79

1. Click the Slide Design button on the Formatting toolbar. Scroll down and then choose the Kimono design template (row 12, column 1).
2. Select the title text. Click the Italic button on the Formatting toolbar.
3. Click the Font Size box arrow on the Font Size button on the Formatting toolbar and then click font size 36.
4. Click the paragraph, Microdisplays the size of stamps. Click the Increase Indent button on the Formatting toolbar to change the paragraph to a second-level paragraph. Then change these three paragraphs to second-level paragraphs: Digital books, Speech recognition, and Control of home systems.
5. Click the Appear as large as regular monitors paragraph. Click the Increase Indent button on the Formatting toolbar twice to change this paragraph to a third-level paragraph.
6. Click File on the menu bar and then click Save As. Type `Trends in Technology` in the File name text box. If drive A is not already displaying in the Save in box, click the Save in box arrow, and then click 3½ Floppy (A:). Click the Save button.
7. Click the Color/Grayscale button on the Standard toolbar, and then click Pure Black and White to display the presentation in black and white.
8. Click the Print button on the Standard toolbar.
9. Click the Close Black and White View button on the Grayscale View toolbar.
10. Click the Close button on the title bar to quit PowerPoint.
11. Write your name on the printout, and hand it in to your instructor.

In the Lab

Note: These labs require you to create presentations based on notes. When you design these slide shows, use the 7 × 7 rule, which states that each line should have a maximum of seven words, and each slide should have a maximum of seven lines.

1 Decades of Nutrition in the Twentieth Century

Problem: You are enrolled in a health class, and one of your assignments is to analyze nutrition and eating habits during the twentieth century. You decide to prepare a presentation for your class discussing food and related health problems during 20-year periods. You first develop the notes shown in Figure 1-80, and then you create the presentation shown in Figures 1-81a through 1-81f on pages PP 1.70 and PP 1.71.

I) Decades of Nutrition
Eating in the Twentieth Century
- A) Presented by
- B) Melissa Ruiz
- C) Health 101

II) 1900 - 1919
- A) Cold breakfast cereals introduced
- B) Ice cream sales soar
  - 1) First ice cream cone served
- C) Hershey introduces its chocolate bar
- D) Plump is preferred body type
  - 1) Slim is considered sickly

III) 1920 – 1939
- A) Kraft introduces Macaroni and Cheese
  - 1) Cooking from scratch begins to decline
- B) Red meat, vegetable intakes increase
- C) Heart disease on the rise
  - 1) Surpasses TB as leading cause of death
- D) Slim becomes preferred body type

IV) 1940 - 1959
- A) First McDonald's Hamburgers opens
  - 1) Home cooking begins to decline
- B) Research links heart disease with high saturated fats
- C) Fewer than 25 percent of Americans have healthy diets

V) 1960 - 1979
- A) Whole grains, Vitamin C gain popularity
- B) Soft drink consumption increases
  - 1) Exceeds milk consumption by 1980
- C) Federal committee finds unhealthy diets
  - 1) Too high in fats, sugar, salt, and meat
  - 2) Too low in grains, fruits, and vegetables

VI) 1980 - 1999
- A) Low-fat snacks flood grocery stores
  - 1) Americans still become more overweight
- B) Omega-3 fats found heart-healthy
  - 1) Found in fish, flaxseed
- C) Fish consumption increases
- D) Dairy and egg intakes decrease

FIGURE 1-80

In the Lab

Decades of Nutrition in the Twentieth Century *(continued)*

Decades of Nutrition
Eating in the Twentieth Century
Presented by
Melissa Ruiz
Health 101

(a) Slide 1 (Title Slide)

1900 - 1919

- Cold breakfast cereals introduced
- Ice cream sales soar
  - First ice cream cone served
- Hershey introduces its chocolate bar
- Plump is preferred body type
  - Slim is considered sickly

(b) Slide 2

1920 – 1939

- Kraft introduces Macaroni and Cheese
  - Cooking from scratch begins to decline
- Red meat, vegetable intakes increase
- Heart disease on the rise
  - Surpasses TB as leading cause of death
- Slim becomes preferred body type

(c) Slide 3

1940 - 1959

- First McDonald's Hamburgers opens
  - Home cooking begins to decline
- Research links heart disease with high saturated fats
  - Fewer than 25 percent of Americans have healthy diets

(d) Slide 4

FIGURE 1-81

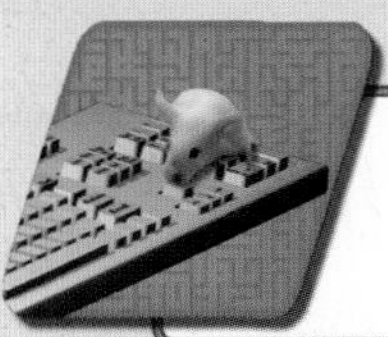

In the Lab

1960 - 1979

- Whole grains, Vitamin C gain popularity
- Soft drink consumption increases
  - Exceeds milk consumption by 1980
- Federal committee finds unhealthy diets
  - Too high in fats, sugar, salt, and meat
  - Too low in grains, fruits, and vegetables

(e) Slide 5

1980 - 1999

- Low-fat snacks flood grocery stores
  - Americans still become more overweight
- Omega-3 fats found heart-healthy
  - Found in fish, flaxseed
    - Fish consumption increases
- Dairy and egg intakes decrease

(f) Slide 6

FIGURE 1-81 *(continued)*

Instructions: Perform the following tasks.

1. Create a new presentation using the Ripple design template (row 19, column 1).
2. Using the typed notes illustrated in Figure 1-80, create the title slide shown in Figure 1-81a using your name in place of Melissa Ruiz. Italicize your name. Decrease the font size of the second paragraph of the title text to 36. Decrease the font size of the paragraph, Presented by, to 28. Decrease the font size of the paragraph, Health 101, to 24.
3. Using the typed notes in Figure 1-80 on page PP 1.69, create the five text slides with bulleted lists shown in Figures 1-81b through 1-81f.
4. Click the Spelling button on the Standard toolbar. Correct any errors.
5. Save the presentation using the file name, Nutrition.
6. Display the presentation in black and white.
7. Print the black and white presentation. Quit PowerPoint.

(continued)

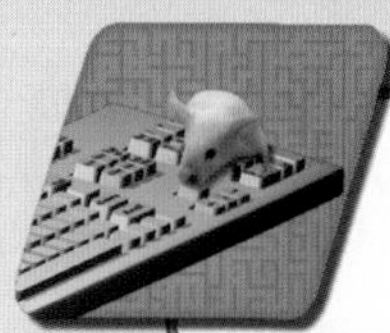

In the Lab

2 Select Electric Products Open House

Problem: You work at Select Electric, a local store featuring a variety of electronic products. Your manager has asked you to participate in the semi-annual open house showcasing the latest consumer electronics. You decide to get involved by developing a PowerPoint presentation that helps customers view key features of various devices. You review the products that will be featured and develop the list shown in Figure 1-82. Then, you select a PowerPoint design template and decide to modify it.

I) Electronics Explosion
  A) Presented by
  B) Select Electric
II) High-Definition TV
  A) Screens from 34 to 61 inches
  B) Some models have two tuners
    1) Picture-in-picture
      a) Watch two shows at once
  C) Inputs maximize digital sources
    1) DVD and satellite
III) Digital Camcorders
  A) Razor-sharp recording
    1) Image stabilization
  B) Crystal-clear audio
  C) Digital still photos
    1) Store on removable memory card
      a) CompactFlash, Memory Stick
IV) Digital Cameras
  A) Megapixels increase clarity
    1) 4.3, 3.3, 2.1 megapixels
  B) Optical and digital zoom
  C) MPEG movie mode
    1) Up to 60 seconds
      a) 15 frames per second

FIGURE 1-82

In the Lab

Instructions: Perform the following tasks.

1. Create a new presentation using the Fireworks design template (row 10, column 2).
2. Using the notes in Figure 1-82, create the title slide shown in Figure 1-83a. Increase the font size of the paragraph, Electronics Explosion, to 48 and change the text font style to italic. Decrease the font size of the paragraph, Presented by, to 28.
3. Using the notes in Figure 1-82, create the three text slides with multi-level bulleted lists shown in Figures 1-83b through 1-83d.

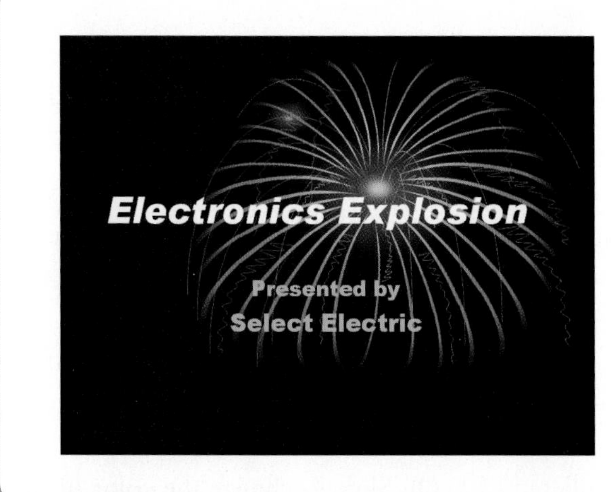

(a) Slide 1 (Title Slide)

High-Definition TV
* Screens from 34 to 61 inches
* Some models have two tuners
  * Picture-in-picture
    * Watch two shows at once
* Inputs maximize digital sources
  * DVD and satellite

(b) Slide 2

(c) Slide 3

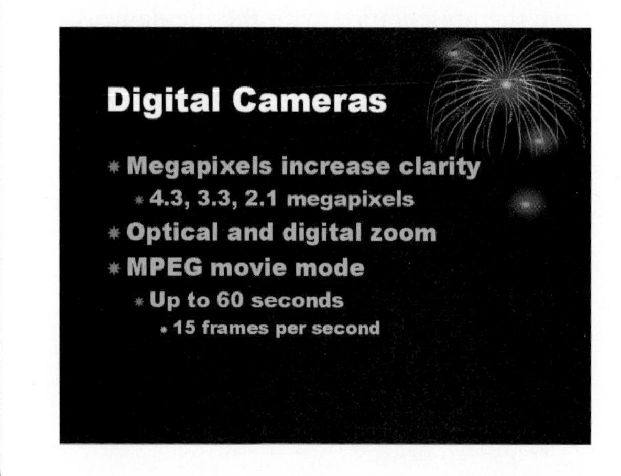

Digital Cameras
Megapixels increase clarity
4.3, 3.3, 2.1 megapixels
Optical and digital zoom
MPEG movie mode
Up to 60 seconds
15 frames per second

(d) Slide 4

FIGURE 1-83

(continued)

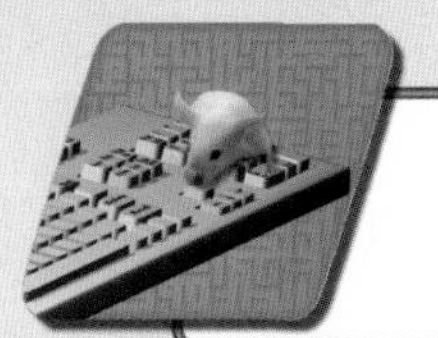

In the Lab

Select Electric Products Open House *(continued)*

4. Click the Spelling button on the Standard toolbar. Correct any errors.
5. Drag the scroll box to display Slide 1. Click the Slide Show button to start slide show view. Then click to display each slide.
6. Save the presentation using the file name, Select Electric. Display and print the presentation in black and white. Quit PowerPoint.

3 West Shore College Job Fair

Problem: Your school, West Shore College, is planning a job fair to occur during the week of midterm exams. The Placement Office has invited 150 companies and local businesses to promote its current and anticipated job openings. The Placement Office director, Bob Thornton, hands you the outline shown in Figure 1-84 and asks you to prepare a presentation and handouts to promote the event.

Instructions: Using the list in Figure 1-84, design and create a presentation. The presentation must include a title slide and three text slides with bulleted lists. Perform the following tasks.

1. Create a new presentation using the Cliff design template (row 4, column 1).
2. Create a title slide titled, West Shore College Career Fair. Include a subtitle, using your name in place of Bob Thornton. Decrease the font size for paragraphs, Presented by, and, West Shore Placement Office, to 28. Italicize your name.
3. Using Figure 1-84 create three text slides with multi-level bulleted lists. On Slide 4, change the color of the diamond bullets from gold to white.
4. View the presentation in slide show view to look for errors. Correct any errors.
5. Check the presentation for spelling errors.
6. Save the presentation with the file name, Career Fair. Print the presentation slides in black and white. Quit PowerPoint.

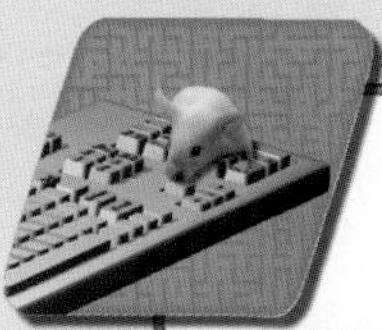

In the Lab

I) West Shore College Career Fair
  A) Presented by
  B) West Shore Placement Office
  C) Bob Thornton, Director
II) Who Is Coming?
  A) National corporations
    1) Progressive companies looking for high-quality candidates
  B) Local companies
    1) Full-time and part-time
      a) Hundreds of jobs
III) When Is It?
  A) Midterm week
    1) Monday through Friday
  B) West Shore College Cafeteria
  C) Convenient hours
    1) 9:00 a.m. to 8:00 p.m.
IV) How Should I Prepare?
  A) Bring plenty of resumes
    1) More than 150 companies expected
  B) Dress neatly
  C) View the Placement Office Web site
    1) Up-to-date information
    2) Company profiles

FIGURE 1-84

Cases and Places

The difficulty of these case studies varies:
▶ are the least difficult; ▶▶ are more difficult; and ▶▶▶ are the most difficult.

Note: Remember to use the 7 × 7 rule as you design the presentations: a maximum of seven words on a line and a maximum of seven lines on one slide.

1 ▶ Fitness Center employees present many classes on a variety of physical and emotional wellness topics. The coordinator, Carol O'Malley, has contacted you to help her prepare a presentation that will be delivered at community fairs and at the local shopping mall. She has prepared the notes shown in Figure 1-85 and has asked you to use them to develop a title slide and additional text slides that can be used on an overhead projector. Use the concepts and techniques introduced in this project to create the presentation.

Enhance Your Physical and Emotional Wellness
At the Mid-City College Fitness Center
Carol O'Malley, director

Mind/Body Programs
- Meditation
  - Various techniques
  - Time to practice included
- Stress Management Workshop
  - Relaxation strategies
  - Four-part series

Lifestyle Programs
- CPR and First Aid
  - Certification and recertification
  - American Red Cross instructors
- Smoking Cessation
  - Eight-session group program
  - Individual consultations

Nutrition Programs
- Nutrition Connection
  - Semester-long program
  - Change your lifestyle to enhance your health
  - Achieve your weight-management goals
  - Increase your self-esteem
- Dining Out: Eat and Be Healthy

FIGURE 1-85

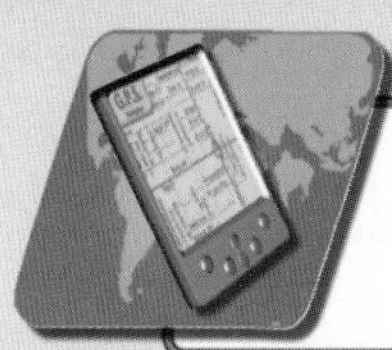

Cases and Places

2 More than 76 million Americans currently carry cellular telephones, and many of these people use their telephones while driving. Although 87 percent of adults believe using a cellular telephone impairs their ability to drive, motorists continue to place and receive calls while driving. Andy Allman, your Lo-Rate Insurance agent, knows you are learning PowerPoint and asks you to help him prepare a presentation that will be delivered at shopping centers and on campus. He has prepared the notes shown in Figure 1-86 and wants you to use them to develop a title slide and additional text slides for a presentation and handouts. Use the concepts and techniques introduced in this project to create the slide show.

Calling All Cars
Using Your Telephone Safely in Your Vehicle
Andy Allman
Lo-Rate Insurance Agency

Cellular telephones distract from driving
37 percent of drivers say they have had a near miss with someone using a cellular telephone
2 percent of drivers have had an accident with someone using a cellular telephone
Some communities have banned cellular telephone use behind the wheel

Your telephone can be a safety tool
More than 118,000 calls placed daily to 911 from cellular telephones
Emergency response times have decreased as 911 calls have increased

Use your telephone responsibly
Place calls before pulling into traffic
Use your telephone's special features such as speed dial and redial
Do not call in hazardous weather or heavy traffic
Do not take notes or look up numbers while driving
Do not engage in emotional or stressful conversations
50 percent of drivers seldom or never use a telephone while driving

FIGURE 1-86

Cases and Places

3 ▶▶ Road Warrior is a business near campus that specializes in quick oil changes, headlight and windshield wiper replacement, flat repair, battery recharging, and interior and exterior cleaning. The owners, Homer and Hank Wilson, want to attract new customers, and they have asked you to help design a PowerPoint advertising campaign for them. Having graduated from your college, they are familiar with the vehicles students drive and the students' financial situations. Students can make appointments to bring their vehicles to the shop or to arrange for on-site service 24 hours a day. Road Warrior also carries a complete line of accessories, including lightbulbs, fuses, air fresheners, and air and oil filters. Many students consult with the technicians to plan for future service and to arrange financing for their repairs. The business is located in Highwood Mall, 1580 North Western Street, West Grove, Michigan. The telephone number is 555-2297. Using the techniques presented in this project, prepare a title slide and four text slides with bulleted lists for the presentation and for handouts.

4 ▶▶ Every year people suffer from more than one billion colds. While no remedy cures the runny nose and sore throat that accompany the common cold, students can reduce their chances of catching a cold and feel better when they are sick. Peter Script, the pharmacist at the drug store near campus, would like you to prepare a short PowerPoint presentation and handouts to educate customers about how to thwart the common cold. He tells you that students should get plenty of rest, drink plenty of fluids, and consume chicken soup when they feel cold symptoms. If their throats are sore, they should gargle with warm salt water or let a lozenge with menthol and a mild anesthetic dissolve slowly in their mouths. Decongestants help relieve a stuffy nose by shrinking blood vessels, but these drugs should not be taken for more than three days. Antihistamines relieve a runny nose, itching, and sneezing by having a drying effect. To avoid a cold, students should stay away from other people with colds, wash their hands frequently and keep them away from their mouths and noses, and dispose of tissues promptly. Using the techniques presented in this project, prepare a title slide and several text slides for their presentation and for handouts.

5 ▶▶ Family reunions are popular ways to unite relatives from all parts of the globe. You have successfully planned three reunions for your family, and your friends have asked you for assistance with their plans. You decide to prepare a PowerPoint presentation to share with them and use as a planning outline. As you reflect on your reunion successes, you recall that the first step is to find the right location for the event. You try to choose somewhere centrally located. You consider a city that everyone can reach by plane or by driving in a few hours, that has adequate accommodations, and a variety of tourist attractions for entertainment, sightseeing, and dining. Avoid cities with adverse weather conditions or with poor airline connections. Favorable cities are Dallas; Washington, D.C.; Las Vegas; and Reno/Lake Tahoe. Cruises and all-inclusive resorts are possibilities. Other planning tips are to use e-mail extensively to send plans to family members simultaneously and to use the Internet to find inexpensive airline tickets and explore the destination's Web site. Using the concepts and techniques presented in this project, prepare a title slide and at least three text slides for the presentation and for handouts.

Cases and Places

6 ▶▶▶ As discussed in the beginning of this project, approximately one-third of college students participate in student activities other than sports. Visit your campus student activities or Student Government offices and discover what activities are among the more popular at school. Find out which events drew the largest audiences this past semester, how much revenue was generated from these events, and what the expenses were for the college. Then, learn which activities are planned for the next semester and for next year. Who plans these events, and how are these individuals appointed or elected to these positions? Using the concepts and techniques presented in this project, prepare a presentation to inform students and staff about campus activities. Create a title slide and at least three additional slides that can be used with an overhead projector and as handouts.

7 ▶▶▶ Dry cleaning expenses can affect a student's budget. Visit two local dry cleaning establishments and obtain the costs of cleaning and pressing a shirt, a pair of pants, a jacket, and a dress. Discover if discounts are available for students and on certain days of the week. Finally, learn how students may reduce cleaning expenses by treating spots on their clothing. Then, using the concepts and techniques presented in this project, prepare a presentation to report your findings. Create a title slide and at least three additional slides that can be used with an overhead projector and as handouts.

Microsoft PowerPoint 2002

PROJECT

Using the Outline Tab and Clip Art to Create a Slide Show

OBJECTIVES

You will have mastered the material in this project when you can:

- Create a presentation from an outline
- Start and customize a new slide show
- Create a presentation using the Outline tab
- Add a slide on the Outline tab
- Create text slides with a single-level bulleted list on the Outline tab
- Create text slides with a multi-level bulleted list on the Outline tab
- Create a closing slide on the Outline tab
- Save and review a presentation
- Change the slide layout
- Insert clip art from the Microsoft Clip Organizer
- Use the Automatic Layout Options button
- Move clip art
- Change clip art size
- Add a header and footer to outline pages
- Add an animation scheme to a slide show
- Animate clip art
- Run an animated slide show
- Print a presentation outline
- E-mail a slide show from within PowerPoint

Plan, Prepare, and Practice

Formula for a Flawless Presentation

Public speaking are two words that strike panic in the hearts of millions of people the world over. The mere thought of standing in front of an audience and trying to maintain composure and focus to convey a message tops the list of absolute fears for the vast majority of people. When asked to describe their experience of public speaking, many individuals recall dry mouths, sweaty palms, queasy stomachs, and shaky knees.

Business News Now
• Sales have increased by an amazing 34%
• Employee productivity is up by 12%
• You just impressed your boss with a great presentation.
Flawless

Now, with the powerful presentation graphics capabilities of PowerPoint, the anxiety of speech-making can be somewhat eased. You have learned that this software helps you organize your thoughts and present information in an orderly, attractive manner. In this project, you will add to your current knowledge of PowerPoint by creating a presentation from an outline, changing the slide layout, and inserting and modifying clip art from the Microsoft Clip Organizer. With the abundant tools available in PowerPoint, your slide shows will have visual appeal and ample content.

While the PowerPoint slide shows help you plan your speeches, they also help your audience absorb your message. People learn most effectively when their five senses are involved. Researchers have determined that individuals remember 10 percent of what they read, 20 percent of what they hear, 30 percent of what they see, and an amazing 70 percent when they both see and hear. That is why it is important to attend class instead of copying your classmate's notes. When you see and hear your instructor deliver a lecture and write your own notes, you are apt to interpret the concepts correctly and recall this information at the ever-important final exam.

The synergy of the speech-graphics combo is recognized in a variety of venues. For example, some college administrators and instructors are requiring students to register for their communications and PowerPoint classes concurrently. The theories of structuring effective communication presentations are deep rooted. Dale Carnegie wrote *How to Win Friends and Influence People* in 1936, and the millions of people who have read that book have learned practical advice on achieving success through communication. He formed the Dale Carnegie Institute, which has taught millions of graduates worldwide the techniques of sharing ideas effectively and persuading others. Microsoft has included Carnegie's four-step process — plan, prepare, practice, and present — in the PowerPoint Help system. Dale Carnegie Training® has incorporated Microsoft PowerPoint to provide powerful presentation tips in its courses and seminars.

In the days prior to PowerPoint, slides and overhead transparencies were the domain of artists in a corporation's graphic communications department. With the influx of Microsoft Office on desktops throughout a company, however, employees from all departments now develop the slide shows.

With proper planning, preparation, practice, and the popularity of PowerPoint for organizing ideas into artful presentations, speakers today successfully deliver their messages with poise and confidence.

Microsoft PowerPoint 2002

Using the Outline Tab and Clip Art to Create a Slide Show

PROJECT

CASE PERSPECTIVE

Cruising has taken on a new meaning for college students. Instead of driving endlessly with a few friends in an old car down boring neighborhood streets, today's students sail endlessly with friends on spectacular ships to exciting destinations. They experience an adventure they will never forget as they snorkel in crystal clear waters among glimmering tropical fish, explore fascinating cities, and watch the sun set from some of the most scenic locations in the world.

Wanting to capitalize on this vacation trend, the Office of Student Activities (OSA) at your school wants to sponsor a college-wide Spring Break cruise to the Caribbean. The Student Activities director, Maria Lopez, has asked you to help with the marketing efforts. She knows you have extensive computer experience and wants you to develop a PowerPoint presentation that advertises the trip and its highlights. The slide show will give an overview of the ports of call, activities, and cruise details. You decide to add clip art and animation to increase visual interest. Then you e-mail the completed presentation to Maria.

Introduction

At some time during either your academic or business life, you probably will make a presentation. The presentation may be informative by providing detailed information about a specific topic. Other presentations may be persuasive by selling a proposal or a product to a client, convincing management to approve a new project, or influencing the board of directors to accept the new fiscal budget. As an alternative to creating your presentation in the slide pane in normal view, as you did in Project 1, PowerPoint provides an outlining feature to help you organize your thoughts. When the outline is complete, it becomes the foundation for your presentation.

Project Two — Enjoy Spring Break in the Caribbean

Project 2 uses PowerPoint to create the five-slide Spring Break presentation shown in Figures 2-1a through 2-1e. You create the presentation from the outline shown in Figure 2-2 on page 2.06.

You can create your presentation outline using the Outline tab. When you create an outline, you type all the text at one time, as if you were typing an outline on a sheet of paper. This technique differs from creating a presentation in the slide pane in normal view, where you type text as you create each individual slide and the text displays in both the slide pane and on the Outline tab. PowerPoint creates the presentation as you type the outline by evaluating the outline structure and displaying a miniature view of the slide. Regardless of how you build a presentation, PowerPoint automatically creates the three views discussed in Project 1: normal, slide sorter, and slide show.

(a) Slide 1

(b) Slide 2

(c) Slide 3

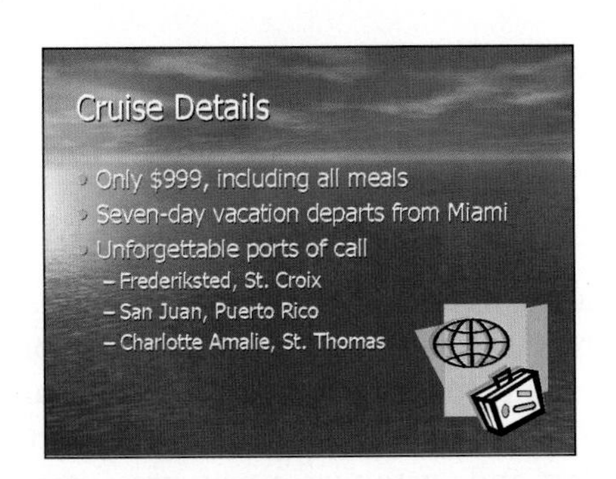

(d) Slide 4

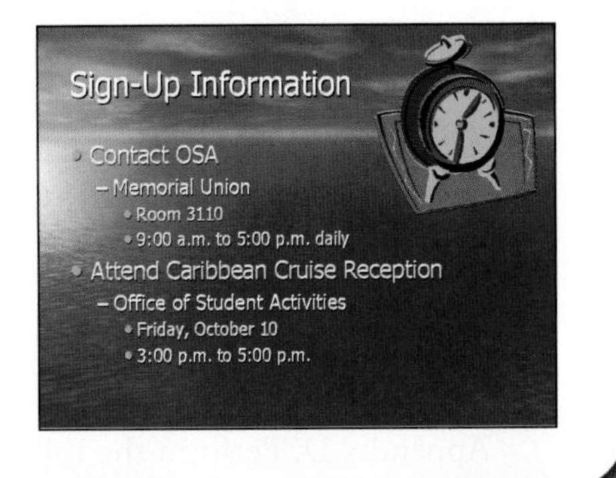

(e) Slide 5

FIGURE 2-1

The first step in creating a presentation on the Outline tab is to type a title for the outline. The **outline title** is the subject of the presentation and later becomes the presentation title text. Then, you type the remainder of the outline, indenting appropriately to establish a structure, or hierarchy. Once the outline is complete, you make your presentation more persuasive by adding **clips**, which are media files of art, animation, sound, and movies. This project uses outlining to create the presentation and clip art to support the text visually.

More About

The PowerPoint Help System

Need Help? It is no further than the Ask a Question box in the upper-right corner of the window. Click the box that contains the text, Type a question for help (Figure 2-3), type `help`, and then press the ENTER key. PowerPoint will respond with a list of items you can click to learn about obtaining help on any PowerPoint-related topic. To find out what is new in PowerPoint 2002, type `what's new in PowerPoint` in the Ask a Question box.

I. Enjoy Spring Break in the Caribbean
   A. Warm Days, Cool Activities
   B. Sponsored by
   C. The Office of Student Activities
II. Onshore Adventures
   A. Golf, play volleyball, swim, and relax
   B. Experience a submarine tour
   C. Try parasailing
   D. Explore a rainforest
III. Onboard Activities
   A. Theaters, fitness center, and stores
      1. Make new friends
      2. Dance to the hits
   B. Indoor and outdoor pools and whirlpools
IV. Cruise Details
   A. Only $999, including all meals
      1. Seven-day vacation departs from Miami
   B. Unforgettable ports of call
      1. Frederiksted, St. Croix
      2. San Juan, Puerto Rico
      3. Charlotte Amalie, St. Thomas
V. Sign-Up Information
   A. Contact OSA
      1. Memorial Union
      2. Room 3110
      3. 9:00 a.m. to 5:00 p.m. daily
   B. Attend Caribbean Cruise Reception
      1. Office of Student Activities
      2. Friday, October 10
      3. 3:00 p.m. to 5:00 p.m.

FIGURE 2-2

Start a New Presentation

Project 1 introduced you to starting a presentation document, choosing a layout, and applying a design template. The following steps summarize how to start a new presentation, choose a layout, and apply a design template. To reset your toolbars and menus so they display exactly as shown in this book, follow the steps outlined in Appendix D. Perform the following steps to start and customize a new presentation.

TO START AND CUSTOMIZE A NEW PRESENTATION

1. Click the Start button on the Windows taskbar, point to Programs on the Start menu, and then click Microsoft PowerPoint on the Programs submenu.
2. If the New Presentation task pane displays, click the Show at startup check box to remove the check mark and then click the Close button on the task pane title bar.
3. If the Language bar displays, click its Minimize button.

4 Click the Slide Design button on the Formatting toolbar. When the Slide Design task pane displays, click the down scroll arrow in the Apply a design template list, and then click the Ocean template in the Available For Use area.

5 Click the Close button in the Slide Design task pane.

6 If the Standard and Formatting toolbars display on one row, click the Toolbar Options button on the right side of either toolbar and then click Show Buttons on Two Rows on the Toolbar Options menu.

PowerPoint displays the Title Slide layout and the Ocean template on Slide 1 in normal view (Figure 2-3).

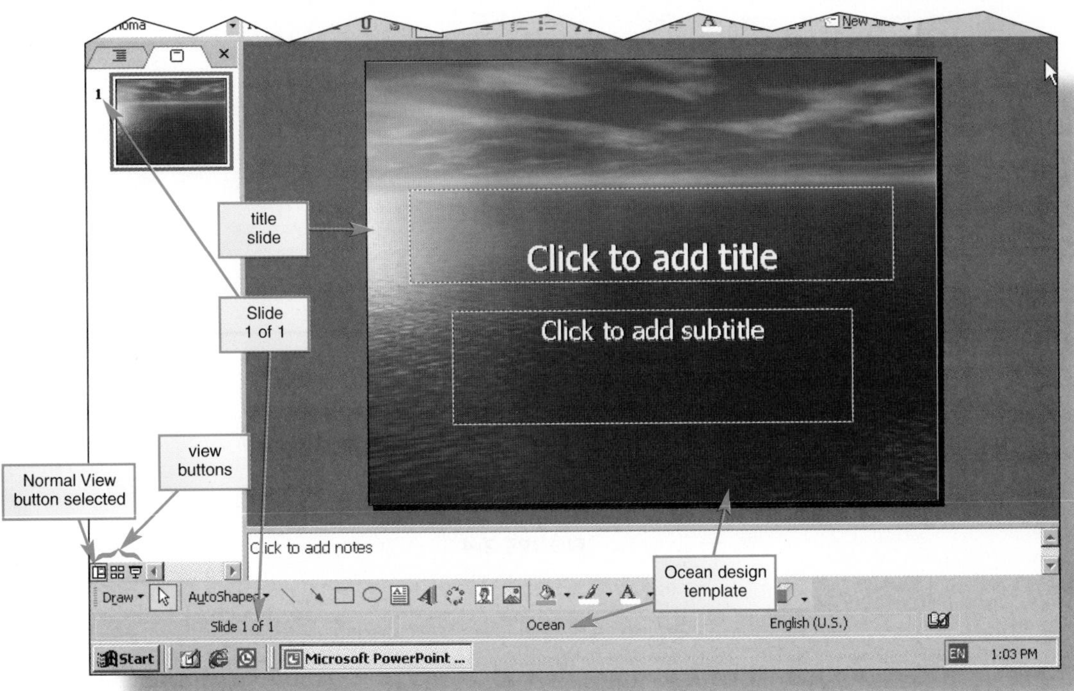

FIGURE 2-3

Using the Outline Tab

The **Outline tab** provides a quick, easy way to create a presentation. **Outlining** allows you to organize your thoughts in a structured format. An outline uses indentation to establish a **hierarchy**, which denotes levels of importance to the main topic. An outline is a summary of thoughts, presented as headings and subheadings, often used as a preliminary draft when you create a presentation.

The three panes — tabs, slide, and notes — shown in normal view also display when you click the Outline tab. The notes pane displays below the slide pane. In the tabs pane, the slide text displays along with a slide number and a slide icon. Body text is indented below the title text. Objects, such as pictures, graphs, or tables, do not display. The slide icon is blank when a slide does not contain objects. The attributes for text on the Outline tab are the same as in normal view except for color and paragraph style.

PowerPoint formats a title style and five levels of body text in an outline. The outline begins with the slide title, which is not indented. The title is the main topic of the slide. Body text supporting the main topic begins on the first level and also is not indented. If desired, additional supporting text can be added on the second through

More About

Text Levels

While PowerPoint gives you five levels of body text to use on each slide, graphic designers suggest you limit your levels to three. The details on all five levels may overwhelm audiences. If you find yourself needing more than three levels, consider combining content in one level or using two different slides.

fifth levels. Each level is indented. Levels four and five generally are used for very detailed scientific and engineering presentations. Business and sales presentations usually focus on summary information and use the first, second, and third levels.

PowerPoint initially displays in normal view when you start a new presentation. To type the outline, click the Outline tab in the tabs pane. Perform the following steps to change to the Outline tab and display the Outlining toolbar.

Steps To Change to the Outline Tab and Display the Outlining Toolbar

1 Point to the Outline tab located in the tabs pane.

The tabs pane consists of the Outline tab and the Slides tab (Figure 2-4).

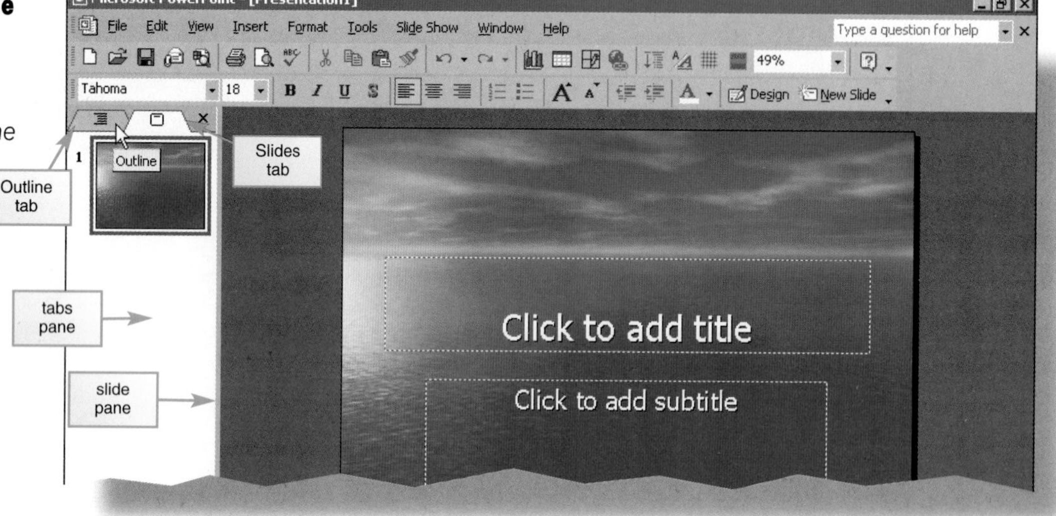

FIGURE 2-4

2 Click the Outline tab.

The Outline tab is selected. The tabs pane increases and the slide pane decreases in size.

3 Click View on the menu bar and then point to Toolbars. Point to Outlining on the Toolbars submenu.

The View menu and Toolbars submenu display (Figure 2-5).

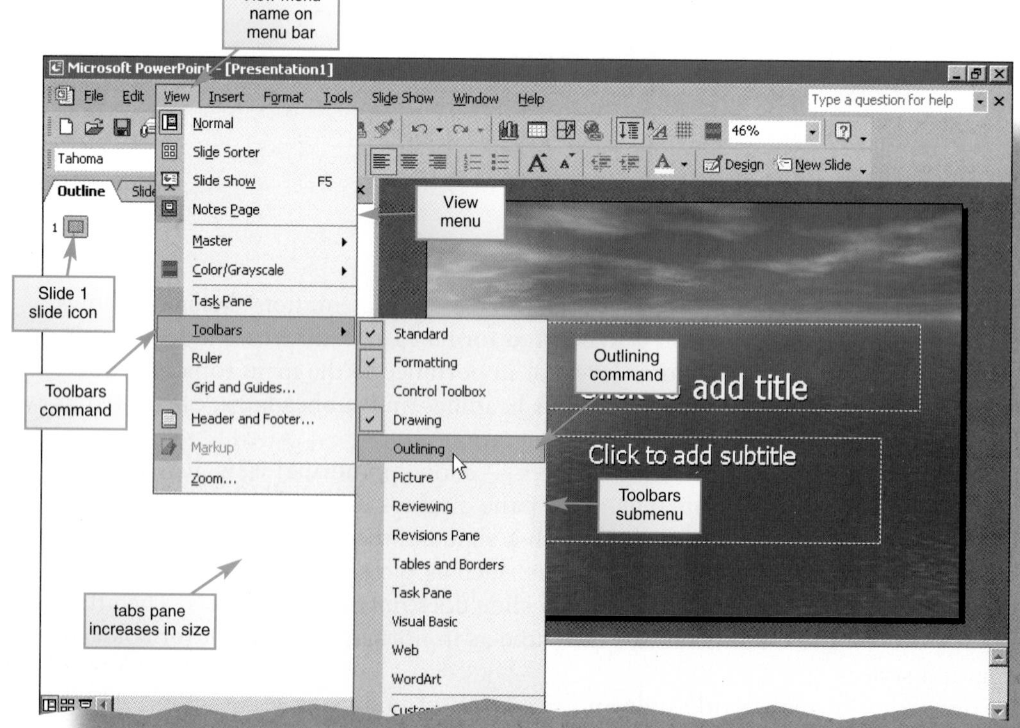

FIGURE 2-5

4 Click Outlining.

The Outlining toolbar displays (Figure 2-6).

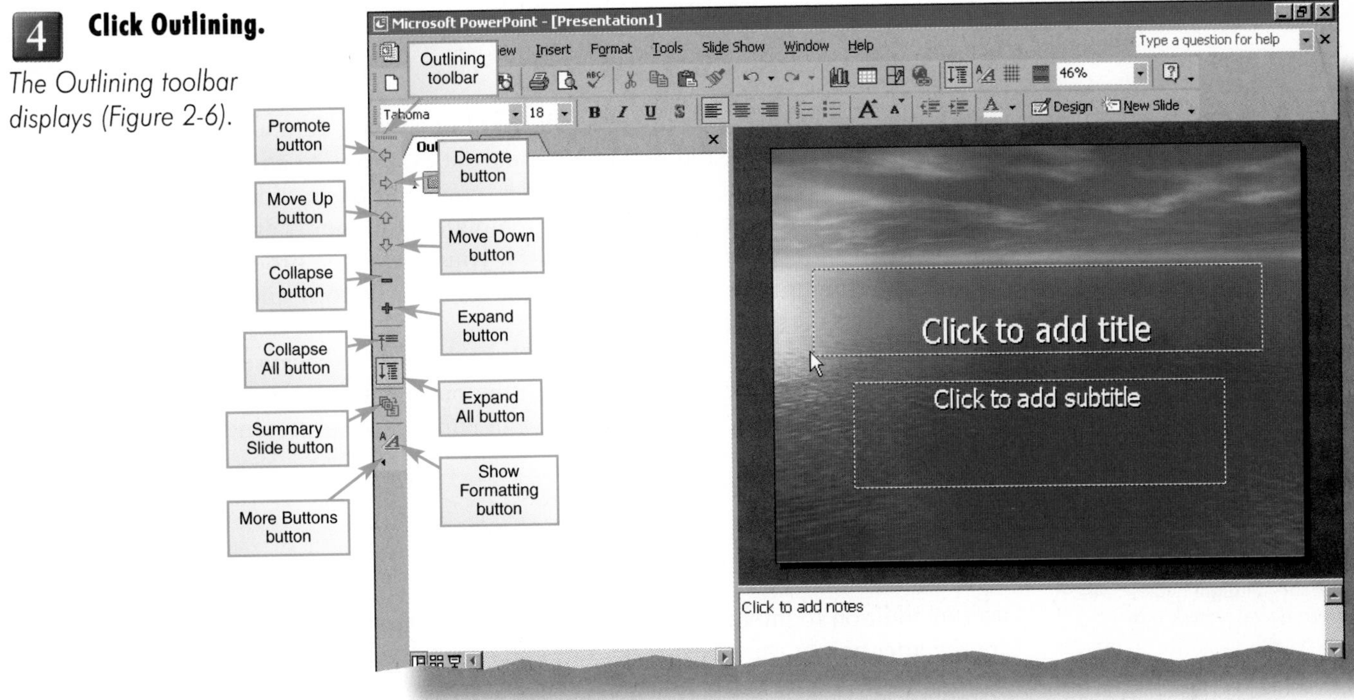

FIGURE 2-6

You can create and edit your presentation on the Outline tab. This tab also makes it easy to sequence slides and to relocate title text and body text from one slide to another. In addition to typing text to create a new presentation on the Outline tab, PowerPoint can produce slides from an outline created in Microsoft Word or another word processing application, if you save the outline as an RTF file or as a plain text file. The file extension **RTF** stands for **R**ich **T**ext **F**ormat.

Table 2-1 describes the buttons on the Outlining toolbar.

Table 2-1 Buttons on the Outlining Toolbar

BUTTON	BUTTON NAME	DESCRIPTION
	Promote	Moves the selected paragraph to the next-higher heading level (up one level, to the left).
	Demote	Moves the selected paragraph to the next-lower heading level (down one level, to the right).
	Move Up	Moves a selected paragraph and its collapsed (temporarily hidden) subordinate text above the preceding displayed paragraph.
	Move Down	Moves a selected paragraph and its collapsed (temporarily hidden) subordinate text below the following displayed paragraph.
	Collapse	Hides all but the title of selected slides. Collapsed text is represented by a gray line.
	Expand	Displays the titles and all collapsed text of selected slides.
	Collapse All	Displays only the title of each slide. Text other than the title is represented by a gray line below the title.
	Expand All	Displays the titles and all the body text for each slide.
	Summary Slide	Creates a new slide from the titles of the slides you select in slide sorter or normal view. The summary slide creates a bulleted list from the titles of the selected slides. PowerPoint inserts the summary slide in front of the first selected slide.
	Show Formatting	Shows or hides character formatting (such as bold and italic) in normal view. In slide sorter view, switches between showing all text and graphics on each slide and displaying titles only.
	Toolbar Options	Allows you to select the particular buttons you want to display on the toolbar.

Smart Quotes

When you type an apostrophe and quotation marks, PowerPoint automatically converts these symbols to "smart quotes," which also are called curly quotes. These symbols are in the shape of a dot and curved line ("") instead of a straight line (' "). If you want to use straight quotes instead, click Tools on the menu bar and then click AutoCorrect Options. Click the AutoFormat As You Type tab, and then click the "Straight quotes" with "smart quotes" check box.

Creating a Presentation on the Outline Tab

The Outline tab enables you to view title and body text, add and delete slides, drag and drop slide text, drag and drop individual slides, promote and demote text, save a presentation, print an outline, print slides, copy and paste slides or text to and from other presentations, apply a design template, and import an outline. When you **drag and drop** slide text or individual slides, you change the order of the text or the slides by selecting the text or slide you want to move or copy and then dragging the text or slide it its new location.

Developing a presentation on the Outline tab is quick because you type the text for all slides on one screen. Once you type the outline, the presentation fundamentally is complete. If you choose, you then can enhance your presentation with objects in the slide pane.

Creating a Title Slide on the Outline Tab

Recall from Project 1 that the title slide introduces the presentation to the audience. In addition to introducing the presentation, Project 2 uses the title slide to capture the attention of the students in your audience by using a design template with an image of water. Perform the following steps to create a title slide on the Outline tab.

To Create a Title Slide on the Outline Tab

1 Click the Slide 1 slide icon on the Outline tab.

The Slide 1 slide icon is selected. You also could click anywhere in the tabs pane to select the slide icon (Figure 2-7).

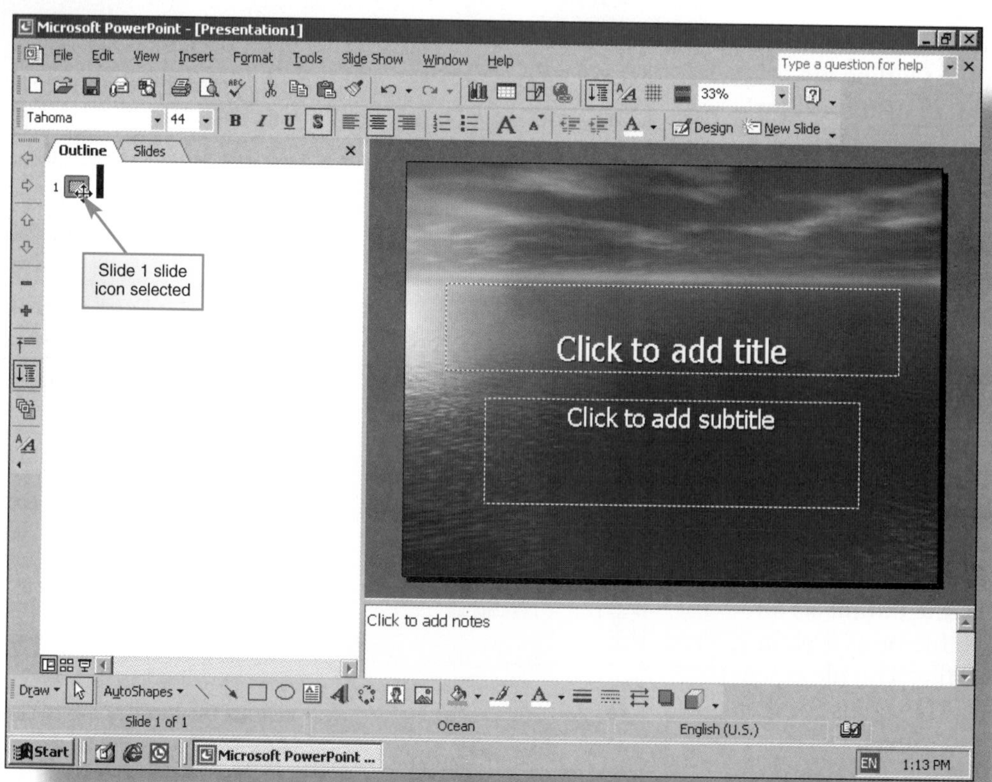

FIGURE 2-7

2 **Type** `Enjoy Spring Break` **and then press SHIFT+ENTER. Type** `in the Caribbean` **and then press the ENTER key. Point to the Demote button on the Outlining toolbar.**

The Demote ScreenTip displays (Figure 2-8). Pressing SHIFT+ENTER moves the insertion point to the next line and maintains the same first level. The insertion point is in position for typing the title for Slide 2. Pressing the ENTER key inserts a new slide.

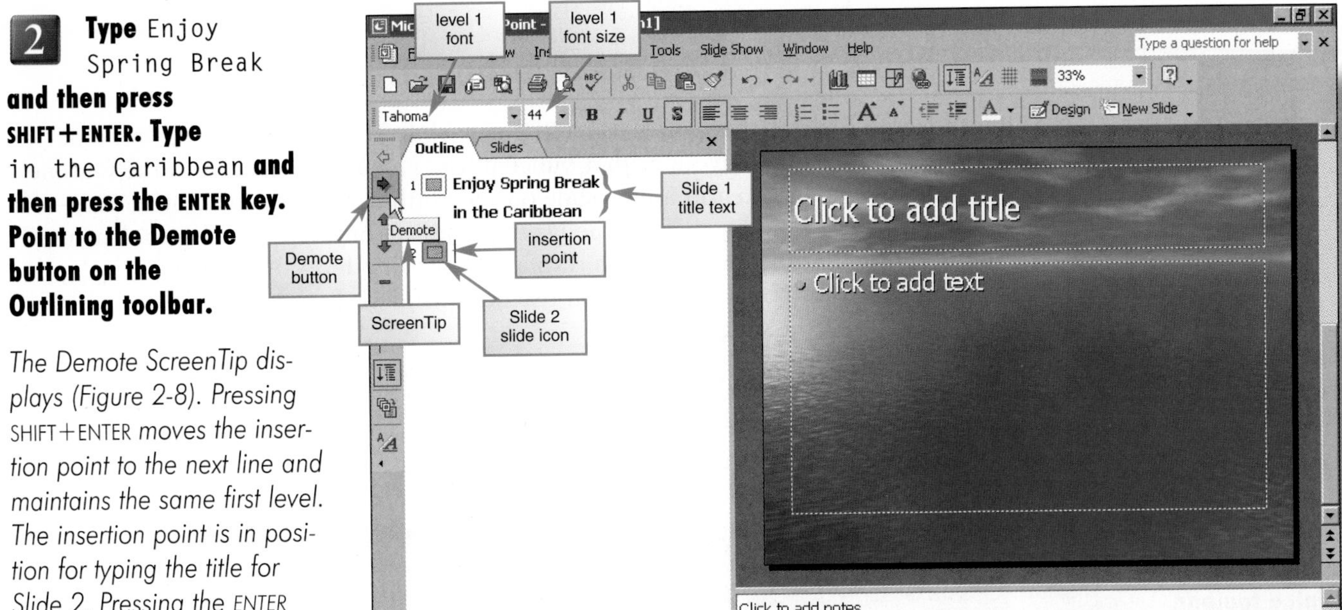

FIGURE 2-8

3 **Click the Demote button on the Outlining toolbar. Type** `Warm Days, Cool Activities` **and then press the ENTER key. Type** `Sponsored by` **and then press the ENTER key. Type** `The Office of Student Activities` **and then press the ENTER key.**

Clicking the Demote button deletes a blank slide. The two paragraphs are subtitles on the title slide (Slide 1) and demote to the second level (Figure 2-9). The second level is indented to the right below the first-level paragraph.

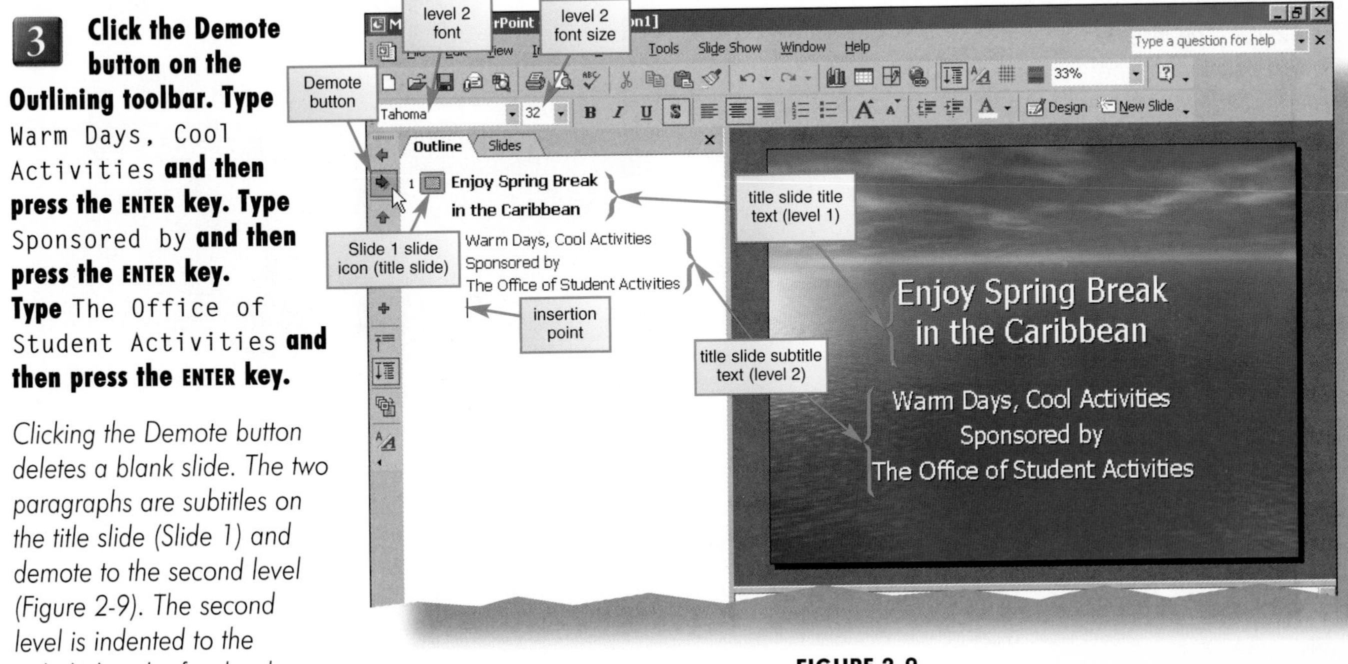

FIGURE 2-9

Other Ways

1. Type title text, press ENTER, click Demote button on Formatting toolbar, type subtitle text, press ENTER
2. Type title text, press ENTER, press TAB, type subtitle text, press ENTER

The title slide text for the Enjoy Spring Break presentation is complete. The next section explains how to add a slide on the Outline tab.

Adding a Slide on the Outline Tab

Recall from Project 1 that when you add a new slide in normal view, PowerPoint defaults to a Text slide layout with a bulleted list. This action occurs on the Outline tab as well. One way to add a new slide on the Outline tab is to promote a paragraph to the first level by clicking the Promote button on the Outlining toolbar until the insertion point or the paragraph displays at the first level. A slide icon displays when the insertion point or paragraph reaches this level. Perform the following step to add a slide on the Outline tab.

Steps To Add a Slide on the Outline Tab

1 Click the Promote button on the Outlining toolbar.

The Slide 2 slide icon displays indicating a new slide is added to the presentation (Figure 2-10). The insertion point is in position to type the title for Slide 2 at the first level.

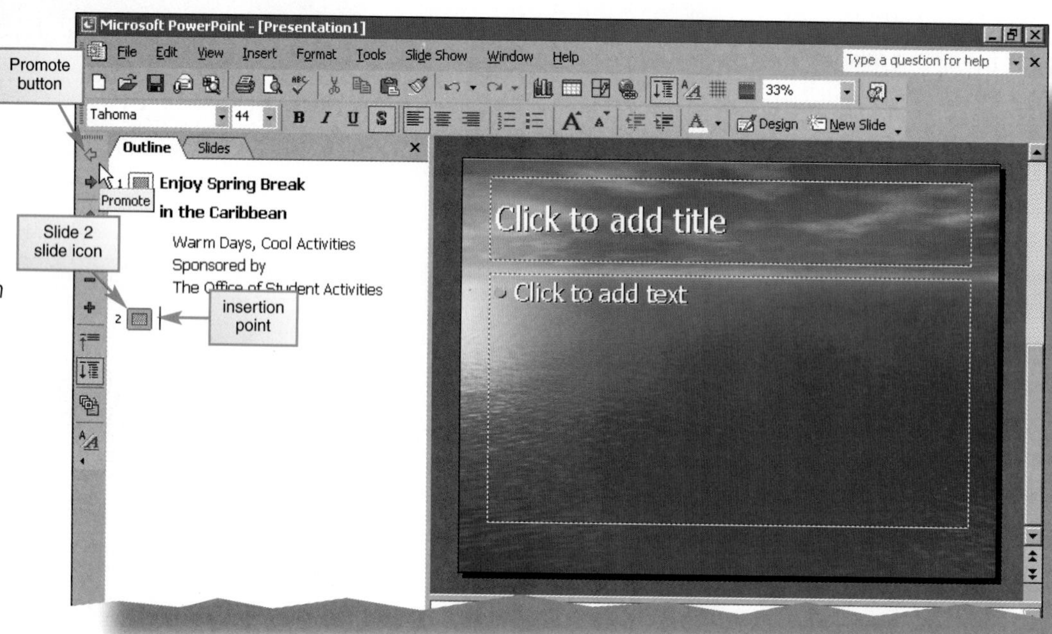

FIGURE 2-10

Other Ways

1. Click New Slide button on Standard toolbar, click OK button
2. On Insert menu click New Slide, click OK button
3. Press CTRL+M
4. Press ALT+I, press N.
5. In Voice Command mode, say "New Slide"

After you add a slide, you are ready to type the slide text. The next section explains how to create a text slide with a single-level bulleted list on the Outline tab.

Creating a Text Slide with a Single-Level Bulleted List on the Outline Tab

To create a text slide with a single-level bulleted list, you demote or promote the insertion point to the appropriate level and then type the paragraph text. Recall from Project 1 that when you demote a paragraph, PowerPoint adds a bullet to the left of each level. Depending on the design template, each level has a different bullet font. Also recall that the design template determines font attributes, including the bullet font.

Slide 2 is the first text slide in Project 2 and describes the activities students can enjoy when the cruise ship docks at various ports. Each of the four major activities displays as second-level paragraphs on the Outline tab and in the slide pane. The following steps explain how to create a text slide with a single-level bulleted list on the Outline tab.

Steps To Create a Text Slide with a Single-Level Bulleted List on the Outline Tab

1 **Type** `Onshore Adventures` **and then press the ENTER key. Click the Demote button on the Outlining toolbar to demote to the second level.**

The title for Slide 2, Onshore Adventures, displays and the insertion point is in position to type the first bulleted paragraph (Figure 2-11). A bullet displays to the left of the insertion point.

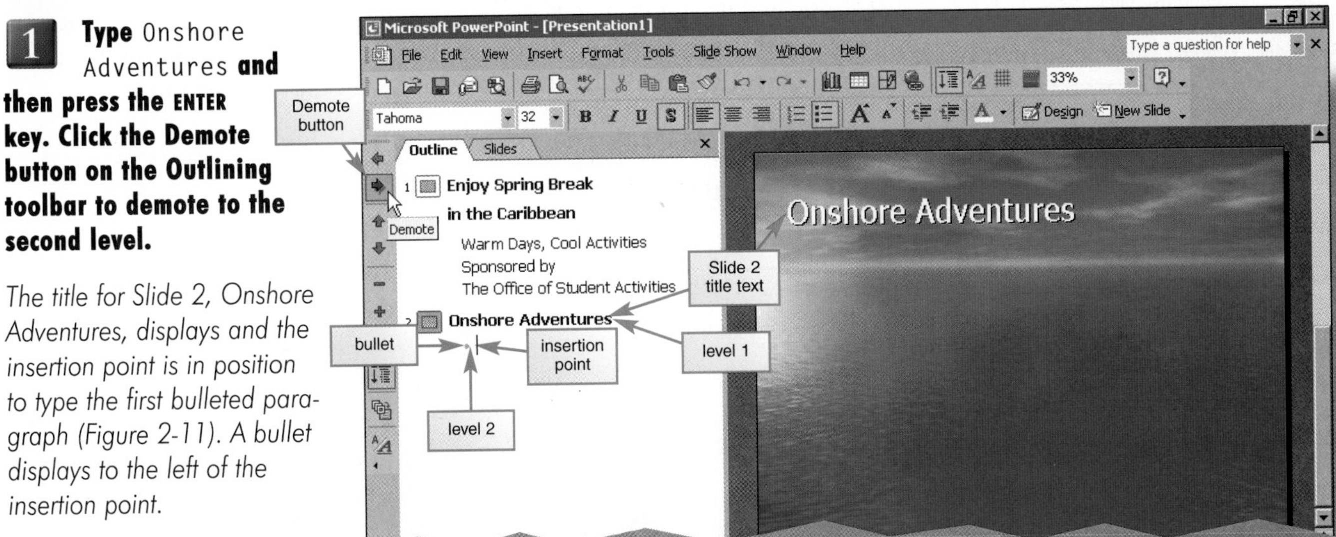

FIGURE 2-11

2 **Type** `Golf, play volleyball, swim, and relax` **and then press the ENTER key. Type** `Experience a submarine tour` **and then press the ENTER key. Type** `Try parasailing` **and then press the ENTER key. Type** `Explore a rainforest` **and then press the ENTER key.**

Slide 2 displays two levels: the title, Onshore Adventures, on the first level; and four bulleted paragraphs and the insertion point on the second level (Figure 2-12).

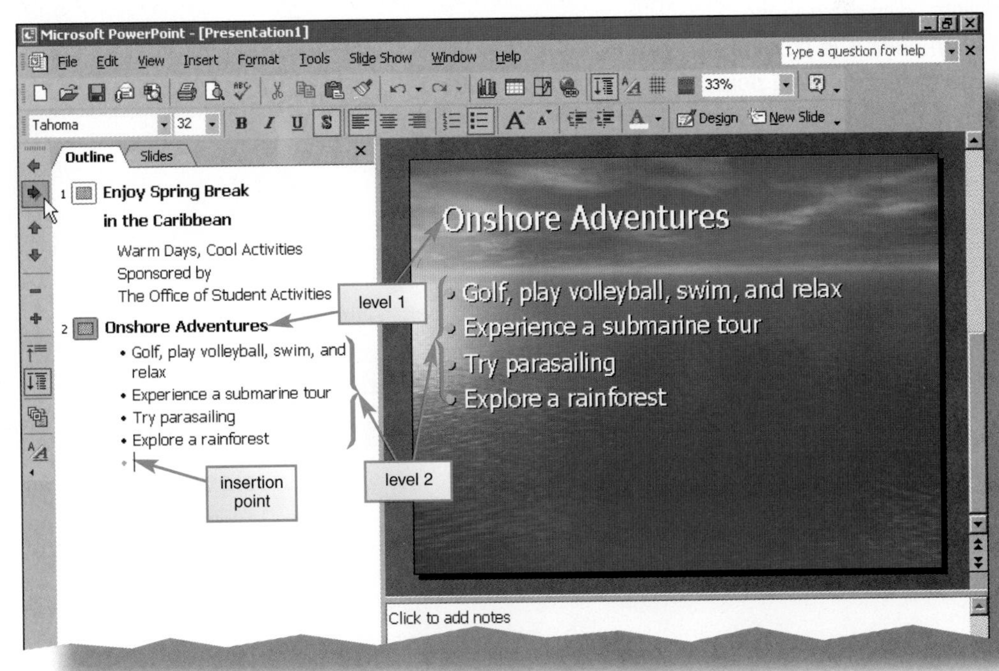

FIGURE 2-12

Slide 2 is complete. The text on this slide abides by the 7 × 7 rule. As you learned in Project 1, this rule recommends that each line should have a maximum of seven words, and each slide should have a maximum of seven lines. All slides in this slide show use the 7 × 7 rule.

Bullets

Besides using bullets, a numbered list can add emphasis to your presentation. When necessary, numbering can show ordered steps or sequences. To make a numbered list, click the Numbering button on the Formatting toolbar

Creating Text Slides with Multi-Level Bulleted Lists on the Outline Tab

The remaining three slides in the presentation contain multi-level bulleted lists. Slide 3 provides information about onboard activities, Slide 4 gives details about the cost and ports of call, and Slide 5 lists information on signing up for the cruise. It is easy and efficient to type the text for these slides on the Outline tab. Perform the following steps to create multi-level bulleted slides on the Outline tab.

Steps To Create a Text Slide with a Multi-Level Bulleted List on the Outline Tab

1 Click the Promote button on the Outlining toolbar. Type `Onboard Activities` **and then press the ENTER key. Click the Demote button on the Outlining toolbar to demote to the second level.**

The title for Slide 3, Onboard Activities, displays and the insertion point is in position to type the first bulleted paragraph (Figure 2-13). A bullet displays to the left of the insertion point in the second level.

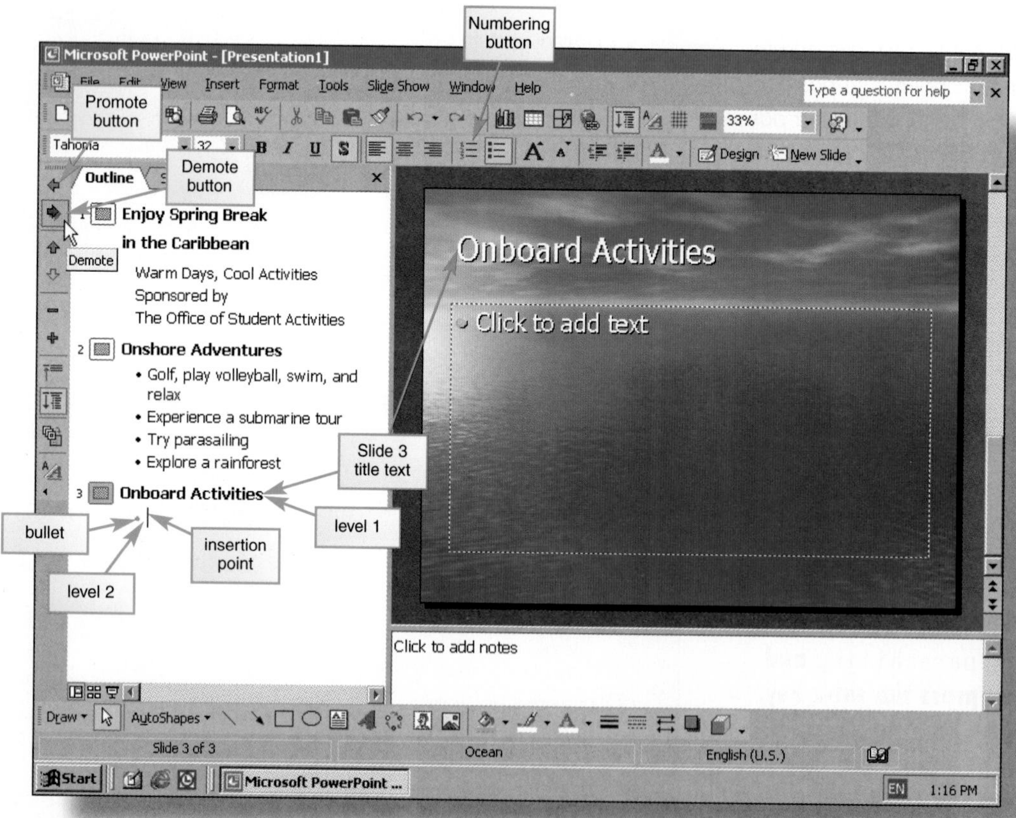

FIGURE 2-13

2 **Type** Theaters, fitness center, and stores **and then press the ENTER key. Click the Demote button on the Outlining toolbar to demote to the third level. Type** Make new friends **and then press the ENTER key. Type** Dance to the hits **and then press the ENTER key. Click the Promote button on the Outlining toolbar to promote to the second level. Type** Indoor and outdoor pools and whirlpools **and then press the ENTER key.**

The text for Slide 3 is complete (Figure 2-14). Pressing the ENTER key begins a new paragraph at the same level as the previous paragraph.

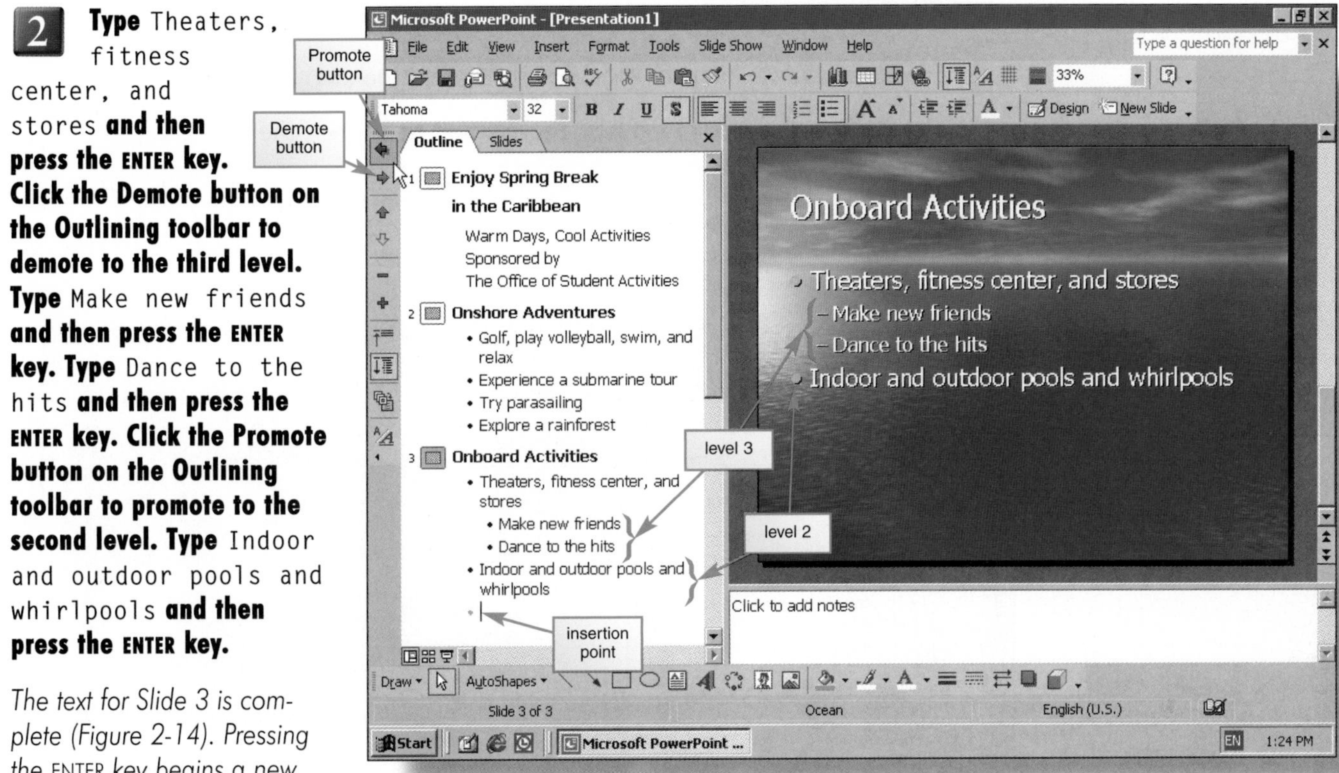

FIGURE 2-14

Entering text on the Outline tab is a quick and efficient process. You can view all the text you type in the outline in the tabs pane to check organization. The last two slides in the presentation give specific information about the cruise itinerary and registration process.

> **More About**
>
> **The Pointing Device**
>
> You can expand or collapse an outline by pointing to a heading and then holding down the SHIFT key as you rotate the wheel on the Microsoft IntelliMouse® pointing device forward or backward.

Creating a Second Text Slide with a Multi-Level Bulleted List

The next slide, Slide 4, provides details about the cost, duration, and itinerary for the cruise. Perform the following steps to create this slide.

TO CREATE A SECOND TEXT SLIDE WITH A MULTI-LEVEL BULLETED LIST

1. Click the Promote button on the Outlining toolbar so Slide 4 is added after Slide 3.
2. Type `Cruise Details` and then press the ENTER key.
3. Click the Demote button on the Outlining toolbar to demote to the second level.
4. Type `Only $999, including all meals` and then press the ENTER key.
5. Type `Seven-day vacation departs from Miami` and then press the ENTER key.
6. Type `Unforgettable ports of call` and then press the ENTER key.
7. Click the Demote button to demote to the third level.

8 Type `Frederiksted, St. Croix` and then press the ENTER key.

9 Type `San Juan, Puerto Rico` and then press the ENTER key.

10 Type `Charlotte Amalie, St. Thomas` and then press the ENTER key.

The completed Slide 4 displays (Figure 2-15). Red wavy lines display below the words Frederiksted and Amalie to indicate those words are not found in the Microsoft main dictionary or open custom dictionaries.

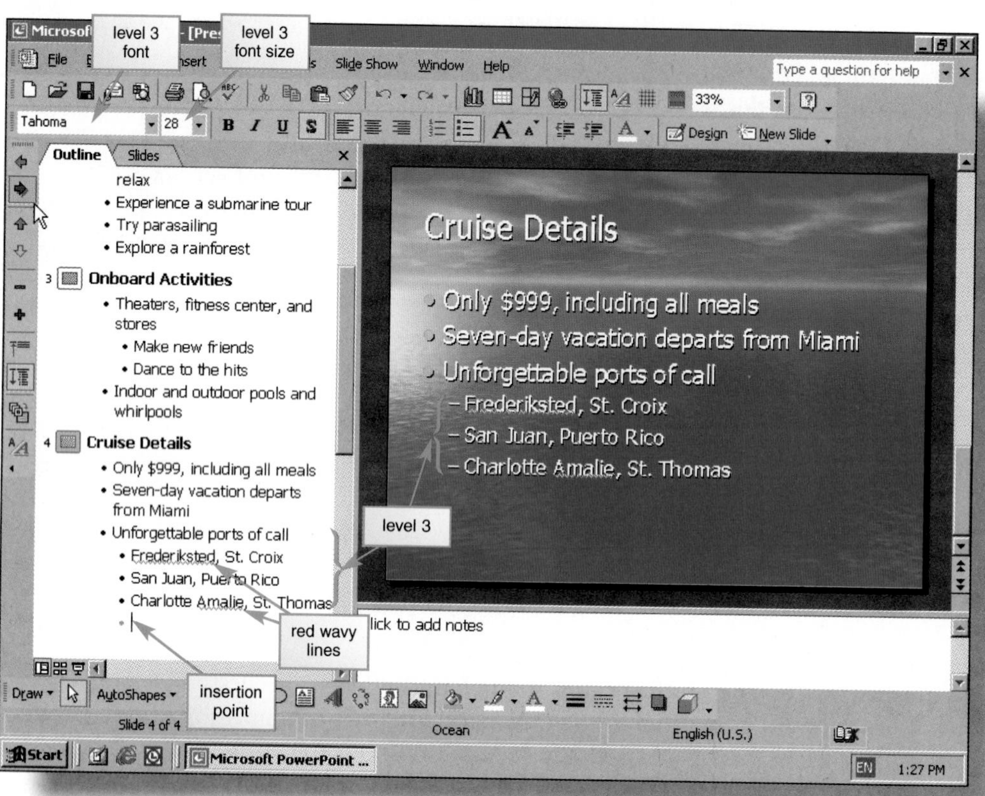

FIGURE 2-15

Creating a Closing Slide on the Outline Tab

Closing Slides

When faced with constructing a new slide show, you may find it helpful to start by designing your closing slide first. Knowing how you want the slide show to end helps you focus on reaching this conclusion. You can create each slide in the presentation with this goal in mind.

The last slide in a presentation is the closing slide. A **closing slide** gracefully ends a presentation. Often used during a question and answer session, the closing slide usually remains on the screen to reinforce the message delivered during the presentation. Professional speakers design the closing slide with one or more of these methods.

1. List important information. Tell the audience what to do next.
2. Provide a memorable illustration or example to make a point.
3. Appeal to emotions. Remind the audience to take action or accept responsibility.
4. Summarize the main point of the presentation.
5. Cite a quotation that directly relates to the main point of the presentation. This technique is most effective if the presentation started with a quotation.

The closing slide in this project uses a multi-level bulleted list to provide contact information for the Office of Student Activities and for a reception held for students desiring additional details. Perform the following steps to create this closing slide.

TO CREATE A CLOSING SLIDE ON THE OUTLINE TAB

1. Click the Promote button on the Outlining toolbar two times to add Slide 5 after Slide 4. Type `Sign-Up Information` and then press the ENTER key.
2. Click the Demote button on the Outlining toolbar to demote to the second level. Type `Contact OSA` and then press the ENTER key.
3. Click the Demote button to demote to the third level. Type `Memorial Union` and then press the ENTER key.
4. Click the Demote button to demote to the fourth level. Type `Room 3110` and then press the ENTER key. Type `9:00 a.m. to 5:00 p.m. daily` and then press the ENTER key.
5. Click the Promote button two times to promote to the second level. Type `Attend Caribbean Cruise Reception` then press the ENTER key.
6. Click the Demote button. Type `Office of Student Activities` and then press the ENTER key. Click the Demote button and then type `Friday, October 10` and press the ENTER key. Type `3:00 p.m. to 5:00 p.m.` but do not press the ENTER key.

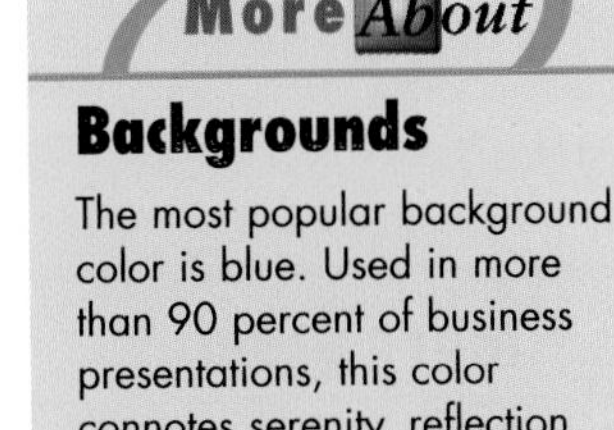

Backgrounds

The most popular background color is blue. Used in more than 90 percent of business presentations, this color connotes serenity, reflection, and proficiency.

The completed Slide 5 displays (Figure 2-16).

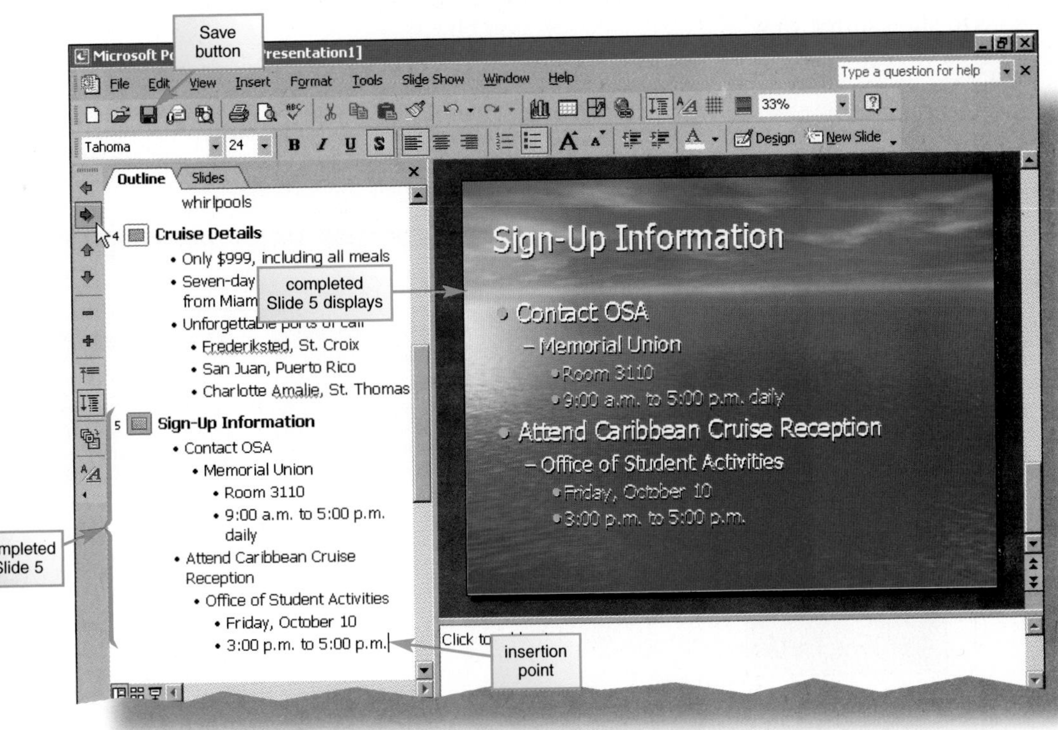

FIGURE 2-16

The outline now is complete and you should save the presentation. The next section explains how to save the presentation.

Saving a Presentation

Recall from Project 1 that it is wise to save your presentation frequently. With all the text for your presentation created, save the presentation using the steps on the next page.

TO SAVE A PRESENTATION

1. Insert a formatted floppy disk in drive A and then click the Save button on the Standard toolbar.
2. Click the Save in box arrow. Click 3½ Floppy (A:) in the Save in list.
3. Click the Save button in the Save As dialog box.

The presentation is saved on the floppy disk in drive A with the file name Enjoy Spring Break. PowerPoint uses the first text line in a presentation as the default file name. The file name displays on the title bar.

> **More About**
>
> **Quick Reference**
>
> For a table that lists how to complete tasks covered in this book using the mouse, menu, shortcut menu, and keyboard, see the Quick Reference summary at the back of this book or visit the Shelly Cashman Series Office XP Web page (scsite.com/offxp/qr.htm) and then click Microsoft PowerPoint 2002.

Reviewing a Presentation in Slide Sorter View

In Project 1, you displayed slides in slide show view to evaluate the presentation. Slide show view, however, restricts your evaluation to one slide at a time. The Outline tab is best for quickly reviewing all the text for a presentation. Recall from Project 1 that slide sorter view allows you to look at several slides at one time, which is why it is the best view to use to evaluate a presentation for content, organization, and overall appearance. Perform the following step to change from the Outline tab to slide sorter view.

Steps To Change the View to Slide Sorter View

1 Click the Slide Sorter View button at the lower left of the PowerPoint window.

PowerPoint displays the presentation in slide sorter view (Figure 2-17). Slide 5 is selected because it was the current slide on the Outline tab. The Slide Sorter View button is selected.

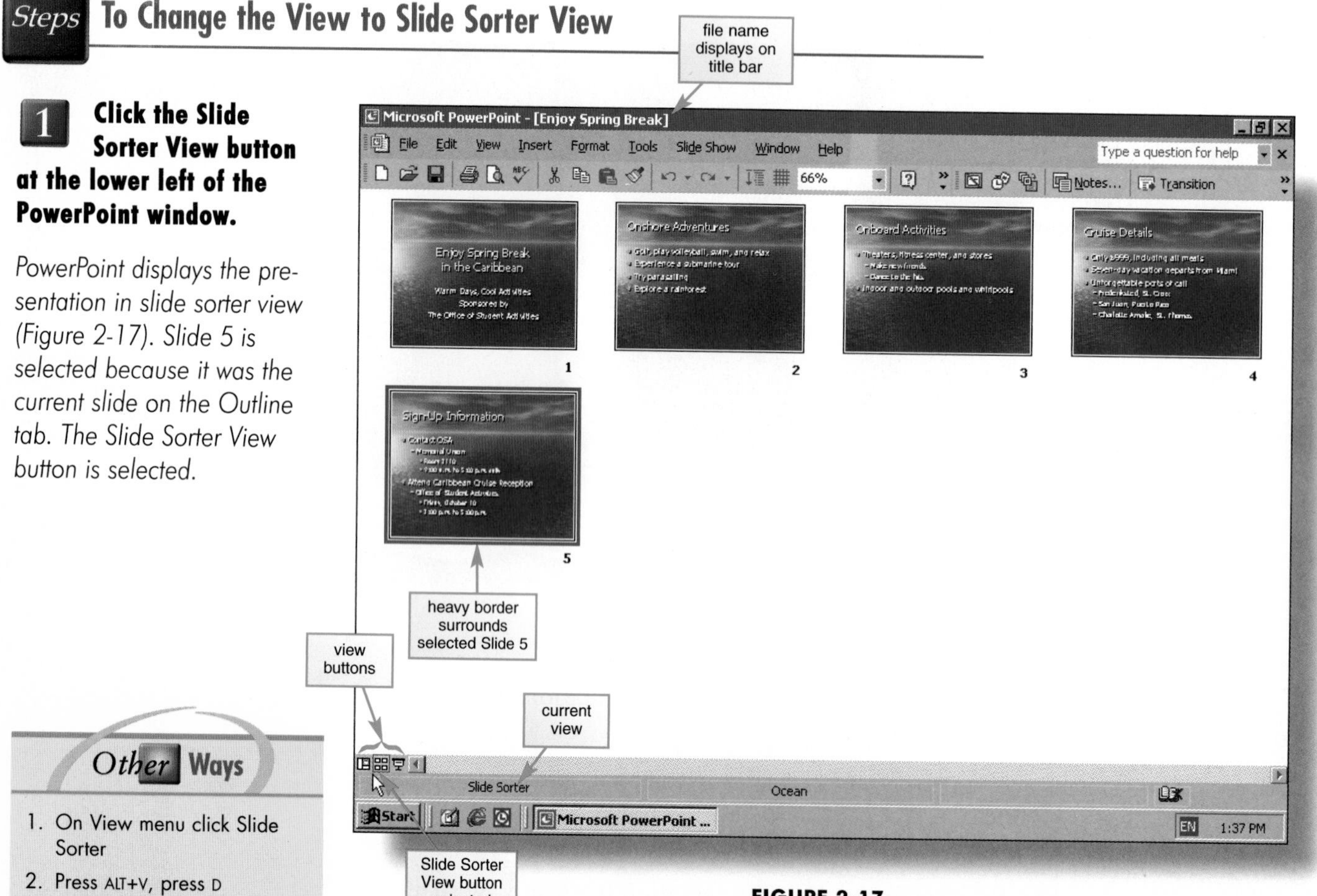

FIGURE 2-17

> **Other Ways**
>
> 1. On View menu click Slide Sorter
> 2. Press ALT+V, press D
> 3. In Voice Command mode, say "Slide Sorter"

You can review the five slides in this presentation all in one window. Notice the slides have a significant amount of space and look plain. These observations indicate a need to add visual interest to the slides by using clips. The next several sections explain how to improve the presentation by changing slide layouts and adding clip art.

You can make changes to text in normal view and on the Outline tab. It is best, however, to change the view to normal view when altering the slide layouts so you can see the result of your changes. Perform the following steps to change the view from slide sorter view to normal view.

More About

Slide Space

Some blank space on a slide can be advantageous. The absence of text, called white space, helps the viewer focus attention on the presenter. Do not be afraid to leave some white space on your slide to give your text and visual elements some breathing room.

To Change the View to Normal View

1 Click the Slide 2 slide thumbnail. Point to the Normal View button at the lower left of the PowerPoint window.

Slide 2 is selected, as indicated by the thick blue border around that slide (Figure 2-18).

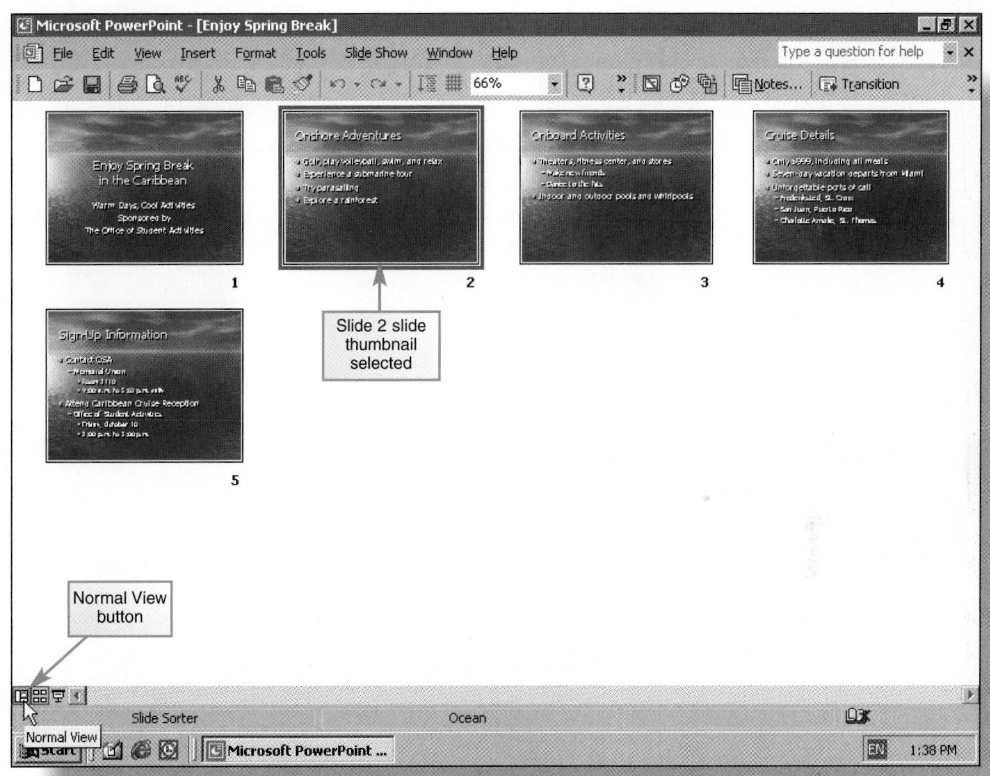

FIGURE 2-18

2 Click the Normal View button. Point to the Slides tab in the tabs pane.

The Normal View button is selected at the lower left of the PowerPoint window. The Slide 2 slide icon is selected in the tabs pane, and Slide 2 displays in the slide pane (Figure 2-19).

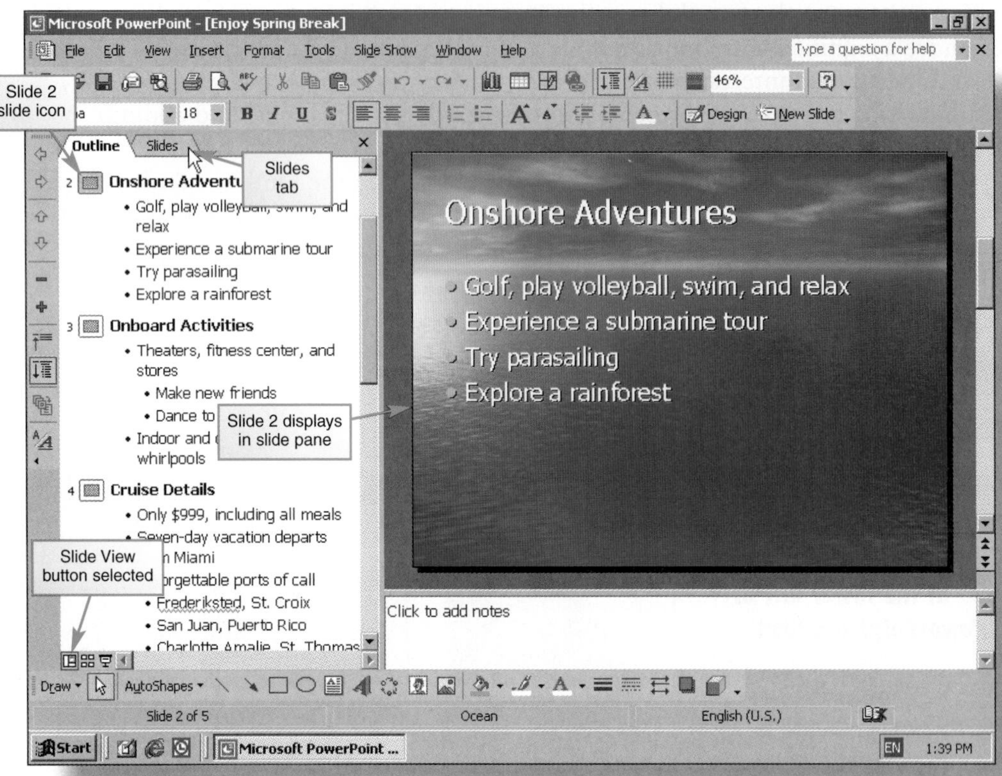

FIGURE 2-19

3 Click the Slides tab.

The tabs pane reduces in size. Slide thumbnails of the five slides display (Figure 2-20).

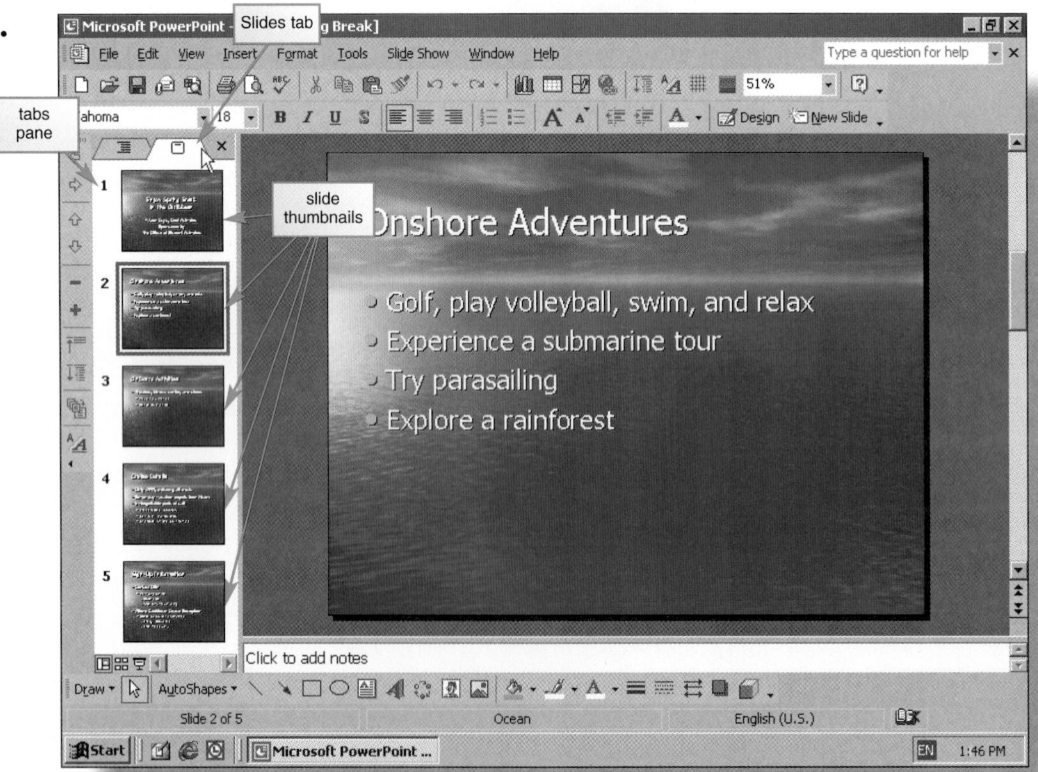

FIGURE 2-20

Switching between slide sorter view and normal view helps you review your presentation and assess whether the slides have an attractive design and adequate content.

Changing Slide Layout

When you developed this presentation, PowerPoint applied the Title Slide layout for Slide 1 and the Title and Text layout for the other four slides in the presentation. These layouts are the default styles. A **layout** specifies the arrangement of placeholders on a slide. These placeholders are arranged in various configurations and can contain text, such as the slide title or a bulleted list, or they can contain content, such as clips, pictures, charts, tables, and shapes. The placement of the text, in relationship to content, depends on the slide layout. The content placeholders may be to the right or left of the text, above the text, or below the text. You can specify a particular slide layout when you add a new slide to a presentation or after you have created the slide.

Using the **Slide Layout task pane**, you can choose a slide layout. The layouts in this task pane are arranged in four areas: Text Layouts, Content Layouts, Text and Content Layouts, and Other Layouts. The two layouts you have used in this project Title Slide and Title and Text — are included in the Text Layouts area along with the Title Only and Title and 2-Column Text layouts. The Content Layouts area contains a blank slide and a variety of placeholder groupings for charts, tables, clip art, pictures, diagrams, and media clips. The Text and Content Layouts have placeholders for a title, a bulleted list, and content. The Other Layouts area has layouts with placeholders for a title and one object, such as clip art, charts, media clips, tables, organization charts, and charts. Some layouts have one, two, three, or four content placeholders.

When you change the layout of a slide, PowerPoint retains the text and objects and repositions them into the appropriate placeholders. Using slide layouts eliminates the need to resize objects and the font size because PowerPoint automatically sizes the objects and text to fit the placeholders. If the objects are in **landscape orientation**, meaning their width is greater than their height, PowerPoint sizes them to the width of the placeholders. If the objects are in **portrait orientation**, meaning their height is greater than their width, PowerPoint sizes them to the height of the placeholder.

Adding clips to Slides 2 and 3 requires two steps. First, change the slide layout to Title, Text, and 2 Content or to Title, Content and Text. Then, insert clip art into each of the two content placeholders. Perform the steps on the next page to change the slide layout on Slide 2 from Title and Text to Title, Text, and 2 Content.

More About

Slide Colors

One in twelve males has color perception difficulties, with the most common problem being distinguishing red and green. For more information on this color deficiency, visit the PowerPoint 2002 Project 2 More About Web page (scsite.com/pp2002/more .htm) and then click Slide Colors.

More About

Customizing Buttons

Customize your toolbars by using buttons that are larger than the ones normally displayed. To enlarge the buttons, click Tools on the menu bar and then click Customize. Click the Options tab and then click the Large icons check box. This setting will affect all of your Microsoft Office programs.

To Change the Slide Layout to Title, Text, and 2 Content

1 Click Format on the menu bar and then point to Slide Layout (Figure 2-21).

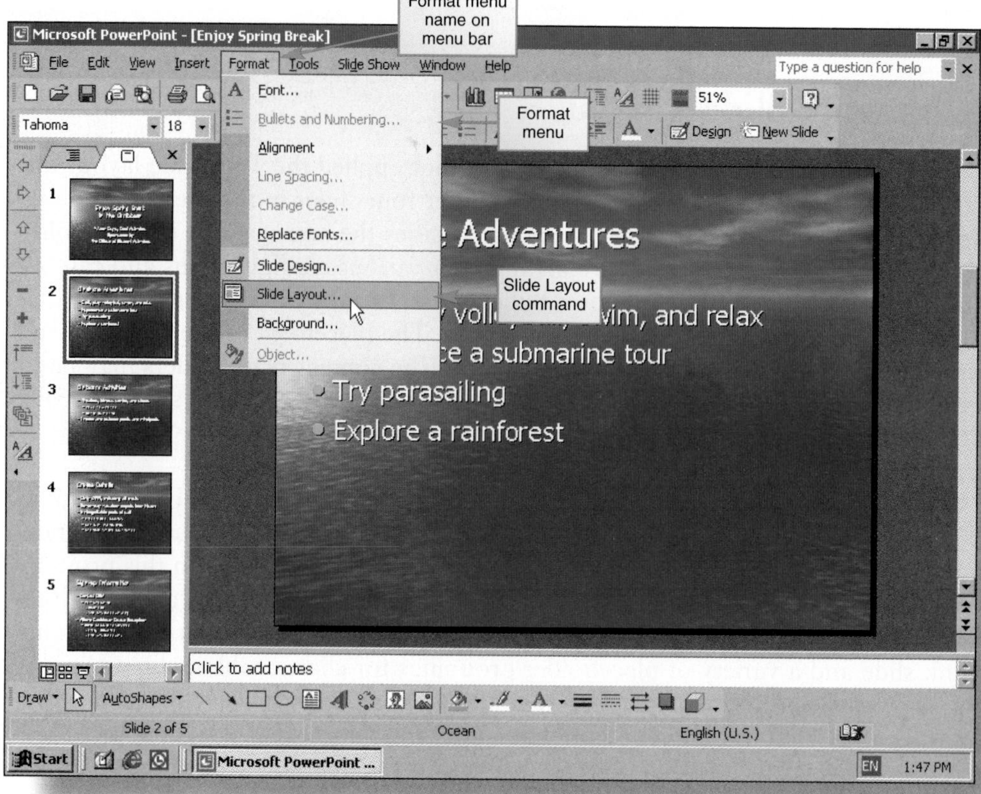

FIGURE 2-21

2 Click Slide Layout. Point to the Title, Text, and 2 Content layout in the Text and Content Layouts area.

The Slide Layout task pane displays (Figure 2-22). The Title, Text, and 2 Content layout is selected, as indicated by the blue box around the template, the ScreenTip, and the arrow button on the right side.

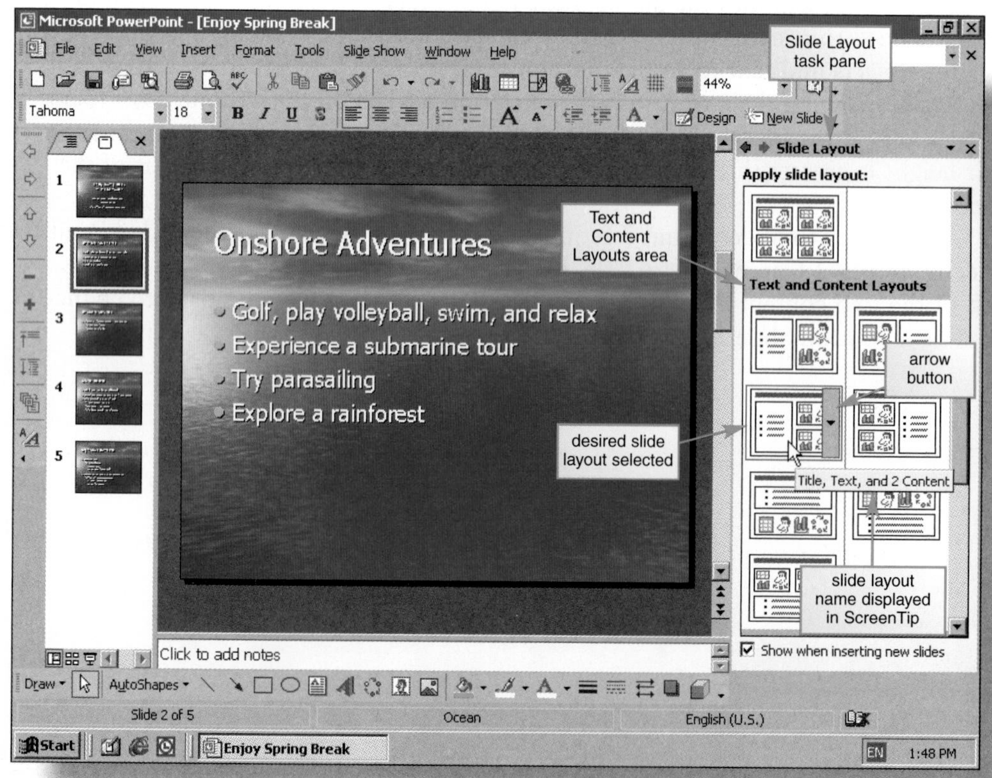

FIGURE 2-22

3 **Click Title, Text, and 2 Content. Point to the Close button in the Slide Layout task pane.**

The layout is applied to Slide 2 (Figure 2-23). PowerPoint moves the text placeholder containing the bulleted list to the left side of the slide and automatically resizes the text. The two content placeholders on the right side of the slide displays the message, Click icon to add content.

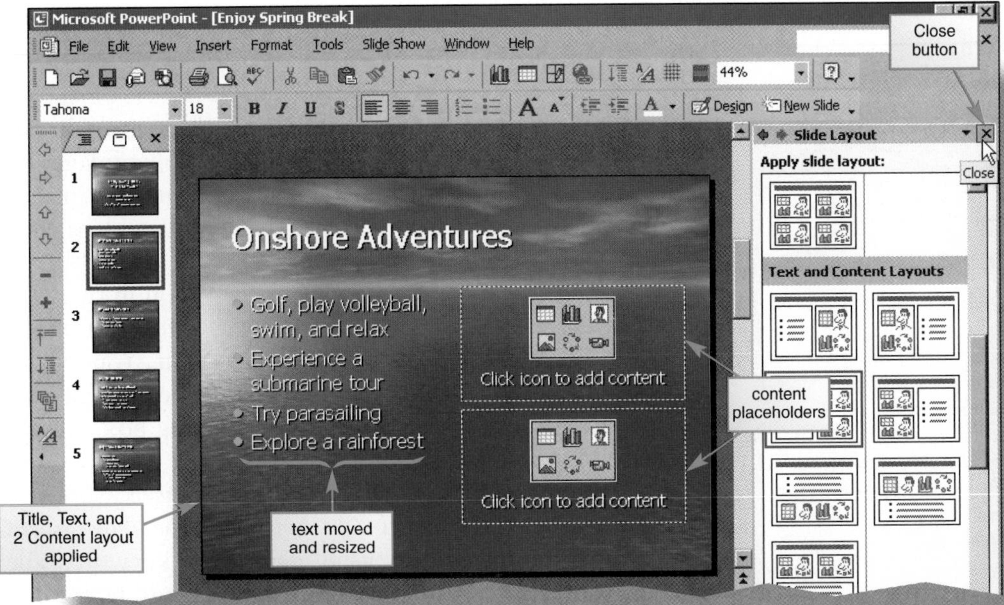

FIGURE 2-23

4 **Click the Close button.**

Slide 2 displays in normal view with the new slide layout applied (Figure 2-24).

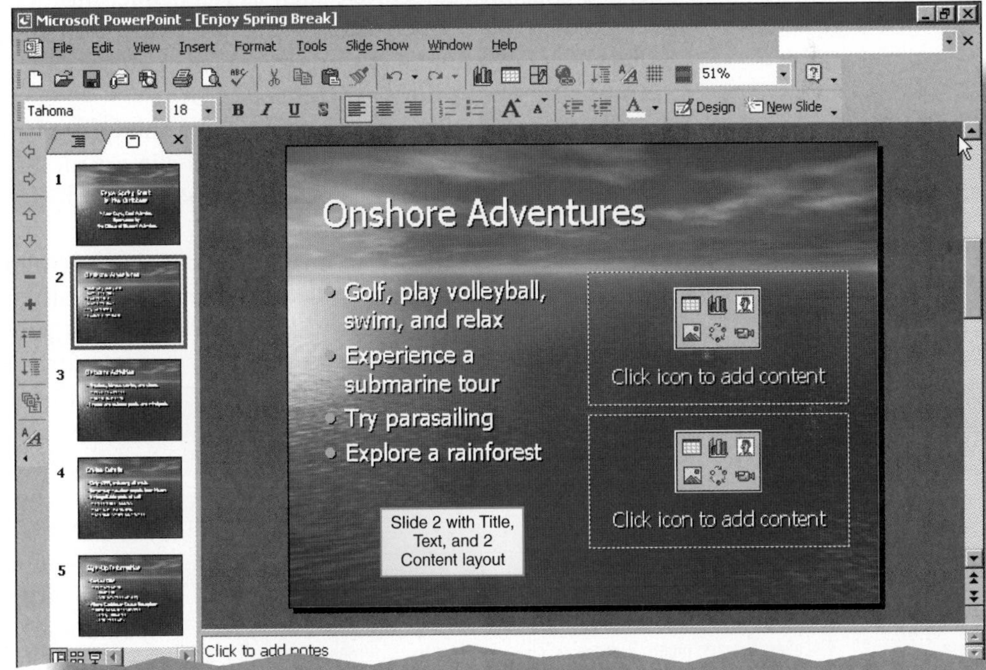

FIGURE 2-24

PowerPoint reduced the second-level text in the Slide 2 text placeholder from a font size of 32 point to 18 point so all the words fit into the placeholder.

Other Ways

1. Right-click slide anywhere except text placeholders, click Slide Layout on shortcut menu, double-click desired slide layout
2. Press ALT+O, press L, press ARROW keys to select desired slide layout, press ENTER
3. In Voice Command mode, say "Format, Slide Layout, Title Text and Two Content, Close"

Adding Clip Art to a Slide

Clip art helps the visual appeal of the Enjoy Spring Break slide show and offers a quick way to add professional looking graphic images to a presentation without creating the images yourself. This art is contained in the **Microsoft Clip Organizer**, a collection of drawings, photographs, sounds, videos, and other media files shared with Microsoft Office applications.

You can add clip art to your presentation in two ways. One way is by selecting one of the slide layouts that includes a content placeholder with instructions to open the Microsoft Clip Organizer to add content. You will add art to Slides 2 and 3 in this manner. Double-clicking a button in the content placeholder activates the instructions to open the Select Picture dialog box, which allows you to enter keywords to search for clips.

The second method is by clicking the Insert Clip Art button on the Drawing toolbar to open the Insert Clip Art task pane. The **Insert Clip Art task pane** allows you to search for clips by using descriptive keywords, file names, media file formats, and clip collections. Specific file formats could be for clip art, photographs, movies, and sounds. Clips are organized in hierarchical **clip collections**, which combine topic-related clips into categories, such as Academic, Business, and Technology. You also can create your own collections for frequently used clips. You will insert clip art into Slides 4 and 5 using this process. You then will arrange the clips on the slides without using a placeholder for content.

Table 2-2 shows four categories from the Office Collections in the Microsoft Clip Organizer and keywords of various clip art files in those categories. Clip art images have one or more keywords associated with various entities, activities, labels, and emotions. In most instances, the keywords give the name of the clip and related categories. For example, an image of a cow in the Animals category has the keywords animals, cattle, cows, dairies, farms, and Holsteins. You can enter these keywords in the Search text box to find clips when you know one of the words associated with the image. Otherwise, you may find it necessary to scroll through several categories to find an appropriate clip.

Depending on the installation of the Microsoft Clip Organizer on your computer, you may not have the clip art used in this project. Contact your instructor if you are missing clips when you perform the following steps. If you have an open connection to the Internet, clips from the Microsoft Web site will display automatically as the result of your search results.

More About

Legal Use of Clips

If you use clips in your slide show, be certain you have the legal right to use these files. Read the copyright notices that accompany the clips and are posted on Web sites. The owners of these images and files often ask you to give them credit for using their work, which may be accomplished by stating where you obtained the images.

Table 2-2 Microsoft Clip Organizer Category and Keyword Examples

CATEGORY	CLIP ART KEYWORDS
Academic	Books; knowledge; information; schools; school buses; apple for the teacher; professors
Business	Computers; inspirations; ideas; currencies; board meetings; conferences; teamwork; profits
Nature	Lakes; flowers; plants; seasons; wildlife; weather; trees; sunshine; rivers; leaves
Technology	Computers; diskettes; microchips; cellular telephones; e-commerce; office equipment; data exchanges

Inserting Clip Art into a Content Placeholder

With the Title, Text, and 2 Content layout applied to Slide 2, you insert clip art into the content placeholder. Perform the following steps to insert clip art of a golfer into the content placeholder on Slide 2.

Steps To Insert Clip Art into a Content Placeholder

1 Point to the Insert Clip Art button in the top content placeholder.

The Insert Clip Art button is selected (Figure 2-25). A ScreenTip describes its function.

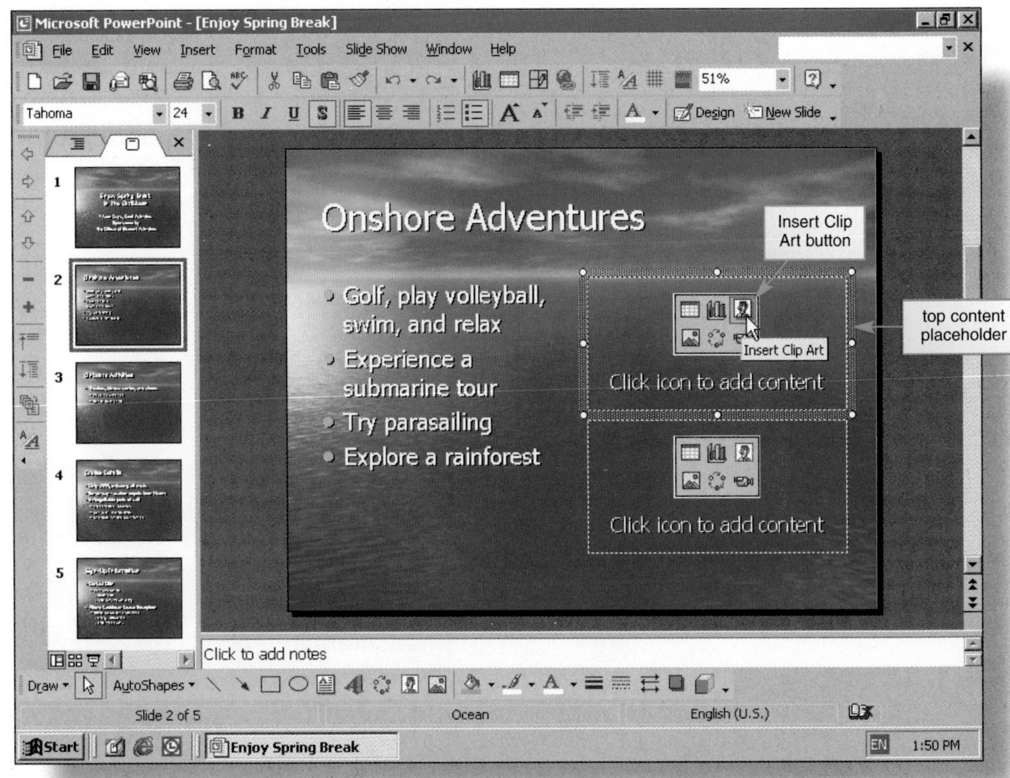

FIGURE 2-25

2 Click the Insert Clip Art button. Type `golf` **in the Search text text box and then point to the Search button.**

The Select Picture dialog box displays (Figure 2-26). The clips displayed on your computer may vary.

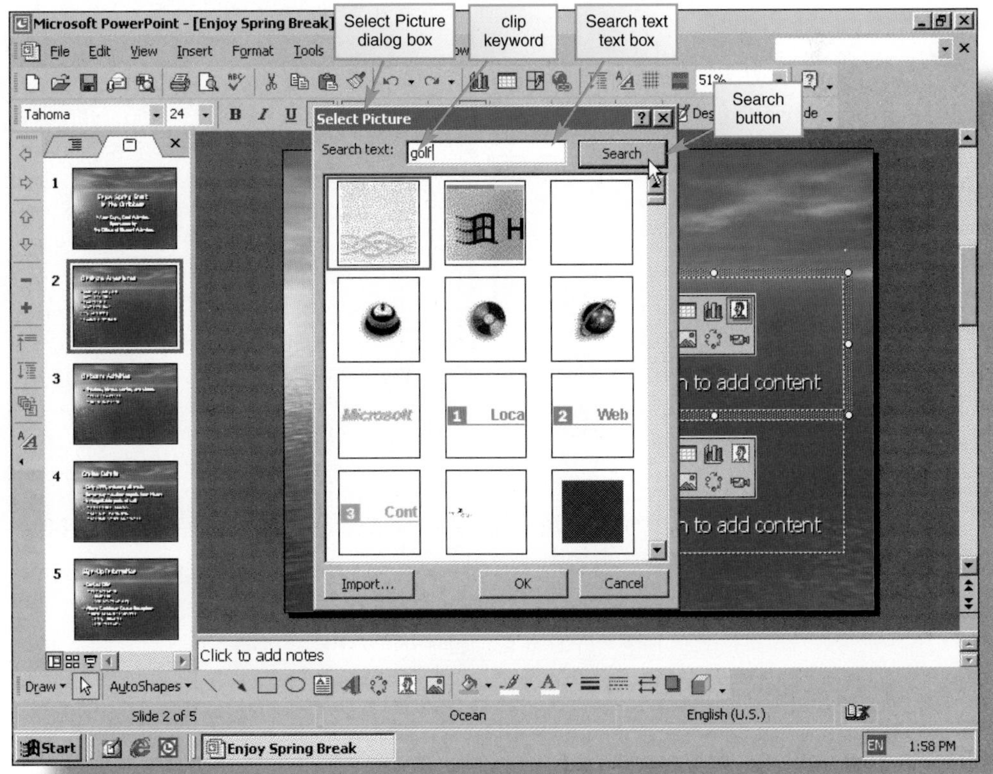

FIGURE 2-26

3 Click the Search button. If necessary, click an appropriate clip and then point to the OK button.

The Microsoft Clip Organizer searches for and displays all pictures having the keyword golf (Figure 2-27). The desired clip of a female golfer displays with a blue box around it. Your clips may be different depending on the clips installed on your computer and if you have an open connection to the Internet, in which case you may need to obtain an appropriate clip from the Internet.

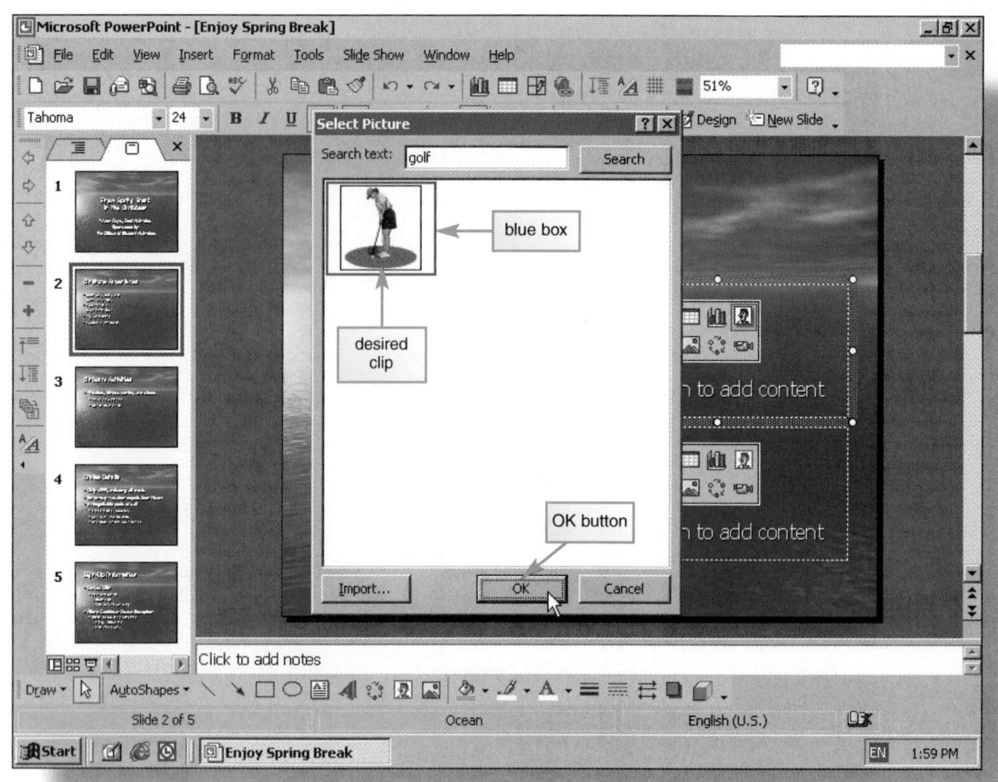

FIGURE 2-27

4 Click the OK button. If the Picture toolbar displays, click the Close button on the Picture toolbar.

The selected clip is inserted into the top content placeholder on Slide 2 (Figure 2-28). PowerPoint sizes the clip automatically to fit the placeholder.

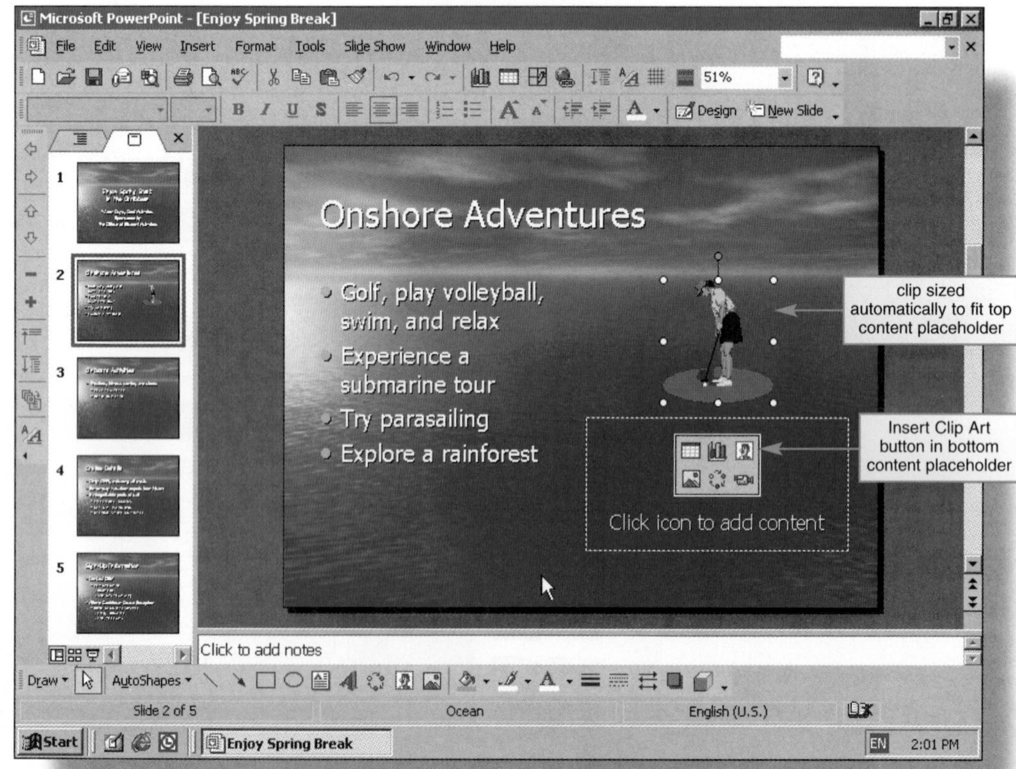

FIGURE 2-28

Inserting a Second Clip into a Slide

Another clip on Slide 2 is required to fill the bottom content placeholder. This clip should be the image of a volleyball. Perform the following steps to insert the volleyball into the bottom placeholder on Slide 2.

TO INSERT A SECOND CLIP INTO A SLIDE

1. Click the Insert Clip Art button in the bottom content placeholder.
2. Type `volleyball` in the Search text text box and then click the Search button.
3. If necessary, scroll down the list to display the desired clip of a volleyball and net, click the clip to select it, and then click the OK button.

The selected clip is inserted into the bottom content placeholder on Slide 2 (Figure 2-29). PowerPoint automatically sizes the clip to fit the placeholder.

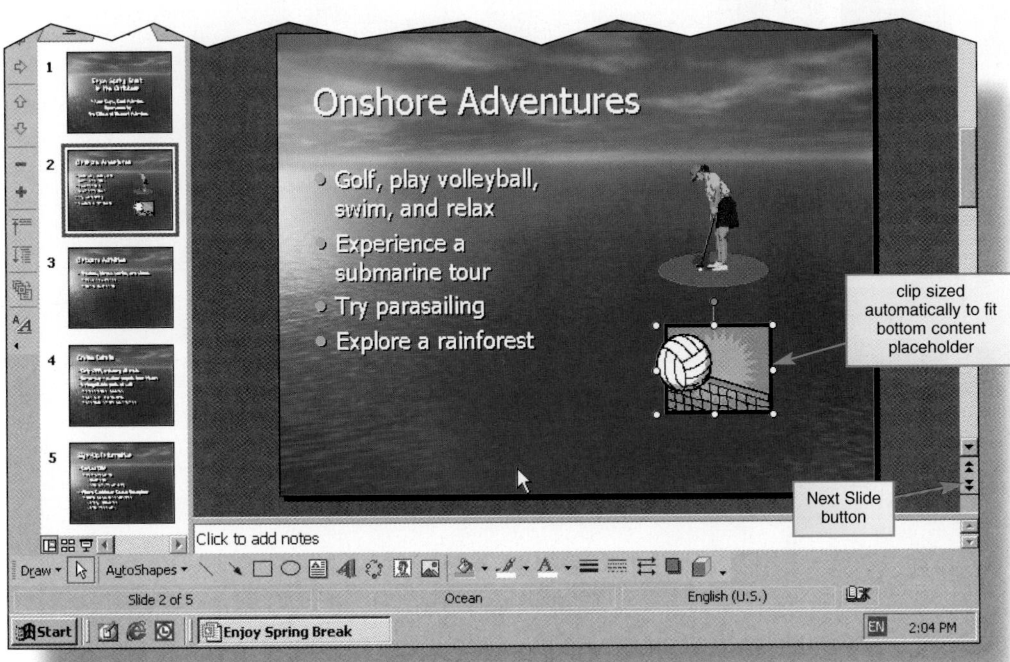

FIGURE 2-29

More About

Design

Consider designing a presentation in black and white and then adding color to emphasize particular areas on the slide. Graphic artists suggest starting with black letters on a white background to concentrate on basic design principles, such as balance, contrast, rhythm, and harmony.

Slide 2 is complete. The next step is to add other clip to Slide 3. This slide uses the Title, Content and Text slide layout so the clip displays on the left side of the slide and the bulleted list displays on the right side. Perform the following steps to change the slide layout and then add clip art to Slide 3.

TO CHANGE THE SLIDE LAYOUT TO TITLE, CONTENT AND TEXT AND INSERT CLIP ART

1. Click the Next Slide button on the vertical scroll bar to display Slide 3.
2. Click Format on the menu bar and then click Slide Layout.
3. Scroll to display the Title, Content and Text slide layout located in the Text and Content Layouts area of the Slide Layout task pane.
4. Click the Title, Content and Text slide layout and then click the Close button in the Slide Layout task pane.

5 Click the Insert Clip Art button in the content placeholder. Type `party` in the Search text text box and then click the Search button.

6 If necessary, scroll down the list to display the desired party clip and then click the clip to select it. Click the OK button.

The selected party clip is inserted into the content placeholder on Slide 3 (Figure 2-30). The slide has the Title, Content and Text slide layout.

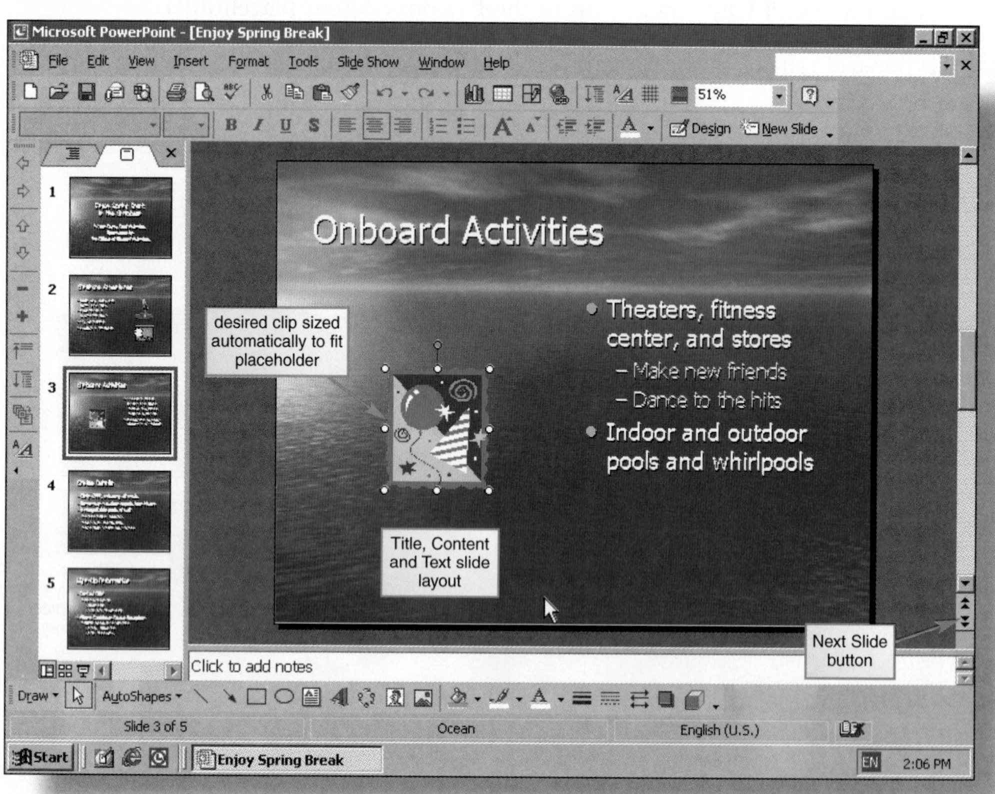

FIGURE 2-30

Changing Clip Art

Be certain you have the legal right to use and modify a clip art image. For example, you cannot use photographs and illustrations to damage people's reputations by representing them falsely, such as inserting a photograph of someone on the FBI's Top Ten Most Wanted list. In addition, corporate logos are designed using specific colors and shapes and often cannot be altered.

Slide 3 is complete. Your next step is to add a clip to Slide 4 without changing the slide layout.

Inserting Clip Art into a Slide without a Content Placeholder

PowerPoint does not require you to use a content placeholder to add clips to a slide. You can insert clips on any slide regardless of its slide layout. On Slides 2 and 3, you added clips that enhanced the message in the text. Recall that the slide layout on Slide 4 is Title and Text. Because this layout does not contain a content placeholder, you can use the Insert Clip Art button on the Drawing toolbar to start the Microsoft Clip Organizer. The clip for which you are searching has a globe and luggage. A few of its keywords are baggage, Earth, global, and globes. Perform the following steps to insert this clip into a slide that does not have a content placeholder.

Steps To Insert Clip Art into a Slide without a Content Placeholder

1 Click the Next Slide button on the vertical scroll bar to display Slide 4. Click Tools on the menu bar and then click AutoCorrect Options. When the AutoCorrect dialog box displays, if necessary, click the AutoFormat As You Type tab. Click Automatic layout for inserted objects in the Apply as you work area if a check mark does not display.

2 Click the Insert Clip Art button on the Drawing toolbar. If the Add Clips to Organizer dialog box displays asking if you want to catalog media files, click Don't show this message again, or, if you want to catalog later, click the Later button.

The Insert Clip Art task pane displays (Figure 2-31).

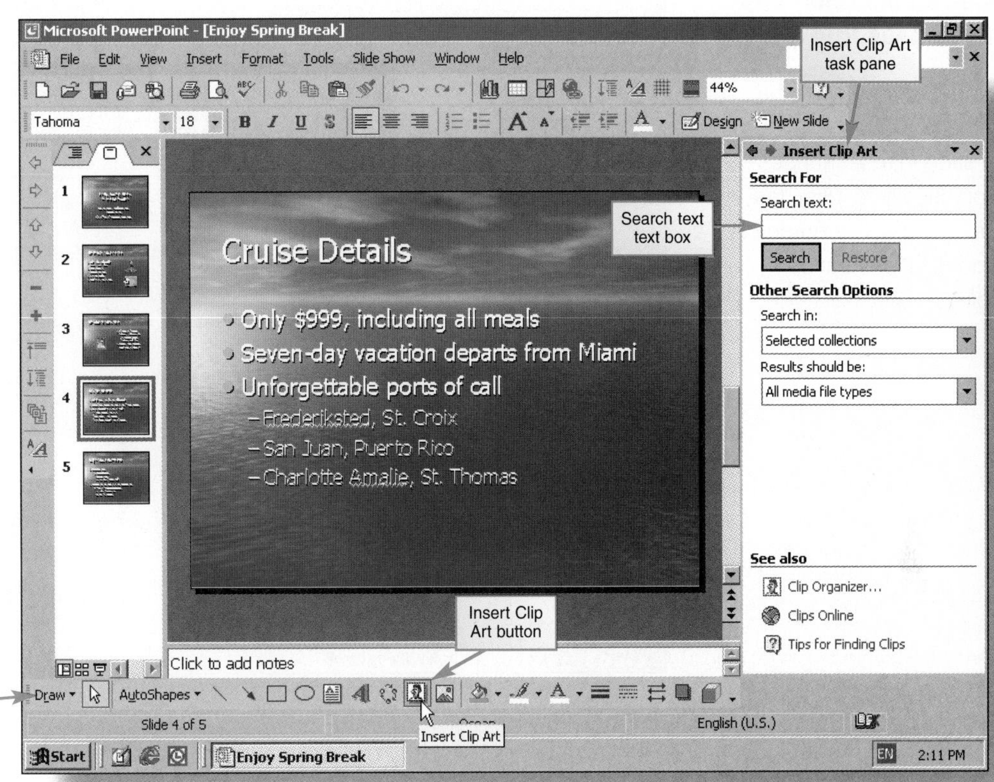

FIGURE 2-31

3 Click the Search text text box. Type `earth` **and then press the ENTER key. If necessary, scroll to display the desired clip of a globe and luggage. Point to this image.**

The clip of a globe and piece of luggage displays with other clips sharing the earth keyword (Figure 2-32). Your clips may be different. The clip's keywords, size in pixels (260 × 247), file size (10 KB), and file type (WMF) display.

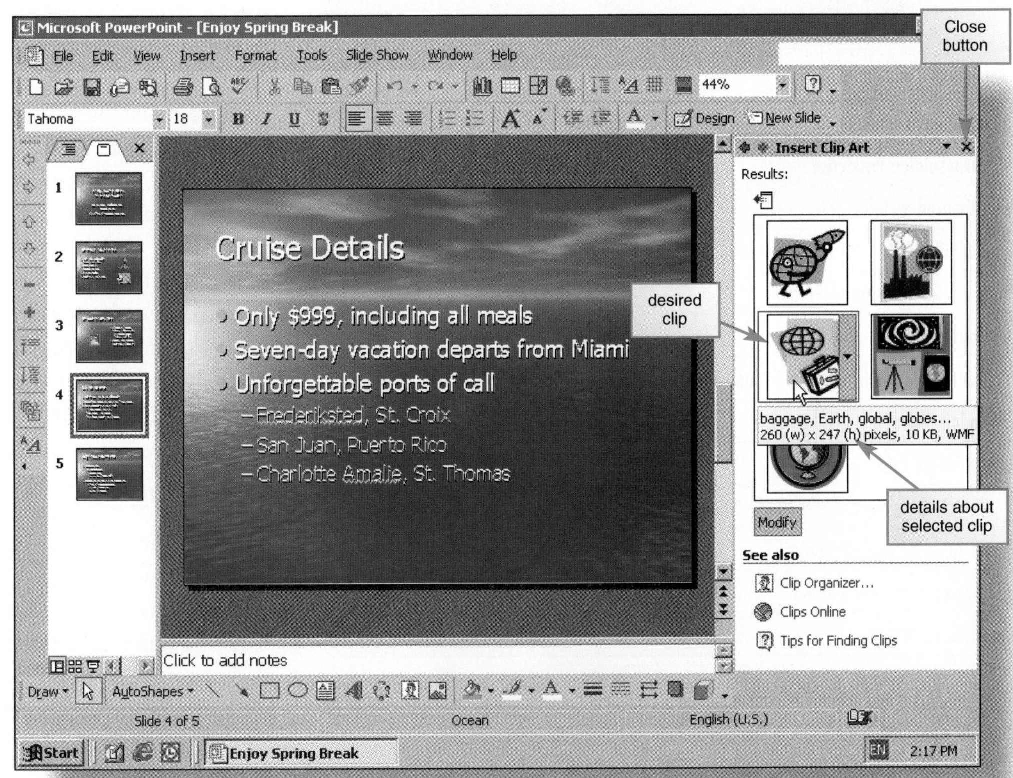

FIGURE 2-32

4 Click the desired clip. Click the Close button on the Insert Clip Art task pane title bar.

PowerPoint inserts the clip into Slide 4 (Figure 2-33). The slide layout changes automatically to Title, Text, and Content. The Automatic Layout Options button displays.

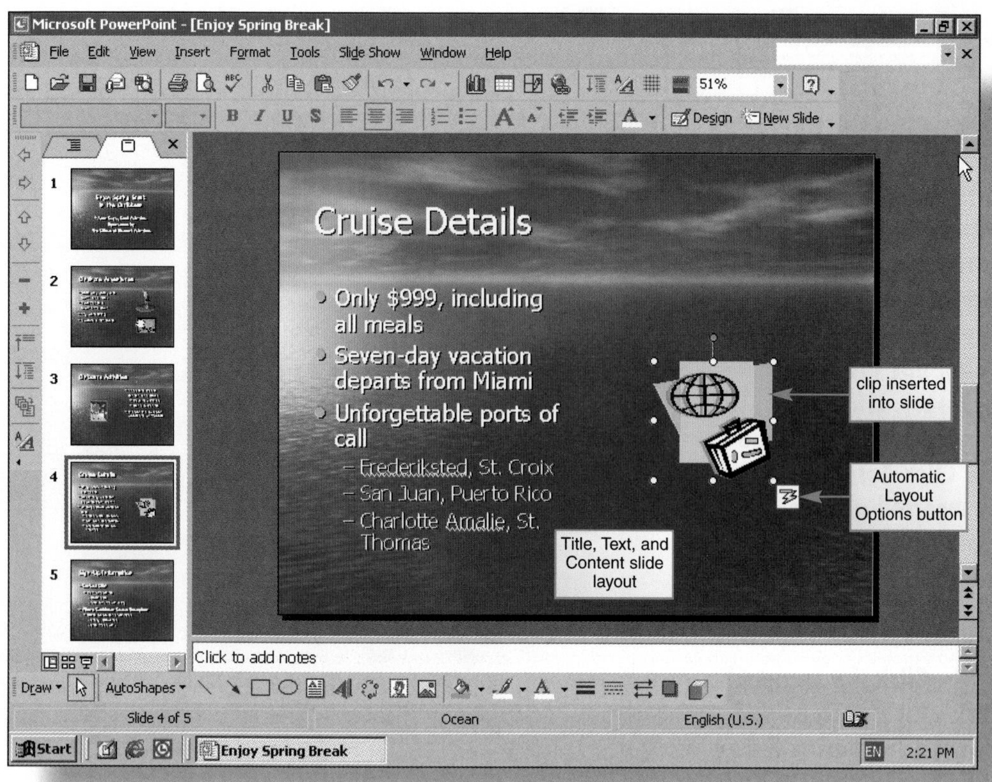

FIGURE 2-33

Table 2-3 Primary File Formats PowerPoint Recognizes	
FORMAT	*FILE EXTENSION*
Computer Graphics Metafile	.cgm
CorelDRAW	.cdr, .cdt, .cmx, and .pat
Encapsulated PostScript	.eps
Enhanced Metafile	.emf
FlashPix	.fpx
Graphics Interchange Format	.gif
Hanako	.jsh, .jah, and .jbh
Joint Photographic Experts Group (JPEG)	.jpg
Kodak PhotoCD	.pcd
Macintosh PICT	.pct
PC Paintbrush	.pcx
Portable Network Graphics	.png
Tagged Image File Format	.tif
Windows Bitmap	.bmp, .rle, .dib
Microsoft Windows Metafile	.wmf
WordPerfect Graphics	.wpg

In addition to clip art, you can insert pictures into a presentation. These may include scanned photographs, line art, and artwork from compact discs. To insert a picture into a presentation, the picture must be saved in a format that PowerPoint can recognize. Table 2-3 identifies some of the formats PowerPoint recognizes.

You can import files saved with the .emf, .gif, .jpg, .png, .bmp, .rle, .dib, and .wmf formats directly into PowerPoint presentations. All other file formats require separate filters that are shipped with the PowerPoint installation software and must be installed. You can download additional filters from the Microsoft Office Update Web site.

Smart Tags

A **smart tag** is a button that automatically appears on the screen when PowerPoint performs a certain action. The Automatic Layout Options button in Figure 2-33 is a smart tag. In addition to the Automatic Layout Options button, PowerPoint provides three other smart tags. Table 2-4 summarizes the smart tags available in PowerPoint.

Table 2-4 Smart Tags in PowerPoint

BUTTON	NAME	MENU FUNCTION
	AutoCorrect Options	Undoes an automatic correction, stops future automatic corrections of this type, or displays the AutoCorrect Options dialog box
	Paste Options	Specifies how moved or pasted items should display, e.g., with original formatting, without formatting, or with different formatting
	AutoFit Options	Undoes automatic text resizing to fit the current placeholder or changes single-column layouts to two-column layouts, inserts a new slide, or splits the text between two slides
	Automatic Layout Options	Adjusts the slide layout to accommodate an inserted object

Clicking a smart tag button displays a menu that contains commands relative to the action performed at the location of the smart tag. For example, if you want PowerPoint to undo the layout change when you add a clip to a slide, click the Automatic Layout Options button to display the Smart Tag Actions menu, and then click Undo Automatic Layout on the Smart Tag Actions menu to display the initial layout.

Using the Automatic Layout Options Button to Undo a Layout Change

The Title and Text layout used in Slide 4 did not provide a content placeholder for the clip you inserted, so PowerPoint automatically changed the layout to Title, Text, and Content. Because the text now violates the 7 × 7 rule with this layout and because you want to place the clip in a location other than the areas specified, you should change the layout to the Title and Text layout.

The **Automatic Layout Options button** displays because PowerPoint changed the layout automatically. If you move your mouse pointer near the changed object or text, the Automatic Layout Options button displays as an arrow, indicating that a list of options is available that allow you to undo the new layout, stop the automatic layout of inserted objects, or alter the AutoCorrect Options settings. Perform the steps on the next page to undo the layout change.

More About

Smart Tags

Microsoft PowerPoint automatically formats or corrects text as you type. For example, if you type a fraction, such as 1/4, the characters change to a fraction symbol. When you place your mouse on the symbol, the AutoCorrect Options button displays. Click the button to see the menu of choices.

More About

Layouts

Placement of text and graphics is important to a good persuasive presentation. Using the Internet for resources, tips, and articles on making clear and interesting presentations will increase your productivity. For more information on presentation design resources, visit the PowerPoint 2002 More About Web page (scsite.com/pp2002/more.htm) and then click Resources.

Steps To Use the Automatic Layout Options Button to Undo a Layout Change

1 Click the Automatic Layout Options button. Point to Undo Automatic Layout.

The Automatic Layout Options list displays (Figure 2-34). Clicking Undo Automatic Layout will reverse the layout change.

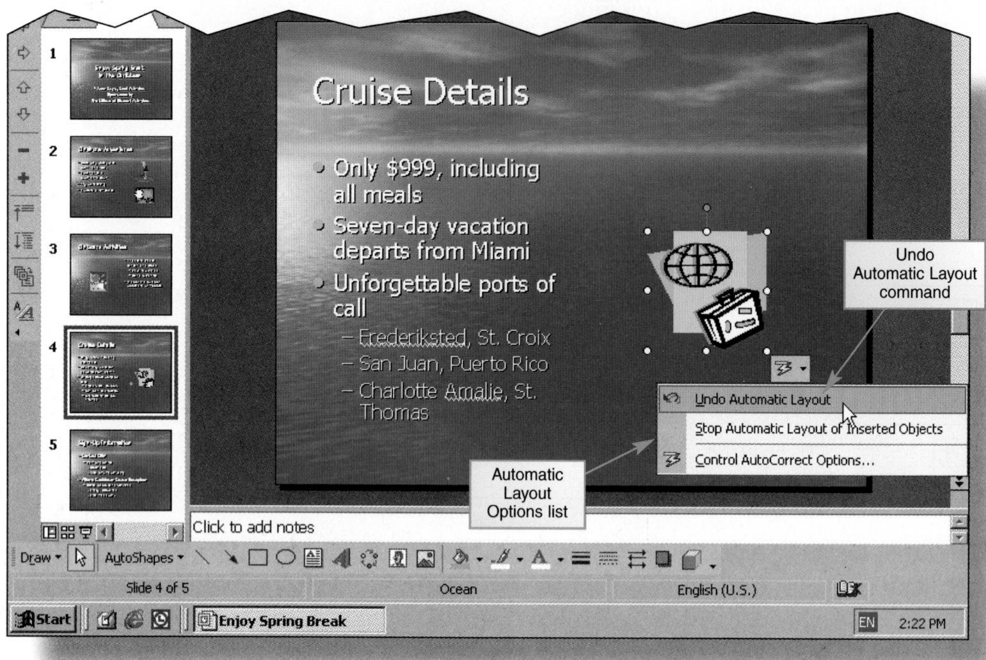

FIGURE 2-34

2 Click Undo Automatic Layout.

The layout reverts to Title and Text (Figure 2-35).

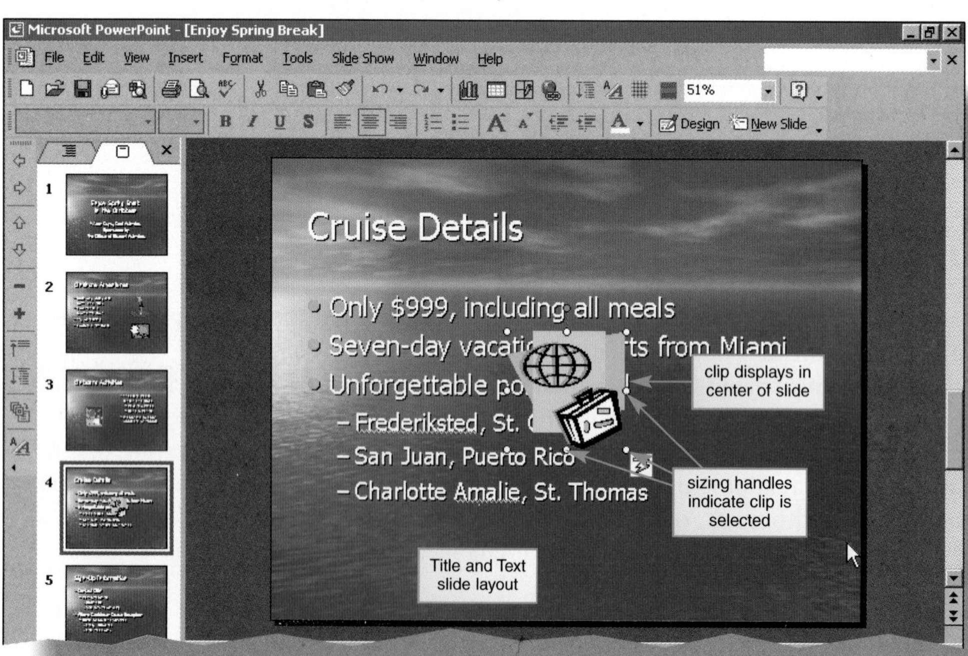

FIGURE 2-35

The desired clip displays in the center of Slide 4, which has the original Title and Text slide layout. The next step is to move the clip to the bottom-right corner of the slide.

Moving Clip Art

After you insert a clip into a slide, you may want to reposition it. The globe and luggage on Slide 4 overlays the bulleted list. You want to move the clip away from the text to the bottom-right corner of the slide. First move the clip and then change its size. Perform the steps below to move the clip to the bottom-right side of the slide.

More About

Voice Commands

Moving clip art with the mouse is easy. Using the Voice Command mode requires that you repeat commands several times to position the clip art. For example, after a clip has been placed in the slide, you must keep repeating the "down" command several times to move the clip art down to the place where you want it to display.

Steps To Move Clip Art

1 With the clip selected, point to the clip and then click.

2 Press and hold down the mouse button. Drag the clip to the bottom-right corner of the slide. Release the mouse button.

When you drag a clip, a dotted box displays. The dotted box indicates the clip's new position. When you release the left mouse button, the clip of the globe and luggage displays in the new location and the dotted line disappears (Figure 2-36). Sizing handles display at the corners and along its edges.

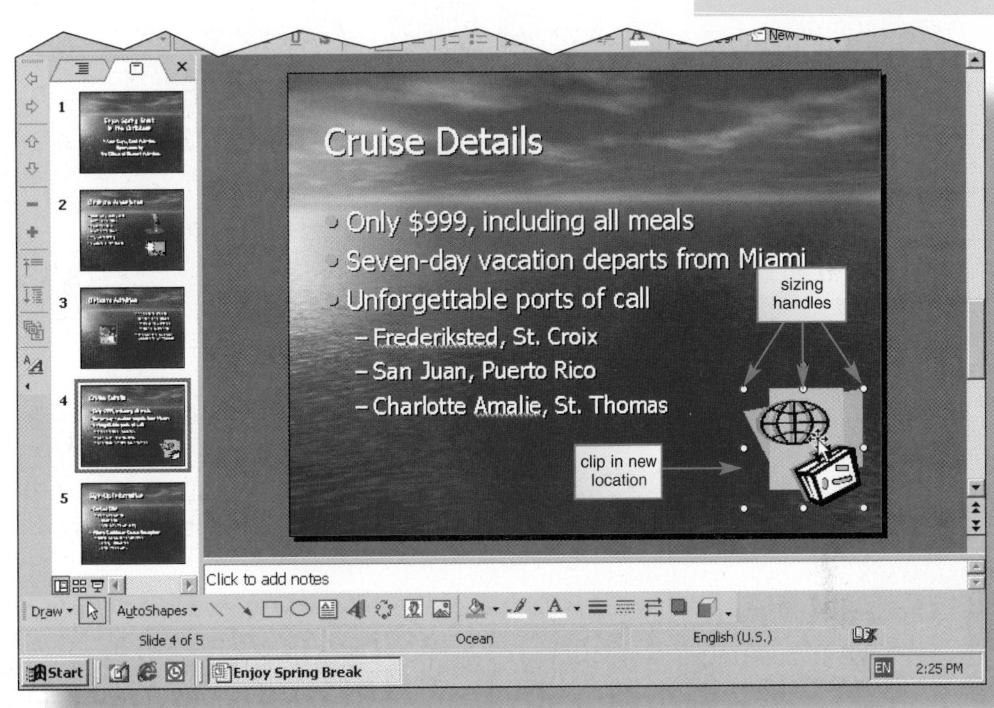

FIGURE 2-36

1. Select clip, press ARROW keys to move to new position

Changing the Size of Clip Art

Sometimes it is necessary to change the size of clip art. For example, on Slide 4 too much space displays around the clip. To make the object fit onto the slide, you increase its size. To change the size of a clip by an exact percentage, use the **Format Picture command** on the shortcut menu. The Format Picture dialog box contains six tabbed sheets with several formatting options. The **Size sheet** contains options for changing a clip's size. You either enter the exact height and width in the Size and rotate area, or enter the height and width as a percentage of the original clip in the Scale area. When the **Lock aspect ratio check box** displays a check mark, the height and width settings change to maintain the original aspect ratio. **Aspect ratio** is the relationship between an object's height and width. For example, a 3-by-5-inch object scaled to 50 percent would become a 1½-by-2½-inch object. Perform the steps on the next page to increase the size of the clip using the Format Picture dialog box.

Steps To Change the Size of Clip Art

1 Right-click the clip. Point to Format Picture on the shortcut menu (Figure 2-37).

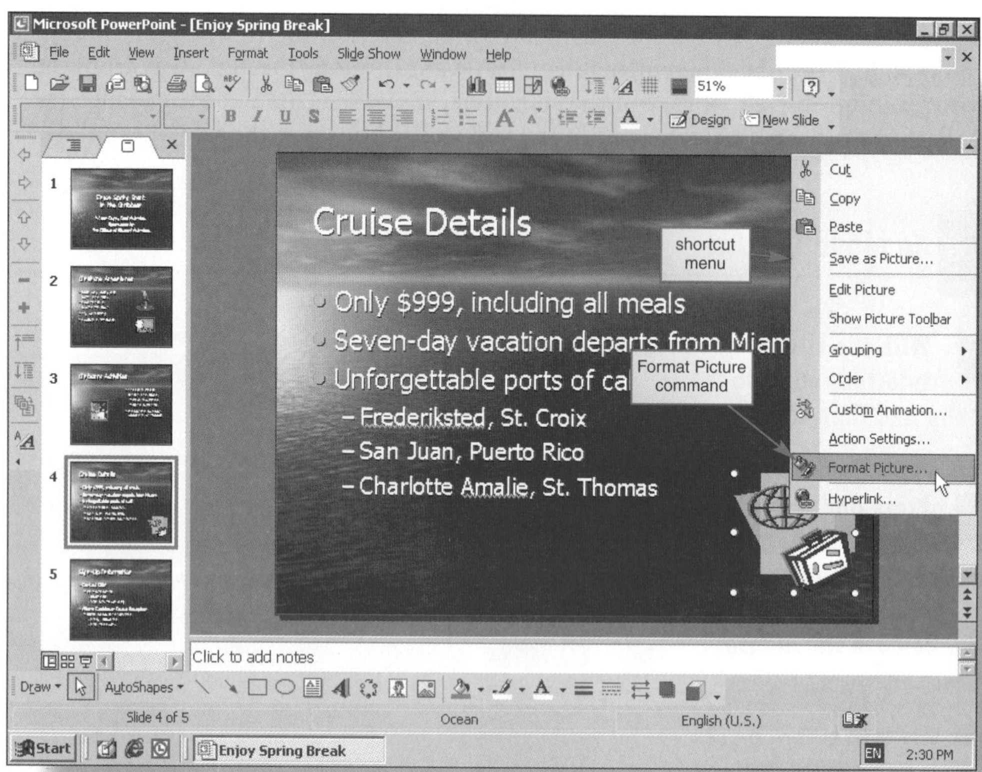

FIGURE 2-37

2 Click Format Picture. Click the Size tab when the Format Picture dialog box displays.

The Size sheet in the Format Picture dialog box displays (Figure 2-38). The Height and Width text boxes in the Scale area display the current percentage of the clip, 100 %. Check marks display in the Lock aspect ratio and Relative to original picture size check boxes.

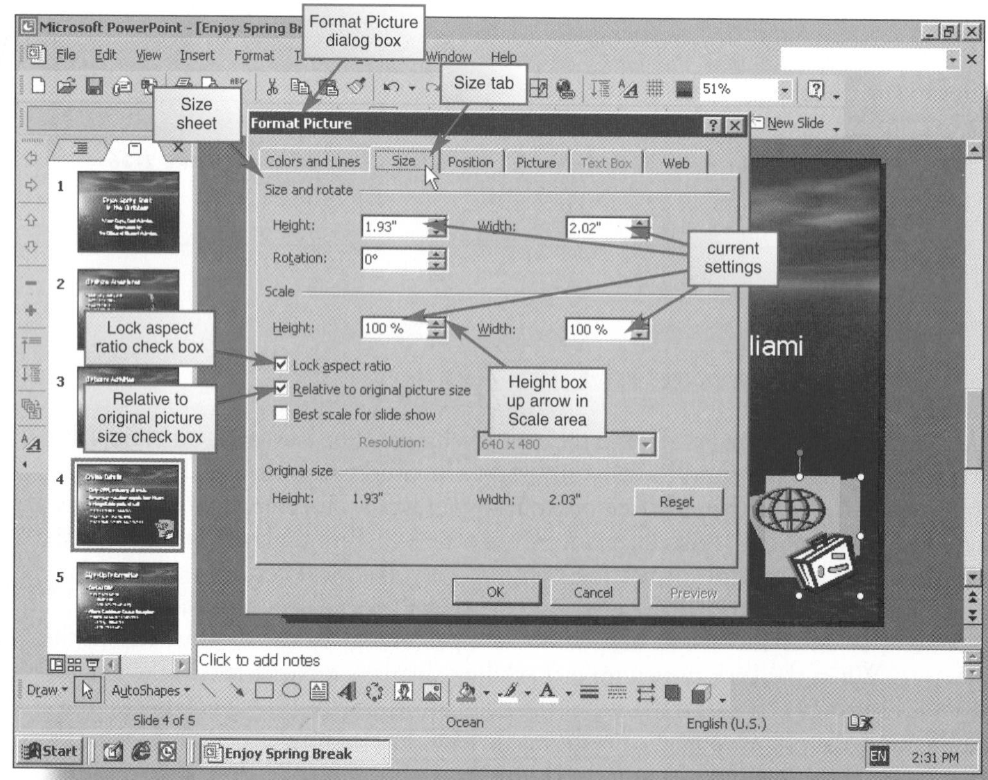

FIGURE 2-38

3 Click and hold down the mouse button on the Height box up arrow in the Scale area until 125 % displays and then point to the OK button.

Both the Height and Width text boxes in the Scale area display 125 % (Figure 2-39). PowerPoint automatically changes the Height and Width text boxes in the Size and rotate area to reflect changes in the Scale area.

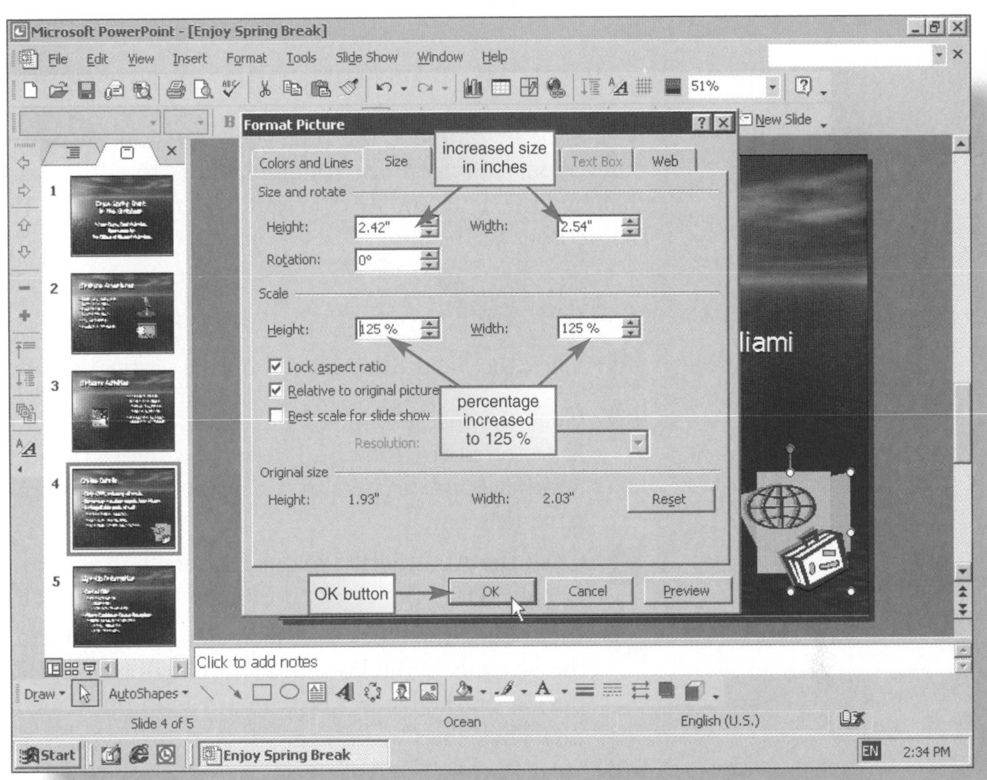

FIGURE 2-39

4 Click the OK button. Drag the clip to the center of the space in the bottom-right corner of the slide.

PowerPoint closes the Format Picture dialog box and displays the enlarged clip in the desired location (Figure 2-40).

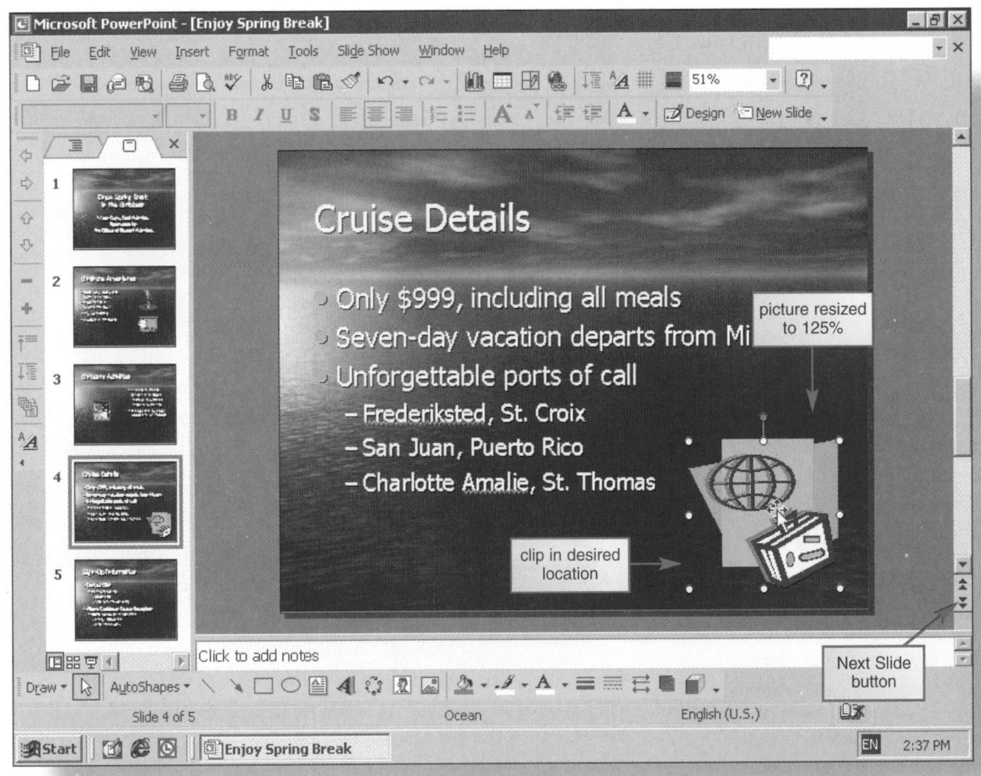

FIGURE 2-40

Other Ways

1. Click clip, on Format menu click Picture, click Size tab, click and hold down mouse button on Height box up or down arrow in Scale area until desired size is reached, click OK button
2. Right-click slide anywhere except the text placeholders, click Slide Layout on shortcut menu, double-click desired slide layout
3. Click clip, drag a sizing handle until clip is desired shape and size
4. Press ALT+O, press I, press CTRL+TAB three times to select Size tab, press TAB to select Height text box in Scale area, press UP or DOWN ARROW keys to increase or decrease size, press ENTER

Inserting, Moving, and Sizing a Clip into a Slide

With Slide 4 complete, the final step is to add the alarm clock clip to the closing slide, Slide 5. Perform the following steps to add an alarm clock to Slide 5 without changing the Title and Text layout, size the clip, and then move it to the upper-right corner of the slide.

TO INSERT, MOVE, AND SIZE A CLIP INTO A SLIDE

1. Click the Next Slide button on the vertical scroll bar to display Slide 5.
2. Click the Insert Clip Art button on the Drawing toolbar. Type `clock` in the Search text text box and then press the ENTER key. Click the alarm clock or another appropriate clip. Click the Close button on the Insert Clip Art task pane title bar.
3. Click the Automatic Layout Options button and then click Undo Automatic Layout. Drag the clock to the upper-right corner of the slide.
4. Right-click the clock and then click Format Picture on the shortcut menu. Click the Size tab in the Format Picture dialog box, click and hold down the mouse button on the Height box up arrow in the Scale area until 150 % displays, and then click the OK button.
5. Drag the clock to the center of the space in the upper-right corner of the slide.

The alarm clock is inserted, moved, and sized into Slide 5 (Figure 2-41).

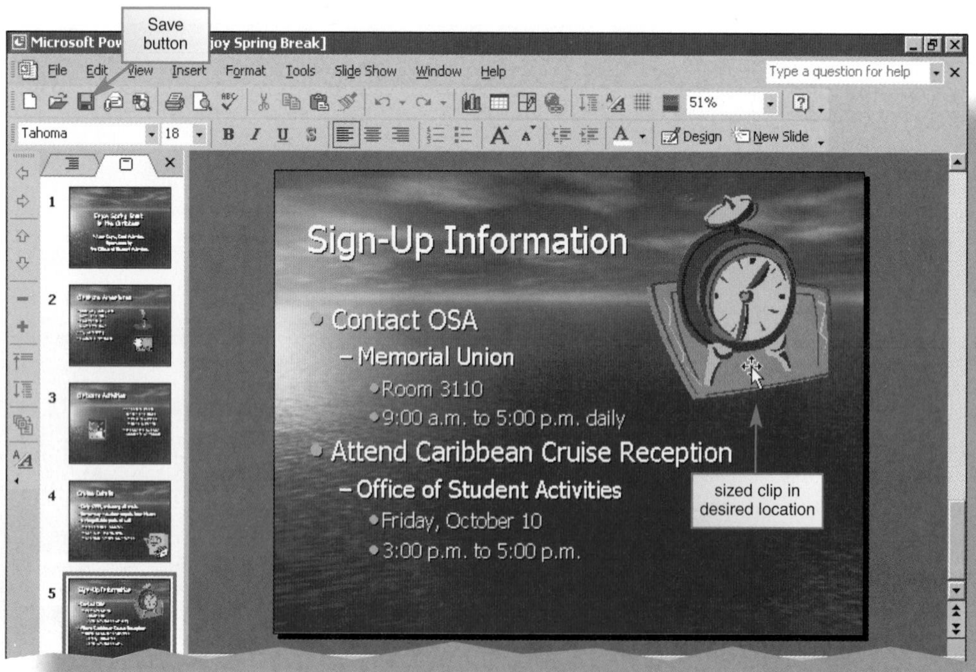

FIGURE 2-41

Saving the Presentation Again

To preserve the work completed, perform the following step to save the presentation again.

Choosing Clip Art

When selecting clip art, consider the direction in which the art faces. To focus the viewer's attention on the center of the slide, images should face in rather than out of the slide. For more information, visit the PowerPoint 2002 More About Web page (scsite.com/pp2002/more.htm) and then click Selecting Clip Art.

TO SAVE A PRESENTATION

 Click the Save button on the Standard toolbar.

The changes made to the presentation after the previous save are saved on a floppy disk.

A default setting in PowerPoint allows for **fast saves**, which saves only the changes made since the last time you saved. To save a full copy of the complete presentation, click Tools on the menu bar, click Options on the Tools menu, and then click the Save tab. Remove the check mark in the Allow fast saves check box by clicking the check box and then click the OK button.

Adding a Header and Footer to Outline Pages

A printout of the presentation outline often is used as an audience handout. Distributing a copy of the outline provides the audience with paper on which to write notes or comments. Another benefit of distributing a copy of the outline is to help the audience see the text on the slides when lighting is poor or the room is too large. To help identify the source of the printed outline, add a descriptive header and footer. A **header** displays at the top of the sheet of paper or slide, and a **footer** displays at the bottom. Both contain specific information, such as the presenter's name or the company's telephone number. In addition, the current date and time and the slide or page number can display beside the header or footer information.

> **More About**
>
> **Using Footers**
>
> Nothing can be more frustrating than having overhead transparencies of your slides get out of order when you are giving a presentation. Help keep them organized by using page numbers and the presentation name in the footer.

Using the Notes and Handouts Sheet to Add Headers and Footers

You add headers and footers to outline pages by clicking the Notes and Handouts sheet in the Header and Footer dialog box and entering the information you want to print. Perform the following steps to add the current date, header information, the page number, and footer information to the printed outline.

Steps To Use the Notes and Handouts Sheet to Add Headers and Footers

1 Click View on the menu bar and then point to Header and Footer (Figure 2-42).

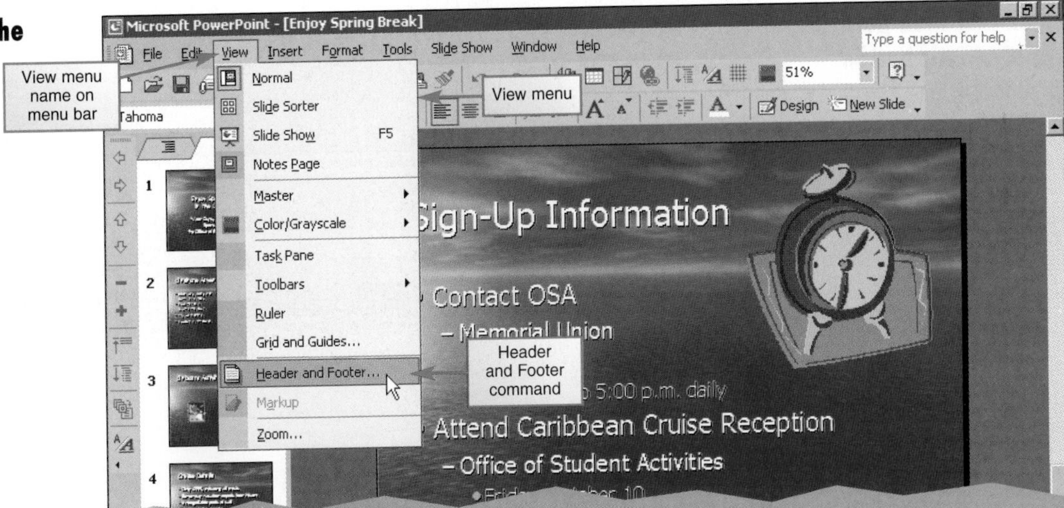

FIGURE 2-42

2 Click Header and Footer. Click the Notes and Handouts tab when the Header and Footer dialog box displays. Point to the Update automatically option button.

The Notes and Handouts sheet in the Header and Footer dialog box displays (Figure 2-43). Check marks display in the Date and time, Header, Page number, and Footer check boxes. The Fixed option button is selected.

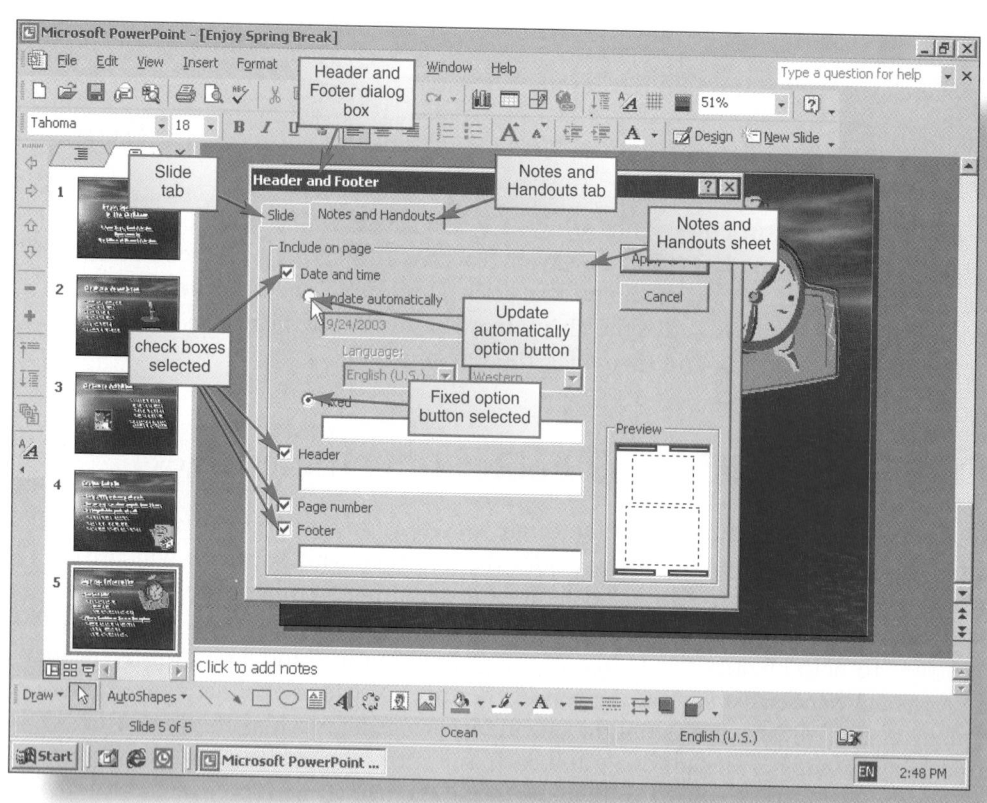

FIGURE 2-43

3 Click the Update automatically option button and then click the Header text box. Type `Spring Break Cruise` **in the Header text box. Click the Footer text box. Type** `Office of Student Activities` **in the Footer text box and then point to the Apply to All button (Figure 2-44).**

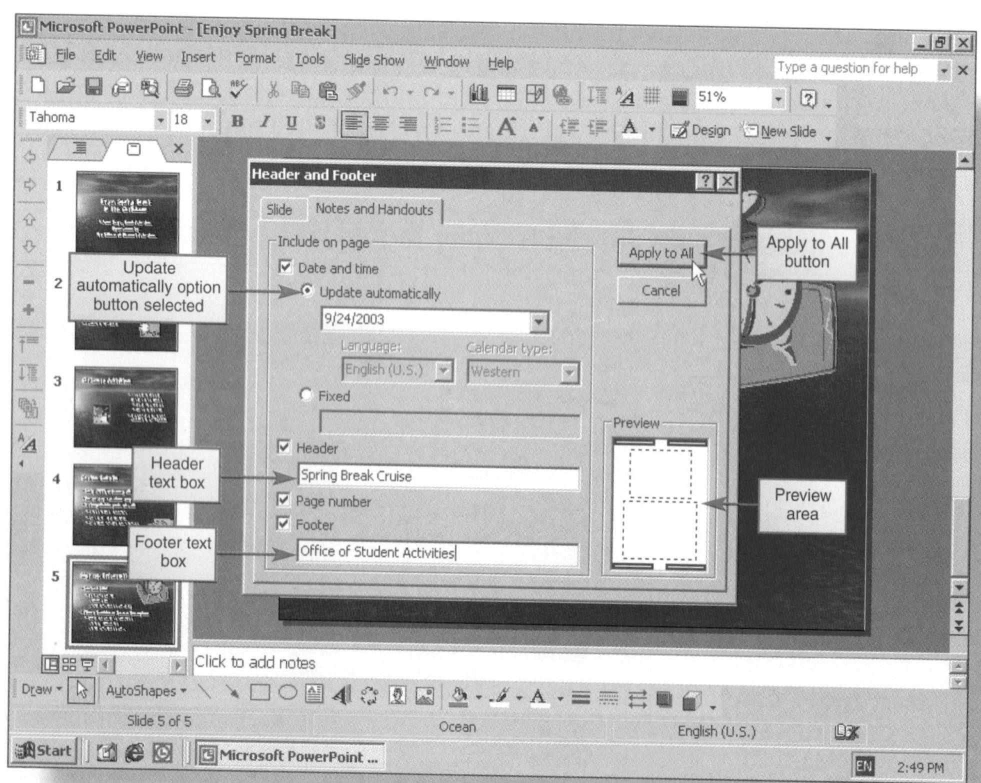

FIGURE 2-44

4 Click the Apply to All button.

PowerPoint applies the header and footer text to the outline, closes the Header and Footer dialog box, and displays Slide 5 (Figure 2-45). You cannot see header and footer text until you print the outline (shown in Figure 2-62 on page PP 2.49).

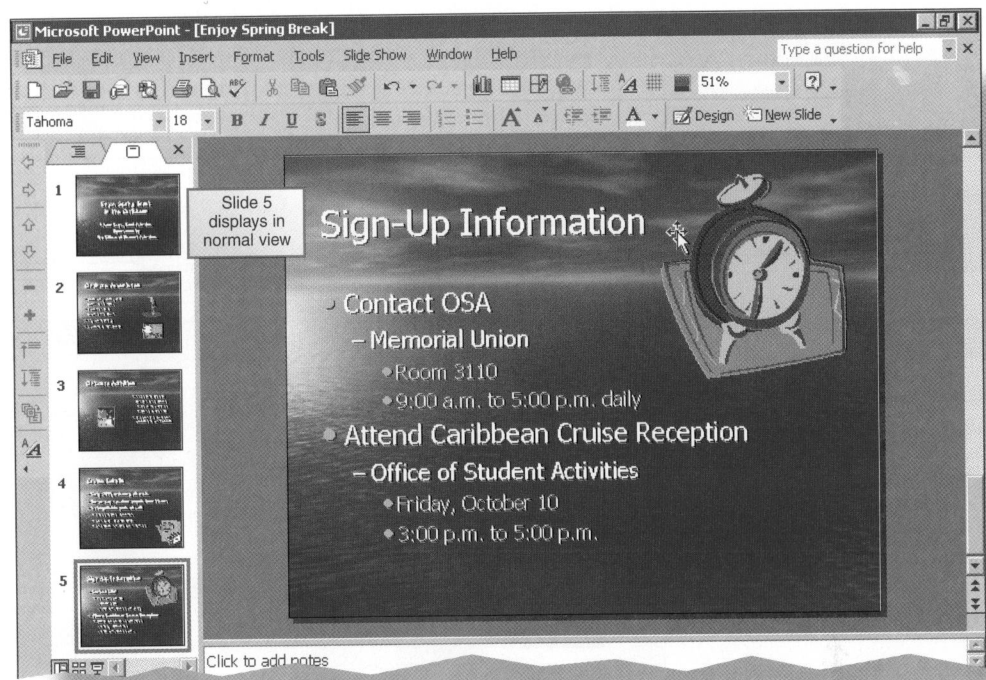

FIGURE 2-45

Applying Animation Schemes

PowerPoint provides many animation effects to add interest and make a slide show presentation look professional. **Animation** includes special visual and sound effects applied to text or content. For example, each line on the slide can swivel as it displays on the screen. Or an object can zoom in from the top of the screen to the bottom. PowerPoint provides a variety of **preset animation schemes** that determine slide transitions and effects for the title and body text. A **slide transition** is a special effect used to progress from one slide to the next in a slide show. PowerPoint also allows you to set your own **Custom animation** effects by defining your own animation types and speeds and sound effects on a slide. The following pages discuss how to add these animation effects to the presentation.

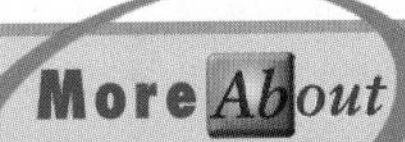

Animation Effects

Graphic designers suggest using a maximum of two different animation effects in one presentation. Any more than two can distract your audience from your important ideas by causing them to fixate on the visual effects and not on the slide content or the speaker. These effects should enhance your ideas in the presentation.

Adding an Animation Scheme to a Slide Show

PowerPoint has preset animation schemes with visual effects that vary the slide transitions and the methods in which the slide title and bullets or paragraphs display on the slides. Not all animation schemes have the slide transition element or effects for both the title and body text. These schemes are grouped in three categories: Subtle, Moderate, and Exciting. The name of the animation scheme characterizes the visual effects that display. For example, the Unfold animation scheme in the Moderate category uses the Push Right slide transition effect, the Fly In effect for the title text, and the Unfold effect for the body text. The Pinwheel scheme in the Exciting category does not use a slide transition effect, but it uses the Pinwheel effect for the title text and the Peek In effect for the body text.

In this presentation, you apply the Float animation scheme to all slides. This effect is added easily by using the Slide Design task pane, which you used earlier in this project to select a design template. Perform the following steps to apply the Float animation scheme to the Enjoy Spring Break presentation.

Steps To Add an Animation Scheme to a Slide Show

1 Click Slide Show on the menu bar and then point to Animation Schemes (Figure 2-46).

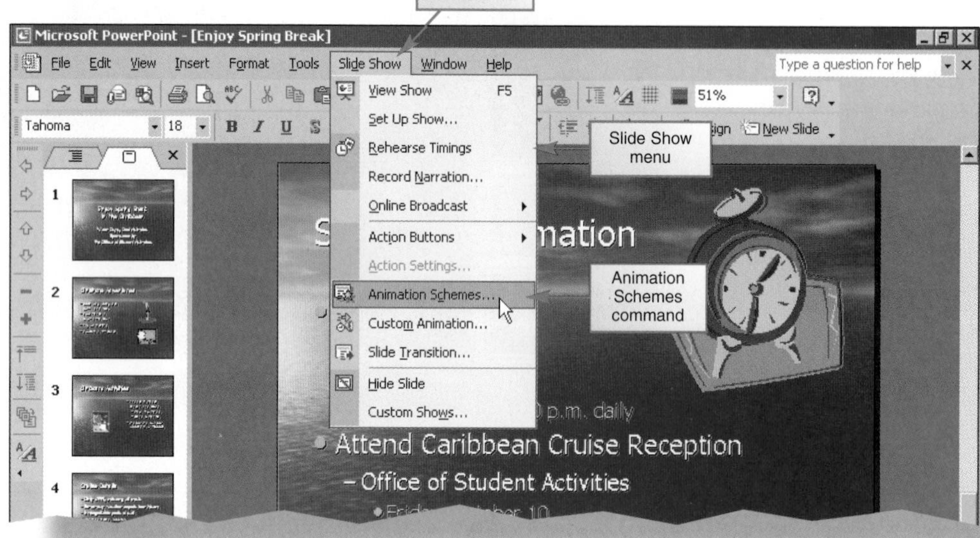

FIGURE 2-46

2 Click Animation Schemes. Scroll down the Apply to selected slides list and then point to Float in the Exciting category.

The Slide Design task pane displays (Figure 2-47). The list of possible slide transition effects displays in the Apply to selected slides area. Exciting is one of the animation scheme categories. The Float ScreenTip shows that the Float animation scheme uses the Comb Horizontal slide transition, the Float effect for the title text, and the Descend effect for the body text.

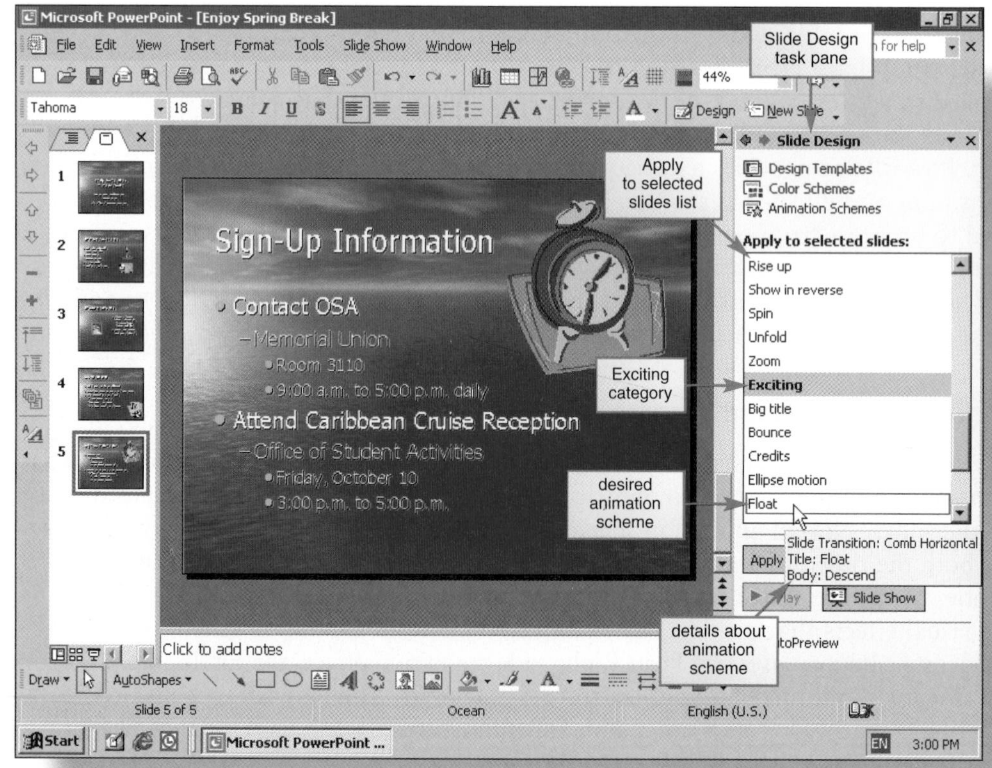

FIGURE 2-47

3 Click Float. Point to the Apply to All Slides button.

PowerPoint applies the Float animation effect to Slide 5, as indicated by the animation icon on the left side of the Slide 5 slide thumbnail on the Slides tab (Figure 2-48). The Float animation effect is previewed because the AutoPreview check box is selected.

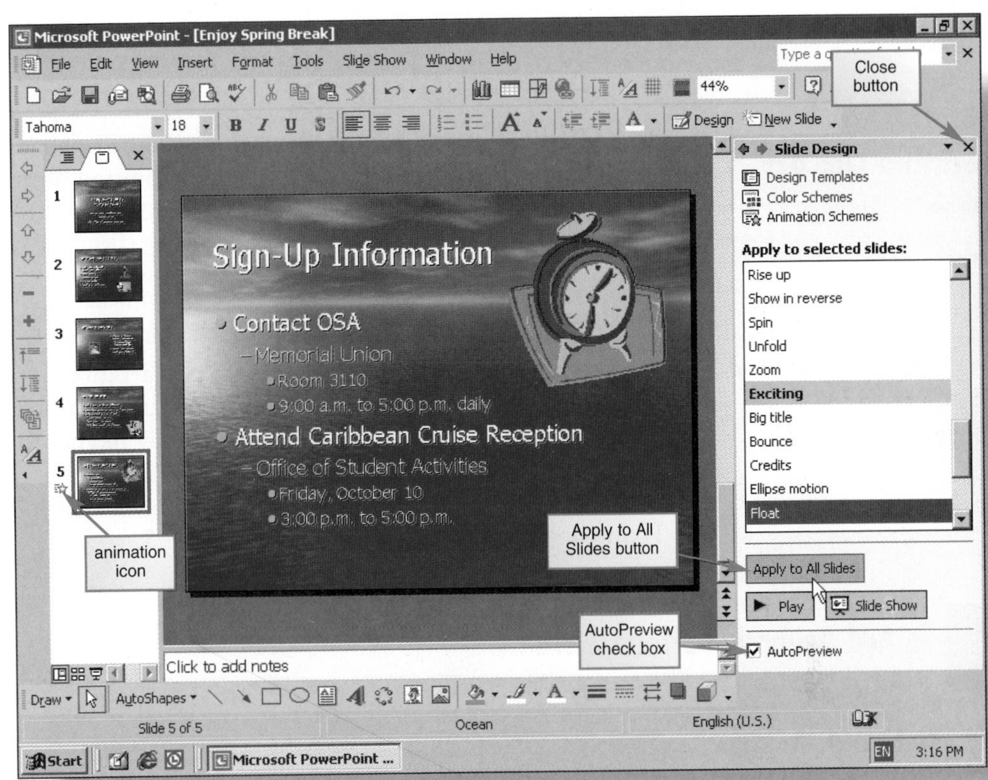

FIGURE 2-48

4 Click Apply to All Slides. Click the Close button in the Slide Design task pane.

The Float animation effect is applied to all slides in the presentation (Figure 2-49).

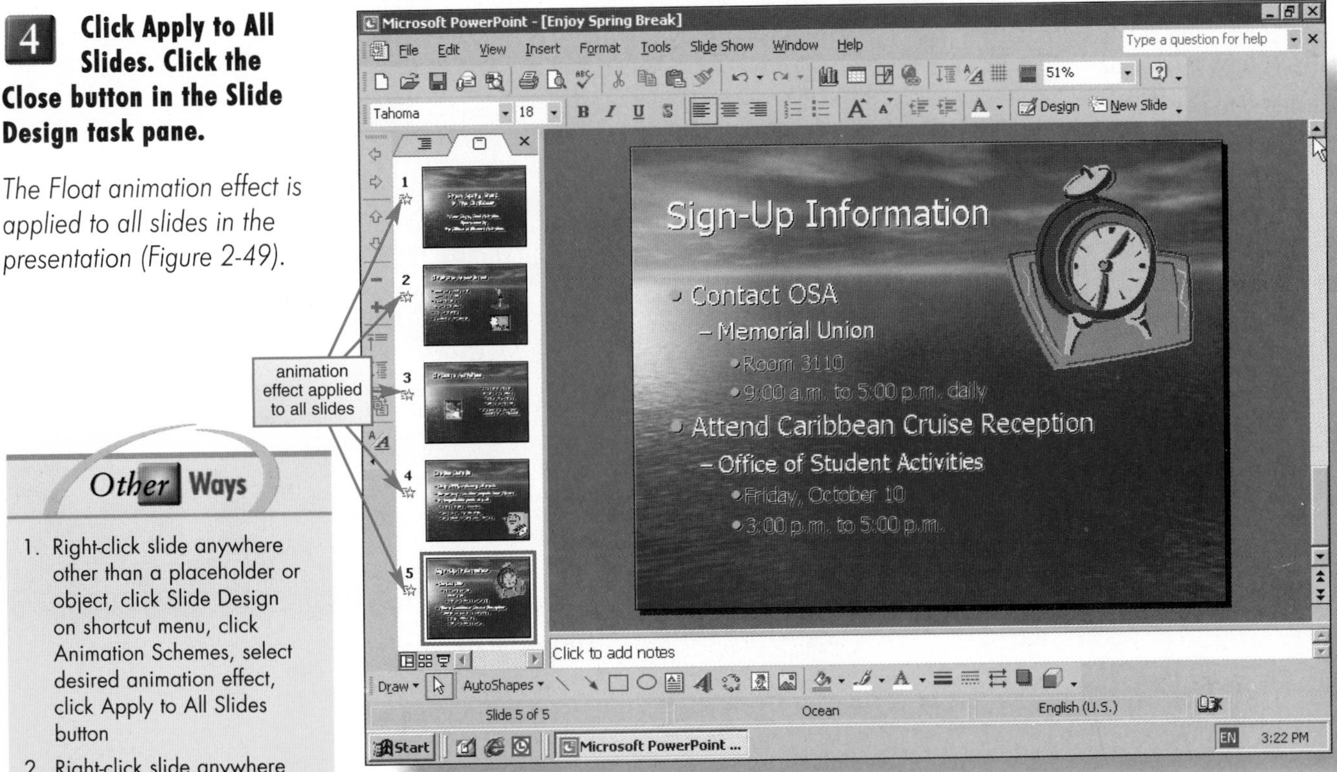

FIGURE 2-49

Other Ways

1. Right-click slide anywhere other than a placeholder or object, click Slide Design on shortcut menu, click Animation Schemes, select desired animation effect, click Apply to All Slides button
2. Right-click slide anywhere except text placeholders, click Slide Layout on shortcut menu, double-click desired slide layout
3. Press ALT+D, press C

Locating Clip Art

Thousands of public domain clips are available on the Internet. Use a search engine and the keywords, clip art and clip+art, to find these Web sites, which often contain bullets, lines, buttons, and sound files sorted into easy-to-navigate categories. You can import these files directly into your presentations.

Animating Clip Art

To add visual interest to a presentation, you can **animate** certain content. On Slide 5, for example, having the alarm clock rise from the bottom of the screen will provide a pleasing effect. Animating clip art takes several steps as described in the following sections.

Adding Animation Effects

PowerPoint allows you to animate clip art along with animating text. Because Slide 5 lists the times when students can gain additional information about the cruise, you want to emphasize these times by having the clip of the alarm clock move from the bottom of the screen to the top. One way of animating clip art is to select options in the Custom Animation dialog box. Perform the following steps to add the Flying animation effect to the clip on Slide 5.

To Add Animation Effects

1 Right-click the clip art image and then point to Custom Animation on the shortcut menu.

The shortcut menu displays (Figure 2-50). The clip is selected, as indicated by the sizing handles that display at the corners and along its edges.

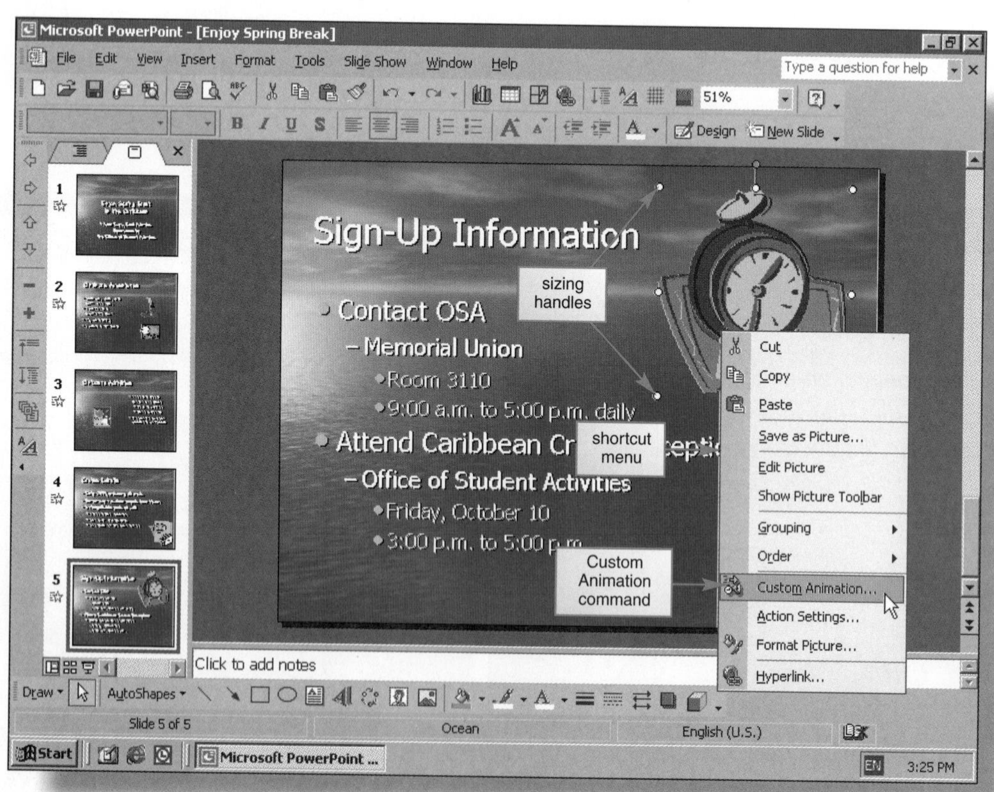

FIGURE 2-50

2 Click Custom Animation. Point to the Add Effect button.

The Custom Animation task pane displays (Figure 2-51). Two animation effects have been applied to the title and body of the slide previously.

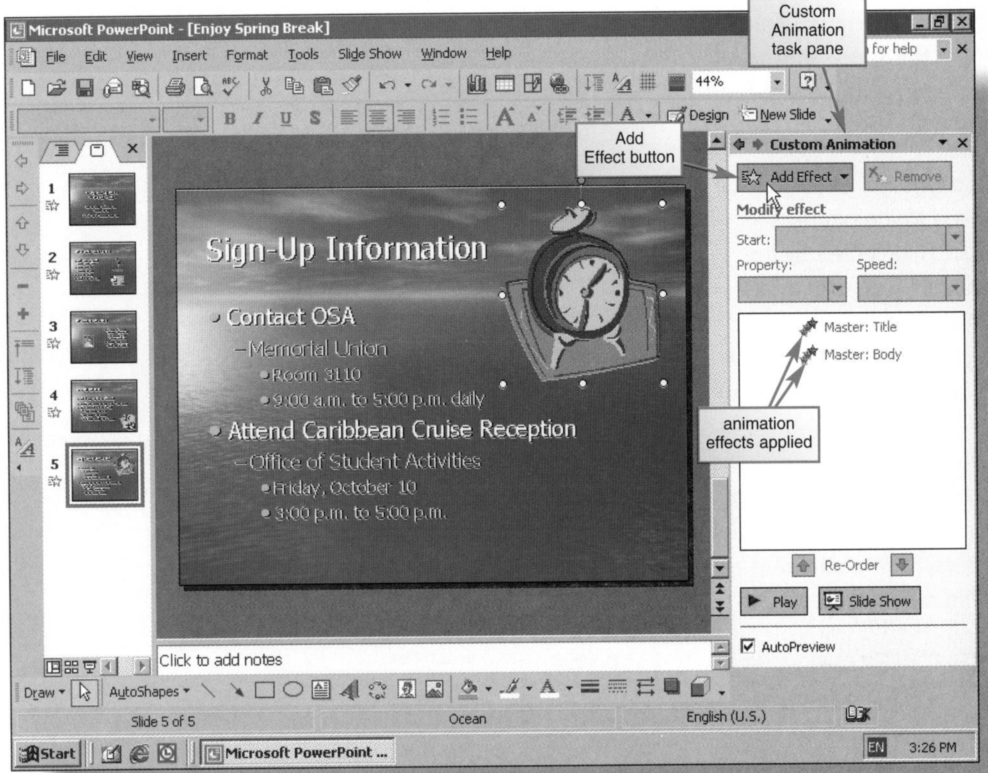

FIGURE 2-51

3 Click the Add Effect button, point to Entrance, and then point to Fly In in the Entrance effects list.

A list of possible effects for the Entrance option displays (Figure 2-52). Your system may display a different list of effects. You can apply a variety of effects to the clip, including how it enters and exits the slide.

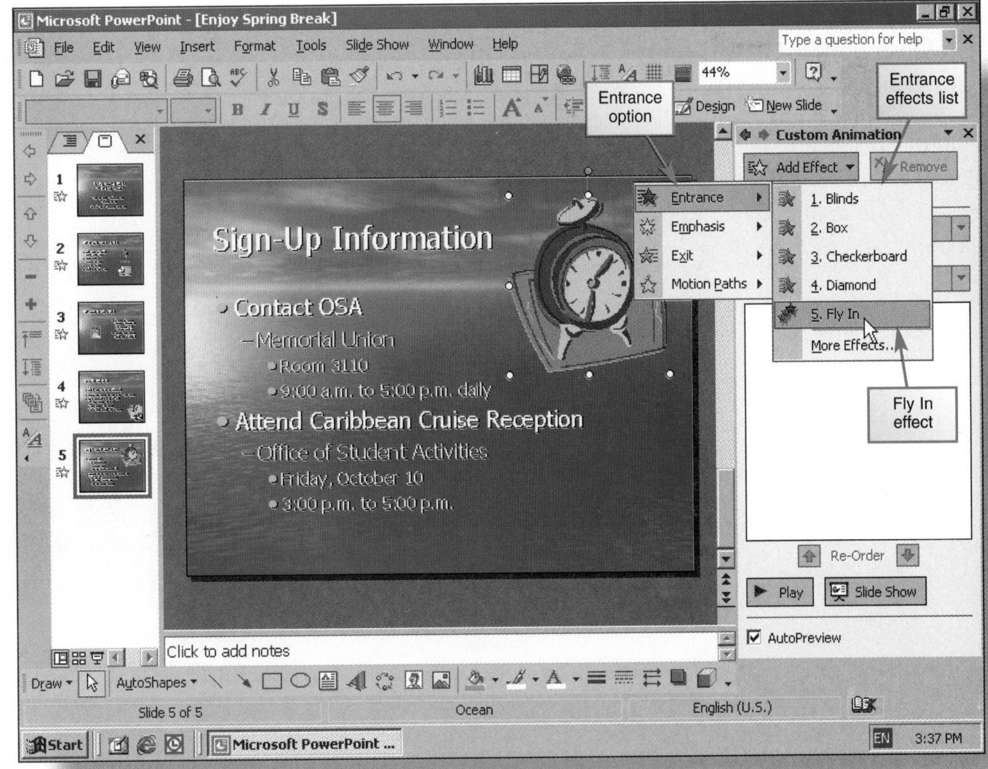

FIGURE 2-52

4 Click Fly In. Point to the Close button on the Custom Animation task pane title bar.

The animation effect is applied to the alarm clock, as indicated by the number 1 icon displaying to the left of the clip and the corresponding 1 displaying in the Custom Animation list (Figure 2-53). You will see this effect when you click the mouse on that slide during your slide show. J0234131 is Microsoft's internal identifier for the alarm clock clip.

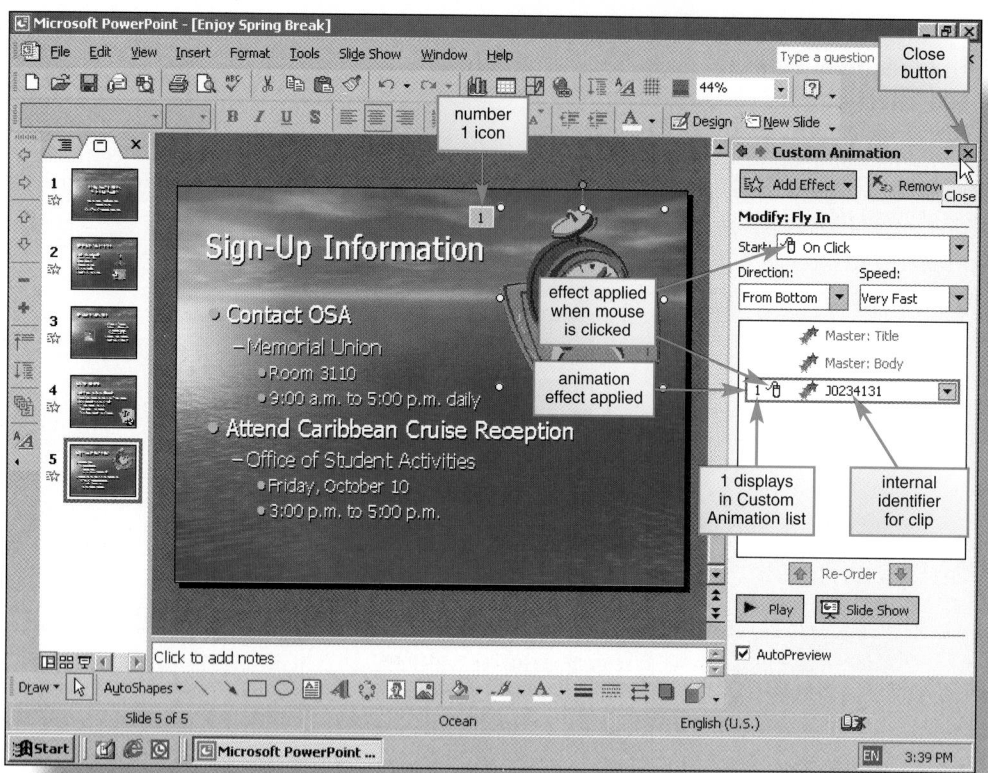

FIGURE 2-53

5 Click the Close button (Figure 2-54).

The alarm clock clip will appear in the presentation using the Fly In animation effect during the slide show.

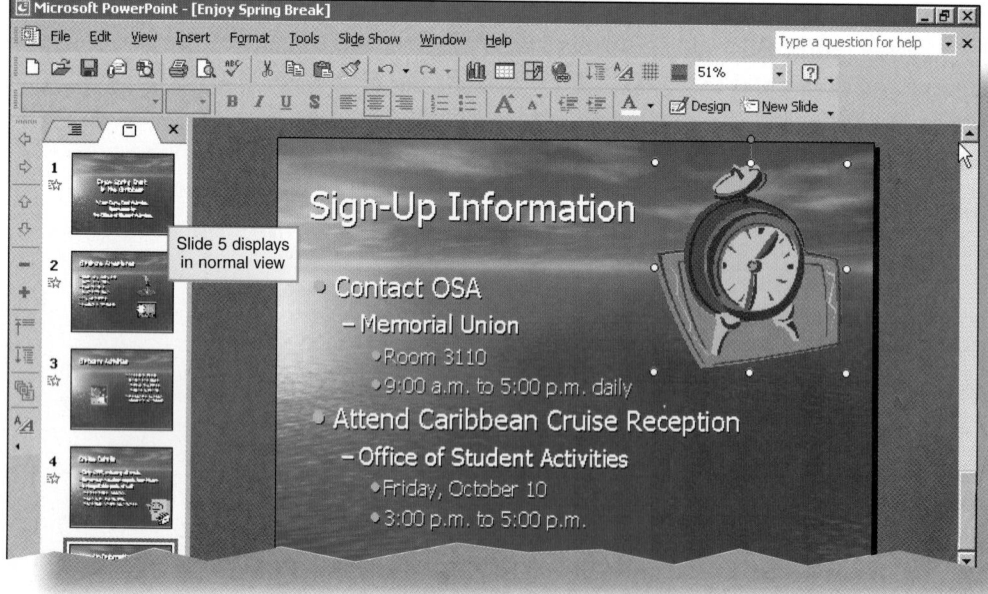

FIGURE 2-54

Other Ways

1. Click clip art, on Slide Show menu click Custom Animation, click desired animation effect, click OK button
2. Press TAB until clip art is selected, press ALT+D, press M, press DOWN ARROW key until desired animation effect selected, press ENTER

When you run the slide show, the bulleted list paragraphs will display, and then the clip art will begin moving from the bottom of the slide and stop at the position where you inserted it into Slide 5.

Animation effects are complete for this presentation. You now can review the presentation in slide show view and correct any spelling errors.

Saving the Presentation Again

The presentation is complete. Perform the following step to save the finished presentation on a floppy disk before running the slide show.

TO SAVE A PRESENTATION

1 Click the Save button on the Standard toolbar.

PowerPoint saves the presentation on your floppy disk by saving the changes made to the presentation since the last save.

Giving a Slide Show

If you are displaying your slide show on a projection system or external monitor, you need to match the resolutions of your computer and the projector. To do this, open the Display Properties dialog box for your computer and click the Settings tab. In the Screen area box, move the slider to adjust the resolution. If you are uncertain of the resolution, try 800 x 600 pixels. When you are using two monitors, you can display your slide show on one monitor and view your notes, outline, and slides on the second monitor.

Running an Animated Slide Show

Project 1 introduced you to using slide show view to look at your presentation one slide at a time. This project introduces you to running a slide show with preset and custom animation effects. When you run a slide show with slide transition effects, PowerPoint displays the slide transition effect when you click the mouse button to advance to the next slide. When a slide has text animation effects, each paragraph level displays in the sequence specified by the animation settings in the Custom Animation dialog box. Perform the following steps to run the animated Enjoy Spring Break presentation.

Steps To Run an Animated Slide Show

1 Click the Slide 1 slide thumbnail on the Slides tab. Click the Slide Show button at the lower left of the PowerPoint window. When Slide 1 displays in slide show view, click the slide anywhere.

PowerPoint applies the Comb Horizontal slide transition effect and displays the title slide title text, Enjoy Spring Break in the Caribbean (Figure 2-55) using the Float animation effect. When you click the slide, the first paragraph in the subtitle text placeholder, Warm Days, Cool Activities, displays using the Descend animation effect.

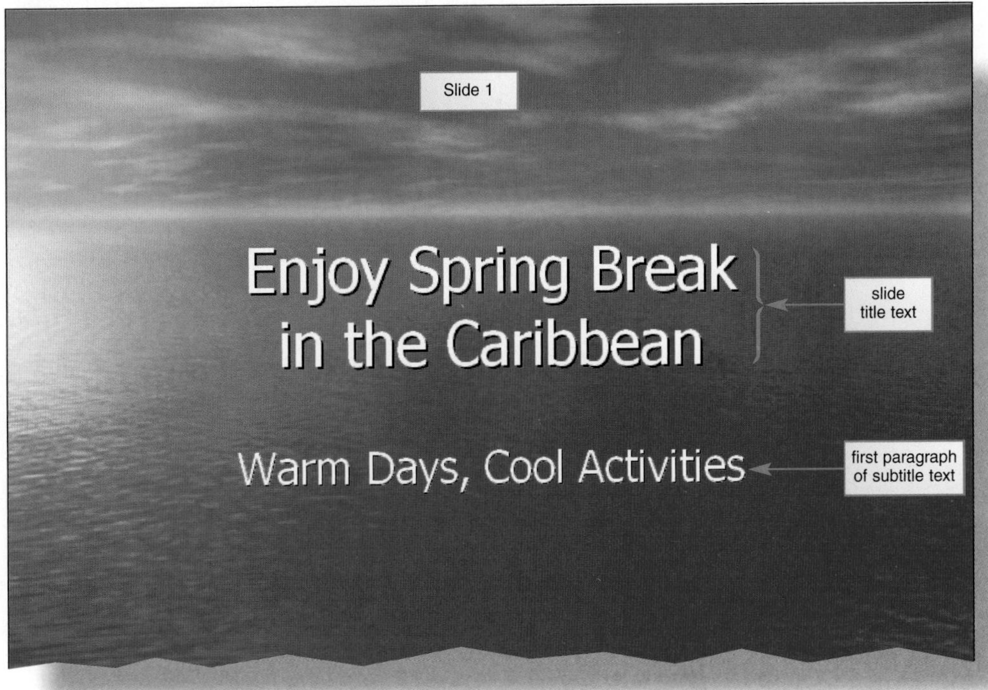

FIGURE 2-55

2 Click the slide again.

PowerPoint displays the second paragraph in the subtitle text placeholder, Sponsored by, using the Float animation effect (Figure 2-56). If the Popup Menu buttons display when you move the mouse pointer, do not click them.

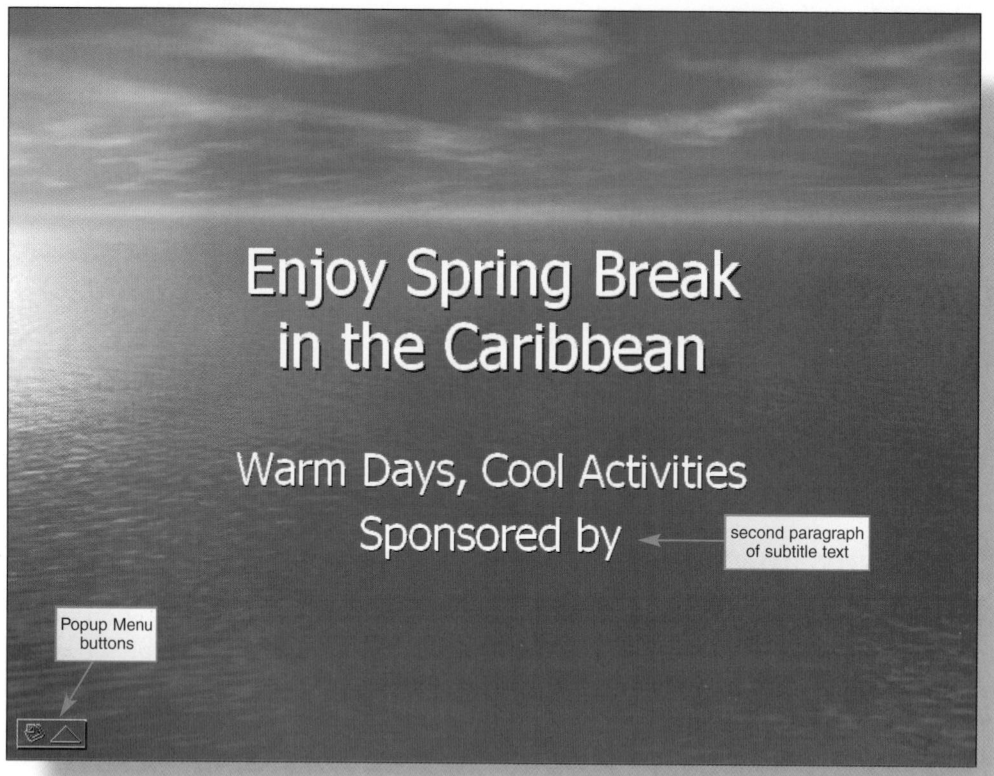

FIGURE 2-56

3 Click the slide again.

PowerPoint displays the third paragraph in the subtitle text placeholder, The Office of Student Activities, below the second paragraph. PowerPoint again uses the Descend animation effect (Figure 2-57).

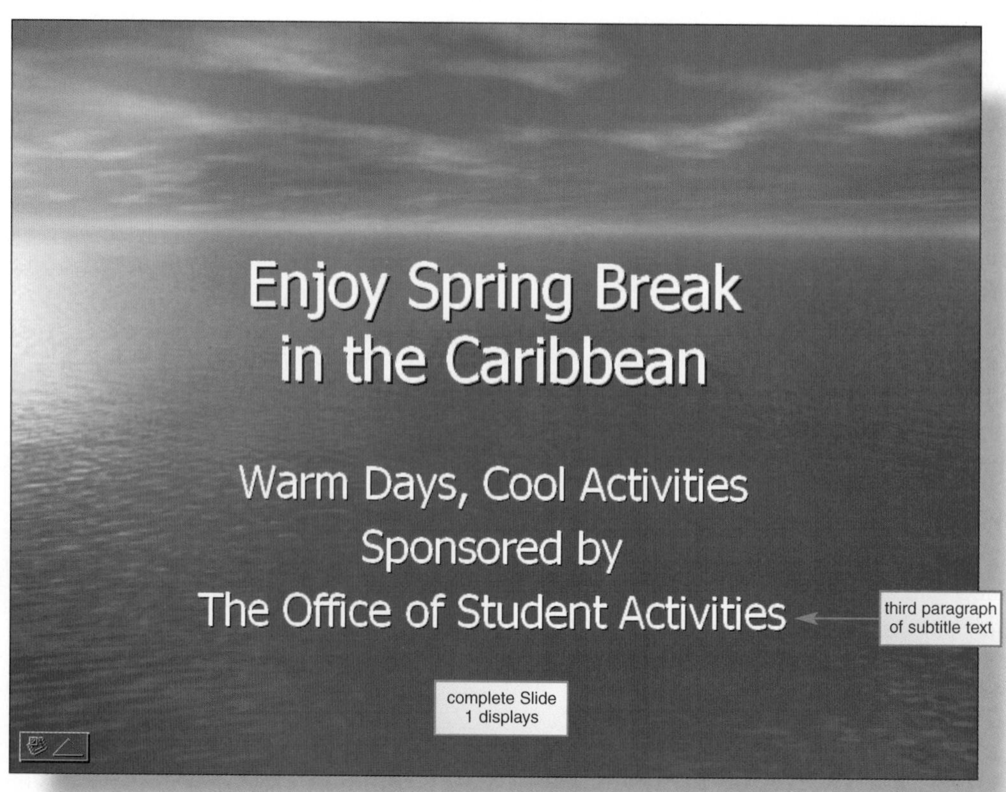

FIGURE 2-57

4 Continue clicking to finish running the slide show and return to normal view.

Each time a new slide displays, PowerPoint first displays the Comb Horizontal slide transition effect and only the slide title using the Float effect. Then, PowerPoint builds each slide based on the animation settings. When you click the slide after the last paragraph displays on the last slide of the presentation, PowerPoint displays a blank slide. When you click again, PowerPoint exits slide show view and returns to normal view (Figure 2-58).

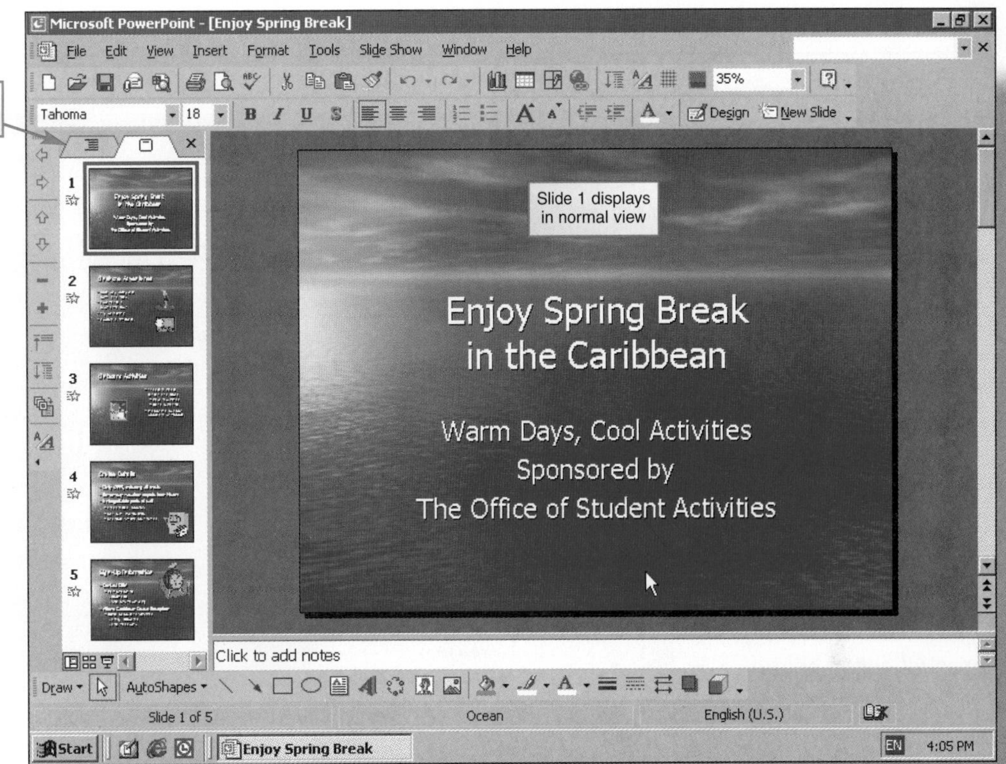

FIGURE 2-58

Other Ways

1. On Slide Show menu click View Show, click slide until slide show ends
2. Press ALT+D, press V, press ENTER until slide show ends
3. In Voice Command mode, say "Slide Show, View Show"

With the presentation complete and animation effects tested, the last step is to print the presentation outline and slides.

Printing a Presentation Created on the Outline Tab

When you click the Print button on the Standard toolbar, PowerPoint prints a hard copy of the presentation component last selected in the Print what box in the Print dialog box. To be certain to print the component you want, such as the presentation outline, use the Print command on the File menu. When the Print dialog box displays, you can select the appropriate presentation component in the Print what box. The next two sections explain how to use the Print command on the File menu to print the presentation outline and the presentation slides.

Printing an Outline

During the development of a lengthy presentation, it often is easier to review your outline in print instead of on the screen. Printing your outline also is useful for audience handouts or when your supervisor or instructor wants to review your subject matter before you develop your presentation fully.

Recall that the Print dialog box displays print options. When you want to print your outline, select Outline View in the Print what list in the Print dialog box. The outline, however, prints as last viewed on the Outline tab. This means that you must select the Zoom setting to display the outline text as you want it to print. If you are uncertain of the Zoom setting, you should return to the Outline tab and review it before printing. Perform the steps on the next page to print an outline from slide view.

More About

Sending Presentations to Word

You can create handouts and other documents by sending your PowerPoint outline to Microsoft Word and then using that text. To perform this action, click File on the menu bar, point to Send To, click Microsoft Word, and then click Outline only.

Steps To Print an Outline

1 Click the Outline tab. Ready the printer according to the printer manufacturer's instructions. Click File on the menu bar and then point to Print.

The File menu displays (Figure 2-59). The Expand All button on the Outlining toolbar is selected, so the entire outline will print. If you want to print only the slide titles, you would click the **Collapse All button** *before you click File on the menu bar.*

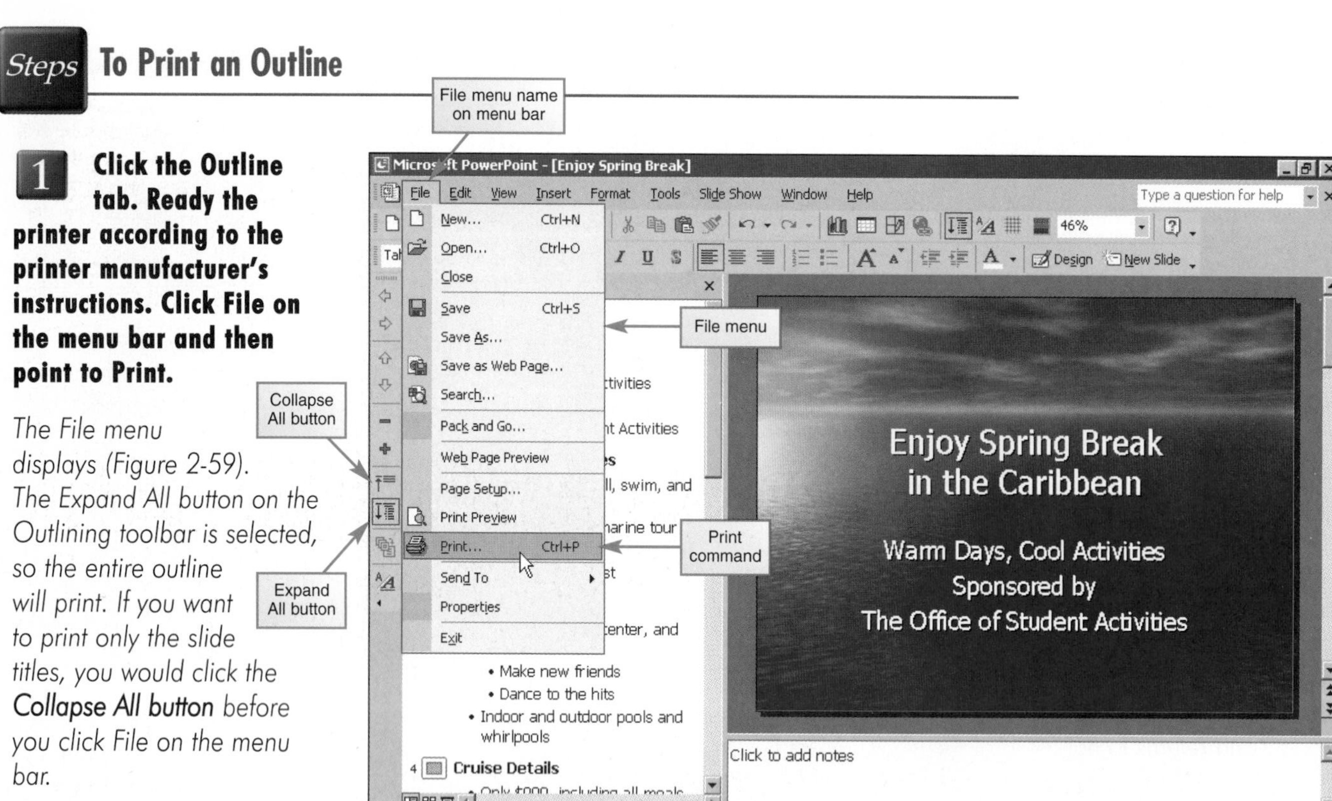

FIGURE 2-59

2 Click Print on the File menu. When the Print dialog box displays, click the Print what box arrow and then point to Outline View.

The Print dialog box displays (Figure 2-60). Outline View displays highlighted in the Print what list.

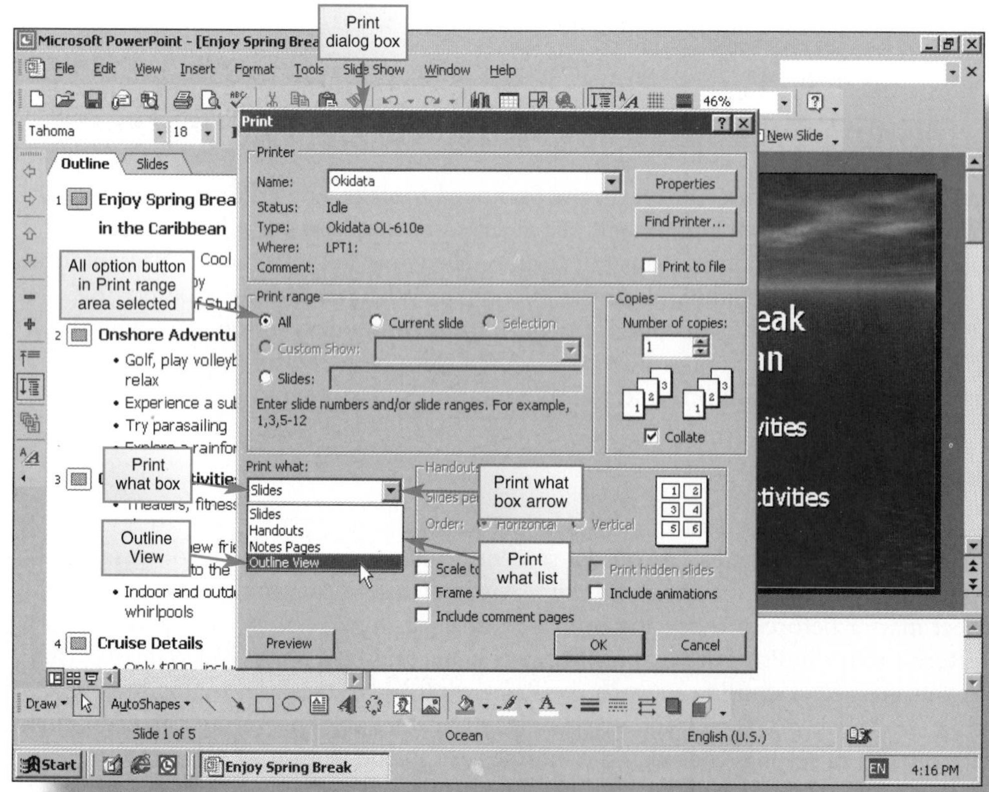

FIGURE 2-60

3 Click Outline View in the list and then point to the OK button (Figure 2-61).

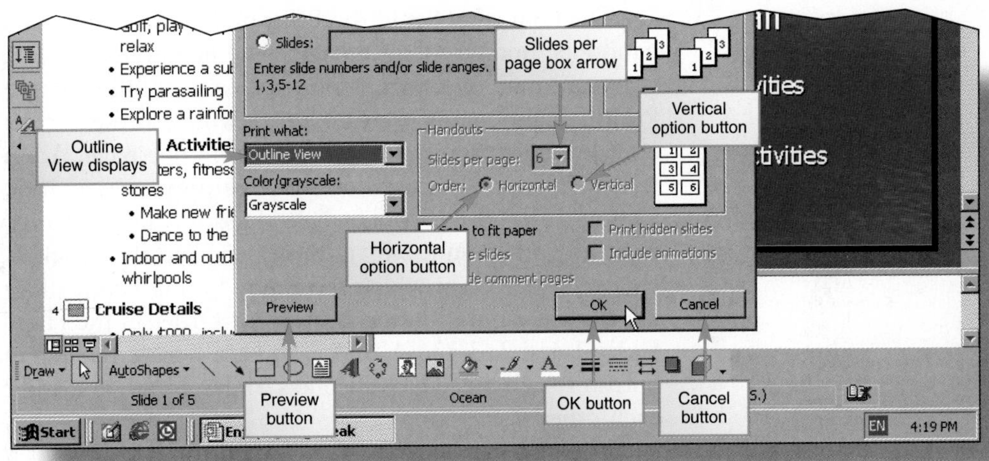

FIGURE 2-61

4 Click the OK button.

To cancel the print request, click the Cancel button.

5 When the printer stops, retrieve the printout of the outline (Figure 2-62).

The five PowerPoint slides display in outline form. The words, Spring Break Cruise, and the current date display in the header, and the words, Office of Student Activities, and the page number display in the footer.

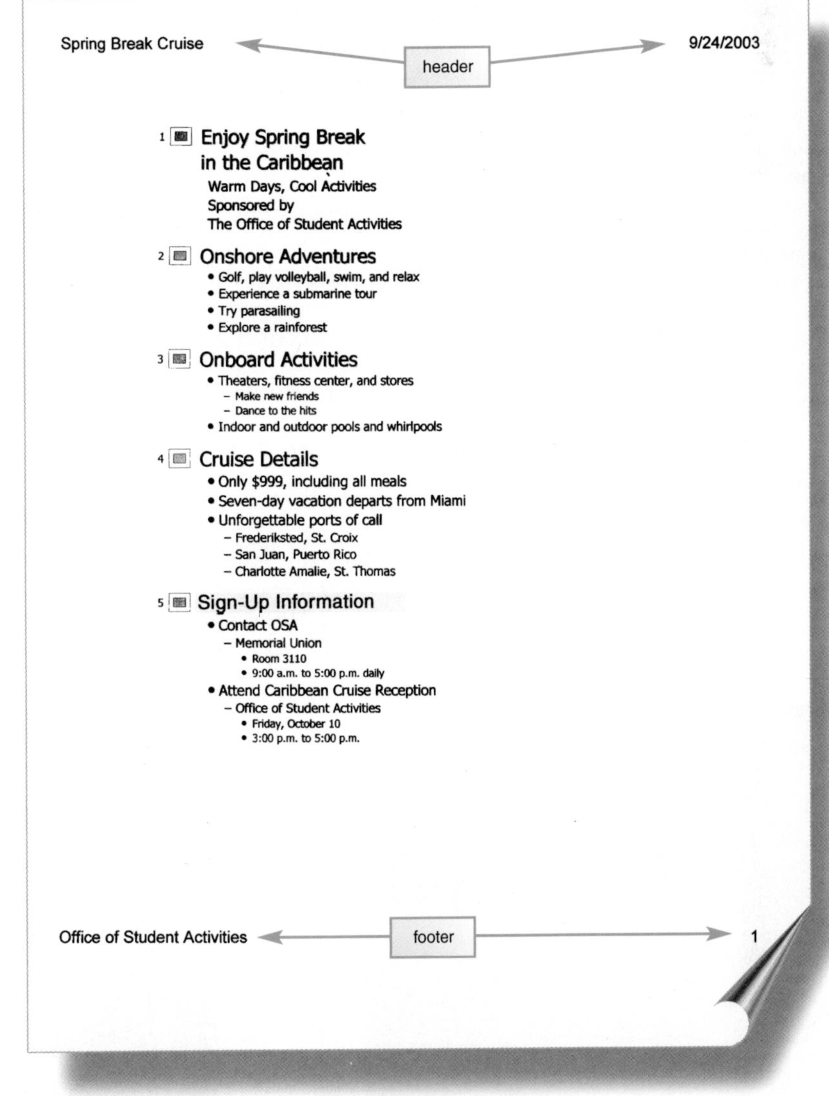

FIGURE 2-62

Other Ways

1. On File menu click Print Preview, click Outline View in Print What list, click Print button on Print Preview toolbar
2. Press ALT+F, press P, press TAB, press W, press DOWN ARROW until Outline View is selected, press ENTER, press ENTER
3. In Voice Command mode, say "File, Print, Print What, Outline View, OK"

The **Print what list** in the Print dialog box contains options for printing slides, handouts, notes, and an outline. The Handouts area allows you to specify whether you want one, two, three, four, six, or nine slide images to display on each page. Printing handouts is useful for reviewing a presentation because you can analyze several slides displaying simultaneously on one page. Additionally, many businesses distribute handouts of the slide show before a presentation so the attendees can refer to a copy. To print handouts, click Handouts in the Print what box, click the Slides per page box arrow in the Handouts area, and then click 1, 2, 3, 4, 6, or 9. You can change the order in which the Enjoy Spring Break slides display on a page by clicking the Horizontal option button for Order in the Handouts area, which displays Slides 1 and 2, 3 and 4, and 5 and 6 adjacent to each other, or the Vertical option button for Order, which displays Slides 1 and 4, 2 and 5, and 3 and 6 adjacent to each other.

You also can click the Preview button if you want to see how your printout will look. After viewing the preview, click the Close button on the Preview window toolbar to return to normal view.

> **More About**
>
> **Printing**
>
> If your printer seems to print slowly, Microsoft suggests clearing at least two megabytes of space on your hard drive and also closing any unnecessary programs that are running simultaneously.

Printing Presentation Slides

At this point, you may want to check the spelling in the entire presentation and instruct PowerPoint to ignore any words spelled correctly. After correcting errors, you will want to print a final copy of your presentation. If you made any changes to your presentation since your last save, be certain to save your presentation before you print.

Perform the following steps to print the presentation.

TO PRINT PRESENTATION SLIDES

1. Ready the printer according to the printer manufacturer's instructions.
2. Click File on the menu bar and then click Print.
3. When the Print dialog box displays, click the Print what box arrow.
4. Click Slides in the list.
5. Click the OK button. When the printer stops, retrieve the slide printouts.

The printouts should resemble the slides in Figures 2-63a through 2-63e.

FIGURE 2-63a Slide 1

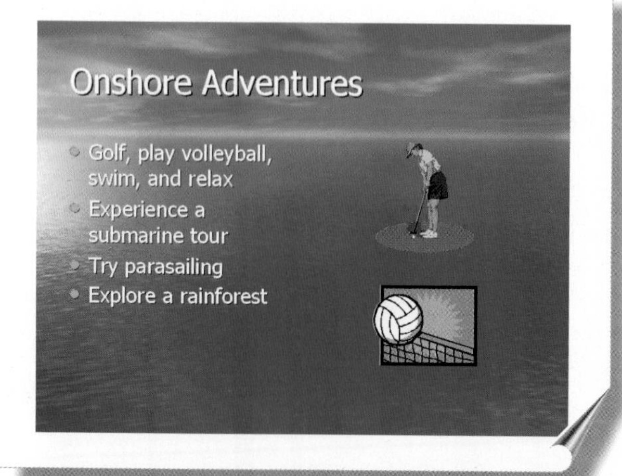

FIGURE 2-63b Slide 2

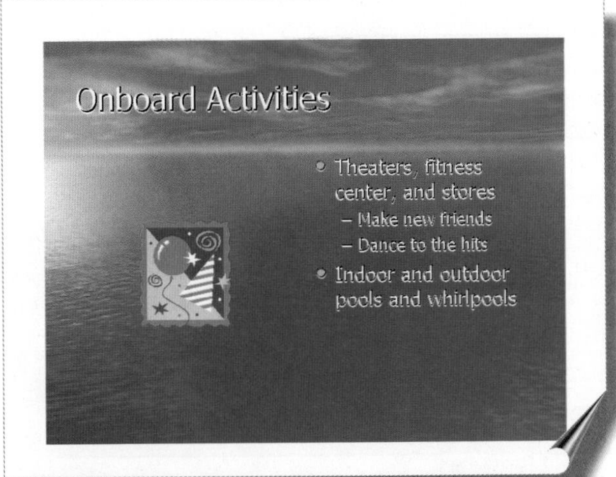

FIGURE 2-63c Slide 3

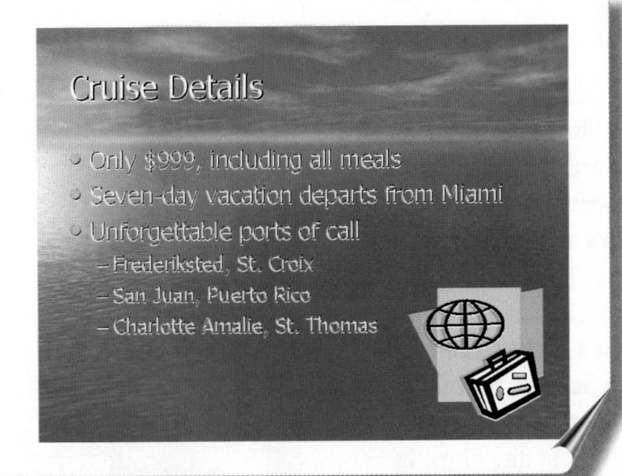

FIGURE 2-63d Slide 4

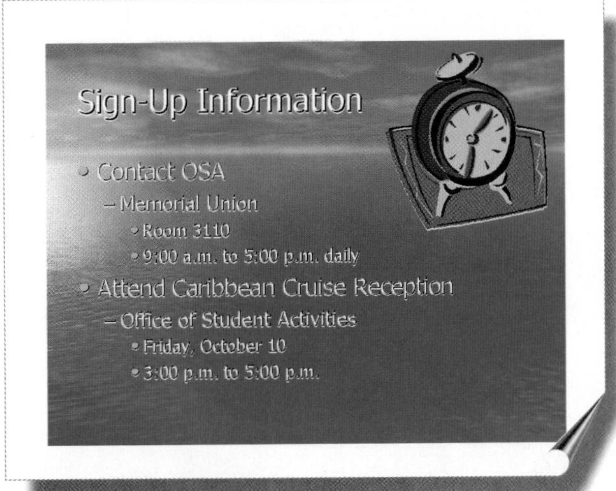

FIGURE 2-63e Slide 5

E-Mailing a Slide Show from within PowerPoint

Billions of e-mail messages are sent throughout the world each year. Computer users use this popular service on the Internet to send and receive plain text e-mail or to send and receive rich e-mail content that includes objects, links to other Web pages, and file attachments. These attachments can include Office files, such as Word documents or PowerPoint slide shows. Using Microsoft Office, you can e-mail the presentation directly from within PowerPoint.

For these steps to work properly, users need an e-mail address and a 32-bit e-mail program compatible with a Messaging Application Programming Interface, such as Outlook, Outlook Express, or Microsoft Exchange Client. Free e-mail accounts are available at hotmail.com. The steps on the next page show how to e-mail the slide show from within PowerPoint to Maria Lopez. Assume her e-mail address is maria_lopez2002@hotmail.com. If you do not have an E-mail button on the Standard toolbar, then this activity is not available to you.

More About

Sending E-Mail

Americans send more than 2.2 billion e-mail messages daily, compared with fewer than 300 million pieces of first-class mail. Professor Leonard Kleinrock sent the first e-mail message in 1969 to a colleague at Stanford University.

Steps To E-Mail a Slide Show from within PowerPoint

1 **Click the E-mail button on the Standard toolbar. When the e-mail Message window displays, type** maria_lopez2002@hotmail.com **in the To text box. Select the text in the Subject text box and then type** Spring Break slide show **in the Subject text box. Click the message body.**

PowerPoint displays the e-mail Message window (Figure 2-64). The insertion point is in the message body so you can type a message to Maria Lopez.

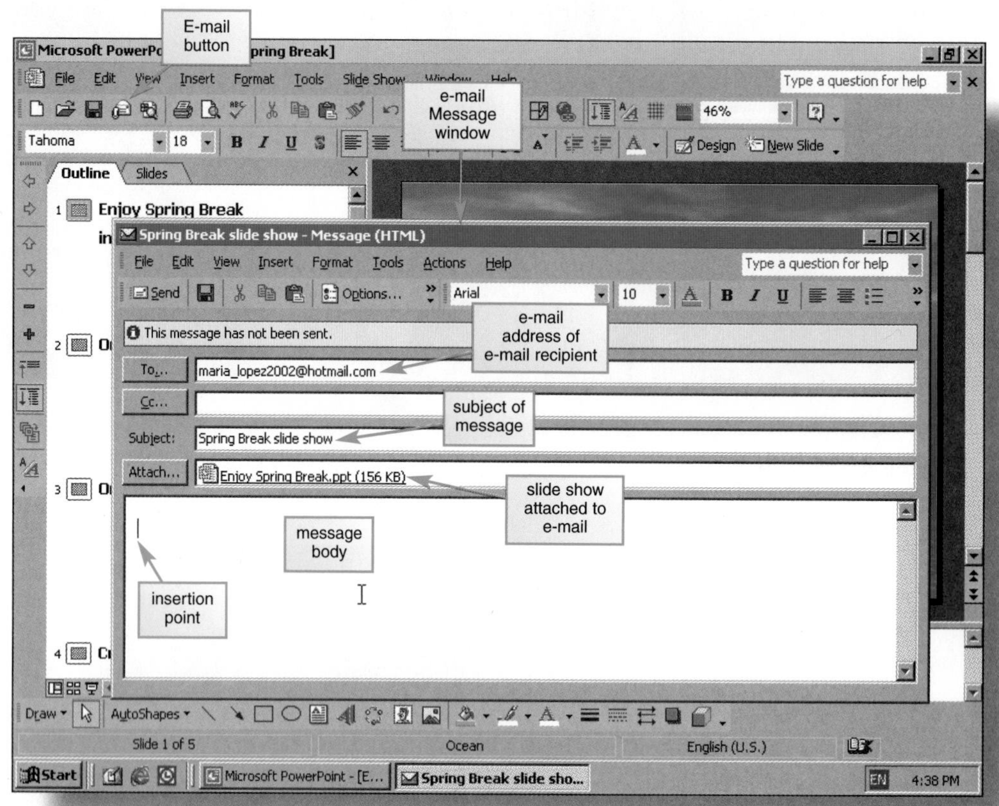

FIGURE 2-64

2 **Type Attached is the PowerPoint presentation you can use to promote the Spring Break cruise. in the message body. Point to the Send button.**

The message is indented to help the recipient of the e-mail understand the purpose of your e-mail (Figure 2-65).

3 **Click the Send button on the Standard Buttons toolbar.**

The e-mail with the attached presentation is sent to maria_lopez2002@hotmail.com.

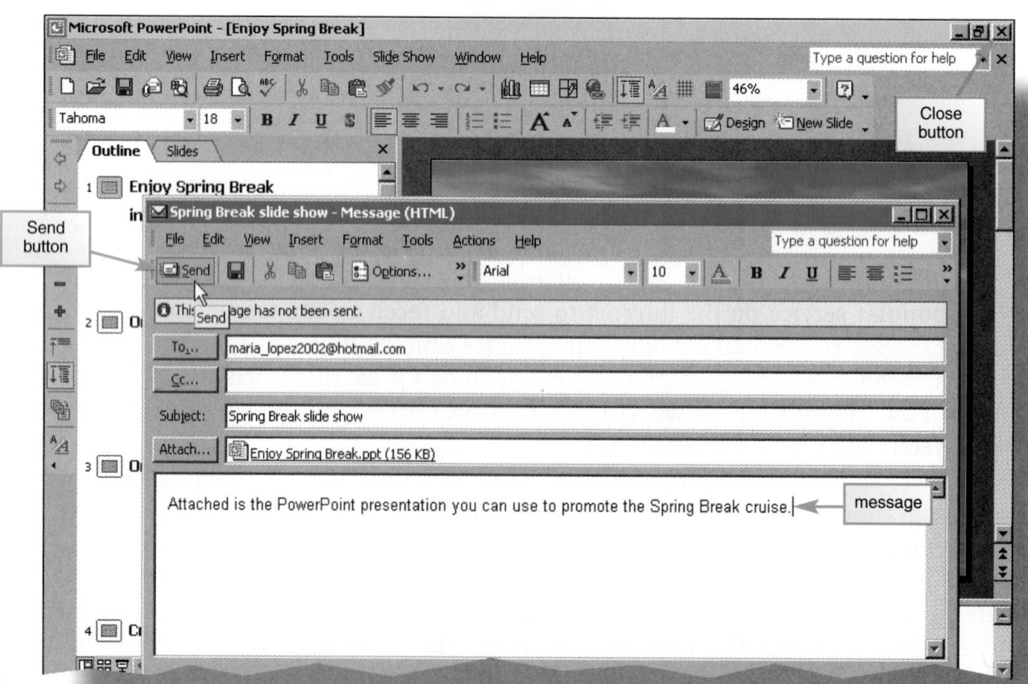

FIGURE 2-65

Because the slide show was sent as an attachment, Maria Lopez can save the attachment and then open the presentation in PowerPoint. You can choose many more options when you send e-mail from within PowerPoint. For example, the **Background command** on the Format menu changes the colors of the message background and lets you add a picture to use as the background. In addition, the **Security button** on the Standard Buttons toolbar allows you to send secure messages that only your intended recipient can read.

Saving and Quitting PowerPoint

If you made any changes to your presentation since your last save, you should save it again before quitting PowerPoint. Perform the following steps to save changes to the presentation and quit PowerPoint.

TO SAVE CHANGES AND QUIT POWERPOINT

1. Click the Close button on the Microsoft PowerPoint window title bar.
2. If prompted, click the Yes button in the Microsoft PowerPoint dialog box.

PowerPoint saves any changes made to the presentation since the last save and then quits PowerPoint.

More About

Microsoft Certification

The Microsoft Office User Specialist (MOUS) Certification program provides an opportunity for you to obtain a valuable industry credential — proof that you have the PowerPoint 2002 skills required by employers. For more information, see Appendix E or visit the Shelly Cashman Series MOUS Web page at scsite.com/offxp/cert.htm.

CASE PERSPECTIVE SUMMARY

The Enjoy Spring Break presentation should help Maria Lopez market the cruise to students at your school. These classmates viewing your presentation will learn about the onshore adventures and onboard activities and discover the details of the trip and how to find more information and register. When Maria runs your slide show, she will describe and expand upon the details you list in your slides. The audience members should have a better understanding of the cruise and the fun they can have during Spring Break this school year.

Project Summary

Project 2 introduced you to the Outline tab, clip art, and animation effects. You created a slide presentation on the Outline tab where you entered all the text in the form of an outline. You arranged the text using the Promote and Demote buttons. Once the outline was complete, you changed slide layouts and added clip art. After adding clip art to slides without using a content placeholder, you moved and sized the clips. You added preset animation effects and applied animation effects to a clip. You learned how to run an animated slide show demonstrating slide transition and animation effects. Finally, you printed the presentation outline and slides using the Print command on the File menu and e-mailed the presentation.

What You Should Know

Having completed this project, you now should be able to perform the following tasks:

- Add a Slide on the Outline Tab *(PP 2.12)*
- Add an Animation Scheme to a Slide Show *(PP 2.40)*
- Add Animation Effects *(PP 2.42)*
- Change the Size of Clip Art *(PP 2.34)*
- Change the Slide Layout to Title, Content and Text and Insert Clip Art *(PP 2.27)*
- Change the Slide Layout to Title, Text, and 2 Content *(PP 2.22)*
- Change the View to Normal View *(PP 2.19)*
- Change the View to Slide Sorter View *(PP 2.18)*
- Change to the Outline Tab and Display the Outlining Toolbar *(PP 2.08)*
- Create a Closing Slide on the Outline Tab *(PP 2.17)*
- Create a Second Text Slide with a Multi-Level Bulleted List *(PP 2.15)*
- Create a Text Slide with a Multi-Level Bulleted List on the Outline Tab *(PP 2.14)*
- Create a Text Slide with a Single-Level Bulleted List on the Outline Tab *(PP 2.13)*
- Create a Title Slide on the Outline Tab *(PP 2.10)*
- E-Mail a Slide Show from within PowerPoint *(PP 2.52)*
- Insert a Second Clip into a Slide *(PP 2.27)*
- Insert Clip Art into a Content Placeholder *(PP 2.25)*
- Insert Clip Art into a Slide without a Content Placeholder *(PP 2.29)*
- Insert, Move, and Size a Clip into a Slide *(PP 2.36)*
- Move Clip Art *(PP 2.33)*
- Print an Outline *(PP 2.48)*
- Print Presentation Slides *(PP 2.50)*
- Run an Animated Slide Show *(PP 2.45)*
- Save a Presentation *(PP 2.18, 2.37, 2.45)*
- Save Changes and Quit PowerPoint *(PP 2.53)*
- Start and Customize a New Presentation *(PP 2.06)*
- Use the Automatic Layout Options Button to Undo a Layout Change *(PP 2.32)*
- Use the Notes and Handouts Sheet to Add Headers and Footers *(PP 2.37)*

Learn It Online

Instructions: To complete the Learn It Online exercises, start your browser, click the Address bar, and then enter `scsite.com/offxp/exs.htm`. When the Office XP Learn It Online page displays, follow the instructions in the exercises below.

1 Project Reinforcement TF, MC, and SA

Below PowerPoint Project 2, click the Project Reinforcement link. Print the quiz by clicking Print on the File menu. Answer each question. Write your first and last name at the top of each page, and then hand in the printout to your instructor.

2 Flash Cards

Below PowerPoint Project 2, click the Flash Cards link. When Flash Cards displays, read the instructions. Type `20` (or a number specified by your instructor) in the Number of Playing Cards text box, type your name in the Name text box, and then click the Flip Card button. When the flash card displays, read the question and then click the Answer box arrow to select an answer. Flip through Flash Cards. Click Print on the File menu to print the last flash card if your score is 15 (75%) correct or greater and then hand it in to your instructor. If your score is less than 15 (75%) correct, then redo this exercise by clicking the Replay button.

3 Practice Test

Below PowerPoint Project 2, click the Practice Test link. Answer each question, enter your first and last name at the bottom of the page, and then click the Grade Test button. When the graded practice test displays on your screen, click Print on the File menu to print a hard copy. Continue to take practice tests until you score 80% or better. Hand in a printout of the final practice test to your instructor.

4 Who Wants to Be a Computer Genius?

Below PowerPoint Project 2, click the Computer Genius link. Read the instructions, enter your first and last name at the bottom of the page, and then click the Play button. Hand in your score to your instructor.

5 Wheel of Terms

Below PowerPoint Project 2, click the Wheel of Terms link. Read the instructions, and then enter your first and last name and your school name. Click the Play button. Hand in your score to your instructor.

6 Crossword Puzzle Challenge

Below PowerPoint Project 2, click the Crossword Puzzle Challenge link. Read the instructions, and then enter your first and last name. Click the Play button. Work the crossword puzzle. When you are finished, click the Submit button. When the crossword puzzle redisplays, click the Print button. Hand in the printout.

7 Tips and Tricks

Below PowerPoint Project 2, click the Tips and Tricks link. Click a topic that pertains to Project 2. Right-click the information and then click Print on the shortcut menu. Construct a brief example of what the information relates to in PowerPoint to confirm you understand how to use the tip or trick. Hand in the example and printed information.

8 Newsgroups

Below PowerPoint Project 2, click the Newsgroups link. Click a topic that pertains to Project 2. Print three comments. Hand in the comments to your instructor.

9 Expanding Your Horizons

Below PowerPoint Project 2, click the Articles for Microsoft Powerpoint link. Click a topic that pertains to Project 2. Print the information. Construct a brief example of what the information relates to in PowerPoint to confirm you understand the contents of the article. Hand in the example and printed information to your instructor.

10 Search Sleuth

Below PowerPoint Project 2, click the Search Sleuth link. To search for a term that pertains to this project, select a term below the Project 2 title and then use the Google search engine at google.com (or any major search engine) to display and print two Web pages that present information on the term. Hand in the printouts to your instructor.

Apply Your Knowledge

1 Intensifying a Presentation by Applying a Design Template, Changing Slide Layout, Inserting Clip Art, and Applying Animation Effects

Instructions: Start PowerPoint. Open the presentation Intramurals from the Data Disk. See the inside back cover of this book for instructions for downloading the Data Disk or see your instructor for information on accessing the files required for this book. Perform the following tasks to change the presentation so it looks like the slides in Figures 2-66a through 2-66d.

(a) Slide 1

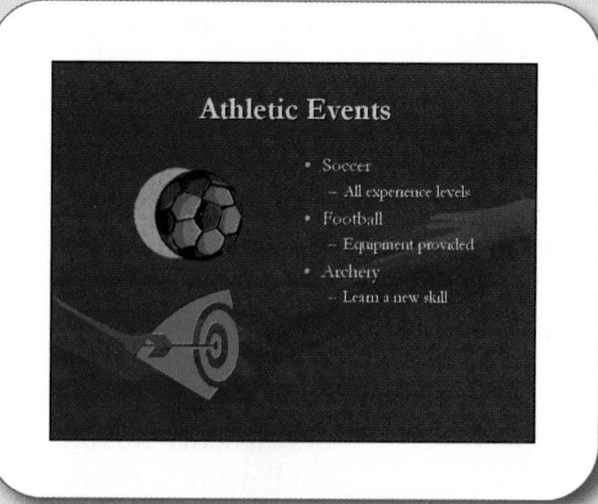

(b) Slide 2

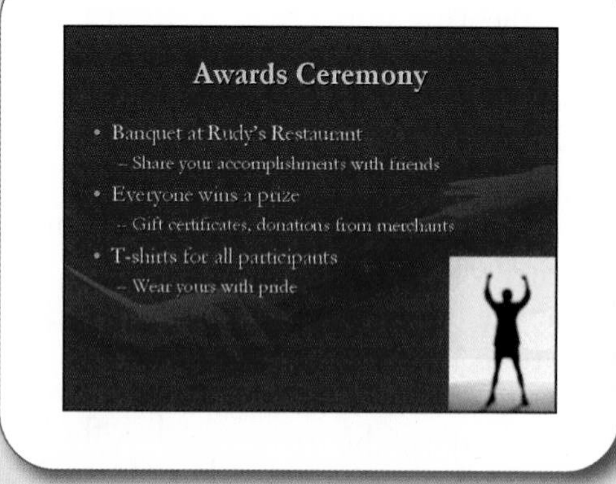

(c) Slide 3

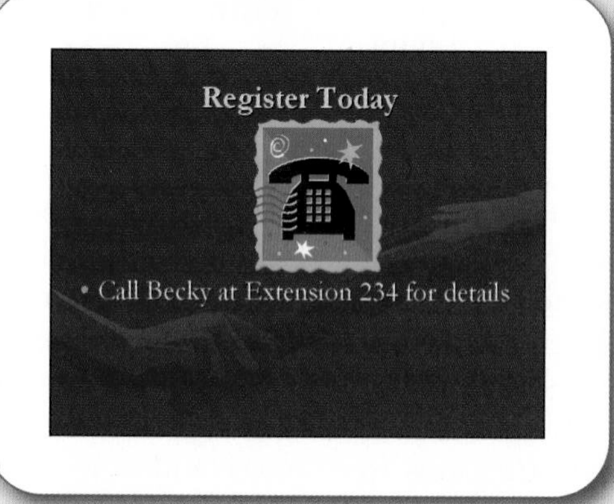

(d) Slide 4

FIGURE 2-66

1. Apply the Teamwork design template. Add the current date and your name to the notes and handouts footer.
2. On Slide 1, increase the font size of the Indulge in Intramurals paragraph to 60 point. Insert the baseball clip shown in Figure 2-66a. Scale the clip art to 130% using the Format Picture command on the shortcut menu. Drag the baseball clip to the top center of the slide, as shown in Figure 2-66a. Apply the Diamond Entrance custom animation effect to the clip.

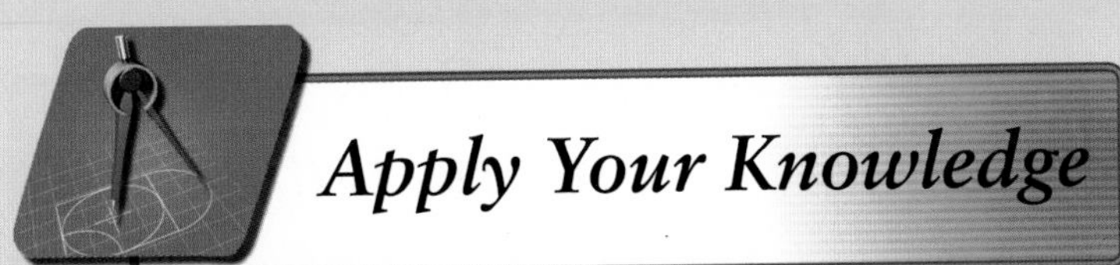

3. Go to Slide 2. Change the slide layout to Title, 2 Content and Text. Insert the sports clips shown in Figure 2-66b. Change the size of both clips to 110%.
4. Go to Slide 3. Insert the clip shown in Figure 2-66c. Increase the clip size to 75%. Drag the clip to the bottom-right corner of the slide. Apply the Spin Emphasis custom animation effect to the clip.
5. Go to Slide 4. Change the slide layout to Title and Content over Text. Insert the telephone clip shown in Figure 2-66d and then center it between the title and the body text. Change the size of the clip to 150%. Apply the Grow/Shrink Emphasis custom animation effect to the clip. Increase the font size of the body text to 40 point.
6. Apply the Bounce animation scheme in the Exciting category list to all slides.
7. Save the presentation on a floppy disk using the file name, Intramurals Publicity.
8. Print the presentation and the outline.
9. Quit PowerPoint.

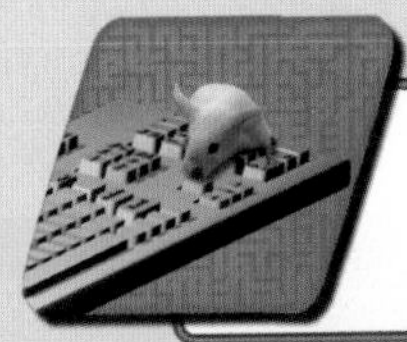

In the Lab

1 Adding Clip Art and Animation Effects to a Presentation Created on the Outline Tab

Problem: One of your assignments in your Health 101 class is to write a research paper and then share your knowledge during a five-minute presentation. You decide to research the topic of keeping your heart healthy. You generate the outline shown in Figure 2-67 to prepare the presentation. You use the outline to create the presentation shown in Figures 2-68a through 2-68d on the next page.

Instructions: Perform the following tasks.

I. Healthy Heart Hints
  A. Presented by Jennifer Korvath
  B. Health 101
II. Healthy Heart Diet
  A. General guidelines
    1) Eat foods that maintain healthy cholesterol levels
    2) Limit saturated fats
      a) In animal products
III. Exercise Benefits
  A. Aerobic activities improve cholesterol levels
    1) Brisk walking, swimming, fencing, and racquet sports
    2) May take year to see significant improvement
  B. Weight training reduces bad cholesterol levels
IV. Decrease Risk Factors
  A. Reduce stress
    1) Mental stress triggers heart disease
  B. Lose weight
    1) Obesity contributes to heart attack risk
  C. Quit smoking
    1) Responsible for 20% of heart disease deaths

FIGURE 2-67

(continued)

In the Lab

Adding Clip Art and Animation Effects to a Presentation Created on the Outline Tab *(continued)*

(a) Slide 1

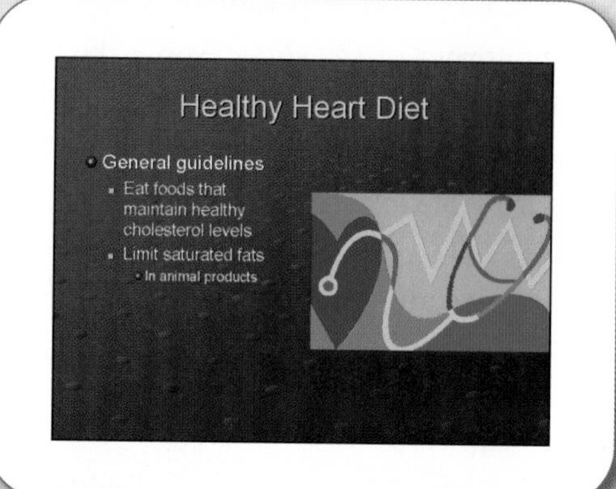

(b) Slide 2

(c) Slide 3

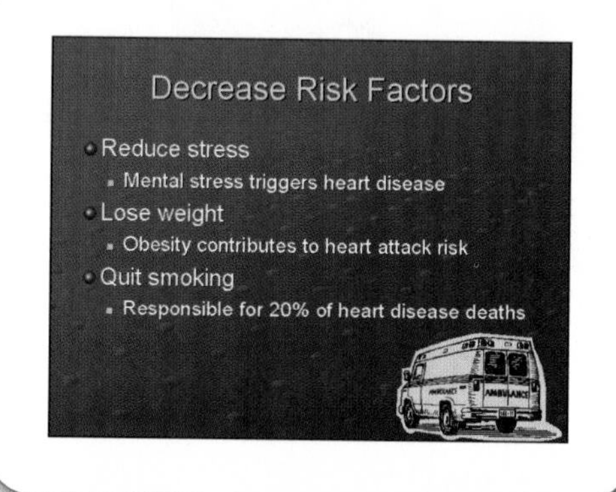

(d) Slide 4

FIGURE 2-68

1. Use the Outline tab to create a new presentation. Apply the Digital Dots design template.
2. Using the outline shown in Figure 2-67, create the title slide shown in Figure 2-68a. Use your name instead of the name Jennifer Korvath. Decrease the font size of the class name to 28 point. Insert the heart clip art. Scale the clip to 75% and then center it at the top of the slide. Add the Box Entrance custom animation effect to the clip.
3. Using the outline in Figure 2-67, create the three text slides with bulleted lists shown in Figures 2-68b through 2-68d.
4. Change the slide layout on Slide 2 to Title, Text, and Content. Insert the heart clip art shown in Figure 2-68b. Scale the clip art to 245% and then move it to the right side of the slide. Add the Checkerboard Entrance custom animation effect to the clip.
5. Change the slide layout on Slide 3 to Title and Text over Content. Insert the clip art shown in Figure 2-68c, scale it to 215%, and then move it to the bottom left of the slide. Add the Right Motion Paths custom animation effect.
6. On Slide 4, insert the ambulance clip art shown in Figure 2-68d. Add the Box Exit custom animation effect.

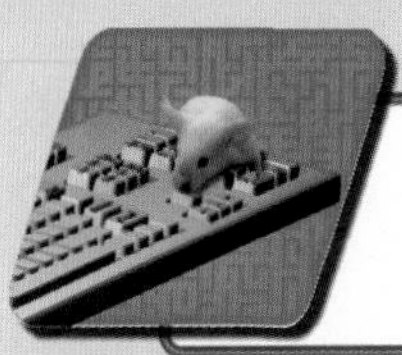

In the Lab

7. Add your name to the outline header and your school's name to the outline footer.
8. Apply the Rise up animation scheme in the Moderate category to all slides in the presentation.
9. Save the presentation on a floppy disk using the file name, Healthy Heart Hints.
10. Print the presentation outline. Print the presentation.
11. Quit PowerPoint.

2 Inserting Clip Art and Animating a Slide Show

Problem: Many students at your school have asked members of the Campus Computer Club for advice on purchasing and upgrading a personal computer. To help these students best, the Club members have decided to prepare a PowerPoint presentation to show to these students. They have given you the outline shown in Figure 2-69. You create the text for the presentation on the Outline tab, and you decide to add animation effects to the slide show. The completed slides are shown in Figures 2-70a through 2-70d on the next page.

Instructions: Perform the following tasks.

1. Use the Outline tab to create a new presentation from the outline shown in Figure 2-69. Apply the Glass Layers design template.
2. On the title slide, increase the font size of Buyer's Guide to 72 point. Decrease the font size of Campus Computer Club to 28 point. Using Figure 2-70a as a reference, insert the clip art shown, scale it to 180%, and then drag it to the lower-right corner of the slide.
3. On Slide 2, insert the clip art shown in Figure 2-70b, click the AutoCorrect Options button to undo the layout change, and then drag the art to the right edge of the slide. Scale the clip to 185%.
4. On Slide 3, change the slide layout to Title, Content and Text. Insert the clip art shown in Figure 2-70c. Scale the clip to 205% and then move it to the location show in the figure.
5. Do not make any changes to Slide 4. On Slide 5, change the slide layout to Title, Text, and Content. Insert the clip art shown in Figure 2-70e. Scale the clip to 210%.

I. Buyer's Guide
- A. Purchasing and Installing a Personal Computer
- B. Campus Computer Club

II. Determine the Type
- A. Desktop
  - 1) Low cost, large screen
- B. Notebook
  - 1) Computing capacity when you travel
- C. Handheld
  - 1) Handle basic organizer-type applications

III. Do Some Research
- A. Talk to friends and instructors
- B. Visit Web sites and read reviews
- C. Use a worksheet to record comparisons

IV. Make the Purchase
- A. Use a credit card
  - 1) Gives purchase protection, extended warranty benefits
- B. Consider an onsite service agreement
  - 1) Available through local dealer or third-party company
  - 2) Technician will arrive within 24 hours

V. Install the System
- A. Read the manuals before you start
- B. Have a well-designed work area
  - 1) Use ergonomic chair and keyboard

FIGURE 2-69

(continued)

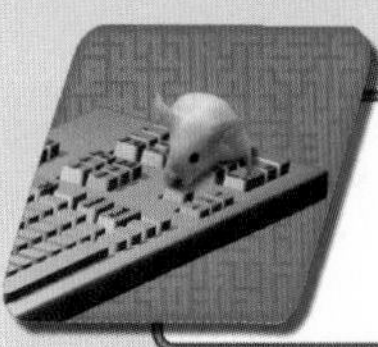

In the Lab

Inserting Clip Art and Animating a Slide Show *(continued)*

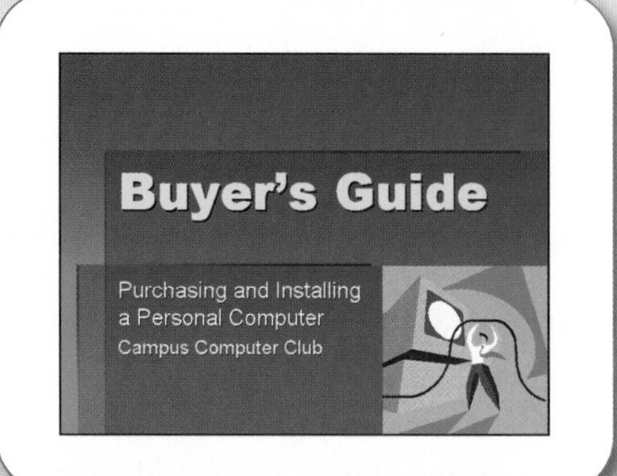

(a) Slide 1

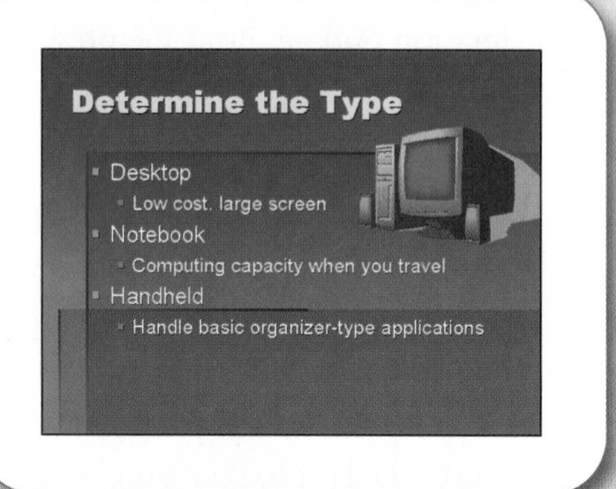

(b) Slide 2

(c) Slide 3

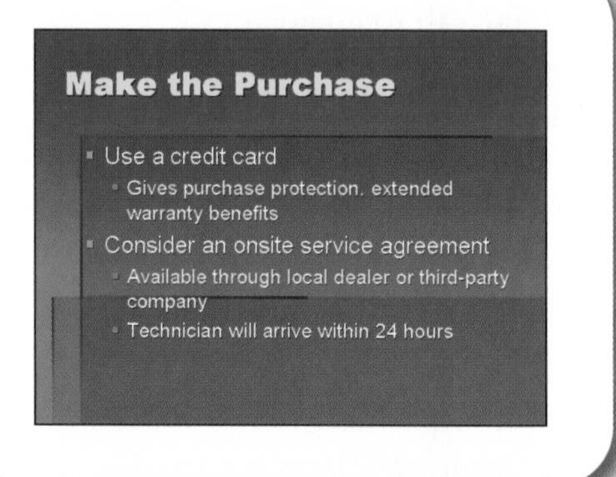

(d) Slide 4

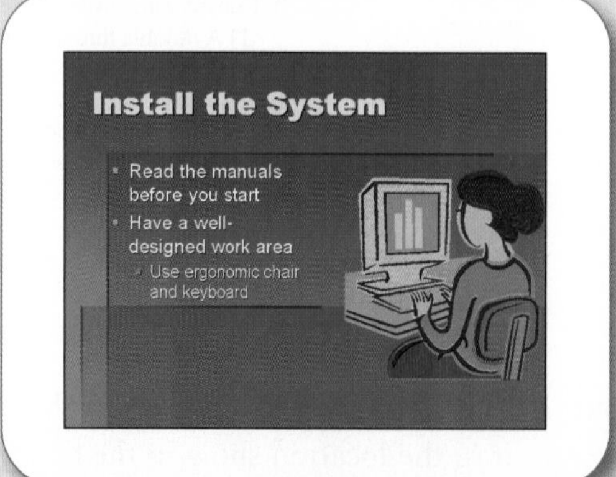

(e) Slide 5

FIGURE 2-70

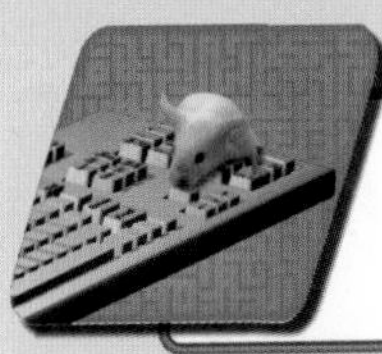

In the Lab

6. Add the current date and your name to the outline header. Include Campus Computer Club and the page number on the outline footer.
7. Apply the Elegant animation scheme in the Moderate category to all slides.
8. Animate the clip on Slide 1 using the Blinds Entrance custom animation effect, the clip on Slide 2 using the Diagonal Down Right Motion Paths effect, the clip on Slide 3 using the Checkerboard Entrance effect, and the clip on Slide 5 using the Box Exit effect.
9. Save the presentation on a floppy disk using the file name, Buyer's Guide.
10. Print the presentation outline. Print the presentation slides. Print a handout with all five slides arranged vertically on one page.
11. Quit PowerPoint.

3 Creating a Presentation on the Outline Tab, Inserting Clip Art, and Applying Slide Transitions and Animation Effects

Problem: Chief Malcolm Snipes from the police department at your school has asked you to help him prepare a lecture on the topic of roadside emergencies. He has helped many students when they call his office for assistance. He knows that nearly 3,000 people die in car accidents every year when their cars are parked on the side of a road or on a median, and many of these fatalities started with a breakdown that could have been avoided. He asks you to prepare a PowerPoint presentation to accompany his talk. The slide show will describe how to pull off the road safely, how to obtain help, what supplies to store in your glove compartment, what supplies to keep in your trunk, and what routine maintenance you should perform. You search for appropriate clip art to add to the slides and are unable to find images that are part of the Microsoft Clip Organizer. You connect to the Internet, obtain clip from Microsoft's Web site, and create the presentation using the outline shown in Figure 2-71.

I. Handling Roadside Breakdowns
  A. Stop Problems, Remain Safe
  B. Presented by
  C. Campus Police Department
II. Pull off the Road Safely
  A. Eliminate distractions
    1) Turn off the stereo
  B. Look in mirrors
  C. Reduce speed slowly
  D. Use turn signal
    1) Not flashers
III. Obtain Help
  A. Place 'Call Police' sign in window
  B. Tie scarf or clothing to door handle or antenna
  C. Stay inside the vehicle
    1) Keep seat belt fastened
IV. Glove Compartment Supplies
  A. 'Call Police' sign
  B. Flashlight
  C. Health insurance card
  D. Pen, message pad
  E. Vehicle registration, insurance
V. Trunk Supplies
  A. Fire extinguisher
  B. Jack and lug wrench
  C. Spare tire inflated properly
  D. Jumper cables
VI. Perform Routine Maintenance
  A. Check oil level, tire pressure weekly
  B. Rotate tires every 5,000 miles
  C. Examine tires for cuts, nails, stones

FIGURE 2-71

(continued)

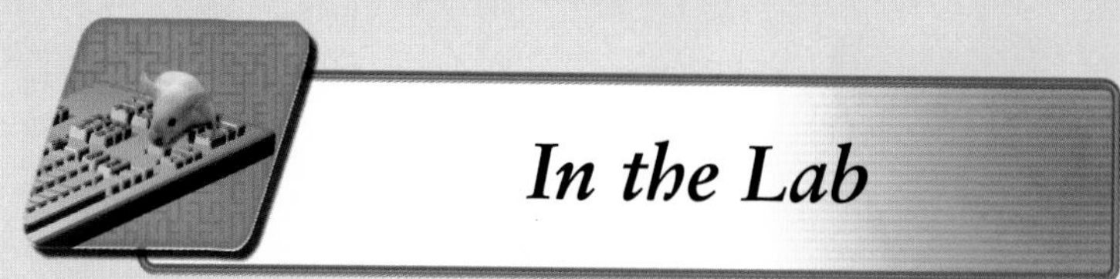

Creating a Presentation on the Outline Tab, Inserting Clip Art, and Applying Slide Transitions and Animation Effects *(continued)*

The clips you find may vary from the clips shown in Figures 2-72a through 2-72f. You then refine the presentation using clip art, animation schemes, and custom animation effects to create the slide show shown in Figures 2-72a through 2-72f.

Instructions: Perform the following tasks.

1. Create a new presentation using the Ripple design template and the outline in Figure 2-71 on the previous page.
2. On the title slide, insert the clip art shown in Figure 2-72a and add the Fly In Entrance custom animation effect. Change the speed to Slow. Size the clip if necessary.
3. On Slide 2, change the slide layout to Title, Text, and 2 Content, and insert the clips shown in Figure 2-72b. Add the Fly In Entrance custom animation effect for the top image and change the Direction to From Top-Right. Add the Fly In Entrance custom animation effect for the bottom image. Size the clips if necessary.
4. On Slide 3, change the slide layout to Title and Text over Content, and insert the clip shown in Figure 2-72c. Add the Grow/Shrink Emphasis custom animation effect. Size the clip if necessary.
5. Change the slide layout on Slide 4 (Figure 2-72d) to Title, 2 Content and Text. Insert the two clip art images shown. Add the Box Entrance custom animation effect to both clips. Size the clips if necessary.
6. On Slide 5 (Figure 2-72e), change the slide layout to Title and 2 Content over Text. Insert the clips shown and add the Fly In Entrance custom animation effect for both. Change the Direction for the fire extinguisher to From Top-Left and for the tire to From Top-Right. Size the clips if necessary.
7. On Slide 6 (Figure 2-72f), change the slide layout to Title, Text, and 2 Content. Insert the clips shown and add the Spin Emphasis custom animation effect to both. Size the clips if necessary.
8. Display your name and the current date on the outline header, and display the page number and the name of your school on the outline footer.
9. Apply the Unfold animation scheme to all slides.
10. Save the presentation on a floppy disk using the file name, Roadside Breakdowns.
11. Run the slide show.
12. Print the presentation outline. Print the presentation slides. Print a handout with all six slides arranged horizontally on one page. E-mail the presentation to Chief Snipes using the address malcolm_snipes@hotmail.com.
13. Quit PowerPoint.

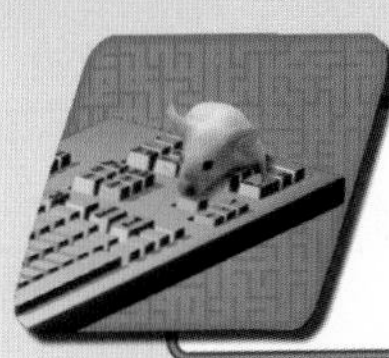

In the Lab

(a) Slide 1

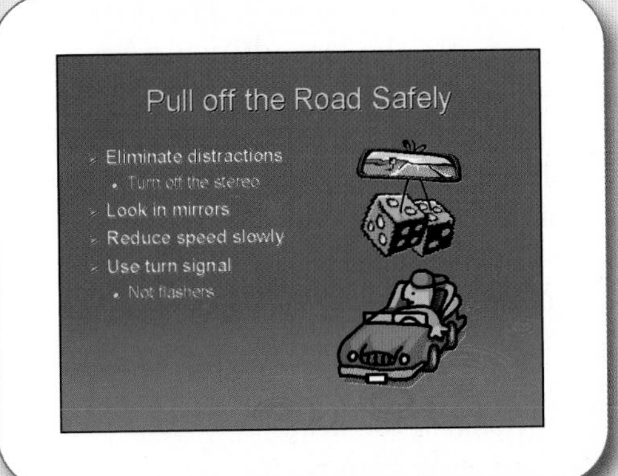

(b) Slide 2

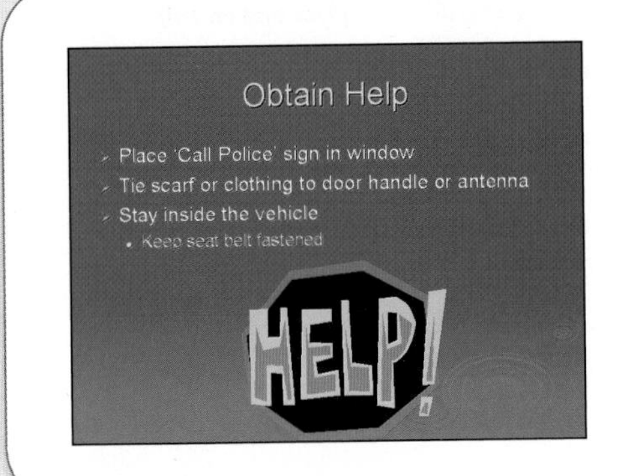

(c) Slide 3

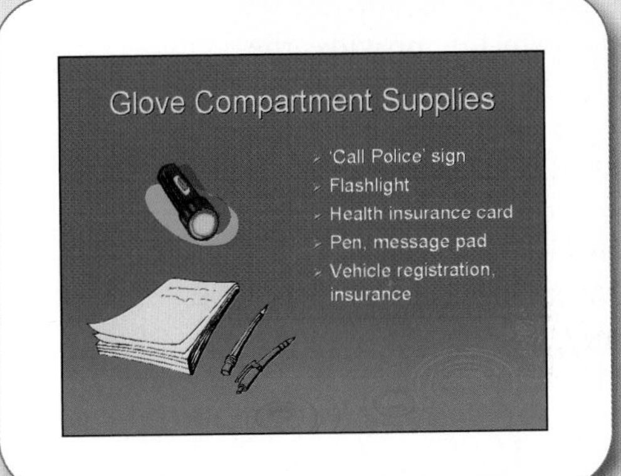

(d) Slide 4

(e) Slide 5

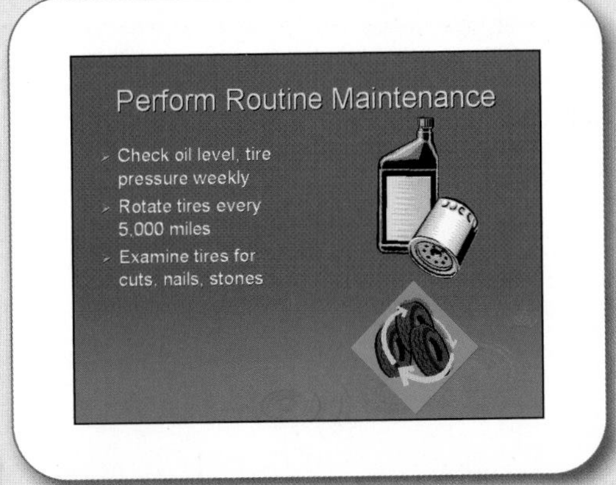

(f) Slide 6

FIGURE 2-72

Cases and Places

The difficulty of these case studies varies:
▶ are the least difficult; ▶▶ are more difficult; and ▶▶▶ are the most difficult.

1 ▶ With the holidays approaching, Janis Lamata, the head librarian at Weber Hills Community Library, wants to present a series of cooking demonstrations. Janis has asked Jean-Luc Richard, the head chef at Chateau la Flambeau Restaurant, to make the presentations. His first program features grilling turkeys and is called, Grilling Is Not Just for Steaks. Jean-Luc provides the outline shown in Figure 2-73 and asks your help in creating a PowerPoint presentation. Using the concepts and techniques introduced in this project, together with Jean-Luc's outline, develop slides for a slide show. Include clip art and animation effects to add interest. Print the outline and slides as handouts so they can be distributed to presentation attendees.

I. Grilling Is Not Just for Steaks
  A. Cooking Turkeys on Your Outdoor Grill
  B. Presented by
  C. Jean-Luc Richard
  D. Head Chef, Chateau la Flambeau Restaurant
II. Before You Start
  A. Pick a turkey less than 24 pounds
    1. Make sure it is thawed completely
  B. Have plenty of fuel
    1. Propane tanks - 5 to 6 hours
    2. Charcoal - 65 to 75 briquettes
  C. Wash hands and utensils thoroughly before touching food
III. Start Cooking
  A. Set grill for indirect grilling and place bird on grill
  B. Cooking times
    1. 12-14 lbs. - 2½ to 3 hours
    2. 15-17 lbs. - 2¾ to 3½ hours
    3. 18-22 lbs. - 3½ to 4¼ hours
  C. No need to turn or baste
IV. Doneness
  A. Cook until meat thermometer reaches 180 degrees
  B. Remove from grill
  C. Let stand 20 minutes
  D. Smoked turkey may appear a little pink
    1. It is cooked thoroughly

FIGURE 2-73

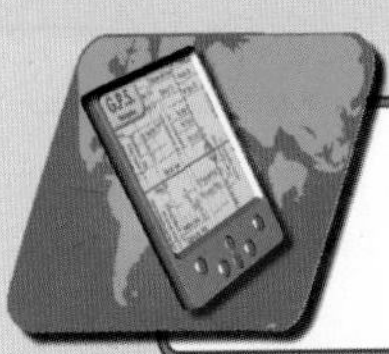

Cases and Places

2 ▸ Dr. Jasmine Lopez wants to make a presentation at the Rest Haven Rehabilitation Center and Clinic where you volunteer on weekends. The presentation is a series of healthy tips for those planning to retire between the ages of 50 and 55 so they can enjoy their retirement for many years. The nursing director, Charles Becker, asks you to create a PowerPoint presentation for Dr. Lopez. The presentation will cover preventive health strategies for those planning early retirement. Dr. Lopez has provided the outline shown in Figure 2-74. Using the concepts and techniques introduced in this project, together with Dr. Lopez's outline, develop slides for a slide show. Include clip art and animation effects to add interest. Print the outline and slides as a one-page handout so they can be distributed to presentation attendees.

I. Staying Healthy as You Age
  A. Presented by
  B. Dr. Jasmine Lopez
  C. Board-certified internist and Director of Adult Health Care
II. Eating to Live Longer
  A. Balance food with physical activity
  B. Eat plenty of whole grains, vegetables, and fruits
  C. Reduce fatty meats
    1. Choose fish and chicken
    2. Concentrate on low-saturated fats
  D. Limit consumption of salt, sugar, and alcoholic beverages
III. Longevity with Vitamins
  A. B vitamins reduce homocysteine protein
    1. Decrease heart disease
  B. As we age, we have difficulty absorbing calcium and vitamins B-12 and D
  C. Vitamin C
    1. Decreases cancer risk by 20%
    2. Reduces the risk of heart attacks by 40%
IV. Do Not Call This a Diet
  A. White blood cells (natural infection fighters) are affected by what we eat
  B. Eat for life
    1. Follow the USDA Food Guide Pyramid
    2. Avoid cooking fats derived from animal products
    3. Avoid trans fats (hydrogenated fats)
      a. They increase triglycerides

FIGURE 2-74

3 ▸▸ Strength training offers many positive benefits. First, it builds power. Athletes who participate in strength training can increase their performance in other sports, such as tennis or golf. Strength training also provides energy. Research shows that strength training increases endurance for runners and swimmers. Another benefit of this training is decreased fatigue. It also improves mood, self-confidence, and self-esteem, which expand beyond sports into personal life. Strength training also helps prevent osteoporosis by strengthening bones and building bone density. It helps burn calories, even while a person is resting, by increasing the body's metabolism for as many as 12 hours after exercising. The training also balances the body by making both sides equally strong. Normally, one side is stronger than the other. A balanced body is less prone to injuries. The director of your campus fitness center wants new members to view a presentation on strength training. Using the techniques introduced in this project, create a slide show about strength training. Include appropriate clip art and animation effects.

Cases and Places

4 ▶▶ As an intern for the Great Lakes Arts Association (GLAA), you have helped the Association's director, Rajish Gupta, with many projects. He asks you to create a PowerPoint presentation for his visits at many community sites. Rajish says the Association's mission is to strengthen the bond between the diverse communities in the Great Lakes area. It also provides opportunities for artistic expression, education, cultural exchanges, and art appreciation. In addition, the Association's commission provides cultural planning, grant writing, information and referral services, and technical assistance. It sponsors exhibits of local, regional, national, and international artists at various locations. Exhibits feature fiber art, photography, paintings, folk art, glass, and sculptures. Educational opportunities include art classes and workshops by prominent artists at local schools, lectures, readings, bus tours narrated by art historians and authorities, and scholarships to send gifted students from low-income families to state colleges and private art schools. Membership levels are student, individual, family, artist, patron, sponsor, benefactor, life member, and organization. Using the techniques introduced in this project, create a presentation about the GLAA. Include appropriate clip art and animation effects.

5 ▶▶ Walking is one of the easiest methods of exercising. Many students have discovered that walking enhances both the body and spirit. Leading researchers believe this form of exercise also prolongs life. Paula Peerman, the director of recreation at your community's park district, wants to organize a walking club and has asked you to help her promote the idea. She wants you to recruit and motivate members by describing various techniques to enhance their walking routines. For example, members can try interval training by increasing their walking speed for 30 seconds and then returning to their normal speed for one minute. They also should walk with a friend to add motivation and help pass the time. If they do not feel like walking on a particular day, they can tell each other they are going to exercise for just a few minutes. Those few minutes might stretch into a half-hour or more. Walkers should swing their arms to increase their heart rates and to burn more calories. Using the techniques introduced in this project, create a presentation about the benefits of walking. Include appropriate clip art and animation effects.

6 ▶▶▶ Bookstores are becoming an integral part of the community. Many have guest speakers, cultural events, and various clubs. Your local bookstore, Bobbie's Books, is sponsoring a book club, where members will meet on four consecutive Monday nights to discuss a famous author. Pick a prominent author, such as Stephen King, Danielle Steel, John Grisham, Michael Crichton, or Margaret Eleanor Atwood. Visit your local bookstore and library, and search the Internet for information about the author. Then, create a presentation to promote Bobbie's Books. Include a short biography of this author, describe his or her best-selling books, discuss critical comments by reviewers, and present relevant Web sites. Include appropriate clip art and animation effects.

7 ▶▶▶ Many homeowners are finding the cost of remodeling prohibitive, so they are taking on do-it-yourself projects. Visit two local lumberyards or building supply stores and collect information about adding a wooden deck to a home. Learn about the different types of wood and stains, the various types of designs, and how to maintain the deck. Then, create a PowerPoint presentation that includes a summary of this information along with a list of the tools and materials needed and the estimated time to complete the project. Add appropriate clip art and animation effects.

Microsoft PowerPoint 2002

Creating a Presentation on the Web Using PowerPoint

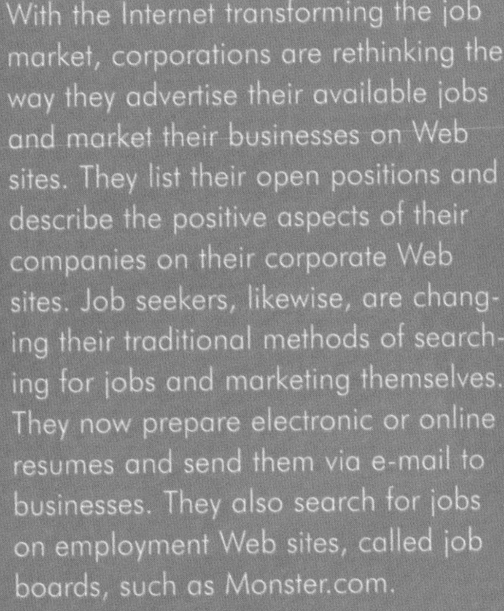

CASE PERSPECTIVE

With the Internet transforming the job market, corporations are rethinking the way they advertise their available jobs and market their businesses on Web sites. They list their open positions and describe the positive aspects of their companies on their corporate Web sites. Job seekers, likewise, are changing their traditional methods of searching for jobs and marketing themselves. They now prepare electronic or online resumes and send them via e-mail to businesses. They also search for jobs on employment Web sites, called job boards, such as Monster.com.

The Placement Center director at Highland College, Tina Natella, wants to teach students how to use the Internet to find careers. She decides the most effective way to disseminate this information is to have you prepare a PowerPoint slide show and then make the presentation available on the World Wide Web to all students. The slide show, called Job Search, will contain this information along with clip art and an animation scheme for visual interest. Tina then wants you to publish the presentation on the Web in a file named Jobs on the Internet.

Introduction

The graphic design power of PowerPoint allows you to create vibrant presentations that convey information in a clear, interesting manner. Some of these presentations are created for small, specific audiences, such as a subcommittee planning a department retreat. In this case, the presentation may be shown in an office conference room. Other presentations are designed for large, general audiences, such as workers at a corporation's various offices across the country learning about a new insurance benefits package. These employees can view the presentation on their company's **intranet**, which is an internal network that uses Internet technologies. On a grand scale, you can inform the entire world about the contents of your presentation by posting your slide show to the World Wide Web. To publish to the World Wide Web, you need an **FTP** (**File Transfer Protocol**) program to copy your presentation and related files to a Web server.

PowerPoint allows you to create a Web page in two ways. First, you can start a new presentation, as you did in Projects 1 and 2 when you produced the Make Friends and Enjoy Spring Break presentations. PowerPoint provides a Web Presentation template in the **AutoContent Wizard** option when you start PowerPoint. The wizard provides design and content ideas to help you develop an effective slide show for an intranet or for the Internet by opening a sample presentation that you can alter by adding your own text and graphics.

Second, by using the **Save as Web Page command**, you can convert an existing presentation to a format compatible with popular Web browsers such as Microsoft Internet Explorer. This command allows you to create a Web page from a single slide or from a multiple-slide presentation.

This Web Feature illustrates opening the Job Search presentation on the Data Disk (Figure 1a) and then saving the presentation as a Web page using the Save as Web Page command. See the inside back cover of this book for instructions for downloading the Data Disk or see your instructor for information on accessing the files required in this book. Then, you will publish your presentation, and PowerPoint will start your default browser and open your HTML file so you can view the presentation (Figures 1b through 1e). Finally, you will edit the presentation, save it again, and view it again in your default browser.

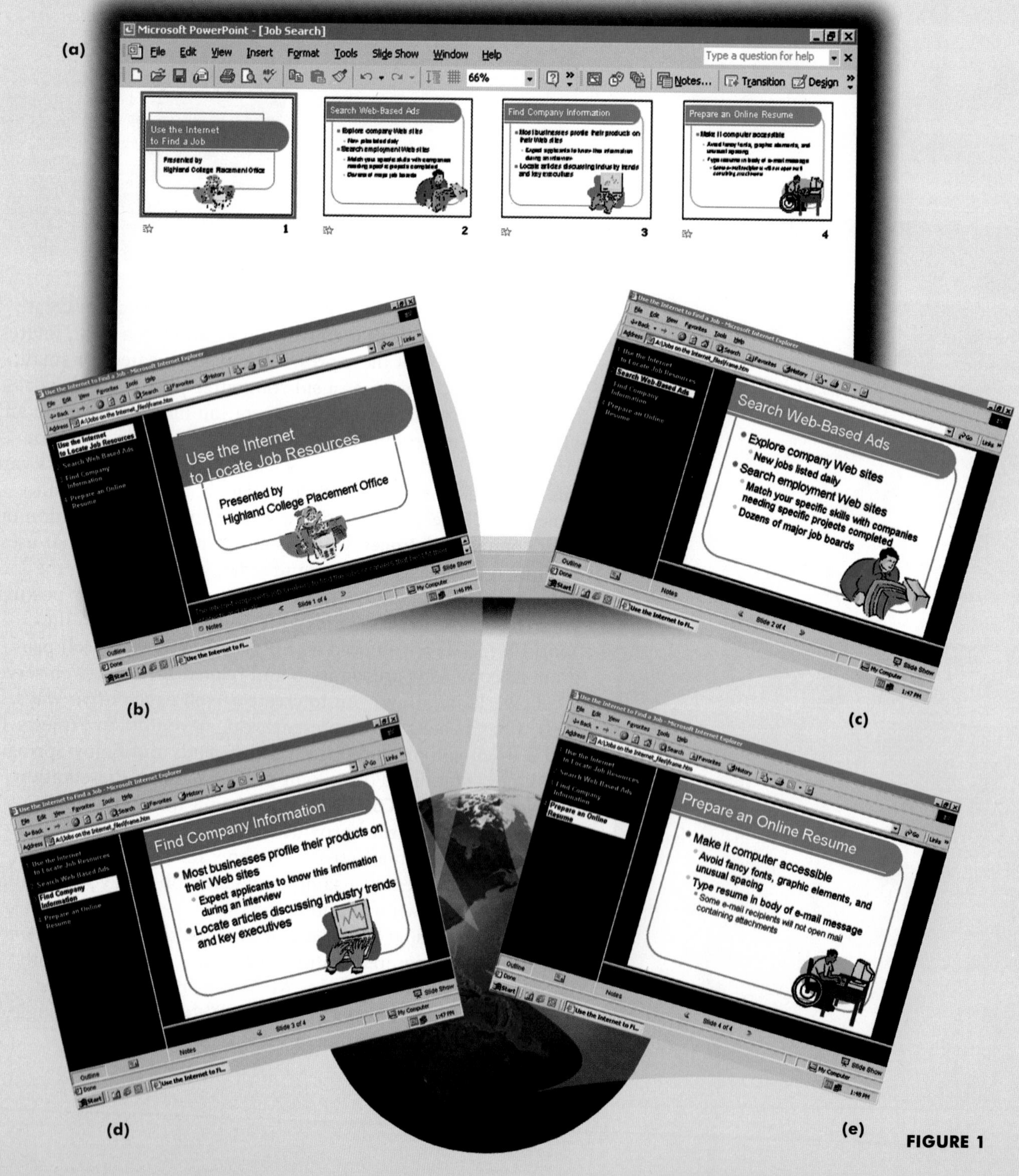

FIGURE 1

You can preview your presentation as a Web page. This action opens the presentation in your default Web browser without saving HTML files. You can use this feature to review and modify your work in progress until you develop a satisfactory presentation.

Because you are converting the Job Search presentation on the Data Disk to a Web page, the first step in this project is to open the Job Search file. Then, you will save the file as a Web page and view the presentation in your default browser. For instructional purposes in this Web Feature, you create and save your Web page on a floppy disk. At times, this saving process may be slow, so you must be patient.

Job Searches on the Internet

Corporations are predicted to spend $4 billion by 2005 on online recruiting and job-placement advertisements, up from $411 million in 1999. Newspaper classified advertising revenues are expected to decrease dramatically. Some human resources personnel claim they can fill vacant positions twice as quickly by posting their ads online rather than placing ads in the newspaper.

Saving a PowerPoint Presentation as a Web Page

Once a PowerPoint slide show is complete, you want to save it as a Web page so you can publish and then view it in a Web browser. Microsoft Internet Explorer and Netscape Navigator are the two more common browsers installed on computers today. PowerPoint allows you to **publish** the presentation by saving the pages to a Web folder or to an FTP location. When you publish your presentation, it is available for other computer users to view on the Internet or by other means.

You can save and then view the presentation in two ways. First, you can save the entire presentation as a Web page, quit PowerPoint, open your browser, and open the Web page in your browser. Second, you can combine these steps by saving the presentation as a Web page, publishing the presentation, and then viewing the presentation as a Web page. In this case, PowerPoint will start the browser and display your presentation automatically. Perform the following steps to save and publish the Job Search presentation as a Web page.

Steps To Save a PowerPoint Presentation as a Web Page

1 Start PowerPoint and then open the Job Search file on the Data Disk. Click the notes pane and then type `The Internet empowers job seekers to find the jobs or careers that best fit their interests and goals.` **as the note. Click File on the menu bar and then point to Save as Web Page.**

PowerPoint opens and displays the presentation in normal view (Figure 2). The File menu displays. The notes frame contains the speaker notes you typed.

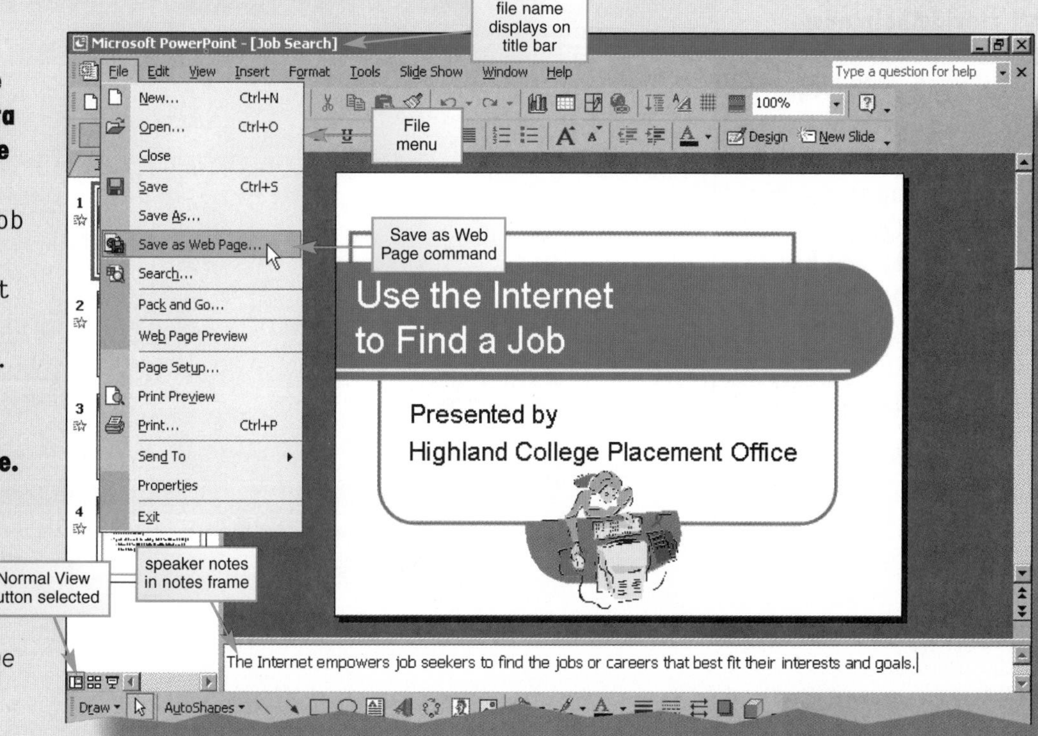

FIGURE 2

2 Click Save as Web Page. When the Save As dialog box displays, type `Jobs on the Internet` **in the File name text box. Point to the Publish button.**

PowerPoint displays the Save As dialog box (Figure 3). Web Page displays in the Save as type box.

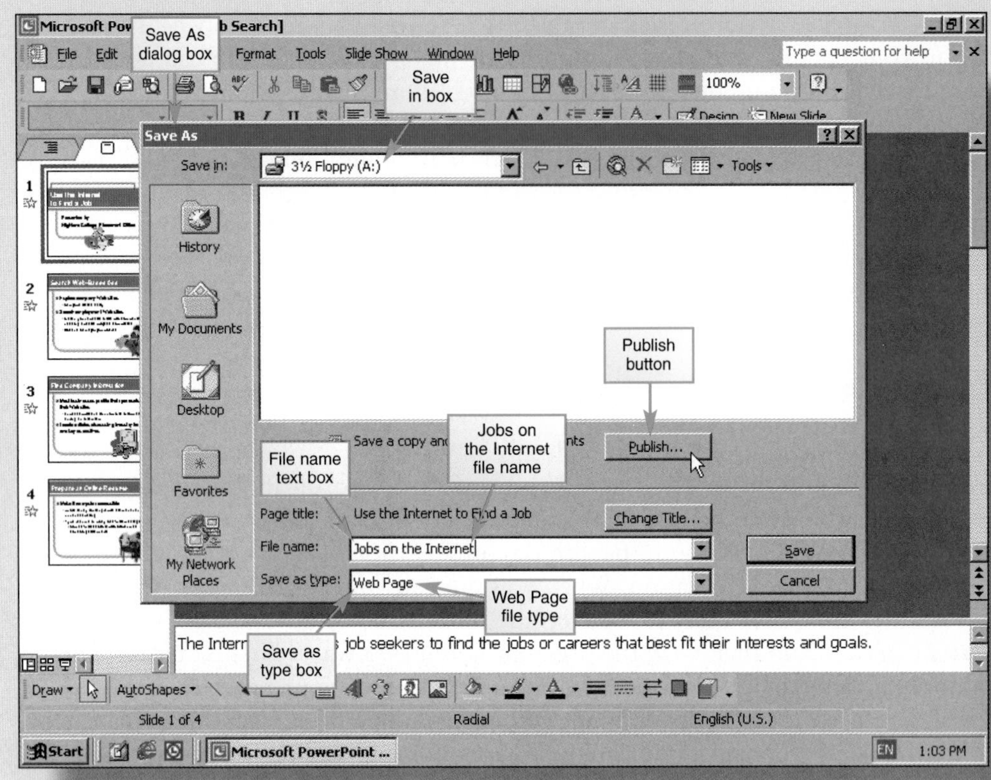

FIGURE 3

3 Click the Publish button. If the Office Assistant displays, click No, don't provide help now. When the Publish as Web Page dialog box displays, triple-click the File name text box in the Publish a copy as area and then type `A:\Jobs on the Internet` **in the text box. If necessary, click Open published Web page in browser to select it. Point to the Publish button.**

The Publish as Web Page dialog box displays (Figure 4). PowerPoint defaults to publishing the complete presentation, although you can choose to publish one or a range of slides. The **Open published Web page in browser check box** *is selected, which means the Jobs on the Internet presentation will open in your default browser when you click the Publish button.*

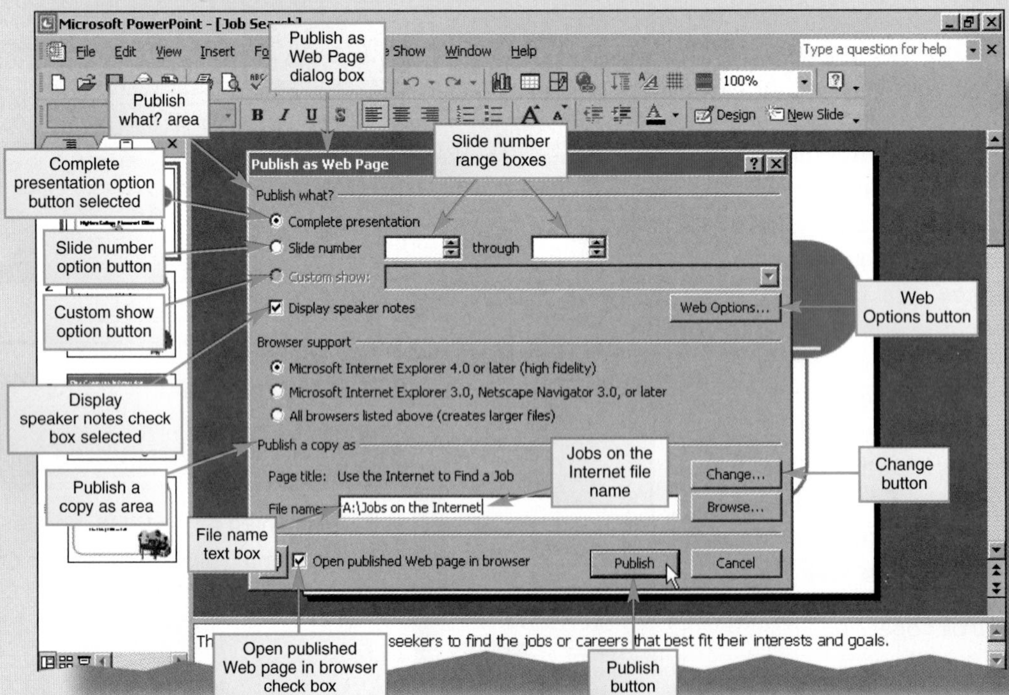

FIGURE 4

4 Click the Publish button.

PowerPoint saves the presentation as Jobs on the Internet.htm on the Data Disk in drive A. After a few seconds, PowerPoint opens your default Web browser in a separate window (Figure 5).

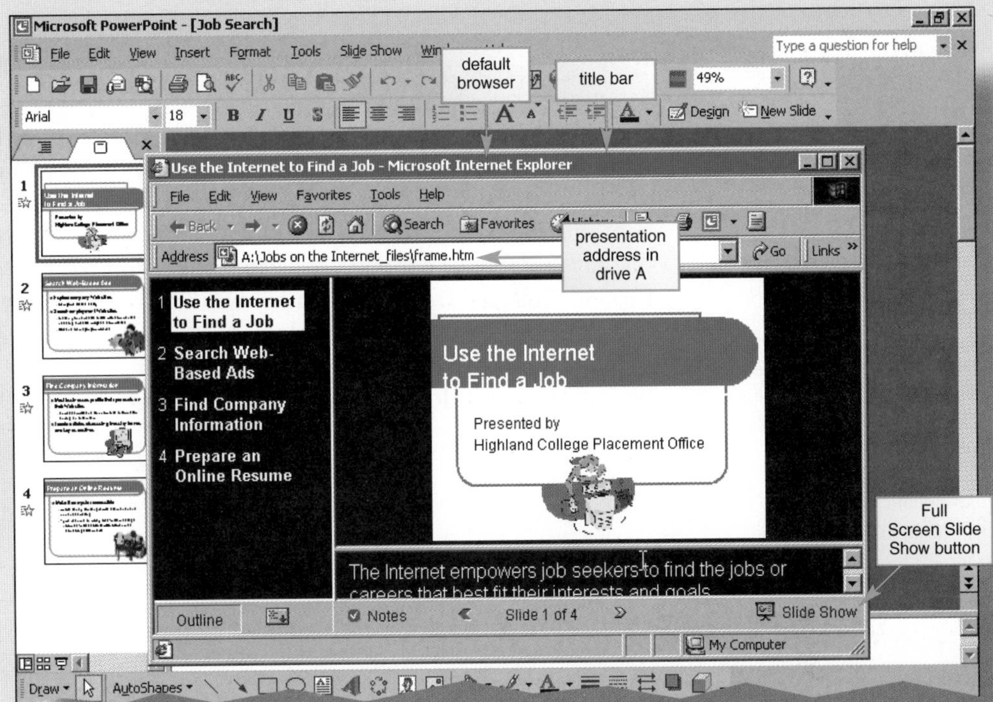

FIGURE 5

Other Ways

1. Press ALT+F, press G, type new file name, press SHIFT+TAB two times, press P, change file name in Publish copy as area; press ENTER
2. In Voice Command mode, say "File, Save as Web Page, [type file name], Publish, [type file name], Publish"

Publishing provides customizing options that are not available when you merely save the entire presentation and then start your browser. The **Publish as Web Page dialog box** provides several options to customize your Web page. For example, you can change the page title that displays on the browser's title bar and in the history list. People visiting your Web site can store a link to your Web page, which will display in their favorites list. To change the page title, you click the Change button in the Publish a copy as area (shown in Figure 4) and then type a new title.

The **Publish what? area** of the Publish as Web Page dialog box allows you to publish parts of your presentation. PowerPoint defaults to publishing the complete presentation, but you can select specific slides by clicking the **Slide number option button** and then entering the range of desired slide numbers in the range boxes. In addition, you can publish a custom show you have created previously. A **custom show** is a subset of your presentation that contains slides tailored for a specific audience. For example, you may want to show Slides 1, 2, and 4 to one group and Slides 1, 3, and 4 to another group.

You can choose to publish only the publication slides, and not the accompanying speaker notes. By default, the **Display speaker notes check box** is selected in the Publish what? area. You typed speaker notes for Slide 1 of this presentation, so they will display in the browser window. If you do not want to make your notes available to users, click the Display speaker notes check box to remove the check mark.

The **Web Options button** in the Publish what? area allows you to select options to determine how your presentation will look when viewed in a Web browser. You can choose options such as allowing slide animation to show, selecting the screen size, and having the notes and outline panes display when viewing the presentation in a Web browser.

With the Job Search file opened and the presentation saved as a Web page, the next step is to view the slide show using your default browser.

More About

Publishing Web Presentations

One advantage of publishing a PowerPoint presentation is the flexibility of using Web discussions to gather comments about the document. Saving the presentation as an .htm or .mht Web-based format provides the most flexibility for reviewers. The .mht format combines multiple pictures and slides into a single file called a Web archive. For more information, visit the PowerPoint 2002 More About Web page (scsite.com/pp2002/more.htm) and then click Publishing.

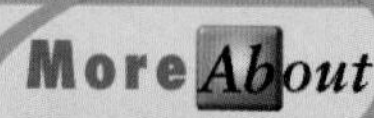

Viewing a Presentation

Presentations to large groups or distributed over many sites can create problems. Publishing the presentation as a Web page allows individuals to see the slides, but recording a broadcast for later viewing on the Internet is another alternative. For more information, visit the PowerPoint 2002 More About Web page (scsite.com/pp2002/more.htm) and then click Broadcasting.

Viewing a Presentation as a Web Page

PowerPoint makes it easy to create a presentation and then view how it will display on an intranet or the World Wide Web. By viewing your slide show, you can decide which features look good and which need modification. The left side of the window contains the navigation frame, which is the outline of the presentation. The outline displays a table of contents consisting of each slide's title text. You can click the **Expand/Collapse Outline button** below the navigation frame to view the complete slide text. The right side of the window displays the complete slide in the slide frame. The speaker notes display in the notes frame below the slide frame. Perform the following steps to view the Jobs on the Internet presentation as a Web page.

To View a Presentation as a Web Page

1 Double-click the Microsoft Internet Explorer title bar to maximize the browser window. Point to the Full Screen Slide Show button.

Slide 1 of the Jobs on the Internet presentation displays in the slide frame in the browser window (Figure 6). The navigation frame contains the table of contents, which consists of the title text of each slide. The notes frame displays the speaker notes.

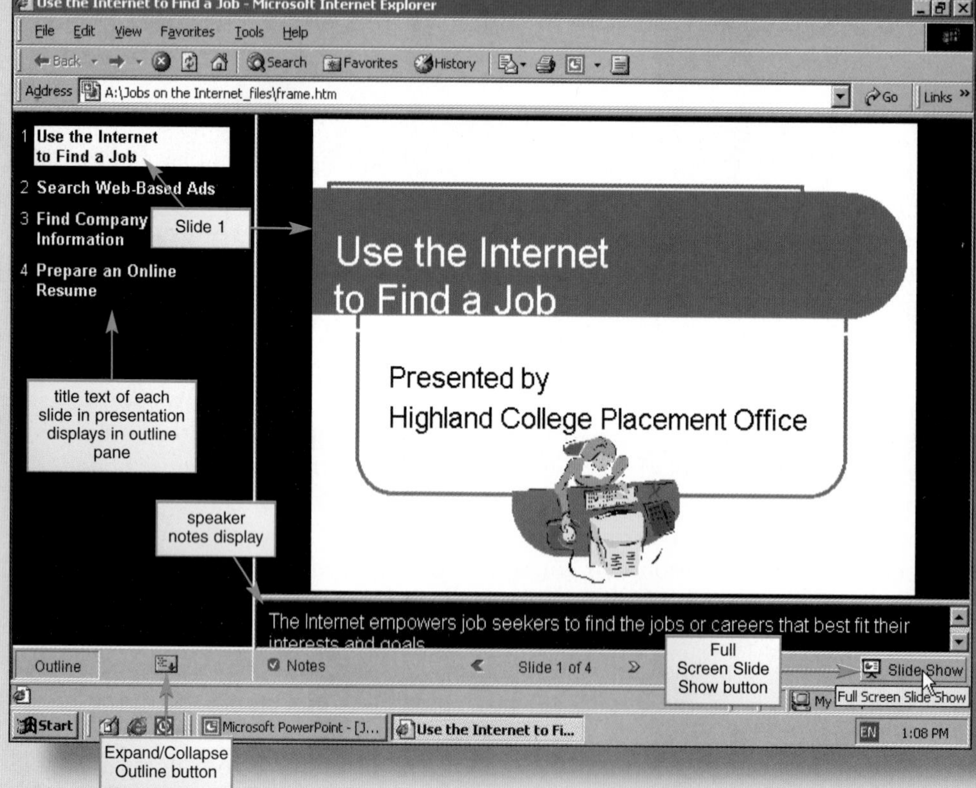

FIGURE 6

2 Click the Full Screen Slide Show button.

Slide 1 fills the entire screen (Figure 7). The Slide 1 title text and computer clip art display.

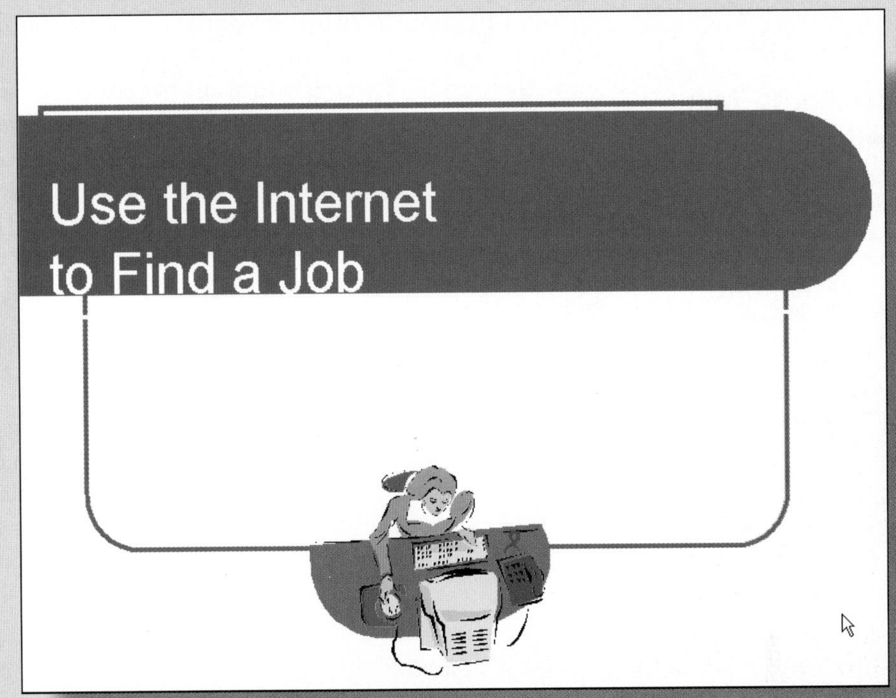

FIGURE 7

3 Click to display the first line of the subtitle text.

The first line of the Slide 1 subtitle text displays.

4 If necessary, continue clicking each slide in the presentation. When the black slide displays, click it. Click the Yes button in the Microsoft PowerPoint dialog box. Point to the Expand/Collapse Outline button below the outline.

Each of the four slides in the Jobs on the Internet presentation displays. The message on the black slide, End of slide show, click to exit., indicates the conclusion of the slide show.

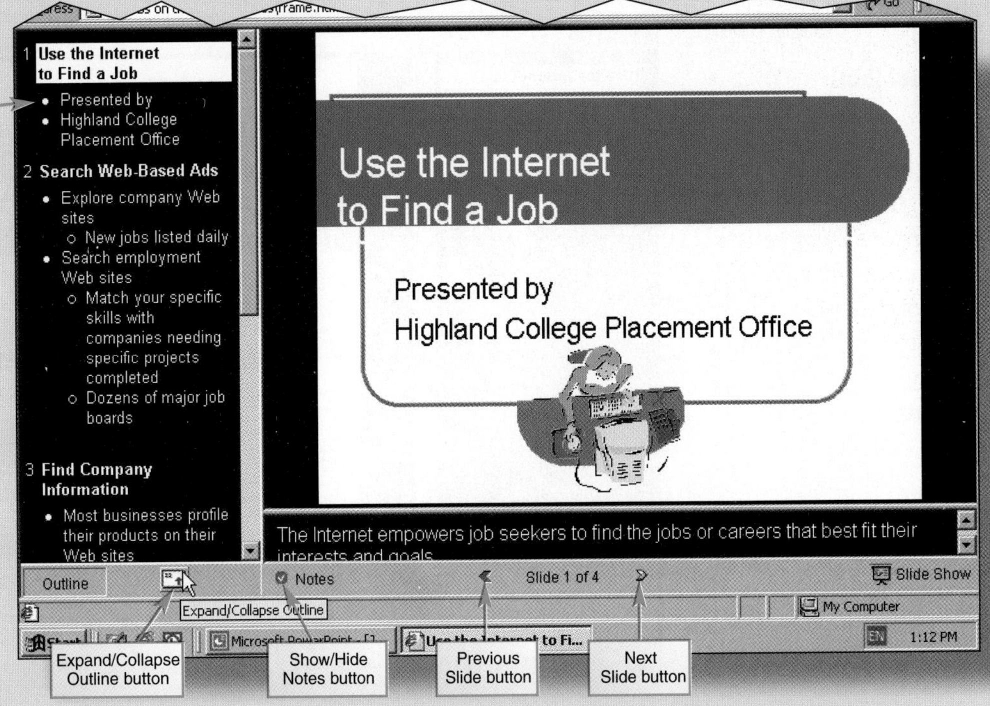

FIGURE 8

5 Click the Expand/Collapse Outline button.

The navigation frame displays the text of each slide in an outline (Figure 8). To display only the title of each slide, you would click the Expand/Collapse Outline button again.

More About

Connecting to Your Audience

As you choose to show or hide your outline and notes, consider the needs of your audience. Some researchers believe listeners are more attentive on Sundays, Mondays, and Tuesdays because they are more relaxed than at the middle and end of a week. Thus, you may need to provide more information via the outline and notes when your audience is less focused.

You can alter the browser window by choosing to display or hide the navigation and notes frames. To hide the navigation frame, click the **Show/Hide Outline button** below the outline. Later, if you want to redisplay the navigation frame, click the Show/Hide Outline button again. Similarly, the **Show/Hide Notes button** below the slide frame allows you to display or conceal the speaker notes on a particular slide.

To advance through the Web page, click the **Next Slide button** below the slide frame. Likewise, to display a slide appearing earlier in the slide show, click the **Previous Slide button.**

Editing a Web Page through a Browser

You may want to modify your Web page by making small changes to the text or art on some slides. In this presentation, you want to change the title text in Slide 1 to reflect the fact that the presentation covers more than finding a job on the Internet; it describes various resources available for planning a career. The following steps change the second line of the title slide to modify Slide 1.

Steps To Edit a Web Page through a Browser

1 Point to the Edit button on the Standard Buttons toolbar.

Slide 1 displays in the browser (Figure 9). The ScreenTip, Edit with Microsoft PowerPoint, indicates you can modify the presentation using PowerPoint directly in the browser window. Your computer may indicate other editing options, such as using Windows Notepad.

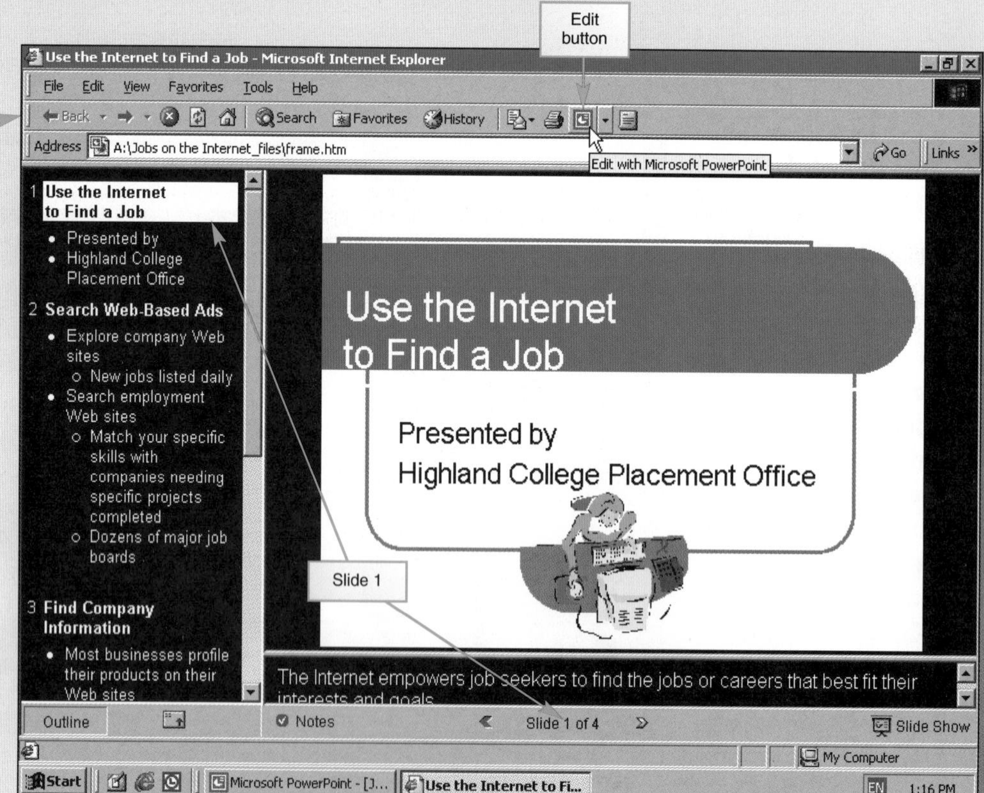

FIGURE 9

2 Click the Edit button. Select the words, Find a Job, in the second line of the title text placeholder.

When you click the Edit button, PowerPoint opens a new presentation with the same file name as the Web presentation file name, as indicated by the title bar and the recessed PowerPoint Jobs on the Internet button on the Windows taskbar (Figure 10). A selection rectangle displays around the title text placeholder. The three words are highlighted.

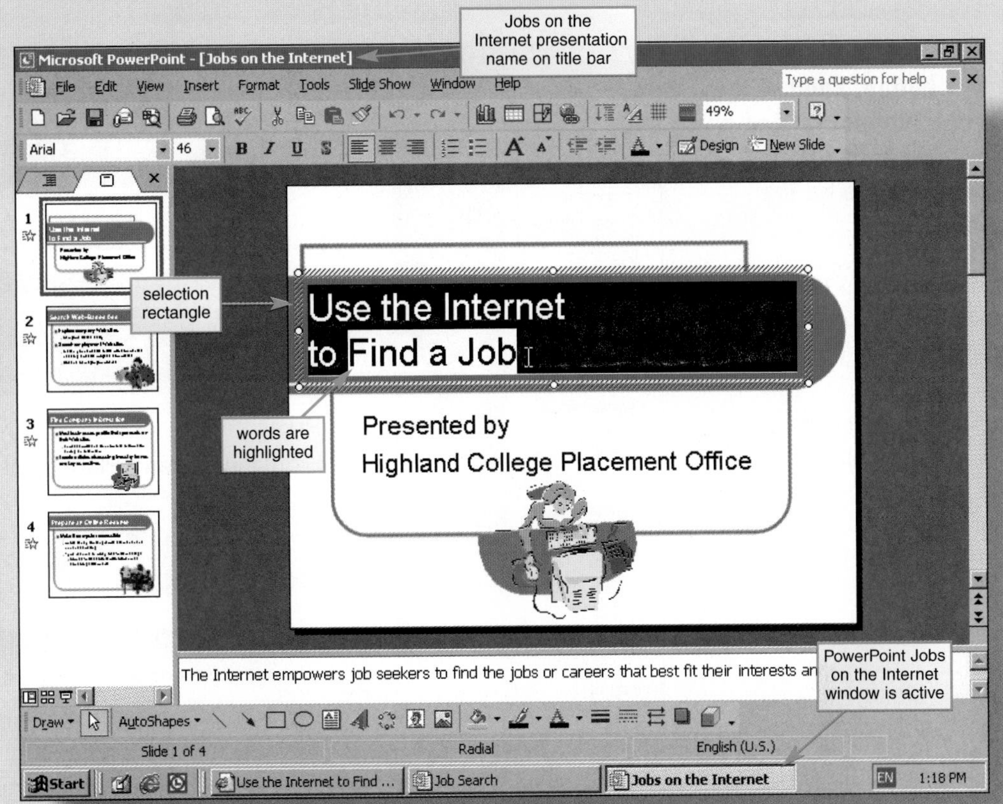

FIGURE 10

3 Type `Locate Job Resources` **and then point to the Save button on the Standard toolbar.**

The second line is modified (Figure 11).

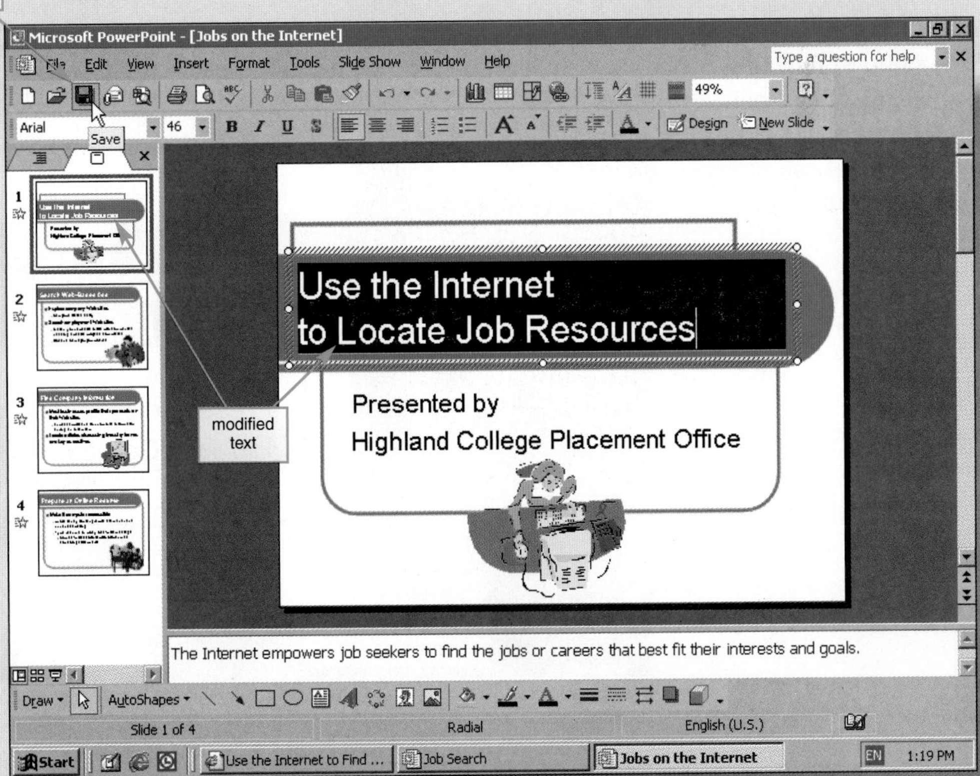

FIGURE 11

4 Click the Save button. Point to the Use the Internet to Find a Job – Microsoft Internet Explorer button on the taskbar.

PowerPoint saves the changes to the Jobs on the Internet.htm file on the Data Disk in drive A. The buttons on the taskbar indicate that two PowerPoint presentations and the browser are open (Figure 12).

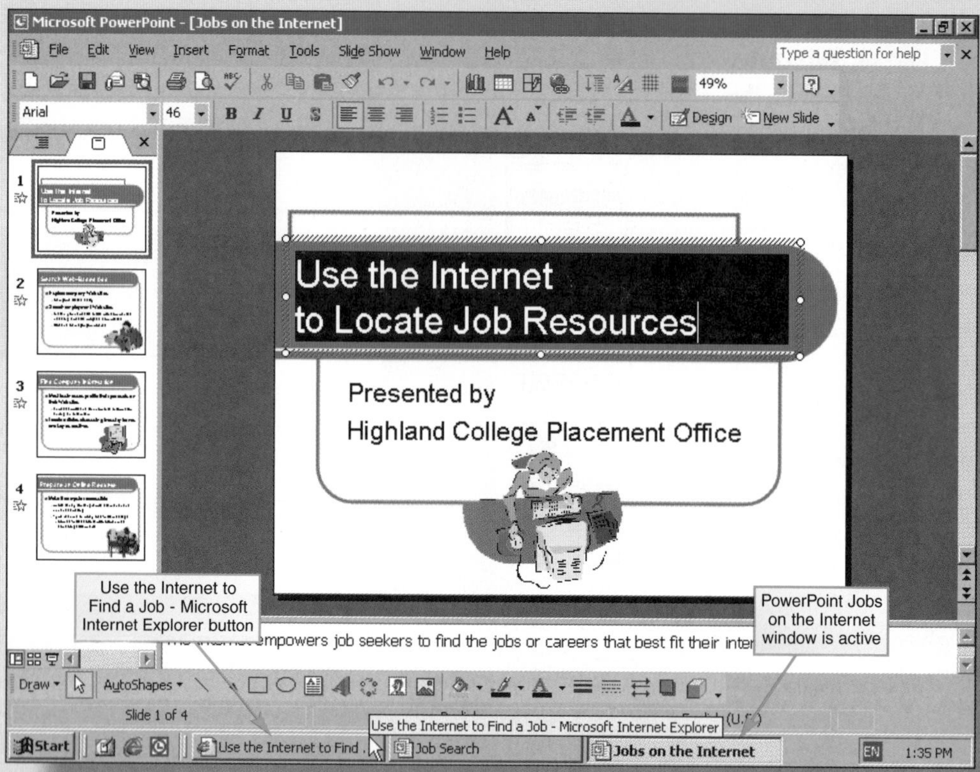

FIGURE 12

5 Click the Use the Internet to Find a Job – Microsoft Internet Explorer button and then point to the Refresh button on the Standard Buttons toolbar.

The browser window displays the title text and clip art on Slide 1 (Figure 13). The **Refresh button** *displays the most current version of the Web page.*

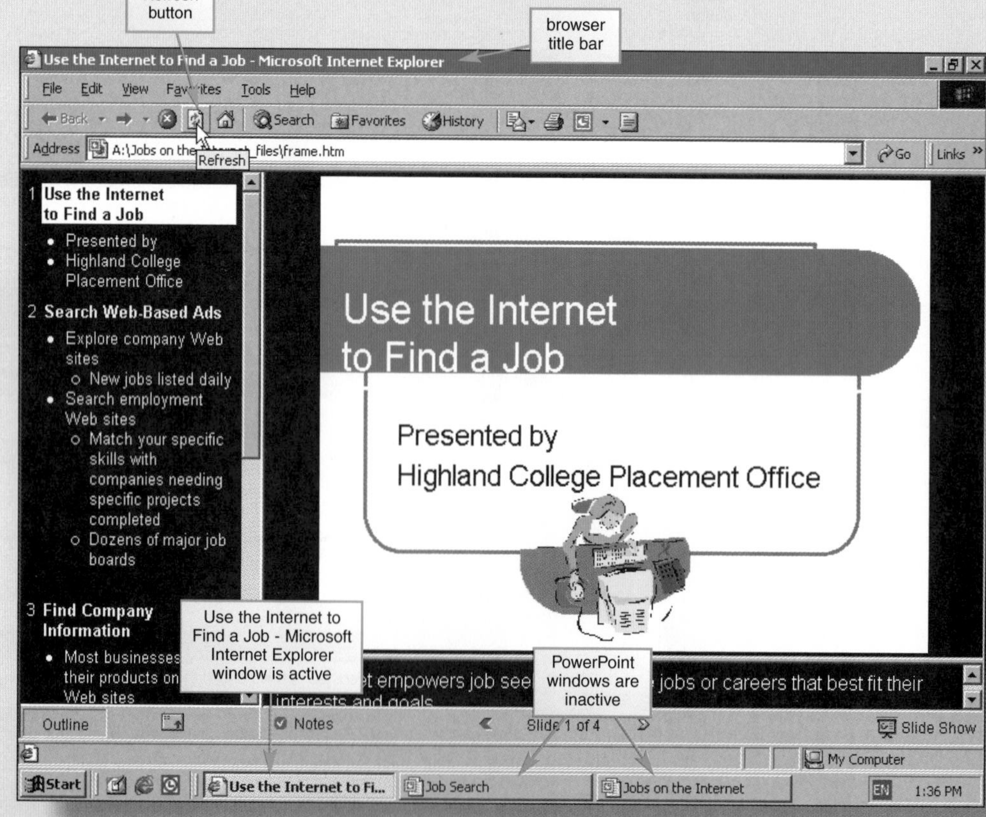

FIGURE 13

6 Click the Refresh button. Point to the Close button on the browser title bar.

The complete Slide 1 displays with the editing change (Figure 14).

7 Click the Close button.

PowerPoint closes the Jobs on the Internet Web presentation, and the PowerPoint window redisplays in normal view with the Jobs on the Internet presentation active.

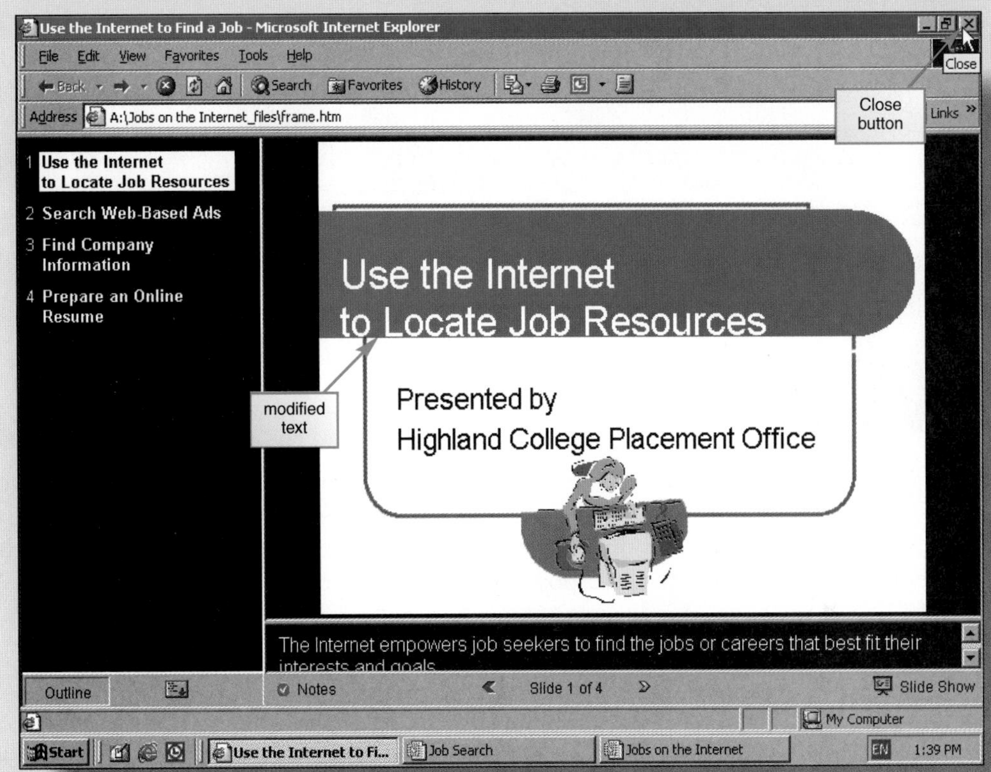

FIGURE 14

The Web page now is complete. The next step is to make your Web presentation available to others on your network, an intranet, or the World Wide Web. Ask your instructor how you can post your presentation.

CASE PERSPECTIVE SUMMARY

Students attending Tina Natella's presentation in the Placement Center should learn information on using the Internet to improve their career searches. The Job Search slide show will help to reinforce the key points presented, including facts about searching Web-based advertisements, finding company information, and preparing an online resume. The students will be able to apply this information when they look for a first job or a new career. Tina can publish your presentation to the World Wide Web so that students who cannot attend the lecture also can gain the useful information presented.

Web Feature Summary

This Web feature introduced you to creating a Web page by saving an existing PowerPoint presentation as an HTML file. You then viewed the presentation as a Web page in your default browser. Next, you modified Slide 1. Finally, you reviewed the Slide 1 change using your default browser. With the Job Search presentation converted to a Web page, you can post the file to an intranet or to the World Wide Web.

What You Should Know

Having completed this Web Feature, you now should be able to perform the following tasks:

- Edit a Web Page through a Browser *(PPW 1.08)*
- Save a PowerPoint Presentation as a Web Page *(PPW 1.03)*
- View a Presentation as a Web Page *(PPW 1.06)*

In the Lab

1 Creating a Web Page from the Make Friends Presentation

Problem: Jennifer Williams, the dean of counseling at Westview College, wants to expand the visibility of the Make Friends presentation you created for the counseling department in Project 1. She believes the World Wide Web would be an excellent vehicle to help students throughout the campus and at other colleges, and she has asked you to help transfer the presentation to the Internet.

Instructions: Start PowerPoint and then perform the following steps with a computer.

1. Open the Make Friends presentation shown in Figures 1-2a through 1-2d on page PP 1.09 that you created in Project 1. (If you did not complete Project 1, see your instructor for a copy of the presentation.)
2. Use the Save as Web Page command on the File menu to convert and publish the presentation. Save the Web page using the file name, Curing Loneliness.
3. View the presentation in a browser.
4. Modify Slide 2 by adding the words, on Campus, to the title.
5. Change the first third-level paragraph to the words, Current events, sports scores, on Slide 4.
6. View the modified Web page in a browser.
7. Ask your instructor for instructions on how to post your Web page so others may have access to it.

2 Creating a Web Page from the Enjoy Spring Break Presentation

Problem: The Enjoy Spring Break presentation you developed in Project 2 for the Office of Student Activities is generating much interest. Students are visiting the office, which has moved to Room 3221, and requesting longer hours for the Caribbean Cruise Reception. Maria Lopez, the student activities director, has asked you to post the presentation to the school's intranet.

Instructions: Start PowerPoint and then perform the following steps with a computer.

1. Open the Enjoy Spring Break presentation shown in Figures 2-1a through 2-1e on page PP 2.05 that you created in Project 2. (If you did not complete Project 2, see your instructor for a copy of the presentation.)
2. Use the Save as Web Page command on the File menu to convert and publish the presentation. Save the Web page using the file name, Caribbean Cruise.
3. View the presentation in a browser.
4. Modify Slide 2 by changing the word, parasailing, to the words, scuba diving, in the third bulleted paragraph.
5. Modify Slide 5 by changing the room number to 3221 and by changing the ending time of the reception to 8:00 p.m.
6. View the modified Web page in a browser.
7. Ask your instructor for instructions on how to post your Web page so others may have access to it.

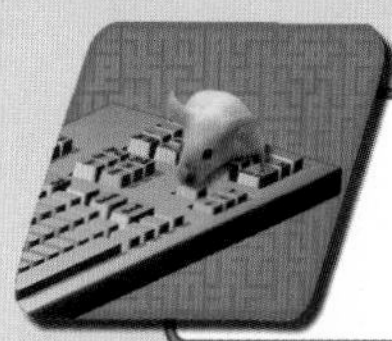

In the Lab

3 Creating a Personal Presentation

Problem: You have decided to apply for an internship at a not-for-profit organization in Chicago. You are preparing to send your resume and cover letter to the executive director, and you want to develop a unique way to publicize your computer expertise. You decide to create a personalized PowerPoint presentation emphasizing your leadership abilities and scholarly achievements. You refer to this presentation in your cover letter and inform the executive director that she can view this presentation because you have saved the presentation as a Web page and posted the pages on your school's server.

Instructions: Start PowerPoint and then perform the following steps with a computer.

1. Prepare a presentation highlighting your leadership abilities. Create a title slide and at least three additional slides. Use appropriate clip art and an animation scheme.
2. Use the Save as Web Page command to convert and publish the presentation. Save the Web page using the file name, Additional Skills.
3. View the presentation in a browser.
4. Ask your instructor for instructions on how to post your Web page so others may have access to it.

2002

Microsoft Outlook

Microsoft Outlook 2002

PROJECT

Schedule and Contact Management Using Outlook

OBJECTIVES

You will have mastered the material in this project when you can:

- Start Outlook
- Open the Calendar folder
- Describe the components of the Calendar - Microsoft Outlook window
- Understand the elements of the Outlook Bar
- Create a personal subfolder
- Enter one-time and recurring appointments
- Use the Date Navigator to move to different days
- Use natural language phrases to enter appointment dates and times
- Move and edit appointments
- Create an event
- Display the calendar in Day, Work Week, Week, and Month views
- Create and print a task list
- Print the calendar in Daily Style, Weekly Style, and Monthly Style
- Create and print a contact list
- Use the find contact feature
- Organize the contact list
- Import and export personal subfolders
- Delete personal subfolders from the hard disk
- Quit Outlook

Productivity Tools

Making the Most of Managing Time and Information

Worldwide communications today consist of cellular technology and satellite systems, the Internet, e-mail exchanges, and personal information managers (PIMs). Barely a thought is given to the incredible advancements made in the primary fields of science and technology that are responsible for this wireless evolution.

Visualize a mere sixty years ago. Television technology became available in many areas of the country, people placed calls using wired telephones with numbers that contained letters of the alphabet in their prefixes, and neighbors shared party lines. Bookkeepers punched numbers on adding machine keypads to perform manual calculations and office workers pounded out correspondence on mechanical typewriters using carbon paper for copies. Using pen and ink, individuals scheduled appointments on paper calendars, convened physically in meeting rooms, and wrote names, addresses, and telephone numbers in their address books.

Now, imagine a period even before technology; the beginning of time. Life was simple and unhurried, no electronic devices existed, timetables revolved around the sunrise and sunset, and very few, if any, engagements, meetings, or appointments needed to be scheduled at all. Although electronic devices are from modern times, even prehistoric man was concerned with timekeeping and calendars. Ice-age hunters in Europe scratched lines and gouged holes in sticks and bones, possibly counting the days between phases of the moon.

More than 4,000 years ago in England, Stonehenge's alignments show its purposes apparently included the determination of seasonal or celestial events. The Egyptians devised a 365-day calendar that seems to have begun in 4236 B.C. — the earliest recorded year in history.

About 1500 B.C., sundials, the first portable timepieces, were designed, which led to the development of horology, or the science of measuring time.

The need to develop newer methods to organize and manage time more effectively continues to expand. Computer users today have no shortage of tools that combine the capabilities of accessing information and conducting worldwide communications using e-mail, videoconferencing, instant messaging, personal information managers, and custom groupware. The Internet and the tremendous quantities of both electronic and paper communications have changed daily life and business, forcing individuals to prioritize their tasks.

Microsoft Outlook 2002 has been designed to answer the problem of electronic information overload. A personal information manager (PIM), Outlook is a central location from which you can create, view, and organize all of your information. The data is stored in folders. A shortcut stores the folder location and allows you to open it quickly using the Outlook Bar.

From Inbox, you can read and send e-mail messages. Calendar provides the tools to create appointments, plan meetings and events, and review tasks. Using Contacts, you are able to store names, addresses, and other data about your business and personal contacts. Tasks simplifies to-do lists and allows you to organize assignments. Journal presents a review of your work history. Notes is an area where you can formulate ideas and save reminders. With this integration, you eliminate the need for weekly planners, daily pocket calendars, sticky notes, and task lists. With its Internet browsing capabilities, Outlook also acts as a Web Address Book and allows you to store, manage, and navigate favorite Web sites.

Using its range of features to help you organize your personal information, Outlook is a valuable productivity tool.

Conceivably in the historic archives of the next millennium, civilization's current technology revolution with its trends toward mobile and wireless connectivity, human computer integration, digital books, intelligent agents, global positioning systems, and robotics may seem as obsolete as the Aztec calendar stone.

Microsoft Outlook 2002

Schedule and Contact Management Using Outlook

PROJECT

CASE PERSPECTIVE

Jamaal Robinson is a student at State University. His busy schedule includes classes, fraternity functions, and extracurricular activities. Jamaal is concerned that he will overlap his school activities and his other activities if he does not keep track of them in an orderly manner. The computer Jamaal purchased for school came with a number of software packages, including Microsoft Outlook. He recently read an article about Outlook and thinks it would be the perfect tool to maintain his personal schedule and contacts. He is unfamiliar with Outlook, however, and needs some direction.

You work part-time at the Help desk in the school's computer lab and are quite familiar with Outlook and its features. Jamaal visits the Help desk and asks you to help him set up his calendar. He plans to schedule his classes, meetings, and other events using Outlook. He read that Outlook allows you to create a single calendar event and set a weekly recurrence pattern, which will help him with this task. Jamaal feels that having his time scheduled should help him to coordinate his school activities and his extracurricular activities more efficiently. With your help, he can accomplish this goal.

What Is Microsoft Outlook?

Microsoft Outlook, an application contained in Microsoft Office XP, is an effective **personal information management** (**PIM**) program that helps you organize your busy schedule, keep track of your contacts, and communicate with others. Most individuals have multiple appointments to keep and tasks to accomplish in a day, week, or month. Outlook assists in maintaining a full schedule such as this, organizing the information in a structured, readable manner. Users easily can track meetings, e-mail messages, and notes with a particular contact. Outlook's Calendar, Contacts, Tasks, and Notes components aid in this organization. Contact information readily is available with the Find option, which can be accessed from the calendar, e-mail, and other Outlook components. PIMs such as Outlook provide a way for individuals and workgroups to organize, find, view, and share information easily.

Files created in Word, Excel, Access, and PowerPoint can be used in an Outlook folder or attached to an e-mail message. Outlook also makes it easy to share data between applications. For instance, a contact list can become the data source for a Word mail merge, or Word can be used as the editor for e-mail messages. Outlook's Inbox and Calendar folders make it easy to update, print, and fax your schedule to anyone, anywhere.

Project One — Personal Information Manager

In Project 1, the basic features of Outlook are illustrated while creating a calendar of classes, meetings, and appointments for Jamaal Robinson. In addition to creating the calendar, you will print it in three views: Day, Week, and Month. Figure 1-1 shows the resulting printouts. Then, you will create a task list for a given day and a contact list.

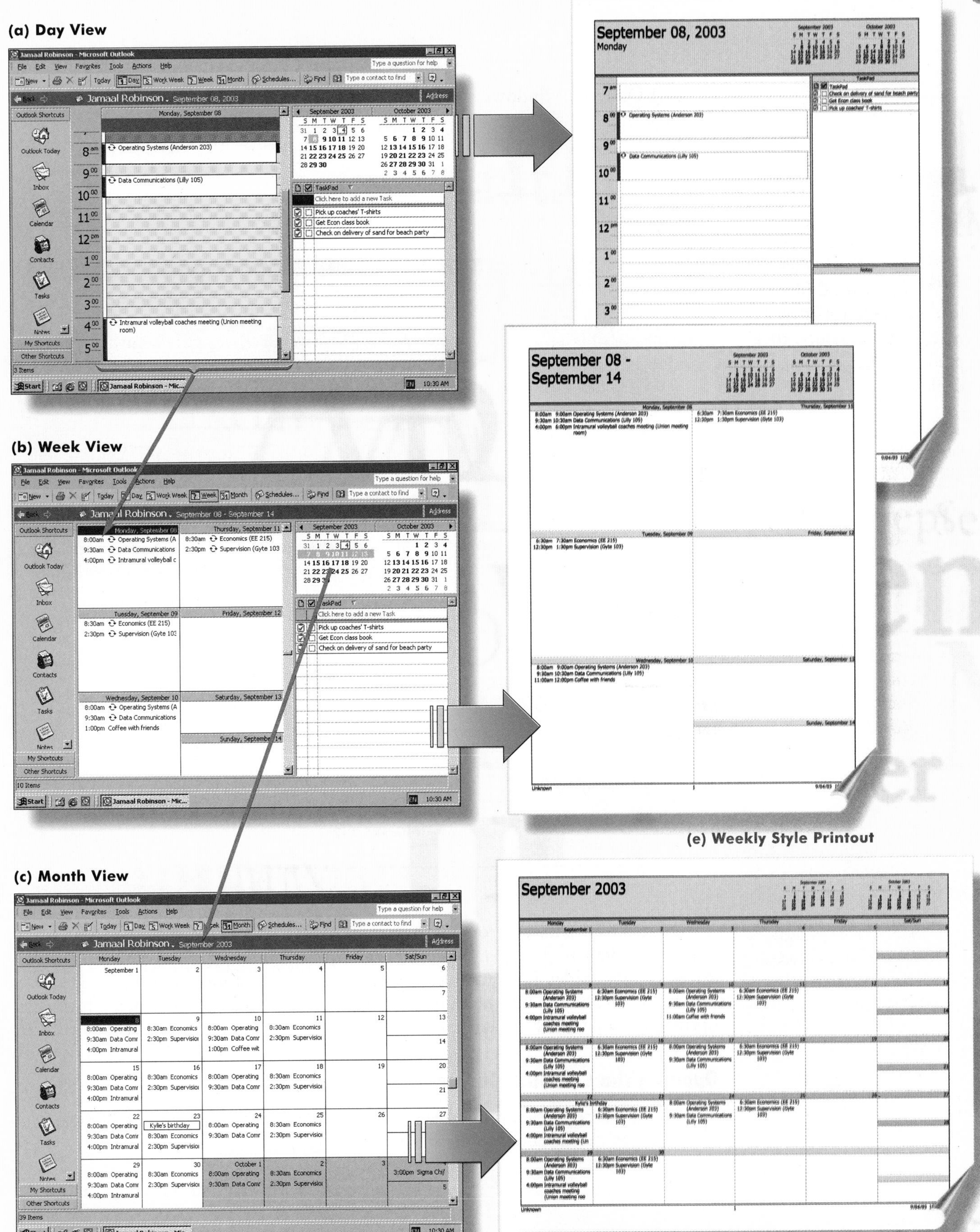
(a) Day View
(b) Week View
(c) Month View
(d) Daily Style Printout
(e) Weekly Style Printout
(f) Monthly Style Printout
September 08, 2003
Monday
September 08 -
September 14
September 2003

FIGURE 1-1

Starting Outlook

To start Outlook, Windows must be running. Perform the following step to start Outlook.

To Start Outlook

1 Click the Launch Microsoft Outlook icon on the Quick Launch toolbar. If necessary, click the Inbox shortcut on the Outlook Bar.

Outlook displays the Inbox folder in the Inbox – Microsoft Outlook window (Figure 1-2).

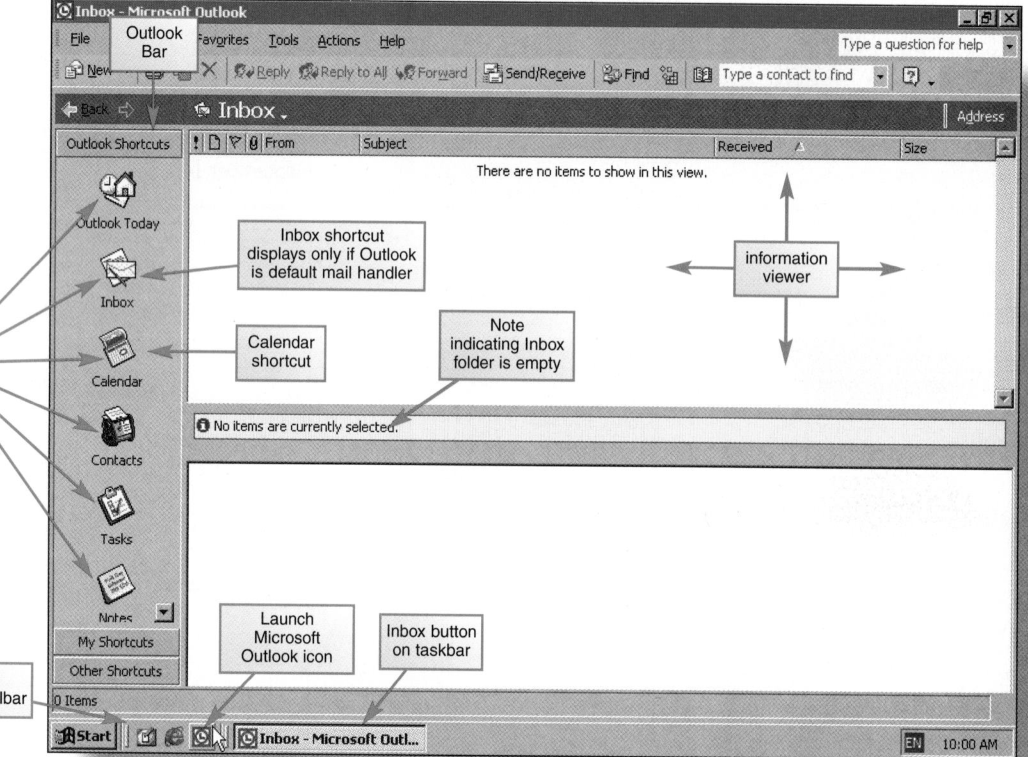

FIGURE 1-2

Other Ways

1. Double-click Microsoft Outlook icon on desktop
2. Click Start button on taskbar, point to Programs on Start menu, click Microsoft Outlook on Programs submenu

Outlook is organized around groups of **items**, such as Outlook Today, Inbox, Calendar, Contacts, Tasks, and Notes. Groups of the same type are stored in the same Outlook folder. For example, all appointments are stored in the Calendar folder, and all contact information is stored in the Contacts folder. When a folder is opened, the items in the selected folder display in the **information viewer** (Figure 1-2).

Opening the Calendar Folder

To begin entering items in Jamaal Robinson's calendar, perform the following steps to open the Calendar folder.

Steps To Open the Calendar Folder

1 Click the Calendar shortcut on the Outlook Bar on the left side of the screen.

Outlook opens the Calendar folder and the Calendar - Microsoft Outlook window opens. When you open the Calendar folder, the Calendar displays in the default Day view (Figure 1-3). The Outlook ***Day view*** *allows you to enter information for one day at a time.*

2 If necessary, click the Maximize button on the title bar to maximize the Calendar - Microsoft Outlook window. If your screen displays a larger appointment area than the one in Figure 1-3, drag the appointment area border to the left.

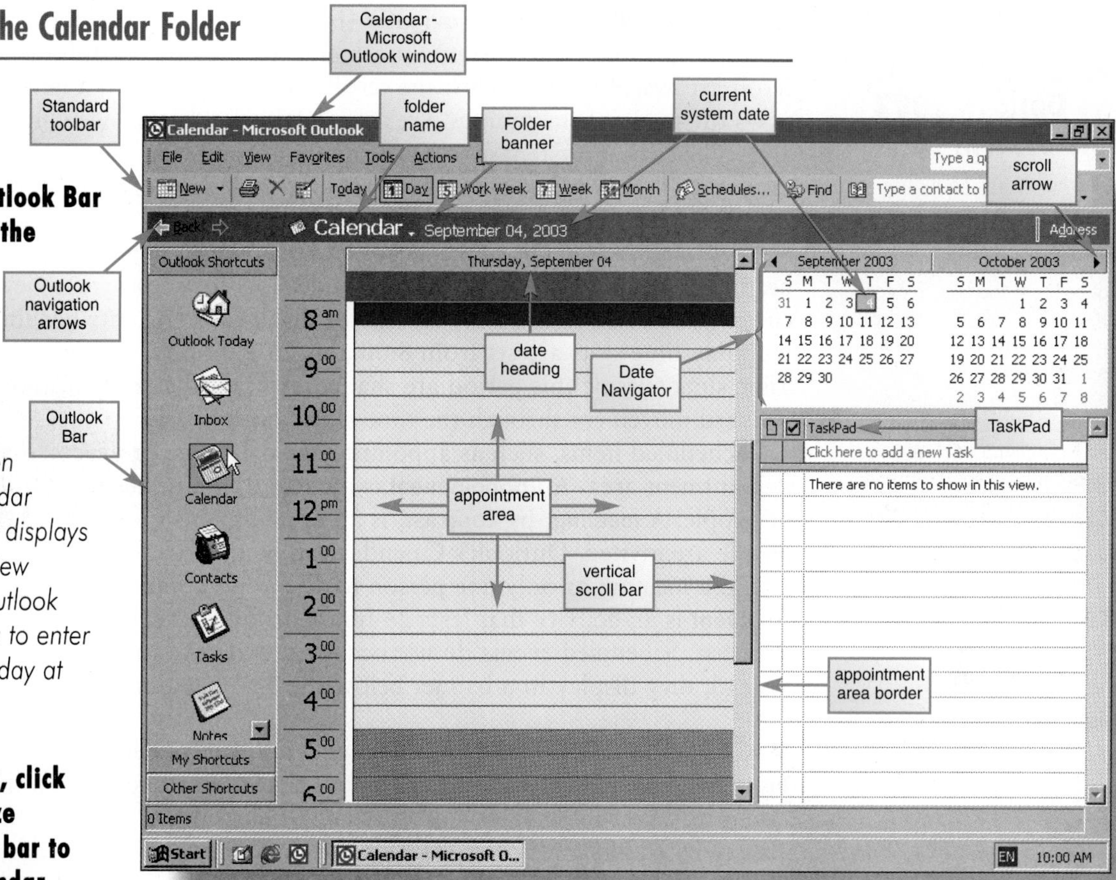

FIGURE 1-3

1. On View menu point to Go To, click Calendar on Go To submenu
2. In Voice Command mode, say "View, Go To, Calendar"

The Calendar - Microsoft Outlook Window

The **Calendar - Microsoft Outlook window** (Figure 1-3) includes a variety of features to help you work efficiently. It contains many elements similar to the windows in other applications, as well as some that are unique to Outlook. The main elements of the Calendar - Microsoft Outlook window are the Outlook Bar, the Standard toolbar, the Folder banner, the Date Navigator, the appointment area, and the TaskPad. The following paragraphs explain some of the features of the Calendar - Microsoft Outlook window.

FOLDER BANNER The **Folder banner** (Figure 1-3) is the horizontal bar just below the Standard toolbar. The Outlook navigation arrows, an icon for the active folder, the name of the active folder, and the selected date display in the Folder banner. When the folder name is clicked, the Folder List showing available folders and subfolders displays.

More About

Personal Information Management (PIM)

For more information about personal information management, visit the Outlook 2002 More About Web page (scsite.com/out2002/more.htm) and then click PIM.

More About

The Outlook 2002 Help System

Need Help? It is no further than the Ask a Question box in the upper-right corner of the window. Click the box that contains the text, Type a question for help (Figure 1-6), type `help`, and then press the ENTER key. Outlook will respond with a list of items that you can click to learn about obtaining help on any Outlook-related topic. To find out what is new in Outlook 2002, type `what's new in Outlook` in the Ask a Question box.

DATE NAVIGATOR The **Date Navigator** (Figure 1-3 on the previous page) includes two monthly calendars (the current month and the previous or following month) and scroll arrows. When you click the scroll arrows to move to a new date, Calendar displays the name of the month, week, or day in the current view in the appointment area. The current system date has a square around it in the Date Navigator. Dates displayed in bold in the Date Navigator indicate days on which an item is scheduled.

APPOINTMENT AREA The **appointment area** (shown in Figure 1-3) contains a date heading and, under the date heading, time slots for the current view. The date currently selected in the Date Navigator displays in the date heading. By default, workday time slots are set from 8:00 a.m. to 5:00 p.m. in one-hour increments. Time slots outside this period are shaded. A vertical scroll bar allows backward or forward movement through the time slots.

Scheduled items, such as appointments, meetings, or events, display in the appointment area. An **appointment** is an activity that does not involve other resources or people. A **meeting**, by contrast, is an appointment to which other resources or people are invited. Outlook's Calendar can be used to schedule several people to attend a meeting or only one person to attend an appointment (such as a class). An **event** is an activity that lasts 24 hours or longer, such as a seminar, birthday, or vacation. Scheduled events do not occupy time slots in the appointment area; instead, they display in a banner below the date heading.

TASKPAD The **TaskPad** (shown in Figure 1-3) displays below the Date Navigator. **Tasks** are personal or work-related duties that need to be tracked through to completion. The TaskPad displays your tasks and their status. You can change the way tasks display by clicking TaskPad View on the View menu or add details to a task by double-clicking the **Tasks shortcut**. When a task is complete, select the check box in the **Complete column** to indicate its completion.

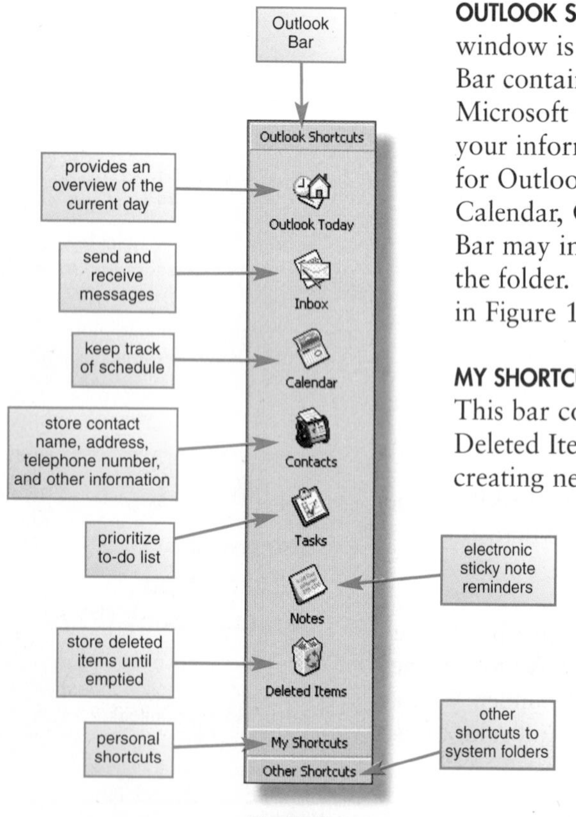

FIGURE 1-4

OUTLOOK SHORTCUTS On the left side of the Calendar - Microsoft Outlook window is a vertical bar called the **Outlook Bar** (Figure 1-4). The Outlook Bar contains shortcuts representing the standard items that are part of Microsoft Outlook. The Outlook Bar is divided into groups to help organize your information. The standard Outlook groups include shortcuts to folders for Outlook Today, Inbox (if Outlook is your default mail handler), Calendar, Contacts, Tasks, Notes, and Deleted Items, although your Outlook Bar may include other shortcuts. When you click a shortcut, Outlook opens the folder. The function performed when you click each folder is illustrated in Figure 1-4.

MY SHORTCUTS Another shortcut bar available in Outlook is My Shortcuts. This bar contains shortcuts to Drafts, Inbox, Sent Items, Outbox, and Deleted Items. Outlook also prompts you to add shortcuts to this bar when creating new folders.

OTHER SHORTCUTS This bar contains shortcuts to My Computer, My Documents, and Favorites. Easy access to these important system components is available through the Other Shortcuts bar.

STANDARD TOOLBAR Figure 1-5 shows the Standard toolbar in the Calendar - Microsoft Office window. The button names indicate their functions. Each button can be clicked to perform a frequently used task, such as creating a new appointment, printing, or changing the current view.

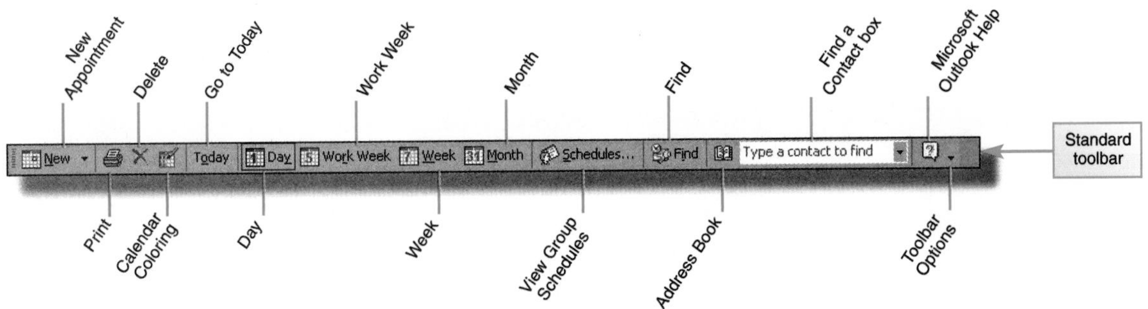

FIGURE 1-5

Creating a Personal Subfolder in the Calendar Folder

If you were the only person using Outlook on a computer, you could enter appointments and events directly into the main Calendar folder, creating a daily, weekly, and monthly schedule. In many office and school situations, however, several people share one computer and therefore need to create separate folders in which to store appointments and events. With Outlook, you can create personal subfolders in which to store your personal calendar and other files. Subfolders then can be saved on the hard disk or a floppy disk. If working on a networked computer, check with your instructor or database manager for the policy on creating and saving subfolders. In this project, substitute your name in place of Jamaal Robinson as you create the personal subfolders. Perform the following steps to create a personal subfolder to store Jamaal Robinson's calendar.

Folders

The Outlook Bar can be used to open any files on your computer or any computer to which you are connected. Click the Other Shortcuts bar on the Outlook Bar and then click My Computer to view or open any files. Files can be viewed as icons, in a table, or in a timeline.

Steps To Create a Personal Subfolder in the Calendar Folder

1 Right-click the folder name, Calendar, in the Folder banner. Point to New Folder on the shortcut menu.

Outlook displays a shortcut menu of tasks associated with the Calendar folder (Figure 1-6).

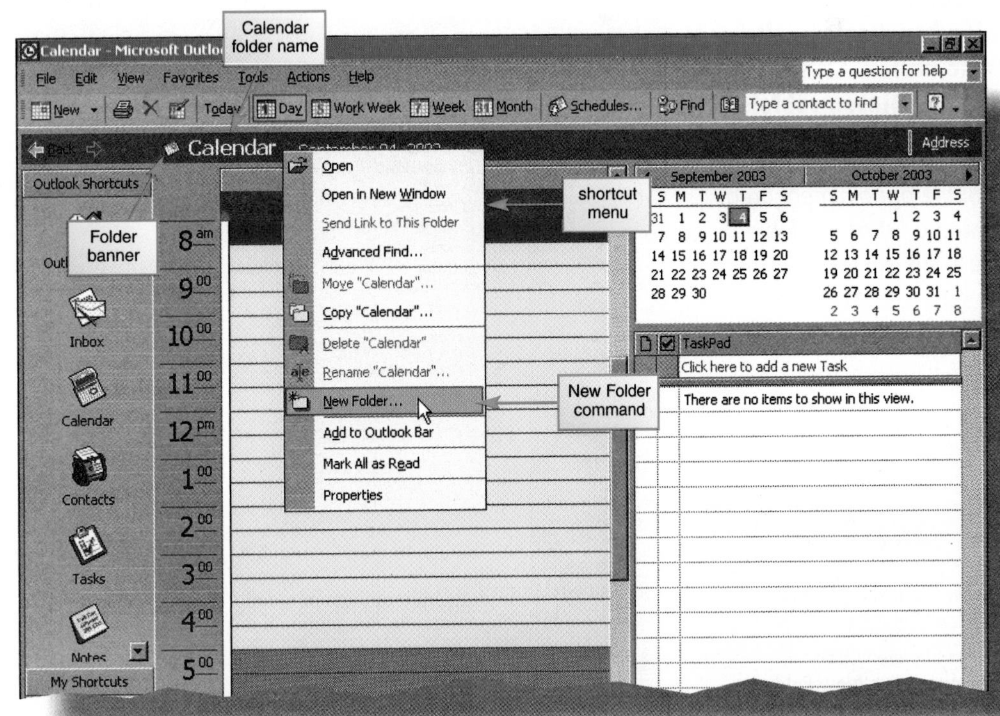

FIGURE 1-6

2 Click New Folder. When the Create New Folder dialog box displays, type Jamaal Robinson **in the Name text box. Point to the OK button.**

The Create New Folder dialog box displays. It contains a text box for the folder name, a list box to indicate what type of items the folder will contain, and a list of folders and subfolders (Figure 1-7).

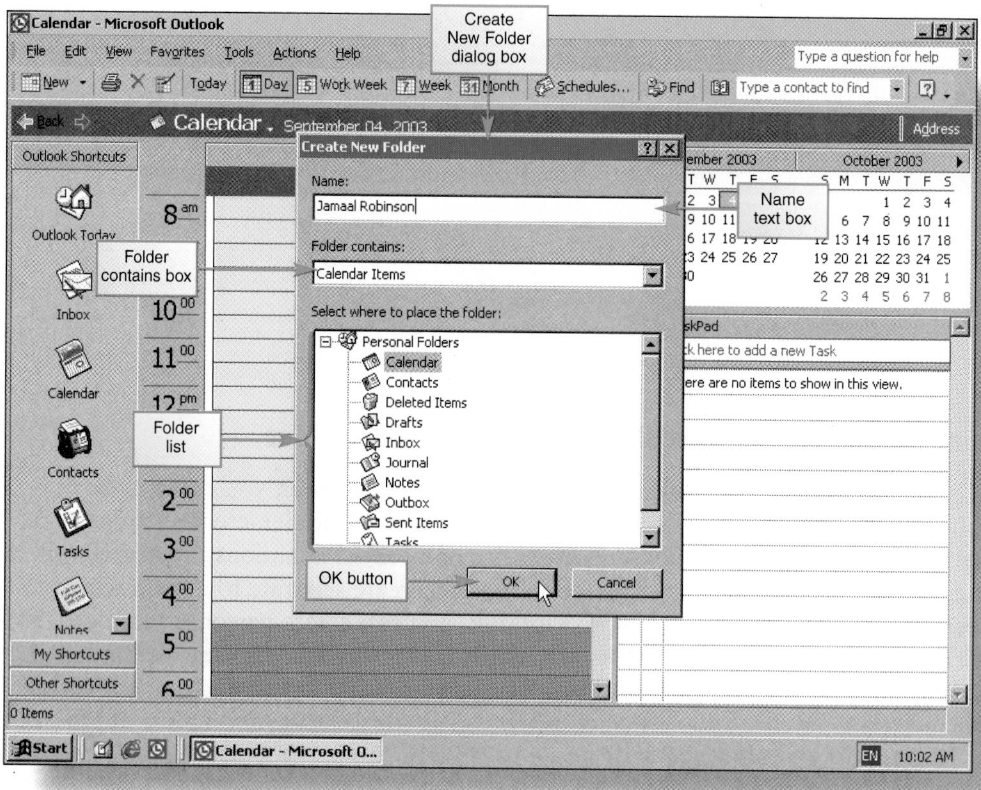

FIGURE 1-7

3 Click the OK button. When the Add shortcut to Outlook Bar? dialog box displays, click the No button. Click the Jamaal Robinson subfolder.

A Folder List displays to the left of the appointment area, showing a list of available folders and subfolders. The new subfolder icon and name, Jamaal Robinson, display (Figure 1-8).

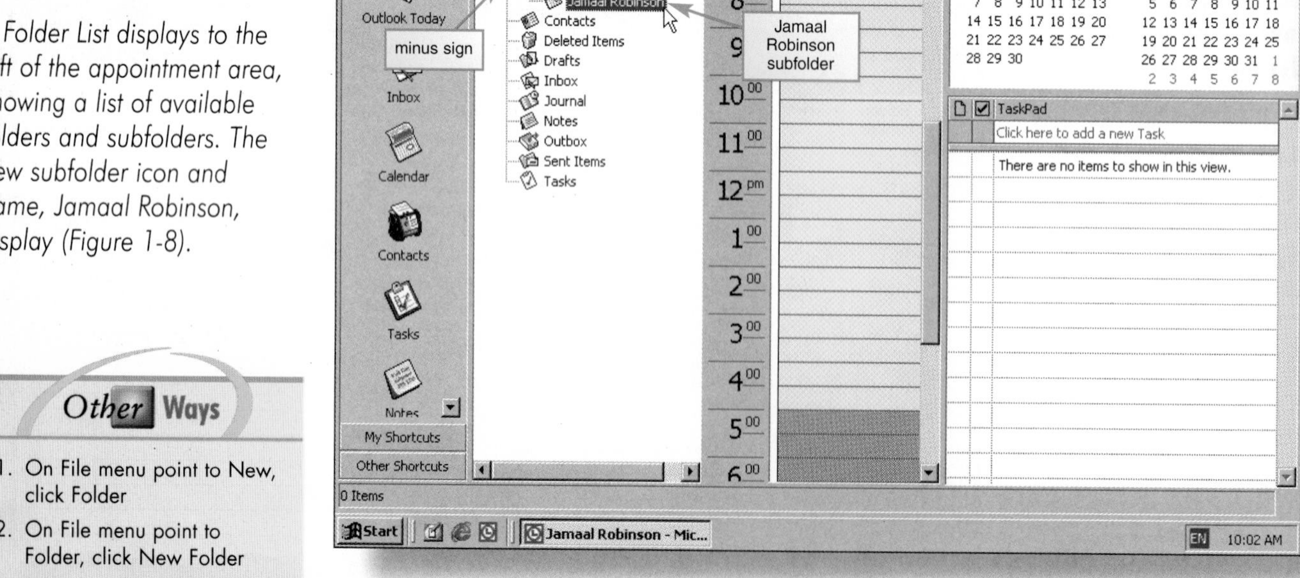

FIGURE 1-8

Other Ways

1. On File menu point to New, click Folder
2. On File menu point to Folder, click New Folder
3. Press CTRL+SHIFT+E
4. In Voice Command mode, say "File, New, Folder"

By clicking the No button in the Add shortcut to Outlook Bar? dialog box, a shortcut for this folder will not be added to the Outlook Bar. In the Folder List, the Calendar now displays with a minus sign to the left. The **minus sign** indicates that the folder is expanded. A **plus sign** to the left of a folder indicates that additional subfolders are contained in the folder.

Changing to a Personal Folder

A personal folder now is created in which calendar information is stored. Perform the following step to change to that folder.

Steps To Change to a Personal Folder

1 **Verify that the Jamaal Robinson folder is selected, and if not, select it. Click the Close button on the Folder List to close the Folder List.**

The Jamaal Robinson folder displays (Figure 1-9). The subfolder name displays on the Outlook title bar and in the Folder banner.

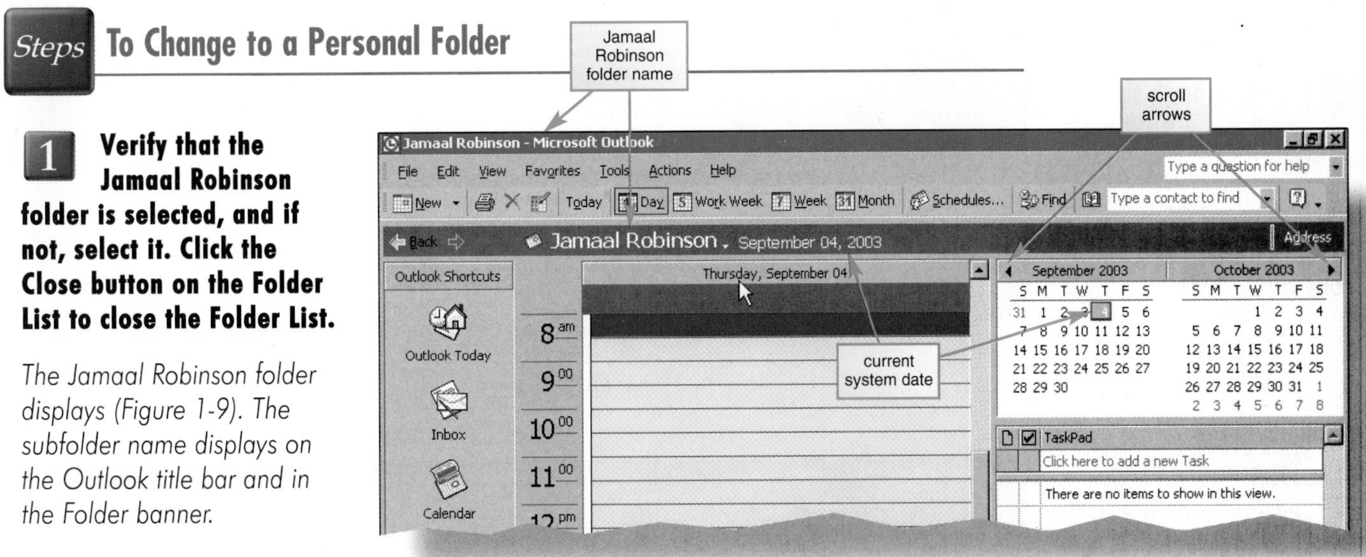

FIGURE 1-9

Figure 1-9 shows the default view for Calendar. If this view does not display on your computer, click View on the menu bar, point to Current View, and then make sure the Day/Week/Month option is selected.

With the Jamaal Robinson personal subfolder open, you now are ready to enter appointments, as demonstrated in the next section.

Entering Appointments Using the Appointment Area

Calendar allows you to schedule appointments, meetings, and events for yourself as well as for others who have given permission to open their subfolders. Students and business people will find that it is easy to schedule resources and people with Outlook's Calendar application.

The next section describes how to enter appointments, or in this case, classes into Jamaal Robinson's personal subfolder, starting with classes for September 8, 2003. Classes and meetings are recurring appointments; coffee with friends is a one-time appointment.

When entering an appointment into a time slot that is not visible in the current view, use the scroll bar to bring the time slot into view. Once you enter an appointment, you can perform ordinary editing actions. Perform the steps on the next page to enter the appointments using the appointment area.

Opening Calendars

Other users can give you access to their calendars. This allows you to make appointments, check free times, schedule meetings, check or copy contacts, or any other tasks that you can accomplish with your own calendar. This is useful if you need to schedule meetings or events that depend on other people's schedules.

To Enter Appointments Using the Appointment Area

1 If necessary, click the scroll arrows in the Date Navigator to display September and October 2003. Click 8 in the September calendar in the Date Navigator to display it in the appointment area.

2 Drag through the 8:00 am – 9:00 am time slot.

The 8:00 am – 9:00 am time slot is highlighted (Figure 1-10).

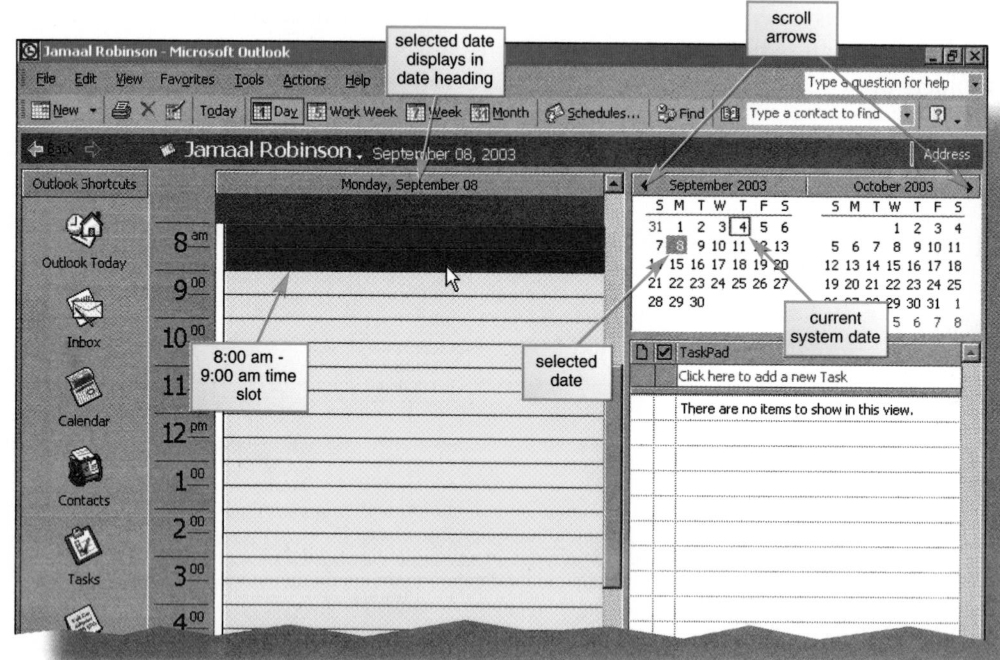

FIGURE 1-10

3 Type `Operating Systems` **as the first appointment.**

As soon as you begin typing, the selected time slot changes to a text box with blue top and bottom borders.

4 Drag through the 9:30 am – 10:30 am time slot. Type `Data Communications` **as the second appointment.**

5 Drag through the 2:00 pm – 3:00 pm time slot. Type `Coffee with friends` **as the third appointment and then press the ENTER key.**

The three appointments display in the appointment area (Figure 1-11).

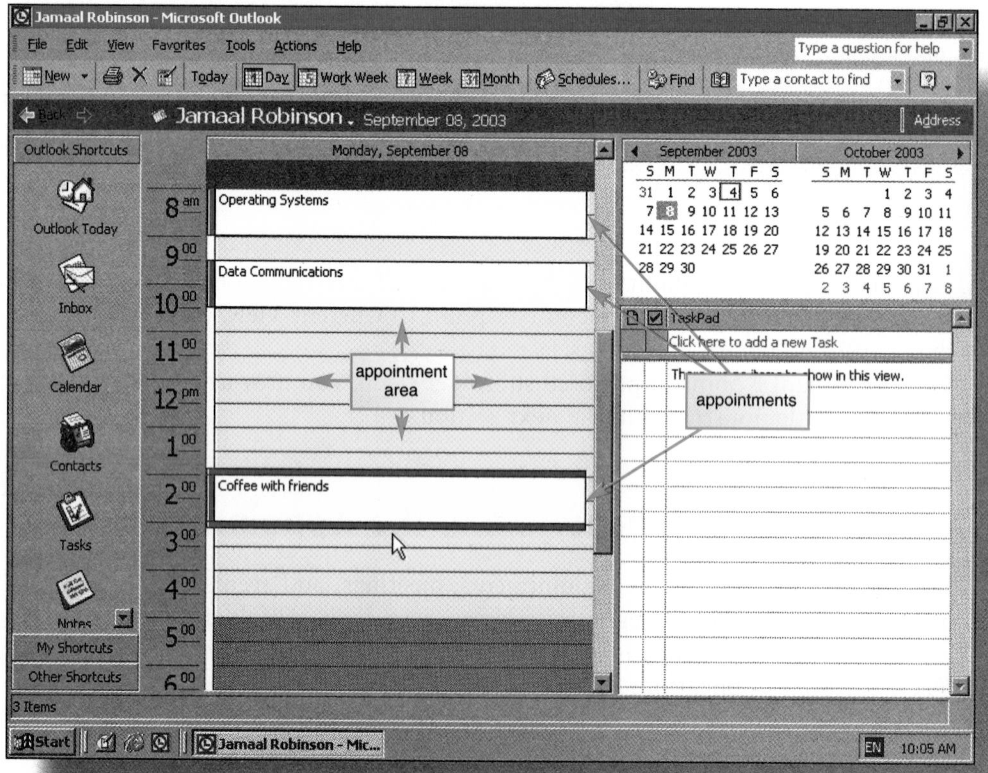

FIGURE 1-11

If you make a mistake while typing and notice the error before clicking outside the appointment time slot or pressing the ENTER key, use the BACKSPACE key to erase all the characters back to and including the error. To cancel the entire entry before clicking outside the appointment time slot or pressing the ENTER key, press the ESC key. If you discover an error in an appointment after clicking outside the appointment or pressing the ENTER key, click the appointment and retype the entry. Later in this project, additional editing techniques are discussed.

More About

Appointments

Appointments can be designated as busy, free, tentative, or out of office. The Private check box in the Appointment window allows you to designate appointments, tasks, meetings, or contacts as private, which prevents viewing by other users with access to your calendar. Private calendar elements are identified with a key symbol.

Entering Appointments Using the Appointment Window

You can enter appointments either by typing them directly into the appointment area as shown in the previous section, or you can enter them using the **Appointment window**. Using the Appointment window is a slightly more involved process, but it allows the specification of more details about the appointment. The following steps describe how to enter an appointment at 4:00 p.m. to 6:00 p.m. using the appointment window.

Steps To Enter and Save Appointments Using the Appointment Window

1 Drag through the 4:00 pm – 6:00 pm time slot and then click the New Appointment button on the Standard toolbar.

The Untitled - Appointment window opens with the insertion point in the Subject text box in the Appointment sheet (Figure 1-12).

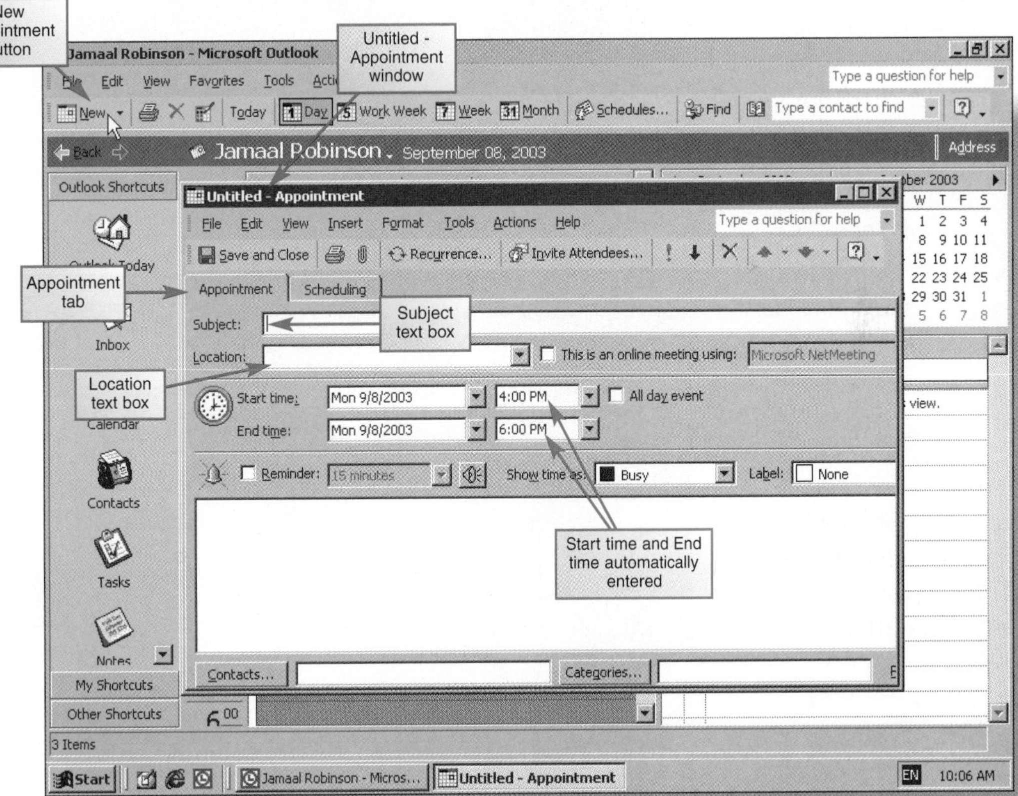

FIGURE 1-12

2 **Type** `Intramural volleyball coaches meeting` **in the Subject text box and then press the TAB key to move the insertion point to the Location text box. Type** `Union meeting room` **in the Location text box. Point to the Save and Close button on the Standard toolbar in the Appointment window.**

Both the subject and location of the appointment display in the appropriate text boxes. Once typed, the appointment subject displays on the Appointment window title bar and on the taskbar button (Figure 1-13). You can click the Reminder check box to instruct your computer to play a reminder sound before an appointment time. A bell icon, called the **Reminder symbol**, *displays next to appointments with reminders.*

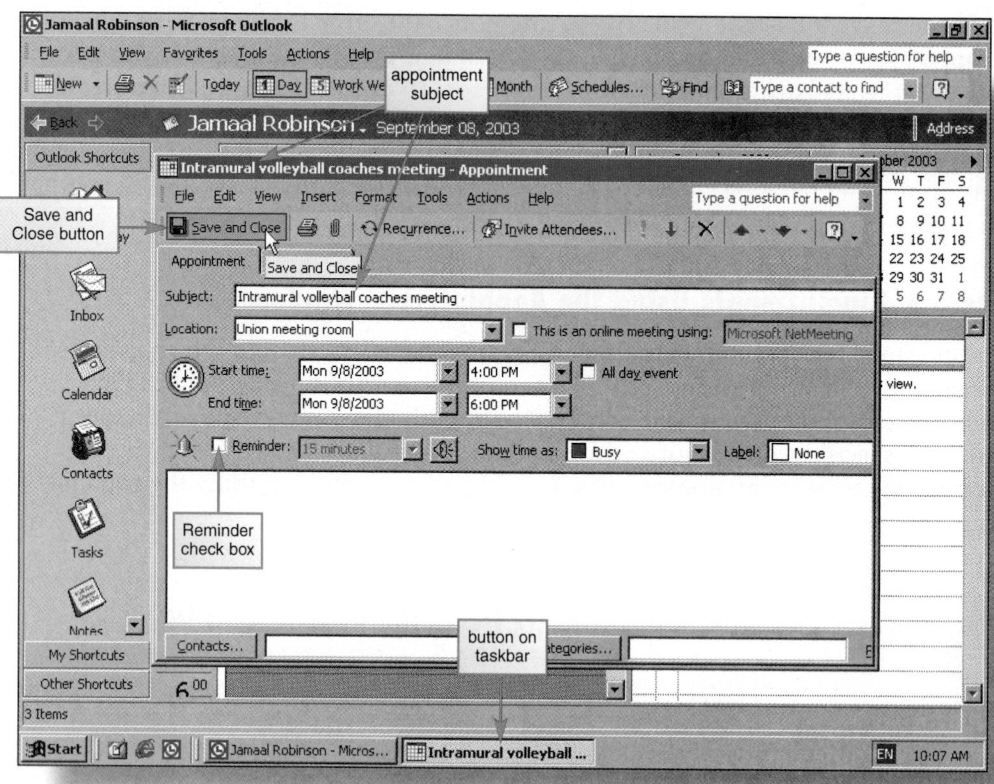

FIGURE 1-13

3 **Click the Save and Close button.**

The schedule for Monday, September 8 displays in the appointment area with the four new appointments entered (Figure 1-14).

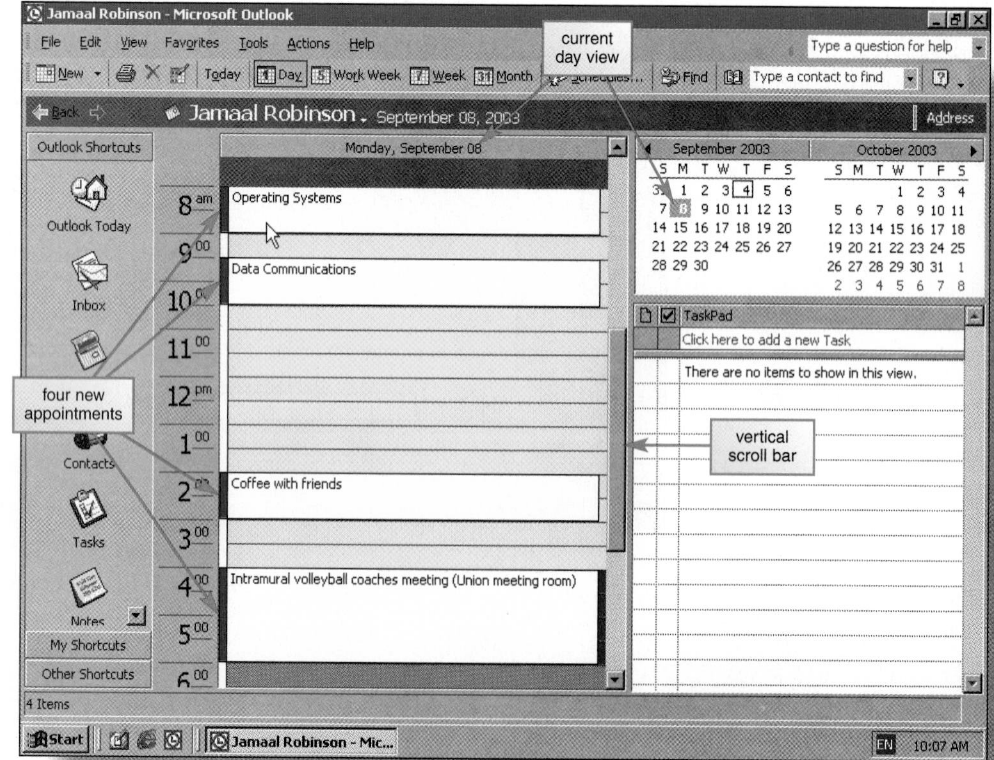

FIGURE 1-14

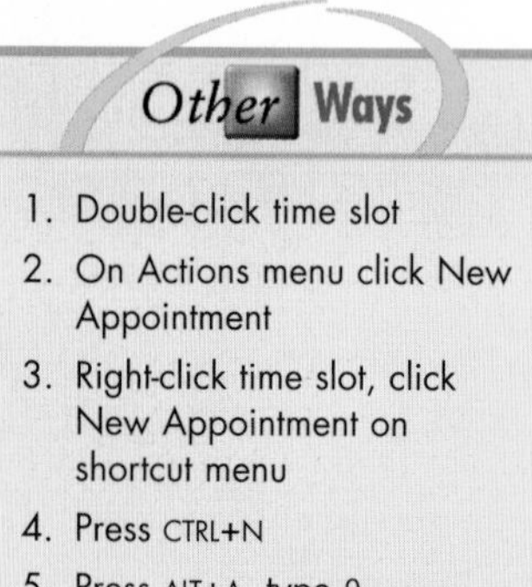

Other Ways

1. Double-click time slot
2. On Actions menu click New Appointment
3. Right-click time slot, click New Appointment on shortcut menu
4. Press CTRL+N
5. Press ALT+A, type 0
6. In Voice Command mode, say "Actions, New Appointment"

Press the TAB key to move through the fields in the Appointment window, or click any text or list box to make a change. Normal editing techniques also can be used to make changes.

Recurring Appointments

Many appointments are **recurring**, or occur at regular intervals. For example, a class held every Monday and Wednesday from 9:00 a.m. to 10:00 a.m. is a recurring appointment. In this project, Jamaal Robinson's college classes and meetings occur at regular, weekly intervals. Typing these recurring appointments for each occasion would be very time-consuming. By designating an appointment as recurring, the appointment needs to be added only once and then recurrence is specified for the days on which it occurs. Table 1-1 lists Jamaal's recurring appointments.

Table 1-1 Recurring Appointments

TIME	APPOINTMENT	OCCURRENCE
8:00 am – 9:00 am	Operating Systems - Anderson 203	Every Monday and Wednesday (30 times)
9:30 am – 10:30 am	Data Communications - Lilly 105	Every Monday and Wednesday (30 times)
4:00 pm – 6:00 pm	Intramural volleyball coaches meeting - Union meeting room	Every Monday (15 times)

Perform the following steps to enter the recurring appointments.

Steps To Enter Recurring Appointments

1 With Monday, September 8, 2003 displayed, double-click the words, Operating Systems.

The Operating Systems - Appointment window opens.

2 Click in the Location text box and then type `Anderson 203` **to set the location of the class. Point to the Recurrence button on the Standard toolbar.**

The symbol on the Recurrence button (Figure 1-15) will become the ***Recurrence symbol*** *that displays beside the appointment in the appointment area.*

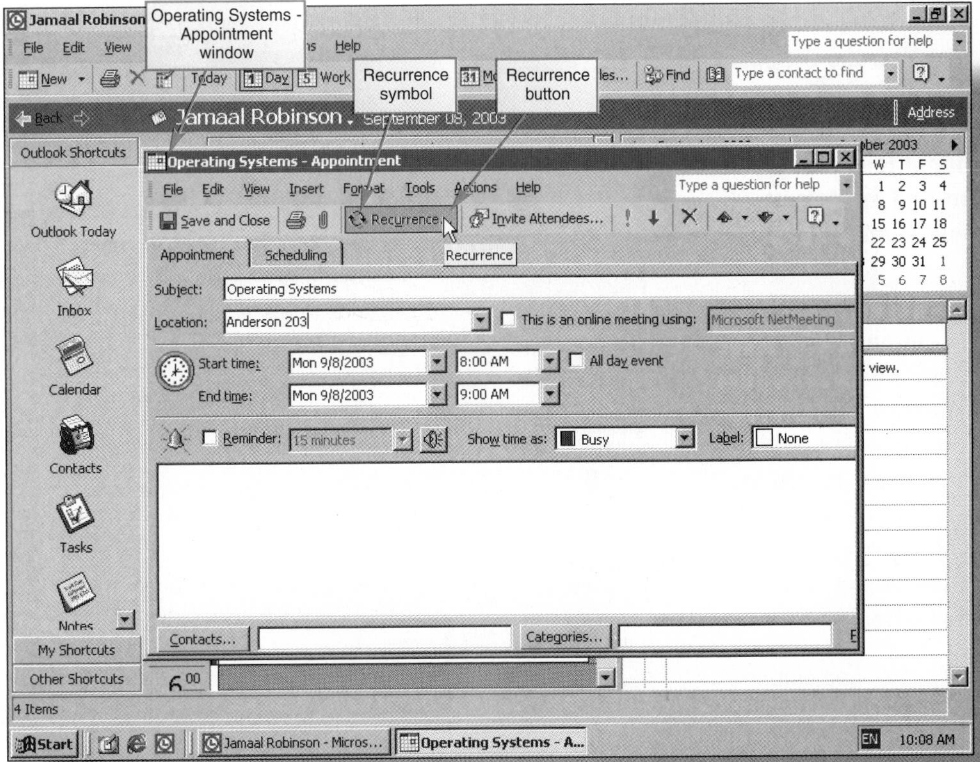

FIGURE 1-15

3 **Click the Recurrence button on the Standard toolbar. When the Appointment Recurrence dialog box displays, click the Wednesday check box to select the days this appointment will recur. Click End after in the Range of recurrence area, double-click the End after text box, and then type** 30 **as the number of occurrences. Point to the OK button.**

The Appointment Recurrence dialog box displays (Figure 1-16). The Operating Systems appointment is set to recur on Mondays (selected as the default) and Wednesday (selected in the step) and end after 30 occurrences.

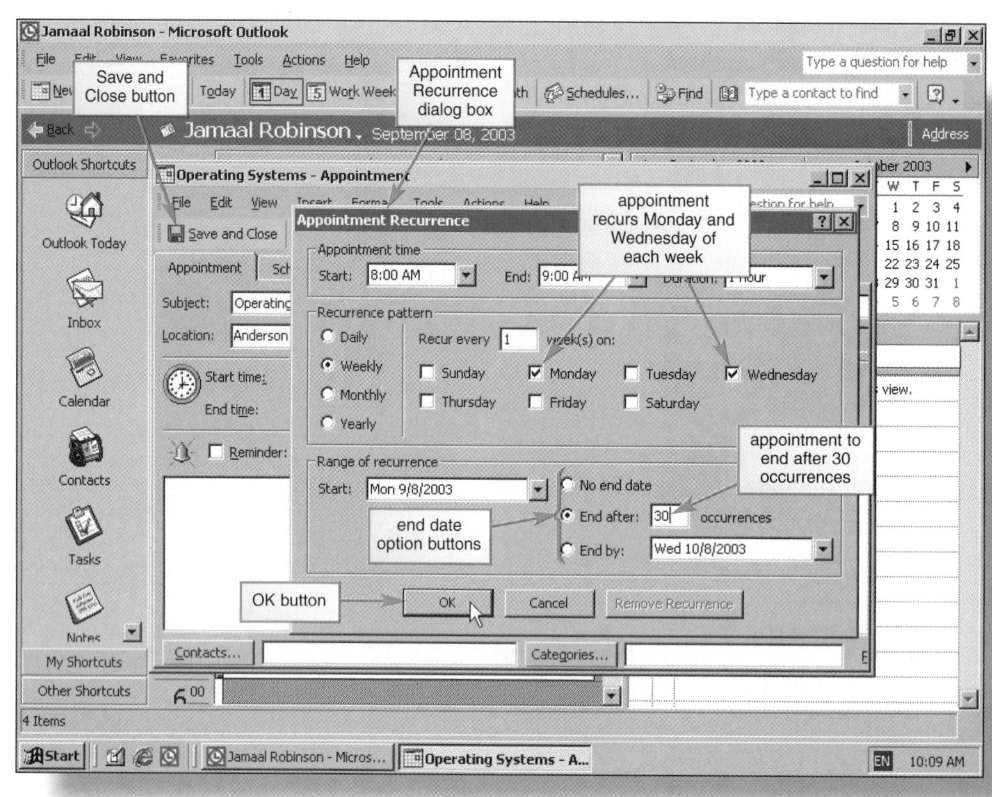

FIGURE 1-16

4 **Click the OK button. Click the Save and Close button on the Standard toolbar in the Operating Systems - Appointment window.**

5 **Repeat Steps 1 through 4 to make the Data Communications and Intramural volleyball coaches meeting appointments recurring. Refer to Table 1-1 on the previous page for the location, range, and ending dates.**

The Monday, September 8 schedule is complete (Figure 1-17). A Recurrence symbol displays beside each recurring appointment.

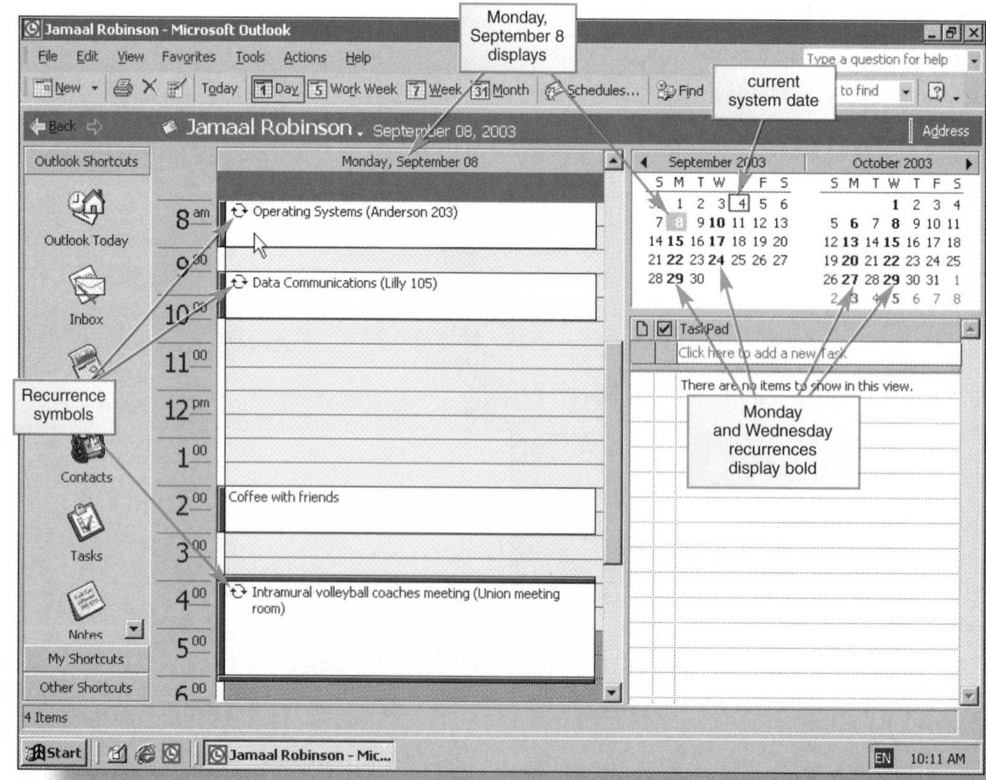

FIGURE 1-17

The Date Navigator serves several purposes when creating appointments. Recurring appointments are assigned to their appropriate dates automatically. Once an appointment is assigned to a date, it displays bold in the Date Navigator (Figure 1-17). You can change these features using the **Customize Current View command** on the Current View submenu of the View menu.

The Date Navigator also allows easy movement and display of a specific date in the appointment area. This allows appointments to be entered on that date. This technique is demonstrated in the next section.

More About

Calendar Coloring

You can color code appointments with one of 10 predefined colors. The different colors can help you to prioritize appointments based on importance. To color code, select the appointment, click the Calendar Coloring button on the Standard Toolbar, and then select a color.

Moving to the Next Day in Calendar and Entering the Remaining Recurring Appointments

With the Monday schedule entered, the next step is to move to the next day in the appointment area and complete the recurring appointments for every Tuesday and Thursday using the appointment information in Table 1-2. Because the recurring appointments start on Tuesday, Tuesday must display in the appointment area. The following steps show how to move to the next day using the Date Navigator and then enter the remaining recurring appointments.

Table 1-2 Additional Recurring Appointments

TIME	*APPOINTMENT*	*OCCURRENCE*
8:30 am – 9:30 am	Economics - EE 215	Every Tuesday and Thursday (30 times)
2:30 pm – 3:30 pm	Supervision - Gyte 103	Every Tuesday and Thursday (30 times)

Steps To Move to the Next Day and Enter the Recurring Appointments

1 **Click 9 in the September 2003 calendar in the Date Navigator. Drag through the 8:30 am – 9:30 am time slot. Point to the New Appointment button on the Standard toolbar.**

Tuesday, September 9 displays in the appointment area (Figure 1-18).

2 **Click the New Appointment button.**

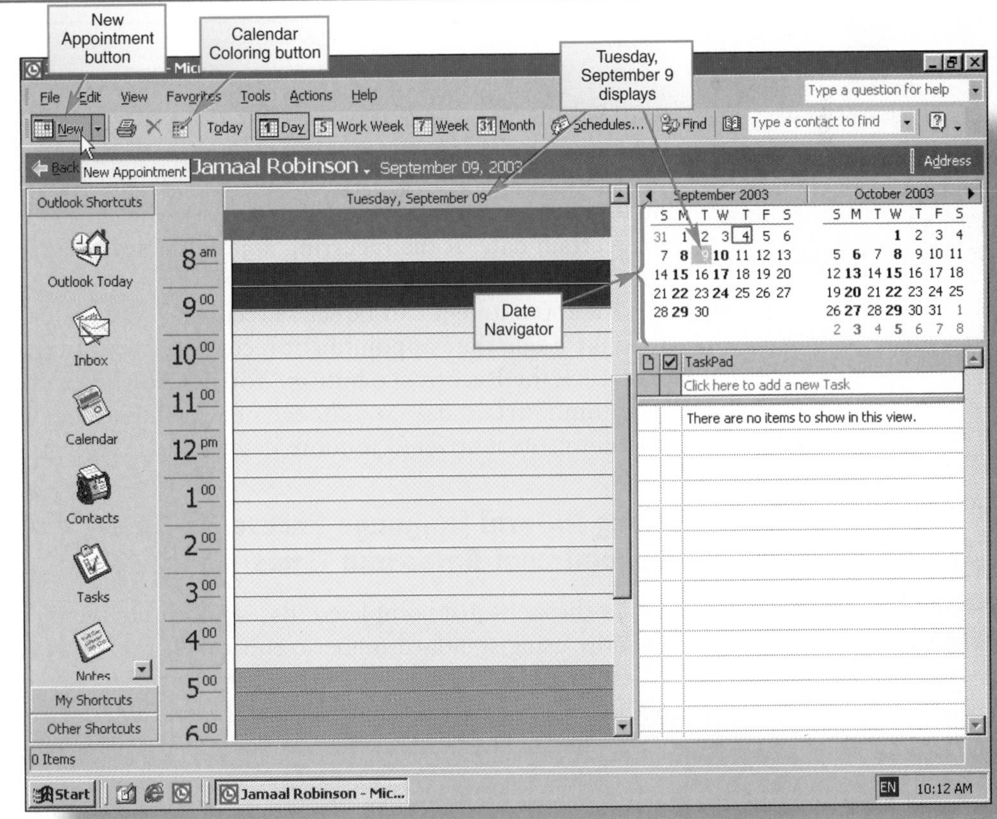

FIGURE 1-18

3 Enter the recurring appointments provided in Table 1-2 on the previous page. Click the Save and Close button in the Appointment window

The appointments for Tuesday, September 9 display (Figure 1-19). These appointments are scheduled to recur on Tuesdays and Thursdays and display in bold on the calendars in the Date Navigator.

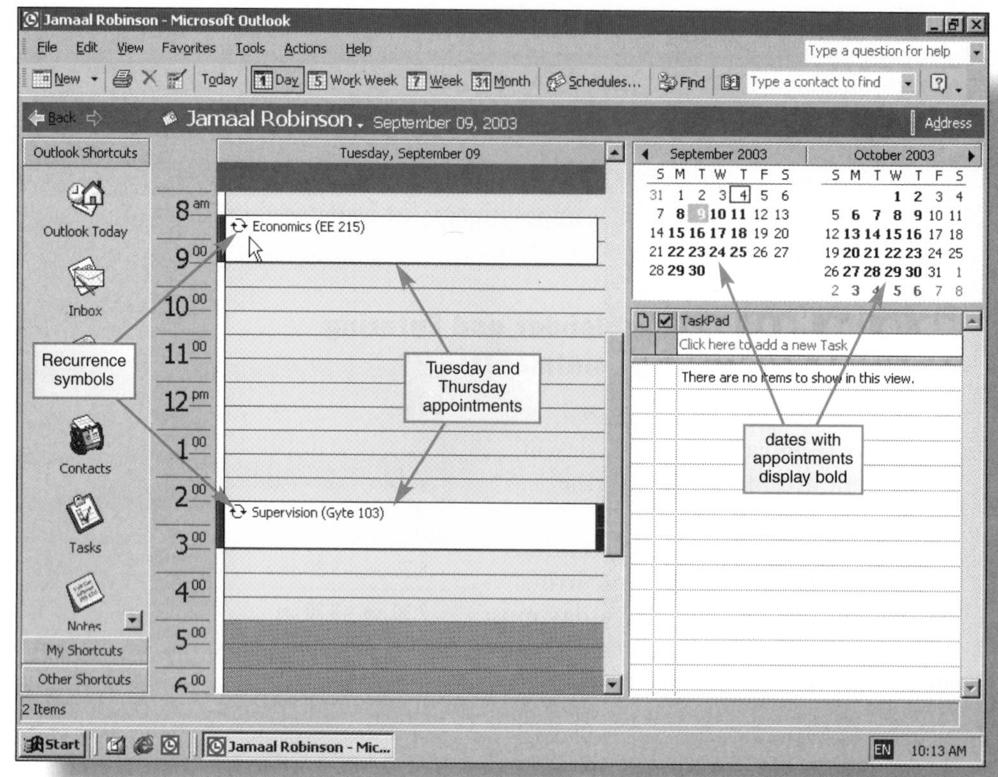

FIGURE 1-19

Other Ways

1. On Actions menu click New Recurring Appointment
2. Press ALT+A, type A
3. In Voice Command mode, say "Actions, New Recurring Appointment"

Daily, weekly, monthly, or yearly recurrence patterns are possible in the Appointment Recurrence options. Outlook also provides three options for the range of recurrence. Appointments can recur every week or choice of weeks for one or multiple days. An appointment can be set to occur a certain number of times or up to a certain date. If the recurring appointment is ongoing, such as office hours, you can select the **No end date option button** (Figure 1-16 on page O 1.18).

An appointment can be set as recurring when it first is entered, or, if you decide to make a one-time appointment recurring later, double-click the appointment and then click the Recurrence button. You can edit recurring appointments to add new days, omit certain days, or change other recurrence details. Editing recurring appointments is covered in more detail later in this project.

More About

The Recurrence Symbol

The Recurrence symbol can be applied to appointments, events, meetings, and tasks. Double-click the item to open its dialog box and then click the Recurrence button.

Using Natural Language Phrases to Enter Appointment Dates and Times

In the steps just completed, dates and times were entered in the Appointment window using standard numeric entries. Outlook's **AutoDate function**, however, provides the capability of specifying appointment dates and times using **natural language phrases**. For example, you can type phrases such as, next Tuesday, two weeks from yesterday, or midnight, and Outlook will calculate the correct date.

In this example, the Sigma Chi/Alpha Delta Pi beach party will be held two weeks from Saturday at the fraternity house, on Saturday, September 27, 2003, from 3:00 p.m. to 7:30 p.m. The following steps describe how to enter the date and time for the party using natural language phrases.

Steps To Enter Appointment Dates and Times Using Natural Language Phrases

1 **With Tuesday, September 9 displayed in the appointment area, click the New Appointment button on the Standard toolbar.**

2 **Type** `Sigma Chi/Alpha Delta Pi beach party` **in the Subject text box and then press the TAB key. Type** `Fraternity house` **in the Location text box and then press the TAB key twice. Type** `two weeks from Saturday` **in the Start time date box for the date.**

The appointment information is entered in the Appointment window. Two weeks from Saturday is entered in the Start time date box (Figure 1-20).

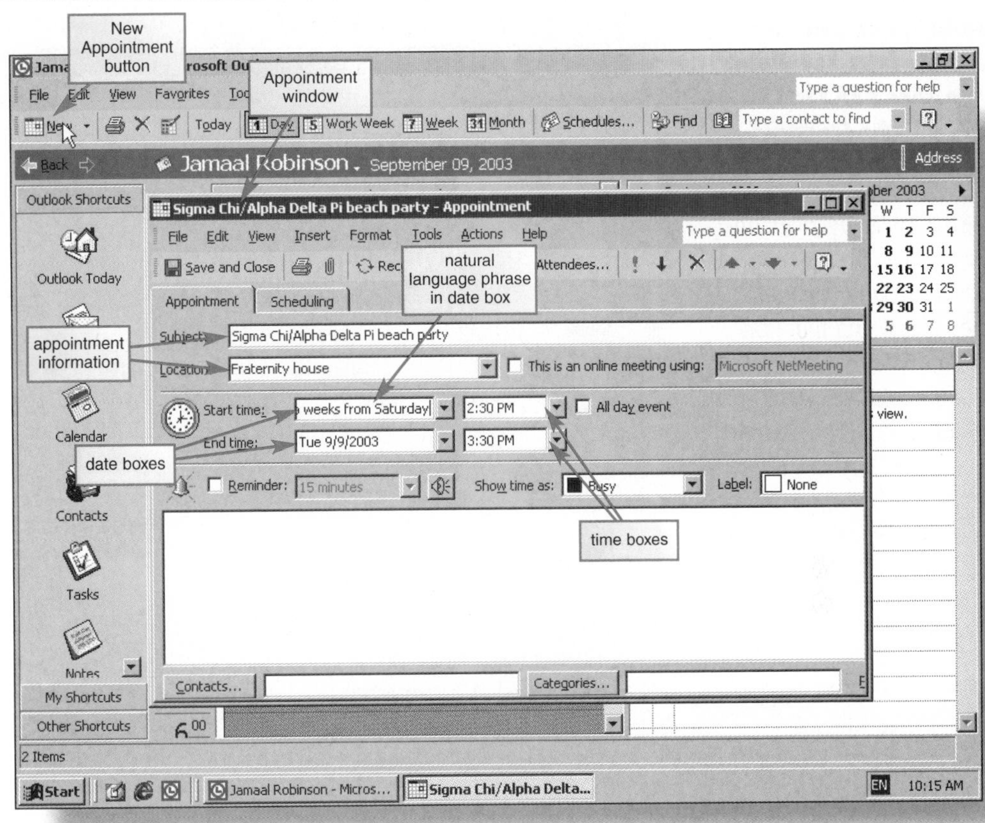

FIGURE 1-20

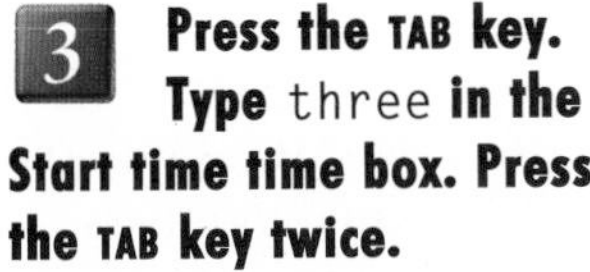

3 **Press the TAB key. Type** `three` **in the Start time time box. Press the TAB key twice.**

Outlook automatically converts the phrase, two weeks from Saturday, into the date, Sat 9/27/2003, in both the Start time date and End time date boxes. It also converts the word, three, into 3:00 PM in the time box (Figure 1-21).

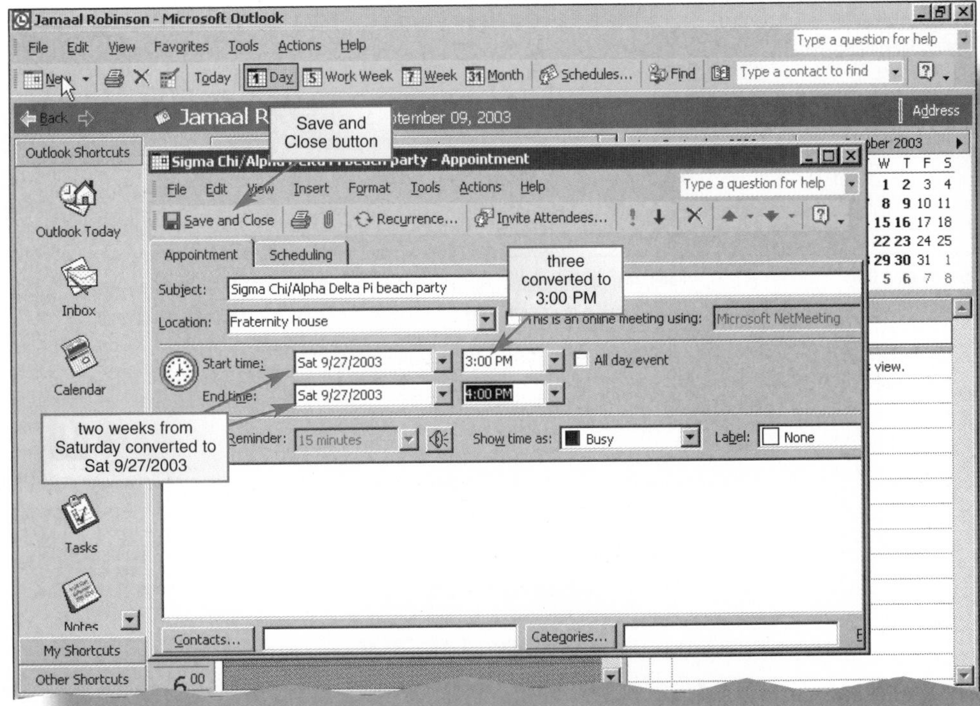

FIGURE 1-21

Type `seven thirty` **in the End time time box and then press the ENTER key. Point to the Save and Close button on the Standard toolbar.**

Outlook automatically converts the words, seven thirty, to 7:30 PM and sets the appointment end time for 7:30 PM. Outlook sets appointments for 30 minutes unless you enter a new End time or drag through a longer time slot in the appointment area before clicking the New Appointment button or changing the default setting.

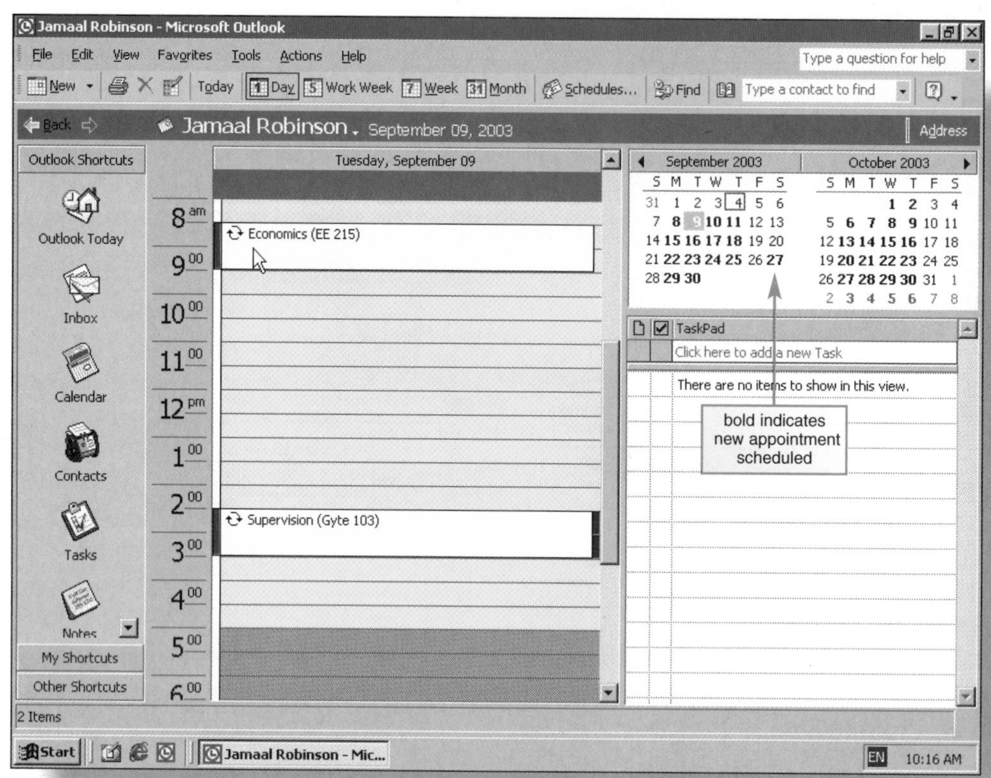

FIGURE 1-22

5 **Click the Save and Close button.**

The Appointment window closes and Tuesday, September 9 displays in the appointment area. The Sigma Chi/Alpha Delta Pi beach party is added to the calendar on Saturday, September 27, 2003 (Figure 1-22).

In addition to theses natural phrases, Outlook can convert abbreviations and ordinal numbers into complete words and dates. For example, you can type Feb instead of February or the first of September instead of 9/1. Outlook's Calendar application also will convert words such as yesterday, tomorrow, and the names of holidays that occur only once each year, such as Valentine's Day. Table 1-3 lists the various AutoDate options.

Table 1-3 AutoDate Options

CATEGORY	EXAMPLES
Dates Spelled Out	• July twenty-third, March 29th, first of December • this Fri, next Sat, two days from now • three wks ago, next week • one month from today
Times Spelled Out	• noon, midnight • nine o'clock a.m., five twenty • 7 pm
Descriptions of Times and Dates	• now • yesterday, today, tomorrow • next, last • ago, before, after ending, following • for, from, that, this, till, through, until
Holidays	• Cinco de Mayo • Christmas, Christmas Day, Christmas Eve • Halloween • Independence Day • New Year's Day, New Year's Eve • St. Patrick's Day • Valentine's Day • Veterans Day

More About

Moving a Recurring Appointment

If a recurring appointment is moved, only the selected instance of the appointment is moved. If all instances of an appointment need to be moved, open the appointment, click Recurrence on the Appointment menu, and then change the recurrence pattern.

Editing Appointments

Because schedules often need to be rearranged, Outlook provides several ways of editing appointments. Edit the subject and location of an appointment by clicking the appointment and editing the information directly in the appointment area, or double-click the appointment and make corrections using the Appointment window. All occurrences in a series of a recurring appointment can be changed, or a single occurrence can be altered.

Editing Appointments

Click Tools on the menu bar and then click Find to locate an appointment for which you cannot remember the details. In the Look for box, click Appointments and meetings. You then may search for any word or subject.

Deleting Appointments

Appointments sometimes are canceled and must be deleted from the schedule. For example, the schedule created thus far in this project contains an appointment on Thursday, November 27, 2003. Because November 27 is Thanksgiving Day, however, no classes will meet and the scheduled appointment needs to be deleted. The following steps describe how to delete an appointment from the calendar.

Steps To Delete an Appointment

1 Click the scroll arrows in the Date Navigator to display November 2003. Click 27 in the November 2003 calendar. Click the first appointment to be deleted, Economics, and then point to the Delete button on the Standard toolbar (Figure 1-23).

Thursday, November 27 displays at the top of the appointment area (Figure 1-23). The blue top and bottom borders indicate the Economics appointment is selected.

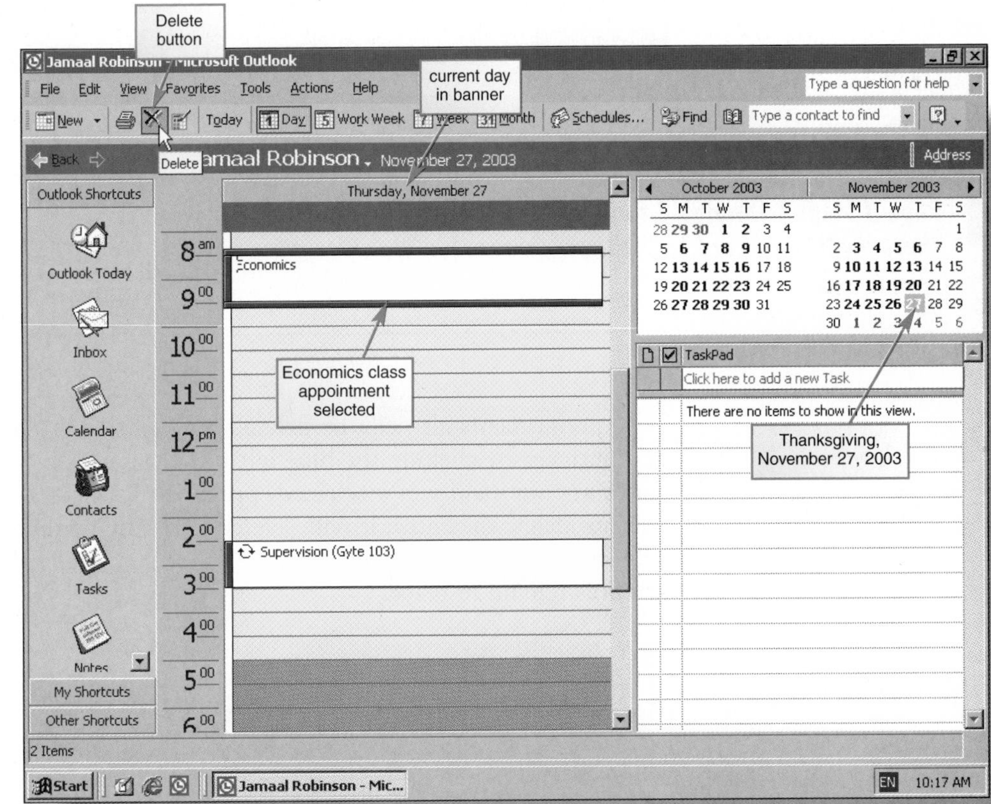

FIGURE 1-23

2 Click the Delete button. When the Confirm Delete dialog box displays, point to the OK button.

Because the appointment selected is a recurring appointment, a Confirm Delete dialog box displays providing the option of deleting all occurrences of the recurring appointment or just this one (Figure 1-24). The Delete this occurrence option button is selected by default.

3 Click the OK button.

The Economics appointment is deleted from Thursday, November 27, 2003. All other occurrences of the appointment remain in the schedule.

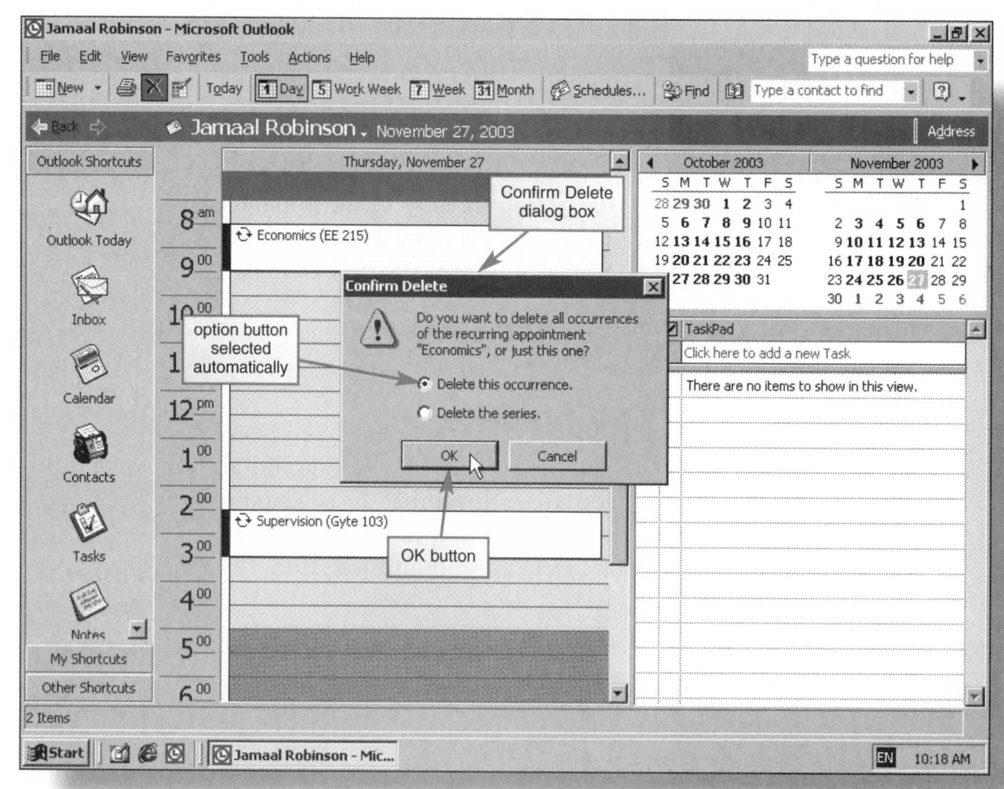

FIGURE 1-24

4 Repeat Steps 1 through 3 to delete the Supervision appointment from Thursday, November 27, 2003.

Other Ways

1. Right-click appointment to be deleted, click Delete on shortcut menu
2. Click blue left border of appointment, press DELETE

Appointments also can be deleted using the DELETE key. First, select the entire appointment by clicking the blue left border and then press the DELETE key. If the entire appointment is not selected, pressing the DELETE key (or the BACKSPACE key) will not delete the entry; it will delete only individual characters of the appointment subject. Even if all the characters are deleted, the time slot remains active and any symbols remain in place.

Moving Appointments to a New Time

Outlook also provides several ways to move appointments. Suppose for instance, that some friends cannot make it for coffee at 2:00 p.m. on Monday, September 8, 2003. The appointment needs to be rescheduled to 1:00 p.m. to 2:00 p.m. Instead of deleting and then retyping the appointment, simply drag it to the new time slot. The following steps describe how to move an appointment to a new time.

Steps To Move an Appointment to a New Time

1 If necessary, click the scroll arrow in the Date Navigator to display September 2003. Click 8 in the September 2003 calendar in the Date Navigator.

2 Position the mouse pointer on the blue left border of the Coffee with friends appointment.

The mouse pointer changes to a four-headed arrow (Figure 1-25).

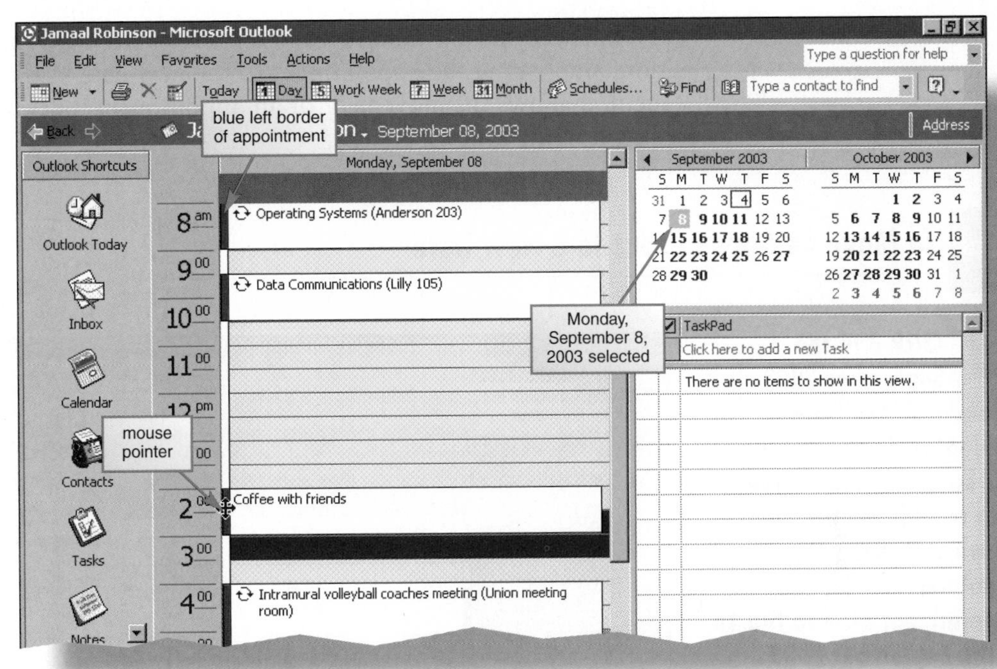

FIGURE 1-25

3 Drag the appointment up to the 1:00 pm – 2:00 pm time slot.

As the appointment is dragged, the mouse pointer changes to a pointer with a small dotted box below it, called the ***drag icon****.*

4 Release the mouse button to drop the appointment in the new time slot.

The appointment is placed in the 1:00 pm – 2:00 pm time slot (Figure 1-26). Outlook automatically allows adequate time for the moved appointment, in this case, one hour.

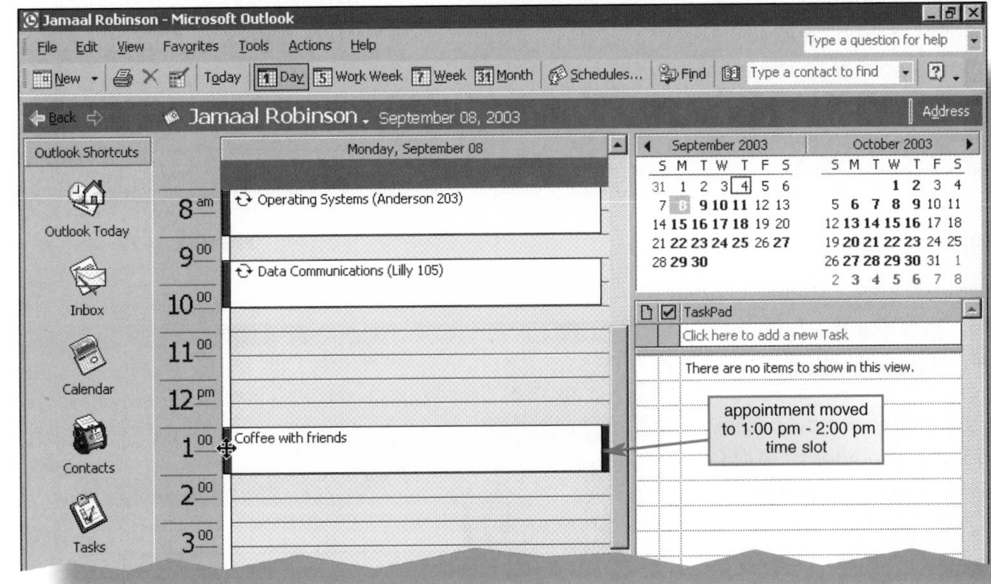

FIGURE 1-26

Other Ways

1. Double-click appointment, edit date in Start date box in Appointment window
2. Click left border of appointment, press CTRL+X, click new date in Date Navigator, click new time slot in appointment area, press CTRL+V

An appointment can be moved to a new time using the Appointment window, as well. Simply type a different time in the Start time or End time time boxes or click one of the time box arrows and select a different time in the list. Natural language phrases also can be used in the time box, which Outlook converts to the appropriate times.

Moving Appointments to a New Date

If an appointment is being moved to a new date but remaining in the same time slot, simply drag the appointment to the new date in the Date Navigator. Using this method allows the movement of an appointment quickly and easily to a new date, as shown in the following steps.

Steps To Move an Appointment to a New Date

1 Click 8 in the September 2003 calendar in the Date Navigator. Click the blue left border of the Coffee with friends appointment to select it. Drag the appointment from the appointment area to the 10 in the September 2003 calendar.

Dragging outside the appointment area causes the mouse pointer to change to the drag icon. A blue border displays around 10 in the September 2003 calendar in the Date Navigator (Figure 1-27).

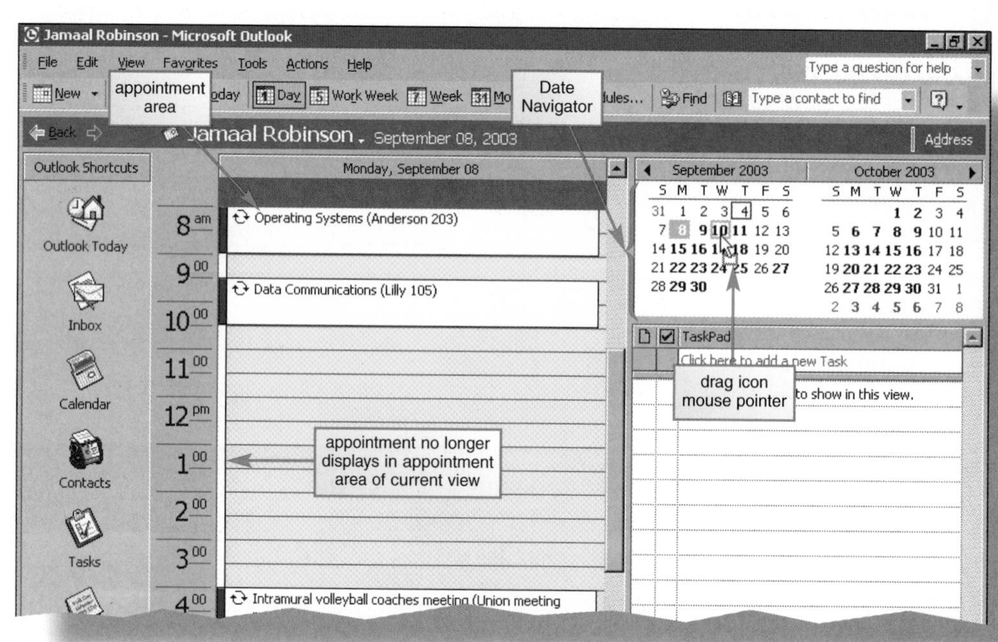

FIGURE 1-27

2 Release the left mouse button.

The appointment moves from Monday, September 8, 2003 to Wednesday, September 10, 2003 (Figure 1-28).

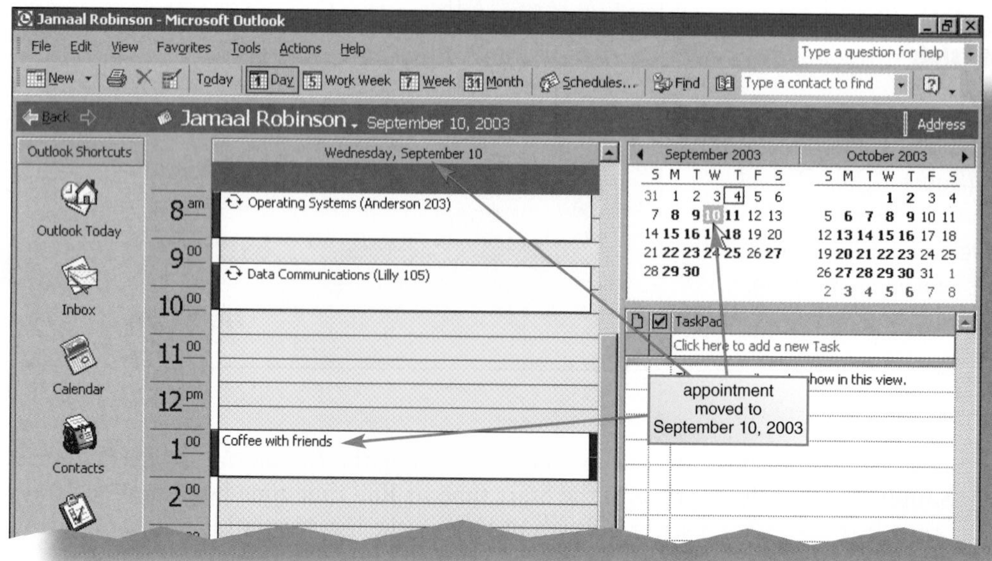

FIGURE 1-28

Outlook provides several ways to move appointments to new dates in addition to the drag and drop method used in the previous steps. Appointments can be moved to new dates by making changes in the Appointment window or by using the cut and paste method discussed in the following section.

Moving an Appointment to a New Month

If an appointment is being moved to a month not displayed in the Date Navigator, it cannot be dragged to a date not displayed. In this case, cutting and pasting the appointment to a new date can be used.

When you cut an item in other Office XP applications, the item that you cut disappears from the screen. In Outlook, the item remains on the screen until it is pasted to another location.

The members of the beach party committee decided to reschedule the party to a date in October. The time of the party is moved from Saturday, September 27, 2003 to Saturday, October 4, 2003. The following steps describe how to move an appointment to a new month using the cut and paste method.

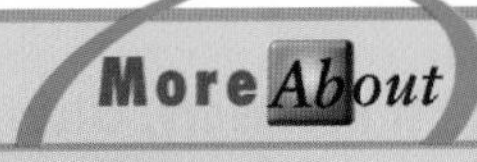

Moving Appointments

To send an appointment to a co-worker, right-click the appointment and choose Forward on the shortcut menu.

Steps To Move an Appointment to a New Month

1 Click 27 in the September 2003 calendar in the Date Navigator. Scroll down to the 3:00 pm time slot. Click the blue left border of the Sigma Chi/Alpha Delta Pi beach party appointment to select it. Click Edit on the menu bar and then point to Cut.

The Edit menu displays (Figure 1-29).

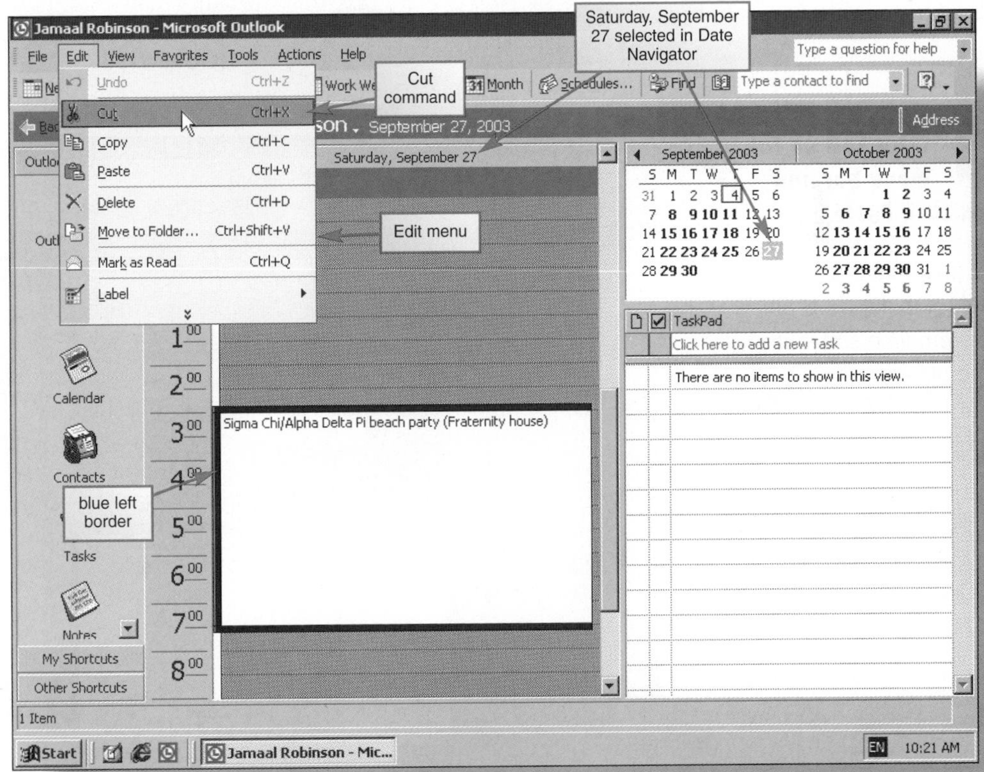

FIGURE 1-29

2 Click Cut.

The appointment is copied to the Clipboard, and the appointment remains on the screen.

3 If necessary, click the right scroll arrow in the Date Navigator to display October 2003. Click 4 in the October 2003 calendar in the Date Navigator.

Outlook displays Saturday, October 4 in the appointment area. The 3:00 pm – 7:30 pm time slot is selected (Figure 1-30).

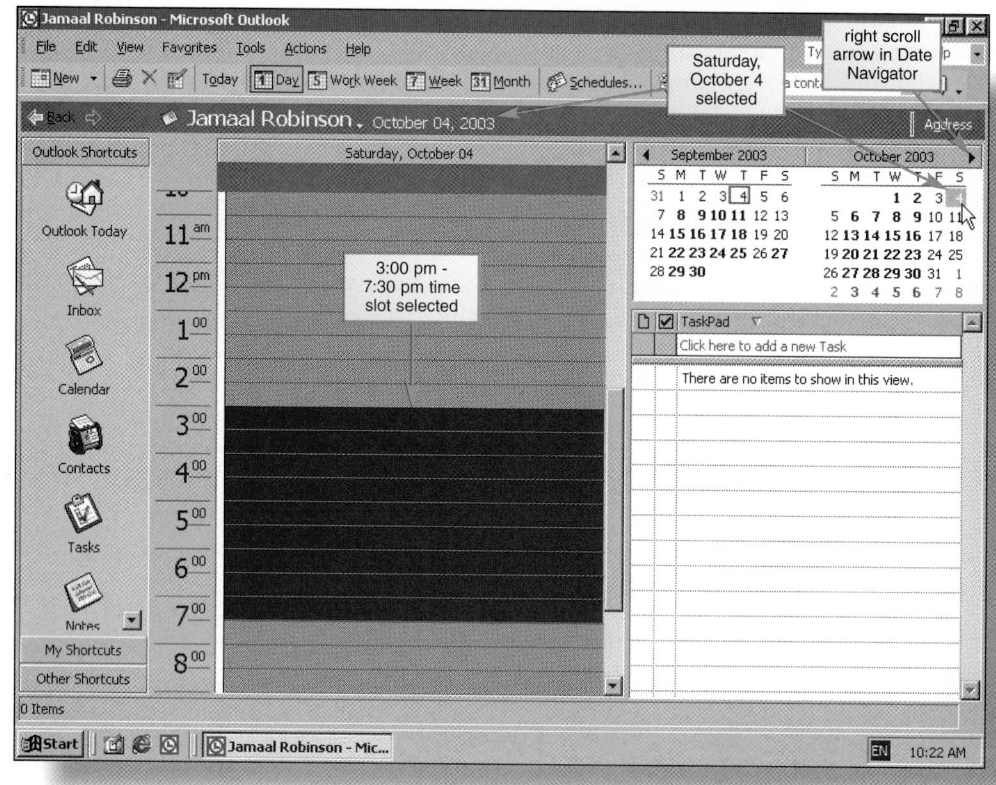

FIGURE 1-30

4 Click Edit on the menu bar and then click Paste.

The appointment now displays in the 3:00 pm – 7:30 pm time slot in the appointment area for Saturday, October 4 (Figure 1-31).

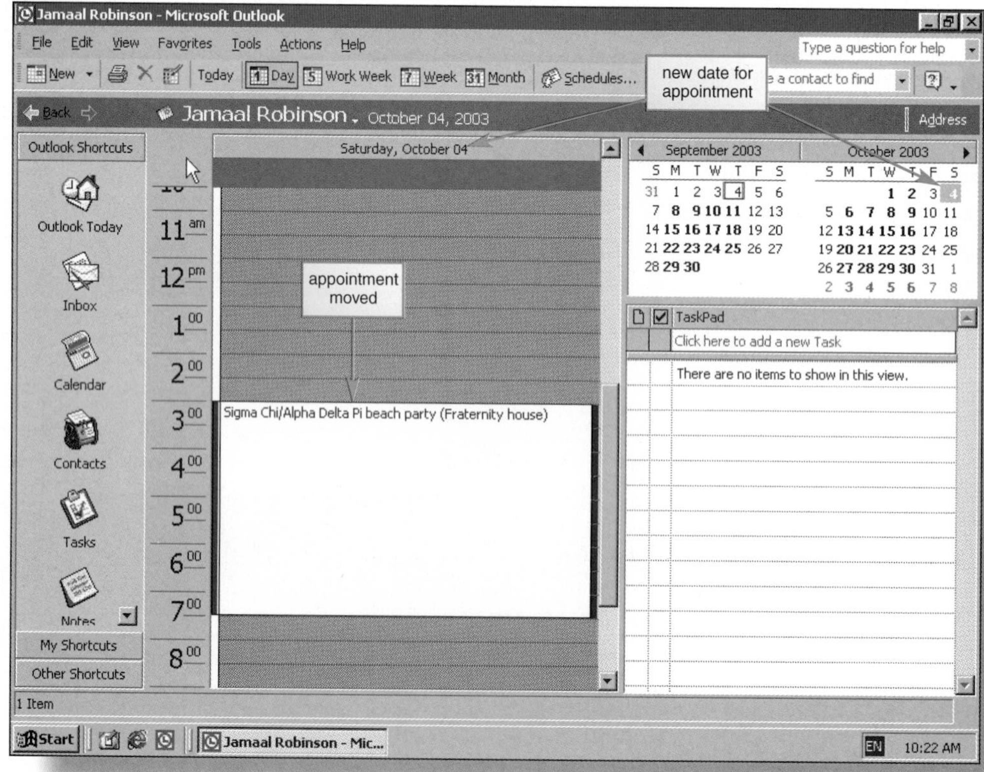

FIGURE 1-31

Either the drag and drop method or the cut and paste method is available for appointment movement. Regardless of the method, the results are the same. An appointment can be moved to a different time on the same day, to a different day, or to an entirely different month.

Locations

As appointments or events are entered with specific locations, the locations automatically are accumulated in a list. This list is accessible through the arrow to the right of the Location text box. Frequently used locations can be selected from this list, thus saving typing time.

Creating an Event

Outlook's Calendar folder allows you to keep track of important events. **Events** are activities that last 24 hours or longer. Examples of events include birthdays, conferences, weddings, vacations, holidays, and so on; they can be one-time or recurring. Events differ from appointments in one primary way – they do not display in individual time slots in the appointment area. When an event is scheduled, its description displays in a small **banner** below the date heading. The details of the event can be indicated as time that is free, busy, or out of the office during the event. The following steps show how to enter a birthday as an event.

Steps To Create an Event

1 If necessary, click the left scroll arrow to display September 2003 in the Date Navigator. Click 23 in the September 2003 calendar in the Date Navigator.

2 Double-click the date heading at the top of the appointment area. When the Untitled - Event window opens, type `Kylie's birthday` **in the Subject text box. Point to the Save and Close button on the Standard toolbar.**

The Untitled - Event window opens (Figure 1-32). Double-clicking the date heading allows all day events to be scheduled. The All day event check box thus is selected by default. The Show time as box indicates Free.

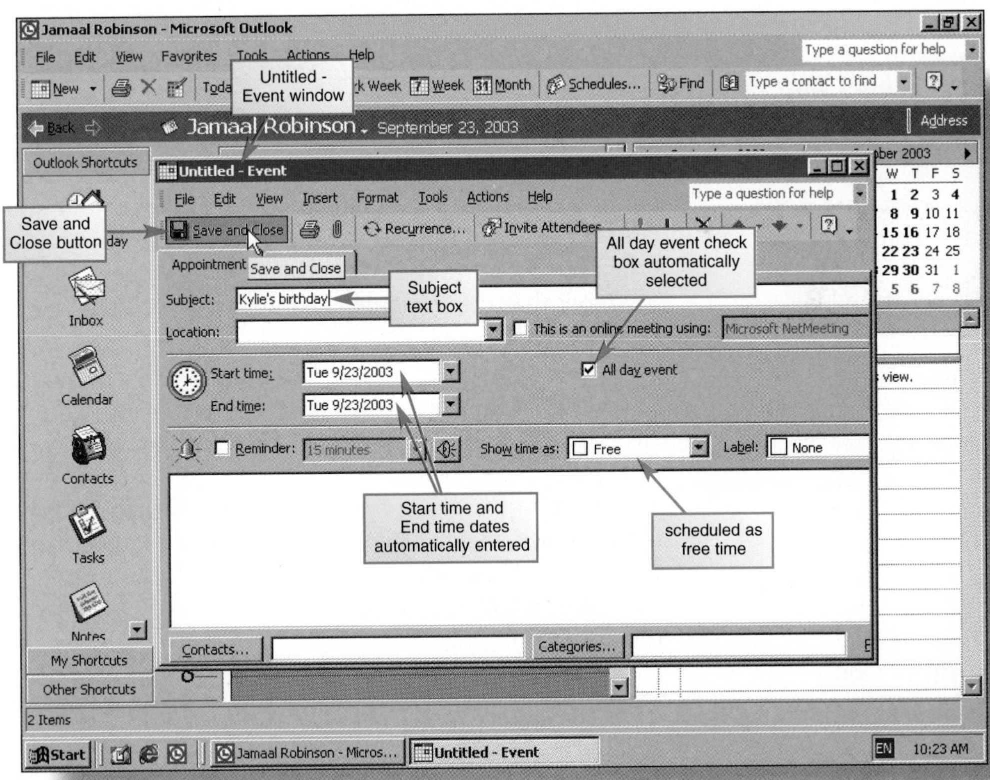

FIGURE 1-32

3 **Click the Save and Close button.**

The Event subject displays in a banner below the date heading (Figure 1-33).

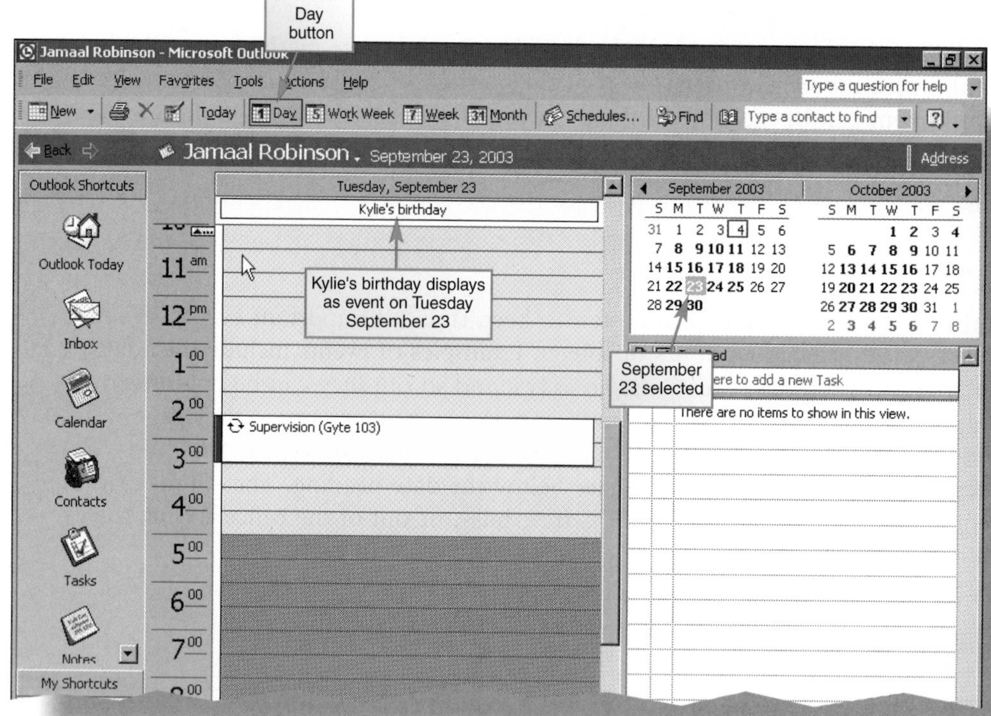

FIGURE 1-33

1. On Actions menu click New All Day Event
2. Right-click appointment area, click New All Day Event on shortcut menu
3. Press ALT+A, type E
4. Press CTRL+N, click All day event check box
5. In Voice Command mode, say "Actions, New All Day Event"

You could use the same steps to enter holidays as annual events; however, Outlook has a folder of typical holidays for various countries that can be added to your calendar automatically. To do this, click Options on the Tools menu. Click Calendar Options, and then click Add Holidays in the Calendar Options sheet.

Now that the schedule is complete, the Calendar can be displayed in various views.

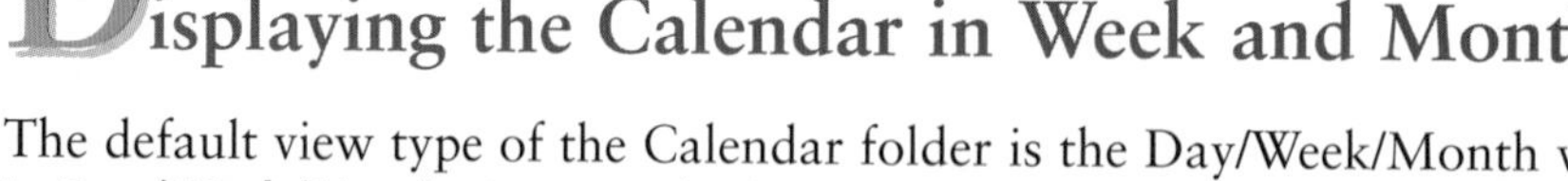

Displaying the Calendar in Week and Month Views

The default view type of the Calendar folder is the Day/Week/Month view. While in **Day/Week/Month view**, Outlook can display calendars in four different views: Day, Work Week, Week, and Month. So far in this project, you have used only the Day view, which is indicated by the selected Day button on the Standard toolbar (Figure 1-33).

Now that the schedule is complete, it also can be displayed in Week or Month view. Although the screen displays quite differently in Week and Month views, the same tasks can be performed as in Day view: appointments and events can be added, edited, or deleted, and reminders can be set or removed.

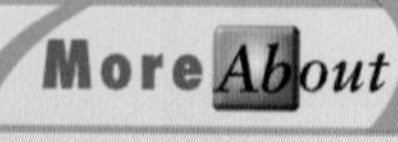

Holidays and Observances

For more information about holidays and observances, visit the Outlook 2002 More About Web page (scsite.com/out2002/more.htm) and then click Calendar.

Work Week View

The **Work Week view** shows five work days (Monday through Friday) in columnar style. The advantage of displaying a calendar in this view is the ability to see how many appointments are scheduled for the Monday through Friday time frame, eliminating the weekends. The following step changes the Calendar view to Work Week view.

Steps To Change to Work Week View

1 Click Tuesday, September 9 in the Date Navigator. Click the Work Week button on the Standard toolbar. If necessary, scroll up in the appointment area until the 8 am time slot displays.

The calendar displays in Work Week view (Figure 1-34). Notice that September 8 through September 12 all are highlighted in the Date Navigator, and the Work Week button is selected.

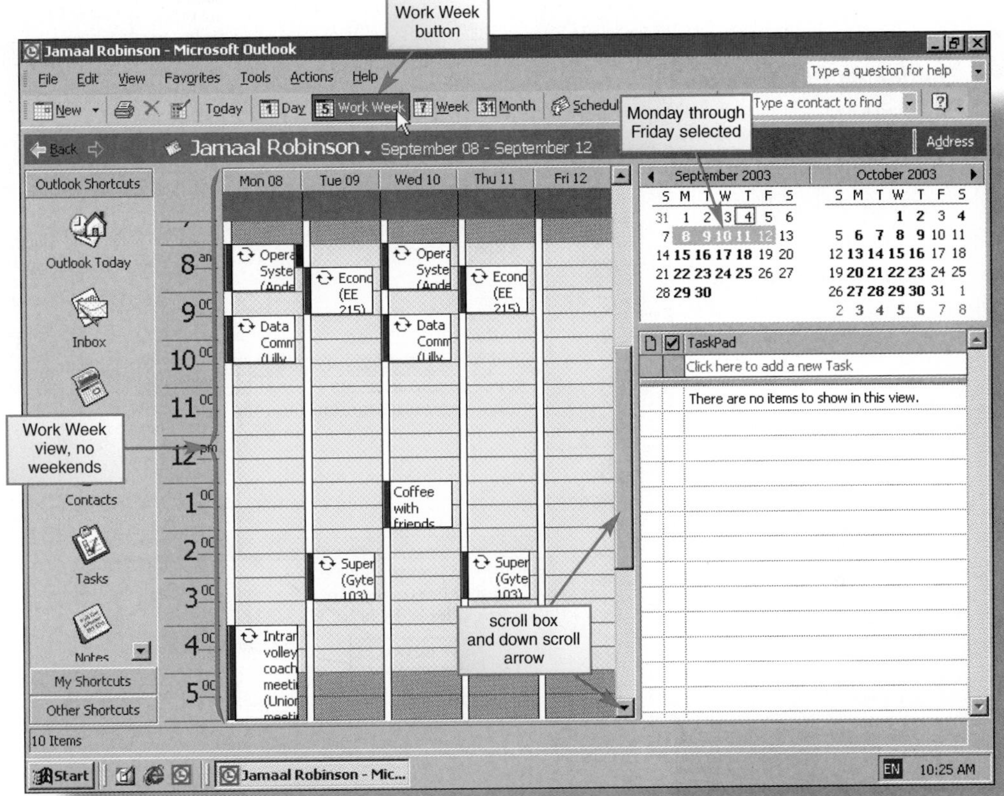

FIGURE 1-34

Other Ways

1. On View menu click Work Week
2. Press ALT+V, type R
3. In Voice Command mode, say "Work Week"

The scroll box and scroll arrows on the vertical scroll bar allow backward or forward movement within the selected week. An individual appointment can be selected by double-clicking it. As shown in Figure 1-34, some appointments may be too long to display horizontally in the appointment area. Dragging the border of the appointment area to the right will increase its width so that more of the appointment text displays.

Week View

The advantage of displaying a calendar in **Week view** is to see how many appointments are scheduled for any given week. In Week view, the seven days of the selected week display in the appointment area. The five days of the work week (Monday through Friday) display in individual frames, while Saturday and Sunday share a single frame. The step on the next page describes how to display the calendar in Week view.

To Change to Week View

1 Click the Week button on the Standard toolbar.

The calendar displays in Week view (Figure 1-35). Notice that the Week button is selected on the Standard toolbar.

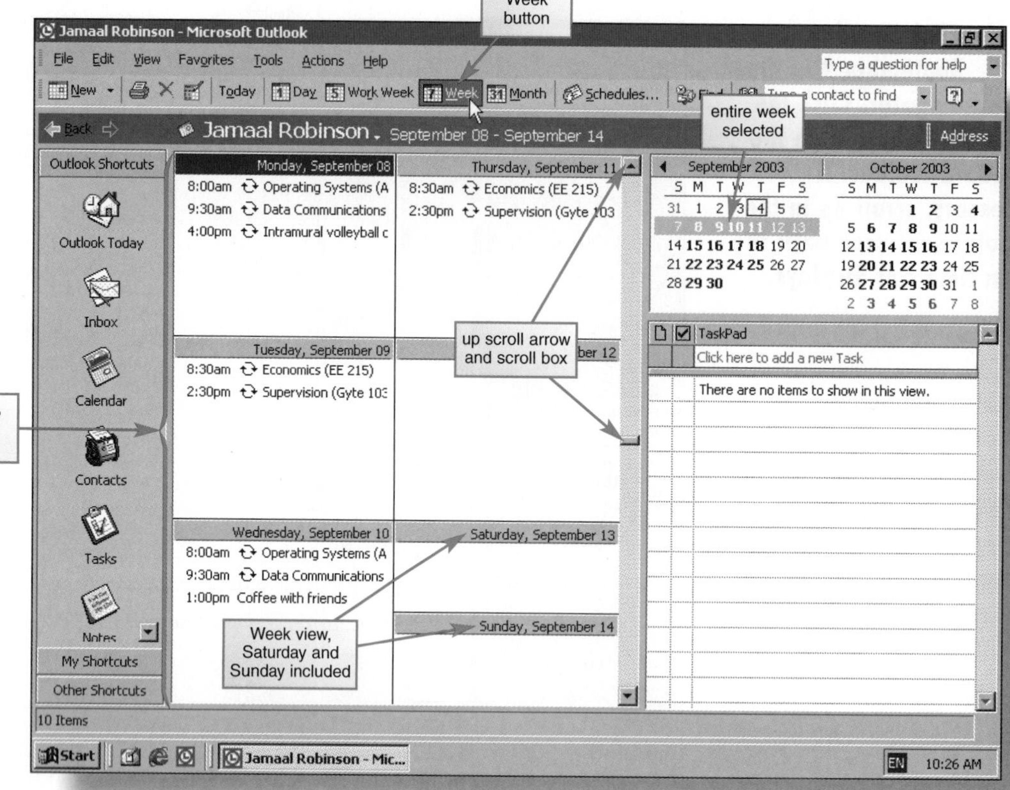

FIGURE 1-35

Other Ways

1. On View menu click Week
2. Press ALT+V, type K
3. In Voice Command mode, say "Week"

The scroll box and scroll arrows on the vertical scroll bar allow backward or forward movement one week at a time. As in Day view, double-click an appointment to view and edit appointment details. As shown in Figure 1-35, some appointments may be too long to display horizontally in the appointment area. Dragging the border of the appointment area to the right will increase its width so that more of the appointment descriptions display. The rest of the Week view is adjusted accordingly to display a single month in the Date Navigator and a narrower TaskPad. If a day contains too many items to display vertically, Outlook will display a down arrow in the lower-right corner of the day frame. Clicking the down arrow returns the calendar to Day view so you can view the rest of the appointments for the day.

Month View

The **Month view** resembles a standard monthly calendar page and displays your schedule for an entire month. Appointments are listed in each date frame in the calendar. The following steps illustrate how to display the calendar in Month view.

Steps To Change to Month View

1 Click the Month button on the Standard toolbar.

The calendar displays in Month view (Figure 1-36).

2 Click the Day button to return to Day view.

Use the scroll box and scroll arrows on the vertical scroll bar to move the Month view forward and backward one week at a time. As you drag the scroll box, Outlook displays the first day of the week in a ScreenTip beside the scroll box. As with Day and Week views, you can add, edit, or delete appointments in Month view. Because the appointments are abbreviated considerably in Month view, however, it is easier to switch back to Day view to make changes.

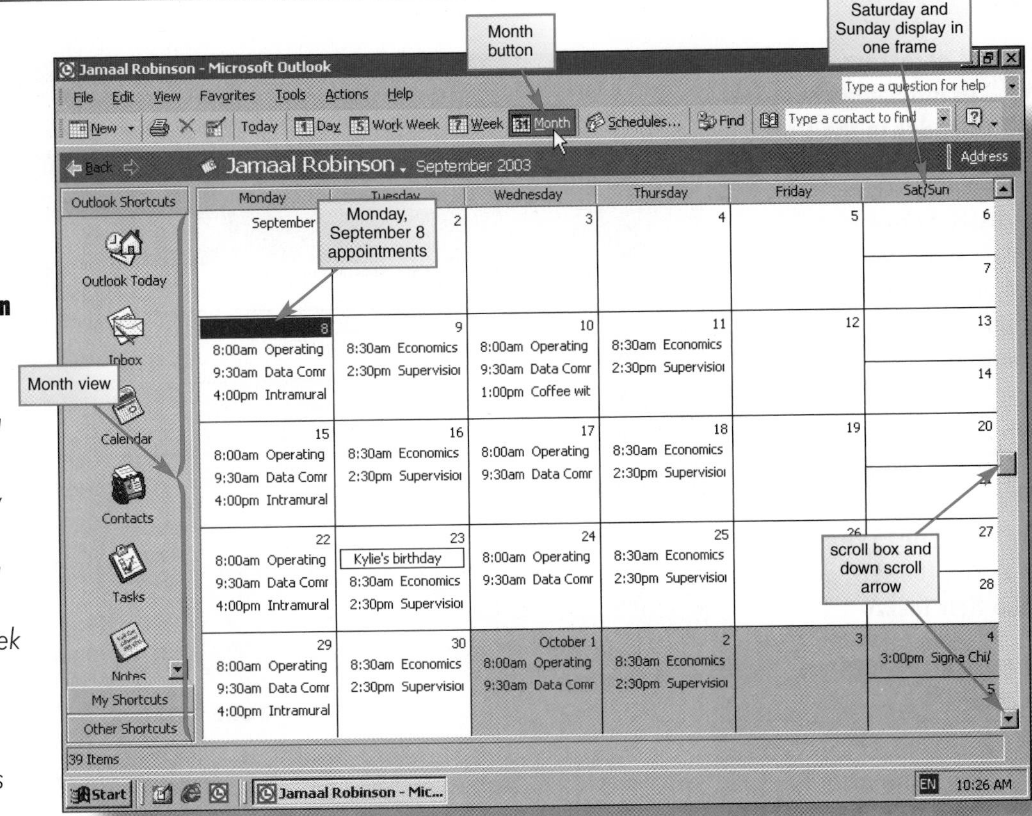

FIGURE 1-36

Other Ways

1. On View menu click Month
2. Press ALT+V, type M
3. In Voice Command mode, say "Month"

Creating a Task List Using the TaskPad

Now that your daily appointments are organized, you can use **TaskPad** in the Calendar window to organize the many duties and projects for each day. The TaskPad, which displays below the Date Navigator in the Calendar window, allows creation of a **task list** of items that need to be tracked through completion. **Tasks** can be simple to do items, daily reminders, assignments with due dates, or business responsibilities. In this project, single-user tasks that occur once are entered, but a Tasks folder also can be created for recurring tasks, group tasks, and assigned or forwarded tasks. Perform the steps on the next page to create a task list using the TaskPad.

More About

Tasks

You can add a task to your Outlook task list from within Word. This is helpful if you have a Word document that must be reviewed, and you want a reminder to do so. From Outlook, you also can assign tasks to other people and track the progress of tasks as they are completed.

Steps To Create a Task List Using the TaskPad

1 If necessary, click 8 in the September 2003 calendar in the Date Navigator.

The TaskPad displays on the right below the Date Navigator. The TaskPad is divided into two main sections, a New Task text box, and the task list.

2 Click the New Task text box and type `Check on delivery of sand for beach party` **as the first task.**

The TaskPad displays (Figure 1-37).

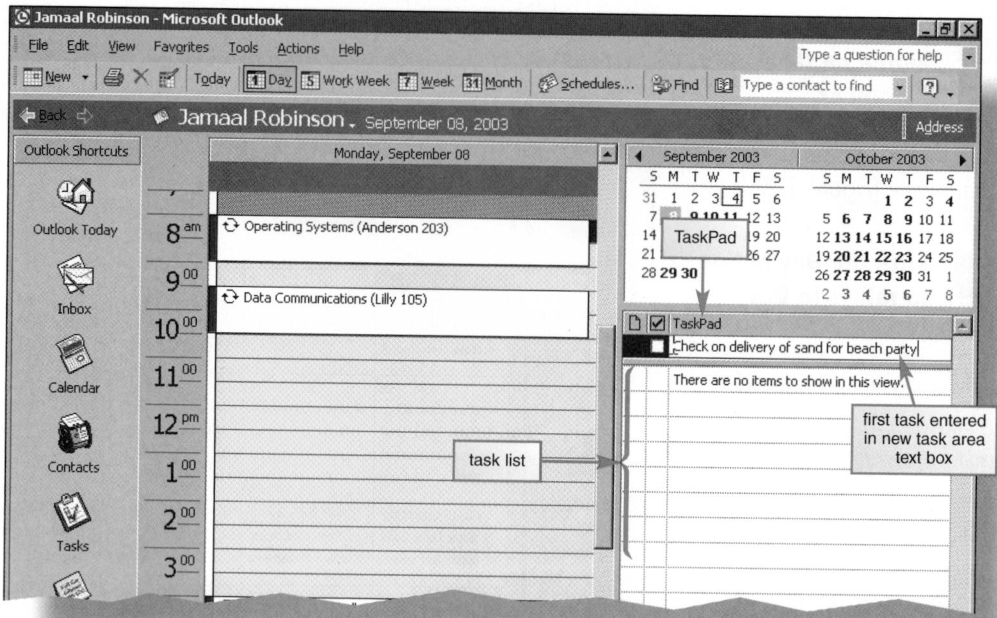

FIGURE 1-37

3 Press the ENTER key. Type `Get Econ class book` **in the text box and then press the ENTER key. Type** `Pick up coaches' T-shirts` **in the text box and then press the ENTER key.**

The task icon displays to the left of each task. As each task is entered, the previous task moves down the list.

4 Click outside the TaskPad.

The TaskPad displays with all the tasks entered in the task list as shown in Figure 1-38.

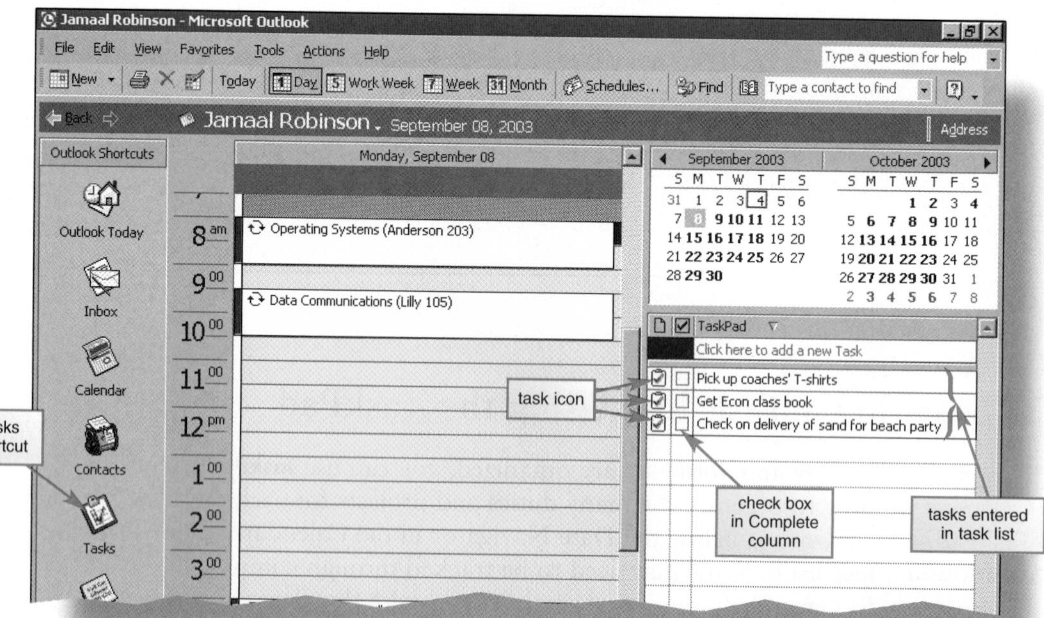

FIGURE 1-38

Other Ways

1. Click New Appointment button arrow on Standard toolbar, click Task
2. On File menu point to New, click Tasks on New submenu
3. Press CTRL+SHIFT+K
4. In Voice Command mode, say "File, New, Tasks"

To add details to tasks, such as due dates, status, and priority, double-click a task in the TaskPad to open a Task window.

When a task is complete, click the check box in the Sort by: Complete column to the left of the task's subject. A check mark called a **Completed icon** will display in the Complete column and a line will be placed through the task indicating it is complete. To delete a task entirely from the TaskPad, select the task and then click the Delete button on the Standard toolbar.

If you have many tasks on various days, or if you assign tasks to others, it is advisable to create a personal Tasks subfolder for your task list. This also is true if you are working in a lab situation or on a shared computer.

More About

Editing Tasks

You can drag a task from the TaskPad to a time slot in the appointment area, thereby making the task an appointment.

Printing a Calendar

All or part of your calendar can be printed in a number of different layouts or **print styles**. The following section describes how to print the calendar in Daily, Weekly, and Monthly Styles.

More About

Printing

The margins, page orientation, or paper size can be changed in the Page Setup dialog box.

Daily Style

A printout of a single day of the calendar, called the **Daily Style**, shows the day's appointments, tasks, and a two-month calendar. Follow the steps to print the calendar in Daily Style.

Steps To Print the Calendar in Daily Style

1 Ready the printer. Click the Print button on the Standard toolbar. When the Print dialog box displays, point to the OK button.

The Print dialog box displays (Figure 1-39). Because the Appointment window was in Day view when the Print button was clicked, Daily Style is selected in the Print style list by default.

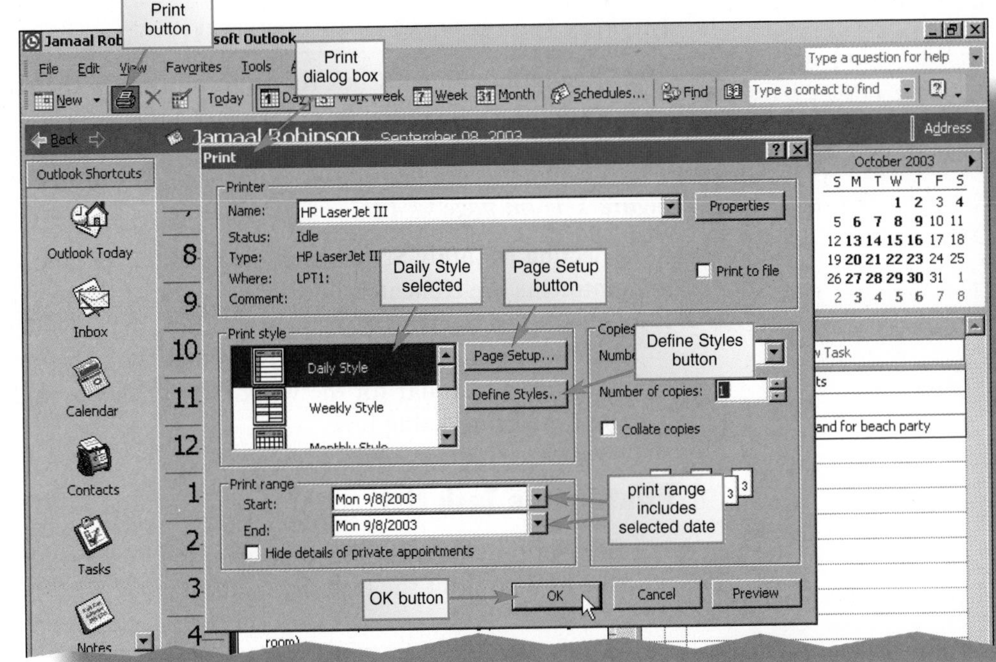

FIGURE 1-39

2 With the Daily Style selected in the Print style list, click the OK button.

The daily schedule of appointments for Monday, September 8, 2003 prints on the printer. The printout should display as shown in Figure 1-1d on page O 1.07.

Other Ways

1. On File menu click Print
2. Press CTRL+P
3. In Voice Command mode, say "File, Print"

The Daily Style printout includes features from the Day view of the Calendar, including appointments, events, tasks, and notes. Dates with appointments print in bold in the two-month calendar. Page numbers and current system dates display at the bottom of the page. The Page Setup button in the Print dialog box allows style modifications to include or omit various features, including the TaskPad and the Notes area. Specific time ranges also can be printed rather than the default 7:00 a.m. to 6:00 p.m.

Weekly Style

To print a calendar in Weekly Style, click the Print button on the Standard toolbar while viewing the calendar in Week view or select the Weekly Style in the Print dialog box, as explained in the following step.

TO PRINT THE CALENDAR IN WEEKLY STYLE

1 Ready the printer. Click the Print button on the Standard toolbar. Click Weekly Style in the Print style list and then click the OK button.

The calendar for the week of Monday, September 8, 2003 through Sunday, September 14, 2003 prints on the printer as shown in Figure 1-1e on page O 1.07.

Monthly Style

The following step prints the calendar in Monthly Style.

TO PRINT THE CALENDAR IN MONTHLY STYLE

1 Ready the printer. Click the Print button on the Standard toolbar. Click Monthly Style in the Print style list and then click the OK button.

The calendar for the month of September 2003 prints on the printer as shown in Figure 1-1f on page O 1.07.

Selecting Monthly Style prints the calendar in landscape orientation. Some appointments are truncated due to that lack of space. The Monthly Style of printout is intended to show the larger picture rather than the detail of a Daily Style printout.

Another useful print style is **Tri-fold Style**, which prints a daily appointment list, a task list, and a calendar for the week. To save styles and setups, use the **Define Styles button** in the Print dialog box.

Printing the Task List

To print only the task list, first open the Tasks folder. The following steps describe how to print the task list by itself.

TO PRINT THE TASK LIST

1 Click the Tasks shortcut on the Outlook Bar to display the task list entered on the TaskPad.

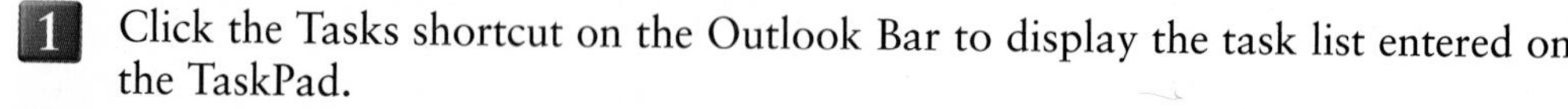
2 Click the Print button on the Standard toolbar. When the Print dialog box displays, click the OK button.

The task list prints (Figure 1-40).

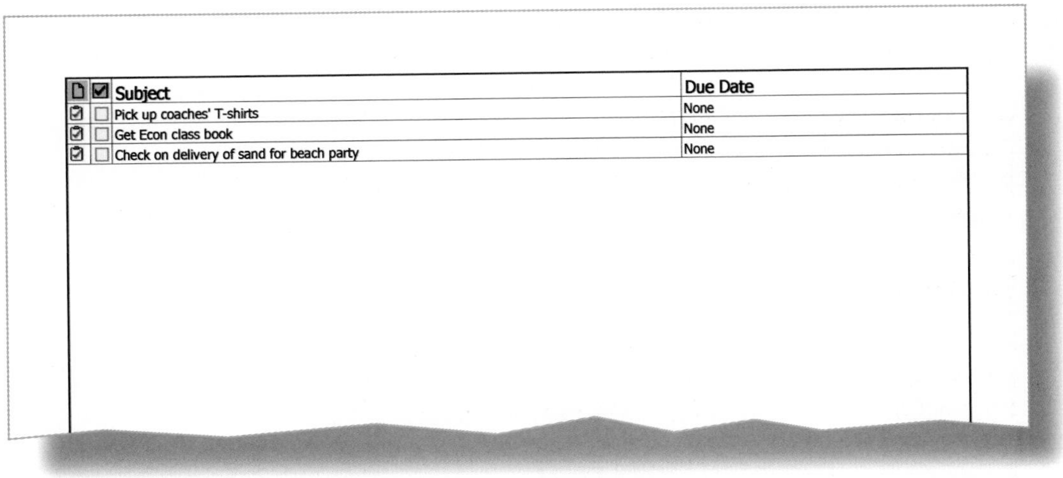

		Subject	Due Date
		Pick up coaches' T-shirts	None
		Get Econ class book	None
		Check on delivery of sand for beach party	None

FIGURE 1-40

Contacts

The **Contacts** component of Outlook allows you to store information about individuals or companies. People with whom you communicate for school, business, or personal reasons are your **contacts**. To help organize information about personal contacts, some people keep the names, addresses, and telephone numbers in business-card files and address books. With Outlook, you can create and maintain important contact information in a **contact list**, which is stored in the Contacts folder. Your contact list is like an electronic address book that allows you to store names, addresses, e-mail addresses, and more. Once the information has been entered, your contact list can be retrieved, sorted, edited, organized, or printed. Outlook also includes a **Find option** that lets you search for a contact name in your address book while you are using the Calendar, Inbox, or other Outlook components.

When the Contacts folder is open, information about each contact displays on an address card in the default **Address Card view**. Each address card includes fields such as name, address, and various telephone numbers, as well as e-mail and Web page addresses. Choose which fields display on the cards using the **View menu**.

In addition to organizing your contacts, Outlook's Contacts can serve many other functions. Contacts can be used to assign a task, send a message, or schedule a meeting with a contact. A contact list also can be used as an e-mail address book or as a database for a mail merge using Microsoft Word 2002. An Internet URL can be accessed through Contacts by clicking a contact's Web page address. If you click the contact's e-mail address, an addressed message box displays ready for use.

Although other forms of maintaining contact information serve a purpose, for example, an address book, using Contacts can be more efficient for the reasons just described. The following sections illustrate how to create and print a contact list with the contact names in Table 1-4 on page O 1.39.

More About

The Internet

Outlook automatically creates a hyperlink when you type a Web page address or e-mail address in the text box of a Contact window. If you are connected to an Internet browser, you can click the hyperlink to go quickly to the destination or send an e-mail message.

Creating a Personal Subfolder in the Contacts Folder

The first step in creating the contact list is to create a personal subfolder. When only one person is working on a computer, a contact list can be stored in Outlook's Contacts folder. If you share your computer with a roommate, lab partner, or co-worker, you likely will want to store your contact list in a personal subfolder. The steps on the next page create a personal subfolder for Jamaal Robinson.

Steps To Create a Personal Subfolder in the Contacts Folder

1 Click the Contacts shortcut on the Outlook Bar. When the Contacts folder opens, right-click the Folder banner and then click New Folder on the shortcut menu.

The Contacts - Microsoft Outlook window opens, and the Create New Folder dialog box displays (Figure 1-41).

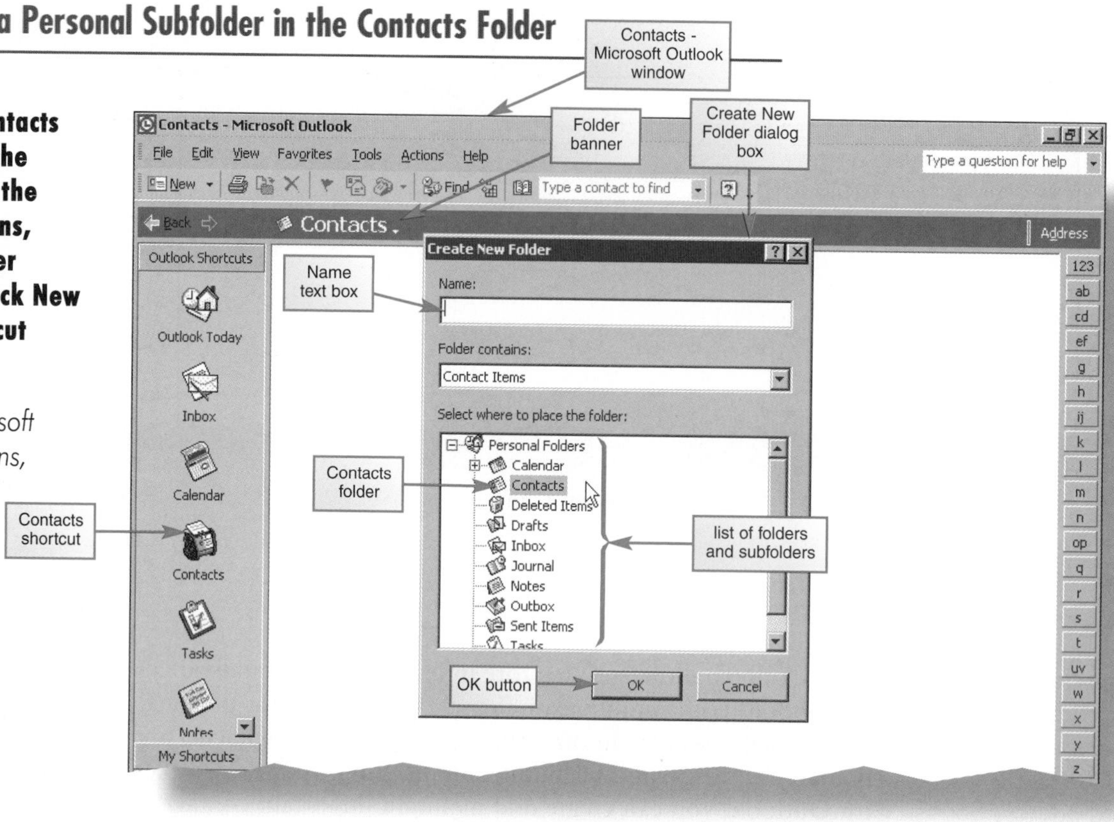

FIGURE 1-41

2 Type `Jamaal's Contacts` **in the Name text box and then point to the OK button.**

The new subfolder, Jamaal's Contacts, becomes a subfolder of the Contacts folder (Figure 1-42). Jamaal's Contacts displays in the Name text box.

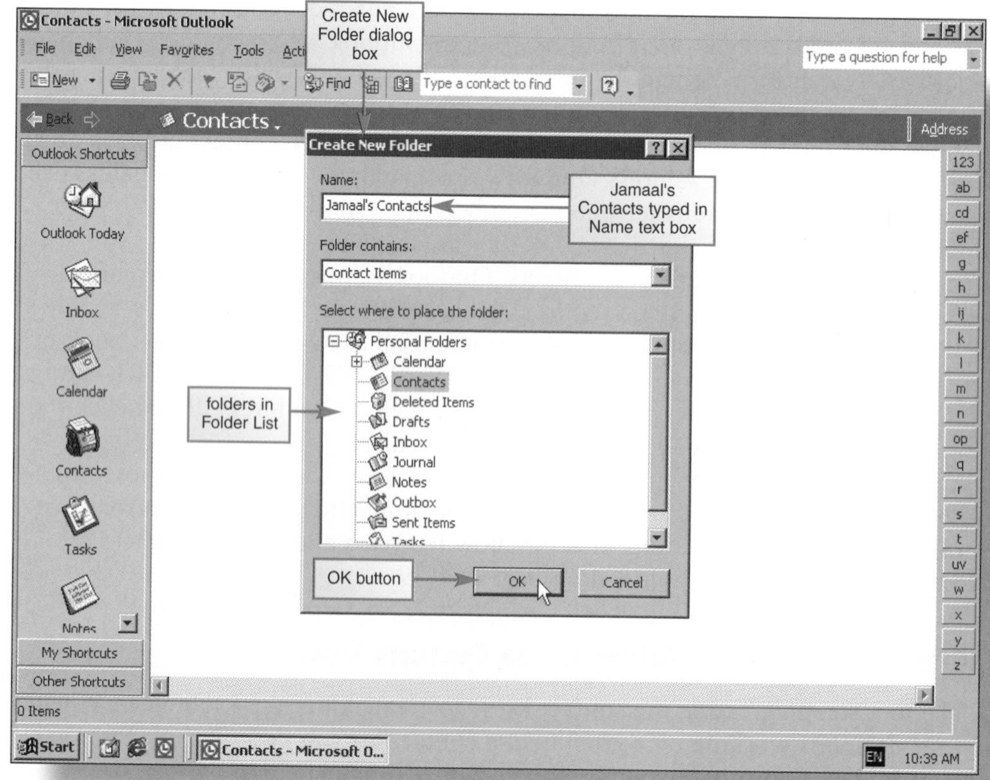

FIGURE 1-42

3 Click the OK button. When the Add shortcut to Outlook Bar? dialog box displays, click the No button.

The Folder List displays to the left of the contact area, showing a list of available folders and subfolders (Figure 1-43).

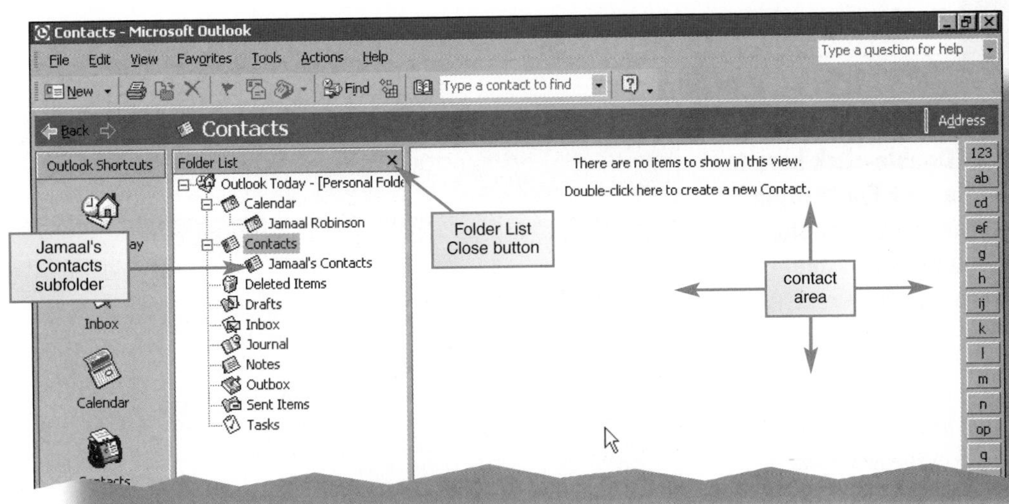

FIGURE 1-43

4 Click Jamaal's Contacts in the Folder List and then click the Folder List Close button.

The Jamaal's Contacts - Microsoft Outlook window opens. Because no contacts have been entered, a message displays (Figure 1-44).

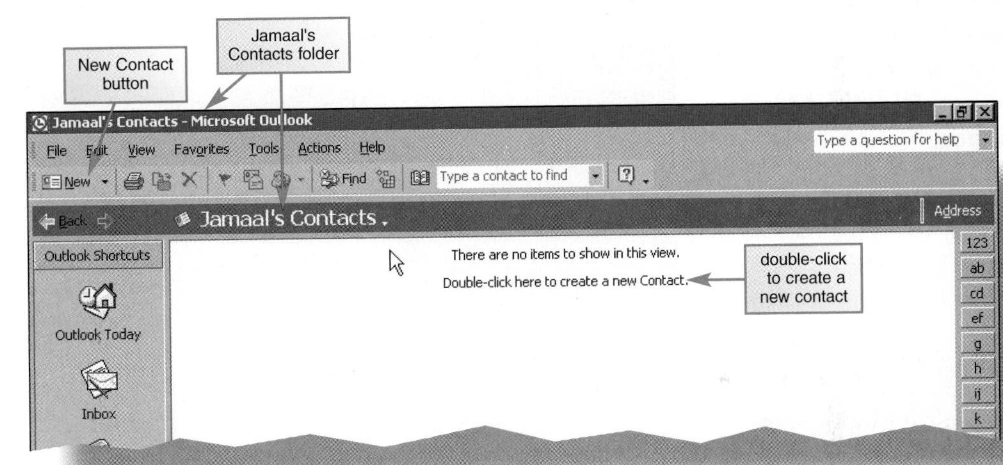

FIGURE 1-44

Other Ways

1. On File menu point to Folder, click New Folder on Folder submenu
2. Press CTRL+SHIFT+E
3. In Voice Command mode, say "File, Folder, New Folder"

With the subfolder created in which the contact list will be stored, you can enter the contact names and other pertinent information provided in Table 1-4.

Creating a Contact List

The steps on the next page describe how to enter the data in Table 1-4 in the contact list.

Table 1-4 Contact Information

NAME	E-MAIL ADDRESS	ADDRESS	TELEPHONE
Dr. Jennifer Craig	jcraig@isp.edu	1683 Elm St. Highland, IN 46322	(219) 555-4456
Dr. Andrew Brinckman	abrinckman@isp.edu	9956 Colonial Dr. Munster, IN 46321	(219) 555-7813
Dr. Courtney Groen	cgroen@isp.edu	188 Ashford Lane St. John, IN 46373	(219) 555-1593
Dr. Ryan Bachman	rbachman@isp.edu	8232 Clay St. Hobart, IN 46342	(219) 555-3571

Steps To Create a Contact List

1 Double-click, Double-click here to create a new Contact., in the contact area as shown in Figure 1-44 on the previous page.

The Untitled - Contact window opens. General contact information can be entered in this window.

2 In the Untitled - Contact window, type `Dr. Jennifer Craig` **in the Full Name text box. Click the Address text box.**

Notice that Outlook automatically fills in the File as box, last name first (Figure 1-45). The Untitled - Contact window changes to the Jennifer Craig - Contact window.

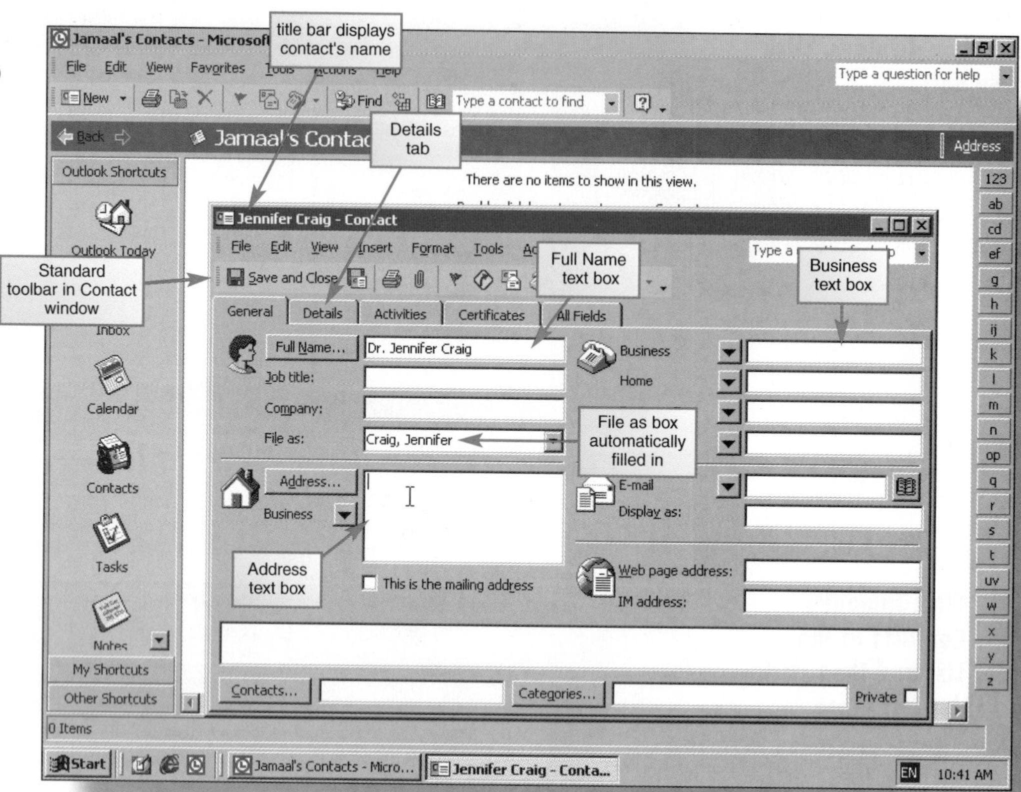

FIGURE 1-45

3 In the Address text box type `1683 Elm St.` **and then press the ENTER key. Type** `Highland, IN 46322` **and then click the Business text box. Type** `2195554456` **in the Business text box and then click the E-mail text box. Type** `jcraig@isp.edu` **in the E-mail text box. Point to the Save and Close button on the Standard toolbar in the Contact window.**

The Contact window displays the information entered (Figure 1-46).

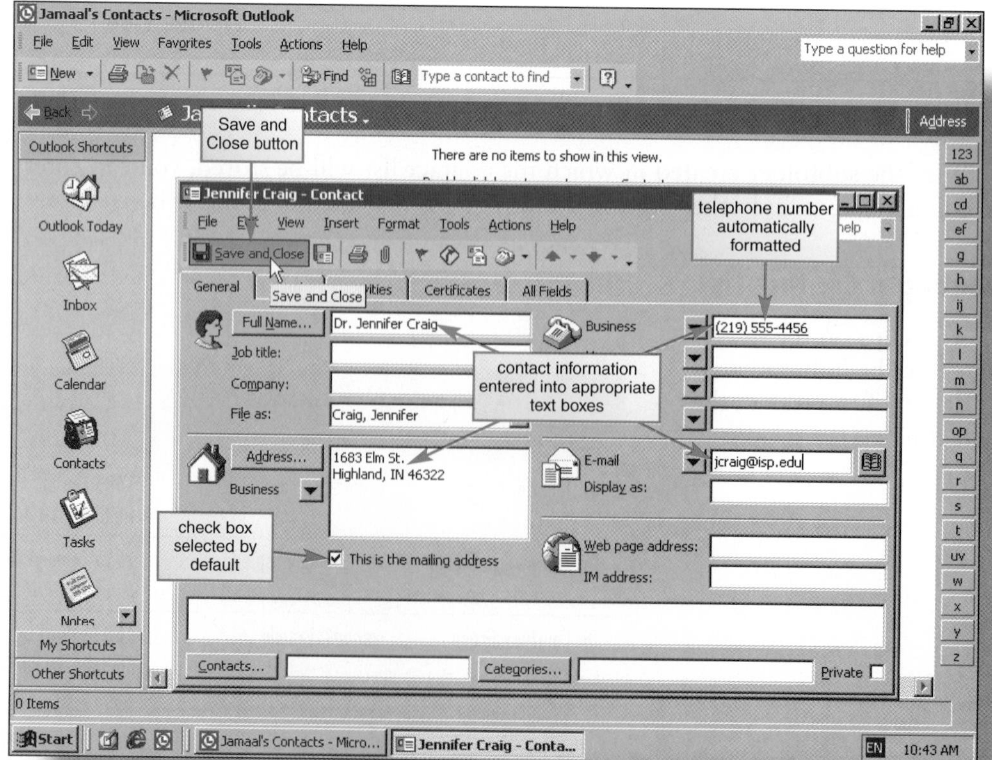

FIGURE 1-46

4 Click the Save and Close button.

The Jennifer Craig address card displays in Address Cards view in the Jamaal's Contacts - Microsoft Outlook window (Figure 1-47). Address Cards is the current view by default.

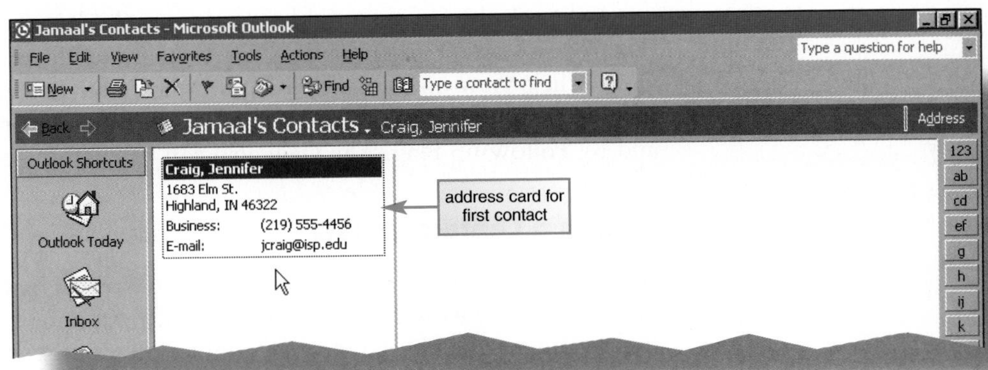

FIGURE 1-47

5 Click the New Contact button on the Standard toolbar. Repeat Steps 2 through 4 to enter the three remaining contacts in Table 1-4 on page O 1.39.

When complete, the contact list should look like Figure 1-48. Outlook automatically lists the contacts in alphabetical order. The phrase, Folder banner, Bac – Gro, indicates the range of contacts currently displayed (Bachman to Groen).

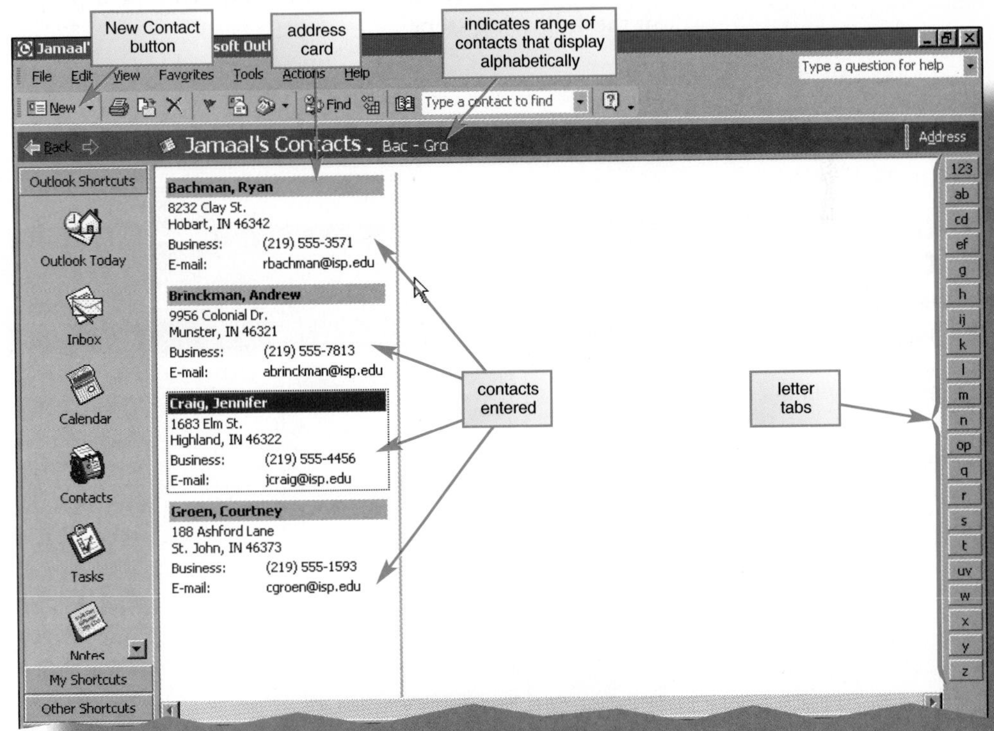

FIGURE 1-48

Other Ways

1. On File menu point to New, click Contact on New submenu
2. On Actions menu click New Contact
3. Press CTRL+SHIFT+C
4. In Voice Command mode, say "File, New, Contact"

Because this contact list is very short, all the names display in Address Cards view. With longer lists, however, you quickly can locate a specific contact by clicking the **letter tab** on the right side of the Microsoft Outlook - Contacts window (Figure 1-48).

Once the contact list is complete, it can be viewed, edited, or updated at anytime. You can make some changes by typing inside the card itself. To display and edit all the information for a contact, double-click the address card to display the Contacts window. Use this window to enter information about a contact, such as home telephone numbers or Web page addresses. Up to 18 different telephone numbers can be stored for each contact categorized by location and type (business, home, fax, mobile, pager, and so on). Clicking the **Details tab** (Figure 1-45) allows you to enter a contact's department, manager's name, nickname, and even birthday information.

Although the Contacts folder displays in Address Cards view by default (Figure 1-48 on the previous page), several other views are available. To change views, click View on the menu bar and select Current View. You can choose views such as Detailed Address Cards, Phone List, By Category, By Company, By Location, and By Follow-up Flag. The view also can be customized.

Finding a Contact Quickly

To find a contact quickly, use the **Find a Contact box** on the Standard toolbar. Enter a first or last name, in full or partially. An e-mail alias also can be used to find a contact quickly. To locate a contact previously searched for, click the find a Contact box arrow, and select a name.

A contact record was created for Andrew Brinckman. This record can be found easily by using the Find a Contact box to type a part of the contact name as shown in the following steps.

Steps To Find a Contact Quickly

1 Click the Find a Contact box on the Standard toolbar. Type `bri` **in the box.**

The letters display in the Find a Contact box (Figure 1-49). The letters, bri, are used to find the contact beginning with those letters.

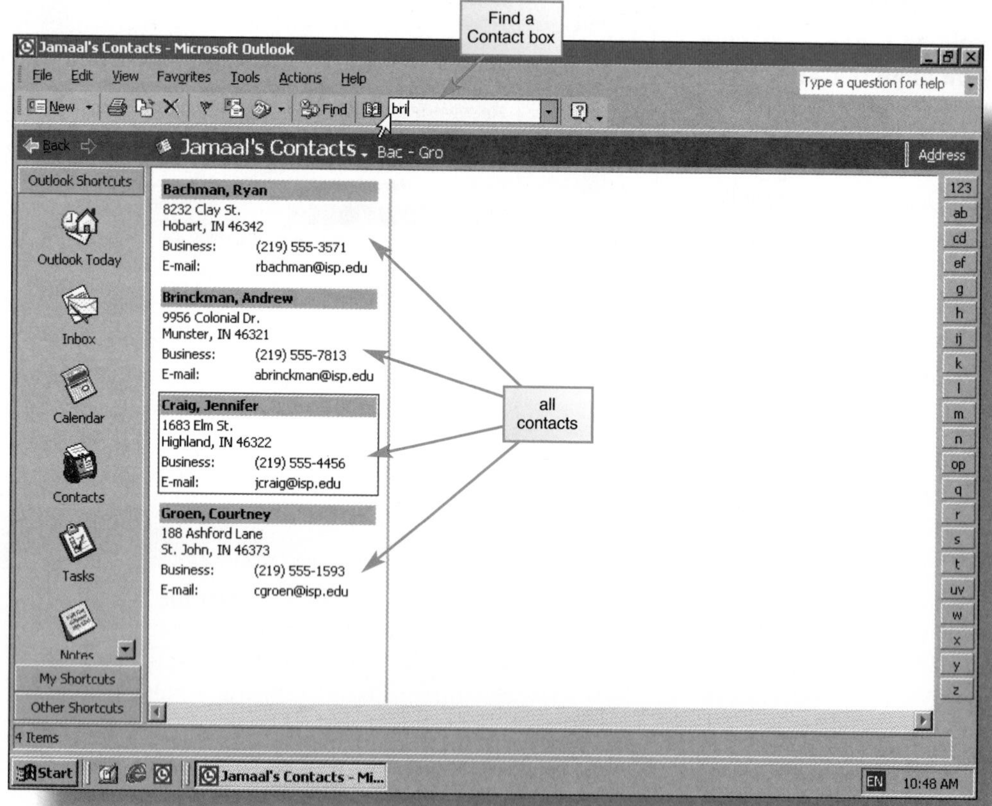

FIGURE 1-49

2 Press the ENTER key.

Outlook opens the Andrew Brinckman - Contact window (Figure 1-50). Currently, only one contact exists with the letters, bri, in its name.

3 Click the Close button in the Andrew Brinckman - Contact window.

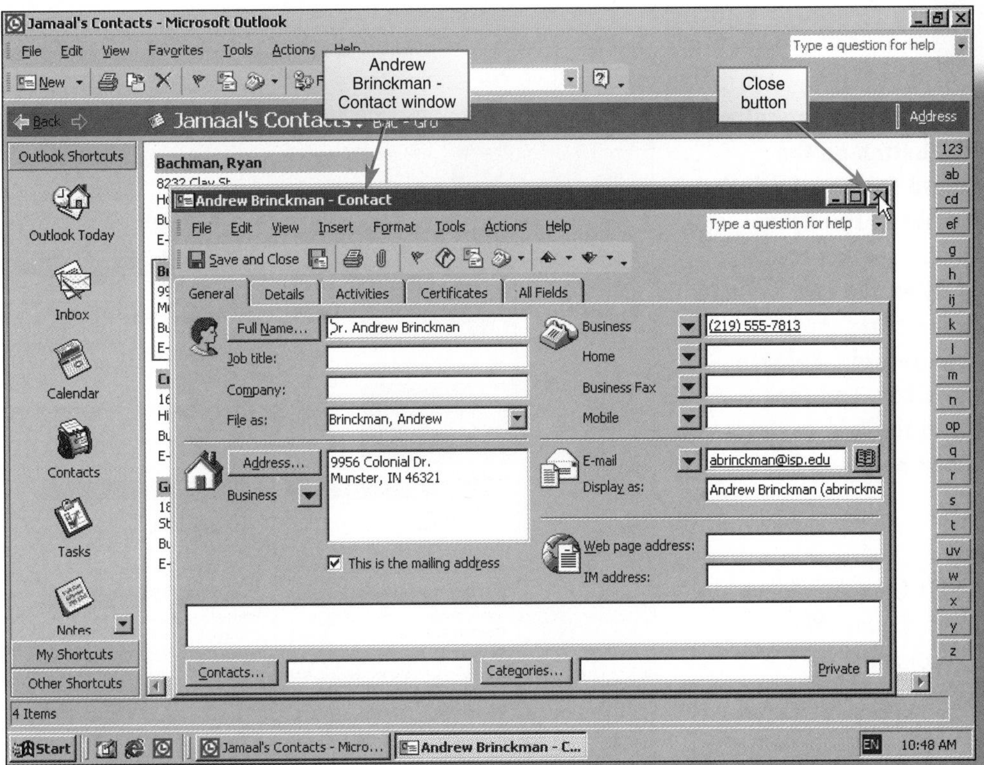

FIGURE 1-50

If more than one contact with the starting letters, bri, exists, a Choose Contact window opens with the list of all contacts beginning with the bri string. The appropriate contact then is selected from this window.

Organizing Contacts

To help manage your contacts further, the contact list can be categorized and sorted in several ways. For example, you can group contacts into categories such as Key Customer, Business, Hot Contact, or even Ideas, Competition, and Strategies. In addition, you may want to create your own categories to group contacts by company, department, a particular project, a specific class, and so on. You also can sort by any part of the address; for example, you can sort by postal code for bulk mailings.

For the contact list created in this project, it is appropriate to organize the contacts in a personal category. You can do this by selecting the contacts and then adding them to the personal category of the contact list. The steps on the next page illustrate this procedure.

Other Ways

1. On Tools menu click Find
2. Press CTRL+SHIFT+F
3. Press CTRL+E
4. In Voice Command mode, say "Tools, Find"

More About

Contacts

You can organize contacts from one or more Contacts folders in a personal distribution list. Outlook also detects duplicates and provides the option to merge the new information with the existing contact entry. You also can filter your contacts list and then use the filtered list to begin a mail merge from Outlook.

To Organize Contacts

1 Click the Organize button on the Standard toolbar. Click the name bar of the Ryan Bachman contact record. Hold down the CTRL key and click the other three contact records. Release the CTRL key, and then point to the Add contacts selected below to box arrow.

The Ways to Organize Jamaal's Contacts dialog box displays (Figure 1-51). All four records are selected.

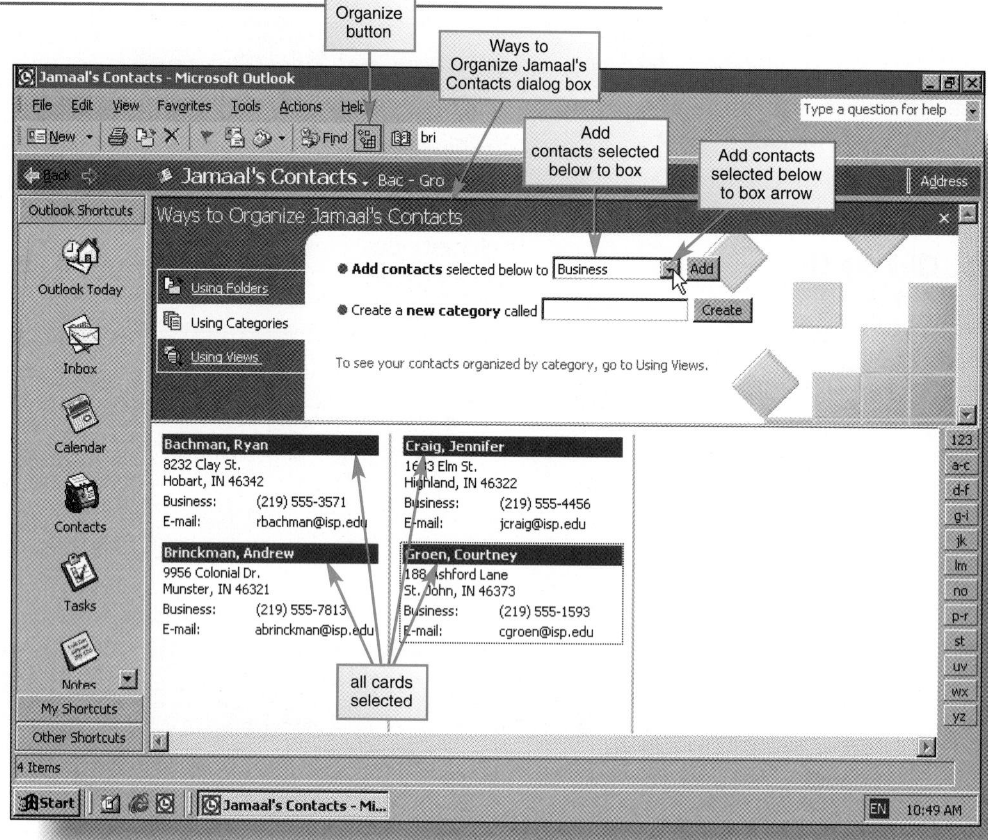

FIGURE 1-51

2 Click the Add contacts selected below to box arrow. Scroll down and point to Personal in the list.

A list of categories displays (Figure 1-52). Personal is selected.

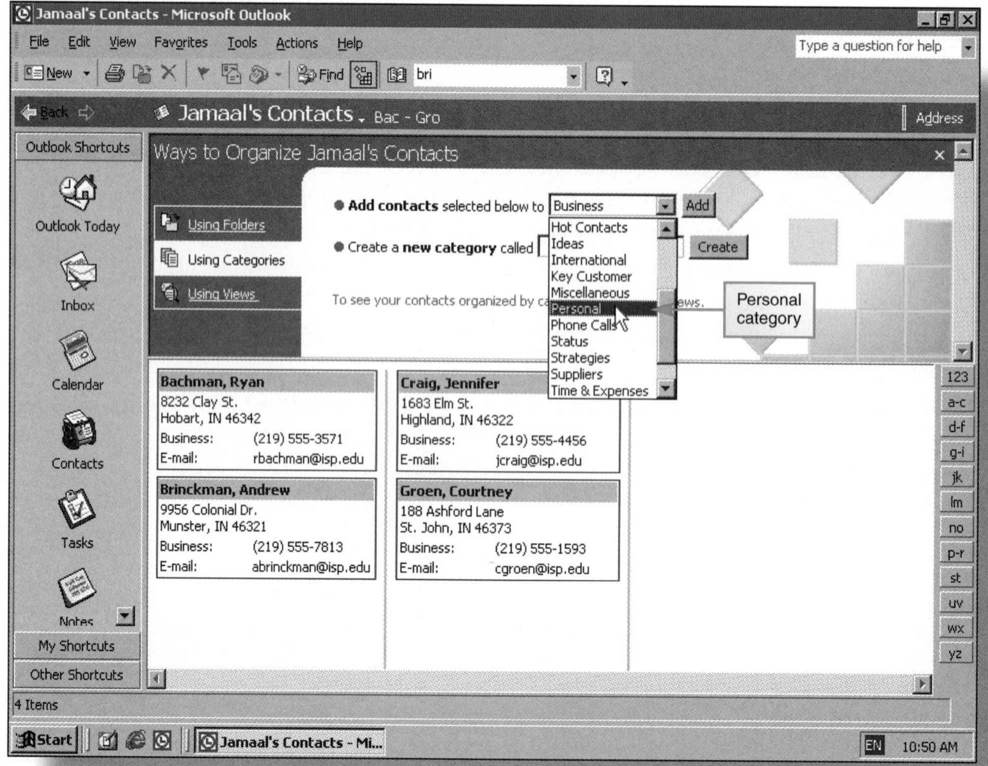

FIGURE 1-52

3 Click Personal and then point to the Add button.

Personal displays in the Add contacts selected below to box (Figure 1-53).

4 Click the Add button. When the word Done! displays to the right of the Add button, click the Close button on the Ways to Organize Jamaal's Contacts dialog box.

The contacts are added to the Personal category.

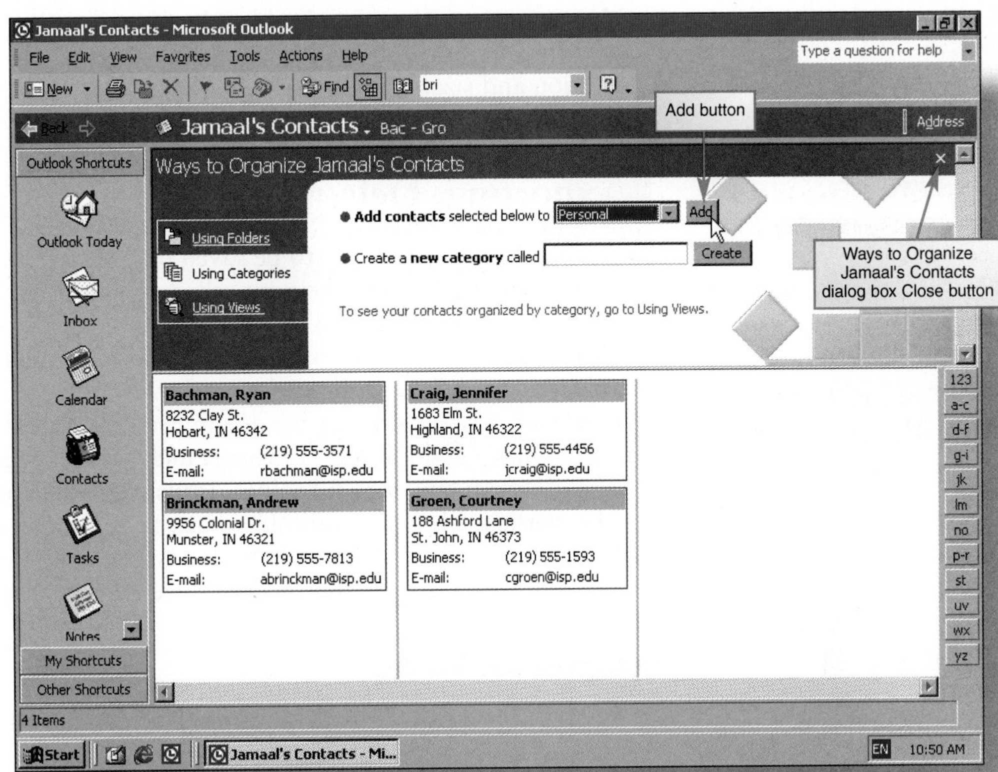

FIGURE 1-53

Other Ways

1. On Tools menu click Organize
2. Press ALT+T, Z
3. In Voice Command mode, say "Tools, Organize"

The contacts now are organized into the Personal contacts list. Organizing contacts in different categories helps make searching for groups of names easier. By putting all instructors into a personal category, it isolates them from all other contacts entered.

Printing the Contact List

Printing the contact list is an easy way to obtain a listing of people you frequently contact. The printed list can be used for business mailings, invitations to social gatherings, or even a telephone or Christmas card list. The following step describes how to print the contact list.

TO PRINT THE CONTACT LIST

1 Ready the printer. With the contact list displaying, click the Print button on the Standard toolbar. When the Print dialog box displays, click the OK button.

The printed contact list should look like the list shown in Figure 1-54.

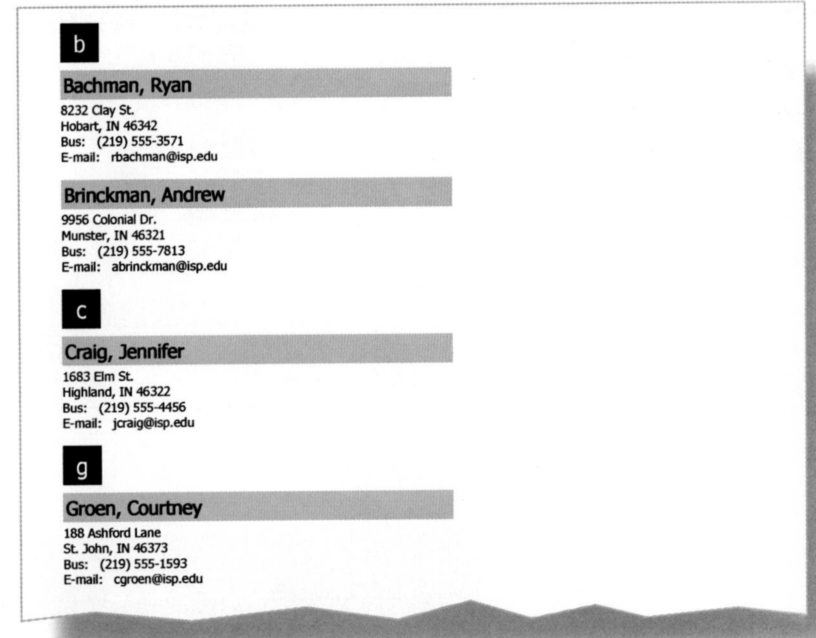
b

Bachman, Ryan
8232 Clay St.
Hobart, IN 46342
Bus: (219) 555-3571
E-mail: rbachman@isp.edu

Brinckman, Andrew
9956 Colonial Dr.
Munster, IN 46321
Bus: (219) 555-7813
E-mail: abrinckman@isp.edu

c

Craig, Jennifer
1683 Elm St.
Highland, IN 46322
Bus: (219) 555-4456
E-mail: jcraig@isp.edu

g

Groen, Courtney
188 Ashford Lane
St. John, IN 46373
Bus: (219) 555-1593
E-mail: cgroen@isp.edu

FIGURE 1-54

A printout can be customized by changing the Print style in the Print dialog box. These styles let you choose from a variety of fields along with choices for paper orientation and size.

Saving

All appointments, events, meetings, and tasks are saved as separate files on your disk. As such, they can be edited, moved, copied, or deleted. These items can be saved together as a group using the Import and Export Wizard.

Exporting, Deleting, and Importing Subfolders

The contact list now is ready to be saved on a floppy disk. Saving your work on a floppy disk allows you to take your schedule to another computer or to merge your contacts as a mailing list with another computer's word processor.

With many application software packages, a single file, such as a letter or spreadsheet, can be saved directly on a floppy disk. With Outlook, however, each appointment, task, or contact is a file in itself. Thus, rather than saving numerous individual files, Outlook uses an **Import and Export Wizard** to guide you through the process of saving an entire subfolder. Transferring a subfolder to a floppy disk is called **exporting**. Moving a subfolder back to a computer is called **importing**. Subfolders can be imported and exported from any Outlook application. Outlook then saves the subfolder on a floppy disk, adding the extension **.pst**.

Exporting Subfolders

Because Jamaal Robinson's contact list is completed, Jamaal's Contacts subfolder is exported first. The following steps show how to export subfolders to a floppy disk.

To Export Subfolders to a Floppy Disk

1 Insert a floppy disk in drive A. Click File on the menu bar and then click Import and Export.

2 When the Import and Export Wizard dialog box displays, click Export to a file in the Choose an action to perform list. Point to the Next button.

The Import and Export Wizard dialog box displays (Figure 1-55). Using this Wizard allows you to perform one of six import and export options available with Outlook.

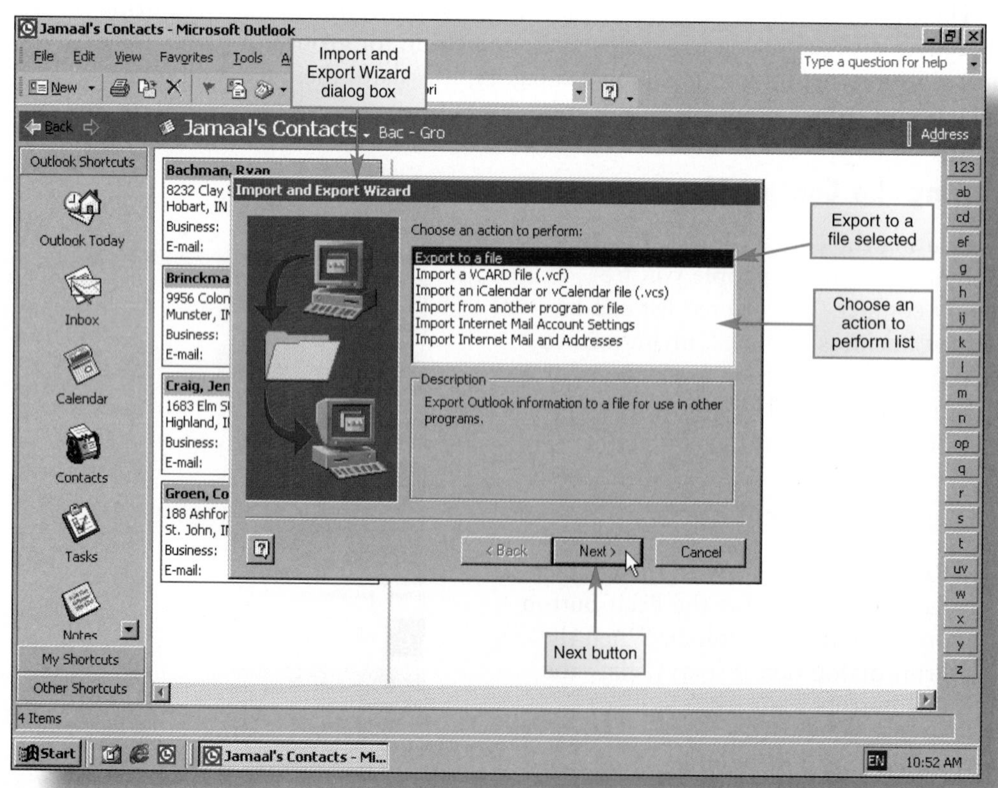

FIGURE 1-55

3 **Click the Next button. In the Export to a File dialog box, click Personal Folder File (.pst) and then click the Next button. If necessary, click the plus sign (+) to the left of the Contacts icon in the Select a folder to export from list. Click Jamaal's Contacts and then point to the Next button.**

The Export Personal Folders dialog box displays (Figure 1-56). The Jamaal's Contacts subfolder is selected as the folder from which to export.

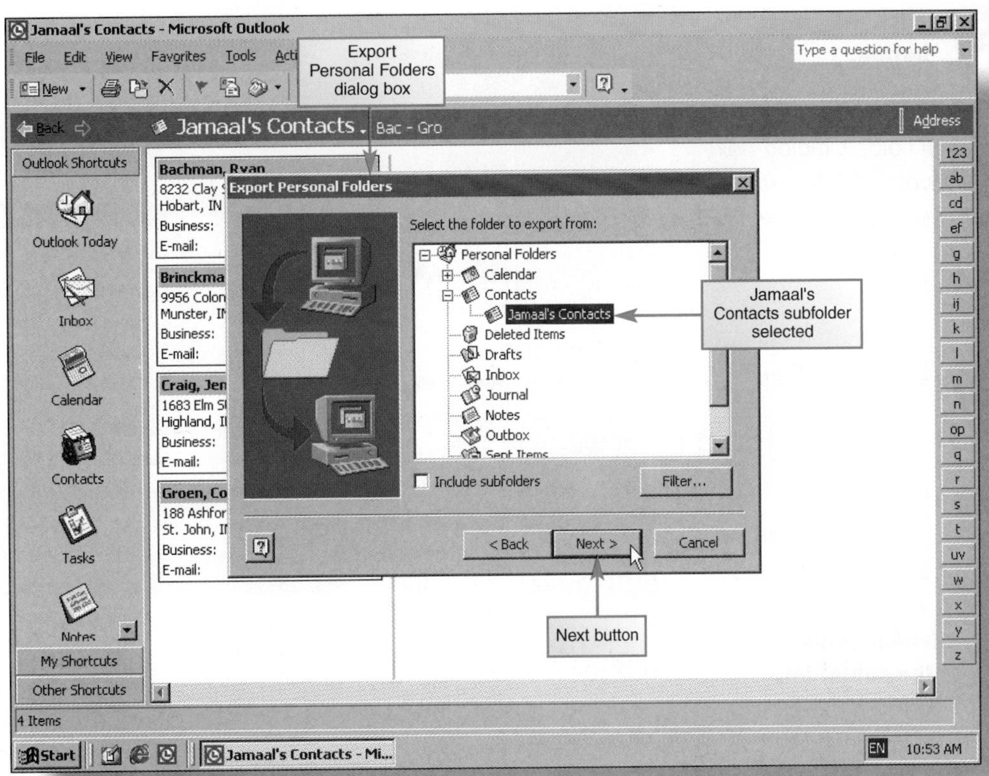

FIGURE 1-56

4 **Click the Next button. Type** `a:\Jamaal's Contacts.pst` **in the Save exported file as text box. (If your floppy drive is not labeled A, type the drive letter accordingly.) Point to the Finish button.**

The Export Personal Folders dialog box displays with the new subfolder name (Figure 1-57). The subfolder will be exported to drive A and saved as Jamaal's Contacts.

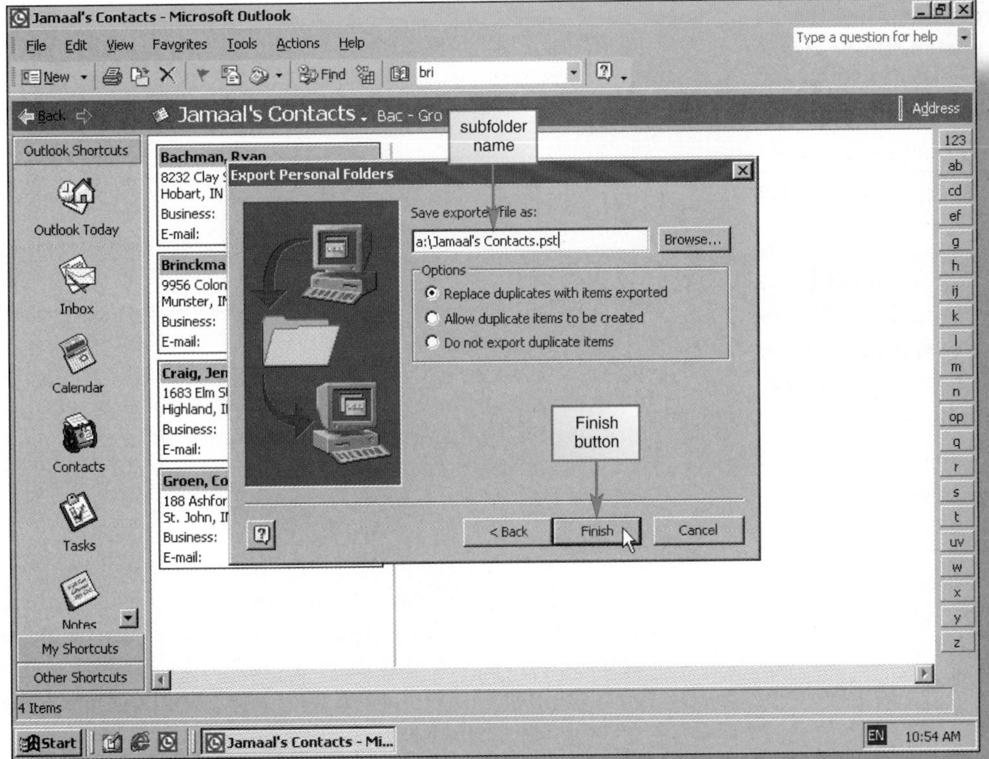

FIGURE 1-57

5 Click the Finish button.

The Create Microsoft Personal Folders dialog box displays as Outlook exports the folder. The subfolder is saved on your floppy disk (Figure 1-58).

6 Click the OK button.

7 To export a Calendar subfolder, repeat Steps 1 through 5. You do not have to open the Calendar folder to export the subfolder. Instead, when the Export Personal Folders dialog box displays, click the plus sign (+) next to the Calendar icon and then click the Jamaal Robinson subfolder. Save the exported file on a floppy disk using the file name, Jamaal Robinson.

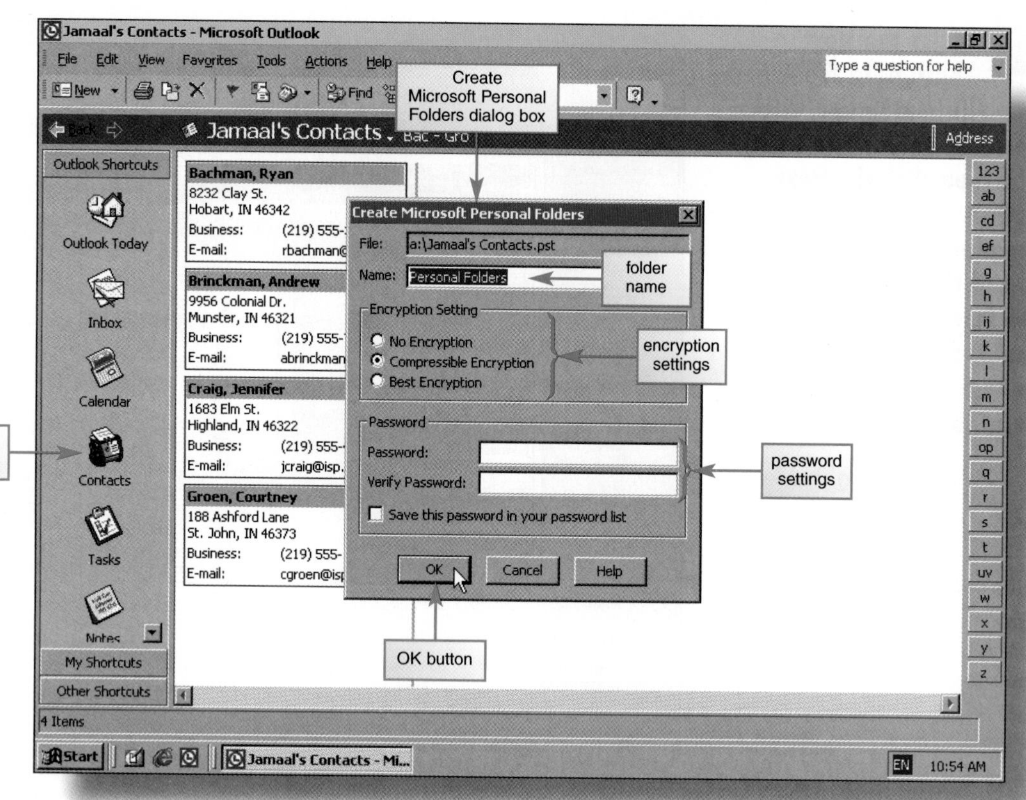

FIGURE 1-58

More About

Folders

To locate a folder or file quickly, use the Folder List. If the Folder List is not visible, click View on the menu bar and then click Folder List.

Subfolders can be exported to a personal folder file, which can be viewed only in Outlook or saved as another file type, such as a text file, which then can be imported into other programs. Importing and exporting folders allows Outlook items to be shared easily. For example, a company Calendar subfolder may be imported to publicize a company meeting, a group Contacts subfolder may be imported to make information about the people who work on a project available to everyone, or a team Tasks subfolder may be imported to help everyone track work on a project.

Deleting Subfolders

The Jamaal's Contacts and Jamaal Robinson Calendar subfolders now have been exported onto a floppy disk. A copy of each still is present on the hard disk of your computer, however, and displays in Outlook's Folder List. To delete a subfolder from the computer entirely, use the Delete command. Perform the following steps to delete a personal subfolder.

To Delete a Personal Subfolder

1 **If necessary, click the Contacts shortcut on the Outlook Bar. Right-click the Jamaal's Contacts folder banner. Point to Delete "Jamaal's Contacts" on the shortcut menu (Figure 1-59).**

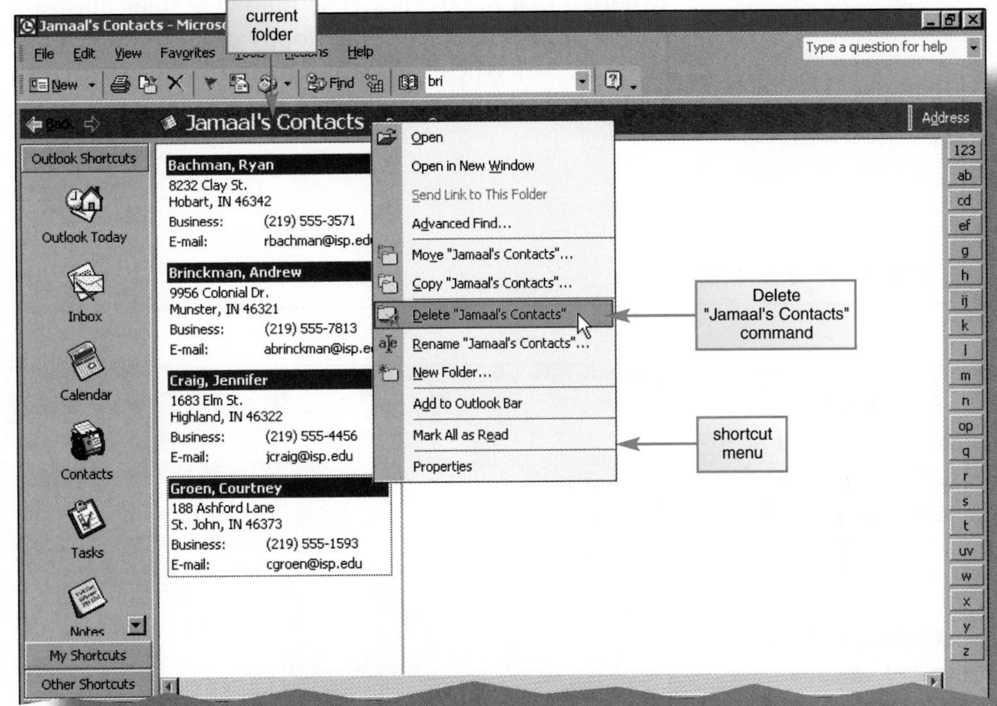

FIGURE 1-59

2 **Click Delete "Jamaal's Contacts". Click the Yes button when the dialog box displays asking if you are sure you want to delete the folder.**

3 **Click the down arrow on the Contacts banner. If necessary, click the plus sign (+) to the left of the Calendar icon in the Folder List to expand the folder list in the Calendar folder. Click the Jamaal Robinson folder.**

4 **Right-click the Jamaal Robinson folder banner. Click Delete "Jamaal Robinson" on the shortcut menu. Click the Yes button when the dialog box displays asking if you are sure you want to delete the folder.**

The Jamaal Robinson folder no longer displays.

Other Ways

1. Click Folder banner, click folder name, click Delete button on Standard toolbar

Outlook sends the deleted subfolders to a special folder called **Deleted Items**. If you accidentally delete a subfolder without first exporting it to a floppy disk, you still can open the subfolder by double-clicking it in the Folder List. To display the subfolder, you may need to click the plus sign (+) next to the Delete Items folder. Once a subfolder no longer is needed, right-click the subfolder in the Folder List and click Delete on the shortcut menu. Deleting a subfolder from the Deleted Items folder permanently removes it from the hard disk. You can delete only subfolders; Outlook's main application folders, such as Calendar and Contacts, cannot be deleted.

Thus far, you have created a schedule, a task list, and a contact list and exported your personal subfolders to a floppy disk. Once a subfolder is created and exported, often it will need to be retrieved or imported from the disk. For example, you might want to revise your office hours, add exam dates to your schedule, or use your schedule on a different computer. To do so, you must import, or retrieve, the subfolder from the floppy disk.

Importing

Other contact lists can be imported through the Import and Export Wizard on the File menu. This wizard allows you to copy information that was created and saved in other applications to Outlook.

Importing Subfolders

Earlier, the Calendar subfolder containing appointment and event files was exported to a floppy disk. The following steps illustrate how to import the same Calendar subfolder from the floppy disk. To import a subfolder, Outlook must be running. Any type of subfolder then can be imported from any application within Outlook. Perform the following steps to import a subfolder.

To Import a Subfolder

1 **Insert the floppy disk containing the calendar and contacts in drive A. Click the Calendar shortcut on the Outlook Bar.**

2 **Click File on the menu bar and then click Import and Export. When the Import and Export Wizard dialog box displays, click Import from another program or file and then click the Next button. When the Import a File dialog box displays, click Personal Folder File (.pst) and then click the Next button.**

3 **In the Import Personal Folders dialog box, type** `a:\Jamaal Robinson.pst` **in the File to import text box or click the Browse button to access the floppy drive and select the Jamaal Robinson subfolder. Point to the Next button.**

The drive, subfolder name, and extension for the subfolder display in the File to import text box (Figure 1-60).

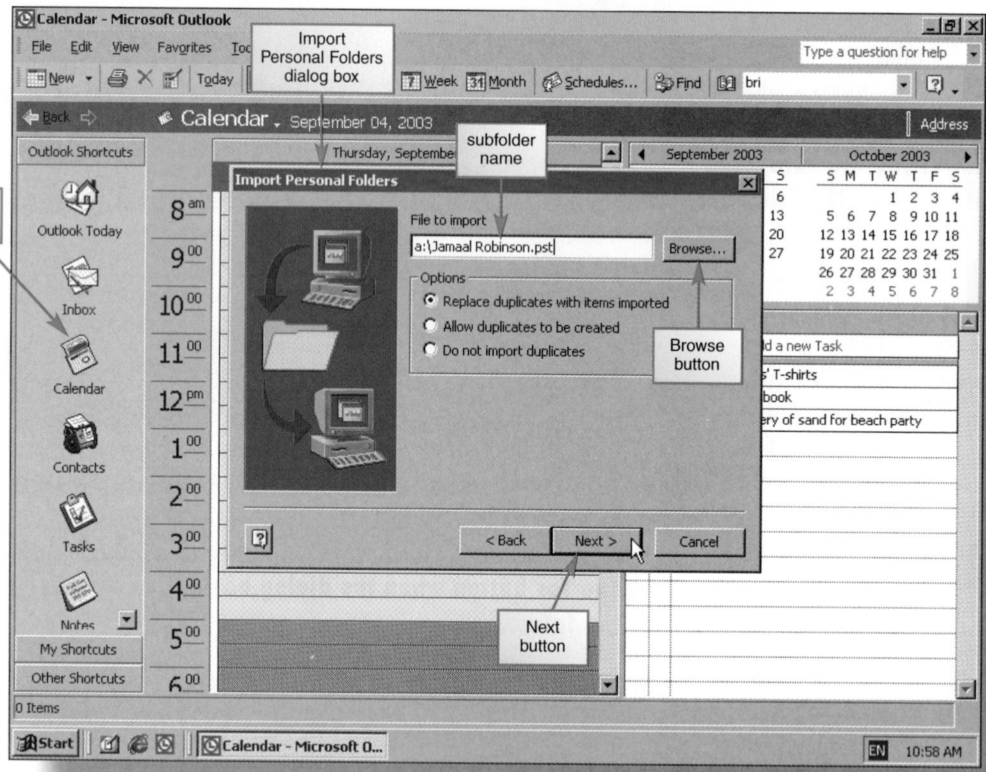

FIGURE 1-60

4 Click the Next button. When the Import Personal Folders dialog box displays, click Calendar in the Select the folder to import from list. Point to the Finish button.

In the Import Personal folders dialog box, you can choose the Outlook folder to import from (Figure 1-61).

5 Click the Finish button.

The subfolder is imported into Outlook as a subfolder of Calendar.

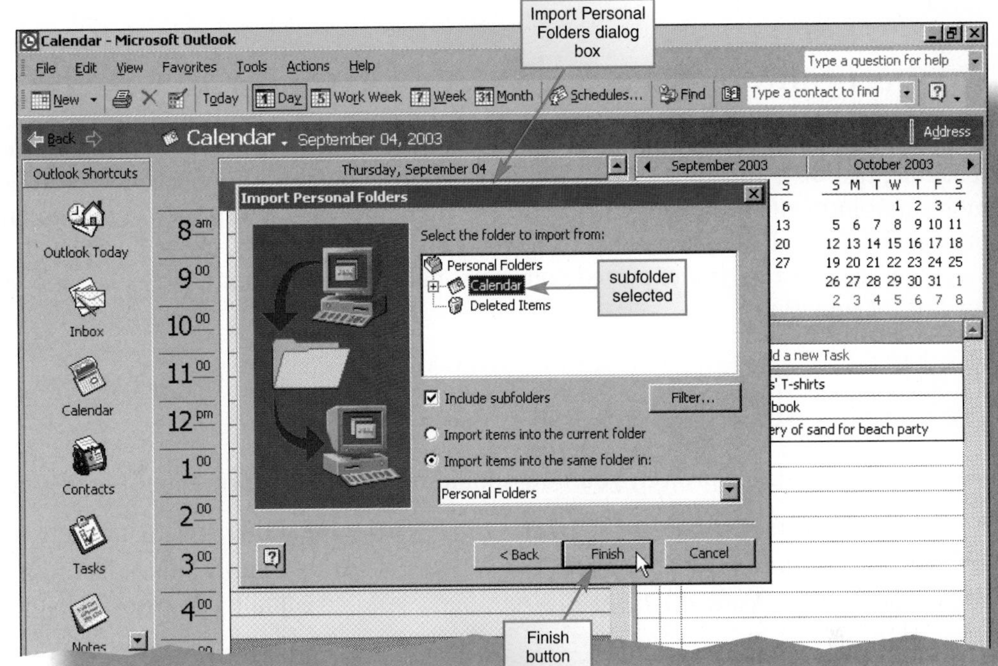

FIGURE 1-61

The Calendar subfolder now can be opened, edited, and printed as described earlier in this project. When changes are complete, the subfolder again can be exported and deleted from the hard disk. In addition to Outlook subfolders, Outlook's Import and Export Wizard allows the import of a Personal Address Book with contact names, addresses, and telephone numbers, or existing information to be brought in from other programs, such as Microsoft Mail or Schedule +.

Microsoft Outlook

For more information about Microsoft Outlook, visit the Outlook 2002 More About Web page (scsite.com/out2002/more.htm) and then click Microsoft Outlook.

Quitting Outlook

The project now is complete and you are ready to quit Outlook. The following step describes how to quit Outlook.

TO QUIT OUTLOOK

1 Click the Close button on the Outlook title bar.

Outlook closes, and the Windows desktop displays.

CASE PERSPECTIVE SUMMARY

Jamaal Robinson's school and meeting schedule, including all his classes and other engagements, are entered in his calendar and saved in a personal subfolder. With your help, he has identified and scheduled all of his recurring appointments, created a task list, and organized his contacts. Now he feels he is prepared to handle his busy workload.

Project Summary

In this project, you learned about personal information management by using Outlook to create a personal schedule, task list, and contact list. You learned how to enter appointments, create recurring appointments, move appointments to new dates, schedule events, and view and print your calendar in different views and print styles. You created a task list to serve as a reminder of tasks to be completed. You also created and printed a contact list. Finally, you exported your personal subfolders to a floppy disk and later imported the subfolders for further updating.

What You Should Know

Having completed this project, you now should be able to perform the following tasks.

- Change to a Personal Folder *(O 1.13)*
- Change to Month View *(O 1.33)*
- Change to Week View *(O 1.32)*
- Change to Work Week View *(O 1.31)*
- Create a Contact List *(O 1.40)*
- Create a Personal Subfolder in the Calendar Folder *(O 1.11)*
- Create a Personal Subfolder in the Contacts Folder *(O 1.38)*
- Create a Task List Using the TaskPad *(O 1.34)*
- Create an Event *(O 1.29)*
- Delete an Appointment *(O 1.23)*
- Delete a Personal Subfolder *(O 1.49)*
- Enter and Save Appointments Using the Appointment Window *(O 1.15)*
- Enter Appointment Dates and Times Using Natural Language Phrases *(O 1.21)*
- Enter Appointments Using the Appointment Area *(O 1.14)*
- Enter Recurring Appointments *(O 1.17)*
- Export Subfolders to a Floppy Disk *(O 1.46)*
- Find a Contact Quickly *(O 1.42)*
- Import a Subfolder *(O 1.50)*
- Move an Appointment to a New Date *(O 1.26)*
- Move an Appointment to a New Month *(O 1.27)*
- Move an Appointment to a New Time *(O 1.25)*
- Move to the Next Day and Enter the Recurring Appointments *(O 1.19)*
- Open the Calendar Folder *(O 1.09)*
- Organize Contacts *(O 1.44)*
- Print the Contact List *(O 1.45)*
- Print the Calendar in Daily Style *(O 1.35)*
- Print the Calendar in Monthly Style *(O 1.36)*
- Print the Calendar in Weekly Style *(O 1.36)*
- Print the Task List *(O 1.36)*
- Quit Outlook *(O 1.51)*
- Start Outlook *(O 1.08)*

More About

Quick Reference

For a table that lists how to complete tasks covered in this book using the mouse, menu, shortcut menu, and keyboard, visit the Shelly Cashman Series Office XP Web page (scsite.com/offxp/qr.htm) and then click Microsoft Outlook 2002.

More About

Microsoft Certification

The Microsoft User Specialist (MOUS) Certification program provides an opportunity for you to obtain a valuable industry credential — proof that you have the Outlook 2002 skills required by employers. For more information, visit the Shelly Cashman Series MOUS Web page at scsite.com/offxp/ cert.htm.

Learn It Online

Instructions: To complete the Learn It Online exercises, start your browser, click the Address bar, and then enter `scsite.com/offxp/exs.htm`. When the Office XP Learn It Online page displays, follow the instructions in the exercises below.

1 Project Reinforcement TF, MC, and SA

Below Outlook Project 1, click the Project Reinforcement link. Print the quiz by clicking Print on the File menu. Answer each question. Write your first and last name at the top of each page, and then hand in the printout to your instructor.

2 Flash Cards

Below Outlook Project 1, click the Flash Cards link. When Flash Cards displays, read the instructions. Type `20` (or a number specified by your instructor) in the Number of Playing Cards text box, type your name in the Name text box, and then click the Flip Card button. When the flash card displays, read the question and then click the Answer box arrow to select an answer. Flip through Flash Cards. Click Print on the File menu to print the last flash card if your score is 15 (75%) correct or greater and then hand it in to your instructor. If your score is less than 15 (75%) correct, then redo this exercise by clicking the Replay button.

3 Practice Test

Below Outlook Project 1, click the Practice Test link. Answer each question, enter your first and last name at the bottom of the page, and then click the Grade Test button. When the graded practice test displays on your screen, click Print on the File menu to print a hard copy. Continue to take practice tests until you score 80% or better. Hand in a printout of the final practice test to your instructor.

4 Who Wants to Be a Computer Genius?

Below Outlook Project 1, click the Computer Genius link. Read the instructions, enter your first and last name at the bottom of the page, and then click the Play button. Hand in your score to your instructor.

5 Wheel of Terms

Below Outlook Project 1, click the Wheel of Terms link. Read the instructions, and then enter your first and last name and your school name. Click the Play button. Hand in your score to your instructor.

6 Crossword Puzzle Challenge

Below Outlook Project 1, click the Crossword Puzzle Challenge link. Read the instructions, and then enter your first and last name. Click the Play button. Work the crossword puzzle. When you are finished, click the Submit button. When the crossword puzzle redisplays, click the Print button. Hand in the printout.

7 Tips and Tricks

Below Outlook Project 1, click the Tips and Tricks link. Click a topic that pertains to Project 1. Right-click the information and then click Print on the shortcut menu. Construct a brief example of what the information relates to in Outlook to confirm you understand how to use the tip or trick. Hand in the example and printed information.

8 Newsgroups

Below Outlook Project 1, click the Newsgroups link. Click a topic that pertains to Project 1. Print three comments. Hand in the comments to your instructor.

9 Expanding Your Horizons

Below Outlook Project 1, click the Articles for Microsoft Outlook link. Click a topic that pertains to Project 1. Print the information. Construct a brief example of what the information relates to in Outlook to confirm you understand the contents of the article. Hand in the example and printed information to your instructor.

10 Search Sleuth

Below Outlook Project 1, click the Search Sleuth link. To search for a term that pertains to this project, select a term below the Project 1 title and then use the Google search engine at google.com (or any major search engine) to display and print two Web pages that present information on the term. Hand in the printouts to your instructor.

In the Lab

1 Creating a Schedule

Problem: You recently accepted a job at an electronics store. You need to give your boss a schedule of your classes for the semester so she will know when you are available to work. You decide to schedule your time in Outlook and then print a month view of the calendar. This calendar is for the Fall semester that begins Monday, August 25, 2003, and ends Friday, December 19, 2003.

Instructions: Perform the following tasks.

1. Create a personal Calendar subfolder called [Your name] Schedule. Using the information in Table 1-5, enter each of the classes as a recurring appointment.
2. Add study time each week to the schedule as a recurring appointment occurring Mondays and Wednesdays from 1:00 p.m. to 3:00 p.m.
3. Schedule your Food Drive Committee meetings beginning August 28, 2003 for three Thursdays from 6:00 p.m. to 7:00 p.m.
4. Your parents' anniversary is September 17, 2003. This should be scheduled as a one-time event.
5. Add a dentist appointment for September 23, 2003 from 3:00 p.m. to 4:00 p.m.
6. All classes are canceled on October 13 and 14, 2003 for Fall Break. Delete the occurrences of classes during these two days, but not all recurring instances.
7. Print a copy of your calendar in Monthly Style for the months of September and October.
8. Export your subfolder to a floppy disk and then delete it from the hard disk.

Table 1-5 Recurring Appointments

CLASS	DAYS	TIME
Electrical Engineering	M, W	7:30 am – 9:00 am
Chemistry	M, W, F	9:30 am – 10:30 am
Technical Report Writing	T, Th	8:00 am – 9:30 am
Operating Systems	T, Th	10:00 am – 11:30 am

2 Creating a Contact List

Problem: You are the volunteer campaign chairperson of a friend's campaign for state representative. Many people have pledged their support by donating money or other services. At the end of the campaign, you would like to personally contact and thank each donor for his or her support. To do so, you need to create and maintain a list of the donors' names, addresses, telephone numbers, e-mail addresses, and type of donation.

Instructions: Create a personal Contacts subfolder in which to store a contact list containing the donors listed in Table 1-6. In the Contact window, enter their donations in the Job Title text box. When the list is complete, print the contact list, export the subfolder to a floppy disk, and then delete it from the hard disk. Submit the printout to your instructor.

Table 1-6 Contact Information

NAME	ADDRESS	TELEPHONE	E-MAIL	DONATION
Kris Davids	354 Rutledge	(219) 555-5686	kdavids@isp.com	Money
Juanita Martinez	8453 Whitcomb	(219) 555-4565	jmartinez@isp.com	Telephone Support
Samantha Stern	7456 Brummitt	(219) 555-2348	sstern@isp.com	Money
Nathan Farmer	4654 Ashford	(219) 555-7410	nfarmer@isp.com	Catering
Denis Marks	678 E. 7th	(219) 555-3647	dmarks@isp.com	Transportation
Lara Carmichael	439 Campbell	(219) 555-9137	lcarmichael@isp.com	Advertising

In the Lab

3 Creating a Calendar and a Task List

Problem: You are the owner of a small auto parts store. Your company has experienced rapid growth during the last several months, and with winter approaching, you need to change to seasonal stock. As the owner, you also have administrative duties to perform, such as staff meetings, payroll, advertising, and sales campaigns. To make your schedule even more hectic, you coach your child's basketball team on Monday nights from 6:00 p.m. to 8:00 p.m. at the Youth Center. You need to create a schedule of appointments as well as a task list to help you keep track of your various jobs and responsibilities each day.

Instructions: Perform the following tasks.

1. Create a personal Calendar subfolder named Creek Side Auto Parts.
2. Enter the appointments in the calendar, using the information listed in Table 1-7.
3. Create a task list containing the following tasks.
   a. Call Katie to confirm auto dealer's visit
   b. Schedule meeting to discuss winter sales goals
   c. Call to check anti-freeze delivery
   d. Sign contract to renew accounting firm agreement
4. Print the calendar for the month of October and submit it to your instructor.
5. Export the personal subfolder to a floppy disk and then delete it from the hard disk.
6. Close all open windows.

Table 1-7 Appointment Information

DESCRIPTION	DATE	TIME
Manager's meeting	Every Monday from October 6, 2003 – November 24, 2003	8:00 am – 10:00 am
Ads for Fall Closeout Sale complete	October 7, 2003	
Brake installation demonstration for customers	October 14 and 16, 2003	8:30 am – 4:30 pm
Payroll verification due	October 17, 2003	
Eric's birthday	October 20, 2003	
Telephone meeting with Susan	October 24, 2003	9:30 am – 10:00 am
Meet with auto dealer about supplier deal	October 27, 2003	11:30 am – 1:00 pm
Meeting with Bob	October 30, 2003	3:00 pm – 4:00 pm

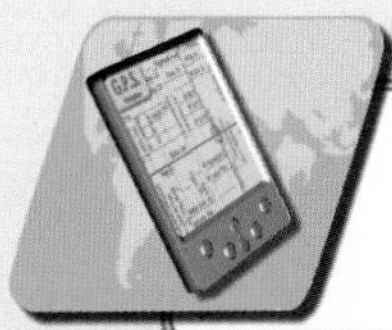

Cases and Places

The difficulty of these case studies varies:
▶ are the least difficult; ▶▶ are more difficult; and ▶▶▶ are the most difficult.

1 ▶ Create a personal schedule for the next month. Include any work and class time, together with study time. Use recurring appointments when possible. All day activities should be scheduled as events. Print the calendar in Month Style and submit to your instructor.

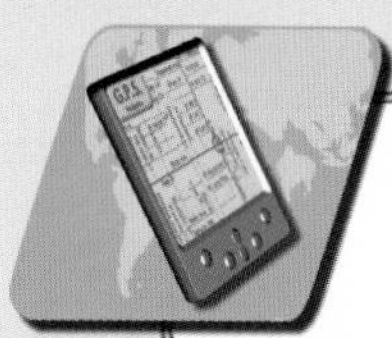

Cases and Places

2 ▶ At work, you are in charge of scheduling for the month of April. Create a schedule of work times for four employees. Jeremy works Mondays, Wednesdays, and Fridays from 9:00 a.m. to 5:00 p.m. Nancy works Tuesdays, Thursdays, and Saturdays from 9:00 a.m. to 5:00 p.m. Nipul works from 12 noon until 9:00 p.m. on Mondays, Wednesdays, and Fridays. Christina completes the schedule working from 12 noon until 9:00 p.m. on Tuesdays, Thursdays, and Saturdays.

3 ▶▶ You work at the school's Writing lab. You need to create a weekly schedule of hours and print it. From Monday through Saturday, the lab is open from 8:00 a.m. to 9:00 p.m. The lab is reserved on Mondays and Wednesdays from 2:00 p.m. to 4:00 p.m. for a Beginning Writing class. It also is reserved on Tuesdays and Thursdays from 1:00 p.m. to 3:00 p.m. for an Advanced Writing class. The lab is closed all day Sunday. Print the schedule in Weekly Style and submit it to your instructor.

4 ▶▶ Create journal entries from your personal schedule for the past week. Comment on activities in which you participated and tasks that you accomplished. Write when the activity was started and ended. Note the problems (if any) associated with the activity. When commenting on completed tasks, include notes about the results of having completed it. Specify what would have happened had the task not been completed when it was. Write a brief summary of your journal and submit it to your instructor.

5 ▶▶ Create a contact list of your family, friends, and colleagues. Include their names, addresses, telephone numbers, and e-mail addresses (if any). Enter the employer for each one, if appropriate. For family members, list birthdays and wedding anniversaries (if any) using the Details sheet. Print the contact list and submit it to your instructor.

6 ▶▶ Use the natural language option in the Start date box to create a list of events for the year. Create a new calendar that contains the following holidays: New Year's Day, Valentine's Day, St. Patrick's Day, Independence Day, Halloween, Veterans Day, Christmas Eve, Christmas Day, and New Year's Eve. For the last four holidays, indicate that you will be out of the office all day. Also, add events for several family or friend birthdays or anniversaries, using the natural language option. For instance, schedule these events by utilizing the phrase, two weeks from today (or something similar) as a start date. Try different phrase options to schedule these. Select two months to print in Monthly Style and submit them to your instructor.

7 ▶▶▶ You recently accepted a position with an international construction company. Your first assignment is to make the main telephone and address file available to everyone in the firm. The file, which currently is maintained in a three-ring binder, contains names, addresses, telephone numbers, fax numbers, e-mail addresses, and Web sites of your company's subcontractors and vendors. You decide to create a contact list using Outlook so everyone can access the same information and automatically dial and send e-mail and access Web sites. Create a contact list that includes at least the names, addresses, and Web sites of seven construction companies. Invent some fictional company names and addresses or look up construction companies on the Web using one of the Internet search engines. Create a Contacts subfolder in which to store the contact list. Print the contact list and submit it to your instructor.

Office XP Integration

PROJECT

Integrating Office XP Applications and the World Wide Web

OBJECTIVES

You will have mastered the material in this project when you can:

- Integrate the Office XP applications to create a Web site
- Add hyperlinks to a Word document
- Embed an Excel chart into a Word document
- Add scrolling text to a Web page created in Word
- Add a hyperlink to a PowerPoint slide
- Create Web pages from a PowerPoint presentation
- Create a data access page from an Access database

A Little Rest and Relaxation

and Amazing Things Happen

Travel brochures entice and invite you to experience exotic locales that can improve your state of mind. Vacations help to eliminate daily stresses, offer opportunities to spend quality time with family and friends, and provide exercise in the great outdoors. Holiday packages are plentiful if you want to explore destination possibilities.

Maybe you are feeling tired and desire a little rest and relaxation away from it all, a haven where you can recapture your spirit in comfort and peace. There you find friendly staff to attend to your every need, nutritious meals, breathtaking views of Chicago's skyline from clean, private rooms tastefully decorated with soothing artwork to promote the healing process. Is this a weekend retreat? you ask. No, this is Chicago's Northwestern Memorial Hospital's Feinberg Inpatient Pavilion, designed with patients' needs in mind.

The hospital's advertising slogan, Making Amazing Things Happen, applied to the efforts of the 4,500 employees, 1,000 physicians, and 800 volunteers involved in planning the state-of-the-art building for more than a decade. The design team formed 125 user groups composed of staff, patients, and their families to develop an ideal patient encounter. They provided input on designing areas that facilitate communication

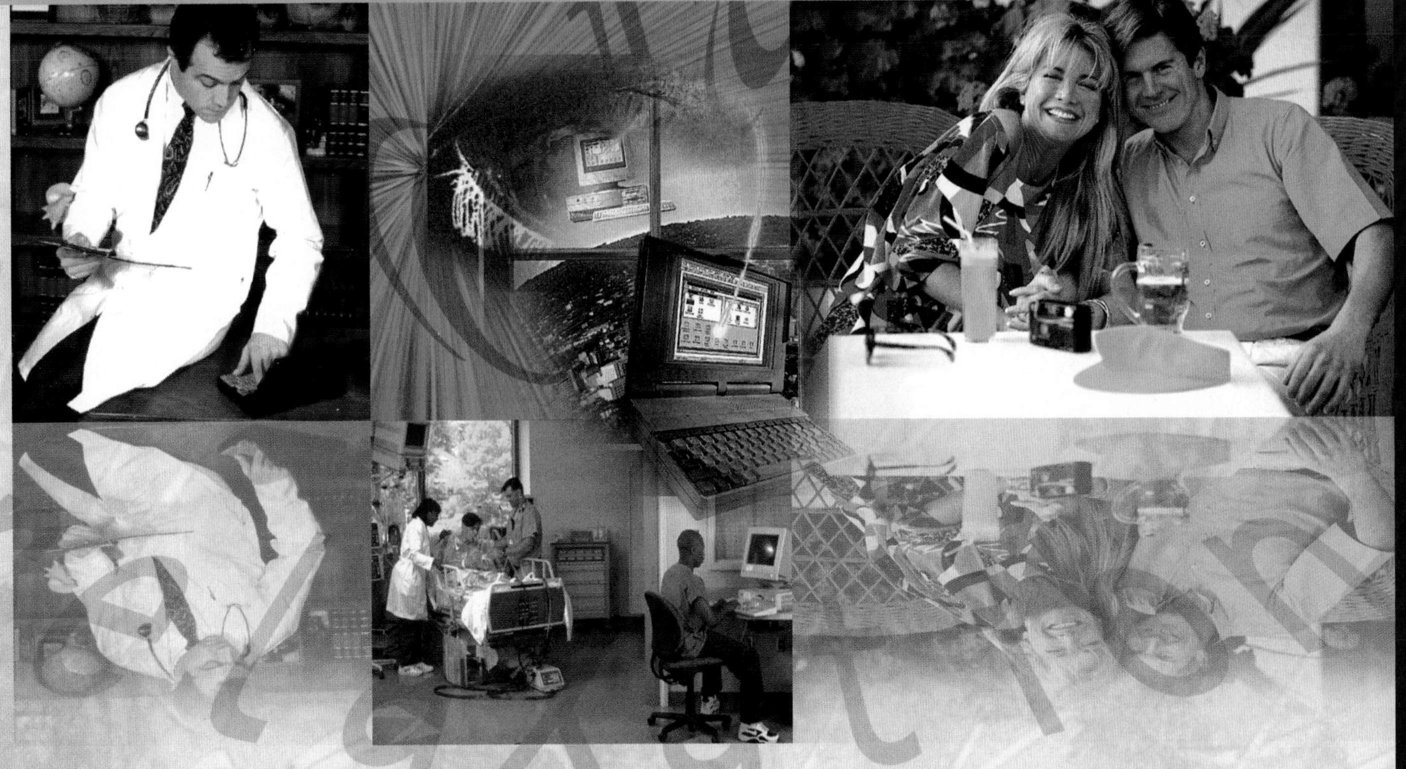

and ergonomics and even staged a mock cardiac arrest to develop optimal working conditions.

The $580 million medical center opened in 1999 and contains the floor area of 44 football fields. Intertwined in this space are 600 miles of fiber-optic and high-speed copper cable that integrate computer functions. Patients are introduced to the innovative computerization techniques the minute they enter the medical center. Instead of registering at a central desk, they proceed directly to a nursing unit on a particular floor. Once the patients are settled in their beds, caregivers complete their registration forms by inputting personal data in notebook computers that are connected to the hospital's computer system through data connections in each private room.

Various medical personnel then can access this data. Doctors use notebook computers to retrieve the records as they make their rounds. Caregivers in the emergency room can retrieve laboratory reports seconds after the tests are complete, which enhances their ability to treat critical patients when seconds matter most. Billing department employees can generate comprehensive statements that detail specific procedures and charges. Students throughout the world can view the latest surgical procedures via teleconferences made possible by special cameras in each operating room.

Another aspect of computer integration throughout the hospital is the use of filmless X-rays. Instead of using the traditional method of exposing and then developing celluloid film, radiology technicians now use the picture archiving and communication system (PACS) to take a digital image. Each of the thousands of X-rays taken monthly is stored on an optical storage system, which eliminates the need to save physical hard copy film in a special room. Caregivers can retrieve these radiology images from workstations throughout the hospital, including intensive care units and the emergency room. When necessary, these files can be transmitted to other medical facilities throughout the world via the Internet.

Northwestern Memorial Hospital integrates its computer applications to maximize patient convenience and minimize costs.

Similarly, in this project, you will utilize the integration features of the Microsoft Office XP applications. Using information already available to you in Word, Excel, Access, and PowerPoint, you will develop a Web site for Garden National Bank as a means for the bank to implement a marketing strategy advertising its benefits and services. This seamless integration makes amazing things happened.

Office XP Integration

Integrating Office XP Applications and the World Wide Web

CASE PERSPECTIVE

Garden National Bank is a community bank managed by Liza Oei. In the past, the bank enjoyed great success by being the only bank in its part of town. Recently, the bank's clientele has been using newer services, such as Internet stock brokers and other local financial service providers.

Liza believes that the bank's business would increase if she implements a marketing strategy that advertises the advantages Garden National Bank has over competitors' services. Garden National Bank offers nationally competitive interest rates and savings plans. In addition, Liza employs highly trained financial advisors and a friendly staff. She is investigating ways to advertise these benefits in an efficient and cost-effective way. She thinks a Web site would be the answer, but she is inexperienced with the Internet. Liza knows that you are studying computer technology and asks you to help her create a Web site advertising Garden National Bank.

Introduction

From your meeting with Liza Oei, you were given four files of information to use to create the Web site for Garden National Bank.

1. A Word document that contains the company logo images and company name (Figure 1-1a on page I 1.06).
2. An Excel workbook with a Bar chart graphically illustrating the bank's breakdown of investments by savings product used by customers (Figure 1-1b on page I 1.06).
3. A PowerPoint slideshow that contains general information about the bank (Figure 1-1g on page I 1.07).
4. An Access database that contains savings product information (Figure 1-1c on page I 1.06).

The Garden National Bank Web site should include the following:

1. A home page with a Bar chart that contains the total asset value per savings product (Figure 1-1e on page I 1.07). Three hypertext links also are included on the home page: About Us, Savings Products, and E-mail Comments.
2. The Savings Products data access Web page (Figure 1-1d on page I 1.06) is created from the Access file. Clicking the Savings Products link on the home page accesses this Web page. On this Web page, visitors can scroll through the savings products, categorized by product category.
3. The PowerPoint Web page (Figure 1-1g on page I 1.07) displays information about the bank. Clicking the About Us link on the home page accesses this Web page.
4. Using the E-mail Comments hyperlink, you can create an e-mail message (Figure 1-1f on page I 1.07). E-mail is sent to the e-mail address `manager@isp.com`.

Integration Project — Garden National Bank Web Site

Many businesses today advertise their products and services on the Internet, as described in the Case Perspective. Companies find it easy to create Web pages using information already saved in spreadsheet, database, or presentation software formats. The Web page creation capabilities of Microsoft Office XP make it simple for you to create an entire Web site using the information available. In Word, a document can be created and saved as a Web page. PowerPoint provides the same capability and adds a navigation structure for browsing. In addition, Access provides a Wizard to create data access pages that enable the Web page visitor to navigate through the database.

The following pages contain a detailed explanation of these tasks.

Adding Hyperlinks to a Word Document

The Web site created for Garden National Bank consists of an initial Web page, called the **home page**, with two hyperlinks to other Web pages, an e-mail link, and a Bar chart. Clicking a **hyperlink**, which can be text or an image, allows you to jump to another location. Text is used (About Us, Savings Products, E-mail Comments) for the three hyperlinks on the Garden National Bank home page (Figure 1-1e on page 1.07). The first hyperlink (About Us) jumps to a PowerPoint Web page that contains staff listings and general information about the bank and its products. A second hyperlink (Savings Products) jumps to a data access page that provides inquiry capabilities for customers to access the Garden National Bank's savings product database. This Web page allows inquiries only; updating the database is prohibited. The third hyperlink (E-mail Comments) creates an e-mail message. In order to place the three hyperlinks to the left of the Bar chart, a table will be created in the Word document.

More About

Web Pages

Making information available on the Internet is a key aspect of business today. To facilitate this trend, the Office XP applications easily allow you to generate Web pages from existing files. An entire Web site can be created with files from Word, Excel, PowerPoint, or Access, using the Save as Web Page command on the File menu.

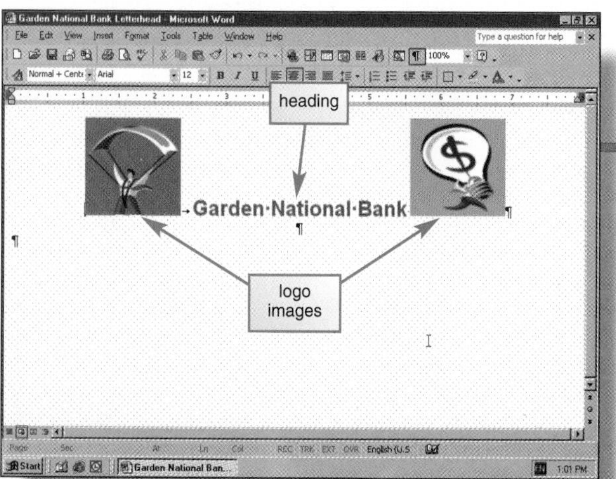

(a) Word Document

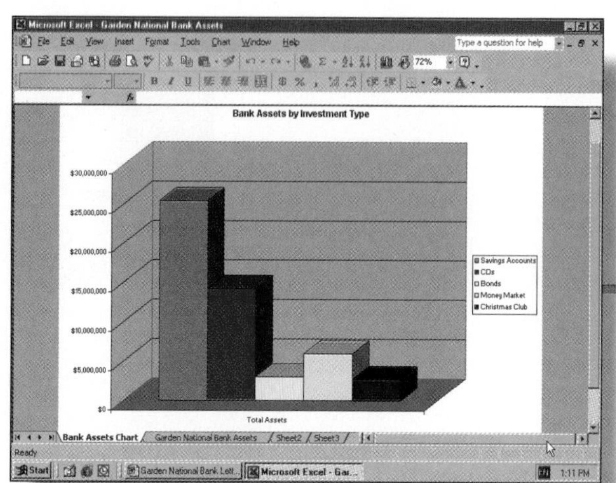

(b) Bar Chart in Excel

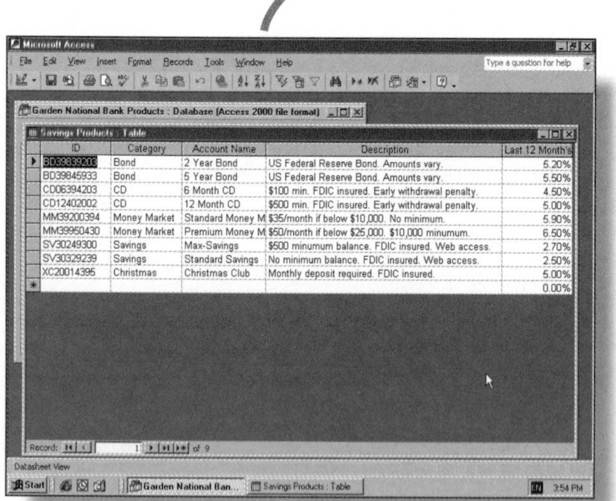
Garden National Bank Products : Database (Access 2000 file format)

Savings Products : Table

ID	Category	Account Name	Description	Last 12 Month's
BD39839203	Bond	2 Year Bond	US Federal Reserve Bond. Amounts vary.	5.20%
BD39845933	Bond	5 Year Bond	US Federal Reserve Bond. Amounts vary.	5.50%
CD06394203	CD	6 Month CD	$100 min. FDIC insured. Early withdrawal penalty.	4.50%
CD12402002	CD	12 Month CD	$500 min. FDIC insured. Early withdrawal penalty.	5.00%
MM39200394	Money Market	Standard Money M	$35/month if below $10,000. No minimum.	5.90%
MM39950430	Money Market	Premium Money M	$50/month if below $25,000. $10,000 minumum.	6.50%
SV30249300	Savings	Max-Savings	$500 minumum balance. FDIC insured. Web access.	2.70%
SV30329239	Savings	Standard Savings	No minimum balance. FDIC insured. Web access.	2.50%
XC20014395	Christmas	Christmas Club	Monthly deposit required. FDIC insured.	5.00%
				0.00%

(c) Access Table

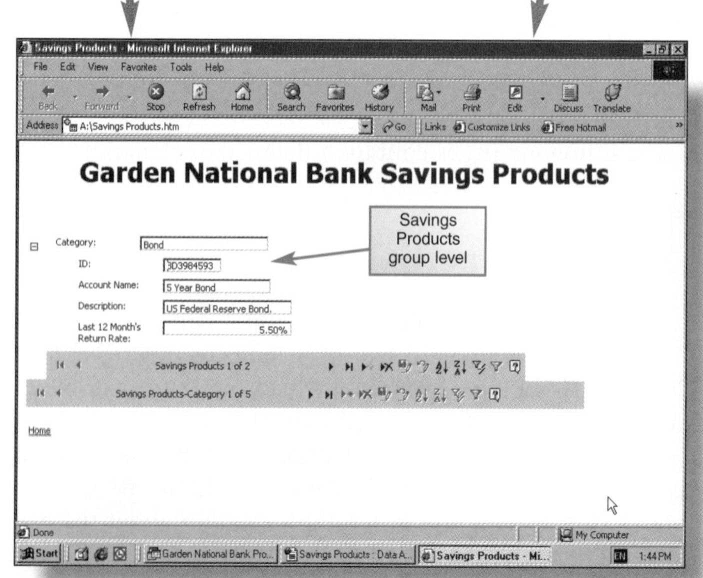

(d) Data Access Page

FIGURE 1-1

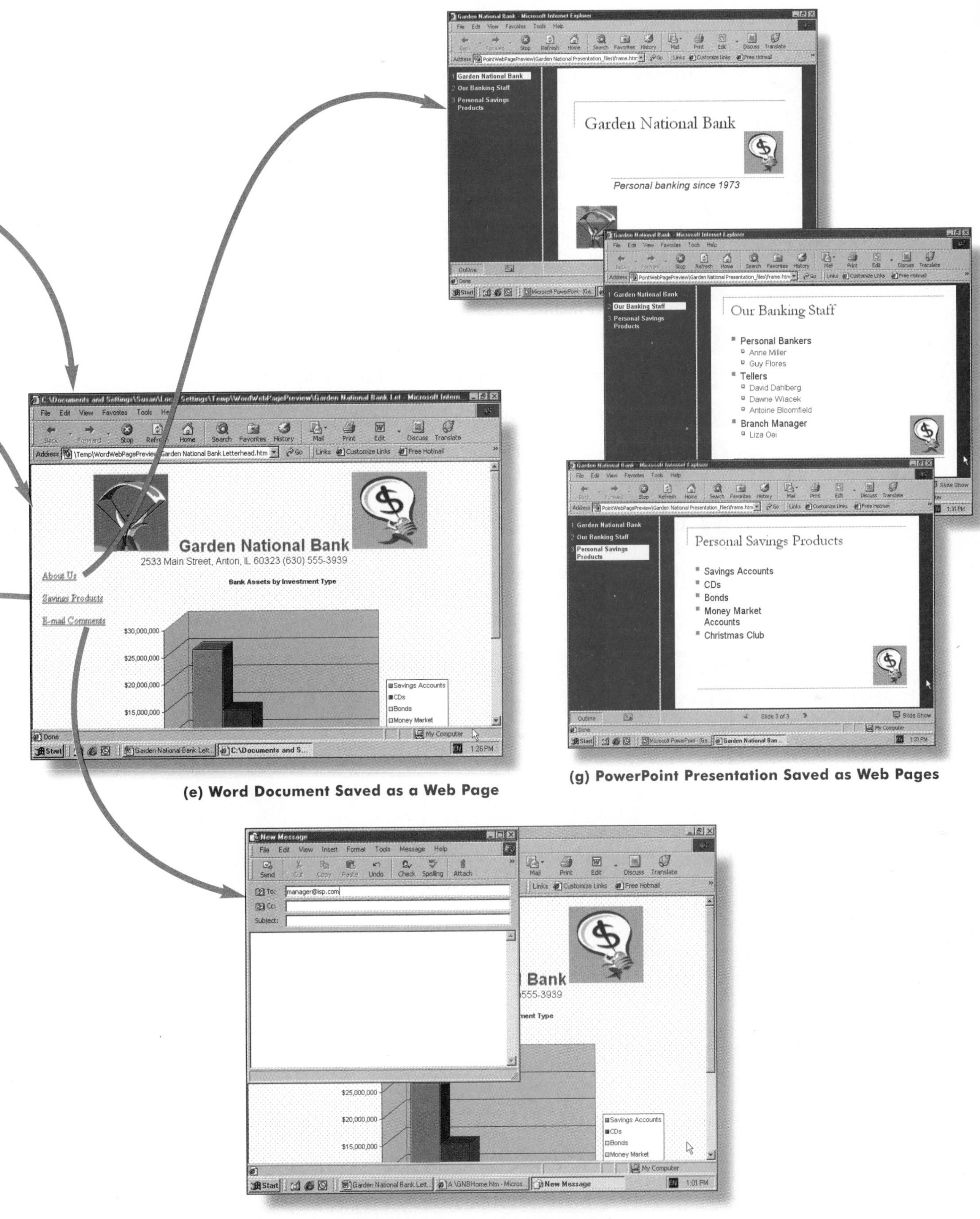

(e) Word Document Saved as a Web Page

(g) PowerPoint Presentation Saved as Web Pages

(f) New E-Mail Message Created from Hyperlink

Starting Word and Opening a Document

The first step in this project is to open the Word document, Garden National Bank Letterhead, and save it with the new file name, Garden National Bank Home Page.

TO START WORD, CUSTOMIZE WORD, OPEN AN EXISTING DOCUMENT, AND SAVE THE DOCUMENT WITH ANOTHER NAME

1. Insert the Integration Data Disk in drive A. See the inside back cover of this book for instructions for downloading the Data Disk or see your instructor for information on accessing the files required in this book.
2. Click the Start button on the Windows taskbar. Click Open Office Document on the Start menu.
3. Click the Look in box arrow and then click 3½ Floppy (A:) in the Look in list.
4. Double-click Garden National Bank Letterhead.
5. If the Language bar displays, click its Minimize button.
6. If the Standard and Formatting toolbars display on one row, click the Toolbar Options button on the right side of either toolbar and then click Show Buttons on Two Rows on the Toobar Options menu.
7. Click File on the menu bar and then click Save As. Type `Garden National Bank Home Page` in the File name text box and then click the Save button in the Save As dialog box.

The document is saved as Garden National Bank Home Page (Figure 1-2).

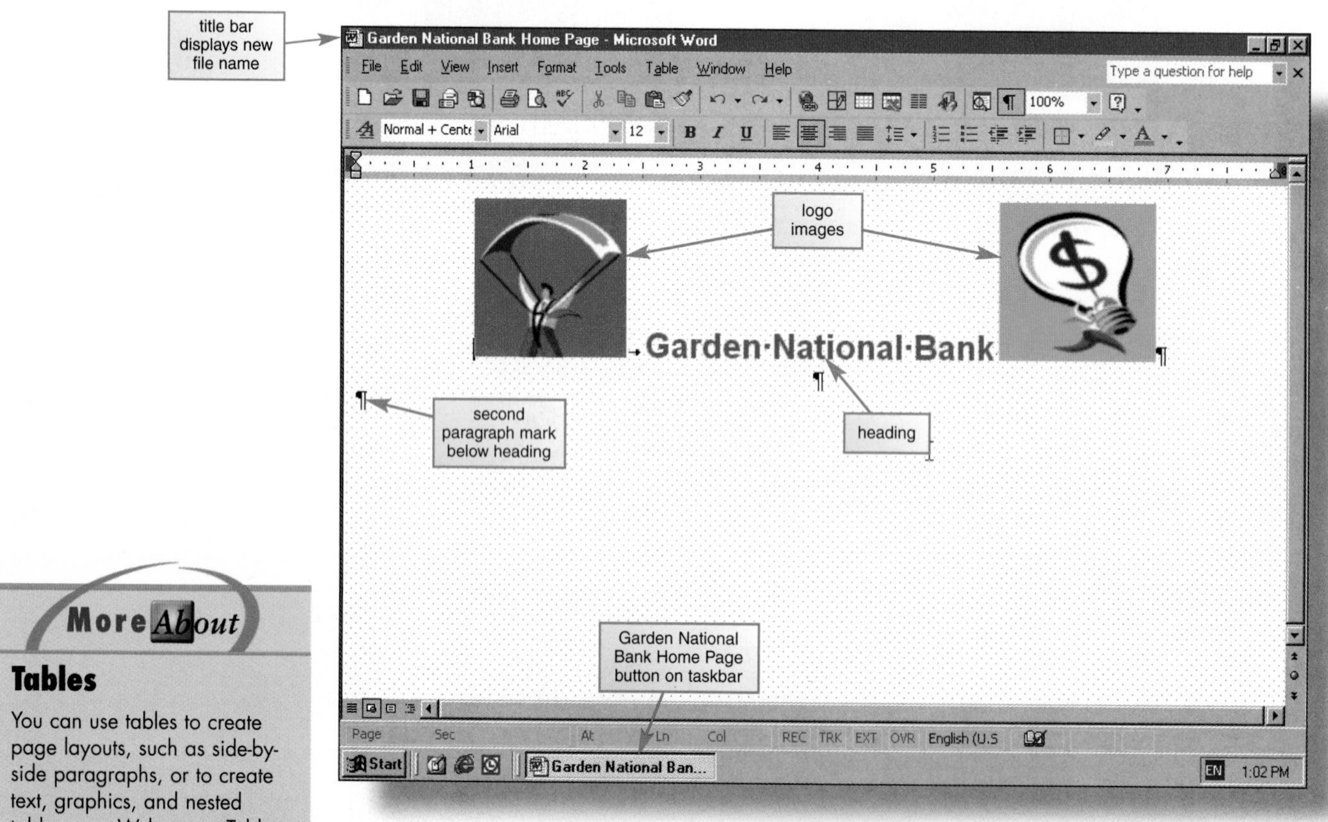

FIGURE 1-2

More About

Tables

You can use tables to create page layouts, such as side-by-side paragraphs, or to create text, graphics, and nested tables on a Web page. Tables are used frequently in Web pages to structure information and images.

Inserting a Table into a Word Document

The next step is to insert a table with two columns and one row. The left column will contain three hyperlinks. The right column will contain the Bar chart.

Perform the following steps to add a table to the Garden National Bank Home Page document.

Steps To Insert a Table into a Word Document

1 Position the insertion point on the second paragraph mark after the heading Garden National Bank. Click Table on the menu bar, point to Insert, and then click Table.

The Insert Table dialog box displays (Figure 1-3).

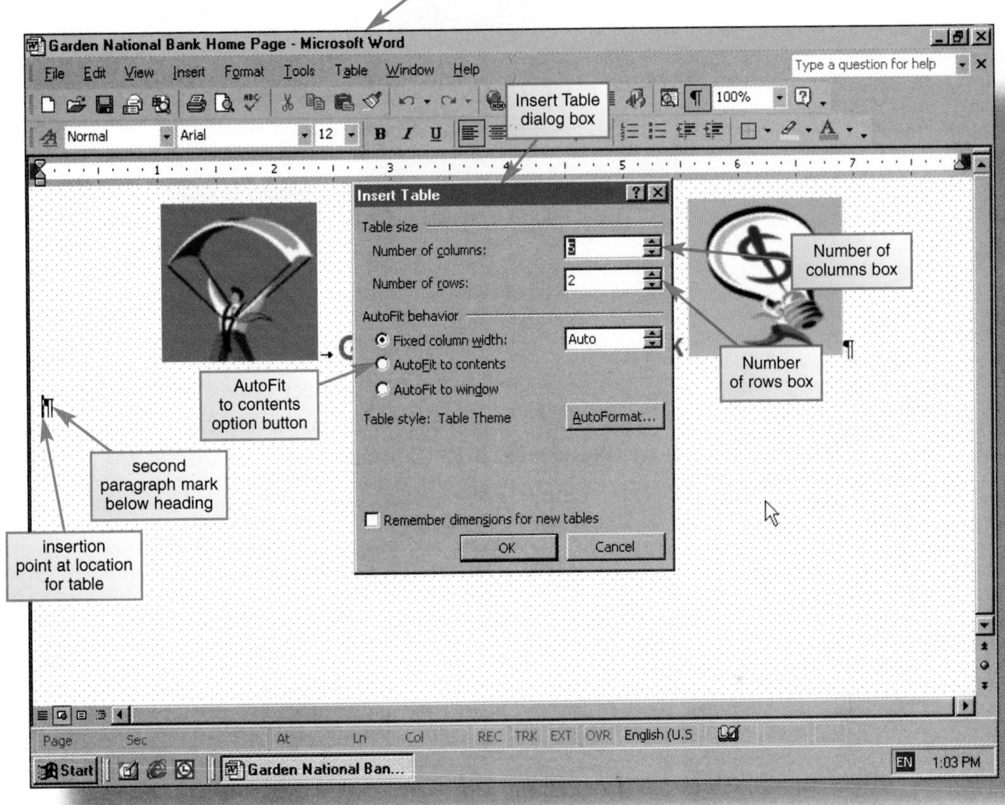

FIGURE 1-3

2 Type 2 **in the Number of columns box and then press the TAB key. Type** 1 **in the Number of rows box and then click AutoFit to contents in the AutoFit behavior area. Point to the OK button.**

The new settings display in the Insert Table dialog box (Figure 1-4).

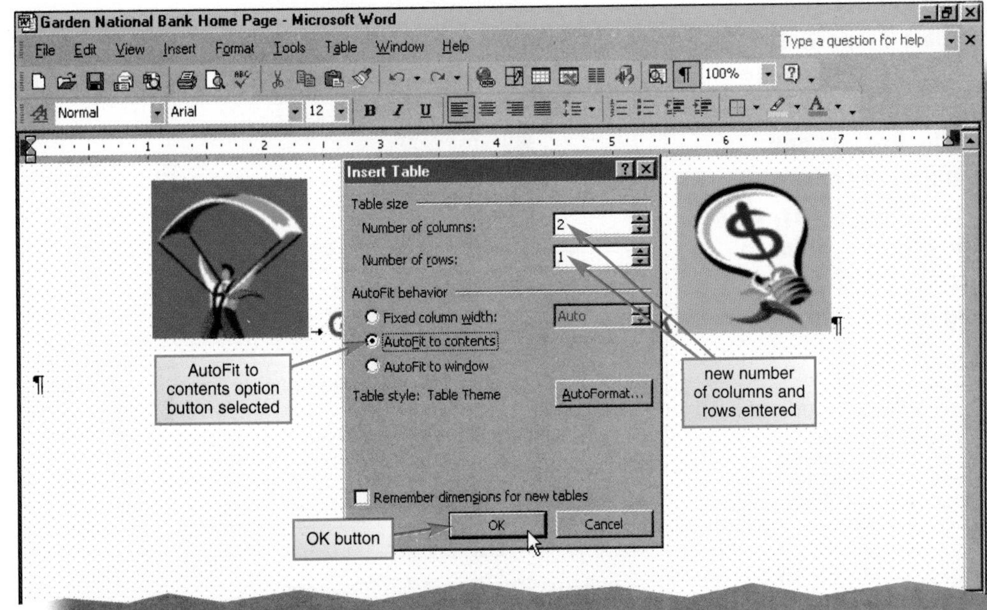

FIGURE 1-4

3 **Click the OK button.**

The table displays in the Word document (Figure 1-5).

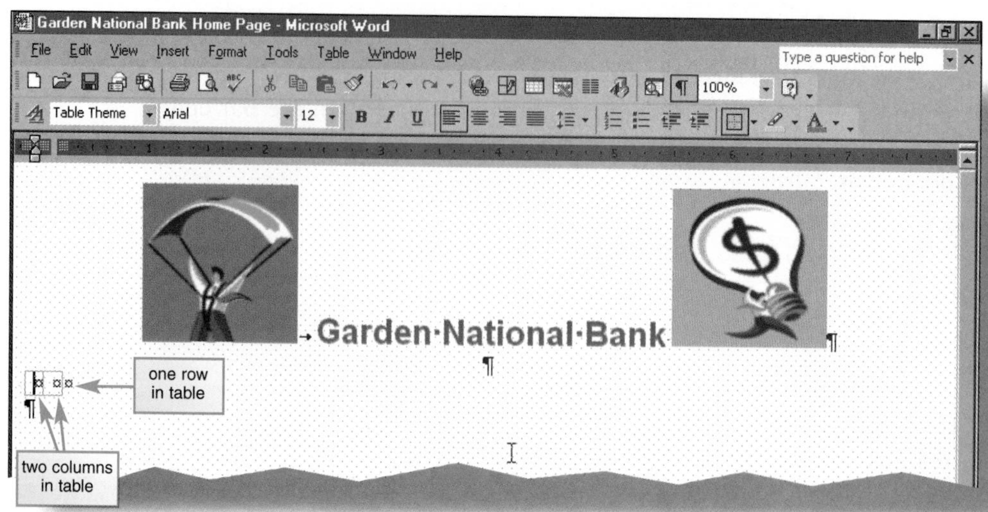

FIGURE 1-5

Other Ways

1. Click Insert Table button on Standard toolbar, drag through one row and two columns, click mouse button
2. In Voice Command mode say, "Insert Table," [drag through one row and two columns, click mouse button]

Step 2 instructed you to select AutoFit to contents. The **AutoFit to contents** option allows you to make the columns in a table automatically fit the contents. If you do not select AutoFit to contents, you can adjust the column widths manually using the sizing handles.

Eliminating the Table Border

The two-column, one-row table has been inserted into the Word document. The table border is not necessary for the Web page. The next steps instruct you on how to remove the border of the table.

Steps To Remove the Table Border

1 **Click Table on the menu bar and then click Table Properties. Click the Borders and Shading button in the Table sheet. When the Borders and Shading dialog box displays, if necessary, click the Borders tab. Point to the None button in the Setting area of the Borders sheet.**

The Borders and Shading dialog box displays (Figure 1-6).

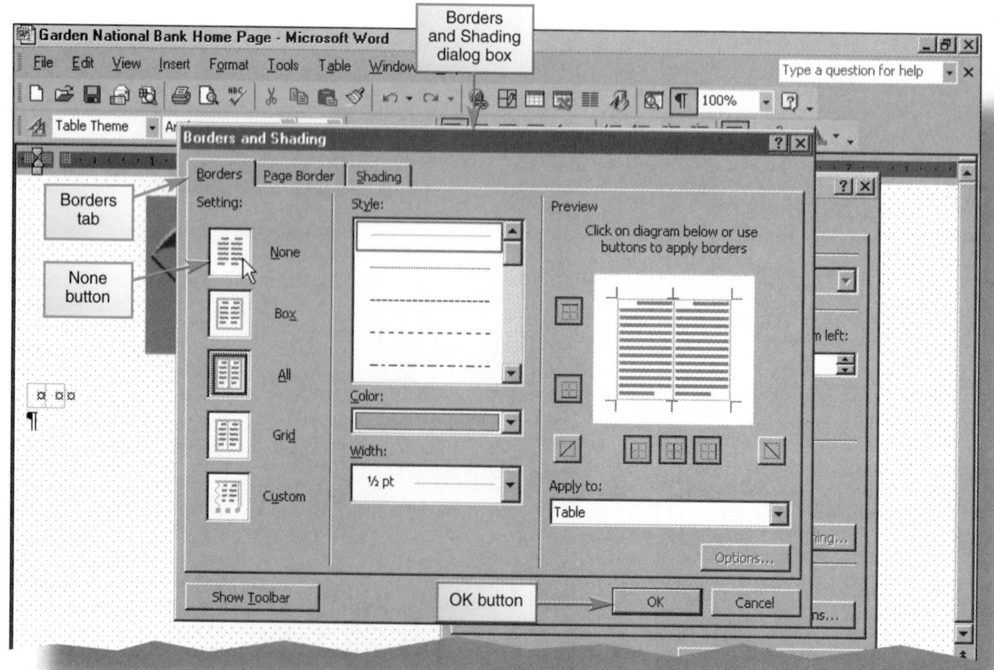

FIGURE 1-6

2 Click the None button in the Setting area and then click the OK button in the Borders and Shading dialog box. Click the OK button in the Table Properties dialog box.

The borderless table displays (Figure 1-7).

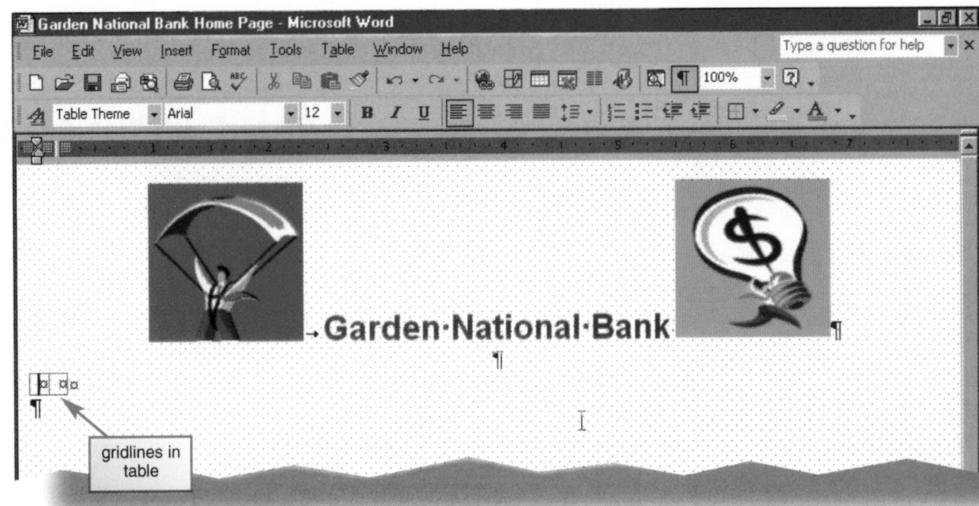

FIGURE 1-7

The border of the table displays with gridlines in the Word document. **Gridlines** can be used as a guide when entering text or images. When the document is viewed in your browser or printed, the table border does not display or print.

Hyperlinks

In addition to the way in which the hyperlinks are created in this project, you can copy and paste text as a hyperlink. Copy the text you want to the Clipboard, click where you want to insert the text, and then click Paste as Hyperlink on the Edit menu.

Inserting the Text for the Hyperlinks

After creating the borderless table, you must insert the three text phrases that will be used as hyperlinks on the home page. These phrases (About Us, Savings Products, and E-mail Comments) allow you to jump to two other Web pages and create an e-mail message. Perform the steps below to add the text phrases that are used as hyperlinks.

To Insert Text for Hyperlinks

1 If necessary, click the leftmost cell in the table.

2 Type `About Us` **and then press the ENTER key twice. Type** `Savings Products` **and then press the ENTER key twice. Type** `E-mail Comments` **as the final text phrase.**

The table displays with the three text phrases that will be used as hyperlinks (Figure 1-8).

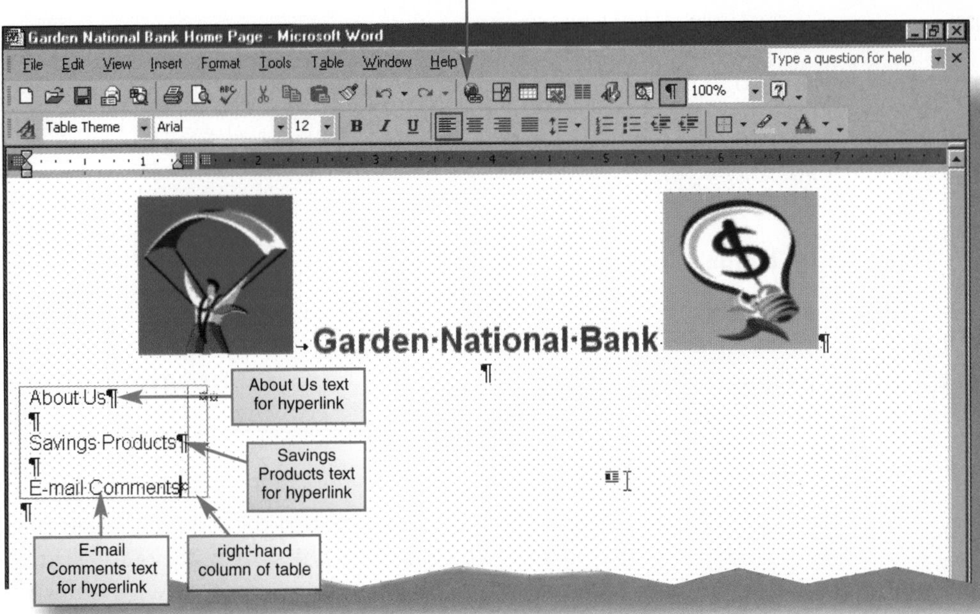

FIGURE 1-8

More About

Hyperlinks

Hyperlinks can link to both external locations and internal locations within the current document. To link to a location inside the current document, select the Place in This Document option in the Link to bar in the Insert Hyperlink dialog box. The Microsoft Office XP application then will provide a list of locations within the current document to which you can link.

With the text phrases added, the next step is to select each text phrase and then insert the corresponding hyperlink.

Inserting a Hyperlink to PowerPoint Web Pages

The **Insert Hyperlink feature** provides the capability of linking to an existing file or Web page, to a place within the current document, to a newly created document, or to an e-mail address. In this project, two text phrases (About Us and Savings Products) will be created that link to Web pages. The About Us hyperlink will jump to a PowerPoint presentation that is saved as a Web page using the Web page name AboutUs.htm. The Savings Products hyperlink will jump to a data access page using the Web page name SavingsProducts.htm. You will create the data access page later from an existing Access database. The third text phrase (E-mail Comments) links to an e-mail address, allowing the Web page visitor to send an e-mail message to the bank manager.

Perform the following steps to create a hyperlink for the first text phrase.

Steps To Create a Hyperlink to PowerPoint Web Pages

1 **Drag through the text, About Us, in the table. Click the Insert Hyperlink button on the Standard toolbar.**

2 **If necessary, click the Existing File or Web Page button on the Link to bar. Type** `a:\AboutUs.htm` **in the Address text box. Point to the OK button.**

The Insert Hyperlink dialog box displays with the name of the Web page in the Address text box (Figure 1-9).

3 **Click the OK button.**

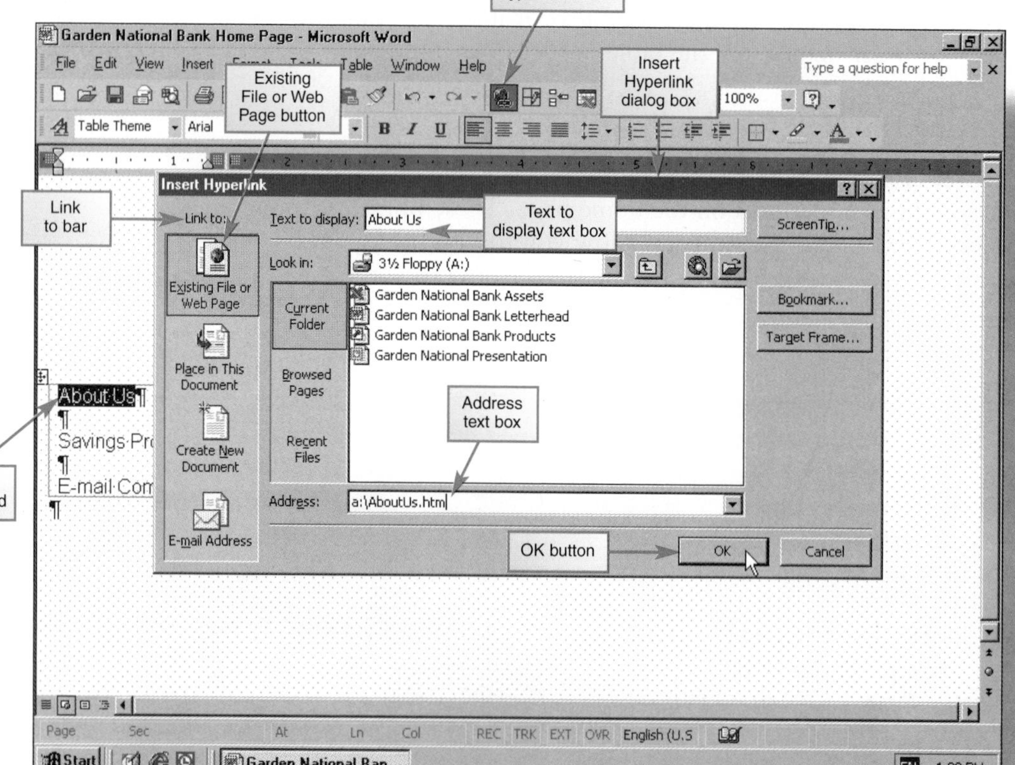

FIGURE 1-9

The hyperlink is assigned to the About Us text phrase. Once the Word document is saved as a Web page and the visitor clicks the text, About Us, the AboutUs.htm file on drive A displays. Perform the following steps to add the other two hyperlinks.

Other Ways

1. On Insert menu click Hyperlink
2. Right-click selected words, click Hyperlink on shortcut menu
3. Press CTRL+K
4. In Voice Command mode say, "Hyperlink"

TO INSERT THE REMAINING HYPERLINKS

1. Drag through the text, Savings Products, in the table. Click the Insert Hyperlink button on the Standard toolbar.
2. Type `a:\SavingsProducts.htm` in the Address text box and then click the OK button.
3. Drag through the text, E-mail Comments. Click the Insert Hyperlink button on the Standard toolbar and then click E-mail Address on the Link to bar.
4. Type `manager@isp.com` in the E-mail address text box and then click the OK button.

The table displays as shown in Figure 1-10.

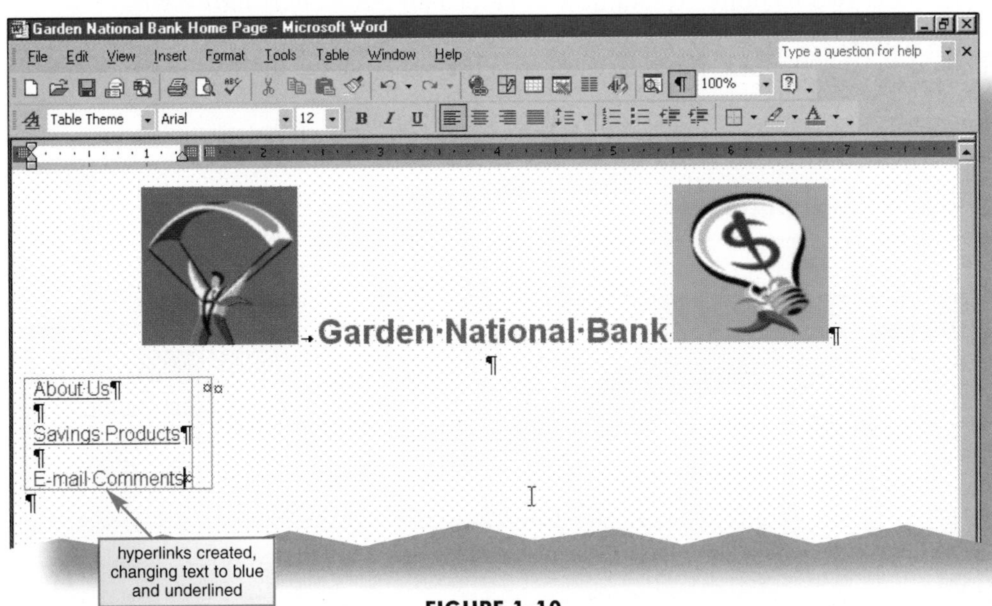

FIGURE 1-10

The three hyperlinks are created. When you click the E-mail Comments hyperlink, it will create an e-mail message to manager@isp.com. The other two hyperlinks (About Us and Savings Products) will not be functional until the corresponding Web pages are created later in this project.

Embedding an Excel Chart into a Word Document

This project uses the **Object Linking and Embedding** (**OLE**) feature of Microsoft Office XP to insert the Excel chart into a Word document. OLE allows you to incorporate parts of a document or entire documents from one application into another.

The Bar chart in Excel is called a **source object** (Figure 1-1b on page I 1.06) and the Garden National Bank Home Page document is the **destination document.** Once an object is embedded, it becomes part of the destination document. This project illustrates using the Paste Special command on the Edit menu to embed the Excel object. The **Paste Special command** inserts an object into Word, but still recognizes the **source program**, the program in which the object was created. When you double-click an embedded object, such as the Bank Assets by Investment Type worksheet, the source program opens and allows you to make changes. In this example, Excel is the source program. With the hyperlinks added to the Word document, the next step is to embed the Bar chart into the Word document. First, open the Excel workbook as shown in the steps on the next page.

More About

Embedded Objects

The advantage of using an integrated set of applications, such as Microsoft Office XP, is the capability of sharing information among applications. The Object Linking and Embedding (OLE) features of Office XP make the integration process more efficient. A chart created in Excel can be included in a Word document using OLE. To edit the embedded object, double-click it. The source program then starts and opens the source object for editing.

TO START EXCEL, CUSTOMIZE EXCEL, AND OPEN AN EXISTING WORKBOOK

1. Click the Start button on the Windows taskbar and then click Open Office Document on the Start menu.
2. Click the Look in box arrow and then click 3½ Floppy (A:) in the Look in list.
3. Double-click the Garden National Bank Assets workbook.
4. If the Language bar displays, click its Minimize button.
5. If the Standard and Formatting toolbars display on one row, click the Toolbar Options button on the right side of either toolbar and then click Show Buttons on Two Rows on the Toolbar Options menu.

The next two sections explain how to embed an Excel chart into a Word document and then resize it. The first section explains embedding a chart into a Word document. Perform the following steps to embed the Excel Bar chart into the Word document.

Steps To Embed an Excel Chart into a Word Document

1 Click the Bank Assets Chart tab.

The Bar chart is active and displays (Figure 1-11).

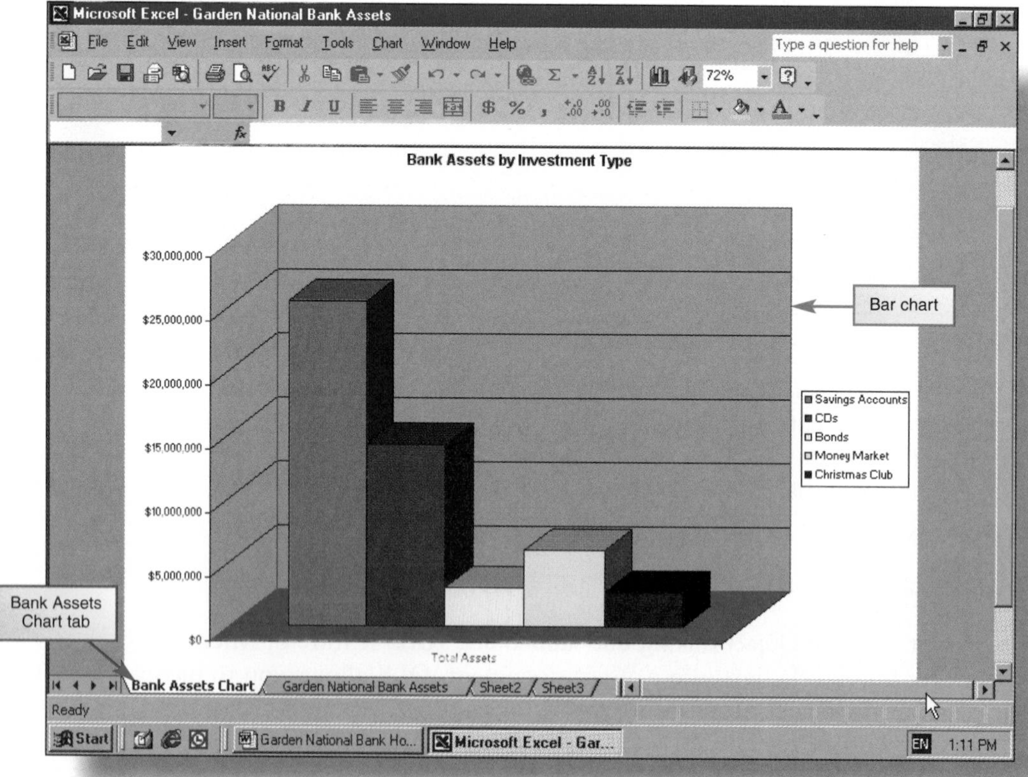

FIGURE 1-11

2 Click the white area around the Chart Area to select the chart and then click the Copy button on the Standard toolbar.

Excel places a copy of the Bar chart on the Office Clipboard. A scrolling marquee displays around the Chart Area (Figure 1-12).

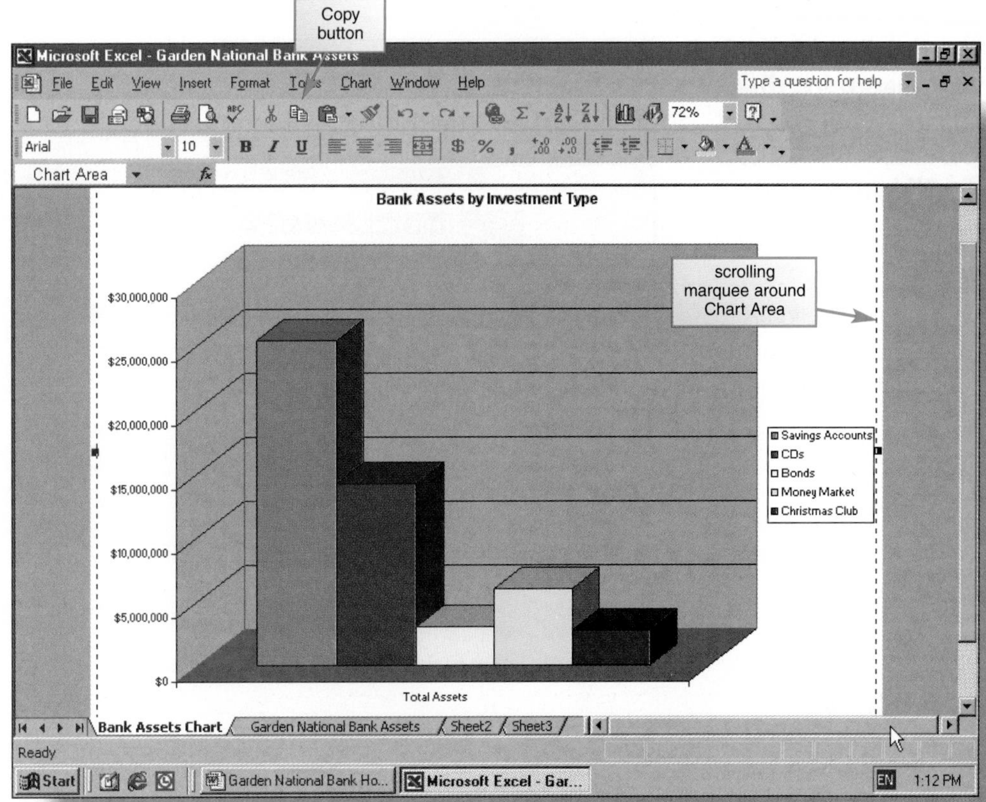

FIGURE 1-12

3 Click the Garden National Bank Home Page button on the taskbar. If necessary, click the right column of the table.

4 Click Edit on the menu bar and then point to Paste Special.

The Edit menu displays and the Paste Special command is highlighted (Figure 1-13).

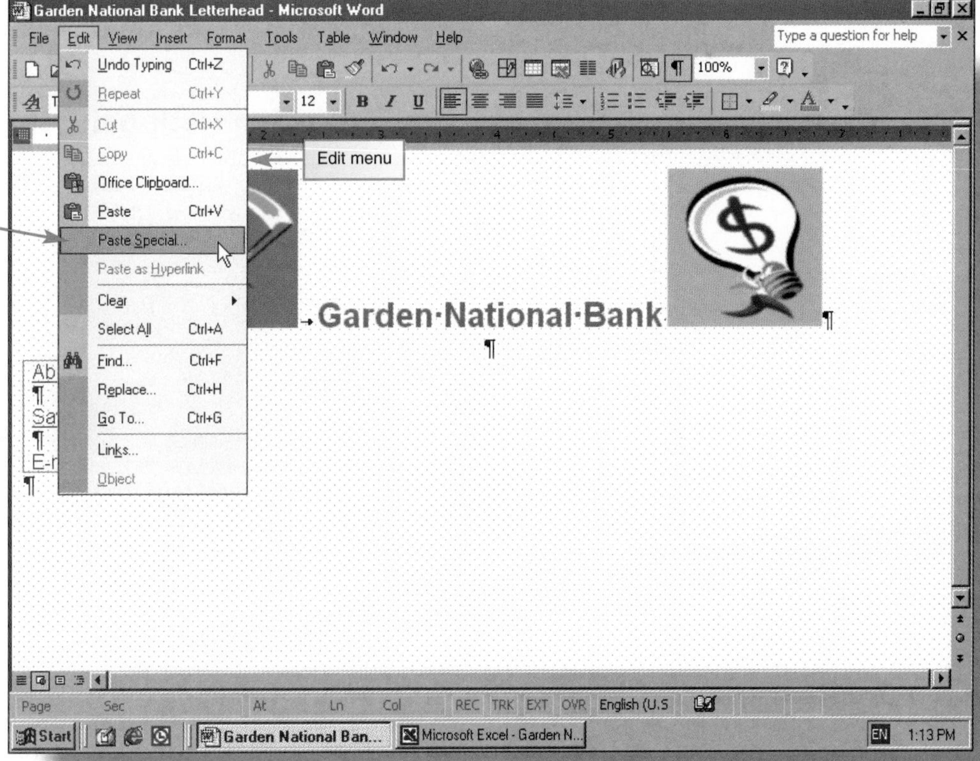

FIGURE 1-13

5 **Click Paste Special. If necessary, click Microsoft Excel Chart Object in the As list. Point to the OK button.**

The Paste Special dialog box displays (Figure 1-14). The Paste option button is selected. Microsoft Excel Chart Object displays in the As list.

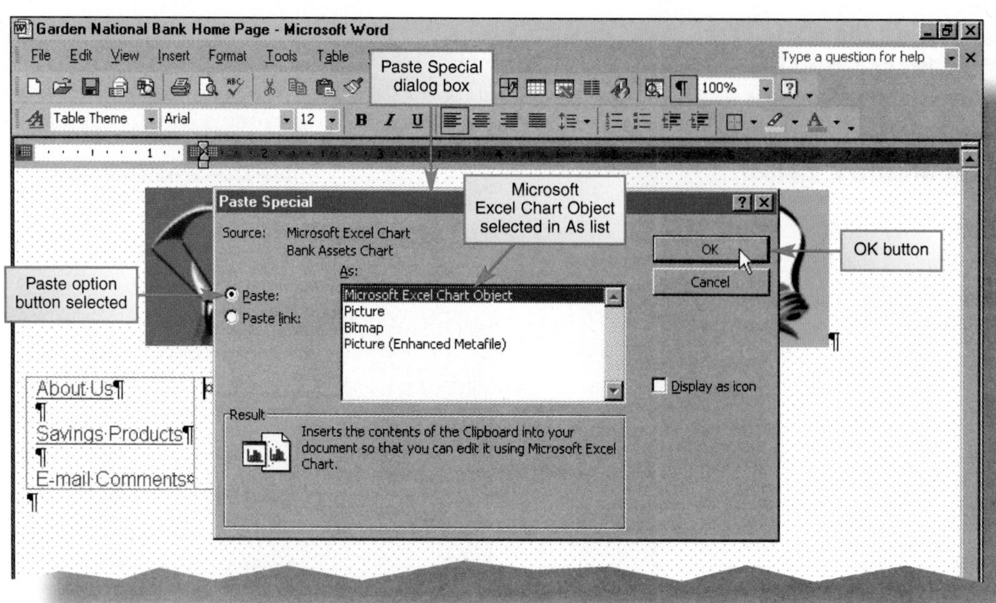

FIGURE 1-14

6 **Click the OK button.**

Word embeds the Bar chart into the document (Figure 1-15).

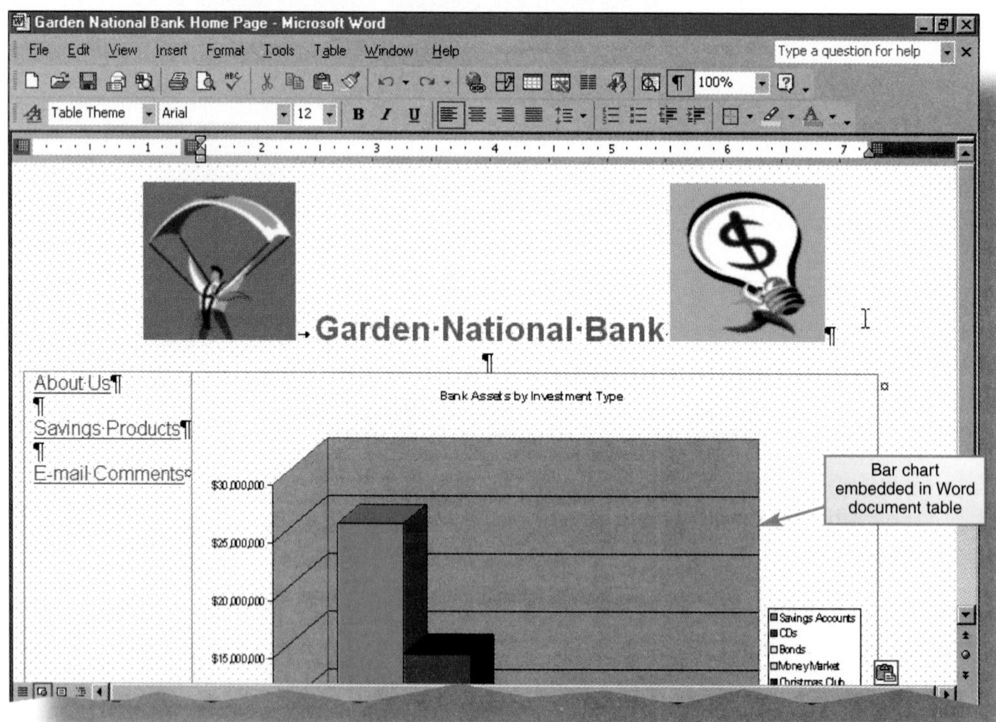

FIGURE 1-15

Other Ways

1. On Edit Menu click Copy
2. Press CTRL+C
3. In Voice Command mode say, "Copy"

Changing the Size of an Embedded Object

The embedded Bar chart exceeds the margins of the Garden National Bank Home Page document. Reducing the size of the Bar chart will improve the layout of the document. In this project, you will use the Format Object dialog box to change the size of the chart.

All Microsoft Office XP applications allow you to use three methods to copy objects between applications: (1) copy and paste; (2) copy and embed; and (3) copy and link. The first method uses the Copy and Paste buttons. The latter two use the Paste Special command. Table 1-1 summarizes the differences among the three methods.

Table 1-1 Copy Methods

METHOD	CHARACTERISTICS
Copy and paste	The source document becomes part of the destination document. An object may be edited, but the editing features are limited to those of the destination application. An Excel worksheet becomes a Word table. If changes are made to values in the Word table, any original Excel formulas are not recalculated.
Copy and embed	The source document becomes part of the destination document. An object may be edited in the destination document using source editing features. The Excel worksheet remains a worksheet in Word. If you make changes to values in the worksheet with Word active, Excel formulas will be recalculated. If, however, you change the worksheet in Excel without the document open in Word, these changes will not display in the Word document the next time you open it.
Copy and link	The source document does not become part of the destination document, even though it appears to be. Instead, a link is established between the two documents, so that when you open the Word document, the worksheet displays within the document, as though it were a part of it. When you attempt to edit a linked worksheet in Word, the system activates Excel. If you change the worksheet in Excel, the changes also will display in the Word document the next time you open it.

More About

Objects

Objects can be nearly any part of an Office XP application or other Windows application. Some examples are Excel worksheets, a paragraph in a Word document, and a slide in a PowerPoint presentation. As long as you use the Paste Special command to paste data on the Clipboard, you can keep data in its native format.

Perform the following steps to reduce the size of the chart using the Object command on the Format menu.

Steps To Change the Size of an Embedded Object

1 If necessary, click the Bar chart to select it. Click Format on the menu bar and then point to Object.

The Bar chart is selected as indicated by sizing handles on the selection rectangle. The Format menu displays, and the Object command is highlighted (Figure 1-16).

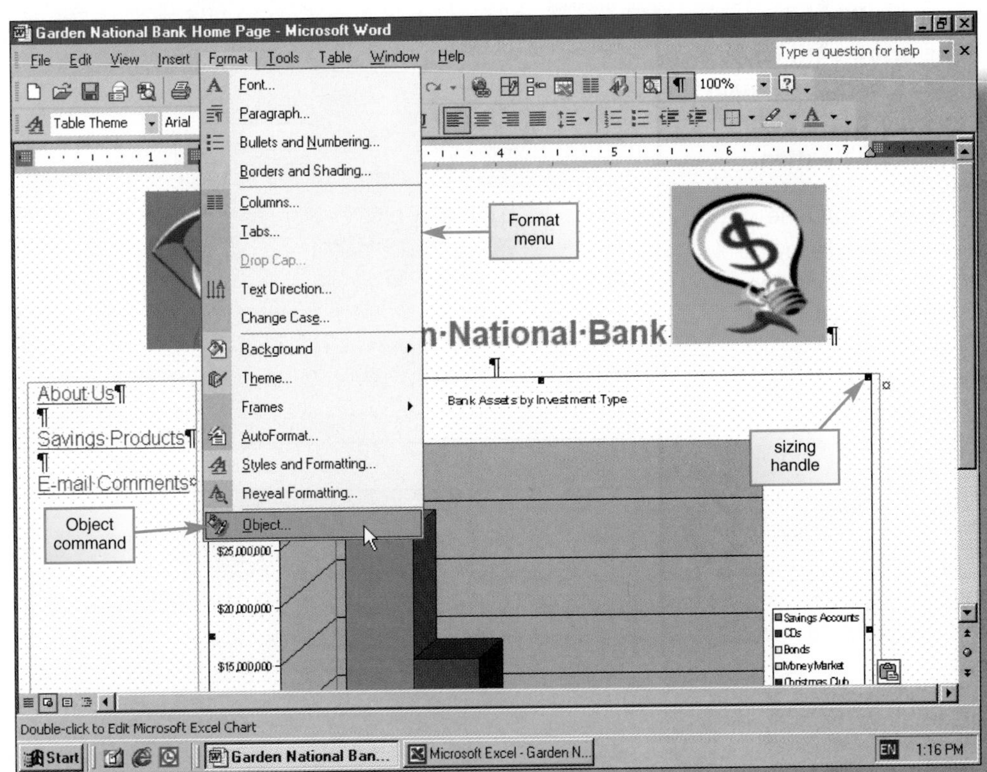

FIGURE 1-16

2 Click Object. If necessary, click the Size tab.

The Format Object dialog box and Size sheet display (Figure 1-17).

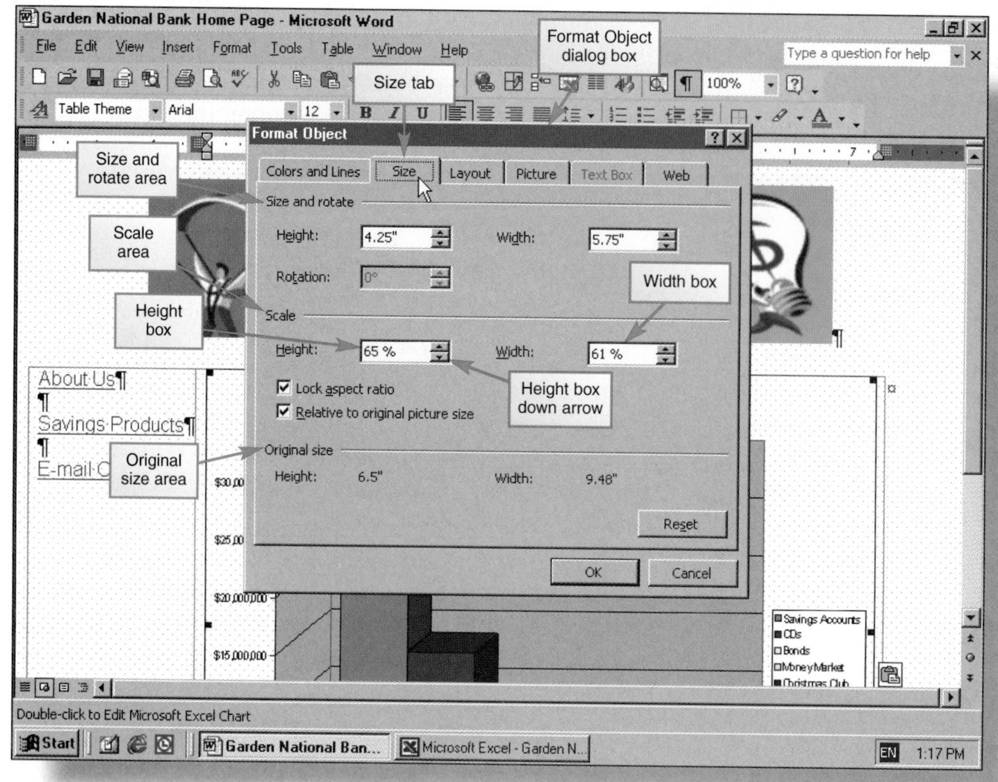

FIGURE 1-17

3 In the Scale area, if necessary, click the Height box up or down arrow or the Width box up or down arrow until 65 % displays in both the Height box and the Width box. Point to the OK button.

The Height box and the Width box both display 65 % (Figure 1-18). Depending on the size of the object when it was pasted into the Word document, you may need to scale either up or down in the Scale area Height and Width boxes. When you change the value in either the Height or Width box, both values change because the Lock aspect ratio check box is selected.

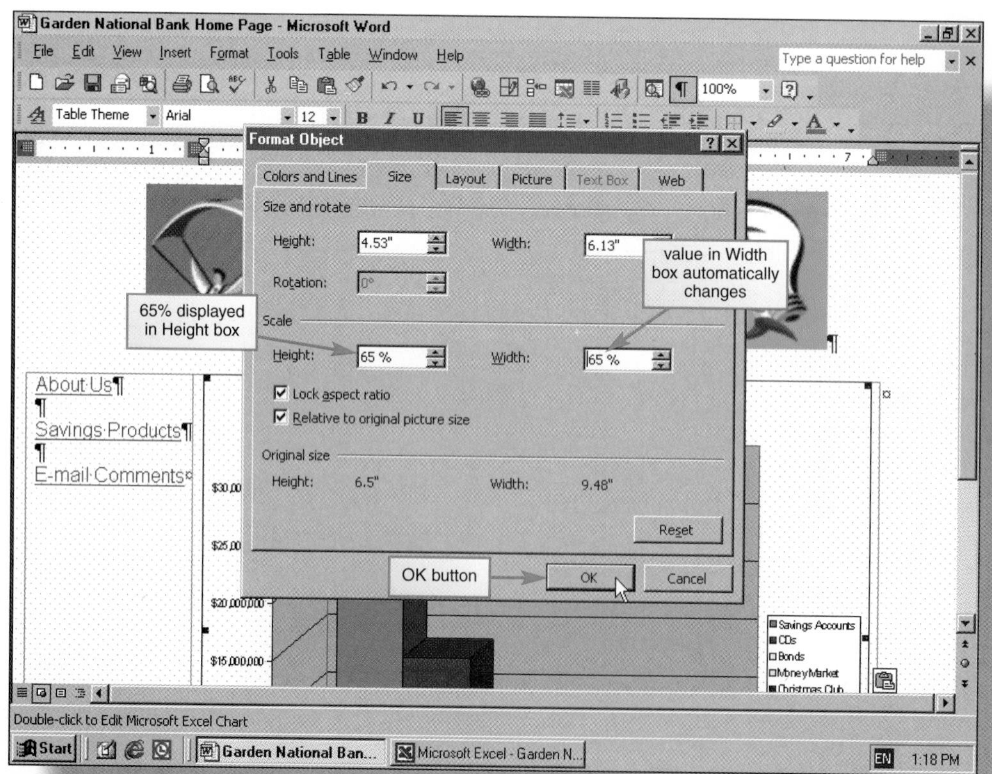

FIGURE 1-18

4 Click the OK button. If necessary, scroll to see the embedded chart.

Word reduces the size of the chart to 65% of its original size (Figure 1-19).

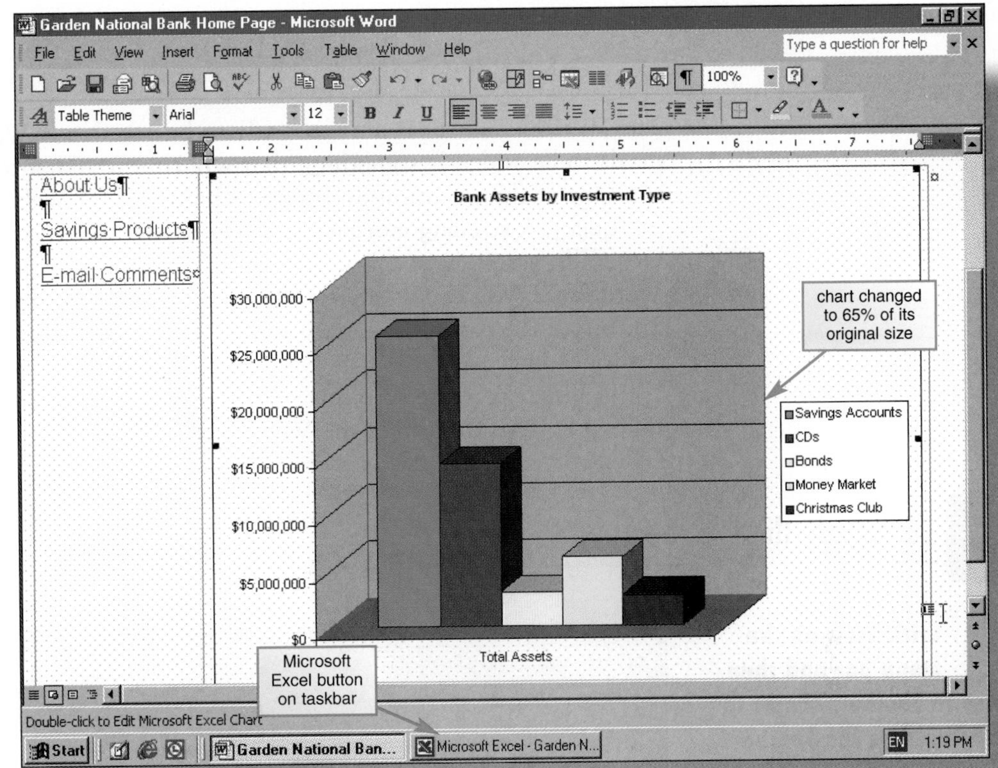

FIGURE 1-19

Other Ways

1. Right-click Bar chart, click Format Object on shortcut menu
2. Select Bar chart, then in Voice Command mode say, "Format Object"

The Format Object dialog box contains two areas that can change the size of an object. The **Size and rotate area** allows you to increase or decrease the height or width of an object in inches. When available, it also allows you to rotate the object in degrees around an axis. The **Scale area** allows you to change the size of an object by a specific percentage while maintaining the height-to-width ratio. The height-to-width ratio is referred to as **aspect ratio**. You change the height and width independently by deselecting the Lock aspect ratio check box. The **Original size area** at the bottom of the Format Object dialog box displays the original height and width of the selected object.

Quitting Excel

With the Bar chart embedded in the Word document, you no longer need the Garden National Bank Sales workbook open. Perform the following steps to quit Excel.

TO QUIT EXCEL

1. Right-click the Microsoft Excel - Garden National Bank Assests button on the taskbar. Click Close on the shortcut menu. If prompted to save changes, click the No button.
2. If the Microsoft Excel dialog box displays regarding saving the large amount of information on the Clipboard, click the No button.

More About

Resizing

To resize an image proportionally from a corner, you can press and hold down the SHIFT key while dragging a corner sizing handle. To resize vertically, horizontally, or diagonally from the center outward, press and hold down the CTRL key while dragging a sizing handle. To resize proportionally from the center outward, press and hold down the CTRL+SHIFT keys and drag a corner sizing handle.

Adding Scrolling Text to a Word Document

The Word document is almost ready to be saved as a Web page. The final item that needs to be added is something that will capture the attention of your Web page visitor. One of the attention-grabbing techniques that Web developers use is scrolling marquees. A **scrolling marquee** is a line of text that moves across the Web page. Generally, scrolling text is used to highlight information about the Web site. With Word 2002, you can create scrolling text using the **Scrolling Text button** on the Web Tools toolbar. A scrolling marquee will be created just below the Garden National Bank heading.

In order to create scrolling text, the Web Tools toolbar must display. Perform the following steps to display the Web Tools toolbar.

Steps To Display the Web Tools Toolbar

1. **Click View on the menu bar and then point to Toolbars. Point to Web Tools on the Toolbars submenu.**

2. **Click Web Tools. If necessary, point to the Web Tools toolbar title bar and drag the toolbar to the center, right side of the window.**

The Web Tools toolbar displays (Figure 1-20).

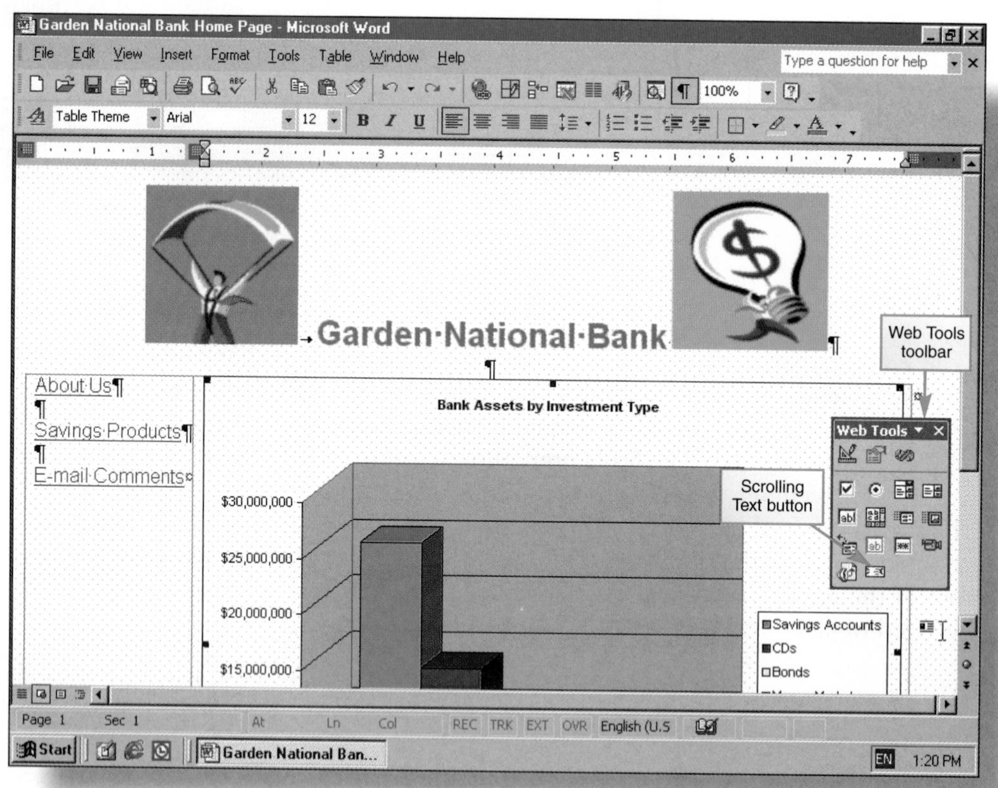

FIGURE 1-20

The **Web Tools toolbar** is used to create the scrolling text that moves under the Web page heading.

Inserting Scrolling Text

A number of options are available for scrolling text. The **behavior** of the text specifies the manner in which the text moves on the Web page. By default, the behavior of the line of text is to scroll. **Scrolling** moves the text in from one side and off the other side of the Web page. Another behavior option is to slide the text. Setting the behavior to **slide** moves the text in from one side of the Web page and stops as soon as the text touches the opposite side. The third option is to set text behavior to alternate. **Alternate** bounces the text back and forth in the margins of the marquee. The default behavior is scrolling text. In this project, the scrolling text behavior is changed to slide, as shown in the following steps.

Steps To Insert Scrolling Text into a Word Document

1 Click the paragraph mark below the Garden National Bank heading and then click the Scrolling Text button on the Web Tools toolbar.

The Scrolling Text dialog box displays (Figure 1-21).

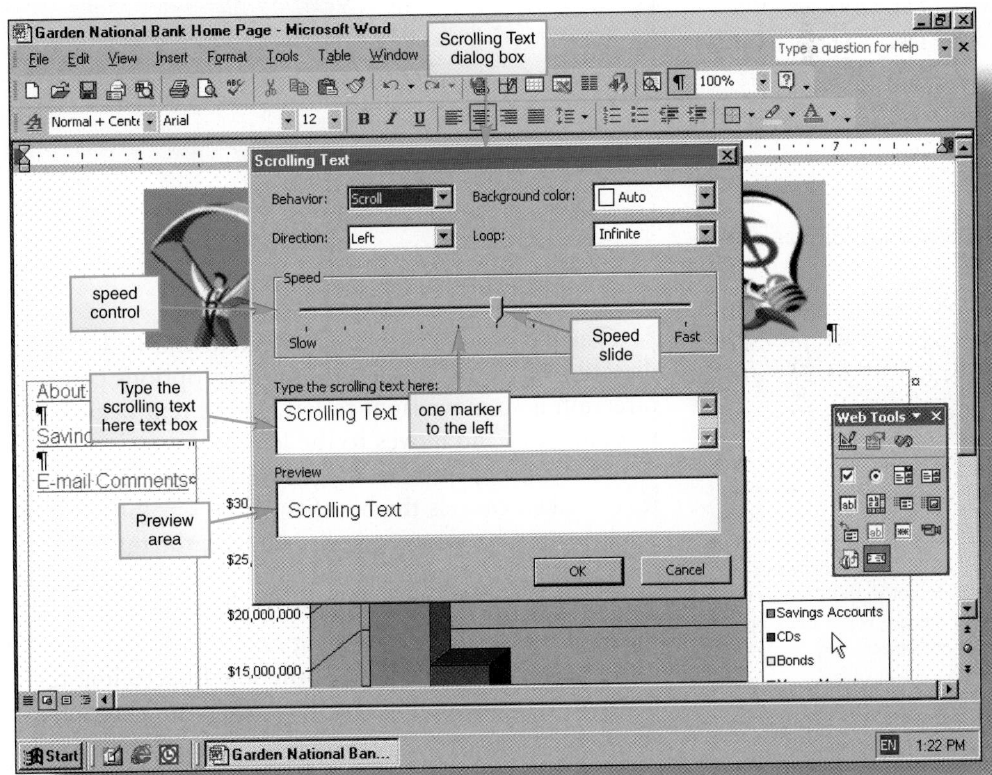

FIGURE 1-21

2 **Click the Behavior box arrow and then click Slide in the list.**

3 **Drag through the text, Scrolling Text, in the Type the scrolling text here text box. Type** `2533 Main Street, Anton, IL 60323 (630) 555-3939` **as the scrolling text.**

4 **Drag the Speed slide one speed marker to the left and then click the OK button.**

The scrolling text displays (Figure 1-22).

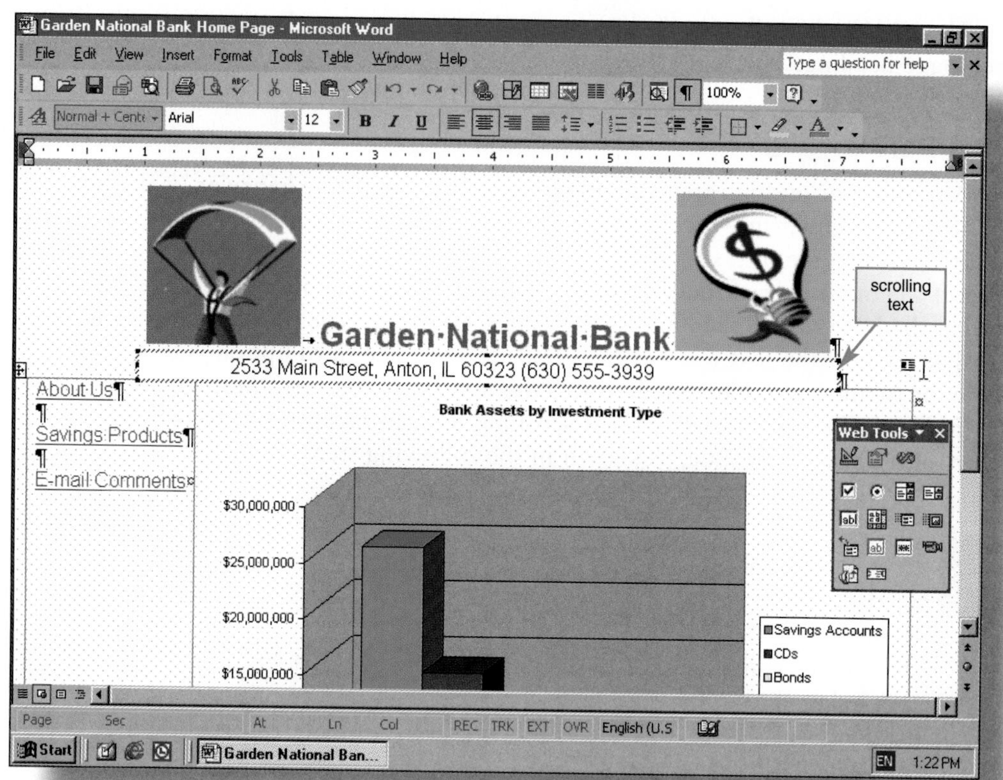

FIGURE 1-22

Scrolling Text

To format the text, use the Font command on the Format menu while you are in Design mode. You turn off Design mode to see the results. In browsers that do not support scrolling text, the text will display but it will not be scrolling.

The **direction** of the text movement can be left to right or right to left. The direction attribute in the scrolling text options controls this movement. The default direction is to move right to left, so the text begins in the right margin of the line of scrolling text and moves to the left.

The **speed** of the scrolling text also can be varied from slow to fast. Scrolling the text too fast cancels the benefits of the scrolling text. If the Web page visitor cannot read the text because it scrolls too fast, the text serves no purpose.

Other options that can be controlled in scrolling text are background colors and the number of times to loop the scrolling text. The **background** attribute determines the color of the line of scrolling text. The background default is a transparent background, so the background of the line of scrolling text displays the background color of whatever is behind it. The **loop** attribute determines the number of times that the scrolling text moves across the Web page. The default is an infinite loop, which means the text will scroll indefinitely, but the loop can be set to a specific number of times.

The default direction, background color, and loop are used for the scrolling text that is inserted into the Word document. Slide was selected as the behavior for the scrolling text. Because of that, the text scrolls from the right margin and stops scrolling when it reaches the left margin. The next section explains how to resize the scrolling text.

Resizing the Scrolling Text

The default for scrolling text is to move the text all the way across the Web page from the right margin of the page to the left margin. Sometimes, it is better to shorten the distance of the scrolling text. In this project, the scrolling text is centered below the Garden National Bank heading of the Word document. The Web page visitor sees the company name with address and telephone number information below it. The Design Mode is used in this project to change the size of the scrolling text. In general, **Design Mode** allows you to rearrange and design the page in a user-friendly manner.

Perform the following steps to change the size of the scrolling text.

To Resize the Scrolling Text

1 Click the Design Mode button on the Web Tools toolbar.

2 If necessary, click anywhere within the scrolling text box to select the text. Point to the center sizing handle on the right side of the text box.

The text box displays as shown in Figure 1-23.

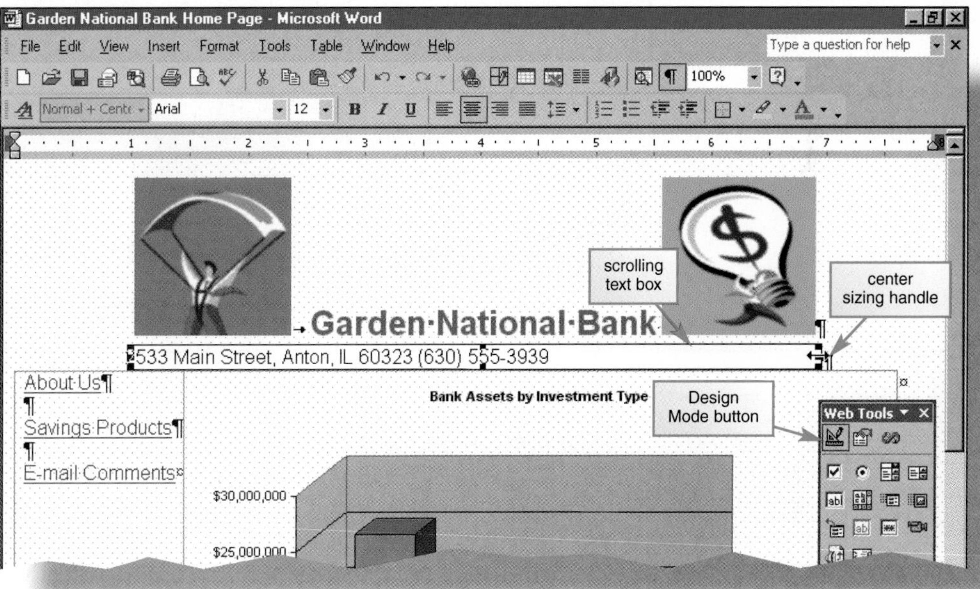

FIGURE 1-23

3 Drag the center sizing handle to the left, so that it is positioned approximately as shown in Figure 1-24.

The dotted line shows the proposed size for the scrolling text.

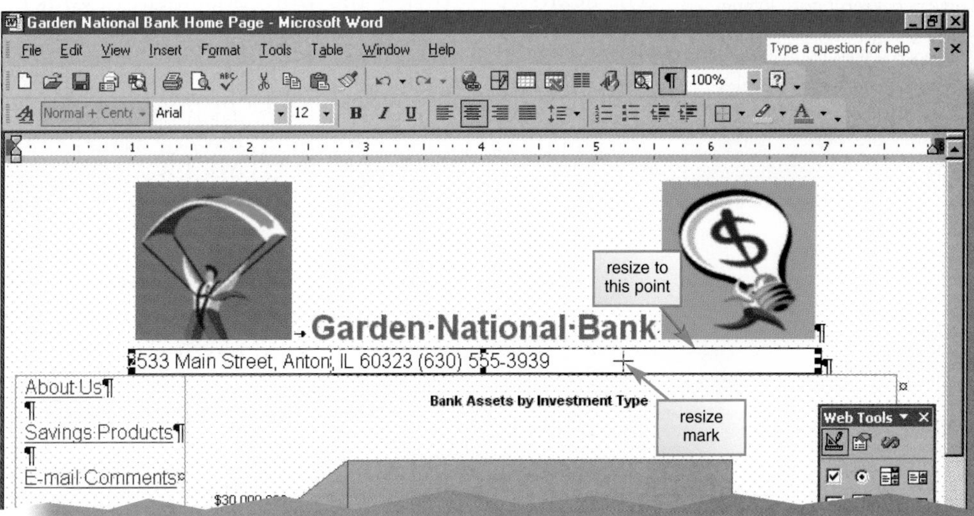

FIGURE 1-24

4 **Release the mouse button.**

The scrolling text box is resized (Figure 1-25).

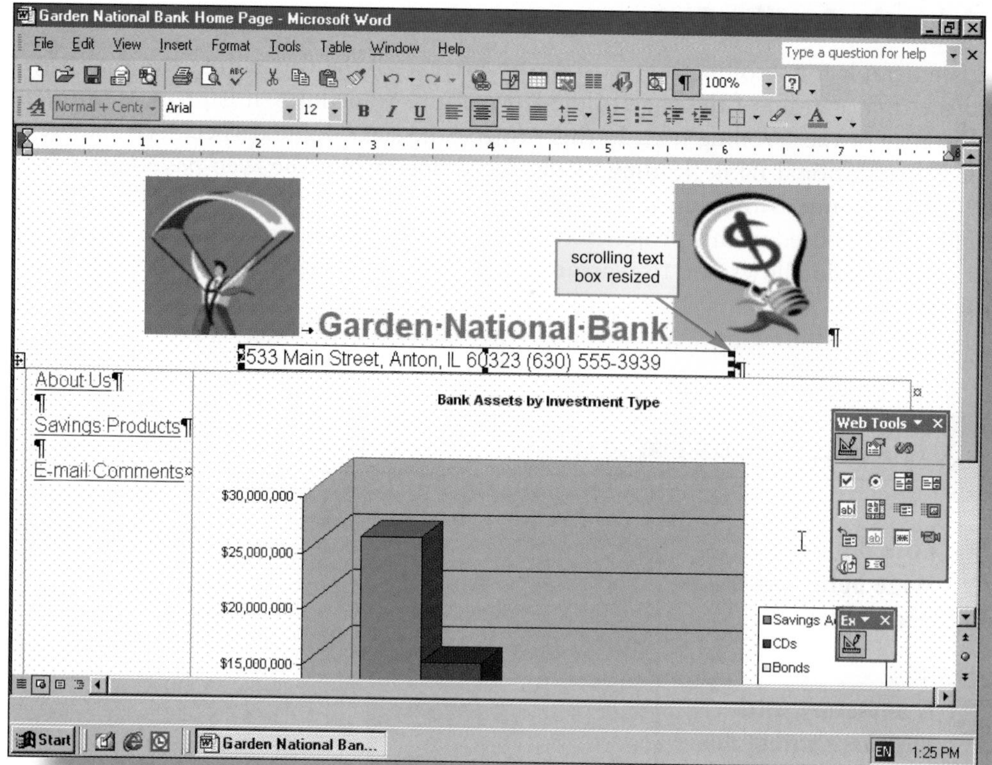

FIGURE 1-25

More About

Web Page Formatting

Because Word provides formatting options that most Web browsers do not support, some text and graphics may look different when you view them on a Web page. When creating documents for the Web, using Web layout view will ensure that your graphics look the way you want them to when they are viewed as Web pages in a Web browser.

The home page for the Garden National Bank Web site is complete. The Web page should be viewed in your browser to verify that it is correct.

Viewing the Word Document in Your Browser and Saving It as a Web Page

The next step is to view the Word document in your browser to verify that all information is accurate. After verifying its accuracy, you then can save the Word document as an HTML file. Saving the Word document as an HTML file makes it possible for it to be viewed using a browser, such as Internet Explorer.

Perform the following steps to preview the document in your browser and then save the Word document as an HTML file.

Steps To Preview the Web Page

1 Click File on the menu bar and then point to Web Page Preview.

2 Click Web Page Preview. If necessary, click the Maximize button on your browser's title bar.

The Web page displays (Figure 1-26).

3 Click the browser's Close button.

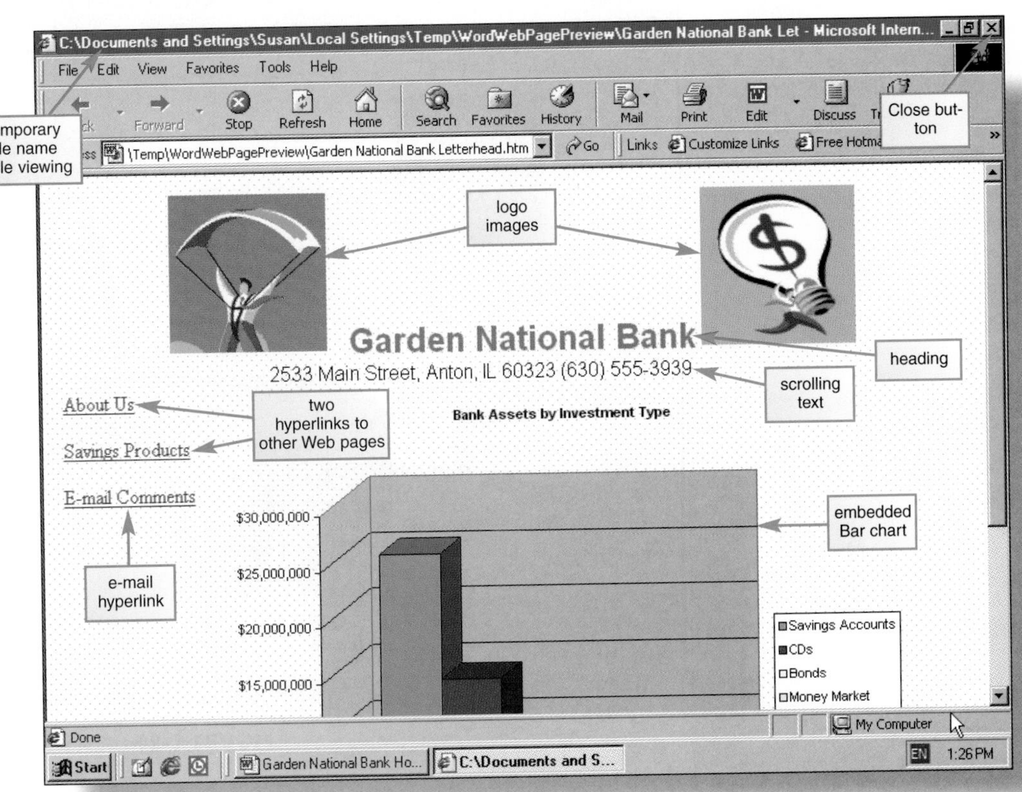

FIGURE 1-26

Other Ways

1. Press ALT+F, B
2. In Voice Command mode say, "File, Web Page Preview"

Verify that the Web page contains all information necessary and displays as shown in Figure 1-26. The Web page consists of a heading with an image and the company name. Below that is a single line of scrolling text that scrolls in from the right margin and stops when it reaches the left margin. Next is a borderless table with three hyperlinks in the left column and a Bar chart in the right column. The E-mail Comments hyperlink should work appropriately when you click it, displaying a new message. The other two links, About Us and Savings Products, do not work because the corresponding Web pages are not available until later in this project.

If the Web page is correct, save it on the Integration Data Disk as an HTML file. If changes need to be made to the Web page, return to the Word document and correct it. Perform the following steps to save the document as a Web page.

TO SAVE A DOCUMENT WITH A NEW FILE NAME

1. Click File on the menu bar and then click Save As Web page.
2. Type GNBHome in the File name text box.
3. If necessary, click the Save in box arrow and then click 3½ Floppy (A:) in the Save in list.
4. Click the Save button in the Save As dialog box.

The GNBHome Web page displays in the Word window (Figure 1-27 on the next page).

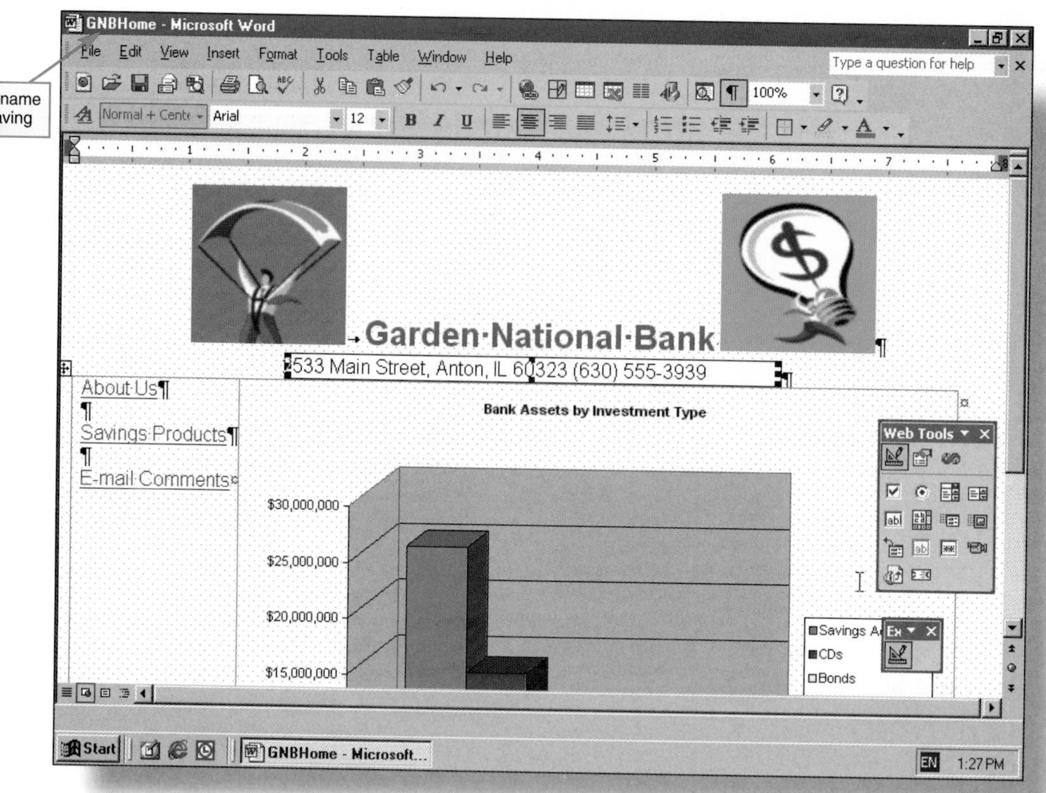

FIGURE 1-27

More About

Web Programming Languages

A number of programming languages can be used to create Web pages. Web pages created using the Save as Web Page command on the File menu can be enhanced with other Web programming languages, such as ASP, DHTML, and JavaScript.

Saving an existing Word document as a Web page allows you quickly to get a Word document ready for copying to the Web or to an intranet. One alternative to this is to directly write the hypertext markup language (HTML) to develop the Web pages. **HTML** is a programming language used for Web page creation. The home page created earlier in this project could be created by writing HTML tags (code). For documents that already are in Word format, the easier method is to use the Word's Save as Web Page command. This essentially creates the HTML code for you and saves it in a file. Perform the following step to quit Word.

TO QUIT WORD

 1 Click the Close button on the Microsoft Word title bar.

The next step in creating the Web site for Garden National Bank is to save a PowerPoint presentation as an HTML file. The following sections describe how to open a PowerPoint presentation, add a hyperlink to the first page, and save the presentation as an HTML file.

Creating a PowerPoint Presentation Web Page

PowerPoint is a powerful software tool often used to assist in the presentation of information to groups of people. **PowerPoint 2002** allows you to create Web pages from an existing PowerPoint presentation, using the Save as Web Page command. The presentation then can be viewed using your browser.

The PowerPoint presentation used in this project consists of three slides (Figure 1-1g on page I 1.07). The first page is a title slide, containing the bank name and graphics. The second slide contains information about the Garden National Bank staff, with names and job responsibilities. The last slide contains information about the Garden National Bank's savings product lines. This information can be used in its present format to enhance a presentation about the bank. As Web pages, you can use this presentation to address a much wider, global audience on the World Wide Web.

Perform the following steps to open an existing PowerPoint presentation.

TO START POWERPOINT, CUSTOMIZE POWERPOINT, AND OPEN AN EXISTING PRESENTATION

1. Click the Start button on the Windows taskbar and then click Open Office Document on the Start menu.
2. Click the Look in box arrow and then click 3½ Floppy (A:) in the Look in list.
3. Double-click the Garden National Presentation name.
4. If the Language bar displays, click its Minimize button.
5. If the Standard and Formatting toolbars display on one row, click the Toolbar Options button on the right side of either toolbar and then click Show Buttons on Two Rows on the Toolbar Options menu.

The first slide of the PowerPoint presentation displays (Figure 1-28).

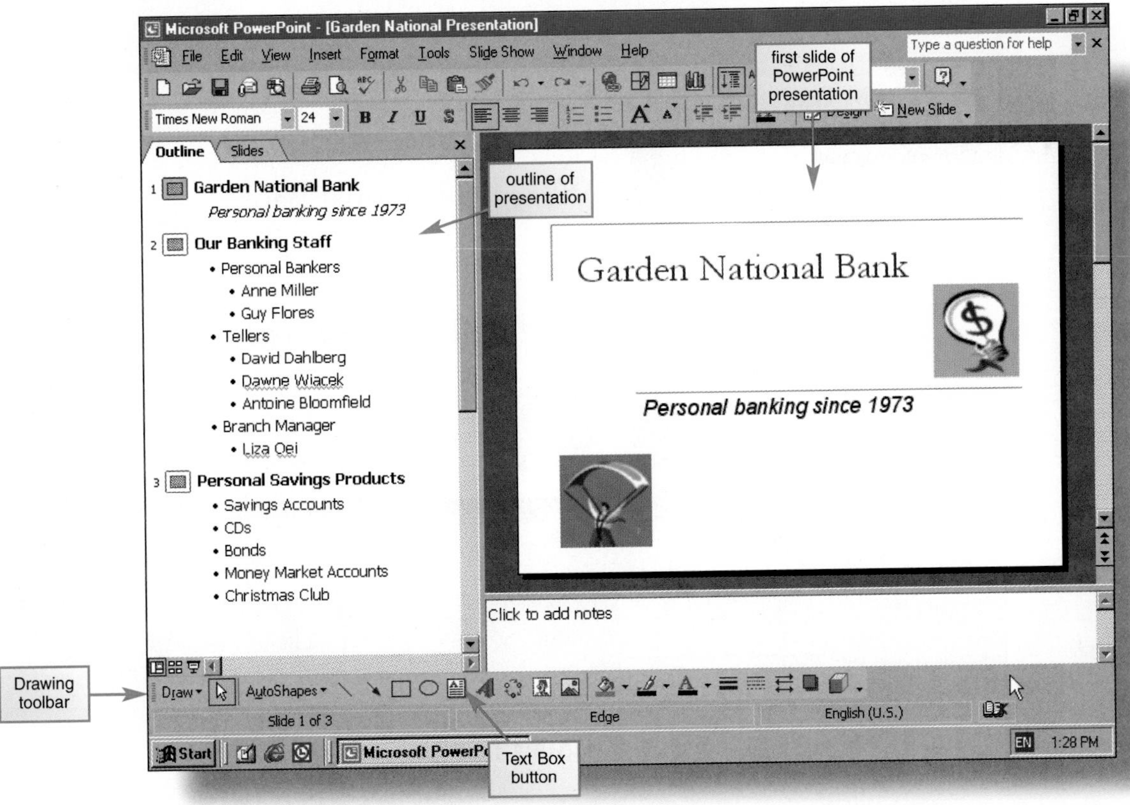

FIGURE 1-28

The PowerPoint presentation now is open. The next step is to add a hyperlink on the first page of the presentation that allows the Web page visitor to return to the Garden National Bank home page.

Keeping Links Fresh

When you create a Web page, it is important to make sure that all of your hyperlinks are functional as time goes on. Links to other pages can become stale, or non-functional, if another Web page creator or an external site takes a page offline. Automated tools can help you identify when pages to which you are hyperlinking no longer are available.

Adding Text for a Hyperlink

One of the more important features of Web sites is their capability of linking from one Web page to another using hyperlinks. In earlier steps in this project, you added three hyperlinks to the Garden National Bank home page. Once Web page visitors link to the PowerPoint Web pages, however, they cannot return to the home page without using the Back button on the browser's toolbar. This is not a convenient way for Web page visitors to navigate through the Web site. In this section, you will add a Home link to the first slide of the PowerPoint presentation (Figure 1-1e on page I 1.07).

Perform the following steps to add the text that will be used as a hyperlink on the PowerPoint Web page.

TO ADD TEXT FOR A HYPERLINK INTO A POWERPOINT PRESENTATION

1. Click the Text Box button on the Drawing toolbar.
2. Click in the lower-right corner of the first page of the PowerPoint presentation.
3. Type `Home` as the hyperlink text.

The text box displays (Figure 1-29).

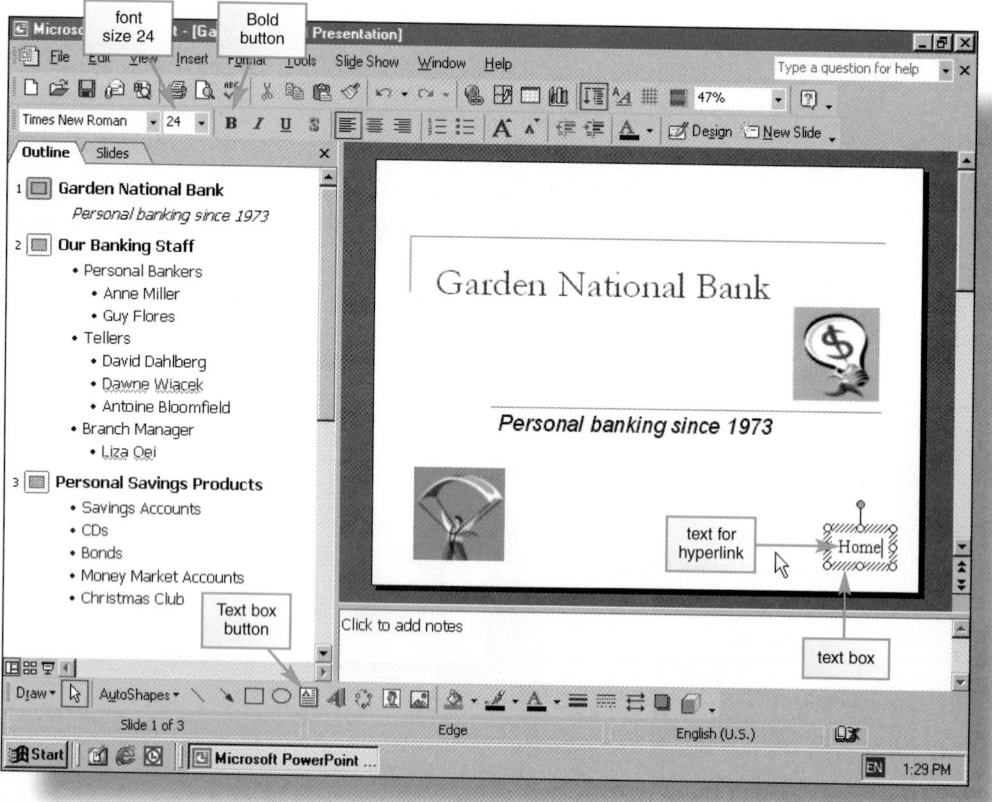

FIGURE 1-29

1. On Insert menu click Text Box
2. Press ALT+I, X
3. In Voice Command mode say, "Insert, Text Box"

Creating a Hyperlink

After you enter the text for the hyperlink, you can create the hyperlink itself. When clicked, the hyperlink jumps to the Garden National Bank home page created previously in this project and saved on drive A. To create the hyperlink, you will use the Insert Hyperlink button on the Standard toolbar.

Perform the following steps to create the PowerPoint hyperlink.

Steps To Insert a Hyperlink into a PowerPoint Presentation

1. **Double-click the word, Home, inside the text box you just inserted.**

2. **If necessary, click the Font Size box arrow and then click 24. Click the Bold button on the Formatting toolbar.**

3. **Click the Insert Hyperlink button on the Standard toolbar.**

4. **If necessary, click the Existing File or Web Page button on the Link to bar. Type** `a:\GNBHome.htm` **in the Address text box. Click the OK button.**

Slide 1 of the presentation displays as shown in Figure 1-30.

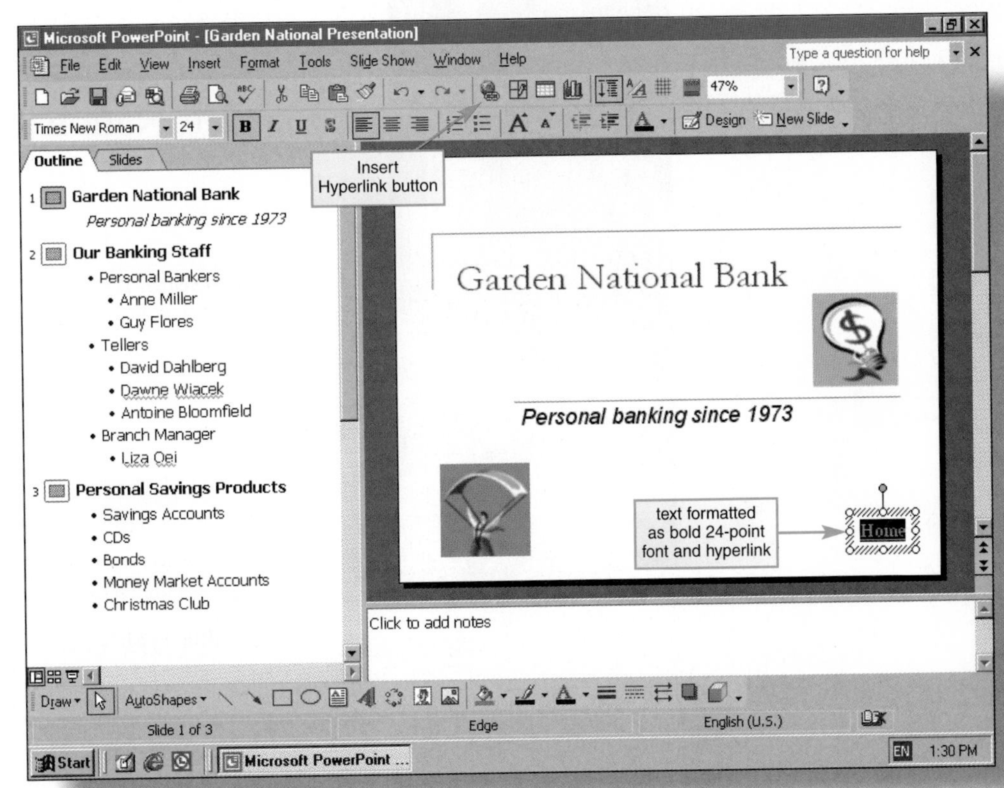

FIGURE 1-30

Other Ways

1. On Insert menu click Hyperlink
2. Right-click highlighted word, click Hyperlink on shortcut menu
3. Press CTRL+K
4. In Voice Command mode say, "Hyperlink"

Viewing and Saving the PowerPoint Web Page

Just as you did in the previous section of this project, view the Web page before saving it. It is important to verify all of the Web page navigation features before you save the file.

TO VIEW THE WEB PAGE IN YOUR BROWSER

1. Click File on the menu bar and then point to Web Page Preview.
2. Click Web Page Preview.
3. If necessary, click the Maximize button on your browser's title bar.

The PowerPoint Web page displays (Figure 1-31 on the next page).

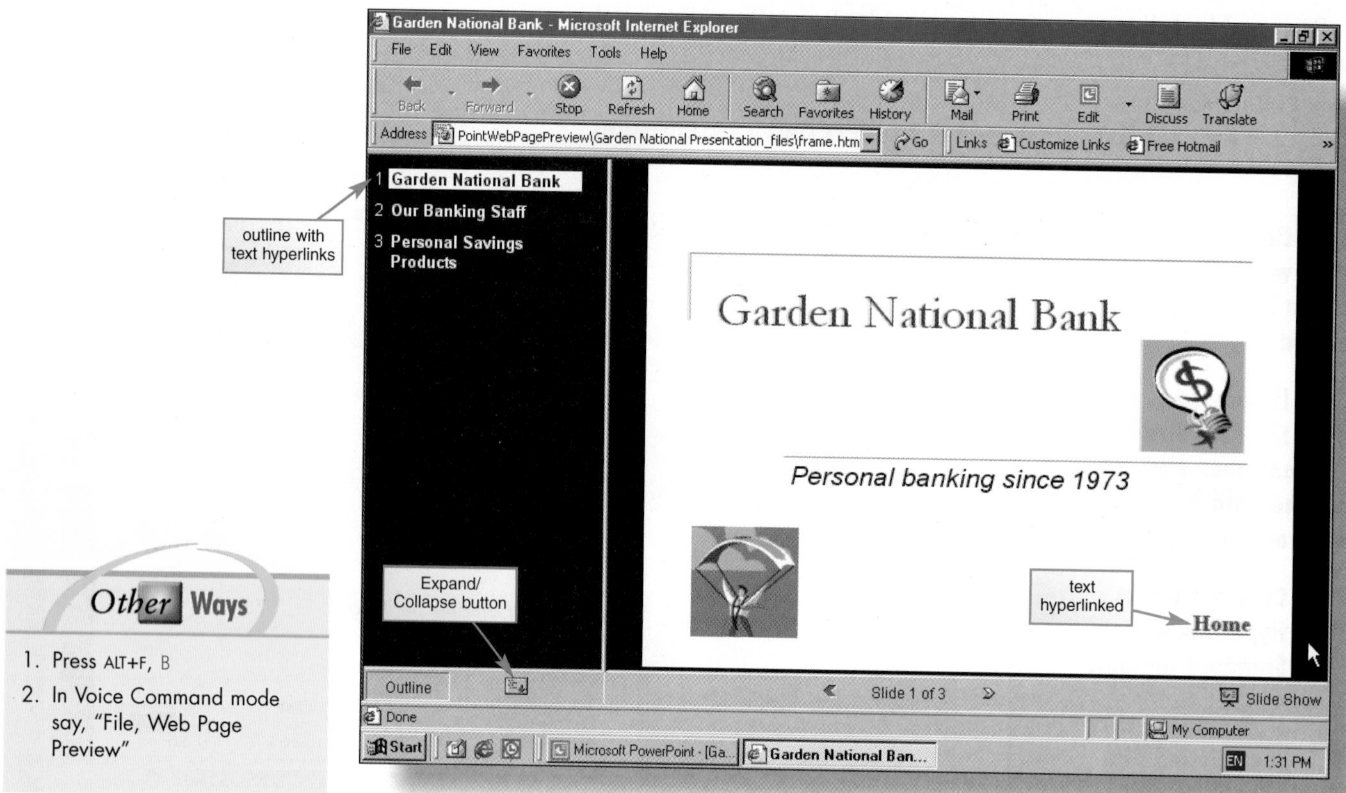

Other Ways

1. Press ALT+F, B
2. In Voice Command mode say, "File, Web Page Preview"

FIGURE 1-31

More About

Outline

The outline pane is displayed by default when you view a presentation in a browser. To hide this pane, click the Outline button while in the browser. Click the Outline button again to redisplay the outline pane.

Slide 1 of the PowerPoint presentation Web page contains a hyperlink to the home page of the Garden National Bank Web site. Although you created this hyperlink by adding a text box to the first slide, you also can create hyperlinks from existing text or images in a PowerPoint presentation. For example, one of the logo images on slide 1 could be used as a hyperlink to the home page of the Web site. Using one of those images, however, does not give the Web page visitor a clear idea of where the hyperlink will lead. It is more appropriate to create a hyperlink to the home page from text — for example, Home — that makes sense to the visitor.

In addition to any hyperlinks that are added to the presentation, PowerPoint automatically creates hyperlinks in the left column of the Web page, called the **outline**. This outline can be expanded or collapsed using the **Expand/Collapse Outline button** below the outline pane and is used to navigate through the Web page presentation (Figure 1-31). The text in the heading of each slide is used as the phrases for these hyperlinks. When you click a link, you jump to that particular slide within the presentation. The ease of navigation within a PowerPoint Web page is valuable to the Web page visitor.

As well as being able to add your own hyperlink text, PowerPoint provides some ready-made action buttons that you can insert into your Web pages. **Action buttons** contain shapes, such as left and right arrows, that can be used to hyperlink to other Web pages within the presentation. You can insert symbols on the action buttons for going to the next (right arrow), previous (left arrow), first (beginning arrow), and last (end arrow) slides. PowerPoint also includes action buttons for playing movies or sounds. You insert these action buttons using the slide master feature of PowerPoint.

Saving the PowerPoint Presentation as a Web Page

The next step is to save the PowerPoint presentation as a Web page. When you save a PowerPoint presentation as a Web page, the Web page is saved in a default folder. All supporting files, such as backgrounds and images, are organized in this folder automatically. The name of the PowerPoint slide show opened in this section is Garden National Presentation. PowerPoint uses the name of the saved Web page and adds the string, files, for the name of the new folder. When the current presentation is saved as a Web page, the folder name that PowerPoint Web creates is AboutUs_files. The default name for the first slide in the presentation is frame.htm. The structure used in the folder organization makes Web page publishing easier because you can keep track of all of the files associated with the Web page. You also can edit the files manually, rather than using PowerPoint.

Perform the steps below to save the PowerPoint presentation as a Web page.

> **More About**
>
> **Web Page Publishing**
>
> The Web pages created in this project all are stored locally on your computer. Typically, a Web page must be published to a server inside the organization or at your ISP. Microsoft offers a Web Page Publishing Wizard to assist in moving all of the related files and directories that comprise a Web site.

TO SAVE THE POWERPOINT PRESENTATION AS A WEB PAGE

1. Click the Microsoft PowerPoint button on the taskbar.
2. Click File on the menu bar and then click Save as Web Page.
3. Type `AboutUs` in the File name text box.
4. If necessary, click the Look in box arrow and then click 3½ Floppy (A:) in the Look in list.
5. Click the Save button in the Save As dialog box.

The PowerPoint presentation is saved as a Web page.

The task of saving the PowerPoint presentation as a Web page is complete. The hyperlink has been added to the first page of the presentation that jumps to the Web site home page when clicked. Standard Web page navigation was added automatically to the presentation that allows the Web page visitor to jump to any slide in the Web page presentation. All of the files necessary for the Web page were saved in a folder named AboutUs_files.

After saving the PowerPoint presentation as a Web page, you can quit PowerPoint and close your browser as shown in the following steps.

TO QUIT POWERPOINT AND CLOSE YOUR BROWSER

1. Click the Close button on the PowerPoint title bar.
2. Click the Close button on the browser title bar.

> **More About**
>
> **Viewing Web Pages**
>
> In addition to Microsoft Windows environments, many environments exist for viewing Web pages. When creating a Web page with special features, such as data access pages, it is important to make sure that the special features are supported within the environment in which the Web page viewers operate. For example, users who view Web pages on Apple Macintosh computers may have a different Web page viewing experience.

Creating a Data Access Page from an Access Database

The next step in the Garden National Bank Web site creation is to use an Access database to create a data access page. A **data access page** is a special type of Web page that is designed for viewing and working with data. Similar to a form, a data access page is connected, or bound, directly to an Access database.

Data access pages are used to analyze data, enter and edit data, make projections, and review data. You also can create a chart using the chart component to analyze trends, show patterns, and make comparisons on the data in the database. Then, you can add spreadsheet controls to allow the inclusion of formulas for calculations.

One of the more common purposes of data access pages is for viewing records in a database via a company's intranet or the World Wide Web. Data access pages provide a method to make inquiries of large amounts of data in a selective way. Groups of records can be expanded or collapsed so that Web page visitors can view the data they want to see.

Perform the following steps to open an Access database.

TO START ACCESS AND OPEN AN EXISTING DATABASE

1. Click the Start button on the Windows taskbar. Click Open Office Document on the Start menu.
2. If necessary, click the Look in box arrow and then click 3½ Floppy (A:) in the Look in list.
3. Double-click the Garden National Bank Products database name.
4. If the Language bar displays, click its Minimize button.

Access starts and opens the Garden National Bank Products : Database window (Figure 1-32).

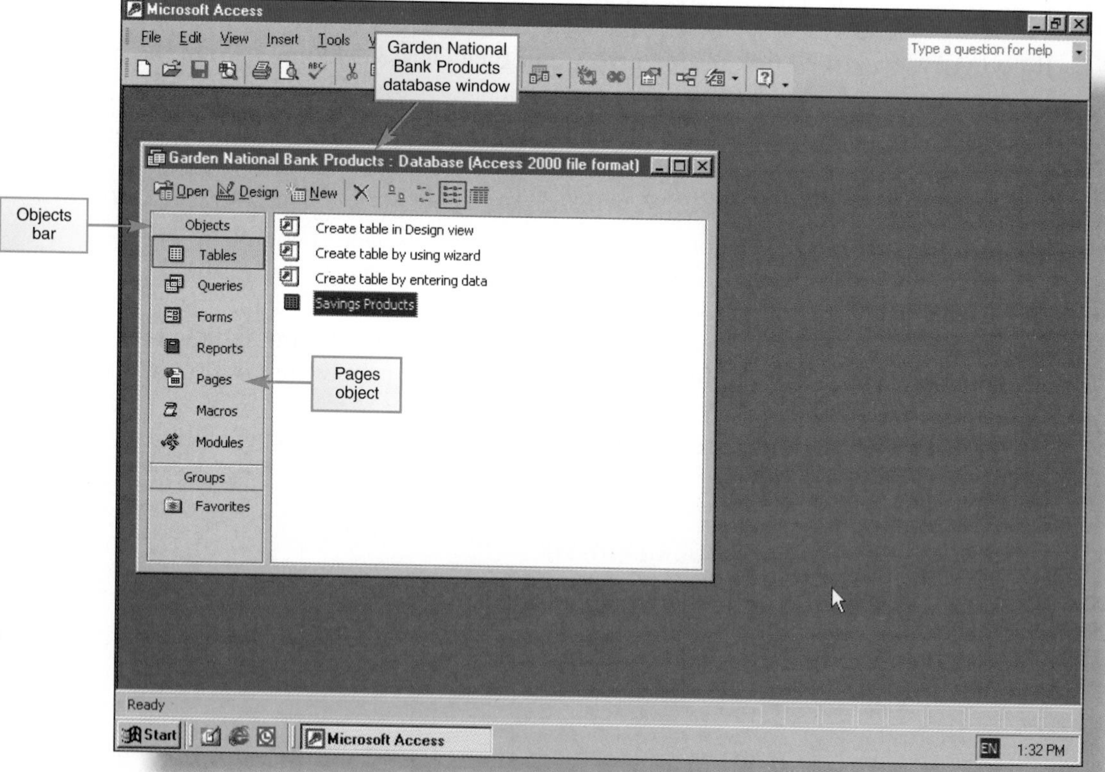

FIGURE 1-32

Creating a Data Access Page Using the Wizard

For the Garden National Bank Web site, you do not want the database to be altered by the Web page visitor in any way. The visitors should be allowed only to view the data. Because of this, you must add a group level to the data access page. Adding **group levels** results in a read-only page. The Web page visitors can view all data and alter that view, but they cannot change the data itself.

Perform the following steps to use the Page Wizard to create a data access page.

Steps To Create a Data Access Page Using the Page Wizard

1 Click the Pages object on the Objects bar.

2 Double-click the Create data access page by using wizard in the list box.

The first Page Wizard dialog box displays (Figure 1-33). The Savings Products table is selected automatically because it is the only table in the database. If more than one table exists, you would need to click the Tables object on the Objects bar and then select the appropriate table before clicking the Pages object in Step 1.

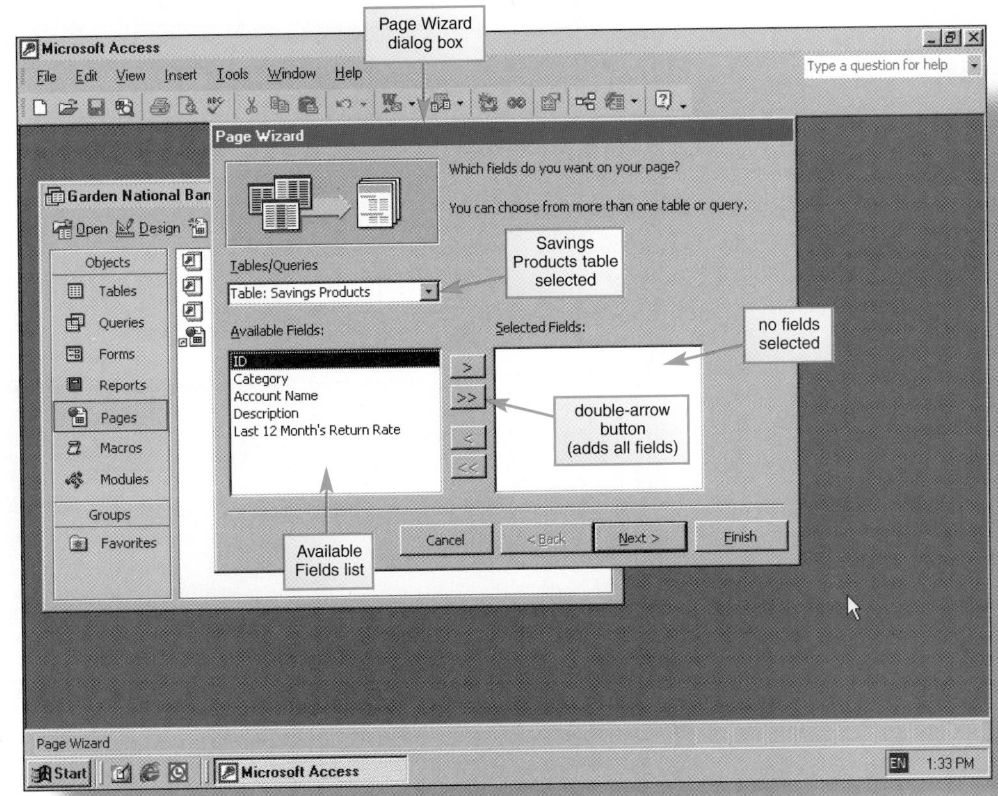

FIGURE 1-33

3 Click the double-arrow button to add all the fields. Point to the Next button.

All the fields in the table are listed in the Selected Fields list (Figure 1-34). This means you want to display all the fields on the data access page.

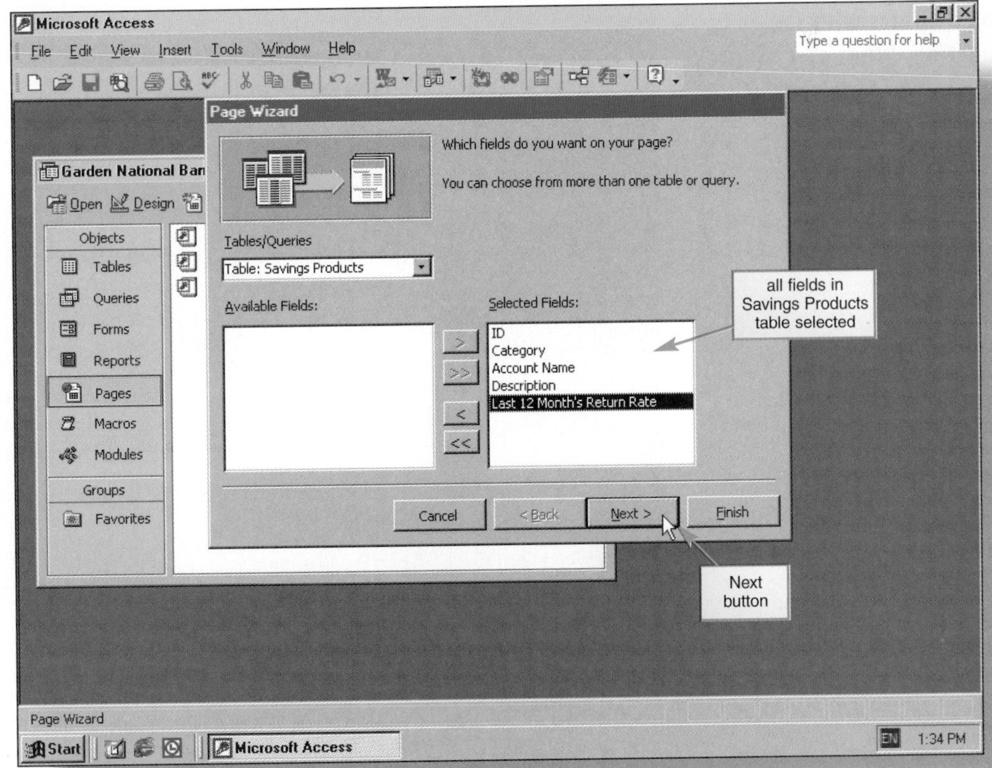

FIGURE 1-34

4 Click the Next button. Double-click Category in the box on the left. Point to the Next button.

Adding a group level, such as Category, prohibits the data access page from being updated. Category displays in the upper-right box indicating it has been selected (Figure 1-35).

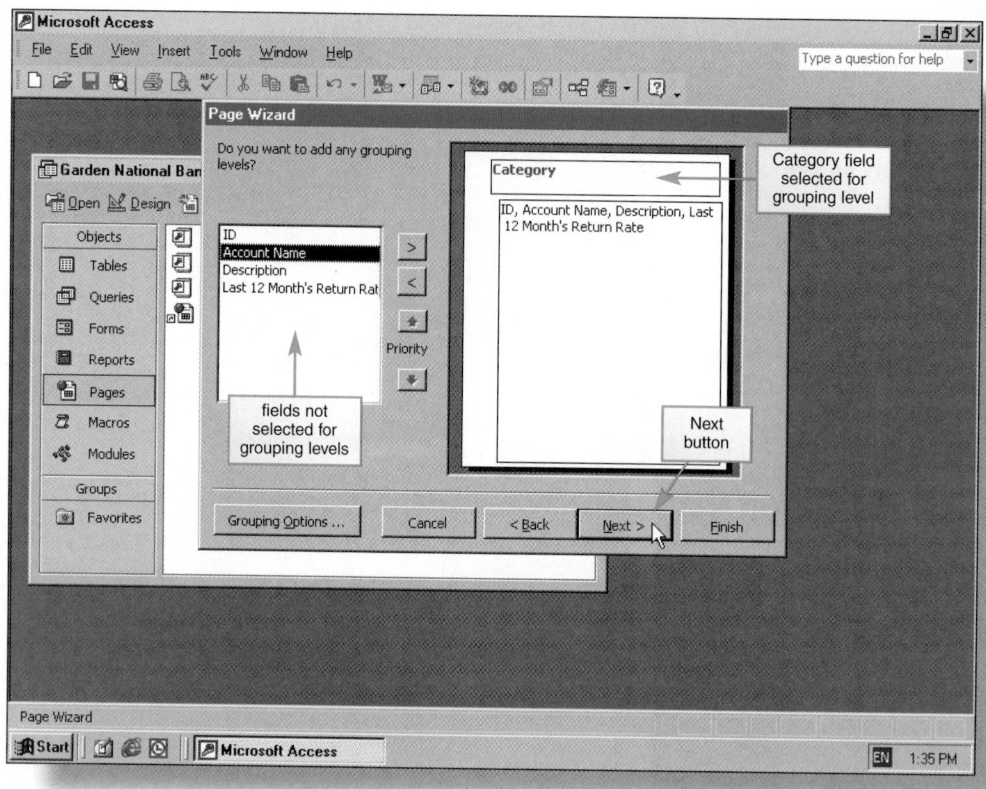

FIGURE 1-35

5 Click the Next button. When the next Page Wizard dialog box displays with the question, What sort order do you want for your records?, point to the Next button.

The next Page Wizard dialog box displays (Figure 1-36).

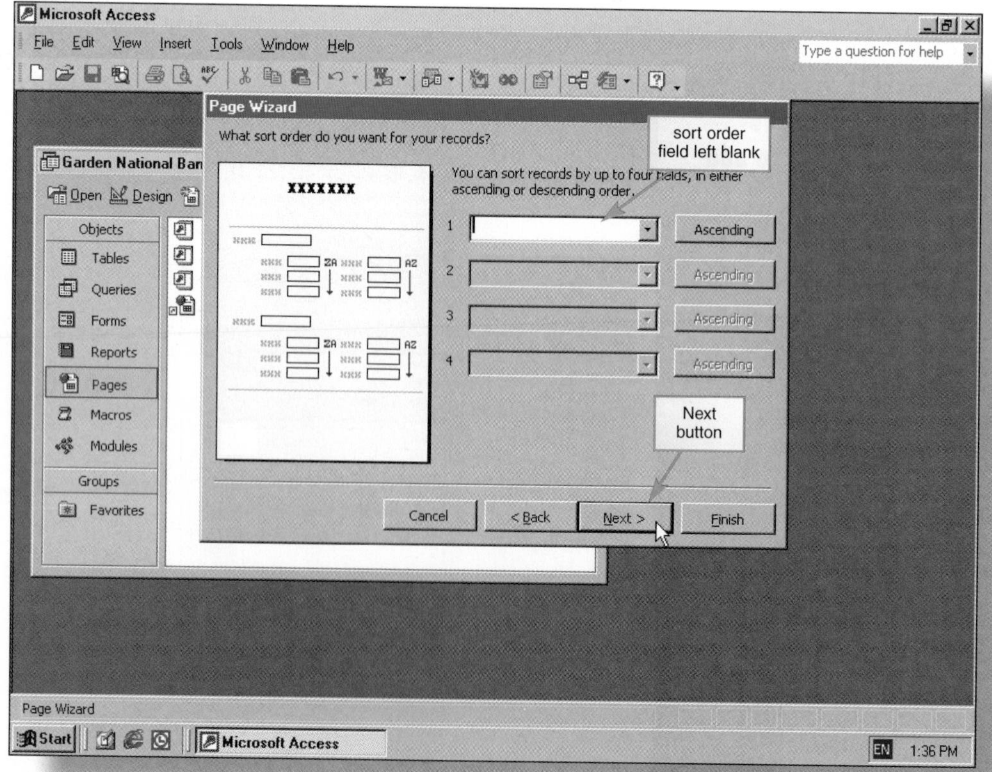

FIGURE 1-36

6 Click the Next button and then type `Savings Products` **in the What title do you want for your page? text box. If necessary, click Modify the page's design to select it. Point to the Finish button.**

The next Page Wizard dialog box displays with the title, Savings Products, in the text box and the Modify the page's design option button selected (Figure 1-37).

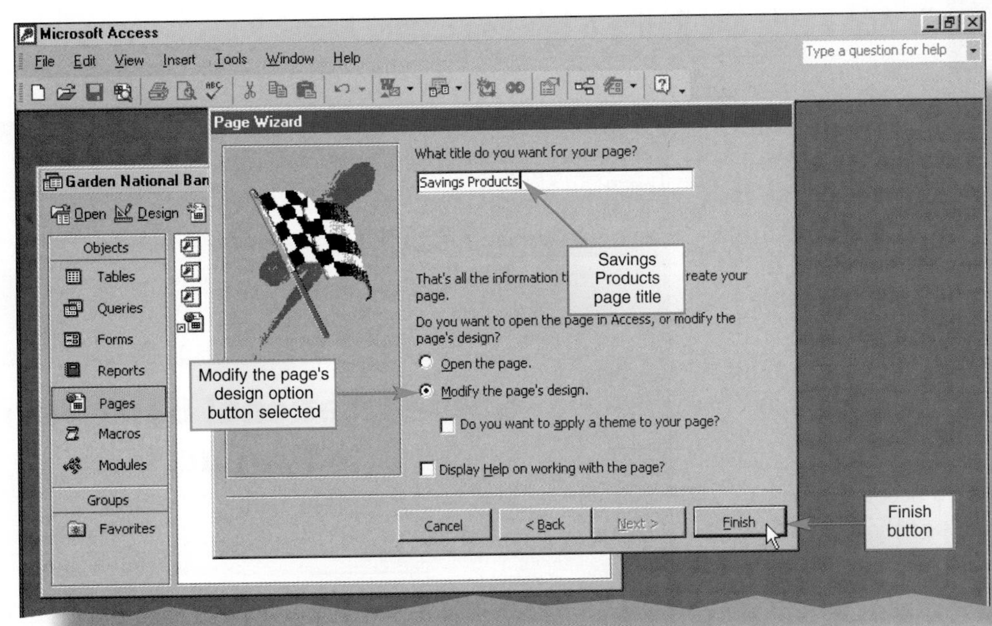

FIGURE 1-37

7 Click the Finish button. If necessary, close the Field List Pane.

Access displays the data access page in Design view (Figure 1-38).

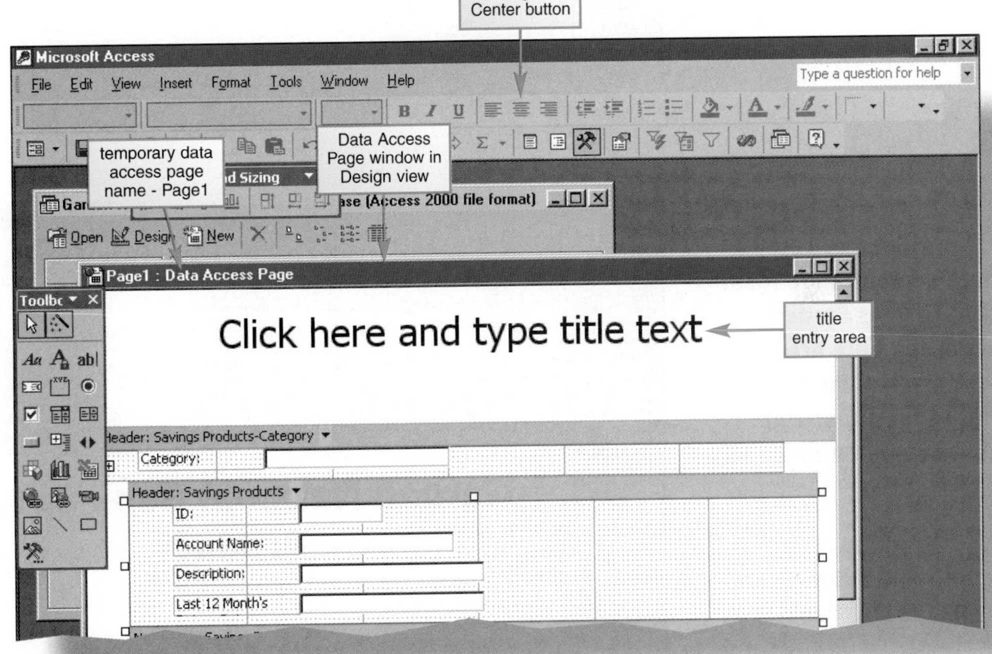

FIGURE 1-38

Adding a Title and Resizing a Label on a Data Access Page

The data access page is created, but additional information can be helpful for the Web page visitor. It is customary to insert a title at the top of the page that tells the visitor the purpose of the Web page. Resizing the Last 12 Month's Return Rate is necessary because the entire text of the label does not show after completing the Data Access Page Wizard. The steps on the next page explain how to add a title and resize a label.

Steps To Add a Title and Resize a Label on a Data Access Page

1 **If necessary, scroll to the top of the data access page. With the data access page in Design view, click anywhere in the Click here and type title text entry area. Type** `Garden National Bank Savings Products` **as the title.**

The data access page displays as shown in Figure 1-39.

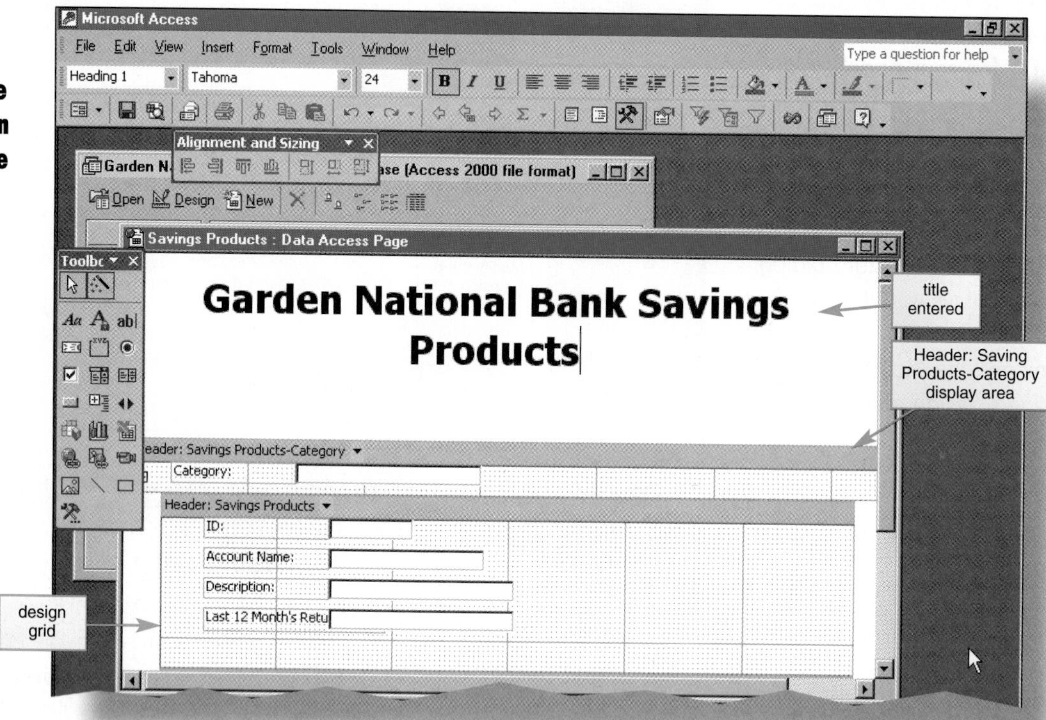

FIGURE 1-39

2 **Click anywhere within the Last 12 Month's Return Rate label in the Savings Products area of the data access page to select the label. Point to the lower-right sizing handle on the label.**

3 **Drag the resize handle straight down so that it doubles in height.**

4 **Release the mouse button.**

The Last 12 Month's Return Rate label is resized, and the data access page displays as shown in Figure 1-40.

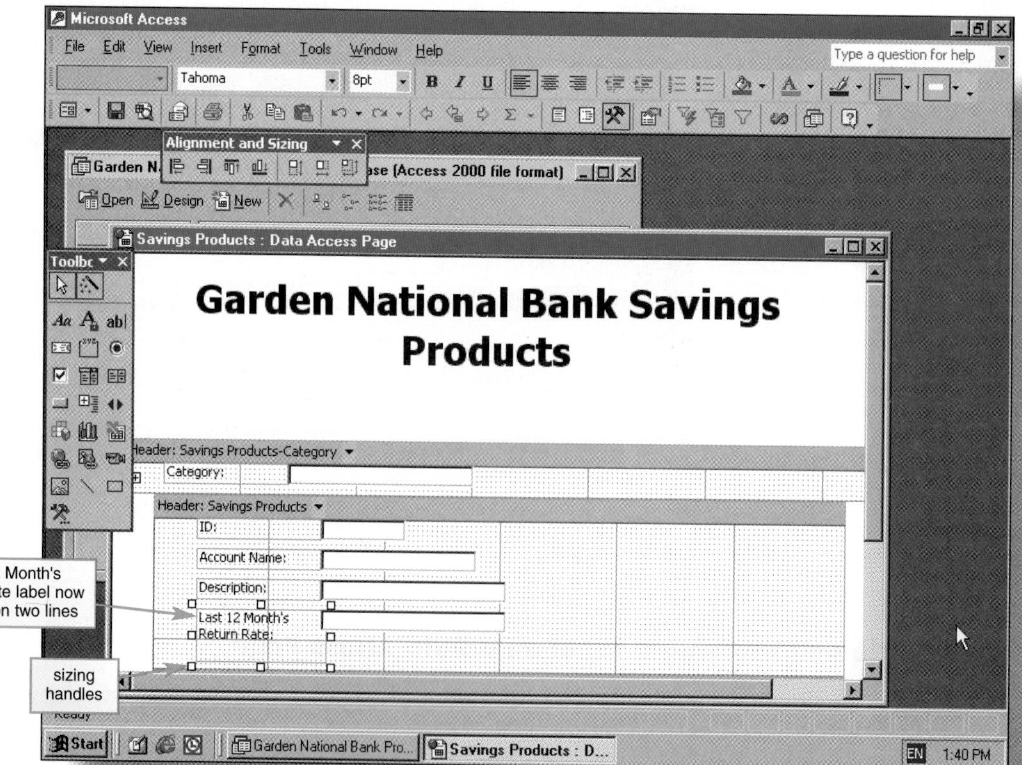

FIGURE 1-40

The data access page is created, a heading is positioned in the header, and the label is resized as shown in Figure 1-1d on page I 1.06. The next step is to add a hyperlink that returns the visitor to the Web site home page.

Data Access Pages

In addition to using Data access pages in a browser, you also can work with a data access page in Page view in Microsoft Access. Data access pages can supplement the forms and reports that you use in your database application. When deciding whether to design a data access page, form, or report, consider the tasks you want to perform.

Adding a Hyperlink to a Data Access Page

Just as you did on the PowerPoint Web page, a hyperlink to the home page should be added to the data access page. This allows the Web page visitor to return to the Garden National Bank home page without having to repeatedly click the Back button on the browser's toolbar. Perform the following steps to add a hyperlink to the data access page.

To Add a Hyperlink into a Data Access Page

1 If necessary, click View on the menu bar and then click Toolbox to display the Toolbox. Scroll down so the bottom of the data access page displays. Click the Hyperlink button on the Toolbox and then point below the Design grid.

The hyperlink mouse pointer displays as shown in Figure 1-41.

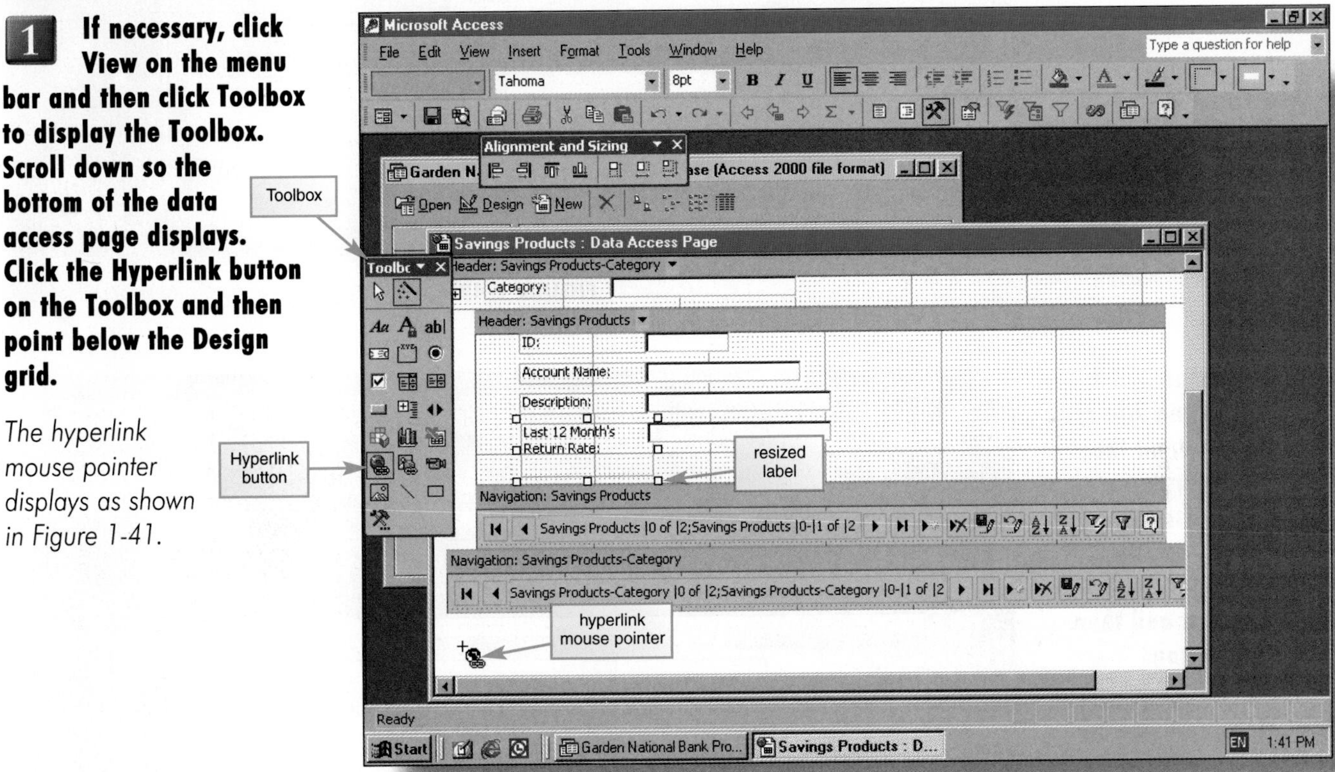

FIGURE 1-41

2 Click below the Design grid.

The Insert Hyperlink dialog box displays (Figure 1-42).

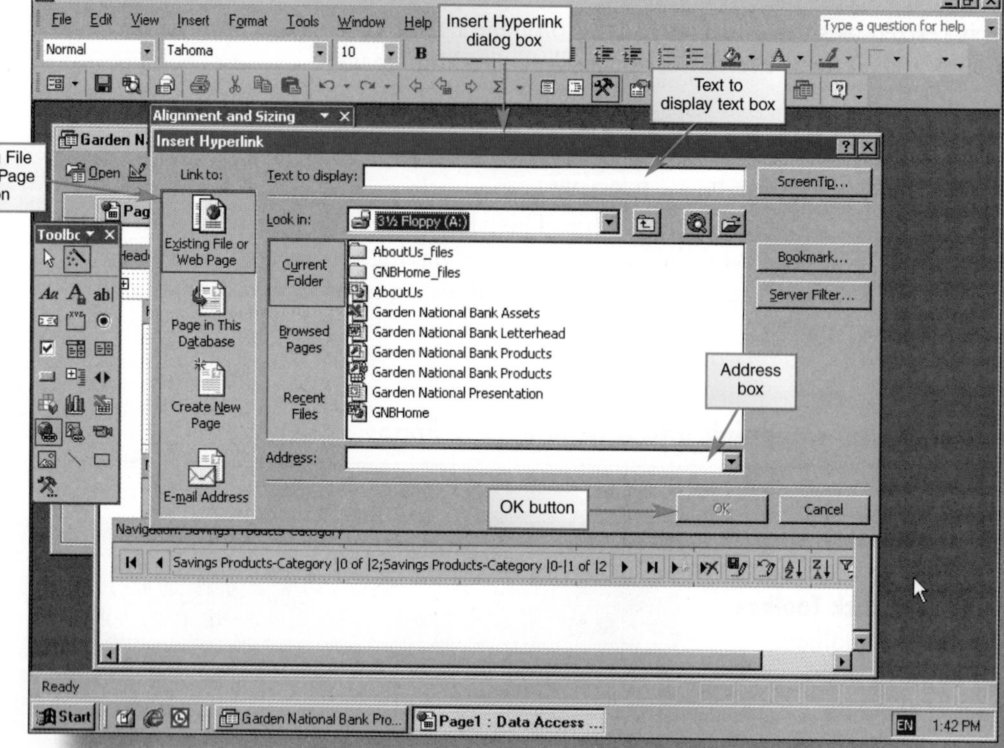

FIGURE 1-42

3 If necessary, click the Existing File or Web Page button on the Link to bar. Type Home **in the Text to display text box. Type** `a:\GNBHome.htm` **in the Address text box and then click the OK button.**

4 Click anywhere on the data access page to deselect the hyperlink box.

The data access page displays as shown in Figure 1-43.

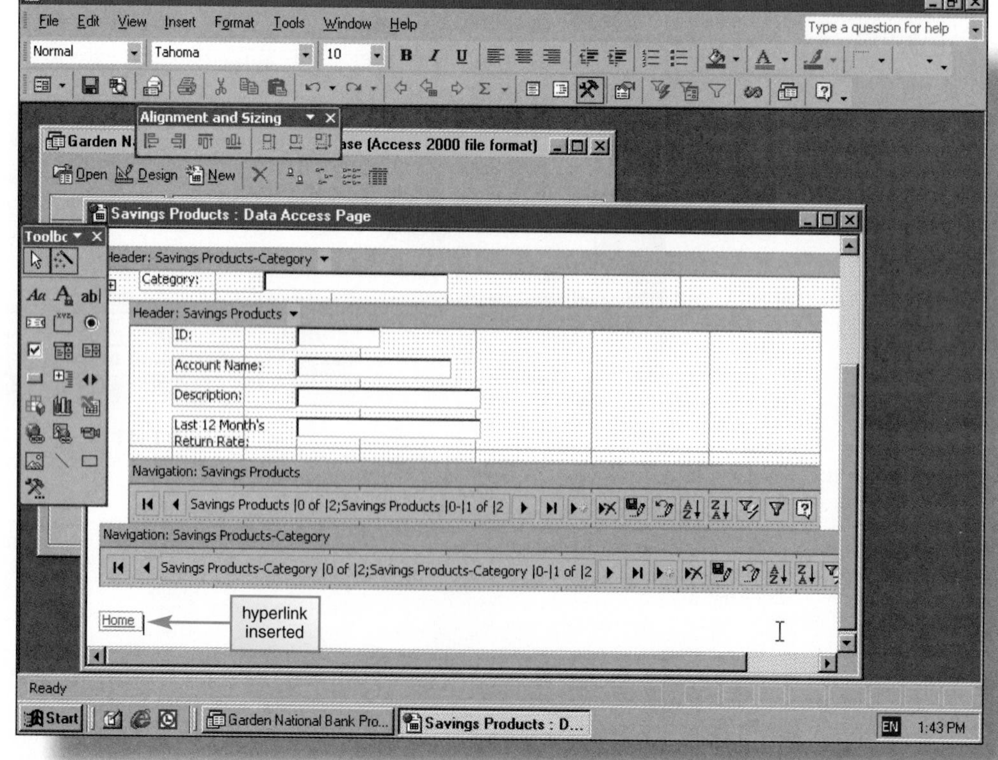

FIGURE 1-43

Other Ways

1. Right-click below Design grid, and in Voice Command mode say, "Hyperlink"

The data access page is complete. In the next section, you will save the page to the Integration Data Disk and view it in the browser.

Database Connections

When a Web page tries to obtain data from a database, such as Access, you must be sure that the database is accessible to the Web page. When publishing Web pages that include Data access pages, you should check with your system administrator to make sure that the Web page will have the proper access to the database.

Saving the Data Access Page and Viewing It

In other sections of this project, you have viewed the Web page, verified that it is correct, and then saved it on a floppy disk. Unlike Word and PowerPoint, you must save a data access page before you can preview it in your browser. As the Web page is being opened in your browser, a Databinding message displays on the status bar of your browser. This indicates that the data access page is connecting to the database that was open when the page was created (Garden National Bank Products).

Perform the following steps to save the file on the Integration Data Disk and then view it in your browser.

TO SAVE THE DATA ACCESS PAGE AND VIEW IT IN YOUR BROWSER

1. Click File on the menu bar and then click Web Page Preview. When the Microsoft Access dialog box displays, click the Yes button.
2. When the Save As Data Access Page dialog box displays, type `SavingsProducts` in the File name text box. If necessary, click 3½ Floppy (A:) in the Look in list.
3. Click the Save button in the Save As Data Access Page dialog box.
4. Click the Expand indicator to the left of the GroupOfProducts-Category to expand the display.

The data access page displays in your browser (Figure 1-44).

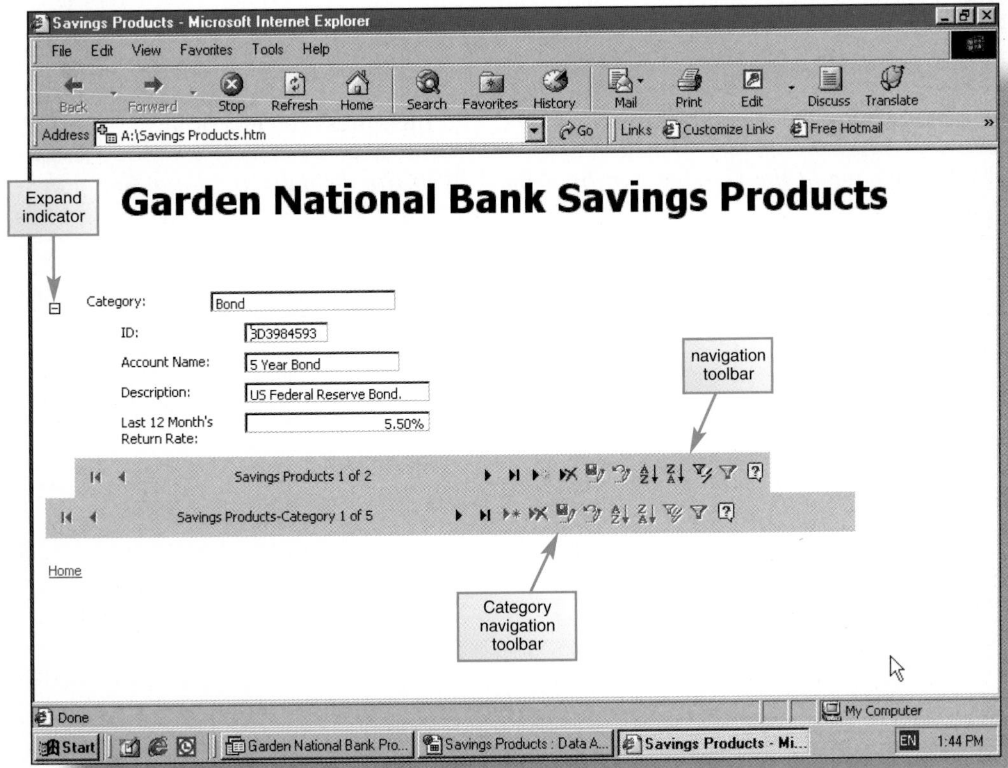

FIGURE 1-44

Once the data access page is saved, you can preview it and then quit Access and close your browser, as shown in the following steps.

TO QUIT ACCESS AND CLOSE YOUR BROWSER

1. Right-click the Garden National Bank Products button on the taskbar and then click Close on the shortcut menu.
2. Click the Close button on the Access title bar to quit Access.

Microsoft Certification

The Microsoft Office User Specialist (MOUS) Certification program provides an opportunity for you to obtain a valuable industry credential — proof that you have the Office XP skills required by employers. For more information, see Appendix E or visit the Shelly Cashman Series MOUS Web page at scsite.com/offxp/cert.htm.

Grouping records on a data access page is similar to grouping records on a report. You can group the data on this data access page in different ways, but the user cannot edit the data. The records in the data access page can be expanded or collapsed, using the Expand and Collapse indicators. This allows users to customize their view of the data and remove extra data from view that may not interest them. Using the **navigation toolbars** on the data access page, you can move, sort, and filter records and obtain Help.

Use the navigation toolbar to verify that the information in the database displays correctly. Click the link to the home page of the Web site to verify it.

Testing the Web Site

The Garden National Bank Web site is complete. To ensure that all the links in the Web site are viable, perform the following steps to open the home page and then thoroughly test the entire Web site.

TO TEST THE WEB SITE

1. Start your browser.
2. Click the Address bar of your browser.
3. Type `a:\GNBHome.htm` in the text box, and then press the ENTER key.

The home page of the Garden National Bank Web site displays as shown in Figure 1-45.

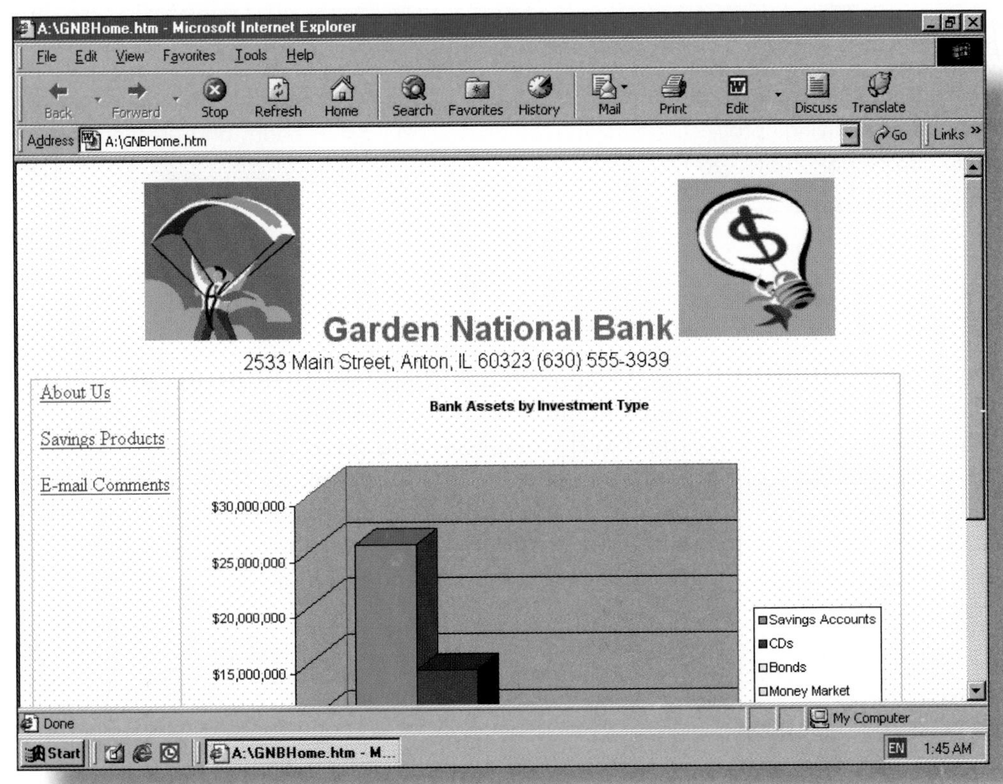

FIGURE 1-45

Verifying the Hyperlinks in Your Browser

All hyperlinks should be tested by clicking them and verifying that they jump to the correct Web page. Three hyperlinks are on the home page: About Us, Savings Products, and E-mail Comments. Perform the following steps to test the links.

TO VERIFY THE HYPERLINKS

1. Click the About Us hyperlink.
2. Click the navigation buttons to view all slides on the Web page.
3. On the first slide on the PowerPoint Web page, click the Home hyperlink.
4. Click the Savings Products hyperlink. Click the Expand and Collapse indicators and then scroll through the database using the navigation toolbars.
5. On the data access page, click the Home hyperlink.
6. Click the E-mail Comments hyperlink.

A new e-mail message displays with manager@isp.com in the To text box.

With the hyperlinks verified, follow these steps to quit the e-mail program and your browser.

TO QUIT E-MAIL AND CLOSE YOUR BROWSER

1. Click the Close button on your e-mail program.
2. Click the Close button on your browser's title bar.

More About

Discussions

The Discussions feature enables you and other people to insert remarks into a Web page. The discussions are threaded; that is, replies to a discussion remark are nested directly below it. You can have multiple discussions in progress simultaneously. You start a discussion from within your browser. The Discussions feature is available only with Microsoft Office Server Extensions, a feature that is set up by a system administrator on a server. Learn more about Discussions in Word Help.

CASE PERSPECTIVE SUMMARY

Liza is very pleased with the new Web site that you helped her create. She thinks it will better educate the community on the benefits of Garden National Bank's savings products and staff. The data access page, chart, and presentation can easily be updated with current information. Now Liza feels better prepared to compete.

Project Summary

This project introduced you to integrating Microsoft Office XP applications. You started this project by opening an existing Word document and creating a two-column, one-row, borderless table. You then inserted three hyperlinks and embedded a Bar chart from an existing Excel worksheet. You saved that document as an HTML file. You then opened an existing PowerPoint presentation and added a hyperlink to the first slide. You saved this presentation as a Web page. Finally, you opened an existing Access database. You used the Page Wizard to create a data access page from that database. You created a group level so that the database could be viewed but not changed. You saved that data access page and viewed and tested all Web pages and hyperlinks in your browser.

What You Should Know

Having completed this project, you now should be able to perform the following tasks.

- Add a Hyperlink into a Data Access Page *(I 1.37)*
- Add a Title and Resize a Label on a Data Access Page *(I 1.36)*
- Add Text for a Hyperlink into a PowerPoint Presentation *(I 1.28)*
- Change the Size of an Embedded Object *(I 1.17)*
- Create a Data Access Page Using the Page Wizard *(I 1.33)*
- Create a Hyperlink to PowerPoint Web Pages *(I 1.12)*
- Display the Web Tools Toolbar *(I 1.20)*
- Embed an Excel Chart into a Word Document *(I 1.14)*
- Insert a Hyperlink into a PowerPoint Presentation *(I 1.29)*
- Insert a Table into a Word Document *(I 1.09)*
- Insert Scrolling Text into a Word Document *(I 1.21)*
- Insert Text for Hyperlinks *(I 1.11)*
- Insert the Remaining Hyperlinks *(I 1.13)*
- Preview the Web Page *(I 1.25)*
- Quit Access and Close Your Browser *(I 1.40)*
- Quit E-mail and Close Your Browser *(I 1.41)*
- Quit Excel *(I 1.19)*
- Quit PowerPoint and Close Your Browser *(I 1.31)*
- Quit Word *(I 1.26)*
- Remove the Table Border *(I 1.10)*
- Resize the Scrolling Text *(I 1.23)*
- Save a Document with a New File Name *(I 1.25)*
- Save the Data Access Page and View It in Your Browser *(I 1.39)*
- Save the PowerPoint Presentation as a Web Page *(I 1.31)*
- Start Access and Open an Existing Database *(I 1.32)*
- Start Excel, Customize Excel, and Open an Existing Workbook *(I 1.14)*
- Start PowerPoint, Customize Powerpoint, and Open an Existing Presentation *(I 1.27)*
- Start Word, Customize Word, Open an Existing Document, and Save the Document with Another Name *(I 1.28)*
- Test the Web Site *(I 1.40)*
- Verify the Hyperlinks *(I 1.41)*
- View the Web Page in Your Browser *(I 1.29)*

In the Lab

1 Creating a Web Page in Word with an Embedded Excel Chart

Problem: As an accountant for Baskin's Heating and Cooling, you have created a worksheet and chart in Excel to analyze the expenses for the past quarter. Create a Web page in Word and embed the chart from the Baskin's Heating and Cooling workbook on the home page. Add a link to a second Web page and an e-mail link to baskinsaccounting@isp.com below the chart. Create a second Web page in Word by embedding the Baskin's Heating and Cooling worksheet.

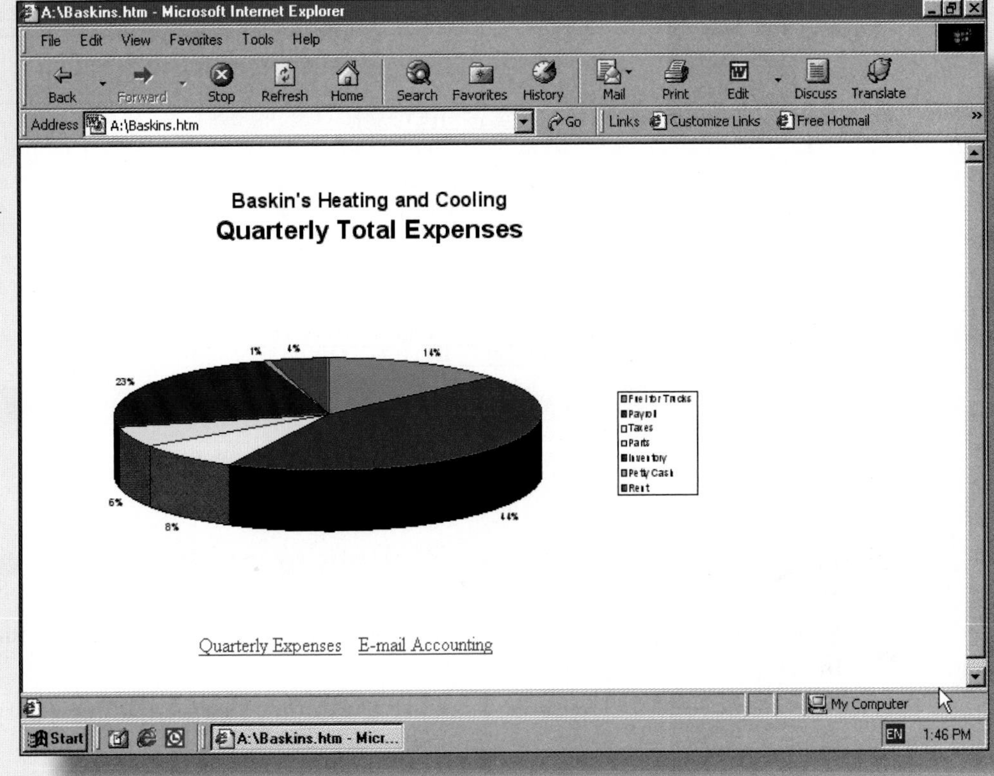

FIGURE 1-46

Instructions: Perform the following tasks.

1. Start Excel by opening the Baskin's Heating and Cooling workbook.
2. Start Word and create a new Web page. Add a title as shown in Figure 1-46. Select the Baskin's Heating and Cooling chart, copy it, and use the Paste Special dialog box in Word to embed the Excel Chart Object.
3. Add two hyperlinks to the bottom of the page in a centered, borderless table. The first hyperlink should jump to the Web page BaskinsExpense.htm, which is created next. The second hyperlink creates an e-mail to baskinsaccounting@isp.com.
4. Save this file as Baskins.htm.
5. Create a new Web page in Word.
6. Embed the Excel worksheet into the Word page. That is, switch to Excel, select the worksheet, copy the worksheet to the Clipboard, switch to Word, and use the Paste Special command on the Edit menu in Word to embed the Excel Worksheet Object.
7. Save this file as BaskinsExpense.htm.
8. View the Baskins.htm file in your browser (Figure 1-46). Print the Web page. Link to the BaskinsExpense.htm page (Figure 1-47 on the next page) and print it.

(continued)

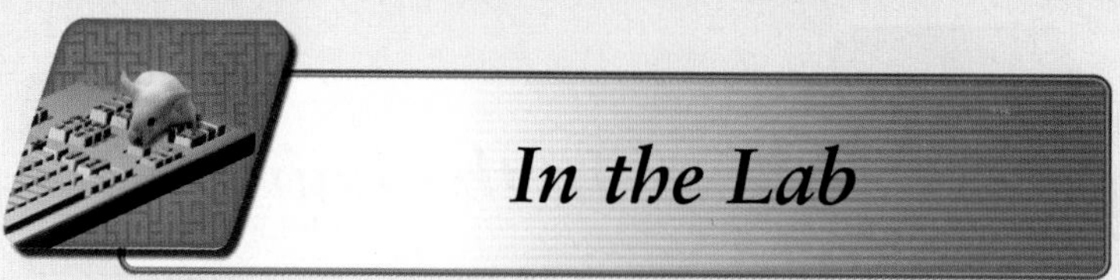

Creating a Web Page in Word with an Embedded Excel Chart *(continued)*

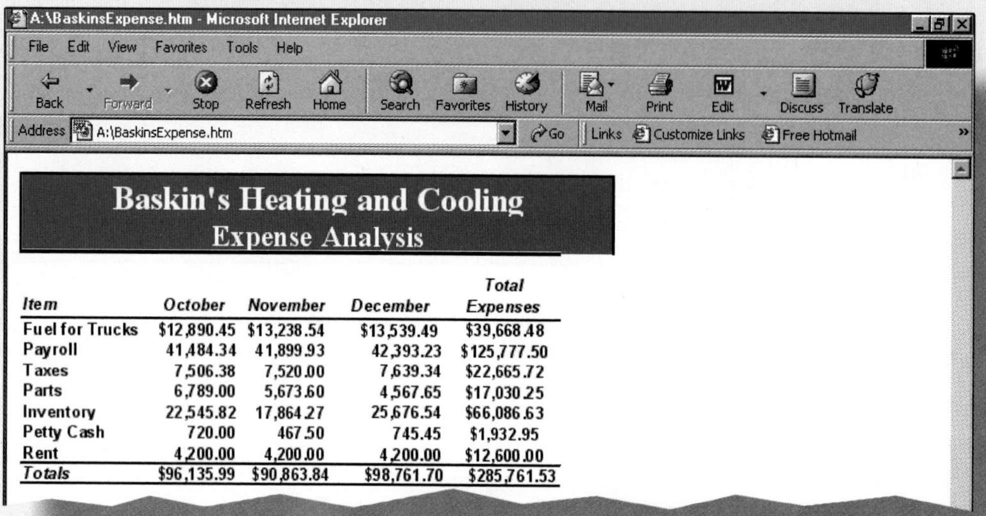

Item	October	November	December	Total Expenses
Fuel for Trucks	$12,890.45	$13,238.54	$13,539.49	$39,668.48
Payroll	41,484.34	41,899.93	42,393.23	$125,777.50
Taxes	7,506.38	7,520.00	7,639.34	$22,665.72
Parts	6,789.00	5,673.60	4,567.65	$17,030.25
Inventory	22,545.82	17,864.27	25,676.54	$66,086.63
Petty Cash	720.00	467.50	745.45	$1,932.95
Rent	4,200.00	4,200.00	4,200.00	$12,600.00
Totals	$96,135.99	$90,863.84	$98,761.70	$285,761.53

FIGURE 1-47

2 Lightning Software Web Site with Data Access Page and Excel Worksheet

Problem: As the manager of Information Technology at Lightning Software, Arthur Bukiet is responsible for loaning laptop computers to those employees who need them on a temporary basis. He would like you to design a site that allows employees to view the availability of laptop computers in inventory. He also wants an e-mail link for questions.

Instructions: Perform the following tasks.

1. Start Word. Create a home page for the Information Technology Department Laptop Loan Program Web site (Figure 1-48). Add a title and a borderless table below the title. In the left column, insert three hyperlinks. The first hyperlink should go to LightningInventory.htm (Lightning Laptops, Figure 1-49). The second hyperlink should go to LightningAvailable.htm (Laptops Available, Figure 1-50 on page I 1.46). The third hyperlink should start an e-mail to `laptop@isp.com`. Type the text in the right column. Save the Web page as LightningLaptops.htm.
2. Start Access by opening the Lightning Inventory.mdb database on the Integration Data Disk. Create a data access page from the Laptop Inventory table. Create a group level using the Operating System field. Add a title as shown in Figure 1-49. Add a link named Home that links to the LightningLaptops.htm home page at the bottom of the data access page. Save the data access page as LightningInventory.htm.
3. Start Excel by opening the Lightning Availability.xls workbook on the Integration Data Disk. Create a Web page from the workbook by using the Save as a Web Page command on the File menu. Use the file name, LightningAvailable.htm.
4. View the LightningLaptops.htm Web page in your browser. Verify that all links operate properly by clicking each one. Print all Web pages.

In the Lab

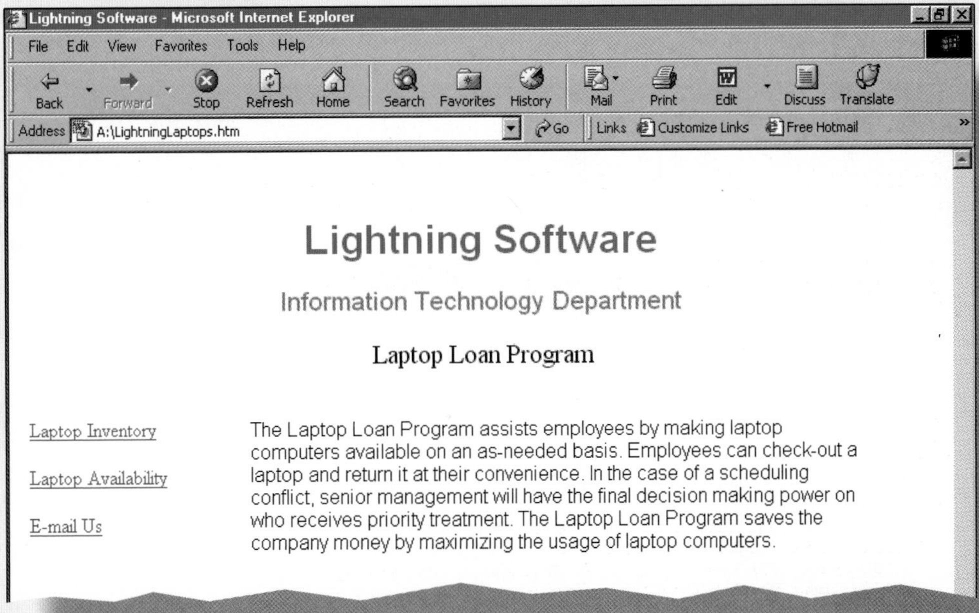

FIGURE 1-48

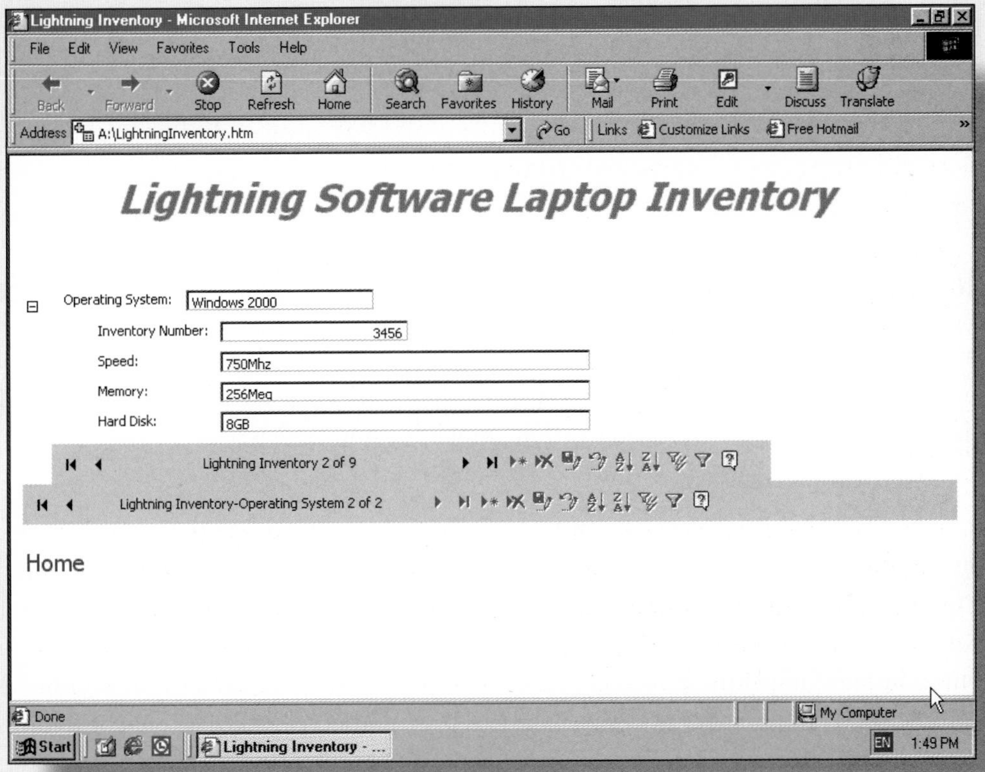

FIGURE 1-49

(continued)

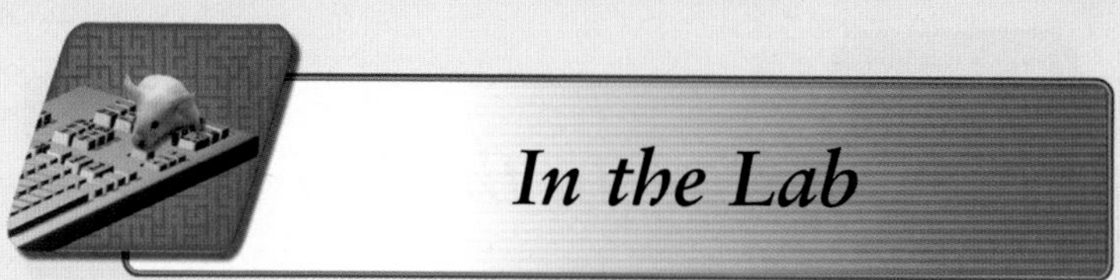

Lightning Software Web Site with Data Access Page and Excel Worksheet *(continued)*

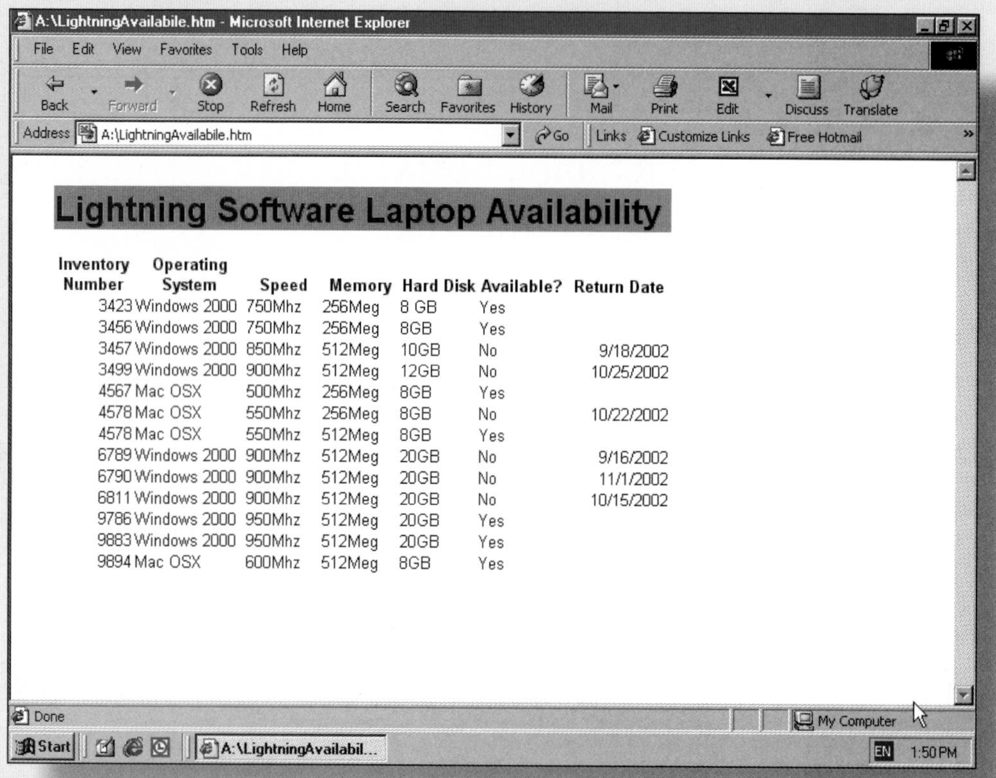

Inventory Number	Operating System	Speed	Memory	Hard Disk	Available?	Return Date
3423	Windows 2000	750Mhz	256Meg	8 GB	Yes	
3456	Windows 2000	750Mhz	256Meg	8GB	Yes	
3457	Windows 2000	850Mhz	512Meg	10GB	No	9/18/2002
3499	Windows 2000	900Mhz	512Meg	12GB	No	10/25/2002
4567	Mac OSX	500Mhz	256Meg	8GB	Yes	
4578	Mac OSX	550Mhz	256Meg	8GB	No	10/22/2002
4578	Mac OSX	550Mhz	512Meg	8GB	Yes	
6789	Windows 2000	900Mhz	512Meg	20GB	No	9/16/2002
6790	Windows 2000	900Mhz	512Meg	20GB	No	11/1/2002
6811	Windows 2000	900Mhz	512Meg	20GB	No	10/15/2002
9786	Windows 2000	950Mhz	512Meg	20GB	Yes	
9883	Windows 2000	950Mhz	512Meg	20GB	Yes	
9894	Mac OSX	600Mhz	512Meg	8GB	Yes	

FIGURE 1-50

3 Sales Meeting Information Web Site Incorporating PowerPoint Web Pages

Problem: As sales manager for Dahlberg Office Supplies, you wish to create a Web page that promotes an upcoming meeting to all of the sales force in the company (Figures 1-51 and 1-52). The specific information for the meeting is located in a PowerPoint presentation, which has four pages.

Instructions: Perform the following tasks.

1. Start Word. Create the Web page as shown in Figure 1-51. Include scrolling text below the Web page title. Insert two hyperlinks. The first hyperlink should link to DahlbergSalesPresentation.htm, and the second should link to an e-mail address at salesmanager@isp.com. Save this Web page as DahlbergSales.htm.
2. Open the PowerPoint presentation Dahlberg.ppt. Add a link named Home at the bottom of the first page of the presentation that jumps to the DahlbergSales.htm Web page. Save the PowerPoint presentation as Web pages on the Integration Data Disk. Name the Web pages DahlbergSalesPresentation.htm.
3. View the Web pages in your browser. Print each page.

In the Lab

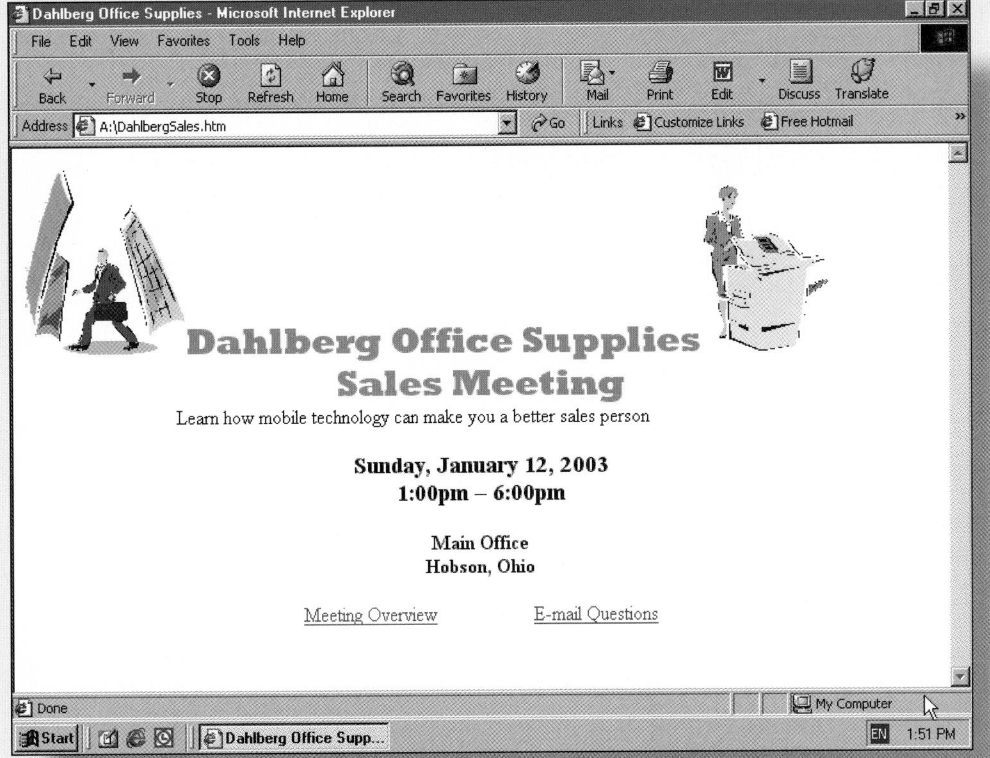

FIGURE 1-51

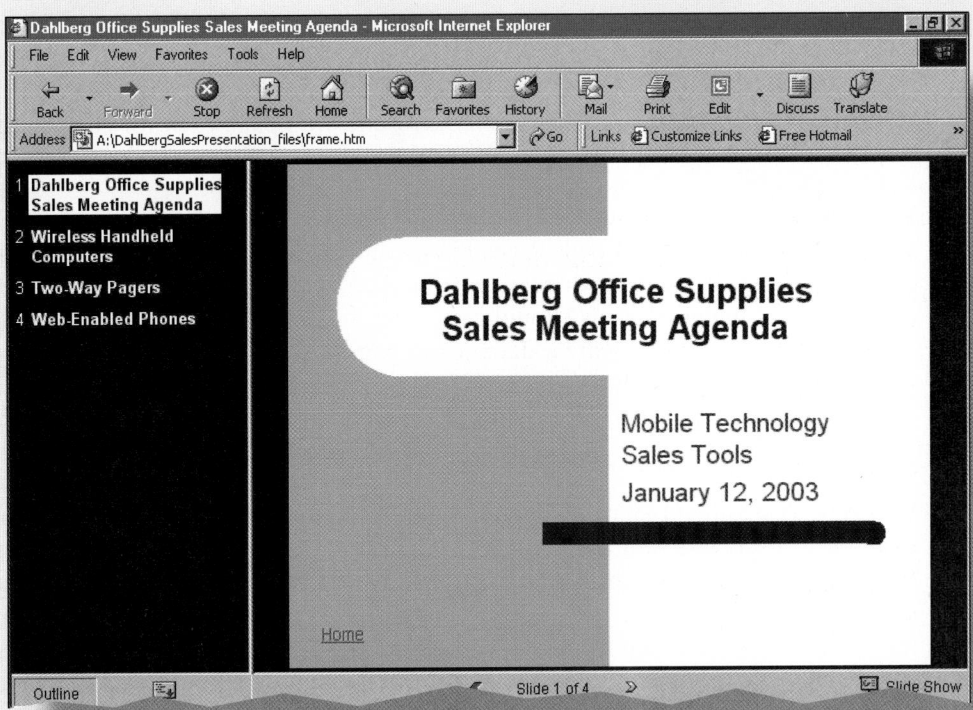

FIGURE 1-52

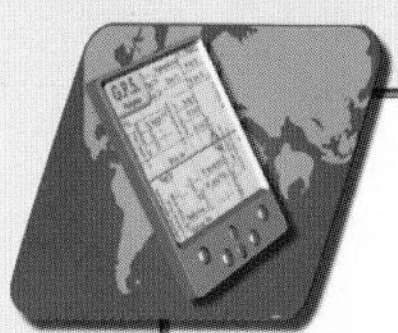

Cases and Places

The difficulty of these case studies varies:
▶ are the least difficult; ▶▶ are more difficult; and ▶▶▶ are the most difficult.

1 ▶ As a volunteer in your school's fund-raising department, you have been asked to create a Web page that shows the different levels of memberships for alumni donations. The membership levels have varying degrees of recognition and rewards. The Founder's Club ($1,000 and above) recognizes donors on a special plaque in the Student Union. The President's Club ($500 to $999) allows donors to have the first chance to purchase premier seats for sporting events. The Executive Club ($100 to $499) allows donors to have special parking privileges at sporting events. The Associate's Club ($10 to $99) recognizes the donors in a yearly Alumni Magazine. Create a worksheet in Excel that summarizes each of these donation levels. Create a Web page using Word that embeds the Excel worksheet; the goal of the Web site is to entice new donors to higher donation levels. Make sure an e-mail address is included on the Web page.

2 ▶ As a member of a mentoring association for local teens, you have been tasked with consolidating information about local colleges for the teens. Research the programs and accreditations of local colleges and determine the following for each: name, location, phone number for admissions office, size of student body, overview of degree types offered, and cost per credit hour. Create an Excel spreadsheet summarizing your data and charts of student body size and cost per credit hour. Using Word, create a Web page and embed the worksheet on the home page of the Web site. Create another Web page, and embed the charts from Excel. Create a link to the Excel chart Web page and a link to each school's Web page.

3 ▶ Your uncle has requested your assistance in gathering inventory data for his antique shop. Create an Access database and add ten items to it with the following information for each item: item number, category, description, year of origin, purchase price, and sale price. From this table, create a data access page with inquiry capability only, using the category as the group level. Include the item number, description, year or origin, and sale price in the data access page. Use a search engine to find relevant links about each category and create links to one Web page each for each category at the bottom of the data access page.

4 ▶▶ As a member of the Blank Pages Book Club, you have been asked to create an online repository of the members' book collections. Create an Access database and add your own book collection to the database. The included fields should be: owner, fiction/non-fiction, genre, publisher, date published, and author. From this table, create a data access page with inquiry capability only, using the genre as the group level. Create a Web page using Word that will act as the home page for the book club and create a link to the data access page. Be sure to include a link to your e-mail address on the Web page.

5 ▶▶▶ As an investment analyst for Millionaire Investments, you recommend stocks to clients. Choose a stock or other investment and gather information about the company, including information about the investment's past performance. Create an Excel 3-D Bar chart to summarize the financial information that you find. Create a PowerPoint presentation that contains at least four major points regarding this investment that you want to convey to potential investors. Embed the Excel chart into one of the PowerPoint slides. Save the PowerPoint presentation as Web pages. Include relevant links to Web pages regarding the investment.

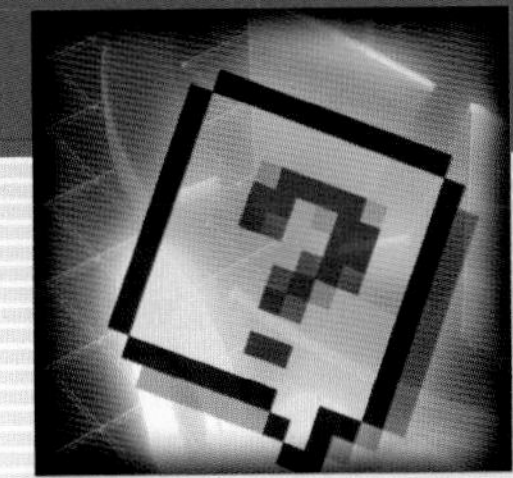

APPENDIX A
Microsoft Office XP Help System

Using the Microsoft Office Help System

This appendix demonstrates how you can use the Microsoft Office XP Help system to answer your questions. At anytime while you are using one of the Microsoft Office XP applications, you can interact with the Help system to display information on any topic associated with the application. To illustrate the use of the Microsoft Office XP Help system, you will use the Microsoft Word 2002 application in this appendix. The Help systems in other Microsoft Office XP applications respond in a similar fashion.

As shown in Figure A-1, you can access Word's Help system in four primary ways:

1. Ask a Question box on the menu bar
2. Function key F1 on the keyboard
3. Microsoft Word Help command on the Help menu
4. Microsoft Word Help button on the Standard toolbar

If you use the Ask a Question box on the menu bar, Word responds by opening the Microsoft Word Help window, which gives you direct access to its Help system. If you use one of the other three ways to access Word's Help system, Word responds in one of two ways:

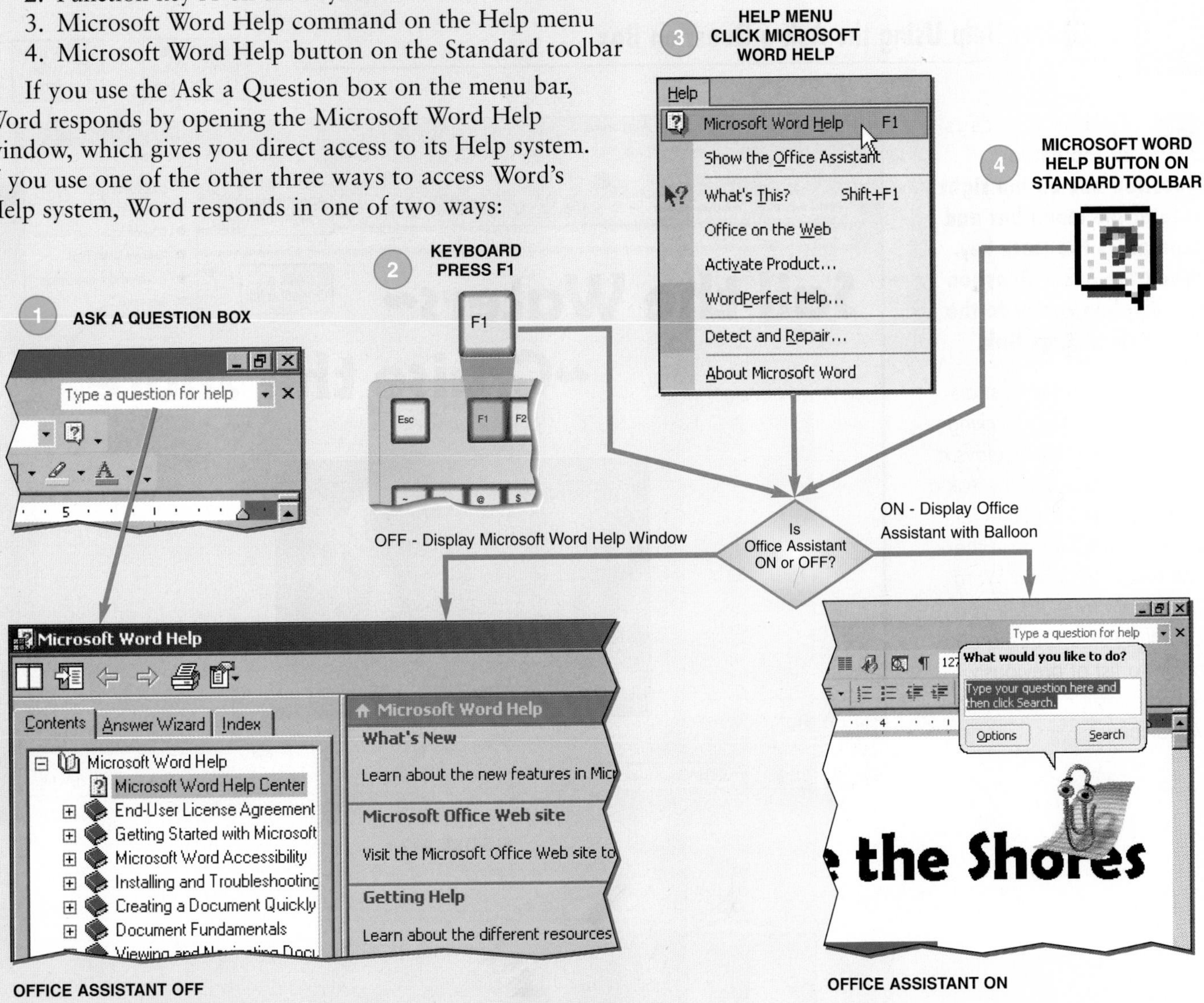

FIGURE A-1

1. If the Office Assistant is turned on, then the Office Assistant displays with a balloon (lower-right side in Figure A-1 on the previous page).
2. If the Office Assistant is turned off, then the Microsoft Word Help window displays (lower-left side in Figure A-1 on the previous page).

The best way to familiarize yourself with the Word Help system is to use it. The next several pages show examples of how to use the Help system. Following the examples are a set of exercises titled Use Help that will sharpen your Word Help system skills.

Ask a Question Box

The **Ask a Question box** on the right side of the menu bar lets you type questions in your own words, or you can type terms, such as template, smart tags, or speech. Word responds by displaying a list of topics related to the term(s) you entered. The following steps show how to use the Ask a Question box to obtain information about how smart tags work.

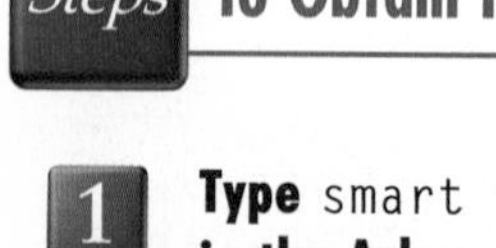

To Obtain Help Using the Ask a Question Box

1 Type `smart tags` **in the Ask a Question box on the right side of the menu bar and then press the ENTER key. When the Ask a Question list displays, point to the About smart tags link.**

The Ask a Question list displays (Figure A-2). Clicking the See more link displays a new list of topics in the Ask a Question list. As you enter questions and terms in the Ask a Question box, Word adds them to its list. If you click the Ask a Question box arrow, a list of previously asked questions and terms will display.

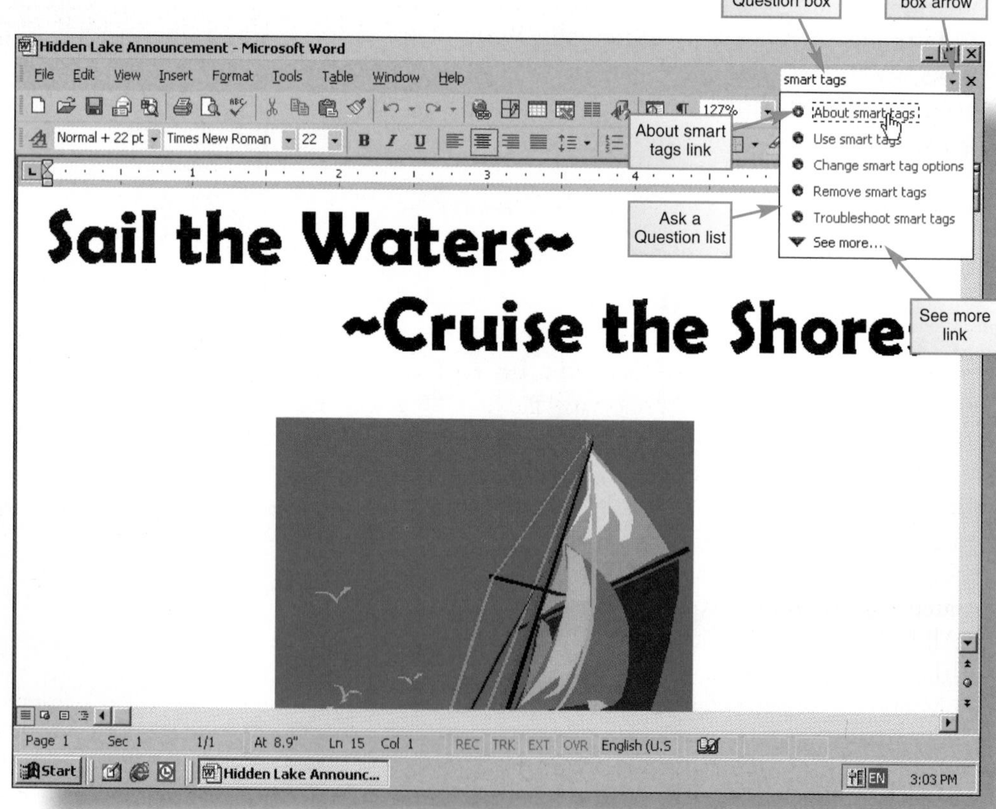

FIGURE A-2

2 Click About smart tags. When the Microsoft Word Help window displays, double-click its title bar to maximize it. If necessary, click the Contents tab.

Word displays and maximizes the Microsoft Word Help window (Figure A-3). A toolbar displays at the top of the window. The left side of the window contains the Contents, Answer Wizard, and Index tabs. The right side of the window contains the About smart tags topic.

3 Click th e Close button on the Microsoft Word Help window title bar.

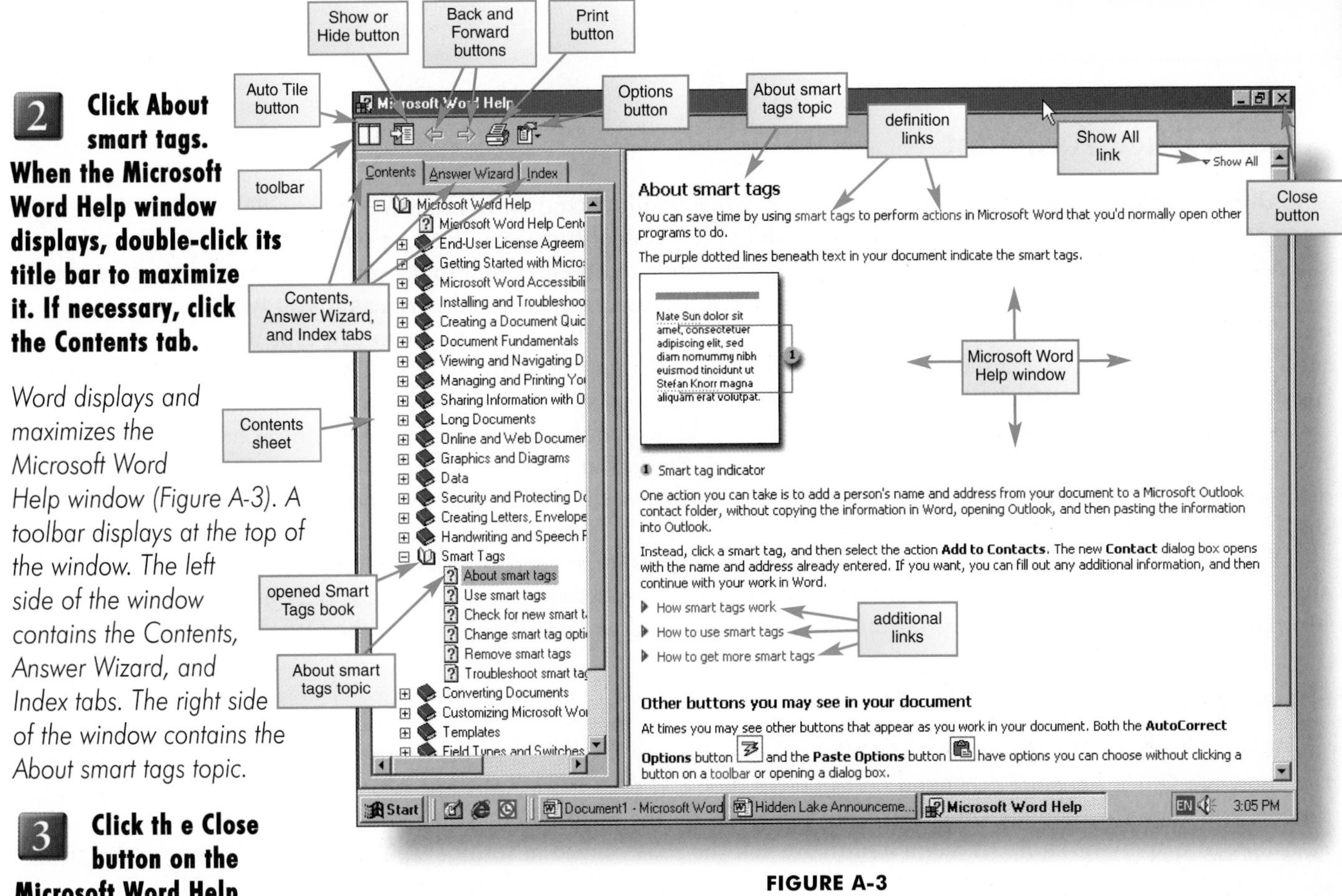

FIGURE A-3

The Microsoft Word Help window closes and the document window is active.

The right side of the Microsoft Word Help window shown in Figure A-3 contains the About smart tags topic. The two links at the top of the window, smart tags and actions, display in blue font. Clicking either of these links displays a definition in green font following the link. Clicking again removes the definition. The How smart tags work link, How to use smart tags link, and How to get more smart tags link also display on the right side of the window. Clicking one of these links displays additional information about the link. Clicking again removes the information. Clicking the Show All link in the upper-right corner of the window causes the text associated with each link to display. In addition, the Hide All link replaces the Show All link.

If the Contents sheet is active on the left side of the Microsoft Word Help window, then Word opens the book that pertains to the topic for which you are requesting help. In this case, Word opens the Smart Tags book, which includes a list of topics related to smart tags. If you need additional information about the topic, you can click one of the topics listed below the Smart Tags book name.

The six buttons on the toolbar in the Microsoft Word Help window (Figure A-3) allow you to navigate through the Help system, change the display, and print the contents of the window. Table A-1 lists the function of each button on the toolbar.

Table A-1 Microsoft Word Help Toolbar Buttons

BUTTON	NAME	FUNCTION
[Auto Tile icon]	Auto Tile	Tiles the Microsoft Word Help window and Microsoft Word window when the Microsoft Word Help window is maximized
[Show icon] or [Hide icon]	Show or Hide	Displays or hides the Contents, Answer Wizard, and Index tabs
[Back icon]	Back	Displays the previous Help topic
[Forward icon]	Forward	Displays the next Help topic
[Print icon]	Print	Prints the current Help topic
[Options icon]	Options	Displays a list of commands

The Office Assistant

The **Office Assistant** is an icon that displays in the Word window (shown in the lower-right side of Figure A-1 on page MO A.01) when it is turned on and not hidden. It has dual functions. First, it will respond in the same way the Ask a Question box does with a list of topics that relate to an entry you make in the text box at the bottom of the balloon. The entry can be in the form of a word, phrase, or question written as if you were talking. For example, if you want to learn more about saving a file, in the balloon text box, you can type any of the following terms or phrases: save, save a file, how do I save a file, or anything similar. The Office Assistant responds by displaying a list of topics from which you can choose. Once you choose a topic, it displays the corresponding information.

Second, the Office Assistant monitors your work and accumulates tips during a session on how you might increase your productivity and efficiency. You can view the tips at anytime. The accumulated tips display when you activate the Office Assistant balloon. Also, if at anytime you see a lightbulb above the Office Assistant, click it to display the most recent tip.

You may or may not want the Office Assistant to display on the screen at all times. You can hide it, and then show it at a later time. You may prefer not to use the Office Assistant at all. Thus, not only do you need to know how to show and hide the Office Assistant, but you also need to know how to turn the Office Assistant on and off.

Showing and Hiding the Office Assistant

When Word initially is installed, the Office Assistant may be off. You turn on the Office Assistant by clicking the **Show the Office Assistant command** on the Help menu. If the Office Assistant is on the screen and you want to hide it, you click the **Hide the Office Assistant command** on the Help menu. You also can right-click the Office Assistant to display its shortcut menu and then click the **Hide command** to hide it. You can move it to any location on the screen. You can click it to display the Office Assistant balloon, which allows you to request Help.

Turning the Office Assistant On and Off

The fact that the Office Assistant is hidden, does not mean it is turned off. To turn the Office Assistant off, it must be displaying in the Word window. You right-click it to display its shortcut menu (right side of Figure A-4). Next, click Options on the shortcut menu. When you click the **Options command**, the **Office Assistant dialog box** displays (left side of Figure A-4).

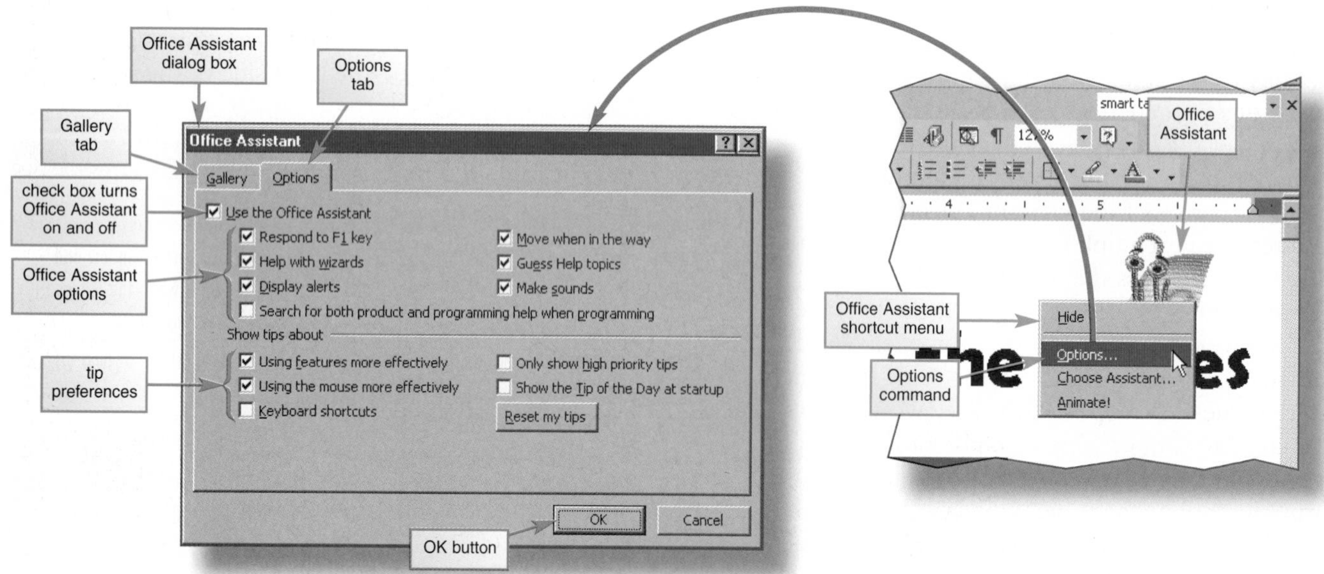

FIGURE A-4

In the **Options sheet** in the Office Assistant dialog box, the **Use the Office Assistant check box** at the top of the sheet determines whether the Office Assistant is on or off. To turn the Office Assistant off, remove the check mark from the Use the Office Assistant check box and then click the OK button. As shown in Figure A-1 on page MO A.01, if the Office Assistant is off when you invoke Help, then Word displays the Microsoft Word Help window instead of displaying the Office Assistant. To turn the Office Assistant on later, click the **Show the Office Assistant command** on the Help menu.

Through the Options command on the Office Assistant shortcut menu, you can change the look and feel of the Office Assistant. For example, you can hide the Office Assistant, turn the Office Assistant off, change the way it works, choose a different Office Assistant icon, or view an animation of the current one. These options also are available by clicking the **Options button** that displays in the Office Assistant balloon (Figure A-5).

The **Gallery sheet** (Figure A-4) in the Office Assistant dialog box allows you to change the appearance of the Office Assistant. The default is the paper clip (Clippit). You can change it to a bouncing red happy face (The Dot), a robot (F1), the Microsoft Office logo (Office Logo), a wizard (Merlin), the earth (Mother Nature), a cat (Links), or a dog (Rocky).

Using the Office Assistant

As indicated earlier, the Office Assistant allows you to enter a word, phrase, or question and then responds by displaying a list of topics from which you can choose to display Help. The following steps show how to use the Office Assistant to obtain Help on speech recognition.

Steps To Use the Office Assistant

1 If the Office Assistant is not turned on, click Help on the menu bar and then click Show the Office Assistant. Click the Office Assistant. When the Office Assistant balloon displays, type `what is speech recognition` **in the text box immediately above the Options button. Point to the Search button.**

The Office Assistant balloon displays and the question, what is speech recognition, displays in the text box (Figure A-5).

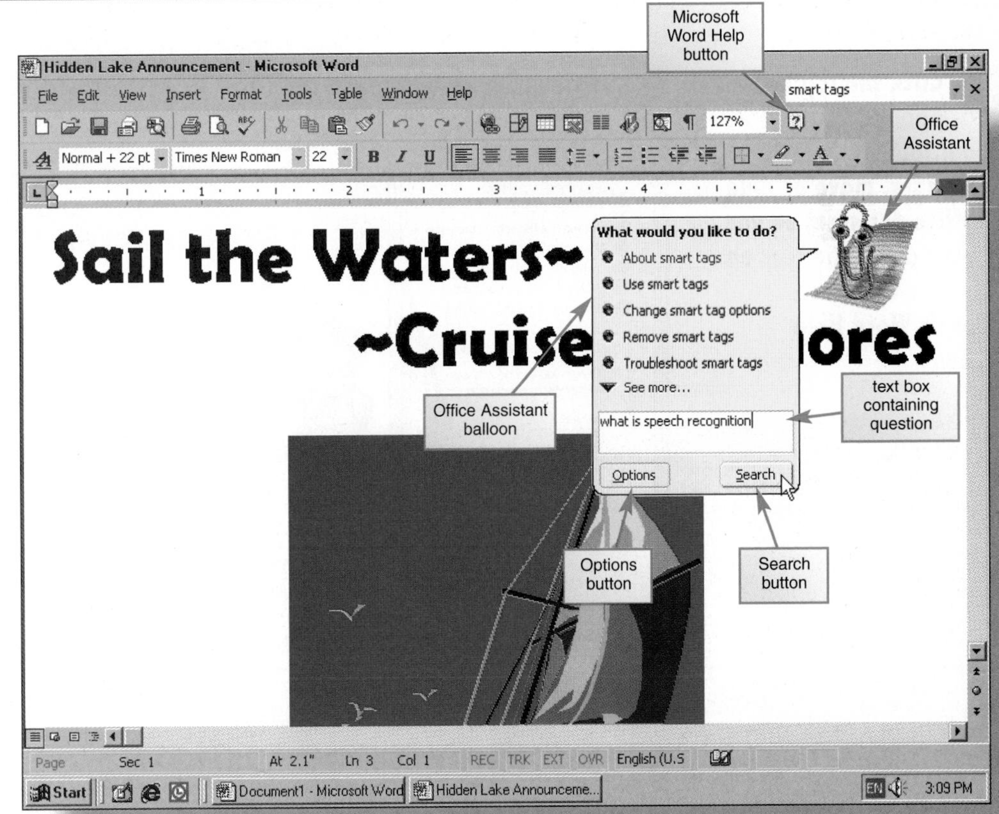

FIGURE A-5

2 Click the Search button. When the Office Assistant balloon redisplays, point to the topic, About speech recognition.

A list of links displays in the Office Assistant balloon (Figure A-6).

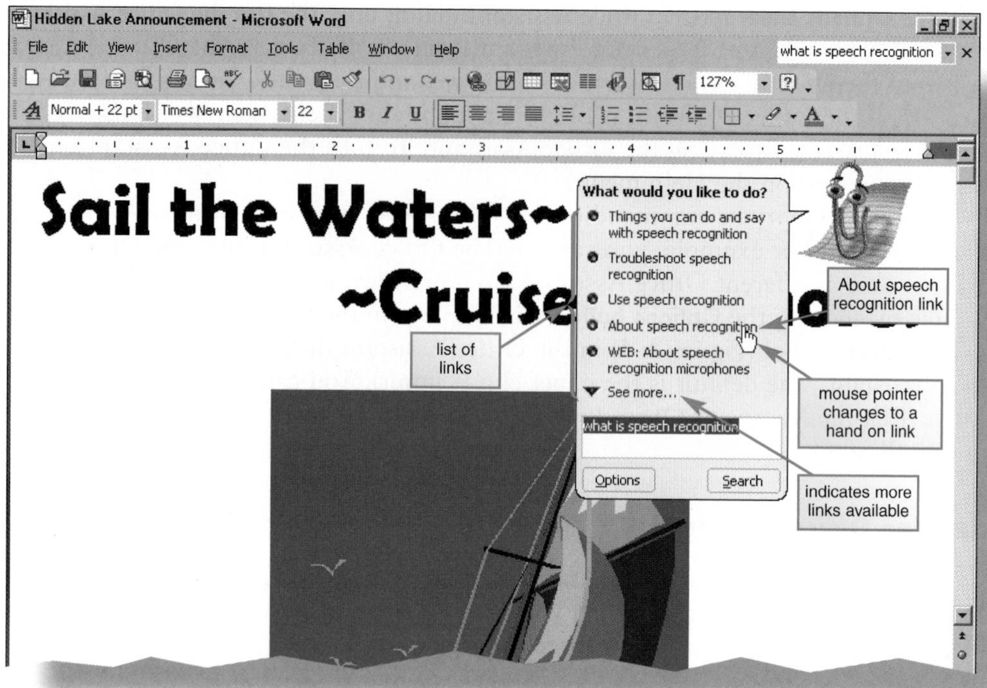

FIGURE A-6

3 Click the topic, About speech recognition (Figure A-7). If necessary, move or hide the Office Assistant so you can view all of the text on the right side of the Microsoft Word Help window.

The About speech recognition topic displays on the right side of the Microsoft Word Help window (Figure A-7). Clicking the Show All link in the upper-right corner of the window expands all links.

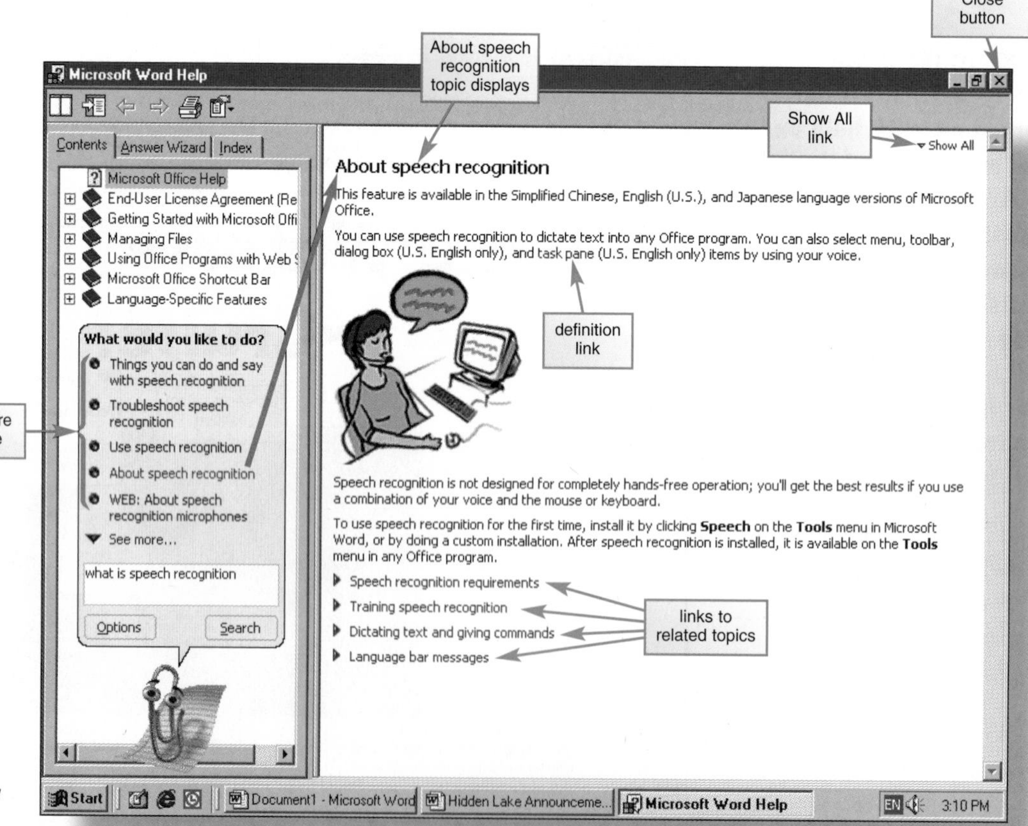

FIGURE A-7

4 Click the Close button on the Microsoft Word Help window title bar to close Help.

The Microsoft Word Help Window

If the Office Assistant is turned off and you click the Microsoft Word Help button on the Standard toolbar, the Microsoft Word Help window displays (Figure A-8). The left side of this window contains three tabs: Contents, Answer Wizard, and Index. Each tab displays a sheet with powerful look-up capabilities.

Use the Contents sheet as you would a table of contents at the front of a book to look up Help. The Answer Wizard sheet answers your queries the same as the Office Assistant. You use the Index sheet in the same fashion as an index in a book to look up Help. Click the tabs to move from sheet to sheet.

Besides clicking the Microsoft Word Help button on the Standard toolbar, you also can click the Microsoft Word Help command on the Help menu, or press the F1 key to display the Microsoft Word Help window to gain access to the three sheets. To close the Microsoft Word Help window, click the Close button in the upper-right corner on the title bar.

Using the Contents Sheet

The **Contents sheet** is useful for displaying Help when you know the general category of the topic in question, but not the specifics. The following steps show how to use the Contents sheet to obtain information about handwriting recognition.

TO OBTAIN HELP USING THE CONTENTS SHEET

1. Click the Microsoft Word Help button on the Standard toolbar (shown in Figure A-5 on page MO A.05).
2. When the Microsoft Word Help window displays, double-click the title bar to maximize the window. If necessary, click the Show button to display the tabs.
3. Click the Contents tab. Double-click the Handwriting and Speech Recognition book in the Contents sheet. Double-click the Handwriting Recognition book.
4. Click the subtopic, About handwriting recognition, below the Handwriting Recognition book (Figure A-8).
5. Close the Microsoft Help window.

Word displays Help on the subtopic, About handwriting recognition (Figure A-8).

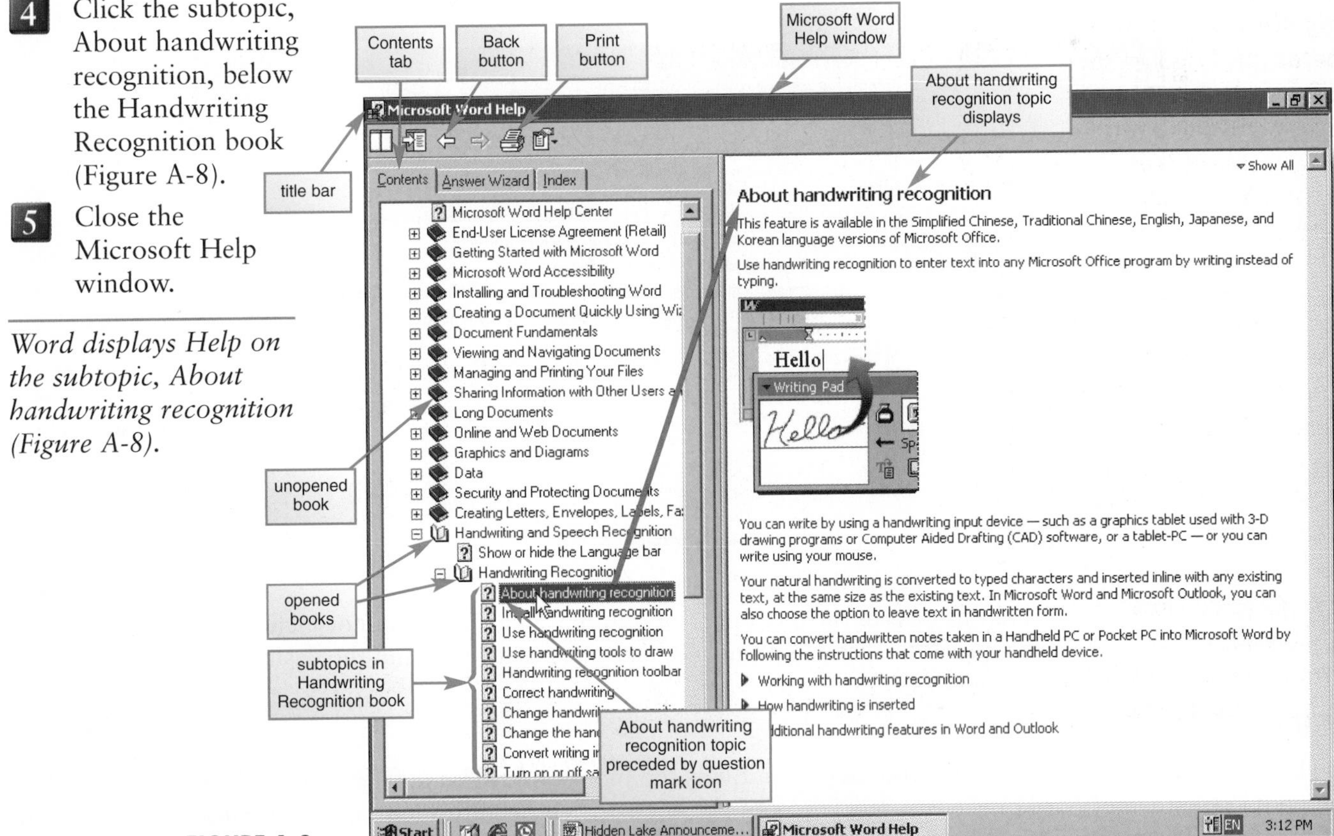

FIGURE A-8

Once the information on the subtopic displays, you can read it or you can click the Print button to obtain a printed copy. If you decide to click another subtopic on the left or a link on the right, you can get back to the Help page shown in Figure A-8 on the previous page by clicking the Back button.

Each topic in the Contents list is preceded by a book icon or question mark icon. A **book icon** indicates subtopics are available. A **question mark icon** means information on the topic will display if you double-click the title. The book icon opens when you double-click the book (or its title) or click the plus sign (+) to the left of the book icon.

Using the Answer Wizard Sheet

The **Answer Wizard sheet** works like the Office Assistant in that you enter a word, phrase, or question and it responds by listing topics from which you can choose to display Help. The following steps show how to use the Answer Wizard sheet to obtain Help on translating or looking up text in the dictionary of another language.

TO OBTAIN HELP USING THE ANSWER WIZARD SHEET

1. With the Office Assistant turned off, click the Microsoft Word Help button on the Standard toolbar (shown in Figure A-5 on page MO A.05).
2. When the Microsoft Word Help window displays, double-click the title bar to maximize the window. If necessary, click the Show button to display the tabs.
3. Click the Answer Wizard tab. Type `translation` in the What would you like to do? text box on the left side of the window. Click the Search button.
4. When a list of topics displays in the Select topic to display list, click Translate or look up text in the dictionary of another language (Figure A-9).
5. Close the Microsoft Help window.

Word displays Help on how to translate or look up text in the dictionary of a different language on the right side of the Microsoft Word Help window (Figure A-9).

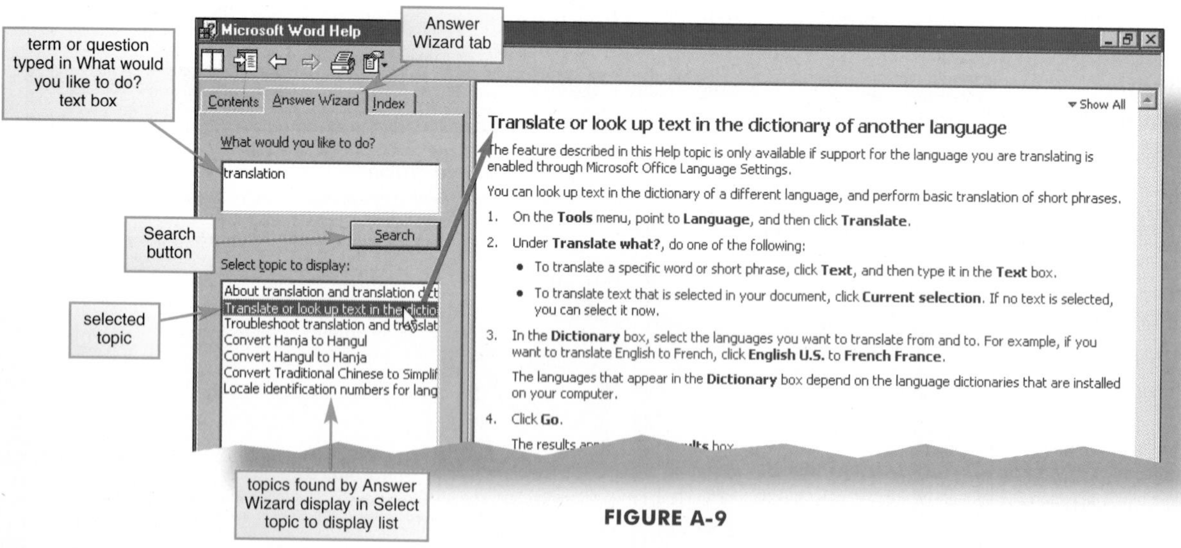

FIGURE A-9

If the topic, Translate or look up text in the dictionary of another language, does not include the information you are seeking, click another topic in the list. Continue to click topics until you find the desired information.

Using the Index Sheet

The third sheet in the Microsoft Word Help window is the Index sheet. Use the **Index sheet** to display Help when you know the keyword or the first few letters of the keyword you want to look up. The following steps show how to use the Index sheet to obtain Help on understanding the readability scores available to evaluate the reading level of a document.

TO OBTAIN HELP USING THE INDEX SHEET

1. With the Office Assistant turned off, click the Microsoft Word Help button on the Standard toolbar (shown in Figure A-5 on page MO A.05).
2. When the Microsoft Word Help window displays, double-click the title bar to maximize the window. If necessary, click the Show button to display the tabs.
3. Click the Index tab. Type `readability` in the Type keywords text box on the left side of the window. Click the Search button.
4. When a list of topics displays in the Choose a topic list, click Readability scores.
5. When the Readability scores topic displays on the right side of the window (Figure A-10), click the Show All link in the upper-right corner of the right side of the window.

Word displays information about readability scores and two links on the right side of the window (Figure A-10). Clicking the Show All link expands the two links and displays the Hide All link. As you type readability into the Type keywords box, Word recognizes and completes the word and automatically appends a semicolon to the keyword.

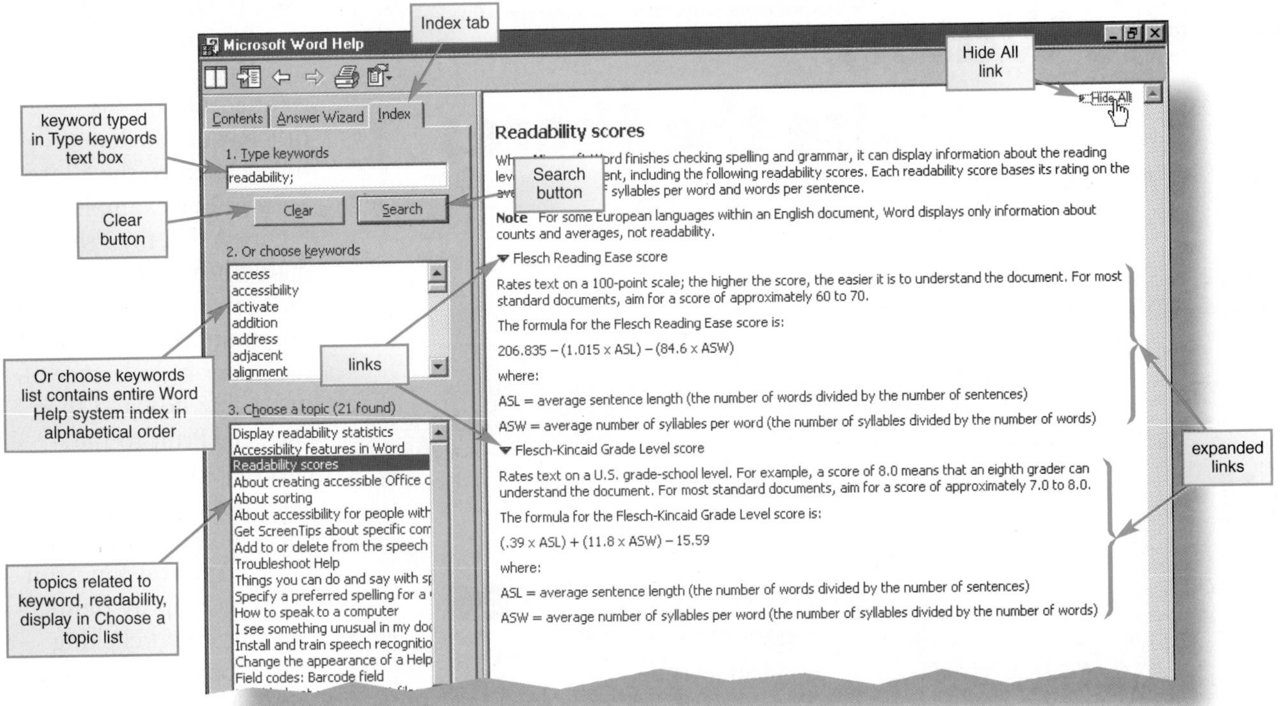

FIGURE A-10

An alternative to typing a keyword in the Type keywords text box is to scroll through the Or choose keywords list (the middle list on the left side of the window). When you locate the keyword you are searching for, double-click it to display Help on the topic. Also in the Or choose keywords list, the Word Help system displays other topics that relate to the new keyword. As you begin typing a new keyword in the Type keywords text box, Word jumps to that point in the middle list box. To begin a new search, click the Clear button.

What's This? Command and Question Mark Button

Use the What's This? command on the Help menu or the Question Mark button in a dialog box when you are not sure what an object on the screen is or what it does.

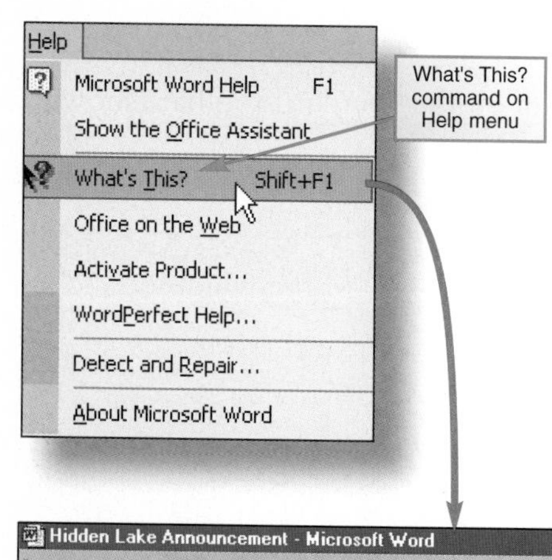

What's This? Command

You use the **What's This? command** on the Help menu to display a detailed ScreenTip. When you click this command, the mouse pointer changes to an arrow with a question mark. You then click any object on the screen, such as a button, to display the ScreenTip. For example, after you click the What's This? command on the Help menu and then click the Zoom box on the Standard toolbar, a description of the Zoom box displays (Figure A-11). You can print the ScreenTip by right-clicking it and then clicking Print Topic on the shortcut menu.

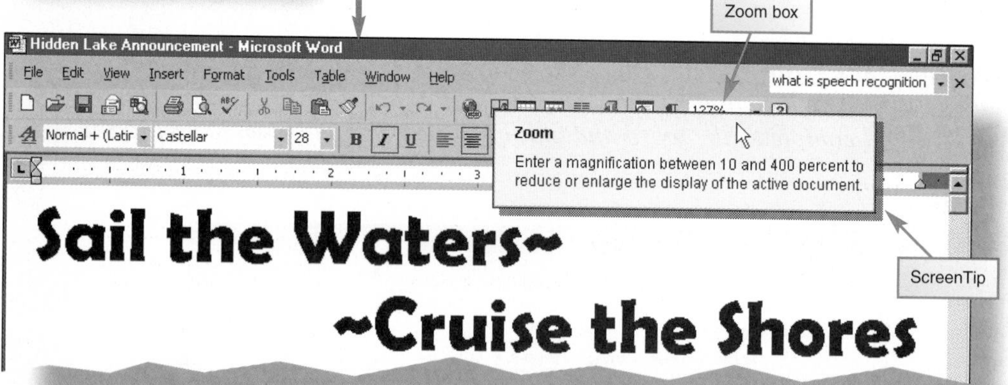

FIGURE A-11

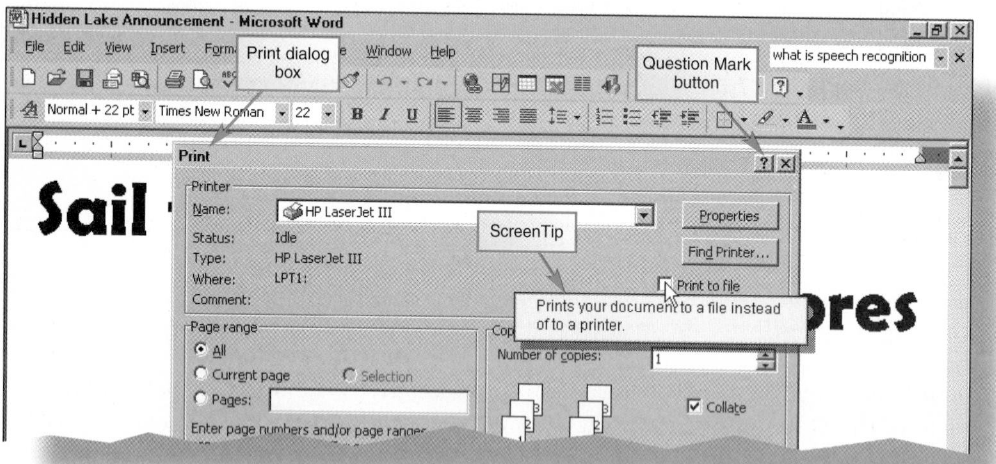

FIGURE A-12

Question Mark Button

Similarly to the What's This? command, the **Question Mark button** displays a ScreenTip. You use the Question Mark button with dialog boxes. It is located in the upper-right corner on the title bar of the dialog boxes, next to the Close button. For example, in Figure A-12, the Print dialog box displays on the screen. If you click the Question Mark button in the upper-right corner of the dialog box and then click the Print to file check box, an explanation of the Print to file check box displays in a ScreenTip. You can print the ScreenTip by right-clicking it and clicking Print Topic on the shortcut menu.

If a dialog box does not include a Question Mark button, press SHIFT+F1. This combination of keys will change the mouse pointer to an arrow with a question mark. You then can click any object in the dialog box to display the ScreenTip.

Office on the Web Command

The **Office on the Web command** on the Help menu displays a Microsoft Web page containing up-to-date information on a variety of Office-related topics. To use this command, you must be connected to the Internet. When you invoke the Office on the Web command, the Assistance Center Home page displays. Read through the links that in general pertain to topics that relate to all Office XP topics. Scroll down and click the Word link in the Help By

Product area to display the Assistance Center Word Help Articles Web page (Figure A-14). This Web page contains numerous helpful links related to Word.

Other Help Commands

Four additional commands available on the Help menu are Activate Product, WordPerfect Help, Detect and Repair, and About Microsoft Word. The WordPerfect Help command is available only if it was included as part of a custom installation of Word 2002.

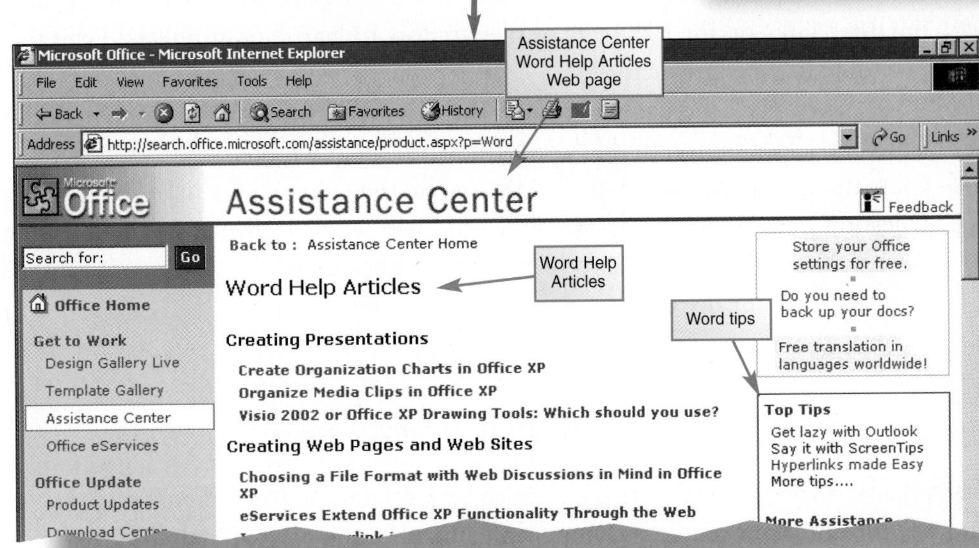

FIGURE A-14

Activate Product Command

The **Activate Product command** on the Help menu lets you activate your Microsoft Office subscription if you selected the Microsoft Office Subscription mode.

WordPerfect Help Command

The **WordPerfect Help command** on the Help menu offers assistance to WordPerfect users switching to Word. When you choose this command, Word displays the Help for WordPerfect Users dialog box. The instructions in the dialog box step the user through the appropriate selections.

Detect and Repair Command

Use the **Detect and Repair command** on the Help menu if Word is not running properly or if it is generating errors. When you invoke this command, the Detect and Repair dialog box displays. Click the Start button in the dialog box to initiate the detect and repair process.

About Microsoft Word Command

The **About Microsoft Word command** on the Help menu displays the About Microsoft Word dialog box. The dialog box lists the owner of the software and the product identification. You need to know the product identification if you call Microsoft for assistance. The three buttons below the OK button are the System Info button, Tech Support button, and Disabled Items button. The **System Info button** displays system information, including hardware resources, components, software environment, Internet Explorer 5, and Office XP applications. The **Tech Support button** displays technical assistance information. The **Disabled Items button** displays a list of items that were disabled because they prevented Word from functioning correctly.

1 Using the Ask a Question Box

Instructions: Perform the following tasks using the Word Help system.

1. Click the Ask a Question box on the menu bar, and then type `how do I add a bullet`. Press the ENTER key.
2. Click Add bullets or numbering in the Ask a Question list. If the Word window is not maximized, double-click the Microsoft Word Help window title bar. Read and print the information. One at a time, click the three links on the right side of the window to learn about bullets. Print the information. Hand in the printouts to your instructor.
3. If necessary, click the Show button to display the tabs. Click the Contents tab to prepare for the next step. Click the Close button in the Microsoft Word Help window.
4. Click the Ask a Question box and then press the ENTER key. Click About bulleted lists in the Ask a Question box. When the Microsoft Word Help window displays, maximize the window. Read and print the information. Click the two links on the right side of the window. Print the information. Hand in the printouts to your instructor.

2 Expanding on the Word Help System Basics

Instructions: Use the Word Help system to understand the topics better and answer the questions listed below. Answer the questions on your own paper, or hand in the printed Help information to your instructor.

1. If the Office Assistant is on, right-click the Office Assistant. When the shortcut menu displays, click Options. Click Use the Office Assistant to remove the check mark, and then click the OK button.
2. Click the Microsoft Word Help button on the Standard toolbar. Maximize the Microsoft Word Help window. Click Getting Help on the right side of the window. Click the five links in the About getting help while you work topic. Print the information and hand in the printouts to your instructor. Close the Microsoft Word Help window.
3. Press the F1 key. Maximize the Microsoft Word Help window. Click the Answer Wizard tab. Type `help` in the What would you like to do? text box, and then click the Search button. Click Guidelines for searching Help. Click the four links on the right side of the window. Print the information and hand in the printouts to your instructor.
4. Click the Contents tab. Click the plus sign (+) to the left of the Document Fundamentals book. Click the plus sign (+) to the left of the Selecting Text and Graphics book. One at a time, click the three topics below the Selecting Text and Graphics book. Read and print each one. Close the Microsoft Word Help window. Hand in the printouts to your instructor.
5. Click Help on the menu bar and then click What's This? Click the E-mail button on the Standard toolbar. Right-click the ScreenTip, click Print Topic on the shortcut menu, and click the Print button. Click Format on the menu bar and then click Paragraph. When the Paragraph dialog box displays, click the Question Mark button on the title bar. Click the Special box. Right-click the ScreenTip, click Print Topic, and then click the Print button. Close the Paragraph dialog box and Microsoft Word window.

APPENDIX B

Speech and Handwriting Recognition and Speech Playback

Introduction

This appendix discusses how you can create and modify documents using Office XP's new input technologies. Office XP provides a variety of **text services**, which enable you to speak commands and enter text in an application. The most common text service is the keyboard. Two new text services included with Office XP are speech recognition and handwriting recognition. The following pages use Word to illustrate the speech and handwriting recognition capabilities of Office XP. Depending on the application you are using, some special features within speech or handwriting recognition may not be available.

When Windows was installed on your computer, you specified a default language. For example, most users in the United States select English (United States) as the default language. Through text services, you can add more than 90 additional languages and varying dialects such as Basque, English (Zimbabwe), French (France), French (Canada), German (Germany), German (Austria), and Swahili. With multiple languages available, you can switch from one language to another while working in an Office XP application. If you change the language or dialect, then text services may change the functions of the keys on the keyboard, adjust speech recognition, and alter handwriting recognition.

The Language Bar

You know that text services are installed properly when the Language Indicator button displays by the clock in the tray status area on the Windows taskbar (Figure B-1a) or the Language bar displays on the screen (Figure B-1b or B-1c). If the Language Indicator button displays in the tray status area, click it, and then click the **Show the Language bar command** (Figure B-1a). The Language bar displays on the screen in the same location it displayed last time.

You can drag the Language bar to any location in the window by pointing to its move handle, which is the vertical line on its left side (Figure B-1b). When the mouse pointer changes to a four-headed arrow, drag the Language bar to the desired location.

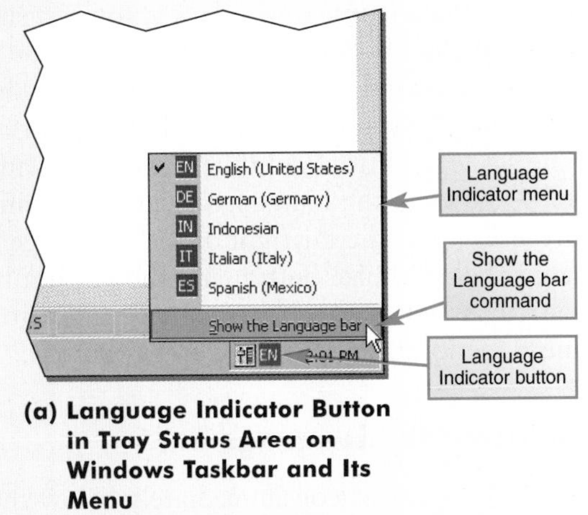

(a) Language Indicator Button in Tray Status Area on Windows Taskbar and Its Menu

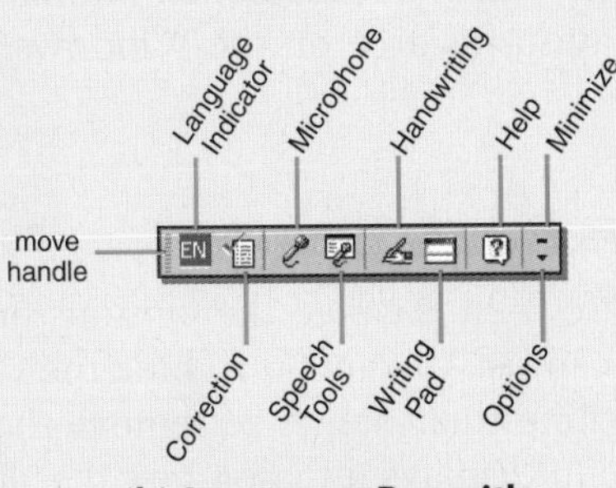

(b) Language Bar with Text Labels Disabled

(c) Language Bar with Text Labels Enabled

FIGURE B-1

If you are sure that one of the services was installed and neither the Language Indicator button nor the Language bar displays, then do the following:

1. Click Start on the Windows taskbar, point to Settings, click Control Panel, and then double-click the Text Services icon in the Control Panel window.
2. When the Text Services dialog box displays, click the Language Bar button, click the Show the Language bar on the desktop check box to select it, and then click the OK button in the Language Bar Settings dialog box.
3. Click the OK button in the Text Services dialog box.
4. Close the Control Panel window.

You can perform tasks related to text services by using the **Language bar**. The Language bar may display with just the icon on each button (Figure B-1b on the previous page) or it may display with text labels to the right of the icon on each button (Figure B-1c on the previous page). Changing the appearance of the Language bar will be discussed shortly.

Buttons on the Language Bar

The Language bar shown in Figure B-2a contains nine buttons. The number of buttons on your Language bar may be different. These buttons are used to select the language, customize the Language bar, control the microphone, control handwriting, and obtain help.

When you click the **Language Indicator button** on the far left side of the Language bar, the Language Indicator menu displays a list of the active languages (Figure B-2b) from which you can choose. When you select text and then click the **Correction button** (the second button from the left), a list of correction alternatives displays in the Word window (Figure B-2c). You can use the Correction button to correct both speech recognition and handwriting recognition errors. The **Microphone button**, the third button from the left, enables and disables the microphone. When the microphone is enabled, text services adds two buttons and a balloon to the Language toolbar (Figure B-2d). These additional buttons and the balloon will be discussed shortly.

The fourth button from the left on the Language bar is the Speech Tools button. The **Speech Tools button** displays a menu of commands (Figure B-2e) that allows you to hide or show the balloon on the Language bar; train the Speech Recognition service so that it can better interpret your voice; add and delete words from its dictionary, such as names and other words not understood easily; and change the user profile so more than one person can use the microphone on the same computer.

The fifth button from the left on the Language bar is the Handwriting button. The **Handwriting button** displays the **Handwriting menu** (Figure B-2f), which lets you choose the Writing Pad (Figure B-2g), Write Anywhere (Figure B-2h), the Drawing Pad (Figure B-2i), or the on-screen keyboard (Figure B-2j). The **On-Screen Symbol Keyboard command** on the Handwriting menu displays an on-screen keyboard that allows you to enter special symbols that are not available on the On-Screen Standard Keyboard. You can choose only one form of handwriting at a time.

The sixth button indicates which one of the handwriting forms is active. For example, in Figure B-1a on the previous page, the Writing Pad is active. The handwriting recognition capabilities of text services will be discussed shortly.

The seventh button from the left on the Language bar is the Help button. The **Help button** displays the Help menu. If you click the Language Bar Help command on the Help menu, the Language Bar Help window displays (Figure B-2k). On the far right of the Language bar are two buttons stacked above and below each other. The top button is the Minimize button and the bottom button is the Options button. The **Minimize button** minimizes (hides) the Language bar so that the Language Indicator button displays in the tray status area on the Windows taskbar. The next section discusses the Options button.

Customizing the Language Bar

The down arrow icon immediately below the Minimize button in Figure B-2a is called the Options button. The **Options button** displays a menu of text services options (Figure B-2l). You can use this menu to hide the Correction, Speech Tools, Handwriting, and Help buttons on the Language bar by clicking their names to remove the check mark to the left of each button. The Settings command on the Options menu displays a dialog box that lets you customize the Language bar. This command will be discussed shortly. The Restore Defaults command redisplays hidden buttons on the Language bar.

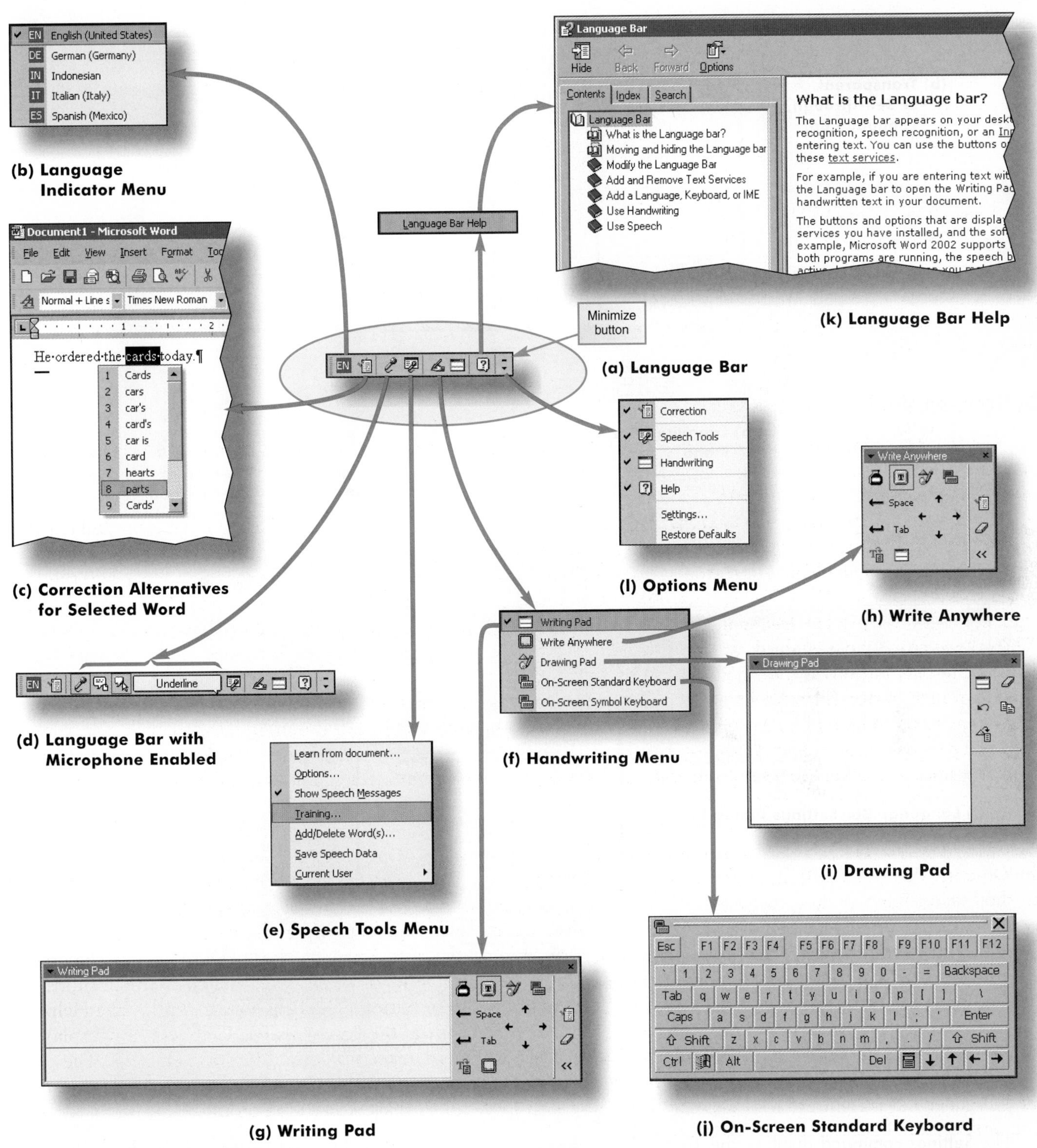

FIGURE B-2

If you right-click the Language bar, a shortcut menu displays (Figure B-3a on the next page). This shortcut menu lets you further customize the Language bar. The **Minimize command** on the shortcut menu minimizes the Language bar the same as the Minimize button on the Language bar. The **Transparency command** toggles the Language bar between being solid and transparent. You can see through a transparent Language bar (Figure B-3b). The **Text Labels command** toggles text labels on the Language bar on (Figure B-3c) and off (Figure B-3a). The **Additional icons in taskbar command** toggles between only showing the Language Indicator button in the tray status area and showing icons that represent the text services that are active (Figure B-3d).

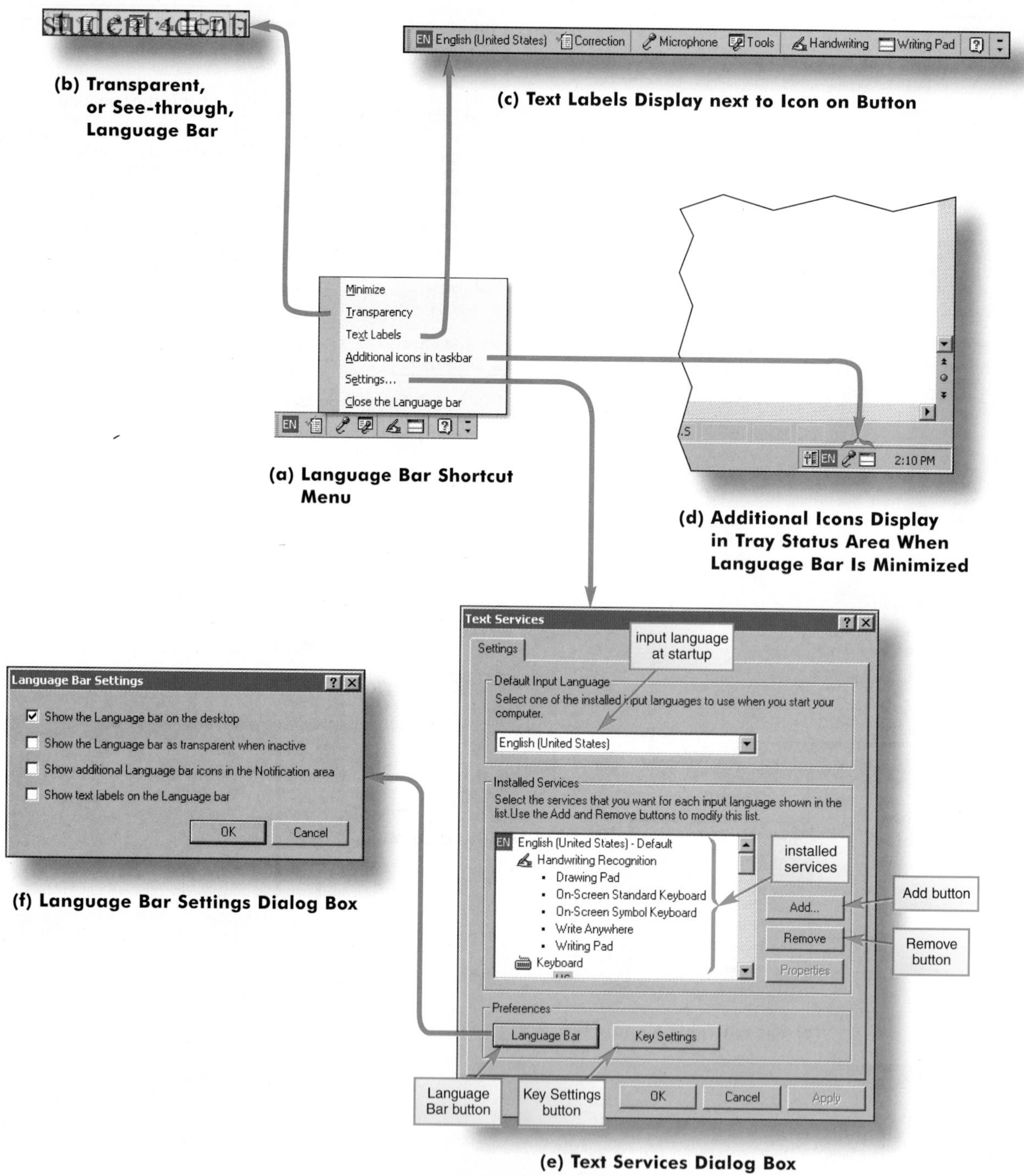

FIGURE B-3

The **Settings command** displays the Text Services dialog box (Figure B-3e). The **Text Services dialog box** allows you to select the language at startup; add and remove text services; modify keys on the keyboard; and modify the Language bar. If you want to remove any one of the entries in the Installed Services list, select the entry, and then click the Remove button. If you want to add a service, click the Add button. The Key Settings button allows you to modify the keyboard. If you click the **Language Bar button** in the Text Services dialog box, the **Language Bar Settings dialog box** displays (Figure B-3f). This dialog box contains Language bar options, some of which are the same as the commands on the Language bar shortcut menu described earlier.

The **Close the Language bar command** on the shortcut menu shown in Figure B-3a closes the Language bar and hides the Language Indicator button in the tray status area on the Windows taskbar. If you close the Language bar and want to redisplay it, follow the instructions at the top of page MO B.02.

Speech Recognition

The **Speech Recognition service** available with all Office XP applications enables your computer to recognize human speech through a microphone. The microphone has two modes: dictation and voice command. The example in Figure B-4 uses Word to illustrate the speech recognition modes of Office XP. You switch between the two modes by clicking the Dictation button and the Voice Command button on the Language bar. These buttons display only when you turn on Speech Recognition by clicking the **Microphone button** on the Language bar (Figure B-5 on the next page). If you are using the Microphone button for the very first time in Word, it will require that you check your microphone settings and step through voice training before activating the Speech Recognition service.

The **Dictation button** places the microphone in Dictation mode. In **Dictation mode**, whatever you speak is entered as text at the location of the insertion point. The **Voice Command button** places the microphone in Voice Command mode. In **Voice Command mode**, whatever you speak is interpreted as a command. If you want to turn off the microphone, click the Microphone button on the Language bar or in Voice Command mode say, "Mic off" (pronounced mike off). It is important to remember that minimizing the Language bar does not turn off the microphone.

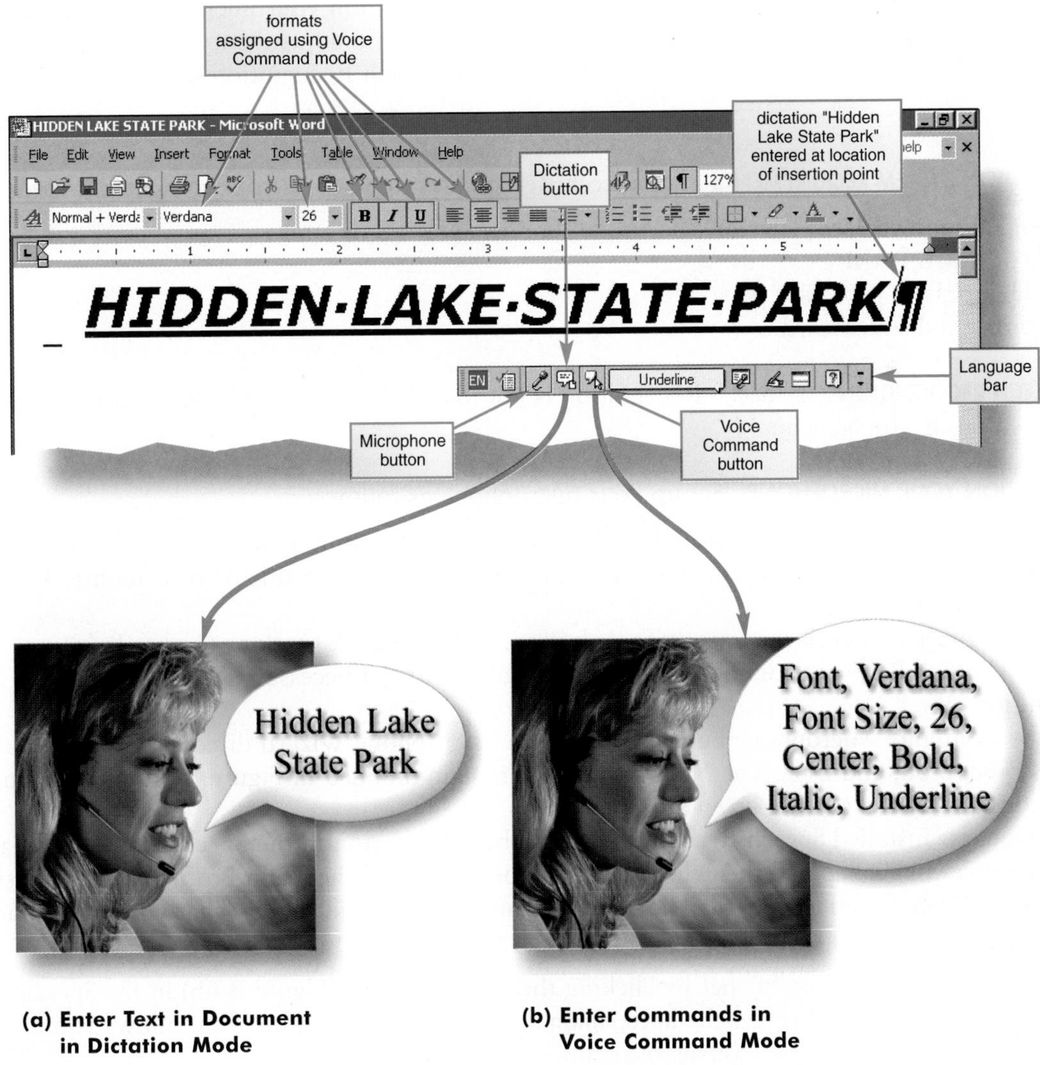

(a) Enter Text in Document in Dictation Mode

(b) Enter Commands in Voice Command Mode

FIGURE B-4

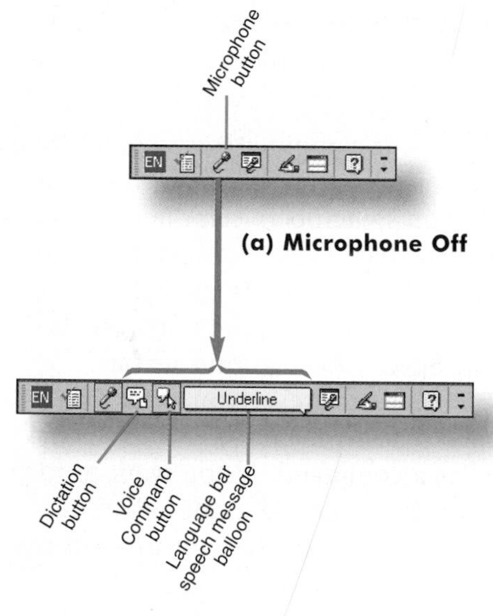

(a) Microphone Off

(b) Microphone On

FIGURE B-5

The **Language bar speech message balloon** shown in Figure B-5b displays messages that may offer help or hints. In Voice Command mode, the name of the last recognized command you said displays. If you use the mouse or keyboard instead of the microphone, a message will appear in the Language bar speech message balloon indicating the word you could say. In Dictation mode, the message, Dictating, usually displays. The Speech Recognition service, however, will display messages to inform you that you are talking too soft, too loud, too fast, or to ask you to repeat what you said by displaying, What was that?

Getting Started with Speech Recognition

For the microphone to function properly, you should follow these steps:

1. Make sure your computer meets the minimum requirements.
2. Install Speech Recognition.
3. Set up and position your microphone, preferably a close-talk headset with gain adjustment support.
4. Train the Speech Recognition service.

The following sections describe these steps in more detail.

SPEECH RECOGNITION SYSTEM REQUIREMENTS For Speech Recognition to work on your computer, it needs the following:

1. Microsoft Windows 98 or later or Microsoft Windows NT 4.0 or later
2. At least 128 MB RAM
3. 400 MHz or faster processor
4. Microphone and sound card

INSTALLING SPEECH RECOGNITION If Speech Recognition is not installed on your computer, start Microsoft Word and then click Speech on the Tools menu.

SET UP AND POSITION YOUR MICROPHONE Set up your microphone as follows:

1. Connect your microphone to the sound card in the back of the computer.
2. Position the microphone approximately one inch out from and to the side of your mouth. Position it so you are not breathing into it.
3. On the Language bar, click the Speech Tools button, and then click Options (Figure B-6a).
4. When the Speech Properties dialog box displays (Figure B-6b), if necessary, click the Speech Recognition tab.
5. Click the Configure Microphone button. Follow the Microphone Wizard directions as shown in Figures B-6c, B-6d, and B-6e. The Next button will remain dimmed in Figure B-6d until the volume meter consistently stays in the green area.
6. If someone else installed Speech Recognition, click the New button in the Speech Properties dialog box and enter your name and then click the Finish button. Click the Train Profile button and step through the Voice Training Wizard. The Voice Training Wizard will require that you enter your gender and age group. It then will step you through voice training.

You can adjust the microphone further by clicking the **Settings button** (Figure B-6b) in the Speech Properties dialog box. The Settings button displays the **Recognition Profile Settings dialog box** that allows you to adjust the pronunciation sensitivity and accuracy versus recognition response time.

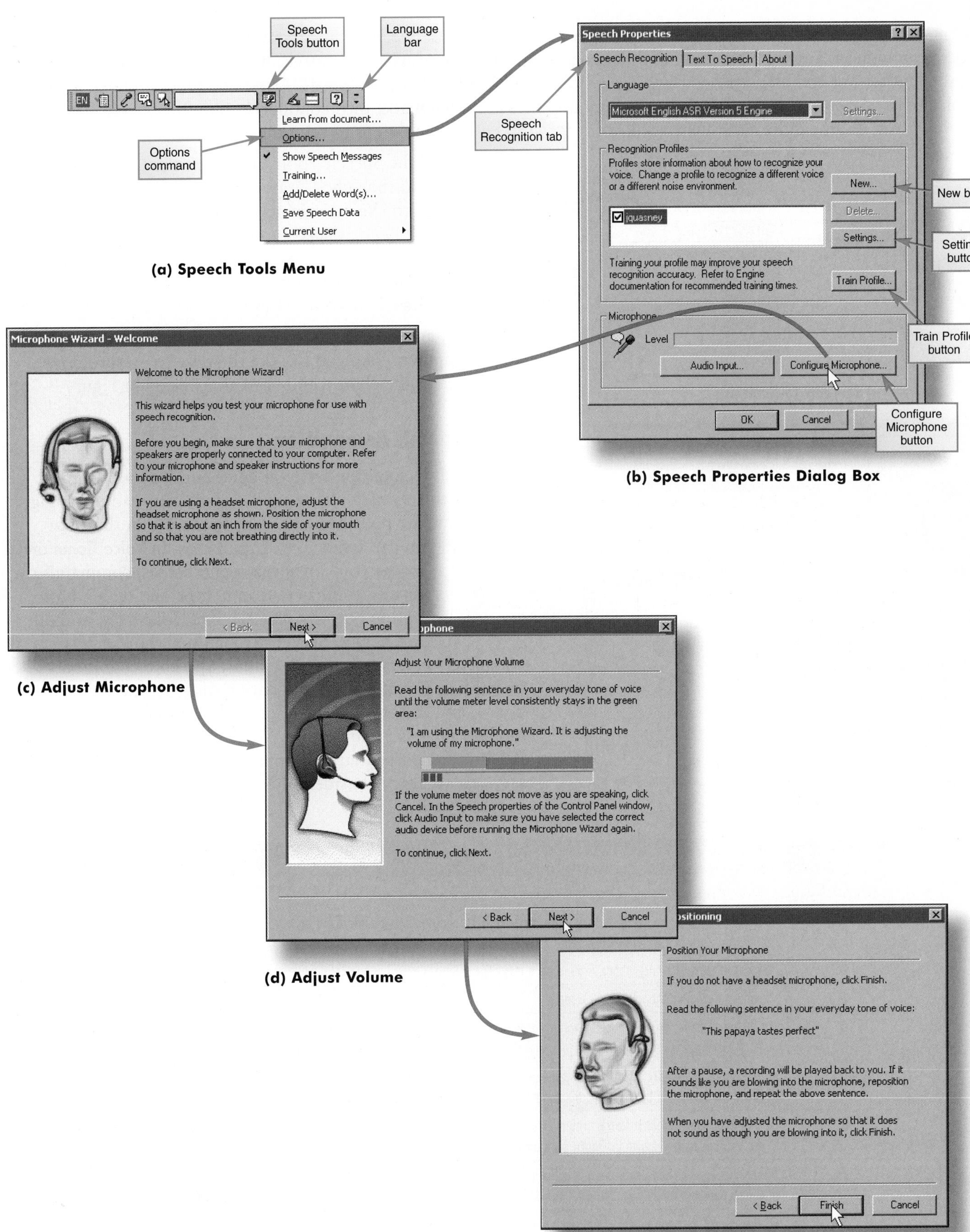

(a) Speech Tools Menu

(b) Speech Properties Dialog Box

(c) Adjust Microphone

(d) Adjust Volume

(e) Test Microphone

FIGURE B-6

TRAIN THE SPEECH RECOGNITION SERVICE The Speech Recognition service will understand most commands and some dictation without any training at all. It will recognize much more of what you speak, however, if you take the time to train it. After one training session, it will recognize 85 to 90 percent of your words. As you do more training, accuracy will rise to 95 percent. If you feel that too many mistakes are being made, then continue to train the service. The more training you do, the more accurately it will work for you. Follow these steps to train the Speech Recognition service:

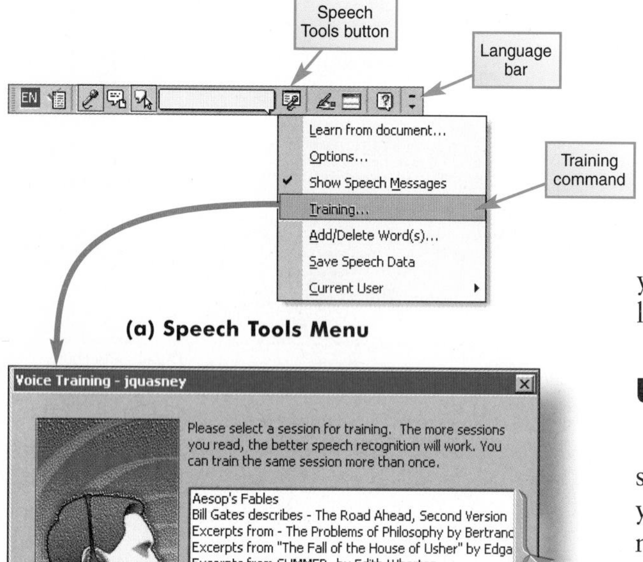

(a) Speech Tools Menu

(b) Voice Training Dialog Box

FIGURE B-7

1. Click the Speech Tools button on the Language bar and then click Training (Figure B-7a).
2. When the **Voice Training dialog box** displays (Figure B-7b), click one of the sessions and then click the Next button.
3. Complete the training session, which should take less than 15 minutes.

If you are serious about using a microphone to speak to your computer, you need to take the time to go through at least three of the eight training sessions listed in Figure B-7b.

Using Speech Recognition

Speech recognition lets you enter text into a document similarly to speaking into a tape recorder. Instead of typing, you can dictate text that you want to display in the document, and you can issue voice commands. In **Voice Command mode**, you can speak menu names, commands on menus, toolbar button names, and dialog box option buttons, check boxes, list boxes, and button names. Speech Recognition, however, is not a completely hands-free form of input. Speech recognition works best if you use a combination of your voice, the keyboard, and the mouse. You soon will discover that Dictation mode is far less accurate than Voice Command mode. Table B-1 lists some tips that will improve the Speech Recognition service's accuracy considerably.

Table B-1 Tips to Improve Speech Recognition

NUMBER	*TIP*
1	The microphone hears everything. Though the Speech Recognition service filters out background noise, it is recommended that you work in a quiet environment.
2	Try not to move the microphone around once it is adjusted.
3	Speak in a steady tone and speak clearly.
4	In Dictation mode, do not pause between words. A phrase is easier to interpret than a word. Sounding out syllables in a word will make it more difficult for the Speech Recognition service to interpret what you are saying.
5	If you speak too loudly or too softly, it makes it difficult for the Speech Recognition service to interpret what you said. Check the Language bar speech message balloon for an indication that you may be speaking too loudly or too softly.
6	If you experience problems after training, adjust the recognition options that control accuracy and rejection by clicking the Settings button shown in Figure B-6b on the previous page.
7	When you are finished using the microphone, turn it off by clicking the Microphone button on the Language bar or in Voice Command mode say, "Mic off." Leaving the microphone on is the same as leaning on the keyboard.
8	If the Speech Recognition service is having difficulty with unusual words, then add the words to its dictionary by using the Learn from document command or Add/Delete Word(s) command on the Speech Tools menu (Figure B-8a). The last names of individuals and the names of companies are good examples of the types of words you should add to the dictionary.
9	Training will improve accuracy; practice will improve confidence.

The last command on the Speech Tools menu is the Current User command (Figure B-8a). The **Current User command** is useful for multiple users who share a computer. It allows them to configure their own individual profiles, and then switch between users as they use the computer.

For additional information on the Speech Recognition service, click the Help button on the Standard toolbar, click the Answer Wizard tab, and search for the phrase, Speech Recognition.

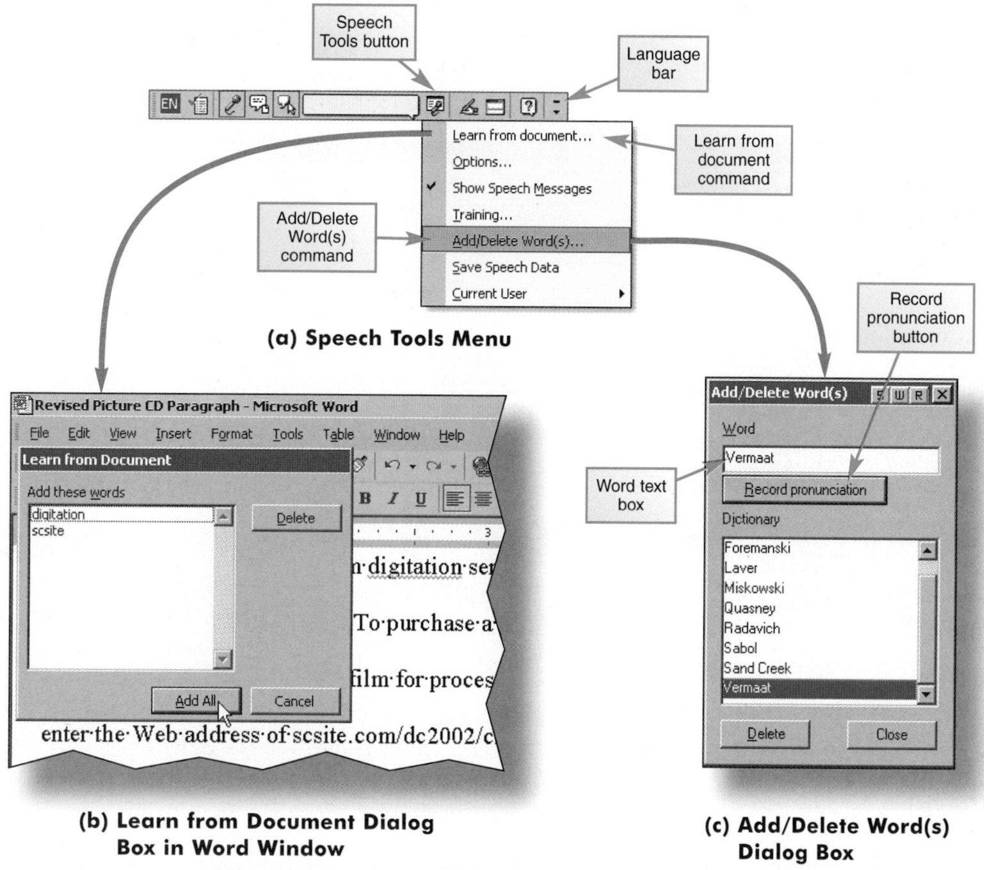

(a) Speech Tools Menu

(b) Learn from Document Dialog Box in Word Window

(c) Add/Delete Word(s) Dialog Box

FIGURE B-8

Handwriting Recognition

Using the Office XP handwriting recognition capabilities, you can enter text and numbers into all Office XP applications by writing instead of typing. You can write using a special handwriting device that connects to your computer or you can write on the screen using your mouse. Four basic methods of handwriting are available by clicking the **Handwriting button** on the Language bar: Writing Pad, Write Anywhere, Drawing Pad, and On-Screen Keyboard. Although the on-screen keyboard does not involve handwriting recognition, it is part of the Handwriting menu and, therefore, will be discussed in this section. The following pages use Word to illustrate the handwriting recognition capabilities available in most Office XP applications.

If your Language bar does not include the Handwriting button (Figures B-1b or B-1c on page MO B.01), then for installation instructions click the Help button on the Standard toolbar, click the Answer Wizard tab, and search for the phrase Install Handwriting Recognition.

Writing Pad

To display the Writing Pad, click the Handwriting button on the Language bar and then click Writing Pad. The **Writing Pad** resembles a note pad with one or more lines on which you can use freehand to print or write in cursive. You can form letters on the line by moving the mouse while holding down the mouse button. With the **Text button** selected, the handwritten text is converted to typed characters and inserted into the document (Figure B-9a on the next page).

Consider the example in Figure B-9a. With the insertion point at the top of the document, the name, Millie, is written in cursive on the **Pen line** in the Writing Pad. As soon as the name is complete, the Handwriting Recognition service automatically converts the handwriting to typed characters and inserts the name into the document at the location of the insertion point.

With the **Ink button** selected, the text is inserted in handwritten form into the document. Once inserted, you can change the font size and color of the handwritten text (Figure B-9b).

To the right of the note pad is a rectangular toolbar. Use the buttons on this toolbar to adjust the Writing Pad, move the insertion point, and activate other handwriting applications.

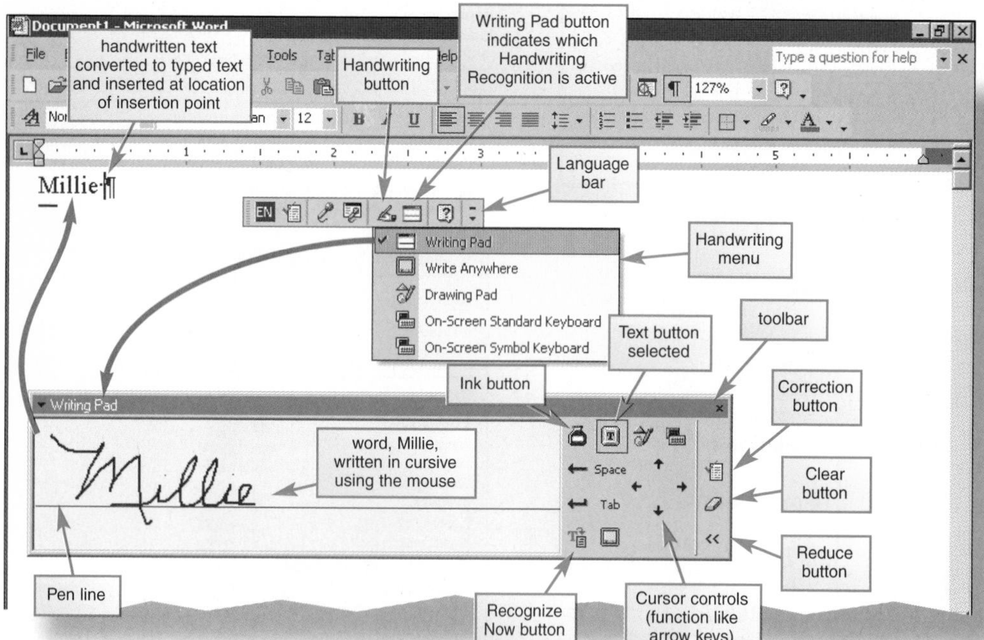

(a) Text Button Selected

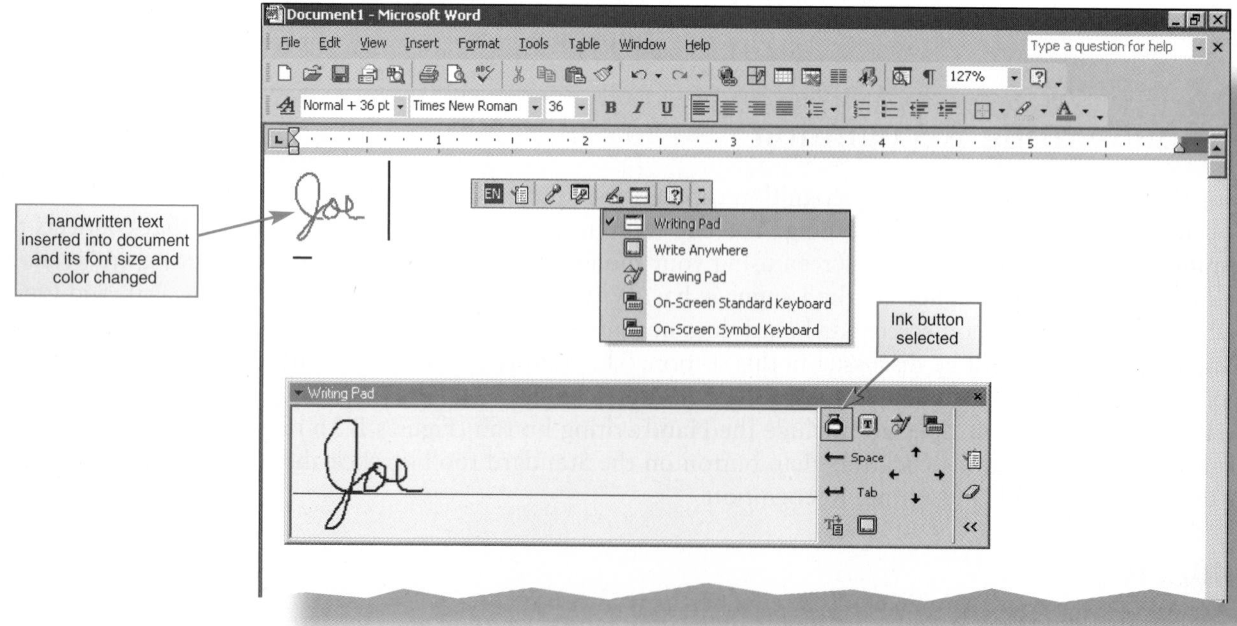

(b) Ink Button Selected

FIGURE B-9

You can customize the Writing Pad by clicking the **Options button** on the left side of the title bar and then clicking the Options command (Figure B-10a). Invoking the **Options command** causes the Handwriting Options dialog box to display. The **Handwriting Options dialog box** contains two sheets: Common and Writing Pad. The **Common sheet** lets you change the pen color and pen width, adjust recognition, and customize the toolbar area of the Writing Pad. The **Writing Pad sheet** allows you to change the background color and the number of lines that display in the Writing Pad. Both sheets contain a **Restore Default button** to restore the settings to what they were when the software was installed initially.

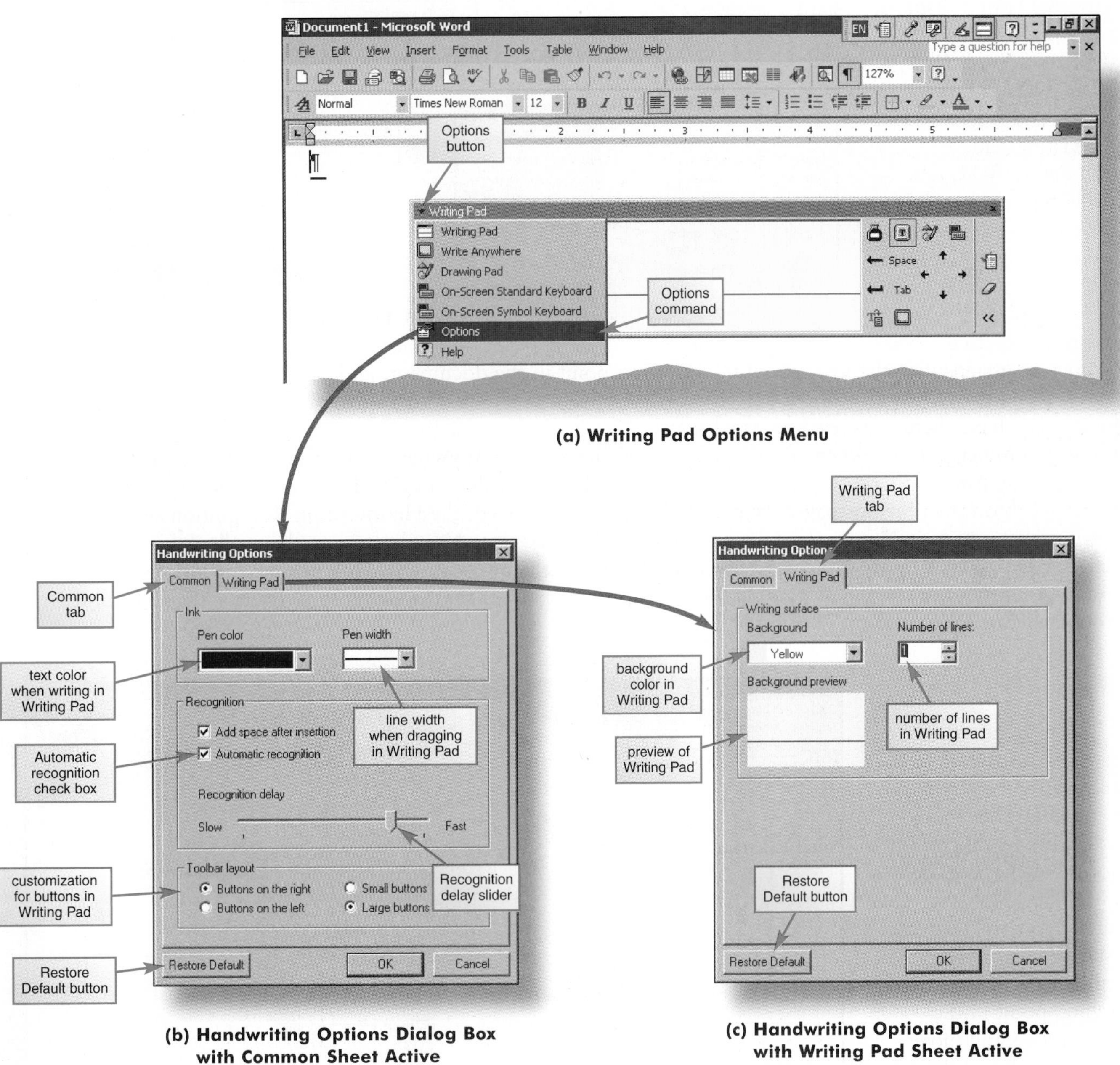

(a) Writing Pad Options Menu

(b) Handwriting Options Dialog Box with Common Sheet Active

(c) Handwriting Options Dialog Box with Writing Pad Sheet Active

FIGURE B-10

When you first start using the Writing Pad, you may want to remove the check mark from the **Automatic recognition check box** in the Common sheet in the Handwriting Options dialog box (Figure B-10b). With the check mark removed, the Handwriting Recognition service will not interpret what you write in the Writing Pad until you click the **Recognize Now button** on the toolbar (Figure B-9a). This allows you to pause and adjust your writing.

The best way to learn how to use the Writing Pad is to practice with it. Also, for more information, click the Help button on the Standard toolbar, click the Answer Wizard tab, and search for the phrase, Handwriting Recognition.

Write Anywhere

Rather than use a Writing Pad, you can write anywhere on the screen by invoking the **Write Anywhere command** on the Handwriting menu (Figure B-11) that displays when you click the Handwriting button on the Language bar. In this case, the entire window is your writing pad.

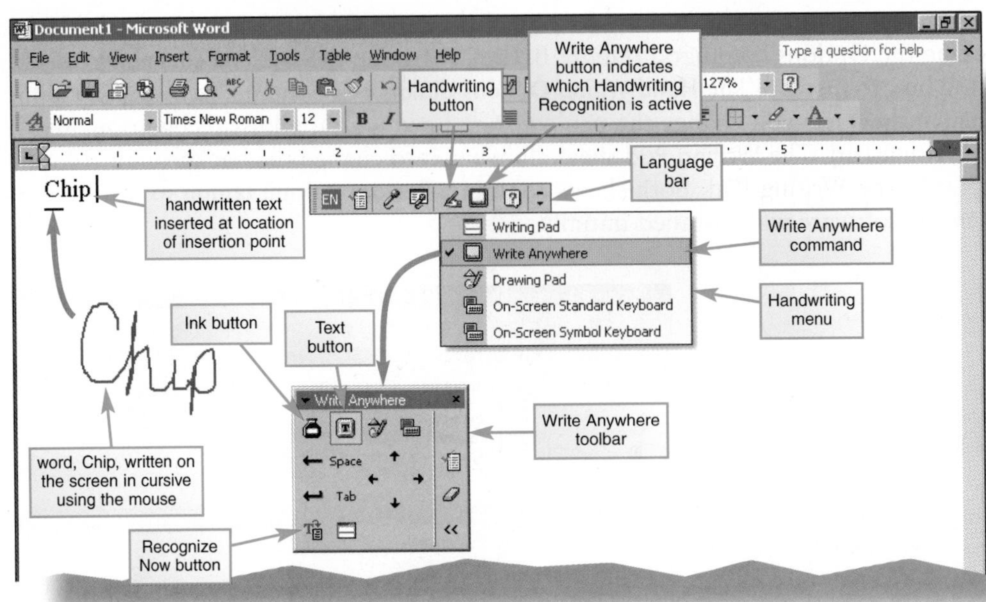

FIGURE B-11

In Figure B-11, the word, Chip, is written in cursive using the mouse button. Shortly after you finish writing the word, the Handwriting Recognition service interprets it, assigns it to the location of the insertion point in the document, and erases what you wrote. Similarly to the Writing Pad, Write Anywhere has both an Ink button and a Text button so you can insert either handwritten characters or have them converted to typed text.

It is recommended that when you first start using the Writing Anywhere service that you remove the check mark from the Automatic recognition check box in the Common sheet in the Handwriting Options dialog box (Figure B-10b on the previous page). With the check mark removed, the Handwriting Recognition service will not interpret what you write on the screen until you click the Recognize Now button on the toolbar (Figure B-11).

Write Anywhere is more difficult to use than the Writing Pad, because when you click the mouse button, Word may interpret the action as moving the insertion point rather than starting to write. For this reason, it is recommended that you use the Writing Pad.

Drawing Pad

To display the Drawing Pad, click the Handwriting button on the Language bar and then click Drawing Pad (Figure B-12). With the **Drawing Pad**, you can insert a freehand drawing or sketch into a Word document. To create the drawing, point in the Drawing Pad and move the mouse while holding down the mouse button.

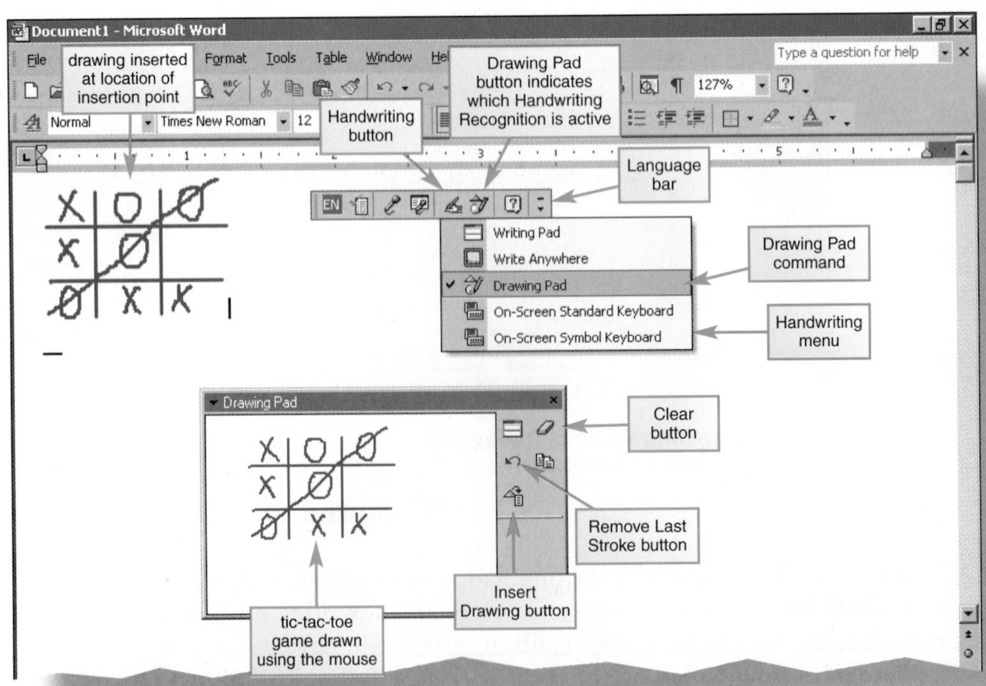

FIGURE B-12

In Figure B-12, the mouse button was used to draw a tic-tac-toe game in the Drawing Pad. To insert the drawing into the Word document at the location of the insertion point, click the Insert Drawing button on the rectangular toolbar to the right of the Drawing Pad. Other buttons on the toolbar allow you to erase a drawing, erase your last drawing stroke, copy the drawing to the Office Clipboard, or activate the Writing Pad.

You can customize the Drawing Pad by clicking the Options button on the left side of the title bar and then clicking the Options command (Figure B-13a). Invoking the **Options command** causes the Draw Options dialog box to display (Figure B-13b). The **Draw Options dialog box** lets you change the pen color and pen width and customize the toolbar area of the Drawing Pad. The dialog box also contains a Restore Default button that restores the settings to what they were when the software was installed initially.

The best way to learn how to use the Drawing Pad is to practice with it. Also, for more information, click the Help button on the Standard toolbar, click the Answer Wizard tab, and search for the phrase, Drawing Pad.

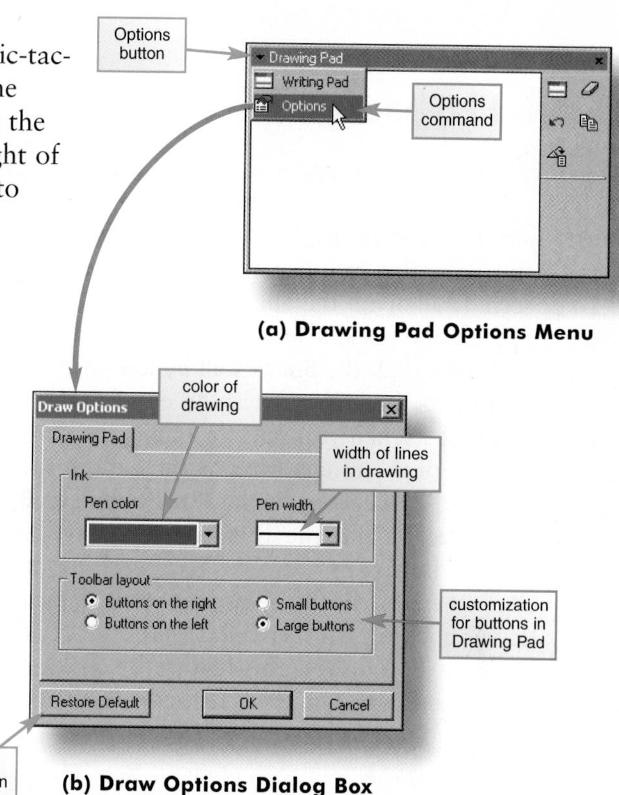

(a) Drawing Pad Options Menu

(b) Draw Options Dialog Box

FIGURE B-13

On-Screen Keyboard

The **On-Screen Standard Keyboard command** on the Handwriting menu (Figure B-14) displays an on-screen keyboard. The **on-screen keyboard** lets you enter characters into a document by using your mouse to click the keys. The on-screen keyboard is similar to the type found on handheld computers.

The **On-Screen Symbol Keyboard command** on the Handwriting menu (Figure B-14) displays a special on-screen keyboard that allows you to enter symbols that are not on your keyboard, as well as Unicode characters. **Unicode characters** use a coding scheme capable of representing all the world's current languages.

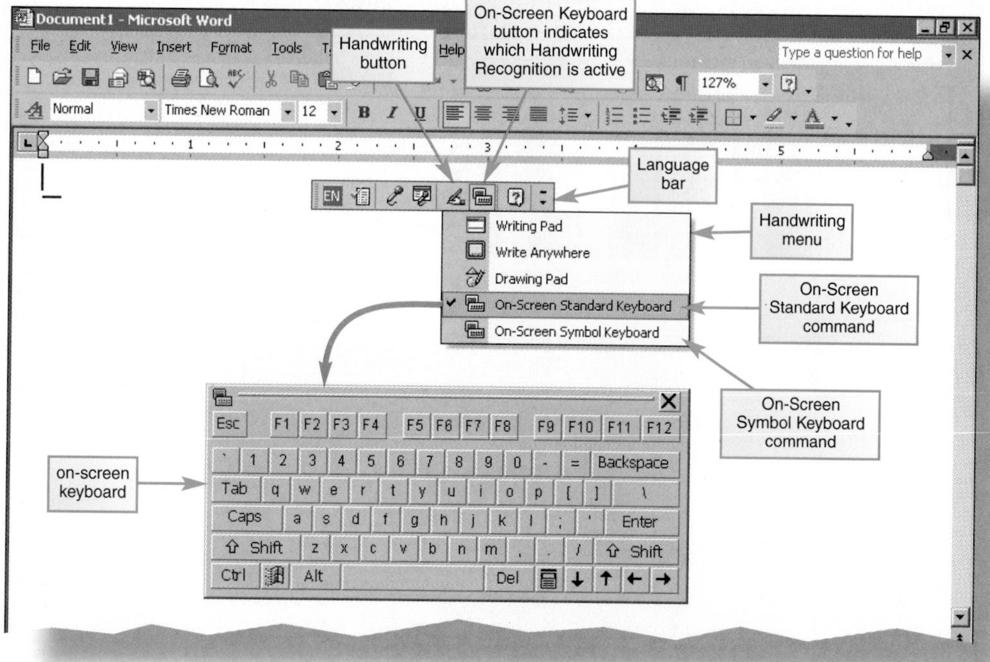

FIGURE B-14

Speech Playback in Excel

Excel is the only Office XP application that supports speech playback. With Excel, you can use **speech playback** to have your computer read back the data in a worksheet. To enable speech playback, you use the **Text To Speech toolbar** (Figure B-15). You display the toolbar by right-clicking a toolbar and then clicking Text To Speech on the shortcut menu. You also can display the toolbar by pointing to Speech on the Tools menu and then clicking Show Text To Speech Toolbar on the Speech submenu.

To use speech playback, select the cell where you want the computer to start reading back the data in the worksheet and then click the **Speak Cell button** on the Text To Speech toolbar (Figure B-15). The computer stops reading after it reads the last cell with an entry in the worksheet. An alternative is to select a range before you turn on speech playback. When you select a range, the computer reads from the upper-left corner of the range to the lower-right corner of the range. It reads the data in the worksheet by rows or by columns. You choose the direction you want it to read by clicking the **By Rows button** or **By Columns button** on the Text To Speech toolbar. Click the **Stop Speaking button** or hide the Text To Speech toolbar to stop speech playback.

The rightmost button on the Text To Speech toolbar is the Speak On Enter button. When you click the **Speak On Enter button** to enable it, the computer reads data in a cell immediately after you complete the entry by pressing the ENTER key or clicking another cell. It does not read the data if you click the Enter box on the formula bar to complete the entry. You disable this feature by clicking the Speak On Enter button while the feature is enabled. If you do not turn the Speak On Enter feature off, the computer will continue to read new cell entries even if the toolbar is hidden.

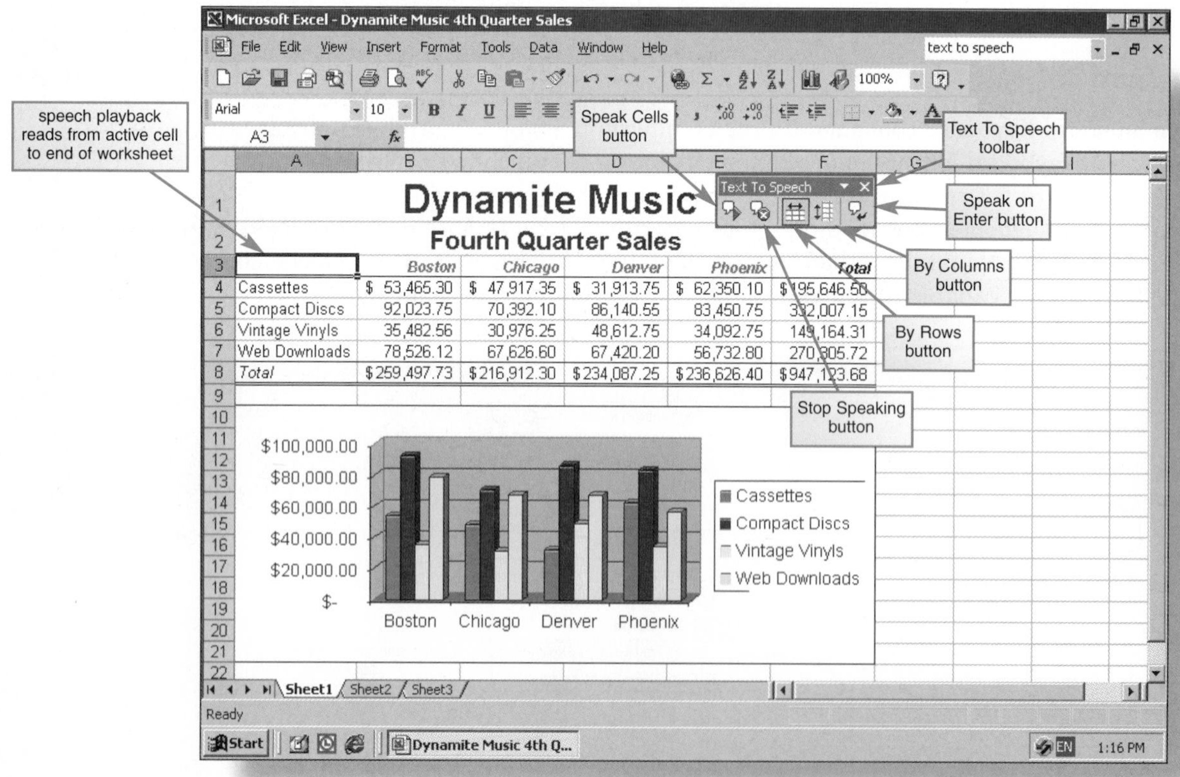

FIGURE B-15

Customizing Speech Playback

You can customize speech playback by double-clicking the **Speech icon** in the Control Panel window (Figure B-16a). To display the Control Panel, point to Settings on the Start menu and then click Control Panel. When you double-click the Speech icon, the Speech Properties dialog box displays (Figure B-16b). Click the Text To Speech tab. The Text To Speech sheet has two areas: Voice selection and Voice speed. The Voice selection area lets you choose between a male and female voice. You can click the Preview Voice button to preview the voice. The Voice speed area contains a slider. Drag the slider to slow down or speed up the voice.

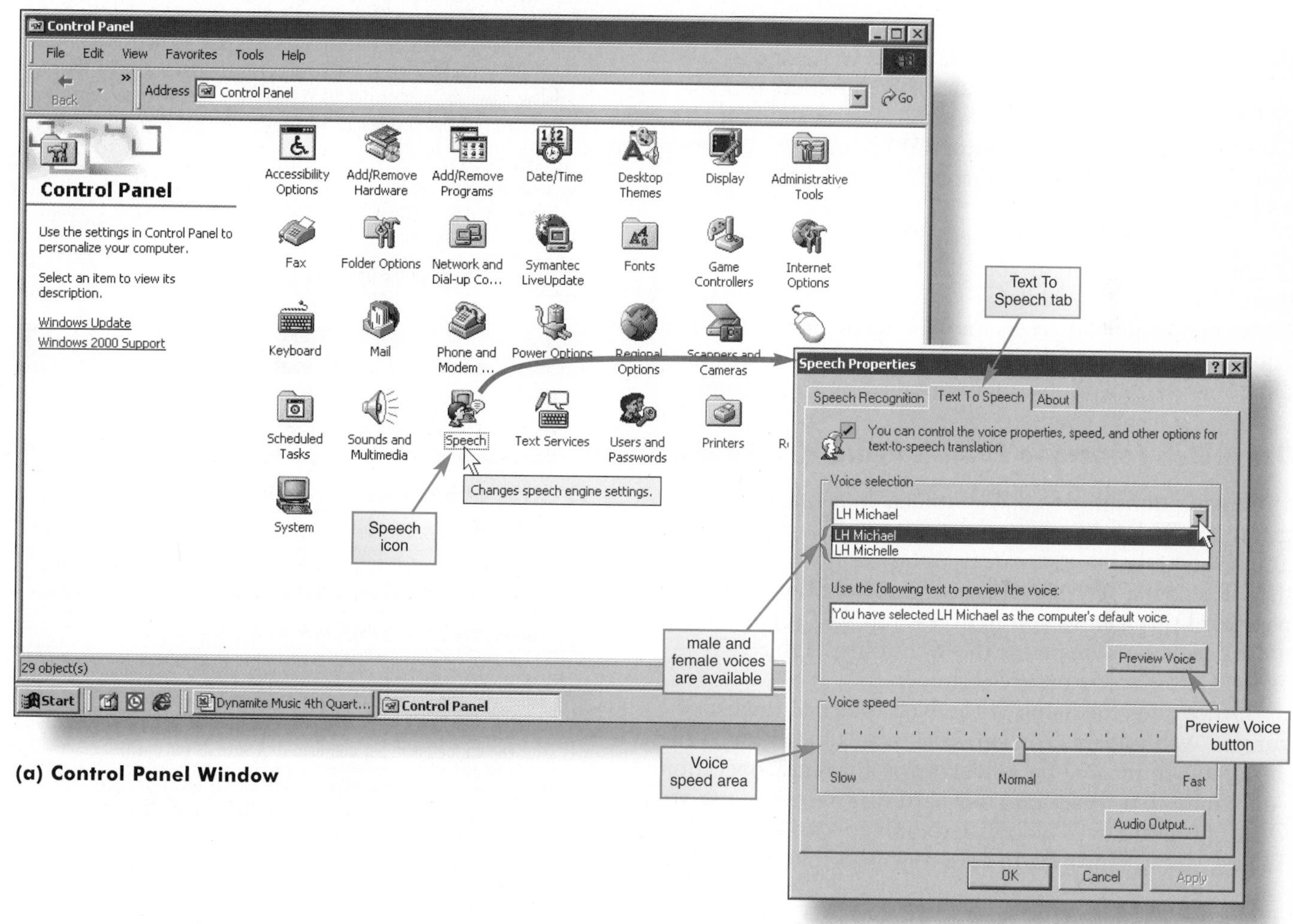

(a) Control Panel Window

(b) Speech Properties Dialog Box

FIGURE B-16

APPENDIX C

Publishing Office Web Pages to a Web Server

With the Office applications, you use the Save as Web Page command on the File menu to save the Web page to a Web server using one of two techniques: Web folders or File Transfer Protocol. A **Web folder** is an Office shortcut to a Web server. **File Transfer Protocol** (**FTP**) is an Internet standard that allows computers to exchange files with other computers on the Internet.

You should contact your network system administrator or technical support staff at your ISP to determine if their Web server supports Web folders, FTP, or both, and to obtain necessary permissions to access the Web server. If you decide to publish Web pages using a Web folder, you must have the Office Server Extensions (OSE) installed on your computer.

Using Web Folders to Publish Office Web Pages

When publishing to a Web folder, someone first must create the Web folder before you can save to it. If you are granted permission to create a Web folder, you must obtain the URL of the Web server, a user name, and possibly a password that allows you to access the Web server. You also must decide on a name for the Web folder. Table C-1 explains how to create a Web folder.

Office adds the name of the Web folder to the list of current Web folders. You can save to this folder, open files in the folder, rename the folder, or perform any operations you would to a folder on your hard disk. You can use your Office program or Windows Explorer to access this folder. Table C-2 explains how to save to a Web folder.

Using FTP to Publish Office Web Pages

When publishing a Web page using FTP, you first must add the FTP location to your computer before you can save to it. An **FTP location**, also called an **FTP site**, is a collection of files that reside on an FTP server. In this case, the FTP server is the Web server.

To add an FTP location, you must obtain the name of the FTP site, which usually is the address (URL) of the FTP server, and a user name and a password that allows you to access the FTP server. You save and open the Web pages on the FTP server using the name of the FTP site. Table C-3 explains how to add an FTP site.

Office adds the name of the FTP site to the FTP locations list in the Save As and Open dialog boxes. You can open and save files using this list. Table C-4 explains how to save to an FTP location.

Table C-1 Creating a Web Folder
1. Click File on the menu bar and then click Save As (or Open).
2. When the Save As dialog box (or Open dialog box) displays, click My Network Places (or Web Folders) on the Places Bar. Double-click Add Network Place (or Add Web Folder).
3. When the Add Network Place Wizard dialog box displays, click the Create a new Network Place option button and then click the Next button. Type the URL of the Web server in the Folder location text box, enter the folder name you want to call the Web folder in the Folder name text box, and then click the Next button. Click Empty Web and then click the Finish button.
4. When the Enter Network Password dialog box displays, type the user name and, if necessary, the password in the respective text boxes and then click the OK button.
5. Close the Save As or the Open dialog box.

Table C-2 Saving to a Web Folder
1. Click File on the menu bar and then click Save As.
2. When the Save As dialog box displays, type the Web page file name in the File name text box. Do not press the ENTER key.
3. Click My Network Places on the Places Bar.
4. Double-click the Web folder name in the Save in list.
5. If the Enter Network Password dialog box displays, type the user name and password in the respective text boxes and then click the OK button.
6. Click the Save button in the Save As dialog box.

Table C-3 Adding an FTP Location
1. Click File on the menu bar and then click Save As (or Open).
2. In the Save As dialog box, click the Save in box arrow and then click Add/Modify FTP Locations in the Save in list; or in the Open dialog box, click the Look in box arrow and then click Add/Modify FTP Locations in the Look in list.
3. When the Add/Modify FTP Locations dialog box displays, type the name of the FTP site in the Name of FTP site text box. If the site allows anonymous logon, click Anonymous in the Log on as area; if you have a user name for the site, click User in the Log on as area and then enter the user name. Enter the password in the Password text box. Click the OK button.
4. Close the Save As or the Open dialog box.

Table C-4 Saving to an FTP Location
1. Click File on the menu bar and then click Save As.
2. When the Save As dialog box displays, type the Web page file name in the File name text box. Do not press the ENTER key.
3. Click the Save in box arrow and then click FTP Locations.
4. Double-click the name of the FTP site to which you wish to save.
5. When the FTP Log On dialog box displays, enter your user name and password and then click the OK button.
6. Click the Save button in the Save As dialog box.

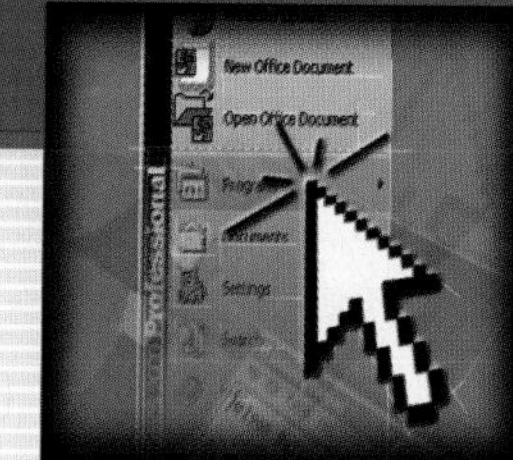

APPENDIX D

Resetting the Word Toolbars and Menus

Word customization capabilities allow you to create custom toolbars by adding and deleting buttons and to personalize menus based on their usage. Each time you start Word, the toolbars and menus display using the same settings as the last time you used it. This appendix shows you how to reset the Standard and Formatting toolbars and menus to their installation settings.

Steps To Reset the Standard and Formatting Toolbars

1 Click the Toolbar Options button on the Standard toolbar and then point to Add or Remove Buttons on the Toolbar Options menu.

The Toolbar Options menu and the Add or Remove Buttons submenu display (Figure D-1).

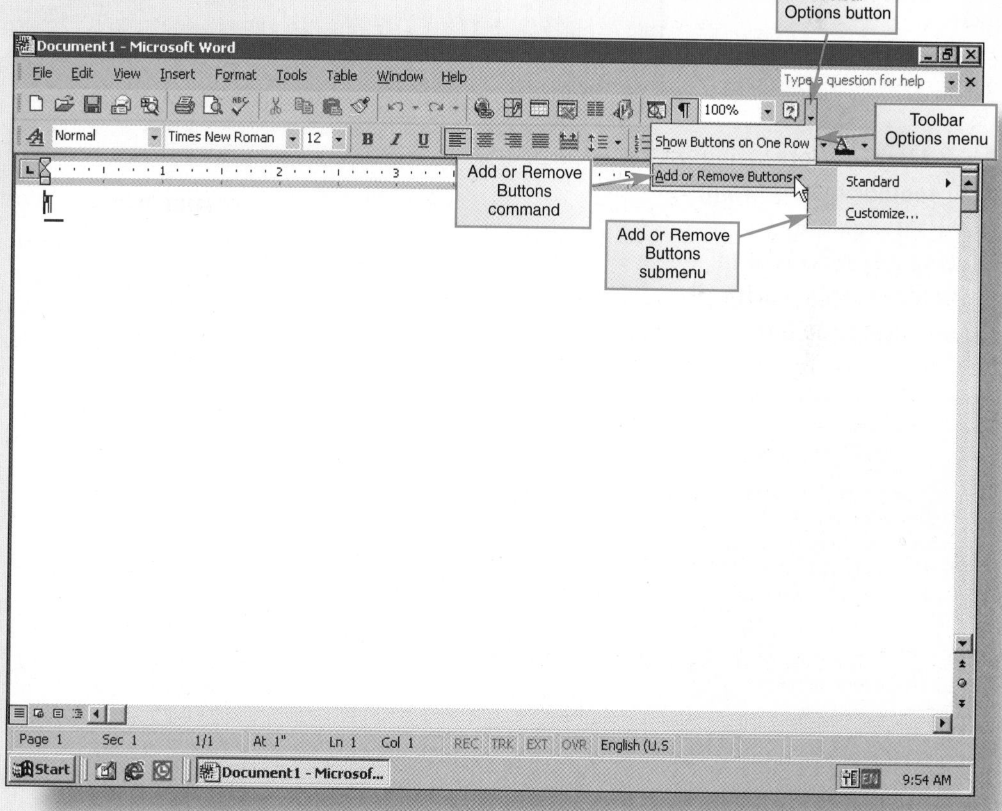

FIGURE D-1

2 Point to Standard on the Add or Remove Buttons submenu. When the Standard submenu displays, scroll down and then point to Reset Toolbar.

The Standard submenu displays indicating the buttons and boxes that display on the toolbar (Figure D-2). Clicking a button name with a check mark to the left of the name removes the check mark and then removes the button from the toolbar.

3 Click Reset Toolbar.

Word resets the Standard toolbar to its installation settings.

4 Reset the Formatting toolbar by following Steps 1 through 3 and replacing any reference to the Standard toolbar with the Formatting toolbar.

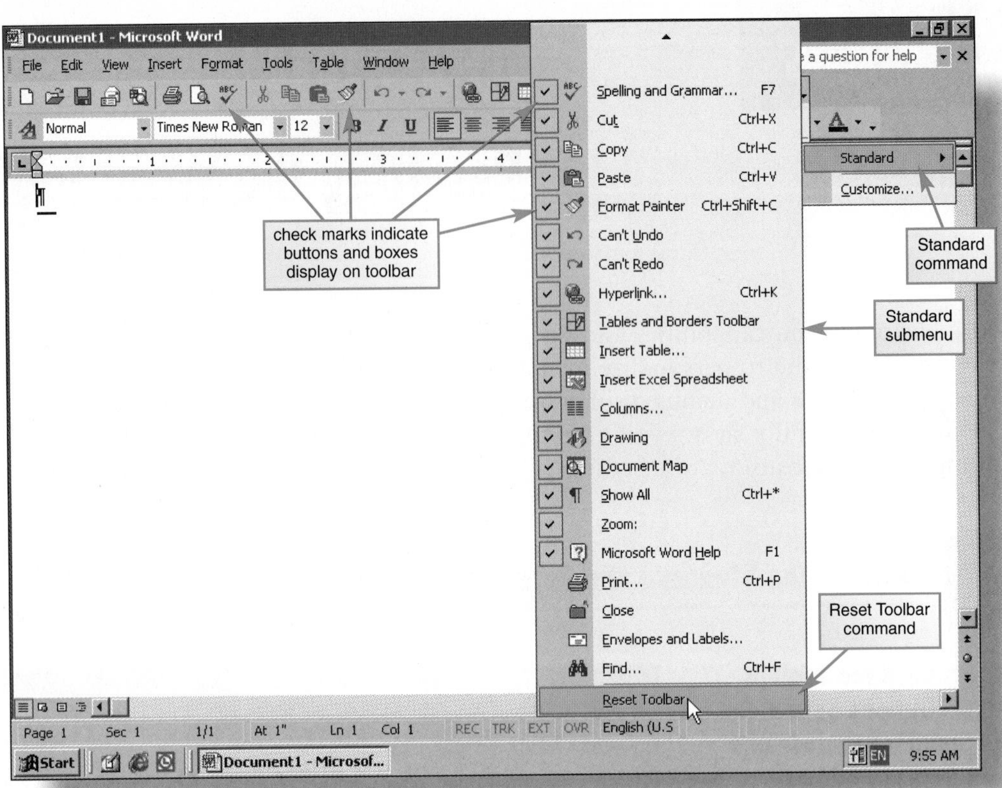

FIGURE D-2

Other Ways

1. On View menu point to Toolbars, click Customize on Toolbars submenu, click Toolbars tab, click toolbar name, click Reset button, click OK button, click Close button
2. Right-click toolbar, click Customize, click Toolbars tab, click toolbar name, click Reset button, click OK button, click Close button
3. In Voice Command mode, say "View, Toolbars, Customize, Toolbars, [toolbar name], Reset, OK, Close"

Steps To Reset Menus

1 Click the Toolbar Options button on the Standard toolbar and then point to Add or Remove Buttons on the Toolbar Options menu. Point to Customize on the Add or Remove Buttons submenu.

The Toolbar Options menu and the Add or Remove Buttons submenu display (Figure D-3).

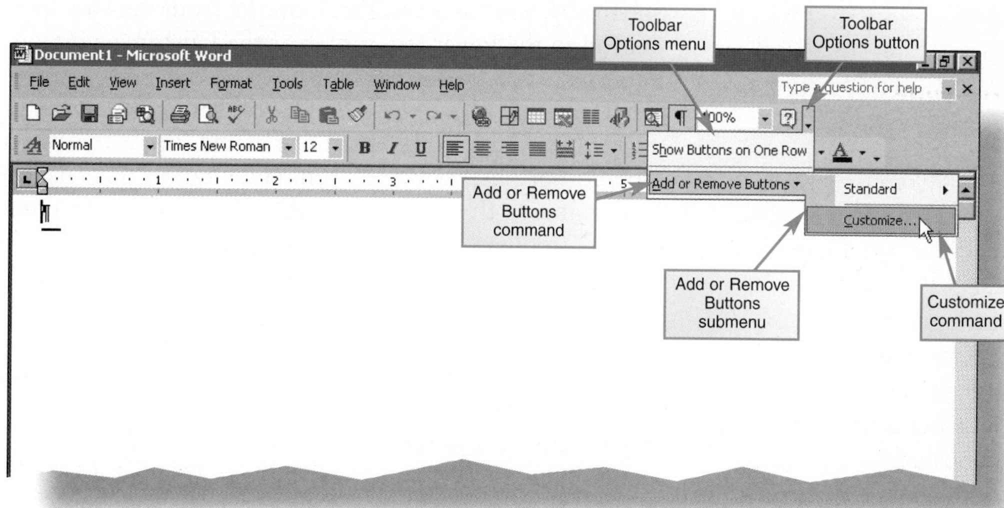

FIGURE D-3

2 Click Customize. When the Customize dialog box displays, click the Options tab and then point to the Reset my usage data button.

The Customize dialog box displays (Figure D-4). The **Customize dialog box** *contains three tabbed sheets used for customizing the Word toolbars and menus.*

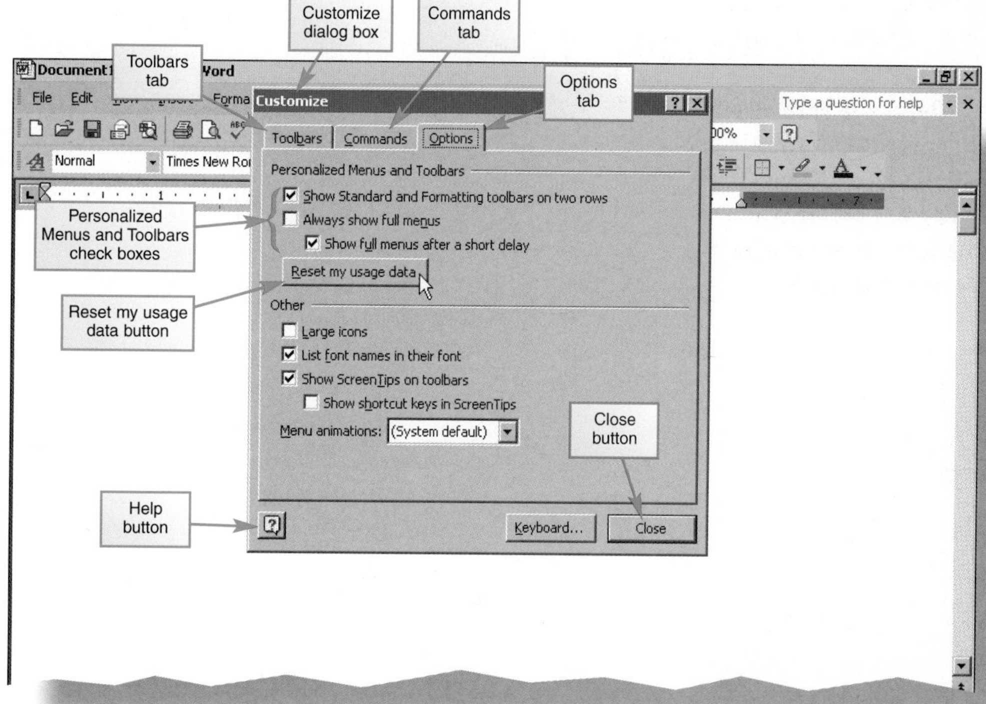

FIGURE D-4

3 Click the Reset my usage data button. When the Microsoft Word dialog box displays, click the Yes button. Click the Close button in the Customize dialog box.

Word resets the menus to the installation settings.

Other Ways

1. On View menu point to Toolbars, click Customize on Toolbars submenu, click Options tab, click Reset my usage data button, click Yes button, click Close button
2. In Voice Command mode, say "View, Toolbars, Customize, Options, Reset my usage data, Yes, Close"

In the Options sheet in the Customize dialog box shown in Figure D-4 on the previous page, you can turn off toolbars displaying on two rows and turn off short menus by removing the check marks from the two top check boxes. Click the Help button in the lower-left corner of the Customize dialog box to display Help topics that will assist you in customizing toolbars and menus.

Using the Commands sheet, you can add buttons to toolbars and commands to menus. Recall that the menu bar at the top of the Word window is a special toolbar. To add buttons, click the Commands tab in the Customize dialog box. Click a category name in the Categories list and then drag the command name in the Commands list to a toolbar. To add commands to a menu, click a category name in the Categories list, drag the command name in the Commands list to the menu name on the menu bar, and then, when the menu displays, drag the command to the desired location in the menu list of commands.

In the Toolbars sheet, you can add new toolbars and reset existing toolbars. If you add commands to menus as described in the previous paragraph and want to reset the menus to their default settings, do the following: (1) Click View on the menu bar and then point to Toolbars; (2) click Customize; (3) click the Toolbars tab; (4) click Menu Bar in the Toolbars list; (5) click the Reset button; (6) click the OK button; and then (7) click the Close button.

APPENDIX E
Microsoft Office User Specialist Certification Program

What Is MOUS Certification?

The Microsoft Office User Specialist (MOUS) Certification Program provides a framework for measuring your proficiency with the Microsoft Office XP applications, such as Word 2002, Excel 2002, Access 2002, PowerPoint 2002, Outlook 2002, and FrontPage 2002. The levels of certification are described in Table E-1.

Table E-1 Levels of MOUS Certification

LEVEL	*DESCRIPTION*	*REQUIREMENTS*	*CREDENTIAL AWARDED*
Expert	Indicates that you have a comprehensive understanding of the advanced features in a specific Microsoft Office XP application	Pass any ONE of the Expert exams: Microsoft Word 2002 Expert Microsoft Excel 2002 Expert Microsoft Access 2002 Expert Microsoft Outlook 2002 Expert Microsoft FrontPage 2002 Expert	Candidates will be awarded one certificate for each of the Expert exams they have passed: Microsoft Office User Specialist: Microsoft Word 2002 Expert Microsoft Office User Specialist: Microsoft Excel 2002 Expert Microsoft Office User Specialist: Microsoft Access 2002 Expert Microsoft Office User Specialist: Microsoft Outlook 2002 Expert Microsoft Office User Specialist: Microsoft FrontPage 2002 Expert
Core	Indicates that you have a comprehensive understanding of the core features in a specific Microsoft Office XP application	Pass any ONE of the Core exams: Microsoft Word 2002 Core Microsoft Excel 2002 Core Microsoft Access 2002 Core Microsoft Outlook 2002 Core Microsoft FrontPage 2002 Core	Candidates will be awarded one certificate for each of the Core exams they have passed: Microsoft Office User Specialist: Microsoft Word 2002 Microsoft Office User Specialist: Microsoft Excel 2002 Microsoft Office User Specialist: Microsoft Access 2002 Microsoft Office User Specialist: Microsoft Outlook 2002 Microsoft Office User Specialist: Microsoft FrontPage 2002
Comprehensive	Indicates that you have a comprehensive understanding of the features in Microsoft PowerPoint 2002	Pass the Microsoft PowerPoint 2002 Comprehensive Exam	Candidates will be awarded one certificate for the Microsoft PowerPoint 2002 Comprehensive exam passed.

Why Should You Get Certified?

Being a Microsoft Office User Specialist provides a valuable industry credential — proof that you have the Office XP applications skills required by employers. By passing one or more MOUS certification exams, you demonstrate your proficiency in a given Office XP application to employers. With over 100 million copies of Office in use around the world, Microsoft is targeting Office XP certification to a wide variety of companies. These companies include temporary employment agencies that want to prove the expertise of their workers, large corporations looking for a way to measure the skill set of employees, and training companies and educational institutions seeking Microsoft Office XP teachers with appropriate credentials.

The MOUS Exams

You pay $50 to $100 each time you take an exam, whether you pass or fail. The fee varies among testing centers. The Expert exams, which you can take up to 60 minutes to complete, consists of between 40 and 60 tasks that you perform online. The tasks require you to use the application just as you would in doing your job. The Core exams contain fewer tasks, and you will have slightly less time to complete them. The tasks you will perform differ on the two types of exams.

How Can You Prepare for the MOUS Exams?

The Shelly Cashman Series® offers several Microsoft-approved textbooks that cover the required objectives on the MOUS exams. For a listing of the textbooks, visit the Shelly Cashman Series MOUS site at scsite.com/offxp/cert.htm and click the link Shelly Cashman Series Office XP Microsoft-Approved MOUS Textbooks (Figure E-1). After using any of the books listed in an instructor-led course, you will be prepared to take the MOUS exam indicated.

How to Find an Authorized Testing Center

You can locate a testing center by calling 1-800-933-4493 in North America or visiting the Shelly Cashman Series MOUS site at scsite.com/offxp/cert.htm and then clicking the link Locate an Authorized Testing Center Near You (Figure E-1). At this Web site, you can look for testing centers around the world.

Shelly Cashman Series MOUS Web Page

The Shelly Cashman Series MOUS Web page (Figure E-1) has more than fifteen Web sites you can visit to obtain additional information on the MOUS Certification Program. The Web page (scsite.com/offxp/cert.htm) includes links to general information on certification, choosing an application for certification, preparing for the certification exam, and taking and passing the certification exam.

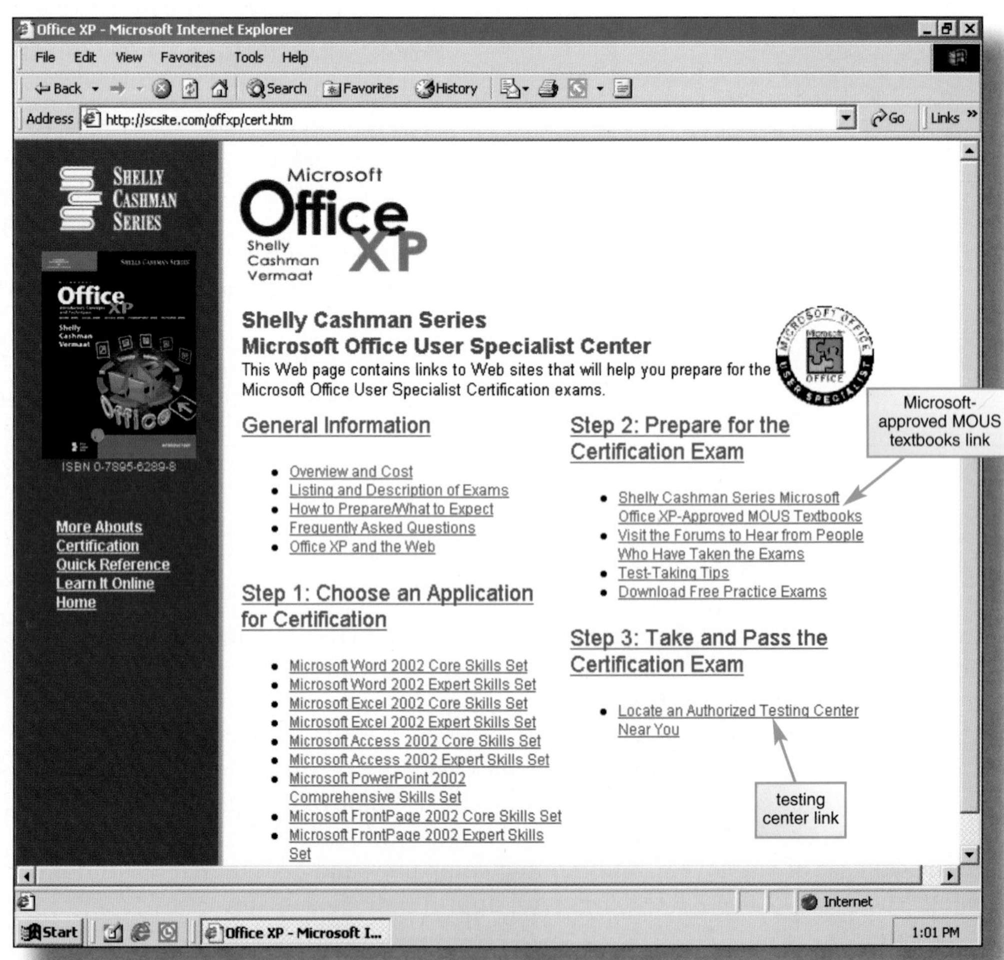

FIGURE E-1

Microsoft Office User Specialist Certification Map

The tables on the following pages list the skill sets and activities you should be familiar with if you plan to take one of the Microsoft Office User Specialist Certification examinations. Each activity is accompanied by page numbers on which the activity is illustrated and page numbers on which the activity is part of an exercise.

Word 2002 Core-level and Expert-level Skill Sets and Activities

Table E-2 lists the skill sets and activities you should be familiar with if you plan to take the Microsoft Word 2002 Core examination. Table E-3 on the next page lists the skill sets and activities you should be familiar with if you plan to take the Microsoft Word 2002 Expert examination. ADV means that the activity is demonstrated in the companion textbook *Microsoft Office XP: Advanced Concepts and Techniques* (ISBN 0-7895-6290-1 and ISBN 0-7895-6386-X). POST-ADV means that the activity is demonstrated in the companion textbook *Microsoft Office XP: Post-Advanced Concepts and Techniques* (ISBN 0-7895-6291-X).

Table E-2 Microsoft Word 2002 MOUS Core-level Skill Sets, Activities, and Locations in Book

SKILL SET	ACTIVITY	ACTIVITY DEMONSTRATED IN BOOK	ACTIVITY EXERCISE IN BOOK
I. Inserting and Modifying Text	A. Insert, modify, and move text and symbols	WD 1.21-26, WD 1.58, WD 2.20-24, WD 2.38-39, WD 2.46, WD 2.48-49, WD 3.19, WD 3.20, ADV	WD 1.64-65 (Apply Your Knowledge Steps 9, 13-14), WD 2.57 (Apply Your Knowledge Steps 1-5), WD 2.59 (In the Lab 1 Step 2), WD 2.61-62 (In the Lab 2 Part 1 Step 2, Part 2 Step 4), WD 2.62-63 (In the Lab 3 Step 2), WD 3.64 (In the Lab 1 Step 2), WD 3.65 (In the Lab 2 Step 1), ADV
	B. Apply and modify text formats	WD 1.20, WD 1.32, WD 1.35, WD 1.36, WD 1.41, WD 1.43, WD 1.45, WD 3.28, ADV	WD 1.66-67 (In the Lab 1 Steps 1, 5, 8-10), WD 1.67-68 (In the Lab 2 Steps 1, 5, 8-10), WD 1.68-69 (In the Lab 3 Steps 1, 5, 7, 9-10), WD 1.70-71 (Cases & Places 1-7), WD 2.57 (Apply Your Knowledge Steps 3, 7), WD 2.60-62 (In the Lab 2 Part 2 Steps 8-9), WD 3.65 (In the Lab 2 Step 1), ADV
	C. Correct spelling and grammar usage	WD 1.22, WD 1.27-29, WD 2.50-52	WD 1.64-65 (Apply Your Knowledge Steps 1-8), WD 1.66 (In the Lab 1 Step 3), WD 1.67-68 (In the Lab 2 Step 3), WD 1.68 (In the Lab 3 Step 3), WD 2.58-59 (In the Lab 1 Step 4), WD 2.60-61 (In the Lab 2 Step 4), WD 2.62 (In the Lab 3 Step 4)
	D. Apply font and text effects	ADV	ADV
	E. Enter and format Date and Time	WD 3.43-44, ADV	WD 3.65 (In the Lab 2 Step 2), ADV
	F. Apply character styles	ADV	ADV
II. Creating and Modifying Paragraphs	A. Modify paragraph formats	WD 1.32, WD 1.37, WD 1.38, WD 2.10, WD 2.17, WD 2.18 Table 2-2, WD 2.19, WD 2.36, WD 2.37-2.38, WD 3.21, WD 3.37-3.38, ADV	WD 1.66-67 (In the Lab 1 Steps 6-7, 11), WD 1.67-68 (In the Lab 2 Steps 6-7, 11), WD 1.68-69 (In the Lab 3 Steps 6-8, 11), WD 1.70-71 (Cases & Places 1-7), WD 2.58-59 (In the Lab 1 Step 1), WD 2.60-62 (In the Lab 2 Step 1), WD 2.62 (In the Lab 1 Step 1), WD 3.64 (In the Lab 1 Step 2) WD 3.65 (In the Lab 2 Step 1), ADV
	B. Set and modify tabs	WD 3.30-32, WD 3.42-43	WD 3.65 (In the Lab 2 Step 2), WD 3.66 (Cases & Places 5)
	C. Apply bullet, outline, and numbering format to paragraphs	WD 3.54-56, ADV	WD 1.68 (In the Lab 3 Step 8), WD 3.64 (In the Lab 1), WD 3.65 (In the Lab 2), WD 3.66 (Cases & Places 5), ADV
	D. Apply paragraph styles	ADV	ADV
III. Formatting Documents	A. Create and modify a header and footer	WD 2.11-15, ADV	WD 2.58-59 (In the Lab 1 Step 1), WD 2.60-62 (In the Lab 2 Step 1), WD 2.62-63 (In the Lab 3 Step 1), ADV
	B. Apply and modify column settings	ADV	ADV
	C. Modify document layout and Page Setup options	WD 2.08, WD 2.14, WD 2.33, ADV	WD 2.59 (In the Lab 1 Steps 1-2), ADV
	D. Create and modify tables	WD 3.49-3.54, ADV	WD 3.63 (Apply Your Knowledge Steps 1-8), WD 3.65 (In the Lab 2), ADV
	E. Preview and Print documents, envelopes, and labels	WD 1.54-55, WD 3.25-26, WD 3.57-58	WD 1.64-65 (Apply Your Knowledge Step 16), WD 1.66-67 (In the Lab 1 Step 15), WD 1.67-1.68 (In the Lab 2 Steps 13, 15), WD 1.68-69 (In the Lab 3 Steps 13, 15), WD 3.64 (In the Lab 1 Step 5), WD 3.65 (In the Lab 2 Steps 5- 6)
IV. Managing Documents	A. Manage files and folders for documents	ADV	ADV

Table E-2 Microsoft Word 2002 MOUS Core-level Skill Sets, Activities, and Locations in Book *(continued)*			
SKILL SET	*ACTIVITY*	*ACTIVITY DEMONSTRATED IN BOOK*	*ACTIVITY EXERCISE IN BOOK*
	B. Create documents using templates	WD 3.08-14, WDW 1.05-08, ADV	WD 3.64 (In the Lab 1 Steps 1-2), WD 3.66 (Cases & Places 1-5), WDW 1.14 (In the Lab 2), ADV
	C. Save documents using different names and file formats	WD 1.30, WD 1.53-54, WDW 1.03, ADV	WD 1.65 (Apply Your Knowledge Step 15), WD 1.66-67 (In the Lab 1 Steps 4, 14), WD 1.67-68 (In the Lab 2 Steps 4, 14), WD 1.68-69 (In the Lab 3 Steps 4, 14), ADV
V. Working with Graphics	A. Insert images and graphics	WD 1.46-49	WD 1.66-67 (In the Lab 1 Step 12), WD 1.67-68 (In the Lab 2 Step 12), WD 1.68-69 (In the Lab 3 Steps 12-13), WD 1.70-71 (Cases & Places 1-7)
	B. Create and modify diagrams and charts	ADV	ADV
VI. Workgroup Collaboration	A. Compare and Merge documents	ADV	ADV
	B. Insert, view, and edit comments	ADV	ADV
	C. Convert documents into Web pages	WDW 1.03, WDW 1.11	WDW 1.14 (In the Lab 1-2)

Table E-3 Microsoft Word 2002 MOUS Expert-level Skill Sets, Activities, and Locations in Book			
SKILL SET	*ACTIVITY*	*ACTIVITY DEMONSTRATED IN BOOK*	*ACTIVITY EXERCISE IN BOOK*
I. Customizing Paragraphs	A. Control Pagination	ADV, POST-ADV	ADV, POST-ADV
	B. Sort paragraphs in lists and tables	WD 2.41-42, ADV	WD 2.60-62 (In the Lab 2 Step 3), ADV
II. Formatting Documents	A. Create and format document sections	WD 3.39, ADV	ADV
	B. Create and apply character and paragraph styles	WD 2.27-31, ADV	WD 2.60-62 (In the Lab 2 Part 2 Step 8), ADV
	C. Create and update document indexes and tables of contents, figures, and authorities	POST-ADV	POST-ADV
	D. Create cross-references	POST-ADV	POST-ADV
	E. Add and revise endnotes and footnotes	WD 2.24-32	WD 2.60-63 (In the Lab 2 Part 1 Step 2, Part 2 Steps 3-4, 7-9), WD 3.62-63 (In the Lab 3 Steps 3-4), WD 2.64 (Cases & Places 1-5)
	F. Create and manage master documents and subdocuments	POST-ADV	POST-ADV
	G. Move within documents	WD 2.43-44, POST-ADV	WD 2.62 (In the Lab 2 Part 2 Step 4), POST-ADV
	H. Create and modify forms using various form controls	POST-ADV	POST-ADV
	I. Create forms and prepare forms for distribution	POST-ADV	POST-ADV
III. Customizing Tables	A. Use Excel data in tables	POST-ADV	POST-ADV
	B. Perform calculations in Word tables	ADV	ADV
IV. Creating and Modifying Graphics	A. Create, modify, and position graphics	WD 1.50-53, WD 3.29-30, ADV, POST-ADV	WD 1.67-68 (In the Lab 2 Steps 12-13), WD 1.68-69 (In the Lab 3 Steps 12-13), ADV, POST-ADV
	B. Create and modify charts using data from other applications	POST-ADV	POST-ADV
	C. Align text and graphics	ADV	ADV
V. Customizing Word	A. Create, edit, and run, macros	POST-ADV	POST-ADV
	B. Customize menus and toolbars	POST-ADV	POST-ADV
VI. Workgroup Collaboration	A. Track, accept, and reject changes to documents	POST-ADV	POST-ADV
	B. Merge input from several reviewers	POST-ADV	POST-ADV

Table E-3 Microsoft Word 2002 MOUS Expert-level Skill Sets, Activities, and Locations in Book			
SKILL SET	*ACTIVITY*	*ACTIVITY DEMONSTRATED IN BOOK*	*ACTIVITY EXERCISE IN BOOK*
	C. Insert and modify hyperlinks to other documents and Web	WD 2.39-40, WD 2.53, WD 3.40, WDW 1.04, WDW 1.10	WD 2.57 (Apply Your Knowledge Steps 6-7), WD 2.58-59 (In the Lab 1 Steps 3, 6), WD 2.60-61 (In the Lab 1 Part 1 Steps 3, 6), WD 2.65 (In the Lab 2 Step 2), WDW 1.14 (In the Lab 2)
	D. Create and edit Web documents in Word	WDW 1.12-13, Appendix C	WDW 1.14 (In the Lab 1-2) POST-ADV
	E. Create document versions	POST-ADV	POST-ADV
	F. Protect documents	POST-ADV	POST-ADV
	G. Define and modify default file locations for workgroup templates	WDW 1.09, WDW 1.12-13, POST-ADV	WDW 1.14 (In the Lab 2), POST-ADV
	H. Attach digital signatures to documents	POST-ADV	POST-ADV
VII. Using Mail Merge	A. Merge letters with a Word, Excel, or Access data source	ADV	ADV
	B. Merge labels with a Word, Excel, or Access data source	ADV	ADV
	C. Use Outlook data as mail merge data source	ADV	ADV

Microsoft Excel 2002 Core-level and Expert-level Skill Sets and Activities

Table E-4 lists the skill sets and activities you should be familiar with if you plan to take the Microsoft Excel 2002 Core examination. Table E-5 on the next page lists the skill sets and activities you should be familiar with if you plan to take the Microsoft Excel 2002 Expert examination. ADV means that the activity is demonstrated in the companion textbook *Microsoft Office XP: Advanced Concepts and Techniques* (ISBN 0-7895-6290-1 and ISBN 0-7895-6386-X). POST-ADV means that the activity is demonstrated in the companion textbook *Microsoft Office XP: Post-Advanced Concepts and Techniques* (ISBN 0-7895-6291-X).

Table E-4 Microsoft Excel 2002 MOUS Core-level Skill Sets, Activities, and Locations in Book			
SKILL SET	*ACTIVITY*	*ACTIVITY DEMONSTRATED IN BOOK*	*ACTIVITY EXERCISE IN BOOK*
I. Working with Cells and Cell Data	A. Insert, delete, and move cells	E 1.32, E 3.16, E 3.18	E 1.57 (Apply Your Knowledge 2nd to last paragraph), E 2.70 (In the Lab 1 Step 14), E 3.78 (In the Lab 3 Part 3)
	B. Enter and edit cell data including text, numbers, and formulas	E 1.08, E 1.16, E 1.19, E 1.21, E 1.49, E 1.51, E 2.07, E 2.16-23, E 2.33-38	E 1.58 (In the Lab 1 Steps 1, 10), E 1.60 (In the Lab 2 Step 5), E 2.70 (In the Lab 1 Step 4), E 2.72 (In the Lab 2 Steps 7-9, 13), E 3.70 (In the Lab 1 Step 7), E 3.77-78 (In the Lab 3 Steps 10-15)
	C. Check spelling	E 2.48-50	E 2.70 (In the Lab 1 Step 10), E 2.73 (In the Lab 2 Step 18)
	D. Find and replace cell data and formats	E 1.35-36, ADV	ADV
	E. Work with a subset of data by filtering lists	ADV	ADV
II. Managing Workbooks	A. Manage workbook files and folders	E 1.46, EW 1.06	E 1.57 (Apply Your Knowledge 1st paragraph), EW 1.15-16 (In the Lab 1 Step 1)
	B. Create workbooks using templates	ADV	ADV
	C. Save workbooks using different names and file formats	E 1.40-44, E 2.24-25, E 2.50, EW 1.06-08, ADV	E 1.58 (In the Lab 1 Step 8), EW 1.15-16, (In the Lab 1 Step 1, In the Lab 2 Step 2), ADV
III. Formatting and Printing Worksheets	A. Apply and modify cell formats	E 1.28-35, E 2.26-43, E 3.32-43, ADV	E 1.58-59 (In the Lab 1 Step 5), E 2.68 (Apply Your Knowledge Step 5), E 2.72 (In the Lab 2 Steps 10, 13-15), ADV
	B. Modify row and column settings	E 2.46, E 2.48, E 3.16-18, E 3.20, E 3.31	E 2.72 (In the Lab 2 Step 10), E 3.70 (In the Lab 1 Step 4), E 3.77 (In the Lab 3 Step 3), ADV
	C. Modify row and column formats	E 2.43-48	E 2.70 (In the Lab 1 Steps 6-7), E 2.72 (In the Lab 2 Steps 10, 13), E 3.70 (In the Lab 1 Steps 2, 4), ADV

Table E-4 Microsoft Excel 2002 MOUS Core-level Skill Sets, Activities, and Locations in Book *(continued)*

SKILL SET	*ACTIVITY*	*ACTIVITY DEMONSTRATED IN BOOK*	*ACTIVITY EXERCISE IN BOOK*
	D. Apply styles	ADV	ADV
	E. Use automated tools to format worksheets	E 1.33-35	E 1.59 (In the Lab 1 Step 5), E 1.60 (In the Lab 2 Step 5), E 1.61 (In the Lab 3 Step 4)
	F. Modify Page Setup options for worksheets	E 2.54, E 2.57, E 3.57, ADV	E 2.68 (Apply Your Knowledge Steps 8-9), E 2.73 (In the Lab 2 Step 19), E 3.71 (In the Lab 1 Step 10), ADV
	G. Preview and print worksheets and workbooks	ADV	ADV
IV. Modifying Workbooks	A. Insert and delete worksheets	ADV	ADV
	B. Modify worksheet names and positions	E 3.54-56	E 3.71 (In the Lab 1 Part 2), E 3.74 (In the Lab 2 Step 11), E 3.75 (In the Lab 2 Part 2 Step 6)
	C. Use 3-D references	ADV	ADV
V. Creating and Revising Formulas	A. Create and revise formulas	E 2.9-13, E 2.17, E 2.22, E 3.25-29	E 2.67 (Apply Your Knowledge Step 1), E 2.70 (In the Lab 1 Step 2), E 2.72 (In the Lab 2 Step 5), E 3.70 (In the Lab 1 Step 7), E 3.74 (In the Lab 2 Step 7), ADV
	B. Use statistical, date and time, financial, and logical functions in formulas	E 1.23-24, E 1.27-28, E 2.16-24, E 3.27-28, ADV	E 2.70 (In the Lab 1 Step 4), E 2.72 (In the Lab 2 Steps 6-9), E 3.68 (Apply Your Knowledge Steps 1-4), E 3.69-70 (In the Lab 1 Steps 1, 7), ADV
VI. Creating and Modifying Graphics	A. Create, modify, position and print charts	E 1.37-40, E 3.43-54	E 1.59 (In the Lab 1 Step 6), E 1.60 (In the Lab 2 Step 6), E 1.62 (In the Lab 3 Part 2), E 2.73 (In the Lab 2 Part 2), E 3.75 (In the Lab 2 Part 2)
	B. Create, modify, and position graphics	E 1.39, E 3.52-54	E 1.59 (In the Lab 1 Step 6), E 1.60 (In the Lab 2 Step 6), E 1.62 (In the Lab 3 Part 2), ADV
VII. Workgroup Collaboration	A. Convert worksheets into Web pages	EW 1.04-05, EW 1.06-08, EW 1.10-12	EW 1.15 (In the Lab 1 Step 2), EW 1.16 (In the Lab 2 Part 1 Step 2)
	B. Create hyperlinks	ADV	ADV
	C. View and edit comments	ADV	ADV

Table E-5 Microsoft Excel 2002 MOUS Expert-level Skill Sets, Activities, and Locations in Book

SKILL SET	*ACTIVITY*	*ACTIVITY DEMONSTRATED IN BOOK*	*ACTIVITY EXERCISE IN BOOK*
I. Importing and Exporting Data	A. Import data to Excel	POST-ADV	POST-ADV
	B. Export data from Excel	POST-ADV	POST-ADV
	C. Publish worksheets and workbooks to the Web	EW 1.04, Appendix C, POST-ADV	EW 1.15 (In the Lab 1 Step 2), EW 1.16 (In the Lab 2 Part 1 Step 2), POST-ADV
II. Managing Workbooks	A. Create, edit, and apply templates	ADV	ADV
	B. Create workspaces	ADV	ADV
	C. Use Data Consolidation	ADV	ADV
III. Formatting Numbers	A. Create and apply custom number formats	ADV	ADV
	B. Use conditional formats	E 2.40-43, ADV	E 2.70 (In the Lab 1 Step 8), E 2.72 (In the Lab 2 Step 14), ADV
IV. Working with Ranges	A. Use named ranges in formulas	ADV	ADV
	B. Use Lookup and Reference functions	ADV	ADV
V. Customizing Excel	A. Customize toolbars and menus	POST-ADV	POST-ADV
	B. Create, edit, and run macros	POST-ADV	POST-ADV
VI. Auditing Worksheets	A. Audit formulas	POST-ADV	POST-ADV
	B. Locate and resolve errors	E 2.25, ADV	E 2.68 (Apply Your Knowledge Step 6), E 2.70 (In the Lab 1 Step 5), ADV
	C. Identify dependencies in formulas	POST-ADV	POST-ADV

Table E-5 Microsoft Excel 2002 MOUS Expert-level Skill Sets, Activities, and Locations in Book			
SKILL SET	*ACTIVITY*	*ACTIVITY DEMONSTRATED IN BOOK*	*ACTIVITY EXERCISE IN BOOK*
VII. Summarizing Data	A. Use subtotals with lists and ranges	ADV	ADV
	B. Define and apply filters	ADV	ADV
	C. Add group and outline criteria to ranges	ADV	ADV
	D. Use data validation	POST-ADV	POST-ADV
	E. Retrieve external data and create queries	POST-ADV	POST-ADV
	F. Create Extensible Markup Language (XML) Web queries	POST-ADV	POST-ADV
VIII. Analyzing Data	A. Create PivotTables, PivotCharts, and PivotTable/PivotChart Reports	POST-ADV	POST-ADV
	B. Forecast values with what-if analysis	POST-ADV	POST-ADV
	C. Create and display scenarios	POST-ADV	POST-ADV
IX. Workgroup Collaboration	A. Modify passwords, protections, and properties	ADV	ADV
	B. Create a shared workbook	POST-ADV	POST-ADV
	C. Track, accept, and reject changes to workbooks	POST-ADV	POST-ADV
	D. Merge workbooks	POST-ADV	POST-ADV

Access 2002 Core-level and Expert-level Skill Sets and Activities

Table E-6 lists the skill sets and activities you should be familiar with if you plan to take the Microsoft Access 2002 Core examination. Table E-7 on the next page lists the skill sets and activities you should be familiar with if you plan to take the Microsoft Access 2002 Expert examination. ADV means that the activity is demonstrated in the companion textbook *Microsoft Office XP: Advanced Concepts and Techniques* (ISBN 0-7895-6290-1 and ISBN 0-7895-6386-X). POST-ADV means that the activity is demonstrated in the companion textbook *Microsoft Office XP: Post-Advanced Concepts and Techniques* (ISBN 0-7895-6291-X).

Table E-6 Microsoft Access 2002 MOUS Core-level Skill Sets, Activities, and Locations in Book			
SKILL SET	*ACTIVITY*	*ACTIVITY DEMONSTRATED IN BOOK*	*ACTIVITY EXERCISE IN BOOK*
I. Creating and Using Databases	A. Create Access databases	A 1.11	A 1.64 (Cases & Places 6)
	B. Open database objects in multiple views	A 1.21, A 1.38, A 1.39, A 3.16, ADV	A 1.58-61 (In the Lab 2, In the Lab 3), A 3.51-57 (Apply Your Knowledge, In the Lab 1-3), ADV
	C. Move among records	A 1.26, A 1.38, ADV	A 1.55 (Apply Your Knowledge Step 5), A 1.59 (In the Lab 2 Steps 9-10), A 1.61 (In the Lab 3 Step 10)
	D. Format datasheets	A 3.21, ADV	A 3.51 (Apply Your Knowledge Step 10), A 3.53 (In the Lab 1 Step 3), A 3.55 (In the Lab 2 Step 11)
II. Creating and Modifying Tables	A. Create and modify tables	A 1.13, A 1.15	A 1.63 (Cases & Places 3)
	B. Add a pre-defined input mask to a field	ADV	ADV
	C. Create Lookup fields	ADV	ADV
	D. Modify field properties	A 3.16, A 3.28, A 3.30, A 3.31, A 3.46, ADV	A 3.51-3.59 (Apply Your Knowledge Steps 2-6, In the Lab 1 Steps 2-3, 11, In the Lab 2 Steps 9, 12, In the Lab 3 Steps 2, 5, 9, Cases & Places 1 -5), ADV
III. Creating and Modifying Queries	A. Create and modify Select queries	A 2.06	A 2.44 (In the Lab 1 Step 2)
	B. Add calculated fields to Select queries	A 2.33	A 2.45 (In the Lab 1 Step 13), A 2.46 (In the Lab 2 Step 12), A 2.47 (In the Lab 3 Step 12), A 2.48 (Cases & Places 2 Part c)

Table E-6 Microsoft Access 2002 MOUS Core-level Skill Sets, Activities, and Locations in Book *(continued)*

SKILL SET	*ACTIVITY*	*ACTIVITY DEMONSTRATED IN BOOK*	*ACTIVITY EXERCISE IN BOOK*
IV. Creating and Modifying Forms	A. Create and display forms	A 1.38, ADV	A 1.56 (In the Lab 1 Step 8), A 1.58 (In the Lab 2 Step 8), A 1.61 (In the Lab 3 Step 12), ADV
	B. Modify form properties	ADV	ADV
V. Viewing and Organizing Information	A. Enter, edit, and delete records	A 1.21, A 1.27, A 3.06, A 3.14, A 3.20	A 1.54-64 (Apply Your Knowledge Step 1, In the Lab 1-3, Cases & Places 1-6), A 1.55 (Apply Your Knowledge Step 5), A 1.59 (In the Lab 2 Steps 9-10), A 1.61 (In the Lab 3 Step 10), A 3.51 (Apply Your Knowledge Step 9), A 3.53 (In the Lab 1 Steps 5, 12), A 3.54 (In the Lab 2 Steps 7, 13), A 3.55 (In the Lab 2 Step 13), A 3.57 (In the Lab 3 Steps 7, 10), A 3.58 (Cases & Places 1-2)
	B. Create queries	A 2.06, A 3.39, A 3.45	A 2.44 (In the Lab 1 Step 2) A 3.59 (Cases & Places 5 Parts a, e)
	C. Sort records	A 2.25, A 3.41, A 3.42	A 2.44 (Apply Your Knowledge Step 14), A 2.46 (In the Lab 2 Step 12), A 2.47 (In the Lab 3 Steps 8-9) A 2.48 (Cases & Places 1 Part c, Cases & Places 2 Part e, Cases & Places 4 Step c), A 3.51 (Apply Your Knowledge Step 15), A 3.53 (In the Lab 2 Step 6), A 3.56 (In the Lab 3 Step 3)
	D. Filter records	A 3.13	A 3.51 (Apply Your Knowledge Step 13), A 3.55 (In the Lab 2 Step 16)
VI. Defining Relationships	A. Create one-to-many relationships	A 3.36-38	A 3.51 (Apply Your Knowledge Step 17), A 3.53 (In the Lab 1 Step 15), A 3.55 (In the Lab 2 Step 18), A 3.57 (In the Lab 3 Step 15), A 3.58-59 (Cases & Places 1-2, 4-5)
	B. Enforce referential integrity	A 3.36-38	A 3.51 (Apply Your Knowledge Step 17), A 3.53 (In the Lab 1 Step 15), A 3.55 (In the Lab 2 Step 18), A 3.57 (In the Lab 3 Step 15), A 3.58-59 (Cases & Places 1-2, 4-5)
VII. Producing Reports	A. Create and format reports	A 1.41, ADV	A 1.55 (Apply Your Knowledge Step 7), A 1.57 (In the Lab 1 Step 9) A 1.59 (In the Lab 2 Step 12), A 1.61 (In the Lab 3 Step 12), ADV
	B. Add calculated controls to reports	ADV	ADV
	C. Preview and print reports	A 1.46, ADV	A 1.55 (Apply Your Knowledge Step 7), A 1.57 (In the Lab 1 Step 9) A 1.59 (In the Lab 2 Step 12), A 1.61 (In the Lab 3 Step 12), ADV
VIII. Integrating with Other Applications	A. Import data to Access	ADV	ADV
	B. Export data from Access	ADV	ADV
	C. Create a simple data Access page	AW 1.02	AW 1.10 (In the Lab 1)

Table E-7 Microsoft Access 2002 MOUS Expert-level Skill Sets, Activities, and Locations in Book

SKILL SET	*ACTIVITY*	*ACTIVITY DEMONSTRATED IN BOOK*	*ACTIVITY EXERCISE IN BOOK*
I. Creating and Modifying Tables	A. Use data validation	A 3.29, A 3.31	A 3.51-3.59 (Apply Your Knowledge Steps 2-6, In the Lab 1 Steps 2-3, 11, In the Lab 2 Steps 9, 12, In the Lab 3 Steps 2, 5, 9, Cases & Places 1-5)
	B. Link tables	ADV	ADV
	C. Create lookup fields and modify Lookup field properties	ADV	ADV
	D. Create and modify input masks	POST-ADV	POST-ADV
II. Creating and Modifying Forms	A. Create a form in Design View	POST-ADV	POST-ADV
	B. Create a Switchboard and set startup options	ADV, POST-ADV	ADV, POST-ADV
	C. Add Subform controls to Access forms	ADV, POST-ADV	ADV, POST-ADV
III. Refining Queries	A. Specify multiple query criteria	A 2.23, A 2.24, POST-ADV	A 2.45 (In the Lab 1 Steps 8-9), A 2.46 (In the Lab 2 Steps 5, 7, 9) A 2.47 (In the Lab 3 Steps 4-5, 7), POST-ADV
	B. Create and apply advanced filters	POST-ADV	POST-ADV
	C. Create and run parameter queries	POST-ADV	POST-ADV
	D. Create and run Action queries	A 3.23, A 3.25, A 3.27	A 3.54 (In the Lab 2 Steps 3-5)

Table E-7 Microsoft Access 2002 MOUS Expert-level Skill Sets, Activities, and Locations in Book			
SKILL SET	*ACTIVITY*	*ACTIVITY DEMONSTRATED IN BOOK*	*ACTIVITY EXERCISE IN BOOK*
	E. Use aggregate functions in queries	A 2.36, POST-ADV	A 2.45 (In the Lab 1 Steps 14-15), A 2.46 (In the Lab 2 Step 13), A 2.47 (In the Lab 3 Step 13, Cases & Places 1 Parts d, e, f, Cases & Places 2 Part f, Cases & Places 4 Parts d, e, f, g), POST-ADV
IV. Producing Reports	A. Create and modify reports	POST-ADV	POST-ADV
	B. Add Subreport controls to Access reports	POST-ADV	POST-ADV
	C. Sort and group data in reports	POST-ADV	POST-ADV
V. Defining Relationships	A. Establish one-to-many relationships	A 3.36	A 3.51-3.58 (Apply Your Knowledge, In the Lab 1-3, Cases & Places 1-2)
	B. Establish many-to-many relationships	POST-ADV	POST-ADV
VI. Operating Access on the Web	A. Create and Modify a Data Access Page	POST-ADV	POST-ADV
	B. Save PivotTables and PivotCharts views to Data Access Pages	POST-ADV	POST-ADV
VII. Using Access Tools	A. Import XML documents into Access	ADV	ADV
	B. Export Access data to XML documents	ADV	ADV
	C. Encrypt and decrypt databases	POST-ADV	POST-ADV
	D. Compact and repair databases	ADV	ADV
	E. Assign database security	POST-ADV	POST-ADV
	F. Replicate a database	POST-ADV	POST-ADV
VIII. Creating Database Applications	A. Create Access Modules	POST-ADV	POST-ADV
	B. Use the Database Splitter	POST-ADV	POST-ADV
	C. Create an MDE file	POST-ADV	POST-ADV

PowerPoint 2002 Comprehensive Skill Sets and Activities

Table E-8 lists the skill sets and activities you should be familiar with if you plan to take the Microsoft PowerPoint 2002 Comprehensive examination. ADV means that the activity is demonstrated in the companion textbook *Microsoft Office XP: Advanced Concepts and Techniques* (ISBN 0-7895-6290-1 and ISBN 0-7895-6386-X). POST-ADV means that the activity is demonstrated in the companion textbook *Microsoft Office XP: Post-Advanced Concepts and Techniques* (ISBN 0-7895-6291-X).

Table E-8 Microsoft PowerPoint 2002 MOUS Comprehensive Skill Sets, Activities, and Locations in Book			
SKILL SET	*ACTIVITY*	*ACTIVITY DEMONSTRATED IN BOOK*	*ACTIVITY EXERCISE IN BOOK*
I. Creating Presentations	A. Create presentations (manually and using automated tools)	PP 1.10-11, PP 1.19-44, PP 2.06, PP 2.07-45, PPW 1.03-05, ADV	PP 1.69-71 (In the Lab 1 Steps 1-3), PP 1.72-73 (In the Lab 2 Steps 1-3), PP 1.74-75 (In the Lab 3 Steps 1-4), PP 1.76-79 (Cases & Places 1-7), PP 2.57-58 (In the Lab 1 Step 1), PP 2.59 (In the Lab 2 Step 1), PP 2.61-62 (In the Lab 3 Step 1), PP 2.64-66 (Cases & Places 1-7), ADV
	B. Add slides to and delete slides from presentations	PP 1.32-33, PP 1.37, PP 1.41, PP 2.12, PP 2.14, PP 2.15, PP 2.17, ADV, POST-ADV	PP 1.69-71 (In the Lab 1 Steps 1-3), PP 1.72-73 (In the Lab 2 Steps 1-3), PP 1.74-75 (In the Lab 3 Steps 1-3), PP 1.76-79 (Cases & Places 1-7), PP 2.57-58 (In the Lab 1 Steps 1-3), PP 2.59-60 (In the Lab 2 Step 1), PP 2.61-62 (In the Lab 3 Step 1), PP 2.64-66 (Cases & Places 1-7), ADV, POST-ADV
	C. Modify headers and footers in the Slide Master	ADV, POST-ADV	ADV, POST-ADV
II. Inserting and Modifying Text	A. Import text from Word	ADV	ADV

Table E-8 Microsoft PowerPoint 2002 MOUS Comprehensive Skill Sets, Activities, and Locations in Book *(continued)*

SKILL SET	*ACTIVITY*	*ACTIVITY DEMONSTRATED IN BOOK*	*ACTIVITY EXERCISE IN BOOK*
	B. Insert, format, and modify text	PP 1.22-24, PP 1.26-28, PP 1.34-43, PP 1.58, PP 2.10-11, PP 2.13-17, ADV, POST-ADV	PP 1.68 (Apply Your Knowledge Steps 2-5), PP 1.69-71 (In the Lab 1 Steps 2-3), PP 1.72-73 (In the Lab 2 Steps 2-3), PP 1.74-75 (In the Lab 3 Steps 2-3), PP 1.76-79 (Cases & Places 1-7), PP 2.56 (Apply Your Knowledge Step 2), PP 2.57-59 (In the Lab 1 Steps 2-3), PP 2.59 (In the Lab 2 Steps 1-2), PP 2.61-62 (In the Lab 3 Step 1), PP 2.64-66 (Cases & Places 1-7), ADV, POST-ADV
III. Inserting and Modifying Visual Elements	A. Add tables, charts, clip art, and bitmap images to slides	PP 2.24-30, ADV, POST-ADV	PP 2.56-57 (Apply Your Knowledge Steps 2-5), PP 2.57-59 (In the Lab 1 Steps 2, 4-6), PP 2.59-60 (In the Lab 2 Steps 2-5), PP 2.61-63 (In the Lab 3 Steps 2-7), PP 2.64-66 (Cases & Places 1-7), ADV, POST-ADV
	B. Customize slide backgrounds	ADV	ADV
	C. Add OfficeArt elements to slides	ADV	ADV
	D. Apply custom formats to tables	ADV	ADV
IV. Modifying Presentation Formats	A. Apply formats to presentations	PP 1.19-21, PP 2.06-07, PP 2.21-23, ADV, POST-ADV	PP 1-68 (Apply Your Knowledge Step 1), PP 1.71 (In the Lab 1 Step 1), PP 1.73 (In the Lab 2 Step 1), PP 1.74 (In the Lab 3 Step 1), PP 1.76-79 (Cases & Places 1-7), PP 2.56 (Apply Your Knowledge Step 1), PP 2.58 (In the Lab 1 Step 1), PP 2.59 (In the Lab 2 Step 1), PP 2.61-62 (In the Lab 3 Step 1), PP 2.64-66 (Cases & Places 1-7), ADV, POST-ADV
	B. Apply animation schemes	PP 2.39-41, ADV, POST-ADV	PP 2.57 (Apply Your Knowledge Step 6), PP 2.59 (In the Lab 1 Step 8), PP 2.61 (In the Lab 2 Step 7), PP 2.62 (In the Lab 3 Step 9), PP 2.64-66 (Cases & Places 1-7), ADV, POST-ADV
	C. Apply slide transitions	ADV	ADV
	D. Customize slide formats	PP 1.26-28, PP 2.42-2.45, ADV, POST-ADV	PP 1.68 (Apply Your Knowledge Steps 2-5), PP 1.69-71 (In the Lab 1 Step 2), PP 1.72-73 (In the Lab 2 Steps 2-3), PP 1.74 (In the Lab 3 Steps 2-3), PP 1.76-79 (Cases & Places 1-7), PP 2.56-57 (Steps 2-5), PP 2.57-59 (In the Lab 1 Steps 2, 4-6), PP 2.59-61 (In the Lab 2 Steps 2-4, 8), PP 2.63 (In the Lab 3 Steps 2-7), PP 2.64-66 (Cases & Places 1-7), ADV
	E. Customize slide templates	ADV	ADV
	F. Manage a Slide Master	ADV	ADV
	G. Rehearse timing	ADV	ADV
	H. Rearrange slides	ADV	ADV
	I. Modify slide layout	PP 2.21-23, ADV	PP 2.57 (Apply Your Knowledge Steps 3, 5), PP 2.58 (In the Lab 1 Steps 4-5), PP 2.59 (In the Lab 2 Steps 2-5), PP 2.62 (In the Lab 3 Steps 2-7), ADV
	J. Add links to a presentation	ADV	ADV
V. Printing Presentations	A. Preview and print slides, outlines, handouts, and speaker notes	PP 1.60-61, PP 2.47-49, PP 2.50-51, ADV, POST-ADV	PP 1.68 (Apply Your Knowledge Steps 7-9), PP 1.71 (In the Lab 1 Steps 6-7), PP 1.74 (In the Lab 2 Step 6), PP 1.74 (In the Lab 3 Step 6), PP 1.76-79 (Cases & Places 1-7), PP 2.57 (Step 8), PP 2.59 (In the Lab 1 Step 10), PP 2.61 (In the Lab 2 Step 10), PP 2.62 (In the Lab 3 Step 12), PP 2.64-66 (Cases & Places 1-7), ADV, POST-ADV
VI. Working with Data from Other Sources	A. Import Excel charts to slides	ADV	ADV
	B. Add sound and video to slides	ADV	ADV
	C. Insert Word tables on slides	ADV	ADV
	D. Export a presentation as an outline	ADV	ADV
VII. Managing and Delivering Presentations	A. Set up slide shows	ADV	ADV
	B. Deliver presentations	ADV	ADV
	C. Manage files and folders for presentations	ADV	ADV
	D. Work with embedded fonts	ADV	ADV
	E. Publish presentations to the Web	PPW 1.03-05, Appendix C	PPW 1.12 (In the Lab 1 Steps 2-3, 6), PPW 1.12-13 (In the Lab 2 Steps 2-3, 6)
	F. Use Pack and Go	ADV	ADV
VIII. Workgroup Collaboration	A. Set up a review cycle	ADV	ADV
	B. Review presentation comments	ADV	ADV
	C. Schedule and deliver presentation broadcasts	ADV	ADV
	D. Publish presentations to the Web	PPW 1.03-05, Appendix C	PPW 1.12 (In the Lab 1 Steps 2-3, 6), PPW 1.12-13 (In the Lab 2 Steps 2-3, 6)

Index

Microsoft Office XP
Quick Reference Summary

In the Microsoft Office XP applications, you can accomplish a task in a number of ways. The following five tables (one each for Word, Excel, Access, PowerPoint, and Outlook) provide a quick reference to each task presented in this textbook. The first column identifies the task. The second column indicates the page number on which the task is discussed in the book. The subsequent four columns list the different ways the task in column one can be carried out. You can invoke the commands listed in the MOUSE, MENU BAR, and SHORTCUT MENU columns using Voice commands.

Table 1 Microsoft Word 2002 Quick Reference Summary

TASK	PAGE NUMBER	MOUSE	MENU BAR	SHORTCUT MENU	KEYBOARD SHORTCUT
1.5 Line Spacing	WD 2.18		Format | Paragraph | Indents and Spacing tab	Paragraph | Indents and Spacing tab	CTRL+5
AutoCorrect Entry, Create	WD 2.23		Tools | AutoCorrect Options | AutoCorrect tab		
AutoCorrect Options	WD 2.22	AutoCorrect Options button			
AutoText Entry, Create	WD 3.45		Insert | AutoText | New		ALT+F3
AutoText Entry, Insert	WD 3.47		Insert | AutoText		Type entry, then F3
Blank Line Above Paragraph	WD 2.18		Format | Paragraph | Indents and Spacing tab	Paragraph | Indents and Spacing tab	CTRL+0
Bold	WD 1.45	Bold button on Formatting toolbar	Format | Font | Font tab	Font | Font tab	CTRL+B
Border, Bottom	WD 3.38	Border button arrow on Formatting toolbar	Format | Borders and Shading | Borders tab		
Bulleted List	WD 3.54	Bullets button on Formatting toolbar	Format | Bullets and Numbering | Bulleted tab	Bullets and Numbering | Bulleted tab	* and then space followed by text, then ENTER
Capitalize Letters	WD 2.18		Format | Font | Font tab	Font | Font tab	CTRL+SHIFT+A
Case of Letters	WD 2.18				SHIFT+F3
Center	WD 1.38	Center button on Formatting toolbar	Format | Paragraph | Indents and Spacing tab	Paragraph | Indents and Spacing tab	CTRL+E
Center Vertically	WD 1.39		File | Page Setup | Layout tab		
Character Formatting, Remove	WD 2.18		Format | Font | Font tab	Font | Font tab	CTRL+SPACEBAR
Clip Art, Insert	WD 1.46		Insert | Picture | Clip Art		
Close Document	WD 1.58	Close button on menu bar	File | Close		CTRL+W
Color Characters	WD 3.28	Font Color button arrow on Formatting toolbar	Format | Font | Font tab	Font | Font tab	
Copy (Collect Items)	WD 3.33	Copy button on Standard toolbar	Edit | Copy	Copy	CTRL+C
Count Words	WD 2.32	Recount button on Word Count toolbar	Tools | Word Count		
Date, Insert	WD 3.43		Insert | Date and Time		
Delete (Cut) Text	WD 1.54	Cut button on Standard toolbar	Edit | Cut	Cut	CTRL+X
Demote List Item	WD 3.56	Decrease Indent button on Formatting toolbar			
Document Window, Open New	WD 3.27	New Blank Document button on Standard toolbar		File | New | Blank Document	CTRL+N

Table 1 Microsoft Word 2002 Quick Reference Summary *(continued)*

TASK	PAGE NUMBER	MOUSE	MENU BAR	SHORTCUT MENU	KEYBOARD SHORTCUT
Double-Space Text	WD 2.09	Line Spacing button on Formatting toolbar	Format | Paragraph | Indents and Spacing tab	Paragraph | Indents and Spacing tab	CTRL+2
Double-Underline	WD 2.18		Format | Font | Font tab	Font | Font tab	CTRL+SHIFT+D
E-Mail Document	WD 2.54	E-mail button on Standard toolbar	File | Send to | Mail Recipient		
Envelope, Address	WD 3.57		Tools | Letters and Mailings | Envelopes and Labels | Envelopes tab		
Find	WD 2.49	Select Browse Object button on vertical scroll bar	Edit | Find		CTRL+F
Find and Replace	WD 2.48	Double-click status bar to left of status indicators	Edit | Replace		CTRL+H
First-Line Indent	WD 2.19	Drag First Line Indent marker on ruler	Format | Paragraph | Indents and Spacing tab	Paragraph | Indents and Spacing tab	
Font	WD 1.36	Font box arrow on Formatting toolbar	Format | Font | Font tab	Font | Font tab	CTRL+SHIFT+F
Font Size	WD 1.20	Font Size box arrow on Formatting toolbar	Format | Font | Font tab	Font | Font tab	CTRL+SHIFT+P
Footnote, Create	WD 2.25		Insert | Reference | Footnote		
Footnote, Delete	WD 2.31	Delete note reference mark in document window			
Footnote, Edit	WD 2.32	Double-click note reference mark in document window	View | Footnotes		
Footnotes to Endnotes, Convert	WD 2.32		Insert | Reference | Footnote		
Formatting Marks	WD 1.24	Show/Hide ¶ button on Standard toolbar	Tools | Options | View tab		CTRL+SHIFT+*
Formatting, Clear	WD 3.39	Styles and Formatting button on Formatting toolbar or Style box arrow on Formatting toolbar			CTRL+SPACEBAR; CTRL+Q
Formatting, Reveal	WD 2.36	Other Task Panes button on open task pane	Format | Reveal Formatting		
Full Menu	WD 1.14	Double-click menu name	Click menu name, wait few seconds		
Go To	WD 2.42	Select Browse Object button on vertical scroll bar	Edit | Go To		CTRL+G
Hanging Indent, Create	WD 2.37	Drag Hanging Indent marker on ruler	Format | Paragraph | Indents and Spacing tab	Paragraph | Indents and Spacing tab	CTRL+T
Hanging Indent, Remove	WD 2.18	Drag Hanging Indent marker on ruler	Format | Paragraph | Indents and Spacing tab	Paragraph | Indents and Spacing tab	CTRL+SHIFT+T
Header, Display	WD 2.12		View | Header and Footer header area		
Help	WD 1.59 and Appendix A	Microsoft Word Help button on Standard toolbar	Help | Microsoft Word Help		F1
Highlight Text	WDW 1.09	Highlight button arrow on Formatting toolbar			
HTML Source	WDW 1.11		View | HTML Source		
Hyperlink, Convert to Regular Text	WD 3.40	AutoCorrect Options button | Undo Hyperlink		Remove Hyperlink	CTRL+Z
Hyperlink, Create	WD 2.40	Insert Hyperlink button on Standard toolbar		Hyperlink	Web address then ENTER or SPACEBAR
Hyperlink, Edit	WDW 1.10	Insert Hyperlink button on Standard toolbar		Hyperlink	
Indent, Decrease	WD 2.18	Decrease Indent button on Formatting toolbar	Format | Paragraph | Indents and Spacing tab	Paragraph | Indents and Spacing tab	CTRL+SHIFT+M
Indent, Increase	WD 2.18	Increase Indent button on Formatting toolbar	Format | Paragraph | Indents and Spacing tab	Paragraph | Indents and Spacing tab	CTRL+M
Italicize	WD 1.41	Italic button on Formatting toolbar	Format | Font | Font tab	Font | Font tab	CTRL+I
Justify Paragraph	WD 2.18	Justify button on Formatting toolbar	Format | Paragraph | Indents and Spacing tab	Paragraph | Indents and Spacing tab	CTRL+J

Table 1 Microsoft Word 2002 Quick Reference Summary

TASK	PAGE NUMBER	MOUSE	MENU BAR	SHORTCUT MENU	KEYBOARD SHORTCUT
Language Bar	WD 1.18	Language Indicator button in tray	Tools | Speech		
Leader Characters	WD 3.30		Format | Tabs		
Left-Align	WD 2.17	Align Left button on Formatting toolbar	Format | Paragraph | Indents and Spacing tab	Paragraph | Indents and Spacing tab	CTRL+L
Line Break, Enter	WD 3.21				SHIFT+ENTER
Mailing Label, Address	WD 3.58		Tools | Letters and Mailings | Envelopes and Labels | Labels tab		
Margins	WD 2.08	In print layout view, drag margin boundary on ruler	File | Page Setup | Margins tab		
Menus and Toolbars, Reset	WD 2.07	Toolbar Options button on toolbar | Add or Remove Buttons | Customize | Options tab	View | Toolbars | Customize | Options tab		
Move Selected Text	WD 2.46	Drag and drop	Edit | Cut; Edit | Paste	Cut; Paste	CTRL+X; CTRL+V
Nonbreaking Hyphen	WD 3.46		Insert | Symbol | Special Characters tab		CTRL+SHIFT+HYPHEN
Nonbreaking Space	WD 3.47		Insert | Symbol | Special Characters tab		CTRL+SHIFT+SPACEBAR
Note Pane, Close	WD 2.31	Close button in note pane			
Numbered List	WD 3.56	Numbering button on Formatting toolbar	Format | Bullets and Numbering | Numbered tab	Bullets and Numbering | Numbered tab	1. and then space followed by text, then ENTER
Office Clipboard Task Pane, Display	WD 3.33	Double-click Office Clipboard icon in tray	Edit | Office Clipboard		
Open Document	WD 1.56	Open button on Standard toolbar	File | Open		CTRL+O
Outline Numbered List	WD 3.56		Format | Bullets and Numbering | Outline Numbered tab		
Page Break	WD 2.35		Insert | Break		CTRL+ENTER
Page Numbers, Insert	WD 2.14	Insert Page Number button on Header and Footer toolbar	Insert | Page Numbers		
Paragraph Formatting, Remove	WD 2.18		Format | Paragraph | Indents and Spacing tab	Paragraph | Indents and Spacing tab	CTRL+Q
Paste	WD 3.35	Paste button on Standard toolbar or click icon in Office Clipboard gallery in Office Clipboard task pane	Edit | Paste	Paste	CTRL+V
Paste Options, Display Menu	WD 2.47	Paste Options button			
Print Document	WD 1.54	Print button on Standard toolbar	File | Print		CTRL+P
Print Preview	WD 3.25	Print Preview button on Standard toolbar	File | Print Preview		CTRL+F2
Promote List Item	WD 3.56	Increase Indent button on Formatting toolbar			
Quit Word	WD 1.55	Close button on title bar	File | Exit		ALT+F4
Redo Action	WD 1.39	Redo button on Standard toolbar	Edit | Redo		
Repeat Command	WD 1.39		Edit | Repeat		
Resize Graphic	WD 1.51	Drag sizing handle	Format | Picture | Size tab	Format Picture | Size tab	
Restore Graphic	WD 1.53	Format Picture button on Picture toolbar	Format | Picture | Size tab	Format Picture | Size tab	
Resume Wizard	WD 3.07		File | New | General Templates | Other Documents tab		
Right-Align	WD 1.37	Align Right button on Formatting toolbar	Format | Paragraph | Indents and Spacing tab	Paragraph | Indents and Spacing tab	CTRL+R
Ruler, Show or Hide	WD 1.13		View | Ruler		
Save as Web Page	WDW 1.03		File | Save as Web Page		
Save Document - New Name	WD 1.54		File | Save As		F12
Save Document - Same Name	WD 1.53	Save button on Standard toolbar	File | Save		CTRL+S
Save New Document	WD 1.30	Save button on Standard toolbar	File | Save		CTRL+S

Table 1 Microsoft Word 2002 Quick Reference Summary *(continued)*

TASK	PAGE NUMBER	MOUSE	MENU BAR	SHORTCUT MENU	KEYBOARD SHORTCUT
Select Document	WD 2.45	Point to left and triple-click	Edit | Select All		CTRL+A
Select Graphic	WD 1.50	Click graphic			
Select Group of Words	WD 1.44	Drag through words			CTRL+SHIFT+RIGHT ARROW
Select Line	WD 1.40	Point to left of line and click			SHIFT+DOWN ARROW
Select Multiple Paragraphs	WD 1.34	Point to left of first paragraph and drag down			CTRL+SHIFT+DOWN ARROW
Select Paragraph	WD 2.45	Triple-click paragraph			
Select Sentence	WD 2.45	CTRL+click sentence			CTRL+SHIFT+RIGHT ARROW
Select Word	WD 1.42	Double-click word			CTRL+SHIFT+RIGHT ARROW
Single-Space Text	WD 2.18	Line Spacing button arrow on Formatting toolbar	Format | Paragraph | Indents and Spacing tab	Paragraph | Indents and Spacing tab	CTRL+1
Small Uppercase Letters	WD 2.18		Format | Font | Font tab	Font | Font tab	CTRL+SHIFT+K
Smart Tag Actions, Display Menu	WD 3.59	Point to smart tag indicator, click Smart Tag Actions button			
Sort Paragraphs	WD 2.41		Table | Sort		
Spelling and Grammar Check At Once	WD 2.51	Spelling and Grammar button on Standard toolbar	Tools | Spelling and Grammar	Spelling	F7
Spelling Check as You Type	WD 1.28	Double-click Spelling and Grammar Status icon on status bar		Right-click flagged word, click correct word on shortcut menu	
Style, Modify	WD 2.28	Styles and Formatting button on Formatting toolbar	Format | Styles and Formatting		
Styles and Formatting Task Pane, Display	WD 3.19	Styles and Formatting button on Formatting toolbar	View | Task Pane		
Subscript	WD 2.18		Format | Font | Font tab	Font | Font tab	CTRL+=
Superscript	WD 2.18		Format | Font | Font tab	Font | Font tab	CTRL+SHIFT+PLUS SIGN
Switch to Open Document	WD 3.32	Program button on taskbar	Window | document name		
Synonym	WD 2.50		Tools | Language | Thesaurus	Synonyms | desired word	SHIFT+F7
Tab Stops, Set	WD 3.31	Click location on ruler	Format | Tabs		
Table AutoFormat	WD 3.53	AutoFormat button on Tables and Borders toolbar	Table | Table AutoFormat		
Table, Insert Empty	WD 3.49	Insert Table button on Standard toolbar	Table | Insert | Table		
Table, Insert Row	WD 3.16		Table | Insert | Rows Above/Below	Right-click selected row; Insert Rows	
Table, Resize Column	WD 3.54	Drag column boundary	Table | Table Properties | Column tab	Table Properties | Column tab	
Table, Resize Column to Contents	WD 3.52	Double-click column boundary	Table | AutoFit | AutoFit to Contents	AutoFit | AutoFit to Contents	
Table, Select	WD 3.53	Click table move handle	Table | Select | Table		ALT+5 (on numeric keypad)
Table, Select Cell	WD 3.53	Click left edge of cell			Press TAB
Table, Select Column	WD 3.53	Click top border of column			
Table, Select Multiple Cells	WD 3.53	Drag through cells			
Table, Select Row	WD 3.53	Click to left of row			
Task Pane, Close	WD 1.10	Close button on task pane	View | Task Pane		
Task Pane, Display Different	WD 1.49	Other Task Panes button on task pane			
Template, Open	WD 3.41		File | New | General Templates		
Toolbar, Dock	WD 2.13	Drag toolbar to dock			
Toolbar, Float	WD 2.13	Double-click between two buttons or boxes on toolbar			
Toolbar, Show Entire	WD 1.16	Double-click move handle on toolbar			
Underline	WD 1.43	Underline button on Formatting toolbar	Format | Font | Font tab	Font | Font tab	CTRL+U
Underline Words, not Spaces	WD 2.18		Format | Font | Font tab	Font | Font tab	CTRL+SHIFT+W
Undo Command or Action	WD 1.39	Undo button on Standard toolbar	Edit | Undo		CTRL+Z

Table 1 Microsoft Word 2002 Quick Reference Summary

TASK	PAGE NUMBER	MOUSE	MENU BAR	SHORTCUT MENU	KEYBOARD SHORTCUT
Web Page Frame, Resize	WDW 1.09	Drag frame border	Format | Frames | Frame Properties | Frame tab		
Web Page Wizard	WDW 1.05		File | New | General Templates | Web Pages tab		
Web Page, View	WDW 1.11		File | Web Page Preview		
White Space, Hide or Show	WD 3.15	Hide or Show White Space button	Tools | Options | View tab		
Zoom Page Width	WD 1.19	Zoom box arrow on Formatting toolbar	View | Zoom		
Zoom Text Width	WD 3.18	Zoom box arrow on Formatting toolbar	View | Zoom		

Table 2 Microsoft Excel 2002 Quick Reference Summary

TASK	PAGE NUMBER	MOUSE	MENU BAR	SHORTCUT MENU	KEYBOARD SHORTCUT
AutoFormat	E 1.33		Format | AutoFormat		ALT+O | A
AutoSum	E 1.23	AutoSum button on Standard toolbar	Insert | Function		ALT+=
Bold	E 1.29	Bold button on Formatting toolbar	Format | Cells | Font tab	Format Cells | Font tab	CTRL+B
Borders	E 2.30	Borders button on Formatting toolbar	Format | Cells | Border tab	Format Cells | Border tab	CTRL+1 | B
Center	E 2.32	Center button on Formatting toolbar	Format | Cells | Alignment tab	Format Cells | Alignment tab	CTRL+1 | A
Center Across Columns	E 1.32	Merge and Center button on Formatting toolbar	Format | Cells | Alignment tab	Format Cells | Alignment tab	CTRL+1 | A
Chart	E 1.37	Chart Wizard button on Standard toolbar	Insert | Chart		F11
Clear Cell	E 1.51	Drag fill handle back	Edit | Clear | All	Clear Contents	DELETE
Close All Workbooks	E 1.45		SHIFT+File | Close All		SHIFT+ALT+F | C
Close Workbook	E 1.45	Close button on menu bar or workbook Control-menu icon	File | Close		CTRL+W
Color Background	E 2.30	Fill Color button on Formatting toolbar	Format | Cells | Patterns tab	Format Cells | Patterns tab	CTRL+1 | P
Color Tab	E 3.55			Tab Color	
Column Width	E 2.44	Drag column heading boundary	Format | Column | Width	Column Width	ALT+O | C | W
Comma Style Format	E 2.34	Comma Style button on Formatting toolbar	Format | Cells | Number tab | Accounting	Format Cells | Number tab | Accounting	CTRL+1 | N
Conditional Formatting	E 2.40		Format | Conditional Formatting		ALT+O | D
Copy and Paste	E 3.14	Copy button and Paste button on Standard toolbar	Edit | Copy; Edit | Paste	Copy to copy; Paste to paste	CTRL+C; CTRL+V
Currency Style Format	E 2.34	Currency Style button on Formatting toolbar	Format | Cells | Number | Currency	Format Cells | Number | Currency	CTRL+1 | N
Cut	E 3.16	Cut button on Standard toolbar	Edit | Cut	Cut	CTRL+X
Date	E 3.22	Insert Function box on formula bar	Insert | Function		CTRL+SEMICOLON
Decimal Place Decrease	E 2.35	Decrease Decimal button on Formatting toolbar	Format | Cells | Number tab | Currency	Format Cells | Number tab | Currency	CTRL+1 | N
Decimal Place Increase	E 2.35	Increase Decimal button on Formatting toolbar	Format | Cells | Number tab | Currency	Format Cells | Number tab | Currency	CTRL+1 | N
Delete Rows or Columns	E 3.18		Edit | Delete	Delete	
Drop Shadow	E 3.40	Shadow Style button on Drawing toolbar			
E-Mail from Excel	E 2.63	E-mail button on Standard toolbar	File | Send To | Mail Recipient		ALT+F | D | A
Fit to Print	E 2.56		File | Page Setup | Page tab		ALT+F | U | P
Folder, New	E W1.06		File | Save As		ALT+F | A

Table 2 Microsoft Excel 2002 Quick Reference Summary *(continued)*

TASK	*PAGE NUMBER*	*MOUSE*	*MENU BAR*	*SHORTCUT MENU*	*KEYBOARD SHORTCUT*
Font Color	E 1.31	Font Color button on Formatting toolbar	Format | Cells | Font tab	Format Cells | Font tab	CTRL+1 | F
Font Size	E 1.30	Font Size box arrow on Formatting toolbar	Format | Cells | Font tab	Format Cells | Font tab	CTRL+1 | F
Font Type	E 2.28	Font box arrow on Formatting toolbar	Format | Cells | Font tab	Format Cells | Font tab	CTRL+1 | F
Formula Palette	E 2.19	Insert Function box on formula bar	Insert | Function		CTRL+A after you type function name
Formulas Version	E 2.56		Tools | Options | View tab | Formulas		CTRL+ACCENT MARK
Freeze Worksheet Titles	E 3.20		Window | Freeze Panes		ALT+W | F
Full Screen	E 1.12		View | Full Screen		ALT+V | U
Function	E 2.20	Insert Function box on formula bar	Insert | Function		SHIFT+F3
Go To	E 1.36	Click cell	Edit | Go To		F5
Goal Seek	E 3.63		Tools | Goal Seek		ALT+T | G
Help	E 1.52 and Appendix A	Microsoft Excel Help button on Standard toolbar	Help | Microsoft Excel Help		F1
Hide Column	E 2.46	Drag column heading boundary	Format | Column | Hide	Hide	CTRL+0 (zero) to hide CTRL+SHIFT+) to display
Hide Row	E 2.48	Drag row heading boundary	Format | Row | Hide	Hide	CTRL+9 to hide CTRL+SHIFT+(to display
In-Cell Editing	E 1.49	Double-click cell			F2
Insert Rows or Columns	E 3.16		Insert | Rows or Insert | Columns	Insert	ALT+I | R or C
Italicize	E 3.42	Italicize button on Formatting toolbar	Format | Cells | Font tab	Format Cells | Font tab	CTRL+I
Language Bar	E 1.16	Language Indicator button in tray	Tools | Speech | Speech Recognition		ALT+T | H | H
Merge Cells	E 1.32	Merge and Center button on Formatting toolbar	Format | Cells | Alignment tab	Format Cells | Font tab | Alignment tab	ALT+O | E | A
Move	E 3.16	Point to border and drag	Edit | Cut; Edit | Paste	Cut; Paste	CTRL+X; CTRL+V
Name Cells	E 1.36	Click Name box in formula bar and type name	Insert | Name | Define		ALT+I | N | D
New Workbook	E 1.52	New button on Standard toolbar	File | New		CTRL+N
Open Workbook	E 1.46	Open button on Standard toolbar	File | Open		CTRL+O
Percent Style Format	E 2.39	Percent Style button on Formatting toolbar	Format | Cells | Number tab | Percentage	Format Cells | Number tab | Percentage	CTRL+1 | N
Preview Worksheet	E 2.51	Print Preview button on Standard toolbar	File | Print Preview		ALT+F | V
Print Worksheet	E 2.51	Print button on Standard toolbar	File | Print		CTRL+P
Quit Excel	E 1.45	Close button on title bar	File | Exit		ALT+F4
Range Finder	E 2.25	Double-click cell			
Redo	E 1.51	Redo button on Standard toolbar	Edit | Redo		ALT+E | R
Remove Splits	E 3.61	Double-click split bar	Window | Split		ALT+W | S
Rename Sheet Tab	E 2.62	Double-click sheet tab		Rename	
Rotate Text	E 3.08		Format | Cells | Alignment tab	Format Cells | Alignment tab	ALT+O | E | A
Row Height	E 2.47	Drag row heading boundary	Format | Row | Height	Row Height	ALT+O | R | E
Save as Web Page	EW 106		File | Save as Web Page		ALT+F | G
Save Workbook – New Name	E 1.41		File | Save As		ALT+F | A
Save Workbook – Same Name	E 2.50	Save button on Standard toolbar	File | Save		CTRL+S
Select All of Worksheet	E 1.52	Select All button on worksheet			CTRL+A
Select Cell	E 1.16	Click cell			Use arrow keys
Select Multiple Sheets	E 3.57	CTRL+click tab or SHIFT+click tab		Select All Sheets	
Series	E 3.8	Drag fill handle	Edit | Fill | Series		ALT+E | I | S
Shortcut Menu	E 2.28	Right-click object			SHIFT+F10
Spell Check	E 2.48	Spelling button on Standard toolbar	Tools | Spelling		F7

Table 2 Microsoft Excel 2002 Quick Reference Summary

TASK	PAGE NUMBER	MOUSE	MENU BAR	SHORTCUT MENU	KEYBOARD SHORTCUT
Split Cell	E 1.32	Merge and Center button on Formatting toolbar	Format | Cells | Alignment tab	Format Cells | Alignment tab	ALT+O | E | A
Split Window into Panes	E 3.60	Drag vertical or horizontal split box	Window | Split		ALT+W | S
Stock Quotes	E 2.58		Data | Import External Data | Import Data		ALT+D | D | D
Task Pane	E 1.08		View | Task Pane		ALT+V | K
Toolbar, Reset	Appendix D	Toolbar Options, Add or Remove Buttons, Customize, Toolbars		Customize | Toolbars	ALT+V | T | C | B
Toolbar, Dock	E 3.38	Drag toolbar to dock			
Toolbar, Show Entire	E 1.14	Double-click move handle			
Toolbar, Show or Hide	E 3.38	Right-click toolbar, click toolbar name	View | Toolbars		ALT+V | T
Underline	E 3.42	Underline button on Formatting toolbar	Format | Cells | Font tab	Format Cells | Font tab	CTRL+U
Undo	E 1.52	Undo button on Standard toolbar	Edit | Undo		CTRL+Z
Unfreeze Worksheet Titles	E 3.32		Windows | Unfreeze Panes		ALT+W | F
Unhide Column	E 2.46	Drag column heading boundary to left	Format | Column | Unhide	Unhide	ALT+O | C | U
Unhide Row	E 2.48	Drag row heading lower up	Format | Row | Unhide	Unhide	ALT+O | R | U
Web Page Preview	EW 1.04		File | Web Page Preview		ALT+F | B
Zoom	E 3.58	Zoom box on Standard toolbar	View | Zoom		ALT+V | Z

Table 3 Microsoft Access 2002 Quick Reference Summary

TASK	PAGE NUMBER	MOUSE	MENU BAR	SHORTCUT MENU	KEYBOARD SHORTCUT
Add Field	A 3.17	Insert Rows button	Insert | Rows	Insert Rows	INSERT
Add Group of Records	A 3.25	Query Type button arrow | Append Query	Query | Append Query	Query Type | Append Query	
Add Record	A 1.21, A 1.27	New Record button	Insert | New Record		
Add Table to Query	A 2.30	Show Table button	Query | Show Table	Show Table	
Apply Filter	A 3.13	Filter By Selection or Filter By Form button	Records | Filter		
Calculate Statistics	A 2.36	Totals button	View | Totals	Totals	
Change Group of Records	A 3.23	Query Type button arrow | Update Query	Query | Update Query	Query Type | Update Query	
Clear Query	A 2.15		Edit | Clear Grid		
Close Database	A 1.25	Close Window button	File | Close		
Close Form	A 1.36	Close Window button	File | Close		
Close Query	A 2.13	Close Window button	File | Close		
Close Table	A 1.25	Close Window button	File | Close		
Collapse Subdatasheet	A 3.40	Expand indicator (-)			
Create Calculated Field	A 2.34			Zoom	SHIFT+F2
Create Data Access Page	AW 1.02	New Object: AutoForm button arrow | Page	Insert | Page		
Create Database	A 1.11	New button	File | New		CTRL+N
Create Form	A 1.35	New Object: AutoForm button arrow | AutoForm	Insert | AutoForm		
Create Index	A 3.47	Indexes button	View | Indexes		
Create Query	A 2.06	New Object: AutoForm button arrow | Query	Insert | Query		
Create Report	A 1.41	New Object AutoForm button arrow | Report	Insert | Report		
Create Table	A 1.15	Tables object | Create table in Design view or Create table by using wizard	Insert | Table		

Table 3 Microsoft Access 2002 Quick Reference Summary *(continued)*

TASK	PAGE NUMBER	MOUSE	MENU BAR	SHORTCUT MENU	KEYBOARD SHORTCUT
Default Value	A 3.30	Default Value property box			
Delete Field	A 1.19, A 3.19	Delete Rows button	Edit | Delete	Delete Rows	DELETE
Delete Group of Records	A 3.26	Query Type button arrow | Delete Query	Query | Delete Query	Query Type | Delete Query	
Delete Record	A 3.14	Delete Record button	Edit | Delete Record	Delete Record	DELETE
Exclude Duplicates	A 2.26	Properties button	View | Properties | Unique Values Only	Properties | Unique Values Only	
Exclude Field from Query Results	A 2.19	Show check box			
Expand Subdatasheet	A 3.40	Expand indicator (+)			
Field Size	A 1.18, A 3.16	Field Size property box			
Field Type	A 1.19	Data Type box arrow | appropriate type			Appropriate letter
Filter Records	A 3.13	Filter By Selection or Filter By Form button	Records | Filter		
Format	A 3.32	Format property box			
Format a Calculated Field	A 2.33	Properties button	View | Properties	Properties	
Include All Fields in Query	A 2.14	Double-click asterisk in field list			
Include Field in Query	A 2.10	Double-click field in field list			
Key Field	A 1.18	Primary Key button	Edit | Primary Key	Primary Key	
Move to First Record	A 1.26	First Record button			CTRL+UP ARROW
Move to Last Record	A 1.26	Last Record button			CTRL+DOWN ARROW
Move to Next Record	A 1.26	Next Record button			DOWN ARROW
Move to Previous Record	A 1.26	Previous Record button			UP ARROW
Open Database	A 1.25	Open button	File | Open		CTRL+O
Open Form	A 3.06	Forms object | Open button		Open	Use ARROW keys to move highlight to name, then press ENTER key
Open Table	A 1.21	Tables object | Open button		Open	Use ARROW keys to move highlight to name, then press ENTER key
Preview Table	A 1.29	Print Preview button	File | Print Preview	Print Preview	
Print Relationships	A 3.39		File | Print Relationships		
Print Report	A 1.46	Print button	File | Print	Print	CTRL+P
Print Results of Query	A 2.11	Print button	File | Print	Print	CTRL+P
Print Table	A 1.29	Print button	File | Print	Print	CTRL+P
Quit Access	A 1.49	Close button	File | Exit		ALT+F4
Relationships (Referential Integrity)	A 3.36	Relationships button	Tools | Relationships		
Remove Filter	A 3.14	Remove Filter button	Records | Remove Filter/Sort		
Resize Column	A 3.21	Drag right boundary of field selector	Format | Column Width	Column Width	
Restructure Table	A 3.16	Tables object | Design button		Design View	
Return to Design View	A 2.12	View button arrow	View | Design View		
Run Query	A 2.11	Run button	Query | Run		
Save Form	A 1.36	Save button	File | Save		CTRL+S
Save Query	A 2.41	Save button	File | Save		CTRL+S
Save Table	A 1.20	Save button	File | Save		CTRL+S
Search for Record	A 3.09	Find button	Edit | Find		CTRL+F
Select Fields for Report	A 1.43	Add Field button or Add All Fields button			
Sort Data in Query	A 2.25	Sort row | Sort row arrow | type of sort			
Sort Records	A 3.41	Sort Ascending or Sort Descending button	Records | Sort | Sort Ascending or Sort Descending	Sort Ascending or Sort Descending	
Switch Between Form and Datasheet Views	A 1.39, A 3.11	View button arrow	View | Datasheet View		
Use AND Criterion	A 2.23				Place criteria on same line
Use OR Criterion	A 2.24				Place criteria on separate lines

Table 3 Microsoft Access 2002 Quick Reference Summary

TASK	PAGE NUMBER	MOUSE	MENU BAR	SHORTCUT MENU	KEYBOARD SHORTCUT
Validation Rule	A 3.29	Validation Rule property box			
Validation Text	A 3.29	Validation Text property box			

Table 4 Microsoft PowerPoint 2002 Quick Reference Summary

TASK	PAGE NUMBER	MOUSE	MENU BAR	SHORTCUT MENU	KEYBOARD SHORTCUT
Animate Text	PP 2.40		Slide Show | Custom Animation | Add Effect button		ALT+D | M
Check Spelling	PP 1.56	Spelling button on Standard toolbar	Tools | Spelling		F7
Clip Art, Add Animation Effects	PP 2.42		Slide Show | Custom Animation		ALT+D | M
Clip Art, Change Size	PP 2.34	Format Picture button on Picture toolbar | Size tab	Format | Picture | Size tab	Format Picture | Size tab	ALT+O | I | Size tab
Clip Art, Insert	PP 2.25	Insert Clip Art button on Drawing toolbar	Insert | Picture | Clip Art		ALT+I | P | C
Clip Art, Move	PP 2.33	Drag			
Delete Text	PP 1.58	Cut button on Standard toolbar	Edit | Cut	Cut	CTRL+X or BACKSPACE or DELETE
Demote a Paragraph on Outline tab	PP 2.13	Demote button on Outlining toolbar			TAB or ALT+SHIFT+RIGHT ARROW
Design Template	PP 1.19	Slide Design button on Formatting toolbar	Format | Slide Design	Slide Design	ALT+O | D
Display a Presentation in Black and White	PP 1.58	Color/Grayscale button on Standard toolbar	View | Color/Grayscale | Pure Black and White		ALT+V | C | U
Edit Web Page through Browser	PPW 1.09	Edit button on Internet Explorer Standard Buttons toolbar	File on browser menu bar | Edit with Microsoft PowerPoint in browser window		ALT+F | D in browser window
E-Mail from PowerPoint	PP 2.52	E-mail button on Standard toolbar	File | Send To | Mail Recipient		ALT+F | D | A
Font	PP 1.25	Font box arrow on Formatting toolbar	Format | Font	Font	ALT+O | F
Font Color	PP 1.25	Font Color button arrow on Formatting toolbar, desired color	Format | Font	Font | Color	ALT+O | F | ALT+C | DOWN ARROW
Font Size, Decrease	PP 1.25	Decrease Font Size button on Formatting toolbar	Format | Font	Font | Size	CTRL+SHIFT+LEFT CARET (<)
Font Size, Increase	PP 1.27	Increase Font Size button on Formatting toolbar	Format | Font	Font | Size	CTRL+SHIFT+RIGHT CARET (>)
Header and Footer, Add to Outline Page	PP 2.37		View | Header and Footer | Notes and Handouts tab		ALT+V | H | Notes and Handouts tab
Help	PP 1.62 and Appendix A	Microsoft PowerPoint Help button on Standard toolbar	Help | Microsoft PowerPoint Help		F1
Italicize	PP 1.26	Italic button on Formatting toolbar	Format | Font | Font style	Font | Font style	CTRL+I
Language Bar	PP 1.18	Language Indicator button in tray	Tools | Speech | Speech Recognition		ALT+T | H | H
Move a Paragraph Down	PP 2.09	Move Down button on Outlining toolbar			ALT+SHIFT+DOWN ARROW
Move a Paragraph Up	PP 2.09	Move Up button on Outlining toolbar			ALT+SHIFT+UP ARROW
New Slide	PP 1.32	New Slide button on Formatting toolbar	Insert | New Slide		CTRL+M
Next Slide	PP 1.46	Next Slide button on vertical scroll bar			PAGE DOWN
Normal View	PP 2.19	Normal View button at lower-left PowerPoint window	View | Normal		ALT+V | N
Open Presentation	PP 1.53	Open button on Standard toolbar	File | Open		CTRL+O
Paragraph Indent, Decrease	PP 1.40	Decrease Indent button on Formatting toolbar			SHIFT+TAB or ALT+SHIFT+ LEFT ARROW
Paragraph Indent, Increase	PP 1.34	Increase Indent button on Formatting toolbar			TAB or ALT+SHIFT+RIGHT ARROW

Table 4 Microsoft PowerPoint 2002 Quick Reference Summary *(continued)*

TASK	PAGE NUMBER	MOUSE	MENU BAR	SHORTCUT MENU	KEYBOARD SHORTCUT
Previous Slide	PP 1.46	Previous Slide button on vertical scroll bar			PAGE UP
Print a Presentation	PP 1.61	Print button on Standard toolbar	File | Print		CTRL+P
Print Outline	PP 2.48		File | Print | Print what box arrow | Outline View		CTRL+P | TAB | TAB | DOWN ARROW | Outline View
Promote a Paragraph on Outline tab	PP 2.14	Promote button on Outlining toolbar			SHIFT+TAB or ALT+SHIFT+LEFT ARROW
Quit PowerPoint	PP 1.52	Close button on title bar or double-click control icon on title bar	File | Exit		ALT+F4 or CTRL+Q
Redo Action	PP 1.23	Redo button on Standard toolbar	Edit | Redo		CTRL+Y or ALT+E | R
Save a Presentation	PP 1.29	Save button on Standard toolbar	File | Save		CTRL+S
Save as Web Page	PPW 1.03		File | Save as Web Page		ALT+F | G
Slide Layout	PP 2.22		Format | Slide Layout	Slide Layout	ALT+O | L
Slide Show View	PP 1.48	Slide Show button at lower-left PowerPoint window	View | Slide Show		F5 or ALT+V | W
Slide Sorter View	PP 2.18	Slide Sorter View button at lower-left PowerPoint window	View | Slide Sorter		ALT+V | D
Task Pane	PP 1.11		View | Task Pane		ALT+V | K
Toolbar, Reset	Appendix D	Toolbar Options button on toolbar, Add or Remove Buttons, Customize, Toolbars tab		Customize | Toolbars tab	ALT+V | T | C | B
Toolbar, Show Entire	PP 1.12	Double-click move handle			
Undo Action	PP 1.23	Undo button on Standard toolbar	Edit | Undo		CTRL+Z or ALT+E | U
Zoom Percentage, Increase	PP 1.45	Zoom Box arrow on Standard toolbar	View | Zoom		ALT+V | Z

Table 5 Microsoft Outlook 2002 Quick Reference Summary

TASK	PAGE NUMBER	MOUSE	MENU BAR	SHORTCUT MENU	KEYBOARD SHORTCUT
Change to Day View	O 1.33	Day button	View | Day		ALT+V, Y
Change to Month View	O 1.33	Month button	View | Month		ALT+V, M
Change to Week View	O 1.32	Week button	View | Week		ALT+V, K
Change to Work Week View	O 1.31	Work Week button	View | Work Week		ALT+V, R
Create a Task	O 1.34	New button			CTRL+SHIFT+K
Create an Event	O 1.29	New button	Actions | New All Day Event	New All Day Event	CTRL +N | ALT+A, E
Create Contact List	O 1.40	New button	Actions | New Contact	New Contact	CTRL+N | ALT+A, N
Create Subfolder	O 1.11		File | New | Folder	New Folder	CTRL+SHIFT+E
Delete an Appointment	O 1.23	Delete button	Edit | Delete	Delete	CTRL+D
Delete Folder	O 1.49	Delete button	File | Folder | Delete	Delete	ALT+F, F, D
Enter Appointments	O 1.14	New Appointment button	Actions | New Appointment	New Appointment	CTRL+N | ALT+A, O
Find a Contact	O 1.42	Find button	Tools | Find		CTRL+E
Import/Export Folders	O 1.46		File | Import and Export		ALT+F, T
Move an Appointment	O 1.25		Edit | Cut | Edit | Paste		CTRL+X | CTRL+V
Move to Next Day	O 1.19		View | Go To | Go to Date	Go to Date	CTRL+G
Open Calendar	O 1.09		View | Go To | Calendar		
Organize Contacts	O 1.44	Organize button	Tools | Organize		ALT+T, Z
Print Calendar	O 1.35	Print button	File | Print		CTRL+P
Print Contact List	O 1.45	Print button	File | Print		CTRL+P
Recurring Appointments	O 1.17	Recurrence button on Standard toolbar in Appointment window	Actions | New Recurring Appointment	New Recurring Appointment	ALT+A, A